# The Complete Guide to Human Resources and the Law

## 2014 Edition

*by Dana Shilling*

*The Complete Guide to Human Resources and the Law* is an invaluable tool for the HR professional who needs to place legal principles and developments in the context of the practical problems he or she faces every day. The law as it relates to human resources issues is an ever-growing, ever-changing body of information that involves not just court cases but also statutes and the regulations of administrative agencies. *The Complete Guide to Human Resources and the Law* brings you the most up-to-date information as well as practical tips and checklists in a well-organized, easy-to-use resource.

### Highlights of the 2014 Edition

The 2014 Edition provides new and expanded coverage of issues such as:

- A discussion of *Liberty University v. Geithner*, 133 S. Ct. 679 (2012). Although PPACA survived a Supreme Court challenge to its fundamental constitutionality, that did not end challenges to the validity of the statute as a whole. The Supreme Court sent this back to the Fourth Circuit to consider challenges to PPACA premised on grounds of religious freedom and equality. [§ 18.01]

- The Supreme Court denied Hobby Lobby's request for an emergency injunction that would have prevented the PPACA contraceptive mandate from taking effect. Supreme Court injunctions are governed by the All Writs Act, which is intended to be used sparingly because it provides a judicial intervention that was denied by the lower courts. The Court refused to consider Hobby Lobby's request that it consider the underlying issue of whether employers can assert a religious objection to covering contraceptives in a health plan: *Hobby Lobby Stores, Inc. v. Sebelius*, 133 S. Ct. 641 (2012). [§§ 18.03[D], 18.19[M]]

- On the last day of the term ending in June 2013, the Supreme Court ruled that § 3 of the federal Defense of Marriage Act (the section restricting "marriage" for federal-law purposes to a union of one man and one woman) was unconstitutional. The decision was based on due process and equal protection grounds. In a companion case, the Supreme Court upheld a California decision

Wolters Kluwer

Law & Business

striking down Proposition 8, the referendum forbidding same-sex marriage in that state: *United States v. Windsor*, 133 S. Ct. 2675 (2013); *Hollingsworth v. Perry*, 133 S. Ct. 2652 (2013). [§§ 2.01[B], 18.01, 18.06[A], 18.06[B]]

- Same-sex marriage is now legal in California, Connecticut, Delaware, the District of Columbia, Iowa, Maine, Maryland, Massachusetts, Minnesota, New Hampshire, New York, Rhode Island, Vermont, and Washington. Civil unions were legal in Colorado, Hawaii, Illinois, and New Jersey and domestic partnerships were registered in Nevada, Oregon, and Wisconsin. [§ 18.06[A]]

- The required FMLA poster and forms were revised. The new poster must be displayed (or similar information provided electronically) starting March 8, 2013, expiring February 28, 2015. The DOL adopted new FMLA forms, including health care providers' certification of the employee's or family member's serious health condition, and the notice of eligibility, employee rights, and employee responsibilities. The new forms reflect the expanded FMLA rights of family members of military personnel and veterans. [§§ 24.04, 38.01[A]]

- A late 2012 per curiam Supreme Court decision held that the Oklahoma Supreme Court should not have invalidated on public policy grounds, the noncompete provisions of two employment contracts. The decision should have been left up to the arbitrator. Because the FAA applies in both federal and state courts, the validity of an arbitration clause is determined by the court system—but if an arbitration clause is valid, then challenges to the validity of the underlying contract are determined by the arbitrator: *Nitro-Lift Technologies, LLC v. Howard*, No. 133 S. Ct. 500 (2012). [§§ 25.02[C], 40.04]

- The Sixth Circuit held that Supplemental Unemployment Benefit payments to employees who are terminated involuntarily because of business cessation are not FICA wages. This creates a circuit split because it disagrees with an earlier Second Circuit ruling: *United States v. Quality Stores, Inc.*, 693 F.3d 605 (6th Cir. 2012). [§§ 1.01, 2.03[A], 3.03[C], 32.01]

- The validity of hundreds of actions taken by the NLRB has been called into question by an early 2013 D.C. Circuit decision. The D.C. Circuit found that the appointments of three NLRB members were unconstitutional because, although described as recess appointments, they were made at a time when the Senate was not actually in recess. If those appointments were invalid, the NLRB lacked a quorum so actions taken without a quorum were invalid: *Noel Canning v. NLRB*, 705 F.3d 490 (D.C. Cir. 2013). [§ 30.01[A]; 30.02[A]. Certiorari was granted as No. 12-1281 on June 24, 2013. In August 2013, the NLRB finally had a five-member board all of whose members were confirmed by the Senate: Chairman Mark Gaston Pierce was confirmed for another term, and five new members were added [§ 30.02[A]].

- In late 2012, the California Supreme Court ruled that a supermarket's privately owned entrance area is not a "public forum" as defined by the California constitution. Therefore, union picketing in such an area did not have protection under the state constitution—but it did have protection under two California labor laws: *Ralphs Grocery Co. v. United Food and Commercial Workers Union Local 8*, 55 Cal. 4th 1083, 290 P.3d 1116, 150 Cal. Rptr. 3d 501 (2012). [§ 30.04[H]]

- Many employers rely on wellness programs to help stem the rising costs of health insurance—but that leaves employers vulnerable to challenges by employees alleging discrimination. The Eleventh Circuit held that the Broward County employee wellness program, which included a risk assessment questionnaire and blood sugar and cholesterol testing, satisfied the ADA safe harbor for insurance plans. Class action plaintiffs described the program as an involuntary medical examination linked to improper disease-related inquiries but the Eleventh Circuit found that the program satisfied the ADA safe harbor for inquiries that are job-related and consistent with business necessity and that are part of a bona fide benefit plan based on underwriting, administering, and classifying risks. There is a safe harbor for insurance plans that maintain a bona fide benefit plan based on underwriting, administering, and classifying risks: *Seff v. Broward County*, 691 F.3d 1221 (11th Cir. 2012). [§§ 18.19[G], 36.10[D]]

- The HHS, the DOL, and the Treasury proposed rules supporting wellness programs, including participatory programs that are generally available without regard to the employee's health status (e.g., rewards for taking a health risk assessment; reimbursement of gym membership). Programs that are contingent on health must be reasonably designed to promote health or prevent disease, and must not be unduly burdensome on participants: <http://www.dol.gov/ebsa/pdf/wellnessproposedregulation.pdf> (Nov. 26, 2012). [§§ 18.19[G], 36.10[D]]

- The Supreme Court drew a distinction between Title VII suits based on personal characteristics (race, color, sex, religion, and national origin) and retaliation suits, requiring retaliation plaintiffs to prove that retaliation was the but-for cause of the adverse job action taken against them: *University of Texas Southwestern Medical Center v. Nassar*, No. 12-484 (June 24, 2013). [§§ 34.02, 34.08, 42.09]

- In a case alleging workplace racial harassment, the Supreme Court defined a "supervisor" narrowly as a person having the authority to take tangible employment action against the plaintiff. Because the alleged harasser was a co-worker and not a supervisor, the Supreme Court held that the employer could only be liable if the hostile work environment was the product of the employer's negligent supervision: *Vance v. Ball State University*, 133 S. Ct. 2434 (2013). [§§ 34.05, 35.02, 42.02]

- The Supreme Court ruled that ERISA preempts Virginia's state law that revokes designation of a spouse as beneficiary when the plan participant's marital status changes. Therefore, death benefits under the federal group insurance program were distributed to a federal employee's first wife, not his second wife (to whom he was married at the time of his death): *Hillman v. Maretta,* 133 S. Ct. 1943 (2013) (June 3, 2013). [§ 12.06[A]]

- An April 2013 Supreme Court decision holds that contract law—enforcing the subrogation provision on an SPD—prevailed over the plan participant's equitable argument that he was not required to reimburse the plan because that would prevent him from receiving full reimbursement of his loss. However, the Supreme Court allowed the concept of "make-whole relief" to be applied to the question of apportionment of attorneys' fees: *US Airways, Inc. v. McCutchen,* 133 S. Ct. 1537 (2013). [§ 13.07, 15.09[A], 15.09[B], 18.17]

**10/13**

---

**For questions concerning this shipment, billing, or other customer service matters, call our Customer Service Department at 1-800-234-1660.**

**For toll-free ordering, please call 1-800-638-8437.**

# THE COMPLETE GUIDE TO HUMAN RESOURCES AND THE LAW

### 2014 Edition

**Dana Shilling**

Wolters Kluwer
Law & Business

This publication is designed to provide accurate and authoritative information in regard to the subject matter covered. It is sold with the understanding that the publisher and the author(s) are not engaged in rendering legal, accounting, or other professional services. If legal advice or other professional assistance is required, the services of a competent professional should be sought.

—From a *Declaration of Principles* jointly adopted by
a Committee of the American Bar Association and
a Committee of Publishers and Associations

Published by Wolters Kluwer Law & Business in New York.

Wolters Kluwer Law & Business serves customers worldwide with CCH, Aspen Publishers and Kluwer Law International products.

Printed in the United States of America

ISBN 978-1-4548-2542-5

1 2 3 4 5 6 7 8 9 0

Certified Chain of Custody
Product Line Contains At Least
20% Certified Forest Content
www.sfiprogram.org
SFI-00756

# About Wolters Kluwer Law & Business

Wolters Kluwer Law & Business is a leading global provider of intelligent information and digital solutions for legal and business professionals in key specialty areas, and respected educational resources for professors and law students. Wolters Kluwer Law & Business connects legal and business professionals as well as those in the education market with timely, specialized authoritative content and information-enabled solutions to support success through productivity, accuracy and mobility.

Serving customers worldwide, Wolters Kluwer Law & Business products include those under the Aspen Publishers, CCH, Kluwer Law International, Loislaw, ftwilliam.com and MediRegs family of products.

**CCH** products have been a trusted resource since 1913, and are highly regarded resources for legal, securities, antitrust and trade regulation, government contracting, banking, pension, payroll, employment and labor, and healthcare reimbursement and compliance professionals.

**Aspen Publishers** products provide essential information to attorneys, business professionals and law students. Written by preeminent authorities, the product line offers analytical and practical information in a range of specialty practice areas from securities law and intellectual property to mergers and acquisitions and pension/benefits. Aspen's trusted legal education resources provide professors and students with high-quality, up-to-date and effective resources for successful instruction and study in all areas of the law.

**Kluwer Law International** products provide the global business community with reliable international legal information in English. Legal practitioners, corporate counsel and business executives around the world rely on Kluwer Law journals, looseleafs, books, and electronic products for comprehensive information in many areas of international legal practice.

**Loislaw** is a comprehensive online legal research product providing legal content to law firm practitioners of various specializations. Loislaw provides attorneys with the ability to quickly and efficiently find the necessary legal information they need, when and where they need it, by facilitating access to primary law as well as state-specific law, records, forms and treatises.

**ftwilliam.com** offers employee benefits professionals the highest quality plan documents (retirement, welfare and non-qualified) and government forms (5500/PBGC, 1099 and IRS) software at highly competitive prices.

**MediRegs** products provide integrated health care compliance content and software solutions for professionals in healthcare, higher education and life sciences, including professionals in accounting, law and consulting.

Wolters Kluwer Law & Business, a division of Wolters Kluwer, is headquartered in New York. Wolters Kluwer is a market-leading global information services company focused on professionals.

# WOLTERS KLUWER LAW & BUSINESS
## SUPPLEMENT NOTICE

This product is updated on a periodic basis with supplements to reflect important changes in the subject matter. If you have purchased this product directly from Wolters Kluwer Law & Business, we have already recorded your subscription for the update service.

If, however, you purchased this product from a bookstore and wish to receive future updates and revised or related volumes billed separately with a 30-day examination review, please contact our Customer Service Department at 1-800-234-1660 or send your name, company name (if applicable), address, and the title of the product to:

**Wolters Kluwer Law & Business**
**Distribution Center**
**7201 McKinney Circle**
**Frederick, MD 21704**

---

**Important Contact Information**

- To order any title, go to *www.aspenpublishers.com* or call 1-800-638-8437.

- To reinstate your manual update service, call 1-800-638-8437.

- To contact Customer Service, e-mail *customer.service@wolterskluwer.com*, call 1-800-234-1660, fax 1-800-901-9075, or mail correspondence to: Order Department – Aspen Publishers, Wolters Kluwer Law & Business, PO Box 990, Frederick, MD 21705.

- To review your account history or pay an invoice online, visit *www.aspenpublishers.com/payinvoices*.

# CONTENTS

*A complete table of contents for each chapter
appears at the beginning of the chapter.*

**PART II**
**PENSION LAW**

**Chapter 4**
**BASIC PENSION CONCEPTS**

# CONTENTS

**Chapter 16**
**EFFECT OF CORPORATE TRANSITIONS ON PENSION AND BENEFIT PLANS**

**Chapter 17**
**PLAN TERMINATION**

# PART IV
# BENEFIT PLANS

# CONTENTS

**Index**

# PREFACE

This book, originally published in 1998, is reissued each year, in revised form, to deal with the cases, statutes, and administrative rulings affecting HR issues. This 2014 edition went to press in August 2013, so it reflects events from mid-2012 to mid-2013.

In this time period, there were few dramatic legal changes but, as usual, changes were made in areas such as tax law and ERISA compliance (including updates to correction programs).

Economic problems continued, affecting business in many ways including hiring and compensation. The process of PPACA implementation was underway (despite delays and challenges to the legality of the statute as a whole), and employers faced questions of how to provide health benefits affordably while still complying with PPACA obligations.

The Supreme Court's June 2013 decision that part of the federal Defense of Marriage Act was unconstitutional requires employers to treat legally married same-sex couples as spouses for various tax and benefit-related purposes; it will take some time for the legal system to define exactly what the implications are depending on the state in which the couples live and where they work.

The 2014 Edition is divided into 43 chapters, in eight parts:

1. Part I: Pay Planning, including compensation planning, bonuses, severance pay, and tax issues.

2. Part II: Pension Law, comprising basic pension concepts, defined benefit plans, and the transition from the predominance of defined benefit plans to the rise of defined contribution and 401(k) plans; cash balance plans; nonqualified plans; and plans for early retirement and retiree health benefits.

3. Part III: Pension Plan Administration, going from the adoption of a plan to disclosures to plan participants, handling claims and appeals, amending the plan, complying with ERISA and tax rules, handling plans in the context of corporate transitions, such as mergers and acquisitions, and terminating a plan.

4. Part IV: Benefit Plans, such as health plans, continuation coverage and portability requirements for health insurance, plans that provide insurance coverage and disability plans.

5. Part V: The HR Function, including hiring and recruitment, HR computing, recordkeeping, corporate communications, employee privacy rights, diversity issues, and work-family issues.

6. Part VI: Employee Relations, not only the major topic of labor law but also occupational safety and health, unemployment insurance, and workers' compensation.

7. Part VII: Substantive Laws Against Discrimination, focusing on Title VII (and sexual harassment, which is considered a form of sex discrimination), age discrimination, disability discrimination, the Family and Medical Leave Act, and wrongful termination suits.

8. Part VIII: Procedure for Handling Discrimination Charges, not only in the context of lawsuits brought by the EEOC, by state regulators, or by private individuals, but by using arbitration and other alternative dispute resolution methods to resolve problems without going to court.

NOTE ON WEB SOURCES: American Lawyer Media's excellent Website, http://www.law.com, uses very long URLs that are hard to cite; so does plansponsor.com. Therefore, for convenience, citations to cases and articles appearing there are simply cited to law.com; do a search for the name of the article if you'd like to retrieve it.

Unfortunately, items on the Web, and Websites themselves, can "go out of print." In some instances, by the time of the current edition of this book was ready for print, items that I had read or downloaded in the past and mentioned in the text are no longer available online or are not available to the general public. In those cases, the item is cited as "Posted to [name of cite] on [date]."

In late 2008, I switched from using the print editions of the New York Times and Wall Street Journal to using the online editions as research sources, so I no longer had access to page numbers. However, the article title should be searchable on the nytimes.com and wsj.com Websites.

PART I
# PAY PLANNING

# CHAPTER 1

# PAY PLANNING

## § 1.01   INTRODUCTION

Since 2008, employers have been facing problems of managing HR functions in a recession. It has often been necessary to lay off workers, let positions go unfilled by attrition, or cut back on benefits.

One of the most significant pay planning issues is the determination of which workers are properly classified as independent contractors, and which ones are common-law employees. For common-law employees, one of the most significant issues is which of them are entitled to receive overtime, and which ones are exempt from overtime requirements because, for example, they are administrative workers or managers. But to escape the need to pay overtime, it isn't enough merely to give a worker an inflated title if his or her work is not really professional, administrative, or supervisory. There have also been a number of cases charging Wal-Mart and other large merchandisers with failure to provide employees with the break time required by law, as well as allegations that employees have been required to "work off the clock" (be paid for less time than actually worked).

Early in 2010, in a suit alleging unpaid overtime and benefits, the Supreme Court ruled that a corporation's principal place of business is its executive office, not where its products are sold. The effect is that fewer cases can be filed in state court—and state courts are less hostile to class actions than federal courts.

Previously, federal courts used various tests. Before 1958, a corporation was only a citizen of its state of incorporation. Congress did not want local businesses to be able to escape state court suits by incorporating out of state, so the federal rules of civil procedure were amended to make a corporation a citizen both of its state of incorporation and where it had its principal place of business. However, the statute did not define the company's principal place of business, and the Courts of Appeals had different standards. [*Hertz v. Friend*, 559 U.S. 77 (2010)]

In March 2010, as part of the economic recovery effort, the Hiring Incentives to Restore Employment (HIRE) Act was enacted, with a 6.2% payroll tax incentive (the employer's share of FICA tax was waived for the period February 3, 2010–January 1, 2011). Employers could also receive a general business tax credit of up to $1,000 per worker if the worker remained on the payroll for at least a year. [Rebecca Moore, *New Law Offers Tax Incentives for Hiring*, plansponsor.com (Mar. 18, 2010). See <http://www.plansponsor.com/New_Law_Offers_Tax_Incentives_for_Hiring.aspx>, discussed in McGuireWood LLP, *IRS Issues Additional FAQs for HIRE Act* (May 6, 2010) (benefitslink.com), for the IRS's three FAQ postings about payroll tax issues in May 2010.]

In late 2010, Congress took another approach to using tax incentives to increase hiring: reducing the employee's, but not the employer's, FICA rate. The Tax Relief, Unemployment Insurance Reauthorization, and Job Creation Act of 2010, Pub. L. No. 111-312 set the employee FICA rate at 4.2%, with the employer rate reverting to 6.2%, plus Medicare tax at a rate of 1.45% each for employer and employee. The wage base at that time was $106,800. The Making Work Pay credit expired December 31, 2010.The Temporary Payroll Tax Cut Continuation Act retained the 4.2% FICA rate for employees through the end of February 2012. This statute imposed a 2% recapture tax (capping the amount of wages eligible for the payroll tax cut at $18,350). A subsequent statue, the Middle Class Tax Relief and Job Creation Act of 2012, enacted February 22, 2012, Pub. L. No. 112-96, retained the 4.2% employee rate—a payroll tax cut that was estimated to benefit 160 million workers—and repealed the $18,350 limitation. However, the payroll tax cut was permitted to expire. [<http://www.irs.gov/pub/irs-pdf/f941.pdf>; see Rebecca Moore, *Payroll Tax Cut Extended, IRS Issues Revised Form*, plansponsor.com (Feb. 24, 2012); Naftali Bendavid and Siobhan Hughes, *Congress Reaches Payroll-Tax Deal*, WSJ.com (Feb. 16, 2012)] High-income employees ($250,000 income on a joint return, $200,000 for single, head of household, surviving spouse with a dependent child, $125,000 for married persons filing separately) are subject to additional Medicare tax; this portion of the tax is applied only to the employee, with no employer match.

The Sixth Circuit held in 2012 that payments to employees who are terminated involuntarily because of business cessation are not FICA wages—i.e., conflicting with the Federal Circuit's earlier holding. The Sixth Circuit held that SUB payments are not "wages" subject to income tax withholding and therefore are not wages for FICA purposes. [*United States v. Quality Stores, Inc.*, 693 F.3d 605 (6th Cir. 2012); see Miller & Chevalier, *The Sixth Circuit's Affirmance of Quality Stores Splits the Circuits as to the FICA Tax Treatment of Severance Pay: Next Steps for Employers?* (Sept. 13, 2012) (benefitslink.com)] On October 18, 2012, the Department of Justice filed a petition for en banc rehearing of this decision. The Sixth Circuit's rules treat en banc rehearings as extraordinary procedures, restricted to cases of exceptional importance to the public or to review opinions that directly conflict with a Supreme Court ruling or an earlier Sixth Circuit precedent. [Mary B. Hevener, David R. Fuller, Steven P. Johnson, Patrick Rehfield, and Robert R. Martinelli, *Quality Stores, Inc. Update*, Morgan, Lewis & Bockius LawFlash (Oct. 24, 2012) (law.com)]

FICA does not apply to work done by "students" who work for their educational institution. A 2004 Treasury regulation says that a full-time employee is not considered a student, even if the work has a training aspect. The regulation uses medical residents as an example of trainees who are considered full-time workers subject to FICA rather than students. The Mayo Foundation for Medical Education and Research sued to challenge the application of this rule to medical residents who are scheduled to work more than 40 hours per week. The Supreme Court upheld the rule, treating it as a reasonable construction of the statute. [*Mayo Foundation for Med. Research v. United States*, 131 S. Ct. 704 (2011); see Buck Consultants FYI, *Supreme Court Upholds Treasury Rule That Medical Residents Are Employees for FICA Purposes* (Jan. 21, 2011) (benefitslink.com)]

## [A]  SEC Regulation of Compensation

At the beginning of 2006, the Securities and Exchange Commission (SEC) voted to increase the amount of disclosure that public corporations must make about the pay packages of top management. The SEC finalized the proposal on July 26, 2006. The final rule requires publication of both tables of top management compensation and narrative disclosure of three years' worth of compensation. Public companies must use the Compensation Discussion and Analysis (which will be filed with the SEC, so the CEO and CFO must certify it) to disclose the compensation for top management. The value of equity-based awards such as stock options must be disclosed, and the SEC required disclosure of timing of option grants, as a way to deter back-dating. A similar disclosure format is required for compensation of directors. The final rule, like the proposal, increases the size of related-person transactions that must be disclosed ($120,000 rather than the prior rule of $60,000). Public companies must disclose the extent to which directors are independent, and must reveal more about officers' and directors' holdings of the company's own stock. [SEC Press Release, *SEC Votes to Adopt Changes to Disclosure Requirements Concerning Executive Compensation and Related Matters*, <http://www.sec.gov/news/press/2006/2006-123.htm> (July 26, 2006), finalizing provisions proposed in Rel. Nos. 33-8655, 34-53185, and IC-27218 (2006).]

Early in 2011, the SEC published the shareholder Say on Pay rules required by the Dodd-Frank Act (Pub. L. No. 111-203). The shareholder vote is nonbinding, but the intention is that corporations would be too embarrassed to continue a policy that was disapproved by its stockholders. The rules also allow shareholders to vote on certain golden parachutes in connection with mergers and acquisitions, and require the corporations to make more extensive disclosures about the compensation packages for top executives. [Rebecca Moore, *SEC Adopts Say on Pay Rules*, plansponsor.com (Jan. 25, 2011)] The compensation packages nearly always obtain shareholder approval.

As of August, there were 2,780 Say on Pay votes in 2013. Only 57 failed. The average vote was 90% for the proposal, 8% against, 2% abstentions. [Steven Hall & Partners, *2013 Say on Pay Voting Results*, <http://www.shallpartners.com/our-thinking/short-takes/2013-say-on-pay-voting-results/> (last accessed May 22, 2013)]

The Conference Board's report, *Proxy Voting Analytics (2008-2012)* available on the organization's Website, shows that, since the say on pay rules took effect, there have been fewer shareholder proposals on executive compensation and shareholders are more engaged with their companies. The say on pay process can be a catalyst for better communications with investors. The specific say on pay mechanism means that it is no longer necessary to launch generic compensation proposals. In 2008, there were 193 shareholder proposals dealing with executive compensation, dropping to 65 in 2011 (the year say on pay took effect), rising again to 92 in 2012. [Catherine Dunn, *Analysis of Proxy Voting*

*Data Looks at Say-on-Pay, Shareholder Engagement,* Corporate Counsel (Jan. 30, 2013) (law.com)]

Say on pay cases usually allege that the corporation announces a pay-for-performance philosophy but actually increases executive compensation despite poor performance. In effect, the plaintiffs question the board's business judgment. If there is an independent compensation consultant in the picture, plaintiffs tend to allege that the consultants breached their contracts by failing to provide adequate advice and aiding and abetting the breach of fiduciary duty in overpaying for poor performance.

According to the Wall Street Journal/Hay Group Survey of CEO Compensation, which uses data from 300 large public companies, for 51 CEOs, at least half of their 2012 compensation was tied to specific targets based on the company's financial performance or its stock market results. In 2009, only about one-third of CEO compensation was subject to performance conditions; the rest came from salaries and stock and option grants that were not subject to performance criteria. Even though over 95% of companies prevail in their "say on pay" votes, corporate policy is now shaped by the desire to avoid offending the company's stockholders. In 2012, median total direct compensation for CEOs rose 6.9%, to $9 million—somewhat less than the median 7.6% shareholder return for those companies. Median net income at a sample of 40 major companies fell 3.9% in 2011, resulting in a 7.6% drop in CEO annual bonuses. For example, Smithfield Foods' income fell 31% and its share price dropped 11%. The CEO's bonus formula was reduced by 34%, although he still received a $4.7 million bonus. He was not granted any stock options for 2011, and some stock awards in the future will be based on the relative performance of Smithfield's stock vis-à-vis its competitors. Farient Advisors (a consulting firm that specializes in pay issues) says that only one-fifth of the companies in the S&P 1500 subjected their equity grants to performance criteria in 2002, whereas almost two-thirds (64%) did so in 2011. In 2013, Johnson & Johnson cut the bonuses its top executives received for 2012 by 10%, reflecting mixed results in the stock market. Shareholder activists now have a new target: determining if the company's compensation structure creates the proper relationship between pay and performance.[Scott Thurm, *'Pay for Performance' No Longer a Punchline,* WSJ.com (Mar. 20, 2013)]

Suits have also been filed against top management, directors, and outside compensation consultants for causes of action such as breach of fiduciary duty, aiding and abetting breach of contract, and unjust enrichment. Fiduciary duty claims may involve the duty of loyalty and perhaps candor, good faith, and independence. These cases usually do not mention the duty of care—perhaps because some state statutes, such as Delaware General Corporation Law § 102(b)(7), provide defenses or allow corporations to indemnify their managers.

Before the shareholder vote, the company should decide how it will disclose a negative shareholder vote, and what will be said in the Form 8-K that discloses the results of the vote. If the vote is negative, some or all independent directors could be directed to examine executive pay, and stock awards and options could be made contingent on performance.

It is not uncommon for companies close to bankruptcy to pay bonuses to management shortly before a bankruptcy filing. The Wall Street Journal's research showed that in, in more than 80 Chapter 11 bankruptcy cases 2007–2012, more than 1,600 insiders received compensation, including bonuses and fees, totaling more than $1.3 billion in the months before the filing. Retention bonuses after a filing are regulated by federal law; those before filing are not. After union protests, Hostess reversed salary increases given to top management five months before the company's bankruptcy filing. [Mike Spector, Tom McGinty and Rachel Feintzeig, *In Trouble and Paying Out*, WSJ.com (Dec. 3, 2012)]

In mid-2011, the D.C. Circuit vacated Rule 14a-11, the proxy access rule, which would have permitted some shareholders to write in their nominees for the board of directors. The D.C. Circuit found that the SEC exceeded its discretion in adopting this rule. [*Business Roundtable & Chamber of Commerce v. SEC*, 647 F.3d 1144 (D.C. Cir. 2011)]

## [B]  TARP Restrictions

Restrictions on executive pay were first imposed by the Emergency Economic Stabilization Act of 2008 (EESA) Pub. L. No. 110-343, which set up a program for the federal government to purchase troubled assets from financial institutions. Institutions that transferred "toxic" assets to the federal government under the Troubled Asset Relief Program (TARP) had to agree to limits on deductions for compensation and bonuses for their top managers. Companies participating in TARP could not use certain types of golden parachutes; had to restrict their severance arrangements for top managers; and had to seek "clawback" (repayment) of certain sums paid to top managers if the payments were based on incorrect financial figures. [See, e.g., Buck Research FYI, *Executive Compensation Under the Emergency Economic Stabilization Act of 2008* (Oct. 20, 2008) (benefitslink.com)]

Additional restrictions were imposed by the American Recovery and Reinvestment Act of 2009 (ARRA), Pub. L. No. 111-5. Limits were imposed on top management's bonuses, retention awards, golden parachutes, and incentive compensation. [See Interim Final Rule, 73 Fed. Reg. 62205 (Oct. 20, 2008), finalized at 74 Fed. Reg. 28393 (June 15, 2009)] The TARP program ended in October 2010.

Public companies are subject to the requirements of Code § 162(m). The general rule is that only $1 million in compensation is deductible for the company's CEO and each of its four other highest-compensated officers. The $1 million limit does not apply to qualified performance-based compensation, that is only paid if the payee meets at least one objective performance goal that was set in advance. The performance-based compensation must have been ordered either by the company's board or a compensation committee consisting of outside directors, and the terms of the plan are disclosed to, and approved by, the shareholders in advance. In mid-2012, the IRS issued guidance on whether dividends on restricted stock, and the equivalent on RSUs, must satisfy the § 162(m) requirements separately to be treated as fully deductible performance-based compensation: Rev. Rul. 2012-19, 2012-28 I.R.B. 16.

Restricted stock is company stock that is released based on a vesting schedule, whereas RSUs are a right to get vested stock in the future. Usually, restricted stock carries voting rights but RSUs do not. Some companies make "dividend equivalent" payments on RSUs: cash payments equivalent to the dividends on the restricted stock for the period between the grant and the vesting date. Rev. Rul. 2012-19 says that, to qualify for exemption from the $1 million exemption, the dividends or dividend equivalents can only be payable if the payee meets performance goals. However, the performance goals for this purpose do not have to be the same ones for granting the underlying restricted stock or RSUs. [Buck Consultants FYI, *IRS Clarifies Treatment of Performance-Based Restricted Stock and Restricted Stock Units* (Aug. 8, 2012) (benefitslink.com)]

The Sarbanes-Oxley Act, EESA, and AARA also call for "clawback": companies must recover from the payee any bonus or incentive compensation that was paid to a top executive on the basis of false financial reporting, and compensation plans must not encourage future false reporting that would lead to higher compensation. The Treasury has the authority to review bonuses, retention awards, etc., paid to top management. If the Treasury deems the payments to have been inconsistent with the purposes of the TARP program, it can negotiate with the company and the recipients of the compensation about appropriate reimbursement to the U.S. government.

## § 1.02   DECISION FACTORS IN SETTING COMPENSATION

A business's compensation policies reflect many factors:

- What the business can afford to pay;

- Competitive factors (other local companies competing for workers, prevailing wages, unemployment rates);

- Impact on cash flow (until recently, cash-poor companies with bright prospects often relied heavily on stock options and/or the potential for an IPO as elements of compensation);

- Effect on future financing (venture capitalists who expect one-third of the shares in a new business, or a business receiving later rounds of funding, will not want too many of the shares to be assigned to employees);

- The compensation package favored by the kind of workers the employer wants to attract. If the objective is to minimize turnover, for instance, workers with families will place a high value on health benefits, whereas more mobile younger workers will tend to favor higher cash compensation and pension portability;

- Tax factors for both employer and employee; the objective is for the employer to get the highest permissible deduction and for the employee to retain as much as possible after taxes.

The year 2012, was the second year in a row that CEO pay in the Russell 300 index increased. In 2011, the median for CEOs' total realized pay was 15% higher than in 2010. In the S&P 500, the average CEO earned $12.1 million, about 12% higher than in 2010; The CEOs at S&P mid-cap companies earned an average of $6.4 million in 2011, up 17% over 2010, and S&P small-cap CEOs earned a 2011 average of $3.5 million, 28% more than 2010. [Catherine Dunne, *Study Shows CEO Pay Up for Second Year in a Row*, Corporate Counsel (May 9, 2012) (law.com)]

Inequality continues to become more marked. In April 2013, the Department of Labor (DOL) reported that, after adjusting for inflation, low-paid workers' wages declined, but compensation of highly paid workers has increased faster than inflation. Using 2013 dollars, the national median wage in 2000 was $819; in 2013, it was $827. The median income of college graduates in 2013 was $1,189 a week—1% less than the median in 2000, using constant dollars. [Floyd Norris, *Wage Disparity Continues to Grow*, NYTimes.com (Apr. 26, 2013)]

According to the Institute for Women's Policy Research, the wage gap between male and female workers remained fundamentally unchanged between 2009 and 2010: women earned 77% as much as men in 2009, 77.4% in 2010. In 2010, women's median weekly earnings for full-time work were 81.2% of what similarly situated males earned; there were more female than male part-time workers, including involuntary part-time workers. The median earnings of Hispanic women were only 54.5% of white men's median earnings; for black women, the corresponding ratio was 62.8%. [Tara Cantore, *Men Continue to Outpace Women in Earnings*, plansponsor.com (Sept. 16, 2011)]

A White House report released March 1, 2011 concluded that, although women are gaining ground economically, men still make more money on the average and women are more likely to be in poverty. Younger women are more likely than younger men to have college degrees or Master's degrees, but there is still a gender gap in compensation. Single-mother households are more common than single-father households, implying more poverty for women. Labor force participation rate for women 20 or over doubled over the past half century, and is stable at 61%. However, women have a disproportionate share of administrative jobs, and fewer higher paying computer and engineering jobs than men. In 2009, on average, women made 75% of male wages. [Conor Dougherty, *Women Advance, Still Lag on Wages*, WSJ.com (Mar. 1, 2011)]

For discussion of the federal Equal Pay Act (29 U.S.C. § 206) see § 34.06[C].

## [A]  Coping with the Downturn

Since the stock market crash of 2008, many businesses looked for ways to cut the size of their workforce, and to reduce the number of hours worked (e.g., by implementing furloughs).

Theoretically, closing the workplace one day a week would cut payroll costs by 14% (for seven-day operation) or 20% (for businesses open five days a week). Non-exempt employees are paid only for actual hours worked. But some exempt employees might become non-exempt if the reduction in hours reduces their compensation below the $455/week federal test. Exempt employees must be paid their full salary for any week in which they work at all. But an exempt worker can trigger payment of a week's salary, even when the office is closed, for example, by checking work-related e-mails, so exempts should be instructed not to do any work during a furlough without advance written approval.

The DOL has issued an opinion letter permitting employers to require exempt employees to use accrued vacation time for a shutdown that lasts less than one workweek. Adopting this expedient will not violate the FLSA or make the worker non-exempt. The DOL's rationale is that employers are not required to provide vacation time at all, so they can offer paid vacation but control when it is taken. However, if an exempt employee who has no available accrued vacation time does any work at all during a week, the employer must pay his or her full salary. [James P. Thomas, Pepper Hamilton LLP, *Department of Labor: Employees May Be Required to Use Accrued Vacation During Shutdown Periods* (Mar. 17, 2009) (benefitslink.com)]

Even before 2012 federal legislation encouraged the development of work-sharing programs (where employees whose hours have been cut can receive partial unemployment insurance benefits), 22 states and the District of Columbia had such programs. A fall 2011 Wall Street Journal article profiles Rhode Island's Pilgrim Screw Company, which had 11 of its 65 employees reduce their workweek by one day a week. Those 11 workers received 20% of the unemployment benefit they would have received if they had been unemployed. As a result of the program, no worker lost his or her job. Although many of the work-sharing programs had been in existence for decades, they were seldom used until the recession when interest in work sharing grew; five states have adopted such programs since 2009. [Justin LaHart, *Work Sharing Gains Traction in Rhode Island, Elsewhere*, WSJ.com (Nov. 21, 2011)]

## § 1.03  BENEFITS AS AN ELEMENT OF COMPENSATION

The accepted rule of thumb is that the cost of benefits adds about one-third to the employee's stated salary.

The size of the benefit package is often directly related to the size of the company. Generally, for any particular benefit, the percentage of companies offering that benefit increases with the size of the workforce, and it is also often true that larger companies offer a more generous benefit package.

In general, unionized workers have access to more benefits than non-unionized workers, and pay and benefits tend to be lower in the South than in other regions.

In December 2012, private industry employers spent an average of $28.89/hour for total employee compensation, consisting of: 70.3% wages and salaries ($20.32) and 29.7% benefits ($8.57). Paid leave benefits represented 6.9% of total compensation, at $1.98/hour, consisting of vacation pay, 3.6% ($1.03), holidays 2.1% (61 cents), and sick leave 25 cents/hour (0.9%). Legally required benefits accounted for 8.2% of compensation, or $2.37/hour, with Social Security the largest amount at 4.7%, $1.36/hour. Workers' Compensation costs averaged 41 cents/hour (1.4%), Medicare 33 cents (1.2%), state unemployment insurance 23 cents (0.8%), federal unemployment insurance 3 cents (0.1%). Private industry employers spent an average of 8.2% of compensation, $2.36/hour for life, health, and disability insurance. Defined benefit and defined compensation plans accounted for 3.6% of pay, $1.05 per hour, with supplemental pay such as overtime premiums and shift differentials accounting for a further 82 cents, or 2.8% of compensation. [BLS Economic News Release, *December 2012 Employer Costs for Employee Compensation*, USDL-13-0421, <http://data.bls.gov/cgi-bin/print.pl/news.release/ecec.nr0.htm> (Mar. 12, 2013)]

Several jurisdictions have mandated various kinds of paid leave. For example, New Jersey requires up to six weeks of paid family leave. [Nevin E. Adams, *Family Leave Bill Gets Thumbs Up in NJ*, plansponsor.com (Apr. 9, 2008); Joao-Pierre Ruth, *State Halves Family Leave Tax on Employees*, NJBIZ.com (Nov. 9, 2010) (benefitslink.com)]

Paid leave bills with various amounts of coverage have been passed in California, Connecticut (limited to non-exempt service workers), Maine, Minnesota, and Washington State. In addition to state requirements, some cities (e.g., San Francisco, Seattle, and Washington, D.C.) have laws requiring employers to provide paid sick leave.) Alaska and the District of Columbia forbid discrimination against caregivers. [Buck Consultants FYI, *Washington State Expands Employee Leave Entitlements* (May 19, 2008) (benefitslink.com); MorganLewis newsletter, *Maryland, District of Columbia Pass New Employee Leave Laws* (Aug. 1, 2008) (benefitslink.com); Mercer Select US, *Washington to Delay Paid Parental Leave Implementation* (May 8, 2009) (benefitslink.com); Morgan-Lewis newsletter, *Maryland, District of Columbia Pass New Employee Leave Laws* (Aug. 1, 2008) (benefitslink.com); Sarah E. Needleman, *Seattle Adopts Paid Sick Leave Mandate*, WSJ.com (Sept. 13, 2011); Jason Stanevich and Jennai Williams, Littler Mendelson ASAP, *Connecticut is First State to Mandate Paid Sick Leave for Service Workers* (June 2011) (benefitslink.com); Jackson Lewis LLP

Workplace Resource Center, *Seattle's New Paid Leave Law* (Aug. 13, 2012) (benefitslink.com)]

In mid-2013, the New York Times reported that, although many business owners dislike paid leave laws, there has been little detrimental effect. Very small businesses are often exempt; and many businesses provided at least some paid sick leave even before the laws were passed. Among businesses that had to implement leave policies, about half said that it was not difficult to administer leave and the leave requirement increased payroll costs by about 1%–2&%. [Robb Mandelbaum, *Paid Sick Leave Laws Generate Concern, But Not Much Pain*, NYTimes.com (July 3, 2013)]

The Centers for Disease Control found that, for the period 2005–2008, the non-fatal injury rate was 2.59 per hundred workers with paid sick leave, 4.18 per hundred workers who did not have access to paid sick leave. Even after adjusting for variables such as the industry, sex, and education, workers with paid sick leave were 28% less likely to have a non-fatal injury. Lower injury rates benefit employers as well as employees, by reducing Worker's Compensation premiums. [Nicholas Bakalar, *Paid Sick Leave May Reduce Work Injuries*, NYTimes.com (Aug. 6, 2012)] Massachusetts, Connecticut, Florida, Georgia, and New Jersey courts have held that forfeiture of discretionary awards does not violate state wage laws (e.g., laws that require weekly payment of wages). [Rebecca Moore, *Court Rules Forfeiture of Incentive Does Not Violate State Wage Law*, plansponsor.com (Feb. 4, 2009)]

## § 1.04  AVOIDING DISCRIMINATION

The Equal Employment Opportunity Commission (EEOC) Compliance Manual contains a section dealing with compensation issues in the context of various antidiscrimination statutes. The EEOC's position is that antidiscrimination laws apply to all aspects of compensation, including salary, overtime, bonuses, options, profit sharing, fringe benefits, and expense accounts. The agency says that employers are never justified in taking race, color, sex, national origin, religion, age, or disability into account in setting compensation.

The EEOC says that equal severance benefits are required for all similarly situated employees, regardless of age. Employers may not deny severance because the employee is eligible for a pension, although sometimes pension benefits can be offset against the severance pay. Denying recall rights to older workers operates as involuntary retirement. Because the cost of providing severance pay does not rise with the employees' ages, employers are not allowed to assert an equal cost defense.

However, retiree health benefits can legitimately be offset against severance if the retiree is eligible for an immediate pension; if he actually receives health benefit coverage; and the retiree benefits are at least comparable to Medicare in type and value. If the retiree is over 65, benefits must be at least comparable to one-fourth the value of Medicare benefits. The offset itself must be reduced by any percentage by which the pension is reduced for retirement before normal retirement age, and by any percentage of the premium that the retiree has to pay for retiree health coverage.

The Compliance Manual says that "if the employer provides additional pension benefits that are enough, or are higher than those necessary to bring an employee up to the level of an unreduced pension, the employer can offset the full amount of those benefits. On the other hand, if the employer offers benefits that are insufficient to raise the employee to an unreduced pension, the employer cannot claim any offset at all."

The Eleventh Circuit reversed the district court's refusal to certify a RICO (Racketeer Influenced and Corrupt Organizations Act) class action in a case alleging that Mohawk used temporary agencies to hire illegal aliens to keep down wages. The Eleventh Circuit found a common question of whether Mohawk acted in concert with others in a pattern of illegal activities to reduce wages. [*Williams v. Mohawk Indus.*, 568 F.3d 1350 (11th Cir. 2009), *cert. denied*, 130 S. Ct. 500 (Dec. 8, 2009); see Fred Schneyer, *Employer May Have to Face More Plaintiffs in Wage and Hour Dispute*, plansponsor.com (June 16, 2009)]

Employers that need to cut costs often use a Reduction in Force (RIF) for this purpose. However, RIFs must be handled carefully to avoid findings that they were used selectively to eliminate employees who were the victims of discrimination. In order to carry out a Reduction in Force that complies with applicable laws, employers must document the preliminary steps to cut costs that were taken before the RIF. Increasing the compensation and benefits of top management when jobs are being cut looks suspicious. Discretionary spending on items such as office parties and corporate jets should probably be reduced before a RIF is instituted.

There are also alternatives such as hiring freezes, shorter workweeks, and furloughs. Management should document the steps that were taken, and that alternatives were considered but were not adopted for reasons that are fully documented. Voluntary exit programs can be used as an alternative to layoffs—either company-wide, in a particular division or unit, or a voluntary early retirement program could be offered to employees with a certain amount of age and service. (The risk is that employees the company wants to retain might opt for early retirement.) The economic necessity for a RIF should be documented (e.g., industry conditions, loss of a major contract, so fewer workers are required).

The ADEA provides a safe harbor for early retirement programs that are truly voluntary, but suits might still be filed if a participant claims the program was not really voluntary or if it is not consistent with the purposes of the ADEA. It is important to train managers not to make statements that could be interpreted as threatening to employees who are reluctant to retire. The most common employee claims about layoffs involve age discrimination, so the employer must be prepared to prove what the criteria were for selecting employees for RIFs, and that the criteria were appropriate and job-related. The least problematic structure is work elimination (eliminating an entire department or function) because personal selections are not made. A number of cases say that it is impossible to prove a prima facie case of discrimination when a whole job or department is eliminated.

If individual selections for RIF are made, there must be well-defined selection criteria that are uniformly applied within a department or group. In unionized businesses, it may be necessary to observe seniority. Performance ratings seem to be objective, but employees can argue that the evaluators were biased in rating performance. It is wise to train line managers not to assume that employees close to retirement age intend to retire, and it is not good practice to ask them about their retirement plans (in case they think they are being forced out of the company). Line managers should document their selection criteria and how employees were chosen for RIF or retained.

Mass layoffs may require notice under the WARN Act or its state counterparts. In unionized businesses, it is an Unfair Labor Practice for management to act unilaterally about wages, hours, and other terms and conditions of employment; it is necessary at least to bargain to an impasse before making changes. The NLRB's position is that a layoff for economic reasons (rather than layoffs based on a fundamental change in the organization's business) require prior bargaining about the decision and its implementation. [Alison B. Marshall and Julie M. Broas, *Getting It Right in Reductions in Force: How to Minimize Legal Risks*, Employee Benefit Plan Review (May 2009) (benefitslink.com)]

## § 1.05 VARIABLE PAY

A variable pay system makes part of the compensation dependent on meeting goals or targets. Because these plans are supposed to create incentives for better work, communication is key. Formal annual review explaining how the award was calculated is useful to pinpoint areas in which employees succeeded and those in which more work is necessary. The most effective plans had "moderate stretch" (i.e., they asked employees to achieve targets that were not impossible, but were not comfortably in view either).

It is important to make it clear whether the variable compensation is a commission on sales or a bonus, and whether the employee is entitled to a specific amount or percentage, or whether the variable pay award is discretionary with management and whether it is contingent on anything (e.g., continued employment with the same company). In some states, sales commissions are considered vested and must be paid when the employee quits or is terminated. [Rebecca E. Ivey and Rebecca Williams Shanlever, Troutman Sanders LLP, *Easy Come, Easy Go: State Rules on Post-Termination Forfeitures of Bonuses and Commissions* (Apr. 12, 2010) (benefitslink.com)]

In mid-2010, the Connecticut Supreme Court ruled that an attorney's year-end bonus was not "wages" as defined by the Connecticut Wage Act, so statutory double damages and attorneys' fees were not available. An amount is treated as wages if entitlement is based on specific definable goals such as billing a certain number of client hours per year—but does not constitute wages if payment of the bonus is discretionary and based on something like the employer's determination that it has had a financially successful year. [*Ziotas v. Reardon Law Firm PC*, 296 Conn. 579 (2010); see Thomas B. Scheffey, *Employers May Benefit from Lawyers' Feud Over Bonus*, Connecticut Law Tribune (June 18, 2010) (law.com)]

In 2012, the New York Court of Appeals held that a job offer to a financial services executive included an oral promise of a guaranteed $175,000 bonus, so when he was fired, the bonus constituted "wages," and he could collect attorneys' fees under the New York statute that calls for an award of attorneys' fees when "wages" are not paid on time. [*Ryan v. Kellogg Partners Institutional Servs.*, 19 N.Y.3d 1 (N.Y. 2012)]

## § 1.06  WAGE AND HOUR ISSUES

The HR department's many and varied responsibilities probably include handling (or outsourcing and supervising) payroll matters, including paying employees subject to the appropriate deductions.

The Fair Labor Standards Act (FLSA) [29 U.S.C. §§ 201–219 and 251–262] regulates wages and hour matters. The FLSA forbids sex discrimination in compensation, sets a minimum wage, requires extra pay when a "non-exempt" worker puts in overtime hours, and sets standards for record keeping and record retention. The Department of Labor's Wage and Hour Division is responsible for administering the FLSA. In mid-2006, the Wage and Hour Division added a feature to its Website: a search engine listing companies that owe back pay to workers; former employees of such companies can submit proof of identity to the Division and collect payments. The site is located at <http://cslxwepl .dol-esa/gov/emploc/>. [Fred Schneyer, *DOL Unveils Back Pay Search Engine*, plansponsor.com (June 1, 2006)] See <http://www.dol.gov/elaws/otcalculator .htm>, the DOL Wage & Hour Division's Web tool for calculating overtime pay, based on various scenarios including bonuses, commissions, and shift differentials. [Adrien Martin, *DOL Unveils Web-based Overtime Pay Calculator*, plansponsor.com (May 9, 2007)]

DOL's Wage & Hour Division (WHD) receives over 35,000 complaints a year, so even though the agency has added 350 new investigators, it cannot fully pursue all complaints. As of December 13, 2010, when the WHD decides not to pursue an FLSA or FMLA complaint, the complainants will be given a toll-free number for the LRIS (the ABA's Lawyer Referral and Information Service). The complainant will be notified of the WHD's determination about the violations at issue and back wages owed, so the complainant's lawyer can use the information. WHD says that it has a procedure to expedite sending relevant case information and documents to complainants and their lawyers. [Rebecca Moore, *DOL Started Attorney Referral System for FLSA Claims*, plansponsor.com (Feb. 7, 2011)]

The Center for Urban Economic Development (University of Illinois), the National Employment Law Project, and the UCLA Institute on Research on Labor and Employment released a 72-page study in September 2009. "Broken Laws,

Unprotected Workers: Violations of Employment and Labor Laws in America's Cities" is based on interviews with workers in New York, Chicago, and Los Angeles. The report estimates that, each week, more than a million workers in the three cities experience at least one pay-based violation, costing them over $56.4 million per week, with widespread failures to pay proper overtime, frequent failures to pay the minimum wage, and failure to provide the full amount (often, to provide any) of statutorily required break time. According to the author, Annette Bernhardt of the National Employment Law Project, violations were found in almost every major industry.

Women were much more likely than men to be the victims of minimum wage violations, and foreign-born workers were almost twice as likely to be victimized as U.S.-born workers. [Tresa Baldas, *Wage-and-Hour Complaints Head for a Company Near You*, Nat'l L.J. (Sept. 9, 2009) (law.com)]

A number of cases involving Starbucks raise questions about appropriate division of tip pools—part of the broader question of who is a "supervisor." In mid-2009, the California Court of Appeal held that shift supervisors should not be considered agents of the owner because they usually do the same work as the baristas and can keep individual tips, so they should be allowed to share in the tip pool. [*Chau v. Starbucks Corp.*, 174 Cal. App. 4th 688 (Cal. App. 2009); see Mike McKee, *Court Dumps Grounds for $86 Million Verdict Against Starbucks*, The Recorder (June 3, 2009) (law.com)]

The First Circuit affirmed class certification and an award of over $14 million in damages ($7.5 million in damages plus 12% prejudgment interest per year, plus $6.6 million treble damages with respect to tips collected by shift supervisors contrary to the July 12, 2008 amendments to the Massachusetts Tips Act) in a suit about Starbucks' policy on tip pooling. The Massachusetts Tips Act forbids having waitstaff share their tips with anyone who is not a member of the waitstaff. The Tips Act says that the waitstaff are workers who do not have any managerial responsibilities. Starbucks took the position that shift supervisors do not have managerial responsibility and spend 90% of their time doing the same work as other baristas, so they are entitled to share the tips. The First Circuit rejected this argument: shift supervisors have to open and close the store, account for cash, and supervise baristas' break schedule. [*Matamoros v. Starbucks*, 699 F.3d 129 (1st Cir. 2012); see Sheri Qualters, *First Circuit Affirms Win for Starbucks Baristas Over Tip-Sharing*, Nat'l LJ (Nov. 12, 2012) (law.com)]

Instead of settling the question of whether assistant store managers should share in the Starbucks tip pool, the Second Circuit certified the question to the New York Court of Appeals. [*Barenboim v. Starbucks/Winans v. Starbucks*, 698 F.3d 104 (2d Cir. 2012)]. The New York Court of Appeals' answer, in 2013, was that shift supervisors, as workers with some supervisory duties, but who primarily serve customers, might be entitled to share in the tip pool. However, assistant managers are not entitled to share tips, because they have too much managerial authority. [*Barenboim v. Starbucks Corp.*, No. 122 (N.Y. 2013)]

California's Labor Code § 351 makes tips the sole property of the employee or employees for whom the tip was left, and it is illegal for employers to take the gratuity. However, California has ruled that this prohibition does not extend to tip pooling required by the employer. A card dealer brought a class action against a casino challenging a mandatory tip pool. The California Supreme Court ruled that there is no private cause of action to sue under Labor Code § 351—enforcement can only be done by the Department of Industrial Relations charging the employer with a misdemeanor. [*Lu v. Hawaiian Gardens Casino, Inc.*, 50 Cal. 4th 592 (2010); see Mike McKee, *Calif. High Court Tips Hand on Suits Over Gratuities*, The Recorder (May 27, 2010) (law.com); Kate Moser, *Calif. Justices Find No Private Right to Sue for Tip-Pooling Violations*, The Recorder (Aug. 11, 2010) (law.com)]

A 2010 New York statute, the New York State Wage Theft Prevention Act (S. 8380), amending New York Labor Law § 195 with respect to wage notice requirements, took effect April 9, 2011. It requires employers to give employees written notice (when they are hired and each year thereafter) of matters such as their regular payday, regular pay rate, overtime rate, commissions, etc. Employees can sue if they do not receive the required notice, and the Commissioner of Labor can also enforce the statute; criminal penalties are possible. Furthermore, the Commissioner can impose a civil penalty of up to $10,000 for retaliation, and retaliation is a misdemeanor. [John P. Furfaro, *New State Laws Cover Wage Notices, Tips, Independent Contractor Status*, N.Y.L.J. (Feb. 4, 2010) (law.com)]

The Southern District of New York certified a class of waiter/captains who alleged that they were forced to share their tips with employees who were not eligible for tips and that they were not given the required extra hour's pay for working over 10 hours in a shift. The plaintiffs brought an FLSA collective action and a putative class action under the New York Labor Law. The Second Circuit affirmed the certification of the class. The FLSA allows the employer to take a tip credit of up to 50% of the minimum wage, but this cannot exceed the tips actually received. As of January 1, 2011, the New York Labor Law limits the tip credit to $2.25. The FLSA forbids employers to use the tip credit if tipped employees are required to share their tips with non-tipped employees, such as managers or employees, who do not provide direct customer service and New York law has a similar provision. FLSA collective actions are opt-in, and New York class actions are opt-out, so the issue in this case was whether it was proper for the federal court to hear the New York claims at the same time. The Second Circuit held that the cases could be combined because they involved the same basic facts. The Third, Seventh, Ninth, and D.C. Circuits have allowed federal courts to combine state class actions with an FLSA collective action. [*Shahriar v. Smith Wollensky Rest. Group*, 659 F.3d 234 (2d Cir. 2011). See also *Knepper v. Rite Aid Corp.*, 675 F.3d 249 (3d Cir. 2012); *Ervin v. OS Rest. Servs. Inc.*, 632 F.3d 971 (7th Cir. 2011); *Wang v. Chinese Daily News*, 623 F.3d 743 (9th Cir. 2010), *vacated on other grounds*, 132 S. Ct. 74 (2011); *Lindsay v. Government Employees' Ins. Co.*, 448 F.3d 416 (D.C. Cir. 2006).]

The FLSA says that suit may be maintained in either state or federal court. In mid-2003, the Supreme Court interpreted this to mean that an FLSA suit for unpaid wages, liquidated damages, interest, and attorney's fees can be removed by the defendant employer from state to federal court. Just because the suit may be maintained in either system doesn't prevent removal, or require a case to remain in the same system from beginning to end. [*Breuer v. Jim's Concrete of Brevard Inc.*, 538 U.S. 691 (2003)]

Employees have a private right of action (that is, they can sue their employers) for unpaid minimum wages and/or overtime, plus liquidated damages, attorneys' fees, and court costs. Courts have the power to order legal and equitable relief against employers who fire employees, or otherwise discriminate or retaliate against them for making an FLSA complaint or participating in a Wage and Hour Division proceeding. [29 U.S.C. § 216]

Not only can employees sue their employers, the Secretary of Labor has the power to sue for unpaid minimum wages and overtime. The funds go directly to the employees who should have received them, not to the Department of Labor (DOL). The court can enjoin the employer against committing any further violations. Willful violations of the FLSA are criminal rather than civil in nature, so prosecution by the federal Attorney General's office is possible, in addition to DOL actions or civil suits by the employees.

After nine years of litigation, the California Supreme Court ruled in April 2012 that employers must provide meal and rest breaks for employees but they are not obligated to make sure that employees actually take the breaks instead of continuing to work. However, this decision was not entirely an employer victory: the California Supreme Court held that workers are entitled to more frequent rest breaks than the employers contended. A concurring opinion points out that class actions remain viable for pressing wage and hour claims. [*Brinker Rest. v. Superior Court (Hohnbaum)*, 53 Cal. 4th 1004 (Cal. 2012). See Scott Graham, *'Brinker' a Win for Employers, but Plaintiffs Cheering, Too*, The Recorder (Apr. 12, 2012) (law .com). Note that the statute of limitations for claims of denial of meal breaks is three years: *Murphy v. Kenneth Cole Prods. Inc.*, 40 Cal. 4th 1094 (Cal. 2007)]

Since *Brinker*, California has continued to hear wage and hour cases. The California Court of Appeal held that it was not an abuse of discretion for a trial court to deny class certification in a case about meal breaks at the Chipotle Mexican Grill fast food chain. Despite the *Brinker* decision, the Court of Appeal held that class certification was inappropriate because Chipotle locations differ greatly in their staffing and shift patterns. Managers determine when employees can take breaks; employees are neither permitted to schedule their own breaks nor refrain from taking the scheduled meal and rest breaks. Without a uniform corporate policy, class certification was unavailable. [*Hernandez v. Chipotle Mexican Grill, Inc.*, 208 Cal. App. 4th 1487, 146 Cal. Rptr. 3d 424 (2012)]

*Gentry v. Superior Court* [42 Cal. 4th 443, 165 P.3d 556 (2007)] held that class action waivers are invalid. The California Court of Appeal held that this ruling is preempted by *AT&T Mobility*. The California Supreme Court will review this ruling in *Iskanian v. CLS Transportation* [No. S204032]. The California Supreme Court will also hear *Duran v. U.S. Bank National Ass'n* [No. S200923] on the issue of whether a case alleging misclassification in order to deny overtime can be decided based on the testimony of 20 employees when the potential class is 10 times larger. [Cynthia Foster, *High Court Queues Up Number of Post-"Brinker" Cases*, The Recorder (Jan. 4, 2012) (law.com)]

Wal-Mart has frequently been accused of labor law violations, such as denying employees legally mandated breaks and forcing them to work off the clock. Such cases raise important issues of when employees' claims are sufficiently similar to justify a class action. [See, e.g., Amaris Elliott-Engel, *Judge Upholds $185 Million Award in Wal-Mart Class Action*, The Legal Intelligencer (Sept. 4, 2008) (law.com) Alison Frankel, *Wal-Mart Loses $6.5 Million Wage-and-Hour Class Action*, The American Lawyer (July 2, 2008) (law.com); *Salvas v. Wal-Mart Stores Inc.*, 452 Mass. 337 (Mass. 2008)]

In 2009 alone, Wal-Mart lost court cases in Minnesota, Pennsylvania, and California and settled 63 suits nationwide for a total of $640 million. [Rebecca Moore, *Wal-Mart Settles with WA Workers Over Pay for Breaks*, plansponsor.com (July 28, 2009).] A class action involving three million Wal-Mart employees, the largest wage and hour class action ever reported, was settled in 2009; the District Court for the District of Nevada's approval also resolved 39 class actions in several states. [Rebecca Moore, *Wal-Mart Wage-and-Hour Settlement Approved in NV*, plansponsor.com (Nov. 4, 2009)] On May 1, 2012, Wal-Mart agreed to pay $4.8 million in back wages and damages to those who received between $30 and $10,800 each, plus $464,000 in civil penalties. The Department of Justice found that more than 4,500 workers were improperly denied overtime, and security guards and vision-department managers were misclassified as exempt between 2004 and 2007. [Shelly Banjo, *Wal-Mart to Pay $4.8 Million In Back Wages, Damages*, WSJ.com (May 1, 2012)]

Wal-Mart argued that the largest class action verdict in Pennsylvania history, the *Braun/Hummel v. Wal-Mart* litigation, should be overturned because the workers alleging underpayment showed only individualized and not class-wide proof. The Pennsylvania Court of Common Pleas affirmed the $185 million award last September, finding that over 186,000 current and former employees in Pennsylvania were denied rest breaks and compensation for off-the-clock work between March 1998 and May 2006. [Amaris Elliott-Engel, *Wal-Mart Seeks Dismissal of Hefty Class Action Award*, The Legal Intelligencer (Aug. 20, 2009) (law.com)]

The District Court for the District of Massachusetts denied a defense motion to compel plaintiffs to respond to written discovery about their immigration status—and ordered a restaurant to answer written questions about potential class members. The plaintiffs claimed that they routinely worked 60–80 hours a week and were not paid for all the hours they worked, and in fact earned less than the minimum wage and did not receive overtime. The court ruled that *Hoffman* does not affect illegal immigrant workers' right to receive back pay, because they are still employees for FLSA purposes. The DOL position is that allowing illegal workers to recover is compatible with federal immigration policy. [*Lin v. Chinatown Rest. Corp.*, No. 1:09-cv-11510-GAO (D. Mass. Mar. 23, 2011); see Sheri Qualters, *Plaintiffs' Immigration Status 'Irrelevant' to Their Wage Claims, Mass. Judge Rules*, Nat'l L.J. (Mar. 28, 2011) (law.com)]

The Seventh Circuit interpreted the FLSA regulations to mean that employees are not doing compensable work merely because they are subject to callout (i.e., being summoned back to work with a phone or beeper to respond to emergencies)—their activities are not restricted as long as the employer has a way to reach them. The court also found that the class action brought by utility workers was inappropriate because the class was not homogenous enough. Either classes should be certified containing similarly situated employees, or the lunch break grievance should be handled through arbitration. [*Jonites v. Exelon Corp.*, 522 F.3d 721 (7th Cir. 2008)]

The Western District of Washington held that a painter who carried work equipment in his truck was not entitled to compensation for direct commuting time spent going to the job site. The court held that most of the equipment was light; carrying it did not change the nature of his commute; and he did not have to do anything with the equipment after the end of the day. The FLSA's illustration for compensable time is a logger who is required to carry a portable power saw or other equipment that is different from ordinary hand tools. [*Kerr v. Sturtz Finishes, Inc.*, No. 2:09-cv-01135-RAJ (W.D. Wash. Aug. 12, 2010); see Rebecca Moore, *Painter Who Carried Equipment in His Truck not Entitled to Compensation*, plansponsor.com (Aug. 27, 2010)]

The prevalence of electronic devices, such as pagers and increasingly sophisticated cell phones, raises questions about the status of workers who are on call, or who can be contacted when they are not in the workplace.

In mid-2009, there were two district court suits dealing with the issue of when hourly workers are entitled to pay for time responding to work telephone calls or e-mails when the employees are "off the clock." In March 2009, an ex-maintenance worker at the C.B. Richard Ellis Group Inc. brought suit in the Eastern District of Wisconsin, charging that he was required to use a work-issued cell phone to take messages. In July 2009, three current and former employees sued T-Mobile USA Inc. in the Eastern District of New York, alleging that they should have been paid for using company-issued smart phones to take work messages after hours.

An appellate court in California reinstated a suit by employees of the medical technology company Lincare Inc. who wanted to be compensated for on-call time spent answering customer questions on the telephone. The DOL position is that workers do not have to be paid merely for carrying pagers—but if they are summoned so often that they cannot use their on-call time for personal pursuits, compensation is due. But as technology gets cheaper, more and more employees are required to be on call electronically; previously, the devices were so expensive that they were only worthwhile for managers. [Michael Sanserino, *Lawsuits Question After-Hours Demands of Email and Cellphones*, WSJ.com (Aug. 10, 2009)]

## [A]   FLSA Litigation

Employers face not only class actions from groups of dissatisfied employees (asserting claims of discrimination and/or violations of state wage and hour laws), but also a special kind of "collective action lawsuit" authorized by FLSA § 216. There are many technical legal differences between class actions and FLSA collective actions.

An FLSA § 216(b) collective action can be brought by one or more employees on behalf of themselves and similarly situated employees; to join, similarly situated employees must opt in. Commencing a collective action requires the plaintiff to show that there is a similarly situated group of employees, although the FLSA does not contain a statutory definition of how similar the group must be. If the court grants conditional certification, it determines whether other similarly situated employees should be notified. The more significant differences appear among the opt-in plaintiffs, the less likely it is that the employees in the group are truly similarly situated.

For five years in a row, the number of federal court wage-and-hour suits increased. There were 7,764 such suits filed between April 1, 2012 and March 31, 2013—about 10% more than the number the year before. There are three main categories of FLSA cases: salaried employees claiming overtime pay; hourly workers who say they were not paid for the full number of hours they actually worked; and restaurant workers alleging tip improprieties. [Catherine Dunn, *Wage-and-Hour Suits Up for Fifth Straight Year,* Corporate Counsel (May 13, 2013) (law.com); for New York trends, also showing a major increase, both in the numbers of cases and the percentage of all civil cases that involve wage and hour claims, see Christine Simmons, *Wage-and-Hour Lawsuits Surge in New York Federal Court,* N.Y.L.J. (Apr. 30, 2013) (law.com).]

There were no Supreme Court wage and hour cases between 2004 and 2012. In June 2012, the Supreme Court ruled that drug "detail" representatives are exempt from overtime because they fall under the exemption for "outside salespersons." [*Christopher v. SmithKlineBeecham Corp.,* 132 S. Ct. 2156 (2012)]

Late in 2003, the Eleventh Circuit held that once a named plaintiff in an FLSA collective action settles his own claims, he will not be allowed to continue the action and notify other class members of a potential case. The Eleventh Circuit distinguished between the FLSA collective action form and the Rule 23 class action, where class members can opt out and the representative plaintiff has the status of a private Attorney General to pursue grievances. [*Cameron-Grant v. Maxim Healthcare Servs. Inc.,* 347 F.3d 1240 (11th Cir. 2003) Another Eleventh Circuit case, *Prickett v. DeKalb Cnty.,* 349 F.3d 1294 (11th Cir. 2003) rules that, if an additional claim is added to an FLSA collective action for overtime pay, workers who opted in initially are not required to opt in again, because it cannot be concluded that they agreed only to the specific claims initially asserted.]

The Supreme Court decided a case about FLSA collective actions. The plaintiff sued on behalf of herself and similarly situated employees. However, the defendant made a settlement offered; the plaintiff ignored it. The Supreme Court held that, since no other employees joined the suit, and the settlement offer would have fully resolved her complaint, the Federal Rules of Civil Procedure required dismissal of the case. There was no longer an active case, because the plaintiff had no personal interest in representing other employees. The Supreme Court drew a distinction between the procedural rules for FLSA collective actions and the rules for class actions. [*Genesis Healthcare Corp. v. Symczyk*, No. 11-1059 (U.S. Apr. 16, 2013)]

In the Fourth Circuit view, the FLSA's anti-retaliation provision protects only employees, not potential employees. Therefore, a plaintiff who said that her job offer was withdrawn after she disclosed her FLSA suit against another company could not sue her potential employer. [*Dellinger v. Science Applications Int'l Corp.*, 649 F.3d 226 (4th Cir. 2011); see Sheri Qualters, *4th Circuit: Anti-Retaliation Provision Of Wage Law Does Not Cover Job Applicants*, Nat'l L.J. (Aug. 15, 2011) (law.com)]

The Seventh Circuit ruled that there is no hard-and-fast rule against certifying a Rule 23(b)(3) class action involving state-law claims in a case that also includes an FLSA collective action, because the FLSA's legislative history does not show an intention to replace other legal procedures. The case was brought by tipped employees who said that Outback Steakhouses maintained policies that violated the FLSA and state wage and hour laws dealing with tips, and employees were not paid for all hours worked. The district court said that a (b)(3) class action, which includes class members unless they opt out, cannot be combined with an FLSA collective action (which required potential plaintiffs to opt in to the action), but the Seventh Circuit disagreed. [*Ervin v. OS Rest. Servs. Inc.*, 632 F.3d 971 (7th Cir. 2011)].

Newspaper reporters in California brought a class and collective action under the FLSA and California labor law. In 2013, the Ninth Circuit held that it was improper to certify a class action for money damages under Rule 23(b)(2) in light of the Supreme Court's *Dukes* decision limiting employment class actions (See § 42.06[A]). The case was remanded to see if there were enough common questions of law or fact to justify a Rule 23(b)(3) class action. The jury ruled that the reporters were not "creative professionals," and therefore they were entitled to overtime. [*Wang v. Chinese Daily News*, No. 08-55483 (9th Cir. Mar. 4, 2013)] Illegal immigrants who worked for Wal-Mart contractors and subcontractors to clean Wal-Mart stores sued Wal-Mart for unpaid overtime, RICO civil damages, and damages for false imprisonment. They sought certification of an FLSA collective action, charging Wal-Mart with knowingly doing business with contractors that hire illegal aliens. The plaintiffs identified Wal-Mart as their employer for FLSA purposes because of its power to hire and fire employees and close supervision of store cleaning. In mid-2012, the Third Circuit rejected class certification and dismissed the RICO and false imprisonment claims. The plaintiffs worked in other places, not exclusively for Wal-Mart, and Wal-Mart hired other contractors and also assigned store employees to cleaning jobs. The false impris-onment charges were dismissed based on Wal-Mart's representation that manag-ers could unlock doors when necessary, and there were emergency exits. The Third Circuit held that an FLSA collective action requires that the plaintiffs be similarly situated, as determined on a case by case basis, using all the relevant factors (similar claims; working in the same corporate location, division, or department; similar compensation and circumstances of employment; whether they all seek similar relief). The Third Circuit did not find enough similarities to certify a collective action: the plaintiffs worked in 180 different stores in 33 states, and the 70 contractors and subcontractors, not Wal-Mart, set wages and hours. The Third Circuit held that bad working conditions and threats of deportation do not constitute involuntary servitude, and there was no evidence that Wal-Mart vio-lated immigration laws. [*Zavala v. Wal-Mart*, 691 F.3d 527 (3d Cir. 2012)]

The Ninth Circuit made it clear in early 2004 that one thing you don't have to worry about is RICO. A plaintiff charged his former employer and its managers with racketeering offenses, charging them with mail fraud for underpaying him and misrepresenting his entitlement to overtime pay. (The alleged wire fraud came in because his paychecks and W-2 forms were mailed, and employees could arrange for direct deposit of their wages.) The Ninth Circuit refused to expand RICO to allow what were essentially basic state contract claims to be brought in federal court. Furthermore, there was no predicate (underlying) RICO offense, because misrepresenting legal consequences, such as entitlement to overtime, does not constitute fraud. [*Miller v. Yokohama Tire Corp.*, 358 F.3d 616 (9th Cir. 2004)]

In mid-2007, using an analysis based on administrative law (federal agen-cies' discretion to promulgate regulations), the Supreme Court upheld 27 C.F.R. § 552.109(a). This is the DOL regulation that says that home care workers who provide companionship services to the elderly and infirm are not covered by mini-mum wage or overtime, whether they are officially employed by the family or by an agency. [*Long Island Care at Home v. Coke*, 551 U.S. 158 (2007). However, about 20 state minimum wage/overtime laws do cover home care workers. This is one of the fastest-growing occupations, with at least 30,000 agencies employing a million workers to care for 12 million patients. See Philip Shishkin, *Political Shift Revives Dispute About Workers' Overtime Pay*, WSJ.com (June 26, 2009)]

In December 2011, the Obama administration proposed regulations to include the approximately two million home care workers under the protection of the FLSA's minimum wage and overtime provisions. The proposal would also require home care agencies to pay for travel between the patients' homes if an aide has multiple clients. Under the proposal, aides hired directly by a patient or patient's family rather than working for a third-party agency would also be cov-ered by the FLSA if they engage in housework or spend more than 20% of their time on activities other than companionship. According to industry experts, at the time of the proposal, almost all home care aides already received minimum wage, but many did not receive overtime. [Steven Greenhouse, *Wage Protection Planned for Home Care Workers*, NYTimes.com (Dec. 15, 2011). The plaintiff in the Supreme Court case died in 2009: see Editorial, *Fairness for Home Care Aides*, NYTimes.com (Dec. 25, 2011); Andrew Council, *Administration Proposes Wage Protections for Home Care Workers*, NYTimes.com (Dec. 16, 2011)]

The first nationwide study of domestic workers, published in late 2012, found that the median wage for nannies, caregivers, and housecleaners is $10/hour. (The study covered workers employed directly rather than through an agency.) Few domestic workers get health insurance or paid sick days. Pay varied greatly depending on ethnicity, immigration status, and whether the worker lives in the employer's household. One-quarter of domestic workers earned less than the state minimum wage. This is not illegal because domestic workers are excluded from minimum wage coverage. Two-thirds of live-in domestic workers did not have any health insurance, and only 4% had employer-paid health insurance. FICA contributions were made on behalf of only 9% of the workers. The Census Bureau's American Community Survey found that 95% of domestic workers are female, 46% are immigrants, 35% are not citizens of the United States, and 54% are non-white. White workers usually earned more than Black, Hispanic, or Asian workers. Illegal immigrants were paid far less than American-born or naturalized workers. [*Home Economics: The Invisible and Unregulated World of Domestic Work*, see Steven Greenhouse, *A Study of Home Help Finds Low Worker Pay and Few Benefits*, NYTimes.com (Nov. 26, 2012)]

Although the heading for this discussion is "FLSA litigation," arbitration is also a possible means of resolving wage and hour disputes. In 2004, the Fifth Circuit confirmed that FLSA claims can be the subject of a compulsory pre-dispute arbitration agreement: there is nothing in the FLSA that requires the court system rather than arbitration to resolve disputes. The limitations on discovery in arbitration do not deprive plaintiffs of substantive rights under the FLSA. [*Carter v. Countrywide Credit Indus. Inc.*, 362 F.3d 294 (5th Cir. 2004); see also *Adkins v. Labor Ready Inc.*, 303 F.3d 496 (4th Cir. 2002) (there is no inherent conflict between the FLSA and the Federal Arbitration Act, and FLSA claims can be subject to mandatory arbitration because the FLSA's statutory language is similar to that of the ADEA, and ADEA claims are subject to mandatory arbitration)]

In contrast, in late 2011, the Southern District of New York ruled that the FLSA collective action is a "unique animal" with a special legislative history designed to permit employees to enforce their own rights without involving the government. Therefore, employers could not mandate the arbitration of FLSA claims for unpaid overtime or minimum wages; the employees had to be allowed to pursue a collective action for this purpose. [*Ranieri v. Citigroup*, 2011 U.S. Dist. LEXIS 135393 (S.D.N.Y. Nov. 22, 2011); see Philip M. Berkowitz, *Developments in Arbitration of Employment Claims*, N.Y.L.J. (Jan. 12, 2012) (law.com)]

A putative class action was filed alleging multiple violations of the California Labor Code with respect to overtime, meal and rest breaks, itemized wage statements, and payroll records. The employer, Legacy, moved to compel arbitration because the named plaintiff signed an arbitration agreement when she was hired.

The California Court of Appeal ruled in 2012 that the arbitration agreement was not, overall, unconscionable, and the plaintiff did not show that requiring her to arbitrate individually violated any state or federal law or public policy. There were some factors supporting a procedural unconscionability argument: the employer supplied a pre-printed form that everyone had to sign, and the arbitration language was not highlighted and appeared on pages 42–43 of the 43-page agreement. But to prevail, the plaintiff would have had to prove both procedural and substantive unconscionability, and was unable to do so. The Court of Appeal held that the agreement did not mention class arbitration, so the employer could not be compelled to arbitrate on a class rather than individual basis. [*Nelsen v. Legacy Partners Residential, Inc.*, 207 Cal. App. 4th 1115, 144 Cal. Rptr. 3d 198 (2012)]

## § 1.07  MINIMUM WAGE

After many years when the federal minimum wage remained steady at $5.15 per hour, and after many attempts in Congress to raise the minimum wage, Title VIII of Pub. L. No. 110-28, The U.S. Troop Readiness, Veterans' Care, Katrina Recovery and Iraq Accountability Appropriations Act of 2007 include provisions entitled "Fair Minimum Wage and Wage Relief." The legislation amends FLSA § 6(a)(1), 29 U.S.C. 206(a)(1), to provide a minimum wage of $5.85 per hour starting 60 days after enactment, rising to $6.55 per hour 12 months later, and $7.25 per hour 24 months after the statute takes effect. The increase was offset by small business tax relief with an estimated value of $4.84 billion over a 10-year period. [See, e.g., Rebecca Moore, *Minimum Wage Bill Passed*, plansponsor.com (May 25, 2007)] See <http://www.dol.gov/whd/regs/compliance/posters/flsa.htm> for the revised wage-and-hour poster. [Rebecca Moore, *Minimum Wage Increase Stages Complete*, plansponsor.com (July 24, 2009)]

The federal minimum wage prevails in the states that either have not enacted a minimum wage law, or set the minimum lower than the federal level. In seven states, the state minimum wage is the same as the federal. [AP, *States With High Minimum Wages*, NYTimes.com (July 24, 2009)]

As of January 1, 2013, 10 states (Arizona, Colorado, Florida, Missouri, Montana, Ohio, Oregon, Rhode Island, Vermont, and Washington) raised their minimum wage. The Rhode Island increase stems from a statute signed by the governor in June 2012, and the other states have automatic annual adjustments. The raises range from 10 to 35 cents an hour, adding up to between $190 and $510 a year for minimum wage workers. The Economic Policy Institute estimated that the increases will add over $183 million to the Gross Domestic Product. [Daniel Massey and Emma Stieglitz, Nat'l Employment Law Project press release, *10 States to Increase Minimum Wage on New Year's Day* (Dec. 19, 2012) (benefitslink.com)]

The Department of Labor permits unpaid internships for trainees, so the trainees can acquire usable job skills. The DOL has set out criteria for acceptable internship programs: for example, the real benefit of the training is to the trainee, not the employer; the training is similar to the curriculum of a vocational school; and trainees do not replace regular employees. The DOL has stepped up investigations, as some companies try to take advantage of the recession by obtaining unpaid labor from "interns." [Steven Greenhouse, *Growth of Unpaid Internships May Be Illegal, Officials Say*, NYTimes.com (Apr. 2, 2010)]

Two men who worked on the film "Black Swan" brought a suit under minimum wage and overtime laws about improper hiring of interns. They said that Fox Searchlight had over 100 unpaid interns who did not receive educational experience but, instead, were assigned to menial tasks that should have been performed by paid employees. The suit asked for back pay and an injunction against further abuse of internship. They won their suit in 2013, when the district court ruled that they were, in effect, regular employees and should have been paid. The judge said that unpaid internships are appropriate only in very limited circumstances—for example, when the work is similar to vocational training; it does not provide immediate benefits to the employer; and interns do not displace paid employees. Whether or not the intern receives academic credit is not relevant to the legal analysis. [Steven Greenhouse, *Interns File Suit Against "Black Swan" Producer* NYTimes.com (Sept. 28, 2011); *Glatt v. Fox Searchlight Pictures*, No. 11 Civ. 6784 (WHP) (S.D.N.Y. June 11, 2013); the ruling grants class certification to Fox Entertainment Group interns. Greenhouse reports that other suits are pending, including a collective action against Hearst Magazines and a suit against Elite Model Management. Charlie Rose's production company made pack pay payments of $1,100 each to almost 200 interns: *Judge Rules for Interns Who Sued Fox Searchlight*,NYTimes.com (June 11, 2013)] ]

## § 1.08   DETERMINING WHO IS AN "EMPLOYEE"

There are many reasons why it becomes necessary to determine if a particular person who performs services is an independent contractor or an employee of the company for which the services are performed. For example, employment status is involved in determining who is allowed to participate in pension and benefit plans; who is entitled to overtime; who is entitled to unemployment benefits and Worker's Compensation; and who can sue under antidiscrimination laws. Although similar factors are used in analyses for different purposes, it is possible that someone will be considered an employee for some purposes but not for others.

If the individual is an employee, the employer will be responsible for paying FUTA taxes and its own share of FICA, and will have to withhold income taxes. In contrast, independent contractors are responsible for their own tax compliance.

Clearly, the company saves money if it can characterize workers as independent contractors, because it saves on taxes and benefits (even if the cash compensation is the same). To prevent abuses, this is an area where the IRS and other regulators are active in determining whether the so-called independent contractor is really an employee.

The Internal Revenue Code specifically identifies some groups as statutory employees, and others as statutory non-employees. [I.R.C. §§ 3121, 3401, 3306, 3508]

The categories of statutory employees are:

- Agents or commission drivers who deliver food products, laundry, or dry cleaning;

- Full-time traveling salespersons who solicit orders for merchandise to be delivered later;

- Full-time life insurance salespersons;

- Corporate officers;

- People who work in their own homes, but under the supervision of someone who supplies the materials to be used in work (e.g., assembling clothing components).

The Ninth Circuit affirmed the NLRB's determination that cab drivers were employees and not independent contractors, because of the substantial evidence of control over their means and manner of performance, and the non-entrepreneurial nature of the job. [*NLRB v. Friendly Cab Co.*, 512 F.3d 1090 (9th Cir. 2008)]

The Fifth Circuit focused on economic reality in deciding whether an insurance company's "sales leaders" were independent contractors: whether the worker is economically dependent on the company it calls an employer, based on the degree of control over the worker, the relative investment by the worker and the company, the degree to which the potential employer determines the worker's opportunity for profit or loss; the permanency of the relationship; and the skill and initiative needed to perform the job. In this case, the insurer controlled the meaningful economic aspects of the business by hiring, firing, and assigning the agents who worked for the sales leaders (most of the sales leaders' income came from a share of the agents' commissions), so not being able to make personnel decisions limited the sales leaders' control over their income. The insurer also assigned geographic territories and controlled sales leads. The Fifth Circuit discounted the fact that the plaintiffs had signed independent contractor agreements: their subjective beliefs about their status could not overcome economic reality. [*Hopkins v. Cornerstone America*, 545 F.3d 338 (5th Cir. 2008)]

Under I.R.C. § 414(n), a long-term leased employee may have to be counted in testing pension and benefit plans for discrimination. A safe harbor is permitted when a company gets less than 20% of its non-highly compensated employees through leasing services, and if those services provide adequate pension coverage for their employees.

*Bronk v. Mountain States Tel. & Tel. Inc.* [140 F.3d 1335 (10th Cir. 1998)] holds that, although the Employment Retirement Income Security Act (ERISA) [29 U.S.C. §§ 1001 *et seq.*] forbids excluding employees from the plan once they have satisfied minimum age and service requirements, it is permissible to draft the plan to deny participation to leased employees, even if they are common-law employees of the sponsor company. The Tenth Circuit position is that I.R.C. § 414(n)(1)(A) merely requires that leased employees be treated as employees; it doesn't require them to be offered plan participation.

Independent contractors can be considered "beneficiaries" under ERISA plans and therefore a suit by a commodities trader that made state insurance and tort law claims about the denial of disability benefits was preempted by ERISA. [*Shyman v. Unum Life Ins. Co.*, 427 F.3d 452 (7th Cir. 2005); see *Ruttenberg v. U.S. Life Ins. Co.*, 413 F.3d 652 (7th Cir. 2005) (another case involving floor traders, for the proposition that independent contractors can be beneficiaries of ERISA plans)]

In 2010, the Eighth Circuit ruled that firing an independent contractor marketing representative and replacing her with a younger common-law employee did not violate the ADEA. The Eighth Circuit held that all factors must be considered to determine if a person is an independent contractor or an employee; the Darden factors are non-exhaustive, and no one factor is decisive. [*Ernster v. Luxco, Inc.*, 596 F.3d 1000 (8th Cir. 2010); see CCH Pensions and Benefits, *Independent Contractors Are Not Protected by ADEA When Terminated* (Mar. 19, 2010) (benefitslink.com)]

## § 1.09  STAFFING ARRANGEMENTS

The U.S. workforce can no longer be divided simply into full-time and part-time workers, or permanent workers and "temps." Many other arrangements have evolved, although, as noted above, the employer's characterization of the arrangement is not always accepted for tax and other legal purposes. Some of the possibilities are:

- Workers who are actually employed by a temporary agency that recruits, trains, and sends workers to companies that are clients of the agency;

- Long-term temporary assignments—where the temporary worker stays at one location for weeks or months, instead of being hired on a daily basis;

- Payrolling—a company wants to hire a specific person, and therefore arranges for a temporary agency to hire that person and be responsible for payment, taxes, and other employment-related matters;

- Part-time workers;

- Independent contractors—who are genuinely self-directed; have clients rather than employers who control their work; and are responsible for their own tax compliance;

- Contract workers—an arrangement usually made with technical workers who are formally employed by a technical services firm. This arrangement is often used for long-range projects, including those that require the contract worker to relocate to the employer's site;

- Leased employees—who are paid by the leasing company, which also handles administrative tasks like tax and Worker's Compensation compliance;

- Outsourcing—delegating a function such as payroll processing, guarding a worksite, or operating an employee cafeteria to a company that specializes in that function.

## § 1.10    SIZE OF THE CONTINGENT WORKFORCE

Clearly, many ways to work have evolved. The BLS uses more than one definition for "contingent workers," the broadest of which is workers "who do not expect their current job to last." The BLS also collects information about "alternative" work arrangements (employment can be both contingent and alternative at the same time).

In March 2013, about 7.6 million workers were "involuntary part-time" workers—i.e., they would have preferred full-time jobs. This was about the same number as in 2012, but three million more than in 2007. Involuntary part-time workers are not counted in the unemployment rate, but it has been estimated that about one-seventh of the workforce is now unemployed, discouraged (i.e., no longer seeking work after extended joblessness), or working on an involuntary part-time basis. About 19% of workers in 2013 worked less than 35 hours a week; this was true of 16.9% of workers at the beginning of the recession. [Catherine Rampell, *Part-Time Work Becomes Full-Time Wait for Better Job*, NYTimes.com (Apr. 19, 2013)]

Since the passage of PPACA, some restaurants, hotels, and retailers have reduced the schedules of hourly workers below 30 hours a week to avoid the pay or play requirement. For example, CKE Restaurants, which owns the Carl's Jr. and Hardee's chains, replaces full-time workers who leave with part-time workers. The HHS said that this trend will peter out: increasing the part-time census means higher turnover and lower morale. The HHS also pointed out that Romneycare did not cause major changes in employment patterns within Massachusetts. [Julie Jargon, Louise Radnofsky, and Alexandra Berzon, *Health-Care Law Spurs a Shift to Part-Time Workers*, WSJ.com (Nov. 4, 2012)]

The Northern District of Illinois held it did not violate the minimum-participation rule (ERISA § 202(a)) to deny pension participation to part time workers. The plaintiffs argued that anyone who worked over 1,000 a year is entitled to pension participation, but the district court said that it is legitimate for an employer to limit participation to certain groups or categories of workers, as long as the classification is not based on age or length of service. (In this case, the defendant, a University, defined only certain groups of employees as benefit-eligible, and the plaintiffs were not hired in benefit-eligible categories.)

[*Krok v. University of Chicago*, No. 11-cv-1-01092 (N.D. Ill. Apr. 3, 2012); see Rebecca Moore, *Court Rules on Eligibility of Benefits for University Employees*, plansponsor.com (Apr. 6, 2012)]

## § 1.11   CO-EMPLOYERS

It's not always possible to say that one company is the employer and the other has no responsibility. Sometimes two companies (such as a leasing company and the company where the individual actually performs services) will be jointly liable—e.g., if the individual is injured at the workplace or harms someone else. Plaintiffs' attorneys are raising new theories of employer liability for wage and hour class actions: for example, citing defendants as joint employers who are responsible for the actions of their contractors, subcontractors, and temporary employment agencies. California Labor Code § 203 requires immediate payment of wages upon termination, raising the question of how the end of a temporary work assignment should be treated.

Enterprise Holdings is the sole stockholder of 38 domestic subsidiaries; the subsidiaries rent cars and Enterprise Holdings does not. The Third Circuit rejected certification of an FLSA collective action because it did not consider Enterprise Holdings to be the joint employer of assistant managers who alleged that they were entitled to overtime pay. Enterprise Holdings recommends HR policies to the subsidiaries (including a recommendation that assistant managers and assistant branch managers not receive overtime pay) but does not mandate these policies. The Third Circuit used an "economic reality" test to determine joint employer status. When two or more employers exert direct or indirect control over a group of employees, they are joint employers, based on, e.g., authority to hire, fire, set work rules, make assignments, discipline employees, and control employee records. [*In re Enterprise Rent-a-Car Wage & Hour Emp't Practices Litig.*, 683 F.3d 462 (3d Cir. 2012)] In 2000, the NLRB ruled that temporary workers could be included in the same bargaining unit as permanent employees, provided that the characteristics of the jobs were similar. But in 2004, the NLRB overturned this decision and ruled that the consent of both the agency supplying the workers and the company where the services are performed is required before temporary workers can be made part of the bargaining unit. [*M.B. Sturgis Inc.*, 331 N.L.R.B. 173 (Aug. 25, 2000), overruled by *Oakwood Care Center*, 343 N.L.R.B. 76 (Nov. 19, 2004)]

The First Circuit remanded a liability insurance case to determine whether a worker referred by an agency was a "leased employee" or a "temporary employee." If he was a leased employee, his employer would not be entitled to defense or indemnification under its Comprehensive General Liability (CGL) insurance policy, which excluded claims of bodily injury to employees. But if he was a temporary employee, the employer would be covered. He had worked for the same employer many times before, and his assignment was for an indefinite duration, but it was possible that other factors would lead to classifying him as a temporary employee hired to cope with a short-term workforce condition. [*Scotts-dale Ins. Co. v. Torres*, 561 F.3d 74 (1st Cir. 2009)]

In the IRS' latest compliance initiative, most companies with leased employees were found to be in compliance with the rules. The few exceptions often used Employee Plans Compliance Resolution System (EPCRS) to correct their failures, so there were few enforcement actions against non-compliant plans. Leased employees must be treated as common-law employees under the minimum participation, minimum coverage, vesting, nondiscrimination, and other pension rules.

The IRS says that there are four requirements for being a leased employee:

1. An agreement between a recipient company and a leasing organization to use the person's service, with a fee to the leasing organization;

2. The worker provides substantially full-time services for at least one year for the recipient, at least 1,500 hours in any 12-month period;

3. The recipient company has primary direction or control over services performed, such as when, where, how, in what order, and by whom services will be performed;

4. Considering all facts and circumstances, the leasing company is the common-law employer of the worker. [Guest Article, Deloitte's Washington Bulletin, *IRS Compliance Initiative Finds Most Plan Sponsors Are Correctly Applying the Leased Employee Rules* (Jan. 17, 2012) (benefitslink.com)]

In a case involving a garment factory with six subcontractors, the Second Circuit applied six factors to determine whether a company that is alleged to be a joint employer "suffers or permits" work to be done on its behalf (those factors were not exclusive; the Second Circuit allowed District Courts to consider any other factors that it finds relevant to the determination):

- Whose premises and equipment were used to perform the work?

- Did garment contractors shift work among the potential joint employers?

- Did the plaintiffs engage in a separate job that was essential to the alleged employer's production process?

- Could contractual responsibility shift to another subcontractor without material changes?

- What was the degree of supervision of the work by the alleged employer or its agents?

- Did the plaintiffs work exclusively or predominantly for the defendant? [*Zheng v. Liberty Apparel Co.*, 355 F.3d 61 (2d Cir. 2003)]

The First Circuit dismissed a sexual harassment case against a parent corporation, on the grounds that the plaintiff was actually employed by a subsidiary corporation. The First Circuit held that the subsidiary, not the parent, issued the plaintiff's W-2 form and had its own accounts, records, and payroll. [*DeLia v. Verizon Commc'ns Inc.*, 656 F.3d 1 (1st Cir. 2011); see Tara Cantore, *Worker for a Subsidiary not Parent Company's Employee*, plansponsor.com (Aug. 29, 2011)]

## § 1.12 APPLICABLE TESTS

### [A] The 20-Factor Test

Determining employee status is not a simple matter. The internal IRS documents used to train tax auditors set out 20 factors to be used to determine if income tax withholding is required:

1. If the employer gives instructions that the employee has to follow;

2. If the employer trains the employee;

   ■ **TIP:** Don't assign independent contractors to take training sessions with employees!

3. If the person renders services that are specific to him or her and can't be delegated to someone else;

4. If the employer provides whatever assistants are needed for the work (someone who provides his own assistants is more likely to be an independent contractor);

5. Whether the services are integrated into the employer's ordinary work, or are separate;

6. If the work relationship continues over time;

   ■ **TIP:** Independent contractors should not be asked to be on call.

7. If the worker is subject to a shift system or other established, structured work hours or work schedule;

8. If the employer demands the worker's full-time commitment;

9. If the worker works for other companies at the same time (if the answer is "yes," it tends to imply independent contractor status, although part-time common-law employees may hold more than one job);

10. If work is done on the employer's premises;

11. If the employer determines the order or sequence of tasks to be done to accomplish the overall task;

12. If the worker has to submit regular oral or written reports;

13. If payment is by time (hour, week, or month) rather than project;

14. If the employer supplies tools and materials;

15. If the worker has to make a significant financial investment to accomplish the tasks;

16. If the employer pays business and travel expenses;

17. If the worker has a profit-and-loss interest in the underlying business of the employer;

18. If the worker gets paid by the employer's customers;

19. The employer's right to fire the worker (as distinct from carrying out the termination provisions of a contract, or refusing to renew the contract) tends to imply employee status;

20. The possibility of the worker's becoming liable to the employer if he or she quits suggests independent contractor status, because this is consistent with remedies for breach of contract.

At a minimum, if the IRS examines records and determines that common-law employees were incorrectly treated as independent contractors, the employer will have to make up the employment taxes that should have been paid but were not. Additional penalties may also be imposed. If the employer filed the required information returns (W-2s and 1099s) and did not intentionally misclassify the worker, then the penalty will be limited to 1.5% of the employee's wages, plus 20% of the FICA taxes that went unpaid because of the incorrect classification.

Those penalties are doubled if the information returns were not filed (unless there was no willful neglect, and there was reasonable cause for failure to file). Even heavier penalties are assessed if the employer not merely was mistaken about filing responsibilities, but deliberately attempted to avoid taxation.

The IRS' Topic 762, Independent Contractor vs. Employee says that evidence for characterization falls into three categories: Behavioral Control (the right, via instructions, training, etc., to direct or control how the work is done); Financial control (whether business expenses are reimbursed; worker's investment in facilities to do the work; how the worker is paid; extent to which the worker can gain profits or risk losses); and the relationship between the parties (e.g., written contract terms; worker's ability to work for others as well; presence or absence of employment-type benefits). [<http://www.irs.gov/taxtopics/tc762.html> (revised Mar. 18, 2010). See also IRS Publication 1779, *Independent Contractor or Employee.*]

Either the worker or the firm can file IRS Form SS-8, available from <http://www.irs.gov/pub/irs-pdf/fss8.pdf> to obtain an IRS determination (for federal income tax and withholding purposes) whether an individual is an employee or an independent contractor. It calls for information such as the firm's business, what the worker does (and his or her job title), and if there is a written service agreement. Part II of the form assesses behavioral control, Part III financial control, and Part IV the relationship between company and worker. Part V assesses the working conditions of salespersons and those who provide services directly to customers.

In 2011, the IRS created a new program, the Voluntary Classification Settlement Program (VCSP), under which employers can voluntarily re-classify workers to resolve past issues instead of waiting to be audited.

The Voluntary Classification Settlement Program (VCSP) was expanded in 2012 so more businesses can use an inexpensive option to re-classify workers. Even employers that are being audited by the IRS (other than employment tax audits) can use the VCSP. The eligibility requirements have been modified so more employers, and especially large employers, can use the program. In general, employers will be ineligible for VCSP if they did not file the required 1099s for the past three years for the workers whom they wish to reclassify, but this requirement was waived until June 30, 2013. The employer must consistently have treated the workers in question as non-employees. Almost 1,000 employers have applied for the program to get partial relief from payroll taxes after reclassification. The ordinary payroll tax statute of limitations applies, whereas participants used to be subject to a special six-year statute of limitations. Application is made on Form 8952 at least 60 days before the employer intends to treat the workers in question as employees. Once accepted in the program, employers pay approximately 1% of the wages paid to reclassified workers in the previous year. No interest or penalties are required, and the employer will not be audited on payroll tax for those workers for past years. However, if the employers are in the temporary relief program for those who did not file 1099s, they must pay slightly more, some penalties will be due, and the 1099s will have to be filed. [Announcement 2012-45, 2012-51 I.R.B. 724, Announcement 2012-46, 2012-51 I.R.B. 725, discussed in IR-2012-23 IRS.gov, keyword VCSP. See *IRS Expands Voluntary Worker Classification Settlement Program; Relief From Past Payroll Taxes Available to More Employers Who Reclassify Their Workers As Employees* (Feb. 27, 2013).]

### [B]  Safe Harbor Treatment

In 1979, Congress passed a safe harbor provision, Section 530 of the Revenue Act of 1978. Under this provision, if an employer treats someone as an independent contractor, the IRS will not be able to reclassify that person as an employee (and will not be able to assess back taxes and penalties) as long as the employer made the characterization reasonably and in good faith. Employers can also apply for a refund of penalties that they believe were improperly assessed.

There are three safe harbor tests for reasonableness:

1. The court system or the IRS has created published authority (e.g., decisions, IRS rulings, or IRS Technical Advice Memorandums) that justifies independent contractor treatment in similar situations;

2. The IRS has already audited the employer, and the audit did not uncover any problems of worker characterization;

3. There is an established practice, within a significant segment of the employer's industry, of treating people who do similar work as independent contractors.

To use the safe harbor, the employer must have treated the person consistently as an independent contractor, including filing Form 1099 as necessary. If the person was treated as a common-law employee at any time after December 31, 1977, the safe harbor will not be available.

## [C] Other Tests of Employee Status

The fundamental test is ability to control work behavior, both as to methods and as to results. This is the test used to determine employee status for ERISA purposes.

State unemployment insurance coverage typically depends either on the common-law right of control, or supplying a worker with a workplace, tools, and materials in addition to control. Most states use an "ABC test": someone who performs services is an employee, and the employer must pay unemployment insurance premiums for that person, unless:

- the person is customarily engaged in an independent trade, business, profession, or occupation;

- no direction or control is given in performing the services;

- the services are not performed in the usual course of the employer's business, or are not performed within any regular business location of the employer.

The employer must pay unemployment insurance plus penalties and interest for misclassified workers.

The FLSA test is based on economic reality. In other words, someone who is not economically dependent on a company, and is not an integral part of its operations, would not be an employee. Factors in the decision include:

- The worker's investment in facilities or equipment;

- Presence or absence of opportunity to earn profits or suffer losses due to managerial or special skills;

- Degree of control others have over the person's work;

- Permanence of the work relationship;
- Skill required to perform the services.

In this case, misclassification can lead to a duty to pay any unpaid minimum wages and overtime, plus liquidated damages, attorneys' fees, and court costs.

## § 1.13   BENEFITS FOR CONTINGENT WORKERS

This issue came to prominence in connection with Microsoft "perma-temps" who were characterized by the company as freelancers and independent contractors, paid through invoices submitted to the accounts payable department rather than through the payroll process. The IRS ruled that these people were really common-law employees. They sued to be held eligible to participate in Microsoft's savings and employee stock ownership plans.

The Ninth Circuit ruled that eligibility for participation depends on being a common-law employee; the form in which payment is rendered is not relevant. The court also rejected the agreement signed by the workers, characterizing them as ineligible for plan participation, on the grounds that an agreement of this type cannot alter employee status. [*Vizcaino v. Microsoft Corp.*, 97 F.3d 1187 (9th Cir. 1996), *aff'd*, 120 F.3d 1006 (9th Cir. 1997), *cert. denied*, 522 U.S. 1088 (1998)]

The Ninth Circuit ruled on the case again in May 1999 [173 F.3d 713 (9th Cir. 1999)], holding that temporary agency workers who also satisfy the common-law control test can be considered Microsoft employees entitled to participate in the stock plan. The case went back to the district court yet again [142 F. Supp. 2d 1299 (W.D. Wash. 2001)], and on January 9, 2000, the Supreme Court again refused to hear an appeal of the decision. [*cert. denied*, 522 U.S. 109 (2000)]

In December 2000, Microsoft agreed to pay $96.9 million to settle the *Vizcaino* case and another pending case. [The settlement agreement can be found at <http://www.bss.com/vizcaino/mssettle.pdf>.]

In March 2003, the Third Circuit decided an important case, holding that to draft a benefits plan to exclude hourly employees does not violate ERISA. [*Bauer v. Summit Bancorp.*, 325 F.3d 155 (3d Cir. 2003)] In this analysis, ERISA allows the employer to deny participation for any reason, as long as ERISA's age and length of service requirements are respected. Of course, if the employer wishes to draft the plan to cover hourly as well as salaried workers, this is permissible.

The Tenth Circuit held that it was reasonable for a pension plan administrator to rely on the method of payment, the plan provisions, and payroll data to deny coverage to a contract worker who was not on the corporate payroll. [*Scruggs v. ExxonMobile Pension Plans*, 585 F.3d 1356 (10th Cir. 2009); see Mercer Select, *Contractor Isn't Eligible "Employee" Under Pension Plan, Appeals Court Says* (Nov. 19, 2009) (benefitslink.com)]

## § 1.14    WORK SCHEDULING

### [A]    Overview

To an ever-increasing extent, new (and usually longer) schedules are replacing the conventional nine-to-five or eight-to-four workday.

Some employees will have to work overtime and weekend hours occasionally. Some will have to work unconventional hours as a long-range or permanent condition of employment. As business becomes more international, it becomes necessary to be able to deal with customers during their workweek—which may occur on a very different schedule from the traditions of the U.S. workplace.

The FLSA allows employers to define the workweek as seven days starting on any day and any time of day—but, once the schedule is established, non-exempt employees must be paid overtime for work in excess of 40 hours per week. The FLSA workweek is not necessarily the same as the calendar week or the business' scheduled or pay week. Workers who are assigned to work, and do work, four 10-hour days in the same workweek are not entitled to overtime under the FLSA. However, if the employee actually works 42 hours in that week, two hours of overtime pay is required even if the employee was not scheduled for the extra work. [John E. Thompson, *The Legal Implications of Nontraditional Workweeks*, Workforce Mgmt. Online (October 2008) (benefitslink.com)]

"Flextime" is a schedule under which employees commit to working at least a certain number of hours per day, week, or month, and also agree to be present at certain agreed-upon times (e.g., for the weekly staff meeting or when customer demand is highest). Otherwise, they can work any schedule that suits their needs and allows them to complete their work tasks. Flextime can work for employees who have work-family problems (e.g., caring for children or elderly relatives). Flextime can be an Americans with Disabilities Act (ADA) "reasonable accommodation" and can also be used by employees taking FMLA leave. The publishing firm BLR said that for exempt employees, 36% were not entitled to flextime in the 2006 survey—a percentage that had declined to 12% in 2010. In 2006, 41% of exempts had some flexible hours, rising to 50% in 2010. In 2006, 10% of exempts had a compressed workweek, declining to 7% in 2010. "Core flex" (some flexibility within a framework of core hours) was available to 9% of exempts in 2006, 20% in 2010. Only 3% of exempts had totally flexible hours in 2006, rising to 11% in 2010. [BLR/HRDaily Advisor Employee Fringe Benefit Survey Series: *Telecommuting, Flextime and Dress Code Practices* (2010) (benefitslink.com)]

There is a basic division between hourly workers, who get more pay if they put in longer hours, and salaried workers, whose compensation does not vary with the number of hours worked.

It is customary, although not legally required, for hourly employees to clock out when they leave the workplace (e.g., for lunch breaks or to do personal errands). They are not normally paid for this nonwork time. Salaried employees are usually not charged for such nonwork time, although personal time is sometimes charged against their sick leave. In a unionized workplace, the Collective Bargaining Agreement (CBA) determines issues like scheduling of meal breaks and when employees have to punch in and punch out.

See § 1.06 above, for discussion of meal and rest breaks.

## [B]   Telecommuting

To an increasing extent, employees are working from home or from other remote locations by "telecommuting," working on a computer and dealing with other employees and clients or customers by telephone or e-mail. Telecommuting is often extremely popular with employees and for years it was hailed as a way for organizations to increase productivity, save money (because less desk space is required at the office), and save energy (because employees do not have to commute as often). However, 2013 saw something of a reversal, with a growing belief that employees are not just more productive but more innovative when they collaborate face-to-face with co-workers.

In 1997, according to the Census Bureau, 9.2 million people (7% of the workforce) worked at home at least one day per week. In 2010, this proportion rose to 9.4% of the workforce. Telecommuting was especially common on Mondays and Fridays, probably to extend the weekend. One-quarter of home-based workers are in management, business, or finance. Nearly half of at-home workers are self-employed. The Census Bureau found that employees who sometimes work at the central location and sometimes work at home tend to earn more than those who only work at the central location. In 2011, more than 8% of non-home workers had a long commute (an hour or more each way) and close to 600,000 workers had a "mega-commute" of 50 miles/90 minutes daily. [Neil Shah, *Census Report Finds More Americans Working Remotely*, WSJ.com (Mar. 5, 2013)]

In the past few years, Aon says that the percentage of organizations offering virtual work arrangements rose from 35% to 45%. However, some major companies have gone in the other direction and rejected working at home. Aon says that the situation must be viewed on a case by case basis to see if working onsite promotes collaboration. Formal guidelines are useful in assessing the effect of telecommuting on recruiting and retaining employees and making them productive. [Aon Hewitt press release, *Banning Work From Home Programs Not One-Size-Fits-All, Says Aon Hewitt* (Mar. 19, 2013) (benefitslink.com)]

Some recent studies show that in knowledge-based industries, employee interaction at the office enhances creativity and innovation. Some office perks are taxable to employees (e.g., free dry cleaning), but providing an on-site gym is probably tax free. Free meals onsite are theoretically taxable if not provided for the convenience of the employer, but this is not a major IRS enforcement priority. [Victor Fleischer, *The Benefits of Working in the Office*, NYTimes.com (Mar. 6, 2013)] Early in 2013, Yahoo ordered all of its employees to work at the office rather than at home on the grounds that face-to-face interaction improves collaboration. Bank of America had a popular remote-work program, but late in 2012 ordered employees in certain categories to return to the office. [Claire Cain Miller and Catherine Rampell, *Yahoo Orders Home Workers Back to the Office*, NYTimes.com (Feb. 25, 2013)]

A 2011 CareerBuilder telecommuting survey says 17% of Americans who telecommute at least part time work one hour or less per day; 35% work 8 or more hours/day, 40% work 4–7 hours. In the organization's 2007 study, only 18% of telecommuters said they worked eight or more hours a day. More than a third (37%) of telecommuters say they are more productive at the office, 29% say they are more productive at home, 34% say it doesn't matter. Ten percent of respondents (an increase from the 2007 level of 8%) telecommute at least once a week. [Tara Cantore, *Most Telecommuters Actually Work When Home*, plansponsor.com (Sept. 15, 2011)]

According to the Telework Research Network, 45% of U.S. workers have jobs that are compatible with at least part-time telework. Almost 80% of employees surveyed said that they would work from home if they were permitted. There are only 2.9 million workers (2.3% of the workforce) who consider home their primary place of work—but a further 50 million workers would like to work at home and could do at least some work from there. Telework Research Network said that current telecommuters save 390 million gallons of gas and avoid 3.6 million tons of greenhouse gases a year and, if all possible telecommuting options were taken, Persian Gulf petroleum imports could be cut by 46%. [*The State of Telework in the U.S.*, <http://www.workshifting.com/downloads/downloads/Telework-Trends-US.pdf>. See Rebecca Moore, *Report Makes Environmental Argument for More Telework*, plansponsor.com (June 28, 2011)]

Congress passed the 2010 Telework Enhancement Act, Pub. L. No.111-292, and the president signed it in December, 2010. The legislation requires federal agencies to determine which employees can telework, and to establish telework policies, including use of telework during disaster recovery. Although the law does not directly affect private companies, the federal government has such a large economic presence that its policies often spread to the private sector. [Rebecca Moore, *House Approves Federal Telework Bill*, plansponsor.com (Nov. 22, 2010); Fred Schneyer, *President Signs Federal Telework Legislation*, plansponsor.com (Dec. 13, 2010)]

There are many practical steps that a company can take to make the arrangement smoother and more productive. The "teleworkers" should sign written agreements clarifying whether they are independent contractors or common-law employees; who they will report to; whether the telework assignment is expected to be temporary or permanent; how often they will be expected to go to the office; how many hours they will work; their work schedule; and promotion possibilities. Telework is most suitable for clearly defined projects with easily measured milestones.

Telecommuting relies heavily on electronics, so it's important to safeguard hardware and data, with backup equipment and an efficient source of online or other data storage.

Make sure the telecommuter has homeowner's insurance (if necessary, in the form of a rider or a separate policy) that covers the computer equipment against theft and damage. This is especially important if the employer supplies the equipment. A "consequential damages" provision that covers lost data and business opportunities is hard to find, but a valuable addition to the policy.

New York ruled in 2003 that a former telecommuter who lived in Florida and submitted work to a Long Island company over telephone lines was not entitled to New York unemployment benefits when the arrangement ended and the employer was no longer willing to allow her to work from home. The "work" occurred at her Florida home. [*Allen v. Comm'r of Labor*, 100 N.Y.2d 282 (N.Y. App. 2003)]

Permitting out-of-state employees to telecommute could create unexpected income tax exposure. Thirty-five states responding to a Bloomberg survey said that their state would find income tax nexus with the out-of-state employer, although that would not be true in Indiana, Kentucky, Maryland, Mississippi, Oklahoma, or Virginia. Twenty-three states said that reimbursing an employee's home office expenses would make that employee subject to income tax, but 18 states said that it would not. [Bloomberg BNA Payroll Library, *Telecommuting Creates Nexus in Many States, Survey Shows* (Apr. 25, 2012) (benefitslink.com)]

New York found that 100% of the earnings of a computer programmer who lives in Tennessee and spends only a quarter of his time in New York were taxable in New York, because he worked at home for his own convenience and not that of his employer. [*Matter of Huckaby v. State Div. of Tax Appeals*, 4 N.Y.3d 427, *cert. denied*, 546 U.S. 976 (2005)]

Telework can also be a lifeline for disabled workers, and it is an important part of the New Freedom initiative, a federal government plan for integration of people with disabilities into the stream of ordinary life. See <http://www.eeoc. gov/facts/telework.html> for the EEOC's fact sheet on using telework to promote full employment opportunity for people with disabilities; how to supervise telecommuters; and the extent to which offering telework options is a reasonable accommodation to disability. But it has generally been held that the ADA does not require employers to grant permission to work at home as an accommodation to disabled employees. [Paul W. Cane Jr., "I Want to Work at Home": *Telecommuting as a Reasonable Accommodation* (special to law.com (Mar. 28, 2005)), citing cases such as *Raffaele v. City of New York*, 2004 WL 1969869 (E.D.N.Y. Sept. 7, 2004); *Dicino v. Aetna U.S. Healthcare*, Civil No. 01-3206 (JBS), 2003 WL 21501818 (D.N.J. June 23, 2003)] However, terminating a telework arrangement could be problematic. According to the D.C. Circuit, permitting a worker disabled by injuries to work at home for up to two days a week could be a reasonable accommodation. Therefore, a new managers' revoking permission to telecommute was discrimination. [*Woodruff v. Peters*, 482 F.3d 521 (D.C. Cir. Apr. 6,

2007); see Fred Schneyer, *FAA Telecommuting Setup Could Be Disabled Worker's Accommodation*, plansponsor.com (May 8, 2007)]

## [C]  Integrated Time Off

An integrated time-off system is an attendance policy that gives the worker the right to take a certain number of days off per year, no matter what the reason for being away from work. The value to the employer is that it keeps people at work because they no longer have an incentive to take sick days for every minor illness just because otherwise they would lose the time. A common system is to provide a certain amount of paid vacation (e.g., one to three weeks a year), six to eight paid holidays, and six sick days a year. Employers vary as to whether they allow unused sick days to be carried over from year to year, or impose a "use it or lose it" rule.

A PTO (Paid Time Off) program integrates vacation and sick days. An Integrated Disability Program (also known as "24-hour coverage") adds disability benefits to the mix. For example, an integrated time-off plan might give the worker 100% pay for days 1–3 of any illness (from the PTO bank), 75% of pay for days 4–90 of the illness from the short-term disability plan, and 66% of pay from the long-term disability plan for an illness lasting over 90 days (as long as the employee satisfies the LTD plan's requirements, of course).

State law determines whether the employer must cash out unused PTO upon termination. If the employer has an established policy, it must be observed; changes in time-off policy must be posted, or employees must be given written notice. If there is no contractual bar, and the employer does not exercise discriminatory animus, an employee who comes to work when sick can be sent home and required to use PTO for the day. However, if the employee's condition is serious, the absence may have to be treated as FMLA leave. The PTO policy should also explain what happens if an employee is not entitled to paid time—can the employee take the time off unpaid, or will discipline be imposed?

PTO systems with a calendar year accrual system need a procedure for handling the employee's first partial year of work: either the time off could be prorated, or the amount of PTO could be based on the month of hiring. Employers must make this point clear to employees, who otherwise might assume that they have a full year's accrual and feel that they're being unjustly deprived of leave.

The plan must specify whether PTO accrues all at once at the beginning of the year or by the month, week, or pay period. Some state laws treat accrued PTO as vested, so forfeitures are illegal. Employers in such states often draft the plan to cap the amount of unused PTO that can be held at any one time: e.g., once three weeks of unused vacation time has accrued, the employee must use some vacation time before any more accrues. Some employers also allow employees to "borrow" against future PTO, although this will create problems if the employee quits, goes on disability leave, or is fired before being able to accrue time off to repay the advances. Advanced, unaccrued PTO is considered a loan or cash advance for FLSA and federal income tax purposes.

The policy should also explain the increments in which PTO can be taken—a full day only, or half days or less? For exempt employees, deductions for personal, vacation, and sick leave can be taken only as full days, and the employer is forbidden to make deductions that exceed the time actually taken. [Keisha-Ann G. Gray, *PTO Bank Questions Answered*, Human Resource Executive Online (Sept. 8, 2008) (benefitslink.com); Jennifer Blum Feldman, *Paid Time Off Perils*, special to law.com (June 19, 2008) See Rev. Rul. 2009-31, 2009-39 I.R.B. 35 and Rev. Rul. 2009-32, 2009-39 I.R.B. 398. discussed in SunGard Relius, *IRS Offers Retirement Plan Options for Paid Time Off*, <http://www.relius.net/news/TechnicalUpdates.aspx> (Oct. 4, 2009); Keith R. Kost, *IRS Gives the Green Light to Contributions of the Value of Unused Leave Time to Retirement Plans*, Pillsbury Advisory (Nov. 11, 2009) (benefitslink.com), for tax issues of contributing PTO to 401(k) plans]

## [D]   Coping with Absenteeism

One-third of employers responding to CareerBuilder's 2011 survey said that workers call in sick more often during the winter holidays—either because they really do get more colds and cases of the flu, or because they use sick days for personal errands. Fifteen percent of employers said they fired someone for taking time off without a legitimate excuse, and 28% have checked up on an employee (of that number, 69% required a doctor's note, 52% called the employee, 19% had another employee telephone to check, and 16% drove by the employee's house). Twenty-nine percent of workers admitted to claiming sick days when they weren't sick. Nearly all (84%) of employee respondents said that they make a phone call to call in sick, 24% send an e-mail, 11% text. [Tara Cantore, *Holiday Season Causes Spike in Absenteeism*, plansponsor.com (Oct. 20, 2011)]

The other side of the coin, however, is "presenteeism"—sick employees who insist on coming in to work when they should be recuperating. They are unlikely to be productive in that situation, and the worst case scenario is that they trigger endless rounds of colds and flu "going around the office."

Epidemiologists suggest that a person with a contagious illness stay home for at least 24 hours after the fever and symptoms abate, The whooping cough epidemic of 2012 was especially severe—and infected persons could infect someone else a day before experiencing symptoms themselves. About half (51%) of respondents to SHRM's survey said that they maintain a paid time-off bank, giving employees access to a specified number of days off for all reasons, up from 42% in 2009. When a flu or other epidemic occurs, some employers temporarily allow employees additional sick leave without reducing their vacation entitlement. [Sue Shellenbarger, *The Art of Calling In Sick—Or Toughing It Out*, WSJ.com (Oct. 23, 2012)]

The winter of 2012–2013 was the worst flu season in several years, which increased advocacy in favor of mandatory paid sick days. According to the BLS, 39% of private sector workers and 11% of state and local government workers are not entitled to paid sick days, although the BLS also said that most full-time private sector workers who are entitled to sick days do not use their full entitlement and that some employers permit an extra sick day during flu season, to encourage workers with contagious illnesses to stay home.

According to the CDC, each flu season causes 3.1 million hospital days and $10.4 billion in direct medical costs each year. It is unclear whether flu is a "serious illness" for FMLA purposes; it probably depends on the state and local leave requirements and the employer's policies.

Requiring employees to get flu shots can create legal problems. There may be disability or religious issues that must be accommodated under the ADA or Title VII. Employers can also offer incentives, such as gift cards, for employees who agree to get flu shots. The shots are also a preventive service that PPACA requires to be provided without copayments. EEOC technical guidance, *"Pandemic Preparedness in the Workplace and the Americans With Disabilities Act,"* permits employers to ask employees if they have cold or flu symptoms such as fever, sore throat, or chills; this is not a disability-related inquiry. Information about employee illnesses must be maintained pursuant to the ADA confidentiality rules. It is also permissible to send employees home if they have symptoms. The EEOC has drafted an employee sample survey for employers to use to ask medical and non-medical questions about the employee's ability to work during a pandemic; the survey avoids questions about chronic conditions. It is permissible for employers to adopt workplace infection control practices such as those set out on the OSHA Web page, "Workplace Safety and the Flu." [Melanie Trottman, *Flu Season Amplifies Calls for Paid Sick Leave*, WSJ.com (Feb. 22, 2013); Jackson Lewis LLP Workplace Resource Center, *Managing Employee Absenteeism and 'Presenteeism' During Flu Season, A Recurring Challenge* (Jan. 15, 2013)(benefitslink.com); Sue Reisinger, *An Outbreak of Flu-Related Legal Issues*, Corporate Counsel (Jan. 18, 2013) (law.com).See *Chenzira v. Cincinnati Children's Hosp. Med. Ctr.*, No. 1:11-CV-00917, 2012 U.S. Dist. LEXIS 182139 (S.D. Ohio Dec. 27, 2012), a religious discrimination suit brought by a vegan who was fired for refusing to take a vaccine that was grown in chicken eggs.]

## [E]  Catastrophe Planning

Employers must be prepared for a variety of adverse events, including the man-made (terrorist attacks) and natural (weather events and epidemics). In addition to practical questions such as determining when the business will be able to open and assembling the necessary staff (when travel conditions may be difficult), the disaster will have employment tax consequences, and many other laws may be invoked as well.

On November 2, 2012, the IRS proclaimed that Superstorm Sandy is a qualified disaster, with the result that disaster relief payments to cover uninsured personal, family, living, or funeral expenses are not taxable income. Uninsured costs of repairing or rehabilitating a personal residence or replacing its contents are covered. An employer-sponsored private foundation can provide disaster relief to employees without losing its tax-exempt status. [Jackson Lewis LLP Workplace Resource Center, *Leave Sharing Programs, Other Steps to Assist Employees Affected by Hurricane Sandy* (Nov. 5, 2012) (benefitslink.com)]

After Superstorm Sandy, many businesses on the East Coast shut down for reasons such as damage to the plant, lack of electric power, and transit disruptions that prevented workers from getting to work. Federal law and New York law both say that employees who did not go to work are not entitled to pay, unless they are covered by a contract that compensates them for the lost days. If a business location is closed due to a disaster, there is no work to pay employees for. Hourly employees are not paid for hours they could not work. Salaried employees might be asked to use their leave to make up for lost time. As long as they are notified in advance, the pay of exempt employees can be reduced for full days that were not worked. Hourly workers who can get to the worksite but cannot put in a full day must be paid for at least four hours at minimum wage, even if the actual duration of work is much less. Salaried employees must be paid for the full day. Employees working at home must be paid for their work, but employers probably will not be able to track this time so it will in effect be on the honor system. [Brendan Pierson, *Worker Absence During Storm Raises Questions for Employers*, N.Y.L.J. (Nov. 19, 2012)]

For disaster leave donation programs, Notice 2006-59 requires a major presidentially declared disaster; state or local declarations do not count. Once again, the recipient must be someone who misses work because of a disaster that causes severe hardship to the employee or family. The donor cannot pick the specific recipient. The maximum donation cannot exceed the leave the donor normally accrues during the year (which may be subject to state or local rules). The leave must be used in connection with the disaster, and the severity of the disaster determines the reasonable period of time during which leave can be taken. At the end of the specified post-disaster period, any unused leave must be returned to the donor. Donor can't specify the recipient. The maximum annual amount of leave donated can't be more than the leave donor normally accrues during the year. The severity of the disaster governs the reasonable period of time post-disaster to use the leave; it must be used for that disaster. Unused leave has to be returned to donor at the end of specified post-disaster period. Check the local rules. [Peter Alwardt, *Tax Considerations in Implementing Donated Leave Policies*, Eisner Amper (Jan. 14, 2013) (benefitslink.com)]

A natural disaster can require the employer to take steps under many different statutes. Under the FLSA, if the worksite is open but an exempt employee chooses to remain at home for weather-related reasons, the DOL considers this a personal absence. For full days when an exempt employee did not report to work, the employer can treat it as unpaid leave or subtract it from the employee's accrued vacation time. If an employee is absent for one or more full days for personal reasons, the employee is still deemed to be salaried (rather than paid by the hour) if salary deductions are made on account of the absence—but the employer must deduct full days, not partial days. The employer is permitted to deduct partial days from the employee's leave bank, but if the leave bank is exhausted, it is not permissible to make salary deductions. Once exempt employees return to work, they can be required to make up the lost time. Non-exempt workers can be required to "catch up" only if they are paid overtime for hours over 40 per week. Employees who are on call and not free to leave (such as maintenance workers assigned to remain onsite during a disaster to perform emergency repairs) must be paid even if they are not given any work assignments. Employees must also be compensated if they are required to wait (e.g., stay in the workplace waiting for power to be restored).

There is a WARN Act exception for closings or layoffs caused by disasters, although the employer must still give as much notice as possible and must explain why less than 60 days' notice was given. USERRA forbids taking adverse employment action against a person (e.g., a National Guard member) who is called up for active duty during an emergency. The employer is entitled to timely notice of the call-up, although it can be given in writing or orally, and can come either from the servicemember or from an officer.

Employers must make decisions about benefit coverage. If coverage will continue during a plant closure, the employer should consult its benefits vendor. If the plan is subject to COBRA, the plan administrator must be notified if any employees lose coverage because they are not working. At that point, the administrator must provide COBRA notice; in practical terms, the notice may not be received if the employee has had to evacuate from the last known address on file with the employer. (The legal obligation is simply to send notice to the last known address.) Someone who is physically or emotionally injured by the disaster may also be entitled to ADA reasonable accommodation, as long the accommodation does not impose undue hardship on the employer.

OSHA obligates employers to protect employees from unreasonable dangers in the workplace, which could mean keeping them out of harm's way before, during, and after a disaster. Employees who are forced to work under unsafe conditions, or who suffer retaliation for refusing or reporting unsafe conditions, may be entitled to whistleblower protection. The National Labor Relations Act may require changes in a workplace that has become unsafe. Refusing to work under dangerous conditions might constitute protected concerted activity, even if only one employee is acting on behalf of others.

Unionized employers may be subject to force majeure clauses in the CBA that explain rights and duties in emergencies. If the disaster causes enough damage to force the employer to go out of business, the employer does not have an obligation to bargain with the union about the decision to go out of business—but effects bargaining will be required. A number of states provide that the employer's Unemployment Insurance experience account will not be charged for layoffs caused by a natural disaster. The Disaster Unemployment Assistance program helps people, including farm owners and the self-employed, who lost jobs as a direct result of a declared disaster. [Duane Morris LLP, *When Disasters Strike: Pay, Leave and Related Issues* (Oct. 31, 2012) (benefitslink.com)]

In practice, most employers excused workers' absences in the immediate aftermath of Sandy. PNC Financial Services paid salaried and hourly employees for the time their bank branches were closed. More than 10,000 workers in hard-hit areas were given five extra paid days off they could use as needed. However, after those five days were used, hourly workers had to use vacation or personal days to get paid, even if they could not get to open bank branches to work. The storm shut down close to 1,000 Starbucks locations; workers were paid for their scheduled hours when the stores were closed. Dunkin' Donuts let each franchisee decide how to handle pay planning issues. A crisis management survey published in 2011 said that it takes an average of 7.8 days to resume business after a hurricane—and close to seven weeks after a flood. For morale purposes, some employers made salary payments that were not legally required or granted hardship loans or advances on 2013 bonuses. [Melissa Korn, Leslie Kwoh, and Rachel Emma Silverman, *Disaster Dilemma: How to Pay Employees Who Missed Work*, WSJ.com (Nov. 7, 2012)]

Under Code § 139 and IRS guidance, when a disaster occurs, the employer can provide cash or benefits to assist employees affected by it. These payments are exempt from federal income and employment tax, and are deductible by the employer. Code § 139(a) provides that qualified disaster relief payments are not included in the employee's gross income; § 1 39(b) defines a qualified disaster relief payment as one that pays or reimburses personal, family, living, or funeral expenses caused by a disaster. A disaster, in turn, is defined as a presidentially declared disaster, a disaster caused by a common carrier accident, terrorism, military action, or anything else determined by the Secretary of the Treasury to be a catastrophic event. Recipients will probably not be taxed on amounts paid by a federal, state, or local government agency. But amounts are excluded from income only to the extent that the same expense is not already covered, e.g., by insurance.

Also covered are the repair or rehabilitation of the employee's personal residence (whether owned or rented) and repair or replacement of the contents of the personal residence required by the disaster. See IRS Publication 3833. However, replacement of lost wages or other income is not considered a qualified disaster relief payment. [Mary Hughes, *Employers May Provide Tax-Free Relief To Employees Hit By Storm, Attorney Says*, Human Resources Report (Nov. 5, 2012) (benefitslink.com)]

IRS Announcement 2012-44, 2012-49 I.R.B. 663, provides relief from some verification procedures under retirement plans for plan loans, hardship distributions, and other pension distributions. Because of this IRS position, ERISA Title I violations will not be charged solely for complying with this announcement. In addition to IRS actions, DOL said that employers would not be penalized for temporary delays caused by being unable to forward contributions to processors in disaster-affected areas. Of course, advance blackout notice does not have to be given if the blackout period is disaster-related. The DOL reminded fiduciaries of EGHPs and COBRA plans to take reasonable steps to preserve benefits in case of deadlines missed due to disaster. [<www.irs.gov/uac/Newsroom/Help-for-Victims-of-Hurricane-Sandy> is the list of covered disaster areas entitled to an extension on filing Form 5500, plus other relief. See EBSA News, *US Department Of Labor Issues Compliance Guidance For Employee Benefit Plans In Wake Of Hurricane Sandy* (Nov. 20, 2012) (benefitslink.com).]

In 2009–2010, the swine flu epidemic was not as serious as projected. Nevertheless, it raised important questions about preparedness for epidemics and other disasters—such as the blizzard conditions in much of the United States in the winter of 2010–2011. Earthquakes and the earthquake/tsunami/nuclear accident in Japan in 2011 also showed the need to plan not only for emergencies but also for catastrophes on a previously unimagined scale.

The CDC's advice to employers about how to decrease flu infections in the workplace:

- Respond based on the severity level that actually occurs;
- Try to reduce transmission among the staff, protect workers who are at the highest risk of complications, maintain business operations, and minimize adverse effects within the supply chain;
- Encourage sick workers to stay home; if they are present in the workplace, encourage them to wash their hands frequently and cover coughs; routinely clean surfaces that employees touch;
- Cancel large meetings whenever possible; allow work from home; reduce non-essential travel;
- Make vaccination more accessible to employees;
- Have a plan if employees who are not sick still must miss work because their children's schools are closed;
- Cross-train workers to cover for colleagues who are sick or caring for sick family members;
- Allow employees with the flu to stay home for at least 24 hours until their symptoms resolve without requiring a doctor's note—doctors will be too busy to give notes, and their offices can become a site of new infection.

[Mark A. Lies II, *Swine Flu: The Employer's Guide to the Legal and Workplace Implications of a Swine Flu Outbreak*, Seyfarth Shaw, <http://www.seyfarth.com/index.cfm/fuseaction/publications.publications_detail/object_id/

b95244cb-af65-40fd-a438-4816472c1849/SwineFluTheEmployersGuidetothe LegalandWorkplaceImplicationsofaSwineFluOutbreak.cfm>. See also <http://www.osha.gov/Publications/influenza_pandemic.html#medium_exposure_risk>; *Guidance for Businesses and Employers to Plan and Respond to the 2009–2010 Influenza Season* (Aug. 19, 2009) (benefitslink.com); see also <www.osha.gov/dsg/topics/pandemicflu/index.html>]

Severe weather conditions in the winter of 2010–2011 highlighted the need for companies to maintain a policy about when employees are required to come to work despite weather problems; when they can work at home; and if they will be paid if it is impossible to get to work. (Another option is to give employees a choice between extra pay and comp time if they are able to come to work despite severe weather conditions.) When a storm is forecast for the next day or day after, advise employees to take work home with them, but let employees wait to come in until after the roads have been plowed. Sometimes it is worthwhile to make a deal with a local hotel near the workplace, where key employees can stay and avoid commuting problems. However, the workload is also likely to be low—if employees can't get to work, neither can customers. [Sarah E. Needleman, *It's Snowing. Do We Get the Day Off?*, WSJ.com (Feb. 4, 2011)] However, this was much less of a concern in the unusually mild 2011–2012 winter season.

## § 1.15   OVERTIME AND OVERTIME PLANNING

### [A]   Generally

One of the major functions of the FLSA is to require "time and a half for overtime" to be paid to all nonexempt hourly employees who work more than 40 hours in a work week. They must receive 150% of their normal pay rate for the additional hours.

According to the D.C. Circuit, the FLSA does not require employers to pay overtime when a worker puts in more than eight hours in a particular day, as long as his or her hours for the week as a whole do not exceed 40. The plaintiff alleged that her CBA required payment of overtime, but even if that is true, the court ruled that it did not have federal subject matter jurisdiction over a contract interpretation claim. [*Fernandez v. Centerplate/NBSE*, 441 F.3d 1006 (D.C. Cir. 2006)]

Certain categories of employees are exempt from the FLSA's minimum wage and overtime provisions. [29 U.S.C. § 213(a)(1)] The major exempt categories are executives, administrators, professionals, and outside salespersons. Whether a person is exempt depends on the actual duties of the job, not the job title. Exemption is based on "primary duties"—what the person does for 50% or more of the work time.

Exempt workers do not have to be paid for weeks in which they do not work at all, but otherwise 29 C.F.R. § 541.118(a) provides that their salary cannot be reduced based on the number of hours worked or the number of hours of absences. The employer cannot reduce the wages of exempt employees for absences that were caused by the employer or the operating requirements of its business. Nor can the employer take deductions to penalize an exempt worker for work place infractions, other than violations of major safety rules.

Specifically, docking a worker's pay for "variations in quantity or quality of work" is appropriate for hourly workers who are entitled to overtime, but not for exempt workers. The real test, however, is whether reductions are ever taken. In 1997, the Supreme Court ruled that police officers were exempt salaried employees, even though the employee manual said that pay could be docked for various disciplinary infractions: the mere possibility didn't make them nonexempt. [*Auer v. Robbins*, 519 U.S. 452 (1997)]

The Middle District of Pennsylvania approved a $20.9 million settlement in Rite Aid's wage and hour class and collective action. The settlement resolves 14 nationwide cases about improper designation of assistant store managers and co-managers as exempt in 4,700 Rite Aid Stores, with 7,426 class members in 31 states. The average class member is expected to receive about $1,845, depending on the number of hours worked during the applicable period. Twelve law firms worked on the case, and they will receive $6.7 million in fees. [*Craig v. Rite Aid*, No. 4:08-cv-2317 (settled M.D. Pa. Jan. 7, 2013; see Gina Passarella, *Class Action Against Rite Aid Settles for $20.9 Million*, Legal Intelligencer (Jan. 9, 2013) (law.com). See also *Knepper v. Rite Aid*, 675 F.3d 249 (3d Cir. 2012) establishing that FLSA collective actions can be combined with class actions.]

## [B] Categories of Exempt Employees

The FLSA defines executives, professionals, and other categories of workers, based on their main responsibilities. However, the statute left many important questions unresolved, and furthermore the existing regulations expressed obsolete concepts about the workplace and the economy. On April 23, 2004, DOL published a 150-page Final Rule amending 29 C.F.R. Part 541, explicating changes in the FLSA § 13(a) overtime exemption for executive, administrative, professional, outside sales, and computer employees: 69 Fed. Reg. 22122 *et seq.* For guidance in somewhat more concise form, see the Wage and Hour Division's FairPay Fact Sheets at <http://www.dol.gov/esa/regs/compliance/whd/fairpay/fact_exemption.htm>.

The Department of Labor's Fair Pay Overtime Initiative site is at <http://www.dol.gov/esa/regs/compliance/whd/fairpay/main.htm>. Additional FLSA information is available at <http://www.wagehour.dol.gov>, and DOL Wage and Hour Opinion Letters can be found at <http://www.dol.gov/esa/whd/opinion/FLSA>.

Until this final rule was promulgated, the minimum salary test for the white-collar exemption under the FLSA had remained pegged at $155 a week since 1976. The Final Rule nearly triples this, to $455 a week. DOL also believed that changes in work categories were necessary because of shifts in the composition of the workforce since 1949—the last time the categories were changed!

The final rule (effective August 23, 2004) provides for both a minimum salary (anyone who earns less than $23,660 a year is automatically entitled to overtime) and a maximum. Employees who earn a total of more than $23,660 in combined U.S. and foreign currency qualify for the white-collar exemption even if their U.S.-currency earnings are below that amount: FLSA 2006-17 (May 23, 2006).

Highly compensated white-collar workers earning $100,000 or more a year are automatically exempt from overtime as long as their salary is at least $455 a week, and as long as they regularly perform at least one duty as an exempt executive, professional, or administrative worker.

The Final Rule applies only to white-collar workers. Blue-collar workers "who perform work involving repetitive operations with their hands, physical skill and energy" (69 Fed. Reg. 22122) are entitled to overtime pay.

In response to criticisms of chain stores and other operations charged with giving low-level personnel "management" titles (to preclude them from overtime eligibility), the amended version of 29 C.F.R. § 541.2 provides that "a job title alone is insufficient to establish the exempt status of an employee. The exempt or nonexempt status of any particular employee must be determined on the basis of whether the employee's salary and duties meet the requirements of the regulations in this part."

The exemptions discussed here all require that the person be compensated on a salary rather than hourly basis, and that the person must earn at least $455 a week. A person is considered to be paid on a salary basis if the set compensation for the pay unit (e.g., week or month) is not subject to reductions based on variations in how much work the person does, or how well the work is performed.

The general rule is that as long as a salaried worker does any work in a pay period, he or she must be paid for the entire period, and deductions must not be taken for time when the employee is ready, willing, and able to work but there is no work for him or her to do. However, employers of salaried workers are permitted to make deductions for full days away from work that the employee takes as personal days; sick days taken under a bona fide plan; unpaid FMLA leave; or when the employee is suspended for violating a major safety rule or for other workplace infractions. Deductions can also be made if the last week a salaried employee works is a partial week.

An individual can also be paid on a fee basis for administrative, professional, or computer-oriented work while remaining exempt from overtime entitlement. The minimum salary test is applied to work done on a fee basis by comparing the compensation and the time spent to complete the assignment with the standard $455 weekly salary.

■ **TIP:** Even if they do not satisfy the salary test, outside salespersons, teachers, lawyers, and doctors are exempt from overtime. See <http://www.dol.gov/esa/regs/compliance/whd/fairpay/fs17g_salary.htm> for discussion of issues about salaried employees. See also Snell & Wilmer's Overtime Compliance Guide and Audit, <http://www.swlaw.com/

publications/files/Overtime_Guide_and_Audit_Web.pdf> for flow charts for determining which employees are entitled to overtime.

A worker will be considered an executive—and therefore not entitled to overtime pay because of executive status—if:

- The person's primary duty is management either of the entire enterprise that employs him or her, or a recognized subdivision or department of the enterprise.

- He or she "customarily and regularly" directs the work of two or more fellow employees (or two full-time equivalents in an enterprise that has some part-time workers).

- He or she has hiring and firing authority, or can make suggestions that "are given particular weight" with respect to (29 C.F.R. §§ 541.100, 541.102).

The C.F.R. defines "management" as activities such as hiring and training employees, appraising their work performance, assigning tasks, budgeting, and complying with legal requirements. Section 541.106 explicates the concept of "concurrent duties" (the issue involved when there is controversy about whether a person is a manager or a rank-and-file worker). If a person otherwise qualifies as an executive, he or she remains exempt despite the performance of concurrent duties (nonexempt work such as waiting on customers, stocking shelves, or cleaning business premises, undertaken by a person whose primary duty is management). However, a person such as a factory supervisor whose main duties are nonexempt does not become an executive merely because he or she occasionally has to make discretionary decisions.

A "business owner" (29 C.F.R. § 541.101) owns a bona fide equity interest of 20% or more in the business that employs him or her, and who is actively employed in the management of the business. A business owner is considered a manager and therefore is not entitled to overtime, even if he or she earns less than $455 a week.

An exempt administrative worker is primarily engaged in "work directly related to the management or general business operations" of the employer company or its customers. See 29 C.F.R. § 541.201—work in "functional areas" such as purchasing, marketing, HR, public relations, etc. The employee must be required to exercise discretion and independent judgment on significant matters. A "New Purchase/Customer Relations Manager" was held by the First Circuit to be an exempt administrative employee, and hence not entitled to receive overtime. 29 C.F.R. § 541.200 defines an administrative employee's primary duty as office or non-manual work related to management or general business operations, using discretion and independent judgment on matters of significance. In this case, although in practice the plaintiff was not required to perform all the duties of the job description he drafted himself, he did have to interact with customers and settle delivery problems, using discretion to meet the individual needs of his customers. [*Cash v. Cycle Craft Co. Inc.*, 508 F.3d 680 (1st Cir. 2007)]

Even though service station managers sometimes perform non-exempt work when they're short-staffed, they remain executives (because of their responsibilities for hiring and firing) as long as non-exempt work is done only infrequently: FLSA 2006-29 (Sept. 27, 2006).

29 C.F.R. § 541.203 provides examples of the administrative worker exemption, e.g., insurance claims adjusters; financial services employees who collect and analyze information about customers' income, assets, and investments; and executive assistants and administrative assistants. There is a specific provision (§ 541.203(e)) clarifying that personnel clerks are typically not exempt from overtime, but human resources managers "who formulate, interpret or implement employment policies" are exempt. A number of cases have been decided on the administrative worker exemption:

- Insurance claims adjusters are exempt because they exercise discretion and make independent judgment after, e.g., investigating and settling claims and making repair adjustments: *Robinson-Smith v. GEICO*, 590 F.3d 886 (D.C. Cir. 2010); *Roe-Midgett v. CC Services, Inc.*, 512 F.3d 865 (7th Cir. 2008); *Miller v. Farmer's Ins. Exchange*, 466 F.3d 853 (9th Cir. 2006), amended 481 F.3d 1119 (9th Cir. 2007); *Harris v. Superior Court (Liberty Mut. Ins. Co.)*, 53 Cal. 4th 170 (Cal. 2011).

- Mortgage loan officers are exempt on the basis of discretion and judgment, even though they use software to help choose the best products for customers: FLSA 2006-31 (Sept. 27, 2006).

- But the Second Circuit held, in 2009 that loan approval underwriters were non-exempt production employees with respect to loans. They simply applied an existing credit policy. It was also relevant that they could earn bonuses for processing more loans per day. [*Davis v. J.P. Morgan Chase & Co.*, 587 F.3d 529 (2d Cir. 2009)]

- The Second Circuit decided a case of first impression in 2010: whether an advertising salesperson is an exempt administrative employee. The court decided that someone who was paid a base salary and commissions, but not overtime, to sell advertising in a publication most of whose revenues came from advertising was a salesperson and not an administrative employee. An employee who makes specific sales to individual customers is considered a salesperson for FLSA purposes, whereas someone who generally encourages greater sales among all customers is an administrative employee. [*Reiseck v. Universal Commc'ns of Miami, Inc.*, 591 F.3d 101 (2d Cir. 2010)]

- Overtime is not required for employees who earn more than 150% of the minimum wage when over half of their compensation comes from commissions. The California Court of Appeal held that employment recruiters were commissioned employees. A commission is a percentage of the price paid for selling a product or service. Recruiting employees for others is a kind of sale, and the firm was paid only if a successful placement was made. [*Muldrow v. Surrex Solutions Corp.*, 208 Cal. App. 4th 1381, 146 Cal. Rptr. 3d 447 (2012)]

Yet another overtime exemption applies to those employed in "a bona fide professional capacity," defined by 29 C.F.R. § 541.300 either as work requiring advanced knowledge acquired by formal education, or "requiring invention, imagination, originality or talent in a recognized field of artistic or creative endeavor." In addition to the traditional "learned professions" (e.g., medicine, law, engineering, teaching, pharmacy), registered nurses, registered or certified medical technicians, and physician's assistants, and dental hygienists are considered to be professionals. 29 C.F.R. § 541.302 defines creative professionals as those whose primary work requires creativity and artistry, e.g., in music, writing, acting, or graphic arts—work that cannot be done by a person with only general "manual or intellectual ability and training."

The Fifth Circuit agreed that nurse practitioners and physician's assistants are not exempt and are entitled to be paid overtime. Although 29 C.F.R. § 541.3(d) specifically calls physician's assistants, nurses, and technologists "learned professionals" who are exempt under the duty requirement, they are not listed as one of the professions that fall outside the "salary basis" exception. They are paid by the hour; they are not licensed to practice medicine; and their work is similar to the work of non-exempt registered nurses. [*Belt v. Emcare, Inc.*, 444 F.3d 403 (5th Cir. 2006); see 69 Fed. Reg. 22,122 (Apr. 23, 2004) for the § 541.3(e) Regulation] Respiratory therapists do not need specialized advanced education and therefore are not a learned profession: FLSA 2006-26 (Sept. 27, 2006).

Systems analysts, computer programmers, software engineers (or people doing the same kind of work, even if their title changes to respond to this fast-moving field) are exempt from overtime under 29 C.F.R. § 541.400. There is an alternative test for computer professionals: a person who earns either the ordinary $455/week salary test, or an hourly rate of $27.63/hour or more, is not entitled to overtime. The Final Rule exempts computer professionals from overtime, but the exemption refers to those who, e.g., design and develop hardware and software, not to people who assemble or repair computers.

According to the Sixth Circuit, a computer help desk employee who does troubleshooting, maintenance, and support is not a "computer professional" exempt under the FLSA, because the work is not analytical enough; programming, software engineering, and systems analysis were not involved, and his work was completely directed by others, not performed with individual initiative.

[*Martin v. Ind. Mich. Power Co.*, 381 F.3d 574 (6th Cir. 2004). See <http://www .dol.gov/esa/regs/compliance/whd/fairpay/fs17e_computer.htm> for the Department of Labor's fact sheet on classification of IT workers; FLSA 2006-12, Nov. 21, 2006 says that help desk employees are non-exempt because the job requires only a high school diploma and does not involve independent judgment, and it does not require the development and analysis skills that justify the computer exception.]

The final white-collar exemption, for Outside Sales staff, is defined by § 541.500 as workers whose primary duty is making sales or getting orders or contracts. The mainstay of such an employee's work is performed outside the employer's place of business. This category does not include mail, telephone, or online sales unless these media are only used to set up a personal appointment. When it comes to "drivers who sell" (§ 541.504), the test is whether sales predominates over delivery (thus making the person exempt) or whether delivery predominates (making him or her eligible for overtime).

The Third Circuit refused to revive an FLSA suit brought by NutriSystem salespersons, even though the DOL agreed with their position and filed an amicus brief. The Third Circuit found that their compensation falls within the FLSA's "retail commission" exception because it was proportional to the cost of products sold. [*Parker v. NutriSystem Inc.*, 620 F.3d 274 (3d Cir. Sept. 7, 2010); see Shannon P. Duffy, *3rd Circuit Refuses to Revive* NutriSystem *Overtime Suit*, The Legal Intelligencer (Sept. 8, 2010) (law.com); Shannon P. Duffy, *No Overtime Pay Due NutriSystem's Phone Sales Force, Federal Judge Rules*, The Legal Intelligencer (Aug. 5, 2009) (law.com)]

The Supreme Court resolved a circuit split about the proper treatment of drug "detailers" in June 2012. The Supreme Court ruled that these pharmaceutical representatives are outside salespersons exempt from overtime. [*Christopher v. SmithKline Beecham*, 132 S. Ct. 2156 (2012); see Marcia Coyle, *A Big Win for Pharma Companies in Overtime Case*, Nat'l L.J. (June 18, 2012) (law.com)]

The final Rule does not affect the eligibility of blue-collar workers for overtime pay. Its examples of blue collar workers are construction workers, carpenters, electricians, plumbers, laborers, etc. (69 Fed. Reg. 22122; 29 C.F.R. § 541.3). As a general rule, public safety workers (e.g., police officers, firefighters, paramedics, Emergency Medical Technicians) are also entitled to overtime. Employers continue to be bound by whatever overtime arrangements they have entered into under Collective Bargaining Agreements, and state laws that are more protective of workers are not preempted by the Final Rule (29 C.F.R. § 541.4). However, the Sixth Circuit held that police officers on airport duty did not prove that they were entitled to overtime pay for times when they were required to wear pagers and stay within a set radius of the airport in order to report when summoned for an emergency. The Sixth Circuit said that the test of whether comp time has to be granted is whether off-duty time is so severely burdened that workers cannot control their use of the time (29 C.F.R. § 553.221(d)). [*Adair v. County of Wayne*, 452 F.3d 482 (6th Cir. 2006); see Fred Schneyer, *Detroit Cops Lose OT Court Fight*, plansponsor.com (July 11, 2006)]

For information about state wage and hour laws (the FLSA does not preempt state laws that offer greater protection to the employee) see DOL's links to state Labor Departments. [<http://www.dol.gov/whd/contacts/state_of.htm>]

### [C] Payment of Overtime

Nonexempt hourly employees must be paid time-and-a-half (150% of their normal pay rate, including commissions) when they work more than 40 hours in any work week. Work time is all the time when the employer controls the employee's actions, including times the employee is required to be on duty or at a prescribed place. However, bona fide meal periods are not considered work time. Ordinary commuting to work is not work time, Work-related travel, such as an assignment to deliver something or go to a meeting at a client's office, is work time.

These are some items that may require compensation or overtime:

- Rest breaks under 20 minutes;
- Down time or on-call time that prevents the employee from carrying out personal business;
- Preparation before shift or clean-up after shift;
- Mandatory classes, meetings, or conventions;
- Travel time other than normal commuting.

The workweek doesn't have to be Monday–Friday, 9–5: it can be defined as any 168 consecutive hours, starting any time. It doesn't have to be the same as the payroll period. Different work groups or individuals can have different workweeks. Usually, once an employer sets a workweek, it has to abide by it—but a permanent change that is not a subterfuge to evade the FLSA's overtime requirements is permitted. [See 29 C.F.R. § 778.104, averaging a long and a short week to see if overtime is payable is not allowed]

### [D] Case Law on Overtime

In a shaky economy, FLSA litigation (and employment discrimination litigation) predictably increases, because many potential plaintiffs are no longer employed and do not fear that filing suit will lead to their discharge. Employers often take the position that the FLSA rules are outdated, and fail to represent the current realities of the workplace, because the statutory categories represent outmoded categories.

Issues often raised in litigation include misclassification of workers as exempt and demands that workers (especially in the retail and restaurant industries) work "off the clock."

Many important cases have reached a verdict or settlement.

The largest overtime pay class action ever to be tried was settled in September 2004 for over $200 million, resolving claims that Farmers Insurance Exchange wrongfully deprived approximately 2,400 Californian claims adjusters of overtime pay. A separate multidistrict case covering claims adjusters nationwide in the District Court for the District of Oregon resulted in a $53 million judgment for the plaintiffs. [*Bell v. Farmers Ins. Exchange*, No. 774013-0 (Alameda Cnty. Superior Court), discussed in Mike McKee, *Huge Settlement Ends Record-Setting Overtime Class Action*, The Recorder (Sept. 7, 2004) (law. com); *In re Farmers Insurance Exchange Claims Representatives' Overtime Pay Litig.*, MDL No. 1439 (D. Or. 2004), discussed in *Insurer Loses to Adjusters on Overtime*, N.Y. Times, May 4, 2005, at C6, and Tresa Baldas, *New Overtime Rules Bring Suits*, Nat'l L.J. (Mar. 17, 2005) (law.com)]

It's important to note that not all employee overtime claims result in victory.

The Seventh Circuit ruled that time (including travel time) spent attending counseling sessions mandated by the employer pursuant to a fitness for duty examination was work time compensable under the FLSA. [*Sehie v. City of Aurora*, 432 F.3d 749 (7th Cir. 2005)]

In a suit for the recovery of unpaid overtime, the California Supreme Court ruled that individual officers, directors, and shareholders were not personally liable. Corporate directors can be jointly liable with the corporation if they personally direct or participate in tortious conduct, but the court declined to impose personal liability in *Reynolds v. Bement* because failure to comply with statutory overtime requirements is not tortious, and there was no allegation that the officers or directors retained the unpaid overtime compensation for their own benefit. [*Reynolds v. Bement*, 36 Cal. 4th 1075 (Cal. Sup. 2005)]

The Supreme Court ruled in March 2011, that it is unlawful to retaliate against an employee who complains about an FLSA violation—even if the complaint is made orally, not in writing, and is made to the employer rather than to a government agency. [*Kasten v. Saint-Gobain Performance Plastics Corp.*, 131 S. Ct. 1325 (2011); see Tony Mauro, *Court Rules for 'Little Guys' Over Corporations in Two Business Cases*, Nat'l L.J. (Mar. 22, 2011) (law.com)]

According to the Eleventh Circuit, punitive damages are not available for violation of the anti-retaliation provision. [*Snapp v. Unlimited Concepts, Inc.*, 208 F.3d 928 (11th Cir. 2000)]

## [E]  Scheduling Workers for Overtime

Sometimes, the employer will have to provide additional incentives, such as meal vouchers or free meals in the employee cafeteria or transportation home, for overtime work. But it is more common for employees to compete to be able to put in extra hours at the higher overtime rate. It is legitimate to assign overtime in order of seniority: to let employees bid for overtime work, with priority to the most senior.

In a unionized workplace, the CBA determines how much notice the company must give when overtime will be required; the extent to which overtime is assigned and when it is voluntary; who gets to bid on it; maximum overtime hours; and meal and rest breaks during overtime. If the employer assigns overtime, the disciplinary procedure should be drafted to specify that refusal to work mandatory overtime is a legitimate subject for discipline.

The FLSA allows employers to maintain a policy under which overtime work must be authorized. (Otherwise, employees would have an incentive to goof off during the day and catch up during better-paid overtime hours). But overtime pay is required if the employer permits or even is aware that nonexempt employees are working more than 40 hours a week.

■ **TIP:**   The amount of overtime can be reduced by

- Planning further in advance;
- Being more realistic about deadlines;
- Coordinating tasks better, so materials and intermediate products are available when the production cycle requires them;
- Coordinating vacation and leave schedules so there will be enough employees available and it won't be necessary for a few workers to put in extra hours to cover for those who are absent.

### [F]   Donning and Doffing; Preliminary and Postliminary Activities

The Portal-to-Portal Act makes the FLSA applicable to the employee's "workweek": the time when he or she is engaged in the principal activities of the job. Walking around within the workplace is not considered to be work time, and neither are "preliminary" and "postliminary" activities prior to and after the employee begins to work.

However, it is often necessary to determine whether "donning and doffing" (putting on and removing required uniforms, equipment, and safety gear) time constitutes work time.

In November 2005, the Supreme Court ruled that putting on and taking off gear that is integral to work is compensable as part of the work day, as is walking between the production area and the area where protective clothing is put on and removed. However, the time employees spend waiting to put on their protective gear is not compensable because it is not closely enough related to the principal activities of the job. [*IBP v. Alvarez*, 546 U.S. 21 (2005)]

A mid-2007 Eleventh Circuit decision held that time spent by workers on an airport construction project in going through security screening, and riding buses provided by the employer from the off-site location where they were required to park for security reasons, was not compensable under the FLSA, because no work-related activity occurred during this time. [*Bonilla v. Baker Concrete Constr., Inc.*, 487 F.3d 1340 (11th Cir. 2007); similarly *Gorman v. Consolidated Edison Corp.*, 488 F.3d 586 (2d Cir. 2007), holds that 10–30 minutes before work going through security and suiting up is not integral; the security requirements are essential to plant operations but not to the principal work activity. They are the equivalent of travel time, which can be extensive but is not compensable. But see *Spoerle et al. v. Kraft Foods Global Inc.*, No. 07-00300, 2007 U.S. Dist. LEXIS 95307 (W.D. Wis. Dec. 31, 2007), holding that wearing safety gear is an integral part of work]

In a donning/doffing suit, the district court granted summary judgment for the employer; the Sixth Circuit affirmed in part, and reversed in part. 29 U.S.C. § 203(o) excludes time changing clothes from work time, if there is a custom or practice under a bona fide CBA of not paying for changing time. The plaintiff said that the required uniforms and standard safety equipment were not "clothes." The Sixth Circuit said that there is a split in authority, but most courts (the Third, Fifth, Eleventh, and Federal Circuits) have ruled that the § 203(o) argument is not an affirmative defense that the employer must prove—the plaintiff must prove that the time should be considered compensable time. [*Franklin v. Kellogg Co.*, 619 F.3d 592 (6th Cir. 2010); see also *Allen v. McWane Inc.*, 593 F.3d 449 (5th Cir. 2010). In early 2011, the Minnesota Court of Appeals ruled that hourly workers at the Turkey Store were not eligible under state law for compensation for time spent putting on and taking off their uniforms and safety equipment: *Rios v. Jennie-O Turkey Store Inc.*, 793 N.W.2d 309 (Minn. App. 2011); see Rebecca Moore, *JennieO Wins Donning and Doffing Suit*, plansponsor.com (Jan. 19, 2011)]

The Seventh Circuit held that time spent changing clothes and showering to remove lime dust and other chemicals after the end of the shift at a paper mill is non-compensable postliminary activity. The C.F.R. defines washing up and changing clothes as non-compensable unless they are integral to employment (29 C.F.R. §§ 785.24(c), 790.7(g)), and the employer had a policy of compensating clean-up after non-routine exposure to hazardous chemicals. [*Musch v. Domtar Indus., Inc.*, 587 F.3d 857 (7th Cir. 2009)]

The Seventh Circuit denied back pay to a former employee who claimed that she worked 15 to 45 minutes before her shift every day without being paid. There was no evidence that her employer knew or had reason to know about the extra work. The plaintiff was a sewing manager, paid by the hour to supervise seven or eight other employees. She said that she regularly spent time before the shift going over schedules, cleaning the work area, and distributing materials. She admitted that she was not ordered to arrive early. Although the work was not de minimis, the Seventh Circuit held that employers do not have to pay for work that they have no reason to know about. [*Kellar v. Summit Seating Inc.*, 664 F.3d 169 (7th Cir. 2011); see Ogletree Deakins, *Seventh Circuit Holds Employer Not Liable Under FLSA for Employee's Off-The-Clock Work* (Dec. 21, 2011) (benefitslink.com)]

## § 1.16  VACATIONS AND VACATION PAY

On the average, U.S. workers get less vacation than European workers. Furthermore, U.S. workers may feel that if they take their scheduled vacation time, they will not be able to complete all the work that falls to them in a downsized workplace.

> ■ **TIP:** Audit requirements may actually require employees with access to the firm's cash and books to take at least two consecutive weeks of vacation. An employee who never uses his or her full allotment of vacation time could be a conscientious person who wants to cope with a backlog, a workaholic who really needs to "get a life" outside the office, a sub-par employee who needs extra time to make up for incompetence, or an embezzler who has to hang around to prevent crooked schemes from unraveling!

The federal Davis-Bacon Act requires government contractors to pay for unused vacation days when an employee terminates but there is no general FLSA provision covering other situations. Most of the states impose a similar requirement for state government employees, but not in the private sector. Some states, however, have rules about this.

In Oklahoma, unused vacation time is payable on termination only if this is agreed on in an established policy. In New Hampshire, vacation, sick, and personal days are wages if the benefits are a matter of employment practice or policy. The Massachusetts statute defines wages to include holiday or vacation pay due under any written or even oral agreement and Wyoming requires employers to pay for unused vacation time accrued under the employer's vacation policy. The Massachusetts Supreme Judicial Court has held that, although employers are not required to provide paid vacation, if they choose to do so they must pay employees for the unused vacation time when their employment is terminated, even if their policy says the vacation time is forfeited. The court did not reach the question of what happens to unused vacation time when an employee quits—the statute the court was interpreting deals only with involuntary termination. [*Electronic Data Systems v. Attorney General*, 454 Mass. 63 (Mass. 2009); see Fisher & Phillips LLP, *Massachusetts Supreme Judicial Court Rules Employers Must Pay Terminated Employees for Any Unused Vacation Time* (June 12, 2009) (benefitslink.com). The statute is Mass. General Laws Chapter 149 § 148.]

A donated leave program, also known as leave sharing or voluntary shared leave, permits employees to donate accrued paid absence (vacation, personal, or sick leave) on behalf of co-workers. The general rule is that income is taxed to the person who earned it, even if the employee donates paid time off instead of money. However, the IRS makes an exception for bona fide leave sharing arrangements for medical emergencies and for leave banks for natural disasters. Rev. Rul. 90-29 defines a medical emergency as the employee's or family member's medical condition requiring prolonged time away from work and substantial loss of income because of exhaustion of paid leave. The employee donating the leave is not taxed on compensation for the leave days. The donee receives his or her normal pay rate and the funds are considered wages of the donee for purposes of FICA, FUTA, and income tax withholding. The donor is not entitled to claim an expense, charitable, or loss deduction for the donated leave. To be valid for tax purposes, the arrangement must be written, administered by the employer, have a procedure for written applications, must limit the donees to people who have exhausted all their paid leave, and must limit use of leave to medical emergencies. (The IRS nevertheless permits plans to give time off after the death of a spouse, child, or parent.) The plan must specify any limits on the amount of leave a person can donate in a year, and must monitor that the leave is actually used as medical leave. [Brendan Pierson, *Worker Absence During Storm Raises Questions for Employers*, N.Y.L.J. (Nov. 19, 2012)]

Federal law doesn't require celebration of holidays, and does not require holiday pay, although some states impose special requirements for employees who do work on a holiday. However, once a company adopts a holiday policy, it must continue to follow it; failure would constitute not paying all wages due. When setting a policy, it is necessary to decide who receives holiday pay—the entire workforce? Managers? Full-time employees only? What happens if the holiday is on a Sunday when the workplace would normally be closed? It is generally legal to have different holiday pay policies for different positions—but it would be discriminatory not to receive the same pay for everyone in the same position. Generally, payment is required only for hours actually worked plus any holiday supplement promised to the employees. Comp time is another possibility, but it must be spelled out. [John Donovan, Fisher & Phillips LLP, *Solutions at Work, Does Your Holiday Policy Need a Tune Up?* (February 2011) (benefitslink.com)]

In the interest of work/life balance, some respondents to Compdata Surveys' Benefits USA 2011–2012 report offer additional paid time off in special circumstances. The survey covered close to 4,500 benefit plans with over six million participants. One-third of respondents offered paid time off in connection with a death in the family, with an average of 3.4 days off allowed. One-third paid employees on jury duty, 17.2% provided paid military leave. Paid maternity, paternity, or adoption leave was provided by 8.6% and 5.1% allowed paid leave for a family illness. Nearly one-quarter (24%) had a leave assistance program to help employees who had exhausted their paid leave; 6.8% had leave banks where other employees could contribute their unused time off, and 5.5% allowed direct transfer of unused leave from one employee to another. [Stephen Miller, *Employers Offering Paid Time Off for Special Circumstances*, SHRM.com (Apr. 16, 2012) (benefitslink.com)]

## § 1.17   GARNISHMENTS AND DEDUCTIONS FOR SUPPORT ORDERS

### [A]   Assignments versus Garnishments

There may be instances in which the HR department is asked to apply some of an employee's wages to a debt, such as consumer debts, student loan debt, and the obligation to support children, and/or an ex-spouse.

An "assignment" is an action undertaken by an individual to direct some of his or her future compensation to creditors. A "garnishment" is a deduction from wages made pursuant to a court order. Federal law doesn't say anything about wage assignments, although many states limit the amount or percentage of each paycheck that can be assigned, permit assignments only for certain classes of debts, or require the spouse's consent to the assignment.

BAPCPA made it harder for many consumer debtors to file for bankruptcy protection. Although the lesser of 75% of wages, or 30 times the minimum wage, is exempt from garnishment, the minimum wage has not kept up with inflation, with the result that only $217.50/week is exempt from seizure under the federal rules. (Some states exempt larger amounts.) Losing 25% of income may make it impossible for the low-wage debtor to pay bills. [Sidney Jones, *More Struggling Borrowers Face Pay Garnishment*, NYTimes.com (Apr. 2, 2010)]

Pensions cannot be assigned before they are received (except through a Qualified Domestic Relations Order (QDRO) See § 12.08). Once a pension payment is made, the recipient can do whatever he or she wants with it, but the "anti-alienation" rules of ERISA prevent advance assignment.

The federal Consumer Credit Protection Act (CCPA) [15 U.S.C. §§ 1671 *et seq.*] puts limits on garnishment. Generally, the maximum permitted garnishment will be 25% of the employee's "disposable" earnings, with stricter limits on garnishments for very low-income workers. "Disposable earnings" is defined as approximately equal to gross income minus Social Security taxes and withheld income taxes. Health insurance premiums and spousal and child support are not deducted, even if the support is ordered by a court. Thus, serious problems can occur if the same individual is subject to garnishment both for consumer debt and support payments.

Garnishment for support rather than consumer debt can be higher [15 U.S.C. § 1673]:

- 50%, if the employee is supporting a spouse or child other than the subject of the order, and the garnishment order covers less than 12 weeks' worth of arrears;

- 55%, if conditions are the same but more than 12 weeks of arrears are involved;

- 60%, if the employee does not have a new family to support, and arrears are 12 weeks or less;

- 65%, if there is no second family and arrears exceed 12 weeks.

There is no limit on garnishments that respond to an order issued by a Chapter 11 or Chapter 13 bankruptcy court, or on a debt due for any state or federal tax. The general rule against alienation of plan benefits doesn't prevent the IRS from garnishing a taxpayer's (or rather, nontaxpayer's) vested interest in qualified benefits when the agency has a judgment for unpaid taxes.

The CCPA says that, if state law limits garnishment more than the federal law does, employees are entitled to the protection of the stricter state-law limits. In other words, the garnishment is limited to what is permitted by state law. Under the CCPA, it's illegal to fire an employee for having one garnishment, but it's lawful to fire if additional garnishments are imposed. [16 U.S.C. § 1674] Willful violation of this provision can be punished by a $1,000 fine and/or one year's imprisonment.

It should be noted that qualified plan benefits can be garnished to collect a criminal restitution order under the Mandatory Victims Restitution Act of 1996, which provides restitution for property losses. Restitution orders have the same status as tax liens, for which plan benefits can also be garnished. [*United States v. Novak*, 441 F.3d 819 (9th Cir. 2006)]

The federal Fair Debt Collection Practices Act (FDCPA) [28 U.S.C. § 3001] lets the federal government collect its judgments by garnishing property held by a third party on the basis of the debtor's "substantial non-exempt interest" in the property. According to the Sixth Circuit, tax levies do not violate ERISA's anti-alienation provisions. [*United States v. Sawaf*, 74 F.3d 119 (6th Cir. 1996)]

In mid-2010, the PBGC revised its regulations on debt collection, to add salary offset and administrative wage garnishment to the acceptable methods of collecting non-tax debts owed to the PBGC. Administrative offset is the process of having amounts that are owed to a business (such as a government contractor) paid to the PBGC instead, to pay the business' debts to the PBGC. Salary offset is withholding of up to 15% of a federal employee's disposable pay to collect debts. Administrative wage garnishment is withholding of wages of a former federal employee who now works for a non-federal employer. The PBGC has to inform debtors of the amount and type of the debt (such as an employer's failure to pay PBGC premiums, or amounts that the PBGC overpaid to an employee), how the PBGC intends to collect the debt, what happens if the debt is not repaid, and how the debtor can make alternate arrangements if the business or individual objects to the PBGC's proposed collection efforts. Under limited circumstances, the PBGC can waive interest, penalties, and administrative costs—but federal law forbids certain types of waivers. [PBGC Proposed Rule, *Debt Collection*, 75 Fed. Reg. 42662 (July 22, 2010)]

## [B]  Student Loan Garnishments

There are separate federal rules at 20 U.S.C. § 1095a with respect to garnishment to repay student loans. Up to 10% of disposable earnings can be garnished to repay those loans. The employee can sign a document agreeing to a higher garnishment level. Before the garnishment order is submitted to the employer, the employee has the right to contest the garnishment and suggest a voluntary repayment schedule. If a person is fired or laid off from a job, and is rehired (by the original employer or someone else) within 12 months after termination, student loan garnishment is deferred until the person has been back in the workforce for 12 months.

The federal provisions do not require employers to change or depart from their normal payment mechanisms to comply with student loan garnishment orders, but if they fail to comply with the order entirely, employers can be penalized by the amount that should have been withheld to satisfy the garnishment, plus costs, fees, and punitive damages.

Federal law forbids an employer to discharge, refuse to hire, or discipline a person because he or she is subject to a student loan garnishment. Employers that violate this rule can be ordered to reinstate the affected employee with back pay, and can also be ordered to pay punitive damages and attorneys' fees.

### [C]  Child Support Collection

State governments are heavily involved in child support enforcement, to prevent children from becoming welfare recipients because their parents do not support them. The federal government also requires state governments to take this enforcement role. Under a federal statute, the Child Support Enforcement Amendments of 1984 [P.L. 98-378], states can lose federal funding if they do not enact laws requiring wage withholding for support arrears. States must also have a procedure for Qualified Medical Child Support Orders (QMCSOs) under which parents who are covered by an Employee Group Health Plan (EGHP) are required to take steps to enroll their children under the plan.

Federal law also requires state-court child support orders to contain a withholding provision, so a withholding order can be issued as soon as a parent falls behind on support, with no need for separate court proceedings. The state child support enforcement agency notifies the employer that a particular employee has child support arrears. The employer is obligated to impose withholding as of the first pay period after 14 days of the date the agency mailed its notice. Once withholding begins, the employer has an obligation to notify the child support agency promptly if the employee quits or gets fired. The notice should give the termination date, the employee's last known address, and the address of the new employer (if known).

The CCPA percentage limits discussed above apply to child support orders. Depending on circumstances, up to 65% of disposable income may be subject to withholding for support. The Child Support Enforcement Amendments allow states to impose a late payment fee of 3 to 6% of the overdue support. Support withholding takes priority over other legal processes (e.g., for consumer debts or student loans) applying to the same income.

Employers must also submit data about newly hired employees to the state unemployment insurance agency within 20 days of hiring. The information is aggregated into a National Directory of New Hires that is used to track down "deadbeat parents" who fail to pay child support.

The basic federal report (which can be made by mail or magnetic tape; state support enforcement agencies can accept telephoned, faxed, and e-mailed reports) consists of:

- Employer's name, address, and Taxpayer Identification Number;
- Employee's name;
- Employee's address;
- Employee's Social Security number.

States may impose additional requirements, such as telephone numbers, driver's license number, and information about the group health plan (to be used in conjunction with a QMCSO). The employer also has to make a quarterly report of wages paid, for use in instituting withholding orders. Failure to make a required report can be penalized by $25 per employee, or $500 for conspiracy with an employee to avoid the requirement.

## § 1.18   USERRA

Under the Uniformed Services Employment and Reemployment Rights Act [38 U.S.C. §§ 4301 *et seq.*] (USERRA), employers have obligations toward their employees who temporarily leave employment to fulfill a military commitment. After the reservist or National Guardsman or -woman returns to civilian life, the employer is obligated to re-employ the person. In this context, uniformed services means the Armed Forces (the Coast Guard is included), the National Guard, and the various service Reserves.

USERRA requires the employee to give the employer advance written or verbal notice of leave, unless this would be impossible, unreasonable, or precluded by military necessity. The statute requires the employer to reinstate the service member after discharge, in the job he or she would have achieved but for the period of military service, applying the "escalator principle" to seniority, status, compensation, and other seniority-related rights. The statute is not clear what re-employment rights apply if the person would have been laid off even absent active military duty. Furthermore, the employer is not obligated to offer the returned service member a job at the same location, and federal law does not require the employer to pay the service member during military leave. The employee can elect to use accrued vacation or other paid leave while he or she is serving, but employers are not allowed to require the service member to use accrued paid leave.

The employer is obligated to make a reasonable effort to provide training to refresh or upgrade the returning service member's skills. Employees who cannot qualify for their former job must be placed in an alternative position. However, re-employment is not required if circumstances have changed so much that it would be impossible, unreasonable, or impose an undue hardship to do it. When active duty lasted 181 days or more, the re-employed person can be fired only for cause during the first year of reinstatement (and only for cause in the first six months after re-employment following service of 30 to 180 days).

If the service member was on active duty for 30 days or less, USERRA requires him or her to report back to work after active duty on the next regular workday. If the military commitment was 31 to 180 days, the general rule is that USERRA requires the employee to apply for re-employment within 14 days of finishing the military commitment. The period to re-apply stretches to 90 days if the service member was on active duty for over 180 days.

Under USERRA, the employer must treat a period of military duty as active service with the employer for eligibility, vesting, and benefit accrual purposes. However, once the service member returns to work, he or she is entitled to benefits attributable to employee contributions only to the extent that he or she actually made such contributions. The employer is not obligated to make contributions to a 401(k) plan while the employee is on active service, but when the service member is re-employed, the employer must make whatever employer contributions would have been made if the service member had continued at work.

For plans that require or accept employee contributions, USERRA gives the employee a period of time equal to the shorter of five years or three times the duration of military service to make the contributions. Once these contributions are made, the employer must make any matching contributions that the plan calls for. However, the employer is not obligated to make contributions that include earnings or forfeitures that would have been allocated to the employee if the contributions had been made during the term of military service.

Veterans with service-connected disabilities are covered both by USERRA (enforced by the Department of Labor) and the ADA (enforced by the EEOC). Both statutes impose an obligation of reasonable accommodation on employers; the USERRA obligation is broader, because it requires employers to make efforts to assist returning veterans to become qualified, e.g., by training or retraining. Some service-related disabilities qualify for accommodation under USERRA even though they are not ADA-level disabilities. Employers are not required to give hiring preference to disabled veterans. Employers can ask applicants if they are disabled veterans, if the inquiry is for affirmative action purposes. [EEOC, *Veterans with Service-Connected Disabilities in the Workplace and the ADA*, <http://www.eeoc.gov.facts/veterans-disabilities-employers.html>] Employer Support of the Guard and Reserve (ESGR), <www.esgr.net>, is a Department of Defense unit, staffed by over 900 volunteers, to provide liaison between Reservists and their civilian workers on USERRA issues. The Website <http://www.AmericasHeroesAtWork.gov>, jointly managed by the DOL Office of Disability Employment Policy and the Veterans' Employment and Training Service, provides resources for employers when veterans with traumatic brain injury or PTSD return to work. The site covers, e.g., implementing accommodations at work and services for veterans. [Rebecca Moore, *DOL Helps Employers with Injured Veteran Issues*, plansponsor.com (Aug. 22, 2008)]

On February 28, 2012, the EEOC released two guidance documents about employment issues for veterans with disabilities. The unemployment rate among post-9/11 veterans was about 12%–13% higher than the overall rate. The revised guidance explains the difference in coverage between the ADAAA and USERRA, and the revised Guide for Wounded Veterans explains the legal implications of service-related disabilities. [CCH Employment Law Daily, *Revised EEOC Guidance Clarifies Interplay Between ADA And USERRA For Employers, Explains Rights To Veterans With Service-Related Disabilities* (March 2012) (benefitslink .com)]

Creditors are legally obligated under USERRA to reduce interest rates to 6% or less on debts owed by those entering military service. The statute allows plan fiduciaries to petition the relevant court to maintain a higher interest rate, based on a showing of the servicemember's ability to pay. USERRA also allows (but does not obligate) the plan to suspend the obligation to make regular payments of plan loans during the term of military service. [See DOL guidelines, <http:// www.dol.gov/ebsa/faqs/faq_911_2.html>. See also the Service Members Civil Relief Act, Pub. L. No. 108-189 clarifying that the 6% interest rate ceiling only applies to obligations incurred prior to entering military service. Therefore, a plan loan made to a plan participant who is already on military duty can charge the plan's normal interest rate. But interest over and above the permitted 6% level must be forgiven, not merely postponed until the servicemember returns.]

Under federal law, USERRA leave does not have to be paid leave (although some state laws do impose a requirement of a period of paid leave). The federal statute allows employees, at their option, to use accrued vacation or other paid leave while they are on active duty, but the employer is not permitted to force them to do so if they prefer unpaid leave and preservation of their leave accrual.

There is no requirement that employers provide pay supplements to prevent servicemembers from suffering a loss of income when they lose their civilian paychecks and get military pay (often much lower). However, some employers elect to do so as a patriotic statement of support for the troops. The time periods vary from three months to several years. The GAO studied past military operations, and concluded that 41% of reservists lost income when called up for active duty, 30% experienced no change, and 29% actually had higher income post-call-up.

■ **TIP:** Reservists don't get much notice before being deployed, and they can be called up for an uncertain period of anywhere from weeks to years, leaving employers to scramble to fill those positions. It is often prudent to cross-train other employees to cover for absent servicemembers.

In addition to the federal requirements, a number of states (e.g., California, Illinois, Indiana, Maine, Minnesota, Nebraska, New York, Rhode Island, and Washington) have enacted statutory employment rights for servicemembers. [See George P. Kostakos and Stephen T. Melnick, *New Rhode Island Law Grants Military Families Unpaid Leave*, Littler Press Releases, Media Advisories, and Newsletters (July 2008) (benefitslink.com)]

Being called for active service is also a COBRA event, requiring notice and giving the service member and family the option of continuing coverage in the employer's plan for up to 24 months by making premium payments. After a service member is deactivated, he or she and family members can also do a kind of reverse-COBRA election by choosing to remain within the TRICARE system for a period of time. [GAO-03-549T, *Military Personnel: Preliminary Observations Related to Income, Benefits, and Employer Support for Reservists During Mobilizations* (Mar. 19, 2003), <http://www.gao.gov/cgi-bin/getrpt?GAO-03-549T>]

While the plaintiff was on active military duty for 15 months, his employer sold substantially all its assets to a successor company. The buyer agreed to make reasonable efforts to employ all of the current employees on a list. The plaintiff was not included on the list. He argued that the COBRA notice he received shortly after deployment, offering continuation coverage due to termination of employment, proved that he was fired for going on active military duty. The District Court for the Eastern District of Arkansas accepted the employer's explanation: that the plaintiff was omitted from the list because he was on leave, and DOL regulations treat active military duty as a leave of absence from work. The language in the COBRA notice came from the COBRA statute, not USERRA, and was not enough to prove a USERRA violation. COBRA does not require reinstatement of health coverage after deployment, whereas USERRA does. [*Dorris v. TXD Servs., LP,* No. 1:10-cv-93-KGB, 96 Empl. Prac. Dec. (CCH) P44,581, 2012 WL 3149106 (E.D. Ark. Aug. 1, 2012); see HighRoads Blog, *Court Examines Interplay of COBRA and USERRA,* HighRoads Blog (Oct. 10, 2012) (benefitslink.com); Gwen Cofield, *COBRA Notice Is Not Culprit in Claim That Termination Violated USERRA,* Smart HR (Aug. 8, 2012) (benefitslink.com)]

As of 2009, two Circuit Courts (the Fifth and Sixth Circuits) had ruled that USERRA cases fall under mandatory arbitration clauses, finding that statutes that provide for lawsuits do not thereby rule out mandatory arbitration of discrimination claims. However, two District Courts have held that USERRA claims are not subject to mandatory arbitration, because the USERRA provision that says the law preempts state laws that eliminate, reduce, or limit USERRA rights forbid mandatory arbitration because the arbitration requirement limits servicemembers' rights under USERRA. [Compare *Landis v. Pinnacle Eye Care,* 537 F.3d 559 (6th Cir. 2008) and *Garrett v. Circuit City Stores,* 449 F.3d 672 (5th Cir. 2006) with *Lopez v. Dillard's, Inc.,* 382 F. Supp. 2d 1245 (D. Kan. 2005) and *Breletic v. CACI Inc.,* 413 F. Supp. 2d 1329 (2006); the issue is discussed in Howard S. Suskin and Benjamin J. Wimmer, *Arbitrability of USERRA Claims: Battle on the Home Front* (special to law.com) (Oct. 15, 2008)]

Note, however, that the California Court of Appeal ruled in late 2007 that USERRA rights cannot be waived by contract. Therefore, a release of rights under a severance agreement could not be enforced to the extent it dealt with allegations that a Marine Reserve captain was terminated because of his military status. (He was fired the day after he returned to work from Reserve duty.) 38 U.S.C. § 4302(b) provides that USERRA supersedes any state law or contract that reduces, limits or eliminates any USERRA right; the court interpreted this to cover suits for wrongful termination and breach of an oral employment contract.

[*Perez v. Uline*, 157 Cal. App. 4th 953 (Cal. App. 2007)] The Sixth Circuit reached a different conclusion in mid-2010, finding that a veteran of the war in Afghanistan could not sue his former employer, IBM, under USERRA, because he negotiated an Individual Separation Allowance Plan under which he received $6,000 for release of all of his employment-related claims. The Sixth Circuit enforced the release because it was knowing and voluntary; the release form was not ambiguous; and there was no evidence of fraud or overreaching. [*Wysocki v. IBM*, 607 F.3d 1102 (6th Cir. 2010)]

The Supreme Court denied certiorari in the Sixth Circuit case of a Nashville police officer who charged that imposing a three-week delay in reinstating him after his discharge from the Army Reserves violated USERRA. The Sixth Circuit ruled in his favor because he satisfied the conditions for reinstatement (discharge under honorable conditions; military service lasting less than five years; prompt request for re-employment), even though the Nashville police department said that its internal policies called for the delay, and the plaintiff was charged with violating Army regulations. The Sixth Circuit held that USERRA rules prevail over internal employment policies. [*Petty v. Metropolitan Gov't of Nashville*, 538 F.3d 431 (6th Cir. 2008), *cert. denied* as *Metropolitan Government of Nashville v. Petty*, No. 08-965, 129 S. Ct. 1833 (Apr. 6, 2009)]

The First Circuit adopted a standard of proof in USERRA cases that is more pro-plaintiff than the rules under Title VII (see § 42.04). In a Title VII case, the burden of proof is always on the employee who charges discrimination. In a USERRA case, the employee has to start the ball rolling by showing that military service was at least a motivating or substantial factor in the employment action that the servicemember complains of. Then the employer has to show, by a preponderance of the evidence that the same adverse action would have been taken even if the employee had not had a military commitment. [*Velazquez-Garcia v. Horizon Lines of P.R., Inc.*, 473 F.3d 11 (1st Cir. 2007)]

Retaliation claims are one of the largest portions of the employment discrimination caseload, and retaliation allegations are also raised in the USERRA context. A California jury awarded $275,000 to a police officer who charged USERRA retaliation. The District Court dismissed the jury award, but the Ninth Circuit reinstated it. [*Wallace v. City of San Diego*, 460 F.3d 1181 (9th Cir. 2006); see Rebecca Moore, *Appellate Court Reinstates Jury Award in USERRA Case*, plansponsor.com (Sept. 20, 2006); Wallace's petition for rehearing was denied by the Ninth Circuit on February 12, 2007 (479 F.3d 616)]

A "cat's paw" is a tool used by someone to accomplish his purpose. In the employment law context, this theory imputes one person's discriminatory animus to the decision-maker, if the decision-maker was influenced by the other person. A USERRA plaintiff alleged that he was fired from his job as an angiography technician because of his association with the military. His ex-employer said that he was fired for his bad attitude, laziness, and insubordination. According to the plaintiff, the hospital's scheduler detested him and wanted to get him fired, and exerted influence on the department head. The Seventh Circuit reversed the jury award of $57,000 to the plaintiff. The Seventh Circuit rejected the cat's paw theory. The decision-maker had no animus against ex-servicemembers. She made an independent investigation, and was not simply manipulated by the scheduler who had it in for the plaintiff. However, in 2011, the Supreme Court permitted use of the "cat's paw" theory of liability. The employer is liable because its agent, pursuing discriminatory animus, intends to and does cause an adverse employment action. [*Staub v. Proctor Hosp.*, 560 F.3d 647 (7th Cir. 2009), *rev'd*, 131 S. Ct. 1186 (2011); Marcia Coyle, *Court Adds Claws to Cat's Paw Claims—But Hisses at Case Over Corporate Privacy*, Nat'l L.J. (Mar. 1, 2011) (law.com)]

## [A]  Regulations

Although USERRA is a 1994 statute, the first proposed regulations were not issued until September 20, 2004, by the Department of Labor's Veterans' Employment and Training Service (VETS). A few months later, on December 10, 2004, President Bush signed the Veterans Benefits Improvement Act of 2004, Pub. L. No. 108-454, amending USERRA Title 38 § 4317 to allow servicemembers to elect and pay for continuation coverage. Another statute, the Heroes Earned Retirement Opportunities Act, Pub. L. No. 109-227, allows active servicemembers to treat combat pay as compensation that can be contributed to an IRA.

The Heroes Earnings Assistance and Relief Tax Act (HEART Act, Pub. L. 110-245) provides financial flexibility for servicemembers. See Notice 2008-82, 2008-41 I.R.B. 853 on Qualified Reservist Distributions (QRDs), special options in health care FSAs for certain military reservists. [JP Morgan Compensation & Benefit Strategies, *IRS Releases Guidance on Health FSA Distributions Under the HEART Act* (Oct. 10, 2008) (benefitslink.com)] Notice 2010-15, 2010-6 I.R.B. 390, provides guidance in question and answer form about the HEART Act of 2008. If an employer provides differential pay to employees called up for active service, it must be included in pension calculations. For persons on active duty for at least six months on or after December 31, 2007, the 10% early withdrawal penalty does not apply to defined contribution plan distributions. The survivor of a deceased servicemember can make a tax-free rollover of the military death benefit and life insurance to the survivor's Roth IRA or education savings account. All qualified plans must provide that the survivors of a person who dies on active service must receive whatever additional benefits would have been provided if the servicemember had returned to work and died while employed. [Rebecca Moore, *IRS Provides Guidance on HEART Act*, plansponsor.com (Jan. 10, 2010)]

USERRA also requires all employers (there is no minimum number of employees for coverage) to give all employees (not just those whom the employer knows to have military commitments) a notice of USERRA rights, benefits, and obligations. The official notice form is available at <http://www.dol.gov/vets/programs/userra/poster.pdf>. The notice of USERRA rights can either be posted, like the mandatory postings dealing with topics such as equal employment opportunity and minimum wages, or be provided to each employee by hand delivery, mail, or e-mail.

Under USERRA, military service is not a break in service when it comes to participation, vesting, or benefit accruals. For either a defined benefit or a defined contribution plan, pension calculations must be based on the pay rate the employee would have received if he or she had not been deployed. If the pay rate is uncertain (for example, it depends on sales commissions) the employer must use the average rate of compensation during the 12-month period prior to military service.

Applying for military service (rather than just performance of military service) is a protected right, so employers are forbidden to discriminate or retaliate on this basis (20 C.F.R. §§ 1002.18–.20). Joint employers are covered by USERRA, and so are a company's successor in interest, even if unaware of the servicemember's re-employment claims (20 C.F.R. §§ 1002.35–.37). The proposals make it clear that USERRA does not just protect full-time permanent workers. Job applicants, temporary, part-time, probationary, and seasonal employees; employees who have been laid off; strikers; employees on leave of absence—but not independent contractors—are covered by USERRA (20 C.F.R. §§ 1002.40–.44). The employer must treat the employee on active service as if he or she were on furlough or leave of absence; if the employer offers more than one type of non-military leave, military leave must provide the same benefits as the most generous of those (20 C.F.R. § 1002.149). If employees request, they must be allowed to apply their accrued vacation, annual or similar paid leave (but not unpaid leave) to their period of active duty, but the employer can't force an employee to use up paid leave while on active duty (20 C.F.R. §§ 1002.151–.153).

The employer must be prompt about re-employing a returned servicemember. Unless there are unusual circumstances, re-employment should occur within two weeks of the application, and for weekend National Guard duty, it should occur on the next regularly scheduled work period (20 C.F.R. §§ 1002.180–.181).

One acceptable alternative is for the employer to use the "escalator principle" and grant the re-employed employee the raises and benefit increases that were reasonably certain to have occurred if he or she had not been called to duty. However, the regulations permit other alternatives, such as returning the employee to the position held before deployment; giving him or her a comparable position to the pre-service or elevator position; or making the nearest possible approximation to one of those. If the person would have been laid off if he or she had remained at work, re-employment to layoff status is permitted (20 C.F.R. § 1002.194).

The appropriate placement of the employee depends on factors such as length of service, the employee's qualifications, and any extent to which military service caused or aggravated an existing disability (20 C.F.R. §§ 1002.196–.197). Sections 225 and 226 require the employer to make reasonable efforts to accommodate disability of persons seeking re-employment and to help the applicant become qualified to perform the duties of the offered job. [Ballard Spahr Andrews & Ingersoll, LLP, *Department of Labor Proposes New Regulations Under USERRA for Military Leave Rights* (Jan. 4, 2005); Lisa N. Bleed and Charles A. Storke, *USERRA Update*, Trucker Huss ERISA and Employee Benefits Attorneys; Faegre & Benson LLP, *Department of Labor Publishes USERRA Notice Just Before the Deadline* (Mar. 11, 2005) (law.com)]

USERRA protects the employment rights of persons who take up to five years' cumulative military leave with the same employer. However, see 20 C.F.R. § 1002.1. There may be exceptions that preclude termination of a person even if more than five years of military leave is taken:

- Service fulfilling an initial period of obligated service, or inability to get released from service, exceeding five years

- Drill weekends and other required drill and training certified as necessary by the military

- Service during war or national emergency or in a critical mission, contingency, or military requirement.

It is prudent for employers to ask employees who are in the National Guard or Reserves about their unit of attachment and commanding officer. All of the services have personnel locators that employers can use to verify that a person is actually in active service. For the Army, the number is (800) 318-5298; for the Air Force (210) 565-2660, the Navy is (901) 874-3383, (800) 268-3710 for the Marines, and (202) 493-1697 for the Coast Guard. [David M. Jaffe, Todd K. Boyer, *Insights: USERRA and the Five-Year Rule*, Littler Press Releases (May 2007) (benefitslink.com)]

In 2005, DOL issued a Final Rule [Notice of Rights and Duties under the Uniformed Services Employment and Reemployment Rights Act, RIN 1293-AA14, 70 Fed. Reg. 75313 (Dec. 19, 2005)] instructing employers to use their best judgment about how to give notice. Non-servicemembers (e.g., spouses who help servicemembers assert USERRA rights) are also protected against retaliation. The Final Rule extends the employer's obligation to make up for omitted pension plan contributions to 90 days or when the contribution would otherwise be made for the year when the employee was on active duty—whichever is later; the prior rules gave employers only 30 days to do this.

PBGC regulations were proposed in August 2009 covering the ERISA requirement that guaranteed benefits be non-forfeitable when a plan terminates. The proposal says that a participant who is covered by USERRA is deemed to have satisfied the reemployment condition as of the termination date if he or she returns to the former job within the USERRA time limits, even if reemployment was after the termination date of the plan. If the plan termination occurs when the plan sponsor is bankrupt, the bankruptcy filing date is treated as the termination date for USERRA purposes. [PBGC Proposed Rule, FR Doc E9-17623, *USERRA*

*Benefits Under Title IV of ERISA*, 74 Fed. Reg. 37666 (July 29, 2009); see CCH Pension & Benefits, *PBGC Issues Proposed Regs on Interaction of USERRA Rules and ERISA Benefit Guarantee* (Aug. 18, 2009) (benefitslink.com)] The rule was finalized in November 2009. [74 Fed. Reg. (Nov. 17, 2009); see *PBGC Unveils USERRA Final Rule*, plansponsor.com (Nov. 16, 2009)]

Veterans Opportunity to Work (VOW) to Hire Heroes Act, Pub. L. No. 112-56, was signed on November 21, 2011. The legislation provides job training and transition assistance to help reduce the unemployment rate for veterans, including a tax credit for hiring veterans. The highest level of credit available for hiring unemployed and/or disabled veterans. The VOW Act amends USERRA to recognize hostile work environment claims based on military status (using the same standards as Title VII). Therefore, EEO policies should be updated to forbid discrimination based on military deployment and veteran status, supervisors should be trained in the new requirements, and the company should adopt a reporting procedure for USERRA complaints. [Laura Broughton Russell, *New Veterans Law Offers Tax Credits to Employers and Recognizes Hostile Work Environment Claims Under USERRA* (Dec. 19, 2011) (benefitslink.com) The IRS has provided guidance: Notice 2012-13, 2012-9 I.R.B. 421]

## [B]   Recent Cases

USERRA has generated a number of important cases..

The First Circuit ruled that USERRA protects servicemembers who have not actually been recalled to active duty, but who have expressed a definite intent to return to active service in the near future. The First Circuit allowed his suit to proceed on his allegation that his Performance Improvement Plan was unfairly extended because of his military service. The plan was extended while he was on leave—an adverse employment action taken because he exercised USERRA rights. [*Vega-Colon v. Wyeth Pharm.*, 625 F.3d 22 (1st Cir. 2010); see Maria Greco Danaher, *1st Circuit -USERRA Coverage May Be Triggered Prior to Formal Military Orders*, Ogletree Deakins newsletter (Nov. 4, 2010) (benefitslink.com)]

The Eleventh Circuit held that the Alabama Department of Mental Health violated USERRA by failing to rehire servicemember Roy Hamilton on a timely basis after return from his 2003 deployment. While he was on active duty, the facility where he had worked was closed. The Eleventh Circuit said that Hamilton's rejection of a transfer to a different city, for family reasons, did not prevent him from being entitled to reemployment. The Eleventh Circuit upheld the jury's $25,000 award for lost pay and benefits. The court held that the department was not entitled to sovereign immunity, because the suit was brought by the Department of Justice rather than by a private individual. [*United States v. Alabama Dep't of Mental Health & Mental Retardation*, 673 F.3d 1320 (11th Cir. 2012); see PLC Labor & Employment, *USERRA Rights May Apply Even if Employee Refuses Position for Other Reasons: Eleventh Circuit* (Mar. 19, 2012)]

Mario Pantuso served six months in Iraq with the Navy. He was turned down for reinstatement by his employer, Safway Services, and sued the company and two supervisors under the state Military and Veterans Code. The California Court of Appeal held that, because that state statute is similarly worded to FEHA, individuals are not liable for discrimination or retaliation. Although some cases have found individual liability under USERRA, the court said that the language of state statute is different from USERRA. [*Haligowski v. Superior Ct.*, 200 Cal. App. 4th 983 (2011); see Shaw Valenza LLP, *No Individual Liability for Supervisors Under Military Service Anti-Discrimination Law* (Nov. 12, 2011) (benefits link.com)]

Two Chicago police officers seeking promotion to sergeant sued under USERRA. The promotion exam was scheduled for March 25, 2006, when the plaintiffs were on active duty. They took the test outside the United States; passed; and were placed on the eligibility list. They sued when the person with the highest score was promoted. The plaintiffs alleged that they would have scored higher if they had not had to travel long distances to take the test, and they should have been given a chance to take the promotion exam at the bases where they were stationed. The Seventh Circuit ruled that USERRA § 4311 does not require accommodation, and the plaintiffs were not entitled to better treatment than employees who were in Chicago on the test date. [*Sandoval v. City of Chicago*, 560 F.3d 703 (7th Cir. 2009)]

The Veterans' Benefit and Improvement Act of 2008, Pub. L. No. 110-389, eliminated that statute of limitations on USERRA claims. However, this law is not retroactive. For cases before it took effect, the statute of limitations is four years. Therefore, a plaintiff who did not file his case within four years was time-barred. Even if the running of the statute of limitations was tolled (suspended) while he was on active duty, he still missed the deadline. There was no evidence of wrongdoing by his employer that would justify equitable tolling. [*Baldwin v. City of Greensboro*, 714 F.3d 828 (4th Cir. 13)]

# CHAPTER 2
# TAX ASPECTS OF PAY PLANNING

## § 2.01 INTRODUCTION

One reason why corporations adopt pension and benefit plans is that, under appropriate circumstances, the employer will get a tax deduction, and the employee will receive valuable benefits—but the employee will not have immediately taxable income as a result of the benefits (or only part of the benefit will generate taxable income).

Therefore, an important part of pay planning is determining what portion of each employee's compensation is taxable, and performing tax withholding, depositing taxes, issuing information returns, and maintaining tax records. In most years, at least one tax bill is enacted that affects employers' tax responsibilities; in some years, there are several bills. In recent years, changes in FICA rules have been especially notable. See § 2.01[A] for a narrative account of recent tax changes.

The pace of change can be fast enough to make it difficult to keep up with current tax rules—and, in fact, there may be several tax rules that apply in the same year, depending on the effective date of the statutes passed during that year.

The basic tax rule is that everything received is taxable income, unless there is a specific exclusion. Therefore, the tax definition of "wages" includes vacation pay, commissions, bonuses, and some fringe benefits, not just straight salary. Severance pay is considered taxable wages, but payments for cancellation of an employment contract are not wages.

Early in 2013, the District Court for the District of Kansas permanently barred marketing of "tool plan" tax schemes to the automotive, construction, and trucking industries. (A permanent injunction was granted, but without admission of guilt.) The "tool reimbursement plan" characterized part of the employee's wages as non-taxable reimbursement for tools that the employee was required to provide as a condition of employment. The plan was sold as a legitimate accountable plan (see § 2.03) for business expenses that would reduce taxes for both employers and employees. The tool rental plan characterized part of wages as rentals paid by the employer to the employee for the required tools. The government considered both schemes fraudulent—the reimbursement plan failed the business connection test because reimbursement did not require proof of purchase date and price; it would be absurd for employer to rent tools from employees. A permanent injunction was granted, but without admission of guilt. [*United States v. Cash Mgmt. Sys.*, Civil No. 2:13-cv-02001EFM-KGG (D. Kan. Jan. 13, 2013); DOJ News Release (Jan. 18, 2013), discussed in EBIA Weekly, *Court Prohibits Promotion of Fraudulent Tool Plans* (Feb. 14, 2013) (benefitslink.com)] These items have been granted exclusions from taxable income:

- Worker's Compensation benefits;

- The employer's contributions to qualified pension plans (but the employee's pretax deferrals placed into 401(k) plans are FUTA and FICA wages);

- Up to $50,000 in § 79 group-term life insurance coverage. Additional coverage is taxable income that must be reported on the W-2 form, but income tax withholding is not required. The excess coverage is not subject to FUTA, but is subject to both the employer and employee share of FICA;

- Certain fringe benefits, e.g., employee discounts, working condition and de minimis fringes, qualified transportation fringes, qualified dependent care assistance within limits, etc.

The IRS issues annual updates of its Publication 15-A, Employer's Supplemental Tax Guide and Publication 15-B, Employer's Tax Guide to Fringe Benefits. See <http://www.irs.gov/pub/irs-pdf/p15a.pdf> and <www.irs.gov/pub/irs-pdf/p15b.pdf> respectively.

[See Code § 7508A as set out in IR-2012-83, <http://www.irs.gov/uac/Newsroom/IRS-Provides-Tax-Relief-to-Victims-of-Hurricane-Sandy;-Return-Filing-and-Tax-Payment-Deadline-Extended-to-Feb.-1,-2013> and Announcement 2012-44, 2012-49 I.R.B. 663 for relief for retirement plans that make loans or hardship distributions to employees affected by Superstorm Sandy.]

When a new employee is hired the employer must use Form I-9 to verify immigration status and that the person can lawfully work within the United States. [See § 23.11 for more information about immigration issues in hiring]

Employer Group Health Plans (EGHPs) that fail to satisfy certain federal requirements must pay excise taxes, which are reported on IRS Form 8928. Self-reporting is required for compliance with the COBRA requirements (including the subsidy program); HIPAA rules; benefits for childbirth, mental health parity, and Michelle's law; and the Genetic Information Nondisclosure Act.

If the employer fails to make contributions to MSAs or HSAs that are comparable as between rank and file and highly compensated employees, the excise tax generally equals 35% of aggregate employer contributions to all employees' MSAs and HSAs for the year. In this situation, Form 8928 is due by the fifteenth day of the fourth month of the year after the year in which a non-comparable contribution was made.

The excise tax is $100 per beneficiary per day for failure to comply with a variety of requirements (dealing with, e.g., pre-existing condition limitations, nondiscrimination in enrollment, minimum hospital stay for childbirth, mental health parity). But the excise tax is waived if the responsible person did not know, and could not have known with due diligence, of the failure; or the failure was reasonable, not caused by willful neglect, and was corrected within 30 days. There are additional penalties for late returns and late payments. [74 Fed. Reg. 45994 (Sept. 8, 2009); IRS Instructions for Form 8928, <http://www.irs.gov/instructions/i8928/ch01.html> See Guest article, Deloitte's Washington Bulletin, *New for 2010: Employers Must Self-Report Excise Tax for Failure to Comply with*

*Group Health Plan Requirements* (Dec. 14, 2009) (benefitslink.com); Jackson Lewis LLP, *New Obligation to Self-Report Excise Taxes for Group Health Plan Failures* (Jan. 14, 2010) (benefitslink.com)]

When a plan complies with PPACA and covers participants' adult children until their 26th birthday that coverage is tax-free for federal purposes—but not necessarily under state law. If state law does not track the federal law, then it may be necessary to report the fair market value of the coverage for state tax purposes.

Only 22 of the states that have state income taxes (plus the District of Columbia) automatically amend their tax rules to conform to federal rules, and in 10 states, EGHPs may have to extend coverage to employees' children even after age 26, in which case the coverage will be taxable unless the child is a dependent or disabled. The 10 states are Connecticut, Florida, Illinois, Nebraska, New Jersey, New York, Ohio, Pennsylvania, and South Dakota. [Buck Research FYI, *States Address Tax Consequences of Health Coverage for Adult Children* (Sep. 16, 2011) (benefitslink.com); Cynthia Lee, Beyond Health Care Reform Blog, *Wisconsin Bill Passed to Conform State Tax Treatment of Coverage of Adult Children* (Oct. 28, 2011) (benefitslink.com)]

Regulations were proposed on August 17, 2011 regarding the implementation of the PPACA premium tax credit. The credit is available to applicable taxpayers (income between 100% and 400% of the federal poverty level) who are enrolled in a qualified plan through an exchange. The general rule is that the credit is the sum of premium assistance amounts for each coverage month in a taxable year. The credit is based on the difference between the premium for the second-lowest-cost silver plan (a plan that provides all benefits designated as "essential" under PPACA, with the plan paying at least 70% of the cost of covered benefits) in the exchange that covers the taxpayer's family and an applicable percentage of household income. The credit does not change based on the plan in which the individual is actually enrolled. Premiums paid on behalf of a taxpayer or his or her family, are considered to be paid by the taxpayer. [Christy Tinnes, Brigen Winters, *Proposed Regulation on PPACA Premium Tax Credit Part III*, plansponsor.com (Oct. 11, 2011)]

IRS regulations for the "shared responsibility" penalty were proposed at the beginning of 2013. The penalty applies to employers who have at least 50 full-time employees or the equivalent that fail to provide affordable minimum essential coverage for employees and their dependents, and who have at least one full-time employee who purchases coverage on an Exchange. The IRS published guidance on "look-back" methods for computing the number of employees for this purpose. The proposal says that an applicable large employer is treated as offering coverage to full-time employees and their families in any calendar for month in which coverage is offered to all except 5%—or five employees, if this is more than 5%. [78 Fed. Reg. 217 (Jan. 2, 2013); see Rebecca Moore, *IRS Proposes Rules for Employer Health Coverage Penalty*, plansponsor.com (Jan. 4, 2013)]

Employers will need to learn these rules—but not right away. In July 2013, the effective date of the employer shared responsibility payment was delayed until January 1, 2015. The mandatory reporting requirement was also delayed for a year until the start of 2015. [Mark J. Mazur, *Continuing to Implement the Aca In a Careful and Thoughtful Manner*, <http://www.treasury.gov/connect/blog/Pages/Continuing-to-Implement-the-ACA-in-a-Careful-Thoughtful-Manner-.aspx> (July 2, 2013)]

A donated leave arrangement, also known as leave sharing or voluntary shared leave, permits employees to donate their own accrued personal, vacation, or paid sick leave days on behalf of other employees. Rev. Rul. 90-29 defines a medical emergency as a medical condition of the employee or a close family member requiring prolonged time away from work and causing substantial loss of income after paid leave is exhausted. The IRS excepts bona fide leave sharing arrangements for medical emergencies and leave banks for natural disasters from the general rule that the person who earns income will be taxed on it. What would otherwise be compensation paid to and taxed to the donor employee is not taxed to the donor. The donor is not entitled to claim a deduction for the leave donation. To be valid for tax purposes, the arrangement must be written; administered by the employer; set up as a leave bank used only for medical emergencies or bereavement; and must have a procedure for potential recipients to make written applications after they have exhausted their paid leave. The plan must specify any limits imposed on the amount of leave that a person can donate in a year, and must ensure that the transferred leave time is actually used as medical leave. It is not permissible to liquidate the leave and give the recipient cash.

Similar arrangements can be used in case of disasters that cause employees to miss work because of personal or family severe hardship. Notice 2006-59 limits favorable federal tax treatment to presidentially declared major disasters; declarations by state and local government do not count for this purpose. The donor must donate time to a bank, rather than specifying the recipient. The maximum amount of leave donated cannot exceed the leave the donor normally accrues during the year. Unused leave must be returned to the donor at the end of the specified post-disaster period. The severity of the disaster determines how long recipients will have to use the leave, and leave from the bank must only be used for that disaster. [Peter Alwardt, *Tax Considerations in Implementing Donated Leave Policies*, Eisner Amper (Jan. 14, 2013) (benefitslink.com)]

## [A]   Changes in Tax Statutes

Although the tax bills since 2005 have not made tremendous changes in the employment tax picture, nevertheless they have made some modifications that are worth noting. The various tax bills since have made changes—often subtle—in employment-related taxes.

Small and medium-sized businesses often forgo targeted tax incentive tax breaks, because they are too hard to understand, cost too much to implement, or risk pushback from the IRS. According to tax consultants, eligible businesses claim only about 5% of the tax breaks they are entitled to. Out of 1.78 million corporate tax returns, only 20,000 claimed any of the approximately 35 main business tax credits. For example, the Work Opportunity Credit was claimed on behalf of only about 20–35% of eligible workers because so much paperwork, including a great deal of information that employers have to get from employees, is required. The small business health care credit was claimed by only 170,300 employers, whereas the estimated number of eligible employers could be anywhere from 1.4 million to 4 million. Corporate taxes were also at a historic low, which made it less important for businesses to capture every available credit. In fiscal 2011, total corporate taxes equaled 12.1% of profits from U.S. activities, the lowest percentage since at least 1972, far below the 25.6% average for the period 1987–2008. [John D. McKinnon, *Firms Pass Up Tax Breaks, Citing Hassles, Complexity*, WSJ.com (July 22, 2012)]

Pub. L. No. 109-264 amends Code § 114(a), to clarify that states do not have the power to tax retirement income paid by certain nonqualified plans to retired partners for past service. This treatment is retroactive to 1996. To qualify, the payments must be substantially equal periodic payments extending over at least 10 years, although payments can be subject to caps or entitled to COLAs and still be considered substantially equal. The test is also satisfied if the payment comes from both a qualified and a nonqualified plan. [No by-line, *Bill Prohibiting States from Taxing Nonresidents Cleared for President*, CCH Pension and Benefits News Story (Aug. 9, 2006) (benefitslink.com)]

As of January 1, 2010, eligible rollover distributions paid directly to a non-spouse beneficiary are subject to 20% mandatory withholding (not 10% voluntary withholding for non-periodic payments) if the amount is not directly rolled over to an IRA. [Elizabeth Thomas Dodd, Groom Law Group Memorandum to Clients, *RE: IRS Pension Distribution Reporting Changes for 2010* (Mar. 3, 2010) (benefitslink.com)]

In accordance with the PPA, the IRS explained how active duty reservists can take withdrawals from their Roth or conventional IRAs without becoming subject to the 10% early withdrawal penalty. (However, in most cases, the withdrawal will be taxable income for the reservist.) The provision is retroactive, so a reservist who incurred a penalty for past withdrawals can file Form 1040X, writing "active duty reservist" on the form and giving the date of call-up, the amount of distribution, and the penalty paid in the Part II Explanation of Changes. The reservist can return part or all of the withdrawal to the IRA. Generally, this must be done within two years of the end of active service, but can be done until August 17, 2008 (i.e., two years from enactment of the PPA) for reservists whose active duty ended pre-PPA. [Fred Schneyer, *IRS Implements Lifting of 10% Early Withdrawal Penalty for Reservists*, plansponsor.com (Sept. 29, 2006)]

The Heroes Earnings Assistance and Relief Tax Act (HEART Act, Pub. L. No. 110-245) allows servicemembers to take qualified reservist distributions, cash distributions from their FSAs that are taxable income but do not trigger the 10% penalty, and provides financial flexibility for servicemembers. See Notice 2008-82, 2008-41 I.R.B. 853 [JP Morgan Compensation & Benefit Strategies, *IRS Releases Guidance on Health FSA Distributions Under the HEART Act* (Oct. 10, 2008) (benefitslink.com)]

The American Recovery and Reinvestment Act of 2009 (ARRA; Pub. L. No. 111-5) enacted a temporary premium subsidy for COBRA premiums, but it was permitted to expire.

The Patient Protection and Affordable Care Act, Pub. L. No. 111-148 (PPACA), the health care reform bill, includes a number of tax-related provisions to finance the expansion of health insurance coverage. Most of the provisions have a deferred effective date to give employers time to gear up for the program.

PPACA §§ 1421 and 10105 provide a tax credit for small employers. The credit can be claimed for tax years beginning after December 31, 2009 if the employer makes non-elective contributions that cover at least half the premium for covering participating employees. A small employer is defined as an employer that maintains a qualified health arrangement, and that has up to 25 full-time equivalent employees (FTEs), whose average wage is not more than twice the dollar amount prescribed for the tax year. The prescribed amount for 2010–2013, is $25,000. The credit is reduced based on the number of employees and their average compensation, and is eliminated at 25 FTEs.

For tax years 2010–2013, the credit is 35% of the employer's total non-elective contributions on behalf of employees to pay premiums for qualified health coverage. However, the credit is capped at the amount that HHS determines is the average small-group premium for the relevant market. That is, employers who pay above-average premiums cannot claim the credit on the full amount paid.

The credit is 50% of total non-elective contributions for premiums for insurance plans purchased through an exchange. Once again, the credit is limited by the average small group premium. [CCH Pension & Benefits, *Health Reform 2010: Small Employer Health Insurance Credit* (Apr. 12, 2010) (benefitslink.com); Fred Schneyer, *IRS Reminds Employers of New Health Coverage Tax Credit*, plansponsor.com (Apr. 1, 2010)] The IRS posted a Small Business Health Care Tax Credit Web page containing resources such as an eligibility guide, a YouTube video, a FAQ, and a webinar. [IRS explanation: <http://www.irs.gov/newsroom/article/0,,id=223666,00.html>; see Rebecca Moore, *IRS Reminds Small Employers about Health Care Tax Credit*, plansponsor.com (Mar. 13, 2012)]

Although the number of businesses eligible for the small business tax credit under PPACA was estimated at between 1.4 million and 4 million, as of May 2012 the GAO said that only 170,000 firms had claimed the credit in 2010. Out of those, only 17% could claim the full credit. The credit refunds 35% of a qualifying employer's health insurance expenses for the period 2010–2013. After 2014, the credit rises to 50% and is available for any two consecutive years of the employer's choice. The full credit is available to companies with 10 or fewer full-time employees and average wages below $25,000; the credit phases down until it is eliminated at the level of 25 employees and average wages of $50,000.

In 2009, the Census Bureau reported that there were 4.6 million companies with fewer than 10 employees and 5.7 million with fewer than 100 employees. The GAO said that the credit was not large enough to persuade small business owners to take the trouble to complete complex paperwork: at least two, perhaps up to eight hours to gather information, plus three to five hours of a tax preparer's time to calculate the credit. At least 360,000 businesses claimed the credit for 2011, but this is still a small share of the eligible businesses. [House Committee on Ways and Means, *Why the Health Care Tax Credit Eludes Many Small Businesses* (Sept. 26, 2012)]

As of March 1, 2013, when automatic budget cuts were imposed as a result of the Balanced Budget and Emergency Deficit Control Act of 1985 mandatory "sequester," the refundable portion of the Code § 45R tax credit was reduced by 8.7%. The reduction is imposed until the end of the fiscal year (Sept. 30, 2013). [Cynthia Stamer, *Sequester Will Cut ACA Small Businesses Health Care Tax Credits*, WSJ.com (Mar. 5, 2013)]

As a result of PPACA, not only does paying above-average premiums restrict the credit for small employers, but also starting in 2018 a 40% excise tax will be imposed on high-cost plans (insured EGHPs and self-funded plans), irrespective of the number of employees covered. The tax is imposed when the premium exceeds $10,200 for individuals, or $27,500 for family coverage; the limits are higher for retirees over age 55 who are not yet Medicare-eligible, and for employees with high-risk jobs. [Lauren Bikoff, Health Reform Talk (CCH) *Inclusion of Cost of Employer-Sponsored Health Coverage on W-2* (Mar. 31, 2010) (benefitslink.com)]

PPACA § 9002 requires that, for tax years beginning after December 31, 2010, employers must disclose the aggregate cost (employer share plus employee share) of employer-sponsored coverage on Form W-2 The costs of long-term care insurance, accident & health, disability income insurance, fixed indemnity insurance, and coverage limited to a specified disease are not included in this figure.

Notice 2012-9, 2012-4 I.R.B. 315, says that the value of EGHP coverage to be reported is based on the COBRA cost of the coverage. In this context, "health coverage" means applicable employer-sponsored coverage, whether it is paid for by the employer or the employee, and whether or not the coverage is taxable to the employee. Long-term care insurance, accident and disability benefits, liability insurance, Worker's Compensation coverage, limited dental or vision insurance under a separate policy, and coverage limited to a specific disease are not treated as applicable employer-sponsored coverage. W-2 reporting is not required for Archer MSA, an H SA of the employee or employee's spouse, or salary reduction contributions to a health FSA. Nor is reporting required for the cost of coverage that is includible under Code § 105(h) [discriminatory self-insured plan] or included in the gross income of a 2% shareholder in an S Corporation.

Any reasonable, consistently applied method can be used to report the cost of coverage for part-year employees. Employers with on-site medical clinics, EAPs, or wellness programs are only required to report the value of this coverage if the program is subject to COBRA and the employer charges a continuation premium. Health coverage that is merely incidental to other benefits does not have to be reported, although the employer can choose to report the full cost of all the benefits.

Fixed indemnity insurance (a policy that pays a particular amount per day of hospitalization, or covers certain expenses for a specific disease) must be included in the cost of coverage on the W-2 if the employer's contribution is excluded from the employee's gross income, or if the employee buys the insurance with a pre-tax salary reduction in a cafeteria plan. But if the employer merely offers the opportunity to purchase an indemnity policy that is not coordinated with other health coverage, and the employee pays with after-tax dollars, then the coverage does not have to be included on the W-2.[Birgit Anne Waidmann, PricewaterhouseCooper *HRS Insight, IRS Provides Guidance on Mandatory Reporting of the Value of Health Coverage on 2012 Forms W-2* (Jan. 6, 2012) (ben efitslink.com); Christine J. Kim, Christine A. Williams, Perkins Coie, *More News From the IRS on W-2 Reporting of Health Coverage Cost* (Jan. 10, 2012) (bene fitslink.com)]

Starting January 1, 2013, PPACA imposes higher Medicare payroll taxes on high-income persons. Instead of 1.45%, the employee share of Medicare tax is 2.35% for those whose income is over $250,000 (married persons filing a joint return) or $200,000 (all other filing statuses). The employer's share of the Medicare tax does not increase. High-income persons also pay a Medicare surtax on their investment income other than tax-exempt bond interest and profits on sale of their principal residence. [CCH Pension and Benefits, *Increased Medicare Taxes Imposed Under Health Reform Law Will Not Be Assessed on Plan Distributions* (Apr. 8, 2010) (benefitslink.com)]

The 3.8% investment surtax applies to gains on nonqualified stock options when they are issued. The surtax also applies to restricted stock when it vests. For high-income taxpayers, tax treatment of dividends depends on whether or not a Code § 83(b) election to accelerate income tax has been made. If there has been an election, the dividends are subject to the 3.8% tax; if not, the dividends are subject to the 0.9% tax. Taxable fringe benefits are also subject to the 0.9% tax. [Laura Saunders, *Tax Report: The New Investment Taxes*, WSJ.com (July 7, 2012)]

Late 2012 proposed regulations deal with the 0.9% Medicare surtax. The proposed regulations require the employer to withhold additional Medicare tax only to the extent that the employee's wages from that employer exceed $200,000 in the calendar year—without considering the employee's filing status or other wages or compensation. The employee cannot request that the employer withhold and deduct additional Medicare tax on wages under $200,000. However, employees who believe that they will be liable for the extra tax (e.g., because of the spouse's income) can request deduction and withholding of additional income tax on Form W-4. If the full amount of additional Medicare tax that a particular employee owes is not withheld by the employer, the employee is liable for the difference and must report it on Form 1040. If a refund or credit on this tax is due, the employee can claim it on Form 1040X or file a claim on Form 843, Claim for Refund [REG-130074-11, <http://www.irs.gov/irb/2012-52_IRB/ar18.html>; see Alistair M. Nevius, *Guidance Issued On Additional Medicare Tax*, J of Accountancy (Dec. 3, 2012) (benefitslink.com)]

The 2013 FICA base is $113,700. FICA taxes are owed on the exercise of nonqualified options or SARS, or when restricted stock vests. For compensation deferred in 401(k) or nonqualified deferred compensation plans, FICA is owed at the time of deferral even though income tax is not owed until the funds are removed from the account. Nonqualified stock options can be exercised without FICA tax consequences on income recognized at exercise if the employee's compensation for the year exceeds the FICA base. Medicare tax and additional Medicare tax are due on all compensation, with no limit. Therefore, 2012 was a good year to exercise nonqualified stock options, because of the payroll tax cut and because the extra Medicare tax had not yet taken effect. [MyStockOptions Blog, *Social Security Yearly Income Cap Will Rise In 2013: Impact On Stock Comp And NQDC* (Oct. 17, 2012) (benefitslink.com)]

The PPACA also imposes a small fee on self-insured plans and issuers of health insurance policies, for plan years that end on or after October 1, 2012 and before October 1, 2019. (The fee will be used to fund research into which treatments are the most effective.) The sponsor of a self-insured plan, or the insurer of a policy covering an insured plan, must pay $1 per person covered under the plan for the first year, and $2 per person for the second year, with subsequent inflation adjustments. The fee is paid on IRS Form 720. [77 Fed. Reg. 22691 (Apr. 17, 2012), <http://www.dol.gov/ebsa/healthreform>; see DOL, *FAQs About Affordable Care Act Implementation Part XI* (Jan. 24, 2013) (benefitslink.com)]

PPACA retains the ability of corporations to receive federal subsidies tax-free if they provide prescription drug coverage for their retirees. The subsidy is 28% of the cost of coverage, subject to a cap of $1,330 per retiree. However, PPACA provides that the subsidy amount will no longer be deductible, starting in 2013. [Kris Maher, Ellen E. Schultz, and Bob Tita, *Deere, Caterpillar: Health-Care Law to Raise Expenses*, WSJ.com (Mar. 26, 2010)]

Stimulus efforts continued with the enactment of the Hiring Incentives to Restore Employment (HIRE) Act, Pub. L. No. 111-147, in March 2010. Under this legislation, employers (other than household employers) who hire unemployed workers after February 3, 2010 and before January 1, 2011 qualified for a temporary 6.2% payroll tax incentive. That is, their share of the Social Security tax on the wages was waived, although the employee's share of FICA still applied, and both employer and employee share of Medicare tax still had to be paid.

If the newly hired workers are retained for at least a year, the business received another general business tax credit of up to $1,000 per worker on its 2011 income tax return. A new hire for an existing position qualified but only if someone is hired to replace someone who quit or was fired for cause. [Rebecca Moore, *New Law Offers Tax Incentives for Hiring*, plansponsor.com (Mar. 18, 2010)]

This was replaced by another payroll tax incentive, a cut in employees' FICA rates. The Temporary Payroll Tax Cut Continuation Act, Pub. L. No. 112-78 (December 2011) reduced the employee FICA rate to 4.2% (or 10.4% for self-employed persons) but subject to a wage cap of $18,350. The Middle Class Tax Relief and Job Creation Act of 2012, Pub. L. No. 112-96, enacted February 2, 2012, extended the 4.2% FICA rate for workers until the end of 2012, and repealed the cap. Form 941 was updated accordingly. [<http://www.irs.gov/pub/irs-pdf/f941.pdf>; see Rebecca Moore, *Payroll Tax Cut Extended, IRS Issues Revised Form*, plansponsor.com (Feb. 24, 2012)] However, there were no further extensions of the FICA cut after the end of 2012.

The Wall Street Journal estimated that the end of the FICA "holiday" meant that a person earning $113,000 or more per year would have to pay an additional $200 per month. [Laura Saunders, *Details of Tax Law Changes Spelled Out*, WSJ.com (Jan. 1, 2013)]

The Small Business Jobs and Credit Act, Pub. L. No. 111-240, also includes some miscellaneous employment-related provisions:

- Employees are no longer required to log personal use of cell phones provided by their employers so they can treat the personal use as taxable income;

- Retirees who own annuities outside their retirement plans can access income from only part of the annuity while leaving the rest invested;

- Balances (known as "eligible rollover distributions") can be transferred from 401(k) to Roth 401(k) plans, beginning on September 27, 2010, but only if the plan includes a Roth 401(k) feature. The transfer is taxable, but income tax on 2010 conversions can be deferred until 2011 and 2012, with half of the taxable amount reported in each of the two years. [Laura Saunders, *Tax Report: Surprise New Tax Breaks*, WSJ.com (Sept. 25, 2010)]

Although the Small Business Jobs and Credit Act of 2010 (SBJCA), Pub. L. No. 111-240, increases tax cuts and credit for small businesses, it also increases the penalty for not providing or filing Form 1099-series forms on time. The penalties depend on whether a Form 1099-R was required from a small business or a large business; whether it was filed late but corrected; or whether the taxpayer intentionally disregarded the filing obligation. The penalties, which can be as high as $100 per form (2011) will be adjusted for inflation in 2012 and every five years after that. [McKay Hochman Company, Inc. E-Mail Alert 2010-16, *Form 1099 Series Penalties Increased* (Oct. 15, 2010) (benefitslink.com)]

The Tax Relief, Unemployment Insurance Reauthorization, and Job Creation Act of 2010 (TRUIRJCA), Pub. L. No. 111-312, was signed December 17, 2010. Major provisions include:

- A one-year cut in payroll tax.

- 100% bonus depreciation on business equipment for 2011, 50% bonus depreciation for 2012.

- Taxpayers can continue to exclude from income the gain from selling qualified small business stock that was held for more than five years.

- The extra $1,000 adoption credit and exclusion provided by PPACA are retained for 2010 only (although subsequent legislation made them permanent). Therefore, in 2011, the maximum amount of adoption assistance or credit was $13,170, and eligibility for the credit phased out between $185,210 and $225,210.

- The enhanced dependent care credit is extended through December 31, 2012. The 35% rate is applied to $3,000 of expenses (or $6,000 if there is more than one qualifying dependent), with the result that the maximum credit is $1,050 for one dependent, $2,100 for two or more. The credit is reduced, but not below 20%, based on the employee's AGI in excess of $15,000.

- Educational assistance (including graduate school tuition) of up to $5,250 can be provided tax-free until December 31, 2012. The Making Work Pay credit expired as scheduled on December 31, 2010, and was not renewed. Payroll tax forgiveness for employers under the HIRE Act also expired on December 31, 2010 and was not renewed.

- The maximum transit assistance/van pooling benefit was $230/month for 2011.

- The Work Opportunity Tax Credit was extended. [CCH Tax Briefing, *Tax Relief/Job Creation Act of 2010 Special Report*, <http://tax.cchgroup.com/downloads/files/pdfs/legislation/bush-taxcuts.pdf> (Dec. 17, 2010);]

In November 2011, the VOW to Hire Heroes Act (Pub. L. No. 112-56) was enacted, including a new tax credit for hiring veterans, up to a maximum of $9,600 per veteran. The credit is available for hiring a qualifying veteran between November 22, 2011 and January 1, 2013. The amount of the credit depends on factors such as the length of time veteran was out of work prior to being hired, the number of hours worked, and the wages paid in the first year post-hiring. The maximum credit is provided for hiring veterans with service-related disabilities.

The statute calls for Form 8850 to be filed with the state workforce agency within 28 days of the veteran's first day at work. The credit is claimed on the employer's tax return, on Form 3800 (as a general business credit) if the employer is a for-profit business, on Form 5884-C if it is a non-profit organization. [Notice 2012-13, 2012-9 I.R.B. 421; VOW to Hire Heroes Act FAQ, <http://www.irs.gov/businesses/small/article/0,,id=253950,00.html> (Feb. 9, 2012); see Laura Saunders, *IRS Extends Deadline to Claim Vet Credit*, WSJ.com (Feb. 9, 2012)]

The "fiscal cliff" tax bill, the American Taxpayer Relief Act of 2012 (ATRA; Pub. L. No.112-240) does not provide guidance for supplemental withholding, so employers should continue using the optional 25% supplemental withholding rate on supplemental wages up to $1 million. Because of the expiration of FICA relief, in 2013 the employer's share of FICA tax is 6.2% of income up to $113,700. Fifty percent bonus depreciation has been extended for one year. [Baker McKenzie Executive Compensation & Employee Benefits, *New Tax Rates in Effect for 2013* (Jan. 3, 2013); Laura Saunders, *High Earners Facing First Major Tax Increase in Years*, WSJ.com (Jan. 1, 2013)]

The ATRA permits in-plant Roth conversions of defined contribution accounts that would not otherwise be distributable, with no income limitations. Under prior law, only amounts that were immediately distributable (e.g., to a participant who had reached age 59 ½) could be converted to Roth status. The provision is effective January 1, 2013,and account balances in existence on that date can be converted. [Rebecca Moore, *Fiscal Cliff Deal Extends Roth Conversions*, plansponsor.com (Jan.3, 2013)]

## [B]   Tax Implications of Same-Sex Marriage

As the number of states permitting same-sex marriage, civil union, or domestic partnership increases (see § 18.06), employers are often faced with the problem of handling tax issues for employees who indicate that they have a same-sex life partner.

In mid-2013, the Supreme Court struck down the federal Defense of Marriage Act (DOMA). DOMA defined marriage, for federal purposes, as a union of one man and one woman. Because the Supreme Court found this statute unconstitutional (on due process and equal protection grounds), same-sex married couples are entitled to file joint income tax returns. There are many other federal consequences, including military spousal benefits and estate tax status as a surviving spouse.

In states that either allow same-sex couples to marry, or that recognize same-sex marriages in other jurisdictions, tax withholding for employees who are married to same-sex partners should be based on: see § 18.06[A] for further discussion of employment consequences of same-sex marriage. [*United States v. Windsor*, 133 S. Ct. 2675 (2013); *Hollingsworth v. Perry*, 133 S. Ct. 2652 (2013)]

There are also issues specific to California, Nevada, and Washington, because they are community property states; domestic partners may qualify for favorable tax treatment. [IRS Q&As for Registered Domestic Partners in Community Property States & Same-Sex Spouses in California, <http://www.irs.gov/newsroom/article/0,,id=245869,00.html>(Sept. 16, 2011); see EBIA Weekly, *IRS Clarifications Affect Employee Benefits for Domestic Partners and Same-Sex Spouses* (Nov. 3, 2011) (benefitslink.com)]

## § 2.02   THE COMPENSATION DEDUCTION

Internal Revenue Code § 162 allows a corporation to deduct its ordinary and necessary business expenses, including reasonable salaries in exchange for personal services rendered to the corporation. Salaries are only reasonable if the person hired is qualified to perform the services, and actually performs them. If vacation pay is treated as deferred compensation, it is not deductible until the year it is actually paid. [See I.R.C. § 404(a)(5)]

The Working Families Tax Relief Act of 2004 (WFTRA) amended § 152(c) to define a "qualifying child" as one who satisfies relationship, residency, and age tests, and who does not provide more than half of his or her own support. The qualifying child must be either under 19 as of the close of the calendar year, a student under 24 at the end of the calendar year, or be permanently and totally disabled at any time during the year. The current version of § 152(d)(1) defines a "qualifying relative" as a relative other than the taxpayer's child (e.g., a dependent parent) who has income below the exemption amount and receives at least half of his or her support from the taxpayer. When it comes to determining the tax impact of employer-provided health coverage, status as a dependent under § 105(b) is determined without regard to § 152(b) and (d). If the employer provides health coverage for someone who is not a qualifying child or a qualifying relative, the value of that coverage will be taxable income for the employee. Domestic partners and same-sex spouses fall into this category (see § 18.06). [Notice 2004-79, 2004-49 I.R.B. 898]

See IRS Publication 503 for rules about the dependent care credit, dependent care assistance programs, and identification of "qualifying individuals" for this purpose. Form 2441 is used to report child and dependent care expenses; taxpayers file it with their Form 1040 to determine the amount of their dependent care tax credit, and to demonstrate that the amount in Box 10 of the W-2 (value of dependent care benefits provided by an employer) are not taxable. Filers of Form 1040A are now required to use this form; previously, the short form included a schedule, Schedule 2, for this purpose. [Form 2441 and instructions, <http://www.irs.gov/pub/irs-pdf/f2441.pdf> and <http://www.irs.gov/pub/irs-pdf/i2441.pdf>. The 2011 Form 2441 (child & dependent care expenses) makes only a few minor changes from the 2010 version. [EBIA Weekly, *IRS Releases 2011 Form 2441 and Instructions* (Oct. 20, 2011) (benefitslink.com)]

Tax breaks for adoption were added by the Economic Growth and Tax Relief Reconciliation Act (EGTRRA), which called for these provisions to expire in 2010. PPACA extends the provisions for one year, so that adoption tax relief does not "sunset" until tax years beginning after December 31, 2011. However, unless Congress provides a further extension, when these provisions sunset, they will return to pre-EGTRRA levels. The exclusion from income will expire, and the adoption credit will be limited to $6,000 and will only apply to adoption of special-needs children.

PPACA increases the maximum adoption credit to $13,170 per child, $1,000 more than the 2009 level, whether or not the adoptee has special needs. This amount will be adjusted for inflation for tax years beginning after December 31, 2010. The adoption credit has also been made a refundable credit (i.e., if the credit reduces the taxpayer's tax liability below zero, he or she can receive a tax refund).

For 2012, the adoption credit and maximum adoption assistance exclusion revert to $10,000 adjusted for inflation. For 2012 that makes the maximum credit $12,650 (whether or not the adoptee has special needs). The credit begins to phase down at AGI of $89,710 and is fully phased out at AGI of $229,710. The adoption credit is no longer refundable. [Rev. Proc. 2011-52, 2011-45 I.R.B. 701.]

See Rev. Proc. 2013-15, 2013-5 I.R.B. 444 for the 2013 adoption credit/ assistance level: $12,970. The credit begins to phase down at AGI of $194,580 and is fully phased out at AGI of $234,580. The ATRA of 2012, Pub. L. No. 112-240, makes the adoption credit/adoption assistance provisions permanent

For 2013, the employer can deduct transportation benefits of up to $245 per employee per month, for both parking and transit passes/van pooling. [Wolters Kluwer Law & Business, *IRS Issues 2013 Adoption and Transportation Benefit COLAs* (Jan. 21, 2013) (benefitslink.com)]

In September 2004, the IRS announced its Tip Rate Determination and Education Program, a voluntary compliance tool for the hospitality industry, had succeeded in its pilot and would be extended indefinitely. The program allows employers to choose among several methods of complying with tip reporting: Tip Rate Determination Agreement; Tip Reporting Alternative Commitment; and Tip Reporting Alternative Commitment Designated by Employer. The IRS intends these methods to be non-burdensome on employers. [<http://www.irs.gov/newsroom/article/0,,id=129379,00.html>; Publication 1875 is the IRs' food and beverage industry tip guide]

For public corporations, § 162(m) does not allow a deduction for over $1 million in compensation paid to "covered employees"—certain senior executives. However, the cap does not apply to "performance-based compensation"— compensation payable solely because the payee has achieved an objective goal (or goals) set in advance. [See Rev. Rul. 2008-13, 2008-10 I.R.B. 518, tightening up the rules for performance-based compensation, with the result that some compensation lost its deductible status; this ruling is discussed in Douglas J. Ellis, *IRS Confirms Controversial New Position on Section 162(m) Performance-Based*

*Compensation    Deduction,*    <http://www.klgates.com/newsstand/Detail.aspx?
publication=4353>.

In mid-2012, the IRS issued guidance on whether dividends on restricted
stock, and the equivalent on restricted stock units (RSUs), must satisfy the
§ 162(m) requirements separately to be treated as fully deductible performance-
based compensation: Rev. Rul. 2012-19, 2012-28 I.R.B. 16. To qualify for exemption from the $1 million exemption, the dividends or dividend equivalents can
only be payable if the payee meets performance goals. However, the performance
goals for this purpose do not have to be the same ones for granting the underlying
restricted stock or RSUs. [Buck Consultants FYI, *IRS Clarifies Treatment of
Performance-Based Restricted Stock and Restricted Stock Units* (Aug. 8, 2012)
(benefitslink.com)]

The Supreme Court refused to review the Eighth Circuit's decision that cash
distribution dividends paid to redeem stock held in an ESOP are not deductible—
Code § 162(k)(1) provides that there is no § 404(k) deduction available for
amounts paid to an ESOP trust to redeem shares of the parent company's stock,
and the facts in this case were fairly similar. [*Nestle Purina Petcare Co. v. Commissioner of Internal Revenue*, 594 F.3d 968 (8th Cir.), *cert. denied*, 131 S. Ct. 86
(Oct. 4, 2010); see Rebecca Moore, *Decision Stands that Nestle Purina Cannot
Deduct Distribution Dividends*, plansponsor.com (Oct. 5, 2010). The comparable
case is *General Mills, Inc. v. United States*, 554 F.3d 727 (8th Cir. 2009)]

## § 2.03   INCOME TAX WITHHOLDING

### [A]   Calculation

A September 2007 IRS press release explains how taxpayers can
request Employer Identification Numbers (EINs) in real time: go to <http://
www.irs.gov>, access the Internet EIN System, and enter the required fields. A
permanent EIN is issued for immediate use if the data passes automated validity
checks. Employers whose application is rejected can correct the information and
then re-submit the application. Once the application is complete, the taxpayer can
view, print, and save the confirmation notice rather than having it mailed. [Nevin
E. Adams, *IRS Now Offers Real-Time EINs*, plansponsor.com (Sept. 25, 2007)]

At the time of hiring, the employer must also have the employee submit
Form W-4 (Employee's Withholding Allowance Certificate) to indicate the filing
status (married filing a joint return, married filing a separate return, single, head
of household) and the number of withholding allowances that he or she claims.
The more withholding allowances, the less that will be withheld from the employee's paycheck.

Although there are other methods, the amount of income tax to be withheld
is usually calculated under either the percentage method or the wage bracket

method. (The calculations will be done by the payroll preparation contractor, if the employer outsources this function.)

Under the percentage method, the IRS tables are used. The number of allowances claimed is multiplied by the amount from the allowance table; the result is subtracted from the employee's wages. The wage rate table gives the actual dollar amount to be withheld.

Under the wage bracket method, tables are used to compute withholding per weekly, semiweekly, or other pay period, based on wage level, marital status, and number of claimed exemptions.

ARRA (Pub. L. No. 111-5) also includes the "Making Work Pay" credit under new Code § 36A, equal to 6.2% of the taxpayer's earned income, up to a maximum of $400 for an individual, $800 for a joint return. This credit expired at the end of 2010.

For income tax purposes, "supplemental wages" means compensation other than, or in addition to, ordinary cash compensation. Bonuses, commissions, overtime pay, severance pay, back pay, taxable fringe benefits, and payments for accumulated sick leave are all supplemental wages.

For payments made after 2004, once a person's supplemental wage income exceeds $1 million, the employer must withhold on the supplemental income at the highest income tax rate (currently, 35%). Employers have an obligation to keep a cumulative record of this income so that they will be aware when the $1 million threshold is crossed.

Regulations were proposed in January 2005, setting out flat rates of withholding for supplemental wages. The employer withholds at a 25% rate for supplemental wages up to $1 million and 35% on any balance paid by the employer or any member of its I.R.C. § 52 controlled group. A payment made by a third party acting as the employer's agent is deemed made by the employer, even if the designation of the agent does not satisfy the I.R.C. § 3504 rules. [70 Fed. Reg. 767, 2005-6 I.R.B. 484, REG-152945-04, RIN 1545-BD96, Notice of Proposed Rulemaking Flat Rate Supplemental Wage Withholding, <http://www.irs.gov/pub/irs-regs/15294504.pdf> (Jan. 5, 2005)]

T.D. 9276 clarifies that compensation can be treated as "supplemental" even if the payee had no regular wages for the year. The category of supplemental wages also includes nonqualified deferred compensation that is included in wages, imputed income when a non-dependent (e.g., a same-sex partner) receives health coverage, and income due to lapse on restrictions on property transferred from employer to employee. Commissions, bonuses, and taxable noncash fringe benefits cannot be treated as regular wages. Under the proposed regulations, commissions could be treated as regular wages if the employee did not receive any other compensation, but T.D. 9276 eliminates this option. [T.D. 9276, 2006-37 I.R.B. 423)]

Rev. Rul. 2008-29, 2008-24 I.R.B. 1149, provides guidance under the supplemental wage regulations for signing bonuses and various kinds of commissions. The ruling describes the "aggregate method": adding supplemental wages to regular wages for the most recent payroll period as if a single payment had been made; tax is calculated under the tax tables, the employer subtracts amounts already withheld from regular wages, and then withholds the rest of the tax from the supplemental wages. For severance pay, the employer can use either the aggregate method or withholding at a 25% flat rate. The employer can use either the aggregate method or the flat rate when it makes a lump sum payment for accumulated vacation pay, or to cash out unused vacation and sick leave. [G.J. Stillson MacDonnell and William Hays Weissman (Littler Mendelson), *IRS Provides Guidance on Proper Income Tax Withholding for Nine Common Supplemental Wage Payment Scenarios* (June 2008) (benefitslink.com)]

The Second Circuit held that back pay is defined as the wages the plaintiff would have earned from the date of discharge to the date of reinstatement, plus lost fringe benefits, whereas front pay is awarded for lost compensation either instead or reinstatement or running from the judgment to the time of reinstatement. In a Title VII case brought by a terminated employee of New York State, the jury awarded back and front pay to the plaintiff. The judgment was sent to the New York State Office of Comptroller for payment. The office treated the judgment as wages, so it made deductions, mostly state and federal taxes, and sent the plaintiff a check for the balance. The plaintiff moved to require the state to pay him the full amount of the judgment, without deductions. The District Court for the Northern District of New York granted the motion, holding that the state did not have the authority to make the deductions without prior court approval. The Second Circuit, however, reversed, holding that the plaintiff received a windfall when he received the full amount. Back pay and front pay are wages subject to FICA and income tax withholding. [*Noel v. New York State Office Of Mental Health Cent. New York Psychiatric Ctr.*, 697 F.3d 209 (2d Cir. 2012)]

The withholding system must distinguish between compensation paid to the employee and reimbursement of legitimate business expenses that the employee incurred on the employer's behalf (reimbursement is not taxable income).

For tax purposes, expense accounts are either "accountable" or "non-accountable" plans. Amounts paid under an accountable plan are not wages for the employee, and therefore are not subject to FICA or FUTA. Withholding is not required. Employees must meet two tests under an accountable plan:

- They paid or incurred deductible expenses in the course of employment;
- They are required to provide adequate accounts of the expenses within a reasonable time of incurring them.

If they receive any amount over and above the expenses, they have an obligation to return it within a reasonable time. The general tax rule is that it is reasonable for employees to be reimbursed within 30 days of spending money; to provide an expense account within 60 days of spending the money; and to return excess amounts within 120 days of the initial advance.

Accounting for a per diem or a fixed allowance (e.g., X cents per mile for business travel) is considered adequate as long as the payment is no higher than the government per diem rates for meals and lodging (see IRS Publication 1542) and the standard mileage rate for travel. [IRS Publication 553]

If these tests are not met, the money is treated as if it were paid under a nonaccountable plan (one which does not require documentation of expenses). Expenses reimbursed under a nonaccountable plan are considered wages, included in income and subject to withholding in the first payroll period after there has been a reasonable time to return any excess funds.

Form 2106 is used for employees to claim business expense deductions for work-related travel, transportation, meals, or entertainment if the employee was reimbursed for deductible work-related expenses. The simplified Form 2106-EZ can be used by employees who use the standard mileage rate for vehicle expenses and who do not receive any expense reimbursement that is not reported as taxable income. The "accountable plan" rules relieve employees from tax on business expense reimbursement if the expenses are business-related, adequately substantiated, and the employee returns any amount of reimbursement that exceeds the expenses. If the reimbursement is less than the actual expense, an employee who can substantiate the actual amount can take a deduction on Form 2106 for the difference.

Rev. Proc. 2011-47, 2011-42 I.R.B. 520, provides the rules governing per diem rates for employees who are reimbursed for meals and incidental expenses or lodging, meals, and incidental expenses when traveling. This procedure updates Rev. Proc. 2010-39, 2010-42 I.R.B. 459. Per diem accounting is not required; taxpayers can use their preferred method of substantiating expenses. Per diem rates are published annually in a notice that lists the rates and high-cost localities, but the Revenue Procedure will not be re-issued annually, only updated as required. [Plansponsor staff, *IRS Publishes Rules on Business Expenses*, plansponsor.com (Oct. 4, 2011)]

For 2012–2013, the special per diem rate for ordinary and necessary business expenses when traveling away from home, is $163 in general, $242 for high-cost localities. Of this amount, $52 ($65 in high cost areas) is treated as having been paid for meals. [Notice 2012-53, 2012–35 I.R.B. 317]

Regulations were proposed in August 2012 under Code § 274(n) dealing with the 50% limit on deductions for food, beverages, and entertainment under a reimbursement arrangement. Only one party in a multi-party arrangement is subject to the limit. In a reimbursement agreement with employees, the 50% limit applies to the employer—unless the reimbursement constitutes taxable wages, in which case the limit applies to the employee. For expenses under an accountable plan, the limit applies only to the employer. For reimbursement arrangements with independent contractors, the agreement governs the way the limit will be applied. If the agreement is silent, the limit applies to the client/customer, but the limit applies to the independent contractor if the independent contractor does not seek reimbursement from, or substantiate expenses to, the client/customer. [Prop.

Regs. at 77 Fed. Reg. 45520 (Aug. 1, 2012); see Elizabeth T. Dold, *Proposed Regulations Clarify the 50% Entertainment Limit for Expense Reimbursement Arrangements*, Groom Law Group (Aug. 31, 2012) (benefitslink.com)]

The 2013 mileage rates are 56.5 cents per mile for business use, 14 cents per mile for charitable use, and 24 cents per mile for work-related moves. For 2013, 23 cents per mile out of the business standard mileage rate represents depreciation. To calculate the allowance under a FAVR (Fixed and Variable Rate) plan, the maximum permitted cost for an automobile is $28,100 or $29,900 for trucks and vans. [Notice 2012-72, 2012-50 I.R.B. 673, IR-2012-95]

All of the employee's taxable income is subject to income tax withholding, except to the degree that a withholding exemption is available. FICA (Social Security) taxes are imposed on the employee's taxable income, up to a certain amount (the amount is $97,500 for 2007, $102,000 for 2008, $106,800 for 2009–2011, $110,100 for 2012, and $113,700 for 2013; each year's wage base must be published in the Federal Register no later than November 1 of the preceding year). The employer and employee are each taxed at a rate of 6.2% on income up to the limit, and Medicare taxes are imposed on all compensation.

AJCA § 251, affecting I.R.C. § 13121(a), 421(b), 423(c), provides that for FICA and FUTA purposes, the definition of "wages" does not include remuneration from exercising an ISO or option to buy stock under an employee stock purchase plan.

CSX Corporation's Reduction in Force program has given rise to extensive federal tax litigation. If payments to RIFed employees qualify as Code § 3402(o) Supplementary Employment Benefits (SUBs), they are not FICA wages, and are not subject to FUTA, but they are subject to income tax withholding. In 2002, the Court of Federal Claims ruled that CSX employees suffered involuntary and complete termination, but payments to employees who stayed on standby recall, subject to active recall, were FICA wages. Lump sums paid to terminated employees in return for surrender of all their employment-related rights were FICA wages. [*CSX Corp., Inc.*, 52 Fed. Cl. 208 (Fed. Cl. 2002), *aff'd*, No. 95-858T (Fed. Cl. Oct. 31, 2003). However, in 2008, the Federal Circuit reversed, holding that the SUB payments were FICA wages, and § 3402(o) is irrelevant because it is limited to income tax withholding and is inapplicable to FICA. *CSX Corp. v. United States*, 518 F.3d 1328 (Fed. Cir. 2008), discussed in Deloitte's Washington Bulletin, *Federal Circuit Rules Supplemental Unemployment Benefits Are Wages for FICA Purposes*, <http://benefitslink.com/articles/guests/washbull080310.html> (Mar. 10, 2008)]

In a contemporary case on a similar issue, the Court of Federal Claims ruled [*Kraft Foods N. Am. Inc. v. United States*, No. 02-342T (Fed. Cl. Nov. 14, 2003)] that certain severance payments could not be treated as nonqualified deferred compensation under Code § 3121(v)(2), even under transition rules that gave employers discretion to adopt reasonable good-faith interpretations of the rules for deferred compensation. (Kraft had applied for refunds of FICA taxes, on the grounds that it was at least reasonable to treat the benefits as nonqualified deferred compensation.) According to the court, the payments were not compensation for specific services and thus were not deferred compensation.

In 2012, the Sixth Circuit created a circuit split, ruling that severance pay is not subject to FICA. The Sixth Circuit held that payments made to employees on their involuntary termination due to business cessation are not FICA wages. The Sixth Circuit interprets Code § 3402(o) to mean that Congress intended to require federal income withholding on payments "other than wages." However, the Sixth Circuit held that supplemental unemployment benefits are not wages that are subject to income tax withholding—nor are they FICA wages.

The Department of Justice requested rehearing en banc, which was denied. En banc rehearings are supposed to be extraordinary measures, and can be granted only if a majority of the active judges in that circuit who are not disqualified vote for rehearing. En banc rehearings permit an entire court panel to fix a precedent-setting error of exceptional importance to the public, or to resolve a direct conflict with Supreme Court precedent.

If the case goes to the Supreme Court and the Court upholds the Sixth Circuit, employers will be entitled to refunds on FICA tax paid on severance benefits. It could be worthwhile for employers who have paid extensive FICA tax on severance to file a refund claim with the IRS, which will extend the period of time for which FICA payments on severance benefits can be recovered. Even if certiorari is denied, employers in the Sixth Circuit may be able to claim refunds. The last date for filing a protective claim for 2009 payments was April 15, 2013; for 2010 payments, it is April 15, 2014. The protective claim is filed on Form 941-X for the open quarters, requesting a refund based on the *Quality Stores* decision. It is filed with a cover letter and Form 8275, saying that the request reflects the Sixth Circuit decision but is contrary to published IRS guidance. The IRS will probably refuse to make the refund—but may agree to use Form 907 to extend the two-year statute of limitations, a common procedure when there has been a circuit split. Extending the statute of limitations creates the possibility of recovering FICA paid in the years covered by the protective claim, plus any subsequent open tax years. [*United States v. Quality Stores*, 693 F.3d 605 (6th Cir. 2012); see Vedder Price Newsletter/Bulletin, *Action Required to Preserve FICA Refund Claim on Severance Pay* (Jan. 16, 2013) (benefitslink.com); Mary B. Hevener, David R. Fuller, Steven P. Johnson, Patrick Rehfield and Robert R. Martinelli, *Quality Stores, Inc. Update*, Morgan, Lewis & Bockius LawFlash (Oct. 24, 2012); Miller & Chevalier, *The Sixth Circuit's Affirmance of Quality Stores Splits the Circuits as to the FICA Tax Treatment of Severance Pay Next Steps for Employers?* (Sept. 13, 2012) (benefitslink.com)]

In mid-2004, district courts in Michigan clashed as to whether early retirement incentive payments offered to teachers in exchange for tenure rights were wages. The Western District said that such payments are wages for FICA purposes; two weeks later, the Eastern District said that because the payments were not wages, the retired teachers could get a refund of FICA withheld on the payments. [Compare *Klender v. United States*, 328 F. Supp. 2d 754 (E.D. Mich. 2004) with *Appoloni v. United States*, *219 F.R.D. 116* (W.D. Mich. 2004); but see *N.D. State Univ. v. United States*, 255 F.3d 599 (8th Cir. 2001)]

The Sixth Circuit resolved the split in mid-2006 by ruling that the payments were FICA wages because "compensation" should be defined broadly, and because eligibility for the payments depended on at least a minimum tenure with the employer, showing that payments were made for services, not for relinquishments of tenure rights. [*Appoloni v. United States/Klender v. United States*, 450 F.3d 185 (6th Cir. 2006); the Federal Circuit earlier ruled that severance payments to retiring employees, reflecting past work, are FICA wages; *Abrahamsen v. United States*, 228 F.3d 1360 (Fed. Cir. 2000). The Western District of Michigan held that severance payments to RIFed employees were not FICA wages. [*United States v. Quality Stores, Inc.*, 2010 U.S Dist. LEXIS 15825 (W.D. Mich. Feb. 23, 2010); see Thomas M. Cryan, Jr. and Marianna G. Dyson, Miller & Chevalier, *Quality Stores Decision Muddies the Waters on the FICA Tax Treatment of Severance Pay* (Mar. 3, 2010) (benefitslink.com)]

Although other courts disagree, the Third Circuit held that the University of Pittsburgh's early retired payments to tenured professors are taxable income, not buyout payments. The Third Circuit deemed tenure to be a form of compensation for past work at the university, so giving up tenure was the equivalent of severance pay and thus FICA wages. [Fred Schneyer, *Payments to Tenured Profs Ruled Taxable Wages*, plansponsor.com (Nov. 5, 2007)]

## [B]  Withholding on Pensions

The general rule is that income tax withholding is required when a plan makes payments to retired employees. There are circumstances under which the retirees can elect to waive withholding, but there are other circumstances in which withholding is mandatory.

For ordinary pension payments in annuity form, the plan can use its regular withholding procedures, based on the number of withholding exemptions on the retiree's Form W-4P. If no W-4P is submitted, the plan should withhold as if the retiree were married and claimed three withholding allowances.

However, if the distribution is a lump sum or other nonperiodic payment and not an annuity, the question is whether it is an "eligible rollover distribution." If it is not, the basic requirement is to withhold at a 10% rate, although the person receiving the lump sum can use the W-4P to claim exemption from withholding. If the recipient of the lump sum expects to be in a high tax bracket, the person can ask for withholding at a rate higher than 10%.

An eligible rollover distribution is an amount that could be placed in the retiree's IRA, Roth IRA, or transferred to another qualified plan. Any such amount that is not rolled over is subject to withholding at a rate of at least 20%. The recipient of the distribution can increase the withholding rate, but cannot lower it below 20% or claim a withholding exemption. See Code § 3405 and the instructions for Form 1099-R. The Pension Protection Act also permits a non-spouse beneficiary of a qualified plan account to roll over inherited funds to his or her own IRA.

One effect of the Economic Growth and Tax Relief Reconciliation Act of 2001 (EGTRRA) [Pub. L. No. 107-16] is to broaden the category of amounts that can be rolled over, and therefore that may be subject to withholding on this basis—although EGTRRA also lowers income tax rates, so 20% may in fact be higher than the retiree's actual tax rate.

Withholding from lump-sum pension distributions is not reported on Form 941. Instead, Form 945 (Annual Return of Withheld Federal Income Tax) is used. The pension withholding amounts should be combined with the other Form 945 amounts, but for nonpayroll withholding only, not payroll taxes. [See Form 945 instructions.] The recipient of the distribution receives a Form 1099-R (Distributions from Pensions, Annuities, Retirement or Profit-Sharing Plans). [See Chapter 12 for further information on distributions from qualified plans.]

## § 2.04 FUTA TAX

FUTA (Federal Unemployment Tax Act) taxes are paid entirely by the employer, on the first $7,000 of the employee's wages that are subject to FUTA. The FUTA tax form is Form 940. IRS discontinued the previous Form 940-EZ (short form) in 2007, but redesigned Form 940 to be more logical and easier to use.

State and federal employment tax is due if an employer pays wages to employees totaling $1,500 or more in any quarter of a calendar year or had at least one employee during any day of a week, 20 weeks in a calendar year, even if the weeks are not consecutive. The 0.2% FUTA surtax expired June 20, 2011, so two rates are used for 2011 taxes: 6.2% of wages through June 30, 6.0% afterwards, applied to a wage base of $7,000. Most employers get a 5.4% offset, making the rate for the first half of 2011, 0.8% of $7,000, or $56 per employee; for the second half, it is generally 0.6% of $7,000, or $42 per employee. [DOL, *Unemployment Insurance Tax Topic: Unemployment Insurance Taxes*, <http://workforcesecurity.doleta.gov/unemploy/uitaxtopic.asp> (Jan. 9, 2012)] The states have their own taxable wage bases: see § 32.06.

There are four quarterly deposit dates for FUTA taxes (April 30, July 31, October 31, January 31) for the quarter ending the previous month. Employers are not required to make a deposit in a quarter in which their liability is $500 or less; they carry it forward until it does reach $500, at which point the deposit must be made either through electronic funds transfer or to an authorized financial institution. Because the maximum amount of FUTA is $56/employee, if the employer made timely payments of state unemployment taxes, in effect an employer with eight or fewer employees will not have to make quarterly FUTA deposits. [IRS,

IRS Issues Final Regulations-FUTA Tax, <http://www.irs.gov/govt/tribes/article/ 0,,id=131902,00.html> (Nov. 5, 2010)]

Form 940 is the annual FUTA tax return, which is due January 31 (or February 10, if all FUTA taxes were deposited when due).

The Supreme Court seldom tackles employment tax issues, but see its 2001 decision in *United States v. Cleveland Indians Baseball Co.* [532 U.S. 200 (2001)] If an employee settles an employment case and receives back pay, for FICA and FUTA purposes the money is taxed in the year in which the wages were actually paid and not the year in which they were earned—whether the tax rates in the year of payment were higher or lower than the rates for the year FYI which the money was earned.

## § 2.05 TRUST FUND TAX COMPLIANCE AND THE 100% PENALTY

The FICA tax withheld from employees' salary (both the OASDI and the Medicare components) is called a "trust fund tax." (Although the employer must pay its FICA share, and must pay FUTA, these are not trust fund taxes.)

Frequently, the employer will collect employee FICA tax from each payroll, but will not have to deposit the tax until the end of the quarter. A cash-strapped company's temptation to "borrow" that money for its own immediate needs is strong. To reduce the temptation, I.R.C. § 6672 imposes a 100% penalty that cannot be discharged in bankruptcy on "responsible persons" who willfully fail to submit the withheld trust fund taxes to the government. The 100% penalty means that the penalty is as large as the amount of taxes that were not properly paid. Furthermore, all of the personal assets of the responsible party can be attached to satisfy the debt.

Tax law creates a very large class of responsible persons, including the corporation's officers, shareholders, and directors, based on their level of responsibility within the corporation. The factors include authority to hire and fire; to decide which creditors will be paid and in what order, control over payroll, and power to deposit federal tax amounts. Top managers will probably be liable because of their degree of control over corporate financial managers. Lower-level managers probably will not be liable unless their duties include actually writing checks (and thus actual knowledge of amounts disbursed or not disbursed). Even parties outside the corporation, such as its bankers and its accountants, can be liable if they have the real control over corporate funds. In an appeal from a conviction for willful failure to pay over payroll taxes, the Ninth Circuit held that "willful" is defined as a voluntary, intentional violation of a known legal duty. [*United States v. Easterday*, 539 F.3d 1176 (9th Cir. 2008)]

The Supreme Court held, early in 2011 that medical residents working over 40 hours a week are not "students" for FICA purposes. Therefore, their compensation is subject to FICA tax. [*Mayo Found. for Med. Educ. & Research v. United States*, 131 S. Ct. 704 (Jan. 11, 2011); see Buck Consultants FYI, *Supreme Court*

*Upholds Treasury Rule That Medical Residents Are Employees for FICA Purposes* (Jan. 21, 2011) (benefitslink.com)]

When a penalty is due, the government can either collect all of it from one responsible person or divide it among several. To avoid liability, an individual has to prove that he or she was incorrectly characterized as a responsible person, or that the failure to pay over the money was not willful. In this context, "willfulness" only means knowledge that the taxes were not submitted, and a failure to correct the situation. If a responsible person finds out that, a payment was missed in one quarter that creates a duty to investigate to find out if other payments were missed as well.

The responsible person's duty is to use all of the corporations "unencumbered funds" to pay trust fund taxes. Unencumbered funds are those not already assigned to a debt that existed before the tax liability arose.

Thanks to the Taxpayer Bill of Rights 2 [Pub. L. No. 104-168] a responsible person is entitled to notice before the IRS imposes the 100% penalty. The notice must also give the names of other responsible persons, the IRs' collection efforts against them, and the success of those efforts. (The other responsible parties who actually pay the IRS can sue other responsible parties to make them pay their fair share.) The recipient of the notice can pay the penalty and sue for a refund, or contest the penalty in federal court. Collection efforts will be suspended until the case is resolved.

TD 9356, 2007-39 I.R.B. 675 took effect Jan. 1, 2009. From that date, Subchapter S corporation subsidiaries, Limited Liability Companies, and certain single-owner entities are required to file employment tax returns and make payments separate from the business owner's return. (Under prior law, the taxpayer could handle all the employment obligations for the employees of a disregarded entity as if the business owner was their employer.) Under the new procedure, taxes paid by the owner are treated as overpayments (although they are not always fully refundable), but the business entity remains liable for the unpaid taxes, penalties, and interest. If no tax return is filed, the statute of limitations never begins to run, so the potential liability extends indefinitely.

IRS policy is to avoid assessing the § 6672 penalty against a responsible person as long as a corporate debtor complies with the terms of its bankruptcy payment plan. However, the IRS might depart from this policy close to the end of the statute of limitations, when failure to enforce might make the debt uncollectable.

Underpaying taxes creates an obligation to catch up on the payments, plus interest. Penalties may also be assessed for, e.g., failure to file, late filing, or serious understatement of the amount of tax.

Code § 6690 imposes a penalty of $50 per failure to furnish a statement required under § 6057(e) to a participant, or for willfully furnishing a false or fraudulent statement. Section 6693 imposes the same penalty for improprieties in connection with statements relating to IRAs, MSAs, or HSAs. Failure to keep records necessary for § 6047(d) reporting is penalized by $50 per person, up to a maximum of $50,000 a year. The administrator of a defined benefit plan who fails to file the actuarial report required by § 6059 is subject, under § 6692, to a penalty of $1,000 per failure (unless reasonable cause for the failure can be shown).

Rev. Rul. 2006-38, 2006-29 I.R.B. 80 sets out the procedures employers can use to calculate their tax obligations under Code § 4975 for delay in submitting employee contributions to 401(k)s and other retirement plans. The "first-tier excise tax" is a 15% penalty on any employer that profits from a prohibited transaction. Employers subject to the tax can apply the 15% rate to any interest they owe on late payments; the interest rate charged is the § 6621(a) rate for underpayments. Rev. Rul. 2006-38 deals only with the first-tier tax, not the 100% "second-tier tax" for failure to correct a prohibited transaction. [Allison Bell, *IRS Explains Taxation of Late Plan Payments*, NU Online News Service (July 5, 2006)]

Furthermore, criminal liability can be imposed in five situations:

- Willful failure to collect or pay over federal tax;

- Willful failure to pay tax, make a return, keep records, or provide mandated information to the IRS is a misdemeanor (not a felony);

- Willful furnishing of a false or fraudulent tax statement, or willful refusal to furnish a required statement;

- Willful tax evasion;

- It is perjury to willfully sign a return or other tax document that the signer knows to be false or inaccurate.

Although these penalties are heavy, in practice the IRS often attempts to collect civil penalties instead of criminal ones, because it's easy to prove that taxes were not paid as required, but hard to prove the state of mind of the person or organization who was supposed to make the payment.

The Voluntary Classification Settlement Program (VCSP) has been expanded so more businesses can clarify the status of their workers as employees or independent contractors and, therefore, report and pay employment-related taxes correctly. The program's eligibility requirements have been modified so more employers, especially large ones, can use the program. Almost 1,000 employers have applied for the program, to get partial relief from payroll taxes when they stop classifying certain workers as independent contractors. Even employers being audited by the IRS (except for employment tax audits) can use VCSP. An employer is eligible to use VCSP for a particular worker if the employer is currently treating the worker as a non-employee; has consistently treated the worker that way, including filing 1099s; if that worker's status is not the subject of a current IRS payroll tax audit, or a DOL, or state agency labor audit; and the worker's status is not currently being contested in court. Under prior law, a special six-year statute of limitations applied to classification cases, but VCSP participants are subject to the regular statute of limitations for payroll taxes. Application is made on Form 8952 and must be made at least 60 days before the employer wishes to treat the worker as an employee. Employers accepted into the program must pay about 1% of the wages paid to the reclassified worker. No interest or penalties are imposed. The employer will not be audited for payroll taxes for those workers for the past year. If the employer is also participating in the temporary relief program for employers who failed to file 1099s, they must issue the 1099s and pay slightly more to resolve their liability. [Announcement 2012-45, 2012-51 I.R.B. 724, Announcement 2012-46, 2012-51 I.R.B. 725 discussed in IR-2012-23, *IRS Expands Voluntary Worker Classification Settlement Program; Relief From Past Payroll Taxes Available to More Employers Who Reclassify Their Workers As Employees* (Feb. 27, 2013)]

### § 2.06 W-2s AND OTHER TAX FORMS

The W-2 form, used to report employee compensation, is a multipart form. Forms are sent to the IRS and to state tax authorities (and city authorities, in cities that impose their own income tax). The employer must also furnish the employee with copies that the employees can use to prepare their tax returns. Of course, the fact that the employer submits the same information to the taxing authorities makes it harder for employees to omit employment income from their tax returns.

For distributions in 2009 and later years, IRS Announcement 2008-56, 2008-26 I.R.B. 1192 requires employers to report the dividends on employer securities distributed from an ESOP on a Form 1099-R that does not report any other distributions. (If the plan makes distributions that are not 404(k) distributions, they must be reported on a separate Form 1099-R.) ESOP distributions that are 404(k) dividends are not subject to the 10% excise tax under Code § 72; not subject to withholding; and are not eligible for rollover. [Announcement 2008-56, Rebecca Moore, *IRS Changes Reporting Requirements for Dividends on ESOP Distributions*, plansponsor.com (June 10, 2008)]

In late 2010, the IRS released final versions of Forms 3921 and 3922 (reporting information about exercise of Incentive Stock Options and options under an Employee Stock Option Plan).

The Form 3921 requires reporting of the grant and exercise date of ISOs, the exercise price per share, the FMV of a share on the exercise date, and the number of shares transferred in exercise of the ISO. Form 3922 requires the grant and exercise date of the option, the FMV of a share on the grant date and the exercise date, the price per share paid on the exercise date, the number of shares to which title was transferred, and the date of the first transfer of title. If the exercise price was not fixed or determinable on the grant date, the exercise price per share, calculated as if the option was exercised on the grant date, must be reported. Failure to file the Form 3921 or 3922 on time is penalized by up to $50 per form (capped at $250,000 per year). Failure to give employees the form is penalized by $50 per form, up to a maximum of $100,000. [Fred Schneyer, *Employee Stock Reporting Deadlines Approaching*, plansponsor.com (Nov. 19, 2010); Vorys, Sater, Seymour and Pease LLP Client Alert, *Reminder—Reporting Required for Exercise of ISOs, ESPP Options* (Nov. 18, 2010) (benefitslink.com)]

As originally enacted, PPACA required that, for taxable years beginning after 2010, the employer must report the aggregate cost of employer-sponsored health coverage on each employee's Form W-2. The information will be used to determine if the employer has met its obligations to provide adequate, affordable health coverage. The cost of providing EGHP coverage, the employer's contributions to the employee's HSA, MSA, or HRA, Medicare supplements and Medicare Advantage plans provided by the employer, and the value of care at employer-sponsored on-site health clinics must all be reported. However, it is not necessary to include salary reduction contributions to a health FSA, long-term care insurance, or certain limited coverages (e.g., stand-alone vision and dental plans). The computation of the value of the coverage is similar to the method used to determine COBRA premiums. [Christy Tinnes and Brigen Winters, *How Should Employers Handle the New W-2 Reporting Requirements?*, plansponsor.com (June 22, 2010)]

Notice 2011-28, 2011-16 I.R.B. 656 grants relief to small employers (those that filed fewer than 250 W-2 forms for the previous year): they will not have to report health insurance cost information until the 2013 forms are filed in 2014. Once the filing obligation begins (or when an employer chooses to report the information voluntarily), the employer must report the aggregate cost of all applicable employer-sponsored coverage—i.e., all EGHP coverage that is excludable from recipients' income under Code § 106. Contributions to an Archer MSA or health savings account are not included (other than salary reduction contributions to a health FSA), but aggregate cost does include the employer's contributions to multi-employer plans and the cost of coverage under an HRA. [Jeffrey Ashendorf, Ford & Harrison Legal Alert, *Health Insurance Information Reporting Further Delayed* (Apr. 5, 2011) (benefitslink.com)]

PPACA § 9006 imposed a requirement, starting January 1, 2012 that companies would have to issue a Form 1099 to any individual or corporation from which they buy over $600 in goods or services in a tax year. [Neil deMause, *Health Care Law's Hidden Tax Change To Launch 1099 Avalanche*, CNN Money.com (May 5, 2010) (benefitslink.com)] However, Congress repealed this requirement in the first quarter of 2011, and President Obama signed Pub. L. No. 112-9, the Comprehensive 1099 Taxpayer and Repayment of Exchange Subsidy Overpayments Act, the repeal legislation, on April 15, 2011. [BNA Tax & Accounting Daily Tax Report, *Obama Signs Measure Into Law Repealing Expanded Form 1099 Rules*, <http://www.bnatax.com/insightsdetail. aspx?id= 2147486071> (Apr. 15, 2011)]

## § 2.07   TAX DEPOSITS

Employment taxes (withheld income taxes, FICA) are usually remitted by the employer either once a month or every other week. The schedule for reporting depends on the size of the employer's tax obligation for the previous year; the IRS notifies employers every November which category they will fall into for the next year. [See Treas. Reg. § 31.6302-1]

The basic reporting form is the quarterly Form 941, but income tax and back-up withholding on nonpayroll amounts are reported once a year on Form 945—Annual Return of Withheld Federal Income Tax. The IRS will notify small employers if they qualify to use Form 944, the annual federal tax return; qualifying employers can, nevertheless, elect to continue to file Form 941. See IRS Publication 15, Employer's Tax Guide for details on filing and reporting.

Penalties of between 2%–15% are imposed for late deposits (rising with the extent of the delay), with the highest penalty imposed on continuing failure to deposit after a demand from the IRS. A failure-to-deposit penalty of 10% is imposed on employers who had an obligation to use EFTPS and did not.

Employers whose annual employment tax liability does not exceed $1,000 do not have to file a quarterly Form 941, and most employers in this category will not have to make monthly or semi-monthly payments. However, the IRS estimates that employers will qualify only if their wage payments are less than $4,000 a year. The IRS created an invitation program under which it notifies very small employers that they can file Form 944 rather than 941. (If they prefer, qualifying employers can still file Form 941.). Employers can request to participate in the Form 944 Program, but they must get the IRS permission before moving to annual filing and once they enter the program, they must file a Form 944 each year until a request to return to filing Form 941 has been made and granted, or until they no longer qualify for the 944 program. Qualifying employers are those whose annual employment tax liability (including FICA, Medicare, and federal income tax withholding) is very small: less than $1,000 for the calendar year. However, agricultural employers and employers of household employees (e.g., nannies, housekeepers) do not qualify. [T.D. 9566, 76 Fed. Reg. 77672 (Dec. 14, 2011)]

Form 944 and associated tax payments are due January 31 of the year after the year for which the return is filed, but employers who have paid all employment taxes accrued to date get an extra 10 calendar days to file. Employers can find out if they qualify by calling (800) 829-0115. New employers who expect tax liability below $1,000 a year can apply to the IRS and indicate on their Form SS-4 that they project a minimal tax liability. If their actual liability exceeds $1,000, they should file Form 944 and then file Form 941 in the future.

An accrual basis taxpayer that meets the "all events test" and the "recurring item exception" under § 461 can treat its payroll tax (FICA and FUTA) liability as incurred in a given year, even if, under § 404, the compensation to which that liability relates is deferred compensation that is not deductible until the following year. The new rule is available if the employer pays the payroll taxes either in the first year, or before September 15 of the second year or the due date of the company's federal income tax for the first year—whichever is earlier. However, companies that want to change their treatment of payroll taxes on deferred compensation must get permission from the IRS. [Rev. Rul. 2007-12, 2007-11 I.R.B. 685; see Fred Schneyer, *Deferred Comp Payroll Tax Scenario Clarified*, plansponsor.com (Feb. 15, 2007)]

## § 2.08 TRANSITION TO ELECTRONIC FILING

For many years, the IRS has been developing rules for electronic filing of tax forms. According to the agency, more than eight million business returns were electronically filed in 2005, with a 99% accuracy rate. By 2006, most business and employment tax returns (including information returns) could be filed electronically. (The TeleFile program, which allowed some forms to be filed over the telephone, was discontinued in mid-2005.)

Business taxpayers can pay all of their federal taxes online or by phone using the Electronic Federal Tax Payment System (EFTPS). EFTPS does not impose any fees. EFTPS is set up to facilitate transmission and processing of tax information submitted by corporations. EFTPS is a highly secure site, using the highest available level of encryption. Users have to enroll on Form 9779, and need a Taxpayer ID, a PIN, and an Internet password to log on. EFTPS users go online or make a phone call at least one calendar day before the due date of a return to input the tax information for their accounts; then the taxpayer directs movement of funds from an approved bank account to the U.S. Treasury account. (Payments can be scheduled in advance, and taxpayers can check the status of any payment made in the preceding 16 months.) [See IRS instructional materials, A Secure Way to Pay Your Federal Taxes, <http://www.irs.gov/efile/article/0,,id= 98005,00.html>, and Publication 4132 (explaining how to enroll in EFTPS and make payments online); Publication 966 (business and individual e-filing rules), Publication 4169, guide to EFTPS for tax professionals, and Publication 4275 (express enrollment for new businesses). Telephone customer service is available at all times, via (800) 316-6541.]

Mid-size and large corporations (with assets of $50 million or more and at least 250 returns—including income tax returns, employment tax returns, and information returns—filed per year) are required to file their Forms 1120 and 1120-S electronically for tax years ending on or after December 31, 2005. The following year, corporations filing 250 returns must file electronically if their assets are $10 million or more. The IRS has revamped its corporate electronic filing system, known as Modernized e-file (MeF). Large corporations must either register with the IRS as a "Large Taxpayer" that prepares their returns in-house or work with an e-file service provider approved by the IRS. [Form 1120/1120S/1120-F e-file, <http://www.irs.gov/Tax-Professionals/e-File-Providers-&-Partners/Form-1120-1120S-1120-F-e-file> (Jan. 29, 2013)]

See    <http://www.irs.gov/uac/Employment-Taxes---Electronic-Filing-and-Payment-Options> (Oct. 15, 2012) for links to the Employment Tax e-file System, which is available to "Reporting Agents," IRS-authorized service providers who file Forms 940, 941, and/or 944 electronically for their clients. Business taxpayers can also file online with the 940, 941, and 944 online filing programs, and all federal tax payments can be made by electronic funds transfer or by credit card. W-2 forms can be submitted electronically, although the Social Security Administration rather than the IRS site is the proper place of filing. The Social Security Administration has online help for employers who file W-2 forms electronically. [*Specifications for Filing Forms W-2 Electronically (EFW2) For Tax year 2012*, SSA Publication No. 42-007, <http://www.socialsecurity.gov/employer/efw/12efw2.pdf#zoom=100>]

## § 2.09  BANKRUPTCY ISSUES

In April 2005 the Supreme Court decided that IRA balances are exempt from creditor claims in bankruptcy because the right to receive IRA funds is "on account of age." Although IRA funds can be withdrawn at any age, there is a substantial penalty on withdrawals prior to age 59½ unless another exemption is available. The Supreme Court resolved a circuit split under which the Second, Fifth, Sixth, and Ninth Circuits took the position eventually adopted by the Supreme Court, but the Eighth Circuit deemed IRA account holders to have unlimited access to their funds, so creditors should be able to reach the funds. (It is likely that the Supreme Court accepted the policy argument that IRAs often receive rollovers from qualified pension plans.) [*Rousey v. Jacoway*, 544 U.S. 320 (2005)]

The Sixth Circuit held that income available to Chapter 13 debtors after repaying a 401(k) loan is projected disposable income that must be paid to unsecured creditors. If the bankruptcy trustee objects, the debtors will not be permitted to use it to make voluntary contributions to the plan. The Bankruptcy Abuse Prevention and Consumer Protection Act of 2005 (BAPCPA) provides a limited exclusion for amounts withheld by an employer from an employee's wages for contributions to a qualified plan, so the Sixth Circuit held that plan loan payments are excluded from debtor's disposable income, but voluntary contributions to a 401(k) plan are not. The Sixth Circuit said that contributions are only excluded from the bankruptcy estate if they were made before the date of the petition. [*In re Seafort*, 669 F.3d 662 (6th Cir. 2012); see CCH Pension & Benefits, *Debtors Could Not Begin Making Post-Petition Contributions to 401(K) Plans Following Repayment of Plan Loans* (Mar. 23, 2012) (benefitslink.com)]

A 2004 Ninth Circuit case involves a Chapter 11 bankruptcy case that was converted to Chapter 13, raising the question of what priority should be awarded to administrative expense claims arising after the petition but before the conversion. The Ninth Circuit read 11 U.S.C. § 348(d) to permit federal employment taxes to retain their administrative-expense priority. The Ninth Circuit treated post-petition tax debt as an administrative expense as long as it relates to taxes incurred by the estate. 11 U.S.C. § 1322(a)(2) requires the Chapter 13 plan to provide full payment of administrative expenses (including penalties and interest) as first-priority claims. Pre-petition, unsecured tax debt generally takes eighth priority, and is paid over the life of the plan without interest. The Ninth Circuit cited cases from other circuits preserving the administrative expense status of tax debt when Chapter 11 cases are converted to Chapter 7, and saw no reason to treat Chapter 11 to Chapter 13 conversions differently. [*In re Fowler*, 394 F.3d 1208 (9th Cir. 2005)]

Although the primary impact of BAPCPA (The Bankruptcy Abuse Prevention and Consumer Protection Act of 2005; Pub. L. No. 109-8) is on individual filings, this legislation has some provisions that affect employment tax planning:

- Clarification that a broad range of retirement savings vehicles will be excluded from the individual debtor's bankruptcy estate—not just government plans and private employer plans subject to ERISA Title I, but also tax-deferred annuities under 403(b) plans, health insurance plans regulated by state law, IRAs (including education IRAs), and funds placed in a § 529 (tuition savings program) a year or more before the bankruptcy filing. In general, the IRA exemption is limited to $1 million, but qualified rollovers into the IRA are not counted for this purpose. Furthermore, protection is granted to employee contributions even before they are deposited into the plan. This wide scope of protection applies even if the debtor is an insider of the employer corporation, and whether the debtor elects the state or federal exemption scheme.

- BAPCA alters the previous treatment of plan loans. It is not a violation of the automatic stay to withhold a debtor-employee's wages to repay a plan loan from a qualified plan.

- Pre-BAPCA, wages, salaries, and commissions for services rendered filing of the bankruptcy petition generally could be paid and claimed as administrative expenses. BAPCA strictly limits payments of retention bonuses and severance payments to corporate insiders.

BAPCA extends the avoidance period (i.e., makes it easier for the bankruptcy trustee to reverse payments) with respect to transfers made to insiders—including certain transfers made under employment contracts that are not in the ordinary course of business.

In 2004, the Sixth Circuit held that an officer of a bankrupt corporation was a responsible person. He was the CEO and majority shareholder and controlled the corporation's financial affairs. He was aware of the tax deficiencies, and nevertheless chose to pay other creditors rather than satisfying the tax obligation. The Sixth Circuit rejected the taxpayer's argument that he did not have control over the funds as a result of lock-box arrangements with lenders. The court ruled that corporate funds can only be considered encumbered by legal obligations imposed by statutes and regulations, not by contractual agreements voluntarily accepted. [*Bell v. United States*, 355 F.3d 387 (6th Cir. 2004)]

## § 2.10  THE INTERACTION BETWEEN §§ 409A AND 415

In May 2005 the IRS proposed new Regulations covering Code § 415 (the previous regulations were published in 1981!). See 70 Fed. Reg. 31214 (May 31, 2005). One of the areas covered by these regulations is the issue of post-separation payments.

The general tax rule is that payments made after an employee's separation from service are not compensation for § 415 purposes. The practical effect is that after an employee is terminated, he or she can no longer defer funds (e.g., severance benefits) paid by the ex-employer by depositing them in a 401(k) or 403(b) or 457 account. However, under the Proposed Regulations, a payment made within the 2½-month period after separation can be deferred in two situations. Either the payment would have been made anyway, even if employment had not terminated, or the payment relates to bona fide vacation, sick leave, or other leave the employee would have had access to if employment had continued.

Code § 409A provision governing nonqualified plans also has implications for the taxation of post-severance compensation (see § 8.02[D] for a more detailed discussion). "Separation pay" is the term used in § 409A for severance pay. It is regulated as defined compensation if there is a legally binding right to payment in a future year—even if there is a substantial risk of forfeiture. However, if the payment is entirely at the payor's discretion, there is no legally binding right to payment, so § 409A will not apply. The Proposed Regulations exempt certain severance payments from § 409A, such as expense reimbursement, payments for involuntary termination or RIF, severance agreements paying less than $5,000 in any tax year, and collectively bargained arrangements. If the payee is a key employee of a public company, payments will probably have to be delayed for six months. [Thomas M. Greene, BNA Tax Management, *Severance ... It's Not What It Used to Be*, <http://www.bnatax.com/tm/insights/greene.htm>; see Notice 2005-1, 2005-2 I.R.B. 274 and Prop. Regs. at 70 Fed. Reg. 57930 (Oct. 4, 2005)]

Dr. Senat Sutardja received a board-approved grant of up to two million stock options on December 10, 2003, well before the effective date of § 409A. The stock price on the grant date was $36.19. The company's compensation committee finalized the grant on December 16, 2003 as 1.5 million stock options, at an exercise price of $36.50, the stock price on that date. On January 16, 2004, when the stock price was $43.64, the 1.5 million share grant was ratified. In January 2006, Sutardja exercised some options. (In the interim, § 409A had taken effect on January 1, 2005.) Subsequently, Sutardja signed an agreement to reform the stock option agreement. He paid $5.35 million between the original and amended exercise prices. Commentator Michael S. Melbinger described this as an attempt to correct an understated exercise price, at a time when there were no § 409A regulations available for guidance. In November 2010, the IRS ruled that the exercise of the option was for less than FMV, and imposed a 20% surtax, plus interest on the underpayment. Under the regulations, discounted stock options are subject to § 409A and must have fixed dates for exercise and payment and must not have any discretionary provisions about the time or form of payment. Sutardja said that the exercise was not deferred compensation under Code § 3121(v) and, therefore, was not deferred compensation for § 409A purposes. The Court of Federal Claims followed a 2005 IRS Notice that treats discounted stock options as deferred compensation despite the language found in § 3121(v).

Sutardja also argued that he did not have a legally binding right to the compensation until he exercised the option, but the Court of Federal Claims ruled that the compensation was earned at the grant of the option, and Sutardja was legally entitled to the compensation as soon as there was no longer a substantial risk of forfeiture and the options had vested. Finally, Sutardja argued that the short-term exemption of § 409A applied because the options were exercised within 2.5 months of the end of the year in which the options vested. The court's interpretation was different: like most plans, this one gave Sutardja a 10-year period in which he could exercise the options; he was not obligated to do so within 2.5 months of the end of the year of vesting. Sutardja pointed to a provision in the grant giving him 30 days after being terminated to exercise the option, saying that this provision made the options at substantial risk of forfeiture until he actually exercised them at a time when he had not been terminated. This argument was also rejected: the Court of Federal Claims said that the 30 days were just a grace period, not a condition creating a substantial risk of forfeiture. The case was remanded to decide the fact question of whether the options were granted at a discount. [*Sutardja v. United States*, No. 11-724T, 2013-1 U.S. Tax Cas. (CCH) P50, 214 (Fed. Claims Feb. 27, 2013); see Jeffrey Cairns, Benefits Notes, *Section 409A Tax Assessed on Discounted Stock Options—Taxpayer Sues for Refund in Federal Court of Claims* (Mar. 7, 2013); Michael S. Melbinger, *If You Thought the IRS Would Not Punish 409A Foot Faults, Think Again*, Winston & Strawn LLP (Mar. 26, 2013) (benefitslink.com); David W. Eckhart, *Sutardja v. United States: When Options Are No Longer Optional*, Whyte Hirschboeck Dudek S.C. Special Report (Mar. 2013)]

# CHAPTER 3

# BONUSES AND SEVERANCE PAY

## § 3.01  INTRODUCTION

Although regular compensation and benefits are the main focus of compensation planning, there are two important types of nonrecurring compensation that also play an important role: bonuses and severance pay.

The 2005 Bankruptcy Reform Act (Pub. L. No. 109-8) limits the ability of a company that is a Chapter 11 debtor to offer retention bonuses and/or severance pay and then claim these payments as an administrative expense in the bankruptcy case. A retention bonus or severance payment to a director, officer, partner, or control person is allowed only if the fact and amount of the payment are both reasonable.

A retention bonus to an insider is allowed only if the insider has, in fact, received a bona fide job offer elsewhere paying at least as much as the insider's job, preventing the insider from taking the offer is essential to the business's survival, and the amount of the bonus is limited to either 10 times the average retention payment made to rank-and-file employees or 25% of any similar payment made to or on behalf of the insider in the previous calendar year. Severance payments to insiders are allowed only as part of a program covering all full-time employees, and insiders must not receive severance that exceeds 10 times the average severance payment to the rank and file.

American Airlines CEO Tom Horton was promised almost $20 million in severance as part of the planned merger between American and U.S. Airways. However, American Airlines was a Chapter 11 debtor, and the U.S. Trustee objected to the severance payment. The bankruptcy court for the Southern District of New York approved the merger in 2013, but rejected the severance payment, holding that it violated Bankruptcy Code § 503(c), which limits severance payments that can be made to corporate insiders. American Airlines argued that this provision did not apply, because the payment would come from a newly-formed business entity. The bankruptcy court, however, held that it was still a severance payment to an insider. Although the bankruptcy court would not permit the payment to be made before the bankruptcy plan was confirmed, it did allow American to include the payment in the Chapter 11 reorganization plan submitted to the bankruptcy court for its approval. [Paul Rubin and Hanh Huynh, *Court to Reassess Severance Payments as Part of Reorganization Plan*, N.Y.L.J. (June 24, 2013) (law.com)]

Hostess' unions were infuriated to discover that executives received pay increases five months before the bankruptcy filing, although the increases were reversed in response to protests. Many companies pay bonuses to top executives shortly before a filing. Federal law regulates post-filing but not pre-filing retention bonuses. It is common for companies to adopt incentive plans that reward executives for staying on and meeting performance targets as the business winds down. The Wall Street Journal's analysis of more than 80 bankruptcy cases over a five-year period showed that more than $1.3 billion in compensation was paid to more than 1,600 insiders in the months before a Chapter 11 filing. [Mike Spector, Tom McGinty, and Rachel Feintzeig, *In Trouble and Paying Out*, WSJ.com (Dec. 3, 2012)]

The Department of Justice, in its role as U.S. Trustee, has been successful in blocking proposed bonuses for executives of Chapter 11 companies. In Hostess' case, the U.S. Trustee challenged about $1.8 million in proposed bonuses for senior managers under the liquidation plan. Similar challenges were posed in other 2012 bankruptcies, such as LightSquared Inc., Eastman Kodak, and Hawker Beechcraft Inc. The Bankruptcy Code requires extraordinary circumstances to pay a retention bonus. [Mike Spector, *Bonuses in Bankruptcy Get Tougher to Collect*, WSJ.com (Nov. 21, 2012)]

## [A]  Limitations on Executive Pay

After many years of assuming that the setting of pay was purely a discretionary act on the part of the paying corporation, limitations began to be imposed: such as § 162(m) limitations on the tax deduction for compensation (see § 3.03[G], below), and restrictions on "shutdown benefits."

Even outside the bankruptcy context, a plan that is "at risk" (i.e., significantly underfunded) may be barred by the Pension Protection Act of 2006, Pub. L. No. 109-280, from providing "shutdown benefits"—payments to employees who are losing their jobs when an operation is shut down. In some cases, the employer will be permitted to make the payments if the employer makes an additional contribution to shore up the plan.

Companies that received Troubled Asset Relief Program (TARP) bailout payments under the Emergency Economic Stabilization Act of 2008 (EESA), as amended by the American Recovery and Reinvestment Act of 2009 (ARRA), were subject to limits on bonuses, incentive compensation, and retention awards as long as they had any outstanding obligations to the federal government. (The TARP program ended in 2010.)

Companies receiving TARP assistance were also forbidden to make "golden parachute" payments to top executives leaving the company. See § 3.03[D] below. EESA and AARA also call for "clawback": companies must recover from the payee any bonus or incentive compensation that was paid to a top executive on the basis of false financial reporting, and compensation plans must not encourage future false reporting that would lead to higher compensation. [Joseph E. Bachelder III, *How Recovery Legislation Amends Executive Pay Limits*, N.Y.L.J. (Apr. 20, 2009) (law.com)]

The Dodd-Frank Act, Pub. L. No. 111-203, was passed to prevent future economic meltdowns. Dodd-Frank Act § 951 requires public companies to allow their shareholders a "say on pay": input into the compensation process for top executives. Shareholders have the right to cast advisory (i.e., non-binding) votes on executive compensation and golden parachutes. As of January 21, 2011, proxy statements must include say on pay resolutions—and a vote on how often say on pay votes will be conducted.

Exchange Act Rule 14a-21(b) requires public companies to hold a say on pay vote at least once every six years as to whether the actual vote will be held every two or every three years. Shareholders must be given a vote on golden parachutes, and parachute arrangements for top executive officers must be disclosed. A separate vote is not required if the golden parachute has already been the subject of a say on pay vote. [Text of rule: <http://www.sec.gov/rules/final/2011/33-9178.pdf>; SEC press release: <http://www.sec.gov/news/press/2011/2011-25.htm> (Jan. 25, 2011); see Rebecca Moore, *SEC Adopts Say on Pay Rules*, plansponsor.com (Jan. 25, 2011); Harpreet S. Bal, Alison M. Kadzik, Susan P. Serota, Brian M. Wong, *SEC Proposes Rules on Say-on-Pay and Golden Parachutes*, Pillsbury Law Advisory (Nov. 17, 2010) (benefitslink.com)]

In mid-2011, the D.C. Circuit vacated Rule 14a-11, the proxy access rule, which would have permitted some shareholders to write in their nominees for the board of directors. The D.C. Circuit found that the SEC exceeded its discretion in adopting this rule. [*Business Roundtable & Chamber of Commerce v. SEC*, 647 F.3d 1144 (D.C. Cir. 2011).]

## § 3.02 BONUSES

For many years, the compensation of executives and professionals was enhanced by bonus amounts—often much greater than their salaries. This was especially true in technology, Internet companies, and financial services firms. Bonus practices became controversial in a recessionary environment, with widespread layoffs and benefit cuts.

A 2012-2013 trend was to reduce the bonuses paid to top management and to increase the degree to which compensation is linked to corporate performance. According to the Wall Street Journal/Hay Group Survey of CEO Compensation, which uses data from 300 large public companies, for 51 CEOs at least half of their 2012 compensation was tied to specific targets based on the company's financial performance or its stock market results. In 2009, only about one-third of CEO compensation was subject to performance conditions; the rest came from salaries and stock and option grants that were not subject to performance criteria. Median net income at a sample of 40 major companies fell 3.9% in 2011, resulting in a 7.6% drop in CEO annual bonuses. For example, Smithfield Foods' income fell 31% and its share price dropped 11%. The CEO's bonus formula was reduced by 34%, although he still received a $4.7 million bonus. In 2013, Johnson & Johnson cut the bonuses its top executives received for 2012 by 10%, reflecting mixed results in the stock market. Shareholder activists now have a new target: determining if the company's compensation structure creates the proper relationship between pay and performance. [Scott Thurm, *'Pay for Performance' No Longer a Punchline*, WSJ.com (Mar. 20, 2013)]

Many compensation plans provide that a bonus is not earned if the employee is no longer employed on the schedule date of payment (e.g., December 31). However, some states forbid forfeiture provisions. Other states distinguish between commissions on sales already made (which cannot be forfeited) and bonuses (based on performance figures for the person or the company as a whole). As a general principle of contract interpretation, ambiguous provisions will be construed against the party that drafted the agreement (and could have made it clearer)—so it is vital to make sure that the contract clearly sets out the intended terms.

A group of former managers of Speedway SuperAmerica (one who quit, two who were fired) sued the former employer under the Indiana Wage Payment and Wage Claims statutes when they did not receive bonuses. The Seventh Circuit held that the bonuses were not "wages" under Indiana law; they were deferred compensation that was forfeited because the plaintiffs did not satisfy the continued employment condition. The Wage Payment Statute, which guarantees timely payment of wages (within 10 days of being earned) applies only to current employees and those who quit voluntarily; the Wage Claims Statute requires payment of full wages due on the regular payday after an employee has been involuntarily terminated. In the Seventh Circuit view, a bonus is a wage only if it is compensation for time worked, not linked to a financial contingency and it is not reasonable to expect bonuses to be calculated within 10 days of the end of employment. [*Harney v. Speedway SuperAmerica LLC*, 526 F.3d 1099 (7th Cir. 2008)]

A 2010 Connecticut Supreme Court case draws a distinction between bonuses that are recoverable as wages under the Connecticut Wage Act (including statutory double damages and attorneys' fees) and discretionary bonuses that are not subject to the wage law. The court found that an attorney's year-end bonus was not "wages" because it was discretionary and not premised on specific, definable goals (such as number of hours billed). [*Ziotas v. Reardon Law Firm P.C.*, 296 Conn. 579 (2010)]

A drug company executive's employment contract said he would be an at-will employee and would receive a grant of 3,000 shares of restricted stock, one-quarter vesting each year. However, any shares not vested at his termination would be forfeited. He also got stock options vesting over four years, and discretionary bonuses. After about 16 months, the executive was told that his job was being eliminated as part of a reorganization. He was allowed to exercise the options that had already vested, but the company would not give him the unvested options or a prorated bonus for the year of his termination. The First Circuit said that, even if the plaintiff was correct that he was promised the rest of his stock options, the contract said otherwise. His options ceased to vest at his termination, and bonus awards are discretionary, and do not have to be made even if the employee performs well. [*Artuso v. Vertex Pharm. Inc.*, 637 F.3d (1st Cir. 2011)]

A financial services executive was approached about changing jobs. He said that he wanted a $350,000 compensation package to move; he signed an employment application stating that he was an at-will employee. He said that he was offered a $175,000 salary plus a $175,000 guaranteed bonus. He started working in 2003, but did not receive the bonus in that year. The managing partner asked him to forego the bonus until the end of 2004 or early 2005; he accepted. On February 3, 2005, he was offered a $20,000 bonus for his work in 2004, which he rejected. He was fired five days later and was offered a separation agreement and a $20,000 payment in return for surrendering all claims. He refused to sign, and sued his ex-employer for failure to pay wages and breach of contract. The New York Court of Appeals held that the jury decided that he was guaranteed a non-discretionary $175,000 bonus, in exchange for quitting his previous high-paid job. The bonus therefore was due and vested and he was entitled to collect it and get an award of attorneys' fees under New York law, which provides for a fee award when wages are not paid on time. [*Ryan v. Kellogg Partners Institutional Servs.*, 19 N.Y. 3d 1 (N.Y. 2012)]

The Ninth Circuit held that conflict of interest must be considered in determining whether an insurer abused the discretion it was granted under a discretionary clause. The plaintiff was rendered a quadriplegic by an accident three months after starting a new job. His salary was $200,000, and he was guaranteed a $300,000 bonus for the first year if he performed as anticipated and had not quit or been terminated for cause. He sued when the employer's LTD plan calculated his benefits based on $200,000 in earnings (i.e., excluding the bonus). The Ninth Circuit, noting that the employer's HR department submitted a claim form describing the plaintiff's compensation as $500,000 (and the premiums were based on that level of compensation) remanded for consideration of whether it was an abuse of discretion to exclude the bonus from the benefit calculation. [*Stephan v. UNUM Life Ins. Co. of Am.*, 697 F.3d 917 (9th Cir. 2012)]

In 2006, the Third Circuit ruled that it does not violate the FMLA to cut an employee's bonus when he or she is on FMLA leave, provided that the reduction is based on specific criteria that are set out in the plan, such as production or number of hours worked. [*Sommer v. Vanguard Group*, 461 F.3d 397 (3d Cir. 2006)]

Rev. Rul. 2011-29, 2011-49 I.R.B. 824, provides criteria under which an accrual-basis taxpayer can deduct employee bonuses in the year the services were performed, even though the bonus is not paid until the beginning of the next year. A deduction can be taken in the year of the services even if it is impossible to identify the specific recipients of bonuses from the bonus pool or the amount payable to each. The regulations under Code § 461(a) say that an accrual-basis taxpayer incurs a liability in the tax year in which the "all events" test is satisfied: all events establishing the fact of liability have occurred, the amount of liability can be determined with reasonable accuracy; and economic performance has occurred, e.g., the obligation to pay a minimum amount of bonuses is fixed at the end of the year. [Mercer Select News, *IRS Rules Favorably On Timing Of Tax Deductions For Some Bonus Pool Arrangements* (Nov. 11, 2011) (benefitslink. com); see Miller Johnson, *New IRS Ruling Discusses Tax Deductions for Cash Bonus Payments* (Dec. 7, 2011) (benefitslink.com)]

## § 3.03  SEVERANCE PAY

### [A]  Generally

There is no federal law requiring that employees receive severance pay, but nevertheless it is very common for employers to provide this type of compensation (unless the employee was fired for misconduct). Severance pay is often defined as a certain number of days or weeks of pay for every year of service with the employer.

The most important characteristic of severance pay is that it is over and above the normal salary or wages earned for past services. Severance payments are by and large discretionary, unlike payment for past services, which must be made when employment terminates. If the employer enters into an express or implied contract to provide severance benefits that contract can be enforced. However, employers typically retain the right to alter their severance pay plans, and this is sometimes done just before a major layoff. Employers may also provide benefits to only certain persons affected by a mass layoff, claiming that the others were terminated for poor performance.

Employees of companies in bankruptcy are at especially high risk of losing severance. Severance payments by bankrupt companies require court approval (and 2005's bankruptcy reform legislation limits payments to insiders), and must compete with other creditor claims.

There are two basic kinds of severance plan: the traditional plan, funded through the employer's general assets or with a trust, and Supplemental Unemployment Benefit (SUB) plans. SUB plans provide additional payments to supplement state unemployment insurance benefits. To receive SUB payments, employees must be eligible for state unemployment benefits, and must verify each week that they continue to be eligible and to look for work. Design changes can save money. A SUB plan resembles unemployment benefits in many ways. Employees have to be eligible for state unemployment to get SUB and they have to verify each week that they're eligible and looking for work. The benefit is often defined as a multiplier of years of service: for example, one to two weeks of benefits for each year that the employee worked for the company. Setting the appropriate level of benefits available under the plan depends on what the company's objective is in adopting the plan: to help employees bridge an income gap until they get a new job? To improve the company's profile after a layoff? There is a potential for a windfall if the employee gets a new job before the severance period ends; SUB plans eliminate this problem because they coordinate with state unemployment benefits, which end when the claimant gets another job. [Philip Parker, *Severance Plans: The Promise and the Savings*, Benefits Quarterly (Second Quarter 2012) (benefitslink.com)]

If the employee turnover is caused by a corporate transition (see Chapter 16), severance-related benefits can be provided under three main structures: a change in control agreement; a severance plan; or a change in control protection plan.

Generally, individual agreements will be offered if the intent is to protect only selected executives, whereas a formal plan should be adopted if there is a broader-based group that might receive severance. (A formal plan will almost certainly be subject to ERISA.) For a change in control provision or retention agreement, the most important questions are which executives are significant enough to be awarded protection, and what will trigger benefits (Termination without cause? Resignation for good cause? Resignation during a window period following a change in control?) The usual term is one to two years after the change in control occurs. For the employee, the most favorable provision is for the employer to reimburse the employee for golden parachute tax penalties imposed under Code § 4999; the intermediate position is for the company and the executive to divide the payment; and the least favorable is for the employee to forfeit severance benefits in any situation in which the employer would lose the deduction as a result of § 280G.

As of mid-2013, several years into a recession, multimillion-dollar severance packages remained frequent. James J. Mulva, departing CEO of Conoco-Phillips, received about $156 million in severance as well as his salary and bonuses. Some severance packages for top management continue for many years. For example, Tyco International's former CEO Edward D. Breen received a $46 million exit package in 2012, plus $55.8 million in deferred shares in 2013 and will receive a $30 million lump sum pension payment in 2016. [Pradnya Joshi, *Golden Parachutes Are Still Very Much in Style*, NYTimes.com (June 29, 2013)]

Departing executives often have access to special terms that are not offered to rank-and-file employees: for example, keeping them in active status in the EGHP while they are receiving severance or paying their COBRA premiums after termination. These special terms are usually set out in a severance agreement. However, if the employer maintains a self-funded group health plan, it is subject to the Code § 105(h) nondiscrimination requirements and it is forbidden to maintain eligibility provisions that discriminate against non-HCEs. Therefore, § 105(h)(7) will probably require the market value of continuation coverage for departing executives to be treated as taxable compensation. The Patient Protection and Affordable Care Act (PPACA) extends the nondiscrimination rules to insured plans, and so, although specific PPACA nondiscrimination rules have not been published, limiting extended coverage to executives or subsidizing COBRA premiums only for them, could be treated as a PPACA violation. [E is for ERISA Blog, *Special COBRA Coverage Terms for the Departing Executive: Pitfalls to Avoid* (Dec. 12, 2011) (benefitslink.com)] If a self-insured plan violates the nondiscrimination rule, the penalties are imposed on the executive, but for non-grandfathered insured plans, the penalty is imposed on the employer. The penalty can be as high as $100 per day of noncompliance for each employee experiencing discrimination, capped at $500,000 or 10% of the employer's EGHPs costs for the previous year. The penalty is waived for employers with fewer than 50 employees, or for employers of any size who had reasonable cause for their position and did not willfully neglect the requirements. [Steven Friedman, Terri Solomon, and Stephanie Kastrinsky, *Employers with Insured Health Plans Must*

*Take Care in Providing Healthcare Subsidies to Departing Executives*, Littler Mendelson (Oct. 29, 2012) (benefitslink.com)]

There are three basic methods for handling insurance continuation in a severance package. The "choice method" gives the exiting employee a choice between making a COBRA election and accepting the alternative in the severance package. The "consecutive coverage" method offers a certain number of months being covered as if he or she were still an active employee, followed by up to 18 months of COBRA coverage. The "concurrent coverage" model treats the alternative coverage as part of COBRA: for example, 12 months coverage at the active-employee rate, with the employee paying the full COBRA premium for the next six months. [*Ten Harmsel v. Pfizer Inc.*, File No. 1:08-CV-880, 2009 WL 1771377 (W.D. Mich. June 18, 2009); see Thompson Newsletter, *Alternative Coverage Case Involving Premium Hike Raises COBRA Issues* (July 29, 2009) (benefitslink.com)]

If there is a formal plan, the employer can protect itself by reserving the right to amend or terminate the plan. If there is a dispute about an informal arrangement, it will probably end up in state court, with the court having broad scope to review the plan administrator's decision. If there is an ERISA plan, then participants must exhaust their administrative remedies within the plan before bringing suit; the suit will have to be filed in federal court; and jury trial will not be available. If the plan document gives the administrators discretion to interpret the plan, the court will review the decision deferentially and is likely to uphold the administrator's decision unless it was arbitrary and capricious. It is permissible to have multiple benefit formulas, as long as the plan does not discriminate in favor of employees in protected classes. A formal plan can be a morale-building tool, because employees know in advance what to expect.

However, the disadvantage is that a formal plan results in loss of flexibility. Individual negotiations with employees are ruled out. The plan requires more administrative time than occasional individual negotiations. It is possible that different treatment of employees will result in discrimination allegations, so it is vital to be able to show a rational business reason for the distinctions. ERISA compliance can be time consuming and costly.

Furthermore, even if the intention is to avoid maintaining an ERISA plan, a de facto plan might be found based on oral representations made to employees; the employer's intention (as manifested by, for example, past practices or maintaining a fund or account to pay benefits). If the plan is deemed to be an ERISA plan even though this was not the employer's intention, penalties might be imposed for reporting and disclosure violations. [Sandra W. Cohen and Carol Buckmann, *ERISA Considerations for Severance Pay Policy Checklists* (February 2011) (benefitslink.com)]

When a termination event does occur, severance benefits can be conditioned on the departing employee signing a covenant not to compete, and not to solicit the ex-employer's customers. Some severance agreements are subject to Code § 409A and its standards for "separation pay arrangements." A plan that is limited to paying lump sums after there has been a termination without cause, with payments completed within two and a half months of termination, would probably be exempt from § 409A. There are § 409A exemptions for collectively bargained plans; plans that are not created under a CBA, and that pay less than twice the participant's annual compensation, with payments completed by the end of the second post-termination calendar year. Benefits that add up to less than $5,000 and are not a substitute for other § 409A benefits are also exempt, as are vacation and sick leave, disability pay, tax-free health benefits, benefits under a qualified retirement plan, and rights accrued and vested before January 1, 2007 and not substantially modified since October 3, 2004. However, it is unusual for separation pay benefits to vest, because they are generally subject to a substantial risk of forfeiture.

In general, an agreement for severance benefits can permit payment at any time within the 90-day period following the event, but only if the employee cannot make a direct or indirect election about when compensation will be paid within this period. The IRS says a release condition in an agreement violates § 409A if the condition operates as an indirect election by the employee about benefit timing. The ADEA requires 45 days' notice for an employee to consider a release and gives him or her seven days after signing to revoke a release, so severance payments are generally not made until after the revocation period has elapsed. Problems can arise if a release is offered late in a year—but not signed until the following year.

IRS Notice 2010-6, 2010-3 I.R.B. 275, says that § 409A is triggered by this "straddle," and it is a major issue in 409A audits. A mid-2011 article suggests drafting releases to provide that if benefits could be paid in two different tax years depending on when the release is signed, benefits will automatically be paid in the later year. [McGuireWoods LLP, *Employee Release Provisions Present Section 409A Trap for the Unwary* (Aug. 31, 2011) (benefitslink.com)]

A Final Rule, 72 Fed. Reg. 16878 (Apr. 5, 2007) addresses the treatment of certain severance benefits vis-à-vis the § 415 limitations on the amounts employers can contribute to qualified plans and the amounts that plan participants can receive under the plan. Under the final regulations, certain amounts paid within two and a half months after severance from employment are considered compensation under § 415 (which means that the employer may be able to deduct them). Payments also qualify if they represent sick leave, vacation days, or other leave that the employee would have been able to take if he or she had continued to be employed. An amount can still qualify as § 415 compensation if it is paid later than 2½ months post-termination, as long as it is paid by the end of the plan's limitation year that includes the date of termination. However, for the employer to take advantage of this rule, the plan must state explicitly that the post-termination payments are included in compensation.

"Terminal leave" can be used if the employer is willing to stretch out a termination date—for example, to allow further vesting of retirement benefits or stock awards, or to extend the period before COBRA starts, perhaps with the result that the terminating employee will be eligible for Medicare once COBRA ends. However, terminal leave can create problems with insurers if they insist that coverage is limited to current active employees—or with the IRS, which might say that § 409A has been triggered. On the other hand, the employer might want to accelerate the termination date so that there is no gap period after an employee's signing a release, and during which further claims might arise.

"Garden leave" is a term used for a transition period during which the employment relationship continues in some way, and the employee is not permitted to get another job. Garden leave is usually a period of weeks or months when the employee is paid to stay home but remains on call in case the employer requires services during a transitional period. Because the individual is still an employee, the duty of loyalty continues to apply. Garden leave is common in, e.g., England and the European Union, where there is a legal requirement of continuing wages during the notice period. So far, garden leave is less popular in the United States, but is gaining popularity in situations in which the employer can demonstrate a reasonable justification (e.g., protecting business interests). The provision could be structured to provide a fixed number of days of continuing salary and benefits followed by severance pay subject to a release of claims and agreements to maintain confidentiality and not to compete, or to solicit the employer's other employees. Executive stock awards, incentive compensation, and supplemental retirement benefits could be restructured into a post-termination package contingent on loyalty agreements. [J. Mark Poerio, Eric Loi, and Peter Haller, *The Basics of Garden Leave—and Why Careful Tilling Is Needed,* BNA Pension & Benefits Daily (Aug. 24, 2011) (benefitslink.com)]

In mid-2009, the EEOC updated its guidance document, "Understanding Waivers of Discrimination Claims in Employee Severance Agreements," reflecting the prevalence of economically motivated layoffs and terminations. The guidance is intended for employees, and generally restates the provisions of the ADEA and OWBPA. The EEOC says that an employer cannot cure a defective waiver by later providing the OWBPA information that was omitted from the original agreement, then restarting the 21- or 45-day period after the employee has signed the agreement. Although some lower courts have required employers to disclose their criteria for choosing employees for a reduction in force, the EEOC did not take a position on this issue.

The Guidance says that an employee who believes he or she has been a victim of discrimination on the basis of any prohibited factor can file an EEOC charge, even if the employee waived all claims, because the EEOC can still investigate and pursue claims made by an employee who signed a waiver. The EEOC's position is that the employee does not have to return severance pay before filing a discrimination charge with the EEOC—although employees can waive their right to recover damages from the employer in a subsequent private suit or EEOC suit, and eventual damages might be reduced to correspond to the severance received. It is settled law that severance does not have to be returned in ADEA cases, but less clear for other statutes. The Guidance says that if an employee challenges the validity of an age discrimination waiver in court, the employer must continue complying with its obligations under the severance agreement, including making any ongoing payments still due. [<http://www.eeoc.gov/policy/docs/qanda_severance-agreements.html> (July 15, 2009) Appendix B, dealing with releases in group layoffs of persons over 40, was revised in April 2010. See Seyfarth Shaw, *EEOC Issues Employee-Friendly Guidance on Separation Agreements* (July 24, 2009) (benefitslink.com); Kevin B. Leblang and Robert N. Holtzman, *Time for Employers to Review Their Severance Agreements*, Metropolitan Corporate Counsel (Feb. 1, 2010) (benefitslink.com). See *EEOC v. Watkins Motor Lines, Inc.*, 553 F.3d 593 (7th Cir. 2009) on the EEOC's right to proceed after a waiver by the complainant]

A county employee, who was told that her job was eliminated in a reorganization, sued the former employer charging that she was offered a less favorable severance package than comparable male employees and that the county found jobs for male employees but not for her. The district court dismissed, holding that there had been no adverse employment action because severance benefits could only create adverse employment action if there was a contract violation. The district court also argued that the employment relationship has ended when severance is paid so there can be no "adverse employment action." The Fourth Circuit rejected these arguments: discriminatory severance is unlawful, and the plaintiff alleged that she was fired only after rejecting the discriminatory severance package so she was an employee at that time. [*Gerner v. County of Chesterfield*, 674 F.3d 264 (4th Cir. 2012). *Hishon v. King & Spalding*, 469 U.S. 69 (1984) stands for the proposition that discrimination must be avoided in all benefits in the employment relationship.]

## [B] Severance Arrangements as ERISA "Plans"

ERISA is not involved in an employer's one-time decision to grant or enhance severance benefits. Nor is there an ERISA component to an employer's payroll practices or payments of extra money for active workers' overtime or holiday work. However, ERISA does come into play if severance payments are made in connection with a "plan," and even an unwritten or informal arrangement might constitute a plan.

Once the severance payment comes within the ambit of ERISA, the degree and nature of regulation depend on whether the plan is characterized as a pension plan or a welfare benefit plan. The arrangement will not be a pension plan (and therefore will not be subject to the stringent rules imposed on pension plans) if:

- Payments are not contingent on the recipient's retirement—i.e., the recipient can retain the payments even if he or she gets another job;

- The total payments do not exceed twice the recipient's compensation for the year just before the termination;

• The payments are completed within 24 months of the termination. If the termination is part of a "limited program of terminations" then payments can be completed within 24 months of the time the recipient reaches normal retirement age, if that is later.

[See DOL Reg. 29 C.F.R. §§ 2510.3-2(b) and 2510.3-1(a)]

The Eastern District of Michigan ruled in mid-2009 that the two primary factors in deciding whether a severance arrangement is an ERISA welfare benefit plan in the determination are whether the employer has discretion over distribution of benefits, and whether there are ongoing demands on the employer's assets. [*Jones v. St. John Health*, Civil No.08-14962, 2009 WL 1034753 (E.D. Mich. Apr. 16, 2009); see *Severance Plan Is Subject to ERISA When Employer Discretion and Ongoing ER Demands on Employer's Assets Are Present*, EBIA Weekly (July 2, 2009) (benefitslink.com)]

The Eighth Circuit ruled in mid-2011 that a one-person employment contract is not an ERISA plan. However, the case was remanded to the district court because the federal system might still have had jurisdiction over part of the complaint. The plaintiff, Schieffer, had an employment contract. Shortly before a merger obtained regulatory approval, Schieffer was terminated without cause, triggering the payment of a lump sum severance payment. Schieffer alleged that he did not receive all the benefits he was entitled to and moved for arbitration. His employer moved to enjoin arbitration, arguing that the employment agreement was an ERISA severance plan so ERISA preempted the demand for arbitration. The Eighth Circuit held that the employment contract was not an ERISA plan because it covered only one person, not a class of employees. However, the other benefits he sought might have been promised by ERISA plans, so the Eighth Circuit sent the case back to see if those demands were preempted by ERISA. [*Dakota, Minnesota & Eastern Railroad Corp. v. Schieffer*, 648 F.3d 935 (8th Cir. 2011); see PLC, *One-Person Employment Contract Not an ERISA Plan: Eighth Circuit* (Aug. 15, 2011) (benefitslink.com)]

The case was remanded to determine whether the contract operated as an amendment to an ERISA plan, or a promise to pay ERISA plan benefits in the future. In 2013, The Eighth Circuit rejected both of these possibilities. The severance agreement only came into operation when the ex-CEO had ceased to be a plan participant. It was also a free-standing agreement; although the amount to be paid was determined by reference to an ERISA plan, the benefits came from the employer's general assets, not plan assets; and making the payments would not affect the administration of ERISA plans. The arbitration demand did not seek benefits due under an ERISA plan—which meant that the determination of underlying rights had to be done by an arbitrator, not the federal courts. When the case got to arbitration, the state law claims (including the double damage claim) could be heard because ERISA preemption did not occur. [*Dakota, Minn. & E. Railroad Corp. v. Schieffer*, 711 F. 3d 878 (8th Cir. 2013). See Jeffrey Russell, Jonathan Potts, and Carrie Byrnes, *Eighth Circuit Clarifies the Scope of ERISA's*

*Application to Severance Arrangements*, Bryan Cave ERISA & Benefits Litigation Blog (Apr. 11, 2013) (benefitslink.com).]

It was not an abuse of discretion for a severance plan administrator to deny severance benefits to a person fired for cause (she accessed company computer files without authorization). The plan defined termination for cause and gross and willful misconduct to include all violations of company policy. [*Johnson v. U.S. Bancorp Broad-Based Change in Control Severance Pay Program*, 424 F.3d 734 (8th Cir. 2005); another employee fired for the same offense was also unsuccessful raising similar claims somewhat later (*Anderson v. U.S. Bancorp*, 484 F.3d 1027 (8th Cir. 2007))]

## [C]   Case Law on Other Severance Pay Issues

The important decision of *United States v. Quality Stores*, 693 F.3d 605 (6th Cir. 2012), holding that severance pay is not subject to FICA tax, creates a circuit split. (Previously, in 2008, the Federal Circuit ruled that severance pay constitutes FICA wages: *CSX Corp. v. United States*, 518 F.3d 1328 (Fed. Cir. 2008)). The Department of Justice petitioned the Sixth Circuit for rehearing en banc, which was denied. A petition for certiorari was expected. If it is granted, and the Supreme Court adopts the Sixth Circuit's ruling, then employers will be entitled to collect tax refunds on FICA paid on severance. Until this issue is resolved, employers that have paid a great deal of severance might consider filing an IRS refund claim, which extends the period of time when the tax payments can be recovered. Employers in the Sixth Circuit may also be entitled to claim a refund if the Supreme Court denies certiorari.

The refund is claimed on Form 941-X for the open quarters, requesting a "Quality Stores" refund. The request is filed with a cover letter and Form 8275, explaining that the request is contrary to published IRS guidance (Rev. Ruls. 56-249 and 90-72) but in accordance with the Sixth Circuit decision. Although the IRS will probably refuse the refund request, it may agree to use form 907 to extend the two-year statute of limitations because the IRS often does this in case of a circuit split. Extending the statute of limitations creates the possibility of recovering FICA paid for the years of the protective claim and any subsequent open tax years. The last day to file a protective claim for 2009 payments was April 15, 2013; the last day for 2010 payments is April 15, 2014. [Vedder Price Newsletter/Bulletin, *Action Required to Preserve FICA Refund Claim on Severance Pay* (Jan. 16, 2013) (benefitslink.com); Mary B. Hevener, David R. Fuller, Steven P. Johnson, Patrick Rehfield, and Robert R. Martinelli, *Quality Stores, Inc.*, Morgan, Lewis & Bockius LawFlash (Oct. 24, 2012) (benefitslink.com)]

For high income executives, FICA tax on severance has little impact if the layoff occurred after the executive had already earned the FICA maximum; the only practical effect is on Medicare tax. Laid-off workers should ask if their former employer is pursuing FICA refunds. The company does not have to inform them until the IRS accepts the claim. At that point, the employer will ask the former employees for consent to include their refund claim. When the IRS refunds the FICA amounts, the employer will distribute the employee share to the former employee. If the employee believes that a refund is due, but the employer did not file for one, the employee may be able to file Form 843 to seek a refund, but this must be done before the statute of limitations expires. Generally this will be three years after the due date for the tax return covering the year the severance was received. If the IRS does make a refund, it will not be taxable to the employee. [Laura Saunders, *Tax Report: When Severance Pay Is Subject to Payroll Tax*, WSJ.com (Oct. 26, 2012).]

Severance package negotiations in a Seventh Circuit case included information about defined benefit pension benefits. (A terminated employee withdrew a potential ADEA suit in light of the severance settlement.) The plan provided five options: a lump sum, a five-year term certain annuity, 50% and 100% joint and survivor annuities, and a straight life annuity. The plaintiff was given accurate information about the lump sum, but the other benefit forms were overstated by almost 64% because the calculations assumed that he was eligible for normal retirement when he was only eligible for reduced early retirement benefits. (He was terminated at age 57½). He signed a severance agreement November 14, 2006 and filled out an election form option for $1,156 a month as a 50% joint and survivor annuity; the correct amount should have been $706.74. The mistake was discovered in January, and an HR clerk filled out a corrected form with the lower figure. Pearson did not return the recalculated form, so the company did not pay his pension and he sued, arguing that the plan was estopped from paying him less than the pension he was promised. The Seventh Circuit held that, to demonstrate extreme circumstances that will justify a departure from the written terms of the plan, a plaintiff must show reasonable, detrimental reliance on a knowing misrepresentation made in writing by the plan. In this case, the Seventh Circuit said that there was no misrepresentation, just a simple error, and the plaintiff was entitled only to the correct pension amount. (However, he might have claims against the employer, but not against the plan.) The Seventh Circuit said that, although Pearson argued that he surrendered his demand for 78 months of health insurance post-termination, worth over $40,000, in return for a written representation that he would receive an $1,156.89 monthly pension, he did not show any realistic chance of bargaining for a better deal, so his claim of economic harm was too speculative to award. [*Pearson v. Voith Paper Rolls, Inc.*, 656 F.3d 504 (7th Cir. 2011); see CCH Pension & Benefits, *Court Rejects Payment of Overstated Pension Benefits; Keeps Severance Pact* (Sept. 23, 2011) (benefitslink.com)]

The Seventh Circuit had to decide whether DHL violated the WARN Act in connection with its November 10, 2009 announcement that five out of its six Chicago-area facilities were going to close. Although the CBA did not provide severance benefits, the Teamsters Union negotiated severance benefits. On

December 5, 2008, each bargaining unit received a severance agreement. Receiving severance was conditioned on waiving all claims, including WARN Act claims. Approximately 500 employees took a severance package, receiving either four or ten weeks' pay. Workers who did not take a severance package retained seniority and recall rights—and the right to sue the former employer. Two laid-off workers sued. The Seventh Circuit held that there was no plant closing because employees who accepted severance should not be counted; without them, the number of layoffs did not reach 33% of the workforce. Under the WARN Act, a voluntary departure is not an employment loss requiring notification. Voluntariness is determined based on whether employees were forced out or coerced. The plaintiffs argued that employees resigned under extreme economic uncertainty and pressure from the employer. The Seventh Circuit said that, although the situation was not perfect, the severance agreements were still voluntary. The agreements and the release were negotiated by the union; were not ambiguous; and informed employees of their right to consult an attorney. [*Ellis v. DHL Express Inc USA*, 633 F.3d 522 (7th Cir. 2011)]

The president/CEO of Capital Bank's employment agreement included a change-of-control severance provision. Another bank negotiated to buy a controlling interest in Capital Bank; the deal initially called for Yarber to remain as president. However, the potential purchaser said that unless Yarber and other Capital Bank executives accepted amendments to their employment agreements waiving the change in control severance payments, the deal would be off. The chairman of Capital Bank's board told Yarber that unless he surrendered the right to receive severance benefits, he would be fired, and shareholders could sue him for breach of fiduciary duty if his recalcitrance led to the deal being called off. Capital Bank was purchased; the purchaser fired Yarber and did not give him severance benefits. He sued Capital Bank, alleging that it violated ERISA to deny him severance benefits; Yarber said the amendment to his contract was invalid because he did not receive any consideration for it. However, the District Court for the Eastern District of North Carolina dismissed Yarber's case, finding that the amendments were valid. The amended contract did not call for severance benefits, and made him an at-will employee as of November 4, 2011, so he had no right to sue. [*Yarber v. Capital Bank Corp.*, No. 5:12-cv-71-D, 2013 WL 1127082 (E.D.N.C. Mar. 18, 2013); see Michael S. Melbinger, *Executive Does the Right Thing—and Gets Screwed For It!* (June 14, 2013) (benefitslink.com)]

A 2010 Sixth Circuit case permits enforcement of a clearly written release of USERRA claims that was part of a severance package, finding that the release was knowing and voluntary and was not obtained by overreaching. The Sixth Circuit allowed USERRA to be released on the same terms as any other employment-related claim. [*Wysocki v. IBM*, 607 F.3d 1102 (6th Cir. 2010); but see *Perez v. Uline*, 157 Cal. App. 4th 953 (2007) holding that USERRA claims cannot be waived by a written release]

To get payments under Pactiv Corp.'s ERISA severance plan, employees had to sign a separation agreement and a release acceptable to the company. There was no noncompete provision in the severance plan. The plaintiff was offered a separation agreement that included a noncompete clause. He refused to sign, and won a court case for the severance payment, which was close to $100,000. The court held that, although employers have some discretion in drafting, the company could not demand a noncompete agreement without amending the severance plan. [Angela Bohmann, *Can I Add a No-Compete Provision to a Severance Agreement?*, Leonard, Street and Deinard Benefits Notes Blog (Nov. 20, 2012) (benefitslink.com)]

Questions often arise as to whether a person who receives severance pay qualifies for unemployment benefits. As a general rule, employees who are in the position of voluntarily quitting their jobs will not be eligible for unemployment; those who receive severance when they lose their jobs through no fault of their own probably will be eligible. West Virginia found unemployment insurance benefits to be available to someone who participates in a voluntary severance program initiated by the employer if the claimant's separation from service is the result of lack of work and termination occurred under a workforce reduction plan. [*Baldwin*, Unempl. Ins. Rep. (CCH) ¶ 8787 (W. Va. 2005)], and also granted benefits to an employee who took a voluntary separation package in the course of downsizing; leaving was attributed to the employer's fault. [*Boggs*, Unempl. Ins. Rep. (CCH) ¶ 8797 (W. Va. Cir. Ct. 2006)] Employees who took a voluntary separation plan were eligible for benefits, based on testimony from a company Vice President and e-mails from the HR department stating that the plan was implemented because of lack of work. [*Verizon North*, Unempl. Ins. Rep. (CCH) ¶ 10,203 (Ohio App. 2006)] The Massachusetts Court of Appeals ruled in 2006 that benefits should have been awarded to claimants who took a voluntary separation package because they had an objectively reasonable belief that they would have been fired if they had not taken the packages. The employer neither announced that employees would be chosen randomly for RIF nor announced criteria for selecting RIF candidates, thus giving employees good cause to cut their losses by taking the package and leaving. [*State Street Bank & Trust Co.*, Unempl. Ins. Rep. (CCH) ¶ 8487 (Mass. App. 2006)]

In contrast, benefits were denied to an office manager who was given the choice of staying at work while she looked for a new job, or leaving immediately with severance pay. When she opted to leave right away, however, she was ineligible for benefits, because she was the one who made the departure decision. [*Arrow Legal Solutions Group PXC*, Unempl. Ins. Rep. (CCH) ¶ 8354 (Utah App. 2006)] A teacher who accepted a $1,000 payment from her school system for early notice of intent to resign or retire was not separated for lack of work, and was not eligible for benefits. She voluntarily quit in order to move to Florida with her husband. Although it is presumed that separation is for lack of work, the school testified that there was work for the following year; the $1,000 payment was an incentive for employees to provide information about their plans so the school district could estimate its hiring needs, not a means to cut back jobs. [*Parma City Schools*, Unempl. Ins. Rep. (CCH) ¶ 10,204 (Ohio App. 2006)]

## [D] Parachute Payment Law and Regulations

A specialized form of severance, the "parachute" payment comes into play in the course of a hostile takeover or takeover attempt. The best-known form is the "golden parachute" for executives—the counterpart of the "golden handcuff" compensation packages that are supposed to keep top managers from leaving companies that depend on their services. A golden parachute arrangement is supposed to deter unwanted takeover attempts, because so much cash severance (and other benefits, such as stock, enhanced pension benefits, and insurance) is owed to the top managers that the acquisition becomes even more expensive—perhaps prohibitively so. A few states mandate the payment of "tin parachutes" to rank-and-file employees when they lose their jobs during a corporate transition.

A "single-trigger" golden parachute agreement gives the executive the right to additional compensation whenever the employer company merges or is acquired. A "double-trigger" agreement doesn't become effective until there has not only been a corporate transition, but the executive has been demoted or terminated and therefore has a real economic injury.

Internal Revenue Code §§ 280G(b) and 4999 impose a 20% excise tax on excess parachute payments—and, furthermore, the payor corporation cannot deduct whatever portion of the payment is not reasonable and therefore does not constitute an ordinary and necessary business expense. (Payments from a qualified pension plan are not considered parachute payments, so they do not affect the excess calculation.)

An excess parachute payment is an amount that:

- Is not reasonable compensation for work done either before the change in ownership and control, or is scheduled to be done after the change; and

- Exceeds three times the "base amount."

A parachute payment is a payment contingent on change in the corporation's ownership or control, or the ownership or control of a significant portion of the corporation's assets. If the executive and corporation entered into a compensation agreement within the year before a change in ownership or control, the payments are presumed to be parachute payments unless there is clear and convincing evidence of a different motivation for the payments.

The base amount is the executive's average annual compensation for the five years just before the change in ownership or control. Bonuses, fringe benefits, pensions, and severance pay as well as cash compensation are used in the calculation.

On August 4, 2003, the IRS issued final regulations dealing with golden parachutes. [68 Fed. Reg. 45745, August 4, 2003] A corporation is exempt from the rules about excess parachute payments if, just before control of the corporation changed, the corporation was not publicly traded and holders of at least 75%

of the voting power of the corporation approved the payment. Furthermore, only one change in ownership or control will be deemed to have occurred with respect to any transaction, even if the language might make it appear that there were multiple changes.

The final rule takes the position that accelerating the vesting of a stock option creates value that counts toward determining whether there has been a parachute payment.

The excise tax on excess parachute payments can be prepaid either in the year of the change in control or any later year—as long as the amount, form, and commencement date of the payments is already known and is reasonably ascertainable under the Code § 3121(v) rules on FICA taxation of nonqualified deferred compensation. However, the excise tax cannot be prepaid on any part of an excess parachute payment that is attributable to continuing to provide health benefits to the recipient of the parachute payment.

### [E]  Parachute Payment Cases

Eligibility to participate in the plan providing parachute payments was the issue in *Habets v. Waste Mgmt., Inc.* [363 F.3d 378 (5th Cir. 2004)] The Fifth Circuit ruled that once the company's Board of Directors exercised its discretion to decide who was a participant in the parachute plan by removing the plaintiff from the list of eligible persons (after he lost his officer status in a corporate restructuring), the plaintiff was no longer entitled to receive parachute payments. Under the plain language of the agreement, only corporate officers were entitled to parachute payments, so termination of his officer status also terminated eligibility for the payments.

An Eighth Circuit case from late 2003 was brought by an executive who, mistakenly believing that she was entitled to severance under a golden parachute agreement, gave her employer a "notice of termination," and took a higher-paid job within the organization that she viewed as a demotion because it carried fewer responsibilities. She believed that the parachute was triggered by the offer of a lesser position, but the Eighth Circuit held that the parachute was never triggered because there was no change in control, and she resigned and was not entitled to severance benefits. [*Curby v. Solutia, Inc.*, 351 F.3d 868 (8th Cir. 2003); see also *Jones v. Reliant Energy-ARKLA*, 336 F.3d 689 (8th Cir. 2003): it is not an adverse employment action to offer a new job in lieu of severance pay.]

### [F]  "Separation Pay" Under § 409A

Under § 409A, which was designed to be a comprehensive regulation of deferred compensation, the IRS calls severance (which was not previously analyzed as deferred compensation) "separation pay." Separation pay is regulated as deferred compensation if there is a legally binding right to payment that arises in one tax year and is paid in a future year, even if there is a substantial risk of forfeiture. The exception is a payment entirely in the discretion of the payor (so there is no legally binding right to receive the funds). A binding contract between employer and employee could give rise to deferred compensation where the employer promises to pay a defined amount when the employee separates from service. But there is no deferred compensation if the employer offers to trade an immediate lump sum for a release, because the right to payment and taxation occur in the same year. The Proposed Regulations exempt certain severance payments from § 409A:

- Payments due to involuntary termination or to participation in a RIF window program where severance does not exceed the § 401(a)(17) limit or twice annual compensation; payments must be completed by the end of the second calendar year after the year of termination.

- Reimbursement of expenses that are either excludable from the employee's gross income or are deductible by the employee as § 162 or § 167 business expenses.

- Severance agreements under which no more than $5,000 is paid in any tax year.

- Collectively bargained severance arrangements covering involuntary termination or RIFs (including voluntarily accepted RIFs or incentives), as long as the program window does not exceed one year, and the program specifies the circumstances under which an employee can terminate and receive severance.

Severance benefits subject to "good reason" provisions are not considered subject to substantial risk of forfeiture, so § 409A probably applies, and neither the safe harbor for involuntary termination nor the one for payment within 2½ months of the end of the plan year will apply.

The Proposed Regulations define separation from service as an employee dying, retiring, or terminating employment. The employment relationship continues during a bona fide leave of absence of less than six months—or longer, if there is a statutory or contractual right to reemployment. Without such a right, the employment relationship is presumed to end on the first day after a six-month absence.

If there is an agreement to continue the relationship after it would normally end, employment is deemed to terminate when the employee provides only insignificant services—i.e., working, and getting paid, less than 20% of pay as compared to the previous three years. (If the employee had worked for the employer less than three years, the comparison is based on the full term of employment.) The "same desk" rule does not apply in the context of § 409A, so if a corporate transaction involves the sale of substantially all of the employer's assets, termination of employment will be deemed to occur even if the employee is rehired by the purchaser of the corporate assets.

Furthermore, severance payments to a key employee of a public company that do not qualify for an exemption must be delayed for six months. [Thomas M. Greene, BNA Tax Management, *Severance . . . It's Not What It Used to Be*, <http://www.bnatax.com/tm/insights/greene.htm>. See Notice 2005-1, 2005-2 I.R.B. 274 and Prop. Regs. at 70 Fed. Reg. 57930 (Oct. 4, 2005). The § 415 Final Regulations at 72 Fed. Reg. 16878 (Apr. 5, 2007) allow payments, made after termination, from a nonqualified unfunded deferred compensation plan, to be treated as compensation if the payments are gross income for the employee, and would have been paid at the same time if the employment relationship had continued.]

Separation pay can be provided without triggering § 409A, for example, by using the short-term deferral and safe harbor exceptions; "stacking"; and integrating the payments with release of claims. Separation pay, for this purpose, is defined as amounts payable only because of separation from service, such as negotiated departure agreements, severance plans, and individual severance plan agreements. Payments are not considered deferred compensation if they are made within 2½ months of the end of the year in which the right to payment vests. For 2009, there is a safe harbor for payments of up to $490,000 (i.e., twice the § 401(a)(17) limit) if the payment is made in case of involuntary termination and does not exceed twice the recipient's annualized compensation. "Stacking" means arranging separation pay so that some fits under the short-term deferral rule, some qualifies for the safe harbor, and some is deferred compensation that complies with § 409A. However, amounts that are not deferred compensation cannot be substituted for amounts of deferred compensation.

The § 409A correction program was originally set up in Notice 2008-113. Notice 2010-6, 2010-3 I.R.B. 275 extends this program to correct document failures as well as operational failures. Correction is required based on certain arrangements that condition separation pay or other forms of severance on employment-related actions that make the separation pay subject to § 409A, such as releasing claims or signing a noncompete agreement. There are limited situations under which separation pay is exempt from § 409A. Even when there is no exemption, the employer can address an existing arrangement without violating § 409A. For example, if the agreement has either a 21- or 45-day period for the employee to complete the employment-related action, followed by a seven-day revocation period, the payment date could be set more than seven days after the end of the revocation period. If the agreement does not provide for payment subject to employee action, it must provide for payment only on a fixed date of either 60 or 90 days after the occurrence of the permissible payment event. [Jeff Minzel, Kurt Linsenmayer, Susan J. Daley, *In 2010 Employers Should Respond to New Developments for Existing and Future Separation Arrangements*, Perkins Coie News (Oct. 29, 2010) (benefitslink.com)]

## [G] Section 162(m) Issues

Code § 162(m) limits (to $1 million) the compensation that a public company can deduct for any executive's compensation in any one year. This general rule is subject to some exceptions—for example, performance-based compensation can be deducted even if it exceeds $1 million. The statutory definition of performance-based compensation is money payable solely as a result of achieving established, objective performance goals set by the company's compensation committee. Compensation will also be considered performance-based if there is a potential for it to be paid on the basis of death, disability, or change in control, but if compensation is in fact paid on such a basis, it will not be considered performance-based. See 76 Fed. Reg. 37034 (June 24, 2011), IRS proposed regulations setting requirements for stock option and stock appreciation awards to qualify as performance-based compensation.

However, Notice 2007-49, 2007-25 I.R.B. 1429 provides that Chief Financial Officers (CFOs) are never subject to § 162(m), even if they are among the corporation's highest earners.

See Morgan Lewis Hot Topics, *Section 162(m) Pitfalls* (Mar. 9, 2010) for a checklist of common problems—e.g., adjusting bonus amounts in light of subsequent events, when the plan does not provide authority for the adjustment—that can cause public companies to forfeit the safe harbor for performance-based compensation. [<http://www.morganlewis.com/pubs/EBHotTopics_Section162m Pitfalls_09mar10.pdf>]

# PART II

# PENSION LAW

CHAPTER 4

# BASIC PENSION CONCEPTS

## § 4.01   INTRODUCTION

This chapter provides a summary and overview of the major ERISA and tax issues that help shape plan design. Many of these subjects are taken up in greater detail in the other chapters in this part of the volume.

In the private sector, employers make part of the employee's compensation available immediately in cash. The employee's total compensation package also includes benefits such as health insurance and fringe benefits, plus deferred compensation that will eventually provide a lump sum or income at the time of the employee's normal, disability, or early or late retirement.

The subject of pensions and benefits is an important one. The retirement market is a hugely significant sector of the economy. According to the Investment Company Institute's publication, *The U.S. Retirement Market, Third Quarter 2012*, in the third quarter of 2012, total United States retirement assets totaled $19.4 trillion. This was 3.5% higher than the June 30, 2012 level. At the end of the third quarter, retirement savings represented more than one-third (36%) of all household financial assets. The level of IRA assets rose 4.3% in the third quarter, reaching $5.3 trillion. Forty-six percent of IRA assets and 57% of defined contribution plan (including 401(k)) assets were invested in mutual funds. [Plansponsor staff, *U.S. Retirement Assets Reach $19T*, plansponsor.com (Dec. 20, 2012)]

Because of the high risk of improprieties or mistakes in handling the funds that the employees rely on for future security, pension plans are administered by fiduciaries. A fiduciary is an individual or institution that takes care of the property of others, and therefore must be held to the highest standards of ethics and prudence. [See Chapter 15 for further discussion of the obligations of plan fiduciaries, and penalties that can be imposed for misconduct or failure.]

In 1974, Congress, concerned about potential abuses of pension plans, passed the Employee Retirement Income Security Act (ERISA). ERISA provides very detailed rules for how pension plans must be administered; how they must accumulate funds for later benefit payments; who qualifies for various kinds of benefits; how those benefits are to be distributed; and how the plan must keep records and communicate with its participants and beneficiaries. ERISA governs not only how ongoing plans operate, but how they can be created and how they can change form by merging with other plans or undergoing termination.

Furthermore, ERISA establishes pensions and benefits as an entirely and inherently federal area of jurisdiction. States are forbidden to legislate in this area, so the question of whether "ERISA preemption" has occurred is an important one.

The bulk of ERISA deals with pension plans, although the statute has less extensive provisions dealing with other types of plans including profit-sharing plans, stock bonus plans, and welfare benefit plans such as health plans, vacation plans, and cafeteria plans.

The legal definition of a pension plan describes it as a plan established and maintained primarily to pay definitely determinable benefits to participants—

usually monthly for the rest of the retiree's life, although lump sum payouts and annuities for a term of years are also permissible. Unlike profit-sharing plans, pension plans normally make distributions only on the basis of retirement, death, disability, or term of employment; hardship distributions are usually not available.

The mid-2006 passage of the Pension Protection Act (PPA), Pub. L. No. 109-280, enacted immense changes. Although the legislation focuses on shoring up the soundness of defined benefit plans, the PPA also has significant provisions about defined contribution and cash balance plans. As it turned out, however, this statute was passed shortly before the economy soured, and the PPA was modified to relieve some of the burden on already hard-pressed employers in stimulus legislation such as EESA, WRERA, and the Preservation of Access to Care for Medicare Beneficiaries and Pension Relief Act of 2010. The Moving Ahead for Progress in the 21st Century Act (MAP-21; Pub. L. No. 112-141) gives the sponsors of defined benefit plans interest rate relief: by allowing them to assume higher interest rates, they can lawfully reduce their contributions to their plans. See § 4.01[B] below.

> ■ **TIP:** In March 2004, the Supreme Court ruled that for the purposes of ERISA Title I, the sole shareholder/president of a Professional Corporation is an employee. As long as there is at least one other plan participant other than the business owner and spouse, then ERISA's anti-alienation provision applies, and the shareholder's creditors cannot reach his or her interest in the pension plan. [*Raymond B. Yates, M.D., P.C. Profit Sharing Plan v. Hendon*, 541 U.S. 1 (2004)]

As a general rule, the employer's tax deduction is taken on a cash basis— for the year in which money was contributed to a qualified plan. Employers that maintain nonqualified plans instead of, or in addition to, qualified plans do not get a deduction until the employee receives benefits from the nonqualified plan and includes them in income.

One of the most important criteria for plan qualification is that the plan must not discriminate in favor of highly compensated employees (HCEs). For the years 2006–2007 HCEs earned $100,000 or more; for 2008, rising to $115,000 in 2012-2013. Yet many companies identify a need for additional benefits to stay competitive in the executive recruiting stakes. It is legal to maintain nonqualified plans limited to, or offering superior benefits for, HCEs (see Chapter 8 for more discussion), but the expenses associated with these plans will not be federally tax deductible.

The Financial Accounting Standards Board (FASB) sets the rules for accounting for pension and benefits. FASB created a new codification of GAAP, reorganizing the thousands of GAAP documents into approximately 90 topics. The previous seven FASB statements relating to retirement and health plans (Nos. 35, 87, 88, 106, 112, 132(R), 158) were reorganized into five topics:

- 712, post-employment compensation other than retirement;
- 715, retirement benefits;
- 960, accounting for defined benefit plans;
- 962, accounting for defined contribution plans;
- 965, accounting for health and welfare benefit plans.

[CCH Pension and Benefits, *FASB Announces New Codification Structure, Superseding All Existing Statements* (June 26, 2009) (benefitslink.com). See <http://www.fasb.org> for the full codification.]

One of the most important questions in plan administration is the standard of review that will be applied when a decision (e.g., denying benefits; altering the terms of the plan) is challenged. In April 2010, the Supreme Court ruled that as long as the plan gives its administrators the power to interpret the plan, then courts must review plan administrators' decisions deferentially—as long as the decisions are reasonable. [*Conkright v. Frommert*, 130 S. Ct. 1640 (U.S. 2010)]

## [A] PPA Changes

The PPA is a wide-ranging statute, and is referenced many times in this book. The major provisions of the PPA (some of which have been amended in light of economic factors) include:

- "At-risk plans" (defined benefit plans that fail to meet the PPA's new standards for adequate funding) are restricted in their ability to make certain types of distributions. If the risk is especially severe, the plan will be required to cease further accruals unless the employer makes additional contributions. The at-risk rules do not apply to plans covering fewer than 500 employees.

- The concept of the "minimum funding standard account" has been replaced by the "basic minimum funding contribution," and a new Code § 430 has been enacted for the purpose; the basic minimum funding contribution is calculated by adjusting the "target normal cost."

- The employer's tax deduction for plan contributions is capped.

- For 2008 and later plan years, plans must set their interest rate assumptions based on corporate bond yields. This requirement has caused compliance problems since the 2008 recession began; it has been the subject of several federal laws providing relief for plan sponsors.

- For plan years beginning after 2007 (collectively bargained plans: 2008) married participants must be given the option of a joint and 75% survivor annuity as well as the well-established joint and 50% survivor annuity. This is referred to as a Qualified Optional Survivor Annuity (QOSA);

- A court order allocating employee benefits order can be a Qualified Domestic Relations Order even if it issued after or revises an earlier order.

- Phased retirement is permitted—a plan can start pension distributions for a person who has reached age 62, but has not reached the plan's Normal Retirement Age, and who works a reduced schedule.

- Congress has given its approval to cash balance plans, but has imposed compliance requirements for new cash balance plans and conversions after mid-2005. The PPA provisions do not retroactively authorize cash balance plans created or converted earlier, and some courts find them age-discriminatory.

The flat-rate PBGC premium is $30 per participant for 2006, $31 per participant for 2007, $33 per participant for 2008, $34 per participant for 2009, and $35 per participant for 2010–2011. The variable-rate premium remains $9/$1,000 of unvested benefits, for 2011 (although plans for fewer than 25 employees are entitled to a premium cap). The Deficit Reduction Act of 2005 surcharge of $1,250 per participant, originally imposed on distress terminations until 2010, has been made permanent.

Pub. L. No. 112-141, MAP-21, requires ongoing increases in the PBGC premiums. This statute increases the single-employer premium to $42 for 2013 and $49 in 2014, at which point inflation indexing will be applied. The 2015 flat-rate premium is $50/participant and the variable-rate premium is $18/$1,000 unvested benefits. But, in 2013 and later years, the variable-rate premium is capped at $400 per participant (as adjusted for inflation). [PBGC *Pension Insurance Premiums Fact Sheet*, <http://www.pbgc.gov/res/factsheets/page/premiums.html> (undated; last accessed Aug. 19, 2013)]

- The obligations of communicating with plan participants have been increased, starting with the 2008 plan year: defined benefit plans must give their participants an annual funding notice no later than 120 days after the end of the plan year. At-risk plans have to give additional disclosures.

- Starting in 2010, companies with fewer than 500 employees can maintain "eligible combined plans," a new type of plan that combines defined benefit and 401(k) components.

- As for defined contribution plans, under the PPA:

- Employers are encouraged to implement automatic enrollment in their 401(k) plans.

- The defined contribution plans of publicly traded companies must offer the opportunity for participants to diversify their 401(k) accounts (to avoid excessive concentration of employer stock), and must be notified of this right.

- It is easier for employers to maintain automatic-enrollment 401(k) plans, as long as the participants are fully vested within two years of enrollment. Immediate participation is not required.

- If the employer/plan sponsor is a public corporation, and the plan holds employer securities, participants must be given at least three other investment options, and must be notified of their right to diversify out of the employer's stock.

- It is not a prohibited transaction for fiduciaries of 401(k) plans to give investment advice to participants, subject to some conditions.

PPA § 303 amends Code § 415(b), so that plan distributions other than straight life annuities are adjusted actuarially to see if they satisfy the assumptions of § 415(b). Pre-PPA, the interest rate assumption for the adjustment could not be lower than the rate specified in the plan or the § 417(e)(3) rate— whichever was lower.

As of August 17, 2006, 401(k) plans can allow distributions for health, tuition, or funeral expenses relating to a "primary beneficiary": that is, a person who is named as a plan beneficiary and has an unconditional right to part or all of the account balance when the plan participant dies. The hardship distribution must be necessary to satisfy the financial need. A § 409A plan can treat a beneficiary on a par with a spouse or dependent to decide whether the participant has incurred an unforeseeable financial emergency.

For distributions after December 31, 2006, PPA § 820 amends Code § 402(c)(11) so that a direct trustee-to-trustee transfer to the IRA of a non-spouse beneficiary can be treated as an inherited IRA and a direct rollover of an eligible rollover distribution, and will not be gross income for the recipient in the year of the distribution. To qualify, the rollover must be made to an IRA established on behalf of the designated beneficiary. Plans are not obligated to offer direct rollovers of distributions to non-spouse beneficiaries, but if they are offered, it must be on a nondiscriminatory basis.

Under pre-PPA law, a defined contribution plan satisfied the § 411(a) minimum vesting rule for employer non-elective contributions as long as vesting occurred on a five-year cliff, or three-to-seven-year graded vesting schedule. PPA § 904, however, requires faster vesting: for plan years beginning after December 31, 2006, vesting must occur vis-à-vis employer non-elective contributions on a three-year cliff or two-to-six-year graded schedule. Plan amendments that change the vesting schedule accordingly must satisfy § 411(a)(10). The plan can maintain separate vesting schedules for employer non-elective contributions, depending on whether or not they are subject to § 411(a)(2)(B).

PPA § 1102 permits notices under §§ 402(f), 411(a)(11), and 417 to be given as much as 180 days before the annuity starting date. However, the plan must revise its 411 notice to take the PPA rules into account. The notice must describe the increase in benefits under a defined benefit plan if receipt is deferred; a defined contribution plan notice must explain the plan's investment options (including associated fees) if distributions are deferred. The notice for either type of plan must reproduce any part of the SPD that contains special rules that could have a material effect on the decision to take benefits right away or defer them.

In mid-2007, the IRS issued a procedure for using plan-specific substitute mortality tables to compute defined balance obligations under Code § 430(h)(3)(C) and ERISA 303(h)(3)(C). [Adrien Martin, *IRS Release Guidelines on Substitute Mortality Table Requests*, plansponsor.com (May 31, 2007)]

Final regulations on this topic were issued in August 2008. See Rev. Proc. 2008-62, 2008-42 I.R.B. 935. The tables, which have separate rates for males and females, and for annuitants and non-annuitants, must be used beginning with 2008 plan years. A small plan (one with under 500 participants) can use a single blended static table for all participants. The PPA also allows certain large employers with adequate experience (at least 1,000 deaths for each sex over a five-year period) to use individualized plan specific tables that accurately reflect the plan's experience. [See Buck Consulting FYI, *IRS Issues Final Regulations on Mortality Tables Under PPA*, FYI_08_07_08a (Aug. 7, 2008) (benefitslink.com) Watson Wyatt Insider, *IRS Finalizes Mortality Tables for DB Plans* (September 2008) (benefitslink.com); CCH Pension & Benefits, *IRS Finalizes Mortality Tables for DB Plans, Substitute Single-Employer Tables* (Aug. 11, 2008) (benefitslink.com); see Notice 2013-49, 2013-32 I.R.B. 127, for updated mortality tables to be used in 2014 and 2015, and tables of minimum present value under § 417(e)(3) for annuity start dates in calendar years 2014 and 2015.]

## [B] Changes Under Recovery Statutes

The PPA was drafted during what, in retrospect, was a robust economy, where employers would be able to shoulder short-term burdens in order to maintain the long-term stability of the pension system. Financial events soon made it necessary to trim the PPA's remedial scheme. The PPA called for plans to become 100% funded within seven years. Congress voted in December 2008 for plans with large investment losses to comply without reaching 100% funding within the seven-year time frame. [Mary Williams Walsh, *Pensions Get a Reprieve in Congress*, N.Y. Times, Dec. 12, 2008]

Congress responded to corporations' pleas for relief by enacting the Preservation of Access to Care for Medicare Beneficiaries and Pension Relief Act, Pub. L. No. 111-192, allowing employers to pick two years to pay only the interest on the funding shortfall, or to amortize the funding shortfalls for any two plan years between 2008 and 2011 over an extended (15-year) period. [See Rebecca

Moore, *Obama Signs Pension Relief Bill*, plansponsor.com (June 25, 2010)] [Gina Chon, *Private-Firm Pensions Face Deadline for Funding Level*, WSJ.com (Apr. 1, 2010)]

The Pension Protection Technical Corrections Act of 2008 (part of the Worker, Retiree and Employer Recovery Act, or WRERA, Pub. L. No. 110-458 (Dec. 23, 2008) provides relief to hard-pressed pension plans in many ways:

- A one-year moratorium (for 2009 only, not 2008) is imposed on the requirement that participants in defined contribution plans and IRAs take minimum distributions from the plan; participants did not want to have to sell securities at a loss to take the distributions (which would have been calculated based on pre-Crash values of their accounts).

- The PPA called for a three-year phase-in of the funding target percentage. Plans falling below the target funding percentage for a year must fund up to the funding percentage for that year—but do not have to reach 100% funding as quickly as originally provided by the PPA.

- Some smoothing is allowed—plans can recognize unexpected gains or losses over 24 months rather than in the year of the event.

- Employers will not be required to comply with all of the PPA's restrictions on accrual of pension benefits.

- The phase-in of full funding is slowed down; the threshold stays at 92% for an additional year.

- An underfunded plan that is not allowed to distribute lump sums is nevertheless permitted to cash out balances that do not exceed $5,000.

- The effective date of the PPA's rules about vesting and interest crediting in collectively bargained plans is delayed.

- Rollovers from Roth 401(k) or 403(b) plans to Roth IRA are not subject to the AGI limit for making Roth IRA contributions. [Fred Schneyer, *Pension Relief Bill with RMD Moratorium Slides Through U.S. Senate*, plansponsor.com (Dec. 11, 2008); Mary Williams Walsh, *Pensions Get a Reprieve in Congress*, N.Y. Times, Dec. 12, 2008 (times.com)]

In addition to PPA technical corrections, WRERA includes relief provisions for employers. The Worker, Retiree and Employer Recovery Act, or WRERA, Pub. L. No. 110-458 includes both PPA technical corrections and relief provisions. The PPA introduced the concept of the "target normal cost." WRERA allows expenses paid directly by the plan to be included in calculating the target normal cost; this is elective for 2009 but mandatory for later years.

WRERA requires the same interest rate assumptions to be used to calculate the funding target and the target normal cost. WRERA gives the IRS expanded authority to issue guidance about determining funded status for years before 2008—which is important for seeing if a plan is at risk.

The PPA includes provisions about cash balance and other hybrid plans (age discrimination rules, conversions, and the whipsaw calculation). WRERA limits the applicability of the new vesting requirements for cash balance plans (such as 100% vesting after three years of service). [Deloitte's Washington Bulletin, *PPA Technical Corrections Affecting Defined Benefit Plans* (Jan. 12, 2009), <http://benefitslink.com/articles/guests/washbull090112.html> (benefitslink.com)]

MAP-21, Pub. L. No. 112-141, signed in July 2012, extends the period for calculating interest rates to 25 years—making recent years, when rates were very low, less influential in the calculation. For 2012, the plan's interest rates must be within 10% of the average benchmark bond rates for the previous 25 years.

Notice 2013-11, 2013-11 I.R.B. 610 provides guidance on MAP-21 funding calculations, such as the 25-year average segment rates to be used to adjust the 24-month segment rates for computing minimum contribution requirements for single-employer defined benefit plans. MAP-21 defines the range within which the segment rates fall. For plan years beginning in 2013, the three segment rates are adjusted to fall within the range of 85%–115% of the appropriate 25-year average rate. The range then increases over time so that, for example, for years beginning after 2015, the rates are 70%–130% of the 25-year average segment rates. [<http://www.irs.gov/pub/irs-drop/n-13-11.pdf>; *see* Rebecca Moore, *IRS Announces New Rates for DB Funding Calculations*, plansponsor.com (Feb. 12, 2013)]

## § 4.02    EXTENT OF COVERAGE

In the more than 30 years since ERISA took effect, the pension sector of the economy has grown mightily, but has changed its characteristics very significantly. There has been a tremendous shift from plans in which the employer makes the contributions, decides how contributions will be invested, and takes the investment risk to plans in which employees bear a far greater burden of making both contributions and decisions. One of the major objectives of the PPA is to improve the soundness of the surviving defined benefit plans by requiring more realistic funding and reporting, although some of the more stringent rules were relaxed by 2008–2009 federal legislation.

In March 2013, 74% of full-time workers in private industry had access to a retirement plan, as did 37% of part-time workers. For all private-industry workers, 64% had access to a retirement plan but only 49% actually participated in the plan. Retirement benefit access was much higher in companies that had 100 or more workers (82%) than companies with one to 99 workers (49%). [Bureau of Labor Statistics, *Employee Benefits in the United States—March 2013*, <http://www.bls.gov/news.release/ebs2.pdf> (July 17, 2013)]

An EBRI Issue Brief published in November 2012 shows that the percentage of workers with employment-based retirement plans was fairly consistent between 2010 and 2011. For all workers (including self-employed persons and part-time and part-year employees), participation was 39.6% in 2009, 39.8% in 2010, and 39.7%

in 2011. For full-time, full-year wage, and salaried workers aged 21–64, the overall participation rate was 53.7%, although with very great differences among sub-groups. Those less likely to participate include non-white, young, female, never-married, less-educated, and lower-wage workers. Workers in the South and the West, and those without health insurance, were also less likely than average to be plan participants. [EBRI Issue Brief, *Employment-Based Retirement Plan Participation: Geographic Differences and Trends, 2011*, is at <http://www.ebri.org/pdf/briefspdf/EBRI_IB_11-2012_No378_RetParticip.pdf>. See Rebecca Moore, *Retirement Plan Participation Rates Stalled*, plansponsor.com (Nov. 27, 2012)]

According to Towers Watson, in 2000, 58 of the Fortune 100 offered a tra-ditional defined benefit plan to new hires—but only 13 did so in 2011. Since 1981, not only have many 401(k) plans been created, but also few defined benefit plans have been created. Furthermore, some companies that were not bankrupt or in serious financial trouble converted defined benefit to defined contribution plans. This move usually reduces the employer's required contribution from 7%–8% of payroll (defined contribution) to the promised match in the 401(k) plan (usually 3%). [Alicia Munnell, *Private Sector Defined Benefit Plans Vanishing*, WSJ.com (Dec. 30, 2011)]

An EBRI fact sheet published in March 2013 shows that in 1979, 7% of U.S. workers participated only in a defined contribution plan and no other plan; in that year, 28% of workers had only a defined benefit plan, and a further 10% had both. The situation changed greatly by 2011, when 31% of workers participated only in a defined contribution plan, 11% participated in both, and a mere 3% of workers had a defined benefit plan only. The fact sheet includes a dramatic graph, show-ing that the proportion of workers with both types of plans has stayed within the 10%–15% range—but defined benefit plan participation plummeted throughout the period as defined contribution plan participation soared.[EBRI Fast Facts #225, *Pension Plan Participation*, <http://www.ebri.org/pdf/FF.225.DB-DC .28Mar13.pdf> (Mar. 28, 2013).

In July 2012, the funded status of the typical corporate pension plan fell 2.9%, to a funded level of 68.7%. This was the lowest level since BNY Mellon started tracking this metric in December 2007. The average funded status dete-riorated because assets increased only 1.2% whereas liabilities increased 5.5%. The rise in liabilities reflected the drop in the corporate discount rate. Aa-rated bonds yielded only 3.64%, and liabilities are calculated based on the yield of long-term investment grade bonds. Lower yields mean larger liabilities. [Mike G. Dunn, BNY Mellon press release, *Funded Status of U.S. Corporate Pensions Falls to Lowest Recorded Level in July, According to BNY Mellon* (Aug. 3, 2012) (benefitslink.com)]

Funded status rebounded somewhat in June 2013, reaching 89.5%—the highest level since June 2011, when it was 91.4%. [News Release, *Funded Status of U.S. Corporate Pensions Rises to 89.5 Percent in June, According to BNY Mel-lon ISSG* (July 2, 2013) (benefitslink.com)]

According to American Investment Planners LLC, 42% of active 401(k) plans did not have an employer match feature in 2011. Five percent of 401(k) plans stopped offering employer matches in 2010, followed by another 2% in 2011. The number of 401(k) plans also declined: from 520,000 active plans in 2009 to 488,000 in 2010 and 472,000 in 2011. [Karen DeMasters, *401(k) Matching Funds Being Eliminated, Study Shows*, Financial Advisor Blog (May 2, 2013) (benefitslink.com)]

Transamerica Retirement Survey's thirteenth annual report examined the preceding five years of 401(k) performance. Catherine Collinson, president of the Transamerica Center for Retirement Studies, said that access to savings plans increased: in 2007, 72% of employers offered 401(k) plans, rising to 82% in 2012, whereas the percentage of companies offering defined benefit plans dropped from 19% to 15% in the same time period. In 2007, the median annual salary deferral rate was 7%, dropping to 6% for 2009–2011, returning to 7% in 2012. Employer matches were more common in 2007 (80%) than in 2012 (70%), but half of the companies that suspended or reduced their match since 2008 have reinstated it. About one-fifth (19%) of employers had a Roth feature in their 401(k) plans in 2007, about one-third (32%) did in 2012.

In 2012, the median account balance was $99,320 for Baby Boomers, $41,821 for members of Generation X, and $15,213 for Echo Boomers. Clearly, this is not enough for retirees to live on, so 56% of workers surveyed expected to work after age 65, and 43% expected to work past age 70 or not to retire at all. [Mary Beth Franklin, *Surprise!401(k)s Rode Out The Great Recession Just Fine*, InvestmentNews (Nov. 14, 2012) (benefitlink.com)]

## § 4.03  EFFECT OF DEMOGRAPHICS ON PLANS

The Baby Boom, people born after World War II, are the largest age cohort in U.S. history. The oldest boomers are already eligible for reduced-level Social Security benefits. That means that soon, employers will not only face the challenge of paying pensions to a very large group of retirees—they will have a smaller group of active workers to generate corporate income and profits. Furthermore, retirees may take priceless and irreplaceable skills and work ethics with them when they leave the workforce.

The population is aging. In 2001, senior citizens made up 12.4% of the population. The fastest-growing demographic group was the "oldest old": people over 85. Senior citizens consume more health services than younger people, so retiree health benefits (see Chapter 9) and the Medicare system will be severely strained.

The PPA provides approval for plans to make in-service distributions starting at age 62, i.e., a person who reduces work effort can continue to draw both a reduced salary and a pension. [*Retirees Continue Working but Not for the Reason You Think*, plansponsor.com (Feb. 24, 2006)] See T.D. 9235, 2007-24 I.R.B. 1386, for Final Regulations defining "Normal Retirement Age" in connection with in-service distributions and phased retirement; issues of early retirement, including phased retirement, are discussed in Chapter 9.

After the recession intensified in 2008, it was anticipated that many Baby Boomers would delay retirement for several years past their original intended retirement date, because of loss of value in their 401(k) accounts, their personal investments, cutbacks by employers, and loss of housing equity.

## § 4.04   INVESTMENT FACTORS

For many years, the strong investment climate allowed plans to reduce or even suspend their contributions to defined benefit plans, because the plans were ample to satisfy the obligation to make future payments.

In the 1990s, many companies found that their investment experience was so favorable that they were able to suspend contributions to their plans, because the plan was already fully funded. This trend later reversed. [John D. McKinnon, *Warning of Pension-Plan Shortfall Raises Pressure for Financial Fix*, Wall St. J., Sept. 5, 2003, at A1] Then, in 2000 and 2001, the dot-com bubble collapsed; the September 11 attack and the Enron scandal also damaged investment results. For the period 2005–2010, the typical average annual return achieved by defined contribution plan participants was 3.7%, for a cumulative return of just over 20%—even considering the recession. Almost all (95%) of participants had positive total return for the five years, but just broke even for 2007–2010. [<https://institutional.vanguard.com/VGApp/iip/site/institutional/research commentary/article/InvResDuringCrisis>; see Tara Cantore, *Vanguard Study Finds DC Plan Account Accumulation Positive Through Recession*, plansponsor .com (Dec. 14, 2011)]

The 2008–2009 declines in the real estate market and financial markets, in conjunction with business problems caused by lack of access to borrowing, placed pension plans under great stress, leading to many plan freezes, plan terminations, and reductions or elimination of employer matching contributions. [Alicia H. Munnell, Jean-Pierre Aubry and Dan Muldoon, *The Financial Crisis and Private Defined Benefit Plans*, No. IB#8-18, Center for Retirement Research at Boston College]

For employees who still are covered by defined benefit plans, decreased funding ratios put their eventual benefit at risk. The SEI's Institutional Group released the results of its 2012 mid-year poll on corporate pension investment. At that point, interest rates were at a historic low and the market was highly volatile; the average funded status of corporate pensions in July 2012 was 68.7% in July— the lowest level reported since 2007. More than half of pension plans surveyed (55%) were either frozen or closed—i.e., no new employees could participate. However, only 1% of plans had begun termination. Approximately one-third of respondents (37%) described their plan as 81%–90% funded, and only 11% said the level of funding was lower than 70%. But about a quarter of plans (27%) fell below the 80% funding level. Forty-four percent of respondents said that they would terminate their plan if it were fully funded, but would continue to offer a 401(k) plan or other alternative benefit. The other 56% reported that their plan was too critical to their benefits structure to be terminated. Forty-three percent expect MAP-21 to be effective in aiding employers with pension plan problems, 21% said it was too early to tell. [Kristen Heinzinger, *SEI Poll Finds Majority of Pensions Frozen*, plansponsor.com (Sept. 13, 2012)]

Freezing or terminating a defined benefit plan can have unforeseen consequences for the sponsor's profit sharing plan, especially if the plan is top-heavy or uses the cross-testing method (for example, a professional firm's cash balance plan). For top-heavy or cross-tested plans, minimum benefits must be provided to non-key, non-HCE employees. If the sponsor has both defined benefit and defined contribution plans, the minimum benefit often includes a 5% top-heavy minimum for all participants who were employed at the end of the year or who worked at least 1,000 hours during the year, with cross-testing based on a 7.5% defined benefit/defined contribution gateway allocation. (Separate defined benefit and defined contribution options are permissible instead of a single 5% figure.)

When accruals in the defined benefit plan stop, the top-heavy minimum benefit falls from 5% to 3% of pay, and allocation is only required for employees who continue to be employed throughout the year. But if the defined benefit plan is terminated and its assets distributed, the defined benefit amounts for active employees are still considered in the top-heavy determination for the remaining plans for up to five years. If there are no more defined benefit accruals to test, the only cross-testing that might be required is for the defined contribution plan itself, so the gateway minimum allocation drops from 7.5% to 5% of pay. Although the ability to reduce the minimum profit-sharing benefit is good for the employer, it will probably have a negative effect on employee motivation, so the employer might choose to keep the profit-sharing rates stable at first and decrease them over time. [Mark Schulte, *Employers Need to Understand Minimum Profit Sharing Benefits for Frozen/Terminated Defined Benefit Plans*, VIA Retirement Plan Blog (Nov. 9, 2011) (benefitslink.com)]

Many pension plans reacted to the financial downturn by freezing defined benefit plans or ceasing or reducing contributions to defined contribution plans—or both. Many employers maintain plans of both types.

## § 4.05   DEFINED BENEFIT/DEFINED CONTRIBUTION

The traditional kind of pension plan, the one usually in effect when ERISA was passed, is the defined benefit plan. In a plan of this type, the employer agrees to provide benefits according to a formula. A typical formula would set the pension level as x% times the number of years the employee worked before retirement times the employee's average pay for his or her last five years working for the employer—or perhaps the average of the three years in which he or she earned the most.

The employer's contributions for all employees go into a single account or trust for the entire plan. However, there must be a separate account balance for each participant who makes voluntary contributions. [I.R.C. § 411(b)(2)(A)]

In some ways, this arrangement is problematic both from the employer's and the employee's point of view. When employees retire, they receive a fixed pension that will probably not be inflation-indexed and will not offer cost of living adjustments. In a highly inflationary environment, they will find that their pension buys less and less over time. Nor will their pension increase if the investment climate is favorable.

From the employer's point of view, defined benefit plans carry heavy burdens, including uncertainty. The employer's commitment is to contribute enough to the plan each year to ensure that the participants will receive the promised level of benefits. Not only does this require elaborate (and expensive) actuarial calculations, it places the investment risk on the employer, who will have to make larger contributions in years in which the value of the plan's securities portfolio declines.

A defined contribution plan is a different, and much simpler, structure. The employer establishes a separate account for each employee who has satisfied the criteria for plan participation. If the plan requires or accepts employee contributions, there will usually be separate subaccounts for employer and employee contributions, but this is not a legal requirement.

The 2008 market crash caused significant losses for 401(k)s, even those managed by reputable firms. As of September 2012, total 401(k) assets were about $3.3 trillion, seven times the level of 20 years earlier, but less than half of private sector workers participate in 401(k) plans, and almost one-quarter of businesses with 100 or more employees do not offer 401(k) plans. Even participants often contribute only 3% of pay. According to the Center for Retirement Research, in 2010 the typical worker in the 55–64 age range had only $54,000 in a 401(k) plan, and total retirement assets, including IRAs, of only $120,000. This is less than one-quarter of the recommended level, and would generate only $7,000 a year in annuity income. The majority (60%) of tax breaks from 401(k) plans go to the top 10% of earners, who would save for retirement even without this incentive. [Steven Greenhouse, *Should the 401(k) Be Reformed or Replaced?*, NYTimes.com (Sept. 11, 2012)]

Towers Watson reported that, for the 12 years preceding 2011 (the last year for which figures are available), defined benefit plans have outperformed 401(k) plans in 11 out of 12 years. The median defined benefit pension plan gained 2.74% in 2011, whereas the median defined contribution plan lost 0.22% of its value. Towers Watson attributed the difference to poor stock market performance in 2011. Most 401(k) balances are invested in stock, whereas defined benefit plan managers often invest in long-term bonds, which performed well in 2011. (Stocks recovered in 2012, which could result in 401(k)s outperforming defined benefit plans for that year when the results are tallied.) 401(k) and other defined contribution plans typically had higher fees than defined benefit plans, contributing to the gap in results. [Matthew Heimer, *Pension Plans Beat 401(k) Savers—Again!*, WSJ.com (May 24, 2013)]

The employer's commitment is to contribute the amount required by the plan formula—generally a simple percentage of compensation. ERISA § 404(c) permits the plan to give control over the assets to the participant. If this is done, the plan's fiduciaries will not be liable for losses that result from the control exercised by the participants.

There is no limit on the number of plans a particular employer can maintain, and it is not uncommon for an employer to maintain both defined benefit and defined contribution plans. Under prior law, § 415(e) imposed a limit on benefits from a combination of defined benefit and defined contribution plans, but that limitation was repealed for limitation years beginning on or after January 1, 2000.

ERISA § 404(c) requires the plan to give participants adequate information about the investment options they have for their accounts. The plan must offer at least three diversified investment types, with materially different characteristics with respect to risk and return.

In a sense, the Social Security system is a kind of pension plan. Both employers and employees pay FICA taxes to fund retirement benefits. Although all earned income is subject to Medicare taxes, the FICA tax phases out at a figure that changes every year. (For 2009–2011, only the first $106,800 of earned income is subject to FICA tax; for 2012, the applicable amount is $110,100, and for 2013, it is $113,700.) The employer makes FICA contributions on all or nearly all of rank-and-file workers' pay, but only on a smaller proportion of the compensation of top earners. The Tax Relief, Unemployment Insurance Reauthorization, and Job Creation Act of 2010, Pub. L. No. 111-312 reduced the employee's share of FICA taxes (but not the employer's share) for 2011, [Plansponsor staff, *Principal Says Tax Holiday an Opportunity to Save*, plansponsor.com (Dec. 17, 2010)]

The Temporary Payroll Tax Cut Continuation Act, Pub. L. No. 112-78, extended the 4.2% FICA rate but subject to a cap of the first $18,350 of compensation. The Middle Class Tax Relief and Job Creation Act of 2012, Pub. L. No. 112-96, enacted February 2, 2012, extended the 4.2% rate until the end of 2012, and removed the cap. The IRS updated Form 941 to reflect the current rates [<http://www.irs.gov/pub/irs-pdf/f941.pdf>; see Rebecca Moore, *Payroll Tax Cut Extended, IRS Issues Revised Form*, plansponsor.com (Feb. 24, 2012)]

The Internal Revenue Code contains "permitted disparity" rules for "integrating" a qualified plan with Social Security (disparities are not permitted in 401(k) plans). Within limits, the employer can reduce its plan contributions on behalf of rank-and-file employees to compensate for the employer's FICA contributions. As long as the permitted disparity rules are satisfied, the plan will remain qualified, and will not be considered discriminatory—even though the practical effect is to cut down on contributions and lower the pension the rank-and-file employees will eventually receive. The 2013 table of covered compensation with respect to permitted disparities appears at Rev. Rul. 2013-2, 2013-10 I.R.B. 533.

## § 4.06   OTHER PLAN TYPES

An Employee Stock Ownership Plan provides employees with shares in the employer company as a form of deferred compensation. Sometimes ESOPs purchase the company. Commentators noted that ESOPs can provide tax and financing advantages that surpass other takeover alternatives. The transaction involves large-scale loans; as the company repays the loans, the interest is tax-deductible and may be large enough to significantly reduce or even eliminate taxable income for the business. The business is also exempt from capital gains taxation on purchases of certain securities that are retained within the ESOP for three years or more—provided that the ESOP owns at least 30% of the employer stock.

Employees are at high risk if their individual pension accounts are heavily invested in employer stock—and the stock does poorly. Because of the ESOP's mission of investing in employer stock, participants have generally been unsuccessful in challenging ESOP fiduciaries when the value of the stock falls. (See § 15.03[C] for discussion of "stock drop" suits in general.)

On November 16, 2009, the IRS released updated ESOP regulations, increasing the flexibility for satisfying the requirements of § 423 (favorable tax treatment for stock acquired under an ESOP option). To qualify for favorable treatment, the employee must hold the stock for at least two years from the grant, and one year from exercise of the option. For nonqualified options, the employee has ordinary income at the time of exercise, equal any excess of fair market value over the exercise price. To be a § 423 plan, the ESOP plan, including the maximum number of shares available, must be approved by the company's stockholders within a period of 12 months before or after the date the plan was adopted. In general, all employees of the corporation must be granted options. Up to $25,000 worth of stock can be optioned for each year the option is outstanding, whether or not the option is exercisable. The exercise price must be at least 85% of the fair market value at the time of grant or exercise. [Sonnenschein Nath & Rosenthal LLP, *IRS Releases Final Regulations on Employee Stock Purchase Plans* (Nov. 17, 2009) (benefitslink.com)]

Hybrid plans are defined benefit plans whose benefits accrue under the formula set by the sponsor rather than as a monthly payment. The benefit is usually defined as a lump-sum account balance and not an annuity benefit payable at NRA. Employers who adopt hybrid plans often do so because funding is predictable and the plan design is easier for employees to understand than other types of defined benefit plans. Although the PPA provided new rules for administration of hybrid plans, sponsors have not received any further guidance since then.

Most hybrid plans are cash balance plans, with the benefit based on a percentage of pay credited annually each year with interest determined based on the plan's interest crediting rate. Another plan design, the Pension Equity Plan (PEP) posts percentage credits to the employee's account each year. The lump-sum balance at retirement is the total of the percentages times the employee's final average pay.

Typically, hybrid plans increase the rate of pay credits as age and/or service increase. To avoid back-loading, IRS rules mandate crediting a minimum interest rate. Employees generally must meet age and service requirements to participate in hybrid plans, such as one year of service plus reaching age 21. The pension can be computed based on salary alone, or salary plus overtime and commission, but most plans include all compensation including overtime, bonuses, and commissions. In late 2010, the IRS issued final and proposed regulations for hybrid retirement plans, including cash balance plans, and Pension Equity Plans (PEPs). The 2010 final regulations deal with subjects such as age discrimination, vesting, conversions from conventional defined benefit plans, and safe harbor rates for crediting interest.

Under the final regulations, a lump sum-based benefit formula is any formula that expresses the accrued benefit either as the current balance of the participant's hypothetical account, or the current value of the accumulated percentage of the participant's final average compensation. Each participant has a hypothetical account that is credited with the employer's hypothetical contributions based on compensation credits (the participant's eligible compensation) plus interest credits (the hypothetical earnings on the account). Usually, compensation credits are defined as a percentage of eligible pay, although the formula may factor in age and years of service. The interest credits can operate as a fixed rate or be based on an extrinsic interest. Compensation credits end when the participant stops working for the employer, but interest rates generally continue until the pension is distributed. The PEP benefit equals a percentage of the final average pay, with the percentage set based on points earned each year by participants.

Under the final regulations, the entire accrued benefit for a plan using a hybrid formula must vest no later than three years of service. Although three-year vesting is required even if only part of the benefit is calculated using the hybrid formula, the final regulations clarify that the three-year vesting requirement does not apply to the traditional defined benefit portion of a floor offset arrangement when a defined benefit plan is combined with a separate hybrid plan. Usually, the defined benefit will be reduced by the value of the hybrid plan account.

The final regulations provide an ADEA safe harbor: the accumulated benefit of any participant must not be less than the accumulated benefit of any similarly situated younger participant. Whether two participants are similarly situated depends on their period of service, their job, compensation, date of hire, and work history. A hybrid plan that does not qualify under the safe harbor must satisfy the general age discrimination rule of Code § 411(b)(1)(H)(i).

To prevent wearaway, the final regulations provide that if an amendment adopted and effective on or after June 29, 2005 eliminates or reduces future benefit accruals, and part or all of the benefit is determined based on the statutory hybrid formula, the benefit after the conversion amendment must at least equal the accrued benefit on the conversion date plus the accrued benefit after the conversion, with no offsets between the two. A plan is considered amended if it changes the conditions of employment, such as a transfer to a different part of the company that has a different plan.

The PPA requires hybrid plans to credit interest at a rate that does not exceed a market rate of return. The final regulations define a market rate as a rate that does not exceed the rate on long-term investment-grade corporate bonds, the rate on certain Treasury bonds; or the actual rate of return on plan assets, if the benefits are indexed; or the rate of return on annuities issued by an insurance company. The rate of benefit accrual can increase as participants earn more, but any year's accrual rate must not exceed one-third more than the previous year's rate. [75 Fed. Reg. 64123 (Oct. 19, 2010) [final regulations], 75 Fed. Reg. 64197 (Oct. 19, 2010) [proposed regulations]. See Proskauer Client Alert, *IRS Issues Cash Balance Plan Guidance*, plansponsor.com (Nov. 19, 2010); Rebecca Moore, *IRS Issues Rules on Hybrid Retirement Plans*, plansponsor.com (Oct. 18, 2010)]

## [A]  Money Purchase Plan

A money purchase plan provides definitely determinable benefits, funded by fixed employer contributions made in accordance with a single allocation formula for all participants. Money purchase plans are subject to the I.R.C. § 412 minimum funding standard. The plan must offer QJSAs and QPSAs. [See §§ 12.05, 12.06] Money purchase plans can accept employee contributions and make plan loans to participants.

## [B]  Profit-Sharing Plan

A profit-sharing plan must have a definite formula, set in advance, for allocating the employer's total contribution among the various plan participants, and for distributing the account money to participants. Distributions can be made after the funds have been in the account for a certain length of time (ERISA requires this to be at least two years), attainment of a stated age (which does not have to be retirement age) or an event such as retirement, termination, illness, or disability. Profit-sharing plans have to have formulas for allocating and distributing employer contributions, but the corporation's Board of Directors can legitimately be given discretion to set the level of contributions each year. Since 1986, it has not been necessary for the contributions to be made from corporate profits, or only in a year in which there are profits. The maximum contribution that the employer can deduct is 15% of the participant's contribution for the year. Profit-sharing plans are allowed to make plan loans.

## [C]  Target-Benefit Plan

A target-benefit plan is a money purchase plan (and therefore subject to the defined contribution rules), but contributions are calculated to fund a specified level of retirement benefits at normal retirement age. The participant receives the aggregate of all contributions plus their earnings, although the actual benefit may be either higher or lower than the target, depending on investment results. The IRS treats these plans as defined contribution plans with respect to the Rev. Proc. 2007-44 filing deadlines. Therefore, opinion and advisory letters for PPA restatements of prototype or volume submitter plans had a January 31, 2012 deadline. Rev. Proc. 2011-49, 2011-44 I.R.B. 608 requires master or specimen plans to have at least 30 sponsors registered as adopting that plan word for word. The only exception is for money purchase plans (when only 10 adopters required). Target benefit plans do not qualify for this exemption. [Suzanne L. Wynn, *Target Benefit Plans: On the Edge of Extinction*, Pension Protection Act Blog (Dec. 13, 2011) (benefitslink.com)]

## [D]  Floor-Offset Plan

A floor-offset plan is a hybrid plan, where the defined benefit portion of the plan guarantees a minimum level of benefits, offset by the annuity the retiree could purchase at retirement with the balance in the defined contribution portion of the plan. *Lunn v. Montgomery Ward & Co. Ret. Sec. Plan* [166 F.3d 880 (7th Cir. 1999)] holds that an employee who retired four years after normal retirement age was not entitled to additional retirement benefits to make up for the reduced duration of benefits. The court upheld the idea of floor-offset plans, finding that this type of plan does not violate ERISA benefit accrual requirements or anti-forfeiture provisions.

## [E]  New Comparability Plan

A new comparability plan is a special type of defined contribution plan (or combination of defined contribution and defined benefit plan) that can increase the allocation for HCEs without violating the antidiscrimination rules. See § 4.22.

The plan document can define the classes used to group the employees in various ways, although a plan amendment is required to change the number or definition of classes, and this cannot be done retroactively. A class could be specified, for example, as all employees born before a certain date, those hired after a certain date, those with a certain number of years of service, those working in a particular department, those with a stated title or type of job, or those assigned to a named region. The IRS and DOL have not issued technical guidance, but if every employee is placed in a separate class, the agencies might rule that the plan has become a deemed 401(k). For example, a medical practice could have three classes: owners, managers, and other employees. To reward productivity, the plan could have different classes for offices depending on their revenue streams and productivity levels. [Mark Papalia, *Class-Based Pensions: A Cost-Saving Alternative for Companies of All Sizes*, Journal of Accountancy (January 2005) <https://www.aicpa.org/PUBS/JOFA/jan2005/papalia.html>]

## [F]  SEP

A SEP (Simplified Employer Pension) is an IRA sponsored by the employer, under a written plan whose contribution formula does not discriminate in favor of HCEs. For 2009–2012, the § 402(k)(2)(C) compensation amount is $550. For 2009–2011, the SEP annual compensation limit (§ 408(k)(3)(C)) is $245,000, rising to $250,000 in 2012 and $255,000 in 2013. [IR-2012-77, *IRS Announces 2013 Pension Plan Limitations*, <http://www.irs.gov/uac/2013-Pension-Plan-Limitations> (Oct. 18, 2012)]

## [G]  SIMPLE

A Savings Incentive Match Plan for Employees (SIMPLE) plan, available only to companies with 100 or fewer employees, involves employer contributions to employees' own IRAs. The SIMPLE IRA offers tax advantages for both employer and employees in small companies, and is easier and less expensive to administer than a 401(k) plan. As a general rule, the company cannot offer any other retirement plan, and all participants must have earned at least $5,000 per year from the company in any two previous years, and expect to earn $5,000 in the current year. The employer can elect two kinds of plan. The most common plan form requires the employer to match employee contributions up to 3% of compensation. The limits remained identical from 2009 to 2012, rising slightly in 2013. As of 2013, employee contributions are limited to $12,000; employees over 50 can make catch-up contributions of up to $2,500. (The $12,000 limit is subject to the aggregate dollar limit of $17,500 for all elective contributions made by a person to all employer-sponsored plans.) The general rule is that the employer can deduct its contributions to the SIMPLE IRA plan.

## [H]  Cafeteria Plans

The underlying purpose of all employee benefits is to motivate employees to do better work. Employees differ in their characteristics and priorities, and it is reasonable to assume that employees will be most strongly motivated by benefits that fit their individual needs. Hence, the Internal Revenue Code, at § 125, regulates "cafeteria plans," giving employees choices from a "menu" of taxable and non-taxable benefits. In the summer of 2007, the IRS withdrew a number of earlier proposals and offered new guidance about cafeteria plans (general rules about qualified and nonqualified benefits in these plans; rules for elections; FSA plan rules; nondiscrimination; substantiating expenses for qualified benefits).

A cafeteria plan must be set out in writing. The written plan document must explain:

- How to make elections
- The employer's contributions under the plan
- The maximum salary reduction permitted under the plan, either as a maximum percentage of contribution or a maximum dollar amount
- The plan year (unless there is a valid business purpose for a shorter plan year, it must be 12 consecutive months)
- If the plan covers paid time off, ordering of non-elective and elective paid time off
- Rules for any Flexible Spending Account included in the plan
- If there is a Health Savings Account, who is eligible to contribute
- Grace period (if any) for health FSA or dependent care assistance

The rules deal with benefits recently added to the roster that cafeteria plans can offer (adoption assistance, HSAs, HSA distributions from health FSAs). The IRS proposed a Regulation clarifying that § 125 is the only way for employers to give employees a choice between taxable and nontaxable benefits without the choice itself creating tax liability for the employees. The proposal adds COBRA premiums and HSA contributions as acceptable qualified nontaxable benefits. The proposed regulations forbid cafeteria plans to offer scholarships, employer-provided meals and lodging, educational assistance, fringe benefits, long-term care insurance, contributions to an Archer MSA, group-term life insurance covering non-employees; or elective deferrals to a 403(b) plan.

All reimbursements under the plan must be individually substantiated by someone other than the employee. If the cafeteria plan discriminates in favor of highly compensated employees, the HCEs have income for tax purposes equal to the highest value of the benefits they could have elected. The Proposed Regulations incorporate some of the safe harbor testing rules of Code § 410(b), with an objective test to determine when the actual election of benefits is discriminatory: when HCEs have higher benefits, measured as a percentage of compensation, than non-HCEs.

PPACA creates a new form of cafeteria plan available to small employers starting in 2011. Like the Simple 401(k) and Simple IRA plan, the Simple Cafeteria Plan insulates small employers from nondiscrimination problems that might otherwise occur. (With only a few employees in a plan, it's likely that most of the benefits will go to key employees.) For this purpose, a small employer is one that, in either of the prior two years, had an average of 100 or fewer employees. For an employer that has been in business for less than two years, eligibility is based on the number of employees it can reasonably be expected to have. If a company grows in size, it can keep its Simple Cafeteria Plan until the end of the plan year in which it reaches 200 employees.

All qualified employees must be eligible to participate if they had at least 1,000 hours of service in the previous plan year. Highly compensated and key employees can participate in the Simple Cafeteria Plan, but the plan must avoid discrimination in their favor in eligibility and benefits. Employees can be excluded if they have not reached age 21 (or a younger age as provided by the plan) by the end of the plan year; if they have not performed at least one year of service; if they are non-resident aliens; or if they are covered by a CBA. All eligible employees must be allowed to elect any benefit in the plan under the same terms and conditions as all other participants.

The employer maintaining the Simple Cafeteria Plan must make a minimum contribution that the participant can apply toward any benefit within the plan. The minimum contribution for non-HCEs must equal or exceed the lesser of a uniform 2% of compensation (whether or not the employee contributes); a match equal to double the employee's contribution; or 6% of compensation. This is the minimum: the employer is permitted to make additional contributions, but the match percentage for HCEs must not be higher than the match rate for non-HCEs. [McKenna Long & Aldridge LLP, *Is a Simple Cafeteria Plan Right for You?*, <http://www.mckennalong.com/publications-advisories-2976.html> (May 16, 2012)]

## [I]   QLACs

The Department of Treasury noted the role of "longevity risk" in the need for retirement income. A 65-year-old woman has a 50-50 chance of living past 86; a 65 year-old man has an equal chance of living past 84. The replacement of defined benefit plans by defined contribution plans as the predominant form leaves many people at risk of outliving their funds. The Treasury and DOL published a package of proposed regulations and rulings in early 2012 to encourage development of lifetime income alternatives. The proposals make it easier for employers to offer combination options (e.g., the employee takes part of the account as a lump sum, but receives an annuity with the rest).

The proposals contemplate the possibility of "longevity annuities"—annuities that protect the very-long-lived by commencing annuity benefits at an advanced age, such as 80 or 85. The proposals allow a lump sum 401(k) distribution to be split: part going to the participant, part deposited with the employer to purchase an annuity. (The proposals assume that group plans can get better deals on annuities than individual investors can.) The proposals also explain how the 401(k) spousal protection rules work when an employee purchases a deferred annuity from the plan.

Under prior law, it was difficult to have a split distribution because the statutory interest rates and mortality tables had to be used for both the lump sum and the annuity, precluding the plan from using its own figures in the annuity calculation. The proposal allows the use of the statutory assumptions for the lump sum only, with the plan's regular conversion factors for the partial annuity.

Prior law also worked against longevity annuities, because the minimum distribution requirements impose penalties if the entire account is not distributed over the individual's predicted life expectancy—which means that people who outlive their predicted life expectancy will have exhausted their accounts. The proposal allows 401(k) (and IRA) plans relief from the minimum distribution requirements for annuities that cost less than the smaller of $100,000 or 25% of the account balance and that start by age 85. This type of distribution is referred to as a QLAC, or "qualified longevity annuity contract." The annuity will be disregarded for RMD purposes until its benefits begin. Longevity annuities must satisfy some requirements for death benefits and cash-out to ensure that they are used only to hedge against longevity risk, and full disclosure of the annuity terms is required.

The proposals give the employer another alternative: the sponsor of a defined benefit plan can permit employees who have 401(k) accounts to roll over all or part of the 401(k) distribution to the defined benefit plan (or a hybrid plan such as a cash balance plan) in exchange for an immediate annuity. The annuity must be at least actuarially equivalent to the sum received by the plan. [Proposed Regulations, 77 Fed. Reg. 5443 and 5454 (Feb. 3, 2012); see *Treasury Fact Sheet: Helping American Families Achieve Retirement Security By Expanding Lifetime Income Choices* (Feb. 2, 2012) (benefitslink.com)]

Rev. Rul. 2012-4, 2012-8 I.R.B. 386 explains how an employer that offers both defined contribution and defined benefit plans can permit 401(k) plan participants who are ready to retire to roll over part or all of the 401(k) account balance to the defined benefit plan, receiving an immediate annuity under the defined benefit plan. The plan must use the same actuarial assumptions (such as interest rates and mortality tables) for annuitized rollovers as for defined benefit distributions. Defined contribution plan participants who elect a rollover are entitled to disclosures about what will happen if the plan terminates without enough money to pay its liabilities. Married participants must furnish notified consent from their spouses. This ruling applies to rollovers made on or after January 1, 2013, but plan sponsors can rely on the ruling for earlier rollovers. Amounts used to purchase a QLAC are excluded from the RMD calculations for the time between the participant reaching age 70 and the start date of annuity payments. The amount that can be used to purchase a QLAC is limited to the lesser of $100,000 or 25% of the account balance. Another IRS proposal permits participants to allocate their benefit between annuity and lump sum payouts rather than requiring an election of only one or the other, and simplifies the associated calculations. [McKay Hochman Company, Inc. *E-Mail Alert 2012-8, Lifetime Income Options* (Aug. 30, 2012) (benefitslink.com)]

## § 4.07   IRA/QUALIFIED PLAN INTERFACE

As the name suggests, an Individual Retirement Arrangement (IRA) is maintained by an individual on his or her own behalf, not by a corporation. However, the two types of plan interact when an IRA is used as a "conduit" for a transfer of funds between two qualified plans, or when distributions from a qualified plan are sheltered from immediate taxation by being rolled over to an IRA.

Employers can maintain a program under which employees authorize payroll deductions to be invested in either regular or Roth IRAs. Such arrangements do not constitute ERISA plans (and therefore do not subject the employer to regulation or potential supervision) if:

- The employer doesn't make any contributions;

- Employee participation in the arrangement is completely voluntary;

- The employer's sole involvement is letting employees participate (without endorsing participation), making the payroll deductions, and forwarding the amounts to the IRA sponsor.

The employer can collect reasonable reimbursement for its services in connection with the employees' IRAs, but no other compensation. The employer can provide educational materials about IRAs and the value of saving for retirement, but must make it clear that the employer's role is purely administrative and does not involve contributions to the plan. It's also permissible for the employer to distribute literature prepared by the IRA sponsor, and even to display its own logo on the materials.

Either the employer can choose a single IRA sponsor or inform employees of criteria for choosing a sponsor. However, it is not permitted for the employer to negotiate special terms for its own employees that are not available to everyone who buys IRAs through that sponsor. The employer should inform employees that there are other ways to fund IRAs; that IRAs are not a suitable investment for everybody; and that IRAs work the same way whether the employee authorizes a payroll deduction or submits the contribution directly to the IRA sponsor.

EGTRRA increases the maximum amount that can be contributed to an IRA (especially by persons over 50) and institutes a tax credit for low-income IRA investors, so IRA options will be more attractive than ever before. Active servicemembers can also base IRA contributions on combat pay.

EGTRRA also creates another option, the "deemed IRA," for plan years beginning after December 31, 2002. A qualified plan can permit employees to contribute to a separate account within a qualified plan. If the separate account meets the criteria for being either a conventional or a Roth IRA, it is treated as an IRA and not a qualified plan—and the employer's qualified plan won't lose its qualified status just because of the IRA subaccounts. The difference between a deemed IRA and the payroll deduction plan described above is that the employer, not the employee, sets up the account, although deemed IRAs can take payroll deductions.

Deemed IRAs are considered IRAs rather than qualified plans, so it is not necessary to satisfy ERISA's coverage and nondiscrimination rules. However, deemed IRAs are subject to ERISA's fiduciary and enforcement provisions, including the requirements for processing claims. Each deemed IRA must be held in a separate account or separate annuity under the plan, and the plan must provide separate accounting for the IRS contributions and earnings.

Under the final rule published in 2004, the deemed IRA account must satisfy the rules for either a traditional or Roth IRA. SEP and SIMPLE IRAs cannot be used as deemed IRAs. Because the employer's qualified plan and the deemed IRA are treated as separate entities, rules such as the minimum distribution requirements must be satisfied separately for each.

The applicable 2013 dollar amount of adjusted gross income for determining the IRA deduction for taxpayers who are active participants in a qualified plan is $92,000 (joint return or qualified widow or widower); for other taxpayers who are not married filing separate returns, the limit is $58,000. The dollar amount for a taxpayer who is not an active participant but who is married to an active participant is $173,000. The traditional IRA deduction phases out for singles and heads of household who participate in a qualified plan between $58,000 and $68,000. The phase-out range for married couples (where the IRA account holder participates in a qualified plan) is $92,000–$112,000. The phase-out range, when, not the account holder but his or her spouse is a plan participant, is $173,000–$183,000.

For Roth IRAs, entitlement to contribute phases out at adjusted gross income of $178,000 to $188,000 (joint returns) or $112,000 to $127,000 (single or head of household returns); the range for married persons filing separate returns is very limited, topping out at $10,000 (2013 figures). [IR-2012-77, *IRS Announces 2013 Pension Plan Limitations*, <http://www.irs.gov/uac/2013-Pension-Plan-Limitations> (Oct. 18, 2012) . The American Taxpayer Relief Act of 2012 authorizes in-plant Roth conversions of defined contribution accounts that are not otherwise distributable, with no income limitation. Under prior law, only amounts that were distributable (e.g., to a participant who had reached age 59 ½) could be converted to Roth form. Although the provision is effective January 1, 2013, prior account balances can be converted. [Rebecca Moore, *Fiscal Cliff Deal Extends Roth Conversions* plansponsor.com (Jan.3, 2013)]

The Saver's Credit, also known as the retirement savings contributions credit, applies to individuals and married persons filing separate returns with incomes up to $29,500 (for 2013 ), joint returns with income up to $59,000, and heads of household with income up to $44,250 . The person claiming the credit must be over 18, not a full-time student, and not the dependent of another taxpayer. The credit is a percentage of the amount contributed, with the highest percentage at the lowest income level. The credit is reported on Form 8800, Credit for Qualified Retirement Savings Contributions. [IR-2012-77] Roth 401(k) plans (i.e., plans that do not give rise to tax benefits at the time funds are deferred, but from which funds can be withdrawn tax-free at retirement) are another option. [See § 6.04[E]] Roth 401(k) plans were first authorized in 2006. There is no income limit on who can contribute. Account-holders do not get a tax deduction for their contributions, but they can withdraw funds from the account tax-free after retirement. Therefore, these plans are best for people who expect to be in a higher tax bracket after retirement than before—although it is very difficult to predict tax trends. If a Roth 401(k) account contains pre-tax matching contributions from the employer, these contributions must be kept in a separate sub-account, and will be taxable when they are withdrawn. Sponsors of prototype Roth IRA plans who wish to accept rollovers from Roth 402A accounts are required to amend their IRA documents. See Final Regulations covering 401(k), 403(b), and Roth IRA plans. [Fred Schneyer, *IRS Puts Out Roth IRA Rollover Final Regs*, plansponsor.com (June 4, 2007)] See IRS Notice 2008-30, 2008-12 I.R.B. 638 for guidance on applying the PPA to Roth IRAs. Distributions from an eligible retirement plan can be rolled over to a Roth IRA, as long as the amount is eligible for rollover (i.e., not a periodic payment, required minimum distribution, or hardship distribution); and the taxpayer includes in gross income any amount that would be includible absent the rollover. However, withholding is not required on the amounts included in gross income. The additional tax under Code § 72(m) does not apply as long as the amount rolled over remains in the account for at least five years.

The PPA increases the extent to which non-spouse beneficiaries will be able to roll over inherited benefits to an IRA, subject to most of the same rules as other eligible rollover distributions. The plan must permit the non-spouse beneficiary to make a direct rollover (a trustee-to-trustee transfer) of the eligible rollover distribution to an inherited IRA. The plan administrator must provide the non-spouse beneficiary with a written notice explaining the direct rollover rules and mandatory 20% withholding if amounts eligible for rollover are not rolled over. The non-spouse beneficiary cannot contribute to the inherited IRA, cannot roll other amounts into or out of the inherited IRA, but can perform a trustee-to-trustee transfer to another inherited IRA in the name of the decedent with the same beneficiary. [CCH Pensions & Benefits, IRS Explains Requirements for Nonspousal Distributions (Jan. 5, 2010) (benefitslink.com). Notice 2009-68, 2009-39 I.R.B. 423, includes sample notice forms]

For the year 2009 only, the obligation to take the Minimum Required Distribution from IRAs was suspended.

## § 4.08 INCIDENTAL BENEFITS

A qualified plan is permitted to offer incidental benefits such as disability, Social Security supplements for early retirees, lump-sum death benefits, incidental death benefits, or 401(h) retiree health benefits. Life insurance can be provided as an incidental benefit as long as the death benefit does not exceed 100 times the estimated monthly retirement benefit under the qualified plan it supplements. However, offering other benefits, such as other medical benefits or layoff benefits, is forbidden, and can lead to loss of plan qualification.

The Tenth Circuit ruled in 2009 that the anti-cutback rule does not apply to a death benefit, or a plan feature that pays a lump sum at retirement that is the actuarial equivalent of a death benefit, so it could lawfully be terminated. The Tenth Circuit ruled that the death benefit was not an accrued benefit, because the plan's definition of accrued benefit excluded death benefits. It could not be a retirement-type subsidy because that means only benefits that continue after retirement. [*Kerber v. Qwest Pension Plan*, 572 F.3d 1135 (10th Cir. 2009); see Stanley D. Baum, *Tenth Circuit Determines That Elimination of a Pension Plan's Death Benefit Does Not Violate ERISA's Anti-Cutback Rule*, ERISA Lawyer Blog (July 22, 2009) (benefitslink.com). See also *In re Lucent Death Benefits ERISA Litigation*, 541 F.3d 250 (3d Cir. 2008)]

## § 4.09  STRUCTURE OF ERISA

ERISA is not an easy statute to understand. A vast variety of plan provisions can legally be embodied in qualified plans, and many of these provisions depend on complex mathematical formulas. Furthermore, ERISA is both a labor law and a comprehensive and difficult piece of tax legislation.

Title I of ERISA, also referred to as the labor title, covers issues such as plan structure, fiduciary conduct, and prohibited transactions. Title II is the tax title, covering the requirements for plan qualification and tax deductions. The Title II provisions are duplicated in the Internal Revenue Code. There is some overlap between the two titles. For instance, prohibited transactions are defined in Title I, but the excise tax penalty is imposed under Title II.

Many of the provisions that are most significant for plan administration are found in Title I, Subtitle B. This subtitle is divided into six parts:

- Part 1: Reporting and disclosure;
- Part 2: Participation and vesting standards;
- Part 3: Funding standards;
- Part 4: Fiduciary responsibility;
- Part 5: Administration and enforcement;
- Part 6: Continuation coverage for health insurance.

Although there are some exceptions, the safest way to operate is just to assume that all benefit plans will be subject to at least some ERISA requirements. For example, a welfare plan (one that provides nonpension benefits such as health insurance or severance pay) is subject to most of the rules on reporting and disclosure, and the fiduciary, administration, and enforcement rules of Parts 4 and 5, but does not have to satisfy the participation, vesting, or funding standards.

## § 4.10  REQUIRED PROVISIONS FOR ALL QUALIFIED PLANS

Although within these confines a tremendous number of variations can be created, ERISA and the I.R.C. impose certain obligations on all qualified pension plans:

- The plan must be in writing [ERISA § 402(a)(1)];

- The employer must intend the plan to be permanent (although mergers and terminations are permitted under appropriate circumstances) [Reg. § 1.401-1(b)(2). Annuity, profit-sharing, and stock bonus plans are also subject to this requirement];

- The plan must provide a procedure for amendments and must indicate who has the authority to amend the plan [ERISA § 402(a)(1)];

- Plan funds must be managed through use of a trust [ERISA § 403(a), I.R.C. § 401(a)], unless they are held in a custodial account that is invested and managed by someone other than the account custodian.

- The plan must be operated for the exclusive benefit of its participants and their beneficiaries. [I.R.C. § 401(a)(2)] If the employer attempts to violate this rule by obtaining reversions of plan assets, an excise tax will be imposed under I.R.C. § 4980 unless an exception to the general rule applies. Even on termination, defined contribution plans generally cannot return any assets to the employer. Independent contractors must not be allowed to participate, because they are not considered employees;

- The plan must have a published funding policy [ERISA § 402(b)(1)];

- Contributions made to the plan, or benefits received under the plan, are subject to the limitations of the I.R.C.;

- Benefits must not be decreased when Social Security benefits increase;

- Employees must be permitted to participate in the plan as soon as they satisfy the plan's minimum participation standards [I.R.C. §§ 401(a)(3), 410];

- The plan must satisfy minimum coverage requirements, and defined benefit plans must satisfy a minimum participation rule;

- Employee contributions and salary deferrals intended for 401(k) plans must be deposited into the plan as soon as possible, always within 90 days [DOL Reg. § 2510.3-102];

- The plan must not discriminate in favor of highly compensated employees (HCEs);

- The plan's vesting schedule must satisfy federal standards—and if the plan is top-heavy (concentrates its benefits on the highest-paid group) it must vest even faster than the basic rule [I.R.C. §§ 401(a)(7), 404(a)(2), 411(b)] EGTRRA, the 2001 tax law, also increased the speed with which employer matching contributions must vest, and the PPA sped up the vesting schedule for employer's non-elective contributions;

- Benefits must be distributed only to participants and their beneficiaries (including "alternate payees" under Qualified Domestic Relations Orders). This is known as the "anti-alienation" rule. In particular, creditors cannot reach pension benefits before they have been distributed;

- Pension benefits must start within 60 days of the end of the plan year in which the individual reaches the plan's normal retirement age (NRA), reaches age 65, terminates service or has 10 years of service—whichever occurs last;

- The plan must furnish Summary Plan Descriptions (SPDs), Summaries of Material Modifications (SMMs) and other disclosure documents [see Chapter 11];

- The plan must designate at least one fiduciary who is responsible for management. Named fiduciaries are allowed to delegate certain plan responsibilities to other people, such as investment managers—but only if the plan specifically permits such delegation;

- The plan must have a procedure for making claims and appealing denials of applications. The claims procedure must be disclosed in the Summary Plan Description [See §§ 10.05, 11.02] but need not be included in the plan document itself;

- Defined benefit plans must pay premiums to the Pension Benefits Guaranty Corporation (PBGC);

- Transfers of assets between plans, and mergers and terminations of plans, are also regulated. [See I.R.C. § 411(d)(3)]

In response to the low level of savings by plan participants, many industry figures recommended that pension plans be permitted to enroll employees automatically in 401(k) plans, so that employees who did not wish to have amounts deducted from their salaries to save for retirement would have to opt out, rather than employees needing to make an affirmative commitment to open 401(k) plan accounts. Automatic enrollment began in the 1990s, and was popularized by the PPA. In September 2006, the Department of Labor released a Proposed Rule implementing relief under the PPA for fiduciaries who invest participants' assets in "qualified default investment alternatives (QDIAs)." The proposal was made to make it easier to design and administer automatic-enrollment plans. [News Release No. 06-1676-NAT U.S., <http://www.dol.gov/ebsaSearch> (Sept. 26, 2006)]

Final rules were issued in 2009 covering Qualified Automatic Contribution Arrangements (QACAs; for single-employer plans) and Eligible Automatic Contribution Arrangements (EACAs; the counterpart for multi-employer plans). The final rules allow employers to increase the percentage rate for automatic contributions during the plan year, not just at the beginning of the plan year, to reflect salary increases or performance evaluations—as long as the increase applies uniformly to all employees.

In a QACA, the employer's safe harbor contribution must be 100% vested after two years of service. Either the contribution must be 3% of pay for all eligible employees (whether or not they contribute), or the employer must match 100% of the first 1% deferred plus 50% of the next 5% deferred, up to a maximum of 3.5% of compensation. Employees must receive notice of automatic enrollment in a plan not less than 30 and not more than 90 days before they become eligible, and before the beginning of each plan year. However, if it is not practicable to give notice on that schedule (e.g., participants are eligible under the plan as soon as they are hired) then the employer can simply give notice as soon as it is practicable. Safe-harbor non-elective and matching contributions under a QACA are not eligible for hardship withdrawals. The QACA rules apply to plan years that begin on or after January 1, 2008; the EACA rules apply to plan years beginning on or after January 1, 2010. [T.D. 9447, 2009-12 I.R.B. 694; see Hodgson Russ LLP Employee Benefits Developments, IRS Publishes Final Automatic Enrollment Rules (May 2009) (benefitslink.com); Jerry Kalish, Auto-Enrollment Alphabet Soup, Employee Benefit News, <http://ebn.benefitnews.com> May 1, 2009; McKay Hochman Company, Inc. E-mail Alert 2009-18, *QDIA Notice Rules* (Nov. 20, 2009) (benefitslink.com); Rebecca Moore, *IRS Issues Final Rules on Automatic Contribution Arrangements*, plansponsor.com (Feb. 24, 2009)]

Contributions to a QACA or EACA are invested in the QDIA (Qualified Default Investment Alternative), selected not just to preserve the safety of the invested capital, but to provide appreciation for participants' long-term retirement needs. Employees must be given notice about the QDIA, and how they can change the investment of their funds.

After earlier proposals about investment advice to plan participants were withdrawn, DOL returned to the subject in 2010, proposing a revised rule limited to implementation of the PPA statutory exemption for certain limited forms of investment advice. Under the 2010 revision, advice can be given two ways: through the use of an unbiased computer model, or when the adviser's fees do not vary no matter what investments the participants choose. The computer model or level fee arrangement has to be chosen by the fiduciary, independent of adviser and its affiliates; qualifications set for the investment expert who certifies the model; investment advisers can't get compensation from affiliates on the basis of their recommendations; and advice arrangements have to be audited each year.

Additional requirements, including fee disclosure, are imposed. [Proposed rule, 75 Fed. Reg. 9360 (Mar. 2, 2010); see Rebecca Moore, *DOL Proposes New Advice Rule*, plansponsor.com (Feb. 26, 2010); Davis & Harman, LLP, *Summary of Investment Advice Regulations* (Mar. 1, 2010) (benefitslink.com); for history of the rule, see Fred Schneyer, *EBSA Delays Advice Rule Again*, plansponsor.com (Nov. 16, 2009) and *EBSA Pulls Back Controversial Advice Mandate*, plansponsor.com (Nov. 19, 2009)]

As the value of pension accounts declined, there was increasing attention to the subject of fees. In good times, high fees often are not noticed—or are accepted as a fair exchange for the excellent investment results obtained. But fees are more noticeable when account balances drop—and it is harder to argue that the mutual fund or other investment vehicle was successful enough to be entitled to high fees.

In 2010, the Supreme Court held that, in a case charging that excessive fees were imposed, the correct legal standard is whether the fees were so excessive that they must have reflected manipulation—they could not have been the result of arm's length bargaining. The case was brought by plaintiffs who alleged that Harris Associates LLP charged plan participants twice as much for managing the fund family they invested in as Harris charged non-ERISA-plan clients for similar investment services. Harris said that its fees were at or only slightly above median fees for comparable mutual funds. The Seventh Circuit ruled that mutual fund managers are only liable for excessive fees if the fees are fraudulent, but the Supreme Court imposed a stricter standard, and remanded the case to the Seventh Circuit for re-hearing using the new standard. [*Jones v. Harris*, 559 U.S. 335 (2010); see Fred Schneyer, *High Court Sides with Investors in Fee Case*, plansponsor.com.] However, the Supreme Court refused to hear the appeal of dismissal of another Seventh Circuit case about excessive 401(k) fees. [*Hecker v. Deere & Co.*, 556 F.3d 575 (7th Cir. 2009); see Fred Schneyer, *U.S. Supremes Turn Away Hecker Fee Case Appeal*, plansponsor.com (Jan. 19, 2010)]

The Supreme Court vacated an Eighth Circuit decision about whether mutual fund fees violated Section 36(b) of the Investment Company Act. The Eighth Circuit had relied on the marketplace to prevent excessively high fees from being imposed. However, the Supreme Court remanded the case to comply with *Jones v. Harris*: *Ameriprise Fin. Inc. v. Gallus*, 130 S. Ct. 2340 (U.S. 2010); see Rebecca Moore, *Supreme Court Sends Investment Adviser Fee Case Back to 8th Circuit*, plansponsor.com (Apr. 6, 2010). On remand, the Eighth Circuit held that the plaintiffs did not show that the fees were so unreasonably high that they could not have been the product of arm's length bargaining. [*Gallus v. Ameriprise,* 675 F.3d 1173 (8th Cir. 2012); see Rebecca Moore, *Ameriprise Wins Excessive Fees Case*, plansponsor.com (Apr. 12, 2012)]

In mid-2008, the DOL proposed regulations requiring the fiduciaries of individual account plans to provide specific disclosures about the plan's investment options—and the fees for these plans: see 73 Fed. Reg. 43014 (July 23, 2008). It was the third set of regulations about defined contribution plan fees—the previous ones were published at 72 Fed. Reg. 64710 and 64731 (Nov. 16, 2007), dealing with Form 5500 reporting requirements, and 72 Fed. Reg. 70988 (Dec. 13, 2007), requiring fiduciaries to obtain specific information about fees, compensation, and conflicts of interest from their service providers.

In July, 2010, DOL issued an interim final rule on fee disclosure, concentrating on the substance of disclosures that must be made and not on their form. This interim final rule deals only with pension disclosure: DOL said that it would issue another rule later covering welfare benefit plan disclosures. "Covered service providers" must provide disclosures—a category that includes not just fiduciaries, brokers, and investment advisers, but also those who receive indirect compensation from a plan. Full disclosure is required of the extent to which the covered service provider will receive compensation from third parties (i.e., not from the plan). [EBSA Interim Final Rule RIN 1210-AB08, <http://www.ofr. gov/OFRUpload/OFRData/2010-16768-Pl.pdf>; see Nevin E. Adams, *DOL Issues New Rules on Fee Disclosure*, plansponsor.com (July 15, 2010)] Regulations were published governing disclosure of fees to plan participants: see 75 Fed. Reg. 64910 (Oct. 20, 2010). Originally, these regulations were scheduled to take effect July 16, 2011, but to give employers more time to update their systems, and to conform to regulations about cost disclosure to the plan itself, their effective date was delayed until April 1, 2012: see 76 Fed. Reg. 42539 (July 19, 2011).]

Another question is the extent to which an account is invested in the employer's securities—a matter that often becomes controversial if the stock price falls, and the value of the account falls with it. T.D. 9484 [2010-24 I.R.B. 748, 75 Fed. Reg. 27927 (May 19, 2010)], effective for plan years beginning on or after January 1, 2011, provides Final Regulations under Code § 401(a)(35), a diversification requirement enacted by PPA § 901. Defined contribution plans subject to these requirements must give each participant who has at least three years of service (and beneficiaries of such participants and of deceased participants) the right to divest employer securities in their accounts and re-invest these amounts. The plan must offer at least three diversified investment options other than employer stock. Divestment/reinvestment must be allowed at reasonable intervals, at least quarterly. [Patrick C. DiCarlo, Alston & Bird LLP Erisa Litigation Advisory, *DOL Proposes Regulations Governing Fee Disclosures to Participants* (July 30, 2008) (benefitslink.com)] "Stock drop" suits are discussed in more detail in, e.g., § 15.03[C] and 15.09[A].

## § 4.11 NORMAL RETIREMENT AGE

Many ERISA and tax rules depend on the concept of drawing a pension at, before, or after the plan's Normal Retirement Age (NRA). The standard NRA remains 65, although perhaps this will change not only as life expectancies increase, but as the Social Security system phases in a higher age for receiving unreduced benefits. (The basic Social Security retirement age is gradually being increased from 65 to 67.)

However, a plan can set the NRA either higher or lower than 65. The plan can choose an NRA lower than 65 if this is customary for the company or for its industry—as long as this choice is not a device to accelerate funding. If the NRA is very low—below 55—I.R.C. § 415(b) requires that maximum pension payable under the plan be reduced, in light of the large number of payments that will be made. However, a profit-sharing plan is allowed to have an NRA lower than 55, even if this is below the industry average.

> ■ **TIP:** If the plan does not specify an NRA, the NRA will be deemed to be the age at which accrued benefits no longer increase solely on account of age or service.

If the plan sets the NRA above 65, or if there is no definition in the plan, then each participant will have an individual NRA. It will be either his or her 65th birthday or the fifth anniversary of plan participation, whichever comes later.

See T.D. 9325, 2007-24 I.R.B. 386, for Final Regulations giving rules for determining whether a plan's NRA is valid if the plan makes in-service distributions under a phased retirement program. In general, the NRA must be set at least as high as the industry standard, although there is a safe harbor if the NRA is at least 62, or is between 55 and 62 and the employer makes a good-faith determination that the NRA is appropriate for the industry.

The Supreme Court declined to review the Seventh Circuit's *Fry v. Exelon* decision from 2009. The Seventh Circuit ruled that a plan sponsor could define NRA other than as a specific age. In that case, Fry took a lump sum in 2003 from a cash balance plan, and later challenged the plan's definition of NRA, saying that it violated ERISA because it was used to avoid the whipsaw calculation. (This was pre-PPA, so there had not yet been a definitive statement that whipsaw is not required.) [*Fry v. Exelon*, 571 F.3d 644 (7th Cir. 2009), *cert. denied*, 130 S. Ct. 1504 (Feb. 22, 2010); see Rebecca Moore, *Supreme Court Lets Stand Alternate Definitions for Retirement Age*, plansponsor.com (Feb. 23, 2010)]

However, in 2013, the District Court for the Southern District of New York held that PriceWaterhouseCooper's cash balance plan did not define NRA appropriately. The plan defined NRA as five "years of service." The district court said that this was not an age. Unlike *Fry,* this case did not use a definition based on the employee's anniversary; the court held that ERISA allows a definition based on the employee's anniversary, but that is not identical to a year of service. [*Laurent v. PriceWaterhouseCooper,*No. 06 Civ. 2280 (JPO) (S.D.N.Y. Aug. 8, 2013)]

In mid-2012, the Fourth Circuit held that increases in benefit accruals to participants who have reached NRA do not violate ERISA's prohibition against backloading in later years of service. (The plan defined NRA as the earlier of age 64 or 60 months of vesting service.) The 133 1/3% test forbids accrual of benefits more than one-third greater than the annual rate of accrual in the previous year.

This rule was adopted to prevent employers from skimping on accrual rates in the early years of service, when turnover is highest. The Fourth Circuit held that anti-backloading rules no longer apply after the participant reaches NRA. [*McCorkle v. Bank of America Corp.*, 688 F.3d 164 (4th Cir. 2012); see Mark Casciari and Justin T. Curley, *The Court Of Appeals For The Fourth Circuit Finds No Backloading Problem With Accrual Increases That Occur After Normal Retirement Age*, Seyfarth Shaw ERISA & Employee Benefits Litgation Blog (Aug. 21, 2012) (benefitslink.com)]

### § 4.12 NORMAL RETIREMENT BENEFIT

The NRB, or Normal Retirement Benefit, is a related concept. It is either the benefit commencing at the NRA or the early retirement benefit (if the plan provides one)—whichever is greater. The early retirement benefit is not adjusted actuarially for this purpose, even though it will be paid for more years than if benefits had commenced at the NRA. Early retirement subsidies are not counted if they continue only until the retiree becomes eligible for Social Security, and if they do not exceed the Social Security benefit.

Not everyone retires on the anniversary of plan participation. If benefits depend on average compensation for, e.g., three or five years, then Treas. Reg. § 1.411(a)-7(c)(5) mandates treatment of the last partial year of service as a full year.

Although there is growing interest in "phased retirement" (a diminishing work schedule creating a transition between full-time employment and full retirement), tax law still has little flexibility in this area. In mid-2004, the Supreme Court ruled that the "anti-cutback" rule of ERISA § 204(g) prohibits a plan from being amended in a way that suspends payments of early retirement benefits the individual has already accrued. In this case, the suit was brought by workers who took early retirement at a time that their pension plan called for suspension of pension payments if they took another job as construction workers. Instead, they worked as construction supervisors. Later, the plan was amended to suspend the benefit payments to anyone who worked in the construction industry at all. The Supreme Court found the amendment improper because workers are entitled to rely on the terms of their pension plan in making career-planning decisions. [*Central Laborers' Pension Fund v. Heinz*, 541 U.S. 739 (2004)]

### § 4.13 PARTICIPATION AND COVERAGE

Both defined benefit and defined contribution plans are subject to "minimum coverage" rules under I.R.C. § 410(b). Remember, one of the main motives in passing ERISA was to prevent plans from concentrating unduly on providing benefits to stockholders and managers. However, it can be difficult to satisfy the various tests in a small company (See § 4.14[A] for top-heavy plan rules) or in a company where there is a great disparity between managers' pay and rank-and-file pay, or where there is a stable group of HCEs but heavy turnover in rank-and-file employees.

To satisfy the minimum coverage rules, the plan must either cover a percentage of the rank and file that is at least 70% of the percentage of highly compensated employees covered by the plan; or the plan must cover a reasonable classification of employees that is not discriminatory. Furthermore, the contributions made on behalf of, or the benefits provided to, the rank-and-file must equal at least 70% of those made or provided to the highly compensated.

Defined benefit plans are subject to a minimum participation rule. On each day of the plan year, the plan must benefit either 40% of all the company's work force, or 50 people, whichever is less. However, plans that are not top-heavy and do not benefit any highly compensated employee or former employee are exempt from the minimum participation rule.

The I.R.C. does not require qualified plans to cover all employees from the time of hiring. It is permissible for a plan to require employees to be at least 21 years old and to have completed one year of service before being eligible for participation. Part-time employees must be covered if they can work 1,000 hours within a 12-month period. If plan benefits become 100% vested after only two years, a qualified plan (other than a 401(k) plan) can require two years of service for participation.

The Northern District of Illinois held that it did not violate the minimum participation rule to deny pension participation to part time workers. An employer may limit participation to certain groups or categories of workers, as long as the classification is not based on age or length of service. [*Krok v. University of Chicago,* No. Case No. 11-cv-01092, 2012 U.S. Dist. LEXIS 46952 (N.D. Ill. Apr. 3, 2012); see Rebecca Moore, *Court Rules on Eligibility of Benefits for University Employees,* plansponsor.com (Apr. 6, 2012)]

## § 4.14 VESTING

### [A] Generally

Participation in a plan is only the first step toward eventually receiving a pension. Vesting is the process of the benefits becoming nonforfeitable. ERISA includes detailed vesting rules to prevent earlier abuses, under which plans were often drafted so that so many years of service were required to achieve a pension that many rank-and-file employees would end up forfeiting their pensions (with the forfeitures going to swell the accounts of highly compensated executives and stockholders).

The normal benefit must always be nonforfeitable at the normal retirement age. It is not required that employees immediately gain 100% ownership of their defined contribution accounts, or the amounts contributed on their behalf to a defined benefit plan. Vesting is the process of moving toward 100% ownership. The Code prescribes minimum funding schedules; employers are always permitted to give employees faster vesting. "Cliff vesting" means that, for a period of time, the employee is not vested at all—but at a certain point, the entire account becomes vesting at once. "Graded vesting" means that part of the account vests each year, until 100% vesting is attained.

There are only two basic vesting schedules allowed by I.R.C. § 411(a):

- Five-year cliff vesting: participants are not vested at all for the first five years of service, but then they are immediately 100% vested as to employer contributions;

- Three-to-seven graded vesting: no vesting at all for three years, but full vesting by seven years of service, increasing proportionately in years 4, 5, and 6.

Top-heavy plans must provide even faster vesting—three-year cliff or six-year graded—but plans with a lot of participants usually are not top-heavy.

The PPA required cash balance plans to provide 100% vesting after three years of service—but WRERA suspended this requirement.

For an example of how vesting works, if a participant leaves employment at a time when he or she is 60% vested, then a participant in a defined contribution plan will be entitled to $60 of every $100 in his or her individual account. A participant in a defined benefit plan will be entitled to an annuity of $60/month for every $100/month that would have been payable if he or she had remained at work until becoming 100% vested.

EGTRRA, the 2001 tax legislation, provides even faster vesting for employer matching contributions (as distinct from the employer's own contributions). Vesting for matching contributions must be either three-year cliff vesting or graded vesting over two to six years (20% in the second year of service, 40% in the third year, etc.). Under the PPA, employer non-elective contributions made for years beginning after December 31, 2006 must satisfy either three-year cliff or two-to-six-year graded vesting.

## [B]  Vesting on Termination

All qualified plans must provide that, if the plan is completely or partially terminated, all affected participants immediately become 100% vested. [I.R.C. § 411(d)(3)] For plans that are not subject to the minimum funding standard of I.R.C. § 412 (for instance, profit-sharing and stock bonus plans), 100% vesting must also occur when the employer completely ceases to make contributions to the plan. A profit-sharing or stock bonus plan is deemed terminated on the day when the plan administrator notifies the IRS of the cessation of contributions.

## [C]  Vesting and Service

For vesting purposes, a year of service is a period of 12 consecutive months during which the employee performs at least 1,000 hours of service. Plans are not required to provide fractional years of service credit—i.e., if someone works only 500 hours, the employer does not have to credit half a year of service.

For the purposes of vesting or participation for accrual purposes, a year of service can be any period of 12 consecutive months that the employer designates. But a year of service for plan eligibility purposes must start on the first day of employment. A plan can have more than one vesting year. If the plan selects a single vesting year for convenience, it doesn't have to be the same as the plan year.

## § 4.15  BREAK-IN-SERVICE RULES

For some pension-related purposes, it makes a big difference whether the individual has been continuously employed by the employer sponsoring the plan, or whether employment has been interrupted: whether the person has been laid off and then recalled, for instance. Interruption of continuous employment is called a "break in service"—a concept that has many implications.

A one-year break in service has occurred when a person renders 501 or fewer hours of service for the employer in a particular year. If someone works more than 501 but less than 1000 hours for the employer in a given year the employer does not have to credit a year of service, but cannot penalize the employee for the break in service.

After someone has had a one-year break, the employer can disregard service before the break for vesting purposes until the employee has come back to work and completed a year of service. After there have been five consecutive one-year breaks in service, a defined contribution plan, or some insured defined benefit plans, can treat the vested benefits as forfeited, and allocate them to other participants.

If the participant was 0% vested before the break in service, the "Rule of Parity" requires the plan to add up the number of years of service before the break. If the number of consecutive one-year breaks is at least five, or is greater than or equal to the aggregate number of pre-break years of service (whichever is greater), the rule allows the pre-break years to be disregarded for vesting purposes, even if the participant is later rehired.

However, under the Retirement Equity Act of 1984 [Pub. L. No. 98-397], a break in service that is caused by parenting leave probably cannot be counted against the employee. A reservist who is called to active military duty does not have a break in service during the active-duty period. [See § 1.18, *infra*, for more about the employment law implications of call-ups of reservists and members of the National Guard]

In its May 18, 2009 decision, *AT&T Corp. v. Hulteen*, 556 U.S. 701, the Supreme Court ruled that AT&T did not commit sex discrimination when it failed to amend its pre-PDA seniority system to equalize the treatment of pregnancy leave taken before the effective date of the PDA with other leave. AT&T was operating a bona fide seniority system and was entitled to avoid liability.

## § 4.16 PLAN LIMITS

One of the basic purposes of ERISA is to prevent plans from unduly favoring executives, managers, and other highly paid employees. One of the ways ERISA furthers this objective is by placing limits on the amount that can be contributed each year to a defined contribution plan, deferred in a 401(k) plan, or provided as a benefit under a defined benefit plan.

The underlying principle is that plan limits are adjusted annually. The adjustment reflects changes in the Consumer Price Index. Starting in 2003, the changes are to be rounded down in $5,000 increments; previously, changes were adjusted in $10,000 increments.

Before 2000, I.R.C. § 415(e) imposed a combined limitation on the allocations to defined contribution plans plus accrued benefits from defined benefit plans. However, as of 2000, plans are permitted to—but not obligated to—impose a combined limitation with respect to employees who participate in both types of plans. Defined benefit plans are allowed to increase benefits (for retirees as well as active employees) to reflect repeal of the combined limitation. See Notice 2007-28, 2007-14 I.R.B. 880, for post-PPA application of the combined limit, and its effect on the employer's maximum deduction.

The breakdown below contains the limitations applicable to various amounts applicable to pension administration for the years 2001–2013. As noted above, figures remained the same in 2009, 2010, and 2011, but were increased in 2012–2013.

1. Maximum annual benefit under a defined benefit plan (§ 415(b)(1)(A)): $140,000/$160,000/$160,000/$165,000/$170,000/$175,000/$180,000/ $185,000/$195,000/$195,000/$200,000/$205,000; the maximum amount is reduced for benefits that begin before age 62, but increased for benefits beginning after age 65.

2. Maximum contribution to a defined contribution plan (§ 415(c)(1)(a)): $35,000 and 25% of compensation/$40,000 and 100% of compensation/ $40,000 and 100% of compensation/$41,000 and 100% of compensation/ $42,000 and 100% of compensation/$44,000 and 100% of compensation/ $45,000 and 100% of compensation/$46,000 and 100% of compensation/ $49,000 and 100% of compensation/$49,000 and 100% of compensation/ $50,000/$51,000 and 100% of compensation.

3. Definition of a "highly compensated employee" under § 414(q)(1)(B): $85,000 a year/$90,000 a year/$90,000 a year/$90,000 a year/$95,000/ $100,000/$100,000/$105,000/$110,000/$110,000/$115,000/$115,000.

4. Limit on annual compensation that can be taken into account in making calculations, as prescribed by §§ 401(a)(17), 404(l): $170,000/$200,000/$200,000/$205,000/$210,000/$220,000/$225,000/$230,000/$245,000/$245,000/$ $255,000.

5. Maximum 401(k) deferral: $10,500/$11,000 plus catch-up contributions for persons over 50/$12,000 plus catch-up contributions/$13,000 plus catch-up contributions/$14,000 plus catch-up contributions/$15,000 plus catch-up contributions/$15,500 plus catch-up contributions/$15,500 plus catch-up contributions/$16,500 plus catch-up contributions/$16,500 plus catch-up contributions/$17,000 plus catch-up contributions $17,500 plus catch-up contributions. For 2009–2011, the catch-up contribution is $2,500 for purposes of Code §§ 401(k)(11) and 408(p), and $5,500 for other purposes. These amounts did not change in 2012 or 2013.

## § 4.17  EMPLOYEE CONTRIBUTIONS

Although 401(k) plans get their basic funding from employees' deferred salary (and may get matching contributions from the employer), pension plans work the other way around. They get their basic funding from the employer, but some plans require and other plans permit employees to make additional contributions to the plan. Internal Revenue Code § 411(c)(2) characterizes employee contributions as mandatory if making the contribution is a precondition of the employer match.

> ■ **TIP:**   The Bankruptcy Abuse Prevention and Consumer Protection Act of 2005 (BAPCPA; Pub. L. No. 109-8) gives employees additional protection against their contributions being seized by their employer's creditors, when the employee has made the contribution but the employer has not yet deposited it into the plan.

Employee contributions are also important in determining whether or not a plan discriminates in favor of highly compensated employees. I.R.C. § 414(g) contains the formula for testing whether the employer's aggregate contributions to the plan on behalf of HCEs are too high. If the plan fails to satisfy the requirements of this section, it will be disqualified, unless the excess contributions made on behalf of the HCEs, plus the earnings on the excess contributions, are returned to the company's employees by the end of the plan year after the year of the excess contribution. A 10% excise also applies to excess employee contributions (e.g., made by HCEs) that are not distributed within two and a half months of the end of the plan year.

Benefits attributable to employer contributions cannot be assigned or anticipated before they are received, except in the form of a QDRO. But employees can withdraw some or all of their voluntary contributions while continuing to be employed and to participate in the plan. Employees must always have the right to withdraw their own voluntary contributions to the plan at any time, without the accrued benefits attributable to employer contributions becoming forfeitable. [I.R.C. § 401(a)(19)] However, if the plan mandates employee contributions, I.R.C. § 411(a)(3)(D) allows the plan to provide that employer contributions will be forfeited if a participant withdraws any mandatory employee contributions at a time when he or she is less than 50% vested. If the benefits are repaid within five years after the withdrawal, or two years after the employee returns to participation under the plan (whichever comes first), the benefits must be restored.

Employees are always 100% vested in their own voluntary contributions to a pension plan. When an employer matches these voluntary contributions, EGTRRA requires vesting in the employer's matching contributions to occur either on a three-year cliff schedule, or a six-year graded schedule, beginning with 20% vesting in the second year of the employee's service.

A 2010 DOL Final Rule allows a safe harbor when a "small plan" (fewer than 100 participants) performs wage withholding or receives contributions from participants and the contribution is deposited within seven business days after the employer received or withheld the money—even if it would have been possible to deposit it sooner. However, if contributions or loan repayments are not deposited in a timely fashion, then losses and interest on late contributions are calculated from the actual date on which they could have been deposited, not from the end of the safe harbor period. [Transamerica Center for Retirement Studies 2010-01, *Department of Labor Final Rule on Definition of Plan Assets: Participant Contributions* (Jan. 22, 2010) (benefitslink.com)]

The significant Supreme Court case of *Hughes Aircraft Co. v. Jacobson* [525 U.S. 432 (1999)] involved a defined benefit plan that mandated employee contributions (most defined benefit plans do not). A large part of the plan was attributable to employee contributions. The Hughes plan operated at a surplus. The employer suspended its contributions in light of the surplus. It also amended the plan to provide for early retirement benefits and to add a new benefit structure for new participants. Under the new structure, employee contributions were no longer required, because the plan was funded by the surplus from the older plan.

The Supreme Court did not accept the contention of the employee plaintiffs that the employer had an obligation to share the plan surplus with the employees who contributed to it, rather than using the surplus to reduce the employer's future obligations. In the Supreme Court's view, in a defined benefit plan, the employer assumes and also controls the risks. Any surplus can properly be used for other obligations—because the employer is always obligated to provide the vested benefits provided by the plan. In this analysis, Hughes did not violate ERISA, because it did not stop providing the vested benefits defined by the plan.

Nor did the Supreme Court accept the argument that Hughes had improperly terminated the old plan. Instead, the court permitted an amendment creating a new benefit structure (and did not treat it as the creation of a second plan) if only one pool of assets funds both obligations. Benefits continued to be paid to longer-serving employees on the basis of the original plan, so the old plan was not terminated merely because the additional benefit structure was added.

## § 4.18  PLAN LOANS

Under the right circumstances, plans are permitted to make loans to participants. These loans can be a useful resource if, for instance, a plan participant wishes to buy a house or pay a child's tuition. Loans to rank-and-file participants are usually permitted. However, a direct or indirect loan to a "party in interest" or a "disqualified person" is a prohibited transaction, unless a prohibited transaction exemption is available to justify the loan.

Under I.R.C. § 72(p), the general rule is that plan loans are treated as distributions—in other words, taxable income to the recipient. But there are certain exceptions. A loan will not be treated as a distribution if it does not exceed $50,000 or half the present value of the employee's nonforfeitable accrued benefit under the plan (whichever is less). (The employee can borrow up to $10,000, even if this amount is more than half the value of the accrued benefit.) Where the participant's account balance is the only security, the loan is theoretically not permitted to exceed half the pledged amount. The DOL Regulations dealing with plan loans do not forbid participants from borrowing funds from their accounts, pledging 50% of the account, and then taking hardship withdrawals, even though these steps have the effect of reducing the security below 50% of the account. [See Reg. § 2550.408-1(f)(2)]

The agreement to take a loan from the plan must call for repayment within five years, in payments made at least quarterly, with level amortization. Plans are permitted to impose variable interest rates on plan loans.

> ■ **TIP:**  BAPCA (Pub. L. No. 109-8), the 2005 bankruptcy reform statute, makes it clear that when an employee files for bankruptcy protection (even a Chapter 13 wage-earner plan), it is not a violation of the automatic stay for the employer to withhold from the employee's wages in order to repay a plan loan from a qualified plan. Plan loans do not qualify for the automatic discharge provision of Bankruptcy Code § 523, and bankruptcy plans are not permitted to materially alter the terms of a plan loan. However, amounts that an employee uses to repay plan loans are not considered "disposable income" and therefore cannot be reached by the employee's other creditors.

For reservists and National Guard members on active duty, federal law limits interest rates on all loans to the service member (including plan loans) to 6%. However, plan fiduciaries have the right to petition the relevant court to permit a higher interest rate. Under USERRA (See § 1.18, *infra*), a pension plan is allowed—but not obligated—to suspend the obligation to make regular repayments of plan loans during active military service.

Publicly traded companies must also be aware of the Sarbanes-Oxley Act [Pub. L. No. 107-204] ban on loans made by such companies to their directors and executive officers; this prohibition took effect on July 30, 2002, although loan arrangements already in effect on that date are exempt as long as their terms are not materially modified after July 30, 2002.

Plan loans made to parties in interest are likely also to constitute prohibited transactions for ERISA fiduciary purpose, subject to a 15% excise tax.

Early in 2009, amendments to Regulation Z were published, exempting most retirement plan loans from the Truth in Lending Act. The Federal Reserve Board's Board of Governors said that plan loans are different from regular loans because there is no third-party creditor to set finance charges, and the principal and interest are reinvested in the participant's account. To qualify for the exemption, which takes effect July 1, 2010, the loan must be made to a plan participant, from fully vested funds in the participant's account, and the loan must comply with Internal Revenue Code requirements, including Code § 72. [Federal Reserve Reg. § 226.3(g), Document E8-31185, 74 Fed. Reg. 5244 (Jan. 29, 2009); see Rebecca Moore, *Plan Loans Exempt from Truth-in-Lending Disclosure Requirements*, plansponsor.com (Mar. 13, 2009)]

Under Federal Reserve Board regulations revised July 1, 2010, loans to plan participants made from fully vested funds in the participant's account in a qualified plan are exempt from TILA, but loans to beneficiaries and QDRO alternate payees require disclosures. The TILA exemption is also unavailable for loans that violate Code § 72(p)—e.g., those that have a term greater than five years, exceed the maximum loan amount, or are not repaid in equal installments. If the plan is subject to the ERISA disclosure requirements, the SPD must disclose the fees or charges that can be imposed on plan loans. [Deloitte's Washington Bulletin, *Most Plan Loans Now Exempt from Truth-in-Lending Act Disclosures* (Aug. 9, 2010) (benefitslink.com)]

The IRS announced relaxation of the verification requirements for plan loans (and hardship distributions) taken in connection with Superstorm Sandy. A plan will not be deemed to violate the Code merely because it made a loan or hardship distribution between October 26, 2012 and February 1, 2013, based on needs caused by Sandy to an employee whose workplace, principal residence, or principal residence of a close family member was in the identified disaster area and whose financial records were destroyed. The usual calculation of maximum permitted hardship distribution will apply. [Announcement 2012-44, 2012-49 I.R.B. 663. This relief is in addition to relief under Code § 7508A provided by IR-2012-83.]

## § 4.19 EMPLOYER'S DEDUCTION

An employer that maintains a qualified defined benefit plan is entitled to deduct the greatest of these three amounts:

- The minimum funding standard as provided by I.R.C. § 412;

- The amount necessary to fund the cost of covering all the employees for their projected future service;

- The amount necessary to fund present and future costs, which may include liabilities stemming from service performed before the plan was established.

In 2007, the IRS published Q&A on the PPA's rules for the employer's deduction for contributions to the retirement plan (Code § 404). If the plan year is not the same as the employer's tax year, the employer can choose to use the deduction limit for the plan year that begins in the tax year; the plan year that ends in the tax year; or a weighted average of the two. For calculating the combined limit when an employer sponsors both defined benefit and defined contribution plans, and the employer's contributions to the defined contribution plan exceed 6% of compensation, the employer contribution to the defined compensation plan minus 6% of compensation is applied to the combined limit. [Notice 2007-28, 2007-14 I.R.B. 880; see Rebecca Moore, *IRS Notice Clarifies PPA Employer Deduction Limitations*, plansponsor.com (Mar. 13, 2007)]

## § 4.20  REVERSIONS

If there were no statutory ban, unscrupulous employers might raid pension assets when they needed cash, or might terminate plans merely to recoup assets or excess assets. To prevent this, defined contribution plans (including profit-sharing and stock bonus plans) usually cannot return any assets to the employer under any circumstances. Even forfeitures (amounts contributed on behalf of employees whose employment terminates before they become vested) are to be allocated to other participants in the plan.

Under appropriate circumstances, employers can receive reversions from a defined benefit plan after satisfaction of all obligations under the plan to employees. Nor may the employer lawfully transfer assets from an overfunded plan to an underfunded plan.

Internal Revenue Code § 4980 imposes an excise tax on the amount of assets reverting to an employer from a qualified plan. The tax rate, for reversions occurring after September 30, 1990, is at least 20%. The rate rises to 50% unless the employer either transfers 25% of the assets in question to a qualified replacement plan, or increases the benefits under the terminating plan to the extent of 20% of the previous benefits to participants. A qualified replacement plan covers at least 95% of the active employees from the terminated plan who continue to be employed.

## § 4.21 FORFEITURES

Depending on the plan, at least some employees—and perhaps the vast majority of the rank-and-file workforce—will terminate employment before they become vested. The contributions made on account of such employees are known as forfeitures.

Under I.R.C. §§ 401(a)(8) and 404(a)(2), defined benefit plans are required to provide that forfeitures will not be applied to increase the benefits any employee would otherwise receive. Instead, favorable plan experience when it comes to forfeitures (or mortality or employee turnover) reduces the amount the employer has to contribute to the plan. In contrast, defined contribution plans are allowed to—and usually do—allocate forfeitures to the accounts of other participants.

If someone leaves employment, and is later rehired by the same company, the eventual retirement benefit must be adjusted actuarially to reflect both periods of employment (unless the break-in-service rules make this unnecessary). Another option is for the plan to give timely notice of its provisions for suspension of benefits, so there is no forfeiture. [Treas. Reg. § 2520.203-3(b)(4)]

When an employee dies, the plan can impose forfeiture of his or her unvested benefits, except if a Qualified Preretirement Survivor Annuity (QPSA) is required. [See § 12.06] Mis-handling of forfeitures is a common target of IRS audits. The IRS requires forfeitures to be used or allocated for the plan year in which they arise—or, in appropriate circumstances, in the following plan year. Forfeitures can be used to pay reasonable administrative expenses of the plan; to reduce the employer's contribution; to restore previously forfeited participant accounts; or to provide additional contributions to participants. Placing the forfeited amounts into a suspense account is not permitted. For two years after the error, mistakes in handling forfeitures can be corrected with the IRS' Employee Plans Compliance Resolution System (EPCRS), a program that allows plans to return to compliance on easy terms. After the two-year period, voluntary correction program (VCP) must be used unless the failure is considered insignificant. VCP must be used if the terms of the plan are incorrect and a retroactive plan amendment is required to correct them. [Chadron J. Patton, *Common Plan Mistakes: Failure to Timely Allocate Forfeitures*, Spencer Fane (Nov. 16, 2012) (benefitslink.com)]

## § 4.22 DISCRIMINATION TESTING

One of the most basic plan concepts is that a plan must be operated for the exclusive benefit of its participants and beneficiaries. Furthermore, one of the main reasons for the creation of ERISA, and its elaborate structure of rules, is to prevent plans from being administered so that company owners, or major executives, get generous benefits while rank-and-file workers get little or nothing. A qualified plan must be "tested" for "discrimination." In this context, discrimination does not mean discrimination on the basis of sex, race, nationality, and so forth; it means allowing a disproportionate share of plan benefits to go to Highly Compensated Employees (HCEs).

A pension, annuity, profit-sharing, or stock bonus plan can lawfully favor HCEs in terms of contributions or benefits, but not both. [See I.R.C. §§ 401(a)(4), 404(a)(2)] Internal Revenue Code § 414(q) says that, for plan years after 1996, an HCE is defined as someone who owned 5% or more of the employer company's stock in either the current or the preceding year—or someone whose compensation for the preceding year was at least $80,000, as adjusted for inflation. For 2013, the adjusted figure is $ $115,000. The employer has the right to choose to use an alternative definition, under which HCEs are those who not only earn more than the adjusted amount, but are also in the top 20% of earners in the company.

The Code used to contain rules called "family aggregation rules" (nicknamed "aggravation rules" because of their complexity) under which the compensation of several members of the family owning a family business had to be combined for purposes including discrimination testing. However, effective for plan years beginning on and after January 1, 1997, the family aggregation rules were abolished by the Small Business Job Protection Act (SBJPA) of 1996. [Pub. L. No. 104-188]

It does not violate the antidiscrimination rules for a plan to be "integrated" with Social Security within limits set by the "permitted disparity" rules of Code § 401(l). In effect, the employer can treat the employee's Social Security benefit (which was partially funded by the employer's FICA contributions) as part of the pension, or the employer can treat its FICA contributions as pension contributions.

The subject of discrimination testing is too complex to be fully laid out in this book. However, it should be noted that the Code includes "safe harbor" provisions for discrimination testing. Plans are not obligated to follow the safe harbor rules; they can set their own formulas. But if they do follow the safe harbor rules, they are sure not to be challenged by the IRS on this issue.

## § 4.23  LEASED EMPLOYEES

Leased employees (hired by a company from an agency that supplies workers) play a significant role in the economy. However, it is often the case that the treatment of a particular individual varies depending on the context. It is simplistic to say that a person is just an employee or a non-employee. Internal Revenue Code § 414(n) requires some people to be treated as employees eligible for plan participation even though they are formally employed by a leasing company rather than by the company for whom they perform services each day.

Section 414(n) refers to "leased employees," who are nominally employed by a "leasing organization" (e.g., an organization that furnishes temporary and contingent workers) but who "perform services" for a "service recipient." Instead of paying the leased employees directly, the service recipient pays the employees' wages (and an agency commission) to the leasing organization, which handles payroll functions including tax withholding.

However, the leased employees will be treated as employees of the service recipient when it comes to determining whether the service recipient's pension plans discriminate in favor of highly compensated employees. If the leasing organization maintains a pension plan for the employees it leases out, its contributions or benefits are treated as if they came from the service recipient for the service recipient's discrimination tests. The leasing organization's plan must count all service by leased employees for the leasing organization (even when they're leased out to a service recipient) with respect to coverage, vesting, contributions, and benefits under its own plan.

Service recipients have to count leased employees when they test their plans under the minimum participation, age and service, vesting, and top-heavy rules. They must be taken into account when computing limits on compensation and benefits and whether contributions to the plan are deductible. Furthermore, the leased employee will be treated as an employee under the Code's rules for fringe benefits such as group term life insurance, accident and health insurance, cafeteria plans, and dependent care assistance. Leased employees also have COBRA rights (they can elect continuation of health coverage).

For I.R.C. § 414(n) purposes, leased employees are those who provide services that last more than a year to a service recipient in conformity with the service recipient's agreement with the leasing organization. As a result of amendments made by the Small Business Job Protection Act of 1996, the test for 1997 and later years is whether the service recipient provides the primary direction or control for the work. (Service for related companies, such as the service recipient's controlled group of corporations, is aggregated with service for the service recipient.)

These rules relate to "substantially full-time service," which is defined as 1,500 hours of service in a 12-month period, or a job that is equivalent to 75% of the hours that the service recipient's actual employees put in during a 12-month period. In other words, after a year of the recipient's full-time work, the leased employee is treated as the service recipient's employee for pension testing purposes. However, if the worker is a common-law employee for other purposes, this safe harbor cannot apply.

Even if leased employees have to be counted in determining whether the service recipient's pension plans are discriminatory, they do not have to be offered participation in the plan until they satisfy any conditions for plan participation lawfully imposed by the plan (e.g., if the employer imposes an age-21 minimum for participation, and a leased employee starts working for the employer at age

19, completing a year of service at age 20, participation can be delayed until the leased employee reaches 21).

To qualify for the safe harbor, the service recipient must get 20% or less of its rank-and-file workforce (that is, workers who are not HCEs) through leasing—and the leasing organization must have its own qualified pension plan that fits particularly stringent criteria. The leasing organization's plan must be a money purchase plan. It must not be integrated with Social Security. The leasing organization's employees must be able to participate as soon as they are hired by the organization. They must be fully vested immediately. Furthermore, the leasing organization must contribute at least 10% of compensation for each plan participant.

Although it is good practice to have individuals you believe to be independent contractors sign waivers agreeing that they are not entitled to participate in pension and benefit plans, these waivers are not sufficient if, under otherwise applicable legal principles, they really are common-law employees. The IRS will issue determination letters as to whether contingent employees are leased employees and, if so, how it affects the plan's qualification.

## § 4.24 COMMUNICATING WITH EMPLOYEES

The subject of communications and notification to employees rates a chapter of its own (see Chapter 11), so here it will merely be noted that the plan administrator is responsible for reporting and disclosure, and can be held liable if appropriate disclosures are not made.

ERISA permits three methods of communication:

- Giving each employee a copy of the plan itself;

- Giving each employee a booklet containing the Summary Plan Description (SPD), describing the features of the plan in understandable language;

- Posting a notice on the bulletin board to inform employees that the company has adopted a plan, and where copies of the plan documents can be consulted.

Nearly all plans adopt the second alternative. The actual plan document is a lengthy, highly technical legal document, and doesn't do much to inform the average employee about rights and obligations under the plan.

■ **TIP:** The very important case of *Amara v. Cigna*, 131 S. Ct. 1866 (2011), discussed in more detail in Chapter 7, holds that the SPD is merely a tool used by the plan to communicate about the plan. If the SPD contradicts the terms of the plan, the plan terms—and not the SPD that the participant actually received—must prevail. The Supreme Court also said that employees cannot sue under ERISA § 502(a)(1)(B) if there are errors in the SPD.

To an ever-increasing extent, employers are permitted to use e-mail and secure Websites to deliver information to employees.

Traditionally, plan communications for defined benefit plans included a Summary Annual Report (SAR). The PPA adopted a new disclosure document, the Annual Funding Notice, to replace the SAR. Defined benefit plans that are not insured by the PBGC (e.g., professional service companies and owner-only plans) are not required to provide an Annual Funding Notice. [Form 5500 Help.com, *Clarification—SARs for Defined Benefit Plans* (Feb. 2, 2009) (benefitslink.com)]

## § 4.25  FIDUCIARY DUTY

A fiduciary is anyone who has charge of someone else's property or finances. Fiduciaries have legal duties to act honestly, prudently, and in the best interests of the owner of the assets. Pension plan fiduciaries have a duty to invest intelligently, selecting a diversified portfolio of appropriate investments that do not involve an excessive degree of risk.

ERISA obligates fiduciaries to administer the plan exclusively in the interests of plan participants and their beneficiaries. Specifically, if there is a situation in which one strategy would be most beneficial to the participants and another strategy would be most beneficial to the corporation sponsoring the plan, the fiduciaries must choose the first course of action, not the second.

If the plan has more than one named fiduciary, they are jointly and severally liable. Someone who alleges fiduciary impropriety can sue any one fiduciary, all of them, or any combination, and can collect the entire amount of liability from each one or from any combination of fiduciaries—no matter which fiduciary was actually at fault. The harshness of this high standard is relieved somewhat by the fact that fiduciaries who are sued can bring fiduciaries who weren't sued into the lawsuit, and can make them pay their fair share.

In recent years, fiduciary liability has been one of the most active areas of employment-related litigation (see Chapter 15 for details). In particular, allegations of breach of fiduciary duty have often been made based on a theory that it was imprudent to retain employer stock as a plan investment, or to fail to warn employees of various factors contributing to decline in the value of the stock. However, these allegations are very seldom successful.

## § 4.26  BANKRUPTCY EFFECTS

Confusion may arise because the Bankruptcy Code uses the term "plan" to refer to the reorganization plan resolving creditors' claims, and not to ERISA plans. A Chapter 11 filing, in which the debtor continues to do business while reorganizing, sometimes affects ERISA plans, and sometimes does not; it is common for employers to modify or terminate ERISA plans as part of the reorganization process. Employee benefit claims against a bankrupt employer may include unpaid wages, vacation pay, severance pay, Worker's Compensation, insurance, and retirement benefits. Claims against the bankruptcy estate for wages and pension or welfare benefits are unsecured claims, and are paid according to the Bankruptcy Code's system of priorities. First priority is given to administrative claims, including wages, salaries, and commissions for services performed after the bankruptcy filing.

Before the 2005 bankruptcy reform legislation was passed, each employee was entitled to a third priority claim of up to $4,925 for wages, salaries, commissions, vacation, sick leave, and severance pay relating to the period 90 days before the bankruptcy filing or 90 days before the cessation of the employer's business—whichever came first. The Bankruptcy Abuse Prevention and Consumer Protection Act of 2005 (BAPCPA), Pub. L. No. 109-8, increased the amount to $10,000 and the period to 180 days before the filing or cessation of business.

Defined benefit plans, including 401(k) plans, are treated the same way as other employee benefits when priorities are set, based on whether the contributions relate to pre- or post-petition services. However, to motivate employees, employers often petition the bankruptcy court for permission to make contributions that were pending at the time of filing such as deferrals withheld from paychecks but not yet deposited into the 401(k) plan trust.

Bankruptcy Code § 1114 provides special protection for retirees' non-pension benefits (health coverage, life insurance, disability insurance). In effect, they become super-priority administrative expenses and a court order is required for the debtor or bankruptcy trustee to modify them. [Kenni B. Merritt, *Employee Benefits in Bankruptcy: The Employer's Perspective and the Employee's Perspective*, Oklahoma Bar J. (January 2005) (benefitslink.com)]

The IRS finalized regulations under the Code § 411(d)(6) anti-cutback rules, effective for plan amendments adopted and effective after November 8, 2012. A single employer defined benefit plan subject to ERISA § 4021 can be amended to eliminate lump sum or other optional forms of benefit that accelerate payment after bankruptcy. The PBGC and the bankruptcy court must determine that the plan would go through a distress or involuntary termination without the elimination of the optional benefit. The PBGC must also determine that the plan isn't sufficient for guaranteed benefits. If the sponsor eliminates an optional form of benefit under these regulations, and the plan does not offer other options with substantial survivor benefits, the sponsor can add other options to provide those benefits as part of the amendment that eliminates the lump sum distribution option. The entire plan amendment is considered together in determining if the amendment can take effect in accordance with § 436(c). [Kristen Heinzinger, *IRS Finalizes Relief for Bankrupt DB Sponsors*, plansponsor.com (Nov. 8, 2012)]

American Airlines' bankruptcy court permitted the airline to eliminate the optional lump sum and installment forms of benefit payment, agreeing with the airline that if pilots could receive a lump sum after American emerges from bankruptcy, there would probably be so many retirements that there wouldn't be enough pilots available. The regulations permit elimination of a bankrupt sponsor's lump sum option if the plan's actuary certifies that the percentage of funding is below 100%; the plan is forbidden to make payments higher than the monthly single life annuity amount because of its status; the bankruptcy court ruled that the amendment is needed to avoid involuntary or distress termination; and the PBGC said that the amendment is needed to avert termination before the end of the bankruptcy case. [Rebecca Moore, *American Allowed to Eliminate Lump Sums*, plansponsor.com (Dec. 14, 2012)]

The Eighth Circuit held that an airline's money purchase plan for pilots, created after the airline's bankruptcy, did not violate ERISA or the ADEA by illegally reducing benefits on account of age. The airline's defined benefit plan was frozen. The new money purchase plan's retirement benefit replaced about 50% of final average earnings or allotted participants the frozen benefit, if that was higher. The benefit was calculated as a target percentage of projected final average earnings, based on age and years of service. A group of older pilots challenged the plan because benefits were linked to age. The Eighth Circuit concluded that the plan does not reduce pensions on account of age. Age is not the only factor in the calculation; seniority, job classification, number of annual pay increases before retirement, and benefits under the frozen plan were also considered. [*Northwest Airlines v. Phillip*, 675 F.3d 1126 (8th Cir. 2012); see CCH Pension & Benefits, *Airline's Post-Bankruptcy Money Purchase Plan Did Not Illegally Reduce Benefits Due To Age* (Aug. 21, 2012) (benefitslink)]

In late 2012, the DOL proposed to extend its Abandoned Plan Program to permit Chapter 7 bankruptcy trustees to distribute assets from bankrupt companies' individual account retirement plans. The proposal sets out streamlined provisions for terminating such plans and distributing their benefits. The Abandoned Plan Program was created in 2006, but applied only to financial institutions holding the assets of abandoned plans. [DOL/EBSA, *Fact Sheet: Proposed Amendments to Abandoned Plan Program* (Dec. 2012) (benefitslink.com)]

There are two kinds of bankruptcy that may have an effect on pension plans: the employer's or an employee's. If the employer is one who seeks bankruptcy protection, an argument could be made under Bankruptcy Code § 547 that the employer's contributions to a qualified plan during the 90 days before the bankruptcy filing are "preferential transfers," and therefore should be returned to the bankruptcy estate and preserved so that creditors can make claims on them.

When it comes to the employee's bankruptcy, a highly relevant case is *Patterson v. Shumate* [504 U.S. 753 (1992)], which provides that ERISA plan law constitutes "applicable non-bankruptcy law" that will permit amounts in the plan to be excluded from the bankruptcy estate. The Supreme Court also held, in its 2005 *Rousey v. Jacoway* decision (544 U.S. 320), that IRAs are more akin to qualified plans than bank accounts from which withdrawals may be freely made. Therefore, the Supreme Court extended the exemption of qualified plans from the bankruptcy estate to IRAs. BAPCA contains a number of provisions affecting both employer and employee bankruptcies:

- Makes the employee's interest in qualified plans and IRAs exempt from the bankruptcy estate. The IRA exemption (which includes both conventional and Roth IRAs) is limited to $1 million—but the $1 million figure does not include amounts rolled over into an IRA from a qualified plan;

- As noted above, limits severance and retention payments to corporate insiders and makes it easier for the business' bankruptcy trustee to set aside preferential payments made to insiders;

- Increases the employer's ability to continue to collect repayments of plan loans from employees who have sought bankruptcy protection;

- Gives the bankruptcy court the power to cancel the employer's modifications of its retiree health benefits made during 180 days before filing of a bankruptcy petition, although if the court is persuaded that the balance of equities favors leaving the modifications in place, they can be affirmed.

Internal Revenue Code § 401(a)(33) forbids certain plan amendments if the plan is covered by ERISA § 4021. Plan benefits may not be increased while the plan sponsor is a bankruptcy debtor. The plan cannot be amended to increase the plan's liabilities because of an increase in benefits, any change in the accrual of benefits, or any change in the rate at which benefits become nonforfeitable. The ban applies only if the amendments in question take effect before the effective date of the employer's plan of reorganization.

The restrictions do not apply if the plan would otherwise have a funded current liability percentage of at least 100%; if the IRS determines that the amendment is reasonable and increases benefits only slightly; or if the amendment is actually required to conform to changes in tax law. The PPA's limitations on activities of "at risk" plans will also affect many companies that are contemplating bankruptcy or have already filed for protection.

## § 4.27 FACTORS IN CHOOSING A PLAN FORM

In deciding which form of plan to adopt, or whether to convert a plan or terminate an old plan and adopt a new one, the employer must balance many considerations, including financial and tax factors and the expected effect of a plan in motivating employee behavior (including retiring at the time most convenient for the employer).

Participants in a defined benefit plan know what their eventual pension will be if they stay with the plan until normal retirement age. If they terminate employment earlier, the vesting rules also control the size of the pension that will be paid later on, when they reach retirement age. This degree of certainty is valuable, but retirees have the problems caused by having a fixed income that does not reflect investment results.

In contrast, defined contribution plan participants know how large their account is at any given time. They can make projections of how large it will grow, based on predictions about interest rates and stock market trends. Market risk shifts from the employer to the employee and future retiree. Defined contribution plans also offer more portability: the contents of the employee's account from Plan A can simply be rolled over to Plan B when the employee stops being a Company A employee and is hired by Company B.

Before the 2008 recession began, there had been a very large-scale shift from defined benefit to defined contribution plans. One effect of the recession, however, was to increase interest in defined benefit plans and in features such as automatic enrollment and investment advice to participants that make defined contribution plans work more like defined benefit plans.

Defined benefits, but not defined contribution plans, are covered by the Pension Benefit Guaranty Corporation (PBGC)'s insurance program. The PBGC insures that employees will receive their pension benefits, at least the part that does not exceed a maximum figure. In exchange, employers must pay insurance premiums to the PBGC. If an underfunded defined benefit plan is terminated, the PBGC takes over part of the obligation to pay benefits.

For 2013, the maximum PBGC guarantee for a 65 year-old retiree rose from $56,000 to $57,477.24. At 62, the annual maximum guarantee is $45,407.04 ($3,783.92 monthly, $3,405.53 joint and survivor). At age 57, the maximum guarantee is $30,462.96 ($2,538.58 a month, $2,284.72 for a joint and survivor benefit); at 50, the maximum guarantee is $20,117.04 ($1,676.42 a month, or $1,676.42 joint and survivor). [PBGC, *PBGC Maximum Insurance Benefit Increases for 2013* (Nov. 27, 2012)]

The 2013 present values of the PBGC guarantee range from $125,539, at age 25, $153,501 (30), $180,229 (35), $230,843 (40), $282,286 (45), $371,638 (50), $476,923 (55), $604,500 (60), $782,324 (65), $1,122,428 (70), $1,704,372 (75), $2,844,680 (80). [Present Value of PBGC Maximum Guarantee, <http://www.pbgc.gov/prac/mortality-retirement-and-pv-max-guarantee/present-guarantee.html> (last viewed Mar. 10, 2013)]

Because of the PPA, the maximum benefit payable to employees of a bankrupt company is determined as of the date of the bankruptcy filing, not the (usually later) date that the plan actually terminates. [<http://www.pbgc.gov/media/key-resources-for-the-press/content/page13542.html>]

Between 1982 and 1999, high stock market returns relieved many employers from the need to make additional contributions to fund their defined benefit plans. Since that time, employers would have to make major contributions to maintain defined benefit plans, leading to the freezing of some plans.

If the defined benefit plan is frozen and replaced with a defined contribution plan, the employer can contribute a flat percentage of pay with or without an employer match of employee contributions. Employer contributions can be tiered based on age, service, or points (a combination of age and service). Conversion to defined contribution form reduces volatility by shifting the market risk to plan participants, although as payroll changes the employer will experience a small amount of volatility.

The cash balance plus defined contribution strategy could replace a defined contribution plan with an 8% annual contribution with a contribution of 4% each to the defined contribution plan and a cash balance plan, improving employees' retirement security through greater diversification.

The Preservation of Access to Care for Medicare Beneficiaries and Pension Relief Act of 2010 (PRA), passed June 24, 2010, Pub. L. No. 111-192, gives plan sponsors some breathing room by giving them more time to amortize large losses in any two plan years between 2008 and 2011. The PPA required amortization of gain or loss over seven years, but PRA allows a nine-year schedule. The first two years are interest-only and both interest and principal are accounted for in years 3–9. The other PRA option is 15-year amortization without triggering the normal benefit restrictions. However, a plan that adopts a relief strategy is subject to limitations on compensating any one employee by more than $1 million, and extraordinary dividends and redemptions are also limited. [Milliman Insight, *Six Ways to Reduce Pension Costs and Combat Volatility* (Sept. 26, 2011) (benefitslink.com)]

Before the PPA, a number of companies adopted cash balance plans (which combine some features of defined-benefit plans with some features more typical of a defined-contribution plan) even though the tax status of these plans was ambiguous, and it was uncertain whether they violated the Age Discrimination in Employment Act. The PPA makes it clear that cash balance plans (as long as they are operated in accordance with the rules!) are tax-compliant and do not discriminate against older workers. (See Chapter 7.) However, this favorable treatment is prospective only. Most courts have ruled in favor of cash balance plans established before the PPA took effect—but some have found ERISA and/or ADEA violations.

An early 2012 article suggests that a company that has maxed out its 401(k) plan but still has steady cash flow and discretionary income that could be used for benefits might consider implementing a cash balance plan. For plan participants in their fifties who got a late start on retirement planning, even if they make catch-up contributions, they could not save as much in a 401(k) plan as in a cash balance plan. A cash balance plan can also be used as a mechanism for a young partner to indirectly buy out an older partner who wants to retire. [Tom Sigmund, Kegler, Brown, *How To Determine If a Cash Balance Pension Plan Is Right for Your Company*, Hill & Ritter Smart Business (Jan. 3, 2012) (benefitslink.com)]

# CHAPTER 5

# DEFINED BENEFIT PLANS

## § 5.01   INTRODUCTION

This chapter deals, in detail, with issues that are specific to defined benefit plans. See Chapter 4 for background issues on pensions, Chapter 6 for defined contribution plans and 401(k) plans, and Chapter 7 for cash balance plans.

One of the most important changes in the employment/retirement landscape has been the transition from the defined benefit plan to the defined contribution plan. Major legislation, the Pension Protection Act (PPA; Pub. L. No. 109-280), has been passed to improve the stability of the remaining defined benefit plans. However, due to financial problems occurring after the passage of the legislation, it was deemed necessary to relax some of the more onerous requirements, by passing the Worker, Retiree, and Employer Recovery Act of 2008 (WRERA; Pub. L. No. 110-458); the Preservation of Access to Care for Medicare Beneficiaries and Pension Relief Act of 2010 (PRA; Pub. L. No. 111-192), and the Moving Ahead for Progress in the 21st Century Act, aka MAP-21 (Pub. L. No. 112-141).

The number of defined benefit plans continues to decline. The DOL reported that there were 103,346 defined benefit plans in 1975—and only 46,543 in 2010. Towers Watson said that, for 400 large companies that have defined benefit plans, the total estimated deficit reached an all-time high of $418 billion, 23% higher than 2011. Companies are responding by buying out pension recipients, transferring pension accounts to third parties such as insurance companies, and increasing their contributions. Some companies, including Boeing, are disclosing "core earnings" separately to exclude pension expenses, so the figures look healthier. [Mike Ramsey and Vipal Monga, *Low Interest Rates Force Companies to Pour Cash Into Pensions*, WSJ.com (Feb. 3, 2013)]

An EBRI fact sheet published in March 2013 shows that in 1979, only 7% of U.S. workers participated only in a defined contribution plan; in that year, 28% of workers had only a defined benefit plan, and a further 10% had both. The situation changed greatly by 2011, when 31% of workers participated only in a defined contribution plan, 11% participated in both, and a mere 3% of workers had a defined benefit plan only. The fact sheet includes a dramatic graph showing that the proportion of workers with both types of plans has stayed within the 10%–15% range—but defined benefit plan participation plummeted throughout the period as defined contribution plan participation soared.[EBRI Fast Facts #225, *Pension Plan Participation*, <http://www.ebri.org/pdf/FF.225.DB-DC.28Mar13.pdf> (Mar. 28, 2013)]

An International Monetary Fund research paper published in mid-2012 concludes that each additional year of life expectancy increases pension liabilities by about 3%–4%, increasing the liabilities of private defined benefit pension plans by $84 billion and doubling the amount of underfunding. [Michael Kisser, John Kiff, Erik S. Oppers, and Mauricio Soto, *The Impact of Longevity Improvements on U.S. Corporate Defined Benefit Pension Plans*, International Monetary Fund WP/12/170 [working paper] (June 2012) (benefitslink.com)]

Starting with the 2008 plan year, the PPA requires defined benefit plans to distribute Annual Funding Notices instead of Summary Annual Reports (SARs). For large plans, the notice is due 120 days after the end of the plan year; for small plans, the due date is the same as the due date for the Form 5500. But plans that are not insured by the PBGC (such as professional service companies and owner-only plans) are not required to provide either an Annual Funding Notice or an SAR. [Form 5500 Help.com, *Clarification SARs for Defined Benefit Plans* (Feb. 2, 2009) (benefitslink.com)]

Hybrid plans are defined benefit plans that accrue benefits under a formula, but define the benefit as a lump sum (the account balance) and not as a monthly payment after retirement. Many employers favor hybrid plans because funding is predictable, and employees find them easier to understand than traditional defined benefit plans. Cash balance plans (see Chapter 7) are the most popular type of hybrid plans. The benefit is based on a percentage of pay credited each year, plus interest at the plan's interest crediting rate. A Pension Equity Plan (PEP) posts percentage credits to the employee's account each year, defining the lump sum balance at retirement as the total of the percentages multiplied by the employee's final average pay. Most (about 75%) hybrid plans increase the rate of pay credits as age and/or service increase, subject to IRS rules that impose a minimum interest credit rate to prevent back-loading. Therefore, if a plan increases pay credits and the sponsor wants a variable interest rate, there must also be a fixed minimum rate, requiring the plan to adopt a combination rate. [Watson Wyatt Insider, *Hybrid Plan Sponsors Concerned About Lack of Regulatory Guidance* (September 2009) (benefitslink.com). On October 19, 2010, the IRS published final (75 Fed. Reg. 64123; corrections at <http://origin.www.gpo.gov/fdsys/pkg/FR-2010-12-28/pdf/2010-32539.pdf>) and proposed (75 Fed. Reg. 64197) regulations on hybrid plans. See § 4.06.]

As a result of PPA § 504, employers must post actuarial information about the funding status of defined benefit plans on their corporate intranet (if they have one; it is not necessary to create an intranet just for this purpose). The posting must include basic information about the plan, and the actuarial information about the plan. However, if the employer chooses to post the entire form rather than just the mandatory information, Form SSA should be removed, because it contains the Social Security numbers of plan participants. The DOL informally indicated that the requirement does not apply to defined contribution plans such as 401(k)s. [Timothy D.S. Goodman, Dorsey & Whitney LLP Resources, *New Law Requires Employers with Defined Benefit Plans to Post Information on Their Intranet* (Nov. 2, 2009) (benefitslink.com)]

The shift from defined benefit to 401(k) plans has gone on since 1981, reflecting both the creation of many 401(k) plans and a halt in the creation of new defined benefit plans. However, until the 2000s, there were few conversions from defined benefit to 401(k) form, and the only companies terminating their defined benefit plans were bankrupt or in serious financial trouble. But the collapse of the dot-com bubble led to low equity prices, declines in asset values, and low interest rates increasing sponsors' liabilities—problems that were exacerbated by the recession beginning in 2008. Towers Watson said that in 2000, 58 of the Fortune 100 offered a traditional defined benefit plan to new hires—whereas only 13 did so in 2011. Shifting from defined benefit to 401(k) form usually reduces the employer's contributions from 7%–8% of payroll to a 3% match. [Alicia Munnell, *Private Sector Defined Benefit Plans Vanishing*, WSJ.com (Dec. 30, 2011)]

Defined benefit plans, in response to investment volatility, changing rules, and longer-lived participants, are looking for "de-risking" strategies. Traditional de-risking strategies include liability-driven investing and annuitizing accrued benefits. Annuitizing is expensive, but has the advantage of placing liability risk on a third party. More modern strategies are annuity buy-ins, where the insurer and plan sponsor share the financial risks. A plan can also cash out retirees completely, placing all the investment risk on them. Two PLRS, Nos. 201228045 and 2012280511, say that this is not a violation of the minimum distribution rules. [Elizabeth Thomas Dold and David N. Levine, *A Look at Retiree Cashouts as the New De-Risking Strategy*, Taxes: The Tax Magazine (Nov. 2012) (benefitslink .com)]

The mid-2011 National Compensation Survey was the first one to include data on domestic partners. It showed that 14% of all civilian workers had access to a defined benefit plan with survivor benefits for unmarried domestic partners (the percentage was the same for same- sex and male/female domestic partners). In private industry, 7% of workers could cover their domestic partners under a defined benefit plan, whereas in state and local government plans, 50% had access to coverage for same-sex and 49% for opposite-sex domestic partners. [News release: <http://www.bls.gov/ncs/ebs/sp/ebs_domestic.pdf >; see Employee Benefits in the United States, March 2011, *Unmarried Domestic Partners Benefit Fact Sheet* (July 26, 2011) (benefitslink.com)]

## [A] PPA and Later Changes

Although it contains other types of provisions, the Pension Protection Act (PPA; Pub. L. No. 109-280) takes defined benefit plan reform as its central mission. Major changes wrought by the PPA include:

- Changing the rules for the interest rate assumptions sponsors must use in plan funding and operations.

- Amending the funding rules, so that plans will have to be 100% funded (earlier law allowed funding at a 90% level). This change is being phased in gradually to give plan sponsors time to adjust.

- Sponsors must meet "funding targets" by making at least the "minimum required contribution" required for the plan, a calculation involving the plan's "target normal cost."

- Contributions over and above the minimum required contribution give rise to "credit balances" which can be applied toward the required minimum contribution for later years.

- Valuation of plan assets can either be at fair market value or "smoothed" over a 24-month period, but values must always fall within 90%–110% of FMV.

- Special rules are imposed on the activities of "at-risk" plans (i.e., those that are at risk of becoming unable to pay benefits as they come due). Plans with fewer than 500 participants are exempt from the at-risk plan rules.

President Bush signed WRERA, the Worker, Retiree, and Employer Recovery Act of 2008, Pub. L. No. 110-458, on December 23, 2008. WRERA provides PPA technical corrections and relief from some of the more onerous PPA requirements. The PPA required plans to become 100% funded within seven years. Businesses asked for temporary relief, but Congress made it permanent, allowing companies with major investment losses to come into compliance without reaching the 100% level within the seven-year time frame. [Mary Williams Walsh, *Pensions Get a Reprieve in Congress*, <http://www.times.com> (Dec. 12, 2008)]

The PPA replaced the concept of the funding standard account with a requirement that contributions each year must be at least as great as the target normal cost (the cost of the benefits that accrued during the year) plus the amount needed to amortize the funding shortfall, as it stood at the beginning of the year, over a period of approximately seven years. Tougher funding requirements were imposed on at-risk plans.

WRERA provides that expenses paid directly by the plan are included in the target normal cost. Under the PPA, the plan's contributions and distributions had to be included in the calculation; WRERA also allows consideration of expected earnings. WRERA requires the same interest rate assumptions to be used to calculate the funding target percentage and the target normal cost.

WRERA expands the IRS' authority to issue guidance about how to determine the plan's funded status for years before 2008, which is important for determining if plan is at risk.

As a result of WRERA, the restrictions on lump sum distributions do not apply to mandatory cash-out of de minimis amounts under $5,000. To determine whether benefit accruals must cease in 2009, the plan can use either its 2008 or 2009 AFTAP—whichever is greater.

Section 415(b) requires benefits that are not in the form of a life annuity beginning between age 62 and age 65 to be converted to that form using actuarial assumptions prescribed by the IRS. The PPA said that the § 415(b) mortality assumptions would be based on the standard table for group annuity contracts, but WRERA requires instead that the table for converting benefit accruals to lump sums under § 407(e) must be used. [Deloitte's Washington Bulletin, *PPA*

*Technical Corrections Affecting Defined Benefit Plans*, <http://benefitslink.com/articles/guests/washbull090112.html> (Jan. 12, 2009). See also T.D. 9467, 2009-50 I.R.B. 760, dealing with post-PPA funding requirements for single-employer defined benefit plans.]

In mid-2010, with financial conditions still hazardous, Congress provided additional relief for defined benefit plans. The Preservation of Access to Care for Medicare Beneficiaries and Pension Relief Act, Pub. L. No. 111-192) (PRA), gives employers two choices. The employer could select two years in which to pay only interest on the plan's funding shortfall (rather than contributing enough to actually reduce the shortfall as required by the PPA), or amortize the shortfall for any two plan years between 2008 and 2011 over 15 years . [Rebecca Moore, *Obama Signs Pension Relief Bill*, plansponsor.com (June 25, 2010). See also Notice 2011-3, 2011-3 I.R.B. 324 (Dec. 22, 2010)]

Important defined benefit plan provisions were included in MAP-21, the Moving Ahead for Progress in the 21st Century Act. (The pension provisions are actually tag-alongs in a highway funding bill.) The Society of Actuaries estimates that the number of large corporate plans funded at a level of at least 80% will rise from the current 62% to 91%. [Hazel Bradford, Pensions & Investments, *Congress Passes Pension Changes in Highway Package* (June 29, 2012) (benefitslink.com)]

MAP-21 extends the period used to calculate interest rates to 25 years, so the recent period, with extremely low interest rates, has a lesser impact on the calculations. For 2012, interest rates must be within 10% of the average of benchmark bond rates for the previous 25 years. The interest-rate change is expected to save the typical defined benefit plan 15%–25% of its contribution requirement. MAP-21 also increases the PBGC premiums and allows overfunded plans to transfer money to a 401(h) plan providing either health benefits or group-term life insurance for retirees. [Rebecca Moore, *Congress Passes Bill With Pension Funding Relief*, plansponsor.com (June 29, 2012); Buck Consultants FYI, *2012 Pension Plan Funding Stabilization Finally a Reality* (July 6, 2012) (benefitslink.com)]

## § 5.02 BENEFIT LIMITS

The limit on the maximum benefit that anyone can receive from a qualified defined benefit plan in a year is set by I.R.C. § 415(b)(1).

The 2012 limit on annual benefits under a defined benefit plan was $200,000; the § 401(a)(17) compensation limit became $250,000, and a highly compensated employee (HCE) is someone who earns $115,000 or more.[IR-2011-103, *IRS Announces Pension Plan Limitations for 2012*, <http://www.irs.gov/newsroom/article/0,,id=248482,00.html> (Oct. 20, 2011)]

For 2013, the annual limit on the annual benefit is $205,000, the compensation limit is $255,000, and the HCE level is still $115,000. [IR-2012-77, *IRS*

*Announces 2013 Pension Plan Limitations; Taxpayers May Contribute Up to $17,500 To Their 401(k) Plans in 2013*, <http://www.irs.gov/uac/2013-Pension-Plan Limitations> (Oct. 18, 2012)]

As a result of the PPA, underfunded plans are restricted in their benefit distribution options: see § 5.10.

## § 5.03　BENEFIT FORMS FOR DEFINED BENEFIT PLANS

All pension plans must provide the basic payment form: a life annuity for single participants, and a QJSA (qualified joint and survivor annuity) for married participants. The basic form of QJSA provides a certain level of benefits while both the former employee and spouse are still alive. When one of them dies, the payment is cut in half, because only one person remains to be supported. Although employers are allowed to offer 50% survivor annuities, they are also allowed to subsidize the survivor annuity so that it is more than 50% of the initial payment, or even so that the payment does not decline when one payee dies. As a result of the Pension Protection Act, employers must now offer married participants not only a choice between a joint and 50% survivor annuity and a single-life annuity, but a choice between a survivor annuity at the 50% level and at the 75% level (Qualified Optional Survivor Annuity, or QOSA).

Internal Revenue Code § 401(a)(25) says that a plan that provides for alternative benefit forms (annuity, installment, lump sum, early retirement) must specify, in a definite form that precludes employer discretion, what actuarial assumptions (such as interest rates and mortality assumptions) are used to calculate equivalencies among different benefit forms. This disclosure obligation does not, however, extend to the plan's funding assumptions.

In a flat benefit plan, the pension is defined as a certain number of dollars per month, or a percentage of average annual compensation or average compensation for the "high three" years. A unit benefit plan defines the pension as compensation times years of participation times a percentage rate. Some plans of this type increase the accrual rate in later years, or are calculated using a "high five" or "final average pay" (the average of the last three years of work, when presumably earnings will be at their peak).

The IRS has ruled frequently on when and how plans can eliminate benefit forms that are hard to administer and are rarely chosen by participants, but the theme of all these rules is that the core benefit forms must remain available to participants. Final Regulations were published under § 411(d)(6) on August 11, 2005, further explaining the benefits and redundant payment forms that can be eliminated from defined benefit plans. The IRS also published proposals in the same document, allowing elimination of benefits that fail a utilization test.

Any benefit outside the core options can be eliminated after four years. The core options are defined as the straight life annuity; the 75% joint and contingent annuity; the 50%/100% joint and contingent annuity; the 10-year certain and life annuity; and an option such as a lump sum or a survivor annuity that would be valuable for a participant with a short life expectancy. [T.D. 9219, 2005-38 I.R.B. 538; see also 71 Fed. Reg. 45379 (Aug. 9, 2006)].

IRS Regulations proposed at 70 Fed. Reg. 31214 (May 31, 2005) unify and systematize the § 415 rules, explaining how to calculate the maximum permitted benefit when a retiree has multiple annuity start dates and how to calculate qualified joint and survivor annuities when the benefit is partly taken as a lump sum and partly in annuity form. The regulations were finalized in 2007: 72 Fed. Reg. 16878 (Apr. 5, 2007). The final rules reflect the changes made by the PPA. [See Sutherland Asbill & Brennan Legal Alert, *Section 415 Final Regulations Clarify Rules*, <http://www.sablaw.com/files/tbl_s10News[ . . . ]> (Apr. 10, 2007)]

The IRS proposed a rule to encourage partial annuity distribution options in defined benefit plans. Proposals published in February 2012 amend § 417(e)(3) to permit combinations of lump sum payments and income streams. Plans that wish to take advantage of this opinion could be amended to allow participants to take a partial lump sum calculated with the statutory actuarial assumptions, plus an annuity using the plan's regular conversion factors. The annuity form is referred to as a Qualified Longevity Annuity Contract, or QLAC. [IRS Proposed Rules, 77 Fed. Reg. 5443 and 5454 (Feb. 3, 2012); see Retirement Town Hall, *IRS Proposes Rule To Encourage Partial Annuity Distribution Options In Pension Plans* (Feb. 9, 2012) (benefitslink.com)] Rev. Rul. 2012-3, 2012-8 I.R.B. 383 explains how the qualified joint and survivor annuity (QJSA) and qualified pre-retirement survivor annuity (QPSA) rules work when a deferred annuity contract is purchased under a profit-sharing plan. Rev. Rul. 2012-4, 2012-8 I.R.B. 386, explains how to satisfy §§ 411 and 415 when a qualified dcfined benefit plan accepts a direct rollover of an eligible rollover distribution from the same employer's qualified defined contribution plan and uses the rollover amount to provide an annuity. [*Treasury Fact Sheet: Helping American Families Achieve Retirement Security By Expanding Lifetime Income Choices*, 020212 Retirement Security Factsheet; Rebecca Moore, *IRS Issues Guidance About Annuities in Retirement Plans*, plansponsor.com (Feb. 2, 2012)]

The Northern District of Texas denied injunctive relief to 41,000 Verizon management retirees who were opposed to Verizon's plan to buy a single-premium group annuity from Prudential to satisfy the obligation to make pension payments. The annuity payment is the same as the current pension benefit. The plaintiffs alleged a violation of ERISA § 510, contending that they would lose ERISA protection because, under 29 C.F.R. § 2510.3-3(d)(2)(ii), a person whose entire benefit is fully guaranteed by an insurance company ceases to be a plan participant. The district court ruled that the plaintiffs failed to show a risk of loss of benefits. The court dismissed the breach of fiduciary duty claim, holding that amending or terminating a pension plan is not a fiduciary act. The plaintiffs said that investing all of the transferred assets with Prudential violated the duty to diversify, but the district court held that there was no duty to diversify in this context: the fiduciary's duty was to be prudent in choosing the insurer. The case as a whole was dismissed in June 2013. The Northern District of Texas ruled that the plaintiffs failed to prove that the pension transfer would deprive them of any benefits or rights—ERISA protects benefits for plan participants, but does not require retention of the original source of payment. The district court did not find the fee to Prudential to be unreasonable. However, the plaintiffs were given leave to replead their case. [*Lee v. Verizon*, No. 3:12-cv-04834-D, 2012 U.S. Dist. LEXIS 173559 (N.D. Tex. Dec. 7, 2012). See Maria Wood, *Judge Disconnects Lawsuit Vs. Verizon Pension Transfer*, LifeHealthPro, <http://www.lifehealthpro.com/2013/06/26/judge-disconnects-lawsuit-vs-verizon-pension-trans> (June 26, 2013)]

In 2008, the Northern District of Illinois held that Verizon was bound by the language in its defined benefit plan document even though a drafting error had possible consequences of $1.67 billion. The cashout value of interests in the predecessor plan was incorrectly drafted, calling for multiplying the balance twice by a variable transition factor based on age and years of service. However, on reconsideration, the Northern District held that the error was an honest mistake, and other actions in administering the plan showed an intent to use the multiplication factor only once. Judge Denlow said that employers would be discouraged from adopting plans at all if they feared that mistakes could have catastrophic consequences that could not be corrected. The Seventh Circuit affirmed in mid-2010 and the Supreme Court denied certiorari. [*Young v. Verizon's Bell Atlantic Cash Balance Plan*, 615 F.3d 808 (7th Cir. 2010), *cert. denied*, No. 10-765 (May 23, 2011), *reh'g denied*, July 25, 2011; see Fred Schneyer, *Verizon Allowed to Fix Plan Drafting Mistake*, plansponsor.com (Aug. 11, 2010)]

## § 5.04  MORTALITY TABLES

Before 2002, the IRS required defined benefit plans to use the 1983 Group Annuity Mortality (83GAM) table for making the actuarial calculations for the value of accrued benefits. [I.R.C. § 417(e)] The mortality tables must be used to make sure that the value of a lump sum benefit is at least as great as the predicted value of an annuity.

Defined benefit plans also have to calculate adjustments of the plan limitations, as required by I.R.C. § 415(b), when the benefit under the plan is paid in any form other than a QJSA, or when the employee retires before age 62 or after age 65.

The PPA imposed additional § 412 funding requirements for defined benefit plans that have unfunded current liability (§ 412(l)(8)). Current liability is determined using the mortality table prescribed by the Secretary, who is required to update the table at least once every ten years. Additional tables are prescribed for disability retirees whose disability satisfies Social Security Act Title II standards: a table for disability occurring before January 1, 1995 and a table for disabilities with later onset. Under § 412(l)(7)(C)(ii)(III), the tables have to be reviewed at least once every five years to reflect trends in mortality rates. The mortality tables have been updated for use in 2014 and 2015: see Notice 2013-49, 2013-32 I.R.B. 127. [TD 9310 RIN 1545-BE72 72 Fed. Reg. 4955 (Feb. 2, 2007)]

Under the PPA, a defined benefit plan must provide that the present value of an accrued benefit, and the amount of any distribution (lump sum or otherwise) must be at least the amount calculated using the Regulations Section 1.417(e)-1(d) appropriate interest rate for the month and the prescribed mortality table.

In May 2007, the IRS explained the procedure for qualifying to use a substitute (plan specific) mortality table to compute defined benefit plan obligations under Code § 430(h)(3)(C)/ERISA § 303(h)(3)(C). The IRS will consider a substitute mortality table adequate if the plan has enough participants; the plan has been maintained long enough to have credible mortality experience; and the chosen table reflects the plan's actual experience and its projected mortality trends for participants. A request to use substitute mortality tables is deemed accepted if 180 days pass without a ruling (unless there is an extension of time by mutual consent). However, a plan sponsor can only use substitute tables for one plan if all of the sponsor's plans (and all plans of the sponsor's controlled group) use the substitute table. [Adrien Martin, *IRS Release Guidelines on Substitute Mortality Table Requests*, plansponsor.com (May 31, 2007)]

Final regulations for defined benefit plan mortality tables were issued in August 2008, incorporating PPA principles: Rev. Proc. 2008-62, 2008-42 I.R.B. 935. These tables are mandatory starting with the 2008 plan year. Small plans (fewer than 500 participants) can use a single blended static table for all participants. Some large employers can use individualized tables that reflect their experience.

## § 5.05   FUNDING THE DEFINED BENEFIT PLAN

### [A]   Funding Requirements

The process of funding a defined contribution plan is quite simple. The employer simply determines a percentage of compensation, and as long as the contribution does not exceed the Code maximum, then there are no further problems. No discretion is involved.

In contrast, funding a defined benefit plan requires subtle decisions about long-range economic and employment trends in order to deposit enough money to yield the correct stream of future benefits to plan participants and their beneficiaries.

Defined benefit, money purchase, and target benefit plans (but not profit-sharing plans, stock bonus plans, or plans under I.R.C. § 412(i) that are exclusively funded by the purchase of individual insurance or annuity contracts) are subject to a "minimum funding" requirement under I.R.C. § 412. Before the PPA, the benchmark was the status of the plan's "minimum funding standard account," but the PPA enacts a new Code § 430, setting out the requirements for "basic minimum funding contributions."

An excise tax of 10% is imposed by I.R.C. § 4971 for failure to meet the minimum funding standard. The excise tax rises to 100% of any deficiency that remains uncorrected a reasonable time after the plan receives notice of deficiency from the IRS.

According to the Supreme Court case, *United States v. Reorganized CF&I Fabricators of Utah Inc.* [518 U.S. 213 (1996)], the 100% assessment is a penalty (and therefore an ordinary unsecured claim) and not an excise tax entitled to seventh priority, if the company subject to it files for bankruptcy protection.

The funded status of the typical corporate pension plan in July 2012 was 68.7%—the lowest figure since BNY Mellon started tracking these figures in December 2007. Plan liabilities increased by 5.5% whereas assets increased only 1.2%. Liabilities are calculated using the yields of long-term investment-grade bonds, so the drop in the corporate discount rate for Aa-rated bonds to 3.64% resulted in higher liabilities. [Mike G. Dunn, BNY Mellon press release, *Funded Status of U.S. Corporate Pensions Falls to Lowest Recorded Level in July, According to BNY Mellon* (Aug. 3, 2012) (benefitslink.com)]

However, Milliman, Inc.'s Pension Funding Index showed a substantial rebound in March 2013. The 100 largest corporate defined benefit plans improved their funding status by $29 billion (a $14 billion decrease in their obligations plus a $15 billion increase in assets). The discount rate increased from 4.16% to 4.22% in March 2013, which reduced pension liabilities. The funded ratio for the 100 plans went from 77% at the end of 2012 to about 83% at the end of the first quarter of 2013. [Kevin McGuinness, *Corporate DB Plans Show $29B Increase*, plansponsor.com (Apr. 23, 2013)]

Underfunding has other implications. The PPA imposes limitations on benefits. If the plan is covered by PBGC insurance, the PBGC must be notified whenever the minimum funding standard is not met. If the plan is terminated (see Chapter 17), then underfunding can make the plan liable to the PBGC for accumulated funding deficiencies.

However, complying with the minimum funding standard doesn't solve all of the employer's problems, because I.R.C. § 4972 also imposes an excise tax on excess contributions to a defined benefit plan.

Therefore, the employer should make sure that its contributions to the defined benefit plan fall within the acceptable range. Contributions should not be small enough to constitute underfunding—especially not small enough to trigger PBGC termination of the plan. But the employer will not want to contribute more than can be deducted, and will particularly want to avoid the excise tax on excess contributions.

## [B]  Deduction Limit

The funding standard serves another purpose: it sets an upper limit on the amount that the employer can deduct under I.R.C. § 404. If the employer overstates its pension liabilities by 200% or more, and therefore takes too large a deduction, with the result that its income taxes are underpaid by 20% or more, then a 20% accuracy-related underpayment penalty can be imposed under I.R.C. § 6662. The penalty will be suspended if the pension overstatement was less than $1,000, or if the plan relied on substantial authority such as Revenue Rulings or IRS Notices.

Pensions are a form of deferred compensation, and any form of compensation is deductible only if it is reasonable and constitutes an ordinary and necessary business expense. Part of the compensation of particularly highly paid employees may have to be disregarded for certain tax-related purposes.

For example, under I.R.C. § 401(a)(17) only $200,000 of compensation (adjusted for inflation in increments of $5,000) can be taken into account. EGTRRA increased this amount from $150,000 (adjusted for inflation; the 2009–2011 level is $245,000, the 2012 level is $250,000, and the 2013 level is $255,000). Even legitimate compensation may have to be deducted over a span of several years, not all at once.

## [C]  Calculating the Contribution

Before the PPA, defined benefit plan actuaries used two basic methods (each of which had variations): the accrued benefit method and the projected benefit cost method. Contributions were made for each participant based on "normal cost" (the actuarial value of benefit units for that year) plus "supplemental liability" (adjustments for service before adoption of a plan, or after a plan is amended). The PPA approach starts with the "target normal cost" and, as [D], below, shows, this is the point of departure for various adjustments.

## [D]  From the Minimum Funding Standard Account to the Minimum Required Contribution

Pre-PPA law required that a "minimum funding standard account" be maintained in all plan years until the end of the year in which the plan terminates. [See I.R.C. § 412(b) and ERISA § 302(b)] Under the pre-PPA rules, the minimum funding standard is met when there is no accumulated funding deficiency at the end of the year. There is no deficiency if, for all plan years, the credits to the funding standard account are at least equal to the total charges.

The minimum funding standard account consists of charges for normal costs, past service liabilities, experience losses in investments, and funding deficiencies. The general rule is that experience losses and funding deficiencies have to be amortized, not deducted currently. The charges to the account are offset by credits for, e.g., the employer's contributions to the plan, investment experience gains, and funding deficiencies that are waived by the IRS. WRERA provides (as an option for 2008, but mandatory for later years) that expenses paid directly by the plan are included in the target normal cost. Under the PPA, the plan's contributions and distributions had to be included in the calculation; WRERA also allows consideration of expected earnings. WRERA requires the same interest rate assumptions to be used to calculate the funding target percentage and the target normal cost.

Internal Revenue Code § 412(l) imposes additional obligations on single-employer plans with 100 or more participants whose "funded current liability" percentage falls below 80% for the current year when it was below 90% for the preceding year. The funded current liability percentage equals the value of the plan assets divided by current liabilities. The underfunded plans are obligated to notify their participants and beneficiaries of the funding deficiency, and must pay an additional PBGC premium. In egregious cases, the PBGC may be able to bring a civil suit against the plan.

The PPA introduced several new concepts and new requirements, calling for employers to achieve 100% funding no later than 2011. The employer's obligation is now the "minimum required contribution," defined as the amount the employer must contribute each year to fund benefits that will be paid in that year, as well as phasing out any existing funding shortfall over seven years. If the plan's assets are lower than its funding target, the minimum required contribution for the year is the "target normal cost" plus the amount needed to amortize the funding shortfall over seven years. The "funding target" is the accrued liability to date: the sum needed to pay all of the claims of participants and beneficiaries, as of the valuation date. The target normal cost, in turn, is defined as the benefit liabilities accruing in the current year, including past service benefits that increased reflecting the employee's higher compensation in the current year. A funding shortfall is any difference between the funding target and the plan assets. The "shortfall amortization installment" is the payment due in each of the seven years to close the gap. However, if the employer contributes more than the required amount, a credit balance is created that can be applied toward the required contribution for later years.

The carried-over balance is also credited with interest, but at the rate used to calculate the plan's liabilities, not the actual interest rate that the plan earns on its investments.

A degree of relief from the requirements for amortizing the shortfall is provided by the Preservation of Access to Care for Medicare Beneficiaries and Pension Relief Act of 2010, which permits employers to elect to pay only the interest on their shortfall for two years, or to amortize the shortfall in any two plan years between 2008–2011 over 15 rather than seven years.

## [E]  Full Funding Limitation

Before 2004, it was necessary to calculate a "full funding limitation" because excise taxes could be imposed if the employer's contribution fell below that amount. EGTRRA reduced the full funding limitation for 2002 and 2003 and provided that the percentage test would expire in 2004, when the FFL would be the difference between the plan's accrued liability and the value of its assets.

## [F]  Funding Procedures

Actual funding of the plan is done by the employer's contributing cash, non-cash property, or its own securities. The valuation of cash is simple; for property and securities, it can be difficult. The prohibited transaction rules (see § 8.03) must be consulted to make sure that contributions do not violate these rules. Wherever possible, transactions should be structured so that the plan trust will not have Unrelated Business Taxable Income (UBTI). In general, plan trusts are not subject to income tax—unless they have unrelated income.

Wherever possible, the employer should avoid contributing depreciated property to the plan. That's because I.R.C. § 267(b)(4) provides that the employer will have taxable gain (capital or ordinary, depending on the facts) if it contributes appreciated property to the plan. But losses on contributions of depreciated property are not recognized, because there is a transfer between the trust grantor and the trust's fiduciary.

> ■ **TIP:**  An employer that wants to use depreciated property in funding can sell the property to a third party, recognize the tax loss, then contribute the cash proceeds of the sale.

The PPA provides that most plans must make their required contribution no later than 8½ months after the end of the plan year. Some plans, however (those with more than 100 participants, and that had a funding shortfall in the previous year) will have to make quarterly contributions (April 15, July 15, October 15, January 15) instead of being permitted to make the whole year's contribution at once. The quarterly installment must equal 25% of the lesser of 90% of the minimum required contribution for the current plan year, or 100% of the minimum required contribution for the previous year.

The Bank of America prevailed in a suit charging the bank with violating ERISA by investing retirement plan assets in affiliated funds. The Fourth Circuit held that the plaintiffs did not have standing to bring the suit. They did not plead any injury in fact or show that they were likely to prevail at trial. The Fourth Circuit said that defined benefit plan participants only have an interest in their own future payments—not the fund's assets in general. The Supreme Court has left open the question of whether there is injury in fact from the possibility that a plan will terminate when a plan is underfunded and the PBGC will not pay full benefits. [*David v. Alphin*, 704 F.3d 327 (4th Cir. 2013); see Plansponsor staff, *Bank of America Wins Suit Over Affiliated Fund Use*, plansponsor.com (Jan. 22, 2013)]

## [G]   Liens Based on Funding Failures

Under I.R.C. § 412(n), a lien can be imposed against the employer, and in favor of the plan subject to PBGC jurisdiction, if the employer fails to make a required contribution to the plan when it is due.

> ■ **TIP:**   The person responsible for making the payment that was missed has an obligation to inform the PBGC within 10 days of the due date that the payment was missed.

The lien covers all of the employer's real and personal property. The lien can be imposed if the plan's funded current liability percentage fell below 100% and the unpaid balance, plus interest, was more than $1 million. It starts on the date the payment should have been made, and runs to the end of the plan year in which the liabilities go over the $1 million mark.

The PBGC can sue in federal district court under ERISA § 4003(e)(1) to enforce the lien against the employer. This power can be exercised at any time until three years after the PBGC knew or should have known of the failure to make the necessary payment (extended to six years if the employer committed fraud or concealment), or for six years after the due date from the payment.

## [H]   Plan Valuation Issues

An actuarial valuation must be performed at least once a year to determine the assets, liabilities, and contribution level for plans subject to I.R.C. § 412. (EGTRRA gives the Treasury the power to adopt regulations that call for even more frequent valuations.) The information is also used to prepare the Schedule B for the 5500-series form.

The basic factors in setting assumptions include:

- Employee compensation;

- Early retirement rate;

- Employee turnover;

- Disability and mortality rates (both before and after retirement);

- (For QJSAs) Life expectancy of employees' spouses;

- Expected percentage return on the plan's investments (interest assumptions may have to be adjusted in the future to reflect the plan's investment record);

- Administrative expenses, defined either as dollars per participant or a reduction in the plan's rate of return.

Within the limits set by I.R.C. § 412 and other relevant provisions, the size of the contribution can be increased or decreased somewhat based on corporate needs. However, the plan's actuarial assumptions must always be reasonable—each individual assumption, not just the aggregate. Courts have the power to overturn a plan's actuarial assumptions, even if the assumptions are not unreasonable. This is especially likely to happen if the plan has applied its own assumptions inconsistently.

> ■ **TIP:** In general, the valuation date has to be within the plan year for which the assets are being valued, or within a month before the start of the plan year—but EGTRRA § 661(a) creates an exception under which the valuation date can sometimes be in the previous year. This exception can only be used if the plan assets, valued as of the prior plan year's date, is at least 125% of the plan's current liability.

ERISA § 302(c) provides that a plan covered by PBGC termination insurance requires IRS approval to change its actuarial assumptions, if the aggregated unfunded vested benefits of all underfunded plans maintained by the employer, or members of the same controlled group, exceed $50 million. Approval for the change is also required if the change in the assumptions raises the unfunded cumulative liability for the current plan year by more than $50 million, or more than $5 million, if this is 5% or more of the current liability.

Before the PPA, plans could use "smoothing" to cope with changes in the valuation of plan assets over time. The PPA requires plans either to value their assets at fair market value (FMV) or to restrict "smoothing" to a 24-month period, during which values fall within the range of 90–110% of FMV.

## [I]   Interest Rates

Internal Revenue Code § 412(l)(7)(C)(i) sets the parameters for the interest rates used to determine the employer's contributions and the plan's current liability.

Under pre-PPA rules, the Department of the Treasury has the power to issue Regulations that lower the permissible range [see I.R.C. § 412(b)(5)] but it is not allowed to fall beneath 80% of the weighted 30-year average Treasury rate.

Factors in the interest rate assumption include:

- The economic components of interest rates;

- Current long-term interest rates;

- The plan's individual actuarial and investment factors;

- Long-range economic trends, especially in the money supply and interest rates throughout the economy.

The basic principle under the PPA—that the present value of a plan's current liabilities must be calculated with an interest rate based on corporate bonds, not Treasury bills—survives. However, the lower the interest rates applied to the calculation, the more the employer must contribute to fund the plan. Congress permitted some funding relief in 2012, under the MAP-21 (Pub. L. No. 112-141). Defined benefit plans consider interest rates stretching back 25 years, so the recent, very low rates, will have less impact on the calculation. For 2012, the interest rates used in the calculation must be within 10% of the average of benchmark bond rates for the previous 25 years.

Employers are allowed to use two approaches to calculate the present value of future pension benefits. The future expected payments can be discounted using a yield curve based on corporate bond data published by the Treasury. The other approach is to use segment rates based on averages from the most recent two years of yield curves. For each year, MAP-21 specifies the range of rates that can be used.

MAP-21 requires plan administrators to disclose additional information if the plan had 50 or more participants on any day of the preceding plan year; the stabilized funding target is less than 95% of the regular funding target; and the plan would have a funding shortfall of $500,000 or more absent stabilization. If all three of those factors are present, the plan's Annual Funding Notice must disclose that the law has changed reducing the employer's contribution. The notice must include a table showing the MAP-21's effect on funding requirements, plan's funding shortfall, and the minimum contribution for the current year and the two years before. [Rebecca Moore, *Congress Passes Bill With Pension Funding Relief*, plansponsor.com (June 29, 2012); Buck Consultants FYI, *2012 Pension Plan Funding Stabilization Finally a Reality* (July 6, 2012) (benefitslink.com)]

Notice 2013-11, 2013-11 I.R.B. 610 provides guidance on MAP-21 funding calculations, such as the 25-year average segment rates to be used to adjust the 24-month segment rates for computing minimum contribution requirements for single-employer defined benefit plans. MAP-21 defines the range within which the segment rates fall. Code § 403 provides that, for plan years beginning in 2013, the three segment rates are adjusted to fall within the range of 85%–115% of the appropriate 25-year average rate. The range then increases over time so that, for example, for years beginning after 2015, the rates are 70%–130% of the 25-year average segment rates. [<http://www.irs.gov/pub/irs-drop/n-13-11.pdf>; see Rebecca Moore, *IRS Announces New Rates for DB Funding Calculations*, plansponsor.com (Feb. 12, 2013)]

The higher the discount rate, the higher the growth rate over the annuity period, so the present value of a lump sum will be lower. A lower discount rate requires a higher lump sum. In a class action about the discount rates used by a pension plan to convert a straight life annuity to a lump sum, the Seventh Circuit ruled in 2013 that the pension plan's segment rate of approximately 5.4% was acceptable. Under the PPA, discount rates can be increased retroactively; this is not a cutback. The plan forbade reduction in accrued benefits (the value of the straight life annuity), it did not forbid a retroactive reduction in the benefits of participants who took a lump sum distribution. [*Dennison v. MONY Life Ret. Income Security Plan*, 710 F. 3d 741 (7th Cir. 2013); see Brian Stolzenbach, Sam Schwartz-Fenwick and Chris Busey, *Seventh Circuit Reads Plan Language To Discount Plaintiffs' Rate Argument*, Seyfarth Shaw ERISA & Employee Benefits Litigation Blog (Mar. 20, 2013) (benefitslink.com)]

## [J] Funding Changes

Rev. Procs. 2000-40 and -41, 2000-42 I.R.B. 357 and 371, provide the procedures under which the sponsor or administrator of a defined benefit plan subject to I.R.C. § 412 or ERISA § 302 can get the Secretary of the Treasury to approve a change in the plan's funding method under I.R.C. § 412(c)(5)(A)—e.g., changing the method of valuing assets, the plan year, or the valuation date.

The IRS has jurisdiction to review the appropriateness of any change that significantly affects the plan's minimum funding requirement or full funding limitation. The agency will approve a change in funding method only if the proposed new method and the form of the transition are both acceptable. The due date for a request is the end of the plan year in which the change will be effective. The IRS has discretion to extend the due date by up to two and a half months if the plan submits a statement giving adequate reason for the delay.

## [K] Minimum Funding Waivers

Waivers from the minimum funding standard are governed by Code § 412(c). The current (i.e., post-PPA) version allows a waiver of all or part of the minimum funding standard if the employer would not be able to satisfy the minimum funding standard without encountering temporary substantial business hardship—and the plan participants would be worse off if the plan were compelled to meet the standard. However, a plan cannot get waivers for more than three years in any 15-year period, and amounts attributable to a waived funding deficiency in one year cannot be waived in the next. For a single-employer plan, if a waiver is granted, the minimum required contribution under § 430 is reduced by the amount of funding deficiency that is waived; this amount is amortized under § 430(e).

Factors in determining whether the employer is undergoing temporary substantial business hardship include whether:

- The company is operating at a loss;
- The industry is experiencing substantial under- or unemployment;
- The industry's sales and profits are declining or already reduced;
- The waiver is the only way for the plan to continue.

The plan can be required to give security for the waiver, to be enforced by the PBGC. The waiver application must be made not later than the fifteenth day of the third month beginning after the end of the plan year. The company applying for the waiver must prove that it has notified affected parties (e.g., plan participants and beneficiaries) of the application. The notice must be given within 14 days before the date of the application for the waiver, and must disclose the sponsor's name; the year for which the waiver is requested; the FMV of plan assets; the present value of vested benefits under the plan; the present value of all benefits if the plan terminated; and the interest rate used in the calculations. Plan participants and beneficiaries must be informed that they can get a copy of the plan's latest annual report, and can submit comments about the waiver application. [IRS EP Examination Process Guide § 9, <http://www.irs.gov/retirement/article/0,,id= 135804,00.html>]

Plans that have obtained a waiver are not permitted to adopt amendments that increase benefits, change accrual of benefits, or change vesting schedules—unless the amendment is required for compliance, repeals another amendment that would be problematic, or is reasonable and has only a minimal effect on plan liabilities.

See 78 Fed. Reg. 20039 (Apr. 3, 2013) for PBGC proposals greatly reducing the number of situations in which "reportable events" must be reported to the PBGC, but application for a minimum funding waiver would continue to be a reportable event.

## [L]  Pension Freezes

As of mid-2012, 47% of corporate defined benefit plans were still active and open to new hires; a further 24% were closed to new entrants, but existing participants continued to accrue benefits. (Thus, according to SEI's Pension Life-cycle Meter, 71% of participants continued to accrue benefits.) One percent of plans were terminating; 28% of plans were frozen but had not commenced the process of termination. [Rebecca Moore, *Majority of DB Participants Still Accruing Benefits*, plansponsor.com (June 13, 2012)]

As research by The Center for Retirement Research at Boston College shows, since the mid-2000s, pension freezes have been common even in plans maintained by companies that are financially sound. Previously, it was very rare for defined benefit plans to be frozen, and then usually in association with bankruptcy or serious financial problems. The researchers attributed the increased acceptability of freezes to:

1. Reducing workers' compensation to be able to compete in the global market.

2. Cutting back pensions because health costs had soared.

3. Financial risks (such as stock market exposure) that made funding defined benefit plans unattractive.

4.  Upper management's lack of interest in rank-and-file pensions because so much of their compensation came from nonqualified plans.

The researchers identified three forms of plan freezes:

1.  Closing the plan to new hires;

2.  A partial freeze that covers new hires and some current employees; or

3.  A total freeze that affects all employees.

Usually, the freeze is accompanied by creation of a 401(k) plan, which reduces the employer's responsibility to making any matching contribution it promises. Pension plan freezes also provide a cosmetic gloss to the company's financial statements. Freezing a pension means that future payment liabilities are eliminated or greatly reduced, resulting in an accounting gain that is considered income for the corporation. Furthermore, if interest rates are low, the discounted present value of future benefits is high (because the role account earnings have in providing future benefits is comparatively small, more money must be set aside at the outset), creating an even more dramatic effect on the corporate bottom line. [Alicia H. Munnell, Francesca Golub-Sass, Mauricio Soto, and Francis Vitagliano, *Why Are Healthy Employers Freezing Their Pensions?* Center for Retirement Research Brief No. 44, <http://www.bc.edu/centers/crr/issues/ib_44.pdf> (March 2006)]

Whether it is more cost effective to terminate or immunize a frozen defined benefit plan depends on factors such as how much it would cost to buy annuities for the participants and how much management time is needed to administer the plan. (Immunization means buying assets to secure benefit payments, such as long-term, high-rated bonds that generate income in amounts and at the time needed to pay benefits.) The PPA, by allowing plan sponsors to make lump-sum calculations based on higher interest rates, reduces the size of lump sum payments, and, therefore, makes it easier to terminate plans than under prior law.

The demographics of the plan's participants greatly affects the decision. In most plans, liability is fairly equal for active participants, ex-employees who terminated when they had vested benefits, and retirees. A young plan is one where liabilities are concentrated on funding future benefits for active employees; a mature plan already has a high volume of retirees receiving benefits. The authors of the article concluded that termination is probably less expensive than immunization in a young plan, but costs are fairly similar for termination and immunization in either a typical or a mature plan.

When a plan terminates, it is common for retirees to want to keep their annuities, but active participants and terminated vested participants often opt for lump sums. [Nathan Zahm and R. Evan Inglis, *Frozen Pension Plans: Is*

*Immunization or Termination the Right Choice?* Vanguard, <https://www.vanguardfrance.fr/content/documents/Articles/Insights/frozen-pension-plans.pdf> (November 2012)]

Closing a defined benefit plan to new employees is not a cure-all for plan problems. Employers often find that they fail nondiscrimination testing. As the plan participants earn more, the disparity between their benefits and the benefits of ineligible employees also grows—particularly because employee turnover is greatest at the lower end of the income scale. Many employers support changing the law to provide that a plan remain permanently exempt as long as it was non-discriminatory at the time of the freeze. Aon Hewitt examined 78 closed plans, finding that half would not face a discrimination problem for at least five years, but 16% already failed testing and 14% would fail within two years. All of the possible responses to a discrimination problem are difficult and expensive: e.g., freezing the defined benefit plan and ending future accruals; excluding HCEs from the plan; adding more participants to the plan; or increasing benefits for employees who are not participants in the plan. [Hazel Bradford, *Closed Pension Plans Face Non-Discrimination Peril*, Pensions & Investments (Feb. 18, 2013) (benefitslink.com)]

## [M]   The Annual Funding Notice

Most plans that are subject to PBGC jurisdiction must provide participants and beneficiaries with annual funding notices—the document that replaced the SAR. PPA § 501(a) amended ERISA § 101(f) to require all PBGC-insured defined benefit plans to provide an annual funding notice to each participant and benefi-ciary, any unions for the workplace, and to the PBGC. Defined benefit plans that are not subject to the PBGC's jurisdiction (e.g., government plans; church plans; plans of professional service employers with 25 or fewer employees) must still file the SAR.

The annual funding notice must be provided to each participant, beneficiary, union, and the PBGC. The DOL will not take action against single-employer plans with liabilities under $50 million for failure to give notice to the PBGC, as long as they respond to the PBGC's request for the information within 30 days. [See 74 Fed. Reg. 17 (Jan. 2, 2009) for the EBSA final rule imposing civil penalties of up to $1,000 per day for each violation of ERISA § 101 or 514(e)(3) committed by not furnishing the annual funding notice, and 75 Fed. Reg. 70625 (Nov. 18, 2010).]

The 2012 pension funding relief bill, MAP-21 (Pub. L. No. 112-141), requires some plans to provide additional information in their annual funding notices. The requirement applies to plans that had at least 50 participants at any time in the previous year; the stabilized funding target is less than 95% than the regular funding target; and, without the relief provided by MAP-21, the plan would have a funding shortfall of $500,000 or more. Plans subject to the requirement must disclose that the law has changed, reducing the employer's required contributions. The funding notice must include a table showing the effect of the law on required contributions and the funding shortfall.

Notice 2012-46, 2012-3 I.R.B. 86, effective November 1, 2012, gives the ERISA § 101(j) notice requirements for single-employer plans subject to benefit limitations under § 436. When the funding status of a single-employer plan falls below a certain level, the administrator has 30 days to provide notice to participants and beneficiaries. The DOL regulations provide that noncompliance can be penalized by up to $1,000 per day for each participant who should have been notified. Notice 2012-46 requires the notice to be understandable by the average participant, containing the plan name, EIN, plan number, and a general description of the payment limitation. The prohibited benefits must be described in detail. The notice must explain when the limitation will cease to apply (e.g., when the AFTAP rises to at least 80%). If the limit is no longer in effect and participants can access distributions that were formerly prohibited, then the plan administrator must send a § 101(j) notice to participants no later than 30 days after the limitations no longer apply. The § 101(j) notice must be in writing and can be given electronically if this is reasonably accessible to the notice recipients. [McGuire-Woods LLP, *IRS Provides Guidance on Notices for Funding-Related Pension Plan Benefit Limitations* (Aug. 28, 2012) (benefitslink.com)]

## § 5.06   BENEFIT ACCRUALS

Another issue in plan administration and compliance is the schedule on which benefits are contributed on the individual's behalf, being added to the pension account so that eventually the participant will receive his or her defined benefit. Vesting is a separate but related concept. Vesting determines the extent to which employees will be entitled to receive the accrued benefit when they retire or employment otherwise terminates.

Defined benefit plans must accrue benefits using one of the three permitted mechanisms:

1.  The 3% rule: at all times, the accrued benefit must be at least 3% of the maximum benefit calculated under the plan's formula, multiplied by the number of years of participation.

2.  The 133.5% test: the accrued benefit payable at Normal Retirement Age equals the normal retirement benefit, and accrual in any plan year does not exceed 133.5% of the accrual for any prior year. In other words, benefits must accrue in a fairly level manner in each year.

3.  The fractional rule: the annual benefit an employee has accrued at the time of separation from service must be proportionate to what he or she would have received by remaining employed until normal retirement age.

Under § 412(i), insured plans whose accrued benefit is always at least equal to the cash surrender value of the insurance are exempt from the minimum funding rules.

The Second Circuit ruled in early 2006 that Xerox unlawfully reduced the pension benefits of persons who left the company and were rehired. Xerox used a "phantom account offset" system under which the lump sum received when the individual left the company for the first time was used to cut the benefits at eventual retirement. The Second Circuit ruled that a plan amendment occurs not when the plan administrator changes the way the plan operates, but when the employees are properly informed of the change. The court ruled that proper information was not provided until 1998, so applying it to anyone who was rehired before that date would be a violation of the anti-cutback rule. [*Frommert v. Conkright*, 433 F.3d 254 (2d Cir. 2006); the same offset method was also disapproved in *Miller v. Xerox Corp.*, 464 F.3d 871 (9th Cir. 2006), *cert. denied*, Mar. 19, 2007]. In its April 21, 2010 decision in this case [559 U.S. 506], the Supreme Court strongly affirmed the powers of plan administrators. According to the Supreme Court, the basic principle comes from *Firestone Tire & Rubber v. Bruch* [489 U.S. 101]. As long as the plan documents give the administrators the power to interpret the plan, courts must uphold the plan administrator's interpretation of plan terms as long as it is not unreasonable. The Supreme Court said that this principle is necessary to carry out ERISA's intention of making plan administration uniform and predictable.

A mid-2012 Fourth Circuit decision holds that increased benefit accruals to participants who have reached normal retirement age (NRA) do not violate the prohibition against backloading in later years. The 133 1/3% test forbids accrual of benefits more than 1/3 greater than the annual rate of accrual in the previous year. The rule was adopted to prevent employers from offering inadequate accrual rates in the early years of employment (when turnover is highest). In this case, the NRA was defined as the earlier of age 64 or 60 months of vesting service. The Fourth Circuit held that ERISA anti-backloading rules no longer apply once the participant reaches NRA. [*McCorkle v. Bank of Am. Corp.*, 688 F.3d 164 (4th Cir. 2012); see Mark Casciari and Justin T. Curley, *The Court Of Appeals For The Fourth Circuit Finds No Backloading Problem With Accrual Increases That Occur After Normal Retirement Age*, Seyfarth Shaw ERISA & Employee Benefits Litigation Blog (Aug. 21, 2012) (benefitslink.com)]

## § 5.07  NOTICES OF REDUCTION OF BENEFIT ACCRUALS

Defined benefit plans (and other plans subject to the I.R.C. § 412 full funding rules) have an obligation under ERISA § 204(h) and I.R.C. § 4980F (a new provision added by EGTRRA) to provide notice of plan amendments that significantly reduce future benefit accruals. The notice must contain the text or a summary of the plan amendment, and the effective date of the amendment. Notice must be given at least 15 days before the effective date of the plan amendment. [See the JCWAA § 411(u) for technical corrections to this provision]

Not only is an excise tax imposed on the failure, but in "egregious" cases (where the employer intentionally refused to give notice, or failed very badly to disclose the needed information) the plan amendment will not be given effect. Therefore, participants will be entitled to the unreduced benefit that was in effect before the plan was amended. See T.D. 9052, RIN-1545-BA08 2003-19 I.R.B. 879. The plan is required to provide notice to plan participants when the rate of future accrual is significantly reduced, or when an early retirement subsidy is modified in a way that operates as a reduction in the rate of future benefit accruals.

In general, the notice must be given at least 45 days before the effective date of the change, but the notice can be as short as 15 days before the effective date for certain merger and acquisition-related transactions of small plans. Also in connection with mergers and acquisitions, where there is a plan-to-plan transfer or merger that affects only the early retirement benefit or subsidy, notice can be given after the effective date of the amendment, but no more than 30 days later.

The notice must be given in a form that is understandable to the average plan participant, providing enough information to understand the effect of the amendment. Excise tax penalties are imposed under ERISA § 204(h)(6) for failure to provide the required notice. See also T.D. 9219, 2005-38 I.R.B. 538.

The Pension Funding Equity Act of 2004, Pub. L. No. 108-218, provides that certain employers who are required to make additional contributions under I.R.C. § 412(l) can elect instead to make lower "alternative deficit reduction contributions" for certain plan years. This relief is available to commercial passenger airlines, steel mills, and 501(c)(5) organizations.

In late 2009, the IRS published T.D. 9472, 2009-51 I.R.B. 850, final regulations about the § 204(h) notice requirements for plan amendments made to conform to the PPA. As long as the PPA compliant amendment is adopted by the last day of the 2009 plan year, it can have retroactive application without violating the anti-cutback rule. It is not necessary to give participants a § 204(h) notice with respect to PPA amendments reflecting mandatory changes in interest rates or mortality assumptions. Nor is a 204(h) notice required for changes to benefits that are not protected benefits, or to protected benefits that can be altered in accordance with § 411(d)(6), or for adoption of a retroactive amendment to comply with PPA § 1107.

Code § 4980F(e)(3) requires notice to be provided within a reasonable time before the plan amendment takes effect. In general, that means 45 days before the effective date (15 days for small or multi-employer plans). However, for some amendments that took effect by December 31, 2008, notice is acceptable if given at least 30 days before the effective date. T.D. 9472 covers amendments required by the PPA's special funding rules for airlines, and for single-employer plans with certain funding shortfalls. Unpredictable contingent event benefits are limited if a plan's AFTAP is, or would be, under 60%, and amendments increasing the plan's liabilities because of a benefits increase are limited if the AFTAP would be under 80%. Certain payments are prohibited when AFTAP is in the 60–80% range; the sponsor is in Chapter 11; and the plan's actuary cannot certify that AFTAP is at least 100%. Benefit accruals cease when AFTAP falls below 60%. [Transamerica Center for Retirement Studies, TCRS 2009-15: *IRS Issues Final Guidance on Section 204(h) Notice Requirements Post PPA* (Dec. 9, 2009) (benefitslink.com)]

The First Circuit held that it was permissible for an employer to eliminate participants' option to move defined contribution plan assets to a defined benefit plan. Although an accrued benefit was diminished, the anti-cutback rule was not violated because ERISA permits this type of benefit to be eliminated. [*Tasker v. DHL Ret. Savings Plan*, 621 F.3d 34 (1st Cir. 2010); see Fred Schneyer, *Interplan Asset Transfer Elimination Upheld*, plansponsor.com (Oct. 7, 2010)]

In late 2012, the Western District of Washington dismissed a case brought by former employees of Airborne Express who claimed that a 2004 amendment that eliminated the right to transfer between defined benefit and defined contribution plans violated the anti-cutback rule by reducing their monthly annuity. The plaintiffs worked for Airborne Express in 2003 when it was acquired by DHL Holdings USA. DHL merged the defined contribution plan into its own plan and eliminated the transfer option. The defined benefit plan had a floor-offset feature and a profit-sharing plan. The benefit formula was based on years of service and final average compensation offset by benefits from the profit-sharing plan (an individual account defined contribution plan). The district court cited an IRS regulation that specifically permits such amendments. The plaintiffs said that they were protected against reductions in their monthly benefit, but the district court held that the regulation does not include that requirement. [*Andersen v. DHL Ret. Pension Plan*, No. C12-439 MJP, 2012 U.S. Dist. LEXIS 157805 (W.D. Wash. Nov. 2, 2012).]

The Eleventh Circuit, noting that Social Security integration (reducing the benefit to coordinate the Social Security benefits the participant receives) is permitted by 29 U.S.C. § 1056(b)), held that it did not violate the anti-cutback rule for a frozen plan to adopt amendments that changed the Social Security integration formula for people who had not yet reached the plan's early retirement age. The change could not affect future benefit accruals because the plan was frozen and there would be no more benefit accruals. The test of an accrued benefit is what a participant would receive by terminating employment at that point, and the plaintiff here was younger than 52, the earliest age at which benefits were available. The right to a future benefit accrual based on additional service is not an accrued benefit, so changing it does not violate the anti-cutback rule. [*Cinotto v. Delta Air Lines Inc.*, 674 F.3d 1285 (11th Cir. 2012)]

In late 2012, the IRS finalized regulations under the § 411(d)(6) anti-cutback rules effective for plan amendments adopted and effective after November 8, 2012. Single-employer defined benefit plans that are subject to ERISA § 4021 can be amended to eliminate lump sum or other optional forms of benefit that accelerate payment after bankruptcy. The PBGC and the Bankruptcy Court must agree that the plan would go through a distress or involuntary termination if the optional benefits are not eliminated. The PBGC must also determine that the plan is not sufficiently funded to provide the guaranteed benefits. If an optional benefit form is eliminated, and the plan does not have other options with substantial survivor benefits, the same amendment that eliminates the lump sum distribution option can also adopt other options to provide survivor benefits. The entire amendment is considered together in determining if the amendment can take effect in accordance with § 436(c). [T.D. 9601, 77 Fed. Reg. 66915 (Nov. 8, 2012), finalizing proposals at 77 Fed. Reg. 37349 (June 21, 2012); see Kristen Heinzinger, *IRS Finalizes Relief for Bankrupt DB Sponsors*, plansponsor.com (Nov. 8, 2012)]

For example, the bankruptcy court permitted American Airlines to eliminate optional lump sum and installment forms of benefit payments, on the grounds that so many pilots would retire if they could get a lump sum when the airline emerges from bankruptcy that it would be difficult to adequately staff the schedule. [Rebecca Moore, *American Allowed to Eliminate Lump Sums*, plansponsor.com (Dec. 14, 2012)]

## § 5.08  PBGC COMPLIANCE

### [A]  PBGC Organization

Formally speaking, the Pension Benefit Guarantee Corporation (PBGC) is organized as a corporation, but it's really a quasi-governmental agency that draws its powers from ERISA § 4002. The PBGC's Board of Directors consists of the Secretaries of Labor, Treasury, and Commerce. The federal court system gives the agency special deference, by giving its cases the earliest possible calendar dates. Employers sued by the PBGC in connection with a plan termination can be required to pay part or all of the agency's litigation costs.

The PBGC protects 43 million employees and retirees. Its single-employer program covers almost 33 million people in 24,000 pension plans; the multi-employer program covers 10 million in 1,500 plans. In FY 2012, the PBGC covered 130,000 American Airlines plan participants; tens of thousands of participants in other plans going through bankruptcy; and 37,000 people whose employer companies emerged from bankruptcy without terminating the plan. The PBGC negotiated $31 million "financial assurance" for over 9,000 people whose plans were at risk because of corporation transactions, $471 million financial assurance for 50,000 people whose companies downsized, and took over 47,000 people in 155 newly failed single employer plans. The PBGC paid out $5.5 billion to almost 887,000 retirees in over 4,500 failed plans. A further 614,000 workers will collect benefits from those plans after they retire. [*PBGC Performance Report*, FY 2012 annual report, < http://www.pbgc.gov/documents/2012-annual-report.pdf>]

In fiscal 2012, the PBGC once again reported a record deficit: $34 billion as of the end of the fiscal year on September 30, versus $26 billion the year before. For most of its existence, the PBGC has operated at a deficit, although there were some surpluses in the late 1990s and early 2000s. The PBGC's pension obligations rose $12 billion, reaching $119 billion, whereas the increase in assets was only $4 billion, bringing the asset level to $85 billion. This was the tenth year in a row with a deficit, and 2012 was a particularly difficult year because of the number and magnitude of bankruptcies and plan terminations. [AP, *U.S. Pension Insurer Runs Record $34B Deficit*, NYTimes.com (Nov. 16, 2012)]

The main task of the PBGC is to guarantee that participants in defined benefit plans will receive a basic benefit even if their plan is insufficiently funded, or if it is terminated.

## [B]   PBGC Premiums

The PBGC stays afloat by charging premiums to employers who maintain defined benefit plans. There are three types of premium: the flat-rate premium; the variable-rate premium (VRP) imposed on insured single-employer plans that have unfunded vested benefits; and a one-time termination premium. For 2010–2011 the flat rate premium for single employer plans rises from $34 to $35; the multi-employer premium remains $9 per employee. [*FAQs: Premiums*, <http://www.pbgc.gov/about/faq/pg/premiumfaq.html>]

The Moving Ahead for Progress in the 21st Century Act (MAP-21; Pub. L. No. 112-141), increases the base annual PBGC premium from the 2012 level of $35 per participant per year in single-employer plans to $42 for 2013, $49 in 2014; and $50 in 2015. The variable-rate premium (VRP) will also be indexed. For 2013, it will be the 2012 premium, indexed for inflation; making the 2013 level $9/$1,000 unfunded vested benefit, rising to $13 in 2014 and $18 in 2015. However, starting in 2013, the VRP will be subject to a cap of $400 per participant. The cap amount will also be indexed for inflation. This statute also increases the PBGC premiums for multi-employer plans. The MAP-21 provides that even if deflation rather than inflation occurs, the PBGC premium will not decrease. The PBGC wanted the power to raise premiums itself, rather than waiting for Congress to pass a statute, but Congress refused to give the PBGC this power. [Rebecca Moore, *Congress Passes Bill With Pension Funding Relief*, planspons or.com (June 29, 2012); Buck Consultants FYI, *2012 Pension Plan Funding Stabilization Finally a Reality* (July 6, 2012) (benefitslink.com); PBGC, *Pension Insurance Premiums Fact Sheet*, <http://www.pbgc.gov/res/factsheets/page/premiums.html> (undated; last accessed August 20, 2013)]

Seventy-seven pages of instructions for filing 2012 PBGC premium packages are available online at <http://www.pbgc.gov/Documents/2012_premium_payment_instructions.pdf>. The forms for 2012 returns have been updated to permit inclusion of the optional information about the preparer of the forms. Disclosure of this information is not mandatory, but the IRS encourages plans to provide it. Trust information on Schedules H and I is also optional. The Schedule SB instructions explain that additional detail is required to add the prior year's excess contributions to the pre-funding balance. Single-employer defined benefit plans are required to follow the guidance contained in Notice 2012-61, 2012-42 I.R.B. 479 about completing the Schedule SB in light of MAP-21 requirements. [Informational (non-filing) copies of forms, schedules, and instructions at www. efast.dol.gov; check this site for availability of the filing versions. See DOL, *U.S. Labor Department Releases Advance Copies Of 2012 Form 5500 Annual Report* (Dec. 4, 2012) (benefitslink.com).]

An additional premium of $1,250 per participant is imposed when a single-employer plan is terminated under ERISA § 4041(c)(2)(B) or 4042. If the plan is terminated while the sponsor's Chapter 11 bankruptcy case is pending, the special premium is not due until the sponsor's bankruptcy discharge or until the bankruptcy case is dismissed.

A PBGC Final Rule was adopted in 2008, explaining how to measure the unfunded vested benefits used to calculate the variable-rate premium.

The PPA made more plans subject to the VRP, because they can no longer claim an exemption on the basis of satisfying the full funding limitation, if they have a shortfall in their funding target as prescribed by the PPA. The Final Regulations make it clear that the number of participants is calculated using the valuation date for the premium payment year, on the theory that this reflects the current funding status better than a valuation based on the first day of the prior year. The UVB calculation is made based on the fair market value of the plan assets on the valuation date—not counting current year contributions from the employer, but assets are not reduced by any credit balances that the plan holds. [PBGC Final Rule, 73 Fed. Reg. 15065 (Mar. 21, 2008); see Harold J. Ashner, Analysis of PBGC's *Final Rule Implementing Variable-Rate Premium Changes*, <http://www.keightleyashner.com/publications/BNA-040408.pdf> (Apr. 8, 2008)]

The PBGC premium is charged for each participant, terminated vested participant, and beneficiary already receiving benefits, other than "lost" beneficiaries (the plan knows they may be entitled to benefits, but can't find them) for whom an insurance company has an irrevocable commitment to pay all the benefits. All defined benefit plans that are subject to PBGC insurance must file Form PBGC-1 each year as a combined annual report and declaration of premium payments.

The premium is paid with Form 1-ES (if the plan has more than 500 participants) or with Form 10-SP (short form for smaller plans). The contributing sponsor and the plan administrator are both liable for the PBGC premium. If the premium is not paid on time, interest runs from the due date, plus a late charge of 5% per month (capped at 100% of the original unpaid premium). The PBGC is also empowered to collect unpaid premiums from what would otherwise be the employer's federal tax refund. If the employer is a federal contractor, the PBGC can seize federal contract payments.

■ **TIP:**   The forms are available online as PDF files. [See <http://www.pbgc.gov/practitioners/premium-filings/content/page1142.html>]

The PBGC proposed a new procedure, to take effect in 2014, that would make it easier for employers to administer the payment process. Prior law set the premium due date based on the size of the plan (small—under 100 participants; medium, 100–499 participants, large, over 500 participants) as well as on the type of premium. The proposal calls for a single, uniform due date, 9½ months after the beginning of the premium payment year, no matter what kinds of premiums are being paid or what size of the organization; for 2014, that would be October 15, 2014 for all premiums. As a result, small plans would have to pay both the 2013 and the 2014 premium in 2014. There are special rules for new plans and terminating plans. The proposal also affects the calculation of the VRP for some small plans. [Buck Consultants FYI, *PBGC Proposes New Premium Rules for 2014*, <http://www.buckconsultants.com/portals/0/publications/fyi/2013/FYI-2013-0725-PBGC-proposes-new-premium-rules-2014.pdf> (July 25, 2013)]

In September 2011, the PBGC relieved defined benefit plan sponsors from certain penalties when the required annual premium payments are not made on time. Under ERISA § 4007 and 29 C.F.R. Part 4007, interest and penalties are applied when the annual premium payments are not made on time. But for plan years beginning after 2010, the PBGC automatically waives payment penalties imposed solely because of lateness of up to seven calendar days. [76 Fed. Reg. 57082 (Sept. 15, 2011); see Rebecca Moore, *PBGC Offers Relief to DB Plan Sponsors*, plansponsor.com (Sept. 14, 2011)]

On January 31, 2012 the PBGC announced a voluntary compliance program for defined benefit plans that have never paid the required PBGC premiums. Penalties—although not interest on the past-due premiums—will be waived. The administrator must notify the PBGC by July 31, 2012 and pay the past due premiums by August 31, 2012 (or a later date set by the PBGC). The PBGC announced that, after the expiration of this program, enforcement efforts will be stepped up, and penalties will be imposed. [<http://www.pbgc.gov/news/press/releases/pr11-55.html>; see PLC, *PBGC Provides Temporary Relief for Defined Benefit Plans That Have Not Paid Premiums* (Feb. 8, 2012) (benefitslink.com)]

The IRS' Employee Plans Compliance Unit (EPCU) launched a Form 5500 non-filer project late in 2011, sending compliance check letters to plan sponsors for whom there is no record of a 5500 or 5500-SF filing with the DOL, or 5500-EZ with the IRS after six to nine months have elapsed since the due date of the return. EPCU asks the sponsor to either file the return or explain why it was not necessary. If a form was required, the IRS sends out a CP 403 Notice (delinquency notice) seeking a response within 30 days. EPCU does not analyze whether employers' explanations for nonfiling are reasonable, although the IRS or the DOL may waive or reduce penalties on a showing of mitigating circumstances that reduced the plan's ability to file the return. [IRS Employee Plans

News, Issue 2011-7 (Oct. 12, 2011); see CCH Pension & Benefits, *EPCU Begins Form 5500 Non-Filer Project* (Nov. 15, 2011) (benefitslink.com)]

All premium information required by ERISA § 4007 must now be e-filed. The plan can file by entering data directly into MyPAA, by uploading data from proprietary software, or by importing data into the MyPAA data entry screens from approved software. MyPAA accepts credit cards, electronic checks, and Automated Clearing House transfers; payments can also be made outside MyPAA. [<http://edocket.access.gpo.gov/2006/pdf/E6-8433.pdf> (no www), 71 Fed. Reg. 31077 (June 1, 2006)]

Electronic filing of Form 5500 and Form 5500-SF (the small plan form), using the EFAST-2 system (the system maintained by the DOL, the IRS, and the PBGC for electronic filing of Form 5500 and Form 5500-SF) has been mandatory since January 1, 2010. To file electronically, the sponsor or the person designated by the sponsor must use either IFILE, a free web-based filing application available at <http://www.efast.dol.gov>, or third-party software that has been approved by the DOL. However, Schedule SSA, the Annual Registration Statement for Deferred Vested Participants, cannot be submitted on EFAST-2, even for delinquent or amended filings for years before 2009. Form 8955-SSA, the Annual Registration Statement for Deferred Vested Participants, must be filed with the IRS. [Seyfarth.com, *Mandatory Electronic Filing of 5500s to Begin in 2010* (Sept. 30, 2009) (benefitslink.com); [EBSA, *Annual Return/Report 5500 Series Forms and Instructions*, <http://www.dol.gov/ebsa/5500main.html>]

Starting January 1, 2012, Forms 5500 and 5500-SF must be signed electronically. Forms that do not have an electronic signature will not be processed and the plan might be penalized. Forms that have an invalid electronic signature will be characterized as "processing stopped." The employer, plan sponsor, or plan administrator must electronically sign the Form 5500 or 5500-SF before submitting the form to the DOL and the IRS. The form can also be signed by an authorized plan service provider who has specific written authorization from the plan administrator. [John Iekel, Smart HR, *Electronic Signatures for Forms 5500 and 5500-SF Mandatory Jan. 1* (Dec. 21, 2011) (benefitslink.com)]

## [C]  Accounting Issues

On the fifteenth of every month, the PBGC updates its Website [<http://www.pbgc.gov/practitioners/interest-rates/content/index.html>] to give the interest rates that should be used in that month for:

- Valuation of lump-sum payments made by the plan;
- Variable rate premiums;
- Valuation of annuity benefits;
- PBGC charges imposed with respect to employer liability, unpaid contributions, and unpaid premiums.

PBGC staff can be reached by e-mail to answer compliance questions about:

- Premium calculations and payments: premiums@pbgc.gov;
- Coverage and standard terminations: standard@pbgc.gov;
- Distress terminations: distress.term@pbgc.gov;
- Early warning program: advance.report@pbgc.gov;
- ERISA § 4010 reporting: ERISA.4010@pbgc.gov;
- Reportable events: post-event.report@pbgc.gov;
- General legal questions: AskOGC@pbgc.gov;
- Problem resolution officer: practitioner.pro@pbgc.gov;
- Other: Ask.PBGC@pbgc.gov.

## § 5.09  REPORTABLE EVENTS

The PBGC doesn't want to be caught by surprise when a plan fails. To this end, plan administrators have a duty to report unusual events to the PBGC that might eventually require the agency to take over payment of pensions. Depending on the seriousness of the event, the PBGC might merely maintain a watchful attitude; or it might seek the appointment of a temporary trustee to manage the plan, or even go to the appropriate federal District Court to seek authority to terminate the plan.

The PBGC regulations identify 19 reportable events. Some of them must be reported 30 days before the event is scheduled to occur; others may be reported after the fact. The events include the following:

- The plan's bankruptcy or insolvency;
- The sponsoring employer's liquidation, bankruptcy or insolvency;
- Notice from the IRS that the plan has ceased to be a qualified retirement plan;
- IRS determination that the plan has terminated or partially terminated;
- Failure to meet the minimum funding standard;
- Receiving a minimum funding waiver from the IRS;
- Inability to pay benefits as they come due;
- DOL determination that the plan fails to comply with ERISA Title I;
- Adoption of a plan amendment that decreases any participant's retirement benefit (except for certain decreases relating to integration with Social Security);

- A reduction in the number of active participants in the plan, to the extent that the number is less than 80% of the census at the beginning of the year or 75% of the number of active participants at the beginning of the preceding plan year;

- Distributing $10,000 or more to a participant who is a "substantial owner" (a definition roughly equal to 10% shareholder in the employer corporation) if the plan has any unfunded, nonforfeitable benefits after the distribution. Distributions made on account of the death of the substantial owner are not counted for this purpose;

- Merger or consolidation of the plan, or transfer of its assets;

- DOL requirement of an alternative method of compliance under ERISA § 110;

- A change of plan sponsor (or the same plan sponsor leaving a controlled group of corporations), if the plan has $1 million or more in unfunded nonforfeitable benefits;

- The controlling sponsor, or a member of its controlled group, engages in a highly unusual transaction, such as declaring an extraordinary dividend or redeeming 10% or more of its stock;

At one time, the sponsoring employer had a duty to report the events to the plan administrator, but now it is only required that the events be reported to the PBGC. ERISA § 4043 requires advance notice of liquidating bankruptcy, extraordinary dividends, transfer of 3% of plan liabilities, or leaving a controlled group of corporations. However, in 2013, the PBGC published proposals to greatly reduce reporting obligations.

In late 2009, the PBGC proposed regulations to conform the agency's rules on reportable events (ERISA § 4043) to the PPA, adding two new reportable events (funding-based benefit limits; transfers to retiree health benefit accounts). [74 Fed. Reg. 61248 (Nov. 23, 2009)] The PBGC published final regulations under ERISA § 4010 on March 16, 2009 (reporting high levels of unfunded vested benefits). The 4010 filing is required so the PBGC will be aware of its potential liabilities if a significantly underfunded plan terminates. The PPA amended § 4010 by requiring a company to file if it fails the "gateway" test: that is, if the funding target attainment percentage of the plan (or any plan maintained by any member of its controlled group) falls below 80%. Filing may also be required when a plan gets a funding waiver, or fails to make the minimum contribution it was required to make. Plans must report their funding target attainment percentages and their funding targets (calculated as if the plan had been at risk for at least five years).. To avoid having to make a 4010 filing, a sponsor can make additional contributions, bringing funding above the triggering 80% level. Reporting under § 4010 is not required if the shortfall for the entire controlled group is less than $15 million. [74 Fed. Reg. 11022 (Mar. 16, 2009),]

In addition to the required report to the PBGC, whenever a defined benefit plan fails to satisfy the minimum funding standard, and there has been no waiver of minimum funding granted, then participants must be notified. Form 200 must be filed with the PBGC within 10 days of the time a failure to meet the minimum funding standard involves $1 million or more.

The 2009 rules were highly controversial and the PBGC has proposed to relax them. The PBGC's latest technical update, Technical Update 13-1, offers some small pension plans relief from the provisions of the proposed amendments dealing with reportable events. The relief is permanent, not just for 2013, but could be superseded if the PBGC issues final rules that are different. The ERISA § 4034.25 waiver of the requirement of reporting missed quarterly contributions is extended for all years in which the plan either has fewer than 25 participants, or has between 25–100 participants and files a simplified notice with the PBGC. However, relief is not available if the quarterly contribution was missed as a result of the plan's financial inability to pay. Technical Update 13-1 applies the assets and liabilities used to calculate the variable rate premium to determine the reporting requirements for events in the next plan year—including eligibility for reporting waivers, extensions, and mandatory advance reporting. [Mark Schulte, *Déjà Vu All Over Again: PBGC Extends Reportable Event Relief for 2013 and Beyond*, VIA Retirement Plan Blog (Jan. 30, 2013) (benefitslink.com)]

In April 2013, the PBGC published a new proposal, under which reporting obligations would be reduced significantly, so that financially sound plans would not have to report most of what would otherwise be reportable events. The PBGC estimated that over 90% of plans and sponsors would no longer have to make most reports. The proposal retains the Technical Update 13-1 relief (i.e., reporting of missed contributions is waived or reduced for plans with under 100 participants as long as the reason for missing the contribution was not inability to pay).

The 2013 proposal relieves "financially sound" plans and plan sponsors of the obligation to report, specifying five criteria for determining soundness. The most important factor is having a good credit rating from a commercial credit reporting company (e.g., Dun & Bradstreet) based on the company's ability to make timely debt repayment. Financially sound plans would not have to make a post-event report for most of the events already covered by a funding-based waiver—for example, an extraordinary dividend or stock redemption; reduction in active participants; or transfer of benefit liabilities.

The other four criteria are safe use of secured debt; two years of positive net income; two years without defaulting on a major loans; and two years of keeping current on pension plan contributions (other than quarterly contributions for which the duty to report has been waived).

The April 2013 proposal includes another safe harbor: plans that were fully funded on a termination basis at the end of the previous year or 120% funded on a premium basis for the previous year would not have to report. Plans with fewer than 100 participants would be given an extra month to report events eligible for these safe harbors.

Small (fewer than 100 participants) plans would not have a reportable event based on the number of participants falling below 80% of the number at the end of the previous year or 75% of the number at the beginning of the previous year. Larger plans would only have to report if the reduction was caused by a single event such as reorganization or mass layoff; if the reduction occurred in a period of 30 days or less; or if the number of participants in the same year falls more than 20%. Large plans can use the financial soundness safe harbor to avoid reporting based on reduction in the number of participants.

The proposal says that there are other reporting obligations that let the PBGC know about a plan's liquidity levels, so reporting is waived for missed contributions that reflect inability to pay benefits when due—unless the plan is exempt from the liquidity shortfall provisions. But reporting is not waived for small plans or under the financial soundness safe harbor.

The requirement to report distributions to substantial owners made when the plan is not fully funded is triggered only when one substantial owner receives distributions that exceed 1% of plan assets or more than 5% of plan assets are distributed to multiple substantial owners.

Reporting is not required if there has been a reorganization within a controlled group of corporations leading to one member of the group ceasing to exist because it has been merged into another member of the group.

However, the proposal eliminates the funding-based waiver for reporting liquidation. Even small plans and plans that qualify for the financial soundness safe harbor must report if they are liquidated.

Prior law makes it a reportable event if 3% or more of a plan's benefit liabilities are transferred within a 12-month period. The proposed regulations make it clear that satisfying benefit liabilities by paying a lump sum or buying an annuity is not a transfer of benefit liabilities for this purpose.

Under the proposal, reporting continues to be required when the plan applies for a minimum funding waiver, and the small-plan and financial soundness safe harbors are not available.

Prior law made it a reportable event when there is a default in payment of over 30 days on a loan of $10 million or more—not only by the plan sponsor, but also by any member of a controlled group of corporations it belongs to. Written notice of default based on reduced cash reserves or a lender's acceleration of a loan is also a reportable event. The proposed regulations not only retain this requirement but also make it stronger: reporting is required when there is a loan acceleration or any kind of default, including a lender's waiver of its right to declare a default. Small plans and plans entitled to the financial soundness safe harbor must still report this event.

The proposed regulations eliminate the sponsor's bankruptcy as a reportable event, because there are many other reliable sources of bankruptcy information available to the PBGC. Reporting of insolvency is not waived for small plans or plans meeting the financial soundness safe harbor.

If this proposal is finalized, in effect in most situations there would be only five situations that would still be reportable events:

- Loan default;
- Failure to make required contributions;
- Applying for a funding waiver;
- Not being able to pay benefits as they fall due;
- Being insolvent; and
- Liquidation.

The proposed regulation has an effective date of January 1, 2014, although the PBGC might publish a rule making the waiver and safe harbor rules effective earlier. [78 Fed. Reg. 20039 (Apr. 3, 2013); see Rebecca Moore, *PBGC Proposed Reduced Reporting Obligations*, plansponsor.com (Apr. 2, 2013); Buck Consultants FYI, *PBGC Reproposes Reportable Event Rules* (Apr. 5, 2013) (benefitslink .com)]

The PBGC has proposed regulations [72 Fed. Reg. 68542 (Dec. 5, 2007)] about disclosures required for distress terminations and terminations initiated by the PBGC after the PPA's enactment date of August 17, 2006. Under ERISA §§ 4041 and 4042, participants and other affected parties are entitled to request information about a pending termination; the plan (or the PBGC, if the agency initiated the termination) must provide the information within 15 business days of the request. ERISA § 4071 imposes a penalty of up to $1,100 a day for failure to make timely disclosure. [Guest article, *PBGC Proposes Rules on New Termination Information Disclosure Requirements*, Deloitte's Washington Bulletin, <http://benefitslink.com/articles/washbull080122a.html> (Jan. 22, 2008)]

## § 5.10   SPECIAL RULES FOR AT-RISK PLANS

The PPA creates a new category, the "at-risk" plan. Plans with under 500 participants are exempt. The determination of risk assumes that all participants who are eligible for benefits in the current plan year or the following 10 years retire as soon as they can and opt for the subsidized early retirement benefit (the benefit with the highest present value of liabilities). A plan is at risk if, in the previous plan year, it was less than 80% funded using the general funding rules and less than 70% funded using the tougher actuarial assumptions for at-risk plans. The 80% requirement is phased in gradually between 2008 and 2011. Plans that were at risk for two of the previous four years must make their calculations subject to an added load factor of $700 per participant, 4% of the funding target and target normal cost.

For at-risk plans, the controls depend on the "adjusted funding target attainment percentage," the ratio of plan assets to the plan's funding target. The funding target is calculated as if the plan had purchased annuities for every participant who was not a Highly Compensated Employee for the two years before the year of the calculation.

At-risk plans are restricted vis-à-vis benefit increases, payments, accruals, and shutdown benefits. The plan cannot be amended to increase benefits if the adjusted funding target attainment percentage is lower than 80%, or if the amendment has the effect of reducing the percentage below 80%. An exemption is available if the plan sponsor makes additional contributions or provides security to bring the plan up to the 80% funding level. The rule is not applied during a plan's first five years in existence. Amendments that increase benefits under a formula that is not based on compensation, and where the increase is not more than the average wage increase for plan participants, are exempt. So are cost of living increases in flat-dollar plans.

If the plan's adjusted funding target attainment percentage is below 60%, or if it is below 100% and the sponsor is bankrupt, then benefits must be paid in life annuity rather than lump-sum form. (This restriction does not apply to plans that were frozen as of September 1, 2005, and continues frozen.) Plans whose adjusted funding target attainment percentage is somewhere between 60%–80% are allowed to make a one-time lump sum payment, limited to the present value of the maximum amount guaranteed by the PBGC to the participant, or 50% of what would otherwise be paid—whichever is smaller. When the adjusted funding target attainment percentage is below 60% (except in the first five years of a new plan's operations), all future benefit accruals must be frozen unless the sponsor makes contributions or gives security to bring the funding up to the 60% level. Shutdown benefits, and other benefits based on an unpredictable contingent event, are forbidden when the target attainment percentage—before or after payment of the benefit—is below 60%.

Plan participants must be notified if funding deficiencies result in restrictions on benefits.

The benefit restrictions do not apply if the plan is fully funded: that is, if they satisfy the percentage requirements of the PPA as modified by WRERA.

The PBGC publishes tables for defined benefit plans to use to administer the partial restrictions imposed on lump sums distributions from plans that fall in the range of 60%–80% funded. The PPA limits lump sums and other accelerated distributions to the lesser of 50% of the benefit otherwise payable or the present value of the participant's maximum guarantee from the PBGC. For benefits with an annuity starting date in 2013, guarantee values are $125,539 at age 25, $153,501 at 30, $230,843 at 40, $371,638 at 50, $782,324 at 65, $1,122,428 at 70, and $2,844,680 at 80. [*Present Value of PBGC Maximum Guarantee*, <http://www.pbgc.gov/prac/mortality-retirement-and-pv-max-guarantee/present-guarantee.html> (last accessed Mar. 10, 2013)]

Notice 2012-70, 2012-51 I.R.B. 712 gives defined benefit plans additional time to comply with § 436. Previously, the deadline was the last day of the last plan year beginning on or after January 1, 2012. Under Notice 2012-70, the deadline for adopting the amendment is the latest of:

- The last day of the plan year for which the plan is first subject to § 436;

- The last day of the plan year beginning on or after January 1, 2013;

- The due date (including extensions) of the employer's tax return for the year that § 436 first applies to the plan.

Notice 2012-70 also extends the relief period for anti-cutback amendments. Sponsors submitting determination letter applications on or after February 1, 2013 for individually designed plans must adopt the § 436 amendment before submitting the application. Cycle B plans, whose filing is before February 1, 2013, are not subject to § 436. [McDermott Will & Emery, *IRS Extends Deadline for Defined Benefit Plans to Adopt Code Section 436 Amendments* (Dec. 13, 2012) (benefitslink.com)]

In March 2011, the PBGC proposed a rule to amend its regulation dealing with benefits payable in terminated single-employer plans. The rule implements PPA § 403, which says that the phase-in period for the guarantee of benefits that are contingent on an "unpredictable contingent event" (the regulation gives the example of a plant shut-down) begins no earlier than the date of the event itself. The rule was necessary because PBGC's guarantee of new pension benefits and benefit increases phases in over a five-year period starting with the later of the date of adoption or the effective date of the change. (This rule was adopted to protect the PBGC against obligations that would be created by plans that knew they were going to terminate adopting new benefits.) The PPA added a new section, ERISA § 4022(b)(8), phasing in the guarantee as if the amendment creating an unpredictable contingent event benefit was adopted on the date of the event, rather than the (usually earlier) date of the plan amendment. The net effect is that the guarantee for benefits that arise from unpredictable contingent events that occur within five years of plan termination is probably lower than the guarantee that would have been available under the pre-PPA law. [PBGC Proposed Rule RIN 1212-AB18, 76 Fed. Reg. 13304 (Mar. 11, 2011) See also PBGC Final Rule, 75 Fed. Reg. 33688 (June 15, 2010) providing that there is no guarantee of benefits earned between the time an employer files for bankruptcy and the date the PBGC takes over the plan; in a bankruptcy situation, benefits are guaranteed only if they were nonforfeitable as of the bankruptcy filing date.]

Some employers who downsized were pursued by the PBGC under ERISA § 4062(e), which gives the agency the power to require immediate escrow payments or posting of bond when cessation of operations results in separation from service of over 20% of participants in a defined benefit plan. Regulations were published in 2006, creating potential liability even on plans that did not terminate. The PBGC could demand that the plan purchase a bond or place funds in escrow to guarantee payments in case the plan later went through an involuntary or distress termination. Section 4062(e) had been on the books since 1974, but was seldom enforced until the 2006 regulations appeared. Additional regulations were proposed in 2010 expanding the definition of "substantial cessation of operations" and explaining the calculations involved. Under the 2010 proposal, the test of whether there has been cessation is whether the employer discontinues all significant activity in the furtherance of the purpose of the operation (maintenance and security are disregarded) and no longer conducts the operation at the facility on an ongoing basis. Section 4062(e) applies to cessation of operations at a facility even if the operation is continued or resumed by another employer at the same facility or another facility (e.g., when corporate assets are sold). [PBGC, *Liability for Termination of Single-Employer Plans; Treatment of Substantial Cessation of Operations*, FR Doc 2010-19695, RIN 1212-AB20, 75 Fed. Reg. 48283 (Aug. 10, 2010)]

In late 2012, the PBGC proposed to concentrate its enforcement efforts under § 4062(e) on the few plans that are at greatest risk. Under the new policy, the PBGC would not take action under § 4062(e) against small (fewer than100 participants) or credit-worthy companies. The PBGC responded to business criticism that the August 2010 proposals subjected companies to enforcement action even though there was little real risk of default. [R. Randall Tracht, Brian J. Dougherty, Lisa H. Barton, and Eric P. Sarabia, *PBGC Changes Enforcement Policy Under ERISA Section 4062(e)* Morgan, Lewis & Bockius (Nov. 13, 2012) (benefitslink.com)]

A March 2012 IRS Private Letter Ruling (PLR) says that participants in a defined benefit plan who stop working with an explicit expectation that they will quickly be rehired by the same employer have not really retired, so they are not eligible for early retirement benefits—and the plan could be disqualified. The ruling was requested by a multi-employer plan in critical funding status that sought to save money by eliminating the subsidized early retirement benefit and was worried that too many participants would retire early to lock in eligibility for the benefit. [Rebecca Moore, *IRS Addresses Agreements to Rehire Retirees*, plansponsor.com (Mar. 5, 2012)]

# CHAPTER 6

# DEFINED CONTRIBUTION AND 401(k) PLANS

## § 6.01 INTRODUCTION

As explored in Chapters 4 and 5, the defined benefit plan not only places the investment risk on the employer (because the employer must adjust its contributions to provide the promised level of benefits—and if the value of the plan's assets declines, and its investment return goes down, the employer must supply additional funds) but also subjects the employer to complex and expensive administrative requirements.

In the 1990s, therefore, the trend was to shift from defined benefit to defined contribution or 401(k) plans. The 401(k) plan form grew fast, because (although employer matches are permitted) the predominant form of funding for these plans is deferral of employee compensation.

In recent years, court cases and regulations have centered on economic factors. Many disappointed plan participants have charged that they were not given adequate investment alternatives, or that they lost potential appreciation because excessive fees were charged. Federal regulators have responded by increasing the amount of disclosure required in connection with defined contribution plans. Service providers (e.g., investment advisors; recordkeepers) must give the plan detailed information about the services they render the plan—and the cost of those services. The plan, in turn, must disclose information about investment costs to plan participants. Under appropriate conditions, service providers can render not just advice to the plan as a whole, but individual advice to plan participants.

The Plan Sponsor Council of America (PSCA) 55th Annual Survey of Profit Sharing and 401(k) plans showed more companies and participants are contributing to 401(k) plans, and at higher rates than in earlier years. More than three-quarters of eligible participants made contributions in both 2010 (76.9%) and 2011 (79.5%). In both years, almost half of plans allowed Roth 401(k) contributions (45.5% in 2010, 49%) in 2011, and in both years, 17.4% of employees who had this option made Roth contributions. In 2010, 41.8% of plans used automatic enrollment, rising to 45.9% in 2011. 401(k) plans offered an average of 19 funds in 2011. The most popular funds were actively managed domestic equity funds, actively managed international equity funds, indexed domestic equity funds, and actively managed domestic bond funds. [Stephen Miller, *Changes in 401(k) Plans Spur Higher Participation*, SHRM (Oct. 15, 2012) (benefitslink.com)]

An EBRI fact sheet published in March 2013 shows that in 1979, only 7% of U.S. workers participated only in a defined contribution plan; in that year, 28% of workers had only a defined benefit plan, and a further 10% had both. The situation changed greatly by 2011, when 31% of workers participated only in a defined contribution plan, 11% participated in both, and a mere 3% of workers had only a defined benefit plan. The fact sheet includes a dramatic graph, showing that the proportion of workers with both types of plans has stayed within the 10%–15% range—but defined benefit plan participation plummeted throughout the period as defined contribution plan participation soared. [EBRI Fast Facts

#225, *Pension Plan Participation*, <http://www.ebri.org/pdf/FF.225.DB-DC.28Mar13.pdf> (Mar. 28, 2013). For more detailed statistics, see <http://bit.ly.WEiMfD>.]

EBRI/ICI said that in 2013, for workers who had less than two years' tenure at their current employer, the average 401(k) balance was $3,426 for workers in their twenties, $8,745 for workers in their thirties, $14,582 for workers in their forties, $20,623 for workers in their fifties, and $25,678 for workers in their sixties. As a result, many plans had a large number of very small accounts. The smaller the average account balance in a plan, the higher the fees: the industry reference guide *401(k) Averages Book* says that in a $10 million plan with an average account balance of $50,000, fees will be 1.22%—but fees will be 1.44% if the average balance is only $10,000. Aon Hewitt reported that in 2011 about half of companies sponsoring IRA plans automatically rolled over accounts of former employees holding less than $5,000 to IRAs, thereby reducing administration costs and associated problems. [Ian Salisbury, *Kicked Out of Your 401(k)? Don't Let the Cash Sit*, WSJ.com (Mar. 25, 2013)]

## § 6.02  DEFINED CONTRIBUTION PLANS

As of early 2012, EBSA oversees about 718,000 private pension plans, of which about 498,000 are individual account plans such as 401(k) plans. [DOL Fact Sheet, *Final Regulation Relating to Service Provider Disclosures Under Section 408(b)(2)* (Feb. 2012)]

The 401(k) plan, also known as a CODA (Cash or Deferred Arrangement) is the most popular type of defined contribution plan, but a variety of defined compensation plan designs can be used, e.g., profit sharing; money purchase; target benefit; ESOP; leveraged ESOP; new comparability plans, as stand-alones or in conjunction with 401(k) plans.

The profit-sharing plan is the most basic defined contribution plan design. The employer does not have to have profits to make contributions, nor is it required that contributions be made whenever there are profits. Allocations can be made by a fixed formula such as a specified percentage of pay; as a flat dollar amount; a formula tied to age and/or years of service (such as X% of pay until the sum of age plus service reaches a certain amount, then a different percentage); a formula related to corporate profits; pro rata contributions by pay, or a completely discretionary amount. A profit-sharing plan can be integrated with Social Security benefits, so that the contribution percentage rises after the participant's income hits the FICA contribution base. In practice, most sponsors of profit-sharing plans do not actually make profit-sharing contributions; the plan is a vehicle for attaching 401(k) savings and matches.

Money purchase pension plans are defined contribution plans that are also pension plans. The formula must be fixed, not discretionary; ERISA rules apply; and the sponsor must meet a minimum funding standard. The contributions can be related to pay, be a flat amount, follow an age-plus-service formula, or other variations. Money purchase pension plans used to be fairly popular, especially among companies that wanted to offer very generous defined contribution plans—more than the 15% of eligible contribution that was once the limit for defined contribution plans. However, true money purchase plans are now obsolete, because a profit-sharing plan contribution can be as much as 25% of compensation.

A target benefit plan is a special money purchase pension plan that mirrors the accruals in a defined benefit plan, reflecting the underlying defined benefit plan formula—but each participant has an account balance which determines the eventual benefit. Target benefit plans were never very popular, and almost no new ones have been created since 1986, when that year's tax bill imposed anti-discrimination regulations that made it difficult to operate a target benefit plan.

An ESOP is a money purchase plan designed to invest primarily in employer securities. This was a popular plan design in the 1980s, but heavy investments in employer stock are now extremely controversial. A Leveraged ESOP (aka LESOP) is partially or wholly financed with loans that the plan sponsor obtains from banks or other lenders. Employees get shares allocated to their LESOP accounts (and can also diversify their investments), then receive shares or cash representing their vested balance when employment terminates. [JP Morgan Compensation & Benefit Strategies, *Rediscovering Defined Contribution Plans—Design Basics*, plansponsor.com (Nov. 13, 2008)]

In 2008, the maximum employer contribution to a defined contribution plan was $46,000 (up from $42,000 in 2005 and $45,000 in 2006). The maximum contribution for 2009, 2010, and 2011 is $49,000. The maximum contribution for 2012 is $50,000; for 2013, it is $51,000. The accrued benefit for a participant in a defined contribution plan equals the balance in the account. The balance, in turn, consists of employer contributions, any mandatory employee contributions that the plan requires, plus any voluntary contributions that the plan permits and the employee chooses to make. Defined contribution plans usually maintain separate subaccounts for the employer and employee component of each employee's account, but this is not a legal requirement.

Former employees of Airborne Express claimed that a 2004 plan amendment violated the anti-cutback rule by eliminating the right to transfer between their employer's defined benefit and defined contribution plans, reducing their monthly annuity. They worked for Airborne in 2003 when it was acquired by DHL Holdings USA. The plaintiffs participated in plans that allowed them to take either lump sums or annuities. They participated in both a defined benefit plan and an individual account profit sharing plan. DHL amended the plan, merging the defined contribution plan into its own plan and eliminating the transfer option. The District Court for the Western District of Washington granted a defense motion to dismiss for failure to state a claim, citing an IRS regulation (§ 1.411(d)-4) that specifically permits amendments of this type, and does not impose a requirement that the monthly benefit not be reduced by the transfer. [*Andersen v.*

*DHL Ret. Pension Plan*, No. C12-439 MJP, 2012 U.S. Dist. LEXIS 157805 (W.D. Wash. Nov. 2, 2012). See also *Tasker v. DHL*, 621 F.3d 34 (1st Cir. 2010).]

The IRS issued final rules applying to loans made on or after January 1, 2004 from qualified defined contribution plans, including loans made to participants who are on military leave (see § 1.18), refinanced loans, and exceptions to the ban on new loans to participants whose earlier loans are in default. A participant who suspends loan repayment during military service and then returns to work must repay the entire loan and its interest in substantially level installments by the end of the original loan term plus the period of military service. If the loan was not a mortgage on the principal residence, repayment must occur within five years plus the period of service, if the original loan term was less than five years. A new loan can be made despite a default based on an enforceable agreement to repay by payroll withholding, or if the plan receives security for the loan in addition to the participant's account balance. [CIGNA's Pension Analyst, *IRS Issues Additional Loan Rules* (September 2003) <http://www.cigna.com/professional/pdf/loanCPA2003.pdf>]

Early in 2009, amendments to Regulation Z were published, exempting most retirement plan loans from the Truth in Lending Act. Effective July 1, 2010, qualifying loans are made to a plan participant, from fully vested funds in his or her account, complying with all tax requirements including the § 72 annuity rules. [Rebecca Moore, *Plan Loans Exempt from Truth-in-Lending Disclosure Requirements*, plansponsor.com (Mar. 13, 2009)]

The Sixth Circuit held that income available to Chapter 13 debtors after repaying a 401(k) loan is projected disposable income that must be paid to unsecured creditors. The debtors will not be permitted to use it to make voluntary contributions to the plan. The 2005 bankruptcy reform law, Bankruptcy Abuse Prevention and Consumer Protection Act (BAPCPA), provides a limited exclusion for amounts withheld by an employer from an employee's wages for contributions to a qualified plan. The Sixth Circuit held that plan loan payments are excluded from debtor's disposable income, but voluntary contributions to a 401(k) plan are not. Contributions are only excluded from the bankruptcy estate if they were made before the date of the petition. [*In re Seafort*, 669 F.3d 662 (6th Cir. 2012); see CCH Pension & Benefits, *Debtors Could Not Begin Making Post-Petition Contributions To 401(K) Plans Following Repayment Of Plan Loans* (Mar. 23, 2012) (benefitslink.com)]

ERISA § 404(c) allows the participant to control the assets in a defined contribution account, including directing the investment of the account. If the participant assumes control, the plan's fiduciaries will not be liable for losses that result from participant control over the funds. Section 404(c) requires the plan to disclose adequate information about their investment alternatives. The plan must offer at least three diversified investment types, with materially different risk and return characteristics. Intent to use the § 404(c) safe harbor for part or all of a plan must be disclosed on Item 8a on the plan's Form 5500—and the form is signed under penalty of perjury. Participants must be allowed to change their portfolios at least once a quarter—more often if volatility requires. Participants must be given the mandatory disclosures (that the plan is a § 404(c) plan; that fiduciaries can be relieved of liability; what the plan's investment options are; and how to give investment instructions for the account). Participants can also request additional information, such as the annual operating expenses for each investment option, copies of financial statements and prospectuses, and the description and value of the assets in the portfolio. [Prudential Retirement Pension Analyst, *Department of Labor Requirements for Participant-Directed Investments* (July 2008) (benefitslink.com)]

The Seventh Circuit agreed with the Fourth Circuit (and the Department of Labor): choosing investment options for the plan, and deciding to retain an investment within the plan, are fiduciary acts that are not entitled to § 404(c) immunity because § 404(c) protects fiduciaries from being blamed for decisions over which they did not have control. However, the Seventh Circuit found for the plan: the stock fund was not worthless, and was not so risky that retaining it in the plan was imprudent. The plan was diversified and offered many other options. [*Howell v. Motorola Inc.*, 633 F.3d 552 (7th Cir. 2011); see EBIA Weekly, *Seventh Circuit Concludes Employer's Selection of Investment Options Is Not Protected Under ERISA Section 404(c)* (Feb. 10, 2011) (benefitslink.com); see also *Lingis v. Dorazil*, 633 F.3d 552 (7th Cir. 2011); see Fred Schneyer, *7th Circuit Stock Drop Rulings Seen as Helping Employers*, plansponsor.com (Jan. 31, 2011)]

The Third Circuit, relying on decisions in the Seventh and Eighth Circuits, allowed dismissal of a breach of fiduciary duty claim alleging that funds with excessive fee profiles (e.g., retail mutual funds) were included in the plan—as long as the fiduciary selected a broad enough range of funds with varying fee characteristics. At the time the complaint against Unisys was filed, the 401(k) plan had 73 different investment options, including 67 individual retail mutual funds with varying characteristics. However, the Third Circuit did not consider whether the 404(c) safe harbor was available, on the grounds that the complaint was properly dismissed so it didn't matter if the safe harbor would have applied. The Third Circuit treated Fidelity as a directed trustee with no contractual authority to control investment options—therefore, it was not a fiduciary for this purpose. All claims against Fidelity were dismissed, because Fidelity did not have knowledge of Unisys' process for selecting investment options. [*Renfro v. Unisys Corp.*, 671 F.3d 314 (3d Cir. 2011); see Richard Black, *The Latest Word on 401(k) Fee Litigation: Third Circuit Narrows Plaintiffs' Ability to Bring ERISA Breach of Fiduciary Duty Claims*, Littler Mendelson ASAP (August 2011) (benefitslink.com); Rebecca Moore, *Court Upholds Decision for Fidelity Unisys in Excessive Fee Case*, plansponsor.com (Sept. 9, 2011)]

But if the § 404(c) safe harbor is not available, a fiduciary can be liable for allowing participants to invest in company stock when it was manifestly imprudent to let them. A Seventh Circuit case held that the plan made no effort to show § 404(c) compliance, and the plaintiff remained 98% invested in employer stock, while its profit margins declined 70–80% over five years. [*Peabody v. Davis*, 636

F.3d 368 (7th Cir. 2011); see Rebecca Moore, *Fiduciaries Showing No Compliance with 404c Breached Duties*, plansponsor.com (Apr. 21, 2011)]

DOL's FAB 2009-03 (September 2009) permits the SPD to be used to satisfy the requirements of ERISA § 404(c), the provision that relieves fiduciaries of liability for investment losses in self-determined accounts. To obtain relief under FAB 2009-03, the plan sponsor must provide a copy of its most recent prospectus either right before or right after a participant's or beneficiary's initial investment in a registered security. Prospectuses must also be provided on request. In January 2009, the SEC published a new summary prospectus option for satisfying the SEC's prospectus rule, and the DOL will accept the short-form summary prospectus under this rule for ERISA § 404(c) purposes if it is the most recent prospectus provided to the plan. The summary prospectus provides key information about mutual funds in which participants and beneficiaries can invest. The summary prospectus must include the mutual fund's name; its ticker symbol; the share class of the stock; the fund's URL and e-mail address; the approximate date the summary prospectus was first used; and a toll-free number for obtaining additional information. The summary prospectus must contain information about the fund's investment objectives, fees and expenses, principal investment strategies, performance, risks of investing in the fund, tax information, and the like.

Selecting an annuity provider has important tax consequences. If a state guaranty association is in the picture, the Advisory Opinion says that the fiduciary should consider whether the annuity provider and the annuity product are covered; the extent of the guarantee; and how likely the guaranty association is to be able to continue to meet its obligations. [DOL Advisory Opinion 2002-14A (Dec. 18, 2002), posted to <http://www.dol.gov/pwba/regs/aos/ao2002-14a.html>]

In September 2007, in order to make annuity distributions more attractive to defined contribution plans, the DOL announced new rules relieving defined contribution plans from the "safest annuity available" rule instituted by Interpretive Bulletin 95-1. DOL Advisory Opinion 2002-14A extended the principle from defined benefit to defined contribution plans that offer annuities as an optional benefit. PPA § 665 mandated the DOL to issue regulations exempting defined contribution plans from this rule. Under September 2007 interim final rules, fiduciaries must select annuity providers with due care and skill, using factors such as the cost of the annuity vis-à-vis the benefits and administrative services offered; the annuity provider's capital, surplus and reserves; its rating; and whether it is covered by a state guarantee program. [Interim final rules, 72 Fed. Reg. 52004 (Sept. 12, 2007); safe harbor for fiduciaries choosing annuity providers, 72 Fed. Reg. 52021 (Sept. 12, 2007), discussed in Guest article, Deloitte Washington Bulletin, *DOL Releases Defined Contribution Plans from* "Safest Annuity Available" *Standard* (Sept. 17, 2007) (benefitslink.com)]

The DOL published final regulations on the selection of annuity providers for individual account plans in late 2008, creating a safe harbor for fiduciary obligations. The fiduciary must perform an objective, thorough, and analytical search to select annuity providers; consider enough information to determine the provider's ability to make all future payments under the contract; the total cost of the annuity contract (including fees and commissions) compared to the benefits of the deal. However, once the provider is selected, the fiduciary does not have to review the appropriateness of the provider. The safe harbor covers only the fiduciary's decision to buy an annuity to distribute the balances of individual account plans—not the selection of a particular investment product. [DOL Reg. § 2550.404a-4, 73 Fed. Reg. 58447 (Oct. 7, 2008); Amendment to Interpretive Bulletin 95-1, 73 Fed. Reg. 58445 (Oct. 7, 2008); Amendments to DOL Reg. §§ 2550.404a-3 and 2578.1, 73 Fed. Reg. 58459 (Oct. 7, 2008); Amendment to PTE 2006-06, 73 Fed. Reg. 58629 (Oct. 7, 2008). See Buck Consultants FYI, *DOL Issues Final Regulations on the Selection of Annuity Providers for Individual Account Plans* (Nov. 7, 2008) (benefitslink.com).]

## [A] § 415 Regulations

In mid-2005, the IRS issued Proposed Regulations on maximum benefits and contributions reflecting the many statutory changes made since the previous set of regulations, which were published in 1981. As usual, the proposals were eventually finalized (in April 2007), with some changes from the proposals. The proposals, dealing with subjects such as computing the plan limits, requirements for employer contributions to the plan, and catch-up contributions by participants over age 40, were published at 70 Fed. Reg. 31213 (May 31, 2005).

Final Regulations under § 415, reflecting the PPA as well as interim changes since the previous set of Final Regulations issued in 1981 (T.D. 7748), were published in the Federal Register for April 5, 2007, effective for limitation years beginning on or after July 1, 2007. For most plans, which are operated on a calendar year, that meant that the new rules would take effect January 1, 2008. Plans can provide that payments in any limitation year will not exceed the § 415(b) limit as of the annuity starting date, and increased pursuant to § 415(d); if this is done, the plan does not require actuarial adjustments for automatic increases unless the benefit is subject to § 417(e)(3).

Under the PPA, compensation used to calculate the "high 3" years does not have to be earned while the employee is an active plan participant. In general, the "high 3" is calculated subject to the annual compensation limit of § 401(a)(17), but the Final Regulations allow grandfathering-in of some additional compensation based on plan provisions that were in effect before April 5, 2007.

In general, money received after severance from employment is not considered § 415 compensation, but the Final Regulations allows inclusion of certain payments under bona fide sick or vacation leave plans—even if the payments are made more than 20½ months after severance from employment or the end of the year.

The Final Regulations allow some payments from non-qualified plans to be treated as § 415 compensation, as well as certain payments to disabled participants. The IRS announced its intentions to revise the rules covering multiple annuity starting dates. Various technical changes are made in the way that defined benefit payouts are adjusted when payment begins between age 62 and age 65. [Final Rule, 72 Fed. Reg. 16878 (Apr. 5, 2007), [American Benefits Council, *Summary: IRS/Treasury Release Final 415 Regulations* [<415_regsummary040407.pdf>]; Rebecca Moore, *IRS Issues Final, Comprehensive 415 Regulations*, plansponsor.com (Apr. 5, 2007)]

## [B]  Pension Protection Act (PPA) Changes

As Chapter 5 shows, the PPA was intended in part to improve the stability of defined benefit plans. Nevertheless, there are important PPA provisions that will affect the operation of defined contribution plans.

One PPA focus is protecting plan participants against excessive risk from declines in the value of the employer's stock. If the employer corporation's stock is publicly traded, then defined contribution plan participants must be given at least three investment options other than employer stock, and participants must have a right to diversify out of their holdings in employer stock—and must be notified of this right. (Because ESOPs are intended to hold employer stock, they are exempt from these requirements.)

The fiduciaries of 401(k) plans are permitted to give investment advice to participants: a prohibited transaction exemption is available if banks, insurance companies, broker/dealers, or registered investment advisers give advice after December 31, 2006. To qualify for the exemption, the adviser either must use an independently verified computer model to make recommendations, or the adviser's compensation must not vary based on the participant's investment choices. The PPA doubles the size of the bond (from $500,000 to $1 million) that fiduciaries must post if the plan they administer holds employer securities.

The PPA also gives small employers (fewer than 500 employees) a new option: maintaining an eligible combined plan that has some features of a defined benefit and some features of a 401(k) plan. An eligible combined plan must comply with the rules for both plan types. The eligible combined plan rules are effective starting in 2010. The plan consists of a single trust, with its assets allocated between a defined contribution plan such as a 401(k) plan, and a defined benefit plan. The plan reports on Form 5500-EZ, which must disclose all the information required of either a defined benefit or contribution plan. The form can be filed either on an official paper form from the IRS; the online form at the IRS site; or with approved software. [Form 5500: <http://www.irs.gov/pub/irs-pdf/f5500ez.pdf>; instructions, <http://www.irs.gov/instructions/i5500ez/ar01.html> or telephone (877) 829-5500. See Plansponsor staff, *The Wait Is Over for 2010 Form 5500 EZ*, plansponsor.com (June 17, 2011).]

## § 6.03  NEW COMPARABILITY PLANS

On October 6, 2000, the IRS published Proposed Regulations at 65 Fed. Reg. 59774-59780 setting the nondiscrimination requirements for "new comparability plans." The regulations were finalized by T.D. 8954, 66 Fed. Reg. 3435 (June 29, 2001). These are defined contribution plans that are allowed to perform cross-testing and demonstrate nondiscrimination under Treas. Reg. § 1.401(a)(4)–(8) by reference to their benefits rather than the employer's contributions, although they must satisfy a "gateway" requirement preserving at least a minimum rate of accrual for non-HCEs. In practice, this is usually done by finding a defined benefit equivalent for the allocations and then arranging them in rate groups.

Some employers find new comparability plans attractive because these plans allow a much higher allocation rate for highly compensated employees than for other employees. For example, a medical group might use three allocation rates in its new comparability plan: the highest for doctors who are also shareholders in the group, the lowest for nonphysician employees, and one in the middle for physicians who are not shareholders in the practice.

The plan document can specify the classes in many ways—by age, hiring date, length of service, type of job, or the location in which they work, for example. The number or definition of classes can only be changed via plan amendment, and the changes must be prospective only, not retroactive. It has been suggested that the IRS and the DOL might treat the plan as a deemed 401(k) plan rather than a new comparability plan if this process were extended to the point that every employee is in a separate class, but the agencies have not issued technical guidance on this point. [Mark Papalia, *Class-Based Pensions: A Cost-Saving Alternative for Companies of All Sizes*, Journal of Accountancy (January 2005) (benefitslink.com)]

## § 6.04  401(k) PLANS

### [A]  Overview

The Cash or Deferred Arrangement (CODA), also known as the 401(k) plan, has achieved prominence as one of the leading forms of plans for providing post-retirement income. Such plans were authorized by a 1978 amendment to the Internal Revenue Code and first became available in 1981. About 75% of 401(k)-eligible employees participate, but less than 10% save the maximum permitted amount. For the typical plan, this is 6% of compensation, and 3% remains the most common employer match. [Jilian Mincer, *As the 401(k) Turns 25, Has It Improved With Age?*, Wall St. J., Nov. 14, 2006, at D2]

Although 401(k) plans are subject to the rules for defined contribution plans, strictly speaking 401(k)s are not conventional pension plans. In a 401(k) plan, the employee agrees to have part of his or her salary, up to the limitation provided by the plan (which, in turn, is subject to limitations under the Tax Code) deferred and placed into an individual account instead of being paid in cash as it is earned. The advantage to the employee (apart from the forced savings aspect) is that the appreciation in value of the account is not taxed until withdrawals begin.

Many 401(k) plans feature an "employer match" (the employer contributes a percentage of what the employee contributes) but this is not a mandatory feature of this type of plan.

In September 2004, the Department of Labor proposed regulations covering the rights of service members returning from active service (see § 1.18) that also affect 401(k) plans. Periods of uniformed service must be counted with respect to 401(k) plan vesting and benefit accrual. Returning service members must be permitted to catch up with voluntary contributions such as elective deferrals that could have been made if they had not been in the military. The employer's obligation to make matching contributions depends on the service member's making the contributions within specified time frames. The Regulations require the employer contributions to be made within 30 days after reemployment for profit-sharing and other contributions for which the employee is not required to participate. [EBIA Weekly, *Proposed USERRA Regulations Address Elective Deferrals, Timing of Employer Contributions* (law.com)]

## [B]   Deferral Limits

Thanks to EGTRRA, and as carried forward by the PPA, the amount that employees can defer will increase after 2001. EGTRRA also includes other novel 401(k) provisions. Participants in 401(k) plans who are over 50 are permitted to make additional "catch-up" contributions, and low-income plan participants are allowed to take a tax credit and not a mere deduction in connection with part of their 401(k) deferrals.

For 2009, 2010, and 2011, the maximum annual contribution to a defined contribution account is $49,000; persons aged 50 and over can make additional catch-up contributions of $5,500. For 2012, the maximum contribution is $50,000; the catch-up contribution limit remains $5,500. The catch-up contribution remains the same for 2013, but the maximum contribution rises to $51,000.

Participants in 401(k) plans are always 100% vested in their deferrals at all times. Employees must be allowed to participate in the cash or deferred part of the plan starting with the first entry date after they have one year of service with the employer. Participants must be re-admitted to the plan immediately if they terminate their jobs but are re-employed at the same company before they have undergone a one-year break in service.

## [C]  Catch-Up Contributions

EGTRRA added a new I.R.C. § 414(v), which allows employees who are age 50 or older to order additional deferrals, over and above the normal limits. These additional amounts are referred to as catch-up contributions. The intent is to make sure that older employees will come closer to getting the same benefit from the enhanced opportunities for deferrals over the course of their careers as younger employees who can make the greater deferrals for a greater number of years. Catch-up contributions can be made for taxable years beginning after December 31, 2001.

The maximum catch-up contribution is $5,000 in 2006–8, $5,500 in 2009–2013. [IR-2011-103, *IRS Announces Pension Plan Limitations for 2012*, < http://www.irs.gov/newsroom/article/0,,id=248482,00.html> (Oct. 20, 2011); IR-2012-77, <http://www.irs.gov/uac/2013-Pension-Plan-Limitations> (Oct. 18, 2012)] EGTRRA § 631 provides that, if all employees who have reached age 50 are permitted to make catch-up contributions, the amount of the catch-up contributions will not be used in calculating the contribution limits. Nor will the catch-up amounts be used in nondiscrimination testing.

A plan participant is eligible to make catch-up contributions as of January 1 of the calendar year in which he or she reaches age 50—irrespective of the plan year.

## [D]  Other EGTRRA 401(k) Changes

Low-income 401(k) plan participants are entitled to a tax credit for their deferrals, for tax years beginning after December 31, 2001. This "saver's credit" was made permanent by the PPA. The "saver's credit" figures, unlike most other pension-related figures, were higher for 2011 than for 2009–2010: $56,500 for joint returns, $42,375 for heads of household, and $28,250 for single persons and married persons filing separate returns [IR-2010-108, <http://www.irs.gov/newsroom/article/0,,id=229975,00.html> (Oct. 28, 2010)] The 2012 saver's credit figures are $57,500 (joint return), $43,125 (head of household), and $28,750 (single/married filing separately). [IR-2011-103, *IRS Announces Pension Plan Limitations for 2012*, < http://www.irs.gov/newsroom/article/0,,id=248482,00. html> (Oct. 20, 2011)] The 2013 figures are $59,000 (joint return), $44,250 (head of household) and $29,500 (single/married filing separately). [IR-2012-77, <http://www.irs.gov/uac/2013-Pension-Plan-Limitations> (Oct. 18, 2012)]

Under current law, a small (under $5,000) balance can be "cashed out"—i.e., even if the employee wants the money to remain within the plan, the employer has the right to close out the account and send such small, hard-to-administer sums to the account owner's last known address. (Tax should be withheld, and an early distribution penalty should be taken if the person is under age 59½.)

## [E]  Roth 401(k)s

Yet another EGTRRA legacy is I.R.C. § 402A, which authorizes "qualified plus contribution programs"—in effect, 401(k) accounts that operate like Roth IRAs. An employee can make an irrevocable designation of part or all of the employee's elective salary deferral as designated Roth contributions. Employees' elective salary deferrals are taxed when they are placed in the account, but can be withdrawn tax-free as long as they have remained in the account for five years and the person withdrawing is at least 59½ or disabled (or the withdrawal is made by the estate of a deceased account holder).

A person who cannot contribute to a Roth IRA because of excess income can nevertheless contribute to a Roth 401(k). Furthermore, the maximum contribution to a Roth 401(k) is the normal 401(k) maximum, which is much higher than the Roth IRA maximum contribution. Roth 401(k) plans are subject to the minimum distribution rules. [Rev. Proc. 2006-53, 2006-48 I.R.B. 997]

Since Roth 401(k) plans were first authorized in 2006, the number of companies offering such plans has expanded rapidly—but the plans are not very popular with employees. According to Vanguard, only 6% of participants who have the option of enrolling in a Roth 401(k) plan actually do; Schwab says 15% do so. [Rachel Louise Ensign, *The Ins and Outs of Roth 401(k) Plans*, WSJ.com (Mar. 4, 2012)]

In 2006, the IRS issued final regulations, covering Roth 401(k) plans, under Code § 402A, applicable to plan years beginning on or after January 1, 2006. [T.D. 9237, RIN 1545-BE05, 4830-01-p, 2006-6 I.R.B. 394; see *Final Regulations on Roth 401(k)s Issued*, Watson Wyatt Insider (January 2006) (benefitslink.com)]

Employers are not permitted to offer a 401(k) plan that accepts only designated Roth contributions: contributing employees must be given a choice between making pre-tax elective contributions and designated Roth contributions.

Employer matches are not permitted, although employers can use automatic enrollment in a Roth 401(k) plan. Designated Roth contributions can be treated as catch-up contributions, and can be collateral for plan loans to participants. [T.D. 9237, RIN 1545-BE05, 4830-01-p, 2006-6 I.R.B. 394; see *Final Regulations on Roth 401(k)s Issued*, Watson Wyatt Insider (January 2006) (benefitslink.com). See also Announcement 2007-59, 2007-25 I.R.B. 1448, explaining how to make mid-year changes in a 401(k) safe harbor plan to implement a Roth program or take advantage of other PPA changes. Regulations were proposed at 71 Fed. Reg. 4320 (Jan. 26, 2006) on Roth 401(k) distribution issues, and T.D. 9324, 72 Fed. Reg. 21103 (Apr. 30, 2007) addresses designated Roth distributions.]

Designated Roth contributions are aggregated with all other 401(k) and 403(b) contributions, so for 2013, the annual contribution limitation is $17,500, plus $5,500 in catch-up contributions by persons aged 50 and over. [IR-2012-77, <http://www.irs.gov/uac/2013-Pension-Plan-Limitations> (Oct. 18, 2012)]

The Small Business Jobs Act of 2010, Pub. L. No. 111-240, allows in-plan Roth conversions for 401(k)s, effective on signing of the bill (September 27, 2010). Employers can amend their plans to permit Eligible Rollover Distributions (ERDs) to be transferred to a designated Roth account in the plan. If the plan did not already offer Roth accounts, the plan must be amended, and the payroll system updated accordingly. This provision benefits sponsors who were concerned about large balances being taken out of the plan, but does not make a major change for participants, who already had the option of rolling over the funds to a Roth IRA. A participant who rolls over an ERD into a designated Roth account in 2010 can either include the rollover amount in income in 2010, or defer taxation by including half of the taxable amount in gross income for 2011 and half for 2012. [*New Law Allows In-Plan Rollovers to Designated Roth Accounts*, <http://www.irs.gov>; Rebecca Moore, *InPlan Roth Conversions Present Challenges*, plansponsor.com (Sept. 28, 2010)]

The American Taxpayer Relief Act of 2012 (ATRA; Pub. L. No. 112-240) permits in-plant Roth conversions of defined contribution accounts that would not otherwise be distributable, with no income limitations. Under prior law, only amounts that were immediately distributable (e.g., to a participant who had reached age 59 ½) could be converted to Roth status. The provision is effective January 1, 2013, but account balances in existence on that date can be converted. [Rebecca Moore, *Fiscal Cliff Deal Extends Roth Conversions*, plansponsor.com (Jan.3, 2013)]

## § 6.05  401(k) ANTIDISCRIMINATION RULES

Understandably, highly compensated employees are in a better position to bypass immediate receipt of part of their salaries than rank-and-file employees. Therefore, the Internal Revenue Code includes detailed provisions for determining whether the plan is excessively unbalanced in favor of deferrals by HCEs.

The IRS Website includes a chart of ten potential mistakes that 401(k) plans can fall into, but that can be retrieved by going through a correction program such as SCP, VCP, or Audit CAP.

1. Is the plan document updated to reflect changes in the law? (The IRS suggests establishing a tickler file to ensure annual review).

2. Is the plan operated in accordance with the plan document? (Due diligence to make sure plan terms are followed is suggested.)

3. Does the plan define compensation correctly for deferrals and allocations?

4. Did the employer make matching contributions for all eligible participants?

5. Does the plan satisfy the applicable nondiscrimination tests?

6.  Were all eligible employees given a chance to opt for elective deferrals? (The plan sponsor must monitor employee census information and apply the participation requirements correctly.)

7.  Are elective deferrals kept within the § 402(g) limit for the year, with any excess deferrals promptly distributed to resolve the problem?

8.  Are employee elective deferrals promptly deposited?

9.  For top-heavy plans, were required minimum contributions made? The IRS says plans should be tested each year to see if they are top-heavy.

10. Were hardship distributions made properly? [IRS chart of *401(k) Plan Potential Mistakes*, <http://www.irs.gov/pub/irs-tege/401k_mistakes.pdf>]

There are two antidiscrimination tests: the ADP test (Actual Deferral Percentage) and the ACP test (Aggregate Contribution Percentage). A full discussion is beyond the scope of this book; you should just be aware that the 401(k) plan will be scrutinized for compliance with at least one of these tests.

The employer can correct the situation in three ways:

- Distributing the excess contributions (and the income allocated to them) out of the plan before the end of the following plan year;

- Recharacterizing the excess contributions as after-tax contributions;

- Making qualified nonelective or qualified matching contributions.

Given the complexity of these rules, the IRS has recognized various safe harbor mechanisms that employers can use to simplify compliance. Companies that use the safe harbor are required to give plan participants notice that is accurate and comprehensive enough to inform them of their rights. The notice must be given a reasonable period (30–90 days) before the beginning of the plan year. Therefore, in a calendar year plan, notice is required on or before December 1 of the previous year.

Another option for employers who do not want to commit to using the safe harbor, but who want to make non-elective contributions, is to give notice, again by December 1 of the preceding year, that the plan may be amended in the next calendar year to provide for safe harbor non-elective contributions, and that the employees will receive a further notice explaining their rights if such an amendment is adopted.

The IRS will generally treat a plan as having lost its status as a 401(k) safe harbor plan if it fails to provide a timely annual safe harbor plan notice for a year. If this status is lost, the plan must satisfy the nondiscrimination requirements from which it was exempted. This could limit highly compensated employees' ability to defer compensation, or could require the plan sponsor to refund some amounts already deferred. Penalties could also be imposed for failure to provide the automatic enrollment or Qualified Automatic Contribution Arrangement (QACA) notice. Failure to give timely Qualified Default Investment Alternative (QDIA) notice forfeits fiduciary protection of the sponsor, plan administrator, or investment company for investment loss. Protection is only restored for amounts invested in the QDIA after compliance with the notice requirements. [McKenna Long & Aldridge LLP, *2011 Year-End Disclosure Reminders for Qualified Defined Contribution Plan Sponsors* (November 2011) (benefitslink.com)]

Current IRS audit policy calls for asking the employer for evidence that participants were given the 401(k) safe harbor notice. The IRS is requiring corrections, and perhaps a closing agreement sanction, from employers that cannot provide the evidence. To protect themselves, employers should keep copies of the notice (including the date it was sent) and the cover letter. If the notice was delivered electronically, the proper evidence would be a copy of the e-mail, the date it was sent, and the list of addressees. Failure to give the safe harbor notice is considered failure to comply with the terms of the plan, not merely a failure to satisfy the statutory requirements under § 401(k). The failure can be corrected under the IRS Self Correction Program, but not under the Employee Plans Compliance Resolution System (EPCRS) (although future versions of EPCRS are likely to include it). If the participant was actually aware of his or her eligibility to defer, the employer can correct the notice failure by giving the notice late, and improving its procedures for the future. But if the participant was not aware of the deferral opportunity, the employer must treat the employer as improperly excluded, and make a corrective contribution equal to 50% of the missed deferral plus any employer match required by the plan. [SunGard Relius, *Failure to Provide Safe Harbor Notice Correction* (Nov. 30, 2012) (benefitslink.com)]

## § 6.06 DISTRIBUTIONS FROM THE 401(k) PLAN

### [A] General Rule

Pre-tax deferrals from a 401(k) plan cannot be distributed to the participant until:

- Retirement,
- Death,
- Disability,
- Separation from service (see below for the abolition of the "same desk" rule),
- Hardship,
- The participant reaches age 59½.

Although profit-sharing plans can make distributions purely because of the number of years the participant has worked for the employer, or the number of years the funds have remained in the account, these are not acceptable rationales for distributions from a 401(k) plan. [I.R.C. § 401(k)(2)(B)(ii)]

EGTRRA enacted § 411(d)(6)(E), providing that the accrued benefit is not reduced by elimination of a form of distribution—if the participant can receive a single-sum distribution at the same time as the eliminated form of distribution, and the single-sum distribution is based on at least as great a portion of the account as the form of distribution that was eliminated. A plan amendment under the Final Regulation can apply only to distributions whose annuity starting date occurs after the adoption of the amendment, not to distributions that have already commenced.

The Heroes Earnings Assistance and Relief Tax Act (HEART Act; Pub. L. No. 110-245) also revives an expired provision that allows reservists called for at least six months of active duty to take money out of their 401(k) and other defined contribution plans before age 59½ without having to pay the 10% penalty for early withdrawals. Employers must also recognize differential pay to called-up employees when they calculate pension benefits. The HEART Act includes the HEROES Act, which protects the (employment-related) survivor's benefits for survivors of servicemembers killed in the line of duty. [Rebecca Moore, *Reservist Benefits Bill Signed Into Law*, plansponsor.com (June 19, 2008)]

The Second Circuit required a profit-sharing plan to give a participant over $1.5 million in assets, earnings, and interest that were wrongly transferred to his ex-wife—even though the plan did not recoup the money from the ex-wife. (The Northern District of New York granted a judgment for the plan against the ex-wife, but the money was not recovered.) The Second Circuit found a legal duty to reimburse the plan participant, finding that undistributed funds held in trust are not considered benefits for purposes of the ban on alienating plan benefits. Furthermore, plan assets can be used to satisfy a judgment against the plan itself. [*Milgram v. Orthopedic Assocs. et.al.*, 666 F.3d 68 (2d Cir. Dec. 23, 2011); see Rebecca Moore, *Plan Must Restore Misplaced Assets Although not Recovered*, plansponsor.com (Jan. 17, 2012)]

Similarly, according to the Tenth Circuit, the ERISA ban on forfeitures does not make the plan liable for third-party wrongdoing. It was not a forfeiture when the plan incorrectly paid benefits to a participant's ex-wife instead of to him. It was the participant's fault that he did not give the plan his current address. His ex-wife learned how to access the benefits, got a user ID, changed the account password, filed a change of address form listing her P.O. box as an address, and withdrew all the money from the account. The participant did not sue his ex-wife; he sued the plan under ERISA § 1132(a)(1)(A) for refusing to distribute the plan funds to him. [*Foster v. PPG Indus. Inc.*, 693 F.3d 1226 (10th Cir. 2012); see Rebecca Moore, *DC Assets Withdrawn Fraudulently Not Forfeited*, plansponsor.com (Dec. 5, 2012)]

Although some employers have added annuities as defined contribution plan options, others are reluctant to do so because there has not been strong demand for them from participants. Young workers are often not interested in annuitizing. The current uncertainty in the market also deters some participants from accepting market risks by taking a lump sum that then has to be invested. There is also a concern about lack of portability: if a plan participant invests in a deferred annuity product, changes jobs, and rolls over the money, expenses already paid may be lost. If, instead of rolling over the amount, the employee leaves the funds in the original plan, he or she will have to manage and track multiple plans. There are also concerns about the size of the fees and charges associated with annuities. [Sharon F. Fountain, *"Annuitizing" a 401(k) – Options for Plan Sponsors and Participants*, Bloomberg BNA (Nov. 30, 2012) (benefitslink.com)]

On the tax front, the Treasury and Department of Labor are working to reduce the risk of employees outliving the balances in their defined contribution plans. Two Revenue Rulings and two Proposed Regulations from 2012 make it easier for plans to offer full and partial lifetime annuities. Rev. Rul. 2012-3, 2012-8 I.R.B. 383, allows defined contribution plans to offer deferred annuities as investments without forcing the entire plan to comply with the QJSA/QPSA (Qualified Joint and SurvivorAnnuities/Qualified Preretirement Survivor Annuities) rules—as long as the deferred annuity contract is accounted for separately. When the tax-deferred annuity reaches pay status, only that investment requires a QJSA. But if the plan permits the participant spouse to waive the QPSA the nonparticipant spouse must receive disclosures and must give notarized consent to the waiver.

Rev. Rul. 2012-4, 2012-8 I.R.B. 386 explains how an employer that offers both defined contribution and defined benefit plans can permit 401(k) plan participants who are ready to retire to roll over all or part of the 401(k) account balance to the defined benefit plan, receiving an immediate annuity under the defined benefit plan. The plan must use the same actuarial assumptions (such as interest rates and mortality tables) for annuitized rollovers that are used to calculate the retirement benefits of defined benefit plan participants. Participants in defined contribution plans who elect a rollover are entitled to disclosures about what will happen if the plan terminates without enough money to pay its liabilities. Married participants must furnish notified consent from their spouses. This ruling applies to rollovers made on or after January 1, 2013, but plan sponsors can rely on the ruling for earlier rollovers.

One of the proposals introduces the QLAC (Qualifying Longevity Annuity Contract), whose payments do not begin until an advanced age such as 80 or 85. Amounts used to purchase a QLAC are excluded from the RMD calculations for the time between the participant reaching age 70 and the start date of annuity payments. The proposal applies to defined contribution plans and IRAs, but the amount that can be used to purchase a QLAC is limited to the lesser of $100,000 or 25% of the account balance. The other proposal permits participants to allocate their benefit between annuity and lump sum payouts, rather than requiring an election of only one or the other, and simplifies the associated calculations. [*Treasury Fact Sheet: Helping American Families Achieve Retirement Security By Expanding Lifetime Income Choices* (Feb. 2, 2012) (benefitslink.com); McKay Hochman Company, Inc. *E-Mail Alert 2012-8, Lifetime Income Options* (Aug. 30, 2012) (benefitslink.com)]

### [B]  Hardship Distributions

Treas. Reg. § 1.401(k)-1(d)(2)(i) defines hardship as an immediate and heavy financial need that cannot be satisfied by reasonable access to the participant's other assets. The hardship withdrawal from the plan must not exceed the amount of the need plus any taxes and penalties that the participant can reasonably expect to incur. Note that, post-PPA, hardship distributions can also be made based on the needs of plan beneficiaries as well as of plan participants.

Certain categories have been identified as automatically satisfying the financial needs test:

- Medical expenses of the employee, spouse, and dependent children;

- Purchase of a principal residence (but not routine mortgage payments);

- Staving off eviction or foreclosure of the mortgage on the principal residence;

- Tuition, room, board, and related expenses for the next 12 months for post-secondary education of the employee, spouse, or dependents.

Employees are expected to seek insurance reimbursement wherever it is available to cope with financial hardship; to liquidate their other assets to the extent this is reasonable; to cease further elective contributions to pension plans; to seek other distributions and nontaxable loans from employer plans; and to engage in commercial borrowing on reasonable terms, before they take hardship distributions from their 401(k) plans.

Under the Final Regulations, 69 Fed. Reg. 78143 (Dec. 29, 2004), a hardship distribution must satisfy both the "events test" (the participant has an immediate and heavy financial need) and a "needs test" (the distribution must be necessary to satisfy the need). A hardship distribution for medical expenses is limited to expenses that would be deductible as medical care under I.R.C. § 213(d), although the 7.5% of AGI limit does not apply. The Final Regulations add two new grounds for distributions: funeral or burial expenses within the immediate family, and expenses for repairs to the principal residence.

The IRS announced relief for taxpayers who wanted to apply retirement assets for financial hardship caused by Superstorm Sandy. The verification requirements for plan loans and hardship distributions have been relaxed. A plan will not be deemed to violate the Code merely because it made a loan or hardship distribution between October 26, 2012 and February 1, 2013, based on needs caused by Sandy to an employee whose workplace, principal residence, or principal residence of a close family member was in the identified disaster area. The usual calculation of maximum permitted hardship distribution will apply. Distributions can be made without the normal documentation, if the storm destroyed the necessary records—but as soon as practicable, the plan administrator must assemble the documentation. However, the announcement does not alter the general rule that a defined benefit or money purchase plan cannot make hardship distributions (other than from a separate account within the plan containing employee contributions or rollovers). [Announcement 2012-44, 2012-49 I.R.B. 663. This relief is in addition to relief under Code § 7508A provided by IR-2012-83.]

## [C]  Elimination of "Same Desk" Rule

One basis on which employees can get distributions from a 401(k) plan is separation from service—i.e., ceasing to be an employee. Before EGTRRA was passed, the "same desk" rule was applied. Under this rule, a person would not be considered separated from service if the original employer had gone through a merger, consolidation, or liquidation, but the employee continued to carry out the same job for the successor company, and thus would not be entitled to a distribution from the plan.

EGTRRA provides, for distributions made after December 31, 2001, that if a corporation sells "substantially all" (defined as 85% or more) of its business assets to an unrelated company, or sells a subsidiary to an unrelated person or company, the selling company's employees have separated from service even if, in practice, they carry out the same tasks for the new employer. [This provision is subject to the EGTRRA sunset date of January 1, 2011. See also Rev. Proc. 2000-27, 2000-21 I.R.B. 1016.]

## [D]  "Orphan" Plans

In addition to plan freezes (see § 5.05[L]), problems arise because of "orphan" or "abandoned" plans—plans in which the sponsor went out of business, without making arrangements to terminate the plan and distribute benefits. The DOL estimates that roughly 1,650 401(k) plans are abandoned each year (about 2% of the total), affecting approximately 33,000 workers and balances of about $850 million. One advantage of a defined contribution plan over a defined benefit plan is that defined contribution plans are designed to be portable. But participants in these "orphan" plans, although they retain ownership of their accounts, often have difficulty in accessing them, because under previous law, if there was no representative of the sponsor company available, the financial institution could not release funds until DOL appoints an independent fiduciary to supervise the distribution. The DOL issued rules in April 2006, effective in late 2006, so that financial institutions holding assets from the defunct plans of bankrupt companies will be able to roll over the 401(k) balances with no requirement of court approval.

The April 2006 document comprises three rules: one describing the procedure to be used by a financial institution to terminate the plan and distribute benefits to the plan's participants; another creating a safe harbor for fiduciaries who make distributions to participants and beneficiaries of "orphaned" plans when there is no election on file covering the method of distribution; and the third creating a procedure for filing a simple terminal report for an abandoned plan. [71 Fed. Reg. 20820 (Apr. 21, 2006); see Rebecca Moore, *DOL Issues Final Rules Regarding Abandoned Plans*, plansponsor.com (Apr. 20, 2006); Robert Guy Matthews, *When Access Is Denied to Your 401(k)*, Wall St. J., Feb. 14, 2006, at D1]

EBSA's Abandoned Plan Program provides standards for determining if a plan is abandoned (e.g., no contributions or distributions for at least 12 consecutive months; the sponsor cannot be located by reasonable effort, no longer exists, or is unable to maintain the plan), with streamlined shut-down and distribution procedures. A Qualified Termination Administrator (QTA), qualified to serve as trustee and hold the assets, determines if the plan is abandoned. The QTA is not required to file Form 5500 on behalf of the abandoned plan, but is obligated to file a summary terminal report, as described on the "abandoned plan program" link at <http://www.dol.gov/ebsa>.

At the end of 2012, the DOL announced its intention to extend the Abandoned Plan Program to help trustees in Chapter 7 bankruptcy cases. Current rules are limited to financial institutions holding assets of abandoned plans. Proposed amendments would let bankruptcy trustees use the program. They often have to act as plan administrators for Chapter 7 companies. The proposed amendments define a Chapter 7 debtor's plan as abandoned on the date the sponsor's bankruptcy proceeding commences (when the Bankruptcy Court enters an order for relief). Under this proposal, the bankruptcy trustee can terminate and wind up the plan or appoint an eligible financial institution to do so. The trustee has an ongoing obligation to monitor the financial institution's performance. The trustee, or the designated financial institution acting on information provided by the trustee, must determine if collecting the delinquent contributions makes economic sense: i.e., if the cost of collection is less than the amount to be collected. If the collection is financially viable, it must be pursued. [DOL/EBSA, *Fact Sheet: Proposed Amendments to Abandoned Plan Program* (Dec. 2012) (benefitslink.com)]

## § 6.07 ADMINISTRATION OF THE 401(k) PLAN

There were a number of reasons why defined contribution plans, especially 401(k) plans, became the dominant form of retirement savings. The initial impetus included lower risk for the employer, and the greater simplicity of operating an individual account plan that does not require the complex actuarial calculations required for a defined benefit plan. However, since the 2008 stock market crash, there has been a trend for employers to attempt to take more control over 401(k) accounts, for example, by moving all participants into target date funds or suggesting automatic deposits of a percentage of their pay. [Eleanor Laise, *Employers Begin Driving Your 401(k)*, WSJ.com (Oct. 17, 2009)]

Defined contribution plans must give their participants a variety of notices:

- Safe harbor 401(k) plan's annual notice about the features of the plan, such as the safe harbor non-elective contribution or matching contribution of the plan; this must be given 30–90 days before the beginning of the plan year;

- Qualified Automatic Contribution Arrangement (QACA) safe harbor 401(k) plans must provide an annual notice on the same schedule;

- Qualified Default Investment Alternative (QDIA) notice of rights and obligations, such as the participant's right to transfer the account to other investments, and when funds will be invested in the QDIA; must be provided at least 30 days before the beginning of the plan year;

- 401(k) automatic enrollment notice, providing information such as deferrals made without an affirmative election, and how the plan invests contributions where there is no election; must be provided 30–90 days before the beginning of the plan year;

- Employer stock diversification notice: information about the right to transfer the participant's investment from employer stock into other investments (if the employer's stock is publicly traded). The notice must be given no later than 30 days before the first date that diversification rights can be exercised.

In general, two or more notices can be combined into a single document as long as the time requirements are satisfied. Electronic distribution is permissible if the electronic disclosure requirements are satisfied—but the defined contribution plan requirements cannot be satisfied in the SPD even if it is distributed annually. [McKenna Long & Aldridge LLP, *2011 Year-End Disclosure Reminders for Qualified Defined Contribution Plan Sponsors* (Nov. 2011) (benefitslink. com)]

## [A] Automatic Enrollment

Even prior to the recession beginning in 2008, there was concern that many employees would not have a secure retirement because many workers would refuse or neglect to take the affirmative steps necessary to open a 401(k) account, select investments, and have the necessary discipline to save part of their compensation. (It also became clear that even workers who faithfully saved their money were at the mercy of market forces that could greatly reduce the value of a 401(k) account.)

In 2000, the IRS gave its blessing for 401(k) plans to operate by automatically enrolling eligible workers rather than by permitting participation only by those workers who took steps to opt in: Rev. Rul. 2000-8, 2000-7 I.R.B. 617.

An automatic plan sets a default savings rate such as 2% to 3% of pay and establishes a default investment, such as a money market or stable value fund. Usually only about 4% of eligible opt out; Hewitt Associates estimates that in a plan where opting in is required, 30% of eligible workers never join. A step-up program gets the employee's advance consent to increasing his or her contributions as income increases.

The PPA makes it easier for employers to operate 401(k) plans that automatically enroll employees and then permit them to opt out, rather than requiring employees to choose to participate in the plan. Automatic-enrollment plans must have employer matches (and the PPA contains a schedule for calculating the required match). Participants in an automatic enrollment plan must be 100% vested after two years, although the employer is not required to offer immediate participation in the plan.

According to Fidelity, about half (51%) of its 401(k) plan participants are in plans that feature automatic enrollment. Most plans (73%) use an age-based life-cycle fund as a default. Since 2006, the percentage of Fidelity's plans with auto-enrollment rose from 2% to 21%. For plans that do not auto-enroll, the average participation rate among eligible employees is 55%, whereas it is 82% for plans with auto-enrollment. This is particularly true of younger employees: only 20% of employees aged 20–24 participate in plans without auto-enrollment, but 76% participate in plans with auto-enrollment. In 2006, the percentage of plans with a Roth 401(k) feature was 4%, rising to 31% in 2011, although utilization remains low: 3% in 2006, only 6% in 2011. [Tara Cantore, *Fidelity Analysis Finds Auto Enrollment Increases Plan Participation*, plansponsor.com (Nov. 30, 2011)]

Final Regulations, effective December 24, 2007, were published at 72 Fed. Reg. 60452 covering investments in Qualified Default Investment Alternatives (QDIAs) for participants who do not direct the investment of their accounts. Under the Final Regulations, fiduciaries are not liable for losses on amounts invested in a QDIA, and the plan's fiduciaries are not liable for decisions made by the managers of the QDIA. A QDIA can mix equity and fixed income investments—for example, in a life cycle or targeted retirement date fund; it can also be a balanced fund or a professionally managed fund. However, a capital preservation fund or other stable value fund can be a QDIA only for the first 120 days after a participant's first elective contribution.

In April 2008, the DOL's FAB No. 2008-03 (Apr. 29, 2008) supplemented the October 24, 2007 final regulations by giving fiduciaries additional guidance on how to administer QDIAs, including notice requirements, asset allocation, and preservation of capital. FAB 2008-03 says that a plan sponsor can have multiple

QDIAs, as long as each satisfies the QDIA requirements. Technical corrections were issued April 30, 2008, explaining when plan sponsors can limit reinvestment in a QDIA and allowing QDIAs to be managed by a committee that is dominated by employees of the plan sponsor—as long as the committee is a named fiduciary. [Clarissa A. Kang, *The Pension Protection Act and Fiduciary Aspects of Automatic Enrollment in 401(k) Plans*, Trucker Huss newsletter (May 2008) (benefitslink.com)]

Two plaintiffs appealed the judgment for the defendant in an ERISA fiduciary breach case based on transfer of their investments from a stable value fund to a QDIA. The Sixth Circuit affirmed the district court. The plaintiffs allocated 100% of their investment in the stable value fund, which was also the default investment for 403(b) participants who did not make an election. The PPA created a safe harbor against fiduciary liability for directing automatic enrollment investments into QDIAs ("investments capable of meeting a worker's long-term retirement savings needs"). The DOL's intention was to give employers an incentive to move away from low-risk but low-return default investments that do not permit employees to keep up with inflation. However, existing stable value fund defaults were grandfathered in. In 2008, the employer changed its default and transferred investments from the old default fund to a new fund. The employer did not know which investments in the stable value fund were defaults and which were affirmatively elected, so it sent a notice to all participants who were 100% invested in the stable value fund telling them that the investments would be transferred if they did not give notice by a specific date. The plaintiffs allege that they never received the notice; the employer said that it was mailed to their correct addresses. They switched their investments when they received the quarterly notice reflecting the change. The plaintiffs argued that the safe harbor is limited to default investments, not investments selected by the participant, and they said they picked the stable value fund as an investment. However, the safe harbor regulations specifically state that they are not limited to default investments. The Sixth Circuit said it was "troubling" that they did not get the notice, but the employer's actions did not violate ERISA: a fiduciary is obligated to take measures reasonably calculated to ensure actual receipt, but it seems that the employer sent the correct number of letters, by first class mail, to the address they had on record. [*Bidwell v. University Med. Ctr.*, 685 F.3d 613 (6th Cir. 2012)]

The IRS Website includes a sample automatic enrollment notice for a hypothetical QACA: <http://www.irs.gov/pub/irs-tege/sample_notice.pdf>, and the DOL announced that using this notice also complies with ERISA. Employees are fully vested in employer matching contributions in two years. Participants can choose among the various investment funds available, but funds are invested in the QDIA if there is no direction, and absent an election, 3% of eligible pay will be deposited into the account. The employer match is dollar-for-dollar up to 1% of eligible pay and 50 cents per dollar for employee deferrals of 1%–6% of eligible pay. DOL says that using this notice also complies with ERISA.

Final IRS rules in T.D. 9447 (2009-12 I.R.B. 694) permit employers to add an automatic enrollment feature to 401(k) plans without performing nondiscrimination testing, but the plan must be a QACA or an EACA (Eligible Automatic Contribution Arrangement—the equivalent for multi-employer plans). T.D. 9447 reflects changes in the law under the Pension Protection Act of 2006 and The Worker, Retiree and Employer Recovery Act (WRERA; Pub. L. No. 110-458).

QACA plans must automatically enroll all employees, with contributions beginning at 3% of salary, rising 1% a year until they reach 6%. An employee who opts out can withdraw from the plan and have contributions end within 90 days. The distribution from the plan is taxable to the employee, but is not subject to the 10% penalty tax on premature withdrawals. The Final Regulations apply to plan years beginning on or after January 1, 2008. [Joanne Wojcik, *IRS Rules on 401(k) Will Help Some Employers*, Business Insurance (Feb. 25, 2009) (benefitslink.com); AICPA, *IRS Issues Final Regs on Automatic Contribution Agreements* (Feb. 25, 2009) (benefitslink.com)]

For QACAs and EACAs, the employer is permitted to increase the percentage of automatic contributions in the middle of the plan year, not just at its beginning, in order to reflect salary increases or performance evaluations, as long as the increases are uniformly applied. Employees must be notified of their automatic enrollment in the plan before they become eligible and at the beginning of each plan year. If it is not practicable to give notice on that schedule (e.g., new hires are immediately eligible for participation) then notice must be provided as soon as practicable. The QACA rules apply for plan years beginning on or after January 1, 2008; the EACA rules apply to plan years beginning on or after January 1, 2010. [Hodgson Russ LLP Employee Benefits Developments, IRS Publishes Final Automatic Enrollment Rules (May 2009) (benefitslink.com) At the beginning of 2009, EBSA published a final rule, effective for plan years beginning on or after January 1, 2008, permitting civil penalties of up to $1,000 per day for each violation of the duty to inform participants of their rights and obligations under a plan with an automatic contribution arrangement. [74 Fed. Reg. 17 (Jan. 2, 2009)]

Notice 2009-65, 2009-39 I.R.B. 413, facilitates automatic enrollment in 401(k) plans by giving two sample plan amendments for adding automatic contribution features to the plan. One of the amendments adds automatic contributions to a 401(k) plan; the other adds an eligible automatic contribution arrangement pursuant to Code § 414(w) (90-day withdrawals).

## [B] Fees

Plan participants disappointed in the returns of their accounts often charge the fiduciaries of the plan with breach of duty, and often the claims include a charge that the fiduciaries allowed the plan to pay excessively high fees, e.g., to brokers and mutual funds. See §§ 15.03[C], 15.15, and 15.17. Plaintiffs frequently allege that retail mutual funds are an unsuitable plan investment; the plaintiffs say that these funds charge fees that are inappropriate when there is little marketing or administration that must be done.

Increased disclosure obligations put pressure on sponsors to have competitive fees. Deloitte/Investment Company Institute's survey for January through August 2011 showed a median participant weighted fee of 0.78% of plan assets, or about $250 per participant—slightly lower than the 0.68% median in the 2009 study. The range was from 0.28% to 1.38% of plan assets; not surprisingly, larger plans and plans with higher average balances tended to have lower fees as a percentage of assets. However, plans with heavy investments in equities tended to have higher fees than plans with a smaller representation of equities. [Joanne Sammer, *Comparing 401(k) Fees in the Age of Disclosure*, Business Finance (Nov. 22, 2011) (benefitslink.com)]

The 12th edition of the 401k Averages Book, says that the average total plan cost for a small 401(k) plan (with 100 participants) is 1.3%, 1.24% of which represents average investment expense. For very large plans, with 1,000 or more participants, the average total plan cost is 1.08%, including 1.05% of investment expense. [Tara Cantore, *Book Reveals Wide Range of 401k Plan Fees*, plansponsor.com (Jan. 17, 2012)]

Fiduciaries must file notices with the DOL to get prohibited transaction relief under ERISA § 408(b)(2)'s fiduciary-level fee disclosure rules when they discover they have not received required notices. The fiduciaries must make a written request to the service provider to get the missing information. If the service provider does not comply within 90 days, the fiduciary must notify the DOL. The procedure was modified in mid-2012. Notice can be given either by mail at DOL, EBSA Office of Enforcement, P.O. Box 75296, Washington, D.C. 20013, or through the link at <www.dol.gov/ebsa/regs/feedisclosurefailurenotice.html>. The site will provide immediate electronic confirmation that notice is received. [Final Rule, DOL EBSA, *Amendment Relating to Reasonable Contract or Arrangement Under Section 408(b)(2)—Fee Disclosure*, 77 Fed. Reg. 41678 (July 16, 2012)]

## [1] Case Law

The Supreme Court held that the correct legal standard in an excessive fund fee case was whether the fees were so disproportionately large that they could not have been the product of arm's length bargaining (the standard used by most federal courts). [*Jones v. Harris*, 559 U.S. 335 (2010); see Fred Schneyer, *High Court Sides with Investors in Fee Case*, plansponsor.com (Mar. 30, 2010); Drinker, Biddle Investment Management Alert, *Supreme Court Rules in Jones v. Harris* (Mar. 30, 2010) (benefitslink.com).

However, the Supreme Court refused to hear the appeal of the dismissal of another Seventh Circuit case about excessive 401(k) fees: *Hecker v. Deere & Co.*

556 F.3d 575 (7th Cir 2009); [see Fred Schneyer, *U.S. Supremes Turn Away Hecker Fee Case Appeal*, plansponsor.com (Jan. 19, 2010)] The Supreme Court vacated an Eighth Circuit decision about whether mutual fund fees violated Section 36(b) of the Investment Company Act. The Eighth Circuit had relied on the marketplace to prevent excessively high fees from being imposed. However, the Supreme Court remanded the case to comply with *Jones v. Harris*, where the standard is whether a fee is so unreasonably large that obviously there was no arm's length bargaining between the fund and its clients. [*Ameriprise Fin. Inc. v. Gallus*, 130 S. Ct. 2340 (U.S. Apr. 5, 2010); see Rebecca Moore, *Supreme Court Sends Investment Adviser Fee Case Back to 8th Circuit*, plansponsor.com (Apr. 6, 2010)] On remand, the Eighth Circuit found that the plaintiffs did not demonstrate a breach of fiduciary duty; the fees were not so high that they fell outside the range of reasonable fees that could have been negotiated at arm's length. [*Gallus v. Ameriprise*, 675 F.3d 1173 (8th Cir. 2012); see Rebecca Moore, *Ameriprise Wins Excessive Fees Case*, plansponsor.com (Apr. 12, 2012)]

Participants in a 401(k) plan sued under ERISA and the Investment Company Act, alleging that the fees on their annuity insurance contracts were excessive. The district court dismissed the Investment Company Act claims, requiring an ownership interest to bring a derivative suit—the plaintiffs were no longer investors in those funds. The district court also dismissed the ERISA claims because the plaintiffs did not make a pre-suit demand on the plan's trustees to make them correct the problem, nor were the trustees named as parties to the suit. The Third Circuit affirmed the Investment Company Act ruling, but reversed on the ERISA question, deciding that ERISA does not require a pre-suit demand, and trustees do not have to be named as parties. [*Santomenno v. John Hancock Life Ins. Co.*, 677 F.3d 178 (3d Cir. 2012)]

The Seventh Circuit refused to overrule its *Hecker* decision in a case in which Exelon employees charged that their 401(k) investment options generated excessive fees. The plan offered 32 funds, 24 of them retail mutual funds with expense ratios of 0.03%–0.96%. The Seventh Circuit affirmed the principle that fiduciaries are not obligated to select only the lowest-cost funds and, because these were retail funds, the fees were set competitively. The Seventh Circuit refused to treat institutional funds as automatically superior to retail funds; institutional funds might be less liquid or less transparent than their retail counterparts, and the retail funds in the plan had below-average expense ratios. A flat fee structure might benefit the participants with the largest balances, but younger employees and those with small accounts could be disadvantaged. [*Loomis v. Exelon*, 658 F.3d 667 (7th Cir. 2011); see Nevin E. Adams, *Another Plan Sponsor Win on Revenue Sharing*, plansponsor.com (Sept. 26, 2011)]

Wal-Mart and Merrill Lynch got final approval of a $13.5 million settlement of a class action about 401(k) fees in a plan all of whose investment options were retail mutual funds. Approximately two million workers and retirees are involved. [*Braden v. Wal-Mart Stores Inc.*, No. 08-cv-3109 (W.D. Mo. settled 2012); see Thom Weidlich, Bloomberg, *Wal-Mart 401(k) Accord Approved* (Mar. 8, 2012) (benefitslink.com); Joshua J. Coleman, *Court Grants Preliminary Approval to Settlement of Wal-Mart 401(k) Fee Lawsuit*, Groom Law Group (Dec. 13, 2011) (benefitslink.com). Coleman says that this is the fifth 401(k) class action to settle; the range of the other settlements is between $13.7 million and $18.5 million plus nonmonetary relief.]

In another recent major case, the plaintiff class was awarded $13.4 million against 401(k) plan fiduciaries who breached their duties by failing to do proper investment research—or follow the plan's stated investment policies—as well as by failing to obtain rebates or monitor the cost of recordkeeping for the plan, plus a further $21.8 million because the funds for the plan were not prudently chosen. It was not enough to monitor the reasonableness of the overall expense ratio because that single metric did not consider either the size of the plan or competitive rates in the market. Fidelity had to pay another $1.7 million for improper administration of investment float on the plan's assets. Although sometimes revenue sharing is permissible, in this case it was applied in a way that did not benefit the plan's participants. [*Tussey v. ABB Inc.* (W.D. Mo. Mar. 31, 2012); see Andrew Holley and Britta Loftus, *The Importance of* "A Deliberative Process," Dorsey & Whitney (Apr. 4, 2012) (benefitslink.com)].

The District Court for the Central District of California denied the plaintiffs' application for attorneys' fees in a suit about the selection of funds in their 401(k) plan. The court held that they had only minimal success because they won in only one of 10 claims against plan fiduciaries who included retail-class funds in the plan. [*Tibble v. Edison Int'l*, CV 07-5359 SVW (AGRx) (C.D. Cal. Aug. 22, 2011); see Rebecca Moore, *Court Denies Attorneys Fees in Institutional Versus Retail Shares Case*, plansponsor.com (Aug. 29, 2011). Fees were awarded in December 2010, but this decision reduces the fee award from $2.5 million to $410,000]

On appeal, this case resulted in a landmark Ninth Circuit decision. The Ninth Circuit held that the six-year statute of limitations began when the decision was made to include the allegedly improper investment in the plan. Although fiduciaries have an ongoing duty to be prudent, the statute of limitations is six years rather than the three years applicable under the "actual knowledge" standard—the plaintiffs did not have actual knowledge of the deficiencies in the selection process. The *Moench* [*Moench v. Robertson*, 62 F.3d 553 (3d Cir. 1995] presumption was applied. The Ninth Circuit held that fiduciaries can be liable based on selecting the plan's investment option; the 404(c) safe harbor does not apply to designating investment options, so the merits of the plaintiffs' claims could be considered. The Ninth Circuit said that revenue sharing is not a prohibited transaction because there is a prohibited transaction exemption that says that revenue sharing does not constitute "consideration" given to the fiduciaries. Including retail funds (rather than only institutional funds) is not per se imprudent and short-term funds can also be included in the portfolio. However, in the case of three specific mutual funds, it was imprudent to include the retail fund rather than its institutional counterpart because the plan failed to analyze the differences between the two. Even though they used a consultant, the fiduciaries still had an obligation to consider all the available share classes for the fund. [*Tibble v. Edison*, 711 F. 3d 1061 (9th Cir. Mar. 21, 2013); see Scott J. Stitt, *An Overview of the Tibble v. Edison Decision From the Ninth Circuit Concerning the Fees Charged to Participants in a 401(k) Plan*, arnlaw.com Mar. 24, 2013 (law .com); The Ninth Circuit denied rehearing in August 2013, but amended its opinion. The amended opinion reaffirms that the statute of limitations is six years for cases about the appropriateness of retaining employer stock in a 401(k) plan. The amended opinion limits the discretion that fiduciaries have with respect to employer stock. In some circumstances, the decision to keep the stock in the plan will not be entitled to deference—for example, if the decision furthers the interests of non-beneficiaries in the plan; fiduciary duty requires protecting the interests of beneficiaries. But the Ninth Circuit did not find those circumstances present in this case. [*Tibble v. Edison Int'l*, No. 10-56406 (9th Cir. Aug. 1, 2013); see Thomas E. Clark, Jr., *Breaking: 9th Circuit Amends Tibble v. Edison Opinion on Rehearing*, FRA Plan Tools (Aug. 2, 2013) (benefitslink.com)]

On the grounds that the change from a pension landscape where defined benefit plans predominated to one dominated by defined contribution plans calls for re-thinking ERISA remedies, the Seventh Circuit allowed a class of defined contribution plan participants to sue under ERISA § 502 in an excessive-fee case, building on the 2008 Supreme Court ruling that individual participants could seek ERISA relief. The Seventh Circuit held that a plan and individual participants can be injured at the same time if the plan's investment advisor charges excessive fees or makes imprudent investment choices. However, although the Seventh Circuit upheld the possibility of ERISA § 502 excessive-fee class actions, the court held that the district court did not certify properly defined classes: they did not have enough similarity of interest among class members because some class members were satisfied with the funds. Furthermore, some fees that were challenged were specific to particular funds, and others were imposed equally on all plan participants, so the classes as certified did not satisfy the "typicality" requirement for class action plaintiffs. [*Beesley v. International Paper Co.*, consolidated with *Spano v. Boeing*, 633 F.3d 574 (7th Cir. 2011); see Rebecca Moore, *Court OKs Class Actions for ERISA Cases*, plansponsor.com (Jan. 24, 2011)]

### [2] Regulations

In late 2010, EBSA published a final rule dealing with disclosure of investment options, including the fees imposed on employees in participant-directed individual account plans. The final rule says that investing plan assets is a fiduciary act subject to ERISA § 404(a)(1), requiring fiduciaries to be prudent and act solely in best interests of plan's participants and beneficiaries. Plan administrators are not liable if they rely, reasonably and in good faith, on information given by a service provider. The plan administrator must make sure that participants and beneficiaries who have investment responsibilities are informed of their rights and responsibilities in connection with their accounts. They must be given the fee and expense information they need to make informed decisions.

Participants must receive performance data, such as one, five, and 10-year historical returns. If the investment does not pay a fixed rate of return, the total annual operating expenses as a percentage of assets, and as a dollar amount per $1,000 invested, must be disclosed. For investments with a fixed rate of return, fees and any restrictions on ability to purchase or withdraw investments must be disclosed. The mandatory information must be given to participants on or before the first date they can direct their investments, then annually thereafter. They must receive general information about the structure and mechanics of the plan, how to give investment instructions, a list of the current investment choices, and fees and expenses for general plan services that can be charged to the account. Participants must receive statements, at least quarterly, showing the dollar amount of fees and expenses actually charged to their accounts, with a description of the services rendered.

This information must be provided in a chart or similar comparison format; DOL drafted a model chart. The final rule differs from previous law by entitling participants to disclosures no matter the size of the plan; previous law applied only to plans with 100 or more participants. Fee disclosure for individual plans extends beyond the fees charged for the plan's investment options, and includes general administrative services such as recordkeeping, accounting, and legal services. Participants must be advised whether the fees are charged pro rata or per capita, so they can determine if some participants pay more than their fair share. Benchmark returns must be compared with a broad-based market index that is not affiliated with the investment firm. [Final Rule, *Fiduciary Requirements for Disclosure in Participant-Directed Individual Account Plans*, <http://www.dol.gov/ebsa/pdf/frparticipantfeerule.pdf> and 75 Fed. Reg. 64910 (Oct. 20, 2010). See Fact sheet, *Final Rule to Improve Transparency of Fees and Expenses to Workers in 401(k)-Type Retirement Plans*, <http://www.dol.gov/ebsa/newsroom/fsparticipantfeerule.html> (Oct. 20, 2010). The model disclosure form is at <http://www.dol.gov/ebsa/participantfeerulemodelchart.doc>. See Fred Schneyer, *EBSA Releases Final 401(k) Fee Disclosure Rule*, plansponsor.com (Oct, 14, 2010); Ryan Alfred, *Reviewing the DOL's Final Rule on Participant Fee Disclosure*, BrightScope Blog (Oct. 18, 2010) (benefitslink.com).]

DOL's FAB 2013-02 gives employers a one-time election to change the deadline for furnishing either the 2013 or 2014 comparison chart, as long as the plan fiduciary determines that the delay is in the best interests of participants and beneficiaries—and no more than 18 months elapses between charts. [FAB 2013-02, <http://www.dol.gov/ebsa/regs/fab2013-2.html>; see EBSA News, *Labor Department Permits 401(k) Plans to Reschedule Annual Disclosures to Employees*, <http://www.dol.gov/ebsa/newsroom/2013/ebsa072213.html> (July 22, 2013)]

In July 2011, EBSA published a rule under ERISA § 408(b)(2), requiring providers to report to plan sponsors on direct and indirect compensation that the sponsors paid for account services. [75 Fed. Reg. 41600 (July 16, 2010)]

A subsequent final rule on this topic was published in February 2012. The rule applies to service providers who are expected to receive $1,000 or more in compensation from defined benefit or defined contribution plans, and to provide certain services or make investment options available in connection with broker-age or recordkeeping. The mandated information must be given, in writing, to the fiduciary for the plan. (Electronic disclosures are permissible if they are readily accessible to the fiduciary.) On request from the plan fiduciary or plan adminis-trator, the service provider must disclose its compensation and other information about the service arrangement. The final regulation is effective July 1, 2012, for both existing and new contracts. [77 Fed. Reg. 5632 (Feb. 3, 2012); DOL Fact Sheet, *Final Regulation Relating to Service Provider Disclosures Under Section 408(b)(2)* (Feb. 2012) (benefitslink.com); Tara Cantore, *Plan Sponsors Must Be Aware of Changes In 408(b)(2) Final Rule*, plansponsor.com (Feb. 7, 2012) and *DoL Issues Final Rule on 401k Fee Disclosure*, plansponsor.com (Feb. 2, 2012)]

A number of procedural decisions have been rendered in cases about 401(k) plan fees, but author Fred Reish could not find a simple pattern in the rulings. His advice to plan committees is that they should:

- Learn about revenue sharing paid to plan's service providers such as the recordkeeper, from investments or other sources, whether or not the arrangement is bundled;

- In bundled arrangements involving affiliated mutual funds, consider both revenue sharing from funds and credit for use of internal funds (such as a mutual fund's payment of subtransfer agent fees to a recordkeeper) in determining the reasonableness of costs;

- Evaluate payments and credits for services provided by the recordkeeper as compared to the marketplace cost of similar services; and

- Switch to lower-cost investments or a less expensive collective trust or separate account if they believe they are paying fees that are too high.

Reish says that ERISA accounts are often used to pay plan expenses during the year, with remaining balance allocated to participants' accts in proportion to their balances. Fiduciaries should make sure that the expense ratios and revenue sharing are appropriate for a plan of comparable size. [Fred Reish, *Just Out of Reish - 'Class' Actions*, plansponsor.com (October 2011)]

## § 6.08  INVESTMENT ADVICE FOR PARTICIPANTS

PWBA Advisory Opinion 2001-09A [(Dec. 14, 2001), <http://www.dol.gov/ebsa/programs/ori/advisory2001/2001-09A.htm>] says that it would not be a prohibited transaction for a company that provides financial services to retain an independent professional to use computer modeling and modern portfolio theory to offer discretionary asset allocation services and recommended asset allocation services in connection with individual account plans—i.e., 401(k) plans. Participants will be given advice about how to allocate assets within their accounts, but would be permitted to either accept or reject the advice.

In effect, this was the approach adopted by PPA Title XI (§§ 601–625). It is not a prohibited transaction for a plan to provide plan participants with investment advice as long as the plan fiduciaries' fees for providing the advice do not vary based on the actual recommendations. There is also a safe harbor for investment advice that is generated by a valid computer model.

In early 2008, the Supreme Court ruled that the purpose of ERISA is to safeguard benefits. Therefore, although the general rule is that ERISA § 502(a)(3) can only be used to provide remedies for the plan as a whole, in a defined contribution plan, a participant can bring suit charging that fiduciary misconduct reduced the value of his or her plan account. [*LaRue v. DeWolff, Boberg & Assocs., Inc.*, 552 U.S. 248 (2008)]

The DOL announced a final rule on improving access to financial advice for 401(k) and IRA accounts, published in the January 21, 2009 Federal Register. However, the effective date of the rule was delayed several times, first to allow the incoming Obama administration to review it, then in light of negative comments. [EBSA Final Rule, *Delay of Effective Date and Applicability Date, Investment Advice—Participants and Beneficiaries*, 74 Fed. Reg. 11847 (Mar. 20, 2009); see Rebecca Moore, *DOL Delays Investment Advice Rules Implementation*, plansponsor.com (Mar. 20, 2009), Fred Schneyer, *DOL Suggests Advice Rule Delay*, plansponsor.com (Feb. 4, 2009); EBSA Final Rule, RIN 1210-AB13, "Investment Advice—Participants and Beneficiaries," 74 Fed. Reg. 23951 (May 22, 2009)]

Finally, in 2010, the DOL withdrew the rule and proposed a revision. Under the revised rule, advice can be given two ways: through the use of an unbiased computer model, or when the adviser's fees do not vary no matter what investments the participants choose. The computer model or level fee arrangement has to be chosen by the fiduciary, independent of adviser and its affiliates; qualifications set for the investment expert who certifies the model; investment advisers can't get compensation from affiliates on the basis of their recommendations; and advice arrangements have to be audited each year. Additional requirements, including fee disclosure, are imposed. [Proposed rule, 75 Fed. Reg. 9360 (Mar. 2, 2010); see Rebecca Moore, *DOL Proposes New Advice Rule*, plansponsor.com (Feb. 26, 2010); Davis & Harman, LLP Summary of Investment Advice Regulations (Mar. 1, 2010) (benefitslink.com); for history of the rule, see Fred

Schneyer, *EBSA Delays Advice Rule Again*, plansponsor.com (Nov. 16, 2009) and *EBSA Pulls Back Controversial Advice Mandate*, plansponsor.com (Nov. 19, 2009)]

Late in 2011, the DOL finalized the ERISA § 408(g) regulations that say it is not a prohibited transaction for fiduciary advisors to give individualized investment advice to participants in individual account plans. Fiduciary advisors qualifying for this exemption include broker-dealers, registered investment advisors, banks, and insurance companies. The effective date is December 27, 2011. The DOL's Fact Sheet on the regulations estimates that about 134,000 defined contribution plans having 17 million participants and beneficiaries will contract with 16,000 investment advisory firms under these rules, and an estimated 3.5 million participants and beneficiaries will access the advice.

Advice must be based on generally accepted investment theories considering historic returns of different asset classes over time, plus information about the individual's age, life expectancy, current investments, assets and income, and investment preferences. The adviser's direct or indirect compensation must not vary based on which options the participant selects. Asset allocations in a computer model must be based on objective criteria, and must not be based on the size of the fee the advisor receives. Before a computer model is used, an eligible investment expert has to certify that it satisfies the requirements.

To use an eligible investment advice arrangement, the plan must have express authorization from a fiduciary. At least once a year, the arrangement must be audited by an independent auditor. The advisor must retain its records for at least six years after furnishing advice. [76 Fed. Reg. 66637 (Oct. 7, 2011); Prudential, *DOL Investment Advice Compliance Advisory* (December 2011) (benefits link.com); Guest Article, Deloitte's Washington Bulletin, *Labor Department Finalizes* "Investment Education" *Regulation* (Oct. 31, 2011) (benefitslink.com)]

## § 6.09  401(k) PLANS RESPOND TO THE ECONOMY

### [A]  Market Effects

In the 1990s, 401(k) plans rose to prominence. At that time, there was a great deal of interest in permitting plan participants to benefit from the bull market. For the period 2005–2010, the typical average annual return achieved by defined contribution plan participants was 3.7%, for a cumulative return of just over 20%—even considering the recession. Almost all (95%) of participants had positive total return for the five years, but just broke even for 2007-2010. [<https://institutional.vanguard.com/VGApp/iip/site/institutional/researchcommen tary/article/InvResDuringCrisis>; see Tara Cantore, *Vanguard Study Finds DC Plan Account Accumulation Positive Through Recession*, plansponsor.com (Dec. 14, 2011)]

The recession caused significant losses to 401(k) accounts, even those managed by reputable firms. In 2012, there was about $3.3 trillion invested in 401(k) accounts, seven times the level of two decades earlier. However, less than half of workers in the private sector participate in 401(k) plans, and close to one-fourth of businesses that have more than 100 employees do not offer 401(k)s. Even among participants, it is common to save only 3% a year, whereas the recommended level for retirement security is 10%–12%. The Center for Retirement Research estimates that, in 2010, the typical worker in the 55–64 age bracket (i.e., approaching retirement age) had an average 401(k) balance of only $54,000, and total retirement assets, including IRAs, of $120,000—less than one-quarter the recommended level of savings, and an amount that would generate only about $7,000 a year in annuity income. Sixty percent of the tax relief stemming from 401(k) plans goes to the top 10% of earners, who are likely to save for retirement even without tax advantages. [Steven Greenhouse, *Should the 401(k) Be Reformed or Replaced?* NYTimes.com (Sept. 11, 2012)] The title of this article would once have been heresy: for many years, 401(k)s were acclaimed as a solution for both employers' and employees' needs. Now some commentators are questioning whether the 401(k) form has failed or is so questionable that it requires major changes—if it can or should survive at all.

However, Transamerica Retirement Survey's 13th annual report examined the preceding five years of 401(k) performance, reaching far more sanguine conclusions. Catherine Collinson, president of the Transamerica Center for Retirement Studies, said that access to savings plans increased: in 2007, 72% of employers offered 401(k) plans, rising to 82% in 2012, whereas the percentage of companies offering defined benefit plans dropped from 19% to 15% in the same time period. Employer matches were more common in 2007 (80%) than in 2012 (70%), but half of the companies that suspended or reduced their match since 2008 have reinstated it. About one-fifth (19%) of employers had a Roth feature in their 401(k) plans in 2007, about one-third (32%) did in 2012. For most of the five-year period, the employee participation rate was approximately 77%. In 2007, the median annual salary deferral rate was 7%, dropping to 6% for 2009-2011, returning to 7% in 2012. In 2012, the median account balance was $99,320 for Baby Boomers, $41,821 for members of Generation X, and $15,213 for Echo Boomers. Clearly, this is not enough for retirees to live on, so 56% of workers surveyed expected to work after age 65, and 43% expected to work past age 70 or not to retire at all. [Mary Beth Franklin, *Surprise! 401(k)s Rode Out The Great Recession Just Fine*, InvestmentNews (Nov. 14, 2012) (benefitlink.com)]

Thanks to investment factors, the average 401(k) account balance increased 10% between 2011 and 2012; the average 2012 balance was $85,212. The average employee contribution in 2012 was $4,845. Only one out of nine (11%) of plan participants made the maximum contribution. [Beth Pinsker, *Americans With Savings in Retirement Plans Have Something to Celebrate*,Reuters Money (June 11, 2013) (benefitslink.com)]

## [B]  Employer Stock and Diversification

During the bull market, publicly traded companies had very strong incentives to use their own stock to compensate employees. Not only could they save cash by offering stock or stock options, but distributing stock to employees reduces the risk of unfriendly takeovers, increases employees' stake in the company and therefore at least theoretically their loyalty, and gives employees the chance to benefit from increases in the value of the stock. The problem is that, in a bear market, employees suffer correspondingly as a result of decreases in the value of the stock. Diversification is a basic principle of investment theory. By law, defined benefit plans cannot be more than 10% invested in the employer's stock; however, employees, especially those who get employer matches in the form of the employer's stock, often have more than one-quarter of their account invested in employer stock. If—like most securities—the value of the employer stock fell, participants would lose much of the value of their account balances. As Chapter 15 shows, many suits have tried (generally unsuccessfully) to penalize plan fiduciaries for retaining employer stock as an investment for an unduly long period.

PPA §§ 507 and 901 enacted a new Code § 401(a)(35) and a related ERISA provision at 204(j), explaining diversification rights for publicly traded employer securities held by a defined contribution plan. Participants (and some beneficiaries) are entitled to notice of the right to diversify their elective deferrals and after-tax contributions. Plans must offer at least three other investment options, with materially different risk and return characteristics. (Because ESOPs are designed to invest in employer stock, they are exempt from these rules.) Plan administrators must notify participants of their rights to divest at least 30 days before the first date the right to divest can be exercised. [IRS Notice 2006-107, 2006-5 I.R.B. 1114 (Nov. 30, 2006), <http://www.irs.gov/pub/irs-drop/n-06-107.pdf>] Failure to provide the statement is penalized by up to $110 per day elapsed without providing the required statement. All defined contribution plans must issue a statement at least annually, and quarterly statements are required for individual account plans (e.g., 401(k)s) whose participants can direct the investment of their account balances. The quarterly statement must disclose:

- The total account balance;
- The amount that is vested; if none is, the earliest vesting date for the participant;
- A breakdown of the value of each of the investments within the account;
- Whatever limitations or restrictions are placed on the right to direct investments by the terms of the plan;
- An explanation of why diversification is important;
- URL for the DOL Website containing investment information;

- (For profit-sharing plans integrated with Social Security) an explanation of plan integration.

The DOL also imposes Civil Money Penalties of up to $100/day for failure to provide notice of the right to sell company stock to diversify. [72 Fed. Reg. 44970 (Aug. 10, 2007); see DOL press release, *U.S. Labor Department Publishes Civil Penalty Rules Under Pension Protection Act* (Aug. 9, 2007)]

Employers can use the general DOL and IRS procedures for distributing statements in electronic rather than hard-copy form. The information can be provided on a secure Website as well as through individual e-mails. But if the sponsor chooses to use a Website to distribute the information, participants and beneficiaries must be given a written notice explaining how to access the information online—and that they can get a free paper copy if they prefer.

Individual account plans that do not permit individuals to direct the investment of their accounts must also furnish annual statements within 45 days of the end of the year. The statements are similar but need not include information about restrictions on investments or the explanation of the importance of diversification. The information can be furnished on a secure Website. [Gregory B. Kuhn, *New Benefit Statement Requirements for Retirement Plans*, <http://www.utzmiller/benefitstatement.pdf?> (Mar. 16, 2007). The DOL URL is <http://www.dol.gov/ebsa/investing.html>]

Regulations proposed in early 2008 were finalized in July 2010, explaining the diversification requirements imposed on plans that invest in publicly traded securities of the employer. Under the Final Rule, a participant who has at least three years of service (or the beneficiary of such a participant, or the beneficiary of a deceased participant) must be given a chance at least every quarter to diversify out of employer securities held in that person's account. The plan must offer at least three investment options other than employer stock, and those three must be diversified and must have materially different risk and return characteristics. [Proposed regulations: Prop. Reg. 136701-07, 2008-11 I.R.B. 616; final regulations, T.D. 9484, 75 Fed. Reg. 27927 (May 19, 2010); see Rebecca Moore, *IRS Issues Final Regs on Diversification Requirements for Company Stock*, plansponsor.com (May 18, 2010)]

As § 15.03[C] shows, "stock-drop" litigation has become very common. That is, plaintiffs whose account value has declined significantly because they invested in employer stock that declined in value frequently bring suits alleging that the plan's fiduciaries were imprudent to retain employer stock as a possible investment.

These plaintiffs face significant difficulties from the *Moench* presumption: that is, in 1995, the Third Circuit held that fiduciaries are presumed to be prudent when they retain employer stock as a plan investment, although this presumption can be disproved if the plaintiffs have enough evidence on their side. [*Moench v. Robertson*, 62 F.3d 553 (3d Cir. 1995)] Late in 2011, the Second Circuit agreed with the Third, Fifth, Sixth, and Ninth Circuits that including employer stock in a plan is presumed prudent unless the plan participants can show that a reasonable fiduciary who carried out an adequate investigation would have found that the employer stock should not have remained in the plan. In this case, although the stock fluctuated in value, there was no cause to disturb the presumption. The Second Circuit also dismissed allegations that the duty of loyalty was violated by inadequate communication with participants, holding that fiduciaries are not obligated to disclose non-public information or forecast declines in the value of the employer's stock. The plaintiffs charged that the SEC filings incorporated into the plan communications were materially false or misleading about the employer's financial condition, but the Second Circuit said that the filings were prepared by the company acting in corporate and not fiduciary status—and issuers of plan communications do not have an obligation to undertake an independent investigation of SEC filings. [*In re Citigroup ERISA Litig.*, 662 F.3d 128 (2d Cir. 2011) and *Gearren v. McGraw-Hill Cos.*, No. 10-792-cv-(L), 2011 WL 4952628 (2d Cir. Oct.19, 2011); see EBIA Weekly, *Another Circuit Court Adopts Presumption of Prudence for Investments in Employer Stock* (Nov. 22, 2011) (benefitslink.com). The presumption has also been adopted by the Eleventh Circuit: *Lanfear v. Home Depot*, 679 F.3d 1267 (11th Cir. 2012)]

The Supreme Court refused to hear the appeal of either *Gearren* (or *Gray v. Citigroup*, a similar stock-drop case involving the presumption). The Second Circuit applied the presumption at the pleading stage, so a defendant's motion to dismiss can be granted if the plaintiffs fail to allege facts showing abuse of discretion. The Second Circuit applied the presumption to ESOPs as well as other types of plans. The circuit split remains because the Sixth Circuit has ruled that the presumption cannot be applied at the evidentiary stage. [*Gearren v. McGraw-Hill Cos.*, 133 S. Ct. 476 (2012); *Gray v. Citigroup*, 133 S. Ct. 475, cert. denied (Oct. 15, 2012); see Susan J. Luken, Schiff Hardin LLP, ERISA Litigation & Benefits Blog, *Supreme Court Allows Moench Presumption to Continue* (benefitslink.com); EBIA Weekly, *Sixth Circuit Concludes Participants Have Plausible Fiduciary Breach Claim for Investments in Employer Stock* (Aug. 23, 2013) (benefitslink.com)]

The Seventh Circuit applied the presumption of prudence—fiduciaries do not have to outsmart the stock market by predicting the performance of employer stock. Nor are they required to apply inside information about the corporation's financial health to plan decisions when that would violate federal securities laws. [*White v. Marshall &Ilsley Corp.*,No. 11-2660 (7th Cir. Apr. 19, 2013)]

The Sixth Circuit held that an employee who sold most of her shares of employer stock at a time when she alleged the share price was artificially inflated by the company's financial misconduct did not have standing to maintain a stock-drop suit. She had no actual injury: if anything, the so-called misconduct benefited her by increasing the price she received for selling the stock. [*Taylor v. KeyCorp.*, 680 F.3d 609 (6th Cir. 2012)]

An important issue, on which there is a circuit split, is the type of plan and whether investment in the employer's stock is required or merely permitted. The

Fifth Circuit has held that the presumption applies to all eligible individual account plans, whether or not the plan mandates investment in employer stock. The Second Circuit affirmed in part, vacated in part a suit against the investment committees of two individual account plans. The participants charged that allowing an employer stock fund as an investment was imprudent. One plan required investment in employer stock, the other didn't. The Second Circuit vacated the district court dismissal and reinstated claims against the plan that permitted but did not require employer stock investment. [*Taveras v. UBS AG*, 708 F.3d 436 (2d Cir. 2013); see Haynes and Boone Blogs, *Second Circuit Reaffirms that Moench Presumption Applies Only When Plan Terms Require Investment in Employer Stock* (Mar. 12, 2013) (benefitslink.com);]

Yet another question is which stage(s) of the case the presumption can be asserted. The Second, Third, and Ninth Circuits have applied the presumption to motions to dismiss, whereas the Sixth Circuit has not. Therefore, the Sixth Circuit permitted profit sharing plan participants to maintain their claim. The defined contribution plan had 20 investment options including the employer stock. The default option for the 4% employer matching contribution was the employer stock, but the matching funds could be moved to other investment options. During the period covered by the lawsuit, the employer's stock price fell by 74%. The Sixth Circuit held that the presumption is not an additional pleading requirement, and is not applicable at the motion-to-dismiss stage of the case. The Sixth Circuit held that it was a fiduciary act to incorporate the SEC filings by reference into the SPD, finding express incorporation of the filings to be a fiduciary communication. [*Dudenhoefer v. Fifth Third Bancorp* 692 F.3d 410 (6th Cir. 2012); see Wolters Kluwer Law & Business News Center, *Sixth Circuit Declines To Apply Presumption Of Prudence At Pleadings Stage* (Nov. 8, 2012) (benefitslink.com)]

The Bank of America won a suit alleging that the bank violated ERISA by investing retirement plan assets in funds affiliated with the bank. The Fourth Circuit held that the plaintiffs did not have constitutional standing to bring the case. They did not plead any cognizable injury in fact that they were likely to prevail on at trial. They did not claim that they were deprived of benefits or likely to be deprived in the future. The plaintiffs alleged that there was a fiduciary breach each time the plan committee overseeing the 401(k) plan met but did not remove bank-affiliated funds from the investment portfolio, but the Fourth Circuit said that the claim was time-barred. The suit was brought in 2006, and the challenge would have to be raised within six years of the initial selection of funds, which occurred in 1999. [*David v. Alphin*, 704 F.3d 327 (4th Cir. 2013); see Plansponsor staff, *Bank of America Wins Suit Over Affiliated Fund Use*, plansponsor.com (Jan. 22, 2013)]

Being able to take advantage of a presumption helps a party's case—but does not guarantee victory if the other side is able to rebut the presumption (in stock-drop cases, by showing that it was not in fact prudent to retain the stock in the plan). The presumption was successfully rebutted in a 2012 Sixth Circuit case. The Sixth Circuit revived a stock drop suit against State Street Bank and Trust holding that, although the *Moench* presumption applied, it was rebutted with evidence that a prudent fiduciary would have made a different investment decision under the same circumstances. In this case, the terms of the plan called for divesting company stock if there was a serious question about the viability of the company as a going concern and GM's auditors disclosed substantial doubts in late 2008, but State Street did not begin divesting GM stock for a further four months. [*Pfeil v. State St. Bank & Trust Co.*, 671 F.3d 585 (6th Cir. 2012); see Rebecca Moore, *Appellate Court Reopens Case Against State Street by GM Participants*, plansponsor.com (Feb. 23, 2012)]

## [C]   Blackout Periods

In certain instances, often associated with corporate mergers and acquisitions, or with the release of corporate earnings and other financial statements, a "blackout period" is imposed, and ordinary activities in connection with plan accounts are suspended. Because of concerns that rank-and-file employees are at risk of losing money during blackouts, the Sarbanes-Oxley Act [Pub. L. No. No. 107-204] not only limits the trading activities of corporate insiders, but also obligates the corporation to provide notice of future blackout periods to the employees at large.

A blackout period, according to § 306(a)(4) of the Act, means a period that lasts more than three consecutive business days, during which at least 50% of the plan's participants or beneficiaries' ability to trade in the employer company's stock is affected. An "individual account plan" means a retirement plan that has more than one participant, and where each participant has his or her own separate account. For instance, a 401(k) plan is an individual account plan, but a defined benefit pension plan is not, because the whole plan has only one account from which benefits are paid.

Certain events that affect trading are not considered blackout periods, so the notice requirement doesn't apply. Under the legal definition, blackout periods are only temporary, so if rights are permanently amended or eliminated, this does not constitute a blackout period, and notice will not be required.

Furthermore, if the plan imposes regularly scheduled blackouts—for instance, every quarter at the time that earnings figures are released—and if the scheduled blackouts have been disclosed to participants and beneficiaries in the Summary Plan Description (SPD) or other plan communications, notice will not be required.

Finally, an event is not a blackout period if it is imposed just because someone becomes—or ceases to be—a participant or beneficiary in an individual account plan because of a corporate merger, acquisition, or divestiture. Limitations on just one person's account (relating to a divorce-related court order or a tax levy, for instance) are not considered blackout periods either, because a blackout period is a mass rather than an individual event.

## [D]  Changes in the Employer Match

Under prior law, the sponsor of a safe harbor 401(k) plan could eliminate or reduce matching contributions under certain circumstances, but could only suspend or cut non-elective contributions by terminating the plan. Proposed regulations published in mid-2009 [74 Fed. Reg. 23134 (May 18, 2009)] allow plan sponsors to reduce or suspend their safe harbor non-elective contributions during a plan year in which they encounter a substantial business hardship. The eligible employees must be notified of the reduction or suspension, and the plan must be amended to provide that anti-discrimination tests must be satisfied for the whole plan year. Substantial business hardship means that the sponsoring corporation is operating at a loss; unemployment or underemployment is common in the sponsor's industry; the industry as a whole is depressed or in a decline; and it is reasonable to predict that the plan cannot be continued without reducing or suspending non-elective contributions. The rules are complex, so sponsors must get legal advice before attempting to alter plan contributions. [See Towers Perrin Governance and Compliance Advisory Insight, *New IRS Regulations Allow Safe Harbor 401(k) Plans to Suspend Non-Elective Contributions* (May 2009) (benefitslink.com)]

In its 55th Annual Survey of Profit Sharing and 401(k) plans, released in late 2012, the Plan Sponsor Council of America (PSCA) reported that in 2010, 91% of companies made matching contributions, rising to 95.5% in 2011. The average employer contribution went from 3.7% (2010) to 4.1% (2011), and the average participant deferral rate rose from 6.2% to 6.4% in the same time frame. [Stephen Miller, *Changes in 401(k) Plans Spur Higher Participation*, SHRM (Oct. 15, 2012) (benefitslink.com)]

American Investment Planners LLC's survey showed that 5% of employers that matched 401(k) contributions dropped the match in 2010, and another 2% did so in 2011, with the result that, in 2011, 42% of active 401(k) plans did not include an employer match. [Karen DeMasters, *401(k) Matching Funds Being Eliminated, Study Shows*, Financial Advisor Blogs (May 2, 2013) (benefitslink .com)]

Another possibility is that employers will impose additional conditions before employees can receive a match. International Foundation of Employee Benefit Plans (IFEBP)'s twelfth annual 401(k) Benchmarking Survey revealed more companies delaying eligibility. In 2011, two-thirds of employers with 401(k) plans made employees eligible for a match as soon as they were hired, but only 56% did so in 2012. This survey shows 21% of respondents stating that they are considering changing the plan design to make all employer contributions discretionary rather than automatic. [Joanne Sammer, *Are 401(k) Matches an Endangered Species?*, Business Finance (May 7, 2013) (benefitslink.com)]

# CHAPTER 7

# CASH BALANCE PLANS

## § 7.01 INTRODUCTION

A cash balance plan is a hybrid pension plan that shares features of a conventional defined benefit plan with characteristics more like a profit-sharing or 401(k) plan. Cash balance plans are subject to the defined benefit plan rules.

The IRS's definition of a cash balance plan, found at 64 Fed. Reg. 56579, is "a defined benefit pension plan that typically defines an employee's retirement benefit by reference to the amount of a hypothetical account balance." In a typical cash balance plan, this account is credited with hypothetical allocations and interest that are determined under a formula set out in the plan.

The plan is drafted so that the corporation's books reflect an individual account for each participant. The employer funds the plan each year, based on a percentage of pay, and subject to the I.R.C. § 415 limit on employer contributions. The pension the employee will eventually receive reflects two elements: an annual benefit credit (a percentage of pay) and annual interest credited at the rate specified by the plan. Because cash balance plans provide individual accounts, the plans are more portable than ordinary defined benefit plans.

At retirement, the employee's retirement annuity is based on the vested account balance. In practice, although in most defined benefit plans accrual is greatest in the later years of employment, in cash balance plans accrual is greatest in the early years. Defined benefit plans often provide early retirement subsidies; cash balance plans seldom do.

Over the past 25 years, many plan sponsors have shifted from defined benefit to cash balance plans to reduce cost volatility, reduce the level of benefits (although many employers offset this by increasing defined contribution benefits) and improve employees' satisfaction with their plans. Kravitz Inc.'s 2012 National Cash Balance Research Report showed a 21% increase in the number of cash balance plans in 2011, which are frequently used in conjunction with defined contribution plans. Nearly all (84%) of cash balance plans are in companies with fewer than 100 employees. Kravitz' research showed that, after combining a cash balance plan and a 401(k), the average employer contribution to employees' retirement accounts was 6% of pay, rather than the 2.3% average for companies having only 401(k)s. [Joanne Sammer, *Is It Time to Consider a Cash Balance Plan?* Business Finance (July 27, 2012) (benefitslink.com)]

The following year, Kravitz, Inc.'s *2013 Cash Balance Research Report,* using 2011 figures, shows that in 2011 1,097 new cash balance plans were created, bringing the total number of cash balance plans to 7,927. In 2011, there were about 11 million cash balance plan participants, with close to $1.5 trillion in assets—much higher than the $713 billion in 2010 assets. The average cash balance plan's assets were $183 million. Annual contributions for 2011 were $30.1 billion. In 2001, cash balance plans represented only 2.9% of all defined benefit plans. The percentage rose steadily, until cash balance plans represented 20% of defined benefit plans in 2011; the projected 2012 percentage was 24%. Virtually all cash balance plans (5,244) now in existence were adopted between

2006-2011 (i.e., after the PPA made it clear that this plan form is legal). Only 1,684 cash balance plans were adopted between 2000 and 2005, 265 between 1990 and 1999, and 82 between 1985 and 1989. [http://cashbalancedesign.com/articles/documents/NationalCashBalanceResearchReport2013.pdf, discussed in Matthew Heimer, *Cash-Balance Plans Grow, 401(k)s Shrink*, WSJ.com (June 13, 2013) and Kevin McGuinness, *Cash Balance Plans Show Decade-Long Growth*, plansponsor.com (June 12, 2013)]

Hybrid plans accrue benefits under the fixed formula set by the employer. A hybrid defined benefit plan usually defines the benefit as a lump sum account balance rather than an annuity benefit payable at age 65. Cash balance plans are the most popular type of hybrid plans. The account balance is the sum of periodic pay credits (a percentage of pay) plus interest credits reflecting the interest rate chosen by the employer.

Pension equity plans (PEPs) post pay credits to participants' accounts, so the lump sum account balance at retirement is the sum of the percentages over the years times final average pay.

The legal status of cash balance plans was highly ambiguous until the Pension Protection Act of 2006 (PPA; Pub. L. No. 109-280) made it clear that a cash balance plan that satisfies the statutory criteria will not be considered discriminatory. (See § 7.07.) However, this relief is prospective only, and cash balance conversions that occurred before June 29, 2005 are not affected by the legislation. As § 7.04 shows, although most courts have ruled in favor of cash balance plans, a few cases have found the cash balance form in general, or specific plans and plan provisions, to violate ERISA or discriminate against older workers.

Although plan amendments cannot reduce benefits earned before the conversion, some conversions have the effect that employees who already earned benefits do not earn additional retirement benefits for varying periods of time after the conversion. This effect, often referred to as "wearaway" or "benefit plateau," continues until the employee's benefit under the ongoing cash balance formula catches up with the employee's protected benefit.

The ERISA Advisory Council defines wearaway as an effect of plan transitions. The employee can get either the frozen benefit under the old plan formula or the total benefit under the cash balance plan—whichever is greater. But for employees who are close to early retirement age, the frozen benefit may be so much larger than the accruals under the new cash balance formula that, in effect, little or nothing will be accrued for a long time, until the benefit under the old rules is "worn away."

Although it is a cash balance plan case, the Supreme Court's mid-2011 decision in *Amara v. Cigna* has much broader implications for ERISA enforcement, looking at the remedies plan participants can receive based on the traditional "equitable" suits that descend from medieval English church court practice. In this case, Cigna performed a cash balance conversion of its plan. Cigna distributed summaries and an SPD stating that the new plan provided an overall improvement in retirement benefits, and that the participants' opening account balance equaled the full value of their accrued benefits. These documents also said that the conversion did not save money for the employer. Plan participants filed a class action charging that many participants were subject to wearaway; that the opening account balance did not reflect the early retirement subsidy, so it offered less than full value; and that the employer saved $10 million a year as a result of the conversion. (Cigna eventually conceded the last point, but said that it spent the money on other benefit plans.) The district court ruled for the plaintiffs, and ordered reformation of the plan to conform to description in the employee communications. The district court ordered the plan to provide beneficiaries their pre-conversion frozen benefits, plus the cash balance benefits they earned after the conversion. The Second Circuit affirmed.

The case went to the Supreme Court, which held that the SPD merely communicates about the plan, and the terms of the SPD are not part of the plan itself. The settlor of the plan sets the terms of the plan; the plan administrator is responsible for communicating with participants. This decision wipes out a long line of cases that hold that, if the SPD conflicts with the plan terms, the SPD should be enforced because it is the document that the beneficiaries saw. The Supreme Court also said that plaintiffs cannot use ERISA § 502(a)(1)(B) to enforce a contract claim for benefits. Asserting a likelihood of harm to a class is not enough to support relief, and (a)(1)(B) does not give courts the authority to reform the terms of a plan.

However, with regard to what constitutes appropriate equitable relief under ERISA § 502(a)(3), the Supreme Court left open the possibility of getting the plan reformed, seeking equitable estoppel, or even getting the trustee to reimburse the plan ("surcharge"). In general, plaintiffs do not have to prove detrimental reliance in equitable proceedings for reformation or surcharge. To win, plaintiffs must show actual harm (e.g., that they lost money), and that the defendants' actions caused the harm. However, they do not have to prove that they actually relied on the provisions of the SPD.

The Supreme Court remanded the case for further proceedings. [*Amara v. Cigna*, 131 S. Ct. 1866 (May 16, 2011). See Edward P. Smith, *Something for Everyone: 'CIGNA Corp. v. Amara'* (special to law.com (June 13, 2011)); Ellen E. Schultz, *Employees Win New Benefit Protections*, WSJ.com (May 21, 2011).]

When *Amara* was remanded, the District Court for the District of Connecticut reformed the plan terms and ordered additional benefits as appropriate equitable relief. The district court said that contract, rather than trust, standards justified reformation, based on fraud on one side and mistake on the other. The Supreme Court used a trust-law analysis, but the district court said that contract analysis conforms better to economic reality. The district court used the "likely harm" standard: once an initial showing of likely harm is made, it is presumed that the participants in the plan were prejudiced. According to the district court, the defective notice misled the employees about the contract, and CIGNA prevented the employees from getting accurate information about changes to the plan and misled them into believing their accrued benefits would be protected. The district court ruled that CIGNA could be required to pay surcharges based on two theories: make-whole relief or unjust enrichment. The make-whole argument would require plaintiffs to prove that they suffered a loss related to CIGNA's breach of fiduciary duty, but if they prove this, CIGNA can show that they would have had the loss even without the breach. Because the district court believed that the plaintiffs received less than their benefits under the cash balance plan plus the benefits under the predecessor plan, the court did not consider the unjust enrichment theory. The district court ordered that the plaintiffs receive full benefits under both plans. [*Amara v. CIGNA Corp.*, No 3:01-cv-2361, 2012 U.S. Dist. LEXIS 180355 (D. Conn. Dec. 20, 2012); see Mark Casciari and Sara Eber, *Amara—The Beat Goes On*, Seyfarth Shaw ERISA & Employee Benefits Litigation Blog (Jan. 10, 2013) (benefitslink.com); Rebecca Moore, *Court Makes Repeat Decision in Amara v. CIGNA Corp*, plansponsor.com (Jan. 23, 2013)]

In October 2011, the PBGC proposed a rule to implement PPA provisions for allocating assets and determining the amount of benefits when a cash balance or other statutory hybrid plan terminates. The PBGC's intention was to give participants more certainty about their benefits when a plan is terminated and trusteed by the PBGC. An applicable defined benefit plan must have provisions for plan termination. If the interest crediting rate is variable, the interest rate applied to accrued benefits at termination is the average of interest rates for the five-year period ending on the date of termination. The interest rates and mortality tables as of the termination date are used to compute plan benefits that are payable as annuities at normal retirement age. Any variable rate must be the average of the five-year period ending on the termination date.

For distress terminations, the proposed termination date determines the benefits. If the proposed termination date is delayed, benefits accrued between the proposed and actual termination dates are recalculated using the interest rate that would have applied before the actual date of termination.

The PPA provides that a defined benefit plan fails to meet accrual requirements related to age if the plan provides for an interest credit in any plan year that exceeds the market rate of return. A plan satisfies the present value requirements if the present value of any participant's accrued benefit equals either the balance in the participant's hypothetical account, or an accumulated percentage of final average compensation.

Under the PBGC's proposed rule, some benefits are calculated differently for valuation than for payment purposes. The PBGC determines if a benefit can be cashed out (*i.e.*, is small enough to be distributed in a lump sum). If, after August 17, 2006, the plan made lump sum payments based on the hypothetical account balance without regard to the present value rules, the PBGC makes a de minimis lump sum determination using the same method as the plan did. The proposed rule says that Category 3 benefits for participants who were eligible to retire three years before plan termination or the sponsor's bankruptcy, but did not retire, are determined based on the account balance and interest rate that would have applied if the person had retired before the applicable date.

For bankruptcy terminations in general, the PBGC determines the hypothetical account balance as of the bankruptcy filing date using the actual crediting interest rate for interest between the bankruptcy filing date and the date of termination. For credits after the plan's determination date and before NRA or the annuity start date, the rate in effect on the termination date is used. [76 Fed. Reg. 67105 (Oct. 31, 2011); see PLC, *PBGC Implements Rules Changing Method for Determining Benefits When Hybrid Plan Terminates* (Oct. 31, 2011) (benefitslink .com); Rebecca Moore, *PBGC Issues Proposed Rule on Hybrid Plan Terminations*, plansponsor.com (Oct. 29, 2011); Deloitte's Washington Bulletin, *PBGC Proposes Rules on Determining Benefits in Terminating Hybrid Plans* (Nov. 7, 2011) (benefitslink.com)]

## § 7.02   CASH BALANCE PLANS: PROS AND CONS

The PPA provision authorizing cash balance conversions was adopted because many employers had already converted their plans to cash balance form, or showed an interest in doing so. Employers wanted to keep the difference between the plan's actual investment return and the rate of return promised to employees. They hoped that the plan could become self-funding without additional employer contributions if the difference were large enough. Perhaps ironically, the development of a positive body of decisions and regulations supporting cash balance plans and cash balance conversions has occurred when financial conditions are not necessarily suitable for conversions.

Sibson Consulting published a report in Spring 2011 suggesting that the IRS final and proposed regulations cleared up some confusion and made cash balance plans more attractive for some employers. Sibson suggested that a simple cash balance plan can be much less expensive for the employer than a defined contribution plan because the discount rate for a cash balance plan is based on the rate of return on investment-grade corporate bonds—and, under conditions prevailing in the first quarter of 2011, the difference between corporate and Treasury bond rates could be as much as 2%, allowing the sponsor to save money. Cash balance plans tend to have less interest rate risk than defined benefit plans.

Cash balance plans, like defined benefit plans but unlike 401(k) plans, cover all employees—so employees will get some employer contributions in a cash balance plan even if they would not get an employer match in a 401(k) plan if they could not save enough money to fund a 401(k) account. Cash balance plans were originally designed to cope with a disadvantage of defined benefit plans: in a defined benefit plan, all of the investment risk falls on the employer. But some employers now feel that shifting all of the investment risk to employees (in a defined contribution plan) is unfair. Combining a cash balance plan with a defined contribution plan places some of the risk on each. [Plansponsor staff, *New Regs May Warrant Reconsidering Cash Balance*, plansponsor.com (Mar. 25, 2011)]

Vanguard's R. Evan Inglis pointed out that sponsors who adopt a cash balance plan instead of a defined benefit plan sometimes fail to realize that they are trading interest rate risk for investment risk. Inglis noted that it is more difficult to invest in assets that match the liability profile of a cash balance plan than a traditional defined benefit plan, which can use long bonds to hedge the inherent risk of funding the pension. Inglis said that cash balance plans are less sensitive to interest rates than defined benefit plans. Although funding liability for cash balance plans is fairly stable and predictable, there are no specific assets that can be matched to a liability, making it difficult to control the funded status of the plan. [Plansponsor staff, *Cash Balance Plans Have Risk Mitigation Challenges*, plansponsor.com (Sept. 3, 2010)]

## § 7.03 "WHIPSAW" AND FINANCIAL FACTORS

The "whipsaw" issue arises because I.R.C. § 417 specifies the interest and mortality assumptions that must be used in converting from annuity to lump sum payment. When a worker covered by a defined benefit plan terminates employment, the sponsor must calculate the present value of any lump sum distribution.

This is done by projecting the account balance that would be available at normal retirement age, using PBGC-authorized interest rate assumptions. The next step is to find the value of the annuity that could be purchased with that sum. Finally, the PBGC interest rate assumptions are used again, to reconvert the annuity to a lump sum that represents the present value of the participant's account.

Applying this so-called whipsaw calculation to some cash balance plans increases the lump sum available to some plan participants. The participants who benefit naturally argue that the calculation has to be applied—and plan sponsors want to argue that they can bypass the whipsaw calculation. The higher the interest rates used, the less likely participants are to complain. Therefore, the whipsaw problem is most acute for disputes about plan actions taken before 1995, because in 1994 the PBGC raised its interest rate assumptions significantly.

The PPA avoids the whipsaw problem by requiring the lump sum distribution to equal the hypothetical account balance, and by specifying the range of interest rates. See § 7.07, below.

The Sixth Circuit held in April 2007 that although the whipsaw calculation is not required after the PPA took effect, it was required before that, and therefore upholds an award of $46 million in benefits and prejudgment interest to a class of 1,250 former employees who retired early and received lump sum distributions. [*West v. AK Steel Corp.*, 484 F.3d 395 (6th Cir. 2007), *cert. denied*, 129 S. Ct. 895 (Jan. 12, 2009)]

The Seventh Circuit held, in late 2011 that, when a district court creates a remedy for participants who were subjected to impermissible whipsaw calculations that did not add future interest credits to their lump-sum distributions, the court does not have to defer to the plan's preferred method for recalculating the lump sums. The plan conceded that unlawful whipsaw had occurred but said that the suit was time-barred or, as an alternative, that the plan's method of calculation should be used. The Seventh Circuit said that the unlawful calculations were part of the plan, so the plan's fiduciaries did not engage in any interpretive discretion to which the court could grant deference. [*Thompson v. Retirement Plan for Employees of S.C. Johnson & Son*, Inc., 651 F.3d 600 (7th Cir. 2011); see CCH Pensions & Benefits, *Deference to Plan's Method for Re-Calculating Distributions Not Required to Remedy Pre-PPA "Whipsaw" Violations* (Oct. 25, 2011) (benefitslink.com)]

For most of the 1990s and 2000s, the Treasury rate was below the guarantees offered by cash balance plans, giving employees an incentive to quit early and take lump sums. In a case interpreting plan language from 2003 (i.e., before the 2007 regulations that now limit the ability to establish a normal retirement age (NRA) lower than age 62), the Seventh Circuit permitted a cash balance plan to define NRA as the completion of five years of service to avoid the whipsaw calculation of lump sum benefits. The language also pre-dated the PPA rules eliminating the whipsaw calculation. The plaintiff was paid the amount of his hypothetical account balance at the time of termination, whereas he thought that his hypothetical balance would be increased by the interest that would have been credited under the plan until he reached 65, discounted to present value using the 30-year Treasury rate. Because the plan set NRA at five years of service—the vesting date—without reference to age, his virtual account balance was also the value of his lump sum. [*Fry v. Exelon*, 571 F.3d 644 (7th Cir. 2009); see Deloitte Washington Bulletin, *Five Years of Service Is a Permissible "Normal Retirement Age" for Cash Balance Plan* (July 20, 2009) (benefitslink.com). Certiorari was denied on February 22, 2010 (No. 09-532); see Rebecca Moore, *Supreme Court Lets Stand Alternate Definitions for Retirement Age*, plansponsor.com (Feb. 23, 2010); for history of the case, see Fred Schneyer, *Appellate Judges Affirm Years-of-Service Definition for Retirement*, plansponsor.com (July 10, 2009)]

However, in 2013, the District Court for the Southern District of New York held that it was invalid for PriceWaterhouseCooper's cash balance plan to set its NRA at five years of service, on the grounds that ERISA's definition is based on plan anniversaries, not years of service. The district court held that the participants were wrongfully deprived of the part of their accrued benefits that was attributable to future interest credits until an NRA that was valid under ERISA. [*Laurent v. PriceWaterhouseCoopers*,No. 06 Civ. 2280 (JPO) (S.D.N.Y. Aug. 8, 2013); see Rebecca Moore, *Court Reiterates Years of Service Is Not Valid NRA*, plansponsor.com (Aug. 12, 2013)]

The Fourth Circuit rejected claims that the Bank of America violated the anti-backloading provision by defining the NRA as the earlier of the first day of the calendar month after the participant reached age 65 or having 60 months of vesting service. The court held that it was not necessary for every employee to have the same NRA and it was permissible to set the NRA on the basis of vesting service to prevent some participants from being entitled to whipsaw distributions. In the Fourth Circuit view, the backloading rules cease to apply once a plan participant reaches NRA. [*McCorkle v. Bank of Am.*, 688 F.3d 164 (4th Cir. 2012); see Rebecca Moore, *Plan Definition of NRA Did Not Lead to Backloading*, plansponsor.com (Aug. 27, 2012)]

The Sixth Circuit held that an ex-employee who challenged the calculation of her lump sum distribution from a cash balance plan was not required to exhaust her administrative remedies under the plan—an appeal would have been futile. According to the Sixth Circuit, participants can go straight to court when they challenge the legality of a plan's entire methodology. The plaintiff admitted that she received the proper amount under the plan's method of calculation—what she objected to was the method. [*Durand v. The Hanover Ins. Group*, 560 F.3d 436 (6th Cir. 2009); see CCH Pension & Benefits, *Legality of "Whipsaw" Lump Sum Calculation Under Cash Balance Plan Can Be Challenged in Court* (Apr. 3, 2009); *French v. BP Corp. North Am. Inc.*, No. 08-216-DLB, 2009 U.S. Dist. LEXIS 104408 (E.D. Ky. Nov. 15, 2009) reaches a similar conclusion.]

Alliant Energy converted its defined benefit plan to cash balance form in 1998. Participants accrued a benefit credit of 5% of salary, plus an interest credit equal to the greater of 4% or 75% of the plan's rate of return for the year. The Western District of Wisconsin found that, between 1998 and 2006, the plan's calculation of lump sums failed to perform the whipsaw calculation that was required at that time, and the 30-year Treasury bond rate did not fairly represent the interest rates promised by the plan. The district court found Alliant liable in 2010. In 2012, the district court ordered Alliant to use an 8.2% interest rate to recalculate payments. The district court approved the calculations resulting in an $18.7 million award to the former participants. [*Ruppert v. Alliant Energy Cash Balance Pension Plan*, No. 08-cv-127-bbc (W.D. Wis. 2011 and Aug. 24, Sep. 5, 2012); see Rebecca Moore, *$18M Judgment Ordered in Alliant Cash Balance Case*, plansponsor.com (Aug. 28, 2012). For background on this case, see Fred Schneyer, *Whipsaw Calculation Case Deemed Class Action*, plansponsor.com (Feb. 17, 2009) and *Alliant Tagged for Pre-PPA Whipsaw Calculation*, planspon sor.com (June 9, 2010).]

## § 7.04   CASE LAW ON CASH BALANCE PLANS

The fundamental age discrimination issue is how ERISA § 204(b)(1)(H)(i) and Code § 411(b)(1)(H), which forbid terminating benefit accrual or reducing the rate of accrual because of a plan participant's attainment of any age, define "rate of accrual." If the rate of accrual is the change, from year to year, in the annuity that the participant can expect at age 65, then cash balance plans are inherently age-discriminatory because of the greater number of years over which younger participants can accrue interest credits. However, if it is merely the pay and interest credits to the hypothetical account, then cash balance plans are not discriminatory, they merely reflect the basic economic concept of the time value of money. [See the chart prepared by the American Benefits Council, *Cash Balance Plan Litigation*, <http://www.americanbenefitscouncil.org/documents/cb_litigation_120706.pdf> (Dec. 7, 2006).]

By mid-2008, five of the courts of appeals (Second, Third, Sixth, Seventh, Ninth) had already ruled that cash balance plans are not inherently discriminatory against older workers. These courts generally held that the higher balance for younger workers was a simple effect of the time value of money. [*Hurlic v. Southern California Gas Co.*, 539 F.3d 1024 (9th Cir. Aug. 20, 2008) [allowing, however, maintenance of a claim that the plan violated ERISA's notice requirements by not providing notice of wear-away]; *Hirt v. Equitable Ret. Plan for Emps., Managers & Agents*, 533 F.3d 102 (2d Cir. 2008); *Register v. PNC Fin. Servs. Group, Inc.*, 477 F.3d 56 (3d Cir. 2007); *Drutis v. Rand McNally & Co.*, 499 F.3d 608 (6th Cir. 2007), *cert. denied*, 129 S. Ct. 68 (2008); *Cooper v. IBM Personal Pension Plan*, 457 F.3d 636 (7th Cir. 2006), *cert. denied*, 127 S. Ct. 1143 (Jan. 16, 2007); see Fred Schneyer, *A Fifth Federal Appellate Court Upholds Cash Balance Plan Designs*, plansponsor.com (Aug. 20, 2008) and *U.S. Supreme Court Denies Cash Balance Challenge Review*, plansponsor.com (Oct. 7, 2008) In June 2010, the District Court for the District of New Jersey ended 12 years of litigation by ruling that AT&T's cash balance plan did not violate ERISA or the ADEA. Nor did the plan violate IRS regulations, requiring subsidized early retirement benefits to be the actuarial equivalent of the standard retirement benefit. The court held that the plan participants did not prove that the plan was "backloaded" (allowed accrual of benefits in any year in excess of 133% of benefits in any prior year): *Engers v. AT&T Inc.*, No. 98-3660 (SRC) (D.N.J. 2010). See Fred Schneyer, *AT&T Cleared in Cash Balance Suit*, plansponsor.com (June 9, 2010).]

Verizon Communications' cash balance plan document included a drafting error (a transition factor for calculating opening balances was used twice instead of once). According to the Northern District of Illinois, the plan's administrative committee should have gone to court to reform the plan documents to correct the mistake; it did not have the power to reform the plan. However, it was not an abuse of discretion to use 120% of the PBGC interest rate instead of 100% to calculate the opening account balance. [*Young v. Verizon's Bell Atlantic Cash Balance Plan*, No. 05 C 7314 (N.D. Ill. Aug. 28, 2008; see Fred Schneyer, *Verizon Hit for Cash Balance Conversion Error*, plansponsor.com (Sept. 2, 2008)] The Northern District re-heard the case in 2009 and ruled that Verizon could correct the error, holding this time that requiring the language to be applied literally would give participants a $1.67 billion windfall. Magistrate Judge Morton Denlow said that employers would be discouraged from adopting plans if they suffered unduly harsh penalties for mistakes. The Seventh Circuit affirmed in 2010. The Supreme Court refused to review the case. [*Young v. Verizon's Bell Atlantic*

*Cash Balance Plan*, 615 F.3d 808 (7th Cir. 2010), *cert. denied*, No. 10-765 (May 23, 2011), *reh'g denied*, July 25, 2011. See Fred Schneyer, *Verizon Escapes $1.6B Pension Liability*, plansponsor.com (Nov. 5, 2009).]

In 2006, the Southern District of New York held that accumulation of benefits based on a percentage of salary for completed years of service discriminated on the basis of age, because participants who join at a later age receive smaller benefits; in 2007, class action status was granted. Nevertheless, the Southern District of New York found that a similar plan was age-discriminatory: [*In re J.P. Morgan Chase Cash Balance Litig.*, 460 F. Supp. 2d 479 (S.D.N.Y. 2006) and No. 06 Civ. 732 (HB) (May 30, 2007)]

The Southern District changed its position in 2009, when it ruled that J.P. Morgan Chase and its predecessors did not violate ERISA when they converted the plan to a cash balance form, rejecting the argument that the plan did not provide "definitely determinable" benefits because it did not specify a method of projecting interest rates. Under ERISA § 402, employers have discretion to choose interest rates, as long as the plan has a written instrument that explains its funding and distribution mechanisms. [*Bilello v. J.P. Morgan Chase Ret. Plan*, No. 07 Civ. 7379 (DLC) (S.D.N.Y. Apr. 24, 2009); see Rebecca Moore, *Court Dismisses Claims Against JP Morgan Cash Balance Plan*, plansponsor.com (Apr. 28, 2009). Despite this ruling, the Southern District of New York approved settlement of two cash balance suits against J.P. Morgan Chase in mid-2010; both cases alleged failure to give adequate notice of conversion. [*In re J.P. Morgan Chase Cash Balance Litigation*, No. 06-cv-0732 (DLC) (THK) (S.D.N.Y. 2010); see Fred Schneyer, *Cash Balance Settlement Gets Court Approval*, plansponsor.com (July 20, 2010)]

The Seventh Circuit cleared Monsanto of class action age discrimination allegations, ruling that the rate of accrual did not decrease because of age. The class action dealt only with the Prior Plan Account (PPA), one of two accounts employees received after the conversion. The PPA accounts were supposed to preserve the accrued balances while also standardizing the disparate provisions of the earlier plans. The PPA's opening balance was calculated with a credit of the actuarial equivalent lump sum for the accrued benefit, discounted by an interest rate of $8\frac{1}{2}\%$ per year, for each month between the participant's age at the time of conversion and age 55. Pay credits were credited each month, but interest credits ceased at age 55. The Seventh Circuit held that the plan was not an "eligible cash balance plan" as defined by IRS regulations (because it distributed lump sums), and in fact operated more like a defined benefit plan. The interest credits were not benefit accruals, because they did not increase the accrued benefit at retirement. If the credits were not benefit accruals, then stopping them could not violate the ban on age-based changes in accruals. [*Walker v. Monsanto Co. Pension Plan*, 614 F.3d 415 (7th Cir. 2010); see Fred Schneyer, *Monsanto Cash Balance Plan Cleared of Age Bias Wrongdoing*, plansponsor.com (Aug. 2, 2010). For background, see Fred Schneyer, *Employer Wins One, Loses One in Cash Balance Case*, plansponsor.com (June 15, 2009). Certiorari was denied, 131 S. Ct. 1678

(Mar. 21, 2011): see Rebecca Moore, *High Court Lets Stand Monsanto Cash Balance Ruling*, plansponsor.com (Mar. 22, 2011)]

The Eighth Circuit held in 2009 that a defined benefit plan that converted to cash balance form in 2000 (i.e., long before the PPA took effect) did not reduce accrued benefits when the discount rate it used to calculate the accrued benefit portion of the opening account balance was 8% at a time when the § 417(e)(3) rate was slightly over 6%. A lower discount rate would have yielded a higher opening balance, and therefore a larger lump sum. At the time of the cash balance conversion, ERISA did not include a definition of "opening account balance." The Eighth Circuit held that using the statutory discount rate to determine the opening balance would have given participants a windfall. However, since the PPA, § 411(b)(5)(B)(iii) has provided that the benefit under the converted plan must be at least as great as the accrued benefit under the old plan, plus the accrued benefit since the conversion. [*Sunder v. U.S. Bancorp Pension Plan*, 586 F.3d 593 (8th Cir. 2009)]

The Sixth Circuit held that the anti-cutback rules prevent a converted cash balance plan from reducing the early retirement subsidy that was available under the pre-conversion defined benefit plan—even though the participant did not become eligible for the subsidy until after the conversion. The case was remanded for the district court to decide whether the participant's benefit was actually reduced. Before the 1998 cash balance conversion, the plan provided early retirement benefits to participants with five years of service who had reached age 55. Nine participants retired after the conversion, electing lump sums. They all filed administrative claims protesting that the lump sum did not include the pre-conversion early retirement subsidy. Only one of the nine made the claim within five years after the distribution. The district court dismissed the eight claims as untimely, and dismissed the one claim it found timely on the merits. The Sixth Circuit agreed that eight claims were time-barred, applying the Kentucky five-year statute of limitations for claims brought under a statute that does not have an explicit statute of limitations. The Sixth Circuit held that it violated ERISA § 204(g) not to include the pre-retirement subsidy in the ninth plaintiff's benefit, because the age condition can be fulfilled either before or after the plan amendment. The case was remanded to decide the fact issue of how to characterize the benefit: whether it was an early retirement benefit or subsidy protected by § 204(g), or an optional benefit form that is only protected from elimination. [*Falllin v. Commonwealth Indus., Inc. Cash Balance Plan*, 695 F.3d 512 (6th Cir. 2012); see Wolters Kluwer Law & Business News Center, *Cash Balance Plan May Not Reduce Pre-Conversion Early Retirement Subsidy* (Oct. 22, 2012) (benefitslink.com)]

The Seventh Circuit affirmed certification of a Rule 23(b)(2) ERISA class action with more than 4,000 current and former participants in a cash balance plan. The plaintiffs made cutback, whipsaw, and wearaway claims covering a 23-year period. The district court certified 10 subclasses. The employer challenged class certification, arguing that *Dukes* (see § 42.06) rules out (b)(2) class actions for monetary, declaratory, or injunctive relief. The employer argued that certification of a (b)(2) class is appropriate only if a single injunction or declaratory judgment could provide relief to all the subclasses. The employer also argued that claims for monetary relief were inappropriate in (b)(2) cases, at least where they are not incidental to injunctive or declaratory relief. The Seventh Circuit rejected these arguments, reading *Dukes* to mean that the requirement of a single injunction or declaratory judgment does not apply where each member in a subclass has the same claim. The Seventh Circuit held that the plaintiffs were seeking a declaration of rights under the plan and reformation of the plan to follow the declaration—any monetary relief would be incidental. It was too early to determine if individualized proceedings would be required at a later stage, but the Seventh Circuit held that it might be possible to bifurcate the case, with subclasses that obtained Rule 23(b)(2) declaratory relief following up with an opt-out (b)(3) proceeding to set relief for the individual members of the class. [*Johnson v. Meriter Health Servs.Emp.Ret.Plan*, 702 F.3d 364 (7th Cir. 2012); see Mark Casciari and Sara Eber, Seyfarth Shaw ERISA & Employee Benefits Litigation Blog, *Rule 23(B)(2) Certification—The Seventh Circuit Strikes Again, This Time In The ERISA Defined Benefit Context* (Dec. 5, 2012) (benefitslink.com); but see *National Life Ins. Co. v. Haddock*, 460 Fed. Appx. 26 (2d Cir. 2012), an unpublished case holding that monetary relief would not merely be incidental to a class action for breach of fiduciary duty.]

## § 7.05 THE CONVERSION PROCESS

At least 15 days' notice must be given in advance of adoption of a plan amendment that significantly reduces the rate of benefit accruals in the future. [See § 11.05 for a discussion of EGTRRA rules increasing the amount of disclosure that participants are entitled to in this situation] The plan may also have to issue a revised SPD and/or a Summary of Material Modification in connection with the conversion.

EBSA's cash balance plan FAQ [<http://www.dol.gov/ebsa/faqs/faq_consumer_cashbalanceplans.html>] Question 11 says that neither ERISA nor the Tax Code obligates employers who convert to a cash balance plan to give employees the option of remaining in the old plan. The employer can simply replace the old formula with the new formula for all participants, as long as the benefits already accrued as of the date of the conversion are not reduced. Or the employer can keep current employees under the old plan formula, applying the new formula only to those hired after the change. Another option is for some employees to be "grandfathered in," or allowed to receive their pensions under the old formula.

The first suit under the Lilly Ledbetter Fair Pay Act (Pub. L. No. 111-2) was filed eight days after the bill was signed. The case involved the El Paso pension plan's cash balance conversion. The plaintiff sought to reverse a January 21, 2009 decision that his age discrimination charge against the conversion was untimely. (The Ledbetter Act provides that an unlawful practice occurs when a violative plan is adopted, when the plaintiff became subject to the practice, or each time the plaintiff was affected by that practice. [Suzanne L. Wynn, Pension Protection Act Blog, *And the Lilly Ledbetter Litigation Begins* (Feb. 11, 2009) (benefitslink.com)]

In 2011, the Tenth Circuit held that the wearaway provision of Tomlinson's cash balance plan did not violate the ADEA § 4(i) accrual requirement, because credits were posted to the accounts of both young and older employees in a nondiscriminatory manner. Many employees were subject to wearaway because it took several years after the cash balance conversion for the minimum benefit to exceed the former benefit, especially for older employees. (The conversion occurred in 1997; wearaway was not forbidden until June 29, 2005.) The Tenth Circuit said that § 4(i) requires equality in inputs (benefit accruals) rather than outputs (accrued benefits), agreeing with the argument that the effect of the time value of money cannot be treated as age discrimination. The Tenth Circuit held that, absent deceit by the employer or failure to explain how the benefits are calculated, an SPD will not be invalidated for failure to inform employees about a wearaway period. [*Tomlinson v. El Paso*, 653 F.3d 1281 (10th Cir. 2011); see CCH Pensions & Benefits, *El Paso Wins Cash Balance Case; No Age Discrimination or Backloading Provisions Were Violated* (Sept. 2, 2011) (benefitslink. com); Rebecca Moore, *Appellate Court Finds Cash Balance Plan not Age-Biased*, plansponsor.com (Aug. 12, 2011)]

## [A] The 204(h) Notice Requirement

ERISA § 204(h), nicknamed the "anti-cutback rule," imposes notice requirements: plan participants and beneficiaries must be informed of plan changes that significantly reduce their entitlement to benefits. T.D. 9472, 74 Fed. Reg. 61270 (Nov. 24, 2009) is a final rule covering the 204(h) notice requirements for plan amendments that reduce accrued benefits. It provides that the effective date of an amendment that is adopted retroactively is the date the amendment goes into effect on an operational basis.

The Tenth Circuit upheld Solvay Chemicals' cash balance conversion, and said that the ERISA § 204(h) regulations did not mandate telling employees in either percentage or dollar terms that the conversion would reduce their future accrual rates. It was permissible to use tables of hypothetical benefit figures, because the data would allow employees to estimate their benefits, and it was clear from the tables that most employees were worse off after the conversion. The Tenth Circuit held that the cash balance plan did not violate the ADEA and satisfied ERISA requirements. However, the Tenth Circuit sent the case back to the district court to determine whether participants could use the information they were given to understand how the early retirement subsidy was calculated, or whether the company committed an egregious failure. [*Jensen v. Solvay Chems. Inc.*, 625 F.3d 641 (10th Cir. 2010)]

The district court found that there was no egregious failure under either standard. The plaintiffs appealed to the Tenth Circuit once again; the Tenth Circuit found no reason to disturb the district court's finding. [*Jensen v. Solvay Chems., Inc.*, No. 11-8092 (10th Cir. July 2, 2013)]

## § 7.06   DECEMBER 2002 REGULATIONS: PROPOSAL AND WITHDRAWAL

In December 2002, the IRS published a set of Proposed Regulations, REG-209500-86, at 67 Fed. Reg. 76123 (Dec. 11, 2002), although the moratorium on cash-balance plan conversions remained in effect. The proposal created the concept of an "eligible cash balance plan," for which the rate of benefit accrual includes additions to the participant's hypothetical account for the plan year, but not previously accrued interest credits. The participant accrues the right to future interest credits without regard to future service at the same time as the accrual of additions to the hypothetical account, for all future periods, including those after normal retirement age. The calculation must use a reasonable rate of interest, and the interest rate must not decrease based on reaching 65 (or any other specific age).

The Proposed Regulations stated that merely converting a defined benefit plan to an eligible cash balance form plan would not make the plan fail under Code § 411(b)(1)(H) as long as there was no wearaway.

The Proposed Regulations' approach to avoiding age discrimination was to forbid plans to stop or reduce accruals after NRA on the basis of age (whether the participant is older, younger, or at the NRA). The mandate of continued accrual of benefits post-NRA is satisfied to the extent that the benefits are distributed to the participant, or are increased actuarially to account for delayed distribution. However, this proposal was politically controversial, and was withdrawn in mid-2004 by Announcement 2004-57, 2004-27 I.R.B. 15 withdrawing the December 2002 Proposed Regulations, in light of the many comment letters received and Congress' interest in passing legislation (which eventually occurred in the form of the PPA).

## § 7.07   CASH BALANCE PLANS UNDER THE PPA AND WRERA

In 2006, Congress resolved legal uncertainties going forward, by providing rules under which cash balance plans can be created, or existing plans can be converted. However, the PPA specifically provides that it does not govern the validity or propriety of cash balance plans already in existence on June 29, 2005, so sponsors who "jumped the gun" by adopting cash balance plans, or making cash balance conversions, in the absence of guidance, may find themselves vulnerable in court. See § 7.04, above.

The statute uses the term "applicable defined pension plan" to refer to cash balance plans. Because other PPA provisions restrict the extent to which pension plans can "smooth" their investment results over several years, many sponsors will have to increase their contributions to defined benefit plans accordingly—a further incentive to convert to cash balance form.

A cash balance plan adopted or converted on or after June 29, 2005 will not be considered discriminatory if participants are 100% vested after three years of service. The plan must calculate interest credits with a rate of return that is not higher than market rates. The rate of return can be set as the greater of a fixed or a variable rate of return, and plans can implement a guaranteed minimum rate of return as long as it is reasonable.

No matter what their ages, all similarly situated employees must have equal accrued benefits. Participants are similarly situated if they have the same position, compensation, date of hire, and terms of service, and differ only in age. This provision adopts the argument that effects of the time value of money do not constitute age discrimination.

The PPA forbids the use of wearaway (adjusting plan formulas in a way that harms long-standing participants) under any plan amendment adopted after June 29, 2005. When a defined benefit plan is converted to a cash balance plan, each participant must receive the benefit accrued before the conversion, calculated under the pre-conversion formula, plus the benefit accrued after the conversion using the cash balance plan formula. Wearaway is also forbidden if a company freezes its defined benefit plan and adopts a cash balance plan. Qualifying participants must be permitted to receive early retirement subsidies.

The PPA eliminates whipsaw by mandating that the lump sum distribution from the plan must be equal to the hypothetical account balance. Cash balance plans are allowed to use a variable interest crediting rate, but the rate must not be higher than the market rate of return, and must be at least zero. Therefore, the account balance never falls below the cumulative total of pay credits.

WRERA, the relief bill for employers harmed by the economic downturn, signed December 23, 2008, eases the PPA's provisions dealing with such matters as age discrimination, conversions, and whipsaw, for cash balance and other hybrid plans. Although the PPA required 100% vesting in cash balance plans after three years of service, WRERA says this only applies if the participant has at least one hour of service after the effective date of the new rules. As a result of WRERA, the whipsaw rules are not applied in determining whether a participant is subject to mandatory cashout; it depends on the balance in the hypothetical cash account. [Deloitte's Washington Bulletin, *PPA Technical Corrections Affecting Defined Benefit Plans*, <http://benefitslink.com/articles/guests/washbull090112 .html> (Jan. 12, 2009) (benefitslink.com)]

At the end of 2007 the IRS proposed regulations implementing the PPA's changes to Code §§ 411(a)(13) and (b)(5), explaining how cash balance plans, as

defined benefit plans, must satisfy the minimum vesting and accrual requirements of § 411. [NPRM REG-104946-07, 2008-11 I.R.B. 596]

In mid-2008, The IRS proposed regulations allowing the same relief permitted by Rev. Rul. 2008-7, to clarify how defined benefit plans, especially hybrid
plans that use a "greater of" benefit formula, can satisfy the anti-backloading test.
In general, they can test each formula separately. This is useful for employers who
want to convert defined benefit to cash balance plans, but still provide pensions for older employees that are more generous than the required transitional
relief. [NPRM, *Accrual Rules for Defined Benefit Plans*; RIN 1545-BH50, 73
Fed. Reg. 34665 (June 18, 2008); see Buck Research FYI, *IRS Proposed Regulations Would Encourage Generosity in Cash Balance Conversion* (July 7, 2008)
(benefitslink.com)]

## [A]   2010 Final and Proposed Regulations

In late 2010, the IRS issued final and proposed regulations for hybrid retirement plans, a category that includes not only cash balance plans but Pension
Equity Plans (PEPs). In the 1990s, hybrid plans grew in popularity, but also
attracted a number of lawsuits, generally charging age discrimination, challenging the calculation of lump sums, or challenging wearaway within the plan. The
IRS issued proposed regulations implementing the Pension Protection Act in
December 2007. The 2010 regulations deal with age discrimination, vesting, conversion from defined benefit to cash balance form, and safe harbor interest crediting rates (final regulations) and alternative rates that constitute a "market rate of
return" (proposed regulations).

In general, a hybrid plan can be described as one that calculates accumulated benefits with a hybrid formula. The final regulations define a lump sum-
based benefit formula as any formula that expresses the accrued benefit as either
the current balance of the participant's hypothetical account, or the current value
of an accumulated percentage of the participant's final average compensation.
Each participant has a hypothetical account, which is credited with the employer's hypothetical contributions based on "compensation credits" (reflecting the
participant's salary) plus "interest credits" (hypothetical earnings from investing
the account). PEPs define the benefit as a percentage of final average pay, with
participants earning points each year to set the percentage. Compensation credits
are usually defined as a percentage of the employee's eligible pay, possibly
adjusted based on age and years of service. When the participant stops working
for the employer, compensation credits end. Interest credits usually continue until
the benefits are distributed.

The 2010 final regulations require the entire accrued benefit of hybrid plans
to vest in no more than three years of service. They cannot use the general five-
year cliff or three-to-seven-year graded vesting. The 2010 final regulations say
that three-year vesting is mandatory even if only part of the benefit is calculated

with a hybrid formula—but this rule applies only if the participant had at least one hour of service on or after January 1, 2008. The three-year requirement does not apply to the traditional defined benefit portion of a floor-offset arrangement combining a traditional defined benefit plan with a separate hybrid plan.

The 2010 final regulations include an ADEA safe harbor, as long as the accumulated benefit of any participant is not less than the accumulated benefit of any similarly situated younger participant. Factors in determining which employees are similarly situated include their period of service, compensation, job duties, date of hire, and work history. The accumulated benefit must be compared in the same form as the plan expresses the benefit (account balance or annuity payable at normal retirement age).

A hybrid plan that does not satisfy the safe harbor must satisfy the general Code § 411(b)(1)(H)(i) age discrimination rule. The final regulations say that the safe harbor can be used if the plan gave the participant a choice between a traditional defined benefit plan and the hybrid plan at the time of conversion; the safe harbor is not limited to plans that used a sum-of or greater-of formula at conversion.

The final regulations protect benefits against wearaway if a defined benefit plan is converted to a hybrid plan by an amendment adopted and effective on or after June 29, 2005. If the amendment eliminates or reduces future benefit accruals, and part or all of the benefit is determined based on a statutory hybrid formula, then the post-amendment benefit must be at least as great as the accrued benefit as of the conversion date plus the accrued benefit after the conversion, with no integration of the two. A plan is considered amended if it changes the conditions of employment that trigger the change to the hybrid plan (e.g., transfer to a different part of the company that maintains a different plan).

The PPA forbids crediting interest at a rate greater than a "market rate of return." The 2010 final regulations define a market rate as one that does not exceed one of these benchmarks:

- The rate of return on investment-grade long-term corporate bonds;

- The rate of certain Treasury bonds shorter than 30 years;

- The actual rate of return on plan assets (if benefits are indexed and the plan's assets are diversified);

- The rate of return on an annuity contract for an employee issued by a licensed insurance company.

It is permissible for the rate of benefit accrual to increase as participants earn more, as long as any year's accrual rate is not more than one-third higher than the previous year's rate. [Final regulations: 75 Fed. Reg. 64123 (Oct. 19, 2010); proposed regulations, 75 Fed. Reg. 64197 (Oct. 19, 2010). See Proskauer Client Alert, *IRS Issues Cash Balance Plan Guidance*, plansponsor.com (Nov. 19, 2010).]

To set "market rates" as required by the PPA, the proposed regulations call for an annual 5% interest cap if interest is credited at a fixed percentage. If interest is credited as either a fixed interest rate or a rate that comes from bond indexes, whichever is higher, the fixed rate must not exceed 4%. Several interest rate formulas are allowable for hybrid plans, including the actual rate of return on the plan's assets (if the assets are diversified); a fixed 5% rate. The proposals would also allow a hybrid plan to use an interest crediting rate after the participant reaches normal retirement age that is sufficient to provide the required actuarial increases—even if that would otherwise exceed the market rate. A hybrid plan can calculate annuity options based on the current account balance, using reasonable actuarial assumptions.. The proposed regulations also provide guidance on the interest crediting rates and annuity conversion rates to be used when a hybrid plan is terminated. [Kendall W. Daines, Mark L. Lofgren, David W. Powell, *Cash Balance Plan Regulations Address Many Knotty Issues*, Groom Law Group (Dec. 15, 2010) (law.com); Rebecca Moore, *IRS Issues Rules on Hybrid Retirement Plans*, plansponsor.com (Oct. 18, 2010)]

The Moving Ahead for Progress in the 21st Century (MAP-21) Act, Pub. L. No. 112-140, allows plan sponsors some relief from interest crediting rules that can make defined benefit and cash balance plans unduly expensive. (See § 5.01[A].) The IRS has not yet issued final rules, but has given some guidance on the timing for final regulations and how relief under MAP-21 may affect the interest credits for some cash balance plans. Notice 2012-61, 2012-42 I.R.B. 479 says that final regulations on market rates will not be effective before January 1, 2014. The notice says that plans that set interest credits on the basis of segment rates can smooth the rates; smoothing is permitted but not required. Plans that use MAP-21 smoothing must use the new rate as of either the first day of the first plan year in which MAP-21 rates are used for funding purposes, or the first day of the plan year that begins in 2012. Once a plan adopts smoothing, it must continue to use it; stopping will trigger the anti-cutback rules. When the final regulations are published, it is possible that they will not permit the use of MAP-21 segment rates—in which case, plans that use them will have to follow IRS' transition procedure to change their rates. [Mark L. Lofgren, *Cash Balance Plans IRS Further Delays Reasonable Interest Rate Rules and Provides Guidance for Plans with Rates Affected by Map-21*, Groom Law Group (Sept. 17, 2012) (benefitslink.com)]

# CHAPTER 8

# NONQUALIFIED PLANS

## § 8.01  INTRODUCTION

### [A]  Generally

One of the most important aspects of maintaining a qualified plan (and therefore obtaining a tax deduction for related costs) is satisfying the Internal Revenue Code's tests for nondiscrimination.

However, it is not illegal for an employer to set up a discriminatory plan, and in fact many types of nonqualified plans have evolved for companies that want to recruit, retain, or motivate senior management and/or persons who own significant amounts of stock in the corporation. Nonqualified plans are also used to provide post-retirement income higher than the levels that can be generated through a qualified plan. Since 2004, sponsors have faced a new set of tax challenges for nonqualified plans under the American Jobs Creation Act (AJCA), Pub. L. No. 108-357, which enacted Code § 409A, and under the Pension Protection Act of 2006 (PPA), Pub. L. No. 109-280. Unlike qualified plans, which are subject to detailed funding and operational requirements under ERISA, nonqualified plans need not be funded in advance. Payments to distribute benefits can be made as they come due, out of the employer's general assets instead of from a special trust. Insurance policies, and other investments that would not be permissible in an ERISA plan, can also be used to fund nonqualified plan benefits.

A deferred compensation plan is a plan or individual agreement to pay compensation to one or more employees in one or more later years for services rendered. Such plans can be taxable or tax-exempt. A nonqualified plan is exempt from most ERISA and IRS requirements, but at the cost of foregoing the tax deductions available to sponsors of qualified plans.

A 2012 article says the five vital things to know about nonqualified deferred compensation (NQDC) plans are:

- Their role in providing incentives to a company's best-performing executives by permitting them to save more when they have maxed out contributions to the other plans—or, an NQDC can operate as a bonus plan, with contributions made only if goals are met. NQDC funds can be accessed while the executive is still working, for example, to pay children's college tuition or buy a second home;

- Eligibility criteria must be set when the plan is designed; if the standards are too broad, the plan might become subject to ERISA. As a rule of thumb, the plan might cover 10%–20% of the employees, based on their title and compensation level, or by their duties;

- Even if the plan is not subject to ERISA, it must satisfy § 409A, and penalties will be imposed on the participants if the plan violates its rules;

- Participants have less security than participants in qualified plans—even a rabbi trust is still subject to the claims of the corporation's creditors;

- NQDCs are good for providing incentives to best-performing executives, permitting them to save more for retirement after they have made maximum contributions to their other plans.

[Pathfinder, *5 Things You Need to Know About Nonqualified Deferred Compensation Plans* (Feb. 29, 2012) (benefitslink.com)]

A late 2011 article points out that nonqualified deferred compensation is very favorable to executives if their share of the company's profits is very small; the executive can cope with the employer's credit risk; and it would be too expensive for the company to provide comparable benefits under a qualified plan. But if those conditions do not apply, the plan does not achieve the desired motivational effect. If the executive is a substantial owner, deferred income will create taxable profits and the corporation's credit risk may be so high that executives insist on a qualified plan. [Jim Van Iwaarden, VIA Retirement Plan Blog, *Deferred Comp Plans: When They're A Great Choice, And When They're Not* (Oct. 12, 2011) (benefitslink.com)]

According to The Newport Group's 2012 edition of "Executive Benefits: A Study of Current Trends," 83% of Fortune 1000 businesses offer NQDC arrangements to their key executives, a percentage that has stayed stable throughout the economic downturn. Three-quarters of respondents say they fund their NQDC plans to establish an asset to hedge NQDC benefit liability, generate income to offset plan expenses, have liquidity to pay benefits, and make the benefits more secure for plan participants. Well over half (61%) have a TPA for the plan, and 51% maintain defined benefit SERPs. Almost half (47%) say that their eligible employees choose to participate. Fixed-rate options are gaining in popularity, probably because NQDC plan participants are cautious. [Newport Group, *Executive Benefits: A Survey of Current Trends*; see Tara Cantore, *Majority of Firms Report Offering NQDC Plans*, plansponsor.com (Feb. 8, 2012); Warren S. Hersch, *Fortune 1000 Firms Lead the Charge in NQDC Plans*, BenefitsPro (Feb. 10, 2012) (benefitslink.com)] In an elective plan, the employees also contribute. A plan with employee deferrals can put aside more money than qualified plans, and can include pay over and above the amount that can be used in qualified plan calculations. (For 2013 the relevant limitations for qualified plans are $255,000 maximum contribution that can be taken into account, $17,500 maximum pre-tax contribution, and $51,000 maximum aggregate employer plus employee contribution.) When there is a deferred compensation plan for executives, the amount of compensation that is deferred and the earnings on those deferrals are not taxed to the executive until they are distributed. Nor does the corporation receive a tax deduction until the employee has the income.

The general practice is for the payor corporation to record the expense on its books when the compensation is earned, even if the tax deduction is not available until a much later year. The general rule of § 409A is that elective participant deferrals are irrevocable, and the election must be made before the beginning of the calendar year in which the services commence. The election must identify the amount to be deferred; the length of the deferral period; and the form of payment. However, for performance-based compensation for services performed over a period of 12 months or more, the initial deferral election can be made at any time up through six months before the end of the performance period. Payments to key employees of public companies triggered by separation from service (other than in case of death, disability, or similar event) must be delayed at least six months after separation. The Code § 83 economic benefit doctrine makes income taxable upon grant if the executive receives tangible, quantifiable value, and there is no substantial risk of forfeiture.

To escape taxation under theories of constructive receipt and economic benefit, benefits under a nonqualified plan must be funded and must be subject to the claims of the corporation's general creditors. If the company becomes insolvent or bankrupt, the executive's right to payment cannot be greater than the right of any other general unsecured creditor.

Corporations with nonqualified deferred compensation plans usually engage in informal funding, e.g., by setting money aside in trusts such as rabbi trusts to cover future payments under the plan. The trusts are assets of the corporation and can be reached by its creditors. Section 409A accelerates income tax and imposes penalties if assets are transferred outside the United States, or if benefit payments are triggered by the corporation's financial problems (i.e., if executives are insulated against the consequences of the company's financial difficulties).

Penalties are also imposed on key executives if the employer sets aside assets to pay nonqualified deferred compensation when the corporation is bankrupt, within six months of termination of an underfunded plan, or if the plan is "at risk" as defined by the PPA and is funded below the 80% level. In many instances, registration exemptions will be available, but absent an exemption, an employee's interest in an elective deferred compensation arrangement is a security that will have to be registered. "Blue sky" compliance (with state securities laws) may also be required. [David Wang and Melissa Rasman, *Elective Nonqualified Deferred Compensation Plans—A Primer*, Hay Group's Executive Edition Newsletter (Feb. 1, 2008) (benefitslink.com)]

In a qualified plan, a "bad boy" clause (one that removes entitlement to benefits) is allowed only for fraud or abuse of fiduciary duty. In a nonqualified plan, benefits can be forfeited by an executive who leaves the company.

Under a qualified plan, the employer gets a current deduction each year as it makes contributions to the plan. The employer's deduction for nonqualified plan expenses is not available until the year in which the participant receives money from the plan and includes it in income. The corporation's general creditors are entitled to make claims against reserves set aside to pay nonqualified plan benefits, but the qualified plan trust is protected against creditors' claims.

## [B]   Structures for Nonqualified Plans

Various structures and funding mechanisms have evolved for providing nonqualified plan benefits to executives, managers, and other favored corporate employees. Objectives include providing incentives for managers by providing generous deferred compensation, and protecting entitlement to these sums against the corporation's creditors.

The most popular structures for nonqualified plans include SERPs, QSERPs, top hat plans, rabbi trusts, and secular trusts, as discussed below. Other structures used for non-qualified plans include:

- Excess benefit plans: plans that provide benefits higher than those permitted by Code § 415. Unfunded excess benefit plans are exempt from ERISA Title I, but that renders them vulnerable to state regulation;

- Integrated plans provide benefits over and above 401(k) plan benefits, using the same investment options and subject to the same employer match rules. The deferral percentage is set by the plan participant. Transfers of both elective deferrals and employer matches are made first to the qualified plan, then to the nonqualified plan;

- Tandem plans combine with qualified plans to accrue more savings for retirement-but usually offer features and investment choices that are different than those offered under the regular qualified plan;

- Wrap plans collect funds throughout the year on behalf of top executives. Once a year, the maximum amount that can be transferred for those executives without violating the nondiscrimination rules is transferred to the qualified plan; the rest is placed in a non-qualified plan.

[See *New Options in Nonqualified Retirement Plans*, < http://institutional. vanguard.com>]

### [1]   SERP

A Supplemental Executive Retirement Plan (SERP), also known as an excess-benefit plan, can be used to defer amounts that exceed the qualified plan limits on behalf of executives. Hay Group says that the most popular formula aims to 60% of the executive's pre-retirement income, which would be impossible under most qualified plans. A performance-based SERP makes accrual of benefits dependent on achievement of one or more performance measures. The measures could be the ones used in the company's incentive programs (e.g., revenues, profitability, or earnings), or could be personalized (a sales target or profitability goal for a particular corporate unit) or depend on other goals or events (developing a product; successful bankruptcy reorganization).

A late 2010 decision holds that the widow of a SERP participant was not entitled to benefits because she did not fit the plan's definition of "spouse," and the definition in the plan prevailed over the language of the SPD. The SERP's provisions required a marriage of at least one year's duration before the participant's death or retirement for the spouse to qualify as a surviving spouse. In this case, the marriage occurred after the participant's retirement. The Northern District of Ohio said that while the SPD's language may have created misrepresentations, it did not alter the terms of the plan, and it was not arbitrary or capricious to say that the survivor did not qualify for the benefits. [*Parr v. Diebold Inc.*, No. 5:09 CV 1041 (N.D. Ohio 2010)]

Because a SERP is a top-hat plan, it is not protected against the claims of the employer's creditors, even if the employer includes an anti-alienation provision in the SERP agreement. Therefore, at least 25% of a bank executive's SERP was subject to garnishment by a creditor of the bank. The state's garnishment law was not preempted by ERISA, because it was a law of general application not related to employee benefit plans. The state Consumer Credit Protection Law protects 75% of a pension or retirement benefit from garnishment, so the judge reserved decision on the fate of 75% of the executive's SERP. [*Sposato v. First Mariner Bank,* No. 1:2012-cv-01569, 2013 WL 1308582 (D.Md. Mar. 28, 2013); see Rebecca Moore, *"Top Hat" Plan Assets Not Protected by ERISA,*planspon-sor.com (Apr. 19, 2013); Jane Meacham, *ERISA Does Not Protect Executive Benefits From Garnishment,*Smart HR (June 7, 2013) (benefitslink.com)]

In the Second Circuit view, early retirement benefits from a SERP are not severance payments that get "administrative expense" (i.e., high) priority in bankruptcy, because the benefits accrue over the entire course of employment—they are not a new benefit earned at termination, and only new benefits can be administrative expenses. [*In re Bethlehem Steel*, 479 F.3d 167 (2d Cir. 2007)]

### [2]  QSERP

A Qualified Supplemental Executive Retirement Plan (QSERP) is a qualified plan used to enhance retirement benefits for executives. The plan must satisfy nondiscrimination requirements and is subject to the I.R.C. § 415 limits. However, the employer's contributions can be integrated with Social Security, reducing the amount the employer has to contribute on behalf of lower-paid employees. To adopt a QSERP, the employer corporation can simply amend the plan documents to include an annual list of people or job titles entitled to additional benefits of $X/year. Usually, QSERP amounts are subtracted from the amounts that would otherwise be payable under nonqualified plans. Because the QSERP is a qualified plan, the employer gets a current deduction, and the employee is not taxed until benefits are actually paid (and the employee has some certainty that they will be paid because of prefunding). If the QSERP is a defined contribution plan, it is subject to the overall limitation on contributions to all defined contribution plans; if the employer is already making close to the maximum contribution under other qualified plans there is little leeway for the QSERP. [Pension Rights Center, *Q-SERPs: How Companies Manipulate the Law to Fund Executive Pay Packages with Workers' Pension Money*, <http://www. pensionrights.org/pubs/facts/Q-SERPS.html> (September 2008)]

For the executive, having a QSERP provides the advantage of securing the benefit (although PBGC limits will apply if the plan sponsor goes bankrupt). QSERPs are not subject to § 409A. Blogger John Lowell, pointed out advantages of QSERP. While the benefit remains in the plan, there has been no constructive receipt under § 83. Benefits payable in lump-sum form can be rolled over to an IRA, further deferring taxation. The executive can wait until just before the benefit commencement date to choose the time and form of benefit distribution. Shareholders benefit because the QSERP is income-neutral or income-positive, and it protects the company from cash flow demands of having to make large payments. [Michael S. Melbinger, *Another Blogger Sings the Praises of QSERPs*, Winston & Strawn LLP Executive Compensation Blog (Sept. 19, 2011) (benefitslink.com)]

### [3] Rabbi Trust

A rabbi trust (so-called because the first one was created by a synagogue for its clergyman) sets aside assets in an irrevocable trust to pay the benefits, although the corporation's creditors can reach the assets. The assets in the trust cannot revert to the employer until all of the obligations to pay deferred compensation have been satisfied. Executives are not taxed until they receive benefits from the trust, because of the risk that creditor claims will prevent benefit payments. A "springing" rabbi trust is set up with only minimal funding. However, if the control of the corporation changes (for instance, because of a merger or acquisition), then the trust provides for funding for payment of benefits. The rabbi trust will not be considered "funded" for ERISA purposes just because it has a spring provision.

A rabbi trust furnishes the greatest permissible degree of protection for participants in deferred compensation plans. Many such trusts are set up with a directed trustee, who follows directions from the sponsor or a committee, and has no discretion over the trust or the plan. A few plans give the trustee full discretion, or discretion for some services. Another option is to increase the trustee's discretion over benefit decisions after a change in control, to relieve participants' anxieties about whether new management will pay the benefits promised by the predecessor. Depending on circumstances, the trustee may have to issue a W-2, Form 1099-R or Form 1099-Misc when the rabbi trust makes distribution. [No by-line, *Special Report: Deferred Compensation: Change Management*, plansponsor.com (magazine article, June 2006)]

One of the effects of the AJCA (see § 8.02[D]) is to ban offshore rabbi trusts.

### [4]  Secular Trust

A secular trust is an irrevocable trust whose assets cannot be reached by the employer's creditors, including its bankruptcy creditors. It offers more protection to the executive's right to receive deferred compensation than a rabbi trust, but has less favorable tax consequences. The price of increased protection for the employee is that the employee has taxable income (taxed using the I.R.C. § 72 annuity rules) equal to the employer contributions to the trust on the employee's behalf. The employer can deduct its contributions to the trust, to the extent they are ordinary and necessary business expenses, in the tax year in which the contributions become taxable income for the employee.

Secular trusts gained in popularity because of economic conditions and the difficulties of complying with § 409A. In general, nonqualified benefits offered through a secular trust are immediately taxable to the employees, but the trust assets are protected from the company's creditors. Rev. Rul. 2007-48, 2007-30 I.R.B. 129, tended to promote the use of secular trusts simply because it was clear what the rules are.

This ruling states that a participant in a secular trust does not have gross income on account of an interest in the trust until accrued benefits vest. The gross income for a given year is the fair market value of the vested part of the account as of the last day of the trust's tax year (whether or not this amount is distributed), plus the amount distributed to the participant during the participant's tax year, minus the participant's investment in the contract (the FMV of the vested portion of the account at the end of the trust's previous tax year), because the participant has already been taxed on the investment in the contract.

The secular trust must maintain separate accounts for each participant (although there can be multiple accounts in one trust). The sponsor corporation can deduct its contributions in the corporate tax year in which the recipients include the funds in the gross income. The income of a secular trust is taxed to the trust itself, not to the sponsor, and the trust can deduct trust income that vests in the participants during the tax year even if the income is not actually paid. [Michael Melbinger, Winston & Strawn LLP, *Protecting Non-Qualified Deferred Compensation—The Secular Trust* (June 9, 2009) (benefitslink.com)]

### [5]  Top Hat Plan

A top hat plan is an unfunded deferred compensation plan limited to managers and/or HCEs. Top hat plans that are pension plans must file a brief notice each year with the Department of Labor, although less disclosure is required than for a qualified plan. An unfunded top hat pension plan is not subject to the ERISA participation, vesting, funding, or fiduciary responsibility rules. The plan must have a claims procedure. Even the modest role that ERISA plays in regulating top hat plans is probably enough to preempt state law, so suits cannot be brought in state court involving claims against top hat plans.

In general, top hat plans are subject to ERISA Part I reporting and disclosure obligations, including annual Form 5500 filing. However, top hat plan sponsors can obtain exemption from annual reporting by filing a statement with the DOL. If the sponsor did not file a timely request for a filing exemption, it can use the DOL Delinquent Filer Voluntary Compliance Program (DFVC) to submit the statement instead of filing the past-due annual reports. The statement goes to DOL, EBSA, Apprenticeship and Training Plan Exemption, 200 Constitution Avenue NW, N-1513 Washington, DC, 20210. A single combined statement can be filed if the sponsor has more than one top hat plan seeking DFVC participation at the same time. There is a $750 penalty for each DVFC submission (for any number of plans filed at once, not per plan) and the penalty is a personal obligation of the plan administrator—plan assets may not be used to pay the penalty. [Prudential Pension Analyst, *DOL Updates Delinquent Filer Voluntary Compliance (DFVC) Program*, <http://www.retire.prudential.com/media/managed/EBSA_Updates_DFVC_Program-Final.pdf> (March 2013)]

In mid-2008, the Second Circuit ruled that it did not violate ERISA or the ADEA for a company (that had reserved the right to terminate) to terminate its top hat plan, even if the plaintiff relied on the representations made in his early retirement package. The plan had become financially untenable, so it was not arbitrary or capricious for the board of directors to terminate it.

The Second Circuit pointed out that many ERISA provisions, such as the fiduciary duty provisions, do not apply to top hat plans. However, the ERISA administration and enforcement provisions do apply to top hat plans, so state law claims such as breach of contract, bad faith, and negligent misrepresentation were preempted. [*Paneccasio v. Unisource Worldwide*, 532 F.3d 101 (2d Cir. 2008)]

The Seventh Circuit ruled in 2011 that the actions of plan administrators had to be reviewed deferentially, because the plan terms gave them discretion. The court held that it was not arbitrary and capricious to describe a discretionary stock-linked payment as a bonus that is not included in the benefit formula. The Seventh Circuit reviewed the decision with deference, even though top hat plan administrators are not ERISA fiduciaries—and even though in 2001, the Third Circuit refused to give deference to interpretations by top hat plan administrators. [*Comrie v. IPSCO, Inc.*, 636 F.3d 839 (7th Cir. 2011); see Mercer Select US, *7th Circuit Says Courts Owe Deference to Top-Hat Plan Administrator's Interpretation* (Mar. 3, 2011) (benefitslink.com)]

A top hat plan, as defined by 29 U.S.C. § 1051(2), is an unfunded plan for a select group of managers or highly compensated employees. That sounds simple enough, but a mid-2006 case from the Third Circuit tackled the question of what "unfunded" means when participants in a nonqualified plan moved in their employer's bankruptcy case to get secured priority status for their benefit claims. All factors must be considered, including tax and non-ERISA law. The DOL has issued an opinion letter if maintaining that a rabbi trust in conjunction with a plan does not make the plan funded. The Third Circuit court said that the plan in question was unfunded because the employer did not set funds aside to pay benefits—

payment could come only from general corporate assets that are subject to creditor's claims. The court concluded that the plan was an unfunded top hat plan and was not entitled to protection as an ERISA plan: the participants were out of luck once the employer filed for bankruptcy protection. [*In re IT Group, Inc.*, 448 F.3d 661 (3d Cir. 2006)]

ERISA does not define "select group of management or highly compensated employees." A recent Eastern District of Kentucky case identified the plan as top hat, because less than 1% of the total workforce was eligible and most of them were high-ranking managers. The district court rejected the argument that the plan also included a few participants who were not top managers, ruling that a top hat plan merely has to be primarily for such employees. [*Cramer v. Appalachian Reg'l Healthcare, Inc.*, No. 5:11-49-KKC, 2012 U.S. Dist. LEXIS 154624 (E.D. Ky, Oct. 29, 2012); see Angela Bohmann, *Do I Have A Top Hat Plan?*, Leonard, Street and Deinard Executive Compensation Blog (Nov. 21, 2012) (benefitslink.com)]

The Sixth Circuit reversed the district court's decision that a nonqualified plan was an ERISA plan but not a top-hat plan. Apparently, the plan was intended to be an unfunded top-hat plan; the author of the article said that an ERISA plan that was not a top-hat plan would create a "tax debacle." The Sixth Circuit ruled that the district court should have remanded the matter to the plan administrator to expand the administrative record. [*Daft v. Advest*, 658 F.3d 583 (6th Cir. 2011) see Ann Caresani, *The Top-Hat Plan Test for Your ERISA Executive Deferred Compensation Plan – Daft v. Advest, Inc.*, Porter Wright (Jan. 13, 2012) (benefitslink.com)]

In a class action about the discount rates used by a top hat plan and a pension plan to convert straight life annuities to lump sums, the Seventh Circuit upheld the lower court's grant of summary judgment for the plan. The top hat plan used a 7.5% discount rate (the pension plan used a rate of approximately 5.4%). As a non-qualified plan, the top hat plan was not subject to the PPA cap on discount rates. The plan terms permitted a 7.5% discount rate to be used by any non-qualified plan, and top hat plans are by definition non-qualified. [*Dennison v. MONY Life Ret. Income Sec. Plan*, No. 710 F.3d 741 (7th Cir., 2013); see Brian Stolzenbach, Sam Schwartz-Fenwick and Chris Busey, *Seventh Circuit Reads Plan Language To Discount Plaintiffs' Rate Argument*, Seyfarth Shaw ERISA & Employee Benefits Litigation Blog (Mar. 20, 2013) (benefitslink.com)]

The Eastern District of Louisiana held in 2012 that a deferred compensation arrangement to pay an executive $9,000 a month for ten years after retirement (or to his survivor) was not an ERISA plan. The single paragraph in the contract describing the arrangement did not create an ERISA plan, much less explain how the plan was to be administered. Therefore, when the executive's widow sued the company when the payments were stopped after seven years, the company could not call the plan an ERISA top hat plan subject to termination at any time. [*Mothe v. Mothe Life Ins.*, No. 2:10-cv-02008-JTM-ALC (E.D. La. Apr. 30, 2012); see

Rebecca Moore, *Employer Cannot Use ERISA to Stop Deferred Compensation Benefits*, plansponsor.com (May 2, 2012)]

Participants in a top hat plan could not recover under ERISA § 502 from the company that bought all of the assets of the bankrupt company that formerly maintained the plan. The buyer did not assume any of the sponsor's liabilities under the plan. At that point the seller was a shell company with no assets, so it was unable to pay benefits. The Seventh Circuit rejected the plaintiffs' arguments that the buyer was a de facto plan administrator, holding that the buyer did not connive with the seller to cheat plan participants, and that the buyer was not just a continuation of the seller. Therefore, the buyer did not have to acquire the liabilities of the unfunded top-hat plan, and the buyer did not violate ERISA § 510 either—it did not interfere with the attainment of ERISA benefits. In the Seventh Circuit view, § 510 refers to employment actions, and many of the plan beneficiaries were former employees or non-employees of the seller. [*Feinberg v. RM Acquisition, LLC*, 629 F.3d 671 (7th Cir. Jan. 6, 2011)]

A commentator suggests that one way to make sure that nonqualified plan benefits are paid to the executives is to put the money in an irrevocable rabbi trust, separate from the corporation's general assets. Rabbi trust assets are subject to the claims of the corporation's general creditors if the company becomes insolvent, but are protected in other situations—including the case of a new or successor employer that does not want to pay the benefits. [Michael S. Melbinger, *How Can SERP and Non-Qualified Plan Participants Protect Themselves Against the Loss of Benefits?*, Winston & Strawn LLP Executive Compensation Blog (Mar. 20, 2011) (benefitslink.com)]

## § 8.02  TAXATION OF NONQUALIFIED PLANS

### [A]  General Considerations

Nonqualified plans can create some subtle tax problems for plan participants. The mere fact that the employer promises to pay benefits in the future doesn't create income for the plan participants, until plan benefits are either actually or constructively received. Constructive receipt is a tax concept roughly equivalent to deliberately turning down money that the taxpayer is entitled to.

Employees are taxed on benefits from nonqualified plans as they are distributed. To the extent that the employee already had to pay tax on amounts not yet distributed, employees are entitled to compute an exclusion ratio (percentage of a distribution that has already been taxed and will not be taxed again).

Nonqualified plan participants are taxed in the year in which rights to property become transferable, or the substantial risk of forfeiture ends, whichever comes first. Sometimes, property rights depend, directly or indirectly, on the plan participant continuing to perform services for the employer. If there is a covenant not to compete, however, property rights might depend on not performing services! Under the IRS Regulations, the facts of each case must be examined to determine whether there is a substantial risk of forfeiture because of a requirement of continued employment or noncompetition.

As for the trust income, there are complex factors (centering around the extent of the employer's contributions and degree of control) that determine ownership of the trust, and therefore whether the employer, the employee, or the trust itself should be taxed on income earned by a secular trust arrangement.

The 2013 FICA base is $113,700. When nonqualified options and Stock Appreciation Rights are exercised, or when restricted stock and restricted stock units vest, FICA taxes are owed. For compensation deferred in a nonqualified deferred compensation plan, FICA is owed at the time of deferral even though income tax is only owed when money is withdrawn from the account. If the employee's compensation for the year exceeds the FICA base, non-qualified stock options can be exercised without FICA tax on the income being recognized at exercise (because maximum FICA tax has already been paid). Medicare tax is due on all compensation, without limit. In 2013, there is also a 2.35% Medicare surtax on high-income taxpayers, so a 2013 exercise may also be subject to this additional tax. In 2013, a high-income taxpayer for this purpose is one with income over $200,000 on a single return, or $250,000 on a joint return. [MyStockOptions Blog, *Social Security Yearly Income Cap Will Rise In 2013: Impact On Stock Comp And NQDC* (Oct. 17, 2012) (benefitslink.com)]

Effective January 1, 2005, transfers of interests in nonqualified deferred compensation and nonstatutory stock options from employee spouse to non-employee spouse incident to a divorce are not "wages" for FICA/FUTA purposes. FICA and FUTA come into play, however, when the options are exercised or the deferred compensation is paid or made available. Nonstatutory options are subject to FICA and FUTA when exercised by the spouse who received them in the divorce. The employee spouse is liable for FICA taxes on the exercise, because the payments relate to the employee spouse's employment. The income the non-employee spouse realizes on exercise of options constitutes wages subject to withholding; the withheld taxes must be deducted from payments to the non-employee spouse. Because the non-employee spouse is by definition not an employee, W-2 reporting is not required. Instead, the employer's obligation is to issue a Form 1099-MISC to the non-employee spouse, and to report the wage withholding on Form 945. [Rev. Rul. 2004-60, 2004-24 I.R.B. 1051. (See § 22.02 and § 22.08 for further discussion of stock options.)]

Under Code § 415, "compensation" includes any nonqualified deferred compensation under § 409A that is includible in the employee's income. [Final Regulations, 72 Fed. Reg. 16878 (Apr. 5, 2007)]

### [B] I.R.C. § 83 Issues

Tax planning for nonqualified plan participants also requires a look at I.R.C. § 83, which sometimes requires employees to include in income amounts that have not been distributed from the nonqualified plan. Section 83 provides that whenever property is transferred to anyone except the employer for the provision of services, the employee's taxable income includes the fair market value of the transferred property, minus any amount paid for the property.

Section 83 doesn't apply to transfers to qualified plan trusts, or to a deferred compensation arrangement that gives the employee a mere contractual right to receive compensation in the future. Many stock option transactions are also exempt from this section. However, § 83 does apply to assets set aside in trusts, escrows, or similar arrangements that are not subject to the claims of the corporation's general creditors.

Where § 83 applies, the employee's tax is based on the value of the employee's income on the plan trust at the time of taxation, and not on the fair market value of the employer's contributions from the trust.

The IRS proposed § 83 regulations in mid-2012, dealing with property transferred in connection with the performance of services, subject to a substantial risk of forfeiture—for example, restricted stock awards. The regulations say that most transfer restrictions (for example, "clawback" provisions and potential liability under Rule 10b-5) do not constitute a substantial risk of forfeiture. The exception is a transfer restriction based on Exchange Act § 16(b) (the ban on short-swing profits), which does create a substantial risk of forfeiture. [77 Fed. Reg. 31783 (May 30, 2012)]

### [C]  Employer's Tax Deduction (Pre-AJCA)

Before the AJCA was enacted, the employer's deduction, as provided by the texts of Code sections 404(a)(5) and 404(d)(2) was not available if the plan provided deferred compensation for shareholders who were not employees of, or independent contractors to, the employer corporation. The employer's deduction for paying deferred compensation occurred in the year the employee received the compensation, not the year of the contribution. Each employee covered by funded, nonqualified deferred compensation arrangements had to have a separate account. Distributions from nonqualified plans were FICA and FUTA wages, but I.R.C. § 3121(v)(2) provided that amounts deferred under a nonqualified deferred compensation plan were taken into account only once—at the later of the time services were rendered, or when there ceased to be a substantial risk of forfeiture of the amounts.

### [D]  AJCA and § 409A

The American Jobs Creation Act of 2004 (AJCA), Pub. L. No. 108–357, adds new I.R.C. § 409A to the Internal Revenue Code. It is effective for amounts deferred after 2004. There is no requirement of common-law employment, so deferred payments to independent contractors and outside directors are also subject to these rules. The I.R.C. § 409A rules supplement those already in place governing economic benefit and constructive receipt of deferred compensation. In effect, amounts deferred under a nonqualified plan are included in the recipient's gross income unless they were previously included in his or her income, or unless they are subject to a substantial risk of forfeiture. Compensation is taxed when I.R.C. § 409A is triggered, or the previous rules apply—whichever comes first.

Compliance with I.R.C. § 409A is critical because the AJCA carries a big stick: unless its requirements are satisfied, all compensation deferred under the nonqualified plan for all taxable years is included in the participant's gross income for the current year, plus interest and a penalty of 20% of the compensation included in gross income. Penalties are also imposed if plan assets are placed into a trust outside of the United States, whether or not the assets are available to satisfy the claims of creditors. Another creditor protection measure applies the penalties if plan assets are placed in a domestic trust triggered by the employer's financial condition.

A plan is considered a nonqualified deferred compensation plan if it is not a qualified pension or welfare benefit (e.g., vacation, sick leave, disability pay, death benefit plan, HSA, HRA, medical reimbursement plan). Whether an option plan is subject to I.R.C. § 409A depends on the terms of the arrangement. If the exercise price for the option is at least as high as the underlying stock's fair market value on the date of the grant, then the option is not considered deferred compensation unless it includes some deferral feature over and above the ability to exercise the option in the future. There is a statutory exemption for ISOs and employee stock purchase plans. By and large, Stock Appreciation Rights (SARs) will be subject to I.R.C. § 409A, although a SAR, that has a fixed payment date, or a non-discounted publicly traded SAR, will be exempt.

I.R.C. § 409A requires elections to defer compensation to be made on or before the end of the taxable year before the year in which the compensation will be earned. For performance-based compensation (e.g., sales commissions) based on services rendered over a period of 12 months or more, the election can be made within the six months before the end of the service period.

Distributions to key employees cannot be made earlier than six months after separation from service, or upon the key employee's death. A key employee is one covered by I.R.C. § 416(I)(l)(c). The AJCA forbids acceleration of distributions. Distributions from a deferred compensation plan can be made only when the person earning the money is separated from service, dies, when a specified time is reached (or when a specified schedule begins), when the corporation changes control, the participant becomes disabled (unable to engage in substantial gainful activity as a result of a condition expected to result in death or last for at least 12 months; or receives income replacement benefits for at least three months under an Accident & Health plan on account of total disability), or there is an unforeseeable emergency (e.g., severe financial hardship to a participant because of illness or accident to the participant or close family member; casualty loss to the participant's property; or results of other events beyond the participant's control; otherwise, elective withdrawals are forbidden, even with a penalty). Even if an unforeseeable emergency has occurred, the amount of the distribution must not exceed the amount needed to cope with the emergency and pay the taxes on the premature distribution. Nor can distributions be made if the hardship could be handled through insurance reimbursement or liquidation of the participant's other assets.

Changes in the form of distribution that have the effect of accelerating payment of deferred compensation are forbidden to the same extent as acceleration of the distribution. However, I.R.C. § 409A is not violated merely because a plan provides a choice between cash and taxable property, if the same amount of income is included in income in the same year irrespective of the participant's election. Therefore, the plan can provide for a choice of a lump sum or a fully taxable annuity contract without falling afoul of I.R.C. § 409A.

The initial election to defer must specify the form of any payment that is supposed to be received at a specified time or on a specified schedule. Exceptions are made to this general rule for payments under a QDRO, payments made to comply with federal conflict of interest requirements, amounts needed to pay FICA taxes, and amounts withheld when there has been an I.R.C. § 457(f) vesting event. A lump sum payment of up to $10,000 is also permitted to a terminated employee.

To prevent an error in one participant's plan from affecting the other participants, the general rule is that all account balance plans for a given employee are considered a single plan, and all non-account-balance plans for him or her are considered a single plan, and any other plans are aggregated into another single plan. The plan aggregation rules are not applied in determining if a payment exceeds $10,000.

If an election is made to defer distribution past its original date, the election must be made 12 months before the scheduled distribution date, and must defer payment for an additional five years.

For an account balance plan, the amount that can be grandfathered is the earned and vested account balance as of December 31, 2004, plus subsequent earnings (as long as the right to the earnings was vested on that date). For a non-account-balance plan, the value of the grandfathered benefit is the present value of the earned and vested benefit that would have been paid at the earliest possible date if the plan participant had voluntarily separated from service on December 31, 2004. Therefore, early retirement subsidies are not grandfathered if they were not payable as of that date, but post-2004 benefits that accrued solely by passage of time are included when the present value of the grandfathered benefit is determined. The employer can use the plan's actuarial assumptions for valuation, as long as the assumptions are reasonable.

A payment (e.g., a bonus) is not subject to I.R.C. § 409A as long as the employer makes the payment no later than the next taxable year after the amount ceases to be subject to a substantial risk of forfeiture. The payment must be made within two and a half months after the end of the employer's tax year or the end of the employee's tax year in which the condition lapses—whichever is later.

I.R.C. § 409A does not apply to payments when all the taxpayers involved use the accrual method. Nor does it apply to payments made to someone who is actively engaged in providing non-employee or non-director services to two or more unrelated recipients. An entity is deemed related if the service provider owns at least a 20% interest in it. Property (such as restricted stock) that is subject to I.R.C. § 83 is not subject to I.R.C. § 409A, but a service provider's enforceable right to receive property in a later year (e.g., under a restricted stock unit plan) can be subject to I.R.C. § 409A.

It does not constitute prohibited acceleration for a company to waive or accelerate the satisfaction of a condition that is a substantial risk of forfeiture, as long as the other conditions of I.R.C. § 409A are satisfied. For example, if a plan will pay a lump sum upon separation from service after at least 10 years, changing the requirement to five years will not violate I.R.C. § 409A. Plans can be amended to allow cashout of up to $10,000. Plans can also be amended so that the entire interest under a future deferral will be distributed in a lump sum whenever the participant's interest in the plan falls below the *de minimis* amount specified by a plan when a distribution event occurs. It is also permissible to accelerate distributions to someone other than the participant to satisfy a QDRO; to the participant to pay FICA and income taxes under § 3121(v); or to a participant to the extent required to pay income taxes generated by a § 457(f) plan's vesting event.

Deferred compensation payments can be accelerated in connection with a change in control (change in ownership or effective control of the company); the change-in-control event must be objectively determinable.

The general rule is that employers cannot use the termination of a nonqualified plan as a means of accelerating distributions. A valuation method that would be acceptable for valuing property in a decedent's estate will be accepted as an I.R.C. § 409A valuation method. The exercise price or base value of non-grandfathered stock options or discounted SARs can be reformed, by means of an amendment adopted by December 31, 2005, to reset the price or value to the fair market value of the stock on the original grant date. (See Notice 2005-1, 2005-2 I.R.B. 274 for detailed discussion of the pre-PPA rules.) [These rules are discussed in, e.g., Haynes & Boone § 409A News Alert, *§ 409A Stock Valuation Guidance for Privately-Held Companies* (Jan. 23, 2006) (benefitslink.com)]

Dr. Senat Sutardja, founder of a business, was granted up to two million options in the company's stock on December 10, 2003—long before § 409A took effect. On the grant date, the stock price was $36.19 a share. The grant was finalized as 1.5 million options, exercise price $36.50 (the stock price on December 16, 2003, when the grant was finalized). The grant was ratified on January 16, 2004, when the stock price was $43.64. Section 409A took effect on January 1, 2005. Sutardja exercised some options in January 2006. Then he signed an agreement to modify the stock option agreement. He paid $5.35 million to the company; HR law expert Michael S. Melbinger said that this payment was an attempt to correct an understated exercise price, undertaken at a time when there were no § 409A regulations for guidance. In November 2010, the IRS ruled that the option was exercised for less than fair market value (FMV), and imposed the 20% surtax plus interest on the underpayment. The regulations, when they were finally issued, made discounted stock options subject to § 409A, and required fixed dates for the exercise of options and for payment of the stock, with no discretionary provisions for time or form of payment. Sutardja argued that the exercise of the options was not deferred compensation as defined by Code § 3121(v) and, therefore, could not be deferred compensation for § 409A purposes. Sutardja also argued that he did not have a legally binding right to the compensation until he exercised the option.

In a February 2013 decision, the Court of Federal Claims followed a 2005 IRS Notice that treats discounted stock options as deferred compensation, despite the language found in § 3121(v). The court ruled that the compensation was earned at the grant of the option and Sutardja was legally entitled to the compensation as soon as there was no longer a substantial risk of forfeiture and the options had vested.

Sutardja argued that the short-term exemption of § 409A applied because the options were exercised within two and a half months of the end of the year in which the options vested. The court pointed to the plan provision (shared with many stock option plans) giving Sutardja a 10-year period in which the options could be exercised. Sutardja cited a provision in the grant giving him 30 days after being terminated to exercise the option. He said that created a substantial risk of forfeiture until he actually exercised the options at a time when he had not been terminated. This argument was also rejected: the Court of Federal Claims treated the 30-day period as a grace period rather than a condition creating a substantial risk of forfeiture. The case was remanded to decide the fact question of whether the options were granted at a discount. [*Sutardja v. United States*, No. 11-724T 227-13, 2013 U.S. Claims LEXIS 126, 2013-1 U.S. Tax Cas. (CCH) P50, 214 (Fed. Claims Feb. 27, 2013); see Jeffrey Cairns, Benefits Notes, Section 409A Tax Assessed on Discounted Stock Options—Taxpayer Sues for Refund in Federal Court of Claims (Mar. 7, 2013); Michael S. Melbinger, *If You Thought the IRS Would Not Punish 409A Foot Faults, Think Again*, Winston & Strawn LLP (Mar. 26, 2013) (benefitslink.com); David W. Eckhart, *Sutardja v. United States: When Options Are No Longer Optional*, Whyte Hirschboeck Dudek S.C. Special Report (March 2013)]

Under § 409A, disability can trigger deferred compensation; many plans provide for 100% vesting on disability. Even if the plan does not make disability a payment trigger, the onset of disability can affect vesting and the timing of payments made for separation from service. If disability leads to full vesting but does not affect the actual payment, then the plan can use any definition it wants and need not satisfy standards under § 409A. But sometimes accelerating vesting can make a plan subject to § 409A. If there is full vesting on disability but payments are not accelerated, and an employee becomes disabled during the first year of a three-year service vesting period, the payment will not be made during the short-term deferral period. Therefore, for that employee, the restricted stock unit is subject to § 409A, whereas if payment had occurred at the point of disability vesting, then the arrangement could be exempt from § 409A under the short-term deferral rule. [Randy L. Gegelman, The Law Firm of Faegre & Benson LLP, *Practical*

*409A: The Impact of Disability on Non-Qualified Deferred Compensation Under Code § 409A* (Mar. 23, 2009) (benefitslink.com)]

## [E] The PPA, 2005 Proposals, and 2007 Final Rules

In 2005, the IRS issued a lengthy and detailed set of proposed regulations [70 Fed. Reg. 58930 (Oct. 4, 2005)] dealing with many aspects of nonqualified plans: valuation; severance pay plans; initial elections to defer compensation; performance-based compensation; commissions; and rules for distributing deferred compensation, including relief for certain delays in distribution.

The basic rule is that a nonqualified stock option is not subject to § 409A if it is granted for at least the FMV of the stock on the date of the grant; it is taxable under § 83; and the option does not have the effect of deferring compensation. Generally speaking, stock appreciation rights (SARs) are treated like stock options.

Severance pay plans are exempt from § 409A if they are collectively bargained; if they are broad-based (i.e., not limited to key employees); or if payments are made within two years after the year of termination of employment. There is a special exception for severance payments that would not otherwise be exempt, but are made within 2½ months of the end of the year of termination of an employee who was involuntarily terminated. An initial election to defer severance resulting from involuntary separation from service can be made at any time before the employee has a legally binding right to the payment, as long as the severance pay is the subject of bona fide arm's-length negotiations. For severance payments under a window program, the initial election to defer the payment can be made until participation in the program becomes irrevocable.

Distributions made to a key employee of a public corporation cannot be made because of separation from service until at least six months have elapsed since the separation.

The plan must have a schedule for making the distribution (e.g., three months after the participant becomes disabled). Employees must make their initial election to defer compensation under a nonqualified plan by the end of the year preceding the year in which the compensation subject to deferral is earned.

The Pension Protection Act of 2006 had a seismic impact on many aspects of the pension and tax world—and nonqualified plans did not escape this phenomenon. Section 116 of the Pension Protection Act (PPA; Pub. L. No. 109–280) amends § 409A to add new categories of compensation that are taxable to the recipient of deferred compensation. The provisions of § 116 apply to transactions after the PPA's enactment date (August 17, 2006).

When a defined benefit plan is "at risk," there will be a "restricted period" during which transfers of funds to a trust or other arrangement in order to pay nonqualified deferred compensation to a "covered employee" will result in the employee being taxed on the amounts transferred, and also on the value of plan assets that are restricted to providing nonqualified deferred compensation. Not only are the assets in question taxable to the employee, the employee will have to pay a 20% excise tax. In some instances, the employee will also have to pay interest on underpayments of tax resulting from this inclusion in income. Furthermore, if the transferred or restricted assets increase in value or accrue earnings, those additional amounts are simply treated as more property transfers taxable to the employee. For this purpose, it is irrelevant whether the assets used for deferred compensation are subject to the claims of the sponsor's general creditors—so rabbi trusts do not protect the employee against taxation.

The definition of covered employees comes from § 162(m)(3) and includes the CEO and the four highest paid executive officers other than the CEO plus officers, directors and 10% stockholders, because the definition incorporates the Securities Exchange Act § 16(a) definition as well. The restricted period means any time when the sponsor company is bankrupt, when its defined benefit plan has at-risk status (see § 4.01[A]) and a 12-month period measured as the six months before and the six months after an involuntary or distress termination of any defined benefit plan maintained by the sponsor. If the payor corporation is publicly traded, it may be subject to SEC rules about management compensation. If the company received federal "bail-out" funds, it may also be subject to limitations on executive compensation, including incentive and deferred compensation. See § 1.01[B].

A plan is considered at risk if its funding status falls below 70% (considering various factors set out in the PPA) and below 80% (when these factors are not considered).

If the employer provides a gross-up (i.e., indemnifies the employee for the extra tax burden), payments of this type will be treated as taxable income to the employee, plus a 20% penalty. The employer will not be permitted to deduct the gross-up payment on its own income tax return. [This issue is discussed, e.g., in Gardner Carton & Douglas Client Memorandum, *Pension Protection Act Restricts Funding of Certain Nonqualified Deferred Compensation Arrangements*, <http://www.gcd.com/PPARestrictsFunding.pdf> (September 2006)]

In April 2007, reflecting public comments as well as the PPA, the IRS published final regulations, defining the types of plans (e.g., short-term deferral of compensation; Stock Appreciation Rights; some health reimbursement arrangements) that are exempt under § 409A. Qualified plans, welfare benefit plans (e.g., disability plans, sick and vacation leave plans) are exempt from § 409A coverage, as are ISOs and other statutory stock options and ESOPs.

The documents for a § 409A plan must reflect the limitations on the amount that can be deferred under or distributed from a nonqualified plan. The plan must be in writing and must disclose the payment schedule, trigger events for payments, amount to be paid, and conditions imposed on making elections under the plan. Most of the time, participants will have to make elections about how much to defer and when and how the deferred compensation will be paid out before the taxable year in which the participant will do the work for which compensation is deferred.

Some participants will find this requirement onerous, because they find it hard to estimate their future earnings, investment and other income, and future needs.

However, under the "bunching" rules, all plans of the same type covering one employee are treated as a single plan (e.g., all of his or her account balance plans or expense reimbursement plans are treated as one plan). Under the proposed regulations, the IRS divided nonqualified plans into four categories; the final regulations have far more categories (account balance plans; non-account balance plans; separation pay arrangements; elective account balance plans; non-account balance plans; separation pay plans; split-dollar insurance arrangements; expense reimbursement or similar plans; stock rights plans; foreign plans; and miscellaneous nonqualified plans not included in any other category.

Nonqualified plans sponsored by public companies must explicitly provide that key employees wait at least six months after separation from service to receive benefits. Short-term deferrals are not covered by § 409A: amounts that are distributed as soon as they vest, or no later than 2½ months after the end of the year to which they refer. Under the final regulations, amounts are exempt from § 409A treatment as separation pay as long as they are completed by the end of the second calendar year after the year of separation, and they do not exceed twice the § 401(a)(17) limit. For larger amounts, only the portion that exceeds this amount is subject to § 409A. Sometimes when an employee leaves for "good reason" (as defined by the final regulations as a material negative change in the employment relationship), separation pay can be treated as involuntary separation pay. Payments can also be accelerated without tax penalty to comply with a QDRO or pay FICA taxes.

Separation from service is deemed to occur either when it is reasonably anticipated that the ex-employee or independent contractor will not work for the employer any more, or will permanently reduce services to a level of 20% or less of the service provided in the previous three years. Separation is presumed to occur if services actually drop below the 20% level—and is presumed not to occur if services remain at the 50% or greater level. To facilitate phased retirement (see § 1.06), a plan can define separation from service as a reduction in services in the range of 20%–50% of previous effort.

Section 409A also applies to substitution of compensation for § 409A deferred compensation—for example, when a say on pay vote leads to some compensation being returned to the employer. [Gary M. Ford, Bloomberg, *Be Ever Vigilant Regarding 409A and Include 409A Interpretive Provisions!*, Benefits Practice Blog (Feb. 3, 2012) (benefitslink.com)]

In general, when a nonqualified plan is terminated and benefits are distributed, there is deemed to have been an acceleration of payments, which results in taxation under § 409A. However, there is an exception if all plans of the same type are terminated, distributions occur over a period of 12 to 24 months—and the sponsor refrains from creating new plans of the same type for a period of three years.

The final regulations expand the kinds of stock that can be exempt from § 409A when used to fund stock options and stock appreciation rights plans; the valuation rules in the final regulations are quite similar to those in the proposed rules. They give participants in nonqualified plans even more choices of how they can receive their payments, including term-certain annuities, "pop-up" annuities (where the benefit increases when the plan participant dies and the benefit continues to be paid to a surviving spouse), and annuities with COLAs or cash refund features.

The final regulations explain how to treat gross-ups under § 409A, and create a safe harbor for treating certain voluntary terminations as involuntary for separation pay purposes. However, the IRS has left some questions unresolved, such as how to calculate amounts of deferred compensation to be included in income; withholding rules if there is taxable income; how to apply § 409A to partner compensation; and which leave programs rate as bona fide plans of sick leave or vacation leave. [T.D. 9321, RIN 1545-BE 79, 73 Fed. Reg. 19234 (Apr. 10, 2007) See also Notice 2007-34, 2007-17 I.R.B. 996 for a discussion of the § 409A consequences of split-dollar insurance plans, and corrections in FR Doc E7-14624, 72 Fed. Reg. 41620 (July 31, 2007).]

Two main ways of structuring separation pay to avoid falling under § 409A are the short-term deferral exception and the separation pay safe harbor.

Employees who are required to release their claims against the employer in order to receive severance should be given releases at or shortly after the termination date, so they will have time to consider the releases and still receive payments within two and a half months if they agree to sign the release. [Randy L. Gegelman and Kathlyn E. Noecker, *Practical 409A: Separation Pay Options Under Code Section 409A* (Mar. 23, 2009) (benefitslink.com)]

Generally, an agreement to provide severance benefits can permit payment at any time within 90 days after the triggering event but only if the employee does not have the capacity to directly or indirectly control when the compensation will be paid. Remember that ADEA releases require 45 days for employees to consider the release and employees have a further seven days after signing to revoke the release, so severance payments are usually delayed until the right to revoke has elapsed. Releases offered in the third quarter of the year, therefore, potentially straddle two years.

The IRS' position, as expressed in Notice 2010-6, 2010-3 I.R.B. 275, effective April 1, 2011, is that this is precisely what § 409A is designed to penalize. This is a common issue in § 409A audits. The way to avoid trouble is to draft releases to say that, if benefits could be paid in more than one tax year depending on when the release is signed, payment will be made in the later year no matter when the release was actually signed. Plans should also be amended by December 31, 2012: Notice 2010-80, 2010-51 I.R.B. 853 says that the transition period for eliminating the "straddle" problem will end then.

Some inadvertent errors can be corrected using IRS correction programs; for the year of a corrective plan amendment, the tax return should include a note that the amendment was adopted in reliance on the correction program.

The IRS will permit the company to drop its requirement that the departing employee sign a release—but that would leave the company vulnerable to suits for things such as discrimination or ERISA violations. The IRS will also permit the payment window to be shortened from 90 days to 30 or 45 days—which makes this tax problem less likely but increases the burden on the company's HR department or benefits administration vendor to process the payment on time. [McGuireWoods LLP, *Employee Release Provisions Present Section 409A Trap for the Unwary* (Aug. 31, 2011) (benefitslink.com); George L. Chimento, Davis Malm & D'Agostine, *Release Me: 4th Quarter Complications for 409A Plans* (Oct. 14, 2011) (benefitslink.com)]

See Rev. Rul. 2010-27, 2010-45 I.R.B. 620, for the types of expenses (illness; funeral expenses; uninsured casualty causing property loss) expenses that could qualify for an unforeseeable emergency distribution from a 409A plan.

The participant must show that the expenses could not otherwise be met by insurance, or by liquidating assets that could be liquidated without severe financial hardship. The distribution must not exceed the amount needed to cope with the emergency (plus taxes). [McGuireWoods LLP Legal Updates, *IRS Issues Guidance on Unforeseeable Emergency Distributions from 409A and 457(b) Plans* (Dec. 30, 2010) (benefitslink.com)]

Not only is § 409A an issue in the corporation's dealings with individual executives, but also it must be considered when there is a change in control of the corporation—for example, in a merger or takeover, when many employees are involved. Section 409A potentially applies to many compensation arrangements in change-of-control situations, such as severance arrangements, stock options, and incentives. Violating the rule leads to accelerated inclusion in income, and a 20% federal penalty. California imposes its own 20% penalty.

Alternative payment methods for a double-trigger severance plan (see § 3.03[A]) could violate § 409A. Some employers fail to realize this because the pre- and post-change severance provisions are found in different documents, such as a company-wide severance plan and an individual change-in-control agreement with a key executive. A double-trigger arrangement typically falls under § 409A if its "good reason" payment trigger is excessively broad—for example, if the executive can resign and collect severance based on a minor reduction in pay or duties, or if the installment payments exceed $490,000 (as indexed for inflation) or extend more than two years after separation from service. An installment or lump sum double trigger violates § 409A unless the definition of change in control complies with § 409A, and it often does not. To avoid this problem, the plan can be structured to make pre- and post-change in control payments in the same way.

Stock options can be assumed in corporate transactions without violating § 409A if the assumption satisfies the rules for assuming ISOs. In general, that means that the economics of the option must be preserved by valuing the consideration paid for the target company's stock, potentially including the earnout. If the calculations are wrong, overvaluing the options violates § 409A and undervaluation causes economic detriment to the holders of the options. [Juliano

P. Banuelos, *Recent Compensation Trends in Mergers and Acquisitions and Section 409A*, Orrick Perspectives (October 2011) (benefitslink.com)]

## § 8.03 PROHIBITED TRANSACTIONS AND CORRECTIONS

Section 409A requires nonqualified plans to provide for payment only on a permitted event, for example death, disability, or separation from service. They must specify that the date of the event is the payment date or specify a fixed schedule or a different payment date that is objectively determinable and not discretionary. A nonqualified plan can also provide that payment is determinable and non-discretionary when it is made, but only if the period begins and ends in the same tax year for the employee or the period is not more than 90 days and the employee does not have the right to designate the taxable year of the payment. (It is common for plans to call for payment within a period of time after an event, because it can be inconvenient to make the payment exactly on the day of the event.)

As a result of these requirements, a nonqualified plan may discover that it has created additional tax liability for the plan and for its beneficiaries.

Notice 2008-113, 2008-51 I.R.B. 1305 provides a correction program for inadvertent, unintentional operational errors in administering § 409A plans. Failures that can be corrected include failing to defer compensation or making incorrect payments of compensation. The correction program is effective for tax years beginning on or after January 1, 2009. [Snell & Wilmer Legal Alert, *IRS Announces Section 409A Correction Program*, <http://www.swlaw.com/Alert_CorrectionProgram_Apr2009.pdf> (April 2009); Fred Schneyer, *IRS Issues Final 409A(a) Relief Procedures*, plansponsor.com (Dec. 5, 2008)] This Notice explains how to correct operational failures; see Notice 2010-6, 2010-3 I.R.B. 275, for guidance on how to correct document failures.

Notice 2010-80, 2010-51 I.R.B. 853, offers additional relief for § 409A plans—more types of plans will be eligible for relief under Notice 2010-6; a new correction method is permitted when there is a failure of payment at separation of service subject to a requirement to release claims; and transition relief is available under Notice 2010-6 to correct plan documents. [Rebecca Moore, *IRS Offers Additional 409A Relief*, plansponsor.com (Nov. 30, 2010); Frank Palmieri, *Employers Should Review Severance Plans in Light of IRS Guidance*, Employee Benefit News (Feb. 1, 2011) (benefitslink.com)]

Nor are tax problems the only potential issues for nonqualified plans. ERISA § 502(i) gives the DOL power to assess a civil penalty against a "party in interest" who engages in a prohibited transaction with a nonqualified plan. The penalty, which is usually assessed in connection with top-hat plans, is 5% for every year or partial year in which the prohibited transaction continues in effect. There is an additional 100% penalty if the DOL issues a notice of violation, but the violation is not corrected within 90 days (or whatever extension of time the DOL grants).

CHAPTER 9

# EARLY RETIREMENT AND RETIREE HEALTH BENEFITS

## § 9.01   INTRODUCTION

The timing of retirement is an individual choice, but employers can take steps to make early retirement either more or less attractive. Sometimes employers pursue early retirement incentives because they find it less expensive to encourage retirement than to maintain a large payroll. At other times, employers want to encourage older, skilled, and experienced employees to remain in the workforce—or they do not wish to devote funds to paying incentives to retire early!

Without careful planning and drafting, early retirement programs can also have a legal downside. The employer must make sure that incentives are available without unlawful discrimination. Furthermore, although it makes sense to ask early retirees to waive their claims against the employer, the waiver must be drafted with due attention to the Older Worker's Benefit Protection Act (OWBPA).

An early retirement program can create risks from two directions. Employees who are eligible may charge that the plan is a subterfuge for forcing them into involuntary retirement. On the other hand, employees who are not offered the incentives can charge that the unavailability of the program was the result of discrimination against them. Furthermore, if the early retirement program changes over time, employees who accepted a first offer may claim that the company should have informed them of the potential for getting a better offer by waiting longer. [This topic is discussed in more detail in Chapter 15, § 15.07, as an issue of fiduciary responsibility to make full disclosure to plan participants]

The questions of early retirement programs and retiree health benefits need to be examined in tandem, because one of the most important questions in deciding whether to retire early is the availability of health coverage. Medicare eligibility depends on age (65 or over) or disability, not employment status. Furthermore, the Medicare system does not provide spousal benefits: each spouse must qualify independently. Therefore, a potential early retiree who is younger than 65 will need retiree health coverage, COBRA coverage, or private insurance. When the insurance coverage pools enacted by the Patient Protection and Affordable Care Act (PPACA) become available, this will be an important resource for coverage of early retirees.

Pursuant to PPACA Section 1102, employers can get partial reimbursement of EGHP (employer group health plan) costs for early retirees and their dependents who are not eligible for Medicare. See § 9.07, below, for further discussion of the ERRP (Early Retiree Reinsurance Program). A mid-2011 Issue Brief by the Center for Retirement Research at Boston College identifies a trend. There are older workers in the workforce as a result of factors such as Social Security changes and lessened availability of pensions and retiree health benefits. Since the mid 1990s, the average retirement age has risen from 62–64 (men) and 60–62 (women). After World War II, the workforce participation rate of older men declined, with a further decline after Medicare and a major increase in Social

Security benefits in 1972. However, labor force participation of men aged 55–64 and 65 and over has increased gradually. Removing the Social Security earnings test has removed one impediment to remaining at work and the delayed retirement credit is also an incentive for longer employment. Workers who have 401(k) plans (now the dominant type of plan) tend to retire a year or two later than comparable workers with defined benefit plans. The decline in retiree health benefits also creates an incentive to remain in the workforce until the age of Medicare eligibility. [<http://crr.bc.edu/wp-content/uploads/2011/08/IB_11-11.pdf>; see Rebecca Moore, *Report Finds Relationship Between Having Pension and Retirement Age*, plansponsor.com (Aug. 16, 2011)]

A mid-2012 article examines the potential effects of PPACA's health insurance exchanges on coverage options for early retirees. The author concludes that the exchanges will probably be beneficial to early retirees. Many of them chose early retirement because of health problems, so the guaranteed availability of coverage and at a premium with limitations on age rating, will be helpful. If the household income of the early retiree is below 400% of the federally defined poverty level, federal subsidies may be available. If household income is below 138% of the poverty level, the early retiree may be Medicaid-eligible. The shared responsibility penalty is not imposed on employers if their pre-65 retirees purchase Exchange coverage. (Exchange coverage is no longer available once a person becomes Medicare-eligible.) However, the early retiree may be better off remaining in the employer's plan, because, in effect, the retiree participates in a larger premium pool that includes many younger employees who qualify for lower premiums. [Jordan Ge, *Health Insurance Exchanges and Early Retiree Health Coverage*, Milliman Benefits Perspectives (June 2012) (benefitslink .com)]

PPA § 841 amends Code § 420: a plan whose assets are at least 120% of current liability is permitted to fund a 401(h) plan with at least two years' worth of estimated retiree health costs. However, a sponsor that chooses to do so must keep the plan funded at a level of at least 120%; if funding drops below this level, the sponsor must withdraw funds from the 401(h) plan until the plan's funding level returns to at least 120%. The PPA also permits transfers to fund the expected future costs of retiree health benefits under a CBA, as long as the employer used at least 5% of its 2005 gross receipts for the purpose of providing retiree health benefits. See § 9.13, below, for more discussion.

## § 9.02  ADEA ISSUES OF EARLY RETIREMENT INCENTIVES

At what point does an incentive provided to motivate early retirement turn into pressure that adds up to "constructive discharge" (the equivalent of firing the employee)? The relevant statute is the Older Worker's Benefit Protection Act, which allows voluntary early retirement incentives but only if they satisfy the objectives of the ADEA: promoting employment opportunities for qualified and willing older workers.

The OWBPA allows employers to subsidize early retirement via flat dollar benefits, extra benefits, or percentage increases. Employees who retire early can be offered a more favorable benefit formula (e.g., adding a certain number of years to the number of years actually worked). It does not violate the OWBPA to impose a "window" period that is the only time that the incentive is available. HHS published an Interim Final Rule, implementing the reinsurance program, on May 5, 2010: see 75 Fed. Reg. 24450 (May 5, 2010).

> ■ **TIP:** The mandates imposed by PPACA on plans that are not "grand-fathered" plans (for example, the requirement of covering employees' children up to age 26) do not apply to plans that cover only retirees, and no active workers. [Seyfarth Shaw LLP, *Health Care Reform Mandates Do Not Apply to Retiree-Only Plans*, <http://www.seyfarth.com/e613f530-2fb9-48e0-8330-44fk5ab6d960_documentupload.pdf> (June 17, 2010)]

A defined benefit plan can pay a "Social Security supplement" starting at the date of early retirement, extending until the first date the retiree will be able to receive reduced Social Security benefits—or, if the employer prefers, until the retiree will be eligible for a full unreduced Social Security benefit.

> ■ **TIP:** The employer can amend the pension plan to raise the NRA from 65 to 67 (a change that the Social Security Administration is gradually implementing), as long as accrued early retirement benefits, including subsidies, are preserved.

Two participants of Washington-Idaho-Montana Carpenters-Employers Retirement Trust filed a complaint against Secretary of Labor Hilda Solis alleging that eliminating subsidized early retirement option violated due process. They argued that distinguishing between early retirees in pay status and those not yet retired was an equal protection violation. The Eastern District of Washington dismissed the case: the mere fact that the early retirement provisions were eliminated pursuant to the PPA did not involve state action and without state action a due process claim could not be maintained. (Although the general rule is that ERISA protects contractual early retirement benefits, PPA allows a pension plan that is in critical financial status to eliminate future early retirement benefits.) [*Arendt v. Solis*, No. 01-11-5135-LRS (E.D. Wash. Mar. 14, 2012) see Rebecca Moore, *Court Dismisses Claim Against Solis for PPA Provision*, plansponsor.com (Mar. 14, 2012)]

A university offered early retirement incentives to both tenured professors and top-level administrators. The North Dakota district court said (and the Eighth Circuit agreed) that payments to the faculty members were not "wages" (and therefore not subject to Social Security taxes) because the payments were made in exchange for property rights in university tenure. The payments to administrators, although similar, were subject to FICA, because the administrators were at-will employees, whereas the tenured faculty could only be dismissed for grave cause. [*N.D. State Univ. v. United States*, 85 A.F.T.R.2d ¶ 2000-332 (D.N.D. Nov. 19, 1999), *aff'd*, 255 F.3d 599 (8th Cir. 2001)]

In 2000, the Federal Circuit ruled that severance payments made to retiring employees are "wages" subject to FICA because they reflect past work. In 2006, the Sixth Circuit held that early retirement incentives exchanging payments for tenure rights were subject to FICA, based on a broad definition of "compensation," and because the payments were made because of the recipients' past services for the employer, not in exchange for surrender of tenure rights. [*Appoloni v. United States/Klender v. U.S.*, 450 F.3d 185 (6th Cir. 2006); *Abrahamsen v. U.S.*, 228 F.3d 1360 (Fed. Cir. 2000). In late 2007, the Third Circuit held that the University of Pittsburgh's early retirement payments to tenured professors were taxable income, not buyout payments. The Third Circuit deemed tenure to be a form of compensation for past work at the university, so giving up tenure was the equivalent of severance pay and thus FICA wages. See Fred Schneyer, *Payments to Tenured Profs Ruled Taxable Wages*, plansponsor.com (Nov. 5, 2007).]

The District Court for the District of Minnesota ruled that the Minnesota Department of Corrections violated the ADEA by maintaining an early retirement incentive plan that had different health and dental plans depending on whether or not the retiree was under 55 at the time of retirement. Those who retired at 55 and under received employer contributions for health and dental coverage until age 65, whereas those who retired after 55 did not receive employer contributions. The district court ruled that this constituted facial discrimination, and ordered damages equal to the premiums that would have been paid from 2001 to 2010 if the plan had not discriminated. [*EEOC v. Minnesota Dep't of Corrs.*, No. Civ 098-05252 PAM/FLN (D. Minn. Apr. 12, 2010); see Rebecca Moore, *Court Finds Early Retirement Incentive Discriminatory*, plansponsor.com (Apr. 12, 2010)]

## § 9.03   DISCLOSURES TO EMPLOYEES

An employee can't make a meaningful decision about whether or not to retire without understanding the choices that will be available in the near future. If the terms of the early retirement program change, people who were not eligible for the improved terms, or who elected early retirement without knowing that they could have gotten a better deal by waiting longer, may charge the employer with fraud, and may charge various parties involved with the plan with violations of fiduciary duty.

The Third Circuit announced a rule in *Fischer v. Philadelphia Elec. Co.* [96 F.3d 1533 (3d Cir. 1996); see also *Bins v. Exxon Co.*, 189 F.3d 929 (9th Cir. 1999), on rehearing, 220 F.3d 1042 (9th Cir. 2000)] that a revised early retirement incentive has received "serious consideration," and therefore must be disclosed to potential early retirees, once senior managers discuss the proposal for purposes of implementation.

The First Circuit held that ERISA preempts state-law claims of negligence, equitable estoppel, and negligent misrepresentation made by an early retiree who blamed his employer's erroneous estimate of his benefits for inducing him to retire early. The plaintiff said that he was not suing over plan administration issues that would be preempted by ERISA, only about the employer's legal obligations to keep proper records. He also said that he sought damages for the employer's negligence, not plan benefits. The First Circuit did not accept this argument, holding that resolution of the claim would require determining whether the plan complied with the record requirements imposed by ERISA. [*Zipperer v. Raytheon Co.*, 493 F.3d 50 (1st Cir. 2007)]

It is a breach of fiduciary duty to inform potential early retirees that lump-sum payouts are available, without also disclosing the I.R.C. § 415 limitations on rollovers and explaining the tax consequences. [*Farr v. U.S. West Commc'ns, Inc.*, 58 F.3d 1361 (9th Cir. 1998)] Given that the fiduciaries' common-law duty of loyalty requires them to deal fairly and honestly with plan participants, it is a violation to give them incomplete information.

Gearlds alleged that his employer negligently induced him to take early retirement by promising health benefits. The district court dismissed the case, arguing that all he asked for was compensatory damages (past and future medical expenses, attorneys' fees, and costs), which are not an available equitable remedy. However, the Fifth Circuit said that *Amara* [*CIGNA Corp. v. Amara* 131 S. Ct. 1866 (2011)] allows relief that makes a plaintiff whole for losses caused by breach of fiduciary duty. [*Gearlds v. Entergy Servs. Inc.*, 709 F.3d 448 (5th Cir. 2013); see Rebecca Moore, *5th Circuit Revives Suit for Retiree Medical Benefits*, plansponsor.com (Mar. 8, 2013)]

To assist older employees in making decisions about Medicare Part D (the prescription drug program that took effect in 2006), employers are required to issue a notice to all Part D-eligible employees (with disclosure to the Center for Medicare and Medicaid services as well) informing them as to whether there is prescription drug coverage under the employer's plan, and whether that coverage is creditable or non-creditable. [See § 9.10[B]]

## § 9.04 EEOC MANUAL ON EARLY RETIREMENT INCENTIVES

Late in 2000, the EEOC updated Section 3 of its Compliance Manual to deal with benefits. [No. 915.003 (Oct. 3, 2000), <http://www.eeoc.gov/policy/docs/benefits.html>] As of press time in 2013, this section of the manual had not been updated. The agency's position is that an early retirement incentive (ERI) program is lawful as long as it's voluntary. The EEOC will not get involved if the employer chooses to:

- Set a minimum age or minimum number of years of service for employees who participate;

- Have a window (i.e., the incentive is only available for a limited time period);

- Limit the ERI to a manager, a department, a particular facility, etc.

However, ERI benefits can't be reduced or denied for older employees versus similarly situated younger employees unless the employer qualifies for one of five defenses:

- Equal cost;

- Subsidizing a portion of the early retirement benefit;

- Integrating the incentives with Social Security;

- (For a university) incentives for a tenured faculty member;

- The plan is consistent with the objectives of the ADEA.

According to the EEOC Compliance Manual (the Manual), an ERI is not voluntary if a reasonable person informed of its terms would conclude that there was no choice but to accept. Relevant factors in the analysis include, e.g., adequate time to decide; absence of coercion; lack of negative consequences for older employees who turn down the offer; and whether a particular employee had legal advice when making the decision.

The Manual provides that it is not coercion for the employer to state that layoffs will be required unless enough people accept the incentives—unless older workers are the only ones at risk of layoff. Nor is it coercion for the employer to make an offer that is "too good to refuse."

The equal cost defense probably will not be available in connection with ERIs, because the cost of early retirement benefits generally does not increase with the employee's age.

The EEOC allows the employer to limit the ERI or pay higher ERI benefits to younger employees where the benefits are used to bring early retirees up to the level of the unreduced pension they would receive at the NRA from a defined benefit pension plan. But the subsidized pension can't be greater than the pension of a similarly situated older employee who has reached NRA.

It is also permissible to offer an ERI to bridge the gap to Social Security eligibility, for a person who has not yet reached the Social Security early retirement age (currently slightly over 62). The supplement can't exceed the Social Security benefit that the employee will eventually receive as an early or normal age retiree.

According to the EEOC, equal severance benefits are required for all similarly situated employees irrespective of their age. Employers may not deny severance on the grounds that the employee is eligible for a pension, although sometimes pension benefits can be offset against the severance pay. Denying recall rights to older workers operates as unlawful involuntary retirement. The cost of providing severance does not rise with the employees' age, so employers are not allowed to assert an equal cost defense in this context.

Retiree health benefits can legitimately be offset against severance if the retiree is eligible for an immediate pension; the retiree actually receives health benefits; and the retiree benefits are at least comparable to Medicare in type and value. If the retiree is over 65, the benefits must be at least comparable for one-fourth the value of Medicare benefits. The offset itself must be reduced by any percentage by which the pension is reduced for retirement before the NRA, and any percentage of the retiree health coverage premium that the retiree has to pay.

In the EEOC view, an ERI ignores age as a criterion (and therefore is consistent with the ADEA's objectives) as long as it gives all employees above a certain age:

- A flat dollar amount (e.g., $20,000);

- Additional service-based benefits, for instance, $1,000 for each year of service;

- A percentage of salary;

- A flat dollar increase in pension benefits, such as an extra $200 a month;

- A percentage increase (e.g., 10%) in pension benefits;

- Extra years of service and/or age used in pension computations.

## § 9.05   ERISA ISSUES

### [A]   Generally

Because one of the primary purposes of ERISA is to make sure that retirement benefits will be paid in accordance with the terms of the plan, ERISA issues often arise when early retirement plans must be construed. Sometimes, ERISA welfare benefit plans will also be involved.

### [B]   Preemption

It is very likely that ERISA will be held to preempt state-court cases about group health plans. In its June 2004 decision in the consolidated cases of *Aetna Health Inc. v. Davila*, and *Cigna Healthcare of Texas, Inc. v. Calad*, 542 U.S. 200 (2004), the Supreme Court found that ERISA § 502(a) completely preempts state-law claims alleging that managed care plans improperly denied care (in one case, it was claimed that the plaintiff was injured by taking a lower-cost drug rather than the safer, more expensive drug that was not covered by the plan; in the other case, alleged premature discharge from hospitalization). [See § 15.18] Preemption is much less likely to be found in the early retirement context. According to the Sixth Circuit, ERISA does not preempt age discrimination claims merely because the plaintiff had already retired and was collecting a pension as of the time of the suit. [*Warner v. Ford Motor Co.*, 46 F.3d 531 (6th Cir. 1995)]

The 1996 case of *Lockheed v. Spink* [517 U.S. 882 (1996)] found (among other issues) that it is not a prohibited transaction (as defined by ERISA § 406) to establish an early retirement program that is conditioned on waiving enforcement of employment claims. Under this analysis, paying benefits under any circumstances shouldn't be treated as a prohibited transaction.

## [C]  Fiduciary Duty

Persons dissatisfied with the terms of an early retirement plan, or the way those terms are applied, often bring suit for breach of fiduciary duty. Whether a breach will be found depends on factors such as whether potential retirees received materially misleading information—possibly whether or not intent to mislead, or even negligence, was present. It does not violate ERISA to deny early retirement to employees who are deemed especially valuable to the company, if the plan gives management discretion as to whether early retirement is in the company's best interests. [*McNab v. Gen. Motors*, 162 F.3d 959 (7th Cir. 1998)] Another General Motors case says that the LMRA and NLRA do not preempt an early retiree's state-law claims that the employer fraudulently induced acceptance of early retirement. [*Voilas v. Gen. Motors*, 170 F.3d 367 (3d Cir. 1999)]

According to a federal magistrate judge, it was a breach of duty to tell ex-workers affected by a merger that they could get lifetime health benefits for $20 a month without disclosing the right to amend the plan. In 2006, the Eastern District of Pennsylvania restored the benefits that were in effect before the plan was modified to eliminate free and low-cost medical coverage. Because the communications about retiree benefits came from corporate agents who had at least apparent authority to discuss benefits, the Eastern District rejected the defendants' contention that the representations were not made in a fiduciary capacity. [*In re Unisys Corp. Retiree Med. Benefits ERISA Litig.*, No. 03-3924 (E.D. Pa. Sept. 29, 2006), discussed in Fred Schneyer, *Unisys Loses Benefits Reduction Fight*, plansponsor.com (Oct. 12, 2006)]

A year later, the Eastern District of Pennsylvania, because of the retirees' detrimental reliance, required Unisys to reinstate free or low-cost retiree health benefits for 12 people who retired from its predecessor corporation. The court did not order back wages or reimbursement of medical premiums that the retirees had to pay since the change in the plan, on the grounds that those measures would not constitute "appropriate equitable relief" under ERISA. [*In re Unisys Corp. Retiree Medical Benefits ERISA Litigation*, No. 03-3924 (E.D. Pa. July 16, 2007); see

Adrien Martin, *Unisys Made Misrepresentations about Health Insurance Coverage*, plansponsor.com (July 23, 2007)]

In the fourth opinion in this case, rendered October 2009, the Third Circuit found that it was a breach of fiduciary duty to give employees the impression that their retiree health benefits would continue for life when, in fact, the employer had the power to terminate the benefits at any time. In this view, employees received "at best a half truth" when the company did not disclose the power to amend the plan. Although the SPD disclosed the right to amend, the Third Circuit said that this was irrelevant because it was not distributed until after the plaintiffs retired, so it could not have affected their knowledge of the plan. The Third Circuit upheld the injunction issued by the district court, because the injunction corrected a violation of fiduciary duty, and the specific provisions in ERISA dealing with equitable relief outweigh the general principle that ERISA does not regulate settlor activity. [*In re Unisys Corp. Retiree Medical Benefits ERISA Litigation*, 579 F.3d 220 (3d Cir. Oct. 19, 2009), *cert. denied*, 130 S. Ct. 1546 sub nom. *Unisys Corp. v. Adair* (Feb. 22, 2010); see Mercer Select US, *Creating the Impression of Lifetime Retiree Health Benefits Is Breach of ERISA's Fiduciary Duties* (Oct. 19, 2009) (benefitslink.com); John R. Richards and Christopher A. Weals, Law360, *Why the 3rd Circ.'s Unisys Decision Defies ERISA* (Jan. 29, 2010) (benefitslink.com)]

A later case, *Bender v. Newell Window Furnishings Inc.*, No. 1:06-CV-113 (W.D. Mich. 2010) held that retiree health benefits, including full coverage of Medicare Part B benefits, were vested for life. The SPD reserved the right to amend the plan, but said that the company hoped to extend the benefits indefinitely. The district court held that a series of CBAs proved that the health benefits were vested. [See Fred Schneyer, *Court Rules for Retirees on Health Benefits*, plansponsor.com (July 9, 2010)]

## [D]   Anticutback Rule

ERISA § 204(g) forbids cutbacks in benefits. On June 7, 2004, the Supreme Court ruled that it is a violation of the anticutback rule to amend a plan to further restrict the type of work that retirees can do without forfeiting their pensions, if the result of the amendment is that early retirement benefits that were already accrued would be suspended. (The plan ruled out benefits for retirees who engaged in post-retirement work as "construction workers"; the plaintiffs were "construction supervisors." Then the plan was amended to rule out benefits for anyone who did any work at all in the construction industry.) [*Central Laborers' Pension Fund v. Heinz*, 541 U.S. 739 (2004)]

The Ninth Circuit ruled that plan trustees improperly suspended early retirement benefits. The trustees said that the retiree engaged in "employment as an electrical contractor," which was forbidden. But the Ninth Circuit held that installing HVAC equipment for an electrical contractor was not the same as being a contractor, and the plan provision only forbade setting up in business as an independent business. [*Brown v. Southern California IBEW NECA Trust Funds*, 588 F.3d 1000 (9th Cir. 2009)]

The IRS has ruled frequently on proper implementation of the anti-cutback rule, starting with T.D. 9052, 2003-19 I.R.B. 879. Participants must receive a "§ 204(h) notice" informing them in plain English if there has been a significant reduction in the rate of future benefit accrual, or whenever an early retirement benefit or early retirement subsidy has been eliminated. Although the basic rule is that notice must be given at least 45 days before the effective date of the amendment, small (under 100 participant) plans can comply by giving notice at least 15 days before the effective date; the 15-day notice period is also adequate for amendments relating to corporate mergers and acquisitions. If the amendment significantly reduces an early retirement benefit or subsidy, but does not significantly reduce the rate of future benefit accruals, the notice can even be given after the effective date of the amendment, as long as it is within 30 days after the effective date.

Before a cash balance conversion in 1998, Commonwealth Industries' defined benefit plan provided early retirement benefits to participants who had reached age 55 and had five years of service. Nine participants retired after the conversion, taking lump sums. They filed administrative claims protesting when they did not receive the pre-conversion early retirement subsidy. However, only one of the nine claimed within five years of receiving the lump sum. The district court held that the other eight claims were untimely and dismissed the one timely claim on the merits. The Sixth Circuit applied the five-year Kentucky statute of limitations for statutes that lack an explicit limitations period, upholding the district court's determination that eight of the claims were time-barred. However, for the ninth claim, the Sixth Circuit held that reducing the early retirement subsidy violated the anti-cutback rule, even though the participant did not become eligible for the subsidy until after the conversion: ERISA § 204(g) allows fulfillment of an age condition either before or after the plan is amended. The case was remanded to decide the fact issue of whether the subsidy was protected by § 204(g), or whether it was an optional form of benefit that the employer could eliminate. [*Falllin v. Commonwealth Indus., Inc. Cash Balance Plan*, 695 F.3d 512 (6th Cir. 2012); see Wolters Kluwer Law & Business News Center, *Cash Balance Plan May Not Reduce Pre-Conversion Early Retirement Subsidy* (Oct. 22, 2012) (benefitslink.com)]

In general, ERISA § 204(h)'s requirements are the same as those under Code § 4980F, but there are additional penalties under § 204(h) for "egregious" failure to provide notice, over and above the excise tax imposed by § 4980F for failure to provide the required notice. [See 69 Fed. Reg. 13769 (Mar. 24, 2004); Proposed Regulations, REG-156518-04, RIN 1545-BE10, 2005-38 I.R.B. 582; T.D. 9219, 2005-38 I.R.B. 538; T.D. 9280, 71 Fed. Reg. 45379 (Aug. 9, 2006)]

The Tenth Circuit found that converting a defined benefit plan to cash balance form had the effect of depriving employees of early retirement subsidies.

The Tenth Circuit remanded the case to the district court for consideration of remedies for the plaintiffs—bearing in mind that remedies for § 204(h) notice failures are available only if the employer's failure to give notice was egregious. An egregious failure means that the circumstances were within the employer's control, and the employer nevertheless intentionally failed to give notice after discovering an unintentional past failure to satisfy the § 204(h) requirements. In this case, the Tenth Circuit ruled that there were no egregious circumstances, only a forgivable omission in the course of drafting the complex notice required by ERISA. [*Jensen v. Solvay Chems.*, No. 11-8092 (10th Cir. July 2, 2013)]

T.D. 9472, 2009-51 I.R.B. 850, is a final rule covering the 204(h) notice requirements for plan amendments that reduce accrued benefits. T.D. 9472 deals with the amendments required by the PPA for single-employer plans with certain funding shortfalls. Unpredictable contingent event benefits are limited if a plan's AFTAP is or would be under 60%. Amendments increasing benefits and therefore the liabilities of the plan are limited if AFTAP is or would be below 80%. Payments are prohibited when AFTAP is in the 60%–80% range and the sponsor is in Chapter 11 and its actuary has not certified that the plan is fully funded; and benefit accruals must stop when AFTAP falls below 60%. [Rebecca Moore, *IRS Issues Final Rule on Certain Notice Requirements*, plansponsor.com (Nov. 23, 2009)]

T.D. 9601, 77 Fed. Reg. 66915 (Nov. 8, 2012) permits a bankrupt sponsor to amend its plan to eliminate optional forms of benefits that accelerate payment after bankruptcy. Approval by the PBGC and the bankruptcy court is required. [Kristen Heinzinger, *IRS Finalizes Relief for Bankrupt DB Sponsors*, plansponsor.com (Nov. 8, 2012)]

## [E]  Other ERISA Issues

Whether a severance plan is an ERISA welfare benefit plan depends on the nature and extent of the employer's role. There is no plan without ongoing administrative responsibility for determining eligibility and calculating benefits. In *O'Connor v. Commonwealth Gas Co.* [251 F.3d 262 (1st Cir. 2001)] the employer wanted to reduce its census before a merger. The plaintiffs charge they were deceived into retiring early because the employer lied about future retirement incentives. The employer provided a one-time severance bonus calculated based on years of service. The First Circuit found that there was no ERISA "plan" because the program lasted only 15 weeks, covered only 300 workers, and involved only simple arithmetic, not discretionary judgment.

The Seventh Circuit ruled that it was not an abuse of discretion for the district court to approve a settlement of an ERISA class action that was less favorable to early retirees than to other members of the class. The Seventh Circuit had already ruled that a defined benefit plan with a cost-of-living adjustment (COLA) must provide the actuarial equivalent of the COLA to participants who receive lump sum benefits. The Seventh Circuit ordered the district court to draft a damage award. The plan argued that the early retirees were not entitled to damages. Then a settlement was reached, giving each early retiree 3.5% of the original lump sum amount. A group of early retirees objected to this amount. The Seventh Circuit held that the district court did not abuse its discretion, and the settlement award was fair to the early retirees because it balanced their risk of continuing to litigate a case where they might lose. [*Williams v. Rohm and Haas Pension Plan*, 658 F.3d 629 (7th Cir. 2011); see CCH Pension & Benefits, *District Court's Approval of Class Action Settlement Less Favorable to Early Retiree Class Members Not Abuse of Discretion* (Nov. 23, 2011) (benefitslink.com)]

The Pension Benefit Guaranty Corporation (PBGC) publishes a table every year in November or December, most recently Table I- 13, 77 Fed. Reg. 71321 (Nov. 30, 2012), for plans with valuation dates after December 31, 2012 and before January 1, 2014, which estimates the probability that a person will retire early from a plan that is being terminated by the PBGC, or in a distress termination initiated by the employer. The table is used to determine the total value of the benefits under the plan by computing the value of early retirement benefits. The likelihood of early retirement is considered low if the monthly benefit is below a certain amount, high if it exceeds a certain amount, and medium if it falls in between.

The table is based on the monthly benefit the worker will receive at "URA" (Unreduced Retirement Age)—either the plan's Normal Retirement Age or the age at which the worker could first receive a benefit that is not actuarially reduced to account for early retirement. For example, if the plan participant reaches URA in 2014, the likelihood of early retirement is considered low if the benefit is under $599 a month; medium if it is between $599 and $2,531 a month; and high if the monthly benefit exceeds $2,531. If the participant reaches URA in 2016, the corresponding figures are $623, $623–$2,633, and over $2,633. If the participant reaches URA in 2023 or later, the figures are $720, $720–$3,046, and over $3,046.

## § 9.06 PHASED RETIREMENT

In many instances, the needs of both employer and employee would be well served by the option of "phased retirement" (a gradual transition out of the workforce) rather than a bright-line test of being either fully active or retired. Employers would certainly save money if they could reduce the full-time payroll yet continue to receive part-time services from older workers, instead of offering them early retirement subsidies.

For many years, phased retirement was quite difficult to implement because of rules limiting "in-service" distributions, other than those made on account of hardship, from defined benefit or 401(k) plans. Many commentators have raised the question of how to structure phased retirement equitably, e.g., by determining that a person is 50% retired, and therefore paying him or her 50% of the salary for the position, and also 50% of the retirement benefits that would be available if the person had completely retired.

Many pension plans (perhaps deliberately to encourage early retirement or as an unintended result of other design features) in effect grant the most rapid accrual of pension benefits when workers are in their fifties; between their mid-fifties and retirement, workers may find that pension accrual is actually negative. That is, even though they will eventually qualify for a larger pension because they work longer, they also receive the pension for one year less for each additional year worked.

The Pension Protection Act of 2006, Pub. L. No. 109-280, includes two major provisions dealing with early retirement and retiree health issues. PPA § 905 amends ERISA § 3(2)(A) and the corresponding Code § 401(a)(36) to permit plans to retain qualification even if they make in-service distributions for the phased retirement of persons aged 62 or older who continue to work on a reduced schedule. This is true even if the recipient of the distributions has not reached the plan's Normal Retirement Age.

In May 2007, final regulations were issued dealing with the definition of "Normal Retirement Age" (NRA) T.D. 9325. Under the proposed regulations (69 Fed. Reg. 65108, Nov. 10, 2004), in-service distributions prior to NRA forbade setting the NRA so low that it was a subterfuge to avoid the requirements for qualified plans, but in-service distributions before NRA could be made in conjunction with bona fide phased retirement.

The final regulations, however, adopt a somewhat different standard: the important factor is not whether the plan's NRA is a subterfuge, but whether it is at least as high as the typical age for the industry. If the NRA is set between 55 and 62, the employer's good-faith determination that the NRA falls within industry norms will be given deference if it is reasonable in light of the facts and circumstances. An NRA below 55 is presumed unreasonable, although not if the employer can prove the contrary. Note that an NRA of 50 will be considered reasonable for public safety employees like police or firefighters. [TD 9325, RIN 1545-BD23, 2007-24 I.R.B. 1386; see, e.g., Rebecca Moore, *IRS Releases Final Rules on In-service Distributions Past Retirement Age*, plansponsor.com (May 22, 2007)]

Phased retirement usually means a reduction of work schedule, for example, beginning at age 62 after at least 10 years of service. Management may impose other requirements, such as limiting phased retirement to specific job categories. The employee's concern is that phased retirement might mean outliving his or her retirement savings. If phased retirement begins before the age at which unreduced Social Security benefits are available, then the retiree will lose Social Security benefits based on the earned income. If the plan allows part-timers to participate, but charges higher premiums, the arrangement might be financially unsustainable for a phased retiree. [Anne E. Moran, *Phased Retirement:*

*Challenges for Employers*, 38 Employee Relations Law Journal 68 (Autumn 2012) (benefitslink.com)]

The IRS issued a Private Letter Ruling (PLR) that says that participants in a defined benefit plan who stop working with the explicit expectation of being rehired quickly by the original employer have not really retired. Therefore, they are not entitled to early retirement benefits. The plan is at risk of disqualification because of this manipulation of the rules. The PLR says that merely requiring a waiting period such as 30 days before resuming employment may not be sufficient to keep the plan compliant with tax law (at least if the employer and plan participant have an understanding that the participant will be rehired.) Nor does re-designating the person as an "independent contractor" make the arrangement valid. Although PLRs cannot be cited as precedent by anyone except the party that obtained the ruling, this PLR is of interest because it describes a popular phased retirement option—and one that other employers might have adopted without this warning. The IRS said that the employees might qualify for in-service distribution of early retirement benefits at age 62, if the plan included this feature. [PLR 201147038; see Rebecca Moore, *IRS Addresses Agreements to Rehire Retirees*, plansponsor.com (Mar. 5, 2012)]

## § 9.07   RETIREE HEALTH BENEFITS: INTRODUCTION

At one time, it was very common for part of the incentive for early retirement to come in the form of health benefits to replace the employer's group health plan. Employers often promised "lifetime health benefits at no cost." However, health care costs rise significantly every year, and employees in poor health are more likely to be interested in health benefits than employees in good health. Therefore, a retiree health benefit program can become a major burden on the employer.

Fidelity's 2012 study found that an average 65-year-old couple retiring in 2012 would need to save $240,000 for out of pocket health costs—a figure that does not reflect inflation. The average rate of health care inflation in the 11 years Fidelity has carried out this survey has been 6% a year, so, using these measures, a 2022 retiree would need $430,000 for health care. The estimate is for acute health care only, not long-term care. Fidelity's figures assume death at age 85, but many people survive longer. The Center for Retirement Research at Boston College projects that 85-year-olds face a further $140,000 in out of pocket health care costs, or $200,000 if long-term care is included. According to EBRI, Medicare covers only 59% of seniors' actual health expenditures. The total consists of 32% for Part B and D premiums, 23% for prescription drug costs not covered by Medicare, and 45% for Medicare copayments, deductibles, and services that are not covered. [Elizabeth O'Brien's Retire Well, *Health-Care Bill In Retirement: $240,000* (Nov. 15, 2012) (benefitslink.com)]

In 2013, the estimate actually declined 8%, to $220,000, because Medicare spending per enrollee rose much less than usual between 2012 and 2013—only 0.4%, whereas between 1985 and 2009 the average annual increase was 7%. [Elizabeth O'Brien, *Retiree Health-Cost Estimate Down, But Still High*,WSJ.com (May 15, 2013)]

According to the Employee Benefits Research Institute (EBRI), the prevalence of retiree health benefits began to diminish seriously in December 1990. One of the precipitating factors was the Financial Accounting Standards Board (FASB)'s release of a standard called SFAS 106, requiring employers to record their unfunded retiree health benefit liabilities on their financial statements—with the result that corporate earnings decreased.

In response, some employers stopped providing retiree health benefits altogether; others put their plans on a defined contribution basis, added age and service requirements, or maintained the level of benefits for current retirees but reduced the benefits that would eventually be available to people retiring in the future.

The Kaiser Family Foundation reported that, in 2013, 28% of companies with 200 or more employees provide retiree health benefits—slightly higher than the 2012 figure of 25%. Among these large employers that provide retiree health benefits, 90% offer health benefits to early retirees, 67% cover Medicare-age retirees, and 4% have a retiree plan that provides prescription drug coverage but no other benefits. [Kaiser Family Foundation, *2013 Employer Health Benefits Survey*, <http://kff.org/report-section/2013-summary-of-findings/> (Aug. 20, 2013)]

The EBRI reported in late 2012 that it is common for workers to realize that they will not receive retiree health benefits from their employer—but more workers expect such benefits than actually are entitled to them. In 2010, 32% of workers expected these benefits, but only 25% of early and 16% of Medicare-eligible retirees actually had access to such benefits. In 1997, 28.9% of the workforce was employed by companies that had coverage for early retirees, a percentage that fell to 17.7% in 2010. Companies that still have retiree health benefits typically have reduced the benefits, raised premiums, made eligibility more restrictive, or a combination of those tactics. [Kristin Heinzinger, *Expectations for Retiree Health Benefits Decreasing*, plansponsor.com (Oct. 23, 2012)]

Some employers have contracts with private-sector exchanges such as Extend Health (which are not the same as the Exchanges required by PPACA: see § 18.19[L]) so that Medicare-eligible retirees can enroll in plans to replace their lost coverage under the company's EGHP. The plan employs counselors to explain financial programs like Medicare Advantage and Medigap insurance. Part or all of the coverage can be funded by the employer depositing amounts into HRAs for retirees. (See § 18.18 for more about HRAs). These exchanges are helpful to employers by making costs more predictable, setting a cap on them, and reducing the burden of administration. Retirees benefit by having access to more plans and rates. [Michelle Andrews, *Some Employers Offer Aid To Retirees After*

*Cutting Their Health Insurance* Washington Post (Oct. 29, 2012) (benefitslink .com)]

FASB's SFAS No. 158 (generally effective for fiscal years ending after December 15, 2006) requires the funded status of all post-retirement plans—including retiree health plans—to be recorded on the company's balance sheet, not just included as a footnote to the financial statements. This FASB document does not require prefunding of retiree health liabilities, but the reporting obligation might provide an incentive to do so.

Among companies continuing to provide some kind of retiree health plans, there has been a strong trend to shift more and more of the costs to the retirees. To reduce the cost of the plan, many employers adopted caps, i.e., maximum amounts that they will devote to retiree health benefits; if costs increase past this point, the additional cost will be entirely passed along to the participants. Another tactic is to impose a combination of age and service requirements for participation in the retiree health plan, e.g., limiting it to persons over 55 with 10 years' service. Or, the amount of financial contribution an employee is expected to make to the retiree health plan could be made proportional to length of service. Or, retirees can be placed into a separate risk pool rather than a shared risk pool with active employees; premiums can be set higher for one group of retirees than another. [Ellen E. Schultz, *Conquering Retirement: When Retirees Face Health-Plan Cuts,* WSJ.com (Apr. 20, 2012)]

The Early Retirement Reimbursement Program (ERRP), created by PPACA, reimburses employers for claims incurred by retirees over 55 who are not Medicare eligible, or incurred by their dependents of any age. [Interim Final Rule: RIN 0991-AB64, 75 Fed. Reg. 24450 (May 5, 2010)] Five billion dollars was appropriated to fund the program. It was scheduled to last until January 1, 2014 or when the money ran out. Reimbursement is limited to 80% of early retiree health care costs in the range from $15,000–$90,000 (2010 figures), but only if the plan implements procedures for saving money on expensive and chronic conditions. All of the federal funds must be used to reduce plan costs, including reducing the premiums, deductibles, and copayments required of early retirees. [Mercer Select US, *HHS to Offset Some Health Costs of Early Retirees in Employer Plans* (Apr. 1, 2010) (benefitslink.com)]

The GAO said that, by June 30, 2011, $2.7 billion in ERRP payments had been approved. Almost half (46%) went to government entities, which was predictable because they are also the most likely employer to provide retiree health benefits. HHS' Center for Consumer Information & Insurance Oversight (CCIIO) approved applications from 6,078 plan sponsors for participation in the program. [GAO report: <http://www.gao.gov/products/GAO-11-875R>; see Rebecca Moore, *ERRP Approvals Consistent with Provision of Benefits in Market*, plansponsor.com (Oct. 31, 2011)]

As expected, the money ran out, and the termination of the ERRP program on January 1, 2014 was announced. [78 Fed.Reg. 23936 (Apr. 23, 2013); see

Kevin McGuinness, *ERRP Will Sunset at Start of 2014*,plansponsor.com (May 17, 2013)]

One important factor in the financial problems of the U.S. auto industry is high retiree health costs. Voluntary Employee Benefit Arrangements (VEBAs; see § 22.07) have been used to remove post-retirement benefit obligation from the car manufacturers' balance sheets. VEBAs are operated through trusts, managed by an independent board of trustees, and funded with cash, cash plus promissory notes, or equity securities. [Haynes Boone newsletter, *Weathering the Storm: Options to Remove Liabilities for High Retiree Medical Costs from a Company's Balance Sheet: VEBAs* (June 19, 2009) (benefitslink.com); Fred Schneyer, *EBSA Proposes ERISA Exemption for Chrysler VEBA*, plansponsor.com (Oct. 2, 2009); Fred Schneyer, *Chrysler VEBA Funded in Post-Bankruptcy Deal*, plansponsor- .com (May 1, 2009); Tresa Baldas, *The Legal Minefield of Cutting Workers' Health Care Benefits*, Nat'l L.J (Feb. 25, 2009) (law.com)]

In 2011 and 2012, VEBAs were running out money and had to cut costs, reduce benefits, and seek additional contributions from sponsors and plan benefi- ciaries. The largest VEBA, the UAW trusts covering more than 820,000 people, had a shortfall of close to $20 billion, according to DOL filings made in October 2011. Because VEBAs are partially funded by employer stock, they are vulner- able to market volatility as well as responsive to increasing medical costs. The UAW proposed to divert 10% of active workers' profit-sharing checks into the VEBA. In 2009, the UAW VEBA cut its ties to auto makers and became an inde- pendent trust—and also reduced prescription benefits and required retirees to make higher copayments. When the UAW VEBA was set up, it was assumed to earn an annual return of 9%, which would provide current benefits for retirees for 80 years, and medical costs were projected as increasing 5% a year. The United Steel Workers union had more than 30 VEBAs, which had good investment returns but could not keep pace with medical inflation. [Sharon Terlep and Mat- thew Dolan, *VEBA Retirement Trusts Face Funding Shortfalls*, WSJ.com (Nov. 7, 2011)]

## § 9.08 THE RIGHT TO ALTER OR TERMINATE RETIREE HEALTH BENEFITS

At one time, it was common for employers to promise their employees that, after the employees retired, they would receive lifetime health benefits without cost. Economic developments in the interim have led many employers to termi- nate their retiree health plans, or to impose premiums and copayment require- ments, or increase retirees' financial responsibilities. It is also common for retirees to sue their ex-employer to roll back these changes.

The general rule is that, as long as the employer drafts the plan to provide that the employer retains the right to amend, modify, or terminate the health benefits, the employer can do so unilaterally. ERISA has rules about vesting of pension benefits (i.e., the circumstances under which the right to a pension becomes nonforfeitable) but ERISA does not provide for vesting of welfare benefits such as retiree health benefits. Furthermore, ERISA preempts state law on this subject, so the states do not have the power to impose vesting requirements. [See, e.g., *Gen. Dynamics Land Sys. Inc. v. Cline*, 540 U.S. 581 (2004) (terminating retiree health benefits did not violate the ADEA).]

Early in 2009 the Sixth Circuit held that the 1998 CBA did not provide a permanent right to retiree medical benefits at no cost, vesting as soon as a worker became eligible for retirement. A group of retirees sued under LMRA § 301 and ERISA, seeking an injunction and a declaratory judgment that they were entitled to health benefits fully paid by Caterpillar. The district court held that the retiree benefits vested when they became eligible to retire or receive a pension, even if they continued working after the CBA expired. However, the Sixth Circuit reversed, drawing a distinction between active workers who will retire in the future and those who have already retired: retirees are usually not represented by a union, but active workers are. [*Winnett v. Caterpillar, Inc.*, 553 F.3d 1000 (6th Cir. 2009). In later proceedings in this case, the Sixth Circuit had to "borrow" a six-year state statute of limitations, because there is no explicit statute of limitations under ERISA § 502 or LMRA § 301. The Sixth Circuit held that the statute of limitations begins when the breach of promise becomes unequivocally clear—in this case, in 1998, so a suit brought in 2006 was untimely under the six-year statute of limitations. *Winnett v. Caterpillar, Inc.*, 609 F.3d 404 (6th Cir. 2010)]

The Sixth Circuit ruled in 2013 that, although retiree health care is a welfare benefit, it is not entitled to the same ERISA protection as pension benefits; employers can surrender the power to alter welfare benefits—in this case, by offering vested healthcare coverage to retired employees and spouses, and by agreeing that the company's CBAs could only be modified with signed, mutual consent of the parties. The case was brought by retired unionized employees who were covered by collective bargaining agreements that addressed healthcare benefits. The parties contested whether the CBAs guaranteed employees and their spouses lifetime healthcare benefits after retirement. After retiring, the employees and spouses continued to receive healthcare insurance from the defendant. When the plaintiffs were between the ages 62 and 65, the defendant paid 80% of the premium costs. When the retirees turned 65, the defendant assumed 100% of premium costs. In 2006, the defendant informed the plaintiffs that the company was instituting a new health care plan that would no longer cover 100% of the premiums. The plaintiffs alleged violations of the Labor Management Relations Act, 29 U.S.C. § 185, and ERISA, 29 U.S.C. § 1132. The district court ruled in plaintiffs' favor as to employee coverage, but in favor of defendant as to spouses. The Sixth Circuit reversed in part, requiring coverage of spouses as well. [*Moore v. Menasha Corp.*, 690 F.3d 444 (6th Cir. 2013)]

The Sixth Circuit held in September 2012 that the right to vested health benefits for life did not prevent management from reducing or restricting the benefits, as long as the changes were reasonable. In this analysis, vesting does not fix the bundle of services for all time. The case was remanded once again for consideration of the reasonableness of the change: whether the new benefits were reasonably commensurate with the old ones, were appropriate in light of changes in health care since the promise was made, and whether the changed benefits were consistent with the benefits that current employees receive. On remand,the district court is required to assess out-of-pocket costs for retirees under the old and new plans, how much retirees must pay for coverage, and the quality of care. [*Reese v. CNH America*, Nos. 11-1359/11-1857, 2012 WL 4009695 (6th Cir., Sept. 13, 2012); see Todd Leeuwenburgh, *Vested Retiree Health Benefits Can Face 'Reasonable' Reductions: 6th Cir.*, Smart HR Blog (Sept. 19, 2012); Wolters Kluwer Law & Business, *Employer Entitled To Make "Reasonable Modifications" To Retiree Health Care Benefits, Sixth Circuit Rules* (Oct. 5, 2012) (benefitslink.com)]

Connecticut Natural Gas Corp's CBA defined the maximum payments CNG would contribute toward retiree health insurance premiums. The union sued, charging that CNG unilaterally changed the method of calculating the contribution, which increased retirees' obligations. The District Court for the District of Connecticut held in mid-2013 that the retiree health benefits were not vested, so there was no ERISA or labor law violation if the employer changed the calculation method. The employee benefits handbook specifically disclosed that the company's contribution was fixed, and consequently retirees might have to pay more cost sharing. Because the benefits were not vested, the change was not a breach of fiduciary duty under ERISA. However, the district court allowed the plaintiffs to pursue another ERISA fiduciary breach claim, one based on failure to provide sufficient information to the retirees about material modification of the plan. The retirees could also pursue claims that the premiums were excessive, because it was possible that the plan collected excessive premiums for its own benefit when it had an obligation to promote the interests of the plan participants. [*Connecticut Indep. Util. Workers Local 12924 v. Connecticut Natural Gas Corp.*,No. 3:12-cv-00961-JBA (D.Conn. June 14, 2013); see Bloomberg BNA, *District Court Issues Mixed Rulings in Retirees' Challenge to Increased Premiums* (June 18, 2013) (benefitslink.com)]

However, there are circumstances under which an employer's promise of retiree health coverage will become an enforceable contract. Under the "promissory estoppel" theory, if the employer makes an unambiguous promise of lifetime benefits, it will no longer be permitted to change the plan.

A limitation on this theory is that the plaintiff might be required to prove that he or she would have obtained comparable medical insurance at his or her own expense if the plan had not been misleading about future health benefits. Employers might also be bound by a promise of lifetime no-cost retiree health benefits if employees actually traded cash compensation or some other benefit in exchange for the employer's promise.

The Ninth Circuit found that retirees were entitled to implied vested contractual rights to fully paid-up retirement and health benefits, so their rights were violated when the board of supervisors cut its benefit contribution to $500 a month. The retirees sued, bringing state-law breach of contract and promissory estoppel claims, and federal constitutional due process and Contract Clause claims. The Ninth Circuit held that retirees plausibly alleged that the county made an express contract with implied terms of lifetime health care coverage. The retirees were given another chance to amend their complaint to state a claim of an implied right to benefits based on an express contract—although the Ninth Circuit ruled that this is a heavy burden to sustain. [*Sonoma Cnty. Ass'n of Retired Emp. v. Sonoma Cnty.*, 708 F.3d 1109 (9th Cir. 2013); see Ronald Kramer, Justin T. Curley, and Barbara Borowski, *Ninth Circuit Breathes New Life Into Retirees' Claim for Lifetime Healthcare Benefits*, Seyfarth Shaw ERISA & Employee Benefits Litigation Blog (Mar. 5, 2013) (benefitslink.com). See also *Retired employees Ass'n of Orange Cnty., Inc. v. County of Orange* (Cal. 2011), holding that an express contract created by county ordinance or resolution can create a vested right to healthcare benefits for retirees.]

Another argument that employers can make to cut back or eliminate retiree health benefits is that the benefits were provided under a particular collective bargaining agreement and do not survive the expiration of that agreement unless the agreement specifically calls for their survival. Retirees are no longer employees, and therefore are not part of the bargaining unit. The bargaining agent does not have a duty to represent retirees—and there is a real potential for conflict of interest between current employees and retirees. Retiree benefits are not included among the mandatory subjects of bargaining. [See § 30.07[A]]

There is a circuit split on the issue of whether the promise to pay retiree health benefits ends when the CBA expires. The Sixth Circuit has decided a number of cases using evidence outside the CBA to show that the retiree benefits vested (but this court has allowed cuts in health benefits for active workers who will retire in the future). In contrast, the Seventh Circuit tends to assume that the promises expire when the CBA ends. The Third and Fourth Circuits will treat retiree health benefits as vested—if there is a clear and express statement in the CBA that they will vest. [See Rebecca Moore, *Early Retirees Non-vested in Health Benefits Lack ERISA Standing*, plansponsor.com (Sept. 23, 2008); Pamela A. MacLean, *Retiree Benefit Cutbacks Roil Courts*, Nat'l L.J. (Feb. 16, 2009) (law.com); but see *Dewhurst v Century Aluminum Co.* 649 F.3d 287 (4th Cir. Aug. 22, 2011), discussed in James P. McElligott Jr., McGuireWoods LLP, *Fourth Circuit Rules for Employer in Retiree Medical Lawsuit* (Sept. 20, 2011) (benefitslink .com): the benefits were not vested under either the plan document or the CBA so they did not show a duty to continue the retiree benefits when the CBA expired.]

The First Circuit ruled in mid-2006, in two related cases involving union and non-union retirees that collectively bargained retiree benefits are not presumed to vest. (The retirees were told that dental benefits were for life, and their surviving spouses could have dental benefits for 12 months after a retiree's death—but the plan documents reserved the usual right to amend, modify, or terminate the plan.) The First Circuit held that, for non-unionized retirees, welfare benefits (in this case dental benefits) do not vest unless the employer gives up the right to amend or terminate the benefits. In this case, far from surrendering such a right, the employer told participants that dental benefits would end at age 65. For union-ized retirees, the fact that management did not negotiate about whether the employer intends to retain the right to modify benefits does not create an infer-ence that benefits will remain at the same level for life [*Senior v. NStar Elec. & Gas Co.*, 449 F.3d 206 [unionized retirees] and *Balestracci v. NStar Elec. & Gas Corp.*, 449 F.3d 848 [non-union retirees] (both 1st Cir. 2006)]

The Sixth Circuit reversed a district court determination that a series of CBAs did not provide vested retiree health benefits. The Sixth Circuit's rationale was that an SPD, issued unilaterally and after the fact, cannot supersede a CBA's amendment provisions. The CBA was ambiguous as to whether retiree health ben-efits had to be maintained at the same level for life. The CBA obligated the com-pany to give each employee an individual contract guaranteeing retiree health benefits until age 65, with reimbursement for Medicare Part B premiums after age 65. The SPD included a reservation of rights clause permitting amendment or modification at any time. The Sixth Circuit found that the CBA was at least ambiguous about supplemental insurance after age 65 and the extent of prescrip-tion drug coverage. Because the CBA's zipper clause forbade amendment with-out mutual signed consent, the CBA could not be unilaterally modified by SPDs. [*Prater v. Ohio Educ. Ass'n*, 505 F.3d 437 (6th Cir. 2007)]

In 2006, the Seventh Circuit permitted insurance benefits described as "life-time" to be terminated, based on the employer's reservation of the right to alter the benefits, and under the principle that when a nonambiguous CBA expires, so does the obligation to provide any benefits that have not vested. In this reading, unless the contract provides for vesting, welfare benefits are presumed to termi-nate when the CBA ends, unless a party can show latent ambiguity in the con-tract. In the Seventh Circuit's view, contract language providing benefits for surviving spouses until their death or remarriage refers only to eligibility, not duration; the duration of the benefit is limited to the CBA term. Statements by company officials that benefits would continue for life were held not to be defini-tive because they could not supplant the CBA language. [*Cherry v. Auburn Gear Inc.*, 441 F.3d 476 (7th Cir. 2006). See also *UAW v. Rockford Powertrain, Inc.*, 350 F.3d 698 (7th Cir. 2003) for the proposition that benefit eligibility ends with the CBA unless the benefits are vested, and *Barnett v. Ameren Corp.*, 436 F.3d 830 (7th Cir. 2006) for the proposition that statements by company officials do not replace the contractual language.]

Another Sixth Circuit case required the restoration of lifetime health ben-efits for retirees—even though the corporation had reorganized in the interim and the employer retained the right to terminate or modify the benefits—because the benefits were vested under a labor contract. Management and union entered into a letter of agreement capping the employer's obligation, but stating that no cov-ered person would have to pay any part of the excess over the cap before a stipu-lated date. After the merger, retirees were billed $56 a month for coverage. The employer and union set up a transition fund, but when it ran out, the premium rose to $290 and then $501 a month, leading the retirees to move for a declaratory judgment that they did not have to pay the increased premiums because of their vested right to lifetime coverage. The Sixth Circuit granted a preliminary injunction because of the risk of harm to the retirees and the likelihood that they would prevail, saying that although welfare benefit plans can expire or be changed at the end of a CBA, courts have the power to interpret ambiguous provisions that might be deemed to create vested benefit rights. (The retirees introduced substantial extrinsic evidence of intent that the benefits last for their lifetimes, including documents about lifetime coverage.) [*Yolton v. El Paso Tenn. Pipeline Co.*, 435 F.3d 571 (6th Cir. 2006). In mid 2011, the case was settled. El Paso continued to deny liability but, to resolve the long-lasting suit, agreed to provide a managed care plan for retirees not eligible for Medicare, to pay for Medicare Supplement coverage for Medicare-eligible retirees, and to continue dental, vision, hearing, and life insurance benefits for the life of all retirees. [*Yolton v. El Paso Tennessee Pipeline Co.*, No. 2:02-cv-75164-PJD-DAS (E.D. Mich. 2011); see Rebecca Moore, *Settlement Approved in Years Long Retiree Benefit Case*, plansponsor .com (Aug. 23, 2011)]

In another successorship case, the Seventh Circuit held that the plant closing agreement promised lifetime benefits. The Seventh Circuit drew a distinction between a plant shutdown agreement, creating an enduring relationship, and a CBA, which is a short-term agreement that is not presumed to create rights after the termination date: *Temme v. Bemis Co Inc.*, 622 F.3d 730 (7th Cir. 2010)]

The Ninth Circuit upheld summary judgment for plaintiffs who were employed by Hughes and then its successor corporation Raytheon, finding that the obligation to pay retirees' health premiums survived the three-year term of each CBA. The CBAs explicitly provided that fully paid coverage would continue until the retirees reached age 65, an obligation that continued after the CBA ended. The Ninth Circuit held that the agreement to pay retiree premiums continued beyond the CBA, although it did not continue for active employees. Raytheon could terminate medical benefits to the extent allowed by the plans, but could not terminate the agreement to continue paying premiums. However, the Ninth Circuit said that the plaintiffs did not introduce proof that would justify punitive damages for breach of the CBA. [*Alday v. Raytheon Co.*, 620 F.3d 1219 (9th Cir. 2010)]

This opinion was withdrawn in May, 2012. The substitute opinion said that Raytheon did not have authority to abrogate benefit obligations that had been collectively bargained. The CBAs before 2003 required the employer to pay health premiums for workers who contributed 3% of their salary to the plan. The principles of contract law made coverage available to age 65. Once again, the Sixth Circuit held that punitive damages were not available. [*Alday v. Raytheon Co.*, 693 F.3d 772 (9th Cir. 2012)]

In January 2013, Raytheon agreed to settle the long-running litigation by reimbursing the *Alday* plaintiffs 100% of the premiums they paid after Raytheon's

2004 policy change. Plaintiffs in a related 2009 case will receive a percentage of their out of pocket medical costs after waiving Raytheon coverage. [GoIAM.org, *IAM, Retirees at Raytheon Win Long Battle for Justice*,<http://www.goiam.org/index.php/imail/latest/10988-iam-retirees-at-raytheon-win-long-battle-for-justice-> (Jan. 29, 2013)]

A class of 277 plaintiffs worked for Westinghouse before Siemens purchased the unit where they worked in late 1997. The Westinghouse plan said that benefits would not be payable to employees who were hired by a purchaser or if their employment ended after 1998. Under ERISA § 208, plan participants cannot be denied benefits when their plan consolidates with another plan or transfers its assets and liabilities to another plan. In this case, however, liabilities were transferred, but ERISA does not provide an entitlement to benefits that did not exist under the original plan. ERISA § 204(g) does not protect the cutback of an early retirement benefit for someone who has not satisfied the conditions for receiving the benefit. These plaintiffs were offered employment by the successor, so they did not qualify. The Third Circuit said that, because Siemens did not establish or maintain the plan, it could not be liable for benefits. [*Shaver v. Siemens Corp.*, 670 F.3d 462 (3d Cir. 2012); see Amaris Elliott-Engel, *3rd Circuit Rejects ERISA Benefits for Siemens Plaintiffs*, The Legal Intelligencer (Mar. 1, 2012) (law.com)]

The Seventh Circuit held that it was a breach of fiduciary duty to increase the retiree health insurance premium without notice to the participants. When the plaintiff retired, the CBA required the plan to apply the value of his accrued but unused sick leave toward his 10% share of the health insurance premium. Without notice, the plan administrator increased the plaintiff's share of the premium to 100% and billed him for additional payments. The Seventh Circuit held that retirees are entitled to notice of changes in the plan; both unwritten and secret modifications are forbidden. Because of the plan's deceptive conduct, the Seventh Circuit upheld an award of restoration of accrued sick leave benefits, plus attorneys' fees. [*Orth v. Wisconsin State Employees Union*, 546 F.3d 868 (7th Cir. 2008); see Robert L. Abell, Kentucky Employment Law Blog, *Retirement Plan Manager Breached Fiduciary Duty by Secretly Increasing Retirees' Medical Insurance Premiums*, <http://www.typepad.com/t/trackback/2757018/34931625> (Oct. 24, 2008)]

The Sixth Circuit ruled that, in arbitration about changes in a corporation's health plan, the union can represent retirees as well as active workers. However, although the union automatically has status to represent the actives, consent of the retirees is necessary. Although retirees are no longer part of the bargaining unit, management and union can still bargain on the subject of retiree health benefits and, once they do that, retirees can have enforceable rights to those benefits. In fact, retirees can have individual rights under LMRA § 301 that active workers do not have (because the union is their sole representative). So they must consent to being represented by the union because when the union represents them, their individual claims are waived. [*Cleveland Elec. Illuminating Co. v. Utility Workers Union of Am., Local 270*, 440 F.3d 809 (6th Cir. 2006)]

The IBEW sought to compel arbitration of a claim that reducing retiree benefits violated the CBA. The Ninth Circuit compelled arbitration, rejecting the employer's argument that the union required the consent of the retirees to pursue the grievance. The Ninth Circuit's rationale was that reductions in retiree benefits also affect the current employees who are represented by the union under an ongoing CBA. Active workers' compensation includes future retirement benefits. [*IBEW Local 1245 v. Citizens Telecommunications Co.*, 549 F.3d 781 (9th Cir. 2008)]

## § 9.09  TAX ISSUES FOR RETIREE HEALTH BENEFITS

Internal Revenue Code § 419A(c)(2) permits the employer to deduct the cost of retiree health benefits as part of a nondiscriminatory funded welfare plan. Key employees' retiree health benefits must be drawn from separate accounts, not the main account. Failure to maintain the separate accounts, or discrimination in furnishing retiree health benefits, is penalized by the 100% excise tax on disqualified benefits imposed by I.R.C. § 4976.

A funded welfare plan can maintain a reserve for future retiree health benefits, funded over the work lives of employees, without violating the account limit. The reserve must use a level-basis actuarial determination, making use of reasonable assumptions and current medical costs.

The Voluntary Employees' Beneficiary Association (VEBA) [I.R.C. § 501(c)(8)] is a possible funding vehicle for retiree health benefits. Caution must be exercised. The VEBA is a tax-exempt organization, so its investment income is subject to taxation. VEBAs are required to use current health costs to calculate the contributions to be made for future retirees. So if costs increase more than anticipated, or if retirees use more health care than expected, the VEBA may be exhausted.

One of the most important functions of ERISA is to make sure that pensions are properly funded in advance of the time that benefits must be paid. However, with respect to retiree health benefits, prefunding is allowed but not required. An argument can be made both for prefunding and for keeping the benefits unfunded.

Unfunded benefits are unsecured and can be changed at any time. They give rise to a large annual expense under the FASB rules. This expense generally increases over time, and can be higher than the pension expense precisely because of the mandate of prefunding pensions. There will also be a large accrued liability on the corporate books. The income received on sums that remain general assets of the corporation (because the money is not dedicated to prefunding retiree health benefits) is taxable. The employer's income tax deduction attributable to the retiree health plan is limited to the annual cost of benefits actually paid in that year.

In contrast, if the plan is funded, the money dedicated to this purpose is protected from diversion. Therefore, the plan is not very flexible. However, the corporation can accelerate its tax deduction, and there is more opportunity to manage the tax deduction. The corporation receives the investment income of a 401(h) account tax-free. Such income reduces the operating expenses of the plan and helps level out the future expenses. That makes the plan's accounting results look more favorable—and therefore the company will have less incentive to cut the benefits in the future.

Early in 2003, the Tax Court held in *Wells Fargo & Co. v. Comm'r* [120 TC 69 (2003)] that employers could deduct the cost of prefunding the present value of retiree medical benefit liabilities for current retirees. The employer deducted the entire amount under Code § 419(c)(2) as a retiree medical benefits reserve, funded over the working lives of the covered employees, actuarially determined on a level basis using assumptions that are reasonable when taken in the aggregate. The Tax Court treated this as a proper deduction, because if the year in which the allocation is first recognized occurs after the employee's retirement, there are no future years to which the benefit can be allocated. Therefore, there are no future normal costs, and the entire present value of the project benefit can appropriately be allocated to the first year.

## § 9.10  MPDIMA AND THE MEDICARE INTERFACE

### [A]  In General

There are two ways a person can qualify for Medicare: either being completely and permanently disabled for a period of at least two years—or reaching age 65. Income and assets are irrelevant—and so is employment status. In other words, people who are still working can be entitled to Medicare benefits (although the employer's group health plan will usually be the primary payor) but a person under 65 who is not disabled will not qualify for Medicare merely because he or she is retired. Nor does Medicare provide benefits for the under 65 spouses of retirees (or retirees' dependent children, if the unusual case but not impossible case that they have any).

The Medicare system includes "secondary payor" rules under which retirees can elect to make Medicare the primary payor for their medical care, with the employer group health plan merely the secondary payor. However, the employer does not have this option, and is not permitted to draft the health plan to make Medicare the primary payor.

Because of its role as secondary payor, Medicare is entitled to seek reimbursement from any entity (including Medicare beneficiaries, health care providers and suppliers, and attorneys) that has received payment from a primary payor. Rules published in 2006 clarify the statutory definitions, including the legal basis for recovery when Medicare paid first although it should have been secondary. If the primary payor is an EGHP or large group health plan, all of the employers that sponsor or contribute to the plan must reimburse Medicare, whether the plan is insured or self-insured. [71 Fed. Reg. 9466 (Feb. 24, 2006)]

If the EGHP fails to make primary payments for active employees of Medicare age, or the Medicare-age spouse of a plan participant, double damages under the Medicare Act or treble damages under the False Claims Act can be imposed. However, the EGHP is exempt from the secondary payor rule if it has fewer than 20 employees; if the participant receives treatment for End Stage Renal Disease; or if the participant is in a large group health plan is disabled. A Medicare regulation dating from February 2006, amending 42 C.F.R. § 411.22, makes it clear that an EGHP must reimburse the Medicare system in any case in which the EGHP was the primary payor, even if it mistakenly paid a health care provider or the beneficiary and did not retain the funds for its own benefit. The Medicare system can seek reimbursement, and perhaps double damages, from anyone responsible for payments, including self-insured EGHPs and Third Party Administrators.

Effective January 1, 2009, the Medicare, Medicaid, and SCHIP Extension Act of 2007 (SCHIP Act; Pub. L. No. 110–173) imposes new Medicare Secondary Payor reporting requirements. EGHPs must find out which participants are Medicare-eligible, and report to CMS for use in the agency's enforcement efforts. Failure is subject to a CMP of $1,000 per day as well as the regular MSP penalties such as the excise tax.

[McDermott Newsletters, *Medicare Secondary Payor Reporting Requirements Will Affect Self-Insured Health Care Providers, Captive Insurers* (Jan. 6, 2009) (benefitslink.com)]

The D.C. Circuit ruled in early 2012 that people over 65 cannot opt out of Medicare Part A while still receiving Social Security benefits. (The suit was brought by plaintiffs who sued that Part A coverage harmed them because it limited their ability to receive private insurance benefits.) The D.C. Circuit said that Part A coverage is automatic with Social Security, and can only be rejected by rejecting Social Security benefits. [*Hall v. Sebelius*, 667 F.3d 1293 (D.C. Cir. 2012); see Spiral Group for HighRoads Blog, *Employees Cannot Opt Out of Medicare Part A Without also Rejecting Social Security Benefits* (Feb. 21, 2012) (benefitslink.com)]

Medicare is only a secondary payor, and not a primary payor, with respect to Worker's Compensation, so employers and insurers must also report WC claims involving Medicare beneficiaries to CMS. If Medicare pays medical expenses for such a worker, it is entitled to be reimbursed if there is a recovery from an insurer or tort defendant. The claims that must be reported are those involving a Medicare beneficiary who has received a settlement, judgment, award, or other medical expense reimbursement on or after July 1, 2009. [Littler, Mendelson Press Releases, *New Medicare Secondary Payor Reporting Obligations for Workers' Compensation Plans*, <http://www.littler.com/PressPublications/Lists/ASAPs/DispAsaps.aspx?id=1359&asapType=National> (April 2009)]

## [B] MPDIMA Statute and Regulations

The Medicare Prescription Drug, Improvement and Modernization Act of 2003 (abbreviated MPDIMA) [Pub. L. No. 108-173], in addition to creating the Health Savings Account plan type discussed in § 18.09, and including provisions for the Medicare Advantage managed-care system to replace the existing Medicare + Choice plans, also enacted the Medicare Part D prescription drug insurance program. MPDIMA includes provisions of special interest to employers. Many employers will take advantage of the availability of prescription drug benefits under Medicare to terminate or cut back their own retiree health benefit programs. To limit the number of employers who will do so, Congress included a program of subsidies for employers who provide prescription drug coverage that is "actuarially equivalent" to the Medicare coverage. That phrase is in quotation marks, because there are significant accounting questions still to be resolved about what constitutes actuarial equivalence for this purpose.

Part D is voluntary: Medicare beneficiaries decide whether or not to enroll. They pay a monthly premium (e.g., $30 a month), then are responsible for an annual deductible of $250 before they receive any coverage under Part D. They are also required to make copayments for certain drug costs. Until 2020, there is a "doughnut hole": at certain levels of drug spending, Part D beneficiaries must pay the full cost of their drugs. Once they have satisfied a certain amount of payment, Part D pays the full cost of additional drugs used by the Part D recipient. As a result of PPACA, the "doughnut hole" is being phased out between 2011 and 2020. For Medicare-eligible individuals who are retired, and who enroll in Part D, Part D (and not the employer's retiree health plan) becomes the primary payor for medications.

Employers can coordinate with Part D in several ways—by paying retirees' Part D premiums, or by providing supplementary coverage when retirees pay their own Part D premiums. [Segal Capital Checkup, *COBRA and the Medicare Part D Retiree Subsidy*, <http://www.segalco.com/publications/capitalcheckup/05606no2pf.zhtml> (May 16, 2006)].

For 2013, the cost threshold is $325, the initial coverage limit is $2,970, the out-of-pocket threshold is $4,750. The minimum copayment under the catastrophic portion of the benefit is $2.65 for generic or multi-source drugs and $6.60 for other drugs. [<http://www.cms.gov/Medicare/Health-Plans/MedicareAdvtgSpecRateStats/downloads/Announcement2013.pdf>; see EBIA Weekly, *CMS Issues Medicare Part D Benefit Parameters for 2013* (Apr. 26, 2012) (benefitslink.com)] 2013 was the third year in a row when the Medicare Part D premium remained essentially unchanged. However, progress toward closing the "doughnut hole" saves Medicare beneficiaries with high prescription drug costs an average of $629. [AP, Yahoo news, *Gov't: Medicare Drug Plan Premiums Stable For* (Aug. 6, 2012) (benefitslink.com)]

The 2014 parameters are somewhat lower than those for 2013. The cost threshold (Part D deductible) is $310, the initial coverage limit is $2,850, the out-of-pocket threshold is $4,550, the minimum copayment under the catastrophic portion of the benefit is $2.55 for generic and preferred drugs, $6.35 for other drugs. For 2014, in the "donut hole" there is a 28% plan benefit (and, therefore, 72% responsibility for the retiree) for generic drugs, and 2.5% benefit (97.5% paid by the retiree) for brand-name drugs. These coinsurance amounts are counted to reach the out-of-pocket maximum. [Buck Consultants FYI, *CMS Releases 2014 Medicare Part D Benefit Parameters*, <http://www.buckconsultants.com/portals/0/publications/fyi/2013/FYI-2013-0409a-CMS-releases-2014-Medicare-Part-D-benefit-parameters.pdf> (Apr. 9, 2013). CMS announced that, as of the first quarter of 2013, 6.3 million Medicare beneficiaries had obtained savings of $6.1 billion on their prescription drugs. [CMS Press Release, *CMS Ensures Greater Value for People in Medicare Drug and Health Plans*, <http://www.cms.gov/apps/media/press/release.asp?Counter=4568> (Apr. 1, 2013)]

MPDIMA requires the plan sponsor to attest to the Department of Health and Human Services at least once a year (more often if the agency requests it) that the actuarial value of the prescription drug coverage under the plan is at least equivalent to Plan D coverage. HIPAA disclosures must be made to both the qualified covered retirees and to HHS as to the extent to which the employer's plan offers creditable coverage (see § 19.05). Disclosure is made by e-filing at <http://www.cms.hhs.gov/CreditableCoverage>. Employers have several choices for handling retiree prescription drug coverage, e.g., include offering drug coverage that is at least the actuarial equivalent of Part D, and receiving the subsidy; creating a wrap-around plan to supplement Part D (foregoing the subsidy) and operating a private drug plan under contract with CMS. (This last option will probably be taken only by very large employers.)

Under the final regulations, to receive the subsidy, an employer must:

- Provide prescription drug coverage under a program that constitutes "creditable coverage" (the concept of creditable coverage is important because it determines whether someone who delays enrolling in Part D because of being covered by another plan will be able to avoid paying the late enrollment penalty);

- Notify eligible participants whether the program qualifies as creditable coverage;

- Satisfy the final regulation's definition of actuarial equivalence;

- Submit an application to CMS by September 30 of each year, disclosing data about plan participants and attesting that the plan is actuarially equivalent to Part D.

- Final Regulations were issued in 2011 to incorporate PPACA changes, clarify the requirements for Part D participation, and explain coordination of Part D benefits with other health benefits. The time for employees to enroll in Part D has been changed from the former period of November 15 to December 31 each year to October 15 to December 7. Therefore, employers must update their notices of creditable coverage to reflect this change. [76 Fed. Reg. 21431 (Apr. 15, 2011); see Buck Consultants FYI, *PPACA Change to Medicare Part D Enrollment Period Impacts Notices of Creditable/Non-Creditable Coverage* (May 20, 2011) (benefitslink.com); *EBIA Weekly, HHS Issues Final Medicare Part D Regulations* (Apr. 21, 2011) (benefitslink.com)]

PPACA, the health care reform bill, maintains the subsidy for companies that provide retiree prescription drug benefits. However, it provides that, starting in 2013, the subsidy will no longer be tax-deductible. [Kris Maher, Ellen E. Schultz, and Bob Tita, *Deere, Caterpillar: Health-Care Law to Raise Expenses*, WSJ.com (Mar. 26, 2010)]

## [C]  Accounting Issues Under MPDIMA

As noted above, PPACA removes the corporate tax deduction, as of 2013, for the retiree health benefit prescription drug subsidy. David Zion, a Credit Suisse analyst, said that the S&P 500 companies will suffer a $4.5 billion loss in first quarter earnings. Large companies said that the loss of this deduction would have a severe negative impact on their earnings. Some of them took a charge against earnings in 2009 to reflect the unavailability of this tax deduction in the future. John Deere & Co. took a $150 million one time charge because of the loss of deduction; Caterpillar Inc. took a $100 million charge (about 40,000 retirees receive drug benefits from the company), and AK Steel took $31 million. The companies say they need the charge now to reflect future tax deductions that will not be available. [Kris Maher, Ellen E. Schultz, and Bob Tita, *Deere, Caterpillar: Health-Care Law to Raise Expenses*, WSJ.com (Mar. 26, 2010)]

## [D]  *Erie* Issues

The Third Circuit in *Erie County Retirees Ass'n v. County of Erie* [220 F.3d 193 (3d Cir. 2000)] ruled that the ADEA applies to retiree benefits, including health benefits. Therefore in this reading, an employer violates the ADEA by offering Medicare-eligible retirees health benefits that are inferior to those offered to employees who are not yet eligible for Medicare, unless the employer can demonstrate that it incurred equal costs or provided equal benefits for both retiree groups. On April 16, 2001, when the case was remanded to the lower court, the Western District of Pennsylvania decided that the plan did not satisfy the equal cost/equal benefit test. [*Erie Cnty.*, 140 F. Supp. 2d 466 (W.D. Pa. 2001)]

Although at first the EEOC adopted the Third Circuit's position, in July, 2003, the EEOC proposed "anti-Erie" regulations allowing employers to reduce or eliminate retiree health benefits when a retiree becomes eligible for Medicare. [68 Fed. Reg. 41542 (July 14, 2003), adding 29 C.F.R. § 1625.32]

The EEOC proposal soon became the subject of litigation. AARP sued the EEOC, and the Eastern District of Pennsylvania permanently enjoined implementation of the regulations in March 2005, holding that the EEOC's rule was not entitled to deference because the EEOC violated the plain language and Congressional intent of the ADEA.

However, after the Supreme Court ruled (in an unrelated case) that federal administrative agencies' regulations are entitled to a high degree of deference, Judge Brody reversed her own earlier decision. In June 2007, the Third Circuit affirmed the District Court's change of policy, and ruled that the EEOC had the power to enact the regulation permitting reduction of retiree health benefits for Medicare-eligible retirees, under the section of the ADEA that allows the EEOC to grant exemptions from ADEA requirements. The Third Circuit considered coordination with Medicare to be necessary, proper, and in the public interest, because the EEOC wanted to prevent retiree health benefits from becoming so expensive that no company could afford to offer them. [*AARP v. EEOC*, 489 F.3d 558 (3d Cir. 2007)] In August 2007, the Third Circuit announced its refusal to review its ruling, [Jerry Geisel, *Review of Retiree Health Care Bias Ruling Denied*, Business Insurance (Aug. 22, 2007) (benefitslink.com)] and in March 2008, the Supreme Court refused to hear an appeal of the Third Circuit decision. [*AARP v. EEOC*, No. 07-662, *appeal dismissed* (Mar. 24, 2008)]

In December 2007, the EEOC issued a final rule reflecting the Third Circuit's decision. The EEOC announced that it was creating a narrow exemption from the ADEA's anti-discrimination rule, to allow retiree health plans to coordinate with Medicare or comparable state health programs. Retiree health benefits can be restricted to employees who are not yet eligible for Medicare, or can supplement Medicare coverage—but not at a level identical to coverage for retirees who are not eligible for Medicare. However, the rule affects only the ADEA, not other issues (such as the status of Medicare as secondary payor for Medicare beneficiaries who continue to be employed). [EEOC Final Rule, 72 Fed. Reg. 72938 (Dec. 26, 2007)]

## § 9.11  SOP 92-6 REPORTS

The American Institute of Certified Public Accountants (AICPA) requires health and welfare benefits to prepare SOP 92-6 reports. SOP stands for "Statement of Position." [See the online newsletter by the Segal Company, *Timing Is Everything: Anticipating and Preparing for Higher Retiree Health Expenditures* (June 2001), <http://www.segalco.com/publications/newsletters/june01.pdf>]

The cash flow projections for the 92-6 project the amount of money needed every year to pay health costs. Although prefunding of welfare benefits is not required, it is often a good idea to create an asset pool (e.g., using a VEBA) to generate tax-free investment income that can be used for future costs.

The 92-6 report deals with issues such as the number of active employees, retirees, spouses, and surviving spouses covered by the plan; the cost of plan benefits; and projections of the cost of providing benefits in the future.

## § 9.12 IMPLICATIONS OF THE EMPLOYER'S BANKRUPTCY

Retiree benefits are often central to bankruptcy cases, because the high cost of providing such benefits adds to the financial stress on the company.

The basic rule, as created by *In re White Farm Equipment Co.* [788 F.2d 1186 (6th Cir. 1986)] is that vesting of welfare benefits is not automatic. It is a subject of bargaining, to be contracted for. In that case, the bankrupt company maintained a no-contributory, non-collectively bargained plan that provided retiree benefits. The plaintiffs were retirees who wanted a declaratory judgment (an official statement) that their claims were both valid under ERISA and allowable as bankruptcy claims.

They also asked the court to order the employer to reinstate the plan retroactively and to resume funding it. But the court found that employee benefits regulation is strictly a federal concern. Furthermore, the employer had reserved the power to terminate the plan and could do so at that time.

Ironically, retirees of bankrupt companies may have more protection for their benefits than retirees of solvent companies. Conversely, bankruptcy may solve some of a company's problems while creating others.

Under 11 U.S.C. § 1113, a company that has filed for Chapter 11 status can ask the bankruptcy court for the right to reject an existing collective bargaining agreement, including provisions covering retiree health benefits. The company must disclose the relevant information to the union and bargain in good faith about the termination.

If the company in Chapter 11 was already paying retiree benefits, the Retiree Benefits Bankruptcy Protection Act of 1988 (RBBPA) [Pub. L. No. 100-334] requires medical and disability payments to retirees to continue, on their original terms, either until the parties agree to modify the benefits or the bankruptcy court orders a modification.

The Act includes standards for bankruptcy courts to use in deciding whether a modification is appropriate. Any modifications proposed by the bankruptcy trustee must be equitable, not just to current and former employees, but also to the company's creditors. The retirees must not have had good cause to reject the proposals. The proposed modifications must be necessary to permit the employer to reorganize in bankruptcy on fair terms.

The RBBPA also requires the employer to negotiate with retiree representatives and to disclose the best available information about the employer's financial condition. Generally speaking, the union will serve as the representative of the retirees, unless the union refuses to do so or unless the court rules that a different representative should be appointed. Any party can petition the court to appoint a committee of retirees to represent benefit recipients who are not covered by a collective bargaining agreement.

The court considering the trustee's proposal does not have the power to order benefits lower than the proposed schedule. Once the parties reach an agreement, or once the court orders changes in the benefits, the authorized representative of the retirees can petition the court for an increase, which will be granted if it appears clearly just to do so.

> ■ **TIP:**   The RBBPA's protection does not apply to retirees, their spouses, or dependents if the retiree's gross income was $250,000 or more in the year before the employer's bankruptcy petition. The only exception is retirees who can prove they are unable to get comparable individual health care coverage. Nor does the RBBPA require bankrupt employers to maintain retiree health benefits that were provided by the union, not the employer, prior to the bankruptcy.

Congress returned to the subject of protection of retiree health benefits when the employer files for bankruptcy protection in the 2005 statute, the Bankruptcy Abuse Prevention and Consumer Protection Act (Pub. L. No. 109-8). § 1403 of this statute amends Bankruptcy Code § 1114. If the corporation, at a time it was insolvent, modified retiree benefits during the 180-day period before the bankruptcy filing, then any party in interest has the right to move for a court hearing. After the hearing, the bankruptcy court is required to order reinstatement of the provisions that were altered—unless the court finds that the balance of the equities clearly favors the modification. That is, if the modification is challenged, it is up to the employer to prove that the modification is fair; the opponents of the change don't have to prove its unfairness.

Under Bankruptcy Code § 1114, first the debtor must try to negotiate or get an agreement to modify the benefits from a union or a court-appointed committee representing the retirees. All affected parties must be treated fairly and equally. The debtor must propose only modifications that are necessary to permit its reorganization. The debtor must release relevant information to the representatives of the retirees, and must bargain with them in good faith.

According to the Seventh Circuit, Bankruptcy Code § 1114 was not intended to be the exclusive remedy for disputes between retirees and their bankruptcy representative. Therefore, state law claims (negligence, misrepresentation, promissory estoppel) by retirees who alleged that their union failed to protect benefits that the union promised would be safe are not completely preempted by the Bankruptcy Code. Because the union's duties in bankruptcy are not identical to the duty of fair representation, the claims also are not preempted by the Labor-Management Relations Act. [*Nelson v. Stewart*, 422 F.3d 463 (7th Cir. 2005)]

Retirees of bankrupt companies have access to the Health Coverage Tax Credit (HCTC), which pays 72.5% of health insurance premiums for retirees after a PBGC takeover of their pension plan. (The HCTC was originally scheduled to expire at the end of 2010 but in fact it was not only extended through 2013 but expanded to pay 72.5% of the premium. Eligible retirees are those aged 55–64 and enrolled in a qualified health plan for which they pay more than 50% of the cost. The program provides comprehensive major medical coverage; in some cases, prescription drugs and dental and vision care are also included. The retiree can either pay the other 27.5% of the premium to the HCTC program, which forwards it to the employer, or pay the health insurer directly each month and take a credit on their federal taxes for 72.5% of the premium. [Ellen E. Schultz, *Conquering Retirement Saving: Retiree Health Plans*, WSJ.com (Jan. 28, 2012)]

A mid-2010 decision of the Third Circuit required Visteon Corporation to comply strictly with § 1114 before terminating retiree health benefits—even though the plan documents reserved the right to modify the plan. Although Visteon argued that it had the right to change the benefit structure when there was no bankruptcy case pending, the Third Circuit said that the plain language of § 1114 forbade the modification. [*IUE-CWA v. Visteon Corp.*, 612 F.3d 210 (3d Cir. 2010) Visteon announced that it would terminate the benefits when it exits Chapter 11 and the benefits are no longer protected under bankruptcy law: see Rebecca Moore, *Visteon Ordered to Restore Retiree Benefits*, plansponsor.com (Aug. 18, 2010)]

In connection with Eastman Kodak's restructuring, bankruptcy judge Allan Gropper permitted termination of retiree health benefits at the end of 2012. In October 2012, Kodak reached an agreement with the court-appointed committee of retirees to eliminate $1.2 billion in liability for medical, life insurance, and survivor benefits by paying $650 million in claims and $7.5 million in cash into a fund for future payments. The Official Committee of Retirees also received a $15 million allowed administrative claim that will have priority status in Kodak's reorganization proceedings. [AP, *NY Bankruptcy Judge Allows Kodak To End Retiree Health Benefits As Part Of Restructuring* (Nov.5, 2012) (benefitslink .com); Rebecca Moore, *Court Approves End to Kodak OPEB*, plansponsor.com (Nov. 6, 2012)]

In 2007, the Supreme Court ruled that a bankrupt company does not have a fiduciary duty to consider merging its pension plan into a multi-employer plan. It is not a violation of ERISA to shut down the plan using a standard termination and to purchase annuities to satisfy payment obligations. [*Beck v. PACE Int'l Union*, 551 U.S. 96 (2007)]

Some courts have refused to apply § 1114 if the retiree benefit plan specifically reserves the right to make unilateral changes. If § 1114 does not apply, then the debtor needs only to satisfy the less stringent "business judgment" standard under Bankruptcy Code § 363. [See, e.g., *In re Delphi Corp.*, No. 05-44481 (Bankr. S.D.N.Y. Mar. 10, 2009), discussed in Arthur Carter, Samuel Glass, Scott Night, Kenric Kattner, Lenard Parkins, Stephen Pezanosky, Sarah Foster, Eric Terry, Haynes and Boone, LLP, *Weathering the Storm: Retiree Benefits and Section 1114* (May 27, 2009) (benefitslink.com)]

A company purchased another company under an asset purchase agreement that included a promise of retiree health benefits for the employees of the acquired company. The benefit could not be reduced or premiums increased without the written consent of the seller—who refused to consent. The purchaser company reorganized in bankruptcy, leading to the rejection of the asset purchase agreement. The purchaser company said that the agreement was no longer in force, so retirees' health premiums could be increased substantially. The retirees sued alleging that the asset purchase agreement amended the retiree health plan and the amendment remained valid after the bankruptcy. The Fifth Circuit held that the asset purchase agreement amended the plan, because any writing that follows certain formalities can amend an ERISA plan. The plan survived bankruptcy, and its terms could only be changed with the consent of the seller company. [*Evans v. Sterling Chemicals, Inc.*, 660 F.3d 862 (5th Cir. 2011); see EBIA Weekly, *Provision in Asset Purchase Agreement Amends Plan and Survives Bankruptcy* (Oct. 20, 2011) (benefitslink.com)]

## § 9.13   401(h) PLANS

### [A]   Basic Principles

The basic principle is that assets must remain within a qualified pension plan until they are distributed to participants or beneficiaries. However, the Code permits transfers of certain assets of overfunded plans to special funds known as 401(h) plans that are segregated to provide retiree health benefits.

A 401(h) plan is a pension or annuity plan that also provides incidental health benefits for retirees: benefits for sickness, accident, hospitalization, or medical expenses. The health-type benefits must be subordinate to the plan's main business of offering retirement benefits. The incidental (insurance and health) benefits must not cost more than 25% of the employer's total contributions to a defined benefit plan.

An employer that maintains a 401(h) plan must maintain separate accounts for retiree health benefits and pension benefits. The transfers are not treated as reversions to the employer, so the § 4980 excise tax is not imposed. The employer must make reasonable and ascertainable contributions to fund the retiree health benefits. These contributions must be distinct from the contributions to fund pension benefits. At first, Code § 420(b)(5) allowed one transfer a year to a 401(h) account for tax years beginning between January 1, 1991–December 31, 2005;

this was extended until December 31, 2013 by the Pension Funding Equity Act of 2004, Pub. L. No. 108-218.

Before making a transfer to a 401(h) plan, the plan administrator must give the DOL at least 60 days' notice, and must also notify participants, beneficiaries and any union representing the participants.

The American Jobs Creation Act of 2004 (AJCA) amends I.R.C. § 420, so that, for tax years after the date of the AJCA's enactment, the determination of whether a 401(h) plan satisfies the minimum cost requirements during the five years after a transfer of pension assets permits the employer to reduce costs only as much as they would have been reduced if the employer had used the maximum amount permitted under current Regulations. In effect, overall benefit costs for all retirees can be cut by the same amount that would have been saved by reducing the number of retirees. [Ellen E. Schultz, *More Retirees May See Health Cuts*, Wall St. J., Oct. 14, 2004, at A5]

The Pension Protection Act of 2006, Pub. L. No. 109-280, permits a plan whose assets are at least 120% of current liability to transfer at least two years' worth of estimated retiree health costs to the 401(h) plan. However, for the year of the transfer, the employer must either make plan contributions sufficient to keep the plan funded at the 120% level, or must recoup money from the 401(h) plan until the 120% level is reached. Transfers to fund the expected cost of retiree health benefits that must be paid in the future under Collective Bargaining Agreements are also permitted, as long the employer used at least 5% of its 2005 gross receipts to provide retiree health benefits.

[PBGC Proposed Rules, *Pension Protection Act of 2006; Conforming Amendments; Reportable Events and Certain Other Notification Requirements*, RIN 1212-AB06 74 Fed. Reg. 61248 (Nov. 23, 2009)]

The Moving Ahead for Progress in the 21st Century Act (MAP-21; Pub. L. No. 112-141) extends the authorization of 401(h) plans, which was supposed to expire in 2013, until December 31, 2021. Plans that achieve more than 125% of their funding target and target normal cost are allowed to transfer excess funds to a 401(h) plan covering either retiree health benefits or retiree group-term life insurance (generally limited to $50,000 per person). The provision for life insurance benefits is added by MAP-21. Life insurance assets must be kept in a separate account within the plan, separate both from the retiree medical account and from the defined benefit plan.

## [B] Final Regulations

Effective June 19, 2001, the IRS issued final regulations on the I.R.C. § 420 minimum cost requirements. [T.D. 8948, R.I.N. 1545-AY43] An employer that significantly reduces its retiree health coverage during a cost maintenance period does not satisfy the I.R.C. § 420(c)(3) minimum cost requirement. The Uruguay

Round Agreements Act of 1994 [Pub. L. No. 103-465] shifted the focus in regulating 401(h) plans from health costs to health benefits, allowing the employer to take into account cost savings recognized in managing retiree health benefit plans, as long as the employer keeps up substantially the same level of coverage for the four years after the transfer as for the year of the transfer itself and the year before the year of the transfer.

# PART III

# PENSION PLAN ADMINISTRATION

CHAPTER 10

# ADOPTING AND ADMINISTERING A PLAN

## § 10.01 INTRODUCTION

The process of creating a plan and getting it approved by the IRS and Department of Labor is exacting. Many alternatives are permitted, and choosing one of them requires projections about the future of the business, the future of the workforce, trends in the economy as a whole, and the laws, court decisions, and regulations that will come into effect in the future. For plans that are subject to ERISA Title I, the Department of Labor must be notified. The IRS does not have to be notified of the intention to adopt a qualified plan, unless and until a determination letter is sought. The employees must always be notified of the adoption of a plan.

Once the plan is in operation, its activities are subject to regulation both on the ERISA and on the tax front.

An ERISA employee benefit plan requires several elements. At a minimum, there must be an intended benefit, an intended beneficiary or group of beneficiaries, a source of financing, a procedure for claiming benefits, and an ongoing administrative scheme.

Plan administration is difficult, painstaking, and mistakes can incur heavy penalties. For these and other reasons, it is common for tasks to be delegated to service providers. Because the term "third-party administrator" (TPA) does not have a uniform definition, it is difficult to estimate how many TPAs there are. An estimate from early 2012 is that about half of all workers covered by private industry plans are covered by plans with some degree of TPA involvement in administration, although some TPAs carry out quite sophisticated tasks, whereas others just process clerical transactions. [Fred Hunt, *Numbers: How Many TPAs are There? Explanation and Legal Liability Factors*, Society of Professional Benefit Administrators (January 2012) (benefitslink.com)]

The PBGC proposed a rule in mid-2009, amending its benefit payment regulations to conform to USERRA amendments. The proposed rule says that as long as a servicemember is re-employed within the USERRA time limits, the servicemember is treated as qualified as of the plan's termination date—even if re-employment occurred after the termination date. The effect is that more servicemembers will be entitled to PBGC-guaranteed benefits. [F.R. Doc E9-17623, *USERRA Benefits Under Title IV of ERISA*, 74 Fed. Reg. 37666 (July 29, 2009)]

Federal Reserve Board (FRB) regulations revised July 1, 2010 exempted most plan loans from Truth in Lending Act (TILA) disclosure requirements. The FRB decided that, in essence, plan loans involve the participant's own money, so there is no third-party creditor whose actions require regulation. Therefore, as of July 1, 2010, TILA does not apply to loans made to a plan participant consisting of fully vested funds from the participant's own account in a qualified plan, although loans made to a plan beneficiary or an alternate payee under a QDRO continue to be subject to TILA. The TILA exception is limited to loans that satisfy Code § 72(p) (i.e., they are amortized levelly over a term of no more than five years, and the loan amount does not exceed the permitted amount). For plans subject to ERISA disclosure requirements, the SPD must disclose the fees and charges that can be imposed on plan loans. [Deloitte's Washington Bulletin, *Most Plan Loans Now Exempt from Truth-in-Lending Act Disclosures* (Aug. 9, 2010) (benefitslink.com)]

The DOL has increased the size of its staff to target violations of the fiduciary, reporting, and disclosure requirements. In 2010, the DOL performed 3112 civil investigations, almost three-quarters of which found at least one violation. A mid-2011 article gives advice about staying out of trouble:

- Deposit participant contributions as soon as possible; this is a major enforcement priority for the DOL. Because most companies have the capacity to transfer funds electronically, the DOL considers the earliest data possible to be within a few days of the pay date—possibly even the same day. Form 5500 requires disclosure of any time when participant contributions were not transmitted on time; the plan must say "Yes" if there were any late deposits, even if they were corrected. The DOL often sends a follow-up letter requiring proof of corrective action.

- Maintain a proper fidelity bond for the plan—at least 10% of the funds handled. (Form 5500 also asks if the plan has a fidelity bond).

- Respond promptly to participants' requests for information; the penalty for failure can be as high as $110 per day, and complaints to the DOL about this issue often trigger investigations.

- Issue the required benefit statements to participants. For defined contribution plans, this probably means a quarterly statement if the participants can direct their investments, annually otherwise. Defined benefit plans must distribute disclosures at least once every three years, and participants and beneficiaries are entitled to make one request for a statement each year.

- Make sure that fees paid by the plan are reasonable; do not use plan assets for inappropriate expenses.

- Respond promptly to any letters from the DOL requesting information.

[Jennifer A. Watkins, *Six Ways to Limit Your Chances of a Visit from the DOL*, Warner Norcross & Judd LLP (Aug. 9, 2011) (benefitslink.com)]

In 2012 and 2013, the PBGC made sweeping proposals reducing reporting obligations for the vast majority of plans under its jurisdiction.

## [A]   Plan Expenses

Running a qualified plan is a difficult business involving the input of many people, including professional advisors. Not all expenses of administration can be paid from the assets of an employee benefit plan. The decision to use plan assets to pay expenses if a fiduciary decision, subject to ERISA fiduciary enforcement.

As long as the plan document allows, or at least does not prohibit, the use of plan assets for this purpose, ERISA allows payment of reasonable administrative expenses. (If the plan document is silent, expenses can be paid by the plan unless the document requires the employer to pay the expenses.) If the employer has retained the right to amend the plan, a prospective amendment can be made to allow payment of expenses from plan assets.

Individual account plans can set out a method for allocating the expenses paid by the plan to participants' accounts. Any allocation method described by the plan is a settler decision, and plan fiduciaries must abide by it. If the plan is silent or unclear, the fiduciaries must select a reasonable method of allocation.

Because businesses are not required to have pension or benefit plans at all, ERISA permits (within limits) the plan to be established, amended, or terminated as the sponsor wishes. Such activities are settlor functions. However, if the employer administers the plan, it acts as a fiduciary. Although settlor decisions are not subject to fiduciary standards, expenses for settlor activities must be paid by the employer—and plan assets cannot be used for this purpose.

Settlor functions include setting up, amending, and terminating a plan, so it is improper for the plan to pay for, for instance, plan design studies, drafting of discretionary plan amendments, determining if the employer satisfies financial accounting standards, and negotiating with a union about proposed plan amendments.

If the plan pays legal expenses, the person who receives the advice will probably find it impossible to deny that the advice was received in a fiduciary capacity—which could make lawyer-client privilege unavailable.

Expenses that probably can properly be paid from plan assets include:

- Providing required disclosures to participants, including SPDs, SARs, required benefit statements, and complying with disclosure requests from participants,

- Communicating with participants about issues such as benefit windows. (Allocation is required if the communication relates to more than one plan, or combines plan and non-plan information,

- Making calculations to implement a plan merger or spin-off,

- Maintaining tax-qualified status (applying for a determination letter; performing nondiscrimination testing; drafting plan amendments needed to comply with ERISA or Internal Revenue Code changes),

- TPA expenses,

- PBGC premiums,

- ERISA bond,

- Fiduciaries liability insurance for the fiduciaries of the plan—but only if the policy gives the insurer recourse against the fiduciary for losses due to breach of fiduciary obligations,

- Making legally required reports, such as Form 5500,

- Enrollment and claims processing,

- Recordkeeping, including preparing audited financial statements,

- Investment management and advice.

The plan can pay the cost of drafting any legally required amendment, but the general rule is that the employer must pay for drafting discretionary amendments, including amendments that relieve the employer of the obligation to pay plan expenses.

## § 10.02  DETERMINATION LETTERS

A determination letter is the IRS' determination that a proposed plan is qualified under I.R.C. § 401(a) or 403(a)—and, if the plan is operated through a plan trust, whether the plan trust is qualified under I.R.C. § 501(a). A qualified plan receives favorable tax treatment: employees are not taxed on contributions to the plan, or increase in the value of these contributions, until the benefits are distributed. From the employer's point of view, it is important that qualified plans give rise to significant tax deductions. Qualified plans are subject to a long list of requirements, and they must be drafted—and operated—in conformity with these rules. The rules change frequently, so the plan must be amended in response to tax code and ERISA changes. There are major negative consequences, including taxes owed and tax penalties, if a plan is ever disqualified.

A plan that has a determination letter and that is amended on a timely basis to conform to changes in the law will probably be able to rebut the IRS' attempts at retroactive disqualification of the plan. [See IRS Publication 794, *Favorable Determination Letter*, < http://www.irs.gov/pub/irs-pdf/p794.pdf> (Oct. 2010)]

The application for a determination letter is made to the IRS Service Center in Covington, Kentucky (P.O. Box 12192; the zip code is 41012-0192). However, if the application is sent by express mail or delivery service, the address is 201 West Rivercenter Blvd., Attn: Extracting Stop 312 Covington, KY 41011 [See IRS, *Determination, Opinion and Advisory Letter for Retirement Plans*, <http://www.irs.gov/retirement/article/0,,id=218529,00.html> (Jan. 12, 2012)]

Interested parties (current employees who will be eligible to participate if the plan is implemented) are entitled to notification that an application has been made. If the plan is collectively bargained, all employees covered by the CBA are entitled to notice. Notice to unionized employees can be given in person (e.g., printed and handed to all employees; slips placed in all pay envelopes), by mailing, or by posting in the usual place for posting employer and/or union notices.

The appropriate time for giving notice to employees is 7–21 days before the IRS gets the application. If the employees are notified by mail, the notices should be mailed 10–24 days before submission of the application.

Employees must be notified because interested parties have the right to comment directly to the IRS about the application. The PBGC or a group of interested parties can also invite the Department of Labor to comment on the application. The PBGC has standing to submit its own comments directly. The comment period runs for either 45 or 60 days after the IRS receives the request for a determination letter.

After 60 days have elapsed, the IRS does its own investigation of the qualification of the proposed plan, including consideration of any comments that have been submitted. A reviewing agent in the relevant IRS Key District Office issues the determination letter (or denies the application). If there are questions about the application, the agent tries to resolve them by telephoning or writing to the company that applied for the determination letter.

If the IRS refuses to issue the letter, there are several levels of review within the IRS, and then the employer has the right to appeal to the Tax Court.

Determination letters are requested on official IRS forms. The IRS charges user fees, depending on the nature of the application. Furthermore, a particular plan may have to apply several times. See Rev. Proc. 2012-6, 2012-1 I.R.B. 197 for the most recent version of the determination letter process.

Nor is initial qualification the end of the process. Plans must continually be amended to keep up with changes in tax law and ERISA—as well as to respond to changes in business and the economic climate.

For an individually designed plan (i.e., one that is drafted to conform to a particular employer's needs), the employer applies for the determination letter. There is a five-year "remedial amendment cycle." The IRS spaces out its workload by having only one-fifth of all individually designed plans apply for determination letters each year. The plan's cycle depends on the last digit in its employer ID number (EIN). Cycle A (plans whose EINs end in 1 or 6) had a due date of January 31, 2012. For Cycle B (EINs ending in 2 or 7), the deadline is January 31, 2013. For Cycle C (EINs ending in 3 or 8), the deadline is January 31, 2014; the Cycle D deadline (EINs ending in 4 or 9) is January 31, 2015, and the Cycle E deadline (EINs ending in 5 or 10) is January 31, 2016.

Master & Prototype and volume submitter plans, which are drafted by a financial service provider, which is also responsible for getting and keeping the plan qualified, are generally reviewed on six-year cycle.

Originally, Rev. Proc. 2011-49, 2011-44 I.R.B. 608 set a January 31, 2012 deadline for the second six-year remedial amendment cycle, but it was extended to April 2, 2012. [John Anderson, *Does Your Qualified Retirement Plan Need to Be Amended This Year?*, Alston & Bird LLP, Employee Benefits & Executive Compensation Advisory (Nov. 7, 2011) (benefitslink.com); Rebecca Moore, *IRS Extends Deadline for Opinion and Advisory Letter Applications*, plansponsor. com (Dec. 22, 2011)]

Announcement 2011-82, 2011-52 I.R.B. 1052 provides that IRS determination letters for qualified plans will no longer consider minimum coverage or most nondiscrimination testing issues. The changes take effect with Cycle B, for submissions made on or after February 1, 2012, with a later effective date for terminating plans. Nor will individual determination letter requests for preapproved plans consider these issues, effective May 1, 2012, when the IRS stopped accepting the Form 5307 Determination Letter application for prototype plans. Volume submitter plans can continue using Form 5307, but only for plans with only minor modifications of pre-approved document language. The coverage and nondiscrimination demonstrations previously filed on Schedule Q have been eliminated. [Mercer Select, *Determination Letters Will No Longer Consider Coverage, Nondiscrimination Testing* (Dec. 19, 2011) (benefitslink.com); Ftwilliam.com, *IRS Eliminates Determination Letters for Pre-approved Plans Without Modifications* (Dec. 19, 2011) (benefitslink.com)]

Between early 2013 and January 31, 2014, Cycle C applications could be filed. Cycle C plans are individually designed plans maintained by an employer whose EIN ends with a 3 or an 8. The determination letter application requires complete restatement of the plan document, including all amendments adopted since the previous restatement. The restatement must also reflect the relevant changes listed in Notice 2012-76 (2012 Cumulative List of Changes in Plan Qualification Requirements), 2012-52 I.R.B. 775. Although the deadline is not until 2014, the IRS notes that documents filed early in a cycle get a faster response. A plan that misses the deadline for applying for a determination letter might be audited and found noncompliant, because its existing determination letter becomes obsolete. Plan administrators should be aware that Notice 2012-70, 2012-51 I.R.B. 712, requires defined benefit plans to be amended by the last day of the 2013 plan year to reflect the restrictions of § 436; for calendar-year plans, the deadline is December 31, 2013, a month earlier than the Cycle C deadline. [Spencer Fane, *IRS Now Accepting "Cycle C" Determination Letter Applications* (Feb. 18, 2013) (benefitslink.com)]

## § 10.03 PROTOTYPE AND MASTER PLANS

The IRS publishes master and prototype plans for the guidance of employers who want to be sure that the plan they adopt satisfies the various requirements for qualification. The significance of the determination letter is that a plan that has one generally will not be disqualified if the IRS subsequently discovers defects in the plan documents. However, this immunity does not extend to operational defects, only to design defects. [Steptoe & Johnson LLP ERISA Advisory, *The 7th Circuit's Big ERISA Day* (Feb. 15, 2011) (benefitslink.com)] A prototype plan has a separate funding mechanism for each employer; a master plan has a single funding mechanism (such as a trust) that covers multiple employers.

It is frequently necessary to amend plans as the tax laws change. The IRS has launched a new cycle for approval of amendments. The IRS divides plans into two groups: the pre-approved and the individually designed. Most pre-approved plans fall into two categories: prototype plans (with very few choices) and volume submitter plans (allowing more options).

The IRS maintains a separate six-year submission cycle for pre-approved plans. For defined contribution plans, volume submitter document sponsors had to submit language for approval by January 31, 2006. The IRS processed all the submissions and issued approval letters for all the approved plans on March 31, 2008, with a filing deadline of April 30, 2010 for all plans using pre-approved documentation.

For individually designed plans, the IRS maintains five-year filing cycles. Cycle A plans, where the last digit of the sponsor's Employer Identification Number (EIN) was 1 or 6, were due January 1, 2007, Cycle B, with EINs ending in 2 or 7, was due January 31, 2008, Cycle C (EINs ending in 3 or 8) was due January 31, 2009, Cycle D (EINs ending in 4 or 9) was due January 31, 2010, and Cycle E (EINs ending in 5 or 0) was due January 31, 2011. [Warner Norcross & Judd LLP, *Deja Vu All Over Again: Remedial Amendment Cycles Recycle* (Feb. 16, 2011) (benefitslink.com)]

As discussed above, a new series of filing cycles has begun: Cycle A (plans whose EINs end in 1 or 6) had a due date of January 31, 2012. For Cycle B (EINs ending in 2 or 7), the deadline is January 31, 2013. For Cycle C (EINs ending in 3 or 8), the deadline is January 31, 2014; the Cycle D deadline (EINs ending in 4 or 9) is January 31, 2015, and the Cycle E deadline (EINs ending in 5 or 10) is January 31, 2016.

The IRS announced in April 2013 that several forms related to pre-approved defined benefit plans had been revised. As of February 1, 2013, plan sponsors and their professional advisors should use the 2013 versions of Form 4461-A (Application for Approval of Master or Prototype or Volume Submitter Defined Benefit Plan and its Attachment 1-A. The user fee for a plan opinion or request for an advisory letter is paid with Form 8717-A. The LRM is the listing of required modifications and information for defined benefits; it has been revised to comply with current law. The IRS encourages sponsors of master and prototype plans not only to use language from the LRM but to identify where in the plan documents it appears. [IRS, *Pre-Approved Defined Benefit Plans— Revised Forms and LRM*, <http://www.irs.gov/Retirement-Plans/Preapproved-Defined-Benefit-Plans-Revised-Forms-and-LRM> (Apr. 25, 2013); see Kevin McGuinness, *IRS Updates DB Forms and Documents*, plansponsor.com (Apr. 30, 2013)]

## § 10.04   ROUTINE TAX COMPLIANCE

### [A]   Necessary Forms

Day-to-day administration of a plan involves creation of tax records and submission of many forms to the IRS and state taxing authorities.

One of the most important forms is Form W-2, disclosing compensation paid to each individual employee. The form must be submitted to the IRS and also to the employee. The normal due date for employee W-2s is January 31 following the end of the year of employment. However, employees who leave during the year have a right to demand that they get a W-2 form within 30 days of the last paycheck (or of the request, if made at a later date). The employer can use IRS Form 8809 to request additional time to file W-2s.

One of the requirements of the health care reform bill, PPACA, is that employers provide information reporting on Form W-2 of the cost of health coverage provided by the employer. This amount is not taxable, but it is relevant to the determination of whether the employer provides adequate coverage, whether it is subject to penalties, and whether the employee is entitled to a subsidy if he or she obtains health insurance through an Exchange. [See § 18.19[K] for more discussion of these issues.]

When PPACA was first enacted, it was intended that the cost of coverage would be reported on the 2011 W-2 forms (distributed in 2012). However, in Notice 2010-69, 2010-44 I.R.B. 576, the IRS recognized that employers need more time to update their payroll systems, so the information does not have to be provided until the 2012 W-2 forms issued in 2013, but can be done voluntarily before then.

Notice 2012-9, 2012-4 I.R.B 315 explains how employers must report the value of EGHP coverage on employees' W-2 forms. At present, this amount does not constitute taxable compensation, but employees must receive this information as part of their decision whether to seek insurance coverage from an Exchange. The value to be reported is based on the COBRA cost of the coverage. Small employers (those who issued fewer than 250 W-2s in 2011) do not have to report the value of health care in 2012, and reporting is not required for MSAs, HSAs, or health FSAs. Someone who would not otherwise get a W-2 form (e.g., a retiree; a former employee who received no compensation that year) does not have to be given a W-2 merely to report health benefits. [Birgit Anne Waidmann, PricewaterhouseCooper HRS Insight, *IRS Provides Guidance on Mandatory Reporting of the Value of Health Coverage on 2012 Forms W-2* (Jan. 6, 2012) (benefitslink. com)]

Other forms include:

- Form W-3: a transmittal form filed with the Social Security Administration consolidating all the W-2 and W-2P forms for the entire company.

The regular due date for any year's W-3 is February 28 of the following year;

- Form W-4P: is used by employees to opt out of withholding or increase withholding on their pension and annuity payments. This form goes straight from employer to employee, no IRS filing is required;

- Forms 941/941E: these are the forms for quarterly returns of federal income tax. Form 941 is used if there are FICA taxes withheld or paid, 941E otherwise. The due date is the end of the month after the close of the calendar quarter being reported on. However, some employers can file an annual Form 944 in lieu of quarterly 941s, if their annual employment tax liability, including income tax withholding, FICA, and Medicare tax, is under $1,000 for the calendar year: [T.D. 9566, 76 Fed. Reg. 77672 (Dec. 14, 2011)]

- Form 945: the report on withheld taxes that are not payroll taxes (e.g., withholding on retirement plan distributions);

- Form 1041: trust income tax return, required if the plan's trust becomes disqualified (or otherwise does not operate as a tax-exempt organization) and if it also has income equal to or greater than $600. The due date is the fifteenth day of the fourth month after the end of the trust's tax year;

- Form 1099-R: 1099-series forms are used to report miscellaneous sums that might otherwise escape the attention of the taxing authorities. The 1099-R is used to report lump sums and periodic distributions. The entire group of a company's transmittal forms requires its own transmittal form, Form 1096. The filing is due by February 28 each year for the preceding year;

  ■ **TIP:**   Within two weeks of making a distribution, the plan administrator must provide each recipient with a written explanation of the tax consequences of taking a lump sum, including how to elect lump-sum tax treatment and how to roll over the sum to another qualified plan or to an IRA.

- Form 5308: form filed in connection with a change in the tax year of a qualified plan or trust;

- Form 5330: excise tax form for failure to meet the minimum funding standard, or for receipt of an impermissible reversion of plan assets. Disqualified persons who engage in prohibited transactions are also required to file this form. There is no fixed due date: the timing depends on the nature of the transaction subject to excise tax. Form 5558 is used to request additional time to file this form;

- Form 8109: the quarterly estimated tax return when a plan trust has unrelated business taxable income (UBTI) [see I.R.C. § 512(a)(1)] from operation of an unrelated trade or business. UBTI is limited to business net income (after deducting the costs of generating the income). It does not include dividends, interest, annuities, loan fees, or royalties;

- Form 8928: used (starting with the 2010 plan year or taxable year) by employers to self-report and pay excise taxes for certain compliance failures of EGHPs—COBRA requirements (including the ARRA premium subsidy, HIPAA rules, mental health parity, the Genetic Information Non-discrimination Act, and failure to make comparable contributions for all employees if there is an HSA or MSA plan. [74 Fed. Reg. 45994 (Sept. 8, 2009), discussed in Guest article, Deloitte's Washington Bulletin, *New for 2010: Employers Must Self-Report Excise Tax for Failure to Comply with Group Health Plan Requirements* (Dec. 14, 2009) (benefitslink. com)]

- Form 8955-SSA, replacing Form 5500 SSA to report information about participants who had deferred vested benefits when they separated from a plan.

See § 18.19 (health care reform) for the forms to be used to comply with the new requirements.

The IRS' project of moving all business tax form filing online is well underway. (The next important planned step is the integration of federal and state tax filings through a coordinated electronic system.) (The TeleFile program, allowing telephone filing of many forms, was discontinued in mid-2005.)

Business taxpayers file taxes via the Electronic Federal Tax Payment System (EFTPS), a highly secure encrypted Website. See <http://www.irs.gov/efile> and IRS Publications 4132, 966, 4169, 4321, 4130, 4276, and 4048. Rev. Proc. 2010-26, 2010-30 I.R.B. 91 provides updated specifications for electronic filing of Forms 1098, 1099, 5498, and W-2G information returns using the FIRE (Filing Information Returns Electronically) system. The new procedure has to be used for preparing tax year 2010 information returns, and information returns for earlier years filed as of January 1, 2011. [CCH Pensions and Benefits, *IRS Updates Specifications for Electronic Filing of Certain 2010 Information Returns, Including Forms 1099-R and 5498* (Aug. 11, 2010) (benefitslink.com)] Notice 1036, <http://www.irs.gov/pub/irs-pdf/n1036.pdf> provides the percentage withholding tables required after February 15, 2013.

For tax years ending on or after December 31, 2005, corporations with assets of $50 million or more that file at least 250 returns a year, including income and employment tax and information returns, are required to file their 1120 and 1120-S forms electronically. The next year, the electronic filing requirement is extended to corporations with assets of more than $10 million who file 250 returns a year. To file electronically, large and mid-size corporations must use the

IRS e-file system Modernized e-File (MeF). W-2 forms also can be submitted electronically, although those forms must be filed with the Social Security Administration rather than the IRS.

On the subject of routine compliance under non-routine circumstances, see Rev. Proc. 2005-27, 2005-20 I.R.B. 1050 for a list of 32 employee benefit issues that are affected automatically whenever the President declares a disaster.

If the contributions to the plan reflect an incorrect amount of compensation, there will be an operational failure, because the operation of the plan will not conform to its terms. A plan is not required to use the same definition of compensation for all types of contributions. For example, discretionary contributions might be allocated based only on base salary, but salary deferral contributions could reflect all compensation, including bonuses and commissions. Compensation errors occur when a payroll processor or TPA does not know the plan's various definitions of compensation, or is not alerted to plan amendments, or if payroll systems are not updated. The Employee Plans Compliance Resolution System (EPCRS) can be used to fix the mistakes. Self-correction without IRS approval is permitted for insignificant errors, or for significant errors that are corrected within two years. However, a plan sponsor is only entitled to self-correct if it has implemented practices and procedures that promote overall tax-law compliance.

The Voluntary Correction Program (VCP) can be used to correct errors, with IRS approval. The VCP submission should explain the plan failure and the proposed correction, including the corrective contributions to be made, and the plan's proposal for improving administration to prevent future errors. The correction method should restore participants to the status they would have been in if there had been no error (for example, making larger contributions, or distributing excess amounts from the plan). If too much compensation was included in the calculations, the correction consists of distributing the excess elective deferrals and earnings to the affected participant, with excess discretionary contributions forfeited as required by the plan document. Forfeitures should either be reallocated to participants based on correct contributions, or transferred to an unallocated account that reduces future contributions.

Conversely, if the error was omitting some forms of compensation from elective deferrals, matches, or discretionary contributions, corrective contributions must be made for the affected participants. For missed salary deferrals, the amount of omitted compensation should be multiplied by the deferral percentage specified in the employee's salary reduction agreement. The missed deferral opportunity is equal to 50% of the omitted compensation. The missed deferral opportunity should be contributed to the employee's account, plus earnings up to the date of the corrective contribution. If discretionary contributions were made to participants for a plan year, the same percentage of omitted contribution should be contributed, plus earnings to the date of correction.

Rev. Proc. 2013-12, 2013-4 I.R.B. 313 updates EPCRS, superseding Rev. Proc. 2008-50 effective April 1, 2013. The VCP submission procedures have been revised to provide rules for plans subject to § 436 restrictions. The safe harbor correction methods and fee structures have been changed.

Rev. Proc. 2013-12 also includes a procedure for using Appendix C, Schedule 1 to correct a failure to adopt a mandatory interim amendment that was required to conform to the PPA or HEART Act. The fee for this program is $375. However, the procedure cannot be used to correct failure to adopt an interim amendment required by a pre-EGTRRA restatement—for example, the 401(k) final regulations. Those failures require correction under Appendix C, Schedule 2, which carries a higher fee. [Sungard Relius, *Correcting a Failure to Adopt an Interim Amendment Under the New EPCRS* (Mar. 19, 2013) (benefitslink.com)]

Rev. Proc. 2013-12 includes model VCP submission documents. These documents are for submissions under Rev. Proc. 2013-12 only, not for submissions made before April 1, 2013 pursuant to Rev. Proc. 2008-50. The documents must be used exactly as published, without modification. The available schedules are:

- Schedule 1, Interim and certain discretionary non-amender failures;

- Schedule 2 Non-amender failures (not covered by schedule 1);

- Schedule 3 SEPs and SARSEPs;

- Schedule 4 SIMPLE IRAS;

- Schedule 5 Plan loan failures;

- Schedule 6 Employer eligibility failure;

- Schedule 7 Failure to distribute excess elective deferrals;

- Schedule 8 Failure to make timely payment of required minimum distributions;

- Schedule 9 correction by plan amendment.

Appendix D is the acknowledgment letter for the filing. Forms 8950 (application for VCP program, including instructions) and Form 8951 (compliance fee) must both be included with the submission.[IRS.gov, updated Jan. 23, 2013 *Correcting Plan Errors—Fill-in VCP Submission Documents*]

Previously, sponsors often used the IRS letter forwarding service to find payees of benefits. For requests postmarked on or after August 31, 2012, however, Rev. Proc. 2012-35, 2012-37 I.R.B. 341 announces that the IRS no longer considers finding missing persons a "humane purpose." Employers must therefore devise other means of finding the payees. The DOL's suggestions are Internet searches, credit reports, and commercial locater services. The Social Security Administration's forwarding service is still available, but at a cost of $25 per letter, whereas the IRS service was free for up to 50 participants. If the plan is terminating, it can use the PBGC's missing participants program, which requires the

employer to submit the amount of the benefit to the PBGC, which looks for par-
ticipants in connection with the termination. The Pension Protection Act man-
dated that the PBGC extend the program to non-defined benefit plans (e.g.,
401(k)s) that terminate, but the PBGC never issued implementing regulations.
[McDermott Will & Emery, *IRS Eliminates Use of Letter Forwarding Service to
Find Missing Participants and Beneficiaries* (Sept. 27, 2012) (benefitslink.com);
Rebecca Moore, *IRS Updates Compliance Resolution System*, plansponsor.com
(Jan. 3, 2013)]

An "operational error" is a failure to comply with the terms of the plan.
Often this can be corrected without IRS involvement and without penalties to the
plan. The sponsor must put the plan and its participants in the position they would
have been in if there had been no error. However, if correction requires a plan
amendment, then it will probably be necessary to use EPCRS, as set out most
recently in Rev. Proc. 2013-12, and to file under the Voluntary Correction Program. However, there are five situations under which a sponsor can use the Self-
Correction Program (SCP) to adopt a retroactive corrective amendment without
making a VCP filing:

- A hardship distribution was made from a plan that did not have a hardship distribution option;

- Making a plan loan where, once again, this option was not included in
  the plan;

- Letting an employee participate in the plan prematurely—before he or
  she satisfied the eligibility requirements;

- Allocating a contribution to correct a violation of the § 401(e)(17) compensation limit;

- Correcting an ADP failure by making a Qualified Nonelective Contribution (QNEC) that would not otherwise be available under the plan.

The plan must comply with the requirements of Code §§ 401(a), 410(b), and
411(d)(6). If the correction is a retroactive amendment to allow hardship distributions or loans, the best practice is to make sure that enough non-highly compensated employees (NHCEs) had access to them to satisfy the nondiscrimination rules. Amendments to change eligibility dates should also
predominantly benefit NHCEs. The general rule is that correcting operational
errors in an individually designed plan by amendment will probably require the
sponsor to make an application for a determination letter reflecting the amendment the next time the plan's cycle requires a determination letter. If the plan terminates before the next cycle, a determination letter including the amendment
will have to be obtained in connection with the termination. But if the plan is an
approved prototype or volume submitter plan, a determination letter is not only
not required for the amendment, the IRS forbids applying for one. [Sungard

Relius, *Self-Correction Program Retroactive Corrective Amendments* (Mar. 29, 2013) (benefitslink.com)]

A forfeiture generally occurs when a participant leaves the employer before becoming fully vested for matching or other employer contributions. The rules permit forfeiture of the non-vested portion, although in practice many plans do not call for forfeiture until there have been five consecutive one-year breaks in service. Mishandling of forfeitures is a common target of IRS audits. The IRS requires forfeitures to be used or allocated for the plan year in which they arise— or, in appropriate circumstances, in the following plan year. Forfeitures can be used to pay reasonable administrative expenses of the plan; to reduce the employer's contribution; to restore previously forfeited participant accounts; or to provide additional contributions to participants. The IRS' position is that forfeitures cannot be used to fund 401(k) safe harbor contributions, because these contributions have to be 100% vested when they are made. Placing the forfeited amounts into a suspense account is not permitted. The most common reasons for not allocating forfeitures on a timely basis are:

- Failure by the sponsor or TPA to monitor the forfeiture account to make sure the allocations are proper;

- Where the plan has both a sponsor and a TPA, each one thinks the other one is monitoring;

- When the plan sponsor incorrectly believes it has more discretion to apply forfeitures than the rules allow;

- When the plan terms do not explain how to handle forfeitures;

- When the sponsor elects not to make discretionary contributions for the plan year; with no contributions to be offset by the forfeited amount, the sponsor does not allocate them;

- When the sponsor does not think of using forfeitures to pay administrative expenses.

In the first two years, mistakes can be corrected with EPCRS. After two years, the VCP must be used unless the failure is considered insignificant. The VCP must be used if the terms of the plan are incorrect and a retroactive plan amendment is required to correct them. [Chadron J. Patton, *Common Plan Mistakes: Failure to Timely Allocate Forfeitures*, Spencer Fane (Nov. 16, 2012) (benefitslink.com)]

In recent years, IRS audits of 401(k) plans often ask the employer for evidence that participants were given the safe harbor notice. Plans that cannot produce this evidence are often asked for corrections and perhaps subjected to a closing agreement sanction. To avoid this problem, the plan should keep a dated copy of the notice and the cover letter sent with it. If the participants were given notice electronically, proper evidence would be a dated copy of the e-mail that was sent and the list of recipients. Failure to give the safe harbor notice is considered failure to comply with the terms of the plan, not just a failure to satisfy the statutory requirements of § 401(k). It is an operational failure that can be corrected under the VSCP, although it is not included in EPCRS. If the participant was aware of his or her eligibility to defer, the employer can correct the failure by giving the notice, even if it is late, and improving its procedures in the future. But if the participant was not aware of the option to defer, the employer must treat the employee as improperly excluded, and make a contribution equal to 50% of the missed deferral, plus any employer match required by the plan and an additional amount to compensate for lost earnings on the amount that should have been contributed. [SunGard Relius, *Failure to Provide Safe Harbor Notice Correction* (Nov. 30, 2012) (benefitslink.com)]

## [B]  Investment-Related Costs

The DOL undertook several measures in 2009–2011 to increase the transparency of defined contribution plan fees. The first step was the new Schedule C requirements that took effect in 2009, enhancing the disclosure that has to be made to the federal government about indirect compensation (revenue sharing) paid to service providers.

The second step was a rule released in July 2010, requiring providers to report to plan sponsors on direct and indirect compensation that the sponsors paid for account services. [EBSA press release, *U.S. Department of Labor Announces Intention to Extend Applicability Date of Section 408(b)(2) Fee Disclosure Regulation* (Feb. 11, 2011) (benefitslink.com); Plansponsor staff, *DoL Extends Applicability Dates for Fee Disclosure Rules*, plansponsor.com (July 13, 2011)] The rule was finalized in early 2012, requiring service providers to give the plan written disclosure of compensation and other information about the arrangement under which services are provided to a defined contribution plan. EBSA published a sample guide to disclosure. The rule took effect July 1, 2012. [77 Fed. Reg. 5632 (Feb. 3, 2012); DOL Fact Sheet, *Final Regulation Relating to Service Provider Disclosures Under Section 408(b)(2)* (February 2012) (benefitslink. com);Tara Cantore, *Plan Sponsors Must Be Aware of Changes in 408(b)(2) Final Rule*, plansponsor.com (Feb. 7, 2012) and *DoL Issues Final Rule on 401k Fee Disclosure*, plansponsor.com (Feb. 2, 2012)]

The DOL requires fiduciaries to be prudent in choosing a fiduciary investment adviser, and must monitor their abilities and qualifications periodically (including whether the adviser continues to comply with securities laws, compliance with the terms of engagement), but the plan's fiduciaries are not obligated to oversee the provision of specific advice. The advisers should be chosen based on an objective process analyzing qualifications, quality of services offered, and the reasonableness of fees. The process must be free of self-dealing, conflict of interest, and improper influence. Advice should be based on generally accepted investment theories. The Pension Protection Act of 2006 (Pub. L. No. 109-280 § 601) adds a prohibited transaction exemption under Code § 4975(d)(17) and ERISA § 409(b)(14) for advice from a fiduciary adviser under an investment advice arrangement.

The DOL published Final Regulations on the selection of annuity providers for individual account plans in late 2008, pursuant to the PPA. Including the option of distributing an individual account plan by purchasing an annuity contract does not trigger the "safest available annuity" standard of Interpretive Bulletin 95-1. However, other fiduciary standards apply. Under the DOL regulations of 2008, fiduciaries can qualify for a safe harbor (for the decision to buy an annuity as a distribution mechanism, not the selection of any particular investment product) by making a thorough, objective, reasoned search before selecting annuity providers, after obtaining enough information to ascertain the provider's ability to comply with the contract, the total cost of the contract including fees and commissions, and how the costs compare to the benefits offered by the transaction. To qualify for the safe harbor, the fiduciary must also retain an appropriate expert to monitor compliance, although the fiduciary is not required to perform ongoing review of the appropriateness of the initial selection. [DOL Reg. § 2550.404a-4, 73 Fed. Reg. 58447 (Oct. 7, 2008); Amendment to Interpretive Bulletin 95-1, 73 Fed. Reg. 58445 (Oct. 7, 2008); Amendments to DOL Reg. §§ 2550.404a-3 and 2578.1, 73 Fed. Reg. 58459 (Oct. 7, 2008); Amendment to PTE 2006-06, 73 Fed. Reg. 58629 (Oct. 7, 2008); Buck Consultants FYI, *DOL Issues Final Regulations on the Selection of Annuity Providers for Individual Account Plans* (Nov. 7, 2008) (benefitslink.com)] See also §§ 6.07[B], 15.15, and 15.17 for discussion of cost issues in the plan context.

## [C]    Satisfying PPA Requirements

The Pension Protection Act (PPA), Pub. L. No. 109-280, although primarily focused on improving the stability of defined benefit plans, has had important effects on other types of plans as well.

Rev. Rul. 2007-67, 2007-48 I.R.B. 1047, held that it does not violate the anti-cutback rule to adopt a plan amendment that adopts the PPA amendments to § 417(e)(3) [actuarial assumptions used in calculating the minimum present value of the accrued benefit]. Accordingly, in the spring of 2008, the IRS proposed amendments to Code § 4980F and ERISA § 204(h), under which a 204(h) notice would not be required if the effect of complying with PPA changes in actuarial assumptions is to reduce a lump sum distribution from a defined benefit plan. [EB095625, REG-110136-07, RIN 1545-BG48, 73 Fed. Reg. 15101 (Mar. 21, 2008). See also Notice 2007-86, 2007-46. I.R.B 990.] However, some cash balance plans must issue 204(h) notices if an amendment to eliminate whipsaw also has the effect of reducing lump sum distributions, and T.D. 9472, 2009-51 I.R.B. 850.

Only about two-thirds of eligible workers participate in 401(k) plans; the PPA promotes automatic enrollment, on the theory that very few workers would actually opt out of a plan once enrolled in it. In September 2006, DOL proposed a regulation explaining the PPA safe harbor for default investments by fiduciaries who have not been instructed by plan participants.

Under the PPA, a plan participant or beneficiary is deemed to have exercised control over the account (thus exonerating the fiduciary) if the fiduciary invests in a "qualified default investment alternative" (QDIA) in a situation where the participant or beneficiary had the opportunity to give investment directions but did not. Notice must be given 30 days before the first investment, and 30 days before each subsequent plan year, explaining the circumstances under which assets will be invested in a QDIA. If the investment gives the plan any materials (e.g., prospectuses for securities), it must be passed along to the participants and beneficiaries.

The participant or beneficiary must be permitted to remove and redirect QDIA funds as often as other plan investments without incurring a penalty—at least quarterly. The plan must offer the broad range of investment alternatives in addition to the QDIA, as required by the ERISA § 404(c) regulations. The QDIA must be diversified, and must be managed by an investment manager or a registered investment company. The QDIA is forbidden to directly invest participant contributions in the employer's stock, and money market and stable value funds are not suitable because their rate of return is too low to provide reliable retirement security. However, life cycle funds, targeted retirement date funds, balanced funds, and professionally managed accounts are all permitted. [<http://www.dol.gov/ebsa>, Fact Sheet, *Proposed Regulation Relating to Default Investment Alternatives Under Participant Directed Individual Account Plans* (Sept. 26, 2006)] [Elayne Demby, *Riding the Tiger: Risky* "Assessment," plansponsor.com (magazine article, February 2008)]

If all of these requirements are satisfied, the fiduciary then qualifies for safe harbor relief. However, the selection of the default investments remains a fiduciary decision—which, in turn, must be prudent, considering fees and expenses. Once selected, the default arrangement must be monitored for continued appropriateness. [Bond, Schoeneck & King, PLLC Employee Benefits Law Information Memo, *Department of Labor Issues Proposed Regulations Regarding Default Investment Options* (November 2006) (benefitslink.com); EBSA FAB 2007-1, discussed in Fred Schneyer, *DOL Sets Out Fiduciary Adviser Selection/ Monitoring Guidelines*, plansponsor.com (Feb. 2, 2007)] Fiduciaries are not liable for losses on amounts invested in a QDIA, and the plan's fiduciaries are not liable for decisions made by the managers of the QDIA. A QDIA can mix equity and fixed income investments—for example, in a life cycle or targeted retirement date fund; it can also be a balanced fund or a professionally managed fund. However, a capital preservation fund or other stable value fund can be a QDIA only for the first 120 days after a participant's first elective contribution.

The DOL announced a final rule on improving access to financial advice for 401(k) and IRA accounts, published in the January 21, 2009 Federal Register, finalizing the August 2008 proposals and implementing the PPA's statutory exemption for investment advice. This rule was withdrawn and replaced by a proposal published in March 2010. Under the March 2010 proposal, advice can be given two ways: through the use of an unbiased computer model chosen by the fiduciary, or when the adviser's fees do not vary no matter what investments the participants choose. Additional requirements, including fee disclosure, are imposed. [Proposed rule, 75 Fed. Reg. 9360 (Mar. 2, 2010); see Rebecca Moore, *DOL Proposes New Advice Rule*, plansponsor.com (Feb. 26, 2010); Davis & Harman, LLP *Summary of Investment Advice Regulations* (Mar. 1, 2010) (benefitslink.com); for history of the rule, see 74 Fed. Reg. 11847 (Mar. 20, 2009) and 74 Fed. Reg. 23951 (May 22, 2009), discussed in Fred Schneyer, *EBSA Delays Advice Rule Again*, plansponsor.com (Nov. 16, 2009) and *EBSA Pulls Back Controversial Advice Mandate*, plansponsor.com (Nov. 19, 2009)]

Final IRS rules in T.D. 9447 (2009-12 I.R.B. 694) permit employers to add an automatic enrollment feature to 401(k) plans without performing nondiscrimination testing, but the plan must be a QACA or an EACA (the equivalent for multi-employer plans). A QACA is a CODA that satisfies the 401(k)(13) rules about notice, automatic deferrals, and matching or nonelective contributions. A QACA must begin automatic contributions at 3% of salary, adding 1% a year until reaching 6%. Company matches and mandatory nonelective contributions vest in two years. If an employer offers a QACA, all employees must be automatically enrolled. If the employer withholds excess contributions from employees who opt out of coverage, the employer must make a corrective distribution by June 30. An employee who opts out can withdraw from the plan and have contributions end within 90 days. The distribution from the plan is taxable to the employee, but is not subject to the 10% penalty tax on premature withdrawals. The Final Regulations apply to plan years beginning on or after January 1, 2008. [Joanne Wojcik, *IRS Rules on 401(k) Will Help Some Employers*, Business Insurance (Feb. 25, 2009) (benefitslink.com); AICPA, *IRS Issues Final Regs on Automatic Contribution Agreements* (Feb. 25, 2009) (benefitslink.com)]

Late in 2011, the DOL finalized the ERISA § 408(g) regulations, which say that it is not a prohibited transaction for fiduciary advisors to give individualized investment advice to participants in individual account plans. To qualify, the advice must be based on generally accepted investment theories considering the individual's investment characteristics as well as the performance of various asset classes over time. Either the adviser's remuneration must be independent of the choices made by the individual, or the advice must be rendered based on a valid computer model. [76 Fed. Reg. 66637 (Oct. 7, 2011); Prudential, *DOL Investment Advice Compliance Advisory* (December 2011) (benefitslink.com); Guest

Article, Deloitte's Washington Bulletin, *Labor Department Finalizes* "Investment Education" *Regulation* (Oct. 31, 2011) (benefitslink.com)]

A mid-2012 final rule revises the procedure for mailing or e-filing certain notices with DOL under the ERISA § 408(b)(2) rules about the fee disclosures that must be made to the plan's fiduciaries. The fiduciaries are required to file these notices to secure a prohibited transaction exemption. If fiduciaries find out that they have not been given the appropriate information, they must make a written request to the service provider to get the missing information. If the service provider fails to comply within 90 days, the fiduciary must either mail a written notice to DOL, EBSA Office of Enforcement, P.O. Box 75296, Washington, D.C. 20013, or use the link at <www.dol.gov/ebsa/regs/feedisclosurefailurenotice.html> The advantage of online filing is that the site gives immediate electronic confirmation that notice is received. [Final Rule, DOL EBSA, *Amendment Relating to Reasonable Contract or Arrangement Under Section 408(b)(2)—Fee Disclosure*, 77 Fed. Reg. 41678 (July 16, 2012)]

## § 10.05    ERISA COMPLIANCE ISSUES

Many compliance issues (e.g., payment of premiums; reporting events that may imperil a plan's future; terminating a plan) involve interaction between plan sponsors and the PBGC. PBGC.gov has been updated, to make the site run faster and make it easier to search. The links have been re-labeled for clarity, and there is a new Resources tab to find reference materials. Many of the guidance documents have been moved to the Resources tab, which includes fact sheets, databooks, and annual reports. [PBGC press release, *PBGC Website Gets New Look with Faster and Easier Navigation Tools* (Jan. 24, 2011) (benefitslink.com)]

An EBSA news release from early 2010 reports that a DOL Administrative Law Judge rejected an appeal by the plan administrators of the 401(k) plan of Airport of an $86,500 civil penalty. EBSA's position is that the plan administrator's bankruptcy did not eliminate the responsibility to file an annual report. The 2004 Form 5500 was improper because it did not include an asset schedule or opinion from an independent accountant. After selling business locations, the plan did not preserve the plan records as required by ERISA. [Plansponsor Staff, *Bankruptcy Doesn't Relieve Plan of ERISA Mandates*, plansponsor.com (Jan. 15, 2010)]

The Summary Plan Description (SPD) for a newly created plan must be filed with the Department of Labor within 120 days of the plan's adoption. (If this is later than the date of establishment, filing must be made within 120 days of the first time the plan covers common-law employees and therefore becomes subject to ERISA Title I.) It is wise to include a disclaimer in the SPD, to the effect that the plan instrument and not the SPD will govern in case of conflict.

ERISA § 104(a)(4)(A) gives the DOL the power to reject an incomplete SPD filing. The plan administrator has 45 days to file again to answer the DOL comments. If the second filing is not made, DOL has the power to sue for legal or equitable relief, or any other remedy authorized by ERISA Title I.

According to EBSA, it is a violation of ERISA's "exclusive purpose" rule for fiduciaries to use plan assets to advance proxy resolutions for political or policy issues that are not connected to increasing the value of the plan assets. Fiduciaries are barred from accepting higher expenses, lower investment returns, or risks to the security of the plan's assets in order to advance any goals that are not directly related to the plan. [EBSA Advisory Opinion 2007-07A; see Rebecca Moore, *Use of Plan Assets for Non-Plan Related Political Issues Violates ERISA*, plansponsor.com (Jan. 3, 2008)]

DOL published a final rule on January 14, 2010, creating a safe harbor for small plan (under 100 participants). The safe harbor explains when funds received from participants or withheld from their wages for contribution to a pension or welfare benefit plan become plan assets under ERISA Title I. In 1988, DOL ruled that the contributions became plan assets on the earliest date they could reasonably be segregated from the employer's general assets, but in any case within 90 days of the employer's receipt of the funds. A 1996 rule reduced the period to the fifteenth business day of the month after receipt.

On February 29, 2008, DOL proposed a seven-business-day rule, which has now been finalized, effective January 14, 2010. Under this version of the safe harbor, a contribution is deemed timely deposited if it placed into the plan not later than the seventh business day after the date of receipt, even if it would have been possible to deposit it more quickly. For a SIMPLE IRA, the maximum period for depositing participants' contributions continues to be 30 days after the end of the month in which the employee would otherwise have received the money in cash form. For a welfare benefit plan, the safe harbor period remains 90 days from the date the employer received or withheld the money. [Transamerica Center for Retirement Studies 2010-01, *Department of Labor Final Rule on Definition of Plan Assets—Participant Contributions* (Jan. 22, 2010) (benefitslink.com); the proposed rule was published at 73 Fed. Reg. 11072 (Feb. 29, 2008)]

Starting with the 2002 plan year, some small plans (usually those having fewer than 100 participants) will be required to get a report from an independent auditor to accompany their Form 5500-series filing, even though they were excused from the audit requirement in earlier years. [65 Fed. Reg. 62957 (Oct. 19, 2000); this issue is discussed in a Reminder from BenefitsLink, *Changed 5500 Rules Will Require 2002 Independent Audit for Some Small Plans*, <http://benefitslink.com/erisaregs/2520.104-41-final.shtml>]

On January 31, 2012, the PBGC announced a voluntary compliance program for defined benefit plans that have never paid required PBGC premiums. Such plans can make the necessary payments without incurring penalties, although interest on the past-due premiums is not waived. However, after the scheduled termination of the program in mid-2012, the PBGC will speed up its enforcement efforts, including imposition of penalties. [ 77 Fed. Reg. 6675 (Feb. 9, 2012); see PLC, *PBGC Provides Temporary Relief for Defined Benefit Plans That Have Not Paid Premiums* (Feb. 8, 2012) (benefitslink.com)]

The 2012 legislation, Pub. L. No. 112-141, the Moving Ahead for Progress in the 21st Century Act (MAP-21), schedules ongoing increases in the PBGC premium. (The PBGC wanted the power to raise premiums itself, without Congressional action, but this was not enacted.) For 2013, the single-employer premium rises to $42, and for 2014, it will be $49. The 2015 single-employer flat-rate premium is $50. The variable-rate premium is $13/$1,000 in unfunded vested benefits for 2014 and $18/$1,000 in unfunded vested benefits for 2015. However, for 2013 and later years, the variable-rate premium will be subject to a cap of $400 per participant. The first year in which plans that previously used the Alternative Premium Funding Target to set the unfunded vested benefit can revoke the election and switch to the Standard Premium Funding Target is 2013 (This is true because 2008 was the first year in which the election could be made—and it had to be maintained for five years.) [Haynes and Boone Blogs, *PBGC Issues Premium Rate Guidance Relating to Changes in 2013* (Oct. 5, 2012) (benefitslink-.com); PBGC, *Pension Insurance Premiums Fact Sheet*, <http://www.pbgc.gov/res/factsheets/page/premiums.html>]

In order to reduce the administrative burdens on plans, the PBGC proposed a new payment procedure for 2014. At that point, the due date for the premium depended on the size of the plan and whether the payment was for a flat- or variable-rate premium. The proposal calls for a uniform payment date for all plans, which would be October 15, 2014. (This means that small plans would have to pay two premiums in 2014, one for 2013 and one for 2014.) There is a penalty of 1% per month for underpayment of the PBGC premium. Under prior law, the penalty is capped at 100% of the unpaid premium; the proposal reduces it to 50% of the premium if correction is made before the PBGC issues a notice that the premium is unpaid. The 100% cap still applies to correction after the PBGC issues its notice. [Buck Consultants FYI, *PBGC Proposes New Premium Rules for 2014*, <http://www.buckconsultants.com/portals/0publications/fyi/2013/FYI-2013-0725-PBGC-proposes-new-premium-rules-2014.pdf> (July 25, 2013)]

Starting with filings covering the 2009 plan year, the DOL requires electronic filing of Form 5500, using EFAST2. (Filings could be made using the original EFAST until June 30, 2010; October 15, 2010 was the last date when paper filings could be accepted, although all late and amended filings must use EFAST2). [Mercer Select US, *Oct. 15 Deadline Completes The Transition to Form 5500 E-filing* (July 28, 2010) (benefitslink.com)]

EBSA announced in early 2013 that migration to the fully electronic EFAST2 system is complete for all filing years and paper filings will no longer be accepted. See the DOL Website for an explanation of which version of the Form 5500/5500SF is required for your plan, and which schedules to use. The announcement, which primarily deals with the Delinquent Filer Voluntary Compliance Program, says that although DFVCP does not offer relief from late filing penalties under the Code or ERISA Title IV, the PBGC has agreed to provide some ERISA § 4071 penalty relief for delinquent filings of annual reports if the conditions of the DFVCP are satisfied. The IRS announced that it would issue separate guidance on penalty relief for Form 5500/5500-SF delinquencies where both DFVCP and IRS requirements are met. [Notice: <http://www.dol.gov/find/20130128>, FAQs at <http://www.dol.gov/ebsa/faqs/faq_dfvc.html>. See Rebecca Moore, *EBSA Updates Delinquent Filer Correction Program*, plansponsor.com (Jan. 28, 2013)]

The EFAST2 FAQ explains how to make a DFVCP filing. The DFVCP allows plan administrators to pay reduced civil penalties if they make the required filings before the DOL gives the administrators written notice of their failure to file timely annual reports under ERISA Title I. (Form 5500-EZ filers and filers of Form 5500 for plans without employees are not eligible for DFVCP because they are not subject to ERISA Title I.) The plan administrator is personally liable for ERISA § 502(c)(2) civil penalties, which cannot be paid from plan assets.

For a small plan (i.e., fewer than 100 participants at the beginning of the plan year), the applicable penalty is $10 per day the annual report is filed after the due date, not counting extension, subject to a cap of $750. If the same plan is delinquent in filing more than one annual report, the maximum is $750 per annual report, up to a maximum of $1,500. For a large plan, the penalty is $10 per day of lateness up to a $2,000 cap; for multiple delinquent filings, the limit is $2,000 per report and $4,000 per plan. All filings for a plan should be submitted together so the submitter gets the benefit of the cap. Payment of the DFVCP penalty waives the right to receive notice of assessment from the DOL—as well as the right to contest the amount of the assessed penalty.

Penalties for plans that do not file a timely annual report and do not participate in DFVCP are $50 per day with no limit; failure to file the annual report is penalized by $300 per day up to $30,000 per year until a complete annual report is filed. If, during the period when the reports were not filed, the plan went from small to large, the large-plan penalties apply. A plan that has received an IRS late-filer penalty letter can participate in DFVCP, but a plan that has received a DOL Notice of Intent to Assess a penalty cannot. [DOL/EBSA, *FAQs about the Delinquent Filer Voluntary Compliance Program* (no date; benefitslink.com). More info about DFVCP: <www.efast.dol.gov.>]

Starting January 1, 2012, Forms 5500 and 5500-SF must be signed electronically by the employer, plan sponsor, or plan administrator. The signer must have a valid EFAST2 user ID and personal ID. If the electronic signature is rejected by the online filing system, it may be necessary to get new credentials. Forms that do not have an electronic signature will not be processed, and the plan might be penalized. Forms that have an invalid electronic signature will be characterized as "processing stopped." Forms can also be signed by an authorized plan service provider (APSP) who has specific written authorization from the plan administrator, including the plan administrator's manual signature on a paper copy of the form. A PDF of the first two pages of the manually signed form must be attached to the filing, so the DOL can add an image of the manual signature to its online database. [John Iekel, *Electronic Signatures for Forms 5500 and 5500-SF Mandatory Jan. 1*, Smart HR (Dec. 21, 2011) (benefitslink.com)]

For 401(k) plans and health and welfare plans, EFAST2 requires the plan administrator's electronic signature to Form 5500. For most single-employer plans that means the employer/plan sponsor. The 2012 instructions clarify that where the plan administrator is an entity, the electronic signature must belong to an individual who is authorized to sign on behalf of the entity. Form 5500 now includes optional information about paid preparers; although the information is optional, the IRS encourages providing it. Schedules H and I have been revised so that the plan can indicate the name and EIN of its trust. If the plan has more than one trust, the one with the highest dollar amount or the one holding the largest percentage of plan assets should be listed. The filing should not give a Social Security Number as identification. If the filer does not have the EIN for the plan trust, the EIN for the Form 1099-R should be used. Form 5500-SF, for certain small plans, has also been revised to include the paid preparer and trust information [<http://www.dol.gov/ebsa/5500main.html>; see EBIA Weekly, *Form 5500 for 2012 Plan Year Released* (Dec. 6, 2012) (benefitslink.com)]

The 2012 instructions for PBGC premium filings take up 77 pages: see <http://www.pbgc.gov/Documents/2012_premium_payment_instructions.pdf>. A one-page guide was published in September 2011. [PBGC, *Information About PBGC Premium Filings*], pointing out that for calendar-year plans, the estimated flat-rate filing was due February 29, 2012 for plans with 500 or more participants, October 15, 2012 for plans with 100–499 participants, and April 30, 2013 for plans with fewer than 100 participants.

The PBGC warned filers not to:

- Use the wrong discount rates to calculate the premium funding target;

- Omit unfunded vested benefit data unless they report that an exemption is available;

- Use the alternative premium funding target without having made an election;

- Calculate the VRP with the standard premium funding target despite having made an alternative election;

- Submit an estimated VRP in a filing without reconciling it with a comprehensive filing; or

- Use a valuation date for the unfunded vested premium that is outside the plan year and therefore invalid.

The PBGC also suggested that filers:

- Log in to their MyPAA accounts at least once a year, because the PBGC deactivates accounts that are never used;

- Update changed information;

- Make sure that filing and payment information is reported;

- Check the confirmation of filing on the Plan Page or check the Account History for the plan. If the Filing Manager Page is visible, the filing has not been submitted; and

- Click buttons only once and give the site time to process the submission; [<http://www.pbgc.gov/documents/updated-premium-mailing-Sept-2011 .pdf>. Questions can be submitted by phone at (800) 736-2444 (select "premium") or by e-mail to premiums@pbgc.gov.]

Form 5500 was updated for 2012 returns to permit submission of optional information about the preparer of the form. The IRS encourages plans to provide this information, although it is not mandatory yet. Trust information on Schedules H and I is also optional, but encouraged. The instructions for Schedule SB have been updated to inform filers that additional detail is needed for the prior year's excess contributions to be added to the prefunding balance. Single-employer defined benefit plans must follow the guidance of Notice 2012-61, 2012-42 I.R.B. 479 about conforming Schedule SB to MAP-21. [Informational (non-filing) copies of forms, schedules, and instructions were posted to <http://www.efast.dol.gov>; check this site for availability of the filing versions. See DOL, *U.S. Labor Department Releases Advance Copies Of 2012 Form 5500 Annual Report* (Dec. 4, 2012) (benefitslink.com).]

The PBGC required MyPAA users to adopt new, stronger passwords no later than August 1, 2012: the new passwords must have between 10 and 24 characters, and must include at least one uppercase character, one lowercase character, one special character, and one numeral. [What's New For Practitioners, <http:// www.pbgc.gov/prac/whatsnew.html> (June 18, 2012)]

Code § 6057(a) requires reporting of certain information about participants who separate from service with deferred vested benefits. Until 2009, this was done on Schedule SSA of the Form 5500. IRS and SSA developed Form 8955-SSA, which is filed directly with the IRS for plan years beginning on or after January 1, 2009.

The information reported on the new form is similar to the Schedule SSA information: participants separated from service when entitled to a deferred vested benefit. The Social Security Administration uses this information to tell retirees who are applying for Social Security what pension plan benefits are available to them. [Jeffrey Ashendorf, *Legal Alert: IRS Replaces Schedule SSA* (Mar. 4, 2011) (benefitslink.com)]

In the January 2013 edition of "What's New in My PAA," the PBGC announced that premium filings for plan year 2013 could be made through My PAA. [PBGC, *Premium Filing MyPAA Pension Benefit Guaranty Corporation*; see http://www.pbgc.gov/prac/prem/online-premium-filing-with-my-paa.html.]

In mid-2010, the PBGC revised its debt collection rules, to add salary offset and administrative wage garnishment to the acceptable methods of collecting non-tax debts owed to the PBGC. The PBGC had previously adopted debt collection regulations in 1994 and 1995 to conform to the Federal Claims Collection Act, Debt Collection Act, and Debt Collection Improvement Act, and to implement the Department of the Treasury's program of offsetting federal debts against tax refunds. Administrative offset is the process of having amounts that are owed to a business (such as a government contractor) paid to the PBGC instead, to pay the business' debts to the PBGC. Salary offset is withholding of up to 15% of a federal employee's disposable pay to collect debts. Administrative wage garnishment is withholding of wages of a former federal employee who now works for a non-federal employer. The PBGC has to inform debtors of the amount and type of the debt (such as an employer's failure to pay PBGC premiums, or amounts that the PBGC overpaid to an employee), how the PBGC intends to collect the debt, what happens if the debt is not repaid, and how the debtor can make alternate arrangements if the business or individual objects to the PBGC's proposed collection efforts. Under limited circumstances, the PBGC can waive interest, penalties, and administrative costs—but federal law forbids certain types of waivers. [PBGC Proposed Rule, *Debt Collection*, 75 Fed. Reg. 42662 (July 22, 2010)]

ERISA § 412 requires all plan officials who handle the plan's money or property to carry a bond of at least 10% of the amount the manager handles, with a minimum of $1,000. The maximum bond required of a plan is $500,000 per plan official—rising to $1 million per official for plans that hold employer securities. EBSA's Field Assistance Bulletin (FAB) 2008-04 provides guidance about the bonding requirements, such as how to calculate the amount of a bond covering multiple plans; if the $1 million maximum for bonds applies; if the plan holds employer securities only because it invests in pooled investment funds; and when third-party service providers that handle plan funds must be bonded. [Rebecca Moore, *EBSA Provides Guidance on Plan Official Bonding Requirements*, plan sponsor.com (Nov. 25, 2008)]

The PBGC published a final rule, effective August 4, 2008, amending 29 C.F.R. Part 4003, formalizing the existing practice of referring some routine appeals to the PBGC's Benefits Administration and Payment Department or the staff of the Appeals Board, not the Appeals Board itself. Referral is appropriate where the claimant says there was a mistake of fact, or asks for a more detailed explanation of benefits. [Rebecca Moore, *PBGC Amends Appeals Procedures*, plansponsor.com (July 3, 2008)]

## [A]  Reportable Events

The PBGC's model of operations requires the agency to be aware of events that could lead a plan to terminate, or be taken over by, the PBGC. Therefore, a number of business and financial events are designated as "reportable events" about which a plan sponsor must advise the PBGC. Some events are reportable in advance; others, promptly after they have occurred. However, in 2012-2013, the PBGC proposed significant reductions in reporting requirements.

In late 2009, the PBGC proposed regulations to conform the agency's rules on reportable events (ERISA § 4043) to the PPA, eliminating most of the automatic waivers and extensions in filing and adding two new reportable events (one dealing with funding-based benefit limits, the other with transfers to retiree health benefit accounts). This proposal called for advance reporting when aggregate unvested benefits exceed $50 million and the plan's funded vested benefit percentage is under 90%. Both advance and post-event notice would be required if the AFTAP fell below 60%. Under ERISA § 4043(c)(12), a report to the PBGC is required if, in any 12-month period, 3% or more of the plan's benefit liabilities are transferred outside the plan's controlled group. (But see below for proposed waivers of this requirement.) Reporting is required because the PBGC is concerned that transfers could reduce the plan's funded percentage—and the transferee might be in even worse financial condition than the transferor.

There are three PBGC forms for reportable events: Form 10 for post-event reporting under Subpart B of the regulation; Form 10—Advance for advance reporting (Subpart C) and Form 200 (subpart D). Previously, Subpart B and C reports did not require the use of official forms, but the proposal makes this mandatory. [PBGC Proposed Rules, *Pension Protection Act of 2006; Conforming Amendments; Reportable Events and Certain Other Notification Requirements*, RIN 1212-AB06 74 Fed. Reg. 61248 (Nov. 23, 2009); see CCH Pension & Benefits, *PBGC Issues Proposed Regs on Reportable Events and Other Notice Rules Reflecting PPA* (Dec. 10, 2009) (benefitslink.com)]

ERISA § 4071 allows the PBGC to impose a penalty of up to $1,100 per day for noncompliance, including failing to contact the PBGC about a reportable event within 30 days of the event, failing to report under ERISA § 4010, failure to give participants the required notices under ERISA § 101(f), and failing to give notification of missing contributions when the shortfall, including interest, is greater than $1 million. The rate for the penalty for late payment of premiums is specified by 29 C.F.R. § 4007.8, but the PBGC has discretion to determine the amount of any information penalty assessed.

Penalties can be waived if there is reasonable cause for the delay, e.g., circumstances beyond the business' control. A partial waiver is also a possibility—for example, if the business could have reconstructed its records after a fire within a month, but in fact took two months. Penalties can be waived if paying the premium would cause undue hardship to the business (although the difficulty or expense the PBGC would incur in collecting the penalty is not a factor). Penalties are also waived if the premium is paid within 30 days of the bill. [Harold J. Ashner, *PBGC Reportable Events: Traps for the Unwary*, Journal of Pension Planning & Compliance (Winter 2007) Volume 32, Number 4 (benefitslink.com); 71 Fed. Reg. 66867 (Nov. 17, 2006)]

Effective December 18, 2006, the PBGC's Final Rule on premium penalties defines "reasonable cause" that will justify waiving premium penalties pursuant to ERISA Section 4007. "Reasonable cause" means situations such as circumstances beyond the responsible party's control; failure to pay in full and/or on time could not have been avoided by using ordinary business care and prudent for an organization of that size; records were destroyed; or reasonable reliance on incorrect advice from a PBGC employee.

Notice 2012-46, 2012-30 I.R.B. 86, effective November 1, 2012, gives the ERISA § 101(j) notice requirements for single-employer plans subject to benefit limitations under § 436. When the funding status of a single-employer plan falls below a certain level, the administrator has 30 days to provide notice to participants and beneficiaries. The DOL can collect a penalty of up to $1,000 per day for each participant who should have been, but was not, notified. The notice must be in plain English and must include the plan name, its EIN and plan number, and a general description of the payment limitation. The prohibited benefits must be described in detail. The notice must explain when the limitation will cease to apply (e.g., when the AFTAP rises to at least 80%). Once the limitations cease to apply, participants will be entitled to additional forms of distributions, so the plan administrator must distribute a § 101(j) notice within 30 days of the date the limitations cease to apply. The notice must be written, but can be given electronically if it is reasonably accessible to the participants who are entitled to notice. [McGuireWoods LLP, *IRS Provides Guidance on Notices for Funding-Related Pension Plan Benefit Limitations* (Aug. 28, 2012) (benefitslink.com)]

The PBGC's latest technical update, Technical Update 13-1, offers some small pension plans relief from the provisions of the proposed amendments dealing with reportable events. The relief is permanent, not just for 2013, but could be superseded if the PBGC issues final rules that are different. The ERISA § 4034.25 waiver of the requirement of reporting missed quarterly contributions is extended for all years in which the plan either has fewer than 25 participants, or has between 25–100 participants and files a simplified notice with the PBGC. However, relief is not available if the quarterly contribution was missed as a result of the plan's financial inability to pay. Technical Update 13-1 applies the assets and liabilities used to calculate the variable rate premium to determine the reporting requirements for events in the next plan year—including eligibility for reporting waivers, extensions, and mandatory advance reporting. [Mark Schulte, *Déjà Vu All Over Again: PBGC Extends Reportable Event Relief for 2013 and Beyond*, VIA Retirement Plan Blog (Jan. 30, 2013) (benefitslink.com)]

ERISA § 4062(e) requires reporting of certain substantial cessations of operations by employers who maintain single-employer plans. An employer that ceases operations at a facility in any location, causing more than 20% of the employees who are participants to be separated from employment will be treated as if it were a substantial employer under a multi-employer plan, and ERISA §§ 4063–4065 will apply. A rule proposed in mid-2010 creates a new Subpart B within 29 C.F.R. Part 4062 to give further details of the calculation.

Under these provisions, the PBGC must be notified within 60 days after withdrawal from the plan. The employer must maintain a specific amount in escrow or a corresponding bond for five years from the date of withdrawal. If the plan terminates during this five-year period, the bond or escrow is applied toward any underfunding. However, § 4063(e) authorizes the PBGC to waive this liability if the sponsors of the plan have an appropriate indemnity agreement, and the PBGC can make alternative arrangements to satisfy the obligation (see § 4067).

The proposal introduces a new term, "active participant base," to describe the baseline number of active participants to be used to determine if there has been a 20% reduction. Section 4062(e) applies to cessation of operations at a facility in any location, even if the employer continues or resumes the operations somewhere else. If the discontinuance is the result of employee action (e.g., a strike or sick-out), then the cessation date is delayed until after the employee action ends; the employer is given a week to resume work. For sudden and unanticipated events not caused by employee action (e.g., natural disasters), the cessation date is deferred for 30 days so work can resume.

The 60-day period for notice does not begin until both cessation and reduction in the number of employees have occurred. Only current employees are included in calculating the number of participants just before cessation. However, an employee does not have to accrue benefits to be considered a participant: the PBGC does not want employers to be able to benefit from plan freezes. [PBGC, *Liability for Termination of Single-Employer Plans; Treatment of Substantial Cessation of Operations*, FR Doc 2010-19695, RIN 1212-AB20, 75 Fed. Reg. 48283 (Aug. 10, 2010)]

However, in 2012, the PBGC launched a pilot program under which § 4062(e) would not be enforced against companies that are small (fewer than 100 participants) or credit-worthy, so that the PBGC can concentrate its enforcement efforts on the truly risky plans. [R. Randall Tracht, Brian J. Dougherty, Lisa H. Barton, and Eric P. Sarabia, *PBGC Changes Enforcement Policy Under ERISA Section 4062(e)* Morgan, Lewis & Bockius (Nov. 13, 2012) (benefitslink.com)]

In 2009, the PBGC made another controversial proposal, this time to reduce the availability of waivers of the reporting requirements. In April 2013, the PBGC published a new proposal, under which reporting obligations would be reduced significantly, so that financially sound plans would not have to report most of what would otherwise be reportable events. The PBGC estimated that over 90% of plans and sponsors would no longer have to make most reports.

The 2013 proposal relieves "financially sound" plans and plan sponsors of the obligation to report. Financial soundness means satisfying five criteria for meeting obligations in full and on time. The primary criterion is the "credit report test"—the company must have a credit rating from a commercial credit reporting company that indicates stability. Financially sound plans would not have to make a post-event report for most of the events already covered by a funding-based waiver—for example, an extraordinary dividend or stock redemption; reduction in active participants; transfer of benefit liabilities. Commercial credit reporting companies such as Dun & Bradstreet usually consider the business' ability to pay its debts as the main test of financial soundness, whereas credit rating agencies focus on the company's financial statements. The PBGC considers ability to pay debts to be a more accurate gauge.

The other four criteria are safe use of secured debt; two years of positive net income; two years without defaulting on a major loans; and two years of keeping current on pension plan contributions (other than quarterly contributions for which the duty to report has been waived).

The proposal also provides another safe harbor where reporting would be waived, if the plan either was fully funded on a termination basis at the end of the previous year, or was 120% funded on a premium basis for the previous year. Plans with fewer than 100 participants would be given an extra month to report events eligible for these safe harbors.

As a general rule, there is a reportable event when the number of participants falls below 80% of the number of participants at the end of the previous year or below 75% of the number at the beginning of the previous year, but the proposal waives reporting of this event for small (fewer than 100 participant) plans. Larger plans would only have to report if the reduction was caused by a single event such as reorganization or mass layoff; if the reduction occurred in a period of 30 days or less; or if the number of participants in the same year falls more than 20%. Large plans can use the financial soundness safe harbor to avoid reporting based on reduction in the number of participants.

The proposal retains the Technical Update 13-1 relief (i.e., reporting of missed contributions is waived or reduced for plans with under 100 participants as long as the reason for missing the contribution was not inability to pay).

The proposal says that there are other reporting obligations that let the PBGC know about a plan's liquidity levels, so reporting is waived for missed contributions that reflect inability to pay benefits when due—unless the plan is exempt from the liquidity shortfall provisions. But reporting is not waived for small plans or under the financial soundness safe harbor.

Prior law required reporting of distributions of more than $10,000 in any year to substantial owners of the sponsor company, unless the plan is fully funded. The proposal does not require reporting of this event unless one substantial owner receives distributions that exceed 1% of plan assets, or distributions to all substantial owners are greater than 5% of plan assets. If the distribution to substantial owner(s) takes the form of an annuity and reporting is required, it is only necessary to make one report, unless the annuity changes.

Reporting is not required if there has been a reorganization within a controlled group of corporations leading to one member of the group ceasing to exist because it has been merged into another member of the group.

However, the proposal eliminates the funding-based waiver for reporting liquidation, and reporting is not waived either for small plans or under the financial soundness safe harbor.

Prior law makes it a reportable event if 3% or more of a plan's benefit liabilities are transferred within a 12-month period. The proposed regulations make it clear that satisfying benefit liabilities by paying a lump sum or buying an annuity is not a transfer of benefit liabilities for this purpose.

Under the proposal, reporting continues to be required when the plan applies for a minimum funding waiver and the small-plan and financial soundness safe harbors are not available.

Prior law made it a reportable event when there is a default in payment of over 30 days on a loan of $10 million or more—not only by the plan sponsor, but also by any member of a controlled group of corporations it belongs to. Written notice of default based on reduced cash reserves or a lender's acceleration of a loan is also a reportable event. The proposed regulations not only retain this requirement but make it stronger: reporting is required when there is a loan acceleration or any kind of default, including a lender's waiver of its right to declare a default. Small plans and plans entitled to the financial soundness safe harbor must still report this event.

The proposed regulations eliminate the sponsor's bankruptcy as a reportable event because there are many other reliable sources of bankruptcy information available to the PBGC. Reporting of insolvency is not waived, however, for small plans or plans meeting the financial soundness safe harbor.

If this proposal is finalized, there would be for most situations, only six reportable events:

- Loan default;

- Failure to make required contributions;

- Applying for a funding waiver;

- Not being able to pay benefits as they fall due;

- Being insolvent;

- Liquidation.

The PBGC retains the power to grant waivers of the reporting requirements in meritorious cases. The 2013 proposal takes the requirements for documentation of reportable events out of the regulations; only the instructions for the reporting form will provide the reporting requirements. However, the rule requires that whatever reportable event notifications are required must be done electronically rather than on paper. The PBGC asked for comments on the pros and cons of this plan.

The PBGC stipulated a January 1, 2014 effective date, although the agency might publish a rule in the Federal Register under which the waiver and safe harbor rules would take effect earlier (30 days after publication of the rule). [78 Fed. Reg. 20039 (Apr. 3, 2013); see Rebecca Moore, *PBGC Proposes Reduced Reporting Obligations*, plansponsor.com (Apr. 2, 2013); Buck Consultants FYI, *PBGC Reproposes Reportable Event Rules* (Apr. 5, 2013) (benefitslink.com)]

The PBGC offered further guidance in May, 2013, defining a creditworthy company as one whose unsecured debt is rated at least Baa3 by Moody's or BBB- by Standard & Poor's. If the company's debt does not have a rating, it is considered creditworthy if its D&B Financial Stress Score is at least 1477 and its secured debt (other than debt to buy real estate or equipment) does not exceed 10% of asset value. However, a company will not be considered creditworthy if the Office of Negotiations and Restructuring finds signs of financial weakness such as lack of ongoing operations or engaging in transactions that will lead to a downgrade. If the PBGC enters into a § 4062(e) settlement, it will suspend obligations under the agreement if the company achieves financial soundness at any time during the five-year period of supervision, but the obligations will be reinstated if the company ceases to be financially sound. [PLC Employee Benefits & Employee Compensation, *PBGC Releases Enforcement Guidelines for ERISA Section 4062(e) Financial Assurance Program* (May 3, 2013) (benefitslink.com)]

# CHAPTER 11

# COMMUNICATIONS WITH EMPLOYEES AND REGULATORS

## § 11.01   INTRODUCTION

Although ERISA does not require corporations to have employee benefit plans at all, if they choose to implement plans, there are many rules that must be followed, including procedural rules. Plan participants must be given enough information from the plan itself to understand their benefits—especially benefits available in multiple forms—so that informed choices must be made.

The Summary Plan Description (SPD) is the main document for communications between the plan and its participants, although other documents may also be required, for example when the terms of the plan are altered. If the plan is materially modified, or if there are changes in the information given in the SPD, the plan administrator has a duty to give participants a Summary of Material Modifications (SMM).

For a calendar-year plan that has undergone a material modification, the SMM must be sent to participants and beneficiaries by July 27 of the following year. Fiscal-year plans have until the 210th day after the end of the plan year.

The due date for the Form 5500 is July 31 (calendar-year plans) and the last day of the seventh month of the plan year after the plan year being reported, for plans that have a fiscal year. This is also the reporting schedule for individual statements of deferred vested benefits, to be sent to plan participants whose employment terminated during the plan year and who were entitled to deferred vested benefits at the time of termination.

For defined benefit plans only, the PBGC Form 1 is due on September 15 (calendar year plans) or eight and a half months after the close of the plan fiscal year being reported on. For most defined benefit plans, the PPA has replaced the former requirement of issuing a Summary Annual Report with an Annual Funding Notice: see § 11.03, below.

Magistrate Judge Denlow allowed Verizon relief from the consequences of a typographical error that led to a class claim of $1.6 billion. When Verizon acquired Bell Atlantic, the new plan was incorrectly drafted: the lawyer drafting the plan included a multiplier in the middle of a sentence, and forgot to delete it from the end of the sentence, so that plan participants argued that they were entitled to have the multiplier applied twice. The magistrate judge allowed correction of the "scrivener's error" because applying the multiplier twice would give plan participants a windfall. His decision was affirmed by the Seventh Circuit in mid-2010. [*Young v. Verizon's Bell Atl. Cash Balance Plan*, 615 F.3d 808 (7th Cir. 2010); Alison Frankel, *Verizon Defeats Billion-Dollar ERISA Class Action Over Lawyer's Typo*, The American Lawyer (Nov. 5, 2009) (law.com) and *In the Case of the Billion-Dollar ERISA Typo, 7th Circuit Upholds Win for Verizon*, The American Lawyer (Aug. 13, 2010) (law.com). The Supreme Court refused to hear the case: *cert. denied*, No. 10-765 (May 23, 2011), *reh'g denied*, July 25, 2011.]

Previously, sponsors often used the IRS letter forwarding service to find payees of benefits. For requests postmarked on or after August 31, 2012, however, Rev. Proc. 2012-35, 2012-37 I.R.B. 341 announces that the IRS no longer considers finding missing persons a "humane purpose." Employers must therefore devise other means of finding the payees. The DOL's suggestions are Internet searches, credit reports, and commercial locater services. The Social Security Administration's forwarding service is still available, but at a cost of $25 per letter, whereas the IRS service was free for up to 50 participants. If the plan is terminating, it can use the PBGC's missing participants program, which requires the employer to submit the amount of the benefit to the PBGC, which looks for participants in connection with the termination. The Pension Protection Act mandated that the PBGC extend the program to non-defined benefit plans (e.g., 401(k)s) that terminate, but the PBGC never issued implementing regulations. [McDermott Will & Emery, *IRS Eliminates Use of Letter Forwarding Service to Find Missing Participants and Beneficiaries* (Sept. 27, 2012) (benefitslink.com)]

Plan documents should state whether it is permissible to pay plan expenses out of the plan's assets. If the document does not give this information, then it is allowable to use plan assets to pay plan expenses unless the plan document obligates the employer to pay the expenses. However, an employer that retained the right to amend the plan can adopt an amendment allowing payment of expenses in the future. An individual account plan can specify the way to allocate expenses paid by the plan to the participants' accounts. An allocation method described in the plan is a settlor decision, so the fiduciary must abide by it. If the plan does not specify, or if it is unclear, the fiduciaries must adopt a reasonable allocation method.

The cost of making required disclosures to participants (such as issuing summary plan descriptions (SPDs), summary annual reports (SARs), and benefit statements) can probably be paid from plan assets. This category includes responding to participants' requests for disclosures, and communications with participants that are helpful but not legally mandated (for example, description of benefit windows). Even if plan communications indirectly benefit the employer, it is probably permissible to use plan assets to pay for plan communications. However, if a communication relates to more than one plan, or includes non-plan information, allocation is required. [Jennifer E. Eller and Andree M. St. Martin, *Paying Employee Benefit Plan Expenses PLC Employee Benefits*, Groom Law Group (February 2012) (benefitslink.com)]

## [A] Communications Requirements Under PPACA

The health care reform act, the Patient Protection and Affordable Care Act of 2010 (PPACA) adds a number of communications and compliance requirements, covering both data that must be provided to plan participants and data to be submitted to regulators. Many of the provisions of PPACA require notices to be furnished, either to specific participants, or as a part of the plan's general benefits materials. Many plans include these notices in the annual enrollment package or the plan's SPD.

All plans, including grandfathered plans, must offer a one-time special enrollment period for adult children who were not covered because of age, or who aged out of the plan, and for persons who lost coverage because they reached the plan's maximum coverage, and notice must be given of the special enrollment period.

PPACA also requires notices of:

- Grandfathered status.

- Patient Protection Model Notice: If the plan requires participants to designate a primary care provider, how to choose one; notice that female enrollees can see an OB/GYN without prior authorization or referral. (Not required for grandfathered plans.)

- Explanation of the external review process; many plans include this in the SPD. (Not required for grandfathered plans.)

- Notice of internal adverse benefit determination.

- Advance notice that coverage will be cancelled or rescinded. [Christy Tinnes and Brigen Winters, *What Notices Are Required by PPACA?*, plansponsor.com (Sept. 21, 2010)]

Another PPACA requirement is notifying all eligible employees of their right to maintain EGHP enrollment of their children up to age 26. In order to remain grandfathered, a grandfathered plan must include an explanation of why the plan is grandfathered in all plan materials that are distributed to existing employees, new hires, and COBRA beneficiaries. The notice must be repeated for each year that the plan maintains grandfathered status, although it can be incorporated into the open enrollment materials furnished to employees and COBRA beneficiaries. [Ben Cohen, Kushner & Company, *Required Health Plan Annual Notices—2010 Edition*, <http://www.kushnerco.com/article.php?fileName=Adult-Child>]

The PPACA requires the employer to give each employee a summary of benefits and coverage (SBC) that explains (in understandable form) the covered benefits, exclusions, cost sharing, and continuation coverage aspects of the plan. A penalty of $1,000 per violation is imposed for non-compliance with this disclosure requirement.

The DOL/HHS/IRS proposed regulations from August 17, 2011 added new rules requiring EGHPs and health insurers to make it easier for consumers to understand and compare health policies. The plan administrator must provide a concise document summarizing the plan's benefits and coverage. The document must be written in plain English and standard terminology must be used. Some documents and information, such as premiums and drug formularies, must be made available online. For plan years beginning on or after January 1, 2014, the summary must indicate whether the plan offers minimum essential coverage.

The summary must include the "coverage facts label," the standardized comparison tool for consumers. Covered expenses must be discussed for three common scenarios (diabetes, breast cancer treatment, childbirth), and the agencies may require up to six more scenarios to be added later. They have provided a template for this disclosure.

The summary must be given to employees and their eligible spouses and dependents at initial enrollment, during each year's open enrollment period, and within seven days after a request. (For insured plans, the summary will probably be prepared by the insurer; self-insured plans that have a TPA should check to see if providing the summary is included in the annual fee, or whether the TPA will do it for an additional fee.) In general, the annual disclosure must be made at least 30 days before health coverage is reissued or renewed. It should be distributed with the open enrollment materials.

Plan enrollees must also be given at least 60 days' notice of any material modifications during the year that affect the information provided in the most recent summary. This is separate from the general requirement of providing a Summary of Material Modifications. [McKenna Long & Aldridge LLP, *Group Health Plans Required to Deliver Summary Documents Beginning in 2012* (Aug. 22, 2011) (benefitslink.com)]

The EBSA released final regulations in early 2012, relating to the SBC. The regulations apply to disclosures given to people who enroll or re-enroll in a group health plan in an open enrollment period beginning with the first day of the first open enrollment period on or after September 23, 2012. Extensive guidance is available online:

- *Summary of Benefits and Coverage Template*:
    <http://www.dol.gov/ebsa/pdf/SBCtemplate.pdf>

- *Sample Completed SBC*: <www.dol.gov/ebsa/pdf/SBCSampleCompleted.pdf>

- *Instructions for Completing the SBC - Group Health Plan Coverage:*
    <http://www.dol.gov/ebsa/pdf/SBCInstructionsGroup.pdf>

- *Instructions for Completing the SBC - Individual Health Insurance Coverage*:
    <http://www.dol.gov/ebsa/pdf/SBCInstructionsIndividual.pdf>

- *Uniform Glossary of Coverage and Medical Terms*:
    <http://www.dol.gov/ebsa/pdf/SBCUniformGlossary.pdf>

- *Automatic Enrollment, Employer Shared Responsibility and Waiting Periods*

    Technical Release 2012-01: <http://www.dol.gov/ebsa/newsroom/tr12-01.html>

    [See Tara Cantore, *EBSA Releases Final PPACA Regulations*, plan sponsor.com (Feb. 9, 2012)]

The Summary of Benefits and Coverage can be distributed electronically to plan participants and beneficiaries who are already covered by an EGHP. DOL electronic disclosure requirements must be satisfied. For eligible people who are not yet enrolled (e.g., newly hired employees), the SBC can be distributed electronically in a readily accessible format, but the plan must make free hard copies available on request. If the electronic distribution occurs via a Website, then the employer must send written notice or e-mail to give the URL for the site and tell employees that they can request free hard copies. [Tracey Giddings and Birgit Anne Waidmann, *Administration Issues Final Rules on PPACA Summary of Benefits and Coverage*, PricewaterhouseCooper HRS Insight No. 12/06 (Feb. 14, 2012) (benefitslink.com)]

Under IRS guidelines, health care cost information must be reported on 2012 W-2 forms (i.e., the ones issued in 2013). Employers are permitted, but not required, to include their HRA contributions in the cost of health care. EAP coverage, wellness programs, and on-site medical clinic costs do not have to be reported if the employer does not charge COBRA beneficiaries premiums for the services. However, the cost of any taxable coverage (e.g., for employees' children who have reached age 26) must be reported. Employees' contribution to flexible spending accounts is not included in the cost figure. [Jerry Geisel, *IRS Issues Guidance on Reporting Health Cover Costs on Employees' W-2s*, Business Insurance (Jan. 4, 2012) (benefitslink.com)]

Starting March 13, 2013, employers must give employees notices about the insurance exchanges and how to contact them. If the employer pays less than 60% of the total cost of health benefits, the employer must inform each employee of possible entitlement to a tax credit if the employee purchases insurance through the exchange. However, the employee loses any employee contribution made for coverage. The employer is not fined if employees in this situation choose to purchase their own coverage through the exchange.

As of January 1, 2014, large employers that offer health insurance must automatically enroll employees in the EGHP, and employees must be given reasonable advance notice and the opportunity to choose different levels of coverage that are available, or to opt out. For plan years beginning on or after January 2, 2014, EGHPs may not impose waiting periods that exceed 90 days.

No later than January 1, 2011, administrators of self-insured plans (and health insurers) must report to the HHS on the "loss ratios"—the amount of premiums devoted to paying claims rather than administrative expenses. In the large group market, if the loss ratio falls below 85%, the plan must give each enrollee a pro rata rebate each year.

As originally enacted, PPACA § 6056 required annual reports by large employers to ascertain whether they satisfied the requirement of providing affordable health insurance to their employees. However, Notice 2013-45, 2013-13 I.R.B. 116, provides transition relief: large employers will not have to make this report until January 1, 2015. [Kristi L. Remington, Barry L. Klein, Virginia Escobar Neiswender, Blank Rome LLP, *Health Care Reform's Impact on Employers* (Mar. 26, 2010) (benefitslink.com)]

## § 11.02  SUMMARY PLAN DESCRIPTION (SPD)

### [A]  Basic Requirements

ERISA § 102 imposes a duty on the plan administrator to furnish a copy of the Summary Plan Description (SPD) to each participant and to each beneficiary receiving benefits under the plan. The SPD must be furnished within 90 days of the time a person becomes a participant or first receives benefits. (For a new plan, the SPD can be furnished within 120 days of the time the plan comes under Title I of ERISA, if this is later than the 90-day period.)

ERISA § 102 requires the SPD to be written in a way that can be understood by the average plan participant. The document must be accurate and comprehensive enough to inform them of their rights and obligations. The Pension and Welfare Benefits Administration (now known as EBSA) published a Final Rule governing SPDs for pension, health, and welfare benefit plans on November 21, 2000. [See 65 Fed. Reg. 70226]

ERISA requires the following items to be included in the SPD:

- The formal and common names of the plan;

- The name and address of the employer (or of the organization maintaining a collectively bargained plan);

- The employer's EIN and the plan's IRS identification number;

- What kind of plan it is;

- How the plan is administered—e.g., by contract or by an insurer;

- The name and address of the agent for service of process (the person designated to receive summonses, complaints, subpoenas, and related litigation documents);

- A statement that process can be served not only on this designated agent, but also on the plan's administrator or trustee;

- The name, address, and title of each trustee;

- Disclosure of whether the plan is a collectively bargained plan, and a statement that the participant can examine the collective bargaining agreement or get a copy of the agreement from the plan administrator;

- Rules of eligibility for participation;

- The plan's normal retirement age;

- Circumstances under which plan benefits can be altered or suspended;

- How to waive the normal payment mechanism (the Qualified Joint and Survivor Annuity) and elect a different payment form, such as a lump sum;

- Procedures for QDROs and QMCSOs, either through a description in the SPD itself or disclosure that a free copy of a separate document will be provided on request;

- A description of the circumstances under which the plan can be terminated, the rights of participants and beneficiaries after termination occurs, and the circumstances under which benefits can be denied or suspended; what will happen to the plan's assets upon termination. (All amendments must be made with the necessary corporate governance steps, such as adoption of a resolution by the Board of Directors);

- If the plan benefits are insured by the PBGC; if they are not, the reason why insurance is not required; if they are, a disclosure that PBGC insurance is in place, how it works, and where to get more information (from the plan administrator or the PBGC; the PBGC's address must be given in the SPD);

- An explanation of the plan's rules for determining service to calculate vesting and breaks in service;

- Do the contributions to the plan come exclusively from the employer, or are employee contributions accepted or mandated?

- Method of calculating the contribution. (A defined benefit plan is allowed to simply say that the amount is "actuarially determined");

- The funding medium and entity for the plan. Usually this will be a trust fund, but sometimes an insurance company is involved;

- The plan's fiscal year;

- How to present a claim for plan benefits;

- If the plan will use the "cutback" rule to change the vesting or accrual rules described in the SPD, participants must be informed which provisions of the plan are subject to modification; when modified, the nature of the modification must be explained;

- Remedies that are available if a claim is denied;

- A statement of the rights of participants and beneficiaries and what protections are available for those rights. A model statement that can be used for this purpose is published at 29 C.F.R. § 2520.102-3.

After reviewing public comments, EBSA decided that the current disclosure requirements give enough information about cash balance conversions and operations, so it was not necessary to impose any special requirements.

SPDs must be given to participants and beneficiaries within 90 days after they achieve that status. For a new plan, all participants must get an SPD 12 days after the plan becomes subject to ERISA reporting and disclosure requirements. If a company offers different benefits to different groups of SPDs, the company can issue a separate SPD for each group.

■ **TIP:** If a significant percentage of the participants in a plan are not literate in English, but are literate in the same non-English language, the SPD must include a notice in that language offering assistance in understanding the English SPD. In this context, a significant percentage means over 25% of the participants in a plan with fewer than 100 total participants, or the lesser of 10% of the participants or 500 people in a large plan.

The best distribution methods are handing the SPDs to the employees at the workplace, or mailing them to employees' homes. It isn't enough to put them out in the workplace, because there's no guarantee that employees will take them.

Because there is no ERISA statute of limitations, it must be borrowed from the relevant state law. The Eastern District of Michigan upheld a three-year limitations period that was contained in the plan document—even though it was not referenced in the letter sent to the claimant denying his claim. The SPD for the plan did not explain how to make a benefit claim, although it did explain how to request plan documents. The district court read these two facts together to conclude that the plaintiff had constructive notice of the limitations period. The case was filed more than a year after the three-year period ended, so the district court found that it was untimely. [*Moyer v. Metropolitan Life Ins. Co.*, Case No.12-cv-10766, 2013 U.S. Dist. LEXIS 27770 (E.D. Mich. Feb. 28, 2013)]

To obtain consistency and convenience, many plans offered by public corporations combine the ERISA SPD with the prospectus required by the SEC. The result is that certain SEC filings, such as annual reports under the Exchange Act, are incorporated by reference into the combined document. In 2013, the Sixth Circuit revived a suit on the issue of whether it was a breach of fiduciary duty to give inaccurate information in the form of incorporated SEC filings. In contrast, the Second Circuit held that SEC filings cannot be treated as misstatements under ERISA because they were not made by the employer in its capacity as plan fiduciary. Incorporating the SEC filings could only give rise to a fiduciary breach claim if the plaintiffs allege intentional or knowing misleading statements by the administrators. As a result of this circuit split, employers in areas covered by the Sixth Circuit (Kentucky, Michigan, Ohio, Tennessee) may want to separate the SPD and prospectus, whereas Second Circuit employers (Connecticut, New York, Vermont) might wish to combine them. [Corie Russell, *ERISA Concerns When Combining SPD, Prospectus*, plansponsor.com (Feb. 28, 2013). Compare *Dudenhoefer v. Fifth Third Bancorp*, 692 F.3d 410 (6th Cir. 2013) with *In re GlaxoSmithKline ERISA Litigation*, 494 Fed. Appx. 172 (2d Cir. 2012)]

A group of Verizon retirees sought to prevent Verizon from transferring part of the pension obligation to Prudential by purchasing annuities for the retirees. The plaintiffs claimed that the decision discriminated against retirees and plan participants for whom the obligation was not transferred, and that the annuity purchase deprived them of the PBGC guarantee because the PBGC does not guarantee annuities. Verizon said that the group was chosen because it was simple to administer: the group was made of retirees who had received fixed benefit payments at least since January 1, 2010. The Northern District of Texas ruled that the plaintiffs were not likely to prevail on the claim that Verizon violated ERISA by failing to disclose in the SPD that the company retained the right to buy annuities for retirees' accounts. The district court held that the SPD only has to explain the current terms of the plan, not potential changes in the terms. Nor did the court believe that the retirees had shown that the annuity purchase would reduce their benefits: the benefits would still be paid in the same form. Furthermore, Verizon retained the right to amend or terminate the plan at its discretion. The district court held that amending or terminating a pension plan is not a fiduciary act. There is a fiduciary duty to select an appropriate annuity provider, but the purchase itself is not subject to the fiduciary duty to diversify. [*Lee v. Verizon,* No. 3:12-cv-04834-D, 2012 U.S. Dist. LEXIS 173559 (N.D. Tex. Dec. 7, 2012); see Kristen Heinzinger, *Court Approves Verizon Pension Buyout*, plansponsor.com (Dec. 7, 2012) In June 2013, the Northern District of Texas dismissed the entire case (although with leave to replead), finding that the plaintiffs did not prove that the transfer deprived them of any benefits or rights. In this analysis, ERISA protects benefits for plan participants, but does not require retention of the original source of payment. See Maria Wood, *Judge Disconnects Lawsuit Vs. Verizon Pension Transfer*, LifeHealthPro, <http://www.lifehealthpro.com/2013/06/26/judge-disconnects-lawsuit-vs-verizon-pension-trans> (June 26, 2013)]

The SPD can also be distributed as an insert in an employee periodical such as one published by the company or the union. If you choose this option, be sure to put a prominent notice on the front page of the periodical, stating that this issue contains an insert that has important legal consequences, and that it should be retained for reference and not discarded.

■ **TIP:**  The statement of participant rights required by ERISA can be incorporated into the SPD.

If a plan is amended—and most are, sooner or later—the plan administrator must issue an updated SPD every five years (measured from the time the plan first became subject to ERISA) reflecting the changes of the past five years. Even if there are no changes at all, the administrator must provide an updated SPD to all participants every 10 years.

If there are any false statements in the SPD, ERISA disclosure regulations have been violated, and the employer could face penalties from the Department of Labor. Most plan participants never see the trust documents for the plan, so they get their information from the SPD.

Until mid-2011, there was a split in authority about which provisions should prevail if the SPD contradicted the plan terms. The Supreme Court settled the question in the very important mid-2011 *Amara v. Cigna* decision, holding that the terms of the plan prevail over the SPD, because the plan terms reflect the intentions of the settlor that adopted the plan. [*Amara v. Cigna*, 131 S. Ct. 1866 (May 23, 2011). See, however, *Koehler v. Aetna Health Inc.*, 683 F.3d 182 (5th Cir. 2012) holding that even post-*Amara*, SPDs must be drafted so participants can understand them—so ambiguities in the plan and SPD must be resolved in favor of the plan participant.]

A 2012 Sixth Circuit plaintiff alleged that her survivor benefits were incorrectly calculated because of a conflict with the SPD. The SPD defines the survivor benefit was 50% of the participant's pension reduced by 50% of the surviving spouse's Social Security benefit, with a minimum benefit of $140 a month. However, the plan document says that 50% of the pension is reduced by 50% of the Social Security benefit, without regard to any offset imposed by law. The Social Security Administration pays only the higher of the old age or the widow's benefit to a person entitled to both. The plaintiff said that Social Security paid her only $458 as surviving spouse. The Sixth Circuit held that SPD language can control over conflicting plan terms—but omitting something from an SPD does not alter the terms of the plan. The Sixth Circuit found that the omission from the SPD was not misleading and the discrepancy between the two provisions was not severe enough to constitute a conflict. [*Lipker v. AK Steel*, 698 F.3d 923 (6th Cir. 2012); see Rebecca Moore, *SPD Omission Not a Conflict with Plan Terms*, plansponsor.com (Dec. 21, 2012)]

## [B] Health Plan SPDs

ERISA § 104(b)(1)(B) requires that plan participants and beneficiaries be notified within 60 days of a material reduction in the services provided under an Employee Group Health Plan (EGHP). Or the plan sponsor can simply provide notices at regular intervals, not more than 90 days apart, of changes in the interim. The SPD for an EGHP must indicate if a health insurer is responsible for financing or administration (including claims payment). If an insurer is involved, the insurer's name and address must appear in the SPD.

In 1998, the Pension and Welfare Benefit Administration (now EBSA) issued a major statement on the SPD requirements for health plans [62 Fed. Reg. 48376 (Sept. 8, 1998)], including disclosures relating to COBRA, insurance portability, and the Newborns' and Mothers' Health Protection Act, and followed it up with a Final Rule. [65 Fed. Reg. 70226 (Nov. 21, 2000)] Calendar-year plans must be in compliance with the Final Rule no later than in the SPDs distributed January 1, 2003.

Group health plans SPDs must include the following:

- Participants' responsibility for cost-sharing (premiums, deductibles, coinsurance, copayments);

- Lifetime or annual caps on plan benefits; any other benefit limits;

- Procedures for Qualified Medical Child Support Orders (QMCSOs);

- Coverage of preventive services;

- Coverage (if any) of established and new drugs;

- Coverage of medical tests, devices, and procedures;

- Which health care providers are part of the network, and how the network is created;

- Circumstances under which network providers must be used; coverage, if any, for out-of-network services;

- How primary care and specialty providers must be selected;

- Conditions for getting emergency care;

- Requirements for preauthorization of treatment and utilization review;

- Information about the required length of hospital stays for childbirth, including descriptions of the federal law and any additional protection furnished by state law;

- Either a description of claims procedures or a statement that a free copy of the claims procedure is available on request;

- The role of health insurance in the plan; the EBSA says "particularly in those cases where the plan is self-funded and an insurer is serving as contract administrator or claims payor, rather than as an insurer";

- Extent to which the sponsor has the right to eliminate benefits or terminate the plan;

- Participants' rights under ERISA.

The SPD can include only a general description of the provider network, as long as the SPD explains that a separate document, available without charge, lists all the network providers.

A health plan's SPD must describe employees' and their families' COBRA rights:

- What constitutes a qualifying event;
- Premiums ex-employees must pay for continuation coverage;
- Notice procedures;
- How to make a COBRA election;
- How long coverage will last.

The SPD for an EGHP must either describe the plan's procedures for validating Qualified Medical Child Support Orders (QMSCO), or must inform participants that a free copy of the plan's QMCSO procedures is available on request. The description should be complete enough to assist potential alternate payees in asserting their rights.

A welfare benefit plan must also have an SPD, containing information such as:

- Plan name;
- Employer's name and address;
- EIN and plan number for annual reporting purposes;
- Contact information for the plan administrator;
- Information about the trustees;
- Who is eligible to participate in the plan;
- Claims procedure;
- Statement of participants' rights under ERISA;
- Where to serve process;
- (For EGHPs) Information about COBRA coverage and HIPAA's rules about preexisting condition limitations.

Failure to provide a participant with a copy of the SPD within 30 days of a request is subject to a penalty of $110 a day.

However, welfare benefit plan participants are entitled to SPDs only if they are "covered by the plan," which happens on the earliest of these dates:

- The date the plan says participation begins;
- The date the person becomes eligible to receive a benefit subject to contingencies such as incurring medical expenses;
- The date of the initial voluntary or mandatory plan contribution.

Therefore, SPDs (and SMMs) must be furnished to employees; retirees covered under the plan; the parent or guardian of a minor child who is the "alternate recipient" under a QMCSO; and spouses or other dependents of deceased participants. Although ERISA doesn't say this, some court decisions require SPDs to be furnished to guardians or other representatives of incapacitated beneficiaries.

Health plans must inform the Centers for Medicare and Medicaid Services (CMS), which plan participants and beneficiaries are eligible for Medicare; and whether the plan offers prescription drug benefits that are at least actuarially equivalent to the coverage under Medicare Part D, the prescription drug program. Actuarially equivalent benefits are referred to as "creditable coverage." (Employers that offer an actuarially equivalent plan may also be able to collect a federal subsidy; see Chapter 9.) The notice must be given at least once a year, before the start of the annual Medicare enrollment period, which is now October 15–December 7 of each year. (The period was extended and moved to earlier in the year by the PPACA.)

Notice must also be given when an employee who is eligible for Medicare enrolls in the health plan, although this can be included in the new-hire package; on request; and when the plan's coverage either becomes creditable or ceases to be creditable.

[See § 11.01[A] for discussion of disclosure requirements added by PPACA (the health care reform bill)]

## § 11.03  SUMMARY ANNUAL REPORT (SAR)/ANNUAL FUNDING NOTICE

One of the administrator's more complex tasks is preparing the plan's annual report, usually on Form 5500. This information is then used to draft the Summary Annual Reports (SARs) that must be distributed to defined contribution plan participants.

The administrator has nine months from the end of the plan year (or two years after the end of the extension, if an extension was granted for filing the underlying Form 5500). DOL regulations [29 C.F.R. § 2520.104b-10(d); see 68 Fed. Reg. 16400 (Apr. 3, 2003)] provide a simple "fill in the blanks" form that must be used for the SAR.

The SAR form consists of a basic financial statement about the plan and its expenses, the net value of plan assets, and whether the plan's assets appreciated or depreciated in value during the year. If the plan is subject to the minimum funding standard, the plan must disclose either that contributions were adequate to satisfy the requirement, or the amount of the deficit. Participants must also be informed of their right to receive additional information, including a copy of the full annual report, a statement of the plan's assets and liabilities, or a statement of the plan's income and expenses. Plans that have simplified reporting requirements can use alternative compliance methods to satisfy the SAR requirement.

Yet another feature of the PPA is that, for most defined benefit plans, the SAR has been replaced by the Annual Funding Notice [ERISA § 101(f) as amended by PPA § 501]. (More precisely, the annual funding notice is required from most defined benefit plans that are subject to PBGC jurisdiction; certain government and church plans and small professional service corporation plans are not insured by the PBGC and continue to issue the SAR.) Before the PPA, multi-employer plans had to issue annual funding notices, but single-employer plans did not.

Notice must be given within 120 days of the end of the plan year (for plans with 100 or more participants) or by the extended date for filing Form 5500 (for smaller plans), to each participant and beneficiary and union, and to the PBGC. However, the PBGC will not take enforcement action against a plan whose liabilities exceed its assets by $50 million or less, as long as the plan provides the mandatory information within 30 days of a request from the PBGC.

DOL issued proposed regulations, RIN 1210-AB 18, in November, 2010, about the annual funding notice. The rule applies to about 29,500 plans, with about 43.9 million participants. The notice must include:

- Plan's funding percentage;

- Funding target attainment percentage for past three years;

- Information about the value of the plan's assets and liabilities, determined as of the date for determining the funding percentage;

- The plan's investment policy and how the assets were invested on the last day of the plan year;

- Description of plan benefits eligible to be guaranteed by the PBGC (and limitations on the guarantee);

- Number of plan participants, divided into three groups: active workers, retired and separated employees already receiving benefits, retired and separated employees not yet receiving benefits;

- Information about material events during the year in which the notice is distributed (i.e., the year after the notice year)—events that are likely to increase or decrease the plan's assets or liabilities by 5% or more, or that are identified by the plan's actuary as having a material effect on the funded percentage;

- A summary of the plan termination rules;

- An explanation of how the participant or beneficiary can obtain a copy of the filed Form 5500 for the plan;

- Disclosure if the plan sponsor had to make a § 4010 filing with the PBGC.

The general requirement is that the notice is to be given within 120 days of the close of the plan year. However, if the plan has 100 or fewer participants, the notice can be given no later than the filing date for the plan's annual report (including any extensions). The proposal includes a model notice form. [75 Fed. Reg. 70625 (Nov. 18, 2010), effective January 18, 2011; EBSA Fact Sheet, *Annual Funding Notice for Defined Benefit Plans* (Nov. 18, 2010) (benefitslink. com), discussed in Buck Consultants FYI, *DOL Proposes Regulations on Annual Funding Notice* (Dec. 14, 2010) (benefitslink.com)]

The Moving Ahead for Progress in the 21st Century Act (Pub. L. No. 112-141, aka MAP-21) helps the sponsors of defined benefit plans by allowing them to calculate their contributions using more favorable interest rate assumptions. However, plans that take advantage of this assistance have additional disclosure obligations. MAP-21 requires plan administrators to disclose additional information if the plan had 50 or more participants on any day of the preceding plan year; the stabilized funding target is less than 95% of the regular funding target; and the plan would have a funding shortfall of $500,000 or more absent stabilization. If all three of those factors are present, the plan's Annual Funding Notice must disclose that the law has changed reducing the employer's contribution. The notice must include a table showing MAP-21's effect on funding requirements, plan's funding shortfall, and the minimum contribution for the current year and the two years before. [Rebecca Moore, *Congress Passes Bill With Pension Funding Relief*, plansponsor.com (June 29, 2012); Buck Consultants FYI, *2012 Pension Plan Funding Stabilization Finally a Reality* (July 6, 2012) (benefitslink.com)]

## § 11.04  INDIVIDUAL ACCOUNT PLAN DISCLOSURES

Defined contribution plans must give their participants a variety of notices:

- Safe harbor 401(k) plan's annual notice about the features of the plan, such as the safe harbor non-elective contribution or matching contribution of the plan; this must be given 30–90 days before the beginning of the plan year;

- Qualified Automatic Contribution Arrangement (QACA) safe harbor 401(k) plans must provide an annual notice on the same schedule;

- Qualified Default Investment Alternative (QDIA) notice of rights and obligations, such as the participant's right to transfer the account to other investments, and when funds will be invested in the QDIA; must be provided at least 30 days before the beginning of the plan year;

- 401(k) automatic enrollment notice, providing information such as deferrals made without an affirmative election, and how the plan invests contributions where there is no election; must be provided 30–90 days before the beginning of the plan year;

- Employer stock diversification notice: information about the right to transfer the participant's investment from employer stock into other investments (if the employer's stock is publicly traded). The notice must be given no later than 30 days before the first date that diversification rights can be issued.

In general, two or more notices can be combined into a single document as long as the time requirements are satisfied. Electronic distribution is permissible if the electronic disclosure requirements are satisfied—but the defined contribution plan requirements cannot be satisfied in the SPD even if it is distributed annually.

The IRS will generally treat a plan as having lost its status as a 401(k) safe harbor plan if it fails to provide a timely annual safe harbor plan notice for a year. If this status is lost, the plan must satisfy the nondiscrimination requirements from which it was exempted. This could limit highly compensated employees' ability to defer compensation, or could require the plan sponsor to refund some amounts already deferred. Penalties could also be imposed for failure to provide the automatic enrollment or QACA notice. Failure to give timely QCIA notice forfeits fiduciary protection of the sponsor, plan administrator, or investment company for investment loss. Protection is only restored for amounts invested in the QDIA after compliance with the notice requirements. [McKenna Long & Aldridge LLP, *2011 Year-End Disclosure Reminders for Qualified Defined Contribution Plan Sponsors* (Nov. 2011) (benefitslink.com)]

In recent years, many IRS audits have asked employers for evidence that the 401(k) safe harbor notice was given to participants. Failure to give the safe harbor notice is an operational failure that requires correction under the IRS Self Correction Program; the Employee Plans Compliance Resolution System is not available. Plans that cannot provide the evidence are required to engage in corrections and possibly pay closing agreement sanctions. Plans should protect themselves by keeping dated copies of the notice and cover letter (for electronic communications, the e-mail, the date it was sent, and a list of addressees). If the plan can't provide the evidence, the IRS is requiring corrections and perhaps a closing agreement sanction. [SunGard Relius, *Failure to Provide Safe Harbor Notice Correction* (Nov. 30, 2012) (benefitslink.com)]

The modern trend is for plans to provide participants with a greater degree of control over the way their pension plan accounts are invested. DOL Reg. § 2550.404c-1(b), dealing with "participant directed individual account plans" (profit-sharing, stock bonus, and money purchase plans) obligates plans to offer at least three diversified categories of investments, with materially different risk and return characteristics, so that overall the participant can choose the balance between risk and return that he or she prefers. Plan fiduciaries are not liable if the participant's own investment choices result in losses, unless obeying the participant's instructions violates the terms of the plan.

Participants are entitled to receive a great deal of information in connection with individual account plans. The burden is on the plan to supply the information, not on the individual participant to request it. The mandated disclosures include:

- A description of the available investment alternatives available under the plan; the general risk and return characteristics of each, including the composition of each portfolio and how they are diversified;

- The designated investment managers for each alternative;

- When and how participants can give investment instructions; any limitations imposed on those instructions (for instance, only four changes in investment per year);

- Fees and expenses that affect the participant's account balance;

- Contact information for a fiduciary (or designee of a fiduciary) who can provide additional information about plan investments on request;

- The fact that fiduciaries are not liable if they follow the participant's investment directions, even if losses result;

- (If participants can invest in securities of the employer) Procedures to maintain confidentiality about the participant's voting and tendering shares of employer stock, and contact information for the fiduciary who monitors the confidentiality provisions.

For most 401(k) plans, participants would have been entitled to receive a comparison chart (showing items such as fees and investment performance for the investment alternatives under the plan) by August 30, 2013. However, the Employee Benefits Security Administration (EBSA) announced one-time relief for plan sponsors. For either the 2013 or the 2014 comparison chart, delivery can be deferred so that this disclosure can be made at the same time as other plan disclosures required later in the year. Deferral requires a finding by the responsible plan fiduciary that the delay is in the best interests of participants and beneficiaries. Even if the plan elects to defer delivery, not more than 18 months can be permitted to elapse between charts. [EBSA News, *Labor Department Permits 401(k) Plans to Reschedule Annual Disclosures to Employees*, <http://www.dol.gov/ebsa/newsroom/2013/ebsa072213.html> (July 22, 2013)]

When a participant invests in publicly traded securities and other assets subject to the Securities Act of 1933 [15 U.S.C. § 77a], the participant must be given a prospectus for the investment either before or right after making the investment. If the plan "passes through" to participants the rights to vote and/or tender the shares, the plan must provide the participant with the proxy materials and other relevant documents, and must provide instructions on how to exercise the rights.

The plan further has a duty to disclose, based on the latest information available to the plan, at least this much information (either to all participants, or on request by a participant):

- For each investment alternative, the fees and operating expenses as a percentage of the average net assets of the investment alternative;

- Whatever prospectuses, financial statements, and reports the plan has about the investment alternative;

- A description of the portfolio of each alternative;

- The value of shares in each alternative;

- The current and past performance of each alternative, net of expenses, calculated on a "reasonable and consistent basis";

- The value of the shares in the individual participant's account.

Since 2010, the DOL has been issuing regulations on two important topics: the information that service providers (such as brokers and investment advisers) must give qualified plans about their fees and services—and the way the plan must disseminate this information to plan participants and beneficiaries.

A 2010 EBSA final rule says that investing plan assets is a fiduciary act subject to ERISA § 404(a)(1), requiring fiduciaries to be prudent and act solely in best interests of plan's participants and beneficiaries. If the participants and beneficiaries have investment responsibility for their own accounts, the plan administrator has a duty to ensure that they are informed of their rights and responsibilities in connection with the investments in their accounts, including fee and expense information.

Participants must be given plan-related information before the first date on which they can direct investments, and then each year afterward. Participants must also receive a statement, at least quarterly, disclosing the dollar amount of plan-related fees and expenses actually charged to their accounts, and why. They must receive one-, five-, and ten-year performance data for their investments. Any fees or restrictions on their ability to purchase or withdraw from an investment must be disclosed. Information must be disclosed in a chart or similar format that facilitates comparisons; the final rule includes a model chart that can be used for this purpose. Participants must also be given whatever materials the plan receives with respect to voting, tender, or other rights with respect to the investment.

On request from a participant, the plan administrator must furnish prospectuses, financial reports, and statements of asset value for that particular investment option. The general disclosure rules at 29 C.F.R. § 2520.104b-1, including the electronic disclosure rules, also apply to material furnished under this final rule. [EBSA Fact Sheet, *Final Rule to Improve Transparency of Fees and*

*Expenses to Workers in 401(k)-Type Retirement Plans* (Oct. 20, 2010); see Haynes & Boone, *Final Participant Fee Disclosure Regulations* (Feb. 8, 2011) (benefits link.com)]

The DOL's final regulations on disclosure of fees and expenses in participant-directed defined contribution plans were released October 20, 2010, although for calendar-year plans, the effective date was delayed until May 31, 2012. Three types of plan information have to be disclosed:

- General plan information,
- Administrative expense information,
- Individual expense information.

As long as the timing requirements are satisfied, the information can be included on the plan's quarterly benefit statements. Certain investment-related information (about fees, expenses, and investment alternatives), in comparative format, must be provided no later than the first date on which participants can direct their investments, and at least once a year after that.

Plan-related information in a pension benefit statement can be given in the same manner as the other information in the statement—including online, if that is otherwise permitted. Investment-related information that is not contained in a pension benefit statement can be provided using the DOL's safe harbor for electronic disclosure or the DOL alternative e-mail method, but not under the IRS electronic disclosure rules. (The alternative e-mail method requires a notice to participants and beneficiaries informing them that they can volunteer to receive information by e-mail, allowing them to submit the e-mail address to be used for this purpose.) Participants must be informed that they can request a free paper copy of the information, and they can opt out of receiving e-mail notices at any time. Once the initial notice is given, it must be repeated annually.

The plan administrator must take reasonable steps to see that the information is received (for example, using a return receipt or notice of non-delivery; conducting reviews or surveys to confirm receipt). The administrator must also take reasonable steps to maintain the confidentiality of the information, and notices must be written in a way that is calculated to be understood. [Prudential Pension Analyst, *DOL Issues Interim Guidance on Electronic Disclosures to Participants* (December 2012) (benefitslink.com)]

In February 2012, EBSA published a final rule on disclosure obligations that plan service providers owe to fiduciaries. The definition of service providers includes registered investment advisors, certain broker-dealers, TPAs, and other providers who receive direct or indirect compensation from plan assets in the amount of $1,000 or more. There were some changes between the Interim Final Rule (IFR) and the final rules. The final rule applies to plans that are defined benefit or defined contribution plans as defined by ERISA, but not to SEPs, SIMPLE plans, 403(b) plans, IRA plans, or welfare benefit plans.

The information must be submitted, in writing, to the fiduciary responsible for the plan. Electronic means of disclosure are permitted as long as the disclosures are readily accessible to the fiduciary. EBSA strongly encourages service providers to furnish a summary or similar tool that helps fiduciaries locate all the required disclosures. Service providers can use Employee Benefits Security Administration (EBSA's) sample guide, published as an appendix to the final rule, as a model. Whenever the individual information changes, the service providers must disclose the change; in any event, disclosure is required within 60 days of the time the service provider learns of the change. Good-faith correction of errors is permitted within 30 days of discovery of an error or omission.

When a plan fiduciary or plan administrator requests, the service provider must divulge information (e.g., compensation) about the service arrangement. The final regulation is effective for both existing and new contracts as of July 1, 2012; the April 1, 2012 effective date in the IFR was extended to give service providers more time to comply. Therefore, the effective date for disclosures to plan participants was also extended, requiring initial written disclosures by August 31, 2012 and a first quarterly statement by November 14, 2012. Failure to comply with these requirements is a prohibited transaction for the fiduciary, whereas compliance secures a prohibited transaction exemption. The final rule requires plan fiduciaries to terminate service arrangements as soon as possible if a provider fails to respond to a fiduciary's request for information within 90 days. [DOL Fact Sheet, *Final Regulation Relating to Service Provider Disclosures Under Section 408(b)(2)* (Feb. 2012) (benefitslink.com); E is for ERISA blog, *401(k) Fee Disclosure Deadlines Extended Three Months; Other Changes Made in Final Regulations Under ERISA 408(b)(2) Guidance Easing Access to Lifetime Payout Options* (Feb. 3, 2012) (benefitslink.com). See also 76 Fed. Reg. 66136 (Oct. 25, 2011) for previous final regulations on this topic.]

A DOL final rule from mid-2012 revises the rules for mailing or e-filing certain DOL notices falling under the ERISA § 408(b)(2) rules for fiduciary-level fee disclosure. Fiduciaries must file these notices to get prohibited transaction relief when they find out that there has been a failure of fee disclosure. The fiduciary must first make a written request to the service provider to get the fee information. If the service provider has not complied within 90 days, the fiduciary must notify the DOL. Notification can be mailed to DOL, EBSA Office of Enforcement, P.O. Box 75296, Washington D.C. 20013, or submitted online at <http://www.dol.gov/ebsa/regs/feedisclosurefailurenotice.html>. The Website provides immediate electronic confirmation that notice is received. [EBSA Final Rule, *Amendment Relating to Reasonable Contract or Arrangement Under Section 408(b)(2): Fee Disclosure*, 77 Fed. Reg. 41678 (July 16, 2012)]

The general rule is that fiduciaries are forbidden to deal with plan assets in their own interest and, unless they qualify for a Prohibited Transaction Exemption, they cannot provide investment advice to participants if the advice results in higher fees for the fiduciaries or their affiliates. The PPA creates an exemption for advisers who receive fees for advice—under an eligible investment advice arrangement, with either level fees or advice generated by a certified, objective computer model. The DOL's 2011 final rule applies to banks, insurance companies, broker-dealers, registered investment advisers, and their affiliates, employees, representatives, and agents. A qualifying arrangement must be based on generally accepted investment theories and consider historical returns. Investments must be suitable for the individual investor, bearing in mind the fees and expenses of the investment. Computer models must also use generally accepted investment theories and analyze historic risks and returns. At least annually, the fiduciary advisor has to get an independent audit, and auditor has to issue a written report within 60 days of completing the audit. [76 Fed. Reg. 66637 (Oct. 27, 2011); see Prudential, *DOL Investment Advice Compliance Advisory* (December 2011) (benefitslink.com); Tara Cantore, *DoL Publishes Final Rule on ERISA Transaction Exemptions*, plansponsor.com (Oct. 28, 2011)]

T.D. 9484, 75 Fed. Reg. 27927 (May 19, 2010) contains the Final Regulations under Code § 401(a)(35)'s diversification requirement. Defined contribution plans that invest in publicly traded employer securities must give certain plan participants and beneficiaries (e.g., those who have at least three years of service) the right to change their investments in the plan out of employer securities. At least three diversified investment options other than the employer's stock must be offered, and covered employees and beneficiaries must be allowed to change their investment choices at reasonable intervals—at least once every quarter.

EBSA published a Final Rule in August, 2007, effective October 9, 2007, amending the ERISA § 502(c)(7) civil penalty rules (29 C.F.R. § 2560.502c-7) in light of the PPA. Civil penalties of up to $100 per day can be assessed for violation of ERISA § 101(m), which obligates the administrators of individual account plans to notify participants and beneficiaries of their right to sell the employer stock in their accounts and reinvest, and to advise them of the importance of diversification. [EBSA Direct Final Rule, RIN 1210-AB23, 72 Fed. Reg. 44970 8/10/07. See <http://www.irs.gov/irb/2006-51_IRB/ar09.html> and Notice 2006-107, 2006-51 I.R.B. 1114, for the content of the model notice.]

## § 11.05 NOTICES OF REDUCTION OF BENEFIT ACCRUALS

Under ERISA § 204(h), plan administrators are required to notify participants, alternate beneficiaries under QDROs, and any union representing the workers whenever a plan amendment significantly reduces future benefit accruals under any qualified plan that is subject to ERISA's minimum funding standards (e.g., defined benefit plans).

The Tenth Circuit has held that a wear-away period does not have to be explicitly disclosed as long as the notice provided by the employer provides sufficiently representative examples of the effects of a plan amendment. A wear-away period is a consequence of a change in the terms of a plan and does not have to be disclosed as a new eligibility requirement. The Tenth Circuit said that plaintiffs who were informed that their benefits would be frozen received adequate notice for § 204(h) purposes. The court said that it would not invalidate an SPD for failure to discuss a wear-away period unless the employer was guilty of deceit or failed to explain the benefit calculation. [*Tomlinson v. El Paso*, 653 F.3d 1281 (10th Cir. 2011); see CCH Pensions & Benefits, *El Paso Wins Cash Balance Case; No Age Discrimination or Backloading Provisions Were Violated* (Sept. 2, 2011) (benefitslink.com); see also *Jensen v Solvay Chemicals*, 625 F.3d 641 (10th Cir 2010) The case was remanded; the district court held once again that the plaintiffs would only be entitled to recover lost benefits if the failure of notice was "egregious." The district court, affirmed by the Tenth Circuit in 2013, ruled that the employer's conduct was not egregious—there was no intention to violate employees' rights, only an unintentional error when drafting a complex notice: *Jensen v. Solvay Chems., Inc.*,No. 11-8092 (10th Cir. July 2, 2013)]

If a plan "egregiously" fails to meet the notice requirement, then the affected participants and alternate payees will be entitled to receive whatever benefits they would have received if the plan had never been amended to cut back the benefits. An "egregious" failure is intentional refusal to provide notice, or simple failure to provide most of the affected individuals with most of the information they are entitled to receive.

An amendment reduces the rate of future benefit accrual if it can reasonably be expected that the annual benefit commencing at NRA (or at the later actual retirement age) will decline because of the amendment. For example, if the plan provides a normal retirement benefit of 50% of the average pay for the highest five years multiplied by the number of years of participation and divided by 20, a change in either the numerator or the denominator of this fraction could produce a substantial reduction.

The required notice must be given in plain English, with enough information for participants and beneficiaries to understand the assumptions that will be used in future calculations, and the effect of the amendment on their benefit entitlement. In general, notice must be given at least 45 days before the effective date of the amendment, but advance notice can be reduced to 15 days if the plan has fewer than 100 participants, or if the amendment was made pursuant to a corporate merger or acquisition. Notice can be given after the effective date (as long as it is no more than 30 days after the effective date) if the amendment reduces or eliminates an early retirement benefit or retirement-type subsidy but does not substantially reduce the rate of future benefit accruals.

If there is an egregious failure (circumstances within the plan sponsor's control that either are intentional or lead to deprivation of information for most of those entitled to receive it), the amendment cannot be used to reduce benefits— affected individuals will continue to be entitled to receive the unreduced benefit as if there had been no amendment.

When a merger or acquisition transaction affects the surviving company's pension and benefit plans, it will probably be necessary to communicate with employees about the effect of the transition on their benefits. Notice will be required if a plan is terminated. A § 204(h) notice will probably be required if there is a potential reduction in benefits under a defined benefit plan or an individual account plan subject to minimum funding standards. In general, the notice must be furnished 45 days before the plan is amended, but a shorter, 15-day notice period is permitted in the mergers and acquisitions context. If restrictions are imposed on participants' ability to access their accounts, a blackout notice is required at least 30 but not more than 60 days before the restrictions take effect. [Principal Financial Group ThoughtCapital, *The Impact of Mergers, Acquisitions and Dispositions on Your Retirement Plan* (July 2010) (benefitslink.com)]

The PPA amended § 417(e)(3) to change the actuarial assumptions to be used in calculating the minimum present value of the accrued benefit. Because Rev. Rul. 2007-67, 2007-48 I.R.B. 1047, held that amendments to conform to the new requirements do not violate the anti-cutback rule, it is not necessary to provide a 204(h) notice if a lump sum distribution from a defined benefit plan is reduced by conformity to the assumptions required by the PPA. On November 24, 2009, the IRS published final regulations under the 204(h) notice requirement for plan amendments reducing accrued benefits, reflecting the PPA changes. The regulations generally apply to amendments effective on or after January 1, 2008. Retroactive amendments to comply with the PPA can be adopted without violating the anti-cutback rule, as long as they are adopted by the last day of the 2009 plan year. A 204(h) notice is not required for amendments reflecting PPA requirements about interest rates and mortality assumptions. Nor is a 204(h) notice required to eliminate a benefit that is not a protected benefit or a protected benefit that can be eliminated or reduced in compliance with § 411(d)(6).

## § 11.06 OTHER NOTICES AND DISCLOSURES

There are many other circumstances under which the plan will be required to communicate with participants and beneficiaries, with the IRS, with the DOL, the PBGC—or all of them!

When an individual account plan is abandoned, 29 C.F.R. § 2578.1 explains how to terminate the plan and distribute benefits. [The Qualified Termination Administrator Special Terminal Report Instructions for Abandoned Plans U.S. Department of Labor <www.dol.gov/ebsa> (June 21, 2006); see also EBSA's Interim Final Rule, *Amendments to Safe Harbor for Distributions from Terminated Individual Account. Plans* for further rules about such distributions, reflecting PPA changes: 72 Fed. Reg. 7516 (Feb. 15, 2007)].

In late 2012, DOL announced its intention to extend the Abandoned Plan program, adding streamlined plan termination and distribution procedures to help bankruptcy trustees distribute the assets from individual account retirement plans maintained by companies in Chapter 7. The assets of such plans are held by custodians such as banks and mutual funds—but the custodians do not have the authority to terminate the plans or distribute their assets, even at the request of participants. Under the proposal, the trustee, as Qualified Termination Administrator (QTA) would be able to hold the assets, wind up the plan (or designate a suitable financial institution to do so), and then file a summary terminal report. The QTA has to determine abandonment; the QTA has to hold assets and be eligible as trustee. [DOL/EBSA, *Fact Sheet: Proposed Amendments to Abandoned Plan Program*, <http://www.dol.gov/ebsa/newsroom/fsAPPamendment.html> (Dec. 2012)]

The Tax Increase Prevention and Reconciliation Act of 2005 (TIPRA; Pub. L. No. 109–222) § 516 targets improper corporate tax shelters by enacting new excise taxes: a Code § 4965(a)(1) tax of $20,000 per approval or other act, on entities and entity managers who get the entity involved in the transaction. Parties to a prohibited tax shelter transaction are required, under § 6033, to disclose not only their own participation but the identity of the other parties to the transaction. There is a penalty of $100 per day of failure to disclose (subject to a limit of $50,000 for any one disclosure) (see § 6652(c)(3)(A)). The Treasury has the power to make a written demand to a plan or its manager, giving a reasonable date for return to compliance. Failure to return to compliance by that date makes the plan manager personally liable for the § 6652(c)(3)(B)(ii) penalty of $100/day, up to a limit of $10,000 per disclosure. [See Notice 2006-65, 2006-31 I.R.B. 102]

In the Southern District of Ohio view, a plan administrator and call center employees were not acting as fiduciaries when they gave the plaintiff inaccurate estimates of her pension entitlement. The defendants did not have any discretionary authority or control over plan management, administration, or the disposition of plan assets. It was not a breach of duty for the employer and pension committee to rely on information from the third-party plan administration firm. The plaintiff was unreasonable to rely on the estimates, in light of the disclaimers in the plan booklet (that estimates might not be exact and that the plan documents control in case of inconsistency between the statement and the plan documents). The written estimate the plaintiff received before electing benefits repeated that the plan documents control, and reserved the employer's right to correct errors. The administrator's Website disclaimed warranties of accuracy or completeness of the contents of the site. The district court held that, at worst, the employer made an honest mistake, and its conduct was not bad enough to justify estoppel. [*Stark v. Mars*, 879 F. Supp. 2d 752 (S.D. Ohio 2012); see Rebecca Moore, *Overestimate of Pension Benefit Not a Fiduciary Breach*, plansponsor.com (Aug. 3, 2012)]

## [A]  Notice of Deferred Benefits

Frequently, an employee will leave for one reason or another ("separation from service") at a time when he or she is entitled to a deferred vested benefit, but is not yet entitled to a retirement pension. The person in that situation is entitled to a notice containing:

- The name and address of the plan administrator;
- The nature, form, and amount of the person's deferred vested benefit;
- An explanation of any benefits that are forfeitable if the employee dies before a certain date.

The notice must be given no later than the date Schedule SSA is to be filed with the IRS. [Schedule SSA is the annual report that I.R.C. § 6057 requires of pension plans and other plans that are subject to the vesting requirements of ERISA Title I, Part 3] The IRS has the power to impose a penalty of $50 per erroneous statement or willful failure to furnish a statement.

Not less than thirty, or more than ninety, days before the annuity start date of any benefit that is immediately distributable before the participant reaches 62 or normal retirement age, the participant must also be given notice of any right he or she has to defer distribution. [See Treas. Reg. § 1.411(a)–11(c)(2)]

## [B]  Rollovers; Withholding Certificate

Not more than 90, and not less than 30, days before making a distribution, the plan administrator must notify the participant of the potential consequences of receiving a distribution that could be made the subject of a rollover. The notice should inform participants of their right to have the distribution deposited into an IRA, or to another qualified plan that will accept it.

Participants must be warned about the 20% withholding that will be imposed on all taxable distributions that are neither rolled over nor transferred— and that the sums that are received are taxable in the year of receipt. Participants must also be told that they can roll over the distribution within 60 days of its receipt to an IRA or another qualified plan. The notice must also provide information about capital gains treatment of lump sums, and the limited circumstances under which five-year averaging will be permitted. IRS Form 1099-R is used to report the taxable component of a designated distribution.

There is also a corresponding notice obligation before a plan makes a distribution that is *not* an eligible rollover distribution; the plan must send the participant IRS Form W-4P, Withholding Certificate for Pension or Annuity Payments. The W-4P informs the participant of the options he or she has with respect to withholding:

- Direct the plan not to withhold;
- Direct withholding based on marital status or the number of allowances;

- Increase withholding on periodic payments (for instance, if the participant has high outside income and might otherwise owe a large balance at the end of the tax year).

## [C]  QJSA/QPSA Notice

Thirty to ninety days before receipt of benefits, a plan that permits payouts in annuity form must provide all participants with a plain English statement. [All participants—vested or otherwise—are entitled to the statement. See I.R.C. § 417(a)(3), Treas. Reg. §§ 1.401(a)(11), and 1.417(e)-1(b)(3)] The notice should contain:

- The terms and conditions of the joint and survivor annuity;
- The participant's right to waive the annuity, including a description of the consequences of the waiver;
- Rights of the participant's spouse;
- Description of the right to revoke the election, and consequences of the revocation.

A comparable explanation must be given about the Qualified Preretirement Survivor Annuity (QPSA), although the timing requirement is more complicated. The notice is due by the latest of:

- The period that begins on the first day of the plan year in which the participant reaches age 32, and ends at the end of the plan year before the participant reaches 35;
- A reasonable time (deemed to mean no more than a year) after a person becomes a plan participant;
- A reasonable time after the employer stops subsidizing the survivor benefit;
- A reasonable time after the I.R.C. § 401(a)(11) survivor benefit provisions become applicable to the participant. This might happen, for example, if a single or divorced person marries and acquires a spouse who could become entitled to a QPSA;
- A reasonable time after separation from service. If the employee leaves before he or she is 35, the period runs from one year before to one year after the separation.

   ■ **TIP:** The plan can accept waivers at earlier stages (as long as the spouse consents), but the plan must give the participant a written explanation of how QPSAs work. The waiver becomes void at the beginning of the plan year in which the participant reaches age 35. If a new waiver is not signed, and the participant dies before retirement age, then the spouse gets a QPSA despite the attempt to waive this form of benefit.

The plan can omit the notice of the right to waive the QPSA/QJSA if the benefit is fully subsidized by the plan, and the participant can neither waive the QPSA/QJSA nor name a nonspouse as beneficiary. The benefit is fully subsidized if not waiving neither lowers the benefit nor results in higher costs for the participant.

A retroactive annuity starting date is allowable only if the plan provides for it and the participant specifically asks for the retroactive starting date. Benefits must be determined in a way that puts the participant in the same position as if he or she had received benefit payments starting on the retroactive annuity starting date. The participant must get a make-up amount to reflect any missed payments (and interest on those missed payments). Furthermore, although commentators requested that this provision should be extended to defined contribution plans, the Final Rule continues to limit the availability of a retroactive start date to defined benefit plans.

If the participant is married, the spouse must consent to the election of the retroactive start date if the survivor payments under the retroactive annuity are less than the QJSA with a start date after the provision of the QJSA explanation. This is true even if the actual form of the benefit elected is a QJSA. But consent is required only if the survivor annuity is less than 50% of the annuity payable during the life of the participant under a QJSA that does not commence retroactively.

As for lump sums, electing a retroactive annuity starting date cannot reduce the size of the lump sum. The distribution must not be smaller than the distribution resulting from applying the applicable interest rate and mortality table to the annuity form that was used determine the benefit amount as of the retroactive start date.

For years beginning on or after January 1, 2007, the PPA increased the period for the notices required under §§ 402(f) [rollover notices], 411 [notice of right to defer] and 417 [notice and election period for annuity distributions from a 401(k) plan] from 90 to 180 days. The election period for waiving QJSA distributions is also extended from 90 to 180 days. [Prop. Treas. Regs §§ 1.401(a)-13, 1.401(a)-20, 1.402(f)-1, 1.411(a)-11, 1.417(e)-1, 73 Fed. Reg. 59575 (Oct. 9, 2008); see EBIA Weekly, *IRS Proposes Regulations Addressing Notice of Participant's Right to Defer a Distribution and 180-Day Notice Period* (Oct. 9, 2008) (benefitslink.com)]

## [D]  QDRO Notices

The general rule is that no one can garnish or otherwise get hold of plan benefits before they are paid. The exception to the rule is that a plan administrator not only has the right, but has the obligation, to comply with valid court orders that direct part of the benefit to the participant's separated or divorced spouse. However, not every divorce-related order must be treated as a Qualified Domestic Relations Order (QDRO).

Once a plan receives a court order, I.R.C. § 414(p) obligates the administrator to review it to see if it is qualified. The plan participant and the alternate payee (nearly always the spouse) must be notified that the plan has received an order and what the plan will do to assess its qualification. Then the administrator carries out that procedure and sends another notice to the participant and alternate payee, if the order has been determined to be qualified and therefore must be obeyed by the plan. EBSA published a Final Rule reflecting PPA changes, clarifying that an order can be QDRO even if it is issued after another domestic relations order, if it revises another DRO, or even if it is issued after the employee spouse's death. [RIN 1210-AB15, 75 Fed. Reg. 32846 (June 10, 2010)]

## [E] Break-in-Service Notice

ERISA's break-in-service rules are complex and difficult for participants to understand. Participants have the right to make a written request (although only once a year) when they are separated from service, or have a one-year break in service. The notice defines their accrued benefits under the plan, and the percentage of the accrued benefits that is nonforfeitable.

## [F] "Saver's Credit"

One effect of EGTRRA was to increase substantially the amount that taxpayers can contribute to IRA accounts (or defer in 401(k) or 403(b) accounts). See the IRS Announcement 2001-106 [2001-44 I.R.B. 416] for a description of the "saver's credit," which is an income tax credit under I.R.C. § 25B for low-income taxpayers who contribute to an IRA or pension plan. The Announcement contains a sample notice that can be given to employees explaining the credit. Although the Saver's Credit as originally enacted had a sunset date, it was made permanent by the PPA.

## [G] FASB Changes

The Financial Accounting Standards Board (FASB) requires employers to disseminate financial statements that accurately reflect their ongoing obligations relating to pension and retiree health plans. As of December 2008, FASB had a proposed staff position, FAS 132(R)-a, in two parts. One applies FAS 157 (Fair Value Measurements) to defined benefit plans; assets must be divided into three risk levels, and plans must disclose their valuation techniques. The other explains additional disclosures of asset categories (e.g., cash, equity securities, debt securities, structured debt, real estate, and derivatives).

The final staff position, FAS 132(R)-1, is effective for fiscal years ending after December 15, 2009. The objective of this rule is to show a plan's investment allocations are made, among what major categories of plan assets, how they are valued, and where risk is concentrated within the plan's asset structure. The plan sponsor must state its overall investment objectives and strategies, including the allocation percentage for each major category of plan assets, the investment goals, the plan's risk management practices, diversification, and which assets are permitted and which are forbidden as investments for the plan. Mutual and hedge fund investments must be disclosed. [JP Morgan Compensation and Benefits Strategies, *FASB Finalizes Rules for Financial Reporting of DB Plan Assets* (Feb. 10, 2009) (benefitslink.com) and *FAS 132 Update* (Dec. 11, 2008) (benefitslink.com)]

In 2009, FASB reorganized thousands of guidance documents into a new organization structure of approximately 90 topics. The previous seven FASB statements relating to retirement and health plans (Nos. 35, 87, 88, 106, 112, 132(R), 158 were reorganized into five topics:

- 712, post-employment compensation other than retirement;
- 715, retirement benefits;
- 960, accounting for defined benefit plans;
- 962, accounting for defined contribution plans;
- 965, accounting for health and welfare benefit plans.

[CCH Pension & Benefits *FASB Announces New Codification Structure, Superseding All Existing Statements* (June 26, 2009) (benefitslink.com). See <http://www.fasb.org> for the full codification.]

## [H] Notices About Funding Problems

Before the enactment of the PPA, ERISA § 4011 required the administrator to notify participants and beneficiaries of the funding standards—and of the fact that the PBGC did not guarantee payment of all the benefits that might have been payable absent a PBGC takeover of the plan. Every year, the PBGC published a Model Participant Notice Form to be used for this purpose, and provided Technical Updates including a worksheet for determining whether notice was required. Technical Update 06-03 explains how to make interest rate calculations for the 2006 participant notice; in general, plans subject to the variable-rate PBGC premium for 2006 had to issue this notice.

For plan years beginning after 2006, PPA § 501 repeals ERISA § 4011. Disclosure is still required, but now it is under Department of Justice jurisdiction as prescribed by ERISA Title I. [FR Doc E7-761, 72 Fed. Reg. 2615 (Jan. 22, 2007). See also Technical Update 06-04 (Aug. 30, 2006, revised Sept. 28, 2006) for further interest rate discussion, and explaining how the PBGC will treat missed quarterly contributions now that the § 4011 notice is no longer required. The Technical Updates can be found at <http://www.pbgc.gov/practitioners/WhatsNew>.]

The PBGC published final regulations under ERISA § 4010 on March 16, 2009. Section 4010 requires notification to the PBGC if a plan fails the "gateway" test: that is, if its funding target attainment percentage drops below 80%. The notice alerts the PBGC to its potential liabilities if the plan terminates with substantial underfunding. Filing may also be required when a plan gets a funding waiver, or fails to make the minimum contribution it was required to make. Filers under § 4010 must also report on any restrictions imposed on benefit payments during the year because the plan was underfunded. If any required payments were missed, leading to imposition of a lien, this must be disclosed. The due date is 105 days after the plan's fiscal year—i.e., April 15 for a calendar year plan. The reporting requirement is waived if the shortfall for the plan's entire controlled group does not exceed $15 million. To avoid making the 4010 filing, a plan sponsor can make additional contributions to bring the funding level above the 80% threshold. [JP Morgan Compensation and Benefits Strategies, *PBGC Finalizes Rules for 4010 Reporting* (Apr. 10, 2009) (benefitslink.com)]

Notice 2012-46, 2012-30 I.R.B. 86 (effective November 1, 2012) explains the ERISA § 101(j) notice requirements for single-employer plans subject to benefit limitations under § 436 because of deficient funding status. The administrator must give the notice to participants and beneficiaries within 30 days of the time the plan's funding status falls below the required level. DOL regulations state that noncompliance can be penalized by up to $1,000 a day per participant entitled to notification. The notice must be understandable to the average plan participant. Notice must be in writing, but can be electronic if it is reasonably accessible to the recipients. The notice must include:

- Plan name;
- Plan number;
- EIN;
- General description of the payment limitations.

For notice of unpredictable contingent event benefits, prohibited payment limitations, and cessation of benefit accruals, the notice must disclose that these measures are required by the plan's AFTAP (and an explanation of the concept of AFTAP) and what the effect is on the benefits, with the prohibited benefits described in detail. If the limitation is caused by the sponsor's bankruptcy, this must be disclosed. Prohibited benefits must be described in detail. The notice must explain that the limitations will end. The administrator must also notify participants and beneficiaries within 30 days of the date that limitations cease to apply because the plan's AFTAP has increased. [McGuireWoods LLP, *IRS Provides Guidance on Notices for Funding-Related Pension Plan Benefit Limitations* (Aug. 28, 2012) (benefitslink.com)]

## [I]  Notice of Termination

Before a standard or distress termination of a pension plan the administrator must give written notice to the parties affected, e.g., the amount and form of the benefit due of the proposed termination date. The notice must explain how the benefit was calculated (e.g., length of service, participant's age, interest rate and other assumptions, and other factors that the PBGC requires to be disclosed).

Defined benefit plans that undergo an involuntary termination (ERISA § 4042) or a distress termination (ERISA § 4041)—that is, that terminate when they are underfunded—must follow up their PBGC filings (Form 600) by notifying plan participants and beneficiaries of the same information that was filed with the PBGC. This notice is due within 15 days of filing the notice of intent to terminate or the involuntary termination disclosures with the PBGC.

Late in 2007, the PBGC published Proposed Regulations on the disclosure requirements for distress terminations and PBGC-initiated plan terminations beginning on or after the PPA's August 17, 2006 enactment date; final regulations were published in November 2008. Plan participants and other affected parties to be given certain information about terminations within 15 business days of the request. (The PBGC is responsible for providing in the information for terminations that it initiates; participants and beneficiaries are not entitled to request information about PBGC-initiated terminations until the plan administrator has received the PBGC's Notice of Determination that the plan should be terminated—presumed to be delivered three days after the PBGC issues it.) Plan sponsors and administrators are required to preserve the confidentiality of information that identifies individual participants or beneficiaries. A court order can be obtained to avoid disclosure of trade secrets or other information exempt from disclosure under FOIA. The penalty for violating these rules can be up to $1,100 a day: see ERISA § 4071. [72 Fed. Reg. 68542 (Dec. 5, 2007) [proposed] and 73 Fed. Reg. 68333 (Nov. 18, 2008) [final], discussed in Guest Article, *PBGC Proposes Rules on New Termination Information Disclosure Requirements*, CCH Pension & Benefits, PBGC *Final Regs Issued on Plan Termination Disclosure Requirements* (Dec. 1, 2008)]

## [J]  PPA Benefit Statement

The PPA obligates plan administrators to issue periodic benefit statements to participants and beneficiaries. The statement requirement took effect on January 1, 2007 for calendar-year plans. Failure to provide the statement is penalized by up to $110 per day elapsed without providing the required statement. All defined contribution plans must issue a statement at least annually, and quarterly statements are required for individual account plans (e.g., 401(k)s) whose participants can direct the investment of their account balances. The first quarterly report was due May 15, 2007. The quarterly statement must disclose:

- The total account balance;
- The amount that is vested; if none is, the earliest vesting date for the participant;
- A breakdown of the value of each of the investments within the account;
- Whatever limitations or restrictions are placed on the right to direct investments by the terms of the plan;
- An explanation of why diversification is important;
- URL for the DOL Website containing investment information;
- (For profit-sharing plans integrated with Social Security) an explanation of plan integration.

Employers can use the general DOL and IRS procedures for distributing statements in electronic rather than hard-copy form. The information can be provided on a secure Website as well as through individual e-mails. But if the sponsor chooses to use a Website to distribute the information, participants and beneficiaries must be given a written notice explaining how to access the information online—and that they can get a free paper copy if they prefer.

Individual account plans that do not permit individuals to direct the investment of their accounts must furnish annual statements within 45 days of the end of the year, starting with January 14, 2008. The statements are similar but need not include information about restrictions on investments or the explanation of the importance of diversification. The information can be furnished on a secure Website.

The PPA's disclosure requirement for defined benefit accounts is a benefit statement furnished at least once every three years. The first statement is required for the 2009 plan year. Only current employees are automatically entitled to statements. The defined benefit account statement contains:

- The participant's total accrued benefit;
- The amount vested (or the date on which vesting will occur);
- (Integrated plans) The formula for integrating the plan with Social Security.

In the alternative, plans can give notice once a year that a statement is available and explain how to access it; in this case, the first notice must be given by

December 31, 2007. Defined benefit plans can give notice electronically, but cannot rely on the availability of the information on a secure Website—individual notice must be given electronically or in hard copy.

The pre-PPA rule, that participants and beneficiaries have the right to request benefit statements, remains in effect, and the employer has 30 days to provide the statement—but the PPA limits the employer's obligation to furnishing one statement per 12-month period. [Gregory B. Kuhn, *New Benefit Statement Requirements for Retirement Plans*, <http://www.utzmiller/benefitstatement.pdf?> (Mar. 16, 2007). The DOL URL is <http://www.dol.gov/ebsa/investing.html>.]

## [K]  Health Plan Notices

When a female beneficiary enrolls in a plan, and each year thereafter, she must receive a notice about availability of benefits available for mastectomy and reconstruction under the WHCRA. [See <http://www.dol.gov/ebsa/publications/whcra.html>]

In plans that are subject to HIPAA's privacy policies, either because the plan receives PHI or because the employer sponsors an FSA or HRA, all participants must receive notice when the policies are adopted. An explanation of how to obtain notice of the plan's privacy practices must be provided at least once every three years.

The Children's Health Insurance Program Reauthorization Act of 2009 (CHIPRA), signed February 4, 2009, obligates employers to amend their plans (by April 1, 2009) to allow special enrollment of employees and dependents who lose eligibility for Medicaid or SCHIP, or who became eligible for state subsidies of their health care premiums as part of a state Medicaid or SCHIP program. A state can either provide coverage to low-income families directly, or subsidize coverage provided by the employer. The subsidy, in turn, can be administered by the state making payments to either the employer or the employee, although employers have the right to opt out of receiving payments (for example, if they are concerned about the difficulties of administering the program).

The CHIPRA imposes notice requirements both on employees (they must inform the health plan within days of becoming eligible under CHIPRA) and on health plans. Plans must notify participants of the potential for premium assistance, and must notify the state of information from participants who disclose their eligibility for premium assistance. To obtain special enrollment, an employee must request coverage within 60 days of either the date of termination of Medicaid or SCHIP coverage or the date the qualifying child or parent is found eligible for assistance. Plan administrators must report to the state the information needed to determine employees' eligibility for premium assistance.

[Norbert F. Kugele, Warner Norcross & Judd LLP, *New Federal SCHIP Law Requires Cafeteria and Health Plan Amendments* (Feb. 10, 2009) (benefits link.com)]

See § 18.19[K] for notice requirements under PPACA (health care reform).

## § 11.07 DISCLOSURE ON REQUEST

In addition to disclosures that must be made, and documents that must be furnished, automatically to all plan participants and beneficiaries, ERISA and the Internal Revenue Code require certain disclosures to be made only if a participant or beneficiary requests them.

Materials that can be requested include:

- A complete copy of the plan's latest Form 5500;

- The plan instrument (that is, the Collective Bargaining Agreement or trust that actually creates the plan);

- The latest updated SPD;

- A report on plan termination;

- Statement of accrued benefits (but the administrator only has to furnish this once in every 12-month period);

- Percentage of vesting; and, for participants who are not fully vested, the schedule on which full vesting will occur.

If a request is made, the information should be mailed within 30 days to the last known address of the requester. The plan is allowed to impose a reasonable charge for the information, based on the least expensive available means of reproducing the documents.

The plan documents, plan description, and latest annual report must be kept on file for participants who want to inspect them, at the plan administrator's principal office. If there is a request to make them available there, copies of the documents must also be kept at the employer's principal office and at each of the employer's locations where 50 or more employees work.

The Department of Labor can impose penalties of up to $110 a day, subject to a maximum of $1,100, for failure to furnish documents on request. The Secretary of Labor has the power to demand documents that were requested by, but not furnished to, plan participants and beneficiaries under 29 C.F.R. § 2520.104a-8. Although some Circuits (such as the Seventh) will impose liability on a "de facto" plan administrator, in the Sixth Circuit, only the official plan administrator can be liable under § 1132(c). The administrator, for penalty purposes, is either the party designated by the plan instrument; the person designated by the sponsor (if the plan instrument does not make a designation) or the party named as administrator in Department of Labor regulations. [*Gore v. El Paso Energy Corp.*, 477 F.3d 833 (6th Cir. Feb. 23, 2007): see Roy Harmon III, *Sixth Circuit Reconciles Opinions on Who Is the "Administrator" for Purposes of Plan Information*

*Requests* (Mar. 9, 2007) (benefitslink.com). See also *Player v. Northrop Grumman Corp.*, 2006 U.S. Dist. LEXIS 62521 (D. Utah Aug. 31, 2006), discussed in *No Statutory Penalties Where Document Request Was Not Made to Plan Administrator*, EBIA Weekly (Sept. 14, 2006), refusing to penalize the employer for failure to provide a copy of the long-term disability policy, because the benefits committee and not the employer was the designated administrator.]

A group health plan participant asked for a copy of the plan's SPD in 2010. Eventually, she was given a copy of the 2006 SPD, although there had been material modifications in the interim. The employer did not respond to a request for a more recent version. The changes since 2006 were only disclosed when the employee's lawyer went to corporate headquarters to inspect the plan documents. The Eastern District of Virginia imposed the maximum $110 per day statutory penalty, for a total of $13,750, when the employee sued for violation of her right to receive a current SPD on written request, but no penalties were imposed for failure to provide a Summary of Material Modifications because the court did not deem that the employee was harmed by this failure. [*Latimer v. Washington Gas Light Co.*, No. 1:11cv571 (GBL/TRJ), 2012 WL 2119254 (E.D. Va. June 11, 2012); see EBIA Weekly, *Court Awards Maximum Statutory Penalty for Failure to Timely Honor Request for SPD* (June 21, 2012) (benefitslink.com)]

## § 11.08   ELECTRONIC COMMUNICATIONS

The Taxpayer Relief Act of 1997 (TRA '97) [Pub. L. No. 105-34] ordered the IRS to create rules for integrating computer technology into plan administration and the disclosure process. Since that time, the IRS, DOL, PBGC, and other agencies have developed rules for using the Internet, e-mail, and other electronic means to communicate with plan participants and beneficiaries—and to file official documents. The basic principle is that the electronic communication must be at least as accessible and understandable as a paper copy, and in general, participants and beneficiaries must not only have the right to receive a hard copy without charge, but must be informed of this right.

Treasury Regulations provide that notices can be delivered electronically only if the consent requirement is met or if the plan qualifies for an exemption. Participants receiving an electronic notice must be informed, in a readily understandable manner, what the subject matter of the notice is and how to access it. The recipient must give explicit consent to electronic delivery and must be informed that he or she can request a paper copy at no charge and withdraw consent. Disclosure is also required about the scope of the consent, how to update contact information, and the hardware and software requirements for using the system. If the hardware/software requirements change, a new consent form is required. PINs or other security devices must be implemented to prevent unauthorized persons from accessing the system or inputting information into it.

Electronic witness affidavits and notarizations are acceptable as long as a notary or plan representative physically witnesses the application of the signature.

Commentator Stephen M. Saxon described the DOL rules for electronic disclosure as "both completely antiquated and ridiculously complex," with the result that paper disclosures still continue to be made. DOL rules about electronic communication of ERISA information can be found in the electronic disclosure safe harbor, the preamble to the final regulation on default investment alternatives, in FAB 2006-03, and in DOL Technical Release 2011-03R (although one of the approaches described in the technical release was temporary, expiring in May 2011). The general safe harbor can be used for any document required by ERISA. Information can either be sent to participants and beneficiaries who have affirmatively consented to electronic disclosure or it can be sent to the computers that employees use as an integral part of their job. Rather than updating the safe harbor, the DOL takes document-specific approaches to electronic disclosure. The specific rules were promulgated without guidance, so they can be withdrawn. According to Saxon, electronic disclosure is not on the DOL's regulatory agenda, so comprehensive reform is unlikely in the short term. [Stephen M. Saxon, Saxon Angle, *The Electronic Age*, plansponsor.com (January 2013)]

EBSA made electronic filing available starting in 2005. [70 Fed. Reg. 51542 (Aug. 30, 2005)] Mandatory e-filing of PBGC documents was originally scheduled for 2006 (large plans) and 2007 (smaller plans) but was deferred based on industry comments. Payments can be made by paper check or by electronic check, credit card, wire transfer, or Automated Clearing House. [Leslie Ziober, *PBGC Says Mandatory E-Filing Begins July 1*, plansponsor.com (June 1, 2006); *Mandatory Electronic Filing of Form 5500 Delayed One Year, Pension and Benefits Alerts*, <http://www.thompson.com/public/printversion.jsp?id=1594&cat=BENE FITS> (July 16, 2007)]

The PBGC announced that both estimated flat-rate filings and comprehensive filings for plan years that begin in 2011 can be submitted electronically using MyPAA, the PBGC's online system. Only electronic, not paper, filing is acceptable. The actual payment of the premium can either be done electronically via MyPAA, by electronic funds transfer, or by check. [*Premium Payment Instructions and Addresses*, <http://www.pbgc.gov> (Dec. 16, 2010)]

T.D. 9294 is the IRS' Final Rule, including a new Reg. § 1.401(a)-21, explaining how, effective January 1, 2007, qualified plans should use electronic means to provide notices to participants and obtain their consent and elections. The rule also applies to notices provided under various welfare benefit plans (accident & health plans; cafeteria plans; educational assistance plans; qualified transportation fringe plans; Archer MSAs; and HSAs). However, T.D. 9294, as an IRS rule, does not apply to ERISA Title I or IV notices (dealing with, e.g., SPDs, COBRA notices, and notices of benefit suspension) because those documents are under DOL or PBGC jurisdiction.

T.D. 9294 applies to the § 402(f) notice of the right to roll over plan distributions; the § 411(a)(11) notice about rights with respect to commencement of benefits; § 417(a)(2) spousal consent elections about QJSAs; and the ERISA § 204(h) notice of significant reduction in the rate of future benefit accrual. Electronic communications must be delivered on a timely basis, provide all the information that was conveyed in the paper form, in at least as comprehensible a manner, alert the recipient to the significance of the information; and explain how to access the information. To comply with eSign, the electronic record must be in a form that can be stored and reproduced for reference (for example, by printing it out). [T.D. 9294, RIN 1545-BD68, 4830-01-p, 2006-48 I.R.B. 980; see Fred Schneyer, *IRS Puts Out Final Rule for Electronic Benefit Notices, Elections*, plansponsor.com (Oct. 19, 2006)]

According to 2009 Census Bureau data, more than three-quarters of households in the United States (76.7%) have some form of Internet access. Out of the 139.1 million workers in the private sector, 111.7 million have some Internet access, and of the remaining 27.4 million workers, approximately 10.6 million live in a household where another member has Internet access. [76 Fed. Reg. 19285 (Apr. 7, 2011); see Rebecca Moore, *DOL Seeks Comments on Electronic Disclosure*, plansponsor.com (Apr. 6, 2011)]

DOL Technical Release 2011-03 allows information about fees in individual account plans to be distributed electronically, and Websites can be used subject to certain safeguards (e.g., those prescribed by the DOL's FAB 2006-03, which allows quarterly individual benefit statements to use the IRS electronic disclosure rules). As long as the plan follows the technical release, the DOL will not take enforcement action merely because fee disclosures were made electronically rather than on paper. There is a general safe harbor for making electronic disclosures, even if the participant has not affirmatively agreed to this, if using a computer or other electronic system is an integral part of the employee's duties.

Under this interim policy, investment information and disclosure of administrative and individual expenses can be included in quarterly benefit statements that are transmitted electronically using FAB 2006-03 standards. However, certain investment data (e.g., a comparative chart of performance data) can be sent under the DOL safe harbor or the alternative e-mail method, but not under FAB 2006-03.

Six conditions are required to justify the use of e-mail:

- The person entitled to the disclosures responds to an initial notice by voluntarily providing an e-mail address;

- The plan submits the request on a clear and conspicuous initial notice;

- The participant or beneficiary must receive an annual notice satisfying most of the initial content notice requirements;

- Electronic delivery uses a method that is reasonably calculated to actually be received;

- Personal information must be kept confidential;

- The notice must be drafted to be understandable to the average participant.

- The notice must explain the rights to receive a free paper copy and/or opt out of receiving notices electronically.[DOL Technical Release 2011-03, <http://www.dol.gov/EBSA/pdf/tr11-03.pdf> (Sept. 13, 2011); see EBSA News, *US Department Of Labor Issues Interim E-Disclosure Policy Under Participant Fee Disclosure Regulations* (Sept. 13, 2011) (benefits link.com); EBIA Weekly, *DOL Issues Interim Policy on Electronic Distribution of Participant-Level Fee Disclosures* (Sept. 15, 2011) (benefits link.com)]

The DOL revised and restated Technical Release 2011-03 in Technical Release 2011-03R. EBSA received many inquiries about whether continuous access Websites can be used to make electronic disclosures, and said that they can be, if the conditions of Technical Release 2011-03 are satisfied. EBSA also said that investment information can either be furnished as part of, or along with, a paper or electronic pension benefit statement. [Technical Release 2011-03R, <http://www.dol.gov/ebsa/newsroom/tr11-03r.html> (Dec. 8, 2011); see Rebecca Moore, *EBSA Revises Electronic Fee Disclosure Rules*, plansponsor.com (Dec. 8, 2011)]

## § 11.09   DISCLOSURE OF DOCUMENTS TO THE DOL and PBGC

ERISA required plan administrators to file all SPDs and SMMs with the Department of Labor (DOL) until it was amended by the Taxpayer Relief Act of 1997. The current version of ERISA § 104(a) requires plan administrators to respond to DOL requests by providing documents relating to an employee benefit plan—including the latest SPD, a summary of plan changes not reflected in the SPD, and the plan instrument.

However, the DOL sees its primary role in this arena as helping participants and beneficiaries get documents from the plan, so the DOL can ask for documents that participants or beneficiaries are entitled to, have requested, but have not received. But the DOL will not ask for documents that the participants and beneficiaries are not entitled to see.

If the plan administrator doesn't respond to the request within 30 days, the DOL has the power (under ERISA § 502(c)(6)) to impose civil penalties of up to $110 a day (but not more than $1,100 per request). Penalties will not be imposed if factors beyond the administrator's control prevent compliance.

The DOL's Final Rule about document disclosure and civil penalties is set out at 67 Fed. Reg. 777–789 (Jan. 7, 2002).

Effective March 3, 2009, the DOL can assess penalties, under ERISA § 502(c)(4) as amended by the PPA, against plan administrators who fail to provide the notices required under the PPA dealing with subjects such as limitations on distributions from underfunded plans; responsibilities of employers that participate in or withdraw from multi-employer plans; and participants' rights and obligations under defined contribution plans that automatically enroll employees as participants.

The amount of the penalty depends on the degree of willfulness. Failing to notify each person entitled to notice constitutes a separate violation. Plan administrators are personally liable for the penalties, and if there are multiple responsible parties, they can be held jointly and severally liable. [Final Regs, 74 Fed. Reg. 17 (Jan. 2, 2009); see EBSA Press release, *U.S. Department of Labor Finalizes Civil Penalty Rules Under the Pension Protection Act* (Dec. 31, 2008) (benefitslink.com); Deloitte's Washington Bulletin, *Procedures for Assessing Civil Penalties Under ERISA § 502(c)(4) Are Finalized*, <http://benefitslink.com/articles/guests/washbull090112a.html> (Jan. 12, 2009)]

Because reportable events occur sporadically, compliance with the reporting rules can be tricky; it's hard to set up a routine. Sometimes reporting is required because of events outside the corporation—for example, occurring in the corporation's controlled group. The penalty for failure to report can be as much as $1,100 a day, although PBGC's penalty guidelines are much lower: $25/day for the first 90 days, followed by $50/day, with relief available for small plans.

A variety of negative financial results must be reported to the PBGC. Events are reportable because they signal plan problems that might lead to termination. When it gets a report, the PBGC can ask for additional information, and can either close the file, continue to monitor the plan, or take action.

In general, the reporting requirements call for post-event reporting; advance reporting is more or less limited to significantly underfunded plans of privately held controlled groups. The reporting obligation is imposed on the plan administrator and the plan sponsor; but a filing by any party is deemed filed for anyone else who is potentially liable. Post-event reports are due within 30 days of the time the reporter knew, or had reason to know that a reportable event had occurred. [Harold J. Ashner, *PGBC Reportable Events: Traps for the Unwary*, J. of Pension Planning & Compliance, Winter 2007, Volume 32, Number 4 (benefitslink.com)]

In late 2009, the PBGC proposed regulations updating § 4043 in light of the PPA, and adding two new reportable events (funding-based benefit limits; transfers to a 401(h) retiree health benefit account). Under the proposal, most waivers of liability and extensions of time are eliminated, because the PBGC believes that it requires notice of potentially troubled plans that may need PBGC intervention later on. [PBGC Proposed Rules, *Pension Protection Act of 2006; Conforming Amendments; Reportable Events and Certain Other Notification Requirements*, RIN 1212-AB06, 74 Fed. Reg. 61248 (Nov. 23, 2009)]

This proposal was extremely unpopular with business, however, and the PBGC has issued two statements greatly reducing the amount of required reporting. The PBGC's intention is to concentrate on the few plans that are genuinely at risk, relieving other, sounder plans of reporting responsibilities.

The PBGC's Technical Update 13-1 offers some small pension plans relief from the provisions of the proposed amendments dealing with reportable events. The relief is permanent, not just for 2013, but could be superseded if the PBGC issues Final Rules that are different. The ERISA § 4034.25 waiver of the requirement of reporting missed quarterly contributions is extended for all years in which the plan either has fewer than 25 participants, or has between 25–100 participants and files a simplified notice with the PBGC. However, relief is not available if the quarterly contribution was missed as a result of the plan's financial inability to pay. Technical Update 13-1 applies the assets and liabilities used to calculate the variable rate premium to determine the reporting requirements for events in the next plan year—including eligibility for reporting waivers, extensions, and mandatory advance reporting. [Mark Schulte, *Déjà Vu All Over Again: PBGC Extends Reportable Event Relief for 2013 and Beyond*, VIA Retirement Plan Blog (Jan. 30, 2013) (benefitslink.com)]

In April 2013, the PBGC published a new proposal, under which reporting obligations would be reduced significantly so that financially sound plans would not have to report most of what would otherwise be reportable events. The PBGC estimated that over 90% of plans and sponsors would no longer have to make most reports.

The 2013 proposal relieves plans that are "financially sound" (using five criteria, primarily having a commercial credit rating agency's report indicating fiscal stability) of the obligation to make most reports. Financially sound plans would not have to make a post-event report for most of the events already covered by a funding-based waiver. Reporting is also waived for fully funded plans.

Small plans would no longer have to report reductions in the number of participants. Larger plans would only have to report this if the reduction was caused by a single event such as a reorganization or mass layoff; if the reduction occurred in a period of 30 days or less; or if the number of participants in the same year falls more than 20%. Large plans can use the financial soundness safe harbor to avoid reporting based on reduction in the number of participants.

The proposal retains the Technical Update 13-1 relief (i.e., reporting of missed contributions is waived or reduced for plans with fewer than 100 participants as long as the reason for missing the contribution was not inability to pay). Reporting is waived for missed contributions that reflect inability to pay benefits when due—unless the plan is exempt from the liquidity shortfall provisions. But reporting is not waived for small plans or under the financial soundness safe harbor.

However, the proposal eliminates the funding-based waiver for reporting the sponsor's liquidation and reporting is not waived for small plans or under the financial soundness safe harbor. Under the proposal, reporting continues to be required when the plan applies for a minimum funding waiver and the small-plan and financial soundness safe harbors are not available. When the sponsor defaults on a loan, or when its lender accelerates a loan, continues to be a reportable event. The proposed regulations eliminate the sponsor's bankruptcy as a reportable event because there are many other reliable sources of bankruptcy information available to the PBGC. But insolvency must be reported. As a result of the relief provided by this proposal, the only reportable events would be: (1) loan default; (2) failure to make required contributions; (3) application for a funding waiver; (4) inability to pay benefits as they come due; (5) insolvency; and (6) liquidation. [78 Fed. Reg. 20039 (Apr. 3, 2013); see Rebecca Moore, *PBGC Proposed Reduced Reporting Obligations*, plansponsor.com (Apr. 2, 2013); Buck Consultants FYI, *PBGC Reproposes Reportable Event Rules* (Apr. 5, 2013) (benefitslink.com) See PLC Employee Benefits & Employee Compensation, *PBGC Releases Enforcement Guidelines for ERISA Section 4062(e) Financial Assurance Program* (May 3, 2013) (benefitslink.com) for May, 2013 guidance from the PBGC about the definition of "creditworthy."]

The fiduciary exception to attorney-client privilege applies to communications between an ERISA trustee and the plan's attorney when the company is the subject of a DOL investigative audit under ERISA § 504. Therefore, the Fourth Circuit required two multi-employer funds to turn over plan administration materials about the decision to invest in entities related to Bernard Madoff. (The investments resulted in a loss of $10 million in plan assets.) The fiduciary exception stems from the trust law rule that advice trustees get about matters of trust administration is for the beneficiaries of the trust, not the trustees themselves. The Fourth Circuit applied the same rule for enforcement actions and government investigations. [*Solis v. The Food Employers Labor Relations Ass'n*, 644 F.3d 221 (4th Cir. 2011); see Tara Cantore, *Fiduciary Exception to Attorney Client Privilege Extends to DoL Audit*, plansponsor.com (Aug. 24, 2011)]

### § 11.10 FORM 5500

Qualified plans must report each year to the IRS, DOL, and PBGC so that these agencies can monitor plan operations and see if the plans remain qualified, are financially sound, and are operated in accordance with all applicable requirements. The basic Form 5500 covers plans with 100 or more participants; single-participant plans can use the less complex Form 5500-EZ. For 2007 and later plan years, the threshold for filing Form 5500-EZ rises from $100,000 to $250,000. Only one filing is necessary—the IRS transmits the information to the DOL and PBGC. [The toll-free telephone hot line for questions about plan coverage, premiums, or terminations is (800) 736-2444]

Form 5500, like the Form 1040, consists of a basic form and various schedules that provide additional information. Form 5500 deals with four main subjects: the plan's financial statements, actuarial data, administrative data, and any benefits covered by insurance. The annual report is due at the end of the seventh month following the end of the plan year. A plan that does not seem likely to complete the report in time should file IRS Form 5558, Application for Extension of Time to File Certain Employee Plan Returns, to get an extension of up to two and a half months. [See <http://www.dol.gov/ebsa/5500main.html> for documents and information about the Form 5500]

But, although some compliance requirements have been eased, some have become more stringent. Starting with the 2002 plan year, some small plans (usually those having fewer than 100 participants) will be required to get a report from an independent auditor to accompany their Form 5500-series filing, even though they were excused from the audit requirement in earlier years. However, audit waivers are available for plans with fewer than 100 participants, or those with participants in the 80–120 range if they filed as a small plan the year before, if at least 95% of plan assets are managed by professionals, as long as participants get additional disclosures in the summary annual report. [See <http//www.dol.gov/ebsa/faqs/faq_auditwaiver.html>]

A "large plan" is one with 100 or more participants as of the beginning of the plan year, and a "small plan" has fewer. If the number of participants at the beginning of a plan year was 80 to 120 and a Form 5500 was filed for the previous plan year, the plan has the right to elect to complete the Form 5500 and the schedules using the same category as the previous year.

The DOL, the IRS, and the PBGC collaborated on the development of the EFAST system for electronic filing of the 5500 series of forms. It has been superseded by the EFAST2 system, which took effect starting with the 2009 plan year. (However, plans that cover only the business owner continue to file Form 5500-EZ or 5500-SF on paper.) Form 5500 can be e-filed using the DOL's IFILE Web-based system, a private Web-based system, or a third-party software application that sends data to the DOL. [SunGard Relius, *Getting Ready for EFAST2*, 2009 (benefitslink.com)]

The EBSA announced in early 2013 that migration to the fully electronic EFAST2 system is complete for all filing years, and paper filings will no longer be accepted. See the DOL Website for an explanation of which version of the Form 5500/5500SF is required for your plan, and which schedules to use. The announcement, which primarily deals with the DFVC program, says that although DFVC does not offer relief from late filing penalties under the Code or ERISA Title IV, the PBGC has agreed to provide some ERISA § 4071 penalty relief for delinquent filings of annual reports if the conditions of the DFVC program are satisfied. The IRS announced that it would issue separate guidance on penalty relief for Form 5500/5500-SF delinquencies where both DFVC and IRS requirements are met. [Notice: <http://www.dol.gov/find/20130128>, FAQs at <http://www.dol.gov/ebsa/faqs/faq_dfvc.html>. See Rebecca Moore, *EBSA Updates Delinquent Filer Correction Program*, plansponsor.com (Jan. 28, 2013).]

Form 5500 was updated for 2012 returns to permit submission of optional information about the preparer of the form. The IRS encourages plans to provide this information, although it is not mandatory yet. Trust information on Schedules H and I is also optional but encouraged. The instructions for Schedule SB have been updated to inform filers that additional detail is needed for the prior year's excess contributions to be added to the prefunding balance. Single-employer defined benefit plans must follow the guidance of Notice 2012-61, 2012-42 I.R.B. 479 about conforming Schedule SB to MAP-21. [Informational (non-filing) copies of forms, schedules, and instructions were posted to <www.e-fast.dol.gov>; check this site for availability of the filing versions. See DOL, *U.S. Labor Department Releases Advance Copies Of 2012 Form 5500 Annual Report* (Dec. 4, 2012) (benefitslink.com).] In the January 2013 edition of "What's New in My PAA," the PBGC announced that premium filings for plan year 2013 could be made through My PAA. [PBGC, *Premium Filing With MyPAA Pension Benefit Guaranty Corporation*, <http://www.pbgc.gov/prac/prem/online-premium-filing-with-my-paa.html>]

The DOL can assess civil penalties of up to $1,100 per day per annual report, running from the date of the failure or refusal to file and until a satisfactory report is filed, against plan administrators who fail or refuse to comply with the annual reporting requirements. A report that is rejected for failure to provide material information has not been "filed."

However, voluntary compliance is usually sought before penalties are imposed. The EBSA sends correspondence asking for additional information if data is omitted, or if the agency thinks corrections are necessary in light of the instructions or to be internally consistent with other data on the form.

The EBSA has discretion to waive all or part of the penalty based on submission of a timely statement showing reasonable cause for failure to file the complete report at the time it was due. Penalties are not assessed during the time when the DOL is considering the statement of reasonable cause.

# CHAPTER 12

# PLAN DISTRIBUTIONS

## § 12.01  INTRODUCTION

One of the major tasks of plan administration is to distribute benefits from the plan to participants and their designated beneficiaries—although sometimes determining the proper beneficiary is not as easy as it sounds. The plan administrator must communicate with participants and beneficiaries of their distribution options with respect to accrued benefits. The plan administrator has a duty to provide whatever forms are necessary to make an election.

The standard form of distribution is a single-life annuity for single participants and a Qualified Joint and Survivor Annuity (QJSA) for married participants. Before the Pension Protection Act (Pub. L. No. 109-280), plans were required to offer joint and 50% survivor annuities (i.e., the annuity payment is cut in half when one of the annuitants dies). The PPA requires plans to offer joint and 75% survivor annuities as well. The payments under a joint and 75% QJSA will be smaller than under a 50% survivor annuity, or under a single-life annuity covering only one spouse.

The plan must also provide for a Qualified Preretirement Survivor Annuity (QPSA) for married persons who die before their pension enters pay status.

But plans can permit other payment forms: lump sums and annuities offering other provisions (but not extending for a term longer than the life expectancy of the employee or the joint life expectancy of the employee and designated beneficiary). [See I.R.C. § 401(a)(9)(A)(ii)] It's up to the plan whether to offer these alternate forms, or just the standard annuities. [See §§ 12.03, 12.09]

A plan can be disqualified if it makes distributions outside the range of permitted events related to separation from service. A defined benefit or money purchase plan can only make distributions when the participant reaches Normal Retirement Age or separates from service. The rules are different for 401(k) plans: distributions can be made at retirement, death, attainment of age 59, disability, severance from employment, or hardship. Termination of service means ceasing to work for any entity that is treated as the same employer under the Code § 411 rules. However, employers are not prohibited from rehiring a former employee who has received a 401(k) distribution, although the IRS may look to whether there was a true termination or if the so-called termination was merely pretextual. The IRS might also accept distributions made to a person who is rehired for substantially different duties, and on a part-time rather than the previous full-time schedule, but there must have been an intervening period when the person was not employed by the employer.

The Heroes Earnings Assistance and Relief Tax Act (HEART Act; Pub. L. No. 110-245) allows reservists called for at least six months of active duty to take withdrawals from a 401(k) or other defined contribution plan before age 59½ without having to pay the 10% penalty. (The withdrawals are taxable income, however.) This provision was included in the Code; expired; and was revived and made permanent by the HEART Act. Differential pay provided to employees who have been called up (i.e., supplements that the employer provides to make up the difference between military pay and what the servicemember earned while working) must be taken into account when calculating pension benefits. The HEART Act also protects survivor benefits under qualified plans for the survivors of servicemembers killed in the line of duty. [Rebecca Moore, *Reservist Benefits Bill Signed into Law*, plansponsor.com (June 19, 2008)]

ERISA, at 29 U.S.C. § 1053(a), requires pension plans to provide that the right to normal retirement benefit is nonforfeitable at NRA. The Supreme Court denied certiorari in *Fry v. Exelon*, 571 F.3d 644 (7th Cir. 2009), 130 S. Ct. 1504 (Feb. 22, 2010). The Seventh Circuit ruled that, before the PPA, it was lawful to define NRA as five years' service rather than a particular age. [Rebecca Moore, *Supreme Court Lets Stand Alternate Definitions for Retirement Age*, plansponsor. com (Feb. 23, 2010) But see *Laurent v. PriceWaterhouseCooper*, No. 06 Civ. 2280 (JPO) (S.D.N.Y. Aug. 8, 2013), disapproving of using five years of service as an NRA.]

According to the Tenth Circuit, the ERISA ban on forfeitures does not make the plan liable for third-party wrongdoing. It was not a forfeiture when a plan incorrectly paid benefits to a participant's ex-wife instead of to him. It was the participant's fault that he did not give the plan his current address. His ex-wife learned how to access the benefits, got a user ID, changed the account password, filed a change of address form listing her P.O. Box as an address, and withdrew all the money from the account. The participant did not sue his ex-wife; he sued the plan under ERISA § 1132(a)(1)(A) for refusing to distribute the plan funds to him. [*Foster v. PPG Indus. Inc.*, 693 F.3d 1226 (10th Cir. 2012); see Rebecca Moore, *DC Assets Withdrawn Fraudulently Not Forfeited*, plansponsor.com (Dec. 5, 2012)]

In light of the volatility of investments, rising PBGC premiums, and longer lifespans for retirees, defined benefit plan sponsors seek "de-risking" strategies. Traditional strategies include liability-driven investing and annuitizing accrued benefits. Annuitization can be costly, but it transfers all liability risk to a third party. Another option is to cash out pension recipients completely, placing all the risk on them. Two recent IRS Private Letter Rulings (201228045, 201280511), state that this can be done without violating the minimum distribution rules. [Elizabeth Thomas Dold and David N. Levine, *A Look at Retiree Cashouts as the New De-Risking Strategy*, Taxes: The Tax Magazine (November 2012) (benefitslink.com)]

However, there has not been a strong demand for annuitization from plan participants: few young workers are interested in annuitizing. There is a concern about the level of fees and limited portability. A participant who invests in a deferred annuity product, changes jobs, and rolls over the balance may lose expenses already paid. But if the participant leaves the money in the ex-employer's plan, the employee will have to track and manage multiple plans. Another possibility is for a 401(k) account to be used like an annuity as a Social Security bridge strategy: that is, benefits are postponed in order to get a higher amount by delaying the start of Social Security benefits. [Sharon F. Fountain,

Bloomberg BNA, *"Annuitizing" a 401(k) – Options for Plan Sponsors and Participants* (Nov. 30, 2012) (benefitslink.com)]

For many years (e.g., DOL Interpretive Bulletin 95-1, Advisory Opinion 2002-14A) the Department of Labor took the position that selecting an annuity provider is a fiduciary decision. In other words, failure to select the safest annuity available could lead to fiduciary liability. Then, in September 2007, to make annuity distributions more attractive, the DOL announced new rules relieving defined contribution plans from the "safest annuity available" rule. PPA § 665 mandated the DOL to issue regulations exempting defined contribution plans from this rule. First the DOL amended Interpretive Bulletin 95-1, effective November 13, 2007, limiting its applicability to defined benefit plans. Under the interim final rules, fiduciaries must select annuity providers with due care and skill, using factors such as the cost of the annuity vis-à-vis the benefits and administrative services offered; the annuity provider's capital, surplus and reserves; its rating; and whether it is covered by a state guarantee program. [Interim final rules, 72 Fed. Reg. 52004 (Sept. 12, 2007); safe harbor for fiduciaries choosing annuity providers, 72 Fed. Reg. 52021 (Sept. 12, 2007), discussed in Guest article, Deloitte Washington Bulletin, *DOL Releases Defined Contribution Plans from "Safest Annuity Available" Standard* (Sept. 17, 2007) (benefitslink.com)]

DOL final regulations on selection of annuity providers for individual account plans (such as 401(k) plans) were published in late 2008, effective December 8, 2008. The PPA limited the application of the Interpretive Bulletin 95-1 "safest available provider" rule to defined benefit plans, raising the question of what standard should be applied to defined contribution plans. To qualify for the safe harbor, the individual account plan fiduciary must perform an objective, thorough, and analytical search to select annuity providers. The selection must reflect a determination that the provider has the ability to make all future payments under the contract, and that the total cost of the annuity contract (including fees and commissions) is reasonable in light of the benefits the contract provides. [DOL Reg. § 2550.404a-4, 73 Fed. Reg. 58447 (Oct. 7, 2008); Amendment to Interpretive Bulletin 95-1, 73 Fed. Reg. 58445 (Oct. 7, 2008); see EBIA Weekly, *DOL Finalizes Annuity Selection Rule and Amendments to Plan Termination Rules for Missing Non-Spouse Beneficiaries* (Oct. 9, 2008) (benefitslink.com); Rebecca Moore, *DOL Issues Final Rules on Missing Benefits and Other PPA Provisions*, plansponsor.com (Oct. 6, 2008)]

The Northern District of Texas refused to enjoin Verizon from removing a group of plaintiffs from the Verizon plan and funding their benefits by purchasing a single-premium group annuity contract from Prudential. Verizon wanted to settle about $7.5 billion in pension liabilities. After the annuity contract is issued, Prudential will make annuity payments to about 41,000 management retirees who were receiving pensions under the plan before January 1, 2010. The annuity payment is the same as the current pension benefit, and carries the same rights (such as survivor benefits) as the current benefit. The plaintiffs said that the proposal violates ERISA § 510 by depriving them of the protections of ERISA: 29 C.F.R.

§ 2510.3-3(d)(2)(ii) says that a person whose entire benefit is fully guaranteed by an insurance company is not a plan participant. The district court held that the plaintiffs did not show a risk of loss of benefits; they would continue to receive the same amount of pension payments. The district court denied the breach of fiduciary duty claim because amending or terminating a pension plan is not a fiduciary act. The plaintiffs also alleged that, because all of the transferred assets were invested in Prudential, the duty to diversity was violated. The district court held that there was no duty to diversify and, in this context, fiduciary duty means prudent selection of an insurer to make annuity payments. [*Lee v. Verizon*, No. 3:12-cv-04834-D, 2012 U.S. Dist. LEXIS 173559 (N.D. Tex. Dec. 7, 2012) The entire case was dismissed In June 2013, although with leave to replead, because the plaintiffs failed to show that altering the source of payment deprived them of any benefits: see Maria Wood, *Judge Disconnects Lawsuit Vs. Verizon Pension Transfer*,LifeHealthPro, <http://www.lifehealthpro.com/2013/06/26/judge-disconnects-lawsuit-vs-verizon-pension-trans> (June 26, 2013)]

The normal payment method for a profit-sharing plan or stock bonus plan is a lump sum, not a periodic payment. When a participant in one of these plans dies, the entire vested balance remaining in the account must go to the beneficiary designated by the participant. The spouse's consent is required if a married participant is to designate anyone other than the spouse as beneficiary.

In 2012, the Northern District of California ruled that it was reasonable for a 401(k) plan to wait two weeks until a scheduled December 31, 2008 valuation was performed before distributing a retiree's balance. The retiree argued that she should have received the 2007 value of her account, which was about $36,000 more than she actually received. The district court held that changing the valuation date did not deprive the plaintiff of vested benefits, although it did force her to accept her share of the plan's investment losses during the year. There was a potential conflict of interest because the plan was for a dental practice and the dentist and his wife and daughters were participants, but because they had only a 10% interest in the plan's assets, the district court did not give this factor much weight. [*Wakamatsu v. Oliver*, No. C 11-00482 CRB, 2012 U.S. Dist. LEXIS 49743 (N.D. Cal. Apr. 9, 2012); see Rebecca Moore, *Retiree Loses Bid to Recover 2008 Losses,* plansponsor.com (Apr. 11, 2012)]

In 2008, the Northern District of Illinois ruled that Verizon was bound by the language in a defined benefit plan document even if there was a drafting error (multiplying the cashout value of an interest in the former plan by a variable transaction factor twice rather than once), but the court ruled in 2009 that Verizon could correct the error and would not be required to provide a $1.67 billion windfall to participants. The 2009 decision treated the error as an honest mistake, and other actions in administering the plan reflected an intent to use the multiplication factor only once. Magistrate Judge Morton Denlow said that employers would be discouraged from adopting plans if they suffered unduly harsh penalties for mistakes. The Seventh Circuit affirmed this decision in August, 2010. [*Young v. Verizon* (N.D. Ill. 2009), *aff'd, Young v. Verizon*, 615 F.3d 808 (7th Cir. 2010).

The Supreme Court refused to hear the case (No. 10-765), denying certiorari on May 23, 2011 and rehearing on July 25, 2011.]

A plan participant discovered that, as a result of a change in plan terms, she had been eligible for a full pension for almost eight years. The pension plan refused to pay her, stating that the plan forbids "retroactive payments." The Fourth Circuit held that it was an abuse of discretion to deny her the payments because the plan explicitly allowed "restorative" benefits to correct administrative errors. [*Helton v. AT&T Inc. Pension Benefit Plan, 709 F.3d 343* (4th Cir. 2013)]

The First Circuit held that, if a company representative, using an online benefits calculator, tells an employee that his retirement benefits will be greater than they actually are, the employee is only entitled to benefits as properly calculated under the plan, not the greater amount calculated by mistake. [*Livick v. Gillette Co.*, 524 F.3d 24 (1st Cir. 2008)]

However, the Seventh Circuit held that ERISA § 502 does not rule out enforcement of a pension plan's recoupment provisions (by suspending benefits to recover a past overpayment). The CBA said that pension and disability benefits were to be reduced by Social Security benefits payable to the employee, and that a grant of retroactive Social Security benefits would be treated as an overpayment that would trigger an obligation to reimburse the plan. The plaintiffs' argument was that the employer had to sue for equitable relief and could not enforce contract remedies, but the Seventh Circuit said that enforcing a contractual provision, like the CBA reimbursement requirement, is not "judicial relief," and employees can be held to clearly disclosed requirements to repay duplicative payments they have received. [*Northcutt v. GM Hourly Rate Emps. Pension Plan*, 467 F.3d 1031 (7th Cir. 2006)]

Under federal law, overpayments must be returned to the pension plan—but the law does not state who must make the payments. Usually, the payor stops or reduces the payments until the overpayments have been recovered. Recoupment is also subject to state trust law, which requires decisions to be made based on equity principles, including "laches" (i.e., if a plan waits too long to recover overpayments, it may be held to have waived the right to repayment). There is no ceiling on the amount a private plan can recoup from later payments, but a multiemployer plan can impose only a 25% reduction, and the PBGC can reduce a pension by only 10% and does not impose interest. [Ellen E. Schultz, *'Overpaid' Pensions Being Seized*, WSJ.com (Aug. 13, 2010)]

Overpayments were caused by a computer glitch. The Sixth Circuit rejected an equitable estoppels claim that would have permitted the plaintiff to continue receiving the excess amounts. The plaintiff could not show that the plan committee intended its representations to be relied on despite knowing the correct value. The plaintiff was not required to repay the overpayments, so she did not incur any detriment. There was no breach of fiduciary duty, because the plan committee was not negligent: the plan committee asked Hewitt Management if the benefit figure was correct, and then reasonably relied on Hewitt's error. [*Stark v. Mars Inc.*,

No. 13a0460n-07 (6th Cir. 2013); see Rebecca Moore, *Retiree Cannot Continue Receiving Pension Overpayments*, plansponsor.com (May 28, 2013)]

It was not a breach of fiduciary duty to decrease a retiree's monthly pension check in order to recoup overpayments made because of miscalculation of the benefit amount. (The pension was not offset by his benefit from another federal contractor, as required by law.) Plan trustees have a duty to make sure that the plan receives all the money it is entitled to, so benefits to other beneficiaries can be distributed. The plan documents also imposed a duty to correct errors. The employee who made the calculation was performing ministerial functions, not acting as a fiduciary. The plaintiff could not show detrimental reliance on the incorrect representation, because he received double payments until the error was discovered. [*Sheward v. Bechtel Jacobs Co. Pension Plan for Grandfathered Employees*, No. 3:08-CV-428 (E.D. Tenn. Mar. 4, 2010); see Rebecca Moore, *Employer Can Reduce Monthly Pension to Fix Error* (Mar. 8, 2010) (benefitslink. com)]

A surviving spouse applied for benefits when her husband, who was receiving a pension, died. The benefit was much smaller than she expected and she sued to receive what she thought was the correct benefit. The issue was whether the survivor benefit would be offset by Social Security benefits. The Sixth Circuit ruled for the plan, holding that SPD language can control over conflicting plan language—but leaving something out of an SPD does not alter the terms of the plan [*Lipker v. AK Steel Corp.*, 698 F.3d 923 (6th Cir. 2012); see John Murray and Violet Borowski, *Sixth Circuit Upholds Plan's Interpretation Of Ambiguous Spousal Benefit Provision*, Seyfarth Shaw ERISA & Employee Benefits Litigation Blog (Dec. 13, 2012) (benefitslink.com); Rebecca Moore, *SPD Omission Not a Conflict with Plan Terms*, plansponsor.com (Dec. 21, 2012)]

It was once common for plan sponsors to use the IRS letter forwarding service to locate the payees of benefits. However, effective for requests postmarked on or after August 31, 2012, the IRS no longer treats finding missing participants a "humane purpose." Plan sponsors will, therefore, have to use costlier and more laborious methods. DOL suggests using Internet search, credit reports, and commercial locater services to find missing participants. The Social Security Administration's forwarding service is still available, but at a cost of $25 per forwarded letter; the IRS used to forward up to 50 letters without charge. A terminating pension plan can use the PBGC missing participants program, paying the benefit to the PBGC, which will try to locate the participant. The PPA mandated the extension of this program to terminating 401(k) plans, but the PBGC never issued regulations. The PBGC also helps participants locate missing benefits. [McDermott Will & Emery, *IRS Eliminates Use of Letter Forwarding Service to Find Missing Participants and Beneficiaries* (Sept. 27, 2012) (benefitslink.com)]

## [A]  Disaster-Related Distributions

The Katrina Emergency Tax Relief Act of 2005 (KETRA), Pub. L. No. 109-73, provided that the 10% penalty on early withdrawals would not be imposed on a "qualified Hurricane Katrina distribution" of up to $100,000 withdrawn by a storm victim from a qualified retirement plan, 403(b) plan, or IRA, although the amounts would be treated as income, recognized over a three-year period. [IRS Publication 4492, *Information for Taxpayers Affected by Hurricanes Katrina, Rita and Wilma*)]

Although qualified hurricane distributions were announced for Hurricanes Katrina, Rita, and Wilma, they were not announced for Hurricane Irene, despite the severe financial impact of that storm. [Keith R. McMurdy, *Employees May Be Eligible for Retirement Funds After Natural Disasters*, Employee Benefit News (Sept. 9, 2011) (benefitslink.com)]

Nor was there a qualified hurricane distribution for Superstorm Sandy. Nevertheless, the IRS announced relief for taxpayers who wanted to apply retirement assets for financial hardship caused by Sandy. The verification requirements for plan loans and hardship distributions have been relaxed. A plan will not be deemed to violate the Code merely because it made a loan or hardship distribution between October 26, 2012 and February 1, 2013, based on needs caused by Sandy, to an employee whose workplace, principal residence, or principal residence of a close family member was in the identified disaster area. The usual calculation of maximum permitted hardship distribution will apply. Distributions can be made without the normal documentation, if the storm destroyed the necessary records—but, as soon as practicable, the plan administrator must assemble the documentation. However, the announcement does not alter the general rule that a defined benefit or money purchase plan cannot make hardship distributions (other than from a separate account within the plan containing employee contributions or rollovers). [Announcement 2012-44, 2012-49 I.R.B. 663. This relief is in addition to relief under Code § 7508A provided by IR-2012-83.]

## [B]  Roth Distributions

The enactment of Roth IRAs and Roth 401(k)s (i.e., accounts that are not tax-advantaged when deposits are made, but permit tax-free withdrawals on appropriate conditions, including retention of the sums within the account for at least five years) created a need for specialized distribution rules.

Proposed regulations on the taxation of Roth 401(k) distributions say that the five-year holding period begins at the beginning of the tax year in which the first Roth 401(k) contribution is made and ends at the end of the fifth tax year. In a direct rollover, the holding period from the sending plan is considered under the receiving plan (this is known as "tacking"—i.e., the earlier holding period is tacked on). However, tacking is not applied if the participant makes an indirect rollover within the 60-day period. Only the taxable part of the distribution can be the subject of an indirect rollover.

Both qualified and nonqualified Roth 401(k) distributions that could otherwise be rolled over can be rolled over directly to another qualified plan that accepts Roth 401(k) contributions. Distributions to a participant can be rolled over to a Roth IRA, and the taxable part of the distribution can be rolled over to another plan that accepts Roth 401(k) funds. Even a person whose AGI is too high to make a Roth IRA contribution can roll funds over into a Roth IRA.

If one Roth plan does a plan-to-plan rollover to another Roth plan, the sending plan must inform the receiving plan that the distribution is a qualified distribution or the amount of the participant's basis and the date the five-year "clock" began to run. Participants are entitled to disclosure of the same information if they receive a distribution.

Partial distributions from a Roth plan allocate taxable income pro rata; that is, if $1,000 in a $10,000 account is income on amounts deposited into the plan, and the account owner receives a nonqualified distribution of $4,000, 10% is attributed to income and therefore is taxable income for the recipient; $3,600 is a nontaxable return of deferred amounts. Only the amount contributed to the account (not earnings) can become a hardship distribution. [71 Fed. Reg. 4320 (Jan. 26, 2006); see SunGard Corbel News Pension Technical Updates, *Roth Distribution Regulations*, <http//www.corbel.com/news/technicalupdates.asp? ID=332&T=P> (Jan. 26, 2006)]

Final rules were published in April 2007, covering Roth 401(k) distribution issues. As in the proposed regulations, the central question is whether the distribution is a qualified distribution and thus excludable from the recipient's gross income. If the distribution is made to a beneficiary or an alternate payee, the participant's age, death, or disability status is the deciding factor, except for rollovers made by a surviving spouse or alternate payee to his or her own employer's Roth plan. Part of a Roth 401(k) distribution can be rolled over directly to a Roth 401(k) or Roth IRA, but a distribution from a designated Roth account can be rolled over only to a 401(k) plan or a 403(b) plan with a Roth feature. [T.D. 9324, RIN 1545-BF04, 72 Fed. Reg. 21103 (Apr. 30, 2007); see Prudential Retirement Pension Analyst, *IRS Issues Final Roth 401(k) Distribution Rules* (Apr. 30, 2007) (benefitslink.com)]

See § 12.10 for Roth account rollover issues.

## [C] PPA Rules

Although the main focus of the Pension Protection Act (PPA; Pub. L. No. 109-280) is on improving the funding mechanisms, and therefore the stability, of defined-benefit plans (including special rules for at-risk plans), this legislation has an impact on many areas of plan operations.

The Pension Protection Act forbids amendments that increase benefits in certain underfunded defined benefit plans (see § 5.10) unless the plan sponsor makes additional contributions or provides security. (This requirement does not apply to a new plan in its first five years of operation.) The PPA limits benefits that can be paid in a lump sum or other alternate form of distribution when a single-employer defined benefit plan is underfunded. For example, if its AFTAP (percentage of funding) is between 60%–80%, the plan cannot make an accelerated distribution that is greater than 50% of the amount otherwise payable, or that exceeds the present value of the maximum PBGC guarantee for the participant—whichever of the two is lower. See Code § 463(d)(3) and ERISA § 206(g)(3)(C). The PBGC publishes present-value tables every year for this purpose.

When an underfunded plan terminates, additional benefit accruals cease and the PBGC's guarantee covers only amounts earned before termination. If the plan terminates when the employer is bankrupt, only the benefits earned before the bankruptcy filing date are guaranteed. The PBGC pays benefits according to the terms of the plan. Most participants will receive their full benefits, but if the benefits exceed the limit on the PBGC guarantee, the PBGC will make estimated benefit payments while it examines the plan records, reducing any benefits that exceed the guarantee. For 80% of participants, the estimated benefit equals the final benefit, but the PBGC will make a single payment (including interest) to catch up if the final benefit is higher than the estimate. Anyone who retired before the PBGC take-over continues to receive the form of benefit already elected. Those who retire after the take-over choose from among the PBGC's annuity options. A participant who is not yet receiving payments from a terminated plan can begin to collect benefits at the plan's Normal Retirement Age. Someone who has already satisfied all the requirements (such as years of service) for early retirement as of the date of plan termination, or the earlier date on which the sponsor filed for bankruptcy protection, can begin early retirement benefits at early retirement age—but only if he or she is no longer employed by the plan sponsor. [PBGC, *PBGC's Guarantees for Single-Employer Pension Plans Fact Sheet*, <http://www.pbgc.gov/res/factsheets/page/guar-facts.html> (no date, accessed Apr. 14, 2012)] For benefits with annuity starting dates in 2013 , the present value of the PBGC's maximum guarantee ranges from $125,537 (age 25), to $153,501 (30), $180,229 (35), $230,843 (40), $282,286 (45), $371,638 (50), $476,923 (55), $604,500 (60), $782,324 (65), $1,122,428 (70), $1,704,372 (75) and $2,844,680 (80). [*Present Value of PBGC Maximum Guarantee*, <http://www.pbgc.gov/prac/mortality-retirement-and-pv-max-guarantee/present-guarantee.html> (undated, last accessed Mar. 10, 2013)]

The PPA also changes the interest rate and mortality table for minimum lump sum benefits, by reducing mortality assumptions (which increases lump sums by about 1%) but by requiring interest rates to be based on corporate bond yields, which will reduce lump sums. [Chicago Consulting Actuaries, *Lump Sums under the Pension Protection Act of 2006* (Nov. 15, 2006) (benefitslink.com)] Valuation issues, including limitations on distributions made by underfunded plans, are addressed by T.D. 9467, *Measurement of Assets and Liabilities for Pension Funding Purposes, Benefit Restrictions for Underfunded Pension Plans* [T.D. 9467, 2009-50 I.R.B. 760]

In late 2011, the PBGC published a proposed rule implementing the PPA rules altering the determination of benefits in a cash balance or other hybrid plan. The regulations are intended to apply to plan years beginning on or after January 1, 2008. When a plan terminates, the variable rate to be used to determine accrued benefits is the average of the interest rates used by the plan in the five years before the date of termination. An average is also used if a variable rate is used to determine the amount of the annuity at NRA. The proposed rule amends the PBGC regulations for terminated plans that are trusteed by the PBGC, conforming the rules for allocating assets and paying benefits under ERISA Title IV to the PPA rules for benefit determinations in statutory hybrid plans. The proposed rule changes the present value calculation for accrued benefits in hybrid plans and offers guidance on benefits after a hybrid plan has gone through a standard termination. Variable interest rates create problems for the PBGC when a plan terminates because a participant's exact benefit can only be determined when he or she starts collecting benefits—so it is hard for the PBGC to decide if the benefit is de minimis and can be cashed out in a lump sum. The PBGC will use the present value methodology if the plan uses the § 417(e) present value rules to calculate the value of the lump sum. [76 Fed. Reg. 67105 (Oct. 31, 2011); see Rebecca Moore, *PBGC Issues Proposed Rule on Hybrid Plan Terminations,* plansponsor.com (Oct. 29, 2011); Deloitte's Washington Bulletin, *PBGC Proposes Rules on Determining Benefits in Terminating Hybrid Plans* (Nov. 7, 2011) (benefitslink.com)]

For plan amendments adopted and effective after November 8, 2012, plan sponsors who are bankruptcy debtors are permitted to amend single-employer defined benefit plans to eliminate certain optional forms of benefits without violating the anti-cutback rule. Under IRS regulations finalized in November 2012, optional forms of benefits, such as accelerated benefits that are greater than what the participant would have received as a single-life annuity, can be eliminated when the plan is not fully funded. The proposed regulations require the bankruptcy court rule that eliminating the optional benefit form is necessary to avoid an involuntary or distress termination. The PBGC's consent to terminate is required, based on the agency's conclusion that the plan is unable to provide the benefits guaranteed under ERISA § 404(d)(2). If the sponsor eliminates an optional form of benefit under these regulations and plan does not offer other options with substantial survivor benefits, the sponsor can add other options to provide those benefits as part of the amendment that eliminates the lump sum distribution option. The entire plan amendment is considered together in determining if the amendment can take effect in accordance with § 436(c). [77 Fed. Reg. 66915 (Nov. 8, 2012); see Kristen Heinzinger, *IRS Finalizes Relief for Bankrupt DB Sponsors,* plansponsor.com (Nov. 8, 2012)]

American Airlines' bankruptcy court permitted the airline to eliminate the optional lump sum and installment forms of benefit payment, agreeing with the airline that if pilots could receive a lump sum after American emerges from bankruptcy, there would probably be so many retirements that there wouldn't be enough pilots available. [Rebecca Moore, *American Allowed to Eliminate Lump Sums* plansponsor.com (Dec. 14, 2012)]

Proposed regulations published in the fall of 2008 cover the PPA requirement that the notice of a participant's rights to defer an immediate distribution also explain the consequences of taking that distribution. A qualified plan cannot distribute benefits before Normal Retirement Age (NRA) without the consent of the participant, so rules are necessary to determine what constitutes valid and informed consent. There is no official format for the disclosures, but all of the information must be given together (e.g., in a list). However, if the required information is already available in other documents that the plan participant can obtain without charge, it is permissible to give cross-references to the other documents instead of repeating the information.

The regulations also deal with the increased period (rising from 90 to 180 days) for giving notice under Code §§ 402(f) [rollover notices], 411 [notice of the right to defer a distribution], and 417 [notice and election periods for 401(k) plans offering annuity distributions]. Cashouts of over $5,000 from a 401(k) plan require the consent of the plan participant, so the participant must be informed of the consequences of deferring versus receiving the distribution immediately (e.g., tax consequences; investment costs; other plan provisions such as availability of retiree health coverage that affect the decision).

PPA § 829 permits a non-spouse beneficiary to roll over a plan distribution to an IRA. [Prop. Treas. Reg. §§ 1.401(a)-13, 1.401(a)-20, 1.402(f)-1, 1.411(a)-11, 1.417(e)-1, 73 Fed. Reg. 59575 (Oct. 9, 2008); see EBIA Weekly, *IRS Proposes Regulations Addressing Notice of Participant's Right to Defer a Distribution and 180-Day Notice Period* (Oct. 9, 2008) (benefitslink.com)]

In a 2013 decision, the Seventh Circuit noted that a higher discount rate means a higher growth rate over the annuity period and a lower present value for lump sums, whereas a low discount rate means a higher lump sum. In a class action about the discount rates used by pension plans and top hat plans to convert a straight life annuity to lump sum, the Seventh Circuit upheld a grant of summary judgment for the plans. The pension plan used a segment rate of approximately 5.4%. The Seventh Circuit pointed out that the PPA allows retroactive increases in the discount rate, subject to a cap, so the change was not a cutback. While the plan forbade reduction in accrued benefits (the value of the straight-life annuity), it did not prevent a retroactive reduction in the benefits of participants who opted for a lump sum. The top hat plan used a higher discount rate (7.5%) but that was permissible because it was a nonqualified plan and the PPA cap did not apply. The plan also permitted a 7.5% discount rate for any plan that is not tax-preferred, a category that includes top hat plans. [*Dennison v. MONY Life Ret. Income Sec. Plan*, 710 F.3d 741 (7th Cir., 2013); see Brian Stolzenbach, Sam Schwartz-Fenwick and Chris Busey, *Seventh Circuit Reads Plan Language To*

*Discount Plaintiffs' Rate Argument*, Seyfarth Shaw ERISA & Employee Benefits Litigation Blog (Mar. 20, 2013) (benefitslink.com)]

### [D]    Hardship Distributions

Economic problems increase the number of employees seeking hardship distributions from retirement plans. To prevent disqualifying the plan, the employer and plan administrators must follow both the plan document and legal requirements before allowing hardship distributions. A hardship distribution is permissible only if the plan allows it; if the employee (in some circumstances, the employee's spouse, dependent, or beneficiary) has an immediate and heavy financial need; and the distribution does not exceed the amount required to meet that need. Employees taking distributions should be required to provide verification of hardship was required by the terms of the plan—and that they have exhausted other loans and distributions from other available plans. The plan terms might also impose dollar limits or require distributions to be made only from salary reduction contributions. [<http://www.irs.gov/pub/irs-tege/fall09.pdf>, *Do's and Don'ts of Hardship Distributions* (Aug. 8, 2011)]

PPA § 826 allows a hardship distribution to be made based on the needs of a primary beneficiary who is not the participant's spouse and who has an unconditional right to receive part or all of the account balance when the participant dies. A § 409A plan can consider the needs of a beneficiary in determining if an emergency has occurred.

The recession has also led to more requests for hardship distributions. Participants in 401(k) plans can receive hardship distributions before age 59½ subject to limitations—but only if the plan provides for them. Plans can be disqualified for making improper distributions. Permissible distributions are made for an immediate and heavy financial need of the participant, determined based on all the facts and circumstances.

The regulations say that family funeral expenses count—but buying a boat or television set does not. The distribution must not be greater than the amount required to satisfy needs that cannot be met by other resources reasonably available to the participant (including resources of the participant's spouse), but it is permissible for the distribution to include taxes and penalties reasonably expected to result from the distribution. Unless it has actual knowledge to the contrary, the plan can rely on the participant's written representation that the need cannot be met by insurance; liquidating other assets; ceasing elective contributions; or taking out a commercial loan or a non-taxable loan from the employer's plan.

Hardship distributions cannot be made from accumulated non-elective employer contributions or qualified matching contributions. The plan administrator has discretion to decide if a request qualifies for a distribution, but discretion must be exercised based on the plan's objective, non-discriminatory standards. The regulations provide a safe harbor set of guidelines that a plan can incorporate (e.g., defining "immediate and heavy financial need"). A distribution can be considered necessary if the employee has already taken all the distributions and non-taxable loans available under all employer-sponsored plans he or she participates in.

An employee who takes a hardship distribution cannot make any elective contribution or after-tax employee contribution to any plan sponsored by the employer for at least six months after the distribution. Administrators should document representations that applicants made about their requests for hardship distributions, and should document why they granted or rejected the application; the source of the distribution; and that it does not exceed the amount needed. [Bruce K. Leigh and Kenneth W. Ruthenberg, Jr., Chang Ruthenberg & Long, *Hardship Distributions and Headaches Down the Road* (2009) (benefitslink.com)]

Rev. Rul. 2010-27, 2010-45 I.R.B. 620 lists examples of expenses that could qualify for an unforeseeable emergency distribution from a 409A plan. The examples include illness or accident suffered by a participant or a participant's spouse, dependents, or beneficiary; an uninsured property loss experienced by a participant or beneficiary; funeral expenses for a participant's spouse or dependent; extraordinary and unforeseeable circumstances stemming from events beyond the control of the participant or beneficiary, such as imminent foreclosure or eviction from the primary residence; heavy medical or prescription drug expenses. To receive an emergency distribution, the participant must show that the expenses could not otherwise be met by insurance, or by liquidation of assets that could be liquidated without severe financial hardship. The distribution must not exceed the amount needed to cover the emergency, plus taxes. Rev. Rule. 2010-27 analyzes three specific requests. Repair of uninsured water damage to a participant's house, or funeral expenses for a participant's son, qualify. But credit card debt does not qualify, because it does not reflect circumstances beyond the participant's control. [McGuireWoods LLP Legal Updates, *IRS Issues Guidance on Unforeseeable Emergency Distributions from § 409A and § 457(b) Plans* (Dec. 30, 2010) (benefitslink.com)]

## § 12.02  CASHOUT

Although it is burdensome for a plan to make periodic payments of a very small sum, and it would be convenient to simply close the books by making a one-time payment, participants cannot be forced to "cash out" (take a lump sum instead of a stream of payments) unless their vested balance is very small—$5,000 or less.

EGTRRA provides for automatic rollovers of cashouts from 401(k) plans in amounts between $1,000 and $5,000 to IRAs.

The calculation of the accrued benefit under I.R.C. § 411(a)(7)(B)(i) does not have to include any service with respect to which the employee has already been cashed out at a level below $3,500.

The 2002 technical corrections bill, the Job Creation and Worker Assistance Act of 2002 [Pub. L. No. 107-147] provides that employers can disregard roll-overs when they determine whether or not the balance exceeds $5,000 and there-fore whether or not it is subject to cashout.

The IRS provided guidance about automatic rollovers, as amended by EGTRRA, in Notice 2005-5, 2005-3 I.R.B. 337; and the Department of Labor did the same in Proposed Regulations at 69 Fed. Reg. 9900 (Mar. 2, 2004) and Final Regulations at 69 Fed. Reg. 58017 (Sept. 28, 2004).

A qualified plan can include a provision cashing out distributions under $5,000; mandatory distributions that exceed $1,000 must be rolled over to an IRA set up by the plan for the participant, unless the recipient makes an affirmative election to roll over the money elsewhere or takes it in cash. Fiduciaries are deemed to have satisfied their duties with respect to rollovers if the plan satisfies the requirements of I.R.C. § 401(a)(31)(B). These rules apply to distributions made without consent of the participant, at normal retirement age or age 62 (whichever is later). An eligible rollover distribution that is a plan loan offset is not subject to the general rules on automatic rollovers. QDROs and distributions to participants' spouses are not covered.

Aon Hewitt said that in 2011 about half of companies sponsoring IRA plans automatically rolled over accounts of former employees holding less than $5,000 in IRAs, whereas only one-third did that in 2005, when cash-outs were forbidden for amounts over $1,000. Establishing IRAs is worthwhile because it spares the expense and complexity of managing a large number of very small accounts. EBRI said that the average 401(k) balance for workers in their 20s with under two years' tenure was $3,426, so this is a relevant consideration. [Ian Salisbury, *Kicked Out of Your 401(k)? Don't Let the Cash Sit*, WSJ.com (Mar. 25, 2013)]

## § 12.03 LUMP SUMS

There is no legal requirement that plans offer lump sum distributions, although it is very common for them to do so for the convenience of retirees who either need a lump sum (to pay the entrance fee to a Continuing Care Retirement Community, for example) or who believe that they can achieve better investment results than a qualified plan, subject to fiduciary requirements, can muster. The interaction between PPA funding requirements and the post-2008 recession made employers less willing to distribute balances, especially large balances, in lump-sum form. Since the stock market decline, the PPA's rules often prevent the 25 highest-compensated employees from taking lump sums, because top earners are forbidden lump sums if the plan assets fall below 110% of liabilities, or if the lump sum represents more than 1% of total plan assets. However, there are loop-holes, such as the executive's promise to repay if the plan terminates when it is insufficiently funded, or setting aside funds in an escrow account. [Jilian Mincer, *Execs Finding It Harder to Get Lump Sums*, WSJ.com (May 12, 2009)] The

Pension Protection Act says that if any defined benefit plan is severely under-funded, or if the plan is underfunded and the plan sponsor is bankrupt, all payouts must be in annuity form—lump sum distribution is forbidden.

In the fall of 2009, the Supreme Court heard arguments about treatment of lump sums received at the time of the first retirement by rehired employees. The plan had two provisions. The "non-duplication" provision called for offsetting the "floor" amount, based on total years of service with the company. The "phantom account provision" further reduced benefits at retirement. The Second Circuit refused to grant deference to the administrator's determination.

The Supreme Court announced its decision on April 21, 2010, strongly affirming the discretion of plan administrators, and holding that, as long as the plan gives administrators the discretion to interpret the plan, courts must defer to the administrators' decisions as long as they are reasonable. (Of course, this principle does not prevent plan participants from bringing suits that claim that the administrators made an unreasonable decision!) [*Frommert v. Conkright*, 129 S. Ct. 2889 (Apr. 21, 2010)]

If a plan offers both lump sums and early retirement subsidies, the plan should specify whether the subsidy can be included in the lump sum, or must be taken in annuity form.

The Seventh Circuit ruled that Cost of Living Increases are accrued benefits required by ERISA (not merely ancillary benefits), and therefore must be included in the calculation of lump sums if annuitants receive COLAs. Failure to do so violates the anti-cutback rule. [*Williams v. Rohm & Haas Pension Plan*, 497 F.3d 710 (7th Cir. 2007); see Rebecca Moore, *COLAs Must Be Included in Lump-Sum Benefits for DB Participants*, plansponsor.com (Aug. 15, 2007); Brian S. King, *Limits on How Plan Benefits Are Provided*, ERISA Law Blog (Aug. 16, 2007) (benefitslink.com)] In March 2008, the Supreme Court refused to hear an appeal of the Seventh Circuit's decision. [Rebecca Moore, *High Court Lets Stand Decision on COLAs in Lump-sum Calculations*, plansponsor.com (Mar. 18, 2008). The case was finally disposed of by a settlement with approximately 18,000 plan participants, with half of the $180 million settlement paid out by September 30, 2010, the other half in September 2011:*Williams v. Rohm & Haas Pension Plan*, No. 4:04-CV-0078-SEB-WGH (S.D. Ind. 2010); see Fred Schneyer, *Rohm and Haas Pension Settlement Gets Final OK*, plansponsor.com (Apr. 14, 2010). The Northern District of Oklahoma followed this reasoning: *Pikas v. Williams Cos. Inc.*, No. 4:08-cv-101-GKF-PJC, 2012 U.S. Dist. LEXIS 150603 (N.D. Okla. Oct. 19, 2012); see Rebecca Moore, *Pension Lump Sums Must Account for COLAs*, plansponsor.com (Jan. 10, 2013)]

The District Court for the District of Columbia upheld the reasonableness of U.S. Airways' policy of paying a lump-sum benefit 45 days after retirement, and held that interest is not due for the interim period. However, the D.C. Circuit reversed in 2011, finding the 45-day delay unreasonable after the PBGC became the trustee after US Airways' bankruptcy. An analysis performed by the airline in the

1990s found that the calculation took a maximum of 21 business days, so the court could find no reason why the PBGC, as trustee, would require 45 days to distribute a lump sum from the plan. [*Stephens v. US Airways Group*, No. 07-1264 (RMC) (D.D.C. Mar. 17, 2010), *rev'd* 644 F.3d 437 (D.C. Cir. 2011), *cert. denied*, 132 S. Ct. 1857 (Apr. 2, 2012); see Rebecca Moore, *U.S. Airways Employees Owed Interest for Delayed Pension Payments*, plansponsor.com (Apr. 3, 2012)]

## § 12.04  ANTI-ALIENATION RULE

The underlying purpose of pension plans is to provide income to retirees and their families once the individual is no longer able to work. This purpose could not be satisfied if the pension became unavailable for some reason. Therefore, pension, annuity, stock bonus, and profit-sharing plans are subject to anti-alienation requirements under I.R.C. §§ 401(a)(13) and 404(a)(2). The benefits under such plans may not be assigned or alienated in advance. But, just as with any legal rule, there are certain exceptions to what seems to be a blanket prohibition.

Federal tax liens under I.R.C. § 6331 can be enforced; they are not considered to violate this provision. [Treas. Reg. § 1.401(a)-13(b)(2)] The anti-alienation provision does not prevent the IRS from proceeding against an interest in ERISA plan benefits. [*United States v. McIntyre*, 222 F.3d 655 (9th Cir. 2000)]

On the grounds that pensions can be invaded to satisfy criminal fines, the Second Circuit held that it is not a violation of ERISA to invade a pension to pay a fine for traveling outside the United States to engage in sex acts with minors. [*United States v. Irving*, 432 F.3d 401 (2d Cir. 2005)]

Once a benefit is in pay status, a participant or beneficiary can make a voluntary revocable assignment of up to 10% of any benefit payment. However, assignments of this type cannot be used to defray the costs of plan administration.

A plan loan is not an improper alienation if:

- The plan includes a specific loan provision;
- Loans are available to all participants on a nondiscriminatory basis;
- The loan is not a prohibited transaction;
- The plan imposes a reasonable interest rate on plan loans;
- The loan is secured by the accrued nonforfeitable benefit. [See I.R.C. § 4975(d)(1) and § 4.18]

The Supreme Court's decision in *Patterson v. Shumate* [504 U.S. 753 (1992)] holds that ERISA's anti-alienation provisions are "applicable non-bankruptcy law" under Bankruptcy Code § 541(c)(1). Therefore, benefits from an ERISA-qualified plan can be excluded from the employee's bankruptcy estate, and will not be available to the employee's creditors.

But because of an earlier Supreme Court decision, *Mackey v. Lanier Collection Agency & Service* [486 U.S. 825 (1988)], pension benefits are protected from creditors, but welfare benefits are not. Creditors are sometimes entitled (within limits) to garnish the wages of debtors, but they cannot garnish future pension benefits. If the plan itself is terminating, creditors cannot garnish employees' interests in the plan, even if one consequence of the termination is that they will receive a lump sum instead of ongoing annuity payments. In 2005, the Supreme Court ruled, in *Rousey v. Jacoway*, 544 U.S. 320, that IRAs are entitled to the same bankruptcy protection as qualified plans. Also in 2005, Congress increased the bankruptcy protection granted to IRAs and qualified plans, via Pub. L. No. 109-8, the Bankruptcy Abuse Prevention and Consumer Protection Act (BAPCA). BAPCA also makes it harder for bankrupt employers to modify their retiree health benefits.

Once the benefits are paid, the anti-alienation provision no longer applies. [See *Robbins v. DeBuono*, 218 F.3d 197 (2d Cir. 2000)] So, unless there is a state law that offers additional protection, the funds can be attached by creditors.

In mid-2003, the Eighth Circuit ruled that a state domestic relations order had higher priority than a prior federal tax lien. Therefore, in a case where the IRS pursued remedies against a divorced airline pilot, the QDRO in the ex-wife's favor prevailed (even though there were technical deficiencies in the order that required it to be reformed twice by the court). The Eighth Circuit read Code § 6323(a) to require the IRS to file a notice of lien to secure its priority in situations like this one, where the ex-wife had the status of a judgment lien creditor. [*United States v. Taylor*, 338 F.3d 947 (8th Cir. 2003)]

## § 12.05 QJSA/QOSA PAYMENTS

The normal method of paying pension plan benefits to married participants is the QJSA, payable for the lives of both the employee and his or her spouse. Once the first spouse dies, the plan can reduce the annuity payable to the survivor—although not more than 50% of the initial payment, for a joint and 50% survivor annuity. Employers can also choose to subsidize the survivor annuity at some level between 50% and 100% of the original payment, and the Pension Protection Act requires a joint and 75% survivor annuity to be offered as an option when a QJSA is required.

In addition to the QJSA/QPSA, a plan can offer term annuities and/or life annuities, and life annuities can include term certain guarantee features.

Why would a couple be willing to waive the standard form and take a payment other than a QJSA? For one thing, the payments might be larger in the short run. The participant might be the first spouse to retire, with additional funds expected in the future from the other spouse's pension. If the spouse who is expected to survive will have ample funds (e.g., from personal assets and insurance on the life of the other spouse), then a reduced or absent survivor annuity may not create problems.

I.R.C. § 417(d) provides that QJSAs are required only if the participant was married for one year or more before plan payments begin, with an exception for participants who marry in the year before payments begin and remain married for one year. To avoid tracking problems, most plans simply offer QJSAs to all married participants whatever the duration of the marriage.

Because of a 1984 federal law, the Retirement Equity Act, the employee spouse cannot waive the QJSA without the written consent of the other spouse. There is a 60-day window for making the waiver, starting 90 days before the annuity start date (the first day of the employee spouse's first benefit period under the plan), ending 30 days before the annuity start date. However, the Small Business Job Protection Act [Pub. L. No. 104-188] amended the Internal Revenue Code to allow QJSA disclosures to be given even after the annuity starting date.

A waiver of the right to receive the pension in QJSA form must be in writing, and must either be notarized or witnessed by a representative of the pension plan. [See Treas. Reg. § 1.417(e)-1(b)(3)] In 2000, when the IRS and DOL were gearing up for implementing electronic filing of notices and disclosures, Proposed Regulations were issued (65 Fed. Reg. 6001) that did not allow a spouse's waiver of the QJSA to be made electronically, because a physical signature and a physical notarization were required. However, the October 20, 2006 Final Rules allow the waiver to be done electronically, as long as there are safeguards for the validity of the signature, and as long as the electronic signature and the verification by the notary can be printed out from the electronic system. [71 Fed. Reg. 61877 (Oct. 20, 2006)]

Furthermore, the waiver must be expressed in a document specifically related to the plan; a prenuptial agreement between the employee and his or her spouse won't work for this purpose. [Treas. Reg. § 1.401(a)-20, Q&A 28] The waiver binds only the spouse who signs it; if the employee and spouse divorce, any subsequent spouse is still entitled to a QJSA unless he or she waives it. [I.R.C. § 417(a)(4)]

According to the Eastern District of Wisconsin, a prenuptial agreement could not waive entitlement to benefits, because ERISA permits only a spouse, and not a prospective spouse, to waive rights in retirement assets. [*John Deere Deferred Savings Plan for Wage Emps. v. Estate of Propst*, No. 06-C-1235 (E.D. Wis. Dec. 28, 2007); see Fred Schneyer, *Pre-Nup Pact Not an ERISA Benefits Waiver*, plansponsor.com (Jan. 4, 2008)]

A business owner was both the sole participant in a plan and the plan representative so the Seventh Circuit held that his spouse's written consent to waive the right to an annuity from the plan was valid, even though her signature was not witnessed. ERISA § 205(C)(2)(A)(iii) requires a spousal waiver of the right to a survivor annuity to be written—and witnessed by a notary or plan representative. After the husband died, the wife sought benefits under the plan. She admitted that she had signed the waiver of joint and survivor annuity, but said the document was invalid because it had not been witnessed. The Seventh Circuit upheld the waiver and awarded benefits to the husband's sons, saying that it would be absurd to invalidate the consent form; the husband obviously knew that his wife had signed the form. [*Burns v. Orthotek, Inc. Employees' Pension Plan and Trust*, 657 F.3d 571 (7th Cir. 2011); see CCH Pensions & Benefits, *Lack Of Witness' Attestation Signature Did Not Invalidate Spouse's Signed Consent to Annuity Waiver* (Nov. 3, 2011) (benefitslink.com)]

In this context, ERISA preempts community property law [*Boggs v. Boggs*, 520 U.S. 833 (1997)], so a spouse who waives the right to a QJSA, can't later assert community property rights in those benefits.

The PPA mandates that plans that have to offer QJSAs must, for plan years beginning after December 31, 2007, offer Qualified Optional Survivor Annuities (QOSAs). A QOSA is a joint and survivor annuity where the survivor receives 75% of the original annuity level (if the QJSA would otherwise provide less) or 50% if the QJSA has a survivor percentage of 75% or more, actuarially equivalent to the single life annuity payable at the same time. If the existing plan terms provide a joint and survivor annuity which satisfies the QOSA percentage requirements, it is not necessary to amend the plan to adopt a QOSA. The requirement is that the QOSA be actuarially equivalent to a single-life annuity; it doesn't have to be equivalent to a QJSA. If the QOSA is actuarially equivalent to the QJSA, the participant's spouse is not required to consent to the participant electing the QOSA. However, spousal consent is required to elect a QOSA which is less valuable than the QJSA. The PPA does not obligate plans to provide an option for the QOSA that works the same way as a qualified pre-retirement survivor annuity does for the QJSA. [Notice 2008-30, 2008-12 I.R.B. 638; see Deloitte Washington Bulletin, *IRS Issues Guidance on PPA Distribution Changes* (Mar. 17, 2008) (benefitslink.com)]

Internal Revenue Code § 417(a)(1)(A)(ii) allows the plan participant to revoke the waiver of QJSA payment at any time before payments begin. The spouse's consent is not required for the revocation, because it has the effect of increasing, not decreasing, the spouse's rights.

It was not an abuse of discretion for a plan review committee to refuse a request to change the beneficiary of a QJSA from the participant's former wife to his new wife. The District Court for the District of Oregon ruled that benefits vested in the ex-wife as soon as the participant retired and began to receive benefits, and could not be re-assigned. In other words, the QJSA designation was "locked in." [*Montgomery v. AGC-International Union of Operating Eng'rs Local 701 Pension Trust Fund, Defined Benefit Plan*, No. 08-3129-CL (D. Or. 2010); see Fred Schneyer, *Annuity Beneficiary Substitution Denial Upheld*, plansponsor. com (Apr. 14, 2010)]

## [A] Section 415 Regulations

Final Regulations under § 415, reflecting the PPA as well as interim changes since the previous set of Final Regulations issued in 1981, were published in the Federal Register for April 5, 2007, effective for limitation years beginning on or after July 1, 2007. Section 415 governs the limitations on benefits that can be provided under defined benefit plans, as well as the contributions that can be made to 401(k) and other defined benefit plans. For most plans, which are operated on a calendar year, that meant that the new rules would take effect January 1, 2008. Plans can provide that payments in any limitation year will not exceed the § 415(b) limit as of the annuity starting date, and increased pursuant to § 415(d); if this is done, the plan does not require actuarial adjustments for automatic increases unless the benefit is subject to § 417(e)(3).

Under the PPA, compensation used to calculate the "high 3" years does not have to be earned while the employee is an active plan participant. In general, the "high 3" is calculated subject to the annual compensation limit of § 401(a)(17), but the Final Regulations allow grandfathering-in of some additional compensation based on plan provisions that were in effect before April 5, 2007. In general, money received after severance from employment is not considered § 415 compensation, but the Final Regulations allows inclusion of certain payments under bona fide sick or vacation leave plans—even if the payments are made more than 2½ months after severance from employment or the end of the year.

The final regulations allow some payments from non-qualified plans to be treated as § 415 compensation, as well as certain payments to disabled participants. The IRS announced its intentions to revise the rules covering multiple annuity starting dates. Various technical changes are made in the way that defined benefit payouts are adjusted when payment begins between ages 62 and 65. [Final Rule, 72 Fed. Reg. 16878 (Apr. 5, 2007), discussed in Sutherland Asbill & Brennan LLP Legal Alert, *Section 415 Final Regulations Clarify Rules*, < http://www.sutherland.com/file_upload/LegalAlertEmpBenSection415FinalRegulationsClarifyRules41007Update.pdf> (Apr. 10, 2007); Rebecca Moore, *IRS Issues Final, Comprehensive 415 Regulations*, plansponsor.com (Apr. 5, 2007). The Final Regulations are based on Proposed Regulations, T.D. 7748, 70 Fed. Reg. 31214 (May 31, 2005).]

## [B] QLACs

In early 2012, the Treasury proposed a rule, explained in a fact sheet, under which workers would have more options for lifetime income to cope with the potential for living to very old age. The proposal would allow employees who take a lump sum 401(k) distribution to transfer part of the sum to the employer's defined benefit plan (provided that the employer has a defined benefit plan and it accepts such contributions) in exchange for an actuarially fair annuity—perhaps a longevity annuity, a life annuity that begins payments at an advanced age such as 85. This option is referred to as a Qualified Longevity Annuity Contract, or QLAC.

Prior law disfavored longevity annuities by mandating minimum required distribution calculations based on distributing the entire sum over the person's actuarially predicted life expectancy—creating the risk of outliving one's assets.

The proposed regulations make it easier for a plan to offer split options by simplifying the calculation of the benefit. Prior law required the statutory interest rate and mortality assumptions to be used for both the lump sum and the annuity, preventing plans from using their own figures in annuity calculations. The proposal would allow the plan's regular conversion factors to be used for the partial annuity, while the statutory factors apply to the lump sum.

The 2012 proposal identifies certain plan and annuity terms that are deemed to protect spousal rights and for which spousal consent will not be required before the annuity begins. At the annuity start date, the insurer issuing the annuity would be responsible for compliance with the consent requirements. [Proposed Regulations, 77 Fed. Reg. 5443 and 5454 (Feb. 3, 2012); see DOT Retirement Security Fact Sheet, *Helping American Families Achieve Retirement Security by Expanding Lifetime Income Choices* (Feb. 2, 2012); see Retirement Town Hall, *IRS Proposes Rule To Encourage Partial Annuity Distribution Options In Pension Plans* (Feb. 9, 2012) (benefitslink.com)]

Under the 2012 proposals, funds used to purchase a QLAC are excluded from the Required Minimum Distribution calculations from age 70 to the annuity start date. QLACs are available for defined contribution plans and IRAs, but the amount that can be devoted to the QLAC is limited to $100,000 or 25% of the account balance, whichever is less. [McKay Hochman Company, Inc. E-Mail Alert 2012-8, *Lifetime Income Options* (Aug. 30, 2012) (benefitslink.com)]

## § 12.06 POST-DEATH PAYMENTS

The terms of the plan, and the fact situation, determine whether payments must continue after the death of the plan participant. For instance, if the employee was unmarried and received a life annuity, or if the employee was married and the employee and spouse validly waived the QJSA in favor of a life annuity, the plan will have no post-death obligations. Usually, however, the plan will be required to make a single or ongoing distributions to a beneficiary designated by the employee, or named as beneficiary under the terms of the plan.

Internal Revenue Code § 401(a)(9)(B) provides that if an employee dies when an annuity or installment pension with a survivorship feature is in pay status, the plan continues distributions in the same manner, but to the beneficiary rather than the retiree. The general rule is that the plan has five years from the death of the employee to complete distribution of the decedent's entire interest.

The five-year rule does not apply if the decedent's interest is payable to a designated beneficiary in life annuity form, or in installments that do not extend past the beneficiary's life expectancy. In this situation, the plan must begin the distributions no later than December 31 of the year following the date of the employee's death.

Qualified plans are required to provide Qualified Preretirement Survivor Annuities (QPSAs) if a vested plan participant dies before benefits begin. [I.R.C. § 401(a)(11)] The QPSA for a defined benefit plan participant who was eligible to retire at the time of death must be at least as great as what the spouse would have received if the employee had retired with the QJSA on the day before the actual date of death.

In the case of a person who was not yet retirement-eligible on the date of death, the defined benefit plan must calculate the survivor annuity that would have been available if the employee had separated from service on the date he or she died, and survived until the plan's earliest retirement date. The QPSA must be at least equivalent to the QJSA that would have been payable if the employee spouse had died the day after retiring with a QJSA on the plan's earliest retirement date.

In a defined contribution plan, the QPSA must be actuarially equivalent to at least 50% of the nonforfeitable account balance as of the time of death.

The designated beneficiary can also be an irrevocable trust that is valid under state law and has identifiable beneficiaries. It's the responsibility of the employee who wants to take this option to provide the plan with a copy of the trust.

According to I.R.C. § 401(a)(9)(B), if an employee dies once payment of an annuity or installment pension has begun, the plan simply continues the distributions in the same manner—unless, of course, they are supposed to stop at the employee's death.

Plans are allowed to reduce pension benefits to fund the QPSA. Therefore, participants (with the consent of the spouse of a married participant) have the right to waive the QPSA in order to prevent this reduction in the pension amount.

The plan must notify participants of the right to waive the QPSA. The notice must be given in the period that starts on the first day of the plan year in which the participant reaches age 32 and ends with the close of the plan year before the plan year in which the participant reaches age 35. [I.R.C. § 417(a)(3)(B)]

The notice must disclose:

- The terms and conditions of the QPSA;

- The effect of waiving it;

- The spouse's right to invalidate the waiver by withholding consent;

- The participant's right to revoke the waiver and reinstate the QPSA

Rev. Rul. 2012-3, 2012-8 I.R.B. 383 explains how the QJSA and QPSA rules work when a deferred annuity contract is purchased under a profit-sharing plan. Rev. Rul. 2012-4, 2012-8 I.R.B. 386 explains when an annuity provided by a defined benefit plan after a rollover can satisfy §§ 411 and 415. [Rebecca Moore, *IRS Issues Guidance About Annuities in Retirement Plans*, plansponsor.com (Feb. 2, 2012)]

The Tenth Circuit ruled in 2009 that the anti-cutback rule does not apply to a death benefit, or a plan feature that pays a lump sum at retirement that is the actuarial equivalent of a death benefit. The death benefit was not an accrued benefit, because the plan's definition of accrued benefit excluded death benefits. Nor was it a retirement-type subsidy, because that term is limited to benefits that continue after retirement. [*Kerber v. Qwest Pension Plan*, 572 F.3d 1135 (10th Cir. 2009); see Stanley D. Baum, *Tenth Circuit Determines That Elimination of a Pension Plan's Death Benefit Does Not Violate ERISA's Anti-Cutback Rule*, ERISA Lawyer Blog (July 22, 2009) (benefitslink.com). See *In re Lucent*, 541 F.3d 25 (3d Cir. 2008) for the proposition that the death benefit was not an accrued benefit.]

## [A] Beneficiary Designation Case Law

Although the broad principle of ERISA preemption is well-settled, there is still tension between federal regulation of pensions and benefits and the traditional state domination of the domestic relations field, so case continue to be decided on issues such as beneficiary designations that have not been updated to reflect the state of the plan participant's family at the time of his or her death.

Federal employees are covered by the Federal Employees' Group Life Insurance Act of 1954 (FEGLIA), which permits employees to name the beneficiary of their life insurance. Death benefits accrue first to the named beneficiary, followed by others in the statutory line of precedence. A Virginia statute revokes the beneficiary designation of a former spouse whenever there is a change in marital status. Another Virginia statutory provision says that, if that provision is preempted by federal law, the ex-spouse will have to compensate the person who would otherwise have received the benefits for the benefits that person lost. Hillman named his first wife Judy Maretta as beneficiary of his FEGLI policy. They divorced and he remarried without changing the beneficiary designation. When Hillman died, Maretta collected the proceeds, and second wife Jacqueline Hillman sued her. The Supreme Court ruled in mid-2013 that state laws are preempted to the extent of any conflict with a federal statute. The relevant federal scheme gives highest priority to the beneficiary by the insured, which must be respected. [*Hillman v. Maretta*, 133 S. Ct. 1943 (2013)]

The Eighth Circuit held that a wife was not properly informed of her waiver of pension rights when she signed a prenuptial agreement. The agreement waived all rights with respect to her husband's separate property, and listed the husband's retirement plan account as an asset. When the husband died, with his parents named as beneficiaries, he had filed for divorce, but the divorce had not yet been finalized. The plan administrator asked the wife to sign a waiver so the benefits could go to the husband's parents. She refused, and the plan asked for court guidance about how to distribute the benefits. The district court awarded the benefits to the parents, but the Eighth Circuit reversed, holding that she prenuptial agreement was not sufficient to satisfy ERISA § 1055(c)(2)(A)(iii)'s requirement for a waiver—leaving the wife as the proper recipient of the benefits. The Eighth Circuit held that the prenuptial agreement did not clearly and expressly inform the wife that she would be entitled to survivor benefits that were waived by the agreement. [*MidAmerican Pension & Emp. Benefits Plan Admin. Comm. v. Cox*, No. 12-3563 (8th Cir. July 12, 2013); see Kevin McGuinness, *Prenup Not Sufficient Notice of Benefits Waiver*, plansponsor.com (July 22, 2013)]

The District Court for the District of Massachusetts ruled that because the Gallaghers never finalized their divorce, the wife was still entitled to benefits under the husband's retirement plan, defining "spouse" as a person the participant is married to, even if estranged. The couple separated in 1989. In 2005, the participant designated his son as beneficiary. The estranged wife and the son both claimed the benefits when the participant died in 2011. The district court said it was not clear whether the plan was an individual account or defined benefit plan. The difference is the wife's entitlement to a QPSA, but the court held that she was definitely entitled to at least half the benefit. [*Gallagher v. Gallagher*, No. 4:12-cv-40027-TSH, 2013 U.S. Dist. LEXIS 26061 (D. Mass. Feb. 26, 2013); see Kevin McGuinness, *Since Divorce Not Final Plan Must Pay Wife*, plansponsor.com (Mar. 15, 2013)]

A divorce court order requiring a plan participant to name his children as retirement plan beneficiaries did not take precedence over his surviving spouse's right to receive a QPSA, because the dissolution agreement in favor of the children did not satisfy the requirements for a QDRO. The agreement did not require action by the plan; did not assign the death benefits to the children; did not specify when the payments began; and did not specifically remove the spouse's right to a QPSA. According to the Ninth Circuit, the QPSA is payable unless the surviving spouse waives it, which was not true in this case. A QDRO can replace the former spouse with the current spouse as payee, but cannot name other beneficiaries without consent of the former spouse. [*Hamilton v. Wash. State Plumbing & Pipefitting Indus. Pension Plan*, 433 F.3d 1091 (9th Cir. 2006), discussed in Rebecca Moore, *Supreme Court Lets Stand QPSA Decision*, plansponsor.com (Oct. 3, 2006)]

Hunter designated his wife as primary beneficiary, and did not designate secondary beneficiaries. When she predeceased him, he did not name a beneficiary. The plan says that in the absence of a valid beneficiary designation, benefits will be distributed to the surviving spouse; if none, the order of distribution is to children, parents, siblings, and the executor of the administrator of the of the estate. The plan distributed the $300,000 benefits to Hunter's six siblings. The stepsons sued to recover the benefits. They said that they were his children as evidenced by Hunter's leaving his estate to his "beloved sons." The Fifth Circuit held that, because the stepson were never adopted, it was reasonable to refuse to treat them as Hunter's children; legal adoption is a reasonable way to determine status as a child of the participant. It cannot be assumed that all stepparents want their stepchildren to inherit from them. The Fifth Circuit said that "equitable adoption" means promises or actions that preclude a person from denying that that person adopted a child. It does not create a parent-child relationship, and is not binding on an ERISA plan. [*Herring v. Campbell*, 690 F.3d 413 (5th Cir. 2012); see Rebecca Moore, *Stepchildren not "Children" for Purposes of Death Benefit*, plansponsor.com (Aug. 20, 2012)]

The widow of a participant in a SERP was not entitled to benefits, because she did not fit the plan's definition of "spouse," and the definition in the plan controls over the language in the SPD. The SERP required the survivor to have been married for at least one year before the participant's retirement, or at least one year before the participant's death, whichever came first; the plan participant married after his retirement. [*Parr v. Diebold Inc.*, No. 5:09 CV 1041 (N.D. Ohio); see Plansponsor staff, *Widow Loses SERP Benefits Bid*, plansponsor.com (Nov. 18, 2010)]

According to the Eastern District of Pennsylvania, a participant in a TIAA-CREF annuity plan substantially complied with the plan's requirements to change the beneficiary from his former wife to the man with whom he lived for 27 years, by sending two written notices of intention to change. (The standard for determining the identity of an ERISA plan beneficiary is whether there has been "substantial compliance" with the requirements for changing the beneficiary.) [*Teachers Insurance and Annuity Association of America v. Bernardo*, No. 09-911 (E.D. Pa. Jan. 26, 2010); see Fred Schneyer, *Court Allows Annuity Contracts Beneficiary Switch*, plansponsor.com (Jan. 29, 2010)]

Shortly after the Supreme Court found the federal Defense of Marriage Act unconstitutional, the District Court for the District of Pennsylvania held that Jean Tobits and Sarah Ellyn Farley became spouses as a result of their 2006 marriage in Canada. The plan provided for payment of benefits to the "surviving spouse" as long as he or she had not waived the right to receive the benefits. Therefore, Tobits, and not Farley's parents, was entitled to the death benefit under Farley's ERISA plan—even though Pennsylvania does not permit same-sex marriages. [*Cozen O'Connor v. Tobits*, Civ. Actions No. 11-0045 (E.D. Pa. July 29, 2013); see Rebecca Moore, *Court Awards Same-Sex Spouse ERISA Plan Benefits*, plansponsor.com (Aug. 5, 2013)]

The Ninth Circuit required a pension trust to recognize a QDRO issued under Washington state law on behalf of a payee who was not married to the plan participant, but had a 30-year quasi-marital relationship with him. The Ninth Circuit gave effect to the court order giving her a 50% interest in the pension benefits, because she was his dependent and therefore an appropriate alternate payee. In this view, ERISA does not define marital property rights, but makes QDROs part of state domestic relations laws; Washington recognizes property divisions between quasi-marital partners. The pension would have been community property if the couple had been married, and a 50-50 division was consistent with state law. [*Owens v. Automotive Machinists Pension Trust*, 551 F.3d 1138 (9th Cir. 2009); see Rebecca Moore, *9th Circuit Finds QDRO Valid for 30-year Quasi-Marriage*, plansponsor.com (Jan. 13, 2009); EBIA Weekly, *QDRO Awarding Pension Benefits to Domestic Partner in "Quasi-Marital Relationship" Upheld on Appeal* (Jan. 29, 2009) (benefitslink.com); CCH Pension and Benefits, *Order Awarding Pension Benefits After 30-Year "Quasi-Marriage" Constituted a QDRO: Court* (Jan. 30, 2009) (benefitslink.com)]

Early in 2009, the Supreme Court held that DuPont correctly paid retirement benefits to a plan participant's ex-wife, even though she renounced her interest in his retirement benefits when they divorced. The plan participant named his daughter as the new beneficiary—but did not remove his wife's name from the beneficiary designation form. A QDRO was executed at the time of the divorce, but not submitted to the plan. The participant died in 2001, with $402,000 in his pension account. The participant's daughter sued the plan, but the plan followed the beneficiary designation. The Supreme Court ruled that the ex-wife did not attempt to direct her interest in the plan to the estate or another potential beneficiary, so her waiver was not the type of assignment or alienation barred by the Retirement Equity Act. The plan had a procedure for waiving benefits, but the ex-wife did not use it—so in the absence of a QDRO, the plan had to distribute benefits according to the beneficiary designation in its records. [*Kennedy v. DuPont*, 555 U.S. 285 (2009); see Rebecca Moore, *High Court Affirms DuPont's Payment to Ex-wife*, plansponsor.com (Jan. 26, 2009)]

*Kennedy* requires benefits to be paid to the beneficiary named in the plan, even if there is a state law waiver that purports to exclude that person. Therefore, the Fourth Circuit required payment of retirement plan funds to Erika Byrd's ex-husband Scott Andochick. The couple separated in July 2006, and their settlement agreement waived his interest in her 401(k) plan. They were divorced in December 2008. Byrd died in April 2011 without changing the benefit designation. [*Andochick v. Estate of Byrd*, 709 F.3d 296 (4th Cir. 2013); see Kevin McGuinness, *Plan Must Pay Ex Husband Despite Estate Suit*, plansponsor.com (Mar. 13, 2013)]

The Northern District of New York held that ERISA does not preempt state "slayer" statutes. Therefore, a son who murdered his father could not collect benefits under his father's employer-sponsored life insurance plan. (The son, who was named as sole beneficiary, argued that his age—he was tried in juvenile court—and extreme emotional disturbance at the time of the killing should permit him to collect the benefits.) The district court held that emotional disturbance only reduces the offense level of the crime—it does not allow a wrongdoer to profit from a crime. The full benefit was awarded to the decedent's other son. [*Union Security Life Ins. Co. v. JJG-1994*, No. 1:10-cv-00369-LEK-RFT, 2011

U.S. Dist. LEXIS 94767 (N.D.N.Y. Aug. 24, 2011); see Rebecca Moore, *Son Who Murdered Father not Entitled to Benefits*, plansponsor.com (Aug. 29, 2011)]

The Eastern District of Pennsylvania awarded life insurance benefits to the spouse of a participant who filed for divorce and then committed suicide. Lisa Marie Mancuso's brother said that she tried to change the beneficiary from her husband to her brother, but the court said that her brother's unsigned, un-notarized e-mail to the insurer was not evidence. Mancuso's brother also argued that the divorce court had jurisdiction to equitably distribute her assets—but the district court pointed out that under Pennsylvania law, life insurance is not marital property that is subject to distribution. The brother said that the slayer statute prevented her husband from obtaining the insurance proceeds, because he drove her to suicide, but he did not actually kill her, so the slayer statute was not applicable. [*Diener v. Renfrew Centers Inc.*, No. 11-4404, 2011 U.S. Dist. LEXIS 108352 (E.D. Pa. Sept. 22, 2011); see Rebecca Moore, *Court Finds no Effort by Participant to Change Beneficiary before Suicide*, plansponsor.com (Sept. 26, 2011)].

## § 12.07  THE REQUIRED BEGINNING DATE

### [A]  Theory and Application

Congress' initial reasons for passing ERISA, and for allowing Individual Retirement Accounts (IRAs) revolved around providing current income for workers for the time period between retirement and their death. Not only was estate planning with qualified retirement benefits not considered important, it was not even considered a worthwhile objective—the benefits were supposed to be used up during the individual's lifetime. Therefore, distributions from qualified plans and IRAs were required to start no later than a Required Beginning Date (RBD). The RBD was defined as April 1 of the year after the year in which the individual reached age 70½. An excise tax penalty was imposed on the failure to make at least the Minimum Required Distribution (MRD) each year.

Over the years, theories in Congress and at the IRS have changed. Estate planning for benefits is now treated as a legitimate objective. Furthermore, although the RBD/MRD requirements remain in effect for IRAs, and for qualified plan participants who are corporate officers or directors, or who own 5% or more of the stock in the employer corporation, they have been abolished for rank-and-file employees. If plan participants choose to defer retirement and remain at work past age 70½, they will no longer suffer a tax penalty for doing so.

For plan years beginning on or after January 1, 1997, I.R.C. § 401(a)(9)(C) sets the RBD for a rank-and-file employee at the later of April 1 following the year in which the individual reached age 70½ or that person's actual retirement date. The plan must make actuarial adjustments to the pensions of persons who continue to work after age 70½.

The eventual pension must be at least the actuarial equivalent of the benefits payable as of the date the actuarial increase must begin, plus the actuarial equivalent of any additional benefits that accrue after the starting date, reduced by the actuarial equivalent of whatever retirement benefits are actually distributed after the annuity start date. Employees who stay at work after age 70½ can be given the option of suspending distributions from the plan until they actually retire.

## [B]  Excise Taxes

The basic tax rule is that amounts received by a plan participant from a plan are taxable income for that year. (Any after-tax contributions made by participants were not deductible when they were made, and will not be taxed again when they are withdrawn. Participants who made after-tax contributions are therefore allowed to calculate an exclusion ratio, so part of each distribution is tax-free to the extent that it can be traced back to past after-tax contributions.)

A 10% excise tax (over and above the normal income tax) is imposed on "premature" distributions. The general rule is that a distribution made before age 59½ is premature. Distributions under a QDRO are not subject to this excise tax. Nor is a distribution considered premature if it is made to a person who has reached age 55 and separated from service. Distributions are not subject to the 10% penalty if they are made after the participant's death, or to employees who are so totally disabled as to be unable to engage in any substantial gainful activity.

The premature distribution excise tax is imposed on lump sums, but not on distributions made over the life, lives, or joint life expectancies of the participant or the participant and one or more beneficiaries. Defined benefit plans are subject to additional rules on this topic. Finally, if a plan participant's unreimbursed medical expenses are high enough to be tax-deductible (over 7.5% of adjusted gross income), plan distributions are not considered premature, even if the participant does not actually use the distributions to pay the medical bills.

Before 1996, plan participants could find themselves between a rock and a hard place. Not only was an excise tax penalty placed on premature withdrawals; a different penalty was imposed on excess lifetime withdrawals from a pension plan but also on excess accumulations of pension benefits within the estate. The SBJPA suspended the tax on excessive distributions for the period 1996–1999, but retained the tax on excessive accumulation in the estate. The Taxpayer Relief Act of 1997 permanently repealed both excise taxes, greatly increasing the financial and estate planning flexibility available to plan participants.

## [C]  Required Minimum Distributions

An IRS Proposed Regulation [66 Fed. Reg. 3928–3954 (Jan. 17, 2001)] covers required minimum distributions from qualified plans, IRAs, and I.R.C.

§ 403(b) and § 457 (government and nonprofit-organization) plans, substantially simplifying the 1987 Proposed Rules under Code § 401(a)(8). The 2001 proposal enacts a single Minimum Distribution Incidental Benefit (MDIB) table, in Treas. Reg. § 1.401(a)(9)-2, to be used to calculate the RMD, with a single table usable whether the beneficiary is a natural person (spouse or non-spouse) or an entity such as a trust or charity. The MDIB table uses the same assumption in all cases: that the beneficiary is 10 years younger than the employee (no matter what their actual ages are). Distributions are made over the predicted life expectancy of a person 10 years younger than the employee. Even greater "stretch-out" is allowed if the beneficiary is the employee's spouse, and is actually more than 10 years younger than the employee, because in that case the calculation of the RMD can be based on the spouse's actual life expectancy. If the employee fails to designate a beneficiary, the RMD is calculated based on the employee's own life expectancy, reduced by one year every year.

The general rule for post-death distributions is that the benefits remaining when the employee dies must be distributed over the life expectancy of the designated beneficiary. The calculation is made in the year the employee dies. If more than one beneficiary is designated (for instance, two or more of the employee's children), then the beneficiary with the shortest life expectancy is treated as the designated beneficiary—whether the employee dies before or after the RBD. If the employee dies without designating a beneficiary, then distribution must be made to his or her intestate distributees, over a period of five years.

The 2002 final rule, Notice 2002-27, 2002-18 I.R.B. 814, makes it easier to distribute benefits to separate accounts with different beneficiaries, slightly simplifies the RMD calculation by eliminating some of the mathematical factors used in the calculation. To clarify that the distribution to beneficiaries must begin in the year of death, Notice 2002-27 requires the beneficiary of a decedent's account to be named by September 30 (rather than December 30) of the year of death. This last change was made to make it clear that distribution to the beneficiaries must start in the year of death.

To prevent abusive planning (e.g., choosing a grandchild as annuitant to stretch out payments), T.D. 9130, 69 Fed. Reg. 33288 (June 15, 2004) forbids use of a joint and survivor annuity with a 100% survivor benefit if the beneficiary is more than 10 years younger than the employee. Additional adjustments are required if the employee starts to receive benefits before age 70 (because the earlier start means that more payments will be made). For annuities with no life contingency, T.D. 9130 lets the recipient change the form that future distributions will take at any time. When a person retires, or when the plan terminates, the form of distribution can be changed prospectively. An employee who marries can change the annuity to a joint and survivor annuity. T.D. 9130 also allows certain payments to children, under Code § 401(a)(9)(F), to receive the same favorable tax treatment as payments to a spouse.

Another Pension Protection Act change allows a non-spouse beneficiary to roll over inherited benefits to an IRA; previously, only a spouse could do this.

[See Notice 2007-7, 2007-5 I.R.B. 395; Robert J. Lowe, "IRS Further Clarifies New Beneficiary Rollover Rules," BNA Tax Management, <http//www.bnatax. com/tm/insights_lowe1.htm> discusses some issues remaining unresolved]

In October 2008, the Department of Labor published final rules on distributions of 401(k) benefits in terminated plans, when the beneficiary is not the participant's spouse and cannot be located. The rules also cover selection of annuity providers and cross-trading of securities by ERISA plans. Under the PPA, certain retirement benefits of deceased participants can be rolled over into an inherited IRA even if the beneficiary is not the deceased participant's spouse. The new rule, which includes a Prohibited Transaction class exemption, requires rollovers into inherited IRAs when a terminated or abandoned defined contribution plan cannot find the non-spouse beneficiaries of a deceased participant. [73 Fed. Reg. 58445 (Oct. 7, 2008); see Rebecca Moore, *DOL Issues Final Rules on Missing Benefits and Other PPA Provisions*, plansponsor.com (Oct. 6, 2008)]

For 2009 only (and not for other years in which many taxpayers needed relief), the Worker, Retiree, and Employer Recovery Act of 2008 (WRERA) suspended the penalties that would otherwise be imposed for failure to take RMDs from qualified plans or IRAs. [Notice 2009-9, 2009-5 I.R.B. 419; see Transamerica Center for Retirement Studies, TCRS 2009-01, *Internal Revenue Service Issues Guidance on Reporting Required Minimum Distributions for 2009* (benefitslink.com); Rebecca Moore, *IRS Modifies 2009 Reporting Requirements for IRA RMDs*, plansponsor.com (Jan. 9, 2009)]

For 2012 and 2013, Qualified Charitable Distributions (QCDs) are permitted. A QCD is a charitable donation, made by a person who has reached age 70½ and therefore would have to take an RMD from his or her IRA or be penalized. The QCD is transferred directly from the IRA to a qualified charity. The donor can exclude up to $100,000 a year in QCDs from gross income for tax purposes, and QCD amounts are deemed to satisfy the RMD requirement. The distributions are reported on IRS Form 1099-R. QCDs cannot be made from SEP or SIMPLE IRAs. [IRS, *Charitable Donations from IRAs for 2012 and 2013*, <http://www. irs.gov/Retirement-Plans /Charitable-Donations-from-IRAs-for-2012-and-2013> (June 27, 2013)]

## § 12.08   DIVORCE-RELATED ORDERS

### [A]   QDROs and QMCSOs

For many couples, one spouse's interest in a retirement plan is a major marital financial asset. In fact, it may be the only significant marital financial asset. Given our society's high divorce rate, plan administrators are often confronted with court orders incident to an employee's separation or divorce—or are faced with conflicting claims after the death of an employee who divorced, remarried, and eventually died without having changed the beneficiary designation from the first to the second spouse.

Although the general rule is that plan benefits cannot be anticipated or alienated, there is an important exception for family law orders that fit the definitions of Qualified Domestic Relations Orders (QDROs) or Qualified Medical Child Support Orders (QMCSOs). [On QMCSOs, see the HHS/DOL Final Rule on National Medical Child Support Notice, 65 Fed. Reg. 82128 (DOL) and 65 Fed. Reg. 72154 (HHS), and the Compliance Guide for Qualified Medical Child Support Orders (Aug. 13, 2003), <http//www.dol.gov/ebsa/publications/qmcso.html>, as discussed at § 18.16.]

Technically speaking, welfare benefit plans are not required to have QDRO procedures, because the QDRO requirements appear in ERISA Title I, Part 2, which does not apply to welfare benefit plans. However, five of the Circuits (the Second, Fourth, Sixth, Seventh, and Tenth) have concluded (in cases about life insurance) that QDRO procedures are required because ERISA doesn't specially say that welfare benefit plans do not have to have QDRO procedures. (The issue for health plans is covered by the QMCSO procedure.)

The Second, Third, Fourth, Seventh, and Tenth Circuits have required top hat plans to enforce QDROs, and the District Court for the District of New Hampshire joined them in late 2009. [*Metropolitan Life v. Drainville*, 2009 U.S. Dist. LEXIS 63613 (D. R.I. July 23, 2009), *MetLife v. Hanson*, 2009 U.S. Dist. LEXIS 92044 (D. N.H. Oct. 1, 2009); see Albert Feuer, *Who Is Entitled to Life Insurance Benefits and Top-Hat Benefits from an ERISA Plan Following a Divorce or a Marital Separation?*, <http://papers.ssrn.com/sol3/papers.cfm?abstract_id=1535733> (Jan. 14, 2010). For cases applying a QDRO-like rationale to divide welfare benefits, see, e.g., *Unicare Life & Health Ins. Co. v. Phanor*, No. 05-11355-JLT (D. Mass. Jan. 30, 2007), as discussed in Fred Schneyer, *Judge Overrides Life Insurance Beneficiary Designation*, plansponsor.com (Feb. 1, 2007); *Deaton v. Cross*, 184 F. Supp. 2d 441 (D. Md. 2002); *Seaman v. Johnson*, 184 F. Supp. 2d 642 (E.D. Mich. 2002)]

Once the administrator determines that a court order has the status of a QDRO, payments can legitimately be made to the alternate payee: i.e., the separated or divorced ex-spouse of an employee.

A QDRO is a court order based on a state domestic relations law (including community property law) dealing with child support, alimony, or marital property rights. No court is allowed to use a QDRO to order a plan to make payments in any type or form not allowed by the plan documents. A QDRO cannot force a plan to pay benefits that have already been assigned to someone else under an earlier QDRO, or to increase the actuarial value of benefits to be paid. The Department of Labor's introduction to the subject of plan administration of QDROs can be found at <http//www.dol.gov/ebsa/faqs/faq_qdro.html>.

To be entitled to recognition by the plan, a QDRO must contain at least this much information:

- The recipient's right to plan benefits;

- The names and addresses of the parties;

- The amount or percentage of the plan benefit to be paid to the alternate payee named in the order;

- The time period or number of payments covered by the order;

- The plan(s) it applies to (the same employee might be covered by more than one plan).

Generally, the alternate payee does not receive distributions under the QDRO before the date the employee would be entitled to them. However, distributions can be made from any plan on the earliest date the participant could get the distribution after separation from service, or when the participant reaches age 50—whichever is later. If the plan is drafted to allow it, QDROs can require immediate distribution, or at a time that is not related to the age of the employee spouse.

For QDROs issued when the employee spouse is still working and has not retired, the payments are calculated based on the present value of the normal retirement benefits already accrued as of that time. Early retirement subsidies are not taken into account. The QDRO can provide for recalculation at the time of retirement, in case an early retirement subsidy is actually paid.

The PPA cleared up the question of whether a later, or even posthumous, court order can be a QDRO by holding that an otherwise qualifying court order must be accepted as a QDRO even if it modifies, or is later in time than, another court order: PPA § 1101. DOL published an Interim Final Rule under PPA § 1001, which says that an order can be a QDRO even if it is later than another order or QDRO, or if it revises the other order. This is true even if the second order involves the same employee but a different alternate payee.

Therefore, a posthumous order, or an order issued after the participant's annuity start date, can be a QDRO. But even after the PPA, a QDRO can only divide benefits as provided by the plan, not require additional forms of benefits. As long as a DRO does not attempt to assign benefits that have already been assigned to a different alternate payee under a different QDRO, an order can be QDRO even if it is issued after, or revises, another DRO. An order can be a QDRO even if it is issued after the participant dies, or after the participant's annuity starting date. However, an order cannot be a QDRO if it orders a plan to provide a type or form of benefit that is not available under the plan. [RIN 1210-AB15, *Final Rule Relating to Time and Order of Issuance of Domestic Relations Orders*, 75 Fed. Reg. 32846 (June 10, 2010); see Rebecca Moore, *EBSA Issues Final Rule on DROs*, plansponsor.com (June 10, 2010)]

The Northern District of New York ruled, in mid-2007, that a QMCSO can require a plan to cover a participant's stepchild. The plan made stepchildren eligible only if they lived with the participant and were claimed as dependents—

which was not true in the case of this stepchild. The employer's position was that the QMCSO was invalid because it required adding a new class of beneficiaries. The Northern District of New York disagreed, because ERISA does not exclude stepchildren as subjects of QMCSOs, and a new type of benefit can be ordered when necessary to comply with the Social Security Act or a state law. New York law requires coverage for children even if they are not claimed as dependents, do not live with the participant parent, or both. Another New York statute makes stepparents financially responsible for stepchildren. [*O'Neil v. Wal-Mart Corp*, No. 8:05-cv-01572-LEK-RFT, 502 F. Supp. 2d 318 (N.D.N.Y. 2007), discussed in *Court Orders QMCSO Coverage for Nonresident Stepchild, Even Though This Exceeded Coverage Ordinarily Provided by Plan*, EBIA Weekly (Aug. 30, 2007)]

## [B] QDRO Methodology

Under the "separate interest" method of distribution under a defined benefit plan, the alternate payee gets future payments based on his or her life expectancy, not that of the plan participant. [See, e.g., *In re Marriage of Shelstead*, 66 Cal. App. 4th 893 (1998)] The nonemployee wife was awarded a 50% community property interest in the employee husband's pension plan. The order said that, if the wife died before the husband, she would be able to designate a successor in interest to receive her community-property share. But the California Court of Appeals decided that, although this was a divorce-related order, it was not a QDRO because it did not settle the rights of an alternate payee, and she could leave her share to anyone, not just another acceptable alternate payee.

Under the "shared payment" method, the alternate payee gets a portion of each pension payment made to the plan participant, so both the participant and the alternate payee use the same timing schedule and form of annuity. The alternate payee gets to take advantage of any early retirement incentives elected by the participant. The enhanced benefit under an early retirement plan is actuarially reduced if the alternate payee is younger than the participant (this is often the case, especially if the participant is male and his ex-wife is younger than he is), but is not increased if the alternate payee is older than the participant.

## [C] The Administrator's Response

When a plan administrator receives a court order, the first step is to determine whether the order is entitled to QDRO status. However, once ERISA compliance is determined, the administrator must comply with the QDRO, without inquiring as to its acceptability under state law. An employee who opposes the terms of the QDRO has to litigate with the ex-spouse in state court; the plan administrator is not liable for complying with the QDRO. [*Blue v. UAL Corp.*, 160 F.3d 383 (7th Cir. 1998)]

The Ninth Circuit held that state courts have the power to decide whether DROs satisfy the federal law QDRO requirements. Therefore, a Nevada Supreme Court decision in a divorce case should not have been disregarded. The case began as a divorce suit, but before the final decree was filed, the husband killed his wife and tried to kill the judge. Before the wife's death, the judge in the divorce case made a verbal ruling that the husband had to pay $500,000 of his 401(k) benefits to the wife, but the DRO was not issued after her death. The husband appealed, arguing that he did not have to pay the benefits because there was no QDRO. After the Ninth Circuit decision, the case was sent back to the district court with instructions to pay the benefits to the wife's estate. [*Mack v. Kuckenmeister*, 619 F.3d 1010 (9th Cir. 2010); see Fred Schneyer, *State Judges Can Rule on QDRO Cases*, plansponsor.com (July 23, 2010)]

The Leveretts divorced, and the decree called for the ex-husband to continue to pay for the ex-wife's health insurance under his military health insurance plan. He notified the plan of his divorce. The ex-spouse was no longer eligible, so the plan terminated the ex-wife's coverage. She moved to amend the divorce decree to re-characterize the couple as legally separated and not divorced, so she could retain eligibility. The motion was granted. The ex-husband appealed. The Alabama Court of Appeals ruled that the court exceeded its discretion by declaring the couple separated rather than divorced. There was no legal basis to reinstate a marriage whose participants had dissolved it. The case was sent back to the trial court to come up with a lawful remedy that was mutually acceptable to the spouses. [*Leverett v. Leverett*, No. 2111042, 2013 WL 1165375 (Ala. Ct. App. Mar. 22, 2013)]

When a plan participant never divorced his first wife, but remarried anyway, and the plan documents listed the second wife as his spouse, the Sixth Circuit had to decide which wife was the surviving spouse. This required determining whether Ohio or Michigan law should be followed. The Sixth Circuit opted for Ohio law, where the second marriage occurred and the decedent lived with the second wife until his death. Under Ohio law, the second spouse has the duty of proving that the first marriage ended. She was unable to do so, because there was no record of a divorce. The Sixth Circuit concluded that the first wife was the valid beneficiary. [*Durden v. Daimler Chrysler*, 448 F.3d 918 (6th Cir. 2006)]

If the administrator believes that a document described as a QDRO is a sham, or at least questionable, PWBA Advisory Opinion #99-13A [(Sept. 29, 1999), <http//www.dol.gov/ebsa/regs/AOs/ao1999-13a.html>] provides guidance.

Administrators are "not free to ignore" information casting doubt on the validity of an order. If the administrator finds that evidence credible, the administrator must make a case-by-case determination of the validity of each order, "without inappropriately spending plan assets or inappropriately involving the plan in the state domestic relations proceeding."

Appropriate action could include informing the court of the potential invalidity of the order; intervening in a domestic relations proceeding; or even bringing suit. However, an administrator who can't get a response within a reasonable time from the agency that issued the order "may not independently determine that the order is not valid under state law." [PWBA Advisory Opinion #99-13A (Sept. 29, 1999), <http//www.dol.gov/pwba/programs/ori/advisory99/99-13a.htm>] ERISA Opinion Letter 94-32A says that it is improper to charge either the participant or the alternate payee a fee for processing a QDRO.

This determination must be made within a reasonable time. The employee and the proposed alternate payee must be notified promptly that the order was received. The administrator must explain to them how the plan will determine the validity of the alleged QDRO. The funds in question must be segregated, and separately accounted for, until the determination has been made. There is an 18-month limit on keeping the funds in the segregated account. [See EBSA Advisory Opinion 2000-09A (July 12, 2000), <http//www.dol.gov/ebsa/regs/AOs/ao2000-09a.html> for a discussion of what to do when an alternate payee is named under a plan that limits beneficiary designations to spouses, minor children, and parents—but not former spouses.]

### [D]   QDRO Case Law: *Egelhoff* and After

The Supreme Court decided, in *Egelhoff v. Egelhoff* [532 U.S. 131 (2001)] that ERISA preempts a Washington State law that made all beneficiary designations (in life insurance as well as qualified plans) invalid when the employee or insured person divorced. The Supreme Court decided that the state law "relates to" ERISA plans, and therefore is preempted, because qualified plans can be regulated only by federal, and not state, law.

In 2002, the Seventh Circuit interpreted *Egelhoff* to mean that state laws cannot be used to displace the designation of beneficiaries made under ERISA, because ERISA preempts the state law completely. [*Metropolitan Life Ins. Co. v. Johnson*, 297 F.3d 558 (7th Cir. 2002)] In light of this decision, the Seventh Circuit refused to allow the state-law remedy of imposing a constructive trust to be used to pay the benefits of a deceased, divorced employee's life insurance plan to his 14-year-old daughter (as required by the terms of his divorce agreement) rather than to his ex-wife (who was still named as the beneficiary in the plan documents). Although the divorce agreement included boilerplate waivers of interest in the other spouse's financial assets, the Seventh Circuit did not believe this was specific or explicit enough to disclaim the ex-wife's interest in the ex-husband's benefit plans. [*Melton v. Melton*, 324 F.3d 941 (7th Cir. 2003)]

The message of the Supreme Court's 1997 ruling in *Boggs v. Boggs*, 520 U.S. 833 (1997) is that, although QDROs are saved from ERISA preemption, other domestic relations orders issued by state courts are preempted.

The Second Circuit required a defined contribution plan to distribute assets to a former participant that were wrongly transferred to his wife after they were divorced—even though the plan did not recover the funds from the wife. The plan erroneously transferred half of the plaintiff's pension account to his ex-wife, giving her about $764,000 more than the divorce settlement entitled her to receive. The plaintiff did not discover this for several years. The plan administrator told the ex-wife to return the excess funds; she refused, and the plan sued her. After two years without resolution, the plaintiff joined the suit. The Second Circuit defined the critical feature of defined contribution plans as placing the risk of investment instability or beneficiary longevity on the employee. The Second Circuit held that if plan funds are treated as benefits that cannot be alienated without violating ERISA as soon as they are credited to a participant's account (as the plan argued) would prevent fiduciaries from debiting amounts that ERISA itself says can be deducted from the account. In this analysis, plan assets only become benefits when they are distributed at retirement—before that point, no one has a claim to any particular assets in the plan trust. [*Milgram v. Orthopedic Assocs. DC Pension Plan*, 666 F.3d 68 (2d Cir. 2011); see Rebecca Moore, *Plan Must Pay Back Assets Wrongly Transferred to ExSpouse*, plansponsor.com (Nov. 30, 2011)]

The Minnesota Supreme Court ruled in April 2013 that a DRO did not qualify as a QDRO because it required payment of a form of benefit that the plan did not allow. The plaintiff did not submit the order for qualification until after her former husband had remarried and retired—by which point the QJSA had vested and become unalterable. The Minnesota Supreme Court held that the election period for QJSAs is 180 days ending on the annuity start date. When the order was submitted, the surviving spouse benefit was payable to the second wife. The DRO was not issued until after the 180-day period had lapsed, so paying a benefit to the first wife would violate the terms of the plan. [*Langston v. Wilson McShane Corp.*, Nos. A10-2219, A11-0683, A11-0684 (Minn. Mar. 27, 2013); see Kevin McGuinness, *DRO Not Qualified After Benefit Payments Start*, plansponsor.com (Apr. 8, 2013) Another case that stresses the importance of obtaining a QDRO before retirement, because it also holds that once the employee spouse retires, the survivor benefit will be paid to the person named as beneficiary on the annuity start date, is *VanderKam v. PBGC*, No. 09-cv-01907 (D.D.C. May 7, 2013); see Carol V. Calhoun, *District Court: QDRO Cannot Change Existing Beneficiary of Joint and Survivor Annuity*, Employee Benefits Legal Resource Site (June 11, 2013) (benefitslink.com).]

### [E] PBGC QDROs

An extensive document published at PBGC.gov explains how the PBGC handles QDROs in the plans under its trusteeship. The document covers subjects such as how to identify alternate payees, how and when to make payments to the alternate payees, and the rights of alternate payees when the employee spouse dies. The total values of the participant's portion and the alternate payee's portion cannot exceed what the PBGC would have paid to the participant if there had been no QDRO. The document includes two basic model QDROs and special orders for child support and surviving spouse benefits.

Courts often consider the percentage of the benefit earned before, during and after the marriage when they divide pension benefits. The PBGC can use this "marital portion" or "marital fraction" analysis for either a shared payment or a separate interest QDRO.

An original signed order, or a certificated or authenticated copy of the order, should be sent to the PBGC QDRO Coordinator, P.O. Box 151750, Alexandria, VA 22315-1750. (Electronic transmission is not acceptable because of the need for a physical signature.) If the PBGC states that an order is not a valid QDRO, the parties will be given 45 days to appeal, and payments to alternate payees will be suspended, and reinstated if the PBGC later determines that the order was a valid QDRO. The PBGC also informally reviews draft orders to see if they would qualify if submitted in that form. Parties must notify the PBGC Customer Contact Center, (800) 400-7242, if any event occurs that affects a benefit: for example, the death of a participant or alternate payee, or the occurrence of an event named in the order, such as a child's majority or the alternate payee's remarriage.

A valid order should:

- Clearly specify the pension plan to which it applies;

- Clearly identify (including Social Security numbers and mailing addresses) the persons to whom it applies; all alternate and contingent payees;

- Specify the start date and amount to be paid to each alternate payee and the duration of payment, and what amount or percentage of the participant's monthly benefit goes to each alternate payee;

- Mandate payment from the PBGC to the alternate payee, rather than the participant receiving payment and then transmitting it to the alternate payee;

- Explain whether shared payments to the alternate payee survive the participant's death;

- Grant the domestic relations court continuing jurisdiction over the order. [*The Division of Pensions Through Qualified Domestic Relations Orders*, <http://www.dol.gov/ebsa/publications/qdros.html>, or by phone at the EBSA hotline, 1-866-444-EBSA (3272). Forms can be ordered by calling the PBGC at (800) 400-7242]

## § 12.09   REDUCTION OF BENEFIT FORMS

Qualified plans must always offer payments in the form of QJSAs, QOSAs, and QPSAs. What if a plan originally adopts additional, optional forms of benefit payments, then later finds that some of them are unpopular or hard to administer? For years beginning after December 31, 2001, as a result of EGTRRA, I.R.C. § 411(d)(6) and ERISA § 204(g) have been amended to make it easier for defined contribution plans to cut back on the number of benefit options that they offer, especially in connection with plan mergers and other transitions.

A defined contribution plan will not be penalized for reducing participants' accrued benefits if the plan adopts amendments that reduce the number of benefit options—provided that the participant is always entitled to get a single-sum distribution that is based on at least as high a proportion of his or her account as the form of benefit that is being eliminated under the plan amendment. EGTRRA obligates the IRS to issue new regulations no later than December 31, 2003, to this effect, applying to plan years beginning after December 31, 2003 (or earlier, if the IRS so specifies).

Under regulations published at 69 Fed. Reg. 13769 (Mar. 24, 2004), redundant optional forms of benefit can be eliminated, as long as another form in the same "family" remains available (the proposal defines six families of optional benefit forms), and as long as the "core" options remain available. A plan amendment changing the availability of benefit forms cannot be effective for any distribution with an annuity start date within 90 days after adoption of the amendment.

The core options that must be preserved are the straight life annuity, the 75% joint and survivor annuity, life and 10-year certain annuity, and the most valuable option the plan provides for participants with a short life expectancy. As a general rule, lump sum payouts cannot be eliminated by making use of this proposal, and plan amendments eliminating non-core options do not apply to start dates within four years after adoption of the amendment. The proposal imposes additional requirements to protect participants when early retirement benefits and subsidies are altered.

T.D. 9472, 2009-51 I.R.B. 850, is a final rule governing notice requirements under 204(h) for plan amendments that reduce accrued benefits. According to the IRS, reducing or eliminating an early retirement benefit or retirement-type subsidy has the effect of reducing future benefit accruals. Code § 4980F(e)(3) requires notice to be provided within a reasonable time before the plan amendment takes effect. In general, this means 45 days before the effective date (15 days for small or multi-employer plans). Unpredictable contingent event benefits are limited if a plan's AFTAP is, or would be, under 60%, and amendments increasing the plan's liabilities because of a benefits increase are limited if the AFTAP would be under 80%. Certain payments are prohibited when AFTAP is in the 60%–80% range; the sponsor is in Chapter 11; and the plan's actuary cannot certify that AFTAP is at least 100%. Benefit accruals cease when AFTAP falls below

60%. [*IRS Issues Final Rule on Certain Notice Requirements*, plansponsor.com (Nov. 23, 2009). See also proposed regulations, 77 Fed. Reg. 37349 (June 21, 2012) for elimination of some optional benefits from single-employer defined benefit plans sponsored by employers that are bankruptcy debtors.]

Notice 2012-46, 2012-30 I.R.B. 86, effective November 1, 2012, gives the ERISA § 101(j) notice requirements for single-employer plans subject to benefit limitations under § 436. When the funding status of a single-employer plan falls below a certain level, the administrator has 30 days to provide notice to participants and beneficiaries. The DOL regulations provide that noncompliance can be penalized by up to $1,000 per day for each participant who should have been notified. Notice 2012-46 requires the notice to be understandable by the average participant, containing the plan name, EIN, plan number, and a general description of the payment limitation. The prohibited benefits must be described in detail. The notice must explain when the limitation will cease to apply (e.g., when the AFTAP rises to at least 80%). If the limit is no longer in effect and participants can access distributions that were formerly prohibited, the plan administrator must send a § 101(j) notice to participants no later than 30 days after the limitations no longer apply. The § 101(j) notice must be in writing and can be given electronically, if this method is reasonably accessible to the notice recipients. [McGuireWoods LLP, *IRS Provides Guidance on Notices for Funding-Related Pension Plan Benefit Limitations* (Aug. 28, 2012) (benefitslink.com)]

Finkl & Sons Co. contemplated voluntary termination of its pension plan, probably in connection with a planned merger but, after preliminary research, decided the plan was too costly. The plan permitted employees to continue working at Finkl after plan termination while still receiving annuities. The plan also included an anti-cutback clause protecting certain benefits from amendments and the plaintiffs charged that the ability to collect an annuity while continuing to work fell into this category. The Seventh Circuit disagreed: neither ERISA nor the plan's terms guaranteed the right to an immediate annuity while still working. A terminated plan can disburse benefits to active employees—but this plan never terminated. [*Carter v. Pension Plan of A. Finkl & Sons Company for Eligible Office Employees*, 654 F.3d 719 (7th Cir. 2011), *en banc reh'g denied* (Sept. 21, 2011)]

Although the First Circuit said that the regulation allowing an amendment that reduced a retiree's benefit nearly by half was not fair, the court nevertheless affirmed dismissal of the retiree's case. The plaintiff, Tasker, worked for Airborne Express, which was acquired by DHL close to the time of the plaintiff's retirement. The plan was amended, eliminating the right to transfer balances from the DHL defined contribution to its defined benefit plan. The applicable regulation permitted elimination of the conversion option, so the amendment did not violate the anti-cutback rule. [*Tasker v. DHL Ret. Sav. Plan*, 621 F.3d 34 (1st Cir. 2010); see Sheri Qualters, *Despite Questioning Fairness, 1st Circuit Rules Against Retiree Who Lost Benefits*, Nat'l L.J. (Oct. 11, 2010) (law.com); *Andersen v. DHL Ret. Pension Plan*, No. C12-439 MJP, 2012 U.S. Dist. LEXIS 157805

(W.D. Wash. Nov. 2, 2012) dismisses a similar case about the elimination of the transfer option.]

The Third Circuit held that a plan amendment that conditioned receipt of health care benefits from a welfare plan on not getting a lump sum from the pension plan violated the anti-cutback rule. Although in general, welfare benefits are not subject to the anti-cutback rule, the Third Circuit held that the amendment had the effect of decreasing an accrued benefit under the pension plan—because the lump sum became less valuable because health benefits had to be surrendered to get it. [*Battoni v. IBEW Local Union No. 102 Employee Pension Plan*, 594 F.3d 230 (3d Cir. 2010); see Stanley D. Baum, *Third Circuit Rules That an Amendment to a Welfare Plan Violates ERISA's Anti-Cutback Rule*, ERISA Lawyer Blog (Feb. 10, 2010) (benefitslink.com)]

## § 12.10  ROLLOVERS

Because of termination of employment, or termination of a plan itself, a person of working age may become entitled to a plan distribution. If he or she does not need the funds immediately, and would encounter an unwelcome income tax liability, one solution is to "roll over" the funds by placing them into another qualified plan or an IRA within 60 days.

The funds that are rolled over are not available to be spent by the plan participant, and therefore the participant is not taxed.

> ■ **TIP:** Although employees have a right to roll over these funds, the qualified plan that is the intended recipient does not have an obligation to accept rollovers. So it makes sense for the distributing plan to require employees to submit a statement that the potential recipient is not only qualified to take rollover contributions, but is willing to do so. The recipient plan is allowed to impose conditions, such as the form in which it will accept rollovers and the minimum amount it will accept as a rollover. The recipient plan is also entitled to set its own distribution rules and does not have to follow the rules of the original plan.

A direct rollover is considered a distribution, not a transfer of assets. [Treas. Reg. § 1.401(a)(31)-1] Therefore, the participant and spouse may have to sign a waiver because plan benefits are not being paid in QJSA form.

Rollovers can be carried out either by the plan administrator of the first plan sending a check or wire transfer to the trustee or custodian of the transferee plan, or by giving the participant a check payable to the IRA, plan trustee, or custodian. The IRS has ruled that the 60-day rollover requirement does not apply to a check for a plan distribution that was made payable to the sponsor of a second plan. The check was mailed to the recipient of the distribution, but made payable to her new employer, but she could not have cashed the check; therefore, it was a direct rollover as defined by § 401(a)(31). Her Form 1099-R showed Code G in

Box 7, showing a direct rollover with no withholding. The IRS said that the distribution was a direct rollover, so the 60-day rule did not apply, and she could deposit the check in the new employer's plan even after 60 days. [Plansponsor Staff, *60-day Rollover Requirement Doesn't Apply to Check Made to New Plan*, plansponsor.com (Apr. 1, 2010)]

A distribution to a spouse, or a QDRO distribution to an ex-spouse, can also be rolled over, but only to an IRA, not to a qualified plan.

PPA § 829(a) enacts Code § 402(c)(11) that permits non-spouse beneficiaries to roll over a distribution they receive from a qualified plan to an IRA.

IRS Notice 2008-30 explains how to make rollovers to Roth IRAs from other types of plans, pursuant to the expanded options for rollovers under the PPA. Funds can be rolled over directly to a Roth IRA, or the individual can take a plan distribution and roll it over to the Roth IRA within 60 days. Any amount that would be includible in the individual's taxable income if there had been no rollover will also be included in his or her gross income. The rollover is exempt from the 10% penalty on early distribution unless the money is distributed from the Roth IRA within five years. [Notice 2008-30, 2008-12 I.R.B. 638; see Deloitte Washington Bulletin, *IRS Issues Guidance on PPA Distribution Changes* (Mar. 17, 2008) (benefitslink.com); Fred Schneyer, *IRS Publishes PPA Distribution Changes Guidance*, plansponsor.com (Mar. 6, 2008); Deborah K. Boling, *New IRS Guidance on Distribution-Related Provisions of PPA*, Employee Benefit Plan Review (June 2008) (benefitslink.com)]

The Small Business Jobs and Credit Act of 2010, Pub L. No. 111-240, permits employers to amend a 401(k) plan to allow an eligible rollover distribution (ERD) to be transferred to a designated Roth account within the plan. (The transfer is taxable, not tax-free.) Transfers can be made after September 27, 2010, from a non-designated Roth account in the same plan, and if other requirements are met. However, in-plan conversions can only be made from amounts that could be distributed under the terms of the plan. Participants who rolled over ERD to a designated Roth account could include half of the taxable amount in their 2011 gross income and half for 2012, or could include it all in their 2010 gross income, depending on which provided better tax results. [<http://www.irs.gov>, *New Law Allows In-Plan Rollovers to Designated Roth Accounts*; see Rebecca Moore, *InPlan Roth Conversions Present Challenges*, plansponsor.com (Sept. 28, 2010)]

The American Taxpayer Relief Act of 2012 includes a provision that could generate tax revenue immediately, adding up to $12.2 billion over 10 years. This legislation authorizes in-plant Roth conversions of defined contribution accounts that are not otherwise distributable, with no income limitation. Under prior law, only amounts that were distributable (e.g., to a participant who had reached age 59 ½) could be converted to Roth form. Although the provision is effective January 1, 2013, prior account balances can be converted. [Rebecca Moore, *Fiscal Cliff Deal Extends Roth Conversions* plansponsor.com (Jan.3, 2013)]

The 402(f) notice must be given when a participant gets a distribution that is eligible to be rolled over to an IRA or another qualified plan. A participant can waive the 30-day minimum notice, but not the 180-day maximum notice requirement. The notice must explain the rollover rules, tax consequences of taking a lump sum, the options for direct rollover (e.g., automatic rollover), the mandatory 20% withholding requirement, and tax consequences of options. Notice 2009-68, 2009-39 I.R.B. 423 includes two updated safe harbor notices replacing the ones issued in 2003—one for designated Roth accounts, one for other accounts. (A participant who has both kinds of accounts must receive both notices.) [*Lock Lord Bissell & Liddell Client Alert, New Lump Sum Distribution Notices Required for 2010* (Dec. 10, 2009) (benefitslink.com); Mary Jo Larson, Warner Norcross & Judd LLP Publications, *New IRS Model Rollover Notices* (Sept. 10, 2009) (benefitslink.com)]

The Southern District of New York held in early 2012 that it was a breach of fiduciary duty to refuse to honor an ex-employee's request for a rollover distribution. Edward Klepeis asked the owner of the employer company, who was also the sole trustee of the plan, to roll over the assets when he quit in January 2005. The plan entitled him to a distribution on his next anniversary date, December 31, 2005. The defendants said that the request did not have to be honored because it was not in proper form, but the district court said that the plan did not require formal claims. There was also a breach of duty in failing to carry out later written rollover requests; neither ERISA nor the plan terms imposed a particular deadline for the request. Eventually, in January 2011, Klepeis was informed that his account had been transferred to an IRA, but by that time, the balance had dropped from $64,000 to $57,000. The district court awarded prejudgment interest running from December 31, 2005 (because, as of that date, he should have been able to invest the balance as he wished), plus attorneys' fees. [*Klepeis v. J&R*, No. 10-cv-0363 (CS)(PED), 2012 U.S. Dist. LEXIS 16441 (S.D.N.Y. Feb. 9, 2012); see Rebecca Moore, *Employer Breached ERISA by Failing to Make Rollover Distribution*, plansponsor.com (Feb. 13, 2012)]

## § 12.11 WITHHOLDING

A designated distribution is any amount of $200 or more that the participant could roll over, but chooses not to. Under I.R.C. §§ 401(a)(3) and 3405(c), plan administrators have to withhold a mandatory 20% of any designated distribution.

All or part of an employee's balance in a qualified plan is eligible for rollover, except:

- A series of substantially equal periodic payments, made at the rate of at least one payment a year, over the life of the employee or the joint lives of the employee and designated beneficiary;

- Payments made for a term of at least ten years [See I.R.C. § 402(c)(4)];

- The RMDs under I.R.C. § 401(a)(8) for officers, directors, and 5% stockholders.

In the case of a partial rollover, withholding applies only to the part that the employee withdraws from the plan, not the part that is rolled over.

For amounts that are neither annuities nor eligible rollover distributions, optional withholding can be done at a rate of 10%. The employee can direct the plan not to withhold. During the six months immediately preceding the first payment, and at least once a year once benefits are in pay status, the plan must notify participants of their right to make, renew, or revoke a withholding election. The employer can either include the withheld amounts in each quarterly Form 941 filing, or use Form 941E to report withholding.

Starting January 1, 2010, eligible rollover distributions paid directly to a non-spouse beneficiary are subject to 20% mandatory withholding, not 10% voluntary withholding for non-periodic payments, unless the funds are directly rolled over to an IRA.

IRS Notice 1036-P, <http://www.irs.gov/pub/irs-pdf/n1036p.pdf>, covering additional withholding for pensions in 2009, provides an optional procedure and tables for calculating additional withholding amounts for pensions, reflecting the Making Work Pay credit.

The plan administrator is responsible for withholding unless the administrator directs that the insurer or other payer of benefits perform this task. [Treas. Reg. § 31.3405(c)-1]

Whenever designated distributions (i.e., those eligible for withholding) are made, the employer and plan administrator become responsible for making returns and reports to the IRS, participants, and beneficiaries.

A penalty of $50 per day is imposed by I.R.C. § 6704(b), up to a maximum of $50,000, for failure to maintain the required records, although the penalty can be waived if the plan has a good excuse for noncompliance. [See I.R.C. § 6047(b) for the required records reports by employers or plan administrators]

## § 12.12   PLAN LOANS AS DEEMED DISTRIBUTIONS

The federal Website firstgov.gov includes FAQs about plan loans:

- Loans are permitted from qualified plans, but not from IRAs or related plans (SEP, SARSEP, or SIMPLE).

- In fact, taking a loan disqualifies the account from being an IRA, and its entire value must be included in the owner's income for the year of the loan.

- Qualified plans are allowed to, but not required, to offer loans. A plan can limit the size of loans.

- The maximum allowable loan is the smaller of A or B, where A is $50,000 and B is $10,000 or half of the participant's vested valance, whichever is greater.

- A participant can have more than one loan outstanding at a time, as long as the aggregate balance does not exceed the permitted maximum.

- Plans that allow loans must specify application procedures and repayment terms for loans.

- Other than loans for purchase of a principal residence, repayment must be completed within five years, via a series of substantially equal payments made at least quarterly and including both principal and interest.

- Loan repayments are not plan contributions: see Reg. § 1.72(p)-1.

- Loan repayment can be suspended for employees who are on active military duty, or during a leave of absence lasting up to one year. However, an employee returning from leave must make up the missed payments either by making a lump sum repayment or increasing the periodic payments so that the loan does not extend past the original five-year term.

- Plan loans are not dependent on hardship, the employee's reasons for wanting the money, or whether the employee could borrow from other sources.

- It is permissible to make loans to owner-employees as long as all participants have equal access to loans.

- A loan that is not repaid according to the plan's terms is taxed as a plan distribution (and cannot be rolled over to an eligible retirement plan), but there is no plan distribution if the repayment terms are followed.

- After a deemed distribution, a default can be remedied by making the missed payment, but the participant's tax basis in the plan is increased by late repayments.

Code § 72(p) sets out the rules under which plan loans that fail to conform to the requirements will be treated as taxable distributions from the plan, rather than as tax-neutral loans. Regulations on this issue were proposed in 2000 and finalized at the end of 2002. [67 Fed. Reg. 71821 (Dec. 3, 2002)] The Final Regulations apply to loans, assignments, and pledges made on or after January 1, 2004 (although plans can adopt the rules earlier). An exemption is available for loans made under an insurance contract that was in effect on December 31, 2003, that is obligated to offer loans to unsecured contract holders.

A loan will not be treated as a deemed distribution if the plan suspends loan repayment when the borrower is on leave of absence for active military service, even if the leave lasts more than a year, as long as repayments resume when the borrower returns from military service, and repayment is complete by the normal term plus the term of military service. Before these regulations were finalized, the Proposed Regulation imposed a limit of only two loans per plan participant; additional loans would be treated as deemed distributions. The Final Regulations remove the two-loan limit, and allow credit card loans to be secured by amounts in a participant's account. Also see the Servicemembers Civil Relief Act, Pub. L. No. 108-189, which limits the interest on plan loans incurred by employees who later go on active military service.

> ■ **TIP:** If a plan loan is made to a party in interest, see Rev. Rul. 2002-43, 2002-28 I.R.B. 85, for an explanation of the calculation of the prohibited transaction excise tax, including situations in which the loan is outstanding for more than one year so multiple prohibited transactions occur. Also note that § 402 of the Sarbanes-Oxley Act [Pub. L. No. 107-204] forbids publicly traded corporations to make loans to their officers and directors. Because this modifies the existing ERISA rule that plans must make loans available to all participants on equal terms, some fiduciaries were worried that they might be charged with violating this provision if they refused plan loans to directors and officers. [See DOL Field Assistance Bulletin 2003-1 (Apr. 15, 2003), <http//www.dol.gov/ ebsa/regs/fab_2003_1.html> for an explanation that denying a loan that violates Sarbanes-Oxley is not a violation of ERISA § 408(b)(1)'s requirement of loan availability to all participants]

Also note that, in early 2009, the Federal Reserve Board amended Regulation Z, so that, as of July 1, 2010, most plan loans are exempt under the Truth in Lending Act. The FRB's rationale is that plan loans are different from ordinary loans because there is no third-party creditor, and the principal and interest are reinvested in the participant's account, so participants are less vulnerable than ordinary borrowers. [Rebecca Moore, *Plan Loans Exempt from Truth-in-Lending Disclosure Requirements*, plansponsor.com (Mar. 13, 2009)]

# CHAPTER 13

# PROCESSING AND REVIEWING CLAIMS AND APPEALS

## § 13.01   INTRODUCTION

All pension and welfare benefit plans that are subject to ERISA Title I are required to maintain a "reasonable claims procedure." An appropriate claims procedure is one that is described in the SPD: does not place undue restrictions or inhibitions on the processing of claims, and satisfies the relevant regulations about filing claims, reviewing submitted claims, and informing participants when a claim is denied. [DOL Reg. § 2560.503]

At the very least, the procedure must give claimants (or their authorized representatives) the right to apply to the plan for review, see the pertinent documents, and submit written comments and issues for resolution.

The plan must give a specific reason if it denies a claim. Claimants must be referred to the relevant plan provision. They must be given information about how to appeal the denial. One of the reasons why the PPACA is so controversial is the extent to which it imposes additional requirements not only for communicating with plan participants about their claims, but also about the timing of claims processing and the addition of a new external claims review step.

In the spring of 2010, the Supreme Court decided *Conkright v. Frommert*, 559 U.S. 506, a suit by a class of Xerox employees who left the company, received lump sums, then were later rehired and eventually retired from Xerox. The Supreme Court granted certiorari on two issues: the amount of deference a district court must give an administrator's interpretation of plan terms outside the context of an actual claim; and whether the Second Circuit applied the correct standard of review (for abuse of discretion or de novo). The court strongly reaffirmed the *Bruch* principle that, if a plan gives administrators the discretion to interpret a plan, then courts must review these decisions deferentially, and a trustee's interpretation of "disputed or doubtful terms" will be upheld if it is reasonable.

## § 13.02   THIRD-PARTY ADMINISTRATORS (TPAs)

About two-thirds of covered workers in the United States get their benefits from plans that use some degree of third-party administration instead of handling all plan administration in house.

A TPA is an outsourcing firm that handles administrative tasks. It could be a consulting firm or a broad-based benefits administration firm. There are no federal licensing rules for TPAs, although some states impose their own requirements.

If the plan has unexpectedly high claims, TPAs usually provide stop-loss protection with back-up insurance that benefits the plan itself (rather than the employees with high expenses). Having a stop-loss plan doesn't turn a self-insured plan into an insured plan for ERISA purposes.

A TPA can be considered an ERISA fiduciary as long as it satisfies the statutory requirement of holding "any authority or control," even if it does not have discretionary control over the assets of the health plan it administers. The Sixth Circuit held that a TPA's authority to write checks on the plan's account (which continued to be exercised to pay the TPA's fees even after the contract with the plan sponsor ended) provided the necessary degree of authority or control to impose liability after the sponsor company went bankrupt and many employees had unpaid medical bills. [*Briscoe v. Fine*, 444 F.3d 478 (6th Cir. 2006)]

The Western District of New York has decided that a TPA was not a fiduciary, because it carried out purely ministerial functions; it did not have discretionary authority, and its nurse merely applied eligibility rules set out in the plan and did not make independent decisions. Therefore, the TPA was not guilty of wrongdoing when benefits were denied. [*Wasmund v. Meritain Health, Inc.*, No. 08-CV-498 (W.D.N.Y. 2008); Fred Schneyer, *Benefits TPA Cleared in New York Legal Battle*, plansponsor.com (Dec. 19, 2008)] However, the Sixth Circuit held in 2012 that a TPA becomes a fiduciary when it exercises practical control over the plan's funds. Therefore, a TPA that failed to pay claims under a self-insured ERISA health benefits plan (the TPA misappropriated the funds) violated its fiduciary duty to act solely in the best interests of participants, [*Guyan Int'l Inc. v. Professional Benefits Administrators Inc.*, 689 F.3d 793(6th Cir. 2012); see EBIA Weekly, *Sixth Circuit Affirms That TPA Breached Fiduciary Duties by Using Plan Assets to Pay Its Expenses Instead of Claims* (Sept. 6, 2012) (benefitslink.com)]

Failure to supervise a TPA can also lead to liability for the sponsor. As a result of a suit brought by the DOL, the president of Clark Graphics was required to restore $505,000 to Clark Graphics' two pension plans, and the plan administrator had to return $567,000 to two plans. The two executives violated their fiduciary duty as trustees when they failed to review or reconcile the participants' trust account statements or ensure that appropriate disclosures were made to participants. [Rebecca Moore, *Employer to Pay $500K for Failing to Monitor TPA*, plansponsor.com (July 18, 2012)]

## § 13.03   HEALTH PLAN CLAIMS

The Department of Labor's Pension and Welfare Benefits Agency (PWBA; later renamed EBSA) published a wide-ranging final ule on claims procedures for health and disability plans, amending 29 C.F.R. § 2560.503-1. [See 65 Fed. Reg. 70246-70271 (Nov. 21, 2000); 66 Fed. Reg. 35887 (July 9, 2001)] The PPACA claims rules (see § 13.03[A], below) build on these rules and add more requirements.

The Final Rule draws a distinction between preservice claims (advance approval of health care services) and postservice claims (where medical care has already been provided). The distinction is made because postservice claims are much less urgent. The employee has already been treated, so the question becomes who will pay the bill, not whether potentially necessary care will be available or not.

Plans are not allowed to impose any fees or costs for appealing a denial. The reviewer cannot be either the person who made the initial denial or someone who works for that person. Whenever there is an issue of medical judgment, such as when treatment is necessary, the plan must consult appropriate health care professionals. The reviewer must examine the claim de novo (from the beginning), not just to see if the initial decision involved an abuse of discretion. The employee is allowed to introduce new facts that they did not provide earlier—even if these facts would not be admissible as evidence in a suit. There can be either a single level of review of denials, or two sequential levels of review, but no additional time is allowed to decide the second level of review.

EBSA's FAQs about the claims procedure regulation make it clear that the regulation only applies to ERISA plans, not government programs such as Medicare or Medicaid. The regulation applies only to coverage determinations that are part of a claim for benefits, such as a preservice or postservice claim. Questions about eligibility for coverage that are not asked in connection with an actual claim are not covered by the claims procedure rules. However, if a person makes a claim and is denied on the basis of non-eligibility for coverage, the claims procedure will apply because there has been a denial. But if a plan requires preauthorization or otherwise requires submission of pre-service claims, EBSA says that the plan may have to treat an inquiry as a claim that has not been properly filed—and may have to explain how to file the claim.

The EBSA says that the time for making an initial claims decision starts when the claim has been filed in accordance with the plan's reasonable filing procedures—even if the plan does not have all the information needed to decide the claim. EBSA forbids plans to extend the time limits if the claim is not a "clean claim" (i.e., one that contains all the necessary information). But EBSA says that claimants can agree to give the plan extra time to decide. If an adverse benefit determination is made, the plan must either set out any rules, guidelines, or protocols used to make the determination in the notice of adverse benefit determination, or make the information available to the claimant on request. This is true even if the rule, criterion, etc. was developed by a third party that says the information is proprietary. Therefore, it is helpful to structure contracts with third parties so that either the employer receives this information routinely, and is authorized to distribute it when adverse benefit determinations are made, or so that the third party has an obligation to provide the information when the employer requests it in connection with an adverse benefit determination.

A plan can set a maximum period for filing initial benefit claims—as long as it is a reasonable limit that does not unduly hamper the right to make claims. The plan can also mandate that request for review of adverse benefit determinations be made in writing—except for requests for expedited appeals of denials of urgent care claims, which can be made orally. In plans where there are two levels of review of adverse benefit determinations, EBSA's position is that the same standards (including time limits) apply to both levels of review. For example, the second-level reviewer cannot grant deference to the first-level reviewer's decision and the second-level review must be done by someone who neither made the first-level decision nor is a subordinate of that person. EBSA says that there cannot be more than two mandatory levels of appeals—but it is legitimate for a plan to offer additional voluntary levels of appeal, such as Alternative Dispute Resolution. However, if claimants choose to sue rather than pursue these voluntary measures after the mandatory appeals have been exhausted, this will not be considered a failure to exhaust administrative remedies. Furthermore, the litigation statute of limitations will be tolled while claimants voluntarily pursue additional levels of appeals. [DOL EBSA, *FAQs About the Benefit Claims Procedure Regulation*, <http://www.dol.gov/ebsa/faqs/faq_claims_proc_reg.html> (undated; last accessed Mar. 16, 2013). See also Technical Release 2011-02, HHS, *Technical Guidance for Non-Federal Governmental Plans*, <http://www.dol.gov/ebsa/newsroom/tr11-02.html? (Aug. 17, 2012), which includes model notices for adverse benefit determinations.]

[See Section [A] below for PPACA's variations on this theme.]

## [A]  PPACA Requirements

Interim final regulations to implement the claims requirements under PPACA (the health care reform bill) were published in July 2010 by DOL, HHS, and the Treasury. These regulations make insurance companies that provide policies for group health plans subject to the requirements to the same extent as EGHPs are. All plans must have an internal appeals process that grants full and fair review of denials (on an expedited basis, for urgent cases). Plan participants must be given detailed information about why claims were denied, and how to initiate an appeal.

Before these rules were published, most—but not all—states had requirements for independent external review of claims (44 states had such requirements), but there was no uniformity so some states offered much more protection to claimants than others. The new rules set standards for state external review procedures, and establish a federal external review procedure for people who are not covered by a state review process. Participants in self-insured plans are covered by the interim final rules.

PPACA requires all group and individual plans to comply with the ERISA claims/appeals procedure. However, certain plans, such as stand-alone vision plans and welfare benefit plans that are not health-related, are not subject to this requirement. As a result of PPACA, group and individual insured plans and self-insured plans must have both an internal claims/appeal process and an external review process. The Treasury, HHS, and the Department of Labor jointly issued interim final regulations (IFR) on July 22, 2010. The IFR was published in the

Federal Register the next day: 75 Fed. Reg. 43330 (July 23, 2010). The IFR supplements, but does not replace, the pre-PPACA claims rules discussed above.

Under PPACA, for covered plans, the appeal and review mandate applies to all adverse benefit determinations. Cancellation or discontinuance of coverage with retroactive effect can be appealed, even if there is no actual benefit denial because of the rescission. Claimants must be notified of the outcome of urgent care claims as soon as possible, considering medical exigencies. The pre-PPACA provision that the time limit is extended if the claimant fails to provide adequate information remains in effect.

Group plans must inform the claimant of any new or additional evidence that the plan used or considered in connection with a claim. Before an appeal can be denied on the basis of a new or additional rationale, the claimant must be informed (without charge) of the evidence supporting the rationale. The information must be provided as soon as possible, definitely early enough for the claimant to respond to it before the final date for submitting information. (The authors of this treatise suggest that a plan that has two levels of appeals might wish to eliminate one to increase the time available for claims processing.)

Under the IFR, the plan must not make the compensation or promotion of people handling claims depend on their denial of a particular claim or a stated percentage of claims, and hiring cannot be based on a propensity to deny claims. If a plan fails to meet all the requirements for internal claims, the claimant is deemed to have exhausted the internal review process—and thus to be entitled to initiate external review or bring suit immediately. In suits under ERISA § 502(a), the case will be reviewed de novo without deference to the claims administrator's decision.

Notices of adverse benefit determinations must include:

- The date of the service

- The name of the health care provider

- Amount of the claim

- The diagnosis and treatment codes, and what they mean

- Other information needed to identify the claim

- The reason(s) for the adverse determination, including the denial code and its meaning, and the standards used by the plan to deny the claim.

In addition to the internal claims process (within the plan), PPACA requires group plans to provide for external review of the plan's claims decisions. If the state has a review process that HHS deems to be acceptable, the state will perform the external review. There will be a federal process, but only for states where there is no adequate state process. PPACA imposes 16 requirements on state external review procedures. For example, it is acceptable to impose a filing fee on the employee claimant, but not more than $25 per claim, capped at $75 per plan year. If the claimant wins, the fee will be refunded. The fee must also be waived in financial hardship cases. The cost of the independent review organization is paid by the plan (or, for insured plans, by the insurer). An important exception to the requirements is that a denial or reduction of benefits based on failure to meet the plan's eligibility requirement will not be subject to external review.

Claimants must be given at least four months after the completion of internal review to request external review, and no minimum requirement for the amount in controversy can be imposed. The external reviewers must be assigned by the state (not by the plan or the claimant) and must either be assigned randomly or in a way that preserves their independence.

The external review decision is binding on the plan and the insurer, but binds the claimant only to the extent that there are no other remedies. In particular, a dissatisfied claimant can still bring a suit under ERISA § 502(a)(1)(B). [Patricia Eschbach-Hall, Jones Day, *Claims and Appeals Procedures: New Internal and External Review Requirements* (August 2010) (benefitslink.com)]

Individuals have four months after a final denial of an internal appeal to request external review. If the claim is urgent, the plan must decide immediately if external review appropriate; for non-urgent claims, the plan has five business days to make the decision. This stage is called "preliminary review," and eligibility depends on whether the person was covered at the time the service was rendered, the type of claim, and if prior appeals have been exhausted. The plan is required to notify the individual of its decision, in writing, within one business day of finishing the preliminary review. The appeal must be referred to an Independent Review Organization (IRO). Within five business days of forwarding the appeal to the IRO, the plan must forward to the participant any information that was considered in the internal appeal. Plan materials such as denial notices and claims procedure documents must be explicit about how participants can request such material.

During the external review process, the plan may reconsider its internal appeal decision if the claimant submits additional information. If the plan reverses the original decision, it must inform the claimant and the IRO within one business day. If the IRO reverses the plan's decision, coverage must be provided immediately.

DOL Technical Release 2010-01 sets out the external review requirements a self-funded plan must meet to qualify for the safe harbor. It has to contract with three IROs, rotating claims assignments among them. The relationship between the plan and the TPA, and which claims are involved must be spelled out clearly. [Christy Tinnes and Brigen Winters, *External Review: To Delete or Not Delegate?*, plansponsor.com (Oct. 18, 2011)]

Sending appeals to a TPA or insurer probably does not constitute external review, because it remains part of the internal claims process, although delegated to a third party. The external review required by PPACA must be done by an independent third party. For an insured plan, that will probably be the state insurance authority; self-funded plans must contract with an independent review organization. [Christy Tinnes and Brigen Winters, Groom Law Group, *What About the New External Review Requirement?*, plansponsor.com (Feb. 22, 2011)]

Some important amendments to the IFR were published in June, 2011, changing the standard for deciding urgent care claims to making a decision as soon as possible consistent with medical needs, but always within 72 hours—rather than the 24-hour limit mandated by the IFR. The amendments say that, when an external reviewer orders benefits, the plan must provide the benefits without delay—even if it intends to seek judicial review. Under the amendments, the only claims eligible for federal external review are claims involving medical judgment or rescission of coverage—not how the participant's diagnosis is coded, or whether care from an out-of-network specialist should be covered. [*Group Health Plans and Health Insurance Issuers: Rules Relating to Internal Claims and Appeals and External Review Processes*, 76 Fed. Reg. 37208 (June 24, 2011); Technical Release 2011-02, <http://www.dol/gov/ebsa/rewsroom/tr11-02.html> and <http://cciio.cms.gov/resources/files/appeals_srg_06222011.pdf> (June 22, 2011); see Amy Goldstein, *Obama Administration Narrows Rules for Patient Health-Care Appeals*, The Washington Post (June 22, 2011) (benefitslink.com); EBIA Weekly, *Important Changes in Amended Regulations on Enhanced Claims and Appeals* (June 20, 2011) (benefitslink.com)]

## § 13.04  HIPAA EDI STANDARDS

One reason for high medical costs is that a lot of time and effort is devoted to processing, transmitting, and analyzing information. A number of different standards evolved for storing and displaying health information. To streamline this process, HIPAA requires a uniform set of EDI standards to be placed into effect for health and welfare funds.

Standard code sets, such as the HCFA Common Procedure System and the CPT-4 [Physicians' Current Procedural Terminology, 4th ed. (Celeste G. Kirschner et al., American Medical Ass'n Annual)] must be applied uniformly. The standards cover both the format and the content of electronic files used to submit health care claims, transmit payment information, coordinate benefits among plans, enroll and disenroll plan beneficiaries, and related tasks.

HIPAA's EDI standards apply to insured and self-insured EGHPs, health insurers and HMOs, but not to small, self-administered health plans with fewer than 50 participants. Employers are covered only if they administer their own health plans.

The Health Information Technology for Economic and Clinical Health (HITECH) Act, part of the economic stimulus bill (Pub. L. No. 111-5), takes effect February 17, 2010. The HITECH Act expands the privacy and security provisions of HIPAA, and includes a new regulatory structure for electronic medical records. Civil monetary penalties (CMPs) for HIPAA violations have increased; for the most egregious violations, the penalty can reach $1.5 million per year.

Persons whose personal health information (PHI) has been disclosed improperly can collect a share of the civil penalties.

Business associates of HIPAA-covered entities are subject to the same privacy rules as the covered entities are, including criminal penalties for violations. HHS' Office of Civil Rights continues to enforce HIPAA compliance, but state Attorneys General have also been given the power to enforce HIPAA by bringing suit in federal district court. [Troutman Sanders LLP, *Keeping Up with Recent Legislation: Numerous Changes to Group Health Plans Required*, plansponsor. com (Feb. 27, 2009)] HHS published extensive proposed regulations (covering more than 50 pages in the Federal Register) in July 2010, implementing the HITECH Act requirements for privacy, data security, compliance, and the imposition of penalties. [RIN 0991-AB57, 75 Fed. Reg. 40868 (July 14, 2010)]

## § 13.05  CASE LAW ON CLAIMS

### [A]  Generally

Many cases have been litigated over questions of the proper way to handle and process claims within a plan—and especially over the standard of review that courts should apply when reviewing the decisions of plan administrators. If review is *de novo*, the court can consider all aspects of the decision, including its reasonableness and correctness. In most cases, however, the plan sponsor drafted the governing documents to reserve discretion—in which case, the court can only determine if the decision-maker acted arbitrarily and capriciously.

### [B]  Experimental Treatment

EGHPs typically refuse to cover experimental treatment, and new forms of treatment are very often more expensive than the ones they replace. There is a long line of cases attempting to distinguish between experimental treatments and those that are novel but are accepted as scientifically valid by the medical community.

In a Wisconsin case involving a clinical trial for specialized chemotherapy for a brain tumor, coverage was denied as experimental. The patient's parents exercised the option of having an independent review organization perform expedited review of the denial. The review organization characterized the proposed treatment as medically necessary and within the standard of care, but still experimental. The state trial court said that Phase II clinical trials were unambiguously excluded from coverage. The state court of appeals reversed, saying that the termination of benefits was arbitrary and capricious; the state supreme court agreed. The denial letter did not provide specific reasons for the denial; the specific plan provision supporting the determination; the review procedures and time limits (including the right to sue); and either an explanation of the scientific or clinical judgment that the treatment was experimental, or a statement that such information will be furnished at no charge on request [*Summers v. Touchpoint Health Plan Inc.*, 2008 WI 45 (Wis. 2008); see Suzanne L. Wynn, *Wisconsin Supreme Court Finds Denial of Health Benefits Arbitrary and Capricious, Lacking Specificity*, Pension Protection Act Blog (May 29, 2008) (benefitslink.com)]

## [C]  Other Exclusions

When a plan's cosmetic-surgery exclusion specifically mentioned gastric bypass and other procedures used primarily to treat obesity, it was reasonable to deny coverage of a gastric bypass that was medically rather than cosmetically indicated (although the procedure on the 470-pound claimant would probably have been covered if the exclusion had not specifically listed gastric bypass). [*Manny v. Central States Pension & Health & Welfare Funds*, 388 F.3d 241 (7th Cir. 2004) See also *Smith v. Medical Benefit Adm'rs Group Inc.*, No. 09-C-538, 2012 WL 1378097 (E.D. Wis. Apr. 19, 2012): the plan document clearly excluded gastric bypass surgery, so the employee did not make a benefits claim. However, he sued for equitable relief when the claims administrator of his EGHP pre-authorized the surgery but denied coverage after the surgery had been performed. The Seventh Circuit held that the plaintiff could not assert a benefit claim because the surgery was clearly excluded. The Seventh Circuit held that ERISA does not permit monetary damages for breach of fiduciary duty—but remanded the case to the district court to see if equitable relief was available.]

A participant in a self-insured health plan sued the plan's claims administrator for refusing to pay the full cost of her breast reconstruction surgery. She charged that the plan's claims procedure was inadequate; the notice of adverse benefit determination was inadequate and untimely; and the WHCRA notice of coverage of post-mastectomy reconstruction was not given. The claims administrator said that it was not a proper defendant, because it had paid the benefits due under the plan and provided WHCRA notice. The District Court for the Northern District of New York refused to dismiss the claims counts because it was unclear whether the claims administrator or the employer (designated as the plan administrator in the SPD) was responsible for final benefit determinations. The benefit denial, a short notation on a check stub, did not satisfy ERISA requirements because it did not explain the denial, refer to the relevant plan provisions, or explain the appeals process. The SPD also called for notice within 30 days, but the plaintiff did not receive it for four months. However, the court held that the SPD adequately explained the WHCRA notice requirement. [*Haag v. MVP Health Care*, 866 F. Supp. 2d 137 (N.D.N.Y 2012); see EBIA Weekly, *SPD Disclosures Provided Adequate Notice of Coverage Required by Women's Health and Cancer Rights Act* (June 14, 2012) (benefitslink.com)]

According to the Second Circuit, it was not arbitrary and capricious to apply the plan's "illegal acts" exclusion to deny coverage of injuries sustained in an accident for which the participant was cited for traffic infractions. The court deferred to the administrator's discretion, even though traffic infractions are not considered crimes in New York; the court nevertheless found this interpretation to be reasonable. [*Celardo v. GNY Auto. Dealers Health & Welfare Trust*, 318 F.3d 142 (2d Cir. 2003)]

Another issue is whether the involvement of alcohol or drugs in an injury will result in claims denial:

- The Sixth Circuit ruled that it was reasonable to conclude that death caused by grossly negligent drunk driving is not accidental, so Personal Accident Insurance benefits could be denied to the beneficiary of a plan participant who died as a result of drunk driving. [*Lennon v. MetLife Ins. Co.*, 504 F.3d 617 (6th Cir. 2007)]

- The First Circuit held that, because a crash death was such a likely result, death with blood alcohol three times the legal limit could not be called accidental. [*Stamp v. Metropolitan Life Ins. Co.*, 531 F.3d 84 (1st Cir. 2008); see Fred Schneyer, *DUI Death as Accident Issue Divides Appellate Court*, plansponsor.com (July 2, 2008)]

- In 2012, the District Court held that driving while intoxicated (.289, over three times the legal limit) was not an accident for the AD&D benefit under an ERISA plan. The Fourth Circuit reversed, holding that a crash after intentionally becoming very drunk and driving was still an accident. The policy did not give the plan enough discretion for review to be for abuse of discretion, and the policy did not have a definition of "accident." The Fourth Circuit said that a crash could not be "anticipated and expected," or even "highly likely"; most drunk drivers are not killed. [*Johnson v. American United Life Ins. Co.*, No. 12-1381, 2013 U.S. App. LEXIS 10528 (4th Cir. May 24, 2013); see Katherine Lange, *Fourth Circuit Reverses District Court and Trend, Finding Death from Driving While Intoxicated to be An "Accident,"* Southeastern ERISA Watch (June 8, 2013) (benefitslink.com)]

In another automobile death case, the Eastern District of Pennsylvania held that accidental death benefits were not payable when a plan participant died in a car accident, because the likely cause was severe hypoglycemia; EMS found that he was in a diabetic coma when the crash occurred, and the accidental death policy excluded direct and indirect results of sickness or disease. The Third Circuit has previously ruled that there is no recovery under a policy with a disease exclusion if pre-existing disease contributed to the death. [*Nally v. Life Ins. Corp. of N. Am.*, CIVIL ACTION NO. 07-0707 2007 WL 4390423 (E.D. Pa. Dec. 14, 2007); Rebecca Moore, *Court Affirms Denial of Accidental Benefits for Diabetic*, plansponsor.com (Dec. 20, 2007)]

## [D]  Timing

One of the most significant questions in tort law is when a potential plaintiff can be expected to be aware that an injury has occurred—and, therefore, when the clock starts for determining whether a claim is timely.

The Fourth Circuit ruled that the time starts for determining disability (including elimination periods) based on proof of total disability; it is an abuse of discretion to make a determination based on a particular date where proof is submitted relating to a different date. [*Evans v. Metro. Life Ins. Co.*, 358 F.3d 307 (4th Cir. 2004)]

In a case in which a plaintiff sued for additional benefits more than ten years after he resigned and received a plan distribution (he said that a break in service should have been included in calculating his benefits), the Ninth Circuit agreed with the employer that the suit was untimely. Even though the plaintiff was not notified of appeal rights or given a full explanation of the reasons behind the benefit denial, he had reason to know that the denial was final, so the six-year statute of limitations expired in 1998. A suit filed in 2003 was untimely. [*Chuck v. Hewlett Packard Co.*, 455 F.3d 1026 (9th Cir. 2006), discussed in *Despite Claims Procedure Violations, Statute of Limitations Began When Employee Had "Reason to Know" of Claim Denial*, EBIA Weekly (Aug. 3, 2006)]

A 2001 long-term disability claim was denied under the plan's claims process. The claimant did not sue at that point. In 2008, he filed another long-term disability claim and sought reconsideration of the 2001 claim. The plan terms limited legal action to three years after the time proof of claim was required. For the 2001 claim, that would be March 12, 2002, ending the statute of limitations period on March 12, 2005. The district court held that a plan's own statute of limitations will be applied if it is reasonable. The district court found it reasonable, so the three-year statute of limitations, not the Ohio 15-year statute of limitations for claims of breaches of a written contract, applied. [*Engleson v. Unum Life Ins. Co. of Am.*, No. 5:09 CV 2969, 2012 U.S. Dist. LEXIS 187548 (N.D. Ohio June 29, 2012); see Haynes and Boone Blogs, *District Court Finds Plaintiff's LTD Claim Time Barred by the Limitations Term in the Plan* (Oct. 11, 2012) (benefitslink .com). *Santaliz-Rios v. Metropolitan Life Ins.*, 693 F.3d 57 (1st Cir. 2012) similarly applies an insurance policy three-year statute of limitations rather than the Puerto Rico 15-year contract statute of limitations. See EBIA Weekly, *Court Enforces Plan-Imposed Limitations Period for Benefits Claims* (Oct. 25, 2012) (benefitslink.com).]

Because there is no ERISA statute of limitations, it must be borrowed from the relevant state law. The Eastern District of Michigan upheld a three-year limitations period that was contained in the plan document—even though it was not referenced in the letter sent to the claimant denying his claim. The SPD for the plan did not explain how to make a benefit claim, although it did explain how to request plan documents. The district court read these two facts together to conclude that the plaintiff had constructive notice of the limitations period. The case was filed more than a year after the three-year period ended, so the district court found that it was untimely. [*Moyer v. Metropolitan Life Ins. Co.*, No. 4:12-cv-10766-GAD-MKM, 2013 U.S. Dist. LEXIS 27770 (E.D. Mich. Feb. 28, 2013)]

In 2013, the Supreme Court granted certiorari in case in which the issue is when the statute of limitations begins for an ERISA suit against a long-term disability plan. The plan required suit to be brought within three years of the time that proof of loss was due. However, it was possible that the claims process would not be completed within three years—so the plaintiff might have a suit rejected as too late, when actually trying to bring the suit would be rejected as too early because administrative remedies had not been exhausted. The Second Circuit held that under Connecticut law, it is permissible for an insurance contract to impose a statute of limitations that is shorter than the state law statute of limitations. According to the plaintiff, the Fourth and Ninth Circuits forbid limitations periods that begin before the legal claim has accrued, but they are allowed by the Second, Fifth, Sixth, Seventh, Eighth, and Tenth Circuits. When it took the case, the Supreme Court said that it would not address the question of the scope of the fiduciary's duties to inform claimants of the time limits for judicial review, or the proper remedy if a fiduciary fails to give proper notice of time limits. [*Heimeshoff v. Hartford Life & Accident Ins. Co.*,No. 12-729, *cert. granted* (Apr. 1, 2013); see Douglas Dahl, *U.S. Supreme Court Agrees to Hear Case on ERISA Statute of Limitations,* Proskauer's ERISA Practice Center Blog (Apr. 16, 2013) (benefitslink.com); Jacklyn Wille, *High Court Agrees to Examine Contractual Limitations Periods Under ERISA*, Bloomberg Pensions & Benefits Daily (Apr. 16, 2013) (benefitslink.com)]

### [E]  Other Issues

Health plan fiduciaries have a duty to consider all pertinent available information and to make a decision based on substantial evidence. The Eighth Circuit reversed the lower court's grant of summary judgment to the employer, because the plaintiff should have been permitted to respond to the independent medical examiner's report to offer evidence that her obesity, alone or in conjunction with post-polio syndrome, rendered her totally disabled.

Especially in a situation in which one party has more resources and more power and is able to draft a document which the other party is not in a position to negotiate, courts will often be faced with allegations that a document is ambiguous, and should be construed in favor of the less-powerful party: here, the plan participant rather than the plan, plan administrator, or insurer.

The general rule is that the reviewing court will look only at the documents themselves. However, if a document is ambiguous, "extrinsic" (outside) evidence can be used to aid in its interpretation.

Estoppel is another legal doctrine, one which holds that in certain circumstances, a party will be "estopped" (prevented) from asserting a right that would otherwise apply—e.g., an employer that prevents an employee from filing a timely claim will not be allowed to reject claims on the grounds that they are untimely.

The doctrines of ambiguity and estoppel are often raised in cases involving plan amendments limiting benefits for those who have already retired. See Chapter 9 for retiree health benefits in general, and Chapter 14 for a discussion of the implications of amending a plan.

## § 13.06 *GLENN* AND THE STANDARD OF REVIEW

If and when a plan participant sues in connection with plan benefits, one of the most important questions is the "standard of review" the court will use to assess the plan administrator's decision. The two possibilities are "de novo" review, under which the court considers the question as if it were a new case, or review to see if the administrator abused his or her discretion. Many more plan decisions will be reversed—and many more claimants will win their cases—if the court can look at all the factors underlying the matter, and not just to see if there was an abuse of discretion.

The basic rule, as set by the seminal case of *Bruch v. Firestone Tire & Rubber* [489 U.S. 101 (1989)], is that plan administrators' decisions will be reviewed on a de novo basis, unless the plan itself is drafted to give the fiduciaries discretion over the way the plan operates. If the plan sponsor reserved this discretion, the court's only role is to see whether the administrators abused their discretion.

The mid-2008 Supreme Court decision in *Metropolitan Life Insurance Co. v. Glenn*, 554 U.S. 105 (U.S. 2008) reaffirms *Bruch*. Wanda Glenn, a Sears employee was diagnosed with heart disease, and received 24 months of disability benefits. The insurer, Metropolitan Life Insurance Co. (MetLife) encouraged Glenn to apply for Social Security disability benefits. The Social Security Administration concluded that Glenn was unable to work, and granted the benefits. MetLife, however, rejected Glenn's application for long-term disability benefits, because the insurer concluded that Glenn was capable of doing sedentary work.

Glenn challenged the denial of benefits. According to the Sixth Circuit, MetLife should not have denied benefits; it was unduly influenced by its conflict of interest (as both payor of the benefits and decision-maker about qualifications). The *Glenn* decision says that there are four principles that determine what standard of judicial review should be applied in ERISA § 1132(a)(1)(B) cases:

- Trust law principles should be applied, as if the plan administrator were a trustee carrying out fiduciary activities.

- The decision will be reviewed de novo unless the plan specifies review for abuse of discretion only.

- Deferential review is appropriate where the plan gives the plan administrator discretion to determine eligibility.

- If the decision-maker has a conflict of interest—such as a dual role in both granting or denying claims and paying claims that are granted—that is a factor in deciding whether there was an abuse of discretion by the decision-maker.

*Glenn* extends the conflict of interest analysis to insurers that administer plans, not just to plan sponsors, a step that the Supreme Court felt justified in taking because insurers that administer ERISA plans must act in the best interests of participants. (Furthermore, a sponsor that has a conflict of interest may act according to that conflict when selecting an insurance carrier.)

After *Glenn*, conflict of interest is a factor in the decision, but does not change the standard of review. Courts have devised many different ways to handle the structural conflict of interest when the institution responsible for paying benefits also evaluates claims. One theory is that there is no conflict of interest if the benefits are funded from a trust. [Nancy Pridgen, *Alston & Bird ERISA Litigation Advisory July, The Circuits Are Split: Does MetLife v. Glenn's "Structural Conflict" Holding Apply When Employee Benefits Are Funded from a Trust?* (Dec. 23, 2009) (benefitslink.com)]

After *Glenn*, all structural and procedural factors must be considered. In mid-2010, the Second Circuit held that Taft-Hartley plans (administered by a board of trustees including both management and union representatives) are inherently conflicted when they consider whether or not to grant benefits to a plan member. In this case, a worker reported chronic pain and weakness after being injured in an automobile accident. The Second Circuit ruled that the plan did not give enough weight to the testimony of her attending physician, and the independent report should not have concluded that the worker was able to perform three occupations. [*Durakovic v. Building Serv 32 BJ Pension Fund*, 609 F.3d 133 (2d Cir. 2010); see Fred Schneyer, *Appeals Panel Declares Taft Hartley Plans Inherently Conflicted*, plansponsor.com (June 30, 2010)]

The Tenth Circuit allowed limited discovery in suits against plan administrators who have conflicts of interest. In general, plaintiffs are not entitled to discovery in cases about their benefits claims, but limited discovery is available when plan officials act as both insurer and administrator. The district court said that discovery was not required because the conflict of interest was obvious, but the Tenth Circuit remanded the case for consideration of the effect of MetLife's conflict of interest. [*Murphy v. Deloitte & Touche Group Ins. Plan*, 619 F.3d 1151 (10th Cir. 2010); see Fred Schneyer, *Court Clarifies ERISA Benefits Disputes Discovery Rules*, plansponsor.com (Sept. 9, 2010)]

## [A]  Statutes Regulating Discretionary Clauses

"Discretionary clauses" give administrators full authority to interpret the terms of the plan, thereby triggering a more deferential standard of review when a denial is challenged. In mid-2009, the Sixth Circuit and the District Court for the District of Colorado ruled that ERISA does not preempt state laws forbidding discretionary language in insurance policies in ERISA plans. The Sixth Circuit found that a Michigan law banning discretionary language is enforceable because it comes under the insurance savings clause; *Miller* says that a law "regulates insurance" if it directly controls the terms of insurance contracts. The Colorado case says that the state law is valid (because it dictates the conditions under which an insurer will pay for a risk that it has assumed) but it did not apply to the plaintiff's case, because the law was not retroactive. [*American Council of Life Insurers v. Ross*, 558 F.3d 600 (6th Cir. 2009)]

An insurer challenged the Montana Insurance Commissioner's interpretation of a state law obligating the commissioner to disapprove insurance contracts containing inconsistent, ambiguous, or misleading clauses, or including conditions deceptively affecting the risk assumed by insurers. The commissioner used this statutory provision to avoid approving contracts with "Firestone" (discretionary) clauses permitting complete discretion over benefit determinations. The insurer's position was that ERISA preempted the commissioner's interpretation. (There was no state law forbidding discretionary clauses that could be challenged, only the insurance commissioner's interpretation.) The Ninth Circuit held that ERISA does not preempt the interpretation, which is a state regulation of insurance and therefore protected by the savings clause. The practice substantially affects the risk-pooling agreement between the insurer and insured. [*Standard Ins. Co. v. Morrison*, 584 F.3d 837 (9th Cir. 2009)]

Cigna helped an engineer get SSA disability benefits (which offset his benefits under the CIGNA plan) after multiple foot surgeries left him unable to work. However, Cigna denied his LTD claim, saying that the definition of disability was different. The Seventh Circuit held that the policy definition was "functionally equivalent" to the SSA's definition, and that the claim denial improperly reflected Cigna's conflict of interest. [*Raybourne v. Cigna Life Ins.Co.*, 700 F.3d 1076 (7th Cir. 2012); see Scott J. Stitt, *The Seventh Circuit Concludes that SSA's Definition of Disability, and Cigna's Definition of Long-Term Disability, Is "Functionally Equivalent."* Arnlaw.com Blog (Apr. 3, 2013) (benefitslink.com)]

## § 13.07  CASE LAW ON CLAIMS PROCEDURAL ISSUES

A fiduciary, including a life insurance company, has a right under ERISA § 502(a) to seek appropriate equitable relief from the courts in order to enforce plan provisions. Therefore, the fiduciary can bring an interpleader action (a suit asking for court guidance on how to dispose of funds whose ownership is disputed) if there are conflicting claims to insurance proceeds—for instance, based on a beneficiary designation and community property law. [*Aetna Life Ins. Co. v. Bayona*, 223 F.3d 1030 (9th Cir. 2000)]

Subrogation (see § 18.17) is another issue that may be involved. It is the right of a party, such as an insurance company or benefit plan that advances money to an injured person to be repaid when the injured person collects damages from the party causing the injury. In a recent Supreme Court case, a plan participant injured in an automobile accident received $100,000 from his own insurer and $10,000 from other sources when he was injured in an automobile accident. After paying his lawyer, he had $66,000 left. His health plan had paid $66,866 of medical expenses for him. He claimed that he was not required to reimburse the health plan, because that would mean that he was not "made whole" for his damages. The Supreme Court held that the SPD for the health plan gave the insurer a right of subrogation, and this right, under contract law, prevailed over McCutchen's equitable arguments about "make-whole" relief. However, the reimbursement provision did not explain how to handle attorneys' fees, so the Supreme Court held that it was possible to apply another equitable doctrine, the "common fund" doctrine to resolve this issue. (This doctrine allows a person who creates a common fund for the benefit of multiple parties to be paid for creating the fund.) [*US Airways, Inc. v. McCutchen*, 133 S. Ct. 1537 (2013); see Sarah Fowles & Angela Marie Hubbell, *Have You Checked Your Plan's Subrogation and Reimbursement Provisions Lately?*, Quarles & Brady LLP Employee Benefits & Executive Compensation Law Blog (April 2013) (benefitslink.com)]

The following month, these principles were applied to a case involving a self-insured medical plan. The District Court for the District of Connecticut allowed the plan to recover benefits that it paid to an employee who settled a case related to the accident that injured him. The plan's reimbursement provision explicitly allowed the plan to recover the full amount of benefits it paid, whether or not the employee had been made whole. Connecticut has a state anti-subrogation statute that forbids employers to seek reimbursement from employees who have received a third-party tort settlement. However, the district court said there were two reasons the statute did not apply. First of all, the law was pre-empted by ERISA; and secondly, the statute did not apply because the plan was self-insured. [*Quest Diagnostics v. Bomani*, No. 11-CV-00951 (D. Conn. June 19, 2013); see Anthony Cacace, *Express Plan Terms Allow Self-Insured Plan to Recover Medical Benefits Paid to Employee Post-McCutchen*, Proskauer's ERISA Practice Center Blog (June 25, 2013) (benefitslink.com)]

It is a reasonable exercise of discretion for an insurer to deny life insurance benefits that violate state law. An employee who quit his job was offered the right to convert his life insurance under an employee welfare plan to a group policy, contingent upon whether he lived in a state that approved such a continuation. The application to convert was denied by the plan's insurer because at that time, the state where he lived (Michigan) did not permit portable term insurance coverage. Three years later, the applicant died, and over a year after that his widow submitted a claim for the death benefits that would have been payable if the conversion application had been accepted. The Sixth Circuit, using the "arbitrary and capricious" standard absolved the insurer as fiduciary of wrongdoing: converting the policy would have been unlawful at the time of the application, and the surviving spouse's claim was also untimely—the three-year statute of limitations started with the original denial of the application. [*Morrison v. Marsh & McLennan*, 439 F.3d 295 (6th Cir. 2006)]

According to the Tenth Circuit, the claims regulation was not violated by failure to disclose documents generated during the administrative appeal process. The point of disclosure is to give claimants enough information to decide whether or not to appeal. At that stage, there was no new factual information or diagnosis to alter the decision process. In the Tenth Circuit analysis, documents have to be produced at only two stages: after the initial claims determination, and after the final decision on appeal (at which point administrative remedies have been exhausted). [*Metzger v. UNUM Life Ins. Co.*, 476 F.3d 1161 (10th Cir. 2007); see *No Deferential Review Where SPD and Certificate, But Not Policy, Grant Discretion to Insurer*, EBIA Weekly (Aug. 24, 2006); *Claimant Has Right to Documents Generated in Administrative Appeal Only After Final Decision*, EBIA Weekly (Mar. 1, 2007)]

A mere request for records and information is not an administrative "appeal"—and it does not satisfy the requirement of exhaustion of administrative remedies. [*Reindl v. Hartford Life and Accident Ins. Co.*, No. 1:11CV167SNLJ, 2012 U.S. Dist. LEXIS 38259 (E.D. Mo. Mar. 21, 2012); see Mike Reilly, *What Constitutes an Appeal? Not a Mere Request for Records*, Lane Powell (Mar. 27, 2012) (benefitslink.com)]

## [A]  HMO and TPA Involvement in Claims

Yet another facet in the complex picture comes from the involvement of HMOs and TPAs in the claims process. The legal questions become much more complex than a simple relationship between employee/plan participant and employer/plan sponsor.

As a general rule, an ERISA plan is the proper defendant if a participant wants to sue for benefits. However, in mid-2013, the Seventh Circuit held that if a health insurer decides all benefit eligibility issues and is the party that legally has an obligation to pay the benefits, an ERISA § 502(a)(1)(B) suit for benefits can be brought against the insurer. In this case, the plaintiffs charged that six insurers violated state law by imposing copayments for chiropractic treatment. [*Larson v. United Healthcare Ins.*, No. 12-1256 (7th Cir. July 26, 2013); see PLC Legal Update, *Insurers Can Be Sued for Benefits Under ERISA: Seventh Circuit*, July 29, 2013 (benefitslink.com). See also Cyr v. Reliance Standard Life Ins. (9th Cir. 2011), also permitting an ERISA § 502(a)(1)(B) suit against an insurer.]

A health plan subject to PPACA has a choice of establishing a direct contractual relationship with an IRO or having the TPA handle the transaction; TPAs frequently have existing IRO relationships. But if the agreement is delegated, the sponsor must ensure that the TPA's contract with the IRO satisfies the requirements of Technical Release 2010-01. The delegation document should spell out the relationship between the plan and the TPA, making it clear what claims are involved. If the TPA that processes medical benefit claims for the plan does not handle prescription drug claims, then the plan must either contract with three more IROs, or delegate the hiring to another party (for example, a pharmacy benefits manager). [Christy Tinnes and Brigen Winters, *External Review: To Delete or Not Delegate?*, plansponsor.com (Oct. 18, 2011)]

In the wake of the Supreme Court's consolidated decision in *Aetna Health Inc. v. Davila*, and *Cigna Healthcare of Texas, Inc. v. Calad*, 542 U.S. 200 (2004), note that plan participants who claim that they were improperly denied necessary health care by a Managed Care Organization will have to bring the cases in federal court. The Supreme Court ruled that ERISA § 502(a) completely preempts state laws purporting to regulate managed care decisions about whether or not to provide treatment.

In the Eleventh Circuit view, whenever an administrator delegates authority to a TPA that is not a fiduciary, the TPA's decisions must be reviewed de novo, but the Tenth Circuit allows the decisions to be reviewed for abuse of discretion. [*Geddes v. United Staffing Alliance Employee Medical Plan*, 469 F.3d 919 (10th Cir. 2006)]

## [B]  Exhaustion of Remedies

Exhaustion of remedies is a traditional legal doctrine under which parties will not be permitted to litigate a claim until they have satisfied the applicable administrative requirements—whether that means filing a claim with a state or federal antidiscrimination agency or using the appeals procedures provided by a health or welfare benefit plan. This is an important doctrine for employers, who can eliminate many suits at their earliest stages if the employees had an obligation to access plan remedies but failed or refused to do so. However, a counterbalancing legal doctrine is that employees do not have to exhaust administrative remedies when doing so would be futile.

When the insurer already concluded that a claimant was ineligible for long-term disability benefits (on the grounds that he could perform the duties of his own occupation), it would have been futile for the claimant to ask for a determination that he could not perform the duties of any occupation in order to get a waiver of life insurance premiums. In other words, the insurer could not require a second exhaustion of administrative remedies when the grounds for denying both claims were similar. [*Dozier v. Sun Life Assurance Co. of Canada*, 466 F.3d

532 (6th Cir. 2006), discussed in Roy F. Harmon III, *Sixth Circuit Applies Futility Exception to Enforce Consistency in Claims Review*, <http://www.healthplanlaw.com>. Similarly, *Paese v. Hartford Life & Accident Ins. Co.*, 449 F.3d 435 (2d Cir. 2006) holds that a finding that someone is not totally disabled from his own occupation implies a determination that he is not totally disabled from any occupation]

# CHAPTER 14

# AMENDING A PLAN

## § 14.01  INTRODUCTION

It is very likely that, no matter how carefully a plan was drafted, amendments will be required over the course of time. The company's line of business or workforce may change. The business may suffer reverses. And it's more than likely that ERISA and the tax code will change in ways that require corresponding amendments to the plan. Each new tax bill that requires amendments includes a schedule for when plans are required to make their conforming amendments. In recent years, there have been major changes in the law such as the passage of the Genetic Information Nondiscrimination Act (GINA), the Americans with Disabilities Amendments Act (ADAA), and the large-scale revision of the FMLA rules. A legal sea change of this kind requires re-examination of the company's plans to see if once-acceptable provisions now violate a tax or other provision.

When employees are fired or laid off, it is possible that the reduction in the workforce will be considered partial termination of a 401(k) or other retirement plan, and an amendment that excludes a group of employees from plan participation could also create a partial termination. When partial termination occurs, the plan is considered to have terminated as to those participants, so their accounts become 100% vested. [Hollands & Hart LLP, *Layoffs May Trigger 100% Vesting in Retirement Plans* (Jan. 9, 2009) (benefitslink.com)]

Plan amendments can be adopted either prospectively or retroactively. Retroactive amendments can be made until the last day (including extensions) for filing the income tax return for the year the plan was adopted.

The Department of Labor must be notified whenever a plan is materially modified or the information called for by ERISA § 102(b) changes. The DOL must receive an updated SPD when the participants and beneficiaries do. The DOL can reject an incomplete submission, giving the plan administrator 45 days for corrections. The 5500-series form filed with the IRS also requires reporting of the plan amendments and changes in the plan description that occurred during the year.

Plans frequently require amendments to keep up with tax law changes. If a plan obtains a determination letter from the IRS, the plan probably will not be disqualified if the IRS subsequently discovers defects in the plan documents. However, this immunity does not extend to operational defects, only to design defects. See § 14.02, below.

An "operational error" is a failure to comply with the terms of the plan. Often, this can be corrected without IRS involvement and without penalties to the plan. The sponsor must put the plan and its participants in the position they would have been in if there had been no error. However, if correction requires a plan amendment, then it will probably be necessary to use the Employee Plans Compliance Resolution System (EPCRS), as set out most recently in Rev. Proc. 2013-12, and to file under the Voluntary Correction Program (VCP). However, there are five situations under which a sponsor can use the Self-Correction Program (SCP) to adopt a retroactive corrective amendment without making a VCP filing:

- A hardship distribution was made from a plan that did not have a hardship distribution option;

- Making a plan loan where, once again, this option was not included in the plan;

- Letting an employee participate in the plan prematurely—before he or she satisfied the eligibility requirements;

- Allocating a contribution to correct a violation of the § 401(e)(17) compensation limit;

- Correcting an ADP failure by making a Qualified Nonelective Contribution (QNEC) that would not otherwise be available under the plan.

The plan must comply with the requirements of Code §§ 401(a), 410(b), and 411(d)(6). If the correction is a retroactive amendment to allow hardship distributions or loans, the best practice is to make sure that enough non-highly compensated employees (NHCEs) had access to them to satisfy the nondiscrimination rules. Amendments to change eligibility dates should also predominantly benefit NHCEs. The general rule is that correcting operational errors in an individually designed plan by amendment will probably require the sponsor to make an application for a determination letter, reflecting the amendment, the next time the plan's cycle requires a determination letter. If the plan terminates before the next cycle, a determination letter including the amendment will have to be obtained in connection with the termination. But if the plan is an approved prototype or volume submitter plan, a determination letter is not only not required for the amendment, the IRS forbids applying for one. [Sungard Relius, *Self-Correction Program Retroactive Corrective Amendments* (Mar. 29, 2013) (benefitslink.com)]

Rev. Proc. 2013-12, 2013-4 I.R.B. 313 includes a procedure for using Appendix C, Schedule 1 to correct a failure to adopt a mandatory interim amendment that was required to conform to the PPA or HEART Act. The fee for this program is $375. However, the procedure cannot be used to correct failure to adopt an interim amendment required by a pre-EGTRRA restatement—for example, the 401(k) final regulations. Those failures require correction under Appendix C, Schedule 2, which carries a higher fee. [Sungard Relius, *Correcting a Failure to Adopt an Interim Amendment Under the New EPCRS* (Mar. 19, 2013) (benefitslink.com)]

Before 2012, there was no limit on health FSAs, but PPACA imposes a $2,500 cap. The cap applies to plan years (not the employees' tax years) beginning after December 31, 2012. A cafeteria plan can be amended retroactively at any time on or before December 31, 2014 to incorporate the cap, but operational compliance with the cap is required after the 2013 plan year. [Christy Tinnes and Brigen Winters, *Second Opinions: ACA Cap on Contributions to Health FSAs*, plansponsor.com (July 18, 2012)]

In most cases, the Internal Revenue Code does not require that employees be notified in advance that the plan will be amended. So they don't have a right to comment on the proposed amendment (although they do have a right to comment on the plan's initial application for a determination letter). The exception is that advance notice is required if the amendment changes the vesting schedules of participants who have three years or more of plan participation, because they have the right to choose between the new and the old schedules. However, ERISA does impose a notice requirement. Once a plan is amended, ERISA §§ 102(a)(1) and 104(b)(1) require participants to get a Summary of Material Modifications (SMM) within 210 days of the end of the plan year in which the change is adopted.

See *Coffin v. Bowater Inc.*, 501 F.3d 80 (1st Cir. 2007): an ERISA plan amendment must be in writing; must be executed by someone authorized to amend the plan; the language must make it clear that the plan is being amended; and any other requirements for amendments set out in the governing documents must be observed. *Halliburton Co. Benefits Comm. v. Graves*, 463 F.3d 360 (5th Cir. 2006) holds that, to amend an ERISA welfare benefit plan, the employer must provide a procedure for amendment, must identify who is authorized to amend, and amendments are effective only if they follow the plan procedure.

The Second Circuit, reversing its own earlier rulings, applied the Supreme Court's *Schoonejongen, Jacobson*, and *Spink* decisions to find that employers and plan sponsors are not acting as fiduciaries when they modify, adopt, or amend plans. This is also true of multi-employer plans, so ex-participants and beneficiaries of the Niagara-Gennessee & Vicinity Carpenters Local 280 Pension and Welfare Funds were unable to recover assets that they said were wrongfully depleted by improper plan amendments that, they alleged, violated fiduciary duties [*Janese v. Fay*, 692 F.3d 221 (2nd Cir. 2012); see Rebecca Moore, *Amending a Plan Not a Fiduciary Act*, plansponsor.com (Sep. 18, 2012)]

The Sixth Circuit held that it is permissible for an employer to make reasonable modifications to its retiree health benefits; even if the retiree health benefits have vested, vesting does not mean that the bundle of services becomes fixed for all time. CNH America's 1998 CBA required all retirees to use managed care, reduced their coverage choices, and required them to pay more for out-of-network care. The Sixth Circuit held that it was lawful for the employer to alter the benefits unilaterally, because health care benefits are not like pension benefits, which can be monetized at retirement. The Sixth Circuit remanded the case, defining reasonable changes are those that maintain benefits reasonably commensurate with the old plan; are reasonable when considered in the context of changes in health care; and are roughly consistent with the types of benefits provided to active employees. [*Reese v. CNH America, LLC*, Nos. 11-1359, 11-1857 and 11-1969 (6th Cir. 2012); see Wolters Kluwer Law & Business, *Employer Entitled To Make "Reasonable Modifications" To Retiree Health Care Benefits, Sixth Circuit Rules* (Oct. 5, 2012) (benefitslink.com)]

## § 14.02   FLEXIBILITY THROUGH AMENDMENT

Before 2005, amendments to retirement plans to comply with changes in the law were submitted to the IRS for approval at irregular intervals. The IRS was often confronted with too many submissions at one time. Therefore, in 2005, a cyclical system was implemented, dividing plans into two groups: pre-approved and individually designed. Most pre-approved plans are either prototype plans or volume submitter plans. A prototype plan has a basic plan document and an adoption agreement. The employer can choose among several plan options offered. A volume submitter plan provides plan language (including some options) that, after approval by the IRS, is used to create plans. Volume submitter plans offer many choices, whereas prototype plans have very few choices and make it difficult to shift the plan to a new provider. Standardized prototype plans are reviewed on a six-year cycle; the first six-year cycle for preapproved defined contribution plans ended April 30, 2010. The six-year cycle for defined benefit plans ends April 30, 2012. Preapproved defined benefit plans should be restated, and perhaps submitted, by that date. See Announcement 2011-82, 2011-52 I.R.B. 1052, which requires submissions to include any EPCRS documentation and any plan amendments adopted since the most recent submission. This announcement provides that user fees will be waived for applications filed in a plan's first five years, or at the end of any later remedial amendment period that begins within the plan's first five years. [The ERISA Law Group, *Does Your Company EIN End With a "2" or a "7," or is Your Plan a Multiple Employer Plan?* (February 2012) (benefitslink.com) The IRS maintains a separate six-year submission cycle for pre-approved plans. Individually designed plans are reviewed on a five-year cycle. The cycle that a particular plan belongs to depends on the last digit in its Employer Identification Number (EIN).

On January 31, 2011, the first completed series of determination letter cycles for individually designed plans ended, and a second series began. Letters issued for Cycle A, ending January 31, 2007, expire on January 31, 2012 unless renewed by a timely new application. See Notice 2010-90, 2010-52 I.R.B. 909 for the required changes for Cycle A.

The due date for Cycle B plans (EIN ending in 2 or 7) is January 31, 2013; for Cycle C (3 or 8) it is January 31, 2014, for Cycle D (4 or 9) it is January 31, 2015, and for Cycle E (5 or 10) it is January 31, 2016. [John Anderson, *Does Your Qualified Retirement Plan Need to Be Amended This Year?* Alston & Bird LLP Employee Benefits & Executive Compensation Advisory (Nov. 7, 2011) (benefitslink.com)]

The deadline for Cycle C applications is January 31, 2014, although they could be filed starting in early 2013. (The IRS has pointed out that documents filed early in a cycle get a faster response than those filed later.) Cycle C plans are individually designed plans whose sponsor's EIN ends in 3 or 8. All amendments adopted after the previous restatement must be incorporated into the plan document, and the relevant changes in Notice 2012-76, 2012-52 I.R.B. 775 (2012

Cumulative List of Changes in Plan Qualification Requirements) must be reflected. The sponsor must formally approve and execute the amended plan document. If a private Cycle C plan fails to file its determination letter application on time, its existing determination letter becomes obsolete—and the plan might be audited and found noncompliant. [Spencer Fane, *IRS Now Accepting "Cycle C" Determination Letter Applications* (Feb. 18, 2013) (benefitslink.com)]

The IRS released revised forms for submitting applications for approval of master or prototype plans or volume submitter defined benefit plans in March 2013. Form 4461-A is used to apply for approval; the user fee is paid with Form 8717-A. A revised Listing of Required Modifications (LRM) was published, updating the LRM issued in 2007. The LRM provides sample language that can be used to draft master or prototype defined benefit plans with assurance that the language will satisfy the IRS. [IRS *Pre-Approved Defined Benefit Plans-Revised Forms and LRM*, <http://www.irs.gov/Retirement-Plans/Preapproved-Defined-Benefit-Plans-Revised-Forms-and-LRM> (Apr. 25, 2013); see Kevin McGuinness, *IRS Updated DB Forms and Documents*,plansponsor.com (Apr. 30, 2013)]

The 2012 rules require all entities that apply for opinion or advisory letters to complete the Certification Regarding Interim Amendments, <http://www.irs.gov/pub/irs-tege/cert_interim_amendments.pdf>, stating that the sponsor or practitioner has made all of the interim amendments required by the IRS, and has communicated them to the employers adopting the plan. A Master & Prototype plan sponsor must maintain records of identifying information for all employers that have adopted the plan (other than those who have stopped maintaining the plan more than three years earlier). [ftwilliam.com, *FAQs for the Next Cycle* (Feb. 2, 2012) (benefitslink.com)]

If a sponsor's EIN or controlled group status has changed since its previous determination letter was issued, then the plan's cycle also changes. For example, if the sponsor of a Cycle D plan merges into a company whose EIN begins with 1 or 6, the plan moves to Cycle A. However, if the cycle change occurs during the Cycle A submission window, an automatic extension to January 31, 2013 is granted. [Steptoe & Johnson LLP ERISA Advisory, *The 7th Circuit's Big ERISA Day* (Feb. 15, 2011) (benefitslink.com)]

Although most plan actions that require communication with the IRS are subject to user fees, Rev. Proc. 2012-8, 2012-1 I.R.B. 235 provides that there is no user fee required if a plan makes an automatic change in its accounting period or accounting method if the change is authorized by a revenue procedure, or if the plan adopts a model amendment word-for-word if the model is published in a revenue procedure that states that the amendment should not be submitted to the IRS. But a $4,000 user fee is required when the change in funding or accounting method is not mandatory. The user fee for most situations is $10,000. In addition to amendments required for tax purposes, amendments for business purposes are common. To preserve flexibility, it's a good idea for the sponsor to draft the plan reserving the right to amend the plan in the future. Plans can be amended to change or eliminate:

- Ancillary life insurance provided in connection with a pension plan;

- Accident or health insurance that is incidental to a pension plan;

- Some Social Security supplements;

- Availability of plan loans;

- Employees' ability to direct investment of their plan accounts or balances;

- The actual investment options available under the plan;

- Employees' ability to make after-tax contributions to the plan, or to make elective salary deferrals to a plan that is not a 401(k) plan;

- Administrative procedures for the plan (although even after the amendments, participants must have a right to fair redress of their grievances);

- Dates used to allocate contributions, forfeitures, earnings, and account balances.

But any amendment must take into account I.R.C. § 411(d)(6), which forbids amendments that reduce accrued benefits, including early retirement benefits and retirement-related subsidies—even if the employees affected by the change consent to it. Furthermore, the general rule is that protected benefits cannot be reduced or eliminated when a plan is merged or its benefits are transferred to another plan.

A current, but not a former, employee can go to court to get a declaratory judgment that a plan has lost its qualification after an amendment. [*Flynn v. C.I.R.*, 269 F.3d 1064 (D.C. Cir. 2001)] The D.C. Circuit considers ex-employees "interested parties" only with respect to termination of a plan.

However, a plan that is subject to the I.R.C. § 412 minimum funding standard can be amended retroactively to reduce accrued benefits—as long as the plan sponsor can prove to the DOL that the sponsor is undergoing substantial business hardship that mandates a cutback in benefits. The amendments must be adopted within 2½ months of the end of the plan year. They must not reduce anyone's accrued benefit for plan years before the beginning of the first plan year that the amendment applies to. IRS approval is required for amendments of this type, and the DOL may have to be notified.

A plan can be amended to change its vesting schedule as long as no participant loses any nonforfeitable accrued benefits.

A defined benefit plan can lose its qualified status if it adopts an amendment that increases plan liabilities, if the result is that the funded current liability falls below 60% for the plan year. The employer can preserve the plan's qualification by posting "adequate" security. Either the corporation must place cash and securities in escrow, or it must obtain a bond from a corporate security company that is acceptable under ERISA § 412. [See I.R.C. § 401(a)(29) and ERISA

§ 307; poorly funded plans are also subject to requirements under the Pension Protection Act of 2006]

Plan amendments also are required when the law changes to permit novel forms of benefit plans and new types of plans (e.g., the introduction of Roth IRAs and Roth 401(k) plans).

## § 14.03   CHANGE IN PLAN YEAR

IRS determination letters are not limited to initial qualification of a plan: They can also be obtained for plan amendments. The current employees who are eligible for plan participation are "interested parties" and must be notified of the application for a determination letter. If the proposed amendment changes eligibility for participation, then all employees at the same workplace as the original interested parties must be notified.

The request for change in a retirement plan's plan year is made on Form 5308. IRS approval is automatic as long as:

- No plan year is longer than 12 months. In other words, a year can be broken up into two short years, but two short years can't be consolidated into a long one;

- The change does not have the effect of deferring the time at which the plan becomes subject to changes in the law;

- The plan trust (if any) remains tax-exempt and does not have any Unrelated Business Taxable Income in the short year;

- Legal approval for the change is granted before the end of the short year;

- (Defined benefit plans) The deduction taken for the short year is the appropriate prorated share of the costs for the full year.

## § 14.04   REDUCTION IN FORMS OF DISTRIBUTION

Although it is not permitted to amend a qualified plan in any way that reduces any participant's accrued benefit, it is permissible to amend a plan to eliminate optional forms of benefits (such as periodic payments other than the required QJSA/QPSA). EGTRRA provides that, for plan years beginning after December 31, 2001, defined contribution plans can eliminate certain forms of benefit payout. See § 12.09 for details.

In particular, if funds are transferred from one qualified plan to another (e.g., in connection with a merger or acquisition), the transferee plan will not be required to provide all the payment options that the transferor plan provided. [See I.R.C. § 411(d)(6)(D) and ERISA § 204(g)(4)] However, if payout forms are eliminated, the plan participants must be allowed to take their distributions in lump sum form.

In 2004, the Supreme Court ruled [*Cent. Laborer's Pension Fund v. Heinz*, 541 U.S. 739 (2004)] that a plan amendment increasing the varieties of postretirement employment that would cause a suspension of benefit payments violated the anti-cutback rule.

This decision was reflected in final regulations published in 2005: T.D. 9219, 2005-38 I.R.B. 538. A plan amendment that decreases accrued benefits or places greater restrictions on the right to receive a benefit protected under I.R.C. § 411(d)(6) is in violation of § 411(d)(6) even if the restriction or condition is acceptable under the § 411(a) vesting rules. However, plans can be amended to restrict the availability of benefits accruing after the date of the amendment.

T.D. 9472, 74 Fed. Reg. 61270 (Nov. 24, 2009) is a final rule explaining § 204(h) notice requirements for airlines and certain underfunded single-employer plans. The PPA imposes limits on certain activities if the plan's funding percentage declines below 80%. Amendments that increase the plan's benefit liabilities are forbidden if the AFTAP is below 80%. Some payments are forbidden when AFTAP is in the range of 60%–80%, or the plan sponsor is in Chapter 11. Benefit accruals must cease when AFTAP falls below 60%. The IRS said that reducing or eliminating an early retirement benefit or retirement-type subsidy has the effect of reducing future benefit accruals. Code § 4980F(e)(3) requires the notice to be provided within a reasonable time before the plan amendment takes effect. T.D. 9472 says that, in general, 45 days before the effective date is reasonable—or 15 days for a small or multi-employer plan. For some amendments that took effect before December 31, 2008, notice is acceptable if given at least 30 days before the effective date.

Plans are not required to issue a 204(h) notice if they are amended to adopt the PPA's interest rates and mortality tables, even if the amendment has the effect of reducing the size of lump sum distributions. The First Circuit held that it was permissible for an employer to eliminate the option for participants to move defined contribution plan assets to a defined benefit plan. The rule change did not violate the anti-cutback rule even though it diminished an accrued benefit, because the change conformed to an ERISA exception. [*Tasker v. DHL Ret. Savings Plan*, 621 F.3d 34 (1st Cir. 2010); see Fred Schneyer, *Interplan Asset Transfer Elimination Upheld*, plansponsor.com (Oct. 7, 2010)]

The Western District of Washington dismissed a case (for failure to state a claim) when ex-employees of Airborne Express charged that a 2004 amendment violated the anti-cutback rule by eliminating their right to transfer between defined benefit and defined contribution plans. They say the loss of this option reduced their monthly annuity. The change occurred in the context of Airborne's 2003 acquisition by DHL Holdings USA. Under both of Airborne's plans, retirees could take either lump sums or annuities. DHL merged the defined contribution plan into its own plan and eliminated the transfer option. However, Reg. § 1.411(d)-4 permits an amendment to eliminate transfers between defined benefit and defined contribution plans. The plaintiffs argued that a 2010 case about the same plan applies only if the amendment does not reduce the monthly benefit, but the district court ruled that the amendment does not include any such limitation. [*Andersen v. DHL Ret. Pension Plan*, No. C12-439 MJP (W.D. Wash. Nov. 2, 2012)]

The Tenth Circuit ruled in 2009 that the anti-cutback rule does not apply to a death benefit, or a plan feature that pays a lump sum at retirement that is the actuarial equivalent of a death benefit, because the plan's definition of "accrued benefit" excluded death benefits. [*Kerber v. Qwest Pension Plan*, 572 F.3d 1135 (10th Cir. 2009); see Stanley D. Baum, *Tenth Circuit Determines That Elimination of a Pension Plan's Death Benefit Does Not Violate ERISA's Anti-Cutback Rule*, ERISA Lawyer Blog (July 22, 2009) (benefitslink.com). See *In re Lucent*, 541 F.3d 25 (3d Cir. 2008) for the proposition that the death benefit was not an accrued benefit]

In contrast, the Tenth Circuit ruled in 2010 that, although welfare benefits are not subject to the anti-cutback rule, a plan amendment that conditioned the receipt of health benefits from a welfare plan on not receiving a lump sum from the pension plan had the effect of amending the pension plan by adding a new condition for receiving an accrued benefit under the pension plan, because a lump sum became less valuable if health benefits had to be surrendered. Therefore, the anti-cutback rule was violated. [*Battoni v. IBEW Local Union No. 102 Employee Pension Plan*, 594 F.3d 230 (3d Cir. 2010); see Stanley D. Baum, *Third Circuit Rules That an Amendment to a Welfare Plan Violates ERISA's Anti-Cutback Rule*, ERISA Lawyer Blog (Feb. 10, 2010) (benefitslink.com)]

## § 14.05 EGTRRA, CHIPRA, and PPACA CONFORMING AMENDMENTS

It is common for plans to require amendments to conform to changes in tax and labor law (or to take advantage of additional options that have opened up for employers). Because these rules are often complex, difficult, and expensive to administer, it is common for the IRS to publish rules giving plans additional time to comply.

PPA § 1107 says that a timely plan amendment that eliminates or restricts a protected benefit is not be considered a cutback if the benefit reduction was mandated by § 436. Sponsors were given additional time to make such amendments by Notice 2010-77, 2010-51 I.R.B. 851 and Notice 2011-96, 2011-52 I.R.B. 915. Notice 2011-96 also provides a sample amendment that sponsors can use to satisfy Code § 436 with respect to the limitations on accrual and payment of benefits under certain underfunded single-employer defined benefit plans. Part 1 of this notice contains provisions applicable to all plans. Part 2 has two alternative provisions; multi-employer plans must adopt one of them. Part 3 contains four optional provisions that can be used to elect certain acceleration distribution mechanisms; any of all of them can be incorporated into Part 1. [CCH Pensions & Benefits, *IRS Issues Sample Plan Amendment to Satisfy Code Sec. 436 Rules* (Dec. 14, 2011) (benefitslink.com); Rebecca Moore, *IRS Provides Sample Plan*

*Amendment for Underfunded Pension Plan Limitations,* plansponsor.com (Nov. 29, 2011)]

Notice 2012-70, 2012-51 I.R.B. 512 gives defined benefit plans additional time to adopt amendments to comply with Code § 436 (the restrictions on amendments and benefits if a plan's funding falls below certain limits). The previous deadline was the last day of the plan year beginning on or after January 1, 2012. The Notice moves the deadline to the latest of:

- The last day of the plan year beginning on or after January 1, 2013;

- The last day of the first plan year in which the plan is subject to § 436; or

- The due date (with extensions) of the employer's tax return for the year that includes the first day of the plan year when the plan becomes subject to § 436.

Sponsors submitting determination letter applications on or after February 1, 2013 for individually designed plans must adopt the § 436 amendment before submitting the application. (Cycle B plans, filed before February 1, 2013 do not have to comply with § 436.) Notice 2012-70 also extends the relief period under the anti-cutback requirements. [McDermott Will and Emery, *IRS Extends Deadline for Defined Benefit Plans to Adopt Code Section 436 Amendments,* Dec. 13, 2012 (benefitslink.com)]

In late 2007, the IRS issued Rev. Rul. 2007-67, addressing mortality tables and interest rates to be used in calculation of the present value of defined benefit plan lump sums. The ruling permits plan sponsors to incorporate the most current mortality table by reference, so that it will not be necessary to adopt an amendment every time the IRS promulgates new tables. [Fred Schneyer, *Lump Sum Distribution Mortality Table Released,* plansponsor.com (Nov. 6, 2007); Brian M. Pinheiro and Jacquelin M. Gray, *IRS Issues Guidance on Interest Rate and Mortality Table for Calculating Lump Sum Distributions from Defined Benefit Plans in 2008,* Ballard Spahr Andrews & Ingersoll, LLP (Nov. 18, 2007) (benefitslink .com)]

The year 2009's SCHIP expansion under CHIPRA, the Children's Health Insurance Program Reauthorization Act, Pub. L. No. 111-3, required amendment of EGHPs and cafeteria plans to cope with the additional enrollment rights (e.g., employees and their dependents entitled to state subsidy for health insurance premiums). Coordination of benefit rules may have had to be changed to reflect broader SCHIP coverage. [Norbert F. Kugele, Warner Norcross & Judd LLP, *New Federal SCHIP Law Requires Cafeteria and Health Plan Amendments* (Feb. 10, 2009) (benefitslink.com)]

PPACA compliance requires the adoption of a number of plan amendments:

- Enrollment of persons under 19 without pre-existing condition limitations;

- Coverage of employees' dependent children to age 26, whether or not they are students or married, and whether or not they are tax dependents of the employees; but see <http://www.dol.gov/ebsa/faqs/faq-aca.html> Q&A #14 for some permitted exceptions;

- Elimination of lifetime limits on essential health benefits (guidance has not yet been issued to define "essential," so plans must use a good-faith reasonable interpretation of the term);

- Restrictions on annual limits on essential health benefits; the limit must be at least $750,000 in 2010, rising to $1.25 million in 2012;

- Elimination of retroactive terminations of coverage;

- Amending FSAs, HRAs, and HSAs to eliminate reimbursement of the cost of over-the-counter drugs unless the participant has a prescription.

Non-grandfathered plans must be amended to provide the following:

- Coverage of some preventive services without cost sharing;

- Free choice of primary care provider (who can be a pediatrician for children enrolled in the plan); women can see an OB/GYN without prior authorization or referral;

- Emergency services must be covered without prior authorization, and emergency services must receive the same coverage whether in or out of network;

- The new external claims review process;

- The requirement of not discriminating in favor of highly compensated employees.

[Christy Tinnes and Brigen Winters, *A 2011 Plan Amendment Checklist*, Groom Law Group, plansponsor.com (Oct. 12, 2010)]

## § 14.06   ERISA 204(h) NOTICE

The plan administrator has a duty to notify employees when a defined benefit plan (or any other plan that is subject to the minimum funding requirement) is amended in a way that significantly reduces the rate at which future benefits will accrue. In effect, this is an early warning system that signals to employees that their eventual pensions may be smaller than anticipated.

EGTRRA supplements the rules found at ERISA § 204(h) with a comparable Internal Revenue Code provision, I.R.C. § 4980F, which also imposes an excise tax on failure to make the required notification. See 67 Fed. Reg. 19714 for additional Proposed Regulations on this topic and T.D. 9052, 2003-19 I.R.B. 879 for final regulations.

The notice must be understandable to the average plan participant, and must give enough information for him or her to understand approximately how much his or her benefit entitlement will be reduced by the amendment. See also Proposed Regulations, 69 Fed. Reg. 13769 (Mar. 24, 2004) for eliminating redundant optional forms of benefits within a "family" of defined benefit payment options.

If the plan is significantly underfunded, and therefore is subject to restrictions on benefit accruals, payments, or shutdown benefits, the Pension Protection Act of 2006 (Pub. L. No. 109-280; PPA) requires the plan administrator to give written or electronic notice to plan participants within 30 days of the point at which the restriction takes effect.

In 2012, the Eleventh Circuit held that it did not violate the anti-cutback rule to amend the plan to change the calculation of the Social Security offset for participants who had not yet reached age 52 (the plan's earliest retirement age). The amendment changed the calculation of the Social Security offset by assuming that the individual earned no income after 2003 and by freezing benefit accruals. The Eleventh Circuit said that, because the plaintiff had not reached age 52 when the amendment was adopted, she did not have a vested benefit that could be protected by the anti-cutback rule. The Eleventh Circuit read *Heinz* to mean that a pension plan can be amended with respect to compensation that will be earned in the future for continued future employment. [*Cinotto v. Delta Air Lines Inc.*, 674 F.3d 1285 (11th Cir., 2012)]

## § 14.07   AMENDMENTS TO A BANKRUPT SPONSOR'S PLAN

Under Bankruptcy Code § 522, funds held in a qualified plan are protected from the plan sponsor's creditors—but only if the plan had a favorable determination letter in effect at the time of filing of the bankruptcy petition.

The general rule is that plan benefits may not be increased while the plan sponsor is a bankruptcy debtor. [See I.R.C. § 401(a)(33)] Amendments are forbidden if the plan's liabilities rise because of the benefit increase, or because of a change in the rate of accrual or nonforfeitability of benefits. However, amendments that take effect after the effective date of the plan of reorganization are allowed. So are amendments to plans, whose funded current liability percentage is 100% or more, or amendments approved by the IRS, or amendments required to maintain compliance with tax law changes.

The Bankruptcy Abuse Prevention and Consumer Protection Act (BAPCPA), Pub. L. No. 109-8, the bankruptcy reform legislation adopted in 2005, alters the treatment of retirement plans in bankruptcy. Bankruptcy Code § 1114, as amended, prevents a Chapter 11 debtor from terminating or modifying retiree welfare benefits without negotiating with retiree representatives. Benefits must be maintained unless the bankruptcy court approves a change. In addition, the court can set aside amendments to a retiree benefit plan made within 180 days before a bankruptcy filing unless the court finds that it is clearly equitable to modify the plan. The Third Circuit required strict compliance with § 1114, so even though the employer retained the right to amend its plan, it could not terminate retiree health benefits while the company was pursuing a bankruptcy reorganization. [*IUE-CWA v. Visteon Corp.*, 612 F.3d 210 (3d Cir. 2010); see Rebecca Moore, *Visteon Must Follow the Rules Before Terminating Retiree Benefits*, plansponsor .com (July 14, 2010)]

The Third Circuit ruled that a plan amendment, adopted just before a Chapter 11 filing that doubled or even quintupled the pension benefits payable to a group, including many corporate insiders, was void because it was a fraudulent transfer. One factor in the court's decision was the fact that the amendment was described to the board of directors as an "administrative formality," when in fact it was a significant modification to the plan. [*Pension Transfer Corp. v. Beneficiaries Under the Third Amendment to the Fruehauf Trailer Corp. Ret. Plan*, 444 F.3d 203 (3d Cir. 2006)]

Also note that, even if the plan's sponsor is not bankrupt, the Pension Protection Act of 2006 (PPA) restricts amendments that increase benefits at a time when the plan is significantly underfunded.

In March 2011, the PBGC proposed a rule to amend its regulation dealing with benefits payable in terminated single-employer plans. The rule implements PPA § 403, which says that the phase-in period for the guarantee of benefits that are contingent on an "unpredictable contingent event" (the regulation gives the example of a plant shut-down) begins no earlier than the date of the event itself. The rule was necessary because PBGC's guarantee of new pension benefits and benefit increases phases in over a five-year period starting with the later of the date of adoption or the effective date of the change. (This rule was adopted to protect the PBGC against obligations that would be created by plans that knew they were going to terminate adopting new benefits.) The PPA added a new section, ERISA § 4022(b)(8), phasing in the guarantee as if the amendment creating an unpredictable contingent event benefit was adopted on the date of the event, rather than the (usually earlier) date of the plan amendment. The net effect is that the guarantee for benefits that arise from unpredictable contingent events that occur within five years of plan termination is probably lower than the guarantee that would have been available under the pre-PPA law. [PBGC Proposed Rule RIN 1212-AB18, 76 Fed. Reg. 13304 (Mar. 11, 2011)]

Certain single-employer defined benefit plans can be amended, starting August 31, 2012, to eliminate some optional forms of benefits without violating the anti-cutback rule, if the plan sponsor is a bankruptcy debtor; the plan is not fully funded; and the bankruptcy court and the PBGC agree that the amendment is necessary. The benefit form can only be eliminated if the PBGC and bankruptcy court determine that, unless the optional form of benefit is eliminated, the plan will have to go through a distress or involuntary termination. The PBGC must also determine that the plan's assets are insufficient to pay guaranteed benefits. If the sponsor uses these regulations to eliminate an optional form of benefit and the plan does not offer other options that have substantial survivor benefits, the sponsor can add more options to provide survivor benefits, as part of the amendment that eliminates the lump-sum distribution option. The entire amendment will be considered in determining if the amendment complies with § 436(c) requirements. [T.D. 9601, 77 Fed. Reg. 66915 (Nov. 8, 2012), finalizing regulations proposed at 77 Fed. Reg. 37349 (June 21, 2012); see Kristen Heinzinger, *IRS Finalizes Relief for Bankrupt DB Sponsors*, plansponsor.com (Nov. 8, 2012)]

## § 14.08   ISSUES HIGHLIGHTED BY THE IRS

IRS' Employee Plans division listed more than a dozen issues that frequently require plan amendments. These issues often prevent the IRS from closing a case until the issues are resolved to the agency's satisfaction:

- Defined benefit plans that do not apply I.R.C. §§ 415(b)(2)(E) and 417(e) properly;

- Defined contribution plans that do not reflect changes in the calculation of the maximum contributions;

- Plans that use the wrong procedure to waive the QJSA;

- Plans that don't meet the effective date requirements of amendments to the Code;

- Plans that can't prove that they complied with earlier tax and pension laws;

- Plans that have not been amended to forbid rollovers of 401(k) plan hardship distributions;

- Plans that do not define "highly compensated employee" properly;

- Top-heavy plans that have not been updated in view of current laws.

[See *Recurring Plan Issues in Determination Case Review*, <http://www.irs.gov/pub/irs-tege/sum01.pdf#page=15>]

Mishandling of forfeitures (which usually occur when a participant leaves the sponsor's employ before becoming fully vested) is a common target of IRS audits. In the first two years, mistakes can be corrected under the EPCRS program. After two years, the VCP must be used unless the failure is considered insignificant. The VCP must be used if the terms of the plan are incorrect and a retroactive plan amendment is required to correct them. [Chadron J. Patton, *Common Plan Mistakes: Failure to Timely Allocate Forfeitures*, Spencer Fane (Nov. 16, 2012) (benefitslink.com)]

# CHAPTER 15

# ENFORCEMENT AND COMPLIANCE ISSUES FOR QUALIFIED PLANS

## § 15.01  INTRODUCTION

The underlying purpose of ERISA, and of various later pieces of legislation, is to make sure that plan participants and their beneficiaries receive the promised benefits. Therefore, the focus of enforcement is to make sure that plans remain sound, and that participants and beneficiaries do not fall victim to outright fraud, mistake, negligence, poor administration, or declines in the sponsoring company's financial fortunes. Certain types of transactions are prohibited—although "prohibited transaction exemptions" can be obtained in cases where payment of benefits is not placed at real risk. [See § 15.15[C]]

Fiduciary conduct is examined on two levels. Fiduciaries must satisfy their affirmative obligations (to choose proper investments for the plan; to diversify investments unless diversification itself is imprudent; to maintain proper liquidity; to obtain a reasonable yield on plan investments; and to make proper administrative decisions). They are also forbidden to engage in prohibited transactions. In addition to private suits by participants and beneficiaries, the Department of Labor (DOL) and the IRS carry out administrative enforcement efforts and become involved in litigation about plan compliance and participant and beneficiary rights.

The PBGC announced late in 2012 that it would not take action under ERISA § 4062(e) against creditworthy companies or small pension plans (those with fewer than 100 participants). Therefore, about 92% of applicable plan sponsors would not be required to give financial guarantees. However, this is a pilot program and may be modified based on the PBGC's experience. The PBGC took this step to concentrate its enforcement resources on companies with a substantial risk of defaulting on their obligations. Regulations were proposed in August 2010, but they were unpopular with the business community and were withdrawn. More favorable proposed regulations were published in March 2012, designating three categories of financial strength; strong, moderately strong and weak. [R. Randall Tracht, Brian J. Dougherty, Lisa H. Barton, and Eric P. Sarabia, *PBGC Changes Enforcement Policy Under ERISA Section 4062(e)*, Morgan, Lewis & Bockius (Nov. 13, 2012) (benefitslink.com)]

In April 2013, the PBGC proposed to modify the reportable event rules under ERISA § 4043, so that plans and sponsors that qualify for a financial soundness safe harbor based on credit reports would be relieved of the obligation to report. [78 Fed. Reg. 20039 (Apr. 3, 2013); see Buck Consultants FYI, *PBGC Reproposes Reportable Event Rules* (Apr. 5, 2013) (benefitslink.com) The PBGC offered further guidance in May, 2013, defining a creditworthy company as one whose unsecured debt is rated at least Baa3 by Moody's or BBB- by Standard & Poor's, or which has a D&B Financial Stress Score of at least 1477 and does not have an excessive amount of secured debt. Certain factors such as lack of ongoing operations or transactions that cause a downgrade prevent a company from being deemed creditworthy. [See PLC Employee Benefits & Employee

Compensation, *PBGC Releases Enforcement Guidelines for ERISA Section 4062(e) Financial Assurance Program* (May 3, 2013) (benefitslink.com)]

A pension plan is a legal entity that can sue or be sued under ERISA Title I. [See ERISA § 502(d)] Unless somebody is found liable in an individual capacity, the plan is responsible for paying all money judgments.

Because the management of plan assets for the sole benefit of participants and beneficiaries is so central to plan operation, the identification, duties, and liabilities of fiduciaries are central to plan enforcement.

ERISA § 402(a)(1) requires all plans either to have a named fiduciary, or to explain in the plan document how fiduciaries will be selected. Under ERISA § 411, a convicted felon is not permitted to serve as plan administrator, fiduciary, officer, trustee, custodian, counsel, agent, consultant, or employee with decision-making authority for 13 years after his or her conviction or the end of his or her prison term, whichever comes later.

Asserting that someone has breached fiduciary duties depends on being able to characterize that party as a fiduciary. Furthermore, the party must have been acting in a fiduciary capacity at the time. In 1995, in a welfare benefit plan case, the Supreme Court said that plan sponsors are generally free to amend or terminate welfare plans. In 1999, the Supreme Court extended this principle to pension plans and made it clear that, when they amend a plan, sponsors are acting as the settlers of the plan trust and not as fiduciaries of the plan.

Citing these cases, the Second Circuit abrogated some of its former decisions and held that employers and plan sponsors are not acting as fiduciaries when they modify, adopt, or amend plans—including multi-employer plans. The suit was brought on behalf of ex-participants and beneficiaries of a union pension and welfare fund. The plaintiffs wanted to recover assets that they claimed were wrongfully depleted by improper plan amendments that violated fiduciary duty. [*Janese v. Fay*, 692 F.3d 221 (2d Cir. 2012); see Rebecca Moore, *Amending a Plan Not a Fiduciary Act*, plansponsor.com (Sept. 18, 2012); see *Curtiss-Wright v. Schoonejongen*, 514 U.S. 73 (1995); *Lockheed v. Spink*, 517 U.S. 882 (1999)]

Investors in Bernard L. Madoff Investment Securities LLC could not recover funds when the firm was liquidated. The Securities Investor Protection Act provides benefits to "customers" of failed brokerage firms, who share in the recovery of the cash and securities in the liquidation. But Judge Denise Cote ruled that ERISA claimants are not customers. In an ERISA-regulated plan, the assets are owned by the plan's trustees, rather than by the participants. [*Securities Investor Prot. Corp. v. Jacqueline Green Rollover Account*, No. 12 civ 1039 (DLC), 2012 U.S. Dist. LEXIS 104024 (S.D.N.Y. July 25, 2012); see Jay Polansky, *Participants in ERISA-Regulated Plans Cannot Recover Funds From Madoff*, plansponsor.com (July 27, 2012)]

Breach of fiduciary duty claims is a very active area of litigation. There are many arguments that the employer and other defendants can raise:

- ERISA preemption;

- Plaintiff's lack of standing to sue;

- Suing the wrong defendant(s);

- Bringing suit after the statute of limitations has run;

- Demand for improper relief—e.g., seeking legal relief when only equitable relief is available; seeking individual relief when relief must be sought on behalf of the plan as a whole.

Courts have come up with many different answers to the question of who is the proper defendant in an ERISA case. ERISA § 502(a)(1)(B) says that a civil action may be brought by a participant or beneficiary to collect benefits under the plan—but does not say who the participant or beneficiary can sue. Section 502(d)(2) says that a money judgment against a plan is enforced only against the plan, unless another person is individually liable. In cases of benefit denial, the plan administrator is the proper defendant. ERISA § 3(16) says that the plan sponsor is the plan administrator, unless the terms of the plan say otherwise. If the plan designates an administrator, then it may be necessary to sue the designated administrator and not the employer—unless the employer has actual control over the operations of the plan.

Depending on the court and the fact situation:

- Only the plan as entity can be sued;

- The plan can be sued, but so can other parties;

- The formal administrator of the plan can be sued;

- A "de facto" plan administrator can be sued, even if he, she, or it is not formally designated as plan administrator, on the basis of control over the plan;

- Plan fiduciaries, including administrators, can be sued;

- An insurer can be sued (perhaps only if there is no plan or plan administrator that could be held liable).

[William F. Hanrahan and Lars C. Golumbic, *ERISA Benefits Litigation: Who Can Be Sued?* <http://www.groom.com/_news/ERISABenefitsLitigation.html> (Summer 2006) (benefitslink.com); Terry Price, *Federal Court Rulings Identify Employers as Liable Party in ERISA Benefits Action*, Employee Benefit News (Sept. 15, 2006) (benefitslink.com)]

The Supreme Court ruled in favor of an employer, acting both as plan sponsor and administrator, that terminated pension plans by purchasing annuities for participants. The union representing the company's employees urged that, instead, the company's plans should be merged into the union's multi-employer plan. The Supreme Court ruled that a bankrupt company does not have a fiduciary duty to consider the merger option. It did not violate ERISA for the company to put the plan through a standard termination and then purchase annuities to cover the payment obligations: terminating the plan in that manner ended the applicability of ERISA to the plan's assets and the employer's obligations. [*Beck v. PACE Int'l Union*, 551 U.S. 96 (2007); see Adrien Martin, *Supreme Court: Plan Mergers Considered an Alternative to Termination*, plansponsor.com (June 12, 2007); *(AP) High Court Goes Against Labor in Pension Case* (June 12, 2007) (law. com)]

In 2010, the Supreme Court strongly reaffirmed the principles of *Bruch* and favored administrators' powers by holding that courts should apply a deferential standard of review to the decisions of plan administrators who are empowered under the plan to interpret plan terms. [*Conkright v. Frommert*, 559 U.S. 506 (2010)]

See § 15.09[C] for the crucial 2011 decision in *Amara v. Cigna*, discussing the remedies available under ERISA § 502.

The final regulations under Code § 415, published in the Federal Register on April 4, 2007 (72 Fed. Reg. 16878) state that annual additions to the plan, for purposes of computing the § 415 limit, do not include payments made to the plan to restore losses due to a fiduciary's action or failure to act that could have been penalized under ERISA or any other applicable law as breaches of fiduciary duty.

Note that the Pension Protection Act of 2006 imposes a penalty of up to $100,000 and/or 10 years' imprisonment for coercive interference with rights under ERISA.

The Second Circuit ordered a profit-sharing plan to repay a participant approximately $1.5 million in assets from his account when half the balance was wrongfully transferred to the participant's ex-wife. The participant was entitled to recover the money even though the plan was unable to recoup it from the ex-wife even after the Northern District of New York granted the plan a judgment against her. The Second Circuit held that undistributed funds held in trust are not "benefits" as defined by the anti-alienation provision and, in any event, ERISA's anti-alienation provision permits plan assets to be used to satisfy a judgment against the plan itself. Paying the judgment was a ministerial function, not a discretionary fiduciary function that could give rise to liability. The Northern District of New York dismissed charges against the plan's TPA, holding that it was not acting in a fiduciary capacity when the mistaken transfer was made. [*Milgram v. Orthopedic Assocs.*, 666 F.3d 68 (2d Cir. 2011); see Rebecca Moore, *Plan Must Restore Misplaced Assets Although not Recovered,* plansponsor.com (Jan. 17, 2012)]

In 2010, the Supreme Court ruled that ERISA plaintiffs who sue under § 502(g)(1) can be awarded attorneys' fees even if they are not the prevailing party in the suit, because that section of ERISA gives the district court discretion to award attorneys' fees to either party. (This is in contrast to § 502(g)(2), a suit alleging that contributions to a multi-employer plan are delinquent; § 502(g)(2) limits fee awards to plaintiffs who obtain a judgment in favor of the pension plan.) This decision makes it likely that more pension plans will have to pay attorneys' fees to plaintiffs who achieve a degree of success in challenges to the plan. [*Hardt v. Reliance Ins. Co.,* 560 U.S. 242 (2010); see Workplace Prof Blog, *ERISA Supreme Court Attorney Fees Case Goes Way of Plaintiffs* (May 24, 2010) (benefitslink.com)]

The Southern District of New York found that it was a breach of fiduciary duty not to honor a former employee's request for a rollover distribution. The defendants said that the request could be ignored because it was not in the proper form—but the court said that the plan did not require formal claims. By the time the account was finally transferred to an IRA in January 2011 (the participant had been trying to get the amount rolled over since December of 2005), the balance had fallen from $75,000 to $64,000. The Southern District of New York awarded prejudgment interest starting on the date of the initial request (because as of that date, he should have been able to invest the balance as he chose) plus attorneys' fees. [*Klepeis v. J&R*, No. 10-cv-0363 (CS)(PED), 2012 U.S. Dist. LEXIS 16441 (S.D.N.Y. Feb. 9, 2012); see Rebecca Moore, *Employer Breached ERISA by Failing to Make Rollover Distribution*, plansponsor.com (Feb. 13, 2012)]

## § 15.02   WHO IS A FIDUCIARY?

In general legal terms, a fiduciary is anyone responsible for another party's money or property. Fiduciaries have a legal duty to behave honestly and conscientiously, and to avoid promoting their own self-interest at the expense of the owner of the assets.

Many types of people who deal with pension and benefit plans are considered fiduciaries under ERISA—including some people who do not think of themselves in that way or do not understand their responsibilities and potential liabilities.

Fiduciary liability extends far beyond embezzlement and other criminal acts. It is even possible for one fiduciary's mistake or wrongdoing to get a group of other fiduciaries into trouble.

An individual, business, or institution that deals with a plan becomes a fiduciary whenever, and to the extent that, he or she:

- Exercises any discretionary authority (i.e., is able to make decisions) or control over the management of the plan;

- Exercises any authority (even if it isn't discretionary) over the management and disposition of plan assets. The distinction is made because the greatest potential for abuse exists when money is at stake;

- Receives direct or indirect compensation for giving the plan investment advice about its assets;

- Has any discretionary authority or responsibility for day-to-day plan administration (as distinct from plan management).

In other words, if a plan hires attorneys, accountants, or actuaries to provide advice, those professionals will usually not become fiduciaries of the plan, because they do not control the direction that the plan takes. They merely provide technical information that the administrator and other fiduciaries use to make decisions.

Just having custody of plan assets doesn't necessarily make the custodian a fiduciary, so a law firm did not become a fiduciary by acting as an escrow agent for funds belonging to one of its clients. (The issue arose when a partner in the law firm embezzled some of the money.) [*Burtch v. Ganz* (*In re Mushroom Transport Co. Inc.*), 382 F.3d 325 (3d Cir. 2004)] A custodian that transfers retirement plan assets at the direction of plan trustees is not a fiduciary, and is not liable under ERISA for the plan's losses, merely because it had check-writing authority. The custodian did not exercise authority or control over the assets. [*Erickson v. ING Life Ins. & Annuity Co.*, 731 F. Supp. 2d 1057 (D. Idaho 2010); see Rebecca Moore, *Court Finds Directed Custodian Not a Fiduciary Under ERISA*, plan sponsor.com (July 29, 2010)]

A financial consulting firm that appraised the employer's stock is not a fiduciary, and is not liable for an Employee Stock Ownership Plan's losses. [*Keach v. U.S. Trust Co.*, 234 F. Supp. 2d 872 (C.D. Ill. 2002)]

■ **TIP:**   If the professional adviser is not a fiduciary, ERISA probably will not preempt state-law malpractice suits brought by the plan.

Similarly, a stockbroker who simply executes the fiduciaries' orders to adjust the plan's investment portfolio is not a fiduciary—but an investment manager who has a role in setting the plan's investment policy is very definitely a fiduciary.

The Ninth Circuit held that being a fiduciary for ERISA purposes does not necessarily entail being a fiduciary as defined by Bankruptcy Code § 523(a)(4), the Bankruptcy Code provision that prevents bankruptcy discharge of debts for fiduciary fraud. [*Hunter v. Philpott*, 373 F.3d 873 (9th Cir. 2004)]

A Third-Party Administrator (TPA) can be considered an ERISA fiduciary even if it does not have discretionary control over the assets of the health plan it administered; the statutory language is "any authority or control." The Sixth Circuit held that a TPA's authority to write checks on the plan's account (which continued to be exercised to pay the TPA's fees even after the contract with the plan sponsor ended) provided the necessary degree of authority or control to impose liability after the sponsor company went bankrupt and many employees had unpaid medical bills. [*Briscoe v. Fine*, 444 F.3d 478 (6th Cir. 2006)]; on remand, the Western District of Kentucky held that the administrative services contract made the employer, not the plan, responsible for paying the TPA's fee, so it was a breach of fiduciary duty for the TPA to pay itself out of plan assets. It was also a breach of fiduciary duty to submit the COBRA premiums and funded claims reserve to the employer, which the TPA knew was in bad financial shape and likely to appropriate the money—which belonged to the plan and the plan participants, not the employer. [*Briscoe v. Preferred Health Plan, Inc.*, CIVIL ACTION NO. 3:02CV-264-S,2008 WL 4146381 (W.D. Ky. Sept. 2, 2008)]

A TPA hired as a health plan claims administrator to pay medical providers misappropriated the money. Many claims were not paid. The TPA had agreements to pay claims under self-insured ERISA health benefit plans funded by both employer contributions and employee payroll deductions. An employer discovered that funds were not accounted for and claims were not paid and sued the TPA. The defendant argued that it was not a fiduciary, there was no harm to the plaintiffs, and the plaintiffs' breach of contract claims were preempted by ERISA. The Sixth Circuit held that a TPA becomes a fiduciary when it exercises practical control over the funds of an ERISA plan. Misappropriating plan assets violates the duty to act solely in the interests of participants. The defendant cited a contract provision describing it as a non-fiduciary, but the Sixth Circuit held that the contract provision could not override ERISA. [*Guyan Int'l Inc. v. Professional Benefits Adm'rs Inc.*, 689 F.3d 793(6th Cir. 2012); see EBIA Weekly, *Sixth Circuit Affirms That TPA Breached Fiduciary Duties by Using Plan Assets to Pay Its Expenses Instead of Claims* (Sept. 6, 2012) (benefitslink.com)]

A TPA that retained part of the money transferred by self-insured employers to pay benefits was sued by sponsors. At an earlier stage of the case, the District Court for the Eastern District of Michigan ruled that the TPA was a fiduciary to the plan, and violated the ERISA ban on self-dealing. The TPA deceived the plans about its charges and how it operated. Although the ERISA statute of limitations for fiduciary breach is six years from discovery of the breach, the district court allowed additional time to sue because of the TPA's fraud and concealment. For breach of the duty of loyalty and for giving the plans false information for submission in Form 5500, the District Court for the Eastern District of Michigan awarded more $5 million in damages, plus attorneys' fees, costs, and interest. [*Hi-Lex Controls Inc. v. Blue Cross & Blue Shield of Michigan*, No. 11-cv-12557-14, 2013 WL 2285453 (E.D. Mich. 2013); see EBIA Weekly, *Court Awards Over $5 Million for TPA's Breach of Fiduciary Duty* (June 6, 2013) (benefitslink.com)]

Sponsors are required to monitor TPA performance. The DOL sued Clark Graphics for ERISA violations. The company's president was ordered to restore $505,000 to Clark Graphics' two pension plans. The plan administrator had to give back $425,000 to the profit sharing plan and $143,000, minus payments made by others, to the defined benefit plan. The business' owners were charged with dereliction of their fiduciary duty as trustees because they did not monitor the activities of the plan administrator, Pension Retirement Planning, which offered third-party record-keeping services to about 50 plans between 2000 and 2010. The owners did not review or reconcile the trust account statements for the plans or make sure that the administrator issued participant statements. Some plan participants did not get correct benefits because of the TPA's failure to maintain accurate records. [Rebecca Moore, *Employer to Pay $500K for Failing to Monitor TPA*, plansponsor.com (July 18, 2012)]

In late 2010, DOL proposed the first update to the definition of "fiduciary" since shortly after ERISA was enacted. DOL wants to restore the simple two-part test for fiduciary status, removing the requirements of a mutual understanding; that advice be given on a regular basis; and that it be a primary basis for investment of the plan assets. Under the proposal, a fiduciary is a party that renders investment advice about any plan assets (or has any authority or responsibility to do so) and receives direct or indirect compensation for the advice. [Nevin E. Adams, Plansponsor Perspectives: *Interests Bearing*, plansponsor (Oct. 23, 2010)]

Because of past problems with incorrect valuation of employer securities, DOL decided to add appraisals and fairness opinions to the definition of advice. It is also possible to become a fiduciary by giving advice to participants and beneficiaries as well as to another fiduciary. DOL asked for comments as to whether it is investment advice to recommend that a plan participant take a distribution that is permitted under the plan.

Explicitly claiming ERISA fiduciary status orally or in writing makes a party a fiduciary, if a fee is received, because claiming the status enhances the party's influence and creates the impression that the advice is valuable. However, mere provision of investment education materials is not advice. Making investments or an investment available without regard to individualized needs of plan or participants does not constitute investment advice as long as the provider discloses in writing to plan fiduciary that it is not undertaking to provide impartial investment advice.

The revised definition says that a party is not a fiduciary if it can show that the recipient of advice knows or reasonably should know that the person giving the advice is selling or buying a security, or acts on behalf of someone who is, and is therefore not impartial. So the person isn't providing impartial investment advice. The advice must also be rendered for a fee to be covered. [FR Doc 2010-26236, 75 Fed. Reg. 65263 (Oct. 22, 2010); see Judy Ward, *DOL Broadens Fiduciary Net*, plansponsor.com (Oct. 22, 2010)]

## § 15.03  FIDUCIARY DUTIES

### [A]  ERISA Requirements

ERISA imposes four major duties on fiduciaries:

- Loyalty;
- Prudence;
- Acting in accordance with the plan documents;
- Monitoring the performance of anyone to whom fiduciary responsibility has been delegated.

The source of the duty of loyalty is the ERISA mandate that plan assets be held for the exclusive benefit of participants and beneficiaries. Once assets have been placed into the plan trust, or used to buy insurance, they can no longer be used for the benefit of the employer.

The duty of prudence requires fiduciaries to behave with the level of care, skill, prudence, and diligence that a hypothetical prudent person would use to handle the same tasks. This hypothetical prudent person is familiar with the plan and its situation—not the "man on the street" who lacks specialized knowledge.

Although trust law requires every asset within a trust to satisfy the prudent person test, DOL Reg. § 2550.404a-1(c)(2) allows the fiduciary to select assets by considering the relevant facts and circumstances, including the role of the individual investment within the portfolio. Relying on expert advice is encouraged, but it does not guarantee that an investment choice will be considered prudent.

In general, it will not be considered a breach of fiduciary duty to make a mistake in calculations. [See, e.g., *Livick v. Gillette Co.*, 492 F. Supp. 2d 1 (D. Mass. 2007), discussed in Rebecca Moore, *Miscalculation of Benefits Not a Fiduciary Breach*, plansponsor.com (June 14, 2007)] The Second Circuit rejected a former employee's argument that it was a breach of fiduciary duty for the administrator of a stock option plan to tell her that she could exercise her options after retirement. Not only were the communications not intentionally false, the Second Circuit said that the advice was not even really wrong. The court ruled that, even if there had been an unintentional misstatement about the consequences for non-ERISA stock option plan, of a retirement decision under an ERISA plan, there would not have been a violation of fiduciary duty. [*Bell v. Pfizer*, 626 F.3d 66 (2d Cir. 2010); see Michael Melbinger, Winston & Strawn LLP, *A $327 Million Stock Option Mistake* (Sept. 2, 2010) (benefitslink.com)]

The Southern District of Ohio dismissed a breach of fiduciary duty claim on the grounds that the plan administrator and call center employees were not acting as fiduciaries when they gave the plaintiff an incorrect estimate of her pension benefits. It was not a breach of duty for the employer or pension committee to rely on information from Hewitt, the plan administrator. The administrator and call center employees did not have any discretionary authority or control over the management, administration, or disposition of plan assets. Disclaimers were included with the information, and the Hewitt Website disclaimed warranties for accuracy and completeness of the site's content, so it would have been unreasonable for the plaintiff to rely on the benefit estimates. There was no cause to apply an estoppel theory because, at worst, honest mistakes were made and there was no intent to deceive the plaintiff or impair the exercise of her rights. [*Stark v. Mars*, 879 F. Supp. 2d 752 (S.D. Ohio 2012; see Rebecca Moore, *Overestimate of Pension Benefit Not a Fiduciary Breach* plansponsor.com (Aug. 3, 2012)]

The Third Circuit ruled that a woman who retired based on alleged misrepresentations about the pension her husband would receive did not make out a case of breach of fiduciary duty. To prove detrimental reliance, there must be both injury and reasonableness. The plaintiff must have engaged in some action; merely expecting continued benefits is not enough. The wife was not a participant in the plan and the couple's retirement decisions did not change their benefits in any way. [*Shook v. Avaya Inc.*, 625 F.3d 69 (3d Cir. 2010); see Stanley D. Baum, *Third Circuit Holds That a Beneficiary's Decision to Retire Is Not the Detrimental Reliance Needed to Establish a Claim for Breach of Fiduciary Duty Under ERISA*, ERISA Lawyer Blog (Nov. 4, 2010) (benefitslink.com)]

However, in 2012, the Eastern District of Wisconsin found an employer and life insurance plan liable on the basis of ERISA estoppel. The temporary administrator of payroll and benefits (filling in for the permanent administrator, who was on maternity leave) incorrectly informed a plan participant that the employer would continue to pay the premiums on his $103,000 life insurance policy after retirement. The SPD accurately informed participants that they had 31 days after employment ended to convert their life insurance to individual coverage and pay the first premium. The SPD said that coverage would end if the policy was not converted—but did not say who had to pay the premiums. The Seventh Circuit also found the employer liable for breach of fiduciary duty. Although the temporary administrator was not an ERISA fiduciary, she was held out as the employer's representative for benefit purposes and the company failed to give her adequate training—making the company liable for breach of fiduciary duty. [*Winkelspecht v. Gustave A. Larson Co.*, No. 10-C-1072, 2012 U.S. Dist. LEXIS 30729 (E.D. Wis. Mar. 8, 2012); see Deidre A. Grossman, Littler Mendelson Employment Litigation Blog, *Unintended Errors in Benefits Communications May Result in Liability under ERISA* (Mar. 14, 2012) (benefitslink.com)]

In an unpublished decision, the Sixth Circuit held that ERISA § 502(a)(2) does not permit a life insurance beneficiary to recover unpaid benefits as a remedy for the plan administrator's fiduciary breach. A Federal Express employee did not convert his group life insurance to individual insurance after he was terminated. To convert the group policy to individual coverage, he would have had to make an election within 31 days of receiving the conversion notice; apply to the insurer; and pay the premiums. After his death, his surviving spouse attempted to collect benefits, alleging that the plan and plan administrator breached their fiduciary duty by not including information about converting the life policy in the COBRA notice he received upon termination. The Sixth Circuit held that there is no obligation (under COBRA or otherwise) to provide a conversion notice about life insurance. The Supreme Court denied certiorari in early 2013. [*Walker v. Federal Express Corp.*, 133 S. Ct. 851 (2013); see Bloomberg BNA Pension & Benefits Daily, *Supreme Court Declines to Review Individual Relief Ruling Under ERISA*, Jan. 8, 2013 (law.com)]

## [B] Diversification

The general rule is that ERISA requires fiduciaries to diversify unless diversification is imprudent (the fiduciary has to prove this). The fiduciary is supposed to select a balanced portfolio that is responsive to current conditions. The portfolio's liquidity and current return must be considered in light of anticipated needs for cash flow. Fiduciaries are not restricted to a "legal list" of investments, and are permitted to take a certain amount of risk, as long as the risk is reasonable in the context of the entire portfolio.

In early 2002, the failure of Enron Corporation highlighted the entire question of investment in employer securities. The basic ERISA rule is that plans can invest in employer securities only if they are "qualifying employer securities" such as stock and eligible debt instruments. Defined benefit plans are subject to additional limitations on holdings of employer securities. [See § 6.09[C] for additional discussion of this issue in the context of 401(k) plans.]

The Supreme Court delayed deciding a case about the ability of Enron shareholders to sue Wall Street investment banks that failed to detect, or at least warn, them of Enron's impending collapse, but eventually denied certiorari early in 2008. [*Univ. of Cal. Regents v. Merrill Lynch*, 482 F.3d 372 (5th Cir.), *cert. denied*, 128 S. Ct. 1120 (2008); see Rebecca Moore, *Supreme Court Delays Decision on Enron Case*, plansponsor.com (June 25, 2007)]

ERISA § 404(c) offers fiduciaries protection against liability. (It covers qualified defined contribution plans and the portions of defined benefit plans that allow direction of investment of individual accounts.) In general, fiduciaries have a duty to diversify and choose investments prudently, but 404(c) indemnifies them for losses in accounts where the participant exercises independent control over the investment of the account, after choosing from among a broad range of investments.

"Broad range of investments" is defined to mean that the participant has the chance to pick investments that will determine the return on the account, and can diversify to reduce risk. There must be at least three main diversified categories of investment choices offered, with materially different risk and return categories, so that the participant can assemble a portfolio with normal and appropriate risk and return characteristics. Employer stock cannot be made one of the core investments. Participants must be allowed to give investment instructions at least once per quarter—more frequently if market volatility requires.

The participant must have a reasonable opportunity to give instructions to an identified fiduciary, who is required to carry out the instructions as given. (Under limited circumstances, the fiduciary can ignore the instructions—for example, if the instruction would be a prohibited transaction or would subject the plan to taxable income.) Under this safe harbor provision, the fiduciary can hire a third-party service provider to carry out the instructions when it is prudent to do so. The participant is also considered to control the account when the fiduciary makes default investments under the default investment safe harbor—but if the plan does not qualify for the safe harbor, it can be held liable for losses in the value of default investments.

Plans that seek to use the safe harbor must disclose that the plan is using § 404(c) to relieve fiduciaries of liability; must describe the investment options and how to give investment directions; and that additional information is available on request (e.g., the annual operating expenses for each investment option, and how to get copies of prospectuses and financial statements). Item 8a of the Form 5500 asks if the plan or any portion of the plan intends to comply with § 404(c); the form must be signed under penalty of perjury. [Prudential Retirement Pension Analyst, *Department of Labor Requirements for Participant-Directed Investments* (July 2008) (benefitslink.com)]

Enhanced diversification rights are mandated by the PPA. In mid-2007, EBSA issued final regulations concerning penalties for plan administrators who fail to inform participants and beneficiaries of their right to diversify out of investments in employer securities. For plan years beginning after December 31, 2006, a civil penalty of up to $100 per day can be imposed under ERISA § 502(c)(7) for failure to provide the notice. [72 Fed. Reg. 44970 (Aug. 10, 2007), discussed in *EBSA Reg. Provides Penalties for Failure to Notify Participants of Stock Diversification Rights Under PPA*, CCH Pension & Benefits (Aug. 21, 2007) (benefits link.com); *EBSA Publishes Final Diversification Fine Rule*, NU Online News Service (Aug. 10, 2007) (benefitslink.com). The corresponding DOL regulation appears at 72 Fed. Reg. 44991 (Aug. 10, 2007).]

The Sixth Circuit held in 2012 that the PPA safe harbor was intended to give employers an incentive to move away from low-risk but low-yielding investments that make it difficult for participants to keep up with inflation. The two plaintiffs allocated 100% of their 403(b) accounts to the stable value fund, which was also the default investment. In 2008, the employer changed its default fund and transferred the plaintiffs' investments from the old to the new default fund. The sponsor did not have records showing which participants retained the default investment and which affirmatively chose to invest in the stable value fund, so it notified all participants who were 100% invested in the stable value fund that their investments would be transferred unless they expressed an intention to retain the stable value investment. The plaintiffs said that they did not receive the notice; the sponsor said that it was mailed to their last known addresses. The plaintiffs argued unsuccessfully that the safe harbor is limited to default investments, not investments selected by the participant, and they said they picked the stable value fund as an investment. However, the safe harbor regulations specifically state that they are not limited to default investments. The Sixth Circuit said it was "troubling" that they did not get the notice, but the employer's actions did not violate ERISA: a fiduciary is obligated to take measures reasonably calculated to ensure actual receipt, but it seems that the employer sent the correct number of letters, by first class mail, to the address they had on record. [*Bidwell v. University Med. Ctr.*, 685 F.3d 613 (6th Cir. 2012)]

T.D. 9484 provides final regulations under Code § 401(a)(35), explicating the PPA's diversification requirements for defined contribution plans that hold publicly traded employer stock. For plan participants who have at least three years of service, their beneficiaries, and the beneficiaries of deceased participants, the plan must allow divestment of employer securities and re-investment in a reasonable menu of choices At least three varied options other than employer stock, each of them diversified, must be offered. Divestment opportunities must be provided at reasonable intervals, at least quarterly. Unless the restriction is required to comply with securities laws, the plan cannot impose conditions on re-investment of employer securities that are not imposed on other investments within the plan. [T.D. 9484, 75 Fed. Reg. 27927 (May 19, 2010); see Rebecca Moore, *IRS Issues Final Regs on Diversification Requirements for Company Stock*, plansponsor. com (May 18, 2010)]

## [C] Stock-Drop Cases and Other Investment Issues

A "stock drop" suit charges a plan's fiduciaries with breach of duty because they retained employer stock as a plan investment without divulging to participants that the stock had declined in value or become risky (e.g., because of the plan sponsor's involvement in derivatives or other risky financial transactions). Another stock drop allegation is that the employer's stock represents too large a part of the plan's investments, and the plan should have been more diversified. Almost all stock drop cases are dismissed. Stock-drop cases frequently are associated with securities law cases, but ERISA cases are easier to bring because securities law requires proof of "scienter" (an enhanced form of intent). Courts of Appeals usually follow three principles:

- The amount of deference fiduciaries receive depends on the amount of discretion the plan design gives them;

- Mere fluctuations in the price of the employer's stock will not show that the fiduciaries were imprudent to keep the stock in the plan; something else has to be present;

- Possible liability factors include breaches of the duty of loyalty (misrepresenting or concealing material facts).

Early in 2011, the Seventh Circuit decided two important stock drop cases. *Lingis v. Dorazil* (and *Howell v. Motorola, Inc.*) agreed with the Department of Labor (and the Fourth Circuit), that the ERISA 404(c) safe harbor applies only to decisions a participant can make—not to the selection of investments available under the plan. However, the Seventh Circuit ruled in favor of the defendants, finding that there was no evidence of imprudence, because prudence is evaluated in the context of the entire menu of plan options, not each option in isolation. The Seventh Circuit also ruled that a release of all claims against the employer in a severance package, in exchange for compensation, can settle claims of fiduciary misconduct. [*Howell v. Motorola Inc.* consolidated with *Lingis v. Dorazil*, 633 F.3d 552 (7th Cir. 2011); see EBIA Weekly, *Seventh Circuit Concludes Employer's Selection of Investment Options Is Not Protected Under ERISA Section 404(c)* (Feb. 10, 2011) (benefitslink.com); Steptoe & Johnson LLP ERISA Advisory, *The 7th Circuit's Big ERISA Day* (Feb. 15, 2011) (benefitslink.com)]

Fiduciaries receive the highest degree of protection if the plan actually requires company stock to be included as an investment option, because the fiduciary had no discretion: see, e.g., *Urban v. Comcast Corp.*, No. 08-733, 2008 WL 4739519 (E.D. Pa. Oct. 28, 2008); *Edgar v. Avaya*, 503 F.3d 340 (3d Cir. 2007). But the level of scrutiny will be higher if the plan gives fiduciaries complete discretion: *Graden v. Conexant Sys. Inc.*, 574 F. Supp. 2d 456 (D.N.J. 2008).

Between these extremes, most courts of appeal agree with the Third Circuit [*Moench v. Robertson*, 62 F.3d 553 (3d Cir. 1995]: the fiduciaries are presumed prudent, so the plaintiff needs more evidence than just a drop in stock prices to overcome this presumption. The "*Moench*" presumption has been applied in the Third, Fifth, Sixth, Ninth, and Eleventh Circuits. It can be rebutted by showing an abuse of discretion by the fiduciary, such as clear risks to the ongoing viability of the employer corporation, or a precipitous drop in value plus evidence of either serious mismanagement or the likelihood of imminent collapse. The greater the plan's duty to invest in the employer's stock, the more the plaintiff must show to prevail. [*Quan v. Computer Sciences Corp.*, 623 F.3d 870 (9th Cir. 2010). The Eleventh Circuit adopted the majority position in *Lanfear v. Home Depot*, 679 F.3d 1267 (11th Cir. 2012).]

Plan fiduciaries are not required to make use of inside information to remove employer stock as a plan investment; using inside information violates securities laws. The Seventh Circuit also held that fiduciaries cannot be expected to "outsmart the stock market." [*White v. Marshall & Ilsley Corp.*, No. 11-2660 (7th Cir. Apr. 19, 2013); see also *Rinehart v. Akers*, No. 11-4232 (2d Cir. 2013)]

For an example of a case in which the presumption was found to be rebutted, the Sixth Circuit revived a stock drop suit about GM common stock, finding that a prudent fiduciary would have made a different investment decision under the same circumstances. The plaintiffs alleged that the plan failed to follow its own requirement of divesting company stock if there was a serious concern about the sponsor's viability as a going concern. GM's auditors revealed substantial doubt about viability in November of 2008, but State Street did not start divesting GM's common stock until March 31, 2009. Unlike the Fifth Circuit, the Sixth Circuit reads § 404(c) to protect fiduciaries from the consequences of decisions made by participants, not the fiduciary itself. (EBIA Weekly pointed out that that recent final regulations under § 404(c) specifically say that § 404(c) is not a defense in allegations of failure to prudently select and monitor any investment or service provider.) [*Pfeil v. State St. Bank and Trust Co.*, 671 F.3d 585 (6th Cir. 2012); see Rebecca Moore, *Appellate Court Reopens Case Against State Street by GM Participants*, plansponsor.com (Feb. 23, 2012); EBIA Weekly, *Sixth Circuit Rules*

*ERISA § 404(c) Protection Not Applicable to Fiduciary's Investment Selection* (Mar. 8, 2012) (benefitslink.com)]

The Ninth Circuit ruled in mid-2013 that the presumption of prudence did not apply to retention of employer stock in the plan when it was known that the company (a drug manufacturer) would be in trouble because of off-label promotion of drugs. The plan did not require or even encourage investment in employer stock, so it was not prudent to retain the stock as soon as the fiduciaries knew or should have known that material misrepresentations about the drugs artificially inflated the price of the stock. Failure to give participants material information about the stock also violated the duties of loyalty and due care. [*Harris v. Amgen,*No. 10-56014 (9th Cir. June 4, 2013)]

The Sixth Circuit revived a dismissed suit about the prudence of retaining employer stock in a retirement plan. The district court dismissed the suit on the grounds that investing in employer stock is presumed prudent in an ESOP, but the Sixth Circuit cited *Pfeil*: the *Moench* presumption does not apply at the motion-to-dismiss stage because it is not an additional pleading requirement. The Sixth Circuit said that ESOP fiduciaries are subject to the same standards as other fiduciaries, except with respect to diversification of the portfolio. The Sixth Circuit held that incorporating SEC filings by reference in the plan's SPD was a fiduciary communication, so the plaintiffs' complaint was adequate because it plausibly alleged that they were furnished misleading information. [*Dudenhoefer v. Fifth Third Bank*, 692 F.3d 410 (6th Cir. 2012); see Rebecca Moore, *Court Revives Fifth Third Stock Drop Suit*, plansponsor.com (Sept. 5, 2012); Wolters Kluwer Law & Business News Center, *Sixth Circuit Declines To Apply Presumption Of Prudence At Pleadings Stage* (Nov. 8, 2012) (benefitslink.com)]

For other recent cases applying the *Moench* presumption, see, e.g.:

- In another ESOP case, the Second Circuit pointed out that, by definition, ESOPs are intended to invest in employer stock [*In re Citigroup ERISA Litig.*, 662 F.3d 128 (2d Cir. 2011) The Second Circuit applied the presumption at the pleading stage, holding that a motion to dismiss can be granted if the plaintiffs have not alleged facts showing abuse of discretion on the part of the fiduciaries. The Second Circuit applied the presumption to ESOPs as well as to other types of plans. There is still a circuit split because the Sixth Circuit does not apply the presumption at the pleadings stage of a case. [*Gray v. Citigroup, cert. denied*, No. 133 S. Ct. 475 (2012); *Gearren v. McGraw-Hill, cert. denied*, 133 S. Ct. 476 (2012); see Rebecca Moore, *High Court Lets Stand Presumption of Prudence Decisions* plansponsor.com (Nov. 8, 2012)]

- Two more stock drop cases were dismissed in March 2013, because the plans (one a 401(k), the other an ESOP) did not give the fiduciaries much discretion about investing in employer stock. Both of them had the employer stock as a default investment. The Southern District of New

York found that, in the 401(k) case, the employer's financial situation was not dire enough to prevent the *Moench* presumption from applying. The ESOP's stated purposes included investing the employer stock. [*Coulter v. Morgan Stanley*, No. 11 Civ. 1849 (DAB), 2013 U.S. Dist. LEXIS 45029 (S.D.N.Y. Mar. 28, 2013) (401(k)); *In re Pfizer ERISA Litigation*, No. 04 civ. 10071 (LTS)(HBP), 2013 U.S. Dist. LEXIS 45868 (S.D.N.Y. Mar. 29, 2013) (ESOP)]

In the Fifth Circuit view, to overcome the presumption, the plaintiff must show that a reasonable fiduciary would have felt duty-bound to divest. [*Kirschbaum v. Reliant Energy*, 526 F.3d 243 (5th Cir. 2008)] In fact, *Nelson v. IPALCO Enters. Inc.*, 480 F. Supp. 2d 1061 (S.D. Ind. 2007), *aff'd sub nom, Nelson v. Hodowal*, 512 F.3d 347 (7th Cir. 2008) held that even a 90% drop in price was not sufficient to overcome the presumption.]

The Sixth Circuit ruled that plaintiffs in a stock-drop case had actual knowledge of the relevant facts more than three years before the suit was filed, so it was time-barred. The employer filed for bankruptcy on October 5, 2000, and sent a letter to all its employees on that date, informing them of the bankruptcy and its effect on their employment, compensation, and benefits. The stock price began falling in 1999, after the Supreme Court ruled against the employer in an asbestos liability case. One of the plaintiffs filed a claim in the bankruptcy proceeding in April 2002 to recoup losses to her investment account, and the class action was filed September 1, 2006. The ERISA statute of limitations is three years if the victim has actual knowledge of the violation—which means knowing the facts themselves, not that the facts add up to a sustainable legal case. The plaintiffs admitted that by October 2000 they were aware of the bankruptcy filing and the worthlessness of their stock, and they were aware of their ability to diversify the holdings in their accounts. [*Brown v. Owens Corning Inv. Review Comm.*, 622 F.3d 564 (6th Cir. Sept. 27, 2010)]

Despite the general lack of success for plaintiffs, there have been some multi-million-dollar settlements in stock drop cases. Wyeth agreed to pay $2 million to settle a case on the prudence of retaining company stock in the 401(k) plan. The plaintiffs alleged that Wyeth was aware that a new drug was ineffective. When investors heard that the FDA gave only conditional approval to sell that drug, Wyeth's stock fell 10% and continued declining. The suit was dismissed in April 2010, but settled pending the plaintiffs' appeal. The settlement obtained preliminary approval on January 3, 2013: <http://www.plansponsor.com/uploadedFiles/Plan_Sponsor/news/Rules,_Regs/HerreraWyethSettlement.pdf>. [Jay Polanski, *Wyeth Settles Stock Drop Suit*, plansponsor.com (Jan. 4,2013)]

The district court certified a Rule 23(b)(2) class of more than 4,000 current and former participants in a cash balance plan who alleged that they were not credited with correct benefits over a period of 23 years. The claims included whipsaw, cutback, and wearaway claims (see Chapter 7). The district court certified 10 subclasses. The employer appealed, arguing that *Dukes* forbids (b)(2) class actions for declaratory, injunctive, or monetary relief. According to the defendant, a (b)(2) class would only be proper if a single injunction or declaratory judgment could provide relief to all the subclasses and claims for monetary relief were incompatible with (b)(2) class certification. The Seventh Circuit upheld certification, ruling that the requirement about relief under a single injunction or declaratory judgment does not apply where each member of the subclass has the same claim. In this case, the plaintiffs were seeking declaration of their rights under the plan and reformation of the plan to follow the declaration, with any monetary relief being incidental. The Seventh Circuit said that perhaps the proceedings could be bifurcated, with sub-classes that obtained declaratory relief under Rule 23(b)(2) following up with a (b)(3) opt-out proceeding to set relief for the individual class members. [*Johnson v. Meriter Health Servs. Emp. Ret. Plan*, 702 F.3d 364 (7th Cir. 2012); see Mark Casciari and Sara Eber, Seyfarth Shaw ERISA & Employee Benefits Litigation Blog, *Rule 23(b)(2) Certification—The Seventh Circuit Strikes Again, This Time In The ERISA Defined Benefit Context* (Dec. 5, 2012) (benefitslink.com). But see *Nationwide Life Ins. Co. v. Haddock*, 460 Fed. Appx. 26 (2d Cir. 2012), an unpublished case that vacated certification of a class action for breach of fiduciary duty on the grounds that the monetary relief would be more than incidental.]

According to the Seventh Circuit, the fiduciaries of a thrift plan did not have an obligation to disclose to plan participants that they had decided to sell their own positions in the company stock. (The fiduciaries made the required SEC filings.) Furthermore, the plan required employer contributions to be held in employer stock, so divestiture was not an option. [*Nelson and Wycoff v. Hodowal*, 512 F.3d 347 (7th Cir. 2008); see Rebecca Moore, *Plan Fiduciaries Not Required to Announce Own Stock Sale to Participants*, plansponsor.com (Jan. 7, 2008)]

Usually, court cases arise when plan participants charge that it was improper to retain employer stock as a 401(k) plan investment, but the opposite allegation was made in a 2008 district of Massachusetts case. Allegations of fiduciary breach against the employer and State Street Bank & Trust were dismissed: the current market price was only one factor to be considered in determining prudence. Other factors were the employer's bankruptcy, the financial performance and outlook of the sponsor company and its entire industry, SEC requirements, and other potential sources of liability, e.g., products liability. [*Bunch v. W.R. Grace & Co.*, D. Mass., No. 04-11380-WGY (Jan. 30, 2008); Rebecca Moore, *Company Stock Price Not Only Factor in ERISA Prudent Rule Standard*, plansponsor.com (Feb. 5, 2008), *aff'd*, 555 F.3d 1 (1st Cir. 2009); discussed in EBIA Weekly, *Employer and Independent Fiduciary "Unquestionably" Satisfied Their Fiduciary Duties in Sales of Employer Stock* (Feb. 19, 2009) (benefitslink.com), and Fred Schneyer, *State Street Validated by Company Stock Suit Ruling*, plansponsor.com (Feb. 2, 2009)]

In 2008, the Ninth Circuit joined the First, Third, Fourth, Sixth, Seventh, and Eleventh Circuits in holding that former employees who have received a full distribution of their benefits under a defined contribution plan have standing to sue under ERISA to recover losses that they say were caused by breach of fiduciary duty. [*Vaughn v. Bay Environmental Mgmt.*, 544 F.3d 1008 (9th Cir. 2008); see *Lanfear v. Home Depot, Inc.*, 544 F.3d 1008 (11th Cir. 2008); *Evans v. Akers*, 534 F.3d 65 (1st Cir. 2008); *In re Mutual Funds Inv. Litig.*, 529 F.3d 207 (4th Cir. 2008); *Bridges v. Am. Elec. Power Co.*, 498 F.3d 442 (6th Cir. 2007); *Graden v. Conexant Sys. Inc.*, 496 F.3d 291(3d Cir. 2007); and *Harzewski v. Guidant Corp.*, 489 F.3d 799 (7th Cir. 2007). For subsequent cases see, e.g., *Harris v. Amgen, Inc.*, 573 F.3d 728 (9th Cir. 2009); But see *Gipson v. Wells Fargo & Co.*, No. 08-4546 (PAM/FLN), 2009 U.S. Dist. LEXIS 20740 (D. Minn. Mar. 13, 2009) holding that a former employee who had her entire account distributed did not have standing to raise a fiduciary breach claim.]

On a related issue, the Sixth Circuit ruled in mid-2012 that a stock-drop plaintiff did not have standing to sue because she could not demonstrate actual injury. She alleged that the company's stock price was artificially inflated because the company failed to disclose its inappropriate tax and lending practices. However, the plaintiff sold over 80% of her company stock holdings at a time when she charged the price was unfairly high—so if there was wrongdoing, she benefited from it rather than being harmed by it. [*Taylor v. KeyCorp.*, 680 F.3d 609 (6th Cir. 2012)]

## [D]  Fiduciary Duties in Health Plans

ERISA's regulation of pension plans is extremely detailed, whereas its regulation of welfare benefit plans (a category that includes health plans) is limited. Nevertheless, ERISA often preempts state regulation, and the Supreme Court has frequently ruled in favor of plan administrators in health cases.

According to the Supreme Court, an HMO is not acting as a fiduciary when, acting through its doctors, it makes a "mixed" decision about medical treatment and health plan eligibility. [*Pegram v. Herdrich*, 530 U.S. 211 (2000)] Therefore, even if plan participants are right that the plan refused them necessary treatments in order to increase its profits, they have not stated a cause of action for breach of fiduciary duty.

The Supreme Court returned to the question of review of HMO coverage decisions in mid-2004: *Aetna Health Inc. v. Davila* and *Cigna Healthcare of Texas, Inc. v. Calad*, 542 U.S. 200 (2004). One of the plaintiffs alleged harm caused by denial of coverage of an expensive arthritis drug; the other claimed that she was prematurely discharged from the hospital, leading to complications of surgery. They sued under a Texas state law dealing with HMO negligence. The Supreme Court held that ERISA completely preempts the state law, because ERISA covers all cases where someone claims that coverage was denied under a plan that is a welfare benefit plan for ERISA purposes. However, in this case, the Supreme Court clarified its earlier *Pegram v. Herdrich* decision. In that case,

HMOs were held not to be fiduciaries to the extent that they act through their physicians to make mixed eligibility and treatment decisions. The 2004 decision says that HMOs are fiduciaries when they make pure eligibility decisions. The consequence is that if patients sue in state court, claiming that they were wrongfully denied health benefits, the case is completely preempted by ERISA and can be removed to federal court.

As long as the employer unambiguously reserved the right to amend the plan in the plan documents, the courts of appeals usually agree that there is no ERISA liability for changing health benefits. However, in 2009, the Third Circuit held Unisys liable for fiduciary breach when it did not remind employees that their retiree benefits could be reduced—even though there was reservation language in the SPD. The Third Circuit ordered the lifetime retiree health benefits at no cost to the retirees restored—an order that remained in effect because the Supreme Court denied certiorari. The Third Circuit found the reservation language in the SPD irrelevant, because it was not distributed until after the participants retired. [*In re Unisys Corp. Retiree Med. Benefits ERISA Litig.*, 579 F.3d 220 (3d Cir. 2009), *cert. denied*, 130 S. Ct. 1546. See John R. Richards and Christopher A. Weals, Law360, *Why the 3rd Circ.'s Unisys Decision Defies ERISA* (Jan. 29, 2010) (benefitslink.com); Rebecca Moore, *Supreme Court Won't Review Whether Unisys Misled Participants*, plansponsor.com (Feb. 23, 2010);]

Until 2006, Menasha Corporation retirees and their spouses continued to receive health insurance from the company. Between ages 62–65, the company paid 80% of the premium; when retirees turned 65, the company paid 100% of the premium. In 2006, however, Menasha informed the plaintiffs that it was adopting a new health plan and premiums would no longer be 100% covered. The plaintiffs sued, alleging violations of the Labor Management Relations Act, 29 U.S.C. § 185 and the Employee Retirement Income Security Act, 29 U.S.C. § 1132. The district court ruled in the plaintiffs' favor as to employee coverage but in favor of defendant as to spouses. The Sixth Circuit reversed in part, ruling for the plaintiffs. Although healthcare is a "welfare benefit," not entitled to the same ERISA protection as pension benefits, certain actions by employers will waive the employers' right to alter welfare benefits. In this case, Menasha waived the right to change the benefits by providing vested healthcare coverage to retired employees and spouses, and by agreeing that CBAs could only be modified with signed, mutual consent of the parties. [*Moore v. Menasha Corp.*, 690 F.3d 444 (6th Cir. 2013)]

The District Court for the District of Connecticut dismissed claims by retirees who charged that their former employer violated ERISA when it changed the method for calculating retiree health insurance premiums. The plan stated that the employer's contribution was fixed, with the retirees responsible for the balance of the costs of health care. The district court ruled that the benefits were not vested, which ruled out a fiduciary breach claim with respect to the altered method of setting premiums. But the district court permitted the suit to proceed on other issues: whether the ex-employer breached its fiduciary duty by not providing proper disclosure of the changed method (a material modification of the plan), and whether the premiums were excessive. If the premiums were excessive, that could mean a breach of the fiduciary duty to operate the plan for the sole benefit of participants and beneficiaries. [*Connecticut Indep. Util. Workers Local 12924 v. Connecticut Natural Gas Corp.*, No. 3:12-cv-00961-JBA (D. Conn. June 14, 2013); see Bloomberg BNA, *District Court Issues Mixed Rulings in Retirees' Challenge to Increased Premium* (June 18, 2013) (benefitslink.com)]

See § 9.05[C] for more discussion of fiduciary issues in retiree health benefit plans.

Financially troubled companies sometimes fail to carry out their obligations to contribute to health plans, and sometimes they misappropriate employee health plan contributions and use them to pay corporate debts instead. In such situations, the employer's bankruptcy often ensues, and the priority of various claims has to be sorted out. The Ninth Circuit has ruled that an employer automatically becomes a fiduciary by breaching its agreement to make contributions, but the Tenth Circuit disagrees, stating that a delinquent employer contributor is just a debtor that owes money to the plan, not a fiduciary. [*Holdeman v. Devine*, 474 F.3d 770 (10th Cir. 2007). Compare *In re Luna*, 406 F.3d 1992 (10th Cir. 2005) with *Northern Cal. Retail Clerks Unions & Food Employers Joint Pension Trust Fund v. Jumbo Mkts., Inc.*, 906 F.2d 1371, 1372 (9th Cir. 1990). On remand, the District Court for the District of Utah held that the CEO did not breach his fiduciary duties. Decisions about plan funding were treated as business and not fiduciary decisions, so ERISA was not involved. Furthermore, the court held that there was no evidence that plan participants would have been better off if the CEO had resigned and another fiduciary had been appointed: *Holdeman v. Devine*, D. Utah 2007; see Rebecca Moore, *CEO Had No Obligation to Resign as Fiduciary of Health Plan*, plansponsor.com (Nov. 7, 2007)]

## § 15.04  DUTIES OF THE TRUSTEE

Usually, pension and welfare benefit plans will be organized in trust form. Every trust must have at least one trustee. ERISA § 403(a) provides that the trustee can be named in the instrument itself, appointed under a procedure set out in the plan, or appointed by a named fiduciary.

The trustee has exclusive authority and discretion to manage and control the plan's assets. If there are multiple trustees, they must jointly manage and control, although ERISA § 403(a) permits them to delegate some duties. Certain fiduciary duties can be delegated—it depends on whether trustee responsibility or other duties are involved.

To implement the requirement that pension plans be operated solely in the interests of participants and beneficiaries, DOL ruled in late 2007 that it is improper for plan fiduciaries to use pension assets for political activities or furtherance of public debates, if the expenditures are not connected to increasing the value of the plan's investments. Fiduciaries who vote proxies must consider only factors that affect the value of plan investments, not general political or ethical factors. [DOL Advisory Opinion 2007-07A, <http://www.dol.gov/ebsa> (Dec. 21, 2007)] In an Interpretive bulletin dated October 17, 2008, the DOL held that pension funds subject to ERISA are not permitted to vote their proxies, and if they do vote, federal prosecution is possible. The DOL's rationale is that exercising fiduciary authority to promote legislative, regulatory, or public policy issues violates the "exclusive purpose" rule. This is a reversal of DOL's 1994 position that shareholders have a duty to vote proxies on the shares held in their portfolios. [John Richardson, *Americans Must Not Vote!* Global Investment Watch (Oct. 27, 2008) (benefitslink.com)]

A plan can be drafted to make its trustee subject to a named fiduciary who is not a trustee—for example, to make the trustee report to an administrative committee. If this is done, the trustee must comply with "proper" directions given by the named fiduciary, if they are in accordance with the plan's procedures and not contrary to law.

If there has been a proper appointment of an investment manager, the trustee does not have to manage or invest the assets placed under the investment manager's control. Crucially, the trustee will not be liable for the acts or omissions of the investment manager. The trustee has a duty to make sure that the manager charges reasonable fees; performance-based fees, rather than flat fees determined in advance, are allowed.

The Supreme Court refused, in early 2007, to hear appeals about the State Street Bank & Trust's performance as directed trustee of United Air Lines' Employee Stock Ownership Plan. Therefore, the Seventh Circuit opinion will not be challenged. The Seventh Circuit ruled that it was not a breach of fiduciary duty to retain the stock, and the participants did not prove when it would have been feasible to sell the stock in order to reduce the risk to participants. [Fred Schneyer, *Supreme Court Refuses United Airlines ESOP Appeals*, plansponsor.com (Feb. 21, 2007)]

Another issue is the extent of liability—including personal liability of individuals who committed the wrongdoing—when there is a failure to remit amounts to a plan on schedule. For example, a company in financial trouble may succumb to the temptation to use insurance premiums or amounts that should be contributed to a pension plan to pay corporate creditors rather than for the specific purpose for which they should have been used.

The Fourth Circuit affirmed the theft convictions of two plan administrators (the company's president and its CFO) who did not deposit the contributions. Once due and payable, contributions become plan assets. An earlier Tenth Circuit ruling is that once an employer has paid wages or salaries to employees, it has a contractual duty to contribute to its ERISA plans; the contractual obligation itself is a plan asset. The defendants fell behind on vendor payments, made false financial statements, and borrowed money when the company was in financial trouble.

They indicated on the Form 5500 that the contributions had been made to two pension plans and a health care plan, but in fact they used the money (over $329,000) to pay the company's bills. [*United States v. Jackson*, 524 F.3d 532 (4th Cir. 2008); see Rebecca Moore, *Unpaid Contributions Constitutes ERISA Theft*, plansponsor.com (May 5, 2008)]

EBSA FAB 2008-1 says that a named or functional fiduciary with authority to appoint trustees for the plan has an obligation to make sure that the proper party takes responsibility for collecting plan contributions (unless the plan makes the trustee a § 403(a)(1) directed trustee with respect to contributions, or a § 403(a)(2) manager has the authority to collect contributions). The FAB defines collecting contributions as a trustee responsibility. If there are multiple trustees, responsibility can be allocated to one of them. Where there is no trustee or investment manager charged with making sure plan contributions are collected on time, the fiduciary with the authority to hire trustees could be liable, on a theory of failure to allocate responsibility, if contributions are not collected on time. [Fred Schneyer, *EBSA: Responsibility for Collecting Contributions Must Be Properly Assigned*, plansponsor.com (Feb. 1, 2008)]

## § 15.05   THE EMPLOYER'S ROLE

Although it might be predicted that the heaviest liability for plan misconduct would fall on the company that sponsors the plan, this is not always the case. The corporation might not be a fiduciary, or might not be acting in a fiduciary capacity in a particular case.

To prevent conflicts of interest, ERISA §§ 403, 4042, and 4044 allow fiduciaries to perform certain actions without violating the duty to maintain the plan for the sole benefit of participants and beneficiaries. Employer contributions can be returned if:

- The contributions were made based on a mistake of fact;

- The plan is not qualified under I.R.C. §§ 401(a) or 403(a);

- The income tax deduction for part or all of the contribution is disallowed;

- The contribution could be treated as an excess contribution under I.R.C. § 4975.

Nor is there a conflict of interest if the fiduciary follows PBGC requirements for a distribution incident to a plan termination.

In mid-2008, the Supreme Court decided *Metropolitan Life Insurance Co. v. Glenn*, 554 U.S. 105 (2008), applying trust law principles to determine the standard of judicial review in ERISA § 1132(a)(1)(B) cases. If the plan administrator has the discretion to determine eligibility for benefits, deferential review will be applied, but if the decision-maker (whether an insurer or a plan sponsor) has a conflict of interest, that conflict of interest will be factored into deciding whether the decision was arbitrary and capricious. However, the mere fact that there is a conflict of interest will not prevent the court from applying a deferential standard of review to the administrator's decisions. [Nancy Pridgen, Alston & Bird ERISA Litigation Advisory July, *The Circuits Are Split: Does MetLife v. Glenn's "Structural Conflict" Holding Apply When Employee Benefits Are Funded from a Trust?* (Dec. 23, 2009) (benefitslink.com)]

If a plan grants the decisionmaker discretion to interpret the terms of the plan, a court reviewing the benefit denial uses the deferential "abuse of discretion" standard rather than the tougher de novo standard. A 2012 Seventh Circuit case involves a plan document that gave discretionary authority to the benefits committee, which was also the plan administrator. The plan administrator exercised its power to delegate by delegating to the insurer. However, the insurer was exiting the market and the policy was administered by an agent who was not named in the plan documents. The Seventh Circuit upheld the denial of benefits because the designation was not arbitrary or capricious. The District Court for the District of Nevada held, also in 2012, that for delegation to be proper, the plan document must provide not merely discretionary authority but an explicit procedure for the named fiduciary to delegate authority. The court carried out de novo review because the plan lacked a delegation procedure—but the court upheld the reasonableness of the claims denial. [*Aschermann v. Aetna Life Ins. Co.*, 689 F.3d 726 (7th Cir. 2012); *Decovich v. Venetian Casino Resort LLC*, No. 2:11-cv-872 JCM (CWH), 2012 WL 3096696 (D. Nev. July 30, 2012); see EBIA Weekly, *Insufficient Delegation of Discretionary Authority Affects Standard of Judicial Review* (Aug. 30, 2012) (benefitslink.com)]

In August 1997, the plan was amended to permit some participants, including Helton, to elect a full benefit at age 55. AT&T sent letters and amended the SPD, but Helton said she didn't get the communications. She was eligible for full pension benefits in October 2001. AT&T said it sent her a pension package with forms to complete (she said she didn't get it) but destroyed her records, pursuant to policy, when the forms were not returned. In 2009, when Helton was close to 65, she asked AT&T how much her pension would be. When she found out about her earlier eligibility, she applied for back payments, which were denied on the grounds that the plan does not provide retroactive payments. The Fourth Circuit did not consider the breach of fiduciary duty claim, finding that it was proper to award relief under ERISA § 1132(a)(1)(B). The plan gave full discretion to the plan committee, so the standard is abuse of discretion. The version of the pension plan in effect when Helton tried to recover lost benefits explicitly allowed "restorative" benefits to correct administrative errors. The Fourth Circuit said that remand to the plan is the appropriate remedy in many cases, but it is not required, especially if there is evidence of abuse of discretion. [*Helton v. AT&T Inc. Pension Benefit Plan*, 709 F.3d 343 (4th Cir. 2013)]

## § 15.06  INVESTMENT MANAGERS

### [A]  Qualified Managers Under ERISA

If the plan so permits, ERISA allows fiduciaries to delegate their investment duties to a qualified investment manager.

There are four categories of qualified investment managers:

- Investment advisers who are registered under the federal Investment Company Act—whether they are independent consultants or in-house employees of the plan;

- Trust companies;

- Banks;

- Qualified insurance companies.

ERISA requires the manager to acknowledge in writing that he, she, or it has become a fiduciary with respect to the plan.

DOL Reg. § 2510.3-21(c) explains who will be deemed qualified to render investment advice:

- Those who give advice about the value of securities or recommend investing, buying, or selling securities (or other property, such as real estate);

- Those who are given discretion to buy or sell securities for the plan;

- Those who give advice, on a regular basis, under an oral or written agreement, if the advice is intended to serve as a primary basis for investing plan funds.

As long as the fiduciaries were prudent when they chose the manager (and continued to review the manager's performance), the fiduciaries will not be liable for acts and omissions committed by the manager.

A broker-dealer, bank, or reporting dealer does not become a fiduciary if its only role is to take and execute buy and sell orders for the plan. [DOL Reg. § 2510.3-21(d)(1)] The investment manager is a fiduciary only as to whatever percentage of the overall investment he or she can influence (except in situations where ERISA § 405(a) makes the investment manager responsible for breaches by co-fiduciaries).

Investment managers, also known as "§ 3(38) managers," actually choose, remove, and replace investments from a plan. A fiduciary safe harbor is available if a plan sponsor or its plan committee is prudent in selecting an investment manager and then monitoring its performance. The safe harbor requires the manager to be a bank, registered investment adviser, or insurance company that has the power to manage, acquire, or dispose of plan assets—and that acknowledges its fiduciary status in writing. The fiduciary must engage in an objective process to discover the adviser's qualifications and manager's experience. The adviser's compensation must be reasonable and disclosed in the service agreement. (Information about advisers can be found on the Form ADV Part 2 that they file with the SEC, and the SEC can also state whether the manager has been disciplined for securities law violations.) The fiduciary should get a written description of the manager's investment process—e.g., whether generally accepted investment theories are used; whether the manager provides reports that can be used to monitor performance; how services will be tailored for the plan's needs; and whether the manager has enough liability insurance for the amount under management. [Fred Reish, *'Safe' Hows,* plansponsor.com (October 2011)]

In mid-2005, DOL and the SEC released suggestions for fiduciaries to help them choose and monitor investment consultants (complementing earlier DOL guidance about doing the same for employee benefit plan service providers such as recordkeepers). The SEC's concern is that investment consultants can experience conflicts of interest, especially in "pay to play" arrangements whereby the consultants are compensated by brokers or money managers for offering access to the consultant's plan clients.

The two federal agencies released a list of issues that a fiduciary must consider:

- Is the consultant registered as an investment adviser? If so, the fiduciary should review the disclosures on Part II of SEC's Form ADV.

- Get written acknowledgment that the consultant is a fiduciary and will comply with fiduciary obligations.

- Find out if the consultant or a related company has relationships with the money managers recommended and whether the consultant receives payments or trades by the money managers that the consultant recommends.

- Ask about the consultant's policy on conflicts of interest.

DOL suggests including questions on these topics in any request for proposals for a new consultant—and perhaps even seeking written answers from existing consultants. The RFP also can be used to obtain representations and warranties of compliance, collect information about the consultant's insurance coverage and willingness to indemnify the client. Plans should determine when the contract can be terminated either for cause or for the convenience of the parties; the plan's right to continue using materials developed by the service provider for the plan; liquidated damages for failure to satisfy contractual standards; and any pending litigation or complaints outstanding against the service provider. [McDermott Newsletters, *Recent Guidance on Selecting and Monitoring Service Providers* (June 27, 2005) (benefitslink.com)]

## [B]  The Role of the Insurer

The Supreme Court's decision in *John Hancock Mutual Life Insurance v. Harris Trust* [510 U.S. 86 (1993)] holds that assets held in an insurer's general account and not guaranteed by the insurer are plan assets subject to ERISA's fiduciary requirements.

DOL issued interim regulations covering insurance contracts sold before December 31, 1998; later contracts are all covered by ERISA fiduciary rules. DOL's Interpretive Bulletin 95-1 says that a fiduciary who chooses annuities to distribute plan benefits has a fiduciary duty to choose the safest available contract, based on factors such as the insurer's size and reputation, the insurer's other lines of business, and the size and provisions of the proposed contracts.

## § 15.07  DUTY TO DISCLOSE

Employees have a right to information about their benefit options, and fiduciaries have a corresponding duty to make complete, accurate disclosure. Furthermore, they need information about the way the plan is expected to evolve, so they can make future plans.

The classic test, stemming from *Fischer v. Philadelphia Electric Co.* [96 F.3d 1533 (3d Cir. 1996)] is that plan participants who inquire must not only be informed about the current structure of the plan—they must be informed of proposals that are under "serious consideration" by management. [Some cases say that, although information must be provided to those who ask for it, it need not be volunteered if there is no request, e.g., *Bins v. Exxon Co.*, 220 F.3d 1042 (9th Cir. 2000); *Hudson v. General Dynamics Corp.*, 118 F. Supp. 2d 226 (D. Conn. 2000). But other cases say that there is a fiduciary duty to give information whenever silence could be harmful to beneficiaries' financial interests. See *Krohn v. Huron Mem. Hosp.*, 173 F.3d 542 (6th Cir. 1999)] The Fifth Circuit refused to adopt the "serious consideration" test: *Martinez v. Schlumberger Ltd.*, 338 F.3d 407 (5th Cir. 2003), even though seven Courts of Appeals use this test. The Fifth Circuit assesses whether the information that was not given would have been material to a reasonable person's decision to retire.

The fiduciary must provide complete and accurate information about the tax consequences of options under a plan. [*Farr v. U.S. West Commc'ns Inc.*, 58 F.3d 1361 (9th Cir. 1998)] But it is not a fiduciary breach to distribute benefits in accordance with the participant's own instructions, even if the fiduciary allegedly gave inaccurate tax advice. [*Glencoe v. TIAA*, 69 F. Supp. 2d 849 (S.D.W. Va. 1999)]

The Seventh Circuit ruled in mid-2010 that an HMO violated its fiduciary duty to plan participants by instructing participants to contact the call center for information—without telling them that they were not entitled to rely on statements from customer service representatives as to whether or not a procedure was covered by the plan. The HMO argued that it was obvious from the plan documents that the procedure (to correct complications of earlier bariatric surgery) would not be covered, but the Seventh Circuit held that the plaintiff acted logically in calling the customer service representative (a course encouraged by the plan) to determine her rights under the plan, and the plan had a duty to administer the plan in participants' best interests. [*Kenseth v. Dean Health Plan Inc.*, 610 F.3d 452 (7th Cir. 2010); see Fred Schneyer, *HMO Found Liable for Coverage Information Gap*, plansponsor.com (June 30, 2010). In subsequent proceedings, the Seventh Circuit held that compensation in money (the cost of the surgery) is not necessarily considered a legal rather than an equitable remedy, so it may be available under ERISA § 502(a)(3): *Kenseth v. Dean Health Plan, Inc.*, No. 11-1560, 2013 WL 2991466 (7th Cir. June 13, 2013); see PLC, *Expanded ERISA Remedies Available in Fiduciary Breach Claims: Seventh Circuit* (June 18, 2013) (benefitslink.com)]

According to the Second Circuit, ERISA § 104(b)(4) requires the plan administrator to provide copies of "plan documents" on request. In 2002, the Sixth Circuit held that affirmatively misleading employees about the continuation of health benefits, inducing them to retire early, is a fiduciary breach, even though not all the plaintiffs asked specific questions about future benefits. The appropriate test is whether the information is materially misleading, whether or not the employer intended to mislead or was negligent in providing the misleading information. [*James v. Pirelli Armstrong Tire Co.*, 305 F.3d 439 (6th Cir. 2002)]

The Fifth Circuit upheld an award of over $243,000 in damages and fees for the employer's failure to provide a copy of the SPD and rollover election forms. The plaintiff, Kujanek orally requested information about rolling over his plan balance (which was about $490,000 when he quit his job in 2007). The plan, relying on SPD language that all requests must be written, ignored his request. He did not receive a distribution until the value of the account had fallen to $306,000. The Fifth Circuit held that his request for a distribution triggered a fiduciary duty to provide the forms. [*Kujanek v. Houston Poly Bag*, 658 F.3d 483 (5th Cir. 2012); see Spencer Fane Britt & Browne LLP Insights, *Federal Appeals Court Upholds $243,000 Damage and Fee Award for Employer's Failure to Provide SPD and Election Forms* (Mar. 1, 2012) (benefitslink.com)]

## § 15.08  PENALTIES FOR FIDUCIARY BREACH

A fiduciary that breaches the required duties can be sued by plan participants, plan beneficiaries, and/or the Department of Labor. Penalty taxes can be imposed for improper transactions involving the plan. Generally speaking, ERISA § 509 grants relief to the plan itself; participants and beneficiaries find their remedies under ERISA § 502(a)(3).

A large, overlapping, and potentially confusing variety of Civil Monetary Penalties (CMPs) can be imposed under various provisions of ERISA. The same action often violates several different sections, with penalties at least potentially assessed for each, such as:

- § 209(b) failure to furnish or maintain records;
- § 502(c)(1)(A) failure to notify participants of their rights to COBRA benefits;
- § 502(c)(1)(B) failure to provide required information on a timely basis;
- § 502(c)(2) failure or refusal to file an annual report;
- § 502(c)(3) failure to notify participants and beneficiaries when the plan fails to satisfy the minimum funding requirements; failure to give notice when excess pension assets are transferred to a 401(h) retiree health benefits account;
- § 503(c)(5) failure or refusal to file information required under ERISA § 101(g);
- § 503(c)(6) failure or refusal to comply with a participant's or beneficiary's request for information subject to disclosure under ERISA § 104(a)(6).

Most penalties are defined as a maximum amount per day—usually $110 or $1100. Courts hearing such cases have the discretion to reduce or even abate the penalty, based on factors such as the employer's inability to pay, its basic good faith, or extenuating factors such as destruction of records in circumstances beyond the employer's control.

The DOL published final regulations, effective March 3, 2009, covering the assessment of penalties under ERISA § 502(c)(4) when plan administrators fail to provide notices as required by the PPA (e.g., limitations on distributions from underfunded plans; employer's potential liability for withdrawal from a multiemployer plan). The amount of the penalty depends on the degree of willfulness, subject to a maximum of $1,000 per violation per day. (Each person entitled to notification is a separate violation.) The DOL sets a tentative penalty level, and notifies the plan administrator. After the notice of assessment is served, the administrator has 30 days to show reasonable cause why the penalty should be reduced. Responsible parties are not only jointly and severally liable, they are also personally liable for the penalties.

Administrators of automatic contribution arrangements must give participants notice of their rights and obligations under the arrangement, including the right not to have elective contributions made on their behalf, and the right to change the percentage contributed. The timing for making the election must be explained, as well as how the contributions will be invested if no election is made. Generally, the due date for the notice is within 30 days of the time a person becomes eligible under the plan. [Final Regs, 74 Fed. Reg. 17 (Jan. 2, 2009); see Deloitte's Washington Bulletin, *Procedures for Assessing Civil Penalties Under*

*ERISA § 502(c)(4) Are Finalized,* <http://benefitslink.com/articles/guests/wash bull090112a.html> (Jan. 12, 2009)]

A fiduciary who is guilty of a breach of duty is personally liable to the plan and must compensate it for any loss in asset value caused by the violation. The fiduciary must also "disgorge" (surrender) any personal financial advantage improperly obtained: see ERISA § 409. However, there is liability only if there is a causal connection between a breach and the loss or the improper profits. Fiduciaries are not expected to guarantee that the plan will never lose money.

A plan can get a court order removing a faithless fiduciary from office. The removed fiduciary can be ordered to pay the plan's attorneys' fees plus interest on the sum involved. But plan participants cannot get an award of punitive damages, no matter how outrageous the fiduciary's conduct (although some courts will order punitive damages payable to the plan itself). In the most serious cases, a fiduciary can be subject to criminal charges instead of, or in addition to, civil penalties.

Plans can have "bad boy" clauses. For example, under ERISA § 206(d) and I.R.C. § 401(a)(13)(C) fiduciaries who are also plan participants can have their pensions reduced if they breach fiduciary duty, if they are convicted of crimes against the plan, or if they lose or settle a civil suit or enter into a settlement with the Department of Labor or PBGC. For example, the DOL obtained a consent judgment from Barstow Truck Parts and Equipment Co. and its president, James M. Rajacich Senior, requiring $118,249 to be returned to the profit-sharing plan. He forfeited his own benefits for misconduct, and was required to return unpaid loan amounts with interest, plus a civil money penalty of $23,650. [Rebecca Moore, *Company President to Restore Plan for Loan Repayments*, plansponsor.com (Dec. 10, 2010)]

## § 15.09 ERISA § 502

### [A] Generally

ERISA § 502 gives participants and beneficiaries, the DOL, and fiduciaries many remedies against abuses and risks to the plan. In fact, an important part of litigation planning is deciding which subsection of ERISA § 502 to invoke— defendants can get a case dismissed if the wrong subsection is charged or if the plaintiff asks for remedies that are unavailable under that subsection.

Under ERISA § 502, "participant" means an employee or ex-employee who is or may become eligible to receive any benefit under the plan. "Beneficiary" either means someone eligible or potentially eligible to receive benefits under the plan terms, or as designated by a participant.

Participants and beneficiaries (but not the DOL, the employer, or the plan itself) can use ERISA § 502(a)(1)(B) to sue for benefits due under the terms of the plan, to enforce rights under the terms of the plan, or to clarify rights to future benefits under the terms of a plan.

Civil actions under ERISA § 502(a)(2) can be brought by participants, beneficiaries, or the DOL when a breach of fiduciary duty is alleged.

The DOL, participants, beneficiaries, or fiduciaries can sue under ERISA §§ 502(a)(3) and (a)(5) to enjoin violations of ERISA Title I, to get equitable relief under Title I, or to impose penalties on PIIs for engaging in prohibited transactions. The remedies under ERISA § 502(a)(3) can include ordering return of misappropriated plan assets, plus the profits improperly earned on them—but this remedy is not available in situations where the defendant did not hold or profit from plan assets.

When plan participants sued John Hancock under ERISA and the Investment Company Act of 1940 (ICA) for charging retirement plans excessive fees on annuity contracts offered to plan participants, the district court granted Hancock's motion to dismiss. The district court ruled that the ICA fee claims were invalid because the participants were no longer investors in the funds and an ownership interest is required to bring a derivative suit. On the ERISA claims, the district court said that participants failed to make a pre-suit demand on the trustees and did not join the trustees as parties. The Third Circuit affirmed on the ICA claim but vacated and remanded on the ERISA counts. An ICA § 36(b) suit is similar to a derivative suit and the recovery goes to the company. FRCP 23.1 requires continuous ownership, and ex-participants no longer have a real interest in getting a recovery. However, ERISA §§ 502(a)(2) and (3) allow a suit by a participant, beneficiary, or fiduciary for injunction, other appropriate equitable relief, to redress violations, or enforce ERISA or the terms of the plan. Pre-suit demand and mandatory joinder of trustees are not required. Unlike some other ERISA sections, § 502(a) does not limit who can be named as a defendant. According to the Third Circuit, mandatory joinder would, in effect, require trustees to sue themselves—which would not further the purposes of ERISA. [*Santomenno v. John Hancock Life Ins. Co.*, 677 F.3d 178 (3d Cir. 2012)]

The question of what constitutes "appropriate equitable relief" is a difficult one, and many cases have been decided on this issue. In particular, the question of whether participants could sue for reduction in value of their own individual accounts—rather than the value of the plan as a whole—was an important litigation issue that was not resolved until 2008, when the Supreme Court ruled that ERISA § 502(a)(2) does not grant a remedy for individual remedies as distinct from injuries to the plan—but it does permit recovery for fiduciary breaches that impair the value of the assets in a particular account, because the goal of ERISA § 409 is to safeguard the benefits that participants are entitled to.

The Third Circuit held that a former employee's signed release of her claims against the employer could interfere with her ability to represent the class of employees in a stock-drop suit, because the defendant might have specific legal defenses against her that did not apply to other participants. The district court had held that the release was void under ERISA § 410 (which says that provisions that purport to relieve a fiduciary from liability are void as against public policy), so she could be the class representative. The Third Circuit, however, said that § 410 deals with agreements that alter the fiduciary's responsibilities, not individual legal releases. But the Third Circuit said that the release did not prevent the plaintiff from bringing a § 502(a)(2) claim on behalf of the plan. [*In re Schering-Plough ERISA Litig.*, 589 F.3d 585 (3d Cir. 2009); see Fred Schneyer, *Employee's Lawsuit Release Could Imperil Class Action Status*, plansponsor.com (Dec. 22, 2009).

Although *Massachusetts Mutual Life Insurance v. Russell* [473 U.S. 134 (1985)] interprets ERISA § 502(a)(3) as limited to remedies for the plan as a whole, the plan in that case was a disability plan providing a fixed benefit, so administrator misconduct could not affect individual accounts unless the whole plan was at risk of default. The plaintiff in that case actually received the full benefit she was entitled to; she sued for damages for delay in claim processing. Furthermore, the Supreme Court read that case as involving a defined benefit plan in a benefits universe dominated by such plans. The *LaRue* case, in contrast, involved a defined contribution plan, for which a participant's entitlement can be reduced by fiduciary misconduct even if the plan as a whole remains solvent. The Supreme Court did not reach the question of whether the make-whole relief was equitable (although a footnote to the decision says that trust law allows claims for lost profits that were lost as a result of a breach of trust by the trustee). The Supreme Court sent the case back to the district court, giving the plaintiff a chance to prove that the fiduciary was to blame for the decline in value of his account. Section 502(a)(2) carries out the purposes of ERISA § 409, which obligated fiduciaries to manage, administer, and invest plan assets properly so that participants and beneficiaries will eventually receive the benefits they were promised under the plan. The Supreme Court decided that, in a defined benefit plan, fiduciary misconduct creates or increases the risk that the plan will default, so the previous decisions look at the effect of misconduct on the entire plan. In a defined contribution plan, misconduct can reduce the value of some but not all accounts— but the misconduct is still the type that ERISA § 409 is intended to deter or redress. [*LaRue v. DeWolff, Boberg & Assocs., Inc.*, 552 U.S. 248 (2008)]

Although technically the result was a victory for LaRue, after the Supreme Court remanded his case, James LaRue apparently ran out of money to continue litigating, so he settled with DeWolff, Boberg. The District of South Carolina's October 21, 2008 order approving the settlement said that the statute of limitations had expired on the events LaRue characterized as fiduciary breaches, so he could not refile later. The case was dismissed with prejudice, although he could bring a further suit for post-2002 events for which the statute of limitations had not run. [Fred Schneyer, *LaRue Bows Out of Legal Fight*, plansponsor.com (Oct. 30, 2008)]

The Seventh Circuit allowed a class of defined contribution plan participants to sue for relief under ERISA § 502, taking the position that the shift from defined benefit plans (the predominant plan type when ERISA was enacted) to defined contribution plans requires re-thinking the remedies available under § 502.

A 2008 Supreme Court decision allows individual defined contribution participants to seek relief; the Seventh Circuit extended this to a plaintiff class in a case alleging excessive fees. The Seventh Circuit held that a plan and its individual participants can be injured at the same time, if excessive fees are charged, or if imprudent choices are included in the plan's investment portfolio. However, the Seventh Circuit, while opening up the potential for class actions, said that the classes actually certified were improperly defined, because they did not have enough similarity because some class members were satisfied with their investment results. It would also be improper to certify a class that involved some fees that are fund-specific and other fees that are imposed equally on all plan participants. [*Beesley v. International Paper Co./Spano v. Boeing*, 633 F.3d 574 (7th Cir. 2011); see Rebecca Moore, *Court OKs Class Actions for ERISA Cases*, plansponsor.com (Jan. 24, 2011); Groom Law Group, *Seventh Circuit Vacates Class Certifications in 401(k) Fee Cases* (Jan. 31, 2011) (benefitslink.com); Fred Schneyer, *7th Circuit Stock-Drop Rulings Seen as Helping Employers*, plan sponsor.com (Jan. 31, 2011)]

However, after *Dukes v. Wal-Mart* (see § 42.06 [A]), all types of employment class actions will be more difficult to maintain.

In 2010, the Sixth Circuit joined the Second, Third, Fifth, Seventh, and Ninth Circuits in allowing equitable estoppel to be used for relief from harsh pension plan provisions, even if the provisions are not inequitable. (Previously, the Sixth Circuit only applied equitable estoppel in the context of welfare benefits.) This case arose when the plaintiff took early retirement after he was told how large a pension the defined benefit plan would pay him. After he had been receiving benefits for about two years, the plan administrator told him that, as a result of a computer error, he was receiving about $500 a month too much, and he had to repay more than $11,000. He sued, taking the position that the Third-Party Administrator made a contract to pay him the amount of benefits originally stated, and that he took early retirement based on those representations. The Sixth Circuit allowed him to assert estoppel based on gross negligence that was severe enough to be tantamount to fraud. However, the Sixth Circuit rejected his ERISA § 502(a)(1)(B) claim, because the benefit election form was not a plan amendment, plan modification, or separate contract providing additional benefits; it merely stated the amount of the benefit. The Sixth Circuit also dismissed the plaintiff's fiduciary breach claim. [*Bloemker v. Laborers' Local 265 Pension Fund*, 605 F.3d 436 (6th Cir. 2010); see CCH Pension & Benefits, *Court Applies Equitable Estoppel Rules to Pension Cases with Unambiguous Terms* (June 14, 2010) (benefitslink.com)]

An ERISA § 502(a)(3) suit for individual equitable relief can be maintained against a company that deceived its employees about benefit safety if they were transferred to a new division that was spun off by the company. The Supreme

Court ruled that the corporation was acting as a fiduciary when it lied about benefit security. [*Varity Corp. v. Howe*, 514 U.S. 1082 (1996)]

A party in interest to a prohibited transaction with a plan can be liable under ERISA § 502(a)(3), even if the defendant is not a fiduciary [*Harris Trust v. Salomon Bros.*, 530 U.S. 238 (2000)]

An employee (in this case, an early retiree) who is misled about the tax consequences of taking a lump sum payout is entitled to rescission as other equitable relief under ERISA § 502(a)(3), but the Fourth Circuit allowed only partial rescission when the employee's unreasonable delay in seeking a remedy was prejudicial to the employer. [*Griggs v. DuPont*, 385 F.3d 440 (4th Cir. 2004)]

ERISA § 502(a)(3) is also used by benefit plans to recover payments made on behalf of plan participants (e.g., when a participant is injured in an accident and later settles or wins a tort case about the accident). See § 18.17 for further discussion of subrogation. [Important recent subrogation cases include *US Airways v. McCutchen*, 133 S. Ct. 1537 (2013), followed in *Quest Diagnostics v. Bomani*, No. 11-CV-00951 (D. Conn. June 19, 2013)]

It was not a breach of fiduciary duty to decrease a retiree's monthly pension check to recoup overpayments made because of miscalculation of benefit amount. The Sixth Circuit held that trustees have a duty to make sure the plan gets all the money it is entitled to, so benefits to other beneficiaries can be made, and plan documents impose a responsibility to correct errors. The court agreed with the defendant; the employee who made the calculation and told Sheward what his pension would be was not acting as a fiduciary. He was performing ministerial functions. (The company did not offset the pension by his benefit from another federal contractor, as was required by law.) Sheward couldn't show detrimental reliance on the misrepresentation, because he got a double payment of benefits until the error was discovered. [*Sheward v. Bechtel Jacobs Co. Pension Plan for Grandfathered Employees*, No. 3:08-CV-428 (E.D. Tenn. Mar. 4, 2010); see Rebecca Moore, *Employer Can Reduce Monthly Pension to Fix Error* (Mar. 8, 2010) (benefitslink.com)]

Section 502(a)(6) authorizes civil actions by the DOL to collect the excise tax on prohibited transactions or the penalty tax on fiduciary violations. State governments (but NOT the DOL) can sue under § 502(a)(7) to enforce compliance with a Qualified Medical Child Support Order (QMCSO). The states have a role to play here because they have traditionally been empowered to deal with family law issues such as child support.

Funds from an insurance contract or annuity purchased in connection with termination of participant status can be secured by a suit under § 502(a)(9). Suit can be brought by the DOL, fiduciaries, or persons who were participants or beneficiaries at the time of the violation—but suit can only be brought if the purchase of the policy or annuity violated the terms of the plan or violated fiduciary obligations.

ERISA § 502(c) allows the Department of Labor to impose a penalty of $110 per day (dating from the date of failure or refusal to furnish the documents) against a plan administrator who doesn't comply with a participant's or beneficiary's request for plan documents within 30 days. Administrators can be penalized even if the failure is not deliberate—but not if it is due to matters beyond their reasonable control.

Both the federal and the state courts have jurisdiction under § 502(e) when participants or beneficiaries bring suit to recover benefits, clarify their rights to future benefits, or enforce rights under any plan that falls under ERISA Title I. Although ERISA does not rule out binding arbitration of claims, any other Title I claim can only be heard in a federal, not a state, court.

ERISA § 502(i) requires the DOL to impose a civil penalty on fiduciaries who violate the fiduciary responsibility provisions of Title I. A nonfiduciary who knowingly participates in a fiduciary violation can also be penalized under this section. The base penalty is 20% of the penalty that the court orders under ERISA § 502(a)(2) or (a)(5). If the fiduciary or person who assisted the fiduciary in the breach settled with the DOL to avoid being taken to court, the base penalty is 20% of the amount of the settlement. The penalty can be reduced or even waived if the person acted reasonably and in good faith. Because the main objective of this section is to safeguard the plan, a reduction or waiver can also be obtained if the fiduciary or helper would not be able to reimburse the plan without severe financial hardship if the full penalty were assessed.

Section 502(k) permits plan administrators, fiduciaries, participants, and beneficiaries to sue the Department of Labor itself in district court in order to compel the agency to undertake an action required by ERISA Title I, to prevent the Department from acting contrary to Title I, or to review a final order of the Secretary of Labor.

Section 502 also permits fiduciaries to ask the court to remove another fiduciary from office, or to issue an injunction against anyone who has violated ERISA Title I or the plan's own terms.

It is mandatory for the DOL to impose civil penalties, under § 502(l), against a fiduciary who knowingly violates the Title I provisions on fiduciary responsibility, and also against anyone who knowingly participates in a violation. The basic penalty is 20% of the court order under §§ 502(a)(2) or (a)(5), or the settlement with DOL in such a case. However, any penalty imposed under § 502(i), or any prohibited transaction excise tax, can be used to offset the § 502(l) penalty. The Secretary of Labor has discretion to reduce or waive the penalty in two circumstances: if the fiduciary acted reasonably and in good faith—or if waiver permits the fiduciary to reimburse the plan for its losses.

## [B]  Issues Under *Knudson, Sereboff,* and *McVeigh*

In 2002, the Supreme Court decided *Great-West Life & Annuity Insurance Co. v. Knudson* [534 U.S. 204 (2002)]. The Supreme Court ruled that a health plan and its administrator cannot sue under ERISA § 502(a)(3) when they claim that beneficiaries violate the terms of the plan by refusing to reimburse the plan for amounts the plan spent on the beneficiaries' medical care. The Supreme Court reached this conclusion because § 502(a)(3) refers to cases that traditionally came under the heading of "equity." Contract suits traditionally were considered suits at "law," not "equity."

After *Knudson*, plans faced three hurdles in bringing claims for restitution. First, the defendant (in many such cases, the plan participant, because the plan itself is the plaintiff) must have been unjustly enriched. In some cases, the defendant will have to have possession of specific property that really belongs to the plaintiff—and equitable relief must be appropriate.

In mid-2006, the Supreme Court revisited ERISA subrogation issues twice. In *Sereboff v. Mid Atlantic Medical Services Inc.* [547 U.S. 356 (2006)], the petitioners were covered by an ERISA plan that included a subrogation provision. The petitioners settled tort claims related to an automobile accident. Their insurer sued under ERISA § 502(a)(3) to recoup medical expenses paid on their behalf. The petitioners set aside part of the tort recovery, corresponding to the insurer's claim. The Supreme Court ruled that the insurer was entitled to recover the amount expended on the petitioners' medical care. The insurer acted as a fiduciary seeking "appropriate equitable relief" to enforce plan terms, as permitted by ERISA § 502(a)(3). Unlike *Knudson*, the disputed funds in this case were in the petitioners' possession and set aside in a separate account. The Supreme Court treated the insurer's claim as equitable not because it was a claim for subrogation, but because it was the equivalent of an action to enforce an equitable lien created by agreement.

A month later, in *Empire Healthchoice Assurance, Inc. v. McVeigh* [547 U.S. 677 (2006)], ruled that an insurer's attempt to recover health care costs paid on behalf of an injured federal employee had to be litigated in state court rather than federal court: there was no jurisdiction under 28 U.S.C. § 1331. Although the worker was covered under the Federal Employees Health Benefits Act, a statute that includes a provision that the terms of the federal plan's insurance contracts will preempt state or local law about health benefit plans, the Supreme Court held that the case for reimbursement does not "arise under federal law" and therefore there is no federal jurisdiction.

In 2013, the Supreme Court ruled in a case in which a plan participant received $110,000 in settlement funds after an automobile accident. He paid a 40% contingent fee to his lawyer, so he had $66,000 after that. His health plan sought to recover the $66,866 it had paid for his care. The plan participant, McCutchen, said that he was not obligated to reimburse the health plan, because if he did, he would not have received any compensation for the injuries he suffered. The Supreme Court ruled that the health plan's SPD clearly and explicitly gave the insurer a right of subrogation. This right, deriving from contract law, prevailed over McCutchen's equitable arguments about "make-whole" relief. However, the reimbursement provision did not explain how to handle attorneys' fees, so the Supreme Court held that it was possible to apply another equitable doctrine, the "common fund" doctrine to resolve this issue. (This doctrine allows a person who creates a common fund for the benefit of multiple parties to be paid for creating the fund.) [*US Airways, Inc. v. McCutchen*, 133 S. Ct. 1537 (2013); see Sarah Fowles and Angela Marie Hubbell, *Have You Checked Your Plan's Subrogation and Reimbursement Provisions Lately?*, Quarles & Brady LLP Employee Benefits & Executive Compensation Law Blog (April 2013) (benefitslink.com)]

Similar issues arose in a mid-2013 Connecticut case; the District Court for the District of Connecticut permitted a self-insured plan to recover the benefits it paid to an injured employee who settled a tort case about the accident. The plan provided that it was entitled to recover 100% of the amount it paid for participants' health care, whether or not the participant was made whole. Although Connecticut has an anti-subrogation statute that forbids employers to seek recovery from third-party tort settlements, the district court did not apply the statute. The court found that the statute was not only preempted by ERISA, it would not apply to a self-insured plan anyway. [*Quest Diagnostics v. Bomani*, No. 11-CV-00951 (D. Conn. June 19, 2013); see Anthony Cacace, *Express Plan Terms Allow Self-Insured Plan to Recover Medical Benefits Paid to Employee Post-McCutchen*, Proskauer's ERISA Practice Center Blog (June 25, 2013) (benefitslink.com)]

Subrogation issues are also discussed in Chapter 18.

### [C]  *Amara v. Cigna*

Cigna employees filed a class action after their plan's cash balance conversion. (See Chapter 7 for more discussion of cash balance plans.) At the time of the conversion, Cigna distributed summaries and an SPD stating that the new plan provided an overall improvement in retirement benefits; that participants' opening account balance equaled the full value of their accrued benefits; and the conversion did not save money for the employer. The employees contested these statements, arguing that the opening account balance was less than full value because it did not reflect the previous plan's early retirement subsidy. They also claimed that many participants were subject to wearaway, and that the employer saved $10 million a year by converting the plan. (Cigna later conceded this point, but said that it spent the money on other benefit plans.)

The district court agreed with the plaintiffs that the plan materials were false and misleading. The district court ruled that there was likely harm even without a showing of detrimental reliance by the plaintiffs (i.e., that they were harmed by relying on the employer's statements). The district court ordered Cigna to reform the plan to conform to the descriptions given to the employees. The district court interpreted ERISA § 502(a)(1)(B) to allow plan participants to sue to obtain benefits that were due under the plan, or to clarify their right to future benefits. The district court ordered the plan to give participants their pre-conversion frozen benefits, plus the cash balance benefits earned after the conversion. However, the district court read § 502(a)(3) to provide only the types of "equitable" relief that traditionally were ordered by equity courts before the two court systems (law and equity) were merged. Therefore, the district court did not order any compensatory damages.

In 2011, the Supreme Court held that the terms of an SPD are not part of the plan itself, and the SPD merely communicates about the plan. The plan's settlor determines the terms of the plan; the administrator provides the SPD. In effect, the Supreme Court overruled the line of decisions allowing enforcement of the terms of the SPD where it conflicts with the plan terms.

The Supreme Court also said that errors in an SPD cannot be enforced through a contractual claim for benefits under ERISA § 502(a)(1)(B). Merely showing likely harm to a class is not enough to support relief. The Supreme Court also held that courts do not have authority under § 502(a)(1)(B) to reform the terms of a plan. These parts of the holding are pro-employer.

But, with regard to what constitutes appropriate equitable relief under ERISA § 502(a)(3), the Supreme Court left open the possibility of obtaining reformation, equitable estoppel, and even surcharge (i.e., requiring the trustee to reimburse the plan). The Supreme Court said that a showing of detrimental reliance is usually not required in equitable proceedings for reformation or surcharges. Plaintiffs must show actual harm and causation—but actual reliance on the SPD would not have to be proved. The Supreme Court vacated the Second Circuit decision, and remanded the case for determination of the availability of equitable remedies. [*Amara v. Cigna*, 131 S. Ct. 1866 (2011)]

On remand, the District Court for the District of Connecticut ordered reformation of CIGNA's cash balance plan, holding that both reformation and surcharge are appropriate equitable remedies. The district court applied the Second Circuit's "likely harm" standard to decide that CIGNA was liable for giving inadequate disclosures of the conversion from the defined benefit to the defined contribution plan. The district court ordered the plan to pay the class members all accrued benefits under both plans. CIGNA argued that the remedies should be based on trust rather than contract principles, but the district court said that the economic reality is that the pension plan stems from the employment contract between employer and employees. The district court held that equity courts have the power to reform contracts that, as a result of mutual mistake or because of one-sided mistake and fraud on the other side, fail to express the parties' intention. The district court ruled that CIGNA engaged in inequitable conduct. The defective notice caused employees to misunderstand the contract. CIGNA not only did not correct their misunderstanding, but also prevented employees from understanding the differences between the old and new plans and misled them into thinking their accrued benefits would be protected. [*Amara v. CIGNA Corp.*, Civil No. 3:01cv2361 (JBA) 2012 U.S. Dist. LEXIS 180355 (D. Conn. Dec. 20, 2012); see Mark Casciari and Sara Eber, *Amara—The Beat Goes On*, Seyfarth

Shaw ERISA & Employee Benefits Litigation Blog (Jan. 10, 2013) (benefitslink. com); Rebecca Moore, *Court Makes Repeat Decision in Amara v CIGNA Corp*, plansponsor.com (Jan. 23, 2013). See also *Helton v. AT&T Inc. Pension Benefit Plan*, 709 F.3d 343 (4th Cir. 2013), holding that a retiree who was not informed of a plan change that would have allowed her to collect a full pension at an earlier age was not barred by *Amara* from recovering the benefits once she became aware of their availability.]

Gearlds alleged that his employer negligently induced him to take early retirement by promising health benefits. The district court dismissed the case, arguing that all he asked for was compensatory damages (past and future medical expenses, attorneys' fees and costs), which are not an available equitable remedy. However, the Fifth Circuit said that *Amara* allows relief that makes a plaintiff whole for losses caused by breach of fiduciary duty. [*Gearlds v. Entergy Servs. Inc.*, 709 F.3d 448 (5th Cir. 2013); see Rebecca Moore, *5th Circuit Revives Suit for Retiree Medical Benefits* (Mar. 8, 2013)]

The Ninth Circuit enforced the less favorable terms of the plan document rather than the more generous terms of the SPD in a case where—unlike *Amara*—there was no evidence of mistake, fraud, duress, undue influence, or intent to deceive. Nor did the plaintiffs show that their position would have been different if they had received accurate SPDs. [*Skinner v. Northrop Grumman Retirement Plan B*, 673 F.3d 1162 (9th Cir. 2012); see Spencer Fane Britt & Brown LLP, *Federal Appeals Court Rejects Equitable Remedies When SPD Promises More Generous Benefits Than Pension Plan Document* (May 18, 2012) (benefitslink.com)]

## § 15.10   ERISA § 510

ERISA § 510 makes it unlawful to interfere with ERISA rights, or to discharge or discriminate against a participant for exercising ERISA rights. The typical examples are firing an employee to prevent benefit accrual, or firing someone in retaliation for making a claim for plan benefits. As the number of layoffs increases, companies are at greater risk that laid-off employees will charge that they lost their jobs to cut benefit costs. Sometimes § 510 claims arise in the context of a wrongful discharge, ADEA, or whistleblower case. Section 510 is enforced under § 502, so the possible remedies are a grant of benefits, reinstatement, or injunctions—but not punitive or compensatory damages. Successful plaintiffs often receive attorneys' fees and costs. Back pay can be allowed as a form of restitution, but money damages are not allowed because § 502 offers only equitable relief.

ERISA preempts state-law wrongful termination claims when the former employee claims termination was motivated by interference with ERISA rights. [*Ingersoll-Rand v. McClendon*, 498 U.S. 133 (1990)] Section 510 applies to welfare benefit plans as well as pension plans. [*Inter-Modal Rail Employees v. Atchison, Topeka & Santa Fe R.R.*, 520 U.S. 510 (1997)] However, refusal to rehire laid off workers who have credited service, as part of a policy of reducing pension obligations, does not violate § 510 because the people who seek to be rehired have not yet been hired or promised benefits. [*Becker v. Mack Trucks Inc.*, 281 F.3d 372 (3d Cir. 2002)]

The Tenth Circuit held that a group of terminated employees who were not rehired after the sale of their employer's facility failed to prove a conspiracy between the employer and the purchaser to violate ERISA § 510 by selling the facility, getting rid of older employees, and depriving them of their pensions. The Tenth Circuit concluded that the seller did not consider pension costs until after the sale. The purchaser of the facility rehired 8,000 out of its 10,000 workers. Both before and after the sale, most of the workers were over 40, but the percentage of over-40 workers rehired was lower than the pre-acquisition workforce. Some of those denied rehiring sued, seeking to represent a class of about 700. The Tenth Circuit held that § 510 is not violated if the employer is motivated by legitimate business reasons, even if the result is that some laid-off workers lose pension eligibility. [*Apsley v. Boeing Co.*, 691 F.3d 1184 (10th Cir. 2012); see Wolters Kluwer Law & Business News Center, *Employees Did Not Prove Intent by Seller and Buyer Companies to Interfere with Employees' Attainment of Benefits* (Oct. 4, 2012) (benefitslink.com)]

Verizon proposed to fund about $7.5 billion in retiree benefits for about 41,000 management retirees by purchasing a single-premium group annuity from Prudential. Verizon said that the annuity payments would be the same as the pension payments. The plaintiffs charged that the transaction violated ERISA § 510 by denying them the protection of ERISA. (29 C.F.R. § 2510.3-3(d)(2)(ii) says that a person is not a plan participant if the entire benefit is fully guaranteed by an insurance company.) The Northern District of Texas denied a TRO and preliminary injunction that would have halted the transaction. The district court said that the annuity provided the same survivor benefits and other rights as the retirees already had. Because the contract terms remained the same, the district court said that they could not show a risk of loss of benefits. Because amending or terminating a pension plan is not a fiduciary act, the fiduciary duty claim was dismissed. Although there is a fiduciary duty to be prudent in selecting an annuity provider, but the annuity purchase itself is not treated as an investment subject to the fiduciary duty to diversify. The plaintiffs argued that all of the transferred assets were invested with Prudential, but the district court said that the duty to diversify did not apply in this context; fiduciary duty meant prudent selection of an insurer. The district court held that an SPD is only required to explain the current terms of a plan, not potential changes. [*Lee v. Verizon*, No. 3:12-cv-04834-D, 2012 U.S. Dist. LEXIS 173559 (N.D. Tex. Dec. 7, 2012); see Kristen Heinzinger, *Court Approves Verizon Pension Buyout*, plansponsor.com (Dec. 7, 2012 The entire case was dismissed in June 2013. The district court found that ERISA protects benefits, but does not require that the original source that provides the benefits be maintained: see Maria Wood, *Judge Disconnects Lawsuit Vs. Verizon*

*Pension Transfer*, LifeHealthPro, <http://www.lifehealthpro.com/2013/06/26/judge-disconnects-lawsuit-vs-verizon-pension-trans> (June 26, 2013).]

When employees charge retaliation in violation of ERISA § 510, there is an important question as to whether the employee must have participated in a formal action or proceeding to be protected. The Second, Third, and Fourth Circuits require a formal proceeding; the Fifth and Ninth say that unsolicited informal complaints are also covered. The Seventh Circuit held that, at least if a plan's anti-relation provision is ambiguous, doubts must be resolved in the employee's favor. Therefore, a plaintiff who made internal complaints and contacted the DOL (but did not make a formal complaint) alleging that funds withheld from his pay were not deposited into his retirement and health savings accounts could bring a § 510 retaliation action when he was fired. The Seventh Circuit said that § 510 applies as long as the employee's grievance is within the scope of § 510, even if the employer did not solicit information and if the employee suffered retaliation because of raising the issue. The employee must have a substantial complaint and a plausible grievance (although he or she does not have to be factually correct); and the complaint must be substantial. [*George v. Junior Achievement of Central Indiana, Inc.*, 694 F.3d 812 (7th Cir. 2012); see Russell D. Chapman, Littler Mendelson Employee Benefits Counsel Blog, *Unsolicited and Informal ERISA Complaints May Be the Basis for ERISA Section 510 Retaliation Claims, Seventh Circuit Holds* (Sept. 10, 2012) (benefitslink.com); see also *Edwards v. Cornell and Son Inc.*, 610 F.3d 217 (3d Cir. 2010), *cert. denied*, 131 S. Ct. 1604 (2011)]

## § 15.11  OTHER ENFORCEMENT ISSUES

### [A]  Generally

Criminal penalties can be imposed under ERISA § 511, making it a crime, punishable by up to one year's imprisonment and/or a fine of $10,000, to use or threaten force, fraud, or violence to restrain, coerce, or intimidate a participant or beneficiary, in order to interfere with or prevent exercise of any right under the terms of the plan or under Title I.

A construction contractor who pled guilty to filing a false Form 5500 was sentenced to a year of federal probation and over $150,000 in penalties and fines. The contractor, who served as trustee of his company's profit sharing plan, admitted to falsifying the document to conceal his conflict of interest in using plan funds to invest in his business. (The plan did not lose money as a result of the improper transactions.) [Fred Schneyer, *Employer Fined for Lying on Form 5500*, plansponsor.com (Apr. 9, 2008)]

ERISA § 409(a) makes a breaching fiduciary personally liable to the plan to make up for losses caused by the breach (such as the difference between what the plan would have earned given appropriate investments, minus its actual earnings).

The breaching fiduciary is also liable for any other legal and equitable remedies the plan chooses to impose.

However, in *Peacock v. Thomas* [516 U.S. 349 (1996)], the plaintiff won an ERISA case against his employer, but could not collect the judgment, allegedly because a corporate officer who was not a fiduciary misappropriated the funds that could have been used to satisfy the judgment. The plaintiff could not "pierce the corporate veil" and make the corporate officer personally liable, for various technical legal reasons. For one thing, the case was not closely enough related to ERISA for the federal courts to get involved. Anyway, a federal court cannot enforce a judgment against someone who was not liable for it in the first place.

The Department of Labor has authority under ERISA § 504(a)(2) to investigate whether a Title I violation has occurred so the employer might be ordered to submit books, papers, and records for DOL examination. This can be done only once per 12-month period unless the DOL has reasonable cause to believe that Title I was violated. The DOL also has subpoena power over books, records, and witnesses under § 504(c), but the subpoena can be enforced only if the agency shows that the investigation has a legitimate purpose, the inquiry is relevant to that purpose, and the government does not already have the information.

For purposes of compliance with a DOL investigative audit under ERISA § 504, the fiduciary exception to attorney-client privilege covers communications about plan administration between an ERISA trustee and the plan's attorney. Therefore, two multi-employer pension funds had to turn over plan administration materials about the decision to invest in entities related to Bernard Madoff. The funds asserted attorney-client and work-product privilege to avoid turning over the materials to the DOL. The fiduciary exception was created under trust law and holds that advice that trustees get about trust administration goes to the trust beneficiaries, not to the trustees. The funds were unsuccessful in asserting privilege because they did not provide privilege logs or say which litigation the documents were prepared for. [*Solis v The Food Employers Labor Relations Ass'n,* 644 F.3d 221 (4th Cir. 2011)]

ERISA § 515 permits a civil action against an employer for delinquency in making contributions. This section does not have a statute of limitations, so most courts that have considered the issue use a six-year statute of limitations (typical for contract cases). The statute of limitations is clear under a similar provision, ERISA § 4003(e)(1) (which correlates with I.R.C. § 412(n)). If an employer fails to make a required contribution to the plan, at a time when the plan's funded current liability percentage is lower than 100% and the employer owes the plan more than $1 million (including interest), then all of the employer's real and personal property becomes subject to a lien in favor of the plan.

The plan that was supposed to, but didn't, make the payment has an obligation to notify the PBGC within 10 days of the payment due date. The PBGC has six years from the date of the missed payment, or three years from the time it knew or should have known about the missed payment, to sue in federal District

Court to enforce the lien. Fraud or concealment by the employer extends the statute of limitations to six years from the PBGC's discovery of the true state of affairs.

Excise taxes are imposed under § 4975 for the employer's failure to make timely payments of elective deferrals into the plan trust. (The excise tax is sent to the IRS with Form 5330.) Small (under 100 participant) plans are entitled to a safe harbor as long as employee contributions are deposited within seven business days of receipt. The safe harbor offers relief from the general rule that employers must deposit contributions as soon as they can be segregated from the employer's assets, but in any case within 15 business days of the end of the month of receipt. [73 Fed. Reg. 11072 (Feb. 29, 2008); see *EBSA Proposes Seven-Day Employee Contrib Safe Harbor*, plansponsor.com (Feb. 28, 2008)]

The Fourth Circuit allowed participants in a defined benefit plan to continue to pursue their fiduciary breach claim even after the plan was turned over to the PBGC. In other words, the right to sue does not end when a plan is terminated, and the PBGC is not the only potential plaintiff. The Fourth Circuit also held that in general, the PBGC cannot make lump sum payments from its own funds, but can do so in its role as statutory trustee. However, state-law claims against the investment manager, such as violation of the Unfair and Deceptive Trade Practices Act, were preempted by ERISA. [*Wilmington Shipping Co. v. New England Life Ins. Co.*, 496 F.3d 326 (4th Cir. 2007)]

## [B]   Sarbanes-Oxley Act and Dodd-Frank Act

The penalty for willful violation of reporting or disclosure rules [29 U.S.C. § 1311] was increased dramatically by the Sarbanes-Oxley Act [Pub. L. No. 107-204]. The maximum penalty under this provision (whether or not the violator is a publicly traded corporation) is $100,000 rather than $5,000 for an individual; ten years rather than one year of imprisonment; and $500,000 rather than $100,000 if the violator is a corporation.

See the DOL final rule [68 Fed. Reg. 3729 (Jan. 24, 2003)] for the effects of the Sarbanes-Oxley Act on penalties. Although the main focus of this rule is on the penalties imposed pursuant to ERISA § 502(c)(7) for failure to provide proper notice of a blackout period, the Sarbanes-Oxley Act made several changes in penalty levels that apply to all ERISA violations, not just those involving corporate governance. The maximum penalty under ERISA § 502(c)(2) is $1,000 per day; starting on the date the plan administrator failed or refused to file the annual report. The maximum penalty under ERISA § 502(c)(5) is $1,000 per day (for violations occurring after March 24, 2003, the penalty can be up to $1,100 a day. [See 68 Fed. Reg. 2875 (Jan. 22, 2003)] Failure to furnish documents on request of plan participants, beneficiaries, or their designates can be penalized by up to $110 a day, subject to a maximum of $1,100 per request.

In all these cases, the plan administrator is entitled to notice and hearing before imposition of the penalty, and the administrator will be permitted to introduce evidence of why it would not be equitable to impose a penalty (e.g., the administrator acted in good faith and the non-compliance was due to factors beyond his or her control).

Sarbanes-Oxley also limits the availability of plan loans to the officers and directors of the sponsor corporation. EBSA issued a Field Assistance Bulletin that such limitations do not violate ERISA. [EBSA Advisory Opinion 2003-04A, <http://www.dol.gov/ebsa/regs/aos/ao2003-04a.html>]

The Dodd-Frank Act, Pub. L. No. 111-203, regulating financial services, was passed after the 2008 stock market crash. In November 2010, the SEC issued a 181-page document to implement the whistleblower program under Dodd-Frank Act § 922. The "bounty" under the Dodd-Frank Act can be 10%–30% of the fines and settlements resulting from enforcement actions triggered by whistleblower claims. The IRS also has a bounty program, which offers a 15%–30% reward from the proceeds of enforcement actions involving more than $2 million or involving taxpayers whose annual gross income exceeds $200,000. The IRS is not required to pay the whistleblower until the accused has exhausted all legal appeals and paid the IRS. Under the SEC and CFTC whistleblower programs, the minimum reward is $100,000, with no cap, if the tip leads to penalties of more than $1 million. The Dodd-Frank program covers almost all kinds of investment fraud; previously, only insider trading was covered. [Jenna Greene, *SEC Proposes New Whistleblower Rules*, The BLT: The Blog of Legal Times (Nov. 3, 2010) (law.com); Jean Eaglesham and Ashby Jones, *Whistleblower Bounties Pose Challenges*, WSJ.com (Dec. 13, 2010). The proposed rules were finalized in 2011: <http://www.sec.gov/rules/final/2011/34-64545.pdf> (May 25, 2011), effective August 12, 2011.]

A mid-2013 Fifth Circuit decision holds that a person who makes an internal complaint about wrongdoing (in this case, possible violations of the Foreign Corrupt Practice Act) is not a whistleblower for Dodd-Frank Act purposes, which requires providing the SEC with information about violations of the securities laws. Therefore, retaliation based on an internal complaint is not covered by the Dodd-Frank Act. [*Asadi v. G.E. Energy LLC*, 2013 WL 3742492 (5th Cir. 2013)]

## § 15.12   LIABILITY OF CO-FIDUCIARIES

If a plan's assets are held by more than one trustee, the general rule is that all the trustees are jointly responsible for management, unless the plan's trust instrument either makes a specific allocation of responsibility, or sets up a procedure for allocating responsibility.

ERISA § 405(c)(1) allows a plan to make an explicit allocation of fiduciary responsibility (other than the responsibility of trustees) among the named fiduciaries. The plan can also have procedures for fiduciaries to designate a party other than a named fiduciary to carry out fiduciary responsibilities under the plan. In general, a fiduciary who designates someone else will not be responsible for the acts or omissions of the designee. The two major exceptions occur when making or continuing the designation violates the designor's duties under ERISA § 404(a)(1), or when ERISA § 405(a) makes the designor responsible for the co-fiduciary's breach.

Every trustee has a legal duty to use reasonable care to make sure the other fiduciaries do not breach their duties. Any fiduciary's misconduct implicates all the others. Fiduciaries are liable for the acts and omissions of their fellow fiduciaries if:

- They knowingly participate in, or knowingly conceal, a breach on another party's act;

- They facilitate someone else's breach by failing to perform their own fiduciary duties as stated by § 404(a)(2);

- They know about a breach by another fiduciary, but fail to take reasonable steps to remedy it.

Under a 1993 Supreme Court case, the plan can also get equitable remedies (but not damages) from a nonfiduciary who cooperated with a fiduciary who breached fiduciary duty. [*Mertens v. Hewitt Assocs.*, 508 U.S. 248 (1993)] Some courts have applied *Mertens* to prevent any claims by plans against nonfiduciaries. This only puts more pressure on the fiduciaries, because then they are the only possible defendants if something goes wrong. But fiduciaries cannot be liable for other fiduciaries' conduct occurring before they themselves became fiduciaries. Nor do they have a duty to remedy breaches that occurred before their tenure or after they cease to be fiduciaries.

Investment advisor Barry Stokes stole millions of dollars from employee benefits plans under his management. The fiduciary accounts for those plans were held in Regions Bank. Stokes' bankruptcy trustee and several of Stokes' clients asserted that the bank negligently or knowingly let Stokes steal from fiduciary accounts at the bank. The Sixth Circuit held that ERISA preempted the plaintiffs' state-law claims—but affirmed the district court's dismissal of the ERISA claims. The Sixth Circuit held that the bankruptcy trustee had standing to pursue ERISA claims against Regions Bank, acting as an ERISA fiduciary rather than as the trustee of the debtor's estate. A plaintiff can obtain both equitable relief and damages from fiduciaries who breach their duty, but can only get equitable relief from nonfiduciaries. However, the Sixth Circuit held that Regions was not a fiduciary even though it had custody of plan assets and earned fees for holding the assets. [*McLemore v. Regions Bank*, 682 F.3d 414 (6th Cir. 2012)]

A non-fiduciary who knowingly participates in a fiduciary's violation of the anti-kickback provision, ERISA § 406(b)(3), can be penalized under ERISA § 502(a)(3) even if the non-fiduciary is not a party in interest. (Section 406(b)(3) forbids fiduciaries to receive consideration from third parties who deal with plan assets.) Ronn Redfearn created a tax-avoidance scheme using welfare plans that paid premiums for life insurance policies, which were used to make tax-free post-retirement payments to owners. Financial planner James Barrett signed up many of his clients. Eventually the IRS found that the arrangement didn't comply with the Code and disallowed the employers' deductions and imposed penalties on them. The employers sued several people involved in the program, including Barrett. The district court described Barrett as a non-fiduciary who could be penalized for knowing participation in ERISA violations. He was ordered to disgorge half the payments he had received. [*National Security Systems, Inc. v. Iola*, 700 F.3d 65 (3d Cir. 2012); see ERISA Litigation Update, *Third Circuit Holds Nonfiduciary Who Is Not a "Party in Interest" May Be Liable For Participation in Fiduciary's Violation of ERISA Section 406(b)(3)* (Dec 13, 2012) (benefitslink.com]

The Fourth Circuit reversed dismissal of a complaint charging 401(k) plan fiduciaries with breach of the duty of prudence when they liquidated two of the plan's investment funds at a loss. The district court dismissed the complaint because it said that the plan's sponsors had amended the plan to eliminate those two funds, and that the amendment was a "settlor act" that did not trigger fiduciary duty analysis. The Fourth Circuit allowed the plaintiffs to pursue their claim because the amendment did not remove the fiduciaries' discretion to maintain the funds, so the decision to liquidate them could be imprudent. [*Tatum v. RJ Reynolds Tobacco Co.*, 392 F.3d 636 (4th Cir. 2004)] But the "settlor act" argument prevailed in a 2010 Eighth Circuit case, which found that plan trustees acted as settlers rather than fiduciaries when they amended an early retirement plan to allow certain laid-off employees access to benefits not available under the original plan. [*Schultz v. Windstream Commc'ns, Inc.*, 600 F.3d 948 (8th Cir. 2010)]

In late 2012, the District Court for the Middle District of Florida ruled that the federal common law of ERISA allows fiduciaries to sue each other for contribution or indemnification. In this case, a group of employees sued the employer and its directors and officers for breaches of fiduciary duty to an ESOP. The district court followed *Lanfear:* the allegations stated a claim of fiduciary breach (failure to be prudent and loyal in managing investments). The employer's stock became worthless after the Office of the Comptroller of the Currency found that the bank's lending practices were unsafe. The defendants sued three of the plaintiffs for contribution or indemnification, charging that they were fiduciaries as a result of their service on the plan's administrative committee. This was a case of first impression in the Eleventh Circuit. The district court held that contribution/indemnification does not constitute appropriate equitable relief under ERISA § 502(a)(3)—but, because ERISA reflects trust and equity principles, including distributing responsibility among responsible parties, the suit is permitted under federal common law. The district court said that ruling the other way would allow fiduciaries to immunize themselves by racing to the courthouse to file the first suit [*Guididas v. Community Nat'l Bank Corp.*, No. 8:11-cv-2545-T-30TBM, 2012 U.S. Dist. LEXIS 158404 (M.D. Fla. Nov. 5, 2012); see Richard Loebl and Mark

Casciari, *Post-Amara: Are Contribution Or Indemnification Among Co-Fiduciaries Available Under ERISA?* Seyfarth Shaw ERISA & Employee Benefits Litigation (Nov. 8, 2012) (benefitslink.com); Rebecca Moore, *Court Finds ERISA Violation from Following Terms of ESOP*, plansponsor.com (June 13, 2012). See *Lanfear v. Home Depot*, 679 F.3d 1267 (11th Cir. 2012).]

## § 15.13  BONDING

The basic rule set down by ERISA § 412(a) is that all fiduciaries, and plan officials who are not fiduciaries but who handle plan assets, must be bonded. Generally, the employer will maintain a single bond covering all of its plans that are subject to ERISA Title I. Recovery on behalf of one plan must not be allowed to reduce the amount available to the other plans below the minimum requirement.

The exceptions are some banks and insurance companies with assets over $1 million, and administrators, officers, and employees who deal with unfunded plans. (An unfunded plan is one whose assets come from the general funds of the employer or a union, even if the funds derive in part from employee contributions.) A bond is not required for amounts characterized as general assets of the employer until they are transferred to the insurers that pay the actual benefits.

Various forms of bonds are acceptable:

- Blanket bond (covering all the fiduciaries and everyone who handles the plan's money);

- Individual bond;

- Name schedule bond (covering a group of named individuals);

- Position schedule bond (covering whoever fills certain jobs or stands in certain relationships to the plan).

The bond must be issued by a corporate surety that holds a Department of Treasury Certificate of Authority. To be acceptable, the bond must not have a deductible, and must cover claims discovered after termination or cancellation of the bond. The amount of the bond must be large enough to cover the plan's potential losses caused by plan officials' dishonesty or fraud. Before the PPA, the bond was required to be 10% of the funds handled, with a minimum of $1,000 and a maximum of $500,000, but, for plans that hold employer stock, and for plan years beginning after January 1, 2007, the Pension Protection Act of 2006 (PPA) increases the maximum to $1 million. If the DOL finds out that a plan does not have the required bond, it can order the company to get a bond; permanently bar the fiduciary from ever serving as an ERISA plan fiduciary; remove the plan administrator and appoint an independent trustee; or impose penalties. [Janelle Sotelo, *Fidelity Bond v. Fiduciary Liability Ins.*, <http://www.preceptgroup.com/blog> (Feb. 19, 2009)]

In 2011, DOL stated that bonding is required for anyone who is considered to handle plan assets: anyone whose duties involve receiving, keeping, and disbursing plan funds, having access to plan funds, or being able to subject the plan to losses by fraud or dishonesty. ERISA § 412, which imposes the bonding requirement, says it is unlawful for any plan official to let any other plan official handle plan property without being bonded first. Therefore, the responsibility of everyone subject to the bonding requirement is to see that everyone else subject to the requirement is bonded. Plan administrators should identify everyone subject to this requirement, and obtain the proper form of bond for each. [Joe Faucher, Reish & Reacher ERISA Controversy Report, *ERISA Fidelity Bonds— Who Needs Them, and Who is Responsible for Securing Them?* (February 2011) (law.com)]

## § 15.14 INDEMNIFICATION

ERISA § 410 says that language in a plan, or in a side agreement with a fiduciary, is void as against public policy if it limits the fiduciary's liability for breach of fiduciary duty. However, the employer (as distinct from the plan) can permissibly indemnify the fiduciary or buy insurance covering the fiduciary. The fiduciary can also buy his or her own insurance coverage. [See § 43.08 for more discussion of fiduciary liability insurance] The sponsor corporation can also agree to use corporate assets to indemnify the fiduciary. This is allowed by the Department of Labor, and it is not considered a prohibited transaction.

## § 15.15 PROHIBITED TRANSACTIONS

### [A] Generally

Objectivity is one of the most important fiduciary characteristics. ERISA bans certain types of transactions between a plan and parties who might lose objectivity because of those transactions. "Parties in interest" and "disqualified persons" are blocked from certain categories of transactions, even if a particular transaction is fair.

Title I of ERISA makes any one of these a prohibited transaction if it occurs between the plan and a party in interest:

- Sale, exchange, or lease of property, including the plan's assumption of a mortgage, or a mortgage placed on the property by a party in interest during the 10 years before the transfer of the property to the plan;

- Extensions of credit;

- Furnishing goods or services;

- Transfers or uses of plan assets for the benefit of a party in interest;

- Acquisition or holding of employer securities that are not qualified, or in excess of the normal limit (usually 10% of the fair market value of the plan assets);

- Use of plan income or assets by a fiduciary in her or her personal interest or for his or her own account;

- Payments to a fiduciary for his or her own account, made by anyone who deals with the plan;

- Conflict of interest: the fiduciary acts on behalf of a party, or representing a party, in any transaction representing the plan—if the interests of the party the fiduciary represents are adverse to the interests of the plan or of its participants and beneficiaries.

## [B]  Parties in Interest

ERISA § 3(14) defines "party in interest" (PII) very broadly:

- Any fiduciary or relative of a fiduciary;

- Plan employees or persons who provide counsel to the plan—or their relatives;

- The plan's service providers and their relatives;

- Any employer or employee organization (e.g., union) whose members are covered by the plan;

- Anyone who owns 50% or more of the employer corporation, whether ownership is direct or indirect; relatives of the 50% owner;

- A corporation, partnership, trust, or estate that is 50% or more controlled by anyone in one of the categories above (unless they are involved only as relatives of a person involved with the plan);

- Employees, officers, and directors of organizations in the list (or anyone with similar powers and responsibilities without the formal title);

- Employees, officers, and directors (or those with similar rights and duties) of organizations in the list;

- Employees, officers, and directors of the plan;

- Anyone who has a direct or indirect 10% share ownership in the plan or an organization closely related to the plan;

- Anyone with a direct or indirect 10% interest in the capital or profits of a partnership or joint venture with anyone on the list.

Any participant, beneficiary, or plan fiduciary can bring suit for "appropriate equitable relief" under ERISA § 406 when an individual or business that is a "party in interest" (e.g., the employees and service providers of the plan) enters into a prohibited transaction—even if this individual or business is not an ERISA fiduciary. [*Harris Trust & Savings Bank v. Salomon Smith Barney*, 530 U.S. 238 (2000)] Therefore, the party in interest can be enjoined by a court, or required to make restitution to the plan, if the prohibited transaction results in financial losses to the plan.

A disqualified person who engages in a prohibited transaction can be required to pay an excise tax, even if he or she didn't know the transaction was prohibited. The excise tax is 15% of the amount involved per year. An additional tax of 100% of the amount involved is imposed when the IRS notifies the disqualified person that the transaction is prohibited, but the transaction is not rescinded within 90 days of receipt of the notice. The excise tax is payable to the IRS. In addition, the Department of Labor can impose a civil penalty that is more or less equivalent to the excise tax if a plan that is not qualified under Title I engages in a prohibited transaction.

The rules for welfare benefit plans are slightly different: The excise tax, under ERISA § 502(i) and I.R.C. § 4975(f)(5), is 5% of the amount of the prohibited transaction, and this amount is cumulated if the prohibited transaction continues over several years. There is a 100% excise tax for failure to correct a prohibited transaction after receipt of notice from the IRS.

### [C]  Prohibited Transaction Exemptions

Because the prohibited transaction rules are so broad, the DOL has the power to grant "Prohibited Transaction Exemptions" for technically improper transactions that in fact are advantageous to the plan and benefit the plan's participants.

Exemptions fall into two main categories: the specific exemptions set out in ERISA § 408, and those granted by DOL and the Treasury after conferring. Before granting an exemption, the federal agency must decide that the proposed exemption is administratively feasible; serves the best interests of participants and beneficiaries; and protects the rights of participants and beneficiaries.

To get an individual exemption, a plan must apply to the relevant agency or agencies, and also give notice to affected parties and publish a notice in the Federal Register. Affected parties can place their comments (positive or negative) on the record. In some cases, a hearing will be required before the exemption is granted (e.g., when a fiduciary seeks permission to deal with the plan for his own account or to represent an adverse party).

ERISA includes statutory exemptions for loans to PIIs who are also plan participants or beneficiaries, as long as the loans are made on fair terms; for payment of reasonable compensation to PIIs for services they provide to the plan, rental of real estate to the plan at reasonable rates, and other deals that are the equivalent of arm's length transactions. There is also a statutory exemption for investing more than 10% of the plan's assets in qualifying employer securities and real property, as long as the plan purchases these items at a reasonable price and does not have to pay a commission to acquire them from the employer. Depending on the type of security, the plan will not be permitted to hold more than 25% to 50% of the entire issue.

"Class exemptions" have also been adopted for frequent transactions that are not harmful to the plan or its participants. Class exemptions have been granted, for instances, in connection with interest-free loans; mortgage loans to PIIs; and hiring PIIs to provide investment advice to the plan.

The Pension Protection Act of 2006 (Pub. L. No. 109-280) grants a Prohibited Transaction Exemption when fiduciaries provide investment advice to 401(k) plan participants after December 31, 2006—as long as the investment advice relies on an independently verified computer model, or the advisor's compensation is not dependent on the investments that the adviser suggests. However, the PPA doubles the size of the bond that fiduciaries must provide if the plan holds employer securities: under previous law, $500,000 was required, and now $1 million is required. (The legislative intent was to improve retirement security by enhancing savings rates and participation rates in 401(k) plans by making it easier to have a 401(k) plan.)

The EBSA issued final regulations in October 2011, spelling out a new prohibited transaction exemption implementing the PPA requirement of improving participants' access to fiduciary investment advice—subject to safeguards to prevent provision of biased advice. In general, the prohibited transaction rules forbid a fiduciary to recommend plan investment options if the fiduciary receives additional fees from the provider of that investment. Under the 2011 final rule, the exemption is limited to investment advice that is given by means of an unbiased computer model, or by an adviser who receives level fees that do not vary based on the selection of investments. The fees must be disclosed, and advisers receiving exemptions are subject to annual compliance audits. This prohibited transaction exemption (PTE) is related to but separate from the DOL's proposal on the definition of fiduciary investment advice, which was withdrawn but the DOL announced its intention to re-propose.[76 Fed. Reg. 66637 (Oct. 27, 2011); see Nicole Bliman, *EBSA Aims to Improve Access to Unbiased Advice*, plansponsor. com (Oct.25, 2011)]

## § 15.16   PAYMENT OF PLAN EXPENSES

One of the EBSA's top enforcement priorities is to make plan sponsors reimburse plans for expenses that were paid out of plan assets but should have been paid by the sponsors themselves. The DOL said that its regional offices would be conducting more plan expense audits than before. If a violation is found, not only must the employer reimburse the plan, but anyone involved in the transaction is subject to a 20% penalty. The Department of Labor can refer the case to the IRS for collection of the excise tax on prohibited transactions.

"Settlor functions" (decisions about establishing a plan or about plan design) are discretionary and not subject to the ERISA fiduciary requirements. Therefore, the expenses of performing settlor functions are not expenses of plan administration, and it is improper to use plan assets to pay them.

DOL Advisory Opinion 97-03A says that plan assets can be used to pay the expenses of terminating the plan itself, if the plan was silent about paying expenses, or if the plan permitted the payment of necessary administrative expenses. Plans that required the sponsor to pay such expenses can be amended to make the plan responsible for the expenses—but only expenses incurred after the amendment.

The DOL provided additional guidance in Advisory Opinion 2001-01A and a separate group of fact patterns. Under this Opinion, formation of a plan is a settlor activity, and the plan should not pay for it. Maintaining qualified status could involve fiduciary activities that the plan can pay for. Depending on whether they are incurred before or after a plan amendment, and whether they are reasonable and necessary for plan administration, these expenses could be legitimate plan expenses:

- Minimum funding valuations;
- Requests for determination;
- Processing fees;
- Preparation and submission of reports required by government agencies;
- Sending copies of such reports to participants;
- Making disclosure to, and communicating with, plan participants;
- Gathering information to make investment decisions for the plan;
- Amending the plan when complying with the law requires an amendment;
- Asset valuations in connection with a plan merger or spinoff (as long as the valuation is done after the plan is amended to cope with the transition);
- Winding up a terminated plan (including preparing valuations for the PBGC and distributing the plan's assets);
- Paying PBGC premiums;
- Preparing and auditing the plan's financial statements;
- Paying investment expenses.

Advisory Opinion 2001-01A says that the following are not allowable expenses that can be charged against the plan:

- Comparing benefit structures;

- Studies for outsourcing services that were previously performed by the sponsor at no cost to the plan;

- Preparing plan amendments that are not required for the sake of compliance;

- Preparing the financial disclosures that the sponsor is required to make under accounting standards;

- Getting valuations as part of deciding whether a merger or spinoff is worthwhile;

- Penalties imposed on the plan administrator;

- Analyses of whether to adopt early retirement incentives;

- Analyses of whether to terminate the plan.

In May 2003, EBSA ruled that it was permissible for a plan to pass along operating costs on a per-participant basis. However, the costs of creating a plan are entirely the financial responsibility of the employer. Cost allocation to individual participants is allowed for calculation of benefits, hardship withdrawals, and QDRO processing. This last is a reversal of a long-standing policy: in 1994 PBGC said that it was not permitted to impose a charge for processing a QDRO. [Kathy Chu, *Employees May Pay More on Retirement Plans*, Wall St. J., June 24, 2003, at D3]

## § 15.17 SERVICE PROVIDERS

Part of the fiduciary's duty of prudence is intelligent and informed selection of service providers for the plan, followed by monitoring of the job that the service providers do. Although it is understandable that fiduciaries will think first of their friends, colleagues, or relatives in selecting a service provider, the baseline is that they must deal only with people who have at least the minimum qualifications and experience to do the tasks they are hired for. A thorough reference check should be performed.

Compensation must be at least reasonably comparable to market rates for the same work. Selection by competitive bidding is helpful. Before retaining a service provider, it is vital to determine whether the fee that is quoted covers all the necessary services, or whether it is possible or likely that additional fees will be incurred, based on the predicted activities of the plan. The fiduciary doesn't always have to select the low bidder, but must be able to justify the selection as providing the best value on balance.

On August 20, 2002, the DOL issued Advisory Opinion 2002-08A, <http://www.dol.gov/ebsa/regs/AOs/ao2002-08a.html>, which permits fiduciaries to cause plans to enter into contracts with actuarial firms and other service providers that contain limitation of liability and indemnification provisions. When service providers are chosen, the fiduciary has an obligation to engage in an objective process to get the information needed to assess the provider's qualifications, the quality of the services offered, and the reasonableness of the fees charged for the services. Soliciting bids is an acceptable way to get this information, including the service provider's policies about indemnification and limitation of liability.

The DOL published a final rule February 3, 2012 about the disclosures a plan's service providers must give the fiduciaries, to show that providers' compensation paid out of plan assets does not exceed what is reasonable. For this purpose, providers include registered investment advisors, certain broker-dealers, TPAs, and others receiving $1,000 or more in direct or indirect compensation from plan assets. The final rules extend the deadline three months, making the compliance date July 1, 2012 rather than April 1, 2012, but the rules say this is probably the last extension.

No form is prescribed for the disclosures (known as the "408(b)(2) notice"), although they must be in writing. Failure to comply with these requirements is a prohibited transaction for the fiduciary, whereas compliance entitles the fiduciary to a prohibited transaction exemption.

If the provider fails to respond to the fiduciary's request for information relating to future services within 90 days, the final rule requires the fiduciary to terminate the service arrangement as fast as it can. The final rule also permits providers to furnish a reasonable, good-faith estimate of compensation or costs that are difficult to itemize—as long as they disclose their calculation method. Disclosures of indirect compensation from third parties to service providers must also disclose the calculation method. [DOL Final Rule, 77 Fed. Reg. 5632 (Feb. 3, 2012); see § 6.07[B] for further discussion of fee disclosure.]

A mid-2012 final rule revises the procedure for mailing or e-filing certain notices with DOL under the ERISA § 408(b)(2) rules for fiduciary-level fee disclosure. Fiduciaries must file these notices to get prohibited transaction relief. Relief is available if, when fiduciaries find out that there has been a discovery failure, they make a written request for the missing information to the service provider. If the service provider does not comply within 90 days, the fiduciary must notify the DOL, either mailing a written notice to DOL, EBSA Office of Enforcement, P.O. Box 75296, Washington, D.C. 20013, or using the link at <www.dol.gov/ebsa/regs/feedisclosurefailurenotice.html>. The advantage of using the Website is that it provides immediate electronic confirmation that notice is received. [Final Rule, DOL EBSA, *Amendment Relating to Reasonable Contract or Arrangement Under Section 408(b)(2)—Fee Disclosure*, 77 Fed. Reg. 41678 (July 16, 2012)]

Fiduciaries must assess the potential risk of loss, and the cost to the plan, if the service provider causes loss to the plan and is indemnified. Furthermore, indemnification or waiver of liability that relates to willful misconduct or fraud is void as against public policy, and it is neither prudent nor reasonable for fiduciaries to agree to such provisions.

ERISA and IRS rules forbid fiduciaries to deal with plan assets in their own interest. Unless a PTE is available, they cannot provide investment advice to participants if the advice increases the fees of the fiduciaries or their affiliates. The PPA created a PTE for advisers who give advice for a fee under an eligible arrangement—one that either has fees that are not affected by the specific advice given, or that are based on a certified, objective computer model. The DOL issued final rules about this PTE on October 24, 2011, effective December 27, 2011. These rules are also referred to as § 408(g) regulations. The DOL's fact sheet on the regulations estimates that 16,000 investment advisory firms will be subject to the exemption, and will offer investment advice to plans with about 17 million participants and beneficiaries, some 3.5 million of whom will access the advice.

The fiduciaries subject to the rule include banks; insurance companies; broker-dealers; registered investment advisers; and their affiliates, employees, representatives, and agents. A party that develops or markets computer programs for financial advice is also deemed to be a fiduciary adviser. The investment advice arrangement must be authorized by a plan fiduciary who is objective, and the fiduciary advisor must obtain an independent audit each year. Arrangements permitted under earlier guidance can still be used.

The final rule says that a fee-leveling arrangement must:

- be based on generally accepted investment theories that consider historic returns of different asset classes over a defined period of time;

- consider the fees and expenses of the recommended investments;

- reflect the adviser's knowledge of the participant or beneficiary's needs—such as age, life expectancy, distance from retirement age, other assets and income sources, and investment preferences; and

- not base the adviser's fees or compensation on the investment options chosen by the participant (although in some circumstances, compensation or bonuses based on the organization's overall profitability will be permitted).

Computer models must employ generally accepted investment theories that consider fees and expenses and historic risks and returns. [76 Fed. Reg. 66637 (Oct. 27, 2011); see Prudential, *DOL Investment Advice Compliance Advisory* (December 2011) (benefitslink.com); Guest Article, Deloitte's Washington Bulletin, *Labor Department Finalizes* "Investment Education" *Regulation* (Oct. 31, 2011) (benefitslink.com)]

## [A] Fees

Nature proverbially abhors a vacuum, and given the general lack of success with stock-drop suits, unhappy plan participants have sought other causes of action. In recent years, they have often alleged that the value of their accounts was impaired by payment of excessive fees.

February 2009 saw the first significant ruling in the wave of ERISA litigation challenging excessive fees. The Seventh Circuit affirmed the dismissal of all claims in *Hecker v. Deere & Co.*, rejecting the plaintiff's theories about excessive fees and improper revenue sharing. In 2006, before the DOL proposals requiring disclosure, fiduciaries had no duty to inform participants about revenue sharing between service providers. As long as a plan offered a sufficient mix of investment options with different fees, it was not a breach of duty to choose one with fees that could be characterized as "excessive"—or to offer multiple choices, some of which might be imprudent. It was also permissible to select all funds from a single management company. The Seventh Circuit treated the DOL safe harbor as an affirmative defense. Certiorari was denied in early 2010 [*Hecker v. Deere & Co.*, 556 F.3d 575 (7th Cir. 2009), *cert. denied*, 130 S. Ct. 1141 (Jan. 19, 2010); see Steve Saxon, Saxon Angle: *Seventh Sojourn*, plansponsor.com (May 2009); Fred Reish and Bruce Ashton, *The New Take on 404(c): Confusion in the Federal Courts* (May 13, 2009) (benefitslink.com).

The plaintiffs alleged that Harris Associates LP charged twice as much for managing a fund family as it charged its independent clients for similar investment services. Harris said that its fees were at or only slightly above the median for comparable mutual funds. In 2010, the U.S. Supreme Court adopted the standard used by most federal courts, and held that the correct legal standard in an excessive fund fee case was whether the fees were so disproportionately large that they could not have been the product of arm's length bargaining. The case was remanded to the Seventh Circuit for reconsideration of its ruling that mutual fund managers can only be held liable if the allegedly excessive fees are fraudulent. [*Jones v. Harris*, 559 U.S. 335 (2010); see Fred Schneyer, *High Court Sides with Investors in Fee Case*, plansponsor.com (Mar. 30, 2010]

The Supreme Court vacated an Eighth Circuit decision about whether mutual fund fees violated § 36(b) of the Investment Company Act. The Eighth Circuit had relied on the marketplace to prevent excessively high fees from being imposed. However, the U.S. Supreme Court remanded the case to comply with *Jones v. Harris*, where the standard is whether a fee is so unreasonably large that obviously there was no arm's length bargaining between the fund and its clients. [*Ameriprise Fin. Inc. v. Gallus*, 130 S. Ct. 2340 (2010); see Rebecca Moore, *Supreme Court Sends Investment Adviser Fee Case Back to 8th Circuit*, plansponsor.com (Apr. 6, 2010)] The Eighth Circuit considered the case twice on remand, in March 2011 and April 2012. The 2012 decision held that the plaintiffs did not prove that the fees were so disproportionately large that they could not have been bargained for and could not be reasonable for the services rendered.

[*Gallus v. Ameriprise,* 675 F.3d 1173 (8th Cir. 2012); see Rebecca Moore, *Ameriprise Wins Excessive Fees Case,* plansponsor.com (Apr. 12, 2012)]

The Seventh Circuit ruled in late 2011 that it is lawful for plan administrators to offer only retail mutual funds as investments, concluding that market competition will keep the fees down to a reasonable level. Exelon's defined contribution plan had 32 investment options, 24 of them retail mutual funds (all no-load, with expense ratios in the range of 0.03%–0.96%). The plaintiffs' theory was that it violated ERISA to require plan participants to pay the same fees as the general public. They also alleged that the plan should have offered institutional-class funds. The Seventh Circuit held that fiduciaries do not have to find the least-expensive funds; their duty is to offer a range of funds. Furthermore, retail funds have greater liquidity than institutional funds, and retail funds do not necessarily charge higher fees. The Seventh Circuit found that ERISA does not impose a duty to make the plan more valuable to participants; it is legitimate for the employer to act in its own interests when deciding how much to contribute. [*Loomis v. Exelon,* 658 F.3d 667 (7th Cir. 2011); see Erin M. Adams, *Win, Win,* Case Sensitive, plansponsor.com (Nov. 28, 2011); Nevin E. Adams, *Another Plan Sponsor Win on Revenue Sharing,* plansponsor.com (Sept. 26, 2011)]

Since 2006, there have been numerous lawsuits about 401(k) plan fees, but no clear trend has emerged. These suits usually allege that a plan paid excessive fees, as a result of practices such as sharing fees with service providers, stocking the plan with actively managed funds instead of lower-fee index funds, and investing in more expensive share classes. The Ninth Circuit held that the six-year statute of limitations began when the decision was made to include the allegedly improper investment in the plan. Although fiduciaries have an ongoing duty to be prudent, the statute of limitations is six years rather than the three years under the "actual knowledge" standard. The *Moench* presumption was applied. The Ninth Circuit held that fiduciaries can be liable based on selecting the plan's investment option; the § 404(c) safe harbor does not apply to designating investment options. The Ninth Circuit said that revenue sharing is not a prohibited transaction; there is a prohibited transaction exemption that says that revenue sharing does not constitute "consideration" given to the fiduciaries. Including retail funds (rather than only institutional funds) is not per se imprudent, and short-term funds can also be included in the portfolio. However, in the case of three specific mutual funds, it was imprudent to include the retail fund rather than its institutional counterpart because the plan failed to analyze the differences between the two. Even though they used a consultant, the fiduciaries still had an obligation to consider all the available share classes for the fund. [*Tibble v. Edison,* No. 711 F.3d 1061 (9th Cir. 2013); see Scott J. Stitt, *An Overview of the Tibble v. Edison Decision From the Ninth Circuit Concerning the Fees Charged to Participants in a 401(k) Plan,* James E. Arnold & Associates, LPA arnlaw.com (Mar. 24, 2013) (law.com) The Ninth Circuit denied rehearing in August 2013, amending the opinion but reaffirming the principle that the six-year statute of limitations applies. The amended opinion noted that there are circumstances in which plan administrators will not be entitled to deference, such as failure to look out for the best interests of plan participants, but did not find such circumstances present. [See Thomas E. Clark Jr., *Breaking: 9th Circuit Amends Tibble v. Edison Opinion on Rehearing*, FRA Plan Tools (Aug. 2, 2013) (benefitslink.com)]

The Fourth Circuit held that plaintiffs did not have standing to sue the Bank of America for investing defined benefit plan assets in funds affiliated with the bank. The plaintiffs did not allege any injury in fact because they did not say that they were deprived or benefits or likely to be deprived of them in the future. The Fourth Circuit has read Supreme Court precedents to mean that defined benefit plan participants only have an interest in their own future payments, not the fund's assets. The Supreme Court has not decided whether the possibility that a plan will terminate while it is underfunded and when the PBGC will not pay full benefits constitutes injury in fact, and the Fourth Circuit was unwilling to rule on that issue in this case. The Fourth Circuit also dismissed similar claims about the 401(k) plan. The plaintiffs alleged that each time the plan committee met and failed to remove the funds that were affiliated with the bank was a new fiduciary breach. However, the Fourth Circuit found that this claim was time-barred, because the statute of limitations was six years from the initial selection of the funds in 1999; the suit was not brought until 2006. [*David v. Alphin*, 704 F.3d 327 (4th Cir. 2013); see Plansponsor staff, *Bank of America Wins Suit Over Affiliated Fund Use*, plansponsor.com (Jan. 22, 2013)]

The Eighth Circuit vacated the dismissal of claims in the *Braden v. Wal-Mart* case, holding that there is a fiduciary duty to disclose material information, and a reasonable finder of fact could conclude that information about revenue sharing would be material to plan participants. *Braden* was subsequently settled. Wal-Mart and Merrill Lynch received final approval of the $13.5 million settlement in late 2011. Merrill, as trustee, agreed to pay $10 million because the plan had only 10 choices, all of them retail mutual funds. Wal-Mart agreed to pay the balance. (The suit had been dismissed in 2008 but was reinstated in late 2009; the Eighth Circuit found it reasonable to infer that the fund selection process was invalid.) The settlement fund is applied first to provide notice of settlement to all class members; then attorneys' fees of up to 30% of the fund; and $20,000 to the named plaintiff. The rest of the settlement was devoted to reducing future plan fees; it was agreed that it would be too costly to compensate the very large class of plaintiffs a small amount apiece. Two years of injunctive relief was also granted, including better financial education for plan participants and removing all retail mutual funds and funds that pay 12b-1 fees from the plan. This was the fifth class settlement in a 401(k) fund selection suit; the other settlements ranged from $13.7 million to $18.5 million plus non-monetary relief. [*Braden v. Wal-Mart Stores Inc.*, No. 08-cv-3109 (GAF) (W.D. Mo. settled Dec. 5, 2012); see Thom Weidlich, *Bloomberg, Wal-Mart 401(k) Accord Approved* (Mar. 8, 2012) (benefitslink.com), William P. Barrett, Forbes, *Wal-mart, Merrill Lynch Agree To Pay $13.5 Million to Settle 401(k) Fiduciary Lawsuit*, Forbes (Dec. 5, 2011) (benefitslink.com)]

The Third Circuit, joining the Seventh and Eighth Circuits, allowed the district court to dismiss an ERISA breach of fiduciary duty claim premised on including funds in the 401(k) plan that had excessive fee profiles—as long as the fiduciary selected a sufficiently broad range of funds with varying fee characteristics. In this case, the plaintiffs said that including retail mutual funds in the plan breached fiduciary duty because the fees were excessive. However, the Unisys 401(k) plan had 73 different investment options, including 67 individual retail mutual funds of varying characteristics, so the Third Circuit found that there was an appropriate range of options. The Third Circuit held that Fidelity was not a fiduciary for the purpose of selecting plan options; it was merely a directed trustee that could not control the investment options. Although the plan sponsor asserted the § 404(c) safe harbor, the Third Circuit refused to rule on this issue because it had already decided that the complaint was properly dismissed. [*Renfro v. Unisys Corp.*, 671 F.3d 314 (3d Cir. 2011); see Richard Black, *The Latest Word on 401(k) Fee Litigation: Third Circuit Narrows Plaintiffs' Ability to Bring ERISA Breach of Fiduciary Duty Claims*, Littler Mendelson ASAP (August 2011) (benefitslink.com); Rebecca Moore, *Court Upholds Decision for Fidelity Unisys in Excessive Fee Case*, plansponsor.com (Sept. 9, 2011)]

When a plan sponsor paid investment management fees directly, not from plan assets, there was no transaction with a party in interest and no self-dealing, and thus no violation of ERISA § 406. The Northern District of California held in late 2008 that it was permissible to offer six investment options at different risk levels (a normal number for plans of that type), and the fiduciaries regularly reviewed investment performance and considered other options. However, the court allowed claims to proceed with respect to a four-month period when investment fees were paid from plan assets. [*Kanawai v. Bechtel Corp.*, No. C 06-05566 CRB (N.D. Cal. Nov. 3, 2008); see Rebecca Moore, *No ERISA Breach Where Fees Not Paid by Plan*, plansponsor.com (Nov. 11, 2008)]

The Eighth Circuit ruled that a participant in an overfunded defined benefit plan did not have standing to sue the plan for fiduciary breach. The plaintiff said that the plan engaged in prohibited transactions when it invested in funds offered by its subsidiaries and affiliates, resulting in abnormally high fees. The plan was always overfunded, and paid all the benefits owed to participants. The existence of the surplus meant that the plan's investment loss did not cause actual injury to the plaintiff's interest in the plan. The court said that a contrary ruling would allow participants to sue on behalf of the plan when they had not experienced injuries. [*McCullough v. Aegon*, 585 F.3d 1082 (8th Cir. 2009); *Court Says Participant in Overfunded DB Plan Has No Standing*, plansponsor.com (Nov. 4, 2009). See *Harley v. Minnesota Mining & Mfg. Co.*, 248 F.3d 901 (8th Cir. 2002)]

After summary judgment was granted for the defendant in an excessive fee class action about a 401(k) plan, the Seventh Circuit reversed in part, on the issue of whether it was prudent to maintain the company stock fund as a unitized fund with no trading limits. The Seventh Circuit also reversed summary judgment for the defendants on the issue of whether it was prudent to pay $43–$65 per participant per year for recordkeeping services, when the plan had not solicited bids for these services since 1995. Relying on an expert can be evidence of prudence, but is not enough, taken by itself, to establish prudence. The company apparently did not take its expert's advice that fees should drop as the size of the plan increased. [*George v. Kraft Foods Global, Inc.*, 641 F.3d 7869 (7th Cir. 2011); see Goodwin Procter, *Seventh Circuit Requires 401(k) Plan Fiduciaries to Stand Trial Where They Did Not Seek an RFP for Plan Recordkeeping Services Every Three Years* (June 16, 2011) (benefitslink.com); Rebecca Moore, *Kraft Suit Plaintiffs Denied Class Status on Remaining Claim*, plansponsor.com (Oct. 31, 2011). The suit was settled for $9.5 million in 2012: No. 1:08-cv-3799 (N.D. Ill. Feb. 29, 2012); see Rebecca Moore, *Settlement Entered in Kraft Excessive Fees Case*, plansponsor. com (Mar. 7, 2012); Rose Bouboushian, *Kraft Settles Claims of 401(K) Mismanagement*, Courthouse News Service (Mar. 6, 2012) (law.com)]

## § 15.18   ERISA LITIGATION

### [A]   Generally

The provisions of ERISA are enforced both by the federal government and by private litigation.

In ERISA litigation, as in many other types of cases involving plans, the basic questions include who can be sued, who is a proper plaintiff (especially in the class action context), the proper court for the case, when the suit must be filed to be timely, and what remedies can be ordered if the case is proved.

Jury trials are usually unavailable in ERISA § 502(a)(1)(B) and (a)(3) cases. Another possibility is that a jury will be empanelled in these cases, but it will only determine the part of the case relating to breach of contract. The judge in the case will decide claims of breach of fiduciary duty.

By and large, ERISA cases are treated like contract cases. Therefore, the damages available to a winning plaintiff basically put the plaintiff in the position he or she would have been in if the contract had been complied with. "Extracontractual" damages (like damages for negligent or intentional infliction of emotional distress) will probably not be available. In most ERISA cases, punitive damages are also ruled out.

In any ERISA action brought by participants, beneficiaries, or fiduciaries, the winning side (whether plaintiff or defendant) can be awarded reasonable costs and attorneys' fees if the court thinks this is appropriate. Usually the attorneys' fee award starts out with the "lodestar" figure. This is the number of hours the winning lawyer spent on the case, multiplied by an hourly rate the court considers reasonable. In rare cases, the lodestar is reduced: if the court thinks the lawyer wasted time, for instance. Sometimes the fee award is greater than the lodestar amount, if the case was especially difficult, the lawyer broke new ground with innovative legal theories, or took on an unpopular case.

Thanks to a 2010 Supreme Court decision, § 502(g)(1) plaintiffs do not have to be the "prevailing party" to be awarded attorneys' fees, because that section (unlike § 502(g)(2)) gives the district court discretion to award attorneys' fees to either side. [*Hardt v. Reliance Ins. Co.*, 560 U. S. 242 (2010); see Workplace Prof Blog, *ERISA Supreme Court Attorney Fees Case Goes Way of Plaintiffs* (May 24, 2010) (benefitslink.com)] But that ruling left questions open, such as whether remand of a benefits decision to the administrator is enough (because it gives the claimant the possibility of receiving additional benefits), or whether a court finding of ERISA violation is required. The "prevailing party" analysis has been replaced by a more fact-intensive consideration of success on the merits—so defendants may have to pay the plaintiff's fees even if the case is settled or withdrawn. [See Renee DeMoss, *Attorney Fee Awards Under ERISA: How Much Success Is Enough?* GableGotwals Insurance Law Update (Sept. 19, 2011) (benefitslink.com)]

As Chapter 40 shows, arbitration assumes an increasingly large role in the resolution of disputes within the U.S. legal system. The Ninth Circuit ruled that the arbitration clause in an investment management agreement between an employer and its investment advisor did not obligate a plan participant to arbitrate fiduciary breach claims. There was no proof that the participant knowingly exploited the agreement that included the arbitration clause. There was no evidence that the agreement, which was not signed by the plan participants, was intended to affect their rights to sue. [*Comer v. Micor Inc.*, 436 F.3d 1098 (9th Cir. 2006)]

## [B] Preemption

In many instances, cases involving benefits will have to be brought in federal rather than state courts, because of ERISA preemption. According to the Seventh Circuit [*Metro. Life Ins. Co. v. Johnson*, 297 F.3d 558 (7th Cir. 2002)], the federal doctrine of "substantial compliance" preempts state law for suits involving alleged changes in the beneficiaries of a plan. In this case, life insurance benefits went to the children of a deceased beneficiary who failed to fully comply with the plan's provisions for beneficiary designation, because the court ruled that the decedent gave proof of his intent and took steps to carry out a change of beneficiary.

In its *Aetna Health Inc. v. Davila*, and *Cigna Healthcare of Texas, Inc. v. Calad*, 542 U.S. 200 (2004), decision, the Supreme Court ruled that ERISA completely preempts HMO participants' claims that they were improperly denied health care.

In general, ERISA will preempt state laws in cases requiring interpretation of plan documents. There is an exception to preemption for "the business of insurance"—so a number of cases deal with the question of whether federal or state courts should handle certain cases in which health or other insurance is involved in a benefit plan.

The preemption issue is very significant in these emotive cases, because if the case can be heard in state court, punitive damages could be available—and a sympathetic jury could impose heavy punitive damages.

In mid-2009, the Sixth Circuit and the District Court for the District of Colorado ruled that ERISA does not preempt state laws forbidding discretionary language in insurance policies in ERISA plans, because of the savings clause (state laws that "regulate insurance" are not preempted). [*American Council of Life Insurers v. Ross*, 558 F.3d 600 (6th Cir. 2009); *McClenahan v. Metro. Life Ins. Co.*, 621 F. Supp. 2d 1135 (D. Colo. 2009); see EBIA Weekly, *ERISA Does Not Preempt State Laws Preventing Insurers From Including Discretionary Language in Insurance Policies* (May 28, 2009) (benefitslink.com)]

But preemption was held not to occur in certain instances:

- A plan brought state claims (e.g., malpractice, breach of contract, promissory estoppel) against its actuary, claiming that the actuary's wrongdoing resulted in the plan being underfunded. However, the actuary was not a fiduciary and the Second Circuit held that ERISA does not preempt state-law negligence claims against nonfiduciaries. But the court also ruled that the remedies under ERISA are the only remedies available—the plan could not get consequential damages against the actuary. [*Gerosa v. Savasta & Co.*, 329 F.3d 317 (2d Cir. 2003)]

- Claims of malpractice, negligent misrepresentation, and breach of contract were brought by ESOP participants against an investment firm they allege undervalued that plan's stock during the process of terminating the plan. (When the company was sold after the plan was terminated, the per-share price was much higher than the price plan participants received for their ESOP shares.) Resolving the charges against the investment firm did not require interpretation of the plan, so the case could be remanded to state court. ERISA's civil enforcement provisions were not triggered because the plaintiffs did not charge fiduciary breach, nor did they seek to recover plan benefits. [*Clark v. Ameritas Inv. Corp.*, D. Neb., No. 4:05CV3251 (Dec. 27, 2005)]

See § 15.09[B] for discussion of developments in the treatment of subrogation and removal of cases to federal court. Also note that, for cases filed after the February 18, 2005, effective date of the Class Action Fairness Act (Pub. L. No. 109-2), the federal system may be the only appropriate venue for certain class actions brought by health plan participants.

## [C]  Exhaustion of Remedies

The court system is supposed to handle major conflicts, not minor everyday disputes that can and should be addressed in less complex and less socially expensive ways. Therefore, plaintiffs often have a legal duty of "exhaustion of remedies." That is, they will not be permitted to bring court cases until they have pursued all the administrative remedies within the system they are challenging. ERISA requires every plan to have a system for pursuing claims and appealing claims denials. So the general rule is that would-be plaintiffs must go through these steps before filing suit. This is not stated in so many words in ERISA itself, but judges have looked to ERISA's legislative history and other labor laws to determine when this requirement should be implied.

Plaintiffs clearly have to exhaust their remedies within the plan when their case involves benefits. Courts are split as to whether ERISA § 510 plaintiffs (interference with protected rights; see above) are required to exhaust their remedies. Exhaustion of remedies will not be required if:

- Going through channels would be futile;

- It was impossible to pursue plan remedies because the defendant wrongfully denied the plaintiff access to the plan's claims procedures;

- Irreparable harm would ensue if exhaustion of remedies was required;

- Participants and beneficiaries did not know how to enforce their rights, because they were deprived of information about claims procedures.

A group of Federal Express drivers obtained certification of an ERISA § 502(a)(1)(B) class action in 2007; they argued that they were really employees who had been mis-classified as independent contractors. In 2010, the Northern District of Illinois dismissed the case for failure to exhaust administrative remedies, although the drivers argued that they were denied access to review and it would have been futile to seek plan remedies when FedEx had always denied that they were entitled to participate in six kinds of plans. [*In re FedEx Ground Package System Inc. Employment Practices Litigation*, No. 3:05-md-00527 (N.D. Ill. 2010); see Rebecca Moore, *Judge Dismisses FedEx Drivers' ERISA Claims*, plansponsor.com (June 30, 2010)]

## [D]  Statute of Limitations

ERISA § 525 permits a civil action against an employer for delinquency in making contributions. This section does not contain an express statute of limitations; most courts use a six-year statute of limitations, treating the case as the equivalent of an action to enforce a written contract.

The statute of limitations for an ERISA § 409 case (breach of fiduciary duty) derives from ERISA § 413. The suit must be brought within three years of the time the plaintiff discovered the alleged wrongdoing, or six years from the date of the last breach or the last date on which the omission could have been cured—whichever is earlier.

The Third Circuit found that ERISA's six-year statute of limitations for fiduciary breaches barred claims about misrepresentations of pension benefits. The statute began to run when the allegedly misleading statements were made, not when the participants relied on the representations to their detriment. [*Ranke v. Sanofi-Synthelabo Inc.*, 436 F.3d 197 (3d Cir. 2006)]

According to the Ninth Circuit, an ERISA cause of action accrues either at the time the claim is actually denied, or when the claimant has reason to know of the denial. Therefore, a suit was untimely even though the pension plan violated its duties under ERISA to give the employee reasons for the denial and a reasonable opportunity for review. He knew that the employer was going to pay benefits below the level he expected, because of a break in service; he also had actual notice that the decision to accept a lump-sum payout would be irrevocable. [*Chuck v. Hewlett Packard Corp.*, 455 F.3d 1026 (9th Cir. 2006); see Rebecca Moore, *ERISA Claim Is Time-barred in Spite of Disclosure Violation*, plansponsor.com (Aug. 4, 2006)]

Similarly, the Sixth Circuit ruled that a suit was untimely where trustees began to worry about their financial advisor some six to seven years before bringing suit. [*Wright v. Heyne*, 349 F.3d 321 (6th Cir. 2003)] The Third and Fifth Circuits start the statute of limitations running with knowledge that the facts constitute a breach of fiduciary duty; the Sixth, Seventh, Ninth, and Eleventh Circuits use the knowledge of the underlying facts; and the Second Circuit uses a hybrid test—knowledge of all the facts necessary to constitute a claim, including expert opinions and understanding of harmful consequences.

The Second Circuit held that the district court properly used New York's borrowing statute to determine limitations period for an ERISA § 502 pension benefits claim. Plan participants living in Pennsylvania said that elimination of many participants through layoffs and divestitures was a partial termination entitling them to accrued benefits. They sued in 2009 concerning benefits claims made in 2003. The suit would have been timely if it were filed in New York, where the statute of limitations would be six years, but the Pennsylvania four-year statute of limitations applied, so the suit was untimely. Because § 502(a)(1)(B) does not prescribe an explicit statute of limitations, the courts usually "borrow" the relevant state statute of limitations. The only reason not to bring this suit in Pennsylvania was that the case was untimely; the Second Circuit deterred forum shopping by applying the Pennsylvania rule. [*Muto v. CBS Corp.*, 668 F.3d 53 (2d Cir. 2012); see CCH Pensions & Benefits, *District Court Properly Applied Forum State's Borrowing Statute to Determine Limitations Period for Pension Benefits Claim* (Mar. 30, 2012) (benefitslink.com)]

Because § 510 does not include an explicit statute of limitations, the First Circuit held that the *state* statute of limitation for the most similar type of case should be applied in § 510 cases. Furthermore, the First Circuit used the state's three-year statute of limitations for personal injury cases, not the six-year statute of limitations for contract cases—so the plaintiff's suit was dismissed as time-barred. [*Muldoon v. C.J. Muldoon & Sons Inc.*, 278 F.3d 31 (1st Cir. 2002)]

According to the First, Third, Seventh, Eighth, Ninth, and District of Columbia Circuits, the six-year statute of limitations under ERISA § 413 "in case of fraud or concealment," can be applied only when both fraud and concealment are charged. The Second Circuit disagrees, allowing the six-year statute of limitations for claims of either fraud or concealment. [*Caputo v. Pfizer Inc.*, 267 F.3d 181 (2d Cir. 2001)]

In a case that did not allege separate dishonest concealment, the Sixth Circuit rejected application of a six-year statute of limitations in a suit against a plan administrator and employer whose pension calculations were allegedly inaccurate. The plaintiffs sued for breach of fiduciary duty, for accounting, restitution, and other ERISA equitable relief; fraud; negligence; and promissory estoppel. The district court found all the claims to be time-barred. The plaintiffs obtained actual knowledge of the events in 2003, so their suit would be timely under a six-year but not under a three-year statute of limitations. The plaintiffs also sued their union, but the Sixth Circuit held that the plaintiffs did not prove that the union was an ERISA fiduciary. The Sixth Circuit held that the non-ERISA claims such as fraud and negligence were preempted by ERISA. [*Cataldo v. United States Steel Corp.*, 676 F.3d 542 (6th Cir. 2012); see Sam D'Orazio, *Case Sensitive:Statute of Limitations*, plansponsor (magazine) (November 2012)]

If the source of the suit is a fiduciary's omission rather than a wrongful action, the time limit is six years from the last date the fiduciary could have cured the problem.

Some courts have upheld the practice of reducing litigation risk by placing a time limitation in the plan documents. The Second Circuit upheld a three-year statute of limitations, running from the time when written proof of loss had to be furnished. The court cited cases from the Fifth, Sixth, Seventh, and Eighth Circuits permitting limitations on statutes of limitations. However, any such requirement in a plan must be disclosed. (In this case, if there had been no limitation in the plan, the six-year statute under state law would have been applied.) [*Burke v. PriceWaterhouseCoopers LLP Long Term Disability Plan*, 572 F.3d 76 (2d Cir. 2009), see ERISA Fiduciary Guidebook, *Second Circuit Upholds Three-Year Limitation Period in Plan Document* (July 12, 2009) (benefitslink.com). See also *Solien v. Raytheon LTD Plan #590*, No. cv 07-456, 2008 WL 2323915 (D. Ariz. June 2, 2008), holding that, although a one-year limitation was reasonable, it could not be enforced because it was not properly communicated to participants.]

Certiorari has been granted in a case on the issue of whether a plan's contractual limitations period can require an employee to file suit before it is possible to exhaust administrative remedies. In this case, the plan required suit to be filed within three years of the time proof of loss was required; it is possible that this time would end before the plan had made a final determination and all internal appeals had been completed. The plaintiff argued that ERISA is designed to require participants to exhaust their administrative remedies before bringing suit. [*Heimeshoff v. Hartford Life & Accident Ins. Co.*,No. 12-729, *cert. granted* (Apr. 15, 2013)]

## § 15.19 CORRECTION PROGRAMS

### [A] Plan Deficiency Aids

One of the central tenets of tax and ERISA enforcement for plans is that, wherever possible, plans should be encouraged to determine where they fall short of compliance, and to correct the problems before regulators detect them. The IRS publishes Alert Guidelines, Explanations, & Plan Deficiency Paragraphs [<http: //www.irs.gov/retirement/article/0,,id=97188,00.html>] so businesses can see the standards that IRS reviewers use when they review retirement plans for compliance. Each worksheet comes with explanatory text. The IRS Checksheets, also known as Plan Deficiency Paragraphs, are standardized text that plans can use to draft provisions that will satisfy IRS requirements.

### [B] Voluntary Correction

The IRS has engaged in ongoing efforts to allow plans to correct failures without losing qualification. The Department of Labor encourages voluntary return to compliance by plan administrators.

The Employee Plans Compliance Resolution System (EPCRS) provides three levels of corrections of inadvertent errors that do not involve deliberate engagement in abusive tax strategies (e.g., inappropriate tax shelters):

- The Self-Correction Program (SCP) allows the least complex types of plans (403(b), SEPs, and SIMPLE IRAs) to correct minor operational failures. These corrections are performed purely in house, do not generate penalties, and need not involve or even be disclosed to the IRS.

- The Voluntary Correction Program (VCP) permits a plan sponsor who detects mistakes before an audit to correct those mistakes and pay a fee that is smaller than the penalties that would be imposed on deficiencies uncovered in an audit.

- The Correction on Audit Program (Audit CAP) permits correction in response to an audit, with sanctions reflecting the extent and seriousness of the deficiency.

EPCRS procedures are revised frequently. Most recently, Rev. Proc. 2013-12, 2013-6 I.R.B. 478 updates EPCRS, superseding Rev. Proc. 2008-50, revising the VCP submission procedures. There are rules for plans subject to § 436 restrictions and the safe harbor correction methods and fee structures have been changed. Under prior law, corrections for missed matching contributions had to be made as qualified non-elective contributions, which were 100% vested immediately. The new rules allow some corrective matching contributions to be made. A plan that provides elective deferrals and non-elective employer contributions can use the self-correction program if it corrects annual additions greater than permitted by § 415(c) by returning elective deferrals to the employees—but the return of elective deferrals must occur within two and a half months after the end of the plan's limitation year. There is also a limited extension of the self-correction program correction period and the 150-day VCP correction period for some plan sponsors trying to find lost participants and who can n longer rely on the IRS' letter forwarding program. Plans must submit Forms 8950 (VCP application) and 8951 (compliance fee) with their VCP submission. The IRS processes fees by converting checks to electronic funds transfers, which take less time to process. Therefore, plans writing checks for VCP fees must be sure that there are available funds to satisfy the funds transfer.

Appendix C to this Revenue Procedure contains the model VCP submission documents, which must be used as published by the IRS without modification. In addition to the Model Compliance Statement, the Revenue Procedure includes schedules dealing with, for example, SIMPLE IRAs, plan loan failures, and failure to distribute excess elective deferrals. [Rebecca Moore *IRS Updates Compliance Resolution System*, plansponsor.com (Jan. 3, 2013); H. Vicky Chen, *Recent Changes to the IRS Employee Plans Compliance Resolution System*, Perkins Coie News 9 (Jan. 23, 2013) (benefitslink.com); Rebecca Moore, *IRS Voluntary Correction Program Forms Available*, plansponsor.com (Jan. 25, 2013); IRS.gov, updated Jan. 23, 2013 *Correcting Plan Errors—Fill-in VCP Submission Documents*; SunGard Relius, *The New EPCRS, Just Released!* (Jan. 3, 2013) (benefitslink.com)]

Rev. Proc. 2012-35, 2012-37 I.R.B. 341 states that, for requests postmarked on or after August 31, 2012, the IRS will no longer forward letters on behalf of retirement plan sponsors, administrators, or trustees of abandoned plans. The IRS changed its policy in light of the other options available to find missing participants. The change affects sponsors and administrators who want to use EPCRS to correct failures requiring payment of additional benefits, so future EPCRS guidance will give an extended correction period for those affected by the change. [Plansponsor staff, *IRS Stops Forwarding Letters for Missing Participants*, plansponsor.com (Sept. 4, 2012)]

See <http://www.dol.gov/ebsa/actuarialsearch.html> for EBSA's online tools for employees and employers. When civil penalties are due for delinquent filings of annual reports, the tools permit plan administrators to return to compliance under the Delinquent Filer Voluntary Compliance Program by filing the overdue reports.

Plan administrators can use the Delinquent Filer Voluntary Compliance Program (DFVCP) to reduce the civil penalties they may be subject to—as long as they make the required DFVCP filings before the DOL gives the administrator written notice of failure to file a timely annual report under ERISA Title I. (Form 5500-EZ filers and filers of Form 5500 for one-participant plans for business proprietors are not eligible for DFVCP because they are not covered by Title I.) An IRS late-filer penalty letter won't keep plan from participating in DFVCP, but a DOL Notice of Intent to Assess Penalty always does.

The EFAST2 FAQ explains how to file a delinquent Form 5500 under DFVCP, and the DOL has posted an online penalty calculator for DFVCP. For a small plan (one with fewer than 100 participants at the beginning of the plan year) the reduced penalty is $10 per day that the annual report was late (not counting extensions), up to a maximum penalty of $750. If there is more than one delinquent annual report filing for the same plan, the penalty is $750 per annual report, subject to a $1,500 per plan maximum. For a large plan that is not eligible for "80/120" relief under 29 C.F.R. § 2520.130-1(d), the penalty is $10 per day of late filing, capped at $2,000, or, for multiple late filings, $2,000 per report and capped at $4,000 per plan.

> ■ **TIP:** All filings for a plan should be sent in the same envelope, to make sure that the per-plan caps will be applied.

DFVCP penalties can be paid by check, sending the check and a paper copy of Form 5500, or Form 5500-SF, or the plan (without attachments or schedules) to DFVCP, P.O. Box 71361, Philadelphia, PA 19176-1361. The penalties can also be paid electronically at <https://www.askebsa.dol.gov/dfvcpay/calculator>.

A plan administrator who does not file a timely annual report and who does not participate in DFVCP can be charged $50 a day (no limits) for late filing and $300 a day for failure to file an annual report, subject to a $30,000 per year limit, until a complete annual report is filed. Plan administrators are personally liable for ERISA § 502(c) civil penalties, and the penalties cannot be paid from the assets of an employee benefit plan.

Paying the DFVCP penalty waives the right to receive notice of assessment from the DOL—and to contest the DOL's assessed penalty amount. However, participating in the DFVCP does not necessarily provide relief from IRS or PBGC late-filing penalties, although the IRS and PBGC both announced that they would issue separate guidance on penalty relief for DFVCP participants. [DOL/EBSA, *FAQs about the Delinquent Filer Voluntary Compliance Program* (benefitslink.com). More info about DFVCP: <http;//www.efast.dol.gov>. See Prudential Pension Analyst, *DOL Updates Delinquent Filer Voluntary Compliance (DFVC) Program*, <http://www.retire.prudential.com/media/managed/EBSA_Updates_DFVC_Program-Final.pdf> (March 2013).]

EBSA announced in early 2013 that migration to the fully electronic EFAST2 system is complete for all filing years and paper filings will no longer be accepted. See the DOL Website for an explanation of which version of the Form 5500/5500SF is required for your plan, and which schedules to use. The announcement, which primarily deals with the DFVC program, says that, although DFVC does not offer relief from late filing penalties under the Code or ERISA Title IV, the PBGC has agreed to provide some ERISA § 4071 penalty relief for delinquent filings of annual reports if the conditions of the DFVC program are satisfied. The IRS announced that it would issue separate guidance on penalty relief for Form 5500/5500-SF delinquencies where both DFVC and IRS requirements are met. [Notice: <http://www.dol.gov/find/20130128>, FAQs at <http://www.dol.gov/ebsa/faqs/faq_dfvc.html>. See Rebecca Moore, *EBSA Updates Delinquent Filer Correction Program*, plansponsor.com (Jan. 28, 2013).]

CHAPTER 16

# EFFECT OF CORPORATE TRANSITIONS ON PENSION AND BENEFIT PLANS

## § 16.01   INTRODUCTION

A qualified plan can change its form for several reasons: by amendment, by termination, or as a response to a change in form in the corporation that sponsors the plan. The sponsoring corporation can merge with or be acquired by another company, and some or all of the first plan's employees can become employees of the new or surviving corporation. The transition may be primarily motivated by corporate needs or primarily to change the form or operation of the plan (e.g., combining several existing plans for ease of administration or to cut costs).

Basic fiduciary principles continue to apply during a transition, and plans must still be maintained for the sole benefit of participants and beneficiaries. Therefore, the Supreme Court decided that plan participants and beneficiaries can sue under ERISA § 502(a)(3) to get equitable relief for themselves, when a company spun off its money-losing divisions to a new, financially unstable corporation and then lied to employees about the safety of their benefits if they transferred to the new corporation. [*Varity Corp. v. Howe*, 516 U.S. 489 (1996)]

However, because pension benefits vest but welfare benefits (including retiree health and insurance benefits) generally do not, ERISA fiduciary duty is not violated by transferring the obligation to pay nonpension retiree benefits to a new company spun off from the former employer. Nor will the courts hear an ERISA contract claim.

A corporate transition can also affect the immigration status of L-1 and H-1B visa holders. If the visa holder's employer is purchased by another corporation in a 100% stock transaction, the purchaser becomes a successor in interest. In an asset transaction, however, it is more difficult to determine if the surviving corporation is a successor in interest. If the new owner absorbs a business unit, business line, or division that is clearly defined, and assumes liabilities (including those related to immigration), then non-immigrant visas, work authorization, and residency cases of non-citizen employees continue uninterrupted, as long as they continue to hold the job to which the visa relates. When the employees are transferred, the new owner should file an amendment with the USCIS, disclosing the change. The deal documents could be structured so that the buyer expressly assumes H-1B liabilities. However, entitlement to the visa can be jeopardized by changes in the worker's job location, duties, or compensation change. It is often necessary for the acquiring corporation to sponsor a new visa for the employees. [Elizabeth Espin Stern, *Don't Forget the Visa Holders*, Legal Times (Oct. 28, 2008) (law.com)]

IRS Form 5310-A, Notice of Plan Merger or Consolidation, Spinoff, or Transfer of Plan Assets or Liabilities is filed to give notice of the combination of two or more plans into a single plan, splitting a plan into two or more spinoff plans, or a transfer of assets or liabilities to another plan. However, Form 5310-A is not filed in certain cases, such as when defined contribution plans are merged, but the sum of the account balances in each plan equals the fair market value of the plan assets; or two defined benefit plans are merged when the total liabilities of the smaller plan are less than 3% of the assets of the larger plan.

## § 16.02  CHOICE OF FORM

### [A]  Generally

Companies considering a merger or acquisition must consider the plan design options that are available for the type of transaction selected. Nondiscrimination testing will probably be required, and there will be compliance requirements for the surviving plan. The presence or absence of golden parachutes, retiree health benefit obligations, and COBRA obligations must be determined. Worker Adjustment and Retraining Notification Act (WARN) [29 U.S.C. § 2101 *et seq.*] notification may also be required if there is a significant reduction in the workforce after the corporate transition. [See § 30.10] Plan discrimination testing must also be repeated after a change of corporate organization. [See § 4.22] Changes in ownership or the form of ownership of a corporation sponsoring a plan will frequently be "reportable events" of which the PBGC must be notified (in case the plan is unable to meet its payment obligations and the PBGC has to take over). The test of whether two companies are alter egos (and therefore one must make up for the other's delinquent contributions to a pension plan) comes from basic corporate law. Does one company control the other so closely that the second corporation has no independent existence? Is the second corporation only a sham used for fraudulent purposes?

For legal purposes, the purchase and sale of a company is usually handled as either a stock or asset sale. The agreement for the transaction should indicate who will become responsible for the retirement plan.

In a stock transaction, the seller conveys its business or ownership interest directly to the buyers, who then own the business, assuming the assets and liabilities of the seller. Unless the seller's retirement plan was terminated before the transaction, it will probably be assumed by the buyer.

In an asset sale, in contrast, the buyer acquires only the assets that it wants, and the seller continues to own the business and any assets that were not purchased. The seller will probably continue to be responsible for the retirement plan unless the buy/sell agreement is to the contrary.

Due diligence includes obtaining plan documents and an inventory of the existing retirement plans and incentive arrangements (e.g., ESOPs and nonqualified plans); learning the plan's investment policies; and what and where the plan's assets are. Some plans are written to make employees in an acquired company automatically eligible for the acquirer's plans, or vice versa. Information can be obtained from past government filings and audits, nondiscrimination tests, employment contracts, and benefit disputes. Acquirers should consider whether there are potential liabilities stemming from plan compliance issues, poorly drafted plan provisions, operational failures, or funding shortfalls.

There are three main options for handling pension and benefit plans in a corporate transition: maintaining separate plans; merging the plan into one or more of the acquirer's plans; or terminating the plans. The acquired corporation could be retained as a separate corporation within the acquirer's controlled group of corporations, or absorbed so that its separate corporate identity ends and its employees have become employees of the acquirer.

If the acquirer's intention is to have separate benefit structures for the acquiring and acquired corporations, it is probably simplest to maintain separate plans. But the acquirer's plan, the acquired company's plan, and all other plans in the controlled group must be able to satisfy the coverage requirements for qualified plans. All employees within the controlled group or affiliated service group must be included in testing.

Combining plans into a single plan can be simpler. It would only be necessary to file one Form 5500, not multiple forms; employee communications are easier if there is only one plan to explain; only one plan document and one SPD are required. However, unifying the benefit structures of two plans can lead to employee hostility (if benefits are reduced) or to additional expense (if benefits in the less generous plan are enhanced).

If plans are merged, participants joining the plan will probably have to be enrolled and given a chance to elect deferrals and investments. If a plan is terminated after an acquisition, it is likely to become the acquirer's responsibility, unless it is an asset sale. For 401(k) plans, the IRS rules about successor plans are unfavorable to plan termination. On the other hand, if a plan is terminated, then distributions can be made and then rolled over to the acquirer's plan or to an ongoing plan. Plan questions also arise when a business location or subsidiary is sold off. Participants who are no longer eligible employees should not be allowed to participate in the selling company's plan after the transaction.

There are three options for dispositions. The retirement plan funds can be distributed to plan participants; the funds and liabilities can be transferred to another plan; or the affected participants can be spun off from the plan into a separate plan, and the plan funds distributed to them. When a subsidiary is sold to an unrelated buyer who does not take control of the plan, plan funds can be distributed to the participants, who will be able to roll over their funds if the unrelated buyer has a qualified plan.

All employers involved in the transaction must agree to any transfer of funds and liabilities to another plan. If they do agree, then all service from the current plan is counted toward the plan to which the assets are transferred. Loans are transferred, and loan terms remain the same—even if the transferee plan does not allow loans.

In designing a new plan, it is important to remember the objectives of the original plan. The definition of "eligible employee" should be reviewed to make sure that employees do not become immediately eligible (unless that was the intention), and employees are not allowed continued participation in a plan for which they are no longer eligible.

It is not legally required that the new plan be identical to the old one, but certain benefits payable under the old plan may be protected, such as normal and early retirement pensions, disability benefits, forms of distribution, and accrued benefits. It may also be necessary to harmonize the vesting provisions of the old and new plans.

Due diligence for an acquisition includes reviewing the nondiscrimination test results for plans that might be acquired. The acquirer's decisions about the plans must be carried out in the buy/sell agreement, and any changes must be communicated to employees. [Principal Financial Group ThoughtCapital, *The Impact of Mergers, Acquisitions and Dispositions On Your Retirement Plan* (July 2010) (benefitslink.com); Lydell C. Bridgeford, *Plan Mergers May Yield Brighter Financial Future* (Feb. 1, 2008) (benefitslink.com)]

The buyer of a company that has a complex, underfunded single-employer defined benefit plan might prefer an asset sale to avoid taking on significant plan liability. The buyer might also prefer an asset sale where the extent of liabilities is not clear after due diligence has been performed. Conversely, a seller that contributes to a multi-employer plan, where withdrawal liability is significant or difficult to estimate, might prefer a stock deal.

In an asset transaction where the seller maintains plans at the parent level for all of its employees, but sells only part of the business, the buyer cannot assume the plan because the seller must continue maintaining it for the other employees. Consequently, the buyer in that situation will either have to merge the relevant part of the plan into its existing plan or structure the deal so that the seller distributes plan assets under § 401(k)(10). If the buyer maintains plans at the parent level, it may prefer to merge or transfer assets from the seller's plan into its own plan so that, after the closing, all of the employees will have a similar benefit structure. Where the buyer's subsidiaries and the purchased entity all have their own retirement plans, the buyer's options include negotiating to assume the plans after the closing; transferring assets; or creating a cloned plan after the closing covering the employees of the acquired entity. [PLC Employee Benefits & Executive Compensation, *Handling Qualified Retirement Plans in Mergers and Acquisitions* (Dec. 18, 2012) (benefitslink.com)]

After it sold a subsidiary company in 1999, Bowater took the position that it was no longer responsible for the subsidiary's benefit plans—either at the time of sale or in 2003, when all of Bowater's plans were consolidated into a single plan that did not cover retirees from the subsidiary, GNP. According to the First Circuit, the sale did not relieve Bowater of the liability (sale of a business often—but not always—terminates the seller's plan responsibilities), but the consolidated plan did by finally giving retirees and their beneficiaries clear notice that they were not entitled to benefits. The court rejected the argument that a promise of lifetime benefits to the retirees was broken: the retiree health benefits were limited to the duration of the CBA. [*Coffin v. Bowater Inc.*, 501 F.3d 80 (1st Cir.

2007); see Adrien Martin, *Court: Sale of Subsidiary Does Not Mean Shedding Benefits Responsibilities*, plansponsor.com (Sept. 10, 2007); *Senior v. NSTAR Elec. & Gas Co.*, 449 F.3d 206 (1st Cir. 2006) (a retiree's labor law rights were based on the language of the CBA in effect at the time of retirement)]

## [B] T.D. 8928

### [1] Generally

T.D. 8928, 66 Fed. Reg. 1843 (Jan. 10, 2001), provides that, when a corporation makes an asset sale (of substantially all the assets of a trade or business, or an asset as substantial as a factory or a corporate division), it is treated as the successor employer if the seller entirely ceases to provide group health plans, and the buyer maintains business operations using the assets. A transfer (e.g., in bankruptcy) is considered an asset sale if it has the same effect as a sale would have.

The plans that the seller maintained before the transaction could be retained, frozen, or terminated. A buyer who adopts an existing plan could agree to assume liability only going forward, with the seller retaining liability for violations of the plan rules that occurred before the sale. As for plans maintained by the buyer before the transaction, the buyer's and seller's plans could merge. [See below for the anticutback rules and the requirement of crediting prior service to the new plan]

Like all rules, this has exceptions. If the transaction is in effect a merger rather than an asset sale, liabilities will be characterized as they would be in a merger. If the buying corporation is a mere continuation of the selling corporation, or if the transaction is a fraud intended to escape liability, the transaction will be disregarded.

If only plan assets, and not the operating terms of the two plans, are merged, then the transaction is not considered a plan amendment that has the effect of reducing plan accruals. However, if the plans merge and one adopts the other's formulas and definitions, the original plan is deemed to have been amended. If benefits are reduced, notice must be given under ERISA § 204.

### [2] ERISA Issues

In most instances, duplicative plans are merged, or some of them are eliminated. The seller's plan generally transfers assets (and related liabilities) either to the buyer's existing plans or to a newly created plan. ERISA does not require employees to be represented in the negotiations; but once the deal is consummated, the surviving and new plans must be operated subject to fiduciary standards, and mandatory communications must be made to employees.

A corporation's decision to terminate or amend a plan, or to spin off part of a plan, is a discretionary "settlor" function, and the plan sponsor does not act as a fiduciary. The amount of assets to be assigned to a spun-off plan, or the decision to transfer employer securities to a new plan created as part of a spin-off, is not a fiduciary decision. However, the fiduciaries of the plan making the transfers must comply with the plan merger and asset transfer standards set out in ERISA § 208.

Many transactions are structured so that the buyer assumes the seller's responsibility for providing unfunded benefits, such as retiree health coverage. The seller's decision to transfer the liability, and the buyer's commitment to accept it, are also settlor functions and therefore cannot give rise to a claim for breach of fiduciary duty. However, ERISA § 208 does require that each participant receive at least as good a benefit package if the plan were terminated just after the transaction as he or she would have received if the plan had terminated just before the transaction. It should also be remembered that plan assets must not be used for purposes other than paying benefits.

The Third Circuit rejected a class action brought by 277 plaintiffs who said they were entitled to pensions from Siemens if their employment ended. The plaintiffs worked for Westinghouse before Siemens bought the unit where they worked in late 1997. The Westinghouse plan said that "permanent job separation" benefits would not accrue if employees were hired by the purchaser or their employment ended after 1998. The Third Circuit said that Siemens did not establish or maintain this plan, so it was not responsible for plan benefits. ERISA § 208 says that participants cannot be denied benefits if their plan consolidates with another plan or transfers its assets and liabilities to another plan. However, this section does not create entitlement to benefits that do not exist under the plan and ERISA § 204(g) does not protect cutback of an earlier retirement benefit for persons who do not satisfy the conditions for the benefit. These plaintiffs were offered employment by Siemens, so they did not qualify under the terms of the plan. [*Shaver v. Siemens Corp.*, 670 F.3d 462 (3d Cir. 2012); see Amaris Elliott-Engel, *3rd Circuit Rejects ERISA Benefits for Siemens Plaintiffs*, The Legal Intelligencer (Mar. 1, 2012) (law.com)]

The District Court for the Southern District of Ohio ruled in early 2013 that Anheuser-Busch does not owe enhanced benefits to ex-employees who took jobs with the company that purchased an Anheuser-Busch subsidiary, Metal Container Corp. Anheuser-Busch was acquired by InBev in 2008. The Metal Container Corp. was sold to Ball Corp. in 2009 and the plaintiffs became Ball employees. The plan said that, for three years after a change in control, the formulas for benefits and forms of payment would not be reduced. Plan participants involuntarily terminated within three years of a change in control received increased benefits. The district court found the denial of enhanced benefits was reasonable, given the intent in creating the plan, and an opinion from outside counsel that the plaintiffs were not involuntarily terminated—they retained their jobs and became employed by the successor corporation. The plaintiffs argued that they were involuntarily terminated because they were not working for an Anheuser-Busch subsidiary, but the court rejected this argument. [*Adams v. Anheuser-Busch Cos. Inc.*, No. 2:10-cv-826, 2013 U.S. Dist. LEXIS 3315 (S.D. Ohio Jan. 9, 2013); see Rebecca Moore, *Anheuser Busch Wins Change in Control Benefits Case*, plansponsor.com (Jan. 11, 2013)]

The Second Circuit held in 2009 that a claim of breach of fiduciary duty cannot be based on oral statements that alter plan terms. Plan participants alleged that they were told that pension accruals after a merger would take pre-merger service into account, but after the merger, accruals reflected only post-merger service. The Second Circuit said that even if those statements had been made, they could not alter the terms of the plan. [*Ladouceur v. Credit Lyonnais*, 584 F.3d 510 (2d Cir. 2009); see Mercer Select US, *Claim for Fiduciary Breach Can't Rest on Oral Statements Altering Plan Terms, Appeals Court Rules* (Oct. 8, 2009) (benefitslink.com)]

On another ERISA issue, the Ninth Circuit ruled in late 2002 that two companies violated ERISA § 510 (the ban on taking adverse employment action against a person to prevent access to plan benefits) when, under an asset purchase agreement, the seller's active employees were hired and given health coverage, but employees who were on extended leave of absence were denied coverage until they returned to work. [*Lessard v. Applied Risk Mgmt.*, 307 F.3d 1020 (9th Cir. 2002)] The Ninth Circuit ruled that it violates § 510 to select for presumptive termination and benefit loss on the basis of being on medical or disability leave. The seller would not have been able to terminate the benefits of employees because they took leave, so the buyer could not either. It was improper to structure the program so that the employees with the worst disabilities received the worst deal. The Ninth Circuit remanded the case to apportion liability between the buyer and seller companies.

The Seventh Circuit held that Abbott Laboratories and its spinoff Hospira, did not violate ERISA § 510 when Hospira was spun off. For a two-year period, Abbott and Hospira agreed not to hire each other's employees. Before the transaction, employees were covered by the Abbott pension plan; afterward, some employees were classified as Hospira employees, and Hospira had a 401(k) plan with an employer match but did not have a pension plan. Non-vested pension rights in the Abbott plan were eliminated for these employees. The no-hire agreement prevented them from retiring from Abbott before the spinoff, taking their pensions, and going back to work for Hospira. The Seventh Circuit held that Abbott and Hospira did not act with intent to interfere with pension benefits. The decision to spin off the division and set a no-hire policy was not motivated by employee benefits. The plaintiffs also sued for breach of fiduciary duty, but this claim failed because Abbott was not involved in the Hospira benefits plan and Abbott disclosed that the spinoff might alter employee benefits. [*Nauman v. Abbott Labs. and Hospira, Inc.*, 669 F.3d 854 (7th Cir. 2012); see Rebecca Moore, *Court Finds Decision to Spin Off Unrelated to Benefits*, plansponsor.com (Feb. 6, 2012)]

A group of terminated employees who were not rehired after their employer's facility was sold sued, alleging a conspiracy by the employer and the purchaser to violate ERISA § 510 by terminating older employees and depriving them of pension benefits. The Tenth Circuit ruled for the employer, holding that pension issues were not even considered until after the sale so they could not have motivated the sale. The acquiror re-hired 8,000 of the 10,000 workers at the facility. Both before and after the sale, most of the workers were over 40: but the percentage of over-40 workers rehired was lower than their share of the pre-acquisition workforce. The plaintiffs moved to certify a class of about 700 people who were not rehired. The Tenth Circuit held that § 510 is not violated if the employer acts on the basis of legitimate business reasons, even if the result is that some laid-off employees lose pension eligibility. [*Apsley v. Boeing Co.*, 691 F.3d 1184 (10th Cir. 2012); see Wolters Kluwer Law & Business News Center, *Employees Did Not Prove Intent By Seller And Buyer Companies To Interfere With Employees' Attainment Of Benefits* (Oct. 4, 2012) (benefitslink.com)]

During negotiations for purchase of a controlling interest in Capital Bank by another bank, Capital's CEO, Yarber, expected to remain as president. However, the potential purchaser said that the deal would be off unless Yarber and other Capital Bank executives acceded to changes in their employment agreements, including waiving their right to severance payments on change in control. Capital's Chairman of the Board threatened Yarber with being fired if he did not give up his right to severance benefits. The chairman told Yarber that shareholders could sue him for breach of fiduciary duty if the deal fell through because of his refusal. The deal did go through, and Yarber was fired and did not receive severance benefits. He brought an ERISA suit against Capital Bank. He said that the amendment to his contract was invalid for lack of consideration. However, the District Court for the Eastern District of North Carolina dismissed Yarber's case, finding that the amendments were valid. The amended contract did not call for severance benefits, and made him an at-will employee as of November 4, 2011, so he had no right to sue. [*Yarber v. Capital Bank Corp.*,No. 5:12-cv-71-D, 2013 WL 1127082 (E.D.N.C. Mar. 18, 2013); see Michael S. Melbinger, *Executive Does the Right Thing—and Gets Screwed For It!* (June 14, 2013) (benefitslink-.com)]

The Ninth Circuit ruled that severance pay provided to an executive who lost her job after a change in control did not constitute "wages and salary" and therefore did not have to be included in the computation of her retirement benefits. The court accepted the plan administrator's argument that the retirement benefit was based on earnings for services rendered. The severance payment in this case represented payment for voluntary termination of employment, waiver of potential claims, and entering into a confidentiality agreement and a covenant not to compete. [*Gilliam v. Nevada Power Co.*, 488 F.3d 1199 (9th Cir. 2007)]

## [C]   Labor Law Implications of Choice of Form

Labor law follows the basic rule that a merger or sale of stock obligates the acquiring company to assume the liabilities of the acquired or selling company. This includes the Collective Bargaining Agreement (CBA). But in an asset sale, the CBA is not assumed unless the purchaser voluntarily takes it on, or unless there is another reason to view the buyer as a successor or surrogate of the seller.

Yet even if the company is not fully bound by its predecessor's CBA, it could still have a duty to bargain in good faith with the existing union, based on continuity linking the old and new enterprises. If a transaction lacks real substance, the successor could be forced to assume the predecessor's labor-law obligations. The main test is whether there has been a significant practical change or whether operations continue despite a nominal change in ownership.

In addition to situations in which one entity replaces another, two or more enterprises can be treated as a "single employer" for labor-law purposes. One might be treated as an alter ego (surrogate) of the other. If a parent company and its subsidiary engage in the same line of business, the NLRB will probably treat them as a single enterprise, not two. Furthermore, "joint employers" that are separate entities but share decision making about labor issues may be treated together by the NLRB.

Either a purchaser must be prepared to take on the predecessor's union contracts and other labor-law obligations, or must structure the transaction to be free of such obligations. Also note that a change in corporate ownership (even if corporate structure remains the same) can lead the state to revoke the privilege to self-insure against Worker's Compensation claims.

A new company that adopts an existing operation can unilaterally change the wage scale, unless it's "perfectly clear" that the new owner will hire all of the old employees. In a "perfectly clear" case where the new owner does not consult with the union and there is no evidence of what would have emerged if there had been negotiations, the employees are given the benefit of the doubt. It is assumed that the former wage rate would have continued and would not have been diminished. So new ownership in a "perfectly clear" case cannot lead to wage cuts unless the union agrees.

In its 1999 decision in *St. Elizabeth's Manor* [329 N.L.R.B. 341 (1999)], the NLRB created a "successor bar" rule under which an incumbent union would be given a reasonable amount of time, after a corporate takeover, to bargain with the successor employer without challenges to the union's majority status. However, the NLRB overruled this decision in mid-2002. Under the new rule, in a successorship situation the incumbent union is entitled to rebuttable presumption of continuing majority status—but if there is evidence to rebut the presumption, an otherwise valid challenge to majority status will be allowed to proceed. [*MV Transportation*, 337 N.L.R.B. 129 (2002)]

When S&F Market Street Healthcare acquired a nursing home previously owned by Candlewood, it offered temporary employment to Candlewood employees. The NLRB treated S&F as a successor employer bound by Candlewood's CBA, because it did not notify employees that their terms and conditions of employment would change. However, the D.C. Circuit ruled in mid-2009 that S&F was not a successor, and it could implement new terms and conditions. Generally speaking, a successor that has not bargained for the CBA is not bound by the substantive terms of a predecessor's CBA, unless it is perfectly clear that the new employer plans to retain all of the former employees. The D.C. Circuit treated this as a narrow exception intended to prevent a new employer from deterring employees from applying for other jobs. In this case, it was obvious that significant changes would be made, and employees were warned that they were offered only temporary at-will employment and not all former employees would be retained. [*S&F Market Street Healthcare LLC v. NLRB*, 570 F.3d 354 (D.C. Cir. 2009)]

A construction company was sold to a non-union employer. To preserve jobs, the union entered into an agreement to withdraw its challenge to the transaction in exchange for the buyer continuing to make timely contributions to the ERISA plan, and the other to hire the existing workforce, with a new CBA to be negotiated. However, neither agreement covered successor liability for delinquent contributions. In early 2011, the Third Circuit held that it is settled law the successor liability can be imposed for delinquent contributions to an ERISA plan in the merger context, but this was not a merger, it was an asset sale. Nevertheless, the Third Circuit held the successor company liable, based on factors such as continuity of operations and workforce, the purchaser's knowledge of the plan, and the employees' inability to obtain relief from the seller corporation. [*Einhorn v. Ruberton Constr. Co.*, 632 F.3d 89 (3d Cir. 2011)]

## [D]  Transitions and Unemployment Insurance

Although it is a comparatively minor cost, the acquirer of a business may wish to take advantage of the amount of FUTA tax already paid by the transferor of the business for the part of the year before the transition. The successor employer can rely on wages paid (and therefore on FUTA payments made) by the predecessor if either one of two circumstances exists. The first is that the transferee acquires substantially all the property used in the transferor's entire trade or business (or in a separate unit of the trade or business). The other is that, whether or not the property was acquired, at least one employee from the old business remains employed immediately after the transfer.

■ **TIP:** A multistate operation will usually be permitted to combine wages paid in the various states for FUTA purposes.

The IRS' view, for FICA and tax withholding as well as FUTA purposes, is that, in a statutory merger or consolidation, the surviving corporation is the same taxpayer and the same corporation as the predecessor corporation(s). Of course, that means that the successor will have to pay any taxes due but unpaid by the predecessor—unless the successor gives the local administrative agency adequate written notice.

However, most state unemployment laws provide that companies remain subject to unemployment insurance laws for at least two years once they have acquired an experience rating—with the result that the transferor may remain liable in a year after it ceases operations, unless it applies to the local administrative agency for a determination that it is no longer an employer.

If the predecessor has acquired a good experience rating, the successor will probably be able to take over the experience rating with the rest of the operation, as long as operations remain more or less the same, at the original business location, and the workforce remains stable. Altering these important factors in effect creates a new enterprise, which will have to acquire its own experience rating.

For example, in 2006 the transferee entity of a nursing home could take advantage of the previous owner's experience rate, even though the transfer occurred by lease agreement rather than sale. [*Jefferson Medical Associates LLC*, Unempl. Ins. Rep. (CCH) ¶ 10,193 (Ohio App. 2006)]

## [E] COBRA Issues

Depending on the structure of the transaction, it is likely that some of the employees of one or both of the companies involved in a transition will lose their jobs. Perhaps as a result of the deal, some individuals will remain employed but will cease to be covered by an Employer Group Health Plan (EGHP). If a COBRA event occurs, unless the organization is too small to be covered, it will be necessary to provide COBRA notice. In the context of a corporate transition, that raises the question of who is responsible for providing the notice.

The crucial question is whether there has been a qualifying event. If there has, the structure of the transaction (stock sale versus asset sale) will determine the allocation of the notice burden. COBRA provides that an M&A qualified beneficiary may have a qualifying event if he or she was last employed by the acquired corporation (in a stock sale) or was last employed in connection with the assets being sold in an asset sale. However, a stock sale is not a COBRA qualifying event if the employee continues to be employed by the acquired organization after the transactions, even if the employee is no longer covered by an EGHP.

An asset sale results in a qualifying event for those whose employment is associated with the purchased assets, unless the buying corporation is a successor employer and the employee is employed by the buying corporation immediately after the sale. There is no COBRA event after an asset sale for people who retain their coverage under the selling corporation's EGHP. A successor employer is either a mere continuation of the former employer company; an entity that results from the merger or consolidation of the employer corporation; or a continuation of the business operations associated with the purchased assets.

If a COBRA event does result, and the selling corporation continues to maintain an EGHP, it is responsible for providing continuation coverage (and COBRA notice) to the M&A qualified beneficiaries. If the selling corporation does not continue to maintain an EGHP, in a stock sale the EGHP of the buying corporation has the COBRA duties. In an asset sale, the EGHP of the buyer corporation is responsible for COBRA only if the buyer corporation continues the business operations associated with the assets without interruption and without substantial change. The buyer and seller corporations can re-allocate the burden by contract—but if the party who agrees to undertake the COBRA obligations fails to do so, the originally responsible party still retains its legal liability. [Kenneth W. Ruthenberg Jr., *Don't Pick up COBRA as Part of Your Next Deal— Negotiating COBRA Liability in Business Transactions* (Sept. 10, 2002) <http:// www.seethebenefits.com/CRLframeset.asp>]

## [F]  Bankruptcy as a Transition

When a bankrupt company operates as a Debtor in Possession under Chapter 11, the benefit plans will usually remain in operation during the reorganization process, but a Chapter 7 liquidating bankruptcy will probably lead to termination of the plans.

The Supreme Court's 2007 *Beck* decision made it clear that a bankrupt company does not have a fiduciary duty to consider the option of merging its pension plan into a union multi-employer plan rather than adopting the company's preferred alternative of carrying out a standard termination and buying annuities to satisfy payment obligations. The Supreme Court's rationale was that terminating a plan is a business decision made by the plan sponsor in its role as settlor of the trust that administers the plan. In this reading, this is not an administrative decision made by the plan's fiduciaries—even if they are the same people as those who carry out the settlor functions. Furthermore, ERISA's termination section (§ 4041) does not discuss mergers. [*Beck v. PACE Int'l Union*, 551 U.S. 96 (2007)]

In 2011, the Third Circuit became the first court of appeals to rule that a claim against a debtor for post-petition liability for withdrawing from a multi-employer pension plan receives administrative expense priority in the company's Chapter 11 bankruptcy case. The Multi-Employer Pension Plan Amendments of 1980 amended ERISA to make employers who withdraw from multi-employer plans liable for their pro rata share of unfunded, vested benefits as of the time of withdrawal.

The Third Circuit balanced Bankruptcy Code and ERISA objectives by apportioning the withdrawal liability between the pre- and post-petition time periods. The post-petition portion can be an administrative expense; the balance was deemed to be a general unsecured claim. The Third Circuit limited the size of the administrative expense claim to prevent the estate from being swallowed up by the withdrawal liability claim. [*In re Marcal Paper Mills, Inc.*, 650 F.3d 311 (3d Cir. 2011).

The PBGC does not get involved in a standard termination because the plan has adequate assets to satisfy its obligations. If a distress termination occurs, the PBGC is required to pay the guaranteed benefits. The PBGC allows distress terminations in Chapter 11 bankruptcy cases if the bankruptcy court makes a determination, under ERISA § 1341(c), that the employer will not be able to pay all of its debts under a reorganization plan and will not be able to stay in business unless the pension plan is terminated.

The court has to decide whether there is any feasible reorganization plan that would preserve the pension plan; it is not restricted to considering the plan proposed by the debtor. An important question is whether financing could be obtained to continue the business—and if the parties that might provide the financing insist on termination of the pension plan. The company must explore alternatives, such as eliminating only some pension plans and maintaining others; exploring funding waivers; freezing future benefit accruals, but not terminating the plan; and looking for non-pension means of saving money.

The PBGC is entitled to press two types of claims against the bankrupt sponsor of the plan: a plan asset insufficiency claim and a claim for unpaid funding contributions accruing after the petition. A plan insufficiency claim is a general unsecured claim to the extent that it involves plan benefits employees earned before the petition. The unpaid funding contributions get priority as administrative expenses. [Daniel J. Morse, *Distress Termination of Pension Plans in Ch. 11*, American Bankruptcy Institute Journal, <http://www.gcd.com/files/Publication/48d1bf73[ . . . ]>]

The PBGC contended—and the D.C. Circuit agreed—that Thunderbird Mining Co. was still trying to get new orders after production at a plant stopped. Therefore, it was not shut down when the pension plan terminated. Eveleth Mines made a Chapter 11 filing. Its wholly owned subsidiary, Thunderbird, ceased production and laid off all the hourly employees except for four. Eveleth told the employees that the closure would be temporary if it received the orders it anticipated. There had been shut-downs in the past, but this time, unlike past layoffs, the plant was not kept in standby condition. The PBGC concluded that the plan had a funded ratio of only 52% and no realistic prospect of adequate funding. The PBGC concluded that the plan would not be able to pay benefits as they came due, and losses would increase unreasonably unless the plan was terminated quickly. The PBGC sued to terminate the plan, effective July 24, 2003. Participants in the Thunderbird plan applied for shutdown pension benefits, arguing that the shutdown was intended to be permanent. The bankruptcy court approved the sale of

Eveleth's assets. However, the purchasers of the assets hired the hourly employees under a new CBA. [*United Steel, Paper & Forestry Workers v. PBGC*, 707 F.3d 319 (D.C. Cir., 2013); see Rebecca Moore, *Court Agrees With PBGC Denial of Shutdown Benefits*, plansponsor.com (Jan. 23, 2013)]

A corporation contemplating bankruptcy will have to determine the future of its plans, including who will serve as administrator and trustee before and after bankruptcy and how benefits will be distributed from a terminated plan.

Severance benefits usually come from the employer's assets, and may have the status of a priority claim in bankruptcy. The Bankruptcy Abuse Prevention and Consumer Protection Act (BAPCA; Pub. L. No. 109-8), 2005's bankruptcy reform legislation, affects the treatment of pensions and employee benefits in several ways.

When an employer files for bankruptcy protection, wage and benefit claims for 180 days (rather than prior law's 90 days) are priority claims, and $10,000 per employee in wages and benefits (raised from the previous level of $4,000) counts as a third-priority claim. The bankruptcy trustee can avoid transfers made to or for the benefit of corporate insiders during two years (rather than one) prior to the filing. Transfers made under an employment contract can be avoided by the trustee—whether or not the transfers caused the employer to become insolvent—if they occurred outside the ordinary course of business. BAPCA also places limits on retention bonuses and severance benefits that can be paid to corporate insiders.

The employer's creditors are not permitted to reach amounts contributed by employees, or withheld from their wages for contribution, to a plan when the amounts are in the employer's hands because they have not yet been placed into the plan.

If the employer modified retiree welfare benefits (e.g., retiree health plans) within the 180 days before filing of the bankruptcy petition, any party of interest can apply for a court order. The modification will be enjoined unless the court rules that the balance of equities clearly supports the modification.

Usually conflicts arise when bankruptcy results in a reduction of benefits. The Third Circuit ruled that plan amendments adopted just before a Chapter 11 filing, which resulted in the doubling or even quintupling of pension benefits for certain participants (including corporate insiders), was invalid as a fraudulent conveyance. The court also criticized the introduction of the amendment to the board of directors as an "administrative formality" as evidence of bad faith and the use of a surplus in the union side of the pension accounts to fund the new benefits. [*Pension Transfer Corp. v. Beneficiaries Under Third Amendment to Fruehauf Corp. Ret. Plan*, 444 F.3d 203 (3d Cir. 2006)]

A later Third Circuit case holds that, even if a company has reserved the right to amend or terminate a plan (e.g., a retiree health plan), the company still must comply with the BAPCPA requirements for obtaining court approval for changes to the plan. [*IUE-CWA v. Visteon Corp.*, 612 F.3d 210 (3d Cir. 2010); see

Rebecca Moore, *Visteon Must Follow the Rules Before Terminating Retiree Benefits*, plansponsor.com (July 14, 2010)]

See Chapter 19 for a discussion of the obligation to provide continuation coverage under COBRA (as modified by the ARRA subsidy program). Even if a health plan is terminated, outstanding claims will have to be satisfied. Under HIPAA (also discussed in Chapter 19) employees are entitled to certificates of creditable coverage showing their date of enrollment in the plan, so they can establish their entitlement to purchase individual coverage.

## § 16.03   THE ANTICUTBACK RULE

Internal Revenue Code § 411(d)(6) forbids amendments that reduce accrued benefits, including early retirement benefits and the availability of additional forms of payment over and above the required QJSA and QPSA. But according to *Board of Trustees of the Sheet Metal Workers Nat'l Pension Fund v. C.I.R.* [117 T.C. 220 (2001)], only employees, not retirees, can "accrue" benefits. Therefore, eliminating post-retirement Cost of Living Increases doesn't violate the anticutback rule, because the benefits weren't "accrued."

In 2004, the Supreme Court ruled [*Cent. Laborer's Pension Fund v. Heinz*, 541 U.S. 739 (2004)] that an amendment increasing the varieties of postretirement employment that would cause the suspension of benefit payments violated the anti-cutback rule. [See T.D. 9219, 2005-38 I.R.B. 538 and T.D. 9280, 72 Fed. Reg. 45379 (Aug. 9, 2006) for Final Regulations reflecting *Heinz*.]

If a plan is spun off, the spin-off plan is required to maintain the old plan's payment options as to benefits accrued before the spinoff.

In a merger, employees are permitted to retain their premerger pay-out options. In practice, this means that if a merged plan wants to have a single pay-out structure, it must improve the less-favorable plan to equal the options under the more-favorable plan.

Section 411(a)(10)(B) requires that individuals who had three years of service before the corporate transition will be entitled to keep the old vesting schedule, if it is more favorable to them than the newly adopted one. Employers have an obligation to inform employees of this option.

According to I.R.C. § 414(l), if plans (even plans maintained by the same employer) merge or consolidate, or if a plan's assets and liabilities are transferred to another plan, each participant's benefit immediately after the transition, calculated on a termination basis, must be at least as great as his or her benefit would have been if the plan had terminated immediately before the transition.

The regulations for this section say that a transfer of assets and liabilities from one plan to another will be treated as a spinoff followed by a merger. This usually means that Form 5310-A has to be filed at least 30 days before the merger, spinoff, or asset transfer.

Section 414(l) requires a plan's actuaries to make reasonable assumptions about expected retirement age, mortality, and interest rates before and after the asset transfer. The termination assumptions that the PBGC uses offer a safe harbor because using them is always deemed reasonable, but their use is not mandatory.

The Secretary of the Treasury has the power to enforce ERISA § 208, which is very similar to I.R.C. § 414(l). The Department of Labor has indirect enforcement powers under ERISA § 208, because of its enforcement powers over fiduciary conduct.

Internal Revenue Code § 414 has separate rules for merging two defined contribution plans; two defined benefit plans; and one plan of each type to make sure that participants' entitlement to benefits is not reduced as a result of the transaction. There are further requirements to be observed if one of the plans is fully funded but the other is underfunded. For defined benefit plans, this section serves two policy purposes. It avoids manipulation of funding by means of moving plan assets between the plans of a controlled group of corporations, and it prevents the dilution of benefits within the ERISA § 4044 priority order for categories of assets during a termination.

The priority order is as follows:

- Assets are allocated to benefits coming from participant contributions;

- Benefits going to individuals who were already getting benefits during the three years before the termination;

- Benefits to persons who could have been getting benefits during that three-year period;

- PBGC-guaranteed benefits;

- Other nonforfeitable benefits;

- Everything else.

The First Circuit ruled in 2010 that it was permissible for a plan to eliminate an option for participants to move assets from a defined contribution plan to a defined benefit rule. The First Circuit held that the rule change did not violate the anti-cutback rule, even though it had the effect of diminishing an accrued benefit. Tasker retired from Airborne in 2004; at about the same time, DHL acquired Airborne and merged Airborne's defined contribution and defined benefit plans into its own plans, which eliminated Tasker's right to transfer his balance between plans. Tasker sued, charging that his actual retirement benefit was lower than estimated because the transfer option had been eliminated. But the First Circuit, although decrying the unfairness of the result, held that, although Tasker's actual pension was only about half of what he had expected, DHL did not violate any of ERISA's statutory requirements. [*Tasker v. DHL Ret. Sav. Plan*, 621 F.3d 34 (1st Cir. 2010); see Fred Schneyer, *Interplan Asset Transfer Elimination Upheld*, plansponsor.com (Oct. 7, 2010)] In another Airborne/DHL case, the District Court for the Western District of Washington held that elimination of the right to transfer did not violate the anti-cutback rule. The district court cited Reg. § 1.411(d)-4 as authority for amending a plan to eliminate transfers between defined benefit and defined contribution plans. The plaintiffs argued that the regulation applies only if the monthly benefit is not reduced by the transfer, but the court noted that there is no such limitation in the language of the regulation. [*Andersen v. DHL Ret. Pension Plan*, No. C12-439 MJP, 2012 U.S. Dist. LEXIS 157805 (W.D. Wash. Nov. 2, 2012)]

## § 16.04   NOTICE OF REDUCTION OF BENEFITS

ERISA § 204(h) requires notices of reductions in future benefits. to be given before the effective date of any amendment that eliminates or reduces an early retirement benefit or early retirement subsidy. An excise tax is imposed on failure to provide proper notice.

Notice is due a reasonable time before the effective date of the plan amendment. The notice can be given before the formal adoption of the amendment, as long as there is no material change before the amendment is finally adopted. If there is an "egregious" failure to provide notice, then the amendment cannot take effect, and individuals affected by the change get the larger of the pre- or post-amendment form of the benefit.

In April 2003, the IRS published Final Regulations on the notice requirements of ERISA § 204(h). [T.D. 9052, RIN 1545-BA08, <http://benefitslink.com/taxregs/204h-final-2003.shtml>] Under the final rule, notice must generally be given 45 days in advance of the event (even if this is earlier than the adoption date of the plan amendment that institutes the cutback). A small plan (one with fewer than 100 participants) is allowed to give less notice: 15 days. The 15-day rule also applies when a § 204(h) amendment is adopted in connection with a corporate acquisition or disposition.

Furthermore, if the amendment is adopted to deal with transfers of liabilities from one plan to another in connection with a transfer, merger, or consolidation of assets or liabilities under Code § 414(l), and the amendment cuts back on early retirement benefits or subsidies but does not significantly reduce the rate of future benefit accrual, the notice can be given after the amendment takes effect—but not more than 30 days afterward. The Final Regulations are in Q&A form, and provide model text that can be used to provide notice.

The IRS modified its position in July 2003, allowing defined contribution plans (including 401(k)s) to reduce alternate benefit forms without 90 days' advance notice—as long as the change was reflected in a timely revised SPD or Summary of Material Modifications. [68 Fed. Reg. 40581 (July 8, 2003)] Similar relief was proposed for defined benefit plans. [69 Fed. Reg. 13769 (Mar. 24, 2004)]

Proposed Regulations [70 Fed. Reg. 47155 (Aug. 12, 2005)] cover the interaction of the anti-cutback rules with the § 411(a) nonforfeitability requirements. There are two ways to reduce or eliminate a benefit: (1) if the benefit is redundant, that is, duplicates another benefit in the same family, 90 days' notice is required; or (2) if the benefit is a core option, such as the straight life annuity and the 10-year certain/life annuity, four years' notice is required. Benefits also can be eliminated when they have been available for a meaningful length of time but no one ever elected them. The IRS returned to this issue with Final Regulations published at 71 Fed. Reg. 45379 (Aug. 9, 2006). This Final Rule also includes a test of utilization to determine whether certain benefit forms (e.g., retirement-type subsidies; optional forms of benefit) are so seldom used that employers are permitted to amend the plan to eliminate them.

T.D. 9472, 2009-51 I.R.B. 850, is a final rule governing notice requirements under § 204(h) for plan amendments that reduce accrued benefits. Code § 4980F(e)(3) requires notice to be provided within a reasonable time before the plan amendment takes effect. In general, that means 45 days before the effective date (15 days for small or multi-employer plans). However, for some amendments that took effect by December 31, 2008, notice is acceptable if given at least 30 days before the effective date. [T.D. 9472, 2009-51 I.R.B. 850]

## § 16.05   THE MINIMUM PARTICIPATION RULE

Initially, minimum participation rules were applied to both defined contribution and defined benefit plans. However, the Small Business Job Protection Act of 1996 [Pub. L. No. 104-188] eliminated this rule for defined contribution plans—now only defined benefit plans are required to have a minimum number or percentage of participants. This is significant in the context of corporate transitions because asset buyers often decline to adopt the seller's plan. If the plan is not adopted, there is a risk that the new plan will fail to cover the mandated number or percentage of employees.

Some relief is available under I.R.C. § 410(b)(6)(C), which allows one year after an acquisition or the disposition of a corporation to satisfy the minimum participation requirement. But after that, the plan is likely to become disqualified—unless it has been terminated in the interim.

A possible strategy is to freeze the plan. However, if too many participants choose to cash out, that creates difficulties. Two or more plans can be merged into a larger plan, offering a benefit structure at least as favorable as the most favorable of the merged plans, no later than the fifteenth day of the tenth month after the end of the plan year.

## § 16.06  IN-SERVICE DISTRIBUTIONS AND REHIRING

The underlying purpose of pension plans is to provide postretirement financial security. Therefore, "in-service distributions" (distributions from the plan while the individual is still working) historically were severely discouraged by the Code. Although many government agency employers had phased retirement plans, few private-sector employers did so. There are some special rules governing taxation of in-service distributions during a transition. Treasury Regulation § 1.401-1(b)(1)(i) provides that defined benefit plans cannot make in-service distributions before the employee's retirement or termination of employment— unless the plan itself is terminated. But a defined contribution plan that is not a 401(k) plan can use the two-year/five-year rule. That is, contributions can be withdrawn from the plan after the contributions have been in the plan for two years, or the participant has five years of plan participation.

> ■ **TIP:** EGTRRA eliminates the "same desk" rule for 401(k) plans. In other words, when there is a merger consolidation, or liquidation, participants in a 401(k) plan will be entitled to take a distribution from the plan even if the successor company hires them and they have not separated from service. Congress intended to increase the portability of pensions in this situation.

Because of the abolition of the same desk rule, distributions can be made from the seller's plan in either an asset or a stock sale, to employees who go to work for the buyer or stay at the subsidiary that has been sold, as long as that subsidiary drops participation in the plan by the time of the sale. Distributions are not allowed if the subsidiary that is the subject of the sale retains the plan, the buyer takes over as plan sponsor, or assets are transferred to a plan maintained by the buyer corporation. In most cases, a plan amendment will be required. It probably makes sense to permit distributions to any participant who is transferred out of the seller's controlled group as a result of a stock sale, sale of assets, or other corporate transaction. Similarly, employees who took substantially similar jobs with the buyer corporation were not "released" from employment and therefore were not entitled to severance pay. [*Cassidy v. Akzo Nobel Salt Inc.*, 308 F.3d 613 (6th Cir. 2002)] The termination plan defined release as permanent separation initiated by the employer for reasons such as lack of work, RIF, or unsatisfactory performance by the employee.

Under the Pension Protection Act, Pub. L. No. 109-280, employees who have reached age 62 can lawfully receive in-service distributions under a phased retirement plan: see § 9.06. See also T.D. 9235, 2007-24 I.R.B. 1386 (Final Regulations on the definition of Normal Retirement Age).

## § 16.07    TAX ISSUES

If, after a merger, liquidation, or reorganization, the surviving company maintains the predecessor corporation's qualified plan, I.R.C. § 381 generally provides that the original plans' tax attributes are passed on to the successor plan. If two qualified plans consolidate, the deductions taken by each employer before the consolidation will not be retroactively disqualified by the consolidation.

The acquiring corporation can keep up the plan for the benefit of those covered by it under the old ownership—with no obligation to cover the workers who were its own employees before the acquisition.

Asset purchases that result in the liquidation of the seller company or acquisition of its assets by the purchaser company, can create "orphan plans" (plans with no sponsor), which create tax problems. Once a plan loses its sponsor, it can lose tax-qualified status. There may also be ERISA fiduciary liability issues about managing, reporting, and distributing assets from the plan. The IRS' Employee Plans Compliance Resolution System (EPCRS; see § 15.19[B]) has a process for correcting errors of orphan plans. [Keith R. McMurdy, *Don't Let Your Plan Become an Orphan*, Fox Rothschild LLP Employee Benefits Legal Blog (Jan. 24, 2012) (benefitslink.com)]

The Sixth Circuit applied labor, not corporation, law to determine whether a company is subject to the FMLA, finding that it is irrelevant for this purpose whether there is a transfer of assets or a merger with the seller. The plaintiff was re-hired by the company that underbid his former employer for a Postal Service delivery contract. The second company did not acquire the previous employer or its assets. The Sixth Circuit did not rule that a merger or transfer of assets is always required to impose successor liability: legal obligations, such as those under a CBA, also count. The Sixth Circuit pointed out that the FMLA defines "employer" to include successors in interest, and the Regulations (29 C.F.R. § 825.107) adopt the Title VII standard for successorship in interest. [*Cobb v. Contract Transp., Inc.*, 461 F.3d 632 (6th Cir. 2006), as discussed in Rosario Vega Lynn, *Workplace Prof Blog: Interesting Case on Successors-in-Interest Under FMLA* (July 11, 2006)]

The risk of acquisition or merger makes corporate recruitment more difficult, because top candidates have a realistic fear that they will lose their jobs during a shake-up. Employment agreements with prominent candidates often include "golden parachutes" (providing generous compensation if the job is lost because of a corporate transition) and "golden handcuffs" (retention bonuses that are forfeited if the individual quits shortly after being hired). Most of these programs only take effect when employees have involuntary job loss; some plans have a "window period" during which payments will be made even if the employee quits voluntarily. See § 1.01[B] for discussion of limitations on golden parachutes and other severance payments to top management of financial services companies receiving federal bail-out funds.

A "stay bonus" for remaining with the new owner is a fixed benefit (and therefore a fixed incremental cost for the business buyer). The bonus is paid after the employee has remained for a certain period of time. It could also be combined with a golden parachute. For instance, the executive could be offered two months' salary as a bonus for staying a year, or given a severance package of three months' salary and outplacement assistance if terminated without good cause within 18 months of the transition.

Internal Revenue Code § 280G does not allow corporations to deduct "excess parachute payments." Any "disqualified person" who receives an excess parachute payment is subject to a 20% excise tax, under I.R.C. § 4999. A parachute payment is a payment of compensation, contingent on a change in ownership, and equal to three times or more of the base amount (roughly speaking, the base amount is the individual's normal compensation).

Code § 409A is the IRS' attempt to control inappropriate deferral of nonqualified deferred compensation. (See § 8.02[D]) Section 409A potentially applies to many compensation arrangements in change of control situations: severance agreements, stock options, and incentive agreements, for example. Violating § 409A can lead to accelerated inclusion in income for the person receiving the compensation, and a 20% federal tax penalty. California imposes its own 20% penalty as well.

A single-trigger arrangement provides benefits upon change in control, even if the executive is not terminated at the time of the acquisition. Double-trigger arrangements, which require an adverse employment action within a specified time of the change in control, are growing in popularity. Post-change in control severance usually is paid in a lump sum, because after the change, the restrictive covenants are less of a concern to the acquired company. The executive also wants to receive the funds in a lump sum to avoid being at the mercy of the acquiring company's CEO and management team.

One potential risk is that alternative payment methods under a double-trigger severance plan could fall under § 409A. The company might fail to recognize this because the pre- and post-change severance arrangements are specified in different documents—for example, the overall severance plan and an individual executive's change-in-control agreement. A double-trigger arrangement typically becomes subject to § 409A if the "good reason" payment trigger is excessively broad—say, if it allows the executive to resign and collect severance based on a minor reduction in pay or duties; if the installment payments exceed $490,000 (indexed for inflation), or the payments extend more than two years after separation from service. Because of economic uncertainty, "earn-outs" have become more popular in private company acquisitions. The earn-out provides for future payments to the seller of the acquired company if the company reaches certain business milestones—typically, within two to five years, although the period could be ten years or even longer. A stock option cash-out or management incentive plan can be subject to an earn-out without violating § 409 as long as payments are made at the same time, and generally on the same terms and conditions, to payments to the shareholders as a whole. To qualify for this treatment, the earn-out payments generally must be made within five years of the transaction's closing date, although § 409A permits limited customized alternatives tailored to the situation of an earn-out that exceeds five years.

Earn-outs are speculative and difficult to value. There are risks: if the earn-out is overvalued, there will be penalties for a § 409A violation, but if it is undervalued, the option-holders will suffer economic harm. Some companies value the earn-out at the time of the assumption, whereas others use an "open transaction" approach, adjusting the options to reflect the earn-out only as it is paid. The issue could also be avoided by requiring option holders to exercise their options just before the transaction. [Juliano P. Banuelos, *Recent Compensation Trends in Mergers and Acquisitions and Section 409A*, Orrick Perspectives (October 2011) (benefitslink.com)]

As well as their tax implications, golden parachutes have ramifications for corporate law and securities regulation. Exchange Act § 14A, enacted by the Dodd-Frank Act, requires a non-binding shareholder vote about golden parachute compensation. The vote cannot be used to overrule the Board of Directors' decision, change the board's fiduciary duties, or restrict the ability of shareholders to include their own proposals in the corporation's proxy materials. The proxy or consent solicitation material for a meeting at which shareholders will be asked to approve an acquisition, merger, consolidation, or the sale or disposition of substantially all assets of the company must disclose any agreements between the party soliciting the proxy and the top managers of either the acquired or acquiring company with respect to the executive's present, deferred, or contingent compensation based on the transaction. Proxy statements must include a separate resolution, subject to shareholder vote, to approve any compensation agreements—unless the shareholders have already approved the agreement through a "Say on Pay" vote. This provision is effective for shareholder meetings that occur after January 21, 2011. [Michael S. Melbinger, Winston & Strawn LLP, *Executive Compensation Blog* (Aug. 12, 2010) (benefitslink.com)]

## § 16.08   THE PBGC EARLY WARNING PROGRAM

PBGC's Early Warning Program is supposed to reduce the agency's risk of loss in the context of corporate transitions by giving the PBGC the power to review transactions of below-investment-grade companies with extensive liabilities and other plans with more than $5 million in unfunded current liability. Certain types of transactions have been identified as potential problem areas: the breakup of a controlled group; a leveraged buyout; major divestiture by a company that retains significantly underfunded pension liabilities; or transfer of significantly underfunded pension liabilities in connection with sale of a business. [This program is discussed in Harold J. Ashner, *Dealing with the Pension Benefit Guaranty Corporation*, Tax Management Compensation Planning Journal,

<http://www.keightleyashner.com/publications/Dealing_with[ . . . ]>    (January 2006)]

RIN 1212-AB03 is PBGC's final rule for calculating the liability when an employer with an underfunded pension plan closes a facility and lays off a significant percentage of its workforce. The final regulations exclude retirees and former employees who separated from service before cessation of operations from the calculations. If the plan is terminated within five years, the liability amount goes to the plan; if there is no termination, the money is returned to the employer. The PBGC refused to enact a small-plan exception, because small companies usually have only one business location, so shutdown would lead to plan termination in any case. [71 Fed. Reg. 34819 (June 16, 2006), discussed in (no by-line) *PBGC Finalizes Regs on Computing Liability When Employer Substantially Ceases Operations*, Pension & Benefits Week (RIA) (June 26, 2006)]

In 2013, the PBGC proposed regulations under which most (perhaps as many as 90%) of plans would qualify for waivers of reporting requirements, based on plan size (fewer than 100 participants) and/or financial soundness.

As a general rule, there is a reportable event when the number of participants falls below 80% of the number of participants at the end of the previous year, or below 75% of the number at the beginning of the previous year, but the proposal waives reporting of this event for small (fewer than 100 participant) plans. Larger plans would only have to report if the reduction was caused by a single event such as reorganization or mass layoff; if the reduction occurred in a period of 30 days or less; or if the number of participants in the same year falls by more than 20%. Large plans can use the financial soundness safe harbor to avoid reporting based on reduction in the number of participants.

Reporting is not required if there has been a reorganization within a controlled group of corporations leading to one member of the group ceasing to exist because it has been merged into another member of the group. Prior law made it a reportable event when there is a default in payment of over 30 days on a loan of $10 million or more—not only by the plan sponsor, but any member of a controlled group of corporations it belongs to. Written notice of default based on reduced cash reserves or a lender's acceleration of a loan is also a reportable event. The proposed regulations not only retain this requirement but make it stronger: reporting is required when there is a loan acceleration or any kind of default, including a lender's waiver of its right to declare a default. Small plans and plans entitled to the financial soundness safe harbor must still report this event. [78 Fed. Reg. 20039 (Apr. 3, 2013); see Rebecca Moore, *PBGC Proposed Reduced Reporting Obligations*, plansponsor.com (Apr. 2, 2013); Buck Consultants FYI, *PBGC Reproposes Reportable Event Rules* (Apr. 5, 2013) (benefitslink.com) In May, 2013 the PBGC gave more guidance about what constitutes a creditworthy company, based on, for example, the rating of the company's debt, its Financial Stress Score, or its debt:asset ratio. See PLC Employee Benefits & Employee Compensation, *PBGC Releases Enforcement*

*Guidelines for ERISA Section 4062(e) Financial Assurance Program* (May 3, 2013) (benefitslink.com).]]

## § 16.09   STOCK OPTIONS

During the late lamented Internet boom, stock options were greatly cherished by employees because of the possibility of purchasing stock for a few dollars and being able to resell it at a much higher price—especially if the company was a start-up with the potential for a high-flying Initial Public Offering. Under current depressed stock market conditions, far fewer employees hold options that can be exercised profitably. However, in the hope that conditions will turn around again, the topic is worth discussing.

Mergers raise many questions about stock options, including:

• Do employees of the acquired company forfeit their outstanding options?

• Are their options bought out?

• Do they receive options in the acquirer company in exchange?

One of the factors fueling the economic boom of the late 1990s and early 2000s was the incentive to mergers and acquisitions offered by "pooling of interest" accounting. When pooling of interest was available, it allowed two companies to exchange equity securities and pool their bookkeeping and accounting thereafter. The net result was that the company's reported earnings would be higher, because there was no need to amortize goodwill as an expense. In contrast, if the transaction had to be accounted for under the purchase method, the acquirer would be deemed to purchase the acquired company, and the financial statements of the combined entity must reflect the fair value of the company's assets and liabilities. However, for most transactions initiated after June 30, 2001, pooling of interest accounting is unavailable—the purchase method must be used instead. For most plans, all outstanding stock options will vest upon a change in control; vested options can be exercised within a limited period, such as 30 or 60 days.

[See § 22.02 for further discussion of stock options]

Treatment of outstanding options is an important part of M&A planning. Whether vesting should be accelerated when there is a change in control is a business decision, separate from consideration of the transaction's effect on outstanding options. The board of directors should be allowed maximum flexibility to decide, at the time of a transaction, whether options that have not already been exercised should be canceled; if the options should be taken over or substituted by the acquiring corporation; or cashed out for the difference between the exercise price of the option and the price per share of the stock to be received in the transaction. One possibility is to cancel the out-of-the-money options without consideration, but to pay cash for the in-the-money options. The acquiring company may wish to assume the target company's options instead of substituting them; substitution could deplete the acquiror's equity incentive plan pool—or could have the inadvertent effect of modifying the awards in a way that triggers § 409A or makes the options non-qualified.

If the acquiring company is a public corporation, the stock exchanges allow the remaining shares under the target company's assumed plan pool to be issued without approval by the shareholders. But the acquiror may prefer to substitute rather than assuming the target's options, if the acquiror wants all of its options to have uniform terms and conditions. Shares underlying substituted options do not have to be registered; there is already a registration statement in effect (which is not true of assumed options). The acquiror may prefer not to assume the options if their terms, or the size of the class qualifying for options, is not consistent with the acquiror's corporate culture. An acquiror that does not pay cash for the underlying stock in the transaction may prefer not to cash out the stock options, so the plan must be flexible enough to permit termination of the options instead. If the options are canceled, the optionees can exercise their vested options until the transaction closes. Cashing out options benefits the acquiror because it does not have to administer the options after the closing; it does not incur a compensation expense; its shareholders' equity is not diluted; and employees can get cash for their equity without having to pay out-of-pocket to fund the exercise price. Holders of options in private companies like cash-outs because the optionees can receive liquidity without having to make an investment.

It must be decided (either when the options are granted in the first place, or when a corporate transition occurs) whether vesting should be accelerated if the transaction constitutes a change of control. The acceleration provisions can be embodied in the incentive plan, or in agreements outside the plan, such as the option award, executives' employment contracts, their severance, or retention agreements. In addition to the conventional single- and double-trigger arrangements, hybrid arrangements are possible, such as partial vesting on change of control, with additional vesting if a second triggering event occurs. Or, vesting might depend on the way the optioins are treated in the transaction. For example, vesting might be accelerated only if the awards are not assumed by the acquiror, which would mean that the optionee would not be able to vest at a later time, even if he or she remains employed. [Pamela B. Greene and Ann Margaret Eames, *Stock Options in Merger & Acquisition Transactions*, Corporate & Securities Advisory (June 6, 2011) (benefitslink.com)]

# CHAPTER 17

# PLAN TERMINATION

## § 17.01  INTRODUCTION

When companies start a pension plan, they usually do so in good faith, and with the intention of keeping the plan in operation as long as it is necessary to provide benefits. However, ERISA and the Internal Revenue Code recognize that sometimes it will be necessary to terminate a pension plan—usually because the sponsoring corporation is ceasing operations, being absorbed by another company, or has financial difficulties so severe that it cannot continue to meet its obligations. There are even some rare circumstances under which the plan is *over* funded, and the employer is able to terminate the plan, distribute its assets, and retain the plan surplus for its own benefit.

Plan termination is usually voluntary, premised on the employer's decision to shut down the plan. However, courts, based on a determination that the economic security of plan participants is at risk, can order involuntary terminations. The legal system provides structures for winding up pension plans in an orderly way. Usually, the plan's assets are applied to purchase annuities that will pay participants' pensions as they become entitled to receive them.

Under the relevant legal and tax rules, a plan termination can be either complete or partial. When a termination occurs, all accrued benefits vest immediately—including benefits that would not vest until later under the plan's normal vesting schedule. This requirement is imposed to reduce the temptation to terminate expensive and inconvenient plans!

Terminating a plan involves both the IRS and the Department of Labor (DOL). Both ERISA and the IRC must be consulted. There are forms to be filed, consents to be secured, and disclosure obligations to the participants and beneficiaries of the plan. Then, the plan's assets are distributed within an "administratively reasonable time" (generally defined as one year or less). But if the process continues for too long, the plan may be treated as if it had not terminated, and reports under I.R.C. §§ 6057–6059 will still be required. Section 6059 applies only to defined benefit plans.

> ■ **TIP:**  Under some circumstances, a Reduction in Force (RIF) is deemed to cause a partial termination (for which vesting will be required). Therefore, before implementing an RIF, the company should determine the pension implications of the program.

A federal agency called the Pension Benefit Guaranty Corporation (PBGC) plays an important role in the termination of defined benefit plans. When a plan termination is contemplated, the plan notifies the PBGC, which has 60 days (or longer, if the plan consents to an extension) to review the proposed termination for any improprieties.

The PBGC also has the power to ask the federal court system to close down a pension plan (even if the employer has not sought to terminate the plan) and supervise the orderly distribution of its assets. The PBGC is not involved in the termination of defined contribution plans, because each participant in such a plan has an individual account that can be distributed to him or her.

There are certain exceptions to these general rules. Benefits are not guaranteed if they become nonforfeitable only because of the termination; nor does the agency guarantee benefits in full if the plan was in effect for less than 60 months before it terminated. If a benefit was scheduled to increase under a plan amendment that was either made or took effect within 60 months prior to the termination, the PBGC will not guarantee the increase.

The PBGC's guarantee applies only to benefits accrued before a plan terminates—and only to benefits accrued before the filing date if the employer is bankrupt when the plan terminates. In general, the PBGC pays benefits according to the terms of the plan, but if an individual's full benefit exceeds the PBGC's limit, the PBGC pays estimated benefits while it examines the plan records, and then reduces benefits to the limit. For about 80% of participants and beneficiaries, the estimated benefit is the same as the final benefit; but if the estimated benefits are lower than the actual benefit, the PBGC will make a single payment (including interest) to catch up. [<PBGC.gov>, *PBGC's Guarantees for Single-Employer Pension Plans Fact Sheet*]

Terminating a plan requires bringing it into conformity with all legal and regulatory changes since the last update and there are usually several federal statutes each year requiring conforming amendments.

The Bankruptcy Court for the Southern District of New York approved plans for Hostess Brands to sell Twinkies and other famous brands and wind down operations. The bankruptcy court ruled that a quick and orderly shutdown was necessary to prevent deterioration of factories and other assets. This was Hostess' second bankruptcy filing; the first was in 2004, with the company leaving bankruptcy in 2009 with 50% more debt than when it filed. According to management, the company was heavily indebted, the union refused to accept cuts, and then two-thirds of the bakeries struck on November 9, 2011. The union said that it had already made substantial concessions in the previous bankruptcy when it had seemed that liquidation was imminent and the company was mismanaged, failing to modernize its facilities or adapt its product line to modern tastes. Hostess's first bankruptcy was in 2004 with $450Million in debt; when it exited in 2009 it had $670Million debt. [Steven Greenhouse and Michael J. De La Merced, *Court Allows Liquidation of Hostess*, NYTimes.com (Nov. 21, 2012)]

Hostess had 115 CBAs (Collective Bargaining Agreement), allowing workers to direct part of their wages directly to the pension plan. Hostess was also supposed to contribute. In August 2011, Hostess announced that it would stop making pension contributions and wages earmarked for pensions were used for operations and other purposes. In the five months preceding the bankruptcy filing, Hostess missed $22.1 million in payments to the main pension fund. Unmade pension payments continued to accrue at a rate of $3–$4 million per month until Hostess rejected its CBAs. This was probably not a violation of federal law because the money was not taken directly from employees. Most Hostess retirees get their payments from multi-employer plans that continued to pay benefits to retirees. The PBGC does not get involved until a plan becomes insolvent, at which point it provides about $12,870 for each employee with at least 30 years of service. [Julie Jargon, Rachel Feintzeig, and Mike Spector, *Hostess Maneuver Deprived Pension*, WSJ.com (Dec. 10, 2012)]

Hostess resumed production of Twinkies and other snack foods in mid-2013, after major changes in operations. The company went from operating 11 factories to having four factories, and from being 79% unionized to 0% unionized. Wages decreased significantly. [Julie Jargon, *Former Hostess Employees Bitter About Wage Cuts*, WSJ.com (July 9, 2013)]

## [A]  New Rules Under the PPA

The Pension Protection Act of 2006, Pub. L. No. 109-280, has affected most areas of pension and benefit law, and plan termination is no exception.

Early in 2007, the PBGC proposed amendments to its regulations to implement the Deficit Reduction Act and the PPA. The proposals affect 29 C.F.R. Part 4006 (premium rates) and 4007 (payment of premiums). The variable-rate premium is capped for employers with 25 or fewer "employees," and the PBGC proposals use the Code § 410(b)(1) definition of employee. This includes certain individuals who are not common-law employees, including leased employees and employees of an affiliated service group. The PBGC's motivation was to deter employers from manipulating the rules to qualify under the cap. The same participant count is used for both flat- and variable-rate premiums. The PPA enacted a new category of premium, the termination premium of $1,250 per participant per year for three years. [CCH Pension and Benefits, *PBGC Proposes to Amend Its Premium Regulations to Implement DRA '05 and PPA '06 Changes* (Feb. 28, 2007) (benefitslink.com)]

See <http://www.pbgc.gov/prac/prem/premium-rates.html> for the premium rates prevailing in 2013, reflecting subsequent legislation including the Moving Ahead for Progress in the 21st Century (MAP-21) Act, Pub. L. No. 112-140.

If a plan is at risk (see Chapter 5 for more discussion), it will be limited in its ability to provide shutdown benefits, unless the employer either makes additional contributions to strengthen the plan, or provides security for the benefits. Participants in at-risk plans are entitled to notification about the limits on distributions. Furthermore if a distress or involuntary termination occurs, the plan must inform the participants (within 15 days of the PBGC filing) of the information contained in the notice to the PBGC (new ERISA § 4041(c)(2)(D), 4042(c)(3)).

The D.C. Circuit agreed with the PBGC that Thunderbird Mining Corporation, a wholly owned subsidiary of Eveleth Mines, was not shut down when its pension plan terminated, so shutdown benefits were not payable. The company was still trying to get new orders after production was stopped at its plant, although production had ceased and all except four hourly employees had been

laid off. Eveleth told the employees that the closure was expected to be temporary but re-opening was conditional on receiving the expected orders. There had
been shutdowns in the past, but during those shutdowns, the plant was kept in
standby condition. The PBGC concluded that the plan had a funded ratio of 52%
and no realistic prospect of adequate funding, so it would not be able to pay
benefits as they came due and losses would increase unreasonably if the plan was
not terminated quickly. The PBGC brought suit calling for a July 24, 2003 termination date. Plan participants asked for shutdown benefits, arguing that the
shutdown was intended to be permanent. The bankruptcy court approved the sale
of the Eveleth assets; the purchaser hired the hourly employees under a new CBA.
[*United Steel Workers v. PBGC*, 707 F.3d 319 (D.C. Cir. 2013); see Rebecca
Moore, *Court Agrees With PBGC Denial of Shutdown Benefits*, plansponsor.com
(Jan. 23, 2013)]

In mid-2008, the PBGC proposed a rule under the PPA, to treat the termination date of a plan that ends when its employer is in bankruptcy as of the date
of the filing of the bankruptcy petition, not the actual date of termination. The
effect of this rule is that the benefits guaranteed by the PBGC will probably be
somewhat smaller, because amounts earned by plan participants after the date of
the bankruptcy filing will not be guaranteed by the PBGC. The rule was finalized
in mid-2011. [Proposed Rule, 73 Fed. Reg. 37390 (July 1, 2008); see *Pension
Guarantees Fact Sheet*, <http://www.pbgc.gov/media/key-resources-for-the-press/
content/page13542.html> Final Rule, 76 Fed. Reg. 34590 (June 14, 2011).]

Some employers that downsized have been required to settle PBGC claims
under ERISA § 4062(c), which allows the PBGC to demand immediate escrow
payments or posting of bond when cessation of operations results in separation
from service of 20% or more of the participants in a defined benefit plan. PBGC
regulations say the amount of liability is the amount by which the plan is underfunded, calculated as if the plan terminated immediately after cessation of operations, multiplied by the percentage reduction in active participants. To satisfy its
claim, the PBGC can demand that the amount of liability be placed into escrow,
or that the employer purchase a bond of up to 150% of the liability amount, to
protect the plan in case there is an involuntary or distress termination. If an involuntary or distress termination occurs, the escrow funds or bond proceeds are considered plan assets. However, if five years passes without an involuntary or
distress termination, then the bond is canceled or the escrow money is returned.
The PBGC is not required to pay interest on the funds. [Final Rule, RIN 1212-
AB03, 71 Fed. Reg. 34819 (June 16, 2006); see Keightley Ashner Client Alert,
*Downsizing Employers with Ongoing Pension Plans May Face an Immediate and
Significant PBGC Liability* (Feb. 19, 2009) (benefitslink.com)]

In effect, the sponsor of a single-employer plan is treated as if it were a
multi-employer plan. In mid-2010, the PBGC proposed amendments to the rules
for termination of single-employer plans to clarify the treatment of substantial
cessation of operations as defined by ERISA § 4062(e). The 2006 final rule
explains how to compute the employer's liability; the 2011 proposal explains

what constitutes a § 4062(e) event. Certain events are treated as predicting that the plan is likely to terminate within five years when it is underfunded—whether or not particular risk factors are present in the case of an individual plan.

The proposal says that § 4062(e) is triggered when "an operation" at a "facility in any location" ceases—even if the employer transfers the operation to another facility. Determining whether "cessation" has occurred depends on whether there has only been a cutback or contraction in the operation—or if the change is so major that the operation can no longer be considered ongoing. The proposal has separate rules for voluntary and involuntary discontinuances of activities. The PBGC must be notified within 60 days after withdrawal from the plan. The employer must maintain a specific amount in escrow or a corresponding bond for five years from the date of withdrawal. If the plan terminates during this five-year period, the bond or escrow is applied toward any underfunding. However, § 4063(e) authorizes the PBGC to waive this liability if the sponsors of the plan have an appropriate indemnity agreement, and the PBGC can make alternative arrangements to satisfy the obligation (see § 4067).

Under the proposal, the "active participant base" means the baseline number of active participants used to determine if a 20% reduction has occurred. If the employer has two or more plans, § 4062(e) applies separately to each, not on an aggregate basis.

Cessation has occurred when the employer no longer conducts the operation at the facility on an ongoing basis, but activity that does not further the purpose of the operation is disregarded, so operations may be considered terminated even if maintenance and security are kept up. Continuance or resumption at another facility or by another employer is disregarded in determining if a cessation occurred.

The § 4062(e) event consists of two parts (cessation and 20% drop in participant count). For discontinuance as a result of employee action (e.g., a strike) the cessation date is delayed until after the employee action ends, plus a week for the employer to resume work. If there is cessation due to a sudden and unanticipated event not caused by employee action, such as a natural disaster, the cessation date is deferred for 30 days.

The 60-day period for notice does not begin until both cessation and reduction in the number of employees have occurred. Only current employees are included in calculating the number of participants just before cessation. However, an employee does not have to accrue benefits to be considered a participant: The PBGC does not want employers to be able to benefit from plan freezes. There is no small plan exemption under this rule. The PBGC says that small plans are adequately protected under the rule, and they have less potential for underfunding and accordingly less exposure. [PBGC, *Liability for Termination of Single-Employer Plans; Treatment of Substantial Cessation of Operations*, FR Doc 2010-19695, RIN 1212-AB20, 75 Fed. Reg. 48283 (Aug. 10, 2010)]

A late 2012 PBGC announcement says that about 92% of plan sponsors will not have to provide guarantees under § 4062(e) enforcement because the PBGC declines to take action against creditworthy companies or small pension plans (fewer than 100 participants). This is a policy change: the PBGC used to enforce all § 4062(e) cases. The PBGC adopted a pilot program, which may be modified in light of the agency's experience. Section 4062(e) requires companies with defined benefit plans to report cessation of operations at a facility where more than 20% of employees have separated from employment so that they can be asked for financial security. The PBGC proposed regulations in August 2010, which were withdrawn after industry protests that many companies are unlikely to default because the plan is small or the plan is strong enough to satisfy its pension obligations. More lenient regulations were proposed in March 2012, dividing companies into three categories of financial strength. [R. Randall Tracht, Brian J. Dougherty, Lisa H. Barton, and Eric P. Sarabia, *PBGC Changes Enforcement Policy Under ERISA Section 4062(e)*, Morgan, Lewis & Bockius (Nov. 13, 2012) (benefitslink.com) See PLC Employee Benefits & Employee Compensation, *PBGC Releases Enforcement Guidelines for ERISA Section 4062(e) Financial Assurance Program* (May 3, 2013) (benefitslink.com) for May, 2013 PBGC guidance on the definition of "creditworthy," based on factors such as the company's bond rating and its debt:asset ratio.]

## § 17.02   TERMINATION TYPES

Once the decision to terminate the plan is made, the date of termination must be chosen. The corporation's Board of Directors will probably have to pass a resolution to this effect. Participants and beneficiaries are entitled to between 60 and 90 days' notice of the impending termination. Benefits will probably be distributed as annuities, lump sums, and/or transfers to IRAs and other qualified plans. If it is determined that the assets are sufficient to satisfy all benefit obligations, then the IRS and PBGC forms are prepared and submitted. The relevant forms include PBGC Form 500 and IRS Forms 5310, 6088, and 8717. Participants and beneficiaries are given an official Notice of Plan Benefits. They are also entitled to 45 days' notice of which insurer will provide the annuities for benefits distributed in this form.

Once the forms are filed, the PBGC has 60 days to raise any concerns it has. The IRS can take as long as 18 months to review filings and issue a determination letter. But once the determination letter has been issued, the funds must be distributed within 120 days.

A sponsor contemplating termination should do a termination planning study, reflecting a variety of interest rate assumptions. Under the PPA, corporate bond interest rates are phased in until 2012. Each 1% change in interest rates can make liabilities 10%–15% larger or smaller. Once the spread between plan assets and the potential cost of termination is calculated, it is possible to determine if the company can afford to fund the shortfall through contributions and/or investment earnings over a selected number of years (e.g., one year; three years; five years).

The three most common funding strategies are:

- Contributing a minimum amount for an ongoing plan each year until termination, with a final contribution when the plan's assets are distributed—typically, 18–24 months after the termination date)

- Contributing a level amount each year until the year of planned termination—e.g., if termination is set for five years in the future, spread the cost evenly over the five-year period

- Fully funding the plan under the PPA rules for ongoing plans, using investment income to make up for the shortfall when the plan is terminated.

The first alternative is probably the most expensive, but it reduces the time frame until termination—and risk increases over time. [*Principal Life Ins Co. Thought Capital*: *Winding Down Your Hard-Frozen Defined Benefit (DB) Plan* (March 2012) (benefitslink.com)]

## [A]  Generally

There are two types of voluntary termination: standard and distress. See 29 C.F.R. Part 4041 for Regulations. A standard termination, governed by ERISA § 4041, is used by plans that have at least enough assets to pay the benefits guaranteed by the PBGC. All terminations are handled as standard terminations unless the PBGC permits a "distress termination," which imposes lower obligations on the plan.

Under ERISA § 4044, there are six priority categories of accrued benefits. When the plan's assets are distributed, all Category-1 claims must be paid, then all Category-2 claims, and so on, until the assets are exhausted. Therefore, in many instances some of the classes will go unpaid. The categories, in descending order of priority, are:

- Voluntary employee contributions made to the plan. (NOTE: These amounts are NOT guaranteed by the PBGC, because they fall outside the definition of "basic benefits.");

- Mandatory contributions that employees made to the plan, plus 5% interest;

- Annuity benefits that derive from employer contributions, if the annuity was or could have been in pay status three years or more before termination of the plan. ("Could have been" refers to the situation in which employees continue to work despite their eligibility for early retirement);

- All other PBGC-guaranteed benefits;
- All other nonforfeitable benefits;
- All benefits that are accrued but forfeitable.

Before a plan administrator can actually make any distributions, there is a legal obligation to determine the plan's ability to pay benefits at the level deemed appropriate by the PBGC. The plan administrator must notify the PBGC if the plan is unable to pay the guaranteed benefits. The PBGC makes its own determination and issues notices. If, on the other hand, the administrator determines that the PBGC-guaranteed benefits, but not all the guaranteed liabilities, can be paid, then the plan should distribute the assets but notify the PBGC.

If the PBGC affirms the administrator's characterization, it will issue a Notice of Liability resolving the issue of the plan's sufficiency. The plan administrator is obligated to provide a new valuation of the plan's liabilities and guaranteed benefits. An enrolled actuary must certify the valuation.

*Hughes Aircraft Co. v. Jacobson* [525 U.S. 432 (1999)], which involved several other pension issues, also affects plan termination. This case involves a plan partially funded by mandatory employee contributions. The employer suspended its own contributions at a time when the plan had a surplus. The employer created a new, noncontributory plan for new plan participants. Participants in the existing plan charged the employer with ERISA violations in connection with the amendment. The Supreme Court held that the employees were not entitled to an order terminating the plan voluntarily because the changes in plan structure did not constitute an ERISA § 4041(a)(1) voluntary termination. As long as a plan continues to provide benefits to participants and to accumulate funds for future payments, termination is not appropriate.

Under the Supreme Court's 2007 *Beck* ruling, it is not a violation of fiduciary duty for a bankrupt company to put the plan through a standard termination (and purchase annuities to satisfy the obligation to pay benefits) in lieu of merging the pension plan into a multi-employer union-run fund. [*Beck v. PACE Int'l Union*, 551 U.S. 96 (2007)]

Also note that the final regulations about nonqualified plans such as top-hat plans provide that terminating and then liquidating a nonqualified plan may be considered a prohibited acceleration of payments that results in the recipient being taxed under Code § 409A. There is an exception to this rule if the employer terminates all the plans of the same type, pays out benefits over a period of one to two years, and refrains from adopting new plans of the same type for three years. [Final Regulations, 73 Fed. Reg. 19234 (Apr. 17, 2007)]

## [B]  Standard Termination

The steps in a standard termination are:

- Plan sponsor decides to terminate the plan, e.g., because the plan is too expensive, or the amount of contributions is too hard to predict.

- Sponsor ensures that the plan has enough assets to satisfy all of its liabilities. It may be necessary for the plan sponsor to make a "top-up" contribution to ensure the necessary level of assets. Or, the sponsor can "freeze and wait," giving 204(h) notice and hoping that the funding gap will be eliminated if the plan's economic condition improves. If the plan is not able to distribute all required benefits in full, a standard termination is unavailable, and only a distress termination or involuntary termination remains possible.

- Standard termination is not permitted if it violates an existing CBA. The PBGC refuses to intervene when a union challenges a proposed standard termination; the challenge has to be resolved as a labor dispute.

- Sponsor decides what replacement benefits participants will receive (e.g., the company could adopt a new 401(k) plan).

- Not only must the legally required notices be issued, plan participants should be kept informed about the rationale for the termination and how it will affect them economically.

- The plan's investment strategy may have to change, e.g., to make sure that there is enough liquidity to distribute benefits. If there are any excess assets remaining after participants receive their benefits, either the remaining funds will revert to the employer (if reversion is allowed) or will be distributed among the participants.

- The plan may have to be amended, e.g., to permit lump sum distributions or to eliminate ancillary benefits such as life insurance that are not protected by ERISA. If the plan is not already frozen, the sponsor will probably want to amend it to freeze benefit accruals as of the planned date of termination, even if the standard termination has not been completed. The PBGC's regulations disregard any amendment adopted after a termination date if it reduces benefits (even optional benefits), unless the amendment was required by the Internal Revenue Code.

- The PBGC requires plans to perform a "diligent search" to locate missing participants. [See, e.g., Harold J. Ashner, *Planning a Standard Termination—A Checklist for Practitioners*, 16 J. of Pension Benefits No. 1 (Winter 2009) (benefitslink.com)]

The appropriate PBGC form for carrying out a standard termination is Form 500 (Standard Termination Notice).

When a plan goes through a standard termination, ERISA § 4050 provides for payment of a designated amount to the PBGC to cover claims from missing participants. The calculation usually depends on the most valuable annuity benefit payable under ERISA assumptions about missing participants, which use the Part 4044 interest assumptions, but with a different mortality table. Until 2007, the PBGC used the table in Rev. Rul. 95-6, but effective February 27, 2007, a blend of mortality rates for healthy males and healthy females (50% each) taken from Part 4044 will be used instead. [RIN 1212-AB08; see (No by-line) *PBGC Revises Mortality Assumptions in Regulations*, CCH Pension and Benefits (Jan. 25, 2007) (benefitslink.com)] See <http://www.pbgc.gov/prac/mortality-retirement-and-pv-max-guarantee/erisa-mortality-tables/erisa-section-4044-mortality-table-for-2013-valuation-dates.html> for the § 4044 mortality table for valuation dates in 2013. To find missing participants, terminating plans can use the PBGC's missing participants program, paying the benefits to the PBGC, which then searches for the participants. Although the PPA mandated that the PBGC extend this program to cover terminating 401(k) plans, the PBGC did not issue implementing regulations. The DOL's suggestions for finding missing participants include commercial locater services, internet searches, and consulting credit reports. Effective for requests postmarked on or after August 31, 2012, the IRS will no longer forward letters from plan sponsors who need to find the payees of benefits. Rev. Proc. 2012-35, 2012-37 I.R.B. 341 states that the IRS no longer considers finding missing participants a "humane purpose." The IRS service was free for up to 50 participants. The ending of this options means employers will have to use a more difficult and expensive method. The Social Security Administration's forwarding service is still available, but it costs $25 per letter. Sponsors and administrators who want to use EPCRS (see § 15.19[B]) and must find missing participants to pay additional benefits will be affected by the change, so the IRS said that it would publish EPCRS guidance with an extended correction period for employers affected by the change. [McDermott Will & Emery, *IRS Eliminates Use of Letter Forwarding Service to Find Missing Participants and Beneficiaries* (Sept. 27, 2012) (benefitslink.com); Plansponsor staff, *IRS Stops Forwarding Letters for Missing Participants*, plansponsor.com (September 4, 2012)]

Within 120 days after the proposed termination date, the plan administrator must submit a Schedule EA-5 of the Form 500, a certificate prepared by a PBGC-enrolled actuary to the PBGC. The certificate estimates the value of the plan assets and the present value of plan liabilities, so that the actuary can certify that assets are adequate to satisfy the liabilities. The administrator must also furnish any other information the PBGC requests. The plan administrator must certify under penalty of perjury that the actuary's certificate is correct, and that the information given to the PBGC has been accurate and complete.

Once all the assets are distributed, the administrator must file PBGC Form 501 within 30 days of the final distribution, to prove that the assets were distributed. The penalty for a late form can be up to $1,100 a day. [See 29 C.F.R. § 4010.13] Late filing can also have the effect of creating a last, short plan year for the plan—thereby reducing the refund of the PBGC premium that the employer would otherwise be entitled to receive.

The ERISA § 204(h) notice of the amendment (including disclosure of its effective date) must be given. [See § 5.07 for further discussion of this issue]

## [C] Notification

The DOL's *Reporting and Disclosure Guide for Employee Benefit Plans* [<http://www.dol.gov/ebsa/pdf/rdguide.pdf> (October 2008; still displayed on the PBGC site in May 2013)] lists the reporting and disclosure requirements for a standard termination, as prescribed by ERISA §§ 4041, 4050, and 29 C.F.R. (Parts 4041 and 4050) as:

- Notice of intent to terminate;
- Standard Termination Notice (Form 500);
- Notice of plan benefits;
- Post-Distribution Certification (Form 501);
- Schedule MP (Missing Participants).

At least 60 days but not more than 90 days before the proposed date of a voluntary termination, the plan administrator must provide notice of the intended termination. [ERISA § 4041(a)(2)] Notice must be given to plan participants; their beneficiaries; alternate payees under domestic relations orders; and the employees' collective bargaining representative (if the workplace is unionized). The notice must give the date of the termination and must explain that the PBGC guarantee ends as soon as the benefits are distributed. The notice must also disclose the name and address of the insurance company chosen to provide annuities to participants. (If the choice has not yet been made, the names and addresses of possible choices must be disclosed.)

■ **TIP:** Selection of the insurer is a fiduciary decision, subject to the normal rules of fiduciary duty. The notice must also identify a contact person who will answer questions about the termination process.

Items to be disclosed include:

- The name of the plan and of its sponsor;
- The plan's tax number;

- The sponsor's Employer Identification Number;

- A statement that service credit and benefits will continue to accrue until the termination, or that benefit accruals have been frozen or will be frozen on a specified date—whichever is applicable;

- A promise to provide written notification of the benefits each affected party will receive under the termination;

- A promise to each retiree that retirement benefits in annuity form will not be affected by the termination;

- Disclosure that standard termination is available if and only if the plan has adequate assets to cover its liabilities to all participants and all beneficiaries of deceased participants;

- A statement that further notice will be given if the termination does not occur as contemplated.

The plan's filing of PBGC Form 500 (Standard Termination Notice) triggers the obligation to issue another notice to participants and beneficiaries, in a comprehensible, nontechnical form. This Notice of Plan Benefits [PBGC Reg. § 4041.23, .24] explains the factors determining benefit entitlement (e.g., age, length of service, wages, interest assumptions), and how payments will be made. It is also necessary to disclose that benefits might be either higher or lower than the estimate.

For benefits already in pay status, disclosure is required of the amount and form of benefits that will be payable. For individuals who have named a retirement date and elected a form for the payout, but whose benefits are not yet in pay status, the projected benefit start date must be announced, with disclosure of the form and amount of benefits payable as of that date, and the date for any scheduled increase or reduction in benefits. If the benefit start date is not known for benefits not in pay status, disclosure is required of the benefits available at normal retirement age or after the death of a participant, with special attention to any benefits that can be paid as lump sums.

PBGC Proposed Regulations dating from December 2007 cover the information disclosure requirements for distress and PBGC-initiated terminations occurring on or after the PPA's enactment date (Aug. 17, 2006). As amended by the PPA, ERISA §§ 4041 and 4042 give plan participants and other affected parties the right to request certain information about a pending termination. The information must be provided within 15 business days of the request. Plan sponsors and administrators are forbidden to divulge information that identifies individual participants or beneficiaries, but the plan must obtain a court order to protect information that the plan characterizes as confidential (e.g., trade secrets).

In a PBGC-initiated termination, the information request can only be made after the plan administrator receives the PBGC's Notice of Determination that the plan should be terminated. The Proposed Regulations assume that the administrator received the notice three days after the PBGC issued it, so queries are proper within three days of this date, even if the notice has not actually been received. ERISA § 4071 imposes a penalty of up to $1,100 per day for failure to make timely disclosure pursuant to a request. When the PBGC receives a request, its obligation is to provide a copy of the administrative record including the trusteeship decision record of termination. The confidentiality rules that prohibit disclosure of individual identities do not apply to the PBGC. [72 Fed. Reg. 68542 (Dec. 5, 2007); see Guest article, *PBGC Proposes Rules on New Termination Information Disclosure Requirements*, Deloitte's Washington Bulletin, <http://benefitslink.com/articles/washbull080122a.html> (Jan. 22, 2008)]

Once the plan assets have been distributed, Form 501 (Post-Distribution Certification) must be given to the PBGC within 30 days of the end of the distribution processes. The PBGC has announced that it will not impose penalties for late submission of this form if it is provided within 90 days after the deadline, including any extensions. Schedule MP, alerting the PBGC to the existence of participants or beneficiaries whose addresses the plan administrator cannot find, is filed with Form 501.

The PPA enacted new ERISA sections, § 4041(c)(2)(D), 4042(c)(3), requiring plan participants to be given the same information about involuntary and distress terminations as the plan furnishes to the PBGC. The new requirement replaces the participant notice formerly required under ERISA § 4011. Plans that were subject to the variable-rate premium in 2006 probably had to issue a participant notice; PBGC Tech Update 06-3 includes a worksheet for determining whether a notice is required. Tech Update 06-4 explains the interest rates to be used in certain reporting and disclosure situations. [See <http://www.pbgc.gov/practitioners/What-New/whatsnew/page15560.html> (Oct. 23, 2006)]

Information about plan termination must also be provided in the Summary Plan Description (SPD) furnished to plan participants. EBSA's Final Rule about SPDs [65 Fed. Reg. 70226–70244 (Nov. 21, 2000)] requires disclosure of:

- A summary of the plan's provisions authorizing the sponsor, or other party, to terminate the plan or eliminate some or all of its benefits;

- Circumstances that might trigger termination or elimination of some benefits;

- The benefits, rights, and obligations of plan participants and beneficiaries if and when the plan is terminated. In pension plan SPDs, the accrual and vesting consequences of plan termination must be disclosed. (This is not an issue in welfare plan SPDs, because such benefits do not vest);

- How the plan assets will be disposed of on termination.

## [D]  Distress Termination

A plan that does not have enough assets to pay all the benefit liabilities can apply to the PBGC for a "distress" termination, which is available only if the plan's sponsors (and the other corporations that are part of a controlled group of corporations with the sponsor) can prove financial hardship, e.g., involvement in voluntary or involuntary bankruptcy or insolvency proceedings. See 29 C.F.R §§ 4041.41–4041.50. If a company makes a Chapter 11 filing, seeking bankruptcy reorganization, a distress termination will be permitted only if the bankruptcy court decides that terminating the plan is necessary, or that the company cannot remain in business and pay its debts if it maintains the plan. [See Daniel J. Morse, *Distress Termination of Pension Plans in Ch. 11*, <http:// www.gcd.com/files/Publication/48d1bf73/[ . . . ]> (March 2006)] The PBGC's *Distress Termination Filing Instructions* are available online at <http://www. pbgc.gov/docs/600_instructions.pdf>.

When the PBGC takes over a plan in a distress termination, the employer is liable to the PBGC for the amount of underfunding, which in most cases will become a general unsecured claim. The PBGC is often one of the debtor's largest unsecured creditors, entitled to a pro rata share of the recovery for the class of general unsecured creditor. It is a basic fact of bankruptcy that the amount of influence a creditor has is proportionate to the size of its claim. The PBGC receives distributions under the debtor's reorganization plan—often in the stock of the reorganized debtor company, which the PBGC sells to recoup some funds. [Ronald Silverman and Scott Seamon, *The Unexpected Guest*, N.Y.L.J. (Dec. 13, 2010) (law.com)]

Distress termination might also be permitted if the sponsor proves to the PBGC that terminating the plan is essential to paying its debts and remaining in operation. A distress termination might also be available if pension costs have become intolerable only because of the decline in the covered workforce—loss of stock market value of the plans' assets would not be considered an acceptable rationale.

DOL's Reporting and Disclosure Guide summarizes the paperwork requirements for distress terminations as:

- Form 600 (Distress Termination Notice of Intent to Terminate), given to the PBGC;

- Notice of Intent to Terminate (given to all other interested parties, such as participants, beneficiaries, unions, and alternate payees; the plan must also disclose whatever information was submitted to the PBGC within 15 days of a request, or whenever the plan updates the information given to the PBGC that was the subject of a previous request);

- Notice of request to bankruptcy court (given to the PBGC whenever the plan asks the Bankruptcy Court to approve plan termination as part of the bankruptcy process);

- Form 601 (Distress Termination Notice for a single-employer plan);

- Form 602 (post-distribution certification) furnished to the PBGC within 30 days of completion of the distribution process; here, too, the PBGC will not assess penalties if the form is furnished within 90 days of the end of the process;

- Schedule MP (Missing Participants).

To request a distress termination, the plan must file PBGC Form 600 and 601 to notify the PBGC and the plan's participants, respectively. Affected participants must get at least 60 days' notice but not more than 90 days' notice. Form 601 must be filed on or before the 120th day after the proposed termination date. The duty to notify participants is more or less the same for standard and distress terminations. A distress termination calls for actuarial certification, using Schedule EA-D of the Form 601.

If the plan has enough assets to pay the guaranteed benefits, the PBGC issues a "distribution notice." Within 15 days of receiving this notice, the plan administrator must give each participant and beneficiary a notice of impending distribution. Unless an extension has been granted, the distribution must begin within 60 days and be completed within 240 days. Then PBGC Form 602 (Post-Distribution Certification) must be filed within 30 days of the completion of distribution of the assets.

As soon as possible after receiving an application for a distress termination, the PBGC is supposed to rule on the application. If the agency turns down the application and the plan has enough assets to satisfy its liabilities, a standard termination is carried out. But if the assets are inadequate and the PBGC is not cooperative, the plan cannot go through a voluntary termination at all.

In late 2008, the PBGC published Final Regulations to implement PPA § 506 (disclosure requirements for distress and PBGC-initiated terminations); information that must be given to participants, beneficiaries, unions, and the PBGC. Under § 4041(a)(2), a plan administrator seeking a distress termination must provide notice of intent to terminate to every affected party. The notice to the PBGC is given on Form 600, Distress Termination, Notice of Intent to Terminate. On written request from an interested party, the plan administrator must provide copies of all of the information submitted to the PBGC. [Final Rule, 73 Fed. Reg. 68333 (Nov. 18, 2008); see CCH Pension & Benefits, PBGC *Final Regs Issued on Plan Termination Disclosure Requirements* (Dec. 1, 2008); see Fred Schneyer, *PBGC Puts Out Distress Termination Info Release Rule*, plan sponsor.com (Nov. 17, 2008). The final regulations are applicable to terminations initiated on or after Aug. 17, 2006, but cover only requests for information made on or after Dec. 18, 2008.]

## [E]  Partial Termination

Full vesting is required when a plan is terminated or partially terminated, but there is no simple definition of "partial termination." The IRS says that partial termination occurs when there is a substantial reduction in the number or percentage of plan participants—e.g., when there has been a significant layoff. Hence, a company considering layoffs must consider whether the action will have implications on the pension plan. An amendment that excludes a group of employees from the plan could also trigger partial termination. Partial termination also requires allocation of forfeitures and other unallocated amounts held by the plan. Whether partial termination has occurred is determined by all the facts and circumstances, but IRS guidance says that partial termination is presumed when there has been 20% turnover. The presumption can be rebutted by showing that this level of turnover is routine. [Holland & Hart LLP, *Layoffs May Trigger 100% Vesting in Retirement Plans* (Jan. 9, 2009) (benefitslink.com)]

The IRS is pursuing both defined benefit and defined contribution plans that have experienced partial termination events. When a partial termination occurs, all affected participants become 100% vested, although usually they will not receive distributions except to the extent they are eligible because of termination of employment. The IRS Employee Plans Compliance Unit's Partial Termination/ Partial Vesting Project uses data from Form 5500 filings to discover partial termination events (involuntary removal of a group of employees from plan participation when there has been a significant reduction in the participant group). A partial termination could be caused by plant shutdown, layoffs, downsizing, restructuring, or a sale that excludes a group of participants from the plan. The determination that a partial termination has occurred is a fiduciary decision generally made by the plan administrator or administrative committee. Although there are IRS guidelines, the determination must be made based on the facts and circumstances of the case.

The IRS uses a rebuttable presumption that there has been a partial termination if there has been a 20% turnover rate within a short period of time. The turnover rate equals the number of participants whose severance from employment is initiated by the employer during the applicable period divided by the sum of the number of participants at the start of the applicable period and the participants added during the applicable period.

The IRS treats any separation from service other than death, disability, or retirement at normal retirement age as employer-initiated, unless the employer can verify that the employee chose to leave or was terminated for cause. Events outside the employer's control, such as economic conditions, are still considered employer-initiated. The employer's normal turnover rate is also a factor: if this year's rate is 22% but the historical rate is 10%, the IRS might be persuaded that the current turnover rate is really only 12%, so there has not been a partial termination. For 401(k) plans, all employees eligible to make elective deferrals are considered participants, whether or not they actually make deferrals. [Lisa B. Zimmer, *Partial Plan Termination . . . What's That?* Warner Norcross & Judd LLP (Nov. 11, 2011) (benefitslink.com)]

If participation levels drop purely as a result of voluntary employee turnover and the employer's actions did not cause the reduction, there has not been a partial termination. However, in some cases employees allege that they were constructively terminated rather than quitting voluntarily or that they were fraudulently induced to take severance. To defend itself, the employer needs records showing whether departing employees quit or were laid off. Despite the Revenue Ruling using a 20% standard for partial terminations, some courts have found a partial termination based on the number rather than percentage of layoffs if they were motivated by a desire to reduce employer contributions or increase forfeitures. [Jeffrey C. Chang, *A Question of Vesting – Determining If Your Plan Has Suffered A Partial Termination*, Chang Ruthenberg & Long (undated, last accessed Mar. 30, 2013) (benefitslink.com)]

The Seventh Circuit rule is that events from more than one plan year can be used to determine if a partial termination has occurred, when an employee alleges that his balances should vest fully because of the termination. [*Matz v. Household Int'l Tax Reduction Inv. Plan*, 227 F.3d 971 (7th Cir. 2000); see also *Sea Ray v. Robinson*, 164 F.3d 981 (6th Cir. 1999)] The Sixth Circuit's rationale in this situation is that, if review was limited to a single year, employers would be able to escape liability by firing some employees in December, some in January. [*Sea Ray*, 164 F.3d 981]

On a related issue, the *Matz* court required counting of both vested and nonvested participants to determine whether a partial termination occurred. However, the Supreme Court ordered the court to reconsider its opinion because of *United States v. Mead Corp.* [533 U.S. 218 (2001)], a Supreme Court case about the extent to which courts have to abide by the rules of administrative agencies. This time, the Seventh Circuit decided that only nonvested participants should be counted in deciding if there has been a partial termination. [*Matz v. Household Int'l Tax Reduction Inv. Plan*, 265 F.3d 572 (7th Cir. 2001)] Litigation in the case continued, and in 2004 the Seventh Circuit adopted the IRS' formula, on the grounds that at-will employees have no reasonable expectation of receiving benefits before vesting occurs, because the at-will employees can be terminated at any time. The Seventh Circuit set 20% as the dividing line: there is a rebuttable presumption that there is no partial termination when reduction in plan participation is below 20%, and a rebuttable presumption of partial termination when plan participation drops by more than 20%. [*Matz v. Household Int'l Tax Reduction Inv. Plan*, 388 F.3d 570 (7th Cir. 2004). See also 441 F.3d 500 (7th Cir. 2006) for class certification issues in this litigation.]

## [F]  Orphan Plans

Although in most cases, termination will be performed by the plan sponsor, an "abandoned" or "orphan" plan is one which no longer has a plan sponsor, or whose sponsor has ceased to conduct business.

When an asset purchase results in the liquidation of the seller company, or when corporate assets are acquired by a buyer, some legacy retirement plans can become orphan plans if they are forgotten or abandoned. The lack of a sponsor may lead to the plan losing its tax-qualified status. There are also fiduciary issues about managing the plan's assets, reporting, and distributions. EPCRS (see § 15.19[B]) includes an orphan plan process. [Keith R. McMurdy, *Don't Let Your Plan Become an Orphan*, Fox Rothschild LLP Employee Benefits Legal Blog (Jan. 24, 2012) (benefitslink.com)]

In March 2005, the DOL issued guidance for winding up of orphan plans by Qualified Termination Administrators (QTAs) who have the power to distribute the benefits from individual account plans when they deem the plan to be abandoned (e.g., there have been no contributions to, or distributions from, the plan over a 12-month period or the sponsor corporation has been liquidated in a Chapter 11 bankruptcy proceeding). A QTA must be a person or entity who could serve as an IRA trustee, such as a bank, insurer, or mutual fund.

The QTA must also notify the DOL that the plan is abandoned, that it intends to serve as QTA, the estimated value of the plan assets, and similar items. The DOL has issued a model notice that can be used for this purpose. There is a safe harbor for balances rolled over to IRAs. [70 Fed. Reg. 12045 (Mar. 10, 2005); see 71 Fed. Reg. 20820 (Apr. 21, 2006), re orphan 401(k) plans] Under 29 C.F.R. § 2578.1, the Qualified Termination Administrator (QTA) has a duty to file the Special Terminal Report for Abandoned Plans (STRAP). The STRAP is an attachment to the final notice, which is sent to the EBSA Office of Enforcement (Abandoned Plan Coordinator). The QTA can file Form 5500 with either Schedule I or Schedule QTA [DOL, *Special Terminal Report Instructions for Abandoned Plans*, Department of Labor, <http://www.dol.gov/ebsa/publications/APterminalreport.html> (June 21, 2006); see also EBSA Interim Final Rule, *Amendments to Safe Harbor for Distributions from Terminated Individual Account Plans and Termination of Abandoned Individual Account Plans to Require Inherited Individual Retirement Plans for Missing Nonspouse Beneficiaries*, RIN 1210-AB16, 72 Fed. Reg. 7516 (Feb. 15, 2007)]

The abandoned plan process requires the use of a Qualified Termination Administrator (QTA), a party eligible to serve as trustee or issuer of an individual retirement plan and who holds the abandoned plan's assets. The QTA must make a finding that the sponsor no longer exists, cannot be found, or can no longer maintain the plan. The plan is officially deemed terminated 90 days after EBSA's Office of Enforcement acknowledges receipt of the notice of plan abandonment.

In order to wind up an abandoned 401(k) plan, the QTA:

- Updates the plan records;

- Calculates benefits payable to each participant and beneficiary;

- Reports any delinquent contributions;

- Uses plan assets to pay the reasonable expenses of serving as QTA;

- Notifies the participants and beneficiaries of the upcoming termination. The notice must include the statement that actual benefits may be more or less than the estimate because of investment gains or losses and administrative expenses. The QTA must explain distribution options to the participants and beneficiaries, warning them that if they do not make an election within 30 days, the QTA will deposit the account balance in an IRA, a federally insured interest-bearing bank account, or send it to the unclaimed property fund of the state of the participant's last known address;

- Distributes the benefits;

- Files the Special Terminal Report for Abandoned Plans;

- Circulates a final notice.

Notice of intent to terminate the plan must be sent, by certified mail, to the former plan sponsor at its last known mailing address. Thirty days after that notice, a second notice of plan abandonment must be given to the DOL, indicating the party's intent to serve as QTA. (A model notice for this purpose can be found on the DOL Website; so can a notice informing participants of their right to roll over 401(k) balances to an IRA.) [Abandoned plan regulation and appendix of forms, <http://ecfr.gpoaccess.gov/cgi/t/text/text-idx?c=ecfr&tpl=/ecfrbrowse/Title29/29cfr2578_main_02.tpl>. See James Baker, *Lost and Found: The Abandoned Plan Rule*, 24 Benefits Law Journal #3 (Autumn 2011) (benefitslink.com)]

In late 2012, the DOL announced its intention to extend the Abandoned Plan Program so that Chapter 7 bankruptcy trustees could use streamlined termination and distribution procedures to distribute the assets of individual account retirement plans of bankrupt companies. The QTA does not have to file a Form 5500 for the abandoned plan, but does have to file a summary terminal report after the plan has been wound up. Under the 2012 proposal, a Chapter 7 plan is deemed abandoned on the date the bankruptcy court enters an order for relief. The trustee, or the trustee's designee using information provided by the trustee, must determine if it makes economic sense to collect the delinquent contributions (in other words, if the cost of collection is less than the amount to be collected). If collection is financially viable, the trustee has a duty to collect the delinquent contributions. [DOL/EBSA, *Fact Sheet: Proposed Amendments to Abandoned Plan Program Dec. 2012* (benefitslink.com)]

## § 17.03   THE PBGC'S ROLE

A great deal of work is required to terminate a plan and wind up its affairs. For most participants, it takes the PBGC about three years to process a termination and provide finalized benefits. Most employees are not subject to recoupment. However, the delays and uncertainty make it difficult for participants in a terminating plan to make financial plans.

The PBGC sends a letter to participants informing them that their plan has been terminated and the PBGC has taken over as trustee. Once the PBGC determines the benefit, it sends a "benefit determination letter" explaining the final benefit amount. The PBGC continues making payments to retirees, with any adjustments required to reflect the limits on the PBGC guarantee

In the case of a single-employer plan, the PBGC guarantees payment of all nonforfeitable benefits. However, the PBGC guarantee is subject to a maximum limitation, with the result that some participants will not receive the full benefit they would have received had the plan not terminated.

Persons who were already retired before the PBGC takeover continue to receive the benefit form they elected. Those who retire later choose among the PBGC's retirement options. Most de minimis benefits (under $5,000) will be cashed out in a lump sum. Monthly benefits under $50 will be paid in a single annual check. Other benefits will be paid monthly. If the plan has adequate assets, some participants will receive more than the basic PBGC guarantee, usually if they retired, or could have retired, three years before the guarantees took effect.

A participant who has not yet commenced benefit payments from a terminated plan can begin benefits at the plan's normal retirement date. A person who has satisfied all requirements (such as years of service) for early retirement as of the date of plan termination (or bankruptcy filing date) can commence early retirement payments at early retirement age—but only if he or she no longer works for the employer.

For benefits already in pay status, the guarantee is based on age at the date the guarantee takes effect but for those not already receiving benefits, the guarantee is based on the age at which payments begin (with adjustments for disabled participants). The maximum guarantee is also adjusted for payment forms other than the single-life annuity. [PBGC.gov, *PBGC's Guarantees for Single-Employer Pension Plans Fact Sheet*] In a standard termination, a fully funded plan terminates; the PBGC does not become a trustee. In a distress termination, the sponsors must apply the limits themselves, so benefits are reduced as of the date of termination. The PBGC sometimes needs years to make the calculations for an involuntary termination.

When the benefit is changed, underpaid retirees usually get a lump sum back payment with interest. Overpaid beneficiaries do not have to pay interest; their future monthly payments are reduced to make up the difference. Under PBGC regulations, the most that the monthly benefit can be reduced is 10% of the monthly benefit, or the amount in excess of the maximum guaranteed benefit—whichever is larger. The PBGC reports that most overpayments are less than $3,000, and the usual repayment amount is about $16 per month. [GAO-10-181T, *PBGC, Workers and Retirees Experience Delays and Uncertainty When Underfunded Plans Are Terminated*, testimony of Barbara D. Bovbjerg (Oct. 29, 2009)]

## [A]  PBGC Guarantee

Defined benefit plans pay premiums to the PBGC annually, providing funds for the federal agency to supervise plan terminations and, if necessary, assume payment of a terminating or terminated plan's obligations to its participants. The Deficit Reduction Act of 2005, Pub. L. No. 109-171, increased the PBGC premium for single-employer plans from its long-held $19 per employee per year to $30. DRA '05 also institutes inflation-indexing of the premium . The 2013 flat-rate premium is $42/participant, rising to $49/participant in 2014 and $50/participant in 2015. The variable-rate premium goes from $9/$1,000 unfunded vested benefits in 2013 to $13 in 2014 and $18 in 2015. However, in all three years, the variable-rate premium is subject to a cap of $400/participant. [PBGC, *Pension Insurance Premiums Fact Sheet*, <http://www.pbgc.gov/res/factsheets/page/premiums.html> (last accessed Aug. 19, 2013)]. In the January 2013 edition of "What's New in My PAA," the PBGC announced that premium filings for plan year 2013 could be made through the online My PAA system. The per-employee flat rate premium is $42 for single-employer, $12 for multi-employer plans. [PBGC, *Premium Filing MyPAA Pension Benefit Guaranty Corporation*]

Certain terminations are also subject to a one-time payment of $1,250. The PBGC guarantee is intended to protect the employees of the plan, not the sponsor corporation. If the assets of a terminating plan are not large enough to pay the benefits, the PBGC makes the payments and then seeks recoupment from the corporation. However, an employer's liability to the PBGC is capped at 70% of its net worth, or 75% of the unfunded guaranteed benefits.

In mid-2013, the PBGC proposed new rules for payment of PBGC premiums. For terminating plans, the premium for the plan's final year would be due on the normal due date; 90 days after the date of the last distribution of benefits; or the date when the plan files a certificate that distributions have been completed—whichever comes first. Under the proposal, plans that go through a standard termination do not have to pay the variable-rate premium for the year the plan closes out, as long as they complete the termination in the premium payment year. The variable-rate premium must be paid, possibly with late-payment penalties, if the standard termination is not completed during that year. [Buck Consultants FYI, *PBGC Proposes New Premium Rules for 2014*, <http://www.buckconsultants.com/portals/0publications/fyi/2013/FYI-2013-0725-PBGC-proposes-new-premium-rules-2014.pdf> (July 25, 2013)]

In April 2009, the Second Circuit held that PBGC termination premiums are not contingent pre-petition claims that can be discharged under Chapter 11. Therefore, companies that terminate their plans post-filing may still have to pay the premium. The Second Circuit ruled that the PBGC's right to termination premiums does not arise until after the discharge, so there was no valid right before bankruptcy decided by non-bankruptcy law (the test of a dischargeable pre-petition claim). Certiorari was denied in late 2009. [*PBGC v. Oneida Ltd.,* 562 F.3d 154 (2d Cir. 2009); see Felice R. Yudkin, *Second Circuit Finds Termination Premiums Non-Dischargeable in Bankruptcy,* Bankruptcy & Restructuring Law Monitor (May 5, 2009) (benefitslink.com); Rebecca Moore, *High Court Lets Stand Decision on Discharging PBGC Termination Premiums,* plansponsor.com (Dec. 15, 2009)]

Form 500 requires employers to explain why the plan is terminating; if there are multiple reasons, they must be ranked in order of importance. The PBGC said that the most common reason was restructuring of the retirement program, followed by the cost of providing the benefits, adverse business conditions, the expense of administering the plan, sale of the company, and liquidation.

The PBGC guarantees "basic benefits." (The PBGC has legal authority to set up a separate trust fund to guarantee nonbasic benefits, but it has chosen not to do so.) The basic benefit guaranteed by the PBGC is a monthly life annuity that lasts for the participant's life. (This is in contrast to the joint and survivor annuity that is the normal payment form for a married participant to receive under an ongoing plan.) The annuity begins at age 65.

Benefits and increases that were not in effect for five years before the termination date/bankruptcy filing date receive only partial, phased-in protection: the PBGC guarantees 20% or $20 per month of the increase (whichever is larger) of the increase for each full year since the increase took effects. Shut-down benefits are phased in depending on the number of years since the plant closing or other shutdown event. [PBGC.gov, *PBGC's Guarantees for Single-Employer Pension Plans Fact Sheet*]

In 2013, the PBGC reported that close to 85% of retirees will receive the full amount of their pensions from plans taken over by the PBGC. For 2013, the maximum PBGC guarantee for a 65 year-old retiree rose from $56,000 to $57,477.24. At 62, the annual maximum guarantee is $45,407.04 ($3,783.92 monthly, $3,405.53 joint and survivor). At age 57, the maximum guarantee is $30,462.96 ($2,538.58 a month, $2,284.72 for a joint and survivor benefit); at 50, the maximum guarantee is $20,117.04 ($1,676.42 a month, or $1,676.42 joint and survivor). [pbgc.gov, *PBGC Maximum Insurance Benefit Increases for 2013* (Nov. 27, 2012]

The 2013 present values of the PBGC guarantee range from $125,539, at age 25, $153,501 (30), $180,229 (35), $230,843 (40), $282,286 (45), $371,638 (50), $476,923 (55), $604,500 (60), $782,324 (65), $1,122,428 (70), $1,704,372 (75), $2,844,680 (80). [*Present Value of PBGC Maximum Guarantee,*

<http://www.pbgc.gov/prac/mortality-retirement-and-pv-max-guarantee/present-guarantee.html> (last viewed Mar. 10, 2013)]

When a plan is to be terminated, the PBGC:

- Determines if the benefit is nonforfeitable and payable in periodic install-ments; if so, it is a guaranteed basic benefit;

- Performs actuarial calculations to convert benefits in other forms to straight life annuities commencing at age 65.

The PBGC has the power to assess penalties if an employer was late in pay-ing its PBGC premiums, or if the employer failed to provide the required notices to employees.

In March 2011, the PBGC proposed a rule to amend its regulation dealing with benefits payable in terminated single-employer plans. The rule implements Pension Protection Act (PPA) § 403, which says that the phase-in period for the guarantee of benefits that are contingent on an "unpredictable contingent event" (the regulation gives the example of a plant shut-down) begins no earlier than the date of the event itself. The rule was necessary because PBGC's guarantee of new pension benefits and benefit increases phases in over a five-year period starting with the later of the date of adoption or the effective date of the change. (This rule was adopted to protect the PBGC against obligations that would be created by plans that knew they were going to terminate adopting new benefits.) The PPA added a new section, ERISA § 4022(b)(8), phasing in the guarantee as if the amendment creating an unpredictable contingent event benefit was adopted on the date of the event, rather than the (usually earlier) date of the plan amendment. The net effect is that the guarantee for benefits that arise from unpredictable contin-gent events that occur within five years of plan termination is probably lower than the guarantee that would have been available under the pre-PPA law. [PBGC Pro-posed Rule RIN 1212-AB18, 76 Fed. Reg. 13304 (Mar. 11, 2011); see Rebecca Moore, *PBGC Proposes Guidance on Limitations on Guaranteed Benefits*, plan sponsor.com (Mar. 10, 2011). The rule was finalized in mid-2011: 76 Fed. Reg. 34590 (June 14, 2011).]

Variable interest rates create serious problems when the plan is terminated because a participant's exact benefit can only be determined at the time benefits begin—but the PBGC needs to know if the benefit amount is de minimis and, therefore, can be made in a single payment. A PBGC proposed regulation, imple-menting PPA § 2006, was published in late 2011.

The proposed regulation explains how to determine the benefits payable when a hybrid plan (e.g., cash balance or pension equity) terminates: a variable rate is used that is an average of rates used in the five years before termination. In a distress termination, the proposed termination date determines the benefits under the plan. If the proposed termination date is deferred, the benefits accrued between the proposed and actual termination dates are recalculated with the interest rate that would have applied before the final termination date. [Proposed Regulations, 76 Fed. Reg. 67105 (Oct. 31, 2011; see Deloitte's Washington Bulletin, *PBGC Proposes Rules on Determining Benefits in Terminating Hybrid Plans* (Nov. 7, 2011) (benefitslink.com)]

Mid-2009 PBGC proposed regulations explain USERRA rights in connection with the ERISA requirement that guaranteed benefits be nonforfeitable when a plan terminates. For USERRA re-employment on or after December 12, 1994, the PBGC proposed to amend 29 C.F.R. Part 4022 to deem participants to have satisfied the conditions for reemployment as of the termination date of the plan as long as the veteran returns to his or her prior job within the USERRA time frame, even if re-employment actually occurs after the plan's termination date. If the plan sponsor is bankrupt at the time of plan termination, the bankruptcy filing date is treated as the termination date for various purposes, including USERRA. [PBGC Proposed Rule, FR Doc E9-17623, *USERRA Benefits Under Title IV of ERISA*, 74 Fed. Reg. 37666 (July 29, 2009); see CCH Pension & Benefits, *PBGC Issues Proposed Regs on Interaction of USERRA Rules and ERISA Benefit Guarantee* (Aug. 18, 2009) (benefitslink.com)]

## [B] Proposal on Payment Forms

Regulations proposed in 2000 and adopted, more or less intact, in 2002 [PBGC No. 02-14 (Dec. 22, 2000) [65 Fed. Reg. 81456 (Dec. 26, 2000), 67 Fed. Reg. 16949 (Apr. 18, 2002)] discuss payment options when the PBGC takes over a plan. Participants can select alternative annuity benefit forms—straight life, five, 10, or 15 years certain and continuous; joint and survivor annuities with various levels of benefits, and "pop-up" annuities that increase if the beneficiary dies before the participant. (Alternate payment forms require the consent of spouses of married participants.) The regulations also discuss inheritance of payments to a deceased participant.

Some changes were made in the definition of "earliest PBGC Retirement Date." The regulations define the "earliest PBGC Retirement Date" as the earliest date the plan participant could retire for the purposes of ERISA Title IV. Usually, this will mean either age 55 or the first date the participant could retire and collect an immediate annuity, whichever is later.

## [C] Penalties and PBGC Enforcement

The PBGC, like the IRS, has the power to assess penalties if required documents are omitted, if documents are filed but are late, if payments are not made, or if payments are made but in an untimely fashion. The PBGC can waive penalties if the failure was due to factors outside the business' control. Penalties can be waived in full or in part, e.g., if there were factors preventing timely full compliance, but the plan was dilatory in getting back into compliance.

Penalties can be waived if payment would impose undue hardship on the business. "Reasonable cause" that might justify a waiver requires a showing that even ordinary business care and prudence would not have permitted full timely payment. Reasonable reliance on incorrect advice from a PBGC employee could give rise to a waiver—but reliance on the plan's own professional advisors will not. [PBGC Final Regulations, 71 Fed. Reg. 66867 (Nov. 17, 2006)]

## [D]  QDROs in Plans Under PBGC Control

Qualified Domestic Relations Orders (QDROs) are discussed in detail at § 12.08. If the PBGC takes over a plan some of whose benefits must be paid to alternate payees (ex-spouses and separated spouses of participants), it issues two standard QDRO forms (Model Separate Interest; Model Shared Payment) for use by domestic relations courts. PBGC QDROs either specify or give the alternate payee discretion to control the time at which benefits begin, how the benefits are paid, the percentage of the pension payment going to the alternate payee, and how long the alternate payments begin.

QDROs cannot require the PBGC to provide any benefit type or option that would not otherwise be available under the plan or that would not otherwise be offered by the PBGC. Nor can the court order increase the amount that the PBGC would have to pay relative to the employee spouse's pension account.

The PBGC's Model Separate Interest form can be used only if the order is entered before the employee's pension is in pay status. It is appropriate when the alternate payee's benefits are fixed and do not depend on when the participant starts to get benefits or the form in which the participant receives them. The effect of this form is to divide the pension account under the PBGC's control into two parts: one for the participant, one for the non-employee alternate beneficiary. The Shared Payment form, in contrast, operates at the level of each individual payment. As each payment comes due, it is divided between the employee and the alternate beneficiary. The alternate beneficiary will not receive benefits after the employee's death unless the order specifically provides for survivor benefits. The PBGC has published a lengthy, detailed, and understandable explanation of how it will divide pensions under its trusteeship when there is a Qualified Domestic Relations Order; see § 12.08 for discussion of this topic. [*The Division of Pensions Through Qualified Domestic Relations Orders*, <http://www.dol.gov/ebsa/publications/qdros.html>, or by phone at the EBSA hotline, 1-866-444-EBSA (3272). Forms can be ordered by calling the PBGC at (800) 400-7242.]

## § 17.04   INVOLUNTARY TERMINATION

### [A]   Basic Procedure

ERISA § 4042 governs involuntary termination proceedings brought when the plan assets are less than the total of guaranteed benefits. The PBGC asks the appropriate federal district court to oust the plan administrator and appoint a trustee to wind up the plan. ERISA § 4062(b)(1) makes the employer liable to the PBGC for the total amount of unfounded plan liabilities on the termination date, plus interest starting on the termination date.

The PBGC is empowered to ask for involuntary termination if:

- The plan has failed to meet its minimum funding standards;

- The plan cannot pay benefits when due;

- The plan has been required to report one or more distributions to a "substantial owner" (10% shareholder);

- The fund's liabilities will increase unreasonably if the plan is not terminated.

In those situations, it is a judgment call: The PBGC decides whether or not to seek involuntary termination. If the situation is even worse (the plan does not even have enough assets to pay its current benefits, much less to keep paying benefits as they come due; the plan has applied for a distress termination but lacks money to fund the guaranteed benefits), the PBGC has an obligation to seek involuntary termination.

If the PBGC brings an involuntary termination proceeding under ERISA Title IV, it will not be a "core proceeding" for bankruptcy purposes. The practical implication is that the District Court reviews all the issues in the bankruptcy case—it does not have to accept the rulings of the Bankruptcy Court. This, in turn, could make a difference in terms of setting the date of plan termination, which determines the interest rates and other calculations to be used. [*In re United Air Lines Inc.*, 337 B.R. 904 (N.D. Ill. 2006); see Daniel J. Morse and Kristin K. Going, "Involuntary Terminations of Pension Plans Under ERISA Are Non-Core Matters," American Bankruptcy Institute Journal <http://www.abiworld .org/InvoluntaryTerminationsofPensionPlans[ . . . ]pdf> (June 2006)]

### [B]   The Role of the Trustee

If the district court appoints a trustee, the plan must be terminated. The PBGC can also force termination of a plan even without such an appointment. If a trustee is appointed, his or her duty is to keep the plan administrator, participants, beneficiaries, unions, and employers with potential ERISA liability informed about the progress of the termination. The trustee has the power to demand turnover of some or all of the plan's records and assets. The trustee has a choice of either continuing the pattern of benefit payments in place before the trustee's appointment, or limiting payment of benefits to the basic benefits.

Under ERISA § 4062(d), the employer is liable for the unpaid contributions to the trustee plan. The employer must provide the trustee with cash, or securities acceptable to the trustee, in an amount equal to:

- The accumulated funding deficiencies under I.R.C. § 412(a);

- Any funding deficiencies that the IRS waived under I.R.C. § 412(c) before the termination date;

- All decreases in the minimum funding standard permitted by I.R.C. § 412(e) before the termination date, plus interest running from the termination date.

Under certain circumstances outlined in ERISA § 4069(b), a successor corporation can become liable for such amounts, if the sponsor reorganizes; the purpose of the reorganization was to evade liability; and reorganization occurred within the five years before a plan termination that would have caused liability. In this context, reorganization means a merger, consolidation, or becoming a division of another company; changing identity, form, or place or organization; or the liquidation of a subsidiary into its parent.

Also note that ERISA § 4062(b) provides that when an employer ceases operations at a facility, leading to separation from service of 20% or more of the total number of plan participants, the employer either has to fund the guaranteed benefits immediately, or make provision for their funding.

## [C] Calculations for Involuntary or Distress Terminations

Under 29 C.F.R. Part 4044, benefits under a plan going through an involuntary or distress termination are calculated based on a determination of the likelihood (low/medium/high) that the participant will retire early in various years. Then, once early retirement benefits are computed, the total value of benefits under the plan can be computed. The process uses the Unreduced Retirement Age, which is either the normal retirement age or the earliest age at which a pension can be paid without actuarial reduction—whichever is earlier.

Table I-13, Appendix D, is used to compute the value of early retirement benefits in an involuntary or distress termination whose valuation date is in 2012.

In this table, "year" means the year in which the unreduced benefit becomes payable. The "low" and "high" benefits are dollar amounts; the "medium" benefits are a range between the two figures.

### TABLE I-13
### SELECTION OF RETIREMENT RATE CATEGORY:

| Year | Low | Medium | High |
|------|-----|--------|------|
| 2014 | <$599 | $599–$2,531 | >$2,531 |
| 2015 | <$611 | $611–$2,582 | >$2,582 |
| 2016 | <$623 | $623–$2,633 | >$2,633 |
| 2017 | <$636 | $636–$2,688 | >$2,688 |
| 2018 | <$649 | $649–$2,745 | >$2,745 |
| 2019 | <$663 | $663–$2,803 | >$2,803 |
| 2020 | <$677 | $677–$2,861 | >$2,861 |
| 2021 | <$691 | $691–$2,922 | >$2,922 |
| 2022 | <$706 | $706–$2,983 | >$2,983 |
| 2023 or later | <$720 | $720–$3.046 | >$3,046 |

[See 77 Fed. Reg 71321 (Nov. 30, 2012)]

The PBGC publishes mortality tables, updated annually, to calculate the present value of annuities in involuntary termination situations. See <http://www.pbgc.gov/prac/mortality-retirement-and-pv-max-guarantee/erisa-mortality-tables/erisa-section-4044-mortality-table-for-2013-valuation-dates.html> for the § 4044 mortality table for valuation dates in 2013.

### § 17.05  PLAN REVERSIONS

Before ERISA, it was legal for an employer to simply wind up a plan and take back its assets. But under current law, a plan provision that calls for reversion (or increased reversion) cannot become effective until the end of the fifth calendar year following the year of adoption. In other words, employers have to wait at least five years to take advantage of a reversion opportunity. Furthermore, if the plan called for mandatory contributions, once the benefits are paid off, assets must be allocated to mandatory contributions before the reversion occurs.

An employer that is entitled to a reversion must pay 50% of the reversion amount as an excise tax. However, if the employer establishes a qualified replacement plan or amends the terminating plan to increase benefits, the excise tax is reduced to 20%. IRS Form 5330 is used to pay the excise tax. It is due the last day of the month after the month in which the reversion occurred.

## § 17.06  EFFECT ON BENEFITS

### [A]  Forfeit of Benefits

Benefits become nonforfeitable when a plan terminates or partially terminates. A defined contribution plan's benefits become nonforfeitable if and when
the employer completely ceases its contributions to the plan. If a defined benefit
plan terminates within 10 years of its creation, I.R.C. § 411(d)(2) imposes limits
on the benefits that can be paid to the 25 highest-compensated individuals covered by the plan. This rule prevails even if it results in the loss of some accrued
benefits.

In the Seventh Circuit view, the employees of a bankrupt company raised a
sufficient claim of breach of fiduciary duty by alleging that the company's executives failed to provide ongoing funding for a health plan that was terminated as
part of the bankruptcy process. The executives were fiduciaries because of their
control over the committee that invested the plan's assets. However, the Seventh
Circuit dismissed claims of breach of fiduciary duty by not giving notice of the
likelihood of plan termination, on the ground that there is no duty to disclose
likely future termination unless plan participants are deliberately misled. [*Baker
v. Kingsley*, 387 F.3d 655 (7th Cir. 2004)]

### [B]  The Anticutback Rule

Whether deliberately or inadvertently, employers sometimes make cutbacks
in a plan, or scale it down. The effect can be inadvertent if the employer lacks the
money to make a required deposit, or simply is ignorant of what the legal requirements are. The consequences are not always those intended by the employer. The
worst-case scenario is that the plan will be treated as partially terminated, and
then retroactively disqualified, obligating the employer to pay back taxes for prior
plan years. Retroactive disqualification also harms employees, who are likely to
owe back taxes. Furthermore, distributions from a disqualified plan cannot be
rolled over to a qualified plan.

A plan is frozen if it is amended to keep the plan trust in existence, but without further contributions or accrual of benefits. A frozen plan is still subject to the
top-heavy plan rules, and still has to provide QJSAs and QPSAs on the same
terms as if it had not been frozen.

If it is uncertain whether there has been a partial termination, Form 5300 can
be filed to request an IRS determination letter. If the IRS rules that there has been
a partial termination, the event must be reported to the PBGC (as must a 20% cut
in the workforce, or a plan amendment that reduces the accrual of benefits by 50%
or more for 50% or more of the workforce).

See 77 Fed. Reg. 37349 (June 21, 2012) for proposed regulations allowing
plan sponsors in bankruptcy to amend their single-employer defined benefit plans
to eliminate optional forms of benefit that are not permitted because the plan is

underfunded. Under the conditions prescribed in the regulations (e.g., approval of the PBGC and bankruptcy court), eliminating the optional benefit forms will not violate the anti-cutback rule.

## § 17.07  REPORTING AND COMPLIANCE

When a plan is terminated, IRS Form 5310 is used to request an IRS determination letter stating that the associated plan trust did not become disqualified or lose its exempt status. Form 6088 must be filed in conjunction with this form, listing up to 25 owners or 5% shareholders of the employer corporation who received any distribution from the plan during the preceding five years.

The general rule is that Form 5310-A must be filed 30 days or more before a transfer of plan assets to another qualified retirement plan because of a merger, consolidation, or change in ownership of assets or liabilities. When two defined contribution plans merge or a defined contribution plan is spun off, or a defined benefit plan engages in a merger or spinoff that has only minimal effects, the Form 5310-A filing is not required.

In the somewhat unlikely case that the trust of a terminating plan has more assets than are needed to pay all the plan benefits, and therefore the employer recovers those excess assets, Form 5319 must be filed by the last day of the month after the month in which the employer recouped the assets. This is also the form the employer uses to pay the excise tax on the recouped funds.

The Form 5500-series annual report must be filed for the year of the merger, consolidation, division, or termination. If a trust is frozen (the plan maintains its assets, although benefit accruals have stopped), the 5500-series filing is required in every year until all the assets have been distributed. Form 8955-SSA is submitted to the IRS to identify separated plan participants who are entitled to deferred vested benefits. For instructions, see <http://www.irs.gov/pub/irs-pdf/i8955ssa.pdf>.

A late-2010 proposed rule, RIN 1210-AB 18, effective January 18, 2011, clarifies the ERISA § 101(f) mandate for annual funding notices for defined benefit plans. It also covers reporting requirements for plans taken over by the PBGC. Because ERISA Title IV imposes separate disclosure requirements in this situation, EBSA believes that a funding notice may be unnecessary or even confusing when the PBGC becomes the trustee of a terminated single-employer plan, or where a terminated single-employer plan has already satisfied all its liabilities. [75 Fed. Reg. 70625 (Nov. 18, 2010); see Fred Schneyer, *EBSA Releases DB Funding Notice Proposed Rule*, plansponsor.com (Nov. 17, 2010)]

## § 17.08  PAYMENT OF EXPENSES

It is appropriate for fiduciaries to use plan assets to pay the expenses of an ongoing plan. However, the decision to terminate a plan is a business decision made by the plan's settlor, and not a fiduciary decision. That means that some of the termination expenses relate to settlor functions—and it violates ERISA to use plan assets to pay settlor expenses. Therefore, allocation is necessary. DOL's ERISA Opinion Letter No. 97-032A (February 1997) recommends that the allocation be made by an independent fiduciary.

These expenses are considered fiduciary expenses that can properly be paid out of plan assets:

- Getting an audit;
- Preparing and filing the final annual report;
- Amending the plan to carry out the termination;
- Calculating benefits;
- Preparing benefit statements;
- Notifying participants and beneficiaries about their rights incident to termination.

However, the cost of maintaining the plan's tax-qualified status—including the cost of getting determination letters—is a settlor expense.

# PART IV

# BENEFIT PLANS

CHAPTER 18

# EMPLOYEE GROUP HEALTH PLANS (EGHPs)

## § 18.01  INTRODUCTION

Health insurance costs are a major planning factor for business. For many years, health care costs, and therefore insurance costs, rose much faster than inflation, until employers faced a heavy burden. In the 1970s and 1980s, there was a vast shift from indemnity insurance [see § 18.12] to some form of managed care. The promise of managed care was that eliminating waste and keeping employees healthier would reduce costs.

However, by the end of the twentieth century, managed care was a problem in and of itself. Insurers began to charge the kind of double-digit annual premium increases that caused so much pain in the 1970s. Many patients were dissatisfied with managed care, charging that they were often denied access to necessary care. Doctors were dissatisfied, with the restrictions on their freedom to prescribe, with the amount of paperwork they had to do, and with both the size and speed of their reimbursement from managed care organizations (MCOs).

Just as there has been a transition from defined-benefit to defined-contribution or employee-funded retirement plans, health plans have shifted from the once-predominant indemnity plan to a heavy dominance of some form of managed care. Some employers have always chosen to self-insure rather than purchase insurance; others have switched to self-insurance to cut costs. A new form that is emerging is the so-called defined contribution or consumer-driven health plan (CDHP). The passage of health care reform legislation, the Patient Protection and Affordable Care Act, Pub. L. No. 111-148, (PPACA) is discussed below, in § 18.19.

In mid-2012, the Supreme Court did not find PPACA unconstitutional. However, that did not end challenges to the validity of the statute as a whole or to the mandate that employer plans cover contraceptives: see § 18.19[M]. Two key PPACA sections (the individual and employer mandates) can be challenged because the Supreme Court sent the case *Liberty University v. Geithner* [(133 S. Ct. 679 (2012)], back to the Fourth Circuit to consider the challenges, which are premised on religious freedom and equality grounds. [Lyle Denniston, SCOTUS Blog, *Way Cleared For Health Care Challenge* (Nov. 26, 2012) (benefitslink. com)]

The Fourth Circuit ruled in 2013 that the requirement that large employers provide health insurance is valid under the Commerce Clause, because it regulates compensation—a term of employment with a substantial impact on interstate commerce. The Fourth Circuit held that the employer mandate does not violate employers' rights under the First Amendment or the Religious Freedom Restoration Act (RFRA). Plans can be drafted to exclude abortion coverage, so the Fourth Circuit rejected the religious argument. The Fourth Circuit also found the mandate that individuals purchase insurance valid under the First Amendment and RFRA. [*Liberty Univ. v. Lew*, No. 12-2346, 2013 WL 3470532 (4th Cir. July 11, 2013); see Lyle Denniston, *Employer Mandate Upheld*, SCOTUS Blog

(July 11, 2013) (law.com); Practical Law Employee Benefits & Executive Compensation, *Health Care Reform's Employer Mandate Is Valid Under Commerce Clause: Fourth Circuit* (July 15, 2013) (benefitslink.com)]

In March 2013, 85% of full-time private-sector workers had access to employer-provided health benefits; only 24% of part-time workers had access. In private industry, workers in the lowest 10% of average earnings paid 29% of the premium for individual and 44% of the premium for family coverage. Higher-paid workers had lower payment responsibilities: for the highest-paid 10% of workers the employee was responsible for 19% of the individual, 27% of the family premium. [BLS, *Employee Benefits In the United States—March 2013* (USDL-13-1344), <http://www.bls.gov/news.release/pdf/ebs2.pdf> (July 17, 2013)]

The Henry J. Kaiser Foundation's *2013 Employer Health Benefits Survey* reports that in 2013, 57% of all firms offered health benefits, but the larger the firm, the more likely it was that health benefits would be offered. For firms with 3—9 workers, only 45% of employers offered coverage, but it was nearly universal in companies with 1,000 or more employees. Availability did not change much between 2012 and 2013. There are various reasons why some employees are not eligible (e.g., they are recent hires; they are part-time workers) and why employees do not accept coverage that is offered (usually because of expense, or because they are covered under a spouse's plan). In 2013, 80% of eligible employees take up coverage, resulting in 62% of workers having employment-related coverage in 2013—the same percentage as in 2012. [<http://kff.org/report-section/2013-summary-of-findings> (Aug. 20, 2013)]

The PPACA imposes a penalty on businesses with 50 or more full-time employees if they fail to provide coverage for full-time employees. This provision led to concern that employers would terminate health coverage for part-time employees because this can be done without incurring a penalty. EBRI's conclusion, however, was that the trend away from full-time and toward part-time employment began before PPACA took effect. In 2007, the percentage of part-time workers was 16.7%, rising to 22.2% in 2011. Between 2007 and 2011, there was a 2.8% decline in the likelihood of full-time workers having employment-related health care coverage, and a 15.7% decline for part-time workers in the same period. The end result was that in 2011, 59.6% of full-time and 15.7% of part-time employees had work-based coverage. [Kevin McGuinness, *Part-Time Employees and Health Coverage*, plansponsor.com (May 22, 2013)]

Federal law makes the EGHP the primary payor and Medicare only the secondary payor for Medicare beneficiaries who continue to be employed. However, this provision is poorly enforced, and in many instances, Medicare ends up paying for health care for working elderly people, where the EGHP should have been the primary payor. One of the provisions of the Medicare, Medicaid & SCHIP Extension Act of 2007, Pub. L. 110-173 § 111, requires EGHPs to report to Medicare Insurers and self-funded EGHPs must report to HHS on situations in which the EGHP had primary responsibility. Failure to make the report is punishable by a civil money penalty of $1,000 per day of noncompliance for each individual for whom reports should have been made—in addition to any other civil money penalty that can be imposed for failure to pay for that individual's care. Reporting is also required for liability insurance (including self-insurance), automobile no-fault insurance, and Worker's Compensation plans, and failure to report is subject to the same penalty [McDermott Newsletters, *Medicare Secondary Payor Reporting Requirements Will Affect Self-Insured Health Care Providers, Captive Insurers* (Jan. 6, 2009) (benefitslink.com); Jessica Forbes Olson & Leslie J. Anderson, Dorsey & Whitney LLP, *New Medicare Secondary Payer Reporting Requirements* (Aug. 14, 2008) (benefitslink.com)]

Reporting to CMS (Centers for Medicare and Medicaid Services) is also required for worker's compensation claims involving Medicare beneficiaries, so Medicare can be reimbursed if it pays medical expenses for a worker who eventually received WC. [Littler, Mendelsohn Press Releases, *New Medicare Secondary Payer Reporting Obligations for Workers' Compensation Plans,* <http://www.littler.com/PressPublications/Lists/ASAPs/Disp Asaps.aspx?id=1359&asap Type=National> (April 2009)]

One of the most important differences between ERISA's pension plan provisions and its welfare benefit plan provisions is that, by and large, welfare benefits do not vest, and can be altered or terminated if the plan document retains the sponsor's discretion to do so. However, in some situations, the employer will be deemed to have a contractual obligation to maintain the plan. In a unionized company, the CBA will impose further limitations on the employer's ability to alter the health plans it maintains. [For the requirements for Summary Plan Descriptions (SPDs) for health plans, see § 11.02[B].]

In mid-2013, the Supreme Court ruled that § 2 of the federal Defense of Marriage Act was unconstitutional, with the result that same-sex married couples became eligible for a variety of federal employment-related benefits. See § 18.06.

## § 18.02 THE HEALTH CARE LANDSCAPE

Although initially the employer group health plan market was divided only between self-insured and indemnity insurance plans, today managed care is dominant. There are many types of managed care plans. At one time the Health Management Organization (HMO) was the dominant managed care form, but today its predominance is yielding to plans that provide somewhat more flexibility and provider choice for patients. The Consumer-Driven Health Plan (CDHP), such as the high-deductible health plan used in conjunction with a Health Savings Account (HSA) is gaining prominence: see § 18.18, below.

"Mini-meds"—the obverse of the HDHP—have also attracted attention. A mini-med is a plan that covers basic medical care, but limits coverage of large expenses. Usually they are designed to provide minimal coverage for employees who would otherwise be uninsured (e.g., part-timers or new hires who haven't qualified for the main plan. Mini-meds are usually employee-pay-all arrangements, where they pay $50–$60 a month for the limited coverage and are required to make copayments. Benefits are capped at low levels.

Transgender people often suffer discrimination, disrespect, and hostility from health care providers. The National Transgender Discrimination Survey reports that 20% of transsexuals say they have been denied medical care because of their gender identity and one-quarter have been verbally harassed in a health care setting; 2% have been physically assaulted when seeking health care. Before PPACA, they were also at risk of losing or being unable to obtain employer-based health coverage because of employment discrimination. Even if they had insurance, insurance companies often denied claims, describing transexuality as an excludible pre-existing condition (even if the health care had nothing to do with gender reassignment). Starting in 2014, PPACA forbids denials for pre-existing conditions, and Title VII extends to health care. HHS has confirmed that, therefore, gender identity discrimination in health care is unlawful. PPACA also includes funding for cultural competency training for healthcare workers to teach them about transgender issues. [Marisa Carroll, *What the Affordable Care Act Means for Transgender People*, The Nation (Aug. 14, 2012) (benefitslink.com)]

HHS' Office of Civil Rights clarified in a letter that the PPACA ban on sex discrimination on health insurance applies to transsexuals and it is discriminatory for an employer or insurer to deny health insurance benefits or coverage on the basis of gender identity or lack of conformity to gender stereotypes. The Office of Civil Rights accepts complaints of PPACA sex discrimination. Violators can lose federal assistance and be subject to other penalties. [Michelle Andrews, *HHS Says Health Plans Cannot Discriminate Against Transgender People*, Kaiser Health News, (Sept. 3, 2012) (benefitslink.com)]

Oregon and California regulators ordered health insurers to stop denying coverage on basis of gender identity. The two states did not require coverage of specific treatment, but required some insurers to pay for hormone therapy, breast reduction, cancer screening, and other medically necessary procedures that are covered for cisgender (non-transgender) insured persons. The rulings affected about one-third of the residents of Oregon and 7% of Californians (the rest of the people in the states are covered by PPOs, Medicare, Medicaid, or HMOs that are not under the supervision of insurance regulators). [AP, *Ore., Calif., Require Transgender Health Coverage*, NYTimes.com (Jan. 11, 2013)]

A lawsuit against the state of Oregon was settled with an agreement requiring insurance coverage for gender reassignment surgery for state employees; the state was required to pay $36,000 and change its policies so that medically necessary treatment for gender reassignment is covered. Hysterectomies were covered for other medical reasons, so they had to be covered for gender reassignment as well. [Rebecca Moore, *Ore. Adds Gender Reassignment to Health Care Coverage*, plansponsor.com (Jan. 25, 2013)]

In early 2012, it was reported that one-third of very large employers provide benefits for transgender employees—five times more than the year before. The Human Rights Campaign's Corporate Equality Index raised consciousness on this issue by publicizing five criteria for benefits for transgendered employees: the availability of short-term leave for transition, mental health counseling, hormone therapy, health care coverage to monitor hormone use, and surgical procedures. The average cost for male to female transition is about $17,000, plus $1,000 for therapy, $1,500 for hormones, and $500 for lab tests and medical visits. [Lisa V. Gillespie, *One-Third of Major Employers Now Offer Transgendered Employees Coverage for Gender-Reassignment Surgery*, Employee Benefit News (Feb. 1, 2012) (benefitslink.com)]

"CAM" is an abbreviation for "complementary and alternative medicine," and a number of insurers offer coverage or discounts. For example, Cigna's Healthy Rewards program offers discounts for acupuncture, chiropractic, massage, natural supplements, and other health and wellness products and services. However, because of the lack of scientific proof for most of these interventions, they are not covered as standard benefits. Companies with drug-free workplace policies are especially interested in modalities such as acupuncture and yoga that can be useful back therapy that gets people back to work without using painkillers that are contraindicated in the workplace. [Kathleen Koster, *Alternative Medicine Reduces Pain, Drives Health Costs Down*, Employee Benefit News (Feb. 1, 2011) (benefitslink.com)]

## § 18.03  BENEFITS MANDATES

### [A]  Generally

One important characteristic of the health care reform legislation is that it phases in a standard package of required health care benefits. But even before the PPACA, there were both federal and state limitations on the principle that employers had complete discretion as to which benefits would be included in their plans.

At the federal level, the Children's Health Insurance Program Reauthorization Act of 2009, Pub. L. No. 111-3 (CHIPRA), requires employers to amend their EGHP and cafeteria plans to allow special enrollment of employees and dependents who either lose their Medicaid or SCHIP eligibility, or have become eligible to participate in the EGHP because the state will provide assistance with the employee's responsibility for health insurance premiums. The employee has an obligation to report to the plan within 60 days of a qualifying event. Amendment was required as of April 1, 2009.

The legislation allows states to subsidize EGHP participation in addition to, or instead of, SCHIP coverage. The state can pay the subsidy to either the employee or the employer. An employer can opt out of state payments, in which case the employee will pay the full employee share of the premium and then look to the state program for reimbursement.

Health plans must provide two new notices—one to plan participants, explaining entitlement to premium assistance; the other, to the state so the state can determine if any employee is entitled to assistance. However, notice does not have to be given until HHS and the DOL develop a model notice; the legislation requires them to do this by February 7, 2010. [Troutman Sanders LLP, *Keeping up with Recent Legislation—Numerous Changes to Group Health Plans Required*, plansponsor.com (Feb. 27, 2009)]

Health and cafeteria plans must be amended to cope with special enrollment rights, and coordination of benefit (COB) rules might have to be changed to reflect SCHIP secondary coverage. [Norbert F. Kugele, Warner Norcross & Judd LLP, *New Federal SCHIP Law Requires Cafeteria and Health Plan Amendments* (Feb. 10, 2009) (benefitslink.com)]

The HITECH Act (Health Information Technology for Economic and Clinical Health Act), part of the economic stimulus bill, expands HIPAA's privacy and security provisions. Business associates of covered entities are subject to the same privacy rules as the covered entities themselves, including criminal penalties. Business associates who discover a breach of the confidentiality or security rules by the covered entity are supposed to either take steps to cure the breach, or terminate their business relationship with the covered entity. Business associates must notify covered entities (who must then notify the affected individual participants) when there has been a breach of unsecured PHI. The covered entity is required to notify HHS—and the news media—if more than 500 people were affected by the breach.

Civil monetary penalties (CMPs) have been increased, and part of a CMP can be distributed to individuals whose PHI was improperly disclosed. The Office of Civil Rights retains its role in enforcing HIPAA compliance, but state attorneys general have been given enforcement powers through suits in federal district courts.

The HITECH Act includes many new regulations for electronic medical records; an accounting must be given of how the records were used and disclosed in the previous three years. The new requirements are generally effective February 17, 2010. [Troutman Sanders LLP, *Keeping Up With Recent Legislation—Numerous Changes to Group Health Plans Required*, plansponsor.com (Feb. 27, 2009)]

In April 2013, the Council for Affordable Health Insurance (CAHI) announced that in 2012 there were 2,271 mandates nationwide—far more than the 850 mandates in existence in 1992 when CAHI began collecting the information. CAHI says that mandates can increase the cost of basic health coverage anywhere from 10% to over 50%.CAHI found that the states varied widely in their mandate practice: Rhode Island imposes 69 mandates, Idaho only 13. The most popular mandates were mammography screening and minimum maternity stay, required by all the states, and breast reconstruction and mental health parity, required in 48 states, whereas only one state mandates cardiovascular disease screening and one state requires organ transplant donor coverage. [Council for Affordable Health Insurance, *CAHI Identifies 2,271 State Health Insurance Mandates*, <http://www.cahi.org/cahi_contents/newsroom/article.asp?id=1115> (Apr. 9, 2013)]

## [B]  Maternity Stays

The Newborns' and Mothers' Health Protection Act of 1996 (NMHPA) [Pub. L. No. 104-204] and the Taxpayer Relief Act of 1997 [Pub. L. No. 105-35] combine ERISA and tax code provisions to mandate that group health plans (both insured and self-insured, whatever the number of participants) provide at least a minimum hospital stay for childbirth. The minimum is 48 hours after a vaginal delivery, 96 hours after a Caesarian section.

Mother and child can be discharged earlier if, after consulting the mother, the mother's attending physician allows it. However, the plan is not allowed to offer financial incentives to the physician or the mother to shorten the stay. If the plan does not provide hospitalization benefits for childbirth, it is not required to add those benefits because of this legislation. The NMHPA does not preempt state laws that require an even longer maternity stay.

Rules to implement the NMHPA were jointly issued by the IRS, Pension and Welfare Benefit Administration, and Health Care Financing Administration (now renamed Centers for Medicare and Medicaid Services). [29 C.F.R. § 2590.711]

Under these rules, when a baby is delivered in the hospital, the stay begins at the time of the delivery (or the last delivery, in a multiple birth). If the mother is admitted to the hospital after giving birth elsewhere, the stay begins at the time of admission. These rules forbid health plans to penalize health care providers for complying with the NMHPA. It is permissible to offer post-discharge follow-up after an early discharge, as long as the services offered do not exceed those that would be provided during the 48- or 96-hour stay required by the NMHPA.

Violation of the NMHPA is subject to the I.R.C. § 4980D penalty of $100 per participant per day, starting when the failure occurs and running until it is corrected. No penalty will be imposed if the failure to provide an adequate postpartum stay was unintentional, and is corrected within 30 days. If the failure is unintentional but is not corrected, the maximum penalty is $500,000 a year, or 10% of the EGHP's expenses for the year before the failure—whichever is less.

In late 2008, the IRS, DOL, and HHS jointly issued final regulations about the length of hospital stays for mothers and newborn infants, effective for plan years beginning on or after January 1, 2009. These rules replace final rules issued in 1998 [63 Fed. Reg. 57546 (Oct. 27, 1998)]. In general, a hospital stay of at least 48 hours (or 96 hours after a Caesarean) must be granted, but the provider of health care can authorize an earlier discharge if the mother or representative of the newborn consents. [Final Regulations, 73 Fed. Reg. 62410 (Oct. 20, 2008), <http://www.dol.gov/ebsa/FAQs/faq_consumer_newborns.html>]

On a related issue, in late 2011, California adopted legislation (SB 299/AB 592 and SB 222/AB 210) to enhance employment and insurance protection for pregnant women, requiring maintenance of at least the same level of insurance benefits during pregnancy-related leave that the employee had before taking leave, and requiring all individual policies to cover maternity services. The California pregnancy disability law applies to all employers of five or more, whereas the FMLA requires 50 employees. It has been argued that this statute is pre-empted by ERISA but a DOL opinion letter dating back to 2005 says that neither ERISA nor the FMLA preempts state laws that offer additional coverage. [Helene Wasserman and Michelle Barrett, *The Stork Has Landed: California Employers Must Maintain and Insurers Must Provide Pregnancy Benefits*, Littler Mendelson (Oct. 19, 2011) (benefitslink.com); Rebecca Moore, *California Extends Pregnancy Health Coverage,* plansponsor.com (Oct. 17, 2011)]

An early 2013 California Court of Appeal decision holds that an employee disabled by pregnancy complications (including prescribed bed rest) was entitled to additional leave as a reasonable accommodation under Fair Employment and Housing Act (FEHA) even though she had used up her California Pregnancy Disability Leave Law and California Family Rights Act leave. The employer gave her 19 weeks of leave, including accrued vacation time. She was fired when she exhausted her leave entitlement but was still on bed rest and could not perform the essential functions of her job. The court of appeal ruled that the plain language of California's Pregnancy Disability Leave Law is that it supplements other FEHA entitlements. [ *Sanchez v. Swissport, Inc.*, 213 Cal. App. 4th 1331 (2013); see Jackson Lewis LLP Workplace Resource Center, *No Statutory Cap on Pregnancy Leave, California Court of Appeal Rules* (Mar. 4, 2013) (benefitslink. com)]

### [C]  Women's Health and Cancer Rights Act (WHCRA)

The Women's Health and Cancer Rights Act (WHCRA) [Pub. L. No. 105-277], became law on October 21, 1998, effective for plan years beginning on or after that date. The Act provides that if an EGHP covers mastectomies, it must also cover reconstructive breast surgery if the patient wants it and her attending physician prescribes it. This includes reconstruction of the mastectomized breast; surgery on the other breast to balance the patient's appearance; prostheses; and treatment of physical complications of mastectomy. Deductibles and co-insurance for reconstructive surgery must be comparable to those imposed on other procedures.

EGHPs (and the insurers and HMOs that provide the medical and surgical benefits) have an ongoing obligation to notify new plan participants of their

WHCRA rights, and to renew the notice annually. (It is not necessary for both the EGHP and insurer or HMO to furnish the notice, as long as one of them does.)

The DOL has furnished this model notice that will satisfy the compliance burden: "Did you know that your plan, as required by the WHCRA, provides benefits for mastectomy-related services including reconstruction and surgery to achieve symmetry between the breasts, prostheses, and complications of mastectomy (including lymphedema)? Call your Plan Administrator [insert phone number] for more information." [<http://www.dol.gov/pwba/pubs>]

It did not violate the WHCRA (or ERISA) for a plan to limit reimbursement for bilateral breast reconstruction performed by non-network surgeons to 150% of the cost of unilateral reconstruction. Nor was the plan required to pay for private duty nurses, because the plan specifically excluded that service. Although plans that cover mastectomy must cover reconstruction "in a manner determined in consultation with the attending physician and the patient," deductibles and coinsurance can be imposed, and the plan can negotiate the level and type of reimbursement with the provider. [*Krauss v. Oxford Health Plans, Inc.*, 517 F.3d 614 (2d Cir. 2008)]

A participant in a self-insured health plan sued the plan's claims administrator for refusing to pay the full cost of her breast reconstruction surgery. She charged that the plan's claims procedure was inadequate; the notice of adverse benefit determination was inadequate and untimely; and the WHCRA notice of coverage of post-mastectomy reconstruction was not given. The claims administrator said that it was not a proper defendant because it had paid the benefits due under the plan and provided WHCRA notice. The District Court for the Northern District of New York refused to dismiss the claims counts because it was unclear whether the claims administrator or the employer (designated as the plan administrator in the SPD) was responsible for final benefit determinations. The benefit denial, a short notation on a check stub, did not satisfy ERISA requirements because it did not explain the denial, refer to the relevant plan provisions, or explain the appeals process. The SPD also called for notice within 30 days, but the plaintiff did not receive it for four months. However, the court held that the SPD adequately explained the WHCRA notice requirement. [*Haag v. MVP Healthcare*, 866 F. Supp. 2d 137 (N.D.N.Y 2012); see EBIA Weekly, *SPD Disclosures Provided Adequate Notice of Coverage Required by Women's Health and Cancer Rights Act* (June 14, 2012) (benefitslink.com)]

## [D]  Contraceptives

A December 14, 2000, EEOC decision [available at <http://www.eeoc.gov/policy/docs/qanda-decision-contraception.html] agrees with the charging parties, a group of female employees, that it violates Title VII for a plan to fail to cover prescription contraceptive drugs and devices when it covers other types of preventive medical care, and when it covers vasectomy and tubal ligation

(permanent surgical methods of contraception). The EEOC treats the distinction as discrimination on the basis of sex (in that only women use birth control pills, diaphragms, and IUDs) and pregnancy.

The EEOC's rationale is that the Pregnancy Discrimination Amendment (PDA) [42 U.S.C. § 2000e(k); see § 34.06] forbids discrimination on the basis of potential as well as actual pregnancy. Employers can lawfully exclude coverage of abortion, but not of contraception. In this case, the employer said that contraception was not covered because only abnormal health conditions were covered— but the plan covered sterilization of healthy persons based on their desire not to procreate in the future.

The EEOC also noted that plans frequently cover vaccination and preventive examinations, which, like contraception, prevent healthy employees from developing unwanted health conditions. The EEOC required the plan to cover the full range of available prescription contraceptives, because a woman employee's needs might change in the course of employment.

In March 2007, the Eighth Circuit ruled against a class of 1,500 female employees protesting the exclusion of contraceptives (prescription or over-the-counter) from the plan. The Eighth Circuit held that contraception is not related to pregnancy for purposes of the Pregnancy Discrimination Act because contraception prevents, rather than treats, pregnancy, and because contraceptives used by both male and female employees were excluded. (However, in practical terms, the case became moot when the plan agreed to cover contraceptives after the suit was filed.) [*In re Union Pacific Railroad Employment Practices Litigation*, 479 F.3d 936 (8th Cir. 2007); see Fred Schneyer, *Union Pacific Ex-Contraceptives Policy Upheld*, plansponsor.com (Mar. 16, 2007)]

A class action of female Wal-Mart employees protesting the exclusion of female contraceptives from the health plan was certified in the Northern District of Georgia in August of 2002. The judge rejected as plaintiffs wives of male employees and female employees who did not use birth control pills, and also dismissed the named plaintiff's claims for compensatory and punitive damages. Wal-Mart's position was that it excluded contraceptive coverage on a gender-neutral basis, for the valid business reason of saving money. In mid-2006, the Western District of Missouri allowed a female employee to sue under Title VII and the PDA when her health plan refused to cover prescription contraceptives for women, because there are no prescription contraceptives for men, and potential pregnancy, unlike fertility, is only an issue for women. [*Stocking v. AT&T Corp.*, 436 F. Supp. 2d 1014 (W.D. Mo. June 5, 2006)]

The California Supreme Court required Catholic Charities of Sacramento, Inc., to cover prescription contraceptives under its health and disability insurance plans. This employer brought suit, challenging the validity of the state statute because it required Catholic Charities to reimburse for contraceptives despite its moral opposition to contraception. The statute offers an exemption for religious employers, but the state Supreme Court rejected that characterization of Catholic

Charities, which was not organized to inculcate religious tenets, was not a non-profit organization, and did not primarily serve and primarily employ members of a particular religion. Therefore, it was subject to the general mandate to reimburse the cost of prescription contraceptives. [*Catholic Charities of Sacramento, Inc. v. Superior Court of Sacramento County*, 32 Cal. 4th 527 (Cal. 2004), *cert. denied*, 543 U.S. 816 (October 2004)] In September, 2010, the United States Conference of Catholic Bishops wrote to HHS to oppose mandatory inclusion of contraception and sterilization as preventive services in individual and group health plans. The bishops described fertility as a healthy condition, and argued that such procedures are risky to women's life and health, and do not prevent abortion because abortion is not a disease. [<http://www.usccb.org/ogc/preventive.pdf>; see Rebecca Moore, *Catholic Bishops Ask HHS Not to Require Coverage of Birth Control*, plansponsor.com (Sept. 23, 2010)]

The Women's Health and Wellness Act, a New York state statute, requires contraceptive coverage in all plans that cover prescription drugs. The statute has a religious exemption, but it is a narrow one (covering only organizations dedicated to religious worship and excluding those that provide, e.g., social services under faith-based control). The New York Court of Appeals upheld the validity of the statute. The language of the religious exception, which limits coverage to employers whose main purpose is promotion of theological values and who primarily employ and serve members of their own faith, is drawn from a California law that also has survived challenge. [*Catholic Charities of the Diocese of Albany v. Serio*, 7 N.Y.3d 510 (2006); see John Caher, *N.Y. Court Rejects Employers' Challenge to Contraception Law*, N.Y.L.J. (Jan. 13, 2006) (law.com). The U.S. Supreme Court refused to hear an appeal of the Court of Appeals decision: Fred Schneyer, *U.S. Supreme Court Rejects NY Contraceptive Coverage Appeal*, plan sponsor.com (Oct. 2, 2007)]

The HHS issued preventive care guidelines for women as an interim final rule (IFR) in August 2011, outlining services that must be covered by non-grandfathered plans, pursuant to the PPACA preventive care rules, for plan years that begin on or after August 1, 2012. (For calendar year plans, that means January 1, 2013.) There is a list of mandated services that must be covered at 100% without cost sharing (although it is permissible to require the services to be obtained within the network for 100% coverage). Plans can also use reasonable management techniques to control the frequency, method, or setting for obtaining a service. The list of mandated services includes well-woman visits, screening for gestational diabetes, HPV testing, STD counseling, breastfeeding support, and screening and counseling about domestic violence. The most controversial provision is that all FDA-approved contraceptive methods must be covered.

The IFR allowed religious organizations the option of buying insurance without contraceptive coverage. [76 Fed. Reg. 46621 (Aug. 3, 2011); List of mandated services: <http://www.hrsa.gov/womensguidelines>; see HealthCare.gov blog, *Affordable Care Act Rules on Expanding Access to Preventive Services for*

*Women,* posted Aug. 1, 2011; Christy Tinnes and Brigen Winters, *Covering Women's Preventive Care Part I,* plansponsor.com (Feb. 8, 2012) and *Agencies Clarify Required Coverage for Contraceptives,* plansponsor.com (Mar. 13, 2013)] The IFR Guidelines for Women's Preventive Services is at [<http://www.hrsa.gov/womensguidelines>; interim final rule, <http://www.ofr.gov/OFR Upload/OFR Data/2011-19684_PI.pdf>; see HealthCare.gov, *Affordable Care Act Rules on Expanding Access to Preventive Services for Women,* posted Aug. 1, 2011] was amended, giving religious employers an extra year to comply. A religious employer is defined as a nonprofit organization whose purpose is inculcation of religious values that primarily serves and employs people belonging to that faith. [76 Fed. Reg. 46621 (Aug. 3, 2011) and *Women's Preventive Services: Required Health Plan Coverage Guidelines* (Aug. 1, 2011) The Guttmacher Institute reported that, in addition to the federal rule, 28 states required full coverage of contraceptives in health plans: Louise Radnofsky, *White House Keeps Rule on Birth Control,* WSJ.com (Jan. 21, 2012)]

The United States Conference of Catholic Bishops announced that, despite the extra year given for compliance, it would sue to challenge the preventive health services rule. [Mary Agnes Carey and Shefali S. Kulkarni, *Bishops Will Sue Feds Over Contraception Rule,* Kaiser Health News (Jan. 20, 2012) (benefitslink.com)] In response, the administration said that religious employers opposed to birth control would not have to pay for it directly: insurers would be required to offer contraceptive coverage without explicit charge to either the religious employer or the employee. [77 Fed. Reg. 8725 (Feb. 12, 2012); see Louise Radnofsky, Laura Meckler, and Carol E. Lee, *Obama Offers Contraceptive Compromise,* WSJ.com (Feb. 11, 2012); BBC News, *Obama Compromise Amid Catholic Contraception Anger* (February 2012) (benefitslink.com). The bishops said this compromise was not adequate because it would not work for religious employers who self-insure. [Louise Radnofsky, *Catholic Bishops Oppose Obama Compromise on Birth-Control Insurance,* WSJ.com (Feb. 12, 2012), <http://www.usccb.org/about/general-counsel/rulemaking/upload/comments-on-advance-notice-of-proposed-rulemaking-on-preventive-services-12-05-15.pdf>; see Rebecca Moore, *Catholic Bishops Still Object to Contraception Coverage Rules,* plansponsor.com (May 18, 2012)]

On February 23, 2012, seven states (Nebraska, South Carolina, Michigan, Texas, Florida, Ohio, and Oklahoma) sued the Obama administration requirement of covering contraception in EGHPs on the grounds that it violates the rights of Roman Catholic institutions to practice their religion. Three religiously affiliated universities and a Catholic TV network had already sued. [Louise Radnofsky, *Seven States Challenge Contraception Rule,* WSJ.com (Feb. 24, 2012)]

On March 16, 2012, the Obama administration announced that the contraceptive coverage requirement would apply to Catholic institutions that self-insure. Students and employees are entitled to access to contraceptive coverage at no cost to them, either provided by the TPA or "some other independent entity." Secretary Sebelius said the money might come from pharmaceutical companies, which sometimes allow rebates on drugs for favored customers. [Robert Pear, *Birth Control Mandate to Apply to Self-Insuring Religious Groups*, NYTimes.com (Mar. 16, 2012)]

Suits about the contraceptive mandate continued to be filed, and gradually decisions were rendered. As of the end of 2013, 35 federal suits had been filed by for-profit businesses, in addition to over 60 suits filed by religious organizations, and 30 of the private-employer cases had been decided. Most of the cases ruled in favor of employers protesting the requirement of contraceptive coverage: 23 cases, including decisions in the Seventh, Eighth, and Tenth Circuits. The Third and Sixth Circuits, and five district courts, ruled against the employers and in favor of the mandate. The Tenth Circuit ruled that business corporations can have religious beliefs that are protected by the Religious Freedom Restoration Act of 1993 (RFRA); the Third Circuit ruled that they cannot.

The RFRA forbids burdens to be imposed on free exercise of religion unless there is a compelling governmental interest. Even if a compelling governmental interest is present, the least restrictive method must be used to achieve it. [Timothy Jost, *Implementing Health Reform: Contraceptive Coverage Litigation Moves Toward the Supreme Court*, Health Affairs Blog (July 29, 2013) (plansponsor .com)]

The Supreme Court denied Hobby Lobby's request for an emergency injunction to prevent the contraception mandate from taking effect: because the lower court rulings were so divided, the Supreme Court refused to decide the case before the situation became clearer. The Supreme Court has only limited powers to issue injunctions, and the Supreme Court found that this case did not qualify. The case was remanded to the Tenth Circuit, which permitted Hobby Lobby to continue litigating against the contraceptive mandate, and held that it would not have to pay fines for not covering contraceptives: *Hobby Lobby Stores, Inc. v. Sebelius*, 133 S.Ct. 641 (2012); *Hobby Lobby v. Sebelius*, No. 12-6294 (10th Cir. June 27, 2013). On remand, the Western District of Oklahoma, which had previously refused to enjoin the contraception mandate, granted a preliminary injunction because the potential penalties outweigh the potential harm to the government if there is no injunction: *Hobby Lobby Stores, Inc. v. Sebelius*, No. 5:12-cv-01000-HE (W.D. Okla. July 19, 2013). [*Monaghan v. Sebelius*, No. 2:12-cv-15488-LPZ-MJH (E.D. Mich. Mar. 14, 2013), similarly grants a preliminary injunction against enforcement of the contraception mandate based on a religious-freedom argument raised by a for-profit corporation.]

## [E] Mental Health Parity

The National Institute of Mental Health says that, in any given year, 26% of adults have a diagnosable mental disorder, and 6% of adults experience a seriously debilitating mental illness. A SHRM survey said that 85% of employers provided at least some mental health coverage. However, the theoretical availability of mental health coverage is only helpful in practice if practitioners are available who take insurance; are accessible to the patient; and are accepting new patients. Even employees who have good insurance coverage may avoid treatment because they do not believe it will be helpful or are afraid of retaliation. [Ron Lieber, *Walking the Tightrope on Mental Health Coverage*, NYTimes.com (Dec. 21, 2012)]

A very controversial 1996 federal statute, the Veterans' Affairs, Housing and Urban Development and Independent Agencies Appropriations Act [Pub. L. No. 104-204], imposed a requirement of parity in EGHPs with more than 50 participants. Under the parity provision, plans that did not impose lifetime or annual limits on medical and surgical benefits could not do so on mental health benefits. Most plans do impose limits—so the limits would have to be the same for mental and physical ailments. In 1996, this requirement was made part of ERISA.

The Mental Health Parity Act was permitted to expire, but obtained a number of short-term extensions, from Pub. L. No. 107-116, Pub. L. No. 107-147, Pub. L. No. 107-313, Pub. L. No. 108-197, Pub. L. No. 108-311, Pub. L. No. 109-151, and Pub. L. No. 109-432.

The stimulus bill, Emergency Economic Stabilization Act (EESA, Pub. L. No. 110-343), makes the mental health parity requirement permanent for companies with 50 or more employees. The mental health parity component of EESA is referred to as the Paul Wellstone and Pete Domenici Mental Health Parity and Addiction Equity Act (MHPAEA). EESA expands the scope of mental health parity by including substance abuse treatment. The financial requirements and treatment limitations for mental health or substance abuse treatment cannot be more restrictive than the predominant requirements or limitations that apply to substantially all of the plan's medical and surgical benefits. It is now unlawful to impose separate treatment limitations on mental health/substance abuse treatment—e.g., frequency of treatment, number of visits, days of coverage. The criteria for determining the medical necessity of mental illness and substance abuse treatment must be disclosed on request to current or potential participants and beneficiaries of the plan, and to contracting providers. Participants and beneficiaries are entitled to request an explanation of denials of mental health and substance abuse benefits.

The definition of "small employer" means one that employed an average of at least two employees (or at least one employee in a state where one-person small groups are permitted), but did not have more than 50 employees during the preceding calendar year. (Employees of corporations in a controlled group are aggregated.)

An exemption from the parity requirement is available after a plan has complied with the parity requirement for the first six months of the plan year, and discovers that the cost of parity is more than 2% of actual total plan costs for the first year, and more than 1% in each subsequent plan year. Actuarial certification of the added costs is required, and plans claiming an exemption must notify participants, beneficiaries, and relevant government agencies. [Edward I. Leeds and

Clifford J. Schoner, Ballard Spahr Andrews & Ingersoll, LLP, *Expansion of Mental Health Parity Requirements* (Oct. 8, 2008) (benefitslink.com); EBIA Weekly, *New Law Expands Mental Health Parity Requirements for Group Health Plans*, EBIA Weekly (Oct. 3, 2008)]

Interim final regulations were published February 2, 2010, with most provisions taking effect January 1, 2011 for most calendar-year plans. The regulations require parity in both quantitative and non-quantitative treatment limitations. A quantitative treatment limitation is something like a limit of only 50 outpatient visits per year, or limits on annual, per episode, or lifetime visits or days of treatment. A non-quantitative limitation affects the scope or duration of benefits in a non-numerical way, for example, by excluding experimental treatment, imposing a prescription drug formulary, determining "usual and customary rates," and imposing "step therapy" protocols (where a more expensive treatment is covered only after a less expensive treatment has been tried and failed). The interim final regulations forbid using the EAP as a gatekeeper only for mental health/substance abuse benefits. The regulations also forbid imposing a "specialist" copayment for mental health that doesn't apply to medical/surgical care. [T.D. 9479, 75 Fed. Reg. 5410 (Feb. 2, 2010); see Groom Law Group, *New Interim Final Regulations on Mental Health Parity and Addiction Equity Act of 2008* (Feb. 15, 2010) (benefitslink.com)]

DOL/HHS FAQs issued in late 2010 clarify that EGHPs maintained by employers with 50 or fewer employees continue to be exempt from the requirements of the MHPAEA. See Alden Bianchi, *Departments of Labor and Health and Human Services Issue Joint Guidance Under the Affordable Care Act and MHPAEA*, Employee Benefits Advisory (Dec. 28, 2010) (benefitslink.com)]

Under EBSA FAQs published November 17, 2011 and interim final rules for the MHPAEA, published February 2, 2012, financial requirements and quantitative treatment limitations for six categories of mental health/substance abuse (MH/SA) benefits cannot be more restrictive than the limitations that apply to at least two-thirds of the medical/surgical benefits in the same classification. The 2011 FAQ says that it is a violation of the MHPAEA to require prior authorization from a utilization reviewer if this is not required for M/S benefits. If the plan has separate utilization reviewers for MH/SA and M/S, they must use consistent standards. [EBSA. *FAQs About Affordable Care Act Implementation Part VII*, <http://www.dol.gov/ebsa/faqs/faq-aca7.html> (Nov. 17, 2011); Sutherland Legal Alert, *Agencies Delay Summary of Benefits and Coverage Requirements, Issue FAQs on Mental Health Parity* (Nov. 21, 2011) (benefitslink.com); FYI, *Further Guidance Issued on Nonquantitative Treatment Limitations* (Dec. 23, 2011) (benefitslink.com)]

Principal Life Insurance, the insurer and claims administrator, denied many hospital charges for treatment of SW, a minor, for an eating disorder, on the grounds that the policy limits had been exceeded. The plan imposed a 10-day limit on inpatient mental health services, so it paid for 10 days of hospitalization in 2006 and only the first 10 days of a hospitalization in 2007. The Eighth Circuit held that there was insufficient evidence to treat the hospitalization as focused on SW's mental rather than her physical health. [*Wrenn v. Principal Life Ins. Co.,* 636 F.3d 921 (8th Cir. 2011); see Roy F. Harmon, *Eighth Circuit Holds Mental Health Treatment Limitation Inapplicable* (Mar. 4, 2011) (benefitslink.com)]

The Ninth Circuit held that insurance coverage of residential treatment for anorexia nervosa was not required by the Blue Shield policy—but was required by the MHPEA. California's mental health parity law requires coverage of medically necessary treatment of severe mental illness, and anorexia is considered a severe mental illness. It would be irrational to pay for 100 days of treatment in a skilled nursing facility that was not suitable for Harlick's condition while excluding suitable and effective care. [*Harlick v. Blue Shield of California,* 656 F.3d 832 (9th Cir. 2011), later proceedings 686 F.3d 699 (9th Cir. 2012)]

Judge Juan R. Sanchez of the Eastern District of Pennsylvania certified a class action suit against Cigna for refusing to cover two kinds of autism therapy that were rejected by the insurer as "investigative or experimental," but are widely accepted by health care professionals. The class was limited to parents who actually filed claims for the treatment and were turned down, excluding those who did not file a claim because of the insurer's characterization of the treatment. There could be as many as 100,000 plaintiffs (given the size of Cigna's participant base and the incidence of autism), making joinder impractical. Sanchez did not find *Dukes* (see § 42.06[A]) persuasive: that case involved multiple employment decisions made by multiple supervisors, whereas this case involved a single decision not to cover those autism therapies. [*Churchill v. Cigna Corp.,* No. 10-6911, 2011 U.S. Dist. LEXIS 90716 (E.D. Pa. Aug. 12, 2011); see Shannon P. Duffy, *Judge OKs Class Challenge to Autism Therapy Denial,* The Legal Intelligencer (Aug. 18, 2011) (law.com)]

## [F]  Other Inclusion Issues

The Supreme Court affirmed, without opinion, the Seventh Circuit's decision in *Doe v. Mut. of Omaha.* [179 F.3d 557 (7th Cir. 1999)] The Seventh Circuit ruled that it is not a violation of Title II of the Americans With Disabilities Act for either an insured or a self-insured health plan to impose a lower lifetime cap on AIDS-related conditions than on other conditions (e.g., $25,000 versus $1 million). The rationale is that Mutual of Omaha didn't refuse to sell policies to people with AIDS, although the policy was worth far less to a person with AIDS or an AIDS-related condition than someone with other health problems.

EGHPs are forbidden to discriminate against employees or their dependents who suffer from end-stage renal disease (ESRD). Internal Revenue Code § 5000 imposes a heavy penalty: 25% of the employer's health care expenses (not just the amount that would have been paid for ESRD coverage in the absence of discrimination). Also note that ERISA § 609(d) requires plans to maintain their coverage of pediatric vaccines at least at the May 1, 1993 level.

In January 2003, the Second Circuit ruled that it is not a violation of Title VII for a plan to exclude coverage of surgical procedures to correct infertility that are performed only on women, because infertility affects male and female participants equally. The district court hearing this case applied the "equal access" standard often used in ADA cases, asking whether all employees have equal access to plan benefits. However, the Second Circuit held that this is not an appropriate standard in a Title VII case, in which the relevant standard is whether sex-specific conditions exist. If they do, the next inquiry is whether excluding coverage of those conditions results in a plan that has inferior coverage for one sex. The Second Circuit said that the Pregnancy Discrimination Act's ban on discrimination on the basis of pregnancy or related conditions does not extend to discrimination on the basis of infertility, because both men and women have reproductive capacity and can be infertile. [*Saks v. Franklin Covey Co.*, 316 F.3d 337 (2d Cir. 2003)]

PPACA requires coverage of adult children up to age 26; by the time it was passed, more than two-thirds of the states had already expanded the age to which dependent coverage would be available, sometimes extending coverage even more than the PPACA requirement; some states require coverage to age 30. These state laws do not apply to self-insured medical plans, but do apply to EGHPs and possibly to stand-alone insured dental and vision plans. (Extending the parent's policy was usually more affordable than buying a policy for the adult child—especially if the adult child had a pre-existing condition.) In the first year, the PPACA opened up coverage options under parental policies, about 6.6 million young adults up to age 26 enrolled in their parents' plan. (Some of those young adults might have already been insured elsewhere.) Most of the benefit went to young adults from higher-income families, because low-income parents often lacked coverage. [Louise Radnofsky, *Millions of Young Adults Join Parents' Health Plans*, WSJ.com (June 8, 2012)]

EGHPs that cover the daughters of participants who have not reached age 26 do not necessarily have to provide pregnancy coverage. The Pregnancy Discrimination Act (see § 34.06) requires EGHPs that cover 15 or more people to provide maternity benefits for employees and their spouses, but does not require dependent coverage. In 2008, approximately 2.8 million women, or 12% of the 15–25 age cohort, became pregnant. In 2007, the average cost of uncomplicated maternity care/delivery was $10,652. Pregnant teenagers are at especially high risk for premature delivery and babies with low birthweight. [Michelle Andrews, *Some Plans Deny Pregnancy Coverage For Dependent Children*, Kaiser Health News (Aug. 6, 2012) (benefitslink.com)]

## [G]  State Mandatory Coverage

PPACA takes the approach of requiring both businesses and individuals to purchase health insurance coverage, or pay a fine—an approach that was already pioneered by several of the states, including California and Massachusetts. [See, e.g., Judy Greenwald, *Californians Vote to Repeal Health Insurance Mandate*, Business Insurance (Nov. 3, 2004); Milt Freudenheim, *Many California Employers Face Health Care Mandate,* N.Y. Times, Sept. 17, 2003, at A14; Jerry Geisel, *Mass. Ups Penalties for Lack of Health Cover*, Business Insurance (Dec. 29, 2008) (benefitslink.com); Steve LeBlanc (AP), *Mass. Governor OKs Landmark Health Bill*, Verizon.net (Apr. 12, 2006); *Massachusetts Health Care Reform: Two Years Later*, <http://www.kff.org/uninsured/7777.cfm> (May 2008)]

Massachusetts' state budget for 2014 includes repeal of the state's employer mandate. Governor Deval Patrick announced that the repeal would be carried out even though the federal employer mandate was delayed until 2015. [Kaiser Health News, *Mass. Employer Health Insurance Mandate Repeal Moves Forward*, <http://www.kaiserhealthnews.org/daily-reports/2013/july/12/health-reform-state -issues.aspx> (July 12, 2013)]

By mid-2007, Rhode Island, Connecticut, and Missouri had joined Massachusetts in requiring some employers to establish cafeteria plans qualifying under Code § 125, and Maine adopted a universal health plan, but it attracted few new subscribers, perhaps because many potential insured persons found the premiums unaffordable. [Sibson Consulting, *More States Enact Cafeteria Plan Mandates* (Aug. 10, 2007) (benefitslink.com); Pam Belluck, *Maine Learns Expensive Lesson as Universal Health Plan Stalls*, N.Y. Times, Apr. 30, 2007, at A1]

Mandates have also been adopted at the local level, e.g., by San Francisco. The Ninth Circuit ruled in September 2008 that San Francisco Administrative Code § 14.3(a), the ordinance requiring a minimum level of employer spending on health care, is not preempted by ERISA [*Golden Gate Rest. Assn v. City & County of San Francisco*, 546 F.3d 639 (9th Cir. 2008)]. The Ninth Circuit declined to review that decision en banc and, on March 29, 2009, the Supreme Court denied the restaurant trade association's request for an emergency order enjoining enforcement of the law. [Jerry Geisel, *Supreme Court Refuses to Stay S.F. Health Spending Law*, Business Insurance (Mar. 30, 2009) (benefitslink.com)]

Before PPACA, the general legal principle was that it was entirely up to employers to decide whether or not to offer insurance coverage. However, some attempts were made to require large employers to provide health insurance. Early in 2006, Maryland passed a bill mandating a minimum level of health care spending by large employers. The bill, nicknamed the "Wal-Mart law," required companies with more than 10,000 employees to either devote at least 8% of payroll to health benefits or make up the difference in taxes. The governor vetoed this "Wal-Mart law" (so-called because Wal-Mart was the only employer subject to it; the other equally large companies already had health plans), but the state legislature overrode the veto. Similar legislation was introduced in about 30 other states. [Tresa Baldas, *Novel Health Benefit Bill Sparks Debate*, Nat'l L.J. (Jan. 24, 2006) (law.com); Matt Brady, *Union Wins Big Employer Health Bill Victory,* NU Online News Service, Jan. 13, 2006] Early in 2007, the Fourth Circuit held that the statute was invalid—imposing Maryland-only requirements, contrary to

ERISA's mandate of uniform national rules. [*Retail Industry Leaders Assn. v. Fielder,* 475 F.3d 180 (4th Cir. 2007), discussed in Michael Barbaro, *Appeals Court Rules for Wal-Mart in Maryland Health Care Case,* N.Y. Times, Jan. 18, 2007, at C4] In response to the Fourth Circuit decision, Maryland's Attorney General announced that the state would not appeal, and would drop its efforts to force Wal-Mart to contribute more toward employee health care costs. [Fred Schneyer, *MD Abandons "Wal-Mart" Health Care Bill Fight,* plansponsor.com (Apr. 17, 2007)]

Although PPACA does not have provisions dealing specifically with the very largest employers, it does impose heavier requirements on "large employers" (those with 50 or more employees) than on smaller employers.

## § 18.04  DENTAL PLANS

Many medium-sized and large companies offer some form of dental coverage. As with most health-related benefits, the prevalence of the benefit increases directly with the size of the company.

Most dental plans offer fee for service coverage, although some plans use HMOs or PPOs. An emerging new form, endorsed by the American Dental Association in 1996, is the direct reimbursement plan: a fee-for-service plan where employees choose their own dentists. The plan sets a limit; up to the limit, the employee is entitled to payment of a percentage of dental expenses, e.g., full coverage of the first $100 in expenses, 50% reimbursement of the next $1,800, phasing out at a plan limit of $1,000 in benefits.

The National Association of Dental Plans Group Purchaser Behavior Study said that separate dental plans are becoming more popular: 59% of respondents had a separate policy, usually purchased from a stand-alone carrier. However, there was a decline in dental policies purchased as a package from the health insurance carrier's dental affiliate or partner. Policy purchasers said that cost was the most important factor in choosing a new dental carrier. Employers said that they offer dental benefits based on requests from employees, the value of dental health in general health, and affordability. However, 21% of employers with fewer than 100 employees in the group (i.e., those who will be eligible to use the Exchanges as soon as they start up) said that they were not likely to continue dental coverage outside the Exchange format. Since 2008, dental policies, like EGHPs in general, have been increasing the amount that employees must contribute toward the cost of their coverage. [Rebecca Moore, *More Employers Offering Dental Benefits,* plansponsor.com (Sept. 15, 2011)]

The basic structure of a dental plan is a schedule of covered procedures and payments for each (which might be defined as dollar amounts or percentages). The dentist who renders the care is paid for each service to covered employees (in a fee-for-service plan) or receives capitated or other prearranged compensation under an HMO or PPO plan. There is an increasing trend to require advance approval of large non-emergency claims.

The general rule is that the percentage of coverage is inversely related to the expected cost of the service. Low-cost procedures like X-rays and examinations get a higher percentage of reimbursement (often, 100%, but limitations to two exams and cleanings per year are also common) than fillings, root canals, and dental surgery (typically reimbursed at an 80% level). Prosthetics and orthodontia are typically reimbursed at a 50% level. Dental plans typically exclude cosmetic dentistry, hospitalization for inpatient dental procedures, and amounts that would be covered by other insurance (including Worker's Compensation). Usually, dental plans impose an annual maximum. [M.P. McQueen, *Health Plans Expand Dental Benefits*, Wall St. J., Sept. 19, 2006, at D1]

## § 18.05  PRESCRIPTION DRUG COVERAGE

Many companies' EGHPs provide at least some coverage of prescription drugs, as a complement to medical treatment. Some employers offer separate prescription drug plans with the objective of saving money by ordering in bulk. Some prescription drug plans also cover employees' dependents—often, with some degree of financial responsibility on the employee's part.

See Chapter 9 for a discussion of the effect of Medicare Part D (prescription drug coverage) on EGHP and retiree health plan operations. Group health plans that cover anyone eligible for Medicare Part D (whether as an active worker, a retiree, a spouse, or a dependent) and that cover prescription drugs must disclose to CMS, within 60 days of the start of each new plan year, whether the prescription drug coverage is creditable or noncreditable, by making an electronic filing at <http://www.cms.hhs.gov/CreditableCoverage>. [Warner Norcross & Judd LLP, *Your Medicare Part D Disclosure to CMS May Be Due Soon*, <http://www.wnj.com/your_medicare_part_d_disclosure_to_cms_may_be_due_soon-1-29-09> (Jan. 29, 2009)]

The typical prescription drug plan covers only outpatient drugs; drugs taken by hospital patients come under the hospital care benefit. The usual plan imposes a copayment on each prescription (e.g., $5–$25). Overall dollar limitations on reimbursement per plan year are common. However, many plans are bedeviled by high increases, such as 15%–20% a year, in prescription drug costs.

Express Scripts 2012 Drug Trend Report uses Express Scripts' claims data for 100 million Americans to track changes in utilization, spending, and unit costs. For the first time in over 20 years, spending on traditional prescription drugs fell in 2012 by 1.5% among people with commercial insurance. However, the cost of specialty medications for more complex diseases rose by 18.4%, so the overall drug trend for year was a 2.7% increase. Although less than 2% of the general population uses specialty medications, this constitutes 24.5% of pharmacy benefit spending. Four of the top 15 diseases with the highest drug spending (inflammatory conditions, multiple sclerosis, cancer, and HIV-related illnesses) use specialty medication. In 2012, utilization of cancer medications increased 3.4% but spending increased 22.3%, in large part because of exceptionally expensive new drugs customized to the patient's genetic profile. [Sharon Frazee, *Prescription Drug Trends: 2012 Drug Trend Report*, Express Scripts (Mar. 5, 2013) (benefitslink.com)]

In an effort to keep costs down, or at least to tamp down the speed of the rate of increase, plan sponsors are altering prescription drug plan design, incorporating features such as imposing higher copayments; imposing a coinsurance percentage instead of a flat amount; requiring doctors to get prior authorization for expensive drugs; requiring a trial of a less expensive drug before a more expensive one is prescribed ("step therapy"); raising the copayment on proprietary drugs when a generic formulation is available ("therapeutic focus"); excluding coverage of drugs prescribed for off-label uses; and having two or even three tiers with a $100 copayment in the highest tier and lower copayments for generics and less expensive branded drugs. [Barbara Martinez, *Drug Co-Pays Hit $100*, Wall St. J., June 28, 2005, at D1]

The majority of retail drug prescriptions are handled by Pharmacy Benefit Management (PBM) companies that permit economies of scale. An article published in early 2012 suggests that employers can obtain the best pricing by using a three-tier structure that makes employees' responsibility for pharmaceutical costs dependent on whether they use retail or mail-order generic purchasing channels and whether they use drugs that are inside or outside the plans' formulary. [Bob Kalman, Buck Consultants, *How To Manage Pharmacy Benefits Plans Part 3: As Pharma Consolidates, Even Smaller Employers Can Negotiate* (February 2012) (benefitslink.com)]

Plans often try to reduce costs by encouraging the use of generic rather than brand-name drugs (e.g., by imposing higher copayments on brand-name drugs; limiting reimbursement to drugs appearing on a formulary set in advance; refusing reimbursement for drugs that are not deemed safe and effective or cost-effective; and requiring prior approval of prescriptions so doctors will test the less expensive drug before prescribing the more expensive alternative).

Early in 2012, commentators pointed out that some important drug patents would expire in the next four years or so, making some extremely popular drugs available as generics for the first time. Since 2007, many employers adopted a three- rather than two-tier cost-sharing system in their prescription drug plans in order to drive more employees toward using generic drugs and drugs in the formulary. Many employers also adopted a percentage coinsurance requirement instead of flat-dollar copayments, so that increases in drug prices would be shifted to employees, protecting the employer. [Bob Kalman, Buck Consultants, *How to Manage Pharmacy Benefits Plans: Part 1: Getting the Plan Design Right* (February 2012) (benefitslink.com)]

The Henry J. Kaiser Family Foundation's report on 2013 health care trends shows that 81% of workers with prescription drug coverage are in plans that have three or even more tiers of cost sharing. The average 2013 copayment in these plans is $10 for first-tier drugs, $29 for second-tier drugs, $52 for third-tier drugs, and $80 for fourth-tier drugs (if the plan has a fourth tier)—almost identical to the 2012 levels. [Henry J. Kaiser Family Foundation, *2013 Employer Health Benefits Survey*, <http://kff.org/report-section/2013-summary-of-findings> (Aug. 20, 2013)]

## § 18.06  DOMESTIC PARTNER BENEFITS, CIVIL UNIONS, AND SAME-SEX MARRIAGE

### [A]  Current Trends

Not all employees fit neatly into the categories of "married" or "single." Some employees live with a domestic partner, whether in a nonmarital cohabitation relationship or with a same-sex partner. An increasing number of companies are offering health or other benefits to the unmarried domestic partners of employees. Because federal law does not recognize same-sex familial relationships, complex federal and state tax issues frequently arise. The federal Defense of Marriage Act (DOMA) specifies that only marriages between a man and a woman are recognized for federal purposes. Some of the states have adopted similar legislation or made it part of their constitutions.

In June, 2013, the Supreme Court ruled that § 3 of the federal DOMA was unconstitutional: it violates due process and equal protection, because it does not serve any legitimate state purpose to disparage same-sex marriages in comparison to male/female marriages, and it deprives same-sex married couples of valuable protections. (Section 3 provides that a same-sex partner cannot be treated as a "spouse" under federal law.) The Supreme Court found that DOMA § 3 improperly interferes with the states' regulation of marriage. The Supreme Court upheld the lower court ruling that invalidates California's Proposition 8 (the referendum forbidding same-sex marriage), on the grounds that the plaintiffs did not have standing to sue when the state of California no longer defended the validity of Proposition 8. [*United States v. Windsor*, 133 S. Ct. 2675 (2013); *Hollingsworth v. Perry*, 133 S. Ct. 2652 (2013). See Marcia Coyle, *Supreme Court Declares DOMA Unconstitutional*, The BLT (Blog of Legal Times) (June 26, 2013) (law.com); N.Y. Times, *Court Strikes Down U.S. Marriage Act*, NYTimes.com (June 26, 2013).]

Supreme Court Justice Kennedy denied request from Prop 8 supporters to stay issuance of same-sex marriage licenses in California. [AP, *Justice Denies Request to Halt Gay Marriages*, NYTimes.com (June 30, 2013)]

These are narrow decisions, and the Proposition 8 decision affects only California. Other cases about same-sex marriage remain in the court system, and may eventually get to the Supreme Court. Eliminating a state DOMA usually requires a popular vote, and perhaps action by the state legislature. Before the *Perry* case was decided, there were eight other federal cases pending in federal and state courts to challenge state bans on same-sex marriage. The Ninth Circuit postponed decision on a Nevada case ( *Sevcik v. Sandoval)* and a Hawaii case ( *Jackson v. Abercrombia);*these cases take up the issue of whether a state denies equal protection by authorizing civil unions but not same-sex marriages. The cases might be decided in 2014, and might be appealed to the Supreme Court. [Geoffrey A. Fowler, *Gay-Marriage Battles Still Loom in States,* WSJ.com (June 26, 2013)]

The general rule is that the employer has discretion to offer—or refuse to offer benefits to domestic partners who do not have the legal status of spouses. The advantage is that the plan can be a powerful motivator; the disadvantages are cost, administrative complexity, and possible offense to employees and recruitment candidates who are offended by nonmarital relationships. However, some states have legalized same-sex marriage and employers may have a legal obligation to provide spousal benefits for same-sex married couples and couples who have registered a civil union or domestic partnership.

In 2011, Mercer found that over half (52%) of employers provided health benefits for domestic partners, much higher than the 31% level for 2010. Coverage of same-sex partners varies by region, from 28% of large firms in the South to 79% of large firms in the West. Over half (58%) of Fortune 500 companies offer domestic partner benefits, some for opposite- as well as same-sex partners. [Julie Appleby, Kaiser Health News, *Many Businesses Offer Health Benefits To Same-Sex Couples Ahead Of Laws* (May 14, 2012) (benefitslink.com)]

As of mid-2013, same-sex marriage was permitted in California, Connecticut, Delaware, Iowa, Maine, Maryland, Minnesota, New Hampshire, New York, Rhode Island, Vermont, Washington, and the District of Columbia. The states recognizing domestic partnerships or civil unions were Colorado, Hawaii, Illinois, Nevada, New Jersey, Oregon, and Wisconsin. [N.Y. Times staff, *How the Rulings Affect Gay Couples,* NYTimes.com (June 26, 2013)] New Mexico state judge Sarah Singleton upheld the action by two county clerks to issue marriage licenses to same-sex couples. New Mexico has neither a DOMA nor a statute authorize same-sex marriage. [AP, *New Mexico: State Judge Rules for Gay Couples,* NYTimes.com (Aug. 23, 2013)]

In mid-2012, the Colorado legislature rejected a bill that would have allowed same-sex civil unions; this occurred six years after Colorado adopted a state DOMA. [Dan Frosch, *Colorado Rejects Same-Sex Civil Unions,* NYTimes.com (May 14, 2012)] However, Colorado passed Senate Bill 11 in 2013, and a civil union bill was signed by Governor John Hickenlooper on March 21, 2013, effective May 1, 2013. The Colorado Civil Union Act covers both same- and opposite-sex couples, offering many quasi-marital rights with respect to inheritance, survivor benefits, and health care decisions. Health plans issued or renewed after January 1, 2014 must treat civil union partners as spouses, but self-insured plans are not required to cover civil union partners, and COBRA coverage is not required under federal law—but is required under Colorado law. [Rebecca Hudson, *Colorado Governor Signs Civil Unions Into Law—How Will the Law Impact Your Employee Benefit Plans?* (Apr. 1, 2013) (benefitslink.com)]

The California Supreme Court authorized same-sex marriage, but the decision was overturned by a voter referendum. On May 26, the California Supreme Court upheld the validity of the referendum, with the result that same-sex marriage was no longer lawful. However, the approximately 18,000 same-sex marriages performed between the May court decision and the passage of Proposition 8 in November remain valid, on the grounds that the voters rejected the creation of any additional same-sex marriages, but Proposition 8's terms do not make it retroactive. [John Schwartz, *California Supreme Court Upholds Ban on Same-Sex Marriage*, <http://www.nytimes.com> (May 26, 2009); (This is the litigation that went to the Supreme Court.)

New Jersey passed a same-sex marriage bill in early 2012, but Governor Chris Christie vetoed it. [Jennifer Maloney, *Gay Nuptials Vetoed in N.J.* WSJ.com (Feb. 18, 2012)] Within a week of Governor Christie's veto of the gay marriage bill, the New Jersey Superior Court allowed seven same-sex couples to argue federal civil rights issues—based in part on the Ninth Circuit's Proposition 8 decision. The New Jersey suit, filed in 2010, says that New Jersey's Civil Union Act does not provide all the rights and benefits of civil marriage. The 2012 decision restores federal claims; in August 2010, the suit was allowed to proceed, but only on New Jersey constitutional claims. [James Campbell, *New Jersey Gay Nuptials Suit Takes a New Turn,* WSJ.com (Feb. 22, 2012)]

> ■ **TIP:**  Although the plan will probably require proof that the alleged domestic partners live together and share their finances, the plan should preserve confidentiality in case the employee doesn't widely publicize that he or she has a same-sex partner. [Mary Beth Braitman, Terry A.M. Mumford, Katrina M. Clingerman, Implementing a Domestic Partner Benefits Policy, Human Resources Winter 2008 Chapter 19, <http://www. thompson.com>; for information on state laws, consult the Human Rights Campaign, <http://www.hrc.org> or DOMA Watch, <http://www. domawatch.org>.]

DOMA also provides that states do not have to recognize same-sex marriages performed in other states or countries. However, some states adopted policies under which same-sex marriages from other jurisdictions will be recognized—even if the state does not authorize same-sex marriages itself. It is also possible for employers to treat employees' same-sex partners as spouses even if the couple is not legally married. Many plans that do this require domestic partners to submit an affidavit of partner status, indicating, for example, that they live together, share their finances, and intend the relationship to continue indefinitely.

## [B] Taxation of Domestic Partner Benefits

Various retirement issues (such as whether a pension will be paid as a QJSA) are governed by federal law. One reason why the Supreme Court DOMA decisions were so significant is that many employment issues depend on whether another person is the employee's "spouse" or not. Spouses are allowed to file joint income tax returns; unmarried cohabitants are not, so the Supreme Court decision makes it possible for married same-sex couples to file jointly.

The general rule is that a same-sex couple will be treated as spouses if they live in the state where they were married, if the state recognizes same-sex marriages—or perhaps if they live in a different state but that state recognizes (gives legal effect to) out-of-state same-sex marriages. However, there are still many and complex issues to be resolved.

In some circumstances, domestic partners who are not married can get favorable federal income tax treatment.

Under Treas. Reg. § 1.106-1, employees are not taxed on coverage provided to their spouse or dependents. However, there is no regulatory language about domestic partners. Therefore, unless the relationship is recognized by the state as spousal, or unless the domestic partner qualifies as a dependent under I.R.C. § 152(a)(8) (i.e., the employee domestic partner provides at least half the support for the other domestic partner), the employee will have taxable income equal to the value of the dependent coverage. However, if the cohabitation relationship is illegal under local law, I.R.C. § 152(b)(5) forbids treatment of the non-employee domestic partner as a dependent of the employee domestic partner.

If the non-employee domestic partner can be claimed as a dependent of the employee domestic partner, then the cost of domestic partner benefits is exempt from FICA and FUTA. But if the cost is taxable to the employee, both FICA and FUTA will apply in addition to income tax. Under Treas. Reg. § 1.61-21(b)(1), the gross income for the employee is the fair market value of the taxable fringe benefit, minus any amount the employee paid for it. Because the employee was taxed at the time the coverage was provided, neither the employee nor the domestic partner will be taxed if, for instance, health insurance or other reimbursement is provided later on.

The IRS issued a Chief Counsel Advice memo in September 2010, stating that if an employee's domestic partner is a dependent for tax purposes, then the value of health coverage for the domestic partner is not FUTA wages. [Chief Counsel Advice 201040012 (Sept. 8, 2010), <http://www.irs.gov/pub/irs-wd/1040012.pdf>; see EBIA Weekly, *Value of Tax-Dependent Domestic Partner's Health Coverage Isn't FUTA Wages* (Oct. 21, 2010) (benefitslink.com)]

Even before the mid-2013 Supreme Court rulings, the IRS granted some favorable tax treatment to registered domestic partners in California, Nevada, and Washington, because these are community-property states. [IRS Q&As for Registered Domestic Partners in Community Property States & Same-Sex Spouses in California, <http://www.irs.gov/newsroom/article/0,,id=2458 69,00 .html> (Sept.

16, 2011)]; see EBIA Weekly, *IRS Clarifications Affect Employee Benefits for Domestic Partners and Same-Sex Spouses* (Nov. 3, 2011) (benefitslink.com)]

### [C] Employer Responsibilities

The current edition of this book went to press shortly after the Supreme Court's DOMA decisions, so the process of adapting to the new rules had just begun and many issues remained unclear. The finding that DOMA § 3 is unconstitutional created a new general rule: for purposes of federal law (including ERISA, the FMLA, COBRA coverage, and income tax) same-sex marriage is treated on a par with male/female marriage. But family law is usually state law, with the definition of "spouse" left up to the states. DOMA § 2 has not been found unconstitutional, so states do not have to give full faith and credit to same-sex marriages from other jurisdictions if they choose not to.

The Supreme Court did not indicate how to handle the issue where a person with a same-sex spouse lives in one state but works in another. Some federal agencies use the rules of the state where the person lives; others use the rules of the state where the marriage was performed. The Social Security Administration determines validity by the place of residence. This is enacted in federal law, so Congressional action is required to change it. But federal agency regulations, like the DOL's FMLA regulations, can be changed administratively by the agency. [Brent Kendall & Jared A. Favolea, *Social Security Rules Defy Same-Sex Decision*, WSJ.com (June 27, 2013)]

Certain fringe benefits (e.g., employee discounts, group term life insurance) are tax-free to employees and their spouses or dependents. When a same-sex partner is considered a spouse, the employer does not have to impute income on the value of health benefits provided to a same-sex spouse, or withhold income tax and pay FICA tax on this imputed income for same-sex married couples. The payroll system will probably require re-programming accordingly.

One important issue that remains uncertain is treatment of same-sex partners who are civil union or domestic partners but not legally married. Treatment of retirement benefits already being paid, in non-QJSA form, to a person who has a same-sex spouse will also have to be resolved. [Vicki Nielsen, *Supreme Court DOMA Decision—Part I: Fringe Benefits and Other Tax Implications*, Ogletree Deakins, <http://blog.ogletreedeakins.com/supreme-court-doma-decision-part-i-fringe-benefits-and-other-tax-implications/> (July 23, 2013); Florence Olsen, *Attorney: DOMA Ruling Touches Most Health and Welfare Benefits*, Bulletin to Management, <http://www.bna.com/attorney-doma-ruling-n17179875364> (July 23, 2013); Prudential Compliance Advisory, *DOMA Decision Answers One Question But Raises Many More*, <http://www.retire.prudential.com/media/managed/DOMADecision-Advisory-0813.pdf> (August 2013)]

## § 18.07  TAX ISSUES IN EGHPs

For both the employer and the employee, the major EGHP tax issues fall under I.R.C. §§ 104–106. It is often in the best interests of both employer and employee for benefits to be provided under a plan of accident and health insurance (A&H). This result is desirable because the employer can deduct its costs of offering such a plan, and the employee does not have taxable income because the plan exists.

See § 18.19[B][6] for PPACA's rules on nondiscrimination in EGHPs. [IRS Notice 2011-1, 2011-2 I.R.B. 259 delays the required compliance date for the PPACA nondiscrimination requirement to insured health plans, until regulations or other official guidance is published, on the theory that employers do not have the necessary compliance information otherwise: Bond Schoeneck & King, PLLC, *Tax Break Extension Legislation Includes Employee Benefits Provisions and IRS Delays Compliance with Nondiscrimination Rules for Insured Group Health Plans* (December 2010) (benefitslink.com)]

Section 104 provides that an employee does not have gross income when he or she receives A&H insurance benefits that the employee paid for, or that derive from employer contributions that have already been taxed to the employee. For years after 1996, amounts paid under other arrangements having the effect of A&H plans will be taxed as if they did, in fact, come from an A&H plan. Section 105 provides that amounts an employee receives from an A&H plan are taxable if they are paid by the employer or stem from employer contributions not already taxed to the employee. If the employer reimburses medical expenses incurred by the employee for him- or herself and family, if the expenses would be deductible under I.R.C. § 213 (medical diagnosis and treatment, rather than cosmetic or experimental procedures), and if they have not already been deducted by the employee, then the employee has no gross income as a result of the medical expense reimbursement.

The employee can rely on I.R.C. § 105 to exclude amounts that were not received from an insurance policy, as long as they were received under a "plan." For this purpose, a plan is a structured arrangement—although it need not be legally enforceable or even written. The purpose of the plan must be to provide benefits to common-law employees (not independent contractors or self-employed persons) in the event of personal injury or sickness. If the plan is not legally enforceable, Treas. Reg. § 1.105-5 imposes the additional requirement that it be communicated to employees before they encounter any covered health expenses.

The third section of the trilogy, I.R.C. § 106, provides that employees do not have gross income if their employers provide them with A&H insurance.

On July 31, 2006, Final Regulations were published explaining comparability testing for employer contributions to HSAs. An employer who contributes to any employee's HSA has to make comparable contributions for all employees with HSAs. The employer's failure to do so is penalized under Code § 4980G by an excise tax of 35% of the aggregate employer contribution to all employee HSAs for the year. [Watson Wyatt Insider, *IRS Issues Final Regulations on Comparable Contributions to HSAs* (September 2006) (benefitslink.com); Nevin E. Adams, *HSA Comparability Rules Published*, plansponsor.com (July 28, 2006).

These excise taxes are reported on Form 8928. The excise tax, $100 per beneficiary per day, is also imposed for failure to comply with other requirements, such as rules about mental health parity and pre-existing condition limitations. [IRS Instructions for Form 8928 (2012), see Maureen Maly and Natalie Kohner, *IRS Updates Form 8928 for Self-Reporting of Excises Taxes Owed for PPACA Failures*, Beyond Health Care Reform Blog (Feb. 6, 2012) (benefitslink.com)]

Small employers (with up to 25 employees and average wages up to $50,000) may be eligible for a tax credit, for 2010–2013 plus any two years after that: See Code § 45R. For 2010–2013, the maximum credit is 35% of the premium paid by an eligible small business (25% of premiums paid by an eligible tax-exempt organization). The credit is computed on Form 8941 and included on the tax return as a general business credit. [See § 18.19[C]; <http://www.irs.gov/newsroom/article/0,,id=220839,00.html>; Fred Schneyer, *Tax Officials Distribute Small Business Health Credit*, plansponsor.com (Dec. 2, 2010)]

Not many businesses have applied for this credit. Although the number of businesses eligible for the small business tax credit under PPACA was estimated at between 1.4 million and 4 million, as of May 2012, the GAO said that only 170,000 firms had claimed the credit in 2010 and only about one-sixth could claim the full credit. The GAO said that the credit was not large enough to persuade small business owners to take the trouble to spend several hours on the paperwork. [House Committee on Ways and Means, *Why the Health Care Tax Credit Eludes Many Small Businesses* (Sept. 26, 2012)] A further complication is that the automatic budget cuts imposed by the federal "sequester" in 2013 reduced the refundable portion of the credit by 8.7%, until the federal fiscal year ends on September 30, 2013. [Cynthia Stamer, *Sequester Will Cut ACA Small Businesses Health Care Tax Credits*, WSJ.com (Mar. 5, 2013)]

The PPACA requires self-insured plans and issuers of health insurance policies to make small payments, reported on IRS Form 720. For plan years ending on or after October 1, 2012 and before October 1, 2019, the fee is $1 per covered person for the first year, $2 per covered person for the second year, with inflation adjustments in subsequent years. The money is used for quality assurance activities. [77 Fed. Reg. 22691 (Apr. 17, 2012); [<http://www.dol.gov/ebsa/healthreform>; see DOL, *FAQs About Affordable Care Act Implementation Part XI* (Jan. 24, 2013) (benefitslink.com)]

## § 18.08   HEALTH-BASED DISCRIMINATION

PPACA's ban on pre-existing condition limitations in health plans builds on a 2001 HHS/IRS interim regulation on discrimination based on health factors.

For questions and answers about the rule, see <http://www.dol.gov/ebsa/faqs/faq_hipaa_ND.html>. This rule implements a HIPAA provision, Code § 9802/ERISA § 702, forbidding discrimination in health coverage. EGHPs and insurers are forbidden to discriminate against, or charge higher premiums to, individual participants or beneficiaries on the basis of individual health factors such as health status, claims experience, or medical history. Note that whether a plan provision complies with HIPAA doesn't determine whether or not it violates the Americans with Disabilities Act (ADA).

Certain plans are exempt from the interim final rule, such as benefits that are not covered by HIPAA (e.g., long-term care insurance); single-participant plans; and self-funded plans that elect under 45 C.F.R. § 146.180 to opt out of the nondiscrimination requirements.

The Genetic Information Nondisclosure Act (GINA, Pub. L. No. 110-233) was enacted on May 21, 2008 and took effect November 21, 2009. It forbids employers to require genetic testing or to consider genetic information for hiring, firing, or promotions, and also forbids health insurers to deny coverage or set premium or deductible levels on the basis of genetic test results. GINA restricts the extent to which employers and insurers can ask for family medical histories. It is unlawful for an EGHP to give financial incentives (e.g., rebates or reduced premiums) for completing family medical histories as part of a health risk assessment. However, an EGHP can request family medical history to determine if an employee should be placed in a wellness or disease management program, as long as the employee gives the information voluntarily, and the information is only requested after plan enrollment and is not used in underwriting. [Steven Greenhouse, *Uses of Medical Histories Are Curtailed Under a New Law*, NYTimes.com (Nov. 15, 2009)]

Extensive interim final regulations covering GINA Title I § 103 were jointly issued by the IRS, DOL, and CMS in 2009. The HIPAA portability provisions already forbade group health plans and group health insurers from imposing pre-existing condition limitations solely based on genetic information. (Of course, the GINA regulations pre-date the restrictions on pre-existing condition limitations enacted by the PPACA.)

The 2009 GINA regulations forbid adjusting premiums or contribution rates for an EGHP because of the genetic information of one or more group members.. Even genetic information that is legitimately acquired cannot be used to discriminate, although a group premium can be increased based on a manifestation of a disease or disorder. Group rates do not have to be reduced by costs relating to benefits for genetic tests and counseling services that are permitted.

GINA Title II forbids employment discrimination based on genetic information, and limits the employer's use of genetic information. It is under the jurisdiction of the EEOC, which issued a Notice of Proposed Rulemaking at 74 F.R. 9056 (Mar. 20, 2009). There is an exception for wellness programs, but only under GINA

Title II, not Title I. [EBSA.gov, *FAQs on the Genetic Information Nondiscrimination Act* (Sept. 15, 2010) (benefitslink.com); see Hewitt Associates, *DOL Updates GINA Information on WebSite* (Sept. 20, 2010) (benefitslink.com)]

The EEOC issued final regulations for GINA Title II, the employment title, effective January 10, 2011. Under the Title II final regulations, an employer is not liable for inadvertent acquisitions of genetic information, or if information is provided voluntarily (e.g., under a wellness program), if family history is obtained to comply with state or local law, as part of an FMLA certification, or some employer leave policies. Nor are employers liable if the information is publicly available, comes from genetic monitoring that is required by law or offered on a voluntary basis, or is acquired by a forensic lab for law enforcement purposes. However, employers must keep exempt genetic information confidential, separate from ordinary personnel records.

GINA Title I and Title II are considered separate, so an employer will not be subject to double liability for Title II claims involving matters enforced under Title I. But it is possible to violate both titles and be penalized, for example, for requiring submission of genetic information to participate in an EGHP. An early 2011 article suggests putting a GINA disclaimer on all forms requesting medical information (such as FMLA forms, WC forms, pre-employment and return-to-work medical forms, ADA forms) so genetic information will not be included on the forms. GINA should be mentioned in the employee handbook, and employees should be informed that genetic information is protected. The required GINA notice should also be posted with the other required notices in the workplace. [Jeffrey Fraser and Sara Tountas, *New GINA Regulations Require Immediate Employer Action*, Miller Johnson newsletter (Jan. 5, 2011) (benefitslink.com) See also 77 Fed. Reg. 5396 (Feb. 3, 2012) for EEOC's final rule on GINA record-keeping requirements; starting April 3, 2012, employers of 15 or more employees must retain all records relating to GINA for at least one year, or until final disposition of any GINA-related discrimination charges.]

On January 17, 2013, HHS published a final rule covering the application of the HIPAA privacy rule to Titles I and II of GINA. Genetic information is considered health information, which cannot be used for underwriting purposes (except for long-term care insurance policies). Effective March 26, 2013, the final rule gives covered entities until September 23, 2013 to comply. [Katherine Georger, *New HIPAA Final Rule Implements GINA Restriction on Use and Disclosure of Genetic Information for Underwriting Purposes*, Holland & Hart LLP News Update, (Jan. 23, 2013) (benefitslink.com)]

In a 2011 case, the Southern District of Ohio found that the plaintiff was not wrongfully terminated after an argument with a co-worker. Nor was he fired because the employer did not want to pay the medical bills resulting from the plaintiff's son's cerebral palsy. The child's diagnosis occurred several months before the termination and this was far from his only altercation with a colleague. The supervisor who fired the plaintiff testified that he was not aware of the plaintiff's insurance claims history or what the insurance premiums were for the family. [*Berry v. Frank's Auto Body Carstar, Inc.*, 817 F. Supp. 2d 1037 (S.D. Ohio 2011); see Plansponsor staff, *Court Finds no Discrimination Based on Health Insurance Use*, plansponsor.com (Sept. 22, 2011)]

## § 18.09  HEALTH SAVINGS ACCOUNTS (HSAs) AND ARCHER MSAs

Current health policy relies heavily on tax-favored accounts that combine a high-deductible health policy (HDHP) with an investment account. Within statutory limits, account holders are entitled to deduct contributions to the investment account and employers' contributions to the accounts are not taxable income for the employee. The intention is that the account, over time, will generate investment returns that, in conjunction with the original deposits, can be applied toward the account holder's medical expenses. There are several kinds of tax-favored health accounts; collectively, they are sometimes referred to as Consumer-Driven Health Plans (CDHPs).

### [A]  MSAs

In addition to imposing health insurance portability requirements, HIPAA enacted I.R.C. § 220, which adds a new type of health plan for taxable years that begin after December 31, 1996. The "Medical Savings Account" (MSA), started out as a small-scale pilot project for the years 1997–2000, designed to terminate once 750,000 accounts had been created. The MSA account is tax exempt as long as it remains an MSA. Account owners do not get a tax deduction when they withdraw funds from the account to pay medical expenses, because the contributions have already received favorable tax treatment. Funds taken from the account for any other purpose are not only taxable income but subject to an excise tax. The tax, formerly 15%, rose to 20% for distributions after 2010. [IRS Publication 969, *Health Savings Accounts and Other Tax-Favored Health Plans*, <http://www.irs.gov/pub/irs-pdf/p969.pdf> (Jan. 14, 2011)]

The Community Renewal Tax Relief Bill of 2000 (H.R. 5652), passed on December 15, 2000, renamed the account the Archer MSA (after Representative Bill Archer, Republican of Texas) and extended its lifetime for a further two years. Then the Job Creation and Worker Assistance Act of 2002 [Pub. L. No. 107-147], extended the availability of Archer MSAs until December 31, 2003.

The Archer MSA program was terminated at the end of 2005, but it was reinstated in December 2006 (with the reinstatement operating retroactively). [Announcement 2007-44, 2007-9 I.R.B. 1238 discussed in (no by-line), *IRS Says Archer MSA Program Can Keep Going*, NU Online News Service (Apr. 18, 2007); EBIA Weekly, *IRS Announces That 2005 and 2006 Are Not Cutoff Years for Archer MSA Program* (Apr. 19, 2007) (benefitslink.com)]

MSAs are subject to limits. For 2013, the deductible must fall between $2,150 and $3,200 (individual coverage), $4,300–$6,450 (family coverage), and out of pocket expenses are capped at $4,300 (individual), $7,850 (family). See Rev. Proc. 2012-41, 2012-45 I.R.B. 539.

## [B]  HSAs Under MPDIMA

Division B of the Medicare Prescription Drug Improvement and Modernization Act of 2003 (MPDIMA; Pub. L. No. 108-173) is called the Health Savings and Affordability Act of 2003. MPDIMA provides for two new kinds of accounts: the Health Savings Security Account (HSSA) and the Health Savings Account (HSA). See § 9.10 for a discussion of the effect of MPDIMA's Medicare prescription drug plan on retiree health benefits and corporate accounting.

HSSAs are designed for uninsured persons or those who are covered only under a high deductible plan. This discussion focuses on the employment-related HSA plan structure, which is much easier to understand in the context of Archer MSAs and other plans than when viewed in isolation.

Starting January 1, 2004, individuals under age 65 who have a qualified health plan can contribute to HSAs, with the maximum contribution limited to the HDHP's deductible. The limit is increased for persons aged 55–65, who are allowed to make catch-up contributions (as originally enacted in 2004, this amount was $500 a year; increases phased in until the amount reached $1,000 in 2009, remaining at that level in 2012). If both spouses are 55 or over, a married couple is allowed to make two catch-up contributions. Eligible individuals (persons covered by an HDHP, and not covered by another plan that duplicates the HDHP's coverage) can receive a tax deduction. [Treasury Dept. Office of Public Affairs JS-1045 *Treasury Secretary Snow Statement on Health Savings Accounts* (Dec. 8, 2003) <http://treas.gov/press/releases/js1045.htm> (no www)]

The HSA itself is a trust created exclusively for the purpose of paying the qualified medical expenses of an eligible person. The term "qualified medical expenses" has the same definition as in Code § 220(d)(2). If funds are paid or distributed out of an HSA, and are used to pay the account beneficiary's qualified medical expenses, they do not constitute taxable income for the beneficiary. However, amounts that are distributed but are used for other purposes not only constitute gross income for the employee, but also are subject to a 15% excise tax penalty. The excise tax is waived if the distribution is made after the beneficiary's death; after the beneficiary becomes totally disabled; or after the beneficiary becomes eligible for Medicare.

For 2013, the annual contribution limit for HSAs is $3,250 (single person) and $6,450 (family). The minimum deductible for an HDHP is $1,250 (single) and $2,500 (family). The out of pocket maximum for a single person is $6,250; for a family, it is $12,500. [Rev. Proc. 2012-26, 2012-20 I.R.B. 933]

For 2014, the limit on the deduction for self-only coverage is $3,300, or $6,550 for family coverage. A high-deductible health plan is one with an annual deductible of at least $1,250 for self-only coverage, $2,500 for family coverage, and the out-of-pocket limit is $6,350 for self-only, $12,700 for family coverage. [Rev.Proc. 2013-25, 2013-21 I.R.B. 1110]

If an employee and his or her spouse have separate self-only HDHP coverage, each can contribute the single-person maximum to a separate HSA. If one spouse has family HDHP coverage, both spouses are considered to have family coverage, so the couple can contribute up to the family maximum, plus an additional $1,000 if one is over 55, $2,000 if both are over 55. Spouses can either establish separate accounts or share an HSA; contributions are allocated 50-50 to each account unless the spouses agree on a different allocation.

The investment firm Devenir said that as of mid-2013, there were over 9.1 million HSA accounts, with a total of $18.1 billion in assets—a 29% increase in both number of accounts and assets since mid-2012. In 2013, the average HSA balance was $1,891. [Devenir press release, *Health Savings Accounts Reach $18.1 Billion in June*,plansponsor.com (Aug. 6, 2013)]

On the compliance front, MPDIMA adds a new Code § 106(e) that states that an employer's contributions to an HSA are considered to be contributions under an Accident & Health plan. The employer's contributions are not subject to FICA or FUTA—but they must be shown on the employee's Form 1099. Failure to provide the mandated reports is penalized under Code § 6693(a). An employer that commits to making HSA contributions for employees, but fails to do so, is penalized under Code § 4980G.

PPACA did not eliminate HSAs; in fact, the Insurance Exchanges will offer them. [Ron Lieber, *Health Savings Accounts Survive Medical Overhaul*, NYTimes.com (Mar. 26, 2010)]

## [C]  IRS Guidance on MSAs and HSAs

Shortly after MPDIMA was passed, the IRS provided guidance in Notice 2004-2, 2004-2 I.R.B. 269 and Notice 2004-50, 2004-33 I.R.B. 196.

A Medicare-eligible person who has not yet enrolled can maintain an HSA, but can no longer contribute to the HSA after enrolling in Medicare.

It is reasonable to limit benefits to the usual, customary, and reasonable charge for those services, and therefore amounts that a patient must pay over and above the usual, customary, and reasonable charge are not included toward the maximum out-of-pocket amount. Although the general rule is that long-term care insurance premiums cannot be paid out of a cafeteria plan, Notice 2004-50 says that the account beneficiary can use HSA distributions to pay LTCI premiums, subject to the Code § 213(d)(1) limits on deductibility of premiums. Joint HSAs are not permitted: each spouse must have a separate account, which can have only one account beneficiary. However, an individual can have multiple HSAs. Tax-free HSA distributions can be used by a retiree over age 65 to pay for self-insured retiree health coverage, and HSA funds can be used to reimburse Medicare premiums deducted from the Social Security benefit; this counts as a qualified medical expense.

## [D]  Plan Comparisons

ERISA and the Internal Revenue Code make it possible for employers to offer a (potentially confusing) variety of tax-advantaged health insurance plans. By far the most popular arrangement is the Health Savings Account used in conjunction with a High-Deductible Health Plan, and this is the arrangement that is most favored under current tax law. (See § 18.10 below for Medical Expense Reimbursement Plans, § 18.11 for Flexible Spending Accounts (FSAs), and § 18.18 for Health Reimbursement Arrangement (HRA) plans.)

The broad distinction between an HRA and an HSA is that HRAs are solely funded by employer contributions and can be used for qualified medical expenses and premiums designated by the employer. Funds also can carry over from year to year. HSAs are tax-exempt trusts or custodial accounts. Contributions are deductible and are not taxable income for the employee if they are made by the employer or made by the employee in the form of pre-tax salary reduction contributions. Any employer can sponsor either type of plan. However, self-employed persons, including partners and owners of more than 2% of the shares in a Sub S corporation, cannot participate on a tax-favored basis in these plans.

HRAs are welfare benefit plans, so ERISA requirements for written plan documents and fiduciary conduct must be followed. SPDs also are required, and Form 5500 must be filed unless there is a small plan or other exemption available. DOL Field Assistance Bulletin, No. 2004-1, says that HSAs are not generally welfare benefit plans if the employer's involvement is limited (the employee pays the full premium; participation is voluntary).

HRA contributions are subject to forfeiture, but HSA contributions are not. Therefore, HSA balances can be rolled over tax-free to another HSA. MSA funds can also be rolled over into an HSA. COBRA and HIPAA apply to HRAs because they are considered EGHPs. COBRA does not apply to HSAs. [See Notice 2004-2, Q&A 35] HIPAA applies to HSAs if, and only if, they are ERISA welfare plans. [Chicago Consulting Actuaries, *HRAs or HSAs, How Does an Employer Decide?* (Nov. 9, 2005) (benefitslink.com); originally published in the Journal of Deferred Compensation (Aspen) (Winter 2005)]

## § 18.10  MEDICAL EXPENSE REIMBURSEMENT PLANS

Medical expense reimbursement plans usually reimburse employees directly for their medical expenses. Payment comes from the employer's resources, not from an insurance policy. Usually, the plan sets a maximum: e.g., only claims of $X per year will be covered. The plan can also be coordinated with insurance, so that the employer pays up to a certain amount, with insurance covering the rest.

The plan must cover employees, although it is not a legal requirement that it cover all employees. The plan can be informal. There is no legal requirement that the plan be in writing, unless it is a "welfare benefit plan" for ERISA purposes. In any case, employees must be given reasonable notice of the plan's existence and of how it operates.

For tax purposes, the most important question is whether the plan shifts risk to a third party (other than the employer and employee). A plan that uses a third-party administrator (TPA) to handle administrative or bookkeeping services does not shift risk to the TPA. The employer's costs of maintaining a self-insured plan will probably be deductible, as ordinary and necessary business expenses.

Internal Revenue Code § 105(h) governs self-insured medical expense reimbursement plans—those whose benefits are not payable exclusively from insurance. Plans of this type must satisfy coverage and nondiscrimination tests to qualify:

- The IRS issues a determination letter stating that the plan is nondiscriminatory;

- The plan covers at least 70% of all employees;

- At least 70% of all employees are eligible for the plan, and 80% or more of the eligible employees are actually covered.

However, the plan need not count employees who are younger than 25 years old, those who have been working for the company for less than three years' service, part-time or seasonal employees, or employees covered by a collective bargaining agreement that made accident and health benefits the subject of good-faith bargaining.

The plan is not discriminatory if the benefits provided for highly compensated employees (HCEs) and their dependents are also provided for other employees. The plan can impose a dollar maximum on the benefits paid on behalf of any individual, but cannot set the maximum at a percentage of compensation, because that would improperly favor HCEs.

If a self-insured medical reimbursement plan is discriminatory, then the HCEs (but not the rank-and-file employees) will have taxable income equal to the employer's plan contributions on their behalf. If taxable income does result from a self-insured medical expense reimbursement plan, the income will be subject to income tax withholding, but not to FICA or FUTA. [See I.R.C. § 3121(a)(2)(B)]

## § 18.11 FLEXIBLE SPENDING ACCOUNTS (FSAs)

An FSA is an arrangement (either stand-alone or part of a cafeteria plan) under which an employer diverts some cash compensation into a separate account, which must be identified for specific use: either for dependent care expenses, or for medical expenses that are not reimbursed by insurance or directly by the employer. The maximum amount of reimbursement that can be made "reasonably available" to a participant during a period of coverage is limited to 500%

of the total premium for the coverage. FSA reimbursement must be made available at least monthly, or when the level of expenses reaches a reasonable minimum amount such as $50.

The amount that can be placed into a dependent care FSA is limited by the Internal Revenue Code's limits on deductible dependent care expenses. Funds targeted for medical care cannot be used for dependent care, and vice versa. A medical expense FSA must last at least twelve months, although a short first year, when the plan is initially adopted, is allowed. Premiums for other health coverage cannot be reimbursed by the FSA.

Before 2012, there was no limit on health FSAs, but PPACA imposes a $2,500 maximum. Benefits USA's 2012/2013 survey says 89.7% of respondents offer an FSA, and 23.6% of employees at those companies enroll in them. [Linda Panszczyk, *Big Change In Store For Health FSAs In 2013*, CCH Benefits Talk blog (Nov. 12, 2012) (benefitslink.com)]

Notice 2012-40, 2012-26 I.R.B. 1046, explains how to apply the cap. The cap applies to plan years (not the employees' tax years) beginning after December 31, 2012. Cafeteria plans can be amended retroactively at any time on or before December 31, 2014 to incorporate the cap, but operational compliance with the cap is required after the 2013 plan year. [Christy Tinnes and Brigen Winters, *Second Opinions: ACA Cap on Contributions to Health FSAs*, plansponsor .com (July 18, 2012)]

To receive reimbursement, the FSA participant must submit a written statement from an independent third party (such as the doctor or medical office administrator) to confirm that a medical expense of $X has been incurred, and that this expense was neither reimbursed by nor eligible for reimbursement under any other plan. [Randy Myers, *Flex Abilities (Flexible Spending Accounts)*, plan sponsor.com (April 2006)] Since 2005, FSAs are allowed to carry over unused amounts from one year to the next.

The Heroes Earnings Assistance and Relief Tax Act (HEART Act, Pub. L. No. 110-245) allows employers to amend their FSA plans so that reservists called up for six months or more of active duty can withdraw their FSA balances as a taxable cash distribution. [Rebecca Moore, *Reservist Benefits Bill Signed into Law*, plansponsor.com (June 19, 2008)] IRS Notice 2008-82, 2008-41 I.R.B. 853 provides guidance on these Qualified Reservist Distributions (QRDs) from FSAs, including a transition rule allowing retroactive plan amendments to cover QRDs made before January 1, 2010. [Rebecca Moore, *IRS Provides Guidance on Reservist FSA Distributions*, plansponsor.com (Sept. 30, 2008)] Rev. Rul. 2010-23, 2010-39 I.R.B. 388, says that a tax-free arrangement can only reimburse OTC drugs if the drugs are prescribed by a physician.

## § 18.12 EGHP STRUCTURES

Originally, indemnity plans were the standard; now, that role is held by managed care plans of various types. Within the managed care category, HMOs were once dominant, but now must share the spotlight with other plan forms that offer greater choice of health care providers. Recently, attention has been given to defined contribution and voucher plans.

Usually, indemnity plans are divided into "basic" and "major medical" models. Basic coverage encompasses surgery, hospitalization, and care provided by physicians during a hospital stay. A major medical plan pays when other coverage is exhausted. A comprehensive major medical plan combines basic and major medical features, whereas a supplemental plan offers pure excess insurance.

The standard model for indemnity insurance calls for the patient to be responsible for paying a deductible each year (e.g., $X, or $X per family member) before the plan has any responsibility for payments. Most plans also impose a co-insurance responsibility: In an 80/20 plan, for example, once the deductible is satisfied, the patient is responsible for 20% of the bill—or 20% of the "schedule amount" that the plan pays for the service, plus the full difference between the actual charge and the schedule amount. It is also typical for indemnity plans to include a "stop-loss" provision that represents the maximum out-of-pocket spending an individual or family will incur under the plan. But the plan, in turn, usually limits its exposure by imposing overall limits on each employee's coverage, whether per year or over a lifetime.

Reimbursement to providers under indemnity plans is generally made on the basis of the table of "usual, customary and reasonable charges" promulgated by the insurer. These are either historical figures or a schedule of charges for various items.

## § 18.13 MANAGED CARE

### [A] Concepts and Models

Managed care was a response to the climate of the 1970s and 1980s, when employers were faced with explosive increases in insurance premiums. Theoretically, managed care will encourage participants to adopt healthier lifestyles and, by deploying preventive care effectively, will detect disease early when it is more likely to be curable.

A common feature of managed care plans is utilization review. Patients may be required to consult a "gatekeeper" primary care physician before they can be referred to a specialist. Nonemergency procedures may have to be approved in advance by a claims reviewer. Patients' operations and hospital stays will be assessed for medical necessity.

In some managed care models, the employee is required to get all care within a closed network of providers; otherwise, reimbursement will not be available for out-of-network care (except in emergencies or when necessary care is not available within the network). But the trade-off is that the employee either gets care within the network at no additional charge, or pays only a small amount per visit, per prescription, or per service.

Managed care plans typically have their own payment schedules, which may be significantly lower than actual health care costs encountered in the community. The managed care plan's reimbursement to the patient may be defined in terms of this schedule, with the result that the patient has very significant copayment responsibilities. If a patient has satisfied the deductible and is charged $1,000 for a procedure and the health plan's schedule amount is $800; it pays 80% of the schedule amount, or $640, making the patient responsible for the remaining $360.

Generally, employees will be given one open enrollment period a year. During this time, employees who have just become eligible will be able to select one of the options available under the plan. Employees who have already selected a plan option will be able to change their selection. Once made, a decision is usually irrevocable until the next open enrollment period. Most open enrollment periods occur in the autumn, but this is by custom; it is not a legal requirement.

In 2011, the PPO remained the most common heath plan design, offered by 79% of employers, whereas 58% offered CDHPs and 38% offered HMOs. About one-third of employers (34%) offered HSAs, versus 18% offering HRAs—but 43% of employees actually enrolled in the HRA versus only 28% in HSAs. Aon Hewitt's explanation is that HRA plan designs are more flexible than HSA designs. The average 2011 enrollment in PPO plans was 69%, 49% in POS plans, 43% in HDHC CDHPs with HRAs, and 28% HDCHDP with HSAs. [Rebecca Moore, *CDHP Use Surpasses HMO Use by Employers*, (Sept. 17, 2012) plansponsor.com]

The Kaiser Foundation reported that in 2012, 16% of covered workers were enrolled in an HMO, 56% in a PPO, 9% in a POS plan, and 19% in a high-deductible plan. Less than 1% were enrolled in the now-misnamed "conventional" (i.e., indemnity) plan. In 2013, 14% of workers were enrolled in an HMO, 57% in a PPO plan, 9% in a POS plan, and 20% in a high-deductible plan; again, less than 1% were enrolled in indemnity plans. [Henry J. Kaiser Family Foundation, *2013 Employer Health Benefits Survey*, <http://kff.org/report-section/2013-summary-of-findings> (Aug. 20, 2013)]

In 2003, the Supreme Court upheld state "any willing provider" laws (statutes requiring MCOs to accept all licensed health care providers who apply; about half the states have such laws). The MCOs' argument was that closed networks control costs by imposing lower fees, but the Supreme Court said that extending the freedom of health care providers to offer care, and making more options available to patients, should be accorded higher priority. [*Kentucky Ass'n of Health Plans v. Miller*, 538 U.S. 329 (2003); see also *Prudential Ins. Co. of Am. v. Nat'l*

*Park Med. Ctr., Inc.*, 413 F.3d 897 (8th Cir. 2005): Arkansas' "any willing provider law," requiring MCOs to open the network to any qualified health provider, "regulates insurance" and therefore is not preempted by ERISA]

## [B]  Health Maintenance Organizations

The Health Maintenance Organization, or HMO, is both a network of providers and a mechanism for financing health care. The theory is that participating providers are paid on a "capitated" basis. That is, they receive a fee "per head" covering all medical services under the plan for a particular employee or dependent of an employee. The theory is that, because providers do not receive more if their patients get additional health services, they will not be motivated to order unnecessary services for purely financial reasons.

In a "staff model" HMO the health professionals are salaried employees of the HMO. In the more prevalent Individual Practice Association (IPA) model HMO, the health professionals enter into contracts with the IPA, and the IPA negotiates with the HMO to set a reimbursement schedule for each service on the schedule.

Under the "group model," the HMO enters into contracts with independent group practices that are responsible for administrative tasks and are usually paid on a capitated basis. The "network model" HMO's doctors practice primarily in fee-for-service mode However, they also agree to provide certain services to HMO patients, once again generally in exchange for a capitation fee.

Federally qualified HMOs must provide an obligatory package of services including both primary and specialty physician services; hospital inpatient and outpatient care; emergency medical treatment; short-term outpatient mental health treatment; referrals and treatment of substance abuse; home health care; and preventive health care. Federally qualified HMOs can also provide additional, optional services such as long-term care, longer-term mental health treatment, dental and vision care; physical therapy; and prescription drugs. Optional services do not have to be provided on a capitated basis, and the HMO can impose fees on such services.

## [C]  Preferred Provider Organizations (PPOs)

A PPO is an administrative structure under which health care providers become "preferred" by affiliating with the structure. Employers negotiate with the PPO to set the rate scale for specified health services. In 2007, the PPO was the managed care form with the most enrollees.

There is no set enrollment period for employees to join a PPO. Nor is there a single centralized entity that has complete financial responsibility for the enrollees' care. Sponsorship of PPOs is quite diverse: They might be created by a hospital or other health care provider, a health insurer, entrepreneur, or group of doctors.

## [D]  Point of Service (POS) Plans

A point of service plan is a hybrid of indemnity and HMO concepts. Participants can select their providers from a network, but they are not obligated to get their care within the network. If they do, their only copayment responsibility is a small amount per visit. Indemnity concepts such as an annual deductible and a co-insurance percentage apply when they choose out-of-network care. POS plans usually impose a high coinsurance percentage, such as 40%, on out-of-network care.

## [E]  Managed Care Cost Reduction Techniques

Utilization review (UR) is a cornerstone of managed care cost-cutting. In traditional fee-for-service medicine, the health care provider determines which treatments will be used, and the payor reimburses for part or all of the care ordered by the provider.

Managed care adds "gatekeepers"—reviewers who determine whether a claim satisfies the requirements of the plan. In many instances, the plan will require prior approval of claims, and will deny or reduce claims for non-emergency services that did not receive this approval in advance. UR also includes concurrent review (e.g., reviewing the need for continued hospitalization while the patient is still in the hospital) and retrospective review (after treatment is completed).

Procedural controls are common. Most plans will pay for a second opinion prior to surgery, but will not pay for surgery unless the second opinion confirms the recommendation for surgery. Cost-cutting techniques also include adopting a fixed payment schedule, and favoring outpatient and home care over hospitalization.

A carve-out is a discount mechanism under which particular forms of medical expense, or high-cost conditions, are managed separately from the rest of the health plan.

Managed care tactics from the 1990s had a resurgence in 2012. For example, choice of doctors and hospitals is being cut back; requiring referrals to see specialists is more common; and procedures such as spinal surgery may require prior authorization. Although these measures were very unpopular with employees, employers are betting that employees will accept these restrictions in order to avoid taking on even more of the burden of health care costs. Insurers are offering both broad PPOs and narrower plans that work like classic HMOs; some plans have tiered designs with employees facing higher bills for non-preferred providers, and still higher bills for care obtained out of network. [Anna Wilde

Mathews, *Remember Managed Care? It's Quietly Coming Back*, WSJ.com (Aug. 2, 2012)]

It is becoming more common for companies to encourage workers to get additional medical opinions before undertaking costly medical treatments—either by incentives (lower deductible on treatment if the patient gets a second opinion) or disincentives (higher premiums or lower reimbursement if the patient does not get a second opinion). There are specialized second-opinion consultants like Advance Medical and Best Doctors; they recommend an alternate treatment 60% of the time. The alternative is usually more conservative (such as medical management) although not necessarily cheaper than surgery. Employers pay the full cost of the second opinion service. Generally, the reviewer only examines the case file and does not see the patient. [Jen Weiczner, *When Your Boss Doesn't Trust Your Doctor*, MarketWatch Bulletin (WSJ.com) (Feb.12, 2013)]

## [F]  Cost Trends

Managed care became popular because of undesirable increases in the cost of indemnity health plans. However, managed care has not lived up to its promise of reducing health care costs. Managed care premiums have always risen much faster than inflation. In response, employers often shifted much or all of the increase to employees, requiring them to pay premiums for the first time, or increasing their premiums, deductibles, and/or coinsurance.

In addition to shifting more of the premium to employees, employers adopted cost cutting measures such as having only high-deductible health plans; imposing a surcharge on spousal coverage if the spouse could be covered elsewhere; reducing the size of the network; imposing extra fees for using certain doctors or hospitals; and giving financial incentives for filling out health risk assessments and achieving goals set by a health coach. [Anna Wilde Mathews, *Choosing the Right Health-Care Plan*, WSJ.com (Oct. 22, 2011)]

Mercer's National Survey of Employer-Sponsored Health Plans showed that 2012 posted the lowest annual average cost increase since 1997 due to factors such as stronger health management programs and moving more employees into CDHPs. The average cost was $10,558 per employee. Only 22% of small (under 500 employees) and 7% of large employers said they were likely or very likely to terminate their health plans when the Exchanges become available. CDHP enrollment rose from 13% of covered employees in 2011 to 16% in 2012. The cost of coverage in an H SA/CDHP was about 20% lower than the cost of PPO coverage: $7,833 and $10,007 respectively. Defined contribution strategies are also popular: that is, the employer decides how much it will contribute, making employees responsible for the balance of the increase. [Mercer, *Employers Held Health Benefit Cost Growth To 4.1%* (Nov. 4, 2012) (benefitslink.com)]

A Towers Watson/National Business Group on Health study reports that, in 2013 employees contribute 42% more to coverage than they did five years ago, whereas employer contribution rose 32% in this period. In 2011, employees paid 34% of the cost of health care in the form of premiums and out-of-pocket spending, a proportion that rose to 37% in 2013. Annual salary increases over the last three years averaged less than 2%, so employees are falling behind. Eighty percent of employees surveyed by Towers Watson said that they would continue to raise employee obligations in the next three years. In 2012, the average employee contribution was $2,658, which was expected to increase 9%, to $2,888, in 2013. [Ann Carrns, *Workers' Share of Health Costs Is Likely to Continue Rising*, NYTimes.com (Mar. 7, 2013)]

The Kaiser Family Foundation said that in 2006, 52% of workers covered by an EGHP paid a deductible for single coverage; 72% did so in 2012. Deductibles are much more common in PPOs than in HMOs. In 2012, 19% of covered employees were enrolled in HDHPs with a savings option. For plans that have a general deductible, the average was $1,097 in 2012—88% more than in 2006. Workers in small firms (those with three to 199 employees) typically have much higher deductibles: (an average of $1,596, versus $875 in larger firms). The average deductible for hospitalization or surgery is $550; the average prescription drug deductible is $145, and many plans also impose copayment requirements for those services. [Matthew Rae, Nirmita Panchal, Gary Claxton, *Snapshots: The Prevalence and Cost of Deductibles in Employer Sponsored Insurance*, Kaiser Family Foundation (Nov. 2012) (benefitslink.com)]

According to the Commonwealth Fund, 80% of working-age Americans live in the 35 states where premiums represent 20% or more of median income. Average premiums for family health insurance rose 62% from 2003–2011 (from $9249 to $15,022/year) in a period when median family income rose only 11%. Health insurance costs rose faster than incomes in all states. In that time period, the employer share of premiums rose 74%, and deductibles increased 117%. [Commonwealth Fund, *State Trends in Premiums and Deductibles, 2003-2011: Eroding Protection and Rising Costs Underscore Need for Action*, <http://www.commonwealthfund.org/Publications/Issue-Briefs/2012/Dec/State-Trends-in-Premiums-and-Deductibles.aspx>; see Wolters Kluwer Law & Business, *Majority Of Americans Live In States Where Health Insurance Premiums Are 20 Percent Or More Of Median Income* (Jan. 2, 2013) (benefitslink.com); Rebecca Moore, *Action Needed to Curb Health Cost Increases* plansponsor.com (Dec. 18, 2012)]

Other cost control measures include imposing a formulary for prescription drugs, using a "tiered" system under which reimbursement is higher for generic than for brand-name drugs, restricting or eliminating family benefits, and performing audits to make sure that ineligible persons are not covered under the plan.

The bulk of cost increases are due to family coverage, so many employers are raising the family premium; refusing to cover spouses who have access to coverage through their own employment; adding larger payments for larger families; or imposing monthly surcharges for family coverage.

## [G] Choosing a Managed Care Plan

Most employers can choose among several or many managed care plan vendors (although they won't be able to take advantage of this to bargain for low prices!). When an employer chooses a plan, cost considerations are important, but they don't tell the whole story. PPACA's Insurance Exchanges are intended to make the health insurance market more competitive, thus lowering premiums.

Employees may initially be glad to sign up with an HMO that imposes low copayments, but they will be dissatisfied if they have to travel too far to find a network provider, or wait too long for appointments. Other possible sources of discontent are difficulties in getting referrals to specialists, and denial of access to prescriptions, tests, and treatments that the patients and/or doctors think are likely to be beneficial.

When an account representative approaches you, collect as much information as you can about the plan, its history, and its results (including references from other subscribers). You can find out how an HMO, PPO, or POS selects the physicians in its network, and how doctors in the network resolve problems among themselves—and with the managed care plan about preferred treatment methods.

Your state insurance department will probably have information about the plan's operations, loss ratios (percentage of premiums used to pay claims rather than profits or administrative expenses) and how complaints have been resolved in the past.

Factors to consider are:

- Number of health care providers in the network or participating in the plan;

- Qualifications of health care providers (board certification or eligibility; hospital affiliations; any past complaints or suits);

- How the provider pattern fits your employee census (Are there too many obstetricians and not enough cardiologists, or vice versa?);

- Quality of hospitals and other facilities involved with the plan;

- Utilization review and other cost-control measures;

- Availability of primary care physicians at off hours (to cut down on the number of emergency room visits);

- Use of claims management to coordinate treatment of serious illness and injury to promote rehabilitation;

- How premiums compare to those of other MCOs—however, a low premium may simply mean that you will face exceptionally large increases in the future;

• Measures the plan takes to promote consumer satisfaction (telephone help lines, clear explanations of claims procedures, swift resolution of claims disputes, periodic surveys to assess consumers' reactions to the plan).

## [H]  Self-Insured Plans

As insurance premiums increase, more and more employers adopt, or at least consider adopting, self-insured plans. However, a self-insured plan has a heavy administrative and disclosure burden. Reinsurance is vital, because even a young and healthy group of employees can incur catastrophically high claims if even one employee is in a serious accident or has a child with major health care needs. Furthermore, health care providers tend to shift costs onto self-payors.

The PPACA requires the DOL to report to Congress each year about self-insured employee health benefit plans, based on data from Form 5500s filed by health plans. (A health plan has to file Form 5500 if it has at least 100 partici-pants and/or holds assets in trust.) About 49,000 Form 5500s were filed by health plans for 2010—a decline of about 3% from the 2009 level. The 2010 forms showed that there were about 19,800 self-insured plans plus about 4,000 plans that combined self-insurance with commercial insurance. In 2010, self-insured plans covered about 30 million participants (27 million active participants) and held assets of about $58 billion. Mixed plans covered almost 26 million partici-pants (21 million active participants) and held assets over $136 billion. About 18,700 self-insured group health plans and 3,400 mixed plans were sponsored by a single employer; about 1,100 self-insured plans and 700 mixed plans were multi-employer plans. The percentage of self-insured or mixed plans dropped from 56% in 2001 to 49% in 2010. Note that most of the plans studied by DOL combine other welfare benefits with health benefits, so the figures include more than just health plans. [Seth Harris (Acting Secretary of Labor) Report to Con-gress: *Annual Report on Self-Insured Group Health Plans*, <http://www.dol.gov/ebsa/pdf/ACAReporttoCongress033113.pdf> (March 2013)]

One coping mechanism is to use a Blue Cross or other entity as a Third-Party Administrator (TPA), which could give your plan access to the insurer's dis-count structure.

In a specific stop-loss plan, the insurer agrees to reimburse the employer or other plan sponsor for any claim that exceeds a specified amount (the "reten-tion"). An aggregate stop-loss plan covers all claims above the retention in a par-ticular year. In effect, a stop-loss plan works like an insurance policy with a very high deductible. But from the insurer's viewpoint, a specified stop-loss plan is more favorable, because although the insurer collects premiums in either case, it has no direct liability to the employees covered by a stop-loss plan, and cannot be sued by them for allegedly improper denials of claims or refusals to pre-approve treatment. A stop-loss plan ends on a particular date, and the insurer is not respon-sible for claims that accrued by that date but have not yet been filed. In contrast, an insured plan is responsible for these "tail" or IBNR (Incurred But Not Reported) claims.

However, the stop-loss premium will be very high if the plan experiences many claims in the early years of self-insurance. Stop-loss insurers have tactics to protect themselves, such as "lasering"–raising the dollar amount the employer is responsible for before stop-loss coverage is available for high-risk employees. Broader self-insurance could create problems for the Exchanges, if companies with a healthy young workforce gamble on remaining self-insured (whereas companies with older, sicker employees join the Exchange). Sometimes stop-loss insurers also avoid state taxes on insurance premiums by creating plans that are self-insured in name only (e.g., with a stop-loss policy that is triggered at only $10,000). For this reason, New York and Oregon forbid the sale of stop-loss coverage to very small groups (under 50 employees). [John Tozzi, *Small Business Makes a Risky Bet on Health Care*, Bloomberg Businessweek (Apr. 5, 2012) (benefitslink.com)]

For the years 2014-2016, PPACA provides a temporary reinsurance program to stabilize premiums after insurers are required to accept all applicants for individual coverage. Insurers and plan sponsors must pay into the stabilization fund; the fee is $63 per person per year. The reinsurance payments will be distributed to insurers in the individual market: $10 billion in 2014, $6 billion in 2015, and $4 billion in 2016. Reinsurance payments will also go to the U.S. Treasury's general funds at the rate of $2 billion each in 2014 and 2015, and $1 billion in 2016. Retiree plans are subject to the fees, but retiree coverage is excluded from the requirement if Medicare is the primary payor and the EGHP is only a secondary payor. Fees must be paid on behalf of active employees who are Medicare enrollees, and when Medicare is the secondary payor. [77 Fed. Reg. 73118 (Dec. 7, 2012); see Segal, *Proposed Rule Would Require Plan Sponsors to Pay Affordable Care Act's Transitional Reinsurance Program Fees* (Dec. 20, 2012) (benefitslink.com)]

## § 18.14  EMPLOYER LIABILITY FOR HEALTH PLAN ACTIONS

### [A]  Generally

The managed care relationship has three parts: the managed care organization (MCO) that provides care; the employer that enters into a contract with the MCO; and the employee or dependent that receives health care. When there is a bad result (whether or not malpractice occurred), the employee might want to sue the employer as well as the MCO.

Initially, employers usually avoided liability because the health plan provided the actual treatment (or claims denial). In many cases, plans escaped liability as well, because ERISA preempts state law but says virtually nothing about the plan's obligations. This state of affairs led to many demands for increased regulation (especially state regulation) to protect health care consumers. Many of these explosive issues are beyond the scope of this book, because they involve the employer and the EGHP only indirectly.

The Supreme Court has tackled some of these issues. *Humana Inc. v. Forsyth* [525 U.S. 299 (1999)] permitted EGHP members to bring a RICO suit for insurance fraud when they alleged that they were overbilled as part of a conspiracy to force them to make excessive copayments. The significance of a RICO suit is that treble damages can be ordered. The defendant claimed that the McCarran-Ferguson Act [15 U.S.C. §§ 1011–1015] (which exempts "the business of insurance" from antitrust regulation) preempts the RICO suit. However, the Supreme Court held that RICO does not invalidate or supersede state insurance laws, so the McCarran-Ferguson Act does not bar the RICO suit.

The Supreme Court returned to EGHP ERISA issues in April 1999, finding in *UNUM Life Ins. Co. of Am. v. Ward* [526 U.S. 358 (1999)] that ERISA does not preempt state "notice-prejudice" laws. These laws prevent insurers from denying claims because they were filed late, unless the delay actually prejudiced the insurer's interests. This decision does not harm employers who administer EGHPs, because it says that although the employer is the insurer's "agent," the employer's role "relates to" an ERISA plan and therefore ERISA preempts suits against the employer with respect to this role.

In mid-2000, the Supreme Court decided, in *Pegram v. Herdrich* [530 U.S. 211 (2000)], that when an HMO, acting through its doctors, makes a mixed decision about medical treatment and health plan eligibility (rather than a purely medical decision about what kind of operation is proper for a particular diagnosis, or a purely financial decision), then the HMO is not acting as a fiduciary. Therefore, even if patients are correct that the HMO refused them necessary and medically valid treatment because the HMO wanted to increase its profits by cutting the amount of care available to subscribers, this would not state a cause of action for breach of fiduciary duty.

In mid-2004, the Supreme Court ruled that ERISA completely preempts HMO participants' claims of improper denial of health benefits. Therefore, any such suits that are filed in state court can be removed to federal court. Only the ERISA remedies, and not state tort remedies such as punitive damages, will be available. In the Supreme Court's view, ERISA contains a complete set of remedies, which Congress intended to be exclusive. However, ERISA stands for "Employee Retirement Income Security Act," and although the statute contains lengthy provisions about pension plans and their administration, it has far less to say about welfare benefit plans such as health plans—and nothing at all to say about the activities of health insurers—who are third parties in the employer/employee relationship anyway. [*Aetna Health Inc. v. Davila, Cigna Healthcare of Tex., Inc. v. Calad*, 542 U.S. 200 (2004)]

The Sixth Circuit held in 2012 that a TPA that is authorized to pay medical claims on behalf of employers is an ERISA fiduciary: a party is a fiduciary to the extent of exercising any discretionary authority or control over plan management, or any authority or control over the management or disposition of plan assets. [*Guyan Int'l Inc. v. Professional Benefits Admins, Inc.*, 689 F.3d 793 (6th Cir. 2012); see Rebecca Moore, *TPA Authorized to Pay Claims Is a Fiduciary* plansponsor.com (Sept. 24, 2012)]

The claims administrator of an EGHP pre-authorized gastric bypass surgery but, after the surgery, coverage was denied. The plan document clearly excluded coverage of the surgery. The plaintiff did not make a claim for benefits. He sued for equitable relief for breach of fiduciary duty (denial of benefits that had already been authorized). The Seventh Circuit held that there was no benefit claim, because of the clear exclusion, and ERISA does not permit money damages for breach of fiduciary duty—but remanded for consideration of equitable relief. [*Smith v. Medical Benefit Adm'rs Group, Inc.*, 869 F. Supp. 2d 990 (E.D. Wis. 2012); see EBIA Weekly, *Preauthorization of Surgical Procedure Not Covered by the Plan Was Not a Fiduciary Breach*, (May 10, 2012) (benefitslink.com)]

## [B] ERISA Preemption Issues

One of the themes of this book is that the balance between state and federal law is critical to the entire subject of employment law. In many cases, plaintiffs who are seeking faster resolution or a greater breadth of remedies will file cases in state court. Often, the employer will then claim that the case can be heard (if at all) in the federal courts, because ERISA preempts the state-law cause of action.

Many older cases became irrelevant in light of the *Davila/Calad* decision, the Supreme Court's ruling that ERISA completely preempts HMO participants' claims of improper denial of health benefits. This ruling rendered invalid the managed care patients' rights laws of eleven states (Arizona, California, Georgia, Maine, New Jersey, North Carolina, Oklahoma, Oregon, Texas, Washington, and West Virginia), and required ERISA plan participants to litigate their claims in federal court (where certain state tort remedies, including punitive damages, are not available). The Supreme Court gave little discussion to ERISA § 514(b)(2)(A), the provision in the statute that exempts from preemption state laws that "regulate insurance." In the Supreme Court view, where there is an overpowering federal policy, even statutes that regulate insurance are preempted. However, to date Congress has had little to say in ERISA about appropriate coverage decisions in managed care plans, or remedies for plan participants who believe they have been wrongfully deprived of health care services. [*Aetna Health Inc. v. Davila*, and *Cigna Healthcare of Tex., Inc. v. Calad*, 542 U.S. 200 (2004)]

The Supreme Court ruled in mid-2006 that certain claims must be litigated in state, not federal, court. [*Empire Healthchoice Assurance, Inc. v. McVeigh*, 547 U.S. 677 (2006)] The injured employee was covered by a plan subject to the Federal Employees Health Benefits Act (FEHBA). FEHBA says that the terms of insurance contracts insuring federal employees preempt state or local law about health benefit plans. Nevertheless, when an insurer sought reimbursement of amounts it spent on the care of a federal employee who received an automobile injury settlement, the Supreme Court required the case to be heard in state court. The Supreme Court ruled that there was no federal jurisdiction under 28 U.S.C. § 1331, because the claim for reimbursement did not arise under federal law, so federal jurisdiction could not be triggered.

## § 18.15   LABOR LAW ISSUES IN THE EGHP

A 1996 NLRB ruling holds that an employer's reservation of the right to "amend or modify" the health plan did not give the employer the power to replace the existing fee-for-service plan with a managed care plan. Such a change is so sweeping that the employer cannot implement it unilaterally without bargaining. [*Loral Defense Systems-Akron,* 320 NLRB No. 54 (Jan. 31, 1996), *aff'd,* 200 F.3d 436 (6th Cir. 1999)]

When negotiations reach an impasse, the employer cannot replace the union-sponsored health (and retirement) plans with employer-proposed plans that did not form part of the pre-impasse negotiations. [*Grondorf, Field Black & Co. v. NLRB,* 107 F.3d 882 (D.C. Cir. 1997)]

A unionized company that wants its employees to pay 30% of the premium thereby has an obligation to release information to the union about the health care claims of non-union employees and their dependents. The information is not confidential, because the employer has opened up the issue of health care costs and cost containment. [*Carr v. Gates Health Care Plan,* 195 F.3d 292 (7th Cir. 1999)]

Although it deducted premiums from an employee's pay, a West Virginia employer failed to remit the premiums to the insurer of the health plan. The employee encountered a very large medical bill, which the insurer refused to pay. The employee sued the employer and its owners (in their role as administrators of the health plan) for breach of fiduciary duty. The Southern District of West Virginia held that the employer and owners were fiduciaries because of their discretionary authority over premium payment. Commingling plan assets (the premiums) with the employer's general assets and using the funds to pay the employer's operating expenses breached the duty of loyalty. Commingling also violated the duty to hold plan assets in trust, and the defendants were also culpable for failing to disclose circumstances that could affect the benefits available under the plan. [*Cook v. Jones & Jordan Eng'g, Inc.,* CIVIL ACTION NO. 5:06-cv-00627, 2009 WL 37376 (S.D. W. Va. 2009); see EBIA Weekly, *Employee Wins Claims for Breach of Fiduciary Duty Against Employer That Failed to Pay Health Plan Premiums to Insurer* (Feb. 12, 2009) (benefitslink.com)]

## § 18.16   QUALIFIED MEDICAL CHILD SUPPORT ORDERS (QMCSOs)

Divorce courts often issue orders explaining how to divide an employee spouse's retirement benefits with the divorcing non-employee spouse. These orders are called Qualified Domestic Relations Orders, or QDROs. [See § 12.08] The counterpart for the EGHP is the QMCSO, which supplements COBRA continuation coverage as an additional means of protecting children against loss of health care coverage as a result of their parents' divorce. [See § 12.08[A]] A QMCSO is a court order that requires a parent covered by an EGHP to take whatever steps are necessary to enroll the child ("the alternate recipient") in the health plan—whether that includes notifying the plan or paying insurance premiums.

A valid QMCSO must identify:

- Every plan it applies to;
- The period of time covered by the order;
- The type of coverage the plan must give each alternate recipient (or a method of determining the coverage);
- The name and last known mailing address of the employee parent and each alternate recipient.

When a health plan receives a document described as a QMCSO, the plan has an obligation to review it to see if it is a valid order. Every health plan must have a written document setting out its procedure for reviewing QMCSOs. Courts do not have the power to order benefits that are not provided under the plan—so, for instance, if a plan does not offer dependent coverage, a QMCSO cannot create this coverage.

The plan administrator must notify the participant and the alternate recipients that the order has been received, and how the plan will analyze the order's validity. If, as usually happens, the plan approves the order as valid, then the participant and alternate recipients must be notified. Because the alternate recipients are children, they can designate a parent, stepparent, or attorney to receive copies of the notice on their behalf.

State governments (but NOT the DOL) can sue under I.R.C. § 502(a)(7) to enforce compliance with a Qualified Medical Child Support Order (QMCSO). The states have a role to play here because they have traditionally been empowered to deal with family law issues such as child support.

A 1998 law, the Child Support Performance and Incentives Act [Pub. L. No. 105-200], requires state child-support enforcement agencies to protect children's rights to medical coverage. The DOL and HHS published a Final Rule giving the text for the National Medical Child Support Notice. [See 65 Fed. Reg. 82128 and 82154 (Dec. 27, 2000)] State agencies have been required to use the form to enforce child support orders since October 1, 2001, either by informing the child support enforcement agency that the employee who is the subject of the order does not have health coverage; has been terminated; or by sending Part B of the form to the plan administrator for coverage of the children under the health plan (if they are eligible).

Employers can be sanctioned under ERISA and state law if they fail to carry out the wage deductions—or, on the other hand, if they fire or discipline employees because they have medical child support obligations.

It is the plan administrator's responsibility to send Part B to the child support enforcement agency. The form indicates whether the administrator deems the notice to be a valid QMCSO and, if so, what coverage options are available and which options the child(ren) has or have been enrolled in.

The IRS (which has jurisdiction over COBRA eligibility questions) has ruled that a child enrolled in an EGHP under a QMCSO who loses coverage as a result of a qualifying event (for instance, the parent is no longer employed; the child marries, ceases to be a full-time student, or reaches age 23) is a qualified beneficiary who is entitled to make a COBRA election.

## § 18.17   THE EMPLOYER'S RIGHT OF SUBROGATION

Subrogation is a legal concept under which a party that advances expenses can recover them when the person who received the funds is reimbursed for those expenses. More specifically, if an EGHP covers the medical treatment of an injured employee, or dependent of an employee, the EGHP will have a legal right to part of the verdict or settlement that the employee receives from suing whoever caused the accident or manufactured the dangerous product.

In the typical subrogation case, a plan participant is injured, and the plan provides funds for treatment of his or her injuries. Then the injured person settles a case, or wins a judgment, against the person responsible for the injuries. In practical terms, that usually means a liability insurance company gets involved. The EGHP then attempts to recover the benefits from the injured person's tort recovery.

For the plan to have a right of subrogation, the plan language, or the insurance covering the plan, must provide this right explicitly. State law must also be consulted to see if limitations are imposed on subrogation—but even if they are, the federal courts may conclude that the state limitations are preempted by ERISA, e.g., *Levine v. United Healthcare Corp.* [402 F.3d 156 (3d Cir. 2005)] Some state laws facilitate subrogation: for instance, by requiring the participant to agree to subrogation as a condition of receiving benefits under the plan.

The Supreme Court decided a subrogation case. [*Great-West Life & Annuity Ins. Co. v. Knudson,* 534 U.S. 204 (2002)] In this case, the plan called for recovery from plan beneficiaries if they recovered any payments from third parties. The plan paid most of the $411,157.11 in medical expenses when a car crash rendered an employee quadriplegic. She settled her tort case; the settlement allocated only $13,828.70 to past medical expenses. The Supreme Court refused to allow the plan to sue under ERISA § 503(a)(3) (civil action to enjoin an act or practice violating the terms of the plan), or to obtain equitable relief to collect more of the funds it had advanced. The Supreme Court refused to permit the plan to bring such a suit, ruling that compelling payment of money due under a contract is not an "equitable" remedy.

The Fourth Circuit ruled that a PPO plan was entitled to recover the $75,000 it had advanced from the personal injury settlement received by two injured plan participants. The Fourth Circuit ruled that, pursuant to *Knudson*, a lien would constitute equitable restitution because there were identifiable funds that, in equity, belonged to the plan and were in the custody of the plan participants. The court also cited the plan's right to reimbursement as clear under the plan documents. Certiorari was granted in late 2005. [*Mid Atl. Med. Servs., LLC v. Sereboff*, 407 F.3d 212 (4th Cir. 2005), *aff'd*, 547 U.S. 356 (2006). The Supreme Court treated the insurer's civil action as "appropriate equitable relief" as defined by ERISA § 502(a)(3)(B) because, unlike the fact pattern in *Knudson*, the injured plan participants agreed to set aside part of their tort recovery (in an amount equal to the reimbursement sought by the insurer), so they became trustees with respect to the funds specifically set aside in case it was determined that the insurer should be reimbursed.]

The "make-whole" doctrine also has to be considered in cases where the injured person has received a recovery, but less than an amount necessary to compensate for all injuries received. This doctrine absolves the injured person of having to reimburse the plan until he or she has been "made whole." Yet another factor is the "common fund" doctrine: whether the EGHP's right of recovery is reduced to account for attorneys' fees paid to the injured person's attorney. The rationale for this doctrine is that without the attorney, there would have been no "common fund" for the injured person and the plan to share, and therefore both of them should contribute toward the fees.

The Third Circuit held that an employee benefit plan was not entitled to full reimbursement of the medical expenses it paid for a participant who was injured in an automobile accident because the participant did not get full relief for his injuries. The plan paid about $67,000 of the injured participant's medical expenses. The other driver was underinsured, so the participant received only $110,000 and, after paying his attorney, was left with less than $66,000. Reimbursing the plan would have left him without any recovery. The Third Circuit said that the plan did not contribute to the cost of recovering the $110,000, so it would be a windfall if it got back all the money it advanced. It held that, subrogation claims in ERISA cases are subject to equitable principles and defenses such as unjust enrichment—even if the plan did not do anything wrong. [*US Airways, Inc. v. McCutchen*, 663 F.3d 671 (3d Cir. 2011).] The Supreme Court vacated and remanded the Third Circuit decision. The Supreme Court reaffirmed what it said in *Sereboff*: contract principles apply, and the terms of the plan are the most important consideration, even if there was no wrongdoing on the employer's part. The common fund doctrine is subject to the terms of the ERISA plan. However, because the plan did not specifically explain how the injured employee's attorney's fees would be handled, the Supreme Court allowed the plaintiff to apply the common fund doctrine to avoid owing the plan more money than the plaintiff actually received. [*US Airways Inc. v. McCutchen*, 133 S. Ct. 1537 (2013); see Ann Caresani, *U.S. Supreme Court Decision: U.S. Airways, Inc. v. McCutchen*, Porter Wright Employee Benefits Law Report (Apr. 16, 2013) (benefitslink.com). Similar principles were applied to a self-insured medical plan: *Quest Diagnostics v. Bomani*, No. 11-CV-00951 (D. Conn. June 19, 2013); see Anthony Cacace, *Express Plan Terms Allow Self-Insured Plan to Recover Medical Benefits Paid to Employee Post-McCutchen*, Proskauer's ERISA Practice Center Blog (June 25, 2013) (benefitslink.com)]

According to the Eighth Circuit, a health plan can recover the "reasonable" value of the services it provided to injured employees. This is defined as the fee-for-service fee schedule. The employer's right of subrogation is not limited to the actual amount that the health plan paid to the health care provider (health plans typically pay providers less than the schedule amount). [*Ince v. Aetna Health Mgmt. Inc.*, 173 F.3d 672 (8th Cir. 1999)]

The factors to consider in drafting a subrogation provision that will provide the most protection for the plan, and enable full recovery, include:

- Scope of obligation—all covered persons (including dependents) have to reimburse the plan; if only the participant has a duty to reimburse, the plan probably will not be able to look to family members for reimbursement.

- Source of recovery: is reimbursement required from all sources including underinsured/uninsured motorist coverage or only from liability coverage?

- Priority of payment: does the plan disclaim the Make Whole Rule or settle the priority of payment?

- Attorneys' fees and costs: does the subrogation provision explicitly disclaim the common fund doctrine? If not, it's likely that the plan's recovery will be reduced by one-third to account for the insured person's attorneys' fees.

- Allocations: Are all amounts received by the injured person presumed to recover medical expenses, or is recovery limited to the extent settlement agreement earmarks amounts for medical expenses? If the latter, then the plan will not have access to judgment or settlement funds allocated to pain and suffering.

- Cooperation: if the plan does not include a clause requiring the participant to cooperate in recovery efforts, the plan may find out that recovery rights have not been protected.

- What is the "res" (fund or other legal entity) from which insurer can recover?

- Does the subrogation provision appear in the plan document, the SPD, or both? If both, the provisions should be consistent between the two.

- Ruling out the common fund doctrine might discourage the injured employee from seeking recovering from the tortfeasor—which means that the plan itself would have to sue the tortfeasor to get back the funds advanced for the employee's treatment.

[Sarah Fowles and Angela Marie Hubbell, *Have You Checked Your Plan's Subrogation and Reimbursement Provisions Lately?*, Quarles & Brady LLP Employee Benefits & Executive Compensation Law Blog (April 2013) (benefitslink.com)]

## § 18.18   DEFINED CONTRIBUTION, CDHP, AND HRA PLANS

A defined contribution health plan, also known as a "consumer-driven" plan, is another way of limiting the employer's exposure to cost increases. The most popular form of CDHP is the Health Savings Account, separately or in tandem with a high-deductible health policy (HDHP).

The employer agrees to give the employee a fixed amount that can be applied to a menu of health care choices. The employer's exposure is limited and is not subject to health care price increases. In effect the voucher works like a defined contribution or 401(k) plan, shifting control to the employees—but also putting them at risk of bad or simply unlucky decisions. The rationale is that greater employee liability for health care costs will lead employees to become better informed and shop for more economical medical care.

In a fixed-dollar contribution plan, the employer offers a choice of health plans and gives each worker a certain amount of compensation to buy insurance. Employees who want a more expensive policy must use their own pretax dollars to pay the difference. In a fixed-percentage contribution plan, the employer's contribution is defined as a percentage of the premium, with the rest paid by the employee.

Employers could also combine a high deductible health plan with a funded or unfunded account for medical expenses. The employer might set up an account in which funds are accumulated on behalf of active employees, to be used for their eventual retiree health expenses.

Defined contribution plans are touted as means of improving employees' consumerism and health care shopping behavior, although that was also an argument used in favor of managed care, which is now failing to control costs.

The National Center for Health Statistics said that in 2007, 15.6% of persons under age 65 who had employment-based health insurance were in HDHPs, rising to 26.9% in 2011 and 27.5% in 2012. In the first quarter of 2012, 29.7% of people under 65 were enrolled in HDHPs, including 10.8% in a CDHP. [*Health Insurance Coverage: Early Release of Estimates From the National Health Interview Survey, January-March 2012,* <http://www.cdc.gov/nchs/data/nhis/earlyrelease/insur201209.pdf>; see Kristin Heinzinger, *Study Shows Jump in Employee Use of HDHPs* plansponsor.com (Oct.1, 2012)]

The Aon Hewitt 2012 Health Care Survey showed CDHPs passing HMOs, becoming the second most common health plan design. In 2011, 58% of employers offered CDHPs, 38% offered HMOs—but 79% of employers offered PPOs, the most popular design. About one-third of employer plans (34%) offer HSAs, whereas only 18% offer HRAs—but more employees enroll in HRAs (43% vs 28%). [Spencer's Benefits Reports, *CDHPs Second Most Common Plan Design Offered By Employers* (Sept. 26, 2012) (benefitslink.com)]

If the arrangement constitutes a Flexible Spending Account, then Internal Revenue Code requirements will have to be satisfied. If the arrangement is trust-funded, it may become an ERISA welfare benefit plan, with additional requirements to meet. Very possibly, the IRS will treat the arrangement as a self-insured medical plan, in which case there may be nondiscrimination, COBRA, and HIPAA compliance obligations. Questions of dependent coverage will have to be worked out.

CDH plans can be combined with HRAs and the plan can be set up so that the employee is required to satisfy a deductible before accessing HRA funds. Another option is for the employer to cover up to 100% of preventive care services, or require employees to use HRA amounts for this purpose. The employer can also impose a cap, such as $3,000 a year, on the amount that can be rolled over from year to year within an HRA.

An HRA is a plan that is 100% funded by employer contributions and provides reimbursement for medical expenses incurred during the 12-month plan year (but not before). In fact, carryover of unused amounts is not only permitted, it is mandatory. The balance in the HRA may be used to provide coverage of medical expenses; and the balance must be used for this purpose if a COBRA event occurs. Distributions for any purpose other than paying medical expenses jeopardizes the exclusion from income of all distributed amounts. Notice 2002-45 says that any expense that qualifies under § 213(d) can be reimbursed from the HRA, including insurance premiums, with one major exception. Because of § 106(c), no amount that constitutes a "qualified long-term care service" under § 7702B(c) can be reimbursed because health FSAs are not allowed to cover long-term care.

The HRA was authorized in 2002 to permit employers to provide employees with pre-tax dollars to pay for medical care and services. The combination of an HRA and an HDHP gives employees both conventional catastrophic coverage after the deductible is met and help with pre-deductible expenses. However, PPACA enacted Public Health Services Act § 2711 which forbids annual dollar limits—and HRAs, by definition, are limited. DOL/HHS/Treasury FAQs posted on the DOL Website on January 24, 2013 says that standalone HRAs are unacceptable because they may violate PPACA's limit of 3:1 for age-related premium disparity. An employer cannot have a "stand-alone HRA" that gives employees a predetermined dollar amount to use to buy health insurance in the individual market. An integrated HRA, paired with an EGHP, is permissible.

A premium-only plan is a cafeteria plan where the contribution is limited to health insurance premiums. An arrangement where employees set aside their own money to pay medical expenses such as copayments and coinsurance with pre-tax dollars is known as a medical FSA. A medical FSA can include employer contributions (usually in the form of flex credits) but employer contributions cannot be used to pay health insurance premiums. The FAQ says that unused amounts credited to an HRA before January 1, 2014 can be used after December 31, 2013 to reimburse medical expenses without violating PPACA. [Timothy Jost, *Implementing Health Reform: Health Reimbursement Arrangements And More*, Health Affairs Blog (Jan. 25, 2013) (benefitslink.com); Alden J. Bianchi and Gary E. Bacher, *Stand-Alone HRAs: DOL, IRS, HHS Put the Brakes On*, Mintz Levin (Feb. 2, 2013) (benefitslink.com)]

Sears Holdings Corp. and Darden Restaurants launched an experiment in the fall of 2013, offering workers a flat sum that they could use to purchase health coverage on an online marketplace (private exchange) operated by Aon Hewitt. Many of them opted for lower-priced plans that created a risk of higher out-of-pocket obligations: in 2012, when employees didn't have access to an exchange, 12% took higher deductible plans rising to 39% in 2013. PPO election dropped from 70% to 47%. One-quarter (26%) took more coverage than the year before, 42% took less. There are also exchanges operated by Mercer and Buck Consultants; Towers Watson & Co. announced that it would expand its existing exchange for Medicare-eligible retirees. [Anna Wilde Mathews, *To Save, Workers Take On Health-Cost Risk*, WSJ.com (Mar. 17, 2013)]

HRA distributions can be made to employees, former employees, COBRA qualified beneficiaries, and spouses or dependents of employees. However, if the HRA makes distributions as bonuses, severance pay, or payments to the estate of a deceased participant, all distributions from that account in that tax year become taxable, even if they were used to pay medical expenses. This result comes from Reg. § 1.105-2, which says that amounts cannot be excluded from income if the taxpayer would be entitled to receive them whether or not he or she had medical expenses.

CMS announced in mid-2011 that the reporting rules for HRAs under the Medicare Secondary Payor rules have changed. HRAs are considered group health plans so they are generally subject to mandatory reporting (see § 9.10[A]) but reports are required if the annual benefit amount under the HRA is less than $1,000—or, starting October 3, 2011, less than $5,000. But when an HRA account is exhausted, a notice of termination must be sent to the employer's Coordination of Benefits Contractor. [CMS Alert, <https://www.cms.gov/MandatoryInsRep/Downloads/HRACoverage.pdf>; see EBIA Weekly, *CMS Raises Threshold for MSP Reporting of HRA Coverage, Reverses Position on Termination Notice* (Sept. 29, 2011) (benefitslink.com)]

## § 18.19 HEALTH CARE REFORM UNDER PPACA

### [A]  Introduction

In March 2010, Congress passed the Patient Protection and Affordable Care Act, Pub. L. No. 111-144. Almost immediately, a package of amendments was passed: the Health Care and Education Affordability Reconciliation Act of 2010, Pub. L. No. 111-152. For convenience, in this book the abbreviation "PPACA" will be used to refer to the main bill, as amended by the reconciliation bill.

The focus of the legislation is on extending insurance coverage to more Americans. This discussion focuses on employers' duties and entitlements under PPACA, although the law naturally has major impact on health care users and providers, on insurers, and on the Medicare and Medicaid programs.

The central goal of PPACA is that, eventually, as many people as possible will be covered by an EGHP or individual policy that provides "minimum essential coverage." The statutory objective is that the subsidies and tax incentives will lead to the creation of many new plans and coverage of a higher percentage of the employee population.

The state insurance exchanges are supposed to help people find coverage. Employers who do not offer compliant health coverage are subject to penalties. The program calls for employers to be taxed if they fail to offer minimum coverage to their employees, or if they offer coverage that does not satisfy federal standards of affordability. At the other end of the scale, there are new taxes on "Cadillac plans" that are deemed to be overly generous. But the program offers carrots as well as sticks for employers: federal subsidies for plans that cover low-income employees, and a special subsidy program for small employers. PPACA has somewhat different rules for "grandfathered plans" (EGHPs (Employer Group Health Plan) already in existence when the law was enacted) and for new plans.

The FPL (federal poverty level) is an important concept for understanding PPACA. Many rights and responsibilities are determined based on whether an employee's household income falls below the FPL, or whether it exceeds 400% of the FPL. For 2013, the FPL for a one-person family is $11,490, for a two-person family, $15,510, and for for a three-person family, $19,530, [See substitute 78 Fed. Reg. 5182 (Jan. 24, 2013); <http://aspe.hhs.gov/poverty/13poverty.cfm > (no www)]

As part of its mission of expanding health insurance coverage, PPACA requires that, for plan years beginning on or after January 1, 2014, health insurance issuers must accept all applications from employers, although enrollment can be restricted to open enrollment periods plus special enrollment periods. (There must be special enrollment periods associated with COBRA qualifying events.) Insurers can only deny renewal if the plan fails to pay its premiums; if the plan sponsor engaged in fraud or intentional misrepresentation of material facts; or if, after proper notice, the issuer has discontinued that type of coverage.

Before PPACA, there were important protections against loss of coverage under COBRA (Consolidated Omnibus Budget Reconciliation Act) (see § 19.02), and a 2009 statute, the American Recovery and Reinvestment Act (ARRA), Pub. L. No. 111-5, made it possible for some workers to receive a subsidy to help them afford COBRA coverage (see § 19.02[F]). According to the Employee Benefits Security Administration (EBSA), PPACA essentially had no effect on the availability or duration of COBRA continuation coverage or the ARRA subsidy. The subsidy expired on May 31, 2010, but persons who were already eligible on that date could get up to 15 months of subsidy. [EBSA, *FAQ on Health Care Reform and COBRA*, <http://www.dol.gov/ebsa/faqs/faq-PPACA .html> (accessed Apr. 23, 2010)]

As a result of PPACA, approximately 16 million people with income of up to 133% of the federal poverty line are potentially Medicaid-eligible, including millions of full-time workers. Medicaid expansion is favorable to employers because it is a source of health coverage for employees that the employers do not have to pay for. PPACA obligates the federal government to pay the full cost of new Medicaid enrollees from 2014–2016 and at least 90% of the cost afterwards. Some state governors resisted Medicaid expansion out of concern about impact on state budgets. The opt-out states say they cannot afford Medicaid administrative costs and fear that the federal government will renege on its commitments. [Louise Radnofsky, *In Medicaid, a New Health-Care Fight*, WSJ.com (Feb. 10, 2013)]

In early 2013, eight Republican governors (those in Florida, Arizona, Michigan, Nevada, New Jersey, North Dakota, and Ohio) reversed their position and said that they would accept the Medicaid expansion for their states. [Abby Goodnough and Robert Pear, *Governors Fall Away in G.O.P. Opposition to More Medicaid*, NYTimes.com (Feb. 21, 2013); Kate Zernike, *Christie Backs Medicaid Help From Federal Government*, NYTimes.com (Feb. 26, 2013) ; Louise Radnofsky, *Arizona Expands Medicaid in Win for Governor Brewer*, WSJ.com (June 13, 2013)]

Tennessee governor Bill Haslam announced that he would join 18 other Republican governors in refusing Medicaid expansion. Haslam wanted to use federal Medicaid funds to purchase private insurance through the Exchanges for up to 175,000 low-income residents of the state. Arkansas and Ohio asked for permission to do the same and lawmakers in other states, such as Florida, Pennsylvania, and Texas considered the idea. [Abby Goodnough, *Governor of Tennessee Joins Peers Refusing Medicaid Plan*, NYTimes.com (Mar. 27, 2013)]

## [B]  Employer Mandates

Although there are a number of employer mandates that took effect as soon as PPACA was passed, or six months later, perhaps the most important PPACA provision is the requirement that employers (other than very small employers) offer either affordable coverage of a package of minimum basic benefits to their employees, or pay a penalty to the federal government (see § 18.19[H] below). As discussed below, the employer shared responsibility payments (aka "pay or play") were supposed to take effect January 1, 2014, but the effective date was postponed until January 1, 2015. See § 18.19[B][3] for discussion of the way in which some rules are relaxed for "grandfathered" plans—those already in existence when PPACA was enacted.

### [1]  Mandates in General

Starting with the first plan year that begins six months after PPACA's enactment, health plans must cover participants' dependent adult children up to the age of 26 if the adult children are not eligible to enroll in another group plan. CHIP (Children's Health Insurance Program) (see § 18.03[A]) has been reauthorized for an additional two years, until fiscal 2015. Starting January 1, 2014, the option under CHIPRA (Children's Health Insurance Program Reauthorization Act), the legislation authorizing this program, of offering a premium subsidy to help employers cover low-income children, if the subsidy is cost-effective, will be available, and will not be limited to children under age 19.

Plans must eliminate lifetime dollar limits and restrictive annual limitations on the essential health benefits. A group or individual insurer is permitted to rescind a policy if and only if there was fraud or intentional misrepresentation of material fact. The enrollee is entitled to prior notice of cancellation of coverage, which is allowed only for nonpayment of premium, plan termination, moving outside the plan's service area, not being in the association anymore if coverage is limited to association members, or discontinuation of that type of coverage (which requires 90 days' notice).

As of January 1, 2014, waiting periods of more than 90 days before a new hire can participate in the health plan are forbidden, and so are annual dollar limits on benefits a participant can receive under the health plan. [Workforce.com, *Understanding Key Provisions in Federal Health Care Reform Legislation* (Mar. 22, 2010) (benefitslink.com)]

Starting January 1, 2014, pre-existing condition exclusions (PCEs) cannot be imposed on any enrollee in a non-grandfathered plan. That is, group health plans and insurers cannot use a person's pre-existing health condition to deny or limit coverage. Eligibility cannot be conditioned on a participant's, or dependent of a participant's, medical condition, claims experience, receipt of health care, medical history, genetic information, or disability. Premiums cannot be increased based on health factors.

All plans must offer preventive services without requiring any cost-sharing by employees: all the preventive services and immunizations recommended by the U.S. Preventive Services Task Force and the Centers for Disease Control, and the preventive services for children (e.g., immunization) recommended by the Health Resources and Services Administration.

Health plans must permit enrollees to choose any available participating primary care provider, including a pediatrician for children covered by the plan. Emergency services in a hospital Emergency Room have to be covered without prior authorization, even if the hospital is not part of the plan's network. Women must be allowed to receive obstetric and gynecological services without a referral from a primary care provider. This requirement is effective for plan years beginning on or after six months from PPACA's enactment date. (The enactment date is March 23, 2010, so six months later is September 23, 2010.)

As originally enacted, PPACA required that, as of January 1, 2014, Employers with over 50 employees would have to provide "free choice" vouchers to employees with income below 400% of the FPL, and who would have high financial obligations under the employer's plan. However, this requirement was repealed in April 2011 as part of the negotiations to pass a budget bill. [Deloitte's Washington Bulletin, *Budget Bill Cuts Into PPACA: Free Choice Vouchers to be Eliminated* (Apr. 18, 2011) (benefitslink.com)]

Group health plans and health insurers have to have an effective claims appeals process, including internal claims appeals and notification to employees. At a minimum, the process must include:

- An established internal claims appeal process;

- Notice to participants of internal and external appeals procedures;

- A provision allowing an enrollee to review his or her file, present evidence and testimony in the appeal, and retain coverage during the appeal.

PPACA gives group health plans and insurers two options for external review: either comply with state external review requirements that include the protections of the NAIC (National Association of Insurance Commissioners) Uniform External Review Model Act, or if the state requirements are less protective or the plan is self-funded so those requirements do not apply, the plan must implement an external review process that satisfies the NAIC requirements. [Christine C. Rinn,

*Health Insurance Reforms Under PPACA: The Future Is Now*, <http://www.crowell.com/PDF/events/hoops-2010/Health-Insurance-Market-Reforms-Under-PPACA.pdf>]

PPACA adds a new ERISA § 715(a), Code § 9815(a)(1) to apply the requirements of the Public Health Service Act (PHS) Part A, Title XXVII to EGHPs and health insurers. Section 2719 of the PHS provides the standards for internal claims and appeals and external review. In general, § 2719 requires an effective internal claims and appeals process, incorporating the DOL claims regulation (29 C.F.R. § 2560.503-1).

In June, 2010, the Treasury, DOL, and HHS issued a joint interim final rule (IFR) detailing the requirements for internal claims and appeals. The rule applies to EGHPs and insurers that offer individual or group policies—but grandfathered plans are exempt. The IFR applies to claims for benefits that are subject to the DOL claims regulation, and to rescissions of coverage (unless the rescission was imposed for failure to pay premiums). The rule applies to eligibility determinations for individual coverage, but apparently does not apply to claims for eligibility alone.

Not only do the DOL claims rules still apply, they have been extended to non-ERISA plans, with some new requirements.

With respect to appeals, plans must automatically disclose any new rationale considered and any new or additional evidence considered in the appeal. This information must be provided as soon as possible, with enough time before the final denial notice for the claimant to respond.

Claims and appeals must be adjudicated in a manner that preserves the independence and impartiality of the decision maker: hiring and compensation must not be based on the likelihood that a person will deny benefits. The rules for the Explanation of Benefits (EOB) have been updated. Denial notices at the initial claim and appeals levels must include more information than previously required, such as the date of the medical service in question, who provided it, the amount of the claim, and the standard the plan used in denying the claim. Final notices must include a discussion of the decision, contact information for consumer assistance, and a description of the internal and external review processes. The notice must be culturally and linguistically appropriate, so it may be necessary to translate the notice if there is a substantial contingent of non-English-speaking workers.

If the plan fails to adhere strictly to all of the internal claims requirements, the claimant is deemed to have exhausted his or her appeals and is permitted to proceed directly to an external appeal or to bring suit. The IFR requires coverage to be continued pending the outcome of the appeal, under the DOL regulations about concurrent claims for ongoing treatment. [Interim Final Rule: 75 Fed. Reg. 43330 (July 23, 2010); see Christy Tinnes and Brigen Winters, *What Internal Claims Procedures Changes Are Required Under PPACA?*, plansponsor.com (Aug. 30, 2010)]

Technical Release 2010-01 was issued August 23, 2010 to explain interim procedures required of self-insured plans' external review. IRS, DOL, and HHS also issued three model notices for internal and external review. [*Availability of Interim Procedures for Federal External Review and Model Notices Relating to Internal Claims and Appeals and External Review Under the Patient Protection and Affordable Care Act; Notice*, 75 Fed. Reg. 52597 (Aug. 26, 2010); EBSA Technical Release No. 2010-01 (Aug. 23, 2010). See EBIA Weekly, *Guidance Provided on Federal External Review Procedures for Self-Insured Plans; Model Notices Issued* (Aug. 26, 2010) (benefitslink.com); Christy Tinnes and Brigen Winters, *External Review: To Delete or Not Delegate*, plansponsor.com (Oct. 18, 2011)]

Some important amendments to the IFR were published in June 2011. The amendment removes the IFR's absolute 24-hour deadline for deciding urgent care claims, reinstating the old standard (decisions must be made as soon as possible consistent with medical needs, and definitely within 72 hours). Plans are bound by a health care provider's characterization of care as urgent. Plan materials may have to be translated if over 10% of the population of the county speaks certain non-English languages. When an external reviewer orders benefits, they must be provided without delay, even if the plan intends to seek judicial review. Under the amended version of the IFR, federal external review is limited to claims involving rescission of coverage or medical judgment. Claims about the coding of the patient's diagnosis, or coverage of care by out-of-network specialists, are not subject to federal external review. [*Group Health Plans and Health Insurance Issuers: Rules Relating to Internal Claims and Appeals and External Review Processes*, 76 Fed. Reg. 37208 (June 24, 2011); Technical Release 2011-02, <http://www.dol/gov/ebsa/rewsroom/tr11-02.html> and <http://cciio.cms.gov/resources/files/appeals_srg_06222011.pdf> (June 22, 2011)]

If a company offers health coverage and has over 200 employees, it must maintain the enrollment of its existing employees, and automatically enroll new full-time employees in the plan—but must give them adequate notice and a chance to opt out of coverage (e.g., to purchase coverage through an Exchange). Automatic enrollment is subject to any allowable waiting periods. [Hinda Chaikind and Chris L. Peterson, *Summary of Potential Employer Penalties Under PPACA (P.L. 111-148)*, Congressional Research Service, <http://www.ncsl.org/documents/health/EmployerPenalties.pdf> (Apr. 5, 2010)]

CMS published a final rule to prevent discrimination against persons with pre-existing conditions, and to prevent the worst abuses by insurers. CMS said that as many as 129 million people—half of the non-elderly population of the United States—have some kind of pre-existing condition. Beginning in 2014, coverage cannot be denied based on pre-existing condition exclusions (PCEs) or other health conditions. Policies in the individual market will be guaranteed available and will be offered during open enrollment periods; policies in the group market will be continuously available year round. The only rating factors allowed in the individual/small group market are age (where premiums for the oldest enrollees cannot be more than three times those for the youngest), family size, geography, and tobacco use (1.5 times higher for tobacco users). Starting in 2017, states have option to permit insurers in the large group market to offer coverage in the marketplace, with the effect that large group health insurers will be subject to the same rating rules. There must be a single, statewide risk pool for the small group market and one for the individual market, unless insurers want a single pool for both. [CMS, *Overview: Final Rule for Health Insurance Market Reform*, <http://www.cciio.cms.gov> undated/ Rules promulgated in November 2012 increase the discretion that states have over plans sold within their borders. States can decide whether tobacco use can be considered in setting premiums. If so, the insurer can charge up to 50% more to tobacco users than non-users. Prescription drug rules are enforced at the state level, so the rules allow states more regulatory options: Louise Radnofsky, *States Get a Say in Health Overhaul*, WSJ.com (Nov. 20, 2012)]

The PPACA enacts Public Health Service Act § 2708, imposing a 90-day limit on plan waiting periods. Notice 2012-58, 2012-41 I.R.B. 436 describes the safe harbors employers can use to determine who is a full-time employee; clarifies the existing safe harbor for current employees; and creates a new safe harbor for newly hired employees.

Notice 2012-59, 2012-41 I.R.B. 443 explains the 90-day waiting period limitation under the Public Health Service Act, including examples of employees who did not meet the guidelines when hired, but who qualify later. The notice says that employers will not be considered non-compliant if a waiting period lasts longer than 90 days—if the employee takes longer than that to make an election, or if the employer does not reasonably expect the employee to satisfy criteria such as minimum number of hours worked per week. Notice 2012-59 clarifies that PPACA does not require offering coverage to particular employees or classes of employees—but it prevents an otherwise eligible employee or dependent from having to wait more than 90 days before coverage becomes effective. Additional guidance is available in DOL Tech Release 2012-02 and the HHS Bulletin, *Guidance on 90-Day Waiting Period Limitation Under Public Health Service Act 2708*. [Alden J. Bianchi, *Guidance on PPACA Employer Shared Responsibility, 90-Day Rules*, Mintz Levin Employment, Labor & Benefits Alert (Sept. 4, 2012) (benefitslink.com); Rebecca Moore, *Guidance Issued About 90-Day Waiting Period* plansponsor.com (Sept. 5, 2012); E is For ERISA Blog, *ACA Update: "Safe Harbor" Guidance on Full-time Employee Status and 90-DayWaiting Periods* (Sept. 4, 2012) (benefitslink.com). See DOL Technical Release 2012-01, *Automatic Enrollment, Employer Shared Responsibility and Waiting Periods*, <http://www.dol.gov/ebsa/newsroom/tr12-01.html> (Feb. 9, 2012).]

Starting January 1, 2011, health insurers and the administrators of self-insured plans must report their "loss ratios" (percentage of premiums used to pay medical claims and not used for administrative expenses or profits) to Health and Human Services (HHS). The minimum required loss ratio for large-group plans (with 100 or more enrollees) is 85% loss ratio. Small-group plans must have an

80% loss ratio. State laws that require higher loss ratios are not preempted. However, HHS has discretion to adjust these percentages if an 80% loss ratio would destabilize the individual market. Health insurers that fail to satisfy the loss ratio standards must give each customer a pro rata rebate. This topic is discussed further at § 18.19[O][4], below.

It is illegal to retaliate against an employee who gets a tax credit, or who provides information about a violation of the employer's obligations under the Fair Labor Standards Act (e.g., automatic enrollment for companies with over 200 employees; providing notice about employees' rights to secure coverage under an Exchange).

PPACA § 1558 amends the Fair Labor Standards Act to prevent employers from retaliating against employees who receive a subsidy or tax credit for using an Exchange. Employees are protected against retaliation if they provided or were about to provide information about PPACA Title I violations to the employer, the federal government, or a state attorney general. Retaliation is also forbidden for testifying or being about to testify in a proceeding about such a violation, assisting in or participating in a proceeding, or objecting to or refusing to participate in a proceeding. Title I is the portion of PPACA that forbids coverage limits, requires coverage of preventive services, the required summary of benefits and coverage, and mandatory inclusion of adult children in the plan to age 26. Retaliation is defined to include discipline, discrimination, threats, and the like with respect to compensation or terms and conditions of employment. Starting in 2014, employees are also protected against retaliation (such as termination of coverage) by EGHP insurers.

Complaints must be filed within 180 after the alleged PPACA violation. Retaliation complaints can be filed with OSHA by going to or calling the local office or sending written complaint to a local OSHA regional or area office. Written complaints can be faxed, sent electronically, or delivered by hand, mail, or commercial carrier. No official form has been published. If the evidence shows retaliation, and settlement is not reached, OSHA orders the employer to reinstate the employee with back pay. OSHA findings become a final order of the DOL unless appealed within 30 days. The general whistleblower rules apply: for example, the employee can go to the district court for review if the DOL has not made a final decision within 210 days of the date the complaint was filed, or 90 days after the written findings of the OSHA investigation were issued. PPACA's anti-retaliation rules do not diminish rights under the CBA, state, or federal law (for example, rights under ERISA § 510 are not reduced by PPACA). [OSHA Fact Sheet, *Filing Whistleblower Complaints under the Affordable Care Act*, <http://www.osha.gov/Publications/whistleblower/OSHAFS-3641.pdf> (February 2013); see PLC Employee Benefits & Executive Compensation, *OSHA Rules Address Retaliation Complaint Procedures under Health Care Reform* (Feb. 25, 2013) (benefitslink.com)]

PPACA amends the Fair Labor Standards Act to require employers to provide break time and a private place other than a restroom stall for employees who are breast-feeding to express and store milk. This PPACA provision does not pre-empt state laws that offer more protection to employees.

## [2] The Essential Health Benefits Package

The essential health benefits package specifies the benefits, cost-sharing standards, and levels of coverage that must be offered for a plan to be PPACA-compliant. (Self-insured plans are not subject to the PPACA provisions dealing with essential health benefits.) Qualified Health Plans (QFPs) have to provide coverage of essential benefits at Bronze, Silver, Gold, or Platinum levels. The difference among the plans is that the Bronze level provides benefits actuarially equivalent to 60% of the full actuarial value of benefits under the plan (i.e., participants can be required to pay 40% of the cost of care); Silver provides actuarial equivalent of 70% of the full actuarial value; Gold, 80% and Platinum, 90% (i.e., the participant pays only 10% of the cost of care). HHS will issue regulations explaining how to calculate actuarial value.

The Obama administration said it would not require a single uniform set of essential health benefits that all insurers must provide. States specify the benefits, within broad categories, so there could be significant variations the way there are in Medicaid and CHIP. Multi-state plans will have problems satisfying the differing benefit definitions prevailing in the various states in which they cover employees.

Individual and small group policies for insured plans must equal the benefits available under a typical employer-sponsored plan. For plan years beginning on or after January 1, 2014, health insurers selling in the individual or small group market must ensure that their coverage includes the essential health benefits package, and that insured persons are not subjected to cost-sharing obligations greater than the permitted levels.

Starting in 2014, the minimum services are:

- Outpatient health care;

- Emergency services;

- Hospitalization;

- Maternity/newborn care;

- Mental health and substance abuse services;

- Prescription drugs;

- Services and devices for physical therapy and rehabilitation;

- Lab tests;

- Preventive and wellness services, including management of chronic disease;

- Pediatric services, including oral and vision care.

This is just a minimum list: plans are permitted to provide additional services. The scope of benefits must be equivalent to a typical employer-sponsored plan; PPACA required the DOL to conduct a survey to define the typical EGHP benefit package.

The design of the benefit package (coverage and reimbursement rates) must not discriminate on the basis of age, disability, or predicted lifespan. Essential health benefits must not be denied based on age, life expectancy, disability, degree of medical dependency, or quality of life. The package must cover the health needs of diverse groups including women, children, and persons with disabilities. The design of the benefit package must not discriminate (e.g., in terms of coverage or reimbursement rates) against anyone on the basis of age, disability, or predicted lifespan. Emergency Room services must be covered even if the facility is not in the insurer's provider network, and the patient's cost-sharing for emergency services cannot be higher than for an in-network facility.

As a general rule, in the small-group market, insured persons cannot be required to pay an annual deductible greater than $2,000 (self-only) or $4,000 (family) coverage. For this purpose, cost-sharing means deductibles, co-payments, and coinsurance, but not premiums or costs of non-covered services. For 2014, total cost-sharing is not permitted to exceed the HSA limitations on out-of-pocket costs (for 2010 and 2011), that means $5,950 for self-only and $11,900 for family coverage: see Rev. Proc. 2009-29, 2009-22 I.R.B. 1050. For 2015 and later years, the amounts will be increased by the same percentage as the change in the average per capita premium for the United States as a whole. [National Conference of State Legislatures, *American Health Benefit Exchanges* (Jan. 26, 2012) (benefitslink.com); Robert Pear, *Health Care Law to Allow States to Pick Benefits*, NYTimes.com (Dec. 16, 2011)]

Catastrophic plans (offering limited coverage for very high expenses, leaving the rest of the financial burden on the insured person) can be offered on the individual market only, not the group market, and only to people who are under age 30 or exempt from the individual requirement of maintaining minimum coverage. Catastrophic plans cover the essential benefit package, but only after the insured person has spent the HSA out-of-pocket limit on care.

HHS proposed regulations on essential health benefits, actuarial value, and accreditation were published on November 26, 2012 then finalized February 20, 2013. Also on February 20, HHS published calculators for determining the actuarial value of individual and small group plans and determining whether large-employer plans satisfy the minimum value requirement. For 2014 only, there is a special transition rule for plans that have different service providers for various benefits, each of which sets a maximum on out of pocket expenses. The group coverage will be deemed compliant as long as the major medical coverage's out-of-pocket maximum does not exceed the PPACA permitted level, and no other separate coverage exceeds the limit. [Timothy Jost, *Implementing Health Reform:*

*The Essential Health Benefits Final Rule,* Health Affairs Blog (Feb. 20, 2013) (benefitslink.com)]

### [3]   Grandfathered Plans

In order to pass the controversial health care reform package, it was necessary to promise plan participants that they would be able to keep their existing health insurance—which requires granting some additional leeway to plans that were in existence on March 23, 2010, when PPACA was enacted. PPACA applies to both insured and self-insured employer plans. However, there are some differences in the rules applied to grandfathered group health plans and new group health plans, with grandfathered plans exempt from some requirements. Grandfathered plans are deemed to provide minimum essential coverage for purposes of the mandate.

A plan continues to be treated as a grandfathered plan even if new employees and their families are allowed to enroll in the plan. Family members are allowed to join grandfathered plans if, on March 23, 2010, the terms of the plan would have allowed enrollment. New employees and their families can enroll in a grandfathered health plan. It is not clear under the statute whether a plan can be modified (e.g., by changing insurance carriers) and retain grandfathered status, but HHS may issue explanatory regulations.

As of the first plan year beginning on or after September 23, 2010 (i.e., six months after PPACA's enactment), grandfathered plans are not allowed to impose lifetime benefit limits; they cannot revoke coverage except for fraud, cannot impose annual dollar limits on essential health benefits as defined by HHS; they must allow coverage of participants' children up to age 26 if the adult child is not eligible for another EGHP; they cannot impose pre-existing condition limitations (PCEs) on enrollees under age 19; and they must offer certain preventive health care services and immunizations without charge to the participant. For plan years beginning on or after January 1, 2014, grandfathered plans are not allowed to impose excessive waiting periods before a new hire can join the plan.

Grandfathered plans are not required to provide the essential benefits without cost-sharing, so if they required deductibles and coinsurance for these benefits before PPACA, they can continue to do so. Nor do they have to offer preventive care services without cost-sharing. They are not required to allow participants to access emergency services without certification and without restriction to in-network providers. Grandfathered plans are not subject to the requirement that participants have a free choice of primary care physician, and do not have to allow the selection of an OB/gyn or a pediatrician as a primary care physician. [McGuire Woods Healthcare Reform Guide, *Installment No. 2, Grandfathered Health Plans—What They Are and Why They're Important,* <http://www.mcguirewoods.com/news-resources/item.asp?item=4719>;   Thompson Hine Advisory Bulletin, *Health   Care   Reform   Impacts   Grandfathered*

*Employer-Sponsored Group Health Plans: Now What?* <http://www.thompsonhi ne.com/publications/pdf/2010/04/employeebenefits2083.pdf> (April 2010)]

Plans retain their eligibility for the special grandfather rules unless they significantly reduce the employer's financial role or significantly increase participants' financial obligations. [Christy Tinnes and Brigen Winters (Groom Law Group), *What Does Being Grandfathered Really Mean?*, plansponsor.com (Oct. 26, 2010). See 75 Fed. Reg. 34537 (June 17, 2010) for HHS/DOL/IRS regulations about retaining grandfathered status when the plan's insurer is changed.]

### [4] Cadillac Plans

Starting January 1, 2018, a 40% excise tax will be imposed on health coverage providers to the extent that the total value of employer-sponsored health coverage for a particular participant is greater than $10,200 (individual) or $27,500 (family coverage). Higher values (an additional $1,650 individual/ $3,450 family coverage) are allowed, and the excise tax is not imposed if the participant is in a high-risk job (e.g., police or firefighter) or is a retiree who is over 55 but not yet eligible for Medicare. The tax is imposed on the insurer (for an EGHP) or the employer (for an HSA, MSA, or self-insured health plan).

A 2013 article reports employers cutting back on plans, for example, increasing deductibles, to avoid their plans being treated as Cadillac plans in the future. Up to 75% of plans might incur Cadillac plan penalties unless employers can reduce costs; the article said that $20 copayments for doctor's office visits and $500 deductibles are likely to be casualties of the move to avert Cadillac plan treatment. The issue is a particular sore point for unionized employees, especially members of public employee unions, who traditionally accepted comparatively low wages in order to secure generous benefit packages. [Reed Abelson, *High-End Health Plans Scale Back to Avoid "Cadillac Tax,"* NYTimes.com (May 27, 2013)]

### [5] Self-Insured Plans

Most of the PPACA requirements apply to self-insured as well as insured group health plans:

- Discrimination based on pre-existing conditions or health status is forbidden;

- If the plan already provides dependent coverage, participants' adult children must be covered until age 26;

- Large plans (over 200 full-time employees) must automatically enroll new hires in one of the plans;

- Participants must be given at least 60 days' notice of any material modifications in the plan's coverage or terms if the modifications are not disclosed in the plan's SPD;

- If the plan covers emergency services at all, it must cover out-of-network emergency services;

- Ban on annual and lifetime benefit limits;

- Coverage must not be rescinded unless the participant committed fraud or intentional misrepresentation of material fact;

- Certain preventive services must be covered without cost-sharing obligations for participants;

- Self-insured plans can qualify as grandfathered plans, and family members of participants can be enrolled without forfeiting grandfathered status;

- The plan must allow a pediatric and OB/GYN services to be obtained without a referral from a gatekeeper;

- The plan must distribute the standardized summary of benefits and coverage, as prescribed by DOL—and failure to do so can be penalized by up to $1,000 per offense;

- Participants are entitled to the claims appeal process (internal and external) set out by PPACA, but self-insured plans are not under the jurisdiction of state insurance ombudsmen, nor do they have to comply with state standards for external review.

However, some PPACA requirements do not apply to self-insured plans:

- They are not required to offer the minimum benefits package specified under PPACA;

- They are allowed to provide better coverage to highly compensated employees than to rank-and-file employees;

- They are not subject to the annual limitation on health plan deductibles;

- The reasonableness of the level of the employer's contributions to fund the plan is not subject to review by the DOL, and self-insured plans will not be subject to the standardized operating rules that DOL will prescribe for health and welfare plans;

- State ombudsmen do not have jurisdiction over complaints against self-insured plans.

When it comes not to requirements but to entitlements, self-funded plans can participate in the federal reinsurance program that helps companies cover the health costs of early retirees (see § 18.19[E]).

### [6]    Nondiscrimination Requirements

PPACA § 2716 makes fully insured group health plans subject to the Code § 105(h) nondiscrimination rules. Previously, only self-insured plans were subject to these rules. To comply, the plan must benefit 70% of all employees, or, if 70% of employees are eligible to participate, 80% of the eligible employees must participate. It is not considered unlawful discrimination to exclude employees with less than three years of service; those under 25; part-time or seasonal employees; employees covered under a CBA (Collective Bargaining Agreement); and non-resident aliens. [Nelson Mullins Riley & Scarborough, LLP, *The Odd Couple: Healthcare Reform and Executive Compensation* (Apr. 15, 2010) (benefitslink.com)]

As long as they remain grandfathered, grandfathered plans are exempt from the nondiscrimination requirement. The nondiscrimination rules do not apply to plans that are exempt from Code § 100/ERISA Part 7, such as stand-alone insured dental and vision plans and stand-alone plans that cover only retirees.

The penalties under the nondiscrimination rules are considered excise rather than income taxes, so if an insured plan discriminates, the highly compensated employees are not taxed on their benefits, but the employer is subject to an excise tax penalty of $100 per day per participant (under Code § 4980D). Small employers—those with fewer than 50 employees—are exempt from the excise tax. The excise tax is capped at 10% of the aggregate amount the employer paid or incurred for the plan during the previous tax year, or $500,000, whichever is less. Excise tax liability is reported on Form 8928. The nondiscrimination requirement can be enforced by the Department of Labor, and participants and beneficiaries have the right to sue to enforce it.

Many executives' employment agreements specify payments on termination. When there is no agreement, the employer often provides severance in exchange for release of claims. There is often a subsidy provided for post-termination health coverage. However, this arrangement creates problems under PPACA. If the health insurance policy or plan allows, the employer may continue to cover the former employee as if he or she were still an active employee for a certain number of months or even years—usually, as long as severance pay continues. When this coverage ends, the former executive is eligible for COBRA. Another approach is to subsidize part of the COBRA coverage, usually by direct payment of the insurance premiums. Before PPACA, self-insured employers had to be careful not to discriminate in favor of HCEs. If HCEs received more coverage than the rank and file, the HCE might be taxed not only on the premiums paid by the employer but on all health coverage. To avoid this result, employers may structure severance so that the departing executive receives a sum of money that can, but need not, be used to pay health premiums; sometimes the employer will gross up the sum, paying an additional amount representing the taxes on the sum. PPACA has extended the nondiscrimination rules to insured group health plans (other than those that are grandfathered in). If a non-grandfathered insured plan violates the non-discrimination rules, the employer (not the HCE) is penalized, up to $100/day per employee suffering discrimination, capped at the lesser of 10% of the employer's EGHP costs for the year before or $500,000. (The penalty is waived for plans covering fewer than 50 employees, if violation had reasonable cause and there was no willful neglect.) [Steven Friedman, Terri Solomon, and Stephanie Kastrinsky, *Employers with Insured Health Plans Must Take Care in Providing Healthcare Subsidies to Departing Executives*, Littler Mendelson (Oct. 29, 2012) (benefitslink.com)]

## [C]  Small Business Tax Credit

For tax years beginning after December 31, 2009, PPACA enacts a new Code § 45R, making a new tax credit available to certain small business employers. A small business, defined as one with 25 or fewer employees, whose average annual wages are under $50,000, is eligible for a tax credit that can be as much as 35% of the non-elective contributions made on behalf of employees for their health insurance premiums. For this purpose, leased employees count in determining the number of employees, but owners of 5% or more of the company's stock and 2% shareholders in S Corporations do not count. To qualify for the credit, the employer must contribute at least half the premium for the coverage, and must make uniform payments on behalf of all employees. However, the credit will be limited if the employer pays an above-average premium for its coverage. For years after 2013, the employer must participate in an Exchange to claim the credit.

The employer receives the maximum amount of credit if it has ten or fewer employees, with average wages under $20,000 (this amount will be adjusted for inflation beginning in 2013). Average wages are rounded down to the next $1,000—that is, a wage of $32,408 is treated as $32,000.

The credit phases down, but is not eliminated, if the employer has more than 10 but fewer than 25 Full-Time Equivalents (FTEs), and is eliminated once the number of FTEs reaches 25. It also phases down as the average wage increases. The number of FTEs is calculated by dividing the number of hours worked by 2,080.

For tax years 2010–2013, the credit is 35% of the employer's total non-elective contributions on behalf of employees for qualified health coverage, subject to a limit based on the average premium for coverage for small groups.

For tax years after 2013, the maximum credit rises to 50% of the non-elective contributions for premiums for purchases from a health insurance exchange, once again subject to the average small-group premium as a limitation. For years after 2013, the qualified arrangement must offer insurance through an Exchange; in earlier years, using an Exchange is optional. [CCH Pension & Benefits, *Health Reform 2010: Small Employer Health Insurance Credit* (Apr. 12, 2010) (benefitslink.com)] Unless Congress extends it, the health insurance credit can be claimed for only two tax years that begin after 2013: for calendar year small employers, this means the years 2014 and 2015.

An IRS news release points out that the credit can be claimed as part of the general business credit, starting with the 2010 income tax return. [Fred Schneyer, *IRS Reminds Employers of New Health Coverage Tax Credit*, plansponsor.com (Apr. 1, 2010)] This credit is a component of the general business credit under Code § 38(b)(36), so it can be carried back one tax year and forward 20 tax years. The credit can also be claimed in full against both regular and AMT (Alternative Minimum Tax) liabilities.

The number of businesses eligible for the small business tax credit was estimated at anywhere from 1.4 million to 5.7 million. However, the GAO reported that only 170,300 firms claimed the credit in 2010 and only 17% claimed the full credit. The White House announced that at least 360,000 businesses claimed the credit for 2011, but this is still a small percentage of those eligible. The GAO attributed the low take-up rate to the complexity of the credit; the financial benefit is not seen as great enough to justify the time investment. Tax preparers said that it took about two to eight hours for their customers to collect the necessary information, and the preparers spent three to five hours calculating each customer's credit. [House Committee on Ways and Means, *Why the Health Care Tax Credit Eludes Many Small Businesses*, <http://waysandmeans.house.gov/news/documentsingle.aspx?DocumentID=310032> (Sept. 26, 2012)]

As of March 1, 2013, when automatic budget cuts were imposed as a result of the Balanced Budget and Emergency Deficit Control Act of 1985 mandatory "sequester," the refundable portion of the Code § 45R tax credit was reduced by 8.7%. The reduction is imposed until the end of the fiscal year (Sept. 30, 2013). [Cynthia Stamer, *Sequester Will Cut ACA Small Businesses Health Care Tax Credits*, WSJ.com (Mar. 5, 2013)]

All wages, including overtime and wages for hours worked in excess of 2,080 a year, are counted to determine average compensation.

A qualifying arrangement is one for which the employer pays health insurance premiums equaling at least 50% of the premium for the coverage. The credit cannot exceed the average premium for the small group market in the relevant state, or area within the state. Multi-state employers apply the average premium limitation separately for each state. [Also see FAQs at <http://www.irs.gov/news room/article/0,,id=220839,00.html>. See Elizabeth Thomas Dold, Christine L. Keller, William F. Sweetnam, Jr. and Brigen L. Winters, Groom Law Group, *IRS Provides Further Guidance on Operation of the Small Business Health Insurance Tax Credit* (Jan. 5, 2011) (benefitslink.com); Fred Schneyer, *Tax Officials Distribute Small Business Health Credit*, plansponsor.com (Dec. 2, 2010)]

Another credit, the Health Coverage Tax Credit (Code § 35), is payable on account of people aged 55 and over who receive their pensions from the PBGC, people who are eligible for Trade Adjustment Assistance (TAA); (see § 19.02[F]), and older workers who receive wage subsidies under the Alternative TAA program or the Reemployment TAA program. The Trade Adjustment Assistance Extension Act of 2011, Pub. L. No. 112-40 modifies the Health Coverage Tax Credit. Before the 2011 amendment, the credit was 65% of qualified health insurance premiums for eligible individuals and families, but the 2011 act retroactively increases the percentage to 72.5%, beginning with coverage months that start after February 2, 2011. (For some months before February 13, 2011, the credit level was 80% of the premium.) Pub. L. No. 112-40 also modified COBRA by extending the maximum COBRA coverage period for TAA and ATAA eligible persons and PBGC payees until the later of their maximum COBRA period or January 1, 2014. But terminated COBRA coverage is not retroactively restored by the statute. The COBRA extension probably does not apply to people whose COBRA coverage lapsed before November 20, 2011. [Allison Ullman, Seth Perretta, and Joel Wood, *Recently Enacted Trade Adjustment Assistance Extension Act of 2011 Affects Health Coverage Tax Credit and COBRA Continuation Coverage,* Crowell & Moring LLP (Nov. 10, 2011) (benefitslink.com)]

## [D]   Extended Coverage of Participants' Children

Before PPACA, many plans offered family coverage: coverage not just of the employee participating in the plan, but of the employee's spouse and children. Traditionally, children were eligible for coverage only until they reached the age of majority or married. Then there was a trend toward covering adult "children" of plan participants: see § 18.03[F] for a discussion of state laws requiring extended coverage, e.g., if the child was a full-time student. The federal "Michelle's Law" also required extended coverage of adult offspring with disabilities.

There are two aspects to coverage of adult children under PPACA. PPACA requires group health plans (including self-insured plans) to allow participants to continue coverage of their children until the child turns age 26, even if the child is not a student and even if the child is married. But for plan years beginning after January 1, 2014, grandfathered group health plans do not have to extend adult dependent coverage if the child is eligible to enroll in another EGHP (e.g., because of the child's own employment or spouse's employment).

The Department of Labor (DOL) and HHS joined together to publish Interim Final Regulations on May 10, 2010, dealing with the requirement of covering adult children until age 26—whether or not the child is a dependent for tax purposes, and whether or not he or she is a student. The regulations forbid charging a higher premium based on the age of the covered child—but permit plans to charge more for family than for single coverage, or to charge more for family coverage based on a greater number of covered individuals. Although married adult children are entitled to coverage, the parent's EGHP is not required to cover the child's spouse or children. Adult children who "aged out" of the plan under its pre-PPACA terms, but who have not reached 26, must be given notice and at least 30 days to enroll in the plan—even if this is not the normal open enrollment period for the plan. Employers must give notice of the new enrollment right. PPACA does not preempt state laws requiring even greater access to the plan. [Proskauer Client Alert, *Health Coverage for Children: Interim Final Regulations*, <http://www.proskauer.com/publications/client-alert/health-coverage-for-children-to-age-26/> (May 11, 2010)]

The other aspect is tax treatment of this coverage. The reconciliation bill amended the Internal Revenue Code to allow plan participants to exclude from income reimbursements they receive for medical expenses of an adult child who has not reached age 27 at the end of the calendar year. (In other words, the age limit is different for tax purposes than for purposes of regulating health plans.) See Notice 2010-38, 2010-20 I.R.B. 682.

Also note that in 10 states (Connecticut, Florida, Illinois, Nebraska, New Jersey, New York, Ohio, Pennsylvania, South Dakota, and Wisconsin) coverage may have to be extended even past age 26. Such coverage is taxable unless the child is a "qualifying child" or "qualifying relative" for federal tax purposes. [Buck Research FYI, *States Address Tax Consequences of Health Coverage for Adult Children* (Sept. 16, 2011) (benefitslink.com); Cynthia Lee, *Wisconsin Bill Passed to Conform State Tax Treatment of Coverage of Adult Children*, Beyond Health Care Reform Blog (Oct. 28, 2011) (benefitslink.com)]

## [E] Retiree Issues

PPACA requires a federal appropriation of $5 billion to reimburse employers for part of the costs that their EGHPs encounter to cover early retirees (aged 55–64) and their dependents for the gap period between retirement and Medicare eligibility. This program is known as Early Retiree Reinsurance Program (ERRP). CMS announced that the Early Retiree Reinsurance Program would stop accepting applications on May 5, 2011, because the money had run out. [CMS report, <http://cciio.cms.gov/resources/files/errp_progress_report_3_31_11.pdf>; see Rebecca Moore, *Early Retiree Reinsurance Program to End* (Apr. 1, 2011) (benefitslink.com)]

The program's termination was announced for January 1, 2014. [78 Fed.Reg. 23936 (Apr. 23, 2013); see Kevin McGuinness, *ERRP Will Sunset at Start of 2014*, plansponsor.com (May 17, 2013)]

PPACA does not eliminate the subsidy that employers receive for furnishing prescription drug coverage to retirees that is actuarially equivalent to Medicare Part D coverage (see § 9.10[B]). However, PPACA reduces the value of the tax break. Qualifying employers continue to receive the subsidy, and the subsidy is not taxable income. However, under pre-PPACA law, the subsidy was deductible to the employer, but starting in 2013 the deduction will no longer be available.

## [F] Cafeteria Plans, HSAs, HRAs, and FSAs

A cafeteria plan can provide a plan through the Exchange only if the employer is considered a "qualified" employer for the Exchange: i.e., an employer with fewer than 100 employees, that makes all of its full-time employees eligible to purchase coverage from the Exchange. This rule is effective for tax years beginning after December 31, 2013. Beginning in 2017, states can allow large employers to use the Exchange as well. In states that permit this option, large employers can also offer Exchange plans under a cafeteria plan.

As a counterpart to SIMPLE IRAs (see § 4.06[G]), PPACA allows certain small employers to provide simple cafeteria plans, which are deemed to satisfy the nondiscrimination rules. For years beginning after December 31, 2010, an eligible employer is one who had an average of 100 or fewer employees in either of the two preceding years, if the employer was in existence throughout the year. If it was not, then the employer can be eligible if it reasonably expects to average 100 or fewer employees on business days during the current year. If the employee census later grows, the employer can maintain an existing Simple Cafeteria Plan as long as it has under 200 employees.

The employer contribution must be at least 6% of the employee's compensation for the year, or twice the employee's salary reduction contribution— whichever is less. The match percentage for HCEs must not be higher than the match rate for non-HCEs. All employees who worked for at least 1,000 hours in the previous year are eligible to participate. Employees can be excluded if they have not reached age 21 (or a younger age as provided by the plan) by the end of the plan year; if they have not performed at least one year of service; if they are non-resident aliens; or if they are covered by a CBA. All eligible employees must be allowed to elect any benefit in the plan under the same terms and conditions as all other participants. [Gary B. Kushner, Kushner & Co., *New Simple Cafeteria Plans* (Aug. 14, 2010) (benefitslink.com)]

HSAs were not eliminated by the reform bill; in fact, it is likely that they will become more popular as a tax-saving measure. [Ron Lieber, *Health Savings Accounts Survive Medical Overhaul*, NYTimes.com (Mar. 26, 2010)]

Starting 2011, reimbursement under FSA, HRA, or HSA is limited to prescription drugs, and is not available for over-the-counter drugs. The additional tax imposed on distributions from an HSA or MSA not used for qualified medical expenses rises, to 20%.

As of January 1, 2013, contributions to an FSA for medical expenses are limited to $2,500 a year (a figure that will be adjusted for inflation). Under pre-PPACA law, there was no limit on FSA contributions, although in practice most employers imposed a limit such as $4,000 or $5,000. This amount will be indexed for inflation in subsequent years. [Workforce.com, *Understanding Key Provisions in Federal Health Care Reform Legislation* (Mar. 22, 2010) (benefitslink. com)]

## [G] Wellness Programs

For PPACA purposes, a wellness program is one that is offered by an employer to promote health or prevent disease. All similarly situated individuals must be allowed to participate in the program, and health status factors must not be used in deciding who qualifies for a rebate or premium discount.

Wellness programs must be reasonably targeted at improving health or preventing illness, and are not allowed to operate as a subterfuge to justify health status discrimination. A reasonable alternative standard must be offered for people whose medical condition keeps them from achieving a stated goal. Pre-PPACA law says that premium discounts for achieving objectives cannot be more than 20% of employee's premium. Under PPACA, starting 2014, the discount can be 30% or even as much as 50%, with wellness discounts extended to the individual market with a ten-state demonstration project beginning July 2014. PPACA allows employees who meet health benchmarks to get waivers of co-payments and deductibles and relief from surcharges. [Roni Caryn Rabin, *Will Health Overhaul Incentives also Penalize Some Workers?*, NYTimes.com (Apr. 12, 2010)]

According to the CDC, smoking causes $190 billion in health costs and productivity losses per year and causes over 440,000 premature deaths. Only about 20% of Americans smoke. PPACA requires health insurance plans to offer products and therapy to help them quit smoking. [Dan Diamond, *About Time? Smokers Face Tough New Rules Under Obamacare*, The Health Care Blog (Jan.25, 2013)]

The Kaiser Family Foundation (KFF) 2012 Employer Health Benefits Report showed that about two-thirds (63%) of firms with health benefits have at least one wellness program, such as nutrition classes, weight loss, or smoking cessation classes. Among firms that have more than 200 employees, over a third ask for completion of health risk assessments—and two-thirds of firms that do this provide financial incentives. [Ann Carrns, *Employers Use Carrots and Sticks to Promote Worker Health*, NYTimes.com (Sept.12, 2012)]

Research by the Principal Financial Group says that participants in comprehensive workplace wellness programs can significantly reduce their health risks in as little as 18 months, especially if they receive personalized health coaching, and reduced health risks can lead to reduced health costs. Almost all participants in a study showed some improvement in their health risk status. One-third (34%) of those receiving individual coaching moved from high risk status to a lower category of risk, measured by factors such as waist size, blood pressure, and tobacco use. [Wolters Kluwer Law & Business News Centers, *Workplace Wellness*

*Programs Can Significantly Reduce Health Risks, Study Finds* (benefitslink.com) (Oct. 2, 2012)]

Mercer's Steven Noeldner concluded that good wellness programs have a 2% positive return by the third year. However, the journal Health Affairs reported two years of tracking the wellness program at a St. Louis hospital system. The rate of hospitalization for employees and their families declined 41% overall for six major conditions—but there were no cost savings because outpatient costs increased. [AP, Study: *Eating Your Broccoli And Getting Fit Might Not Cut Health Care Costs For Your Employer*, Washington Post (Mar. 4, 2013) (benefitslink.com)]

Wellness programs usually provide incentives in forms such as gift cards, HSA contributions, or reductions in employee obligations. According to the National Business Group on Health, the median incentive in 2011 was $250, and the projected median for 2013 is $450. The Kaiser Family Foundation (KFF) said that in 2011 approximately 27% of large firms with wellness programs offered financial incentives, a proportion that rose to about 41% in 2012. KFF also said that 11% of large firms required employees whose health assessment showed risks to either take steps (such as entering a health management program) or be penalized. A few large firms base rewards and penalties on biometric outcomes such as cholesterol level or BMI. The privacy problems can be reduced somewhat by tracking health metrics for the whole workforce, not just those that appear to have health problems. [Jonnelle Marte, *Get Paid to Stay Healthy*, MarketWatch date? (benefitslink.com)]

Employers say that incentives didn't work to improve wellness, so now they're imposing penalties. CVS Caremark levied a $600 fine on employees who don't report weight, cholesterol, and BMI levels to the company's benefits consultant; General Electric charges self-identified smokers an extra $50/month premium; Honeywell International has a $1,000 penalty for having certain kinds of surgery (e.g., back surgery, hip replacement) without going to the company's support program that stresses non-surgical management; Michelin North America makes health coverage up to $1,000 a year more expensive based on high cholesterol or a large waist measurement; Mohawk Industries charges a $100/month penalty for not having health risk assessments. Until 2012, Michelin credited an automatic $600 toward deductibles and made wellness action plans optional. Now only workers who satisfy their standards for blood sugar, blood pressure, cholesterol, and waist size qualify for the full $1,000 credit toward annual deductibles; nonconforming workers have to have health coaching, and their credit is lower. Most companies allocate 5%–10% of employee premium costs for incentives, which is likely to increase. Lew Maltby (National Workrights Institute, a nonprofit advocacy group) says that this is a pay cut by another name—and a significant invasion of privacy. An Aon Hewitt survey says 60% of employers plan to impose penalties in the next few years for employees who don't take steps to improve their health. CIGNA says that 70% of health costs are related to chronic conditions brought on by lifestyle choices like being overweight or sedentary.

[Leslie Kwoh, *When Your Boss Makes You Pay for Being Fat*, WSJ.com (Apr. 5, 2013) and *If Workers Are Out of Shape, Should Companies Make Them Pay?* WSJ.com (Apr. 5, 2013)]

Joint HHS, DOL, and Treasury proposed rules on wellness programs, reflecting PPACA provisions, were released, effective for plan years beginning on or after January 1, 2014. The rules support wellness programs, including participatory programs that are generally available without regard to the individual's health status. Examples include reimbursement for gym memberships, rewards for attending a free monthly health seminar, or rewards simply for filling out a health risk amendment. Programs that are contingent on health (i.e., the reward is triggered by meeting specific health standards such as giving up smoking) must be reasonably designed to promote health or prevent disease, and must not be overly burdensome on participants. They must be made reasonably available to all similarly situated individuals. Alternative means to qualify must be provided for employees who have a medical reason for being unable to satisfy the health-related standard. Under the final rules, the employer can offer a reward of up to 30% of the health coverage (an increase from 20% in the proposed rules), and smoking cessation programs can offer a reward of up to 50% of the cost of health coverage. The rules were finalized in 2013, via T.D. 9620, 2013-27 I.R.B. 1.The HHS, DOL, and the Treasury jointly issued final rules, endorsing the value of wellness programs in reducing reduce chronic illness and disciplining health care costs, but placing limits on underwriting practices that might discriminate on the basis of health status. The rules permit participatory wellness programs that are available to employees without regard to health status (e.g., rewards for taking health information seminars or completing a health questionnaire; paying for health club memberships). Rewards for meeting a health goal (e.g., quitting smoking; meeting a target for weight or blood cholesterol) are acceptable if they are non-discriminatory. The final rules are effective January 1, 2014. [See DOL's report on wellness programs, <http://www.dol.gov/ebsa/pdf/work placewellnessstudyfinal.pdf>, discussed in Plansponsor staff, *Wellness Program Final Rules Issued*, plansponsor.com (May 29, 2013)]

An important mid-2012 decision held that the Broward County employee wellness program satisfied the ADA safe harbor for insurance plans. The program included a finger stick for glucose and cholesterol and an online health risk assessment questionnaire. The information was used to find employees who had asthma, hypertension, diabetes, congestive heart failure, and kidney disease. Employees who have one of those diseases can participate in a coaching program that gives them copayment waivers for some medications. Participation in the program was not required to get insurance coverage but, until January 1, 2011, non-participating employees were charged $20 per biweekly paycheck. A class action was filed describing the program as an involuntary medical examination and disability related inquiry. However, the ADA permits inquiries that are job-related and consistent with business necessity. There is a safe harbor for insurance plans that maintain a bona fide benefit plan based on underwriting, administering, and classifying risks. The Eleventh Circuit held that the wellness program, as a term of the group health insurance plan, satisfied the ADA safe harbor. [*Seff v. Broward Cnty.*, 691 F.3d 1221 (11th Cir. 2012)]

## [H] Penalties for Failure to Offer Affordable Coverage

A large employer (one with over 50 employees) is subject to a fine (the "assessable payment") if it fails to offer its full-time employees and their dependents the opportunity to receive minimum essential coverage under a plan sponsored by the employer—but only if at least one full-time employee has enrolled in an Exchange and received a premium tax credit or cost-sharing reduction. Large employers can avoid the assessable payment by providing their employees vouchers for purchasing coverage from an Exchange.

The assessable payment, also known as the employer shared responsibility payment or the "pay or play" obligation (Internal Revenue Code § 4980H), was originally scheduled to begin January 1, 2014. However, on July 2, 2013, the Obama administration announced a one-year delay in the effective date of this requirement. The applicability of the individual mandate to maintain insurance was not delayed. The same announcement also delayed the Code § 6055 reporting requirement for self-insured plans and insurers with respect to minimum essential coverage. [Notice 2013-45, 2013-3 I.R.B. 116; see Reed Abelson & Katie Thomas, *Health Law Delay Puts Exchanges in Spotlight*, NYTimes.com (July 3, 2013); John D. Martini, *Obama Administration to Delay Employer Reporting Requirements and "Shared Responsibility" Payments Until 2015*, JD Supra Law News, <http://www.jdsupra.com/legalnews/obama-administration-to-delay-employer-r-50627> (July 5, 2013); Tina Bull, *PPACA's Employer Reporting Requirements & Penalties Delayed*, PSA Perspective <http://www.psafinancial.com/2013/08/ppacas-employer-reporting-requirements-penalties-delayed> (Aug. 1, 2013)]

The basic payment is $166.67 per month, multiplied by the number of full-time employees the employer has in that month, minus 30. If the employer has more than 50 employees, and offers coverage, but at least one employee receives a premium subsidy after purchasing coverage through an exchange, then the employer is fined an annual amount calculated as $3,000 per employee receiving the credit, or $2,000 per employee (after the first 30 employees have been disregarded)—whichever is less. [Rebecca Moore, *Mercer Estimates 38% of Employers to Be Penalized for Unaffordable Coverage*, plansponsor.com (Apr. 27, 2010)]

The penalty imposed on the employer for failure to provide affordable coverage is calculated based on the employer's contribution to self-only coverage, not family coverage. But if an employee buys coverage through an Exchange and receives a premium tax credit, the employer will not be penalized as long as it otherwise satisfies the requirement of affordable coverage. A plan is considered affordable for dependents if the employee's contribution for his or her own coverage does not exceed 9.5% of household income. One problem is that the employer is not necessarily aware of the employee's household income level. The proposal says that regulations will be published including a safe harbor based on the employee's W-2. The employer will not have to pay a penalty if the employee's required contribution does not exceed 9.5% of that employee's W-2 wages from that employer. [Christy Tinnes and Brigen Winters, *Proposed Regulation on PPACA Premium Tax Credit* series, plansponsor.com (Sept. 20, Sept. 27, Oct. 11, 2011)]

Although many employers found PPACA confusing, one clear take-away was that keeping the employee census below 50 (and especially below 30, when the $2,000 "pay or play" penalty does not apply) can be desirable for the employer. [Reed Abelson and Steven Greenhouse, *Small Employers Weigh Impact of Providing Health Insurance*, NYTimes.com Nov. 30, 2012]

Nine percent of respondents to a mid-2012 Deloitte survey said they plan to drop health coverage as soon as the Exchanges are available, and more companies may do so later. This is much lower than McKinsey's 2011 survey results that 30% of employers would definitely or probably stop offering insurance after 2014. The CBO's estimate is that about 7% of workers would lose coverage by 2019. However, the Deloitte survey found that one-third of respondents might drop their health plans if they have to provide more benefits than their current level; if the "Cadillac" tax takes effect in 2018; or if paying the penalties is cheaper than providing insurance. [Louise Radnofsky, *Deloitte: One in 10 U.S. Employers to Drop Health Coverage*, WSJ.com (July 24, 2012)]

Some restaurants, hotels, and retailers reduced the schedules of hourly workers below 30 hours a week to avoid being subject to the shared responsibility payment. However, HHS said that this would not be a major problem: shifting to part-time workers means that an employer will have more turnover and lower morale. The agency also said that the history of Massachusetts' Romneycare plan shows that employers adapted without large-scale cutbacks in staffing. [Julie Jargon, Louise Radnofsky, and Alexandra Berzon, *Health-Care Law Spurs a Shift to Part-Time Workers*, WSJ.com (Nov. 4, 2012)]

Nevertheless, choosing to pay the penalty is not a simple decision. It means that the employer will lose out on tax deductions, and employees will no longer have tax-free income in the form of health benefits. This may make recruitment and retention difficult. Recordkeeping and reporting will still be required to calculate the penalty. Employees who do not have EGHP coverage are likely to patronize the Exchanges—which will require a great deal of information from the employer. [Thom Mangan, *PPACA: Play Or Pay? 7 Reasons Why 'Pay' Is Not The Easy Answer*, Employee Benefit Adviser (Jan. 15, 2013) (benefitslink.com)]

In late 2012, the Obama administration explained that employers are required to offer coverage to employees and their children, but "dependent" means children only; it is not required that coverage be offered to employees' spouses. Employers will not be penalized if family coverage is not affordable. The IRS said that employers would receive a one-time reprieve if they do not offer coverage to the dependents of full-time employees—provided that they take steps in 2014 to come into compliance so that, in 2015 when dependent coverage is required, it will be provided. [Robert Pear, *Employers Must Offer Family Health Care, Affordable or Not, Administration Says*, NYTimes.com (Dec. 31, 2012)]

The proposed regulations treat children up to age 26 as dependents—but spouses are not considered dependents because they are not explicitly named by PPACA. All employers in a controlled group are aggregated to determine if an employer is subject to the penalty. However, the penalty is applied separately to each member of the controlled group, so compliant members will not be penalized. Although dependents must be offered coverage, the employer does not have to subsidize their health coverage the way employee health coverage is subsidized. [Mark Stember, Kilpatrick Townsend Health & Welfare Blog, *Employer Penalty Guidance*, (Dec. 31, 2012) (benefitslink.com); Janet Adamy, *Under Health Law, Employers Must Insure Workers' Dependents*, WSJ.com (Dec. 29, 2012)]

The IRS issued proposed regulations and an FAQ on the Code § 4980H "shared responsibility" (aka "pay or play") obligation at the beginning of 2013. [78 Fed. Reg. 217 (Jan. 2, 2013); see Rebecca Moore, *IRS Proposes Rules for Employer Health Coverage Penalty*, plansponsor.com (Jan. 4, 2013); Christy Tinnes and Brigen Winters, *Second Opinions: Employer Shared Responsibility Requirements Proposed Regs, Part I*, plansponsor.com (Jan. 16, 2013) and *Part II* plansponsor.com (Jan. 30, 2013)]

## [I] The CLASS Act

The Community Living Assistance Services and Support (CLASS) Act was intended to facilitate saving by employees for the cost of home care. However, the program never took effect.

In October 2011, HHS announced that the CLASS Act program was financially unsustainable and would not be implemented. [Rebecca Moore, *Repeal of Long-Term Care Provision of Health Reform Heads to House*, plansponsor.com (Jan.19, 2012)] At the beginning of 2013, as part of the "fiscal cliff" deal to resolve the budget crisis, the CLASS Act was formally repealed.

## [J] PPACA Effects on Employees

The intention of PPACA is to provide most people with at least the minimum benefits package, with limits on employee payments responsibilities, through their employment. The health care reform legislation provides both "carrots" and "sticks"—many employees will be able to receive premium credits or vouchers to help them pay for insurance; temporary high-risk pools followed by

Insurance Exchanges will be available to cover workers who do not receive employment-related insurance coverage.

### [1]  Premium Credits

PPACA allows workers with household income between 100% and 400% of the federal poverty level (FPL) to receive a refundable tax credit if their employer fails to offer creditable coverage and if the employees purchase coverage under an Exchange. The premium credit is defined as 2% of income for taxpayers whose income equals 100% of FPL, increasing to 9.5% of income for employees whose income is in the 300%–400% FPL range.

On August 17, 2011, the IRS proposed regulations on this tax credit. A taxpayer will not be eligible for the tax credit if he or she is eligible for "minimum essential coverage," including coverage under an eligible employer-sponsored plan that pays at least 60% of the cost of a plan that provides the minimum essential benefits. (A person who could enroll in an employer's plan, but chooses not to, does not qualify for the premium tax credit.)

Generally, the credit is the sum of premium assistance amounts for each month of the tax year and represents the difference between the premium for an officially selected benchmark plan and a percentage of the taxpayer's household income. (That is, the credit does not depend on the actual plan selected by the taxpayer.) Christy Tinnes and Brigen Winters, *Proposed Regulation on PPACA Premium Tax Credit*, plansponsor.com (Sept. 20, Sept. 27, Oct. 11, 2011)]

HHS proposed regulations on the process that the Exchanges will use to verify whether people who apply for advance payment of premium tax credits are either enrolled in an EGHP or are eligible for employer-sponsored coverage that satisfies the affordability and minimum value standards. The applicant for advance payment of the premium tax credit must submit an attestation form, which the Exchange uses to determine eligibility. [Proposed Regulations, 78 Fed. Reg. 4593 (Jan. 22, 2013); see EBIA Weekly, *HHS Proposes Process for Exchanges to Verify Employer-Sponsored Health Coverage* (Jan. 17, 2013); <http://www.ofr.gov/inspection.aspx>, discussed in CMS press release, *Proposed Rule For Strengthening Medicaid, The Children's Health Insurance Program And The New Health Insurance Marketplace* (Jan. 14, 2013) (benefitslink.com)]

### [2]  Individual Penalties

Although PPACA provides rights for individuals, including greater access to health insurance because they cannot be turned down for coverage because of PCEs, the law also imposes individual personal responsibility requirements. Starting in 2014, a "shared responsibility payment" is imposed for each month that a person fails to maintain minimum essential health coverage for themselves and their dependents. The penalty is imposed on the taxpayer, so in effect dependent children are exempt from the penalty. The coverage can be obtained either through an EGHP or by purchasing an individual policy; the Exchanges exist to make it easier to obtain individual coverage.

The penalty is the larger of a flat dollar amount per person, reaching $695 in 2016 (at which point it will be indexed for inflation), or a percentage of household income, starting at 1.09% in 2014, 2.0% in 2015, reaching 2.5% in 2016 and then indexed for inflation. For families, the penalty per child is half the individual penalty, subject to a cap amount no matter how large the family is. Married couples are jointly liable for the penalty. But the federal government will not bring criminal prosecutions or impose liens or levies for failure to pay it. [Congressional Budget Office, *Payments of Penalties for Being Uninsured Under the Patient Protection and Affordable Care Act*, <http://www.cbo.gov/ftpdocs/113xx/doc11355/Individual_Mandate_Penalties-04-22.pdf> (Apr. 22, 2010); Rebecca Moore, *CBO Says Four Million Likely to Pay Penalty for Being Uninsured*, plan sponsor.com (Apr. 22, 2010)]

### [3]   Taxes on High-Income Participants

Although the focus of this discussion of PPACA is on the employer's point of view, certain provisions affecting individuals are crucial to understanding PPACA. One of the ways that the health care reform program will be funded is through increasing the Medicare tax imposed on plan participants with especially high income.

Before PPACA, the FICA payroll tax was imposed on all earned income up to the FICA limit (for 2010-2011, this is $106,800, for 2012, it is $110,100, and for 2013, it is $113,700), and the Medicare tax was imposed on all income without the limit. (For employees, the employer and employee each pay 1.45%; self-employed persons pay 2.9%.) Starting in 2013, the 1.45% Medicare payroll tax rises to 2.35% for high-income persons. Only the employee's share, not the employer's share, rises. For this purpose, a high-income taxpayer is one with total earned income plus investment income greater than $250,000 (joint return) or $200,000 (other returns). Although in general self-employed persons can deduct half of the regular FICA tax, the additional Medicare tax is not deductible. Elective contributions are generally subject to FICA tax, but the additional Medicare tax does not apply to elective contributions or to earnings on qualified plans, including 401(k) plans. Tax-exempt bond interest and profits on the sale of the taxpayer's principal residence are not included in gross income, so they are not included in the Medicare tax base.

The reconciliation bill imposes an additional Medicare tax equal to 3.8% of certain investment income (the smaller of net investment income, or modified AGI minus $250,000 for joint returns, $125,000 for married persons filing separate returns, and $200,000 for other filing statuses). CCH noted that it is not clear whether this tax is imposed only on net investment income over the threshold or all investment income of persons whose income is higher than the threshold amounts. [CCH Pension and Benefits, *Increased Medicare Taxes Imposed Under Health Reform Law Will Not Be Assessed on Plan Distributions* (Apr. 8, 2010) (benefitslink.com); Kristi L. Remington, Barry L. Klein, Virginia Escobar Neiswender, Blank Rome LLP, *Health Care Reform's Impact on Employers* (Mar. 26, 2010) (benefitslink.com)]

IRS Q&As published in mid-2012 state that the employer must withhold on wages or compensation over $200,000 in a calendar year, no matter what marital status is claimed on the employee's Form W-4. [Alden J. Bianchi, *IRS Issues Q&As on Affordable Care Act's Additional Medicare Tax*, Mintz Levin Employment, Labor & Benefits Advisory (Aug. 31, 2012) (benefitslink.com)]

## [K]  Recordkeeping, Reporting, and Disclosure

PPACA imposes many information requirements on health plans—communication with employees about their health plans and communication with regulators to ensure that employers satisfy their obligations (and also to claim the financial assistance they are entitled to).

Many of the provisions of PPACA require notices to be furnished, either to specific participants, or as a part of the plan's general benefits materials. See <http://www.dol.gov/ebsa/healthreform> for model notices for several of these forms. Many plans include these notices in the annual enrollment package or the plan's SPD.

All plans, including grandfathered plans, must offer a one-time special enrollment period for adult children who were not covered because of age or who aged out of the plan, and for persons who lost coverage because they reached the plan's maximum coverage, and notice must be given of the special enrollment period.

PPACA also requires notices of:

- Grandfathered status;

- Patient Protection Model Notice: If the plan requires participants to designate a primary care provider, how to choose one; notice that female enrollees can see a OB/GYN without prior authorization or referral. (Not required for grandfathered plans);

- Explanation of the external review process; many plans include this in the SPD (Not required for grandfathered plans);

- Notice of internal adverse benefit determination;

- Advance notice that coverage will be cancelled or rescinded. [Christy Tinnes and Brigen Winters, *What Notices Are Required by PPACA?*, plansponsor.com (Sept. 21, 2010)]

As a parallel to the Summary Plan Description for a pension plan (see § 11.02), the employer must give each employee a one- to four-page summary of health care benefits that explains the covered benefits, exclusions, cost sharing, and continuation coverage. For readability, the summary must be in 12-point or larger type. This document is referred to as the Summary of Benefits and Coverage (SBC). The document must be printed either in the official colors or in gray-scale. PPACA says that this explanation must be "culturally and linguistically appropriate" for the beneficiary who receives it. If the health plan changes, the employer must update the summary to reflect material modifications, at least 60 days before the change. A material modification is anything that a reasonable participant would consider an important change—whether the benefit is enhanced or reduced. Satisfying this requirement also satisfies the ERISA requirement of providing a Summary of Material Modification (SMM)—but as Buck Consultants points out, this is a shorter time frame than the requirement for the ERISA SMM, so a timely SMM might violate the PPACA requirement.

The summary must be provided to job applicants when they apply, to enrollees before they enroll or re-enroll, and to the policyholder or certificate holder when the policy is issued or the certificate is delivered. Not only must the SBC be distributed when an employee enrolls in the plan, but also it must be furnished as soon as possible after a request (definitely within seven days). The SBC can be furnished either on paper, or electronically as long as the DOL's electronic disclosure safe harbor (see 29 C.F.R. § 2520.104b-1) is satisfied. Willful failure to provide an SBC is subject to a fine of $1,000 per failure (each person affected constituting a separate offense) and is also subject to an excise tax of $100 per day per person affected under Code § 4980D.

The new standards preempt state requirements that are less protective, but states have the power to impose separate additional disclosure requirements on health insurers.

The insurers of insured plans provide the SBC to the plan, and the plan and the insurer are jointly responsible for giving participants the SBC, but only one has to furnish the SBC, not both. The plan administrator is responsible for providing SBCs to participants of self-insured plans. Although grandfathered plans and HRAs are required to furnish the SBC, the requirement does not apply to retiree-only plans or plans such as stand-alone vision and dental plans that are exempt from HIPAA requirements.

The SBC must include:

- A uniform glossary of insurance and medical terms so that consumers may compare health coverage and understand the terms of (or exceptions to) their coverage;

- A description of the coverage, including cost sharing for each category of benefits;

- Exceptions, reductions and limitations on coverage;

- Cost-sharing provisions of coverage, including deductibles, coinsurance and co-payment obligations;

- The renewability and continuation of coverage provisions;

- A "coverage facts label" that includes examples to illustrate common benefits scenarios (including pregnancy and serious or chronic medical conditions);

- For coverage beginning on or after January 1, 2014, a statement of whether the plan provides minimum essential coverage and whether the plan pays at least 60 percent of the total cost of benefits;

- A statement that the SBC is only a summary and that the plan document, policy or certificate of coverage should be consulted to determine the governing contractual provisions of coverage;

- Contact information for questions and for obtaining a copy of the plan document or insurance policy, certificate or contract of insurance;

- For plans that maintain one or more provider networks, an Internet address for obtaining a list of network providers;

- For plans that use a prescription drug formulary, an Internet address for obtaining information on prescription drug coverage;

- An Internet address for obtaining the uniform glossary.

An important difference between the proposed and final regulations is that the final rule removes the requirement of specifying the premium or cost of coverage of a self-insured plan. [Buck Consultants FYI, *Final Guidance Issued on Summary of Benefits and Coverage* (Mar. 1, 2012) (benefitslink.com); PWC HRS Insight, *Administration Issues Final Rules on PPACA Summary of Benefits and Coverage* (Feb. 14, 2012) (benefitslink.com); Greg Gautam and Nancy Campbell, Snell & Willmer Legal Alert, *Four-Page Benefit Summary Requirement for Group Health Plan Arrives in 2012* (Nov. 9, 2011) (benefitslink.com); Christy Tinnes and Brigen Winters, Groom Law Group, *What is Required in the Summary of Benefits and Coverage Part II*, plansponsor.com (Sept. 13, 2011) FAQs at <http://www.dol.gov/ebsa/faqs/faq-aca7.html>; see Ilyse Schuman, Employee Benefits Council, *Agencies Issue Eighth Set of FAQs on Affordable Care Act Implementation* (Mar. 21, 2012) (benefitslink.com)]

Starting March 13, 2013, employers must give their employees (and new employees as they are hired) information about how the Insurance Exchanges work and how to contact them. If the employer pays less than 60% of the actuarial value of the total cost of health benefits, the employer also has a duty to inform employees that they may be eligible for a tax credit if they buy insurance through an Exchange—but that they will lose any employer contribution made to provide health coverage for that employee. Employers are not fined if employees in this situation purchase their coverage from the Exchange. [Laura Meckler and Janet Adamy, *Key Part of Health Law to Be Clarified*, WSJ.com (Mar. 25, 2010)]

PPACA § 9002 requires employers to disclose the aggregate cost of employer-sponsored coverage on Form W-2, whether the employee or employer pays. The cost calculation is similar to the one used for COBRA premiums. However, the cost of long-term care insurance, accident and health, or disability income insurance is not included. Salary reduction contributions to FSAs under a cafeteria plan and contributions to MSAs or HSAs are not considered employer-sponsored coverage, so they do not have to be disclosed on the Form W-2. The employer is only obligated to report the total amount, not to furnish an itemized breakdown. Reporting is purely informational: the cost of coverage (other than "Cadillac plan" coverage, as of 2018) is not a taxable item. [Lauren Bikoff, Health Reform Talk (CCH), *Inclusion of Cost of Employer-Sponsored Health Coverage on W-2* (Mar. 31, 2010) (benefitslink.com)]. See Notice 2012-9, 2012-4 I.R.B. 315, for information about how to report the cost of coverage.

Once the "pay or play" requirement takes effect, large employers that fail to provide coverage as required by PPACA must file a return with HHS, disclosing that they do not provide coverage; the number of their full-time employees; and other information as required by HHS. Large employers that do provide coverage must report to HHS the number of full-time employees; the name of everyone who has the option to enroll in coverage; the number of months of coverage each received; the length of any waiting period; the number of months that coverage was available; the monthly premium for the lowest-cost option; the plan's share of covered health expenses. The employer must also give employees notice about the availability of coverage under the Exchanges. [Hinda Chaikind and Chris L. Peterson, *Summary of Potential Employer Penalties Under PPACA (P.L. 111-148)*, Congressional Research Service, <http://www.ncsl.org/documents/health/EmployerPenalties.pdf> (Apr. 5, 2010)]

PPACA compliance requires the adoption of a number of plan amendments:

- Enrollment of persons under 19 without pre-existing condition limitations;

- Coverage of employees' dependent children to age 26, whether or not they are students or married, and whether or not they are tax dependents of the employees; but see <http://www.dol.gov/ebsa/faqs/faq-aca.html> Q&A #14 for some permitted exceptions;

- Elimination of lifetime limits on essential health benefits (guidance has not yet been issued to define "essential," so plans must use a good-faith reasonable interpretation of the term);

- Restrictions on annual limits on essential health benefits; the limit must be at least $750,000 in 2010, rising to $1.25 million in 2012;

- Elimination of retroactive terminations of coverage;

- Amending FSAs, HRAs, and HSAs to eliminate reimbursement of the cost of over-the-counter drugs unless the participant has a prescription.

Non-grandfathered plans must be amended to provide:

- Coverage of some preventive services without cost sharing;

- Free choice of primary care provider (who can be a pediatrician for children enrolled in the plan); women can see an OB/GYN without prior authorization or referral;

- Emergency services must be covered without prior authorization, and emergency services must receive the same coverage whether in- or out of network;

- The new external claims review process;

- The requirement of not discriminating in favor of highly compensated employees.

[Christy Tinnes and Brigen Winters, Groom Law Group, *A 2011 Plan Amendment Checklist*, plansponsor.com (Oct. 12, 2010)]

## [L]  Health Insurance Exchanges and High-Risk Pools

One of the main drivers behind the legislation was the perception that many individuals and small businesses found it difficult to buy and maintain health insurance. PPACA's response to this problem is the creation of health insurance exchanges: the SHOP Exchange (Small Business Health Options Program) and an individual exchange. All policies offered by the exchanges must meet the federal standards for essential health benefits. For this purpose, a small employer is one that has between one and 100 employees, although until 2016, a state has the option to limit the small-group market to employers with fewer than 50 employees. Starting in 2017, states also have the option to allow companies with more than 100 employees to purchase insurance from the SHOP Exchange. Starting in 2016, two or more states can join in a Health Care Choice Compact, offering at least two qualified health plans that are available in more than one state. The intention is that competition across state lines will be more vigorous and will result in lower premiums.

On July 11, 2011, HHS issued proposed regulations on the establishment of exchanges and Qualified Health Plans (QHPs). The proposal explains the general requirements a state exchange must meet to be approved by HHS, the minimum requirements health insurers must satisfy to participate in an Exchange, and how small employers can obtain coverage through the SHOP Exchange. Future guidance will deal with subjects like which benefits are "essential health benefits" and determining the actuarial value of coverage offered by an Exchange.

The SHOP exchanges must allow a qualified employer (i.e., a small employer that makes all of its full-time employees eligible for Exchange coverage) to select the level of coverage for which QHPs will be available to employees. HHS regulations published March 11, 2013 indicated that insurers were not ready to launch the SHOP as scheduled in 2014. The SHOP was supposed to give businesses with up to 100 employees a competitive market where they can purchase coverage for their employees. The delay does not affect the exchanges maintained by 16 states and the District of Columbia, only to the federal Exchanges. [Drew Armstrong, *Small-Business Insurance Market Delayed*, Treasury & Risk (Apr. 1, 2013) (benefitslink.com)]

As of the beginning of 2013, 18 states were conditionally approved to run their own state-based exchanges: California, Colorado, Connecticut, the District of Columbia, Hawaii, Idaho, Kentucky, Maryland, Massachusetts, Minnesota, Nevada, New Mexico, New York, Oregon, Rhode Island, Utah, Vermont, and Washington. Two states (Arkansas and Delaware) were conditionally approved to operate exchanges in conjunction with the federal government. [Center for Consumer Info & Insurance Oversight (CCIIO) *State Health Insurance Marketplaces* (Jan. 3, 2013) (benefitslink.com)]

Montana, which has a Democratic governor, announced that it would not set up its own Exchange. Six states with Republican governors confirmed that they would not have state exchanges: New Jersey, Tennessee, North Carolina, Ohio, Virginia, and Missouri. By February, Illinois, New Hampshire, Michigan, and Iowa had partnership exchanges. [Louise Radnofsky, *Six More States Reject Role In Health-Care Exchanges*, WSJ.com (Feb. 15, 2013)]

Even before PPACA, most of the states responded to problems in the health insurance market by setting up high-risk pools so that people with pre-existing conditions could still purchase insurance. After PPACA, 27 states opted to maintain high-risk pools. The Commonwealth Fund estimated that about 6 million out of the 50.7 million uninsured people might qualify for pool coverage. [Rebecca Moore, *HHS Secretary Takes First Step to Establish High-risk Insurance Pools*, plansponsor.com (Apr. 5, 2010); Kevin Sack, *High-Risk Insurance Pools Draw Fewer Takers Than Projected*, NYTimes.com (Nov. 4, 2010)]

## [M]  Timeline

Another way to look at health care reform is to consider when the various provisions take effect, so your health plan can be amended, and the administration of the plan adapted, to satisfy the statutory requirements. Shortly after the passage of PPACA, the Kaiser Family Foundation published an excellent chart summarizing the timetable for implementing the new law. [Kaiser Family Foundation, *Health Reform Implementation Timeline*, <http://www.kff.org/health reform/upload/8060.pdf> (Mar. 25, 2010)]

Provisions taking effect in 2010 include:

- The subsidy program for small employers takes effect;

- The subsidy program for coverage of non-Medicare-eligible retirees begins;

- All individual and group policies must cover employees' adult children up to age 26;

- A temporary nationwide high-risk pool will be set up to cover people with pre-existing conditions; this pool will be replaced by the Exchanges in 2014;

- Lifetime maximums on coverage are forbidden, although, until 2014, annual maximums can be imposed, subject to limits set by HHS;

- EGHPs must provide coverage for preventive care, without imposing cost-sharing on plan beneficiaries: e.g., immunizations, preventive care for children, Pap smears, etc.;

- Insurers can only rescind coverage on the basis of fraud, not because the individual makes expensive claims;

- Health plans must report their loss ratios.

Provisions taking effect in 2011 include:

- If loss ratios are less than 85% (large group plans) or 80% (individual and small group plans), then the insurer must give rebates to consumers;

- HRAs and health FSAs can no longer cover over-the-counter drugs that are not prescribed by a doctor. HSAs and MSAs can still cover them, but not on a tax-free basis;

- New uniform rules on verifying eligibility and claims status will be published.

Provisions taking effect in 2012 include:

- New uniform rules for electronic funds transfers and health care payments take effect.

Provisions taking effect in 2013 include:

- The Consumer Operated and Oriented Plan (CO-Op) program goes into effect, with the objective of creating non-profit health insurance companies run by members;

- The uniform rules on claims and eligibility verification take effect.

Provisions taking effect in 2014 include:

- The temporary high-risk pool and the temporary reinsurance program for employees over age 55 end; the American Health Benefit Exchanges and Small Business Health Options Program (SHOP) exchanges go into operation;

- Employers can offer financial rewards to employees who participate in wellness programs;

- Companies with over 200 employees can auto-enroll employees into health plans offered by the employer, although employees can opt out of these plans;

- Persons whose income is below 133% of the federal poverty level are eligible for Medicaid;

- Persons whose income does not exceed 400% of the federal poverty level are protected by a sliding scale of maximum out of pocket payments;

- Limits are imposed on waiting periods for coverage and deductibles for small-group health plans;

- Medicare tax rate increases to 2.35% for high-income taxpayers ($250,000 for joint returns, $200,000 for other returns). High-income taxpayers are also subject to a 3.8% assessment on their unearned income;

- FSA contributions for medical expenses are limited to $2,500 per year (adjusted for inflation);

- Uniform rules about health plan enrollment, disenrollment, and premium payments will be published;

Provision taking effect in 2016 is:

- States can get together to create "health choice compacts" where insurers can sell policies in any state within the compact; the objective is increasing competition and thereby decreasing premiums.

Provision taking effect in 2018 is:

- Insurers have to pay an excise tax on "Cadillac plans" (EGHPs that cost more than $10,200 for individual or $27,500 for family coverage).

## [N] The Future of PPACA

The PPACA is an extremely controversial statute, and its legality became the subject of many challenges. In mid-2012, the Supreme Court decided a case about the legality of the "individual mandate" (i.e., the requirement that individuals either maintain health insurance coverage—under an EGHP or by individual purchase—or pay a monetary penalty). The Supreme Court's majority found that Congress exceeded its power under the Commerce Clause when it imposed the individual mandate. However, the mandate was upheld as a valid tax, so most of the PPACA was not struck down. There was one exception: the provision imposing financial penalties on states that reject Medicaid expansion was found invalid. [*National Federation of Independent Business v. Sebelius*, consolidated with *Dep't of HHS v. Florida*, and *Florida v. Dep't of HHS*, 132. S. Ct. 2566 (2012). See John H. Cushman Jr., *Supreme Court Lets Health Law Largely Stand*, NYTimes.com (June 28, 2012)]

At press time in 2013, challenges to PPACA continued, often premised on religious freedom arguments. The Supreme Court remanded the case of *Liberty University v. Lew* to the Fourth Circuit to consider challenges to PPACA's individual and employer mandates. The Fourth Circuit found PPACA to be constitutionally acceptable, because the Commerce Clause permits Congress to regulate compensation in interstate commerce. The Fourth Circuit rejected religious arguments, finding PPACA to be a neutral law of general applicability that does not substantially burden free exercise of religion. [*Liberty Univ. v. Lew*, No. 12-2346, 2013 WL 3470532 (4th Cir. July 11, 2013)]

Small business owners and individuals in six states sued the IRS under the Administrative Procedures Act to prevent expansion of health care subsidies, arguing that the state exchanges prevent low-income residents in those states from obtaining subsidies. The IRS said that tax credits are available whether a person buys coverage on a federal or a state Exchange. [*Halbig v. Sebelius*, No. 1:13-cv-00623-RWR (D.D.C. filed May 2, 2013); see Jenna Greene, *Small Business Owners Sue IRS Over Obamacare*, The BLT (Blog of Legal Times) (May 2, 2013) (law.com)]

## [O]  Implementing Regulations

After the passage of PPACA, HHS and the other agencies involved in health law enforcement issued several major regulations. Several of them took the form of interim final regulations (IFRs). Frequently, HHS, DOL, and the Treasury joined in issuing regulations affecting all of their areas of responsibility. (For state laws passed in the first half of 2011 to conform to PPACA, see CCH Benefits, *States Move to Implement Health Reform Provisions*, <http://www.hr.cch.com/news/benefits/072011.asp> (July 20, 2011). For example, Delaware, Kentucky, Minnesota, and Virginia adopted statutes requiring health plans to cover participants' adult children up to age 26; Hawaii, Indiana, Maryland, and Oklahoma passed protective laws for employees with preexisting conditions; and Connecticut, Georgia, Idaho, and Maine imposed medical loss ratios that insurers must satisfy.)

### [1]  T.D. 9491

T.D. 9491, 75 Fed. Reg. 37188 was issued by HHS, DOL, and the Treasury on June 28, 2010. This rule deals with pre-existing condition exclusions (PCEs), limits on policy benefits, rescission, provider choice, and emergency services.

T.D. 9491 expands the definition of PCE used in earlier regulations, so now it includes denying either inclusion in the plan or coverage for a particular benefit. PCEs also include limitations and inclusions based on information about health status, such as information deriving from health exams or pre-enrollment questionnaires. [T.D. 9491, 75 Fed. Reg. 37188 (June 28, 2010)]

DOL published a model notice that can be used to inform employees of their right to re-enroll in the plan if they lost coverage after exhausting the lifetime maximum benefit: <http://www.dol.gov/ebsa/lifetimelimitsmodelnotice.doc>; this information can also be included in enrollment materials for the plan as long as the information is displayed prominently. According to T.D. 9491, once a person is covered under a plan, coverage cannot be rescinded except as a result of fraud or an intentional misrepresentation of material fact.

### [2]  T.D. 9489

T.D. 9489, 2010-29 I.R.B. 55, provides a set of Interim Final Rules for grandfathered plans, (i.e., those already in existence when PPACA was signed), effective July 12, 2010. To take advantage of its grandfathered status, an eligible plan must include a statement in plan materials explaining that the plan is grandfathered, describing plan benefits, and giving contact information for questions and complaints. T.D. 9489 includes a model notice that can be used for this purpose, including disclosure that a grandfathered plan does not provide all of PPACA's consumer protections, such as providing preventive health services without cost sharing by the plan participant—but that even grandfathered plans are subject to certain PPACA requirements, such as eliminating lifetime dollar limits on benefits. The notice must inform its recipients that they can direct their questions about requirements for grandfathered plans, and how plans can lose grandfathered status, to the health plan administrator—and must give contact information for the administrator.

### [3]  T.D. 9493

T.D. 9493 is another tri-agency IFR, published July 19, 2010. It deals with the required coverage of preventive services, effective September 17, 2010. Plans that provide care through a network of providers can either refuse to cover preventive services out-of-network, or can impose cost-sharing requirements on out-of-network preventive services. However, in-network preventive services must be provided without any kind of cost sharing: no deductibles, coinsurance, or copayments. The preventive services requirements apply to plans that are not grandfathered, or that lose their grandfathered status. [T.D. 9493, 2010-35 I.R.B. 273, 73 Fed. Reg. 41726 (July 19, 2010). See <http://www.HealthCare.gov/ center/regulations/prevention.html> for a list of preventive care services that PPACA-compliant plans must offer without imposing cost-sharing on participants.]

### [4]  Loss Ratios

A health insurance company's loss ratio is the percentage of the premiums that it collects that it distributes in the form of benefits. The higher the loss ratio, the more of the premium is used to provide health care; the lower the ratio, the more of the premium that goes toward the insurer's operating costs and profits.

The PPACA appropriates $250 million for states to sanction insurers who demand unreasonable premium increases. [*Health Insurance Rate Review: Lowering Costs for American Consumers and Businesses*, <http://cciio.cms.gov/ resources/factsheets/rate_review_fact_sheet.html>] Rebates are required if MLR falls below 85% (large group) or 80% (small group). Rebates can take the form of a premium credit, a check for a lump sum, or a lump sum reimbursement to the account the enrollee used to pay the premium. A CMP of $100/day can be imposed for each individual affected by the violation of the reporting and rebate requirements. [75 Fed. Reg. 74864 (Dec. 1, 2010); see CCH Pension & Benefits, *Medical Loss Ratio Rules will Affect 64 Million Covered by Group Plans* (Nov. 29, 2010) (benefitslink.com)]

According to HHS, the factors in determining the reasonableness of a premium increase include whether the insurer's loss ratio is at least 80%, and whether it offered substantial evidence for the necessity of the increase. Insurers must post on their Websites if their proposed increase exceeds the threshold, and insurers whose increases are deemed unreasonable must post this fact on their sites and explain why they sought such a large increase. They must also disclose their spending on medical care, expected future claims costs, and administration (including executive compensation). [PPACA § 1003; Regulations at 75 Fed. Reg. 81009 (Dec. 23, 2010) and 76 Fed. Reg. 29964 (May 23, 2011)]

DOL Technical Release 2011-04 explains how EGHPs should treat rebates that they receive from insurers that failed to meet the loss ratio requirement. The first rebates were due on August 1, 2012. If the policy is owned by the health plan or a trust, the policy—and the rebates—are plan assets. If the employer is the policyholder and the policy and plan documents describe part or all of the rebate as property of employer that will be respected. But if the ownership of the rebate is ambiguous, factors such as who paid the premiums will be consulted. If the entire premium is paid from trust assets, the entire rebate becomes a plan asset. (Funds allocable to employee contributions are also considered plan assets.) But if the employer pays the full premium, no part of the rebate becomes a plan asset. The employer cannot recover a rebate that exceeds the total premiums and expenses paid by the employer.

Rebates that are plan assets can either be distributed to all participants, including ex-participants; but if it is not cost-effective to include ex-participants, the rebate can be allocated entirely to current participants. And if distributing the rebate is not cost-effective, the funds can be used to pay future premiums or enhance benefits. The technical release says that it might be permissible to use rebates from a policy to reduce expenses for the same participants and beneficiaries covered by another policy under the same plan—but it violates the duty of loyalty to use rebates from one plan for the benefit of participants in another plan. [Guest article, Deloitte's Washington Bulletin, *Labor Department Advises ERISA Plans How to Handle Medical Loss Ratio Rebates* (Dec. 12, 2011) (benefitslink. com)]

Since PPACA passed, the number of states with authority to reject unreasonable increases has risen from 30 to 37. In early 2012, HHS said that independent experts determined that premiums in Alabama, Arizona, Pennsylvania, Virginia, and Wyoming were unreasonable because not enough was spent on medical care and quality improvement. New Mexico rejected a request for a 9.7% premium increase, reducing it to 4.7%; Connecticut limited a proposed 12.9% increase to 3.9%; and New York reduced a 12.7% increase to 8.2%. [<http://companyprofiles.healthcare.gov.> For general rate review information, see <http://www.healthcare.gov/law/features/costs/rate-review/> and Rebecca Moore, *HHS Deems Rate Hikes in Five States Unreasonable*, plansponsor.com (Jan. 13, 2012)]

The KFF estimated that about $1.3 billion in rebates would be issued under PPACA, with $426 million going to purchasers of individual policies, $541 million to large employers (an average of $72 per person) and $377 million to smaller employers (an average of $76 per person). Goldman Sachs estimated that there would be $1.2 billion in rebates. When employers receive a rebate, they are supposed to pass through part of the rebate to the employees. However, self-insured plans do not get rebates and the KFF estimated that in 2011, 60% of employees who had work-related coverage were in self-insured plans. [Anna Wilde Mathews, *Health Insurers Plan Over $1 Billion in Rebates*, WSJ.com (Apr. 27, 2012)]

### [5]  Waivers

Until 2014, HHS has the power to permit plans to set limits on annual benefits so that coverage can continue with minimal impact on premiums. On June 28, 2010, the Federal Register published an interim final regulation (IFR) allowing EGHPs to impose an annual limit on essential benefits—but the limit must be at least $750,000 (for years beginning between September 30, 2010 and September 23, 2011), at least $1.25 million (years beginning between September 24,

2011 and September 23, 2012) and at least $2 million (years beginning between September 24, 2012 and January 1, 2014).

Waivers are not available with respect to lifetime dollar limits on essential benefits, only on annual limits.

The administration allowed "mini-med" plans (plans with low benefit caps) relief on benefit limits and loss ratios on the theory that without these one-year waivers employees would lose coverage or would have to pay much higher premiums, and at least low-wage earners would have some access to insurance in the interim until the Exchanges begin in 2014. [Janet Adamy and Avery Johnson, *Rules Eased for Some Health Plans*, WSJ.com (Nov. 23, 2010)]

On June 17, 2011, the administration announced that it would stop granting new waivers. (At that point, the number of waivers had reached 1,433.) Organizations that already had a waiver, and anyone who got a waiver approved by September 22, 2011, could retain a one-year waiver and apply for extensions through 2013, but no further applications would be taken after September 22, 2011. [Janet Adamy, *Obama Administration to End New Waivers Under Health Law*, WSJ.com (June 18, 2011)]

# CHAPTER 19

# HEALTH INSURANCE CONTINUATION AND PORTABILITY (COBRA AND HIPAA)

## § 19.01  INTRODUCTION

The two dominant mechanisms for providing health insurance coverage in our society are employee group health plans (EGHPs) and the Medicare system for senior citizens and the disabled. However, there are many instances in which a person has lost coverage under one EGHP and is not (or is not yet) covered by another one, and is not eligible for Medicare. Individual health coverage is expensive—and furthermore, the ex-employee or a member of his or her family might have a medical condition that makes insurance harder to obtain or raises its cost even higher.

Two federal statutes, the Comprehensive Omnibus Budget Reconciliation Act (COBRA) and the Health Insurance Portability and Accessibility Act (HIPAA) work together to make the transition between EGHPs, or from EGHP coverage to individual health coverage, at least somewhat smoother. Both statutes impose responsibilities on the employer, so the health plan administrator must be aware of these duties. If the health care reform bill remains in effect, it will create a new paradigm under which, for the first time, employers have a duty to provide health insurance, and individuals have a duty to purchase health insurance.

As part of the ongoing attempt to stimulate the economy, Congress passed the ARRA, American Recovery & Reinvestment Act of 2009 [Pub. L. No. 111-5, Title III] early in 2009, providing subsidies for COBRA premiums. See § 19.02[F]. This was a temporary program that expired in 2010.

The Supreme Court refused to review an unpublished Sixth Circuit case about conversion of group to individual life insurance after an employee's termination. The Sixth Circuit held that people who were denied life insurance benefits under policies that were not converted could not sue the plan administrator for breach of ERISA fiduciary duty. In this case, the employee took a leave of absence after a disabling stroke in 2001, and was fired in March 2002 when he could not return to work after the leave of absence. To convert his group policy to individual coverage, he would have had to have made an election within 31 days of receiving conversion notice; apply to the insurer; and take over premium payments. The Sixth Circuit held that COBRA does not require the employer to provide notice of the right to convert group life insurance. The requirement of COBRA notice applies only to health insurance. [*Walker v. Federal Express Corp.*, 133 S. Ct. 851 (2013); see Bloomberg BNA Pension & Benefits Daily, *Supreme Court Declines to Review Individual Relief Ruling Under ERISA* (Jan. 8, 2013) (law.com)]

Not strictly in the COBRA context, but dealing with issues of continued coverage, the Children's Health Insurance Program Reauthorization Act of 2009 (CHIPRA; Pub. L. No. 111-3, signed February 4, 2009) requires employers to amend their plans to permit special enrollment of employees and dependents if they lose their Medicaid or SCHIP coverage—or if they become eligible under Medicaid or SCHIP for the state to assist them with paying EGHP premiums and other financial responsibilities. [CHIPRA, Pub. L. No. 111-3; see EBIA Weekly,

*New Law Establishes Additional Special Enrollment Rights, Notice, and Disclosure Obligations for Group Health Plans* (Feb. 4, 2009) (benefitslink.com)]

CHIP has been financed until 2015, and PPACA did not alter this. PPACA essentially leaves the COBRA system intact (although the provision in the House version of the legislation that would have extended COBRA subsidies until 2014 when the exchanges become available was not adopted in the final version).

When employers report the value of health coverage on employees' W-2 forms, the reported value is based on the COBRA cost of the coverage, whether or not any part of the coverage is taxable. [Notice 2012-9, 2012-4 I.R.B. 315; see Birgit Anne Waidmann, *IRS Provides Guidance on Mandatory Reporting of the Value of Health Coverage on 2012 Forms W-2*, PricewaterhouseCooper HRS Insight (Jan. 6, 2012) (benefitslink.com)]

## § 19.02  COBRA CONTINUATION COVERAGE

Continuation coverage is the right of a "qualified beneficiary" (i.e., a former employee or his or her spouse and dependents) to maintain coverage under the employer's group health plan after a "COBRA event." Some of the important legal questions include which employers are subject to COBRA; which employees, ex-employees, and their family members are permitted to make a COBRA election; and what the employer's responsibilities are to furnish notice of COBRA rights.

### [A]  Qualifying Events

A COBRA event is either personal or work-related and poses a threat to coverage under the ordinary circumstances:

- The employee is terminated or has hours reduced (unless termination is for gross misconduct);

- The employee divorces or becomes legally separated;

- The employee's dependent child ceases to be covered by the plan (usually because of "aging out");

- The employee's employer files for bankruptcy protection;

- The employee becomes Medicare-eligible (which entitles the employee's spouse to COBRA coverage);

- The employee dies (obviously, this is only a COBRA event for the survivors).

Although COBRA does not define "gross misconduct," the standard is probably the same as "willful misconduct"—substantial and willful disregard of the employer's best interests. [See, e.g., *Chatterjee v. School Dist. of Philadelphia*, 170 F. Supp. 2d 509 (E.D. Pa. 2001); *Lloyd v. Hanover Foods Corp.*, 72 F. Supp. 2d 469 (D. Del. 1999); *Pomales v. Celulares Telefonica, Inc.*, Civ. No. 02-1256 (D.P.R. 2005); see Rebecca Moore, *Termination for Gross Misconduct Not COBRA Qualifying Event*, plansponsor.com (May 19, 2006)]

For example, the District Court for the District of Kansas held that a nurse, who was fired for "mooning" a male colleague who had insulted her, could not be denied COBRA. Her conduct violated work rules but did not impair the interests of the hospital or violate criminal laws. The District Court for the District of Massachusetts upheld denial of COBRA coverage to a one-time college professor who used fraudulent credentials to get hired, misused a college credit card, and plead guilty to charges of fraud including student aid fraud. The district court held that this conduct was outrageous enough to be characterized as gross misconduct, and showed reckless disregard of the college's best interests. [*Compare Stormont-Vail Health Care Inc. v. DOL-EBSA*, No. 10-4052-RDR, 2010 WL 2132004 (D. Kan. May 27, 2010), *with Moore v. Williams College*, No. 09-cv-30208-MAP, 2010 WL 1375401, discussed in Fred Schneyer, *Professor's COBRA Denial Suit Thrown Out*, plansponsor.com (May 28, 2010)]

An employee who did not return to work after an injury was not fired immediately. However, because she was no longer receiving a paycheck, she stopped making payroll deduction contributions under the employer's plan. About three months after the injury, the employer, in its role as plan administrator, said that coverage would be terminated unless the employee submitted a check for the missed contributions. She did not, and was told that she would be fired because she was unable to work. After her termination, the employer retroactively canceled the coverage, effective more than two months before the termination date. She received a COBRA notice shortly after termination, but alleged that she should have been notified when she failed to return to work because termination of coverage was caused by non-payment of premiums. The District Court for the District of Massachusetts found that the COBRA notice was timely, but denied summary judgment for the employer because the plaintiff's argument, that her hours were returned to zero when she did not return to work, triggered COBRA entitlement. The court said that her argument of having to send a check instead of having premiums deducted from her paycheck was a loss of coverage might be valid. [*Barnett v. Perry*, No. CCB-11-cv-00122, 2011 WL 4593743 (D. Mass. Nov. 16, 2011); see EBIA Weekly, *Court Considers Whether Reduction of Hours to Zero Triggered COBRA Notice* (Dec. 1, 2011) (benefitslink.com)]

An employee terminated after taking FMLA leave for multiple surgeries did not receive a COBRA notice for almost 10 months. According to the employer, as a result of a clerical error, her group coverage continued after her termination. The employer denied that she was COBRA-eligible because she had an individual policy. The Eastern District of Pennsylvania ruled that employees are not required to prove harm as a result of notice failures. The court also said that individual coverage did not make her ineligible under COBRA, which refers to coverage under another group plan, or an individual plan with high employer involvement. [*Fleck v. WILMAC Corp.*, CIVIL ACTION NO. 10-05562, 2012 WL 1033472 (E.D. Pa. Mar. 27, 2012); see EBIA Weekly, *Individual Policy Did Not Preclude Employee From Receiving COBRA Coverage* (Apr. 12, 2012) (benefitslink.com)]

The Eastern District of Arkansas held that sending a COBRA notice shortly after an employee went on military deployment was not evidence that the employee was fired for military service, contrary to USERRA requirements (see § 1.18). The notice referred to "termination of employment" that could have been either voluntary or involuntary. The district court said that, under DOL regulations, an employee on active military service is considered to be on leave of absence. [*Dorris v. TXD Servs., LP*, No. 1:10-cv-93-KGB, 2012 WL 3149106, 96 Empl. Prac. Dec. (CCH) P44,581 (E.D. Ark. Aug. 1, 2012); see HighRoad blog, *Court Examines Interplay of COBRA and USERRA* (Oct. 10, 2012) (benefitslink. com); Gwen Cofield, *COBRA Notice Is Not Culprit in Claim That Termination Violated USERRA*, Smart HR (Aug. 8, 2012) (benefitslink.com)]

Whenever a "qualifying event" occurs, anyone who performs services for the employer and is covered by the EGHP must be given COBRA rights—including partners, self-employed people who are allowed to participate in the plan, and eligible independent contractors.

If a cafeteria plan includes health benefits, COBRA applies only to benefits actually elected by a plan participant, not those that he or she declines. COBRA does not apply to Flexible Spending Accounts, Medical Savings Accounts, or to plans that are substantially limited to qualified long-term care services, because these are not deemed to be conventional health plans. The District Court for the District of Kansas ruled that a long-term disability plan does not have to give COBRA notices; although it is a welfare benefit plan, it is not a "group health plan," because a group health plan provides medical care rather than benefits for persons who are unable to work. [*Ernisse v. L.L. & G., Inc.*, Case No. 07-2579-JAR, 2008 WL 4499974 (D. Kan. Sept. 29, 2008); see EBIA Weekly, *Employer Was Not Required to Provide a COBRA Election Notice for Its Long-Term Disability Plan* (Oct. 16, 2008) (benefitslink.com)]

When a person makes a COBRA election, health insurance coverage continues under the EGHP—but the employee, not the employer, pays the premium. (The employer can also agree to subsidize the COBRA premium, e.g., as an early retirement incentive.) The employer can impose an administrative charge of up to 2% of the premium, but no other fees or charges. The COBRA premium is set once a year, in advance.

The increased number of layoffs means that many people receive a smaller severance package than they expected. It used to be common for companies to pay COBRA premiums or offer six months to a year of post-termination health coverage but that is now rare. [Anna Prior, *Employers Cut Back on Aid to Laid-Off Workers*, WSJ.com (Aug. 9, 2009)]

There are three basic methods of structuring continuing coverage in a severance package. The "choice method" gives a choice between COBRA coverage and an alternative set out in the severance package; consecutive coverage offers a certain number of months of coverage as if the ex-employee were still active, followed by 18 months of COBRA coverage; or concurrent coverage (e.g., 12 months of coverage at the active rate, followed by six months of COBRA coverage, for a total of 18 months of continuation coverage). The plan and paperwork for the severance must make it clear how the coverage is structured.

## [B]  Covered Businesses

Businesses are subject to COBRA if they have 20 or more employees on a typical workday, and if they maintain a group health plan (either insured or self-insured). Most of the states (all except Alabama, Alaska, Arizona, Delaware, Hawaii, Idaho, Indiana, Michigan, Montana, Virginia, and Washington) have COBRA expansion statutes that require companies with fewer than 20 employees to provide the equivalent of the federal COBRA notice and continuation coverage rights.

The length of the required period of continuation coverage ranges from four months (Arkansas) to 36 months (in California, Minnesota, Nevada, New Hampshire, North Dakota, South Dakota, and Texas). [Kaiser Family Foundation, *Expanded COBRA Continuation Coverage for Small Firm Employees, 2010*, See <http://scorecard.assetsandopportunity.org/2013/measure/expanded-cobra-coverage>]

The District Court for the District of Idaho held that an employer violated COBRA by providing only three months of COBRA coverage rather than the required 18 months. Although the employer had fewer than 20 employees, it was part of a controlled group with over 20 employees. The district court rejected the employer's argument that the employee signed a COBRA election form agreeing to three-month coverage and paid only three months of premiums. [*Warnecke v. Nitrocision LLC*, No. 4:10–cv–00334–CWD. 2012 WL 5987429 (D. Idaho Nov. 29, 2012); see Gwen Cofield, Smart HR blog, *Common Control Means COBRA's Small Employer Exception Does Not Apply* (Dec. 7, 2012) (benefitslink.com)]

The 20-employee figure does not include employees working "under the table." Furthermore, the District Court for the District of Arizona ruled that vacation and holiday pay can be considered in determining whether someone has worked 1,250 hours and therefore is a full-time employee eligible for COBRA, but vacation and holiday pay do not count as hours worked for determining the number of full-time employees and thus whether the employer is subject to COBRA. [*Galati v. D & R Excavating, Inc.*, No. CV 04-1684-PHX-NVW, 2006 U.S. Dist. LEXIS 28723 (D. Ariz. 2006)]

The Sixth Circuit held, in mid-2007, that in rare cases it will be possible for an employer with fewer than 20 employees to be sued under COBRA—for example, if the employer's statements or behavior would lead a reasonable plaintiff to believe that he or she had COBRA coverage. But the actual plaintiff lost her case. She alleged that she overheard corporate managers talking about providing benefits to another employee; but even if this conversation did take place, no one said anything about COBRA coverage for the plaintiff. [*Thomas v. Miller*, 489 F.3d 293 (6th Cir. 2007), discussed in Roy F. Harmon III, *COBRA Requirements May Apply to Employers Having Less Than 20 Employees* (June 28, 2007) (benefitslink.com)]

The Northern District of Ohio found an employer grossly negligent for not knowing that it was not subject to COBRA because it had fewer than 20 employees. The district court refused to dismiss a qualified beneficiary's equitable estoppels claim. A corporate officer was laid off in early 2009. After receiving a COBRA notice, he made the election and paid premiums for 13 months. He filed a complaint with the Department of Labor against his former employer (the court record did not explain what kind of complaint). The DOL informed the company that it was not subject to COBRA, so the insurer retroactively terminated the plaintiff's coverage. He was reimbursed for the premium payments, but had more than $7,000 of medical expenses. The district court held that in general, a mere mistake will not support a claim for equitable estoppel—but the employer knew how many employees it had and the insurance contract made the employer responsible for complying with state and federal law. [*Hanysh v. Buckeye Extrusion Dies, Inc.*, No. 4:11 CV 528, 2012 WL 3852569 (N.D. Ohio Sept. 5, 2012); see Gwen Cofield, *Employer Can't Pin COBRA Compliance on Insurer, Court Points Out*, Smart HR (Sept. 18, 2012) (benefitslink.com)] Self-insured plans are subject to COBRA, too. The "premium" for them is a reasonable estimate, using reasonable actuarial assumptions, of the cost of providing health coverage for employees similarly situated to the qualified beneficiary.

Continuation coverage must be the same as active employees receive, although continuation coverage can change as the underlying plan changes. If the employer terminates or reduces coverage in an EGHP, qualified beneficiaries must be allowed to elect coverage under whatever plan the employer continues to maintain for similarly situated active employees. The employer cannot condition continuation coverage on submission of evidence of insurability. [See I.R.C. § 4980B(f)(2)(D)]

## [C]  Family Rights

The employee's spouse and children may also have independent rights to maintain coverage: for instance, after a divorce, when the former employee dies, or when the former employee becomes eligible for Medicare. (In this situation, the former employee no longer has COBRA rights—but, because Medicare does not cover spouses or dependents, these family members have COBRA rights.)

The one-time employee can exercise the COBRA election on behalf of his or her spouse and children, and the spouse can exercise the election on behalf of the children. However, only plan participants, not their beneficiaries, are entitled to receive penalties if the plan administrator fails to provide COBRA notice. [*Wright v. Hanna Steel Corp.*, 270 F.3d 1336 (11th Cir. 2001)]

As a result of the Supreme Court's June, 2013 decision striking down part of the federal Defense of Marriage Act (DOMA; see § 18.06), same-sex married couples are entitled to spousal coverage under COBRA. If a state "mini-COBRA" law is in effect, it may also require coverage of registered domestic partners or civil union partners.

## [D]  Duration of Coverage

COBRA specifies minimum obligations that employers must meet; they always have discretion to provide additional coverage. The basic duration of COBRA continuation coverage for ex-employees is 18 months, starting with the qualifying event. In some instances, ARRA will increase the duration of coverage: see § 19.02[F]. However, if the ex-employee satisfies the Social Security Administration definition of total disability (basically, is incapable of substantial gainful activity), the employee and family members are entitled to 29 months of continuation coverage, not 18. But for the 11 months after the end of the normal 18-month term, the employer can lawfully charge the employee 150% of the premium, not just the normal 102%.

Qualified beneficiaries can get 29 months of continuation coverage with respect to the same qualifying event if they are qualified with respect to a termination of employment or a reduction in hours; they became disabled within the first 60 days of COBRA continuation coverage; and they give the plan administrator a copy of the determination of disability within 60 days of the date it was issued and also within the initial 18-month COBRA period.

Notification is crucial. The District Court for the Northern District of Ohio held in 2013 that COBRA coverage of the participant's spouse would not be extended to 29 months when the notification was not given, even though the plan administrator had actual knowledge that the participant was disabled. The plan explicitly required notice of disability as a condition of the extension. [*Rayle v. Wood Cnty. Hosp.*, No. 3:12-cv-02052-0, 2013 WL 1654898 (N.D. Ohio 2013). See EBIA Weekly, *Actual Notice of Employee's Disability Insufficient to Extend COBRA Coverage When Plan's Notice Procedures Were Not Followed* (May 16, 2013) (benefitslink.com)]

If the qualifying event is the ex-employee's becoming eligible for Medicare, his or her qualified beneficiaries are entitled to 36 months of continuation coverage. See Rev. Rul. 2004-22, 2004-10 I.R.B. 553, providing that Medicare entitlement is not a second qualifying event for a beneficiary who would not have lost coverage under the plan as a result of Medicare entitlement. If the plan does not terminate coverage for the employee's spouse, the spouse is entitled to only 18 months of continuation coverage because there has not been a second qualifying event.

However, COBRA entitlement ends if:

- The employer terminates and does not replace the EGHP for active employees (in effect, there is no longer any plan whose coverage can be continued);

- The qualified beneficiary fails to pay the COBRA premium;

- The qualified beneficiary gains coverage under another EGHP;

- The employee becomes eligible for Medicare (although family members still have COBRA rights).

Utah held that although COBRA eligibility can be terminated based on qualifying for Medicare, it cannot be terminated based on qualifying for Medicaid; public policy is to prevent insurers from transferring responsibility to the Medicaid program, which is publicly funded. [*Mellor v. Wasatch Crest Mut. Ins. Co.*, 2009 Utah 5 (Utah 2009); see EBIA Weekly, *Health Plan Insurer Could Not Terminate COBRA Coverage When Qualified Beneficiary Became Covered Under Medicaid* (Feb. 12, 2009) (benefitslink.com)]

The Supreme Court ruled, in *Geissal v. Moore Med. Group* [524 U.S. 74 (1998); on remand, 158 F. Supp. 2d 957 (E.D. Mo. 2001). In 2003, the Eighth Circuit required Moore to pay the Geissal estate over $200,000 in attorneys' fees and court costs, 338 F.3d 926 (8th Cir. 2003)], that the employer can terminate COBRA coverage if the employee gains access to other coverage AFTER making a COBRA election, but cannot terminate COBRA eligibility on the basis of coverage (for instance, coverage under a spouse's plan) that the employee had access to before the COBRA election.

## [E]   COBRA Regulations

The IRS published important Proposed Regulations at 63 Fed. Reg. 708 (Jan. 7, 1998), adopted as 26 C.F.R. § 54.4980B-1 to conform COBRA to HIPAA (see below), the Small Business Job Protection Act [Pub. L. No. 104-188], and various other statutes. As a result of these changes, qualified beneficiaries can get 29 months (rather than the basic 18 months) of COBRA coverage with respect to the same qualifying event if:

- They are all qualified with respect to a termination of employment or a reduction in hours;

- They became disabled (as defined by the Social Security Administration) within the first 60 days of COBRA continuation coverage;

- They gave the plan administrator a copy of the determination of disability within the initial 18-month COBRA period and also within 60 days of the date the determination was issued.

During the 11-month extension, the employer can charge a premium that is 150% of the applicable premium, whereas the employer is limited to charging 102% of the premium during the 18-month basic COBRA period. Charging 150% is not considered premium discrimination on the basis of health status, so I.R.C. § 9802(b) is not violated. If there is a second qualifying event during a disability extension, then COBRA coverage can last for 36 months, with the 150% premium charged until the end of the 36-month period.

HIPAA entitles children born to, or adopted by, covered employees during a period of COBRA coverage to be covered by COBRA. The child's maximum coverage period runs from the date of the employee's qualifying event, and not from the child's birth or adoption. The effect is that the child's COBRA coverage ends at the same time as the coverage of other family members.

## [F]    TAAP and ARRA Subsidy Programs

Acknowledging that the high cost of COBRA premiums can be burdensome on people who have lost their jobs, Congress has enacted two subsidy programs to reduce these costs.

The earlier program, the Trade Act of 2002 [Pub. L. No. 107-210] enacted a tax credit under Code § 35: workers who were displaced by factors such as overseas business or imports could qualify for a tax credit equal to 65% of the COBRA premium. The credit was refundable (i.e., persons with no tax liability could receive a refund). The credit could be submitted to the health plan, so the qualifying individuals would have to pay only 35% of the COBRA premium. The Trade Act credit applied only to persons not covered by other government or private insurance programs; aged 55–64 and receiving guarantee payments from the PBGC; or unemployed and entitled to Trade Adjustment Assistance benefits under the Trade Act. [Jerry Geisal, *Congress Extends Health Premium Subsidies*, workforce.com (Oct. 1, 2008) (benefitslink.com)]

The Trade Adjustment Assistance Program (TAAP) was expanded in May 2009. Benefits include unemployment benefits, retraining, and 80% of the cost of medical insurance for workers who lost their jobs because of their employer's overseas move or foreign competition.

The economic stimulus plan enhanced TAAP, so that displaced workers can receive as much as 156 weeks of training and up to 156 weeks of cash payments. The tax credit for health insurance premiums rises from 65% to 80%. A wage subsidy of up to $12,000 (rather than the $10,000 under prior law) is provided for up to two years so workers over 50 can be re-employed at a reduced salary. Unemployment benefits can be paid for two and a half rather than two years.

White-collar workers as well as manufacturing workers can qualify for benefits. Late 2010 legislation, H.R. 6517, extended the federal Health Coverage Tax Credit Subsidy for health insurance premiums, but only for six weeks (through February 12, 2011). [Jerry Geisel, *Obama Signs Extension of Health Insurance Tax Credit*, Business Insurance (Dec. 30, 2010) (benefitslink.com)] Congress did not take further action, so the credit reverted to the 65% level on February 13, 2011. [Jerry Geisel, *Health Insurance Subsidy Reverts to 65%*, Business Insurance (Feb. 22, 2011) (benefitslink.com)]

Pub. L. No. 112-40, the Trade Adjustment Assistance Extension Act of 2011 (October 21, 2011), reauthorized the TAA program until December 31, 2013. Coverage for TAA/ATAA eligible individuals and people who receive pensions from the PBGC is extended until the later of their maximum COBRA period or January 1, 2014. However, it does not appear that terminated COBRA coverage is revived by this legislation.

For months beginning after February 12, 2011, this statute also increases the Health Coverage Tax Credit (HCTC); (see Code § 35) to 72.5% of the health insurance premiums of eligible individuals and their families. (The previous level was 65%, although for months before February 13, 2011, it was 80%). In general, the HCTC is available to persons eligible under TAA or the Alternative Trade Adjustment Assistance Program (ATAAP), and to retirees who receive their pensions from the PBGC and who have lost employer coverage. It is not clear, but apparently some people who received the 65% credit will be eligible for the additional 7.5% for certain months. The HCTC is scheduled to expire January 1, 2014, when the Exchanges are expected to be in operation. [See Allison Ullman, Seth Perretta, and Joel Wood, *Recently Enacted Trade Adjustment Assistance Extension Act of 2011 Affects Health Coverage Tax Credit and COBRA Continuation Coverage*, Crowell & Moring LLP (Nov. 10, 2011) (benefitslink.com); EBIA Weekly, *Legislation Amends the Health Coverage Tax Credit* (Oct. 27, 2011) (benefitslink.com)]

Pub. L. No. 111-5, the American Recovery and Reinvestment Act of 2009 (ARRA), created a temporary program to provide up to nine months of federally funded COBRA subsidies (later extended to 15 months by the Department of Defense Appropriations Act of 2010, Pub. L. No. 111-118). Employers advanced 65% of the COBRA premium and later claimed a payroll tax credit; the employees paid the other 35%. After two extensions, under the Temporary Extension Act of 2010 (TEA), Pub. L. No. 111-144 and the Continuing Extension Act of 2010, Pub. L. No. 111-157, the program expired in 2010. [Walecia Konrad, *Patient Money: Health Law Preserves COBRA Plan*, NYTimes.com (Apr. 2, 2010); Bucks Editors, *How the Health Care Bill Affects COBRA*, Bucks Blog NYTimes.com (Mar. 24, 2010)]

## § 19.03   COBRA AND THE FMLA

Taking FMLA leave [see Chapter 38] is not in and of itself a COBRA-qualifying event. But if an employee who was covered by the EGHP before or during the FMLA leave fails to return to work after the FMLA leave, there is a qualifying event for this person (and any dependent at risk of losing health coverage) as of the last day of the FMLA leave. The employer is not allowed to make the ex-employee reimburse the employer for health premiums paid during the leave.

However, there is no qualifying event if, while the employee is on leave, the employer eliminates EGHP coverage for the entire group of workers the person on leave belonged to. The rationale is that the worker would have lost health coverage even if he or she had not taken leave.

The qualifying event for an employee who does not return to work occurs on the last day of the FMLA leave, and the regular COBRA notice must be given. The qualifying event occurs even if the employee had an obligation to pay health insurance premiums during the leave but failed to do so. State laws that require a longer leave than the 12-week FMLA period are disregarded in determining whether a qualifying event has occurred.

## § 19.04   COBRA NOTICE

### [A]   Generally

One of the most important tasks in COBRA administration is timely issuance of the proper notices, as provided by I.R.C. § 4980B(f)(6)(A) and ERISA § 606. There are three types of COBRA notice: one given to employees as soon as they become eligible for participation in the health plan (informing them of COBRA rights they might have in the future), the one given to a qualified beneficiary in connection with a COBRA event, and the notice of rights under ARRA. The employer has an obligation to notify the plan administrator when employment-related qualifying events occur, such as when an employee is terminated or laid off, or when the company files in Chapter 11 for bankruptcy protection. The responsibility for reporting personal qualifying events, such as divorce or separation, rests on the qualified beneficiary.

There are three timing requirements. The employee must give notice to the plan that a qualifying event has occurred within 60 days of the event. At that point, the employer has 30 days to notify the plan administrator that there has been a qualifying event for which COBRA notice must be provided; and the plan administrator has a further 14 days to actually issue the notice.

A COBRA notice should explain:

- Who can be a qualified beneficiary;

- What events trigger the right to continuation coverage;
- How and when to elect coverage;
- The right to reject the coverage (e.g., for financial reasons);
- Rights of the other qualified beneficiaries if one qualified beneficiary waives the election;
- Obligation to pay the premiums on time;
- How long the coverage will last;
- Events that will allow the employer to terminate continuation coverage;
- If the health plan satisfies PPACA's minimum coverage and affordability standards;
- How to purchase coverage on a health insurance Exchange;
- Eligibility criteria for premium tax credits under PPACA.

Notice must be furnished to covered employees and covered spouses on the earlier of two dates: 90 days from the first date of coverage (or the date on which the plan first becomes subject to COBRA, if that happens later), or the date on which the plan administrator has to provide a COBRA election notice.

The election notice must be furnished within 44 days of the qualifying event—or the date the qualified beneficiary ceases to be covered under the plan, if the plan's terms date the start of COBRA coverage from the loss of plan coverage.

Plans must provide notice when coverage is unavailable. The notice of unavailability must be given within 14 days of receiving notice of a qualifying event when the plan denies coverage—whether or not the notice was given in proper form. Termination notices must be given as soon as practicable after the plan administrator determines that continuation coverage is ending.

See DOL Tech Release 2013-02 (May 8, 2013), <http://www.dol.gov/ebsa/newsroom/tr13-02.html> for a model form that can be used to satisfy the requirement of informing employees of their COBRA rights consistent with PPACA. [See PLC Employee Benefits & Executive Compensation, *DOL Issues Model Exchange Notices, Updated COBRA Election Notice and Related Guidance* (May 2013) (benefitslink.com)]

Although the COBRA notice must be written, an oral waiver of the election has been held to be valid and enforceable. [*Hummer v. Sears, Roebuck & Co.,* 1994 U.S. Dist. LEXIS 3659 (E.D. Pa. Mar. 21, 1994)] However, in 2002 the Eighth Circuit ruled that while the initial COBRA notice (given when a person becomes eligible for health plan participation) must be in writing, the notice about the availability of the COBRA election can be given orally to a terminating employee. [*Chesnut v. Montgomery,* 307 F.3d 698 (8th Cir. 2002)]

A recurring issue is what must be done to demonstrate an adequate attempt to furnish notice.

Mailing to the employee's last known address is generally considered sufficient, at least if the Post Office does not return the notice. Even if the employee does not in fact receive the notice, the employer is not liable if a proper attempt to notify was made:

- Notice was not sent to the plaintiff's last known address when it was sent to the P.O. Box he used when he was on active military duty, but the box was no longer active. The district court held that, because letters to the P.O. Box were marked "undeliverable" and the employer sent at least one letter to the correct address before the COBRA notice was mailed, the employer did not act in good faith when it failed to follow up on the returned letters. [*Boddicker v. Esurance Ins. Servs., Inc.*, CIV. 09-4027-KES, 2011 WL 6372863 (D.S.D. Dec. 20, 2011); see EBIA Weekly, *Court Imposes Statutory Penalties for Failure to Send COBRA Election Notice to Employee's Last-Known Address* (Jan. 5, 2012) (benefitslink.com)]

- The Southern District of Illinois required a case to go to trial when there was a factual dispute over the employee's last known address. The employee informed the employer about a change of address, which was entered into the payroll system. (The system for insurance purposes was separate.) Later, however, the employee herself put the wrong address on her health insurance enrollment form. The TPA sent COBRA notice to the address in the insurance records, but the plaintiff had moved. EBIA Weekly suggests asking all employees to confirm their current address in writing and having the employer confirm that the entity that gives the notices has that address. [*Munsamy v. Rittenhouse Senior Living of Indianapolis, LLC*, No. 1:10-cv-294-RLY-TAB, 2012 WL 1035019 (S.D. Ind. Mar. 27, 2012); see EBIA Weekly, *COBRA Claim Continues to Trial to Resolve "Last-Known Address" Issues* (May 17, 2012) (benefitslink. com)]. The Eastern District of Arkansas ruled against a former employee who said that he was not given COBRA notice. The employer created a presumption of receipt of the notice by submitting its log of notices, date-stamped by the Postal Service. The employer stated that whenever its TPA was notified of a COBRA qualifying event, it processed, printed, and mailed the election notice to the beneficiary, then showed the log to a USPS clerk who verified that the mailed items corresponded to the log entries. The employee's testimony that he did not receive the notice could not overcome the presumption of receipt. [*Hearst v. Progressive Foam Techs., Inc.*, 2010 WL 143751 (E.D. Ark. Jan. 12, 2010); see EBIA Weekly, *COBRA Election Notice Presumed Received Based on Date-Stamped Evidence of Mailing by U.S. Postal Service* (Feb. 25, 2010) (benefitslink.com)]

Although an employee received COBRA notice 64 days after termination, it was dated much earlier, suggesting that it was actually sent within the 44-day time frame. The employer continued to pay the premiums for two months, until the end of the month when the notice was received. The Eastern District of Michigan refused to impose penalties because the employee did not lose anything as a result of the arguable untimeliness of the notice. EBIA's comment is that the statute merely requires the employer to furnish the notice within 44 days, even when it received later—but many courts have imposed statutory penalties even without a showing of prejudice. [*Pethers v. Metro Lift Propane*, No. 09-CV-10516, 2010 WL 3023887 (E.D. Mich. July 29, 2010); see EBIA Weekly, *Court Refuses to Award Penalties for Late COBRA Election Notice Without Showing of Harm or Prejudice* (Aug. 19, 2010) (benefitslink.com)]

The District Court for the District of Idaho held that the duty to provide COBRA notice falls on the plan administrator; in this case, the employer was not the administrator and, as long as it notified the administrator of a qualifying event, the employer was not liable for the administrator's alleged failure to send the notice to the right address. [*Mirceau v. Idaho*, 2011 WL 3439178 (D. Idaho 2011); see EBIA Weekly, *Employer Was Not Responsible for Providing COBRA Election Notice* (Sept. 8, 2011) (benefitslink.com)]

The District Court for the District of Maryland treated the employer, not the TPA, as the plan administrator responsible for providing COBRA notice. The SPD named the employer as plan administrator, and the TPA's service agreement said that it merely provided administrative and claims processing services.. According to the TPA's record, the notice was sent five days after the end of the 44-day election period, but no penalties were assessed because the employee did not show prejudice from the delay. Furthermore, the employee received a new package offering a retroactive election when it was discovered that the first notice had not been received. [*Myers v. Carroll Indep. Fuel Co.*, Civil Action No. RDB 09-1633, 2011 WL 43085 (D. Md. Jan. 6, 2011); see EBIA Weekly, *Court Declines to Impose Penalties Against TPA for Late Election Notice* (Jan. 20, 2011) (benefitslink.com)]

Department of Labor Advisory Opinion 99-14A allows the health plan to satisfy the notice requirement by sending a single notice to multiple beneficiaries living at the same address: e.g., one first-class letter covering the employee, spouse, and dependent children. But there must either be a separate election notice in the mailing for each qualified beneficiary, or an explanation of their independent rights to elect coverage. [See <http://www.dol.gov/ebsa/regs/AOs/ao1999-14a.html>; see, e.g., *McDermott v. Case Windham Pub. Schs.*, 225 F. Supp. 2d 180 (D. Conn. 2002), *Starr v. Metro Sys. Inc.*, 2004 U.S. Dist. LEXIS 15744 (D. Minn. Aug. 10, 2004)—but an administrator who is on notice of the employee's divorce cannot treat notice to the employee as notice to his or her ex-spouse: *Phillips v. Saratoga Harness Racing Inc.*, 233 F. Supp. 2d 361 (N.D.N.Y. 2002)]

Qualified beneficiaries must be given a period of at least 60 days to either accept or waive continuation coverage. The election period must begin no later than the time EGHP coverage would end if there were no election. In other words, notice must be given early enough to prevent any gap in coverage. The Eleventh Circuit has ruled that if the COBRA notice fails to specify the 60-day period, then the right to make the election extends indefinitely. [*Branch v. G. Bernd Co.*, 955 F.2d 1574 (11th Cir. 1992)] The Fifth Circuit ruled that an employer can have a COBRA election period of any length, as long as the period is at least 60 days. Participants in a plan that failed to set an election deadline could therefore make a COBRA election at any time during the 18 months following the qualifying event. [*Lifecare Hosps. Inc. v. Health Plus of La. Inc.*, 418 F.3d 436 (5th Cir. 2005)]

If an ex-employee needs only a certain number of months of COBRA coverage (usually the waiting period for eligibility in a new plan), COBRA does not permit the ex-employer's plan to require the ex-employee to pay for a full 18 months of retroactive coverage. [*Popovits v. Circuit City Stores Inc.*, 185 F.3d 726 (7th Cir. 1999)]

The first premium payment is not due until 45 days after the election. Qualified beneficiaries get an automatic grace period of at least 30 days, during which coverage cannot be terminated for nonpayment of premiums—even if the underlying EGHP has a shorter grace period. But if the plan provides a longer grace period, the employee must be permitted to take advantage of it.

There is no statute of limitations in the COBRA statute, so a basic issue in these cases is when the cause of action accrued. The Western District of Kentucky wanted to borrow the statute of limitations from the most analogous state statute, the Kentucky Unfair Claims Settlement Practices Act, but that law didn't have a statute of limitations either, so the magistrate judge applied the statutory five-year default, which is used in cases where no other time period is prescribed. [*Gilbert v. Norton Healthcare, Inc.*, 2012 U.S. Dist. LEXIS 17553 (W.D. Ky. Feb. 10, 2012); see Roy F. Harmon III, *Five Year Limitations Period For COBRA Notification Lapse* (Feb. 20, 2012) (benefitslink.com)]

## [B] Penalties for Notice Failure

The Internal Revenue Code and ERISA § 502(g) impose a penalty of $110 per day per beneficiary for noncompliance, subject to a maximum of $220 per family per day. There is also a limit of the smaller of $500,000 or 10% of the amount the employer paid (or incurred obligations for) its EGHPs in the preceding year. Furthermore, a health plan that does not conform to COBRA does not generate I.R.C. § 162 "ordinary and necessary business expenses." Therefore, the employer is denied a deduction for health plan costs.

The penalty is imposed on the employer. It can also be imposed on the individuals responsible for administering the plan or providing benefits under it, if those individuals have contractual responsibility for running the plan. A third-party administrator (TPA) would fall into this category unless factors beyond the administrator's control prevented the notice from being given.

There is a cap of $2 million for all plans administered, for an administrator who fails to satisfy all the COBRA requirements, but who is not guilty of willful neglect and who did have reasonable support for his or her decisions.

The penalty can be reduced or waived if no one had reason to know that the appropriate notices were not given, or if the failure to notify was corrected within 30 days after a responsible person became aware of the failure.

In addition to the statutory penalties, any person or organization can be sued under ERISA Title I by someone who lost coverage because of the defendant's actions or inaction.

In the Hostess bankruptcy case, the Eighth Circuit held that Hostess did not have to pay penalties for initial and election notice failures because, in effect, the plaintiff received two years of free health coverage. Because of an inefficient clerical system, Hostess could not prove that plaintiff Sean Deckard received an initial COBRA notice or that he received an election notice when he was terminated in September 2006. His termination was not processed for almost two years, so he remained in the health plan (receiving about $19,000 worth of benefits) without having to pay premiums. When Hostess discovered the mistake, his coverage was cancelled retroactive to his termination, and the health insurer tried to recover the benefits from health providers, who moved against Deckard. Hostess reinstated his coverage. CIGNA returned about $2,400 recovered from health providers; Deckard got back approximately $230 of the $693 he had been required to pay. Deckard filed a claim in the Hostess bankruptcy case seeking COBRA penalties for the six months when the coverage was cancelled. The Eighth Circuit held that penalties were inappropriate: Hostess had acted in good faith, Deckard's damages were not related to lack of notice, and he benefited by receiving two years of free health coverage. [*In re Interstate Bakeries Corp.*, 609 F.3d 1069 (8th Cir., 2013); see Gwen Cofield, *COBRA Penalties Not Needed Due to 'Free' Coverage*, Smart HR blog, (Feb.1, 2013) (benefitslink.com)]

Books-a-Million was ordered to pay heavy penalties because the Northern District of Alabama found its COBRA notice procedure inefficient and unwieldy. A second trial on attorneys' fees was ordered. The process required the benefits department to manually cross-reference three lists to determine who was entitled to COBRA notice. The plaintiff, Tondelaya Evans, was given conflicting information, and Books-a-Million could not prove that a COBRA notice was sent. The penalty was $75 per day for 506 days (a total of $37,950), because of the employer's bad faith and intentional withholding of notice after there had been many chances to correct the notice failure. [*Evans v. Books-A-Million*, Civil Action No. CV-07-S-2172-S, 2012 U.S. Dist. LEXIS 154596 (N.D. Ala., Oct. 29, 2012) and

2012 WL 5954118 (N.D. Ala., Nov. 28 2012); see Gwen Cofield, *COBRA Penalties of $126K Assessed Due to Notice Failure COBRA Penalties and Legal Costs Due to Notice Failure, Evasive Answers Rise to $126K*, Smart HR blog (Dec. 3, 2012) (benefitslink.com)]

The Southern District of New York held that an employer's mistake in not sending a COBRA notice for four months did not constitute retaliation for the employee's filing a Title VII charge with the EEOC. The employer successfully argued that, when the mistake was discovered, the ex-employee was offered retroactive COBRA coverage, and she did not make a COBRA election after receiving notice. The district court limited Title VII claims to actions that affect current employmenet or the ability to be employed in the future, and this plaintiff was not seeking employment: she had filed for Social Security Disability benefits. [*Thompson v. Morris Heights Health Ctr.*, No. 09 civ 7239 (PAE), 2012 WL 1145964 (S.D.N.Y. Apr. 6, 2012); see EBIA Weekly, *No Title VII Retaliation Claim for Employee Who Received Late COBRA Notice* (Apr. 19, 2012) (benefitslink.com)]

IRS Form 8928 must be filed to self-report any failure to satisfy the Code § 4980B requirements to provide COBRA continuation coverage. The form must be filed by any employer, group health plan, plan administrator, or plan sponsor that is subject to the excise tax for failure to provide continuation coverage. Form 8928 is due by the due date for the responsible party's federal income tax return. Interest is charged on taxes not paid by the due date (even if the responsible party obtained an extension of time to file by using Form 7004), and there are also penalties for late filing of returns and late payment of the tax. [Form 8928 instructions, <http://www.irs.gov/instructions/i8928/ch01.html> (December 2009)]

Until 2010, there was little IRS enforcement of compliance with COBRA rules, but now that self-reporting on Form 8928 is required, the IRS has stepped up audits of COBRA compliance. On March 26, 2012, the IRS posted information for IRS examiners to use in assessing COBRA compliance, instructing the examiners that they must request copies of the employer's COBRA manual, COBRA notices, health plan documents, and the company's internal audit procedures. Examiners also have the power to request many other documents, such as data about everyone who has had a qualifying event and how beneficiaries receive COBRA notice. If coverage was denied on the grounds of gross misconduct, the examiner can check with local unemployment benefits administrators to see if those benefits were denied for misconduct as well. Examiners are also allowed to contact COBRA-qualified beneficiaries for information about the plan. [Thompson Media, *15 Things the IRS May Ask Employers in a COBRA Coverage Audit* (Mar. 28, 2012) (benefitslink.com)]

## § 19.05  HEALTH INSURANCE PORTABILITY

### [A]  Coverage

An important focus of the PPACA is to permit previously uninsured individuals, or individuals who once had insurance coverage but had to drop it, to resume their insured status. The PPACA also restricts the use of pre-existing condition exclusions (PCEs): denials or limitations of coverage based on the applicant's or insured person's health status. However, an earlier statute already tackled some of the same concerns.

The Health Insurance Portability and Accountability Act of 1996 (HIPAA) [I.R.C. Chapter 100, §§ 9801–9806], also known as the Kennedy-Kassebaum Act, copes with the situation in which a person leaves employment with one employer, gets another job, and experiences health care bills before he or she is covered by the new employer's plan, or where the new plan might exclude coverage of the ailment as a pre-existing condition.

For plan years beginning after June 30, 1997, the HIPAA "creditable coverage" requirement in effect allows coverage to carry over from one plan to the other, as long as employees use COBRA (or other means) to make sure that there is never a gap of 63 days or more in coverage.

Although plans can control costs by imposing pre-existing condition limitations, the scope of the limitation is restricted. Under HIPAA, the most stringent definition of "pre-existing condition" that a plan can apply is a mental or physical condition for which medical advice, diagnosis, care, or treatment was sought during the six-month period before the enrollment date. In general, the maximum duration for a pre-existing condition limitation is 12 months from the enrollment date for the current health plan. The enrollment date is the earlier of the first day of the waiting period for enrollment or the date of actual enrollment. Late enrollees (who fail to enroll in the plan during the open enrollment period, or the first period of eligibility) can be subject to an 18-month rather than a 12-month pre-existing condition limitation.

The Genetic Information Nondiscrimination Act (GINA, Pub. L. No. 110-233) requires genetic testing information to be kept separate from other medical data.

"Creditable coverage" means coverage from another EGHP, from individual health insurance, from Medicare Part A or B, or from Medicaid. Health plan coverage ceases to be creditable, and therefore is not portable to a new plan, if there is a break of 63 days or more during which the employee is completely without health insurance. The so-called affiliation period (the waiting period after a new employee enrolls in a new health plan) is not considered a period of being uninsured.

The mental health parity requirement applies to HIPAA.

## [B] Nondiscrimination Requirements

HIPAA forbids discrimination in benefits in health plans. (In this context, discrimination is closer to the Title VII sense than the pension plan sense of not favoring highly compensated employees.) Under HIPAA, it is unlawful for a plan to base its rules for eligibility or continued eligibility, or its definition of the waiting period, on an employee's or dependent's:

- Health status;
- Physical or mental health condition;
- Claims experience;
- Past receipt of health care;
- Medical history;
- Genetic information;
- Evidence of insurability;
- Disability.

None of these factors can be used to increase the premium or other contribution that an individual plan participant has to pay, when compared to other similarly situated participants. HIPAA does not limit the premiums or co-payments that employers can require participants to pay. It is also legitimate to offer employees discounts, rebates, or reductions in their co-payment obligations based on their participation in health promotion and disease prevention programs (such as smoking cessation or weight loss programs).

Almost six years after interim and proposed regulations were issued, DOL, HHS, and the IRS teamed up again to issue Final Regulations covering HIPAA's nondiscrimination rules for wellness programs. The Final Regulations, appearing in the Federal Register on December 13, 2006.

The final rule allows health incentives under wellness plans that satisfy certain criteria. (See § 18.19[G]) Wellness programs are acceptable if they are available to all similarly situated individuals, and either the sponsor does not offer rewards, or the rewards are not dependent on health status. Acceptable provisions include reimbursement of gym membership and health risk assessments that are not punitive. Programs that do not fit into one of these safe harbors can still qualify under HIPAA—e.g., as long as the program is reasonable, and the reward does not exceed 20% of the total cost of coverage paid by the employer and employee. [Lockton Compliance Alert, *Feds Finally Finalize HIPAA Nondiscrimination Regulations, Clarify Wellness Programs*, <http://www.?2007_Final%20Nondiscrim%20Regs_Inc@20Wellness_v2.pdf> (Jan. 9, 2007); Rebecca Moore, *Feds Clarify HIPAA Rules for Wellness Rewards*, plansponsor.com (Dec. 13, 2006)]

It is common for executives' employment agreements to specify their entitlement to various kinds of payments on termination. When there is no agreement, the employer often provides severance benefits, including subsidized health care coverage, in exchange for release of employment-related claims. Sometimes the employer will continue to cover the ex-employee as if he or she were still an active employee for a certain number of months or years—often, as long as severance pay continues. When this coverage ends, the ex-employee is eligible to make a COBRA election. Another approach is to subsidize COBRA coverage, usually by the employer making direct premium payments to the insurer. Before PPACA, self-insured employers had to be careful to avoid discrimination in favor of HCEs. If the company paid 18 months of premiums for HCEs but only one month for rank and file workers (or no payment at all for non-HCEs), the HCE might be taxed not only on the premiums but on all health benefits. To avoid this, employers often made cash severance payments that could, but did not have to be, used to pay COBRA premiums. Some employers "gross up" these amounts (increase the payment to account for the ex-employee's tax obligations). Pre-PPACA, the non-discrimination rules did not apply to insured plans. But, as a result of PPACA, all non-grandfathered insured group plans are now subject to anti-discrimination requirements and penalties are imposed on the employer, not the employee receiving the discriminatory benefits. The penalty can be as much as $100 per day of noncompliance times the number of employees suffering discrimination, with a cap of the lower of $500,000 or 10% of the employer's aggregate cost of EGHPs for the preceding year. The penalty is waived for small employers (fewer than 50 employees) or if the employer acted with reasonable cause and did not neglect the requirements. The nondiscrimination rules were supposed to take effect on the first day of the plan year after the year in which the IRS issued regulations—but, as of late 2012, the regulations had not been issued. [Steven Friedman, Terri Solomon, and Stephanie Kastrinsky, Littler Mendelson, *Employers with Insured Health Plans Must Take Care in Providing Healthcare Subsidies to Departing Executives* (Oct. 29, 2012) (benefitslink.com)]

## [C]  Insurers' Obligations

One of Congress's rationales in passing HIPAA was that employers, especially small companies, often had difficulty getting insurance—and once they had insurance, they often faced cancellation of coverage or at least excessively high rate increases.

HIPAA imposes obligations on insurers with respect to group health policies. The rules are different for "small employer" coverage (2–50 employees) and "large employer coverage" (groups of more than 50 employees). HIPAA's general requirement is that insurers who sell small employer coverage within a state must sell to all small employers who want to purchase the coverage, although there is no corresponding obligation to sell to would-be large-group buyers.

In either the small- or the large-group market, the insurer has an obligation to renew coverage or continue it in force as long as the purchase chooses, unless the purchaser:

- Stops paying the premiums;

- Commits fraud related to the policy;

- The insurer withdraws from the relevant market within the state;

- Plan enrollees move outside the service area for a network plan;

- (In a plan based on association membership) enrollees cease to be members of the association;

- The purchaser violates the rules on participation or contributions to the plan.

If an insurer discontinues one kind of group coverage but maintains others, all affected plan sponsors, participants, and beneficiaries are entitled to 90 days' notice of the discontinuance. The plan sponsor must be given the option to purchase the other coverage that the insurer offers in that market.

The insurer must act uniformly, without considering the existing or potential health problems of plan participants and beneficiaries, or the claims experience of the plan sponsor. An insurer that chooses to discontinue all of its coverage in the small- or large-group market must give state insurance regulators 180 days' notice of intent to discontinue. An insurer that withdraws will be barred from re-entering the market for five years. This requirement is imposed to prevent insurers from leaving and re-entering the market purely based on their own needs.

The Ninth Circuit held that Montana's "little HIPAA" law, Code § 33-22-526, is preempted by ERISA, but did not decide whether a state statute that provided more protection than HIPAA would be preempted. [*Fossen v. Blue Cross and Blue Shield of Montana, Inc.,* 660 F.3d 1102 (9th Cir. 2011); see Haynes and Boone Blogs, *Ninth Circuit Holds that Federal HIPAA Preempts Montana's "Little HIPAA" Law* (Feb. 2, 2012) (benefitslink.com)]

As the various PPACA provisions take effect, HIPAA's insurance provisions will be less significant, although the privacy rules will retain their significance. For example, PPACA's insurance Exchanges (also known as the Marketplace) are designed to make it easier for both individuals and businesses to compare insurance plans and obtain coverage. At first, the business Marketplace will be limited to small business purchasers, but PPACA is drafted so that eventually large businesses will also be able to get Marketplace coverage.

## [D]   Exceptions to the Portability Rule

Plans of certain types are not subject to the portability rules, because they are not deemed to be health benefit plans:

- Plans that offer accident and/or disability insurance;
- Liability insurance plans;
- Insured plans that provide medical benefits that are secondary or incidental to other benefits;
- Limited scope plans providing, e.g., dental, vision, or long-term care benefits;
- Coverage that is limited to a specified disease or illness;
- Fixed-indemnity plans (e.g., hospitalization insurance);
- Medicare Supplementary (Medigap) insurance.

Plans that cover only a single current employee are not subject to portability requirements.

Flexible Spending Accounts (FSAs) are "excepted benefits" under ERISA §§ 732 and 733(c) and I.R.C. §§ 9831 and 9832(c). Therefore, health insurance portability is not required for these plans. [See the "clarification of regulations" jointly issued by the IRS, the Pension and Welfare Benefit Administration, and the Department of Health and Human Services at 62 Fed. Reg. 67688 (Dec. 29, 1997)] The FSA is excepted from HIPAA if the employee's maximum FSA benefit for the year does not exceed twice the employee's salary reduction election for the year, as long as the employee has other EGHP coverage and as long as the FSA provides at least some benefits that are not "excepted benefits."

## [E]   Penalties and Enforcement

Health plans are subject to a penalty tax, under I.R.C. Chapter 100, for failure to comply with the HIPAA portability rules.

HHS' interim final rule, effective November 30, 2009 for violations occurring on or after February 18, 2009, increases the HIPAA CMP schedule. Penalties range from $100 to $50,000 per violation, with a cap of $1.5 million for all violations of the same requirement in a calendar year. Under prior law, lack of knowledge of the violation was an affirmative defense. The Interim Final Rule allows covered entities and their associates to be penalized up to $50,000 even if they did not know there was a violation. If the entity did not know of the violation, the range is $100 to $1.5 million, but if there was reasonable cause for the violation and there was no willful neglect, the minimum penalty is $1,000. In the presence of willful neglect, where the violation was corrected within 30 days of discovery, the minimum is $10,000; the minimum is $50,000 if willful neglect was not corrected within 30 days. [74 Fed. Reg. 56123 (Oct. 30, 2009). ] The 2010 Notice of Proposed Rulemaking, 75 Fed. Reg. 40868 (July 14, 2010) discussed in § 19.05[F], below, also discusses CMPs.

## [F] Data Privacy and Security

As discussed in § 26.07, HIPAA also penalizes misuse of Protected Health Information (PHI). "Covered entities"—typically, an insurer or self-insured plan—are not permitted to use or disclose PHI without the consent of the subject of the information. [See 45 C.F.R. Parts 160 and 164 and HHS's FAQ at <http://www.hhs.gov/ocr/hipaa/privacy.html>. Information about privacy enforcement was added in April 2007: see <http://www.hhs.gov/ocr/privacy/enforcement>] The privacy rules are limited to health plans, not other welfare benefit plans (including disability plans), and PHI can lawfully be used for payment, treatment, or health care operations. In an insured EGHP, the insurer rather than the plan is the covered entity. The covered entity must provide privacy notices to plan members explaining their rights to data confidentiality.

A final enforcement rule was published, at 71 Fed. Reg. 8390 (Feb. 16, 2006), effective March 16, 2006, covering the HIPAA privacy, security, and EDI rules and the rules about unique identifiers.

The Health Information Technology for Economic and Clinical Health (HITECH) Act, part of the economic stimulus bill, takes effect February 17, 2010. The HITECH Act expands the privacy and security provisions of HIPAA, and includes a new regulatory structure for electronic medical records. The HITECH Act increases the civil monetary penalties (CMPs) that can be imposed for violations and the individuals whose PHI has been disclosed improperly can collect a share of the civil penalties.

Business associates of HIPAA-covered entities are subject to the same privacy rules as the covered entities are, including criminal penalties for violations. A business associate that discovers that a covered entity with which it has a business relationship has breached the security or confidentiality rules is supposed to take steps to cure the breach—or terminate the contract. Notice must be given to individuals whose PHI was improperly disclosed; and if 500 or more people were affected by the breach, disclosure to HHS and the news media is also required. Covered entities and their business associates who use electronic health records are required to provide an accounting of how the electronic records were used and disclosed in the previous three years. HHS' Office of Civil Rights continues to enforce HIPAA compliance, but state Attorneys General have also been given the power to enforce HIPAA by bringing suit in federal district court. [Troutman Sanders LLP, *Keeping up with Recent Legislation: Numerous Changes to Group Health Plans Required*, plansponsor.com (Feb. 27, 2009)]

Many courts have held that there is no private cause of action for violation of HIPAA's privacy rules: enforcement must come from the government—HHS for civil actions, the Department of Justice for criminal cases. [See, e.g., *Acara v. Banks*, 470 F.3d 569 (5th Cir. 2006); *Walker v. Gerald*, CIVIL ACTION NO. 05-6649 SECTION "B," 2006 WL 1997635 (E.D. La. June 27, 2006); *Makas v. Miraglia*, 05 Civ. 7180 (DAB)(FM), 2007 WL 152092 (S.D.N.Y. Jan. 23, 2007); *Univ. of Colo. Hosp. Auth. v. Denver Publ. Co.*, 340 F. Supp. 2d 1142 (D. Colo. 2004); *Lester v. M&M Knopf Auto Parts*, 04-CV-850S, 2006 WL 2806465 99 (W.D.N.Y. Sept. 28, 2006); *Gliatta v. Stein*, 2006 WL 2482019 (W.D.N.Y. Aug. 25, 2006); *Johnson v. Kachelmeyer*, 03-CV-356S, 2006 WL 625837 (W.D.N.Y. Mar. 9, 2006); *Cassidy v. Nicolo*, 03-CV-6603-CJS, 2005 WL 3334523 (W.D.N.Y. 2005)]

The Northern District of Georgia dismissed a HIPAA claim against a third-party administrator (TPA) that allegedly improperly gave the plaintiff's employer information from her FMLA file, which included medical and therapy records. The employer wanted the information in connection with a separate sex discrimination suit filed by the plaintiff. The contract between the employer and the TPA said that information collected under the FMLA plan would only be used to administer that plan, not for employment-related actions unless authorized by the employee. The Northern District said that the TPA was neither a covered entity nor a business associate of a covered identity because FMLA and STD plans are not covered entities. Other claims against the TPA were also dismissed, although the decision did not address the merits of claims against the employer. [*Floyd v. SunTrust Banks, Inc.*, CIVIL ACTION NO. 1:10-CV-2620-RWS , 2011 WL 2441744 (N.D. Ga. June 13, 2011); see EBIA Weekly Archives, *TPA's Disclosure of FMLA File to Employer Was Not Subject to HIPAA Privacy Rule* (June 30, 2011) (benefitslink.com)]

Data confidentiality protects the patient against improper disclosure of PHI by health care providers and insurers. The related subject of "data security" is tackled by a final rule appearing at 68 Fed. Reg. 8333 (Feb. 20, 2003). Covered entities are required to carry out technical, physical, and business procedures to protect PHI from unauthorized access (e.g., by hackers), and to have compliance programs so their employees carry out the program.

After issuing interim final rules in 2009 [RIN 009-AB56, 75 Fed. Reg. 42740 (Aug. 24, 2009) and a 2010 Notice of Proposed Rulemaking dealing with privacy, security, and enforcement [RIN 009-AB56, 75 Fed. Reg. 40868 (July 14, 2010), at the beginning of 2013 HHS' Office of Civil Rights (OCR) published an omnibus restatement of the HIPAA privacy and security rules, reflecting the HITECH Act Amendments. Covered entities and their contractors and subcontractors are subject to civil and criminal penalties for violations of the privacy, security, and breach notification rules. Security breaches must be reported to HHS each year, and large-scale breaches must also be reported to the individuals involved and to the news media. There are requirements for using encryption and destruction of obsolete information to prevent unauthorized persons from accessing protected health information (PHI). Penalties assessed for failure to notify individuals of breach of their PHI and failure to notify the media when required have increased. The penalty ranges between $100 and $50,000 per violation in situations where the covered entity did not know of the violation (and could not have known by exercising reasonable diligence). If there was reasonable cause for the violation, and there was no willful neglect, the penalty range is $1,000 to $50,000. Where willful neglect occurred, the penalty range is $10,000–$50,000 if the violation was corrected on a timely basis—and at least $50,000 for offenses of willful neglect that were not timely corrected. However, in each penalty category, there is a cap of $1.5 million on total penalties for all violations of the same provision. The actual penalty imposed within the penalty range for a particular offense depends on factors such as the nature and extent of the violation and the extent of the harm it caused.

This rule makes some changes to conform HIPAA to the Genetic Information Nondiscrimination Act (GINA) Title I (health coverage) and Title II (employment). For example, GINA treats genetic information as health information and health plans must be informed that it is forbidden to use or disclose genetic information for underwriting purposes. (However, the information can be used for underwriting of long-term care insurance.) The final rule became effective on March 26, 2013 and covered entities must comply by September 23, 2013 [78 Fed. Reg. 5566 (Jan. 25, 2013) Cynthia Marcotte Stamer, Solutions Law Press HR & Benefits Update, *OCR Publishes Long-Anticipated Omnibus Restatement of HIPAA Privacy, Security, Breach Notification & Enforcement Rules* (Jan. 13, 2013) (benefitslink.com); Katherine Georger, Holland & Hart LLP News Update, *New HIPAA Final Rule Implements GINA Restriction on Use and Disclosure of Genetic Information for Underwriting Purposes* (Jan. 23, 2013) (benefitslink. com)]

In early 2011, HHS' Office for Civil Rights (OCR) issued a Notice of Final Determination imposing a $4.35 million CMP on a health center in Maryland. The penalty was imposed for violations of the HIPAA privacy rule and refusal to cooperate with the OCR investigation. OCR received many complaints that the health center denied them access to copies of their PHI, making it difficult for them to get health care because their new doctors could not get necessary information. The more stringent provisions of the HITECH Act were applied for periods after February 18, 2009. The penalty for denying access to individuals' information was $1.35 million; the penalty for non-cooperation was $1.5 million each for the years 2009 and 2010. According to EBIA, this was the first CMP imposed for a HIPAA privacy violation, although some earlier cases had been settled. [HHS Notice of Final Determination (Feb. 4, 2011); HHS Notice of Proposed Determination (Oct. 20, 2010); HHS News Release (Feb. 22, 2011), available at <http://www.hhs.gov/ocr/privacy/hipaa/news/cignetnews.html>. See EBIA Weekly, *HHS Assesses $4.35 Million in First-Ever Civil Penalty for HIPAA Privacy Rule Violations* (Feb. 24, 2011) (benefitslink.com)]

The District Court for the District of Connecticut entered a protective order in an FMLA retaliation case. The plaintiff said that she was fired for taking leave after her husband's surgery; the employer said that she was fired for leave abuse (claiming FMLA leave while vacationing in Mexico). The employer sought discovery of the husband's medical records, which the plaintiff said were both protected by HIPAA and irrelevant, because he was not a party to the suit. The district court entered the protective order, permitting disclosure of the husband's condition only for the period between the surgery and the plaintiff's termination. The employer was forbidden to use the information for non-litigation purposes and ordered to return or destroy the data after the resolution of the suit. [*Tavares v. Lawrence & Mem'l Hosp.*, No. 3:11-CV-770 (CSH),2012 U.S. Dist. LEXIS 146614(D. Conn. Oct. 10, 2012); see Wolters Kluwer Law & Business News Center, *Husband's Medical Records Must Be Disclosed To Former Employer In Employee's Lawsuit Based On FMLA* (Nov. 2, 2012) (benefitslink.com)]

In 2012, BlueCross BlueShield (BCBS) of Tennessee agreed to pay HHS $1.5 million to settle HITECH charges about a 2009 data breach. Fifty-nine unencrypted hard drives were stolen from a disused Chattanooga call center. The drives contained PHI (such as Social Security numbers and diagnoses) for more than a million BlueCross customers. However, there is no indication that the data was misused. BCBS reported the breach as required, and has spent over $17 million since then on investigations and improving its systems. The settlement requires a 450-day correction program for review and improvement of security procedures. More settlements can be expected in the future—since opening its breach notification Website in February 2010, HHS has gotten an average of 17 breach reports a month, and many of the breaches are under audit. [HHS Website for reporting breaches: <http://www.hhs.gov/ocr/privacy/hipaa/administrative/breachnotificationrule/brinstruction.html>; see Beth Moskow-Schnoll, Jean C. Hemphill, Evan W. Krick, and Edward I. Leeds, *Data Breach Leads to First HITECH Enforcement Settlement*, Ballard Spahr (Mar. 19, 2012) (benefitslink.com); Shannon Green, *$1.5M HHS Data Breach Settlement Is First Under HITECH Law*, Corporate Counsel (Mar. 21, 2012) (law.com)]

On June 26, 2012, HHS settled its first HIPAA enforcement action against a state agency when the Alaska DHHS agreed to pay $1.7 million and improve its security procedures. HHS received a HITECH Act breach report after a USB drive, possibly containing PHI was stolen from an agency employee's car. The investigation showed that the agency had inadequate security, did not do risk analysis, did not train its workers in security measures, or encrypt data as required. [PLC, *Theft of USB Flash Drive Results in $1.7 Million HIPAA Security Settlement* (June 27, 2012) (benefitslink.com)]

In late 2102, HHS settled HIPAA charges against the Massachusetts Eye and Ear Infirmary when a personal laptop containing unencrypted PHI of patients and research subjects was stolen. The Infirmary agreed to pay $1.5 million over a three-year period, and to comply with a correction plan to improve security measures and usage of portable devices. HHS news release, <http://www.hhs.gov/ocr/privacy/hipaa/enforcement/examples/meei-agreement.html> (Sept. 17, 2012); see EBIA Weekly, *Unencrypted Laptop Leads to $1.5 Million HIPAA Security Settlement* (Oct. 11, 2012) (benefitslink.com)]

On January 2, 2013, the OCR announced that the Hospice of North Idaho was required to pay a $50,000 penalty for potential violations in connection with theft of a laptop containing unencrypted PHI. This was the first settlement in a case where the breach involved fewer than 500 people. [Cynthia Marcotte Stamer, Solutions Law Press HR & Benefits Update, *OCR Publishes Long-Anticipated Omnibus Restatement of HIPAA Privacy, Security, Breach Notification & Enforcement Rules* (Jan. 13, 2013) (benefitslink.com)]

Idaho State University agreed to a $400,000 settlement of Office of Civil Rights charges when electronic health information of at 17,500 patients was vulnerable to unauthorized access for a period of 10 months. The university failed to perform accurate assessments or analyses; did not have adequate security procedures; and dismantled firewalls that could have protected the patients' privacy. [Kim Stanger, *Idaho University to Pay $400,000 for HIPAA Violations*, Holland & Hart News Update (May 22, 2013) (benefitslink.com)]

In late 2011, a pilot program of HIPAA privacy and security audits of health plans and providers was launched with a small number of audits to refine the audit protocols. Subsequent audits, to be completed by the end of 2012, will rely on the revised protocols. Covered entities that receive HIPAA audit notification letters are given only 10 business days to produce the information and documents. All audits include fieldwork at the site, on 30–90 days' notice. Most visits last three to 10 business days and include interviews of key personnel. Companies under audit are required to give the auditor a copy of its privacy and security policies. The entity is given 10 business days to review the draft report and discuss it with the auditor. A final audit report is submitted to HHS within 30 days after the reviewed entity comments.

The list of entities that have been audited will not be made public, nor will audit findings be disclosed in a way that discloses the identity of the reviewed entity. The results are supposed to be used to find entities that require technical assistance rather than to impose penalties—although, if serious compliance problems are uncovered, HHS might address them. [Christine A. Williams, *HIPAA Audits Come With Short Turnaround Times*, Perkins Coie News (Dec. 19, 2011) (benefitslink.com)]

# CHAPTER 20

# DISABILITY PLANS

## § 20.01  INTRODUCTION

Because of an acute illness, a chronic illness, or an injury (work-related or otherwise), many working-age individuals will go through brief, extended, or permanent periods during which they are unable to perform their normal jobs. The rate of disability in the United States is increasing for many reasons: the aging of the workforce; greater incidence of obesity and sedentary lifestyles; and medical improvements that make it possible for people to survive for many years despite significant impairments. [M.P. McQueen, *Workplace Disabilities Are on the Rise*, Wall St. J., May 1, 2007, at D1] Many employers either provide disability insurance under an ERISA plan, or give employees the option to purchase disability coverage on their own, at a lower premium than they could find in the ordinary individual market.

There are both public (Social Security Disability Income; Worker's Compensation) and private systems for dealing with disability. The Supreme Court ruled that the Commissioner of Social Security reasonably construed the definition of disability to deny benefits to a claimant who was healthy enough to do her former job (elevator operator) even though that job no longer exists in significant numbers within the national economy. [*Barnhart v. Thomas*, 540 U.S. 20 (2003)] Some states require employers to provide disability benefits; in other states, employers often do this as an employee benefit. Benefits are analyzed as short-term disability (STD) or long-term disability (LTD), with separate standards for each.

Returning to the subject of disability in 2008, the Supreme Court upheld the Kentucky state retirement system's practice of calculating disability retirement benefits by including extra years of service for those who became disabled before normal retirement age, but not for those who were disabled after normal retirement age. The Supreme Court did not consider this to be age discrimination; depending on the age at hire, some younger workers did better than older workers, and some older workers did better than younger workers, under the system. The court held that, in drafting the ADEA, Congress considered it acceptable to consider age when setting disability benefit formulas. [*Kentucky Ret. Systems v. EEOC*, 554 U.S. 135 (2008)]

In 2013, 14 million people received federal disability benefits each month, and the program was criticized as an undue burden on the federal government (which spends more on disability benefits than on welfare plus food stamps). Some commentators said that people who were capable of working applied for disability benefits because, for example, they were laid off in a factory closing. [Chana Joffe-Walt, *Unfit For Work: The Startling Rise Of Disability In America*, Planet Money (NPR) (Mar. 24, 2013). But see Brad Plumer, Harold Pollack: *What 'This American Life' Missed On Disability Insurance*, WonkTalk Blog (Mar. 28, 2013) (benefitslink.com): Harold Pollack, the University of Chicago School of Social Service Administration's expert on disability policy, says that the federal system is quite stringent, and most applicants are rejected. Less than 50% of applicants who are denied subsequently get jobs, so the federal system is not removing qualified workers from the workforce.]

The University of California (Berkeley)'s Jesse Rothstein did not find a correlation between reductions in unemployment benefits and rising disability claims. In 2008 and 2009, unemployment benefits were extended, but the number of disability claims continued to rise. In mid-2013, unemployment benefits had been reduced, and the number of people exhausting their unemployment benefit eligibility increased, but the number of disability applications stayed flat or declined. His conclusion is that there is no large cohort of able-bodied workers using the disability system to hide from a poor job market. Rothstein suggested that ability to work is not completely independent of the job market: a person who is disabled from heavy work might be able to perform a desk job—if desk jobs are available. [Ben Casselman, *Are Long-Term Unemployed Taking Refuge in Disability?*, WSJ.com (June 14, 2013)]

Because disability claims are administered by the same insurance company that pays claims that are granted, the legal system had to determine the effect of this conflict of interest on the standard of review. Should a court review a claims decision deferentially, or only see if there was an abuse of discretion and sustain the decision if it was not arbitrary and capricious? This is discussed in *Metropolitan Life v. Glenn*, 554 U.S. 105 (2008). See § 20.07 for post-*Glenn* case law, and Chapter 13 for the subject of claims in general.

Under the FMLA, although the provisions about substituting paid for unpaid leave do not apply when an employee receives disability benefits during an FMLA leave, the employer and employee can, by agreement, supplement disability benefits by running paid leave concurrently with FMLA leave. (See Chapter 38.)

Reed Group studied almost 112,000 FMLA claims closed between 2008 and 2011, finding that employees who take intermittent leave for themselves or to care for family members are almost three times as likely to file an STD claim within six months as employees taking continuous FMLA leave. Reed Group found that about half (51%) of FMLA claims were for intermittent leave. One-fifth (21%) of employees taking intermittent leave filed an STD claim within six months, whereas only 8% of those taking continuous FMLA leave did. [PR Newswire, *Reed Group Study Finds Employees Taking Intermittent Family Medical Leave Are Three Times More Likely to File for Short-term Disability*, MarketWatch WSJ.com (Aug. 7, 2012)]

## § 20.02  EMPLOYMENT-BASED PLANS

Usually, a short-term disability (STD) is defined either as one that lasts less than six months, or one that lasts less than a year. Long-term disability benefits typically terminate after a period of years (e.g., five years) or at age 65, when the employee would presumably be retiring anyway.

A typical arrangement is for the employer to self-insure for short-term disability, but to buy long-term disability (LTD) insurance (possibly with the covered employees contributing part of the cost). It is also typical for STD and LTD plans to use different definitions of disability. The long-term plan has more restrictive definitions, because the employer's possible exposure is greater.

Using an "own occupation" definition (the person is disabled when unable to carry out the duties of the pre-disability occupation) makes it easier to qualify for benefits than using an "any occupation" definition (benefits stop as soon as the person is able to return to any work, or any work suitable to his or her education and training). Another frequent plan design is for the definition to start out as "own-occ" but switch after two years to inability to perform any occupation suitable to the individual's education and training.

Some disability plans have adopted tactics used in the acute health market, such as reducing benefits (replacing 50% rather than 60% of salary) and shifting costs to employees. The Social Security Administration estimates that a 20-year-old has a 30% chance of becoming disabled by retirement age, and 90% of disability claims are illness-related. Group plans often impose a benefit cap, such as $5,000 a month. According to LIMRA, only 47% of employers offer LTD coverage, but companies with 100 or more employees usually provide some disability benefits. About 50 million working Americans (approximately one-third of the workforce) have some disability insurance. LIMRA figures show that, among employers offering disability coverage, 49% paid the full premium in 2002, but only 37% did so in 2010. In 2002, 41% of LTD programs were voluntary (i.e., employees paid 100% of the premium), a percentage that rose to 50% in 2010. When employees must pay the full premium, only about 40% elect the coverage. A typical voluntary program cost about $350 a year in 2010. Individual disability policies, which can be more comprehensive than group policies, typically cost $600 to $2,000 a year. [Michelle Andrews, *Employers Increasingly Trimming Or Cutting Disability Benefits*, Kaiser Health News (Sept. 20, 2011) (benefitslink. com)]

Benefits from group disability plans are offset by Social Security Disability Income; benefits from individual policies are not.

Plaintiff Hannington's disability benefits under an ERISA plan were offset by his service-related disability compensation under the Veterans' Benefits Act (VBA). The ERISA plan paid 60% of pre-disability salary, reduced by "other income" as defined by the plan. The "other income" provision covers disability benefits under the Social Security Act, Railroad Retirement Act, or "any other similar act or law." The plan administrator was also the insurer, so there was a conflict of interest. The district court held that the VBA benefits were not "similar to" the Social Security Act or Railroad Retirement Act, so they should not have offset the benefits under the ERISA disability plan. Because of the conflict of interest, the First Circuit reviewed the plan's decision de novo and concluded that the VBA benefits are not "similar" to the SSA or RRA benefits because they are based on military service rather than employment. The VBA benefit is funded by

Congressional appropriations; the ERISA benefits are funded by taxes on employ-ers and employees. Congress did not enact a provision requiring offset of VBA benefits against SSA or RRA benefits The First Circuit held that the offset was improper, because the VBA benefits did not constitute "other income" as defined by the ERISA plan. [*Hannington v. Sun Life & Health Ins. Co.*, 711 F.3d 226 (1st Cir. 2013)]

The Council for Disability Awareness (CDA) reported that 2011 was the third consecutive year in which the number of employees with private disability income insurance declined. The CDA's suggested explanation was that employ-ees may be gambling that they can get away without having disability insurance because they do not understand the risks involved. However, the number of LTD (long term disability) claims continued to rise. In 2011, the top LTD carriers paid $9.3 billion in benefits, 2% more than in 2010. The CDA says that, by far, the leading cause of disability claims is disease of the musculoskeletal system and connective tissue—for example, arthritis and osteoporosis. [Tristan Lejeune, *Long-Term Disability Claims Rise As Coverage Falls*, Employee Benefit News (Sept. 4, 2012) (benefitslink.com) ]

LTD plans usually replace 60%–70% of pre-disability income; 60% is the most common level. The plan may also limit income replacement from all sources, including Worker's Compensation and Social Security, to a percentage such as 75% of pre-disability income. Many group plans offset (reduce) disability benefits to account for government benefits and damages received from tort suits or settlements (e.g., if the employee was injured in an accident or by a defective product), whereas individual policies generally do not require benefit offsets. The Ninth Circuit held that it was not an abuse of discretion for a plan to deduct SSDI (Social Security Disability Income) payments from the benefits paid by two LTD plans. The plain language of the plan explained the plan's right to be reimbursed for overpayments, and defined other sources of income (specifically including Social Security benefits) as overpayments. The Ninth Circuit also allowed a double offset of the SSDI benefit from two separate plans. [*Renfro v. The Funky Door LTD Plan*, 686 F.3d 1044 (9th Cir. 2012)]

Another cost-saving measure for a group plan is to have benefits start after a waiting period, so that the plan covers situations in which work ability is impaired for a long time, but not ordinary illnesses and minor injuries (which are probably covered by sick leave anyway).

A Taft-Hartley plan is a temporary disability plan jointly run by employers and a union. The plan's goal is to assist employees who are in financial need because of a disability, while also helping them return to work as soon as possible (if they can be rehabilitated adequately). A 2010 Second Circuit decision treats Taft-Hartley plan benefit decisions as inherently subject to a conflict of inter-est when they make benefit decisions. The Second Circuit ruled that the plan did not give enough weight to the testimony of the attending physician of an employee, injured in an automobile accident, who claimed ongoing pain and weakness. The court also said that the independent report should not have concluded that the worker was capable of performing three occupations. [*Durakovic v. Building Serv. 32 BJ Pension Fund*, 609 F.3d 133 (2d Cir. 2010); see Fred Schneyer, *Appeals Panel Declares Taft Hartley Plans Inherently Conflicted*, plansponsor.com (June 30, 2010)]

Highly compensated employees, who often experience crushing income loss after disability (because disability benefits are capped at a level far below their pre-disability income) can be good subjects for corporate disability buy-up policies—supplemental group disability plans providing additional income replacement.

The buy-up plan could be either employer paid, in which case the employer can deduct the premiums and the employee does not have taxable income because of the premium payments, but benefits will be taxable when received; or the employer sponsors the plan, allowing insurers to sign up employees who pay for their own coverage but can then receive benefits tax-free. The second approach is more popular. A disability buy-up can also be included in a cafeteria plan, so that premiums are paid with pre-tax dollars but benefits are taxable. In this case, the coverage will be portable, and employees can take it with them when they change jobs. In a hybrid plan, the employer pays the premiums for a select group of employees; other employees can participate by paying premiums.

Buy-up plans are structured with two tiers. The first tier is a guaranteed issue policy issued at standard rates without underwriting. The second tier has limited underwriting, which may lead to higher premiums or some coverage restrictions. [Stanley B. Siegel, *Corporate Disability Buy-Ups*, <http://www.aicpa.org/pubs/jofa/dec2002/siegel.htm>]

As an incentive for rehabilitation, the plan may continue benefits at a low level while the individual engages in a trial period of re-employment, or undertakes part-time or lower-level work in an attempt to re-enter the workforce. [See Chapter 37 for a discussion of the Age Discrimination in Employment Act (ADEA) [29 U.S.C. §§ 621 *et seq.*] implications of disability plans]

## § 20.03  STATE MANDATES

In five states (California, Hawaii, New York, New Jersey, and Rhode Island), employers are required to provide TDI (Temporary Disability Insurance) coverage for between 26 and 52 weeks of non-occupational temporary disability for industrial and commercial workers. Either the state administers a fund from which employer contributions are distributed to disabled employees, or the state maintains a fund but gives employers the choice of self-insuring, buying insurance, or paying into a union-sponsored disability plan.

TDI benefits are offset (that is, reduced) by Worker's Compensation and unemployment benefits.

## § 20.04   COMPLIANCE ISSUES

### [A]   ERISA Compliance

For ERISA purposes, most disability arrangements are welfare benefit plans, and therefore subject to disclosure, filing, and fiduciary requirements. Some disability plans, however, are top-hat plans that only cover executives, so the employer's disclosure obligations are more limited. If a plan is maintained only to comply with Worker's Compensation or state mandates, then ERISA § 4(b)(3) exempts the plan from ERISA compliance obligations. ERISA compliance is also excused in situations where an employer makes payments out of its general assets to an employee who is out of work for medical reasons. [See 29 C.F.R. § 2510.3-1(b)(2)]

The Middle District of Florida held that Lockheed Martin did not violate the ERISA ban on interference with benefits (ERISA § 510) when it terminated an employee for excessive absence. The plaintiff did not prove that she was terminated because of the cost of her STD benefits; she had been put on a performance improvement plan for excessive absences and poor work even before she applied for STD. She was only terminated after being denied STD (for lack of proof that her condition made it impossible for her to work) and then refusing to either return to work or provide medical documentation of her inability to return. [*Mundale v. Lockheed Martin Corp.*, No. 8:08-CV-217-T-24-TBM (M.D. Fla. Jan. 26, 2009); see Rebecca Moore, *Court Finds No Interference of Benefits in Excessive Absence Termination*, plansponsor.com (Feb. 5, 2009)]

The Eastern District of California ruled in early 2013 that a Worker's Compensation release did not release an ERISA disability claim. The release did not explicitly mention the ERISA plan or ERISA claims. Teresa Duncan made an LTD claim under an ERISA plan and received disability benefits between 2005 and 2010. She settled her Worker's Compensation claim in 2008 and gave a release of all claims, saying she would not "be able to go back to the defendant for additional treatment or disability payments." The district court held that the standard language in Worker's Compensation releases applies only to Worker's Compensation claims, and there was no mention of ERISA. [*Duncan v. Hartford Life and Accident Ins. Co.*, No. 2:11-cv-1536-GEB-CKD, 2013 WL 506465 (E.D. Cal. Feb. 8, 2013); see Mike Reilly, *Releases Should Explicitly Release ERISA Claims and ERISA Plan*, Lane Powell Boom: The ERISA Law Blog (Feb. 26, 2013) (benefitslink.com)]

If the employee pays all the premiums for LTD insurance, and the employer's only role is to administer the payments (without giving its approval of the policy), then ERISA does not preempt a suit by the employee against the insurer claiming bad faith termination of benefits. There are two tests for deciding whether ERISA preempts litigation about a disability policy:

- Was there a "plan, fund or program"? In this case, a plan was clearly present—but it was not an ERISA plan;

- Does the arrangement qualify for the ERISA safe harbor? The safe harbor is available if the employer does not make any contributions to the plan; the plan is completely voluntary; the employer does not profit from the plan (although it can legitimately receive a reasonable administrative fee); and the employer allows one or more insurers to publicize the availability of the program, but does not endorse or recommend it.

An employer's offering a group supplemental LTD policy with a group discount was enough employer involvement to create an ERISA plan. The plaintiff applied for an individual policy through a hospital plan that gave discounts to medical residents. Several years after leaving the hospital's employ, McCann collected LTD benefits. When the benefits were terminated, McCann sued the insurer for breach of contract, treating it as group insurance exempt from ERISA under the safe harbor regulation, 29 C.F.R. § 2510.3-1(j). Defendant Provident said that it was an ERISA plan. The Third Circuit position is that an ERISA plan exists if a reasonable person would be able to ascertain the intended benefits, financing, and claims procedure. The safe harbor exempts group insurance plans if participation is voluntary and the employer does not make any contributions, confining its involvement to collecting premiums and submitting them to the insurer. The Third Circuit found that there was an ERISA plan even though the policy did not take effect until after McCann left employment. [*McCann v. UNUM Provident*, 3:11-cv-03241-MLC-TJB, 2013 WL 396182 (Jan. 31, 2013); see D. Ward Kallstrom and Michelle M. Scannell, *It's an ERISA Plan? District Court Construes Group Discount as Employer Contribution under DOL Group Insurance Safe Harbor Analysis* Seyfarth Shaw ERISA & Employee Benefits Litigation Blog (Feb. 15, 2013) (benefitslink.com). The definition of ERISA plan comes from *Shaver v. Siemens Corp.*, 670 F.3d 462 (3d Cir. 2012).]

Even arrangements that are exempt from ERISA (and therefore from federal ERISA suits) as payroll practices are vulnerable to state-court suits charging, for example, bad faith. [*Street v. Ingalls Mem'l Hosp.*, 2007 U.S. Dist. LEXIS 18643 (N.D. Ill. Mar. 15, 2007); see EBIA Weekly, *Short-Term Disability Payment Policy Not an ERISA Plan; No Interest on Delayed Payments* (Mar. 29, 2007)]

The Southern District of Ohio held that ERISA preempts the Wisconsin statute about benefit substitutions, which allows employees to substitute any other kind of paid or unpaid leave provided by employer for part of their family leave or medical leave. An ALJ held that an insurance company violated the substitution provision by denying short-term disability benefits to a plan participant. The insurance company sued for declaratory and injunctive relief. The district court held that the requirement of paying STD benefits was expressly preempted by ERISA § 514(a), and there was conflict preemption with ERISA § 502(a)'s civil enforcement provisions. Accordingly, the district court granted a permanent injunction against application of the substitution provision. [*Sherfel v. Gassman*, No. 2:09-cv-00871-JLG-TPK, 2012 U.S. Dist. LEXIS 187548 (S.D. Ohio Sept. 28, 2012); see Matthew R. Madara, Bloomberg BNA Pension & Benefits Blog, *Court Holds That Wisconsin FMLA Substitution Law Is ERISA-Preempted* (Oct. 4, 2012) (benefitslink.com)]

ERISA does not preempt state "notice-prejudice" laws. Such laws prevent insurers from denying a claim on the basis that the insured person did not give timely notice of the covered event, unless the delay really causes harm to the insurer. [*Daug v. UNUM Life Ins. Co.*, 1999 WL 238236 (10th Cir. 1999); *Cisneros v. UNUM*, 134 F.3d 939 (9th Cir. 1999)]

## [B]  Tax Issues

Whether an employer can get a tax deduction for the cost of its disability plan depends on satisfying I.R.C. § 162 (ordinary and necessary business expenses). The employer's contributions must also satisfy I.R.C. § 104.

From the employee's viewpoint, the key section is I.R.C. § 106, which excludes employer coverage under an accident and health insurance (A&H) plan from the employee's gross income. This section is usually interpreted to include the premiums that the employer pays to maintain an insured disability plan, as well as the value of coverage under a self-insured disability plan. After a disability occurs, the benefits received by the employee under A&H or disability insurance must be included in income to the extent that they are attributable to previously excluded employer contributions. Amounts paid directly by the employer to the employee are also includible in gross income.

However, benefits paid for permanent loss (or loss of use) of a body part or its function, or for disfigurement, are not included in the employee's income, as long as the benefit is computed without regard to absence from work.

## [C]  ADA Compliance

It should also be noted that a disability plan that imposes lower limits for mental health care than for care of physical ailments may violate the Americans with Disabilities Act (ADA). The Mental Health Parity Act [42 U.S.C. § 300gg] makes it unlawful for employee group health plans to set lower limits for mental health care than for treatment of physical illnesses. This statute, however, is not applicable to disability plans.

Early in 2000, the Supreme Court affirmed (without opinion) [528 U.S. 1106 (2000)] the Seventh Circuit's decision in *Doe v. Mutual of Ohio* [179 F.3d 557 (7th Cir. 2000)] It does not violate the ADA's public accommodations title for an insured or self-insured health plan to impose a lower cap on benefits for AIDS-related illnesses or conditions than for other ailments. The Supreme Court would not grant privileged status to diseases that cause ADA disability over other diseases that do not.

ADA Title IV immunizes insurer and benefit plan decisions based on underwriting, classifying, or administering risk, as long as the decisions are not a subterfuge to escape ADA compliance. Decisions that have actuarial support are likely to qualify for this safe harbor.

## [D]  EEOC Compliance Manual

EEOC directives do not have the force of law. Even Regulations promulgated by this agency have often been invalidated by court decisions. However, you should consult Section 3 of the EEOC's Compliance Manual, issued October 3, 2000 [<http://www.eeoc.gov/policy/docs/benefits.html>] for EEOC policy on what constitutes discrimination on the basis of age or handicap, and what "equal" benefits mean in the context of disability benefits.

The revised Compliance Manual permits employers to reduce long-term disability benefits to account for Social Security Disability Income, Worker's Compensation, and other non-age-based government benefits. LTD benefits paid to older workers can also be reduced by pension benefits that come from employer contributions, under two conditions. Either the employee voluntarily opts to receive the pension (at any age) or has reached age 62 of the plan's normal retirement age (whichever is later) and is eligible for a full, unreduced pension. In plans partially funded by employee contributions, the employer is only permitted to reduce benefits that can be traced back to its own contributions, not employee contributions.

The EEOC position is that disability retirement benefits are not equal if they are calculated on the basis of the number of years the employee would have worked until NRA, because that approach favors younger employees. But disability benefits under government programs can legitimately be used to reduce disability benefits paid by the employer.

## [E]  Other Compliance Issues

Disability benefits are not considered "medical care," so when an employee is terminated, the right to COBRA continuation coverage [see Chapter 19] extends to the employee group health plan but not to the long-term disability plan.

The District Court for the Northern District of Ohio held in 2013 that even the plan administrator's actual knowledge that a former employee was disabled (and received Social Security disability benefits) was not enough to extend her husband's COBRA continuation coverage duration from 18 to 29 months, where the plan explicitly provided that coverage would only be extended if the plan participant provided notice of disability to the plan administrator. [*Rayle v. Wood Cnty. Hosp.*, No. 3:12-cv-02052-0, 2013 WL 1654898 (N.D. Ohio 2013). See

EBIA Weekly, *Actual Notice of Employee's Disability Insufficient to Extend COBRA Coverage When Plan's Notice Procedures Were Not Followed* (May 16, 2013) (benefitslink.com)]

The Family and Medical Leave Act [Pub. L. No. 103-3; see Chapter 38] may entitle the employee to claim unpaid leave for personal medical needs, or the need to care for a sick family member.

The Supreme Court ruled in May 2010 that an employee, who applied for LTD benefits from a plan insured by Reliance Standard, was entitled to attorneys' fees when the trial court found that the benefit denial was an abuse of discretion. The court remanded to give Reliance 30 days to reconsider; if it did not, judgment would be entered for the plaintiff. Reliance granted the benefits, but argued that an attorneys' fee award was inappropriate because the plaintiff received only a remand, not court-ordered benefits. The Supreme Court held that the relevant ERISA section gives the district court discretion to award attorneys' fees to either side—fee awards are not limited to prevailing parties. [*Hardt v. Reliance Standard Life Ins.,* 560 U.S. 242 (2010); see Marcia Coyle, *High Court Smooths Path to Plaintiff Fees in Disability Cases,* Nat'l L.J. (May 25, 2010) (law.com). See also *Williams v. Metropolitan Life Ins. Co.,* 609 F.3d 622 (4th Cir. 2010), awarding attorneys' fees to a disability claimant who had a degree of success in arguing that she suffered ongoing pain and loss of function in her hands and wrists, and eventually received LTD benefits for carpal tunnel syndrome.]

## § 20.05   CASE LAW ON "TOTAL DISABILITY"

In many instances, the question is not how to interpret the plan—the question is whether or not the claimant satisfies the plan's definition of "total disability." It may be inability to perform the applicant's own occupation, or any occupation for which his or her education and training qualifies him or her—or the definition may shift depending on the length of the period of disability.

Even if the question is ability to engage in "any gainful occupation," most courts will require consideration of the individual's earnings history and the availability of jobs in the relevant geographic area. The Utah Supreme Court held that an injured worker's past earnings can be considered in a permanent total disability case. The claimant, a building engineer, had a lower back injury in 2001. The ALJ found him permanently and totally disabled, in part because the only available employment paid less than the state's average weekly wage. The injured worker's former employer and its insurer said that under Utah law, the determination of available work is based only on the employee's age, education, work experience, medical capacity, and residual functional capacity. The Utah Supreme Court held that past work experience also includes consideration of the wages the worker earned prior to becoming disabled. [*LPI Servs. v. McGee,* 2009 UT 41 (Utah Sup 2009); see Rebecca Moore, *Utah Court Says Wages Can Be Considered in Disability Determination,* plansponsor.com (July 27, 2009)]

The Second Circuit held that the fact that an employee continues to work does not prevent him from showing that he was disabled, if there is evidence that the disability was very severe. In this case, an office administrator who suffered a head injury experienced a decline in work performance and ability to interact with others, and was fired about a year after the accident. She was treated for headaches, mood changes, sleep disorder, and impaired memory. The Second Circuit rejected the insurer's conclusion, that the disability was only partial or temporary, for lack of evidence. [*O'Hara v. National Union Fire Ins.*, 642 F.3d 110 (2d Cir. 2011)]

The First Circuit held that denial of benefits on the basis of an unwritten exclusion was unreasonable. The plaintiff was an anesthesiologist who obtained LTD benefits for part of an inpatient stay to treat her addiction to Fentanyl. At that point, her claim was denied on the grounds that the risk of relapse was not a continuation of disability. The district court awarded benefits for the 36-month maximum term under the plan, and the First Circuit affirmed. The First Circuit held that the plaintiff's risk of relapse was significant, because the plaintiff had a bad back and a stressful job with convenient access to drugs—and the insurer should have written in an exclusion for relapse if that was the intention in designing the policy. However, the Fourth Circuit has reached the opposite conclusion: that no matter how significant the risk of relapse, the risk, without an actual relapse, will not support a disability claim. [*Colby v. Union Sec. Ins. Co. & Mgmt. Co. for Merrimack Anesthesia Assocs. Long-Term Disability Plan*, 705 F.3d 58 (1st Cir. 2013); see Ron Kramer and Jim Goodfellow, *First Circuit: Unwritten Risk of Relapse Exclusion is Unreasonable, Creates Split with Fourth Circuit*, Seyfarth Shaw ERISA & Employee Benefits Litigation Blog (Feb. 4, 2013) (benefitslink.com)]

## § 20.06  EFFECT OF PLAN AMENDMENTS

In late 1999, the Eighth Circuit offered yet another lesson in the importance of careful drafting of plan documents. Ceridian Corporation used to pay insurance premiums for disabled individuals as part of its long-term disability plan. When it discontinued this practice, a group of disabled ex-employees sued. The SPD reserved the right to amend the plan, but did not specify whether it could be amended with respect to people who were already disabled at the time of the change. [*Barker v. Ceridian Corp.*, 193 F.3d 976 (8th Cir. 1999)] The Eighth Circuit held that the SPD provision was ambiguous. That opened the way for testimony about the company's intentions. The Eighth Circuit ordered Ceridian to continue paying for insurance for the group of ex-employees already disabled at the time of the change in the plan.

The Sixth Circuit held that it was not an abuse of discretion to amend a multi-employer pension plan to impose a two-year cap on occupational disability benefits: the plan did not provide vested welfare benefits. The plaintiff was injured at work in 1990, and began to receive disability benefits under the Indiana Laborer's Pension Fund. In 2001, he was informed that benefits under the Total and Permanent Disability Benefit category were canceled, but he would receive Occupational Disability benefits until the plan's early retirement age. The plan gave the trustees authority to determine benefit eligibility and amend the plan—but amendments reducing vested benefits were restricted. In 2004, the occupational disability benefit was amended to cut off benefits at early retirement age or December 31, 2006, whichever came first. The Sixth Circuit ruled that welfare benefits can be terminated at any time as long as termination is consistent with the terms of the plan. [*Price v. Board of Trustees of the Indiana Laborer's Pension Fund*, 707 F.3d 647 (6th Cir. 2013); see Bloomberg BNA, *Sixth Circuit Upholds Plan Amendment Retroactively Limiting Disability Benefits* (Feb. 19, 2013) (benefitslink.com)]

According to a 2006 Second Circuit decision, the standard for judicial review of an administrator's benefit determination is the SPD that was in effect when the plaintiff became disabled—and not the amended SPD in effect when the application was denied. (The later SPD granted discretion to the plan administrator; the earlier one did not.) The right to benefits vested when the plaintiff became disabled, so the second SPD could not apply. [*Gibbs v. Cigna*, 440 F.3d 571 (2d Cir. 2006)]

## § 20.07  CLAIMS PROCEDURES AND THE STANDARD OF REVIEW AFTER *GLENN*

### [A]  Generally

See Chapter 13 for a discussion of claims procedures, including the additional requirements imposed by PPACA, the health care reform statute. Also see Chapter 11 for discussion of which documents (e.g., guidelines used in analyzing claims) participants are entitled to receive on request.

### [B]  De Novo or Abuse of Discretion?

When a case gets to court, the question is whether the plan administrator's decisions will be reviewed "de novo" (the court examines all aspects of the case for the first time) or whether the administrator's decisions will be valid.

Before the Supreme Court's 2008 decision in *Metropolitan Life v. Glenn*, 554 U.S. 105 (2008), the courts of appeals developed a number of different standards for reviewing claims decisions. In many cases, benefit claimants asserted that courts should perform de novo review of benefit determinations because the decision was made by an insurer that had a conflict of interest because it both made the claims decision and paid the benefits, so extending more benefits would reduce its profitability. However, in many of these cases, the plan was drafted to give the plan administrator discretion to make decisions—which would make the standard of review whether the decision-maker acted arbitrarily and capriciously.

*Glenn* involved a claimant who received 24 months of disability benefits for heart disease. The plan administrator, MetLife, had discretionary authority. MetLife encouraged Glenn to apply for SSDI benefits, which she received. Then MetLife concluded that Glenn was capable of working, and terminated her benefits. The Supreme Court found that MetLife's conflict of interest was one factor in reviewing the decision, but all facts and circumstances must be considered. *Glenn* applied the same analysis whether the plan was self-administered by the employer or was administered by an insurance company that had a financial interest in the outcome of its determinations.

After *Glenn*, conflict of interest is a factor in the decision, but decisions are not automatically reviewed de novo if there was a conflict of interest. The Fourth Circuit ruled that before *Glenn*, it used a modified abuse of discretion standard that reduced the amount of deference accorded to decision-makers who had a conflict of interest. After *Glenn*, its new test is whether the decision to terminate disability benefits was reasonable and whether there was an abuse of discretion.

In the view of the District Court for the District of Massachusetts, an insurer's applying the plan's 24-month limit for certain disabilities was reasoned and supported by substantial evidence, not arbitrary and capricious. The standard of disability was inability to earn 80% of pre-disability income (first two years of benefits), 60% of pre-disability income (after the first two years). Benefits were provided up to age 67 if the onset of disability occurred before age 62. There was a 24-month limit for neuromuscular and soft tissue disorders, with six specific conditions excluded. The plaintiff suffered spinal fractures in a car accident, which may have been caused by an epileptic seizure that occurred when he did not take his medication. The participant said that he was disabled by a combination of disabilities, some of which were not subject to the limitation. The plaintiff asserted that he had radiculopathy, one of the excluded conditions. However, the district court agreed with the insurer that the disability was predominantly caused by neuromuscular and soft tissue factors, and the evidence of radiculopathy was weak. [*Brien v. Metropolitan Life Ins. Co.*, No. 1:11-cv-10395-DJC, 2012 U.S. Dist. LEXIS 135790 (D. Mass. Sept. 21, 2012); see Bloomberg BNA Pension & Benefits Daily, *Limitations Provision Upheld Against Long-Term Disability Plan Participant* (Sept. 25, 2012) (benefitslink.com)]

Spradley, a 37-year veteran at Owens-Illinois took early retirement at age 55 because of a disability. About nine months before his retirement, he submitted a claim stating that the Social Security Administration found him to be permanently and totally disabled as of March 1, 2008. The plan says that PTD (permanently and totally disabled) life insurance benefits are payable to a person who becomes permanently and totally disabled before age 65, files a claim within 12 months of leaving employment, and is unable to engage in significant gainful activities—or who is under 65 and receives SSDI. Spradley received a denial letter that referred only to health insurance, not the PTD life insurance he applied for. He appealed the denial, which was upheld on the grounds that health insurance is available only to active employees. He brought an ERISA suit. The defendant argued that PTD life insurance is available only for temporary disability. The district court ordered payment of benefits. On appeal, the question is whether the plan administrator's denial was arbitrary and capricious. The Tenth Circuit found that the denial was inappropriate, and the district court should have entered judgment for the plaintiff based on the record instead of remanding for further proceedings—which would only give the plan a chance to fabricate more excuses. [*Spradley v. Owens-Illinois Hourly Employees Welfare Benefit Plan*, 686 F.3d 1135 (10th Cir. 2012)]

Cigna helped an engineer apply for SSA disability benefits after he had multiple surgeries on one foot and ongoing, disabling pain. Cigna denied his LTD claim, asserting that the policy used a different definition of "disability" than the federal system. The Seventh Circuit rejected this argument, finding the two definitions functionally equivalent and attributing the claim denial to Cigna's conflict of interest. [*Raybourne v. Cigna*, 700 F.3d 1076 (7th Cir. 2012); see Scott J. Stitt, *The Seventh Circuit Concludes that SSA's Definition of Disability, and Cigna's Definition of Long-Term Disability, Is "Functionally Equivalent."* Arnlaw.com Blog (Apr. 3, 2013) (benefitslink.com)]

## [C]  The Treating Physician Rule

When the Social Security Administration decides whether an applicant is entitled to receive SSDI benefits, it uses the "treating physician" rule. In other words, the opinion of a physician who actually treats the claimant is given more weight than the opinion of a physician-reviewer who looks at the patient's medical file but doesn't actually examine the patient. There was a Circuit split as to whether this rule should be applied in the context of an ERISA plan.

The Supreme Court resolved the Circuit split through its May 2003 decision in *Black & Decker Disability Plan v. Nord.* [538 U.S. 822 (2003)] The Supreme Court ruled that the Social Security rule does not have to be followed in cases involving private ERISA plans rather than public benefits. According to the Supreme Court, neither the ERISA statute nor the Department of Labor's regulations demand any special deference for the opinion of the treating physician. Furthermore, in January 2005, the Sixth Circuit ruled that not only is the treating physician rule not mandatory, but an ERISA plan administrator is not bound by the Social Security Administration's determination that a person is totally and completely disabled to the extent that payment of SSDI benefits is justified. The court ruled that it was not arbitrary and capricious for the plan to base its conclusion that the plaintiff was not disabled on the opinions of an independent neurologist and psychiatrist who reviewed the plaintiff's medical records. [*Whitaker v. Hartford Life & Accident Ins. Co.*, 404 F.3d 947 (6th Cir. 2005)]

## § 20.08  APPEALS OF CLAIM DENIALS

The Ninth Circuit said that it was "illogical" and "implausible" to refuse to grant LTD payments to a Honda employee who was disabled by Chronic Fatigue Syndrome (CFS) and who qualified for Social Security disability payments. His claim was denied on the grounds that there were no objective physical findings substantiating his illness, although he submitted medical evidence of having an unusually severe case of CFS. The Ninth Circuit found an abuse of discretion: disregarding ample medical evidence and insisting on objective findings where there is no objective medical test available. [*Salomaa v. Honda*, 642 F.3d 666 (9th Cir. 2011); see Tim Hull, *Man with Controversial Illness Can Get Benefits*, Courthouse News Service (Mar. 10, 2011) (benefitslink.com)]

Because a disability claimant must exhaust administrative remedies before bringing a suit and those remedies typically include an internal appeal. It is important to define "appeal." In 2012, the Eastern District of Missouri held that it is not an appeal to send the plan a letter stating that the claimant's lawyer was reviewing the records and obtaining medical information for an appeal of termination of long-term disability benefits. Benefits were terminated November 25, 2008; on December 12, 2008, the claimant's lawyer sent a letter asking for copies of all of the claimant's medical records; on July 8, 2009, the lawyer sent another letter disagreeing with the adverse decision and asking the insurer to review the case and advise the lawyer of any further determination. The district court said that the December 12 letter was not an appeal of the termination, merely a request for records. Although the July 8 letter was a request for an appeal, it was untimely, because the plan required appeals to be filed within 180 days of notice of termination of benefits. [*Reindl v. Hartford Life and Accident Ins. Co.*, No. 1:11CV167 SNLJ,, 2012 U.S. Dist. LEXIS 38259 (E.D. Mo. Mar. 21, 2012); see Mike Reilly, *What Constitutes an Appeal? Not a Mere Request for Records*, Lane Powell (Mar. 27, 2012) (benefitslink.com)]

Eligibility determinations for an LTD plan were delegated to Reliance Standard Life Insurance by the employer, which was the plan's sponsor and administrator. The loss of the administrative file for a disability benefits claim is not necessarily fatal to review of decision terminating benefits. The plaintiff, Schorsch was not given plan documents or an SPD. In 1993, Schorsch was totally disabled by an auto accident. In 2006, Reliance requested an independent medical examination. Based in part on surveillance, Reliance determined that Schorsch could work a medium-duty job, and terminated her disability benefits. Schorsch's attorney sent a notice of intent to seek reconsideration, but did not submit a request for review. When Schorsch sued for resumption of the benefits, Reliance admitted that it had lost the administrative record of her claim. However, the Seventh Circuit held that Scorsch failed to exhaust her administrative remedies, and held that the insurer's errors were relevant only if Schorsch had reasonably relied on them when she did not seek review of the termination. The termination letter provided adequate notice of the reasons for the decision and how the review process worked. Because the employer was not the insurer's agent, the Seventh Circuit declined to penalize the employer for the loss of the documents. [*Schorsch v. Reliance Standard Life Ins. Co.*, 693 F.3d 734 (7th Cir. 2012); see Mike Reilly, *Failure to Exhaust Defense Trumps Missing Administrative Record*, Lane Powell BOOM: The ERISA Law Blog (Aug. 30, 2012) (benefitslink.com)]

Robert Fier, a casino manager, participated in his employer's AD&D policy and LTD plan, both ERISA plans. In 1992, Fier was shot and became a quadriplegic. In 1993, he returned to work, in a job accommodating his physical limitations; the salary was the same as before the shooting. In 1997, he was assigned to a new job, which paid $20,000 less. In that year, he claimed and was awarded LTD benefits. He received about $150,000 in benefits between 1997 and late 2004, when the insurer said that the benefits should have ended in 1998, when Fier returned to work at the same salary as before disability ensued. The Ninth Circuit held that the LTD policy was not ambiguous: it said that benefits ended at the earliest of the insured's death; cessation of disability; or earning more than 80% of pre-disability earnings. Therefore, Fier was not eligible for LTD benefits between 1993 and 1997 because he earned his full salary, and was not entitled to the benefits after 1998 because the new job was with another employer. He was not entitled to AD&D benefits, because he had lost the use of his limbs but not the limbs themselves. [*Fier v. Boyd Group*, 629 F.3d 1095 (9th Cir. 2011); see Robert McKennon, *Ninth Circuit Holds Tight to Erisa Interpretation Rule That Courts Will "Not Artificially Create Ambiguity Where None Exist*," California Insurance Litigation Blog (Jan. 7, 2011) (benefitslink.com)]

The Sixth Circuit held that termination of LTD benefits was supported by substantial evidence. Guardian Life Insurance decided that a former CEO who had several operations for a herniated disk was able to return to work; was participating in a new venture; and, although he was not getting paid yet, had an employment agreement promising him a $115,000 salary. (His previous salary was $140,000.) The Sixth Circuit held that, to terminate LTD benefits, it is not necessary that the insured earn as much as before the disability, as long as he or she is able to perform the major duties of a consistent occupation. [*Schwalm v. Guardian Life Ins. Co. of Am.*, 626 F.3d 299 (6th Cir. 2010); see Stanley D. Baum, *Sixth Circuit Upholds a Plan Administrator's Termination Of Disability Benefit Due To Substantial Evidence Showing No Disability As Defined by the Plan*, ERISA Lawyer Blog (Nov. 22, 2010) (benefitslink.com)]

LTD benefits were wrongfully denied when the claimant's doctors ordered indefinite restrictions forbidding the claimant to pinch with more than five pounds of force, kneel, or squat. The employer said that an indefinite restriction was not a permanent one, so she was not disabled. The Eighth Circuit ruled that the denial was an abuse of discretion, because in context, it was clear that the plaintiff had a permanent disability. It was not an abuse of discretion for the district court to award attorneys' fees to the plaintiff because this was not a close case—the employer obviously refused to give credence to the medical evidence. [*Rote v. Titan Tire Corp.*, 611 F.3d 960 (8th Cir. 2010)]

The Third Circuit ruled in mid-2009 that it was not arbitrary and capricious to consider ALS a pre-existing condition (defined by the policy as one for which medical treatment or advice was rendered within three months before the coverage date) for a policy with an effective date of coverage of July 1, 2006. ALS was not definitively diagnosed until March 27, 2007, the day before Doroshow applied for LTD benefits—but earlier, on May 16, 2006, Doroshow's doctor said that he had a motor neuron disease but the doctor did not think it was ALS. The Third Circuit found it reasonable to say that Doroshow received advice about ALS in the three months before the coverage date. In general, ruling out a condition is not advice or treatment for that condition, in this case an ALS diagnosis was under consideration. Doroshow had a family history of ALS, so he had a suspected condition without a confirmatory diagnosis, which can be considered a pre-existing condition. [*Doroshow v. Hartford Life & Accident Ins. Co.*, 574 F.3d 230 (3d Cir. 2009)]

The Ninth Circuit held that conflict of interest must be considered in determining whether an insurer abused the discretion it was granted under a discretionary clause. The plaintiff was rendered quadriplegic by an accident three months after starting a new job. His salary was $200,000, and he was guaranteed a $300,000 bonus for the first year if he performed as anticipated and had not quit or been terminated for cause. He sued when the employer's LTD plan calculated his benefits based on $200,000 in earnings (i.e., excluding the bonus). The Ninth Circuit, noting that the employer's HR department submitted a claim form describing the plaintiff's compensation as $500,000 (and the premiums were based on that level of compensation) remanded for consideration of whether it was an abuse of discretion to exclude the bonus from the benefit calculation. [*Stephan v. UNUM Life Ins. Co. of Am.*, 697 F.3d 917 (9th Cir. 2012)]

The Seventh Circuit said that it was not arbitrary and capricious to decide that an HIV-positive person could perform sedentary work despite his fatigue, neuropathy, and opportunistic infections. The plaintiff's viral load had decreased and four health professionals said that he could at least attempt sedentary work (although two health professionals disagreed). The plaintiff admitted that there were days when he was healthy enough to do a full day's work. The Seventh Circuit found that it was not irrational for the insurer to consider the effect of AIDS treatment and longer and healthier lifespans for HIV-positive persons. [*Jenkins v. Price Waterhouse LTD Plan*, 564 F.3d 856 (7th Cir. 2009)]

The Ninth Circuit held that the statute of limitations for filing an ERISA claim for denial of protected benefits is four years (for contract claims) even if the insurance plan or ERISA itself does not have an explicit time limit. Withrow became permanently disabled in 1986 and was approved for disability benefits in 1987. In 1990, she began a series of inquiries about whether her benefit payment was correctly canceled; the insurer never replied. In 2003, Withrow filed an internal appeal with the insurer, seeking an increase. This request was denied early in

2004. Withrow sued the insurer for denial of ERISA benefits in February 2006. An ERISA claim accrues either at the point of benefit denial or when the claimant had reason to know the claim was denied, so Withdrow's claim was held to have accrued in 2004 when her attorney was informed that the claim was denied. [*Withrow v. Bache Halsey Stuart Shield Inc., Protection Plan,* 655 F.3d 1032 (9th Cir. 2011); see Thomas E. Donahue, Michael B. Horrow, Nichole D. Podgurski, Jason A. Cole, *California's 9th Circuit Rules Timing Critical for Filing ERISA Claims,* Donahue & Horrow LLP (undated) (benefitslink.com)]

After leaving his job as a result of mental disability, Santaliz-Rios received monthly benefits for two years. At that point, the limit was reached and benefits were terminated. Santaliz-Rios filed an internal appeal, citing an exception that would allow his benefits to continue. The appeal was denied. He sued, withdrew the suit, and sued again five years later. The trial court dismissed the suit based on the insurance policy's three-year statute of limitations for claims against the insurer. The First Circuit affirmed. There is no ERISA statute of limitations, so courts use the most analogous local statute of limitations. The Puerto Rico statute of limitations for contracts is 15 years—unless the parties adopted a reasonable shorter period. The First Circuit found the three-year limitation reasonable. [*Santaliz-Ríos v. Metropolitan Life Ins. Co.,* 693 F.3d 57 (1st Cir. 2012); see EBIA Weekly, *Court Enforces Plan-Imposed Limitations Period for Benefits Claims* (Oct. 25, 2012) (benefitslink.com)]

A 2001 long-term disability claim was denied under the plan's claims process. The claimant did not sue at that point. In 2008, he filed another long-term disability claim and sought reconsideration of the 2001 claim. The plan terms limited legal action to three years after the time proof of claim was required. For the 2001 claim, that would be March 12, 2002, ending the statute of limitations on March 12, 2005. The district court held that a plan's own statute of limitations will be applied if it is reasonable. The district court found it reasonable, so the three-year statute of limitations, not the Ohio 15-year statute of limitations for claims of breaches of a written contract, applied. [*Engleson v. UNUM Life Ins. Co. of Am.,* No. 5:09 CV 2969, 2012 U.S. Dist. LEXIS 187548 (N.D. Ohio June 29, 2012); see Haynes and Boone Blogs, *District Court Finds Plaintiff's LTD Claim Time Barred by the Limitations Term in the Plan* (Oct. 11, 2012) (benefitslink.com)]

# CHAPTER 21

# INSURANCE FRINGE BENEFITS

## § 21.01   INTRODUCTION

In addition to plans in which insurance operates behind the scenes (health plans; pension plans funded by insurance contracts), some fringe benefit plans exist to provide insurance coverage to employees. This chapter covers life insurance and long-term care insurance (LTCI) fringe benefits.

## § 21.02   LIFE INSURANCE FRINGE BENEFITS

Life insurance is a very popular benefit. Not only do many employers offer it, but when it is available it is almost universally chosen. According to BLS' National Compensation Survey, in March 2013, 57% of workers had access to workplace life insurance benefits, and 55% participated—so the take-up rate was 97%. Higher-paid workers were more likely to have access. Workers in the highest-paid 25% had a 84% access rate and 83% participation rate, whereas workers in the lowest-paid quadrant had an access rate of 22% and a participation rate of 20%. Full-time workers were much more likely to have access to life insurance and to participate than part-time workers, as is true of nearly all benefits. [BLS Economic News Release, *Table 5. Life Insurance Benefits: Access, Participation, and Take-Up Rates*, <http://data.bls.gov/cgi-bin/print.pl/news.release/ebs2.to5.htm> (last accessed Aug. 26, 2013)]

Among workers with basic life insurance entitlement through work, only 5% had to contribute for the coverage. There were differences by region, type of industry, and whether the workers were union or non-union, but the differences were slight.[BLS, *Life Insurance Plans: Employee Contribution Requirements, Private Industry Workers, National Compensation Survey, March 2012*, <http://www.bls.gov/ncs/ebs/benefits/2012/ownership/private/table13a.pdf> (last accessed Mar. 23, 2013)]

### [A]   Favorable Tax Treatment

The Internal Revenue Code authorizes several mechanisms under which employers can provide life insurance to employees at little or no income tax cost to the employees. (These mechanisms are distinct from the "key-person" insurance coverage that pays benefits to the corporation itself when it becomes necessary to replace a top executive or creative person.) The basic rule is that, if the employer pays the premiums and the insurance proceeds go to the beneficiary designated by the employee, the employee will have taxable income and the employer will be able to deduct the cost of providing the insurance. (The employer gets a deduction only for "ordinary and necessary business expenses.") However, the Code also provides certain relief measures that limit or eliminate the tax cost of these fringe benefits.

In mid-2005, the IRS issued T.D. 9223 to forbid abusive transactions involving "springing value" life insurance policies transferred to employees. The transactions are abusive because the purpose is to have an employee who has received a policy from a § 412(i) plan taxed at the cash surrender value of the policy, which is low. T.D. 9223 makes the employee taxable on the full fair market value (FMV) of the transferred life insurance contract. [*Final Regulations: Value of Life Insurance Contracts When Distributed from a Qualified Retirement Plan*, 2005-39 I.R.B. 591 (Aug. 26, 2005); 2004 Proposed Regulations were published at 69 Fed. Reg. 7384; see also Rev. Proc. 2004-16, 2004-10 I.R.B. 559, and Rev. Rul. 2004-20, 2004-10 I.R.B. 546]

An individual insurance contract plan is exempt from the minimum funding requirement of I.R.C. § 412 if it satisfies six requirements:

1.  It is funded exclusively by the purchase of individual annuity and/or insurance contracts from a licensed life insurance company, although purchases can be made either directly by the employer or through a trust or custodial account.

2.  The contract provides for level premium payments, either annual or more frequent.

3.  The benefits under the plan equal benefits provided under each contract at the plan's Normal Retirement Age, guaranteed by the carrier to the extent premiums have been paid.

4.  The premiums payable for the current and all previous plan years were paid before lapse (or the contract is reinstated).

5.  There has never been a security interest at any time during the plan year affecting rights under the contract (although a security interest created after the distribution of the contract to the participant is permissible).

6.  There are no policy loans outstanding at any time during the plan year prior to distribution of the policy.

The employer can deduct contributions used to pay premiums on the insurance contract if the plan holds the contract until the employee's death or until the contract is distributed or sold to the employee (e.g., at retirement).

The IRS targets plans involving specially designed life insurance policies whose cash surrender value is temporarily set far lower than the premiums paid. Such policies are distributed or sold to employees at the artificial cash surrender value; the "springing" feature then returns the value of the policy to something more commercially realistic. The Final Regulations carry over the principle from the 2004 proposal that a property distribution is included in the recipient's income at FMV, including the value of all rights under the agreement, including supplemental agreements (whether or not they are guaranteed). A transfer of property to a plan participant for less than FMV is considered a distribution by the plan to the extent of the difference.

Announcement 2005-80, 2005-46 I.R.B. 967, lists § 412(i) defined benefit plans and 20 other tax-saving devices that are deemed improper by the IRS. Section 412(i) plans tend to use life insurance policies with a guaranteed return to fund defined benefit plans because reporting is simplified by having a guaranteed return. The § 412(i) programs targeted by the IRS include plans in which the life insurance death benefits are greater than the benefits specified in the plan documents, or those in which the rights of plan participants to buy life insurance contracts under the plan are extremely unequal. [See Allison Bell, *Settlement Offer Could Affect Small DB Pension Plans*, NU Online News Service (Oct. 28, 2005)]

## [B]  Employee-Owned, Employer-Paid Insurance

It is common for employers to pay the premiums for life insurance owned by the employees covered by the plan. Treas. Reg. § 1.1035-1 gives the employer an income tax deduction for the cost of the plan, provided that the employer is not the beneficiary, and also limited by the I.R.C. § 162 "ordinary and necessary" rule.

The premiums that the employer pays are taxable income for the employee, but the insurance proceeds are not taxable income for the beneficiary who receives them. [See I.R.C. § 101] If the employee borrows against the policy, interest on the loan (unlike most forms of personal interest) is deductible.

■ **TIP:** Employer-pay life insurance plans are not subject to nondiscrimination requirements, so it is perfectly legitimate for the employer to furnish insurance to the employees the employer particularly wants to motivate, without making the plan available to the whole workforce.

Most group life insurance policies include a "portability" (also known as "right of conversion") provision under which employees can convert their employment-related coverage to an individual policy. Employers have a responsibility to tell employees about the right to convert group to individual life insurance at termination of employment, and the right to apply for waiver of premium if the employees become disabled or are absent from work. Failure to give the required information can subject the employer to liability. The employer should inform the departing employee to contact the insurer as soon as possible, because the group plan may impose a deadline for conversion and submission of the first individual premium payment. [Ford & Harrison Practical Insights: *Liability for Termination of Group Life Insurance Coverage* (October 2009) (benefitslink. com)]

In an unpublished decision, the Sixth Circuit held that ERISA § 502(a)(2) does not permit a life insurance beneficiary to recover unpaid benefits as a remedy for the plan administrator's fiduciary breach. A Federal Express employee did not convert his group life insurance to individual insurance after he was terminated. To convert the group policy to individual coverage, he would have had to have made an election within 31 days of receiving the conversion notice; apply to the insurer; and pay the premiums. After his death, his surviving spouse attempted to collect benefits alleging that the plan and plan administrator breached their fiduciary duty by not including information about converting the life policy in the COBRA notice he received upon termination. The Sixth Circuit held that there is no obligation (under COBRA or otherwise) to provide a conversion notice about life insurance. The Supreme Court denied certiorari in early 2013. [*Walker v. Federal Express Corp.*, 133 S. Ct. 851 (2013); see Bloomberg BNA Pension & Benefits Daily, *Supreme Court Declines to Review Individual Relief Ruling Under ERISA* (Jan. 8, 2013) (law.com)]

The Western District of Wisconsin held that the SPD for a group life insurance plan adequately explained, in plain language, the right to accelerate life insurance benefits (to collect benefits while the insured person is still alive but severely ill). Therefore, the employer did not violate its fiduciary duty even though it did not remind the employee's wife (who became his surviving spouse) of the availability of the accelerated benefits option. [*Pfeil v. Edward Kraemer & Sons Inc.*, No. 09-cv-wmc (W.D. Wis. June 1, 2010); see Rebecca Moore, *Failure to Mention Benefit Option Explained in SPD No Fiduciary Breach*, plansponsor. com (June 8, 2010)]

## [C] Company-Owned Life Insurance (COLI)

Under this variation, the policies are owned by the company itself, and can be used to finance death benefits paid under the employer's benefit plans. Cash-value insurance can be used to finance retirement benefits. The beneficiary of the plan, or the estate of the deceased employee, does have income under I.R.C. § 101(a), because the death benefits are deemed to be paid directly by the employer and not by an insurer.

When the employer owns the COLI policy and uses it only to fund the death benefit, the employee does not have taxable income during his or her life from either the policy's cash surrender value or the premium payments that the employer makes—as long as the employee's beneficiary is only an unsecured creditor with respect to the proceeds of the policy.

Usually, the corporation is not entitled to a deduction for the premiums it pays for COLI, because of the employer's interest as a beneficiary. However, there is an exception to this rule for premiums paid for certain annuity contracts used in connection with COLI plans.

For COLI policies issued after August 17, 2006, the PPA enacts a new Code § 101(j). In general, employers will have income if they receive insurance proceeds on the lives of employees and former employees (minus the costs, such as premiums, that the employer paid for the policy). Insurance proceeds are not taxable if the employer satisfied notice and consent requirements:

- Before the policy was issued, the employer gave written notice to the potential insured of the intention to purchase insurance on the employee's life, and the maximum size of policy that could be purchased.

- The potential insured consents in writing to the coverage (including the possibility that it will continue after the person ceases to be employed).

- The employer discloses that the proceeds of the policy will go to the employer, not the employee's family.

If these disclosure and consent requirements are satisfied, then the employer can exclude the policy proceeds from gross income as long as the insured was employed by the company at any time during the 12 months before his or her death, or the insured was a director or HCE when the policy was issued. Nor does the employer have taxable income to the extent that policy proceeds are paid to the insured's family or to the beneficiary (including a trust) designated by the employee. Insurance proceeds used to buy out the interest of the decedent's family in the business are also excluded from the employer company's income. In other words, proceeds of "key-person" policies will generally be excluded. Post-PPA COLI ownership imposes a duty of filing information returns about the policy. [Bond, Schoeneck & King PLLC Tax Law Information Memo, *Tax Law Change Affects Taxation of Proceeds from Employer-Owned Life Insurance* (October 2006) <http://www.bsk.com>]

In late 2007, the IRS issued temporary and proposed regulations to carry out the PPA provisions about employer-owned life insurance. The death benefit excluded from the policyholder's gross income is limited to the sum of the premiums and other amounts paid for the contract. An exception is available if notice and consent requirements are met—that is, the insured was an employee within 12 months of the time of death, is a highly compensated employee, the benefits are paid to the insured's family, trust, or estate or are used to buy out the decedent's business interest, and the policyholder filed a Code § 6039I information return for each year the contracts were owned. [72 Fed. Reg. 63838 (Nov. 13, 2007), discussed in Sutherland Asbill & Brennan LLP, *Legal Alert: IRS Implements Information Reporting for Employer-Owned Life Insurance* (Nov. 19, 2007)] For tax years ending on or after November 14, 2007, a policyholder owning employer-owned life insurance contracts issued after August 17, 2006 must attach Form 8925 to the income tax return. The form discloses the number of employees covered by employer-provided life insurance contracts; whether each one consented in writing, in advance, to be insured and for coverage to continue after employment ends. [Sutherland Asbill & Brennan LLP, *Legal Alert: IRS Issues Forms to Report Employer-Owned Life Insurance* (Feb. 7, 2008)]

The IRS published final regulations under Code § 6039I (added by the PPA), for reporting on COLI. The regulations took effect November 6, 2008. The amount of death benefits excluded from gross income cannot exceed the sum that the policyholder paid for the contract. Exceptions are made for some COLI that satisfies notice and content requirements—e.g., policies used to fund a buyout of a deceased business owner's interest. The holder of the COLI policy must file a return showing the employer's total number of employees; the number insured by COLI; the total amount of insurance in force at the end of the year; the policyholder's name, address, taxpayer ID, and type of business; and either a statement that the policyholder obtained consent from all the insureds, or the number of insureds for whom consent was not obtained. [T.D. 9431, RIN 1545-BG58, 4830-01-p, 2008-41 I.R.B. 1235, *Information Reporting on Employer-Owned Life Insurance Contracts*] [Nevin E. Adams, *IRS Sets Out Limits for Employer-Owned Life Insurance Expense*, plansponsor.com (May 26, 2009)]

Notice 2009-48, 2009-24 I.R.B. 1085, explains Code § 101(j), the rules for employer-owned life insurance enacted by the PPA. When an employee dies, the employer can recover tax-free only the portion of the death benefits equal to the premiums paid by the employer. However, for certain highly compensated employees, where the employer notifies the insured and obtains his or her consent, death benefits paid to a family member or trust or used to buy an equity interest in the employer company are tax-free. The notice must disclose the face amount of the insurance either as a dollar figure or as a multiple of the employee's salary; it is not adequate to say that the policy's face amount is the maximum for which the employee could be insured.

For employer-owned contracts issued after August 17, 2006, there is a reporting obligation under § 6039I. Notice 2009-48 says that a contract is not employer-owned if it is owned by a related person who is not engaged in a trade or business (e.g., the policy is used to buy out the ownership interest of the decedent), or if it is owned by a qualified plan or VEBA. An insurance contract owned by a rabbi trust or other grantor trust is considered to be owned by the employer. Split-dollar is considered employer-owned except to the extent that death benefits are paid to a family member or a trust. [Buck Research FYI, *IRS Provides Guidance on Employer-Owned Life Insurance After PPA* (June 15, 2009) (benefitslink. com)]

One factor impelling Congress to regulate COLI was the belief that COLI carried the potential for abuse. In 2002 and 2003, a series of articles in the *Wall St. J.* severely criticized COLI (calling it "janitor insurance" or "dead peasant insurance"), because in some instances, a corporation collects significant insurance benefits on the lives of low-paid workers who had little or no personal or company-provided insurance and whose families therefore were left poorly provided for. Insurance benefiting the company when nonkey employees die was criticized as unfair, because the insurance is sometimes maintained on retirees and other ex-employees, so companies benefit by the death of persons who are no longer employees at all, much less key employees. (Initially, corporations were only deemed to have an insurable interest in the lives of key employees, but this rule was changed in the 1980s.)

This type of insurance can also be used by corporations for financial manipulation. Corporations can deduct the insurance premiums they pay for this purpose; and, because they are insurance policies, the buildup of cash value is not taxed, and increase in cash value can be used to improve the financial results on the company's books. The insurance proceeds are not taxable income, so the company can get a windfall if someone dies after a short period of employment. The insurance can also be used as collateral for loans, or policy loans can be taken against the insurance. [Theo Francis, *Workers' Lives: Best Tax Break?*, Wall St. J., Feb. 19, 2003, at C1; Ellen E. Schultz and Theo Francis, *Death Benefit: How Corporations Built Finance Tool Out of Life Insurance*, Wall St. J., Dec. 30, 2002, at A1; Theo Francis and Ellen E. Schultz, *Tax Advantages of Life Insurance Help Lift Income*, Wall St. J., Dec. 30, 2002, at A8]

### [D]   Section 79 (Group-Term Life)

Internal Revenue Code § 79 allows an employer to establish a written, non-discriminatory plan to provide term life insurance policies to a group of employees. (Term life insurance is pure insurance, with no cash value.) Employees can receive up to $50,000 worth of coverage under the plan with no tax consequences to them. But if the employer provides coverage over $50,000, the employee does have taxable income. The calculation is based on an official IRS table. The excess coverage is subject to FICA tax but not FUTA tax or income tax withholding. [I.R.C. § 3121(a)(2)]

The table was revised effective July 1, 1999. [See 64 Fed. Reg. 29788 (June 3, 1999)] At press time in 2013, this table was still current, according to the IRS Website.

| Employee's Age | Prior Law | Revised Rates |
|---|---|---|
| Up to 25 | .08 | .05 |
| 25–29 | .08 | .06 |
| 30–34 | .09 | .08 |
| 35–39 | .11 | .09 |
| 40–44 | .17 | .10 |
| 45–49 | .29 | .15 |
| 50–54 | .48 | .23 |
| 55–59 | .75 | .43 |
| 60–64 | 1.17 | .66 |
| 65–70 | 2.10 | 1.27 |
| >70 | 3.76 | 2.06 |

A Section 79 plan must either be available to all employees, or to groups of employees defined in a way that does not allow selection of employees based on individual characteristics. So the plan can condition eligibility on factors related to age or employment, but not on the amount of the corporation's stock that the person owns. Nor can the amount of coverage be based on individual factors (although it can be proportionate to compensation). As a general rule, Section 79 plans must cover at least ten employees.

To satisfy the nondiscrimination test, the plan must benefit at least 70% of the sponsoring company's employees, and not more than 15% of the participants may be key employees. If the group-term life insurance plan is part of a cafeteria plan, it must also satisfy the I.R.C. § 125 rules. If the plan fails the nondiscrimination test, then highly compensated employees will have to include the full cost of coverage (not just the coverage over and above $50,000) in income.

The IRS' mid-2007 cafeteria plan proposals include a simplified rule for calculating the cost of group-term life insurance. There is a safe harbor for premium-only cafeteria plans that do not discriminate as to eligibility. The proposal also includes a simplified rule for calculating the cost of group-term life insurance: the amount taxable to the employee is based entirely on the cost of any excess coverage under Table I of the § 79 regulations. [72 Fed. Reg. 43938 (Aug. 6, 2007)]

The Moving Ahead for Progress in the 21st Century Act (MAP-21; Pub. L. No. 112-141) allows sponsors of over-funded defined benefit pension plans to use Code § 401(h) to transfer funds from the pension plan to an account to provide retiree benefits: either health benefits or group-term life insurance (generally limited to $50,000 per person). Section 401(h) was scheduled to expire on December 31, 2013, but MAP-21 not only extended its applicability until December 31, 2021 but also added group-term life to health benefits as a possible 401(h) benefit. The life insurance assets must be kept in a separate account within the 401(h) plan, segregated both from the general assets of the defined benefit plan and the retiree health benefit account.

## [E]   Split Dollar

A split dollar plan is a benefit arrangement that divides ownership, and possibly premium payments, between an employer and an employee. Each year the employer makes a contribution equal to the policy's increase in cash value for the year. Under the "endorsement method," the employer owns the policy. The policy is endorsed to allocate cash value and death benefit between employer and employee. Under the "collateral assignment" method, either the employee or a third party owns the policy and then assigns it to the employer. At the employee's death, the employer receives either the cash value of the policy or an amount representing the premiums paid; the rest of the benefits go to the employee's designated beneficiary. If the plan is an "equity split dollar plan," the employer is entitled to repayment of the premiums it paid, while the rest of the proceeds go to the designated beneficiary.

Split dollar plans became popular as a way to enhance the compensation of top executives without angering the shareholders by disclosing the full value of the compensation package, and while giving executives the security of benefits backed by the insurer's resources. [For historical perspective on split dollar, see, e.g., Theo Francis and Ellen E. Schultz, *Insurers Move to Protect Executive Policy*, Wall St. J., Dec. 30, 2002, at C1]

However, beginning in 2001, the IRS launched an attack on split dollar as a compensation mechanism. Another factor was the Sarbanes-Oxley Act's ban on personal loans to the directors and officers of public corporations, a provision that brought new sales of corporate split dollar policies to a halt because of uncertainties as to whether split dollar arrangements would be treated as interest-free loans to executives.

Notice 2007-34, 2007-17 I.R.B. 996, explains the interface between split-dollar insurance and non-qualified plans. Insurance arrangements that provide nothing but death benefits, or that generate amounts that are included in income, are exempt from taxation under § 409A. The cost of current life insurance protection is excluded from § 409A, even if there are additional economic benefits under the arrangement. But policy cash value that is available to the employee, and is payable in a year after the year of service is likely to be deferred compensation under § 409A. Split-dollar loans generally do not give rise to § 409A deferred compensation—unless, for example, loan amounts are waived, cancelled, or forgiven. Notice 2009-48, 2009-24 I.R.B. includes split-dollar contracts in the definition of employer-owned life insurance subject to Code § 60391. [See Nevin E. Adams, *IRS Sets Out Limits for Employer-Owned Life Insurance Expense*, plansponsor.com (May 26, 2009)]

### [F]  Case Law on Life Insurance Fringe Benefits

Life insurance plans, like other employee benefit plans, often give rise to disputes about benefit eligibility and whether a survivor beneficiary has been properly designated.

Spradley, a 37-year veteran at Owens-Illinois, took early retirement at age 55 because of a disability. About nine months before his retirement, he submitted a claim stating that the Social Security Administration found him to be permanently and totally disabled as of March 1, 2008. Under the plan, PTD life insurance benefits are payable to persons who are unable to engage in substantial gainful activities because of a permanent and total disability commencing before age 65, and who file a claim within 12 months of leaving employment—or who are under 65 and receive SSDI. Spradley received a denial letter that referred only to health insurance, not the PTD life insurance he applied for. He appealed the denial, which was upheld on the grounds that health insurance is available only to active employees. He brought an ERISA suit. The defendant argued that PTD life insurance is available only for temporary disability. The district court ordered payment of benefits. On appeal, the question was whether the plan administrator's denial was arbitrary and capricious. The Tenth Circuit found that the denial was inappropriate, and the district court should have entered judgment for the plaintiff based on the record instead of remanding for further proceedings—which would only give the plan a chance to fabricate more excuses. [*Spradley v. Owens-Illinois Hourly Emps. Welfare Benefit Plan*, 686 F.3d 1135 (10th Cir. 2012)]

The Northern District of Ohio held that a divorce decree making the employee's child the sole beneficiary of a life insurance policy is a QDRO. The district court noted that welfare benefit plans can have QDROs: see 29 U.S.C. § 1144(b)(7), and life insurance plans are welfare benefit plans. (The employee remarried, then designated his second wife as 100% beneficiary of his life insurance, despite the divorce decree.) [*Metropolitan Life Ins. Co. v. Darkow*, No. 5:09CV02482, 2010 U.S. Dist. LEXIS 77187 (N.D. Ohio July 30, 2010); see Rebecca Moore, *Divorce Decree Naming Child as Life Insurance Beneficiary Is a QDRO*, plansponsor.com (Aug. 4, 2010)]

Dennis Hall designated one of his four children as beneficiary of his employment-related life insurance policy in 1991. In 2001, he married Jane, but did not change the beneficiary form. In early 2010, when he was diagnosed with cancer, he told his employer that he wanted to change the beneficiary, and was given a change of beneficiary form but did not complete it. In 2011, when he learned his condition was terminal, he had his daughter complete a will form for him that named his wife as beneficiary of the life insurance. He died that day. Insurer MetLife refused to pay the benefits to Jane. The beneficiary designation on file, from 1991, did not name Jane. Because the plan gave MetLife discretion over eligibility decisions, the denial was reviewed for abuse of discretion. The district court held that it was not unreasonable to refuse to pay the benefits to Jane: the plan required participants to give the employer a signed change of beneficiary form within 30 days of the date the form was signed, and the employer never received a form naming Jane as beneficiary. [*Hall v. Metropolitan Life Ins. Co.*, No. 0:11-cv-01269-DWF-LIB (D. Minn. Jan. 15, 2013); see Kathy Sherby & Stephanie L. Moll, *Rock, Paper, Scissors: Life Insurance Beneficiary Designation Beats Will*, Lexology (May 9, 2013) (benefitslink.com)]

The Sixth Circuit held that an insurer is not obligated to provide life insurance benefits that are contrary to state law (in this case, portable term insurance, which was illegal in Michigan), so the District Court was correct to dismiss a surviving spouse's claim. When the decedent resigned from his job, he was given the right to convert the life insurance under an employee welfare plan to a group policy—contingent upon whether he lived in a state that approved such a continuation. When the widow's claim for death benefits that would have been payable if the policy had been converted was denied, she sued for the life insurance benefits and statutory penalties for failure to provide plan documents. The Sixth

Circuit held that the insurer, as fiduciary, did not act arbitrarily or capriciously in refusing what would have been an illegal conversion. Furthermore, the benefit claim accrued at the time of the original denial of conversion, not the date when the surviving spouse attempted to access plan benefits, so the claim was untimely under the applicable three-year statute of limitations. [*Morrison v. Marsh & McLennan*, 439 F.3d 295 (6th Cir. 2006)]

In a 2012 Fourth Circuit case, a life insurance/accidental death & disability plan was offered, with coverage for employees' children. The plaintiff, McCravy, filed a claim after her daughter died. The claim was denied, on the grounds that the daughter was no longer eligible for coverage after she reached age 19—but the plan continued to accept premiums for the coverage. The Fourth Circuit ruled that McCravy was entitled not only to a return of the premiums but also to a surcharge, as equitable relief under ERISA § 502(a)(3). [*McCravy v. MetLife,* 690 F.3d 176 (4th Cir. 2012); see Rebecca Moore, *4th Circuit Uses High Court Decision to Allow for Surcharge*, plansponsor.com (July 16, 2012)]

## § 21.03  LONG-TERM CARE INSURANCE PLANS

Long-term care insurance (LTCI) is private insurance, sold by life and health insurers, that covers the cost of home and institutional care for the frail elderly and disabled. There is an increasing trend for employers to offer group long-term care insurance plans as an employee benefit—and to permit employees not only to purchase coverage for themselves and their spouses, but for their parents. Individual coverage for senior citizens can be difficult to find, and is often expensive when it is available.

LTCI and benefits services provider EM-Power Services says that reasons for employers to offer workplace LTCI include:

- Reductions in health costs caused by caregiver stress;

- Better productivity, because caregivers miss less work;

- Helping employees avert family financial problems—the high cost of long-term care; depletes the savings even of affluent families;

- An LTCI program can be provided at little or no cost to the employer;

- The providers of LTCI can educate employees about elder care issues.

[Amanda McGrory, *5 Reasons To Offer LTCI In 2012*, Benefits Pro (Jan. 23, 2012) (benefitslink.com)]

Despite the obvious needs of an aging society and the burden on employee caregivers, the role of long-term care insurance is dwindling as part of the overall health care package, according to HighRoads' Long-Term Care Benefits Program Pulse Survey. About half of the respondents (51%) provided LTCI—71% on a group basis, the rest individual policies. About half of those who dropped LTCI from their plan said that their carrier left the market, but 96% of companies offering LTCI said they planned to maintain it. Among respondents who did not offer LTCI, 40% said they planned to do so in the future, but as a voluntary program. [HighRoads, *Long-Term Care Coverage for Employees Continues to Decline as More Insurers Leave, Says HighRoads Study* (Mar. 7, 2012) (benefitslink.com)]

Work-related LTCI coverage usually is completely paid for by the employee. The employer's role is purely to administer the plan, and make it easier for employees to get insurance (frequently without proof of insurability) and at lower, group rates than if they purchased policies individually. Workplace LTCI sales can either take the form of a master policy with certificates issued under it, or a group discount of perhaps 5–10% for purchase of individual policies. [NU Online News Service, *Insurer Sees Employers Backing LTC Plans* (Jan. 30, 2007)] The continuing viability of workplace LTCI has been questioned by some commentators, because a number of once-important insurers have stopped selling group LTCI. As of mid-2012, Genworth and Prudential were the only remaining companies that still sold true group LTCI plans (where the employer or plan sponsor buys a master policy). Genworth also sold individual workplace LTCI policies, but Prudential had stopped selling individual policies. [Richard W. Samson, Employee Benefit Adviser, *Is This The End of Group Long-Term Care?* (July 1, 2012) (benefitslink.com)]

Certain kinds of LTCI are tax-favored: for policies that satisfy federally prescribed criteria, LTCI premiums are tax-deductible (within limits), and a certain amount of benefits can be received under the policy even if the insured person has no taxable income. (If the policy is an indemnity policy that pays the full cost of care, then the entire amount is tax-free—but indemnity policies are rare.) The cost figures for this purpose are adjusted every year.

For 2013, the potentially deductible long-term care insurance premium is limited to $360 (person under 40), $680 (ages 40–50), $1,360 (ages 50–60), $3,640 (60–70), and $4,550 (over 70). The periodic payment that can be received under a long-term care insurance policy is $320. [ Rev. Proc. 2012-45, 2012—45 I.R.B. 539]

Starting in 2013, fewer taxpayers will be able to claim medical expense deductions, because even qualified medical expenses are deductible only to the extent that they exceed 10% of Adjusted Gross Income (AGI). Previously, qualified expenses over 7.5% of AGI were deductible. Senior citizens, who usually have higher medical expenses than younger people, get a relief provision: the 10% limit does not apply to persons aged 65 or over until 2017.

# CHAPTER 22

# OTHER FRINGE BENEFITS

## § 22.01  INTRODUCTION

This book has already dealt with issues of setting and administering current compensation (pay planning), deferred compensation (pension planning), and the provision of several of the major types of fringe benefits: health plans, disability coverage, and life insurance plans.

This chapter traces their tax, ERISA, and state-law consequences. The availability of benefits tends to fluctuate based on employers' needs: when employees are hard to recruit, benefits often become more generous—especially if employers can put together a package of benefits that are low or moderate in cost, but highly valued by employees. However, the economic decline beginning in 2008 not only created something of a buyer's market for employment, but also reduced the amount of funds many corporations had available for benefits and other compensation.

For tax purposes, the most relevant sections include I.R.C. § 162 (allowing a deduction for all of the employer's ordinary and necessary business expenses, including the employer's contributions to unfunded welfare benefit plans) and I.R.C. §§ 419 and 419A, which set limits on the deductions.

In general, employers will be able to deduct direct payments of benefits or expenses. Employers can make contributions that bear a reasonable actuarial relationship to the amounts that will be needed to pay benefits in the future. In some circumstances, a statutory safe harbor allows deductible contributions.

If a funded welfare plan earns income (e.g., from investments), that income will probably be taxed to the employer that maintains the plan. Unrelated business taxable income (UBTI) earned by the plan will almost certainly be taxed to the employer. [See Chapter 1, §§ 1.08, 1.12 for a discussion of some of the issues of determining who is an "employee" who is or might be eligible for plan participation]

The American Taxpayer Relief Act, Pub. L. No. 112-40 (ATRA; popularly known as the "fiscal cliff" bill) does not provide guidance about supplemental withholding so employers should continue using the optional 25% supplemental withholding rate on supplemental wages up to $1 million. This legislation extends the exclusion of up to $5,250 per year in education assistance from the recipient's gross income after its scheduled expiration date in 2012. The exclusion has been made permanent. ATRA also makes favorable tax treatment of employer assistance with adoption costs permanent. [Baker McKenzie Executive Compensation & Employee Benefits, *New Tax Rates in Effect for 2013* (Jan. 3, 2013) (benefitslink.com)]

Under Rev. Proc. 2013-15, 2013-5 I.R.B. 444, for tax years that begin in 2013, the maximum adoption assistance is $12,970, whether or not the adoptee has special needs, and whether the taxpayer excludes employer-provided assistance from gross income or claims a credit. For 2013, the adoption credit phases down if the claimant's AGI exceeds $194,580 and is eliminated at an AGI level of $234,580. [Wolters Kluwer Law & Business, *IRS Issues 2013 Adoption And Transportation Benefit COLAs* (Jan. 21, 2013) (benefitslink.com)]

## § 22.02  STOCK OPTIONS

### [A]  Generally

Stock options give employees (either a broad base of employees, or top executives only) the right to purchase stock in the employer corporation at a particular price at a stated time. The intention is that the exercise price will be far below the market value of the shares. However, under current conditions, many options are "underwater" (see § 22.02[G])—that is, they are almost certain not to be exercised, because the holder of the option would have to pay far more than the market price to exercise the option.

According to the Wall Street Journal/Hay Group Survey of CEO Compensation, which uses data from 300 large public companies, for 51 CEOs, at least half of their 2012 compensation was tied to specific targets based on the company's financial performance or its stock market results. In 2009, only about one-third of CEO compensation was subject to performance conditions; the rest came from salaries and stock and option grants that were not subject to performance criteria. For example, Smithfield Foods' income fell 31% and its share price dropped 11%. Its CEO was not granted any stock options for 2011 and some of his future stock awards will be based on how Smithfield's stock performs in comparison to the stock of its competitors. Farient Advisors (a consulting firm that specializes in pay issues) says that only one-fifth of the companies in the S&P 1500 subjected their equity grants to performance criteria in 2002, whereas almost two-thirds (64%) did so in 2011. [Scott Thurm, *'Pay for Performance' No Longer a Punchline*, WSJ (Mar. 20, 2013)]

For tax purposes, stock options are divided into statutory and non-statutory options. Statutory options are granted as part of an employee stock purchase plan or incentive stock option program; all other options are non-statutory. The distinction is significant because the two types of options are taxed differently. The IRS says that options granted under an Employee Stock Ownership Plan (ESOP) or an Incentive Stock Option (ISO) plan will generally be statutory options, whereas other options are non-statutory. A person receiving a grant of statutory options generally does not have income either at the time of the grant or when the option is exercised, although exercise of an ISO may be subject to Alternative Minimum Tax. See the instructions for Form 6251.

But when the stock obtained via the option is sold, the taxpayer's income or loss will be treated as a capital gain or capital loss (depending on whether the stock was sold for more or less than the option price). If the stock is sold before the holding period expires, then the income from the sale will be ordinary income. The employer must issue Form 3921 when an ISO is exercised, to give the employee the information needed to determine if any tax is payable because of an ISO-related transaction. The employer must issue Form 3922 when an employee sells or otherwise transfers stock acquired via an ESOP option.

For non-statutory options, the primary tax question is whether the fair market value of the option can be readily determined (e.g., if it is actively traded on an established market.) The IRS says that most non-statutory options do not have a readily determined fair market value, so granting the option is not a taxable event—but the fair market value of the stock minus the amount paid for it constitutes taxable income when the option is exercised. The employee will have income or loss (generally capital rather than ordinary) on selling the stock obtained under the option. [IRS Topic 427, *Stock Options*, <http://www.irs.gov/taxtopics/tc427.html>, Last updated Jan. 4, 2013. See IRS Publication 525, *Taxable and Nontaxable Income*, for guidance on classifying options.]

For practical and tax reasons, the employer will probably want to impose some limitations on the options. A typical restriction is the employee's obligation to put (resell) the stock back to the corporation on termination of employment. An arrangement like this includes a method of calculating the put price (e.g., book value or a set P/E ratio).

A stock bonus plan is very similar to a profit-sharing plan from both the labor law and tax perspectives. However, distributions are generally made in the employer's common stock rather than in cash. Employees must be given put options obligating the employer to repurchase shares of stock that are not readily tradeable on an established market.

An Employee Stock Ownership Plan (ESOP) is a stock bonus plan or a plan combining stock bonus and money-purchase features. ESOPs invest primarily in the employer's common stock. The Internal Revenue Code contains additional rules for leveraged ESOPs that borrow the funds used to purchase the stock. ESOPs are often adopted as a defense against hostile takeovers of the issuing corporation. Furthermore, because ESOPs are designed to invest in employer stock, fiduciaries of such plans are not vulnerable to "stock-drop" suits that are common in 401(k) plans when the value of the employer's stock has declined, and plan participants charge that fiduciaries should have removed the stock from the list of available plan investments, or at least diminished its importance.

In mid-2008, regulations were proposed under Code § 423 for ESOPs. Usually, an ESOP works by issuing options allowing participating employees to purchase employer stock. The employee makes an election to have a particular amount or a percentage of after-tax wages deducted from pay and accumulated. After the regular purchase period ends, the option is exercised and the shares are purchased at the option price. If the conditions under the Code are satisfied, the employee does not have income—and the employer does not have a compensation deduction—at the time the shares are acquired. The employee must be employed at the time of the grant, and up to three months before the exercise, and the employee must hold the shares for one year from the transfer of the shares, or two years from the grant of the option, whichever is later. (This is also true of ISOs.)

Section 423 forbids employees to acquire shares at a rate exceeding $25,000 in fair market value of stock for each calendar year in which an option remains outstanding and exercisable, calculated the same way as the $100,000 limitation on ISOs. [73 Fed. Reg. 43875 (July 29, 2008); see Faegre & Benson LLP, *IRS Issues Proposed Regulations for Employee Stock Purchase Plans* (Aug. 1, 2008) (benefitslink.com)]

On November 16, 2009, the IRS finalized these 2008 proposed regulations. The final regulations took effect January 1, 2010. Under § 423, stock acquired under an Employee Stock Purchase Plan (ESPP) option receives favorable tax treatment as long as statutory requirements are satisfied. The employee is not taxed (but the employer does not receive a deduction) when the option is exercised, if the purchase price is at least 85% of the FMV of the stock when the option was granted or when it is exercised (whichever is less); the plan and the offering satisfy the § 423 requirements; and the employee holds the stock for at least two years from grant and one year from exercise of the option. For nonqualified options, the employee has ordinary income at the time of exercise, equal to any excess of fair market value over the exercise price.

The final regulations divide the statutory requirements into those that must be satisfied by the plan and those that can be satisfied separately by each offering under the plan. If an offering fails to satisfy the § 423 requirements, stock purchased in that offering does not receive favorable tax treatment, but it does not disqualify other offerings that comply with the rules. An employer can make multiple, successive, or overlapping offerings. The terms of the options can vary from offering to offering. For example, the offering for one subsidiary can include highly compensated employees, while a simultaneous offering in another subsidiary excludes them.

Most ESPPs accumulate employees' contributions in an unfunded account that is used to buy the stock at a set price on a set date.

The plan, including the maximum number of shares available, must be approved by stockholders within 12 months before or after the adoption date of the plan. The regulations clarify some questions about which company's shareholders must approve the plan in a mergers and acquisitions context. Other than the four statutory exceptions, options must be granted to all employees of any corporation whose employees receive any options. Up to $25,000 worth of stock can be optioned for each year the option is outstanding, whether or not the option is exercisable. The exercise price must be at least 85% of the FMV at the time of grant or exercise.

An option is considered granted only when the maximum number of shares that can be purchased under the option is determinable. If the plan uses an open formula, where the number of shares depends on the share price and accumulation account at the date of exercise, the option is only considered granted when it is exercised—unless the overall maximum number of shares is stated from the outset. Offerings do not have to be made available to citizens or residents of non-U.S. jurisdictions where the offering is illegal under local law, or complying with local law would violate § 423. The plan, including the maximum number of shares available, must be approved by stockholders within the 12 months before or after the date of adoption. The plan must provide that options can be granted only to employees, not independent contractors, and anyone who owns 5% or more of the company's stock must not receive options under the plan. The plan cannot allow for redemption more than 27 months from the date of the grant (or five years, if the option price is at least 85% of the FMV at the date of exercise).

The final regulations make some changes from the proposed regulations. For example, if the exercise price of options is not determinable on the grant date—for example, if it is based on the fair market value on a later date—then the participant's tax liability when the shares are sold may depend on the exercise price per share, determined as if the option had been exercised on the grant date. Therefore, Form 3922 requires the company to report information for this calculation.

Form 3921 (ISOs) reports:

- Grant and exercise date of the ISO;
- Exercise price per share;
- FMV of a share on the exercise date;
- Number of shares transferred in exercise of the ISO.

Form 3922 (ESOP shares) reports:

- Grant and exercise date of the option;
- FMV of a share on the grant date and exercise date;
- The price paid per share on the exercise date;
- Number of shares to which title was transferred;
- Date of the first transfer of title;
- (If the exercise price was not fixed or determinable on the grant date) Exercise price per share, calculated as if the option had been exercised on the grant date.

An option issuer's failure to make a timely Form 3921 or 3922 filing is penalized by up to $50 per form (capped at $250,000 per year). Failure to give employees forms relating to their options is penalized by $50 per form, up to a maximum of $100,000 per year. Electronic filing is mandatory if the employer files 250 or more forms. [Fred Schneyer, *Employee Stock Reporting Deadlines Approaching*, plansponsor.com (Nov. 19, 2010); Vorys, Sater, Seymour and Pease LLP Client Alert, *Reminder—Reporting Required for Exercise of ISOs, ESPP Options* (Nov. 18, 2010) (benefitslink.com)]

Stock appreciation rights (SARs) are really a form of cash compensation. The grantee of SARs gets money from the corporation, based on the price of the company stock. If, for instance, a corporate Vice President has SARs for 1,000 shares, the corporation will pay him or her the difference between the FMV of those shares at the time of exercise and the FMV at the time of grant. SARs are not usually issued by themselves. Generally they accompany qualified or non-qualified stock options. Often, they can be exercised with the stock options, giving the employee some of the cash needed to pay for the optioned shares. A restricted stock plan grants stock outright, although with restrictions that defer taxation until the restrictions lapse. SARs provide compensation, in the form of cash and/or stock, pegged to the appreciation in value of the stock between the grant date and the exercise date. If the intention is to give the executive additional flexibility, SARs can be combined with incentive stock options. Phantom stock plans entitle the plan participant to receive cash and/or stock equal to the value of a hypothetical award of shares, although the participants do not actually receive ownership of the shares, only compensation equal to their value. [Sverre Roang, *Executive Compensation: Besides Stock Options, What Else Is There?*, Wisconsin Technology News (Apr. 2, 2008), <http://wistechnology.com/articles/4658>]

A public company must satisfy the requirements under Code § 162(m) for restricted stock and restricted stock units (RSUs) to be fully deductible. Under § 162(m), the general rule is that a public company is limited to a $1 million compensation deduction apiece for its CEO and four other highest compensated officers. But there is an exception: the $1 million limit does not apply to qualified performance-based compensation that is only paid if the payee meets at least one objective performance goal that was set in advance. The performance-based compensation must have been ordered either by the company's board or a compensation committee consisting of outside directors and the terms of the plan are disclosed to, and approved by, the shareholders in advance. In mid-2012, the IRS issued guidance on whether dividends on restricted stock and the equivalent on RSUs must satisfy the § 162(m) requirements separately to be treated as fully deductible performance-based compensation: Rev. Rul. 2012-19, 2012-28 I.R.B. 16.

Restricted stock is company stock that is released based on a vesting schedule, whereas RSUs are a right to get vested stock in the future. Usually, restricted stock carries voting rights but RSUs do not. Some companies make "dividend equivalent" payments on RSUs: cash payments equivalent to the dividends on the restricted stock for the period between the grant and the vesting date. Rev. Rul. 2012-19 says that to qualify for exemption from the $1 million exemption, the dividends or dividend equivalents can only be payable if the payee meets performance goals. However, the performance goals for this purpose do not have to be the same ones for granting the underlying restricted stock or RSUs.

Public corporations should not only review their stock compensation plans for compliance, they should check the tax consequences of other documents, such as severance plans and golden parachutes, involving employees who receive grants of restricted stock and/or RSUs. [Buck Consultants FYI, *IRS Clarifies*

*Treatment of Performance-Based Restricted Stock and Restricted Stock Units* (Aug. 8, 2012) (benefitslink.com)]

As long as stock options are issued "at the money" rather than at a discount, they are not subject to Code § 409A (the tax provisions dealing with certain non-qualified plans).

Nor does I.R.C. § 409A apply to stock appreciation rights (SARs) that are issued by a public company if the rights are settled in employer stock; they are not discounted, and therefore do not have the effect of deferring compensation.

Dr. Senat Sutardja received a board-approved grant of up to two million stock options on December 10, 2003, well before the effective date of § 409A, from a corporation of which he was a co-founder. The stock price on the grant date was $36.19. The company's compensation committee finalized the grant on December 16, 2003 as 1.5 million stock options, at an exercise price of $36.50, the stock price on that date. On January 16, 2004, when the stock price was $43.64, the $1.5 million share grant was ratified. In January 2006, Sutardja exercised some options. (In the interim, § 409A had taken effect on January 1, 2005.) Subsequently, Sutardja signed an agreement to reform the stock option agreement. He paid $5.35 million between the original and amended exercise prices. Commentator Michael S. Melbinger described this as an attempt to correct an understated exercise price, at a time when there were no § 409A regulations available for guidance. In November 2010, the IRS ruled that the exercise of the option was for less than FMV (fair market value) and imposed a 20% surtax, plus interest on the underpayment. Under the regulations, discounted stock options are subject to § 409A and must have fixed dates for exercise and payment and must not have any discretionary provisions about the time or form of payment. Sutardja said that the exercise was not deferred compensation under Code § 3121(v) and, therefore, was not deferred compensation for § 409A purposes. The Court of Federal Claims followed a 2005 IRS Notice that treats discounted stock options as deferred compensation, despite the language found in § 3121(v).

Sutardja also argued that he did not have a legally binding right to the compensation until he exercised the option, but the Court of Federal Claims ruled that the compensation was earned at the grant of the option and Sutardja was legally entitled to the compensation as soon as there was no longer a substantial risk of forfeiture and the options had vested. Finally, Sutardja argued that the short-term exemption of § 409A applied because the options were exercised within 2.5 months of the end of the year in which the options vested. The court's interpretation was different: like most plans, this one gave Sutardja a 10-year period in which he could exercise the options; he was not obligated to do so within 2.5 months of the end of the year of vesting. Sutardja pointed to a provision in the grant giving him 30 days after being terminated to exercise the option, saying that this provision made the options at substantial risk of forfeiture until he actually exercised them at a time when he had not been terminated. This argument was also rejected: the Court of Federal Claims said that the 30 days were just a grace period, not a condition creating a substantial risk of forfeiture. The case was remanded to decide the fact question of whether the options were granted at a discount. [*Sutardja v. United States*, 109 Fed. Cl. 358 (Fed. Claims 2013); see Jeffrey Cairns, *Section 409A Tax Assessed on Discounted Stock Options – Taxpayer Sues for Refund in Federal Court of Claims*, Benefits Notes (Mar. 7, 2013); Michael S. Melbinger, *If You Thought the IRS Would Not Punish 409A Foot Faults, Think Again*, Winston & Strawn LLP (Mar. 26, 2013) (benefitslink.com); David W. Eckhart, *Sutardja v. United States: When Options Are No Longer Optional*, Whyte Hirschboeck Dudek S.C. Special Report (March 2013)]

A junior stock plan is another motivational device. Executives are given the right to buy junior stock (stock in the employer corporation with reduced dividend rights and voting powers). Owners of junior stock can convert it to ordinary common stock by achieving specified performance goals.

In 2011, the Supreme Court of Texas held that it is lawful for an employer to require an employee to give a covenant not to compete in exchange for letting the employee exercise stock options—as long as the non-compete agreement is reasonable in time, geographic area, and scope of activity, whether or not the employee had access to confidential information. The state Supreme Court said that stock options that are reasonably related to goodwill or other protectable interests such as confidential information and trade secrets create the necessary connection between the non-compete clause and the business interests. In this case, the stock options were ancillary to the protection of goodwill, so the agreement could be legitimate. The case was remanded to the trial court to determine the reasonableness of the agreement. [*Marsh USA Inc. v. Cook*, 2011 Tex. LEXIS 465 (Tex. June 24, 2011); see John L. Utz, *Noncompete as Condition for Option Exercise in Texas*, Utz, Miller & Eickmann LLC (Sept. 20, 2011) (benefitslink.com)]

The Idaho Supreme Court ruled that stock options are not wages under state law—so it was not a violation of state law to fire an employee for intending to exercise his stock options. The court defined "wages" under state law to mean compensation for services rendered, determined on the basis of time, task, piecework, or commissions—categories that do not include stock options. Therefore, firing someone for reasons related to stock option exercise did not violate the public policy exception to employment at will, because "wages" meant only monetary compensation paid on a periodic basis, not non-monetary compensation paid in stock. [*Paolini v. Albertson's Inc.*, 143 Idaho 547 (2006); see Adrien Martin, *Idaho Court Rules Stock Options Are Not Wages*, plansponsor.com (Jan. 30, 2007)]

The Northern District of Illinois permitted two ex-employees to pursue a claim that the company breached a stock option contract by allowing options to expire during a two-year blackout period. (The blackout period was extended by an accounting restatement.) During the blackout period, only accredited investors could exercise options, so the plaintiffs and 54 others could not exercise their remaining vested options after leaving the company in 2007. The other 54 employees accepted an offer of cash reimbursement, so they did not sue. The

Northern District of Illinois held that releases signed by the plaintiffs did not apply to the options: the releases only applied to claims that had already arisen when the releases were signed and the options expired after the releases were signed. The district court also refused to dismiss claims under the Illinois Wage Payment and Collection Act, holding that stock options can be considered "other compensation"—even though most courts have held that options and other equity awards are not subject to state wage payment laws. [*Rawat v. Navistar Int'l*, No. 08-cv-04305 2012 U.S. Dist. LEXIS 1566 (N.D. Ill. Jan. 4, 2012); see Michael Melbinger, Winston & Strawn LLP Executive Compensation Blog, *Litigation Over Unexercised Options that Expired* (Feb. 6, 2012) (benefitslink.com)]

The California Supreme Court held that Citigroup's voluntary employee compensation plan, allowing employees to elect to take some of their compensation in reduced-price shares of restricted stock, did not violate the California Labor Code's requirement of prompt payment of "earned wages" when an employee quits or is fired. Incentive compensation is not like vacation pay (compensation for past services, which vests pro rata as soon as the employee performs substantial services). Incentive compensation is an inducement for the employee to continue working and achieving goals. [*Schachter v. Citigroup, Inc.*, 47 Cal. 4th 610 (Cal. 2009); see Morgan, Lewis & Bockius LawFlash/Client Alert, *California Supreme Court Affirms Employer's Right to Offer Voluntary Equity Plan* (Nov. 5, 2009) (benefitslink.com); Ethan Lipsig and Jeffrey D. Wohl, Paul, Hastings, Janofsky & Wohler, *California Supreme Court Upholds Forfeiture of Incentive Compensation* (November 2009) (benefitslink.com)]

See § 1.01[A] for discussion of advisory "say on pay" votes that public corporations must hold as a result of the Dodd-Frank Act (Pub. L. No. 111-203), the extensive package of financial services regulatory legislation that was enacted in July 2010.

## [B]   Incentive Stock Options (ISOs)

Internal Revenue Code § 422 creates a specially tax-favored category of Incentive Stock Options (ISOs). An ISO plan is permitted to discriminate in favor of highly compensated employees. However, favorable tax consequences are available to the employee only if he or she retains the shares for at least one year from the exercise of the option and two years from the grant of the option.

ISOs must be granted pursuant to a plan that states the aggregate number of shares that can be issued under option, and indicates which employees can receive them. The corporation's shareholders must approve the plan, during the time period running from 12 months before to 12 months after the adoption of the plan. Options can only be granted during the 10-year period after the adoption of the plan, but the corporation can simply adopt further ISO plans after the initial 10-year period expires.

The option price must be at least equal to the fair market value of the stock at the time the option is granted. In other words, ISOs cannot be issued at a bargain price, although NQSOs can be. The employees must wait for the stock's value to appreciate to benefit from the options.

Employees themselves can only exercise ISOs, during their lifetimes. Employees are only allowed to transfer ISOs by will or intestacy. If, at the time of the grant, the grantee owns 10% or more of the corporation's stock, the option price must be set higher, and only five years can be given to exercise the option, not ten.

Furthermore, the aggregate fair market value of each employee's stock cannot exceed $100,000 (measured as of the date of the grant of the option) in the first calendar year for which the options are exercisable. The $100,000 limit does not have to be written into the ISO plan document. It is applied automatically, and amounts over $100,000 simply are not characterized as ISOs.

Section 251 of the American Jobs Creation Act of 2004 (Pub. L. No. 108-357) amends I.R.C. § 3121(a), § 421(b), and § 423(c) to provide that FICA and FUTA "wages" do not include remuneration derived from exercising an Incentive Stock Option or an option to buy stock under an ESOP. (Nor does this remuneration count toward the person's future Social Security benefits.) The spread (the difference between the stock's FMV and the option price) is not income at the time of the exercise. However, if the statutory holding period is satisfied, it does constitute capital gain once the stock is disposed of. This treatment is effective for stock acquired through options exercised after the enactment of the AJCA.

The Tax Relief and Health Care Act of 2006 (TRHCA; Pub. L. No. 109-432) changed the reporting requirements for stock transferred under an ISO or an employee stock purchase plan (ESPP). The current rule is that the employer must report to the IRS when shares are transferred pursuant to an ISO or ESPP if the option price is in the range of 85%–100% of the value of the stock. The first reports will be due early in 2008, and shares transferred in 2007 under previous arrangements must also be reported. The IRS has stated that there will be a $50 penalty for failure to file a required statement. The issuer must also provide a written statement to each employee for whom an information return is filed; the statement is due January 31 of the year following the calendar year of the transfer. [Powell Goldstein LLP Client Alert, *New Reporting Requirements for Incentive Stock Options and Employee Stock Purchase Plans*, <http://www.pogolaw/files/news-alerts/2156/Report+Requirements-Stock+Options_2.07.pdf> (Feb. 12, 2007)] [David Rogers, *Tax Bill Spells Relief for Tech-Bubble Options Gains Ensnared in AMT*, Wall St. J., Dec. 13, 2006, at A6]

Code § 425 provides that an ISO loses its entitlement to favorable tax treatment if it is modified, unless the modified option meets the ISO requirements as of the date of the modification, or unless changes are made in connection with a corporate transaction. As long as the option itself provides for employer discretion (e.g., to pay a bonus or make a loan when an option is exercised), the exercise of discretion is not a modification of the option.

An out-of-the-money option has no economic value and, therefore, does not operate as an incentive to the option-holder. Therefore, in bad economic times, repricing is common: companies either reduce the exercise price of the employees' outstanding stock options to the current price or raise the exercise price to provide tax benefits for the holders of the options. Section 409A requires an ISO's exercise price to be at least equal to the stock price on the date of the option grant. For a private company, it must be at least equal to the fair market value of the stock, calculated by reasonably applying a reasonable valuation method reflecting the facts and circumstances at the date of valuation. Otherwise, discount stock options—those granted at an exercise price below the stock price on the grant date—are subject to ordinary income tax plus a 20% penalty tax when they vest, measured on the difference between the stock price at the time of vesting and the exercise price.

Notice 2008-113, 2008-51 I.R.B. 1305, provides that outstanding discount stock options that otherwise satisfy § 422 can be turned into ISOs by increasing the exercise price to the stock price at the option grant date. But repriced options satisfy § 409A only if the discount price was erroneously set on the date of the grant; the options are repriced before the employee exercises them; and repricing occurs not later than the last day of the employee's tax year in which the options were granted. However, if the employee is not an "insider" as defined by Securities Exchange Act § 16 at any time during the year of the grant, options can be repriced until the last day of the employee's tax year immediately following the year of the grant.

Employees must be given the choice of whether or not to take the repricing offer; if they refuse, the options continue to be treated as discount options. Accepting the offer provides the tax benefits of an ISO, but does not necessarily maximize the future profit that can be obtained from the option. [Jin Dong Park, *Upward Stock Option Repricing*, J. of Accountancy (September 2011) (benefitslink.com)]

## [C]  Nonqualified Stock Options (NQSOs)

Nonqualified stock options (NQSOs) are stock options that do not satisfy the I.R.C. § 422 rules. Sometimes NQSOs are issued "in the money": that is, the price at which the option can be exercised is lower than the current value of the stock, not just the anticipated future value of the stock at the time the option can be exercised.

There is no tax effect at the time of the grant of an NQSO, as long as the option itself does not have a readily ascertainable market value (i.e., the options are not traded actively). When the option is exercised, the employee has taxable income, equal to the FMV of the stock minus the consideration paid for the option. However, if the stock received by exercising the option is not transferable, and is subject to a substantial risk of forfeiture, then income is not taxed until the condition lapses. At that time, the amount of gain is determined, using the then-current FMV of the stock.

The FMV of the stock at the time of the exercise of the option, minus the price of the option, is a preference item for Alternative Minimum Tax purposes.

The American Jobs Creation Act of 2004, Pub. L. No. 108-357, changed the tax effectiveness of discount stock options (non-qualified stock options with an exercise price lower than the stock's fair market value on the grant date). Under prior law, the question was whether the discount was so deep that the grant should be treated as direct issuance of the stock. For example, if options were granted to buy $10/share stock for a penny a share, that would be treated as a direct grant; but if the exercise price for the same stock were $8, the option feature would be recognized, and there would be a taxable event only at exercise of the option.

The AJCA subjects discount stock options to the I.R.C. § 409A deferred compensation rules (see Chapter 8). Deferred compensation can be paid only on the occurrence of specified events: death, separation from service, disability, change in control, unforeseen financial hardship, or the arrival of the date specified in the plan. The taxable income equals the option spread (the exercise price minus the current FMV of the stock). The spread is also subject to a 20% excise tax penalty.

The First Circuit decided, in 2008, that a stock option plan was not required to permit NQSOs to be exercised a week after the plan's deadline (three years post-retirement). Delaware law requires strict observance of the terms and conditions of stock option plans. There was no cause for estoppel here, because when he retired, the plaintiff was aware of his retirement date and of the three-year requirement, and his employer did not deprive him of information needed to exercise the options. [*Mariasch v. The Gillette Co.*, 521 F.3d 68 (1st Cir. 2008). The strict-observance rule comes from *First Marblehead Corp. v. House*, 473 F.3d 1 (1st Cir. 2006); later proceedings, upholding the jury verdict that the president of a financial services company reasonably relied on misrepresentations that the options had a duration of ten years, no damages were awarded because he would not in fact have exercised the options during the three months before they expired, because the company was in financial trouble at that time and the president did not have the $80,000 cash that would have been required to exercise the options: 541 F.3d 36 (1st Cir. 2008)]

### [D]  Option Taxation Under I.R.C. § 83

Internal Revenue Code § 83 governs all transfers of property in exchange for performance of services, so it is important to stock option taxation but also has broader applicability. Under I.R.C. § 83, the person who performs the services has taxable income, at ordinary income (not capital gains) rates at the time that the rights in the property become transferable or are no longer subject to a substantial risk of forfeiture.

The amount of ordinary income to be recognized equals the fair market value (FMV) of the property minus any amount the employee paid for it. The options can be made forfeitable if the employee leaves before a certain number of years of employment. That motivates the employee to stay longer by offering tax incentives: There is no taxable income until the restriction lapses.

The point at which an option becomes subject to I.R.C. § 83 depends on whether it has an ascertainable market value (for instance, if it is traded on an established market). If so, and if the option is vested, it is taxed as soon as it is granted—not at the later point when it is exercised. Options that have no ascertainable FMV do not become subject to I.R.C. § 83 until they are exercised, on the theory that an option with an FMV can be sold as a separate asset.

Therefore, the employee faces taxation at two stages. The first is when the option can be exercised and the stock purchased; the second is when the stock is sold. (Gains from the sale of stock are capital gains; they do not generate ordinary income.)

Stock options are vested when the stock is transferable and there is no longer a substantial risk of forfeiture. (Sometimes stock awarded to employees is endorsed on its face to prevent transfer.) Section 83 holds that property is subject to a substantial risk of forfeiture if the right to receive the property is conditioned on future performance of substantial services ("earn-out restriction").

There's no bright-line test for when services are substantial; it depends on factors such as the regularity with which services are supposed to be performed and the amount of time needed to perform them. A retiree whose consulting agreement allows him or her to keep the stock while failing to perform the services is not performing substantial services.

Under I.R.C. § 83, refraining from performing services (e.g., under a noncompete clause) can also give rise to a substantial risk of forfeiture.

For purposes of the Exchange Act of 1934's ban on "short-swing" profits earned by officers, directors, or 10% shareholders of public companies, Internal Revenue Code § 83(c)(3) provides that rights are not vested at any time that the person receiving stock options cannot sell the stock without violating the short-swing profit rules. That means that the insider who gets a stock option has no income either for six months or until the first day that the stock can be sold. Regulations were proposed under § 83 in mid-2012, stating that a transfer restriction such as a lock-up agreement, "clawback" provision, or potential liability under Exchange Act Rule 10b-5 does not constitute a substantial risk of forfeiture—but an Exchange Act § 16(b) transfer restriction does constitute a substantial risk of forfeiture. When the substantial risk is based on a condition related to the purpose of the transfer, both the likelihood that the event will occur, and the likelihood that the forfeiture provision will actually be enforced, must be taken into account. The proposed regulations are effective for transfers of property on or after January 1, 2013, but taxpayers can rely on them for transfers after May 30, 2012. [77 Fed. Reg. 31783 (May 30, 2012); see Michael S. Melbinger, *New Proposed Regulations Under Code Sec. 83 (Taxation of Amounts Subject to a Risk of Forfeiture)*:

*Just Clarifications, or Potentially Significant Changes?* Winston & Strawn LLP Executive Compensation Blog (May 30, 2012) (benefitslink.com)]

The health care reform law, PPACA, imposes additional taxes on high-income earners: AGI over $200,000 on a single return, $250,000 on a joint return. For these high earners, an additional Medicare tax of 0.9% is imposed on wages, self-employment income, and taxable fringe benefits. In addition, there is a 3.8% surtax on net investment income. The investment surtax applies to gains on non-qualified stock options when they are issued, and on restricted stock when it vests. Tax treatment of dividends on restricted stock depends on whether a § 83(b) election to accelerate income tax was made. If it was made, the 3.8% tax applies to the dividends, but if it was not made, then the dividends are subject to the 0.9% tax. [Laura Saunders, *Tax Report: The New Investment Taxes*, WSJ.com (July 7, 2012)]

In the usual stock option situation, until the option vests, the corporation is still considered the owner of the stock. The dividends on the stock are considered additional compensation for the employee. On the other hand, the corporation can deduct these dividends (as employee compensation) even though under ordinary circumstances a corporation cannot deduct the dividends that it pays.

The employee has the right to elect immediate taxation in the year of the transfer of the property, even if I.R.C. § 83 would not otherwise impose tax. This is a reasonable choice where otherwise the appreciation on the stock would be taxed as compensation.

> ■ **TIP:**    If the employee pays the tax right away and later has to forfeit the options (e.g., by quitting his or her job), the tax already paid is not refundable.

The employer can deduct the compensation that the employee includes in income under I.R.C. § 83 (as long as the compensation is reasonable). The deduction is taken in the employer's tax year that includes the year in which the employee includes the sum in his or her income. Nearly all employees pay taxes on a calendar-year basis, whereas most corporations operate on a fiscal year. The employer gets an immediate deduction if the property is vested as soon as it is transferred, or if the employee exercises the election to be taxed immediately.

To sum up the ISO/NQSO distinction, when an individual is granted NQSOs:

- (At time of grant) If there is no readily ascertainable FMV, there is no tax effect;

- (At time of grant) If there is an ascertainable FMV, § 83 governs taxation;

- (At time of exercise) The employee has taxable income equal to the FMV of the stock minus consideration paid for the option. However, if the stock received on exercise of the option is nontransferable and subject to a substantial risk of forfeiture, taxable income is not a factor until the condition lapses. At that point, gain is determined based on the FMV at the time of the lapse. If the employee actually sells the stock purchased under the option, then he or she will have capital gain or loss on the sale;

- The employer gets a deduction equal to the individual's gain.

If the employee gets ISOs instead of NQSOs:

- (At time of grant) The employee has no taxable income;

- (At time of exercise) The employee has no income;

- (At time of disposition of stock) The employee has capital gain or loss, with consequences depending on the length of the holding period;

- The employer does not get a deduction. [I.R.C. § 421(a)(2)]

If an employee disposes of shares obtained under an ISO within two years of the grant of the option or one year of exercising the option, any gain is ordinary income, and the employer is entitled to a tax deduction equal to this amount.

Taxpayers have often raised the argument that there is no taxable transfer of non-statutory options until the sale of the shares, if they financed the purchase with margin debt, because their own capital is not at risk until then. However, this argument has been rejected by the Tax Court and by the Fifth and Ninth Circuits, the Court of Federal Claims, and the Western District of Washington. [*Racine v. Comm'r*, 92 T.C.M. 100, 102 (2006); *Facq v. Comm'r*, 91 T.C.M. 1201 (2006), *Cidale v. United States*, 475 F.3d 685 (5th Cir. 2007); *United States v. Tuff*, 469 F.3d 1249 (9th Cir. 2006); *Facq v. United States*, 363 F. Supp. 2d 1288 (W.D. Wash. 2005); *Palahnuk v. United States*, 70 Fed. Cl. 87 (Fed. Cl. 2006)]

The Eighth Circuit ruled in 2010 that Nestle Purina Petcare could not deduct cash distribution, redemptive dividends paid to ESOP participants. Employees leaving the company had to instruct the ESOP trust to convert the value of the preferred stock allocated to the account into cash and/or shares of employer common stock. When participants chose to take cash, the trust could require that the employer pay the trust a "redemptive dividend" to purchase the stock. The employer wanted to deduct over $9 million in redemptive dividends, but the Tax Court said that the payments were not deductible dividends: § 162(k)(1) rules out a § 404(k) deduction for amounts paid to an ESOP trust to redeem shares of the corporation's stock, and the Eighth Circuit affirmed. [*Nestle Purina Petcare Co. v. Comm'r*, 594 F. 3d 968 (8th Cir. 2010); see CCH Pension and Employee Benefits, *Payments by Employer to Redeem Stock Held by ESOP Were Not Deductible as Dividends* (Mar. 29, 2010) (benefitslink.com)]

## [E]   Securities Law Issues for Stock Option Plans

Federal securities laws and state Blue Sky Laws must be consulted before offering stock options (or any other form of securities-based compensation). Public companies have an established obligation to disclose option transactions to their shareholders, and to reflect them in SEC filings and on proxy statements. The Exchange Act also forbids insiders to take short-swing profits.

For fiscal years ending on or after March 15, 2002, and for proxies for shareholder meetings or shareholder actions on or after June 15, 2002, the SEC has imposed additional disclosure requirements on reporting companies that offer stock compensation plans. Disclosure is now required of plans offering equity compensation, whether or not approved by security holders.

For each category, the reporting company must put a table in the Form 10-K (the annual report) and in the proxy statement whenever shareholders are asked to approve a compensation plan that includes securities. The table should have three columns:

Number of securities to be issued on exercise of outstanding options, rights, and warrants;

- The weighted average exercise price for the outstanding options, rights, and warrants;

- Securities not reflected in the first column, still available to be issued in the future under equity compensation plans. [See *New Disclosure Rules for Stock Plans*, Watson Wyatt Insider, <http://www.watsonwyatt.com/us/pubs/insider/showarticle.asp?ArticleID=9588&Component=The+Insider>]

The SEC adopted a Final Rule in late 2007 exempting certain stock options from registration under Exchange Act § 12(g). The rule provides one exemption for public companies that are required to file reports under the Exchange Act ("reporting companies"), another for non-reporting companies (e.g., smaller or private corporations). The exemption is limited to stock options issued as compensation, and does not extend to the underlying stock. [72 Fed. Reg. 69554 (Dec. 7, 2007)]

The SEC's 2006 Final Rule on disclosure of executive compensation requires public corporations to discuss stock options in the Compensation Discussion and Analysis disclosed to stockholders. Effective for fiscal years beginning on or after December 15, 2006, annual reports, proxy statements, and registration statements will have to give far more detail about option grants to and exercises by top management. A Summary Compensation Table is required, giving dollar amounts for stock awards and stock option awards (measured as of the grant date, using FAS 123R; see below). If the closing market price on the grant date is higher than the exercise price, the closing price must be disclosed. To prevent abusive back-dating of options, the date that the decision to make the grant of options must be disclosed, if it is different than the stated grant date. If the exercise price of an option is different from the closing market price on the grant date, the methodology for calculating the price must be disclosed. [SEC Press Release, *SEC Votes to Adopt Changes to Disclosure Requirements Concerning Executive Compensation and Related Matters*, <http://www.sec.gov/news/press/2006/2006-123.htm> (July 26, 2006)]

The 2010 financial services reform package, the Dodd-Frank Act (Pub. L. No. 111-203), extends the availability of "clawback": i.e., funds that the corporation can recoup from executives who received stock options or other incentive compensation during the three years before the company had to restate erroneous financial statements. [Christine Hurt, *Dodd-Frank Forum: Executive Compensation & Incentive-Based Compensation*, The Conglomerate, <http://www.theconglomerate.org/2010/07/doddfrank-forum-executive-compensation-incentivebased-compensation> (July 19, 2010)]

## [F] Accounting Issues

Traditionally, the Financial Accounting Standards Board (FASB) did not require corporations to expense their stock options; the cost merely had to be reflected in the footnotes to the financial statement. Expensing means that the cost of the options is deducted in the year the option is offered. Although taxpayers usually want to increase their deductions to cut their tax bills, there is a countervailing pressure on corporations to report high earnings, so anything that depresses their earnings is unattractive.

This position has evolved since 2004, when FASB 123(R), *Share-Based Payment*, required expensing of stock options and other forms of share-based compensation beginning in July 1, 2005 (public corporations) and January 1, 2006 (non-public corporations). A February 3, 2006 amendment (FAS 123(R)-4), clarifies that stock options and SARs did not have to be classified as liability awards merely because the plan permits contingent cash settlements based on an event outside the employee's control (e.g., a corporate change in control). [Ellen Sheng, *Stock-Option Cuts to Hit Employees in Lower Ranks*, Wall St. J., July 13, 2005, at D3. Technical corrections were issued in August 2006: see FAS 123R-f, <http://www.fasb.org/fasb_staff_positions/prop_fsp_fas123r-f.pdf>]

FASB 123(R) did not require any particular model (such as the popular Black-Scholes model) to be used in valuing options, but did mandate that valuation reflect issues such as vesting schedules, employee turnover, and expected time of exercise. [Keith Sellers, Yingping Huang and Brett A. King, *Are Your ESO Values on Target?*, Journal of Accountancy, <http://www.aicpa.org/pubs/jofa/mar2008/eso_values.htm> (March 2008)]

In mid-2009, FASB re-organized thousands of documents into a new classification of approximately 90 topics. Seven FASB statements about retirement and health plans (Nos. 35, 87, 88, 106, 112, 123(R), 158 were reorganized into five topics:

- 712, post-employment compensation other than retirement;
- 715, retirement benefits;
- 960, accounting for defined benefit plans;
- 962, accounting for defined contribution plans;
- 965, accounting for health and welfare benefit plans.

[CCH Pension and Benefits, *FASB Announces New Codification Structure, Superseding All Existing Statements* (June 26, 2009) (benefitslink.com). See <http://www.fasb.org> for the full codification.]

Accounting Standards Codification (ASC) Topic 718, *Stock Compensation*, sets out a general rule that equity awards granted to employees must be accounted for at fair value, measured at the time of grant (for awards settled in stock) and at the time of settlement or exercise (for awards settled in cash). Fair value is the same as the underlying value of the stock if it is a "full-value" award (e.g., restricted stock and performance shares). If it is an "appreciation" award, such as a stock option or stock appreciation rights, value is estimated under an option pricing model.

Subtopic 718-40 provides guidance for ESOP transactions; Subtopic 718-50 offers guidance for share-based payment transactions with Employee Stock Purchase Plans (ESPPs). A share-based payment arrangement is considered equity if the terms of the award call for settlement solely in company stock—e.g., stock options, ESPPs, stock-settled SARs, restricted shares, and performance shares. Compensation cost for equity awards is based on award's fair value at grant, minus anything paid by the employee; the corporation makes a corresponding credit to its equity, usually paid-in capital. Topic 718 explains how to choose inputs to the option pricing model; estimates must be reasonable, supportable, and determined consistently between periods. Topic 718 says that non-public companies must use the same principles to value equity awards as public companies, unless it is impossible to calculate a fair value. If it is impossible, the historical volatility of an index for the relevant industry (not a broad index like the S&P 500) should be used. [Frederic W. Cook & Co., *Accounting for Stock Compensation Under FASB ASC Topic 718* (Apr. 5, 2010) (benefitslink.com)]

## [G]  Backdating; Coping with Underwater Options

An option is said to be "underwater" if the value of the stock on the open market declines below the exercise price given in the option. In that case, of course, the employee will not have any advantage from exercising the option. For example, if an employee is given the right to buy 5,000 shares of the company's stock for $50 a share on a specific date on the future, but on that date, the stock is worth only $30 a share, the option is essentially worthless. The corporation can take various measures to alter the options plan so that the grantee of the options will be able to exercise them at a gain. Generally speaking, the grantees will find this a more satisfying tactic than the corporation's shareholders will.

The conventional method of repricing options is to cancel the options and replace them with new options with a lower strike price—or amend the original options to change the strike price. However, in 2003, the New York Stock Exchange and NASDAQ changed their rules to require shareholder approval to reprice options. A newer tactic is to allow a re-grant of a smaller number of new options intended to have the same current value as the old options. This can be more acceptable to shareholders than one-for-one exchanges, because fewer shares are being reallocated, so the effect of dilution is less. This approach can also fit in better with FASB rules. Another possibility is to cancel options and replace them with restricted stock units or phantom stock. Finally, some companies choose to calculate the current value of the underwater options, cancel them, and pay cash for the canceled vested options. [JP Morgan Compensation & Benefit Strategies, *Our Stock Options Are Underwater, We Might Re-Price Them*, <http://www.jpmorgan.com/cm/Satellite?c=JPM_Content_C&cid=1159382867977[ . . . ]> (Apr. 14, 2009) (benefitslink.com)]

One coping mechanism for price volatility, of doubtful legitimacy, is "backdating": deliberate alterations of grant dates to take advantage of lower stock prices that put options in the money when they're issued. Backdating is sometimes analyzed as breach of fiduciary duty by management. The Internal Revenue Code requires the FMV of options to be set in good faith. Allegations of backdating have been raised in many securities law cases, and some executives have been indicted—and a few convicted—on criminal charges such as fraud and criminal violations of the securities laws.

By mid-2009, at least 225 companies disclosed federal or internal investigations of options practices, and more than 140 companies announced that their financial results would be restated. James Treacy, the former CEO of the Monster Worldwide Website was convicted of securities fraud and conspiracy, for altering option grants to make them appear to have been made when the stock price was low. The prosecution also charged that the option grants should have been accounted for as compensation expenses, but were not. [Fred Schneyer, *Jury Convicts Former Monster Exec in Options Backdating*, plansponsor.com (May 14, 2009)]

In 2009, the Ninth Circuit dismissed the backdating conviction of Brocade's former CEO, Gregory Reyes, and ordered a new trial because the prosecution was guilty of misconduct (false assertions during closing arguments that misled the jury). [Zusha Elinson, *9th Circuit Tosses Reyes' Backdating Conviction due to Prosecutorial Misconduct*, The Recorder (Aug. 19, 2009) (law.com)] At the retrial in 2010, the jury found Reyes guilty on nine out of ten felony counts. [Kate Moser, *In Retrial, Former Brocade CEO Found Guilty of Most Counts*, The

Recorder (Mar. 29, 2010) (law.com)] Reyes' conviction was upheld by the Ninth Circuit. He was fined $15 million and sentenced to 18 months in prison. In August 2011, Reyes settled the SEC case against him for $850 million and agreed not to serve as director of a public company for a decade. [Ginny LaRoe, *9th Circuit Upholds Reyes' Backdating Conviction*, The Recorder (Oct. 13, 2011) (law.com)]

After four years of litigation, former executives of KLA-Tencor Corp. settled a derivative suit alleging backdating of stock options. The defendants and their insurer agreed to pay about $33 million to KLA-Tencor, with two-thirds of the funds coming from the insurer and the remaining third from the executives. The company settled a securities class action in 2008 for $65 million. The $33 million figure for the derivative suit does not include the value of canceled and repriced options, although this is usually a component of settlements in backdating cases. [Zusha Elinson, *After Delays, KLA Backdating Suit Settles*, The Recorder (Mar. 10, 2010) (law.com)]

## [H]  Change of Control Issues

One of the numerous issues that has to be resolved in a merger or acquisition (see Chapter 16 for a general discussion) is what will happen to stock options in the transition. The problem is especially acute when only part of a company (for instance, a division or subsidiary) is sold, and there are arguments pro and con as to whether the plan's "change in control" threshold (which would lead to immediate vesting of options) has been reached. A common provision says that unvested options are forfeited when a person terminates employment other than in a change-of-control situation, and employees of the merged or acquired company are given a limited time (such as three months) to exercise their stock options; under the original option plan, they might have had as much as ten years to exercise the options.

Many kinds of compensation arrangements in a change in control situation (for example, stock options, severance arrangements, and incentive plans) can create problems under Code § 409A, the provision dealing with nonqualified plans. If § 409A is triggered, then the amounts must be included in income in the year they are paid even though the purpose of the arrangement was to defer taxation. Furthermore, there is a 20% federal tax penalty—plus an additional 20% penalty on transactions in California. An article from late 2011 reports that double-trigger arrangements have become more popular than single-trigger plans. Double trigger plans often provide severance protection both before and after the change in control. Usually, severance before the change is paid in installments to coordinate with the imposition of restrictive covenants after the employee leaves the company. But after the change, restrictive covenants are of less concern, so severance is usually paid as a lump sum.

There are significant § 409A risks for double trigger severance plans with alternative payment methods. Some companies fail to recognize this because the pre- and post-transaction severance provisions are in different documents—such as a company-wide severance plan and an individual change-in-control agreement with a top executive. This problem can be avoided by drafting both agreements with a consistent definition.

A double trigger arrangement typically comes under § 409A if its "good reason" is excessively broad, allowing the executive to quit and collect severance when there has been only a minor reduction in pay or duties). Section 409A may also be triggered if the installment payments exceed $490,000 (as adjusted for inflation) or extend for more than two years after separation from service, if the definition of change in control falls afoul of the statutory definition in § 409A.

Because of economic uncertainty, there are now more "earn-outs" in acquisitions of private companies. This arrangement provides for future payments to the sellers of the acquired company if the business achieves certain financial milestones. Typically, the arrangement lasts from two to five years, although the earn-out period could be as much as 10 years or even longer. A stock option cash-out plan or management incentives that would otherwise be paid at the time of the acquisition can be made subject to the earn-out without violating § 409A, as long as the payments are made at the same time and under the same general terms and conditions as payments to the other shareholders. However, the § 409A exception applies to payments made within five years of the transaction's closing date—with limited alternatives permitted for earn-outs that extend longer than five years.

Stock options can be assumed in corporate transactions without § 409A penalties if the assumption satisfies the rules for assuming Incentive Stock Options (ISOs). In general, that means that the economics of the option must be preserved: valuing the consideration paid in the acquisition of the target company's stock, potentially including the earn-out. Because earn-outs are speculative, it's very possible that calculation assumptions will eventually be proved wrong, so there is a risk of future § 409A penalties if the transaction is over-valued. If it is under-valued, on the other hand, the option-holders will suffer economic detriment. Some companies value the earn-out at the time of the assumption, whereas others keep the transaction open and adjust the option to reflect the ongoing earn-out payments. The entire issue can be avoided by requiring option holders to exercise their options immediately before the transaction. [Juliano P. Banuelos, *Recent Compensation Trends in Mergers and Acquisitions and § 409A,* Orrick Perspectives (October 2011) (benefitslink.com)]

Whether there should be accelerated vesting on change in control is a business decision, separate from the effect of the transaction on outstanding options. The plan should give the board of directors maximum flexibility to decide how to handle options. They could be taken over or substituted by the acquiring corporation. The acquired corporation could choose to cancel options that have not been exercised or cash them out for the difference between the exercise price of the option and the per-share price of the stock that will be received in the transaction. One common strategy is to cancel out of the money options but pay cash for in the money options.

The acquiring corporation might prefer assuming the acquired company's options instead of substituting them because substitution would reduce the acquiror's equity incentive plan pool. Substitution could also lead to modifications that make the options non-qualified or trigger the application of § 409A. But the acquiror may prefer to substitute if it wants to have uniform terms and conditions for all its options. If the acquiror is a public company, it will not be necessary to register the shares underlying substituted options (because there is already a registration statement in effect)—which is not true for the assumed options. However, the acquiror might not want to assume the options if the amount or availability of the options conflicts with the acquiror's corporate culture.

If the options are canceled, optionees can exercise their vested options until the time the transaction closes. However, many options are "underwater" (i.e., the exercise price is actually higher than the stock price). This provides an incentive to cancel the options so the acquired company can re-allocate the cost of the options more productively among its stockholders and employees.

If the options are cashed out, the acquiring company benefits by not having to administer them after the closing and employees can get money for their options without having to spend money to exercise options.

It is common for vesting of options to be accelerated if there is a change of control. Vesting provisions can be incorporated in the stock option plan itself or in other agreements, such as employment contracts, severance plans, and retention agreements. A single-trigger arrangement accelerates vesting and allows option awards to be exercised as soon as there is a change in control. A double-trigger arrangement requires something else to happen in addition, such as the optionee being fired without cause or resigning for good reason within a specified time after the transaction. [Pamela B. Greene, Ann Margaret Eames, *Stock Options in Merger & Acquisition Transactions,* Corporate & Securities Advisory (June 6, 2011) (benefitslink.com)]

The Second Circuit rejected the argument that it was a breach of fiduciary duty for the administrator of a stock plan to tell an ex-employee that she could exercise her options after retirement. In general, stock option plans are not covered by ERISA. The plaintiff argued (unsuccessfully) that part of her entitlement to exercise options depended on her eligibility for benefits under an ERISA pension plan. The plan provided that options terminated when employment ended for any reason, including retirement—unless the option holder retired under the regular retirement provisions of the pension plan. In that case, options (other than options granted within one year of retirement) could be exercised during the rest of the ten-year life of the option grant. The plaintiff was eligible for a special retirement benefit, but not for regular retirement. The Second Circuit held that even if the administrator gave inaccurate information about the consequences of retirement decisions under an ERISA plan on non-ERISA plans, there was no violation of fiduciary duty. [*Bell v. Pfizer*, 626 F.3d 66 (2d Cir. 2010); Fred Schneyer, *Pfizer Cleared in Stock Options Suit*, plansponsor.com (Aug. 31, 2010)]

The Fifth Circuit held that one-time Merrill Lynch trader John Young was not entitled to an award under the long-term incentive compensation plan after he quit his job. Young was granted about 15,000 restricted stock units in 2006 that were not exercised. In general, employees lost their rights to unexercised stock units on termination. Young argued that he had left for good cause after a change in control (Merrill's January 1, 2009 merger with Bank of America)—an eventuality contemplated by the plan. Young received his 2008 bonus in December 2008, after the merger was signed but before it was consummated. He left Merrill about a month after the merger and would have had good cause for resignation if his 2008 bonus had been paid after the merger. According to Merrill, the date the merger was consummated was the date of the "change in control." The Fifth Circuit said that the plan committee had the discretion to interpret the terms of the plan and Young did not prove that his interpretation was obviously the correct one. [*Young v. Merrill Lynch*, 658 F.3d 436 (5th Cir. 2011); see Tara Cantore, *Appeal Court Reverses Lower-Court Ruling Denying Former Employee Plan Benefits*, plansponsor.com (Sept. 14, 2011)]

A 2012 Eighth Circuit case permits several former executives to receive performance share and restricted stock awards. The plan, required employment throughout the full three-year performance period to receive a full award, but prorated awards would be made in case of retirement or involuntary termination. The plan did not define these terms. The plan gave the Executive Compensation Committee authority to administer the plan and make final, binding determinations. The company was sold, and the office where the plaintiffs worked was closed, before the three-year period ended. They were offered jobs in another city, but did not want to move. A senior executive who was not part of the Compensation Committee decided that the plaintiffs forfeited their awards because they rejected a transfer. The Compensation Committee did not review this decision. The Eighth Circuit held that the plaintiffs were entitled to the award: they should have been treated as retired (because the plan did not impose any age limit on retirement), and it was improper for someone outside the Compensation Committee to make the determination. [*Schaffart v. ONEOK, Inc.*, 686 F.3d 461 (8th Cir. 2012); see PLC, *Terminated Executives Entitled to Payment Under Equity Awards: Eighth Circuit* (July 9, 2012) (benefitslink.com)]

## § 22.03  CAFETERIA PLANS

### [A]  Plan Characteristics

A cafeteria plan, as defined by I.R.C. § 125, is a written plan under which the employer offers a "menu" of benefits, permitting employees to choose between cash and a group of benefits. The plan must offer at least one taxable and one nontaxable benefit. Other than a 401(k) plan, the cafeteria plan may not offer any pension or deferred compensation benefits.

The I.R.C. § 125 requirements for a valid cafeteria plan are

- All plan participants are employees (although the Proposed Regulations allow ex-employees to be included in the plan, as long as it is not predominantly for their benefits). Spouses and children of employees can receive benefits under the plan, but cannot actively participate (e.g., by choosing the benefits);

- The participant chooses between cash and one or more benefits, although the amount of cash does not have to be as great as the entire cost of the nontaxable benefit [Prop. Reg. § 1.125-1];

- The plan does not discriminate in favor of highly compensated employees (HCEs);

- The benefits provided to HCEs do not exceed 25% of the total benefits for the year;

- The election to take benefits rather than cash must be made before the beginning of the plan year;

- Changes in the election must conform to the Regulations.

The allowable benefits include:

- Accident and health plans;

- Group-term life insurance;

- Disability coverage, including accidental death and dismemberment (ADD) plans;

- Dependent care assistance;

- Benefits that fail nondiscrimination tests and therefore are not part of a qualified plan;

- Vacation days;

- Group automobile insurance or other taxable benefit purchased by the employee with after-tax dollars.

Cafeteria plans are not permitted to include long-term care insurance. Neither can Flexible Spending Accounts (see § 18.11) because FSAs are not allowed to be used to pay insurance premiums.

For plan years that begin on or after January 1, 2013, employee contributions to health FSAs that are made by salary reductions under a Code § 125 cafeteria plan are limited to $2,500 a year. This limitation does not apply to the employer's contribution to the plan, or to employee salary reduction contributions to a cafeteria plan that are used to pay the employee's share of health insurance premiums. Cafeteria plans that include FSAs can be amended to reflect this statutory limitation at any time until the end of calendar 2014, but operational compliance is required after the 2013 plan year. [Code § 125(i); Notice 2012-40, 2012-26 I.R.B. 1046; see Christy Tinnes and Brigen Winters, *Second Opinions: ACA Cap on Contributions to Health FSAs*, plansponsor.com (July 18, 2012)]

The nontaxable benefits that can be included in a cafeteria plan are group-term life insurance, medical expense reimbursement, and accident and disability benefits as defined by I.R.C. § 106, dependent care assistance, and paid vacation days.

In a pretax premium plan, a "mini cafeteria" salary reduction plan is used to provide after-tax dollars for the employees to pay insurance premiums. The most common application is health insurance coverage for dependents, in plans where the employer covers employees but dependent coverage is on an "employee pay all" basis. The employer adopts a plan that allows the employee, before the start of the plan year, to elect a reduction in compensation sufficient to pay the employee's share of the premium. These salary reductions are not subject to the employer share of FICA.

A cafeteria plan must be designed as a "use it or lose it" plan: Unused benefits cannot be carried over to subsequent years. Participants can be given a chance to use their vacation days, sell them back to the employer for cash, or buy extra vacation days—as long as the plan is not used to defer the receipt of compensation to a later plan year. [See Prop. Reg. § 1.125-1, Q&A 7]

If a cafeteria plan fails nondiscrimination testing, then the HCEs will have taxable income. The test for discrimination in benefits is whether contributions are made for each participant in a uniform relationship to compensation. If contributions for each participant are equal to the cost of coverage that the plan incurs for HCEs, or if contributions for each participant are at least equal to 75% of the cost for the similarly situated plan participant who has the highest cost of benefits, the plan satisfies the nondiscrimination tests.

Nontaxable cafeteria plan benefits are not subject to employer or employee FICA taxes. However, amounts placed into a 401(k) plan are subject to both employer and employee shares of FICA and FUTA.

Generally, participants will be given a 30-day period at the end of every year to make the election for the following year. The period might close a few days, or even a month, before the end of the year to give the plan administrators time to process the election request.

Cafeteria plans must be in writing, describe all benefits under the plan, apply uniformly to all participants, and be adopted on or before the first day of the plan's first plan year. Retroactive adoptions and amendments are forbidden.

The only permissible benefits for cafeteria plans are:

- Up to $50,000 group-term life insurance on the lives of employees;

- Accident and Health plans, including health Flexible Spending Accounts and payment of individual A&H premiums or COBRA premiums under an A&H plan;

- Contributions to a Health Savings Account (HSA distributions can be used to pay for long-term care or premiums of qualified long-term care insurance policies);

- Dependent care assistance;

- Adoption assistance;

- 401(k) contributions;

- Short- and long-term disability coverage

However, cafeteria plans are forbidden to offer:

- Scholarships;

- Tuition reduction;

- Employer-provided meals and lodging;

- Educational assistance;

- Long-term care insurance;

- Athletic facilities;

- Commuting benefits;

- Working condition fringe benefits;

- De minimis benefits;

- Employee discounts;

- Cell phones provided by the employer;

- MSA contributions;

- Group-term life insurance on non-employees (e.g., employees' parents).

The written plan document must explain how employees can make elections, the maximum salary reduction the plan will allow, the employer's contributions, and rules for any FSAs and HSAs included in the plan. The Proposed Regulations incorporate some of the safe harbor testing rules of Code § 410(b), with an objective test to determine when the actual election of benefits is discriminatory: when HCEs have higher benefits, measured as a percentage of compensation, than non-HCEs. [IRS Publication 15-B (2013 edition), <http://www.irs.gov/publications/p15b/ar02.html#en_US_2013_publink1000193630>]

ERISA § 403 does not require cafeteria plans to be managed by a trust (although the terms of the plan itself can require trust management). However, if the plan allows after-tax contributions for the purchase of benefits, such contributions must be placed into trust unless they are used to buy insurance policies.

## [B]  Cafeteria Plans After HIPAA

Proposed and Temporary Regulations for bringing cafeteria plans into conformity with HIPAA were published at 62 Fed. Reg. 60165 and 60196 (Nov. 7, 1997). Then, in March 2000, the IRS replaced the 1997 Temporary Regulations with T.D. 8878, 65 Fed. Reg. 15548, 2000-15 I.R.B. 857 (Mar. 23, 2000). These Regulations, which were supposed to be final, clarified the circumstances under which employees participating in cafeteria plans can change their elections in connection with accident, health, or group-term life insurance coverage. For example, a change might be needed when a Qualified Medical Child Support Order (QMCSO) is granted, or when the person gains or loses eligibility for Medicare or Medicaid.

At the beginning of 2001, the IRS revised this Treasury Decision. [See T.D. 8921, 66 Fed. Reg. 1837 (Jan. 10, 2001)] T.D. 8921 modifies the T.D. 8878 Final Regulations by allowing cafeteria plan participants to increase or decrease their coverage whenever they have a change-of-status event.

Changes were always allowed on the basis of marriage or divorce. Thanks to T.D. 8921, changes are also permitted when a dependent is born or adopted. An employee who decreases or cancels coverage under the cafeteria plan because of coverage under a spouse or dependent's plan has to certify that he or she is getting other coverage.

The cafeteria plan election can be changed to conform to a domestic relations order, but only if the spouse or former spouse actually provides coverage for the child; T.D. 8921 also allows elections to be changed when the employee's responsibility for payments under the plan increases or decreases significantly. The plan's payment for dependent care cannot be greater than what the employee earns.

The Simple Cafeteria Plan is a new plan form created by the health care reform statute. Small employers can set up Simple Cafeteria Plans starting in 2011. PPACA (the health care legislation) defines a small employer as one that averaged 100 or fewer employees in each of the previous two years. (For employers that have not been in business for two years, a reasonable estimate is used.) The advantage of the Simple Cafeteria Plan over a conventional cafeteria plan is that the employer is not subject to the requirements of nondiscrimination testing. All qualified employees must be eligible to participate if they had at least 1,000 hours of service in the previous plan year, but employees can be excluded if they are younger than 21 (or an even younger age stipulated by the plan), or if they are covered by a CBA. Highly compensated and key employees can participate in the

Simple Cafeteria Plan, but the plan must not discriminate in their favor. All eligible employees must be allowed to elect any benefit in the plan under the same terms and conditions as all other participants. The employer sponsoring the plan must make at least a minimum contribution that the participant can apply toward any benefit within the plan. The minimum contribution for non-HCEs must equal or exceed the lesser of a uniform 2% of compensation (whether or not the employee contributes); a match equal to double the employee's contribution; or 6% of compensation. [Gary B. Kushner, Kushner & Co., *New Simple Cafeteria Plans* (Aug. 17, 2010) (benefitslink.com)]

## § 22.04  EDUCATION ASSISTANCE

Employers offer education assistance both because anything that employees consider a valuable benefit is a good motivator, and because a better-educated workforce promotes efficiency and productivity. However, the tax status of this benefit has fluctuated over the past decades.

There were no Code provisions allowing employees to receive educational assistance tax-free before I.R.C. § 127 was enacted in 1978, as a five-year pilot project. It was extended several times, and finally made permanent by the Economic Growth and Tax Relief Reconciliation Act (EGTRRA), which also removed the earlier limitation of the assistance to undergraduate-level education. Under I.R.C. § 127, employees can exclude from income up to $5,250 in benefits under an educational assistance program. The benefits should not be included in Box 1 on Form W-2, because they do not constitute taxable income. [The version of Publication 970, Tax Benefits for Education, for calculating 2012 returns, is available at <http://www.irs.gov/pub/irs-pdf/p970.pdf>]

Although many EGTRRA provisions were scheduled to expire in 2011, legislation passed at the end of 2010 revived many EGTRRA provisions, including educational assistance. This benefit, at the $5,250 level, can be offered tax-free to employees until the end of 2012. [Tax Relief, Unemployment Insurance Reauthorization, and Job Creation Act of 2010, Pub. L. No. 111-312 (Dec. 17, 2010); see EBIA Weekly, *2010 Tax Relief Act Extends Various Benefits, Including Higher Transit/Vanpool Limit, Adoption, and Education Assistance* (Dec. 23, 2010) (benefitslink.com)]

The "fiscal cliff" legislation, the American Taxpayer Relief Act of 2012, extends the educational assistance provision, at the $5,250 level, indefinitely. See IRS guidance at <http://www.irs.gov/uac/Tax-Benefits-for-Education:-Information-Center > (Feb. 13, 2012).

Benefits USA's 2011/2012 survey found a rapid increase in the percentage of companies offering tuition reimbursement to all their employees. In 2009, only 34.9% offered reimbursement to all employees, rising to 45.3% in 2010 and 51.7% in 2011. About one-third (32%) provide reimbursement for management employees, 31.7% to technical and professional employees, 30.6% to administrative employees, and only 25.8% to hourly employees. Two-thirds (65%) impose work requirements, such as working for 15 months after receiving tuition reimbursement, and 87% of employers limit the courses of study that will be reimbursable. [Tara Cantore, *More Employers Offer Employee Tuition Reimbursement*, plansponsor.com (Oct. 18, 2011)]

In late 2011, EdLink, the ROI Institute and Capella University published a study, "Tuition Assistance Value Study" to see if private-sector organizations thought having a tuition assistance program was worth it. Nearly all employees who used the programs said that their job satisfaction, efficiency, and productivity were enhanced. Ninety-six percent said that education was worthwhile and a good use of the employer's resources; more than 94% said that they got knowledge that was useful for their jobs. [Tara Cantore, *Organizations Find Value in Offering Tuition Assistance Programs*, plansponsor.com (Nov. 1, 2011)]

## § 22.05  EMPLOYEE ASSISTANCE PROGRAMS (EAPs)

The purpose of the Employee Assistance Program (EAP) is to help employees cope with stress and other problems. The theory is that sympathetic listening, and referrals for whatever professional services are needed, will ease employees' anxieties and make them more productive. EAPs can offer any combination of one-on-one counseling, information and referral, hotlines and crisis intervention, and informational seminars.

EAPs typically deal with problems such as substance abuse, dependent care, and problems with spouses and children. Many companies have found that early intervention makes it possible to shorten the damage and amount of time that would otherwise be involved, for instance, when the employee "hits bottom" with a drug or alcohol problem, or when an untreated mental illness requires inpatient hospitalization in a crisis. Each dollar invested in EAP services is estimated to return anywhere from two to eight dollars in health and productivity savings.

EAPs also take a role in coordinating an employee's return to work after recuperating from an accident or illness (which may include a shortened or flexible schedule, intermittent FMLA leave, or other accommodations).

The services can be provided in house by the HR department, or contracted out to outside vendors. The second course is more expensive, but it may make the EAP more credible to employees, or may reassure employees that their confidentiality will be protected.

## § 22.06  MISCELLANEOUS FRINGES

Employees do not have taxable income if they receive certain minor fringe benefits provided by the employer on a nondiscriminatory basis to all employees. Under I.R.C. § 132, the benefits are not taxed to the employees. FICA, FUTA, and federal income tax withholding are not required, and the employer share of these taxes does not have to be paid. Generally, the employer will be able to deduct the cost of the program (which is supposed to be nominal, in any case) as long as it fits the definition of an ordinary and necessary business expense.

The categories of miscellaneous fringe benefits authorized under I.R.C. § 132 are:

- No-additional-cost services of the employer company (e.g., air travel for an airline employee; a simple will prepared by a law firm for a non-attorney staffer). The employee must gain access to services normally sold to customers, but the employer must not incur any substantial cost. In effect, the employees are given access to the business's excess capacity;

- Employee discounts; the discount must not exceed the gross profit percentage for goods, or 20% of the cost of services;

- De minimis fringe benefits, such as free beverages at work or small Christmas presents—anything too trivial to account for separately;

- An on-premises eating facility such as a low-cost cafeteria that prepares meals on premises for the convenience of the employer (because employees can take shorter meal breaks because the subsidized dining facility is available). The facility must be owned or operated by the employer, must generate revenue at least equal to its operating costs, and must provide meals during the workday or right before or right after it. It must also be in or near the workplace, and must be operated by the employer (possibly through a contract with a third-party management company);

- Working condition fringe benefits—goods or services the employee could deduct if he or she paid for them personally. Typical examples are business travel and the use of company cars;

- An on-premises gym for the exclusive use of employees and their families;

- Reimbursement of employment-related moving expenses that would be deductible if the employee paid them directly (but have not in fact been deducted by the employee).

In some years, the transportation fringe benefit has been set at a different level depending upon whether the benefit covers parking or transit passes and vanpooling. For 2013, however, the benefit is the same for both, and the limit is $245 per month: Rev. Proc. 2013-15, 2013-5 I.R.B. 444. [See Wolters Kluwer Law & Business, *IRS Issues 2013 Adoption And Transportation Benefit COLAs* (Jan. 21, 2013) (benefitslink.com)]

The Emergency Economic Stabilization Act, Pub. L. No. 110-343, added a new bicycle commuting benefit under Code § 132. Employers can provide employees with tax-free reimbursement of up to $20 a month for each month in which the employee regularly bicycles to work, starting with December 31, 2008.

Reimbursable costs include buying a bicycle that is regularly used for commuting, and repairing and storing it. [Rebecca Moore, *Economic Stabilization Plan Includes Bicyclist Benefit*, plansponsor.com (Oct. 29, 2008); EBIA Weekly, *Bicycle Commuting Fringe Benefit Added to Code Section 132(f)* (Oct. 29, 2008) (benefitslink.com)]

Under Reg. § 1.132-6(e)(1), de minimis fringes include items such as:

- Occasional typing of personal letters by employees;

- Occasional meals, picnics, or cocktail parties for employees or their guests;

- Birthday or holiday gifts of low value;

- Theater or sports tickets;

- Coffee or snacks provided in the workplace.

However, these are not de minimis:

- Season tickets;

- Country club membership;

- The use of employer-provided vehicles more than one day per month;

- Weekends at facilities owned or leased by the employer.

Reg. § 1.132-6 says that if a benefit is too valuable or is provided too often to be considered de minimis, then the value of the entire benefit must be included in the recipient's gross income, unless it is excluded for another reason (for example, it qualifies as a no-additional-cost fringe or a working-condition fringe benefit).

Under Code § 132(e)(1), cash and benefits that are equivalent to cash, such as gift certificates, are not de minimis because they have a readily ascertainable value, and it is not impracticable for the employer to account for them. A de minimis fringe benefit must be offered in the form of goods or services and not cash—even if it represents an item that would be de minimis if it were distributed in kind. [Bruce M. Bird and J. Harrison McCraw, *De Minimis Fringe Benefit Rules: Current Guidance and Tax Implications*, CPA Journal (April 2006) (benefitslink.com)]

Another Code section, I.R.C. § 119, governs meals and lodging furnished on premises for the convenience of the employer, e.g., a room for a hotel manager who must be around to handle problems as they arise. Such benefits are not taxable income for the employee.

Decline in the real estate market made it difficult for corporations to relocate employees and has led to changes in relocation benefits. "Loss on sale" benefits used to be common (reimbursement for losses when employees had to sell their homes in order to relocate) but have lost popularity because it has become so difficult for corporations to re-sell such homes. So there has been a move to offering assistance with renting out the old home and renting (instead of buying) a home in the new location. The recruitment process for an out-of-town candidate might include consultation with a relocation manager. A lump sum for the move might be offered, or the company might agree to assume some home-sale losses subject to a cap. Or, instead of relocating, an employee or new hire might be permitted to telecommute or stay in hotels or corporate housing part of the time while remaining in his or her current home. [Heather O'Neil, *Relocation Benefits Are on the Move*, Workforce (Feb. 6, 2012) (benefitslink.com)]

### § 22.07  VOLUNTARY EMPLOYEE BENEFIT ASSOCIATIONS (VEBAs)

A Voluntary Employee Benefit Association (VEBA), as defined by I.R.C. § 501(c)(9), is a trust that is funded by employer contributions (with or without employee contributions) and is used to pay benefits to employees who voluntarily exercise the option to participate in the association. VEBAs provide life, sickness, accident, or similar benefits to employee members and their dependents and designated beneficiaries. Benefits that can be offered by a VEBA safeguard or improve health or protect against a contingency that threatens the employee's earning power. But VEBAs are not allowed to offer reimbursement of commuting expenses, profit sharing, or stock bonuses.

The trust itself is not a taxable entity, but VEBA benefits constitute taxable income to the employee unless they are specifically exempted.

The VEBA must be controlled by its employee membership, by a bank or other independent trustee, or by fiduciaries chosen by or on behalf of the membership. A VEBA is considered a welfare plan under ERISA, and therefore is subject to ERISA Parts 1 (notice and reporting), 4 (trust and fiduciary responsibility), and 5 (enforcement).

The Sixth Circuit ruled that the portion of the VEBA contribution used to fund long-term disability benefits was deductible, but the portion used to fund post-retirement benefits and medical benefits for union members was not deductible, because the employer failed to satisfy the I.R.C. § 419A(c)(2) requirements for accumulating assets to prefund the benefits. [*Parker-Hannifin Corp. v. Comm'r*, 139 F.3d 1090 (6th Cir. 1998)]

The VEBAs are at risk of market volatility, because of their partial funding by employer stock and because they also experience large increases in medical costs. Many VEBAs are running out of money so they have to cut costs, reduce benefits, and seek additional funding from sponsors and beneficiaries. According to DOL filings from October, 2011, the largest VEBA, covering over 820,000 former auto workers and their families, is almost $20 billion short. The United Steel Workers Union's 30 VEBAs have been hard-hit by medical cost inflation. The UAW retirees have above-average benefits, providing some leeway for cuts. In 2009, the UAW VEBA severed its ties to the auto makers and became an independent trust—resulting in higher copayments for retirees and reduced prescription drug benefits. [Sharon Terlep and Matthew Dolan, *VEBA Retirement Trusts Face Funding Shortfalls*, WSJ.com (Nov. 7, 2011)]

## § 22.08  FRINGE BENEFIT PLANS: TAX COMPLIANCE

### [A]  Reporting Requirements

The reporting requirements for a fringe benefit plan are set out in I.R.C. § 6039D. The plan must report:

- Number of employees at the employer company;
- Number of employees eligible to participate in the plan;
- Number actually participating;
- Number of highly compensated employees in each of the above categories;
- The plan's total cost during the year;
- The employer's name, address, and Employer Identification Number;
- The nature of its business.

If any fringe benefits are taxable, the employer can either add them to the regular wages for a payroll period, or withhold federal income tax at the rate for supplemental wages. [The relevant IRS publication is 15-B, Employer's Tax Guide to Fringe Benefits.]

### [B]  The Employer's Tax Deduction

When it comes to pensions, the tax rules are devised to make sure that the employer contributes enough to fund the plan. In contrast, when it comes to welfare benefits, the tax focus is preventing excessive prefunding of benefit plans. So the relevant Code sections (I.R.C. §§ 419 and 419A) specify a maximum funding level for welfare benefit trusts. If this level is exceeded, the trust is no longer tax-exempt.

Although the employer receives a tax deduction for maintaining a welfare benefit trust, the deduction is limited to the "qualified cost" of the benefit plans for the year. That means the direct cost of funding benefits, plus whatever amount I.R.C. § 419A permits to be added to the account for the year as a safety cushion.

Reference should also be made to I.R.C. § 4976, which imposes a 100% excise tax on disqualified benefit distributions made from funded welfare benefit plans. For instance, retiree health and life insurance benefits for highly compensated employees are supposed to be kept in a separate account from comparable contributions for rank-and-file employees.

Therefore, benefits paid to HCEs from the general account would be disqualified. VEBA benefits to HCEs that violate nondiscrimination requirements are also disqualified, as are amounts that revert to the employer. (An erroneous contribution which is withdrawn by the employer after a determination that it is not deductible is not considered a reversion.)

## § 22.09   ERISA REGULATION OF WELFARE BENEFIT PLANS

### [A]   Creation and Administration

Although most of the attention goes to ERISA's regulation of pension plans, ERISA also covers welfare benefit plans—a category roughly equivalent to fringe benefit plans. An ERISA welfare benefit plan is created (generally by a corporate resolution passed by the Board of Directors and managed by the relevant corporate officials) and administered to provide one or more of these benefits to plan participants and their beneficiaries:

- Medical benefits;
- Health care;
- Accident insurance;
- Disability benefits;
- Death benefits;
- Supplemental unemployment benefits;
- Vacation benefits;
- Training (e.g., apprenticeship);
- Day care centers (but not dependent care spending reimbursement accounts);
- Scholarships;
- Prepaid legal services;
- Any benefit described in the Labor-Management Relations Act § 302(c) [29 U.S.C. §§ 141–144, etc.] other than death benefits, pensions, or insurance coverage for pensions or death benefits.

The people receiving the benefits must be common-law employees and not independent contractors. For this purpose, employee status depends on agency principles such as who controls and supervises the person, and whether the person can recognize profit or loss from the work relationship. It does not depend on the "reasonable expectations" of the parties. [*Mut. Ins. Co. v. Darden*, 503 U.S. 318 (1992)]

Welfare benefit plans are subject to ERISA Title I. The Eleventh Circuit has ruled that a Title I plan exists if circumstances lead a reasonable person to ascertain the intended benefits, intended beneficiaries, financing sources, and procedure for receiving benefits under the plan. [*Donovan v. Dillingham*, 688 F.2d 1367 (11th Cir. 1982)] A plan can be deemed to exist even if the ERISA rules are not observed, and in fact, even if there is no written instrument.

Severance pay plans are sometimes treated as pension plans, but are more likely to be characterized as welfare benefit plans. DOL Advisory Opinion 84-12A says that a severance pay plan is not a pension plan if:

- Its benefits are not contingent on the employee's retirement;
- Total payments do not exceed twice the employee's compensation for the year before the termination;
- Payments are completed within 24 months after termination of service for the employer.

Under a similar analysis, bonus programs are not treated as pension plans for ERISA Title I purposes unless the payments are systematically deferred at least until termination of employment. DOL Reg. § 2510.3 says that an employer plan that supplements retirement benefits (e.g., until early retirees can qualify for Social Security benefits) can be either a pension or a welfare benefit plan, depending on its terms and how it is administered.

ERISA Title I does not apply to certain payroll practices:

- Extra pay for nonstandard working hours (overtime, shift premiums, holiday premiums);
- Compensation paid when the employee is on sick leave, taking a sick day, or otherwise medically unable to work;
- Compensation paid for other absences, such as vacation days, sabbaticals, and military leave.

In mid-2004, EBSA issued an advisory opinion as to whether a vacation pay plan was a "welfare benefit plan" as defined by ERISA § 3(1). The plan provided paid vacation to eligible employees, based on average hours worked, length of service, and level of employment. EBSA opined that 29 C.F.R. § 2510.3-1 draws a distinction between a welfare benefit plan and a payroll practice, such as paying vacation benefits out of the employer's general assets. The factors in the determination of a welfare benefit include whether the employee's right is contingent on a future occurrence or whether the employee undertakes some risk other than ordinary employment risk. If there is a VEBA or trust involved, ERISA coverage depends on whether the trust is a bona fide separate fund; whether it has a direct legal obligation to pay plan benefits; if the employer's obligation to make contributions is legally enforceable; and whether the contributions are actuarially determined or established via collective bargaining. EBSA concluded that the trust was just a pass-through vehicle for the distribution of ordinary vacation pay. [EBSA Advisory Opinion 2004-08A, 7/2/04, <http://www.dol.gov/ebsa/regs/aos/a02004-08a.html>]

## [B]  ERISA Case Law on Welfare Benefits

A brokerage firm created an association of small firms (under 225 employees) so the members could maintain a self-funded health benefit plan. The Third Circuit ruled that the members lacked the requisite commonality of interest, and therefore the plan was not an "employee welfare benefit plan" as defined by ERISA. [*Gruber v. Hubbard Bert Karle Weber Inc.*, 159 F.3d 780 (3d Cir. 1998)]

Where failure to make complete disclosure could be harmful to benefit participants, a benefit plan administrator had a fiduciary duty to give complete and accurate information about the plan. If it is clear that a participant is unaware of important features of the plan, it is not enough simply to answer questions. [*Krohn v. Huron Mem'l Hosp.*, 173 F.3d 542 (6th Cir. 1999)]

Until 2006, Menasha Corporation retirees and their spouses continued to receive health insurance from the company. Between ages 62–65, the company paid 80% of the premium; when retirees turned 65, the company paid 100% of the premium. In 2006, however, Menasha informed the plaintiffs that it was adopting a new health plan, and premiums would no longer be 100% covered. The plaintiffs sued alleging violations of the Labor Management Relations Act, 29 U.S.C. § 185, and ERISA, 29 U.S.C. § 1132. The district court ruled in the plaintiffs' favor as to employee coverage, but in favor of defendant as to spouses. The Sixth Circuit reversed in part, ruling for the plaintiffs. Although healthcare is a "welfare benefit," not entitled to the same ERISA protection as pension benefits, certain actions by employers will waive the employers' right to alter welfare benefits. In this case, Menasha waived the right to change the benefits by providing vested healthcare coverage to retired employees and spouses, and by agreeing that CBAs could only be modified with signed, mutual consent of the parties. [*Moore v. Menasha Corp.*, 690 F.3d 444 (6th Cir. 2013)]

# PART V

# THE HR FUNCTION

CHAPTER 23

# HIRING AND RECRUITMENT

## § 23.01  INTRODUCTION

Efficient hiring practices benefit the company at all levels. Prompt, economical selection of the best person to do the job (whether from inside the company or brought in from outside) will keep operations running smoothly and encourage innovation that will keep the business competitive.

On the downside, bad hiring practices create many kinds of risks such as employment discrimination charges, or charges of negligent hiring or retention (if an employee commits a crime or sexual harassment). Or, a poorly chosen employee can be inefficient, make costly mistakes and have to be replaced, generating additional costs.

The Hiring Inventives to Restore Employment (HIRE) Act was enacted in March 2010. The law provides a payroll tax incentive to employers who hire previously unemployed workers between February 3, 2010 and January 1, 2011: a federal tax credit equal to the 6.2% employer share of FICA tax. The credit could be claimed by creating a new position, but not by firing one worker and replacing him or her. Qualifying workers must have been unemployed or worked only limited hours in the 60 days before being hired. [Rebecca Moore, *New Law Offers Tax Incentives for Hiring*, plansponsor.com (Mar. 18, 2010)]

This credit was not renewed after it expired. However, the Tax Relief, Unemployment Insurance Reauthorization, and Job Creation Act of 2010 (TRUI; Pub. L. No. 111-312) provided a different kind of payroll tax cut: reduction of the employee (not the employer) share of FICA tax to 4.2%. The Middle Class Tax Relief and Job Creation Act of 2012, Pub. L. No. 112-96, extends the 4.2% payroll tax rate until the end of 2012, but it was not extended further. [Naftali Bendavid and Siobhan Hughes, *Congress Reaches Payroll-Tax Deal*, WSJ.com (Feb. 16, 2012); Josh Mitchell and Naftali Bendavid, *Tax Bill Passed by Congress Broadens Jobless Program*, WSJ.com (Feb. 18, 2012)]

In November 2011, Congress passed the VOW to Hire Heroes Act of 2011, including a new tax credit for hiring veterans. On February 9, 2012, the IRS published guidance for claiming the credit (up to $9,600 per veteran for for-profit companies, $6,240 for tax-exempt organizations) and extended some deadlines. The credit is claimed on Form 8300 (for-profit corporations) or Form 5884-C (not-for-profits). The size of the credit depends on factors such as how long the veteran was out of work before being hired, the number of hours worked, and the wages paid in the first year. The maximum credit is provided for hiring veterans with service-connected disabilities. In general, Form 8850 is supposed to be filed with the state workforce agency within 28 days of the veteran's start date. [Notice 2012-13, 2012-9 I.R.B. 421; see Laura Saunders, *IRS Extends Deadline to Claim Vet Credit*, WSJ.com (Feb. 9, 2012)]

## § 23.02  PRODUCTIVE HIRING

The recession has increased the number of applicants for most jobs, and gives many hiring managers a choice among many qualified (or overqualified) candidates—but when a company seeks to keep payroll manageable, it is important to select the right candidate.

Current employees can be a great starting point for recruitment (and many companies offer bonuses if a current employee recruits someone who is hired and completes a minimum period satisfactorily), but they should not be the only source of recruitment—especially if you want a diverse workforce.

College and graduate school recruitment should not be restricted to those nearby, or only to a small class of Ivy League schools. If nationwide recruitment is a cost problem, the Internet allows nationwide recruiting and low cost. However, resumes posted on the Internet are no more or less truthful than those delivered by traditional means, so reference checks are still required.

See § 25.02[C] for a discussion of recent cases about the effect of covenants not to compete on hiring. However, the opposite tack could also be problematic. The Justice Department started investigating hiring practices at major corporations, especially in the technology sector, to see if companies have violated antitrust laws by agreeing NOT to recruit each other's employees, with the possible result that workers such as computer engineers are deprived of chances to change their jobs to earn more money. The Department of Justice concluded that there are significant competitive concerns about these agreements. The Department of Justice settled with six tech companies in 2010: the settlement requires the companies to avoid anti-competitive hiring practices. A class action filed in California Superior Court charges Lucasfilm Ltd., Adobe, Apple, Google, Intel, Intuit, and Pixar with fixing employees' pay, capping pay packages offered to employees, and limiting opportunities for employees to be hired by competitors. The class action seeks restitution for lost compensation, plus antitrust treble damages. [Thomas Catan and Brent Kendall, *U.S. Steps Up Probe of Tech Hiring*, WSJ.com (Apr. 10, 2010) The class action is *Hanrahan v. Lucasfilm Ltd.* (California Superior Court, pending); see Shannon Green, *They Want Theirs: Tech Employees File Suit in Wake of Antitrust Pact*, Corporate Counsel (May 6, 2011) (law.com)]

## § 23.03  ANALYZING JOB REQUIREMENTS

In many cases, poor hiring decisions are made because of lack of insight into the real demands of the job. A candidate is chosen who matches the formal, written job description, but there's a mismatch, because the real job isn't very much like the job description. Often, people are hired on the basis of technical skills, but those skills are seldom used on a day-to-day basis.

The job should be analyzed to see how much time is spent on various tasks, such as working with machinery, writing and analyzing reports, or supervising other workers.

It is important to understand the physical demands of the job, to see who can meet them without accommodation, and what accommodations can reasonably be made to the needs of individuals with disabilities. [See § 36.05 for a discussion of reasonable accommodation.]

The job must be identified as exempt or nonexempt for wage and hour purposes. Sometimes it makes economic sense to restructure job duties so that the job becomes exempt from overtime requirements. However, the change must be real, not just a meaningless title.

There should be a written job description indicating:

- Job title;
- When it has to be filled;
- Why the organization needs someone for that position at all (perhaps the duties could be delegated to existing employees, outsourced, or assigned to temporary or part-time employees);
- Required educational qualifications;
- Necessary skills;
- Standards for defining inadequate, satisfactory, good, and excellent performance; the educational qualifications, skills, and experience that are really needed to perform the job; and standards (as objective as possible) for defining inadequate, satisfactory, good, and excellent performance.

The job description should indicate reporting relationships (whom the job-holder reports to; who reports to him or her). It should explain the promotion potential for the job, including conditions (such as getting an MBA or meeting performance goals). If your company has a grading system, the job grade should be indicated. The job description should also include the salary range.

## § 23.04  RECRUITMENT

It is probably worthwhile to consider promoting existing employees to fill important positions, although sometimes it is necessary to look outside—or desirable to get new skills and viewpoints. Even a policy of promoting from within requires recruiting, to fill entry- and mid-levels that have been vacated by the promoted employees.

CareerXRoads reported that in 2009, over half of job openings (51%) were filled by people who worked for the company already. Of the 49% filled externally, 27% of hires came from referrals, about the same percentage as in 2008, with about one hire per 15 referrals. Websites produced about 22% of external hires, job boards 13%. Among external hires coming from job boards, 42% came from CareerBuilder.com, 12% from Monster.com, and 10% from aggregation sites that advertise openings from multiple job boards. Craigslist produced 2.8% of external hires. Nearly half of respondents to CareerXRoads' survey (48%) expected to hire more people in 2010 than in 2009; 11% expected fewer hires, and the rest expected the number to remain level. [Sarah E. Needleman, *Internal Hires, Referrals Were Most Hired in 2009*, WSJ.com (Feb. 19, 2010)]

The Web and social media (blogs, MySpace, Facebook, etc.) are gaining in importance as recruiting and hiring sources.

The Associated Press reported in February, 2012 that some job applicants are being pressured to turn over their Facebook and other social media passwords so employers can investigate potential hires. In March 2012, Senators Charles Schumer (D.N.Y.) and Richard Blumenthal (D. Conn.) asked the Department of Justice and EEOC to investigate whether it is illegal for employers to seek this information. [Todd Ruger, *Senators Ask Feds to Investigate Employer Requests for Social Media Passwords*, The BLT: The Blog of Legal Times (Mar. 26, 2012) (law.com)]

[See § 27.05 for more discussion of the HR implications of social networking]

In most companies, job postings literally are posted on a bulletin board, leaving the notice up for five to ten days. More and more companies are using the corporate Intranet for this purpose. The posting should explain the nature of the job (although another advantage of recruiting from within is that the applicants will be fairly familiar with it already); the qualifications required; and whether there are any limitations. For instance, seniority is a very significant factor in promotions in a unionized workplace. Some companies have a policy that employees are not allowed to apply for internal vacancies unless they have held their current job for at least six months with satisfactory or better performance appraisals. The usual policy is to keep the application confidential from the applicant's immediate supervisor, until there is the possibility that the promotion will be offered.

The state employment service can be a good resource for low-level jobs, and even some higher-level technical jobs. Unemployment benefits are not available to workers who have voluntarily quit, or who were fired for wrongdoing, so workers receiving benefits are probably not unstable or a bad risk merely on account of being unemployed. Also, people who are employed but want a new job sometimes register with the state employment office because it has contacts with a wide range of employers and because it does not charge jobseekers a fee. To fill higher-level positions, if a local company has had a major downsizing recently, check with the company that handles their executive outplacement.

If you hire someone who held a senior position at one of your competitors, it is possible that the individual had an employment contract with the company that contained a covenant not to compete. Another possibility is that, when his or her severance package was negotiated, a covenant not to compete was signed at that time. Therefore, it is important to find out if a job applicant is subject to such an agreement, and whether taking the job that is offered would violate it.

Even without a covenant not to compete, a competitor could charge that you hired its ex-employee to misappropriate the competitor's customer lists and trade secrets. If you recruited the ex-employee, you might be charged with interference with contractual relationships. So make it part of the interview process to make a record about the circumstances of the contact.

The Seventh Circuit rule is that it's improper to refuse to hire someone merely because of their union sentiments, membership, or activities [*Bloedorn v. Francisco Foods Inc.*, 276 F.3d 270 (7th Cir. 2001)], or even because they're union "salts" (people "salted" into the workforce to spread pro-union ideas). [*Hartman Bros. Heating & Air Conditioning Inc. v. NLRB*, 280 F.3d 1110 (7th Cir. 2002)] However, the Seventh Circuit found that the company's hiring procedure was not tantamount to a refusal to hire or consider pro-union applicants. As long as an employer is not motivated by anti-union animus, for labor law purposes it can freely exercise its business judgment when deciding whom to hire. [*NLRB v. Louis A. Weiss Mem'l Hosp.*, 172 F.3d 432 (7th Cir. 1999)] Even the NLRB itself takes the position that preferring current employees, ex-employees, and people referred by management cannot be interpreted as anti-union discrimination. [*Custom Topsoil, Inc.*, 328 N.L.R.B. 446 (1999). See Chapter 30 for more about labor law concepts]

## § 23.05 SEARCH FIRMS

Businesses often retain search firms for top executive and professional positions, although this can be a costly option.

There are two main types of firms in the search professional. Contingency firms are usually used to find candidates for jobs paying $40,000–$80,000 a year; an executive search firm usually gets involved only with jobs paying $75,000 a year or more. A search firm works directly for the company seeking to hire an executive. Usually, its contracts require the company to pay for its services whether or not a candidate is hired. In contrast, a contingency firm's clients include both job seekers and companies looking to hire someone, and the company pays a fee if and only if hiring results.

A search firm's fee can be anywhere from 25% to 100% of the first year salary. Contingency firms usually charge less, perhaps 20% to 33% of the first year's salary. Only cash compensation, not bonuses or stock options, is included in the calculation. Both kinds of firms often give refunds if the new hire leaves or has to be discharged during a probationary period such as 90 days.

Many companies are not familiar with search firms, so they do not know what to expect or how to assess the quality of the firm's performance. John Marra, president of the recruitment firm Marra Peters & Partners, has some suggestions:

- Be clear on the criteria you use to judge the firm's performance;

- Get references from past clients and follow them up;

- Tell the search firm what you expect the successful candidate to accomplish the first six months and the first year after hiring, and how you will assess the new hire's performance;

- Ask the search firm to send only candidates who are a good match with your requirements;

- Get the search firm's promise to keep working with you until the vacancy is satisfactorily filled (if necessary, after someone has been hired, terminated after a probationary period, and a new search performed).

Some of the provisions to look for in a recruitment contract are:

- Clarification that the firm does not have the authority to hire someone on behalf of your company, or to promise terms and conditions of employment—only your company's authorized agent can do that;

- A statement that your company is committed to equal employment opportunity principles;

- The firm's agreement that it will be responsible if it commits discrimination in referring candidates to you—and that it will indemnify your company for any liability resulting from its discriminatory referrals;

- A clear statement of the firm's responsibilities, including screening candidates and checking their references;

- Recruiting expenses that your company agrees to pay;

- Whether you have to pay if you hire a candidate obtained through another channel, or only if the recruiter sends the successful candidate to you;

- The recruiter's promise not to contact or solicit your new hire for a period of at least two years.

## § 23.06  JOB APPLICATIONS

Frequently, the first real contact between the corporation and the potential employee occurs when the applicant submits a formal job application. The application is a legal document that can have serious consequences: both as a source of promises that the employer can be held to, and as a source of information whose correctness the applicant can be held responsible for. For example, false statements on an application can constitute "after-acquired evidence" of wrongdoing that can limit the damages available to a successful employee plaintiff. [See § 42.10[C]]

It often makes sense to have a candidate fill out a job application even if he or she has submitted a resume. The resume only includes the information the candidate wants to disclose. The application form is standard, and resumes are very variable, so it is easier to compare applicants if you have the same information about each. The application might ask for:

- Positions held with the last three or four employers;
- Dates of employment;
- Job title;
- Salary;
- Name of immediate supervisor;
- Why the candidate left that job (unless he or she is still employed);
- Permission to contact the supervisor for a reference.

■ **TIP:** In several states (e.g., California, Delaware, Minnesota, Wisconsin), if you require applicants to sign their applications, the state privacy law also requires you to give them a copy of the completed application, or lets employees copy personnel files including job applications.

The application should make it clear that the form is a legal document that can have serious ramifications. It is important to require the applicant to state that all the information given on the application is complete and accurate—and that it will be grounds for discipline or dismissal if the applicant is hired and the employer later finds out that false information was given on the application.

There should be a separate signature line if the employer wants to get a credit report to indicate release of this information. Applicants should be informed when reference checks will be done. The form should clarify that application is being made for at-will employment. If the job offer is conditional on the applicant's passing a physical examination and/or drug and alcohol testing, this should be indicated on the application.

Check state law about which questions are permissible, and which are ruled out by antidiscrimination laws.

See 70 Fed. Reg. 58,947 (Oct. 7, 2005) for DOL's Office of Federal Contract Compliance Programs' Final Rule covering federal contractors' records maintenance obligations with respect to Internet-based job applications. If possible, contractors should collect data on the gender, race, and ethnicity of applicants (including those who apply online). Contractors are required to maintain records of Internet-based expressions of interest that resulted in the contractor considering an applicant for a particular job. [Tresa Baldas, *New Web Hiring Rules Cause Corporate Consternation*, Nat'l L.J. (Dec. 7, 2005) (law.com)]

OfficeTeam reported that 43% of managers responding to its poll said job seekers often lie on resumes; 7% said that dishonest or exaggerated information appeared on resumes very often, 36% said it appeared somewhat often, 48% said not very often, and 8% said resumes were never falsified. Twenty-one percent of workers said they knew someone who was less than truthful, usually with respect to job duties, job experience, or education. [Tara Cantore, *Lying on Resumes not a Rare Occurrence*, plansponsor.com (Sept. 29, 2011)]

## § 23.07  ESTABLISHING TERMS AND CONDITIONS

The interview should stress the at-will nature of employment if your company wants the flexibility to terminate employees without a formal structure. Train interviewers to avoid statements such as "If you do a good job, you'll be set for life here" or "We never lay anybody off, no matter how tough the economy gets." Interviewers should also avoid statements about corporate procedure ("We go through all the channels before anybody gets fired") unless they accurately reflect corporate policy and practice.

Interviewers are agents of the company, and even if the employee handbook says that the company is only obligated if there are written contracts, in fact the company is likely to be held accountable for promises made by the interviewer (for instance, about vacation terms, the availability of leave, and education benefits). Even if the interviewer is not a common-law employee of the company, the agency relationship is likely to create liability for the company if the interviewer is guilty of discrimination. [See, e.g., *Halpert v. Manhattan Apartments Inc.*, 580 F.3d 86 (2d Cir. 2009); see Mark Hamblett, *2nd Circuit: Employer May Be Held Liable for Contractor Age Bias,* N.Y.L.J. (Sept. 14, 2009) (law.com)]

Many companies set a salary range rather than an explicit pay rate for a particular job. Interviewers should understand whether or not they can negotiate a salary with a promising candidate, or if that matter will have to be referred to a higher-up. Interviewees should always be told clearly who else is involved in the interview process, what the powers are of each person, and who has the power to actually make a job offer.

## § 23.08  REFERENCE CHECKS

Reference checks have become much more common, as prices have fallen and employers have become more sensitive to potential problems and liability related to the hiring process.

Reference checks on employees (rather than applicants) can also be useful. A lack of candor can be a valid reason for denying a raise or promotion, and "after-acquired evidence" discovered as late as the preparation for a discrimination suit can be used to reduce the recovery a plaintiff can obtain.

In early 2011, the Supreme Court unanimously upheld the federal government's background check procedure for workers employed by federal contractors. Although the Ninth Circuit granted an injunction against enforcement of the procedure, finding that the questions about counseling and drug treatment were too broad, and persons listed as references were asked open-ended questions that were not detailed enough, the Supreme Court held that the process was reasonably related to security needs, and the Privacy Act controls inappropriate releases of information. [*NASA v. Nelson*, 131 S. Ct. 746 (2011); see Rebecca Moore, *High Court Rejects Federal Contract Workers Challenge to Background Checks*, plansponsor.com (Jan. 20, 2011)]

SHRM's 2010 survey showed 73% of major employers always check criminal records, and 19% do so for some job candidates. Almost half of major companies perform credit checks for some jobs (typically, positions of financial trust); 13% perform a credit check on all potential hires. The EEOC's position is that a blanket refusal to hire based on credit reports or criminal records is illegal if it has a disparate impact on racial minorities. According to the Department of Justice, 38% of prisoners, and 12% of the U.S. population, is black. In 2008, the incarceration rate for African-Americans was six times that for whites, and the incarceration rate for Latinos was 2.3 times that for whites. The EEOC says that a lawful use of criminal history must consider the nature of the job, the seriousness of the offense, and how long ago it happened. [Sam Hananel, *EEOC Warns Against Illegal Job-Screening Tactics* (AP) (Aug. 12, 2010) (law.com)]

The EEOC included these principles in Enforcement Guidance published in April, 2012. [EEOC Enforcement Guidance, *Consideration of Arrest and Conviction Records In Employment Decisions Under Title VII of the Civil Rights Act of 1964*, <http://www.eeoc.gov/laws/guidance/arrest_conviction.cfm> (Apr. 25, 2012); see Steven Greenhouse, *Equal Opportunity Panel Updates Hiring Policy*, NYTimes.com (Apr. 25, 2012)]

The EEOC has brought several suits (e.g., against BMW and Dollar General) alleging discriminatory use of background checks. In mid-2013, however, the District Court for the District of Maryland dismissed the agency's suit against Freeman Co., finding that the EEOC did not prove discrimination against black applicants in Freeman's use of criminal record checks or credit checks. The district court found that Freeman's practices were reasonable and satisfied the company's need for an honest work force. [*EEOC v. Freeman Co.*, No. 09-CV-2573 (D.Md. Aug. 9, 2013)]

Usually, a criminal-record check starts with a trace on the applicant's Social Security number, which generates a list of previous addresses. (Of course, this implies that the applicant was operating "on the books" and using his or her own name!) A complete search looks for outstanding wants and warrants (misdemeanors as well as felonies), motor vehicle reports, credit reports, academic qualifications, and verification of past employment.

A good criminal record check goes back at least seven years. Because many court systems have automated records going back only one to six years, it is often necessary for the research firm to do a manual search (which often costs extra). It is also common for misdemeanor and felony records to be kept in different places, which could also lead to higher fees for separate searches. [Merry Mayer,

*Background Checks in Focus*, HR Magazine, Jan. 2002, at 59] Federal contractors, especially defense contractors, must also be alert to the question of which employees will require a security clearance.

There are large nationwide databases, such as Esteem (First Advantage Corporation), HireRite, and GIS, that track employees accused of theft. Tens of thousands of businesses subscribe to these databases and consult them before hiring. However, sometimes employees make written statements when questioned by store security without being aware that they have confessed to theft—or that the information will remain in databases. Employees may be described as having confessed to theft when they did not report thefts by others or when they made cash register mistakes. The FTC is studying these databases to determine whether they violate the Fair Credit Reporting Act, and whether accused thieves are given an appropriate chance to dispute the charges. Companies that perform background checks do not always give credence to the theft admissions submitted by employers. [Jessica Silver-Greenberg, *Retailers Track Employee Thefts in Vast Databases*, NYTimes.com (Apr. 2, 2013)]

Given the limited job market and employers' greater insistence on background checks, it became more common for employees and job applicants to seek to have their criminal records cleared, especially for minor charges many years earlier. In most states, felony convictions cannot be expunged, but misdemeanor convictions can be expunged after a successful appeal. Furthermore, it is impossible for a court system to remove all records of an arrest or conviction from the Internet, so the information may still be revealed by Web searches (e.g., social media such as Facebook). Under EEOC rules, it is lawful for an employer to make decisions based on convictions, but not on arrests not leading to conviction; approximately 60% of men have been arrested at least once. Some states (Wisconsin, California, Hawaii) forbid discrimination on the basis of arrest record. In New York, usage of criminal records is based on a number of factors: for example, how serious the offense was, when it was committed, the age of the convicted person, and whether he or she shows evidence of rehabilitation. [Douglas Belkin, *More Job Seekers Scramble to Erase Their Criminal Past*, WSJ .com (Nov. 11, 2009); Tresa Baldas, *As Michael Vick Returns to NFL, Employment Lawyers Push Criminal Records Checks*, Nat'l L.J. (Aug. 13, 2009) (law.com)]

## § 23.09 NONDISCRIMINATORY HIRING

Federal law bans discrimination in employment, which definitely includes hiring. Discrimination on account of age, sex, race, disability, religion, and/or national origin is banned. However, even a company that strives to avoid deliberate prejudice can find it hard to eradicate "disparate impact"—apparently neutral practices that actually disadvantage members of one group more than others. For instance, a minimum height requirement screens out more women and certain ethnic groups than white males. That does not mean that employers cannot impose height requirements, as long as it really is necessary to be taller than a certain height to do the job properly.

Other potential sources of disparate impact include:

- Educational standards;

- Pre-employment testing;

- Requirements of military service;

- Referrals from your current workforce (who tend to know people of their own ethnic group);

- Rules about facial hair (which could disadvantage religious applicants, or black men who have ingrown hairs that make shaving painful);

- Refusing to hire anyone who has ever been arrested, filed for bankruptcy, or had a child out of wedlock.

Your attorney should review hiring practices to make sure that they are not discriminatory and that all requirements can be justified in terms of the practical needs of the business and skills that will actually be used on the job. For each position, you should also determine the physical capacities that are central to the job, those that are sometimes used but are peripheral, and those that are never invoked by the job.

If employees request flextime (for parenting needs, as an accommodation to disability, as a religious accommodation, or simply for convenience), you should either be able to grant the request or demonstrate a legitimate business reason why conventional business hours or standard shifts must be observed.

There are two important criteria for assessing interview questions:

- Do the questions relate to legitimate workplace issues, rather than just satisfying curiosity?

- Are they asked uniformly, rather than only to a group of people chosen on the basis of preconceived notions? For instance, it is discriminatory to ask a woman if her husband "lets" her travel on business, but not discriminatory to discuss the amount of travel required with all applicants, including the number of overnight or prolonged stays required, and to ask all candidates if they are able to travel that much.

Equal employment opportunity law assumes that many candidates will be interviewed for each opening, and there are many reasons why the successful candidate will be selected. There is no reason to collect a great deal of information about candidates who have no real chance of selection. Therefore, some questions are acceptable when a conditional job offer is made that would not be allowed at a first-stage interview.

For instance, marital status and having children are very relevant to participation in an employee group health plan, but irrelevant if the person is not going to get a job offer. So this information should either be requested only after hiring, or collected on a separate sheet of paper and not consulted until after hiring. [See § 36.09 for a discussion of acceptable and unacceptable pre-employment inquiries and tests in the disability context.]

It is not acceptable to ask an interviewee about his or her history of receiving Worker's Compensation benefits, but anyone who gets a conditional job offer can be asked about past injuries that may require accommodation.

There are also circumstances under which the company's commitment to equal employment opportunity must be put into writing: if the company is a federal contractor, for instance.

## § 23.10  PRE-EMPLOYMENT TESTING

It is legitimate for an employer to test job applicants to see if they have relevant skills. Title VII permits the use of professionally developed ability tests that are not designed or administered with a discriminatory motive. A valid test is one that is neither explicitly nor implicitly discriminatory against protected groups; one that tests skills that are actually used in the job; and one that has been validated by psychologists or other experts so that it really offers insight into the issues needed for effective hiring.

A Supreme Court case, *Albemarle Paper Co. v. Moody* [422 U.S. 405 (1975)], holds that if a test has a disproportionate negative effect on a minority group, the test is permissible only if professionally accepted methods verify the test's ability to predict important elements of work behavior. As *Griggs v. Duke Power Co.* [401 U.S. 424 (1971)] says, the point of pre-employment testing is to measure the applicant's performance in the context of a specific job, not in the abstract. Even if the company's pre-employment test is valid, it is discriminatory to give the test only to minority-group members.

However, in 2009, another Supreme Court case (dealing with a promotional exam for firefighters) endorsed properly validated and professionally drafted tests. New Haven, Connecticut refused to certify the test or use the test results to make up a promotion list, because almost all of the highest scoring candidates were white, and the city was afraid of lawsuits from minority firefighters. However, a suit was filed by white firefighters who said they were improperly denied promotions. The Supreme Court said that refusing to certify the test constituted intentional discrimination against the higher scoring white and Hispanic firefighters. Even if it had been sued by minority firefighters, the city could have defended itself by citing the Title VII provision that allows the use of valid, job-related tests that are implemented as a matter of business necessity. [*Ricci v. DeStefano*, 129 S. Ct. 2658 (U.S. June 29, 2009)]

Pre-hire assessments of traits such as personality, cognitive ability, and competency are increasing: about 48% of companies used them in 2010, rising to 56% in 2011. Some companies use the tests only for executives, some for all new hires—but generally only after a short list of candidates has been compiled. [Ruth Mantell, *Job Seekers Are Getting Tested*, WSJ.com (Sept. 11, 2011)] If your company adopts a pre-employment test and monitors the results, discovering that the test has an adverse impact on women and/or members of minority groups, then you should either get rid of the test, change it to remove the adverse impact, or do a validity study that confirms both that the test is a business necessity and that it accurately predicts the skills needed for successful job performance. The Civil Rights Act of 1991 [Pub. L. No. 102-166] says that it is not acceptable to grade minority applicants' tests on a "curve," or to have a lower passing grade for minorities.

Publications about psychological testing are good for finding out which tests have already been validated. Three types of validation are accepted:

- Criterion-related (the test is an accurate predictor of work behavior or other criteria of employee adequacy);

- Content-related (the test accurately duplicates the tasks that will actually be called for in the workplace);

- Construct-related (the test identifies general mental and psychological traits needed to do the job, such as the ability to remain cool under pressure and respond courteously to angry customers).

Some job applicants challenge online pre-employment tests for bias. The employer can be liable if the effect of the test is to exclude protected groups; the company must be able to prove that the traits that are measured are relevant to job performance. For example, Vicky Sandy, who is hearing-impaired, scored low on a 50-question test about cheerfulness, empathy, and self-confidence that Kroger asks cashier applicants to take. She complained to the EEOC that she was discriminated against by being required to take a test that is biased against the hearing-impaired, even those who can work effectively and the EEOC investigated her claim. The EEOC included pre-employment tests in its draft enforcement plan for 2012–2016 (issued Sept. 4, 2012). In 2011, only 164 out of almost 100,000 EEOC complaints referred to testing—perhaps because employees seldom see the test results, so they blame other factors if they are not hired or promoted. In July 2012, Leprino Foods Inc. (a food processor that is a government contractor) settled DOL hiring discrimination charges by agreeing to pay $550,000 in back pay to black, Hispanic, and Asian applicants who were rejected as laborers because they failed the WorkKeys pre-hire test. The DOL's Office of Federal Contract Compliance Programs (OFCCP) said that the test, which involves math and observation skills, is not relevant to the entry-level jobs for which it was used. [Joseph Walker, *Debating the Legality of Big Data in Hiring*, WSJ.com (Sept. 19, 2012)]

## § 23.11 IMMIGRATION ISSUES

### [A] Employment Requirement

If an alien wishes to enter this country on the basis of employment, he or she must not only have a definite job offer from a U.S. employer, but the employer must have "labor certification." [<http://workforcesecurity.doleta.gov/foreign/hiring.asp>] That is, the Department of Labor must certify that the job is "open" because the company cannot recruit a qualified U.S. worker at the prevailing wages. First, the employer must use the State Employment Service and post and advertise the job opportunity. The employer must interview any applicants who come through that route, and must file a recruitment report with the DOL explaining why none of those applicants was suitable for the position.

However, certain occupations are considered "shortage" occupations because of a documented difficulty in filling the jobs: nursing, physical therapy, and people of demonstrated exceptional ability in business, science, or the arts. Multinational executives, outstanding university-level teachers, researchers, and people whose jobs are in the national interest do not displace American workers, so labor certification will not be required for such jobs.

Immigration law is basically a federal area, as the Supreme Court pointed out in June 2012, when it struck down most of Arizona's immigration law. The Arizona law made it a misdemeanor for an illegal alien to apply for work, or to work as either an employee or as an independent contractor. The Supreme Court noted that Congress chose not to make it a crime for illegal immigrants to work in the United States. However, the Supreme Court did uphold the part of the Arizona statute that allows the police to check the immigration status of people who have been detained. [*Arizona v. United States*, 132 S.Ct. 2492 (2012); see Marcia Coyle, *Supreme Court Trims Arizona Immigration Law*, NYTimes. com (June 25, 2012). Alabama enacted a statute, the Beason-Hammond Alabama Taxpayer and Citizen Protection Act, with similar immigration provisions. The Eleventh Circuit held that federal immigration law preempts this statute, which made it a crime for unauthorized aliens to work in the United States: *United States v. Alabama*, 691 F.3d 1269 (11th Cir. 2012), rendering the law unenforceable.]

South Carolina's immigration laws were also held to be preempted by federal immigration law. [*United States v. South Carolina*,Nos. 12-1096, 12-1099, 12-2514, 12-2533 (4th Cir. July 23, 2013)]

## [B]  Immigration Categories

Employment-based immigration is regulated under the Immigration Act of 1990. [Pub. L. No. 101-649] There are various categories of employable immigrants, e.g.:

- Priority workers (individuals of extraordinary ability and/or vocational responsibility);

- Professionals with advanced degrees and/or exceptional ability;

- Other workers (skilled workers, professionals without advanced degrees; unskilled workers who have DOL certification that there is a shortage of U.S. workers with similar skills);

- Special immigrants (e.g., religious workers sent to the U.S. by a religious hierarchy);

- Immigrants who have the financial capacity to invest at least $1 million within the United States, employing at least 10 U.S. workers;

- H-1B "specialty occupation" workers who reside temporarily within the United States, and work here, but do not become citizens;

- H-2 temporary non-agricultural workers.

According to the USCIS Website, employers can use the Petition for Nonimmigrant Worker (I-129) not only for H-1B workers but P-1 athletes and entertainers, H-1C registered nurses, P-2 artistic exchange candidates, H-2 temporary laborers, H-3 alien trainees, Q-1 international cultural exchange program participants, O-1 aliens with extraordinary ability, and L-1 intracompany transferees. The H-1B classification is divided into H-1B1 (specialty occupations requiring theoretical and practical application of professional skills) and H-1B2 (exceptional services in a cooperative research and development project administered by the Department of Defense). [USCIS, Temporary Benefits Employment Categories and Required Documentation, <http://www.uscis.gov/portal/site/uscis/menuitem.5af9bb[. . . ]>]

In May 2010, the DOL launched a new Website, the H-1B Advisor, to assist employers and potential H-1B visa holders in understanding the requirements of the program. [<http://www.dol.gov/elaws/h1b.htm>; see Fred Schneyer, *DOL Puts Up H-1B Web Site*, plansponsor.com (May 17, 2010)]

Although DOL policy, including 2010 amendments to the regulations, requires employers to reimburse H-2B workers (non-agricultural temporary workers) visa, travel, and recruitment expenses, the Fifth Circuit held in 2010 that this is not required by the FLSA itself. Therefore, the Fifth Circuit dismissed an FLSA collective action brought by a group of hotel workers who said that these costs were "tools of the trade" that should have been reimbursed. [*Castellanos-Contreras v. Decatur Hotels LLC*, 622 F.3d 393 (5th Cir. 2010); see Jackson

Lewis LLP, *Federal Appeals Court Rules Employers Need Not Reimburse H-2B Workers* (Oct. 22, 2010) (benefitslink.com)]

### [C]  Employer Responsibilities: No-Match Letters and E-Verify

U.S. labor and immigration law places a burden on the employer (or on an agency that gets a fee for recruitment or making referrals) to determine whether job applicants are legally permitted to work in this country. No later than three business days after hiring, the employer must ascertain if the new hire is a U.S. citizen or a legal immigrant who is not only permitted to reside in this country but to work here. Presidential Executive Order 12989 [61 Fed. Reg. 6091 (Feb. 13, 1996)] debars federal contractors from getting further federal contracts after they have been caught knowingly hiring illegal aliens.

The employer responsibilities stem from the Immigration Reform and Control Act of 1986 (IRCA). [7 U.S.C. § 1324a] The employer is responsible for checking documents presented by potential new employees to demonstrate their identity and authorization to work within the United States. (There are people who are lawfully permitted to enter and reside in this country, but not to work here, so there is more to the matter than distinguishing illegal aliens from lawful immigrants.)

The information must be obtained in a way that is not discriminatory against dark-skinned people, or people whose first language is not English.

Both the U.S. Citizenship and Immigration Services (USCIS) and the DOL are entitled to inspect a company's immigration-related forms, but to enter a workplace they must either have a warrant or give 72 hours' notice.

Employment of immigrants requires the employer to work with both the DOL's Employment and Training Administration and the USCIS, which is part of the Department of Homeland Security. Employers can obtain permission to hire foreign workers on either a temporary (e.g., nurses; seasonal agricultural workers; specialized professional workers) or a permanent basis, depending on the facts of the case and the conditions within the U.S. labor market. The overarching policy is that employment of a foreign worker depends on proof that there is a shortage preventing the hiring of U.S. workers for the job. Furthermore, the law requires lawful immigrant workers to receive at least the prevailing wage for their jobs, so immigrant workers cannot be used to depress wages.

The Department of Labor published a Final Rule, effective March 28, 2005, now found at 20 C.F.R. § 656.10 and 20 C.F.R. § 656.15.

Labor certification is the process of petitioning DOL's Employment and Training Administration; the ETA certifies to the USCIS that permitting the person the employer wishes to hire is appropriate because no U.S. worker is available to fill the job. The application is ETA Form 9089, Alien Employment Certification, describing the job duties, qualifications, and experience required. The employer should submit Form 9089 in duplicate, signed by the alien and by an authorized official of the employer company. If the petition for an alien worker (see below) is approved, then the USCIS will forward one copy of the Form 9089 to the Chief of the Division of Foreign Labor Certification.

The employer must obtain a prevailing wage determination from the state workforce agency (to show that the employer is not hiring immigrants in order to depress the wages paid for the job). If the employer has a collective bargaining unit, the employer must either notify the union or post a notice for at least ten consecutive calendar days, to disclose that labor certification is being sought. If the employer normally uses in-house media, such as an employee newsletter, to announce job openings, the same means must be used to inform employees that labor certification is being sought. Notice of this type should be given not more than 180 and not less than 30 days before the Form I-140 petition is filed.

After labor certification is obtained, the employer files USCIS Form I-140, Immigrant Petition for an Alien Worker, on behalf of the alien worker. [The DOL's explanation of the process can be found at *Hiring Foreign Workers*, <http://www.workforcesecurity.doleta.gov/foreign/hiring.asp> and *Permanent Labor Certification*; see also USCIS, *Guidance for Schedule A Blanket Labor Certifications Effective February 14, 2006*, <http://www.uscis.gov/graphics/lawsregs/handbook/afm_ch22_021406.pdf> (Feb. 24, 2006)]

It is illegal to knowingly hire an ineligible person. Knowledge includes constructive knowledge (reasonable inferences from facts and circumstances, to the degree that a person acting with reasonable care would have to be aware). According to USCIS regulations [see 8 C.F.R. § 274a], these circumstances create an inference of constructive knowledge:

- The employer actually has some information that the person is not eligible for U.S. employment;

- The applicant refuses to complete the I-9 form, or does it improperly;

- The employer acts with "reckless and wanton disregard" of the consequences of hiring ineligible persons.

However, accent and appearance are not acceptable sources of constructive knowledge. Once the employer knows that the hiree is (or has become, because of a change of status) ineligible to work in the United States, continuing employment is unlawful. [See 8 U.S.C. § 1324a]

The federal crime of "aggravated identity theft" (18 U.S.C. § 1028A(a)(1)) carries a mandatory two-year prison sentence if a person convicted of certain crimes committed the crime by knowingly using someone else's means of identification. In a mid-2009 Supreme Court case, the petitioner was a Mexican citizen who, to establish eligibility to work in the United States, gave his employer false Social Security and alien registration cards with his name and identification numbers that belonged to other people. He was arrested for immigration offenses and aggravated identity theft. His argument was that the numbers were chosen at random, and he did not know that they belonged to other people. The Supreme Court ruled that, to convict, the prosecution must show that the defendant knew the identification numbers belonged to someone else. [*Flores-Figueroa v. United States*, 556 U.S. 646 (2009)]

E-Verify is an electronic program for ascertaining employees' right to work in the United States. It began as a voluntary program, although several states (e.g., Arizona, Georgia, Minnesota, South Carolina) passed laws requiring employers in those states to use E-Verify. [Rebecca Moore, *House Bill Would Extend Use of Federal E-Verify Program*, plansponsor.com (Aug. 5, 2008)]

Because of a suit brought by business groups, the DOJ delayed the effective date of mandatory E-Verify until February 20, 2009 (after the deadline for filing final motions and briefs in the suit). [Rebecca Moore, *Department of Justice Delays Effective Date for E-Verify Requirement*, plansponsor.com (Jan. 9, 2009)]

Mandatory status was delayed yet again, to May 21, 2009, so that the incoming Obama administration could review the rule. [Miriam Jordan, *White House Holds Off on Tightening Immigration Checks*, WSJ.com (Jan. 30, 2009). The suits in question were *Chamber of Commerce of the U.S. v. Napolitano*, No. 08-cv-3444AW (D. Md.) and *AFL-CIO v. Napolitano*, No. 07-cv-4472CRB (N.D. Calif.). [Pamela A. MacLean, *Controversial "E-Verify" Immigration Program on Hold*, Nat'l L.J. (Feb. 3, 2009) (law.com)]

In mid-2009, Department of Homeland Security Secretary Janet Napolitano announced the administration's support for a regulation requiring federal contractors to enroll in E-Verify within 30 days of getting a federal contract, and to use it to check employees' work authorization. The administration concluded that E-Verify is more effective than the No-Match Rule, and the latter was rescinded. Any business receiving a federal contract or subcontract, including ARRA funds, must use E-Verify, with full implementation beginning September 8, 2009. DHS announced that it had new processes to reduce typographical errors and initial mismatches, and to connect to naturalization databases to verify the status of naturalized citizens. [Homeland Security Press Release, *Secretary Napolitano Strengthens Employment Verification with Administration's Commitment to E-Verify*, <http://www.dhs.gov/ynews/releases/pr_1247063976814.shtm> (July 8, 2009)]

The E-Verify requirement for federal contractors affected about 169,000 contractors and subcontractors and their 3.8 million workers. The requirement will be written into all new and renewed federal contracts, and new work orders under existing contracts. [Cam Simpson, *Judge Rejects Bid to Delay E-Verify Mandate*, WSJ.com (Sept. 8, 2009)]

In addition to the federal requirement, at least 10 states mandate their own contractors to use E-Verify As of February 2011, only about 11% of the 7.7 million employers in the United States used E-Verify, either because it is required of them as federal contractors, or voluntarily. [Miriam Jordan, *U.S. Expands Crackdown on Firms Hiring Illegal Immigrants*, WSJ.com (Feb. 17, 2011)]

The Obama administration adopted a new enforcement strategy: "silent raids" under which federal agents examine employment records to find undocumented workers. [Julia Preston, *Illegal Workers Swept From Jobs in "Silent Raids,"* WSJ.com (July 9, 2010); Miriam Jordan, *U.S. Expands Crackdown on Firms Hiring Illegal Immigrants*, WSJ.com (Feb. 17, 2011). In mid-2011, ICE said that 2,393 companies were being audited, the largest number to date, although ICE does not disclose the names of companies under audit. In mid-2009, American Apparel paid about $35,000 in fines, and over a quarter of its workforce was found to be working illegally. ABM had 1,250 undocumented workers out of a total of about 100,000 nationwide and paid $108,000 in civil penalties. [Miriam Jordan, *Immigration Audits Drive Illegal Workers Underground*, WSJ.com (Aug. 15, 2011)]

In 2011, federal agents raided 15 locations of the restaurant chain Chuy's Mesquite Broiler, arresting the owners, the bookkeeper, and 40 suspected illegal immigrants. (In its fiscal year ending September 30, 2010, ICE filed 180 criminal charges against corporate executives—the highest level to date.) The indictment charges the owners with having separate payrolls: one for legal workers as waiters, the other for illegal immigrants in the kitchen who were paid under the table without any deduction of employment taxes. Chuy's was charged with employing 360 illegal workers, and under-reporting and failing to pay at least $400,000 in FICA and Medicare taxes.

Civil fines for violating federal immigration laws on employment were raised in February 2008. Civil penalties under the INA are adjusted for inflation, and the previous adjustment was in 1999, so the average increase was about 25%. The maximum penalty for knowingly employing an unauthorized alien rose from $275 to $375. The maximum penalty for first violations rose from $2,200 to $3,200, and the civil penalty for multiple violations went from $11,000 to $16,000 (all penalties on a per-worker basis). [Rebecca Moore, *DOJ Announces Higher Civil Fines for Employer Immigration Violations*, plansponsor.com (Mar. 3, 2008)]

## [D]   Employment Verification Documents

Hired individuals prove their eligibility to work within the United States either by showing that they are U.S. citizens (e.g., showing a U.S. passport or birth certificate evidencing birth within the United States) or by showing that they have a so-called green card. (The document, Form I-551, is no longer actually green.)

Since 1997, the Immigration and Naturalization Service has issued Form I-766, a tamper-resistant card issued to aliens whose immigration status permits work within the United States. The I-766 is a List A Employment Authorization Document (EAD): that is, it establishes both the job applicant's identity and his or her entitlement to work.

There are three categories of documents. List A documents can be used to prove both identity and employability; List B documents prove identity only; List C documents prove employability only.

A DOL Proposed Rule establishes a 45-day window during which employers must file an application with the Department of Homeland Security after labor certification has been granted for a particular non-citizen worker. However, the application is not transferable, and a new labor certification application must be filed if the person for whom the certification was applied for is unavailable to take the job. Previous practice accommodated the long period for getting approval by allowing substitutions. [71 Fed. Reg. 7655 (Feb. 13, 2006); see *DOL Proposes Barring Name Substitutions by Employers on Green Card Applications*, 74 L.W. 2492 (Feb. 21, 2006)]

In November 2007, the Department of Homeland Security released new I-9 forms for the determination that new hires are authorized to work in the United States and changed the roster of documents that can be used to establish identity and/or work authorization. [<http://www.uscis.gov/files/form/I-9.pdf>; see Fred Schneyer, *DHS Releases New Job Eligibility Form*, plansponsor.com (Nov. 16, 2007)]

## [E]  H-1B and H-2B Visas

The H-1B visa is a non-immigrant visa for temporary workers in "specialty occupations." This means jobs that apply a highly specialized body of knowledge in both a theoretical and a practical way. Most H-1B visa holders work in high-tech businesses, such as software development. The initial duration of the visa is three years, although it can be extended for three more years. The worker must have at least a bachelor's degree in his or her specialty field, or must have equivalent qualifications and expertise. If the job requires a state license, the visa holder must have the license.

H-1B workers must be paid either the salary the employer would otherwise pay for the job, or the prevailing wage in the area. This requirement is designed to prevent employers from hiring foreign workers simply to lower wage costs. Willful violation of this requirement or the layoff requirement can be penalized by a $35,000 fine and three years' debarment from federal contracts.

Employers usually recruit workers from foreign students in the United States on student visas and about to graduate from a program that gives them the necessary specialized skills. Immigration law requires the employer to wait until the student graduates before making a job offer. You can get around this problem by having the student get permission from the Immigration and Naturalization Services to add a year of PGPT (post-graduate practical training) to his or her student visa, so you can apply for the H-1B visa during this extra year. The holders of student visas are required to leave the United States by July of the year in which they graduate, unless they have PGPT authorization.

II-1B visa holders may not be hired until the employer has first attempted to recruit qualified U.S. workers, although a more qualified H-1B applicant can legitimately be preferred to a less-qualified U.S. citizen. Employers are also forbidden to terminate U.S. workers for the purpose of replacing them with H-1B workers. Temporary agencies and other suppliers of contingent workers are forbidden to make any placements of H-1B workers with any company that has displaced U.S. workers.

The DOL regulation not only protects U.S. jobs, but also it protects the H-1B workers from exploitation. They must be given benefits on the same basis as their U.S. counterparts. Whenever their employer places them in a nonproductive category (e.g., there is a temporary lull in work), they must be kept at full salary. It is unlawful for employers to require H-1B workers to reimburse them for the cost of filing the employment petition, or to penalize workers for terminating their work assignment prematurely.

To encourage reporting of misconduct, protection is extended to applicants, employees, and ex-employees who assist the Departments of Labor and Justice in their investigations. In fact, H-1B whistleblowers can be permitted to remain in the United States for up to six years.

Also see the H-1B Visa Reform Act of 2004, enacted as part of Pub. L. No. 108-447, the appropriations act, adding an additional 20,000 H-1B visa slots for visa holders with a Master's Degree or higher from an institution in the United States, and permitting expedited processing for an additional fee. Interim Final Rules were published in mid-2005. [70 Fed. Reg. 23775 (May 5, 2005), discussed at 73 L.W. 2636, 2666. See also <http://www.foreignlaborcert.doleta/gov/foreign/h01b.asp>]

On March 19, 2008, USCIS issued an interim final rule that forbids employers to file more than one H-1B petition for a particular employee in a fiscal year. Duplicate petitions will be rejected and the filing fees will not be refunded. The purpose of the rule is to prevent employers gaming the system by making multiple applications in the hope that one of them will be accepted. The interim Final Rule does not apply to applications made by related employers (e.g., a parent company and a subsidiary) to transfer an alien from one job to another.

Only 65,000 new H-1B visas can be granted per year, but the first 20,000 H-1B petitions filed on behalf of aliens who have earned master's or higher degrees in the United States are exempt from the 65,000 cap and subject to a separate "20,000 cap." H-1B petitions are entirely exempt from the numerical limitations if the alien will work in certain educational institutions, their affiliated nonprofit organizations, or nonprofit or governmental research institutions, so employers can make H-1B applications for exempt workers even if no regular H-1B visa numbers are available. [USCIS, *Fact Sheet: Changes to the FY2009 H-1B Program*, <http://www.uscis.gov/portal/site/uscis/template.PRINT/menuitem. 5af9bb959[ . . . ]>. USCIs' *Handbook for Employers* (Form M-274, Nov. 1, 2007) was posted to <http://www.uscis.gov/files/nativedocuments/m-274.pdf>]

It took almost a year for all of the FY 2003 visas to be used; then H-1B visas became far more popular. It took 300 days for all the visas to be granted in 2010, about 250 days in 2009 and 2011—but less than a week in 2007 and 2008. In 2013, demand heated up once again, and it was expected that all visas would be taken up in the first few days of availability. As a result, USCIS was expected to randomly select applications for processing. [Miriam Jordan, *Visa Demand Jumps*, WSJ.com (Apr. 1, 2013)] Once laid off, H-1B visa holders must leave the United States unless they can find a qualifying new job almost immediately. There is no grace period: aliens who do not have another job must either leave within a few days of losing their jobs, or convert their visas to a B1/B2 tourist visa which does not allow them to work (but gives them a little time to sell their homes and arrange for the return to their home countries [Miriam Jordan, *Slump Sinks Visa Program*, WSJ.com (Oct. 29, 2009); Mona Sarika, *Homeward Bound*, WSJ.com (Nov. 9, 2009)]

In 2012, the H-2B program was changed to improve job opportunities for Americans while protecting foreign temporary workers. Most H-2B workers are employed by seasonal small businesses such as seafood fishing and processing, hotels and landscaping, and amusement parks. The extensive new rules took effect April 23, 2012.

A new electronic registry was created for posting jobs that employers want to fill with H-2B workers. The recruitment period for Americans is expanded; the employer must hire any qualified local worker who applies up to three weeks before the start of the H-2B contract. The process of labor-market certification has changed. It used to be sufficient to state that there was a search for U.S. workers. Now formal consultation with the state workforce agency is required to demonstrate that U.S. workers were unavailable. Once a migrant worker completes half the contract period, the employer is obligated to pay the guest worker's transportation costs from the home country to the United States. The employer is responsible for all visa fees and must pay for travel home when the job is completed or if the worker is dismissed early. A provision that is particularly unpopular with employers requires foreign workers to be paid for three-quarters of the period of the contract even if there is no work for them. Foreign recruiters are not allowed to charge fees to workers who come to the United States under the H-2B program. [Julia Preston, *Rules Revised for H-2B Guest Worker Program*, NYTimes.com (Feb. 10, 2012)]

For Form 9142 filings between January 18, 2009 and April 23, 2012, each season the employer submits an application on form 9142, a copy of the job order, and additional documents, which the Employment & Training Administration (ETA) uses to check job opportunities. Submission must be made 75–90 calendar days before the employer's date of need; this time frame can be waived for good cause. Both the job contractor and the end employer must declare themselves joint employers, and both must sign Appendix B agreeing to comply with H-2B rules.

The employer must provide copies of any agreements with international recruiters and must disclose the name and location of subcontractors who recruit

H-2B workers. A new recertification rule has been added. If a U.S. worker does not appear, or abandons the job before the job order ends, the employer can ask the ETA for expedited re-certification so an H-2B worker can be hired.

The job order must be disclosed to all H-2B workers in a language they can understand. The offered wage is the minimum wage or the prevailing wage (if that is higher) and must be paid for the full employment period certified in the application. The employer must pay H-2B workers every two weeks—or more frequently, if that is the prevailing practice. The employer must provide, without charge, all tools, supplies, and equipment needed for the job and must guarantee employment for at least three-quarters of the workdays in each 12-week period. The employer is obligated to keep accurate records of hours and pay and give workers an earnings statement on or before every payday.

H-2B workers cannot be used to replace strikers or workers who have been locked out. The employer must not lay off U.S. workers in the same occupation and area of intended employment from 120 days before the first date of need to the end of the assignment. Lawful job-related layoffs, for example at the end of the work season, are permissible as long as the H-2B workers are laid off before their U.S. counterparts. The terms and conditions offered to U.S. workers must not be less favorable than those offered to H-2B workers and employers cannot impose restrictions only on the U.S. workers.

It is unlawful for an employer or an employer's agent or attorney to seek or collect any of the costs of certification, such as application costs, legal fees, or recruitment fees; of course kickbacks are forbidden. The employer must pay, or reimburse the worker for, all visa-related expenses in the first workweek.

The employer must post a worker's rights poster in English and in other appropriate languages. [Note that 20 C.F.R. § 655.20(m) just says that the poster must be provided in any language spoken by a significant portion of workers who are not fluent in English, but doesn't state a procedure for determining this].

The 2012 rules forbid employers to retaliate against workers who file complaints, testify, or vindicate the rights of other workers. Employers are forbidden to hold or confiscate workers' immigration documents. The ETA has the power to revoke labor certification for various reasons, including fraud, willful misrepresentation of material fact, substantial failure of the terms and conditions of employment, and non-cooperation with the DOL or its sanctions. Civil monetary penalties of up to $10,000 per violation can be assessed. [Department of Labor Wage and Hour Division (WHD), *H-2B Side-by-Side Comparison of the 2009 and 2012 Rules*, <http://www.dol.gov/whd/immigration/H2BFinalRule/H2BSide BySide.htm> (February 2012)]

## [F]  Case Law on Immigration Issues in Employment

Undocumented aliens are employees entitled to vote in representation elections, even if their status has been challenged under the IRCA. [*NLRB v. Kolkka*,

170 F.3d 937 (9th Cir. 1999)] But an illegal alien is not an "employee" for Worker's Compensation purposes, and therefore cannot receive Comp benefits for an on-the-job injury. [*Granados v. Windson Dev. Corp.*, 257 Va. 103, 509 S.E.2d 290 (1999)], or back pay in a suit alleging unfair labor practices. [*Hoffman Plastic Prods. Inc. v. NLRB*, 535 U.S. 137 (2002) ; *Palma v. NLRB*,No. 12-1199 (2d Cir. July 10, 2013)]

The Second Circuit permitted an award of lost earnings—using United States and not home country rates—to an undocumented worker crippled in a fall, because the injury was caused by the employer's violation of scaffolding requirements, not by the employee's ineligibility to work legally in the United States. [*Madeira v. Affordable Hous. Found. Inc.*, 469 F.3d 219 (2d Cir. Nov. 14, 2006). See also *Majlinger v. Cassino Contracting Corp.*, 25 A.D. 3d 4, 802 N.Y.S.2d 56 (2d Dept. 2005) allowing compensation for lost U.S. earnings at U.S. rates, holding that this does not conflict with IRCA; *Flores v. Limehouse*, 2006 U.S. Dist. LEXIS 30433 (D.S.C. May 11, 2006) holding that IRCA does not preempt claims by undocumented workers against their employers under RICO and federal and state labor law—even if the workers obtained employment fraudulently; *Rosa v. Partners in Progress, Inc.*, 868 A.2d 994 (N.H. 2005) (for undocumented worker to be able to make a tort claim, the employer must have known or have a duty to know the worker's employment was illegal)]

California Labor Code § 1171.5 says that immigration status is irrelevant to liability issues under the state's labor and employment laws. IRCA preempts state or local laws that impose criminal penalties for employing ineligible aliens, but does not preempt state Worker's Compensation laws. In this reading, the purpose of the Worker's Compensation law is remedial and humanitarian, not penal, and it does not impose penalties for employing aliens, so it does not conflict with and is not preempted by IRCA. Although WC benefits cannot be paid as a direct result of fraudulent misrepresentation, that principle is not applied where use of fraudulent documentation to obtain employment did not cause the physical injury. [*Farmers Brothers Coffee v. Workers' Comp. Appeals Board and Ruiz*, 133 Cal. App. 4th 533 (Cal. App. 2005)]

In 2011, the District Court for the District of Massachusetts granted the plaintiffs' motion to make a restaurant answer written questions about possible members of the class—but denied the defendants' motion to require the plaintiffs to answer questions about their immigration status. Restaurant workers claimed that they were paid less than the Massachusetts minimum wage, because they routinely worked 60–80 hours per week but not only did not receive overtime but also were not paid for all of the hours they worked. The district court ruled that allowing recovery by illegal aliens is compatible with federal immigration policy, and there is a consensus that FLSA recoveries are not discretionary—wages must be paid even if the worker is undocumented. [*Lin v. Chinatown Rest. Corp.*, No. 09-11510-GAO, *2011 U.S. Dist. LEXIS 30626* (D. Mass. Mar. 23, 2011); see Sheri Qualters, *Plaintiffs' Immigration Status 'Irrelevant' To Their Wage Claims, Mass. Judge Rules*, Nat'l L.J. (Mar. 28, 2011) (law.com). See also *NLRB v. Domsey*

*Trading Corp.*, 636 F.3d 33 (2d Cir. 2011), discussed in Rao Tiliakos, *Questioning Board Applicants Seeking Backpay About Their Immigration Status is Permitted*, Tri-State Employment Blog Employer (Feb. 25, 2011) (benefitslink.com), holding that, in an NLRB compliance hearing about alleged unlawful termination of strikers, the employer has the right to cross-examine plaintiffs about their immigration status, and expert testimony about immigration is admissible.]

Nor, according to the Ninth Circuit, does IRCA preempt California labor laws that forbid employers to fire employees without good cause because it is possible to comply with both laws—for example, by obtaining an H-1B visa for the plaintiff, or granting his request for unpaid leave to resolve his work status. Although the defendant argued that it would have been a violation to continue to employ the plaintiff once his E-1 visa was terminated, the Ninth Circuit held that a person on suspension is not "employed" because he or she does not get paid for performing services. In the Ninth Circuit view, although *Hoffman* requires immediate termination of workers who have no possible claim to legal status, it does not apply to a person who can obtain work authorization relatively quickly. [*Incalza v. Fendi N. Am. Inc.*, 479 F.3d 1005 (9th Cir. 2007). See also *Zamora v. Elite Logistics, Inc.*, 449 F.3d 1106 (10th Cir. 2006), holding that it is a defense in a TVII suit that the employee was put on leave without pay until his immigration status was resolved]

Tennessee ruled that the survivors of a deceased worker can be "dependents" who receive Worker's Compensation benefits even if they are foreign nationals, not Tennessee residents, if they were actual dependents on the money sent by their deceased son. [Adrien Martin, *Foreign Nationals Can Be Dependents for TN Workers' Comp [sic] Benefits*, plansponsor.com (Jan. 23, 2007)]

It was an unfair labor practice to contact the INS right after the union won an election, telling eleven employees that they could not work until they straightened out their immigration status. This was a departure from the employer's normal practice. The NLRB said that, although IRCA compliance is important, it must not be used as a smokescreen for anti-union animus. [*Nortech Waste*, 336 N.L.R.B. 79 (2001)]

In 2004, the Seventh Circuit ruled that employees cannot state a RICO claim by alleging that the employer deliberately hired illegal aliens to keep wages down. In such a situation, the defendant company is the "enterprise," so there is no one for it to conspire with for RICO purposes. [*Baker v. IBP Inc.*, 357 F.3d 685 (7th Cir. 2004)] The Eleventh Circuit, however, disagreed, ruling that both RICO and state law claims were raised by allegations that the employer conspired with temporary agencies to hire illegal workers and use false documentation, with the objective of lowering wages and escaping Worker's Compensation responsibilities. The Supreme Court granted certiorari in December of 2005, but dismissed certiorari as improvidently granted in June 2006 and sent the case back to the Eleventh Circuit to resolve some minor issues. [*Williams v. Mohawk Indus. Inc.*, 411 F.3d 1252 (11th Cir. 2005), *cert. granted but dismissed as improvidently granted*, 547 U.S. 516 (2006)]

In September 2008, the Ninth Circuit upheld the Legal Arizona Workers Act, a 2007 Arizona state law penalizing employers who hire illegal aliens, by revoking their state business licenses. The Supreme Court upheld this law in mid-2011, holding that federal immigration law does not preempt the state law, because it is possible for employers to comply with both. IRCA forbids states to impose any criminal or civil sanctions for hiring illegal immigrants, other than through licensing and similar laws—but the Arizona statute is a licensing law because it is enforced by taking away the licenses of companies that hire undocumented workers. [*Chamber of Commerce v. Whiting*, 131 S. Ct. 1968 (2011); see Tony Mauro, *In Blow to Business Groups, Justices Uphold Arizona Law on Hiring Foreign Workers*, Nat'l L.J. (May 26, 2011) (law.com)]

After almost a decade, Wal-Mart prevailed in an FLSA/RICO suit about the company's relationships with contract janitorial services that hire immigrants, allegedly including illegal immigrants. The suit charged Wal-Mart with knowingly transacting with contractors with an illegal workforce. The plaintiffs contended that Wal-Mart supervised the workers and had authority over hiring and firing. The Third Circuit held that there were too many differences among the plaintiffs to certify an FLSA class action because in order to certify the class, the district court must make a finding that the members of the collective action are similarly situated. The plaintiffs worked for 70 contractors and subcontractors, in 180 stores in 33 states, and their wages and hours were set by the contractors, not directly by Wal-Mart. The cleaners did not work only for Wal-Mart nor did Wal-Mart use those contractors for all cleaning tasks, which were often assigned to store employees. The fact that they are immigrants is not enough; there must be a common practice on the employer's part that violates the FLSA. The Third Circuit held that there was no evidence that Wal-Mart itself trafficked or helped workers to stay in the United States illegally. [*Zavala v. Wal-Mart Stores Inc.*, 691 F.3d 527 (3d Cir. 2012)]

The civil rights division of the Department of Justice settled with FTD about a job applicant's allegations that the company retaliated against him for exercising his rights under the Immigration and Nationality Act anti-discrimination provision. The plaintiff, an immigrant legally entitled to work in the United States, said that his job offer was rescinded after a background check showed an error in his Social Security Number. He provided documents showing his legal status and said that refusing to hire him could violate Immigration and Nationality Act, which forbids discrimination on the basis of citizenship status or national origin in hiring, firing, and recruiting. It also forbids document abuse, including unfair practices in the verification process. FTD stopped communicating with him once he mentioned legal rights. The Department of Justice said that legal immigrants should not be penalized for database errors. The DOJ's Civil Rights Division's Office of Special Counsel for immigration-related unfair employment practices enforces this INA provision. In this case, the penalty was $1,800 in back pay, $3,000 in civil penalties, plus DOJ training on the INA provision. The Office of Special Counsel posts descriptions of cases (but does not divulge the name of the parties) at <http://www.justice.gov/crt/about/osc/htm/LORs13.php>, to alert employers to enforcement trends. The DOJ also offers free Webinars on immigration employment issues at < http://www.justice.gov/crt/about/osc/webinars.php> [Sue Reisinger, *FTD Case Offers Lessons on Immigration Discrimination*, Corporate Counsel (Feb. 22, 2013) (law.com).]

## § 23.12 ADA COMPLIANCE IN HIRING

In 2012, more than 20 years after passage of the ADA, only 17.9% of persons with disabilities were employed, versus 63.7% of non-disabled persons. Most accommodations are free or cost only a few hundred dollars. [Peggy Klaus, *Disabilities Can Be Workplace Assets*, NYTimes.com (Feb. 4, 2012)]

For ADA purposes, some pre-employment inquiries are simply unacceptable; others are permissible only after a conditional job offer has been made.

The EEOC's Technical Assistance Manual for implementation of the ADA defines these pre-hire questions as improper:

- Have you ever been treated for these diseases?

- Have you ever been hospitalized? Why?

- Are there any health factors that prevent you from doing the job you applied for? (However, if the inquiry is restricted to specific job functions, it is permissible to ask about ability to perform those particular functions, and about potential accommodations.)

- How much sick leave did you take last year?

- Are you taking any prescribed medications?

- Have you ever been treated for substance abuse?

When it comes to pre-employment testing, it is discriminatory to give a test in a form or manner that requires the use of an impaired sensory, speaking, or manual skill, unless the point of the test is the degree to which that skill is present. So an assembly-line job may legitimately require manual dexterity. But if the point is to test keyboarding speed, a hearing-impaired person may have to be given a test that includes nonverbal commands as to when to start and stop. It may be necessary to have a test read aloud to a blind or dyslexic person, or to have a sign language interpreter. Every effort should be made to administer the test in a room that is wheelchair-accessible.

■ **TIP:** Tell applicants if there will be a test as part of the interview process. Then it is up to them to explain the nature of any accommodation they need to take the test.

Pre-employment medical examinations are allowed only if the candidate has already met the other criteria, and a conditional job offer has been extended. The examination must be required of everyone in that job category who gets a conditional offer. Once the offer has been made, it is acceptable to ask about past injuries and Worker's Compensation claims.

To avoid violating the Genetic Information Nondiscrimination Act (GINA), it is important to avoid asking about family medical history, because such inquiries can constitute requests for forbidden genetic information.

On January 17, 2013, HHS published a final rule covering the application of the HIPAA privacy rule to Titles I (health coverage) and II (employment) of the Genetic Information Nondiscrimination Act (GINA). Genetic information is considered health information, which cannot be used for underwriting purposes (except for long-term care insurance policies).Covered entities must comply no later than September 23, 2013. [Katherine Georger, *New HIPAA Final Rule Implements GINA Restriction on Use and Disclosure of Genetic Information for Underwriting Purposes*, Holland & Hart LLP News, (Jan. 23, 2013) (benefitslink.com)]

Post-offer medical examinations are considered nondiscriminatory, and therefore it is not necessary to provide proof of business necessity. But if the applicant with a disability is in fact qualified for the job, and the offer is withdrawn subsequent to the examination, the employer must show job-related business necessity for canceling the offer, and must also prove that reasonable accommodation to the disability could not be made without undue hardship.

In late 2005, the EEOC issued an Advisory Letter stating that there is an exception to the ADA's ban on disability-related inquiries before making a job offer if the employer has an affirmative action program for people with disabilities. To qualify, the employer's program must include an interview that gives the person with a disability a real opportunity to compete for a job; the information sought must not be greater than what is needed to determine eligibility for the interview; and the applicant must voluntarily provide the information. [EEOC Advisory Letter, <http://www.eeoc.gov/policy/docs/preemp.html> (Nov. 8, 2005)]

For active employees, medical examinations and inquiries about the nature and severity of disability can be required only if they are job-related and consistent with business necessity: For instance, someone has been ill or injured, and the question is fitness to return to work.

The ADA also requires disability-related information to be kept confidential. In fact, it should be collected and maintained on separate forms, and even stored in files separate from general personnel information, although there are certain exceptions to the general rule of confidentiality: GINA also contains confidentiality requirements for genetic information, which must be kept separate from other health information.

- Supervisors and managers can be informed about work restrictions or accommodations that are needed;

- If emergency treatment might be required for a disabled employee (e.g., an epileptic might have a seizure; a diabetic might go into insulin shock or coma), first aid and safety personnel can be informed, so they will be prepared;

- A special post-September 11 rule allows collection of information about special needs for evacuation in an emergency;

- Government officials investigating ADA compliance are entitled to information about the number of employees with disabilities, and the nature of the disabilities.

The ADA forbids employers to ask about prescription drug use unless the workers have been seen to compromise safety or appear unable to function. (There is an ADA exception: public safety workers such as police and firefighters, who are required to report prescription drug use that could create a threat to public safety.) Even jobs that are subject to federal drug testing requirements (e.g., bus and truck drivers) are tested for only six categories of drugs, and powerful drugs like Xanax, Vicodin, and OxyContin are not included. Many states have drug-free workplace laws, but their provisions vary widely and tend to focus on illegal drugs.

A 2010 Sixth Circuit case involves seven former employees of Dura Automotive Systems, who said that the company's drug testing policy (which led to terminations for taking prescription drugs) violated the ADA. The Sixth Circuit said that the relevant section of the ADA, 42 U.S.C. § 12112(a)(6), makes it unlawful to discriminate against a Qualified Individual with a Disability (QIWD) by using qualification standards that tend to screen out persons with disabilities—unless the standard is job-related and consistent with business necessity. The Sixth Circuit ruled that only a QIWD can sue under this section, although any employee can bring suit under other ADA sections. In this case, at least six of the seven plaintiffs were not disabled as defined by the ADA (the seventh might have had a record of disability), so they could not sue. The case arose before the ADAAA took effect (see § 36.03) so that law did not apply. [*Bates v. Dura Auto. Systems Inc.*, 625 F.3d 283 (6th Cir. Nov. 3, 2010)]

If an employee or a job applicant is a veteran and possibly disabilities may be service-related, then both the ADA and USERRA (see § 1.18) may be involved. In fact, USERRA actually requires more of employers, by imposing a duty to assist veterans in becoming qualified for jobs, whereas the ADA just protects the rights of individuals with disabilities who are qualified for the job they hold or have applied for. Both statutes require employers to provide reasonable accommodation.. The EEOC guidance says that an employer seeking to hire someone with a service-connected disability can ask if he or she is a disabled veteran—if the employer has an affirmative action obligation, or voluntarily seeks to benefit individuals with disabilities. It is also acceptable to recruit through organizations for veterans with disabilities. But before asking for applicants to voluntarily describe themselves as disabled veterans, the employer must explain that the information will only be used for affirmative action purposes, and will be kept confidential. Although the ADA does not require affirmative action for disabled veterans, it is acceptable for an employer to give a preference to disabled veterans. Recruiting material can be made handicap-accessible, and advertisements can state explicitly that disabled veterans are welcome to apply. [EEOC, *Veterans with Service-Connected Disabilities and the Americans with Disabilities Act (ADA): A Guide for Employers*, <http://www.eeoc.gov/facts/veterans-disabilities-employers.html> (Feb. 29, 2008)]

EARN is the Department of Labor's Employee Assistant Referral Network [<http://www.earnworks.com>], a resource for putting employers in touch with qualified individuals with disabilities. DOL also maintains a Job Accommodation Network for information about how to make workplace accommodations affordable. [<http://www.jan.wvu.edu>] The DOL points out that even in the boom times of the 1990s, only about 48% of persons with disabilities were employed. But one in five Americans has a disability, and the BLS projects that there will be only 20 million workers available to fill 55 million new jobs by 2008, so employers will have to become more flexible about finding talent in unconventional places.

The tax code provides various employer incentives, such as the § 44 disabled access credit, available for small businesses that make their premises accessible; and the § 190 barrier removal deduction for removing physical, structural, and transportation barriers on business premises. The § 190 deduction can be taken by any size business, but is not available for construction of new premises, only retrofitting; it is limited to $15,000 a year, but larger amounts can be depreciated.

### § 23.13   CREDIT REPORTING IN THE HIRING PROCESS

A federal law, the Fair Credit Reporting Act (FCRA) [15 U.S.C. §§ 1681a *et seq.*], as amended by the Consumer Credit Reporting Reform Act of 1996 (CCRRA) [Pub. L. No. 104-208], governs the use of credit reports and investigative credit reports not only for making loans and approving credit card applications, but in the employment context as well.

The FCRA provides that a consumer report is a written or oral communication from a consumer reporting agency, dealing with a consumer's entitlement to credit, "character, general reputation, personal characteristics, or mode of living."

An investigative credit report is different in that it involves personal interviews with people who have personal knowledge of the individual. The CCRRA requires employers to give job applicants a written disclosure statement, and to get their consent in writing, before requesting either a consumer report or an investigative consumer report. Furthermore, if the employer wants an investigative report, it must explain to the applicant (via a written disclosure mailed no later than three days after the report is requested) that this type of report covers matters like character and conduct.

The FCRA [see 15 U.S.C. § 1681b(3)(B)] says that "employment purposes" are legitimate reasons for requesting a credit report or investigative credit report. "Employment purposes" means "evaluating a consumer for employment, promotion, reassignment or retention as an employee." Because the FCRA specifically authorizes the use of credit reporting information in the hiring process, doing so is not employment discrimination.

An "adverse action" includes "denial of employment or any other decision for employment purposes that adversely affects any current or prospective employee." When the credit report is negative, leading to adverse action, the employer must provide oral, written, or electronic (for instance, fax or e-mail) notice of the adverse action. It must also explain how to review the credit report file, correct errors (the negative report might refer to someone else with a similar name, or someone who has appropriated the job applicant's identity) and contest items that the consumer believes to be untrue. Notice must be given after the employer makes the decision, but before the adverse action is implemented.

The CCRRA also imposes an obligation on the employer. Before it gets any reports from a reporting agency, it must give the agency a statement that the employer complies with the various consumer protection requirements of credit reporting law.

As a result of a later statute, the FACTA (Fair and Accurate Credit Transactions Act of 2003; Pub. L. No. 108-159), 15 U.S.C. § 1681a has been amended to add a new subsection (x). Under the new law, a communication is not treated as a consumer report—and therefore is not subject to the FCRA requirements—if the purpose of the communication is job-related and not related to the person's creditworthiness.

To qualify for the FACTA exemption, the communication must be made to an employer as part of an investigation of suspected employment-related misconduct, or in compliance with laws or regulations (including the rules of a self-regulatory organization such as a stock exchange), or under the employer's pre-existing written policies. Reports of this type must not be disclosed to anyone except the employer or its agents, government officials, or self-regulatory organizations, unless disclosure is mandated by law. Furthermore, once the employer gets the information, if the information is the basis of any adverse action against the person, the employer must provide the person with a summary of the communication—but does not have to disclose the sources furnishing the information.

Effective July 21, 2011, the Dodd-Frank Act (Pub. L. No. 111-203) requires employers to disclose whenever credit scores have had an adverse effect on the employer's assessment of a job applicant.

In late 2010, the Third Circuit ruled that it does not violate the bankruptcy law provision 11 U.S.C. § 525(b) to avoid hiring a person because of his previous bankruptcy. (The situation would be different if someone who was already an employee was fired for filing a bankruptcy petition.) [*Rea v. Federated Investors*, 627 F.3d 937 (3d Cir. 2010)]

However, the EEOC's position is that discrimination on the basis of credit history is illegal, because of the disparate impact that such discrimination has on minorities. Employers who face Title VII disparate impact suits may be able to defend themselves by showing the procedure is job-related and consistent with business necessity. But even then, plaintiffs can still prevail by showing that there is an alternate practice that would achieve the same result without discriminatory impact.

In addition to federal laws regulating the use of credit checks, state law may be more stringent. For example, Hawaii, Illinois, Oregon, and Washington forbid most usage of credit history in employment decisions, with an exception for substantially job-related use of information, and usage that is disclosed in writing to the employee or job applicant.

Background checks performed by third-party credit reporting agencies can create problems for employers, unless the employer satisfies the FCRA's notice, authorization, and disclosure requirements before taking adverse employment action. Here, too, state laws must be consulted. For example, California requires additional protection of job applicants. [Carla Rozycki and Emma Sullivan, *Avoid Credit History Pitfalls When Making Employment Decisions*, special to law.com (Mar. 17, 2011) (law.com)]

# CHAPTER 24

# RECORDKEEPING

## § 24.01  INTRODUCTION

### [A]  Employer Responsibility in General

Employee records are important in setting compensation, assuring that it is paid appropriately, and administering benefit plans. Proper records are necessary to handle insurance matters, comply with court orders, fill out tax returns and other government documents, and demonstrate EEO and immigration compliance. For a general introduction to federal requirements, see <http://www.dol.gov/compliance/topics/recordkeeping.html>.

Employers cannot evade their responsibility for remittances to benefit funds by failing to keep required records. The Ray Haluch Gravel Company's 2005 CBA required the company to make payments to benefit funds. In 2007, the union demanded additional remittances on behalf of employees whose work records were incomplete. The First Circuit held that it was certain that one employee's account was underpaid: the evidence showed that 75% of the work he did was covered by the CBA, so 75% of his work should have resulted in earning benefits. Other, unidentified employees were also entitled to benefit contributions. The union argued that the lack of proper records about the work performed by the employees shifted the burden of proof to the employer. The First Circuit agreed that burden-shifting was logical in this case because employers have an incentive to under-report the amount of work completed by employees because less work means lower contributions by the employer. The First Circuit remanded the case for calculation of the amount to be remanded. [*Central Pension Fund of the Int'l Union of Operating Eng'rs & Participating Employers v. Ray Haluch Gravel Co.*, 695 F.3d 1 (1st Cir. 2012); see Meg Hunt, *Burden of Proof* plansponsor.com (Jan. 22, 2013)]

In addition to determining its internal needs for gathering, processing, and deleting information, the company must be aware of legal requirements for record retention, and limitations on document destruction. Destroying documents that are subject to discovery in a court case is at least a civil offense, and may constitute contempt of court or even a criminal offense, depending on circumstances.

All documents in personnel files should be date-stamped when they are received, because it may be necessary to determine what was in the file at a particular time.

> ■ **TIP:** If it is legal and practical to destroy a document, make sure that all paper copies have been destroyed, as well as all computer files (including back-ups, copies on disks, and data uploaded to an Internet site for safekeeping). Just because someone has deleted a file does not mean that it has even been removed from that computer, much less from the entire network.

Whether the records are on paper or electronic, the goal of the corporate record retention policy should be to store and manage information on- and off-site in a systematic and cost effective manner. When necessary, the system must be able to handle litigation-related requests for documents, and managing risk. The policy must satisfy the statutory and regulatory requirements for record retention, applicable statutes of limitations, and best practices for business. Publicly traded companies are subject to additional requirements imposed by the Sarbanes-Oxley Act (for example, communications with the company's audit firm must be retained). The Public Company Accounting Oversight Board (PCAOB) requires accountants to retain audit work papers for at least seven years. Early in 2003, the SEC covered record retention issues in Exchange Act Release No. 47241.

A Sarbanes-Oxley provision enacted at 18 U.S.C. § 1519 calls for imprisonment of up to 20 years for knowing alteration, destruction, mutilation, falsification, or cover-up of records or documents with the intent to obstruct investigation of any matter under the jurisdiction of a federal department or agency. Even document destruction that occurred before a proceeding commenced can be prosecuted.

Courts have imposed major—even multi-million-dollar—sanctions on companies that destroyed key evidence in violation of court orders. Litigation parties that destroy evidence have also been precluded from introducing their own evidence as a penalty. It is increasingly clear that once litigation begins, a "litigation hold" should be placed on destruction of paper and electronic documents. Once the company becomes aware of impending litigation, employees should be informed of the possibility. They should receive copies of the relevant court orders, and be informed of the penalties for destruction of evidence.

However, if a company has a reasonable policy for when documents should be retained and when they should be destroyed, and the policy is consistently applied, then courts will probably find that it is unreasonable to expect the company to produce documents destroyed pursuant to the policy.

As Chapters 6 and 15 show, a current major litigation topic is whether defined contribution plans select the correct menu of investment options for plan participants—and whether the plan pays excessive fees for the investments in the plan or services to the plan. Even the cost of recordkeeping can create hazards for fiduciaries. In a Western District of Missouri class action, the plaintiffs were awarded $21.8 million against the plan's fiduciaries for failure to choose funds prudently and in accordance with the plan's published policies—and a further $13.4 million for failure to obtain rebates or monitor the cost of recordkeeping. [*Tussey v. ABB Inc.* No. 2:06-CV-04305-NKL (W.D. Mo. Mar. 31, 2012); see Andrew Holley and Britta Loftus, *The Importance of* "A Deliberative Process," Dorsey & Whitney (Apr. 4, 2012) (benefitslink.com)]

## [B] 2002 DOL Final Rule

The Department of Labor published Final Rules Relating to Use of Electronic Communication and Recordkeeping Technologies by Employee Pension and Welfare Benefit Plans, updating 29 C.F.R. Part 2520, at 67 Fed. Reg. 17264 (Apr. 9, 2002). This document provides final rules under ERISA Title I for using electronic media to disclose benefit plan information to participants (a topic discussed in Chapter 27) and enacts a safe harbor for using electronic methods of disclosing and maintaining records. The final rule is effective October 9, 2002.

Under the Final Rule, 29 C.F.R. § 2520.107-1, electronic media can be used for maintenance and retention of records, if:

- The system has reasonable controls to ensure integrity, accuracy, authenticity, and reliability of the records.

- The records are maintained in reasonable order, in a safe and accessible place, so they can reasonably be inspected.

- The records can readily be converted into legible and readable hard copy from electronic form.

- The electronic data is labeled, securely stored, and backed up so it can be recovered if the main data repository is destroyed or corrupted.

- The employer retains paper copies of any data that cannot be seamlessly transferred to the electronic system.

The Final Rule permits destruction of paper records that have been transferred without error to the electronic system, unless there is a requirement (under the terms of the plan or an applicable law) that duplicate or substitute records be maintained in paper form.

See § 27.06 for more discussion of electronic media in pension and tax contexts.

## [C] CHIPRA and ARRA Rules

The Children's Health Insurance Program Reauthorization Act of 2009, Pub. L. No. 111-3, which expands the state children's health insurance program, allows states to subsidize coverage provided by employers through their existing EGHPs. Plan administrators must report to the state the information needed to determine which plan participants are entitled to premium assistance from the SCHIP program. Employers therefore must create and maintain records about employees' eligibility for subsidy, and records for administering the subsidies. Employers must distribute the HHS model notice to inform employees about premium assistance. Failure to give notice is penalized by $100/day/participant. [Norbert F.

Kugele, Warner Norcross & Judd LLP, *New Federal SCHIP Law Requires Cafeteria and Health Plan Amendments* (Feb. 10, 2009) (benefitslink.com)]

The federal premium subsidy for COBRA premiums under the American Recovery and Reinvestment Act of 2009, Pub. L. 111-5, now expired, also created requirements for retaining records of employee terminations, employees electing COBRA at termination, and employees not electing COBRA but entitled to a notice of their eligibility for the subsidy, and of employee income (to demonstrate eligibility for the subsidy). [Notice 2009-27, 2009-16 I.R.B. 838; see Edward I. Leeds, Ballard Spahr Andrews & Ingersoll, LLP, *Stimulus Package Modifies COBRA, HIPAA, and Other Welfare Benefit Provisions* (Feb. 17, 2009) (benefitslink.com); Michael S. Melbinger, Winston & Strawn LLP, *All Employers' Severance Plans and Agreements Affected by ARRA* (Feb. 20, 2009) (benefitslink.com)]

### [D] PPACA (Health Care Reform) Requirements

One reason that PPACA is unpopular is because of the recordkeeping and notice burden. Participants must be notified of their right to keep their adult children in the plan until they reach age 27. The plan must keep track of the facts supporting its entitlement to grandfathered status—or causing loss of that status. When the health insurance exchanges are in operation, it will be necessary for employers to prove that they offer at least minimum required coverage or that they are exempt from the requirement. Otherwise, penalties will be imposed. [Christy Tinnes and Brigen Winters, *What Notices Are Required by PPACA?*, plansponsor.com (Sept. 21, 2010)]

PPACA will eventually require the cost of providing EGHP coverage to be reported on employees' W-2 forms. The reporting is purely informational because the cost of EGHP coverage is not generally taxable. (The exception is the 40% excise tax imposed on Cadillac plans beginning in 2018.) PPACA § 9006 added a requirement that all corporate businesses must issue a Form 1099 to any individual or corporation from which they purchase more than $600 in goods or services in a tax year. This was an immensely unpopular provision because of the vast amount of paperwork it was expected to generate. In February 2011, the Senate voted not to repeal the entire PPACA statute, but did vote to amend this provision (S. 223). The House had already approved similar legislation (H.R. 4 and H.R. 705), and President Obama signed it as Pub. L. No. 112-9, which eliminates the requirement for payments to corporations and for the acquisition of property. [Janet Adamy, *Senate Votes Down Health-Care Repeal*, WSJ.com (Feb. 3, 2011); Plansponsor staff, *Senate Passes Repeal of HCR 1099 Rule*, plansponsor.com (Feb. 21, 2011)]

## § 24.02 OSHA RECORDS

### [A] Injury and Illness Recordkeeping

Complying with the Occupational Safety and Health Act [see Chapter 31] requires constant accumulation of data on a day-by-day basis, followed by compilation of annual records.

Effective January 1, 2002, OSHA changed the reporting requirements found in 29 C.F.R. Part 1904 ("Recording and Reporting Occupational Injuries and Illnesses"). The new requirements are simplified, streamlined, and work better with computer technology than the old requirements. The new forms can be downloaded from <http://www.osha.gov> or ordered by telephone from the OSHA publication office at (202) 693-1888. The Final Rule appears at 66 Fed. Reg. 5916 (Jan. 19, 2001). Although most of the changes went into effect as scheduled, the effective date of the rules about hearing loss and reporting of musculoskeletal disorders were delayed until January 1, 2003. [See 66 Fed. Reg. 35113 (July 3, 2001)]

Under the prior rules, employers were required to make incident reports on Form 101, Supplementary Record of Occupational Injury and Illnesses. The replacement form is Form 301, the Injury and Illness Incident Report.

The prior rules called for the employer to collate all the 101 forms to create the annual Form 200, Log and Summary of Occupational Injuries and Illnesses. The new forms are 300, Log of Work-Related Injuries and Illnesses, and 300A, Summary of Work-Related Injuries and Illnesses. [See 29 C.F.R. § 1904.4]

The forms are used to report new cases of work-related illness or injury. The OSHA 301 Incident Report must be completed within seven calendar days of receiving information about the incident. The OSHA 300 log requires a short description of each incident. The OSHA 300-A summary is compiled at the end of the year, using this log.

All businesses have to make a report of OSHA if an incident in the workplace results in a death, or if three or more workers are hospitalized. However, it is not necessary for companies in low-hazard businesses such as retail, service, finance, real estate, or insurance to maintain OSHA illness and industry records unless OSHA specifically requests such records. [See <http://www.osha-slc.gov/OshStd_data/1904_New/1094_0002.html> for information about the exemption]

OSHA issued compliance manual CPL 2-0.131 in late 2001, which has been somewhat amended as CPL 02-00-135. [*Recordkeeping Policies & Procedures Manual* (Dec. 30, 2004), <http://www/osha.gov/pls/oshaweb/owadisp.show_document[ . . . ]>, more easily reached by selecting "Recordkeeping" in the A–Z listing at the OSHA home page]

■ **TIP:** In a "privacy concern case" (e.g., one involving mental illness, sexual assault, HIV status, or other sensitive issues), the employee's name should not be entered on the OSHA 300 Log. Effective January 1, 2004, other illnesses can also be treated as privacy concern cases, and the employee's name omitted at the request of the employee. [68 Fed. Reg. 38607 (June 30, 2003)]

The Occupational Safety and Health Review Commission (OSHRC) heard oral arguments in November 2010 (the first oral arguments allowed in four years) in a case about the length of time in which a company can be cited for OSH reporting violations. OSHA said that the DOL has six months from the time it discovers, or should have discovered, the facts needed in order to issue a citation. However, the DOL policy is that an inaccurate log entry violates the law until it has been corrected, or until the five-year period for record retention has expired—and the statute of limitations does not begin with the date the entry was or should have been made. OSHRC held that failure to keep proper records can be treated as a continuing violation of OSHA's five-year record retention requirement, and fined the company $13,300 for recordkeeping violations. [*Secretary of Labor v. AKM LLC dba Volks Constructors* OSHRC No. 06-1990, 2011 WL 896347 (OSHRC Mar. 11, 2011)]

Then, however, the D.C. Circuit reversed OSHRC in an unpublished decision, and ruled that the statute of limitations for recordkeeping violations is only six months, not five years. The D.C. Circuit rejected the continuing violation theory, holding that all the violations charged were separate events. Although it enunciated a six-month statute of limitations for pure recordkeeping violations, the D.C. Circuit left the way open for tolling the statute of limitations for a genuine ongoing violation, such as continuing to require employees to use unsafe equipment. [*Sec'y of Labor v. AKM LLC dba Volks Constructors*, No. 11-1106, 2012 WL 1142273 (unpublished) (D.C. Cir. Apr. 6, 2012); see Jenna Greene, Blog of Legal Times, *D.C. Circuit: Limit for OSHA Violations Is Six Months, Not Five Years* (Apr. 6, 2012) (law.com)]

## [B]  Asbestos, Lead, and Noise Monitoring Records

If the workplace noise level is high, the employer not only must monitor exposure, but must maintain records for two years. Records of employees' hearing tests must be retained at least as long as they work for the employer. Exposure monitoring records and asbestos and lead medical surveillance records should be retained for at least 30 years after termination of employment of the individual monitored.

Asbestos monitoring records should indicate:

* Each monitored employee's name, Social Security number, extent of exposure;

* If a respirator was worn; if so, what kind;

- Date the asbestos level was monitored;
- The workplace operation or process that was monitored;
- How the samples were taken and evaluated;
- Evidence supporting the scientific validity of the sampling methodology;
- How long the sampling process lasted; number of samples taken; sampling results.

For each employee subject to medical surveillance, the record should give his or her name and Social Security number, the employee reports of asbestos-related medical conditions; and a written report from the doctor who performs the surveillance, indicating whether the employee actually is suffering effects of asbestos exposure.

For testing of lead rather than asbestos, the employer must maintain written records of tests determining whether the ambient lead level exceeds the Permissible Exposure Limit (PEL). The test record should indicate:

- Name and Social Security number of each monitored employee;
- Date of the test;
- Area that was monitored;
- Previous airborne lead readings taken at the same place;
- Employee complaints that might be related to lead exposure;
- Any other evidence suggestive of lead exposure.

## [C]  OSHA Postings

Employers must post a notice of OSHA rights, as mandated by 29 C.F.R. § 1903.2(a). Failure to post is subject to a civil penalty of up to $7,000 per violation, but normally the penalty will be $1,000.

An employer who receives an OSHA citation must post a copy of the citation near each place where a violation occurred. The copy must be left in place for three working days or until the violation is corrected—whichever comes first. Posting is also required if the employer contests a citation or files a petition for modification of abatement. Failure to make these postings can result in a $1,000 fine.

## § 24.03  TITLE VII RECORDKEEPING AND NOTICE REQUIREMENTS

The Equal Employment Opportunity Commission (EEOC) requires companies with 100 or more employees to file an annual report. The Employer Information Report (EEO-1) is a simple two-page form that tracks the composition of the workforce. The due date is September 30 of each year. A copy of the most recent report must be kept on file at every company required to file (either at the "reporting unit" or the company's or division's headquarters). The EEOC also has the right to require other reports about employment practices if the agency thinks additional reports are necessary to carry out Title VII or the Americans With Disabilities Act.

The federal Website GovDocs has been updated to incorporate the Genetic Information Nondiscrimination Act (GINA; see § 34.01[B]), and the EEOC released its GINA-compliant poster; see <http://www.govdocs.com> or <http://www.eeoc.gov/employers/upload/eeoc_self_print_poster.pdf> (accessed May 27, 2010) or call (888) 273-3274. GovDocs has compliance materials such as electronic posters for all the states, and automatically sends new posters to subscribers when there are changes. [David L. Woodard and Susanna Knutson Gibbons, Poyner Spruill LLP, *Check Your Posters—Passage of the Genetic Information Nondiscrimination Act Imposes New Obligations and Posting Requirements on Employers* (Mar. 1, 2010) (benefitslink.com); Rebecca Moore, *GovDocs Updates Labor Law Materials*, plansponsor.com (Nov. 2, 2009) and *EEOC Updates Notice to Employees*, plansponsor.com (Oct. 27, 2009)]

The EEOC published a final rule on February 3, 2012 extending the Title VII and ADA recordkeeping requirements to entities covered by GINA. As of April 3, 2012, employers with 15 or more employees must retain all personnel and employment records for at least one year, and retain documents about any GINA charges until those charges have been disposed of. Documents include requests for accommodation, application forms, hiring, promotion, demotion, transfer, layoff, and termination data and records of pay, tenure, training, and apprenticeship. Records must be retained for at least a year after any employee's involuntary termination. [77 Fed. Reg. 5396 (Feb. 3, 2012); see PLC Labor & Employment, *EEOC Issues Final Rule Extending Title VII and ADA Recordkeeping Requirements to GINA* (Feb. 2, 2012) (benefitslink.com)]

Records of application forms, requests for accommodation, and other employment-related data must be preserved for one year. The one-year period starts either when the data is collected or the personnel action is taken, whichever is later. Personnel records of fired employees must also be kept for one year after employment ends. [Press Release, *Recordkeeping Guidance Clarifies Definition of* "Job Applicant" *for Internet and Related Technologies* (Mar. 3, 2004), <http://www.eeoc.gov/press-3-3-04.html>; a notice appeared in the March 4, 2004, Federal Register]

Under a final rule published in late 2005, a person is considered an "Internet applicant" if the federal contractor accepts expressions of interest in a job through the Internet, e-mail, the employer's Website, or a resume databank. The applicant must have used the Internet or related means to submit an expression of interest in the job; the contractor must have considered the person for a particular position; the expression of interest must have demonstrated that the applicant had at least the basic qualifications for the job; and the person must have never removed him- or herself from consideration for the job before receiving a job offer. Contractors are not required to maintain records of electronic expressions of interest unless the contractor actually considered the person for a particular job. Federal contractors are permitted to have rules under which they reject general expressions of interest in working for their company that are not submitted for a particular position. It also is lawful to reject expressions of interest that do not meet the contractor's requirements. [70 Fed. Reg. 58945 (Oct. 7, 2005)]

The EEOC proposed revisions to the EEO-1 form in mid-2003 [68 Fed. Reg. 34965 (June 11, 2003)] and finalized them in late 2005. [70 Fed. Reg. 72194 (Nov. 28, 2005)] Except in cases in which the employer cannot get Internet access, filing must be done electronically; see the instructions at <http://www. eeoc.gov/eeo1survey/howtofile.html>. The revised EEO-1 form increases the five racial/ethnic categories to seven: There is a new "two or more races" category, and the "Asian or Pacific Islander" category has been divided into "Asian" and "Native Hawaiian or other Pacific Islander." The category "Black" has been changed to "Black or African American," "Hispanic" is now "Hispanic or Latino," and the job category of "Officials and Managers" has been divided into an Executive/Senior Level category and a First/Mid-Level Officials and Managers group. Business and financial occupations are now to be disclosed as Professionals rather than as Officials and Managers. The EEOC wants racial and ethnic categories to be determined by employees' self-identification, not visual identifications made by the employer.

In September 2006, the Office of Federal Contract Compliance Programs eliminated the federal contractor's EEO survey, because it more or less duplicated the information collected on the EEO-1. [71 Fed. Reg. 53032 (Sept. 8, 2006); see Rebecca Moore, *EO Survey Eliminated for Federal Contractors*, plansponsor.com (Sept. 11, 2006)]

If a discrimination charge is made, all records relating to the employment action involved in the charge must be retained until there has been a final disposition of the charge. According to 29 C.F.R. § 1602.14, this means that either the case is over, or the employee's time to sue has elapsed.

Users of pre-employment tests must maintain records about the validation of the test, including statistical studies to determine if the test has adverse impact on protected classes of applicants and employees.

Employers also have to make records that are relevant to charges of unlawful employment practices and maintain those records. [See 42 U.S.C. § 2000e-8(c)]

A general overview on posting requirements appears in the DOL's "eLaws Power Advisor," <http://www.dol.gov/compliance/topics/posters.htm>.

One of the many notices that must be posted in the workplace is the official EEOC notice about equal employment opportunity and how to file a charge. [42 U.S.C. § 2000e-10] If the employer willfully violates this requirement, a fine of up to $100 can be imposed for each separate offense.

Other mandatory posters include:

- Employee Rights Under the Fair Labor Standards Act
- Job Safety and Health: It's the Law
- Employee Rights and Responsibilities under the Family and Medical Leave Act
- Equal Employment Opportunity Is the Law
- Migrant and Seasonal Agricultural Worker Protection Act Notice
- Employee Rights for Workers with Disabilities Paid at Special Minimum Wages
- Employee Polygraph Protection Act Notice
- Your Rights Under USERRA (revised July 2008)
- Genetic Information Nondiscrimination Act information

In late 2010, the NLRB announced that companies would be required to post notices on its bulletin boards to inform employees of their rights to unionize. Electronic posting is also required if the employer primarily communicates with employees electronically (e.g., by e-mail). The notice form can be obtained from the regional NLRB office, or online. [Notice of Proposed Rulemaking, 75 Fed. Reg. 80410 (Feb. 22, 2010); see <http://www.nlrb.gov/publications/rules-regulations/ notice-proposed-rulemaking>. See also Steven Greenhouse, *U.S. Proposes Posted Notice of the Right to Unionize*, NYTimes.com (Dec. 21, 2010); Fred Schneyer, *NLRB Proposes Workplace Notice Rule*, plansponsor.com (Dec. 23, 2010)]

The posting requirement was supposed to take effect November 14, 2011, but it was delayed, first until January 31, 2012, then until April 30, 2012, in response to business criticisms. [Steven Greenhouse, *N.L.R.B. Tells Companies to Ease Right to Unionize*, NYTimes.com (Aug. 25, 2011); Tara Cantore, *NLRB Postpones Required Date to Post Employee Rights,* plansponsor.com (Dec. 27, 2011) and *NLRB Postpones Implementation Date for Notice Posting Rule*, plan sponsor.com (Oct. 5, 2011)]

Two Circuit Courts (the Fourth and the D.C. Circuits) have found the posting requirement inappropriate and unenforceable. The Fourth Circuit said that Congress intended the NLRB's powers to be limited, dealing only with Unfair Labor Practices and representation elections—and that the NLRB's powers are triggered only by a complaint or an election petition. In this analysis, posting requirements imposed by other agencies such as OSHA and the EEOC are based on statutory authorization from Congress, whereas the NLRB has not been given this power. Rather than uphold part of the posting requirement but remove the NLRB's power to treat failure to post as an Unfair Labor Practice, the Fourth Circuit struck down the entire regulation, concluding that the NLRB would not want to have a purely advisory rule that it was unable to enforce.

[*Chamber of Commerce v. NLRB*, No. 12-1757 (4th Cir. June 14, 2013); see Jenna Greene, *Fourth Circuit Strikes NLRB Poster Rule*, The BLT (Blog of Legal Times (June 14, 2013) (law.com); *Nat'l Ass'n of Mfrs. v. NLRB*, No. 12-5068 (D.C. Cir. May 5, 2013)]

## § 24.04 FMLA RECORDS

Federal law does not impose any specific form for keeping FMLA records, so any paper or electronic method can be used to record the necessary information:

- Basic payroll data for each employee, such as hours worked; pay rate; supplemental wages or wage deductions; total compensation paid;

- Dates on which FMLA leave was taken;

- Hours of leave (if less than a day was taken);

- Copies of the employee's notice to the employer of impending leave;

- Copies of the employer's disclosure materials about FMLA rights;

- Documentation of the employer's leave policy;

- Records of payment of premiums for employee benefit plans;

- Records of any dispute about when employees are entitled to leave or reinstatement after a leave.

ERISA § 209(a)(1) requires employers to maintain records "sufficient" to determine benefits due to their employees. Nurse Mary Henderson brought a class action suit against the University of Pittsburgh Medical Center, alleging that the employer did not keep records of the hours she worked. She charged that nurses were required to work through their 30-minute unpaid meal breaks, and were required to come to work 20–40 minutes before official start of their shifts to review patient records. The district court dismissed her case for failure to state a claim, holding that the defendant was only required to keep records of wages paid, not hours worked. On appeal, the Third Circuit agreed. Henderson also made ERISA claims (she said that she was denied retirement credits for the hours she worked without pay). The Third Circuit said that an employer's recordkeeping duties depend on how contributions are allocated under the payment plan, and in this case, the contributions were based only on compensation paid, not on hours worked. [*Henderson v. UPMC*, 640 F.3d 524 (3d Cir. 2011)]

■ **TIP:** Because employee medical records, including certification of serious medical condition and fitness to return to work, are confidential, they should be kept physically separate from the employee's other records, to prevent unauthorized access to the data. [See § 26.07 about privacy requirements]

The required FMLA poster and forms were revised; the new versions expire February 28, 2015. The new poster must be displayed starting March 8, 2013 in all business locations, even if there are no FMLA-eligible employees at that location. The information can also be given electronically.

The DOL stopped publishing the model forms as appendices to the FMLA regulations. Instead, they appear on the DOL site, making it possible for the agency to amend the forms without going through the Office of Management and Budget. The new regulations instruct employers about their GINA confidentiality obligations: it is permissible to disclose genetic information or family history that is consistent with the FMLA.

Employers are permitted to adapt the forms rather than using them unaltered, provided that the employer's version does not call for disclosure of more information by the employee or health care provider than the FMLA regulations permit.

The new forms added in 2013 are:

- WH-380-E certification of health care provider of serious health condition (employee);

- WH-380-F health care provider certification for family member's serious health condition;

- WH-381 notice of eligibility, rights, and responsibilities;

- WH-382 designation notice;

- WH-383 reserved;

- WH-384 certification of exigency of military family leave;

- WH-385 certification of serious injury or illness of a servicemember for military family leave;

- WH-385-V certification of serious injury or illness of a veteran for military caregiver leave.

[*Airline Flight Crew Technical Corrs. Act*, Pub. L. No. 111-119; see Jackson Lewis LLP, *Workplace Resource Center Labor Department Releases New FMLA Model Forms and Notice Poster* (Feb. 27, 2013) (benefitslink.com); Jeff Nowak, *Employers Must Begin Using Updated FMLA Forms and Poster Starting March 8, 2013*, Franczek Radelet FMLA Insights (Feb. 28, 2013) (benefitslink.com)]

## § 24.05  IMMIGRATION RECORDS

The information collected to verify identity and eligibility to work in the United States [see § 23.11[D]] must be retained for three years after the date of hiring. Records should be retained for three years from the date of recruiting or referral with respect to applicants who were not hired or who did not accept a job offer. Certifications of employment eligibility furnished by state employment services must also be retained for three years. For former employees, the record-retention period is the later of three years after hiring, or one year after termination.

## § 24.06  EMPLOYMENT TAX RECORDS

Newly hired employees should be asked to provide a W-4 (withholding exemptions) form, so the appropriate number of exemptions can be used to withhold income taxes. An employee about to retire should be asked for Form W-4P to determine whether pension withholding should be done, and if so, in what amount. Note that, in recent years, the FICA and FUTA payroll taxes have been adjusted several times, so it is essential to use the appropriate withholding tables for the pay period. IRS Publication 15, Employer's Tax Guide, requires at least the following information to be collected by the employer and made available for IRS review on request:

- Dates and amounts of all payments of wages and pensions;
- Fair market value of any wages paid other than in cash (e.g., in merchandise or services);
- Each employee's name, address, Social Security number, and job title;
- Dates each employee started and terminated employment;
- Dates and amounts of any payments made by the employer, or by an insurer or other third party, to employees who were out sick or injured;
- Copies of W-4 and W-4P forms;
- W-2 forms sent to employees but returned as undeliverable;
- Copies of all tax returns;
- Records of dates and amounts of tax deposits.

The Pension Protection Act of 2006, Pub. L. No. 109-280, adds a new section to the Internal Revenue Code, § 6039I, requiring the owners of employer-owned life insurance contracts issued after the PPA took effect to report to the IRS each year on the number of employees the company has, how many of them are covered by company-owned life insurance, the amount of insurance in force under those insurance policies, the nature of the company's business, and that all employees covered under the COLI program have consented to being covered (or the number of employees who are covered but did not provide a written consent form). Businesses with COLI programs are required to keep any records necessary for determining if the PPA COLI rules have been complied with.

For tax years ending on or after November 14, 2007, a policyholder owning employer-owned life insurance contracts issued after August 17, 2006 must attach Form 8925 to the income tax return. The form discloses the number of employees covered by employer-provided life insurance contracts; whether each one consented in writing, in advance, to be insured and for coverage to continue after employment ends. [Sutherland Asbill & Brennan LLP, *Legal Alert: IRS Issues Forms to Report Employer-Owned Life Insurance* (Feb. 7, 2008)]

## § 24.07   UNEMPLOYMENT INSURANCE RECORDS

FUTA records must show the total amount of remuneration to employees in the calendar year, the amount of wages subject to tax, and the contributions made to the state unemployment insurance funds of each state in which the company does business. The records must be kept open to inspection by the IRS and state unemployment tax officials.

Records must be organized by pay period (dates the period starts and ends; total remuneration including commissions paid in the period) and by employee. The records to be kept for each worker include:

- Name;
- Social Security number;
- Date of hiring (or rehiring) and termination;
- Place of work;
- Wages for each payroll period;
- Wage rate;
- Date wages were paid;
- Amount of expense reimbursement granted;
- Time lost when worker was unavailable for work.

Although unemployment insurance information can be released to government agencies other than the employment security agency (child support enforcement agencies, for example), in general the information is confidential and should not be disclosed to unauthorized parties.

## § 24.08   RECORD-RETENTION REQUIREMENTS

Various state and federal laws require retention of records (about individual employees and summaries reflecting the entire corporate experience). The enterprise should draft its record-retention policies to comply with statutory requirements:

- Title VII: Personnel and employment records as well as EEO-1 reports must be kept for six months. Records relating to a discrimination charge must be retained until the charge is disposed of;

- Equal Pay Act: Records of a pay differential imposed on the basis of sex must be kept for two years;

- FMLA: Records must be retained for three years;

- FICA/FUTA: Records of withholding and paying these taxes must be retained for four years;

- ERISA: There are two record retention provisions. Section 107 requires the filer or certifier of certain information (for example, Form 5500) to maintain sufficient records to explain, corroborate, substantiate, or clarify the filing or certification. Relevant records might include plan documents, e-mails, work records, or spreadsheets. Such records must be maintained for six years after the date they were filed (including any amendments). But ERISA § 209 requires all such information to be retained for as long as it might be relevant to determining benefit entitlement—which is tantamount to requiring them to be retained indefinitely. Retention is the responsibility of the employer, not its TPA. Section 107 does not impose money penalties for violations and the § 209 civil penalty is small, but failure to retain required information might be deemed a breach of fiduciary duty, or might embroil the employer in a costly suit over benefits. [Jewell Lim Esposito, *How Long to Retain ERISA Plan Records? Forever,* Employee Benefits Unplugged (Aug. 30, 2011) (benefitslink.com)];

- Federal contractors: Information about the employer's contractor status must be retained for three years;

- OSHA: The record-retention requirement for employee exposure to toxic substances is very long: 30 years;

- Tax records: The minimum retention period is four years;

ADEA: 29 C.F.R. § 1627.3(b)(2) requires a benefit plan that is subject to the ADEA to be kept on file while the plan is in operation, and for at least one year after its termination.

# CHAPTER 25

# CORPORATE COMMUNICATIONS

## § 25.01	INTRODUCTION

Communications within the corporation, and from the corporation to outsiders, have tremendous practical and legal consequences. To avoid trouble, everyone in a position to speak for the corporation should be aware of these potential ramifications and should be very careful about what is communicated (because not only are there things that should not be said, but items that must be accurately disclosed in various contexts) and in what form.

## § 25.02	EMPLOYMENT CONTRACTS

### [A]	Basic Considerations

Labor law aspects of Collective Bargaining Agreements between an employer and a union are discussed in Chapter 30. For employees who are not union members, there are both advantages and disadvantages to entering into a written employment contract. The written contract reduces uncertainty, and that is good—but it also limits flexibility, and that can create problems. An individual written employment contract should cover issues such as:

- Duration of employment;

- Renewal provisions (including the amount of notice to be given);

- The duties the employee will perform;

- Promotion possibilities;

- Compensation and benefits, including contingent compensation—contingent on results and/or bonuses and stock options;

- Rights in inventions and other intellectual property developed by the employee during the contract term; treatment of intellectual property developed while the contract is in force but not during working hours, or not of the type the employee was hired to produce;

- Covenant not to compete with the employer, and agreement not to solicit its employees and customers, even after termination of employment. To be enforceable, these agreements must be reasonable in both duration and geographic scope, and must not be so severe that they prevent the individual from earning a living;

- Severability: If any contract provision is invalid, that provision will be removed from the contract, and the rest of the contract will remain valid and enforceable;

- Alternative Dispute Resolution: Whether disputes about the contract will be resolved by an arbitrator, mediator, or other decision maker other than a court.

## [B]  Employment Contract Case Law

Individual employment contracts are usually analyzed under the same rules as ordinary commercial contracts, so it is relevant whether there was a meeting of the minds; each side obtained consideration; and there was no mistake about the terms. (Relief for one or both parties may be available if there was a mistake, especially mutual mistake.) The Statute of Frauds is another fundamental contract rule, one that says that a contract that lasts a year or more can only be enforced if it is in writing.

The Fifth Circuit upheld the dismissal of state-law claims relating to William Sullivan's hiring as CEO of Leor Energy. Sullivan and Leor reached a tentative agreement, including duties, salary, and equity. Leor's attorneys drafted an employment agreement, but this draft was never signed. Sullivan worked on a deal for Leor; after the deal was signed, Sullivan was fired without cause. The unsigned contract was not enforceable because of the Statute of Frauds. According to Sullivan, the Statute of Frauds did not apply because the contract could have been performed within one year. However, the draft called for a fixed term of employment of approximately 30 months, with a noncompete agreement lasting 12 months after termination of the agreement. Texas law says that just because it is possible that a contract could be terminated within a year (Sullivan's contract allowed either side to terminate the agreement) does not mean it is not for a fixed term of over one year. Sullivan also asserted that the Statute of Frauds did not apply because he had partially performed the agreement, but the Fifth Circuit held that the "partial performance" exception only applies when not applying it would mean that fraud was tolerated. In this case, Sullivan was paid a salary for his work, so he was not defrauded. [*Sullivan v. Leor Energy LLC*, 600 F.3d 542 (5th Cir. 2010)]

In 2012, the New York Court of Appeals took up the case of a financial executive, Ryan, who was offered a new job. He said that he needed a $350,000 compensation package to change jobs. He was promised 2003 compensation of $175,000 in salary and a $175,000 guaranteed bonus to be paid in late 2003 or early 2004. He accepted and signed an employment application describing him as an at-will employee. The employee handbook reiterated the at-will nature of the job, but said that the handbook itself was not a contract. Ryan did not receive a bonus in 2003. In early 2004, he was asked to defer his bonus for a year, and he reluctantly accepted. Early in 2005, he was offered a $20,000 bonus for 2004, and this time he rejected it. He was fired within a week and offered a $20,000 separation payment in exchange for release of all claims. He did not sign this agreement, but brought suit for breach of contract and failure to pay wages. The jury found a breach of an oral agreement to pay a guaranteed $175,000 bonus, but did not find willful withholding of compensation. The court of appeals held that it was clear that Ryan was an at-will employee, so it was lawful to terminate him, but he was entitled to the bonus. There was no Statute of Frauds problem, because the contract could be performed within a year, and the consideration for the promise of the bonus was Ryan's quitting his existing, lucrative job. The bonus therefore was due and vested, and constituted "wages"—and, under New York law, Ryan was entitled to an attorneys' fee award because his wages were not paid on time. [*Ryan v. Kellogg Partners Institutional Servs.*, 19 N.Y. 3d 1 (N.Y. 2012)]

Under New York common law, at-will employees cannot sue for wrongful discharge. In 2012, the New York Court of Appeals refused to make an exception for hedge fund compliance officers. The plaintiff said that he was fired for objecting to improper trading. The Court of Appeals ruled that state common law is not required to take a more active role merely because there are federal law compliance requirements. The plaintiff could not make use of federal whistleblower protection because there was no evidence that he told anyone outside the firm about the alleged misconduct. [*Sullivan v. Harnisch*, 19 N.Y.3d 259; 969 N.E.2d 758; 946 N.Y.S.2d 540 (2012)]

## [C]  Noncompete Case Law

States differ in their approach to covenants not to compete, and some states forbid or disfavor them, whereas others will enforce them—but in any case, a covenant not to compete will be enforced only if it is reasonable in its geographic scope and duration. The California Business and Professions Code makes most noncompetes unenforceable. A 2012 New Hampshire statute says that a noncompete is void if it is not given to job applicants or promotion candidates before the job or promotion offer. The state legislatures in Massachusetts, Minnesota, and New Jersey are considering bills to limit the duration or extent of noncompetes.

The *Wall Street Journal* published two articles about noncompetes in mid-2013, noting that the frequency of employers requiring noncompete agreements has increased—and so has the number of cases challenging these agreements. In 2000, 72.5% out of 1,000 employment contracts for CEOs included a noncompete, a percentage that rose to 78.7% in 2010. Critics of noncompetes say that they suppress innovation by making it difficult or impossible for creative employees to start their own businesses, because they are likely to be accused of using the ex-employer's proprietary information. Top executives may be out of the workforce for prolonged periods to avoid violating a noncompete; or their new employers may have to pay large sums to an ex-employer to avoid claims, or may have to reimburse the employees for extensive severance benefits they gave up to take the new job. Venture capital availability is greater in states that limit noncompetes than in those (e.g., Florida and Massachusetts) that favor enforcement of such clauses. It is also difficult for startups to find talented applicants with relevant experience who are not bound by noncompetes. In 2012, there were 760 published court opinions in cases about noncompetes, 61% higher than the number ten years earlier. The total number of lawsuits is probably much higher, because many of these cases are settled and do not yield a published opinion.

Another option for employers is a suit for misappropriation of trade secrets, although these cases can be expensive for both plaintiffs and defendants because it is likely that extensive discovery will be required. [Joann S. Lublin, *Companies Loosen the Handcuffs on Non-Competes*, WSJ.com (Aug. 12, 2013); Ruth Simon & Angus Loten, *Litigation Over Noncompete Clauses Is Rising*, WSJ.com (Aug. 14, 2013)]

The only real protection for employees is not signing a noncompete—but the potential employer may insist. Employees could offer to sign an intellectual property protection agreement instead, although many potential employers would reject that option. Employees who plan to leave can protect themselves by avoiding going on the record with disparaging comments about the former employer and use their best efforts until they leave, so the employer has no motivation to sue them. [Elizabeth Dilts, *How Employees Can Negotiate Around a Non-Compete Agreement*, Corporate Counsel (July 23, 2012) (law.com)]

Late in 2012, the Supreme Court held that the Oklahoma Supreme Court was wrong to hold that the noncompete provisions in two employment contracts were void because they violated public policy. The decision should have been left up to the arbitrator. The clause referred to any "dispute, difference or unresolved question." When two employees quit and went to work for a competitor, Nitro-Lift demanded arbitration. The ex-employees sued in Oklahoma state court to enjoin enforcement of the noncompete agreement, which they said was null and void. The Oklahoma Supreme Court asked the parties to show why the state law limiting the enforceability of noncompete agreements should not be applied. The Supreme Court held that the FAA applies in both federal and state courts and attacks on the validity of the contract (rather than on the validity of the arbitration clause) must be resolved by the arbitrator. The validity of the arbitration clause is determined by the court. If the arbitration clause is valid, then the validity of the rest of the contract is decided by the arbitrator. [*Nitro-Lift Techs., LLC v. Howard*, No. 133 S. Ct. 500 (2012)]

In 2011, the Supreme Court of Texas held that it is permissible for an employer to require an employee to sign a covenant not to compete in exchange for letting the employee exercise stock options as long as the noncompete agreement is reasonable in time, scope of activity, and geographic area. It is not necessary that the employer actually give the employee access to confidential information. In Texas, a noncompete agreement is enforceable if it is part of, or ancillary to, an otherwise enforceable agreement. Consideration such as stock options that is reasonably related to goodwill, trade secrets, confidential information, or other protectable interests creates the necessary connection between the noncompete and the business' interests. It is not necessary that the options themselves motivate the employer to require the noncompete. In this case, the stock options were reasonably related to protecting corporate goodwill, so the noncompete was ancillary to an agreement. The Texas Supreme Court remanded the case to determine the reasonableness of the underlying agreement. [*Marsh USA Inc. v. Cook*, 354 S.W.3d 764 (Tex. 2011); see John L. Utz, *Noncompete as Condition for Option Exercise in Texas*, Utz, Miller & Eickmann LLC (Sept. 20, 2011) (benefitslink.com)]

EMC sought a preliminary injunction to prevent Christopher Blotto from competing, soliciting EMC's employees or customers, or using confidential business information. The district court granted a preliminary injunction with respect to the confidential information only, denying it for competition and solicitation, on the grounds that the one-year term of the noncompete had already expired. The First Circuit affirmed, holding that, when a time period has expired, even if the delay was caused by legal proceedings, an injunction is not the proper remedy; damages are. Because the employer drafted the agreement, it could have provided that the one-year term would be suspended during litigation or that it would not start until there was a preliminary finding of impropriety. [*EMC Corp. v. Arturi*, 655 F.3d 75 (1st Cir. Aug. 26, 2011)]

Frequently, employment agreements forbid raiding or soliciting employees from the former workplace. Some New York cases treated these provisions like covenants not to compete—but they are actually quite different. An agreement that forbids a former employee from going to work for a competitor could be challenged as hindering the employee's ability to earn a living but an anti-raiding clause does not, making it inherently more reasonable and less restrictive than a noncompete. However, in late 2012, the Western District of New York applied the test of reasonableness to a no-raid clause. To be reasonable, such a clause might be limited only to personnel with whom the employee worked in the previous year or two, or only if the employees who leave the employer actually go to work for a competitor. [*Renaissance Nutrition v. Jarrett*, No. 08-CV-800S, 2012 WL 42171 (W.D.N.Y. Jan. 9, 2012); see Lloyd B. Chinn and Rebecca L. Berkebile, *Evaluating the Enforceability of Anti-Raiding Provisions*, N.Y.L.J. (Dec. 10, 2012) (law.com)]

The Supreme Court of Illinois held that it was an invasion of privacy when North American Corp. hired investigators to find out if ex-employee Kathleen Lawlor had raided its clients after she changed jobs. The investigators hired a detective agency that claimed to be Lawlor in order to get her phone records. The court said that North American Corp. was vicariously liable for the tort of invasion upon seclusion. The company's counterclaims against Lawlor for breach of fiduciary duty were dismissed but Lawlor was originally awarded $1.75 million in punitive damages, later reduced to $65,000. [*Lawlor v. North Am. Corp.* (Ill. 2013); see Leigh Jones, *Company Held Liable for Privacy Invasion in Employee Probe*, Nat'l L.J. (Mar. 5, 2013) (law.com)]

The Eleventh Circuit upheld the grant of an injunction for violation of a covenant not to complete. According to the Eleventh Circuit, if a restrictive covenant is enforceable, it creates a rebuttable presumption of irreparable injury. However, the Eleventh Circuit held that $1,659,000 in damages was excessive because the plaintiff did not establish that the defendant's solicitation of a former client cost the plaintiff the contract. To receive damages, the former employer must show that it sustained a loss, and its lost profits were directly caused by the defendant's breaches of the restrictive covenants. In this case, the former employer tried to recover "ill gotten gains" from the new employer—which wasn't even a party to the suit. [*Proudfoot Consulting Corp. v. Gordon*, 576 F.3d 1223 (11th Cir. 2009) See also *Environmental Servs., Inc. v. Carter*, 9 So.3d 1258 (Fla. Dist. Ct. App. 2009) holding that a non-compete provision that forbade the employee from performing services for any customer of the ex-employer that the employee had business-related contact with during employment was justified by the former employer's business interest in maintaining client relationships]

California law actually forbids noncompete agreements, although, in the right case, California might agree with the 20 states that accept the "inevitable disclosure" doctrine—i.e., that an ex-employee can be enjoined from going to work for a competitor of the former employer, if the inevitable result would be disclosure of the ex-employer's trade secrets, even if the ex-employee does not intend to do so.

In mid-2008, the California Supreme Court found most covenants not to compete invalid under California law, because the state law gives workers freedom to compete and solicit their former clients when they change jobs. Employers can only restrain former employees from engaging in their trade or profession if the agreement falls within one of the statutory exceptions.

However, California has adopted the Uniform Trade Secrets Act, which allows protection of some information, including client lists. The California Supreme Court also dismissed the plaintiff's claim that requiring him to sign the noncompete agreement interfered with his economic advantage, because it did not try to release any statutory claims that could not be waived. (The plaintiff was an accountant who worked for Arthur Andersen until the firm went under; his division was sold to another financial services company that required employees to release all their claims against Arthur Andersen; he refused to sign, was fired without severance, and his job offer was rescinded.) [*Edwards v. Arthur Andersen*, 44 Cal. 4th 937 (Cal. 2008); Cheryl Miller, *Calif. High Court Brightens Rule Against Non-Compete Pacts*, The Recorder (Aug. 11, 2008) (law.com); Rebecca Moore, *Noncompetes Invalid Under California Law*, plansponsor.com (Aug. 8, 2008). See Labor Code § 16600.]

Also note that even though California law bars covenants not to compete, a California court does not have the power to issue an injunction forbidding the parties in a California suit from bringing suit in a different state to enforce the covenant not to compete. [*Advanced Bionics Corp. v. Medtronic Inc.*, 29 Cal. 4th 697, 59 P.3d 231, 128 Cal. Rptr. 2d 172 (2002)] The theory is that judges should respect the powers of other judges, especially those in other states.

Because California law forbids strict noncompete arrangements, Marissa Mayer did not have a noncompete agreement when she left Google for Yahoo. There are at least three categories of states regarding noncompete agreements: those that generally enforce noncompetes, but overbroad clauses are restricted; states that will not enforce noncompetes at all; and states whose laws are so idiosyncratic that special drafting is required. Drafting should reflect the employee's actual duties: for example, for technical workers, the focus should be on confidentiality, whereas non-solicitation clauses are more important for salespersons. [Elizabeth Dilts, *Mayer Didn't Have a Non-Compete, But Your Competitor Might*, Corporate Counsel (July 20, 2012) (law.com)]

New York considers noncompete agreements an unreasonable restraint on trade. To enforce one, the employer must show that the covenant is reasonable in duration and scope, does not harm the public interest, does not subject the employee to undue hardship, and is no broader than needed to protect the employer's protectable interests. An employee on "garden leave" (i.e., paid to remain at home and not take another job) is still subject to the duty of loyalty to the employer. The "employee choice" doctrine says that courts will not analyze the reasonableness of a covenant that gives an employee a choice between competing (and forgoing benefits) and not competing (and receiving benefits). It is common for employers to require job applicants to disclose terminations for cause. Failure to disclose could justify firing the new employee. In other words, it is often rational for employees to quit before they can be terminated for cause. [Alexandra Wald and Nathaniel P.T. Read, *To Quit or Not to Quit?* N.Y.L.J. (Nov. 13, 2012) (law.com)]

Bimbo Bakeries, manufacturer of Thomas' English Muffins, sued Chris Botticella, who claimed that he was retiring but in fact took a job with a rival company. Bimbo says that Botticella is one of only seven people who know the trade secrets for making the muffins. Botticella signed a confidentiality agreement when he managed a Thomas' English Muffins plant; Bimbo did not allege that Botticella stole any secrets, but applied for an injunction, arguing that he will inevitably disclose confidential information and trade secrets. California law forbids inevitable-disclosure claims against departing employees; suit is premature until there has been improper disclosure of trade secrets. However, inevitable disclosure is recognized in some states, such as Pennsylvania. A Temporary Restraining Order was issued, forbidding Botticella to take the job with Hostess. [*Bimbo v. Botticella*, No. 2:2010 cv 00194 (E.D. Pa. 2010); see Tresa Baldas, *Bimbo Bakeries Seeks Limits on Its Departing Muffin Man*, Nat'l L.J. (Jan. 27, 2010) (law.com)]

The Third Circuit upheld the injunction in July 2010, on the grounds that Bimbo proved that, without an injunction, it was likely that its trade secrets would be misappropriated. It is not necessary to show that it would be "virtually impossible" for the ex-employee to perform the new job without using the ex-employer's trade secrets. [*Bimbo Bakeries USA Inc. v. Botticella*, 613 F.3d 102 (3d Cir. 2010); see Shannon P. Duffy, *Court May Block Executive's Start Date at Competitor Due to Muffin Trade Secrets* (July 28, 2010) (law.com)]

The general rule is that employees who are not bound by employment agreements or termination agreements containing noncompete clauses are free to compete with the employer after they leave. A top executive may be considered a fiduciary as to the employer. A principle of corporate law called the "corporate opportunity doctrine" imposes a duty on a current employee to disclose to the employer whenever a business opportunity arises that is appropriate for the corporation, and it is improper for an executive to take personal advantage of the opportunity at the corporation's expense.

Three weeks after quitting as a WEC project director, Mike Miller made a presentation to a potential WEC customer on behalf of a competitor. The customer entered into a contract with the competitor. WEC charged that Miller, on behalf of the competitor, downloaded proprietary WEC info to his own computer and used it in the presentation. WEC sued Miller, his assistant, and ARC under the Computer Fraud and Abuse Act (CFAA). The Fourth Circuit held that the CFAA does not apply to this situation. To maintain a civil suit under the CFAA, at least one of five additional factors must be proved. WEC had policies forbidding unauthorized use of proprietary information, and forbidding downloading proprietary information to a personal computer. However, Miller's authorization to access the information in the first place was not restricted. Like the Ninth Circuit, the Fourth Circuit held that the CFAA does not cover misappropriation of trade secrets or violation of corporate use policy committed by a person who had access to the information. [*WEC Carolina Energy Solutions LLC v. Miller*, 687 F.3d 199 (4th Cir. 2012)]

## § 25.03  EMPLOYEE HANDBOOKS

### [A]  Generally

Employee handbooks are traditional in large corporations, as a means of creating a uniform culture and distributing information to what can be a large, diverse, and widely disseminated group of employees. Handbooks are useful in training new hires about the employer's expectations. They provide a ready reference about work rules—and employee discipline often revolves around claimed infractions of these rules, so employees must be informed of the rules.

Not all handbooks are printed; more and more companies are using the Web or an intranet to provide information.

Employee handbooks can be extremely useful, but unless they are drafted carefully and kept up to date, they can create at least as many problems as they solve. Sometimes, statements made in a handbook will be deemed to create a binding contract—although this is not necessarily what the employer wished to do.

Furthermore, once the employer is deemed to have created a contract, some courts will say that the employer can no longer amend that contract whenever it wants to, without providing additional consideration to the employees in return for the change. Although some courts say that the fact that the employee continues to work for the employer provides consideration, others require the employees to get some additional benefit if the employer wants to alter the contract.

■ **TIP:** Many federal and state statutes limit the policies that employers can adopt. For example, a policy against leaves of less than one day could violate the Family and Medical Leave Act, or might be a refusal to make a reasonable accommodation required by the Americans with Disabilities Act.

Typical subjects for coverage in the handbook include:

- Training;
- Benefits (health plan, dental plan, disability, etc.);
- Access to profit-sharing plans;
- Defined benefit, defined contribution, 401(k), and other pension plans;
- Stock options;
- Vacations, leave (including sick leave, pregnancy, and military leave), holidays, and time off;
- Explanation of employees' statutory rights under, e.g., the Family and Medical Leave Act (FMLA), ADA, USERRA, etc.;
- Employer's policy of checking all references provided;
- Policy of employing only U.S. citizens and noncitizens who can lawfully work within the United States;
- Drug-free workplace policy, including circumstances under which drug testing will be required;
- Policies about e-mail and Internet use in the workplace;
- Policies about employment of both spouses in a couple, or more than one family member;
- Antiharassment policy; commitment to investigate charges; alternative reporting procedures if the supervisor is the alleged harasser;
- Policies about conflict of interests and acceptance of gifts from suppliers;
- Confidentiality of the employer's intellectual property;
- Employees' patent rights (if any) in inventions they develop while they are working for the employer;
- What will be considered a disciplinary offense;
- Discipline procedure (e.g., oral reprimand, followed by a written warning; suspension after two written warnings for the same offense; retention of warnings in the personnel record for at least a year; and termination; immediate termination will be permitted in the case of a serious, dangerous, or criminal act).

## [B]   At-Will Employment

For employees who are not unionized, and who do not have individual employment contracts, it is often a good idea to put a disclaimer in the handbook:

- Employees are hired at will;

- They can be fired when the employer sees fit; it is not necessary for the employer to demonstrate good cause for the discharge;

- The information in the handbook is for guidance only, and does not bind the employer to a contract.

To be legally effective, a disclaimer must be clear and conspicuous. It cannot be buried in small print somewhere in the back of the book. In fact, the first page is an excellent location. When a disclaimer is issued, it does not apply to people who were already employees and working under the old policy.

The mere fact that the employer has a system of progressive discipline, spelled out in the handbook, does not mean that the employee is no longer an at-will employee. However, it makes sense to include a disclaimer explaining the function of the disciplinary system.

The more specific a provision is, the more likely that courts are to construe it as creating a formal contract. However, in order to win when they charge breach of this implied contract, employees may have to show detrimental reliance (i.e., that they relied on the provision, and this reliance was harmful for them). At the very least, employees will have to prove that they read the handbook, because it is hard to claim reliance on an unread provision.

A terminated employee charged that his termination violated public policy, because he was retaliated against for complaining about harassment by his supervisors. His supervisors said that his work performance was unacceptable. The stated reason for his termination was intentional falsification of delivery records. The plaintiff, Semple, had signed an employment contract indicating at-will status, and he also received an employee manual explaining the grounds for termination. The Eighth Circuit upheld summary judgment for the employer. There was violation of a substantial public policy as found in a statute or judicial decision. Semple could have sued Federal Express for breach of contract if he believed that the company violated its own procedures. Although Semple asserted that the employee handbook created an employment contract, which was breached by firing him, the handbook itself said that it did not create a contract. [*Semple v. Federal Express Corp.*, 566 F.3d 788 (8th Cir. 2009)]

## [C]   Orientation Checklists

It is a good idea to provide orientation to train new hires. It is even better to standardize the orientation process, with standard documents for welcoming and instructing new employees. Both the employee and the supervisor handling the orientation should sign the document, so that later on the employee will not be able to claim that lifetime employment was promised if the document clearly states that employment is at will.

The orientation checklist should cover subjects such as:

- The company's equal employment opportunity policies;

- The company's position on unionization and union activity (get legal advice before promulgating a policy!);

- Which unions (if any) that are already recognized as bargaining agents for the employees;

- The terms of the formal probation process (if there is one);

- What a new hire has to do to become a permanent employee, but make sure that no promises are made of indefinite tenure or lifetime employment;

- The new employee's job title, duties, and promotion path;

- The compensation and benefit package for the job (including vacation days, vacation banking, disability benefits, sick leave, options under the group health plan, and severance pay);

- Work rules;

- Circumstances under which the employee can be terminated.

Even if the manual indicates the employees will be on probation for a certain length of time after being hired, they will still be entitled to good faith and fair dealing from the employer. In fact, some courts will allow probationary employees to sue for wrongful termination, if the employer did not offer them long-term employment after the end of the probation period.

## [D]   Legal Consequences of Handbooks

The Minnesota Supreme Court ruled that it is a matter of contract whether an employer must pay all terminating employees for all their accrued vacation and Paid Time Off (PTO). Minnesota Statutes § 118.13(a) makes all wages earned and unpaid at discharge immediately due and payable on demand. However, in this case, the company handbook said that employees who were terminated for misconduct or failed to give proper notice would not be paid for PTO. When an employee was terminated for misconduct and was denied payment for accrued PTO, she sued to recover what she characterized as wages. However, the state Supreme Court held that employers can impose contractual conditions on collecting wages at termination, and in this case, the plaintiff violated the conditions. In most instances, employers do not want to characterize handbook provisions as contractual, but this is one situation in which contract status is useful to the employer. [*Lee v. Fresenius Med. Care, Inc.*, 741 N.W.2d 117 (Minn. 2007), *reversing* 719 N.W.2d 222 (Minn. App. 2006); see Melissa Raphan and Megan McKenzie, Dorsey & Whitney LLP, *Benefits & Compensation, Minnesota Supreme Court Rules on Employer's Vacation Pay Liabilities* (Nov. 20, 2007)]

Early in 2004, the NLRB ruled that it violates federal labor law to promulgate a handbook provision that restricts employee communications with other employees and the press about the terms and conditions of employment (such as wages and grievances). The employer could not forbid discussion of company issues in public areas other than the casino floor. Discussions on the casino floor, however, could be banned by analogy with the retail sales area of a store. It was improper for the handbook to forbid communicating any information about the company to the media without management approval; even a rule that is never enforced can have a chilling effect. [*Double Eagle Hotel & Casino*, 341 NLRB No. 17 (Jan. 30, 2004)]

Denial of unemployment benefits was proper for a claimant who was terminated for absenteeism. When she was hired, she signed an acknowledgment that she received the company handbook, which included the employment policy. Her position was that she was entitled to benefits—that her actions could not be willful or wanton because she misinterpreted the attendance policy. But the employer gave the claimant coaching warning her that she was at risk of termination for noncompliance, and it was therefore just to terminate her when she did not improve, and denial of unemployment benefits was also justified for violation of a known employer policy when the potential consequences were also known. [*Jackson*, Unemp. Ins. Rep. (CCH) ¶ 8317 (Del. Super. Ct. 2008)]

## § 25.04  WORK RULES

Some organizations are small enough, informal enough, or simple enough in operation that they do not need written work rules. But in the larger organization, or even a small operation where the work rules could become an issue, a written list of rules (in the handbook or set out separately) can be very useful.

The work rules document should make it clear that the employer is the only one to make work rules and that the employer has the right to modify them at any time. The rules themselves are not a contract with the employees that has to be negotiated, or that has to be maintained in its original form.

Work rules deal with issues such as:

- Workplace safety and security (not letting in unauthorized persons; wearing protective equipment in construction areas or where hazardous chemicals are present);

- Emergency procedures in case of fires, chemical spills, etc.;

- Where (if anyplace!) smoking is allowed in the workplace; if smoking is banned inside the workplace, limitations on going outside for smoking breaks;

- Requirement of on-time arrival and staying until the end of the work day or shift;

- Dress and grooming rules—are uniforms required for any job titles? Which days are "casual" days, and what is acceptable business casual clothing? Are there any limitations or bans on facial hair, hairstyles, makeup, or jewelry? (Make sure that these rules do not violate employees' rights to reasonable accommodation of their religious practices);

- Availability of paid and unpaid leave; how to request leave. Some companies maintain a no-fault absence policy, under which employees get a certain number of days off no matter what the reason is, but discipline can be imposed for excessive absence. A paid leave bank is similar, but allows unused days to be carried over or cashed out. Get legal advice about harmonizing your leave policy with legal requirements for disability and unpaid family leave;

- Bans on horseplay, substance abuse, possession of alcohol in the workplace, and removing products or materials (even waste or spoiled items) without permission;

- Bans on harassment, fighting, and weapons;

- Control of solicitation within the workplace. A "no-solicitation" rule can be very helpful, not only in restricting union activity, but in improving efficiency and avoiding conflict among employees. It can get pretty expensive to come to work each day if you are asked to contribute to everyone's favorite charity and chip in for presents for people who are getting married, leaving the company, having a baby, in the hospital, etc. An effective no-solicitation rule must be appropriately communicated to employees, it must be nondiscriminatory, and it must be applied uniformly. So if one employee is given permission to sell raffle tickets for the Catholic Church, while another is denied permission to raise money for the NAACP (or vice versa), it will appear that the employer is guilty of discrimination;

- The extent to which employees are permitted to inspect their own personal records or show them to an attorney, union representative, etc. Check your state law: It probably requires employees to have access to their records, and also protects privacy rights by limiting disclosure of personal information to anyone except the employee without the employee's consent. [See § 26.07 for rules on privacy of health records];

- Ethical standards imposed on employees: for example, when they are allowed to accept gifts from a potential supplier; use of inside information; lobbying, political activities, and donations;

- How to find additional work-related information and answers to questions: for instance, through the HR department, the Employee Assistance Program, or the corporate intranet.

■ **TIP:**   Even though the work rules are not contractual in nature, it is a good idea to have employees sign a notice stating that they received a copy of the work rules and had a chance to read and become familiar with them. The notice may come in handy later if the employee claims that he or she never saw the rules or didn't understand them.

## § 25.05   SYSTEMS OF PROGRESSIVE DISCIPLINE

One approach to at-will employment is for the employer to take and maintain a consistent position that only the employer determines the quality of the employee's work performance. Employees can therefore be disciplined or fired based on the employer's sole determination that their work is unsatisfactory. In a unionized workplace, it is almost certain that the collective bargaining agreement will require a system of progressive discipline, where all the steps, from a verbal warning through levels of reprimands, must be followed before the employee can be fired.

There are various reasons why even a nonunion workplace might have a progressive discipline system. It could improve efficiency. Sometimes, employees really do not know that their work is below par, so it is better to show them how to improve instead of firing them. Also, if the employer voluntarily adopts a progressive discipline system, this could make employees less interested in unionizing.

The downside is that having specific rules to follow limits the employer's flexibility. Even in a nonunion setting, the disciplinary system may be treated by courts as a contractual obligation, so that once the system is set up, it has to be maintained in the future.

Usually, a system of progressive discipline begins with an oral warning explaining why the supervisor is dissatisfied with the employee's performance. The next step is a written warning. If performance is still unsatisfactory, discipline proceeds to a probationary period or suspension (usually unpaid, lasting three–five days), then demotion or termination.

All the steps, including oral warnings, should be documented in the employee's personnel record. The written warning should include a place for the employee's signature, indicating that the document has been read. The employee should be given a copy for reference. It is often helpful to let the employee include a brief written statement giving his or her side of the story.

It is important to monitor the reasons for an employee's lateness or absence. Discipline or discharge could constitute a violation of a statute if the employee has been injured (and qualified for Worker's Compensation), is disabled as defined by the ADA, or is taking care of a sick family member and therefore is entitled to FMLA leave.

All investigations should be documented, to show that the employer is acting on the basis of facts and not discrimination against members of a protected group.

An objective party should review all termination decisions. The best time is after tempers have had a chance to cool, but promptly enough to demonstrate the employer's efficiency and involvement. Before a termination, review the process to see that the employee received the appropriate warnings; the investigation gave enough weight to the employee's explanation; and the employee was treated fairly, objectively, and on a par with other similarly situated employees.

In general, employees who are discharged for cause are not entitled to severance pay (see Chapter 3). However, the employee handbook may have been written in such general terms that it constitutes a contract to pay severance benefits, even in connection with a discharge for cause. Severance policies that are written and communicated to workers may become welfare benefit plans subject to ERISA. If there is no formal plan, and the employer has not entered into an express or implied contract, then it is completely at the employer's discretion to grant or withhold severance benefits.

## § 25.06  EMPLOYEE EVALUATIONS

Regular evaluations of employee performance can be critical in making sure that the organization meets its goals. Employees who are not performing up to par can be identified and given the training, encouragement, or whatever they need to improve. When it's time to award merit raises and bonuses, the performance appraisal should identify the stars.

A well-done performance appraisal identifies real problems in employee performance and gives insights into solutions. Some of the basic issues for performance reviews include:

- Whether the quantity of work performed by the employee has been satisfactory;

- Quality of the work;

- The employee's knowledge of the job;

- His or her dependability, initiative, and adaptability;

- The extent to which the employee has learned new skills, and seems likely to be able to acquire the skills that will be needed in the future;

- The extent of the employee's cooperation, attendance, and punctuality;

- Areas in which the employee needs to improve.

However, performance appraisals must be carefully done. If they're mishandled, the result is often to subject the employer to liability for wrongful termination or employment discrimination. There are many reasons why the appraisal process itself doesn't work well:

- Managers do not have time to do a thoughtful job of appraising performance, so they decide to err on the side of generosity;

- The appraisals do not seem to actually be used for anything, so managers put down whatever seems uncontroversial—or simply update the previous year's forms without much thought;

- In a large work group, managers may not know very much about what individual employees are doing;

- Managers want to be liked by the employees who report to them; they're afraid that a tough-minded appraisal could create hostility and reduce motivation;

- Ambitious managers want to give themselves an indirect pat on the back, hoping that they will be seen as outstanding leaders if all their subordinates are doing a great job;

- A bad appraisal could be attacked as the product of racism, sexism, sexual harassment, or retaliation. However, the answer is **not** to give everyone good marks because it looks very suspicious if the employer claims that someone who got a long line of excellent appraisals was fired for poor performance.

At a minimum, the employee should be shown a written performance appraisal, be given an opportunity to discuss it, and should be asked to sign a statement that he or she has read the document. Some states make it a legal requirement that the employee must be allowed to add comments; it is a good idea anyway.

The modern form of appraisal is the "360-degree review," which has input from more than one person, including co-workers and customers. However, it can be hard to gather all the necessary information, and not everyone will be candid. An alternative might be to have more frequent but informal reviews: for instance, at the end of every project, or every quarter or twice a year.

## § 25.07 MANDATORY PREDISPUTE ARBITRATION PROVISIONS

Employers, faced with the delay, high costs, and significant risks of employment litigation, often seek to require in advance that employees will raise any discrimination claims using the arbitration process rather than litigation (see Chapter 40).

However, it takes skillful drafting to use the employee handbook for this purpose. Cases like *Paladino v. Avnet Computer Techs. Inc.* [134 F.3d 1054 (11th Cir. 1998)], *Phox v. Allied Capital Advisers* [74 Fair Empl. Prac. Cas. (BNA) 809 (D.D.C. 1997)], and *Trumbull v. Century Mktg. Corp.* [12 F. Supp. 2d 683 (N.D. Ohio 1998)] have refused to enforce these provisions, because they did not give the employees enough notice of their rights.

To have a chance of enforcement, a handbook provision must make it clear which statutes are covered, and clearly and explicitly indicate that arbitration is the sole remedy. It makes sense to have the employee sign a document when he or she receives the handbook—not only stating that the handbook has been received, but that the employee haes read its contents and understands them.

In recent years, most cases have come down on the side of arbitration, even if it is compelled by a mandatory predispute arbitration clause (i.e., if employees had to agree to arbitrate their claims as a condition of being hired)—a proposition that was approved by the Supreme Court in *Circuit City v. Adams.* [532 U.S. 105 (2002)] The jurisdiction and the facts of the case will determine whether the fact that the employee continues to work after the arbitration requirement has been imposed constitutes acceptance of the terms of the arbitration provision. [For example, *In Re Dallas Peterbilt Ltd.*, 196 S.W.3d 161 (Tex. 2006); *In re Dillard Dep't Stores, Inc.*, 198 S.W.3d 778 (Tex. 2006); *Hardin v. First Cash Fin. Servs. Inc.*, 465 F.3d 470 (10th Cir. 2006); *Berkley v. Dillard's Inc.*, 450 F.3d 775 (8th Cir. 2006), hold that continued employment constitutes acceptance, but *Leodori v. CIGNA Corp.*, 814 A.2d 1098 (N.J. 2003), says that it does not]

The Supreme Court ruled in 2009 that a labor union could require arbitration of a grievance brought by workers who said they were demoted because of age discrimination—the Supreme Court rejected drawing a distinction between collective bargaining agreements (CBAs) and individual contracts that contain arbitration clauses. [*14 Penn Plaza LLC v. Pyett,* 556 U.S. 247 (2009)] Another Supreme Court decision—in a consumer protection rather than an employment case—has been read to mean that federal law supports arbitration so strongly that state rulings about the unconscionability of arbitration agreements will be preempted. [*AT&T Mobility LLC v. Concepcion,* 131 S. Ct. 1740 (Apr. 27, 2011)]

In a decision covering all employees whose employers are engaged in interstate commerce (whether or not the company is unionized—about 25% of nonunion workers are subject to arbitration clauses), the NLRB ruled in early 2012 that requiring employees to waive collective actions and class arbitration and arbitrate all employment disputes individually violates the NLRA. The NLRB said that it was not bound by *AT&T Mobility* because that case does not apply to rights specifically guaranteed to employees by the NLRA. [*D.R. Horton and Michael Cuda,* 357 NLRB No. 184, Case 12-CA-25764 (Jan. 3, 2012). See also *Raniere v. Citigroup Inc.,* 2011 U.S. Dist. LEXIS 135393 (S.D.N.Y. Nov. 22, 2011): employers cannot enforce mandatory arbitration of FLSA collective actions for minimum wage or unpaid overtime, discussed in Philip M. Berkowitz, *Developments in Arbitration of Employment Claims*, N.Y.L.J. (Jan. 12, 2012 (law.com); Scott Graham, *AT&T Mobility Doesn't Apply in the Workplace, Says NLRB*, Corporate Counsel (Jan. 9, 2012) (law.com); Steven Greenhouse, *N.L.R.B. Backs Workers on Joint Arbitration Cases*, NYTimes.com (Jan. 6, 2012)]

If your company is a federal contractor, however, its post-2009 ability to enforce mandatory arbitration clauses is severely limited. A provision in the federal spending bill for the Department of Defense for the years 2009–2010 (§ 8116) forbids defense contractors holding contracts or subcontracts over $1 million to enforce mandatory arbitration clauses. The defense contractor cannot be paid by the federal government unless it agrees not to enter into or enforce any employment contract making it a condition of employment for an employee or independent contractor to agree to arbitrate Title VII claims or many other tort claims. The Department of Defense has the power to grant a waiver for national security reasons, although the waiver must be disclosed to the public. [David Ingram, *Obama Signs Into Law Restriction on Arbitration Clauses*, Nat'l L.J. (Dec. 22, 2009) (law.com)]

The fact that a statute can be enforced through federal lawsuits does not rule out arbitration, so the Fifth Circuit upheld mandatory arbitration of USERRA claims brought by a Marine reservist who said he was harassed and eventually fired because of his military status. [*Garrett v. Circuit City Stores*, 449 F.3d 672 (5th Cir. 2006). See § 1.18 for more discussion of USERRA]

However, an employer seeking to enforce an arbitration agreement must be careful to abide by the agreement itself. In late 2005, for example, the Ninth Circuit ruled that an employer that unilaterally imposed an arbitration policy had to arbitrate an employee's claims of wrongful termination (the employer said that she was fired for falsifying a time sheet). The employee sued in state court; the employer removed the case to federal court and sought to compel arbitration, but the federal courts refused to compel arbitration because the employer had failed to cooperate with the requirements of AAA arbitration required by the arbitration policy. [*Brown v. Dillard's Inc.*, 430 F.3d 1004 (9th Cir. 2005)]

The Ninth Circuit initially ruled that employees can't be fired for refusing to accept predispute arbitration [*Duffield v. Robertson Stephens*, 144 F.3d 1182 (9th Cir. 1998)] but then, in 2002, the Ninth Circuit decided another case overturning the *Duffield* decision. [*EEOC v. Luce, Forward, Hamilton & Scripps*, 303 F.3d 994 (9th Cir. 2002)] The 2002 ruling was upheld on appeal in 2003, affirming the validity of mandatory predispute arbitration clauses. [345 F.3d 742 (9th Cir. 2003)] [For history of this case, see two articles by Jason Hoppin (both available from law.com): Jason Hoppin, *9th Circuit Grapples with Duffield*, The Recorder (Mar. 28, 2003) (law.com); Jason Hoppin, *Employer Can Insist on Arbitration Agreement*, The Recorder (Sept. 4, 2002) (law.com)]

An important focus in recent cases that accept the basic validity of predispute arbitration agreements is whether a particular agreement contains unfair terms that place too great a burden on employees who might seek to arbitrate grievances. The significant California case of *Armendariz v. Found. Health Psychcare Servs., Inc.* [24 Cal. 4th 83 (2000)] imposes fairness requirements (the arbitrator's award must be appealable, and employees must not be required to pay unaffordable sums to arbitrate a claim). However, it has been held that *Armendariz* only applies to arbitration of claims of employment discrimination barred by federal or state statutes, and not to claims that someone was wrongfully terminated in violation of public policy. [*Little v. Auto Stiegler, Inc.*, 29 Cal. 4th 1064, 63 P.3d 979, 130 Cal. Rptr. 2d 892 (2003)]

Even if part of an arbitration clause is ruled to be unfair, that doesn't necessarily mean that the employer loses everything. A number of cases allow the invalid part of the clause to be severed, and the rest of the clause to be enforced. [See, for instance, the *Little* case mentioned above, and *Spinetti v. Serv. Corp. Int'l*, 324 F.3d 212 (3d Cir. 2003)]

## § 25.08 DEFAMATION

A hostile or unflattering statement that a company or one of its agents makes about a job applicant, employee, or former employee could become the focus of charges, or even a lawsuit. However, there are several circumstances under which negative statements are legally protected. For one thing, the statements might have been demonstrably true. They might have been made without malice, or in a privileged context.

Slander is defined as communicating a defamatory statement orally or otherwise informally. Libel means communicating a defamatory statement more broadly ("publishing" it). A defamatory statement is one that attributes serious misconduct to someone else. The victim of slander or libel can sue and obtain tort damages, unless the statement was privileged in some way.

The basic rule is that a plaintiff not only has to prove that defamation occurred, but also that some actual damages were suffered because of the defamation. But there are some statements so negative that they are automatically presumed to damage the reputation of the person about whom they are made. A plaintiff who proves such "defamation per se" can win without proving actual damages (concrete injury attributable to the defamation).

To support a suit, the alleged slander or libel must be a statement of fact, not a mere opinion or a general, imprecise statement ("Marcia is hard to work with"; "Steve seems to be working through some problems in his life."). A pure opinion cannot be defamatory, because it is not a statement of fact, but a statement of fact backing up that opinion can be defamatory. A corporation is liable for the statements of its employees and agents, as long as they were acting within the scope of their employment.

Truth is always a defense to a defamation charge: For instance, it is not defamatory to say that an employee was fired for stealing office supplies if this is what actually happened. If the employer believes a statement is true, and the statement is communicated without malice, then the employer is entitled to a defense. The jury, not the judge, decides whether or not a statement was communicated with malice.

A statement has not been "published" to the extent that a libel charge can be made if it is communicated only to the plaintiff, or to someone who is acting on behalf of the plaintiff (including a friend or an investigator who calls to find out what the employer is saying about the employee). Courts take different positions about communications that stay within the employer corporation. Some courts say that this is so narrow that no publication has occurred, whereas others accept the plaintiff's argument that dissemination was broad enough to constitute libel.

Although employers are hesitant to communicate about employees, technology like e-mail, blogging, and social networking makes it easier to disseminate information—positive or negative—about employees. Not only references, but performance reviews, outplacement interviews, and written or electronic conversations can give rise to defamation suits. Former employees, who may feel that they have little chance of getting another job in the current economy, also have less to lose, may be more likely to file a defamation suit. More and more suits involve "defamation by conduct" such as subjecting an employee to an undeserved investigation of alleged wrongdoing. Attorneys for employers suggest making sure that corporate policies are applied evenly (e.g., requiring all terminated employees to turn in their company laptops immediately) so no one can claim to have been singled out unfairly.

## § 25.09  PRIVILEGED STATEMENTS

### [A]  Generally

Some kinds of communication are essential to the operation of businesses and the legal system, so they are afforded special treatment. They are referred to as "privileged," and by definition cannot be defamatory.

Restatement of Torts (2d) § 596 permits a privilege when the publisher and the recipient of the information share a common interest, such as making sure that honest, qualified individuals are hired and retain their jobs.

In addition to absolute privilege, "qualified" privilege exists in some circumstances. A qualified privilege is one that can be taken away under some circumstances, whereas an absolute privilege survives all kinds of challenges. If the employer asserts a qualified privilege, it has the burden of proving that it is entitled to the privilege.

If a corporation has an audit committee, discussion of possible embezzlement or securities violations are probably entitled to qualified privilege as long as they remain within the committee, and are not disclosed (other than to law enforcement officials, which is the subject of another privilege). If there has been an investigation about workplace matters, disclosing the results of the investigation to the employees at large would probably also be privileged.

Even though they are not law enforcement officials, the EEOC and unemployment officials are close enough so that communications to them are privileged. There is at least a qualified privilege to make statements in the course of processing a union grievance or issuing dismissal letters required under a collective bargaining agreement. In fact, in some states (Michigan, New Mexico, Louisiana, Missouri) the privilege is absolute, not qualified.

California [Cal. Civ. Code § 47(c)] gives employers a qualified privilege for statements made without malice and on the basis of credible evidence. Alaska presumes [Alaska Stats. § 09.65.160] that employers act in good faith when they discuss their employees with other prospective employers. However, if the employer acts recklessly, maliciously, or contrary to the employee's civil rights, the privilege is no longer available.

In any state, employers are probably entitled to a qualified privilege when they make good-faith comments on employee performance to someone who has a legitimate right to the information. However, some degree of caution must be exercised. Not all co-workers necessarily have a legitimate interest in performance appraisals.

The Connecticut Supreme Court ruled in mid-2009 that an employer cannot necessarily assert qualified privilege in a defamation suit brought by an employee merely by saying that the employer thought the statement was true. Apple Health Care, an extended care facility, fired admissions counselor Laure Gambardella for stealing from a patient. The Connecticut Supreme Court held that there was no evidence for the theft charge (the niece of a deceased patient said Gambardella could take the items). The charge was discussed in front of co-workers at a meeting about firing Gambardella. The Connecticut Supreme Court held that an employer's qualified privilege is defeated by actual malice or malice in fact, and upheld the $224,000 defamation damages ordered by the trial court. [*Gambardella v. Apple Health Care*, 291 Conn. 620 (Conn. 2009); see Fred Schneyer, *Employer Loses Privilege in Defamation Case*, plansponsor.com (May 14, 2009)]

There is a qualified privilege to protect the safety of employees who might hurt themselves, or might be hurt by others. (Communications that are privileged in the context of a defamation suit are probably also privileged if the employee sues for violation of privacy instead of, or in addition to, defamation.)

However, even if a privilege initially exists, it can be sacrificed—most typically, by failure to act in good faith, or by making statements without proof and with reckless disregard as to whether or not they are true.

The conventional viewpoint was that the EEOC prefers for in-house investigations of discrimination charges to be kept confidential. However, a July 2012 NLRB ruling, in the case of Banner Estrella Medical Center, says that a blanket policy mandating employees to keep HR investigations confidential violates NLRA § 7 because it burdens protected concerted activity. However, it is permissible to require confidentiality if the facts of the case require it: for example, to protect witnesses, avoid cover-ups, and prevent destruction of evidence. Employers should protect themselves by having formal policies. The complainant should be asked if he or she wants the investigation to remain confidential (and this is usually the case). The employer should protect itself by getting a written statement of this intent. [Catherine Dunn, *NLRB Rules on Keeping Employees From Discussing HR Investigations*, Corporate Counsel (Aug. 31, 2012) (law.com).]

### [B] Attorney-Client Privilege

The term "privilege" is also applied to communications that are privileged in the sense of being protected from disclosure. To do a good job, lawyers must learn all the facts of the situation, not just the facts that put their clients in a favorable light. Certain information is privileged if a client communicates it to a lawyer. The lawyer cannot be required to disclose this information—in fact, in most instances, it is unethical for the lawyer to disclose the information without the client's consent.

The factors that determine the availability of attorney-client privilege include:

- Whether the client approached the lawyer specifically to seek legal advice (as distinct from a casual chat, or when the lawyer played another role, such as giving business advice or serving as a director of a company);

- Whether the lawyer is acting as a lawyer, not a director or business advisor;

- Whether the communication relates to the lawyer-client relationship;

- Whether the client intends the information to be confidential;

- Whether the client did anything (deliberately or inadvertently) to remove the privilege; for instance, material distributed by the corporation will not be privileged.

It can be hard to determine the status of corporate documents.

A report might be confidential only if it were drafted specifically as a confidential document for transmission to the attorney.

The EEOC was not allowed to introduce a report prepared by the employer's attorneys about their investigation of a sexual harassment charge.

If the primary purpose of a communication is to get legal advice, a secondary business motive will not take away the privilege. But the privilege will be waived (that is, surrendered) if the corporation voluntarily distributes the document to non-attorneys, or discloses or allows the disclosure of a significant part of the document. For instance, if a corporation issues a press release about a development, or sends an employee to read a technical paper at an industry conference, it will not be able to argue that the press release or the technical paper is confidential.

However, a statement made by an employee who is not acting as an agent of the employer, but is simply an independent witness to an event probably will not be confidential, no matter why the statement was made.

In addition to the attorney-client privilege, the law of evidence contains a separate "work product" privilege. Work product is material prepared by attorneys and their employees as part of representing a client. Work product is also confidential and cannot become part of the discovery process before litigation.

In December 2006, Deputy U.S. Attorney General Paul McNulty issued a memorandum stating that the DOJ supports the recognition of limited waiver of attorney-client privilege, under confidentiality agreements that would give prosecutors access to the results of internal company investigations without making the material vulnerable to discovery in civil suits. Under the memorandum, there are two categories of protected materials. For the first category (factual information like witness statements or interview memoranda), the prosecutor has to ask the U.S. attorney to approve a waiver request, and the U.S. attorney is required to consult the Justice Department's Criminal Division. For the second category of material, including attorney work product and attorney-client communications, the U.S. Attorney needs written consent from the Deputy Attorney General.

There are four factors that prosecutors must show to demonstrate legitimate need to access these materials. The policy allows prosecutors to consider a corporation's refusal to surrender Category 1 material in the decision whether or not to bring charges against the corporation. Refusal to provide Category 2 materials cannot be a factor in bringing criminal charges, but favorable consideration can be given for provision of such material. Reimbursing employees' legal fees is supposed to be a factor in the prosecution decision only in the most extreme cases.

Corporate defense lawyers did not feel that the memorandum solved the problems created by the original Thompson memo. The guidelines have no enforcement mechanism if prosecutors violate them. Corporations can still be given incentives for surrendering confidential information. The government can still raise the argument that a corporation advanced attorneys' fees to an employee in order to impede the government investigation. The Association of Corporate Counsel's 2006 survey showed that almost three-quarters of corporate attorneys say that government agencies expect waivers from the companies they investigate. In the past five years, 51% of corporate outside counsel and 30% of in-house counsel said they had been asked to trade waivers of privilege for leniency in prosecution. [Pamela A. McLean, *McNulty Memo on Attorney-Client Privilege Blasted for Lack of Change*, National Law Journal (Jan. 26, 2007) (law.com); Marcia Coyle, *The "McNulty Memo": Real Change, or Retreat?*, Nat'l L.J. (Dec. 20, 2006) (law.com); Lynnley Browning, *Judge's Rebuke Prompts New Rules for Prosecutors*, N.Y. Times, Dec. 16, 2006, at C4]

The New Jersey Supreme Court ruled that the attorney-client privilege outweighs corporate policy about use of workplace computers. Therefore, a plaintiff suing her employer had a reasonable expectation that e-mails to and from her lawyer using her personal, password-protected Yahoo account, would be private even though they were sent on a laptop owned by the company. [*Stengart v. Loving Care Agency Inc.*, 990 A.2d 650 (N.J., 2010); see Michael Booth, *Privilege Trumps Company E-Mail Surveillance*, N.J.L.J. (Apr. 1, 2010) (law.com)]

## [C]  Self-Critical Analysis

When a company finds out that misconduct may have occurred and launches an investigation, the company has to decide if it should report any misconduct that it discovers to the authorities. If the company's stock is publicly traded, disclosure will probably be required by the securities laws and the company will be liable under the anti-fraud provisions of federal securities laws. Financial institutions are required to file a Suspicious Activities Report with the FinCEN (Financial Crimes Enforcement Network) when they become aware of potential illegalities. Federal regulations make government contractors subject to debarment or suspension for knowing failure to make timely disclosure of credible evidence of fraud, conflict of interest, bribery, or False Claims Act violations in connection with performance of a government contract.

If the corporation itself is clearly a victim (e.g., of embezzlement or theft of trade secrets) then self-reporting can result in help from the authorities. There are more advantages than disadvantages in reporting offenses committed by an employee with little corporate exposure (e.g., a criminal act carried out on company property, but not related to the criminal's employment). The stronger the evidence, the stronger the case for reporting—especially since the likelihood that regulators will discover the wrongdoing also increases. The Department of Justice Principles of Federal Prosecution of Business Organizations permit prosecutors to treat timely, voluntary disclosure of wrongdoing as a mitigating factor, and cooperation with the authorities can affect the decision of what crimes to charge. The DOJ's Antitrust Division offers amnesty to the first corporation to confess to an antitrust violation—and turn in the other co-conspirators. [Michael B. Mukasey and Andrew J. Ceresney, *Should Corporations Self-Report Wrong doing?*, N.Y.L.J. (Oct. 1, 2010) (law.com)]

Companies that want to improve diversity and eliminate discrimination often make studies of their employment and HR practices. Can discrimination plaintiffs require the company to disclose those documents, and use them to prove that the company used discriminatory employment practices?

Several federal courts have recognized a "self-critical analysis privilege": in other words, that these reports are internal documents that should not have to be revealed to plaintiffs, because companies should be encouraged to be candid about their discrimination problems instead of suppressing what they know to avoid embarrassing disclosures in lawsuits.

The opposite view is that the documents were prepared as part of the company's Title VII compliance program, would eventually be reported to the EEOC, and therefore could not reasonably be described as privileged. Even under this argument, a distinction might be drawn between a self-critical analysis that a company originated voluntarily and one that is mandated by the EEOC or by federal contract regulators. Or the court might require the company to produce hard information like statistics about workplace diversity, but permit the analytical part of the report to remain confidential.

It also helps to control dissemination of sensitive documents. The fewer people who have access to the document, and the more they agree that the company needs to analyze its performance in order to improve, the less likely they are to disclose the document in a way that is harmful or embarrassing to the corporation.

## § 25.10   DUTY TO COMMUNICATE

Not only are there situations in which an employer becomes liable for defamation or other disclosures; sometimes the employer can get into trouble for failing to communicate. There might be a duty to disclose dangerousness, so that other employers will not hire someone who puts their other employees or customers at risk. A subsequent employer may sue if the first employer fails to reveal relevant information, such as a job applicant's dismissal for stealing or workplace drug dealing.

Employers have a legal duty to protect customers and co-workers. That makes them negligent if they know that someone is dangerous, but they still retain him or her as an employee. This is true even if the risk is of conduct outside the scope of employment. An employer who knows that an employee has violent tendencies can be liable because of workplace assaults committed by that person, even if the assaults are not only not part of the job, but are contrary to the employer's policy and work rules. However, if the injured person is a fellow employee, it is very likely that the employee's only remedy will be through the Worker's Compensation system. [See § 33.03 for the concept of WC exclusivity]

Employers can be sued for negligent hiring or negligent entrustment if they hire someone for a safety-critical job but fail to check that person's references. In some contexts (such as hiring workers for a nursing home or day care center) there may be a duty to consult a special database maintained by the state or by a licensing organization to list individuals who are ineligible for employment because they have been convicted of a crime.

An employer will probably be exempt from liability for negligent hiring if a thorough investigation is performed before hiring; but if an employer fails to discover information that would have been disclosed by an ordinary background check, liability is a possibility.

Discrimination plaintiffs sometimes add a negligent hiring claim to their complaints. Their theory is that the employer was negligent in hiring and/or retaining a supervisor who was racist, sexist, or otherwise prone to engage in discriminatory conduct. The advantage to the plaintiff is that, although the discrimination claim is subject to the Civil Rights Act of 1991 (CRA '91) cap on damages (see § 42.12[B]), the negligent hiring claim is not. Also, it is hard to introduce evidence into a discrimination case about acts of discrimination or harassment carried out against employees other than the plaintiff, but this is relevant evidence in a negligent hiring case.

The employer might also be liable for negligent supervision, if the court or jury accepts the argument that the supervisor would not have been able to carry out the act of discrimination or harassment if the employer had managed the facility better.

## § 25.11  RESPONSES TO REFERENCE CHECKS

The employer has to steer between two hazards: neither committing defamation, nor failing to disclose information that must be divulged. One approach that often works is just to confirm the start and end dates of a former employee's employment, and then say that it is against company policy to discuss ex-employees. Another possibility is to disclose only information that is fully documented by HR files.

> ■ **TIP:** If your state gives employees the right to review their files and make their own comments, make sure that any response to an inquiry includes the employee's comments. For instance, "Ms. Jones was dismissed for excessive lateness and poor performance. However, she said that other people were late just as often, and we should have been more sympathetic about her performance because her mother had just died." That way, the questioner gets both sides of the story.

According to employment lawyer Wendy Bliss, it is perfectly legitimate for a former employer to provide information about the candidate's performance as a member of a work team, and the adequacy of his or her work habits. But information should be disseminated only if it is truthful, work-related, and can be supported by documentation. Bliss suggests that employers should have a written policy about what kind of information will be given in references—and who will be allowed to provide this information. Information should not be released without a signed consent and release form (including a liability waiver) from the employee.

If an employee's resignation or termination is being negotiated, one area of negotiation is what will be said in response to reference checks.

It may be easier to get reference check information by asking about a job candidate's strengths and accomplishments as an employee, rather than stating or implying that you want negative information. No one is going to sue for defamation for being described as "hard working," "effective," or "creative"!

The growing trend toward outsourcing functions opens new risks if background checks are omitted, but the law is not clear as to whether the employer or the staffing agency is responsible for performing the checks. Hence, employers who are concerned about liability risks should either perform or make sure that the staffing agency performs background checks on:

- Anyone working in a customer's home;
- Anyone working with children or vulnerable adults (e.g., the elderly or disabled);
- Anyone with access to bank accounts, Social Security numbers, trade secrets, or other confidential information.

The employer's contract with the agency should include a warranty that the agency has performed background checks on all agency workers and certification that the check did not show anything precluding placement of the worker. The agency should warrant that background checks were performed in accordance with the FCRA and state laws. Employers should make sure that the agency maintains adequate liability insurance and should seek indemnification from the agency. [Tresa Baldas, *Outsourced Employees Triggering More Suits*, Nat'l L.J. (Feb. 22, 2006.) (law.com)]

## § 25.12  NEGOTIATED RESIGNATIONS

In some cases, an employee has been guilty of misconduct so serious (securities fraud or embezzlement, for example) that immediate removal is needed to reduce the risk to the corporation. In other cases, it will be less clear that employment must be ended—situations that fall under the Hollywood euphemism "creative differences." In such a situation, both parties benefit if they negotiate a resignation. The employee will leave on a stipulated date, and will release the company from all claims of employment-related discrimination. [See Chapter 37, § 37.07[A] for the specific problems of drafting a release that will satisfy the provisions of the Older Workers Benefit Protection Act (OWBPA). Pub. L. No. 101-433]

A resignation agreement is a contract and therefore is subject to the ordinary rules of contract law. For instance, if the employer deliberately misleads an employee, or subjects him or her to undue influence, the resignation agreement will be void and the employer will not be able to enforce it against the employee. The implications of the agreement are serious enough that first-line supervisors should not be allowed to negotiate. Either a trained HR staffer or an attorney should take on this role.

The agreement covers issues such as:

- The employee represents that he or she has not already filed any charges, or instituted litigation against the employer. If legal action is already in the works, settlement discussions or conciliation from the antidiscrimination agency is in order, but it is too late to negotiate a simple resignation agreement;

- The employee waives all claims against the employer. Drafting the proper, enforceable language is an intricate legal task;

- The employee agrees to treat the resignation as voluntary, and therefore not to apply for unemployment compensation;

- The employer should state that it does not admit liability of any kind, but is only using the agreement to clarify the issues;

- The employer should specify the kind of reference it will give the employee, and how it will handle reference checks from potential future employers;

- The employee should waive any merit-based bonuses that would otherwise be payable in the year of the resignation;

- The employee should agree to return all materials in his or her possession containing trade secrets or other proprietary materials of the employer, and should agree to refrain from using the employer's proprietary/trade secret information in any later employment;

- The employee should agree to keep the terms of the agreement confidential.

## § 25.13  RELEASES

An employee who has already filed discrimination charges may be willing to settle those charges, receiving some consideration in exchange for releasing the employer from further threat of suit by that employee. (However, a suit brought by another employee, or by the EEOC, continues to be a risk.) During the negotiations before a resignation, the employer and employee could agree on a severance package that winds up their relationship, making it clear that the soon-to-be-ex-employee will not bring any discrimination charges.

A release is a contract, a legal agreement for surrendering claims that already exist. A release can be quite general, simply referring to "all claims" or quite specific, spelling out a whole laundry list of claims. A release of liability could be combined with reasonable covenants not to compete and provisions about the employer's intellectual property.

Courts might refuse to enforce a release that is too general, on the grounds that it is not specific enough to inform employees of their rights. But a release that is too detailed can put ideas into the heads of employees who had no real intention of bringing suit—or who didn't know the vast and exotic variety of ways in which they can make trouble for the employer!

Before payments of pensions and benefits begin, the plan might require the potential participant or beneficiary to sign a release stating that the plan has computed the amounts of benefits correctly, or that the participant or beneficiary waives all claims against the plan except the right to receive benefits as specified by the plan.

Courts are split as to whether such mandatory releases are enforceable. If all plan participants and beneficiaries have to sign, the release becomes part of ordinary plan administration, and there is no additional consideration for it. The employer gets something (freedom from suits and other claims) but doesn't give up anything in return (the benefits would be available under the plan anyway).

All contracts require consideration to be enforceable. Each party must receive something under the contract. In a typical release situation, the employer provides additional benefits (e.g., extra severance pay; outplacement assistance; early retirement incentives) over and above normal severance. The employee offers the employer a release of all claims, thus sparing the employer the risk of having to defend against charges. If each party gets something of value, the court probably won't worry about exact equivalence, as long as the parties knew their rights and understood all the implications of the release.

A general release covers all claims in existence at the time of the release; a limited release covers only the types of claims named in the release itself.

■ **TIP:**   A release covering an injured worker who is entitled to Worker's Compensation is valid only if it is approved by a Worker's Compensation judge. Special care is required in drafting the release. If the worker releases claims relating to compensable physical injury, he or she will still have the right to bring suit on other grounds, such as claims that the employer acted in bad faith or intentionally inflicted emotional distress on the employee.

A Worker's Compensation release that did not explicitly mention ERISA claims or the ERISA plan did not release the employer from an ERISA disability claim. Teresa Duncan received disability benefits under an ERISA long-term disability plan from 2005 to 2010. She settled her WC claim in 2008 and released all claims. The release form said she would not "be able to go back to the defendant for additional treatment or disability payments." The Eastern District of California held in early 2013 that the standard language in WC releases applies only to WC claims, not ERISA claims. [*Duncan v. Hartford Life &Accident Ins. Co.*, No. 2:11-cv-01536-GEB-CKD, 2013 WL 506465 (E.D. Cal. Feb. 7, 2013); see Mike Reilly, Lane Powell Boom: The ERISA Law Blog, *Releases Should Explicitly Release ERISA Claims and ERISA Plan* (Feb. 26, 2013) (benefitslink.com)]

The Seventh Circuit ruled in early 2011 that WARN Act claims can be waived in a voluntary general release. The Seventh Circuit upheld the release because the release (and the severance agreements in connection with closing DHL Express shipping facilities) were negotiated by the union; were not ambiguous; and suggested consulting a lawyer before signing. [*Ellis v. DHL Express Inc. USA*, 633 F.3d 522 (7th Cir. 2011)]

However, as the FMLA regulations provide (see Chapter 38), the Department of Labor says that it is invalid for employees to give an advance release of claims that might arise under the FMLA in the future. But with respect to FMLA claims that have already arisen, it is legitimate for employers to offer—and employees to sign—a release of existing claims. Supervision by the Department of Labor, or by a court, is not required.

The Seventh Circuit held in mid-2013 that the plaintiff knew, when he signed a release to get separation benefits, that he was not entitled to pension benefits. In 1996, his former employer amended its pension plan to exclude employees in certain departments. In 1999, the plaintiff was transferred to one of those departments. In 2000, he received a Statement of Individual Benefits that said that, because of his classification, he could not participate in the plan. Therefore, he could not allege that he was entitled to additional benefits because he was not informed of a plan amendment that affected his eligibility. The Seventh Circuit said that pension claims for additional benefits, as distinct from pension entitlements to benefits that have already vested, are outside the reach of ERISA's anti-alienation provision, so they can be waived by a release. [*Hakim v. Accenture United States Pension Plan*, No. 11-3438, 2013 WL 2249454 (7th Cir. May 23, 2013); see Rebecca Moore, *Release of Claims Bars Lawsuit for Pension Benefits*, plansponsor.com (June 10, 2013)]

In mid-2009, the EEOC published a guidance document in Question & Answer form covering waivers of discrimination claims in severance agreements. The EEOC noted that older employees are often targeted because they earn more than less experienced, younger co-workers.

The document is intended for employees, and includes sample language and examples of adequate consideration and knowing and voluntary waivers. In general, it re-states existing principles rather than breaking new ground. To be valid, waivers must be knowing and voluntary, written clearly enough for employees to understand them, must not be induced by improper conduct on the employer's part, and the employee must be given access to counsel and given enough time to consider the terms. Employees must receive some additional consideration for signing the waiver that they would not otherwise receive. Waivers must not give up the right to pursue remedies for future acts of discrimination. Waivers should not limit employees' right to testify or participate in EEOC proceedings. [EEOC, *Understanding Waivers of Discrimination Claims in Employee Severance Agreements*, <http://www.eeoc.gov/policy/docs/qanda_severance-agreements.html> (July 15, 2009). See *EEOC v. Watkins Motor Lines, Inc.*, 553 F.3d 593 (7th Cir. 2009): the EEOC can continue to investigate and pursue claims made by a person who signed a waiver. The guidance is discussed in Kevin B. Leblang and Robert

N. Holtzman, *Time for Employers to Review Their Severance Agreements*, Metropolitan Corporate Counsel (Feb. 1, 2010) (benefitslink.com)]

States take varying approaches about what can be covered by a general release. Some states say that they can cover all claims, known or unknown, but other states say that a general release is not effective for claims that the employee did not know about or suspect at the time the release was signed. Under this theory, people can only give up claims that they know about and decide are worth less than the benefits under the release.

The California Court of Appeal ruled that USERRA rights (see § 1.18) cannot be eliminated by a contract; 38 U.S.C. § 4302(b) says that USERRA supersedes any state law or contract that reduces, limits, or eliminates any rights under the statute. Therefore, a release of rights in a severance agreement was unenforceable to the extent that it dealt with allegations he was terminated because of his military status. California Civil Code § 1542 provides that a general release does not extend to claims of material importance that the creditor does not know about at the time of the release. The plaintiff said that the release was invalid because it did not include an explicit waiver of § 1542, but the court of appeals held that although it is good practice to include a § 1542 waiver, it is not absolutely necessary: a proper release will be enforced if it is knowing and voluntary. [*Perez v. Uline*, 157 Cal. App. 4th 953 (Cal. App. 2007)]

However, a 2010 Sixth Circuit decision holds that a release under IBM's Individual Separation Allowance Plan prevented an ex-employee from asserting USERRA claims. The court found that the release was enforceable because it was knowing and voluntary; there was no evidence of fraud or overreaching; and the release form was not ambiguous. [*Wysocki v. IBM*, 607 F.3d 1102 (6th Cir. 2010)]

Although it is common for employment, change in control, and severance agreements to condition payment of severance or other compensation on the employee's signing a general release of all claims against the employer, the documents must be carefully drafted in light of Code § 409A. (See § 8.02[D]) In general, § 409A allows a severance agreement to permit payment at any time during the 90 days after the event—but only if the employee does not have a direct or indirect election about when to receive the benefits.

Executives can create problems for their former employers if they do not sign the release until the calendar year after employment ends. Problems can be averted by drafting releases to say that if benefits could be paid in two different tax years, depending on when the employee signs the release, benefits will automatically be paid in the later year, no matter when the release is signed.

A new rule took effect April 1, 2011. If the payment window between an event and the deadline for payment overlaps the end of a calendar year, generally payments cannot begin until the year in which the payment window ends. For most plans, problems did not start until the fourth quarter of 2011, because the payment window for § 409A plans is usually 90 days or less, so payments in the first three quarters will not overlap two calendar years. But some plans do allow payments to be made either in the year of the event or the following two and a half months. Penalties will be imposed if payments that were supposed to be made in 2012 were made in 2011, unless a correction procedure is available. The rule allows the payment window to be shortened from 90 days to a shorter period (e.g., 30 or 45 days), which could be a good tax move although it increases the problems of administration.

A further complication is that ADEA releases generally require 45 days notice, and employees must be given seven days after signing to revoke their consent. Therefore, severance payments are generally reserved until after the revocation period ends. [McGuireWoods LLP, *Employee Release Provisions Present Section 409A Trap for the Unwary* (Aug. 31, 2011); George L. Chimento, *Release Me: 4th Quarter Complication for 409A Plans* (Oct. 14, 2011) (benefits link.com)]

## § 25.14  SARBANES-OXLEY AND DODD-FRANK NOTICES

The Sarbanes-Oxley Act of 2002 [Pub. L. No. 107-204] became law in July 2002. It is a wide-ranging piece of legislation; many of the issues it covers are outside the scope of this book because they involve corporate governance and accuracy in accounting. However, the Sarbanes-Oxley Act also deals with "blackout periods" in individual account plans such as 401(k) plans. If a blackout period does occur, the corporation is required, by Sarbanes-Oxley Act § 306(b), to provide advance notice to plan participants that their ability to control their plan accounts will be limited during the blackout period, and a plain English explanation of the effect on their rights. [See 68 Fed. Reg. 3715 (Jan. 24, 2003) for DOL's Final Rule on this subject]

The general rule is that the notice must be given at least 30 days, but not more than 60 days, before the start of the blackout period, although exceptions are recognized if circumstances make it unfeasible to give the notice at the regular time. The notice must disclose the start and end dates of the blackout period and explain the extent to which participants' ability to change their plan investments or get distributions or loans from the plan will be affected. The notice must be written, rather than verbal, but it can be distributed electronically.

Civil money penalties of up to $100 per participant per day can be imposed on the plan administrators as individuals if the required notice is not given (although DOL also has discretion to suspend penalties if the imposition of penalties would be unjust). The Final Rules for Sarbanes-Oxley civil penalties were published by the DOL at 68 Fed. Reg. 3729 (Jan. 24, 2003).

The notice must be in writing—so a speech to the workforce wouldn't count—but it can be handed to participants, mailed, or distributed electronically. [See 68 Fed. Reg. 3729 (Jan. 24, 2003) for the text of a model notice that can be used to comply with the disclosure requirement] The model notice ("Important Notice Concerning Your Rights Under the [Plan Title] Plan") includes:

- The reason why a blackout period is imposed;

- The extent of the restrictions, including the statement "whether or not you are planning retirement in the near future, we encourage you to carefully consider how this blackout period may affect your retirement planning as well as your overall financial plan";

- The expected beginning and ending dates of the period; a toll-free telephone number or URL the participants can access to check to see if the blackout period is still in effect;

- A warning of the need to check and perhaps re-balance the participant's overall investment strategy because of the effect of the trading restrictions

- (If the full 30-day notice is impossible) The reason why the regular notice could not be given;

- Name, address, and telephone number of a contact person who can answer questions about the blackout period and its effects.

Sarbanes-Oxley is one of several statutes giving protection to whistleblowers: persons who disclose corporate wrongdoing to law enforcement authorities. Corporations are forbidden to retaliate against whistleblowers. Under Sarbanes-Oxley Act § 906, the standard for "adverse employment actions" does not require the employee to suffer tangible consequences as a result of protected activity. The DOL Administrative Review Board ruled that Sarbanes-Oxley § 301, which requires public companies to maintain procedures for anonymous, confidential submission of employee complaints, is a term and condition of employment. Therefore, publicizing an employee's whistleblower activity is an adverse action. In late 2005, Menendez filed a confidential SEC complaint raising concerns about Halliburton's accounting practices. Early in 2006, an e-mail to the company's internal audit committee repeated this information, giving Menendez' name and contact information. The SEC told the company that its accounting practices were under investigation and the company's General Counsel allegedly told some managers that the company was acting on Menendez' information. Menendez took paid administrative leave and resigned before his scheduled return date. He said that Halliburton retaliated against him for the internal and SEC complaints and violated his expectation of confidentiality. The Administrative Review Board held that § 806 explicitly covers non-tangible activities because whistleblowers are entitled to broad protection. [*Menendez v. Halliburton, Inc.*, Case Nos. 09-002 and 09-003 (DOL Admin Review Board Sept. 13, 2011); see Plansponsor staff, *DoL Adopts New Standard for SOX Whistleblower Cases*, plansponsor.com (Sept. 29, 2011). The most recent form of whistleblower protection derives from PPACA § 1558, which amends the Fair Labor Standards Act to protect employees against retaliation for disclosing violations of PPACA Title I. [OSHA Fact Sheet, OSHAFS-3641.pdf?, *Filing Whistleblower Complaints under the Affordable Care*

*Act*; see PLC Employee Benefits & Executive Compensation, *OSHA Rules Address Retaliation Complaint Procedures under Health Care Reform* (Feb. 25, 2013) (benefitslink.com)]

Although it is predominantly aimed at preventing future stock market crashes, the Dodd-Frank Wall Street Reform and Consumer Protection Act, Pub. L. No. 111-203, has some implications for corporate governance and corporate communications. The Dodd-Frank Act and the SEC's final whistleblower rules affect three aspects of corporate internal investigations:

- Teaching employees about internal corporate controls;
- Performing the investigation;
- Dealing with regulators.

For almost a decade, internal investigations were based on Sarbanes-Oxley, including its requirement for internal controls such as "up the ladder" reporting requirements and the role of independent directors, especially the audit committee, in ensuring compliance. Both internal and outside investigators need strategies for handling the consequences of reporting violations to regulators before there has been an in-house investigation. Employees must learn to use the internal reporting mechanisms.

The possibility that employees will go straight to regulators in the hope of collecting rewards puts pressure on businesses to report their own violations, to achieve cooperation credit, and to avoid negative response from shareholders. If the whistleblower goes to the company first and the company itself gives the SEC information leading to a successful investigation, the whistleblower gets credit for all of the information provided by the company. But if the whistleblower interferes with the internal investigation, the reward for the whistleblower will be reduced. It is unlawful to penalize whistleblowers whether or not the SEC ever investigates the complaint if the reported conduct actually violated the law or the whistleblower received an award. However, if an employee's knowledge of potential investigations comes from an attorney during an interview in an internal investigation, Rule 21F-4(b)(4)(vi) says that the information is not original and cannot support a whistleblower complaint. [Final Regulations, 76 Fed. Reg. 34,300 (June 13, 2011), effective Aug. 12, 2011; see Steven S. Sparling and Arielle Warshall Katz, *Internal Investigation Strategies in a Post Dodd-Frank World*, N.Y.L.J. (Aug. 11, 2011) (law.com)]

In 2013, the Fifth Circuit ruled that a claim of retaliatory termination for making an internal report of possible securities law violations did not fall under the Dodd-Frank whistleblower provisions, which require volunteering information to the SEC or participating in an SEC investigation. [*Asadi v. G.E. Energy LLC*,2013 WL 3742492 (5th Cir. 2013)]

# PRIVACY ISSUES

## § 26.01   INTRODUCTION

For the employee, a significant part of each working day is spent in the workplace. The employer takes on some of the roles of the government. Do employees have the same civil rights with respect to their employers as citizens have with respect to their governments? In some ways, the answer is "Yes," but in other ways, the legal system balances the employer's need for honesty, sobriety, and efficiency in the workplace against the employees' desire for privacy. Many (if not most) constitutional rights are limitations on government power, not the power of private entities such as employers.

Many of the topics in this book are either completely regulated by federal laws, or federal laws are dominant, but in the privacy arena, state laws are very significant. Most states have laws on access and copying of personnel files, so that employees can view and copy their own files, but access by outsiders is restricted.

The Supreme Court ruled that a corporation does not have a right of "personal privacy," using the ordinary definition of "personal." The Freedom of Information Act (FOIA) mandates that federal agencies make their records and documents publicly available. However, there is an exception for law enforcement records whose disclosure could reasonably be deemed an unwarranted invasion of personal privacy. A competitor of AT&T made a FOIA request for documents that AT&T gave the FCC during an investigation. Although the Third Circuit agreed with AT&T that the corporation had a privacy right that could prevent disclosure of the documents, the Supreme Court reversed in March 2011—although a corporation has the legal status of a "person," the concept of "personal privacy" is limited to human beings, and has traditionally been applied only to individuals. [*FCC v. AT&T*, 131 S. Ct. 1177 (2011); see Marcia Coyle, *Court Adds Claws to Cat's Paw Claims—But Hisses at Case Over Corporate Privacy*, Nat'l L.J. (Mar. 1, 2011) (law.com)]

In a case brought by a pilot who concealed his HIV status (the FAA would not issue medical certificates to HIV-positive people) and who was fired and indicted for making false statements to a government agency when his status was uncovered in a federal investigation of invalid FAA certifications, the Supreme Court held that the suit could not be maintained against the federal Department of Transportation. The Privacy Act sets standards for management of federal records and allows suits for actual damages when an intentional or willful violation affects an individual. The Supreme Court held that the Privacy Act does not unequivocally authorize damages for mental and emotional distress—so there was no clear waiver of sovereign immunity, and the plaintiff could not sue the federal agency. [*FAA v. Cooper*, 132 S. Ct. 1441 (2012)]

An early 2011 Second Circuit ruling holds that it does not violate an employee's right of privacy to disclose that she has fibromyalgia: unlike HIV/AIDS or transexuality, it is not a condition that creates a constitutionally protected privacy right. In the Second Circuit, privacy rights in medical information vary based on the condition. There is no history of discrimination against sufferers from fibromyalgia. Nor did the plaintiff allege that disclosing her condition exposed her to discrimination or intolerance. The issue is not the seriousness of the condition, but the extent of the risk of discrimination. The court also held that the investigators had a right to publicize investigations into potential fraud or misconduct. [*Matson v. Board of Educ. of City Sch. Dist of N.Y.*, 631 F.3d 57 (2d Cir. 2011)]

It is not uncommon for employees to violate company policy and access employer files to obtain confidential information for use in a suit filed by the employee. The plaintiffs may rationalize this as self-help discovery. In many instances, the employer only discovers that this has occurred after the plaintiff has filed suit and referenced the contraband documents or even attached them as an exhibit to the complaint. A line of cases is emerging to state that employees do not have a right to access confidential employer information. Self-help discovery is not considered protected concerted activity under the NLRA, so firing an employee for doing this is not unlawful retaliation. Courts often use a balancing test, comparing the employer's legitimate interest in protecting proprietary information against the employee's right to discover the information needed for litigation. The test uses questions such as whether the evidence was obtained through improper means, whether the employer consistently applied a policy that the employee violated, the degree of relevance of the information to the employee's claim, and whether there was a risk that relevant evidence would be lost or destroyed if the employee did not take it. [Connie Bertram, *Using Confidential Documents in Claims Against Your Employer*, Corporate Counsel (Aug. 14, 2012) (law.com); see *JDS Uniphase Corp. v. Jennings*, 473 F. Supp. 2d 705 (E.D. Va. 2007), holding that even employees who claim whistleblower status are not entitled to use proprietary corporate information to make their cases.]

## § 26.02 POLYGRAPH TESTING

There are many problems with using polygraphy ("lie detector tests") in the workplace setting. These tests are expensive and not very reliable. The real test is whether the employee is nervous, and a practiced liar may be far less nervous than a timid but honest employee.

There are outright bans on polygraph testing in the workplace in Massachusetts, Michigan, Minnesota, and Oregon. Alaska, Connecticut, Delaware, Hawaii, Maine, Nebraska, New Jersey, New York, Rhode Island, West Virginia, and Wisconsin forbid employers to require, request, or even suggest testing. In one of these states, it violates public policy to fire someone for refusing to take a polygraph test, because the test cannot be demanded as a condition of employment. In Illinois, Maine, Michigan, Nevada, New Mexico, and Virginia, testing is not forbidden, but polygraph operators have to be licensed.

The Federal Employee Polygraph Protection Act of 1988. [Pub. L. No. 100-347, 29 U.S.C. § 2001; EPPA] forbids most private employers from using polygraph tests for pre-employment screening. In the workplace itself, it is permissible to polygraph employees but only in the course of an ongoing investigation about economic loss or injury to the employer's business. (In this context, drug tests and written or oral "honesty tests" are not considered polygraph examinations.)

Under the federal law, an employee can be asked to submit to polygraph testing only if:

- He or she has access to the property involved in the inquiry;

- The employer has a reasonable suspicion about the employee's involvement;

- Before the examination, the employer provides the employee with a specific written statement about the nature of the investigation and the basis for the employer's suspicion of the employee.

The employer is required to keep these statements on file for three years after they are issued.

The employer must advise the employee of his or her rights:

- To refuse the test or stop it after it has begun;

- To seek representation by a lawyer or other person (such as a union representative);

- To review the questions before the test;

- To review the results before the employer uses them as a premise for adverse employment action.

The employee must be notified that test results may be turned over to prosecutors.

In an EPPA suit, the Fourth Circuit held that the polygraph does not have to be the sole reason for the discharge for EPPA to be violated, but the employer is automatically liable (unless an exception applies) if the polygraph was the sole reason for the discharge. There is an exception for ongoing investigations of economic loss or injury to the employer's business, when the employer reasonably suspects the employee is involved. There is a Department of Labor regulation, 29 C.F.R. § 801.4(c), that says that it violates EPPA for an employer to receive polygraph information from law enforcement, but the Fourth Circuit held that the regulation is invalid, because employers have to participate actively to be held liable. [*Worden v. Suntrust Banks Inc.*, 549 F.3d 334 (4th Cir. 2008)]

An Eleventh Circuit case arose when a bank branch manager was fired after $58,000 disappeared from two ATMs at the bank. Surveillance cameras showed the plaintiff and his four employees repeatedly violated the bank policy requiring two people to be present whenever cash was handled or secure areas were accessed. The ex-manager was fired after refusing to take a polygraph test. The bank said that he was fired for violating the two-person access policy, not for his refusal. The Eleventh Circuit affirmed summary judgment for the defendant on the polygraph claim, holding that an inventory shortage by itself is not enough to justify a polygraph but if there is additional evidence of theft and reasonable suspicion, it is lawful to ask for the test. Mere access or opportunity is not tantamount to reasonable suspicion, but other evidence (such as information from co-workers) can justify a polygraph request. [*Cummings v. Washington Mut.*, 650 F.3d 1387 (11th Cir. 2011)]

In 2006, the Eleventh Circuit ruled that a company did not violate the Employee Polygraph Protection Act by accepting the union's proposal that miners who were fired for theft be allowed to take a polygraph test so they could clear their names and be rehired. The company was not liable because the proposal was for the employee's own good, and there was no evidence that the company exerted pressure on the union to propose the testing. Nor was the union liable, because it acted on behalf of its members. [*Watson v. Drummond Co.*, 436 F.3d 1310 (11th Cir. 2006)]

## § 26.03   DRUG USE IN THE WORKPLACE

### [A]   A Pervasive Problem

Drug use in the workplace, and the effects of off-premises drug use at work, are significant problems. Many employers, because of the nature of their business (e.g., public transportation and public safety) or because they are federal contractors, are subject to legal mandates to maintain a drug-free workplace.

Drug users (primarily users of illegal drugs, but sometimes of prescription drugs) are likely to be impaired during working hours. They may use or even deal drugs in the workplace. If they can't afford to pay for their drugs, they are very likely to steal, embezzle, or commit industrial espionage to get drug money. Employees who are already breaking the law by illegal drug use may lose their inhibitions against committing other crimes as well.

Federal law requires drug testing for some categories of workers, such as truckers and workers in environmental cleanup. These jobs require hard physical labor, with high turnover. Employers find that many applicants fail drug tests, especially tests for abuse of prescription drugs. Nationwide, the rate of positive workplace drug tests has declined somewhat in the 2010s, but trucking and pipeline workers' positive test rates are rising. Quest Diagnostics said that there were 1.5% positive tests in those industries in 2009, 1.8% in 2011. About one-quarter of federally mandated tests that were positive in 2011 showed amphetamine use; 3.1% were positive for oxycodones. Random on-the-job tests were twice as likely to be positive for oxycodones than were pre-employment tests—and post-accident tests are three times higher than pre-employment results, suggesting that these drugs are especially bad for safety. The sensitivity and quality of the test is also an issue: a Texas drilling company found that there was a 34% drop in safety incidents that required medical treatment after it used hair follicle tests, which are more sensitive than urinalysis. [Kris Maher, *Wanted: Drug-Free Workers*, WSJ. com (Jan. 8, 2013)]

DOT rules require mass transit, aviation, rail, and motor carrier workers who fail a drug test (or refuse to take one) to successfully complete drug treatment and pass a series of urine tests before they can return to any safety-sensitive duties. In 2008, the regulations were amended to require the urine testing to be done by direct inspection (by a person of the same sex as the worker). The D.C. Circuit upheld the regulations, finding that they were not arbitrary and capricious. It was rational for the Department of Transportation to require direct inspection because cheating on drug tests is so widespread. It was not irrational to impose the direct inspection method for return-to-duty tests but not examinations after an accident, because of the differing likelihood of cheating. There is a compelling public interest in transportation safety, so the procedure falls under the Fourth Amendment exception for warrantless searches that promote a compelling public interest. [*BNSF Railway Co. v. United States Dep't of Transp.*, 566 F.3d 200, 1378 (D.C. Cir. 2009); the DOT regulations were published at 73 Fed. Reg. 62,910 (Oct. 22, 2008)]

United Insurance Company of America agreed to pay $37,000 to resolve the EEOC's disability discrimination suit about Craig Burns, a recovering drug addict who had been in a methadone program since 2004. He was offered a job as an insurance agent in January 2010, contingent on passing a drug test. When the test was positive for methadone, he provided a letter from his treatment program explaining that his methadone use was legal. The offer of employment was withdrawn. The EEOC filed suit in August 2011 in the Eastern District of North Carolina. United Insurance agreed to a two-year consent decree calling for training on the need for individualized assessment of ADA disability and how to determine if the direct threat defense applied. [Tara Cantore, *United Insurance to Pay $37K for Failing to Hire Recovering Addict*, plansponsor.com (Jan. 25, 2012)]

The abuse of legal substances, such as alcohol and prescription drugs, also creates problems for employers. A 2010 Sixth Circuit case arose when Sue Bates, a 22-year veteran, was fired by Dura Automotive System when a drug test showed hydrocodone, which she was taking legally under a prescription. Six other employees who were fired for using prescription drugs joined as plaintiffs. Dura gave them a chance to transition to drugs without the 12 substances that the employer tested for, but refused to accept letters saying that the prescriptions did not affect the employees' work performance. The Sixth Circuit ruled that six out of the seven plaintiffs were not disabled for ADA purposes (the seventh one might have had a record of disability). The ADA forbids imposition of qualification

standards that tend to screen out individuals with a disability, unless those qualifications are job-related and consistent with business necessity. The Sixth Circuit's interpretation of this provision is that only a qualified individual with a
disability (QWID) can sue under this section. (The case arose before the ADAAA
took effect—and before the 2011 regulations that avoid using the term "Qualified
Individual With a Disability.") [*Bates v. Dura Auto Sys. Inc.*, 625 F.3d 283 (6th
Cir. 2010)]

Under the Federal Drug-Free Workplace Act, [41 U.S.C. § 701] companies
with federal procurement contracts over $25,000 (and many companies are fed-
eral contractors) must certify to the contracting agency that they will provide a
drug-free workplace. The contract will not be awarded if they do not make the
certification.

The contractor-employer's obligations are to:

- Notify employees that using, possessing, and selling drugs is prohibited,
  and what the penalties will be if these rules are violated;

- Set up a drug-free awareness program;

- Order employees to abide by the program and notify the employer if they
  are convicted of a drug offense (even one occurring off-premises);

- Notify the contracting agency within ten days of receiving such a report
  from an employee;

- Impose penalties on all employees convicted of drug violations that are
  related to the workplace;

- Continue to make a good-faith effort to keep drugs out of the workplace.

If the employer is a defense contractor, it must do regular drug tests on
employees in "sensitive positions," in other words, those with access to classified
information.

In an increasing number of states, medical marijuana is either legal or under
consideration. In October 2009, the Department of Justice announced that it
would not prosecute medical marijuana users, leaving enforcement in the hands
of state and local governments. Nevertheless, federal law permits discharge or
other adverse job action when an employee tests positive for marijuana, even
medical marijuana. A Colorado state law forbids firing employees for lawful off-
duty behavior, which might include medical marijuana use.

In addition, if a medical marijuana user has a disability for ADA purposes,
adverse employment action on this basis could violate the ADA. In 2003, the
U.S. Supreme Court held that even in a state that permits medical marijuana, an
employer can penalize an employee who tests positive for drugs, and in 2005 the
Supreme Court permitted the federal government to enforce the Controlled
Substances Act's prohibition of medical marijuana even if the usage conforms
to state law. [See also *Roe v. TeleTech Customer Care Mgmt. (Colorado), LLC*,

171 Wash. 2d 736, 257 P.3d 586 (Wash. 2011) and *Emerald Steel Fabricators Inc. v. Bureau of Labor & Indus.*, No. BOLI 3004, LA A130422 (Or. Apr. 14, 2010); see Fred Schneyer, *Oregon Employer Cleared in Medical Marijuana Hiring Case*, plansponsor.com (Apr. 16, 2010)—both cases denying remedies to persons who were not hired because of their medical marijuana use.]

Wal-Mart fired store manager Joseph Casias, who tested positive for medical marijuana he was legally permitted to smoke (because he has an inoperable brain tumor). Similar suits have been filed in California, Montana, Oregon, and Washington. When Casias sued, the Sixth Circuit held that medical marijuana statutes merely protect the user against being arrested for using illegal drugs—they do not confer employment rights. Employers do not have a duty to accommodate medical marijuana use because it violates federal law and could create safety risks. However, the Michigan statute, unlike the California or Oregon laws, protects medical marijuana users against adverse employment consequences. [*Casias v. Wal-Mart Stores, Inc.*, 694 F.3d 428 (6th Cir. 2012); for background see Tresa Baldas, *Wal-Mart Manager Sues Over Right to Smoke Pot for His Health*, Nat'l L.J. (June 30, 2010) (law.com).]

Even though medical and recreational marijuana are legal in Colorado, it is still lawful for businesses to fire people who test positive for marijuana. The plaintiff is a quadriplegic who is authorized for medical marijuana use and said that he was never under the influence of marijuana at work. He sued for lawful activity discrimination; the Colorado Court of Appeals held that marijuana use is not lawful because it violates federal law. He appealed to the Colorado Supreme Court. ACLU attorney Emma Anderson expected to see more suits in Arizona, Connecticut, Delaware, Maine, Nevada, and Rhode Island, because those states have laws forbidding employment discrimination against medical marijuana users. [*Coats v. Dish Network*, 2013 COA 62 (Colo. App. Apr. 25, 2013); see Nathan Koppel, *Legal Pot Use in Colorado Could Still Get You Fired*, WSJ.com (Apr. 25, 2013); Gregory J. Millman, *Medical Marijuana Poses Litigation Risk to Employers*, WSJ.com (Aug. 15, 2013)]

In some cases, medical marijuana users, although not violating the law, will develop problems associated with marijuana use that require referral to the Employee Assistance Program or other mental health/substance abuse resources.

## [B]  Case Law on Drug Testing

Pre-employment drug testing is more likely to be upheld by the courts than testing of current employees, on the theory that employees have a legitimate right of privacy. (For example, in late 2003 West Virginia ruled that because of the lower expectation of privacy, it is permissible to require job applicants to take a drug test even though state law bars mandatory testing of employees. [*Baughman v. Wal-Mart Stores Inc.*, 215 W. Va. 45 (W. Va. 2003)]) In 1997, the California Supreme Court took the position that urine testing for drugs can be required of persons who have received conditional job offers, but not employees who are under consideration for promotions. [*Loder v. Glendale, Cal.*, 14 Cal. 4th 846, 927 P.2d 1200 (1997)]

Cases in Arizona and California say that it does not violate public policy to discharge a worker based on his or her refusal to take a drug test. [*AFL-CIO v. Cal. Unemployment Ins. Appeals Bd.*, 23 Cal. App. 4th 51, 28 Cal. Rptr. 2d 210 (1994); *Hart v. Seven Resorts Inc.*, 191 Ariz. 297 (Ariz. App. 1997)] In a Fourth Circuit case, two employees charged that, although they were nominally fired for refusing to take a drug test, the real reason was that they were union activists. The court held that neither imposing the drug testing requirement nor firing the two workers violated the National Labor Relations Act.

In *Smith v. Zero Defects Inc.*, [132 Idaho 881 (1999)] the employer's policy called for termination of any employee testing with a detectable level of alcohol or illegal drugs. The plaintiff tested positive for amphetamines during a random test; he was not impaired at that particular time. However, Idaho (like Nebraska, Nevada, Oklahoma, and Utah—but unlike Arizona, Kansas, Oregon, and Washington) considers violation of an employer's zero-tolerance policy to be misconduct that is serious enough to prevent the employee from getting unemployment insurance benefits, even if he or she was not impaired at the time of the test. In other words, off-duty drug use can be serious enough to block unemployment benefit eligibility.

An arbitrator's award, requiring reinstatement of an employee who was fired after failing a drug test, could not be enforced, because it violated the well-established public policy against allowing drug users to keep safety-sensitive jobs. [*Exxon Corp. v. Esso Worker's Union*, 118 F.3d 841 (1st Cir. 1997)] However, two years later, the Tenth Circuit upheld an award reinstating a truck driver who admitted to smoking marijuana two days before an accident. The arbitrator read the CBA's requirement of discharge only for "just cause" to require proof of on-the-job drug use, drug dealing, or impairment, not just off-hours drug use. [*Kennecott Utah Copper Corp. v. Becker*, 195 F.3d 1201 (10th Cir. 1999)]

Current substance abuse is not a disability for ADA purposes (although it is unlawful to discriminate against someone who is now clean and sober because of a past history of substance abuse).

The ADA has a safe harbor [42 U.S.C. § 12114(b)] for people who have completed a rehab program. Just entering a program isn't enough; the safe harbor is for people with a history of staying clean.

Courts have come to varying conclusions as to whether or not a person fired for failing a drug test will be entitled to unemployment benefits, or will be deemed to have been terminated for misconduct. For example, an Idaho employee who failed a drug test was held ineligible for benefits: the employer clearly communicated its legitimate business interests in maintaining a drug-free workplace and in employees refraining even from off-premises use of illegal drugs. [*Desilet*, Unempl. Ins. Rep. (CCH) ¶ 8499 (Idaho 2006)]

But if the drug-free workplace policy is not explicit enough [*Comer*, Unempl. Ins. Rep. (CCH) ¶ 8635 (Mo. App. 2006)], or if the employer fails to demonstrate the validity of the test itself [*Owen County*, Unempl. Ins. Rep. (CCH) ¶ 8607 (Ind. App. 2006)], then benefits might be available.

An unemployment insurance claimants who successfully appealed a denial of benefits could not get damages against his ex-employer under the state drug testing law, because the statute made an exception for drug tests required by federal law, and he had worked for a government contractor with a federal testing mandate. [*Welcher*, Unempl. Ins. Rep. (CCH) ¶ 9085 (Ia. App. 2006)]

## [C]   Tobacco Issues

Tobacco is a drug, albeit a legal one. Some employers are providing incentives to encourage employees to stop smoking (e.g., paying for smoking cessation classes or offering a bonus); others are imposing penalties on those who smoke (e.g., higher insurance premiums), even outside the workplace, or requiring nicotine testing as part of the pre-employment drug test. It is becoming increasingly common for employers to increase the health care cost obligations of employees who smoke, are overweight, and/or have high cholesterol. Towers Watson found that, of 248 major employers, 19% imposed such penalties in 2011—twice as many as two years earlier. Mercer reported that about one-third of employers with 500 or more employees offer financial incentives for participating in wellness programs. Wal-Mart has imposed a $2,000 annual surcharge on some smokers, which can be avoided only if their doctor attests that quitting would be impossible or medically contraindicated; some other companies waive the extra charge if the employee enrolls in a tobacco cessation program. [Reed Abelson, *Smokers Penalized with Health Insurance Premiums*, NYTimes.com (Nov. 16, 2011)]

At least 30 states have "lawful activities" statutes that protect employees who smoke away from the worksite from discrimination. However, some companies refuse to hire smokers; others fire employees who are found to smoke (even off-site), and sometimes employers deliberately refrain from asking job applicants because they assume smokers will lie. [Jeremy Smerd, *Smoker? Can't Work Here, More Firms Say*, workforce.com (Nov. 9, 2007) (benefitslink.com)]

## § 26.04   CRIMINAL RECORD AND CREDIT CHECKS

A federal law, the Fair Credit Reporting Act (FCRA), [15 U.S.C. § 1681] as amended by the Consumer Credit Reporting Reform Act of 1996, [Pub. L. No. 104-208] governs the access of businesses to credit reports. Although credit reports are most commonly used in the context of loans or merchandise sales, it is also fairly common for potential employers to run a credit check before making a job offer.

Under the FCRA, employers must notify applicants before they seek credit information as part of the application process. A civil penalty is imposed for ordering a credit check without the mandatory notification. The employer must also notify applicants and employees before any negative employment-related action is taken on the basis of an investigative credit report.

The FCRA allows credit reporting agencies to disclose the information they have gathered to companies that use the information for "employment purposes," i.e., evaluating the subject of the credit report for employment, promotion, retention as an employee, or reassignment. The reporting agency is allowed to furnish a report discussing the job applicant's or employee's creditworthiness, standing, character, and reputation.

As a result of the Dodd-Frank Act, Pub. L. No. 111-203, starting July 21, 2011, employers have been required to inform job applicants whenever the employer has obtained the applicant's credit scores, and those scores have had an adverse effect on the employer's decision on the application.

In addition to federal regulation of the use of credit reports, some states impose additional requirements on employer use of credit reports.

2003 legislation, the Fair and Accurate Credit Transactions Act (FACTA; Pub. L. No. 108-159) amends 15 U.S.C § 1681a, enacting a new subsection (x) under which a communication will not be treated as a consumer report (and therefore will not be subject to FCRA requirements) if it is a job-related communication not related to the creditworthiness of the individual. The communication must be made to the employer as part of an investigation of suspected workplace misconduct, or under the employer's pre-existing policies or under any law or regulation. To qualify for the exemption, the information must be disclosed only to the employer or to government officials or self-regulatory officials—unless broader disclosure is mandated by law. If the employer uses the information as the basis of any adverse action against the subject of the investigation, the subject must be furnished a summary of the information. The employer, however, is not obligated to disclose the sources of the information.

Under the Intelligence Reform and Terrorism Prevention Act of 2004, Pub. L. No. 108-458 (Dec. 17, 2004), private employers can access the FBI criminal records database to obtain information about employees or applicants for private security jobs. The statute applies to full-time or part-time, uniformed or non-uniformed, armed or unarmed personnel, but not to persons hired to monitor electronic security systems. Section 6403 of the statute provides that, on the written consent of the employee or applicant, the employer can submit fingerprints or other means of identification to the state's investigative agency for a background check. (States can opt out of the background check system by passing a law, or if the state governor issues an order to this effect.) The United States Attorney General has the power to respond to a request from the state agency to view the FBI data. Then the state investigative agency notifies the employer whether, in the previous 10 years, the employee or applicant has been convicted of a felony, an offense involving dishonesty, or a false statement. Employers must be notified of offenses involving physical force against another person in the previous 10 years, as well as any unresolved felony charges within the previous 365 days. The employer has an obligation to disclose the information to the employee. [See also § 23.08]

The Supreme Court unanimously upheld the standard background check procedure that the Department of Commerce requires of government contractors. The standard background check requires employees to answer whether they used, possessed, supplied, or manufactured illegal drugs in the past year. If so, they must provide information about any treatment or counseling received. Employees are also required to sign a release for personal information from schools and employers. The government submits a questionnaire to employees' references, asking about adverse information and reasons to question the employee's honesty or truthfulness. The Supreme Court found these inquiries reasonable, and the Privacy Act limits disclosure of the information to the public. [*NASA v. Nelson*, 131 S. Ct. 746 (2011); see Rebecca Moore, *High Court Rejects Federal Contract Workers Challenge to Background Checks*, plansponsor.com (Jan. 20, 2011)]

The increasing prevalence of outsourcing to cut labor costs raises questions about whether the employer or the staffing agency is responsible for background checks. Clearly, both are at risk of being sued in connection with any harm caused by an outsourced worker. It is prudent for employers to get background checks at least on anyone who works in clients' homes; has access to trade secrets, bank accounts, or Social Security numbers; or works with children or the elderly. Employers that work through agencies should get the staffing agency to agree to indemnify the worksite employer, carry adequate insurance, and name the worksite employer as an additional insured. [Tresa Baldas, *Outsourced Employees Triggering More Suits*, Nat'l L.J. (Feb. 22, 2006) (law.com)]

The EEOC's position expressed in April 2012 enforcement guidance, is that a blanket refusal to hire based on the applicant's credit reports or criminal records is illegal if it has a disparate impact on racial minorities. The Department of Justice reported that the percentage of black people in the prison population is more than three times as high as the percentage of black people in the overall population. In 2008, the incarceration rate for Latinos was 2.3 times, and for African Americans, six times as high as for Caucasians. The EEOC's position is that employer's considering criminal history must consider the nature of the job, how serious the offense was, and how long ago it occurred. [EEOC Enforcement Guidance, *Consideration of Arrest and Conviction Records In Employment Decisions Under Title VII of the Civil Rights Act of 1964* <http://www.eeoc.gov/laws/guidance/arrest_conviction.cfm> (Apr. 25, 2012); see Steven Greenhouse, *Equal Opportunity Panel Updates Hiring Policy*, NYTimes.com (Apr. 25, 2012)]

But the EEOC lost a suit in the District Court for the District of Maryland, which dismissed an EEOC suit against Freeman Co., one of several companies sued by the EEOC for discriminating against black applicants in their use of criminal record and credit checks. The district court ruled that Freeman's practices were reasonable and were justified by the need to hire and retain honest workers. [*EEOC v. Freeman Co.*,No. 09-CV-2573 (D.Md. Aug. 9, 2013)]

Although the Third Circuit was uncomfortable with "bright-line" tests (refusal to hire any person with a criminal conviction), the court accepted the employer's business necessity defense because the plaintiff did not rebut testimony about risk due to hiring convicted persons. [*El v. Se. Penn. Transit Auth.*, 479 F.3d 232 (3d Cir. 2007)]

In addition to records of convictions, large-scale databases track accusations of theft placed against employees. The FTC is studying these databases to determine whether they violate the Fair Credit Reporting Act, and whether accused thieves are given an appropriate chance to dispute the charges. [Jessica Silver-Greenberg, *Retailers Track Employee Thefts in Vast Databases*, NYTimes.com (Apr. 2, 2013)]

## § 26.05   GENETIC TESTING

In addition to a variety of state laws, Congress adopted protection against genetic discrimination in the Genetic Information Nondisclosure Act (GINA; Pub. L. No. 110-233). The statute forbids discrimination on the basis of genetic predisposition to disease, but not disease already manifested. Genetic discrimination cases require use of the Title VII process, including the requirement of a Right to Sue letter. The federal law does not preempt more protective state laws. [Jane Zhang and Shirley S. Wang, *Bill on Genetic Bias Advances*, Wall St. J., Apr. 25, 2008, at A11]

Title I of GINA applies to group health plans maintained by private employers, as well as to unions, government employers, and insurers. Title II applies to entities covered by Title VII. GINA Title II prohibits the use of genetic information in employment and restricts the acquisition and disclosure of genetic information. The EEOC was empowered to issue regulations under Title II of GINA, and to enforce it, effective November 21, 2009, for employers of 15 or more employees.

The EEOC proposed regulations on March 2, 2009, clarifying the definition of "genetic information" and providing guidance on proper use of the information. A party subject to Title II of GINA is permitted to obtain genetic information only if it was:

- Acquired inadvertently (e.g., volunteered by the employee, or overheard);

- Aggregate information, not individually identifiable, stemming from genetic counseling at a wellness program;

- Information given to an employer to certify eligibility for leave;

- Information from genetic monitoring required by law (e.g., by OSHA);

- Voluntarily authorized in writing by the employee.

There is a limited exception for information obtained by law enforcement or the military to assist in genetic identification, and for publicly available information.

In order to prevent genetic markers for a disease being treated as preexisting conditions, the regulations define "manifestation of disease" as a condition that has been or reasonably could be diagnosed by a health care professional. Therefore, the presence of a genetic marker, even one that assures that the individual is certain to develop the disease in the future, is not a manifestation of disease.

However, even if the employer has obtained the information legitimately, the information must be kept confidential and must not be used to discriminate. Genetic information (except publicly available information) must be kept in a separate, confidential file rather than in an ordinary personnel file.

Genetic information can be disclosed only to the person it relates to; to an occupational health researcher carrying out research pursuant to federal regulations; or in response to a court order that specifically calls for information. However, information may not be disclosed in response to a discovery request that is not under a court order (e.g., a party in a lawsuit asks for the information). Disclosure is permitted to government officials assessing the company's GINA compliance, in connection with a request for leave, or to officials investigating contagious disease or an imminent hazard of death or life-threatening illness.

Employers should make sure that doctors avoid questions about family medical history in post-offer, pre-employment medical examinations and fitness for duty exams. Nor may genetic information be obtained in connection with the interactive process of establishing reasonable accommodation to disability.

■ **TIP:**  The EEOC says that the best practice for an employer asking for documentation of disability is to state in the request that genetic information, including family medical history, should not be provided.

Employers were required to begin posting the official GINA information no later than November 21, 2009. [RIN 3046-AA84, 74 Fed. Reg. 9056 (Mar. 2, 2009); see Margaret Hart Edwards, *Proposed Regulations Under Federal Genetic Information Nondiscrimination Act (GINA) Suggest Employer Action Now*, LittlerASAPs, <http://www.littler.com/PressPublications/Lists/ASAPs/DispAsaps.aspx?id=1344&asapType=National> (March 2009)]

The EEOC published a final rule on recordkeeping requirements under GINA. As of April 3, 2012, companies with 15 or more employees must retain all personnel and employment records relating to GINA for at least one year. If charges are filed under GINA, relevant documents must be retained until final disposition of the case. If an employee is involuntarily terminated, records must be kept for a year after termination. The relevant documents in this context include requests for accommodation; application forms; records of hiring, promotion, demotion, transfer, layoff, and termination; and records about terms of employment, e.g., pay, training, and tenure. [77 Fed. Reg. 5396 (Feb. 3, 2012), finalizing the Notice of Proposed Rulemaking, 76 Fed. Reg. 31892 (June 2, 2011).]

On January 17, 2013, HHS published a final rule covering the application of the HIPAA privacy rule to GINA Titles I (health coverage) and II (employment). The final rule specifies that genetic information is considered health information, which cannot be used for insurance underwriting purposes other than for long-term care insurance policies. [Katherine Georger, *New HIPAA Final Rule Implements GINA Restriction on Use and Disclosure of Genetic Information for Underwriting Purposes*, Holland & Hart LLP News Update (Jan. 23, 2013) (benefitslink.com)]

The EEOC settled a GINA case against Fabricant, Inc. in May, 2013 for $50,000. This was the EEOC's first suit under this statute. The EEOC filed its first class action GINA suit in the same month. Genetic discrimination is one of the six priorities listed in the EEOC's Strategic Enforcement Plan. [*EEOC v. Founders Pavilion*,No. 6-13-cv-06250 (W.D.N.Y. filed 2013); see Sue Reisinger, *EEOC Gets Tough With Companies on Genetic Privacy*,Corporate Counsel (May 23, 2013) (law.com)]

## § 26.06  SEARCHES AND SURVEILLANCE

### [A]  Constitutional Limits on Employees

Although the Constitution puts limits on unreasonable searches and seizures, the focus is on the activities of public agencies such as the police and the military. Therefore, it is very unlikely that the actions of a private employer would have a constitutional dimension, or that the employee would be able to invoke the Fourth Amendment as protection against searches and seizures.

It is becoming more common for employers to use tracking devices (such as sensors that employees wear around their necks, or placed on furniture) to find out how employees work and what can be done to enhance productivity. Companies that use these devices handle privacy issues by letting employees opt out of tracking or by pointing out that employees' movements can already be tracked with smartphones and ID badges. [*Tracking Sensors Invade the Workplace*, WSJ. com (Mar. 6, 2013)]

However, an employer's surveillance activities might constitute an invasion of privacy, which could furnish grounds for a suit by an employee.

An employer can legitimately order a workplace search if there is a good reason in the first place (such as getting evidence of embezzlement, theft of products, or other work-related misconduct) and the scope of the search is appropriate to satisfying that purpose. But, because the employer controls the workplace but employees control their own personal possessions such as coats and handbags, get legal advice about how to handle a search.

Surveillance programs are most likely to survive legal challenge if:

- They are created in response to a real problem (e.g., inventory shrinkage) or a real threat (e.g., potential employer liability);

- Employees are accurately informed of the purposes and content of the program;

- Surveillance is restricted to the least intrusive method that is still effective.

The Third Circuit ruled that Labor Management Relations Act (LMRA) § 301 does not preempt state laws about wiretaps and privacy, so state tort claims about workplace surveillance are not ruled out. Suit was brought to protest audio and video surveillance of the time clock area that was imposed without notice to the employees. The court held that it is not necessary to interpret the CBA to determine whether surveillance violated employee rights; merely looking at the CBA to see if it has a surveillance clause is not a contract interpretation. Tort claims are preempted by LMRA § 301 only if they involve a duty of care imposed by a CBA. [*Kline v. Sec. Guards Inc.*, 386 F.3d 246 (3d Cir. 2004)]

The First Circuit says that it does not violate the Fourth Amendment for a public employer to use silent video cameras for surveillance of the work area. In this case, the work environment was an open space with no assigned offices, cubicles, workstations, or desks, so the court concluded that it would not be reasonable to assume that privacy would be available in such an environment. [*Vega-Rodriguez v. P.R. Tel. Co.*, 110 F.3d 174 (1st Cir. 1997)]

The Supreme Court of Illinois held that it was an invasion of privacy when North American Corp. hired investigators to find out if ex-employee Kathleen Lawlor had raided its clients after she changed jobs. The investigators hired a detective agency that impersonated Lawlor in order to get her telephone records. The court said that North American Corp. was vicariously liable for the tort of invasion upon seclusion. The company's counterclaims against Lawlor for breach of fiduciary duty were dismissed. Lawlor was originally awarded $1.75 million punitive damages, but the court reduced the punitive damage award to $65,000. [*Lawlor v. North Am. Corp.*, 2012 IL 112530 (Ill. Oct. 18, 2012), *reh'g denied* (Jan. 28, 2013); see Leigh Jones, *Company Held Liable for Privacy Invasion in Employee Probe*, Nat'l L.J. (Mar. 5, 2013) (law.com)]

However, in a unionized company, it might be an unfair labor practice to install surveillance devices, at least without the consent of the union. In 1997, the NLRB decided [*Colgate-Palmolive Co.*, 323 N.L.R.B. 82 (1997)] that installation of hidden surveillance cameras is a mandatory bargaining subject, not a management decision. To the NLRB, only subjects like product lines and capital investments are management prerogatives.

Early in 2002, the Supreme Court permitted unionized employees to sue in state court for invasion of privacy because of video surveillance of company bathrooms. The employer, a trucking company, said that the cameras were installed to frustrate drug dealing and drug use, and were not aimed at urinals or bathroom stalls. The issue in *Consolidated Freightways v. Cramer* [534 U.S. 1078 (2002)] was whether LMRA § 301 preempts the state law forbidding undisclosed videotaping of employees. The Supreme Court held that it does not, so state-law suits can go forward—even though the case might be interpreted as involving interpretation of a collective bargaining agreement (the usual test for LMRA § 301 preemption).

The NLRB ruled that it was a violation of federal labor law to install hidden surveillance cameras, without bargaining in a room where the employer suspected illegal drugs were sold. The NLRB ordered the company to bargain on the issue. [*Anheuser-Busch Inc.*, 324 NLRB No. 49 (July 22, 2004)]

In 2005, the D.C. Circuit ruled that surveillance, as a subject plainly germane to the work environment, is a mandatory bargaining subject because it is not within the core of entrepreneurial control. However, the court ruled that while the employer must bargain over the use of cameras and the general reason why surveillance is necessary, the employer is not obligated to inform the union of the location of the cameras or when they will be in use. The D.C. Circuit remanded the case to determine whether the employees observed on the videotape would be entitled to individualized relief if the employer discovered their misconduct unlawfully. [*Brewers and Maltsters v. NLRB*, 414 F.3d 36 (D.C. Cir. 2005); *Nat'l Steel Corp. v. NLRB*, 324 F.3d 928 (7th Cir. 2003) (also treats surveillance cameras as a mandatory bargaining subject)]

Video surveillance of employees is fairly common—e.g., to determine if employees are performing tasks that they claim are impossible because of job-related injuries. Sometimes employers use surveillance to monitor suspected abuse of FMLA leave. Investigators have found some employees engaging in sports, doing yard work, or holding another job. According to attorneys for the employees, the surveillance constitutes harassment, intimidation, and interference with FMLA rights. They point out that a person can have a serious health condition without being absolutely bedridden—and surveillance often operates during hours when the employee would not be at work. Employers say that FMLA leave, especially intermittent leave, is often abused.

However, such surveillance is usually upheld by the courts. For example, *Vail v. Raybestos*, 533 F.3d 904 (7th Cir. 2008) upheld surveillance of an employee who took leave for migraines and was found to run a lawn service on the side; the court said that the surveillance provided the employer with an honest suspicion about the validity of the leave request. In *Crouch v. Whirlpool*, 447 F.3d 984 (7th Cir. 2006), the Seventh Circuit upheld the validity of videotaping a suspected leave abuser, who was caught doing yard work and flying to Las Vegas when he was off work due to a knee injury. The pending case *Wiemer v. Honda*, No. 2:06-cv-00844 (S.D. Ohio), involves an employee who suffered a concussion, then was fired after he was videotaped building a new porch for his house. He sued for FMLA retaliation, claiming that he was waiting for clearance from his doctor to return to work. [Tresa Baldas, *Spying Employers Raise Legal Hackles*, Nat'l L.J. (Aug. 19, 2008) (law.com)]

The Pennsylvania Superior Court ruled in mid-2010 that it was not an invasion of privacy to tape a WC claimant while he was praying at his mosque. The court said that WC claimants have a diminished expectation of privacy and know that they might be investigated. Pennsylvania law is not clear about the amount of privacy required in religious settings; the lower court treated the mosque as a public place. The plaintiff was praying right in front of a plate glass window, and the investigator was lawfully present in the parking lot across from the mosque. [*Tagouma v. Investigative Consultant Servs. Inc.*, 2010 Pa. Super. 147 (Pa. Super. Aug. 10, 2010); see Rebecca Moore, *Videotaping Workers Comp Claimant Praying not Invasion of Privacy*, plansponsor.com (Aug. 16, 2010)]

## [B] Wiretapping

Wiretapping, and other forms of interception of wire, oral, and electronic communications, including e-mail (or electronic or mechanical interception of conversations) are covered by the federal Omnibus Crime Control and Safe Streets Act of 1968. [18 U.S.C. §§ 2511 *et seq.*] Interceptions by the employer are regulated. Interceptions are prohibited only if the employee had a reasonable expectation that the communication would not be subject to interception.

For instance, if a telephone salesperson has known from the beginning of the job that contact with customers is subject to monitoring, there would be no reasonable expectation of privacy. But even if interception of calls is legitimate, the employer must cease the interception if it is clear that a particular call is personal and not business-related. One of the parties to a communication has a right to intercept it; so does anyone with explicit or implicit consent to intercept.

The federal statute imposes penalties for improper interception that can be as high as $10,000. Punitive damages can be imposed on an employer that acted wantonly, recklessly, or maliciously.

The Connecticut Supreme Court ruled in early 2010 that fire inspectors do not have a private right of action under the state's electronic monitoring statute. The law requires prior written notice to employees before electronic monitoring of activities. However, the statute does not provide any specific civil or administrative remedy to employees who are monitored contrary to the law. The state labor commissioner can impose a penalty if an administrative hearing shows a violation, but there is no mechanism for employees to report violations, much less to bring suit. [Rebecca Moore, *Fire Inspectors Cannot Sue Over City's GPS Monitoring*, plansponsor.com (Feb. 1, 2010)]

## [C] Internet and E-Mail Monitoring

Apart from the fact that employees are not supposed to use the company computer system for personal purposes, employee e-mails can subject the employer to liability (in the context of sexual or racial harassment, for example, or concealment of improprieties). See § 27.06for discussion of the human resources implications of social networking.

State and federal wiretap statutes typically include a "provider exception," under which the provider of communications is allowed to intercept messages on the system. An employer is clearly a provider when it owns the equipment on which the employees communicate.

Most employers have broad policies that warn employees that e-mails can be monitored, usually stated in the employee handbook or displayed on the log-in screen for the e-mail system. Software is now available to mechanize e-mail monitoring, so the IT department will not have to do so manually. E-mail monitoring usually begins only after there has been a problem, such as an allegation of harassment or misuse of proprietary information. Employees should probably be informed that their e-mail has been read, which has the effect of reinforcing the employer's e-mail policy. [Shannon Green, *When Should Employers Be Monitoring Employee Email?* Corporate Counsel (Mar. 13, 2013) (law.com)]

In late 2007, the NLRB voted 3-2 to permit employers to restrict the use of the company e-mail system for union organizing campaigns and distributing union news, on the grounds that personal use of the e-mail system can be restricted. However, to be valid, a ban on personal use must be evenly applied, not limited to union applications. [The Guard Publishing Company d/b/a The Register-Guard and Eugene Newspaper Guild, CWA Local 37194. Cases 36–CA–8743-1, 36–CA–8849-1, 36–CA–8789-1, and 36–CA–8842-1] The D.C. Circuit upheld the NLRB's Unfair Labor Practice decision when a newspaper disciplined the union president for sending three union-related e-mails to co-workers. Although the newspaper's e-mail policy forbade using the system for commercial ventures, religious or political causes, or outside organizations, the NLRB found that personal e-mails were common and did not result in discipline. The D.C. Circuit said that the policy did not rule out sending union e-mails that merely clarified facts about a union rally and did not call for action. [*Guard Publishing Co. v. NLRB*, 571 F.3d 53 (D.C. Cir. 2009)]

According to the Iowa District Court, discharge for violation of the corporate e-mail policy constitutes disqualifying misconduct that will prevent the receipt of unemployment insurance benefits (and therefore will not result in deterioration of the employer's experience rating). [*Mercer*, Unempl. Ins. Rep. (CCH) ¶ 9042 (Iowa Dist. Ct. 2002) (the discharged employees continued sending sexually explicit e-mails after receiving a warning—also e-mailed—from their supervisor; they had signed the employer's procedures for Internet, e-mail, and telephone usage at work, so they were familiar with the rules)]

In June 2010, the Supreme Court made its first ruling on privacy issues related to workplace texting. However, the Supreme Court kept its ruling narrow. It decided that it was reasonable, under the Fourth Amendment, for the city of Ontario to perform an audit of employees' messages on pagers owned by the city to determine if the city should upgrade to a plan giving employees more minutes on their pagers. The Supreme Court declined to decide the broader issue of whether the plaintiff, a police sergeant who sent private messages (some of them sexually oriented) on his work-issued pager, had a reasonable expectation of privacy in those text messages. The decision concentrated on whether the search of the pagers was legitimate, work-related, and not excessive in scope; because it was, the Supreme Court ruled in favor of the city. [*Ontario v. Quon*, 130 S. Ct. 2619 (2010); see Tony Mauro, *Supreme Court Allows Search of Employee's City-Owned Pager*, Nat'l L.J. (June 18, 2010) (law.com)]

Some cases hold that employees have a greater expectation of privacy when:

- The employer allows some personal use of the electronic network, but imposes imprecise standards such as "subject to the highest standards of morality" (e.g., *Bowman v. Butler Township Board of Trustees*, 2009 Ohio 6128 (Ohio App. Nov. 20, 2009);

- The employer is a multi-national corporation, and reviews electronic communications of employees located in the European Union, even though they are protected by EU law (Directive 2002/58/EC);

- The employee was disciplined for communications not made during work hours, and not made on the employer's system (e.g., N.Y. Lab. Law § 201-d(2)(a); Cal. Lab. Code §§ 1101–1102);

- The company is subject to a collective bargaining agreement that limits electronic monitoring, and the employer fails to comply.

However, in some circumstances there might even be a duty to monitor—for example, if the employer is on notice of unlawful usage of the network that could be harmful to others such as accessing child pornography, or creating a hostile work environment by displaying pornography on the corporate computer system. See, e.g., *Doe v. XYC Corp.*, 887 A.2d 1156 (N.J. Super. 2005). Note also that FTC guidelines at 16 C.F.R. Part 255 that took effect December 1, 2009 make employers liable for failure to create and enforce policies restricting employees from endorsing the employer's products on a blog or social networking site without disclosing the employee's relationship to the employer. [Daniel L. Prywes, *Electronic Privacy and the Supreme Court*, The Corporate Counselor (Feb. 9, 2010) (law.com)]

A number of states (including California, Colorado, and New York) have statutes that forbid employers from disciplining employees for lawful conduct that they engage in off company premises. However, there are exceptions for conduct reasonably related to the employee's job, or when the conduct creates a conflict of interest for the employer (for example, with respect to trade secrets) or impairs the employer's business interests. Several states (Connecticut, Louisiana, New York, South Carolina, Washington, and the District of Columbia) forbid discipline on the basis of engaging in political activities or speech.

Proskauer Rose's second annual "Social Media in the Workplace Around the World 2.0" report says that, in 2012, more than two-thirds of employers (68.9%) had specific social media policies whereas only about half did a year earlier (55.1%). Looking at a group of 250 multinational corporations, social media monitoring rose from 27.4% in 2010 to 35.8% in 2011. More than half (52.1%) of employers allowed employees to access their personal social media accounts on company equipment, during work time, for non-work purposes; the percentage was 48.3% in 2011. About one-third of employers (31.3% in 2011, 35% in 2012) have taken disciplinary action against one or more employees because of misuse of social media. Employers have wide latitude to regulate employees' use of social media on behalf of the corporation. For example, a sound policy would require employees to have the company's permission to set up a work-sponsored account, and the employer should disclose clearly that it owns the content, connections, screen names, and passwords for the account—and has the right to monitor communications on the corporate network, other than communications involving protected activity (e.g., union organization). Employees are required to respect the confidentiality of trade secrets and proprietary information, even when they are using personal accounts outside the workplace. [Catherine Dunn, *More Employers Creating Social Media Policies for the Workplace*, Corporate Counsel (Nov. 29, 2012) (law.com).]

Six states—most recently California and Illinois—have laws forbidding employers to ask employee or job applicants for their social networking passwords. [Steven Greenhouse, *Employers' Social Media Policies Come Under Regulatory Scrutiny*, NYTimes.com (Jan. 21, 2013); see also Todd Ruger, *Senators Ask Feds to Investigate Employer Requests for Social Media Passwords*, The BLT: The Blog of Legal Times (Mar. 26, 2012) (law.com)]

The NLRB started coming to grips with social media issues in October 2010.

An August 18, 2011 Office of General Counsel memo cleared up some issues about social media in the workplace, although there are still no appellate decisions to provide final guidance. Social media policies are generally tested under a reasonableness standard to see if they are impermissibly vague or overbroad or if they chill employees' exercise of their rights under the NLRA.

In 2011, more than 100 employers, including Wal-Mart and a BMW dealership, had been the subject of worker charges about social media. The NLRB found merit in about half the complaints, and usually filed a civil complaint that was sent to an ALJ. Of 39 cases reviewed in November 2011, 51% were sent to an ALJ and 14 were still under review. The other charges were settled, withdrawn, or remained under investigation in an NLRB regional office.

An NLRB ALJ ordered Hispanics United of Buffalo to reinstate five employees who were fired after posting Facebook complaints about work. The ALJ held that the terminated employees engaged in protected concerted activity because they discussed job performance and staffing levels. It was not required that they make a formal effort to change working conditions or communicate their concerns to the employer. One employee put a co-worker's allegation that the organization didn't do enough to help its clients on Facebook. Other employees replied, saying they did the best they could under adverse conditions. The five respondents were fired for harassing the original poster. [Tara Cantore, *Employer Ordered to Reinstate Employees Fired for Facebook Posts*, plansponsor.com (Oct. 17, 2011).]

The NLRB's analysis asks whether the activity was concerted (done with or on the authority of other employees). Posts surveying co-workers about workplace issues and sharing concerns about income tax withholding at the workplace have been held to be concerted activity—but complaining to a relative about compensation and tip practices or personal complaints about a dispute with a supervisor have been held not to be concerted activity. Once other employees reply, the possibility of concerted activity becomes stronger. The NLRB has found protected activity when employees asked co-workers about their commissions or the implications of work disputes. However, tweets about public safety issues by a newspaper reporter or an employee's derogatory comments about mental patients when he was alone on the night shift have been held not to be protected.

Initially protected activity can lose protection if the employee is guilty of severe disloyalty or if the statement is reckless or maliciously untrue. The employer can also prevail even if the activity is protected and protection has not been lost—if the adverse action would have been taken even absent protected concerted activity. [Michael C. Schmidt, *Deciphering the NLRB's Stance on Social Media Issues,* N.Y.L.J. (Oct. 24, 2011) (law.com). The NLRB's *Operations Management Memo* discusses seven social media cases: NLRB, Memorandum OM 12-31, *Acting General Counsel Issues Second Social Media Report* (Jan. 24, 2012) (benefitslink.com)]

A third NLRB social media report, issued May 30, 2012, focuses on whether the employer's restrictions chill the rights granted to employees by NLRA § 7—i.e., whether employees are forbidden to discuss workplace conditions or criticize the employer. [<http://www.mynlrb.gov/link/document.aspx/09031d4580a375cd>; see Jenna Greene, *NLRB Report on Social Media Highlights Overbroad Employer Restrictions*, The BLT (May 30, 2012) (law.com)]

A March 2012 Advice Memorandum from the NLRB's Office of the General Counsel said that Giant Food's social media policy constrained protected employee activity to the extent that it forbade use of the employer's logo, graphics, and trademark, and forbade photographing or video-recording the facility. However, it was legitimate for the policy to encourage employees to report violations of the policy to management. [*Giant Food LLC*,Cases 05-CA-064793, 05-CA-065187, and 05-CA-064795, <http://www.nlrb.gov/case-05-CA-064793> (Mar. 21, 2012)]

Another issue is whether the employer is entitled to access e-mails sent on its system that the employee claims are entitled to attorney-client privilege (for example, when an employee communicates with his or her attorney about a Title VII suit against the employer). See, e.g.,

- E-mails were not privileged because the employee was aware of the employer's policy (that the e-mail system was restricted to use for business only, and the employer retained the right to access and disclose communications on the system) *Scott v. Beth Israel Med. Ctr. Inc.*, 17 Misc. 3d 934 (N.Y. Sup. 2007).

- E-mails sent to the employee's lawyer on a personal, password-protected, Web-based Yahoo account on a laptop issued by the employer were held to be privileged in *Stengart v. Loving Care Agency Inc.*, 973 A.2d 390 (N.J. Super. A.D. July 29, 2009), *aff'd*, 201 N.J. 300 (2010). Although the employee handbook reserved the right to review, intercept, and disclose anything in the company "media system" at any time, the court ruled that "media system" was an ambiguous term that would not justify access to personal data—especially since company policy allowed occasional personal use of company computers. The court said that public policy supports attorney-client privilege in e-mails.

- E-mails to the employee's attorney were privileged although sent on the employer's computer, because there was no policy against personal use, and the employee password-protected the e-mails and kept them in a separate folder: *People v. Jiang*, 131 Cal. App. 4th 1027, 33 Cal. Rptr. 184 (2005).

- *Pure Power Boot Camp Inc. v. Warrior Fitness Boot Camp*, LLC, 587 F. Supp. 2d, 548 (S.D.N.Y. 2008) holds that it violated the Stored Communications Act to access a former employee's Hotmail e-mails from the company computer without consent. Although the employee was on notice that company computers could be searched for evidence of personal use, he did not know that his Web-based e-mail accounts like Hotmail could be included. The court held that the company policy did not waive privacy rights in Web-based accounts. [Anthony E. Davis, Attorney-Client Privilege in Work E-Mails N.Y.L.J. (Nov. 5, 2009) (law. com); on the *Stengart* affirmance, see Michael Booth, *Privilege Trumps Company E-Mail Surveillance*, N.J.L.J. (Apr. 1, 2010) (law.com)]

## [D]  Identification Numbers

It is convenient, but not always good policy, to use Social Security numbers as employee IDs. Business is becoming more and more internationalized, so overseas personnel will not have Social Security numbers. The European Union's privacy requirements are quite stringent, and must be obeyed when doing business outside of the United States. [See Susan J. Wells, *You've Got Their Numbers— And They Want Them Back*, HR Magazine, Dec. 1998, at 3] Wells suggests choosing an identification system that does not rely on Social Security numbers or nine-digit numbers that could be confused with Social Security numbers. For most companies, a six-digit number (which allows 999,999 options!) will be satisfactory. It's better to assign numbers at random, not sequentially. If the numbers are assigned based on hiring dates, a hacker who knows when some people were hired could guess other employees' numbers. Your payroll and database programs impose standards: You may have to start each ID number with a number not a zero, blank space, or character such as an asterisk or ampersand.

## [E] How-Tos for Employers

Attorney Jonathan A. Segal. [Jonathan A. Segal, *Security vs. Privacy*, HR Magazine, Feb. 2002, at 93; *Searching for Answers*, HR Magazine, March 2000, at 59] provides some useful guidance for employers:

- Notify employees that working areas in the workplace are not private, and employees and their belongings are subject to search there, to rebut later charges that employees felt their reasonable expectation of privacy was violated or that private information about them was made public;

- Inform employees that their cars can be searched when they are parked on company property;

- Make it clear that the employer has the right to search employees' lockers, even if they are locked (providing the locks can reinforce this message as well as making it easier to open them when needed);

- Reserve the right to search all employees, not just individuals on the basis of reasonable suspicion. However, given the potential for hostility, in practice searches should only be done in emergencies, or on a reasonable suspicion basis;

- Impose a work rule that refusal to be searched will be considered serious misconduct that justifies termination;

- Tell workers that they do not have an expectation of privacy in their e-mails, voice mails, computer hard drives, network access, and Web usage histories on company computers, even if they have been issued, or have chosen, a password;

- Put a message on the voice mail system indicating that messages can be recorded and reviewed. This puts outsiders as well as employees on notice that there is potential for monitoring;

- Ask employees for their written consent to monitoring of telephone conversations and voice mail;

- Inform employees that mail that they have addressed to them at the workplace can be opened by the employer—even if it is marked Personal or Confidential. (Federal law makes it illegal to obstruct mail delivery—but the Post Office's position is that once mail is delivered to the workplace, it has been delivered, so the employer does not obstruct mail delivery by opening mail before the employee gets it.)

Segal points out the need to balance reserving legal rights against employees' (and perhaps customers') reactions to a full-surveillance program. He stresses the absolute need for documentation: why a search was ordered, and what it found, for instance; or the nature of an emergency that required broad-based searches without individual suspicion.

He counsels employers to rely on observed or alleged behavior, and not profiling characteristics such as race, religion, or union advocacy. Wherever possible, searches of female employees should be performed by women, and searches of male employees by males. There should be a witness to all searches, and the shop steward should be allowed access if he or she wishes to be present.

To avoid later claims of harassment or battery, don't touch employees who refuse to be searched, and don't detain employees (which could constitute false imprisonment) except in security emergencies where it is necessary to detain the employee until the police arrive.

Even if the employer has the right to monitor conversations, or to open mail, the best policy is to terminate observation once it is clear that the communication is personal.

## § 26.07   HIPAA PRIVACY RULES

Congress passed the Health Insurance Portability and Accessibility Act (HIPAA). [Pub. L. No. 104-191], covering many issues related to health insurance and health care. The statute ordered Congress to issue federal health care privacy standards by August 21, 1999. However, Congress failed to meet this deadline, which gave the Department of Health and Human Services the right to draft regulations.

HHS published a Final Rule on HIPAA enforcement in February 2006. [71 Fed. Reg. 8390 (Feb. 16, 2006), discussed in Segal Capital Checkup, *Final HIPAA Enforcement Rule*, <http://www.segalco.com/publications/capitalcheckup/031509no2.html> (Mar. 15, 2006)] HIPAA enforcement relies largely on HHS investigation of complaints of violations and efforts to obtain voluntary compliance by conciliation. Civil monetary penalties are imposed only if conciliation fails. HHS also carries out compliance reviews independent of complaints.

The HITECH Act (Health Information Technology for Information and Clinical Health Act; part of the American Recovery and Reinvestment Act of 2009, Pub. L. No. 111-5), took effect February 17, 2010, strengthening the privacy and security provisions of HIPAA, and increasing civil monetary penalties for HIPAA violations.

In an FMLA retaliation case, the employer fired the plaintiff for abusing her leave by vacationing in Mexico after her husband had surgery. The employer tried to obtain the medical records of the plaintiff and her husband. The plaintiff's attorney objected, so the employer narrowed the request down to information from the surgeon who operated on the husband, and recommended a warm climate for recovery, and said his wife was an essential person to his recovery. The plaintiff's attorney argued that the husband's medical records were protected by HIPAA—and were not even relevant because he was not a party to the suit. The District Court for the District of Connecticut agreed, entering a protective order permitting disclosure only of the husband's condition during the period between his back injury and the plaintiff's termination. The employer was forbidden to use the information for any non-litigation purpose, and was required to return it or destroy it after resolution of the suit. [*Tavares v. Lawrence & Mem'l Hosp.*, 2012 U.S. Dist. LEXIS 168221 (D Conn. Nov.27, 2012); see Wolters Kluwer Law & Business News Center, *Husband's Medical Records Must Be Disclosed To Former Employer In Employee's Lawsuit Based On FMLA* (Nov. 2, 2012) (benefitslink. com)] In a somewhat similar situation, the Eastern District of Michigan granted summary judgment for an employer who fired an employee for FMLA abuse based on vacation pictures posted to Facebook showing her engaging in physical activities. The plaintiff first claimed that she used a wheelchair in the airport to and from the trip, and then admitted this was a lie. Her dishonesty was a legitimate, non-FMLA-related reason to fire her: *Lineberry v. Detroit Med. Ctr.*, No. 11-13752 (E.D. Mich. Feb. 5, 2013).]

After issuing interim final rules in 2009 [RIN 009-AB56, 75 Fed. Reg. 42740 (Aug. 24, 2009)] and a 2010 Notice of Proposed Rulemaking dealing with privacy, security, and enforcement [RIN 009-AB56, 75 Fed. Reg. 40868 (July 14, 2010)], at the beginning of 2013, HHS' Office of Civil Rights (OCR) published an omnibus restatement of the HIPAA privacy and security rules reflecting the HITECH Act Amendments. Covered entities and their contractors and subcontractors are subject to civil and criminal penalties for violations of the privacy, security, and breach notification rules. Security breaches must be reported to HHS each year and large-scale breaches must also be reported to the individuals involved and to the news media. There are requirements for using encryption and destruction of obsolete information to prevent unauthorized persons from accessing protected health information (PHI).

Penalties for failure to notify individuals of breach of their PHI and failure to notify the media when required have increased. The penalty ranges between $100 and $50,000 per violation in situations where the covered entity did not know of the violation (and could not have known by exercising reasonable diligence). If there was reasonable cause for the violation and there was no willful neglect, the penalty range is $1,000 to $50,000. Where willful neglect occurred, the penalty range is $10,000–$50,000 if the violation was corrected on a timely basis—and at least $50,000 for offenses of willful neglect that were not timely corrected.

However, in each penalty category, there is a cap of $1.5 million on total penalties for all violations of the same provision. The actual penalty imposed within the penalty range for a particular offense depends on factors such as the nature and extent of the violation and the extent of the harm it caused. [78 Fed. Reg. 5566 (Jan. 25, 2013); see Cynthia Marcotte Stamer, Solutions Law Press HR & Benefits Update, *OCR Publishes Long-Anticipated Omnibus Restatement of HIPAA Privacy, Security, Breach Notification & Enforcement Rules* (Jan. 13, 2013) (benefitslink.com); Katherine Georger, Holland & Hart LLP News Update, *New HIPAA Final Rule Implements GINA Restriction on Use and Disclosure of Genetic Information for Underwriting Purposes* (Jan. 23, 2013) (benefitslink. com)]

There is no private right of action for violation of the HIPAA privacy rules (i.e., employees cannot sue if they claim their PHI was improperly disclosed or used). Instead, enforcement is the province of government agencies—HHS in the civil context, the Department of Justice in the criminal arena. However, under the HITECH Act, aggrieved individuals can receive a share of civil penalties collected for privacy breaches involving their data. [See, e.g., *Acara v. Banks*, 470 F.3d 569 (5th Cir. 2006); *Walker v. Gerald*, CIVIL ACTION NO. 05-6649 SECTION "B" (2), 2006 WL 1997635 (E.D. La. June 27, 2006); *Makas v. Miraglia*, 05 Civ. 7180 (DAB)(FM), 2007 WL 152092 (S.D.N.Y. Jan. 23, 2007)] A HIPAA privacy rule violation could be admissible as evidence in a private civil suit for, e.g., RICO violations or negligent infliction of emotional distress. [See, e.g., *Acosta v. Byrum*, 638 S.E.2d 246 (N.C. App. 2006). But in *Vavro v. Albers*, Civil Action No. 05-321, 2006 WL 2547350 (W.D. Pa. Aug. 31, 2006), a RICO claim failed in a case where the plaintiff charged that his property interest in his Personal Health Information was held to be violated. The court found it would be impossible to estimate the value of such intangible injuries. This issue is raised by Roy Harmon III, *HIPAA Violations as a Basis for Private Causes of Action* (Feb. 6, 2007) <http://www.healthplanlaw.com>]

In late 2011, the HHS launched a pilot program for HIPAA privacy and security audits of health plans and providers, with the intention of refining the process to undertake more audits in 2012. Covered entities that receive HIPAA audit notification letters are given only 10 business days to produce the information and documents. Entities to be audited receive 30–90 days; auditors spend three to 10 business days at the site interviewing personnel. Companies under audit are required to give the auditor a copy of its privacy and security policies. The entity is given 10 business days to review the draft report and discuss it with the auditor. A final audit report is submitted to HHS within 30 days after the reviewed entity comments. The results are supposed to be used to find entities that require technical assistance rather than to impose penalties—although, if serious compliance problems are uncovered, the HHS might address them. [Christine A. Williams, Perkins Coie News, *HIPAA Audits Come with Short Turnaround Times* (Dec. 19, 2011) (benefitslink.com)]

If the EGHP is funded by insurance and the employer-plan sponsor has no access to PHI, the insurer has full responsibility for privacy compliance. A plan sponsor that does have access to PHI has an obligation to amend the plan document to institute privacy procedures under which participants can inspect (and, if necessary, correct) their PHI and control disclosure of the PHI to others. The plan sponsor must give the plan a certificate of complying amendments and safeguards. The plan must have a privacy officer, and it must modify contracts with business associates to make sure that PHI is protected.

A self-insured or self-administered plan doesn't have an insurer in the picture to handle privacy concerns, so the plan document must be amended to control dissemination of PHI; privacy safeguards and certification are required; a privacy officer must be appointed; and business associates' access to PHI must be controlled.

■ **TIP:** The privacy rules apply only to health plans, not to other types of welfare benefit plans (for instance, short-term and long-term disability plans, Worker's Compensation, and sick pay) even though administering these plans requires insight into the health status of employees.

With one important exception (self-insured plans) EGHPs are not directly affected by the privacy rules. The theme of the HIPAA privacy rules is that the individual must give specific authorization before a covered entity can use protected health information for any reason other than payment, treatment, or health care operations. State health care laws are not preempted if they furnish even greater protection of patient confidentiality.

A covered entity is a health plan, health care clearinghouse, or health care provider that ever transmits health information electronically. PHI means all individually identifiable information that is transmitted or maintained in any form by a covered entity. A group health plan is permitted to disclose PHI to a plan sponsor only if the sponsor certifies to the plan that it will comply with the privacy rules about use and disclosure of the information.

A fully insured group health plan is not required to issue the Notice of Privacy Practices to its plan participants. The HMO or issuer of the plan has this responsibility. However, a self-insured plan does have to provide the Notice. For people already in the group, notice is required as of the plan's compliance date (and within 60 days after a material revision). New participants get the notice at enrollment. The notice must be written in plain English or otherwise effectively communicate how PHI can be used, and explain when the individual must authorize disclosure of information about him- or herself.

Enforcing this Regulation is the responsibility of the Department of Health and Human Services' Office of Civil Rights, which handles a spectrum of tasks from providing technical guidance and doing compliance reviews to complaint investigations, assessing civil penalties, and making referrals for criminal prosecution.

Although employers and plan sponsors of insured plans are not directly subject to these rules, they do have to restrict the way in which they collect and use personal information. When employers and sponsors receive PHI from a covered entity such as an insurer or HMO, the plan sponsor must agree to control re-use of the information. Employers are not permitted to use PHI for employment-related functions or functions for other benefit plans. The plan document must explain how PHI can be used and disclosed, and must describe the security measures adopted (e.g., having a firewall; restricting access to authorized persons).

Businesses that are covered entities under the general privacy rule are also covered entities under the security rule, and therefore obligated to ensure the confidentiality and integrity of electronic PHI (and its availability to properly authorized persons).

CHAPTER 27

# THE ROLE OF THE COMPUTER IN HR

## § 27.01  INTRODUCTION

Corporate human resource functions have always been number-intensive, from calculating a payroll to preparing reports on the nature of the workforce. Therefore, the HR department was an "early adopter" of all kinds of technology, going as far back as tabulating machines, through mainframe computers using punched cards, to the desktop PC, to today's networked systems. (Ironically, computer networks have something in common with the old-style mainframe with "dumb terminals" linked to it.)

Not only are computers used within the business, and not only are functions such as payroll preparation and tax reporting compliance often outsourced by electronic means, computerized communications continue to gain in importance. The Internet provides vast information and calculation resources for the HR department.

A corporate intranet (private computer network) can be developed to transmit information to, and receive information from, employees. Instead of printing a lengthy employee manual, then reprinting it to respond to changes in laws and corporate policy, the material can be input in a form that a computer can use and displayed on the intranet, with access limited to authorized persons.

An intranet can be set up with various levels of security, possibly password-protected, so that all employees have access to basic information like the employee handbook and work rules, but only those who need to know have access to salary information and employee performance ratings. Intranets can also be used for training, for job postings within the organization, and to advise employees how to save for retirement and manage their benefits.

In addition to functions performed on the employer's computer system, functions accessing the Internet and using mobile devices are extremely significant, both for their business potential and for the problems they might create—not least of which is the amount of work time that employees spend on personal computing and social networking. In response to the age of social networking, the NLRB maintains its own Facebook page, YouTube channel, and Twitter feed.

Some companies allow BYOD—"bring your own (smart) device." It can improve employee satisfaction to allow them to use the devices they have chosen, and it saves the company some money—but there are associated risks. A BYOD policy means that the device, the data, and the networks belong to different people. There is a risk that employees will put proprietary, confidential, or privileged information on their devices—including information that belongs to a customer or client rather than the employer. The employee could back up information to the cloud, and have the information intercepted. On the other hand, if the company decides to ban BYOD, limit it, or limit stored data, the policy must be communicated to employees. Employees should be informed which devices they can bring to work and which platforms and networks are allowed. The policy should make it clear which data is company-owned, and inform employees that the company can access and control the data while it is on the employee's device.

The company should reserve the right to remove its data when the employee leaves the company. The company should forbid employees to modify device hardware and software, including "jailbreaking" telephones. Employees should also be required to use data safeguards, such as PIN or password protection and self-locking devices that shut off after a specified period of inactivity. [Cynthia Larose and Narges Kakalia, *Integrating Employees' Smart Devices Into the Workplace*, N.Y.L.J. (Dec. 13, 2012) (law.com)]

## § 27.02  INTERNET RESEARCH

Many Websites specialize in providing information about the HR function. The Society for Human Resources Management (SHRM) has a secure commerce server for online book orders, so credit card orders are safe. [See <http://shrmstore.shrm.org> (no www)] HR Magazine's site has a "conference room" for online chat with other HR professionals. The articles archive for HR Magazine appears at <http://www.shrm.org/hrmagazine/articles> (members only).

Law firm Websites are also an excellent source of up-to-date information about court cases, new tax rulings, and compliance matters.

If you need information about outplacement, or need to find an experienced professional in your area, see the Association of Career Firm's site, <http://www.aocfi.org>. The International Foundation of Benefit Plans can be found at <http://www.ifebp.org>.

The best government sites, such as <http://www.irs.ustreas.gov> are full of useful forms, explanations, and news summaries, as well as offering the full text of new regulations. It is worth scheduling time to regularly review the Pension and Welfare Benefit Administration and Occupational Safety and Health Administration sites to monitor ongoing developments; to see if you want to post an official comment on a proposal or testify at a hearing; or if there are new forms and publications available. The IRS launched its Retirement Plan Navigator in September 2009 to help small businesses choose plans, maintain the tax-qualified status of plans, and use correction programs if necessary. The site provides side-by-side comparisons of plan features of IRAs, 401(k)s, profit-sharing plans, defined benefit plans, and tax-exempt plans. [<http://www.retirementplans.irs.gov>; see Fred Schneyer, *IRS Site Helps Employers Navigate Retirement Plan Waters*, plansponsor.com (Sept. 18, 2009)]

The Department of Labor has an immense bank of information online. Their main site is <http://www.dol.gov>. The Bureau of Labor Statistics reports the relative strengths of various employment sectors and employment cost trends. [See <http://www.bls.gov>] It also disseminates statistics on occupational safety and health. [See <http://www.bls.gov/bls/safety.htm>. OSHA's home page is <http://www.osha.gov>] Federal contracting compliance information is available from the Employment Standards Administration. [See <http://www.dol.gov/esa/ofcp_org.htm>] The DOL has revised its Employment Law Guide, explaining the major laws that it enforces, and helping small businesses to develop wage, benefit, health and safety, and anti-discrimination policies. The update covers increases in minimum wages and FMLA expansions. The guide is a companion to the online FirstStep overview advisor, <dol.gov/elaws/firststep>; the law guide is <dol.gov/compliance/guide/index.htm>. [Fred Schneyer, DOL Workplace Law Manual Gets Freshened Up, plansponsor.com (Nov. 30, 2009)] In May 2010, the DOL launched a new Website, the H-1B Advisor, to assist employers and potential H-1B visa holders in understanding the requirements of the program. [<http://www.dol.gov/elaws/h1b.htm>; see Fred Schneyer, *DOL Puts Up H-1B Web Site*, plansponsor.com (May 17, 2010)], and a Disability Nondiscrimination Law Advisor (part of the eLaws series) for employers to make sure their policies do not discriminate against persons with disabilities. The Disability Advisor contains a series of questions; the employer's answers generate a list of federal anti-discrimination laws that are likely to apply. [<http://www.dol.gov/elaws/odep .htm>; see Fred Schneyer, *DOL Launches Disability Law Web Site*, plansponsor .com (May 5, 2010)]

The Employee Benefits Security Administration, a subagency of DOL, has its site at <http://www.dol.gov/ebsa>. For Worker's Compensation information, see <http://www.dol.gov/esa/owcp_org.htm>. The Wage and Hour Division's Web presence is <http://www.dol.gov/esa/whd>. See <http://www.doleta.gov> for the DOL's Corporate Citizenship Resource center, with profiles of companies that have implemented exceptional work-family programs. See <http://www.pbgc .gov> for coverage of the expansion of PBGC information technology. See <http://www.dol/gov/elaws/ERISAFiduciary.htm> for information about ERISA compliance, tools for plan officials, and an overview of the most common compliance errors reported by EBSA. [Fred Schneyer, *EBSA Unveils Fiduciary Education Web Site*, plansponsor.com (Oct. 9, 2007)]

## § 27.03   RECRUITING VIA THE INTERNET

If your corporation has a Website, it's easy and inexpensive to add an area for posting job opportunities. You can include an electronic form so even candidates who do not have an electronic resume can submit their qualifications. The form can be used for initial screening of applicants.

To an ever increasing extent, performing a Web search on candidates' names is becoming a normal part of recruitment and hiring—for example, to see if inconsistent resumes have been posted to help-wanted sites, or to check out the candidate's blog (which might, for instance, include indiscreet material about the candidate's current employer, or negative comments about a competitor or an industry as a whole). Corporations also establish and update their own blogs or encourage employees to do so. A 2006 Wall St. J. article puts the matter in a nutshell by saying "Employee blogs can put a human face on companies. But that's not always a good thing." Small companies can get extremely valuable publicity at low cost. However, corporate image specialists warn that having a lot of employee blogs can create conflicting messages about what the company is like, and lawyers warn about liability potential and security problems about new products, trade secrets, and proprietary formulas. Companies need to have policies about when employees can post to their blogs at work—and what they can say when they're posting from home. Even anonymous blogs can be tracked back, so many company policies require employees to use their real names on work-related blogs. [William M. Bulkeley, *The Inside View*, Wall St. J., Apr. 3, 2006, at R7]

Federal contractors who accept Internet-based job applications are subject to DOL's Office of Federal Contract Compliance Programs' Final Rule on record-keeping. The Final Rule covers jobs for which the contractor accepts expressions of interest via the Internet, e-mail, employer Websites, or resume databanks. Federal contractors are required, wherever possible, to obtain data on the sex, race, and ethnicity of their employees and job applicants—including those who apply over the Internet. An Internet applicant is one who uses the Internet or related technology to submit an expression of interest and who demonstrates at least basic qualifications for the position, who the federal contractor has considered for a particular position, and who never took him- or herself out of consideration for the job before an offer was made. The rule requires federal contractors to maintain records of Internet-based expressions of interest that resulted in the contractor considering the applicant for a particular job (the OFCCP decided it would be too burdensome to make them retain records of non-specific applications). It is acceptable for federal contractors to discard expressions of interest that do not relate to a particular position or that do not meet the contractor's standards for submitting applications. [70 Fed. Reg. 58,945 (Oct. 7, 2005)]

## § 27.04   BENEFITS MANAGEMENT ONLINE

There are many reasons to limit the corporate content that is publicly available on the Internet: Premature disclosure of confidential information could result in loss of privacy, premature release of corporate plans, exposure of trade secrets, securities law violations, or the like. Corporations also generate a tremendous amount of information that is not security-sensitive, but is not of interest outside the organization.

The cost of implementing an intranet depends on the scope of the project, and whether the project requires full-scale programming or can be implemented wholly or partially with off-the-shelf commercial software packages. Another important question is whether the in-house information technology staff can handle the job, or whether a consultant will be needed.

Guardian Life Insurance Co. of America said that, in the past five years, the proportion of employees using some kind of Web-based technology to enroll in benefits programs is up 165%. Five years ago, 12% used a computer only to enroll, now 40% do so; 58% of benefit programs were paper-only five years ago, a percentage that has dropped to 36%. In 2005, 11% of plans used a combination of computer and paper enrollment, now 21% do so. Almost all respondents (92%) said that convenience was the top reason to access benefits online, 87% said it saves time, 73% said it gives them more control. Three-quarters of women and 61% of men cited the environmental advantages of reducing paper usage. [Rebecca Moore, *Benefits Enrollment Increasingly Going Paperless*, plansponsor.com (Mar. 18, 2010]

## § 27.05  LEGAL IMPLICATIONS OF E-MAIL AND SOCIAL NETWORKING

The benefits of e-mail in providing a simple method of communications are obvious. However, unencrypted e-mail is not secure. It is much more like a post-card that can be read by anybody than it is like a sealed letter—much less a coded message. Merely clicking a "delete" icon does not remove a message completely and permanently from the entire computer system, network, or service provider that offers e-mail service. So a message that is embarrassing or worse (e.g., one involving racial epithets, sexual harassment, or evidence of corporate wrongdoing) can be found by hostile parties—including plaintiffs' lawyers.

In mid-2010, the Supreme Court decided a case involving text messaging on an older technology (pagers). However, the court refrained from making a broad ruling about employees' expectation of privacy in personal text messages sent from the workplace. Instead, the Supreme Court held that it did not violate the Fourth Amendment for the city of Ontario to perform an audit of employees' messages on city-owned pagers to determine if the city should upgrade to a plan giving employees more minutes on their pagers. The plaintiff was a police sergeant who alleged that it was an unlawful search for the city to examine personal messages that he sent on his city-owned pager. Finding that the search of the pagers was legitimate, work-related, and not excessive in scope, the Supreme Court ruled in favor of the city. [*Ontario v. Quon*, 130 S. Ct. 2619 (2010); see Tony Mauro, *Supreme Court Allows Search of Employee's City-Owned Pager*, Nat'l L.J. (June 18, 2010) (law.com)]

The Minnesota Court of Appeals held, in late 2010, that it is reasonable for an employer to expect that employees will not use work computers to view pornography even if there is no express policy forbidding it. A terminated employee appealed denial of unemployment benefits, taking the position that he was not guilty of misconduct because there was no rule in the employee manual against viewing pornography on work computers. The court said that such behavior is not job-related, so employers are entitled to assume that employees will refrain from doing this even if they do not break any laws. [*Brisson v. City of Hewitt*, 789 N.W.2d 694 (Minn. App. 2010); see Rebecca Moore, *Employer Can Expect No Dirty Pic Viewing Even with No Policy*, plansponsor.com (Nov. 4, 2010)]

If a company provides e-mail access at work, it should inform employees of the company's policies with respect to e-mail. A reasonable e-mail policy might involve

- Disclosure that the company has the right to monitor employee e-mail. [See § 26.06[C] for a discussion of privacy issues] It would be illegal to fire, or otherwise take action against, an employee who uses e-mail to engage in protected concerted activity such as complaining about safety risks. Threatening or inflammatory messages are not protected under labor law, but a direct protest to management certainly would be. Employee-to-employee communications are probably protected unless they actually threaten the harmonious and efficient operation of the business enterprise;

- Restriction of e-mail to business use. Inexpensive software is available to uninstall or disable games on office computers or networks, and to track usage (e.g., to see if gambling or pornographic sites are being accessed). However, although such measures may increase productivity, they must be balanced against the resentment employees may experience;

- No forwarding of copyrighted materials (for example, newspaper stories or cartoons);

- No use of obscene or suggestive language or slurs against any group;

- No discussion of matters that might have legal consequences (e.g., price fixing or industrial espionage);

- Asking employees to think before they send a message if there is anything in the message that they would not want publicized, or that could put the employer in a bad light.

Most employers maintain broad policies that warn employees that their e-mails can be monitored. The warning is usually conveyed in the employee handbook or on a screen displayed when employees log into the e-mail system. However, in practical terms, employers usually worry more about Internet use than e-mail. Software is now available for e-mail monitoring, saving the effort of having the IT department review the messages manually, but few employers use it. Many employers only begin to review e-mail after a problem has emerged, such as an alleged violation of the anti-harassment policy; alleged hate speech; or misuse of confidential or proprietary information. [Shannon Green, *When Should Employers Be Monitoring Employee Email?* Corporate Counsel (Mar. 13, 2013) (law.com)]

About three-quarters of lawsuits against corporations are employment suits, and e-mail often becomes a battleground, as the opponents seek discovery of communications made by their opponents. Usually, employers have a heavier burden because most of the relevant information, such as evaluations of employees who claim they were discriminated against, are generated by the employer, are stored on the employer's servers, or both. Employers are in a difficult position when employees raise claims of retaliation, because carrying out routinely scheduled document destruction can look as though the employer was suppressing evidence.

Electronic discovery is often helpful to employers, because once e-mails (and corporate-issued cell phones) are examined, evidence can come to light of wrongdoing by the employee—violating e-mail policies, accessing pornography at work, resume fraud, or even embezzlement. In cases alleging violation of covenants or misuse of trade secrets, the employer can examine computers, cell phones, pagers, and Blackberrys to determine how the information was used.

However, the flow of information does not go in only one direction. It is not uncommon for employees who contemplate a lawsuit to engage in "self-help discovery" by accessing the employer's files to find confidential information that they hope to use in their cases. The emerging legal consensus is that employees do not have a right to do so and that it is lawful to terminate an employee for misuse of confidential information. The court will probably apply a balancing test to compare the employer's legitimate interest in protecting proprietary information against employee's right to investigate information needed for a suit. Factors to be considered are the propriety or impropriety of the means used to obtain the evidence, if the employer maintained a disclosed and consistently applied policy that the employee violated, the impact on the company, the relevance of the information to the employee's case, and the risk that the evidence would be lost or destroyed if the employee did not access it. [Connie Bertram, *Using Confidential Documents in Claims Against Your Employer* Corporate Counsel (Aug. 14, 2012) (law.com)]

In some cases, the employee's use of the employer's e-mail system, or a company-supplied laptop, to communicate with his or her attorney will remove attorney-client privilege from the communications—especially if the employer has a policy of forbidding non-work related e-mails; monitors e-mails, and has warned employees that their communications are subject to examination. However, it is less likely that employers will be granted discovery of communications made using a laptop that was supplied by the employer but is not connected to the employer's computer network. [A. Michael Weber, *E-Discovery Keeps an Eye on the Job*, N.Y.L.J. (Apr. 21, 2008) (law.com)]

The New Jersey Supreme Court ruled that the attorney-client privilege outweighs corporate policy about use of workplace computers. Therefore, a plaintiff suing her employer had a reasonable expectation that e-mails to and from her lawyer using her personal, password-protected Yahoo account would be private even though they were sent on a laptop owned by the company. (Marina Stengart was going to quit her job and sue Loving Care Agency for constructive discharge and hostile work environment.) The court said that even if the company's policy manual had been clearly written to ban any personal use of company computers, and that the employer could read employees' e-mails, the policy would not be enforceable. The court said that although companies can monitor use of their computers to protect their assets, and employees can be disciplined or fired for excessive personal use during work time, there is no need to read the specific contents of employees' privileged personal communications. [*Stengart v. Loving Care Agency Inc.*, 201 N.J. 300 (N.J. 2010); see Michael Booth, *Privilege Trumps Company E-Mail Surveillance*, N.J.L.J. (Apr. 1, 2010) (law.com)]

Employers should draft and publicize social networking policies, information employees that, for example, they can be fired for social networking abuse, and warning them not to divulge confidential or trade secret information in their posts. Employees should be told not to go online during work hours for non-work purposes, and informed how to act if they might be perceived as spokespersons for the company. The policy should also explain the risk of charges of defamation, harassment, discrimination, and invasion of privacy if social networking is misused.

Employees' social networking sites can provide information about what they did when they were on sick leave, and of the true nature of their qualifications. For example, Facebook postings can show employees engaging in physical activities contrary to their representations when they applied for FMLA leave, Worker's Compensation, and/or disability benefits. Proskauer Rose's second annual "Social Media in the Workplace Around the World 2.0" report says that in 2012, 68.9% of employers claimed to have specific social media policies, versus 55.1% in 2011. In 2011, 48.3% of employers allowed employees to use company equipment to access their personal social media accounts for non-business reasons during working hours. This percentage rose to 52.1% in 2012. In both years, about one-third of employers (31.3% in 2011, 35% in 2012) said they had taken disciplinary action against an employee because of misuse of social media. Employers have wide latitude to regulate social media that represents the company. Employees should be required to get the company's permission to set up a work-sponsored account. For work-sponsored accounts, it should be clear that the content, connections, screen names, and passwords are the property of the employer. Employees should be put on notice that the employer has the right to monitor communications on the corporate network, but will not read communications that deal with concerted activity (e.g., union-related messages). Employees should also be warned that the corporate code of conduct governing off-work conduct (for example, maintaining confidentiality of trade secrets) applies online as well. [Catherine Dunn, *More Employers Creating Social Media Policies for the Workplace*, Corporate Counsel (Nov. 29, 2012) (law.com).]

Lawyers who represent employers warn of liability risks in friending subordinates on social networking sites: for example, harassment, wrongful termination, and discrimination (especially if only some employees who make friending requests are friended). Social networking sites contain a great deal of information about users—some of it negative for employment purposes, and it could be argued that this information was used against the employee. For example, an employee whose membership in a gay rights group appears in his profile might charge discrimination if he is fired, even if the employer says that his work was sub-par. Profiles could also contain religious affiliations and disability information. Office Team, a staffing service, says that 48% of executives do not want to be friended by their subordinates, and 47% do not want to be friended by their own bosses. [Tresa Baldas, *Lawyers Warn: Bosses Who "Friend" Are Begging to Be Sued*, Nat'l L.J. (Oct. 23, 2009) (law.com); Fred Schneyer, *Can Your Boss Be Your Facebook Friend?*, plansponsor.com (Aug. 20, 2009)]

With respect to social media, the NLRB's question is whether the employer's social media policy impairs the protected right of engaging in concerted mutual aid activities. Employer policies must be reasonable. The NLRB also assessed whether the social media activity is concerted (multiple employees act together), whether the activity is protected (i.e., involves workplace terms and conditions), and whether the employee has forfeited protection (e.g., by making maliciously untrue statements or lying to customers about product quality). It is a defense for the employer that the action would have been taken even if there had been no protected concerted activity: for example, there was a valid, non-discriminatory reason to discipline or terminate the employee. [Michael C. Schmidt, *Deciphering the NLRB's Stance on Social Media Issues*, N.Y.L.J. (Oct. 24, 2011) (law.com). See, e.g., Rebecca Moore, *NLRB Supports Car Dealership Facebook Firing*, plansponsor.com (Oct. 4, 2011)]]

In 2011, the NLRB said that over 100 employers had been the subject of worker charges involving social media. Most were filed by non-union employees. In about half the cases, the NLRB found merit, usually resulting in filing a civil complaint against the employer, which is heard by an ALJ. Social media statements that can be interpreted as threats are not protected; neither are posts that are derogatory to other employees. [Melanie Trottman, *When a Facebook Rant Gets You Fired*, WSJ.com (Dec. 2, 2011)]

Lafe Solomon, acting general counsel of NLRB, has released a second report on the social media cases his office has reviewed. The "Operations Management Memo" covers 14 cases, half of them with questions about an employer's social media policies. Five policies were found unlawfully broad, one lawful, and one lawful as revised. The other cases were about employees who were fired for posting to Facebook. The NLRB concedes that "mere gripes" are not protected if they do not relate to group activity—but advises employers to avoid any policy broad enough to prohibit protected activity like discussing wages and working conditions. [<http://www.nlrb.gov>, NLRB, *Acting General Counsel Issues Second Social Media Report* (Jan. 25, 2012) Solomon's third report concentrates on whether an employer's restrictions on social media can reasonably be considered to impair employees' rights under NLRA § 7, such as the right to free discussion of working conditions: <http://www.mynlrb.gov/link/document .aspx/09031d4580a375cd>, discussed in Jenna Greene, BLT, *NLRB Report on Social Media Highlights Overbroad Employer Restrictions* (May 30, 2012) (law.com)]

A March 2012 Advice Memorandum from the NLRB's Office of the General Counsel points out that social media guidelines are a mandatory bargaining subject. It violates NLRA § 8(a)(1) for an employer to adopt a work rule that reasonably tends to discourage employees from exercising their rights to protected collective activity. Under this standard, Giant Food's social media policy constrained protected activity to the extent that it forbade use of the employer's logo, graphics, and trademarks, and forbade photographing or video-recording the facility. Employees' references to the employer's logo and trademarks are non-commercial and do not interfere with the employer's business use of its trademarks. Employees were not allowed to refer to "non-public information" in their postings; the General Counsel said that this term was so vague that employees might be discouraged from permissible discussions of working conditions. However, it was legitimate for the policy to forbid defaming or discrediting the company's products or services, and it was legitimate to encourage employees to report violations of the policy to management. [*Giant Food LLC*,Cases 05-CA-064793, 05-CA-065187, and 05-CA-064795, <http://www.nlrb.gov/case-05-CA-064793 (Mar. 21, 2012)]

Some employers protest that the NLRB is extending union concepts to non-unionized employees. The NLRB's May 30, 2012 report on social media says that the key question is whether the employer's restrictions can reasonably be interpreted as having a chilling effect on employees' exercise of NLRA § 7 rights—for example, if employees are forbidden to discuss working conditions or criticize the employer. [See Jenna Greene, *NLRB Report on Social Media Highlights Overbroad Employer Restrictions*, The BLT (May 30, 2012) (law.com)]

Six states, including California and Illinois, have laws that forbid employers from asking employees or job applicants for their social networking passwords. [Steven Greenhouse, *Employers' Social Media Policies Come Under Regulatory Scrutiny*, NYTimes.com (Jan. 21, 2013)]

Social media often make such information available online. Some states, including New York, California, and Colorado, have laws forbidding "lifestyle discrimination" (based on lawful off-premises activity). However, the statutes may be interpreted to mean that disloyalty to the employer and material conflicts of interest with the employer's interests are not protected. Social media use probably will not be protected unless it is union-oriented or at least involves concerted action about working conditions. [Karlee S. Bolanos and Kyle W. Sturgess, *Will Lifestyle Discrimination Statutes Protect Employee Social Media Use?*, N.Y.L.J. (Mar. 30, 2011) (law.com)]

An employee fired on the basis of online conduct may have a claim for invasion of privacy—although the employer might prevail on an argument that activity on social networking sites is not really private. Information that is posted subject to restrictions might still be considered private: see, e.g., the *Pietrylo* case, involving a private, invitation-only MySpace discussion group where restaurant employees could talk about their jobs. One of the members allowed restaurant managers to use her access information; after viewing the discussion group, they fired the plaintiff and another employee.

## § 27.06   FEDERAL RULES ON DIGITAL COMMUNICATIONS

Many of the rules affecting HR functions were drafted before the heyday of the personal computer, when plan administration generated mounds and mounds of paper (but nothing but paper). Two trends coalesced in the 1980s: personal computing and the drive to make government more efficient and reduce unnecessary paperwork. Obviously, the often-proclaimed Paperless Office never arrived, but to an increasing extent, documents are not only being created on computers but also distributed and retained electronically.

Department of Labor regulations [29 C.F.R. § 2560.104b-1] create a safe harbor for using electronic methods of satisfying the obligation to give various notices to government agencies, plan participants, and beneficiaries under the plan. The overriding objective is finding a method that is reasonably calculated to make sure that the information actually gets into the hands of those who are entitled to it.

Materials that are subject to disclosure (either mandatory or on request by a participant or representative) can be disclosed through electronic media, as long as the delivery system is reasonably calculated to result in actual receipt of the information (for instance, by using a system that "bounces" undelivered e-mail messages). The electronic communication must use content, format, and style consistent with the requirements for paper documents. When documents are furnished electronically, participants and beneficiaries must also receive a notice (whether hard-copy or electronic) explaining the significance of the document if it is not immediately apparent. Recipients must also be advised that they have the right to request a paper copy of the document. Furthermore, electronic distribution is permitted only for plan participants who have effective computer access at work, and for participants and beneficiaries who have expressly consented (whether electronically or on a paper document) to receiving digital documents. Documents can properly be furnished online only to people who have provided an e-mail address, given affirmative consent, or confirmed consent electronically, in a manner that shows they can effectively access the means the plan will use to communicate the information.

A valid consent requires advance provision of a clear and conspicuous statement (digital or hard-copy) of the kind of documents covered by the consent; that consent can be withdrawn at any time without financial penalty; how to withdraw consent; how to get hard copies of electronic documents; and the hardware and software requirements for accessing digital documents.

The Summary of Benefits and Coverage (SBC) required by the PPACA (see § 18.19[K] can be distributed electronically to plan participants and beneficiaries who are already covered by an EGHP. DOL electronic disclosure requirements must be satisfied. For eligible people who are not yet enrolled (e.g., newly hired employees), the SBC can be distributed electronically in a readily accessible format, but the plan must make free hard copies available on request. If the electronic distribution occurs via a Website, then the employer must send written notice or e-mail to give the URL for the site and tell employees that they can request free hard copies. [Tracey Giddings and Birgit Anne Waidmann, *Administration Issues Final Rules on PPACA Summary of Benefits and Coverage,* PricewaterhouseCooper HRS Insight 12/06 (Feb. 14, 2012) (benefitslink.com)]

The PBGC's Web-based MyPAA (My Plan Administration Account Authentication Records) system was launched in February 2004. Plans can set up an account with the PBGC, which can be used, e.g., to make filings, pay premiums, make the reports of events required under 29 U.S.C. § 1343, or ask the PBGC questions. [71 Fed. Reg. 31077 (June 1, 2006), discussed in Harold J. Ashner, *PBGC Issues Final Rule Mandating E-Filing of Premium Information*, BNA Pension & Benefits Reporter (June 13, 2006) [<http://www.bna.com> (E-filing_BNA061306.pdf). The PBGC announced that My Plan Administration Account (MyPAA) is ready to accept premium filings for plan years beginning in 2009. Information about e-filing, with FAQs and Demos, is on the PBGC's site at the MyPAA page. Electronic filing of Form 5500 became mandatory starting with the 2009 plan year. Companies that maintain a corporate Intranet are also required to post part of Form 5500 on the Intranet, beginning with the 2008 annual report. [Seyfarth.com, *Mandatory Electronic Filing of 5500s to Begin in 2010* (Sept. 30, 2009) (benefitslink.com)]

The PBGC required MyPAA users to adopt new, stronger passwords, 10-24 characters long, containing at least one each of uppercase, lowercase, special characters, and numerals. The new password had to be adopted no later than August 1, 2012. [What's New For Practitioners, <http://www.pbgc.gov/prac/whatsnew.html> (June 18, 2012)]

As of January 1, 2010, all Form 5500s and 5500-SFs must be filed with EFAST-2 approved third party software, or e-filed. Schedule Schedule SSA, the Annual Registration Statement for Deferred Vested Participants, cannot be submitted on EFAST2, even for delinquent or amended filings for years before 2009: Form 8955-SSA must be filed with the IRS. Consult the EFAST-2 FAQ to see if you qualify for filing Form 5500-SF electronically. [EBSA, *Annual Return/Report 5500 Series Forms and Instructions* (benefitslink.com); <http://www.dol.gov/ebsa/5500main.html> undated; accessed August 9, 2012]

An employer maintaining a one-participant plan can file Form 5500-EZ on paper with the IRS, or file Form 5500-SF electronically with the DOL. The IRS' online Employee Plans Newsletter published December 20, 2011 says that, as of January 1, 2012, filing of Form 5500-SF will not be publicly disclosed on the DOL Website (previously, some one-participant plans that did not want such disclosure refrained from e-filing). The 5500 and 5500-SF must be electronically signed by the plan administrator or by a preparer who was authorized to sign on behalf of the plan administrator. In the past, sometimes preparers tried to avoid late filing penalties by submitting unsigned forms if they could not find the plan administrator or get permission to sign before the filing deadline. The DOL would process the form, but in "filing stopped" status, and the administrator would have to amend the document and re-file it with the proper electronic signature. As of January 1, 2012, the DOL will no longer process unsigned forms; they will be classified as "unprocessable" and subject to late filing penalties. If an invalid e-sig is attached (for example, based on credentials that have not been activated) the form will be classified as "filing stopped," and an amended form with a valid signature will have to be filed. [SunGard Relius, *New Form 5500 Guidance* (Dec. 22, 2011) (benefitslink.com)]

In mid-2009, the IRS released specifications for using the FIRE (Filing Information Returns Electronically) system for electronic filing of Forms 1098, 1099, 5498, and W-2G for 2009. The specifications appear in Publication 1220. Three new forms were published: Form 3921 (exercise of a qualified Incentive Stock Option under § 422(b); Form 3922 (transfer of stock acquired through an ESOP); and Form 8935, an airline payments report. [CCH Pension and Benefits, *IRS Issues Electronic/Magnetic Media Specs for 1099s* (July 14, 2009) (benefitslink.com)]

See <http://www.dol.gov/ebsa/actuarialsearch.html> for EBSA's online tools for employees and employers. When civil penalties are due for delinquent filings of annual reports, the tools permit plan administrators to return to compliance under the Delinquent Filer Voluntary Compliance Program by filing the overdue reports. The civil penalty assessment can be reduced by voluntarily paying a reduced penalty, which can be calculated on the site with the Department of the Treasury's financial management system and paid with a credit or debit card. For information about the Delinquent Filer Voluntary Compliance Program, call (202) 693-8360 or go to <http://www.dol.gov/ebsa/Newsroom/0302fact_sheet .html>. For electronic calculation and payment of civil penalties: see <http:// www.dol.gov/ebsa/calculator/dfvcpmain.html>. [Nevin E. Adams, *DOL Tool Makes It Easier to Pay Fines*, plansponsor.com (Sept. 22, 2008)]

Commentator Stephen M. Saxon described the DOL rules for electronic disclosure as "both completely antiquated and ridiculously complex"; the problems associated with these rules inspire some sponsors to continue to issue mandatory disclosures in paper form. The DOL has several approaches to electronic communication of ERISA information. Two of them are found in the electronic disclosure safe harbor, one in the preamble to the final regulations on default investment alternatives, one in FAB 2006-3, and the fifth in DOL Technical Release 2011-03R. The Technical Release described two approaches, but one was temporary and expired in May 2011. A general safe harbor is available for any ERISA-required document. Information can be sent digitally to any participant or beneficiary who has affirmatively consented to electronic delivery. Under the 2002 safe harbor for electronic delivery of information to employees who have computer access, the employer must determine which employees use a computer as an integral part of their jobs. They can be notified electronically. Other employees must affirmatively consent to electronic disclosure—even if, in practice, the employer knows that the employees use company computers during work hours and the employer knows their personal e-mail addresses. Saxon says that updating the electronic disclosure rules is not included in DOL's published regulatory agenda, so it will probably not happen in the near future. [Stephen M. Saxon, *Saxon Angle, The Electronic Age* (January 2013) (plansponsor.com)]

T.D. 9294 is the IRS' Final Rule, explaining how, effective January 1, 2007, qualified plans should use electronic means to provide notices to participants and obtain their consent and elections. The rule also applies to notices provided under various welfare benefit plans (accident & health plans; cafeteria plans; educational assistance plans; qualified transportation fringe plans; Archer MSAs; and HSAs). However, T.D. 9294, as an IRS rule, does not apply to ERISA Title I or IV notices (dealing with, e.g., SPDs, COBRA notices, and notices of benefit suspension) because those documents are under DOL or PBGC jurisdiction. [T.D. 9294, RIN 1545-BD68, 4830-01-p, 2006-48 I.R.B. 980; see Fred Schneyer, *IRS Puts Out Final Rule for Electronic Benefit Notices, Elections*, plansponsor.com (Oct. 19, 2006)]

The DOL regulations on disclosure of fees and expenses in participant-directed defined contribution plans were published October 20, 2010, but the effective date was delayed until May 31, 2012 for calendar-year plans. DOL Technical Release 11-03 provides an interim policy for electronic disclosures. The rule was estimated to affect about 72 million plan participants. The DOL has announced that it will not take enforcement action with respect to participant-level fee disclosures that satisfy Technical Release 11-03.

The final rules on fee disclosure require disclosure of three types of plan information: general information, administrative expenses, and individual expenses. If the plan's quarterly benefit statements satisfy the timing requirements, they can be used to provide these disclosures. Participants and beneficiaries must also be given certain investment-related information (fees, expenses, and investment alternatives) in comparative format, no later than the first date they can direct investments and at least once a year afterward. Investment-related information that is not contained in a pension benefit statement can be provided using the DOL electronic disclosure safe-harbor method or its alternative e-mail method, but not under the IRS electronic disclosure rules.

The administrator must take reasonable steps to ensure that the information is received: for example, using a return receipt feature or requiring notice of non-delivery, or undertaking reviews or surveys to confirm receipt of the information. The administrator must also take reasonable steps to maintain confidentiality. Notices must be written in a manner calculated to be understood by participants.

The initial notice to participants must be delivered on paper unless the recipient is part of a group that has had an e-mail address on file and used that address for dealing with the plan in the 12 months before the initial notice. Annual notices must be delivered on paper unless there is evidence that the recipient interacted with the plan electronically during that time. [DOL Technical Release

2011-03, <http://www.dol.gov/EBSA/pdf/tr11-03.pdf> (Sept. 13, 2011); see EBSA News, *US Department of Labor Issues Interim E-Disclosure Policy Under Participant Fee Disclosure Regulations* (Sept. 13, 2011) (benefitslink.com); EBIA Weekly, *DOL Issues Interim Policy on Electronic Distribution of Participant-Level Fee Disclosures* (Sept. 15, 2011) (benefitslink.com); Prudential Pension Analyst, *DOL Issues Interim Guidance on Electronic Disclosures to Participants* (December 2012) (benefitslink.com)]

DOL Technical Release 2011-03R revises and restates Technical Release 2011-03, updating the agency's policy on use of electronic media for disclosure to participants. Disclosure can be made via Websites that offer continuous access, subject to certain conditions. Investment information can be furnished as part of, or along with, a pension benefit statement either on paper or in electronic form. The DOL will not take enforcement action solely because a plan administrator provides required disclosures in electronic form, as long as the disclosure complies with the rules. [<http://www.dol.gov/ebsa/newsroom/tr11-03r.html>; see Rebecca Moore, *EBSA Revises Electronic Fee Disclosure Rules*, plansponsor .com (Dec. 8, 2011)]

In April 2011, the EBSA published a Request for Information seeking public comment about the DOL's standards for electronic distribution of required disclosures, at that point nearly 10 years old. The EBSA asked about employees' Internet access, employers' current practices for furnishing notices online, how to handle privacy, spam and spam filters, and whether ERISA and tax disclosure requirements should be unified into a single standard. According to 2009 Census Bureau figures, 76.7% of households in the United States have at least some Internet access. Among the 139.1 million private-sector workers, 111.7 million have some Internet access, and about 10.6 million of the remaining workers live in a household where one member has at least some Internet access.

The IRS has also issued guidance on using electronic media in plan communications: final regulations in 2000 covering participant notices and consents to plan distributions; 2003 final regulations about 204(h) notices; and 2006 final regulations about electronic notices in retirement plans and employee benefit arrangements. [EBSA Proposed Regulation, 76 Fed. Reg. 19,285 *Request for Information Regarding Electronic Disclosure by Employee Benefit Plans* (Apr. 7, 2011)]

## [A] Data Security

The recession increased the problems caused by leaks of sensitive or confidential corporate information—so much so that some companies assume that they should make public announcements at the same time as distributing information internally, because the information will leak almost instantly. Yahoo and several large law firms experienced disclosures of pending layoffs or release of internal memoranda about cost cuts when the information turned up on blogs or

Internet news sites. For example, a Portland law firm was e-mailed by a legal Website for comment only 41 minutes after the first employees were notified that they were laid off, and the firm said that only three or four people knew about the planned layoffs. Another blog disclosed salary cuts at a different law firm before all the employees were notified. The American Management Association surveyed 586 employees, 14% of whom admitted to sending confidential or potentially embarrassing corporate e-mails to someone outside the company. Employers are protecting themselves with technical fixes, such as software that blocks certain e-mail addresses and scans e-mail attachments to see if sensitive information is included. [Dana Mattioli, *Leaks Grow in World of Blogs*, WSJ.com (July 20, 2009)]

After issuing interim final rules in 2009 [RIN 009-AB56, 75 Fed. Reg. 42740 (Aug. 24, 2009)] and a 2010 Notice of Proposed Rulemaking dealing with privacy, security, and enforcement [RIN 009-AB56, 75 Fed. Reg. 40868 (July 14, 2010)], at the beginning of 2013 HHS' Office of Civil Rights (OCR) published an omnibus restatement of the HIPAA privacy and security rules, reflecting the HITECH Act Amendments. Covered entities and their contractors and subcontractors are subject to civil and criminal penalties for violations of the privacy, security, and breach notification rules. Security breaches must be reported to HHS each year and large-scale breaches must also be reported to the individuals involved and to the news media. There are requirements for using encryption and destruction of obsolete information to prevent unauthorized persons from accessing protected health information (PHI). Penalties for failure to notify individuals of breach of their PHI and failure to notify the media when required have increased. The penalty ranges between $100 and $50,000 per violation in situations where the covered entity did not know of the violation (and could not have known by exercising reasonable diligence). If there was reasonable cause for the violation and there was no willful neglect, the penalty range is $1,000 to $50,000. Where willful neglect occurred, the penalty range is $10,000–$50,000 if the violation was corrected on a timely basis—and at least $50,000 for offenses of willful neglect that were not timely corrected. However, in each penalty category, there is a cap of $1.5 million on total penalties for all violations of the same provision. The actual penalty imposed within the penalty range for a particular offense depends on factors such as the nature and extent of the violation and the extent of the harm it caused.

This rule makes some changes to conform HIPAA to the Genetic Information Nondiscrimination Act (GINA) Title I (health coverage) and Title II (employment). For example, GINA treats genetic information as health information and health plans must be informed that it is forbidden to use or disclose genetic information for underwriting purposes. (However, the information can be used for underwriting of long-term care insurance.) The final rule is effective March 26, 2013 and covered entities are given until September 23, 2013 to comply. [78 Fed. Reg. 5566 (Jan. 25, 2013); see Cynthia Marcotte Stamer, Solutions Law Press HR & Benefits Update, *OCR Publishes Long-Anticipated Omnibus Restatement of*

*HIPAA Privacy, Security, Breach Notification & Enforcement Rules* (Jan. 13, 2013) (benefitslink.com); Katherine Georger, Holland & Hart LLP News Update, *New HIPAA Final Rule Implements GINA Restriction on Use and Disclosure of Genetic Information for Underwriting Purposes* (Jan. 23, 2013) (benefitslink .com)]

In late 2011, the HHS launched a pilot program of audits of health plans and providers to see if they satisfy the HIPAA's security and privacy standards. More audits followed in 2012 based on the protocols developed in the pilot. The HHS investigators do fieldwork at the site of the audited company. The purpose of the audits is to discover which entities require technical assistance to meet the security and privacy standards, although penalties might be imposed if the HHS finds serious compliance problems. [Christine A. Williams, *HIPAA Audits Come with Short Turnaround Times*, Perkins Coie News (Dec. 19, 2011) (benefitslink.com)]

An HHS Website for reporting security breaches was established in February 2010; since then, the HHS has received an average of 17 breach reports a month, many of them leading to audits.

Security breaches can have serious financial consequences for companies that break the rules: BlueCross BlueShield of Tennessee agreed to pay the HHS $1.5 million to settle HITECH charges about a 2009 data breach. Fifty-nine unencrypted hard drives were stolen from a disused call center in Chattanooga; the drives contained protected data, including Social Security numbers and diagnoses, of more than a million BlueCross subscribers. However, there is no indication that the data was misused. BCBS reported the breach as required, and has spent over $17 million since then on investigations and improving its systems. The settlement requires a 450-day correction program for review and improvement of security procedures. [HHS Website for reporting breaches: <http://www .hhs.gov/ocr/privacy/hipaa/administrative/breachnotificationrule/brinstruction .html>; see Beth Moskow-Schnoll, Jean C. Hemphill, Evan W. Krick, and Edward I. Leeds, *Data Breach Leads to First HITECH Enforcement Settlement,* Ballard Spahr (Mar. 19, 2012) (benefitslink.com); Shannon Green, *$1.5M HHS Data Breach Settlement Is First Under HITECH Law*, Corporate Counsel (Mar. 21, 2012) (law.com)] See § 19.05[F] for more discussion of HIPAA security rules.

It can be difficult to safeguard business data when employees are terminated. The Computer Fraud and Abuse Act (CFAA) gives employers a civil claim against former employees who seek competitive advantage through wrongful use of information from the employer's computer system. The former employee is liable for accessing a protected computer without authorization, or in excess of authorized access, if it is done knowingly and with intent to defraud, as long as the access furthers the intended fraud and the person obtains anything of value. If a civil violation of the CFAA is proven, then the court can award compensatory damages and/or equitable relief such as an injunction. The statute of limitations is two years from the date of the access or the date it was discovered. The CFAA does not define "without authorization," but 18 U.S.C. § 103(e)(6) defines "exceed authorized access" as using permission to access a computer to obtain or alter information in a way that the user is not allowed to do.

Courts have interpreted this definition differently. Some decisions (e.g., *LVRS Holdings LLC v. Brekka,* 581 F.3d 1127 (9th Cir. 2009) narrowly interpret the statute and limit its application to situations in which the person accessing was an outsider who had no permission to access the system at all—so an employee who exceeds his or her authorized access would not be covered.

Employers can protect themselves against data misuse by:

- Setting up a security system that flags unauthorized access to, or use of, data;

- Having new hires sign a confidentiality agreement that specifically references data protection;

- Exploring the technical feasibility of preventing transmission of certain crucial data to PCs or electronic devices;

- Including discussion of what kinds of remote access are permitted in your firm's telecommuting policy;

- Enforcing the information security policy, and impose even-handed discipline on all detected violations of the policy;

- As soon as possible after a resignation or termination, revoking the individual's log-in privileges on your computer system.

[Carolyn M. Plump, *Can the CFAA Protect Your Business Data?* The Legal Intelligencer (Dec. 10, 2009) (law.com)]; Nick Ackerman, *When Workers Steal Data to Use at New Jobs,* Nat'l L.J. (July 7, 2009) (law.com). Compare *Intl Airport Ctrs. LLC v. Citrin,* 440 F.3d 418 (7th Cir. 2006) with, e.g., *Shamrock Foods Co. v. Gast,* 535 F. Supp. 2d 962 (D. Ariz. 2008); *Lasco Foods Inc. v. Hall,* 600 F. Supp. 2d 1045 (E.D. Mo. 2009). *United States v. Mitra,* 405 F.3d 492 (2005) defined "computers" very broadly, so that wireless networking stations and cell phones might also be subject to the CFAA.]

In 2012, the Ninth Circuit adopted a very narrow construction of the CFAA. The court held that the federal law does not penalize violations of employer computer policies or Website terms of service. The defendant in this case worked at an executive search firm; the firm accused him of allowing accomplices to access the employer's database to get information that could be used to help the defendant set up a business competing with his ex-employers. The Ninth Circuit majority said that the federal statute does not criminalize exaggerating on dating sites or using work time for personal Internet use. However, the two dissenting judges said that this case was about deliberate fraud on an employer and the statute penalizes actions undertaken with "intent to defraud." [*United States v. Nosal,* 676 F.3d 854 (9th Cir. 2012); see Ginny LaRoe, *With 9-2 Ruling, Circuit Narrows Scope of Computer Fraud and Abuse Act,* The Recorder (Apr. 10, 2012) (law.com)] Similarly, the Fourth Circuit ruled in mid-2012 that it did not violate the CFAA for an employee to download proprietary information into his own computer then use it in a presentation to a potential customer—on behalf of a competitor of his ex-employer, three weeks after quitting his job. Although the CFAA does include a civil provision, it does not apply to misappropriation of trade secrets or violating an employer's usage policy at a time when the individual was entitled to access the computer. [*WEC Carolina Energy Solutions LLC v. Miller*, 687 F.3d 199 (4th Cir. 2012)]

The Seventh Circuit permitted the application of the federal Computer Fraud and Abuse Act, and civil penalties, in the case of an ex-employee who maliciously erased files from the ex-employer's computer system when he left to set up his own business. The statute, intended to penalize computer hacking, applies to transmission of computer code with the intention of damaging a computer system. [*International Airports Ctrs. v. Citrin*, 440 F.3d 418 (7th Cir. 2006); see Pamela A. MacLean, *Erasing Computer Files Might Create Employee Liability*, Nat'l L.J. (Mar. 29, 2006) (law.com). An earlier Seventh Circuit ruling on the Computer Fraud and Abuse Act, *United States v. Mitra*, 405 F.3d 492 (2005) defined "computers" expansively, so that wireless networking stations and cell phones might also be included in the statute's reach.]

# Chapter 28

# WORK-FAMILY ISSUES

## § 28.01 INTRODUCTION

Employees who have children or who have care responsibilities for their parents seek to balance their roles at work and at home. Even employees who do not have family responsibilities seek work-life balance. There are new kinds of families developing (single parents, blended families, grandparents raising grandchildren). Greater involvement of fathers in hands-on child care also increases the demand for FMLA leave or flexible hours for fathers; however, paternity leave has never really caught on. [See Chapter 38]

The Census Bureau's American Community Survey said that the proportion of pregnant women who work increased, from 56%–57% in the 2004–2007 period to 61% of pregnant women and new mothers in 2008. The EEOC received 5,587 complaints of pregnancy discrimination in 2007, rising to 6,285 in 2008 and falling slightly to 6,196 in 2009. Carla Moquin, president of the advocacy group Parents in the Workplace, said that she was aware of 150 companies with babies-at-work programs; a program of this type makes workers more willing to return to work after a short maternity leave instead of taking more time off. [Sue Shellenbarger, *Handling the Office Baby Boom*, WSJ.com (Jan. 13, 2010)]

The Census study published in 2011 showed that about one-fifth of first-time mothers quit their jobs: 16% during pregnancy, 6% in the first three months after birth. But women who worked during pregnancy were more likely to return to work within three to five months than women who did not. Four-fifths of women who worked during pregnancy had returned to work with the same employer within a year of delivery. About 70% had the same number of hours per week, pay, and skill level after giving birth.

Census data shows that 42% of working women who had their first child in the period 1996–2000 received paid leave (maternity leave, sick leave, or vacation time), a percentage that rose to 51% for the period 2006–2008. About 24% of women younger than 22 had paid leave, versus 61% of women over 25. More than half (56%) of full-time workers, but only 21% of part-time workers, had access to leave. Forty-two percent of maternity leaves were unpaid. [Bureau of the Census, *Maternity Leave and Employment Patterns of First-Time Mothers: 1961-2008*, <http://www.census.gov/prod/2011pubs/p70-128.pdf>; see Rebecca Moore, *Paid Maternity Leave Use Trending Up*, plansponsor.com (Nov. 14, 2011)]

California adopted new laws, SB 299/AB 592 and SB 222/AB210 to enhance insurance and employment protection during pregnancy. SB 299 amends FEHA, effective January 1, 2012, to require employers to provide the same level of insurance benefits during pregnancy-related leave as the employee had before taking leave; employers are permitted to increase benefits during pregnancy. Even employees who are not eligible for FMLA leave may be entitled to continue their health benefits. The California law applies to all employers of five or more employees, versus 50 employees required for FMLA coverage. [Helene Wasserman and Michelle Barrett, *The Stork Has Landed: California Employers Must*

*Maintain and Insurers Must Provide Pregnancy Benefits*, Littler Mendelson (Oct. 19, 2011) (benefitslink.com)]

The EEOC received almost 6,300 complaints of pregnancy discrimination in 2008, falling to 5,800 in 2010. The EEOC filed 20 pregnancy discrimination suits in FY 2011; there were 16 such suits in 2009 and more than 20 in both 2007 and 2008. In the past decade, the EEOC has filed a total of 268 pregnancy suits, mostly for wrongful termination. Two hundred sixteen of the suits have been resolved, generally by settlement, and the EEOC secured a total of more than $42 million for the plaintiffs. [Melanie Trottman, *Agency Makes New Push to Help Pregnant Workers*, WSJ.com (Feb. 16, 2012)]

"Maternal depression" is an umbrella term for perinatal (during pregnancy) depression, postpartum depression (just after birth) and postpartum psychosis (an actual psychotic episode shortly after birth). Pregnancy is a risk factor for depression because of hormone fluctuations, stress, and anxiety about adding a child to the family. Depression causes serious disruption in the workplace and generates a high level of medical costs. The National Business Group on Health recommends that employers ask their health plans to include routine screening for maternal depression as part of pregnancy and postpartum care. Employers should encourage their insurers to distribute information about depression, or should make it available to employees themselves. Including visiting nurse services in the maternity care package reduces stress on new mothers—and the visiting nurse is in the best situation to detect maternal depression and refer the mother to appropriate psychological and/or psychiatric care. The employer can also support new mothers by offering parenting classes and including information and referral about maternal depression in health fairs. [Nat'l Business Group on Health Issue Brief, *Maternal Depression: What Employers Need to Know and What They Can Do*, <http://www.businessgrouphealth.org/pdfs/NBGH%20Maternal%20Depression_IB-Final.pdf> (January 2011)]

A March 2013 report published by Pew Research Social & Demographic Trends shows that between 1965 and 2011, there were major changes in the way working parents handled family and work tasks. As of 2011, approximately 60% of two-parent households with minor children had two working parents. In 1965, the average number of hours mothers spent on paid work was six hours, combined with 32 hours of housework and 10 hours of child care (a total of 51 hours a week). In 1965, fathers spent an average of 42 hours a week on paid work, four hours on housework, and 2.5 hours on child care (total of 49). In 2011, the picture was very different. Mothers averaged 21 hours of paid work, 18 hours of housework, and 14 hours of child care (53 hours total). Fathers averaged 37 hours of paid work, 10 hours of housework, and 7 hours of child care (54 hours total). Mothers' preference for work scheduling has changed significantly. Almost one-third of mothers of children under 18 said in 2012 that they wanted to work full time; in 2007, only 20% said so. More than half of working mothers of children under 18 found work/life balance somewhat or fairly difficult (56%) with 43% found it not difficult or not too difficult. Men found it somewhat easier:

there was a 50-50 split between those finding it not difficult or not too difficult, and those finding it somewhat or very difficult. Forty percent of working mothers and one-third of working fathers of children under 18 report feeling constantly rushed. Nearly half (46%) of fathers and 23% of mothers felt that they do not spend enough time with their children—perhaps because, on the average, mothers spend twice as much time each week on child care as fathers do. [Kim Parker and Wendy Wang, *Modern Parenthood: Roles of Moms and Dads Converge as They Balance Work and Family*, <http://www.pewsocialtrends.org/2013/03/14/modern-parenthood-roles-of-moms-and-dads-converge-as-they-balance-work-and-family/> (Mar. 14, 2013)]

Aon Hewitt's latest survey found that 13% of respondent companies offered paid paternity leave. Yahoo gives new fathers eight weeks of paid paternity leave (new mothers can get 16 weeks of paid maternity leave). The Bank of America offers 12 weeks of paid paternity leave, and Ernst & Young offers six weeks. Businesses do not find this to be an expensive benefit—because few fathers take advantage of it. About 85% of new fathers take off some time after their child's birth, but it is usually limited to one or two weeks. A study published in 2012 by the Universities of Virginia and Connecticut found that 69% of mothers but only 12% of fathers accessed paid leave when it was offered. [Jen Wieczner, *88% of Dads Pass on Paid Paternity Leave*,WSJ.com (May 9, 2013); Lauren Weber, *Why Dads Don't Take Paternity Leave*,WSJ.com (June 12, 2013)]

Concerns have been raised that there are many "off-ramps" for mothers to leave the workforce, but fewer "on-ramps" to return. Charlotte Hanna, who worked at Goldman Sachs' orientation program for new analysts and associates, said that after she returned from her first maternity leave in 2005, Goldman demoted her and made her feel unwelcome in an all-male environment. She was fired in February 2009, a week before she was supposed to return from her second maternity leave. The complaint for her suit filed in the Southern District of New York in 2010 says that she was hired in 1998, became a vice president in 2000, and was well-regarded. She used a program allowing part-time work after maternity leave, but she said she hit a glass ceiling and was systematically excluded from operations and social functions. The complaint alleges that 75% of those selected for termination in her group had recently taken maternity leave. Her suit was dismissed on November 20, 2010, pursuant to a confidential settlement; terms were not disclosed. [*Hanna v. Goldman Sachs & Co.*, No. 10-02637 (S.D.N.Y. settlement 2010); see Bob Van Voris, *Goldman Sachs Settles Lawsuit Over Pregnancy Bias With Former Vice President*, Bloomberg <http://www.bloomberg.com/news/2010-11-05/goldman-settles-lawsuit-over-pregnancy-bias-with-former-vice-president.html> (Nov. 5, 2012); Jonathan Stempel, *Judge Dismisses "Mommy Track" Lawsuit Against Goldman Sachs*, Insurance Journal, <http://www.insurancejournal.com/news/national/2010/11/05/114640.htm> (Nov. 5, 2010)]

McKinsey & Co. reached out to women who quit several years ago, assuming that they might have left to start families but are now ready to return. Other major consulting firms also have programs for current and former employees, promoting flexible hours and maintaining contact with former employees. Bain & Co. says that more than 80% of its female partners have used flextime. Goldman Sachs' "returnship" program offers short-term jobs for professionals who took a few years off, usually mothers of young children. [Leslie Kwoh, *McKinsey Tries to Recruit Mothers Who Left the Fold*, WSJ.com (Feb. 19, 2013)]

The first lawsuit under Family Responsibilities Discrimination (FRD) was brought in 1971. There were only eight such cases in the 1970s. Between 1986 and 1995, the Hastings College of the Law Center for WorkLife Law found that there were 97 lawsuits alleging discrimination on the basis of family responsibilities. The number rose to 481 cases in the decade 1996–2005. About 93% of FRD plaintiffs are women. Most allege that they suffered discrimination because of their care needs as parents, but some are caregivers for their parents. The largest award to a successful FRD plaintiff was $25 million, but the average award is about $100,000; employees get settlements or win at trial in about half of FRD cases. [The Hastings study is called *Litigating the Maternal Wall: U.S. Lawsuits Charging Discrimination Against Workers with Family Responsibilities*; see Lisa Belkin, *Family Needs in the Legal Balance*, N.Y. Times (July 30, 2006, section 1, p.1) and Fred Schneyer, *Strong Rise Seen in Family Responsibilities Discrimination Suits*, plansponsor.com (July 10, 2006). See also Dee McAree, *"Sex-Plus" Gender Bias Lawsuits Are on the Rise*, Nat'l L.J. (Mar. 14, 2005) (law.com); discussing, e.g., the suit filed in the Southern District of New York by 12 woman employees alleging a pattern of disparate pay and promotions and denial of access to the management development program after they took FMLA leave for child birth: *Velez v. Novartis*, No. 04 Civ. 09194 (GEL) The case was settled in 2010 for $175 million. See Grant McCool & Jonathan Stempel, *Novartis Settles Gender Bias Class Action for $175 Million*, Claims Journal, <http://www.claimsjournal.com/news/national/2010/07/16/111632.htm> (July 15, 2010).]

The Center for WorkLife Law, in its report, "Family Responsibilities Discrimination: Litigation Update 2010," said that family responsibility discrimination plaintiffs are much more likely to win their cases than other plaintiffs. Although discrimination plaintiffs overall win less than 30% of their cases, family responsibility discrimination plaintiffs won 50.7% of their cases, sometimes receiving high damages. Lawsuits alleging discrimination against caregivers almost quadrupled between 2000 and 2010.

Out of more than 2,100 caregiver discrimination cases tracked by the Center for WorkLifeLaw, there were four verdicts or settlements over $10 million (two of them were class actions). Twenty-one cases had verdicts or settlements over $1 million, usually because of high punitive damages. The average verdict or settlement was $578,316. Nearly all (88%) of caregiver-discrimination plaintiffs were women, and female plaintiffs won 51.6% of their cases whereas only 41.9% of male plaintiffs were successful. The Center for WorkLifeLaw noted that many cases reflect the "new supervisor syndrome" (which also operates in other types of workplace discrimination cases): the plaintiff was doing fine and receiving adequate accommodations, until the new supervisor canceled the accommodations. Some caregiver discrimination plaintiffs say their work situation deteriorated when they became pregnant with twins or triplets, or when they were expecting a second child, and management decided that they were not committed to their jobs. Some plaintiffs have alleged preemptive elder care discrimination, charging that a supervisor tries to get rid of them before they devote too much time to caring for their parents. [Preventing Discrimination Against Employees with Family Responsibilities: A Model Policy for Employers, <http://www .worklifelaw.org/pubs/Model_Policy_for_Employers.pdf>; see Seyfarth.com, *Caregiver and Family Responsibilities: A Continuing Challenge for Employers* (June 4, 2010) (benefitslink.com); Rebecca Moore, *Caregiver Discrimination Can Be Costly for Employers*, plansponsor.com (Mar. 2, 2010)]

In a case settled in 2009, Rachel Robinson applied for FMLA leave when her mother had a brain tumor. She took 18 days of leave, then a further 10 days— but then was told to "draw a line" between work and caregiving. She was fired three days later; her mother died within less than a month.

Hastings said that five states and 67 localities forbid discrimination against caregivers and there is a move to extend the protection already given to parents to workers with family responsibilities of all kinds. [Paula Span, *When Work Makes You Choose*, NYTimes.com (Sept. 14, 2012)]

The First Circuit (reversing the district court) permitted a plaintiff to pursue a sex discrimination claim when she charged that she was denied promotion to Team Leader, despite an excellent evaluation, because she is the mother of four small children. The Supreme Court, and several circuits, including the First Circuit itself, have ruled that adverse job action against mothers is a form of sex discrimination based on stereotyping. [*Chadwick v. WellPoint Inc.*, 561 F.3d 38 (1st Cir. 2009); see Rebecca Moore, *Mother of Young Children Can Pursue Sex-Bias Claim Against WellPoint*, plansponsor.com (Mar. 30, 2009)]

The Families and Work Institute says that 20% of families have a child with some significant physical or mental health problem. Data from the Archives of Pediatric and Adolescent Medicine shows the incidence of disabling conditions affecting children and teenagers rose from 2% in 1960 to 7% today.

The federal Maternal and Child Health Bureau says that 30% of parents have to quit their jobs or cut back on working hours if they have a child with a disability.

MetLife found that 29% of parents in this group have made no financial plans for their child's future, less than half have designated a guardian for their child to serve after their own deaths, and close to two thirds experience barriers in getting information they need. Employers can furnish valuable information about, e.g., Medicaid planning, creating trusts to manage the assets of persons incapable of self-care, and tax issues. However, parents in this situation may be afraid to raise the issue, in case they suffer discrimination based on prejudice against persons with disabilities or because of a perception that the company's health plan will become too costly to be afforded. [Kelley M. Butler, *It Takes a Village: Employers Have Key Role in Supporting Employees with Special-Needs Children*, Employee Benefit News, Jan. 2006, <http://www.benefitnews.com/pfv .cfm?id=8461>; Sue Shellenbarger, Employers Begin to Provide Assistance for Parents of Children with Disabilities, Wall St. J. (Oct. 13, 2005, at D1); MassGeneral has a manual about workplace benefits, online at <http://www .massgeneral.org/ebs>] Having a special needs child is extremely stressful for working parents, and is likely to lead to health problems and absenteeism. [Paul Gallagher, *Sick Kids Add to Workplace Anxiety*, Human Resource Executive Online (Aug. 5, 2009) (benefitslink.com)]

Nor is child care the only issue. People in mid-life are sometimes called the "sandwich generation" because they have responsibilities for aging parents as well as growing children. The Department of Labor Women's Bureau is a good resource for work-family issues. [See <http://www.dol.gov/wb/childcare/ b2bintro.htm>] So is the National Partnership for Women and Families. [See <http://www.nationalpartnership.org>]

Work-life programs have gained prominence since 2001, as hard-pressed companies looked for ways to motivate employees without burdening themselves with very high capital obligations. There are several broad categories of work-life programs:

- Family-friendly benefits such as day care, information and referral services (I&R), offering leave in excess of FMLA requirements, lactation rooms, adoption assistance, and domestic partner benefits;

- Alternative work arrangements and time off (flextime; telecommuting; temporary or project-based work; paid time off for volunteer activities; sabbaticals);

- Health and wellness benefits;

- On-site amenities (an ATM or bank branch; concierge service);

- Financial assistance (tuition reimbursement; personal use of frequent flyer miles earned at work; prepaid legal services).

[The categories come from Tara Pickering, *Work/Life Programs: Not Just Another Employee Benefit*, The CEO Refresher, <http://www.refresher.com/ !tpworklife.html>]

However, WorldatWork reported in 2011 that although employers are offering work-life programs, some of them penalize the employees who use them. WorldatWork's survey showed that 80% of employers say that they support family-friendly workplaces, but when employees are questioned, they say that they were punished or overtly or subtly discouraged from using such programs. More than half of managers surveyed say that ideal employees are available at all times and close to one-third believe that employees who use flexible hours will not advance within the organization. [Kelley M. Butler, *Employers Penalize Workers For Using Work-Life Programs,* Employee Benefit News (Sept. 12, 2011) (benefitslink.com)]

Joan C. Williams, founding director of the Center for Work-Life Law (Hastings) coined the term "flexibility stigma"—being punished by one's employer for actually using the policies promulgated by the employer. Williams says that women and men are affected differently by the stigma. The risk for women is that they might be seen only as mothers, and treated as if they are not competent or committed to work. But men may encounter even more prejudice if they are seen as feminine and not ambitious enough. The 2012 National Study of Employers performed by the Families and Work Institute shows that work-family options have nominally increased between 2005 and 2012, but employers have cut back on things like sabbaticals and easy moves between full- and part-time—measures that would allow employees to spend significant time away from the workforce. In May 2013, Vermont passed a statute, modeled after practices in the United Kingdom and Australia that gives employees the right to request flexible working arrangements without retaliation for making the request. The law allows applications twice a year, but does not require the employer to grant the request—only to refrain from retaliating against the employee for making it. [Tara Siegel Bernard, *The Unspoken Stigma of Workplace Flexibility*, NYTimes.com (June 14, 2013)]

## [A]  Paid Leave Requirements

It has traditionally been the employer's prerogative to decide whether leave will be paid or unpaid. The FMLA requires employers to grant leave, within limits, when an employee has a serious health condition or cares for a family member who does However, there is no requirement that the employer pay employees who have taken FMLA leave.

An increasing trend is for states to pass laws requiring paid leave for certain health or family events. So far, these programs are funded by payroll taxes on employees so they do not impose a direct financial burden on employers but, nevertheless, it is inconvenient to have to replace the work of employees on leave and to do the paperwork associated with the paid leave program.

In May 2011, Connecticut enacted a law, effective January 1, 2012. All service businesses with 50 or more employees must allow all service workers to accrue one hour of paid sick time for every 40 hours worked, and up to 40 hours of accrued time can be used in any year for the worker's own illness, care of a spouse or child, or personal needs caused by family violence or sexual assault. Service workers covered by the law are defined as non-exempt hourly employees; the law lists covered workers such as child care workers, retail clerks, registered nurses, secretaries, waiters and waitresses. [Connecticut S.B. 913; see Jason Stanevich and Jennai Williams, Littler Mendelson ASAP, *Connecticut is First State to Mandate Paid Sick Leave for Service Workers* (June 2011) (benefitslink.com); AP, *Connecticut Becomes First State Requiring Paid Sick Time*, WSJ.com (July 5, 2011)]

Seattle, San Francisco, and Washington, D.C. also require paid sick leave. Seattle's Sick/Safe Leave Law covers all employers that have at least one full-time employee in Seattle and more than four employees in all locations. Employees who work in Seattle for more than 240 hours in a calendar year are covered. Companies with up to 250 employees must provide one hour of leave for every 40 hours worked; larger companies must provide an hour of leave for every 30 hours worked. The leave can be taken for the employee's or close family member's health care. "Safe leave" can be used when the workplace is closed for safety reasons or when the employee or close family member is a victim of domestic violence or stalking. Noncompliant employers can be sued, and the city's civil rights office can seek reinstatement, two years' back pay, attorneys' fees, and up to $10,000 for emotional distress damages on behalf of covered employees. [Jackson Lewis LLP Workplace Resource Center, *Seattle's New Paid Leave Law* (Aug. 13, 2012) (benefitslink.com)]

The SHRM said that about one-third of small businesses (under 50 employees) offered paid time off for illness in 2011—a smaller percentage than the 39% who did so in 2009. Accountant Daniel L. Haynes estimated that a 30-employee firm paying an average of $10/hour would incur costs of $18,700 to provide seven paid sick days per employee. Mercer said that while the direct cost of incidental absences was only about 2% of payroll in 2010, that percentage almost doubled if indirect costs (such as paying other workers overtime to cover and doing paperwork) were taken into account. [Sarah E. Needleman, *Debate Over Sick Leave Intensifies*, WSJ.com (Mar. 1, 2012)]

It is not clear whether employees can claim intermittent FMLA leave for fertility treatment; if the employee is entitled to leave, then taking intermittent leave for fertility treatment cannot be used as a negative factor in hiring, promotion, or discipline. It is possible that denying the leave might be considered to violate the ADA or PDA. [Keisha-Ann G. Gray, *Procreation Problems*, Human Resource Executive Online (Nov. 2, 2010) (benefitslink.com)]

A 2010 report by the Congressional Research Service says that although 61% of private sector employers offer paid sick leave as part of the compensation package, only 8% of employees have access to paid time off to deal with family matters. [Linda Levine et. al., Congressional Research Service, *CRS Issue Statement on Labor Standards and Labor Relations*, <http://pennyhill.net/documents/labor_stan dards_and_labor_relations.pdf> (Jan. 11, 2010)] In 2010, the Bureau of Labor Statistics says that 67% of all workers were entitled to paid sick leave; 86% to unpaid family leave; and only 11% to paid family leave—although there were wide variations in access by the type of job, whether or not the employee was unionized, and whether the employee was high- or low-paid. [Bureau of Labor Statistics, *Table 32, Access, Civilian Workers, National Compensation Survey, March 2010*, <http://www.bls.gov/ncs/ebs/benefits/2010/ownership/leave_all .pdf>]

## [B]  Leave for Military Families

Also note that the National Defense Authorization Act, signed on January 28, 2008, extends the requirements of the FMLA for families of military service members. An employee can use up to 12 weeks of unpaid leave when his or her spouse, child, or parent is called up or is on active duty in the armed forces. If the service member is seriously injured, his or her family member can take up to 26 weeks of FMLA leave to care for the injured service member. [Fred Schneyer, *FMLA Expansion for Military Family Headed to White House Again*, plansponsor.com (Jan. 23, 2008)] The 2008 revision of the FMLA final regulations makes it clear that intermittent or reduced leave can be taken for military family leave. See § 38.01[A]. [Jennifer Haskin, Will, Faegre & Benson LLP, *Managing Intermittent Leave Under the FMLA* (June 18, 2009) (benefitslink.com)]

Military-related FMLA leave was further expanded by the Defense Department Fiscal Year 2010 authorization bill, also known as the National Defense Authorization Act, signed October 28, 2009. Under prior law, an employee covered by the FMLA could take up to 12 weeks of leave in a 12-month period because of a qualifying exigency resulting from the employee's spouse, child, or parent being called to, or serving on, active duty. The expanded entitlement allows a worker whose spouse, parent, or child is a reservist to take FMLA leave for a qualifying exigency arising from deployment to a foreign country on active duty. There is also a new leave right when an employee's spouse, parent, or child who serves in the regular armed forces is deployed to a foreign country. A military caregiver can take up to 26 weeks of leave per 12-month period to care for a parent, spouse, child, or relative to whom the employee is next of kin, when the servicemember is under treatment for a serious injury or illness incurred in the course of service (or that began before active duty but was aggravated by active duty). The same categories of relatives can take leave to care for an ill or injured veteran who was on active duty within the five years before the date of treatment. The Secretary of Labor can issue regulations defining qualifying illness or injury. [Kilpatrick Stockton LLP, *President Obama Signs Legislation Expanding Family and Medical Leave Act* (Oct. 30, 2009) (benefitslink .com)]

DOL's Wage and Hour Division issued a Notice of Proposed Rulemaking in early 2012 to implement the 2008 FMLA amendments. [DOL Wage and Hour Division FMLA NPRM; DOL Wage & Hour Division News Release, *Labor Secretary Hilda L. Solis announces proposed rulemaking to implement statutory amendments to Family and Medical Leave Act* (Jan. 30, 2012) (benefitslink.com)]

Notice 2010-15, 2010-6 I.R.B. 390, provides guidance in question and answer form about the HEART Act of 2008. The survivor of a deceased servicemember can make a tax-free rollover of the military death benefit and life insurance to the survivor's Roth IRA or education savings account. All qualified plans must provide that the survivors of a person who dies on active service must receive whatever additional benefits would have been provided if the service-member had returned to work and died while employed. [Rebecca Moore, *IRS Provides Guidance on HEART Act*, plansponsor.com (Jan. 10, 2010)]

Final regulations under the National Defense Authorization Act permit 15 (rather than the earlier limit of five) days of rest-and-recuperation FMLA leave to be taken by an eligible employee. [Jeff Nowak, *DOL Issues Final Rule Implementing FMLA Amendments Expanding Military Family Leave and Leave for Airline Flight Crew Members*, Franczek Radelet FMLA Insights (Feb. 7, 2013) (benefitslink.com)]

Some states, e.g., California, Illinois, Indiana, Maine, Minnesota, Nebraska, New York, Rhode Island, and Washington have their own states providing leave rights to the families of servicemembers. [Buck Consultants FYI, *Washington State Expands Employee Leave Entitlements* (May 19, 2008) (benefitslink.com); George P. Kostakos, Stephen T. Melnick, *New Rhode Island Law Grants Military Families Unpaid Leave*, Littler Mendelson Press Releases (July 2008) (benefitslink.com)]

## [C]   EEOC Guidance on Best Practices About Caregivers

The EEOC defines "best practices" as "proactive measures that go beyond federal non-discrimination requirements" to remove barriers to equal employment opportunity. In May 2007, the EEOC issued Enforcement Guidance on employers' responsibilities toward workers who are caregivers for family members.

Although discrimination against caregivers is not per se forbidden, the EEOC warns that in some situations, placing an employee caregiver in an unfavorable position could constitute unlawful disparate treatment that violates Title VII or the Americans With Disabilities Act's ban on discrimination for associating with a person with a disability. The EEOC said that the Guidance does not create a new protected category; it explains the EEOC's enforcement priorities when caregiving is an additional element in an allegation of discrimination, and warns against making employment decisions based on stereotypes—e.g., that women, but not men, will have caregiving responsibilities.

The document points out that African-American women are particularly likely to combine paid work and family responsibilities, and lower-income workers are likely to encounter times when they have care responsibilities but cannot afford to hire someone to take care of the child or elder. However, the EEOC notes that there will probably be no violation of Title VII if employment decisions reflect poor or declining work performance and not assumptions or stereotypes—even if the employee's work is sub-par because of caregiving responsibilities. [EEOC Enforcement Guidance: *Unlawful Disparate Treatment of Workers with Caregiving Responsibilities* Number 915.002 <http://www.eeoc.gov/policy/docs/caregiving.html> (May 23, 2007)]

In April 2009, the EEOC followed up with a 13-page document to help employers adopt work-life policies that will assist employees who are responsible for the care of vulnerable children, parents, and other dependents. The EEOC's suggestions include:

- Train managers about laws affecting caregivers, e.g., the ADA, the EPA, the FMLA, and the PDA;

- Train managers about the text and application of your company's work-life policies;

- Include caregiving in your equal employment opportunity policy—with a broad definition of the people for whom your employees might provide care;

- Do not be influenced by stereotypes (e.g., that mothers of small children are not committed to their careers; that men should not take parenting leave); ask male and female applicants the same questions about their family obligations;

- Allow flexible schedules, formal or informal, where this does not impair operations;

- Communicate job openings and promotions equally; do not assume that caregivers will not want to apply for a job with long hours or a lot of travel;

- Help employees maintain their skills while on leave, facilitate return to the workforce, and include them in recruiting efforts;

- If your organization has non-exempt employees who work overtime, distribute overtime in a family-friendly way (e.g., optimize the use of volunteers instead of ordering caregivers to work overtime assignments when they may not have child care or elder care available);

- Reassign duties that pregnant or caregiving employees cannot handle;

- Allow the use of sick leave or personal days for caregiving needs—even if your company is not legally subject to the FMLA or related state laws; allow free use of intermittent leave for very short-range caregiving needs (such as taking a parent to a medical appointment);

- Provide information and referral services for caregivers; provide services through the EAP; and/or host workplace support groups for caregivers;

- Have an effective complaint procedure for caregivers who suffer discrimination;

- Enforce an anti-retaliation policy that protects caregivers.

[EEOC, *Employer Best Practices for Workers with Caregiving Responsibilities*, <http://www.eeoc.gov/policy/docs/caregiver-best-practices.html> (Apr. 24, 2009)]

## § 28.02   EMPLOYER-PROVIDED DAY CARE

One option, perhaps the most appreciated by employees, is for the employer to maintain an on-site day care center. Calculating the costs and benefits of running a day care center can be difficult. Initial expenses can be high, but this perk is valuable in recruiting good employees and retaining employees who need quality care for their children.

On-site care is only feasible for large companies—and probably is more workable outside big cities because metropolitan rents are often prohibitive. An employer-sponsored day care center has to be licensed. It will be subject to ongoing inspections. The employer company could become liable if, for example, a child was injured on the premises, or several children developed a contagious illness. The standard Worker's Compensation insurance policy also excludes injuries that occur in an employer-operated day care center.

It can be convenient for the employer to contract out daily operations to an experienced provider of high-quality child care, although this adds further expenses. The employer can also co-sponsor a nearby child care center that offers care to employees of several companies.

However, it is much more common for employers to reimburse employees for some of their child care expenses. [See § 28.07 for a discussion of child care fringe benefits and their tax implications. A smaller-scale program gives employees "I&R" (information and referral) to child care resources, but does not actually furnish services or funds.]

The Home Depot corporate headquarters in Atlanta, where 5,000 employees work, has an on-site child care center with capacity for 278 children. Home Depot employees who work at nearby stores can also use the facility. The day care center, plus a dependent care hotline, are operated by contractor Bright Horizons, which specializes in employer-sponsored on-site child care and back-up care. Home Depot's summer camp accommodates 48 school-age children. Home Depot also has a comprehensive system of back-up care outside the Atlanta area. Employees who have worked for Home Depot for a year or more can get up to 10 days of back-up care for any dependent, including a sick parent. There is a copayment obligation, but it is much lower than the cost of paying for the care out of pocket. [Andrea Davis, *Home Depot Goes Big With Child Care Center*, Employee Benefit News (Sept. 15, 2012) (benefitslink.com)]

The Tax Relief, Unemployment Insurance Reauthorization, and Job Creation Act of 2010, Pub. L. No. 111-312 extends until the end of 2012 the federal tax credit available to employers who furnish child care services. This legislation defines the credit as 25% of qualified child care expenditures and 10% of child care information and referral expenditures. The credit is capped at $150,000 per year.

The American Taxpayer Relief Act of 2012, Pub. L. No. 112-240, extended the availability of this credit once again. The credit is claimed on Form 8882.

## § 28.03   BREAST FEEDING IN THE WORKPLACE

Breast feeding for at least the first six months of life, and preferably a year, is the medical recommendation for newborn babies. So either new mothers must choose bottle feeding; delay their return to work until they are ready to stop breast feeding; or participate in a workplace lactation program that either allows them to feed their babies at the workplace or gives them an appropriate private place to pump and store breast milk. Workplace lactation programs are a good value for employers, because they aid employee retention. Furthermore, breast-fed babies are often healthier than formula-fed babies, so their parents need less time off to deal with babies' illnesses. The demands of a lactation program are modest. Participating employees need a private, reasonably quiet and pleasant place to express breast milk and a refrigerator or cooler to keep it cool, plus a sink to wash up. Typically, employees will need two 30-minute, or three 20-minute, breaks to express milk.

A number of states have laws requiring employers (or employers with a minimum number of employees) to provide lactation support, such as:

- Adequate breaks to express milk;
- A private place that is not a toilet stall to express milk;
- Refrigeration for expressed milk.

Some of these laws impose fines for violation of the requirements; some allow employees to bring private suits to enforce these rights.

At the time of passage of the Patient Protection and Affordable Care Act (PPACA) in March 2010, there were workplace lactation laws in 24 states: Arkansas, California, Colorado, Connecticut, Georgia, Hawaii, Illinois, Indiana, Maine, Minnesota, Mississippi, Montana, New Mexico, New York, North Dakota, Oklahoma, Oregon, Rhode Island, Tennessee, Texas, Vermont, Virginia, Washington, and Wyoming, as well as in the District of Columbia and Puerto Rico. [Sarah Andrews and Mike Ossip, Morgan Lewis LawFlash, *Healthcare Reform Law Requires Reasonable Break Times and Locations for Nursing Mothers*, <http://www.morganlewis.com/pubs/WashGRPP_NursingMothers_LF_07apr10 .pdf> (Apr. 7, 2010) (benefitslink.com)]

The PPACA enacts new 29 U.S.C. § 207(r)(1), requiring all employers subject to the FLSA to provide reasonable breaks to express breast milk for mother of infants up to a year old. A private space other than a restroom must be provided. [Rebecca Moore, *What to Do if Employee Prefers Bathroom for Expressing Milk*, plansponsor.com (Oct 29, 2010).]

Companies with fewer than 50 employees are exempt if the requirement would create undue hardship (significant difficulty or expense for the employer). Although in general, the FLSA requires pay for breaks of less than 20 minutes, the new federal requirement says the break time can be either paid or unpaid. The new law does not preempt state laws that give greater protection to employees. The PPACA provision on breast-feeding amends the FLSA, with the result that employees who are exempt under the FLSA (as executives, professionals, administrative workers, outside salespersons, or computer professionals) are not covered. [Sarah Andrews and Mike Ossip, Morgan Lewis LawFlash, *Healthcare Reform Law Requires Reasonable Break Times and Locations for Nursing Mothers*, <http://www.morganlewis.com/pubs/WashGRPP_NursingMothers_LF_07apr10.pdf> (Apr. 7, 2010) (benefitslink.com); Jackson Lewis, *Health Care Reform Act Requires Employers to Provide Breaks for Breastfeeding* (Mar. 26, 2010) (benefitslink.com)] DOL's Wage and Hour Division published Fact Sheet #73, *Break Time for Nursing Mothers Under the FLSA* in July 2010: [<http://www.dol.gov/whd/regs/compliance/wndfs73.pdf>; see Chad W. Moeller, Neal, Gerber & Eisenberg LLP, *DOL Sheds Light on Break Time for Nursing Mothers Law; Asks Employers for Input* (Feb 9, 2011) (law.com); John E. Thompson, Fisher & Phillips, *DOL Publishes Guidance On FLSA Lactation-Break Requirement*, LLP Blog (July 22, 2010) (benefitslink.com)]

The Fact Sheet says that the FLSA does not require pay for breaks taken to express milk—but if the employer already provides paid breaks, nursing mothers must be allowed to use their paid breaks to express milk. The general FLSA requirement—that employees must be paid for break time unless they are completely free from work duties—continues to apply in this context. The reasonableness of break time depends on the duration and frequency of permitted breaks, and the employer's obligation depends on the individual employee's needs. On an average, DOL expects that two to three breaks will be required in an eight-hour shift, including time to get to the lactation area (which must be located conveniently enough that the mother is not deterred from taking breaks), any waiting time if the area is full, time to get the breast pump and set it up. The employer must provide a place to store the pump and an insulated container to store the milk. The lactation area need not be reserved exclusively for use by nursing employees, as long as it is private and suitable for expressing breast milk.

In May 2013, the Fifth Circuit became the first Court of Appeals to decide a case about lactation discrimination. The Fifth Circuit treated lactation as a medical condition related to pregnancy and childbirth because it was a physiological state caused by childbirth. The plaintiff did not ask for accommodation of lactation; she alleged that she was fired merely for saying that she wanted to express milk at work. The Fifth Circuit treated this as sex discrimination that violated Title VII. [*EEOC v. Houston Funding II*, 717 F.3d 425 (5th Cir. May 30, 2013).

See William Metke, *Fifth Circuit Holds that Lactation Discrimination Violates Title VII* (May 31, 2013) (benefitslink.com).]

The district court for the Northern District of Iowa ruled that, although PPACA amended the FLSA to mandate that employers give employees reasonable time to express breast milk, there is no private right of action against employers for violating that rule. (Aggrieved employees can file a complaint with the Department of Labor, but cannot file a suit because there are no unpaid wages to sue for.) The plaintiff said that she was allowed to express milk in the store office but subsequently found that there was a video camera there. She was not allowed to cover the camera while pumping milk. However, employees can sue for FLSA retaliation if they are disciplined for complaining about the employer's policies: 29 U.S.C. § 115(a)(3), the FLSA anti-retaliation provision, covers informal as well as formal complaints. [*Salz v. Casey's Mktg. Co.*, No. 11-cv-3055 (N.D. Ohio July 19, 2012); see Lawrence E. Dube, Human Resources Report, *Court Tosses PPACA Lactation Rights Claim But Agrees FLSA Barred Employer Retaliation* (July 23, 2012) (benefitslink.com); Michael P. Maslanka, *Can An Employee Sue If An Employer Doesn't Provide A Place To Express Milk?* Work Matters (benefitslink.com) (Aug. 31, 2012)]

In 2011, the IRS reversed its previous holding and said that breast pumps and supplies to assist lactation qualify as medical care under Code § 213(d), because they affect a structure or function of the mother's body. Therefore, they can be deductible medical expenses. If an FSA, MSA, HRA, or HSA reimburses the cost of these items, the employee does not have taxable income. [IRS Ann. 2011-14, 2011-9 I.R.B. 532]

Concluding that working mothers are the fastest-growing segment of the workforce, the National Business Group on Health released a 71-page toolkit, "Investing in Workplace Breastfeeding Programs and Policies," in early 2011. The kit was developed in conjunction with HHS's Office on Women's Health and Health Resources Services Administration's Maternal and Child Health Bureau. The kit has ten major sections, including the business case for workplace lactation programs, the available options, experience of major employers, and resources for communicating with employees. [<http://www.businessgrouphealth.org/index.cfm>; see Fred Schneyer, *NBGH Offers Employers Help on Nursing Mothers Rules*, plansponsor.com (Feb. 3, 2011)]

## § 28.04  ADOPTION ASSISTANCE

Under I.R.C. § 137, as amended by EGTRRA, employers can establish a written adoption assistance program, providing benefits for employees who adopt children. More than 100,000 Americans adopt children each year, so the question is whether the company will offer adoption assistance, and whether employees will get paid leave for adoption.

The tax code provides for two types of assistance. Within limits, certain employees can receive adoption assistance payments from their employers without those benefits being subject to income taxes. There is also a tax credit for adopting a child. Under prior law, more favorable tax treatment was extended when the adoptee had special needs, but current law offers the same treatment whether or not the adoptee has special needs.

PPACA increases the maximum adoption credit to $13,170 per child, $1,000 more than the 2009 level, whether or not the adoptee has special needs. This amount will be adjusted for inflation for tax years beginning after December 31, 2010. The adoption credit has also been made a refundable credit (i.e., if the credit reduces the taxpayer's tax liability below zero, he or she can receive a tax refund). For employer-sponsored adoption assistance programs, the maximum exclusion also goes up $1,000, to $13,170, once again whether or not the adopted person has special needs.

Under the Tax Relief, Unemployment Insurance Reauthorization, and Job Creation Act of 2010, Pub. L. No. 111-312 (TRUI), the extra $1,000 adoption credit and exclusion provided by PPACA are retained. The PPACA increases in the adoption credit—increasing the maximum credit and the phase-out amounts, and making the credit refundable—expire after the 2011 tax year. TRUI says that the adoption credit is not refundable for 2011 or 2012. But the EGTRRA enhancements remain until 2012. Therefore, for tax years beginning in 2012, the limit for the adoption tax credit and income exclusion reverts to $10,000 as adjusted for inflation. [Rev. Proc. 2010-40, 2010-46 I.R.B. 663; IRS News Release IR-2010-108 <http://www.irs.gov/newsroom/article/0,,id=229975,00.html> (Oct. 28, 2010); see EBIA Weekly, *2011 Cost-of-Living Adjustments for Adoption Assistance, Archer MSAs, and Control Employees* (Oct. 28, 2010) (benefitslink.com)]

The 2013 adoption credit, whether or not the child has special needs, is limited to $12,970. It phases out between modified Adjusted Gross Income of $194,850 and $234,580. These figures also apply to adoption assistance programs. [Rev. Proc. 2013-15, 2013-5 I.R.B. 444]

Adoption assistance can be offered under a cafeteria plan—a structure that provides tax benefits for employees with no direct cash outlay by the employer. Adoption assistance programs provided to members of the armed forces are automatically treated as qualified, even if they would not otherwise satisfy the § 137 rules. But illegal adoptions, adoptions involving surrogate mothers, adoption of a stepchild, or adoption of an adult do not qualify under § 137. [See the adoption assistance FAQs at <http://benefitsguides.com/portals/benefits_guides/adoption/adoption_assistance_faqs.html>]

## § 28.05   CORPORATE ELDER CARE ACTIVITIES

Everybody knows that the U.S. senior citizen population is growing, and soon the huge Baby Boom generation will reach retirement age. The vast majority of care provided to assist elderly people with their illnesses and limitations imposed by aging is unpaid, informal care from family members and friends.

A survey by Coupon Cabin shows that 26% of older baby boomers support adult children financially or the children live with them. Over one-fifth (21%) have supported aging parents financially, and 18% have elderly parents living with them. Close to half (42%) of baby boomers postponed retirement for financial reasons. [Rebecca Moore, *Family Pressures Thwart Boomers' Retirement Plans*, plansponsor.com (Feb. 20, 2013)]

Bankers Life and Casualty reported in 2013 that nearly all baby boomers who cared for a parent or spouse (88%) found that the experience was more difficult than they expected; 34% said it cost more financially, 33% experienced more relationship impact, 57% needed more emotional strength, and 52% said it took more time than they expected. Forty percent of middle-income ($25,000–$75,000 household income) baby boomers have been caregivers—77% of them caring for a parent, the rest for a spouse with a disability. Forty-four percent of women and 32% of men in this cohort report having been caregivers. [Bankers Life & Casualty Co. Center for a Secure Retirement, *Retirement Care Planning: The Middle-Income Boomer Perspective*, <http://www.centerfora secureretirement.com/media/139741/retirement-care-study.pdf> (Aug. 2013); see Kevin McGuinness, *How Adult Caregiving Can Impact Retirement*, plansponsor .com (Aug. 27, 2013)]

A study by Agingcare.com, published in November 2012 asked 285 caregivers (89% female, 11% male) about their experiences with elder care. One-third said the experience was mostly negative, 9% found it mostly positive, and the plurality (58%) found it equally positive and negative. A quarter said that being a caregiver damaged their relationship with their parents, 32% said it improved the relationship, and 43% said it had no or only minor impact. But 90% of caregivers said that caregiving affected their other relationships, such as with their spouse, children, and co-workers. Only one-seventh of caregivers (14%) were not involved in their parents' finances at all, and 60% were fully involved in their parents' decision-making process. Forty-one percent provided monthly financial assistance to their parents, and 24% of those providing financial help gave $500 or more a month, and another 24% gave $250–$499 a month. Among caregivers who help parents financially, 92% assist with day to day expenses, 44% with housing, 24% with prescription drug costs, and 23% with other health costs. [Agingcare.com/eHealth, *Caregiver Survey*, <http://news .ehealthinsurance.com/_ir/68/20125/eHealth-CareGiverReport_FINAL_.pdf> (November 2012)]

An early 2011 Wall St. J. article reports that, to serve the 43 million caregivers, about 10% of companies provide eldercare benefits. Flextime is also gaining in popularity. Caring.com's February 2011 survey showed close to 75% of caregivers saying that they had to drop out of the workforce or change jobs because of care needs. The MetLife Juggling Act survey showed 40% of caregivers reporting that caregiving limited their chances to advance in their careers. A federal survey, the Disability and American Families study, showed that household income in households where there is a caregiver were 15% lower than in households with no caregivers. Catey Hill, *Best Careers for Family Caregivers*, WSJ.com (Feb. 24, 2011)]

Federal legislation, the National Alzheimer's Project Act, Pub. L. No. 111-375, calls for the creation of a national strategic plan to fight Alzheimer's Disease. The law sets up an advisory council from all federal agencies dealing with health, science, and aging, as well as a coordinated national plan to improve early diagnosis and coordination of care, and to research new treatments. [Pam Belluck, *Caring for the Patient With Alzheimer's*, NYTimes.com (Jan. 2, 2011)]

In mid-2010, the National Institute on Aging published an Alzheimer's caregiver guide, available as a PDF file online. Print copies can be ordered from the Institute's Website. The mission of the National Institute on Aging's Alzheimer's Disease Education and Referral Center includes answering questions, sending out publications, providing local referrals, and disseminating information about clinical research trials. Its phone number is (800) 438-4380. [Paula Span, *Caregiving and Alzheimer's: A Road Map*, NYTimes.com (June 14, 2010)]

Caring for the disabled elderly has an immense impact on the caregivers' family life—and on their productivity as employees. The MetLife Mature Market Institute regularly performs and publishes research about the effect of caregiving on the workplace. A MetLife study, published in mid-2011, shows that the average lifetime wages lost to caregivers who leave the job market early is $149,693 for women, $89,107 for men, and women lose $131,351 in Social Security benefits, men lose $142,609, and both lose $50,000 in pensions. [2011 *MetLife Study of Caregiving Costs to Working Caregivers*, discussed in Sara Kelly, *Workers Lose 300k in Wages and Benefits When Caregiving*, plansponsor.com (June 14, 2011)]

The Alzheimer's Association looked specifically at the effect of Alzheimer's caregiving on employment. Almost half (44%) of the 14.9 million unpaid Alzheimer's caregivers held part- or full-time jobs, but worklife was significantly affected for most of them. Seventy percent of male, and 61% of female, caregivers said they had to take time off, get to work late, or leave early because of caregiving needs. Eighteen percent of male and 21% of female caregivers had to take a leave of absence; 11% of males and 14% of females had to shift to part-time work; 6% of males and 12% of females had to quit their jobs; 11% of men and 12% women had to take a less demanding job; and 14% and 11% respectively, had to turn down a promotion that would have interfered with their caregiving needs. Loss of job benefits was reported by 8% of men and 11% of women. Three percent of men and 10% of women opted for early retirement, and 8% of men and 9% of women said that their work deteriorated so much as a result of caregiving that they were at risk of being fired. [Alzheimer's Association, *2011 Alzheimer's Disease Facts and Figures*, <http://www.alz.org>]

In early 2012, there were an estimated 43 million caregivers taking care of persons who are aged 50 and older; almost a quarter of the caregivers reported difficulty in coordinating care and combining it with work. The National Alliance for Caregiving's June 2011 analysis of data from the U.S. Health and Retirement Study estimates that caregivers age 50 and over sacrifice a lifetime average of $303,880 in wages, pensions, and Social Security benefits (because quitting a job or reducing hours also affects pensions and Social Security benefits). The National Alliance says that, because caring for a person with Alzheimer's Disease is so stressful, being an Alzheimer's caregiver can increase the caregiver's own health bills by an average of $4,766 a year—which means that these caregivers also lose time at work for their own health needs.

Genworth Financial and AARP introduced a new service for AARP members: families of older adults suffering from dementia and other illnesses can assess needs and develop a care plan online, on the phone, or in person with a registered nurse. The fees for the program depend on which services are used, starting at $12.99 for six months of online access, through $149 for a phone assessment, service plan, plus six months' online access, to $489 for an in-home visit. The "service finder" option, giving local information and quality ratings, negotiating discounts for participants, and coordinating the start of care costs $295 over the telephone, $665 in person.

Employees who do not consider themselves caregivers will not access specialized services, so one important role the HR department can play is helping employees recognize that they are caregivers; the realization often comes only after they have been engaged in caregiving for a while as occasional small tasks increase to a major commitment. [Carol Harnett, Human Resource Executive Online, *Caring for the Caregivers* (Feb. 13, 2012) (benefitslink.com)]

## § 28.06   THE CORPORATE ELDER CARE ROLE

One problem with corporate elder care efforts is that they often use a child-care template that is not very effective—child care doesn't require tangling with the Medicare Part D labyrinth, for example! Another problem is that, in a time of soaring benefit costs, corporations are far more willing to provide low-cost I&R than more costly benefits such as paying for geriatric care management or offering paid leave to employees with elder care problems. The I&R system could be limited in scope and could be poorly edited, so that obsolete listings remain, or poor-quality providers are not eliminated. Even if the I&R system is excellent, employees still face a lot of hard work in creating and managing the elder care plan.

A 2010 article lists ten tips for helping employees with their eldercare problems:

1. Encourage employees over age 40 to talk to their parents about elder planning, including discussing their parents' medical and financial information;

2. Link employees to community resources, such as the Area Agency on Aging and social service agencies;

3. Have books, tapes, etc. on elder care on hand and available as resources;

4. Inform employees about financial and health care proxies;

5. Remind employees that a child assisting parents with financial matters should know the parents' bank accounts, online banking passwords, insurance, etc.;

6. Plan for long-term care, possibly including long-term care insurance in the plan—especially if the employer offers an LTCI plan (see § 21.03) LTCI;

7. Support caregivers by offering counseling or other resources;

8. Encourage employees to take advantage of respite options;

9. Maintain policies and procedures for dealing with caregiving-based absenteeism;

10. Involve the EAP's care managers or private Geriatric Care Managers—especially for long-distance caregivers. [Carolyn Rosenblatt, *10 Tips for Helping Employees With Aging Parents*, workforce .com (April 2010) (benefitslink.com)]

Under an I&R plan, the HR department, Employee Assistance Program, or other relevant department maintains listings of nursing homes, home health agencies, government agencies for the aging, and other resources.

Other elder care resources that employers can provide include:

• Seminars about relevant topics such as Medicare and Medicaid;

• Support groups for caregivers;

• Hotlines giving elder care information;

• Subsidized phone consultations with resource or elder care experts (including those in other geographic areas, where employees' relatives live);

• Directories and other publications;

• Caregiver fairs, providing exhibits from public agencies as well as voluntary organizations and for-profit service vendors;

• Counseling from a psychologist or clinical social worker;

- Subsidies for adult day care for the parent;

- Respite care;

- Emergency care (including care in the home of the elderly person);

- Paratransit, such as wheelchair-accessible vans, to provide transportation to medical appointments and other trips that would otherwise require the employee's services as driver;

- Subsidizing the cost of pagers that the parent can use to contact the employee in an emergency;

- Case management—services of social workers or geriatric care managers (GCMs), who advise the employee about creating and managing a complete elder care plan (The employer could pay care managers to provide in-home assessments of the care needs of employees' elderly relatives; the care manager produces a written report and research recommendations, saving employees a lot of research time. Ceridian Lifeworks estimates that employers can save three dollars for every dollar spent on a program like this.);

- "Elder-proofing" services to make a senior citizen's home safer;

- Monthly or other regularly scheduled seminars for caregiver employees;

- Special outreach efforts during May (Older Americans Month) and October (National Caregivers Month);

- Discounts on eldercare-related products such as incontinence supplies and nutritional supplements;

- An in-house elder care coordinator (especially if the company has a large workforce, or a workforce with a preponderance of middle-aged and older people who can be expected to have elder care needs);

- Adding elderly dependent parents to the coverage of dependent care accounts.

For the unionized workplace, see the AFL-CIO's worksheet, "Bargaining for Eldercare," available at <http://www.aflcio.com>.

In March 2012, the National Alliance for Caregiving published a report on *Best Practices in Workplace Eldercare,* <http://www.caregiving.org/pdf/research/ BestPracticesEldercareFINAL.pdf>. The authors are Donna L. Wagner, Andrea Lindemer, Kelly Niles Yokum, and Mary DeFreest. This report says that the pioneering model for corporate eldercare was the same "resource and referral" model already in use for child care. In 1997, 23% of the employers surveyed used this model. As the 1990s ended, employers began to innovate, adding interventions tailored to individual needs—for example, providing access to elder law attorneys and geriatric care managers. More caregivers gained access to flexible schedules. There were some experiments with on-site support groups for employees, and even adult day care centers in the workplace, but the experiments were seldom used and were not cost-effective.

This report cites the SHRM for the proposition that corporate eldercare activities have declined significantly: in 2007, 22% of employers surveyed offered eldercare referrals, but only 9% did in 2011. In 2007, one-third of employers offered paid family leave; only one-quarter did in 2011.

The Health Insurance Portability and Accountability Act (HIPAA) of 1996 [Pub. L. No. 104–191] cleared up some previously murky tax questions. It enacted Code § 7702B, which provides for tax deductions for some LTCI purchasers. In effect, HIPAA places "qualified" long-term care insurance plans on the same footing as Accident & Health (A&H) plans, so the employer will be entitled to a tax deduction (if it does contribute to the premiums) and employees will not have taxable income on account of employer contributions. But HIPAA also makes it clear that LTCI cannot be provided through either a cafeteria plan or a flexible spending account.

Rev. Proc. 2012-41, 2012-45 I.R.B. 539, defines the qualified long-term care insurance policy premiums that can be deducted for 2013 by individual taxpayers, ranging from $360 a year for people who have not reached age 40 to $4,550 for those who are 70 years or older. Up to $320 a day in benefits from a qualified policy can be received tax-free.

## § 28.07   DEPENDENT CARE ASSISTANCE PLANS

The Internal Revenue Code recognizes, and gives favorable tax treatment to, plans under which the employer makes direct payments to provide dependent care to employees, or the employer reimburses employees for certain dependent care expenses. [I.R.C. § 129] The employer is not obligated to pre-fund the plan. It can pay benefits as they arise, out of current income, with no need to maintain a separate account. However, the employer is required to provide reasonable notice to eligible employees that the program is in existence and how it operates.

Employees do not have taxable income because of participation in an I.R.C. § 129 plan. However, the plan cannot pay more for dependent care than the employee earns. (In other words, the plan can't be set up as a perk for employees who are, in essence, on parenthood leave and earn very little.) Furthermore, in effect the plan only assists employees who are single parents, or who are part of a two-career couple, because the employee will have taxable income if the I.R.C. § 129 benefits exceed the income of the employee's spouse, unless that spouse is a full-time student or disabled.

In addition to these limitations, the maximum employer contribution to an I.R.C. § 129 plan that can be excluded from income is $5,000 per employee. This is further reduced to $2,500 in the case of married employees who file separate returns. The § 129 amounts are not indexed for inflation, so those numbers remain current.

For this purpose, dependent care expenses are household services and other expenses that are incurred to permit the employee to hold a job outside the home. In the I.R.C. § 129 context, "dependents" means dependent children under age 15, or a spouse or other dependent (e.g., an aging parent) who is physically or mentally incapable of self-care.

The Code defines a qualified dependent care assistance plan as a written plan for the exclusive benefit of employees, subject to a classification created by the employer but approved as nondiscriminatory by the IRS. To be considered nondiscriminatory, not more than 25% of the contributions to the plan or benefits received from the plan may relate to shareholders, 5% owners, or their families. The average benefits provided under the plan to employees who are not highly compensated must be 55% or more of those provided to highly compensated employees.

If the plan fails to be qualified for this reason, then HCEs (but not other employees) will have taxable income as a result of plan participation. Every year, by January 31, employees must be given a written report of the amounts paid or expenses incurred by the plan for that employee's dependent care in the previous year. An employer-provided day care center is deemed to be a welfare benefit plan, but a dependent care plan that involves reimbursement of employees' dependent care expenses is not.

Dependent-care plans are linked to the Code provisions for a dependent care credit that taxpayers can take. The credit is a sliding-scale percentage (a higher percentage for lower-income people) of qualifying dependent care expenses up to a maximum. The Child and Dependent Care Tax Credit was extended through December 31, 2012 by the Tax Relief, Unemployment Insurance Reauthorization, and Job Creation Act of 2010 (Pub. L. No. 111-312). It was still listed as available by the IRS Website on January 13, 2013: <http://www.irs.gov/taxtopics/tc602.html> (Jan. 13, 2013).

# CHAPTER 29
# DIVERSITY IN THE WORKPLACE

## § 29.01  INTRODUCTION

It can no longer be assumed that all employees in an organization will be young, able-bodied, Anglo-Saxon males. Greater diversity within a workplace allows recruitment of the best available talent and the widest variety of viewpoints and inputs—but also creates potential for misunderstanding and conflict among employees.

The U.S. Census Bureau projections released in late 2012 project that in the half century after the 2010 census (source of the figures adjusted to create the projections), there will be no single majority racial group. Non-Hispanic whites will be the largest single group, but will no longer have majority status. The senior citizen (65 and over) population is projected to more than double, from 43.1 million (2012) to 92.0 million (2060). The non-Hispanic white population is expected to reach its peak in 2024, at approximately 200 million. In 2012, about 1/6 of U.S. residents are Hispanic—a proportion that is expected to almost double by 2060, with the Hispanic population rising from 53.3 million (2012) to 128.8 million (2060). The projection for the African-American population is an increase from 42.1 million to 61.8 million (13.1% to 14.7% of the population) over the half-century period. The Asian population is expected to rise from 15.9 million people/5.1% of the U.S. population in 2012 to 34.4 million/8.2% in 2060. As the population ages and senior citizens become a larger proportion of the populace, the size of the working-age (18–64) population is expected to go from 197 million to 239 million from 2012–2060—but the percentage of working-age people will probably decline, from 62.7% of the populace to 56.9%. [Census Bureau press release, *U.S. Census Bureau Projections Show a Slower Growing, Older, More Diverse Nation a Half Century From Now*, <http://www.census.gov/newsroom/releases/archives/population/cb12-243.html> (Dec. 12, 2012)]

The HR department's mission is to promote efficiency and cooperation—not to eliminate differences or even prejudices. A company's workforce doesn't have to worship together, enjoy the same sporting events, celebrate the same holidays, or even like each other. They do have to understand the factors shaping other peoples' behavior, strive to avoid offending others, be tolerant of unintended offensive remarks and actions, and work together harmoniously and productively.

ERGs are Employee Resource Groups, also known as employee networks and affinity groups. According to Mercer's Equality, Diversity and Inclusion practice, they are emerging in many companies, not just for traditional affinity groups such as race and gender but also for intentionally inclusive ones like multicultural or multigenerational groups and groups based around a common interest (e.g., the environment). Study participants said the most common ERG categories were women (reported by 93% of respondents), race/ethnicity (90%), LBGT (84%), disability (52%), generational (48%), multicultural (43%), working parents (35%), military (34%), religion (16%), adoptive parents (13%), elder care (11%), and interfaith (9%). Study respondents said between 1% and 20% of their world-wide workforce participated. Survey participants said a typical budget was $7,203 per 100 ERG members. Annual spending at some companies runs into six fig-ures, even without counting non-financial resources such as the cost of providing facilities and technologies. Survey respondents said they assigned an average of 1.4 full-time equivalents to manage their ERGs. [*ERGs Come of Age: The Evo-lution of Employee Resource Groups*, <http://www.mercer.com/ERGreport>; see Rebecca Moore, *Study Finds Rebirth of Employee Resource Groups*, plansponsor .com (Jan. 26, 2011)]

There are pros and cons for employers that already have employee resource groups for female and minority employees to adopt similar programs for gay employees. A number of major businesses (e.g., Chubb Corporation, Merck, Ernst & Young, Lehman Brothers Holdings) are training their managers in preventing workplace discrimination against gay and lesbian employees. Chubb's training is a two-hour session for all managers, led by one gay and one straight employee, covering topics such as how to deal with transgender employees and discussion of case studies. [Sarah E. Needleman, *More Programs Move to Halt Bias Against Gays*, Wall St. J., Nov. 26, 2007, at B3]

The Human Rights Campaign, which published its first Corporate Equality Index in 2002, finds that the corporate world (especially law firms and large banks) has become much more gay-friendly over the course of the decade. In the 2002 edition, 13 businesses out of 319 had a perfect score for equal treatment policies about sexual orientation. Since then, more criteria have been added, resulting in 190 out of 636 businesses (including 55 law firms and 22 financial services companies) earning a perfect score. Most participants scored 80% or more, with policies forbidding sexual-orientation and gender identity discrimina-tion and providing benefits for domestic partners. However, Exxon Mobil man-aged to score minus 25%. [Tiffany Hsu, *Study: Workplace Friendlier to Gays*, Los Angeles Times (Dec. 12, 2011) (benefitslink.com)]

There are 54 million persons with disabilities—the largest minority group in the United States, but the DOL says that only 22% of working-age persons with a disability are employed, whereas 70% of working-age non-disabled persons are employed. A special advertising section in the N.Y. Times in Spring 2010 profiles New Jersey organizations serving the employment needs of persons with disabilities.

Hire Disability Solutions (West Nyack, New Jersey) offers training, staff-ing, and recruitment and connecting national employers with appropriate candi-dates.

EmployME! Is a public-private partnership sponsored by the New Jersey Institute of Technology to train adults with physical disabilities for information technology jobs. Candidates are trained for 18 weeks in classrooms equipped with assistive technology and, after training, get placement assistance and individual job coaching. EmployME! Can be reached at (800) 624-9850.

The Think Beyond the Label campaign, <http://www.thinkbeyond thelabel.com>, is a 38-state collaboration with Medicare Infrastructure Grants to raise awareness of the business case for small- and medium-sized businesses to hire people with disabilities. The Website contains information about hiring people with disabilities.

Winston-Salem Industries for the Blind operates a factory where all the workers are visually impaired, many of them totally blind. Almost 70% of blind adults of working age are unemployed. Blind workers receive training in using adaptive devices, such as audio alerts that inform them when to remove a part from a machine or sewing machines equipped with a metal strip for lining up material to be sewn together. Winston-Salem Industries for the Blind was established in 1938 after the Roosevelt administration ordered federal agencies to buy supplies made by blind workers. Winston-Salem Industries is now looking for more private-sector work as its military and other government contracts are reduced. [Nicole LePorte, *Hiring the Blind, While Making a Green Statement*, NYTimes.com (Mar. 25, 2012)]

Rutgers, the state university of New Jersey, maintains several research organizations on disability employment issues, including the John J. Heldrich Center for Workforce Development, <http://www.heldrich.rutgers.edu>, which studies workplace best practices and offers research assistance to industry. The Heldrich Center set up the National Technical Assistance and Research Center to Promote Leadership for Increasing Employment and Economic Independence of Adults With Disabilities, which is working with the states of Connecticut, Maryland, and Massachusetts to create state models for creating jobs for persons with disabilities. [Special advertising section, *Diversity & Disability Hiring*, N.Y. Times, Mar. 21, 2010, Business p. 10]

## § 29.02  THE GLASS CEILING

Unfortunately, some people are actively and consciously hostile to those different from themselves. They engage in whatever discriminatory actions they think they can get away with. However, overt hatred and resentment are not the only factors that block full advancement for qualified women and members of minority groups. There are other, subtler forces at work, sometimes affecting people who on a conscious level are objective and tolerant.

The prejudices of the past cast a long shadow. If law and business schools used to discriminate against minorities and women, then the supply of members of these groups with professional degrees, and with decades of business experience, will be limited. If a company hardly ever recruits women or members of minority groups for its training program, and if its policy is to promote from within, then it will look to its (overwhelmingly white male) middle managers when it's time to fill senior posts.

These subtler barriers to advancement are sometimes called the "glass ceiling": Advancement up to a point is reasonably easy, but there are invisible barriers to achieving the really top jobs. See the reports of a federal commission convened under the Glass Ceiling Act, a provision of the Civil Rights Act of 1999. [Pub. L. No. 102-166]

According to the main report, "Many judgments on hiring and promotion are made on the basis of a look, the shape of a body, or the color of skin." [*A Solid Investment: Making Full Use of the Nation's Human Capital*, <http://www.ilr.cornell.edu/library/catherwood/collections . . . >]

Although the Glass Ceiling report acknowledges that some factors (such as educational systems and social attitudes) are beyond corporate control, the report identifies some factors that business can control:

- Whether recruitment is narrow or broad-based;

- Extent of outreach efforts;

- Degree to which new hires are assigned to marginal areas or staff jobs that have less promotion potential than more central, line jobs;

- Presence or absence of mentors;

- Whether good performance is rewarded with access to training and prime assignments;

- Access to social events and informal networks (e.g., social and sporting events);

- Help and support from colleagues, versus hostility and demeaning treatment;

- Whether evaluations are objective or merely reflect prejudices.

Certain characteristics are shared by successful diversity programs:

- The CEO actively supports the program;

- The program is comprehensive and inclusive;

- The program has a genuine goal of advancing the most talented people, whatever their background;

- Results are reviewed, and managers are accountable for results;

- The company has long-range relationships with community organizations, not a single effort that is quickly abandoned;

- Recruitment is genuinely diverse;

- Recruiters consult sources such as <www.diversityee.com>, <www .newsjobs.com>, <www.diversity-services.com>, and <www.Hire Diversity> to obtain resumes from people from a wide variety of backgrounds;

- The program makes out a business case for diversity and communicates it to employees.

In early 2013, more than half of the Wall Street workforce was female, but only 3% of finance chief executives were female. Women held only 19% of corporate board seats and 16% of executive-suite jobs. Most women in senior positions run divisions like asset management, marketing, or HR—which do not contribute as much to corporate revenue as divisions such as trading or investment banking. [Jessica Silver-Greenberg, *A Suite of Their Own*, Dealbook, NYTimes.com (Apr. 2, 2013)]

To reduce the gender gap in financial services, major banks are experimenting with networking and mentorship to encourage women to seek for promotion. Irene Dorner, chief executive of HSBC USA, said that there is not just a "glass ceiling" but a "sticky floor" problem caused by women who do not try to achieve major corporate roles. Dorner's take on diversity, as told to the New York Times: "I think that you are insane commercially if you run any corporation and you turn down the opportunity for different views, innovation and a different way of thinking." [Andrew Ross Sorkin, *Women in a Man's World*, Dealbook, NYTimes.com (Apr. 2, 2013)]

## § 29.03  DIVERSITY TRAINING

Corporations frequently attempt to defuse hostilities within the workplace by offering (or requiring) diversity training. Usually, it is provided by outside contractors. The training could be a voluntary initiative by management, part of a negotiated settlement with the EEOC or a state antidiscrimination agency, or part of the settlement of a court case. The mission of the training is to make employees examine their assumptions and to relate to other employees in a more professional manner.

The goals of diversity training include:

- Finding areas in which the organization is defective;

- Setting goals for improvement;

- Identifying specific steps for reaching the goals;

- Training employees to carry out those steps.

However, diversity training is not without risks and disadvantages. The program can wind up furnishing evidence for a Title VII or other discrimination suit. A well-intentioned program to promote understanding and harmony can worsen the anger and resentment already simmering below the surface. Employees can feel that discussion of other religions or lifestyles is an insult to their own deeply held beliefs. A 2004 case illustrates this risk. AT&T Broadband maintained a diversity policy requiring all employees to "recognize, respect, and value differences." A fundamentalist Christian employee refused to sign the certificate, because his religion teaches that some differences are sinful and do not deserve to be valued. The District of Colorado found that he put the employer on notice of his religious objection to the policy, requiring the employer to start the interactive process of accommodation; not doing so violated the employee's right to religious accommodation. [*Buonanno v. AT&T Broadband LLC, 313 F. Supp. 2d 1069* (D. Colo. 2004)] An attempt to reach out to traditionally disfavored groups could be construed as reverse discrimination. And, in any event, a diversity training program (which could be viewed as purely cosmetic) is no substitute for effective hiring or for making sure that no one is subjected to a hostile environment in the workplace.

In 2007, the District Court for the District of Columbia held that the existence of a diversity policy cannot be used as evidence of reverse discrimination. The white male plaintiff alleged unsuccessfully that promoting a woman rather than promoting him was discriminatory, and the diversity policy encouraged promotion of women and thereby discriminated against men. The Seventh Circuit held that it was not discriminatory to forbid an employee to form a religious affinity group when race, national origin, gender, and sexual orientation groups were permitted. The company policy forbade groups engaging in religious or political advocacy, and the Seventh Circuit held that the policy was acceptable because it was applied even-handedly to all religious groups. [David K. Haase, *The Legal Pitfalls of Diversity Policies* (special to law.com) (Jan. 2, 2008). See *Jones v. Barnhanke*, 493 F. Supp. 2d 18 (D.D.C. 2007); *Moranski v. GM*, 433 F.3d 537 (7th Cir. 2005)]

## § 29.04  DIVERSITY AUDITS

The prospect of performing a diversity audit raises a similar mix of questions. A company that has central-office commitment to diversity might have very different conditions at the shop-floor level. Furthermore, a multi-unit company can find it difficult to maintain uniform policies throughout.

A well-designed audit can pinpoint the problems and lead to their resolution. However, a badly designed survey does not generate any useful information, but it does generate data that could be damning if a plaintiff discovers it. Doing a diversity audit shows that management cares about the issue. However, that could backfire, if employees expect real change that doesn't come.

■ **TIP:** If a lawyer performs or supervises the audit, there is at least a possibility that potentially embarrassing material can be protected by attorney-client confidentiality. But don't forget that confidentiality is sacrificed if the information is publicized.

Labor lawyers Christine Amalfe and Heather Akawie Adelman give some suggestions for an effective diversity audit:

- The first step is advice from a qualified employment lawyer;

- Concentrate on facts, not subjective comments, when collecting information;

- Destroy the individual survey responses and interview notes once statistical data has been compiled;

- Mark the finished report "privileged and confidential";

- Keep the reports separate from other HR information;

- Control distribution, and do not disclose the results to anyone who does not have a legitimate need to know.

## § 29.05 ENGLISH-ONLY RULES

In many (if not most) workplace situations, the ability to speak and understand English fluently is a valid job qualification. However, a person can be fluent in English even though it is not his or her first language. He or she may be more comfortable speaking other languages. According to the 2000 U.S. Census, 18% of the residents of the United States (47 million people) spoke a language other than English when they were at home. However, this has not frequently been raised as a legal issue: In 1996, the EEOC received a mere 32 complaints about English-only policies, up to only 155 in 2004. [Miriam Jordan, *Employers Requiring "English Only" at Work May Face Bias Suits* and *Employers Provide Language Aid*, Wall St. J., Nov. 8, 2005, at B1, B13]

If the employer bans languages other than English in the workplace, it is easy for national-origin minority groups to show disparate impact.

In some contexts, it is also required that management communicate with workers in languages other than English: for example, the PPACA requires distribution of health plan communications in other languages based on the county population that is literate only in a non-English language.

Many states have enacted statutes making English the official language of the state. In 2013, Alabama, Alaska, Arizona, Arkansas, California, Colorado, Florida, Georgia, Hawaii, Idaho, Illinois, Indiana, Iowa, Kansas, Kentucky, Louisiana, Massachusetts, Mississippi, Missouri, Montana, Nebraska, New Hampshire, North Carolina, South Carolina, South Dakota, Tennessee, Utah, Virginia, and Wyoming had "official-English" laws. [Chart, <http://www.us-english.org/view/13> (accessed Apr. 3, 2013)]

Most of these statutes include certain exceptions (e.g., the criminal trial of a person who does not speak English; when health and safety requires communication in another language). About 40 cities also had similar laws of their own. In June 2010, Tennessee adopted a bill permitting workplace English-only policies if the company has legitimate business reasons for the policy. [Rebecca Moore, *TN Bill Permits English-Only Policies in Workplaces*, plansponsor.com (June 29, 2010)]

An employer who imposes an English-only rule must be able to demonstrate job-relatedness and business necessity: for instance, that there is no other way to meet customer needs or communicate in an emergency. But it would be hard to establish business necessity for forbidding employees to converse in other languages during meals or breaks, or when they are in the restroom or a locker room.

Where a high percentage of employees or customers speak languages other than English, or where the company does a good deal of business in non-English-speaking countries, bilingual employees (whether native speakers or those who have learned the language) can be invaluable. The question then becomes whether the pay rate should be higher for bilingual employees.

In September 2000, the EEOC arranged a settlement of close to $200,000 with an Illinois company that agreed to provide back pay for seven Hispanic workers who quit or were fired under the company's English-only rule, plus punitive damages. [No by-line, *Employer's English-Only Policy Brings a Settlement of $192,500*, N.Y. Times, Sept. 2, 2000, at A12] Years later, the EEOC obtained a settlement from Skilled Healthcare Group, Inc. (a nursing home chain) calling for payments of up to $450,000 plus other relief for a class of 53 Hispanic employees and former employees who were subjected to disparate treatment and harassment and were discriminated against in work assignments, promotion, and pay because of their national origin and Spanish language. The facilities had an English-only policy that covered breaks as well as on-duty hours and even forbade the employees to speak Spanish to Spanish-speaking facility residents of the chain's facilities. [Rebecca Moore, *Nursing Home Group to Pay $450K for National Origin Discrimination*, plansponsor.com (Apr. 21, 2009)]

## § 29.06  PROMOTING DIVERSITY

Steps to take to promote equality in the workplace—or simply to avoid getting sued—include:

- Broaden your recruitment efforts. Don't recruit only at the nearest colleges, or only at the Ivy League. Low-cost public colleges attract some excellent students who can't afford private institutions, so don't rule them out as sources of recruitment;

- Reward managers who increase the diversity of their workforces (with raises, bonuses, and promotions);

- Compare your diversity efforts to those of competitors;

- Provide newly hired female and minority candidates with the training, access to information, mentoring, and networking that they need to succeed;

- Remind employees to avoid ethnic slurs and statements that could create a hostile environment in all written documents, e-mail, and voice mail messages—and also remind them that supposedly deleted materials can often be restored!

Many businesses find that diversity is a market advantage if they do business internationally, or if many of the customers within their markets are, e.g., black, Asian, or Latino. Having employees who literally speak the customers' language, or are familiar with their customs and preferences, improves sales. There is also a danger that someone unfamiliar with language and culture will offend business partners or potential customers, so a diverse team minimizes such risks. [Kelley Holland, *How Diversity Makes a Team Click*, N.Y. Times, Apr. 22, 2007, Business, p. 16; Julie Bennett, *West Coast Makes Diversity a Corporate Imperative*, Wall St. J. (special advertising section), Jan. 30, 2007, at B9]

Some companies are appointing a CDO, a Chief Diversity Officer, to handle matters such as recruitment, ethics, and legal compliance to improve the diversity of the company's workforce. The CDO is also responsible for seeing that mentoring, good assignments, and leadership training are available to employees from groups that have been disadvantaged in the workplace. About a quarter of CDOs report directly to the CEO; the rest report to HR or another department. CDOs who report to the CEO probably have greater power and influence. [Leslie Kwoh, *Firms Hail New Chiefs (of Diversity)*, WSJ.com (Jan. 5, 2012)]

Another area of concern is diversity on the board of directors. In early 2013, institutional investors filed shareholder resolutions with 20 major companies protesting the absence of women from the companies' boards. The Thirty Percent Coalition Institutional Investor Committee approached companies including Hartford Financial, Lowe's Companies, and Urban Outfitters Inc. Calvert Investments analyst Christine DeGroot said that female and minority directors help companies widen their customer base and add new perspectives to the board. Making a commitment to adding women and minority directors shows that a company recognizes the value of diversity. [The Thirty Percent Coalition's Website is <http://www.30percentcoalition.org>; see Rebecca Moore, *Institutional Investors Encourage Corporate Board Diversity*, plansponsor.com (Feb. 28, 2013).]

# PART VI

# EMPLOYEE RELATIONS

# CHAPTER 30

# LABOR LAW

## § 30.01  INTRODUCTION

In the broadest sense, labor law covers the entire relationship between employers and employees. However, the term is usually used in a much narrower sense: to mean the body of law dealing with whether a union will be allowed to organize a workplace; union elections, challenges to elections, and decertification of a union that is guilty of misconduct or that no longer represents employee interests; negotiating a Collective Bargaining Agreement (CBA); interpretation of the CBA; and strikes. Labor law sets rules for conduct by both management and unions.

In most cases, labor law is a matter of federal law. Congress has preempted this issue, in the interest of creating a single, uniform body of law that prevails throughout the country.

Between 2010 and 2011, there was little change in the percentage of U.S. workers belonging to unions; in previous years, there had been large declines. In 2010, there were 14.7 million union workers, or 11.8% of the workforce, rising slightly to 14.8 million union members, or 11.9% of the workforce, in 2011. Between 2010 and 2011, there were about 110,000 new union members in the private workforce—but a decline of 61,000 in the number of unionized government employees. Fiscal 2011 saw only 1,594 union elections conducted by the NLRB, the lowest number ever recorded; six years earlier, there were 2,669 elections. [Melanie Trottman and Kris Maher, *Unions See Little Change in Membership*, WSJ.com (Jan. 27, 2012)]

The easiest kind of operation for a union to organize is a large factory with many well-paid blue collar workers who believe they can improve their job security and enhance their pay and benefits by unionizing. The workers must be secure enough to be able to make a credible threat of going out on strike. They have to believe that they will be able to survive economically during a strike, that they will be rehired afterwards, and that the employer needs to end the strike quickly for its own economic benefit.

But there are many instances in which these conditions are not met, and either workers are afraid to unionize, or believe that they have nothing to gain (and in fact may lose by becoming the pawns of a corrupt union, or may undergo job loss if the employer goes out of business or relocates in another state or a foreign country). Recently, unions have been concentrating on organizing service workers, whose jobs can't be relocated easily, and putting pressure on employers to recognize unions by consent, rather than having a representation election. (There are still about 3,000 representation elections each year, and the results are pretty evenly divided between union and employer victories.)

A fast food organization drive began in late 2012 in New York City. Forty organizers strove to unionize chains such as McDonald's, Wendy's, Dominos, and Taco Bell, with a goal of a $15 hourly wage. This was the largest-scale initiative to date. The New York Department of Labor said that the median pay for fast food workers in New York City is about $9 an hour, or $18,500 a year for full-time work. [Steven Greenhouse, *Drive to Unionize Fast-Food Workers Opens in N.Y.*, NYTimes.com (Nov. 28, 2012)]

Although the Second Circuit held that employees could not be compelled to arbitrate their ADEA claims, despite the arbitration clause in their CBA, the Supreme Court reversed, holding in the spring of 2009 that federal law mandates the enforcement of CBA clauses that unambiguously require union members to arbitrate their ADEA claims. [*14 Penn Plaza LLC v. Pyett*, 556 U.S. 247 (2009); the Supreme Court already held that ADEA claims are arbitrable, in *Gilmer v. Interstate/Johnson Lane Corp.*, 500 U.S. 20 (1991)] The Supreme Court returned to the question of arbitrability in 2010 on another labor law issue, this time deciding that when a CBA's no-strike clause had to be interpreted, it was up to the district court and not the arbitrator to decide when the CBA had been officially ratified. [*Granite Rock Co. v. Int'l Brotherhood of Teamsters*, 130 S. Ct. 2847 (2010)]

Early in 2012, the NLRB held that it violates the NLRA for an employer to require that employees waive class arbitration of grievances because employees always have the right to take collective action about grievances, whether in court or in arbitration. This decision covers all employers operating in interstate commerce, whether or not their employees are unionized. However, the NLRB did not decide whether an employer can require employees to arbitrate instead of litigating collective actions. [*D.R. Horton Inc. and Michael Cuda* (NLRB 2012); see Scott Graham, *AT&T Mobility Doesn't Apply in the Workplace, Says NLRB*, Corporate Counsel (Jan. 9, 2012) (law.com)]

Similarly, in late 2011, the Southern District of New York ruled that the FLSA collective action is a "unique animal" with a special legislative history designed to make it easier for employees to enforce their own rights without involving the government. The FLSA's opt-in procedure balances the need for enforcement of small claims against protecting employees from unwanted inclusion in cases in which they do not want to participate. The district court held that employers cannot mandate arbitration when employees bring collective actions for unpaid minimum wages or overtime. [*Raniere v. Citigroup Inc.*, 827 F. Supp.2d 294 (S.D.N.Y. 2011); see Philip M. Berkowitz, *Developments in Arbitration of Employment Claims*, N.Y.L.J. (Jan. 12, 2012) (law.com)]

## [A]   Challenges to the NLRB Itself

As long as the NLRB has been in operation, businesses and unions that object to NLRB decisions have been challenging the correctness, appropriateness, and validity of those decisions. However, in recent years, the NLRB has confronted significant challenges to the way that the organization is constituted and whether it has had the power to issue valid decisions at certain crucial time periods.

In January 2008, the appointment of two NLRB commissioners expired and no one was appointed to replace them, so the NLRB had two members rather than the statutorily prescribed level of five. More than 400 decisions were issued by the two-member NLRB. In mid-2010, the Supreme Court ruled that the NLRB did not have the authority to issue decisions when it had only two members, so all of these decisions were invalid. As a result, many cases were sent back to the NLRB for reconsideration after it once again had a quorum. [*New Process Steel v. NLRB*, 130 S. Ct. 2635 (2010), discussed in Marcia Coyle, *High Court Finds Hundreds of Labor Cases Were Improperly Decided*, Nat'l L.J. (June 18, 2010) (law.com). For an example of a challenge based on the Supreme Court's decision, see *NLRB v. Talmadge Park*, 608 F.3d 913 (2d Cir. 2010).

At the beginning of 2012, the NLRB swore in three new members: Richard Griffin, Sharon Block, and Terence Flynn. These were all recess appointments. [Melanie Trottman, *Labor Board Swears In New Members*, WSJ.com (Jan. 10, 2012)] Terence Flynn resigned on May 27, 2012 after allegations that he leaked internal NLRB information. Flynn denied wrongdoing. [Steven Greenhouse, *Labor Board Member Resigns Over Leak to G.O.P. Allies*, NYTimes.com <http://www.nytimes.com/2012/05/28/business/gop-labor-board-member-terence-flynn-quits-over-leak.html?_r=1> (May 27, 2012)]

An immensely significant D.C. Circuit decision from early 2013 holds that the recess appointments of Sharon Block, Terence Flynn, and Richard Griffin to the NLRB were unconstitutional. The D.C. Circuit ruled that recess appointments are only permitted at times when the Senate is in recess and, therefore, cannot vote on nominations. The D.C. Circuit held that the president does not have the discretion to decide when the Senate is in recess and, during the time the appointments were made, the Senate met in pro forma session every third day and so was not in recess. Without those three members, the NLRB did not have a quorum, potentially invalidating hundreds of actions. [*Noel Canning v. NLRB*, 705 F.3d 490 (D.C. Cir. 2013); see Mike Scarcella, *D.C. Circuit Declares NLRB Recess Appointments Unconstitutional*, Nat'l L.J. (Jan. 25, 2013) (law.com)]

This decision caused vast uncertainty. Companies were not sure whether to appeal NLRB rulings, or reopen cases that were closed in 2012 by the Board whose composition was found defective by the D.C. Circuit. Every 2012 decision involves at least one member who was a recess appointment. The NLRB announced that it would continue its usual operations. Companies seeking review of NLRB orders can file either in their own circuit or in the D.C. Circuit—after *Noel Canning* it is far more likely that challengers will go to the D.C. Circuit because it has already ruled against the legality of the composition of the Board. When this edition went to press in April 2013, it was uncertain whether the Supreme Court would expedite its consideration of this issue, with a ruling in mid-2013 or whether hearing would be delayed to late 2013 or even 2014. [Sue Reisinger, *After DC Circuit Ruling, What Happens to NLRB Decisions and Its GC?*, Corporate Counsel (Jan. 29, 2013) (law.com)]

By March 2013, at least 87 employers and three unions had cited this case in all stages of NLRB cases and in federal appeals. Another argument is that at least 10 NLRB regional directors were named by the invalidly appointed NLRB members, so the regional directors' decisions should also be struck down. Approximately 600 NLRB decisions and orders have been issued since January 2012, and another 1,400 cases could be challenged if a 2010 recess appointment is found invalid. [Melanie Trottman and Kris Maher, *Companies Challenge Labor Rulings*, WSJ.com (Mar. 8, 2013)]

For example, the Fourth Circuit ruled in mid-2013 that although the NLRB made out its case of unfair labor practices in two refusal-to-bargain cases, the NLRB lacked the power to enter orders because the recess appointments were invalid, and therefore the NLRB lacked a quorum. [*NLRB v. Enterprise Leasing Co. Se. LLC*,Nos. 12-1514, 12-2000, 12-2065 (4th Cir. July 17, 2013). The National Chamber Litigation Center maintains a Recess Appointments Litigation Resource Page tracking the progress of the numerous cases dealing with this issue: <http://www.chamberlitigation.com/recess-appointments-litigation-resource-page> (last accessed Sept. 12, 2013)]

The NLRB announced that, rather than apply to the D.C. Circuit for en banc rehearing, it would request that the U.S. Supreme Court grant certiorari. [Marcia Coyle, *NLRB to Appeal Recess Case Directly to Supreme Court*, The BLT (Mar. 12, 2013) (law.com)] Certiorari was granted on June 24, 2013, as No. 12-1281. [See Brent Kendall, *Supreme Court to Consider Obama Recess Appointments*, WSJ.com (June 24, 2013)]

Eventually, in August 2013, the Senate confirmed enough NLRB members to bring the Board up to its full strength of five members—the first time this had been true since August 21, 2003. Chairman Mark Gaston Pierce was confirmed for another five-year NLRB term. Four new members were added: Nancy Schiffer, a senior attorney for unions; Harry I. Johnson, III, formerly a partner in the law firm Arent Fox LLP; Kent Hirozawa, one-time chief counsel to Chairman Pearce; and Philip A. Miscimarra, ex-partner in Morgan Lewis &Bockius LLP. Pearce's term lasts until August 27, 2018. Schiffer's term ends December 16, 2014. Johnson's ends August 27, 2015, Hirozawa's ends August 27, 2016, and Miscimarra's ends December 16, 2017. [NLRB Press Release, *The National Labor Relations Board Has Five Senate-Confirmed Members*, <http://www.nlrb.gov/news-outreach/news-releases/national-labor-relations-board-has-five-senate-confirmed-members> (Aug. 12, 2013)]

## § 30.02  SOURCES OF LABOR LAW

### [A]  Generally

The NLRA was supplemented in 1947 by the Labor-Management Relations Act (LMRA) [29 U.S.C. §§ 141–144, etc.], popularly known as the Taft-Hartley Act. The LMRA extends the powers of the NLRB. It outlaws certain kinds of strikes, including jurisdictional strikes, strikes to enforce unfair labor practices (rather than strikes to protest them), and secondary boycotts. A secondary boycott is an attempt to pressure a neutral company to keep it from dealing with a company that the union has a dispute with.

To induce a nationwide laundry company to hire only union members and to improve working conditions, a union used a variation of secondary picketing by targeting a group of hospitals that used the laundry company. The union sent postcards to prospective patients saying that the hospital used a company that didn't clean the linens thoroughly enough to be safe. The hospitals, saying that its laundry hygiene was adequate and the postcard campaign hurt its business, sued the union for defamation, trade libel, and interference with prospective economic relations. The jury found for the hospital, and ordered the union to pay a $17 million judgment. However, the California Court of Appeal ruled in 2010 that the court should have instructed the jury that the union acted with actual malice; either knowing that its statements were false, or recklessly disregarding whether they were true or not. The court of appeal treated the postcard campaign as a labor dispute communication, because it exerted pressure on hospitals to stop using the laundry service. [*Sutter Health v. Unite Here*, 186 Cal. App. 4th 1193 (2010)]

The Landrum-Griffin Act, known as the Labor-Management Reporting and Disclosure Act of 1959 [Pub. L. No. 86-257], forbids hot-cargo agreements (agreements not to carry the merchandise of a company involved in a labor dispute). It allows prehire agreements in the building and construction industries, and makes it an unfair labor practice to picket in order to force an employer to recognize or bargain with a union.

The Labor-Management Reporting and Disclosure Act (LMRDA) requires employers to make an annual filing, using the LM-10 form, to disclose payments over $250 per year made to unions and union officials. The LM-10 form is due 90 days after the end of the employer's fiscal year. [DOL, *Form LM-10-Employer Reports—Frequently Asked Questions*, <http://www.dol.gov/esa/regs/compliance/olms/LM10_FAQ.htm>, discussed in Dechert On Point, *Department of Labor Issues New LM-10 Guidelines*, <http://www.dechert.com/library/Labor_and_EB_03-06.pdf> (Mar. 2006)]

The Norris-LaGuardia Act severely limits the situations in which an employer can secure an injunction against a union, but does not completely rule out all injunctions. Although federal law usually preempts state law in the labor arena, the states do have a limited role in protecting their own legitimate interests. They can pass certain labor laws that will not be federally preempted: For instance, there is a legitimate state interest in preventing violence, so states can regulate how and when picketing can be done. States can legislate in areas such as minimum wages, child labor, and employment discrimination.

States can also cope with issues that are only peripheral to the main purposes of the LMRA. This category includes defamation suits brought by employers against unions, suits dealing with continuation of welfare benefits during strikes, and internal union affairs. States are also allowed to legislate in the area of union security, for instance by passing right-to-work laws forbidding union shops and agency shops. [See § 30.06]

The National Labor Relations Board's (NLRB) jurisdiction is limited to work performed in the United States; the agency has no jurisdiction over temporary work assignments in Canada. [*Asplundh Tree Expert Co. v. NLRB*, 365 F.3d 168 (3d Cir. 2004)]

Although public employee unions are outside the scope of this book, Wisconsin's Governor Scott Walker signed a bill in early 2011 limiting bargaining rights for most government workers. The Wisconsin Circuit Court enjoined the law, holding that the statute was not passed with adequate notice under the Open Meetings Law, but that decision was reversed in mid-2011 by the Wisconsin Supreme Court, which held that the law was validly passed and limitations could be imposed on public employee bargaining rights. This is a significant decision in light of the budgetary problems of many state and local governments—problems that are also found in the private sector. [Amy Merrick, *Judge Voids Wisconsin Antiunion Law*, WSJ.com (May 27, 2011); Monica Davey, *Wisconsin Court Reinstates Law on Union Rights*, NYTimes.com (June 14, 2011)]

## [B]  NLRA Section 7

The National Labor Relations Act of 1935 (NLRA), also known as the Wagner Act, is one of the bedrock federal labor statutes. The NLRA establishes the National Labor Relations Board (NLRB) as a kind of referee between management and unionized labor.

Section 7 of the NLRA says that employees have the right to engage in "protected concerted activities." In other words, they can act together to form a union, join a union, present grievances, bargain collectively, go on strike, and picket peacefully.

In the July 2012, *Banner Estrella Medical Center* case, the NLRB said that a blanket policy mandating employee confidentiality with respect to HR investigations violates NLRA § 7 because it burdens protected concerted activities. This position was surprising to many commentators, who said that the previous belief was that EEOC rules required confidentiality of investigations. The NLRB ruled against blanket policies, but confidentiality requirements can be imposed on a case by case basis as needed, for example, to protect witnesses and prevent coverups and destruction of evidence. Companies should review their practices, devise formal policies about confidentiality factors, and ask complainants whether they want confidentiality. This is usually the case; the company should protect itself by getting a written statement to this effect. [Catherine Dunn, *NLRB Rules on Keeping Employees From Discussing HR Investigations*, Corporate Counsel (Aug. 31, 2012) (law.com).]

## [C]   Unfair Labor Practices

Either a union or an employer can be guilty of an "unfair labor practice" (ULP) as defined by the NLRA and the LMRA. The NLRB has the power to issue a "cease and desist" order if it deems that an unfair practice has occurred. The NLRB also has powers to order positive actions, such as ordering an employer to bargain with a union.

NLRA § 8 defines unfair labor practices to include:

- Refusal to engage in collective bargaining—whether the recalcitrant party is management or union;

- Employer domination of a union;

- Retaliation against employees for filing charges with the NLRB or testifying before the agency;

- Discrimination against employees based on either union activities or refusal to join a union. In this context, discrimination includes firing, refusal to hire, refusal to reinstate, demotion, discrimination in compensation, discrimination in work assignments etc. However, if a union security clause is in place, employees can be required to pay union dues or the equivalent of dues, but they cannot be required to actually join the union;

- Deliberately inefficient work practices that require the employment of excessive numbers of workers ("featherbedding");

- Certain practices occurring during strikes or picketing.

The LMRA penalizes unfair labor practices by unions, including:

- Restraining or coercing employees when they exercise their right to bargain collectively, choose a representative, or vote against unionization;

- Causing an employer to discriminate against any employee;

- Refusing to participate in collective bargaining, once the union becomes the authorized bargaining representative for the employees;

- Engaging in strikes or concerted activity for the purpose of boycotting one employer, forcing another employer to recognize an uncertified union, forcing any employer to recognize a particular union when a different union is actually the authorized bargaining representative, or when a determination of jurisdiction still has to be made;

- Requiring union members in a union shop to pay excessive initiation fees or excessive dues;

- Featherbedding.

A ULP is an employment decision that interferes with the right to organize or discourages union membership. The test of such a decision is whether or not the action was motivated by anti-union animus.

The NLRB considers it a ULP to promulgate work rules that are likely to chill exercise of § 7 rights—even if the rules are never enforced. A rule that explicitly restricts § 7 activity violates the NLRA, and so does a rule that an employee would reasonably construe to prohibit § 7 activity, if the rule was promulgated in response to union activity, or the rule has been applied to restrict the exercise of § 7 rights. The Seventh Circuit held that a hospital unlawfully interfered with nurses' rights to organize and discriminated against a union activist nurse by forbidding solicitation in "patient care areas"—including the breakroom. The NLRB conceded that bans on solicitation in patient areas are valid, but the Seventh Circuit ruled that it was improper to define the breakroom as a patient care area because it was across the corridor from patient rooms. The facially valid anti-solicitation rule was applied in a discriminatory fashion: union solicitation was forbidden, but charitable solicitations and product sales were permitted. [*St. Margaret Mercy Healthcare Ctrs.*, 519 F.3d 373 (7th Cir. 2008)]

It is not an unfair labor practice for an employer to put work rules in the employee handbook against abusive and threatening language and limiting solicitations and distributions within the workplace; pro-union employees can make their point of view known without threatening their opponents, so the rules do not interfere with protected collective activity. [*Adtranz ABB Daimler-Benz Transp. v. NLRB*, 253 F.3d 19 (D.C. Cir. 2001)]

Early in 2010, the Fourth Circuit upheld the NLRB's determination that a trucking company committed Unfair Labor Practices (threatening to discharge employees for engaging in protected concerted activity; firing one employee for engaging in protected concerted activity). In 2007, the company announced fuel surcharges that reduced the drivers' net pay. Drivers who protested were told they could "clean out their trucks" (an action associated with termination of employment) if they were unhappy. A truck driver who "shouted" at a supervisor was discharged for "disorderly conduct." The owner later said that it was the last straw after various incidents of misconduct, but no other incidents were disclosed to the fired driver. There are precedents that it is unlawfully coercive to tell employees they can quit their jobs when they protest about conditions; protected activity is not incompatible with continued employment. [*Alton H. Piester, LLC v. NLRB*, 591 F.3d 332 (4th Cir. 2010)]

To avert worker protests at Wal-Mart stores over Thanksgiving (one of the major retail weekends of the year) Wal-Mart filed a ULP complaint against the union planning the protest. The protesters charged that they were underpaid and had bad working conditions. Wal-Mart applied for an injunction against rallies and picketing at stores and warehouses. According to Wal-Mart, the worker coalition sought recognition of a union, so federal law allows only 30 days of protests before collecting signatures for an election. The organization, OUR Walmart, said that the protests are not an organizing campaign but an attempt to publicize retaliation against workers who complained about pay and working conditions. [Shelly Banjo and Ann Zimmerman, *Wal-Mart Seeks to Head Off Worker Protests*, WSJ.com (Nov. 16, 2012)]

## [D]   LMRA Preemption

Many cases turn on whether § 301 of the Labor-Management Relations Act (LMRA) should be applied. This section gives federal District Courts jurisdiction over suits for violations of a collective bargaining agreement, as well as suits by one union against another. This section is often applied to bring labor questions into the federal courts—and keep them out of state courts when issues such as wrongful termination and unfair employee discipline are raised.

The most important issue in deciding whether LMRA preemption exists is the relationship between the controversy and the collective bargaining agreement. State laws are preempted whenever it is necessary to interpret the CBA. However, the Supreme Court decided in 1994 that a mere need to refer to the CBA is not enough to justify preemption. The underlying dispute must really involve searching out the meaning of the terms of the contract. [*Lividas v. Bradshaw*, 512 U.S. 107 (1994)]

If the CBA includes a contractual grievance or arbitration provision (and most do), then potential plaintiffs have to exhaust their remedies (complete the entire process) before bringing suit under § 301.

Preemption has been found in cases such as:

- Failure to rehire, negligent and intentional infliction of emotional distress (because deciding the case required interpretation of the CBA's seniority provisions);

- A claim that a worker was denied reinstatement after a period of disability in retaliation for filing a Worker's Compensation claim, because the issue here was the management's exclusive right to hire and fire under the CBA "management rights" clause;

However, preemption was not found in these situations, on the grounds that the court did not have to interpret the CBA to decide the case:

- Retaliatory discharge;

- Discharge of an employee for reasons violating public policy;

- False imprisonment (unreasonable detention of an employee by a security guard);

- Claims about oral contracts other than the CBA (for instance, a verbal promise of lifetime employment) or implied contracts;

- Claims under state antidiscrimination laws on issues that are not normally bargained away during contract negotiations;

A Whirlpool manager charged that he was terminated, in violation of public policy, for refusing to fire employees who were engaged in unionizing activity—i.e., that he was fired for refusing to commit unfair labor practices. The Sixth Circuit ruled that this claim was preempted by the National Labor Relations Act, so it should have been raised before the NLRB. In fact, Lewis did file an NLRB charge, but the agency found that the charge was without merit. [*Lewis v. Whirlpool Corp.*, 630 F.3d 484 (6th Cir. 2011)]

In 2012, the Fifth Circuit held that LMRA preemption should not have been applied in a case where a group of former employees raised tort claims against their ex-employer based on hearing loss that they said was caused by failure to abate workplace noise. The plaintiffs raised only state-law tort claims and the charges could be resolved without interpreting the CBA at all. [*McKnight v. Dresser, Inc.*, 676 F.3d 426 (5th Cir. 2012)]

## § 30.03   EMPLOYEE STATUS

### [A]   Definition of Employee

The NLRA defines the rights of "employees," so an important basic question is who fits into this category. Independent contractors are not employees, but common-law employees under the employer's control in terms of hiring, firing, work methods and results, provision of tools and materials, and employee discipline, are also employees for NLRA purposes.

Employee status is maintained during a temporary layoff, if the worker reasonably expects to be recalled in the future. A sick or injured worker continues to be an employee either until he or she takes another permanent full-time job, or is permanently unable to return to work for physical reasons.

In some contexts, retirees will not be considered employees once they are off the company's active payroll and have no right to be rehired or any reasonable expectation of being rehired. A postal service union in Texas sued the Postal Service for CBA violations. It took ten years for the suit to be resolved through arbitration. The union decided to divide the settlement between active workers and retirees, with the retirees getting half as much as active workers. Two retirees filed Unfair Labor Practices charges against the union. The NLRB said that the union did not breach its duty of fair representation, because unions breach this duty to retirees only if the union discriminates, acts arbitrarily, or acts in bad faith. The NLRB noted that the union's counsel said that it was not necessary to give retirees any part of the settlement, so the union should not be penalized for exceeding its legal obligation. [Adrien Martin, *Texas Labor Union Was Not Required to Represent Retirees*, plansponsor.com (Aug. 15, 2006)]

In other instances, however, retirees will continue to be treated as members of the bargaining unit, on the theory that the union bargained for a compensation package covering both active workers and retirees. This is a particularly significant question in terms of retiree health benefits promised "for life" when the employer later claims that the promise expired with the CBA. See § 9.08.

## [B]  Part-Time and Temporary Workers

Temporary or casual workers will probably not be considered employees. Part-time workers are considered employees, although sometimes it is inappropriate to put them in a bargaining unit with full-timers, if their interests are adverse. In August 2000, the NLRB ruled that temporary workers can be included in the same collective bargaining unit as permanent employees, as long as the characteristics of the job are similar. [*M.B. Sturgis Inc.*, 331 N.L.R.B. 173 (Aug. 25, 2000)]

This reverses earlier NLRB decisions saying that temporary workers could be organized in a bargaining unit with permanent workers only if neither the "supplier employer" (the temp agency or other company that supplied the workers) nor the "user employer" (the place where the work was actually performed) objected. As you can imagine, one or both usually did object!

The NLRB ruled that the union has the right to show that the two companies are really joint employers of the workers, because they both determine the terms and conditions of employment. However, the user employer can rebut the union's contention by showing that the supplier employer maintains the real control over the workers.

The Seventh Circuit held that seasonal employees at a factory were eligible for inclusion in the bargaining unit with permanent employees, based on shared interests and the seasonal workers' reasonable expectation of future employment. The seasonal workers constituted a large part of the workforce; they came from a definable, static group of workers (the local Hispanic population), and all new permanent hires came from the pool of seasonal workers. The Seventh Circuit reached this conclusion although the seasonal employees did not receive the same benefits as the permanent employees; and the employer did not try to recruit former seasonal workers when new workers had to be hired. [*Winkie Mfg. Co. v. NLRB*, 348 F.3d 254 (7th Cir. 2003)]

## [C]  Supervisors

The text of the NLRA [29 U.S.C. § 152] says that "supervisors" such as foremen and forewomen are not "employees," for the common-sense reason that supervisors promote management interests and therefore do not fit in well with rank-and-file workers, who have different and often opposing interests.

A supervisor is someone who has a formal job title indicating supervisory status, has been held out as a supervisor by management, or is perceived as a supervisor by rank-and-file workers. A supervisor makes independent, individual judgments, can reward or discipline employees (up to and including firing them) and has authority to adjust employee grievances.

To be a supervisor, someone must have supervisory authority on a consistent basis (whether or not it is exercised). Sporadic or limited authority, such as power to take over in an emergency, doesn't make a rank-and-file worker into a supervisor. Courts have expanded the statutory definition, so that managers are not considered employees either, because of their discretion and ability to set corporate policy.

In mid-2001, the Supreme Court resolved a conflict about the status of Registered Nurses in nursing homes. Because the RNs direct the activities of non-RN staff, they are supervisors and cannot be organized in the same unit as the other staffers. [*NLRB v. Kentucky River Cmty. Care Inc.*, 532 U.S. 706 (2001)]

Late in 2006, the NLRB ruled that employees who have been permanently designated as shift supervisors are not entitled to unionize, but also nurses who work supervisory shifts on a rotating basis are not supervisors. An employee is a supervisor if he or she has subordinates; decides what task will be done next or who does it; and this direction reflects independent judgment. The authority to direct work and correct mistakes must come from the employer, and the supervisor must be at risk of adverse consequences because of his or her direction of subordinates. Therefore, in three 2006 cases, the NLRB found that "lead persons" in a factory did not exercise supervisory authority, and charge nurses did not supervise nursing assistants because they could not control their hours or give them assignments. [*Oakwood Healthcare Inc.*, 348 NLRB 37 (Sept. 29, 2006); *Golden Crest Healthcare Center*, 349 NLRB 39 (Sept. 29, 2006); *Croft Metals Inc.*, 348 NLRB 38 (Sept. 29, 2006). See Fred Schneyer, *Three NLRB Cases Define "Supervisor" Under Union Law*, plansponsor.com (Oct. 3, 2006)]

In 2013, the Sixth Circuit, reversing the NLRB, held that Registered Nurses (RNs) at a nursing home were supervisors because of their power to use independent judgment to assign, direct, and discipline Certified Nurse Assistants at the facility. The Sixth Circuit held that merely reporting misconduct is not supervisory authority, but it is not necessary for a worker to have the power to hire and fire to be considered a supervisor. [*GGNSC Springfield v. NLRB*, Nos. 12-1529, 12-1628 (6th Cir. July 2, 2013)]

## [D]  Union Organizers

A paid union organizer can qualify as a protected "employee" under the NLRA. The fact that he or she is paid a salary by the union does not deprive him or her of the protection of federal labor law. This concept has been extended to treat a volunteer union organizer who is not paid by the union as an employee.

[*NLRB v. Town & Country Elec. Inc.*, 516 U.S. 85 (1995); *NLRB v. Fluor Daniel*, 102 F.3d 818 (6th Cir. 1996)]

In general, the LMRA prevents employers from making payments to any union representative, but this rule is not violated by continuing to provide full pay and benefits to a long-tenure employee who served as shop steward and worked full-time representing employees who had grievances. The Ninth Circuit held that it was in the employer's best interests to have grievances handled expeditiously. The shop steward was an employee of the company and not the union because the company controlled his work week; he reported to the company's HR director; and his workplace was the shop floor, not the union hall. [*International Ass'n of Machinists v. B.F. Goodrich*, 387 F.3d 1046 (9th Cir. 2004)]

In appropriate cases, the employer can assert the defense that the union "salts" who applied for jobs were not entitled to be hired because they had a disabling conflict with the employer's interests. However, according to the D.C. Circuit, the disabling conflict defense can only be asserted if a union organizer seeks work while engaged in an economic strike against the employer, or if what is described as protected union organizing activity is actually a cloak for unlawful conduct aimed at sabotage or driving the employer out of business. [*Casino Ready Mix v. NLRB*, 321 F.3d 1190 (D.C. Cir. 2003)] In this case, the union salts responded to an advertisement, and were clearly qualified for the job, so refusal to assign work to them was unlawful discrimination. However, in 2003 the Seventh Circuit held that a construction company's hiring system, which gave preference to former employees and referrals from trusted sources did not violate the LMRA. The union "salts" were not hired—but that was not because of their union affiliation, but because they were walk-ins, the lowest-priority category in the employer's classification. [*International Union of Operating Eng'rs, Local 150 v. NLRB*, 325 F.3d 818 (7th Cir. 2003)]

## § 30.04  ELECTIONS, CERTIFICATION, AND RECOGNITION

### [A]  Generally

To gain "certification," and thereby become the bargaining agent for the employees (whom the employer must deal with), a union has to win an election supervised by the NLRB. There is a one-year period after the certification election during which no rival union is allowed to seek certification.

A union organizing campaign begins with a petition for certification. Typically, the petition is filed by the union or by an individual employee who is a union supporter. Most organizing work is done by pro-union employees, because employers can and usually do bar non-employees from soliciting on business premises during working hours. [But see § 30.04[H] for exceptions to this rule] If there are two or more unions trying to organize the same workplace, the employer is allowed to express a preference for one over the other.

A certification petition is valid only if at least 30% of the employees in the bargaining unit indicate their interest. Acceptable indications of interest are:

- Authorization cards;
- Union membership cards;
- Applications for membership;
- Records of union dues;
- Employee signatures on certification petitions.

It is a serious unfair labor practice for employers to retaliate against workers because of their union activism, so it is important to document good business reasons for any disciplinary action taken against less-than-optimal workers who also happen to be union activists.

The employer has the right to request a representation election when a majority of the employees have submitted signed authorization cards designating a particular union as their bargaining agent. However, an employer that engages in serious ULPs forfeits the right to call for an election, and can be compelled to bargain with the union, because an employer loses the right to call for an election if it engages in conduct that is likely to disrupt the election. [*NLRB v. Orland Park Motor Cars*, 309 F.3d 452 (7th Cir. 2002)]

Current law allows "card check" (certification of a union based on employees checking a box on a card, in lieu of a full-scale election) only if the employer consents. Legislation has been introduced in Congress, the Employee Free Choice Act, which would expand the availability of card check. In the fiscal year ending September 30, 2009, the number of representation elections fell 16%, continuing a trend. But when elections are held, the percentage of union victories has increased from 60% in 2008 to 63.8% in 2009. Because a union that loses a representation election must wait a year before holding another election, unions often defer seeking an election unless they believe they are likely to win. [Kris Maher, *Card Check Grows in Union Organizing*, WSJ.com (Oct. 12, 2009)]

Several states, Arizona, South Carolina, South Dakota, and Utah, have adopted state constitutional amendments in November 2010 requiring secret ballot elections for unionization. The NLRB said that it would file suit against those states, because the amendments are preempted by the NLRA, which permits card check organization under appropriate circumstances. [Melanie Trottman, *Labor Board Warns on Secret Ballots*, WSJ.com (Jan. 15, 2011); Steven Greenhouse, *Labor Board to Sue 4 States Over 'Card Check' for Unionizing*, NYTimes.com (Jan. 14, 2011)]

On November 30, 2011, the NLRB passed a resolution that limits appeals of union organizing elections in order to speed up the election process. About 90% of elections are held on consent, with an average time of 38 days between the filing of the petition and the election. The resolution limits pre-election litigation about contested elections to matters directly related to the election. Appeals are deferred until after the election, because many disputes are mooted by the result of the election. [Matthew Huisman, *NLRB Votes to Streamline Union Organizing Elections*, Nat'l L.J. (Nov. 30, 2011) (law.com) The rule was finalized at 76 Fed. Reg. 80138 (Dec. 22, 2011).]

The NLRB chairman's resolution includes six procedural amendments intended to reduce unnecessary litigation related to elections, such as a limitation of pre-election hearings to evidence relevant to the question of whether an election should be held and consolidating two levels of appeals into a single post-election procedure. [NRLB press release: <http://www.nlrb.gov/publications/r ules-regulations/notice-proposed-rulemaking/proposed-amendments-nlrb-election-rules-an/> (Dec. 1, 2011)]

Then, in May 2012, the District Court for the District of Columbia found that this rule was invalidly promulgated because the NLRB did not have a quorum when the rule was adopted. The NLRB had three members at that time; two members (both Democrats) voted for the rule, the one Republican member did not vote at all. The district court said that without three actual votes being cast, there was no quorum. [*Chamber of Commerce of the United States v. NLRB*, No. 1:11-cv-02262-HEB (D.D.C. May 14, 2012); see Melanie Trottman, *Judge Rejects New Rule,* WSJ .com (May 15, 2012)]. In response, the NLRB suspended implementation of the new rule. [<http://www.nlrb.gov/news/nlrb-suspends-implementation-representation-case-amendments-based-court-ruling> (May 15, 2012)]

## [B]  Consent Elections

The NLRB is responsible for determining the validity of the representation petition. If the employer does not oppose holding the election, the election is a consent election. The employer and union sign a contract permitting an election. The NLRB will probably have to accept the consent agreement's definition of the appropriate bargaining unit, unless it violates the law (for instance, by including guards in a mixed bargaining unit).

Within seven days of the time that the appropriate NLRB Regional Director approves a consent agreement, the employer has a duty to submit the "Excelsior List" to the Regional Director. This is a list of the names and addresses of every worker eligible to vote in the consent election. The Regional Director distributes the list to all interested parties. [The name comes from the NLRB case of *Excelsior Underwear Inc.*, 156 N.L.R.B. 271 (1986)]

■ **TIP:**  It is an unfair labor practice for an employer to recognize a union that does not represent the majority of workers. So the employer has a duty to at least examine the authorization cards before agreeing to a consent election. But if an NLRB hearing is anticipated, it is better not to examine the cards. Disciplinary actions will be less vulnerable to challenge if the

employer did not know which employees expressed pro-union sentiments, and therefore could not have retaliated against them on this basis.

## [C]  NLRB Hearings

If the employer objects, but the NLRB finds that there is reasonable cause
to believe that the union might be an appropriate representative for the employees, the NLRB holds a nonadversary hearing to determine if there is a question of
representation. (Employers who are dissatisfied with the Regional Director's
decision can appeal to the central NLRB for review.) This type of hearing cannot
be used to raise claims of unfair labor practices by either side.

In most instances, the hearing will result in setting a date for a secret ballot
election under NLRB supervision. The NLRB will then certify the result: whether
or not the union has secured a majority vote.

A union will be certified as bargaining representative for the unit if it wins
the votes of a majority of the voters (not a majority of those eligible to vote). But
the election will not be valid unless a "representative number" of eligible employees actually voted. There is no bright-line test for whether the number of voters
was representative. Many factors, such as the voter turnout, adequacy of the
employees' notice of the election and opportunity to vote, and the presence or
absence of unfair practices by the employer, are considered to see if there was a
high enough turnout.

## [D]  Election Procedure

Usually, the election will be held at the workplace, because that is accessible to all employees. However, if there is good cause shown for holding an election somewhere else, or for allowing voting by mail, the NLRB will supervise the
out-of-plant election. Elections are held by secret ballot. The voters enter the voting location, have their employee status checked, and then mark their ballots in a
closed booth where their selections are not visible. The ballots are collected for
later tallying.

According to *San Diego Gas & Electric* [325 NLRB 218 (1998)], voting by
mail should be allowed not only in the tense situation of an election during a
strike or picketing, but also whenever potential voters would have to travel a significant distance to the polls and are so scattered that simply relocating the poll-
ing place would not be effective. Another indicator for mail balloting is a
workforce with varying schedules, so that they cannot be assembled in one place
at a particular time.

Before a certification or deauthorization election, the employer must post an
election notice in a conspicuous place in the workplace. The notice must be up
for at least three full working days before 12:01 a.m. of the day scheduled for the
election. Failure to post the notice can result in the election results being set aside.

The notice must give the date, time, and place of the election, and must show a sample ballot so employees will know how to mark it to indicate their choice.

If there are objections to the eligibility of certain voters, or to the mechanics of the election, either the employer or union can file an objection with the NLRB within seven days of the ballot tally. There is no absolute right to get a hearing on the validity of the election: The NLRB Regional Director decides when one is needed.

The NLRB held that a worker who put an X in the "Yes" box but also wrote in a question mark nevertheless expressed a preference for the union—with the result that the UAW won the election by one vote. [*Daimler-Chrysler Corp.*, 338 NLRB No. 148 (Apr. 18, 2003)]

If an employer relies on the results of an invalid election to change policies within the workplace, the Ninth Circuit said that the appropriate remedy is to hold a new election. [*Gardner Mech. Servs. v. NLRB*, 89 F.3d 586 (9th Cir. 1996)] A bargaining order is improper unless there is proof that it would be impossible to hold a valid election.

## [E]  Voter Eligibility

The simple answer is that all "employees" in the "bargaining unit" are entitled to vote in a representation election. However, it can be hard to determine the appropriate bargaining unit, and there are some questions about who retains employee status.

A worker who has taken a voluntary leave of absence is entitled to vote unless the relationship with the employer has been severed. If the employee on leave retains seniority and is still in the employer's pension and benefit plans, he or she is probably an eligible voter. Employees on sick leave, disability leave, or maternity leave are entitled to vote, unless they have been formally or constructively terminated from employment. [*Home Care Network Inc.*, 347 NLRB 80 (Aug. 2, 2006)] In 2008, the D.C. Circuit ruled that a bargaining unit member is presumed to remain a member of the unit while on sick leave, long-term disability, or worker's compensation, unless the employer proves that the person has resigned or been terminated.[*Abbott Ambulance of Illinois v. NLRB*, 522 F.3d 447 (D.C. Cir. 2008)]

For laid-off workers, the question is whether they have a reasonable expectation of recall (determined as of the date of the election, not the date of the NLRB pre-election hearing). A person who was lawfully fired before the date of the election is not eligible to vote, but someone who is unlawfully discharged for union activity retains employee status, and therefore is entitled to vote.

Economic strikers (see § 30.09[B] for characterization of strikes) who have not been replaced as to the date of the election are entitled to vote. During the 12 months after the beginning of an economic strike, economic strikers are still entitled to vote if they have been replaced—even if they are not entitled to immediate reinstatement after the strike ends. Employees who are on the preferential reinstatement list are also entitled to vote. But if the election is held more than 12 months after the beginning of a strike, replaced economic strikers are not entitled to vote, even if they still have a reasonable expectation of recall.

Replacement workers hired during an economic strike are entitled to vote in the election, but only if they were employed before the eligibility cutoff date for the election. Unlike economic strikers, unfair labor practice strikers are always eligible to vote in representation elections, but their replacements are never entitled to vote.

## [F]  Electioneering and Communications

During a certification campaign, both employer and union are entitled to communicate their viewpoints to employees. The employer is considered a "person" entitled to exercise free speech rights, subject to limitations of accuracy and fairness. If the employer overreaches, the election results will be set aside, and the employer will have to go through the whole process again, perhaps with more employee sympathy for the union. In egregious cases, the employer might have to answer charges of an unfair labor practice.

The "critical period" is the time between the filing of a representation petition and the election itself. (For a runoff or rerun election, the critical period begins at the first election, and even conduct occurring before the certification petition was filed might be considered relevant as to the fairness of the election.) The NLRB will observe the conduct of both sides, and has the power to invalidate elections, even if the misconduct is not serious enough to constitute an unfair labor practice. The employer is held responsible for the conduct of its agents, including its lawyers and labor relations consultants.

■ **TIP:**  An employer can avoid liability for an inappropriate statement by an agent if it repudiates the statement promptly, admitting that it was out of line, restating it in proper form, and giving at least as much publicity to the retraction as to the original communication.

Certification elections are supposed to provide "laboratory conditions" (i.e., pure and untainted) for workplace democracy. Employers are not allowed to conduct pre-election polls, or even ask employees their opinions about unionization, if the inquiry is too close to the time of the election. However, it is accepted labor law that employers can call a meeting of workers on company time for management to assert its arguments against unionization. If the union is permitted to solicit employees during meals and other breaks, the employer can call a mass meeting without giving the union equal time to reply.

During the 24-hour period just before the election, neither management nor union is allowed to make speeches to massed employees on company time. If the employer does this, it is not an unfair labor practice, but it could lead to invalidation of the election. The employer is allowed to distribute printed materials to workers during this time. The employer can also conduct antiunion meetings away from the workplace during the 24-hour period, as long as attendance is voluntary and employees choose to come in on their own time.

These are examples that have been found to constitute unfair labor practices by the employer:

- Announcing benefits on election day;

- Explicitly promising benefits if the union loses;

- Threatening to withhold benefits if the union wins;

- Announcing new benefits during the critical period to show that the employer offers a better deal than the union—unless the benefits were decided before the representation petition was filed, or there is economic justification for providing them at that time;

- Delivering paychecks at the voting site for a decertification election, rather than at the workplace. The NLRB requires a legitimate business reason-for changing the procedure for delivering paychecks within 24 hours of an election. Usually, a higher voter turnout is good—but in a decertification election, increased turnout benefits the employer rather than the union;

- Telling employees that unless they returned to work the next day without a union contract, the business would be closed down, and its equipment would be leased, was a threat (an unfair labor practice) and not just a permissible prediction of future events. It was a threat because it referred to events wholly within the employer's control;

- The Seventh Circuit ruled that it was a violation of federal labor law to threaten stricter enforcement of rules and possible plant closure if the union won the election—but it was legitimate to forbid posting union literature on a bulletin board where personal notices were allowed but there was a consistently applied ban on materials from any group or organization.

However, these have been held not to be improper practices by the employer:

- Delaying pay raises until after the election, as long as timing is the only issue—raises will be paid no matter who wins the election;

- Distributing fact-based (not coercive or threatening) handbills during an organizing drive, saying that unionization would lead to long, bitter negotiations and possibly an ugly strike

- Announcing two new floating holidays the day before the election. The timing of the announcement was logical within the company's fiscal year; it was just a coincidence that it was right before the election.

The NLRB imposes a five-part test, all of which must be met, to determine when it is legitimate for an employer to ask employees to appear in an anti-union video. Direct solicitation is considered improper, but it is permissible to make a general announcement seeking volunteers, with a guarantee that employees who do not wish to participate will not be penalized. The Third Circuit approved the NLRB test, finding it to be a rational balance between the employer's right of free expression and employees' right to be free of coercion. Employees must not be pressured into making a decision while a supervisor is present. The employer must not have engaged in other forms of coercion or unfair labor practices during the union campaign and the process of seeking employees to appear in the video must not be used to spy on the union. [*Allegheny Ludlum Corp. v. NLRB*, 301 F.3d 167 (3d Cir. 2002)]

## [G]  Buttons and Insignia

The right to free speech extends to employees in the workplace to the extent that workers must be allowed to wear union buttons. They must be allowed to wear union buttons to the poll, even though blatant electioneering like this would not be allowed in a general election.

Wearing union insignia is protected by NLRA § 7, and interfering with this right violates § 8(a)(1), unless the union materials cause a real safety hazard, or there is a real risk of violence between union supporters and opponents. The mere possibility of violence is not enough.

There is a partial exception. Employees who work with the public, and who are required to wear a uniform, can be forbidden to wear all kinds of jewelry, including union buttons. They can be required to wear the standard uniform, not a union T-shirt. But the employer must be careful to communicate the uniform policy, and to enforce it across the board, not just against union insignia.

A hospital that required employees to wear a uniform, and banned all pins except for professional association pins and hospital service awards could lawfully forbid a carpenter from wearing a union button. The Fifth Circuit held that the hospital's interest in maintaining a tranquil and peaceful atmosphere outweighed the carpenter's First Amendment free speech rights. [*Communications Workers of Am. v. Ector County Hosp. Dist.*, 467 F.3d 424 (5th Cir. Oct. 5, 2006)] The NLRB found it permissible for a hospital to forbid nurses to wear "RNs Demand Safe Staffing" buttons in areas where they could be seen by patients or their family members. [*Sacred Heart Medical Center*, 347 NLRB 48 (June 30 2006)] A hotel could forbid room service workers from wearing union buttons in public areas, but not in non-public areas, where management's argument that guests were entitled to a luxurious fantasy atmosphere would not apply. [*Starwood Hotels*, 348 NLRB 24 (Sept. 29, 2006)]

The Starbucks dress code actually required employees to wear a variety of buttons and badges. Two union activist employees were fired for dress code violations. The Second Circuit vacated one termination and remanded the other. Discharge was upheld for an employee who, in addition to dress code violations, frequently missed work and was not well informed about current products. Discharge was remanded for further proceedings in the case of an employee discharged after a profane outburst in a Starbucks store while the worker was off-duty. It was remanded because the outburst was about union matters, and the NLRB was instructed to consider whether protected collective activity is limited to situations in which employees wear their work uniforms. [*NLRB v. Starbucks Corp.*, 679 F.3d 70 (2d Cir. 2012)]

## [H]  Access by Non-Employees

In most instances, a workplace is private property, not a public space. Therefore, union organizers do not automatically have a right to leaflet or distribute literature if this is contrary to the wishes of the employer or other owner of the property.

An exception might occur in a "company town" situation, where in effect all property is owned by the employer, so there is no public space where the union can distribute literature. [See, e.g., *Lechmere v. NLRB*, 502 U.S. 527 (1991)] Another exception might be a place that is so remote geographically that the union has no reasonable means of communicating with employees outside the workplace.

The Ninth Circuit ruled that the California Constitution requires private shopping centers to respect free speech rights, so a rule against distribution of literature naming a mall tenant, owner, or manager was invalid and could not be used to ban distribution of handbills criticizing Disney and Capitol Cities/ABC. [*Glendale Assocs. Ltd. v. NLRB*, 347 F.3d 1145 (9th Cir. 2003)] A later case, in contrast, holds that it is not a violation of California law for a stand-alone grocery store on private property to bar union organizers from distributing literature. [*Waremart Foods v. NLRB*, 354 F.3d 870 (D.C. Cir. 2004)]

California law protects reasonable speech in privately owned shopping centers, but does not require shopping centers to allow expressive activities that interfere with normal business opportunities. The D.C. Circuit couldn't figure out whether forbidding all expressive activities on the premises that did not have a permit violated the NLRA, so it sent the case to the California Supreme Court for a determination of whether a mall can impose a rule against urging customers to boycott any of the tenants of the mall. [*Fashion Valley Mall LLC v. NLRB*, 451 F.3d 241 (D.C. Cir. 2006)]

In late 2012, the California SupremeCourt ruled that a supermarket's privately owned entrance area is not a "public forum" as defined by the California constitution. Therefore, union picketing in such an area did not have protection under the state constitution. However, two California labor laws protected picketing. This decision conflicts with the D.C. Circuit's decision in 2004 that one of those statutes, the Moscone Act (which forbids injunctions against peaceful picketing) is unconstitutional because it grants greater protection to labor speech than to other forms of speech. [*Ralphs Grocery Co. v. United Food and Commercial Workers Union Local 8*, 55 Cal. 4th 1083, 290 P.3d 1116, 150 Cal. Rptr. 3d 501 (2012)]

The Sixth Circuit found that it was an Unfair Labor Practice for a non-union nursing home to require employees distributing union literature to leave non-working areas of the premises. The court found that the rights of employees who worked at other sites to receive the information outweighed the employer's property rights. There was no proof that nursing home residents would be any more distressed by the presence of union organizers than any other stranger. [*First Healthcare Corp. v. NLRB*, 344 F.3d 523 (6th Cir. 2003)]

The Third Circuit has found that the NLRA is not violated when an employer denies access to its property to union representatives who want to distribute handbills accusing the employer of using underpaid nonunion labor. In this context, the employer's property rights clearly prevail over the union's free speech right—especially because general information aimed at the public, not an actual certification election, was involved. [*Metropolitan Dist. Council of Phila. v. NLRB*, 68 F.3d 71 (3d Cir. 1995)] In contrast, where employee interests outweighed the employer's security and property rights concerns, the D.C. Circuit ruled that off-site employees must be allowed to distribute pro-union handbills in the plant parking lot. [*ITT Indus. v. NLRB*, 413 F.3d 64 (D.C. Cir. 2005)]

Can a business located in a shopping mall forbid the distribution of union literature in that mall? The Eighth Circuit says that a business that is just a tenant (and therefore does not have exclusive rights to the corridor outside its business location) cannot forbid union handbilling. But the Sixth Circuit says that a mall owner can ban solicitation by union representatives who are not employed at the mall, even if other kinds of solicitation (e.g., for charity) are allowed. [*O'Neil's Markets v. United Food & Commercial Workers*, 95 F.3d 733 (8th Cir. 1996); *Cleveland Real Estate Partners v. NLRB*, 95 F.3d 457 (6th Cir. 1996); *Riesbeck Food Mkts. Inc. v. NLRB*, 91 F.3d 132 (4th Cir. 1996)] Reasonable restrictions on the time, place, and manner of expressive activities can be imposed. Courts give more scrutiny to content-based restrictions on expressive activities than to those that are content-neutral. [*United Brotherhood of Carpenters & Joiners Local 848 v. NLRB*, 540 F.3d 957 (9th Cir. 2008)]

The New Jersey Supreme Court ruled early in 2009 that it violated First Amendment rights for a city to forbid temporary signs on public streets (including the rubber inflatable rat used at labor protests). A union official was fined $100 plus $33 in court costs for putting up the rat to protest a non-union building project. The ordinance, banning portable signs, inflatable signs, pennants, streamers, banners, and balloons, was too restrictive of speech and expression. The court ruled that public streets and sidewalks are forums with special entitlement to First Amendment protection, the ordinance was invalid because it was content-based; did not advance government interests; and was not narrowly tailored. The township said that the ordinance promoted aesthetics and public safety, but the New Jersey Supreme Court held that those considerations were not enough to support a content-based restriction. Because many other towns have similar ordinances, the decision had wide-ranging impact. [*State v. DeAngelo*, 197 N.J. 478, 963 A.2d 1200 (N.J. 2009); see Michael Booth, *Court Knocks Down Sign Ordinance That Banned Giant Rat Balloon at Labor Rally*, N.J.L.J. (Feb. 9, 2009) (law.com)]

Picketing is a particularly confrontational practice and has the potential to create conflict and danger, especially when persons who wish to enter the premises are told not to cross the line. The District Court for the District of Maryland ruled that it was permissible for a union to display a large banner outside the offices of a law firm that hired a nonunion subcontractor, treating the banner as purely informational—the equivalent of leafletting—not a confrontational barrier. [*Gold v. MidAtlantic Regional Council of Carpenters*, 74 L.W. 1432 (D. Md. Dec. 22, 2005)] The Ninth Circuit ruled that the NLRB was not entitled to a preliminary injunction to prevent a union from putting "Labor Dispute" banners outside stores that hire nonunion contractors because banners do not threaten, coerce, or restrain employees or potential customers. [*Overstreet v. United Bhd. of Carpenters & Joiners of Am.*, 409 F.3d 1199 (9th Cir. 2005)]

## § 30.05   THE APPROPRIATE BARGAINING UNIT

Even after winning an election, a union cannot be certified unless it is organized as the appropriate bargaining unit for the enterprise. NLRA § 9(b) gives the NLRB power to determine the appropriate bargaining unit. The basic standard is whether there is a community of interest among the unit members, not just employees in general (who can be expected to want higher wages and better benefits). Neither employer nor union can tell in advance what will be considered the appropriate unit, or how large the unit will be.

The appropriateness of a bargaining unit depends on the duties, skills, and working conditions of the employees who are supposed to have common interests. If there are competing proposed bargaining units for the same company, their relative popularity with employees is highly significant.

A union can be organized by employer, craft, or plan, or a subdivision of one of these categories. A union decision to organize as a craft unit is legally protected. The NLRB does not have the power to decide that a different unit would be more appropriate.

Employees and supervisors cannot be in the same bargaining unit. In fact, in many instances, supervisors cannot unionize at all, because they are considered a part of management. As a general rule, professionals and nonprofessionals cannot be included in a unit, but this rule can be waived if a majority of the professional employees vote to be included. (The nonprofessionals do not get veto power over inclusion of professionals.)

Determination of professional status does not depend entirely on job title. The factual determination is whether the work is predominantly intellectual, is not routine, requires discretion and independent judgment, mandates specialized knowledge, and cannot be standardized as to time. Professionals can still be unionized, but they must consent to inclusion in a nonprofessional bargaining unit instead of having their own.

If plant guards are unionized, they must have their own bargaining unit. They cannot be organized with other employees, because the employer would not feel very secure during a strike if several guards were union activists—much less if one of them was the shop steward!

The advance of technology, reducing the need for skilled work, creates difficult collective bargaining problems. When Wal-Mart decided to sell prepackaged meat in its stores instead of having the meat cut onsite, the D.C. Circuit upheld the NLRB: the meat department in the Jacksonville store was no longer an appropriate bargaining unit, so Wal-Mart did not have a general duty to bargain, but still had to bargain over the effect of the conversion on the employees of the meat department. Historically, meat department bargaining units were treated as presumptively appropriate, because of the workers' specialized skills and expertise. However, the NLRB no longer presumes appropriateness, because of the prevalence of packaged meat. Effects bargaining was required because the conversion eliminated the bargaining unit. [*United Food and Commercial Workers v. NLRB*, 519 F.3d 490 (D.C. Cir. 2008)]

In mid-2011, the NLRB sided with unions in several cases about organization and representation. In each case, the three Democrats voted against the one Republican on the board. In the *Specialty Healthcare* case, the NLRB ruled that it was permissible to organize a group consisting only of nursing assistants at a long-term care health facility. Management wanted to include other nonprofessionals in the unit to prevent the creation of "mini-bargaining units" targeting small groups of pro-union workers. The NLRB said that an employer that believes the proposed bargaining unit excludes some workers must prove that the excluded workers have an overwhelming community of interest with the workers in the unit. In the case of *Lamons Gasket Company* the NLRB ruled that employees opposed to the union cannot immediately challenge the employer's recognition of a card-check vote. The NLRB decision in *UGL-Unicco Service Company* says that, when a company is sold, neither the new owner, the employees, nor a rival union can immediately challenge the existing union. The incumbent union must be given a fair chance, over a reasonable time, to prove its mettle in collective bargaining. All three of these cases overturned decisions made earlier, when the NLRB was under Republican control. [Melanie Trottman, *Labor Board Rulings Likely to Rile Business*, WSJ.com (Aug. 31, 2011)]

## § 30.06  UNION SECURITY

### [A]  NLRA Prohibitions

Closed shops (where only union members can be hired) are illegal. The NLRA also forbids "preferential hiring" situations under which the employer is obligated to hire only union members unless the union is unable to fill all vacancies with qualified workers.

However, the LMRA authorizes "union shops," where all current employees must be union members, and new hires can be required to join the union after hiring (within seven days in the construction industry, within 30 days in other industries), and "agency shops," where payment of initiation fees and union dues is mandatory, but actual membership is optional. "Union security" measures are available to a union that is the bona fide bargaining representative of the employees in the bargaining unit and there has not been a deauthorization election certified in the year preceding the effective date of the union security agreement.

It is not a breach of a union's duty of fair representation for it to enter into a CBA that contains a union security clause that echoes the wording of NLRA § 8(3)(a). [*Marquez v. Screen Actors Guild*, 525 U.S. 33 (1998)] The plaintiff claimed that she should have been notified of her right not to join the union and to pay the union only for its representational activities.

If the union wants "automatic dues checkoff" (deduction of dues from the paycheck, so the union doesn't have to bill the member), it must have its members provide a written assignment lasting until the contract expires, or for one year, whichever comes first.

In 2011, the Second Circuit held that the Newspaper Guild's right to dues checkoff survived the expiration of the CBA—but so did the arbitration requirements of the CBA, so a dispute about checkoff had to be arbitrated, not litigated. [*Newspaper Guild CWA of Albany v. Hearst Corp.*, No. 10-2402 (2d Cir. May 17, 2011)]

Under the NLRA [29 U.S.C. § 169], employees who have a religious objection to unionization cannot be forced to join or support a union—even if the workplace is subject to a union security measure. However, to prevent financial windfalls, the employee can be required to contribute the equivalent of the initiation fee to a nonreligious charity of the employee's choice. *Commc'ns Workers of Am. v. Beck* [487 U.S. 735 (1988)] says that employees who do not want to join a union, but who are subject to a union security clause in the CBA, can be charged fees that can be traced back to collective bargaining, contract administration, and pursuing grievances. But they can prevent the union from using their money for political or other "nonrepresentational purposes."

It was a ULP for a union to fail to inform members of their legal rights under *Beck* if they resigned from the union; by not honoring resignations made during a strike; and by improperly assessing a second initiation fee when ex-members rejoined the union. [*International Bhd. of Teamsters Local 492*, 346 N.L.R.B. 37

(Jan. 31, 2006)]. A union can include organizing expenses as an element in the agency fees charged to nonmembers. The NLRB allows this [see *United Food & Commercial Workers*, 329 N.L.R.B. 69 (Sept. 30, 1999)] because of the positive effect of unionization on a company's wage scales, benefiting workers who do not join. In June, 2007, the Supreme Court ruled that it is permissible for a state to require unions that represent public employees to get affirmative consent from non-members of the union before using their agency fees for political purposes. (In other words, a state can forbid the union to use the agency fees this way unless the non-member employee opts out.) [*Davenport v. Washington Educ. Assn*, 551 U.S. 177 (2007); see Fred Schneyer, *U.S. Supreme Court Deems WA Union Fee Law Constitutional*, plansponsor.com (June 19, 2007)]

The Supreme Court returned to the subject of agency fees early in 2009. The CBA between the State of Maine and the union representing its employees requires non-member employees who are represented by the union to pay a "service fee" equal to the part of the union dues devoted to representational activities such as collective bargaining and contract administration. These funds cannot be used for politics, lobbying, or public relations. A group of petitioners brought suit to avoid being charged for any part of the service fee that covers nationwide litigation that does not directly benefit the union local. The district court and First Circuit upheld the imposition of this part of the fee. The Supreme Court ruled early in 2009 that the First Amendment permits a local union to charge non-members for the expense of national litigation that they could be required to pay for if it were local: i.e., the suit relates to collective bargaining rather than political issues, and the union local has a reasonable expectation that other locals will contribute. [*Locke v. Karass*, 555 U.S. 207 (2009)]

A "Hudson notice" (the name comes from *Chicago Teachers Union v. Hudson* [475 U.S. 292 (1986)]) informs non-members of a union of the "fair share" fees that they are charged to cover their fair share of the union's cost of negotiating and enforcing the CBA. Courts disagree about what constitutes an adequate Hudson notice, and how the union must present the figures. Executive Order 13202, mandating that federal agencies awarding contracts can neither require nor prohibit the contractors from entering into or adhering to agreements with unions, has been upheld by the D.C. Circuit. The court found this to be proprietary action, not regulation, and therefore to be a constitutional exercise of presidential power that is not preempted by the NLRA. [*Bldg. & Constr. Trades Dep't v. Allbaugh*, 295 F.3d 28 (D.C. Cir. 2002)]

A June 2012 Supreme Court case deals with a special assessment imposed on non-Union employees in a public sector agency shop. The special assessment, a 25% increase in monthly dues and removal of the previous cap on dues to create a "fight-back" fund to oppose legislation disfavored by the Union, was held to violate the non-members' First Amendment rights by forcing them into association and speech they did not endorse. The Supreme Court ruled that a separate Hudson notice should have been given. The Supreme Court said that a compulsory subsidy for private speech is permissible only when the fees are a necessary part of the larger purpose that led to the creation of the association. It is unlawful to charge the fee to non-Union members unless they opt out: the charge can only be imposed on non-members who affirmatively opt in to paying it. [*Knox v. SEIU*, 132 S. Ct. 2277 (2012)]

During the Bush administration, Executive Order 13201 required federal contractors to post a "Beck notice" to inform employees that they are not obligated to join a union; that they can object to use of their money for non-representation purposes, and can seek a refund of money used in this manner. [69 Fed. Reg. 16375 (Mar. 29, 2004)]

Shortly after his inauguration, President Obama signed three orders to expand the union rights of employees of federal contractors, and to reverse Bush administration policies. The first order (E.O. 13496) revoked E.O. 13201. E.O. 13201 required posting a notice of the right not to join a union. E.O. 13496 requires posting of a balanced notice of employee rights under the NLRA. E.O. 13496 applies to companies that have more than $100,000 in federal contracts. The second order holds that, when a federal agency changes the contractors who provide services to a federal building, the incoming contractor must offer jobs to the outgoing contractor's non-supervisory employees. The third order denies reimbursement of money spent on supporting or deterring employees' rights to unionize or bargain collectively. [<http://www.edocket.access.gpo.gov/2009/pdf/E9-2485.pdf>; see Laura Meckler, *Obama to Reverse Bush Labor Policies*, <http://www.wsj.com> (Jan. 30, 2009)]

Another Obama administration move was the NLRB's publication of regulations requiring employers to display a poster about the right to unionize, bargain collectively, distribute union literature, and be free of retaliation for collective action to improve wages and working conditions. (In effect, this is the converse of the Beck notice.) Agricultural, rail, and airline employers are exempt from these rules. Originally, the requirement was supposed to take effect November 14, 2011. [Steven Greenhouse, *N.L.R.B. Tells Companies to Ease Right to Unionize*, NYTimes.com (Aug. 25, 2011). In response to protests by business groups, the NLRB postponed the effective date of the notice-posting requirement to January 31, 2012, then postponed it once again to April 30, 2012. [Tara Cantore, *NLRB Postpones Implementation Date for Notice Posting Rule*, plansponsor.com (Oct. 5, 2011) and *NLRB Postpones Required Date to Post Employee Rights*, plansponsor.com (Dec. 27, 2011)]

Both the D.C. and the Fourth Circuit ruled in 2013 that the posting requirement was invalid. The D.C. Circuit held that the posting rule violates employers' expressive rights. Instead of severing the provision that failure to post is a ULP, the D.C. Circuit invalidated the entire rule, concluding that the NLRB would not want to have a purely voluntary rule that it could not enforce. The Fourth Circuit stated that the NLRB's powers are limited, not extensive, and the NLRB has power to act only when triggered by a certification petition or an Unfair Labor Practices charge. According to the Fourth Circuit, other agencies such as the EEOC and OSHA derive their authority to require posting from their governing statutes, and the NLRA does not authorize a posting requirement. [*Chamber of Commerce v. NLRB*, No. 12-1757 (4th Cir. June 14, 2013); see Jenna Greene, *Fourth Circuit Strikes NLRB Poster Rule*, The BLT (Blog of Legal Times (June 14, 2013) (law.com); *Nat'l Ass'n of Mfrs. v. NLRB*, No. 12-5068 (D.C. Cir. May 5, 2013)]

The Ninth Circuit upheld California Gov't Code §§ 16645–16649 (forbidding companies that receive state grants over $10,000 from using the money to assist, promote, or deter union organizing). The court found that the statute does not violate the First Amendment, does not undermine federal labor policy, and is not preempted by the NLRA. [*Chamber of Commerce v. Lockyer*, 463 F.3d 1076 (9th Cir. 2006)] Certiorari was granted in late 2007. According to the United States Solicitor General, New York, Florida, Illinois, Maine, Massachusetts, Minnesota, North Dakota, Ohio, and Rhode Island have similar laws, and bills of this type have been introduced in New Jersey and Michigan. [The Supreme Court ruled that the California law was preempted by federal labor law. According to the Supreme Court, federal labor law promotes wide-open debate on labor matters, as long as employers refrain from coercion. [*Chamber of Commerce v. Brown*, 554 U.S. 60 (2008)]

The converse of union security is a state "right to work" law that says that unwilling employees cannot be compelled to join unions or pay dues. Early in 2012, Indiana became the twenty-third "right to work" state (i.e., a state forbidding union contracts that obligate non-members to pay representation fees). It was the first state to adopt such a law in more than a decade and the only Midwestern state in that category; most right to work states are in the South (e.g., Alabama, Arkansas, Florida, Georgia, Louisiana, Mississippi, North Carolina, South Carolina, Tennessee, Texas, Virginia). [Monica Davey, *Indiana Becomes 'Right to Work' State*, NYTimes.com (Feb. 1, 2012). According to a graphic in Kris Maher's article, *Despite Win, Right-to-Work Bills Face Long Slog*, WSJ.com (Dec. 13, 2013), Arizona, Idaho, Iowa, Kansas, Nebraska, Nevada, North Dakota, South Dakota, Oklahoma, Utah, and Wyoming were also right to work states.]

In late 2012, Michigan became the 24th right to work state, as a result of a statute affecting hundreds of thousands of private and public sector union members. (However, the police and fire unions are not affected by the law.) The right to work law means that non-union workers are not required to pay union representation fees. [Matthew Dolan and Kris Maher, *Michigan Approves Union Curbs*, WSJ.com (Dec. 12, 2012);Kris Maher, Q&A: *How Michigan's 'Right-to-Work' Law Will Work*, WSJ.com (Dec. 11, 2012)].

The economic effect of right to work laws is complex. According to the Wall Street Journal, right to work states tend to have lower wages but a higher rate of job creation. Private-sector employees in right to work states earned an average of $738.43 a week in 2012, 9.8% less than workers in states without such laws. Some economists said that lower wages were offset by lower cost of living in right to work states. The DOL said that private employment rose 4.9% in right to work states versus 3.9% in the other states, with the gain especially noticeable for factory work—but factory jobs pay 7.4% less in the right to work states. But the National Institute for Labor Relations Research reported that employees in right to work states earned more: $675 weekly average rather than $660 in the other states. [Neil Shah, Ben Casselman, *'Right-to-Work' States Tend to Have Lower Wages, More Jobs*, WSJ.com (Dec. 15, 2012) and *Laws' Scant Effect On Wages*, WSJ.com (Dec. 12, 2012)]

## [B]  Hiring Halls

Under a union security option, the employer decides who to hire, but the union may be able to get hirees to join or pay dues. A hiring hall works differently. It is a mechanism under which the union selects workers and sends them to the employer, based on the employer's requisition (for six plasterers and two electricians, for example). The union decides which union or nonunion workers will be referred for the job.

An exclusive hiring hall is a relationship under which the employer gets all its workers through union referrals. This is not considered a union security arrangement, so it is legal in the right-to-work states. A nonexclusive hiring hall makes union referral only one of the ways in which the employer can find new workers.

The NLRA provides that it is unlawful for a union to give preference to union members over equally qualified nonmembers in the operation of a nonexclusive hiring hall. The operation and structure of a hiring hall is a mandatory bargaining subject.

In a situation in which union members testified that they often got work for themselves without union referral, the union was not operating an exclusive hiring hall. Therefore, it was a ULP for the union to pressure management to avoid hiring persons who were not referred by the union, or to fire employees for that reason. Enforcement of a hiring hall arrangement depends on the terms of the CBA. Therefore, once the NLRB shows discriminatory conduct that could have affected employee rights, the burden shifts to the employer or union to show that it acted in compliance with the CBA. [*NLRB v. Local 334, Laborers Int'l Union*, 481 F.3d 875, 1639, 1714 (6th Cir. 2007)]

## § 30.07  THE COLLECTIVE BARGAINING PROCESS

## [A]  Basic Issues

Under the NLRA, the purpose of certifying a union is to provide an ongoing process of collective bargaining between employer and union on important work-related issues, leading to the adoption of a union contract, or Collective Bargaining Agreement (CBA). Even after a CBA is in place, it is still necessary to bargain on "mandatory" issues, and allowable to bargain on "permissive" issues. [See 29

U.S.C. § 158(a)(5)] There are some subjects on which it is illegal to bargain. For instance, it is illegal to implement a closed shop, even if both employer and union are willing.

Mandatory bargaining subjects include:

- Drug testing;
- Dues checkoff (the employer's practice of deducting union dues from paychecks, then forwarding these amounts to the union);
- Work rules;
- Bans on moonlighting by employees;
- Transfers of work out of the bargaining unit;
- Contracting out work done by employees in the bargaining unit (contracting out work done by nonunionized employees is not a mandatory subject of bargaining);
- Bonuses;
- Medical insurance;
- Clauses that forbid strikes and lockouts.

Mandatory bargaining subjects are those that materially or significantly affect the terms or conditions of employment. Issues that have a remote or incidental effect on the work environment are permissible subjects of bargaining.

Where bargaining is required, the employer has a duty to meet with the union at reasonable times to confer over the terms and conditions of employment (such as wages and hours). Insisting that bargaining sessions be held during regular business hours and making negotiating committee members use paid leave to attend the sessions was a management ULP because it interfered with the right to bargain collectively. [*Ceridian Corp. v. NLRB*, 435 F.3d 352 (D.C. Cir. 2006)]

Refusal to bargain is an unfair labor practice. On the other hand, certain issues are established as managerial prerogatives that can be decided unilaterally, without bargaining:

- Complete termination of operations;
- Sale of an entire business;
- A partial closing that has business motivations, and is not the result of anti-union animus;
- Relocation of bargaining-unit work that is motivated by a basic change in the nature of the employer's operations, where the work at the new location is significantly different from the work at the old one.

The basic rule is that bargaining is required if a decision is undertaken to save labor costs, but not if the employer takes on a program of modernization or environmental compliance that costs more than the potential savings on labor costs. Even if the employer has the right to make a decision without union involvement, it has an obligation to engage in "effects bargaining": that is, it must notify the union that the decision has been made, and must bargain about the effects the change will have on union members.

Changing the methods of production is considered a managerial prerogative, although employees who believe that they are adversely affected by the change can file a grievance or seek effects bargaining about the change.

A Gissel bargaining order (stemming from *NLRB v. Gissel Packing Co.*) [395 U.S. 575 (1969)] is an order compelling management to bargain in good faith with a union. Early in 2003, the D.C. Circuit upheld an NLRB order requiring a movie theater chain to bargain with union locals before making the theaters "manager-operated" and firing the union projectionists. Although technological improvements have greatly reduced the amount (and skill level) of the work done by projectionists, eliminating a job classification does not come under the heading of "new or improved work methods" that can be introduced without bargaining. Transfer of work always requires bargaining if it results in loss of bargaining unit jobs. [*Regal Cinemas Inc. v. NLRB*, 317 F.3d 300 (D.C. Cir. 2003)]

Bargaining must be done in good faith. Neither side is obligated to make concessions or give in where it thinks surrender would be imprudent. If the bargaining process comes to an impasse—i.e., neither side is introducing new proposals or yielding on proposals already on the table—then the employer can lawfully cease negotiating and simply put its own proposals into place.

"Regressive bargaining"—withdrawing an offer if the union is unable to meet the employer's time frame—has been upheld by the NLRB in *White Cap, Inc.* [325 NLRB 220 (1998)], unless it is done specifically for the purpose of avoiding a contract. Where the employer has a legitimate business reason for wanting to resolve the issue quickly, regressive bargaining is permissible.

After a collective bargaining agreement expires, there is nothing left to be enforced under contract law. But labor law [NLRA § 8(a)(5)] obligates the employer to maintain the status quo, at least until an impasse is reached and the employer can start implementing its own proposals unilaterally. The employer cannot take advantage of a bargaining impasse to unilaterally impose new provisions, or any provisions more favorable to its own cause than the provisions that were on the table during negotiations.

The Seventh Circuit has ruled (in a case involving a union's request for information about hidden surveillance cameras in the workplace) that the right to bargain about a mandatory bargaining subject can only be waived by a clear and unmistakeable expression of an intention to waive. [*Nat'l Steel Corp. v. NLRB*, 324 F.3d 928 (7th Cir. 2003)] The cameras are mandatory bargaining subjects because, like drug and alcohol tests, they involve the terms and conditions of employment. Furthermore, the employer was merely ordered to bargain and provide the union with information about the cameras; it was not forbidden to use security cameras or ordered to make public disclosure of the location of the cameras. The deployment of hidden surveillance cameras was also treated as a mandatory bargaining subject by *Brewers & Maltsters v. NLRB*, 414 F.3d 36 (D.C. Cir. 2005), because subjects plainly germane to the work environment are mandatory bargaining subjects, unless they are at the core of entrepreneurial control of the workplace. (See § 26.06 for additional discussion of workplace surveillance.)

A growing issue (see §§ 26.06 and 27.05) is the extent to which employers can monitor employees' social media activities.

The NLRB began to confront social media issues in late 2010. Since then, what has emerged as the major question is whether employees use social media to discuss or protest working conditions (which constitutes protected activity) or whether they merely discuss personal issues (which is probably not protected, especially if there are issues of misuse of the employer's proprietary information.)In general, employer policies are tested for reasonableness: are they too broad or impermissibly vague? Do they prevent employees from exercising their rights under the NLRA?

Finally, employers are entitled to a defense if they would have taken adverse action against the employee even without the protected concerted activity. [Michael C. Schmidt, *Deciphering the NLRB's Stance on Social Media Issues*, N.Y.L.J. (Oct. 24, 2011) (law.com); NLRB acting general counsel Lafe Solomon published several reports on this issue: <http://www.nlrb.gov/news-outreach/news-releases/acting-general-counsel-releases-report-employer-social-media-policies>, *Acting General Counsel Issues Second Social Media Report*, (Jan. 25, 2012). Solomon's third report was issued May 30, 2012: <http://www.nlrb.gov/news/acting-general-counsel-releases-report-employer-social-media-policies> A March 2012 Advice Memorandum from the NLRB's Office of the General Counsel finds a social media policy unlawfully constrained protected concerted activity to the extent that it forbade use of the employer's logo, graphics, and trademarks, and forbade photographing or video-recording the facility. Forbidding employees to refer to "non-public information" was so vague that employees might be discouraged from permissible discussions of working conditions. But it was legitimate to encourage employees to report violations of the policy to management, and legitimate to forbid defamation or discrediting the company's products or services. [*Giant Food LLC*,Cases 05-CA-064793, 05-CA-065187, and 05-CA-064795, <http://www.employmentlawwatch.com/uploads/file/July%202013%Advice%Memorandum.pdf> (last accessed Mar. 21, 2012)] (See Chapter 27).]

## [B]  Typical CBA Clauses

Although the actual contract that emerges from bargaining will reflect the individual needs of the business, and the comparative strengths of management and union, the following are issues that are often addressed in Collective Bargaining Agreements:

- Description of the bargaining unit;
- Management rights;
- Workday and workweek;
- Overtime;
- Classification of jobs for wage purposes;
- Compensation, bonuses, health, and other benefits;
- Paid time off (who is eligible, scheduling time off, who must be notified, which paid holidays are provided);
- Sick leave (number of days available; waiting period; doctors' notes; discipline for misusing sick leave);
- Seniority (what counts as a break in continuous service; effect of corporate transitions on seniority);
- Subcontracting;
- Plant closing and successorship;
- Severance pay;
- Hiring halls;
- Union security;
- Access to premises by non-employee union staff;
- Progressive discipline (the steps such as reprimands, conferences, and written warnings that will be provided before an employee is discharged);
- Drug testing;
- Grievance procedures (scope of disputes covered; how employees can present grievances; whether binding arbitration is required).

## [C]    Bargaining on Modification, Termination

The employer has an obligation to notify the union whenever it intends to modify or terminate a CBA. The employer must also notify the Federal Mediation and Conciliation Service of the intended action. Sixty days before the contract is scheduled to expire (or 60 days before the intended modification or termination), the employer must notify the union, inviting it to negotiate a new or amended contract. Notice to the FMCS is due 30 days after the notice to the union. Failure to give the required notice is an unfair labor practice. [29 U.S.C. § 158(d)]

The 60-day notice period is referred to as the cooling-off period. The contract remains in effect during this period, and neither strikes nor lockouts are permitted.

Employers need not volunteer information, but they have a duty to provide the union with whatever information (other than confidential or privileged information) the union requests in order to represent the employees adequately. Information relating to wage rates and job descriptions is presumed relevant. The union has to show a specific need for access to the employer's nonpublic financial information—e.g., if the employer claims inability to afford a wage increase. [*Lakeland Bus Lines Inc. v. NLRB*, 347 F.3d 955 (D.C. Cir. 2003)]

## § 30.08    ELECTIONS AFTER CERTIFICATION

Representation elections are not the only kind that can be ordered and supervised by the NLRB. Federal labor law allows a rerun or runoff election to be held to redress an improper election. Once a union is in place, employees can ask that it be deauthorized or decertified. The employer also has the right to challenge a union's majority status.

A rerun election is held if there were election improprieties, or if two unions competed for representation; the ballot included a "no union" choice, and "no union" got as many votes as the other alternatives. (If there is only one union on the ballot, a tie vote means that the union loses, because it failed to attract a majority of the voters.)

A runoff election is held if no choice gets a majority. Only one runoff election can be held, although there could be both a rerun and a runoff election in the same organizing campaign.

A deauthorization petition is filed by a group of employees who want to remove the union's authority to enter into a union shop contract. Therefore, there are no deauthorization petitions in right-to-work states, because there aren't any union shops either. When a majority of the bargaining unit (not just a majority of the voters) vote for deauthorization, the union remains the authorized bargaining representative for the employees, but the employees no longer have to pay union dues.

The purpose of a decertification petition is to remove the union's bargaining authority. The petition can be filed by an employee, a group of employees, or someone acting on behalf of the employees. The employer does not have the right to file a decertification petition, but it does have a free-speech right to inform employees of their right to remove a union that they feel has not represented them adequately.

A decertification petition requires a showing of interest by 30% of the employees in the bargaining unit. Most petitions that are filed get the necessary vote (a majority of actual voters, not eligible voters) and therefore result in decertification of the union.

Decertification petitions cannot be filed at certain times: one year after certification of a union; a reasonable time after an employer's voluntary recognition of a union; or within 12 months of another decertification petition.

The employer has the right to petition the NLRB to determine that the union has lost its majority status. The employer must offer objective evidence of the change, such as employee turnover so heavy that few of the original pro-union workers remain; the union's failure to process employee grievances; or a strike that yielded no benefits for employees. If an employer has information that leads it to doubt the union's majority status, it is an unfair labor practice to enter into a contract with this union and then try to disavow the contract based on those doubts. The appropriate action is to refuse the contract. [*Auciello Iron Works Inc. v. NLRB*, 517 U.S. 781 (1996)]

In 2001, the NLRB issued a decision, *Levitz Furniture Co. of the Pacific*, [333 NLRB 105 (2001)] eliminating the good faith-reasonable doubt standard in withdrawal-of-recognition cases. Under *Levitz*, the employer must show that the union has actually lost majority status to justify unilateral withdrawal of recognition from an incumbent union. Nor can the employer cite employee discontent with the union arising after an unlawful refusal to bargain as evidence of reasonable uncertainty about majority status, because the refusal to bargain itself taints the employer's relations with the union, which can only be repaired through good-faith bargaining. [*Marion Hosp. Corp. v. NLRB*, 321 F.3d 1178 (D.C. Cir. 2003); *Prime Servs. Inc. v. NLRB*, 266 F.3d 1233 (D.C. Cir. 2001)]

The general rule, known as the CBA bar, is that no union election can be held while a collective bargaining agreement is in force. However, if there has been a substantial increase in personnel since the contract was signed, a new election may be proper if the union no longer represents a majority of the current workforce.

There used to be another "bar" in effect, the "successor bar" rule of *St. Elizabeth's Manor* [329 NLRB 341 (1999)], under which an incumbent union would be given a reasonable amount of time after a corporate takeover to bargain with the successor employer without challenges to its majority status. However, in 2002, the NLRB overruled that decision [*MV Transportation*, 337 N.L.R.B. 129 (July 19, 2002)] and now takes the position that the incumbent union gets a rebuttable presumption of continuing majority status, but that will not bar an otherwise valid challenge to majority status. It violates federal labor law for an employer to withdraw recognition of a union prematurely, without engaging in bargaining for a reasonable period of time. (However, pursuing reasonable bargaining will remove the taint of an earlier refusal to bargain.) In this case, there were only five bargaining sessions, and apparently the parties were close to reaching agreement when recognition was withdrawn, so the D.C. Circuit upheld the NLRB's ruling against the employer. [*Lee Lumber & Building Materials Corp. v. NLRB*, 310 F.3d 209 (D.C. Cir. 2002)]

## § 30.09  STRIKES

### [A]  Right to Strike

The NLRA gives employees the right to engage in "protected concerted activities"—joining together to organize, protest, and otherwise assert their interests in a lawful manner. This includes going on strike if a new contract cannot be negotiated, or based on a union's claim that working conditions are bad enough to justify a strike.

A striking union's gamble is that the employer will need to maintain continuous operations and therefore will grant significant concessions before the employees lose too much income by stopping work. But at other times employers actually benefit from strikes, if they can save payroll for a while, shut down an unproductive location, relocate to a lower-cost area (in another state or even another country) or bringing in "striker replacements."

Violence, sabotage, and threats are not protected activity. If a threatened strike would imperil the national health or safety, the President of the United States can order the U.S. Attorney General to petition the appropriate federal court for an 80-day cooling-off period, during which the strike is enjoined.

Secondary strikes and secondary boycotts—actions taken against one employer to put pressure on another employer that does business with the first employer—are banned by NLRA § 8(b)(4). A company that is the victim of a secondary strike or boycott can sue for damages under LMRA § 303.

### [B]  Types of Strike

Employees can lawfully engage in a work stoppage in three situations:

- An economic dispute with the employer;
- A claim that the employer has committed unfair labor practices;
- A claim that workplace conditions are so unreasonably dangerous that they should not be required to continue work.

An "unfair labor practices" strike is caused in whole or part by unfair labor practices. There must be a causal connection between the strike and the employer practices. If the practices are simply cost-related (such as shift changes), then the strike should be characterized as an economic strike. But a strike that begins as an economic strike can be converted to an unfair labor practices strike if the employer acts unfairly or refuses to accept legitimate offers for return to work.

The main difference between an economic strike and an unfair labor practices strike is the extent of employees' reinstatement rights after the strike ends and they want to go back to work. Some issues are areas of managerial prerogative, so employees cannot lawfully strike to challenge management's decisions in these areas.

29 U.S.C. § 143 makes it a protected concerted activity for employees to refuse to work if there is measurable, objective evidence of undue hazards (not just a subjective feeling that something is wrong). The employees must also articulate goals that the employer can respond to: replace a defective machine or install guard rails, for instance, not just "make the workplace safer." [See Chapter 31 for information about occupational safety and health]

According to a mid-2002 Sixth Circuit decision, the right to engage in a good-faith work stoppage due to abnormally dangerous conditions applies whether or not the employees have a no-strike clause in their CBA, and the employer does not have the right to hire permanent replacements in such a situation. However, in this particular case, the Sixth Circuit found that the workers' belief that conditions were abnormally dangerous was not objectively supported. It's true that NIOSH found that the workers had high uranium levels, but the levels were within limits permitted by the state and by the Nuclear Regulatory Commission. [*TNS Inc. v. NLRB*, 296 F.3d 384 (6th Cir. 2002)]

If the underlying strike is lawful, then a sympathy strike (workers outside the striking bargaining unit refuse to cross the picket line) is probably protected concerted activity as defined by the NLRA. A 2003 decision of the Ninth Circuit says that a no-strike provision in a CBA does not bar a sympathy strike for another bargaining unit within the same local union, because the CBA clause did not clearly and unmistakeably waive the right to call a strike in support of fellow union members. [*Standard Concrete Prods. Inc. v. Gen. Truck Drivers Office, Food & Warehouse Union*, 353 F.3d 668 (9th Cir. 2003)]

In contrast to those protected activities, a sitdown strike (an illegal takeover of the employer's premises) is unlawful. A wildcat strike, called by the rank and file without authorization from the union, is not protected activity if the workers want to usurp the union's role as sole bargaining representative for the workers.

A collective bargaining agreement can lawfully be drafted to include a no-strike clause. It is not protected concerted activity to call an economic strike in violation of a no-strike clause. Therefore, the employer can legitimately fire the strikers and deny them reinstatement after the strike ends.

Because of the special risks involved, NLRA § 8(g) requires unions at health care facilities to give at least 10 days' notice before a strike, picket, or concerted refusal to work. The employer must be notified of the date and time the action will commence. The NLRB ruled that starting the strike four hours later than the time stated in the notice violates the notice requirement. Unions are not permitted to make unilateral extensions of strike notices. Therefore, it was not an unfair labor practice to fire nurses involved in the strike. [*Alexandria Clinic PA*, 339 NLRB No. 162 (Aug. 21, 2003)]

## [C]   Lockouts and Other Employer Activity

The lockout is the employer's counterpart to the union's strike. In a strike, the employees refuse to come to work. In a lockout, the employer refuses to let them in. An employer that undertakes a lockout for business reasons can hire replacement workers. It can enter into a temporary subcontract for the duration of the lockout. However, the employer is not allowed to use the lockout to permanently contract out work formerly performed by employees. Lockouts are lawful if and only if they have a business motivation, not if they are used to prevent the workers from organizing a union, or to avoid bargaining with an incumbent union. However, a lockout is a justified response to a strike that violates a CBA no-strike clause.

It is an unfair labor practice for an employer to institute a lockout that is inherently destructive of the rights of employees. It is also an unfair labor practice to institute a lockout without having legitimate economic business justification (not just the employer's convenience). The mere possibility of a strike if contract negotiations break down is not a sufficient justification for a lockout during collective bargaining; and it might be treated as an unlawful refusal to bargain. Lockouts are analyzed even more stringently outside the strike context, because the union's power is weaker and there is less need for the employer to counter-balance it.

Employers are allowed to close a business, or shut it down temporarily, with economic motivations. But doing it to harm the union is an unfair labor practice. A "runaway shop" (transferring work between existing locations or opening a new location) is an unfair labor practice if it is based on antiunion motivation rather than a desire to enhance profitability.

During a strike, the employer is not permitted to alter the terms and conditions of employment that affect strikers. However, once a CBA expires, the employer is allowed to change those terms as they affect striker replacements.

The NLRB held that, after a 14-year lockout, it was not a violation of the NLRA to require a four-week retraining period before reinstating strikers. Nor was it a violation to limit the opportunities for overtime during the training period. The Ninth Circuit upheld the NLRB's decision: there had been an election that resulted in rejection of both the competing unions that wanted to unionize the company, so management had little to gain by anti-union animus. The overtime policy had only minimal impact on employee rights. Restricting the overtime opportunities for untrained workers was reasonable, because the employer pays more for overtime hours and can expect the work to be done by employees who understand the work processes. [*Fresh Fruit & Vegetable Workers Local 1096 v. NLRB*, 539 F.3d 1089 (9th Cir. 2008)]

## [D]  Striker Replacements

During a strike, employers are entitled to keep their operations open by hiring replacements. Employers can always hire replacements for jobs that are described as temporary stopgaps until the strike ends. The question is whether the employer can hire permanent replacements, outsource functions formerly performed by employees, or keep the replacements and deny reinstatement to the strikers post-strike.

It is not an unfair labor practice to discharge strikers who have lost their employee status, and therefore their protection under the NLRA. The NLRA protects only lawful strikes that are conducted in a lawful manner, are called for a protected purpose, and are authorized by the bargaining unit representative (if there is one).

A strike is lawful if it occurs after the expiration of a CBA, if it is either an economic or an unfair labor practices strike, or if it demands concessions from the employer. Wildcat strikes, sitdown strikes, and strikes contrary to a CBA no-strike clause are not protected. Excessive violence removes employee status, although a minor instance of violence would not prevent the perpetrator from being considered an employee.

In an economic strike, the employer can permanently replace the strikers and keep the replacement workers after the end of the strike. However, strikers are entitled to reinstatement after the strike if they have not been replaced. Delay in reinstating them counts as an unfair labor practice. Even after being replaced, an economic striker is still considered an employee. If the former economic striker makes an unconditional application for reinstatement, the employer must reinstate him if the replacement worker quits or is terminated. If no jobs are available at the time of the application, the employer must reinstate the ex-striker when a job becomes available.

However, the former striker does not have to be reinstated if:

- He or she gets regular and substantial employment somewhere else;
- The employer has a legitimate business reason (violence or sabotage during the strike, for instance) for denying reinstatement;
- The job itself has been eliminated (e.g., due to new technology).

The NLRB's position, which has been upheld by the Seventh Circuit, is that the main issue is whether the replacement workers have a reasonable expectation of recall after being laid off. Strikers are entitled to reinstatement if the replacements did not have a reasonable expectation of recall—unless the employer can prove that the job is vacant or there is good cause not to rehire the striker. A "Laid-law vacancy," otherwise known as a "genuine job vacancy," occurs if the replacement worker cannot reasonably expect recall after layoff.

Unless there is a legitimate and substantial business reason to depart from the rule, a reinstated economic striker must be treated equally with nonstrikers and permanent replacements, with the same benefits, including paid vacations and accrual of seniority. Normally, reinstatement should return the worker to status quo, but he or she can be demoted for a legitimate business reason such as a risk of sabotage.

## [E]   Subcontracting

When a strike is imminent, employers who have a pressing business reason, and who are not acting out of antiunion animus, can legitimately subcontract out work that was performed by the bargaining unit, even though employees are displaced. NLRA § 8(a)(3), which penalizes employer actions that are intended to discourage union membership, can be invoked even if there is no direct proof of the employer's motivation—if the employer's action is inherently destructive of important rights of the employees. Subcontracting is a mandatory bargaining subject, so the employer can act unilaterally if a bargaining impasse has been reached.

## § 30.10   THE WARN ACT

The Worker Adjustment Retraining and Notice Act (WARN Act) [29 U.S.C. § 2101] requires employers of 100 or more full-time employees (or a combination of full- and part-timers adding up to at least 100 people and 4,000 work hours a week) to provide notice of a plant closing or mass layoff. At least 60 days' notice must be given to employees, unions, and the federal government. The Act defines a plant closing as employment loss (termination, prolonged layoff, serious cutback in work hours) affecting 50 or more workers during a 30-day period.

A mass layoff has a lesser effect on the individual workers (e.g., potential for recall) and affects 500 people or one-third of the workforce. Anyone rehired within six months, or anyone who elected early retirement, should not be counted in determining if a mass layoff has occurred.

A reduction in force (RIF) may require compliance with the WARN Act or a related state statute (e.g., in California, Connecticut, Illinois, Maine, New Hampshire, New Jersey, New York, Tennessee, and Wisconsin). Penalties imposed for non-compliance can wipe out the savings associated with reducing payroll.

Even employers who qualify for the faltering company exception or the unforeseen business circumstance exception still must give as much notice to employees as is practicable, and the notice itself must explain why the full 60 days of notice was not given.

The faltering company exception applies if the company proves that it was actively seeking capital or new business 60 days before the shutdown; there was a realistic chance of obtaining it; the financing would have been enough to avert shutdown; and giving the notice would have made it impossible to secure the financing.

The unforeseen business circumstances exception requires events that are beyond the employer's control—for example, sudden, dramatic, and unexpected conditions such as unexpected termination of an important contract, a major supplier goes on strike, or the government orders closing of a site without time to prepare. However, this exception is seldom applied when a company was simply in bad financial condition and its finances continued to deteriorate.

In mid-2011, the District Court for the District of Minnesota ruled that U.S. Steel did not violate the WARN Act because the unforeseeable business circumstances exception applied to recession-oriented layoffs. Although 340 workers were laid off in December 2008 without receiving 60 days' notice, they were eventually recalled (some of them laid off and recalled twice). The district court held that employers are not required to operate at a detriment for 60 days merely because it is possible to give notice. Furthermore, 60 days before the actual layoff date, the company was operating at full capacity. [Sheri Qualters, *U.S. Steel Off The Hook Under WARN Act Because of Economic Crisis*, Nat'l L.J. (Aug. 19, 2011) (law.com)]

Companies that plan RIFs should consider implementing an ERISA severance plan. If there is a plan in place, employees must exhaust the internal claims procedure before suing, and the employer can reserve the discretion to construe the plan terms as long as the employer does not act arbitrarily and capriciously. ERISA claims can be removed to federal court—thus escaping tougher state laws on severance. Furthermore, claims under an ERISA plan can be removed to federal court, and states tend to have tougher laws on severance.

Another consideration is that an employer's action in laying off an employee for no fault of his or her own may make it impossible to enforce covenants not to compete. [These points are raised by Steven J. Friedman, Gerald T. Hathaway, Bruce R. Millman, Michael Weber, Ellen N. Sueda, *And You Thought the Bailout Was Bad: Employment Law Risks in the Current Financial Crisis* (October 2008) (benefitslink.com). On the unforeseeable business circumstances exception, see, e.g., *Childress v. Darby Lumber Co.*, 357 F.3d 1000 (9th Cir. 2004)]

According to the Ninth Circuit, for WARN Act purposes, the "site of employment" for construction workers is the actual job site and not the company headquarters. Therefore, since the site did not have 50 or more workers, the WARN Act did not apply. (There were 33 employees at headquarters plus three outside administrators, and 162 construction workers at sites in seven states.) [*Bader v. Northern Line Layers*, 503 F.3d 813 (9th Cir. 2007)]

Although the WARN Act refers to a "group" of laid-off employees, employers cannot avoid the application of the act by performing layoffs one at a time. All economically motivated layoffs within a 90-day period are aggregated toward the 50-employee figure. [*Hallowell v. Orleans Reg'l Hosp.*, 217 F.3d 379 (5th Cir. 2000)]

If the employer fails to give the required notice, each affected employee is entitled to up to 60 days' back pay (work days, not calendar days) and benefits. A federal civil penalty of up to $500 can also be imposed for every day that the failure to give notice continued. A union can sue for damages on behalf of its members.

The Eighth Circuit ruled that the seller of a business was protected by the WARN Act's sale-of-business exclusion. The buyer promised to hire a substantial number of the seller's employees (and in fact did so), so the seller believed that fewer than 50 employees would lose their jobs. A seller is responsible for providing WARN Act notice up to and including the sale date, but at that point, the purchaser becomes responsible for giving notice of a plant closing. In the Eighth Circuit view, only the party actually causing employment loss must give notice. When a business is sold as a going concern, the sale-of-business exception creates a presumption that the buyer is the employer if the seller continues to employ its employees on the day of the sale. [*Wilson v. Airtherm Prods. Inc.*, 436 F.3d 906 (8th Cir. 2006)]

The Ninth Circuit, interpreting the meaning of "voluntary departure" under the WARN Act, said that an employee who leaves a job because the business is closing has an employment loss and does not depart voluntarily. Gee West told its employees that the business would close in two weeks, and unless a buyer was found by then, the entire workforce except for a few accounting and business office staffers would be terminated. Gee West said that it was impossible to give more notice—they wanted to sell the business, and thought it would be unattractive if the employees left. The company closed two days before the announced closing date because there were too few employees to maintain it. No buyer was found for the business. In a suit for failure to give WARN Act notice, the district court said that 120 employees departed voluntarily, leaving fewer than 50 employees—so notice was not required. The Ninth Circuit reversed, stating that the WARN Act was passed precisely to protect employees against sudden and unexpected job loss. In this analysis, departures caused by termination of the business are not voluntary. The WARN Act includes a faltering business exception precisely for the situation of a business that wants to preserve its sale options. [*Collins v. Gee West Seattle LLC*, 631 F.3d 1001 (9th Cir. 2011)]

DHL Express announced in late 2009 that five of its six Chicago-area facilities would close. To get severance benefits, employees had to waive all of their claims against the employer, including WARN Act claims. Two of the laid-off workers sued under the WARN Act. The district court held that the WARN Act was not applicable, ruling that there was no plant closing, because the five facilities were not a single site, and the layoffs did not reach 33% of the workforce. Although the plaintiffs alleged that employer pressure and extreme economic uncertainty negated voluntariness, the Seventh Circuit ruled that the severance package was voluntary. The agreements and release were negotiated by the union; were unambiguous; and suggested that employees consult a lawyer. The Seventh Circuit ruled that WARN Act claims can be waived by a voluntary general release. [*Ellis v. DHL Express Inc. USA*, 633 F.3d 522 (7th Cir. 2011)]

A company that provided payroll management services for other companies was not a WARN Act "employer" and could not be held liable for failure to provide notice, because it did not order the closing. [*Administaff Cos., Inc. v. New York Joint Board, Shirt & Leisurewear Div.*, 337 F.3d 454 (5th Cir. 2003)]

A WARN Act event may result in "substantial cessation of operations" as defined by ERISA § 4062(e), which may require giving notice to the PBGC.

## § 30.11  LABOR LAW ISSUES OF SHARED LIABILITY

### [A]  Possible Scenarios

There are many situations in which more than one company may be deemed to be a particular person's "employer." Sometimes, both companies will be liable, or the actions of one will be attributed to the other, with respect to unfair labor practices, defining the appropriate bargaining unit, or enforcing a collective bargaining agreement.

Vested benefits under a collective bargaining agreement are transferable when the employer transfers employees to another one of its locations, which is covered by another CBA with another union. [*Anderson v. AT&T Corp.*, 147 F.3d 467 (6th Cir. 1998)]

When one company merges with or takes over another, it is common for many or all of the first company's employees to be retained. Whether the acquirer is now the employer, and whether it is bound by the former employer's CBA and other promises to its workers is a factual question, depending on whether or not real operational changes were made.

In connection with CBAs, a "successor company" is one that continues the same business and hires at least half of the old employees. A successor employer is not bound by the predecessor's contracts, but does have an obligation to recognize and consult with the union. The Supreme Court has ruled that a new company becomes a successor if it is clear that all the former employees will be retained. [*NLRB v. Burns Int'l Sec. Servs. Inc.*, 406 U.S. 272 (1972)] *Canteen Corp. v. NLRB* [103 F.3d 1355 (7th Cir. 1997)] holds that a company can also be treated as a successor employer if it fails to give employees enough information about the new wages and working conditions to make a meaningful choice about accepting a job offer from the new employer.

After a merger or the purchase of a business, a successor has a duty to bargain collectively and can be liable for unfair labor practices committed by the predecessor if there is "continuity of identity" with the ex-employer, such as using the same facility to produce identical products and services, using the same or substantially the same labor force, without changes in job description, working conditions, supervision, equipment, or production methods.

An alternate test is whether there is a new corporate entity to replace the predecessor, whether there is a hiatus in the enterprise's operations, and whether the employment relationship with the prior workforce was terminated. If it is perfectly clear under the *Burns International* standard that the new owner will hire the entire existing workforce, then the incoming employer has a duty to consult with the union about wage scales. It cannot unilaterally impose cuts. If there is no such consultation, it is presumed that the negotiations would have continued the prior wage scale.

Generally speaking, a successor that has not bargained for the CBA is not bound by the substantive terms of a predecessor's CBA, unless it is perfectly clear that the new employer plans to retain all of the former employees. The D.C. Circuit treated this as a narrow exception intended to prevent a new employer from deterring employees from applying for other jobs. In this case, it was obvious that significant changes would be made, and employees were warned that they were offered only temporary at-will employment and not all former employees would be retained. [*S&F Market Street Healthcare LLC v. NLRB*, 570 F.3d 354 (D.C. Cir. 2009)]

Another possibility is that two or more enterprises might be deemed to be "alter egos" (substitutes) for one another, even if they are not formally under common control. Alter egos may be held liable for each other's unfair labor practices. The test is whether transferring business from one alter ego operation to another benefits the transferor by eliminating labor relations obligations. The alter ego theory became part of labor law to prevent "double-breasting": the practice of pairing commonly owned firms, one with a union and one nonunionized. If the double-breasted firms are actually alter egos, a federal district court can require the nonunion firm to abide by the union firm's labor agreements, even if there has been no NLRB determination of a single bargaining unit.

Two or more entities organized as legally separate entities might be treated as a "single employer" if there is an integrated enterprise. The factors that determine integration include common ownership, common management, integrated business operations, and centralized control of labor relations.

These tests are similar to the tests to see if companies are alter egos. The difference is that the two alter ego companies are not considered a single enterprise, so all their employees are not necessarily in the same bargaining unit.

A parent company and its subsidiary would probably be treated as a single employer if they were fundamentally in the same industry or business enterprise.

This would be manifested by sharing supervisory, technical, and professional personnel; sharing workforce and equipment; having common officers and directors; and operating under the same labor relations policies.

The NLRB might group separate entities together as "joint employers" if they "codetermine" (i.e., make decisions jointly) about essential terms and conditions of employment. Under this theory, the crucial factor is not whether the companies have overlapping ownership, but whether they make joint decisions about hiring and firing, working conditions, compensation, and supervision of employees.

## [B]  Agents of the Employer

An employer company will be liable for the actions of any "agent" of the company acting in the employer's interest. For example, a labor consultant is considered the employer's agent, but a Chapter 7 bankruptcy trustee is not. The determination uses factors similar to those used in deciding if someone is a common-law employee. The employer's degree of control is crucial: the right to hire and fire the agent; furnishing tools and materials; prescribing what the agent will do and how to do it.

Someone can become an agent of the company either by actual agency (explicitly granted) or apparent agency (where a principal says that the agent can speak for it, or knowingly lets the agent exercise authority). An employer is responsible for the actions performed by a supervisor in the course of actual or apparent authority. Even if a supervisor acts without authority, the employer can become liable by ratifying the supervisor's action (i.e., offering support for it after the fact). In general, however, the employer will not be responsible for actions for someone who is not an employee, or perhaps not a supervisory employee, unless the employer initiates, promotes, or ratifies the conduct. If the agent's improper conduct was an isolated, unpremeditated act, or if the employer repudiates the conduct, it is possible that the employer will be relieved of liability.

In general, the NLRB will blame the employer for an unfair labor practice only if it was committed directly by the employer, or by the employer's agent. But in a representation proceeding, a finding of agency is not required to set aside an election if the election was unfair enough to prevent employees from exercising a rational, unforced choice.

## § 30.12  EMPLOYER DOMINATION

In Europe, "codetermination," where union representatives collaborate closely with management, and where joint management-labor committees play an important decision-making role, is well accepted. However, under U.S. law, employer domination of a labor organization is an unfair labor practice. [See

NLRA § 8(a)(2)] Although this provision was originally enacted to bar "sweetheart unions" (formed or taken over by the employer), it has been applied more broadly.

It was a violation of the NLRA for an employer to unilaterally implement a workplace ethics program (WEP) (after consulting with the employees, but not bargaining with the union). Under the WEP, employees could invoke either the WEP process or the grievance procedure to review management decisions about discharge, discipline, or demotion, although the WEP yielded when arbitration was invoked. Grievance procedures are a mandatory bargaining subject, and the CBA already contained a grievance procedure. The Eleventh Circuit held that the employer would have been required to bargain to eliminate the existing grievance procedure, so they could not use the workplace ethics program to perform an end-run around the CBA's grievance procedure. [*Ga. Power Co. v. NLRB*, 427 F.3d 1354 (11th Cir. 2005)]

To avoid NLRB characterization of a work team or quality circle as an unduly dominated "labor organization," the employer should consider these steps:

- Look for a neutral meeting place away from the workplace, such as a local library, Rotary club, or City Hall;

- Rotate membership of the team, to involve as many people as possible and get new viewpoints;

- Focus the team on productivity and workplace issues, not compensation;

- Don't use the team to avoid contract negotiations;

- Employee representatives, not management, should draft the bylaws under which the team operates.

## § 30.13   NLRB JURISDICTION

The National Labor Relations Board has the power to get involved in a situation if:

- It is a labor dispute—i.e., there is any controversy about conditions of employment or representation of workers. Strikes, walkouts, picketing, and employer refusals to bargain are labor disputes;

- It affects interstate commerce. The threshold is so low that virtually any business will be deemed to affect interstate commerce;

- Employers and employees, rather than independent contractors and their clients, are involved;

- The dispute involves working conditions.

The NLRB cannot initiate proceedings on its own: it only has the power to respond to a representation petition or unfair labor practice (ULP) charge. When it has issued a complaint or filed an unfair labor practices charge, the NLRB can ask a federal District Court to issue a temporary injunction. In fact, the agency has an obligation to seek an injunction if it charges unlawful secondary activity (such as striking one employer to put pressure on another), some forms of improper activity, or certain boycotts. However, permanent injunctions are very rare, because of the Norris-LaGuardia Anti-Injunction Act.

Theoretically, the NLRB has jurisdiction over all unfair labor practice claims that require interpretation of a CBA that is still in effect. In practice, the NLRB often declines to exercise its jurisdiction, allowing the parties to use the contract's grievance arbitration machinery, to proceed with ongoing arbitration, or to enforce an arbitration award. However, it is up to the NLRB to intervene or stay out. The employer and union cannot deprive the NLRB of jurisdiction by agreeing to arbitrate.

Except in extraordinary circumstances, courts do not have jurisdiction over any issues that were not raised before the NLRB [*NLRB v. Saint-Gobain Abrasives, Inc.*, 426 F.3d 455 (1st Cir. 2005)]

Documents such as briefs, motions, and requests for permission to appeal in representation cases can be filed electronically at the NLRB e-filing home page, <http://gpea.nlrb.gov>; (no www)>, by filling out a form, attaching the document to the form, and e-mailing it to the NLRB's Office of the Executive Secretary. The agency prefers files in .pdf format, but .doc and .txt files are also acceptable.

## § 30.14    LABOR LAW IMPLICATIONS OF BANKRUPTCY FILINGS

The general rule is that the "automatic stay" on litigation as soon as a bankruptcy petition is filed will protect the company that files from being sued. However, because the NLRB is considered a unit of the federal government exercising its regulatory powers, NLRB unfair labor practices hearings are exempt from the automatic stay. However, the bankruptcy court has the power to enjoin the NLRB from doing anything that would prevent the reorganization of the bankrupt company.

Part of the bankruptcy process is a decision about which executory contracts (i.e., contracts to be performed in the future) will be carried out by the reorganized company and which can and should be rejected. The company seeking bankruptcy protection can petition the court to allow it to assume or reject a CBA. The court's standard for granting a rejection request is whether it would be fair to reject the contract, or whether the union unreasonably refused to accept contract modifications proposed by the employer. The employer does not have to prove that the proposed plan of reorganization will fail unless the contract can be rejected.

However, if the collective bargaining agreement expires while bankruptcy proceedings are pending, the whole issue becomes moot, because there is nothing for the employer to either accept or reject.

The Bankruptcy Abuse Prevention and Consumer Protection Act of 2005, Pub. L. No. 109-8 (BAPCPA), includes various provisions not only extending the exemption of individual debtor's retirement accounts from the bankruptcy estate, but altering the treatment of retirement plans in corporate bankruptcy. The employer's bankruptcy estate does not include funds that the employer withheld or funds received by the employer from employee wages to be paid to ERISA plans, such as defined contribution plans or benefit plans. [See BAPCPA § 323]

Bankruptcy Code § 1114, as amended by BAPCPA § 1403, permits the bankruptcy court to set aside modifications of retiree health plans that the employer made within the 180 days before filing, unless the court finds that the balance of equities clearly supports the changes. (Section 1114 is the provision that requires Chapter 11 debtors to negotiate with retiree representatives rather than unilaterally modifying or terminating retiree welfare benefits. After a bankruptcy filing, the benefits must be maintained unless the bankruptcy court orders or permits modification.)

BAPCPA raises the amount of wages and benefits earned by an employee before the employer's bankruptcy filing, but not paid before the filing, that can be treated as a priority claim. The amount is now $10,000, rather than $4,925 in unpaid wages and benefits per employee, earned within 180 days before the filing (rather than only 90 days pre-filing under prior law). BAPCPA also limits the amount of severance or retention bonuses that can be paid to insiders of a bankrupt company.

The Southern District of New York Bankruptcy Court approved plans for Hostess Brands to wind down, selling Twinkies and other famous brands. The court said that a quick and orderly shutdown was necessary to prevent deterioration of Hostess' assets. This was the second time that Hostess had filed for bankruptcy protection—the company filed in 2004, when it had $450 million in debt, and exited in 2009 $670 million in debt. There was a strike affecting two-thirds of Hostess' bakeries on November 9, 2012 after Hostess called for a round of cuts. The union said that it had already made extensive concessions in the previous bankruptcy case, and that Hostess, which has had six CEOs since 2002, had been mismanaged, with facilities allowed to become obsolete and products not tailored to the current health-conscious environment. The Teamsters accepted concessions but the bakery workers' union refused, saying that it would set a precedent but would not be enough for Hostess to survive. [Steven Greenhouse and Michael J. De La Merced, *Court Allows Liquidation of Hostess*, NYTimes.com (Nov. 21, 2012)]

In 2013, Hostess resumed production of Twinkies, relieved of union contracts and $1.3 billion in debt as a result of the second bankruptcy. Hostess went from having 19,000 employees, 79% union members, to having about 1,800 employees and no union. Some former employees were re-hired, but at lower pay.

The *Wall Street Journal* quoted one ex-employee who declined to return, because, instead of his previous $16.53/hour wage, he was offered $11/hour to start, with a chance to get an increase to $14/hour. [Julie Jargon, *The Twinkie Returns, With Less Baggage*, WSJ.com (July 8, 2013) and *Former Hostess Employees Bitter About Wage Cuts*,WSJ.com (July 9, 2013)]

The Eastern District of Missouri's bankruptcy court allowed Patriot Coal Corporation to cut pay and benefits of workers, retirees, and beneficiaries. Patriot argued that, unless it could cut labor costs by $150 million a year, it would have to liquidate, with even worse consequences for its 21,000 workers, retirees, and beneficiaries. The bankruptcy court agreed that the concessions were necessary for the business to survive. The union said it would appeal in federal court. Approximately 1,700 union miners had their pay cut from $26.80 to $20 per hour, and they were moved to a health plan that requires them to pay 10% of the premium, whereas before they did not have to make premium payments. Patriot said that it would remain in the union pension plan only if the union agreed to reduce the employer's contribution rate. Otherwise, it would withdraw from the plan, leaving the miners with only a 401(k) plan. Patriot also proposed to create a Voluntary Employee Benefit Association (VEBA) (see § 22.07) to shift its retiree health liabilities for 8,100 retirees and beneficiaries. [Kris Maher & Jacqueline Palank, *Bankruptcy Judge Allows Patriot Coal to Scrap Union Contracts*, WSJ .com (May 29, 2013)]

# CHAPTER 31

# OCCUPATIONAL SAFETY AND HEALTH

## § 31.01 INTRODUCTION

The federal Occupational Safety and Health Act and the agency that administers it, the Occupational Safety and Health Administration (both abbreviated OSHA) have as their mission protecting employees against unreasonably hazardous workplaces. All employers must satisfy the "general duty standard" of maintaining a workplace that is reasonably free of recognized dangers. Additional standards are imposed in some circumstances, particularly in the construction industry. OSHA's 10 regional and 90 local area offices are responsible for the safety of 130 million workers in over eight million worksites. The agency has approximately 2,200 inspectors, or one for every 59,000 workers. In fiscal 2011, 40,648 federal and 52,056 state plan inspections were performed. OSHA's FY 2012 budget was $583,386,000, slightly more than the 2011 level of $573,096,000. In FY 2011, there were 40,648 total federal inspections and 52,056 18(b) state plan inspections. [OSHA, *Commonly Used Statistics*, <http://www.osha.gov/oshstats/commonstats.html> (last accessed Feb. 27, 2013)]

OSHA also protects whistleblowers under a number of statutes, not just those concerned with conventional safety and health issues; see § 31.09[C] below. Employees are also entitled to whistleblower protection in the context of securities law, and if they report PPACA violations—or if they experience retaliation because they use the insurance Exchanges to obtain health coverage.

Employers are not held to an impossible standard of a hazard-free workplace, but they must be prepared to deal with known hazards (including disease and chemical toxicity as well as accident). They must use the reasonably available methods and technology to keep the dangers within bounds.

There were 4,609 fatal work injuries in 2011, a drop from the 4,690 fatal injuries in 2010. The rate was 3.6/100,000 full-time employees in 2010, falling to 3.5/100,000 in 2011. In 2011, there were 458 workplace homicides and 242 suicides. There were 152 incidents with more than one fatality; 354 people died in these incidents. Falls, slips, and trips caused 666 deaths in 2011, 219 workers died when struck by falling objects, and 192 were killed by vehicles or mobile equipment. [OSHA Economic News Release, *Census of Fatal Occupational Injuries Summary, 2011* <http://www.bls.gov/news.release/cfoi.nr0.htm> (Sept. 20, 2012). For demographic analysis of fatalities, see <http://wwww.bls.gov/iif/oshcfoil.htm>. The number of fatal workplace injuries was 7% lower in 2012 than in 2011, although fatal injuries in private-sector construction rose by 5%, and fatal injuries in oil/gas extraction rose 23%. There were 4,383 workplace fatalities in 2012, a rate of 3.2/100,000 full-time equivalent workers. The reduction in fatalities is generally positive, of course, but it may be affected by negative trends such as declines in jobs and hours worked, and perhaps greater fear by workers that they will suffer retaliation if they report injuries. [Melanie Trottman, *Workplace Fatalities Fell 7% in 2012, Report Shows*,WSJ.com (Aug. 22, 2013); James R. Hagerty, *Workplace Injuries Drop, But Claims of Employer Retaliation Rise*, WSJ.com (July 22, 2013)]]

In 2011, there were 117 non-fatal occupational injury cases per 10,000 full-time equivalent workers—the same rate as in 2010. The median number of missed workdays was also the same in both years (8). Almost 20% of the non-fatal injuries occurred in only five occupations: nursing aides/orderlies, attendants; laborers; janitors/cleaners; truck drivers; and police and sheriffs' officers. One-third of the 2011 injuries were classified as musculoskeletal disorders (e.g., back injuries). [OSHA Economic News Release, *Nonfatal Occupational Injuries and Illnesses Requiring Days Away from Work, 2011*, <http://www.bls.gov/news.release/osh2.nr0.htm> (Nov. 8, 2012)]

Studying data from the period 2005–2008, the Centers for Disease Control found that the non-fatal injury rate was 2.59 per 100 for workers who had access to paid sick leave, 4.18 for workers without sick leave entitlement. Even after adjusting for factors such as industry, sex, and educational level, workers with paid sick leave were 28% less likely to suffer a non-fatal injury, although it is also true that correlation is not the same as causation; there could be many explanations for this finding. [Nicholas Bakalar, *Paid Sick Leave May Reduce Work Injuries*, NYTimes.com (Aug. 6, 2012)]

The California Court of Appeal ruled in 2011 that Cal OSHA regulations apply only to employees, so an independent contractor air conditioning servicer could not use those standards to prove negligence per se. (He charged the owner of a condominium complex with negligence per se because the ladder from which he fell did not have the state-mandated safety mechanisms.) [*Iversen v. California Village HOA*, 194 Cal. App. 4th 107 (2011)]

## § 31.02  OSHA POWERS

Under the OSH Act, OSHA has the authority to inspect workplaces, order correction of violations, and impose penalties if correction does not occur as mandated. It has been held that it is not a violation of the OSH Act, or the Fourth Amendment's ban on unreasonable searches and seizures, for an OSHA compliance officer to videotape a construction site from across the street before going to the site and presenting his credentials. The theory is that looking at a site (to determine if fall protection techniques were adequate) is not a "search," so no warrant is required. [*L.R. Willson & Sons Inc. v. OSHRC*, 134 F.3d 1235 (4th Cir. 1998)]

The OSH Act also requires employers to keep records of workplace injuries and to use this information to generate annual reports (which must be disclosed to the workforce as well as being submitted to OSHA).

All employers whose operations affect commerce among the states are subject to OSHA. There is no minimum number of employees. However, small-scale or low-risk enterprises are entitled to relaxation of some reporting requirements.

■ **TIP:** An employer who would be damaged by full compliance with OSHA requirements can petition the Secretary of Labor for a temporary or permanent "variance" that protects the company against noncompliance penalties. Variances are effective only for the company that applies for them. It is no defense against a charge of noncompliance that a variance was granted to a different company in a similar situation.

The OSH Act interacts with various other statutes. It is probably a violation of public policy to discharge a worker because he or she filed a Worker's Compensation claim after suffering an occupational injury; to retaliate against a whistleblower who reported unsafe conditions to OSHA; or to take steps against someone who cooperated in an OSHA investigation.

Federal labor law says that a walkout premised on unsafe working conditions will not be treated as a strike. Furthermore, it is a protected concerted activity for workers to complain about safety conditions in the workplace, and therefore the employer cannot use this as a premise for employee discipline. However, state courts will not necessarily consider an OSHA violation relevant evidence of neglect if the employer is sued.

## § 31.03   OSHA REGULATIONS

The main authority for federal regulation of workplace safety comes from the OSH Act itself. OSHA's agency rules appear in the Code of Federal Regulations. In addition to the General Duty Clause, OSHA enforces more specific guidance in the form of the General Industry Standards that cover most industrial workplaces, and the Construction Standards.

The General Industry Standards deal with topics such as:

- Condition of floors (this is called the "walking/working" standard);
- Number and design of entrances and exits;
- Noise control;
- Radiation safety;
- Proper handling of hazardous materials (known as "hazmats")—toxic chemicals and toxic wastes;
- Personal Protective Equipment (PPE) such as respirators, hard hats, steel-toed shoes, work gloves, etc.;
- Fire prevention and safety;
- On-site first aid and medical treatment;
- Requirements for guards on machinery;
- Proper use of tools and other hand-held equipment;
- Welding and cutting;
- Control of electrical hazards;

- Design and maintenance of lifts and powered platforms;

- Access to employees' health records.

The Construction Industry Standards overlap with the General Industry Standards. The two rules sometimes treat the same topics, but the construction rules tend to be more stringent in this case. The construction standards also cover control of asbestos, welding and cutting, scaffolding, steel construction, and the use of masonry and concrete in construction.

After several workers died in accidents with cranes, the DOL performed its first update of crane regulations in 2008—the first time in nearly 40 years (the previous version was released in 1971). Training requirements were increased, and a nationwide certification test for crane operators was instituted. [News item, *New Federal Rules to Require Crane Operators to Pass Test*, Wall St. J., Sept. 19, 2008, at p. A13]

See also CPL-02-00-135, *Recordkeeping Policies and Procedures Manual*, <http://www.osha.gov/pls/oshaweb/owadisp.show_document . . . > (Dec. 30, 2004) for the employer's obligations for maintaining OSHA records.

## § 31.04  CONTROLLING PHYSICAL HAZARDS

### [A]  Personal Protective Equipment

An important part of the employer's duty of providing a safe workplace is to furnish protective equipment and to make sure that machinery is guarded and that, where appropriate, moving parts will stop before employees are injured.

The legal system treats PPE (Personal Protective Equipment) as essential to workplace safety. Wherever possible, employers should eliminate hazards directly, by reducing the likelihood of falls, falling objects, burns, chemical exposure, etc. But it is not always possible to remove the hazard, and even when it is physically possible, the cost may be prohibitive.

In such situations, the employer has a duty to provide PPE, and the employee has a complementary duty to use it. The employer must provide suitable equipment, in sizes that fit the workers, and must train them in how to use the equipment. The obligation exists whenever a reasonable person, familiar with workplace conditions and industry practices, would require PPE. The industry standard is not a defense, however, if the employer knew or should have known that dangerous conditions were present—for instance, if injuries had occurred in the past under similar circumstances.

A respiratory protection rule took effect October 5, 1998. The standard, known as 1910.134, covers respirator use in general industry, shipyards, longshore work, and construction, but not in agriculture. For guidance to employers, OSHA issued compliance directive CPL 2-0.120, explaining how to analyze workplace hazards, select respirators, when to change the chemical cartridges in respirators, and how to make sure respirators fit properly. [See <http://www.osha.gov>]

At last, final rules were published in November 2007, taking effect six months after publication. The rules require the employer to pay for almost all mandatory PPE (the exceptions being ordinary clothing, weather gear, logging boots, prescription safety glasses, and ordinary safety-toe boots). The rule does not create obligations for employers to provide PPE in any additional situations. [72 Fed. Reg. 65341 (Nov. 15, 2007); see Fred Schneyer, *Feds Finalize Protective Gear Payment Rule*, plansponsor.com (Nov. 16, 2007)]

OSHA imposed the maximum fine of $140,000 for safety violations that led to the fatal electrocution of a Verizon technician in Brooklyn in 2011. OSHA also issued 10 citations for failure to follow safety rules. Verizon did not provide life-saving equipment and did not require protective helmets and gloves to be used during dangerous tasks. Douglas Lalima's death was not reported as required, and the technicians were not adequately trained for working near high-voltage lines. Verizon denied any wrongdoing and said that it would appeal the finding. [Hannah Miet, *Verizon Fined $140,000 After Electrocution Death*, NYTimes.com (Mar. 19, 2012)]

## [B] Lockout/Tagout

OSHA's lockout/tagout rule (29 C.F.R. § 1910.147) applies in nonconstruction workplaces where the machinery has potentially dangerous moving parts. The rule imposes obligations on employers to immobilize machinery while it is being serviced, cleaned, repaired, etc. The rule does not apply to normal operation of the machinery, because in those situations the equipment and work routines are supposed to prevent injuries due to moving parts.

To comply with the lockout/tagout rule, machinery could be equipped with a trip control ("panic button") so it can be shut down quickly in an emergency. Blades and other dangerous parts can be protected with guards that protect workers' bodies from contact and prevent scrap materials from becoming projectiles. If guards are impractical, machinery could be equipped with sensing devices that turn off the machine if a body part goes beyond the safe point. Machinery can also be designed to require two hands to operate, so that it will not work when a hand is within reach of moving parts.

## [C] Bathroom Breaks

The OSHA general industry sanitation standard [29 C.F.R. § 1910.141] requires the presence of toilet facilities in the workplace. An April 6, 1998, letter from OSHA forbids employers to impose unreasonable restrictions on bathroom use. OSHA inspectors who receive complaints on this issue are directed to investigate the reasonableness of the employer's policy.

Female workers (especially pregnant women) need more bathroom breaks than male workers, although older male workers may need to use the restroom more often because of prostate enlargement.

## § 31.05  CONTROLLING EXPOSURE TO HAZARDOUS CONDITIONS

### [A]  Generally

The employer must limit employees' exposure to hazardous materials (e.g., asbestos, lead) and conditions (e.g., potentially damaging noise levels). Hazardous substances must be stored properly. Employees must be warned about their presence and taught how to handle the materials safely.

Other laws, such as environmental laws and laws requiring notification to the community of the presence or accidental release of hazardous substances, are also triggered when dangerous materials are used in a workplace. The company must have an emergency-response plan that involves coordination with fire departments and other community resources.

There is no simple solution to the problems of controlling materials that are dangerous from the environmental or workplace safety points of view—without significantly raising manufacturing costs and perhaps impairing competitiveness. A major investigative article in the New York Times in early 2013 discusses "unintended consequences" in regulation. The chemical n-propyl bromide (nPB) is now used six times as often as it was used 15 years ago, despite more than a decade of warnings that nPB causes neurological damage to workers who inhale it. OSHA performed 15 inspections at two locations of the Royale Comfort Seating factories in North Carolina beween 1996 and 2011, finding many times that workers were exposed to dangerous concentrations of nPB, were not give respirators, and did not receive proper ventilation. However, five fines were imposed, the largest of which was only $14,000. Several workers have settled Worker's Compensation cases for neurological damage, and Royale has spent almost half a million dollars in settlements and plant upgrades. However, OSHA has found that vents were covered and filters were not changed, resulting in dangerously poor air quality. A vice president of another cushion manufacturer, Franklin Corporation, said "There are people lined up out there for jobs. If they start dropping like flies, or something in that order, we can replace them today." OSHA director David Michaels said "I'm the first to admit this [OSHA regulation of disease rather than injury] is broken." The nPB based glues were adopted not only because they are inexpensive but to replace another chemical, TCA, that OSHA condemned as unsafe. The EPA listed nPB as a relatively benign chemical that does not damage the ozone layer. However, the EPA expressed concerns about the use of the substance in factories that cannot be ventilated adequately to prevent harm to workers. The nPB-based glue is also less flammable than acetone-based glue. OSHA has never imposed an exposure standard for nPB, and was reluctant to regulate small employers in North Carolina, an economically hard-pressed state. The Times article says that OSHA responded promptly to worker complaints by coming to the plants for inspections, but often reduced the penalties to make the employer more cooperative. [Ian Urbina, *As OSHA Emphasizes Safety, Long-Term Health Risks Fester*, NYTimes.com (Mar. 30, 2013)]

After OSHA issued a citation when a supervising employee worked on a dangerous ledge without fall protection (violating 29 C.F.R. § 1926.501(b)(1)), the Administrative Law Judge (ALJ) upheld the citation and imposed a $5,000 penalty (plus $4,000 for incorrect usage of fall protection by other employees)—but the Fifth Circuit reversed, finding that the decision was based on an error of law. In the Fifth Circuit view, failure to comply with a specific regulation, even if there is substantial danger, is not enough to constitute a violation of the OSH Act. Employers are not strictly liable; they are liable only if they knew or should have known there was a violation. According to the ALJ, the supervisor knew that working without a harness was dangerous and violated OSHA regulations and company safety policy, so his knowledge would be imputed to the employer. But in the Fifth Circuit view, although a company is usually liable for acts of supervisors performing their duties, making a company liable just because a supervisor was aware the he was violating OSHA regulations would be an improper imposition of strict liability. The Fifth Circuit does not impute the supervisor's knowledge of his own misconduct to the employer if the employer's safety policy, training, and discipline make it unforeseeable that the supervisor would break the rules. The burden is on the DOL to prove that the employer should be held responsible. Employee misconduct is an affirmative defense, requiring proof that the employer not only made, but adequately communicated, work rules designed to prevent violations, and has taken steps to detect and correct violations if they do occur. [*W.G. Yates & Sons Const. Co. Inc. v. OSHRC*, 459 F.3d 604 (5th Cir. 2006). Although the Sixth Circuit imputes a supervisor's knowledge of his own misconduct to the employer, the Third and Tenth Circuits disagree: see the cases cited in *Danis-Shook Joint Venture XXV v. Sec'y of Labor,* 319 F.3d 805 (6th Cir. 2003).The Fifth Circuit's analysis of the employee misconduct affirmative defense derives from *Frank Lill & Son, Inc. v. Sec'y of Labor*, 362 F.3d 840 (D.C. Cir. 2004)]

The First Circuit upheld a $33,700 fine for violations of the excavation safety rules. One of the trench diggers was a foreman, thus ruling out the unpreventable employee misconduct (UEM) defense. An employer can be charged with constructive knowledge of safety violations that supervisors know or should know about and the site superintendent was at the site several times an hour. [*P. Gioioso & Sons Inc. v. OSHRC,* No. 675 F.3d 66 (1st Cir. 2012)]

## [B]  PELs

A PEL, or Permissible Exposure Limit, is set for certain hazardous substances such as asbestos and lead. A PEL is a level of contact with the substance that employees can encounter without becoming endangered. The employer has an obligation to monitor the plant environment to determine the level of the regulated substance, to provide appropriate safety equipment (e.g., face masks and respirators) and to train employees in safety techniques.

OSHA rules require that employees have access to showers, changing rooms, eye baths, first aid, and other measures for preventing long-term contamination. Where necessary, the employer must provide protective clothing and appropriate containers for collecting contaminated clothing for treatment or disposal. Employees must not be permitted to smoke or eat in any environment where asbestos, lead, etc., are present. Warning signs must be posted in danger areas.

The employer's basic job is to keep employee exposure below the PEL. In some instances, this is impossible. When exposure reaches the "action level" defined by OSHA, the employer must take additional steps, such as periodic medical testing of employees to see if they have suffered environmental injury or illness.

## [C]  Noise Levels

In workplaces where the noise level routinely exceeds 85 decibels per eight-hour shift, the employer has an obligation to create and maintain a comprehensive program for hearing conservation. The environmental noise level must be monitored; employees' hearing must be tested (with a baseline reading within six months of initial exposure to high occupational noise levels, and an annual checkup after that), and they must be trained to protect themselves against hearing loss. If any audiometric test shows that an employee's hearing has deteriorated, the employer's obligation is to notify that worker within 21 days and then make sure that the worker uses hearing protection devices in the future.

In the October 19, 2010 Federal Register, OSHA published a proposed interpretation of "feasible administrative or engineering controls" in the context of workplace noise. However, in January 2011, OSHA withdrew the document because of industry complaints about potential costs, saying that it is studying other approaches to abating noise hazards in the workplace. According to the Bureau of Labor Statistics (BLS), since 2004, almost 125,000 workers have had significant, permanent work-related hearing loss, with over 22,000 hearing loss cases occurring in 2008 alone. OSHA said that it continues reviewing comments on the proposal, holding a meeting about occupational hearing loss prevention, consulting experts from the National Institute for Occupational Safety and Health and the National Academy of Engineering, and teaching businesses about effective, inexpensive technical controls. [Fred Schneyer, *OSHA Takes More Time on Noise Standard*, plansponsor.com (Jan. 19, 2011)]

The Fifth Circuit ruled that hearing-loss claims based on charges that the employer failed to monitor noise exposure or protect employees against excessive noise could be heard in state court. The claims were not subject to LMRA

§ 301 preemption (i.e., the doctrine that cases about interpretation of a CBA must only be heard in the federal system) because the state (Louisiana) had a body of workplace law about the duty to protect employees from injury. The case could be resolved using these principles without even consulting the CBA. Furthermore, Louisiana forbids CBA provisions that eliminate rights to workplace safety. [*McKnight v. Dresser, Inc.*, 676 F.3d 426 (5th Cir. 2012)]

## [D]  Workplace Violence

Workplace violence can occur among co-workers or other persons entering the workplace. One quarter of those reporting abuse said they were attacked by customers, clients, or patients; 15% said they were victimized by co-workers; and 13% alleged that bosses or supervisors were responsible. The balance of the incidents involved outsiders (e.g., a spouse going to the workplace to threaten or attack an employee). [News Articles, *Survey: Outsider Most Often Workplace Violence Perpetrators*, plansponsor.com (Jan. 27, 2005)]

Late in 2004, the U.S. Supreme Court applied the intentional infliction of emotional distress cause of action against an employer who failed to provide a safe workplace. The plaintiff sued after she was kidnapped from work and raped by her former lover. She informed her employer that she had an order of protection against him and asked not to be assigned to remote locations where she was vulnerable. Her supervisor ignored her concerns and tried to reconcile the couple. After the attack, the plaintiff complained to the employer about the supervisor's facilitation of the attack. She was required to continue reporting to him. The Supreme Court dismissed her constitutional claims but upheld the intentional infliction of emotional distress element of the case because the employer's actions (granting access to the attacker; refusing to let her work in a safer location) inflicted distress over and above that suffered directly from the incident. Worker's Compensation exclusivity did not apply, because the employer's conduct was intentional rather than negligent. Furthermore, most states do not cap damages for intentional infliction of emotional distress. [*Gantt v. Security USA, Inc.*, 543 U.S. 814 (2004)]

## § 31.06  ERGONOMICS

Ergonomics is the study of the mutual adaptation between tools and the human body. Ergonomically efficient tools will reduce the number, or at least the degree, of injuries associated with tool use.

OSHA has made several attempts to impose ergonomic requirements on industry. This has been an extremely controversial quest. Congress's appropriation bills for OSHA between 1996 and 1998 actually forbade the agency to adopt ergonomics standards.

The Occupational Safety and Health Review Commission (OSHRC) issued an April 1997 decision that was the first declaration that the Secretary of Labor can properly cite ergonomic hazards under the general duty clause. [*Sec'y of Labor v. Pepperidge Farm Inc.*, 65 L.W. 2725 (OSHRC Apr. 26, 1997). See also *Reich v. Arcadian Corp.*, 110 F.3d 1192 (5th Cir. 1997)]

In March 2001, both Houses of Congress used a little-known federal statute called the Congressional Review Act of 1996 (CRA) to repeal the ergonomics regulations and prevent OSHA from enacting substantially similar regulations in the future. [See Steven Greenhouse, *House Joins Senate in Repealing Rules on Workplace Injuries,* N.Y. Times, Mar. 8, 2001, at A19]

A decade later, in 2011, DOL withdrew a proposal that would have required more logging of workplace musculoskeletal disorders. OSHA also withdrew another proposal re workplace noise that would have required installing noise-abating equipment. [Melanie Trottman, *Labor Department Withdraws Record-keeping Proposal*, WSJ.com (Jan. 25, 2011)]

## § 31.07   VARIANCES

The OSH Act permits employers to petition for variances that will excuse them from having to comply with requirements that are particularly onerous. A variance can only be granted if employees will not be exposed to undue risk or danger.

The C.F.R. includes rules for "national security variances" and "experimental variances," but most of the variances granted are classified as either "temporary" or "permanent."

Grounds for a temporary variance are that the company will eventually comply with a new regulation, but cannot do so by its scheduled effective date because of a shortage of staff, materials, or equipment. (Being unable to afford to comply is not considered good cause for a variance.) A temporary variance lasts up to one year. It can be renewed twice, for up to 180 days at a time. The application must demonstrate that the employer is doing everything it can to comply as soon as possible, and that employees are being protected from undue hazards in the meantime.

A permanent variance is granted to an employer whose work methods are unconventional but still provide at least as much protection for employees as the OSHA regulations do. A company asking for a permanent variance can also apply for an interim variance.

The original plus six copies of the variance application and supporting documents must be filed. The documents must be signed by an authorized representative of the company, such as a corporate officer or the corporation's attorney.

Employees are entitled to notice of the variance application. They can ask that a hearing examiner conduct a hearing on the application.

Variance applications are reviewed, and then granted or denied, by the Assistant Secretary of Labor of Occupational Health and Safety in Washington.

Anyone affected by a variance after it is granted can petition for modification or revocation of the order granting the variance. After a temporary variance ends, the employer can petition to have it renewed or extended.

## § 31.08  DIVISION OF RESPONSIBILITY

For OSHA purposes, companies are responsible for the safety of their "employees." A company that has all its work done by leased employees or independent contractors will not be subject to OSHA unless the arrangements are only a subterfuge to avoid liability. What counts is the economic reality of the work relationship, including the degree of control over the work, who signs the paycheck, and whether payment is a regular salary or a per-project amount. The power to change working conditions or fire the employee is considered especially significant. If several employers are involved (e.g., a temporary employment agency and its clients), OSHA responsibilities will be allocated based on actual job performance and working conditions. The basic rule is that the general contractor has primary OSHA responsibility for a construction worksite.

OSHA liability of general contractors can derive from several theories:

- A construction contract provision under which the general contractor agrees to provide safety equipment;

- The general contractor's role of controlling conditions because it is in charge of the site;

- The general contractor is the only party involved with the specialized knowledge to abate the hazards;

- The general contractor's actual knowledge of the hazards (by observation or by notice from a subcontractor), creating a duty to cope with the hazards.

In doubtful cases, OSHA cites all possibly responsible parties and then allows them to make arguments why they are not liable. However, both a company that creates a hazard and the actual employer of the employees exposed to the hazard (and who were not protected by their employer) can be found liable.

OSHA uses a two-step test to see whether the Construction Standard should be applied to nonconstruction companies. The tests are ability to direct or control trade contractors, and a degree of involvement in the multiple activities that are needed to complete a construction project.

The Seventh Circuit vigorously affirmed the dismissal of the indictment charging the defendant with a violation of OSH Act § 17(e) after the electrocution death of two employees of the defendant's wholly owned subsidiary. OSHA asserted that the defendant was culpable because it oversaw its subsidiaries' safety programs and provided safety training to employees of the subsidiaries. However, notwithstanding the corporate affiliation, the Seventh Circuit ruled that unless it would be possible to pierce the corporate veil, the parent corporation should not be deemed culpable for deaths of persons employed by another entity. [*United States v. MYR Group, Inc.*, 361 F.3d 364 (7th Cir. 2004)]

## § 31.09  OSHA ENFORCEMENT

### [A]  Generally

Unlike ERISA enforcement (where federal jurisdiction preempts the state role), OSHA enforcement is coordinated between the states and the federal government. States have discretion to shape the degree of their occupational safety enforcement involvement. They can draft regulatory plans; if the Department of Labor believes the plan does enough to protect worker safety, it becomes an "approved state plan."

OSHA examined the operation of the OSH programs operated by 25 states and territories (out of the total of 27 that have approved state plans). As of September, 2010, 40% of the workplaces in the United States were subject to state OSH plans; the rest were subject to federal OSHA. OSHA started collecting data after deficiencies were found in Nevada's program when many construction-related fatalities were reported. OSHA identified some states that had requirements that offered workers more protection than the federal standards: e.g., California, Minnesota, Oregon, and Washington. OSHA found that Hawaii had problems related to inadequate staffing and funding cutbacks. A federal takeover was a possibility if the state was unable to work out a strategy acceptable to OSHA for improving its regulation of worker safety. [OSHA news release, *Agency Calls for Corrective Action to Keep Workers Safe*, <http://www.dol .gov/opa/media/press/osha/OSHA20101325.htm> (Sept. 29, 2010). The states and territories in question are Alaska, Arizona, California, Connecticut, Hawaii, Indiana, Iowa, Kentucky, Maryland, Michigan, Minnesota, Nevada, New Jersey, New Mexico, New York, North Carolina, Oregon, Puerto Rico, South Carolina, Tennessee, Utah, Vermont, the Virgin Islands, Virginia, Washington, and Wyoming. However, in Connecticut, Illinois, New Jersey, New York, and the Virgin Islands, the state plans cover only public employees, not those in the private sector. The reports themselves are available at <http://www.osha.gov/dcsp/osp/ efame/index.html>. See <http://www.osha.gov/dcsp/osp/index.html> for information about state plans in general]

In states that do not have an approved state plan, OSHA has primary responsibility for safety enforcement. State governments, however, are allowed to regulate issues that the OSH Act does not cover (such as boiler and elevator safety) as well as broader safety issues (such as fire protection in buildings that are open to the public).

One important function of state OSH agencies is offering free on-site consultations about how to maintain a safer workplace. The consultation is a simulated inspection, but the inspector is only authorized to point out problem areas and suggest solutions, not to issue citations or penalize the company. The consultation begins with an opening conference with the employer, proceeds to a walk-through and identification of safety problems, and ends with a closing conference about how to solve those problems.

## [B]  Inspections

Inspections are a central part of OSHA's enforcement function, because direct evidence about workplace conditions is necessary.

A "programmed inspection" takes place on a routine basis, when workplaces are chosen at random from a list of sites with above-average injury rates.

Inspections can also be made based on written complaints from employees, former employees, or their representatives, such as attorneys and union staff. Complaints are made to OSHA's area director or Compliance Officer (CO). OSHA investigates the complaint and sends a copy of the complaint to the employer. (The complainant can request that his or her name be suppressed on the employer's copy.) Depending on the nature of the complaint, OSHA will either send the employer a letter describing the hazard that has been charged and giving a date for abatement, or schedule an inspection. The inspection probably will be scheduled if the employer ignores a letter from OSHA or if there is evidence of other safety problems.

OSHA is supposed to respond to a complaint of imminent danger within one day, to an allegation of a serious hazard within five working days, or within 30 working days if the complaint is less serious. A serious hazard is one that creates a reasonable expectation that it could cause death or irreversible bodily injury.

Generally speaking, OSHA inspections are made on an unannounced basis. However, the employer is entitled to notice if an imminently dangerous situation is alleged (because abatement is more important than detecting violations), if special arrangements are needed for the inspection, or if the inspection will be made outside normal business hours.

The CO shows credentials at the workplace and asks for permission to inspect. If permission is refused, the CO cannot perform a search without an administrative search warrant granted by a court, based on OSHA's showing that it has reason to believe that violations of the General Duty Clause or a more specific standard have occurred. However, courts need far less proof to authorize an administrative search than a search in a criminal case.

Most employers grant permission, so the CO explains the procedure in the opening conference with the employer. Next is the "walk-through" (employer and employee representatives are allowed to comment). At this stage, the CO makes notes on any hazardous or noncompliant conditions prevailing in the workplace.

At this point, the inspector often points out trivial violations that can be corrected on the spot: mopping up a pool of water that could cause a slip, for instance. At this stage, the CO usually asks to see the business's logs, summary reports, exposure records, training records, and other safety-related paperwork.

If the inspection is based on a complaint, the employer has the right to review the complaint, and can instruct the CO to limit the inspection to the issues raised by the complaint. Employers who take this option should make a written record of the scope of authorization, give a copy to the inspector, and retain a copy for their records.

The last part of the inspection is the "closing conference" when the CO reveals findings about potential OSHA violations.

COs do not have the power to issue citations during an inspection. The CO must return to the OSHA office and confer with the Area Director about the level of citation (if any) that should be issued in response to each perceived deficiency.

The procedure is slightly different in the construction industry. A "targeted inspection" is a short-form inspection that concentrates on the major hazards to construction workers' safety: falls, falling objects, electrical hazards, and vehicle accidents. The CO decides whether to do a focused or a full inspection during the opening conference. At sites where the general or prime contractor has a workable safety plan and designates a representative to work with OSHA, only a focused inspection will be performed. In contrast to a nonconstruction inspection, citations can be issued during a focused inspection if there are serious violations, or nonserious violations that are not abated immediately.

## [C]  Whistleblowers

OSHA is responsible for receiving and processing whistleblower complaints charging violations of a number of environmental statutes in addition to the OSH Act. [See Final Regulation, 69 Fed. Reg. 52,103 (Aug. 24, 2004)]

The OSHA Fact Sheet, *Your Rights as a Whistleblower*, requires complaints to be filed in writing or by telephone. For most statutes (the OSH Act, Clean Air Act, CERCLA, Federal Water Pollution Control Act, Safe Drinking Water Act, Solid Waste Disposal Act, and Toxic Substances Control Act), the complaint must be filed within 30 days of the incident. However, longer reporting periods are permitted for the International Safe Container Act (60 days), Asbestos Hazard Emergency Response Act and Sarbanes-Oxley Act (90 days) and 180 days under the Surface Transportation Assistance Act, Energy Reorganization Act, and Pipeline Safety Improvement Act. In general, if the state has a state OSH plan, retaliation complaints are supposed to be filed with the state agency, although dual filing with OSHA is acceptable.

The OSHA announced in mid-2011 that it would take additional measures to strengthen its whistleblower protection program, which covers close to two dozen statutes. OSHA performed an internal review in response to the GAO's

2009 and 2010 audits of the whistleblower program. The program has been restructured to report directly to the Assistant Secretary of Labor rather than being part of the Directorate of Enforcement. Twenty-five new investigators were hired. OSHA also stepped up its training efforts, including a national training conference for investigators from federal and state plans. The agency announced that it would reissue its Whistleblower Investigations Manual to reflect developments since 2003, when the last edition was published. [OSHA News Release 11-1136-NAT 2011 and internal review report, <http://www.whistleblowers.gov/report_summary_page.html>; see DOL, *OSHA announces measures to improve Whistleblower Protection Program* (Aug. 1, 2011) (benefitslink.com)]

The Department of Labor ordered the Union Pacific Railroad Co. to pay $400,000 in punitive damages, $90,315 in compensatory damages, $34,900 in attorney's fees, and more than $90,000 back pay to three employees. OSHA found that the company violated the whistleblower provisions of the Federal Railroad Safety Act by firing two employees and suspending one for reporting a work-related injury and discussing concerns about safety hazards in the workplace. The railroad was also ordered to train managers, supervisors, and employees about whistleblowers' rights. [Tara Cantore, *Union Pacific Fined for Retaliation against Whistleblowers*, plansponsor.com (Aug. 26, 2011)]

In a case of first impression, the First Circuit ruled in early 2012 that employees of privately held companies that are contractors or subcontractors for public companies are not entitled to Sarbanes-Oxley whistleblower protection against retaliation. The First Circuit heard consolidated cases brought by former employees of contractors or subcontractors for Fidelity mutual funds. The funds are publicly traded but have no employees. The First Circuit said that if it wanted to protect such employees, the Sarbanes-Oxley Act could have specified the protection. Although the Dodd-Frank Act increased the scope of protection, it did so only for employees of subsidiaries of public companies and statistical rating organizations. [*Lawson v. FMR LLC*, 670 F.3d 61 (1st Cir. 2012); see Sheri Qualters, *No SOX Protection For Whistleblowers Working For Contractors Of Public Companies*, Nat'l L.J. (Feb. 6, 2012) (law.com)]

PPACA § 1558 forbids employers to retaliate against employees if they receive a health insurance tax credit or reduced cost sharing because they purchase their health insurance from an Exchange. Retaliation is also forbidden against employees who report violations of PPACA Title I. Complaints must be filed within 180 days of the alleged violation. Complaints can be filed by telephoning or going to the local OSHA office or sending a written complaint (faxed, sent electronically, or delivered by hand, mail, or commercial carrier) to the OSHA regional or area office. There is no official form for the complaint. If the evidence shows retaliation, and settlement is not reached, OSHA orders employer to reinstate the employee with back pay. OSHA findings become a final order of the DOL unless appealed within 30 days. Either side can request an ALJ hearing, which can be appealed to DOL Administrative Review Board. If there is no final agency order within 210 days from filing of complaint, or 90 days of employee receiving OSHA findings, employee can sue in district court. [OSHA Fact Sheet, *Filing Whistleblower Complaints under the Affordable Care Act*, <https://www.osha.gov/Publications/whistleblower/OSHAFS-3641.pdf> (last accessed Aug. 29, 2013)]

OSHA issued interim final rules for handling of retaliation complaints on February 22, 2013. The rule deals with the time limits and procedures for employee complaints, and how the complaints will be investigated and reviewed. PPACA Title I includes the ban on coverage limits, the requirements of preventive services and of furnishing a summary of benefits and coverage, and the mandate of covering adult children up to age 26. Employees are protected against retaliation when they provide information (to the employer, to the federal government, or to the state Attorney General) about acts or omissions the employee reasonably thinks violate PPACA Title I. They are also protected if they testify, assist, or participate in a proceeding about Title I. Starting in 2014, employees are protected against retaliation (such as termination of coverage) committed by insurers. The PPACA retaliation rules do not diminish employee rights under a Collective Bargaining Agreement or federal or state law. For example, these rights are in addition to the rights established by ERISA § 510. [<http://www.dol.gov/find/20130222/OSHA2013.pdf>; see PLC Employee Benefits & Executive Compensation, *OSHA Rules Address Retaliation Complaint Procedures under Health Care Reform* (Feb. 25, 2013) (benefitslink.com)]

## § 31.10  OSHA CITATIONS

### [A]  Categories of Violations

The CO's comments during an inspection are not official OSHA pronouncements, and the employer cannot be penalized for failing to respond to them. However, penalties can be imposed for failure to respond to a written citation from the OSHA Area Director that is sent within six months after the date of the alleged violation that is cited. The citation form lists the violations, classified by seriousness, imposes penalties, and sets a date for abating each violation. Usually, the citation will be Form OSHA-2, sent by certified mail, although other forms can be used.

OSHA violations are generally divided into four categories: de minimis (trivial), nonserious, serious, and other. Penalties are heavier on willful violations or repeat violations within a three-year period. Criminal penalties might be imposed in the very worst cases, such as the preventable death of an employee.

### [B]  Penalties

Penalties are set under OSHA § 17 (29 U.S.C. § 666). [For OSHA's Field Inspection Reference Manual, CPL 2.103, Section 8-Chapter IV Post Inspection Procedures, see <http://www.osha.gov>]

It's hard to predict what penalty will be imposed for any particular OSHA violation. There are many factors involved, primarily the gravity of the violation. However, the size of the business, the employer's past history of violations, and whether or not the employer acted in good faith are all important considerations.

The statute imposes penalties as follows:

- Willful or repeated violations of the OSH Act or regulations: penalty of up to $70,000 per violation, minimum penalty of $5,000 per willful violation;

- Penalty of up to $7,000 per serious violation;

- Penalty of up to $7,000 per day for failure to correct a cited violation, although the period is suspended until any review proceeding instituted in good faith is completed;

- Up to $10,000 and/or six months in prison if a violation caused an employee's death (first offense); up to $20,000 and/or one year in prison for repeated violations resulting in employee deaths;

- A fine of up to $1,000 and/or six months in prison for giving advance notice of an inspection;

- Fine of up to $10,000 and/or six months imprisonment for knowing false statement, representation, or certification;

- Fine of up to $7,000 per violation of the posting requirement.

The gravity of a violation depends on two factors: the severity of the damage that the violation could cause and how probable it is that the violation will result in occupational injury or illness.

The multifactorial penalty analysis also reflects factors such as the number of workers exposed, how close they were to the danger, how frequently they were exposed, and how long exposure continued, whether appropriate PPE was used to reduce the risk, and other working conditions.

Civil penalties are payable to the Secretary of Labor for deposit into the U.S. Treasury; the United States can bring suit to recover penalties. The proper court is the district court for the district in which the violation is alleged to have happened, or where the employer is headquartered.

OSHA has the discretion to reduce penalties greatly, to reflect good faith, small business size (no reduction can be made on this basis if the enterprise has more than 250 employees), and previous acceptable history with regard to occupational safety and health violations.

Failure-to-abate penalties are applied when a cited violation becomes a final order, and the employer fails to correct the violation. Normally, the maximum failure-to-abate penalty will be limited to 30 times the daily proposed penalty for that violation.

Penalties are greater for repeat violations. If the employer has fewer than 250 employees, the penalty based on the gravity of the violation (GBP) is doubled for the first repeated violation, and quintupled if a violation was previously cited twice. For employers of over 250, the GBP is multiplied by five for a first repeated violation, by 10 for a second repeated violation. (The overall potential for harm is greater in a larger workplace, which explains the difference.) [No by-line, *OSHA Targets High Injury Workplaces*, plansponsor.com (Mar. 15, 2007)]

29 U.S.C. § 666(e) imposes penalties whenever a willful violation of an OSHA standard leads to the death of any employee. This penalty can be assessed against the culpable employer on a multiemployer worksite, even though the deceased worker was employed by one of the other companies at the site. [*United States v. Pitt-Des Moines Inc.*, 168 F.3d 976 (7th Cir. 1999)] OSHA imposed a $7,000 fine on Wal-Mart when temporary worker Jdimyta Damour was trampled to death at the store when its post-Thanksgiving sale began. Damour, who had no crowd control experience, was knocked down and asphyxiated by the crowd. Wal-Mart settled separately with the Nassau County DA's office agreeing to improve its crowd control, set up a victim compensation fund, and provide jobs for teenagers. [Rebecca Moore, *Wal-Mart Fined for Trampling Death of NY Worker*, plansponsor.com (June 2, 2009). OSHRC upheld the citation and penalty in 2011, finding that workers were placed at risk by the store's failure to have reasonable and effective crowd management practices, including adequate training to manage a large crowd safely: Rebecca Moore, *Judge Upholds Penalty against WalMart for Worker Trampling*, plansponsor.com (Mar. 28, 2011)]

The "unit of prosecution" issue is how many charges should be filed for multiple similar violations. The OSHA regulations were amended in 2008 to provide that failure to provide respirators or workplace training is considered a separate violation for every employee who was not trained or who did not receive a respirator [29 C.F.R § 1910.9(a) and (b)]. Thirty-three other standards were also amended the same way. The regulations were amended in response to *Chao v. OSHRC*, 401 F.3d 355 (5th Cir. 2005), which held that failing to train eleven employees, and to provide them with respirators, constituted two violations, not 22 (eleven respirator, eleven training). The amendment was challenged by three trade associations that claimed the Secretary did not have authority to issue the amendments, because OSHRC is the only body that has the jurisdiction to set units of prosecution. In 2010, the D.C. Circuit rejected this argument, because setting the unit of prosecution is up to the legislatures, not the courts, and the Secretary of Labor is Congress' stand-in for these matters. [*National Ass'n of Home Builders v. OSHA*, 602 F.3d 464 (D.C. Cir. 2010). For the 2008 amendments, see 73 Fed. Reg. 75,568 and 75,583 (Dec. 12, 2008)]

In 2011, OSHRC accepted the DOL's argument that failure to keep proper records can be treated as a continuing violation of OSHA's five-year record retention requirement. Therefore, penalties could be imposed for violations that occurred over four years before OSHA issued a citation, whereas the construction company defendant argued that OSHA had only six months to bring charges. In addition to the initial failure to log employees' injuries and illnesses as they occurred, OSHRC ruled that AKM LLC failed to meet its obligations to retain the records for five years. [*Secretary of Labor v. AKM LLC dba Volks Constructors*, OSHRC No. 06-1990, 2011 WL 896347 (OSHRC Mar. 11, 2011); see Joseph P. Curtin, William M. Hill, and Peter McCarthy, Mintz Levin OSHA Advisory, *Decision Drastically Expands OSHA's Power to Punish Recordkeeping Violation*, <http://www.mintz.com/newsletter/2011/Advisories/1010-0311-NAT-LIT/web .htm> (Mar. 31, 2011)] The following year, however, the D.C. Circuit reversed. The statute of limitations is six months after the "occurrence of any violation." OSHA treated it as a continuing violation. The D.C. Circuit rejected this theory, pointing out that there were separate violations, although it left open the possibility of tolling for a true ongoing violation such as requiring workers to use unsafe equipment [*Sec'y of Labor v. AKM LLC dba Volks Constructors*, No. 11-1106, 2012 WL 1142273 (D.C. Cir. Apr. 6, 2012); see Jenna Greene, *D.C. Circuit: Limit for OSHA Violations Is Six Months, Not Five Years* Blog of Legal Times (Apr. 6, 2012) (law.com). Rehearing was granted, so the case was "depublished."]

Even though OSHA violations can result in serious injuries or death, penalties are much lower than under other federal laws involving less serious matters. In a 2001 case, there was a sulphuric acid tank explosion at a refinery. OSHA imposed a penalty of $175,000 because a worker was killed. However, the EPA imposed $10 million in penalties for the same incident, because fish and crabs were killed. If PAWA is adopted, employers would be liable for the death of a worker based on "knowing" rather than "willful" acts. PAWA also strengthens protection for whistle-blower employees. PAWA gives injured employees and their families the right to more information about OSHA proceedings, and to interact with OSHA and contest citations if they believe that stronger penalties are appropriate. Current OSHA policies mandate enforcement of any fatality or any incident resulting in hospitalization of three workers; PAWA would reduce this to two hospitalizations. [Testimony, <http://www.osha.gov/pls/oshaweb/owadisp.show_ document?p_table=TESTIMONIES&p_id=1062> (Mar. 16, 2010)]

In fiscal 2012, the highest proposed penalties included:

- $1.01 million against Piping Technology and Products, Inc. (Houston, Texas) for 13 willful violations of lockout/tagout requirements, and 17 serious violations such as failure to guard machinery. OSHA became aware of the situation when a worker complained about dangerous conditions.

- $758,000 against All-Feed Processing & Packaging Inc. (Galva, Illinois) for 13 willful citations and 10 other citations for failure to require respirators and maintaining dangerous levels of dust. OSHA issued citations on five occasions during 10 inspections since 2000.

- $702,000 against Tribe Mediterranean Foods (Taunton, Massachusetts); after a worker was crushed to death in a machine, the company was cited for nine willful violations, three repeat violations for failure to inspect machinery and six violations involving lack of machine guards.

However, proposed fines are often reduced in the course of litigation or a settlement with the employer. [Safety + Health, *Penalty Box*, <http://www.nsc.org/safetyhealth/Pages/OSHA-Top-10-Penalty-Box-.aspx> (undated; last accessed Mar. 18, 2013)]

OSHA publishes regional news releases discussing penalties imposed against particular employers, giving the identity of the employer, the amount of the penalty, and why it was applied: e.g., J.C. Stucco and Stone (Lansdowne, Pennsylvania) was fined $73,150 for four repeat and two serious safety violations including fall hazards. [Region 3 News Release 13-330-PHI (osha 13-020, <http://www.osha.gov/pls/oshaweb/owadisp.show_document?p_table=NEWS_RELEASES&p_id=23760> (Mar. 11, 2013). See <http://www.osha.gov/stopfalls> for English and Spanish resources on fall prevention, including fact sheets, posters, and videos.]

Criminal penalties mandated by courts, not directly by OSHA, can be imposed, under OSHA § 17(f)–(h), for giving advance notice of an inspection that is supposed to be made unannounced, for giving false information, or assaulting or interfering with the work of a CO.

OSHA criminal prosecutions are extremely rare, even in cases of obvious disregard of worker safety. About a hundred companies are cited each year for fatal accidents involving workers, but there are never more than a dozen prosecutions in any year. Between 1982 and 2002, according to the *N.Y. Times*, there were over 170,000 occupational deaths. OSHA investigated 1,242 "horror stories": workplaces where willful violations resulted in preventable deaths. Yet even in these worst-case scenarios, OSHA tried to prosecute only 7% of the cases. Out of 2,197 workplace deaths, 1,798 involved rules violations that could have been prosecuted but only 196 cases were referred to prosecutors, who rejected 92 of them. Out of the 81 convictions in the 104 prosecutions that did occur, only 16 prison sentences were imposed. [David Barstow, *U.S. Rarely Seeks Charges for Deaths in Workplace*, N.Y. Times, Dec. 12, 2003, at A1]

It does not constitute double jeopardy to impose administrative penalties on an employer after it has been convicted of criminal OSHA violations because the administrative penalties are clearly civil and cannot result in imprisonment. [*S.A. Healy Co. v. OSHRC*, 138 F.3d 686 (7th Cir. 1998)]

## § 31.11    OSHA APPEALS

Employers don't have to agree with an OSHA citation. There are several administrative steps that can be taken to protest—although these administrative remedies do have to be exhausted before filing suit.

If an employer challenges a citation, OSHA has to prove that the employer failed to live up to some applicable standard. The agency also has to prove that feasible corrective measures existed that could have brought the employer into compliance. If the standard has a time element (for example, the noise exposure standard does), then OSHA also has to prove that the condition existed long enough and intensely enough to constitute a violation.

OSHA has to prove that the employer knew about the condition or could have become aware by exercising due diligence. It is not necessary to prove that the employer was aware of the standard and deliberately chose to violate it. A supervisor's or foreman's knowledge will be attributed to the employer, unless the employer maintained work rules that satisfied the OSHA standard, communicated those rules to employees, and enforced the work rules.

OSHA is entitled to prove the employer's knowledge (and therefore does not have to prove actual knowledge) in some situations:

- Another employee has already been injured by the same hazardous conditions;

- Several written employee complaints have already been made to OSHA;

- The employer knows that employees habitually omit safety equipment, or otherwise allow hazardous conditions to be present in the workplace;

- The employer doesn't provide enough training;

- The employer doesn't enforce its own safety rules;

- The hazards would easily have been discovered if the employer had performed an adequate inspection.

An employer that receives an OSHA citation has 15 days to file a Notice of Contest, disputing that there was a violation, demanding a fair period of time to abate the violation, or challenging the size of the penalty. If the employer is not sure whether or not to contest, it can schedule an informal conference with the OSHA area director to discuss OSHA's position on workplace conditions and how to improve them. The 15-day limit is strictly applied: OSHRC does not have jurisdiction to review a notice of contest filed after the 15-day period expires. [*Chao v. Russell P. LeFrois Builder, Inc.*, 291 F.3d 219 (2d Cir. 2002)]

There is no official form for the Notice of Contest; it is simply a letter stating in plain English that the employer disagrees with the citation and wants to contest some or all of the violations, to ask for a smaller penalty, and/or ask for more time to comply. If the Notice of Contest is not filed within the required 15 days, the citation becomes final, and no court has the power to reverse it or even to review it.

> ■ **TIP:** If an employer appeals in bad faith, knowing that the citation is valid, the whole period of time until the challenge is resolved is treated as a period of noncompliance, with additional penalties for each day.

Another factor is whether the citation will affect other cases. For instance, some courts allow an OSHA citation, especially an uncontested one, to be introduced as evidence of dangerous conditions (e.g., in a Worker's Compensation hearing). Contesting the violation can help clear the employer's name.

When a notice is filed, an OSHA Administrative Law Judge (ALJ) will set a date for a hearing. Although the hearing is informal, it is still governed by the Federal Rules of Evidence. The ALJ's decision becomes final 30 days after it is rendered, unless it is contested.

All Notices of Contest, and all ALJ decisions, are automatically passed along to the Occupational Safety and Health Review Commission (OSHRC). OSHRC has the power to order review of part or all of an ALJ decision. The employer, or any other party adversely affected by the decision, can file a Petition for Discretionary Review. Although it has the power to raise the level of a violation, OSHRC usually doesn't do so.

The employer can raise many arguments to OSHRC:

- The CO got the facts wrong;
- The employer did not know, and had no duty to know, that the violation had occurred;
- The inspection itself was improper—for example, the inspection was really a search, requiring a warrant that had not been obtained;
- OSHA applied the wrong standard;
- The standard itself was invalid, because it was not properly promulgated, or was so vague that employers could not reasonably be expected to understand and comply with it;
- The real cause of the violation was misconduct by employees, beyond the employer's control; this misconduct is unlikely to recur;
- Complying with the OSHA requirement actually increased the hazards to employees rather than decreasing them, but the employer was unable to get a variance.

OSHRC issues an order after considering the employer's arguments and defenses. The employer has 60 days from the date of the OSHRC order to file a further appeal. The employer can now go to federal court, because administrative remedies have been appealed. In fact, the employer can bypass the District Court (the lowest tier in the federal court system, where federal cases normally begin) and appeal either to the Court of Appeals for the Circuit where the violation is alleged to have occurred, or to the District of Columbia Circuit.

OSHRC's obligation, under the OSH Act, is to impose a penalty of $5,000 to $70,000 for each willful violation. The ALJ found that two related companies committed many willful violations of 29 C.F.R. § 1904.2(a) by refusing to record work-related accidents and illnesses. However, the ALJ grouped the violations so that each company was treated as having committed one willful violation, and was assessed with one penalty of $70,000 rather than the $9,000 each for 82 violations, and $8,000 for each of 52 violations, sought by the DOL. The Fifth Circuit agreed with the DOL: ALJs can select a per-violation penalty from within the statutory range, but are not permitted to manipulate the number of violations. DOL can group willful violations at the charging stage—but OSHRC does not have the authority to group per-instance willful violations at the penalty stage. [*Chao v. OSHRC/Chao v. Jindal United Steel Corp.*, 480 F.3d 320 (5th Cir. 2007); the penalty statute is 29 U.S.C. § 666. The circuit courts review OSHRC penalty determinations for abuse of discretion: *Chao v. OSHRC*, 401 F.3d 355 (5th Cir. 2005)]

The Secretary of Labor and OSHRC, both of which are part of the Department of Labor, came into conflict about interpretation of asbestos regulations. The OSHRC found that nine asbestos violations were "not serious," and reduced the overall penalty from $16,875 to $3,150.The Third Circuit reversed OSHRC, finding that the secretary did not have to show that the work in this case could have exposed employees to harmful amount of asbestos. It is presumed that violating Class II asbestos requirements exposes employees to substantial amounts of asbestos. There was a possibility of actual exposure to harmful levels of asbestos, which is all that is required to impose liability. The test is whether secretary demonstrates that the employees did a particular type of asbestos work; there is a presumption under the regulations that the work generates significant asbestos exposure; the employer had actual or constructive notice of the conditions; and the conditions violated the regulations. [*Sec'y of Labor v. Conoco-Phillips Bayway Refinery*, 654 F.3d 472 (3d Cir. 2011). The standards come from *Sec'y of Labor v. Trinity Indus.*, 504 F.3d 397 (3d Cir. 2007)]

OSHA issued citations to the Loretto-Oswego Residential Healthcare Facility for violating employee safety standards (e.g., with respect to eye protection, hepatitis vaccination, training, and electrical equipment). The citations were settled except for one issue: whether some violations were repeated, which depends on whether Loretto-Oswego and two other entities were a single employer for OSH Act purposes. The penalty would be $54,250 for repeat violations, $11,250 otherwise. The three entities shared a president/CEO and CFO/COO. However, the power to hire, fire, and discipline Loretto-Oswego's employees was delegated to its licensed administrator. Nevertheless, the ALJ found repeat violations based on the three entities operating as a single employer. OSHRC reversed. The Department of Labor petitioned for review of the OSHRC decision. Review was denied by the Second Circuit, which deferred to the OSHRC findings, holding that there was substantial evidence of the independence of the facilities. [*Solis v. Loretto Oswego Residential Heath Care Facility,* 692 F.3d 65 (2d Cir. 2012)]

OSHA sought a multi-million-dollar fine against the Imperial Sugar refinery in Georgia, where 13 workers died and 40 were injured when sugar dust exploded in 2008. OSHA alleged that the company was aware of hazards as early as 2002 (including similar conditions at another plant), but failed to correct them. The proposed $8.7 million fine is the third-largest proposed penalty in OSHA history. The penalties include more than $5 million for 120 violations at the plant where the fire occurred and $3.7 million for 91 violations at the other plant. OSHA cited 118 egregious violations. However, ventilation and dust come under the general duty clause, and OSHA cannot issue per-instance violations without a specific standard. [Shaila Dewan, *OSHA Seeks $8.7 Million Fine Against Sugar Company,* N.Y. Times, July 26, 2008, at p. A11]

On September 3, 2009, laborer Nick Revetta died in an explosion at the U.S. Steel plan in Clairton, Pennsylvania when leaking gas ignited and pushed him into a steel column that crushed his head. A co-worker said that potential ignition sources were not properly insulated and safety practices had been deteriorating for five years in order to save money. Based on the co-worker's complaint, OSHA settled the proposed fine of $32,400 for $19,800. The only penalty imposed related to Revetta's death was $10,763 in unrelated fines imposed on an insulation contractor working near the explosion. Ten months later, another explosion hospitalized 17 workers. According to OSHA, U.S. Steel allowed contractors to use a shortcut that was responsible for the explosion; U.S. Steel denied this. In January 2011, OSHA issued 12 violations, one willful, and proposed a $143,000 fine. U.S. Steel appealed. There was a settlement with OSHA on October 26, 2012, calling for a payment of $78,500: [*Solis v. U.S. Steel,* OSHRC Docket No. 11-0361, <http://www.osha.gov/pls/oshaweb/owadisp.show_document?p_table= CWSA&p_id=2206>]

It is a positive trend that the number of workplace fatalities has declined significantly, but this is partially a result of the smaller number of hours worked rather than improved safety. The U.S. fatality rate is six times that of the United Kingdom, where safety rules are tougher. It would take OSHA 130 years to inspect every workplace in the United States. For fiscal 2012, a target of 42,250 inspections (5.6% higher than the previous year's goal) was set, but only 1,118 inspections were actually performed. [Emma Schwartz, Center for Public Integrity, *In U.S. Steel Town, Fatal Gas Explosion Goes Unpunished By OSHA,* iWatch News (May 21, 2012) (benefitslink.com)]

SHRM editor Roy Maurer provided some advice about reducing fines. One important measure is to request an informal conference, which can result in lower penalties, more time to abate hazards, and reclassification or even deletion of some citations. Fines can be reduced by up to 10% if the employer has not had any willful, serious, repeat, or failure-to-abate citations in the preceding five years.

But employers do not qualify for this "Clean History" relief if they have had any of these major citations at any worksite in the United States. Recently, OSHA updated its Field Operations Manual to make it harder for employers to get penalty reductions. The employer must have had an inspection within the previous five years—with no violations being noted at the inspection. Penalties can be reduced 15% under the "quick fix" program if the employer corrects hazards within 24 hours of the inspection. The violation must not have been worse than "moderate-gravity serious," and the employer must undertake substantial permanent corrective actions to qualify. Sometimes OSHA will reduce penalties further and/or structure an installment payment plan, if the employer can show financial hardship; there is no official definition of hardship, so negotiation may be possible. OSHA sometimes reduces penalties based on "Enhanced Abatement" (improvements are extended throughout the corporation, or an external auditor is consulted). Safety improvements can also trigger penalty reductions, although expensive engineering controls might be required. [Roy Maurer, *How to Contest and Reduce OSHA Fines,* <http://www.shrm.org/hrdisciplines/safetysecurity/ articles/Pages/Contest-Reduce-OSHA-Fines.aspx > (undated; last accessed Mar. 18, 2013)]

## § 31.12  ABATEMENT

Abatement—removal of hazardous conditions—is the rationale for the whole OSHA process. An uncontested citation, a citation for which the contest period has expired, and a citation where the employer's challenge was partially or wholly unsuccessful, all give rise to abatement responsibilities.

Employers are required to abate violations within the shortest reasonable interval for correction. The CO orders an abatement date. Ordinarily, this will not be more than 30 days, although the initial abatement date could be more than 30 days from the date of the inspection if structural changes are needed, or if abatement relies on components that take a long time to deliver. [See OSHA Field Inspection Reference Manual CPL 2.103, at <http://www.osha.gov>]

> ■ **TIP:**  If a citation notes several violations, only some of which are contested, the appropriate action is to correct the uncontested violations, notify the OSHA area director that correction has occurred, and pay the penalties for the uncontested violations. With respect to contested citations, abatement and payment of fines will be suspended until there is an OSHRC final order.

OSHA reinspects the premises. If the same conditions are detected, penalties of up to $1,000 a day can be imposed. The employer, however, can contest penalties in the same way as an original citation.

The employer is entitled to file a Petition for Modification of Abatement (PMA) with the OSHA Area Director, no later than the scheduled abatement date, if factors beyond the employer's control prevent abatement. The PMA explains what the employer has done to cure the problem, how much additional time is required and why, and what the employer will do to protect employees until full abatement is achieved. The PMA must be posted and served on the employer's workforce, because they have the right to contest it.

If the PMA is uncontested, the Secretary of Labor has the power to approve it. OSHRC holds a hearing on contested PMAs, to determine if the employer did in fact act in good faith and was really unable to achieve full compliance. The employer does not have to comply with the underlying citation during the time that the PMA is under consideration.

## § 31.13   OSHA CONSULTATION

State OSH agencies, working under grants from the federal OSHA, offer free on-site consultation services to identify and eliminate potential safety problems before they become real ones. The consultants are also available by telephone for advice and discussion. On-site visits are followed up by a written analysis of workplace hazards and suggestions for correction.

The consultants do not have the authority to impose penalties, but participating employers must agree to take steps to correct whatever problems the program uncovered.

Consultations cannot take place while an OSHA inspection is already underway, but if a consultation is scheduled, there is a good chance that OSHA will cancel a scheduled inspection, unless it is investigating a fatality or serious accident, or it is suspected that employees are in imminent danger.

An employer that has completed a consultation, made corrections based on the recommendations, and who posts a notice of correction where employees can see it, is entitled to request one year's immunity from scheduled OSHA inspections.

OSHA gives priority to scheduling consultation in industries with high hazards. The names of companies engaging in consultation will not be disclosed to state or federal enforcers unless the employer refuses to correct imminent hazards that are discovered during the process. [See 29 C.F.R. § 1908.5; for a map of locations, see <http://www.osha.gov/dcsp/smallbusiness/consult_directory.html>]

## § 31.14   VOLUNTARY PROGRAMS

Under the title of Voluntary Protection Programs (VPP), OSHA has three incentive programs (Star, Merit, and Demonstration) for employers with good safety records, who are supposed to serve as examples for other companies. Participants qualify for participation by proving that they maintain safe workplace and provide ongoing safety training for workers. OSHA and state authorities do not do programmed inspections at participating companies, although inspections will still be made if a complaint is registered.

Employers can apply to OSHA for VPP certification. They must complete applications that demonstrate their qualifications for participation. OSHA sends an inspector to check the company's safety records and site conditions, and expects that participants will show continuous improvement in their safety performance.

VPP began in 1982. The Star Program is for sites that are at or below the national average injury rate for their industry. OSHA reviews accident rates every year, and re-evaluates the participants every three to five years. Merit sites have the potential to reach Star status within three years, but in the meantime, they need help with their safety management. OSHA evaluates the site every 18–24 months. The Star Demonstration program is for sites that have reached Star levels, to test alternative means of promoting safety in the workplace. OSHA evaluates Star Demonstration sites every 12–18 months. [OSHA Fact Sheet, *Voluntary Protection Programs*, <http://www.osha.gov/OshDoc/data_General_Facts/fact sheet.vpp.pdf>. (August 2009); see also OSHA, *All About VPP,* <http://www.osha.gov/dcsp/vpp/all_about_vpp.html> (]undated; last accessed Mar. 18, 2013)]

# CHAPTER 32

# UNEMPLOYMENT INSURANCE

## § 32.01 INTRODUCTION

In the late 1990s, the subject of unemployment insurance was something of a backwater: a topic of limited interest in a booming, full-employment economy. However, starting in mid-2001, and accelerating after the September 11 attack, unemployment insurance, and especially the employer's experience rating and funding obligations, became far more interesting. The economic travails since 2008 have placed significant stress on the unemployment system.

Unemployment compensation (UC also known as Unemployment Insurance, or UI) is a state-administered insurance system. Employers make contributions to a fund. The State Employment Security Agencies (SESAs) that administer the system receive federal funding. In exchange, they must perform investigations and other managerial tasks.

Each state creates an Unemployment Insurance Trust Fund from employer contributions. In a few states, employee contributions are also required. However, FICA tax imposes equal (and substantial) burdens on both employer and employee, but unemployment tax is almost exclusively a responsibility of the employer. The theory is that in good times, unemployment will be low, and the fund will accumulate a surplus that can be used in bad times to pay unemployment insurance claims.

The Department of Labor's unadjusted and seasonally adjusted data on the number of unemployment insurance claims can be found at <http://www.dol.gov>. A map with UI contact and other information is posted to <http://www.servicelocator.org/OWSLinks.asp>.

Unemployment payments peaked in 2010, when 12 million people received benefits; in March 2013, the total number of people receiving benefits under all federal and state programs was less than half that figure (5.6 million). The average state allotment in February 2013 was 55 weeks of benefits. In early 2013, there was a general trend of reduction in unemployment benefits, but it was not uniform throughout the United States. For example, benefit duration in Michigan dropped below one year for the first time since 2007, although Michigan's unemployment rate was almost 9%. In 2011, Michigan reduced its regular state benefits from 26 weeks to 20 weeks, which triggered a reduction in federal benefit eligibility. Eighteen other states also had entitlement of fewer than 52 weeks of benefits for new applicants. North Carolina passed a law, effective July 1, 2013, reducing benefits to 20 weeks. To a certain extent, the reductions reflect a positive factor: lower overall unemployment rates. In January 2010, the rate may have been as high as 10%, but the reported national unemployment rate in February 2013 was 7.7%. The average duration of unemployment in March 2013 was 36.9 weeks—but one-quarter of the unemployed had been out of work for a year or more.

The National Employment Law Project (NELP) reported in February 2013 that seven states permanently have reduced state UI benefits: Arkansas, Florida, Georgia, Illinois, Michigan, Missouri, and South Carolina. In these states, the maximum duration of state benefits is 18 weeks (Georgia), 19 weeks (Florida), 20 weeks (Michigan, Missouri, and South Carolina) or 25 weeks (Arkansas and Illinois). In the other states, the maximum duration of state benefits is 26 weeks. Reduction in the state benefit also reduces availability of federal benefits. [National Employment Law Project Policy Brief, *One-Two Punch: As States Cut Employment Benefit Weeks*, <http://nelp.3cdn.net/115f0e07e648c2397d_p4m6b3rnj.pdf> (Feb. 2013)]

The Wall Street Journal reported that the states with the worst unemployment problem were not necessarily those offering the greatest duration of benefits, and vice versa. The longest duration of benefits was 86 weeks in Alaska, but Alaska's unemployment rate was 6.7%, below the national average, whereas Michigan, Florida, Georgia, and South Carolina offer a below-average duration of benefits despite severe unemployment. States are motivated to reduce benefits if they owe money to the federal unemployment system and need to repay it; retaining the same level of benefits would require increases in employer contributions, a politically unpopular move. [Ben Casselman, *Jobless Aid Shrinks Unevenly*, WSJ.com (Mar. 19, 2013)]

Federal spending is subject to limits imposed by the "sequester," as a result of the Budget Control Act of 2011, which mandates that the federal government make $85 billion in budget cuts for the 2013 fiscal year. NELP reported in May 2013 that the sequester does not affect the regular state UI benefits received by approximately 3 million private-sector workers and over 50,000 federal workers and servicemembers. However, the sequester affects almost two million workers receiving Emergency Unemployment Compensation (EUC; see 32.02[B]). As of May 3, 2013, 23 states made sequester cuts in EUC benefits, an average of $155 a month. The sequester also reduces federal funding given to the states to manage both unemployment programs—and funds for helping the unemployed find new jobs. [National Employment Law Project Briefing Paper, *The Sequester's Devastating Impact on Families of Unemployed Workers and the Struggling Unemployment Insurance System*, <http://nelp.3cdn.net/e981ef2022538ced66_bfm6b85we.pdf> (May 3, 2013)]

In early 2013, after the automatic cuts under the budget sequester took effect, about 3.8 million people who were unemployed for more than six months faced a cut of approximately 11%, or $32 a week, in the federal unemployment benefit. Before the cuts, the average benefit was $292. The DOL estimate is that on September 30, 2013, $2.3 billion will be cut from the federal benefits, the 14–47 weeks of aid after the state benefits run out, which usually happens after 26 weeks. In January 2013, more than one-third (38.1%) of the unemployed had been out of work for more than six months; the worst-hit were workers over 45. The Urban Institute's 2012 survey showed that workers in their 50s were 20% less likely to be rehired than workers in the 25–34 age range. [Editorial, *As the Budget Cuts Hit Home*, NYTimes.com (Mar. 1, 2013)]

Although the policy that UI beneficiaries must be able to work and available to work had been in existence for a long time, the Department of Labor formalized it in a Final Rule promulgated early in 2007. The publication did not require any new action by the states. [DOL Final Rule, 72 Fed. Reg. 1890 (Jan. 16, 2007)]

> ■ **TIP:** The Medicare Prescription Drug Improvement and Modernization Act [Pub. L. No. 108-173] provides that one type of "qualified medical expense" that can be withdrawn from a Health Savings Account (HSA) without tax penalty is a premium paid for health insurance by a person receiving federal or state unemployment benefits.

The Federal Circuit reversed the Court of Federal Claims, which held that Supplemental Unemployment Benefit (SUB) payments are not FICA wages because Code § 3402(o) covers only income tax withholding and not FICA. The Federal Circuit found that § 3402(o) was irrelevant, and the payments made during a 1980s Reduction in Force were FICA wages. [*CSX Corp. v. United States*, 518 F.3d 1328 (Fed. Cir. 2008), discussed in Deloitte's Washington Bulletin, *Federal Circuit Rules Supplemental Unemployment Benefits Are Wages for FICA Purposes*, <http://benefitslink.com/articles/guests/washbull080310.html> (Mar. 10, 2008)] A circuit split was created in 2012 when the Sixth Circuit held that severance pay is not subject to FICA. The United States requested rehearing en banc, which was denied. It is likely that the Supreme Court will take on a case to resolve the split. [*United States v. Quality Stores*, 693 F.3d 605 (6th Cir. 2012)]

Some help-wanted advertisements stipulate that the company will not hire unemployed persons, only those who already have another job. California, Connecticut, Florida, and other states are considering laws to forbid discrimination against the unemployed; New Jersey was the first state to actually pass such a law. Since December 2009, more than 40% of the unemployed have been looking for work for more than six months. According to the DOL, in January 2012, 5.5 million people had been unemployed for more than six months, more than four million for over a year. [Shelly Banjo, *Measures Aim to End Bias Against Long-Term Jobless*, WSJ.com (Feb. 24, 2012)]

## § 32.02  ELIGIBILITY FOR BENEFITS

### [A]  Generally

Two of the most important determinants in entitlement are whether the employee worked long enough before termination to qualify for benefits; and the reason for termination. The "base period" is the period of time used to analyze whether the job continued long enough.

In most states, the base period is the first four of the preceding five completed calendar quarters. Some states allow the four most recent quarters of employment to be counted. The difference is whether the most recent months of employment (which might have higher earnings) will be counted. Theoretically, only persons who earned at least a minimum amount during the base period can collect UI benefits. In practice, these limits are so low that nearly all employees meet them.

The rationale for the UI system is to provide benefits for employees who lose their jobs through "no fault of their own." But in this context, an employee will not be considered to be at fault even if the employer was justified in firing him or her—for instance, if an employee is fired for incompetence but there was no crime or wrongdoing. For example, in *Time Warner Cable*, Unempl. Ins. Rep. (CCH) ¶ 8314 (Miss. App. 2006), benefits were held to have been correctly paid to a claimant who was terminated for lack of knowledge and judgment needed in his job. Inefficiency, unsatisfactory conduct, and good-faith errors do not constitute misconduct.

In general, benefits will not be available to anyone who quit voluntarily without good cause. However, states vary as to whether employees who quit will be entirely denied UI benefits, or whether benefit eligibility will merely be delayed. If the employer's conduct has been so abusive as to constitute constructive discharge, then the employee will be deemed to have had good cause to resign. For example, the District of Columbia Court of Appeals ruled that a laundry manager was entitled to benefits when she quit, because she had been subjected to frequent verbal abuse. Decision factors include whether the insults were habitual; if the employee was insulted in front of other people; if the insults were related to job duties; and whether the employee protested the abuse to a supervisor or executive. [*Imperial Valet Servs. Inc. v. Alvarado*,No. 12-CV-1173, 2013 WL 3820947 (D.C. App. 2013); see Zoe Tillman, *Verbal Abuse Is "Good Cause" to Quit, D.C. Court Says*,The BLT (Blog of Legal Times) (July 25, 2013) (law-.com)]

However, there are situations where the employee is considered to have acted with good cause, even if the employer was not at fault. Many states interpret quitting a job to follow a spouse who has gotten a job elsewhere to constitute good cause.

Pennsylvania ruled that a claimant quit work without good cause when her husband was relocated to Ohio. The claimant failed to show that the move to Ohio caused insuperable problems for commuting, or that maintaining two residences caused economic hardship. The Pennsylvania Commonwealth Court did not necessarily treat maintaining the family unit as good cause to quit. [*Sturpe*, Unempl. Ins. Rep. (CCH) ¶ 12,433 (Pa. Commw. 2003)]

Yet another issue is the treatment of persons who have accepted severance packages (see Chapter 3 for more discussion of severance benefits). The Massachusetts Court of Appeals ruled in 2006 that benefits should have been awarded to claimants who took a voluntary separation package because they had an objectively reasonable belief that they would have been fired if they had not taken the packages. The employer neither announced that employees would be chosen randomly for RIF nor announced criteria for selecting RIF candidates, thus giving employees good cause to cut their losses by taking the package and leaving. [*State Street Bank & Trust Co.*, Unempl. Ins. Rep. (CCH) ¶ 8487 (Mass. App. 2006); see also *Johnson v. Unemployment Compensation Bd. of Review* (Pa. Commonwealth 2005), discussed in Asher Hawkins, *Bought-Out Verizon Workers Denied Jobless Aid*, The Legal Intelligencer (Mar. 10, 2005) (law.com)]

Employees who took a voluntary separation plan were eligible for benefits, based on testimony from a company Vice President and e-mails from the HR department stating that the plan was implemented because of lack of work. [*Verizon North*, Unempl. Ins. Rep. (CCH) ¶ 10,203 (Ohio App. 2006)]

In contrast, however, an office manager was given the choice between staying on while she looked for a new job, or leaving immediately and receiving severance pay. When she opted to leave right away, she was ineligible for benefits, because she was the one who made the departure decision. [*Arrow Legal Solutions Group PXC*, Unempl. Ins. Rep. (CCH) ¶ 8354 (Utah App. 2006)]

Benefits are also denied to persons who are guilty of "misconduct detrimental to the best interests of the employer." This is interpreted in an industrial rather than moral light, so improper activities are likely to rule out UI benefit eligibility even if they are not criminal in nature. Poor job performance would not be treated as "misconduct," unless it demonstrated gross negligence or willful disregard of the employer's best interests.

Depending on the state, disqualifying misconduct might also have to be work-related. Excessive absence or insubordination might be treated as misconduct. Benefits were properly denied to a claimant who was terminated for excessive absences. On her first day at work, she signed an acknowledgment of receiving the company handbook, including the attendance policy. The claimant asserted that she misinterpreted the policy, so her actions could not be deemed willful or wanton, but the Delaware Superior Court ruled that denial of benefits was correct because the employer coached her about the policy and warned her that she was at risk of termination for continuing to violate it. [*Jackson*, Unempl. Ins. Rep. (CCH) ¶ 8317 (Del. Super. Ct. 2008)]

Being intoxicated on business premises would almost certainly be considered misconduct. For example, Kansas denied benefits for disqualifying misconduct on the basis of the claimant's repeated insubordination to a supervisor in an open area where other workers could hear the interaction, which also involved an unprovoked barrage of vulgar and abusive language. [*Siler*, Unempl. Ins. Rep. (CCH) ¶ 8265 (Kan. App. 2003)] Denial of benefits for work-related misconduct was proper when the claimant gave a supervisor's personal phone number to a former employee who used it to leave an obscene and threatening message. The claimant was present when the call was made, and lied about it afterward, so even if his only involvement was having bad judgment in distributing the number, lying about it was work-related misconduct that ruled out benefits. [*Schwartz*, Unempl. Ins. Rep. (CCH) ¶ 8427 (Tenn. App. 2008)]

A truck driver whose blood alcohol concentration exceeded the legal limit was guilty of disqualifying misconduct, even though he was not convicted of driving under the influence and did not lose his license; he should have known that duty to his employer precluded driving while impaired. [*Risk*, Unempl. Ins. Rep. (CCH) ¶8557 (Minn. App. 2003)] Being stopped for a non-work-related DUI, resulting in surrender of the driver's license when the claimant's job at a tire shop required a valid license, constituted disqualifying misconduct. [*Gummert*, Unempl. Ins. Rep. (CCH) ¶9126 (Iowa Dist. Ct. 2008)]

A fired legal secretary could obtain benefits: it was not disqualifying misconduct to fail to complete a project before leaving for vacation because it was merely an isolated incident of bad judgment or ordinary negligence, not intentional disregard of the employer's interests. [*Aspen Ridge Law Offices*, Wyo. Sup. Unempl. Ins. Rep. (CCH) ¶8209 (Wyo. 2006)]

New York granted unemployment benefits to a Whole Foods Market employee who violated store policy by taking a sandwich out of the trash at the end of his shift. Employees are required to get their supervisors' consent before taking food; servings are usually sample-sized, and must be logged and accounted for. Initially, unemployment benefits were denied on grounds of misconduct. The employee said that his previous supervisor allowed employees to take damaged food that was going to be thrown out and written off. The ALJ sided with the employee, because he had a good record, did not take the sandwich out of the store, and this was an isolated instance of poor judgment that should not be considered misconduct. [Rebecca Moore, *Reason for Denying Unemployment Benefits Sounded Fishy*, plansponsor.com (Mar. 20, 2009). See also Rebecca Moore, *Dillards Tries to Block Unemployment Benefits for Hot Dog* "Thief", plansponsor.com (July 29, 2011):

The Indiana Court of Appeals reversed disqualification of Nolan Koewler, who was fired for eating two hot dogs that were left over after a company picnic. The Review Board concluded that he had been fired for theft, but the Court of Appeals noted that although employees including Koewler were told to put the leftovers away, they were not aware that it was supposed to be saved for Labor Day. Furthermore, the food had been supplied for consumption by employees, and Koewler was not aware that employees were no longer supposed to consume food items. But see Tara Cantore, *Dumpster Diving Employee Can't Get Unemployment,* plansponsor.com (Aug. 25, 2011): An employee fired for taking soup from a dumpster, a violation of the store policy against employees taking anything from the store without paying for it, was terminated for misconduct and, therefore, did not qualify for unemployment benefits.]

Continued eligibility requires the claimant to make a serious search for work. Benefits will be terminated if the claimant receives but rejects a legitimate job offer for suitable work. Benefits will not be paid in any week in which the claimant receives a pension, annuity, retirement pay, or any other private or government payment based on past work history. But benefits can be paid in a week in which the claimant receives a distribution from a profit-sharing plan, because that is not treated as compensation for work. The general rule is that a claimant who has recovered from an injury must return to the employer and offer to work. However, the Iowa District Court ruled in 2008 that a worker who knew that he was only able to do light work, that his employer had no light duty assignments to offer, and someone else had already been hired to replace him was not required to make a futile offer of his unsuitable services in order to receive benefits. [*Riner*, Unempl. Ins. Rep. (CCH) ¶ 9133 (Iowa Dist. Ct. 2008)]

Benefits can be paid based on job loss due to a material change in working conditions imposed by the employer, if the employee has a valid reason for being unable to work under the new conditions. (This is referred to as "voluntary with good cause attributable to the employer.") A published job description can be evidence of the original nature of the job, and therefore whether material change has occurred. If a job is described as a day-shift position, a change to a night or swing shift might well be considered material.

In mid-2003, the New York Court of Appeals ruled that the employee's physical presence is critical, not the location of the employer on whose behalf the work was done. So a worker who telecommuted from Florida could not collect New York unemployment benefits, even though her employer was located in Long Island and work was directed and controlled from New York. [*Allen v. Comm'r of Labor*, 100 N.Y.2d 282 (N.Y. 2003); see John Caher, *N.Y. Court First to Rule on Telecommuting*, New York Law Journal, July 3, 2003 <http://www.law.com>; Al Baker, *Telecommuter Loses Case for Benefits*, N.Y. Times, July 3, 2003, at B1]

Strikers were held to be entitled to benefits after the date that permanent replacements were hired. (The employment relationship is severed when employees have been notified that they have been replaced, or their positions are permanently filled by someone else.) [*M. Conley Co.*, Unempl. Ins. Rep. (CCH) ¶ 10,186 (Ohio 2006)] School district employees were properly denied benefits during a work stoppage. When CBA negotiations reached an impasse, the employer implemented its best and final offer, which was not so unreasonable that employees would feel constrained to strike. Therefore, the work stoppage was a strike, not a lockout, and benefits were unavailable. [*Tietz*, Unempl. Ins. Rep. (CCH) ¶ 10,178 (Ohio App. 2005)] Union members did not get benefits: their work stoppage was not caused by a lockout, and they had the opportunity to return to work when the employer hired permanent replacement workers. [*Magnode*, Unempl. Ins. Rep. (CCH) ¶ 10,195 (Ohio App. 2006)]

## [B]  BAA-UC

The Department of Labor created a program called BAA-UC (BAA stands for Birth and Adoption) [20 C.F.R. Part 604], through a Notice of Proposed Rulemaking at 64 Fed. Reg. 67972 (Dec. 3, 1999), finalized, without significant changes, at 65 Fed. Reg. 37209 (June 13, 2000). The program allowed new parents to receive unemployment benefits for a one-year period beginning with the week of birth or adoption, because they would be treated as being "able and available for work" during this time period. The DOL regulations gave states the ability to opt in to the program, but no state elected to do so.

A lawsuit [*LPA, Inc. v. Chao*, 211 F. Supp. 2d 160 (D.D.C. 2002)] challenged the BAA-UC program as inconsistent with federal law. Although the suit was dismissed on procedural grounds, it caused the DOL to re-think the program. After review, the DOL decided that the BAA-UC experiment was a bad decision and an invalid interpretation of the rules about availability for work. It would also put additional strain on already hard-pressed state unemployment insurance funds. Therefore, the DOL decided to terminate the experiment, publishing a Notice of Proposed Rulemaking for this purpose at 67 Fed. Reg. 72122 (Dec. 4, 2002).

## [C]  Federal Statutes Extending UI

A federal statute, 42 U.S.C. § 177(a), the Robert T. Stafford Disaster Relief and Emergency Assistance Act, establishes the Disaster Unemployment Assistance (DUA) program. Up to 26 weeks of benefits can be furnished after a major disaster declared by the President, for unemployment caused by that disaster for which no other benefits are available. DUA eligibility ceases when the state agency finds that unemployment is no longer directly traceable to the major disaster. The minimum weekly amount of benefit is 50% of the state's average UI benefit. The maximum is set by state law.

The DUA benefit is considered a UC benefit. It cannot exceed the maximum benefit payable under the state's UC law. Qualifications for DUA are that the claimant no longer has a job, cannot reach the place of work, is unable to start a promised job; is the household breadwinner; has become head of the household because the former head of the household died in the disaster; or is unable to work because of an injury caused by the disaster. [DOL, *Disaster Unemployment Assistance* fact sheet, <http://workforcesecurity.doleta.gov/unemploy/disaster.asp> (updated July 23, 2010)]

The November 2001 rule provides a definition of "unemployment as a direct result" of a major disaster [20 C.F.R. § 625.5(c)]—DUA benefits are limited to the immediate result of the disaster itself, not more remote consequences of a chain of events that was started or made worse by the disaster. Examples of direct results are unemployment caused by damage to or destruction of the physical worksite, lack of access to the worksite because the government has ordered it closed, or lack of work and lost revenues caused to a business that got the majority of its income from the premises that were damaged, destroyed, or shut down. But "ripple effects" (for instance, if an office building is closed, workers who can't come in to work don't stop at a coffee shop for snacks) are not covered.

Beneficiaries can include, for example, workers at airports closed by government orders.

Major disaster declarations were issued for Superstorm Sandy for Connecticut, New Jersey, and New York on October 30, 2012, triggering availability of initial Disaster Unemployment Assistance (DUA) claims until February 4, 2013. Benefits were available to employed and self-employed persons who were unemployed as a result of the storm, or were unable to reach their jobs because they could not travel. It is available for up to 26 weeks as long as unemployment continues to be a result of the disaster. [DOL News, *Hurricane Sandy Disaster Unemployment Assistance (DUA)*, <http://www.ows.doleta.gov/unemploy/docs/DOL_news_sandy.pdf> (last accessed Mar. 10, 2013)]

In addition to this federal law, some states have state "optional trigger" laws that let them provide a 13-week extended benefit period for workers who have used up their regular benefits during a period of high unemployment. The weekly amount of Extended Benefits (EB) is the same as the claimant's regular unemployment compensation. The Basic EB program requires states to provide up to 13 weeks of additional benefits, based on unemployment rates. States have the option to provide the additional 13 weeks of EB if unemployment is high, but not as high as the level where EB is mandatory in states where unemployment is high and rising. In addition, in some states with extremely high unemployment, there is a voluntary program adding seven more weeks of EB after the claimant has exhausted other unemployment benefits (not counting Disaster Unemployment Assistance or Trade Readjustment Allowances). However, not everyone who qualifies for regular benefits qualifies for EB. [Unemployment Insurance Extended Benefits, <http://workforcesecurity.doleta.gov/unemploy/extenben.asp> (July 23, 2011)]

Although in general, EB is 50% state and 50% federally funded, ARRA included a provision under which the federal government temporarily took over 100% funding of EB. This provision was renewed by Pub. L. No. 111-312, the 2010 tax bill, until January 4, 2012—so several states could offer EB benefits again. [DOL, *100% Federal Funding of Extended Benefits (EB) Extended to January 4, 2012*, <http://www.ows.doleta.gov/unemploy/supp_act_eb.asp> (accessed Mar. 25, 2011)] Subsequently, the American Taxpayer Relief Act of 2012 (ATRA), Pub. L. No. 112-240, extended 100% federal funding of EB until December 31, 2013. [DOL, *100% Federal Funding of Extended Benefits (EB) Extended to December 31, 2013*, <http://workforcesecurity.doleta.gov/unemploy/supp_act_eb.asp> (Jan. 16, 2013)]

A program of Temporary Extended Unemployment Compensation was established under the Job Creation and Worker Assistance Act of 2002 (JWCAA). [Pub. L. No. 107-147] The program was originally scheduled to end as of January 1, 2003. It was extended to June 1, 2003 by Pub. L. No. 108-1 (which doesn't have a short title), and once again to December 31 by Pub. L. No. 108-26 (The Unemployment Compensation Amendments of 2003 Act). However, that was the final extension, and the program ended December 2003.

Emergency Unemployment Compensation (EUC) is a federal temporary extension of benefits for people who have collected all their regular state benefits. Although the basic unemployment programs are jointly funded by federal and state governments, EUC is wholly federally funded. The program was created by Pub. L. No. 110-252, the Supplemental Appropriations Act of 2008, and has been expanded since then in light of ongoing economic problems. Pub. L. No. 110-449, the Unemployment Compensation Extension Act of 2008, expanded the reach of the program, as did the Worker, Homeownership, and Business Assistance Act of 2009, Pub. L. No. 111-92. The program was extended (saved from termination) by ARRA, Pub. L. No. 111-5, and then by the Department of Defense Appropriations Act, Pub. L. 111-118, the Temporary Extension Act of 2010, Pub. L. No. 111-144, Continuing Extension Act of 2010, Pub. L. No. 111-157, and the Unemployment Compensation Extension Act of 2010, Pub. L. No. 111-205.

EUC was preserved from elimination by the Middle Class Tax Relief and Job Creation Act of 2012, Pub. L. No. 112-96—but that law not only imposes some limitations on persons receiving UI benefits, it phases down the maximum duration of benefits from 99 weeks to 66 weeks (or 73 weeks, in states with high unemployment).

In the period 2006–2010, state and local governments' inflation-adjusted spending on unemployment compensation more than tripled. Before the 2008 recession, it was common for persons in states that did not have high unemployment to exhaust benefits after 13 weeks, although federal law had some extended benefit triggers based on local markets. By mid-2008, these provisions had been triggered nationwide. In 2007 and the first half of 2008, no emergency or extended benefits were paid. At that point, about one-quarter of UI benefits were emergency or extended; by the end of 2009, emergency and extended benefits represented the majority of UI benefits. [Casey B. Mulligan, *How Unemployment Benefits Became Twice as Generous*, NYTimes.com (Nov. 2, 2011)]

EUC is organized into four tiers (a tier is a set of extra weeks of benefits provided after the basic state benefits have been exhausted). The duration of the various Emergency Unemployment Compensation (EUC) tiers has been amended several times. The 2013 tiers are:

- Tier I: 14 weeks;

- Tier II: 14 weeks if the state unemployment rate is 6% or higher;

- Tier III: 9 weeks if the state unemployment rate is 7% or higher;

- Tier IV: 10 weeks if the state unemployment rate is 9% or higher.

Therefore, counting the maximum of 26 weeks of state unemployment benefits, the maximum number of weeks of unemployment compensation is 73. This reflects a reduction: in 2010, for example, the maximum number of weeks of benefits was 99.[Alison Doyle, "Unemployment Tiers," <http://jobsearch.about.com/od/extended/a/unemployment-tiers.htm?> (undated; accessed Mar. 22, 2012)]

EUC was extended under the Tax Relief, Unemployment Insurance Reauthorization, and Job Creation Act of 2010, Pub. L. No. 111-312, so that benefits are available for weeks of unemployment ending on or before January 3, 2012, with benefits available up to June 9, 2012. [DOL, *Emergency Unemployment Compensation (EUC) Extended to January 3, 2012*, <http://www.ows.doleta.gov/unemploy/supp_act.asp>] The American Taxpayer Relief Act extended the expiration date of this program until Jan. 1, 2014, but it does not provide additional weeks of benefits to claimants who had already used up all their entitlement. [DOL, *Emergency Unemployment Compensation (EUC) Extended to January 1, 2014*, <http://workforcesecurity.doleta.gov/unemploy/supp_act.asp> (last accessed Mar. 10, 2013)] The extension benefited approximately two million long-term unemployed people who would have lost benefits at the beginning of 2013, as well as millions of others whose state benefits expire in 2013. Because the EUC extension was considered an emergency measure, the cost did not have to be offset by cuts in other programs: Christine L. Owens, National Employment Law Project press release, *Statement on Congress's Renewal of Unemployment Insurance*, <http://www.c-spanvideo.org/program/309633-4> (Jan. 2, 2013).

The Middle Class Tax Relief and Job Creation Act of 2012, Pub. L. No. 112-96, includes many provisions dealing with UI:

- § 2101: UI benefits are available only to people who are able to work, available to work, and are actively seeking work;

- § 2102: Up to ten states can work with the DOL on demonstration projects to get the long-term unemployed back into the workforce;

- § 2103: Recovery of state and federal overpayments is now mandatory;

- § 2105: States are allowed to pass laws imposing a drug testing requirement in connection with unemployment—but only if the applicant was fired from his or her most recent job because of drug use, or the only suitable work for the applicant is in an industry that conducts regular drug tests pursuant to DOL regulations;

- §§ 2122, 2123: Reauthorization of EUC until January 2, 2013, but with the maximum duration scaling down from 99 weeks to 73 weeks;

- § 2141: EUC and Extended Benefits use the same standard for work search (able and available to work and actively seeking work);

- § 2142: Eligibility of long-term benefit recipients will be re-assessed;

- § 2144: Eligible states can remain entitled to federal EUC funds through the end of the fiscal year by modifying their UI benefits;

- § 2161-2163: Work-sharing provisions

- § 2181-2183: Grants to allow states to set up self-employment assistance programs for the long-term unemployed. The existing Self-Employment Assistance (SEA) program receives additional funding and DOL technical assistance

[United States Senate Committee on Finance, *Summary of the Middle Class Tax Relief and Job Creation Act of 2012*, <http://www.finance.senate.gov/news room/chairman/release/?id=c42a8c8a-52ad-44af-86b2-4695aaff5378> (Feb. 16, 2012); Josh Mitchell and Naftali Bendavid, *Tax Bill Passed by Congress Broadens Jobless Program*, WSJ.com (Feb. 18, 2012); Naftali Bendavid and Siobhan Hughes, *Congress Reaches Payroll-Tax Deal*, WSJ.com (Feb. 16, 2012)]

The STC program (for Short-Time Compensation; also known as work-sharing) provides partial unemployment benefits to persons who are still working at the same job, but whose hours have been reduced from full- to part-time.

The Middle Class Tax Relief and Job Creation Act of 2012 encourages states to have STC programs, but the programs must be consistent with the federal definition. The federal government will reimburse up to 100% of certain state STC costs for up to three years. The Middle Class Tax Relief Act also set up a temporary federal STC program. States that do not already have their own STC program can sign a two-year contract with DOL to operate an STC program. Half of the STC benefit costs under this program will come from employers, the other half from the federal government. [DOL, *Unemployment Compensation: Federal-State Partnership*, <http://www.ows.doleta.gov/unemploy/pdf/partnership.pdf> (April 2012). This document says that 25 states had STC programs—but did not say which states they are, and the information is not readily available from the DOL Website.] To receive a grant under this program, states must submit an application to DOL, which made grants of almost $100 million to the states to set up STCs or improve existing STCs. The DOL intended one-third of each grant to be used to implement or improve an STC, the other two-thirds to enroll employers in the program. [DOL, *What's New in Workforce Investment?*, <http://doleta.gov/usworkforce/whatsnew/eta_default.cfm?id=5810> (Aug. 16, 2012)]

In late 2011, the Wall Street Journal wrote about the Pilgrim Screw Company, which avoided layoffs by having 11 of its 65 employees cut their hours by one day per week. The workers whose hours were reduced received one-fifth of the unemployment benefit from the state. Twenty-two states and the District of Columbia have work-sharing programs that provide partial unemployment benefits. Many of these programs have been around for decades but were seldom used until recently; five states added work-sharing programs since 2009. [Justin LaHart, *Work Sharing Gains Traction in Rhode Island, Elsewhere*, WSJ.com (Nov. 21, 2011)]

ARRA allowed about 500,000 part-time and low-income workers to receive benefits for the first time. According to the Department of Labor, only 36% of the unemployed actually receive benefits, because applicants must be involuntarily unemployed, and most states denied benefits to a person who is only looking for part-time work. ARRA provided federal funding for states to offer benefits to seekers of part-time work; those who left the workforce for compelling reasons such as caring for a sick child; applicants who have benefit-eligible dependents; and workers who undertook training after exhausting their benefits.

States vary greatly in their "recipiency rate" (the percentage of the unemployed who receive benefits). The national average is 36%, ranging from a low of 18.2% in South Dakota to 61.4% in Idaho. [Nat'l Employment Law Project, *Millions of Jobless Workers to Get Critical Aid in American Recovery & Reinvestment Act*, <http://nelp.3cdn.net/8dcffc4d1cea59f8b6-9im6bn1qh.pdf> (Feb. 14, 2009); Catherine Rampell, *Stimulus Bill Would Bestow New Aid to Many Workers*, N.Y. Times, Feb. 14, 2009]

Unemployment benefits, retraining, and health insurance subsidies are available under the Trade Adjustment Assistance Program (TAAP) to workers who lost their jobs when their employer moved outside of the United States, or because of foreign competition. A brochure available on the DOL Website (as updated through February 19, 2013) explains that benefits are triggered by filing a petition with DOL, either online or at an American Job Center. The petition can be filed either by an employer, a union official, a job center operator or partner (such as a state workforce agency), or by three or more workers from the same firm. DOL investigates to determine if the layoff is eligible (i.e., was caused by increased importation, outsourcing of production, loss of business from a customer that is also TAAP-eligible, or a declaration of trade injury made by the International Trade Commission. If the DOL certifies eligibility, the state will notify the eligible workers that they can apply for benefits, such as up to 130 weeks of training, wage subsidies, job search allowance, reimbursement for the cost of relocating for a new job, and a tax credit for 72.5% of the premium the individual pays for health insurance. [DOL brochure, *The Trade Adjustment Assistance Program: Back to Work After a Trade-Related Layoff*, <http://www.doleta.gov/tradeact/pdf/2011_brochure.pdf>]

## [D] Case Law on Benefit Eligibility

There are a number of reasons why benefits will be denied: that the individual was not totally unemployed; that he or she voluntarily quit his or her past job rather than being involuntarily employed; that he or she was guilty of misconduct (which generally means something worse than sheer incompetence).

A nurse working under an intermittent employment contract was not entitled to benefits after the contract expired: A person who chooses to work under a fixed-term contract is not involuntarily unemployed when the contract ends. [*Brinkman*, Unempl. Ins. Rep. (CCH) ¶ 10,179 (Ohio App. 2005)]

According to Louisiana's District Court, providing a false Social Security number and false information about one's criminal record constitutes material misconduct. The job was coordinator of environmental health and safety, so the employer had the right to expect honesty and integrity, and the employer's work rules spelled out a zero-tolerance policy for document falsification. [*Sheppard*, Unempl. Ins. Rep. (CCH) ¶ 9043 (La. Dist. Ct. 2002)]

Benefits were denied on the basis of disqualifying misconduct when a machinist used small amounts of scrap materials and a few minutes of time on the employer's machinery for a personal project without permission; the ALJ was wrong to say that the employer's interests were not substantially harmed. [*Doerfer Acquisition Co.*, Unempl. Ins. Rep. (CCH) ¶ 9051 (Iowa Dist. Ct. 2003)]

A New York lower-level appellate court held in 2009 that a woman who did not tell her employer about her clinical depression could not receive unemployment benefits or charge that her ADA rights were violated when she was fired for excessive absences. The failure to disclose constituted disqualifying misconduct. Although the employer warned her for more than a year that her job was at risk unless her attendance improved, she failed to take reasonable steps to protect her job. The ADA permits employers to inquire about potential health problems at work that are related to a business necessity—and attendance is generally considered an essential function of a job. [*Anumah v. Commissioner of Labor*, 2009 N.Y. Slip Op. 01893 (N.Y.A.D. 2009); see Joel Stashenko, *Woman Who Failed to Disclose Depression Cannot Collect Unemployment Benefits, Appeals Court Rules*, N.Y.L.J. (Mar. 27, 2009) (law.com)]

The Mississippi Court of Appeals denied benefits, on the grounds of disqualifying misconduct, to two claimants who participated in an unauthorized strike that violated the no-strike provision of their Collective Bargaining Agreement (CBA). [*Berry*, Unempl. Ins. Rep. (CCH) ¶ 8284 (Miss. App. 2001)], but union members are entitled to unemployment benefits during a lockout by the employer. [*Schott Glass Technologies Inc.*, Unempl. Ins. Rep. (CCH) ¶ 12,436 (Pa. Commw. 2003)]

According to the Delaware Superior Court, benefits were properly denied for a claimant who failed to update her leave of absence form as required by company policy. When she failed to update the form, the employer sent a letter telling her to come to the office to fill out the form, but she did not. Even if she believed, as she said, that her doctor was faxing updates about her condition, she failed to satisfy the employer's requirement that placed the burden on the employee. [*Norman*, Unempl. Ins. Rep. (CCH) ¶ 8316 (Del. Super. Ct. 2008)]

Accepting benefits for total disability without actually having the claimed physical limitations was a falsehood in disregard of the employer's interest and standards, and therefore disqualifying misconduct that precluded receipt of UI benefits. [*Downey*, Unempl. Ins. Rep. (CCH) ¶ 12,505 (Pa. Commw. 2006)]

An individual who has a reasonable expectation of reemployment (absolute certainty is not required) will not be required to make a formal search for other work. [*Thomas*, Unempl. Ins. Rep. (CCH) ¶ 9510 (Wis. Cir. 2000)] The claimant, #2 on the seniority list of a unionized workplace where the Collective Bargaining Agreement stipulated recall on the basis of seniority, could reasonably expect to be called back to work when the workplace re-opened after it was purchased. So he could collect unemployment benefits in the interim, even if he didn't make a job search.

Ability to work is another important criterion. The claimant in *Daniels* [Unempl. Ins. Rep. (CCH) ¶ 9022 (Iowa Dist. Ct. 2000)] was seven months pregnant when her doctor told her to find a job she could do sitting down. She worked as a blackjack dealer, required to stand for her entire seven-hour shift. Her employer put her on medical leave; unemployment benefits were denied because of her medically based inability to work. A pregnant security guard had good reason—health concerns—to leave her job when accepting reassignment would have required taking three buses to work, and her obstetrician advised her not to take buses during her third trimester. [*Gibson*, Unempl. Ins. Rep. (CCH) ¶ 8979 (Fla. App. 2006)]

A New Jersey claimant received $600 a week in benefits from October 10 to December 11, 2010. On December 15, she went to Jamaica and the Virgin Islands, returning to New Jersey December 31, 2010. She argued that she applied for jobs online, but the New Jersey Appellate Division held that she was not available to start work right away—it is impossible for a person outside the United States to be "ready, willing, and able" to work. The only exceptions to the immediate availability requirement are jury duty, job training programs, and family funerals. [*Vialet v. Board of Review*, DOCKET NO. A-1226-11T2, 2012 N.J. Super. Unpub. LEXIS 2420 (Oct. 26, 2012); see Charles Toutant, *Online Job Seeker Overseas Held Ineligible for Unemployment Pay*, N.J.L.J. (Oct. 29, 2012) (law.com)]

Benefits were available to a worker who discovered, when she returned to work after maternity leave, that her job had been filled by someone else, and the employer violated the FMLA (see Chapter 38) by failing to reinstate her in her former job or offer her an equivalent position. [*Bordon*, Unempl. Ins. Rep. (CCH) ¶ 8634 (Mo. App. 2006)]

The Iowa District Court held that a claimant left work for good cause when a hostile work environment caused physical and emotional symptoms. Her illness was attributable to the work environment and not to her job duties, so she was entitled to benefits and not disqualified by her failure to give notice to her employer. [*Wagner*, Unempl. Ins. Rep. (CCH) ¶ 9132 (Iowa Dist. Ct. 2008)] The Michigan Circuit Court deemed it good reason to quit after the claimant's request for a raise was turned down after she was given more office duties and an additional day of janitorial work. The employer's alteration of working conditions by increasing her duties constituted good reason to quit. [*Express Plumbing Heating/ Mechanical Inc.*, Unempl. Ins. Rep. (CCH) ¶ 10,211 (Mich. Cir. Ct. 2008)]

## [E]  Cases Involving Drugs

Missouri held that an employee was not disqualified from benefits when he was fired after a positive marijuana test. Because the company's drug-free workplace policy did not use the word "misconduct," the Missouri Court of Appeals held that he was not on notice that drug use would preclude receipt of benefits. However, the court remanded the case for determination under the general misconduct standard, and to apply the state law holding that an employer does not have to show a demonstrable impact of drug use on the employee's ability to do his or her job. [*Comer*, Unempl. Ins. Rep. (CCH) ¶ 8635 (Mo. App. 2006)]

The Indiana Court of Appeals reversed the denial of benefits to a claimant who was fired after failing a random drug test. The employer did not show that the claimant knowingly violated a rule. Although the policy of discharging employees who tested positive was reasonable and was uniformly applied, the employer failed to disclose what test was used, what the cutoff levels were, or why the test should be considered valid, so it was impossible to determine if the claimant really used drugs. [*Owen County*, Unempl. Ins. Rep. (CCH) ¶ 8607 (Ind. App. 2006)] The Oregon Court of Appeals said that it was not disqualifying misconduct for an employee to refuse when the employer ordered him to take a drug test on his own time, without compensation, after being written up for insubordination. [*Andrews*, Unempl. Ins. Rep. (CCH) ¶ 8878 (Or. App. 2000)] The court held that the employer's policy of requiring a drug test after all reprimands was not reasonable in cases where there was no evidence of drug use.

The Michigan Court of Appeals held in 2008 that a positive marijuana test was disqualifying misconduct even though the employer did not establish the chain of custody for the specimen. An unemployment benefits board can rely on evidence that is not admissible in court. Because there was no evidence that the test was inaccurate, denial of benefits was supported by substantial evidence. [*Ciaravino*, Unempl. Ins. Rep. (CCH) ¶ 10,213 (Mich. App. 2008)]

A claimant's successful appeal of denial of benefits did not entitle him to a civil remedy against his former employer under the state drug testing law. The state statute ruled out remedies where the drug test was required by federal law, and his ex-employer was a defense contractor. [*Welcher*, Unempl. Ins. Rep. (CCH) ¶ 9085 (Iowa App. 2006)]

## § 32.03  CALCULATION OF BENEFITS

## [A]  Basic Calculation

The actual benefit depends either on the claimant's average weekly wage, or the wage earned in the quarter of the base period when wages were highest. For partial weeks of unemployment, a reduced benefit is available, although the various states use different calculation methods.

Individual claimants are usually assigned a 52-week "benefit year," beginning when the claim is filed, although some states use the same benefit year for all claimants. Usually, a one-week waiting period is imposed before benefits become payable. Most states limit the payment of basic benefits to 26 weeks, although a few states permit 30 weeks of payments. Once claimants use up the basic benefit, they must wait until the next benefit year before starting another base period and therefore qualifying for unemployment benefits all over again. So someone who receives benefits in a particular benefit year will have to be re-employed and work for at least a second base period before qualifying for a second benefit period.

## [B]  Benefit Offsets

Benefit offsets may be applied in two situations: if the unemployment benefit is reduced because other income is received, or if the UI benefits offset other amounts that the person would otherwise be entitled to receive.

As noted above, payments (e.g., pension, IRA) reduce entitlement to unemployment compensation if they can be traced to work done by the employee in the past. The offset is applied only to a plan maintained or contributed to by the company that was the employer during the base payment period, or the employer that is chargeable with the unemployment claim. So if the pension was earned at Company A, but the worker became unemployed while working for Company A, pension will not offset the unemployment insurance benefit.

States differ in their treatment of rollovers. Some states (e.g., New York and North Carolina) require a reduction of unemployment benefits because of rollovers; the other states do not. The Department of Labor's interpretation is that rollovers should not reduce unemployment benefits, but each state is permitted to set its own unemployment rules; this is not an exclusively federal area of regulation. [See Dori R. Perrucci, *When Pension and Unemployment Checks Don't Mix*, N.Y. Times, Jan. 13, 2001, at Bus. 8] Furthermore, reduction is necessary only for amounts based on the claimant's own past work history, not when a person receiving benefits gets a distribution as a surviving spouse.

A claimant's failure to report part-time income was caused by mistake and bad communications, rather than fraudulent intent, so he was required to repay the overpayment but was not subject to fraud penalties. [*Orzel*, Unempl. Ins. Rep. (CCH) ¶ 8655 (N.J. Super. Ct. 2006)]

About half the states deny unemployment benefits in weeks in which Worker's Compensation benefits are also received, or consider the Comp benefit income that reduces the benefit. (There is also a question of whether someone whose condition is bad enough to justify Comp benefits is "ready and able" to work even if he or she wants to work.)

Vacation pay also generally offsets unemployment benefits although an exception might be made if the claimant is deemed to be on vacation involuntarily rather than choosing to take time off.

Back pay awarded in a Title VII case generally is not reduced by UI. However, some courts, like the Second Circuit, say that courts that hear Title VII cases have discretion to reduce the award to account for UI received. A nurse for the Federal Department of Veterans Affairs was terminated, appealed her termination, and received unemployment benefits in the interim before she was reinstated with back pay. The plain language of the Federal Back Pay Act provides that people who receive a back pay award are deemed to have performed services during that period. Hence, the claimant had remuneration and it was proper to order payback of unemployment benefits received in the interim. [*Braselton*, Unempl. Ins. Rep. (CCH) ¶ 10,221 (Ohio App. 2008)]

## § 32.04  EXPERIENCE RATING

### [A]  Determination of Rating

The unemployment insurance rate that employers pay to help fund the system is partially based on their "experience" (the number of claims against them). The more claims, the higher the insurance rate. Seasonal businesses in particular often have a regular pattern of laying off workers who rely on UI until they are rehired.

The standard rate is 5.4%, although many employers qualify for a more favorable experience rate because of their record of few discharges and layoffs. The treatment of new employers varies from state to state. Some states impose a higher initial rate, until the employer can demonstrate its compliance with filing and payment requirements and its low experience of unemployment. On the other hand, some states have a special low rate for new employers until and unless they demonstrate bad claims experience. Some states even allow a zero rate (no tax at all) on employers with especially good claims experience. But all employers may become subject to the standard rate, and perhaps even additional "subsidiary contributions" if the state as a whole has a high unemployment rate and consequently has a low balance in its UI fund. A few states (Alaska, New Jersey, Pennsylvania) also require employee contributions to the system.

Employers in over half the states owe billions of dollars to the federal government for UI benefits. Thirty-five of the states borrowed federal money because their UI trust funds were too small to cope with recession-related unemployment. Seven of them opted to cut benefits to unemployment claimants to repay the federal loan. One problem with the current system is that the wage bases are so low, making it difficult for states to collect significant amounts. In over half of the states, the base is $15,000 or less. Federal law merely requires the state base to be as high as the federal base, which has been unchanged (at $7,000) since 1983. In

1983, that was 40% of the average wage, but it is now less than 20% of the average wage, and a small fraction of the FICA base. States are allowed to make voluntary repayments of federal loans at times when their UI contributions are greater than outgoing benefit payments. Theoretically, states can use general revenues to repay the federal government, but that is difficult when unemployment is rife and states have large and growing deficits. [Jasmine Tucker, *Employers in Many States Face Tax Hike to Help Repay Federal UI Loans*, National Academy of Social Insurance (Feb. 3, 2012) (benefitslink.com); Sara Murray, *Benefits Tax Hits Businesses Twice*, WSJ .com (Sept. 28, 2011)]

There are four basic methods of experience rating:

- Variations in payroll over time (showing whether the workforce has increased or decreased);

- Reserve ratio;

- Benefit ratio;

- Ratio of benefits to wages.

Some states use hybrid methods. States often permit joint filing and risk pooling: joint payment by a group of employers who get a combined experience rate for the group as a whole. A further refinement is a distinction between "charging" and "noncharging" claims. Some claims are not charged against the last employer's experience rating: for instance, claims for very brief periods of unemployment, or cases where the employee spent very little time working for the last employer. In some states, the employer is not charged for benefits paid after a period of disqualification based on voluntary quitting or misconduct, or when benefits are terminated because of the claimant's failure to seek suitable work. The rationale is that employers should not be penalized for circumstances beyond their control.

Another question is whether all employers in the base period, or only the last one in the series, will be charged with the claim. If more than one employer is charged, they might be charged with the most recent employer charged first, or the charge might be divided proportionate to the amount of wages they paid during the base period.

States vary greatly in their UI wage bases. The wage base is $7,000 in Arizona and California; $7,700 in Louisiana; $8,000 in Alabama, Florida, Kansas, and Virginia; $8,500 in Maryland, New York, and Pennsylvania; $9,000 in the District of Columbia, Nebraska, Ohio, Tennessee, and Texas; $9,300 in Kentucky, $9,500 in Georgia, Indiana and Michigan; $10,500 in Delaware;

$11, 300 in Colorado; $12,000 in Arkansas, Maine, South Carolina, and West Virginia; $12,900 in Illinois; $13,000 in Missouri and South Dakota; $14,000 in Massachusetts, Mississippi, New Hampshire, and Wisconsin; $15,000 in Connecticut; $16,000 in Vermont; $20,100 in Oklahoma; $20,200 generally, but $21,700 for some employers, in Rhode Island; $20,900 in North Carolina; $22,900 in New Mexico; $23,800 in Wyoming; $26,000 in Iowa; $26,900 in Nevada; $27,900 in Montana; $29,000 in Minnesota; $30,300 in Utah; $30,900 in New Jersey; $31,800 in North Dakota; $34,100 in Oregon; $34,800 in Idaho; $36,900 in Alaska; $39,600 in Hawaii; and $39,800 in Washington State. (In 2012, Hawaii had the highest wage base, but it traded places with Washington State in 2013.) [*Significant Provisions of State Unemployment Insurance Laws Effective January 2013*, <http://www.ows.doleta.gov/unemploy/content/sigpros/2010-2019/January2013.pdf>]

Each year's edition of *Significant Provisions* also includes state-by-state data about the weekly benefit amount, number of benefit weeks available, and the minimum, maximum, and new employer rates of unemployment tax.

"SUTA dumping," to avoid the federal State Unemployment Tax Act, is the practice of transferring employees from a unit with high turnover (which increases unemployment tax liability) to one with low turnover, then eliminating the first unit and creating a new unit for further transfers. According to Kelly Services, the practice began in the mid-1990s, but was fairly rare then because the economy was booming; it gained attractiveness after the 2001 stock market crash. [Michael Schroeder, *Tax Dodge Faces Extinction*, Wall St. J., Aug. 4, 2004, at A4] Congress considered this practice such a threat to the soundness of the unemployment insurance system that it passed legislation, the SUTA Dumping Prevention Act of 2004, Pub. L. No. 108-295.

## [B]  Collateral Estoppel

Two related legal doctrines, collateral estoppel and res judicata, may come into play in contesting unemployment claims. An employer's unsuccessful contest of one worker's claim could harm the employer in later lawsuits. Legal advice is required as to the comparative risk of letting a claim go through without opposition (which will increase the employer's experience rating and therefore its rates) or contesting the claim but losing and being at a disadvantage when similar claims are made later.

The doctrine of res judicata refers to a matter that has already been tried. If one court has already dealt with a case, a higher court may handle an appeal of the matter, but a different court, which is not in the same line of authority, will not decide a matter that has already been decided. The doctrine of res judicata applies only to the same legal issues and the same or closely related parties. So if one employee sues his or her employer for race discrimination, the defense of res judicata will not be available if a different employee sues another employer for race discrimination. But Employee A's suit against Company B may have "collateral estoppel" effect on Employee C's suit against Company B, because Employee A's suit involves decisions on some basic issues about Company B's policies.

Either side can use collateral estoppel. In a later court case, the employer says that the administrative decision proves that the employee was guilty of misconduct, so terminating the employee was not wrongful. [See Chapter 39 for wrongful termination suits] The employee might assert that having received unemployment benefits proves that he or she did not quit and was not guilty of misconduct. Usually, administrative decisions in an unemployment matter will be granted collateral estoppel effect—but some states say that only a court decision can have that effect.

According to the Third Circuit, the ALJ's holding of misconduct in his unemployment compensation hearing did not prevent the employee from bringing suit for wrongful discharge. The station agent says that he put $80 for a ticket change fee in a drawer near the boarding gate, but the money was not entered into the computer system. The passenger complained when he was charged again for the fee that he paid in cash. The ticket agent was fired for violating the airline's rules. The unemployment ALJ denied benefits for questionable conduct and violation of procedure. In the Virgin Islands, the rule is that an unemployment insurance finding of misconduct does not preclude a wrongful discharge claim, because the two laws have different objectives. The facts and issues are different, and the wrongful termination statute does not refer to misconduct, so finding that the employee was guilty of misconduct does not resolve the issue of wrongful termination. [*Gonzalez v. AMR*, 548 F.3d 219 (3d Cir. 2008)]

## [C]  Planning Steps to Reduce Unemployment Tax Liability

The unemployment insurance system is designed to stabilize employment, so it penalizes employers who dislocate workers unnecessarily. Terminated employees often find it much easier to get a new job if their employment record indicates that they quit instead of being fired. Agreeing to treat the termination as a resignation can benefit both employer and employee, if the employer's experience rate stays low. But employees must understand the effect that the characterization of the termination will have on their UI application.

Companies can take various steps to reduce their experience rating and therefore their liability for unemployment tax:

- Understanding the nature and interaction of the federal and state payroll taxes;

- Reducing FUTA payments appropriately to compensate for state tax payments;

- Making sure taxes are paid when due;

- Reviewing state experience records for correctness;

- Understanding the experience rating system and the claims appeal procedure;

- Transferring employees within the organization instead of terminating them, to reduce unemployment claims;

- Analyzing operations to see if they could be made more consistent, less seasonal (thus avoiding layoffs and terminations);

- Firing unsatisfactory employees quickly, before they become eligible for benefits;

- Holding exit interviews with employees who quit, with a view to resolving problems that lead to resignations;

- Scheduling layoffs for Fridays, not earlier in the week wherever possible, because all the states provide benefits for partial weeks of employment;

- Maintaining adequate documentation of misconduct (which will also be useful if the terminated employee makes discrimination or wrongful termination claims);

- Monitoring all benefit claims and appealing claims that the company believes to be unfounded (e.g., employees who quit asserting involuntary termination).

The laws in over half the states (Arkansas, Arizona, Colorado, Georgia, Indiana, Kansas, Kentucky, Louisiana, Maine, Massachusetts, Michigan, Minnesota, Missouri, Nebraska, North Carolina, North Dakota, New Jersey, New Mexico, New York, Ohio, Pennsylvania, South Dakota, Texas, Washington, Wisconsin, West Virginia) allow employers to make intentional overpayments of unemployment insurance taxes resulting in a lower tax rate for the next tax period; sometimes the numbers work out so that a small voluntary contribution produces a large reduction in future liabilities. [Equifax Workforce Solutions, *State Unemployment Tax Savings—Voluntary Contributions*, <http://www.talx.com/News/ TaxIntelligence/ETS-Tax-Intelligence-Voluntary-Contributions-November-2012. pdf> (November 2012)]

## § 32.05  ADMINISTRATION AND APPEALS

Traditionally, states required in-person application for unemployment benefits; now virtually all the states permit claims to be filed remotely (e.g., via telephone or the Internet). If and when an ex-employee applies for UI benefits, the employer is asked for the reason for the termination. The employer is given a certain number of days to contest the claim. Once this period elapses, the employer can no longer protest the granting of benefits. If the employer objects to the grant of benefits, the state agency that administers unemployment benefits will assess the matter. The decision can be appealed to an Administrative Law Judge, an administrative board, and finally through the state court system (the federal courts are not appropriate for these questions).

If the employer fails to meet its burden of proof about the employee's disqualification at the administrative hearing, the case will not be remanded to give the employer another chance—and a remand will probably not be granted to submit additional evidence [Holmes, *Unempl. Ins. Rep.* (CCH) ¶ 8664 (La. App. 2001)], so it's important to prepare well for the initial administrative hearing.

## § 32.06  FUTA COMPLIANCE

Employers (but not employees) have an obligation to make payments under the Federal Unemployment Tax Act (FUTA) to fund the federal program of unemployment insurance. The general rule is that the basic federal FUTA tax rate is 6.2%, but this tax is imposed only on the first $7,000 of wages. The states set their own taxable wage bases. Starting with calendar 2010, the 6.2% FUTA rate drops to 6.0%. Most employers actually pay a lower rate, because they qualify for a 5.4% credit for state employment taxes they have already paid. This is sometimes referred to as the "normal credit" or "90% credit." Sometimes the company will qualify for an even lower FUTA rate if its experience rating is good. The additional credit equals the difference between the basic state rate of 5.4% and the employer's actual experience rate. However, the full credit can be claimed only in states that the Department of Labor certifies as compliant with federal requirements. To qualify for the full credit, the employer must make all state contributions by January 31 (the due date for Form 940). For 2010 and later years, the effective tax rate therefore can be as low as 0.6%. [*Unemployment Insurance Tax Topic: Unemployment Insurance Taxes*, < http://workforcesecurity.doleta.gov/unemploy/uitaxtopic.asp> (Jan. 9, 2012)]

The employer reports its FUTA liability on IRS Form 940. See IRS Tax Topics, Topic 759 for an explanation of depositing FUTA taxes and filing Form 940. [<http://www.irs.gov/taxtopics/tc759.html>] In 2006, the IRS discontinued the short-form Form 940-EZ, but redesigned Form 940 to be more logical and easier to use.

# CHAPTER 33

# WORKER'S COMPENSATION

## § 33.01  INTRODUCTION

The states administer the Worker's Compensation ("Worker's Compensation" or WC) system to provide income to individuals who are unable to work because of employment-related illnesses and injuries. WC benefits, like unemployment insurance benefits, are funded by insurance maintained by the employer.

The WC system balances the interests of employers and employees: the employees' need for continuing income; the employer's need to have claims resolved quickly, in an administrative system that is not prone to make large sympathy awards the way the jury system is. Employers have a duty to make a prompt report of all accidents to the agency that administers the WC system. If an employee claims job-related injury or illness, the claim is heard by a WC tribunal. Depending on the state, this may be referred to as a board or a commission. The tribunal decides if the claim is valid. If so, benefits are awarded: reimbursement of medical expenses, plus weekly income.

WC benefits do not begin until a waiting period (typically three to seven days) has elapsed. This serves to distinguish genuine temporary disability from minor incidents without lasting consequences. However, most state WC laws also provide that, if a disability continues for a period of time (set by the state at anywhere from five days to over seven weeks), retroactive payments dating back to the original date of the injury will be granted.

The weekly benefit is usually limited to half to two-thirds of the pre-accident wage, subject to fixed minimum and maximum payments (often keyed to the state's average income) and also subject to an overall limitation on payments. In some states, additional payments are available if the worker has dependent children—especially in cases where the work-related incident caused the death of the worker. A burial benefit is also paid in death cases. Depending on the state it ranges between $1,000 and $5,000.

In late 2011, the California Supreme Court had to determine how to calculate cost of living increases under a 2002 statute and decided that COLAs are prospective from January 1 of the first year after the date of initial receipt of payments—unfortunately for the claimant because the court of appeal had treated all COLAs as retroactive to January 1, 2004, no matter when the injury occurred. [*Baker v. Workers' Comp Appeals Bd. and XS*, 52 Cal. 4th 434 (Cal. 2011); see Rebecca Moore, *Employers Win in CA Workers Comp COLA Case*, plansponsor .com (Aug. 12, 2011)]

In 1999, the Supreme Court decided a Worker's Compensation case, *American Manufacturers Mut. Ins. Co. v. Sullivan.* [526 U.S. 46 (1999)] Under Pennsylvania's WC Act, once liability is no longer contested, the employer (or its insurer) has an obligation to pay for all reasonable or necessary treatment. However, an insurer or a self-insured employer is permitted to withhold payment for disputed treatment pending utilization review by an independent third party. The Supreme Court ruled that private insurers doing utilization review are not "state actors" subject to the Due Process clause of the Constitution. Employees have no property rights until treatments have been found reasonable and necessary. Therefore, the insurer has no obligation to notify employees, or to hold a hearing, if it withholds benefits until review has been completed and a decision made in the employees' favor.

The Pennsylvania Superior Court ruled in 2010 that it was not an invasion of privacy to tape a WC claimant while he was praying: claimants have a diminished expectation of privacy and are aware that they may become the subjects of an investigation. Pennsylvania does not have an explicit rule about the amount of privacy required in religious settings; the Superior Court agreed with the trial court that the mosque was a public place, and the investigator had a right to stand in the parking lot across from the mosque to observe the claimant praying in front of a plate glass window. [*Tagouma v. Investigative Consultant Servs. Inc.*, 2010 Pa. Super. 147 (Pa. Super. 2010); see Rebecca Moore, *Videotaping Workers Comp Claimant Praying not Invasion of Privacy*, plansponsor.com (Aug. 16, 2010)]

A 2010 press release issued by the New York State Insurance Department reports that Alexis Muniz was sentenced to restitution and three years' probation when a Facebook posting showed that she stole $8,975 in WC benefits, collected while she was working full time. She boasted on her Facebook page about how much she earned as an apartment manager. [Fred Schneyer, *Facebook Posting Reveals Workers Comp Theft*, plansponsor.com (Sept. 14, 2010)]

## § 33.02  CLASSIFICATION OF BENEFITS

### [A]  Type and Degree of Disability

If the initial tribunal accepts the contention that the worker is genuinely disabled, and the disability is in fact work-related, benefits are awarded based on the type and degree of disability.

There are four categories:

- Permanent total disability;
- Permanent partial disability;
- Temporary total disability;
- Temporary partial disability.

Permanent disability payments can be based on wage loss, earning capacity, physical impairment, or some combination. A "schedule injury" is loss of a finger, toe, arm, eye, or leg. The schedule determines the number of weeks of benefits payable for such an injury. Death benefits are also available to the survivors of persons killed in work-related incidents. For injuries such as back strains related to lifting, the tribunal must make a case-by-case determination of the number of weeks of disability that can be anticipated, and the seriousness of the disability.

Benefits can be granted for either "disability" or "impairment." The difference is that disability is defined to mean loss of wages, whereas impairment is permanent partial disability that does not cause wage loss.

The concept of Maximum Medical Improvement (MMI) comes into play in the case of a temporary disability. MMI is a doctor's opinion that there is no reasonable medical probability of further improvement in function (as determined based on factors such as current and proposed treatment, history of improvement, and pre-existing conditions). Most states impose an obligation on the employer to notify the employee that MMI has been reached, and the employee is likely to lose benefits within 90 days unless he or she returns to work or finds other employment. Benefits can be extended past the MMI if the claimant makes an honest effort yet cannot find suitable work.

The New York Court of Appeals ruled in mid-2012 that the Workers' CompensationBoard can draw an inference that reduction in future earnings is the result of the disability, whether the claimant has completely stopped working or merely stopped working at the job held before the disability occurred. But this inference is merely permitted—it is not mandatory that the Board find this way. A Board's finding that a claimant failed to make a reasonable search for suitable work is a fact determination, so it must be upheld by an appellate court as long as it is supported by substantial evidence. [*In re Zamora v. N.Y. Neurologic Assocs.*, 19 N.Y.3d 186, 970 N.E.2d 823, 947 N.Y.S.2d 788 (2012). See *Burns v. Varriale*, 9 N.Y.3d 207, 879 N.E.2d 140, 849 N.Y.S.2d 1 (2007) on attachment to the labor force.]

In addition to making wage-based payments, the employer must provide the employee with reasonable and necessary medical treatment, continued as long as the injured employee's medical condition requires. Most states include chiropractic in the definition of medical care. Many include home health attendants as well.

In two 2009 cases, the Utah Supreme Court allowed employers and insurers to reduce Worker's Compensation medical expenses to reflect only the work-related portion of a claimant's injury. One case involved carpal tunnel syndrome, which the ALJ found to be only 10% work-related. The other case involved a lower back injury. The Utah Supreme Court interpreted state law to mean that, because medical benefits compensate the injured worker, only the part of the medical benefit reflecting the work-related part of the injury should be the responsibility of the WC system. [*Ameritech Library Servs. v. Utah Labor Comm'n*, 2009 UT 20 (2009); *Dale T. Smith Sons v. Utah Labor Comm'n*, 2009 UT 19 (2009); see Rebecca Moore, *UT Court Says Employers Can Apportion Worker's Comp*, plansponsor.com (Apr. 10, 2009)]

However, at about the same time, the Utah Supreme Court also held that it is unconstitutional to reduce Workers' Compensation benefits to offset Social

Security benefits. The agency argued that coordinating the benefits served the valid purpose of keeping the insurance fund solvent, but the Utah Supreme Court said that reducing Workers' Compensation benefits for disabled persons over 65 does not achieve this objective, and that Social Security benefits and Workers' Compensation benefits serve different purposes and are not substitutes for one another. (The law that was struck down provided that someone who qualified for both benefits, and who had received 312 weeks of Workers' Compensation, the Workers' Compensation benefits would be reduced by 50% of the Social Security benefit.) [*Merrill v. Utah Labor Comm'n*, 2009 UT 74 (2009); Rebecca Moore, *Social Security Offset of Workers' Comp Unconstitutional*, plansponsor .com (Apr. 28, 2009)]

A 2011 Georgia Court of Appeals decision permitted aggravation of an injured employee's condition by light duty work to be treated as a new injury because the job responsibilities changed and the claimant was not performing his normal or ordinary duties. The claimant was an assistant pressman who suffered a work-related neck and arm injury in October 2002. He had carpal tunnel surgery and received WC benefits, including permanent partial disability. He returned to light duty work (including quality control and fulfillment) in mid-2003 with a permanent restriction on lifting, pushing, or pulling over 15 pounds. He said that the work exceeded his medical restrictions 40% of the time but his supervisors refused to modify the assignment. He was laid off in April 2008 and had lumbar fusion surgery in October 2008. He filed a claim for medical and temporary total disability benefits, which was granted because he worked under strenuous new circumstances that exceeded his light duty restriction. [*R.R. Donnelley v. Ogletree*, 312 Ga. App. 475 (2011); see Tara Cantore, *Employee Eligible for New Comp Claim Based on New Injury*, plansponsor.com (Oct. 24, 2011)]

## [B] Compensable Injuries

Whether an incident is covered by WC depends on several factors, e.g., employee status and the connection between employment and the injury.

It is significant whether the injured person is a common-law employee rather than an independent contractor. Early in 2002, California ruled that even a hirer of an independent contractor can be liable to the contractor (or employees of the contractor) if, for example, the hirer provides unsafe equipment or makes another affirmative contribution to the injury—merely controlling safety conditions at the site is not enough to impose liability. [*McKown v. Wal-Mart Stores Inc.*, 27 Cal. 4th 219, 38 P.3d 1094, 115 Cal. Rptr. 2d 868 (2002); *Hooker v. DOT*, 27 Cal. 4th 198, 38 P.3d 1081, 115 Cal. Rptr. 2d 853 (2002)]

The California Court of Appeal struck down a state statute that mandates a payment of $250,000 to the estate of employees without dependents if their death is work-related. According to the court, the statute is unconstitutional: making estates automatic beneficiaries would require an amendment to the state

Constitution, because California law does not permit expansion of the class of WC beneficiaries past the list provided in the state Constitution. Furthermore, the policy reason for having WC laws is to support workers or their dependents after job-related injury or death, and payments to the estate do not serve this purpose. [*Six Flags, Inc. v. Workers' Comp Appeals Bd.*, 145 Cal. App. 4th 91 (2006); see Rebecca Moore, *CA Court Denies Workers' Comp to Estate*, plansponsor .com (Nov. 29, 2006). The statute is Labor Code § 4702(a)(6)(B)]

Sometimes injuries occurring outside the workplace will be covered—e.g., if the employer sent the employee to make a delivery or perform an errand, and the injury occurred in that place or en route. Injuries occurring during employer-sponsored athletics, or at a company picnic or holiday party, are probably compensable. Injuries on company premises during scheduled breaks are probably compensable, but employees take unscheduled breaks at their own risk because such injuries are considered to occur outside working hours. If employees are engaged in work-related tasks, injuries occurring at home can be compensable. [*A.E. Clevite, Inc. v. Tjas*, 996 P.2d 1072 (Utah App. 2000) (worker who became a paraplegic when he slipped while salting down his driveway so it would be safe for the expected delivery of a work-related package)]

In 2007, Georgia upheld the award of WC benefits to the dependent 11-year-old son of a worker killed in the crash of a company vehicle, even though the decedent was a Florida resident who was delivering his family's furniture to a storage facility while he was on sick leave. Georgia applied the "continuous employment" doctrine: benefits are available whenever an employee is required to live and work within an area accessible to the job site. The decedent had to take a temporary residence in Georgia to supervise a construction job. The Georgia court did not deem his medical leave status to make the continuous employment doctrine inapplicable. [*Ray Bell Constr. Co. v. King*, 281 Ga. 853 (2007); see Adrien Martin, *Workers' Comp Award Upheld on Grounds of "Continuous Employment*," plansponsor.com (Mar. 29, 2007); Alyson M. Palmer, *Ga. High Court Ruling May Widen Workers' Comp Net for Traveling Employees*, Fulton County Daily Report (Mar. 29, 2007) (law.com)]

The Maine Supreme Judicial Court held that a worker who was injured when returning to work from a lunch break was entitled to benefits, because the staircase where she fell was part of the workplace. The employer said that under the "coming and going principle," the injury was not compensable because an accident off premises when an employee goes to or from work is not in the course of employment. But the Maine court granted benefits because injury occurred during an "insubstantial deviation" from employment; she was not reckless; and she did not violate work rules. [*Fournier v. Aetna, Inc.*, 2006 ME 71, 899 A.2d 787 (2006); see Rebecca Moore, *Worker Who Fell Returning from Lunch Is Entitled to Benefits*, plansponsor.com (June 16, 2006)]

Early in 2010, the South Carolina Supreme Court ruled that a packing house seasonal worker who broke an ankle in the barracks provided by his employer was entitled to Worker's Compensation, even though he was not working at the time the injury occurred. The court ruled that migrant workers did not earn enough to be able to afford other housing (and there were no short-term rentals available anyway), so in effect they were required to live on the grounds of the packing house. The living arrangement accommodated the employer's work schedule, which varied with weather and crop conditions. The plaintiff was injured in a fall before his first day of work, when he fell on a sidewalk that was wet with water from the outdoor sink used to wash clothes. The court cited decisions in four other states applying the "bunkhouse rule," where WC benefits are available to injured workers who are hurt on the employer's premises when they are required to be there. [*Pierre v. Seaside Farms*, 386 S.C. 534, 689 S.E.2d 615 (S.C. 2010), see Fred Schneyer, *SC High Court Rules for Injured Migrant Worker*, plansponsor .com (Feb. 17, 2010)]

The Pennsylvania Workers' Compensation Appeal Board denied benefits to the surviving spouse of a sales manager who died days after being found injured in his home office. The denial was based on the grounds that he was not acting in the scope or course of employment when he was injured. His wife said that he fell at the front entrance to the home on a day when he had been working, and eventually died of blunt force head injuries. The appeal board said that it was unknown what he was doing when he fell so it could not be assumed to be a work-related injury. [Rebecca Moore, *Spouse of Worker Found Dead in Home Office Denied Benefits*, plansponsor.com (Sept. 6, 2011)]

Whether an incident is covered by WC may also depend on whether it results from an "accident" (an unexpected occurrence with a definite time, place, and occasion) and whether there is any reason to remove the incident from coverage (e.g., the employee's substance abuse was a causative factor).

Connecticut allowed benefits for an employee whose shoulders were dislocated when fellow-workers tried to restrain him during a seizure to prevent him from hurting himself. The court attributed the injury to the restraint, not the seizure. The employer's argument was that awarding WC benefits would discourage co-workers from trying to offer aid, but the court said that potential good Samaritans would not distinguish between potential WC and non-WC cases. [*Blakeslee v. Platt Bros. & Co.*, 279 Conn. 239 (Conn. 2006), discussed in Adrien Martin, *Employee Awarded Workers Comp for Injuries from Helpful Coworkers*, plansponsor.com (Aug. 1, 2006)]

One of the most vital factors is the employer's degree of control over the employee's activities. A Missouri case [*Leslie v. School Servs. & Leasing Inc.*, 947 S.W.2d 97 (Mo. App. 1997)] holds that a job applicant injured during training had not become an "employee," and therefore was not covered by WC. In this case, the potential employer didn't require her to take the training, didn't control her activities during the training process, and in fact didn't even guarantee her a job if she completed the training successfully.

In 2004, the New Jersey Supreme Court ruled that injuries occurring during a recreational or social activity can come under WC provided that the employee believed that he or she was required to engage in the activity. [*Lozano v. De Luca*

*Constr. Co.*, 178 N.J. 513; 842 A.2d 156 (N.J. Super. Ct. App. Mar. 2004). Note that N.J.S.A. § 34:15-7 allows payment of WC benefits for recreational injuries sustained through activities that are a regular incident of employment and produce benefit for the employer over and above improved employee fitness and morale]

At-work assaults raise difficult questions. The general rule is that injuries caused by assaults are compensable if the job increases the risk of encountering dangerous people (e.g., convenience store clerks are at risk of being robbed). But if the assault occurred for personal reasons, for instance if an abusive spouse commits an assault at the victim's workplace, the fact that the assault occurred at work will not necessarily render the injury a compensable one, if it is not work-related in any way. The WC system is essentially a no-fault system, so it will not be necessary to decide if the employer was at fault in not having a better security system. Virginia refused to apply WC exclusivity in the case of a paramedic who had a seizure and died three days after a co-worker deliberately shocked her with live defibrillator paddles, because an assault or horseplay is purely personal and not attributable to the employer. [*Hilton v. Martin, Va.*, 275 Va. 176 (2008), discussed in Fred Schneyer, *VA Paramedic's Death Ruled Outside Workers' Comp Coverage*, plansponsor.com (Feb. 12, 2008)]

The Delaware Supreme Court allowed an employee injured by horseplay to bring a personal injury suit against the co-workers who injured him. The court used the four-part "Larson Test" (named after the treatise Larson's Workers' Compensation Law): the scope and seriousness of the deviation of the conduct from employment activities; if the conduct was separate from work duties or commingled with them; if the nature of the job typically includes horseplay; and whether the employer tolerated horseplay. In this case, a pipefitter/welder sued three co-workers for wrapping him in duct tape; he had to have back and knee surgery and counseling after the injury. He sued the co-workers for more than $74,000 in medical expenses and $142,000 lost wages and also sought future medical expenses. The Delaware Supreme Court remanded the case for a determination of whether the prank fell outside the scope of employment. [*Grabowski v. Mangler*, 938 A.2d 637 (Del. 2007). See Sheri Qualters, *A New Test for Workplace* "Horseplay," Nat'l L.J. (July 19, 2007)] On remand, the Delaware Supreme Court upheld summary judgment for the defendants. The injuries occurred at a time when there was no work to be done; horseplay was so frequent as to be an accepted part of the workday; and the prank was performed quickly without substantial abandonment of duties. [*Grabowski v. Mangler*, 956 A.2d 1217 (Del. 2008)]

*Schmidt v. Smith* [155 N.J. 44, 713 A.2d 1014 (1998)] says that bodily injury caused by sexual harassment is covered by the employer liability section of the Worker's Compensation insurance policy, because this section of the policy is designed to make funds available to compensate employees for their work-related injuries, even those for which Worker's Compensation payments are not available.

The Pennsylvania Supreme Court, without really exploring the policy issues, upheld a lower court's determination to uphold an award of Worker's Compensation benefits to an illegal alien, on the grounds that the employer did not show that the injured person failed to satisfy the requirements of a section of the Worker's Compensation Act. However, if the employer applies for suspension of such benefits, the employer does not have to make a showing of job availability. [*Reinforced Earth Co. v. WC Appeals Bd. (Astudillo)*, 810 A.2d 99 (Pa. 2002)] In contrast, *Granados v. Windson Dev. Corp.* [257 Va. 103, 509 S.E.2d 290 (1999)], held that an alien who was hired after submitting forged immigration documents could not become a lawful employee entitled to Worker's Compensation, because no employment contract could be formed.

In mid-2005, the Eleventh Circuit ruled that an allegation that an employer hired illegal workers as part of a conspiracy to reduce wages and cut the number of WC claims stated RICO and state-law claims. [*Williams v. Mohawk Indus. Inc.*, 411 F.3d 1252 (11th Cir. 2005). Certiorari was granted in December 2005, but the case was never heard: certiorari was dismissed as improvidently granted in June 2006, and the case was remanded to the Eleventh Circuit: No. 05-465 547 U.S. 516 (June 5, 2006)]

The Second Circuit approved an award of lost earnings to an undocumented alien worker after he was crippled in a fall attributed to violations of the scaffolding requirements for work sites. New York case law specifically rejects the concept that the damages should be limited on the basis of what the worker would earn in his or her home country. The jury awarded $638,671.63 in compensatory damages, including about $93,000 for incurred expenses, $46,000 for past pain and suffering, $40,000 for lost earnings, $230,000 for future pain and suffering over the plaintiff's predicted life expectancy, and $230,000 for 26 years of future lost earnings. [*Madeira v. Affordable Hous. Found. Inc.*, 469 F.3d 219 (2d Cir. 2006). See *also Majlinger v. Cassino Contracting Corp.*, 25 A.D.3d 4, 802 N.Y.S.2d 56 (2d Dept. 2005) allowing compensation for lost U.S. earnings at U.S. rates, holding that this does not conflict with the federal immigration statute, IRCA; *Flores v. Limehouse*, No. 2:04-1295-CWH 2006 U.S. Dist. LEXIS 30433 (D.S.C. May 11, 2006) holding that IRCA does not preempt claims by undocumented workers against their employers under RICO and federal and state labor law—even if the workers obtained employment fraudulently; *Rosa v. Partners in Progress, Inc.*, 868 A.2d 994 (N.H. 2005) (for undocumented worker to be able to make a tort claim, the employer must have known or have a duty to know the worker's employment was illegal)]

When an illegal alien worker was injured in a fall from a roof, the Louisiana Court of Appeal found three parties, including Vaughan Roofing, liable for providing WC benefits. When Vaughan Roofing appealed, the Supreme Court denied certiorari, refusing to decide whether I.R.C. preempts the state ruling that illegal workers are entitled to WC benefits. [*Vaughan Roofing & Sheet Metal LLC v.*

*Rodriguez, cert. denied,* 131 S. Ct. 1572 (2011); see Plansponsor staff, *U.S. Supreme Court Turns Away Illegal Immigrant Case,* plansponsor.com (Mar. 2, 2011)]

Tennessee awarded survivor benefits to foreign nationals (Mexicans) who were dependents of a worker who died in a work-related accident, although the court found they were not wholly dependent on remittances from their son and therefore the case remanded to determine the correct benefit to be paid. [*Fusner v. Coop Constr. Co.,* 211 S.W.3d 686 (Tenn. Sup. 2007); see Adrien Martin, *Foreign Nationals Can Be Dependents for TN Workers' Comp [sic] Benefits,* plansponsor.com (Jan. 23, 2007)]

Ohio ruled that David Gross, a teenager who suffered severe burns when cleaning the pressure cooker at work, could collect WC even though he was fired for breaking the safety rules. Previously, the Ohio Supreme Court ruled against Gross, on the grounds that termination for misconduct constituted voluntary abandonment of employment. However, the case went to the Tenth Circuit and then was sent back to state court, and this time, the worker received an award based on the no-fault nature of the WC system. [Adrien Martin, *Worker Who Broke Safety Rules Gets Workers' Comp,* plansponsor.com (Sept. 28, 2007)]

If the incident is covered, the next question is whether WC exclusivity applies. [See § 33.03]

## [C]  Problems of Co-Employment

There are many reasons for employers to use temporary, contingent, part-time, or leased workers. In some cases, employee leasing results in lower WC costs. For employers who do not self-insure, the insurance rate has a lot to do with past experience. The smaller the workplace, the greater the impact that a few claims—especially a few very large claims—will have on its experience rating. That is one of the motivations for using leased workers to replace some or all of a company's common-law employees. [See § 1.09 for more about employee leasing]

Although a large leasing company will not qualify for small business discounted rates, a leasing company can offer the services of a broad range of workers, some in low-risk occupations such as office work.

In its initial years, a leasing company will probably qualify for low rates, because there has not been enough time for many accidents to happen. Abuses of the system are possible, if companies dissolve and re-form to manipulate their experience rates. Just for this reason, some states (e.g., Arizona, California, Colorado, Florida, Nevada, New Hampshire, New Mexico, Oregon, South Carolina, Texas, and Utah) disregard the presence of leasing companies, and still require the underlying employer to buy WC insurance and maintain its own experience rating.

Furthermore, state courts may decide that the leasing company or temporary agency's client is the actual employer, because it has real control over the worker's activities and therefore is legally responsible for compensation for injuries. Both companies might also be treated as co-employers.

Another possibility is that, if the underlying employer takes the position that the leasing company is the true employer, the underlying employer might be treated as a third party that can be sued for tort claims and cannot assert WC exclusivity. The underlying employer might be sued for negligence or for violating established safety rules, and might be forced to pay damages (including punitive damages). Nor would the employee's WC benefits be used to offset the underlying employer's liability in this situation.

The National Association of Insurance Commissioners (NAIC) has drafted an Employee Leasing Registration Model Act under which leasing firms must register with the state before they purchase WC insurance. At the time of registration, they must disclose their ownership and their past WC history. Registration will not be permitted if the company has had its insurance policies terminated in the past for failure to pay premiums.

The "borrowed servant" doctrine says that if an employer lends an employee to someone else to perform a "special service," the recipient of the special service is considered the employer of the borrowed employee if the recipient can control the details of the work. According to the Eighth Circuit, this requires a contract for hire and the employee's consent to the special employment relationship—and the burden of proof is on the party citing the doctrine. Therefore, an employee of the Truck Crane Service Co., injured on a job site operated by Maguire Tank Inc., and who received WC benefits from Truck Crane, nevertheless could sue Maguire Tank. Maguire Tank did not direct or control the injured person's actions. He merely worked there for a day and was not instructed in how to do his job by Maguire Tank employees. In fact, the injury occurred after the job was finished and part of a crane that was being prepared for shipping fell and injured the plaintiff's arm. [*Lundstrom v. Maguire Tank Inc.*, 509 F.3d 864 (8th Cir. 2007)]

In New York, Workers' Compensation Law § 11 forbids an employee to sue his or her employer or co-employer, except under limited circumstances. An employee cannot bring a tort suit against his or her special employer (an employer into whose service the worker has been transferred for a limited time). However, so-called special employers have lost a number of cases in New York because they have failed to prove this defense. It should be raised in the defendant's answer to the complaint. The defense is established by showing that there existed a true employment relationship with the alleged special employer based on factors such as the right to hire and fire, set hours and salary, or supervise and control the employee's work. The most significant factor is who directs the employee's work; setting work hours and training the employee are also significant. A general employer's power to fire the worker does not necessarily preclude a finding of special employment. A person who is a general employee of one employer can be a special employee of another—even if the general employer continues to pay the worker's wages and benefits and maintains WC insurance. The general employment is presumed to continue, but the presumption can be overcome by showing that the general employer surrendered control to the special employer. Usually, the existence of special employment status is a question of fact, but the determination can be made as a matter of law if there are undisputed facts that compel this conclusion, and there is no triable issue of fact. [Eugene O. Morenus and Eileen M. Baumgartner, *Re-Examining the Basics of the Special Employment Defense*, N.Y.L.J. (Nov. 1, 2010) (law.com)]

In Delaware, a general contractor does not have a duty to protect the employees of its independent contractors against the hazards of the contract, unless the general contractor actively controls the manner or method of performing the work, voluntarily undertakes responsibility for safety measures, or controls the premises where the work is done. In a case where a worker was seriously injured after a fall from a roof (he was not wearing a safety harness although he owned one and it was at the job site), Delaware held that the general contractor was not liable, even though it made checklists, informed the independent contractor of safety problems, and even finally terminated the contract because of the safety issues. Delaware held that the Restatement (2d) of Torts § 411 does not create a cause of action by employees of an independent contractor, against the general contractor for failure to use due care in selecting an independent contractor. By and large, employees are restricted to the Worker's Compensation system for work-related injuries, and it would be unfair to permit employees of an independent contractor to sue the general contractor when the general contractor's own employees would be limited to WC for their own comparable injuries. [*Urena v. Capano Homes, Inc.*, 930 A.2d 877 (Del. 2007)]

The Texas Supreme Court ruled that if a general contractor provides Worker's Compensation insurance to a subcontractor, the general contractor cannot be sued for negligence by the subcontractor's employees. A premises owner can be deemed a general contractor if it fits under the definition in the WC Act. [*Entergy v. Summers*, 282 S.W.3d 433 (Tex. 2009); see Fred Schneyer, *General Contractor Deserves Workers' Comp Liability Coverage*, plansponsor.com (Apr. 6, 2009)]

In a choice of law case, an employee of a Nebraska subcontractor was injured while performing demolition work in Kansas. He received WC benefits from his Nebraska employer, but could also have collected from the Kansas general contractor. When he sued the general contractor for negligence in the District Court for the District of Kansas, the question was whether the WC exclusivity provision of Kansas WC law applied; if it did, the suit would have to be dismissed. If it did not, Nebraska law would allow a suit against a responsible third party even if WC benefits had already been received. The Tenth Circuit applied the legal principle of "lex loci delicti": the law of the place where the tort occurred. Under Kansas law, the sole remedy would be WC, and after collecting WC from the direct employer, he could not sue the general contractor for negligence. [*Anderson v. Commerce Constr. Servs. Inc.*, 531 F.3d 1190 (10th Cir. 2008)]

## [D]   How the WC System Handles Disease Claims

WC benefits are also available if an employee develops a work-related disease. However, occupational diseases create some difficult problems of analysis. Disease is covered only if there is a close connection between onset of the disease and the work environment. This is fairly clear for "brown lung" disease and cotton mills, but more difficult if the claim is that nonsmoking employees have been harmed by cigarette smoke exhaled by customers and co-employees who smoke.

Depending on the state, benefits may also be available if workplace conditions aggravate a disease that the individual already had. In California, Florida, Kentucky, Maryland, Mississippi, North Dakota, and South Carolina, WC benefits will be available but will be reduced to compensate for the pre-existing condition. If, for instance, the worker's condition was 25% due to workplace factors, 75% due to the preexisting condition, only 25% of the full benefit will be payable.

Occupational disease creates difficult questions involving "long tail" claims: claims made on the basis that it took years, or even decades, for the symptoms caused by occupational exposure to hazardous substances to manifest themselves. During this long period of time, the employee could have held several jobs (involving exposure to different hazards) and/or engaged in behavior such as smoking that is hazardous or compounds other hazards.

The general rule under the legal system is that claims are timely if they are filed within a reasonable time after the individual first experiences disability or symptoms, and could reasonably be expected to draw a connection between work exposure and illness.

Another question is whether the employee's exposure was extensive enough to trigger the claimed symptoms. The epidemiology (disease pattern) for similar exposures should be studied to see if the employee's alleged experience is typical. Furthermore, one disease claim by an employee could trigger a wave of related claims from other employees who actually are ill, believe themselves to be ill because they have developed psychosomatic symptoms, or who just hope for easy money.

Asbestos-related disease is "bodily injury by disease" rather than "bodily injury by accident" under WC and employer liability insurance policies. Asbestos exposure is not an accident because it is not violent and because it develops over a latency period rather than right away. [*Riverwood Int'l Corp. v. Employers Ins. of Wausau*, 420 F.3d 378 (5th Cir. 2005)]

In a case of separate but concurrent illnesses, only one of them occupational, the Connecticut Supreme Court permitted segregation of lung damage caused by smoking from the respiratory problems caused by working with asbestos—and reduction of the WC award to compensate for damage caused by cigarettes. This is a change from the previous practice of awarding full compensation for blended injuries. WC law requires an injury to have arisen from or occur in the course of employment, but the employer "takes the employee as he finds him." In this case, the Connecticut Supreme Court agreed that the claimant would have been entitled to full compensation if, when he was hired, he had smoking-related emphysema as a preexisting condition, but in this case the two concurrent lung injuries were separate. [*Deschenes v. Transco*, 288 Conn. 303 (Conn. Sup. 2008); see Thomas B. Scheffey, *Workers' Comp Award in Asbestos Case Reduced to Account for Cigarette Usage*, Connecticut Law Tribune (Aug. 14, 2008) (law.com)] An appellate court in New Jersey upheld a $7.5 million jury award to a former Exxon worker and his wife. The court found Exxon liable for Bonnie Anderson's mesothelioma not only because she worked there for 12 years, but because she washed her husband's work clothes for 24 years. The court rejected Exxon's argument that her claim was barred by WC exclusivity, because Exxon took on a separate, independent role with respect to Ms. Anderson's non-occupational exposure to asbestos. (Occupational exposure was ruled out, because her work as an electrician did not involve contact with asbestos.) New Jersey's rule is that employers have a duty to protect the spouses of employees, as well as employees, from asbestos exposure. [*Anderson v. A J Friedman Supply Co. Inc.*, 416 N.J. Super. 46 (2010)]

## [E]  Psychological Injuries

By and large, the WC system deals with palpable physical injuries and diseases, although in some circumstances mental and emotional illnesses can be compensable. Emotional and mental injuries are analyzed in three categories:

- Mental-physical—physical impact of mental conditions, such as chest pains and high blood pressure;

- Physical-mental—such as suffering a phobia after being involved in an accident or developing "AIDS-phobia" after a needle-stick incident;

- Mental-mental—injuries with no physical component.

In all the states, mental-physical and physical-mental injuries are compensable as long as a causal connection between the two is established. Compensability of mental-mental injuries is less clear-cut. Some states, including Alabama, Florida, Georgia, Kansas, Minnesota, Montana, Nebraska, Ohio, Oklahoma, and South Dakota refuse to compensate cases where there is no demonstrated physical involvement. In the other states, it may be necessary to prove a connection to a severe, unpredictable event, and compensability may depend on whether the onset was gradual or sudden.

The Ohio Court of Appeals ruled in 2010 that WC benefits were available to a bank employee who experienced psychological injuries when she saw a police officer shot to death. Ohio has held that a psychiatric injury caused by a compensable injury to a third party is covered by WC, even if the claimant was not physically injured by the incident. [*Rader v. Fifth Third Bancorp.* 09 AP_821 (Ohio App. 2010); see Rebecca Moore, *Bank Worker Who Witnessed Murder Entitled to Workers Comp*, plansponsor.com (Apr. 2, 2010). The court relied on *Bailey v. Republic Engineered Steels Inc.* 91 Oh. St. 3d 38, 741 N. E. 2d 121 (Ohio 2001)]

Rigoberto Garcia suffered a traumatic head injury after falling from a 24-foot ladder while picking avocados. He filed a WC claim for psychiatric injury. He had been employed for about two months at the time of the injury. California's Labor Code § 3208.3(d) generally bars psychiatric injury claims by people employed for less than six months, with an exception for psychiatric injury caused by a sudden and extraordinary employment condition. The California Court of Appeal denied the claim, ruling that falling off a ladder is an occupational hazard of the job. [*State Comp. Ins. Fund v. Workers' Comp. Appeals Bd.*, 204 Cal. App. 4th 766 (Cal. App. 2012)]

The Nevada Supreme Court permitted survivors to file a WC claim if a suicide is closely enough connected to a workplace injury. To prevail, the survivors must show that the industrial injury caused a psychological ailment severe enough to override rational judgment, and that caused the suicide. In this case, a bartender suffered chronic back pain after a workplace fall, and one of his doctors testified that he committed suicide because of the pain. [*Vredenburg v. Sedgwick CMA*, 188 P.3d 1084 (Nev. Sup. 2008); Fred Schneyer, *Nevada High Court Sanctions Worker's Comp Claims for Suicide*, plansponsor.com (July 28, 2008); suicide can be compensable, even if the worker suffered from pre-existing depression, as long as a work-related injury was at least a contributing cause of the suicide: *Altes v. Petrocelli Elec. Co.*, 270 A.D.2d 767 (N.Y. Sup. 2000)]

## § 33.03   WC EXCLUSIVITY

The WC system gives employers the protection of "worker's compensation exclusivity"; in other words, in the normal work-related injury or illness case, the employee's only remedy against the employer is to collect compensation benefits. Tort lawsuits are not permitted. However, exclusivity applies only against the employer. If the employee is injured by a product manufactured by the employer, the employee can sue the employer in its capacity as manufacturer. Suits against other manufacturers, or non-employer parties responsible for hazardous conditions at the workplace, are also a possibility. The employer itself can sue the third party in order to recover the medical benefits that the employer provided on behalf of the employee.

WC is essentially a no-fault system, so negligence by any party is usually irrelevant. However, in some states, a worker's failure to use safety equipment can reduce (but not eliminate) the benefits that would otherwise be payable after an accident. Sometimes, the employer's wrongdoing will take the case out of WC exclusivity. Some (but not all) courts would allow an ordinary tort suit against an employer that deliberately concealed information about workplace hazards.

Compensation benefits will be granted only if the employee has medical evidence to prove the connection between the job and the disabling condition. Furthermore, the employee must be incapacitated by the condition, so benefits will not be awarded to a person who stoically continues to work despite pain. Courts have reached different conclusions as to whether a person is permanently and totally disabled only if there is absolutely no job he or she can perform, or whether "human factors" such as job availability within a reasonable commuting distance must be considered.

There are three categories of workplace assaults for WC purposes. There is an inherent connection if the assault is related to employment, e.g., occurs in connection with an employee's termination. An assault might occur in the course of an inherently private dispute not related to employment, such as violence committed by the employee's spouse or partner. A "neutral force" random assault is committed on an employee outside the employment relationship. Inherent connection assaults are compensable under WC; private dispute assaults are not; neutral force incidents might be depending on circumstances. The "street risk" doctrine requires proof either that employees were indiscriminately exposed to dangers from the public, or the employee was assaulted because of his or her connection with the employer. The Tennessee Supreme Court ruled that WC benefits were not available for the widow of an employee whose murder at the workplace remained unsolved. The decedent opened the store; when the store owner arrived at 6 am, he found the body. The court treated the death as a "neutral force assault." The "street risk" doctrine did not apply because the premises were not open to the public at the time of the killing; his job did not involve public contact; and there was no evidence that members of the public were more likely to be close to the store in the early morning than at other times. [*Padilla v. Twin City Fire Ins. Co.*, 324 S.W.3d 507 (Tenn. 2010); see Rebecca Moore, *TN High Court Denies Benefits for Widow of Murdered Employee*, plansponsor.com (Oct. 11, 2010)]

WC exclusivity applies, and the victim does not have the right to bring tort claims against the employer in cases of rape or robbery by an unknown assailant. The Florida Court of Appeals ruled that the parents of a 16-year-old store employee who charged that she was raped by her manager cannot pursue a negligence suit against the store. (Their theory was that the store was negligent in hiring the manager.) The court of appeals held that it was possible that the family had a WC claim, but that would preclude a civil suit. [*John and Jane Doe v. Footstar Corp.*, 980 So. 2d 1266 (Fla. App. 2008); Fred Schneyer, *FL Appellate Court Upholds Sexual Assault Civil Claim Dismissal*, plansponsor.com (May 12, 2008)]

The Utah Supreme Court allowed a worker in a refinery plant who suffered a permanent seizure disorder caused by exposure to toxic gases to sue her employer, Chevron, for damages. The injury fell under the "intentional injury" exception so WC exclusivity did not apply. The plaintiff was ordered to neutralize toxic sludge in an open-air pit, only hours after another worker set off toxic alarms and several workers were sent home sick, after the same process was performed. The intentional injury exception is triggered when an employer orders a task that is reasonably certain to cause injuries. The test distinguishes between intentional acts that result in injuries that were unknown or unexpected (where WC exclusivity applies) and intentional acts resulting in known or expected injuries (where tort suits are permitted). But the actor must have known or expected that injury would result from the action; it is not enough for the plaintiff to show merely that some injury was substantially certain to occur at some time. The worker's supervisors did not warn her about the earlier incident or tell her to wear respiratory protection. Chevron was ordered to pay the worker's medical expenses and pay $7,880 for the temporary total disability caused by the incident [*Helf v. Chevron USA Inc.*, 2009 UT 11 (2009); see Rebecca Moore, *Utah Court Says Worker Can Sue for Damages Above Workers' Comp*, plansponsor .com (Feb. 17, 2009). See also *Turner v. PCR, Inc.*, 754 So. 2d 683 (Fla. Sup. 2000)]

In a suit against the parent company of the company that owned and operated a factory where two workers were severely burned when flammable vapors were ignited, the First Circuit held that to sue a parent company, the employee must establish, by specific facts, that the parent company (either expressly or by implication) assumed primary responsibility for workplace safety. The employee has the burden of presenting specific facts to show such an express or implied duty. [*Mendez-Laboy v. Abbott Labs. Inc.*, 424 F.3d 35 (1st Cir. 2005)]

Although, in general, injuries incurred when going to and returning from work are not covered by WC, the District of Columbia has a "traveling employee" exception that makes WC exclusive for injuries of a person for whom travel is integral to the job. However, relocating to accept a new assignment does not make a person a "traveling employee." For example, an employee who was sent to the Philippines for a two-year assignment was kidnapped, imprisoned, and tortured. Although he worked under an employment contract in which job-related injuries were only covered by WC, the D.C. Circuit ruled that his injuries were not work-related, nor were they a reasonable and foreseeable part of the work, so he could sue his employers for negligence and intentional infliction of emotional distress. [*Khan v. Parsons Global Servs. Ltd.*, 428 F.3d 1079 (D.C. Cir. 2005).

The Texas Supreme Court ruled that a drug sales representative was acting in the scope of her employment (and therefore entitled to WC benefits when she was severely injured in an automobile accident) when driving to a storage unit containing drug samples, after a dinner with clients. The representative usually worked out of her home, but kept samples in a storage unit provided by the employer near her home: *Leordeanu v. American Prot. Ins. Co.*, 330 S.W.3d 239 (Tex. 2010); see Fred Schneyer, *TX Drug Rep Wins Workers Comp Appeal*, plansponsor.com (Dec. 9, 2010)]

The New Jersey Appellate Division extended the "coming and going" rule to grant full WC benefits to an off-site employee who was seriously injured during a five-mile trip to the deli for coffee, because a coffee break is a minor deviation from employment that does not prevent payment of full benefits. An alternative argument was that he was on an authorized "mission" for the employer (going to the union hall to discuss plans for a new project) and was required to be away from the workplace on business. It was reasonable for him to take his coffee break instead of interrupting the union official or simply doing nothing, and in a secluded rural location, it was reasonable to drive five miles to find good coffee. [*Cooper v. Barnickel Enters. Inc.*, 411 N.J. Super. 343; (N.J. App. Div. 2010); see Michael Booth, *Employee Injured in Five-Mile Drive for Coffee Is Eligible for Workers' Comp*, N.J.L.J. (Jan. 14, 2010) (law.com). See also *Sager v. O.A. Peterson Constr. Co.*, 182 N.J. 156 (2004): compensation was awarded when carpenter was injured on way to job site after dinner break in an extended work day, on the grounds that an employee who is doing what he is supposed to be doing, whether on or off premises, is acting in the course of employment.]

The Nebraska Supreme Court found that an employer can be liable for injuries suffered by an employee walking from the employee parking lot to the workplace. Walking from the lot through a city-owned alleyway to get to work was in the course and scope of employment—so the railroad employer was liable under the FELA when the plaintiff stepped into a hole in the alleyway. The railroad knew that its employees used the alleyway, and even encouraged its use by posting signs to keep the public out. In a FELA "traversing" case, the issue is not whether the employer owns or has control over the premises where the injury occurred, but whether the commuting employee encounters risks that the general public does not face, and the injury occurs near the job site when going to or returning from the job site within a reasonable time before or after the workday. [*Holsapple v. Union Pac. R.R Co.*, 279 Neb. 18 (Neb. 2009); see Rebecca Moore, *Employer Found Liable for Employee Injury While Walking from Parking Lot*, plansponsor.com (Dec. 16, 2009)]

The Connecticut Court of Appeals said that a slip-and-fall suit against individual corporate officers of the victim's employer should not have been dismissed, because the defendants were not entitled to a Worker's Compensation exemption. The plaintiff fell in Dymax's parking lot in 2005, suffering a fractured hip and other injuries. After receiving Worker's Compensation benefits, she sued the individual corporate officers because they owned the parking lot and leased it to the corporation. The court of appeals held that, in their role as parking lot owners, the defendants were not entitled to assert WC exclusivity. In some other states (but not in Connecticut), there is a "dual-capacity" doctrine, permitting a suit for injuries sustained while the employer or a co-employee was acting in a non-employment capacity. In this case, the plaintiff was employed by Dymax, not by the Bachmanns as individuals, and her suit asserted a premises liability claim rather than a WC claim. [*Roy v. Bachmann*, 121 Conn. App. 220 (2010); see Fred Schneyer, *Corporate Officers Open to CT Injury Lawsuits*, plansponsor .com (May 18, 2010)]

## § 33.04 ALTERNATIVES FOR INSURING WC

### [A] Types of Available Insurance

Depending on state law and the employer's own financial status and risk category, there are several ways to cope with the obligation to provide benefits for injured employees.

- Buying insurance from a state-run fund that is the sole source of WC coverage within the state;

- Buying insurance from a commercial carrier. Nearly all privately purchased policies will follow the form of the "standard policy"—the Worker's Compensation and Employers' Liability Policy developed by the national Council on Compensation Insurance (NCCI);

- Buying insurance from a state fund that competes with commercial carriers;

- Self-insurance (most employers who take this option combine it with third-party administration, reinsurance, or both);

- Insurance through a captive insurer owned by the employer;

- Participating in an assigned risk pool (depending on circumstances, this can be either mandatory or voluntary).

The Supreme Court ruled in mid-2006 that in the context of Chapter 11 bankruptcy, premiums owed to a WC insurer are not unpaid contributions to an "employee benefit plan" and therefore are not accorded priority under 11 U.S.C. § 507(a)(5). [*Howard Delivery Serv. Inc. v. Zurich Am. Ins. Co.*, 547 U.S. 651 (2006)]

In September 2007, a New York State law took effect requiring employers who have any employees in New York to maintain full Worker's Compensation coverage within the state. Previously, a multi-state employer could cover its New York employees with an "all states" endorsement to its WC policy unless the employer exceeded limits on the amount of money earned by its workers within the state or other limitations. The penalty for non-compliance is $1,000 for every ten days of lack of coverage, and criminal penalties can also be imposed. There is also a private right of action for employees who do not receive the appropriate WC coverage. [Rebecca Moore, *Law Mandating Workers Comp Coverage for NY Employees in Effect*, plansponsor.com (Sept. 13, 2007)]

### [B] State Funds

The states of North Dakota, Ohio, Washington, West Virginia, and Wyoming have monopolistic state funds, i.e., all covered employers have to buy their coverage from the fund. Until July 1, 1997, Nevada was in this category, but now it maintains a state fund but allows private coverage.

The states that have competitive state funds (i.e., the employer chooses whether to purchase coverage from the state funds or a private insurer) are Arizona, California, Colorado, Idaho, Louisiana, Maine, Maryland, Michigan, Minnesota, Montana, New Mexico, Nevada, New York, Oklahoma, Oregon, Pennsylvania, Rhode Island, Texas, and Utah. State funds set their own rates, which can be low because the fund has very low marketing expenses.

Texas allows employers to self-insure for WC, but they must be careful to provide benefits at least roughly comparable to the benefits that would be available under an insured plan. In *Reyes v. Storage & Processors Inc.* [995 S.W.2d 722 (Tex. App. 1999)], the court said that employers cannot require arbitration of claims for work-related injuries if the benefits they provide are substantially less generous than Comp benefits.

## [C]  Assigned Risk Pools

In any situation in which people or organizations have a legal obligation to maintain insurance coverage, some of them will not be insurable under normal underwriting standards. Assigned risk pools are created to issue coverage. In the WC context, the NCCI administers the National Worker's Compensation Reassurance Pool. It covers about 25% of all employers, making it the largest single WC insurer in the United States.

This WC assigned risk pool has some unusual features. Commercial insurers have to support it by paying "residual market assessments" of approximately 14 cents on every premium dollar they receive. But because of this heavy assessment, commercial insurers are less willing to grant discounts to their insurable customers, thus driving more employers to see the assigned risk pool as an attractive alternative.

## [D]  Self-Insurance and Captive Companies

In all the states except North Dakota and Wyoming, employers who satisfy certain criteria (e.g., being financially capable of paying all WC claims that arise in the course of operations; posting bond or establishing an escrow) can elect to self-insure.

> ■ **TIP:**  Self-insurance is considered a privilege. It can be revoked by the state if an employer fails to file the necessary reports, does not maintain the required amount of excess insurance, or otherwise fails to keep up its end of the bargain. A change in corporate ownership might also lead to revocation of the privilege, even if the corporate structure remains the same.

In practice, self-insurance is practical only for very large companies with six- or seven-figure WC premium obligations; about one-third of the WC market is now self-insured because some economic giants have taken this option.

More than half the states impose a requirement that self-insured companies maintain reinsurance (excess coverage). It is prudent for companies to do this even if it is not required. Self-insured employers generally must show that they have arranged for claims administration, employee communications, and safety programs. These functions are usually performed under a Third Party Administration (TPA) arrangement. An effective TPA should have 24-hour-a-day claims service; low turnover (experienced representatives do a much better job than novices); a high proportion of employees who have obtained professional certification in loss control; quick settlement of claims; and a low average final cost per claim.

In a pure self-insurance arrangement, the employer sets up reserves and pays all WC claims from these reserves. In a group arrangement, several companies join forces. Each one is jointly and severally liable for all Comp claims within the group. Most of the states permit group self-insurance; nationwide, there are over 250 group self-insurance pools. In a limited self-insurance arrangement, the employer is responsible for the Self-Insured Retention (SIR), which is roughly equal to a deductible, and excess insurance pays the rest.

Excess coverage can be written on a per-occurrence or per-loss basis, covering an aggregate amount for the year or per accident per payment year. (The payment year is a relevant concept because the consequences of an injury might extend over several years.) Specific excess insurance limits the employer's liability for claims for any occurrence where the exposure exceeds the SIR. Aggregate excess insurance copes with the possibility of a bad year. The employer has to pay the amount in the aggregate retention or loss fund. This is usually expressed as a percentage, such as 125%, of the reinsurance premium for the year. Aggregate excess coverage usually stops at $1 million or $2 million, so the employer will be at risk once again if the exposure is greater. Specific excess insurance is both easier to obtain and less expensive than aggregate insurance.

To self-insure, the company must file an application with the state (this typically costs $100–$1,000). The employer may have to post a letter of credit as security, and the lending bank will impose fees. Excess insurance and TPA fees each costs about 8%–13% of the amount that would otherwise be the WC premium. States also impose taxes on self-insurance arrangements—about 1%–4% of the premium that would have been charged by an insurer, incurred losses, or paid losses.

Working through a captive insurance company (one that does business only with a company that is its sole shareholder, or a small group of cooperating companies) is another option. The advantage of this arrangement to the employer is the ability to keep the underwriting income (deposits that are the equivalent of premiums, plus investment income), but the company will also have to pay the expenses of the captive insurer.

## [E]   High-Deductible Plans

A high-deductible plan combines features of both insurance and self-insurance. To reduce its premiums, the employer agrees to accept a higher deductible. Usually, it falls between $100,000 and $1 million, but policies are available with deductibles up to $5 million. Any employer can purchase a high-deductible policy. Unlike self-insurance, there are no financial qualifications imposed by the state.

When a claim is made under a high-deductible plan, the insurer pays the full claim, then bills the policyholder for payments made that fell within the deductible. Bills are usually sent on a monthly basis. Employers who buy high-deductible policies are generally required to create an escrow fund equal to about three months' potential loss payments, and must submit a letter of credit in an amount equal to the deductible. At the end of the first year of high deductible coverage, the letter of credit is adjusted upward or downward to reflect experience. Paid losses are billed until all claims have been closed. The high-deductible insurer may require indemnification or a hold-harmless agreement offering remedies against the employer if, for instance, legislation is passed subjecting the insurer to increased losses that fall within the deductible.

## § 33.05   SETTING THE WC PREMIUM

There are 600 industry classifications, each identified by a four-digit number. An employer's basic WC premium is the "manual rate" for its industry classification. The manual rate is the average cost of WC coverage for the classification, based on the number of claims in the past three years for injuries serious enough to cause lost work time. The rate is sometimes expressed as a percentage of total payroll, but is usually defined as a number of dollars per $100 of payroll. Large employers may qualify for premium discounts, because the administrative expenses are fairly similar for policies of all sizes.

The manual rate is only one factor in setting an individual employer's rate. Experience rating (the employer's actual claims experience for the previous two years) can increase or decrease the base premium that will be imposed in the future. States can also adopt retrospective rating, under which past losses are used to adjust the premium already charged for a particular year, so that either the employer is entitled to a refund or will have to make additional payments.

WC policies have both general inclusions, which recur in many industries (for workers in employee cafeterias, and repair and maintenance crews, for instance) and general exclusions that are written out of ordinary industry classifications (for instance, construction activities performed by employees; running an employer-operated day care center).

## § 33.06   BAN ON RETALIATION

Due to a lower reported injury rate, and some state laws making it harder to qualify for WC benefits, the average cost of WC per $100 payroll fell from $2.67 in 1994 to $1.79 in 2012—a rare commodity that cost less in the later year! But, although the number of workplace injuries reported to OSHA dropped by nearly one-third in the decade ending in 2013, one factor in the decline is not better safety practices, but greater fear of retaliation against employees who report their injuries. In 2012, there were approximately 100 state and federal suits charging Worker's Compensation retaliation, about twice as many as 10 years earlier. [James R. Hagerty, *Workplace Injuries Drop, But Claims of Employer Retaliation Rise*, WSJ.com (July 22, 2013)]

Nearly all the states have passed statutes making it illegal to retaliate against an employee, either specifically for filing a Worker's Compensation claim or for filing any "wage claim" or "wage complaint," a broad category that includes WC. The states are Alabama, Arizona, California, Connecticut, Delaware, Florida, Hawaii, Idaho, Illinois, Indiana, Kansas, Kentucky, Louisiana, Maine, Maryland, Mississippi, Michigan, Minnesota, Missouri, Montana, New Hampshire, New Jersey, New Mexico, New York, North Carolina, North Dakota, Ohio, Oklahoma, Rhode Island, South Carolina, South Dakota, Texas, Vermont, Virginia, Washington, West Virginia, Wisconsin, and Wyoming.

Even in the minority of states that do not have a statute, it is very likely that courts will treat retaliatory discharge as an illegal violation of public policy.

The Tenth Circuit found it likely that UPS retaliated against an injured worker by denying him the opportunity to return to work with lifting restrictions. However, because the plaintiff suffered only monetary harm, the Tenth Circuit found the $2 million district court judgment excessive. After a 2003 injury, the company doctor told plaintiff Jones that he could not lift more than 20 pounds over his head, and carriers must be able to lift 70 pounds routinely. In 2004, two doctors cleared Jones to lift 70 pounds, but a UPS occupational health manager told them not to remove the lifting restrictions. Jones said that UPS retaliated against him for filing a WC claim. The Tenth Circuit found the retaliation claim valid (the occupational health manager intentional interfered with the medical evaluations to prevent his return to work) and found punitive damages appropriate, but said that $2 million was excessive because the manager's conduct did not involve disregard for health or safety. The Tenth Circuit affirmed the $630,000 award of actual damages. [*Jones v. United Parcel Serv. Inc.*, 674 F.3d 1187 (10th Cir. 2011); see Tara Cantore, *Appeals Court Says Judgment in Retaliation Suit Excessive*, plansponsor.com (Oct. 26, 2011). Rehearing was granted March 5, 2012.]

Discharge is not the only employment action that can give rise to retaliation charges: A retaliatory demotion, that results in a pay cut, is also wrongful, and can give rise to a lawsuit. [*Brigham v. Dillon Cos. Inc.*, 935 P.2d 1054 (Kan. Sup. 1997)]

The Ninth Circuit ruled that it is not retaliation to fire a worker for lying about previous occupational injuries on a questionnaire. Although the state's Right to Privacy in the Workplace Act forbids employers to ask prospective employees if they have ever filed a Worker's Compensation claim, it is permissible to ask about previous occupational injuries, time lost from work because of work-related injuries, or medical treatment for those injuries, even though it wouldn't be difficult to extrapolate from those disclosures that a Comp claim had been filed. [*Carter v. Tennant Co.*, 383 F.3d 673 (9th Cir. 2004)]

## § 33.07  ADMINISTRATION OF WC

### [A]  Generally

In most states, employers are required to participate in the WC system (although Texas and New Jersey allow private employers to opt out of the system entirely, as long as they notify the Compensation Commission and their employees that they have left the system). The tradeoff is that injured employees have the right to bring tort suits against employers who are outside the WC system, whereas in most cases workers who are injured in a WC-covered workplace will not be allowed to sue the employer.

Some states allow employees to opt out of WC coverage as long as they do so in writing, within a reasonable time after starting a new job, and before any accident or injury has occurred. Corporate officers are often given the option of leaving the WC system.

In about a third of the states, the state itself runs the WC fund. Those states give employers three choices for handling their responsibilities:

- Pay into the state fund;
- Buy insurance from a private carrier;
- Self-insure by maintaining a segregated fund that contains enough money to handle the expected compensation claims.

In states with no state fund, employers can either buy insurance or self-insure.

The insurance premium depends on the level of risk: A coal mine is much more likely to have occupational injury claims than a boutique. The nationwide average premium is about 2.5% of compensation.

The general rule is that employees are obligated to notify the employer within a short time (usually about five days) after an injury or the onset of an illness. Employers should encourage reporting, because such information is needed for WC and other purposes (OSHA reports, improving safety conditions).

In some WC systems, the employer notifies its WC insurer, which then files the report. In other systems, the employer (whether it has insurance or is self-insured) is responsible for notifying the compensation board. If the employer fails to make the necessary report, the employee will probably be given additional time to pursue his or her claim.

If the employer agrees that the injury or disease is work-related and accepts the employee's characterization of its seriousness, the claim is uncontested. Most states follow the "agreement system" under which a settlement is negotiated by the parties, or by the employee and the employer's WC insurer. In some states, the agency that administers WC claims must approve all settlements, even in uncontested cases. Most settlements involve payment of ongoing benefits at a continuing rate: either a percentage of the employee's pre-accident income, or a percentage of the state's average income. However, there is an increasing trend to settle WC cases for a lump sum.

However, some uncontested cases are treated as "direct payment" cases. Either the employer or the insurer initiates the process, by making the statutory initial installment payment to the employee. Under this option, the employee does not have to sign anything or agree to anything—unlike the agreement system, which results in a written agreement.

WC settlements cover only the matters specifically set out in the agreement, so agreements must be drafted carefully. Employers are allowed to settle claims that have already accrued, but not future claims (such as claims for future medical expenses), because employees cannot be required to give up future claims that are hard to quantify in advance.

Generally, any settlement between employer and employee will be final. However, there are grounds for which agreements can be set aside, such as fraud, mutual mistake of fact (both sides believe something about the employee's condition that turns out not to be accurate), or mistake of law (misinterpretation of the legal rules and their consequences). Usually, the mere fact that the employee did not have a lawyer is not enough to invalidate a settlement—unless, perhaps, the employer prevented the employee from seeking legal advice. Just to be on the safe side, employers should inform employees that they have the right to be represented by counsel.

Contested cases are heard and decided by the agency administering the system. However, there are comparatively few contested cases. In most cases, it is quite clear that there has been an injury. Because WC is a no-fault system, it is not necessary to apportion blame.

In some states, mediation is either an option that is available (but only if both sides agree); in other states, it is compulsory. In mediated cases, a neutral mediator has at least one informal meeting with the parties. Sometimes, the meeting is held off the record, so both sides can speak freely, without having to restrict what they say to things that would help their case in formal legal proceedings. If necessary, the mediator arranges more meetings, until the mediator is either able to facilitate a settlement, or it is clear that an impasse has been reached.

In some states, when mediation fails, binding arbitration can be applied; in other states, the case is sent to the Comp board for adjudication.

Appeal rights are granted to dissatisfied employers and employees. Usually, parties get 30 days to file for an appeal, although the requirements of different states range from 10 days to one year. Grounds for appeal include improprieties in the process and changed circumstances (such as unpredictable improvement or deterioration in the employee's condition) that were unknown at the time of the award.

After exhaustion of remedies (the process of going through all the administrative appeals), the case can be taken to court by a dissatisfied party. The Texas WC Act provides for two kinds of judicial review of the decisions of the WC appeals panel: one covering eligibility for benefits and compensability, the other handling everything else. The widow of an employee who died when he fell off a ladder during roof repairs sought review of the panel's decision that the decedent was an independent contractor rather than an employee of one of three companies. (Two of the companies subscribed to WC, the third did not.) The Texas Supreme Court ruled in late 2007 that the question of employee status is a question of compensability. The defendants said that if one of the possible employers is not a subscriber to WC, then the question is one of coverage, and compensability doesn't arise until that question is resolved. However, the court ruled that coverage and compensability questions are not necessarily mutually exclusive. The main issue is whether there was a compensable injury. [*Morales v. Liberty Mut. Ins. Co.*, 241 S.W.3d 514 (Tex. 2007)]

Many state laws entitle the employee to an additional payment of 10%–20% if the employer is late in making a required payment. Civil fines may also be imposed, and the unpaid amounts could operate as a lien on the employer's assets.

## [B]   Responding to an Accident

Even before there have been any accidents, your workplace should have an effective procedure in place, and should hold regular drills to make sure everyone can handle the procedure. Make sure that employees learn first aid and CPR. Keep plenty of first aid kits around, with fresh supplies, in convenient locations. It's important to provide first aid for all minor incidents, and immediate medical care in more serious cases.

Somebody must be designated to take charge of taking the injured worker to a doctor's office or hospital emergency room, or to call an ambulance. Someone must be in charge of filing the initial accident report (and an OSHA incident report if necessary). [See § 24.02[A]] Some insurers have 24-hour telephone lines that can be used for WC and OSHA reporting, and to assign a case manager to review utilization of care and the injured person's potential for rehabilitation. There is clear evidence that the earlier and more aggressively rehabilitation can be pursued, the more likely it is that the employee will be able to return to work (or at least to limited duties or a less strenuous job) instead of becoming permanently disabled.

In addition to immediate accident reports, some states require a yearly report of all workplace incidents, similar to the OSHA annual report. [See § 24.02[A]] Follow-up status reports may also be required on individual accidents. Employers who fail to make mandatory reports can be subject to fines; there may even be criminal penalties.

As Chapter 18 shows, managed care dominates the U.S. health care system. It also plays a role in WC cases. Some states such as Connecticut, Florida, and Ohio make managed care involvement in WC cases compulsory. Many other states have laws authorizing managed care as an option in WC cases: Arkansas, California, Georgia, Kentucky, Massachusetts, Minnesota, Missouri, Montana, Nebraska, Nevada, New Hampshire, New Jersey, New York, North Carolina, North Dakota, Oregon, Pennsylvania, Rhode Island, South Dakota, Utah, and Washington.

## § 33.08   WC IN RELATION TO OTHER SYSTEMS

Because WC cases involve physical injury, in an employment context, both health care and employment law can be implicated—for example, ERISA and the ADA.

The U.S. Supreme Court rejected an appeal of a decision that allowed employees with WC claims to pursue a RICO case against their employer. Plaintiffs said that the self-insured Cassens Transportation relied on its claims adjuster and poorly qualified doctors to get medical examinations that would deny WC claims. The case was remanded to the trial court for further proceedings. Business groups wanted the decision reversed, because they saw it as opening the door for bringing WC claims (which are usually heard in state courts) into the federal court system. [*Brown v. Cassens Transp. Co.*, 546 F.3d 347 (6th Cir. 2009); see Fred Schneyer, *Workers Comp RICO Claim Gets Second Chance*, plansponsor. com (Dec. 9, 2009)]

The Longshore and Harbor Workers' Compensation Act (LHWCA) provides a compensation scheme for disability or death caused by injury on the navigable waters of the United States. Benefits for most disabilities are subject to a cap of twice the national average of weekly wage for the fiscal year of the initial award of benefits. In cases where the employer contests liability or the employee contests employer's actions, the dispute goes to the DOL Office of Workers' Compensation Programs (OWCP). The OWCP attempts conciliation; if there is no resolution, there is an ALJ hearing resulting in a compensation order. After Roberts was injured in 2002, his employer, Sea-Land, voluntarily paid benefits until 2005. Roberts filed an LHWCA claim, which was controverted. In FY 2007, the ALJ awarded benefits at the statutory maximum rate—for 2002. Roberts said that it should have been set at the 2007 rate, because that was when he was "newly awarded compensation." In 2012, the Supreme Court ruled that the date that counts is the date worker becomes disabled because this is when entitlement to benefits is triggered, no matter when—or even whether—a compensation order issues. [*Roberts v. Sea-Land Servs., Inc.*, 132 S. Ct. 1350 (2012)]

The Bankruptcy Code (11 U.S.C. § 509(a)(8)(E)(ii)) gives priority to certain non-dischargeable amounts owed by a debtor to the state if the amounts are an excise tax incurred on a transaction that occurred in the three years before filing of the bankruptcy petition. In 2009, the Ninth Circuit ruled that amounts an employer was legally obligated to pay to the California self-insurance security fund, to reimburse the fund for WC benefits paid to the employer's workers, were not excise taxes, so the self-insurance security fund could not claim the priority for these amounts. [*In re Lorber Indus. of California*, 564 F.3d 1098 (9th Cir. May 4, 2009)]

The Medicare system is a secondary payor with respect to Worker's Compensation: that is, if a Medicare beneficiary also receives WC, the WC system is required to pay for the care first, with Medicare responsible only for amounts not covered by WC. Employers and insurers have a duty to report WC claims involving Medicare beneficiaries who have received a settlement, judgment, award, or other reimbursement of medical expenses on or after July 1, 2009 to the Center for Medicare and Medicaid Services. [Littler, Mendelson Press Releases, *New Medicare Secondary Payer Reporting Obligations for Workers' Compensation Plans*, <http://www.littler.com/PressPublications/Lists/ASAPs/DispAsaps.aspx?id=1359&asapType=National> (April 2009)]

A Worker's Compensation release that did not explicitly mention ERISA claims or the ERISA plan did not release the employer from an ERISA disability claim. Teresa Duncan received disability benefits under an ERISA long-term disability plan from 2005 to 2010. She settled her WC claim in 2008 and released all claims. The release form said she would not "be able to go back to the defendant for additional treatment or disability payments." The Eastern District of California held in early 2013 that the standard language in WC releases applies only to WC claims, not ERISA claims. [*Duncan v. Hartford Life & Accident Ins. Co.*, 2 :11-cv-01536-GEB-CKD, 2013 WL 506465 (E.D. Cal. Feb. 8, 2013); see Mike Reilly, *Releases Should Explicitly Release ERISA Claims and ERISA Plan*, Lane Powell Boom: The ERISA Law Blog (Feb. 26, 2013) (benefitslink.com)]

## [A]  Taxation of WC Benefits

Generally speaking, WC insurance premiums paid by employers, or WC benefits received by employees, are not taxable income for the employee. Therefore, the employer does not have to perform tax withholding on these amounts, or withhold or pay FICA or FUTA tax on them. However, in a limited range of situations, WC benefits will be taxable: e.g., if they are paid to a person who has returned to work in a light-duty position; if they reduce Social Security benefits; or if state law calls for payment of non-occupational disability benefits. [See Chapter 20 for the related topic of disability benefits provided under a fringe benefit plan]

The amount that the employer pays in WC premiums is tax deductible. So are loss amounts paid by a self-insured employer. However, reserves maintained in order to satisfy the deductible under a WC policy are not tax-deductible.

## [B]  ERISA

The general tenor of court decisions on this subject is that WC benefits can legitimately be used to offset accrued benefits that derive from the employer's contribution to a pension plan—but only if a statute specifically provides this, or if the plan has been drafted to include this specific provision. ERISA preempts state WC laws to the extent that they "relate" to an ERISA plan.

In 1992, the Supreme Court decided that a state law relates to an ERISA plan if it refers to or has a connection with the plan, even if the effect is indirect, and even if the law was not designed to affect the plan. Therefore, a law requiring employers to provide health insurance to employees who received or were eligible for WC was preempted. [*District of Columbia v. Greater Wash. Bd. of Trade*, 506 U.S. 125 (1992)]

ERISA preempts an Illinois law that forbids making claims on WC awards, because the state law related to ERISA-regulated benefit plans. Therefore, the Southern District of Illinois permitted an EGHP to seek reimbursement for medical bills it paid before determining that accident claims were work-related, where the injured person settled a case and received a recovery for medical bills that were paid by the EGHP. At least one of the settlements was drafted stating that it did not cover health benefits, but the Southern District found this provision to be a subterfuge to prevent recovery, and refused to give it effect. [*Graphic Communications National Health and Welfare Fund v. Tackett*, Case No. 07-cv-0123-MJR, 2008 WL 2020504 (S.D. Ill. May 9, 2008); see Adam V. Russo's Subrogation Blog, *Law Prohibiting Liens Against WC Settlements Preempted by ERISA* (Aug. 15, 2008) (benefitslink.com) and *District Courts States That Worker's Compensation Must Reimburse ERISA Plan* (June 4, 2008) (benefitslink.com)]

## [C]  The ADA

A person might claim disability discrimination and also claim eligibility for WC benefits, at the same time or at different times.

The right to get WC benefits is considered a privilege of employment for ADA purposes [see, e.g., *Harding v. Winn-Dixie Stores*, 907 F. Supp. 386 (M.D. Fla. 1995)], so a case can be brought premised on alleged discrimination in this area. However, the ADA does not have the strong preemptive power that ERISA does to rule out state-law claims. In 1998, for instance, a case was allowed to proceed even though the ADA's standard of proof is higher for employees with pre-existing conditions. [*Baley v. Reynolds Metals*, 153 Or. App. 498, 959 P.2d 84 (1998)]

The EEOC announced late in 2009 that it had settled with Sears for $6.2 million, in what was then the single largest ADA settlement for a single suit. The EEOC charged that Sears violated the ADA by imposing an inflexible policy calling for termination of anyone who took a WC leave that lasted more than 12 months. The EEOC filed a similar complaint against UPS, also involving a policy under which WC leave over 12 months led to termination. [Rebecca Moore, *Sears Settles Disability Discrimination Suit for $6.2M*, plansponsor.com (Oct. 2, 2009); Lynne Marek, *Sears Agrees to Multimillion-Dollar Settlement Over Firing of Disabled Workers*, Nat'l L.J. (Sept. 30, 2009) (law.com)]

## [D]   Second Injury Funds

Although they predate the ADA, in a way "second injury funds" serve the same purpose as the ADA: promoting the employment of people with disabilities. Second injury funds (which exist in, for example, California, Missouri, New Jersey, and Washington State) deal with the situation in which a permanent disability is compounded by a later injury to become either a permanent partial disability that is more serious than before, or a permanent total disability. In states that do not have these funds, an employer who hires someone whose pre-existing condition deteriorates because of occupational factors, would be responsible for all of the employee's WC benefits, even though the occupational factors may be comparatively less important than the pre-existing condition.

When there is a second injury fund in the picture, the employer is responsible only for the economic consequences of the later injury. The second injury fund, which is publicly funded, takes on the rest of the economic burden.

The first injury must have been serious enough to be compensable, but need not actually have come under the WC system. For instance, the second injury fund could get involved if a work-related injury aggravates an existing condition caused by a non-work-related automobile accident or a birth defect.

■ **TIP:**   To collect from the fund, the employer may have to certify that it knew about the pre-existing condition at the time of hiring. This, in turn, requires asking questions in a way that does not violate the ADA.

The Wyoming Supreme Court held that the Medical Commission's denial of benefits for foot injuries, and a second compensable injury to the claimant's wrist and hip when he fell when his injured foot gave out, was arbitrary and capricious and made without substantial evidence. The "odd lot" doctrine allows a finding of permanent total disability for a worker who, although not altogether unable to work, in practice cannot be employed regularly in the existing labor market. The claimant did light duty work for 13 years, but could not carry out any gainful occupation for which he was reasonably suited by experience and training because the condition of his injured leg deteriorated. A subsequent injury is compensable if the initial compensable injury turns into a condition requiring further treatment, and the second injury is causally related to the first. [*Nagle v. State of Wyoming*, 2008 WY 99, 190 P.3d 159 (Wyo. 2008)]

### [E]   Social Security Disability Income

In many states, the Social Security Disability Income (SSDI) system is considered the primary payer whenever an employee is injured seriously enough to meet the Social Security Administration's stringent definition of total disability. The states in this category are Alaska, Arkansas, California, Colorado, Florida, Louisiana, Maine, Massachusetts, Michigan, Minnesota, Missouri, Montana, Nevada, New Jersey, New York, North Dakota, Ohio, Oregon, Utah, Washington, and Wisconsin.

When SSDI is involved, the payments from the federal agency reduce the WC benefit dollar-for-dollar, until the combination of SSDI and WC reaches the level of 80% of the worker's pre-accident earnings. However, SSDI reduces only the part of the benefit that represents lost income, not the part that goes to medical care or legal fees.

The Pennsylvania Commonwealth Court ruled that an employer asserting that a worker on disability can get other employment and earn income has the burden of providing evidence of actual available jobs. Kraft employee Leonard Anterola went on disability after a 2004 knee injury. Three years later, Kraft petitioned to change the employee's disability benefits because they claimed that he could get another job. The WC judge modified the benefits; the appeal board overturned the modification; and Kraft brought suit and lost. [Fred Schneyer, *Disability Change Requires Stronger Job Proof*, plansponsor.com (Feb. 2, 2010)]

## § 33.09   TECHNIQUES FOR LOWERING COMP COSTS

Employers can reduce their costs via good planning—sorting valid from invalid claims, and finding more economical ways to handle the valid claims. Companies have had some success by educating workers that everyone is responsible for reducing injuries and maintaining a safer workplace. Focusing on getting injured workers back to work as soon as possible also helps cut costs. Departments can be made responsible for their own injury rates, and be made responsible for keeping their rates at least as low as those for comparable operations.

HR policies that are associated with lower WC rates include:

- Increasing employee involvement (e.g., through the use of quality circles). The more employees get involved, the more careful they will be about identifying potentially dangerous conditions, finding ways to correct them—and the more motivation they will have to return to work quickly after an injury;

- Strengthening grievance and conflict resolution procedures if dangerous conditions are alleged, and to resolve claims;

- Reducing turnover: Experienced workers are less likely to get hurt than novices;

- Training workers better—especially in lifting and safe handling of hazardous materials;

- Using health maintenance and wellness programs.

The National Institute of Occupational Safety and Health (NIOSH) defines three areas in which employers can be proactive to cut Comp costs:

- Using engineering controls, such as workstation layout, choice of tools, work methods, to tailor the job to fit employee capabilities and limitations;

- Reducing risk exposure through administrative controls, such as more rest breaks, better training, task rotation;

- Supplying workers with Personal Protective Equipment (PPE), although scientific consensus has not been reached on which devices are effective.

An article in CCH's Worker's Compensation newsletter gives some useful tips for spotting claims that might be fraudulent:

- Delayed reporting of injury;

- Accidents of a type that might be staged;

- The worker claiming injury was on probation or has been identified as having a poor work record;

- The alleged injury is not consistent with the worker's assigned duties;

- The injury is reported just after a weekend or holiday—showing that the injury might have been incurred away from the workplace, or work might have exacerbated a non-work-based injury.

Sometimes, a WC insurance premium quote will be inaccurate, and the premium can be reduced simply by:

- Checking to see if payroll is stated accurately, because the higher the payroll, the higher the premium;

- Making sure that employees are assigned to the lowest risk classification that accurately reflects their duties;

- Having your insurance agent review the calculations.

# PART VII

# SUBSTANTIVE LAWS AGAINST DISCRIMINATION

# CHAPTER 34

# TITLE VII

## § 34.01  INTRODUCTION

Title VII, passed as part of the Civil Rights Act of 1964, is the main federal civil rights statute that bans discrimination in employment. It has been enacted at 42 U.S.C. §§ 2000e *et seq.* (By the time Title VII came around, the United States Code was pretty much "full-up," leading to some very odd section numbers. Title VII starts with just plain § 2000e, which is divided into subsections running from § 2000e(a) to 2000e(n). The next section is § 2000e-1, with additional sections up to § 2000e-17.)

Title VII is supplemented by other civil rights statutes: Sometimes other parts of the United States Code (such as 42 U.S.C. §§ 1981, 1983, and 1985) are invoked in employment discrimination suits. Disability discrimination is barred by the Americans with Disabilities Act. [See Chapter 36] Age discrimination is barred by the Age Discrimination in Employment Act. [See Chapter 37]

In a sense, the Family and Medical Leave Act, [29 U.S.C. §§ 2601 *et seq.*] discussed in detail in Chapter 38, is also an antidiscrimination statute as well as an employee benefits statute, because it prevents discrimination against individuals who are ill or who must cope with illness as part of their family responsibilities. Note that any federal, state, or local law that creates special rights or preferences for veterans continues in force and is not repealed by Title VII [42 U.S.C. § 2000e-11] a provision that is more prominent in the post-9/11 environment.

The areas of discrimination forbidden by Title VII are race, color, religion, sex, and national origin. These are known as "suspect classifications," because employers are not supposed to discriminate for reasons involving these classifications. It is very common for Title VII suits to involve multiple allegations (e.g., that the plaintiff suffered discrimination and/or harassment because of sex and race, or national origin and religion). In many instances, employees who say they have been discriminated against also say that their employer or ex-employer retaliated against them for protesting the violation of Title VII. Many cases also combine Title VII allegations with allegations under other statutes (e.g., sex and age discrimination under the ADEA).

Also see 42 U.S.C. § 2000e-2(h), which says that it is not an unlawful employment practice for an employer to abide by FLSA § 6(d) [29 U.S.C. § 206(d)] which allows certain differences in the minimum wage.

Title VII enforcement has two aspects: public (governmental) and private (suits brought by employees, job applicants, ex-employees, or groups of people in these categories). Section 2000e-5 gives the Equal Employment Opportunities Commission (EEOC) the power "to prevent any person from engaging in any unlawful employment practice" that is banned by 42 U.S.C. § 2000e-2 or 2000e-3.

State laws still remain in force, although state laws are not permitted to require or even allow anything that is treated as an unlawful employment practice under Title VII [42 U.S.C. § 2000e-7]

## [A]    The Ledbetter Act

In 2007, the Supreme Court decided the case *Ledbetter v. Goodyear Tire*, 550 U.S. 618 (2007); see § 42.05[A]. The Supreme Court dismissed Ledbetter's charge that she was the victim of sex discrimination in compensation, holding that to be timely it would have to have been filed within 180 days of the employer's adoption of the discriminatory pay practice.

The first legislation signed by President Obama after his inauguration was the Lilly Ledbetter Fair Pay Act of 2009, Pub. L. No. 111-2, legislation designed to reverse the effect of this Supreme Court decision. Congress found that the short time frame impaired the rights that Congress intended to provide for employees. Under the Ledbetter Act, a discrimination charge is timely if it is filed within 180 days (or within 300 days, in a state with a work-sharing agreement with the EEOC) of any of these events:

- Adoption of a discriminatory practice;

- Employee becomes subject to that practice;

- Employee is affected by application of the practice—including every paycheck reflecting discrimination.

The Ledbetter Act applies to Title VII, the ADA, the ADEA, and the Rehabilitation Act. An employee who succeeds in pursuing a pay discrimination claim under Title VII, the ADEA, or the Rehab Act can recover back pay for up to two years before the filing of the charge, if the compensation discrimination was similar or related to discriminatory acts during the charge filing period.

The Ledbetter Act takes effect as if it had been passed the day before the Supreme Court decision was handed down—so the Act applies to all compensation discrimination claims that were pending on that date, or filed after *Ledbetter* was decided. (It did not, however, require Goodyear to pay Ms. Ledbetter herself any additional compensation.) The statute makes it an unlawful practice to apply a discriminatory policy when "wages, benefits, or other compensation is paid," but does not explain the degree to which benefits are covered. For example, pension and retiree benefits are often paid many years after retirement. [Erin Kilgore, *Lilly Ledbetter Fair Pay Act Revives Pay Discrimination Claims*, Louisiana Law Blog (Feb. 13, 2009) (law.com); Sheryl Gay Stolberg, *Obama Signs Equal-Pay Legislation*, <http://www.nytimes.com> (Jan. 30, 2009); SCOTUS Blog, *Congress Overturns Court on Job Bias*, <http://www.scotusblog.com/wp/court-over turns-court-on-job-bias> (Jan. 28, 2009); Janell Grenier, Benefitsblog, *Lilly Ledbetter Fair Pay Act of 2009 Passes: Benefits Impacted*, <http://www.benefits counsel.com/archives/002025.html> (Jan. 28, 2009)]

## [B]  GINA

The Genetic Information Nondiscrimination Act of 2008 (GINA; Pub. L. No. 110-233, signed May 21, 2008, effective November 21, 2009) extends the protective provisions of Title VII to discrimination based on genetic information. Employers are forbidden to deny hiring, discharge anyone, or discriminate in pay or working conditions on the basis of the results of genetic testing. Health insurers are not permitted to deny coverage or set premiums or deductibles based on genetic test results. The EEOC proposed regulations under GINA prohibit hiring, firing, or other personnel decisions based on genetic predisposition to a disease. Employers are forbidden to deliberately acquire genetic information from employees or job applicants. The "water cooler" exception immunizes a supervisor who inadvertently discovers an employee's condition from statements made by other employees, or if a doctor's note contains the information. Genetic information includes tests of an individual and the individual's medical history and family medical history—but does not include information about a current disease or condition. A person's sex, age, or drug or alcohol test results are not considered genetic information. [Neil Roland, *EEOC Proposes Rules to Bar Genetic Discrimination*, workforce.com (Feb. 26, 2009) (benefitslink.com)]

Family health information can be requested if there are no financial consequences, but there must be no financial benefit or penalty associated with family health information. EGHPs are not permitted to provide incentives, such as lower premiums or rebates, for including family medical histories in health risk questionnaires. GINA and its regulations do permit EGHPs to request family medical histories in order to see if an employee should be placed in a wellness program or a program to manage a disease such as hypertension, but the employees must give the information voluntarily, and the group plan must not use the information for underwriting or request the information before enrollment in the plan. [Steven Greenhouse, *Uses of Medical Histories Are Curtailed Under a New Law*, NYTimes.com (Nov. 15, 2009); Watson Wyatt Insider, *EEOC Proposes Procedural and Administrative Regulations on Genetic Information* (July 2009) (benefitslink. com)]

Unlike HIPAA, GINA does not exempt plans that have fewer than two participants who are current employees. The regulations under GINA Title I took effect January 1, 2010 for calendar-year plans.

On January 17, 2013, HHS published a final rule covering the application of the HIPAA privacy rule to Titles I (health coverage) and II (employment) of the Genetic Information Nondiscrimination Act (GINA). The final rule is effective March 26, 2013; covered entities have until September 23, 2013 to comply. The final rule clarifies that genetic information is considered health information, which cannot be used for underwriting purposes (except for long-term care insurance policies). [Katherine Georger, *New HIPAA Final Rule Implements GINA Restriction on Use and Disclosure of Genetic Information for Underwriting Purposes*, Holland & Hart LLP News Update (Jan. 23, 2013) (benefitslink.com)]

Even pre-GINA, HIPAA forbade imposing Pre-Existing Condition Exclusions (PCEs) solely based on genetic information. HIPAA also forbade discrimination in eligibility, benefits, or premiums for individual policies based on health factors (including genetic information). GINA Title I (prohibiting discrimination in EGHP coverage) broadens the underwriting protection, and forbids insurers to demand genetic tests and restricts the collection of genetic information. The premiums for a plan or group of similarly situated individuals within a plan must not be changed based on the genetic information of one or more individuals in the group. However, premiums can be increased for the group based on an actual disease or disorder experienced by a person in the group. A health care provider treating an individual can legitimately request genetic tests. A plan or insurer can request genetic test results to determine if a claim is payable—but only the minimum amount of information needed to process the claim. [*FAQs on the Genetic Information Nondiscrimination Act*, <http://www.dol.gov/ebsa/faqs/faq-GINA.html> (no date)]

GINA Title II is the employment title. The EEOC issued final regulations on GINA Title II, effective January 10, 2011, and published two question and answer documents, one targeted at small business. The regulations state that an employer is not liable for acquiring genetic information if the information was acquired inadvertently; if the information was provided by the employee voluntarily (including information given in connection with a wellness program); family history information obtained to comply with FMLA certification, the employer's leave policy, or state or local law; publicly available information; or information acquired in connection with law enforcement. Employers who receive exempt genetic information must keep it confidential, typically in a file that is separate from the employee's personal records. It is possible for an employer to violate both Title I and II by the same action, but will not be subject to double liability. Employment attorneys Jeffrey Fraser and Sara Tountas suggest including disclosures about GINA on all forms that call for employees to submit medical information (e.g., FMLA requests, disability forms, pre-employment and return to work medical forms), so genetic information will not be provided inadvertently. [<http://eeoc.gov/laws/types/genetic.cfm>; see Plansponsor staff, *EEOC Issues Final Regs on Genetic Info NonDiscrimination*, plansponsor.com (Nov. 9, 2010); Jeffrey Fraser and Sara Tountas, *New GINA Regulations Require Immediate Employer Action*, Miller Johnson newsletter (Jan. 5, 2011) (benefits link.com)]

The EEOC published a final rule on recordkeeping requirements under GINA. As of April 3, 2012, companies with 15 or more employees must retain all personnel and employment records relating to GINA for at least one year. If charges are filed under GINA, relevant documents must be retained until final disposition of the case. If an employee is involuntarily terminated, records must be kept for a year after termination. The relevant documents in this context include requests for accommodation, application forms, records of hiring, promotion, demotion, transfer, layoff, and termination; and records about terms of employ-ment, e.g., pay, training, and tenure. [77 Fed. Reg. 5396 (Feb. 12, 2012)]

The EEOC launched its efforts to enforce GINA in mid-2013. In May 2013, the EEOC settled its first GINA suit. Fabricut, Inc. agreed to pay $50,000 and pro-vide other relief because its post-job-offer medical exam required a job applicant to provide her family medical history, resulting in refusal to hire her for a clerical job because Fabricut believed that she was prone to developing carpal tunnel syn-drome. EEOC general counsel David Lopez warned employers that GINA pro-hibits requests for family medical history. The EEOC filed a class action suit in the Western District of New York, also involving unlawful collection of genetic information. The employer is liable even if the inquiries are made by a third-party medical provider, so it is important to supervise the practices of third parties. [*EEOC v. Fabricut, Inc.*, No. 13-CV-248-CVE-PJC (N.D. Okla., settled May 7, 2013); see EEOC Press Release, *Fabricut to Pay $50,000 to Settle EEOC Disability and Genetic Information Discrimination Lawsuit*, <http://www.eeoc.gov/eeoc/newsroom/release/5-7-13b.cfm> (May 7, 2013). The class action suit is *EEOC v. Founders Pavilion*, No. 6:13-cv-06250 (W.D.N.Y. pending); see Sue Reisinger, *EEOC Gets Tough With Companies on Genetic Privacy*, Corporate Counsel (May 23, 2013) (law.com)]

## § 34.02  TREATMENT/IMPACT

Title VII discrimination claims are divided into two categories, each of which has its own requirements for drafting complaints and proving the case, and its own defenses that the employer can assert to win its case.

The two categories are disparate treatment and disparate impact. A disparate treatment case alleges that persons were singled out for inferior treatment because of the group they belong to. A disparate impact case alleges subtler forms of dis-crimination.

For instance, an allegation that a police department refused to hire Hispan-ics would be a disparate treatment claim. A disparate impact claim might chal-lenge the police department's requirement that all newly hired officers be over 5'10" tall, on the grounds that more Hispanics than people from other back-grounds are unable to meet this requirement, and therefore a requirement that seems at first glance to be acceptable actually discriminates against members of a protected group.

Under Title VII's discrimination (but not its retaliation) provisions, a "mixed motive" case can be maintained. That is, if an employer has several motivations for making an employment decision or adopting an employment practice, Title VII forbids practices that are partially motivated by discrimination against a pro-tected group, not just those where discrimination is the sole motivation. [See 42 U.S.C. § 2000e-2(m)] In mid-2013, the Supreme Court ruled that mixed-motive cases are proper for discrimination based on personal characteristics (race, color, religion, sex, or national origin) but not for retaliation. [*University of Tex. Sw. Med. Ctr. v. Nassar*,No. 12-484 (U.S. June 24, 2013)]

Under the Supreme Court's June 2003 decision [*Desert Palace, Inc. v. Costa*, 539 U.S. 90 (2003)], a Title VII plaintiff can obtain a mixed-motive jury instruction without necessarily showing direct evidence of discrimination, because the statute does not specifically require direct evidence. Therefore, the general rule of civil litigation—allowing proof by direct and/or circumstantial evidence—applies.

In response to *Smith v. City of Jackson*, 544 U.S. 228 (2005), the Supreme Court's ruling that ADEA disparate impact claims can be brought, but the employer is not liable if the disparate impact is the result of a reasonable factor other than age, the EEOC proposed new regulations, holding that an employment practice with disparate impact on older individuals violates the ADEA unless it is justified by an RFOA. The person challenging the practice has the burden of identifying the specific practice that creates the impact; citing a generalized policy is not sufficient. But once the RFOA exception is raised, it is an affirmative defense—that is, the employer must prove it. [73 Fed. Reg. 168087 (Mar. 31, 2008)] The Supreme Court agreed that RFOA is an affirmative defense: see *Meacham v. Knolls Atomic Power Labs*, 554 U.S. 84 (2008).

The Supreme Court pointed out that Title VII and the ADEA have different language and different requirements, deciding, in mid-2009, that mixed-motive ADEA cases require the plaintiff to prove, by a preponderance of the evidence, that age was the "but-for" cause of the unfavorable employment action: in other words, that the action would never have been taken but-for the plaintiff's being over 40. [*Gross v. FBL Fin. Servs., Inc.*, 557 U.S. 167 (2009)]

After the Supreme Court's *Lewis v. City of Chicago* decision (holding that plaintiffs in disparate impact cases do not have to prove deliberate discrimination; see § 34.04[D]), the District Court for the District of Columbia revived a claim in attorney Yolanda Young's suit against the firm Covington & Burling. In 2012, however, the district court dismissed the suit, finding a legitimate, non-discriminatory reason (lack of work) for Young's termination. Young was one of 170 staff attorneys hired in the period 2005 to 2008 to review documents. No staff attorney has ever been hired as an associate, counsel, or partner of the firm. The district court said that Young never applied for a promotion, so she couldn't claim she was denied promotion, and no staff attorney was ever promoted so failure to promote Young was not discriminatory. [*Young v. Covington & Burling LLP* No. 09-464 (RBW) (D.D.C. 2012); see Zoe Tillman, *Judge Dismisses Former Covington Staff Attorney's Discrimination Suit*, The BLT: The Blog of Legal Times (Mar. 7, 2012) (law.com)]

In a similar case brought by an African-American contract attorney, the Southern District of New York granted summary judgment for the law firm. The plaintiff's case relied on statistical evidence that black contract lawyers billed fewer hours than other full-time contract attorneys. The court held that individual private plaintiffs must prove that they were individually subjected to intentional discrimination. In this reading, pattern or practice evidence cannot be used outside the context of a class action, because it forces employers to prove that they did not discriminate, whereas it is up to the plaintiff to prove discrimination. [*Simmons-Grant v. Quinn Emanuel*, No. 1:11-cv-07706 (dismissed, S.D.N.Y.); see Christine Simmons, *Quinn Emanuel Wins Dismissal of Bias Suit*, N.Y.L.J. (Jan. 9, 2013) (law.com) See also *Chin v. Port Auth.*, 685 F.3d 135 (2012) on pattern-or-practice claims.]

The District Court for the District of Massachusetts required arbitration of a gender bias case against CIGNA Healthcare. The plaintiff alleged that CIGNA's evaluation and promotion practices violated Title VII and Massachusetts anti-discrimination law and that her job was downgraded whereas similarly situated male co-workers received a higher classification. CIGNA argued that the charge had to be arbitrated; the plaintiff said that she had never waived the right to litigate class-based or pattern-or-practice claims. However, the court ruled that pattern-or-practice claims are a method of proving discrimination in a class action, not a separate cause of action. [*Karp v. CIGNA Healthcare Inc.*, 882 F. Supp. 2d 199 (D. Mass. 2012); see Sheri Qualters, *Judge Sends Gender Bias Case Against CIGNA To Arbitration*, Nat'l L.J.( Apr. 19, 2012) (law.com), The Second Circuit reached the same conclusion, compelling arbitration of claims by three Goldman Sachs executives who wanted to assert a pattern-or-practice claim in court: *Parisi v. Goldman, Sachs & Co.*, 710 F.3d 483 (2d Cir. 2013).]

## § 34.03 TITLE VII COVERAGE

Title VII bans "unlawful employment practices." Unlawful employment practices discriminate against an employee or job applicant on the basis of the individual's race, color, religion, sex, or national origin. [42 U.S.C. § 2000e-2(a)] Note that Title VII does not ban sexual-orientation discrimination, but some applicable state and local statutes do.

Unlawful employment practices on the part of the employer are defined by 42 U.S.C. § 2000e-2(a) as:

- To fail or refuse to hire;

- To discharge;

- To discriminate with respect to compensation, terms, conditions, or privileges of employment;

- To limit, segregate, or classify employees or job applicants in a way that deprives or tends to deprive them of employment opportunities, or otherwise adversely affects their status as employees.

Title VII also bans discriminatory practices by employment agencies and labor unions, but their activities are outside the scope of this book.

In late 1998, the Fourth Circuit joined the Third, Fifth, Seventh, Eighth, Tenth, Eleventh, and D.C. Circuits in ruling that only employer companies, and not individuals, can be held liable under Title VII. [*Lissau v. S. Food Serv.*, 159 F.3d 177 (4th Cir. 1998); see also *Fantini v. Salem State College*, 557 F.3d 22 (1st Cir. 2009)]

An important—and growing—part of the employment discrimination caseload is the "retaliation" case. Section 2000e-3(a) makes it unlawful for an employer to discriminate against anyone who has opposed an unlawful employment practice or who has "made a charge, testified, assisted, or participated in any manner in an investigation, proceeding, or hearing" under Title VII. [See § 34.08 for more about retaliation cases]

It is also an unlawful employment practice to indicate "any preference, limitation, specification, or discrimination" based on race, color, religion, sex, or national origin in a help-wanted ad, unless belonging to a particular group is a Bona Fide Occupational Qualification (BFOQ). [See 42 U.S.C. § 2000e-3(b)]

It might be a BFOQ to be male or female (e.g., because of authenticity, for an actor or actress; for privacy, for a restroom attendant); to be under 40 (in a job where public safety depends on youthful reactions) or even to belong to a particular religion (e.g., to work in a kosher slaughterhouse). Race is never a BFOQ. In the disability context, it is a BFOQ not to pose a safety risk to oneself or others. Where safety or efficiency is involved, it may be possible to raise a "business necessity" defense for a discriminatory business practice.

## § 34.04   EXCEPTIONS TO TITLE VII COVERAGE

### [A]   Definition of Employer

Perhaps the most important exception is found in 42 U.S.C. § 2000e(b), which defines an "employer" as a natural person or business engaged in an industry affecting commerce—and having 15 or more employees for each work day in 20 or more weeks either in the year in question or the preceding calendar year. So a very small business will be exempt from Title VII. Possibly some businesses with even more than 15 employees will escape coverage because their business does not "affect commerce," but most businesses do sell or at least attempt to make interstate sales, so their business will be deemed to "affect commerce."

The 15-employee figure is calculated based on the number of people on the payroll, not the number of full-time employees. [*Walters v. Metro. Educ. Enters., Inc.*, 519 U.S. 202 (1997)]

Whether a company has 15 employees or not is a substantive element of the Title VII claim (in this case, a sexual harassment charge), not a jurisdictional prerequisite. The practical significance of this 2006 Supreme Court ruling is that the number of employees is an issue that can be waived if it is not raised on time, whereas questions of subject matter jurisdiction can be raised at any time. The

Supreme Court decided that the 15-employee requirement is not jurisdictional because it is not found within the part of the Title VII statute that grants jurisdiction to the federal courts. [*Arbaugh v. Y&H Corp.*, 546 U.S. 500 (2006)]

Suit could be brought under Title VII against a U.S.-based parent corporation, even though it had only six employees, because its wholly owned Mexican subsidiary had at least 50 employees. Even though the Mexican employees would not be protected by Title VII, the Ninth Circuit ruled in 2002 that they should be included in the count. [*Kang v. U Lim Am. Inc.*, 296 F.3d 810 (9th Cir. 2002)]

As shown below, there is a "ministerial exception" to accommodate First Amendment freedom of religion (see § 34.07). Another exception is allowed under 42 U.S.C. § 2000e-2(e) if religion, sex, or national origin is a bona fide occupational qualification "reasonably necessary to the normal operation" of the business. Educational institutions sponsored by a religious organization (e.g., Notre Dame or Yeshiva University) or institutions "directed toward the propagation of a particular religion" are permitted to base hiring and other employment decisions on religion—parochial schools can, but do not have to, employ staffers of other religions.

According to the Seventh and Eighth Circuits, Congress took a valid action in 1972 when it abrogated sovereign immunity and made the states subject to Title VII, so Title VII disparate impact suits can be brought against a state employer. [*Nanda v. Board of Trustees of the Univ. of Ill.*, 303 F.3d 817 (7th Cir. 2002); *Okruhlik v. Univ. of Ark.*, 255 F.3d 615 (8th Cir. 2001)]

## [B] Aliens

Section 2000e-1 provides that Title VII does not apply to the employment of "aliens." In August 1998, the Fourth Circuit reversed its earlier ruling. Now *Egbuna v. Time-Life Libraries, Inc.* [153 F.3d 184 (4th Cir. 1998)] holds that it is necessary to be a U.S. citizen or an alien holding a valid work visa, to be a "qualified" individual. So an alien who does not have legal worker status in the United States cannot make out a Title VII prima facie case.

Furthermore, an employer does not violate Title VII if it (or a corporation it controls) takes an action with respect to an employee in a foreign country that is necessary to avoid violating that country's law—even if the action would be barred by Title VII if it were taken in the United States. The factors in whether an employer controls a corporation include whether there is common management, ownership, or financial control, and whether the two organizations have related operations. See also § 23.11 on immigration and nationality issues in hiring.

42 U.S.C. § 1981 applies only to conduct within the United States, so this provision does not cover allegations of racial discrimination made by a non-U.S. citizen who was transferred to South African by his U.S. employer. However, he could use § 1981 to charge discrimination while he worked in the United States. [*Ofori-Tenkorang v. Am. Int'l Group Inc.*, 460 F.3d 296 (2d Cir. 2006)]

## [C]  National Security

42 U.S.C. § 2000e-2(g) enacts a national security exception. It does not violate Title VII to fire or refuse to hire someone who has not met, or no longer meets, security clearance requirements "in effect pursuant to or administered under any statute of the United States or any Executive order of the President."

Engineer Hossein Zeinali, who is of Iranian descent, sued Raytheon for terminating him after the Department of Defense denied him a security clearance. The district court dismissed the race/national origin discrimination charges, holding that the federal courts do not have jurisdiction over security clearance cases. The Ninth Circuit reversed and allowed Zeinali's suit to proceed, because he did not dispute the validity of the denial—only whether it was legitimate for Raytheon to require a security clearance. He produced evidence that non-Iranian engineers without security clearances were allowed to work, so he raised a triable issue about whether having a security clearance was a bona fide requirement for engineers. [ *Zeinali v. Raytheon Co*, 636 F.3d 544 (9th Cir. 2011); see Rebecca Moore, *9th Circuit Revives Iranians Bias Lawsuit Against Raytheon*, plansponsor .com (Apr. 5, 2011)]

## [D]  Seniority Systems

Employers are permitted, under 42 U.S.C. § 2000e-2(h), to abide by "bona fide seniority or merit systems," or to base compensation on quantity or quality of production, or to pay different rates at different locations—even if the result is to provide different standards of compensation or different terms, conditions, or privileges of employment. However, employers are not allowed to impose such differences in treatment if they are "the result of an intention to discriminate" on the basis of race, color, religion, sex, or national origin.

Also see 42 U.S.C. § 2000e-5(e)(2), which says that the unlawful unemployment practice occurs, with respect to a seniority system that was adopted "for an intentionally discriminatory purpose," whether or not the purpose can be discerned from the face of the provision, either when the seniority system is adopted, when the potential plaintiff becomes subject to the seniority system, or when the seniority system is applied in a way that injures the potential plaintiff.

The Lilly Ledbetter Act, Pub. L. No. 111-2, was passed to reaffirm these statutory principles and to overturn a Supreme Court decision that restricted the time to file discrimination suits.

A 2009 Supreme Court decision [*AT&T Corp. v. Hulteen*, 556 U.S. 701 (2009)] holds that AT&T abided by the terms of a bona fide seniority system, and therefore was not guilty of sex discrimination even though the pensions of some female workers were reduced because, before the passage of the Pregnancy Discrimination Act (PDA), AT&T treated pregnancy leave less favorably than other forms of temporary disability leave. (Once the PDA took effect, AT&T changed its policies, so the question was the effect of past discrimination.)

Section 2000e-2(h) also allows employers to use validated pre-employment tests of ability, as long as testing is not designed, intended or used to discriminate. The subject of test scores is taken up again in 42 U.S.C. § 2000e-2(l), which states that it is an unlawful employment practice to adjust scores or use different cutoff scores in hiring or promotion tests, based on the race, color, religion, sex or national origin of the test taker.

Also in 2009, the Supreme Court ruled that a city should not have refused to certify a promotional test for firefighters. The city argued that, because certifying the test would make the city vulnerable to lawsuits from minority firefighters who scored poorly, the test should have been discarded. The Supreme Court, however, held that refusing to certify the promotion list discriminated against high-scoring firefighters (mostly white and Hispanic), so the employer should have relied on its properly validated test. [*Ricci v. DeStefano*, 129 S. Ct. 2658 (2009). CNN reported that payouts to 20 firefighters (19 white, one Hispanic) finally began in 2011; the 20 received $2 million for back pay, attorneys' fees, and pension credits. See Rebecca Moore, *Award Finally Decided in Connecticut Firefighters Suit*, plansponsor.com (Aug. 3, 2011)]]

The following year, the Supreme Court heard another challenge to a firefighters' promotional exam, this time brought by black and Hispanic firefighters. The Supreme Court ruled that challenges to the test were not untimely, although they were brought a number of years after the original test—because, when an employer continues to use an employment practice with disparate impact on a protected group, each use of the practice (i.e., each time a class of firefighters is promoted based on the original test results) can be challenged. [*Lewis v. City of Chicago*, 130 S. Ct. 2191 ( 2010)]

## § 34.05  RACIAL DISCRIMINATION

### [A]  Basic Protections

The first equal opportunity laws were bans on racial discrimination. The Civil Rights Act of 1866, enacted at 42 U.S.C. § 1981, was passed to give former slaves the same rights as "white citizens." There is no requirement of a minimum number of employees for a § 1981 suit, and the EEOC and state antidiscrimination procedures do not have to be invoked before bringing suit under this provision.

The Civil Rights Act of 1991 generally requires plaintiffs to proceed under § 1981 if they have claims of racial discrimination, before using Title VII. Compensatory and punitive damages are not available under Title VII for any plaintiff who can get such damages under § 1981.

There have been some major recent cases about race discrimination. The quest to have a completely race-neutral workplace is a difficult one, and claims have been raised both by majority and minority groups that their rights have been violated.

In mid-2013, the Supreme Court used standards similar to those for sexual harassment cases (see § 35.02) in a case of racial harassment of an African-American employee. The Supreme Court held that the employer is strictly liable if harassment is committed by a supervisor and involves a tangible employment action (e.g., hiring, firing, reassignment) against the victim. If the harasser is a supervisor, but there is no tangible employment action, then the employer can assert an affirmative defense under *Faragher/Ellerth*: that the employer took reasonable care to prevent and correct harassment, but the plaintiff unreasonably failed to take advantage of this procedure. A supervisor is a person authorized to take tangible employment actions against the plaintiff. However, in this case, the harasser was a co-worker of the plaintiff's. In cases of co-worker harassment, the Supreme Court held that the employer is liable only if it was negligent in controlling working conditions. [*Vance v. Ball State Univ.*, 133 S. Ct. 2434 (2013); see Marcia Coyle, *Supreme Court Makes It Harder to Prove Job Bias Claims*, Nat'l L.J. (June 24, 2013) (law.com)]

Even a single racial slur by a supervisor in the presence of another supervisor can be severe enough to create a hostile work environment. [*Taylor v. Metzger*, 706 A.2d 685 (N.J. 1998), although a later case, *Jordan v. Alternative Res. Corp.*, 458 F.3d 332 (4th Cir. 2006), holds that a single racial slur uttered by a colleague (it was directed at a TV news report, not at the plaintiff) was not enough to create a hostile work environment. Therefore, the employee could not prove a retaliation case when his job was eliminated several months later: the incident was isolated and did not alter the terms and conditions of employment]

The Eighth Circuit found that there was a racially hostile work environment when white co-workers refused to work with the plaintiffs (who are black); there were many racist graffiti in the workplace that remained for months without being removed; rail cars were spray-painted with racist threats; and co-workers displayed Confederate flags and even swastikas. The plaintiffs complained, but management did not help them. The plaintiffs also alleged that white co-workers falsely accused them of safety violations that could have gotten them fired, and that they were disciplined for infractions that white workers were not punished for. [*Watson v. CEVA Logistics, Inc.*, 619 F.3d 936 (8th Cir. 2010)]

After Judges Carnes and Pryor decided that calling a black man "boy" could be racist, they were open to the possibility that bananas could be used for racial harassment, but had other questions about a racially hostile work environment case. Plaintiff Reginald Jones cited bananas being left in his truck as one instance of racial harassment; the site manager said that banana peels were probably garbage left by kids—but there were no banana peels or other garbage on any other driver's truck. Jones said that he had seen co-workers wearing Confederate insignia. UPS said that it responded promptly and appropriately and a manager urged

Jones not to resign when he said he was considering it. The Northern District of Alabama granted summary judgment for the employer, denying that bananas had racial connotations and finding that the conditions were not severe and pervasive enough to create a hostile environment. The Eleventh Circuit vacated summary judgment and remanded the case, because a reasonable trier of facts could conclude that the work environment was racially hostile. [*Jones v. UPS Ground Freight*, 683 F.3d 1283 (11th Cir. 2012).

The Eighth Circuit dismissed the Title VII portion of a racial harassment claim, because the employer's racial slurs against several groups, amounting to about one outburst per month over a two-year period, were not severe or pervasive enough to create a hostile work environment. However, the § 1981 claim (termination as retaliation for objecting to the slurs) was permitted to go to trial. [*Bainbridge v. Loffredo Gardens Inc.*, 378 F.3d 756 (8th Cir. 2004)]

The often-cited case of *Herrnreiter v. Chicago Hous. Auth.* [315 F.3d 742 (7th Cir. 2002)] was brought by a white auditor who was transferred by his black supervisor from the agency's investigation division to its auditing division. The Seventh Circuit held that there was no actionable racial discrimination (even though the plaintiff preferred the investigator's job) because he was not demoted to an objectively inferior position or prevented from exercising his professional skills.

There have been a number of major settlements of racial discrimination and harassment cases (e.g., nooses or swastikas displayed in the workplace, hate graffiti, display of minority employees' names on a "hit list") and racially hostile work environments. Settlements usually included injunctions, training, posting of information about the settlement, and monitoring by the EEOC to prevent further offenses. In many of these cases, the employer denied wrongdoing, but stated that it wished to settle to avoid prolonged litigation.

- Allied Aviation Services, which fuels planes at airports, agreed to a $1.9 million settlement of a Title VII racial harassment suit brought by the EEOC on behalf of 15 black and Hispanic plaintiffs at one airport. The case was so egregious that EEOC filed its own suit after the investigation, which seldom happens. [Eric O'Keefe, *Contractor at Airports Settles Suit in Bias Case*, N.Y. Times, Mar. 12, 2008, at C4]

- Pepsi Beverages settled EEOC race discrimination charges, agreeing to pay $3.13 million and provide job offers and training. Most of the settlement goes to black job applicants, more than 300 of whom were denied access to permanent jobs. Pepsi also agreed to offer jobs to qualified applicants who still want to work there. The EEOC said that Pepsi's criminal background check procedure, which ruled out everyone who had ever been arrested even if no conviction resulted, discriminated against black applicants. Employment was also denied to people convicted of certain minor offenses. [Tara Cantore, *Pepsi to Pay $3.13M to Resolve Race Bias Charge*, plansponsor.com (Jan. 12, 2012)]

• Merrill Lynch settled a long-running suit (it lasted for eight years, including two Supreme Court appeals) by agreeing to pay $160 million to a class of 700 black brokers. It was the largest race discrimination settlement in any suit against a U.S. employer. It is difficult to certify an employment class after *Dukes* (see §§ 34.06[A], 42.06[A]) but it was possible in this case because of Merrill Lynch's highly centralized control and uniform operations. [*McReynolds v. Merrill Lynch*, No. 11-01957 (7th Cir. settled 2013)/ *McReynolds v. Merrill Lynch*, No. 05-cv-06583 (N.D. Ill. settled 2013); see Patrick McGeehan, *Merrill Lynch in Big Payout for Bias Case*,NYTimes.com (Aug. 27, 2013)]

## [B]  Reverse Discrimination

Although most discrimination suits are brought by members of protected groups charging that they were discriminated against by members of the dominant group, a reverse discrimination suit is brought by members of the dominant group charging that they were discriminated against for being, e.g., white, male, or non-disabled. This issue is intimately related to the question of when, if ever, affirmative action is appropriate: see § 34.05[C], below.

The city of New Haven, Connecticut, gave an examination for firefighters to be promoted to the jobs of lieutenant and captain. Far more white than minority firefighters passed the exam. The city, fearing that it would be sued by minority candidates, discarded the exam and did not promote anyone. The city was sued by white and Hispanic firefighters alleging that their superior test scores entitled them to promotion. The Supreme Court held that the city violated Title VII by refusing to certify the test and make promotions based on the test results, intentionally discriminating against the white and Hispanic firefighters without evidence that it would be liable if it did not make up for past disparate impact. If it had been sued by minority firefighters who charged a violation of Title VII, the Supreme Court said the city could have asserted the Title VII provision allowing valid, job-related tests. [*Ricci v. DeStefano*, 129 S. Ct. 2658 (2009)]

The EEOC announced settlement of a sex discrimination suit against Pure Weight Loss ($16.8 million back pay, $3.15 million in punitive damages) brought by men who had been discriminated against since 1997. In 2002, the EEOC sued, charging discrimination against male job applicants and retaliation against a female employee who protested the discriminatory policy. However, because the company is in Chapter 7, the consent decree gives the EEOC a $20 million claim in the bankruptcy. [Rebecca Moore, *L.A. Weight Loss Settles Gender Discrimination Suit for $20M*, plansponsor.com (Dec. 8, 2008)]

## [C]  Affirmative Action and Quotas

A very important question in employment law is how to balance the rights of current employees and applicants against the desire to have a workplace that is truly representative and does not reflect past discrimination.

According to 42 U.S.C. § 2000e-2(j), Title VII does not require employers to grant preferential treatment to any individual or any group because the workforce is imbalanced in terms of the number or percentage of workers from groups that have been discriminated against in the past. In other words, employers do not have to use quotas in hiring, promotion, etc.

In 1977, the Supreme Court decided that it is unlawful to perpetuate the present effects of past discrimination, although bona fide seniority systems can be left in operation. [*Teamsters v. U.S.*, 431 U.S. 324 (1977)] Under this approach, preferential hiring of women and minorities might be acceptable to correct an imbalance in the workforce that results from past discrimination. It might also be acceptable to set goals to remove past discrimination and to remove the barriers that existed in the past to prevent racially neutral hiring, but the hiring system must not exclude white applicants.

Cases in the late 1990s say that employers should not set up affirmative action programs merely to enhance diversity within the workplace, but an affirmative action program might be an appropriate corrective measure if there is a history of racism in a particular industry. [*Johnson v. Transp. Agency of Santa Clara County*, 480 U.S. 616 (1987); *Eldredge v. Carpenters Joint Apprenticeship and Training Comm.*, 94 F.3d 1366 (9th Cir. 1996); *Schurr v. Resorts Int'l Hotel*, 196 F.3d 486 (3d Cir. 1999)]

The Supreme Court agreed to hear the case of *Piscataway Twp. Bd. of Educ. v. Taxman* [#96-679, *cert. dismissed*, 522 U.S. 1010 (1997)] involving the important issue of whether a well-qualified employee can be laid off to promote the goal of diversity in the workplace. However, the case was settled out of court in late November 1997, so the Supreme Court did not issue a decision.

In the past two decades or so, affirmative action has been most prominent in the context of government contracts. In 1995, the U.S. Supreme Court decided that race-based preferences in government contracting are permissible only if the actual contractor has been the victim of discrimination—not merely that he or she belongs to a group that has historically been economically disadvantaged. [*Adarand Constructors Inc. v. Pena*, 513 U.S. 1108, and 515 U.S. 200 (1995)] The case continued to bounce up and down the court system with various decisions that had more to do with technical legal issues than with the rights and wrongs of affirmative action. The case was supposed to be reheard by the Supreme Court, but in November 2001, the Supreme Court dismissed certiorari as having been improvidently granted. [*Adarand Constructors v. Mineta*, 534 U.S. 103 (2001)]

## [D]   Executive Order 11246

Executive Order 11246 requires government contractors and contractors on federally assisted construction projects worth over $10,000 to have a policy of furthering equal employment opportunity. If the contractor or subcontractor has more than 50 employees, and the contract is worth over $50,000, the company must have a formal affirmative action program, which must be submitted to the Office of Federal Contract Compliance Programs (OFCCP) within 30 days of the OFCCP's request to see the program.

Contracts over $1 million require a pre-award audit of the affirmative action program. [See 41 C.F.R. Part 60] There are separate, slightly different, rules for construction contractors.

A company charged with reverse discrimination because of its affirmative action program can cite as a defense that it followed the EEOC's Guidelines on Affirmative Action. To qualify for this defense, the employer must have a written plan. It must act reasonably, taking actions based on self-analysis that leads to a reasonable conclusion that there are actual problems of job bias that require correction. The plan of action must be tailored to eliminate inequality. It must last only as long as it takes to eliminate the effects of past discrimination.

## [E]   National Origin Discrimination

Since the September 11 attack, there has been an increase in attention to the related problems of national origin discrimination against people of Middle Eastern and South Asian origin and religious discrimination against Muslims. As the EEOC points out, immigrants are now a substantial part of the workforce.

The EEOC responded to the increasing threat of national origin discrimination by issuing guidance on national origin discrimination. National origin discrimination is often intertwined with other types of discrimination: e.g., based on religion and/or having a native language other than English.

According to the guidance document [EEOC, National Origin Discrimination, <http://www.eeoc.gov/origin/index.html> (modified Mar. 29, 2006); the EEOC also issued a new § 13, "National Origin Discrimination," as part of the agency's manual, replacing transmittals 622 on Citizenship, Residency Requirements, Aliens and Undocumented Workers, and 623, Speak-English-Only Rules and Other Language Policies], national origin discrimination means less-favorable treatment imposed because of someone's country of origin, ethnicity, or accent, or belief that someone has a particular ethnic background. Discrimination on the basis of marriage or other association with people of a disfavored nationality is also covered.

The EEOC position is that employers have a responsibility to prevent or at least correct ethnic slurs that create a hostile work environment. Employment decisions may be made on the basis of accent only if a person's accent materially interferes with job performance. Fluency in English can be imposed as a job requirement only if it is required to do the job; English-only rules are permissible only if they are adopted for non-discriminatory reasons such as promoting the safe or efficient conduct of the business. The agency's stance is that all antidiscrimination laws apply whether or not the discriminatee is a citizen, although remedies are limited for those who do not have authorization to work in this country.

The EEOC has discussed harassment and discrimination against Asians. [EEOC, *Questions and Answers About Employer Responsibilities Concerning the Employment of Muslims, Arabs, South Asians, and Sikhs* (July 16, 2002) <http://www.eeoc.gov/facts/backlash-employer.html> (modified Mar. 21, 2005)] The agency position is that it is impermissible to deny employment (e.g., to people who wear turbans, headscarves, or other religious dress) even if the employer believes that customers will be hostile to such workers. A manager or supervisor who learns about ethnic slurs or harassment in the workplace should tell the harassers to stop doing this, and discipline anyone who is found to have committed harassment. If employees ask for the use of space for prayer, the employer can turn down the request only if the space is legitimately required for business needs. (Employers have a duty of reasonable accommodation to religious practice, whereas they merely need to avoid discrimination on the basis of national origin.) Nor can background checks be made more stringent based on an applicant's country of origin.

The relevant factors in determining whether national origin harassment has occurred include whether physical threats were made or workers were intimidated; whether the conduct was hostile and patently offensive; the frequency of the conduct; the context in which it occurred; and whether management acted appropriately after learning of the conduct.

The Supreme Court denied *certiorari* in a First Circuit case brought by an Afghan Muslim immigrant who charged that he was fired for discriminatory reasons, and that he suffered a hostile work environment after 9/11. The jury found that harassment occurred, but the First Circuit denied damages for lack of proof of lost wages or out of pocket payments for medical treatment or therapy. Therefore, the plaintiff's contention, that the jury should have been instructed on the option of awarding punitive damages in the absence of compensatory damages, was not reviewed by the Supreme Court. [*Azimi v. Jordan's Meats, cert. denied,* 549 U.S. 1279 (2007); see Adrien Martin, *Supreme Court Rejects Discrimination Case by Muslim Immigrant,* plansponsor.com (Mar. 19, 2007)]

The Ninth Circuit ruled that a CEO's insistence on calling an employee "Manny" or "Hank" rather than his Arabic name, Mamdouh el-Hakem, constituted intentional hostile work environment discrimination forbidden by 42 U.S.C. § 1981, even in the absence of racial epithets. [*El-Hakem v. BJY Inc.,* 415 F.3d 1068 (9th Cir. 2005)]

A state university professor alleged that he was the lowest-paid faculty member in his department because of discrimination based on his national and tribal origin (he is black, an immigrant from Nigeria, and a member of the Igbo tribe). His department chair is black and an immigrant from Ghana who belongs to a different tribe. The university argued that Professor Onyiah's salary fell within the "salary grid" range for his position and he could have negotiated for higher pay within the grid range. The Eighth Circuit said that the six professors cited as comparators were not really comparable. They were hired at a time when the grids were not used to establish salaries and they were not hired by the same decision-maker as Onyiah. The Eighth Circuit did not decide whether tribal affiliation is a form of national origin because Onyiah did not include tribal affiliation discrimination in his complaint, so the university was not on notice of this allegation. [*Onyiah v. St. Cloud State Univ.*, 684 F.3d 711 (8th Cir. 2012)]

The Tenth Circuit permitted Hispanic employees who said that an English-only policy caused them to be taunted by native English speakers to maintain hostile environment discriminatory impact claims. In the court's view, the employer anticipated that this would happen and had no justification for imposing the policy. [*Maldonado v. Altus*, 433 F.3d 1294 (10th Cir. 2006)] The Sixth Circuit reversed summary judgment for the employer in a case alleging denial of promotion because of speech characteristics and accent. (EEOC regulations say that denial of opportunity on linguistic grounds can be evidence of national origin discrimination.) The plaintiff filed suit as a race discrimination claim, but the Sixth Circuit re-characterized it as a national origin claim. Evidence that managers treated the plaintiff's accent as a bar to promotion was considered direct evidence of discrimination—so the case was remanded to permit the employer to show it would have made the same decision absent discrimination. [*In re Rodriguez*, 487 F.3d 1001 (6th Cir. 2007); see Carla J. Rozycki and David K. Haase, *Statements About Employee's Accent May Be Direct Evidence of Discrimination* (July 18, 2007) (special to law.com). However, the Southern District of New York reached the opposite conclusion in *Altman v. New York City Dept. of Educ.*, No. 06 CV 6319, 2007 WL 1290599 (S.D.N.Y. May 1, 2007), where remarks about accent were not facially discriminatory because English fluency was legitimately related to job performance in the job of teaching English as a second language.]

## [F] EEOC 2006 Guidance

In April 2006, the EEOC revised § 15 of its compliance manual with respect to race and color discrimination. Studies show that racial prejudice persists in hiring—for example, white people with criminal records were three times as likely to be offered employment as black people with similar records, temporary agencies preferred white to black applicants, and interviews were 50% more likely to be given based on the same resume if it showed a "white" rather than a "black" surname. [In *El-Hakem v. BJY, Inc.*, 415 F.3d 1068, 1073 (9th Cir. 2005), the Ninth Circuit held that names are often a proxy for race and ethnicity.]

Title VII does not define "race," and neither does the EEOC; federal race/ethnicity data is collected using the OMB's categories (American Indian/Alaska native; Asian; Black (African-American); Native Hawaiian or Other Pacific Islander; and White, plus the ethnic category of Hispanic/Latino). This guidance says that Title VII generally covers:

- Racial or ethnic ancestry; the EEOC notes that race and national origin can overlap, but are not the same thing;

- Perceived race, even if the perception is incorrect;

- Association with someone of a particular race;

- Subgroup or "race plus," e.g., treating black women who have pre-school children worse than white women with pre-school children;

- Physical characteristics associated with race, such as skin color, hair, facial features, height and weight;

- Race-linked illnesses (for example, sickle cell anemia and diabetes). An employer who applies facially neutral standards that exclude the treatment of conditions for which certain ethnic groups are disproportionately at risk must show that the standards are based on generally accepted medical criteria;

- Cultural characteristics related to ethnicity, such as name, dress and grooming practices, accent or manner of speech;

- Reverse discrimination. The EEOC does not require a heightened standard of proof when Caucasian employees raise reverse-discrimination claims, but the ultimate burden of persuasion always rests with the plaintiff.

The EEOC notes that color discrimination can be intra-racial, for example, a black manager's favoring lighter-skinned black subordinates over darker-skinned subordinates.

A complaint can involve any combination of race, color, and national origin; EEOC policy is for complaints to list all allegations that can reasonably be made. Discrimination is also forbidden if it is based on the intersection of two or more protected categories (e.g., Latinos with a disability).

The EEOC's position is that disparate impact analysis applies to all objective or subjective criteria for recruitment, hiring, promotion, or layoff, as well as grooming standards and education requirements. Proof of a disparate impact case begins with a statistical showing that the policy or practice causes significant disparate impact to a protected group. Then the employer has the burden of showing the practice is job-related and consistent with business necessity. Finally, the burden shifts to whether the person challenging the policy or practice can show a less discriminatory alternative method for satisfying the business need.

In assessing arrest records, the employer must evaluate not only the relationship between the charge and the job, but whether or not the arrested person was actually guilty. For conviction records, the employer must consider the nature and gravity of the offense(s); the length of time elapsed since the conviction or completion of the sentence; and the nature of the job. The EEOC considers a blanket refusal to hire anyone who has ever had a conviction of any kind to be inappropriate because it is not job-related or consistent with business necessity. For the EEOC's most recent statement of these principles, see EEOC Enforcement Guidance, *Consideration of Arrest and Conviction Records In Employment Decisions Under Title VII of the Civil Rights Act of 1964* < http://www.eeoc.gov/laws/ guidance/arrest_conviction.cfm> (Apr. 25, 2012)]

The EEOC has brought several suits (e.g., against BMW and Dollar General) alleging discriminatory use of criminal records as part of background checks. In mid-2013, however, the District Court for the District of Maryland dismissed the agency's suit against Freeman Co., approving the records check policy as a reasonable means of recruiting an honest work force, and finding that the EEOC failed to prove race discrimination. [*EEOC v. Freeman Co.*, No. 09-CV-2573 (D.Md. Aug. 9, 2013)]

The EEOC says that appearance and grooming standards must be neutral, consistently applied, and adopted for nondiscriminatory reasons. Racial or ethnic attire that conforms to the dress code must be allowed. Employers can require hairstyles that are neat, clean and well-groomed, as long as racial differences in hair texture are respected, and the standards are equally applied. A no-beard policy is not acceptable vis-à-vis employees who have problems with shaving. Although there has not been a high volume of court decisions on this issue, some employers must handle the question of whether Islamic head coverings can be forbidden—or how to handle head coverings in an environment where employees are required to wear protective headgear or sanitary head coverings as part of the job.

The guidance says that Title VII allows diversity outreach. Affirmative action is action to overcome past or present barriers to equal employment opportunity, and can be court-ordered after a discrimination finding, negotiated as a remedy in a consent decree or settlement agreement, or created pursuant to government regulation. Voluntary affirmative action plans are permitted, for example, to eliminate a manifest imbalance in a job category that has traditionally been segregated. Courts ruling on a voluntary affirmative action plan look at whether it involves a quota or inflexible goal; whether the plan is flexible enough to make each candidate compete against all other qualified candidate; if the plan is unnecessarily harmful to interests of third parties, and whether the plan is temporary and will end when the goal has been met.

Race-based conduct by a supervisor, co-worker, or non-employee who is nevertheless under the employer's control (for example, a customer or business partner) can constitute unlawful harassment if unwelcome and severe or pervasive enough to alter terms and conditions of employment as viewed by a reasonable person in the victim's position. The more severe, the less pervasive it has to be, and vice versa, so a single incident would create an abusive environment only if very severe (e.g., physical).

Employers are generally liable for the acts of supervisors. However, in hostile environment cases when there was no tangible action against the victim, the employer can raise the affirmative defense that it used reasonable care to prevent harassing behavior, or that any harassment was promptly corrected—but the employee unreasonably failed to make use of these procedures. If the harasser is high enough in rank to serve as proxy for the employer (e.g., if the harasser is an owner, president, partner, or corporate officer) then the affirmative defense is not available even for a hostile environment claim. For harassment committed by co-workers or customers on the employer's premises, the employer is liable if it knew or should have known about the conduct and did not take prompt corrective steps. [See <http://www.eeoc.gov/policy/docs/race-color.html> (last revised Feb. 8, 2011). See also Section 13: *National Origin Discrimination* (2002), posted to <http://www.eeoc.gov/policy/docs/national-origin.html>, and *Guidelines on Discrimination Because of National Origin*, at 29 C.F.R. § 1606.1.

## [G]  Association Discrimination

"Association discrimination" is the claim that persons of one group were subjected to workplace discrimination because of their association with persons of another group.

Early in 2011, the Supreme Court held that Title VII forbids retaliation against a discrimination complainant that takes the form of punishing an associate of that person. In this case, Miriam Regalado filed an EEOC sex discrimination charge against North American Stainless in 2002. Three weeks after the charge was filed, Regalado's then-fiance (they subsequently married) was fired. The Supreme Court's majority opinion says that the Title VII anti-retaliation provision covers any action by an employer that would prevent a reasonable worker from making or pursuing a discrimination charge. There are no hard and fast lines, but firing a close family member is almost always covered by Title VII, a mild reprisal against an acquaintance is not covered, and courts must decide the intermediate cases. A suit can be brought by anyone within the "zone of interests" protected by the law. [*Thompson v. North Am. Stainless*, 131 S. Ct. 863 (2011); see Marcia Coyle, *Court Says Third Parties Can Sue in Retaliation Cases* (Dec. 7, 2010) (law.com)]

The Second Circuit allowed such a case to proceed, holding that Title VII can be violated by firing a white man for associating with a person of another race (in this case, his black wife). Taking adverse action because of an interracial relationship reflects discrimination because it embodies stereotypes about how white people should behave. [*Holcomb v. Iona College*, 521 F.3d 130 (2d Cir. 2008); see Mark Hamblett, *2nd Circuit Allows Bias Claim of White Man with Black Wife*, N.Y.L.J. (Apr. 2, 2008)]

In a race discrimination and retaliation case, three white employees charged that they suffered discrimination for their friendship with and advocacy of black co-workers. The Sixth Circuit affirmed the dismissal of all of the charges except for one plaintiff's hostile environment discrimination charge, because the plaintiffs failed to show a high enough degree of association to justify an association discrimination claim, and most of their assertions of hostile work environment and retaliation were not proved. The Sixth Circuit held that, although Title VII and § 1981 forbid association discrimination, there is no Sixth Circuit precedent about how closely the employees must associate before a discrimination case can be sustained.

However, the Seventh Circuit ruled in 1998 that the degree of association is irrelevant; the key inquiry is whether discrimination occurred and, if so, if it was because of the employee's race. But harassment is actionable only if it is directed toward the plaintiffs or others who associated with or advocated for African-American employees—and only to the extent that the plaintiffs were aware of it. The Seventh Circuit applied the *Faragher/Ellerth* analysis to racial harassment. An employee has engaged in "opposing activity" when he or she complains about unlawful practices to a manager, the union, or to other employees; and retaliatory harassment committed by supervisors because of an employee's opposition to unlawful conduct violates Title VII. [*Barrett v. Whirlpool Corp.*, 556 F.3d 502 (6th Cir. 2009). The Seventh Circuit case is *Drake v. 3M*, 134 F.3d 878 (7th Cir. 1998)]

## § 34.06  SEX DISCRIMINATION

### [A]  Generally

Discrimination on account of sex is unlawful, except if there is a gender-based (bona fide occupational qualification) BFOQ. The Sixth Circuit held that being female is a BFOQ for working as a correctional officer in a women's prison. [*Everson v. Mich. Dep't of Corrs.*, 391 F.3d 737 (6th Cir. 2004)] In 1983, the Supreme Court decided that it constitutes sex discrimination for a health plan to provide less comprehensive benefits to male employees and their wives than to female employees and their husbands. [*Newport News Shipbuilding v. EEOC*, 462 U.S. 669 (1983)] Note, however, that in mid-2009, the Supreme Court ruled that AT&T did not commit sex discrimination by failing to adapt its pension plan to correct pre-Pregnancy Discrimination Act discrimination in treatment of pregnancy leave. [*AT&T Corp. v. Hulteen*, 556 U.S. 701 (2009)]

Karla Gerner said that the county, her employer, offered her a less favorable severance package than comparable male employees. The district court dismissed, holding that there had been no adverse employment action because severance benefits could only create adverse employment action if there was a contract violation and, in any event, severance benefits are paid after termination and after the employment relationship is over. The Fourth Circuit reversed. Any benefit—even one that the employer is not legally obligated to provide—might be discriminatory. Gerner testified that she was fired only after rejecting the discriminatory severance package, so she was an employee at that time. [*Gerner v. County of Chesterfield*, 674 F.3d 264 (4th Cir. 2012). *Hishon v. King & Spalding*, 469 U.S. 69 (1984) stands for the proposition that discrimination must be avoided in all benefits in the employment relationship.]

On a showing of enough circumstantial evidence that women suffer more bullying and harassment than men, female employees can maintain a Title VII gender-based discrimination action, even if the harassment takes the form of shouting, screaming, foul language, and invading employees' personal space rather than a direct solicitation of sexual activity. [*EEOC v. Nat'l Educ. Ass'n Alaska*, 422 F.3d 840 (9th Cir. 2005); the Eleventh Circuit reached a similar conclusion in 2009, and affirmed that holding en banc in 2010: *Reeves v. C.H. Robinson*, 569 F.3d 1290 (11th Cir. 2009), *aff'd en banc*, 594 F.3d 798 (2010); see Alyson M. Palmer, *11th Circuit: "Sex Specific" Profanity Could Win Harassment Case*, Fulton County Daily Report (Jan. 22, 2010) (law.com) and *In Code and in Specifics, Judges Debate Lewd Office Talk*, Fulton County Daily Report (Oct. 7, 2009) (law.com)]

The Seventh Circuit upheld the termination of a man (the only male respiratory therapist out of seven) who was fired for accessing hacking sites and pornography on the office computer system. The plaintiff alleged that, as the only male, he was targeted for investigation when inappropriate sites were accessed. The Seventh Circuit held that it was reasonable to suspect him because he was logged on to the computer when the inappropriate sites were accessed, and he even admitted accessing 17 of the 31 sites. (He denied going to the hacking sites, and said malware must have gotten loaded onto his computer accidentally.) He did not show that women were allowed to violate the hospital's acceptable computer use policy with impunity. [*Farr v. St. Francis Hosp. & Health Ctr.*, 570 F.3d 829 (7th Cir. 2009)]

It violates the Fourteenth Amendment's guarantee of Equal Protection to apply a facially neutral state law in a way that reflects sexual stereotyping. Therefore, a male state trooper should have been granted a 30-day parental leave when his child was born. (Leave was denied on the basis that only women can be primary caregivers for infants.) However, *Knussman v. Md.* [272 F.3d 625 (4th Cir. 2001)] holds that an award of $375,000 in emotional distress damages was disproportionate to the actual damages that the trooper suffered.

A Ninth Circuit decision holds that it is illegal sex discrimination for an airline to set its weight limits for female flight attendants based on tables for persons with a medium frame, while using tables for a large frame to set limits for male flight attendants. The court treated this as disparate impact discrimination not qualifying for a BFOQ defense. The airline called it a grooming standard (which can permissibly differ by sex), but the court said that requiring women flight attendants to be thinner than males of the same height did not improve their ability to do their jobs. [*Frank v. United Airlines*, 216 F.3d 845 (9th Cir. 2000)]

According to the Sixth Circuit, a company's anti-nepotism policy (requiring one spouse to resign when two employees marry) was rational. However, firing someone for criticizing the policy could be a violation of the employee's right of freedom of thought. In *Vaughn v. Lawrenceburg Power Sys.* [269 F.3d 703 (6th Cir. 2001)], the bride agreed to resign, then the groom was fired for agreeing with the statement, "I take it you do not fully agree with our policy." The Sixth Circuit said that antinepotism rules get heightened scrutiny under the First Amendment right of freedom of association if, but only if, they place a direct and substantial burden on the right to marry. [See also *Montgomery v. Carr*, 101 F.3d 1124 (6th Cir. 1996)]

In 2010, the Ninth Circuit certified the largest employment discrimination class ever, including over a million plaintiffs. A class of women charging Wal-Mart with sex discrimination was initially certified in 2004. Extensive litigation ensued about the composition of the class. The Ninth Circuit certified one of the larger classes, but a smaller class was remanded for further analysis.

In mid-2011, however, the Supreme Court issued a ruling that will make it far more difficult for employees of large companies to bring class action discrimination suits. The Supreme Court held that the would-be class members failed to prove that there was a common, company-wide policy of discrimination. In the Supreme Court view, although the plaintiffs alleged that the Wal-Mart corporate culture discriminated against women, the official policy of the chain was to give local managers significant discretion. The Supreme Court's majority opinion said that the plaintiffs complained of millions of employment decisions, not a single employment decision that could properly be addressed in a class action. The Supreme Court also criticized the demand for back pay, and ruled that Wal-Mart was entitled to individual determinations of back pay eligibility for class members, rather than extrapolation from a sample of employees. Some commentators suggested that companies could protect themselves against class actions by delegating to managers. [*Wal-Mart Stores Inc. v. Dukes*, 131 S. Ct. 2541 (2011); see Tony Mauro, *Supreme Court Erects Major Barriers to Class Actions in Wal-Mart Ruling*, Nat'l L.J. (June 20, 2011) (law.com); Brian Zabcik, *In-House and Labor Lawyers Respond to the Supreme Court's Wal-Mart Decision*, Corporate Counsel (June 22, 2011) (law.com)]

After the Supreme Court ruling, the plaintiffs re-filed a narrower suit, with over 90,000 plaintiffs, against Wal-Mart in the Central District of California, limited to California stores; it is expected that there will be many other suits in other places, rather than another attempt to launch a nation-wide suit. [Andrew Martin, *Women File New Class-Action Bias Case Against Wal-Mart*, NYTimes.com (Oct. 27, 2011)]

Seyfarth Shaw's Annual Workplace Class Action Litigation Report, published January 14, 2013, showed that *Dukes* had a major effect on private class actions. The top 10 employment discrimination class action settlements of 2012 aggregated approximately $49 million. This was the lowest figure since 2006, and far below the pre-*Dukes* 2010 total of $346 million. Employers have become much tougher during settlement litigations. The EEOC reacted by increasing its focus on systemic investigations. [Shannon Green, *Workplace Class Action Litigation Report Outlines a Post-Dukes World*, Corporate Counsel (Jan. 14, 2013) (law.com)]

Although a class was certified about alleged sex discrimination in Costco's promotion practices and corporate culture, after *Dukes* was decided, the Ninth Circuit overturned the certification of the class. The Ninth Circuit said that the district court should have considered if the claims for monetary relief require individual determination. If so, a Rule 23(b)(3) class action is required, and a (b)(2) class action is inappropriate. [*Ellis v. Costco Wholesale Corp.*, 657 F.3d 970 (9th Cir. 2011); see Karen Talley, *Costco Wins Appeal in Gender-Bias Suit*, WSJ.com (Sept. 16, 2011); Rebecca Moore, *9th Circuit Uses WalMart Decision to Deny Class in Costco Case*, plansponsor.com (Sept. 26, 2011)] On remand, however, the district court once again certified a class of 700 women alleging denial of promotion opportunity to assistant manager and general manager positions. The defendant said that each of the named plaintiffs was denied promotion for personal reasons. However, the district court said that concerns about personal and family needs are universal, not specific to each plaintiff, so any defense based on personal or family circumstances is best handled by class treatment. [*Ellis v. Costco*, 285 F.R.D. 492, 96 Empl. Prac. Dec. (CCH) P44,630 (N.D. Cal. 2012); see Cynthia Foster, *Judge Certifies Class Suing Costco for Gender Bias* The Recorder (Sept. 25, 2012) (law.com)]

In May 2010, a jury in the Southern District of New York found pharmaceutical company Novartis systematically discriminated against a class of 5,600 female sales representatives in terms of pay and promotion, and also practiced pregnancy discrimination. In July 2010, Novartis agreed to settle the case for a payment of $152.5 million (including about $60 million in back pay) to be paid to the plaintiff class, plus $22.5 million that Novartis agreed to spend on programs to avoid discrimination in the future. The settlement replaces both the compensatory and punitive damage awards, and Novartis agreed not to appeal. The settlement, one of the largest ever achieved in an employment class action, received final approval by the Southern District of New York on November 30, 2010. [*Velez et al. v. Novartis Corp.*, No. 04-09194 (S.D.N.Y. 2010); see Gerald L. Maatman, Jr. and Scott Velasquez, Seyfarth Shaw, *Record Gender Discrimination Class Action Settlement and Fee Award Given Final Approval*, <http://www.workplaceclassaction.com/settlement-issues/record-gender-discrimination-class-action-settlement-and-fee-award-given-final-approval> (Nov. 30, 2010)]

EEOC Enforcement Guidance published in May 2007 stresses that, although the EEOC does not consider being a caregiver for family members to be a separate new protected category, sometimes discrimination on the basis of care-giving will violate existing protection under Title VII and/or the Americans With

Disabilities Act. The EEOC says that it may take enforcement steps when a care-giver (male or female) is subjected to stereotyping in hiring or in the work environment. [EEOC Enforcement Guidance: *Unlawful Disparate Treatment of Workers With Caregiving Responsibilities* Number 915.002, <http://www.eeoc.gov/policy/docs/caregiving.html> (May 23, 2007). In April 2009, the EEOC published additional guidance on this topic at <http://www.eeoc.gov/policy/docs/caregiver-best-practices.html> (Apr. 24, 2009); see <H1>§ 28.01[C]]

### [B]   The Pregnancy Discrimination Act (PDA)

Section 2000e contains vital definitions for understanding federal antidis-crimination law. Sex discrimination includes, but is not limited to, discrimination "because or on the basis of pregnancy, childbirth, or related medical conditions." [42 U.S.C. § 2000e(k)]

This part of Title VII is referred to as the Pregnancy Discrimination Act (PDA). Under the PDA, women "affected by pregnancy, childbirth, or related medical conditions" have to be treated the same way as "other persons" who are not affected by such conditions, but who are comparable in their ability or inability to work. In other words, the PDA does not treat pregnancy itself as a disability, but to the extent that a particular pregnant worker does encounter disability, the employer must treat it the same way as other non-occupationally related disability.

The PDA requires equal treatment for "all employment-related purposes," including fringe benefits—a category that includes the all-important health benefits. However, employers do not have to provide health coverage if they would not otherwise. Employers have the discretion to provide abortion benefits, and are required to cover medical complications of abortion, but do not have to cover elective abortions, only abortions in situations where the mother's life would be endangered by carrying the fetus to term.

A late 2010 article says that it is possible that refusing to allow an employee to take intermittent FMLA leave for fertility treatment might violate the PDA. While pregnancy itself is not an ADA disability, under the ADAAA, it might be possible to argue that a pregnant employee was regarded as disabled. An unpublished Sixth Circuit case treats in vitro fertilization (IVF) as a serious heath condition because it requires the employee to take drugs that require medical monitoring, and involves outpatient surgical procedures. The Southern District of Illinois held that a department manager who was demoted, and lost pay and benefits, after having IVF, established a prima facie case of sex discrimination under the PDA, even though the employer argued that she was demoted because of poor work. [Keisha-Ann G. Gray, *Procreation Problems*, Human Resource Executive Online (Nov. 2, 2010) (benefitslink.com). See *Culpepper v. BlueCross/BlueShield of Tennessee*, 321 Fed. Appx. 491 (6th Cir. 2009); *EEOC v. Menard, Inc.*, 2010 U.S. Dist. LEXIS 5467 (S.D. Ill. Jan. 22, 2010)]

The Ohio Supreme Court ruled in mid-2010 that it did not constitute pregnancy discrimination to terminate an employee for taking maternity leave, because under the company's neutral leave policy, the employee had not been employed long enough to qualify for leave. The Ohio Civil Rights Commission argued that maternity leave has to be provided even if a non-pregnant employee would not be entitled to leave, but the Ohio Supreme Court held that the Pregnancy Discrimination Act and its Ohio counterpart merely require pregnant employees to receive the same treatment as non-pregnant employees with a similar ability or inability to work. [*McFee v. Nursing Care Mgmt. of America, Inc.*, No. 201-Ohio-2744 (Ohio June 22, 2010); see Sue Marie Douglas and Meredith C. Shoop, *Ohio Supreme Court Rules Neutral Leave Policy Not Direct Evidence of Sex Discrimination* (June 2010) (benefitslink.com)]

As a threshold question, to succeed, the plaintiff must be a common-law employee, not an independent contractor. [See, e.g., *Alberty-Velez v. Corporacion de Puerto Rico Para La Difusion Publica*, 242 F.3d 418 (1st Cir. 2003). The Ninth Circuit ruled in mid-2010 that insurance agents who sell financial products such as annuities are independent contractors for Title VII purposes (and for ERISA and ADEA purposes). The plaintiff in this case decided when and where to work, maintained an office for which she paid rent, scheduled her own time off; did not receive pay for vacations or sick days; was entirely paid on a commission basis; had the right to sell products other than those sold by the alleged employer; and paid taxes as a self-employed person. [*Murray v. Principal Fin. Group, Inc.*, 613 F.3d 943 (9th Cir. 2010)] The Eighth Circuit rejected a pregnancy discrimination suit brought by a doctor whose contract to provide emergency medical services at a hospital was terminated. The court found that the doctor worked as an independent contractor, not an employee: she decided which shifts to work and which patients to see, did not receive employee benefits, and paid her own license fees and employment taxes. Her contract, which was terminable by either party at any time, was labeled "Independent Contractor Physician Service Agreement." Therefore, as a non-employee, she was not protected by Title VII. [*Glascock v. Linn Cnty. Emergency Medicine PC*, 698 F.3d 695 (8th Cir. 2012)] On May 18, 2009, The Supreme Court held that it was not a violation of the PDA for AT&T not to revise its plan retroactively. AT&T acted under a valid seniority system, and thereby qualified for an exception to Title VII. The Supreme Court refused to apply the Ledbetter Act (§ 34.01[A]), because the original system of service credits was not discriminatory, and therefore employees were not "affected by application of a discriminatory compensation decision or other practice," as the Ledbetter Act says, and without such an effect, the Ledbetter Act does not apply. [*AT&T v. Hulteen*, 556 U.S. 701 (2009)]

If pregnant employees are covered by the plan, the pregnant wives of employees must be covered (in a plan with dependent coverage), and vice versa. However, it is permissible to exclude the pregnancy-related conditions of dependents other than the spouses of employees, as long as the exclusion is applied equally for male and female employees and their dependents.

A policy of restricting light-duty assignments to workers injured on the job who took Worker's Compensation leave was held to be neutral and equitably applied. Therefore, the Sixth Circuit dismissed a pregnant trucker's discrimination case when she was denied light duty after her obstetrician imposed a 20-pound lifting limitation. Pre-pregnancy, she had been able to lift 200 pounds, as the job required. There was no evidence of anti-pregnancy animus, or anyone seeking to get her fired to take her job, and a man recovering from non-work-related surgery would also have been denied a light-duty assignment, so the Sixth Circuit found that the PDA was not violated. [*Reeves v. Swift Transp. Co.*, 446 F.3d 637 (6th Cir. 2006); see Fred Schneyer, *Pregnant Trucker Loses Discrimination Suit Battle*, plansponsor.com (Aug. 29, 2006); earlier, the Fifth Circuit reached a similar conclusion in *Urbano v. Cont'l Airlines*, 138 F.3d 204 (5th Cir. 1998)]

Transferring a pregnant employee from traveling to offer computer technical support to the help desk was an adverse employment action because it reduced her pay, the work was less technical, and the job was considered a demotion. The plaintiff was fired, and the Eleventh Circuit found that her pregnancy was a motivating factor. The plaintiff's supervisor admitted that one reason for the transfer was concern about her pregnancy; she had suffered a previous miscarriage. However, the Eleventh Circuit said that even well-intentioned actions can violate the law. [*Holland v. Gee*, 677 F.3d 1047 (11th Cir. 2012)]

An early 2013 California Court of Appeal decision holds that an employee disabled by pregnancy complications was entitled to additional leave as a reasonable accommodation under FEHA even though she had used up her California Pregnancy Disability Leave Law and California Family Rights Act leave. She had a high risk pregnancy and was prescribed bed rest. The employer gave her 19 weeks of leave, including accrued vacation time. She was fired when she was still on bed rest, couldn't perform the essential functions of her job, and had exhausted her leave entitlement. The court of appeal ruled that the plain language of California's Pregnancy Disability Leave Law is that it supplements other FEHA entitlements. [ *Sanchez v. Swissport, Inc.*, 213 Cal. App. 4th 1331, 153 Cal. Rptr. 3d 367 (2013); see Jackson Lewis LLP Workplace Resource Center, *No Statutory Cap on Pregnancy Leave, California Court of Appeal Rules* (Mar. 4, 2013) (benefitslink.com)]

The First Circuit ruled that a job application was ambiguous as to whether people who applied but were not hired were subject to the arbitration clause. Therefore, the First Circuit refused to mandate arbitration in a case where a job applicant asserted pregnancy discrimination. The court concluded that there was a valid arbitration agreement—but the conditions under which it would come into play (the plaintiff being hired and having a dispute with her employer) never occurred. [*Gove v. Career Sys. Dev. Corp.*, 689 F.3d 1 (1st Cir. 2012)]

In mid-2013, the Fifth Circuit became the first Court of Appeals to rule on lactation discrimination. The Fifth Circuit held that discriminating against an employing for breast-feeding or expressing milk is unlawful sex discrimination.

The plaintiff charged that she was fired merely for saying that she wanted to express milk at work. The Fifth Circuit ruled that lactation is a medical condition related to pregnancy and childbirth because it is a physiological state caused by childbirth. [*EEOC v. Houston Funding II*,717 F.3d 425 (5th Cir. 2013); see William Metke, *Fifth Circuit Holds That Lactation Discrimination Violates Title VII*, Workplace Prof Blog (May 31, 2013) (benefitslink.com)]

## [C]   The Equal Pay Act (EPA)

The Equal Pay Act [29 U.S.C. § 206] is related to the Title VII provisions that forbid sex discrimination, but it is not a part of Title VII. The EPA covers all employers with *two* or more employees. It forbids discrimination in compensation, including all forms of benefits, on the basis of sex—if the two jobs are of equal skill, effort, and responsibility and are performed under similar working conditions. In other words, the statute does not apply to "comparable worth" claims under which women claim that a typically female job is of greater value to society than a higher-paid but different job typically performed by men (e.g., child care workers and parking lot attendants). See § 34.06[B] for discussion of the Supreme Court's 2009 *Hulteen* decision, finding that it was not illegal for a pension plan to continue to reflect the effect of pre-Pregnancy Discrimination Act pay inequalities.

Cost-based defenses are not allowed under the EPA, [see 29 C.F.R. § 216(b)] which says that even if it costs more to provide benefits to women than to men, the employer must either eliminate the benefit or provide it to everyone.

The EPA imposes civil penalties on employers who violate it; even criminal penalties, as prescribed by Fair Labor Standards Act § 216(a), are a possibility. Punitive damages are not allowed, but double back pay is. A winning plaintiff can get costs and attorney's fees.

A 2006 Tenth Circuit case explores the differences between Title VII and the EPA. The plaintiff, a marketing service consultant with a law degree, charged that she was paid less than male employees doing the same work. The Tenth Circuit ruled that a claim of salary discrimination can be brought either as a Title VII intentional-discrimination case or an EPA wage discrimination case. It is not necessary to prove intent in an EPA case, whereas a woman charging wage discrimination under Title VII must prove that the employer intentionally paid her less than a similarly situated male employee. The Title VII case uses the familiar *McDonnell-Douglas* analysis. In an EPA case, the plaintiff makes out a *prima facie* case by showing that men earned more for substantially equal work. If this is done, the burden of persuasion shifts to the employer to justify its action using a seniority system; a merit system; pay based on quantity or quality of work; or a pay disparity based on any factor other than sex. [*Mickeson v. N.Y. Life Ins. Co.*, 460 F.3d 1304 (10th Cir. 2006)]

The Eighth Circuit rejected an employer's contention that it applied "factors other than sex" to pay a male new hire $62,500 (the salary that he said he "required") while paying $45,000 to a female manager who was promoted one level above the man. In fact, he was hired to replace her when she was promoted. The Eighth Circuit said that the issue was not whether the new hire was entitled to be paid a market rate—but the employer's failure to justify paying the plaintiff much less than the market rate for her job. [*Drum v. Leeson Electric Corp.*, 565 F.3d 1071 (8th Cir. 2009)]

A state agency gave lateral hires a salary at least as high as they had earned in the past, plus a raise if the salary scale under the new job permitted it. A female worker brought suit, charging that this practice discriminated against women. The plaintiff alleged that she and a man with a different title did the same work, but he earned more because the process of setting initial salaries favored him, and the agency's practices maintained the salary gap. Seventh Circuit precedent is that past wages are a "factor other than sex" that will justify pay differentials because federal courts are not entitled to set standards for business practices. As long as an employer has a reason other than sex, it is not up to the court to inquire whether the reason is a good one. In the Seventh Circuit view, men's higher wages reflect the greater amount of time women spend on child-rearing, something that the Seventh Circuit did not interpret as discrimination. In the case at bar, the plaintiff failed to introduce expert testimony showing that the previous employers' salary scales were discriminatory. [*Wernsing v. DHS, State of Ill.*, 427 F.3d 466 (7th Cir. 2005), citing, e.g., *Covington v. S. Ill. Univ.*, 816 F.2d 317 (7th Cir. 1987). Other circuits, however, have held that past wages constitute a "factor other than sex" only if the employer has an acceptable business reason for using past wages to set starting pay for new hires: *Aldrich v. Randolph Cent. Sch. Dist.*, 963 F.2d 520 (2d Cir.), *cert. denied*, 506 U.S. 965 (1992); *EEOC v. J.C. Penney Co.*, 843 F.2d 249 (6th Cir. 1992); *Kouba v. Allstate Ins. Co.*, 691 F.2d 873 (9th Cir. 1982); *Glenn v. Gen. Motors Corp.*, 841 F.2d 1567 (11th Cir. 1988)]

A contrary result was reached in a 2006 Sixth Circuit Case. Nurse practitioners working for the federal Department of Veterans' Affairs (DVA) brought suit under the EPA and Title VII, alleging they (95% of whom are female) are paid less than physician's assistants (most of whom are male) for performing jobs of equal skill, effort, and responsibility under similar working conditions. The District Court granted summary judgment to the agency, accepting the affirmative defense that it was merely following the two separate statutes that set pay for the two types of health practitioners. The nurse practitioners were required to have master's degrees, whereas the physician's assistants didn't even have to have a bachelor's degree. (In fact, one woman who was qualified as both an NP and a PA worked as a PA because it paid more.) The Sixth Circuit reinstated the suit, noting that the DVA advertised for either an NP or a PA for certain jobs, and the two kinds of workers often filled in for one another. Both statutes allowed the DVA to increase salaries to cope with recruitment problems. The DVA chose to do so for PAs but not for NPs, even though recruitment problems were equally severe. [*Beck-Wilson v. Principi*, 441 F.3d 353 (6th Cir. 2006)]

A nurse charged a hospital with paying a man more for substantially equal work performed under substantially equal conditions. The jury ruled for the defendant. The Eighth Circuit denied the plaintiff's motion for a new trial. The EPA is a strict liability statute (the employer's motivation for unequal pay is irrelevant). The employer's exercise of business judgment is a defense in a Title VII case, but not an EPA case. Therefore, business judgment jury instructions are inappropriate in a pure EPA case, although they can be given in a case that combines EPA and Title VII violations. The Eighth Circuit ruled that the jury instructions were questionable because they included wording that might have implied a business judgment defense—but the Eighth Circuit found that the jury instructions correctly defined other important concepts, and were not defective enough to affect the plaintiff's rights. [*Bauer v. Curators of Univ. of Missouri*, 680 F.3d 1043 (8th Cir. 2012)]

## [D] Sexual Orientation and Gender Behavior Discrimination

Although there are a number of state and local laws banning discrimination in the workplace on the grounds of sexual orientation, Title VII does not forbid discrimination on the basis of actual or perceived homosexuality or bisexuality. [See also § 18.06 for health plan issues for employees with same-sex spouses or life partners.] A number of state laws, however, do forbid sexual orientation discrimination.

Shortly after the Supreme Court decision that found the federal Defense of Marriage Act Amendment unconstitutional, the *New York Times* pointed out that fewer than half the states had laws forbidding employment discrimination on the basis of sexual orientation or gender identity. According to a report published in June 2013 by the Center for American Progress and the Human Rights Campaign, at that time 21 states and the District of Columbia had laws against sexual orientation discrimination; 16 of them and the District of Columbia forbade discrimination on the basis of gender identity or expression. [Tara Siegel Bernard, *Fired for Being Gay? Protections are Piecemeal*,NYTimes.com (May 31, 2013). According to the Movement Advancement Project, *Percent of LGBT Population Covered by Laws*, <http://www.lgbtmap.org/equality-maps/employment_non_discrimination_laws> (undated; last accessed June 1, 2013), the states of California, Colorado, Connecticut, Illinois, Iowa, Maine, Massachusetts, Minnesota, Nevada, New Jersey, New Mexico, Oregon, Rhode Island, Vermont, Washington, and the District of Columbia forbid sexual orientation and gender discrimination. Delaware, Maryland, New Hampshire, New York, and Wisconsin forbid sexual orientation discrimination but not gender identity discrimination.]

Kentucky Baptist Homes for Children, Inc. was sued over its policy of refusing to employ lesbian and gay employees. The suit charged violations of Title VII and the Kentucky Civil Rights Act and the establishment clause of the First Amendment. The Sixth Circuit upheld the district court's dismissal of the employment discrimination claim, but reinstated the First Amendment claims. The agency fired one of the plaintiffs when it discovered she is a lesbian, then promulgated a policy against employing gay people. The other plaintiff is a lesbian who said that she was denied the opportunity to apply for a job there. The plaintiffs, and six taxpayers, objected to the use of public funds at a religious agency. The Sixth Circuit held that sexual-orientation discrimination is not forbidden by Title VII or the corresponding Kentucky law, and rejected the argument that the plaintiffs were discriminated against because of the employer's religious objection to homosexual conduct, treating that aspect of the case as a pure allegation of sexual-orientation discrimination. [*Pedreira v. Kentucky Baptist Homes for Children Inc.*, 579 F.3d 722 (6th Cir. 2009)]

In some instances, the case revolves around whether a person suffered adverse employment action not because of sexual activities or sexual orientation, but because a male employee was perceived to lack masculinity or a female employee to be unfeminine. (As discussed below at § 34.06[E], however, the highly feminine behavior of a woman becoming a mother also gives rise to workplace litigation.)

Employee plaintiffs have asserted theories of gender non-conformity bias that derive from the discussion of sex stereotyping in *Price Waterhouse*. [*Nichols v. Azteca Rest. Enters. Inc.*, 256 F.3d 864 (9th Cir. 2001); *Higgins v. New Balance Athletic Shoe Inc.*, 194 F.3d 252 (1st Cir. 1999)] Although Title VII does not cover transsexuality, transsexual plaintiffs now raise claims that they are discriminated against because they present themselves as the "other" sex and do not conform to gender stereotypes. [This issue is discussed in *Price Waterhouse, Sex Stereotyping, and Gender Non-Conformity Bias*, 73 LW 2211 (Oct. 19, 2004)] The Sixth Circuit dismissed claims by a private police officer who charged that he was harassed by co-workers because of their perception that he was gay, insufficiently masculine, or both, after he helped a gay doctor with an investigation at the hospital where he worked. The Sixth Circuit said that he failed to make a case, because at most he charged harassment on the basis of perceived homosexuality, and even actual homosexuality is not a suspect classification under Title VII. [*Vickers v. Fairfield Med. Ctr.*, 453 F.3d 757 (6th Cir. 2006)]

The Eighth Circuit held that a female-to-male transsexual who was turned down for a part-time job as a package handler did not prove that hiring was denied because of the plaintiff's membership in a protected group. There was no evidence that the interviewer knew that the plaintiff was transsexual. When it is not clear that a person belongs to a protected group, the plaintiff must prove that the defendant was aware of the plaintiff's status or thought that the plaintiff was a member of the protected group. The Eighth Circuit believed UPS' explanation that Hunter was not hired because of his poor work history and unimpressive interview performance. [*Hunter v. UPS Inc.*, 697 F.3d 697 (8th Cir. 2012)]

Although Title VII does not cover sexual orientation discrimination, the
Third Circuit permitted an effeminate gay man to pursue a Title VII claim of
harassment based on his failure to conform to gender stereotypes. The Third Circuit said that the case should not have been dismissed, but should have gone to a
jury, because it was uncertain whether the case involved sexual orientation or gender discrimination (but affirmed dismissal of his charge that he was harassed for
not conforming to his co-workers' religious beliefs). [*Prowel v. Wise Business
Forms Inc.*, 579 F.3d 285 (3d Cir. 2009); see Shannon P. Duffy, *3rd Circuit
Revives Gay Man's Title VII Suit*, The Legal Intelligencer (Aug. 31, 2009) (law.
com)]

The Ninth Circuit upheld the termination of a casino bartender for refusing
to wear makeup. She was fired after close to 20 years of working there and gar-
nering excellent ratings. (She objected to makeup as demeaning and personally
offensive.) The Ninth Circuit held that the plaintiff did not have a cause of action
under Title VII: she failed to show that the grooming policy imposed greater burdens on female than on male bartenders. For example, she failed to prove the
amount of time and money women had to invest to comply with the policy. In the
Ninth Circuit, the rule is that employers can impose different grooming standards
on men and women, as long as one sex is not burdened more than the other. [*Jes-
persen v. Harrah's Operating Co.*, 392 F.3d 1076 (9th Cir. 2004)] The case was
reheard en banc (i.e., by all the judges of the Ninth Circuit) and affirmed on the
grounds that no triable issues of fact were raised. [444 F.3d 1104 (9th Cir. 2006)]
The full court affirmed the three-judge panel's decision, agreeing that the plaintiff failed to show that the company's appearance policy imposed a greater burden on women. Although the en banc panel left the door open for claims that
makeup requirements and other appearance standards can be unlawful sexual stereotyping, in this case it was held that the plaintiff failed to create any triable
issues of fact.

A hotel desk clerk, whose new boss said she did not have the "pretty Midwestern girl look" that was required, was terminated for "thwarting the interview
procedure" and hostility to company policy. The plaintiff had short hair, didn't
wear makeup, and wore loose, unfeminine clothing. Before the new Director of
Operations took over, the plaintiff Brenna Lewis, had good evaluations, and her
direct supervisor was forced to resign for sticking up for Lewis. The Eighth Circuit reversed the grant of summary judgment for the defendant, and remanded the
case for further proceedings, holding that women bringing Title VII suits do not
have to provide evidence of being treated differently from similarly situated
males. In this case, the Director of Operations was the primary decision-maker
with the authority to hire and fire. She consistently required front-desk workers
to be pretty, and not "tom-boyish." However, the Eighth Circuit's opinion does
not state whether Lewis either is or was perceived as a lesbian, or as a female-
to-male transsexual. [*Lewis v. Heartland Inns of Am.*, LLC, 591 F.3d 1033 (8th
Cir. 2010). On the issue of sex stereotyping, see also *Chadwick v. WellPoint, Inc.*,
561 F.3d 38 (1st Cir. 2009)]

The Obama administration changed the federal job Website, usajobs.gov, to forbid discrimination on the basis of gender identity (transsexuality). The federal government had taken this position informally for several years, but this is a written statement. The federal government is the largest employer in the United States, so its HR decisions have a lot of impact. [*U.S. Job Site Bans Bias Over Gender Identity*, NYTimes.com (Jan. 5, 2010)] In mid-2009, Federal Express amended its anti-discrimination policy to include gender identity. The change was adopted voluntarily, before the shareholder meeting at which a resolution to that effect had been submitted. [Fred Schneyer, *FedEx Adds Gender Identity to Discrim Policy*, [sic] plansponsor.com (July 16, 2009). Wal-Mart added gender identity and expression to its non-discrimination policy in 2011; sexual orientation was already covered under the company's Discrimination and Harassment Prevention Policy: see *WalMart Adds Transgender Protections*, plansponsor.com (Sept. 29, 2011)]

In 2005, the Sixth Circuit upheld a jury award of $320,000 in damages to a transsexual police officer who was denied promotion to sergeant, and the district court added $527,888 in attorneys' fees and $25,837 in costs. The Sixth Circuit ruled that a reasonable jury could conclude that there had been intentional discrimination because, although the plaintiff's scores during probation were not good, they were better than those of another person who became a sergeant; he was the only person not to become a sergeant after the probationary period in seven years; that the other police officers knew that the plaintiff was in the process of transitioning to being a woman; and that he was often criticized for lacking command presence, which could reasonably be interpreted to mean that he was not masculine. [*Barnes v. City of Cincinnati*, 401 F.3d 729 (6th Cir. 2005)] The Supreme Court denied certiorari (546 U.S. 1003). [Gina Holland (AP), *Supreme Court Avoids Transsexual Police Officer Case* (Nov. 8, 2005) (law. com)] On transsexuals as a protected class, see *Smith v. City of Salem, Ohio*, 378 F.3d 566 (6th Cir. 2004).

In 2007, the Northern District of Indiana held that while there was no Title VII cause of action for discrimination against a transgendered employee, an employee who was transitioning from male to female could proceed on claims that he was terminated for failure to satisfy male gender stereotypes. The plaintiff was fired for wearing makeup in addition to the prescribed uniform. However, the Northern District held that the plaintiff could win only by proving that the employer was motivated by stereotypes about male and female behavior, not the plaintiff's transsexual status. [*Creed v. Family Express Corp.*, No. 3:06-CV-465RM, 2007 WL 2265630 (N.D. Ind. Aug. 3, 2007), discussed in Carla J. Rozycki and David K. Haase, *Employers Should Be Mindful of Sex-Stereotyping Claims in Dealing with Gender Identity* (Sept. 5, 2007) (special to law.com)]

The Eleventh Circuit ordered the Georgia General Assembly to reinstate Vandiver Elizabeth Glenn, a transgender woman who worked as an editor for the assembly but was fired after telling her supervisor that she would be changing her name and working dressed as a woman. The Eleventh Circuit said that discrimination on the basis of gender nonconformity is sex-based discrimination that is reviewed using heightened scrutiny under the Equal Protection clause of the Constitution. [*Brumby v. Glenn*, 663 F.3d 1312 (11th Cir. 2011); see Alyson M. Palmer, Daily Report, *Transgender Woman's Sex Bias Claim Upheld* (Dec. 8, 2011) (law.com)]

It is common for transgender people to suffer discrimination, respect, and hostility from health care providers. Before PPACA, transgender people who suffered employment discrimination were also deprived of employer-based coverage. Individual insurers often refused to cover them or treated transsexual identity as an excludible pre-existing condition. Furthermore, transgender people who had insurance often found that health care claims were rejected as pre-existing conditions because the insurer treated all health care as related to their gender identity. Starting in 2014, PPACA forbids denials for pre-existing conditions. HHS has confirmed that this provision forbids discrimination based on gender identity. PPACA includes funding to train health care workers in cultural competency when dealing with LGBT patients. [Marisa Carroll, *What the Affordable Care Act Means for Transgender People*, The Nation (Aug. 14, 2012) (benefitslink.com)]

A letter from HHS' Office of Civil Rights clarifies that PPACA's ban on sex discrimination in health insurance extends to discrimination against transsexuals: it is unlawful discrimination for an employer to deny health insurance coverage or benefits based on gender identity or failure to conform to gender stereotypes. Discrimination complaints can be submitted to the Office of Civil Rights and violators can lose federal financial assistance and be subjected to other penalties. However, insurers are not always required to cover surgery for transition.

For the Human Rights Campaign to give an employer a perfect score for trans-inclusive benefits, the employer must offer transgender employees equal health care without excluding any form of necessary care, and transition benefits are included. In 2011, 85 companies got a perfect score, and 207 did in 2012 even though the standard was raised. According to the National Business Group on Health, in 2010, 14% of the organization's members covered surgery for transition, and 32% covered non-surgical care such as hormones and counseling. [Michelle Andrews, *HHS Says Health Plans Cannot Discriminate Against Transgender People*, Kaiser Health News (Sept. 3, 2012) (benefitslink.com)]

Regulators in Oregon and California ordered health insurers to stop denying coverage on the basis of gender identity. Insurers were ordered to pay for hormone therapy, breast reduction, cancer screening, and other medically necessary procedures on the same basis whether or not the patient is transsexual. The decision affects about one-third of citizens of Oregon and 7% of Californians. Most Californians are not affected by the decision because they get their health care through HMOs, which are under a different system of supervision. [AP, *Ore., Calif., Require Transgender Health Coverage*, NYTimes.com (Jan. 11, 2013)] The state of Oregon settled a lawsuit by agreeing to provide insurance coverage for gender reassignment of state employees; the state agreed to pay $36,000 in damages and provide coverage for all types of reassignment surgery. The suit alleged that, because hysterectomies are covered under the plan, denying coverage when a hysterectomy is part of reassignment is discrimination on the basis of gender. [Rebecca Moore, *Ore. Adds Gender Reassignment to Health Care Coverage*, plansponsor.com (Jan. 25, 2013)]

## [E] "Sex-Plus" Discrimination

The sex-plus cause of action asserts that the plaintiff suffered discrimination on the ground of sex and other factors—*e.g.*, motherhood. Title VII does not list parenthood as a protected category. The Pregnancy Discrimination Act and Family and Medical Leave Act are limited to pregnancy and childbirth, and do not forbid bias against women who act as primary caregivers of their children. In 2004, the District Court for the District of Connecticut ruled that child care is gender-neutral and hence not protected under Title VII. [*Guglietta v. Meredith Corp.*, 301 F. Supp. 2d 209 (D. Conn. 2004). However, in a failure to hire/failure to promote case, the same district treated interview questions about child care arrangements as evidence of bias: *Senuta v. Groton, Conn.*, 2002 U.S. Dist. LEXIS 10792 (D. Conn. Mar. 5, 2002)]

The first lawsuit for Family Responsibilities Discrimination (FRD) was brought in 1971, with only eight such cases in the 1970s. Between 1986 and 1995, the Hastings College of the Law Center for WorkLife Law found that there were 97 lawsuits alleging discrimination on the basis of family responsibilities. The number rose to 481 cases in the decade 1996–2005. About 93% of FRD plaintiffs are women. Most allege that they suffered discrimination because of their care needs as parents, but some are caregivers for parents. The largest award to a successful FRD plaintiff was $25 million, but the average award is about $100,000; employees get settlements or win at trial in about half of FRD cases. [The Hastings study is called *Litigating the Maternal Wall: U.S. Lawsuits Charging Discrimination Against Workers with Family Responsibilities*; see Lisa Belkin, *Family Needs in the Legal Balance*, N.Y. Times, July 30, 2006, section 1, p. 1 and Fred Schneyer, *Strong Rise Seen in Family Responsibilities Discrimination Suits*, plansponsor.com (July 10, 2006). The Center for WorkLife Law has issued an updated report, *Family Responsibilities Discrimination: Litigation Update 2010*, <http://www.worklifelaw.org/pubs/FRDUpdate.pdf> (undated)]

A 2009 First Circuit decision permits an employee to pursue a sex discrimination claim that she was denied a promotion because she is the mother of four young children. (The district court had ruled in the employer's favor.) Several Circuits, including the First, have ruled that adverse job action on the basis of being a mother is sex discrimination based on stereotyping. In this case, in effect the plaintiff was told that her work was completely satisfactory, but she would not be promoted because she had young children and was going to school part-time. The plaintiff brought suit after the "team leader" job went to a woman with less experience and a lower performance evaluation than the plaintiff (3.84 versus 4.40). [*Chadwick v. WellPoint Inc.*, 561 F.3d 38 (1st Cir. 2009); see Rebecca Moore, *Mother of Young Children Can Pursue Sex-Bias Claim Against WellPoint* (Mar. 30, 2009)]

## § 34.07 RELIGIOUS DISCRIMINATION AND REASONABLE ACCOMMODATION

### [A] Employer's Duties and Obligations

Religious issues can arise in the workplace in many contexts: employees' need for time off for prayer, or to observe a Sabbath or attend services or religious events; wearing of religious dress; men wearing beards for religious reasons; and religious objections to joining a union.

The EEOC issued a 97-page revised version of the Compliance Manual § 12 (religious discrimination) on July 22, 2008. The EEOC issued accompanying guidance online: Questions and Answers and a Best Practices document for employers.

The Compliance Manual says that Title VII forbids differential treatment of employees on the basis of their religious beliefs or practices, including atheism. Religious beliefs include moral and ethical beliefs, and are not required to reflect the concept of a deity. Religious harassment, including association-based harassment, is also forbidden. Employers must provide reasonable accommodation of needs based on an employee's sincerely held religious belief, unless the cost or burden to the employer would be more than minimal. As examples of required accommodation, the EEOC lists scheduling changes; changing the tasks assigned to a worker; and allowing religious dress and beard or hairstyles. Employers must not favor expressions of some religions over others. Retaliation is also forbidden. [Revised § 12 of the Compliance Manual, <http://www.eeoc.gov/policy/docs/religion.pdf> Questions and Answers: Religious Discrimination in the Workplace <http://www.eeoc.gov/policy/docs/qanda_religion.html> Best Practices for Eradicating Religious Discrimination in the Workplace <http://www.eeoc.gov/policy/docs/best_practices_religion.html>]

Bilan Nur, a Somali sales representative, was awarded $287,000 in damages by an Arizona federal court when she was unlawfully terminated for refusing to take off her head covering during her holy month of Ramadan. The award consisted of about $25,000 in back pay, $16,000 in compensatory damages, and $250,000 in punitive damages. She had previously been permitted to wear the head covering at work; she was willing to wear a scarf with the corporate logo; and wearing a scarf was not even a violation of the company dress code. In fact, the judge granted summary judgment for the plaintiff because the employer's liability was so clear-cut; the jury's only job was to set the damages. [Fred

Schneyer, *Alamo Hit with $287,000 Jury Award in Muslim Discrimination Case*, plansponsor.com (June 7, 2007)]

In mid-2012, the MTA (New York City's public transportation authority) agreed to a settlement under which Muslim and Sikh employees can wear religious headgear, as long as the headgear is in the MTA's uniform color—navy blue. The employees will not be required to affix MTA logos to the headgear, which had been a point of contention in the past. Eight current and former employees were awarded a total of $184,500 in damages for past denial of reasonable accommodation. [Matt Flegenheimer, *MTA Agrees That Workers May Wear Religious Headgear*, NYTimes.com (May 30, 2012); Ted Mann, *MTA Settles Bias Lawsuit*, WSJ.com (May 31, 2012)]

After the United States' invasion of Afghanistan in 2001, a Muslim salesman (Mohommed Rafiq) charged that his managers, despite repeated protests, called him "Taliban" managers and co-workers told him to go back home and mocked his religious requirements for daily prayers and halal food. A supervisor ordered him to attend a United Way meeting and gave him a written warning for his "militant stance" and "acting like a Muslim extremist." Rafiq complained to the general manager after an argument with a finance manager and was fired. The EEOC brought a hostile work environment suit, which was dismissed by the district court for lack of evidence of severe and persistent harassment and failure to prove deterioration in quality of life caused by the severity of the harassment. The Fifth Circuit reversed, holding that the pattern of harassment alleged was explicitly based on religion and national origin, and was severe enough to impair daily life. [*EEOC v. WC&M*, 496 F.3d 393 (5th Cir. 2007); see Adrien Martin, *Appeals Court Reinstates Houston Muslim Car Salesman's Discrimination Claims*, plansponsor.com (Aug. 14, 2007)]

A Jewish police officer alleged repeated workplace harassment, including frequent anti-Semitic remarks. He was not allowed to wear a yarmulke because it violated the uniform policy, but another officer was allowed to wear Christian religious symbols on his uniform. A New Jersey jury found a hostile work environment but did not award damages, and ruled that the delay in the plaintiff's promotion to corporal was not discriminatory. Both sides appealed. The New Jersey Supreme Court applied the same test for a hostile environment based on religion as for one based on sex or race: whether a reasonable person would consider the antagonistic, degrading, or demeaning acts and comments in his or her presence to be severe or pervasive enough to alter the working conditions for the worse. In this case, the plaintiff was repeatedly subjected to humiliating anti-Semitic comments, not the mere "ribbing" that the defense characterized it as. [*Cutler v. Dorn*, 196 N.J. 419 (N.J. July 31, 2008); see Michael Booth, *Religious Slurs May Amount to Hostile Workplace, N.J. High Court Says*, N.J.L.J. (Aug. 5, 2008) (law .com); Rebecca Moore, *Anti-Semitic Slurs Create Hostile Work Environment*, plansponsor.com (Aug. 8, 2005)]

Religion includes belief and all forms of religious observance and practice. The Eastern District of Wisconsin held that a sincerely held belief that takes the place of religion in the employee's worldview could constitute a religion, whether or not it involves concepts of God or an afterlife. Therefore, it was a violation of Title VII to demote a supervisor for expressing his sincere religious views in favor of white supremacy in a non-work-related newspaper article. The concept of reasonable accommodation applies only to religious observance or practice, not religious ideas. [*Peterson v. Wilmur Commc'ns Inc.*, 205 F. Supp. 2d 1014 (E.D. Wis. 2002)] However, the California Court of Appeals held that it does not constitute religious discrimination to refuse to hire a vegan who refused to be vaccinated with a vaccine grown in chicken embryos, because beliefs about harming animals are secular, not a religious philosophy, because they were deemed to lack a spiritual or otherworldly component. [*Friedman v. S. Cal. Permanente Med. Group*, 125 Cal. Rptr. 2d 663 (Cal. App. 2002)]

The Seventh Circuit reversed summary judgment for the employer, and permitted a Nigerian immigrant to pursue his religious discrimination claim when he was denied unpaid leave to return to Nigeria to perform funeral rites for his father. Adeyeye, who believed that his family's spiritual well-being depended on performance of the rites, took time off without authorization and was fired when he returned from the trip. The Seventy Circuit held that there were genuine questions of material fact precluding summary judgment; Adeyeye informed his employer that he sincerely believed in his funerary obligations, even if the beliefs, a mixture of Christian and animist, was not a conventional religion. Furthermore, the employer frequently hired temporary replacements when regular workers were unavailable, so granting the requested leave would not have imposed undue hardship on the employer. [*Adeyeye v. Heartland Sweeteners*, No. 12-3820 (7th Cir. July 31, 2013); see Sheri Qualters, *Worker Denied Funeral Leave Has Religious Bias Claim*, Nat'l L.J. (Aug. 1, 2013) (law.com)]

Employers do not have an obligation to incur "undue hardship on the conduct" of their business if they can demonstrate that they are unable to make reasonable accommodation to an employee's or applicant's religious observance or practice. [42 U.S.C. § 2000e(j)] In fact, a 1977 Supreme Court case holds that investing more than a minimal amount in accommodation can actually represent an illegal preference in favor of the employee who receives the accommodation. [*TWA v. Hardison*, 432 U.S. 63 (1977)]

Except in very limited cases (being a priest or minister, for example) religious beliefs are irrelevant to employment and cannot be used as a hiring criterion. Employers are not supposed to prefer one religion over another, or even to prefer organized religion over atheism or agnosticism.

Initially, the Third Circuit held in favor of a woman who claimed that she was subjected to sex discrimination and retaliation when she was fired from her job as a university chaplain. In September 2006, however, the Third Circuit reversed itself and upheld the dismissal of her sex discrimination charges. The Third Circuit joined seven other circuits in applying the ministerial exception to any claim whose resolution would limit a religious institution's designation of who will perform spiritual functions. However, the Third Circuit did permit the plaintiff to pursue claims for breach of contract, because contracts are voluntary and Title VII has mandatory application. [*Petruska v. Gannon Univ.*, 462 F.3d 294 (3d Cir. 2006); see Shannon P. Duffy, *3rd Circuit Reverses Itself on Groundbreaking Sex Discrimination Ruling*, The Legal Intelligencer (Sept. 8, 2006) (law .com)]

The Supreme Court unanimously endorsed the ministerial exception (i.e., held that the First Amendment prevents courts from interfering when a church takes employment action against a minister). This was the first Supreme Court case on this issue, although all 12 Circuits have recognized the principle. The Court left open the possibility of suits for breach of contract or tortuous conduct. The Court said that the ministerial exception is not a jurisdictional bar but an affirmative defense: that is, an employer that asserts the defense has the responsibility for proving that it applies. [*Hosanna-Tabor Evangelical Lutheran Church v. EEOC*, 132 S. Ct. 694 (2012); see Tony Mauro, *Unanimous High Court Finds For Church In EEOC Fight*, Nat'l L.J. (Jan. 11, 2012) (law.com)]

AT&T Broadband maintained a diversity policy requiring all employees to "recognize, respect, and value differences." A fundamentalist Christian employee refused to sign the certificate, because his religion teaches that some differences are sinful and do not deserve to be valued. The District of Colorado found that he put the employer on notice of his religious objection to the policy, requiring the employer to start the interactive process of accommodation; not doing so violated the employee's right to religious accommodation. [*Buonanno v. AT&T Broadband LLC*, 313 F. Supp. 2d 1069 (D. Colo. 2004)]

Employees will probably have to be permitted to wear forms of dress, jewelry, and hairstyles required by their religion. The exception might be a situation in which the employer can show a genuine safety hazard that cannot be accommodated in another way. For example, a "no-beard" policy could not be enforced against an employee whose religion requires him to grow a beard, unless the beard is unsanitary or creates a hazard of getting caught in machinery—and there is no method of securing the beard that would preserve safety and cleanliness.

Probably the most common religious accommodation issue involves work assignments when the employee is supposed to observe a Sabbath, attend religious services, study the scriptures, teach in a religious school, or the like. The consensus is that the employer has to accommodate activities (or non-activities, like avoiding work on the Sabbath) that are mandated by an organized religion, but not employee's personal wishes about religious observance.

The EEOC considers it unlawful discrimination to set overtime rates in a way that disadvantages employees who observe a Sabbath other than Sunday. [See Guidelines, 29 C.F.R. Part 1605] The EEOC considers acceptable accommodations to include voluntary substitution of one employee for another, swapping shifts, lateral transfers, changes of job assignment, and flextime (i.e., the employee makes up the time devoted to religious observance).

However, employers are not required to accommodate religious observance by violating the seniority rights of a nonobservant employee. In the view of the

EEOC, it would be undue hardship for the employer to have to pay overtime to other employees to cover for the religious employee or to have an untrained or inexperienced person covering for the religious employee.

When it comes to union security, the National Labor Relations Act, at 29 U.S.C. § 169, provides that if an employee belongs to a religion that has traditionally objected to unions, then the employer cannot require the employee to join or support a union, even if the operation is an agency shop or participates in another union security arrangement. However, the employee's religious objection can be accommodated by requiring him or her to contribute an amount equivalent to the union initiation fee and dues to a charitable organization that is neither a union nor religious in nature. That way the employee does not benefit financially from the antiunion belief, but is not required to perform a religiously repugnant act. The Sixth Circuit upheld the dismissal of a suit brought by a worker who had a religious objection to joining a union. The union told him to donate the equivalent of his agency fees (see § 30.06[A]) to one of three charities chosen by the UAW. The arrangement required him to pay $100 more to charity as a religious objector than he paid in agency fees as an objecting non-member. The Sixth Circuit ruled that, in a religious accommodation case, it is necessary to prove discharge or discipline; merely losing some pay did not constitute an adverse employment action. [*Reed v. Int'l Union, United Auto, Aerospace and Agricultural Implement Workers of America*, 569 F.3d 576 (6th Cir. 2009)]

The Second Circuit reversed the lower court and ruled that offering a shift change on Sundays is not a reasonable accommodation to an employee's Sabbath observance. The proposed schedule change allowed him to attend church, but did not satisfy his religious mandate to avoid working at all on Sunday. [*Baker v. Home Depot*, 445 F.3d 541 (2d Cir. 2006); see Rebecca Moore, *Schedule Change on Sundays Not Accommodation for Observing Sabbath*, plansponsor.com (Apr. 25, 2006); Tom Perrotta, *2nd Circuit Revives Suit Over Man's Refusal to Work on Sunday*, N.Y.L.J. (Apr. 25, 2006) (law.com). See also Fred Schneyer, *Wal-mart Accused of Religious Bias*, plansponsor.com (Oct. 4, 2010): the EEOC sued Wal-Mart for back pay, compensatory and punitive damages, and injunctive relief because a 2009 change in the store scheduling system deprived a Mormon store manager of the accommodation of his Sunday Sabbath that he had received since 2005.]

States are not allowed to pass laws that give employees an absolute right to get their Sabbath day as a day off—that would be an unconstitutional establishment of religion. [*Estate of Thornton v. Caldor, Inc.*, 472 U.S. 703 (1985)] However, an employee who is fired for refusing to work on the Sabbath is entitled to collect unemployment benefits. [*Hobbie v. Unemployment Appeals Comm'n of Florida*, 480 U.S. 136 (1987)] Some state laws, including New York's Human Rights Law, make it clear that employees who get time off for religious observances must make up the time at another time that is religiously acceptable.

## [B]  Steps Toward Religious Accommodation

Employers should extend at least the same tolerance to religious garb as to "fashion statements." Where there are actual risks (such as robes getting caught in machinery), document the risk, and work with religious leaders to find out what kinds of safety garments are compatible with religious needs.

Bulletin board postings or the corporate intranets can be used to get volunteers to cover for workers taking prayer time or observing religious holidays. A diverse workforce really helps here—Christian employees can cover the holidays of non-Christian religions, and vice versa. Optional or floating personal days can be used for religious observance.

Because Islam requires five daily prayers, several occurring during the normal work day, it can be difficult to accommodate Muslim employees in a production line environment. Part of the prayer obligation is keyed to sundown, so it does not occur at the same time every day, making it harder to schedule prayers. The need for Muslims to wash their hands and feet before prayer can cause hazardous wet conditions in the washrooms (or hallways, if water is tracked). One simple solution is to install a special self-draining basin, or arrange to have the floors mopped more often.

Although it is often impossible to arrange the menu in the employee cafeteria to conform to all dietary requirements, it is a reasonable gesture to provide some vegetarian alternatives, and to make sure that people whose religion bans the consumption of pork or beef will have other menu choices available.

A growing concern for many employers is how to balance some employees' desire to evangelize for their faith against the desire of other employees to maintain their existing religion (or lack thereof) and lifestyle. Cases have been brought alleging a religiously hostile environment caused by unwanted attempts at religious conversion.

Employees who are not allowed to preach in the workplace can invite co-workers to a church service, prayer meeting, Bible study group, etc., that meets outside the workplace, so their religious expression can be continued elsewhere. The Ninth Circuit permitted a government agency employer to restrict prayer meetings and displays of religious symbols in the workplace: employees were allowed to discuss religion with one another, but not with clients, and could display religious items but not where they would be visible to clients. Prayer meetings were permitted in the break room or outside the office, but not in the conference room, which could only be used for business purposes. The Ninth Circuit concluded that the employer had found an appropriate balance between employees' religious rights and the agency's duty of religious neutrality. [*Berry v. Dep't of Social Servs., Tehama Cnty.*, 447 F.3d 642 (9th Cir. 2006); see Rebecca Moore, *Employer's Restrictions of Religious Activity Not Discriminatory*, plan sponsor.com (May 2, 2006)]

## [C]   Case Law on Reasonable Accommodation

The Second Circuit ruled in 2003 that an employer's rejection of an employee's proposed accommodation of religious needs is a discrete act. Therefore, the statute of limitations is 300 days from the occurrence of the act; the statute of limitations does not restart with every scheduled prayer time that the employee was forced to work. Once an employer rejects a proposed accommodation, the facts to make the case are in existence; the decision is not re-implemented periodically. [*Elmenayer v. ABF Freight Sys. Inc.*, 318 F.3d 130 (2d Cir. 2003)]

The Fourth Circuit concluded that reasonable accommodation was provided to the religious beliefs of a worker with a Saturday Sabbath who was also forbidden to work on seven religious holidays. In this case, the seniority-based bidding system for work shifts operated as a significant accommodation in and of itself, as a neutral method of reducing the number of days that an employee must work when he or she prefers not to, whether for religious or any other reason. The plaintiff also had access to holidays and unpaid time off that could be used neutrally for any reason including religious observance. The plaintiff also failed to switch shifts with another employee. Employers are not required to violate the CBA or the seniority system to accommodate religious needs. [*EEOC v. Firestone Fibers & Textiles Co.*, 515 F.3d 307 (4th Cir. Feb. 2008)]

According to *Weber v. Roadway Express Inc.* [199 F.3d 270 (5th Cir. 2000)], the employer had no obligation to accommodate a Jehovah's Witness truck driver who wanted to be assigned only male driving partners, because his religion forbade him to take overnight trips with any woman other than his wife. The employer would have encountered a serious burden to reconfigure the schedules. Although the employer had accommodated nonreligious requests in the past, it did so only consistent with business needs and did not have an obligation to encounter undue hardship to accommodate the truck driver.

Late in 2003, the Seventh Circuit granted a rehearing in a case holding that a social service agency was not required to accommodate the employee's desire to wear a head covering for religious reasons. [*Holmes v. Morton County Office of Family & Children*, 349 F.3d 914 (7th Cir. 2003)] A temporary employment agency did not violate Title VII when it refused to place a Muslim woman who wears a "khimar" head covering at a printing plant that forbids any kind of head covering as a safety risk. The agency offered the worker, Asthma Suliman, seven other potential placements, which she turned down, so the Eighth Circuit concluded that there had been no adverse job action. Suliman did not have a guarantee or reasonable expectation of being placed with a particular employer, and offering the other jobs was a reasonable accommodation to Suliman's religious practice. [*EEOC v. Kelly Servs., Inc.*, 598 F.3d 1022 (8th Cir. 2010). The Third Circuit upheld dismissal of an EEOC suit on behalf of a class of Muslim women prison employees who wanted to wear khimars. The prison's uniform policy forbade all non-standard head coverings. The court ruled that, despite the plaintiffs' belief that covering their heads is religiously mandated, the khimars create at least a small risk that prisoners could use the head coverings as weapons against prison employees, and theoretically khimars could be used to smuggle drugs or could be used by prisoners to impersonate prison employees. [*EEOC v. Geo Group Inc.*, 616 F.3d 265 (3d Cir. 2010)]

The Council on American-Islamic Relations (CAIR) filed an EEOC race discrimination complaint when an Abercrombie & Fitch manager fired a Muslim employee who refused to stop wearing hijab. CAIR alleged that when the employee was hired, she was told she could wear a hijab as long as it was white, gray, or navy blue (the colors of the store uniforms). Then she was told that hijab did not fit the company "look."—although Abercrombie & Fitch paid $50 million to settle an EEOC suit based on requiring an Anglo-Saxon "look." [Amanda Bronstad, *Abercrombie & Fitch Draws EEOC Complaint for Banning Islamic Head Scarf*, Nat'l L.J. (Feb. 26, 2010) (law.com)]

A petroleum company reached a $125,000 religious discrimination settlement with the EEOC after the company enforced its dress code and refused to let a Rastafarian employee wear the headwrap required by her religion. [Adrien Martin, *RaceTrac Settles Religious Discrimination Suit for $125,000*, plansponsor. com (Jan. 22, 2007)] The Seventh Circuit held that it did not constitute religious discrimination to fail to hire an applicant as a security guard because he wore dreadlocks, finding that he did not prove that he mentioned his religious beliefs or that the belief was the reason for the refusal to hire him. (The defendant said that it did not know that he wore dreadlocks for religious reasons.) [*Lord Osunfarian Xodus v. Wackenhut Corp.*, 619 F.3d 1109 (7th Cir. 2010)]

## § 34.08   RETALIATION

Section 8 of the EEOC Compliance Manual (used by EEOC offices), EEOC Directives Transmittal 915.003 (May 20, 1998), covers retaliation. There are three essential elements in a retaliation claim that the EEOC will pursue:

- The charging party engaged in protected activity, such as opposing discrimination or participating in the Title VII complaint process;

- The employer took adverse action against the charging party;

- There was a causal connection between the protected activity and the employer's adverse action.

A retaliation complaint might be proper if the charging party had a reasonable good-faith belief that the employer committed discrimination (even if this belief was incorrect), and the charging party used a reasonable means to protest this to the employer.

It is illegal to retaliate against a charging party if he or she, or someone closely associated with him or her, participated in any statutory enforcement proceeding. This includes any investigation, proceeding, hearing, or suit under any of the statutes enforced by the EEOC. It is unlawful for one employer to retaliate on the basis of a complaint against another employer.

The Supreme Court resolved several questions about the retaliation cause of action in its June 22, 2006, decision in *Burlington Northern & Santa Fe Ry. Co. v. White*, 548 U.S. 53 (2006). The Supreme Court ruled that retaliation against employees who engage in protected concerted activity is unlawful, whether or not the form the retaliation takes is employment-related. The Supreme Court reached this conclusion based on differences in the statutory language covering the substantive ban on discrimination and the anti-retaliation provision. However, to be actionable, the retaliatory measures must be severe enough that a reasonable employee might have been deterred from pursuing discrimination charges. In the case at bar, there was actionable retaliation because even though the petitioner's job classification did not change, she was assigned less attractive work (more arduous, dirtier, more strenuous) to punish her for complaining about workplace sexual harassment.

In 2013, the Supreme Court made it more difficult for employees to assert Title VII retaliation claims. As a result of this decision, to prevail, the plaintiff must prove that retaliation is the "but-for" cause of the adverse employment action that the employee complains about. It is not enough that retaliation is one of the factors supporting the employer's decision. The Supreme Court therefore mandated a higher standard of proof than the one used by the EEOC. It is also the ADEA standard of proof that the Supreme Court mandated in 2009, in its *Gross v. FBL Financial Services* decision.

The Supreme Court's rationale is that Title VII's retaliation provision is separate from the basic provision forbidding discrimination. Mixed-motive cases are acceptable in cases involving discrimination on the basis of the five personal characteristics listed in Title VII: race, color, religion, sex, and national origin. The Supreme Court majority found that the language of the Title VII retaliation provision has more in common with the ADEA than with the rest of Title VII. [*University of Tex. Sw. Med. Ctr. v. Nassar*, No. 12-484 (U.S. June 24, 2013); see Marcia Coyle, *Supreme Court Makes It Harder to Prove Job Bias*, Nat'l L.J. (June 24, 2013) (law.com)]

The Second Circuit ruled that Title VII's retaliation provisions include both an "opposition" and a "participation" clause. It is unlawful for an employer to retaliate against an employee who opposes the employer's unlawful employment practices. But adverse job action imposed for participation in an employer's internal investigation of harassment charges, with no connection to a formal EEOC investigation, does not entitle the employee to maintain a Title VII retaliation suit. [*Townsend v. Benjamin Enters.*, 679 F.3d 41 (2d Cir. 2012)]

The Southern District of New York held that it did not constitute Title VII retaliation to fail to give a timely COBRA notice to a plaintiff who was terminated (allegedly because she filed an EEOC charge). The employer acknowledged the lack of timely notice, but said that she was offered retroactive COBRA coverage but did not make a COBRA election when the notice was available. The

Southern District of New York held that the plaintiff failed to show that the defective notice was retaliatory. The plaintiff was not looking for another job (she had applied for Social Security Disability benefits), so the court restricted the application of Title VII to actions affecting current employment or the ability to obtain future employment. [*Thompson v. Morris Heights Health Ctr.*, No. 09 Civ. 7239 (PAE) (THK) 2012 WL 1145964 (S.D.N.Y. Apr. 6, 2012); see EBIA Weekly, *No Title VII Retaliation Claim for Employee Who Received Late COBRA* Notice (Apr. 19, 2012) (benefitslink.com)]

The EEOC might seek temporary or preliminary relief such as injunction if the retaliation places the charging party at risk of irreparable injury and there is a substantial likelihood that the retaliation claim will succeed. The compliance manual notes that all of the statutes enforced by the EEOC make both compensatory and punitive damages available to victims of retaliation.

Retaliation complaints under 42 U.S.C. § 1981 are cognizable. A defendant argued that it was not fair to apply § 1981 in the retaliation context, because it has a longer statute of limitations than Title VII and awards are not subject to the CRA '91 damage caps, but the Supreme Court held that this "end run" is allowed for discrimination claims and should also be allowed for retaliation. [*CBOCS West Inc. v. Humphries*, 553 U.S. 442 (2008)]

Although Title VII retaliation damages are subject to the statutory cap, there is no cap on ADEA or EPA damages.

CHAPTER 35

# SEXUAL HARASSMENT

## § 35.01 INTRODUCTION

Sexual harassment is the subjection of an employee to unwanted sexual contact, propositions, or innuendoes. Sexual harassment occurs in two forms: either "quid pro quo" harassment, where an employee is threatened with job detriment for not complying with a sexual proposition or offered job benefits for compliance, or "hostile environment" harassment, where the atmosphere in the workplace is offensive.

Sexual harassment is considered a form of sex discrimination and therefore is forbidden by Title VII. The EEOC has adopted a two-part test. Conduct is unwanted if the employee did not solicit or initiate the conduct, and the employee finds it undesirable or offensive.

The Fourth Circuit refused to apply disparate impact analysis in sexual harassment cases, and ruled late in 2002 that the alleged sexual harassment was not actionable because co-workers would have subjected the plaintiff to the same offensive behavior and vulgar language if she had been male. [*Ocheltree v. Scollon Prods. Inc.*, 308 F.3d 351 (4th Cir. 2002), *on reh'g*, 335 F.3d 325 (4th Cir. 2003)] On rehearing, the court found that a reasonable jury could have found the conduct to be sexually discriminatory against the sole female worker, in the context of a pervasively harassing work environment. However, punitive damages were denied because of lack of proof of employer knowledge sufficient to support punitive damages. The Ninth Circuit also permitted a gender-based harassment action to be maintained based on a showing that women were subjected to a greater degree of bullying, shouting, cursing, and invasion of personal space, even though the perpetrator was not attempting to solicit sexual activity from employees. [*EEOC v. Nat'l Educ. Ass'n Alaska*, 422 F.3d 840 (9th Cir. 2005)]

In late 2012, the Iowa Supreme Court ruled that it was legal for a dentist to fire an assistant he thought was attractive because he and his wife considered her a threat to their marriage. The court found this legitimate because termination was based on feelings and emotions, not her gender. [Nelson v. Knight, No. 11-1857, 2012 Iowa Super. LEXIS 111 (Dec. 21, 2012); see AP, *Iowa—Court Upholds Firing of Woman Whose Boss Found Her Attractive*, NYTimes.com (Dec. 21, 2012)]

The sexual harassment cause of action requires that the victim suffer tangible job action, not merely lack of friendliness or exclusions from workplace social activities. In a 2006 sexual harassment retaliation case, *Burlington Northern & Santa Fe Ry. Co. v. White*, the Supreme Court ruled that retaliation liability is broader than liability for workplace discrimination: retaliation can be actionable even if the employee's job classification and compensation do not change, as long as the retaliatory measures are severe enough to be daunting to a reasonable employee. [548 U.S. 53]

There is a circuit split on the issue of whether rejecting a supervisor's sexual advances is a protected activity for labor law purposes. In 2007, the Fifth Circuit held that rejection of a single advance is not protected, but this conflicts with a 2000 Eighth Circuit ruling that being able to reject unwanted propositions is a clear example of protected activity. In 2008, the Seventh Circuit held that a man who claimed that his supervisor threatened to fire him if he ended a consensual affair with her did not show protected conduct. (The supervisor denies that there was ever a sexual relationship). The supervisor said that the plaintiff was fired for his hostile attitude and unwillingness to work his full shift. In the Seventh Circuit reading, protected conduct requires only the plaintiff's reasonable good-faith belief that the practice he opposed violated Title VII. But in this case, he did not show that he believed the supervisor's conduct was illegal—he merely said that he wanted to end the affair. Therefore, the employer was entitled to JMOL. [*Tate v. Executive Mgmt. Servs. Inc.*, 546 F.3d 528 (7th Cir. 2008); also cf. *LeMaire v. L.A Dept of Transp & Dev*, 480 F.3d 383 (5th Cir. 2007) with *Ogden v. Wax Works, Inc.*, 214 F.3d 999 (8th Cir. 2000)]

Although one or more individuals may commit sexual harassment, it is the employer company that has the legal liability. The only way the employer can avoid liability is by carrying out appropriate investigations of allegations of harassment and by taking appropriate steps to deal with harassment accusations that are well founded.

In 2010, the Ninth Circuit held that a recently widowed male employee was entitled to pursue a charge of hostile environment discrimination continued by ongoing, unwelcome sexual advances from a married female co-worker. His co-workers mocked him as being unmanly or homosexual for rejecting these advances and supervisors did not respond to his complaints. He became depressed, and his work deteriorated to the point that he was fired. The Ninth Circuit held that it cannot be assumed that a heterosexual male will welcome sexual propositions from any and all females. The employer was liable in this case because the victim informed management that the overtures were unwelcome. Perhaps the conduct was not very severe, but it was repetitive, and continued and accelerated over a six-month period. [*EEOC v. Prospect Airport Servs. Inc.*, 621 F.3d 991 (9th Cir. Sept. 3, 2010)]

## § 35.02   THE EMPLOYER'S BURDEN

In this context, two of the key cases are *Burlington Indus., Inc. v. Ellerth* [524 U.S. 742 (1998)] and *Faragher v. City of Boca Raton.* [524 U.S. 775 (1998)] If the action that the plaintiff complains of had adverse employment effect on the victim, the employer is absolutely liable. The employer is still liable even if no adverse employment effect occurred—unless the employer can assert as a defense that it maintained proper antiharassment and grievance policies.

The *Ellerth* case involved a sales representative who felt threatened by repeated remarks and gestures from a manager (not her immediate supervisor). She was not deprived of job benefits. Although she knew the company had an antiharassment policy, she did not complain about the harassment while it was occurring. She quit her job but did not attribute her resignation to harassment. Three weeks later, she sent a letter to the company explaining why she resigned.

The Supreme Court's decision was that the supervisor's threats of adverse job action created a hostile work environment. In such a situation, the employer becomes vicariously liable for the supervisor's conduct by:

- Failing to stop it after learning about it;

- Giving the supervisor apparent authority over the victim, thus making harassment possible;

- Allowing the supervisor to actually take adverse job action against the victim.

However, the other side of the coin is that the employer can be free of liability by taking reasonable care to maintain a workable complaint procedure, if the plaintiff fails to use the procedure.

In the *Faragher* case, a lifeguard sued her municipal employer and two supervisors for creating a hostile environment (including lewd touching of female employees). The employer did have an antiharassment policy, but it was not publicized to the employees. The employer didn't supervise the conduct of the supervisors themselves, and didn't create a procedure for reporting to someone other than the supervisor who committed the harassment. Therefore, the Supreme Court held that the employer was legally responsible for the hostile environment, because it failed to communicate the antiharassment policy and didn't track the conduct of supervisors.

In 2003, the Third Circuit (contrary to holdings in the Second and Sixth Circuits) held that the *Ellerth/Faragher* affirmative defense would not be available to employers in situations where the employee was able to prove constructive discharge. The Supreme Court reversed the Third Circuit in mid-2004. The Supreme Court settled a contentious point by holding that the test of constructive discharge is objective (whether a reasonable person would feel compelled to resign) rather than subjective (the individual employee's personal reaction to the situation). The Supreme Court also noted that, although firing an employee is always an official act (and therefore the affirmative defense is not available), constructive discharge is not always an official act of the employer company. Therefore, the company should be given the chance to assert and prove the affirmative defense. [*Suders v. Easton*, 325 F.3d 432 (3d Cir. 2003), *rev'd sub nom. Pa. State Police v. Suders*, 542 U.S. 129 (2004)]

The Second Circuit ruled in 2012 that the *Ellerth/Faragher* affirmative defense cannot be used where the alleged harasser is high enough in the corporate hierarchy to be considered a proxy or alter ego of the organization. In this case, the alleged harasser was a corporate executive and the husband of the company president. The president took over the investigation, hiring an outside HR consultant who said that the charges were unfounded. [*Townsend v. Benjamin Enters. Inc.*, 679 F.3d 41 (2d Cir. 2012)]

It is not always simple to determine whether an individual accused of harassing conduct is a supervisor or not. In mid-2013, the Supreme Court decided a case about the definition of "supervisor" and the employer's burden. The case involved racial rather than sexual harassment, but it relied heavily on *Ellerth/Faragher*,so it will certainly be influential in sexual harassment cases. In a case of harassment by a supervisor, where there was tangible employment action taken against the plaintiff (such as firing or reassigning him or her) then the employer is strictly liable. If the harasser is a supervisor (defined as someone who has the authority to take tangible employment actions against subordinates) and there is no tangible employment action, the *Faragher/Ellerth* affirmative defense can be raised. But if, as in this case, the harasser is considered a co-worker rather than a supervisor, the employer is only liable if the hostile work environment can be attributed to the employer's negligence. [*Vance v. Ball State Univ.*, 133 S. Ct. 2434 (2013); see Marcia Coyle, *Supreme Court Makes It Harder to Prove Job Bias Claims*, Nat'l L.J. (June 24, 2013) (law.com)] Although many cases involve the conduct of supervisors (because of their ability to affect working conditions), employers have also been held liable, in appropriate cases, for harassment committed by nonsupervisory, fellow employees, and by customers.

In what could be the first case of its type, the New Jersey Court of Appeals ruled that a business owner who says that a customer insisted that she have sex with him or he would not place an order could use the New Jersey Law Against Discrimination to sue for discriminatory refusal to do business on the basis of gender. The court found that quid pro quo harassment in business unlawfully interferes with women's ability to earn a living. [*J.T.'s Tire Service v. United Rentals North Am., Inc.*, 411 N.J. Super. 236 (N.J. App. Div. 2010); see Mary Pat Gallagher, *N.J. Court Allows Business-to-Business Sex Harassment Suit*, N.J.L.J. (Jan. 11, 2010) (law.com)]

A male waiter charged harassment after he terminated his sexual relationship with a female supervisor. (The supervisor conceded that there had been a relationship, but denied that she harassed him in order to get him to resume the relationship.) The Seventh Circuit held that there was a material issue of fact about the hostile work environment, and remanded to see if there was a basis to find the employer liable. The Seventh Circuit held in early 2010 that the same rules apply for males alleging harassment by females as for females alleging harassment by males: if there was a consensual relationship in the past, the question is whether, by both subjective and objective standards, there was a hostile work environment. The Seventh Circuit found that dismissal six months after complaints to Turner's supervisors were not close enough in time to suggest retaliation—especially since Turner received a positive evaluation in the interim.

However, he also received at least ten reprimands for poor workplace behavior. [*Turner v. The Saloon, Ltd.*, 595 F.3d 679 (7th Cir. 2010)]

The employer's burden rests with the employer—harassed employees can't sue their unions for involvement in the employer's failure to redress sexual harassment. If one union member accuses another of harassment, the union has a duty to give both of them fair representation at the disciplinary hearing—but the union does not have an obligation to investigate or remedy discrimination. [*Thorn v. Amalgamated Transit Union*, 305 F.3d 826 (8th Cir. 2002)]

## § 35.03   APPROPRIATE EMPLOYER RESPONSES

### [A]   Statutory and Case Law

Most companies are aware of the potential risk of sexual harassment litigation. After the landmark *Ellerth* and *Faragher* cases, the employer must prevent severe, pervasive unwelcome physical and verbal conduct to prevent the development of a hostile, intimidating, or offensive environment. Supervisors and managers must be trained to recognize and report harassment. There must be a chain of command that can bypass an alleged harasser. Employees must believe that their complaints will be taken seriously. Top management must be involved, to prove that the company takes these matters seriously.

If customers commit the harassment, the Tenth Circuit analyzes the situation as if the harassers were co-employees (not supervisors). So the employer will not be strictly liable for the actions of customers, but will be liable if its negligence permitted the harassment to continue. [*Lockard v. Pizza Hut Inc.*, 162 F.3d 1062 (10th Cir. 1998)]

It is important to look behind supervisors' write-ups to make sure that the lateness, poor work habits, etc., actually occurred—and that one subordinate was not singled out for conduct that was not punished in employees who did not become sexual targets.

Sexual harassment charges require conduct that was unwanted, but some courts weaken the employer's defense in consensual cases. A Seventh Circuit case was brought by a teenage store employee who filed an EEOC charge about inappropriate sexual advances from her 25-year-old shift supervisor, who was convicted of aggravated sexual abuse. The trial court rejected the claim, stating that she engaged in a consensual sexual relationship, but the Seventh Circuit permitted her lawsuit to advance because of her status as a minor. [*Jane Doe v. Oberweis Dairy*, 456 F.3d 704 (7th Cir. 2006); see also *Jane Doe v. Haronmar Inc.*, filed in Broward Circuit Court (Fla.) (June 2007); see Jordana Mishory, *Teen Sues McDonald's Franchisee Over Sex with Boss*, Daily Business Review (June 21, 2007) (law.com)]

The district court made a similar ruling in a case in which a teenage fast-food worker was subjected to sexual harassment by a manager who had had sexual relations with several other employees. The manager fired her for missing a shift (after he re-scheduled her without notice), then rehired her and continued the harassment. The young woman complained repeatedly to shift supervisors and to an assistant manager, who repeatedly frustrated her attempts to file a formal complaint. When the worker's mother came to the restaurant to complain, she was fired again, this time permanently. The district court ruled for the employer, on the grounds that the worker did not invoke the company's complaint procedure, and retaliation for her mother's conduct was not actionable.

In this case, however, the Seventh Circuit reversed, ruling that the reasonableness of an employer's complaint mechanism only affects the employer's liability for damages, not a claim of unlawful termination. The age and sophistication of the complainant are very relevant to the determination of whether the complaint mechanism is adequate. Although employers do not have to have a tailored procedure for each individual, if the business plan is to hire teenage part-time workers, the complaint procedure should be comprehensible to them. At a minimum, employees should have been informed of a toll-free telephone number in the HR department to report complaints; the plaintiff here first was told there was no number to call, then given a wrong number. Furthermore, because a minor has to bring suit by means of a representative, retaliation based on the actions of a young worker's representative should be actionable. [*EEOC v. V&J Foods, Inc.*, 507 F.3d 575 (7th Cir. 2007), discussed in Fred Schneyer, *Appellate Panel Restores Teenager's Sex Harassment Suit*, plansponsor.com (Nov. 7, 2007)]

The Third Circuit held that an employer can be held liable only for hostile work environment sexual harassment committed by co-workers (rather than by supervisors) if the plaintiff charging sexual harassment reports it to a "management level" employee. The Third Circuit defined "management level" employees as those who have authority to hire, fire, and discipline employees, or who are specifically assigned to deal with sexual harassment charges. The plaintiff made her charges to two supervising technicians who, according to the Third Circuit, did not have the necessary authority to put the employer on notice of the charges. After an investigation of the allegations, the entire work team, including the plaintiff herself, was disciplined for violating the work rules against vulgar language in the workplace. The plaintiff was later fired for fabricating data on her machine maintenance logs. [*Huston v. Procter & Gamble Paper Products Corp.*, 568 F.3d 100 (3d Cir. 2009)]

The employer's failure to investigate a claimant's repeated reports of sexual harassment made her resignation a voluntary quit with good cause attributable to the employer, so benefits were available. [*Yaeger*, Unempl. Ins. Rep. (CCH) ¶ 8915 (Fla. Dist. App. 2001)]

## [B]   EEOC Enforcement Guidance

The EEOC's position about what employers should do is summed up in its 20-page guidance available online. [*Enforcement Guidance: Vicarious Employer Liability for Unlawful Harassment by Supervisors*, Number 915.002 (June 18, 1999), <http://www.eeoc.gov/policy/docs/harassment.html> (last accessed Mar. 24, 2013)]

The Guidance makes employers responsible for preventing harassment of all kinds—harassment based on sex (including derogation of women or men because they are women or men, even if the harasser is not seeking sexual gratification); race, color, religion, national origin, age, disability, or protected activity such as enforcing legal rights.

Under this Guidance, the employer will not be liable if harassment does not subject the employee to tangible disadvantages, as long as the employer uses reasonable care to prevent harassment. The employer is also free of liability if it takes reasonable steps to correct harassment that has already occurred, provided that the employee is also at fault by failing to take advantage of the policies and procedures in place.

Employers are liable for the actions of "supervisors": i.e., those with the authority to direct daily work activities, or with authority to recommend or implement tangible employment decisions.

Merely having a policy isn't enough: It must really be enforced. The EEOC encourages employers to terminate harassment even before it reaches the severe, protracted level that would justify a lawsuit.

Under the EEOC interpretation, the employer is always liable when a harassing supervisor subjects an employee to tangible employment action. A tangible employment action means a significant change in employment status such as firing, denial of a promotion, reassignment, an undesirable work assignment. An unfulfilled threat, a trivial effect, or causing hurt feelings doesn't count.

This is the minimum that the EEOC will accept as a satisfactory corporate anti-harassment policy:

- Clear explanations of what constitutes prohibited harassment;

- Assurances that employees who report harassment will not suffer retaliation;

- A clear explanation of a workable procedure for investigating complaints promptly, fairly, and thoroughly (with alternatives so that no one will be expected to report harassment to the person who committed it);

- A confidentiality procedure for complaints;

- Assurance of fast, appropriate response when the investigation shows that harassment has occurred.

Adequate responses to confirmation of a harassment allegation include:

- A warning or an oral or written reprimand to the harasser;

- Training and counseling the harasser about why the conduct violated the employer's policy;

- Transferring, reassigning, demoting, suspending, or, in appropriate cases, firing the harasser;

- Monitoring to make sure harassment has ended;

- Allowing the victim to take leave to get out of the range of harassment;

- Correcting the victim's file to remove unfair evaluations;

- Having the harasser apologize to the victim;

- Checking to make sure that there is no retaliation for reporting the harassment.

### [C] Internal Investigations of Harassment Allegations

An article by two Winston & Strawn attorneys [Susan Schenkel-Savitt and Jill H. Turner, *Effective Investigation of Sexual Harassment Claims*, archived at <http://www.lawnewsnetwork.com>] gives some insights into appropriate investigation of sexual harassment charges. [For more how-tos for internal investigations, see Jonathan A. Segal, *HR as Judge, Jury, Prosecutor, and Defender*, HR Magazine, October 2001, at 141]

Employers can't just summarily fire everyone accused of harassment, because some of those charges could be fabricated; the result of honest misunderstanding; or the accused person's misconduct might not have been serious enough to justify termination. Overreaction on the employer's part could constitute wrongful termination. [See Chapter 39] A mechanism for unbiased internal investigations is necessary, to strike the proper balance between the rights of accusers and accused persons.

Whoever conducts the investigation may have to testify later on, so an in-house or outside attorney who normally represents the corporation could be a poor choice. Attorneys are not allowed to serve as witnesses in cases where they are also representing a party.

However, choosing an attorney rather than someone else can be a good choice, because communications between attorney and client are privileged (opposing parties in litigation can't get hold of them). An attorney's "work product"—the materials drafted by the attorney while preparing the case—is also protected. Similar privileges are not extended to other professionals. If the company will want to assert confidentiality at the pretrial and trial stages, it will have to be sure to keep the materials confidential. Access must be limited to the people involved in the investigation; there must be no general distribution.

The investigator must determine:

- Who claims to have been the victim of harassment (in many cases, harassment involves a number of people);

- Everyone who is accused of committing harassment, contributing to a hostile work environment, or participating in a cover-up;

- Everyone who is claimed to be a witness—and the extent to which their recollection tallies with the complainant's;

- Detailed information about the alleged acts of harassment or the duration and nature of the hostile environment;

- Whether the acts occurred on company property, at company functions, or elsewhere;

- Did the complainant make a prompt report of the alleged harassment? To whom was it made? If there was no report, was there any justification for failing to report at or close to the time of the incident?

The investigator should follow up by contacting witnesses and checking matters of fact. For instance, if an incident is charged on a particular date, the investigator should verify whether the alleged harasser was out of town at the time.

The interview with the alleged harasser is very important. It is up to the employer whether or not to reveal the name of the person making the allegation. To protect the employer against later claims by the alleged harasser, the investigator should make it clear that an investigation is underway, and no conclusions have yet been reached as to the validity of the accusation. The accused person must be given a full, fair chance to get his or her own story on the record.

Additional rounds of interviews may be needed to follow new lines of investigation or confirm disputed facts. The end product of the investigation should be a confidential written report to the person with corporate-level HR responsibility.

Whenever it is determined that an allegation is well founded, the company has a responsibility to take action. The appropriate action is proportionate to the seriousness of the conduct and serves to deter future harassment. The action should also be proportionate to steps the employer has taken in similar cases in the past. The harasser's employment record may provide either mitigation factors (such as a long history of good performance) or aggravating factors (past instances of discipline, especially prior instances of harassment).

If the employer determines that a sanction short of dismissal is appropriate, steps should be taken to keep the harasser and victim apart, but without retaliating against the victim for having complained! The employer should also follow up (and keep written records) to make sure that the disciplinary action has served to prevent future harassment incidents.

## § 35.04   HOSTILE WORK ENVIRONMENT HARASSMENT

### [A]   Generally

A hostile work environment is one where actions are taken to make an employee feel unwelcome. Harassment cases have been recognized dealing with race, religion, disability, and age, as well as cases in which women are made uncomfortable by, e.g., unwanted touching, crude propositions, dirty jokes, pin-ups, etc. Hostile work environment sexual harassment cases have been recognized for many years, dating back to the Supreme Court case of *Meritor Sav. Bank v. Vinson.* [477 U.S. 57 (1986)]

A single act of harassment, if it is severe enough, can create a hostile work environment. The Seventh Circuit permitted a claim of co-worker harassment, who alleged unwelcome physical contact with intimate parts of her body, to proceed to trial. But she did not show that the alleged comments by her supervisor were severe or pervasive enough to create a hostile environment: the court said that she did not show that she felt humiliated or physically threatened, and she did not allege that her work performance was affected. [*Berry v. Chicago Transit Auth.*, 618 F.3d 688 (7th Cir. 2010); see Rebecca Moore, *Court Must Consider Uncorroborated Evidence in Hostile Workplace Suit*, plansponsor.com (Aug. 25, 2010)]

It can be difficult to predict what conduct will be considered sufficiently outrageous to create a hostile environment, because different courts have reached very different conclusions. There is often disagreement about the seriousness of conduct that constitutes harassment, how severe and prolonged it must be, and the extent of injuries that the complainant must suffer before having a sustainable case.

The Eleventh Circuit permitted a female sales representative to pursue a hostile work environment suit because of very frequent use of anti-female language ("bitch" "whore") even though it was not specifically directed at the plaintiff herself. The plaintiff also alleged that there was a lot of workplace discussion about sexual topics, and sexually suggestive radio shows were frequently played in the workplace. Ingrid Reeves resigned her job in 2004 and brought suit. The Northern District of Alabama granted summary judgment for the employer, finding that Reeves herself was not the individual target, so the harassment was not "based on" her sex. A three-judge panel of the Eleventh Circuit reversed this decision in 2008, and was upheld by an en banc panel (of all the judges on the court) in 2010. [*Reeves v. C.H. Robinson*, 594 F.3d 798 (11th Cir. 2010); see Alyson M. Palmer, *11th Circuit: "Sex Specific" Profanity Could Win Harassment Case*, Fulton County Daily Report (Jan. 22, 2010) (law.com) and *In Code and in Specifics, Judges Debate Lewd Office Talk*, Fulton County Daily Report (Oct. 7, 2009) (law.com)]

A sexual harassment plaintiff who charged that her boss' sexual innuendoes offended and humiliated her could not prevent the jury from hearing about dirty jokes and sexual content in her own e-mails on the work computer. The plaintiff made a motion to exclude some e-mails that she said were irrelevant or not probative. The Eastern District of Pennsylvania excluded one e-mail that dealt with health issues, including the plaintiff's use of anti-depressants, but admitted the rest because a hostile environment sexual harassment claim has both objective and subjective components. One element is whether a reasonable employee would have found the work environment offensive; the other element is how the plaintiff felt personally. Therefore, the e-mails were relevant to the extent to which the plaintiff found sexual jokes and bad language to be offensive. [*Seybert v. Int'l Group Inc.*, No. 07-3333 (E.D. Pa. Oct. 13, 2009); see Shannon P. Duffy, *Dirty Jokes on Sex Harassment Plaintiff's Computer Ruled Fair Game*, The Legal Intelligencer (Oct. 23, 2009) (law.com); Rebecca Moore, *Dirty Joke Emails of Plaintiff Can Be Used in Sexual Harassment Case*, plansponsor.com (Oct. 23, 2009)].

The California Court of Appeal reversed a verdict for the defense, holding that the trial court should have admitted "me too" evidence that the defendant, a lawyer, exhibited gender and racial bias by harassing and berating other women working in his office. The court of appeal found exclusion of this evidence prejudicial to the plaintiff. [*Pantoja v. Anton*, 198 Cal. App. 4th 87 ( 2011); see Kate Moser, *Court OKs 'Me Too' Testimony in Sex Harass Suit Against Lawyer*, The Recorder (Aug. 9, 2011) (law.com)]

## [B]   Retaliation

As Chapter 34 discusses, allegations of retaliation for filing discrimination claims are in themselves a major litigation area.

The Supreme Court's 2009 *Crawford* decision, which holds that employees are protected against retaliation if they respond to questioning in an employer's internal investigation—not just if they volunteer information about illegalities in the workplace—began as a sexual harassment case. The plaintiff charged her employer with retaliating against her for testifying in an investigation of charges raised by another employee; Crawford said that she had also been harassed by the same supervisor. [*Crawford v. Metropolitan Gov't of Nashville & Davison County, TN*, 555 U.S. 271 (2009); see Rebecca Moore, *Employees Questioned in Workplace Sexual Harassment Investigations Are Protected*, plansponsor.com (Jan. 26, 2009)]

The First Circuit held that a reasonable jury could believe that the drug company manager plaintiff, Collazo, opposed sexual harassment when he helped a co-worker pursue harassment charges. Although the employer's internal inquiry cleared the alleged harasser, a plaintiff does not have to prove that the conditions he or she opposed actually violated Title VII—only that he or she had a good faith reasonable belief that they did. Management argued that Collazo was fired for performance problems, and because his job was eliminated in a reorganization, but the First Circuit refused to allow reorganization to be used as an excuse for discriminatory or retaliatory termination. Nor was he given any counseling or progressive discipline for the supposed performance problems. Although other employees were transferred, Collazo was the only person terminated, and the only person not given a chance to transfer. Collazo did not get any verbal or written warnings or counseling in the months before his termination, supposedly for deficient performance. [*Collazo v. Bristol-Myers Squibb Mfg. Inc.*, 617 F.3d 39 (1st Cir. 2010)]

## § 35.05  SAME-SEX HARASSMENT

For several years, courts were divided about whether sexual harassment of a male employee by a male supervisor, or a female employee by a female supervisor, was barred by Title VII. Perhaps this reflects a stereotype of sexual harassment as only something that is perpetrated by males against females. Questions were raised as to whether same-sex harassment could be described as occurring "on account of sex," because the harasser is of the same sex as the victim.

The uncertainty was resolved by the Supreme Court in *Oncale v. Offshore Servs. Inc.* [523 U.S. 45 (1998)], which brought same-sex harassment into the ambit of Title VII.

In 1997, 12% of harassment charges were filed by men, a proportion that rose to 16% in FY 2011. Sparks Steak House agreed to pay $600,000 to settle EEOC charges of male/male harassment of waiters by managers. The harassment continued despite complaints from the waiters. The primary harasser, the maitre d'hotel, was given a last chance agreement, but was not fired. [Jenna Greene, *NYC Steakhouse Settles with EEOC over Male-on-Male Harassment Charges*, The BLT (Nov. 16, 2012) (law.com)]

On its own motion, the Eleventh Circuit decided to re-hear *Corbitt v. Home Depot*. The district court and the Eleventh Circuit dismissed the sexual harassment claim (in July and December 2009), but both times the retaliation claim was allowed to proceed. Two male plaintiffs alleged ongoing harassment from a male supervisor, who had a reputation for being vindictive. They were fired after complaining about the harassment, which the district court characterized as insufficient to alter the terms and conditions of employment. [The three decisions are 573 F.3d 1223 (July 10, 2009), 589 F.3d 1136 (Dec. 4, 2009) and 598 F.3d 1259 (Mar. 10, 2010). See Tresa Baldas, *Sex Harassment Suit Given Surprise Third Shot at 11th Circuit*, Nat'l L.J. (Mar. 17, 2010) (law.com)] But before the en banc court could render an opinion, the case was settled in July 2010. [*Corbitt v. Home Depot*, 611 F.3d 1379 (11th Cir. 2010); see Alyson M. Palmer, *Male Employees' Sex Harassment Case Settles Before Full 11th Circuit Rules* (special to law.com (July 30, 2010)]

An oil rig worker said that a bisexual male co-worker harassed him by not only insisting on describing his sexual activities with women, but also propositioning the plaintiff and subjecting him to unwanted sexual touching. The Sixth

Circuit held that the plaintiff failed to provide proof of the alleged harasser's sexual orientation, which was necessary to create the inference that the plaintiff was harassed "because of his sex." The Sixth Circuit requires proof of at least one of three elements in a same-sex harassment case: (1) credible evidence that the alleged harasser is homosexual; (2) clear evidence that the harasser is generally hostile to the presence of members of the plaintiff's sex in the workplace; or (3) in a mixed-sex workplace, with worse treatment by the harasser of one sex than the other. All of the oil rig workers were male and there was no evidence that the alleged harasser was hostile to males as a group. Therefore, the Sixth Circuit required proof of the alleged harasser's sexual orientation, and held that a suggestion that he was bisexual was not enough to prove the plaintiff's case. [*Wasek v. Arrow Energy Servs., Inc.*, 682 F.3d 463 (6th Cir. 2012)]

The Tenth Circuit, reversing the district court, held that it is possible for women to create a work environment that is hostile to other women (e.g., lewd jokes and offensive touching directed by lesbians against the heterosexual female plaintiff). However, the Tenth Circuit dismissed the retaliation claim because, at worst, there was one instance of discipline, in a situation that could be interpreted as management's attempt to prevent future harassment. [*Dick v. Phone Directories Co.*, 397 F.3d 1256 (10th Cir. 2005)] The Eighth Circuit disagreed, affirming summary judgment for the employer in a case in which a heterosexual female employee said that another heterosexual female employee subjected her (and other women) to unwanted rude, vulgar, and sexually charged behavior, such as sexual innuendo and groping. The plaintiff said that co-worker also engaged in similar conduct toward male employees. The plaintiff said that she complained about 100 times to at least 12 managers, but management denied that she had complained and refused to transfer her out of the baking department. Because the co-worker treated males and females in the same vulgar and inappropriate way, the Eighth Circuit said that the plaintiff could not prove that the conduct was motivated by sexual desire, that harassment was motivated by general hostility to the presence of women—or men—in the workplace, or that the harasser targeted only one sex for harassment. [*Smith v. HyVee Inc.*, 622 F.3d 904 (8th Cir. 2010)]

## § 35.06  ORIENTATION AND PERCEIVED ORIENTATION

Although a number of states and cities have their own laws against sexual-orientation discrimination, Title VII itself does not forbid discrimination on the basis of homosexual or bisexual orientation. [*Higgins v. New Balance Athletic Shoes Inc.*, 194 F.3d 252 (1st Cir. 1999); *Bibby v. Philadelphia Coca-Cola Bottling Co.*, 260 F.3d 257 (3d Cir. 2001)] The *Bibby* case says that three kinds of same-sex harassment are illegal: unwanted sexual advances made toward an employee of the same sex; harassment because the harasser believes that women or men do not belong in that type of workplace; or harassment for failure to behave with appropriate masculinity or femininity.

Although Title VII does not cover transsexuality, some transsexual plaintiffs now raise claims that they are discriminated against because they present themselves as the "other" sex and do not conform to gender stereotypes. [See, e.g., *Tronetti v. TLC Healthnet Lakeshore Hosp.*, 03-CV-0375E(Sc), 2003 WL 22757935 (W.D.N.Y. Sept. 26, 2003); *Barnes v. Cincinnati*, 401 F.3d 729 (6th Cir. 2005), *cert. denied*, 546 U.S. 1003 (2005); *Price Waterhouse, Sex Stereotyping, and Gender Non-Conformity Bias*, 73 LW 2211 (Oct. 19, 2004)]

A transgender plaintiff, Maya Perez, sued Burlington Coat Factory, alleging years of physical and verbal abuse and retaliatory discharge. The California statute, FEHA, has covered gender identity since 2004. Perez alleged that co-workers taunted her and engaged in pushing, shoving, groping, and other forms of physical harassment. Perez also says that customers were verbally abusive and threatening, and that co-workers and supervisors observed harassmentbut did not intervene until it had escalated. [Evan Hill, *Rare Transgender Employment Discrimination Lawsuit Filed Against Burlington Coat Factory*, The Recorder (Feb. 26, 2009) (law.com)]

Although Title VII does not cover sexual orientation discrimination, the Third Circuit permitted an effeminate gay man to pursue a Title VII claim of harassment based on his failure to conform to gender stereotypes. The Third Circuit said that the case should not have been dismissed, but should have gone to a jury, because it was uncertain whether the case involved sexual orientation or gender discrimination (but affirmed dismissal of his charge that he was harassed for not conforming to his co-workers' religious beliefs). [*Prowel v. Wise Business Forms Inc.*, 579 F.3d 285 (3d Cir. 2009); see Shannon P. Duffy, *3rd Circuit Revives Gay Man's Title VII Suit*, The Legal Intelligencer (Aug. 31, 2009) (law.com); on harassment on the basis of perceived effeminacy, see also *EEOC v. Grief Bros. Corp.*, No. 02-CV-468S, 2004 WL 2202641 (W.D.N.Y. Sept. 30, 2004); *Doe v. City of Belleville*, 119 F.3d 563 (7th Cir. 2001); *Nichols v. Azteca Rest. Enters. Inc.* [256 F.3d 864 (9th Cir. 2001)]

Two mid-2002 cases reached opposite conclusions. The Ohio Court of Appeals agreed that a gay male worker stated a cause of action for severe emotional distress and depression affecting his work performance as a result of continuous harassment, graffiti, and unwelcome sexual remarks. [*Tenney v. GE Corp.*, 2002 Ohio 2975 (Ohio App. 2002)] But, in the Florida Court of District Appeals view, a lesbian did not state an emotional distress claim by alleging a severe and pervasive pattern of harassment by supervisors, including derogatory comments about homosexuality and abusive conduct directed to her as a lesbian, because the court did not find the conduct sufficiently outrageous to be actionable. [*DeLaCampa v. Grifola Am. Inc.*, 819 So. 2d 940 (Fla. Dist. App. 2002)]

A male AT&T Mobility worker lost his case alleging that hostile comments by his supervisor created a hostile work environment. The Sixth Circuit held that he did not prove that he was subjected to unwanted sexual conduct or communications on the basis of sex that substantially interfered with the conditions of employment. The Sixth Circuit characterized the supervisor's statements as teasing or name-calling, insufficient to create an actionable hostile work environment. Plaintiff Kalich contended that the supervisor targeted him for homophobic insults because he knew or suspected Kalich was gay—but in Michigan, sexual orientation is not a protected classification. The Sixth Circuit concluded that the supervisor did not have any sexual interest in Kalich, and treated him rudely and unpleasantly but that was how he treated everyone, irrespective of sex. Furthermore, the Sixth Circuit found that AT&T Mobility was entitled to the *Faragher/Ellerth* defense, because it investigated Kalich's allegations promptly, finished the investigation within 10 business days, and it transferred the alleged harasser and gave him anti-discrimination training and a final warning.[*Kalich v. AT&T Mobility*, 679 F.3d 464 (6th Cir. 2012)]

## § 35.07   WRONGFUL DISCHARGE CLAIMS

Employers often fear that they may be caught between two fires. If they do not respond to allegations, they face EEOC charges and/or lawsuits. But if they fire an alleged harasser, he or she may sue for wrongful termination. It is a delicate balance, but the employer can avoid liability by carrying out a thorough investigation in each case and taking proportionate steps against anyone found to have committed harassment. A complete "paper trail" is very important here (as in many other contexts).

When discriminatory discipline is charged, the question is whether different discipline is imposed for the same offense. A black female employee did not have a discrimination claim when she was fired for groping the genitals of male co-workers, when a white female was not fired for exposing her breasts on request, because the black female had engaged in conduct contrary to the wishes of its recipients, justifying a higher level of discipline. [*Wheeler v. Aventis Pharm.*, 360 F.3d 853 (8th Cir. 2004)]

Another implication of wrongful termination law is that in Maryland, an employee discharged for refusing to have sexual intercourse with a harasser can pursue a tort claim for abusive discharge in addition to the sexual harassment charges. The additional tort claim can be pursued because the state has a public policy against prostitution—and having sex to keep a job is, in effect, prostitution. [*Insignia Residential Corp. v. Ashton, Md.*, 755 A.2d 1080 (Md. 2000)]

## § 35.08   DAMAGE ISSUES

The Seventh Circuit allows a sexual harassment plaintiff to get punitive damages in cases in which there were no compensatory damages. [See *Timm v. Progressive Steel Treating Inc.*, 137 F.3d 1008 (7th Cir. 1998)] This might occur, for instance, where a company fails to establish a complaint procedure and then blames the plaintiff for failure to go through channels. In this case, the plaintiff mitigated her damages so effectively that she got a higher-paying job, and therefore could not collect a back pay award.

The Supreme Court has imposed a general rule, for all kinds of cases, that punitive damages should not be more than nine times compensatory damages. Late in 2003, the District of Columbia Court of Appeals struck down an award of $4.8 million in punitive damages in a sexual harassment retaliation case, finding it to be unconstitutionally excessive (26:1 ratio). The award was also improper because it reflected the defendant's nationwide conduct, not just its treatment of the individual plaintiff. Furthermore, the most relevant civil penalty under the local Human Rights Act was only $50,000 for multiple offenses. [*Daka Inc. v. McCrae*, 839 A.2d 682 (D.C. App. Dec. 24, 2003)]

The Seventh Circuit affirmed a jury award of $15,000 in compensatory and $50,000 punitive damages to a nursing home employee who experienced lewd remarks and inappropriate touching from residents. Her supervisor told her to get a security escort before cleaning the rooms of those residents, but the security guards always said they were too busy to accompany her. The Vice President of Operations said that the nursing facility was the residents' home and nothing was going to change, and it was the employee's fault for making residents want to touch her. Pickett, the employee, thought that this conversation meant that she was fired, so she left the building (which violated the work rules). The next day, when she reported for work, she was told that she had been fired. After she filed an EEOC charge, she was offered reinstatement, which she eventually accepted. The Seventh Circuit held that the jury was justified in believing Pickett's contention that a business can be responsible for sexual harassment committed by third parties, such as customers or nursing home residents, so the question was whether Pickett provided enough evidence of harassment; the Seventh Circuit said she did. The award of compensatory damages was not obviously excessive, was comparable to awards in similar cases, and the $15,000 jury award fell well within the $200,000 cap on damages. It was not unreasonable for the jury to assume that management was aware of federal laws, so punitive damages were justified. [*Pickett v. Sheridan Health Care Ctr.*, 610 F.3d 434 (7th Cir. 2010)]

The EEOC won a class action against grocery store KarenKim. The 10 members of the class were awarded a total of $10,000 in compensatory damages and $1.25 million in punitive damages for verbal and physical harassment committed by Allen Manwaring. Manwaring had been the manager of the store. He was fired, but continued to be present at the store because he was the store owner's romantic partner, and continued to do business with the store as a produce contractor. The EEOC asked for 10 years of injunctive relief to prevent a repetition of the harassment. The Second Circuit agreed with the EEOC that a permanent injunction is appropriate where relief is needed and there is a risk of repeated violations. Because there was a risk that the store owner would re-hire Manwaring, the Second Circuit allowed an injunction forbidding KarenKim to re-employ Manwaring or to allow him to enter the store's business premises. [*EEOC v. KarenKim, Inc.*, 698 F.3d 92 (2d Cir. 2012)]

Normally, the question is whether the defendant will have to pay the plaintiff's legal fees and costs—but, in rare cases, a prevailing defendant will be entitled to a fee award. The EEOC brought a suit on behalf of more than 200 female truck drivers who said that they suffered sexual harassment, including rape in some cases, by male drivers assigned as trainers by their employers, CRST Van Expedited Inc. The District Court for the Northern District of Iowa not only dismissed the EEOC suit but also ruled that the defendant was the prevailing party in the suit—so the EEOC would have to pay almost $5 million of CRST's legal fees and litigation expenses. The district court found that the EEOC completely mishandled the preparation of the case and entirely failed to prove its pattern-or-practice theory. The district court gave the EEOC only three months for discovery, ruling that any woman for whom the EEOC did not get a deposition would be dismissed from the case. The EEOC took only 150 depositions, so 120 potential plaintiffs were excluded from the case. The district court dismissed all of the plaintiffs' claims because the EEOC did not investigate or attempt conciliation in each individual case. The district court also said that the trainers were not supervisors, so CRST was not vicariously liable for any harassment that occurred.

The EEOC appealed to the Eighth Circuit, which upheld most of the district court's findings. However, the Eighth Circuit ruled that claims of two of the plaintiffs should not have been dismissed. Therefore, CRST was no longer a prevailing defendant, and the EEOC did not have to pay its fees and costs right away (although it might have to at a later stage of the case). The Eighth Circuit held that the EEOC had an obligation to investigate thoroughly before filing suit and to attempt conciliation of each claim. [*EEOC v. CRST Van Expedited Inc.*, 679 F.3d 657 (8th Cir. 2012); *en banc reh'g denied* (June 8, 2012). However, the Eighth Circuit remanded the case to the Northern District of Iowa—which once again ordered the EEOC to pay close to $5 million to CRST for attorneys' fees, court costs, and other expenses, reinstating the finding that CRST was a prevailing defendant. The district court criticized the EEOC for the inadequacy of its investigation and its failure to attempt conciliation, and found the EEOC's pattern or practice claim unreasonable because of the lack of statistics or legal citations to back up the charges. The district court found that the EEOC brought 153 individual claims that were frivolous, unreasonable, or groundless. [*EEOC v. CRST Van Expedited, Inc.*, No. 07-CV-95, 2013 U.S. Dist. LEXIS 107822 (N.D. Iowa Aug. 1, 2013); see Gerald L. Maatman, Jr. and Howard M. Wexler, *Time to Pay Up! EEOC Ordered to Pay $4.694 Million in Fees and Costs for Pursuing "Unreasonable" and "Groundless" Claims*, Lexology.com, <http://www.lexology.com/library/detail.aspx?g=b02607dc-df4c-4db0-b6e8-d41731e59635> (Aug. 3, 2013)]

See also *EEOC v. Great Steaks, Inc.*, 667 F.3d 510 (4th Cir. 2012): the jury ruled for the defendant in an EEOC suit charging hostile environment sexual harassment. The Fourth Circuit held that the defendant was not entitled to an award of attorneys' fees under Title VII, the Equal Access to Justice Act, or the federal statute against "vexatious litigation." The Fourth Circuit held that, although a prevailing defendant does not have to prove the plaintiff's subjective bad faith to receive a fee award, the plaintiff must either have made a groundless, unreasonable, or frivolous claim, or must have prolonged the litigation after it was clear that the suit was inappropriate. In this case, even though the EEOC's case was not strong enough to win, it was not worthless.]

## § 35.09  LIABILITY OF INDIVIDUALS

Sexual harassment charges are not really very similar to charges of, say, environmental pollution, commercial fraud, or tax evasion. Although a corporation is only an artificial person, so individuals must commit its wrongful acts, in some cases individuals who commit a tort or a crime are doing so on behalf of the corporation. People who commit sexual harassment may be echoing a corporate culture that tolerates such things, but they are not benefiting the corporation!

Nevertheless, the language of Title VII, like most antidiscrimination statutes, refers only to "employers," and with few exceptions, courts have ruled that only the employer corporation, and not the individual, is liable for harassment. [No individual liability: *Carrisales v. Dep't of Corrs.*, 90 Cal. Rptr. 2d 804 (Cal. 1999); *Smith v. Amedisys Inc.*, 298 F.3d 434 (5th Cir. 2002). But see *Speight v. Albano Cleaners*, 21 F. Supp. 2d 560 (E.D. Va. 1998), where the individual supervisor was held liable, but the corporation was not held liable]

*Reno v. Baird* [957 P.2d 1333 (Cal. 1998)] holds that an individual manager, although potentially liable for harassment, is not an "employer" under California's antidiscrimination statute. Although the state's Fair Employment and Housing Act defines "employer" to include "any person acting as an agent of an employer, directly or indirectly" the *Baird* court interpreted this language to make employers liable for the action of their agents, not to make agents personally liable.

## § 35.10  INTERACTION WITH OTHER STATUTES

It is a familiar theme throughout this book that legal concepts do not exist in isolation, and a single case may trigger many statutes and regulations.

According to the Kentucky Supreme Court, there is an exception to Worker's Compensation exclusivity for injuries occurring through the "deliberate intention" of the employer. Therefore, although a suit against the employer for the physical and psychological consequences of sexual harassment would not necessarily be barred by WC exclusivity, nevertheless plaintiffs must make a choice. Either they can bring a tort suit (for instance, for intentional or negligent infliction of emotional distress; battery) or file for Worker's Compensation benefits. Acceptance of the Comp benefits rules out a suit involving the same injuries. [*Am. Gen. Life & Accident Ins. Co. v. Hall*, 74 S.W.3d 688 (Ky. Sup. 2002)]

The Bankruptcy Abuse Prevention and Consumer Protection Act of 2005 (BAPCA; Pub.L. No. 109-8) denies a discharge in a Chapter 13 case for civil damages awarded against the debtor when the debtor's willful or malicious injury resulted in personal injury or death to a plaintiff.

A "top-hat" (executive benefit) plan called for payment of benefits on termination, with no qualifications. Because the plan did not mandate forfeiture when an employee was fired for cause, someone who was fired for sexually harassing employees was eligible for the benefits. [*Fields v. Thompson Printing Co.*, 363 F.3d 259 (3d Cir. 2004)]

The Second Circuit required a makeup artist to arbitrate her sexual harassment claims against her employer, Atlantic Video, and against ESPN, even though ESPN did not sign the arbitration agreement. The plaintiff alleged that she was harassed by ESPN personnel, and that Atlantic Video and ESPN engaged in concerted action to allow the harassment to continue. [*Ragone v. Atlantic Video*, 595 F.3d 115 (2d Cir. 2010)]

Luciano Manganella, former president of Jasmine Co. Inc. was accused of sexual harassment by several employees. He sought defense and indemnity from Jasmine's liability insurer. The First Circuit held that he was not entitled to them because an arbitration involving Manganella and the company that purchased Jasmine established that his conduct was excluded from coverage under the exclusion for conduct showing wanton, willful, reckless, or intentional disregard of law. Jasmine Co. was sold in July 2005. Manganella entered into a stock purchase agreement and an employment contract. Seven million dollars of the purchase price was placed into escrow as security against major breaches of Manganella's employment contract (including breaches of the purchasing corporation's code of conduct). Jasmine purchased the insurance policy shortly after an employee filed sexual harassment charges in 1998, based on Manganella's conduct. Jasmine launched an investigation in May 2006 when there were additional charges against Manganella, and Manganella was fired shortly thereafter. The dismissal letter said that he violated the purchaser's code of conduct by sexually harassing four employees and downloading pornography on company computers. Lerner and Manganella went to arbitration on the question of whether the purchaser could recover the $7 million. The arbitration panel decided that Manganella committed sexual harassment—but he was entitled to retain the $7 million because the purchaser did not give him notice or opportunity to remedy the violation. The Southern District of New York confirmed the arbitration award. While the arbitration was pending, another employee filed Massachusetts sexual harassment charges against Manganella, Jasmine, and the purchaser. Manganella applied for but was turned down for liability insurance coverage. The insurer said that the harassment began before the retroactive date of the coverage. The First Circuit held that the arbitration had already determined the question of whether Manganella acted with wanton or willful neglect of legal obligations, so he was not entitled to insurance coverage. [*Manganella v. Evanston Ins. Co.*, 700 F.3d 585 (1st Cir. 2012)]

CHAPTER 36

# AMERICANS WITH DISABILITIES ACT (ADA)

## § 36.01   INTRODUCTION

Since its passage in 1990, the Americans With Disabilities Act (ADA) has been contentious and controversial. In recent years, the Supreme Court and the lower courts have greatly limited the scope of this Act, especially in the employment arena. Employers nearly always prevail in these cases, for a variety of reasons, such as lack of proof that:

- The plaintiff was a Qualified Individual With a Disability (QIWD). NOTE: 2011 EEOC guidance does not use the term QIWD; see § 36.04[F] below;

- The plaintiff suffered adverse employment action;

- The plaintiff sought reasonable accommodation;

- A reasonable accommodation could have met the plaintiff's needs without unduly burdening the employer.

Perhaps the suit can be dismissed because it was brought against an employer who is not subject to the ADA, or on grounds of untimeliness.

The ADA starts at 42 U.S.C. § 12101 (regulations at 29 C.F.R. § 1630.1). Title I is the employment title; Title II deals with public services (i.e., provided by government aIII with public accommodations, and Title IV with miscellaneous issues, some of which relate to employment.

Major legislation, the ADA Amendments Act of 2008, or ADAAA, was passed in 2008 to clarify some disputed ADA issues, and reverse some of the harsher effects of recent Supreme Court precedents. See § 36.03, below. A number of decisions hold that the ADAAA is not retroactive [See, e.g., *EEOC v. Agro Distribution, LLC*, 555 F.3d 462 (5th Cir. 2009)], so there will be a period of time when pre-ADAAA cases continue to be decided by the legal system.

In fiscal 2012, the EEOC received 26,379 charges of disability discrimination, representing 26.5% of all charges. [EEOC, *Charge Statistics FY 1997 Through FY 2012*, <http://www1.eeoc.gov//eeoc/statistics/enforcement/charges.cfm?> (undated, last accessed Mar. 18, 2013]

The ADAAA has reduced the number of cases dismissed at the summary judgment stage—and this, in turn, has led to higher settlements. In FY 2012, 26.5% of EEOC charges included an ADA allegation. Overall, the number of charges fell, but the number of ADA charges increased by over 600. ADA charges have increased each year since the ADAAA: in 2008, there were 19,453 charges; there were 26,379 in 2012. Pre-ADAAA, in 2007, EEOC settlements were $1.6 million for anxiety disorder charges, rising to $6.4 million in 2012; for back impairments, the figures are $3.8 million in 2007, $10 million in 2012. Giving employees fixed amounts of leave in addition to their FMLA entitlement is easy to administer but risky—it doesn't provide individual case by case accommodation. The article warns against a hard and fast rule that employees must be able to return to full duty after leave; light duty might be required as an accommodation. HR personnel should be trained to consider leave requests on an individual basis. Language in a no-fault or fixed leave policy should disclose possible eligibility for additional leave if that would be a reasonable accommodation. [Shannon Green, *Disability Act Charges and Awards Skyrocket*, Corporate Counsel (Mar. 27, 2013) (law.com)]

## § 36.02   REACH AND RANGE OF ADA TITLE I

According to 42 U.S.C. § 12101, Congress went on record that the over 43 million employees with disabilities (a number that is increasing as the population ages) have a history of social alienation and discrimination in important areas such as work, housing, public accommodations, health services, and education. Congress declared that people with disabilities are a minority group that has suffered discrimination—and that our national goal in dealing with people with disabilities should be "to assure equality of opportunity, full participation, independent living, and economic self sufficiency." The legislative purpose is given as providing "clear, strong, consistent, enforceable standards addressing discrimination against individuals with disabilities."

A "covered entity," as defined by 42 U.S.C. § 12111(2), means an employer, an employment agency, a union, or a joint labor-management committee.

Only employers who have at least 15 employees in each working day in each of 20 or more weeks in the current or preceding year are subject to the ADA. [42 U.S.C. § 12111(5)]

In an April 22, 2003, decision, the Supreme Court ruled that four physicians who were shareholders and directors of a medical PC were probably not "employees," using the economic reality test. The doctors controlled business operations; they were not subject to the control of others. If so, the professional corporation had fewer than 15 "employees," and the PC's bookkeeper could not bring suit under the ADA, whether or not it was true that she was terminated because of disability. [*Clackamas Gastroenterology Assocs., PC v. Wells*, 538 U.S. 440 (2003)]

An employer with fewer than 15 employees, although exempt under the ADA, can be sued under the Rehabilitation Act. [*Schrader v. Fred A. Ray, MD PC*, 296 F.3d 968 (10th Cir. 2002)]

Individuals are nearly always exempt from being sued under antidiscrimination suits (only the employer company is liable). *Alberte v. Anew Health Care Servs.* [588 N.W.2d 298 (Wis. App. 1998)] permits an ADA suit against an individual who was president, administrator, and 47.5% shareholder in a company accused of disability discrimination. In this reading, the president was the company's agent and personally liable for both compensatory and punitive damages. But this ruling is an anomaly. Far more typically, in mid-2007, the Eleventh Circuit held that individuals cannot be sued for violating the ADA's ban on retaliation in employment, nor under the Florida state statute that forbids HIV/AIDS discrimination. (The plaintiff brought suit against his employer company and three of its officers as individuals.) The Eleventh Circuit concluded that the language of the employment provisions of the ADA is similar to that of Title VII and the ADEA, where individual suits have been ruled out, and cited the Southern District of Florida's conclusion that the state anti-discrimination statute also rules out suits against individuals. [*Albra v. Advan, Inc.*, 490 F.3d 826 (11th Cir. 2007)]

A U.S. citizen who works outside the United States can count as an employee entitled to protection under the ADA. [42 U.S.C. § 12111(4)] However, it is not unlawful for a workplace outside the United States to comply with local law, even if the result is discrimination. Foreign operations of a foreign company that is not controlled by an American employer are exempt from the ADA. [42 U.S.C. § 12112(c)]

Section 12115 requires employers to post notices of ADA rights "in an accessible format" in the workplace.

The ADA does not invalidate or limit the remedies, rights, and procedures of any state or federal law that provides additional protection of the rights of individuals with disabilities. [42 U.S.C. § 12201]

"Mixed-motive" cases (where disability discrimination is alleged to be only one factor in the employer's decision) can be brought in some circuits, where it is not necessary for the plaintiff to allege that the employer was solely motivated by disability discrimination. [*McNely v. Ocala Star-Banner Corp.*, 99 F.3d 1068 (11th Cir. 1996)] However, the Sixth Circuit does not allow mixed-motive cases: to sue there, the plaintiff must allege that disability must have been the sole cause for the employment decision. [*Hedrick v. W. Reserve Care Sys.*, 355 F.3d 444 (6th Cir. 2004)] On the other hand, the Ninth Circuit does permit mixed-motive ADA cases. [*Head v. Glacier Nw.*, 413 F.3d 1053 (9th Cir. 2005)]

Most of the circuits allow hostile environment claims in the ADA context, because the ADA uses the same language as Title VII "terms, conditions and privileges of employment" so the concept of the hostile work environment has been extended to cover the ADA as well as Title VII. [*Shaver v. Indep. Stave Co.*, 350 F.3d 716 (8th Cir. 2003); *Flowers v. S. Reg'l Physician Servs. Inc.*, 247 F.3d 229 (5th Cir. 2001); *Fox v. Gen. Motors Corp.*, 247 F.3d 169 (4th Cir. 2001)] To win a hostile environment suit, the plaintiff must show that he or she is a member of the protected group; that unwelcome harassment occurred; that it resulted from membership in the protected class; and it was severe enough to affect the terms, conditions, or privileges of employment. [*Reedy v. Quebecor Printing Eagle, Inc.*, 333 F.3d 906 (8th Cir. 2003)] In the *Shaver* case, the plaintiff had severe epileptic seizures, and at least some of his colleagues treated him as stupid or mentally ill for that reason or because he had had brain surgery resulting in removal of part of his skull. There is evidence that he was taunted, but the Eighth Circuit concluded that the verbal harassment was not severe enough to rise to the level of an objectively hostile work environment. The plaintiff was upset, but not threatened or traumatized.

Although Congress specifically stated in 42 U.S.C. § 12202 that states are NOT immune from ADA suits, the Supreme Court held in 2001 that Congress had no right to abrogate the states' "sovereign immunity" (freedom from being sued) with respect to ADA Title I cases that seek money damages rather than injunctions, because there was no documentation of a past history of disability discrimination perpetrated by the states themselves. [See *Board of Trustees of the Univ. of Ala. v. Garrett*, 531 U.S. 356 (2001)] In 2002, the Supreme Court held that punitive damages are not available in a suit for discrimination against disability discrimination committed by a public body, or by an agency that receives federal funding. [*Barnes v. Gorman*, 536 U.S. 181 (2002)] The Fifth Circuit later ruled that Congress did not properly abrogate the states' sovereign immunity with respect to ADA Title II either [*Reickenbacker v. Foster*, 274 F.3d 974 (5th Cir. 2001)], and the Second Circuit agrees. [*Garcia v. SUNY Health Sciences Ctr.*, 280 F.3d 98 (2d Cir. 2001)] *Gibson v. Ark. Dep't of Corrs.* [265 F.3d 718 (8th Cir. 2001)] says that although the states themselves are immune from suits for damages under the ADA, state officials can be sued to get prospective injunctive relief. It has also been held that states can be held liable for retaliation against employees who exercise ADA rights. [*Roberts v. Pa. Dep't of Pub. Welfare*, 199 F. Supp. 2d 249 (E.D. Pa. 2002). See Shannon P. Duffy, *States Not Immune From ADA Retaliation Suits*, The Legal Intelligencer (Feb. 27, 2002) (law.com)]

However, the Fifth Circuit ruled that the Eleventh Amendment does not give the states immunity against ADA suits brought by the United States itself seeking victim-specific relief for individuals. In this situation, the individuals themselves would not be able to sue—but one consequence of a state ratifying the U.S. Constitution is consent to being sued by the United States itself and by other states. [*United States v. Miss. Dep't of Pub. Safety*, 321 F.3d 495 (5th Cir. 2003)]

## § 36.03 FORBIDDEN DISCRIMINATION

It is unlawful to discriminate against a qualified individual with a disability (QIWD) because of that person's disability, with respect to the terms, conditions, and privileges of employment: e.g., job application, hiring, promotion, discharge, compensation, and training. [See 42 U.S.C. § 12112]

Section 12112 goes on to enumerate seven types of action that constitute disability discrimination:

- Limiting, segregating, or classifying applicants or employees in ways that affect their opportunities, because of disability;

- Entering into a relationship (for instance, with an employment agency) that results in disability discrimination;

- Using standards, criteria, or methods of administration that either discriminate or perpetuate discrimination by another party under the same administrative control (e.g., another division in the same company);

- Denying jobs or benefits to a qualified person who has a relationship or association with someone else who has a disability (e.g., refusing to hire someone merely because he or she is married to a person with a disability who has high medical bills that might result in higher EGHP premiums);

- Failing to make a reasonable accommodation to known physical or mental limitations of an employee or applicant who is a QIWD—unless the accommodation would work undue hardship on the employer; or denying employment opportunities to QIWDs if the denial is based on the need to accommodate;

- Using employment tests or other standards or criteria that screen out people with disabilities—but a defense is available for job-related measures that are consistent with business necessity;

- Using tests that are biased by an applicant's or employee's impairment (speech difficulties, for instance) and therefore fail to reflect the job aptitudes that the test is supposed to assess.

It is also unlawful to retaliate against anyone who opposed any act of disability discrimination, or who made a charge, testified, assisted, or participated in an investigation, administrative proceeding, or court case. It is unlawful to interfere with the ADA investigation process, or to "coerce, intimidate, threaten, or interfere with" anyone because of enforcement of ADA rights. [42 U.S.C. § 12203]

The ADA Amendments Act of 2008, ADAAA (Pub. L. No. 110-325), was signed September 25, 2008 and took effect January 1, 2009. Congress passed the legislation to reverse various Supreme Court decisions that made it very difficult for ADA claims to succeed because they ruled that a variety of impairments were not ADA "disabilities." As a result of the ADAAA, the central question is not whether the plaintiff has a disability, but whether the employer reasonably accommodated disabled applicants and employees.

The ADAAA adds two lists of major life activities, although the statute specifies that these lists are illustrative, not comprehensive. Major activities of daily living include self-care, manual tasks, seeing, hearing, eating, standing, walking, sleeping, breathing, working, concentrating, thinking, learning, and communicating. The second list is of major body systems (e.g., circulatory, digestive, excretory, reproductive) whose impairment can constitute a disability. An impairment is considered a disability even if it is episodic or in remission, as long as it substantially limits a major life activity during a relapse.

The definition of being "regarded as" having a disability is expanded to forbid employers to discriminate based on their perception of a mental or physical impairment—whether or not the plaintiff can establish that the impairment actually limits or is perceived to substantially limit a major life activity. A "regarded as" claim cannot be based on a transitory impairment—one that actually lasts, or is expected to last, six months or less. Employers do not have a duty to provide reasonable accommodation for a perceived disability. Except for ordinary glasses and contact lenses, mitigating measures are not taken into account in determining whether a person has a disability. [EEOC Notice *Concerning the Americans With Disabilities Act (ADA) Amendments Act of 2008*, <http://www.eeoc.gov/ada/amendments_notice.html> (Mar. 10, 2009); see Lawrence A. Lorber, Fredric C. Leffler and Samantha Morris, *Get Ready to Re-Learn the ADA*, Legal Times (Oct. 20, 2008) (law.com)] See § 36.04[F] for EEOC guidance about the ADAAA.

## [A]  Association

The ADA also forbids discrimination in fringe benefits on the basis of an employee's relationship to or association with a person who has a disability.

The EEOC says that the ADA association provisions forbid employers to discriminate based on stereotyping of people who associate with someone who has a disability: e.g., that a person whose child has a disability will take excessive time off work or that a person who worked or lives with HIV-positive people will develop AIDS. The EEOC does not treat the belief that the person's association with a person with a disability will increase the company's health insurance costs as a legitimate business motivation—but does not require employers to enhance their insurance program to make it more disability-friendly. Employees who seek leave to care for family members with a disability must be treated equally with employees who seek leave for other reasons. [EEOC, *Questions and Answers About the Association Provision of the Americans With Disabilities Act*, <http://www.eeoc.gov/facts/association_ada.html> (Oct. 17, 2006). Some of these situations can involve the FMLA, but this guidance is limited to ADA implications.]

*Trujillo v. PacifiCorp.*, 524 F.3d 1149 (10th Cir. 2008), allowed an ADA association discrimination suit to proceed where a married couple were terminated, allegedly for falsifying their time records. According to the plaintiffs, they were fired because their son's terminal illness was very costly for the employer's self-insured medical plan.

The District Court for the District of Kansas permitted ADA and ERISA claims to proceed in a case brought by an employee who was fired about a year after his wife was diagnosed with end-stage renal disease. The plaintiff alleged association discrimination (being fired because of the cost of his wife's disability) and claimed that the employer violated ERISA § 510 by firing him for exercising his rights under an ERISA plan. The employer, alleging that the plaintiff was terminated for poor work performance, moved for summary judgment, which was denied. The district court found factual issues remained to be resolved because the employer was aware of the wife's health issues and had tried to remove her from the health plan. [*Bideau v. Beachner Grain, Inc.*, Case No. 10-2390-JTM, 2011 WL 4048961 (D. Kan. Sept. 13, 2011); see EBIA Weekly, *Employee Terminated Following Spouse's Medical Diagnosis Can Pursue ADA and ERISA Claims* (Oct. 13, 2011) (benefitslink.com)]

EEOC Enforcement Guidance published in mid-2007 points out that, although employees who are caregivers for children or elderly or disabled family members are not entitled to separate protection against discrimination, subjecting a caregiver employee to negative employment actions could violate the ADA's ban on discrimination on the basis of association with a person with a disability. [EEOC Enforcement Guidance: *Unlawful Disparate Treatment of Workers with Caregiving Responsibilities* Number 915.002, <http://www.eeoc.gov/policy/docs/caregiving.html> (May 23, 2007). See also EEOC, *Employer Best Practices for Workers with Caregiving Responsibilities*, <http://www.eeoc.gov/policy/docs/caregiver-best-practices.html> (Apr. 24, 2009)]

## § 36.04  DEFINING "DISABILITY"

### [A]  Generally

According to 42 U.S.C. § 12102, there are three forms of disability:

- A physical or mental impairment that substantially limits one or more of the major life activities of such individual;

- A record of such an impairment;

- Being regarded as having such an impairment (even if the impairment is only perceived and does not exist).

According to the statute, transvestism is not a disability [42 U.S.C. § 12209], nor are homosexuality, bisexuality, transsexualism, pedophilia, exhibitionism, gender identity disorders, compulsive gambling, kleptomania, pyromania, or current use of illegal drugs. [42 U.S.C. § 12211]

A QIWD is defined by 42 U.S.C. § 12111(8) as one who can perform the essential functions of the job (with or without accommodation). The employer's determination about which functions of a job are essential is entitled to consideration. Written job descriptions used in advertising or job interviews are considered evidence of the essential functions of the job. In other words, these descriptions must be drafted with care!

The EEOC's position is that determining which functions are essential to a job is a complex process involving several factors, e.g.:

- Expertise or skill needed to do that task;

- Other employees available to perform that function (as individuals or as a team);

- If that function is the entire rationale of the job;

- Time spent on that particular function;

- Qualifications of people who held the same job in the past;

- What would happen if the individual did not perform the function in question;

- What the Collective Bargaining Agreement (if there is one) says about the function as it relates to the job.

The First Circuit held that a restaurant assistant manager who did not recover fully after shoulder surgery was not a qualified individual with a disability, so her failure-to-accommodate/wrongful termination ADA case was properly dismissed. She was unable to perform the many manual tasks required of assistant managers. When she reported to work with a medical release imposing permanent lifting restrictions, she was told that she had been fired because she had used up her FMLA leave but was still disabled. The First Circuit ruled that no reasonable jury could believe that Richardson was able to perform the essential functions of the job. The First Circuit found that the job description made physical tasks central to the job, and Richardson's WC claim was based on her suffering injuries due to repetitive manual work. The First Circuit did not require the interactive process, holding that there was no reasonable accommodation that would have permitted Richardson to do the assistant manager's job. [*Richardson v. Friendly Ice Cream Corp.*, 594 F.3d 69 (1st Cir. 2010)]

The Tenth Circuit ruled that a function that is rarely required in the normal course of the employee's duties can be an essential job function if the consequences of hiring someone who cannot perform that function are serious enough: e.g., a prison physician's assistant who had several physical impairments that prevented her from complying with a newly adopted policy requiring all inmate-contact personnel to take physical safety training. [*Hennagir v. Utah Dep't of Corrs.*, 587 F.3d 1255 (10th Cir. 2009)]

A Central District of Illinois jury awarded $100,000 in compensatory damages, $115,000 in back pay, and $500,000 in punitive damages against AutoZone for failure to provide reasonable accommodation to a sales manager with a disability. Pursuant to the CRA '91 cap, the punitive damages were reduced to $200,000. The manager was required to mop floors and perform other tasks violating the medical restrictions stemming from permanent neck and back injuries. The jury accepted the EEOC's position that these tasks were not an essential function of the sales manager's job and could have been assigned to other people. [Rebecca Moore, *Court Awards $600K in AutoZone EEOC Case*, plansponsor. com (June 6, 2011); earlier proceedings, *EEOC v. AutoZone Inc.*, 630 F.3d 635 (7th Cir. 2010)] Autozone appealed to the Seventh Circuit, seeking to reduce the compensatory and punitive damages to $10,000 each. The Seventh Circuit refused, holding that the district court did not abuse its discretion, because the compensatory damages were not excessive; the punitive damages were reduced because of the cap; and the ratio between compensatory and other damages was not excessive. The Seventh Circuit held that Autozone's conduct was reprehensible enough to justify reasonable punitive damages, because it forced Shepherd to undergo significant, and eventually disabling, pain. However, the Seventh Circuit ordered a remand to reduce the indefinite injunction to what it deemed a more reasonable three-year term. [*EEOC v. Autozone, Inc.*, 707 F. 3d 824 (7th Cir. 2013)]

In June 1999, the Supreme Court decided three major employment-related cases, concluding that an individual is not disabled if the condition has been corrected, e.g., through medication or an assistive device. [*Murphy v. United Parcel Serv.*, 527 U.S. 516 (1999); *Sutton v. United Air Lines*, 527 U.S. 471 (1999); *Albertsons v. Kirkingburg*, 527 U.S. 555 (1999)]. The ADAAA, however, says that ordinary eyeglasses and contact lenses are the only ameliorative measure that can be considered in determining whether a person has an ADA disability.

BAE Systems fired Ronald Kratz II in October 2009; he had worked for the company since 1994. He counted and wrapped parts, made computer entries, and drove a forklift. He was morbidly obese, weighing over 600 pounds. Kratz said that his work was adequate, but that one of the company's HR officials said that Kratz' weight made it impossible for him to perform his duties and he could not be transferred to another job. The EEOC brought an ADA suit, alleging that Kratz could have been reprimanded rather than fired for not wearing a seatbelt on the forklift (other employees were not fired for not wearing a forklift seatbelt) and that Kratz was fired two weeks after requesting a seatbelt extender and not getting one. [Tara Cantore, *EEOC Sues BAE Systems for Firing Obese Employee*, plansponsor.com (Sept. 30, 2011)]

In a suit filed under the Montana Human Rights Act, the Montana Supreme Court held that severe overweight, even without an underlying medical condition, can constitute a disability protected by state law. The court's analysis was based on the EEOC's ADA compliance manual, which says that severe obesity (more than 100% over normal weight) constitutes an impairment even without other physiological conditions. [*BNSF Railway Co. v. Feit*, No. OP 11-0463, 2012 MT 147 (Mont. July 6, 2012). See Kathryn McGovern, Smart HR, *Montana on Obesity: No Underlying Condition Necessary to Prove a Disability* (Aug. 2, 2012) (benefitslink.com). See also *EEOC v. Resources for Human Dev. Inc.*, 827 F. Supp.2d 688 (E.D. La 2011): there is no explicit requirement of physiological impairment in cases where an individual's weight is outside the normal range and obesity substantially limits a major life activity. In 2013, the American Medical Association defined obesity as a disease; commentators believed that this would be ammunition for ADA suits. For example, shortly thereafter, a severely obese Missourian sued his ex-employer for firing him because it incorrectly regarded him as limited in the activity of walking. [*Whittaker v. America's Car-Mart, Inc.*, No. 1:13-cv-00108 (E.D. Mo. pending); see Richard Cohen, *After AMA Declares Obesity a Disease, The First Suit Is Filed Under the ADA to Declare Obesity a Disability*, Fox Rothschild Employment Discrimination Report (July 26, 2013) (benefitslink.com)]

The Second Circuit described the New York City Human Rights Law as broader than federal law. The Second Circuit remanded to the district court the question of whether the New York law treats obesity as a disability. The plaintiff in this case charges that he was fired by a karate school because of his obesity. The Second Circuit also ruled that ADA retaliation plaintiffs can only sue the employer corporation, not individuals, because the ADA uses Title VII remedies. [*Spiegel v. Schulmann*, 604 F.3d 72 (2d Cir. 2010); see Mark Hamblett, *Judge to Determine if Obesity Constitutes a Disability in Karate Teacher's Suit Over Firing*, N.Y.L.J. (May 12, 2010) (law.com)]

## [B]  Attendance

The question is often raised whether predictable, regular attendance is a fundamental job qualification. If it is, then it does not violate the ADA to fire, refuse to hire, etc., a person who cannot satisfy attendance requirements because of disability. [See, e.g., *EEOC v. Yellow Freight Sys., Inc.*, 253 F.3d 943 (7th Cir. 2001) (granting an unlimited number of sick days is not a reasonable accommodation)] A person whose physical or mental condition precludes working more than 40 hours a week has been held not to be ADA disabled, [*Tardie v. Rehabilitation Hosp. of R.I.*, 168 F.3d 538 (1st Cir. 1999)] given that there are many jobs available that do not require a commitment of over 40 hours a week. Also see *Davis v. Fla. Power & Light*, [205 F.3d 1301 (11th Cir. 2000)] finding that mandatory overtime was an essential function of the job, and it would violate the collective bargaining agreement to provide a no-overtime or selective-overtime arrangement for a disabled worker.

The Fourth Circuit held in 2012 that a maintenance engineer who was able to work eight hours a day, but could not work overtime or rotating shifts, was not disabled. He received long-term disability benefits from May to October 2004, then returned to work; his employer and the union negotiated a new day-shift job with base hours of eight hours a day rather than 10. According to the Fourth Circuit, the First, Third, Fifth, and Eighth Circuits have all ruled that an employee who can work 40 hours a week but not overtime is not substantially limited for ADA purposes. This is a pre-ADAAA case, so the issue is whether the plaintiff was significantly restricted in his ability to perform an entire class of jobs, or a broad range of jobs in various classes. [*Boitnott v. Corning Inc.*, 669 F.3d 172 (4th Cir. 2012)]

In the Eighth Circuit view, firing a dialysis technician who suffered from depression for attendance problems did not violate the ADA. For disabilities that are not open and obvious (including many mental disabilities), the initial burden is primarily on the employee to identify the disability, explain his or her limitations, and suggest reasonable accommodation. The Eighth Circuit held that, because she failed to inform her employer (a hospital) of her specific limitations, the duty to accommodate was not triggered. Allowing absences would not be a reasonable accommodation because the patients she treated were very sick and could not postpone treatment. Permission to take sudden unscheduled absences would have been for the employee's personal benefit, not relevant to the duties of the job. [*Rask v. Fresenius Med. Care N. Am.*, 509 F.3d 466 (8th Cir. 2007); see Rebecca Moore, *Employer Did Not Violate ADA by Not Excusing Unannounced Absences*, plansponsor.com (Dec. 31, 2007). See also *Rehrs v. The Iams Co.*, 486 F.3d 353 (8th Cir. 2007): after a change from fixed to rotating shifts, the Eighth Circuit accepted the employer's argument that ability to rotate shifts was an essential function of the job of warehouse technician because it gave all employees additional opportunities for training and career development, and allowing some employees to work straight shifts as an accommodation would undermine the team concept and burden other workers by having to take on more night shifts.]

Evidence that the plaintiff never missed work precluded a determination that he was substantially limited in the major life activities of standing and sitting. [*Pegram v. Honeywell Inc.*, 361 F.3d 272 (5th Cir. 2004)]

## [C]   Infertility

A 1996 case says that reproduction is not a major life activity, but in 1997, the Northern District of Illinois disagreed, even though reproduction does not directly affect employment. [Compare *Krauel v. Iowa Methodist Med. Ctr.*, 95 F.3d 674 (8th Cir. 1996), with *Erickson v. Bd. of Governors, Nw. Ill. Univ.*, 911 F. Supp. 316 (N.D. Ill. 1997), *later proceedings*, 207 F.3d 945 (7th Cir. 2000)]

The plaintiff in *Saks v. Franklin Covey Co.* [117 F. Supp. 2d 318 (S.D.N.Y. 2000)] was covered by a self-insured health plan that excluded "surgical impregnation procedures." She sued under Title VII, the ADA, and the Pregnancy Discrimination Act. The court ruled that infertility might be a disability, because it interferes with the major life activity of procreation.

However, the ADA claim was dismissed because all employees got the same coverage; infertile employees were not singled out for inferior coverage of reproductive services. The plan also qualified for the safe harbor for bona fide employee benefit plans. The Title VII claim failed because both male and female infertility were excluded. Surgical procedures were excluded for both female employees and wives of male employees. The PDA claim failed because infertility treatments were equally unavailable to pregnant and nonpregnant employees and beneficiaries.

The Second Circuit affirmed the dismissal in 2003 [*Saks v. Franklin Covey Co.*, 316 F.3d 337 (2d Cir. 2003)], although using a slightly different rationale. The District Court looked at the question of whether all employees have equal access to plan benefits. The Second Circuit said that this standard, often used in ADA cases, was wrong because this was really a Title VII case. Therefore, the correct standard is whether sex-specific conditions exist. If they do, the question becomes whether excluding coverage for those conditions results in a plan with inferior coverage for one sex.

A late 2010 article says that it is possible that refusing to allow an employee to take intermittent FMLA leave for fertility treatment might violate the ADA or the Pregnancy Discrimination Amendment (PDA). Pregnancy itself is not an ADA disability, but under the ADAAA, it might be possible to argue that a pregnant employee was regarded as disabled.

According to the Northern District of Illinois, it did not violate the ADA to refuse to pay for infertility treatment for an employee's spouse, because the law does not extend to dependents of an employee if the dependents do not perform services for the employer. [*Niemeier v. Tri-State Fire Prot. Dist.*, 2000 U.S. Dist. LEXIS 12621 (N.D. Ill. Aug. 24, 2000)] Furthermore, non-employees can't sue the employer under Title VII or the PDA. The employee had standing (the legal right to pursue the PDA claim), but the claim itself was invalid, because the plan did not cover fertility treatment for either sex.

## [D]  Psychiatric Disability

ADA regulations [29 C.F.R. § 1630.2(h)(2)] define mental impairment to include developmental disability, learning disabilities, organic brain syndrome, and neurological disease, as well as mental or psychological disorders. The examples given by the EEOC are major depression, bipolar disorder, panic disorder, obsessive-compulsive disorder, post-traumatic stress disorder, schizophrenia, and personality disorders.

The psychiatric profession's official compendium, the Diagnostic and Statistical Manual of Mental Disorders (DSM), is the first step in identifying mental disorders. However, certain disorders are included in the DSM but excluded from ADA coverage—for instance, current drug and alcohol abuse, compulsive gambling, certain sexual disorders, and kleptomania.

Furthermore, persons who are troubled but not classically mentally ill may seek treatment such as family therapy. Such individuals are not impaired for ADA purposes. A mental illness impairment may be present yet not covered by the ADA, if it is mild enough not to substantially limit the impaired person's ability to work and carry out other major life activities.

The National Institute of Mental Health says that 5.7 million adult Americans are affected by bipolar syndrome each year, and it is one of the ten top causes of disability. The EEOC's position is that people with bipolar syndrome are unfairly stereotyped as to work ability. In one of the first trials involving employees with bipolar disorder, the EEOC prevailed in a 2012 case in which a receptionist took medical leave to manage a flare-up of her condition. Despite company policy permitting 18 months of leave, she was fired after five months. The EEOC sued the supermarket chain King Soopers Inc. on September 18, 2012 for firing a bipolar worker. In December 2011, King Soopers paid $80,000 to settle another EEOC case; the chain did not stop bullying of a developmentally disabled worker. [Ashley Casas, *EEOC Sues Food Retailer for Firing Bipolar Worker*, The BLT

(Blog of Legal Times) (Sept. 19, 2012) (law.com.)] In another case involving a worker with bipolar disorder, the District Court for the Eastern District of Washington required Cottonwood Financial to pay $56,500 for unlawfully terminating store manager Sean Reilly because it regarded him as unable to work because of his psychiatric condition. Reilly was awarded $6,500 in back pay and $50,000 for emotional pain and suffering. [See EEOC press release, *EEOC Wins Disability Discrimination Suit Against Payday Lender "The Cash Store,"* <http://www1.eeoc.gov/eeoc/newsroom/release/3-28-12a.cfm> (Mar. 28, 2012)]

As the baby boom generation ages, it will become more common for employers to have to cope with employees who have Alzheimer's disease or other dementias. It has been estimated that 500,000 people under age 65 have early onset Alzheimer's disease, and no one knows how many of them are still in the workforce. Early onset Alzheimer's can cause personality changes (such as obsession or apathy) that create problems at work as well as in their families, although similar symptoms could have many other causes, such as depression and thyroid problems. In some cases, an employee with early onset Alzheimer's might be disciplined or fired for poor performance when he or she should be offered reasonable accommodation or perhaps disability retirement.

The Alzheimer's Association of the National Capital Area created a pilot project for corporate assistance to Alzheimer's caregivers, but the organization was not aware of any corporation with an existing policy or program to help these caregivers. [Beth Baker, *When Alzheimer's Strikes Reasonable Accommodations Might Include Flexible Schedule, Reminders, or Help from a Co-worker,* workforce.com (benefitslink.com)]

An epileptic who was fired after several incidents of aggressive and threatening behavior was neither disabled nor regarded as disabled. The Eighth Circuit held that he did not show that epilepsy substantially limited major non-work life activities. Although the plaintiff's former employer told him to get anger-management therapy, the Eighth Circuit did not deem this to mean that the employer regarded him as having an emotional condition that was substantially limiting. [*Brunke v. Goodyear Tire & Rubber Co.*, 344 F.3d 819 (8th Cir. 2003)]

## [E]  *Williams* and "Impairment"

Early in 2002, the Supreme Court decided *Toyota Motor Manufacturing, Kentucky, Inc. v. Williams.* [534 U.S. 184 (2002)] The court held that the plaintiff, who had carpal tunnel syndrome, was not disabled for ADA purposes. She was able to care for herself and perform ordinary daily tasks. In this view, merely having an impairment does not make a person disabled, nor does being unable to perform the tasks associated with that person's specific job, as long as the person can perform other tasks.

*Williams* is one of the cases that the ADAAA is designed to reverse.

The Lilly Ledbetter Fair Pay Act, Pub. L. No. 111-2, also applies to the ADA, so a suit can be brought within 180 days (or, if the state has an anti-discrimination agency, 300 days) of each time that an employee is subjected to discriminatory conduct under the ADA—even if the conduct is the result of a policy that was adopted much earlier.

## [F]   EEOC Guidance

The EEOC proposed regulations in September 2009 to implement the ADAAA.

Under the proposal, actions based on an impairment include actions based on symptoms of an impairment. Reasonable accommodation is not required in "regarded-as" cases. An impairment that substantially limits one life activity does not have to be shown to limit others. For example, a diabetic whose endocrine system is substantially limited does not also have to show substantial limitation in eating; a person whose normal cell growth is limited by cancer doesn't have to show limitation in working. The examples of episodic or remitting impairments include epilepsy, hypertension, multiple sclerosis, asthma, cancer, depression, bipolar syndrome, and post-traumatic syndrome disorder.

The DOL lists certain impairments as consistently meeting the definition of disability: deafness, blindness, intellectual disability, amputations, use of a wheelchair, autism, cancer, cerebral palsy, diabetes, epilepsy, multiple sclerosis, muscular dystrophy, and major mental illness. However, the EEOC's position is that the fact that a condition does not appear on the list does not mean it is not a disability. Some conditions are disabling for some people but not others, depending on their seriousness: for example, asthma, learning disabilities, back injuries.

The fact that a claimant got another job does not rule out that person's having a substantial limitation in working. Under the proposed regulations, a person with a disability can usually establish coverage by showing a limitation in major life activities other than working, so it will generally be unnecessary to consider whether there is a limitation in working. The new definition of "regarded as disabled" is an adverse action taken by an employer because of an actual or perceived impairment. The employee need not prove that the employer perceived him or her as substantially limited in the ability to perform a major life activity.

Previously, in 2006, the EEOC issued FAQs about the ADA implications of deafness and hearing impairment in an aging population. The EEOC warns employers to assess hearing-impaired workers' abilities on a case-by-case basis, and not to assume that hearing impairment always means that the worker compromises workplace safety. Lip-reading and sign language interpretation are not considered mitigating measures, because they do not improve the person's hearing.

The EEOC says that it is inappropriate to ask questions about hearing tests, hearing aids, and occupationally caused hearing loss during pre-job-offer interviews. However, it is legitimate to direct all job applicants to information (*e.g.,* an HR person; part of the company Website) about reasonable accommodations in the application process.

The EEOC lists sign language interpreters; special telephones; telephone headsets; vibrating or flashing emergency notifications; assistive software; writing notes; assistive listening devices; and devices that translate speech into writing as examples of reasonable accommodation for those with hearing loss. Changing the employee's work area (e.g., away from an area with ambient noises that interfere with a hearing aid) can also be a reasonable accommodation. In some instances, allowing an employee to trade an assignment with another employee to avoid a task that is a small part of the job, and that is difficult for a hearing-impaired person to perform, will be considered a reasonable accommodation. But a solution that deprives the hearing-impaired worker of real-time access to events (e.g., furnishing written minutes after a meeting) is not adequate. [EEOC, *Questions and Answers About Deafness and Hearing Impairments in the Workplace and the Americans With Disabilities Act*, <http://www.eeoc.gov/facts/deafness.html> (July 26, 2006)]

UPS policy did not provide interpreters for deaf employees at short meetings. A deaf worker sued, charging that it was not a reasonable accommodation to have someone give him written summaries of the meetings instead of having an interpreter. (The employee has limited reading skills; he repeatedly complained that he did not understand various written materials, but was merely told to look up difficult words in a dictionary.) The district court dismissed the suit but the Ninth Circuit reversed, saying that UPS did not provide effective accommodations. The case was settled in late 2011 for $95,000 plus three years of non-monetary relief (appointing an ADA coordinator, investigating disability discrimination complaints promptly, and providing accommodation to deaf and hearing-impaired employees. [*EEOC v. UPS Supply Chain Solutions*, 620 F.3d 1103 (9th Cir. 2010); see Fred Schneyer, *Deaf UPS Clerk Gets New Shot with ADA Suit*, plansponsor.com (Aug. 30, 2010)] Settlement: *EEOC v. UPS Supply Chain Solutions*, No. CV 06-06210 ABC (Ex); see Tara Cantore, *UPS Unit to Pay $95K to Settle Disability Discrimination Lawsuit*, plansponsor.com (Dec. 15, 2011)]

In 2006, the Ninth Circuit ruled that excluding all deaf people from driving UPS package cars violated the ADA [*Bates v. UPS*, 465 F.3d 1069 (9th Cir. 2006); see Rebecca Moore, *UPS Violates ADA with Policy Against Deaf Drivers*, plans ponsor.com (Oct. 11, 2006)] Then the case returned to the Ninth Circuit. The en banc panel re-heard the case and reversed the earlier panel decision, vacating class certification and the injunction against UPS. The en banc panel held that UPS can show business necessity by relying on a government safety standard— DOT's hearing acuity requirement for drivers of large trucks—even if the standard was not drafted for the conduct at issue. However, the en banc decision still requires UPS to prove business necessity for refusing to let hearing-impaired people drive trucks. In this reading, an employer seeking to raise a business necessity defense must show that the qualification standard is job-related, consistent with business necessity, and cannot be reached by reasonable accommodation. However, the ADA has no equivalent of a BFOQ defense. Job-relatedness requires the employer to show that the standard fairly and accurately measures the individual's actual ability to perform essential functions of the job. [*Bates v. UPS*, 511 F.3d 974 (9th Cir. 2007); see Dan Levine, *9th Circuit Switches Gears on UPS Drivers in Closely Watched Class Action*, The Recorder (Jan. 2, 2008) (law.com)]

## § 36.05  REASONABLE ACCOMMODATION

### [A]  Employer's Obligation

Employers have an obligation to engage in an interactive process of reasonable accommodation, to permit employment or continued employment of qualified individuals with disabilities. However, it is not required that employers undergo undue hardship in making such accommodations.

Section 12111(9) says that the category of reasonable accommodation may include making existing facilities readily accessible and usable by QIWDs. It can also include job restructuring, part-time or other altered work schedules, reassignment to a *vacant* position (in April 2002, the Supreme Court ruled that it is not in general "reasonable" to reassign an employee if the reassignment violated an established seniority system—but the employee can demonstrate that an exception should be made in his or her individual case: *U.S. Airways v. Barnett*, 535 U.S. 391 (2002)). Other possible reasonable accommodations include acquiring or modifying equipment, providing training, making readers or interpreters available, etc.

It is an established principle that employers are not required to provide indefinite leaves of absence or unlimited sick days as a reasonable accommodation to disability. [See, e.g., *Wood v. Green*, 323 F.3d 1309 (11th Cir. 2002), *cert. denied*, 540 U.S. 982 (2003)]

According to the First Circuit, ability to lift more than 50 pounds is an essential function of nursing. Therefore, the employer does not have to accommodate a nurse with a back injury, either by assigning other employees to help her lift, or by reinstating the position of "medicine nurse" (which did not involve lifting) after the position had been abolished. [*Phelps v. Optima Health Inc.*, 251 F.3d 21 (1st Cir. 2001)]

"Auxiliary aids and services" is defined by § 12102 to mean interpreters or other effective methods of communicating with hearing-impaired people, readers, taped texts, and other ways to deliver texts to the visually impaired, acquiring or modifying adaptive equipment or devices, or "other similar services and actions."

An undue hardship is an action that requires significant difficulty or expense. [42 U.S.C. § 12111(10)] This determination is made based on factors such as the cost of the accommodation and how it compares to the employer's budget.

The employer must retain records about requests for accommodation for one year after the request or personnel action, whichever is later. [29 C.F.R. § 1602.14]

The Ticket To Work and Work Incentives Improvement Act of 1999 [Pub. L. No. 106-170] allows disabled persons to retain Medicare and/or Medicaid coverage for their health needs after they return to the workforce.

There is evidence that modest investments in accommodation can be very productive. The Job Accommodation Network, part of the Department of Labor's Office of Disability Employment Policy, has a series of worksheets online, including one about the favorable cost-benefit status of disability accommodations, concluding that more than half of accommodations didn't cost the employer anything, and the average expense for those that did had a cost of about $600.

Accommodations for disability resembled those sought by employees looking for work-family balance (e.g., flexible work schedules, better computer software, ergonomic workstations, and the availability of telecommuting).

## [B]  EEOC Enforcement Guidance

On October 17, 2002, the EEOC released a major enforcement guidance. [*Enforcement Guidance: Reasonable Accommodation and Undue Hardship Under the Americans With Disabilities Act*, <http://www.eeoc.gov/policy/docs/accommodation.html>] The EEOC has retained this document on its Website, but warns that it should be interpreted in light of the ADAAA.

Under the Guidelines, employers need not eliminate essential job functions. Employers do not have to provide items used for both work and nonwork tasks; employees are responsible for furnishing their own prostheses, eyeglasses, and hearing aids.

Employees who want accommodation must make a clear request but need not use the term "reasonable accommodation," as long as it is clear what they mean. Employers must act on reasonable verbal requests but can ask to have them confirmed by a written memorandum.

The employer can demand reasonable documentation of, for instance, the nature, severity, and duration of the impairment, which activities are impaired, and the extent to which the employee's functional ability is limited. But documentation cannot be required if the disability and accommodation are obvious, or if the employee has already furnished adequate information. The employer can choose its preferred (usually the most cost-effective) reasonable accommodation, and need not follow the employee's suggestion.

Using accrued paid leave, or unpaid leave, is a reasonable accommodation, but employers do not have to offer additional paid leave to employees with a disability. Employees should be allowed to exhaust paid leave before taking unpaid leave. Unless it is an undue hardship, the employer must keep the job open during leave. A leave request need not be granted if the employer can keep the employee at work via a reasonable alternative accommodation.

The EEOC position is that employers should consider ADA and FMLA entitlement separately and then determine whether the two statutes overlap. The EEOC's example is an ADA-disabled person who needs 13 weeks of leave. The FMLA requires only 12 weeks of leave, but the EEOC says the ADA requires the employer to provide the 13th week unless that would be an undue hardship.

If there is a vacant position available for transfer, the employer does not have to train the person with a disability as an accommodation, unless training would be offered to a nondisabled employee. The EEOC position is that a transfer is a reasonable accommodation, so it must be offered even if the employer does not normally provide transfers. It is not enough to allow the disabled employee to compete for a vacant position; it should be offered to any QIWD who wants the transfer as an accommodation.

Final regulations about the ADAAA were published in the Federal Register on March 25, 2011. [76 Fed. Reg. 16977] Under these final regulations (which cover the "Appendix," also known as the Interpretive Guide), a disability is a physical or mental impairment substantially limiting one or more major life activities; a record or history of disability; or being regarded as having a disability. (These three potential litigation areas are sometimes referred to as the three "prongs" of the ADAAA.)

The regulations provide principles for determining whether a person has a disability. An impairment does not have to prevent or severely or significantly restrict performance of a major life activity to be considered a disability. The final regulations state that whether an impairment is a disability should be broadly construed to the maximum extent allowed by law. If an impairment is substantially limiting when it is active, then it is a disability even if it is episodic or in remission. Other than ordinary eyeglasses or contact lenses, mitigating measures are not taken into account in making disability determinations.

An important change is that the final regulations make "individual with a disability" and "qualified individual" separate terms, and the term QIWD, which occurs frequently in earlier ADA cases, is no longer used. In order to focus on whether or not there was discrimination, and not whether the charging party fits within the definition of disability, the final regulations now forbid discrimination on the basis of disability, not discrimination against a QIWD.

Under the 2011 final regulations, major life activities include major bodily functions, such as the functions of the immune system; normal cell growth; and brain, neurological, and endocrine functions. Certain conditions, such as diabetes, epilepsy, bipolar disorder, and being HIV+ are considered to be impairments. The final regulations make it easier for employees to make out a case of regarded-as-disabled liability, because the focus has shifted from the employer's beliefs about the nature of impairment and to the way the employer treated the individual. It's also easier to establish regarded-as liability; now the focus is on treatment of the plaintiff and not on the employer's beliefs about the nature of the impairment. [The regulations, fact sheets, and Q&A can be found at <http://www.eeoc.gov/ laws/statutes/adaaa_info.cfm>; see Rebecca Moore, *EEOC Announces Final ADA Amendments Act Regs*, plansponsor.com (Mar. 24, 2011)]

The Q&A clear up some difficult and/or disputed points:

- Q6: In general, plaintiffs do not have to use a particular "prong" of the definition of disability to challenge an employer's action, and to win, a plaintiff need only prove discrimination under one "prong." Claims of failure to hire, failure to promote, unlawful termination, and harassment can be brought under any one of the three. But, because accommodation is not required in regarded-as cases, plaintiffs alleging denial of reasonable accommodation must allege either actual disability or a record of disability;

- Q9: To be covered under the disability or record-of-disability prong, it is only necessary to be substantially limited (or have a record of substantial limitation) in one major life activity;

- Q10: The effects of impairment lasting less than six months can still be substantially limiting;

- Q12: Psychotherapy, behavioral therapy, physical therapy, have been added to the list of examples of mitigating measures;

- Q15: The positive effects of mitigating measures cannot be considered in determining whether a person has a disability, but negative effects—such as medication side effects—can be;

- Q16: However, either positive or negative effects of mitigating measures can be considered to see if a person is entitled to reasonable accommodation, or poses a direct threat;

- Q25: A covered entity regards a person as having a disability if the covered entity takes an unlawful action based on an impairment, or based on an impairment the entity believes the individual has, unless the impairment is minor and transitory (expected to last less than six months). This is a change from the original ADA definition. Now, the legality of the employer's action is a separate question from the merits of the charging party's or plaintiff's claim to have a disability, so a defense (even a successful defense) does not eliminate the charging party's or plaintiff's chance to get a trial on the claim. Under the final regulations, an employer can defend against a regarded-as claim by showing that the impairment (actual or perceived) is both transitory and minor. However, this defense cannot be raised when it is objectively untrue—e.g., claiming that a serious condition such as bipolar disorder is transitory and minor;

- Q31: The ADAAA does not change Worker's Compensation laws or federal or state disability programs;

- Q32: A non-disabled person cannot raise a reverse claim of being denied employment opportunity or reasonable accommodation because of not having a disability. [Questions and Answers on the Final Rule Implementing the ADA Amendments Act of 2008, <http://www.eeoc.gov/laws/regulations/ada_qa_final_rule.cfm>] The EEOC also has publications dealing specifically with small business issues.

For general information about ADA and small business, see <http://www.eeoc.gov/eeoc/publications/adahandbook.cfm>. To find nearest Small Business Liaison, see <http://www.eeoc.gov/employers/contacts.cfm>. There is also a set of Q&A for small business, overlapping with the general Q&A. Q2 of the small business document says that the ADAAA applies to private employers that have 15 or more employees. The ADAAA change in the definition of disability applies to employers who are federal contractors or who get federal financial assistance (i.e., are subject to the Rehab Act), whether or not they have 15 employees. Q26 states that the interactive process for providing reasonable accommodation has not been altered by the final regulations. [EEOC, *Questions and Answers for Small Businesses: The Final Rule Implementing the ADA Amendments Act of 2008*, <http://www.eeoc.gov/laws/regulations/adaaa_qa_small_business.cfm>]

## [C]   Case Law

It is very common for summary judgment to be granted to the employer in ADA cases—often on the grounds that the plaintiff did not have a disability for ADA purposes, or that he or she was not qualified, but sometimes on the grounds that there was no reasonable accommodation possible, or that the employer either provided reasonable accommodation or attempted to do so, but the interactive process was frustrated by the employee. A number of cases, however, resulted in summary judgment at the district court level, which was then reversed by the court of appeals, and the case sent back to the district court for a full trial.

Some courts say that the employee must take the first step by requesting accommodation. [*Gaston v. Bellingrath Gardens & Home Inc.*, 167 F.3d 1361 (11th Cir. 1999); *Mole v. Buckhorn Rubber Prods. Inc.*, 165 F.3d 1212 (8th Cir. 1999)] Taylor v. Phoenixville Sch. Dis. [174 F.3d 142 (3d Cir. 1999)] adopts the EEOC position that, as soon as an employee asks for reasonable accommodation, the employer has a duty to engage in an interactive process with the employee and must cooperate with the employee to find out if the employee really is ADA-disabled, finding out what accommodations the employee wants, and determining if they are practical. The employer can decide which reasonable accommodation to offer; it is not obligated to accept the employee's suggestions.

The Seventh Circuit decided that it does not violate the ADA to refuse a software engineer's request to work at home as an accommodation to the fatigue and pain caused by treatment for cancer. In fact, in the Seventh Circuit view, most jobs require supervision, teamwork, and interaction with others, so working at home will rarely constitute a reasonable accommodation. [*Rauen v. United States Tobacco Mfg. Ltd.*, 319 F.3d 891 (7th Cir. 2003); working at home was not a reasonable accommodation for an employee traumatized by witnessing a fatal workplace shooting incident: *Mason v. Avaya Commc'ns, Inc.*, 357 F.3d 1114 (10th Cir. 2004)]

Note, however, that the D.C. Circuit found in 2007 that revoking a disabled worker's previously given permission to work at home two days a week was discriminatory, because the telecommuting arrangement constituted a reasonable accommodation. [*Woodruff v. Peters*, 482 F.3d 521 (D.C. Cir. April 6, 2007); see Fred Schneyer, *FAA Telecommuting Setup Could Be Disabled Worker's Accommodation*, plansponsor.com (May 8, 2007)]

According to *Donahue v. Consol. Rail Corp.* [224 F.3d 226 (3d Cir. 2000)], the employer need not engage in the interactive process if the employee failed to show that there were any available jobs he or she could have done with reasonable accommodation.

Furthermore, a person who claims that his or her injury prevents full-time work, and therefore is allowed to work a part-time schedule, is estopped from claiming that the employer refused accommodation, because the person is unable to work full-time even with accommodation. [*DeVito v. Chicago Park Dist.*, 270 F.3d 532 (7th Cir. 2001)]

The employer faces difficult problems if it believes that the employee is engaging in leave abuse, or is sincere but mistaken in his or her estimated return-to-work date. For example, the District Court for the Southern District of Indiana refused to grant summary judgment for the employer on an ADA failure to accommodate claim made by a worker who suffered post-partum anxiety and depression. The plaintiff, Crystal Wirstiuk, took 12 weeks of FMLA leave after the birth of a baby. After she exhausted her FMLA leave, she applied for and was granted 30 days leave. After the 30 days were up, she submitted a note from her doctor indicating that she could return to work in another 30 days. The employer denied the second extension, because the employer did not believe that she would return after the extension. Wirstiuk was terminated. However, the employer offered Wirstiuk's job on a permanent basis to the person who was filling in for her temporarily. That employee accepted, but said she couldn't start the job for three months. The employer got another temporary employee to fill in. As a result, the district court concluded that granting Wirstiuk the second extension would not impose undue hardship on the employer, because there was no reason not to continue to use temporary workers. Subsequently, the case was settled, with the employer agreeing to pay $90,500 to settle her ADA charge. FMLA expert Jeff Nowak's comment on this case was that an employer that doubts whether an employee who requests multiple extensions will actually return to work should

ask the employee to submit a doctor's note explaining why the initial exten-
sion(s) did not have the effect of getting the employee in shape to return to work.
[*EEOC v. Midcontinent Indep. Transmission Sys. Operator*, No. 1:11-cv-1703-
WTL-DML (S.D. Ind. May 30, 2013); on the settlement, see EEOC press release,
*MISO To Pay $90,500 To Settle EEOC Discrimination Lawsuit*, <http://
www.eeoc.gov/eeoc/newsroom/release> (July 11, 2013). The case is discussed in
Jeff Nowak, *Failure to Provide Additional Leave as ADA Accommodation Could
Prove Costly to Employers*,FranczekRadelet FMLA Insights (June 10, 2013)
(benefitslink.com).]

The EEOC position [29 C.F.R. § 1630.2(o)], echoed by several appellate
cases, is that reassignment to a job that the employee can handle constitutes a reasonable accommodation. [*Dalton v. Subaru-Isuzu Auto., Inc.*, 141 F.3d 667 (7th
Cir. 1998); *Cravens v. Blue Cross/Blue Shield*, 214 F.3d 1011 (8th Cir. 2000); *Aka
v. Wash. Hosp. Ctr.*, 156 F.3d 1284 (D.C. Cir. 1998)] The disabled person in search
of accommodation must be able to prove his or her ability to handle the new job.
[*DePaoli v. Abbott Labs.*, 140 F.3d 668 (7th Cir. 1998)] The Second Circuit said
that as long as a comparable job is available, it is not a reasonable accommodation to offer an ADA plaintiff reassignment to a part-time job (with much lower
compensation and benefits) or to another location (resulting in loss of seniority).
[*Norville v. Staten Island Univ. Hosp.*, 196 F.3d 89 (2d Cir. 1999)]

The EEOC used the ADAAA in suits filed in Georgia, Maryland, and Michigan, involving diabetes, cancer, and severe arthritis. The Georgia suit was brought
against Eckerd Corporation, which refused to allow a cashier with severe arthritis
in her knee to sit on a stool after permitting this accommodation for seven years.
She was fired shortly after the newly hired manager said he didn't like the idea of
a cashier sitting down. The Maryland defendant is Fisher, Collins & Carter, which
fired two diabetic, hypertensive employees after they were ordered to complete a
questionnaire about their health status and medication use; the EEOC alleges that
they were RIFed because of their disability when less qualified non-disabled
employees were retained. The Michigan case says that IPC unlawfully fired an
employee instead of letting him work part-time during cancer treatment. [Rebecca
Moore, *New Definition of Disability Opens Door for EEOC Suits*, plansponsor
.com (Sept. 10, 2010)]

## § 36.06  DEFENSES

### [A]  Primary Defense

The primary defense, under 42 U.S.C. § 12113, is that the employer's criterion, standards, or tests may screen out individuals with a disability, but are nevertheless appropriate because they are job-related and consistent with business
necessity, and the employer cannot achieve the same goals via reasonable accommodation. Qualification standards can lawfully rule out employment of anyone

who poses a direct threat to the health or safety of others. According to 42 U.S.C. § 12111(3), a "direct threat" is a significant risk to the health or safety of others that cannot be eliminated by reasonable accommodation.

Furthermore, the Secretary of Health and Human Services publishes a list of infectious and communicable diseases that can be transmitted by food handling. If the risk cannot be eliminated by reasonable accommodation, then an employer can legitimately refuse to assign or continue to assign someone who suffers from such a disease to a food handling position. This provision does not preempt state public health laws about food safety. The Supreme Court greatly increased the applicability of this exception in a June 2002 decision [*Chevron USA Inc. v. Echazabal*, 536 U.S. 73 (2002)] by allowing employers to use it in the context of danger to a job applicant or employee whose own physical condition would be endangered by workplace conditions. In 2012, the Supreme Court gave an expansive interpretation to the "ministerial exception" (the principle that courts will not intervene in a congregation's selection of religious ministers). Cheryl Perich, who taught at a religious school, argued that she was fired in retaliation for threatening to file an ADA suit. (Perich suffers from narcolepsy.) The Supreme Court accepted the employer's argument that Perich, as a "called" teacher (who led prayers and religious activities as well as teaching secular subjects) was a religious minister, so the exception applied. [*Hosanna-Tabor Evangelical Lutheran Church v. EEOC*, 132 S. Ct. 694 (2012).]

## [B]  Drug and Alcohol Exception

Congress must have been concerned about the potential for claims of disability on the basis of substance abuse, because there are several statutory references. According to 42 U.S.C. § 12111(6), a "drug" is a controlled substance as defined by federal law, and "illegal use of drugs" means using controlled substances, but does not include drugs taken under the supervision of a licensed health professional.

Section 12114 says that an employee or job applicant who is currently engaging in the illegal use of drugs is not a qualified individual with a disability. However, a person who is in rehab, has completed a rehab program, or otherwise stopped using drugs can be considered a qualified individual with a disability. So can a person who is not in fact using illegal drugs, but who is incorrectly perceived to be.

However, a 2013 Fifth Circuit ruling permits enforcement of a corporate policy calling for termination of employees who reject treatment for drug or alcohol problems or who start but fail to complete a treatment program. Leave was granted for a factory worker to be treated for Vicodin addiction. He went through detox but left the program before receiving addiction treatment. The employer said he could be reinstated if he completed the program. He returned to the program, but for only one day, when he checked himself out again. The Fifth Circuit agreed with the district court: summary judgment for the employer was proper in the worker's ADA and FMLA suit. The safe harbor does not protect everyone who enters a treatment program—only those who remain drug-free for a significant amount of time. [*Shirley v. Precision Castparts Corp.*, No. 12-20544 (5th Cir. Aug. 12, 2013); see Kathryn McGovern, *Employee Who Left Drug Rehab Not Entitled to ADA, FMLA Protections*,Thompson SmartHR Blogs (Aug. 23, 2013) (benefitslink.com)]

The plaintiff in the Supreme Court case of *Raytheon v. Hernandez* [540 U.S. 44 (2003)] was forced to resign after he tested positive for cocaine, thus violating a workplace conduct rule. More than two years later, after he said he had stopped using drugs, he applied to be rehired. Rehiring was denied, on the basis of a corporate policy against rehiring anyone who had been terminated for misconduct. The employee who rejected his application said that she did not know he was a former addict when she denied the application.

The Supreme Court held the no-rehire policy was neutral and satisfied the *McDonnell-Douglas* requirements. On remand, the Ninth Circuit found that there was a genuine issue of material fact as to whether the decision to refrain from rehiring him was disability-based, and therefore the Ninth Circuit reversed the grant of summary judgment for the defense. [362 F.3d 564 (9th Cir. 2004)]

Employers are allowed to forbid the use of alcohol or illegal drugs at the workplace, can enforce the requirements of the Drug-Free Workplace Act, can make a rule that employees not be under the influence of alcohol or drugs when they are at work (even if they used the substances outside the workplace), and can adopt reasonable procedures (including drug testing) to make sure employees are not currently abusing substances. Drug testing is not considered a "medical examination" for ADA purposes. Many of these provisions are repeated in 42 U.S.C. § 12210.

A "last chance" agreement, where reinstatement after rehab is conditional on continued good performance (and perhaps on passing periodic drug tests) has been upheld as a reasonable accommodation to the disability of alcoholism. [See, e.g., *Longen v. Waterous Co.*, 347 F.3d 685 (8th Cir. 2003);)]. The Seventh Circuit affirmed summary judgment for the employer on ADA (and FMLA) claims brought by an employee who was already on a Last Chance Agreement and who was fired after coming to work drunk and failing a blood alcohol test. (The Last Chance Agreement subjected her to periodic suspicionless drug/alcohol test, and said that refusing to take a required test was grounds for dismissal.) The Seventh Circuit ruled that she did not show that she had an alcoholism disability, because alcohol did not substantially limit her major life activities. She sought help from the EAP for an alcohol problem, but said it had not yet affected her work. She was fired for coming to work drunk, a violation of the employer's legitimate expectations. According to 42 U.S.C. § 12114(c)(4), alcoholic employees can be held to same qualifications standards as other employees, even if the unsatisfactory performance is related to alcoholism. The Seventh Circuit held that the employer did not fail to accommodate—in fact, it gave her time off for AA meetings. [*Ames v. Home Depot USA Inc.*, 629 F.3d 665 (7th Cir. 2011)]

The New Jersey Law Against Discrimination treats alcoholism as a protected disability. The New Jersey Appellate Division reinstated a disability bias suit by a research technician who was fired after a positive alcohol test. The Appellate Division held that she was tested, and then fired, because of her voluntary disclosure of alcoholism, making the testing direct evidence of discrimination. In 2007, she told the company nurse that she was an alcoholic and was going into rehab to be treated for drinking and depression (her husband had died). On Oct 29, 2007, she signed an "after care contract" with the employer, agreeing not to drink and be randomly tested for at least two years. She also agreed to three years of monitoring, with a positive test grounds for discipline, probably termination. She passed nine tests from late 2007 to mid-2008 but tested positive in August 2008 (but at a level below the legal definition of drunk driving). The Appellate Division found direct evidence of hostility: the two-year abstinence requirement and two years of testing, imposed only on alcoholics. The court said that the reasonableness of the requirement had to be measured in context of job performance. [*A.D.P. v. ExxonMobil Research & Eng'g Co.*, A-4806-10 (N.J.A.D. Oct. 26, 2012); see Mary Pat Gallagher, *Alcoholic Tested Without Cause Can Proceed With Bias Claim*, N.J.L.J. (Oct. 29, 2012) (law.com)]

The Ninth Circuit held that the association representing longshoremen did not violate the ADA (or California's anti-discrimination law) by adopting a "one-strike" rule in response to drug-related injuries and fatalities. The rule disqualified from longshore employment anyone who tested positive for drugs or alcohol when tested by the association. The plaintiff, Lopez, applied to be a longshoreman in 1997. At that time, he used drugs and alcohol, and tested positive for marijuana. In 2002, he stopped using drugs and alcohol. In 2004, he re-applied and was disqualified because of the earlier positive drug test. He brought suit under the ADA, charging that he was discriminated against as a former drug addict who was now abstinent. The Ninth Circuit rejected the argument, finding that there was no proof that the association intentionally discriminated against him on this basis, or that the rule had disparate impact on recovered drug addicts. The rule did not target addicts as distinguished from casual drug users; it disqualified anyone who was unable to pass the drug/alcohol test. [*Lopez v. Pacific Maritime Ass'n*, 636 F.3d 1197 (9th Cir. 2011); see Rebecca Moore, *Failed Drug Test Can Haunt Applicants Later*, plansponsor.com (Mar. 4, 2011)]

> ■ **TIP:** A substance abuser entering a rehab program (at least if it is an inpatient program) may be entitled to FMLA leave. Reasonable ADA accommodation may require providing additional leave after the 12 weeks of FMLA leave have been used up.

The United Insurance Company of America agreed to pay $37,000 to resolve the EEOC disability discrimination lawsuit concerning Craig Burns, a recovering drug addict who had been in a methadone program since 2004. Burns was offered a job as an insurance agent in January 2010, contingent on passing a drug test. When the test was positive, he sent a letter from his treatment program saying that he was legally taking methadone as part of a program. The offer of employment was withdrawn. The EEOC brought suit in the Eastern District of North Carolina in August 2011. The defendant also agreed to a two-year consent decree requiring training about the need for individualized assessment of ADA disability and how to determine direct threat. [Tara Cantore, *United Insurance to Pay $37K for Failing to Hire Recovering Addict,* plansponsor.com (Jan. 25, 2012)]

## § 36.07 "REGARDED AS" LIABILITY

The ADA covers qualified individuals who actually do not have a disability, but who are discriminated against because of the perception that they do. The ADAAA expands the definition of "regarded as" to forbid discrimination on the basis of the employer's perception of a mental or physical impairment—whether or not the plaintiff can prove that the impairment actually limits or is perceived to limit a major life activity. However, a "regarded as" claim can only be based on a long-lasting impairment, not one that lasts or is expected to last for less than six months. The ADAAA resolved a circuit split by holding that reasonable accommodation is not required in "regarded-as" cases.

The First Circuit ruled that an intermittently disabling condition (in this case, remitting and relapsing multiple sclerosis) can be a handicap, and the plaintiff, Susanna Sensing, was regarded as disabled after she took medical leave after a major flare-up of the disease. She was not allowed to return to work although she had a doctor's note releasing her to work without restrictions. Her supervisor refused to let her work, saying that if she fell down, it would cost the restaurant hundreds of thousands of dollars. Sensing was offered only one-third the number of hours at a half her original pay. She applied for unemployment because she did not think that this would provide a living wage. The First Circuit held that applying for unemployment did not prove job abandonment; she needed to support herself while waiting for the employer to schedule an independent medical exam. The case was remanded to the district court: a reasonable jury could conclude that the restaurant did not need to fire her for safety reasons, and it appeared suspicious that the employer ignored three doctors' notes clearing Sensing to return to work and never scheduled the independent medical examination that the restaurant said was necessary for her to return to work. [*Sensing v. Outback Steakhouse of Florida, Inc.,* 575 F.3d 145 (1st Cir. Aug. 11, 2009)]

The Seventh Circuit upheld the district court's dismissal of a meat packing plant laborer's challenge to the employer's return to work policy. The policy, which was subsequently changed, would not permit employees to return to work after a non-work-related injury if they were not 100% recovered and had any work limitations. The plaintiff had a hip replacement operation. After her 12 weeks of FMLA leave were exhausted, her doctor imposed a permanent restriction on heavy lifting, squatting, crawling, and climbing. The plant's doctor refused to clear her because she could not lift 50 pounds. The Seventh Circuit ruled that her hip problems did not substantially limit major life activities because she obtained other jobs after being fired. The court held that the employer did not regard her as disabled by her lifting limitation, and the plaintiff did not prove that there were suitable vacant positions in the plant that could accommodate her disability. [*Kotwica v. Rose Packing Co. Inc.*, 637 F.3d 744 (7th Cir. 2011)]

According to the Second Circuit, a trucking company did not violate the ADA by refusing to hire drivers who used prescription drugs with side effects that could impair their driving ability. According to the Second Circuit, the trucking company did not perceive such persons as disabled. Furthermore, the EEOC's regulation, 29 C.F.R. § 1630.2(j)(3)(i) says that inability to perform a particular job is not the equivalent of a substantial limitation in the activity of working; being a truck driver is not a class of job or a broad range of jobs. The fact that the defendant company did not have any less demanding driving jobs to offer (that might have been performed safely by prescription medication users) does not prove that the defendant regarded the applicants as unfit for any driving position at all. [*EEOC v. JB Hunt Transport*, 321 F.3d 69 (2d Cir. 2003)

## § 36.08 DISABILITY AND THE BENEFIT PLAN

### [A] Employer's Obligations and Challenges

Under the ADA, employers are permitted to make benefit plan decisions that are consistent with underwriting, reasonable risk classifications, or actual or reasonably anticipated experience. If the employer does not normally provide health benefits, it has no obligation to provide special insurance coverage for the disabled or to adopt a plan that covers both disabled and nondisabled employees.

Three Circuit Courts (the Sixth, Seventh, and Eleventh) have ruled that a totally disabled retiree or ex-employee is not "qualified" (because he or she is unable to perform job functions) and therefore cannot sue for fringe-benefit discrimination. [*Morgan v. Joint Admin. Bd. Ret. Plan*, 268 F.3d 456 (7th Cir. 2001); *EEOC v. CAN Ins. Cos.*, 96 F.3d 1038 (7th Cir. 1997); *Parker v. Metro. Life Ins. Co.*, 99 F.3d 181, *aff'd*, 121 F.3d 1006 (6th Cir. 1997); *Gonzalez v. Garner Food Servs., Inc.*, 89 F.3d 1523 (11th Cir. 1996)]

The Eighth Circuit dismissed ADA claims by an employee with multiple sclerosis who was fired the day after her employer learned that its health premiums were going to increase by about 30%. The Eighth Circuit held that she did not prove that the employer's explanation—her poor job performance—was pretextual. The Eighth Circuit found that there was no evidence that the manager who fired the plaintiff was even aware that the premium had increased, much less that he blamed the plaintiff for the additional costs. [*Libel v. Adventure Lands of Am.*, 482 F.3d 1028 (8th Cir. 2007); see Adrien Martin, *Court: No Proof That Firing Was Discriminatory*, plansponsor.com (Apr. 23, 2007)]

### [B]   EEOC Compliance Manual

In 2000, the EEOC redrafted its Compliance Manual Section 3, which can be found at <http://www.eeoc.gov/policy/docs/benefits.html>. As of press time in 2013, the EEOC had not issued a new version of this document. The employer must provide "equal" benefits for all employees, irrespective of disability. However, benefits can be "equal" even if there are certain distinctions drawn on the basis of disability. The employer is entitled to employ practices that reflect sound actuarial principles or are related to actual or reasonably anticipated experience.

The employer can rebut charges of disability discrimination by proving that disparate treatment is necessary to maintain the solvency of the plan, because covering the disabilities at issue would cost enough to threaten the fiscal soundness of the plan, and there is no way to change the plan without affecting disabilities.

In the EEOC view, it violates the ADA to:

- Exclude an employee from participation in a service or disability retirement plan because of disabilities;

- Have a different length of participation requirement in the same plan because of disability;

- Provide different levels of types of coverage within a plan (although coverage levels can be lower in disability than in service retirement plans).

Service retirement benefits can legitimately be denied to any employee who voluntarily took disability retirement.

### § 36.09   QUESTIONS AND MEDICAL TESTS

The general ADA rule is that employers are not permitted to ask job applicants or perform medical exams to find out if the applicant has a disability or to discover the nature and severity of the disability. However, it is permissible to tell the applicant what the job entails and ask about ability to perform these tasks. So "have you ever had any back problems?" is not a legitimate question, but "This job involves lifting 25-pound weights several times an hour, and sometimes involves lifting up to 100 pounds—can you handle that?" is acceptable.

Once the company decides to extend a job offer, then it is permissible to require a medical examination, as long as all employees (whether or not they have a disability) are subject to this requirement, and the results of the examination are kept in separate medical files and kept confidential, disclosed only to persons with a genuine work-related need to know.

Furthermore, any medical examination or inquiries must be job-related and consistent with business necessity. Voluntary medical examinations (including taking medical histories) are allowable if they are part of a program available to all employees at a work site, and an employer can ask about an employee's ability to perform job-related functions. [42 U.S.C. § 12112(d)]

Before requiring employees to get flu shots employers should consider whether there are disability issues requiring ADA accommodation. EEOC technical guidance, "Pandemic Preparedness in the Workplace and the Americans With Disabilities Act," says the employers are permitted to ask employees if they have cold or flu symptoms, because this is not a disability-related inquiry, but employers should refrain from asking about chronic illnesses. Information about employee illnesses is subject to the ADA's confidentiality rules. [Jackson Lewis LLP Workplace Resource Center, *Managing Employee Absenteeism and 'Presenteeism' During Flu Season, A Recurring Challenge* (Jan. 15, 2013) (benefitslink .com)]

The Sixth Circuit held that psychological counseling an employee was required to undergo (her supervisor thought she might be depressed) could be considered a medical examination, so she could maintain a 42 U.S.C. § 12112(d)(4)(A) claim [the ban on requiring a medical examination to see if an employee has a disability]. The factors include whether the examination was performed by a health care professional, and whether it was designed to find mental impairments. [*Kroll v. White Lake Ambulance Auth.*, 691 F.3d 809 (6th Cir. 2012). See Elliott T. Dube, *Counseling Refused by Employee Could Be Considered 'Medical Examination' Under ADA*, Bloomberg BNA Human Resources Report (Aug. 31, 2012) (benefitslink.com)]

Use of the Minnesota Multiphasic Personality Inventory (MMPI) as part of a battery of tests required for promotion violated the ADA. The test results were not interpreted by psychologists. The company claimed the tests were scored to determine personality traits, but the practical result was that employees with mental health disorders were denied consideration for promotion. The Seventh Circuit ruled that the MMPI is considered a medical examination because it was designated to diagnose mental illness and, as applied in practice, it impaired the job opportunities for persons with mental illnesses. [*Karraker v. Rent-a-Center, Inc.*, 411 F.3d 831 (7th Cir. 2005)]

A related issue is when genetic information reveals disability or the potential to develop a disability. Title I of the Genetic Information Nondiscrimination Act (GINA; Pub. L. No. 110-233) applies to the group health plans of private employers, and to unions, government employers, and insurers. Title II applies to entities covered by Title VII. The EEOC is the agency in charge of enforcing GINA, and it proposed regulations on March 2, 2009 clarifying the rules for acquiring and disseminating genetic information.

See 29 C.F.R. Part 1635 for final regulations, effective January 10, 2011, under GINA Title II.

GINA defines manifestation of disease to mean a condition that has been, or reasonably could be, diagnosed by a health professional. Merely testing positive for a genetic trait is not considered a manifestation, even if the person tested is certain to develop the disease eventually—a requirement that was adopted to prevent positive markers being classified as preexisting conditions. Employers that require a medical examination after a job offer has been made and before the new hire starts work should make sure that the doctors administering the physicals do not ask about family medical history unless the GINA requirements are satisfied. The same is true of fitness for duty examinations. The EEOC says that the best practice is, when an employee is asked to provide documentation of disability, the request should tell the employee not to provide genetic information (including family medical history). [RIN 3046-AA84, 74 Fed. Reg. 9056 (Mar. 2, 2009); see Margaret Hart Edwards, *Proposed Regulations Under Federal Genetic Information Nondiscrimination Act (GINA) Suggest Employer Action Now*, Littler ASAPs, <http://www.littler.com/PressPublications/Lists/ASAPs/DispAsaps.aspx?id=1344&asapType=National> (March 2009)]

The EEOC's first settlement of a suit about genetic information involved an applicant who was not hired for a clerical job because the employer regarded her as likely to develop carpal tunnel syndrome because of family medical history information that she disclosed in response to an improper inquiry. The employer, Fabricut, Inc. agreed to pay $50,000 and provide other relief. [*EEOC v. Fabricut, Inc.*, No. 13-CV-248-CVE-PJC (N.D. Okla., settled May 7, 2013); see EEOC Press Release, *Fabricut to Pay $50,000 to Settle EEOC Disability and Genetic Information Discrimination Lawsuit*, <http://www.eeoc.gov/eeoc/newsroom/release/5-7-13b.cfm> (May 7, 2013). See Sue Reisinger, *EEOC Gets Tough With Companies on Genetic Privacy*,Corporate Counsel (May 23, 2013) (law.com).]

## § 36.10   INTERACTION WITH OTHER STATUTES

In 2003, the Supreme Court held that, in a suit under the Federal Employers Liability Act (FELA), damages for mental anguish (fear of developing cancer after exposure to asbestos) can be recovered if the plaintiff has already suffered another actionable injury (e.g., asbestosis). Pain and suffering associated with physical injury is actionable, even though independent claims for negligent infliction of intentional distress often are not. Here, the plaintiffs did not seek damages for the increased risk of future cancer. Instead, they sought compensation for their current injuries, which include experiencing fear. However, to win a case of this type, the plaintiff must prove that the alleged fear is genuine and serious. Although this case deals specifically with a federal employment statute, it's an important indication of the Court's thinking on these topics. [*Norfolk & Western Railway Co. v. Ayers*, 538 U.S. 135 (2003)]

On February 28, 2012, the EEOC released two guidance documents protecting veterans with disabilities. The unemployment rate for post-911 veterans is about 12%, 3% higher than the overall rate. The ADAAA requires reasonable accommodation to the impairments of veterans, including traumatic brain injuries and PTSD. Revised guidance for employers explains how the ADA treats recruitment, hiring, accommodation of veterans' disabilities, and the differences in coverage between the ADAAA and USERRA. The revised Guide for Wounded Veterans explains to injured veterans the rights and protections they are entitled to. [CCH Employment Law Daily, *Revised EEOC Guidance Clarifies Interplay Between ADA and USERRA for Employers, Explains Rights to Veterans with Service-Related Disabilities* (March 2012) (benefitslink.com)]

## [A]   The Rehabilitation Act

The ADA is a successor statute to the Rehabilitation Act of 1973 (29 U.S.C. §§ 793 *et seq.*; "Rehab Act"). There are many circumstances in which the HR department will have to apply the ADA in conjunction with other laws—typically, the FMLA and ERISA.

The Rehab Act applies to federal contractors and subcontractors whose government contract involves more than $2,500, and to federal programs and federal grantees. It does not apply to businesses that are not involved in government contracting.

Rehab Act § 503 protects qualified handicapped applicants against discrimination in employment practices. However, one reason that the ADA was passed is that the Rehab Act does not contain a private right of action. In other words, handicapped persons who charge that they were victims of discrimination cannot sue the alleged discriminators. Another section, § 504, does carry a private right of action, but only for discrimination solely on account of handicap in a federally financed program or activity.

Rehab Act § 503 imposes an affirmative action requirement. Federal contractors must have goals for hiring and promotion of qualified handicapped individuals. However, the Department of Labor does not have the power to enforce this requirement by bringing administrative prosecutions against companies that violate it.

The Ninth Circuit held that the Rehab Act protects independent contractors as well as common-law employees. [*Fleming v. Yuma Reg'l Med. Ctr.*, 587 F.3d 938 (9th Cir. 2009); see Tresa Baldas, *9th Circuit Widens Split on Rights of Independent Contractors*, Nat'l L.J. (Nov. 30, 2009) (law.com)]

## [B]    The ADA and Disability Benefits

Although independent contractors are not covered by the ADA, the Seventh Circuit allowed ADA (and ADEA) claims to proceed when brought by a terminated employee who was promised consulting work and charged that he was denied the promised work in retaliation for pressing discrimination charges. The consulting arrangement grew out of the employment relationship, and loss of access to consulting could deter other employees from pursuing discrimination charges. [*Flannery v. Recording Indus. Ass'n of Am.*, 354 F.3d 632 (7th Cir. 2004)]

A February 12, 1997, EEOC Notice No. 915.002, sets out the EEOC's position that employees can legitimately make ADA claims (based on the assertion that they are qualified to perform essential job functions) at the same time that they apply for disability benefits (which are premised on inability to do gainful work).

This position was adopted by the Supreme Court. [*Cleveland v. Policy Mgmt. Sys. Corp.*, 526 U.S. 795 (1999)] According to *King v. Herbert J. Thomas Mem'l Hosp.* [159 F.3d 192 (4th Cir. 1998)], actually receiving disability benefits (as distinct from just applying for them) prevents an age-discrimination plaintiff from claiming she was able to perform the job at the time of her discharge.

Applying for SSDI does not automatically preclude an ADA suit, a plaintiff who has sworn to his or her inability to work will be required to reconcile that with the position taken in the ADA suit that he or she is qualified to work. [*Gilmore v. AT&T*, 319 F.3d 1042 (8th Cir. 2003); *Lane v. BFI Waste Sys. of N. Am.*, 257 F.3d 766 (8th Cir. 2001)]

On a related issue, late in 2003 the Supreme Court decided that it was reasonable for the Commissioner of Social Security to use that agency's definition of "disability" to deny benefits to a claimant who had recovered to the point of being healthy enough to do her former job—as an elevator operator—even though that job no longer exists in significant numbers within the national economy. [*Barnhart v. Thomas*, 540 U.S. 20 (2003)]

## [C]    The FMLA

A person with a "serious health condition" (as defined by the FMLA) may also be a QIWD. FMLA leave, although unpaid, is easier to obtain than medical leave as a reasonable ADA accommodation, because employers with 50 or more employees have to grant FMLA leave to eligible employees. Reinstatement after FMLA leave is automatic, but ADA reinstatement requires showing of ability to perform essential work tasks (with or without reasonable accommodation).

It is unclear how much leave must be provided, after FMLA leave is exhausted, as a reasonable accommodation under the ADA. Once an employee has exhausted all leave provided by the employer, including FMLA leave, the employer must assess if the employee is covered by the ADA. If so, the employer must engage in the interactive process, and may have to reassign the employee to a vacant job as a reasonable accommodation.

A June, 2013 seminar brought together plaintiff and defense-side lawyers to discuss the interaction between the ADA and the FMLA. The FMLA permits a maximum amount of leave, whereas the ADA gives employees more leeway. Employers must assess their communications with employees to make sure that they satisfy the requirements of both statutes. The FMLA requires leave to be granted to qualified employees; there is no exception for situations that cause undue hardship to the employer. The ADA's definition of "disability" is not identical to the FMLA's definition of a "serious health condition," so it is possible that an employee who has exhausted FMLA leave will not be ADA-eligible. According to the seminar, an emerging issue is whether pregnancy-related conditions must be treated the same way as workplace injuries—for example, whether pregnant employees are entitled to light-duty assignments. [D.C. Bar Labor & Employment Law Section seminar (June 11, 2013), discussed in Lydell C. Bridgeford, *Attorneys for Both Plaintiffs, Employers Offer Views on Leave Under the ADA, FMLA*, Bloomberg BNA (June 25, 2013) (benefitslink.com)]

For example, a 2012 Eastern District of California case involved a bank teller with rheumatoid arthritis. She took a leave of 10 weeks and one day. Five months later, she was hospitalized with a kidney infection. She was in the hospital for 16 days and required unpaid recovery time that lasted longer than 12 weeks. Five weeks into her second leave, she was notified that she had exhausted her leave entitlement. Two months before she could return to work without restrictions, she was informed that she would be replaced. She applied for two jobs within the company, including two that would require relocation because she indicated willingness to move. She was not offered a job, and was fired a few months later. She claimed that she was a QIWD because she could perform the essential functions of the job with the reasonable accommodation of an additional, but finite, leave of absence, and transferring her to a job she could do was a reasonable accommodation. She sued under the ADA and FEHA. The district court denied summary judgment for the employer on discrimination and failure to accommodate, but granted summary judgment for the employer on California and FMLA violations. The district court held that holding a job open is a reasonable accommodation and may be required if an employee can return to work in a short period of time. [*Maharaj v. California Bank & Trust*, No. 2:11-cv-00315-GEB-EFB, 2012 WL 5828552 (E.D. Cal., Nov. 15, 2012); Daniel Cafaro, *Extended FMLA Leave May Be Protected under ADA, Court Says*, Smart HR (Dec. 10, 2012) (benefitslink.com). See *Kranson v. Federal Express Corp.*, No. 11-cv-05826-YGR (N.D. Cal. Oct. 1, 2012) [holding the job open as reasonable accommodation.] However, the situation is different if the employee is unable to provide a return-to-work date.

It has been held that it is lawful to terminate an employee who cannot provide a reasonable estimate of when he or she will be able to resume all of the essential functions of the job. In a case brought by a supervisor of released felony offenders, the written job description listed 18 essential functions, including field-work at supervisees' homes. The court said that to show that a request for a leave of absence is reasonable, the employee must provide an estimated date for resuming essential duties, with reassurance that the employee can perform all the essential functions in the near future. [*Robert v. Board of Comm'rs of Brown Cnty.*, 691 F.3d 1211 (10th Cir. 2012); see Jeff Nowak, *An "Indefinite Reprieve" of Essential Functions of Job Not a Reasonable Accommodation under the ADA*, Franczek Radelet FMLA Insights (Sept. 5, 2012) (benefitslink.com)]

The EEOC's position is that it violates the duty of reasonable accommodation to terminate employees who are unable to return to work or unable to return to full duty at the end of the FMLA leave. This is not necessarily the position that the courts will take, but there have been a number of settlements on this issue, and some employers have agreed to drop policies requiring termination after a certain amount of leave. The employer may be able to show undue hardship because of the cost of giving extended leave (although this argument is harder to sustain when leave is unpaid) or the operational difficulties of changing work schedules or hiring temporary employees to fill in. COBRA allows employers to provide COBRA notice to an employee on extended leave after FMLA leave has been used up, shifting the premium payment obligation to the employee.

The EEOC position is that the employer must hold the job open as an accommodation unless this is an undue hardship. It may also be required to hold open a vacant equivalent position the employee is qualified for, or even vacant non-equivalent jobs the employee is qualified for. However, if the employee fails to apply or reapply for extended leave, it may be possible to terminate the employee for job abandonment. There may also be medical information that justifies denial of further leave. If there is a need to replace an employee who is on extended leave, the employer should document the reasons why this is necessary.

DOL Wage & Hour Division Interpretation No. 2013-1 clarifies FMLA leave rights for employees who want leave to care for an adult son or daughter who has an ADA disability. The ADAAA's broad definition of disability is used to determine if the adult child is disabled. It is not required that the disability occurred before the child reached age 18. An employee can take FMLA leave to care for a disabled adult adopted or foster child, stepchild, or even a person for whom the employee is in loco parentis.[Spencer Fane Britt & Browne LLP, *FMLA Leave for Employees with Adult Disabled Sons and Daughters* (Jan. 22, 2013) (benefitslink.com). Administrative Interpretation 2010-3 defines "in loco parentis" as having day to day responsibility of care for the individual, or an obligation of financial support.] A former associate at the Dechert law firm blamed the firm's macho culture for discrimination committed against him for taking FMLA leave to care for his children (including a newborn) and his mentally ill wife. The District Court for the District of Massachusetts dismissed his state-law claim of discrimination based on association with a handicapped person. The district court said that the Massachusetts law does not cover association discrimination. Although the plaintiff was told that association claims can be pursued, the district court said this was just an agency interpretation that does not have the force of law. [*Ayanna v. Dechert*, No. 10-12155-NMG (D. Mass. Jan. 6, 2012); see Sheri Qualters, *In Bias Suit By Former Dechert Associate Against Firm, Judge Tosses Disability Claim*, Nat'l L.J. (Jan. 10, 2012) (law.com)] The retaliation allegation was scheduled to go trial in February 2013 but, immediately before the scheduled trial, a sealed, confidential settlement was reached. [Sheri Qualters, *Dechert and Former Associate Settle "Macho Culture" Retaliation Case*, Nat'l L.J. (Feb. 11, 2013) (law.com)]

A 2011 article recommends that if an employee's mental or physical condition precludes performing the essential functions of the job with or without reasonable accommodation, the employee should be placed on leave. An FMLA notice should be issued to anyone who misses three or more days at work. Before FMLA or other legally guaranteed leave ends, or when an employee who is not eligible for guaranteed leave applies for leave, the employer should engage in the interactive process to determine if reasonable accommodations are available to return the employee to work. The article suggests requiring that employees re-apply for extended leave at intervals (perhaps every three, six, or twelve months, depending on administrative convenience) but employees should not be terminated for failure to return to work unless they have also failed to apply for extended leave. Employers can tell employees that they must either return to work or be considered to have abandoned the job, if the medical evidence shows that the employee is able to perform the job. But extended leave is a reasonable accommodation if the employee cannot currently perform the essential functions of the job but might be able to do so in the future. Extended leave would not be required if the medical evidence shows that the employee will never be able to return to work, or if the employee has applied for LTD benefits on the basis of permanent total disability.

If the employee has applied for SSDI, the employer should document the interactive process and that the employee is unable to return to work because some courts have held that it is not inconsistent to apply for SSDI and also raise an ADA claim, because SSDI focuses on what the employee is unable to do, whereas the ADA focuses on ability to work with reasonable accommodation. [Kerry Notestine & Kelley Edwards, *Recent EEOC Lawsuits Highlight Importance of Adopting Comprehensive Procedures for Managing Employee Leaves*, Littler Mendelson Insights (February 2011) (benefitslink.com)]

The First Circuit ruled that an employee's seven-week trip to the Philippines with her seriously ill husband, for a faith healing pilgrimage, was not covered by the FMLA. The employee also raised a claim of association discrimination under the ADA, which also failed: it did not violate the ADA to demand verification of her husband's condition, and a paperwork requirement is not an adverse employment action for ADA purposes. [*Tayag v. Lahey Clinic Hosp.*, 632 F.3d 788 (1st Cir. January, 2011).

### [D]  HIPAA and Wellness Programs

Under HIPAA, a plan may not discriminate among similarly situated persons based on their health status, so differences in costs or premiums are forbidden. However, "adherence to programs of health promotion and disease prevention" (i.e., wellness programs) can lawfully give rise to premium discounts or reduced payment responsibilities. Wellness programs can include, for example, assessment of the health risks affecting individual employees, health screening, integration with the corporate attendance program, and diet or exercise plans.

DOL, HHS, and the IRS published final HIPAA regulations about wellness programs in the December 13, 2006 Federal Register. Wellness programs are acceptable if they are available to all similarly situated individuals, and either the sponsor does not offer rewards, or the rewards are not dependent on health status.

DOL's Field Assistance Bulletin FAB 2008-02 provides a checklist for testing a wellness program's HIPAA compliance: [<http://www.dol.gov/ebsa/regs/fab2008-2.html>; see JP Morgan Compensation and Benefits Strategies, *DOL Provides Further Guidance on Wellness Programs* (Mar. 10, 2008) (benefitslink.com)]

The three agencies issued a second set of joint final rules for wellness programs in mid-2013, reaffirming the agencies' belief in the value of these programs in alleviating chronic illness and keeping health care costs in check. The 2013 regulations (effective January 1, 2014) limit underwriting practices that might discriminate on the basis of health status. The final rules are effective January 1, 2014. The rules permit participatory wellness programs that are available to employees without regard to health status (e.g., rewards for taking health information seminars or completing a health questionnaire; paying for health club memberships). The program can offer rewards for meeting a health goal (for example, quitting smoking; meeting a target for weight or blood cholesterol) but the rewards must not discriminate against employees with health problems.[T.D. 9620, 2013-27 I.R.B. 1. See Plansponsor staff, *Wellness Program Final Rules Issued*, plansponsor.com (May 29, 2013).]

The Patient Protection and Affordable Care Act (Pub. L. No. 111-148), the health care reform program adopted in 2010, encourages wellness programs, so this will continue to be a significant issue. See § 18.19[G].

The Broward County employee wellness program satisfies the ADA safe harbor for insurance plans. The program included a finger stick for glucose and cholesterol, and an online health risk assessment questionnaire. The information was used to find employees who had asthma, hypertension, diabetes, congestive heart failure, and kidney disease. Employees who have one of those diseases can participate in a coaching program that gives them copayment waivers for some medications. Insurance coverage was not dependent on participation in the wellness program, but, until it was suspended January 1, 2011, a $20 charge was deducted from each biweekly paycheck of non-participants. The program became the subject of a class action that characterized it as an involuntary medical examination/disability-related inquiry contrary to the ADA. The Eleventh Circuit applied the safe harbor for insurance plans that have a bona fide benefit plan based on underwriting, administering, and classifying risks. The wellness program was a term of the group health insurance plan, so it fell within the ADA safe harbor. [*Seff v. Broward Cnty.*, 691 F.3d 1221 (11th Cir. 2012)]

## § 36.11  ADA ENFORCEMENT

The EEOC has enforcement power over the ADA. [42 U.S.C. § 12111(1)] The remedies available for disability discrimination are also available in retaliation cases. [42 U.S.C. § 12203(c)] ADA charges must be filed with the EEOC or the state agency. [See § 41.03 for an explanation of the process] The charge must be filed within 180 days of the last discriminatory act (in nondeferral states) or within 300 days of the last act (in deferral states). The Title VII investigation and conciliation procedures will be followed, and the ADA remedies are equivalent to Title VII remedies, with the distinction that reasonable accommodation can be ordered as an ADA remedy.

The EEOC and the federal courts have discretion to make an attorneys' fee award to the prevailing party. If the United States loses a case, it can be required to pay attorneys' fees—but if the United States wins, the other party cannot be required to compensate the government for the costs of the case. [See 42 U.S.C. § 12205]

In late 2012, shortly before trial was scheduled to begin, Rite Aid agreed to pay $520,000 to settle EEOC charges of discrimination and retaliation against an epileptic employee. Rite Aid initially argued that epilepsy is not an ADA disability and it did not regard the worker as disabled. The employee had to be hospitalized twice as a result of seizures in the workplace, and he almost hit an employee when he had a seizure while driving a forklift. Judge Catherine Blake denied summary judgment for Rite Aid, holding that it was not clear whether the employee was regarded as disabled when he was placed on administrative leave. [Jenna Greene, *Rite Aid Settles EEOC Charges Regarding Employee With Epilepsy*, Nat'l L.J. (Nov. 8, 2012) (law.com)]

## § 36.12  THE ADA PRIMA FACIE CASE

Once a disabled employee makes out a prima facie case, the burden then shifts to the employer to prove, by a preponderance of the evidence, that it either offered the plaintiff reasonable accommodation or was unable to do so because of undue hardship. [*Cmty. Hosp. v. Fail*, 969 P.2d 667 (Colo. Sup. 1998)]

## § 36.13  DAMAGES

Although, in the vast majority of cases, employers prevail in ADA cases, there is still the risk that high damages will be awarded in the few cases in which plaintiffs win. The Third Circuit upheld a $2.5 million jury verdict ($2 million compensatory, $500,000 punitive damages) for a multiple sclerosis sufferer who was denied reasonable accommodation. The jury verdict was divided into $2 million compensatory and $500,000 in punitive damages, but was not allocated between federal and state damages. The ADA damage cap was $300,000; the state law does not include a damage cap. The District Court applied the cap amount only to the punitive damages, thus lowering them from $500,000 to $300,000, and apportioned all the compensatory damages to the state-law claim. (The state law doesn't allow punitive damages, so the court didn't allocate any of the punitive damages to the state claim.) In this view, the CRA '91 damage cap limits only the federal damages, not damages received under a state claim—even one that is virtually identical to a federal claim that is subject to the cap. [*Gagliardo v. Connaught Labs, Inc.*, 311 F.3d 565 (3d Cir. 2002)]

The Fourth Circuit upheld a jury award of $8,000 in compensatory and $100,000 in punitive damages to a deaf former package handler at FedEx who was denied reasonable accommodation. Despite numerous requests, he was denied sign language interpreters at employee meetings and training sessions. In the court's view, his supervisors' indifference to the need to accommodate his disability meant that his safety, and perhaps the safety of others, was jeopardized. [*EEOC v. Federal Express Corp.*, 513 F.3d 360 (4th Cir. 2008); see Fred Schneyer, *Deaf Former FedEx Package Handler Wins ADA Award Appeal*, plansponsor.com (Jan. 25, 2008); certiorari was denied: see Rebecca Moore, *Supreme Court Declines Review of FedEx ADA Case*, plansponsor.com (Oct. 9, 2008)]

Although the Second, Eighth, and Tenth Circuits have upheld jury verdicts granting compensatory and punitive damages, the Seventh Circuit interpreted the Civil Rights Act of 1991 to allow compensatory and punitive damages for ADA claims only if they fall under §§ 12112 or 12112(b)(5). Retaliation claims are provided for by § 12203—and therefore the remedies are limited to the equitable relief provided by 42 U.S.C. § 2000e-5(g)(1). Because the plaintiff was only entitled to equitable remedies, she had no right to a jury trial. [*Kramer v. Banc of Am. Sec., LLC*, 355 F.3d 961 (7th Cir. 2004)]

## § 36.14  ARBITRATION OF ADA CLAIMS

*Wright v. Universal Mar. Serv. Corp.* [525 U.S. 70 (1998)] involves an injured stevedore who was denied employment because potential employers deemed him to be permanently disabled. The plaintiff sued under the ADA without first filing a grievance or going through arbitration under the collective bargaining agreement.

The lower federal courts dismissed his case because of his failure to exhaust grievance remedies, but the Supreme Court unanimously reversed. Although ADA claims are subject to compulsory arbitration under the U-4 (securities industry employment agreement), the Supreme Court treated this case differently because Wright's claims arose under a statute, not a contract. Contract claims are presumed to be subject to arbitration, but statutory claims are not.

For a CBA to rule out litigation of a claim under an antidiscrimination statute, *Wright* says that the CBA must be very clear on that point. A generalized arbitration clause that fails to specify the antidiscrimination statutes that it covers will not be enough to keep disgruntled employees out of the court system.

According to *EEOC v. Waffle House Inc.* [534 U.S. 279 (2002)], the EEOC can pursue an ADA case, including victim-specific relief, even though the employee him- or herself was covered by a mandatory predispute arbitration requirement and would not have been able to sue the employer because of this requirement. [See Chapter 40 for fuller discussion of arbitration and ADR]

# CHAPTER 37

# AGE DISCRIMINATION IN EMPLOYMENT ACT

## § 37.01  INTRODUCTION

The Age Discrimination in Employment Act (ADEA), unlike Title VII and the ADA, is found in Title 29 of the United States Code starting at Section 621. (Title VII and the ADEA are in Title 42). In other words, Congress considered the ADEA to be labor law instead of civil rights law. [See § 41.06[A] for a discussion of EEOC procedure for filing discrimination charges, and § 42.11 for a discussion of procedural issues arising in private ADEA lawsuits filed by an employee or class of employees]

Congress defined its purpose in passing the ADEA as protecting older people who want to stay in the workforce and are still capable of working from discrimination involving "arbitrary age limits." The ADEA's aim is to "promote employment of older persons based on their ability rather than age; to prohibit arbitrary age discrimination in employment; to help employers and workers find ways of meeting problems arising from the impact of age on employment." [29 U.S.C. § 621]

The basic rule is that anyone over age 40 is protected by the ADEA [29 U.S.C. § 631], so the protected group is not restricted to senior citizens. In a limited range of situations, being under 40 is a bona fide occupational qualification (BFOQ). In other cases, adverse employment action against an older person could be legally justified by a Reasonable Factor Other than Age (RFOA). State age discrimination suits have been upheld when young people are deprived of employment opportunities because of their youth because this, too, is discrimination "on account of age." [*Bergen Commercial Bank v. Sisler*, 157 N.J. 188 (N.J. 1999); *Zanni v. Medaphis Physician Servs. Corp.*, 240 Mich. App. 472 (2000)]

In fiscal 2012, the EEOC received 22,857 age discrimination charges and resolved 27,335 charges. In most cases, the EEOC found no reasonable cause: 19,234 charges, 70.4% of the total. There were 2,001 settlements (7.3%), 1,280 withdrawal with benefits (4.7%), 4,045 administrative closures (14.8%), and a roughly equal number of merit resolutions (4,051; 14.8%). The EEOC reported that there were 343 successful and 427 unsuccessful conciliations, and that $91.6 million in monetary benefits were obtained for employees, a figure that does not include benefits obtained in litigation. [EEOC, *Age Discrimination in Employment Act (includes concurrent charges with Title VII, ADA and EPA (FY 1997-FY 2012)*, <http://www.eeoc.gov/eeoc/statistics/enforcement/adea.cfm> (last accessed Mar. 26, 2013)] But formal complaints may not tell the whole story. The AARP's 2013 survey reported that about two-thirds of older employees claim that they have experienced age discrimination themselves, or seen it happen at their workplace. Fifty-eight percent believed that discrimination begins when workers reach their fifties. Nineteen percent said that their age was the reason why they lost out on a job they applied for; 12% said they were passed up for promotion, and 9% said they were fired, laid off, or refused training because of age. Older workers had an average duration of unemployment (as of April 2013) of 50.2 weeks—much longer than the average 36.9 weeks of unemployment for workers under 55. Employers may have an incentive to get rid of older workers, because their experience means that they tend to have high salaries—and health insurers may raise premiums in groups with a high representation of older workers. But, as PPACA comes on line and restricts the extent to which age can be used to set premiums, this last factor may become less significant. [The AARP survey is *Staying Ahead of the Curve: 2013*, <http://www.aarp.org/work/on-the-job/info-01-2013/staying-ahead-curve-work.html>; see Ann Carrns, *Older Workers Say Age Bias Is Common*,NYTimes.com (May 8, 2013); Matthew Heimer, *Boomers Fuel Surge in Age-Bias Complaints,* WSJ.com (July 24, 2013)]

See § 7.04 for discussion of cases considering whether cash balance plans are inherently discriminatory against older employees; nearly all cases have held that they are not, for various rationales (e.g., that the asserted favoritism toward younger employees merely reflects the economic principle of the time value of money).

The Supreme Court denied certiorari in *Drutis v. Quebecor World (USA)*, 555 U.S. 816, a Sixth Circuit case on the issue of whether cash balance plans violate the ADEA. The Supreme Court also refused to hear a challenge to the Seventh Circuit's decision on the IBM cash balance plan. [Fred Schneyer, *U.S. Supreme Court Denies Cash Balance Challenge Review*, plansponsor (Oct. 7, 2008)]

The Pension Protection Act of 2006, Pub. L. No. 109-280, amends ADEA § 4(i) (29 U.S.C. § 623(i)). For post-PPA time frames, a plan is not guilty of age discrimination if the participant's accrued benefit is at least as great as the benefit of a similarly situated younger individual who is either a plan participant or potential plan participant. Two participants are considered to be similarly situated if they are the same as to date of hire, period of service, position, compensation, work history, etc., and differ only in their age. In making this determination, the subsidized part of any available early retirement benefit is disregarded. The accrued benefit can be expressed as an annuity payable at NRA, the current value of the accumulated percentage of the employee's final average compensation (the measure used by many defined benefit plans) or the balance of a hypothetical account (i.e., a cash balance plan). [The IRS published final regulations about this safe harbor in late 2010: 75 Fed. Reg. 64123 (Oct. 19, 2010)]

The Lilly Ledbetter Fair Pay Act, Pub. L. No. 111-2 (signed Jan. 29, 2009), amends the ADEA (as well as Title VII, the ADA, and the Rehabilitation Act), to reverse the Supreme Court's *Ledbetter v. Goodyear Tire & Rubber*, 550 U.S. 618 (2007) ruling about the timing of discrimination suits. The Ledbetter Act adds a new ADEA § 7(d)(3), providing that an unlawful employment practice is deemed to occur when it is initially adopted; when a person first becomes subject to the practice—or each time the person is affected by the practice, e.g., every time he or she receives a paycheck that is unfairly low because of discrimination. Depending on whether or not the state has a work-sharing agreement with the EEOC, suit must be brought either within 180 days or 300 days of the last act covered by the Act. A successful plaintiff can recover back pay for up to two years before the date the charge was filed. The Act became effective as if it had become law the day before the Supreme Court *Ledbetter* decision—with the result that any cases that were pending on May 28, 2007, or have been filed since then, can take advantage of the statute's timing rules.

The first federal suit filed under the Ledbetter Act was an ADEA suit filed early in February by Wayne Tomlinson to challenge a cash balance conversion. Tomlinson wanted to reverse a January 21, 2009 decision that his age discrimination suit was untimely.

The District Court for the District of Colorado initially decided in 2009 that Tomlinson's ADEA suit was time-barred. However, on August 28, 2009, the district court reversed its earlier decision and reinstated the ADEA claim. Accrual of pension benefits could plausibly be deemed to be affected by application of a discriminatory compensation decision. Although the court did not find a separate violation each time a pension check was paid, the decision to convert, the actual conversion, and subsequent pension accruals could be treated as separate.

The EEOC Compliance Manual § 2-IVC.4, Compensation Discrimination, has been amended to allow suit 180 or 300 days after receipt of compensation affected by a discriminatory practice, and says the time frames apply to "all forms of compensation, including the payment of pension benefits," but the EEOC "strongly encourages" suit within 180 or 300 days of retirement to make sure that the suit is timely. [*Tomlinson v. El Paso Corp.*, Civil Action No. 04-cv-02686-WDM-MEH, 2009 WL 2766718, 2009 U.S. Dist. LEXIS 4214 (Jan. 21, 2009), *amended by* 2009 U.S. Dist. Lexis 77341 (D. Colo. Aug. 28, 2009); see Suzanne L. Wynn, *And the Lilly Ledbetter Litigation Begins*, Pension Protection Act Blog (Feb. 11, 2009) (benefitslink.com); Randy L. Gegelman and Amy C. Taber, *Tomlinson Reversal May Suggest Fair Pay Act Is Fatal to Ripeness Arguments in ADEA Pension Cases*, The Law Firm of Faegre & Benson LLP (Oct. 21, 2009) (benefitslink.com)] Then, in mid-2010, the district court dismissed the ADEA claims in the suit, finding that even if the ADEA claim was timely, it was not meritorious—El Paso Corp. did not reduce the accrual rate on account of age. [*Tomlinson v. El Paso Corp.*, No. 04-cv-02686-WDM-MEH (D. Colo. 2010); see Fred Schneyer, *Court Dismisses Cash Balance ADEA Charges*, plansponsor.com (July 28, 2010)

In mid-2011, the Tenth Circuit held that El Paso Corporation's cash balance plan did not violate the ADEA or ERISA. The Tenth Circuit adopted the argument that the time value of money is not age discrimination. Claims under ADEA § 4(i) would have to be based on discrimination in input (cash balance credits) rather than output. The only input that varied with age was the pay credit, which increased as the employee got older. [*Tomlinson v. El Paso Corp.*, 653 F.3d 1281 (10th Cir. 2011); see Rebecca Moore, *Appellate Court Finds Cash Balance Plan not Age-Biased*, plansponsor.com (Aug. 12, 2011) and CCH Pensions & Benefits, *El Paso Wins Cash Balance Case; No Age Discrimination or Backloading Provisions Were Violated* (Sept. 2, 2011) (benefitslink.com).]

Another recent trend is to bring disparate impact ADEA claims, charging that a seemingly age-neutral policy in fact has unfair effects on older workers. It was not clear, until the Supreme Court's *Smith v. City of Jackson* decision in 2005 that disparate-impact ADEA claims were allowable. [Tresa Baldas, *Age Bias Suits on the Rise with Older Employees Working Longer*, Nat'l L.J. (Mar. 16, 2007) (law.com), *discussing, e.g., Mody v. Gen. Elec.*, No. 3:04 CV 358 (D. Conn. 2006); *Hogan v. City of Hollywood*, No. CACE04014128 (Fla. Cir. Ct. 2006)]

## § 37.02  ADEA EXCEPTIONS

The ADEA bars job discrimination, so a discharge for good cause will not violate the ADEA. As is true of many other labor and anti-discrimination laws, the ADEA exempts very small businesses. The definition of "employer" is limited to industries affecting commerce and having 20 or more employees for each workday in each of 20 or more weeks in the current or previous year. [29 U.S.C. § 630(b)]

The ADEA applies to employees of the United States branch of a foreign corporation that has 20 or more employees worldwide; there need not be 20 employees at the U.S. branch. [*Morelli v. Cedel*, 141 F.3d 39 (2d Cir. 1998)] The number of employees at several small affiliates of a larger corporation can be aggregated for the 20-employee test if the parent company directed the discriminatory act or policy; the original larger enterprise was split up to avoid liability; and the corporate veil can be pierced (i.e., the parent can be held liable for the subsidiaries' debts, torts, and breaches of contract). [*Papa v. Katy Indus. Inc.*, 166 F.3d 937 (7th Cir. 1999)]

Although the general rule under the ADEA is that no one can be compelled to retire simply because of that person's age, there is an important exception. Under 29 U.S.C. § 631, a person who has been a "bona fide executive or high policy maker" for two years just before retirement, can lawfully be compelled to retire at 65, as long as he or she is entitled to aggregate retirement benefits that are the equivalent of an annuity of $44,000 a year or more. EEOC Guidelines [29 C.F.R. § 1625.12(d)] define a bona fide policymaker as the manager of an entire enterprise, or at least a customarily recognized department or subdivision. He or she must direct the work of at least two employees, and must hold a job that regularly involves the exercise of discretionary power. At least 80% of work time (or at least 60% in a retail or service business) must be spent on managing the business rather than on routine tasks. The Higher Education Amendments of 1998 [H.R. 6 (Oct. 7, 1998)] reinstate a traditional ADEA exception. Under the Amendments, it is lawful to require tenured faculty members to retire solely on the basis of age. Although this act affects a small group of individuals, it is significant in showing a possible trend toward restricting the scope of the ADEA and other civil rights legislation.

In late 2007, the mandatory retirement age for commercial pilots was raised from 60 to 65, in conformity with other nations' rules, by the Fair Treatment for Experienced Pilots Act, Pub. L. No. 110-135. The law firm of Kelley Drye & Warren, after being sued by the EEOC, changed its policy and stopped requiring partners to change their status at age 70. Instead of being equity partners sharing in the firm's profits, they would become "life partners" who received payments each year, plus a bonus if they continued to practice law for the firm. The case was settled in April 2012: the firm agreed to pay "life partner" Eugene D'Ablemont $574,000, and also agreed not to reduce partners' compensation because of their age. [*EEOC v. Kelley Drye & Warren*, No. 0655 cv-10 (2d Cir. Settled 2012); see Brian Baxter, *Kelley Drye Settles EEOC Age Discrimination Suit Involving Firm Partner*, AmLaw Daily (Apr. 10, 2012) (law.com)]

Note that, in 2007, the law firm of Sidley Austin settled with a group of ousted partners for $27.5 million; the Seventh Circuit held that the former partners were employees entitled to protection under anti-discrimination laws. The settlement is discussed in the EEOC Management's Discussion and Analysis for FY 2008, <http://www.eeoc.gov/eeoc/plan/archives/annualreports/par/2008/managements_discussion.html> (Nov. 26, 2008)].

## § 37.03  FORBIDDEN PRACTICES

### [A]  Statutory Prohibitions

Under 29 U.S.C. § 623, employers are forbidden to:

- Discriminate because of age (by firing or failing or refusing to hire, or in any other way) against anyone in connection with "compensation, terms, conditions, or privileges of employment";

- Use age to "limit, segregate, or classify" employees that reduce employment opportunities or "otherwise adversely affect" status as an employee;

- Reduce any employee's wage rate to comply with the ADEA;

- Discriminate against an employee or job applicant because of that person's protests about age discrimination, or in retaliation for that person's bringing an ADEA charge or involvement in someone else's ADEA charge;

- Publish Help Wanted ads that indicate "any preference, limitation, specification, or discrimination, based on age."

Section 623 also forbids age discrimination perpetrated by employment agencies and unions, but those provisions are outside the scope of this book.

The EEOC has ruled that the ADEA applies to apprenticeship programs. Early in 2005, the Fourth Circuit upheld this rule as valid and not contrary to the

Congressional intent in passing the ADEA. [*EEOC v. Seafarers Int'l Union*, 394 F.3d 197 (4th Cir. 2005)]

Only significant employment actions will support a suit.

The Eighth Circuit affirmed dismissal of an ADEA suit, finding that a small reduction in hours, negative performance reviews, and allegations of differential treatment as compared to younger employees (e.g., he claimed that younger workers were given advance notice of inspections) were inadequate to constitute adverse employment actions [*Baucom v. Holiday Cos. Inc.*, 428 F.3d 764 (8th Cir. 2005)]

In a case of first impression for the Circuit, the Fifth Circuit ruled in 2011 that a hostile work environment suit can be brought under the ADEA. The plaintiff, Dediol, established that: he was over 40; subjected to harassment; it was severe enough to create an objectively intimidating, hostile, or offensive work environment; there was a rationale for imposing liability on the employer. He was also permitted to pursue constructive discharge and religiously hostile work environment claims. The harassment began when the 65-year-old plaintiff asked for time off to volunteer at a church event. At first, permission was granted, but Dediol's supervisor rescinded the permission, insulted Dediol, and threatened to fire him if he attended the event. Subsequently, age- and religious-based insults were common, and the supervisor threatened Dediol and tried to provoke him into fighting. In response to the threats, Dediol stopped coming to work, and was fired for job abandonment. [*Dediol vs. Best Chevrolet Inc.*, 655 F.3d 435 (5th Cir. 2011); see Rebecca Moore, *Court Says Worker Can Claim Hostile Work Environment under ADEA*, plansponsor.com (Sept. 15, 2011)]

An Alameda County judge approved age discrimination claims of 130 employees laid off by the Lawrence Livermore National Laboratory, finding that they provided adequate evidence of disproportionate termination of employees older than age 40 and reassignment of their duties to younger workers. The ex-employees had an average age of 54 and an average tenure of 20 years at the laboratory. This decision affects a group of consolidated suits filed in 2009 after the lab was privatized. The first trial, covering five plaintiffs, was expected in early 2013. [Shelley Eades, *Judge OKs Age Bias Claims Against Lawrence Livermore Lab*, The Recorder (Oct. 17, 2012) (law.com)]

## [B]   Supreme Court Precedents

A Supreme Court case, *Public Employees Ret. System of Ohio v. Betts* [492 U.S. 158 (1989)], held that the ADEA did not apply to employee benefits. In 1990, Congress amended the statute, adding a new § 630(l), extending the ADEA ban on age discrimination in "compensation, terms, conditions, or privileges of employment" to cover "benefits provided pursuant to a bona fide employee benefit plan."

To win, the ADEA plaintiff does not have to show that he or she was replaced by someone under 40; it may even be possible to win by showing age-motivated replacement by another person over 40 (for instance, choosing someone who will retire soon, thus removing two older workers from the workplace). [*O'Connor v. Consol. Coin Caterers Corp.*, 517 U.S. 308 (1997)]

The Tenth Circuit refused to impose a bright-line test (where an age difference of five years or less would rule out age discrimination), and permitted an ADEA action to proceed when a 62-year-old was replaced by a 57-year-old. The small gap in ages would make it harder for the plaintiff to prevail, but it was only one factor for the jury to consider. [*Whittington v. Nordam Group Inc.*, 429 F.3d 986 (10th Cir. 2005)]

In 2004, the Supreme Court ruled that one group of over-40 workers could not use the ADEA to charge they were the victims of discrimination in favor of another group of over-40 workers who were older than they were. (This was a retiree health benefits case about grandfathered benefits.) The Supreme Court concluded that the ADEA permits employers to favor their oldest group of workers, even at the expense of younger workers who are nevertheless over 40 and covered by the ADEA. [*General Dynamics Land Systems, Inc. v. Cline*, 540 U.S. 581 (2004); see also *Lawrence v. Town of Irondequoit*, 246 F. Supp. 2d 150 (W.D.N.Y. 2002), permitting employers to enhance retiree health benefits for persons over 80.

The EEOC adapted its ADEA regulations to conform to *Cline* and provide that it is lawful to favor the oldest employees over younger, but still, ADEA-eligible, employees. The agency revised § 1625.2 so that its caption is "discrimination prohibited by the Act," rather than "Discrimination between individuals protected by the Act." Asking for a date of birth or age on a job application is not a per se violation, but will be closely scrutinized by the EEOC because it could have the effect of discouraging older applicants.

The final rule, published in mid-2007, states that employers are not required to prefer older individuals, and applicable state or local laws forbidding preferences for older individuals remain valid. [72 Fed. Reg. 36873 (July 6, 2007)]

A group of Mississippi police officers objected to a plan that gave higher percentage raises to police officers with *fewer* than five years' service. Because the veteran officers tended to be older than those with shorter tenure, they alleged that the practice had a disparate impact on older officers, even though it did not explicitly categorize them on the basis of age. The U.S. Supreme Court ruled in the spring of 2005 that the plaintiffs did not have a valid claim—but the Court clarified that, under the right circumstances, disparate-impact ADEA cases can be valid, because the ADEA's statutory language is very close to that of Title VII. However, employers who are charged with disparate impact age discrimination can raise a defense that the disputed practice is based on reasonable factors other than age (RFOA), whereas there is no similar defense in race or sex discrimination cases.

The plaintiffs in this case were unsuccessful because they failed to identify the specific aspect of the pay plan that harmed the interests of older workers. The defendant, on the other hand, had a reasonable explanation for its adoption of the practice: to retain the newer officers, their compensation had to be brought closer to market norms. [*Smith v. City of Jackson, Miss.*, 544 U.S. 228 (2005)]

As of March 2009, the Second, Third, and Eighth Circuits imposed a requirement of direct evidence to prove ADEA cases, and the First, Fifth, Seventh, Ninth, and Tenth did not. The Supreme Court granted certiorari in *Gross v. FBL Financial* to resolve the split. In mid-2009, the Supreme Court decided that in order to win, a mixed-motive ADEA plaintiff must prove by a preponderance of the evidence that age was the "but-for" cause of the challenged employment action: that it would never have occurred but-for the plaintiff's age. The burden of persuasion is always on the plaintiff, and can be met by either direct or circumstantial evidence. The burden of persuasion never shifts to the defendant. This is not the same standard applied in Title VII, but the Supreme Court stressed the difference in wording and legislative history between the ADEA and Title VII. [*Gross v. FBL Fin. Servs., Inc.*, 129 S. Ct. 1606 (2009); see Russell E. Adler, Law Firm of Pepper Hamilton LLP, *Supreme Court Ruling Increases Burden on Employees in Age Discrimination Cases* (June 19, 2009) (benefitslink.com)] *St. Mary's Honor Ctr. v. Hicks* [509 U.S. 502 (1993)] says that the plaintiff always has the "ultimate burden of persuasion." So if the judge or jury (whichever is responsible for determining the facts of the case) does not believe the employer's explanation of the reasons behind its conduct, the plaintiff could still lose—if he or she fails to provide adequate evidence. The *Hicks* standard is sometimes called "pretext-plus": The plaintiff has to do more than show the defendant's excuses are a mere pretext for discrimination.

Although the ADEA statute explicitly waives sovereign immunity, permitting suits by state employees, the Supreme Court ruled that Congress violated the Eleventh Amendment by abrogating sovereign immunity without demonstrating a history of violations of this type committed by state employers. [*Kimel v. Florida Bd. of Regents*, 528 U.S. 62 (1999)]

The Supreme Court's June 2000 decision in *Reeves v. Sanderson Plumbing Prods. Inc.* [530 U.S. 133 (2000)] is a narrow procedural one. It holds that an ADEA plaintiff can defeat a motion for judgment as a matter of law (a procedural technique for terminating a lawsuit without a full trial) by establishing a prima facie case plus enough evidence for a reasonable court or jury to find that the employer's defense is merely pretextual. It is not required that the plaintiff introduce any further evidence at this stage, unless a rational finder of fact would not be able to find the defendant's conduct discriminatory. However, *Reeves* had little practical impact on the litigation climate [see 69 L.W. 2185 (Oct. 3, 2000)]; it certainly didn't issue in a new pro-plaintiff era.

In 2002, certiorari was granted in *Adams v. Fla. Power*, No. 01-584, on the issue of whether ADEA disparate impact claims are cognizable, but later that year, certiorari was dismissed as improvidently granted: 535 U.S. 228 (2002). The

Supreme Court finally resolved the issue in 2005, ruling, in *Smith v. Jackson*, 544 U.S. 228, that disparate impact claims are cognizable.

The Supreme Court permitted an ADEA suit to proceed, after the complainant filed a Form 283 intake questionnaire with the EEOC, but did not file the official Form 5 (charge). The EEOC did not carry out informal dispute resolution with the employer. The Supreme Court held that a valid ADEA charge requires only a few items of information (the name of the charging party, the nature of the allegation, and a request that the EEOC settle a dispute or take remedial action). In this case, the employer was aware that the plaintiff and 13 other employees had alleged age discrimination. The Court remanded the case to the district court, holding that the lower court can make up for the deficiency by attempting to reconcile the parties in a settlement. (The EEOC stated that it has improved its procedures to make sure the same problem will not recur.) [*Federal Express Corp. v. Holowecki*, 552 U.S. 389 (2008); see Mark Sherman, AP, *Supreme Court Says FedEx Employees Can Sue Over Age Discrimination* (Feb. 28, 2008) (law.com); Fred Schneyer, *Supreme Court Clears FedEx Age Discrimination Case for More Hearings*, plansponsor.com (Feb. 28, 2008); see also *Holender v. Mutual Indus. North Inc.*, 527 F.3d 352 (3d Cir. 2008), in which the Third Circuit allowed a suit to proceed based on the filing of a two-page document, including an EEOC Form 5 ("Charge of Discrimination"). The Third Circuit deemed the document to be a valid charge because it contained the information required by the regulations.]

In February 2008, the Supreme Court did not really resolve the question of whether testimony of bias exhibited by a different supervisor is admissible to show a corporate culture of discrimination. The Court did not adopt the district court's outright ban on testimony by employees of other supervisors, but neither did it adopt the Tenth Circuit's position that such testimony should always be admitted. The Supreme Court required a fact-based inquiry based on balancing relevance against prejudice, and stated that, in general, the courts of appeals should defer to the district court's determination (because the district court hears all of the testimony instead of just seeing the record on appeal). Instead of reversing, the Tenth Circuit should have sent the case back to the district court. Because the two statutes use similar language, the ruling also applies to "different-supervisor" testimony in Title VII cases. The likely result of this decision is that employers will have to fully litigate more cases: fewer cases will be disposed of at the summary judgment stage, because plaintiffs will be able to offer a broader range of evidence at the early stages. [*Sprint/United Mgmt. Co. v. Mendelsohn*, 552 U.S. 379 (2008); see, e.g., Fred Schneyer, *Supreme Court Reverses Age Discrimination Ruling on Procedural Grounds*, plansponsor.com (Feb. 27, 2008)] Before the Supreme Court decision, Sprint settled ADEA charges brought by 1,700 employees laid off between October 2001 and March 2003 for $57 million; the employees were expected to receive between $4,226 and $35,738 each. The company denied wrongdoing but wanted to reduce its legal fees by settling the case. [Rebecca Moore, *Sprint Settles Age Discrimination Suits for $57M*, plan sponsor.com (Sept. 18, 2007)]

The Supreme Court also ruled in 2008 that:

- Federal employees can use the counterpart of the ADEA that covers federal workers to assert age-based retaliation claims. [*Gomez-Perez v. Potter*, 553 U.S. 474 (2008)]

- The employer always has the burden of production and the burden of proof when it comes to the affirmative defense of reasonable factors other than age (RFOA). [*Meacham v. Knolls Atomic Power Labs*, 554 U.S. 84 (2008)]

## [C]  Employee Status

ADEA cases are limited to the employment context, not all aspects of economic life. Therefore, it could not be an ADEA violation to use age to refuse an automobile dealership to an applicant; dealers are contractors, not employees. [*Mangram v. GM Corp.*, 108 F.3d 61 (4th Cir. 1997)]

Salespersons who are independent contractors are not covered by the ADEA. [*Oestman v. Nat'l Farmers Unions Inc.*, 958 F.2d 303 (10th Cir. 1992)] The Eighth Circuit ruled in 2010 that it was not a violation of the ADEA to fire an independent contractor marketing representative and replace her with a younger employee. [*Ernster v. Luxco, Inc.*, 596 F.3d 1000 (8th Cir. 2010); see CCH Pensions and Benefits, *Independent Contractors Are Not Protected by ADEA When Terminated* (Mar. 19, 2010) (benefitslink.com)]

The critical test of employee status is whether the economic realities of that person's situation are more like employment or more like another relationship (such as being a partner in a partnership). [*EEOC v. Sidley Austin Brown & Wood*, 315 F.3d 696 (7th Cir. 2002). The shareholders in a professional corporation are not counted in determining if the PC has 20 "employees" for business purposes. [*Schmidt v. Ottawa Med. Ctr. PC*, 322 F.3d 461 (7th Cir. 2003)]

> ■ **TIP:**  In April 2003, the Supreme Court ruled (although in an ADA rather than an ADEA case, and a case brought by someone who was an ordinary employee rather than by a shareholder-director) that doctors-shareholders in medical PCs are NOT employees, and are not counted in determining if the business has enough employees to be subject to an anti-discrimination statute. [*Clackamas Gastroenterology Assocs., PC v. Wells*, 538 U.S. 440 (2003)]

## [D]  Occupational Qualifications and RFOAs

Being under 40 can be a bona fide occupational qualification (BFOQ) for a narrow range of jobs, usually involving public safety (e.g., the strength, agility, and quick reaction time required of police officers and firefighters), [see 29 U.S.C. § 623(f)(1)] but most ordinary private sector jobs will not give rise to a BFOQ defense.

The First Circuit held that forced retirement of police officers in Puerto Rico did not violate the ADEA, and the older officers were not entitled to keep their jobs by passing a skills test. There is a safe harbor for mandatory retirement of police officers and firefighters when they reach the age of retirement as defined by their employer as of March 3, 1983; for age limits imposed after the 1996 ADEA amendments, the safe harbor protects a requirement of retiring at age 55 or the post-1996 limit, whichever is higher. [*Correa-Ruiz v. Fortuno*, 573 F.3d 1 (1st Cir. 2009); see Rebecca Moore, *PR Mandatory Retirement Age for Police Not Discriminatory*, plansponsor.com (July 9, 2009)]

Reasonable factors other than age (RFOA) can offer a defense, as long as the employer used objective, job-related criteria to make the employment decision, and applied those criteria uniformly. Courts have often accepted arguments that the employer's decision was not really age-based, but was inspired by factors that merely tend to go along with age: for instance, the tendency of salaries to rise with experience. Employers in search of cost cutting might discharge higher-paid older workers in order to replace them with lower-paid workers.

The RFOA is an affirmative defense—i.e., one that the employer has to prove, not one that the plaintiff must disprove, and the employer has the burden of production and the burden of proof on the RFOA defense. [*Meacham v. Knolls Atomic Power Labs*, 554 U.S. 84 (2008)]

The EEOC Regulations say that, if the RFOA has a disparate impact on over-40 workers, the employer must prove that it has a business necessity for the action. The EEOC issued an NPR on March 31, 2008, in response to the *Smith v. City of Jackson* decision. Based on the comments received, the EEOC decided to issue further guidance, and about two years later, in February 2010, the EEOC published a Notice of Proposed Rulemaking (NPR) to define "reasonable factors other than age" under the ADEA. The determination of whether an employment practice is based on RFOA is made based on the facts and circumstances, and whether the employer responded prudently to the facts of the case.

RFOAs must be objectively reasonable (assessed from the point of view of a reasonable employer acting under similar circumstances), and the employer must manifest prudence and awareness of responsibilities under the ADEA. A reasonable factor is one that an employer that uses reasonable care to avoid limiting the employment opportunities of older persons would use. Reasonableness is affected by the design of the practice, which must be reasonably administered to further a legitimate business purpose. The NPR permits consideration of job performance, skill sets, and flexibility in deciding who will be affected by a RIF—as long as the employer has made reasonable efforts to be accurate and fair, and has taken steps to ameliorate avoidable harm.

The EEOC suggests training managers to avoid age stereotypes; identifying the specific skills the employer wants to retain after the RIF has been completed;

and comparing possible preventive and corrective steps (to avoid or redress harm) to the burden of undertaking those steps. However, the NPR says that if harm is severe, reasonableness includes consideration of whether the employer was aware of other, not unduly burdensome, measures that could have been taken to reduce harm. The NPR does not always require employers to adopt the practice that imposes the least harm on the protected group. [75 Fed. Reg. 7212 (Feb. 18, 2010); see Rebecca Moore, *EEOC Defines Reasonable Factors Other Than Age*, plansponsor.com (Mar. 2, 2010)]

In 2012, the EEOC issued a Q&A, explaining what employers must do to use a Reasonable Factors Other Than Age (RFOA) defense when practices that are neutral on their face but might have disparate impact on older workers are challenged. The employer is only required to prove an RFOA after an employee has identified a specific business practice with disparate impact on older workers. An RFOA is reasonably designed when administered to achieve a legitimate business purpose—for example, a physical test for police patrol officers.

Whether the factors are indeed reasonable depends on, e.g.,

- Their relation to the employer's stated business purpose;

- The extent to which the factor is accurately defined and fairly and accurately applied (application includes training managers and supervisors);

- Limits on supervisors' discretion, especially when the criteria are vulnerable to negative age-based stereotypes;

- The extent to which the employer assessed the adverse impact of the practice on older workers;

- The degree of harm to workers over 40—not just the number of people affected and the extent of the injury, but the employer's measures to reduce harm, balanced against the burden of the actual and potential measures

The EEOC stresses that these are not elements that all employers must prove in every case, merely characteristics of reasonable practices.

The EEOC said that, unlike an employment test that has been challenged under Title VII, it is not necessary for the employer to produce a validation study about the RFOA.

The EEOC says it is not unreasonable to use subjective decision-making (e.g., ranking an applicant or employee's qualities such as flexibility and willingness to learn new things), but it is useful to give supervisors evaluation criteria to help them avoid age-based stereotypes. The EEOC said that employers are not obligated to discover and use the least discriminatory method of achieving the purpose—but attempts to limit harm to older persons are not irrelevant. [EEOC, *Questions and Answers on EEOC Final Rule on Disparate Impact and "Reasonable Factors Other Than Age" Under the Age Discrimination in Employment Act of 1967*, <http://www.eeoc.gov/laws/regulations/adea_rfoa_qa_final_rule.cfm>; see Rebecca Moore, *EEOC Issues Final Rule Under ADEA*, plansponsor.com (Mar. 30, 2012)]

It is a defense to an age discrimination charge if an employer follows the provisions of "a bona fide seniority system that is not intended to evade" the ADEA's purposes. [29 U.S.C. § 623(f); 29 C.F.R. § 1625.8] However, even a valid seniority system cannot be used to impose involuntary retirement on an employee who is capable of working and wants to continue. Furthermore, older seniority systems (and retirement plans) are not "grandfathered in." Section 623(k) requires all seniority systems and benefit plans to comply with the ADEA, no matter when they were adopted.

## § 37.04 IMPLICATIONS FOR BENEFIT PLANS

### [A] Generally

At one time, it would have been accurate to say that the ADEA covered only hiring, firing, and salary, but not employee benefits, based on a Supreme Court decision. [*Public Employees Ret. Sys. of Ohio v. Betts*, 492 U.S. 158 (1989)] In 1990, however, Congress passed a statute, the Older Workers Benefit Protection Act (OWBPA) to make it clear that the ADEA covers all of the terms and conditions of employment, including the full compensation package. Therefore, in the current legal environment, it is important to discover how the ADEA interacts with ERISA, insurance laws, and other laws affecting compensation and benefits.

Section 623(i) takes up the question of how the ADEA interacts with employee benefit plans. Employers are forbidden to "establish or maintain" a pension plan that requires or even permits age-based termination or reduction of pension credits. In a defined benefit plan, benefits must continue to accrue at the same rate. In a defined contribution plan, the employer's allocations must be made to all employees' accounts on the same basis, irrespective of their ages. [29 U.S.C. § 623(i)(1)] People who count as "highly compensated employees" for tax purposes are not entitled to this protection. [See 29 U.S.C. § 623(i)(5)]

The ADEA provides various defenses and safe harbors for employers. Voluntary early retirement plans are allowable as long as they are consistent with the ADEA's purpose of protecting employment rights for older workers. [29 U.S.C. § 623(f)(B)(2)]

It is permissible for a plan to put an upper limit on the amount of benefits a plan can provide to anyone, or to limit the number of years of employment that can be taken into account, as long as these provisions are imposed without regard to age. [29 U.S.C. § 623(i)(2)] For instance, if the plan does not permit crediting of more than 30 years of service, this is an allowable age-neutral provision because it applies to employees with more than 30 years' tenure whether they started working for the company at age 18 or age 40.

Once an employee has reached the plan's Normal Retirement Age (NRA) and has started to receive a pension, then the employer's obligation to continue accruing benefits is satisfied by the actuarial equivalent of the pension benefits themselves. [29 U.S.C. § 623(i)(3)(A)]

Section 623(i)(3)(B) says that, for employees who have reached NRA but have not started to draw a pension (typically, employees who defer their retirement and are still working), and whose benefits have not been suspended pursuant to ERISA § 203(a)(3)(B) or I.R.C. § 411(a)(3)(B), the employer's obligation to keep accruing benefits is satisfied by making an actuarial adjustment to the pension that the employee eventually receives, so that he or she gets a larger pension because of deferred retirement.

Because the ADEA covers persons over age 40, the protected group includes many people who will voluntarily elect early retirement. Section 623(l) says that it does not constitute age discrimination for a pension plan to set a minimum retirement age as a condition for being eligible for either early or normal retirement.

A defined benefit plan can lawfully provide early retirement subsidies, or supplement the Social Security benefits of retirees who get a reduced benefit because they retire before the plan's NRA. [29 U.S.C. § 623(l)(1)(B). With respect to retiree health benefits, also see 29 U.S.C. § 623(l)(2)(D)]

There is no ADEA violation if a departing employee's severance pay is reduced to account for the value of retiree health benefits, and/or the value of additional pension benefits that are made available because of a contingency that is not based on age to a person who is already eligible for a full retirement benefit. [29 U.S.C. § 623(l)(2)] For this purpose, severance pay is defined to include certain supplemental unemployment insurance benefits. [See 29 U.S.C. § 613(l)(2)(C) and I.R.C. § 501(c)(17)]

> ■ **TIP:**  If the employer says that retiree health benefits will be provided, and reduces severance pay accordingly, but fails to provide retiree health benefits, 29 U.S.C. § 623(l)(2)(F) lets employees sue for "specific performance" (i.e., to make the employer provide the benefits). This is an additional right, over and above any other remedies the individual has.

In mid-2003, the EEOC reversed its earlier position and proposed Regulations under which employers would be allowed to coordinate retiree health benefits with Medicare: i.e., it would not be considered an ADEA violation to reduce or even eliminate retiree health benefits at the point at which the ex-employees become eligible for Medicare; the rule was finalized in 2004. [68 Fed. Reg. 41542 (July 14, 2003)]. The EEOC's authority to promulgate this rule was upheld by the Third Circuit (and certiorari was denied) based on a 2005 Supreme Court administrative law decision requiring deference to an agency's reasonable interpretation of statutes within the agency's scope of operations. [*AARP v. EEOC*, 489 F.3d 558 (3d Cir. 2007); see Jerry Geisel, *Review of Retiree Health Care Bias Ruling*

*Denied*, Business Insurance (Aug. 22, 2007) (benefitslink.com); *AARP v. EEOC*, *appeal dismissed* 128 S. Ct. 1733 (Mar. 24, 2008). The administrative law case is *National Cable & Telecomm. Ass'n v. Brand X Internet Servs.*, 545 U.S. 967 (2005)]

In December 2007, the EEOC issued a Final Rule reflecting the Third Circuit's decision; the EEOC said that it permitted a narrow exemption from the anti-discrimination rule. The Final Rule permits employers to limit retiree health benefits to retirees who are not yet eligible for Medicare, or to supplement Medicare coverage without making that coverage identical to the coverage that non-Medicare-eligible retirees receive. Companies that offer prescription drug coverage do not have to make it identical for Medicare-eligible and non-eligible retirees. However, the rule affects only the ADEA, not other issues (such as the status of Medicare as secondary payor for Medicare beneficiaries who continue to be employed). [72 Fed. Reg. 72938 (Dec. 26, 2007)]

## [B] Case Law on Pension and Benefit Issues

Another of 2008's many Supreme Court age discrimination rulings held that it was not age discrimination for a public retirement system to add years to the disability retirement formula (resulting in a higher benefit) only for employees who became disabled before Normal Retirement Age, not for those—like the plaintiff—who continued to work after Normal Retirement Age, and subsequently became disabled. The Supreme Court held that the difference in treatment was not motivated by age, because age and pension status are distinct. [*Kentucky Ret. Sys. v. EEOC*, 554 U.S. 135 (2008)]

The Seventh Circuit ruled in mid-2010 that a cash balance plan provision that cut off interest credits when a participant reached age 55 did not discriminate against older workers. According to the Seventh Circuit, the interest credits, which were designed to reverse the 8.5% annual discount applied to opening account balances, were not benefit accruals, so discontinuing them did not violate ERISA's ban on age-related cuts in accruals. The plan offered a lump sum cash balance, so it was not an "eligible cash balance plan" under the Treasury regulations. [*Walker v. Monsanto Co. Pension Plan*, 614 F.3d 415 (7th Cir. 2010); Fred Schneyer, *Monsanto Cash Balance Plan Cleared of Age Bias Wrongdoing*, plan sponsor.com (Aug. 2, 2010)]

The Eighth Circuit used the familiar rationale that correlation is not causation to hold that plan contributions to a frozen plan on behalf of airline pilots were not reduced "on account of age," although the contributions were based on projected final average earnings for the plaintiffs, and the projected earnings could not be calculated without considering the pilot's age. Many factors, not just age, could reduce projected final average earnings: for example, seniority and position, the number of annual pay increases the pilot had received, and benefits under the frozen plan. [*Northwest Airlines, Inc., v. Phillips*, 675 F.3d 1126 (8th Cir.

2012), see Asset International Inc., *Northwest Pilots' Pension Plan Found Non-Discriminatory* (Apr. 10, 2012) (benefitslink.com); CCH Pension & Benefits, *Air-line's Post-Bankruptcy Money Purchase Plan Did Not Illegally Reduce Benefits Due To Age* (Aug. 21, 2012) (benefitslink.com)]

## § 37.05  HEALTH BENEFITS

If the employer maintains a group health plan, the plan must cover over-65 employees on equal terms with younger employees. Either the cost per employee must be the same, irrespective of age, or the employer must offer equal benefits.

Under ADEA § 3(f)(2), an employer can abide by the terms of a bona fide employee benefit plan without violating the ADEA or the OWBPA. A bona fide plan is one which:

- Existed before the challenged employment action occurred;

- The terms of the plan are observed;

- The plan is not used to force anyone into involuntary retirement;

- (Except for voluntary early retirement plans) the costs incurred, or the benefits paid, are equivalent for older and younger employees.

For EEOC regulations on this subject, see 29 C.F.R. § 1625.10.

Under ADEA § 4(f)(2), the employer is allowed to compare costs quoted on the basis of five-year age brackets (e.g., employees aged 30–35). Comparisons must be made using adjacent age brackets: not the costs of employees 65–70 versus those of employees aged 20–25, for instance.

ADEA § 4(l)(3)(B) allows long-term disability benefits to be reduced by pension benefits for which the individual is eligible at age 62 or normal retirement age. Also see Regulations at 29 C.F.R. § 1625.10(f)(1)(ii). The EEOC says it will not pursue an ADEA claim in situations where disability benefits stop at 65 for disabilities occurring before 60, or stop five years after a disability that occurred after age 60.

In a staff informal letter released in November, 2011, the EEOC Office of Legal Counsel explained that the ADEA exemption for coordination with Medicare is limited to retiree benefits, and does not apply to benefits for current active employees. Eliminating EGHP eligibility for current employees when they become eligible for Medicare is an age-based action, so it must satisfy the equal benefit or equal cost test. The availability of Medicare benefits for older employees does not justify depriving older employees of any non-Medicare benefit that is available to younger employees. Equal cost can be analyzed either benefit-by-benefit or for the whole benefit package; eliminating health benefits for Medicare-eligible employees will probably make it impossible to prove equal spending. The EEOC's interpretation is that spending more on another benefit for older employees violates 29 C.F.R. § 1625.10(f)(2)(iii).

Medicare law requires employers who are secondary payors to provide to provide same group coverage to workers and dependents with Medicare as to those without Medicare, so the EEOC says that even without ADEA considerations, Medicare law may prohibit eliminating health coverage for Medicare-eligible actives. [EEOC Informal Discussion Letter, <http://www.eeoc.gov/eeoc/foia/letter s/2011/adea_coordinating_medicare.html>; see CCH Pension & Benefits, *ADEA Exemption for Coordination of Health Benefits with Medicare Does Not Permit Employer to Terminate Current Employees' Benefits* (Nov. 18, 2011) (benefitsli nk.com); EBIA Weekly, *EEOC Letter Addresses Coordination of Current Employees' Health Benefits with Medicare* (Nov. 3, 2011) (benefitslink.com)]

## § 37.06   PROVING THE ADEA CASE

The Tenth Circuit ruled that in order to exhaust their administrative remedies, private-sector employees have a duty to cooperate with the EEOC's investigation of their age bias charges before they file suit. [*Shikles v. Sprint/United Mgmt. Co.*, 426 F.3d 1304 (10th Cir. 2005)]

The California Supreme Court ruled in mid-2010 that age-based remarks can be admitted into evidence in California cases even if they were not made by the decisionmaker, or were outside the direct context of the employment decision, because such remarks can be relevant circumstantial evidence of discrimination. In other words, California rejected the federal "stray remarks" doctrine that excludes statements outside the official decision-making process. Google said that he was fired because he did not fit in with the corporate culture. The plaintiff, who was hired at age 52, alleged that co-workers described him as an obsolete old fuddy-duddy who lacked new ideas. [*Reid v. Google Inc.*, 50 Cal. 4th 512, 235 P.3d 988 (2010); see Kate Moser, *Calif. High Court Hands Win to Workers in Google Age Bias Ruling*, The Recorder (Aug. 6, 2010) (law.com); Fred *Schneyer, Court Rejects Stray Remarks Doctrine in Google Ageism Case*, plansponsor.com (Aug. 9, 2010). This case is cited in Kate Moser, *In Ugly Economy, Age Bias Claims Are a Tough Sell*, The Recorder (Aug. 11, 2010) (law.com), which notes that although *Reid* makes it easier for cases to get to the jury, jury awards still tend to be modest, and employers can still get summary judgment if the only evidence is indirect and circumstantial.]

The Eleventh Circuit ruled in early 2013 that the "cat's paw" theory of liability (developed in the context of USERRA: see § 1.18) is not applicable in ADEA cases. "Cat's paw" liability (also known as "subordinate bias theory" is the principle that the employer can be liable if the actual decision-maker was manipulated by someone else who had a discriminatory intent against the plaintiff. The Eleventh Circuit held that this concept is not applicable to ADEA cases because the ADEA requires but-for causation, whereas USERRA plaintiffs can win by showing that discrimination against servicemembers was one of several motivating factors in the adverse employment decision. [*Sims v. MVM, Inc.*, 704 F.3d 1327 (11th Cir. 2013)]

The Tenth Circuit permitted a school principal's ADEA suit to proceed, finding that she presented enough evidence that transferring her from the job of executive director of curriculum to school principal was the result of unlawful age bias. The plaintiff was 60 years old when the transfer occurred; she had been asked about her expected retirement date; and a person 13 years younger was hired with a different title but with the same responsibilities as her former job. At first, the plaintiff's salary was not affected, but her vacation benefits were cut. Then, after a year, her salary was reduced $17,000, which also affected her retirement benefits. The city argued that she was not demoted, but the Tenth Circuit said that she was, because she lost professional prestige and was moved to a lower position within the hierarchy. [*Jones v. Oklahoma City Pub. Schs.*, 617 F.3d 1273 (10th Cir. 2010); Fred Schneyer, *School Principal Age Bias Suit Revived*, plan sponsor.com (Aug. 25, 2010)]

The Ninth Circuit affirmed summary judgment for the employer in an ADEA case brought by a 66-year-old and a 47-year-old laid off by a television station. However, the court ruled that plaintiffs can make out a prima facie case of disparate-treatment age discrimination purely by statistics, by showing a stark pattern that cannot be explained by anything other than discrimination. In this case, the television station had to cut its budget, and persuaded the court that it was necessary to lay off general-assignment reporters based on the dates their contracts expired—and that on-camera news anchors, whatever their age, had to keep their jobs so viewers would not know that the station was financially troubled. The station also benefited by the "same-actor" inference: i.e., the plaintiffs were laid off by the person who hired them, must have known their ages, and presumably would not have hired them if he objected to working with people over 40. [*Schechner v. KPIX TV CBS*, 636 F.3d 1018 (9th Cir. 2012)]

The Fifth Circuit ruled that lack of expertise in the particular type of transaction that was central to the job was a legitimate, non-discriminatory reason justifying hiring a younger candidate as staff counsel rather than the 68-year-old plaintiff. To win the case, the plaintiff would have had to show that no reasonable and impartial person could have chosen the younger candidate—and that was not true here. [*Moss v. BMC Software*, 610 F.3d 917 (5th Cir. 2010); see Mary Alice Robbins, 5th *Circuit Upholds Summary Judgment for Company in Attorney's Age Discrimination Suit*, Texas Lawyer (July 12, 2010) (law.com)]

## [A] Damage Issues

A New Jersey jury awarded $10 million in punitive damages to a former executive of Avaya, Inc., but the trial judge remitted the punitive damages to $3.7 million. Then the New Jersey Appellate Division further reduced the punitives by another $1.25 million, corresponding to the emotional damage award, using the argument that emotional damage awards frequently include a punitive element. In this case, the plaintiff did not allege physical harm or a need for treatment. The final award was $2.465 million in punitive damages, $743,000 compensatory damages, $325,500 in back pay, $167,500 front pay, and $250,000 for emotional distress. [*Saffos v. Avaya, Inc.*, No. A-3189-08 (N.J.A.D. 2011); see Mary Pat Gallagher, *Court Further Slashes Punitives Award In Age Discrimination Suit vs. Avaya*, N.J.L.J. (Mar. 8, 2011) (law.com)]

The Tenth Circuit allows a plaintiff in a race/age discrimination case to receive the statutory maximum damages on a Title VII compensatory damage claim (see § 42.12[B] for discussion of the CRA '91 damage cap), plus ADEA back pay and liquidated damages. On the issue of front pay, both Title VII and the ADEA make this available as a remedy. Reinstatement is the preferred remedy, but this is not always practical—particularly since in this case, the defendant corporation's financial condition was deteriorating, so any job might be short-lived. Furthermore, where there is a hostile environment that renders reinstatement inappropriate, even an unconditional offer of reinstatement in a comparable job does not prevent an award of front pay as an alternative to reinstatement. [*Abuan v. Level 3 Commc'ns, Inc.*, 353 F.3d 1158 (10th Cir. 2003)]

Marymount Manhattan College settled an ADEA suit by paying $125,000 to Patricia Catterson, a faculty member who was denied a tenure-track job as assistance professor; a less qualified younger applicant was hired instead. The college administration said that the younger candidate "was at the right moment of her life for commitment to a full-time position." [*Catterson v. Marymount*, No. 12-cv-2388 (JPO) (S.D.N.Y. settled 2013); see Jay Polansky, *Marymount Manhattan College Settles EEOC Suit* plansponsor.com (Jan. 7, 2013); Rebecca Moore, *EEOC Sues College for Not Hiring 64-Year-Old*, plansponsor.com (April 23, 2012)]

Computer Systems LLC settled an EEOC case by agreeing to pay $32,500 to a 60-year-old who was RIFed while a less qualified 34-year-old with the same job classification was retained. [*EEOC v. Computer Sys. LLC*, No. 2:11-cv-1178 (E.D. Wis. 2012); see Rebecca Moore, *Employer to Pay for Terminating 60-Year-Old*, plansponsor.com (Nov. 1, 2012)]

As Chapter 40 shows, arbitration is involved for an ever-increasing proportion of employment disputes—although the court's caseload continues to be increased by cases examining the question of whether a particular dispute should be litigated or arbitrated.

In April 2009, the Supreme Court extended its line of pro-arbitration decisions by ruling that federal law mandates enforcement of a CBA clause that clearly and unmistakably obligates union members to arbitrate their ADEA claims. [*14 Penn Plaza LLC v. Pyett*, 546 U.S. 247 (2009); the Supreme Court already held that ADEA claims are arbitrable, in *Gilmer v. Interstate/Johnson Lane Corp.*, 500 U.S. 20 (1991)]

## § 37.07  WAIVERS OF ADEA RIGHTS

### [A]  Requirements for Valid Waiver

It makes sense for employers to make it part of the severance process to request that terminating employees sign a waiver of their rights to bring suit for discrimination allegedly occurring in the course of the employment relationship. However, in order to be valid and enforceable, a waiver of ADEA rights must be strictly tailored to satisfy the requirements of the Older Workers Benefits Protection Act, a 1990 statute that has been enacted as 29 U.S.C. § 626(f)(1). Furthermore, waivers do not prevent the EEOC from carrying out an age discrimination investigation or bringing suit against the employer. It is unlawful for ADEA waivers to prohibit employees from filing charges with the EEOC or participating in EEOC investigations.

A waiver is not valid if it is not "knowing and voluntary" on the part of the employee. No one can surrender legal rights without receiving full disclosure of the implications of the document he or she signs. The ADEA provides a definition of what is required before a waiver will be considered knowing and voluntary:

- The agreement that contains the waiver must be written in understandable terms;

- The waiver specifically mentions ADEA rights or claims;

- Only claims that have already arisen are waived—not claims that might arise in the future;

- The employee receives something in return for the waiver; it is not enough that the employee receives severance or other benefits that would be provided even if there had been no waiver;

- The document includes a written warning that the employee should consult a lawyer before signing the agreement;

- The employee gets at least 21 days to think over the employer's severance offer. If the agreement is offered to an entire group (*e.g.*, in connection with a layoff or incentives for voluntary departure) then the offer must remain open for at least 45 days;

- When incentives are offered to a group, everyone in the group must get an understandable notification of the features of the program: who can participate; eligibility factors; time limits; and the ages and job titles of everyone eligible or chosen for the program, vis-à-vis the ages of workers in the organizational unit or job classification who were not eligible or selected. (This was included in the law to make it easier for potential plaintiffs to decide if age was an improper factor in selecting employees for the program.)

Waivers are also used when charges have been filed, and then the employer and employee agree on a settlement. In this case, the waiver is only considered knowing and voluntary if all the rules noted above have been observed, and the employee has been given a reasonable time to consider the offer.

Getting a waiver does not provide complete protection for the employer. Sometimes the employee will go to court and sue anyway, claiming that the lawsuit is permissible because the waiver was defective in some way. Section 626(f)(3) provides that it is up to the employer to prove that the waiver satisfied the various requirements and therefore was knowing and voluntary. The employee is not required to prove that the waiver was invalid.

## [B] EEOC Rules

The EEOC's rule on waivers, can be found at 29 C.F.R. § 1625.22. A valid ADEA waiver must:

- Be embodied in a written document that contains the entire agreement (the agreement cannot be written but supplemented by oral discussion);

- Be written in plain English, appropriate to the signer's educational level;

- Information about exit incentives must also be understandable;

- Be honest and accurate, not misleading;

- Specify that it relates to ADEA claims;

- Advise the employee to consult an attorney before signing.

In general, waivers can release existing claims but not those that might arise in the future. However, the Final Rule allows an otherwise valid waiver to include the signer's agreement to retire, or otherwise terminate employment at a specified future date.

For the waiver to be valid, the signer must receive consideration specific to the waiver, which he or she would not receive otherwise. Therefore, normal severance pay is not adequate to support a waiver. Nor does it constitute valuable consideration if the employer restores a benefit that was wrongfully terminated in the past. However, the Final Rule says that it is not necessary to give greater consideration to over-40 employees who sign waivers than to under-40 employees, even though the older employees waive an additional range of claims (those arising under the ADEA).

Despite the existence of waivers, a certain number of employees will nevertheless bring age discrimination claims against the employer, claiming that the waivers were invalid and therefore did not constitute a knowing and voluntary waiver of the right to sue.

The Supreme Court's decision in *Oubre v. Entergy Operations Inc.* [522 U.S. 422 (1988)] says that such a person can bring suit under the ADEA even without tendering back (returning) the severance pay received under the agreement that included the allegedly invalid waiver. The rationale is that the defective waiver does not qualify for ratification by the ex-employee, so it is not necessary to return the consideration to avoid ratification.

The EEOC published Final Regulations to implement *Oubre*. [See 29 C.F.R. Part 1625 as amended by 65 Fed. Reg. 77438 (Dec. 11, 2000), effective January 1, 2001], and published guidance in mid-2009 in Question and Answer form, *Understanding Waivers of Discrimination Claims in Employee Severance Agreements*, <www.eeoc.gov/policy/docs/qanda_severance-agreements.html> (July 15, 2009). The EEOC's position is that the existence of a valid waiver is an affirmative defense for the employer. That means that the employer has the burden of proving the validity, but the employee can produce evidence that the waiver was not knowing and voluntary. The EEOC analyzes covenants not to sue in the same way as waivers, and in fact believes they may be even more damaging to employee rights because employees might be deterred from bringing suit with respect to wrongdoing occurring after the covenant was signed.

According to the agency, ordinary contract principles about ratification and tender-back do not apply to employment waivers, because ex-employees might not be able to afford to give back the consideration even if they have a valid claim against the former employer.

Tender-back is not required even if the waiver seems to be lawful, and even if the employee does not allege fraud or duress. Once the case is resolved, the trial court may have to determine the employer's entitlement to restitution, recoupment or set-off. However, the employer can only recover the amount of consideration paid for the waiver, or the amount the plaintiff is awarded for winning the case—whichever is lower. Employees who file suit in bad faith can also be required to pay the employers' attorneys' fees.

The guidance points out that waivers cannot be used to limit an employee's right to testify or participate in any EEOC proceedings. It is not acceptable for an employer to cure a defective waiver by subsequently providing the information that was omitted, then re-starting the period of time to sign the waiver. The EEOC did not take a position as to whether employers must disclose the criteria under which employees were selected for RIF, although some lower courts have required this: see § 37.07[C], below. [Kevin B. Leblang and Robert N. Holtzman, *Time for Employers to Review Their Severance Agreements*, Metropolitan Corporate Counsel (Feb. 1, 2010) (benefitslink.com); Seyfarth Shaw, *EEOC Issues Employee-Friendly Guidance on Separation Agreements* (July 24, 2009) (benefitslink.com)]

## [C]   Case Law on ADEA Waivers

*Oubre*, and EEOC's regulations issued in response, make it clear that ADEA waivers and releases can be enforceable—but only if they satisfy all of the requirements of the OWBPA. If restrictions are imposed on the employee's right to sue—including challenges to the validity of the release itself—it is possible that the release will be deemed to violate the OWBPA. The release must be understandable.

Cases on these issues include:

- *Syverson v. IBM*, 472 F.3d 1072 (9th Cir. 2006): IBM's standard release was invalid because it was not understandable—the use of terms "release" and "covenant not to sue" was confusing, and so was the statement that the covenant did not apply to actions based solely on the ADEA, and did not rule out filing an EEOC charge. It was not sufficient for the release to suggest consulting a lawyer, because language that requires a lawyer to be understood is not "calculated to be understood" by participants and beneficiaries, as required by the statute.

- *EEOC v. Lockheed Martin Corp.*, 444 F. Supp. 2d 414 (D. Md. 2006): offering severance benefits in exchange for a release from an employee who had filed an EEOC charge was unlawful retaliation, so the agreement was invalid.

# CHAPTER 38

# THE FAMILY AND MEDICAL LEAVE ACT (FMLA)

## § 38.01  INTRODUCTION

The Family and Medical Leave Act (FMLA) was enacted on February 3, 1993, as 29 U.S.C. §§ 2601–2654. Congress stated an intention to aid families in which both parents, or the single parent, work outside the home, and to minimize sex discrimination by making leave available in a gender-neutral manner.

The FMLA focuses on two subjects: health care (whether for the employee's own serious health condition or for a family member for whom the employee is a caregiver) and parenting a newborn or newly adopted child. 29 U.S.C. § 2601(a)(2) says that "it is important for the development of children and the family unit that fathers and mothers be able to participate in early childrearing and the care of family members who have serious health conditions."

Under appropriate circumstances, qualifying employees can take up to 12 weeks of leave a year, whether the leave is taken all at once, in several blocks, or intermittently in small units. FMLA leave can be important for preserving the job (and benefits) of someone who has used up all of his or her sick days and is too sick to maintain a normal work schedule, but not sick enough to obtain disability benefits or file for disability retirement.

Employers have the option of providing paid leave under these circumstances, but it does not violate the federal statute for the employer to provide only unpaid FMLA leave. [See § 38.06[G] for state-law developments]

> ■ **TIP:**  Providing unpaid leave to an employee who is exempt from the Fair Labor Standards overtime requirements does not convert the employee from exempt to nonexempt. [29 U.S.C. § 2612(c)]

Leave can be taken, under 29 U.S.C. § 2612, for a total of 12 weeks in any 12-month period (not necessarily a calendar year), when the employee has or adopts or fosters a child (but this leave can only be taken during the first year after the child's birth or after the adoption or foster care placement) or for a serious health condition suffered by the employee or his or her spouse, parent, or child. If the employee is the sick person, the serious health condition must prevent the employee from performing the functions of the job. The FMLA also includes provisions for leave for family members of military personnel.

The employer must give employees at least 60 days' notice of changes in the method of calculating the leave year. [29 C.F.R. § 825.200(d)] The 12-week limit applies per year, not per illness. Therefore, an employee who uses up the allowance is not entitled to additional leave based on events later in the same leave year.

As defined by 29 U.S.C. § 2611(9), a reduced leave schedule is a partial leave under which the employee does work, but for less than the usual number of hours per workday or workweek.

It is unlawful for employers to interfere with employees' exercise of FMLA right or to discriminate or retaliate against them for exercising such rights, charging the employer with FMLA violations, or participating in an investigation. [29 U.S.C. § 2615]

The FMLA does not modify federal or state antidiscrimination laws. [See 29 U.S.C. § 2651(a)] Employers always have a legal right to set up their own policies that are *more* generous than the FMLA: § 2653, and the federal statute does not preempt state and local laws that require employees to offer even more leave than the FMLA does. [29 U.S.C. § 2651(b)] In mid-2005, the DOL issued an opinion that says that state family leave laws are not preempted by the FMLA if they offer more generous benefits than the federal law. [DOL Advisory Opinion 2005-13A, <http://www.dol.gov/ebsa/regs/aos/ao2005-13a.html> (May 31, 2005)]

Employers do not have the power to draft their benefit plans or programs to limit FMLA rights, nor can a Collective Bargaining Agreement be used to cut back FMLA rights. [See 29 U.S.C. § 2652(b)]

In mid-2012, the DOL published a 20-page FMLA guide, "Need Time? The Employee's Guide to the Family and Medical Leave Act," to explain FMLA rights—and obligations—to employees. [<http://www.dol.gov/whd/fmla/employee guide.pdf> (undated); see Jeff Nowak, *DOL's New Employee Guide to the FMLA Issued: What's the Impact on Employers?*, Franczek Radelet FMLA Insights (June 29, 2012) (benefitslink.com)]

Commemorating the 20th anniversary of the FMLA, DOL published a survey on FMLA use, concluding that the FMLA is not unduly burdensome on employers and few employees are guilty of misuse. Asked about the FMLA's effect on the business' absenteeism, worker turnover, and morale, 91% said that compliance either has no noticeable effect on the business—or has a positive effect. Only 10% of workers fail to return after FMLA leave, which the DOL interprets to mean that there is little risk that employers will lose their investment in the workers. [*Family and Medical Leave Act in 2012: Final Report*, <http://www.dol.gov/asp/evaluation/fmla/fmla2012.htm>, discussed in DOL Wage & Hour Division, WHD News Release: *Family And Medical Leave Act Benefits Workers And Their Families, Employers* (Feb. 4, 2013) (benefitslink.com)]

FMLA Title I covers private employment. The statute also has a Title II, covering federal employees. Although the Supreme Court has ruled that Congress exceeded its power when it made state government employers subject to the ADA and ADEA, the Supreme Court reached the opposite conclusion with respect to the FMLA provisions permitting leave to care for a sick family member, finding that Congress validly abrogated state sovereign immunity when it comes to family leave. [*Nevada Dep't of Human Resources v. Hibbs*, 538 U.S. 721 (2003)]

In March 2012, a divided (5-4) Supreme Court held that the states have not waived sovereign immunity and cannot be sued under the FMLA "self-care" provision (i.e., leave taken to care for the employee's own serious health condition) for monetary damages. The Supreme Court held that Congress could not remove states' immunity from suit because there was no widespread evidence of sex discrimination or sex stereotyping that prevented women from taking leave to care for their own illnesses. The four dissenting justices (Ginsburg, Breyer, Sotomayor, and Kagan) identified the whole FMLA as legislation directed at sex discrimination. [*Coleman v. Court of Appeals of Maryland*, 132 S. Ct. 1327 (2012); see Adam Liptak, *Supreme Court Rules on Family Leave Act Suits*, NYTimes.com (Mar. 21, 2012)]

## [A]  2008–13 Changes

By 2008, it was clear that the FMLA was in need of clarification and amplification.

Additional protection was added to the FMLA for the families of military servicemembers—the first extension of the FMLA's requirements in the 15 years the law had been in effect. The extension provides up to 12 weeks of unpaid leave when an employee's spouse, child, or parent is called up or is on active duty in the armed forces, and up to 26 weeks when a child, parent, or spouse is injured seriously enough during military service to be unable to continue his or her duties. [Mark Schoeff, Jr., *Employer FMLA Frustrations May Rise with First Extension*, workforce.com (Dec. 27, 2007) (benefitslink.com); Rebecca Moore, *Bush Vetoes FMLA Expansion for Military Families*, plansponsor.com (Jan. 2, 2008); Fred Schneyer, *FMLA Expansion for Military Family Headed to White House Again*, plansponsor.com (Jan. 23, 2008). A one-page form for posting the military family leave information can be found at <http://www.dol.gov/esa/whd/fmla/NDAA Amndmnts.pdf>; see Proskauer Rose LLP Alert, *DOL Issues Proposed Revised FMLA Regulations and Expanded FMLA Leave to Family of Military Servicemembers* (February 2008) (benefitslink.com)] See below for additional protection added in 2010.

EBSA issued a massive Notice of Proposed Rulemaking in February 2008, making many clarifications and some changes in FMLA rules. [DOL, EBSA, Notice of Proposed Rulemaking to Amend the FMLA (RIN 1215-AB35) (Feb. 11, 2008) *DOL Proposes Revisions to Current FMLA Implementation Rules*, CCH Benefits (Feb. 19, 2008); Proskauer Rose LLP Alert, *DOL Issues Proposed Revised FMLA Regulations and Expanded FMLA Leave to Family of Military Servicemembers*, <www.proskauer.com> (February 2008); Allison Bell, *Labor May Cut Light Duty Work from FMLA Leave Total*, NU Online News Service (Feb. 11, 2008)]

In light of the many comments received in response to the proposal, the FMLA regulations were revised for the first time in 2008, covering more than 200 pages in the Federal Register. The regulations took effect January 16, 2009 (60 days after the November 17, 2008 posting date).

The extensive new rule retains the six definitions of "serious health condition" for which FMLA leave may be available, and provides regulatory guidance.

If the leave involves more than three consecutive calendar days of incapacity plus two health care visits, the two visits must occur within 30 days of the period of incapacity. If the employee asserts a chronic serious health condition, at least two visits per provider per year must be made. The right to reinstatement is in abeyance while an employee works on light duty—but voluntarily accepting a light duty assignment is not FMLA leave. An employer is justified in denying a "perfect attendance" award to an employee who was on FMLA leave, but only if FMLA leave is treated on a parity with other types of leave.

Under the new rules, when an employee requests FMLA leave, or the employer knows that a requested leave may qualify under the FMLA, the employer must notify the employees of their eligibility to take FMLA leave within five business days. (This period can be extended if there are extenuating circumstances; the previous rule gave the employer only two days.)

Notice must be provided about the employee's FMLA rights and responsibilities (such as providing medical certification and paying premiums to continue benefits) when an employee's eligibility is determined at the beginning of the first instance of leave for each reason in the 12-month leave period. All FMLA leave taken for the same reason is considered a single leave. The employee remains eligible for leave for that reason throughout the 12-month period. If the employer believes additional information is needed to complete the medical certification, it must give the employee written notice, and must allow seven calendar days for submission of the information. The employer is justified in refusing to grant leave if the employee fails to submit the complete certification within the cure period. If the employer requests certification, the employee must provide it even if the employee substitutes paid leave for FMLA leave.

[Jeff Nowak, *DOL's Model FMLA Forms Now Approved Through 2015*, Franczek Radelet FMLA Insights (Feb. 14, 2012) (benefitslink.com)]

The new military family leave benefit allows relatives of seriously injured or ill members of the military to take up to 26 weeks off work per year. The definition of family members is broader than in the FMLA in general; the military provision includes siblings and cousins. Servicemembers can make a written designation of a blood relative who would not otherwise be covered to take military caregiver leave. An employee can take more than one leave for different servicemembers, or for a subsequent injury or illness of the same servicemember—but the total military FMLA leave in any 12-month period cannot exceed 26 weeks.

In addition to leave granted when the servicemember is injured or ill, when a servicemember of the National Guard or Reserves is called up or released to civilian life, family members can take 12 weeks of FMLA leave. Leave can be taken for a "qualifying exigency" such as short-term deployment, counseling, making legal and financial arrangements, R&R, military events, and post-deployment activities. Intermittent leave can be taken by military family members. An optional Form WH-384 has been published so employees can certify their claims to a qualifying exigency.

In general, the new rules are considered to be pro-employee, but the final rule modifies a provision that was interpreted to allow some employees to wait up to two days after an absence to notify their employers, even if notice was possible earlier. The final rule requires employees to use the employer's procedures for giving notice and calling in during sick leave, unless unusual circumstances make it impossible to follow the procedures.

If the FMLA leave includes more than three consecutive days of incapacity plus two doctor visits, the two visits must be made within 30 days of the period of incapacity. "Periodic visits" to a health care provider means at least two a year. The "serious illness" form asks the health care provider for the frequency and duration of illness. The final rule clarifies that, although the employer cannot force employees to provide a diagnosis, it is legitimate for the employer to ask. However, the employee's direct supervisor is no longer permitted to contact the employee's health care provider to get medical certification.

To make it easier to administer FMLA leave, the new rules allow the employer to require notice within two days of the absence, or within five days of the leave request. The HR department is permitted to contact the health care provider.

The previous rules allowed employers to demand a fitness for duty exam before the employee returned to work; the final rule obligates the employer to notify employees if an exam is required before returning; the notice must list the essential functions of the employee's job (to show that the employee has recuperated enough to perform them).

Employer and employee can mutually agree to retroactively classify qualifying leave as FMLA leave. The updated rules clarify that it does not violate the FMLA for an employer to use its procedures for requesting medical information under the ADA, paid leave, or Worker's Compensation in the FMLA context.

The DOL's news release explaining the new rules says that the rule has been updated to reflect *Ragsdale*, removing the former "categorical" penalties that required employees who had already taken 30 weeks of leave to receive an additional 12 weeks of leave; the *Ragsdale* court said that the law requires only 12 weeks of leave. The final rule eliminates the penalty, but says that employers can be held liable if an employee suffers individual harm as a result of the employer's failure to satisfy the notification rules. The employer's failure to provide the required written notice can be treated as interference with the employee's FMLA rights, and the potential damages include "any other relief tailored to the harm suffered."

The DOL's position is that prospective waivers of FMLA claims are invalid, but employees can voluntarily agree to settle an FMLA claim that has already matured without DOL supervision or court approval.

If there is no written employee handbook or similar written description of benefits and leave entitlement, a general FMLA notice must be given to each new hire at the time of hiring. If a significant percentage of the workforce is not literate in English, the employer must provide the general notice in a language they can read. The notice can be posted electronically by satisfying the general electronic notice requirements—but paper copies must be posted where employees who do not have computers can see them.

The employer is permitted to require a new medical certification for each new leave year. If the employee asserts a continuing, open-ended condition, the employer can require recertification of the need for leave every six months (the previous rule was that recertification could be required when the minimum duration specified by the employee had elapsed). If circumstances (the seriousness of the condition, or frequency or duration of absences) change, recertification can be required more often.

The previous regulations required employees to try to schedule their intermittent or reduced schedule leave in a way that did not disrupt the employer's operations; now employees are required to "make a reasonable effort" to avoid undue disruption. The employer must account for the intermittent or reduced schedule leave in increments no greater than the shortest period used for other kinds of leaves (sick leave; vacations) and not less than one hour. The general rule is that the employer is not permitted to reduce the employee's leave entitlement by more than the amount of leave actually taken. However, sometime it is impossible to start or stop part-way through a shift, in which case the entire period the employee must be away from work counts against his or her FMLA entitlement. The revised rules permit temporary transfer of employees who need intermittent or reduced schedule leave, if the need for leave is foreseeable (based on planned medical treatment) or if such leave is permitted for the birth or adoption of a child. However, employers are not allowed to impose temporary transfers when employees have frequent and unpredictable absences caused by a chronic condition.

When an employee is ready to return to work after FMLA leave, the employer can ask for more than a simple statement of ability to return to work. If reasonable safety considerations are involved, the employer can ask for a fitness for duty certificate for intermittent leave.

If the nature of the workplace makes it physically impossible for employees to start working part-way through a shift, then an entire shift can be designated as FMLA leave. If the employee works a schedule that varies from week to week, entitlement to leave is calculated based on the weekly average for the preceding 12 months (the previous rule was that only 12 weeks were averaged).

Merely calling in sick is not enough to trigger FMLA obligations: the employee must provide enough detail for the leave request for the employer to determine if the leave qualifies under the FMLA. If the employee does not adequately explain, the employer is justified in denying leave. If the leave is for an FMLA-qualifying reason for which leave has already been taken, the employee must specifically reference this reason or need for FMLA leave.

The regulations say that if employer and employee disagree about whether a leave qualifies, they should resolve the dispute by discussion—and the discussion, and its outcome, must be documented.

Although the provisions about substituting paid for unpaid leave do not apply when an employee receives disability benefits during an FMLA leave, the employer and employee can, by agreement, supplement disability benefits by running paid leave concurrently with FMLA leave; this is also true for Worker's Compensation benefits. The employer can consider FMLA leave when awarding bonuses for perfect attendance.

On October 28, 2009, President Obama signed the Defense Department Fiscal Year 2010 Authorization Bill, expanding FMLA entitlement for military families. After the expansion, an employee whose spouse, parent, or child is a reservist can take FMLA leave for a qualifying exigency arising from deployment to a foreign country on active duty, with a new right to leave based on the deployment of the employee's spouse, parent, or child who serves in the regular armed forces to a foreign country.

Military caregiver leave has been expanded to 26 weeks per 12-month period in order to care for a parent, spouse, child, or relative to whom the employee is next of kin, if the servicemember is under treatment for a serious injury or illness incurred in the course of service (or began before active duty but was aggravated by active duty). Furthermore, leave can be taken for the same classes of family members when the family member is a veteran being treated for a qualifying illness or injury when the veteran was on active duty during the five years before the date of treatment. The Secretary of Labor has the power to define which illnesses and injuries qualify. The legislation does not include an effective date, so presumably it took effect as soon as the law was signed—except for leave for caregivers of veterans, which requires action by the Secretary of Labor to become effective. [Kilpatrick Stockton LLP, *President Obama Signs Legislation Expanding Family and Medical Leave Act* (Oct. 30, 2009) (benefitslink.com); Jeff Nowak, *DOL Issues Final Rule Implementing FMLA Amendments Expanding Military Family Leave and Leave for Airline Flight Crew Members*, Franczek Radelet FMLA Insights (Feb. 7, 2013) (benefitslink.com)]

In March, 2013, the DOL released revised FMLA forms and a new poster. The forms expire February 28, 2015. The poster must be displayed, starting March 8, 2013, even in locations where there are no FMLA-eligible employees. [Jackson Lewis LLP Workplace Resource Center, *Labor Department Releases New FMLA Model Forms and Notice Poster* (Feb. 27, 2013) (benefitslink.com)]

As of March 8, 2013, employers are required to use the updated notice/certification forms and post the new FMLA poster. DOL no longer prints model forms in the appendices to the FMLA regulations: they are posted on the DOL Website, so they can be changed without obtaining the approval of the Office of Management and Budget. DOL has developed a new certification form for leave occasioned by the serious injury or illness of an eligible veteran. Employers are permitted to adapt the forms rather than using them as published by DOL—as long as the employer's version does not call for disclosure of more information than the standard forms require. The updated regulations confirm that employers have obligations to keep genetic information confidential. The new forms are:

- WH-380-E, health care provider's certification of an employee's serious health condition;

- WH-380-F, the counterpart for a family member's serious health condition;

- WH-381, notice of eligibility, rights, and responsibilities;

- WH-382, designation notice;

- WH-384, certification of need for military family leave (number WH-383 is reserved);

- WH-385, certification of servicemember's serious injury or illness;

- WH-385-V, the counterpart for a veteran's serious injury or illness.

[Airline Flight Crew Technical Corrections Act, Pub. L. No. 111-119; see Jeff Nowak, *Employers Must Begin Using Updated FMLA Forms and Poster Starting March 8, 2013*, Franczek Radelet FMLA Insights (Feb. 28, 2013) (benefitslink. com)]

## § 38.02   FMLA ELIGIBILITY ISSUES

Like most federal employment discrimination laws, the FMLA exempts very small employers. The FMLA applies only to employers engaged in interstate commerce or activities affecting commerce (but most employers fit into this category)—and only if, in the current year or the previous calendar year, there were at least 50 employees on each workday of 20 or more workweeks. Furthermore, the FMLA does not apply when there are fewer than 50 people at that worksite and the total number of employees at all of the employer's sites within a 75-mile radius is less than 50. Anyone who acts on behalf of the employer, whether directly or indirectly, also counts as an employer. So does the successor in interest of a past employer. [29 U.S.C. § 2611(4)]

According to the Fifth Circuit, the definition of an eligible employer subject to the FMLA (at least 50 employees within 75 miles of the worksite) is not a jurisdictional requirement of an FMLA case. The Fifth Circuit remanded a case to see if the employer would be forbidden to raise the defense that it was not covered by the FMLA if the employee was told by the company that she was covered by the Act and relied on this statement. [*Minard v. ITC Deltacom Commc'ns Inc.*, 447 F.3d 352 (5th Cir. 2006)]

The 75-mile requirement was interpreted by the Tenth Circuit as surface miles, not linear miles as the crow flies, so in this case, the surface measurement was 75.6 miles so the employer was not subject to the FMLA. [*Hackworth v. Progressive Cas. Ins. Co.*, 468 F.3d 722 (10th Cir. 2006)]

The Sixth Circuit held, in mid-2006, that whether a company is subject to the FMLA is measured under labor rather than corporate law, and it is irrelevant whether a company transfers its assets or merges with another company. [*Cobb v. Contract Transp., Inc.*, 452 F.3d 543 (6th Cir. 2006), discussed in Rosario Vega Lynn, *Interesting Case on Successors-in-Interest Under FMLA*, Workplace Prof Blog (July 11, 2006) (benefitslink.com). The FMLA regulations, at § 825.107, use the Title VII test for liability of successor employers.]

Even after it is established that an employer is covered, not all employees are entitled to take FMLA leave. Comparatively veteran employees have FMLA rights, but new hires do not. Eligibility is limited to an employee who not only has worked for the employer for at least 12 months, but put in at least 1,250 hours for that employer in the preceding year. [See 29 U.S.C. § 2611(2)(A)]

The 1,250 hours are counted back from the time the employee went on FMLA leave, not from the time the employer fired the employee or took other adverse action. Therefore, a plaintiff who took three leaves that she claimed satisfied FMLA requirements, and therefore did not work 1,250 hours during the year before her discharge, was still entitled to bring an FMLA suit. [*Butler v. Owens-Brockway Plastic Prods. Inc.*, 199 F.3d 314 (6th Cir. 1999)]

The number of hours of FMLA leave an employee will be entitled to depends on his or her regular workweek. For a fluctuating schedule, the employer must average the scheduled hours for the 12 months before the beginning of the leave period—including hours when the employee was on leave. However, if the employee is exempt under the FLSA (does not receive overtime pay for work over 40 hours a month) it is likely that the employer does not track working hours. The burden is on the employer to disprove the employee's assertion of how many hours he or she worked. FMLA expert Jeff Nowak suggests that employers have employees complete a standard leave-of-absence form for any absence, including a place for exempt employees to specify the number of hours worked in the previous year. Employers should have a procedure for discussing this figure with the employee if the employer thinks it is inaccurate. [Jeff Nowak, *FAQ: How Many Intermittent FMLA Leave Hours is an FLSA-Exempt Employee Entitled To?* Franczek Radelet FMLA Insights (Sept. 19, 2011) (benefitslink.com)]

The Eleventh Circuit ruled in 2012 that the FMLA protects a request made before eligibility is achieved for leave to be taken post-eligibility. The plaintiff was fired after requesting FMLA leave for upcoming childbirth. She was fired after taking time off when her doctor ordered bed rest. The Eleventh Circuit cited 29 C.F.R. § 825.110(d)(4), which says that FMLA eligibility is determined when leave begins and the plaintiff would have been FMLA-eligible when the baby was due. The court also pointed out that FMLA policy is for employees to give employers notice of health events that can be announced in advance (e.g., elective surgery, childbirth), and removing FMLA protection would give employees an incentive not to provide notice—leading to additional inconvenience for employers. [*Pereda v. Brookdale Senior Living Communities Inc.*, 666 F.3d 1269 (11th Cir. 2012); see Lara J. Peppard, Ogletree Deakins, *Pregnant Employee Terminated Prior to Becoming Eligible for Leave Can State Causes of Action Under*

*FMLA* (Jan. 12, 2011) (benefitslink.com)—a reversal of its earlier position, in *Walker v. Elmore County Bd. of Ed.*, 379 F.3d 1249 (11th Cir. 2004).]

A Seventh Circuit plaintiff sued under the FMLA after being fired for receiving more than eight points under the no-fault attendance policy. She said that two of the absences were actually FMLA leave, for which she could not be penalized. However, she was not employed for 1,250 hours during the preceding 12 months, unless she was allowed to toll the 12-month period by adding in time worked during 56 days that preceded the time period, when she was on FMLA leave. The Seventh Circuit ruled that she was not entitled to tolling; the 1,250 hour requirement must be applied strictly. Bailey also charged FMLA retaliation, on the grounds that taking FMLA leave is not allowed to result in the loss of any employment benefit accrued before the date on which leave commenced. Although the Seventh Circuit found that removal of absenteeism points under a rolling no-fault policy was an employment benefit, it did not accrue before the leave commenced, and the FMLA statute says (§ 2614(a)(3)(A)) that employment benefits do not accrue during a period of leave. Forgiveness of attendance points, like seniority, accrues only when an employee is at work, not when he or she is on leave. [*Bailey v. Pregis Innovative Packaging, Inc.*, 600 F.3d 748 (7th Cir. 2010)]

In *Ragsdale v. Wolverine Worldwide* [535 U.S. 81 (2002)], the Supreme Court ruled that the DOL regulation [29 C.F.R. § 825.700(a)] is invalid to the extent that it requires employers to disclose the relationship between FMLA leave and the employer's own leave policies. The revised regulations reflect this decision: see § 38.01[A], above.

Under most anti-discrimination suits, the suit must be brought against the employer corporation, and not against individual decision-makers. However, in 2010 the Eastern District of Pennsylvania refused to dismiss claims against three HR executives and a manager accused of conspiring to find an excuse to fire a worker soon after discovering that he needed leave to have surgery, finding that the plaintiff provided evidence that the three had the power to hire and fire. Cases in Utah, Minnesota, and Kansas have limited individual liability under the FMLA to corporate officers, but the Eastern District found them inconsistent with Third Circuit precedent and held that an individual who exercises control over FMLA leave is potentially liable. [*Narodetsky v. Cardone Indus.*, No. 09-4734 2010 U.S. Dist. LEXIS 16133 (E.D. Pa. Feb. 24, 2010); see Shannon P. Duffy, *Federal Judge OKs FMLA Claims Against Individuals*, The Legal Intelligencer (Mar. 2, 2010) (law.com)]

## § 38.03  WHEN LEAVE IS AVAILABLE

An eligible employee can take FMLA leave for his or her own serious health condition or the serious health condition of an eligible family member.

The statute itself defines "serious health condition" as an "illness, injury, impairment, or physical or mental condition" that requires either inpatient care (in a hospital, nursing home or hospice) or at least continuing treatment by a health care provider. [29 U.S.C. §§ 2611(6) and (11)]

Qualifying family members are spouse (husband or wife only—not cohabitant), child (including adopted or foster child) who is either under 18 years old or mentally or physically disabled, or parent (biological parent or someone who played a parental role—but NOT a mother- or father-in-law, even though many individuals become caregivers for their in-laws). [See 29 U.S.C. §§ 2611(7) and (12)]

As a result of the Supreme Court's June 2013 decisions invalidating the federal Defense of Marriage Act, a legally married same-sex spouse counts as a husband or wife for this purpose.

The FMLA regulations define "child" as a son or daughter who, at the time of the leave, is under 18 or incapable of self-care because of a physical or mental disability (using the same definition as the ADA). Disability is defined as a need for assistance or supervision with three or more activities of daily living (ADLs) or instrumental activities of daily living (IADLs). In the case of *Salas v. 3M,* the district court refused to dismiss an FMLA suit involving an employee's adult daughter whose learning disabilities might have been caused at birth. *Serednyj v. Beverly Healthcare* holds that complications of pregnancy can be a disability, but if they end with birth, they are not substantially limiting. *Novak v. MetroHealth Medical Center* held that two weeks of postpartum depression was not sufficient to constitute a disability. *Patton v. Ecardio Diagnostics LLC* involved an adult child who broke both legs and suffered holes in the lungs and bladder in an automobile accident and had to spend a year in a wheelchair. [Jeff Nowak, *Best Practices: FMLA Leave to Care for an Adult Child*, Franczek Radelet FMLA Insights (Oct. 6, 2011) (benefitslink.com)]

A DOL Wage and Hour Division Administrator's Interpretation from mid-2010, reflecting the ADA Amendment Act's altered definition of disability, says that a foster child, stepchild, or child for whom the employee stands "in loco parentis" is a "son or daughter" for FMLA purposes, so the employee is entitled to take FMLA leave in connection with the child's birth, to bond with the child, or to care for the child—even if there is no biological or formal legal relationship between the employee and the child. [<http://www.dol.gov/whd/opinion/admin Intrprtn/FMLA/2010/FMLAAI2010_3.htm> (June 22, 2010).

A parent might also qualify for FMLA leave under the expanded definition of military caregiver. If the servicemember's disability continues over a span including at least two years, the parent might qualify for 26 weeks of FMLA leave in the first year, and an additional 12 weeks in the second year. The age at which the disability began is irrelevant for FMLA leave purposes. In 2013, DOL reiterated that leave can be taken to care for an adopted or stepchild, foster child, legal ward, or even someone who has the day to day responsibility of caring for the child or has a financial obligation to support the child. [DOL Wage and Hour

Division, Administrator's Interpretation No. 2013-1, Fair Labor Standards Act (Jan. 14, 2013). See Administrator's Interpretation 2010-3 for the in loco parentis relationship. See Spencer Fane Britt & Browne LLP, *FMLA Leave for Employees with Adult Disabled Sons and Daughters* (Jan. 22, 2013) (benefitslink.com)]

Travel time to care for an out-of-state family member is an FMLA gray area. If it is clear that an employee will be needed to care for a family member on a certain date, then travel to arrive by that time is probably part of protected leave. The line seems to be drawn between direct care (covered by the FMLA) and indirect care (e.g., fixing up a relative's house; not covered). [Jeff Nowak, *Does Travel Time Count as FMLA Leave?*, Franczek Radelet FMLA FAQ (Feb. 23, 2011) (benefitslink.com)]

The Eleventh Circuit held that it was permissible to fire an employee who was out of work for four weeks (after being given two weeks' leave) to assist her daughter, who was having a baby. The leave request did not mention either the FMLA or pregnancy complications. Pregnancy in and of itself is not a serious health condition, so a valid FMLA request must assert the need for a caregiver as a result of complications. [*Cruz v. Publix Super Mkts. Inc.*, 428 F.3d 1379 (11th Cir. 2005)]

According to 29 C.F.R. § 825.119(a), FMLA leave can be taken when an employee receives treatment for substance abuse after a referral by a health care provider, but absence caused by use of a substance by a person who is not under treatment is not covered by the FMLA. However, in a recent case, a customer service representative told his employer, John Crane, Inc., that he needed help for alcoholism. The Southern District of Texas ruled in early 2011 that an employee does not have to be enrolled in a rehab program for every day of leave to qualify under the FMLA. Employers should not promise a full 12 weeks of leave when the rehab process is expected to be much shorter, and employees should be given ample warning that they must return to work to avoid discharge. [*Picarazzi v. John Crane, Inc.*, Civil Action No. C-10-63, 2011 U.S. Dist. LEXIS 11432 (S.D. Tex. Feb. 7, 2011); see Jeff Nowak, *Mishandling FMLA Leave for Alcohol Treatment Causes Employer to Fall Off the Wagon*, Franczek Radelet FMLA Insights (Feb. 21, 2011) (benefitslink.com)]

In 2013, the Fifth Circuit dismissed FMLA and ADA claims filed by a plaintiff who was granted leave to treat his Vicodin addiction. He completed detox, but quit the program before receiving addiction treatment. The employer had a corporate policy of terminating employees who reject treatment for drug or alcohol problems or who start but fail to complete a treatment program. The plaintiff argued that he was entitled to be reinstated after he left the rehab facility, but the Fifth Circuit held that the right to reinstatement is not absolute. It was appropriate for the employer to fire him for violating the company policy that requires completion of a rehab program for which leave is granted. The employer was willing to live up to its obligations (providing leave so he could be treated for his drug dependency). The plaintiff did not live up to his obligation (completing the treatment). [*Shirley v. Precision Castparts Corp.*,No. 12-20544 (5th Cir. Aug. 12,

2013); see Kathryn McGovern, *Employee Who Left Drug Rehab Not Entitled to ADA, FMLA Protections*,Thompson SmartHR Blogs (Aug. 23, 2013) (benefitslink.com)]

The Seventh Circuit upheld dismissal of FMLA (and ADA) claims brought by an employee who tested positive for alcohol. The employee was on a last chance agreement after ongoing alcohol problems and a drunk driving arrest. She was tested for alcohol because she appeared to be under the influence of alcohol at work. The plaintiff did not prove she was entitled to FMLA leave. Although substance abuse is considered a serious health condition, this is true only if the employee receives inpatient treatment or is under continuing care from a health care provider. The plaintiff's FMLA retaliation claim failed because she did not show a connection between her alleged request for leave and a materially adverse action. The blood alcohol test could not have been retaliatory, because it was permitted by the Last Chance Agreement, and she was terminated for violating that agreement. [*Ames v. Home Depot USA Inc.*, 629 F.3d 665 (7th Cir. 2011)]

If both spouses work for different employers, each one is entitled to 12 weeks of leave when a child is born or adopted, but if they work for the same employer, the employer can legally require them to split a single 12-week leave period, or to share the 12 weeks when they are caring for the same sick child. [See 29 U.S.C. § 2612(f). The FMLA regulations create a loophole: 29 C.F.R. § 825.120(a)(3) says that if both parents are married and work for the same employer, they are entitled to a combined 12 weeks of baby bonding leave per leave year. However, if they work for the same employer but are not married, each of them can get 12 weeks of leave. Some state laws, e.g., California's, limit the leave to a combined 12 weeks for both parents, whether or not married. [Jeff Nowak, *Where FMLA Bonding Leave Is at Issue, Unmarried Parents Have More Generous Leave Rights*, Franczek Radelet FMLA Insights (Mar. 23, 2011) (benefitslink.com)]

## § 38.04   THE EMPLOYER'S OBLIGATION

It is the employer's responsibility to determine if the FMLA applies, so when an employee calls in sick it is necessary to find out if the employee is likely to miss more than three consecutive days of work, if the employee has a chronic condition that manifests intermittently, if he or she is caring for a family member with a serious health condition, or has pregnancy complications.

To avoid discrimination, there should be a standard list of questions that are asked of everyone who calls in sick: for example, the specific reason for the absence, which job duties the person cannot perform, if he or she has already taken leave for the same condition and when; if he or she is seeing a doctor; when he or she discovered the need for time off; and when he or she will return to work. If FMLA leave has already been taken for the same condition, find out if recertification is appropriate; if there seems to be a pattern of abuse (e.g., an excessive number of Monday and Friday absences); 29 C.F.R. § 825.308(e) permits the employer to check with the employee's doctor to see if three-day weekends are consistent with the medical need for leave. [Jeff Nowak, *Suffering from Super Bowl-Induced FMLA Leave?*, Franczek Radelet FMLA Insights (Feb. 7, 2011) (benefitslink.com)]

Nowak counsels, in the situation where a leave request is denied (particularly at holiday time) and then, at the last minute, the employee requests FMLA leave for a flare-up of a chronic condition, that the employer send a cover letter to the employee. The letter should explain that the FMLA request covers time for which leave was denied, so the employer requires confirmation of the medical need for leave in light of the employee's pattern of leave use. If the employee fails to provide certification, or the certification is dubious, it is legitimate for the employer to ask for clarification or a second opinion. If there is already a certification on file, asking for FMLA leave on days when leave was denied could be considered a significant change in circumstances justifying a recertification request. [Jeff Nowak, *An Employee Requests and is Denied Vacation Leave but Later Takes FMLA Leave for the Same Time Period. What Recourse Does an Employer Have?*, Franczek Radelet FMLA Insights (Jan. 8, 2013) (benefitslink.com)]

The FMLA regulations state that if there is a temporary cessation of one week or more (e.g., a school vacation) then those days that employer activity has ceased do not count against the FMLA entitlement—even if the employee would not have been healthy enough to work. With respect to holidays, if an employee observes a holiday that falls on Friday or Monday and takes the whole week off, the whole workweek should be counted as a full week of FMLA leave. However, if the employee works any part of the workweek, then the holiday cannot be counted as FMLA leave: see 29 C.F.R. § 825.200(h). This section also applies to calculation of FMLA leave when the operation is shut down by a natural disaster. If the employer is shut down for a week or more, the lost days do not reduce the employee's FMLA leave entitlement, even if it is obvious that the employee would not have been able to work during the downtime. [Jeff Nowak, *Calculating FMLA Leave for Holidays, Breaks and Plant Shut Downs*, Franczek Radelet FMLA Insights (Nov.10, 2011) (benefitslink.com) and *Hurricane Sandy and the FMLA (Part II): How Do Employers Calculate FMLA Leave When the Workplace Closes Because of the Storm?*, Franczek Radelet FMLA Insights (Nov. 2, 2012) (benefitslink.com)]

FMLA expert Jeff Nowak warns against allowing employees to make up time they took off under the FMLA. The regulations do not make it clear whether such policies are unlawful, but there is certainly a risk that forcing employees to make up the time will be considered FMLA interference, by "chilling" the employee's willingness to take FMLA leave. Nowak says that if the employer does permit employees to work to make up wages they lost by taking FMLA leave, the policy should make it clear that the time will be counted toward the FMLA allotment. If the FMLA leave was taken concurrently with paid leave such as sick or vacation days, Nowak suggests having a policy forbidding make-up time for paid leave. But if the policy allows make-up time for non-FMLA leave, it would violate the FMLA to deny make-up time for FMLA leave. [Jeff Nowak, *Can an Employer Require an Employee to Make Up Time Taken as FMLA Leave?*, Franczek Radelet FMLA Insights (Apr. 5, 2012) (benefitslink.com)]

## [A]   Benefits

The employer must reinstate the employee after leave, and must maintain all employee benefits during leave. [See 29 U.S.C. § 2615(c) for health coverage requirements] However, the employee does not accrue seniority or additional benefits. FMLA leave is not considered a break in service when pension eligibility is determined.

"Benefits" means all of the employer's benefits (not just those offered under ERISA plans), e.g., "group life insurance, health insurance, disability insurance, sick leave, annual leave, educational benefits, and pensions." [29 U.S.C. § 2611(5)]

When employees are on FMLA leave, the EGHP must maintain their coverage at the original level. If employees are required to pay part of the EGHP premium under normal circumstances, the plan can require them to continue contributing during FMLA leave. Furthermore, if the employee is more than 30 days late paying the premium, health insurance coverage can legitimately be terminated. If coverage is terminated in this manner, but the employee returns to work and is reinstated, then he or she is entitled to immediate reinstatement in the EGHP, with no need to satisfy plan requirements a second time.

If the employee quits instead of returning from leave, the employer is entitled to recover the health premiums expended on the employee's behalf during the leave period. But if the employee files a health claim for treatment during the leave period, a claim that would otherwise be allowable cannot be denied because the employee later terminates employment.

Nowak warns that a policy of recovering health insurance premiums only from new mothers who do not return from maternity leave, but not from other non-returning employees, could violate the PDA. [Jeff Nowak, *When Employee on FMLA Leave Indicates They Will Not Return From FMLA Leave, What Should an Employer Do?*, Franczek Radelet FMLA Insights (June 22, 2012) (benefits link.com)]

## [B]   Reinstatement

Section 2614 takes up the subject of reinstatement in more detail. It provides that an employee who returns from leave not only must not lose any benefits because of taking leave, but must be reinstated either in the old job or an equivalent new one. The second job is equivalent to the first if it provides equivalent terms and conditions of employment (benefits, pay, etc.) The right to be rehired in one's former position is not absolute; an employee can be fired if his job has been eliminated when a number of positions were consolidated. [*Yashenko v. Harrah's N.C. Casino Co.*, 446 F.3d 541 (4th Cir. 2006); see Fred Schneyer, *Court: FMLA Job Protection Not Absolute*, plansponsor.com (Aug. 28, 2006)]

The FMLA creates an exception for employees earning in the top 10% of the employer's workforce. It is not necessary to reinstate them after leave if reinstatement would cause "substantial and grievous economic injury" to the employer, and the employer promptly notifies the employee that reinstatement will be denied.

However, taking FMLA leave does not entitle any employee to anything he or she would not have been entitled to by remaining at work without taking leave.

An employee who returns from FMLA leave and is ready to work is entitled, in the Sixth Circuit view, to immediate reinstatement, not reinstatement a month later. The statute does not provide the employer with additional time to adjust to the employee's return. Therefore, insisting that an employee take a longer leave than the employee could certify to be medically necessary could be treated as interference with FMLA rights. [*Hoge v. Honda of Am. Mfg. Inc.*, 384 F.3d 238 (6th Cir. 2004)]

A number of cases hold that if an employee has committed misconduct serious enough to justify termination, the fact that the employee requests or takes FMLA leave does not make it unlawful for the employer to fire the employee. See, e.g.,

- Engaging in unauthorized employment during leave, contrary to the terms of the employee handbook. [*Pharakhone v. Nissan N. Am. Inc.*, 324 F.3d 405 (6th Cir. 2003)]

- Refusal to sign a performance improvement plan covering issues that had been reported even prior to the FMLA leave. [*Cole v. State of Illinois*, 562 F.3d 812 (7th Cir. 2009)]

- Issuance of a county auditor's report recommending the plaintiff's immediate termination for acts of fraud and impropriety; the report was issued while the plaintiff was on leave for knee surgery. [*Simpson v. Office of the Chief Judge of the Circuit Court of Will County*, 559 F.3d 706 (7th Cir. 2009); *Edwards v. Harleysville National Bank*, Civ. Action No. 07-3987 (E.D. Pa. 2008), discussed Shannon P. Duffy, *Judge: FMLA Doesn't Shield Worker from Being Fired for Other Reasons*, The Legal Intelligencer (Oct. 17, 2008) (law.com) also holds that termination for embezzlement was permissible after the employee announced a plan to take medical leave]

- Although intent is not required for an interference claim, the Tenth Circuit found that termination two days after a request for FMLA leave was justified by the employee's lack of improvement after receiving mixed feedback in his performance review. The retaliation claim required circumstantial evidence of a retaliatory motive, which the plaintiff could not provide. [*Brown v. ScriptPro LLC*, 700 F.3d 1222 (10th Cir. 2012); see Wolters Kluwer Law & Business, *Evidence Of Employer's Dissatisfaction Is Sufficient To Forestall Employee's FMLA Claim* (Jan. 18, 2013) (benefitslink.com)]

The employer can justify termination based on its honest belief (even if it is mistaken) that the employee deliberately misused FMLA leave.

In most states (although California is an exception), employers can defend against FMLA charges by alleging an honest belief that the employee was abusing leave. However, a complete investigation is required. Tools for fighting abuse include medical certification and recertification and requiring second or even third opinions. If the employee will have an ADA disability after FMLA leave ends, the interactive process (see § 36.05) should begin during the leave. Employers who claim that the leave request is an undue hardship must be able to document the hardship—for example, by showing loss of productivity, lower morale because workers are overburdened, lost sales, or deterioration in customer service. [Jeff Nowak, *Best Practices for Employers When Administering FMLA Leave: A Recap of our Webinar*, Franczek Radelet FMLA Insights (Dec. 12, 2012) (benefitslink.com)]

The "honest belief" defense was also allowed in an interference/retaliation case when a company, suspecting FMLA misuse, placed 35 employees under surveillance and fired one whose car remained in his driveway, and who did not leave the front door of his house, on days that he took leave to visit his mother in a nursing home. (He said that his brother picked him up from the back door.) However, Nowak cautions that the employer must do a meaningful investigation before disciplining an employee for leave misuse: *Scruggs v. Carrier Corp.*, 688 F.3d 821 (7th Cir. 2012); Jeff Nowak, *Employer's "Honest Suspicion" of FMLA Abuse Enough to Dismiss FMLA Claims*, Franczek Radelet FMLA Insights (Aug. 8, 2012) (benefitslink.com)]

Summary judgment for the employer was granted in an FMLA interference/retaliation case, where the employer had a reasonable, honest belief that an employee abused FMLA leave, on the basis of the vacation pictures she posted to Facebook. Lineberry, who is a nurse, went on FMLA leave after a work injury. Her doctor said that she could take the vacation she had already planned and paid for because it was less stressful than her work duties. However, her Facebook postings showed her engaging in physical activities. After complaints from some of her co-workers about FMLA abuse, Lineberry's doctor revised his estimate and cleared her to return to work two weeks earlier than his previous estimate. During an investigation, Lineberry admitted that she had lied when she claimed to have used wheelchairs in the airports during her trip. She was fired for dishonesty and falsifying or omitting information in employment records. The district court upheld the termination because she admitted to lying about wheelchair use—a legitimate, non-FMLA related reason for firing her. [*Lineberry v. Detroit Med. Ctr.*, No. 11-13752, 2013 U.S. Dist. LEXIS 15540 (E.D. Mich. Feb. 5, 2013); see Jackson Lewis LLP Workplace Resource Center, *Termination Upheld Where Employee's Facebook Photos Showed She was Dishonest While on FMLA Leave* (Mar. 13, 2013)(benefitslink.com)]

Anyone who is on FMLA leave can be laid off during a RIF, if he or she would have been laid off anyway. [*O'Connor v. PLA Family Health Plan Inc.*, 200 F.3d 1349 (11th Cir. 2000)]

## [C]  Interference

Under the FMLA regulations, discouraging an employee from using FMLA leave can constitute unlawful interference. After back surgery, a hospital housekeeper's immediate supervisor called her every week asking for a return to work date to the point that the worker asked her supervisor if her job was at risk. The supervisor told her to return as soon as possible; she went back to work three weeks post-surgery. She was fired when a surveillance camera showed her opening a desk drawer in an office she was not assigned to clean. (The camera was installed after reports of thefts.) She sued, charging that she was denied the full benefit of FMLA leave by having to return before she was fully recovered, and that she was fired in retaliation for taking leave. The Western District of Arkansas dismissed the retaliation claim, but allowed the case to proceed to trial on the interference claim because there was evidence that she was discouraged from taking as much leave as she needed. [*Terwilliger v. Howard Mem'l Hosp.*, No. 09-CV-4055, 2011 U.S. Dist. LEXIS 8577 (W.D. Ark. Jan. 27, 2011); see Maria Danaher, Ogletree Deakins Employment Law Matters, *Employer's Frequent Calls to Employee During FMLA May Create Interference with That Leave*, <http://www.employmentlawmatters.net/2011/02/articles/fmla/employers-frequent-calls-to-employee-during-fmla-may-create-interference-with-that-leave> (Feb. 14, 2011)]

Employees on FMLA leave cannot be asked to work—a proposition that requires a definition of "work." The District Court for the Northern District of Ohio permitted an FMLA interference case to continue based on allegations that, while respiratory therapist Julie Vess was on leave to recover from surgery, there were frequent work-related telephone calls. She alleged that she was expected to schedule and train other therapists, discuss work with her replacement and with her supervisor, and submit evaluations of the therapists that she supervised. The district court said that FMLA interference includes denial of any benefits protected by the FMLA, including the right not to work while on leave. The district court said that the only work tasks that can be required are having the person on leave transmit "institutional knowledge" to new staff, disclose computer passwords, close out assignments, and name other employees who can substitute for the worker on leave. [*Vess v. Select Med. Corp.*, No. 3:11 CV 2549 (N.D. Ohio

Mar. 15, 2013); see Daniel Cafaro, *Consider Limiting Work Calls to Employees on FMLA Leave*, Smart HR (Apr. 18, 2013) (benefitslink.com)]

The Eighth Circuit permitted a nurse to pursue an FMLA interference claim. She was fired for job abandonment shortly after being sent home by the HR director after she had a panic attack. The Eighth Circuit found that there were factual issues as to whether her employer was aware of her condition. She had the panic attack when she was apprehensive about being assigned to a new unit when she was not trained to do the work. She was threatened with termination and losing her license for patient abandonment if she did not take the assignment. The panic attack was severe enough for her to want to take an ambulance to a hospital. The HR director told her to go home and return the next day to negotiate the assignment. The next day, she saw her doctor, who prescribed medication, suggested therapy, and gave her a note covering an absence for the rest of the week. She submitted the doctor's note and asked for FMLA forms, but was told that she had been fired for walking off the job. The ex-employer's argument was that she had already been fired when she requested leave so she had no FMLA rights. (The opinion did not discuss the implications of the HR director sending the plaintiff home, or whether it could be considered patient abandonment for a nurse to reject an assignment he or she is not qualified to perform.) The employer also argued that it was not aware of the plaintiff's anxiety disorder, but the Eighth Circuit noted that the FMLA has explicit provisions for a need for leave that arises unexpectedly. [*Clinkscale v. St. Therese of New Hope*, 701 F.3d 825 (8th Cir. 2012), *reh'g denied*, No. 12-1223 (Jan. 3, 2013); see Jackson Lewis LLP, *Nurse who Suffered Panic Attack and was Sent Home Can Pursue FMLA Interference Claim* (Nov. 27, 2012) (benefitslink.com)]

Swimming instructor Beverly Ballard was the primary caregiver for her terminally ill mother. A charitable organization offered her mother a six-day make-a-wish trip to Las Vegas. Ballard applied for six days off to care for her mother. The request was denied, but she went anyway. She sued for FMLA interference after she was fired for the unauthorized absence. The Northern District of Illinois held that it didn't matter where Ballard provided the care that her dying mother required. The district court held that the FMLA does not require that the family member receive medical treatment at the time the employee provides care, and the FMLA's legislative history refers to care rendered during the end stage of a terminal illness. The district court held that summary judgment for the employer was unavailable because there was a fact issue as to whether Ballard gave adequate notice of her intention to take leave. [*Ballard v. Chicago Park Dist.*, No. 10 C 1740, 2012 U.S. Dist. LEXIS 141055 (N.D. Ill. Sept. 29, 2012); see Jeff Nowak, *What!?! Time Caring for Mom in Las Vegas is FMLA Leave*, Franczek Radelet FMLA Insights (Nov. 26, 2012) (benefitslink.com)]

A Southern District of New York plaintiff charged interference with his right to continue coverage during an FMLA leave taken just before his termination. He claimed that his coverage lapsed because the employer neither paid the premiums nor notified him of his obligation to pay. The employer denied that it had any obligations. The employer sent a letter explaining the premium payment process—to the employee's former address. The Southern District of New York ruled that the employer was not obligated to pay the employee's share of premiums while he was on leave; the employer only has to maintain coverage under the same conditions as if the employee were still at work. The court refused to decide the FMLA claim until evidence was submitted as to whether coverage actually lapsed. [*Rodriguez v. Atria Senior Living Group, Inc.*, 887 F. Supp. 2d 503 (S.D.N.Y. 2012); see EBIA Weekly, *Court Addresses FMLA's Health Coverage Continuation and Employer Notice Requirements* (Sept. 27, 2012) (benefitslink. com)]

Hotel housekeeper Sonia Figueroa, who was eligible for FMLA leave, often missed work for health reasons. The HR department, anticipating that she would continue to take intermittent leave in the future, told her she could not return to work without medical certification of a serious health condition and need for medical leave. She told the HR department that she saw no need to complete the forms because she was healthy enough to perform her job. When the HR department continued to repeat its requests, Figueroa assumed that she had been fired and sued for FMLA interference. The Eastern District of Pennsylvania did not rule on the question of whether it is legal to place an employee on involuntary FMLA leave, but held that she had no cause of action for FMLA interference because she was not unable to work at the time she was told not to come to work. [*Figueroa v. Merritt Hospitality*, No. 11-1807, 2011 U.S. Dist. LEXIS 107465 (E.D. Pa. Sept. 21, 2011); see Business Management Daily, *Can FMLA Leave Be Involuntary? Court Punts* (Dec. 19, 2011) (benefitslink.com)]

## § 38.05  INTERMITTENT LEAVE

Section 2612(b) governs intermittent leave and leave that produces a reduced work schedule. The FMLA provides the equivalent of 12 weeks of work: up to 480 hours a year for full-time workers, and an equivalent prorated amount for part-time workers, such as 240 hours a year for someone who works a half-time schedule. The FMLA regulations [see 29 C.F.R. § 825.205(b)] refer to the actual number of hours the employee usually works in a week; or in an average week, if the schedule varies. Therefore, a person who is exempt from receiving overtime benefits but who typically works longer than 40 hours a week can get additional intermittent leave because of this work history.

Reed Group studied over 112,000 FMLA claims closed between 2008 and 2011 and concluded that employees who take intermittent leave for themselves or to care for family members are almost three times as likely to file a short-term disability claim within six months as employees not taking FMLA leave. About half (51%) of FMLA claims were for intermittent leave. One-fifth (21%) of employees taking intermittent leave filed a short-term disability claim 51% of

FMLA claims were for intermittent leave. 21% of employees taking intermittent leave filed an STD claim within six months(usually musculoskeletal or behavioral health) vs. 8% of those taking continuous FMLA leave. [PRNewswire, *Reed Group Study Finds Employees Taking Intermittent Family Medical Leave Are Three Times More Likely to File for Short-term Disability*, MarketWatch (WSJ. com) (Aug. 7, 2012)]

Employers are not obligated to grant intermittent leave for cosmetic procedures. The general rule is that leave to care for a newly born or adopted child must be taken in a block of time off, and not on an intermittent or reduced schedule—unless the employer agrees to the special schedule. Intermittent leave for parents can be denied unless the child has a serious health condition, or unless a pregnant employee has severe morning sickness or needs time off for prenatal care. Leave premised on a serious health condition can be taken intermittently or on a reduced schedule when it is medically necessary.

It is permitted for the employer to use health-related intermittent/reduced leave to offset birth or adoption leave taken by the employee in the same year, but only to the actual extent of intermittent or reduced leave that was taken.

When a health-related intermittent leave can be predicted, based on scheduled medical treatment, the employer can lawfully transfer the employee to an available alternative position—as long as:

- The employee is qualified for the position;

- The two jobs are equivalent in pay and benefits;

- The second job provides a better accommodation to the changed work schedule than the first job did;

- Once the need for intermittent leave ends, the transferred employee must be offered reinstatement in the former job or a comparable job. It violates the FMLA for employers to use transfers deliberately to discourage the use of FMLA leave or to retaliate against employees who take or request leave.

Filings in Rachel Robinson's case allege that she applied for FMLA leave when her mother had a brain tumor. Her manager insisted that the leave be intermittent rather than continuous. After 18 days leave, Robinson was granted a further 10 days—but was ordered to "draw a line" between work and caregiving. She was fired three days later. Her mother died three weeks after that. Robinson's suit was settled in 2009. The Hastings Center has a database of over 3,000 published state and federal cases on caregiver discrimination, and its hotline is popular, especially with parents. [Paula Span, *When Work Makes You Choose*, NYTimes.com (Sept. 14, 2012)]

*Human Resource Executive Online* points out that employees are only entitled to intermittent or reduced schedule FMLA leave if it is medically necessary for their own serious health condition or to care for a family member.

Employers are not required to grant intermittent or reduced schedule leave for the birth or adoption of a child. Although determination of an employee's eligibility for FMLA leave can be made only once per 12-month period for all related intermittent absences involving the same health condition, the article recommends that employers re-evaluate eligibility at the beginning of each 12-month period. Under the revised FMLA regulations, it is probably permissible to require call-in before the beginning of the shift. If employees fail to comply with the call-in procedure, it is legitimate to impose discipline, as long as the discipline does not discriminate against employees who take FMLA leave. Employers are justified in asking for more information if employees call in sick without providing enough information to determine if the leave qualifies under the FMLA. However, the employer does not have a duty to inquire further if an employee calls in sick—but if an employee mentions the FMLA, the employer can ask why the employee is taking time off, what the symptoms are, if the employee has a medical appointment, and when the employee plans to return to work. [David B. Calzone, *Managing Intermittent Leave*, Human Resource Executive Online (May 24, 2010) (benefitslink.com)]

An employer that is dubious about the authenticity of a certification can ask the health care provider if he or she prepared the certification, and what it means. The employer can also ask for a second opinion—and, if it conflicts with the initial opinion, can ask for a third opinion to resolve the conflict. However, the employer must pay for the second and third opinions, and the third opinion is binding. [Daniel Cafaro, *7 Best Practices in FMLA Intermittent Leave Administration*,Smart HR (Apr. 12, 2013) (benefitslink.com)]

## § 38.06  RELATING FMLA LEAVE TO OTHER LEAVE

### [A]  Generally

The simplest example is in the case of an employer that does not offer any form of paid leave. If the employer is subject to the FMLA, it must offer unpaid leave to FMLA-eligible employees. More difficult issues arise when the employee is entitled both to FMLA leave and to some form of paid leave (e.g., vacation; sick leave).

In a controversial 2007 decision, the Seventh Circuit ruled that it violates the FMLA to make an employee use paid sick and vacation leave, even if the employee was also receiving disability benefits under a multi-employer plan. (See 29 C.F.R. § 825.207(d)(1).) Therefore, the Seventh Circuit allows an employee who takes FMLA leave to extend the 12 week allotment under the FMLA by any other paid leave offered by the employer. The employer's theory was that the regulation applies only to benefits under the employer's own temporary disability plan, not a third-party plan, but the Seventh Circuit held that the regulation does not distinguish based on the type of disability plan. [*Repa v. Roadway Express*,

477 F.3d 938 (7th Cir. 2007); see Carla J. Rozycki and David K. Haase, *7th Circuit Rules on FMLA Leave with Disability Benefits*, special to law.com (Mar. 7, 2007) and Fred Schneyer, *Employer Can't Force Paid Leave Substitution Under FMLA*, plansponsor.com (Mar. 7, 2007)]

The Southern District of Ohio held that ERISA preempts the Wisconsin statute about benefit substitutions, which allows employees to substitute any other kind of paid or unpaid leave provided by employer for part of their family leave or medical leave. The plaintiff wanted to substitute short-term disability leave under an ERISA plan for part of her FMLA leave to bond with a new baby. Her employer denied the request because she did not meet the plan's definition of disability. An ALJ held that an insurance company violated the substitution provision by denying short-term disability benefits to a plan participant. The insurance company sued for declaratory and injunctive relief. The district court held that the requirement of paying STD benefits was expressly preempted by ERISA § 514(a) and there was conflict preemption with ERISA § 502(a)'s civil enforcement provisions. The state law was preempted because it forced employers to use their general assets to pay benefits that were not available under the plan; it gave the employees an alternative enforcement mechanism other than the plan's claims procedure; and it prevented multi-state employers from offering uniform FMLA benefits in the states where it did business. Accordingly, the district court granted a permanent injunction against application of the substitution provision. [*Sherfel v. Gassman*, No. 2:09-cv-00871-JLG-TPK, 2012 WL 4499245 (S.D. Ohio Sept. 28, 2012); see Matthew R. Madara, *Court Holds That Wisconsin FMLA Substitution Law Is ERISA-Preempted*, Bloomberg BNA Pension & Benefits Blog (Oct. 4, 2012) (benefitslink.com)]

State law may require employers to provide intermittent leave on more generous terms than the FMLA does. If the employee is also a qualified person with a disability as defined by the ADA, then it may be necessary to grant even more than the equivalent of 12 weeks' intermittent leave as a reasonable accommodation.

Sometimes it is hard to distinguish between leave taken because of complications of pregnancy and leave taken to prepare for parenting. Under Wage and Hour Division regulations, FMLA leave is not available after the employee has taken a disability leave for pregnancy-related complications. However, if there is a post-delivery period when the mother is physically unable to work, that period can be counted as a leave for serious illness, even though it also represents parenting leave. This is especially significant if both parents work for the same employer and would otherwise have to split a single 12-week leave period.

If the state has a law obligating employers to provide paid or partially paid maternity leave, employees are entitled to unpaid FMLA law in addition to the paid leave required by state law. Furthermore, if the state has an FMLA-type law that extends coverage in circumstances that the federal law does not provide for (e.g., taking care of a friend or parent-in-law), the state-required leave is treated as if it were taken for non-FMLA purposes and therefore does not reduce the 12-week FMLA allowance.

A late 2010 article says that it is an open question whether intermittent FMLA leave is available for fertility treatment, because the statute and regulations are silent and there is no clear judicial rule. It is possible that denying the leave might be considered to violate the ADA or PDA. If the employee is covered by the FMLA, then taking intermittent leave for fertility treatment cannot be used as a negative factor in hiring, promotion, or discipline. If leave is requested after a miscarriage or the death of a newborn, some decisions hold that bereavement leave is not covered by the FMLA, unless the bereaved employee has a serious health condition as a result of bereavement. [Keisha-Ann G. Gray, *Procreation Problems*, Human Resource Executive Online (Nov. 2, 2010) (benefitslink.com)]

Taking a cross-country trip to fetch a more reliable family car during his wife's pregnancy, and his regular phone calls to her during the trip, did not constitute caring for her, so the employee was not entitled to FMLA leave for the trip. [*Tellis v. Alaska Airlines*, 414 F.3d 1045 (9th Cir. July 12, 2005)]

A seven-week trip to the Philippines, accompanying a seriously ill husband who consulted a faith healer, was not covered by the FMLA, so it was lawful to fire the employee for taking unapproved leave. The retaliation claim failed because the plaintiff not merely obtained FMLA leave when her husband received conventional medical care, but also because a pilgrimage to a spiritual healing center (much less tourism) is not protected by the FMLA. [*Tayag v. Lahey Clinic Hosp. Inc*, 632 F.3d 788 (1st Cir. 2011); see Sheri Qualters, *Spiritual Healing Not Covered by Leave Act, 1st Circuit Rules*, Nat'l L.J. (Jan. 28, 2011) (law.com)]

Statutes governing medical leave typically define the amount of medical leave that must be granted. Conditions that require long-term absences are often severe enough to trigger protection against disability discrimination. Worker's Compensation might also be involved if the illness or injury is work-related.

Many companies maintain a formal policy that sets a maximum length of available medical leave (e.g., six months or a year), with termination for employees who are unable to return to work after exhausting their leave allowance. Multi-state companies must make sure that the policy is acceptable under the laws of all the states in which they do business. Calendar-year employers might face situations in which an employee succeeds in taking 12 weeks' leave in each of two calendar years.

It is common for state medical leave laws to use the FMLA definitions and to provide that leave under the state law runs concurrently with the federal FMLA leave. However, Connecticut and the District of Columbia require access to 16 weeks of leave over a two-year period. California requires up to 12 weeks' leave in a 12-month period, with a separate four-month leave requirement for disability related to pregnancy and childbirth. Both the ADA regulations and case law have recognized leave as an effective accommodation to disability. However, employers are not required to provide an infinite amount of leave; there must be a reasonable expectation that granting leave will permit the employee to recover to the point that the employee can perform the essential functions of the job (or perhaps of another available job). Some cases require leave only if there is a determinable date for return to work. [Chuck Rice and James H. Coil III, *Limits on Limited Medical-Leave Policies*, Kilpatrick Stockton LLP Employment Relations Today (Autumn 2005)]

The California Court of Appeal held in 2013 that an employee disabled by the complications of a high-risk pregnancy was entitled to additional leave as a reasonable accommodation under the California civil rights law FEHA, even though she had used up her California Pregnancy Disability Leave Law and California Family Rights Act leave. Her employer allowed her 19 weeks of leave, including accrued vacation time. She was fired when, at the end of that time, she was still on bed rest and could not perform the essential functions of her job. According to the court of appeal, the plain language of the Pregnancy Disability Leave Law is that it supplements and does not replace other FEHA entitlement. [*Sanchez v. Swissport, Inc.*, 213 Cal. App. 4th 1331, 153 Cal. Rptr. 3d 36 (2013); see Jackson Lewis LLP Workplace Resource Center, *No Statutory Cap on Pregnancy Leave, California Court of Appeal Rules* (Mar. 4, 2013) (benefitslink. com)]

Failure to comply with the FMLA, which allows part-time hours (in conjunction with intermittent leave), can be deemed to violate Title VII: *Orr v. City of Albuquerque*, 417 F.3d 1144, 1151 (10th Cir. 2005); see also *Mickeson v. N.Y. Life Ins. Co.*, 460 F.3d 1304 (10th Cir. 2006): refusing to permit an employee to return to work on a part time basis accelerated depletion of her FMLA leave, so the employee was deprived of salary and benefits, and therefore encountered an adverse job action.

## [B] ADA Interface

An employer can satisfy both the FMLA and the ADA by offering a reduced work schedule to a disabled employee until he or she has used the 12 weeks of FMLA leave. After FMLA leave, employees are entitled to reinstatement in a job equivalent to the original job. The FMLA permits the employer to demand a physical exam to determine if a worker can be reinstated after a health-related FMLA leave. To satisfy the ADA as well, the examination must be job-related, not a comprehensive inventory of all physical conditions.

Although the two statutes were designed to accomplish different goals, workers sometimes find that FMLA leave is more accessible than taking time off as an ADA reasonable accommodation. Remember, FMLA leave is available when the employee is the sick person—not just when the employee is a caregiver.

Furthermore, if the company employs at least 50 people and the employee has put in the necessary 1,250 hours in the previous 12 months, entitlement to

FMLA leave is automatic. The employer's discretion as to what constitutes a reasonable accommodation is not a factor. The right to reinstatement is also automatic. Employers can raise a defense of unreasonable hardship in ADA cases—but not in FMLA cases.

Lawyers representing employers and employees met at a June, 2013 seminar to consider the interplay between the ADA and the FMLA. There is a maximum amount of leave allowable under the FMLA; the ADA does not have specific leave allotments. The two statutes use different definitions: an ADA "disability" is not necessarily the same thing as a "serious health condition" under the FMLA. Therefore, not every employee who exhausts FMLA leave will be entitled to ADA accommodation. Employers must review their forms used to communicate with employees to make sure that they provide accurate information about both statutes. [D.C. Bar Labor &Employment Law Section seminar (June 11, 2013), discussed in Lydell C. Bridgeford, *Attorneys for Both Plaintiffs, Employers Offer Views on Leave Under the ADA, FMLA*, Bloomberg BNA (June 25, 2013) (benefitslink.com)]

Absences that qualify under the FMLA or ADA should not be counted against an employee's record under a no-fault attendance policy. For example, Wal-Mart was unable to get summary judgment in an FMLA interference/retaliation suit filed by a department manager who alleged that her FMLA leave was a factor in disciplining and then firing her. The district court found that Wal-Mart did not apply its progressive discipline policy uniformly; the plaintiff's earlier performance evaluation showed 14 attendance occurrences without any discipline imposed. [*Green v. Wal-Mart Stores, East, LLP*,No. 3:11-cv-440, 2013 WL 3223629 (S.D. Ohio June 25, 2013); see Daniel Cafaro, *Walmart on Trial for Counting FMLA-Qualifyng Absences Against Employee*, Smart HR (July 11, 2013) (benefitslink.com)] Worker's Compensation defines disability in terms of specific injuries, such as the loss of hands or feet. The Worker's Compensation laws do not make explicit provision for leaves of absence, but denying reasonable time off could be interpreted as illegal retaliation for filing a Comp claim. However, it is lawful to fire someone who receives Worker's Compensation benefits as long as there is a legitimate non-retaliatory reason for the termination. Recipients of Worker's Compensation benefits are not guaranteed reinstatement if they recover from their injuries. If a work-related injury is also a disability, reasonable accommodation may be required under the ADA.

The EEOC's Enforcement Guidance on Reasonable Accommodation and Undue Hardship specifically says that no-fault leave policies that make termination automatic after a certain amount of leave has been taken violate the ADA.

An employee's job protection does not necessarily end once FMLA leave is used up. The employer must then consider if the employee is covered by the ADA. If so, the employer must engage in the interactive process and reassignment to a vacant position for which the employee is qualified may constitute reasonable accommodation. A bank teller with rheumatoid arthritis required two extensive periods of leave. During her recovery, she applied for other jobs within the company and said that she was willing to relocate. She was not offered a new job and was fired. The plaintiff said that she could perform the essential functions of the job with the reasonable accommodation of a finite leave of absence and was willing to transfer to other available jobs. The Eastern District of California granted summary judgment for the employer on FMLA and corresponding California law, other than failure to rehire after the plaintiff was released for work. The district court denied summary judgment for the employer on ADA and FEHA discrimination counts and failure to accommodate. The district court held that holding a job open is a reasonable accommodation that may be required if the employee is expected to be able to return to work quickly. [*Maharaj v. California Bank & Trust*, No. 2:11-cv-00315-GEB-EFB, 2012 WL 5828552 (E.D. Cal., Nov. 15, 2012); see Daniel Cafaro, *Extended FMLA Leave May Be Protected under ADA, Court Says*, Smart HR (Dec. 10, 2012). (benefitslink.com). *Kranson v. Federal Express Corp.*, No. 11-cv-05826-YGR (N.D. Cal. Oct. 1, 2012) says that holding the job open can constitute reasonable accommodation.]

However, some courts have ruled that indefinite leave is not required as a reasonable accommodation. [Kerry Notestine and Kelley Edwards, *Recent EEOC Lawsuits Highlight Importance of Adopting Comprehensive Procedures for Managing Employee Leaves*, Littler Mendelson Insights (February 2011) (benefitslink.com)]A 2012 case permits terminating an employee who is unable to give a reasonable estimate of when he or she will be able to resume all essential functions of the job. The plaintiff was a supervisor of felony offenders. The written job description included 18 essential functions, including fieldwork at the homes of persons under supervision. The plaintiff's joint problems required her to use a wheelchair. She took a long leave of absence, returned, then required additional leave for surgery. She was granted additional leave after her FMLA entitlement ended on July 5. She was terminated because she was unable to return to work at full capacity. She brought an ADA failure to accommodate/FMLA retaliation suit. The court held that a request for a leave of absence is reasonable only if the employee can estimate when he or she can resume essential duties. The plaintiff's doctor estimated that she could walk with a cane in a few weeks—but that did not mean that she would be able to perform casework. In this case, the employer prevailed largely because of the detailed job description. [*Robert v. Board of Comm'rs of Brown Cnty.*, 691 F.3d 1211 (10th Cir. 2012); see Jeff Nowak, *An "Indefinite Reprieve" of Essential Functions of Job Not a Reasonable Accommodation under the ADA*, Franczek Radelet FMLA Insights (Sept. 5, 2012) (benefitslink.com)]

## [C]  COBRA and HIPAA

An IRS Final Rule, published starting at 64 Fed. Reg. 5160 (Feb. 3, 1999), provides that merely taking FMLA leave is not a COBRA qualifying event. However, a qualifying event does occur with respect to an employee (and any dependents of the employee who are at risk of losing health coverage) who fails to return to work at the end of the FMLA leave. The typical example is a new mother who does not return to work after the end of maternity leave.

Under the Final Rule, the COBRA qualifying event occurs on the last day of the FMLA leave. The employer is not allowed to condition the COBRA election on the employee paying the EGHP back for premiums paid on his or her behalf during the leave. However, if the employer has actually terminated coverage under the group plan for the whole class of employees that the employee belonged to before the FMLA leave, continuation coverage does not have to be offered to employees who do not return from leave. The HIPAA rules jointly released in late 2004 by the Treasury, DOL, and HHS (69 Fed. Reg. 78800, Dec. 30, 2004, amending 26 C.F.R. §§ 54.9801 to .9807, 29 C.F.R. §§ 701–708, and 45 C.F.R. § 146.20) provide important new guidance on the relationship between the FMLA and HIPAA's portability rules. HIPAA's protection ends if the individual goes for 63 days or more without "creditable coverage." The 2004 rule holds that a period of FMLA leave when the person on leave has not continued group health coverage does not count toward the 63-day period for the person on leave or his or her dependents.

The Northern District of Georgia dismissed a suit charging a Third-Party Administrator (TPA) with improperly giving information from the plaintiff's FMLA file, which contained medical and therapy records, to her employer. (The employer wanted the information in connection with a sex discrimination suit filed by the plaintiff, who refused to give the information directly.) The TPA's contract with the employer said that information collected under the FMLA plan would only be used to administer the plan and not for employment-related actions without the employee's authorization. The district court dismissed the HIPAA claim because the TPA was neither a covered entity nor a business associate of one—FMLA and short-term disability plans are not covered entities. [*Floyd v. SunTrust Banks, Inc.,* No. 1:10-cv-2620-RWS, 2011 WL 2441744 (N.D. Ga. June 30, 2011); see EBIA Weekly Archives, *TPA's Disclosure of FMLA File to Employer Was Not Subject to HIPAA Privacy Rule* (June 30, 2011) (benefitslink.com)]

A March 2013 case finds the TPA liable under a different legal theory. The plaintiff alleged that he submitted certification for leave from November 22–January 15, and the TPA accepted the certification but granted only four weeks of leave (about half of his request) and said he would have to provide additional medical information to extend his leave. He did not provide the information and was fired. The FMLA claim was dismissed because the TPA was not a proper defendant—but the plaintiff argued tortious interference with his employment relationship, causing his employer to fire him even though he submitted proper certification. The court held that the facts were adequate to suggest denial of meritorious leave so that the TPA could reduce FMLA leave and enhance its own profits. [*Arango v. Work & Well Inc.*, No. 11 C 1525, 2013 U.S. Dist. LEXIS 35904 (N.D. Ill. Mar. 15, 2013); see Jeff Nowak, *Court Rules That Third Party Administrators Can Be Held Liable for FMLA-Related Violations*, Franczek Radelet FMLA Insights (Mar. 18, 2013) (benefitslink.com)]

In an FMLA termination case, where the employer said that the employee abused leave by vacationing in Mexico and the plaintiff said that she had to take care of her husband when his surgeon recommended recuperating in a warm climate, the employer sought discovery of the plaintiff's and husband's medical records. The plaintiff's attorney objected, so the employer narrowed the request to information about the surgery. The plaintiff argued that her husband's medical records were not only protected by HIPAA, but were not relevant because he was not a party to the suit. The district court agreed and entered a protective order, permitting disclosure of the husband's condition only for the time between his back injury and the plaintiff's termination. The employer was forbidden to use the information for any non-litigation purposes, and ordered to return or destroy the information after conclusion of the suit. [*Tavares v. Lawrence & Mem'l Hosp.*, No. 3:11-CV-770 (CSH), 2013 U.S. Dist. LEXIS 48655 (D. Conn. Apr. 3, 2012); see Wolters Kluwer Law & Business News Center, *Husband's Medical Records Must Be Disclosed To Former Employer In Employee's Lawsuit Based On FMLA* (Nov. 2, 2012) (benefitslink.com)]

## [D]  Cafeteria Plans

The IRS published final regulations, effective October 17, 2001, applicable for cafeteria plan years beginning on or after January 1, 2002, explicating the FMLA obligations of cafeteria plans. [See T.D. 8966, R.I.N. 1545-AT47, 66 Fed. Reg. 52676]

The employer must offer coverage under any group health plan as long as the employee is on paid or unpaid leave, on the same conditions as coverage would have been provided if the employee had continued to work during the leave period.

When the employee is on unpaid FMLA leave, the employer must either allow the employee to revoke the coverage or continue coverage but stop contributing premiums to the plan. The employer can then maintain the coverage by taking over both the employer and the employee share of the premium. The employer can recover the employee share of contributions when the employee returns from the leave. If the employee does not return, 29 C.F.R. § 825.213(a) permits the employer to recover both the employer and the employee shares of the premium from the employee. However, an employee who directed that premium payments be discontinued cannot be required to make contributions until after the end of unpaid leave.

## [E]    Fair Labor Standards Act

A 1998 Opinion Letter from the Department of Labor [Opinion Letter #89 (1998)] says that salaried workers who are exempt from the FLSA (and therefore are not entitled to overtime pay) are not entitled to FLSA protection merely because their employer docks their paychecks to reflect unpaid FMLA leave, even though pay deductions for absence are more characteristic of FLSA-covered wage workers than of "exempts."

## [F]    USERRA

Under the Uniformed Services Employment and Reemployment Rights Act [38 U.S.C. §§ 4301 *et seq.*] (USERRA), the Department of Labor indicated in mid-2002 that National Guard members and reservists who are called to active duty, and then released from active duty and return to their civilian jobs, are entitled to count their active duty service toward the 1,250 hour "work" requirement for FMLA eligibility. See § 1.18[A]. See § 31.01[A] for discussion of FMLA rights of the families of servicemembers: leave may be available either to assist the servicemember with deployment or return to civilian life, or to care for a sick or injured servicemember.

## [G]    State and Local Paid Leave Laws

California was the first state to require paid leave, under S.B. 1661 (2002), effective for leave taken on or after July 1, 2004. Eligible employees (caring for a newborn or newly adopted child or a family member—including a domestic partner—with a serious health condition) can access up to six weeks' paid leave per twelve-month period, under the Family Temporary Disability Insurance program. The leave must run concurrently with FMLA leave and its state equivalent—it does not increase leave entitlement, it merely establishes some circumstances under which leave must be paid. The program is completely funded by deductions from employees' salary; employers are not required to contribute. Eligible workers can receive up to 55% of their wages.

New Jersey's Family Leave Insurance Law, also known as the Paid Leave Act, took effect July 1, 2009. Covered employers (there is no minimum number of employees) must provide up to six weeks of paid family leave, or 42 days of intermittent leave in any 12-month period, so covered employees can care for a sick family member (employee's child, spouse, domestic partner, civil union partner, parent with serious health condition, or child born or adopted within the previous year)—but not for the employee's own serious health condition. The employee receives two-thirds of his or her weekly pay, subject to a statutory maximum. [Mintz, Levin, Cohn, Ferris, Glovsky and Popeo, P.C. Labor and Benefits Alert: *Employers Must Provide Paid Leave to New Jersey Employees*

*Effective July 1, 2009* (June 23, 2009) (benefitslink.com)] A Connecticut statute passed in May 2011 and taking effect January 1, 2012 requires service businesses with 50 or more employees to allow service workers (i.e., hourly non-exempt employees) to accrue paid sick leave. Covered workers can use up to 40 hours of accrued leave in any year for a serious illness, caregiving for a spouse or child, or needs related to family violence or sexual assault. [Connecticut S.B. 913; see Jason Stanevich and Jennai Williams, Littler Mendelsohn ASAP, *Connecticut is First State to Mandate Paid Sick Leave for Service Workers* (June 2011) (benefitslink .com); AP, *Connecticut Becomes First State Requiring Paid Sick Time,* WSJ.com (July 5, 2011)]

The National Conference of State Legislatures reported that in 2011, 20 states introduced bills dealing with family leave—but only four bills passed, leaving California and New Jersey as the only two states with a general requirement of paid family leave. California requires group health coverage to be maintained while employees are on maternity leave (S. 299, enacted October 5, 2011). North Dakota doubled the amount of family leave (from 40 to 80 hours) available to state employees (Laws 2011 Chapter 435, signed April 26, 2011). Although Washington passed a law calling for paid family leave, its effective date has been delayed twice, now until 2015 (S. 5091, enacted May 25, 2011). Wisconsin passed a bill forbidding local government from requiring employers to provide paid leave: Act 2011-16, enacted May 5, 2011. [National Conference of State Legislatures, *2011 Family Leave Legislation,* <http://www.ncsl.org/issues-research/labor/2011-family-leave-legislation.aspx> (undated; as of March 31, 2013, the document remained on the Website and had not been updated)]

## § 38.07 NOTIFYING THE EMPLOYER

No one schedules an emergency, of course. However, treatment for some serious health conditions is scheduled in advance (e.g., elective surgery). Section 2612(e) requires the employee to give at least 30 days' notice before leave based on the expected due date of a baby, or the expected placement date for adoption or foster care. If the date of birth or placement is less than 30 days from the time the employee decides to apply for FMLA leave, the employee must give as much notice as is practicable.

The FMLA imposes a duty on employees taking leave based on planned medical treatment to make reasonable efforts to schedule the treatment in the way that causes the least disruption to the employer (as long as this does not endanger the sick person's health). The employee should provide at least 30 days' notice before the leave is scheduled to begin—but if the need for the treatment becomes known less than 30 days in advance, the employee must provide as much notice as is practicable.

## § 38.08   CERTIFICATION OF HEALTH CARE LEAVE

Employers have the right, under 29 U.S.C. § 2613, to require employees to prove that their request for medical leave is supported by a health care provider. This process is called certification. Employees have a duty to furnish the employer with a copy of the certification document, in a timely manner.

FMLA regulations require the employee to return the medical certification form to the employer within 15 calendar days of receiving the blank form, unless there are circumstances that prevent the employee from submitting the form despite diligent good faith efforts: see 29 C.F.R. § 825.305(b). Before taking adverse action against the employee based on failure to return the certification, the employer must make sure that it has notified the employee of the need to return the form and has inquired if anything prevented the return. FMLA expert Jeff Nowak recommends sending a letter to the employee as soon as the fifteenth calendar day passes, offering assistance if the employee needs help completing the form and setting a firm seven-day deadline to receive the form. A telephone call (documented by the employer) should follow if the form is not received. If the employee fails to provide the certification, FMLA leave can be denied after the fifteenth day until certification is received, and days after Day 15 can be treated as unexcused absences. 29 C.F.R. § 825.313(b) says that leave is not FMLA leave if the employee never returns the certification; Nowak reads this to mean that the entire absence, from the first day, is not FMLA leave. [Jeff Nowak, *FMLA FAQ: How Do Employers Count Unexcused Absences When FMLA Medical Certification is Not Returned?*, Franczek Radelet FMLA Insights (Oct. 11, 2012) (benefitslink.com)]

A mid-2013 case from the District Court for the Eastern District of Wisconsin involves an employee who provided medical documentation that he suffered from the serious health condition of depression, with periodic flare-ups that would prevent him from working. His doctor estimated he would have about four episodes in a six-month period, lasting two to five days apiece. What actually happened was that Hansen had 10 episodes in three months. His employer denied several leave requests and terminated him for attendance violations, on the grounds that he used up the leave approved under his medical certification. The district court denied summary judgment for the employer in Hansen's FMLA interference/retaliation suit. FMLA expert Jeff Nowak said that the employer made many mistakes. Estimates of future leave requirements are not enforceable. Once there was an initial medical certification on file, the employer's only recourse was to obtain recertification (which is permitted when there is a substantial change in the frequency or duration of absences). But Hansen's employer did not seek recertification; it contacted Hansen's doctor improperly, and merely asked the doctor to confirm the previous certification, when it should have asked for a medical opinion that the ongoing absences were caused by Hansen's serious medical condition. The employer should have given the doctor a new form to complete, explaining whether Hansen's pattern of absences was consistent with his health condition and need for leave. However, the only time the employer is permitted to contact the health care provider directly is when it believes that the employee submitted a falsified certification. [*Hansen v. Fincantieri Marine Grp.*, No. 12-C-032 (E.D. Wis. June 14, 2013); see Jeff Nowak, *Employee Fired for Absences Exceeding His Certification Can Raise a Viable FMLA Claim*, Francezk Radelet FMLA Insights (June 20, 2013) (benefitslink.com)]

The FMLA regulations say that the requirement of "continuing treatment by a health care provider" can be satisfied with at least three days of incapacitation, but they do not indicate whether medical testimony is required. A 2010 Third Circuit case holds that the employee's own testimony about the length of incapacitation, in conjunction with medical evidence, can be used to prove eligibility. The Third Circuit held that some medical evidence is required; the employee's unsupported testimony is not enough. The plaintiff was fired for violating the employer's policy requiring a call-in on sick days. The employer said that she did not qualify for FMLA leave because of the lack of proper notice, and because she did not prove three days of incapacitation. The Third Circuit remanded the case to the district court for further proceedings. [*Schaar v. Lehigh Valley Health Servs., Inc.*, 598 F.3d 156 (3d Cir. 2010); see Rebecca Moore, *Employee's Own Testimony Can Help Prove FMLA Eligibility*, plansponsor.com (Mar. 16, 2010)]

## § 38.09  DISCLOSURE TO EMPLOYEES

Employers have an obligation to post the standard EEOC notice to inform employees of their rights under the FMLA. Failure to do so can result in a civil penalty of up to $100 per offense. [29 U.S.C. § 2619] The notice, which must be at least 8½ × 11", can be obtained from the local office of the DOL Wage and Hour Division, or can be enlarged and copied from 29 C.F.R. Part 825, Appendix C. Employers who employ a significant number of people who are literate in a language other than English must also post a translation of the notice into that language.

In a recent Third Circuit case, the plaintiff was fired four days after calling in before her shift to say that she was in the emergency room accompanying her mother. Her supervisor merely entered "sick mom" in the log without additional explanation. The Third Circuit held that, while the plaintiff did not provide enough information to indicate that leave was required to care for her mother's serious health condition, the employer had an obligation to inquire, and the timing of her termination raised an inference of FMLA interference. [*Lichtenstein v. University of Pittsburgh Med. Ctr.* 691 F.3d 294 (3d Cir. 2012); see Jeff Nowak, *When Has an Employee Provided Sufficient Notice of the Need for FMLA Leave?*, Franczek Radelet PC FMLA Insights (Sept. 13, 2012) (benefitslink.com)]

The Sixth Circuit held that an employer that did not explain how it calculated FMLA benefits could not terminate an employee for violating the policy.

Leave was approved from April 27–June 27, 2005 for a non-work-related shoulder injured. The employee's doctor cleared him to return to work on June 13, 2005. The employer asked why he did not return to work. He said he would return on June 27; his shoulder was still painful. He came to work on June 17, submitting a doctor's note supporting an extension of leave until July 18. He was fired, because the company treated all absences since June 13 as unexcused, so he exceeded the firing level of absences. The Sixth Circuit said that he was vulnerable to being fired if the company calculated backwards from the date of using leave, but not if the company allowed 12 weeks of leave per calendar year. But, because the company failed to disclose its calculation method, it was unlawful to fire the plaintiff. The court awarded liquidated damages, more than $312,000 in back pay and attorneys' fees. [*Thom v. American Standard*, 666 F.3d 968 (6th Cir. 2012); Judy Greenwald, *Employer Did Not Communicate FMLA Policy and Cannot Fire Worker: Appeals Court*, Business Insurance (benefitslink.com)]

Companies that have employee handbooks must include FMLA information in the handbook. Even if there is no handbook, employees who actually request leave are entitled to a written explanation of their rights. Employees must be notified, e.g.,

- That the requested leave reduces the employee's "bank" of FMLA leave for the year;

- Whether the employer requires medical certification of the serious health condition; consequences if the certification is not provided;

- The fact that employees who are entitled to paid leave have a right to substitute paid leave for FMLA leave; the conditions under which the employer will substitute paid leave on its own initiative;

- The employee's right to be reinstated in a comparable job after returning from leave;

- The method for the employee to pay health premiums while he or she is on FMLA leave;

- Disclosure of the employee's obligation to reimburse the employer for premiums if the employee does not return to work after the leave;

- Any requirements for proving fitness for duty before returning to work;

- (For key employees) limitations on the right to reinstatement.

## § 38.10 ADMINISTRATIVE REQUIREMENTS

The Department of Labor's investigative authority under the FMLA is the same as its authority under FLSA § 11(a), including subpoena power. Employers have a duty to make and retain records showing FMLA compliance. The general rule is that the DOL can only require employers and employee plans to submit books and records once a year, unless the DOL is investigating a charge made by an employee, or has reason to believe that there has been an FMLA violation. [29 U.S.C. § 2616]

## § 38.11 FMLA ENFORCEMENT

### [A] Litigation and Arbitration

A mid-2011 article suggested that the FMLA's specific rules might support class actions even in the post-*Dukes* environment. For example, former AT&T employees Beard and Guerrero charged AT&T with treating FMLA-covered absences as occurrences under the attendance plan and subjecting employees who take FMLA leave to harassment, denial of promotion, and termination. The plaintiffs proposed a narrowly defined class of non-managerial employees plus first-level managers of call centers who took FMLA leave and were in the lowest 30% vis-a-vis attendance. In another case, current and former Sysco employees sued in Chicago, charging that the FMLA was violated by excessive demands for medical information in FMLA certification and adverse employment action, including termination, for failure to provide the information. [Jeff Nowak, *Life After Wal-Mart v. Dukes: Is the FMLA the New Breeding Ground for Class Actions?*, Franczek Radelet FMLA Insights (Aug. 9, 2011) (benefitslink.com)]

The D.C. Circuit reinstated part of a legal secretary's suit alleging FMLA interference with leave when she was ill (she suffered from Graves' Disease, fibromyalgia, and depression) and to care for her husband, who had cancer. The D.C. Circuit said that it was only necessary to prove that her FMLA rights had been infringed, not that she was denied leave entirely. When the plaintiff's FMLA leave ran out, she asked the HR manager what her job status was. She was offered a word processing job, but could not take it because she had trouble typing. She asked for a receptionist's job that was being held open for another employee on disability leave. The plaintiff was denied the opportunity to transfer, and was eventually fired. [*McFadden v. Ballard Spahr Andrews & Ingersoll, LLP*, 611 F.3d 1 (D.C. Cir. 2010); see Fred Schneyer, *Court Reinstates FMLA Claim Against Law Firm*, plansponsor.com (July 1, 2010)]

It is very common for employment discrimination plaintiffs to charge retaliation, either as their sole cause of action, or because they say that the employer retaliated against them for making an internal complaint or filing charges with an anti-discrimination agency. The FMLA is no exception.

A law firm associate, Ayanna, used paternity and FMLA leave to care for children and his mentally ill wife after birth of his second child; four months later his job was terminated. His December 2010 complaint said that men at the Dechert firm were required to satisfy stereotypes that men do not take care of their families. Summary judgment was denied on the FMLA claim because the judge held that a reasonable jury could find that he received a low rating and was fired for "personal issues" because he had taken leave. There was an issue of fact as to whether he was denied work in retaliation for taking leave or whether there was an agreement he could reduce hours during a temporary work assignment in Germany. However, the district court had previously dismissed his state sex discrimination claim for lack of evidence that he was fired for being a male caregiver. His state-law handicap discrimination claim was dismissed in January 2012 on the grounds that the district court did not recognize claims by non-handicapped employees based on their association with a handicapped person. Just before trial was scheduled to begin in Ayanna's FMLA retaliation case, a confidential settlement was reached. [*Ayanna v. Dechert*, Civil Case 10-12155-NMG (D. Mass. settlement 2013); see Sheri Qualters, *Dechert and Former Associate Settle "Macho Culture" Retaliation Case*, Nat'l L.J. (Feb. 11, 2013) (law.com)]

The Seventh Circuit rejected the possibility of suing under the FMLA on a theory that a supervisor's actions made the employee's existing health condition worse. The Seventh Circuit held that the cause of an injury is irrelevant under the FMLA, and refused to grant front pay. The alleged conduct that caused his condition to worsen occurred after his second unprotected leave (his FMLA entitlement had been used up during his first leave; the second leave was provided voluntarily by his employer, as a courtesy). If retaliation occurred, it happened after he was no longer eligible under the FMLA. The court said that, although in general stress is bad for health, the FMLA does not cover all health-related issues. [*Breneisen v. Motorola*, 656 F.3d 701 (7th Cir. 2011); see William Hoffman, *7th Cir. Rejects FMLA Claim that Supervisor Worsened Illness*, Thompson Smart HR Share Blog (Sept. 22, 2011) (benefitslink .com); Michael Mishlove, *Employee Whose Boss Gave Him Heartburn Has No Remedy Under the Family Medical Leave Act*, The GSH 60-Second Memo (Nov. 2, 2011) (benefitslink.com)]

The FMLA ban on retaliation can be invoked by a worker who claims he or she suffered retaliation for asking for FMLA leave; it is not required that leave was actually granted. The Third Circuit said that employers should not be given an incentive to fire employees for exercising their legal rights. The Third Circuit sent the case back to the District Court, for a jury to determine whether the defendant had constructive notice of the hours that the plaintiff worked at home (and which put her over the 1,250 hour mark for eligibility under the FMLA). But the court rejected the plaintiff's argument that she would be entitled to FMLA leave if the employer failed to advise her about the eligibility rules, because that argument was based on a DOL regulation that was rejected by the courts and that the agency had to revise. [*Erdman v. Nationwide Ins. Co.*, 582 F.3d 500 (3d Cir. 2009); see Shannon P. Duffy, *3rd Circuit Ruling Broadens Protection of FMLA*, The Legal Intelligencer (Sept. 24, 2009) (law.com)]

A retaliation claim may even be sustainable if the plaintiff was not eligible for FMLA coverage. The Eastern District of Pennsylvania permitted an FMLA retaliation claim to proceed under the following circumstances The plaintiff, a nursing assistant, said that she was fired for taking intermittent leave for her son's serious health condition after the employer granted her leave request. After granting the request, the employer discovered that the plaintiff was not eligible for FMLA leave because she worked less than 1,250 hours the year before. Nevertheless, the suit was allowed to proceed because the employer led her to believe that she was FMLA-eligible. [*Medley v. County of Montgomery*, No. 12-1995, 2012 U.S. Dist. LEXIS 99006 (E.D. Pa. July 17, 2012; County motion for summary judgment denied Jan. 25, 2013; CIVIL ACTION NO. 12-1995, 2013 U.S. Dist. LEXIS 10580, 96 Empl. Prac. Dec. (CCH) P44,743). See Daniel Cafaro, *Employer 'Mistake' Leads to FMLA Retaliation Claim*, Smart HR (July 26, 2012) (benefitslink.com).]

The Seventh Circuit allowed an FMLA retaliation case to proceed to the jury when the AMA changed its plan to eliminate one job for budgetary reasons and instead eliminated the job of a veteran employee who had applied for FMLA leave. The Seventh Circuit held that referring to FMLA leave in an e-mail recommending the employee's termination could be deemed retaliation and a reasonable jury could conclude that he was fired for requesting leave. [*Shaffer v. AMA*, 662 F.3d 439 (7th Cir. 2011); see Jeff Nowak, *Supervisor's Inadvisable Email Creates Basis for FMLA Claim*, Franczek Radelet FMLA Insights (Oct. 31, 2011) (benefitslink.com); Rebecca Moore, *Employer Email Could Show FMLA Bias*, plansponsor.com (Nov. 1, 2011)]

See also *Richardson v. Monitronics Int'l*, 434 F.3d 327 (5th Cir. 2005) holding that although mixed-motive retaliation cases are possible—if the employer's action was at least partially motivated by retaliation for exercise of FMLA rights—the employer can win by showing that there was cause to fire the employee even if FMLA rights had never been used. *Mauder v. Metro. Transit Auth.* [446 F.3d 574 (5th Cir. 2006)] holds that it was not retaliation to terminate an employee who was already on a corrective action plan, and Type II diabetes and medication side effects causing uncontrollable diarrhea did not constitute a "serious health condition."

Not only do employers face FMLA suits from employees or groups of employees; they can also be sued by the Department of Labor, which can sue on behalf of employees to recover the same kind of damages employees would get. If the DOL wins an FMLA case, the damages got to the employee, not to the government agency (unless it is impossible to locate the employees within three years). [See 29 U.S.C. § 2617(b)] The Secretary of Labor has the power to investigate and try to resolve complaints of FMLA violations, to the same degree as investigations and resolutions of violations of FLSA §§ 6 and 7. But employees are no longer allowed to bring FMLA suits once the DOL starts a suit. [29 U.S.C. § 2617(a)(4)]

FMLA claims can become the subject of arbitration as well as litigation. The Seventh Circuit found that where a Collective Bargaining Agreement included broad anti-discrimination language, the arbitrator did not exceed his powers by interpreting the FMLA as well as the CBA. [*Butler Mfg. Co. v. United Steelworkers*, 336 F.3d 629 (7th Cir. 2003)]

## [B]  Releases

The 2009 revision of the FMLA rules provides that, while employees cannot waive FMLA claims that arise in the future, if a claim has already arisen, a release does not require DOL or court supervision to be valid. Previously, the Fifth Circuit held that public policy favors enforcement of waivers, and an employee who keeps the money paid for a release ratifies the release. [*Faris v. Williams WPC-I, Inc.*, 332 F.3d 316 (5th Cir. 2003)], whereas the Fourth Circuit required DOL supervision of all FMLA releases, whether retrospective or prospective. [*Taylor v. Progress Energy Inc.*, 493 F.3d 454 (4th Cir. 2007)]

## [C]  Damages

If the employees win, 29 U.S.C. § 2617(a) provides that the court can order damages equal to the wages and benefits that the employee lost as a result of the violation. Even employees who have not lost compensation can receive damages to compensate them for financial losses (such as costs of hiring someone to care for sick relatives), but damages of this type are limited to 12 weeks' salary for the employee-plaintiff.

Furthermore, winning FMLA plaintiffs can receive double damages: their damages (plus interest) and also an equal amount of liquidated damages. However, if the employer can prove that it acted in good faith and reasonably believed that it was in compliance with the FMLA, the court has discretion not to order double damages.

In a case of first impression, the Ninth Circuit ruled that FMLA front pay, which is awarded either in lieu of reinstatement, or to make up for compensation that was lost between the court's judgment and the plaintiff's reinstatement, is an equitable remedy. Therefore, the amount is determined by the judge, not the jury, and the judge also decides if reinstatement is practical. (The Fourth, Fifth, and Tenth Circuits had already ruled that the judge determines if front pay is available and, if so, how much.) Under the FMLA, liquidated damages are mandatory unless the employer proves both its good faith and that it had reasonable grounds for believing it acted lawfully. However, liquidated damages are not automatically payable in every case in which front pay is ordered, because it is possible for an employer to act in good faith, but for reinstatement to be impractical because of the friction caused by the plaintiff's extensive usage of FMLA leave. [*Traxler v. Multnomah County*, 596 F.3d 1007 (9th Cir. 2010)]

An employee who has received an FMLA back pay award is not precluded from receiving liquidated damages for retaliation. The Tenth Circuit held that wages that are temporarily lost but restored after a significant delay must be treated as "lost or denied" for purposes of calculating FMLA liquidated damages. [*Jordan v. U.S. Postal Service*, 379 F.3d 1196 (10th Cir. 2004)]

Although most of the remedies are equitable ones, the Southern District of Georgia allows jury trials in FMLA cases, because they are allowed in Fair Labor Standards Act cases, and the two statutes contain many similar provisions. [*Helmly v. Stone Container Corp.*, 957 F. Supp. 1274 (S.D. Ga. 1997)] So does the Sixth Circuit. [*Frizzell v. Southwestern Motor Freight*, 154 F.3d 641 (6th Cir. 1998)]

In addition to money damages, courts in FMLA cases can award the appropriate equitable relief for the case, including hiring, reinstatement, and promotion. FMLA winners are entitled to receive reasonable costs, defined to include attorneys' fees and expert witness fees. Section 2617(a)(3) makes this automatic for plaintiffs who win, not a matter of discretion for the court.

This is not true of all federal statutes. Some of them do not allow attorneys' fee awards at all, others allow a fee award to any prevailing party (plaintiff or defendant) or leave it up to the court whether an award should be made, or limit fee awards to cases in which the losing party's conduct has been outrageous.

# PART VIII

# PROCEDURE FOR HANDLING DISCRIMINATION CHARGES

# CHAPTER 39

# WRONGFUL TERMINATION AND AT-WILL EMPLOYMENT

## § 39.01   INTRODUCTION

Employees always have the right to quit their jobs, no matter how inconvenient their departure may be for the employer (although employment contracts can require a certain amount of notice, can obligate the employee to compensate the employer for economic loss caused by a resignation, and can impose reasonable restrictions on re-employment and use of the employer's proprietary information).

The employer's right to fire an employee is not so simple and clear-cut. Some employees have written contracts that specify the conditions under which they can be terminated. Unionized employees are covered by collective bargaining agreements (CBAs). In CBAs or individual employment contracts, if the agreement sets out a termination procedure (such as a warning, then a chance for the employee to respond to charges, a suspension, and then termination), then it is a breach of contract to terminate the employee without following the procedure.

Employers may also find that they are subject to responsibilities under implied contracts. The employer's written documents that it issues such as the employee handbook or even its oral statements are deemed to constitute a legally enforceable contract, then the employer will have to abide by that contract.

A supervisor is a representative of the employer when he or she is acting in the scope of his or her job, in a situation in which he or she is authorized to act. The supervisor's conduct will then have legal implications for the employer. A supervisor's negligence or outrageous conduct (such as abusive treatment of an employee that results in emotional distress) can be imputed to the employer. In many instances, the supervisor will *not* be personally liable, e.g., under federal and state antidiscrimination statutes or for inducing a breach of contract.

Even if termination is justifiable, however, it must be carried out in a reasonable manner, avoiding intentional infliction of emotional distress. The employer must also avoid both actionable defamation (destructive false statements) and depriving another employer of the accurate information needed to make a rational hiring decision.

"Constructive discharge" is the legal concept that an employee who responds to intolerable conditions by quitting is entitled to be treated as if he or she had been fired, because the employer's conduct was the equivalent of a discharge. To prove constructive discharge, the employee does not have to prove that the employer intended to force a resignation, only that it was reasonably foreseeable that a reasonable employee would quit under the same circumstances. The Supreme Court's mid-2004 decision, *Pennsylvania State Police v. Suders*, 542 U.S. 129 [(2004)] makes it clear that the test of constructive discharge is objective, not subjective, based on the behavior of the hypothetical reasonable employee rather than the personal reactions of the plaintiff. In a pregnancy discrimination/FMLA case, the Sixth Circuit ruled that a threat of demotion coupled with other factors can constitute constructive discharge. [*Saroli v. Automation & Modular Components, Inc.*, 405 F.3d 446 (6th Cir. 2005)]

The fact situation is not one that is likely to be repeated frequently, but it should be noted that at the end of 2004, the U.S. Supreme Court ruled that it did not violate a police officer's First Amendment or Fourteenth Amendment rights to fire him for selling videos (and police paraphernalia) on the Internet. The videos featured the officer in police-related pornographic scenarios. The Supreme Court held that he was not expressing himself on matters of public concern or commenting on police department operations. [*City of San Diego v. John Roe*, 543 U.S. 77 (2004)]

The vast majority of employees do not have a written contract. They are legally defined as "at-will" employees who work "at the will of the employer." However, at-will employers are not permitted to discharge employees for reasons that violate an antidiscrimination statute, or for reasons contrary to public policy.

Employees who want to bring suit under federal antidiscrimination laws (Title VII, the ADA, the ADEA, and the FMLA) have to satisfy elaborate procedural requirements. [See Chapters 40 and 41] Employees who charge the employer with wrongful termination merely have to go to state court and file a complaint. This is much easier to do, so employers may find themselves fighting on two fronts, or may be able to raise the argument that a wrongful termination case should be dismissed because the employee was required—but failed—to use the procedure for a discrimination suit.

## § 39.02  EMPLOYEE TENURE

Some state court cases consider it an implied promise of continuing employment once an employee has worked for the employer for a long time (say, a decade or more), and a number of states impose an implied covenant of good faith and fair dealing in the employment context.

The Connecticut Court of Appeals ruled that it is permissible to terminate an at-will employee even before work begins: either side can terminate the relationship at any time for any reason, not conditioned on work actually beginning. (The plaintiff was hired for a sales job and asked to submit references; when he reported for work, he was told that there were issues about his references.) He sued, claiming a breach of the employment contract and the contract to hire him, charging that the offer letter constituted negligent misrepresentation. [*Petitte v. DSL.net, Inc.*, 102 Conn. App. 363 (Conn. App. 2007); see Rebeca Moore, *Court Upholds Firing Before Work Commenced*, plansponsor.com (Aug. 22, 2007)]

New York's highest court ruled that an at-will employee can be fired at any time unless there is a statutory ban, an express limitation in an individual employment contract, or the firing reflected a constitutionally impermissible rationale. Therefore, a group of five financial services money managers who claimed fraudulent inducement because they were not informed of the merger that led to their termination could not sustain a fraudulent inducement claim. [*Smalley v. Dreyfus Corp.*, 10 N.Y.3d 55 (2008); see Fred Schneyer, *NY Court: "At-Will" Workers Can Be Fired Anytime*, plansponsor.com (Feb. 14, 2008); Joel Stashenko, *Terminated At-Will Workers Lose Bid to Press Tort Action Against Dreyfus Corp.*, N.Y.L.J. (Feb. 14, 2008) (law.com)]

The New York Court of Appeals held in mid-2012 that a hedge fund compliance officer who was fired after confronting his boss about allegedly improper trades was an at-will employee not entitled to common-law protection against wrongful termination. Compliance was only part of his job, and the court held that his regulatory and ethical obligations as compliance officer were not so intertwined with his employee responsibilities for separation to be impossible. [*Sullivan v. Harnisch*, 19 N.Y.3d 259 (N.Y. 2012); see John Caher, *At-Will Doctrine Denies Protection for Compliance Head*, N.Y.L.J. (May 9, 2012) (law.com)]

## § 39.03   PROMISSORY ESTOPPEL

The theory of "promissory estoppel" is sometimes decisive in employment cases. The theory is that the employer's promise to the employee estops (precludes) the employer from disavowing that promise, often because the employee has "undergone detrimental reliance" (suffered in some way after relying on a statement or implication from the employer).

The classic example is a top executive recruited from another company, who gives up a high salary and stock options, has expenses of relocation, and then is fired shortly after taking up the new job. However, employees who allege oral promises of permanent employment may find that their claims are barred by a legal doctrine, the Statute of Frauds that requires contracts lasting a year or more to be in writing if they are to be enforceable.

## § 39.04   PUBLIC POLICY

### [A]   Generally

A whole line of cases permits employees to sue when they are fired for a reason contrary to the public policy of the state. In other words, it is unlawful to fire an employee for doing something that is acceptable or even admirable. For instance, no matter how inconvenient the timing is for the employer, it is not permitted to fire an employee for serving jury duty.

The First Circuit ruled that for a safety engineer to inform his supervisors about potential overtime violations with respect to the security guards he supervised was part of his job duties. Doing so was not protected activity under the Fair Labor Standards Act, so firing him for raising the issue could not be retaliation in violation of the FLSA. [*Claudio-Gotay v. Becton Dickinson Caribe Ltd.*, 375 F.3d 99 (1st Cir. 2004)]

It violates ERISA § 510 to fire an employee merely to prevent access to pension or welfare benefits. [See Chapter 15]

The First Circuit joined the Fifth, Seventh, and Ninth Circuits: In a retaliatory discharge case, the plaintiff must show specific intent to interfere with ERISA benefits. The courts have held that the contrary result would give every discharged employee who had ever exercised benefit rights the opportunity to sue his or her employer. In the First Circuit case, a software engineer was notified that he was one of about 500 employees about to be let go due to a RIF. A week before the scheduled date of the layoff, plaintiff Kouvchinov applied for short-term disability benefits for depression. He received the benefits, and then found another job. He lost the second job for unethical conduct (his new employer was informed that he was working while continuing to collect disability benefits). He brought suit under ERISA § 510, for interference with ERISA benefits. [*Kouvchinov v. Parametric Tech.*, 537 F.3d 62 (1st Cir. 2008); see Ross Runkel, *Workplace Prof Blog: 1st Cir.: Intent Required in ERISA Retaliatory Discharge Case*, <http://www.typepad.com/t/trackback/89778/32252014> (Aug. 11, 2008)]

Certiorari was denied in a Third Circuit decision holding that it did not violate ERISA § 510 to fire an HR director for her unsolicited comments to management about what she perceived to be ERISA violations (such as misrepresentation) in the company health plan. The Second and Fourth Circuits have ruled similarly—that protection under § 510 is limited to testimony in a formal inquiry such as a federal investigation. However, the Fifth and Ninth Circuits agree with the DOL, that informal, unsolicited comments are protected. [*Edwards v. A.H. Cornell & Son, Inc.*, 610 F.3d 217 (3d Cir. 2010), *cert. denied*, 131 S. Ct. 1604 (2011); see Jewell Lim Esposito, *Companies Can Safely Fire Someone Who Alleges Internal ERISA Violations*, Employee Benefits Unplugged Blog (Mar. 23, 2011) (benefitslink.com)]

The Eighth Circuit affirmed summary judgment for the employer in a case where the plaintiff signed an employment contract describing him as an at-will employee. He also received an employee manual that covered acceptable conduct and termination. According to the plaintiff, he was harassed by his supervisors; the supervisors said that he did a poor job. He was fired for intentional falsification of delivery records. He said that this was pretextual, and the real reason was that he complained of harassment. He said that his termination violated public policy, because retaliation against those who make harassment complaints violates public policy. The Eighth Circuit disagreed: there was no violation of a substantial public policy expressed in a statute or judicial decision. Alleging that a company violated its own policies is a contract claim. [*Semple v. Federal Express Corp.*, 566 F.3d 788 (8th Cir. 2009)]

Thom DeFranco worked for StorageTek in Colorado. In 2004, he agreed to take a two-year overseas assignment. He claimed that three StorageTek employees verbally assured him that on his return he would have a permanent job. He signed a "secondment agreement" identifying him as an at-will employee. In 2005, StorageTek was acquired by Sun. DeFranco alleged that he was promised permanent employment with Sun, but he was RIFed in 2006. He sued for breach of contract and promissory estoppel. The Tenth Circuit ruled for the defendants: he acknowledged his at-will employment status. The Second Agreement stated that a job was not guaranteed on his return. After the acquisition, Sun sent him a memo stating that DeFranco was an at-will employee, and the memo itself superseded any promises made by StorageTek. DeFranco refused to sign this memo. The Tenth Circuit held that he did not prove any special services, so he was an at-will employee whose job could be terminated at any time. [*DeFranco v. Storage Tech. Corp.*, 622 F.3d 1296 (10th Cir. Oct. 20, 2010)]

A 2010 Sixth Circuit case was brought by an employee who charged that he was fired for refusing to participate in a market allocation conspiracy in the packaged ice industry. (His former employer plead guilty to antitrust charges and agreed to pay a $9 million fine, and three executives plead guilty to individual charges.) He said that he was blackballed and was unable to find another job since exposing the conspiracy. The Sixth Circuit ruled that he was not covered by the Crime Victims' Rights Act: although preventing a person from getting a job may be the subject of a civil action, it is neither inherently criminal nor an inherent part of the antitrust conspiracy. The plaintiff filed a separate RICO suit alleging that he was fired for refusing to participate in the scheme, and because he cooperated with federal authorities. [*In re McNulty*, 597 F.3d 344 (6th Cir. 2010); see Tresa Baldas, *6th Circuit: Whistleblower Not a* "Crime Victim" *Even if He's Been Blackballed*, Nat'l L.J. (Mar. 3, 2010) (law.com)]

Michigan has a Medical Marihuana [sic] Act that says that qualifying patients who have been issued a registry card by the state cannot be prosecuted for using medical marijuana. The state law says that qualifying patients must not be denied any right or privilege "including [ . . . ] disciplinary action by a business." However, in 2012 the Sixth Circuit held that it is not unlawful, and does not constitute wrongful termination, to fire an employee who tested positive for medical marijuana. [*Casias v. Wal-Mart Stores, Inc.*, 695 F.3d 428 (6th Cir. 2012)]

The Colorado Court of Appeals ruled in mid-2013 that, although medical and recreational marijuana are legal in Colorado, it is still lawful for businesses to fire people who test positive for marijuana. The court rejected a suit for "lawful activity" discrimination brought by a quadriplegic who is authorized to use medical marijuana. The court of appeals held that using marijuana violates federal law, so it is not a protected lawful activity. This issue is likely to arise in Arizona, Connecticut, Delaware, Maine, Nevada, and Rhode Island, because those states ban employment discrimination on the basis of medical marijuana use. [*Coats v. Dish Network*,2013 COA 62 (Colo. App. Apr. 25, 2013); see Nathan Koppel, *Legal Pot Use in Colorado Could Still Get You Fired*, WSJ.com (Apr. 25, 2013); Gregory J. Millman, *Medical Marijuana Poses Litigation Risk to Employers*,WSJ.com (Aug. 15, 2013)]

A black co-worker complained about the two Confederate flag stickers on the (white) plaintiff's toolbox. The plaintiff refused to remove the stickers, and was fired under the corporate anti-harassment policy. In 2003, the Fourth Circuit held that the workplace is not a Constitutionally protected forum for political discourse, so there was no right to display a Confederate flag within the employer's privately owned workplace, although once off the employer's premises he could display the flag on his own home or vehicle. But in 2004, the Fourth Circuit reheard the case and reversed its earlier opinion, sending the case back to the South Carolina state court (where it was originally filed, then removed on Constitutional grounds) because there was no substantial question of federal law. [*Dixon v. Coburg Dairy, Inc.*, 330 F.3d 250 (4th Cir. 2003), *rev'd*, 369 F.3d 811 (4th Cir. 2004)]

In the case of a drug company manager who said that he was fired for helping one of his subordinates fight sexual harassment by another supervisor, the First Circuit held that a reasonable jury could believe that the plaintiff, Collazo, opposed sexual harassment. Although the employer's internal inquiry cleared the alleged harasser, a plaintiff does not have to prove that the conditions he or she opposed actually violated Title VII—only that he or she had a good faith reasonable belief that they did. Management said that he was fired for poor performance and because his job was eliminated in a reorganization, but these arguments were dubious because he was not given any counseling or progressive discipline for the alleged performance problems, and he was the only employee who was terminated and not given a chance to transfer to a new job during the reorganization. [*Collazo v. Bristol-Myers Squibb Mfg. Inc.*, 617 F.3d 39 (1st Cir. Aug. 5, 2010)]

The Maryland Court of Appeals ruled in mid-2003 that it does not violate public policy to fire an employee after she tried to contact an attorney before signing off on her unfavorable performance appraisal. There is no real public policy that creates a "right to counsel" in the employment context, in the sense of the right to consult an attorney (although employees in a unionized workplace do have a right to bring a union representative to an investigatory interview that could result in discipline). [*Porterfield v. Mascari II Inc.*, 374 Md. 402 (Md. App. 2003)]

## [B]  Whistleblower Employees

The case of the "whistleblower" employee is more complex. Employees (often those who are dissatisfied for other reasons) go to the press, or file complaints with enforcement agencies, about some aspect of corporate conduct they find unsatisfactory. In some instances, firing (or taking other adverse employment action) against whistleblowers violates public policy, because in appropriate cases, whistleblowers are exposing violations of law or other improprieties.

At the end of 1998, the Supreme Court held that an action under 42 U.S.C. § 1985 (damage to person or property) can be maintained by an at-will employee who alleges that he was fired for assisting a federal criminal investigation of the employer company. [*Haddle v. Garrison*, 525 U.S. 121 (1998)]

Early in 2012, the District Court for the District of Columbia said that Stephen Shea, who had already been awarded $13.7 million for exposing Verizon's fraudulent billing scheme, was entitled to 20% of the $93.5 million settlement in the case—more than $18.8 million in total. [Mike Scarcella, *D.C. Judge Orders Government to Pay Whistleblower Millions More*, Blog of Legal Times (Feb. 24, 2012) (law.com)]

The Supreme Court ruled in 2010 that a whistleblower cannot bring a False Claims Act suit based on information that has already been disclosed in county or state reports. (Previous law said that information in congressional, federal administrative, or GAO reports is already known, and therefore cannot form the basis of a "qui tam" whistleblower action.) [*Graham County Soil & Water Conservation Dist. v. U.S. ex. Rel. Wilson*, 559 U.S. 280 (2010). See *Rockwell Int'l Corp. v. United States*, 549 U.S. 457 (2007) for the principle that the whistleblower must be the original source of the information, having direct and independent knowledge of the facts of the case. The Supreme Court extended this principle in 2011. *Schindler Elevator Corp. v. United States ex. rel. Kirk*, 131 S. Ct. 1885 (2011), ruling that releasing documents pursuant to a FOIA request is a "report" that makes the documents public, so the information in the documents will not support a whistleblower award.]

However, the health care reform act, the Patient Protection and Affordable Care Act (PPACA), Pub. L. No. 111-148, deals with the subject of whistleblower protection. It says that only federal, and not state or local disclosures, will rule out a False Claims Act qui tam action. PPACA § 1558 amends the Fair Labor Standards Act to provide that it is unlawful to discharge or discriminate (in compensation or working conditions) against anyone who has given information to the federal government or a state attorney general, testified or is about to testify, or assisted in a proceeding involving an alleged violation of the health care reform law. OSHA interim final rules were published February 22, 2013 covering complaints made by employees who say they suffered retaliation for receiving a subsidy or tax credit in connection with using a health insurance Exchange (rather than being covered by an EGHP). The general OSHA whistleblower procedures apply in this situation. [<http://www.dol.gov/find/20130222/OSHA2013.pdf>; see PLC Employee Benefits & Executive Compensation, *OSHA Rules Address Retaliation Complaint Procedures under Health Care Reform* (Feb. 25, 2013) (benefitslink.com)]

The First Circuit upheld dismissal of a suit against Federal Express brought by a driver who tried to get OSHA involved in investigating his exposure to fumes in his delivery truck. He alleged a sustained campaign of harassment after he raised the issue, but the court disagreed: there were legitimate performance problems with his work, and he was never subjected to intolerable conditions tantamount to constructive discharge. He was permitted to file OSHA complaints and take FMLA leave. It was not intolerable to have a supervisor take a "check ride" to observe his performance; in fact, during this time, the supervisor advised him of a possible tuition reimbursement that he might qualify for. [*Meuser v. Federal Express Corp.*, 564 F.3d 507 (1st Cir. 2009)]

The Department of Labor ordered the Union Pacific Railroad Co. to pay $400,000 in punitive damages, $90,315 in compensatory damages, $34,900 in attorney's fees, and more than $90,000 back pay to three employees. OSHA found that the company violated the whistleblower provisions of the Federal Railroad Safety Act by firing two employees and suspending one for reporting a work-related injury and discussing concerns about safety hazards in the workplace. The railroad was also ordered to train managers, supervisors, and employees about whistleblowers' rights. [Tara Cantore, *Union Pacific Fined for Retaliation against Whistleblowers*, plansponsor.com (Aug. 26, 2011)]

In addition to its workplace safety responsibilities, OSHA is responsible for enforcing several federal whistleblower statutes, although the Sarbanes-Oxley Act is the only one that deals with financial wrongdoing rather than health and safety.

In mid-2011, OSHA announced additional measures to strengthen whistleblower protection under 21 statutes. In 2009 and 2010, the GAO audited the whistleblower program and OSHA prepared an internal review. OSHA moved the whistleblower protection program from the Directorate of Enforcement, making it report directly to the assistant secretary of labor. OSHA hired 25 new investigators and held a national training conference in September 2011. Plans were announced to issue a new edition of the Whistleblower Investigations Manual, reflecting the statutory changes since 2003, when the previous edition was issued. [OSHA News Release 11-1136-NAT 2011US; see <http://www.whistleblowers.gov>, and *Department of Labor's OSHA Announces Measures to Improve Whistleblower Protection Program* (Aug. 1, 2011) (benefitslink.com). The internal review report was posted to <www.whistleblowers.gov/report_summary_page.html>]

The federal Sarbanes-Oxley Act [Pub. L. No. 107-204] (also discussed in this book in connection with 401(k) plans and corporate communications—notices to employees about "blackout" periods that restrict their abilities to trade their plan accounts) includes two provisions to protect whistleblowers.

In 2013, the Second Circuit clarified the standard for analyzing Sarbanes-Oxley whistleblower retaliation claims (18 U.S.C. § 1514A). J. Scott Bechtel, VP of technology commercialization for Competitive Technologies Inc., said that he was fired for saying the company should make more Sarbanes-Oxley disclosures. CTI said he was fired as part of a cost-cutting drive. He filed an OSHA whistleblower complaint. In 2005, OSHA found reasonable cause to believe CTI violated OSHA and ordered Bechtel reinstated with back pay and compensatory damages. Eventually, the ALJ dismissed Bechtel's complaint in 2011. The Second Circuit said that Bechtel had to prove by a preponderance of the evidence that he was engaged in protected activity; that CTI knew it; and that the protected activity was a contributing factor in the adverse employment action. The employer can rebut with clear and convincing evidence it would have done the same thing without protected activity. [*Bechtel v. Administrative Review Bd.*, 710

F.3d 443 (2d Cir. 2013); see Mark Hamblett, *Standard for SOX Whistleblower Retaliation Claims is Clarified*, N.Y.L.J. (Mar. 6, 2013) (law.com)]

The economic stimulus bill ARRA (American Recovery and Reinvestment Act), Pub. L. No. 111-5, includes the McCaskill Act, which gives Sarbanes-Oxley whistleblower employees the right to a jury trial. Employers that receive federal stimulus funds are required to notify employees of their rights as whistleblowers. Any employer (other than a federal agency) that receives stimulus funds is forbidden to fire, demote, or otherwise discriminate against an employee who makes disclosures to a supervisor, regulatory agency, law enforcement agency, grand jury, or court, if the information represents the employee's reasonable belief that the information proves gross mismanagement or waste of stimulus funds. [Maribeth L. Minella, *Delaware Employment Law Blog*, <http://www.delaware employmentlawblog.com/2009/02/stimulus_package_provides_for.html> (Feb. 27, 2009)]

Under § 806 of the Sarbanes-Oxley Act, 18 U.S.C. § 1514A is amended to provide that publicly traded companies are forbidden to "discharge, demote, suspend, threaten, harass, or in any other manner discriminate against an employee in the terms and conditions of employment" because the employee has engaged in any lawful act to provide information to the government or participate in an investigation of securities fraud or corporate wrongdoing. (The lawful acts condition is important—whistleblowers are not protected if they commit burglaries or hack computer systems to get this information, for example.)

Someone who believes that he or she has been discriminated against for whistleblowing can file a complaint with the Secretary of Labor; if, after 180 days, the Secretary has not issued a final decision, the whistleblower can sue in federal District Court (even if the amount in controversy is below the $75,000 usually required to get to federal court). The Sarbanes-Oxley Act provides for whatever relief is necessary to make a successful whistleblower claimant whole—i.e., compensatory damages, reinstatement with whatever seniority the person would have had without discrimination, back pay plus interest, and compensation for special damages such as attorneys' fees, expert witness fees, and costs.

Also see Sarbanes-Oxley Act § 1107, which provides for fines and/or up to 10 years' imprisonment, for knowing harmful actions, taken with intent to retaliate against someone who provided truthful information about Sarbanes-Oxley violations to any law enforcement officer. This provision covers all actions, including interference with any person's lawful employment or livelihood.

Companies can take steps to encourage employees to report internally rather than immediately contacting outside agencies. The company should have a clear reporting chain, and make sure that information is transmitted to the proper decision-maker. The reporting mechanism should be easy to use and should be explained to employees. Reports should be encouraged, because they can be instrumental in saving the company's reputation by solving problems before they become untenable. In some cases, it is worth allowing customers, suppliers, and consultants to report internally because their outsider perspective can be useful—

and they might otherwise be encouraged to seek bounties. [Alexandra Wrage, *8 Ways to Encourage Whistleblowers to Report Internally*, Compliance Insider (May 10, 2012) (law.com)]

The Second Circuit held that whistleblower claims under the Sarbanes-Oxley Act are arbitrable, rejecting the plaintiff's arguments that arbitration does not provide adequate accountability or transparency and does not furnish information that would encourage other employees to make meritorious claims of their own. [*Guyden v. Aetna Inc.*, 544 F.3d 376 (2d Cir. 2008); see Mark Hamblett, *Whistleblower Claims Arbitrable Under SOX, 2nd Circuit Determines*, N.Y.L.J. (Oct. 6, 2008) (law.com)]

The First Circuit held that an employee's allegations about improprieties in the return process were merely his opinion, and accepted his employer's argument that he was legitimately fired for poor work performance and being disruptive. In the First Circuit view, Sarbanes-Oxley whistleblowing requires an allegation of violations of SEC rules or mail, wire, securities, or bank fraud. Disagreements over corporate policy are not covered; and it is not unlawful for a company to adopt policies that it believes further its efficiency. [*Day v. Staples Inc.*, 555 F.3d 42 (1st Cir. 2009), see Fred Schneyer, *Corporate Inefficiency Allegations Not Protected by SOX*, plansponsor.com (Feb. 12, 2009)]

In a case of first impression, the First Circuit ruled in early 2012 that employees of privately held companies that are contractors or subcontractors for public companies are not entitled to Sarbanes-Oxley whistleblower protection against retaliation. The First Circuit heard consolidated cases brought by former employees of contractors or subcontractors for Fidelity mutual funds. The funds are publicly traded but have no employees. The First Circuit said that, if it wanted to protect such employees, the Sarbanes-Oxley Act could have specified the protection. Although the Dodd-Frank Act increased the scope of protection, it did so only for employees of subsidiaries of public companies and statistical rating organizations. [*Lawson v. FMR LLC*, 670 F.3d 61 (1st Cir. 2012); see Sheri Qualters, *No SOX Protection for Whistleblowers Working for Contractors of Public Companies*, Nat'l L.J. (Feb. 6, 2012) (law.com)]

The Dodd-Frank Wall Street Reform and Consumer Protection Act of 2010, Pub. L. No. 111-203, includes an incentive provision for whistleblowers, even if the claim involves a privately held corporation not subject to Sarbanes-Oxley. If whistleblowers voluntarily provide information that leads the federal government to recover more than $1 million for a violation of the federal securities laws (including the Foreign Corrupt Practices Act, abbreviated as FCPA), the SEC has discretion to award them between 10% and 30% of the part of the recovery over and above $1 million. Awards are only available for providing original information, not already available through existing investigations or reports—and that the SEC did not already have. Several very large FCPA penalties had been assessed shortly before the Dodd-Frank Act passed, such as $1.6 billion imposed on Siemens AG and $335 million against Snamprogetti Netherlands B.V. [See Bethany Hensbach,

*Whistleblower Provision Likely to Increase FCPA Risk*, <http://www.government contractslawblog.com/2010/08/articles/fcpa/whistleblower-provision-likely-to-increase-fcpa-risk> (Aug. 4, 2010)]

The SEC published final rules about the whistleblower program in May 2011. The rules enhance rewards for employees who go through channels within their company before approaching the SEC, because they receive a reward of 10%–30% of any penalty in excess of $1 million collected because of the whistleblower's information. Employees have up to 120 days after making an internal complaint to go to the SEC. Employees who approach the SEC directly, without giving the employer a chance to correct the problem, get lower rewards. Whistleblowers can get credit if they report a minor violation that would not otherwise qualify for a bounty, if their complaint leads to an internal investigation that uncovers additional wrongdoing that the company discloses to the SEC. [Final rules for the program: <http://www.sec.gov/rules/final/2011/34-64545.pdf> (May 25, 2011) and 76 Fed. Reg. 34300 (June 13, 2011)]

The Dodd-Frank whistleblower program officially took effect August 12, 2011. The SEC launched a new Web page. [<http://www.sec.gov/whistleblower>; see SEC Press Release 2011-167, *SEC's New Whistleblower Program Takes Effect Today*, <http://www.sec.gov/news/press/2011/2011-167.htm> (Aug. 12, 2011)]

The SEC's whistleblower rules under the Dodd-Frank Act affect three aspects of corporate internal investigations:

- Teaching employees about the corporation's internal controls;
- Performing the investigation;
- Dealing with regulators.

Dodd-Frank protects whistleblowers whether or not the SEC actually investigates the complaint, if it found any violations, or the whistleblower actually received an award. However, if the employee does not learn about the potential violation that he or she reported from a corporate attorney in the course of a corporate investigation, Rule 21F-4(b)(4)(vi) says that the whistleblower is not the source of the information, and therefore cannot receive an award. [Steven S. Sparling and Arielle Warshall Katz, *Internal Investigation Strategies in a Post Dodd-Frank World*, N.Y.L.J. (Aug. 11, 2011) (law.com)]

In general, the SEC does not have jurisdiction over qualified plans, but SEC Rule 240.21F-2(b)(1) defines a whistleblower as a person who reasonably believes that he or she has information about a securities law violation and reports the information as described in Exchange Act § 21F(h)(1)(A). It is not necessary that there actually was a violation only that the whistleblower reasonably believed that there was. See, e.g., *Kramer v. Trans-Lux Corp.*, a retaliatory discharge case brought by a member of a corporate pension committee who charged he was fired because of his complaints about the actions of the pension plan's trustee. Kramer discussed these issues with his supervisor, the company's CFO, and the board's audit committee, and eventually went to the SEC and the PBGC. The district court found that it was reasonable of him to believe that pension administration implicates federal securities laws. [*Kramer v. Trans-Lux Corp.*, No. 3:11-cv-01424-SRU, 2012 WL 444820 (D. Conn. Sept. 25, 2012); see Michael S. Melbinger Winston & Strawn LLP Executive Compensation Blog (Oct. 22, 2012) (benefitslink.com)]

The Fifth Circuit held in mid-2013 that it is necessary to contact the SEC with information about securities law violations to be a Dodd-Frank whistleblower. A person who charges retaliation for filing an internal complaint (in this case, alleged violations of the Foreign Corrupt Practice Act) is not a whistleblower and not protected under the Dodd-Frank Act. [*Asadi v. G.E. Energy LLC*,2013 WL 3742492 (5th Cir. 2013)]

Some states have statutes extending specific protection to whistleblower employees. However, some of these statutes apply only to government workers, not employees of private-sector companies. The trend in some courts is to limit the number of situations in which employees will be considered protected whistleblowers.

A state whistleblower suit cannot be removed to federal court merely because the wrongdoing alleged by the whistleblower consisted of submitting false claims to the federal government. The Sixth Circuit ruled in 2006 that there was no private cause of action under the False Claims Act, so there was no substantial federal question that would justify removal under 28 U.S.C. § 1441(b). Alleging a federal law that has no private cause of action as an element of a state law cause of action does not state a claim "arising" under federal law. [*Eastman v. Marine Mech. Corp.*, 438 F.3d 544 (6th Cir. 2006)]

## [C]  WC Claimants

Retaliation against employees who have filed Worker's Compensation claims is unlawful, because public policy favors injured employees receiving income to replace the income lost when they are injured.

Although the number of injuries reported to OSHA has fallen by almost one-third in the past decade, one theory is that there may be some injuries that occur but are not reported because the injured employees fear retaliation. In 2012, there were about 100 state and federal cases alleging Worker's Compensation retaliation, about twice as many as the number ten years earlier. In 2012, OSHA issued a warning to employers that retaliation is illegal, and said that it is inappropriate to offer prizes or bonuses for meeting safety goals if the effect of the program is to deter injured workers from reporting. [James R. Hagerty, *Workplace Injuries Drop, but Claims of Employer Retaliation Rise*, WSJ.com (July 22, 2013)]

Similar considerations apply with respect to unemployment benefits, which also require an administrative determination of eligibility. An airline station agent claimed that a customer gave him $80 in cash for a ticket change fee, and he put it in a cash register near the boarding gate, but the amount was not entered into the computer system. The passenger was charged the same fee again, and complained. The agent was fired for violating airline rules. When he applied for unemployment benefits, the Administrative Law Judge found him guilty of misconduct for questionable conduct and violation of airline procedure. When he sued his former employer for wrongful termination, the airline argued that the ALJ's finding ruled out a wrongful termination suit. However, the Third Circuit held that local (Virgin Islands) precedent is that an unemployment finding of misconduct does not rule out a wrongful termination suit—the two laws have different objectives, and the relevant facts for a finding are different. The wrongful termination statute does not refer to misconduct, so even if the employee was guilty of misconduct, this does not prevent the termination from being found wrongful. [*Gonzalez v. AMR*, 549 F.3d 219 (3d Cir. 2008)]

In mid-2011, the Ohio Supreme Court held that a machine shop worker who was fired within an hour of reporting a workplace injury—but before he could apply for WC benefits—could sue his ex-employer under the state law forbidding retaliation for making WC claims. [*Sutton v. Tomco* (Ohio 2011); see Sara Kelly, *Court Rules on Injured Worker's Wrongful Termination*, plansponsor.com (June 10, 2011)]

## § 39.05   PREEMPTION ARGUMENTS

Preemption is the legal doctrine under which passage of a federal law limits or eliminates the state's power to regulate that subject. ERISA preempts state wrongful termination claims based on alleged termination to avoid paying pension benefits. All such claims must be brought in federal court, under ERISA § 510, and not in state court.

The Family and Medical Leave Act preempts common-law claims of retaliatory discharge when an employee says he or she was fired as punishment for taking FMLA leave. [*Hamros v. Bethany Homes*, 894 F. Supp. 1176 (N.D. Ill. 1995)]

The Sixth Circuit upheld the dismissal of a wrongful termination suit brought by a former Whirlpool executive. Lewis charged that he was fired, in violation of public policy, because he refused to commit the Unfair Labor Practice of firing employees for engaging in union activism. The Sixth Circuit held that Lewis' claim was preempted by the NLRA, so he should have raised his claim before the NLRB. (In fact he did, but the NLRB found that his charge was without merit.) Supervisors are generally excluded from coverage under the NLRA, but there is a cause of action for termination or other discipline for refusing to commit Unfair Labor Practices—but the NLRB has exclusive jurisdiction over such claims. [*Lewis v. Whirlpool Corp.*, 630 F.3d 484 (6th Cir. 2011)]

However, National Labor Relations Act §§ 7 and 8 do not so completely preempt state wrongful discharge claims that the state claims can be removed to federal court. In 2005 the Fourth Circuit held that preemption depends on a preexisting federal cause of action, and the wrongful discharge case was not based on the right to bargain collectively or the ban on unfair labor practices. [*Lontz v. Tharp*, 413 F.3d 435 (4th Cir. 2005)]

Preemption arguments can also be used in state court. If the employee is covered by a state antidiscrimination law that is not preempted by federal law, the employer may be able to get a wrongful termination suit dismissed, because the employee should have sued for discrimination. From the employer's viewpoint, the best-case scenario is that the employee waited too long, so the discrimination charges must be dismissed.

# ARBITRATION AND ADR

## § 40.01   INTRODUCTION

Taking a case to the court system is time-consuming, expensive, and often frustrating. Therefore, companies encounter non-litigation means of dispute resolution in many contexts. In addition to commercial arbitration, which is beyond the scope of this book, unionized companies will often wind up arbitrating labor disputes.

Alternative Dispute Resolution (ADR) methods are supposed to be informal, governed more by justice and fairness than by strict rules of legal procedure. Depending on the ADR method, either one person or a panel of people will either assist the parties to work out their own solution (mediation) or will make a decision (arbitration). It has been estimated that an employment lawsuit takes an average of a year and a half from the date the case is filed to resolve, versus only one year for arbitration. Once the case gets to the arbitrator, 90% of arbitration hearings are completed in two days or less.

Both unionized and nonunionized companies often find mediation or arbitration a superior alternative to litigation when employees make claims that they have suffered employment discrimination. In fact, employers often use various methods to make sure that all claims will have to go through arbitration. The question is when and how it is legitimate to impose an arbitration requirement on employees. If the employees freely choose arbitration over litigation, this problem does not arise, but nevertheless, the employer will still have to find a way to present its case effectively to the arbitrator.

The "first principles" of arbitration are that arbitration should be independent of the court system and should provide flexibility and respect the rights of the parties.

The federal statute known as the Railway Labor Act was enacted to resolve labor disputes. It requires minor disputes to be arbitrated before two labor and two industry representatives, plus a neutral referee to break tie votes. First, the parties must engage in "on-property proceedings" (going through the full grievance procedure under the CBA), and try to get a settlement "in conference." If they cannot agree, either side can refer the matter to the National Railroad Adjustment Board for arbitration. An arbitrator's order can be reviewed by the courts for failure to comply with the requirements of the Railway Labor Act, for not confining itself to matters within the jurisdiction of the Board, or for fraud or corruption. There was a circuit split over whether NRAB proceedings can also be reviewed for due process violations as well as these statutory grounds for review. In late 2009, the Supreme Court ruled that statutory and not Constitutional analysis should be applied. As long as a respondent does not seek to modify the Board's judgment, it can cite any information that appears in the record to support the Board's judgment. The Supreme Court held that the requirement to "conference" the dispute is not jurisdictional, so it is not necessary to prove that the dispute was conferenced before the Board hears a dispute. [*Union Pac. R.R. Co. v. Brotherhood of Locomotive Eng'rs*, 558 U.S. 67 (2009)]

## § 40.02  GRIEVANCES AND DISCIPLINE

### [A]  "Progressive Discipline"

The typical Collective Bargaining Agreement (CBA) for a unionized company spells out a system of "progressive discipline" under which employees whose work performance is unsatisfactory will be warned, offered guidance and training, and given a series of escalating penalties before being fired. Progressive discipline is sometimes used in nonunionized environment, although less frequently.

The system must make it clear to employees what the employer's expectations are and what the employer intends to do if the rules are violated. Once employees have been told what they are doing wrong, they should be given a reasonable amount of time to correct it. There should be a monitoring process to sort out the employees who have made adequate progress from those who have not. The time period should probably be between 30 and 90 days: Too long a period may make the arbitrator believe that the employer is stringing together isolated, unrelated incidents to make a case.

Employees who have been subject to discipline are likely to feel that they were unfairly singled out—and in some cases, this will result in discrimination or wrongful termination charges. An important HR function is creating a legally sustainable system of progressive discipline, and making sure that supervisors understand the system and apply it objectively.

A legally sustainable disciplinary system should be:

- Consistent—not only must discrimination be avoided but employees should not be subjected to supervisors' whims or penalized when the supervisor has a bad day;

- Well documented—an arbitrator or court should be able to see that each step reflects the employer's own rules;

- Clear—employees should know that if they fail to meet X goals in Y days, they will be put on probation, lose wages, or be terminated;

- Appropriate—the degree of the sanction should reflect the severity of the error or misconduct;

- Reciprocal—employees should get a chance to give their side of the story to an objective decision maker who isn't already committed to management's viewpoint.

Arbitrators will examine the "step formula" under the system and see if it was followed. For example, if the first step results in a determination that the employee was at fault, then he or she might be verbally admonished, whereas by the fourth step, dismissal could be appropriate. If the step formula is not followed, the arbitrator is likely to reverse the decision or substitute a lesser penalty, and there's a good chance that the courts will uphold the arbitrator.

Presenting grievances to the employer is one of the clearest cases of concerted activity protected by the NLRA, whether or not the employees are unionized. However, they must in fact act in concert, or one employee must present a shared grievance. One person pressing his or her own agenda is not protected under the NLRA. For NLRA purposes, a grievance must be something that relates directly to the terms and conditions of employment.

Once they have made a complaint, employees are required to return to work within a reasonable time. In fact, one of the bywords of labor arbitration is "obey now, grieve later."

## [B] Grievance Records

It makes sense to buy or design standard forms for keeping track of employee grievances, although there is no specific federal requirement for making such records or keeping them for a particular length of time. The grievance form should contain:

- Identification of the CBA that creates the grievance procedure and the specific clause of that contract that has to be interpreted;

- Date the grievance was submitted;

- Grievance case number;

- Name, department, shift, and job title of the employee who submits the grievance;

- What the employee says is wrong;

- Records of statements by witnesses;

- Documentary evidence relevant to the grievance;

- Whether the employee was represented (e.g., by the shop steward or a fellow employee);

- Written decisions by the first-level supervisor or others involved in processing the grievance;

- A signed statement by the union representative as to whether the union considers the grievance to be adequately resolved;

- Signatures of the employee and all decision makers.

It can be very helpful to analyze past grievances to see how patterns change over time.

## [C] NLRB Deference

Although the NLRB has the power, under the NLRA § 10(a), to prevent unfair labor practices, the NLRB will defer to grievance arbitration (i.e., will not interfere) if several criteria are satisfied:

- Understanding the meaning of the CBA is central to resolving the dispute;

- The dispute came up during an ongoing collective bargaining relationship;

- The employees do not claim that the employer prevented them from exercising all their rights under labor law;

- The employer has agreed to a broad-based arbitration clause—in fact, one broad enough to cover the existing dispute.

## § 40.03 MEDIATION

A mediator is a neutral third party who listens to both sides and helps the parties themselves work out a solution that is acceptable to both of them. The American Arbitration Association has a set of uniform Employment Mediation Rules. Parties can trigger this procedure by writing a request to the AAA for mediation, or by filing a Submission to Mediation form, also with the AAA.

One reason that the procedure for filing discrimination charges is so elaborate is that part of the EEOC's job is to attempt mediation of the charge. [See Chapter 41]

## § 40.04 ARBITRATION VS. LITIGATION

Opponents of mandatory arbitration state that the process is pro-employer, not only because it restricts discovery and limits the remedies available to a successful plaintiff, but because there is a risk that arbitrators will (consciously or unconsciously) favor employers. Employers are much more likely to need to choose arbitrators in the future than employees, who typically are involved in only one case.

Many cases have arisen in the court system because one party wants to litigate a dispute and the other says that arbitration is required. The court system then has to determine what parts of the dispute—if any—must be resolved by judges, and what parts are to be decided by arbitrators. The Supreme Court rendered two major decisions on this issue in mid-2010.

The first one was brought by an account manager who sued his former employer, charging that he was subjected to racial discrimination and retaliation. The employer cited the mandatory arbitration agreement to show that the case had to be arbitrated. Jackson, the plaintiff, argued that the arbitration agreement was unconscionable under state law and therefore unenforceable.

The arbitration agreement gave the arbitrator sole authority to resolve disputes about the interpretation, applicability, enforceability, or formation of the agreement. The Supreme Court ruled that it is up to the arbitrator, not the court system, to decide the unconscionability of the entire agreement—if the agreement includes a "delegation clause" that gives the arbitrator this power. In this case, however, the Supreme Court said that Jackson used a mistaken strategy. He challenged the validity of the agreement as a whole, and did not challenge the validity of the delegation clause until his case had reached the Supreme Court, by which time it was too late to raise a new argument. [*Rent-a-Center West v. Jackson,* 130 S. Ct. 2772 (2010); see Marcia Coyle, *High Court Restricts Judges' Role in Deciding Arbitration Fairness,* Nat'l L.J. (June 22, 2010) (law.com)]

Shortly thereafter, when the Supreme Court returned to the question of arbitrators' powers, the Supreme Court ruled that it was up to the district court and not the arbitrator to decide when a CBA had been officially ratified. (The dispute was about whether a strike was unlawful because it violated the no-strike clause in the CBA—which, in turn, required determining when the contract took effect.) The Supreme Court ruled that a court can order arbitration only based on a finding that the parties agreed to arbitrate that type of dispute—including resolving any issues about the validity of the arbitration clause. Because the federal system favors arbitration, there is a presumption of arbitrability—but it applies only if there is a valid arbitration agreement and a question about whether the agreement covers the actual dispute between the parties. The Supreme Court said that in that situation, the court should order arbitration only if the presumption of arbitrability has not been rebutted by the party seeking to litigate the dispute. [*Granite Rock Co. v. Int'l Brotherhood of Teamsters,* 130 S. Ct. 2847 (2010).

Although it is not an employment decision (it involves consumers who wanted to bring a class arbitration about sales tax charged on "free" cell phones), the 2011 Supreme Court decision in *AT&T Mobility LLC v. Concepcion,* 131 S. Ct. 1740 (2011) has often been interpreted to mean that the federal policy in favor of arbitration is so strong that state rulings that arbitration agreements are unconscionable will be preempted.

In a late 2012 summary ruling, the Supreme Court held that the Oklahoma Supreme Court was wrong to hold that the noncompete provisions in two employment contracts were void. (The state court said that the provisions violated the state's public policy against noncompete clauses.) The Supreme Court said that the decision should have been made by the arbitrator. The employment contracts included an arbitration clause covering "any dispute, difference or unresolved question." The two plaintiffs quit their jobs and went to work for a competitor. Their former employer Nitro-Lift demanded arbitration. The plaintiffs sued in Oklahoma state court to enjoin enforcement of the noncompete clauses, which they alleged were null and void. The trial court ordered arbitration, but the Oklahoma Supreme Court asked the parties to show why the state law limiting enforceability of noncompete agreements should not apply. The Supreme Court held that federal substantive law under the FAA applies in both state and federal courts. If an arbitration clause is severable, then its validity is determined by the court system. But attacks on the validity of the contract, not just the validity of the arbitration clause, are resolved by an arbitrator. If the arbitration clause is valid, the validity of the rest of the contract is decided by the arbitrator. [*Nitro-Lift Techs., LLC v. Howard*, 133 S. Ct. 500 ( 2012)] The Northern District of California struck down an arbitration agreement that it held was unconscionable.The plaintiff was required to sign the agreement on the day she was fired. She had already signed several employment agreements, beginning with the day she was hired—but those agreements did not have arbitration clauses. The arbitration clause was placed in the agreement without warning, and it was coercive because the plaintiff got the impression that she would not receive her final paycheck if she refused to sign the agreement. The district court said that the rule in the Ninth Circuit is that an agreement that, like this one, is both substantively and procedurally unconscionable, if unenforceable. [*Lou v. Ma Labs.*, No. 12-5409 (N.D. Cal. May 17, 2013);see Vanessa Blum, *Judge Strikes Arbitration Agreement in Suit Against Ma Labs*, The Recorder (May 16, 2013) (law.com)]

The NLRB rejected an arbitration agreement that required employees to waive the option of class arbitration on the grounds that filing a class or collective action about wages, hours, or working conditions is protected concerted activity, whether it occurs in court or before an arbitrator. The NLRB held that employees, whether or not they are unionized, cannot be forced to waive class arbitration. The NLRB said that *AT&T Mobility* was not relevant because it is a consumer class action case, whereas here the employees wanted to enforce substantive workplace rights granted by the NLRA. Furthermore, in the NLRB's view, *AT&T Mobility* involved a conflict between the FAA and state law, triggering the Supremacy Clause of the Constitution—whereas here there is a possible conflict between two federal statutes (the FAA and the NLRA). This decision is subject to review by the Eleventh Circuit or D.C. Circuit. [*D.R. Horton Inc. and Michael Cuda* Case No. 12-CA-25764 (N.L.R.B. Jan. 3, 2012); see Scott Graham, *AT&T Mobility Doesn't Apply in the Workplace, Says NLRB*, Corporate Counsel (Jan. 9, 2012) (law.com); Philip M. Berkowitz, *Developments in Arbitration of Employment Claims*, N.Y.L.J. (Jan. 12, 2012) (law.com)].

*Raniere v. Citigroup Inc.*, 2011 U.S. Dist. LEXIS 135393 (S.D.N.Y. Nov. 22, 2011) says that employers cannot mandate arbitration of FLSA collective actions for unpaid minimum wage or overtime, on the grounds that the FLSA collective action is a unique mechanism designed to permit employees to enforce their rights themselves without government involvement.]

Shortly before a merger obtained regulatory approval, an employee who had an employment contract was terminated without cause, triggering payment of a lump-sum severance benefit. The employee said that he did not receive all the benefits he was entitled to, and sought arbitration. The employer moved in the District Court for the District of South Dakota to enjoin arbitration, asserting that the employment contract was an ERISA severance plan, so ERISA preempted the demand for arbitration. The Eighth Circuit held that the employment contract was not an ERISA plan because it covered only one person, but remanded the case because parts of the complaint might be subject to ERISA preemption because of its relation to other plans that are ERISA plans. [*Dakota, Minnesota & Eastern Railroad Corp. v. Schieffer*, 648 F.3d 935 (8th Cir. 2011); see PLC, *One-Person Employment Contract Not an ERISA Plan: Eighth Circuit* (Aug. 15, 2011) (benefitslink.com)]

## § 40.05 LABOR ARBITRATION

### [A] Grievance Arbitration and Contract or Interest Arbitration

Arbitration and mediation have a long history as means to settle disputes between labor and management without a strike and without litigation. By agreeing to arbitrate an issue, in effect the union agrees not to strike over that issue. The employer agrees not to take unilateral action.

The two main types of labor arbitration are grievance arbitration (also known as rights arbitration), used when there is a disagreement about interpretation of an existing contract, and contract or interest arbitration, invoked when the parties are not sure which provisions should be included in a new, renewed, or reopened CBA. However, this promotes a somewhat different mind-set from the type of arbitration discussed later in this chapter, where the focus is not on avoiding a strike dealing with an entire bargaining unit, but a court case involving one person's discrimination charge.

Nearly all collective bargaining agreements allow for an in-house grievance procedure, but if that does not resolve the problem, then final, binding arbitration, resulting in a decree that can be enforced by the court system, is the last part of the procedure.

Organizations such as the American Arbitration Association and the Federal Mediation and Conciliation Service maintain lists of qualified arbitrators, who are familiar both with the conditions in a particular industry and with arbitration rules and practices. If there will be only one arbitrator, then both sides will have to agree on an acceptable arbitrator. If there are three arbitrators, usually each side selects one arbitrator, and the two arbitrators select the third.

As a preliminary step, the employer and union try to agree on a statement of the issues involved in the grievance. If they cannot even agree on that, the arbitrator may have to draft the statement.

■ **TIP:** If the employer wants to discharge or discipline an employee, it will proceed first in arbitration; in other matters, the union usually proceeds first.

## [B]  Arbitrability

If it is not clear whether a company has agreed to submit a particular issue to arbitration, then the issue is arbitrable. This principle comes from "The Steelworkers' Trilogy," three cases decided by the Supreme Court in 1960. [*Steelworkers v. American Mfg. Co.*, 363 U.S. 564 (1960); *United Steelworkers of Am. v. Warrior Gulf Navigation Co.*, 363 U.S. 574 (1960); *United Steelworkers of Am. v. Enter. Wheel & Car Corp.*, 363 U.S. 593 (1960)] If a CBA contains both an arbitration clause and a no-strike clause, any dispute that involves the application and interpretation of the CBA is arbitrable unless arbitration is specifically ruled out by the terms of the contract.

Under the Steelworkers' Trilogy, the language of the CBA is the first thing the arbitrators consult, but this is not the only factor in the analysis. The "law of the shop" (practices that have evolved in that particular operation) can be considered. Factors such as the effect of the arbitrator's decision on productivity, morale, and workplace tensions are also legitimate considerations. Courts can't review the merits of an arbitration decision or whether a different resolution would have been more sensible. All the court can do is decide whether the arbitration award "draws its essence" from the arbitration agreement.

However, because of a later Supreme Court case [*First Options of Chicago, Inc. v. Kaplan*, 514 U.S. 938 (1995)], the court system rather than the arbitrator decides whether a party agreed to arbitrate a particular type of dispute, if there is no clear, unmistakable evidence of the parties' intentions. There is no right to re-arbitrate an issue already considered by the NLRB in an unfair labor practice proceeding.

When Cooper Tire & Rubber signed a CBA, it also signed a side letter limiting its contributions to retiree health benefits. When a dispute arose about one of the terms of the side letter, the union went to federal court to compel arbitration of the retiree's grievance about the benefits. Management's position was that the side letter covering retiree health benefits did not have an arbitration clause. The Sixth Circuit analyzed the case using a "scope" test: that is, unless the parties agreed to the contrary, disputes about a side agreement are arbitrable if the subject matter of the side agreement falls within the scope of the arbitration clause in the CBA. Therefore, the union had standing to arbitrate on behalf of retirees and their survivors. However, the Sixth Circuit vacated the order certifying a class action, because the district court should have required the union to get the consent of the class members to being represented by the union. [*United Steelworkers of Am. v. Cooper Tire & Rubber Co.*, 474 F.3d 271 (6th Cir. 2007).

The "scope" test is also used in the Third, Seventh, and Ninth Circuits. Other courts have used different formulas: in the Second, Fourth, and Eighth Circuits, if the side agreement deals with matters that are not similar to the subject matter of the CBA, then the side agreement is merely collateral to the CBA and is not covered by its arbitration clause. But if the subject matter of the side agreement is integral to the CBA, then side-agreement disputes are arbitrable. [See, e.g.,

*United Steelworkers v. The Duluth Clinic, Ltd.*, 413 F.3d 786, 788 (8th Cir. 2005)]

## [C]  Potentially Arbitrable Issues

Many issues have been found potentially arbitrable. In fact, because collective bargaining and arbitration are complementary processes, the list is similar to the list of issues that are mandatory bargaining subjects:

- Sale of a business;
- Relocation of operations;
- Contracting out bargaining unit work;
- Temporary shutdowns;
- Discharge of an individual employee;
- Layoffs;
- Recalls after a layoff;
- Disputes about work assignments (including assigning supervisors to bargaining unit work);
- Work schedules;
- Classification of work;
- Compensation, including bonuses, overtime pay, incentive pay, and severance;
- Vacation, sick leave, and holidays;
- Seniority systems;
- Safety disputes;
- No-strike clauses.

## [D]  The Process of Labor Arbitration

In most instances, when management and union hit a deadlock over a grievance or dispute, resort to arbitration will be automatic. However, depending on needs and comparative bargaining power, the arbitration clause might be drafted to allow only the union to invoke arbitration. Employees might also be given the right to invoke arbitration in situations where the union declines to press an employee grievance.

■ **TIP:**  Even if the CBA does not include a formal arbitration clause, management and union can sign a "submission agreement" agreeing to be bound by the arbitration decision on a one-time basis.

Arbitration clauses usually call for the involvement of either the Federal Mediation and Conciliation Service (FMCS) or the American Arbitration Association (AAA). However, the parties can agree on other ways to resolve disputes if they so choose.

Arbitration begins with a "demand": Either side invokes the CBA arbitration clause and notifies the appropriate agency. The FMCS can be called in by either management or union to assist in the negotiating process. The FMCS can also offer its services, but cannot demand to be made part of the process. FMCS will not mediate a dispute that has only minor effect on interstate commerce if there are other conciliation services (e.g., state agencies) available. The FMCS can also refuse to intervene on behalf of parties who have a record of noncooperation with arbitration, including failure to pay arbitration fees.

Once an arbitration award is rendered, it is usually final, binding, and not subject to judicial review by any court. In other words, agreeing to submit to arbitration is a very significant decision that cannot be undertaken casually. It will probably be impossible to get any kind of review or have the decision set aside. However, a serious irregularity in the process, such as proof that the arbitrator was not impartial, may justify setting aside the award.

The mission of the Federal Mediation and Conciliation Service (FMCS) is to assist in contract negotiation disputes between employers and their unionized employees. The FMCS also assists in mediation of discrimination cases and grievances before they reach the arbitration stage. Parties can request an arbitrator online, at <http://www.fmcs.gov> or can download request forms from the site and then fax them or mail them to the FMCS. [The FMCs' FAQ is at <http://www.fmcs.gov/internet/faq.asp?categoryID=336>; the agency's policies and procedures are at <http://www.fmcs.gov/internet/itemDetail.asp?categoryID=197& itemID=16959>]

## [E]  Case Law on Labor Arbitration

In late 2000, the Supreme Court decided that, in a unionized workplace, an arbitrator's decision is enforceable by the court system as long as the arbitration award draws its essence from the Collective Bargaining Agreement (CBA). So, unless the arbitrator's decision actually violates a statute or regulation, it must be enforced—even if it violates public policy. [*E. Associated Coal Corp. v. UMW*, 531 U.S. 57 (2000)]

Arbitration awards are quite hard to overturn. For example, a court cannot overturn an award merely because it believes the arbitrator made the wrong decision, or misinterpreted the facts of the case. One of the rare cases in which an award was overturned involved a new zero-tolerance drug policy adopted by an oil refining company for all its facilities nationwide. The policy was challenged by the union, which claimed that it was impermissible to adopt such a policy unilaterally, without bargaining. One arbitrator upheld the policy. The other arbitrator upheld most of the policy, but disapproved of the potential for firing employees immediately, without a chance for rehabilitation. The employer sought to have the district court vacate the award, but the district court upheld. The Third Circuit reversed the district court, finding that the arbitrator exceeded his discretion by attempting to substitute his own discretion in an area of legitimate management prerogative. The Third Circuit held that the award did not draw its essence from the collective bargaining agreement. [*Citgo Asphalt Refining Co. v. Paper, Allied-Industrial Chemical, & Energy Workers Int'l Union Local No. 2-991*, 385 F.3d 809 (3d Cir. 2004)]

## [F]   Just Cause

One of the distinctive features of a collective bargaining agreement is that it means that employees no longer work at the will of the employer. Therefore, they cannot be discharged, or even subjected to lesser forms of discipline, without just cause. So the arbitrator's task becomes to determine whether the employer did, indeed, act with just cause. The arbitrator must determine if the employee really did whatever the employer claims he or she did; whether the employer offered the employee due process before imposing discipline; and whether the discipline was reasonable and not out of proportion to the offense. Usually, arbitrators divide offenses into very serious offenses such as assaulting someone at work, stealing, or creating a safety hazard (which will justify dismissal) and less serious rules, which are appropriate for progressive discipline such as admonition, notations in the permanent record, or suspension with or without pay.

The New Jersey Supreme Court ruled in mid-2010 that, if a CBA does not define what constitutes just cause to discipline an employee, it is up to the arbitrator to supply a definition—and the parties to the arbitration will be bound by what the arbitrator says. Therefore, the court upheld an arbitrator's award, reinstating a high school custodian on the grounds that progressive discipline required him to suspended instead of fired. The New Jersey Supreme Court ruled that, because the CBA was ambiguous on this point, the arbitrator did not exceed his authority by ruling that progressive discipline was an essential element of just cause. [*Linden Board of Education v. Linden Educ. Ass'n on Behalf of John Mizichko*, 202 N.J. 268, 997 A.2d 185 (2010); see Michael Booth, *Arbitrator Can Fashion Discipline in Labor Dispute, N.J. High Court Rules,* N.J.L.J. (June 10, 2010) (law.com)]

## [G]   Contract Interpretation

When arbitrators interpret a contract, their job is to find out what the parties meant. If the language of the contract is plain, clear, and unambiguous, the arbitrator has to follow it—even if the arbitrator doesn't think that the contract as written is very sensible or fair. In fact, if the arbitrator doesn't follow this "plain meaning rule," a court is likely to decide that the arbitrator's award is invalid and not entitled to be enforced by the court system.

In fact, if a contract (any kind of contract, not just a CBA) is supposed to represent the whole agreement between the parties, a legal principle called the "parol evidence rule" says that evidence of anything said or written before or during the negotiations cannot be introduced to contradict the written contract or vary its terms. ("Parol" is an archaic term for "word" or "speech.") However, parol evidence can be used to explain terms that are unclear or ambiguous.

## § 40.06   ARBITRATION OF EMPLOYMENT DISCRIMINATION CLAIMS

### [A]   Employer-Imposed Clauses

The reputation of arbitration has had its ups and downs. A Supreme Court case, *Alexander v. Gardner-Denver* [415 U.S. 36 (1974)] allowed an employee to litigate after pursuing arbitration remedies, on the grounds that the arbitration provision in the plaintiff's CBA did not offer enough protection for statutory claims—i.e., claims that arise under Title VII, the Americans With Disabilities Act, or other antidiscrimination law.

In 1991, however, the Supreme Court took a different tack. The important case of *Gilmer v. Interstate/Johnson Lane Corp.* [500 U.S. 20 (1991)] allowed an employer to impose mandatory arbitration (under the U-4 securities industry employment agreement) for ADEA claims. The Supreme Court said that it wasn't really contradicting the earlier *Gardner-Denver* decision, because that involved a union contract that the plaintiff was subject to along with all the other union members, whereas Gilmer signed the U-4 agreement as an individual.

Under *Gilmer*, an arbitration clause can be valid as long as the process provides a written award rendered by a neutral arbitrator, and as long as discovery and adequate remedies are available under the arbitration process.

In April 2009, the Supreme Court extended its line of pro-arbitration decisions by holding that an arbitration clause in a CBA prevented employees from litigating ADEA claims when building service employees were re-assigned to lower-paid jobs as porters and cleaners. The union withdrew age discrimination charges because it had consented to the new contract under which the reassignments were made. The individual workers affected by the reassignments filed ADEA charges with the EEOC, and received right to sue letters. The Second Circuit refused to compel arbitration, taking the position that a CBA provision cannot be enforced if it prevents ADEA suits. The Supreme Court reversed, finding that federal law favors arbitration, mandating enforcement of a CBA provision that clearly and unmistakably obligates union members to arbitrate claims. Opponents of the decision said that the Supreme Court allowed unions to bargain away their members' rights to pursue discrimination cases in court. However, the

Supreme Court held that union and management mutually agreed on the contract's provisions in bargaining, and the clause would have to be upheld unless the ADEA forbids arbitration. In the Supreme Court view, the ADEA does not contradict the general federal policy of supporting arbitration. [*14 Penn Plaza LLC v. Pyett*, 556 U.S. 247 (2009)]

The *Gilmer* case was the "opening bell" for recognition of employers' right to impose predispute arbitration requirements: That is, employees would be covered by employment agreements, job handbooks, or other means of ensuring that they would have to arbitrate discrimination claims instead of litigating them.

The Civil Rights Act of 1991 and the Americans with Disabilities Act (ADA) both include language favoring arbitration and other forms of Alternative Dispute Resolution (ADR) as means of handling discrimination charges. For the ADA provision, see 42 U.S.C. § 12212: Wherever it is lawful and appropriate, ADR (including settlement negotiations, conciliation, facilitation, mediation, fact-finding, minitrials, and arbitration) is "encouraged" when ADA charges are asserted. Similarly, in 2004 the Fifth Circuit ruled that there is no reason why arbitration of Fair Labor Standards Act claims cannot be compelled. [*Carter v. Countrywide Credit Indus., Inc.*, 362 F.3d 294 (5th Cir. 2004)] The Fifth Circuit agreed with the District Court that the contract provision requiring the employer and employee to split the costs of arbitration was invalid—but also agreed with the District Court that the proper remedy was to sever this invalid provision and enforce the rest of the agreement.

The two main ADR methods are arbitration (a trusted person or panel renders a decision) and mediation (a trusted person helps the parties reach a mutually acceptable decision).

■ **TIP:** If an employer offers to arbitrate, and the employee refuses, this could be treated as evidence of the employer's good faith—preventing the employee from collecting damages for breach of the covenant of good faith and fair dealing.

Stephen Mayers sued his ex-employer and its parent corporation under FEHA (the California anti-discrimination law) charging age and disability discrimination and retaliation for taking leave. The defendant moved to compel arbitration based on his employment application, employment agreement, and acknowledgment of receipt of the employee handbook, which all required submission of employment claims to final and binding arbitration. The California Court of Appeal found the arbitration requirement unconscionable and refused to enforce it. Although the agreement said that arbitration of employment-related claims would be governed by AAA rules, Mayers was never given a copy of these rules or told how to obtain them. The provision allowed the arbitrator to award attorneys' fees to the prevailing party, which exposed Mayers to a greater risk of having to pay the employers' counsel fees than if he had brought suit under FEHA. The court of appeal said that the unconscionable terms were central to the agreement and could not be severed. The court ruled that *AT&T Mobility* did not apply because it interpreted that case to be about whether arbitration of a particular kind of claim can be required. [*Mayers v. Volt Mgmt. Corp.*, 203 Cal. App. 4th 1194 (Cal. App. 2012)]

The First Circuit ruled that a job application was ambiguous as to whether people who applied but were not hired were subject to the arbitration clause. Therefore, the First Circuit refused to mandate arbitration in a case where a job applicant asserted pregnancy discrimination. The court concluded that there was a valid arbitration agreement—but the conditions under which it would come into play (the plaintiff being hired and having a dispute with her employer) never occurred. [*Gove v. Career Sys. Dev. Corp.*, 689 F.3d 1 (1st Cir. 2012)]

The District Court for the District of Massachusetts sent a gender bias case against CIGNA Healthcare to arbitration, but held that the plaintiff, who said that the company's evaluation and promotion practices violated Title VII and Massachusetts state law, could not compel CIGNA to participate in class arbitration. The plaintiff alleged that her salary and title were reduced without explanation in 2003, and in 2004, her job was downgraded again, but similarly situated male co-workers were not downgraded. In the district court's view, a pattern or practice claim is a method of proving discrimination in a class action, not a freestanding cause of action. The plaintiff would have to prove causation in arbitrating her individual claim even if she established a widespread pattern of sex discrimination. The district court concluded that permitting a class action suit in a case where there was a valid arbitration clause would allow the Title VII burden-shifting rule to outweigh the Federal Arbitration Act. [*Karp v. CIGNA Healthcare Inc.*, No. Civ-A 11-10361-FDS, 2012 WL 1358652 (D. Mass. Sept. 14, 2012); see Sheri Qualters, *Judge Sends Gender Bias Case Against CIGNA To Arbitration*, Nat'l L.J. (Apr. 19, 2012) (law.com). *Parisi v. Goldman, Sachs & Co.*, No. 11-5229 (2nd Cir. Mar. 21, 2013) reaches a very similar conclusion in a case brought by three financial executives who charged the existence of a pattern at Goldman, Sachs of limiting compensation and promotion opportunities advancement for female managers.]

But, despite the almost universal judicial approval of mandatory arbitration, the executive branch took a step in 2009 that, in practical terms, greatly limited the practicality of mandatory arbitration clauses. A provision in the federal spending bill for the Department of Defense for the years 2009–2010 (§ 8116) forbids most defense contractors to enforce mandatory arbitration clauses. The defense contractor cannot be paid by the federal government unless it agrees not to enter into or enforce any employment contract making it a condition of employment for an employee or independent contractor to agree to arbitrate Title VII claims or many other tort claims. The provision took effect for federal subcontractors six months later. However, the holders of contracts and subcontracts under $1 million are exempt. The Department of Defense has the power to grant a waiver for national security reasons, although the waiver must be disclosed to the public.

[David Ingram, *Obama Signs Into Law Restriction on Arbitration Clauses*, Nat'l L.J. (Dec. 22, 2009) (law.com)]

## [B]  AAA Arbitration

The American Arbitration Association (AAA) has long been respected for its work in dispute resolution. The AAA's National Rules for the Resolution of Employment Disputes (promulgated in 1993; amended in 1995 to increase due process protection for employees) cover about three million workers.

The due process standards for fair arbitration require that:

- The employee's role in selecting the arbitrator(s) is equal to the employer's role;

- Each side has a right to counsel;

- The arbitrator can order whatever discovery he or she thinks is necessary;

- The parties are entitled to the same remedies in arbitration that they could get from the court system;

- The arbitrator will provide a written opinion explaining the reasons behind his or her decision;

- Attorneys' fees will be awarded in the interests of justice, so the employee does not have to be successful enough to be considered the "prevailing party" to get a fee award.

■ **TIP:**  The employer can indicate in employment applications, the employee handbook, and/or employment contracts that employment disputes will be resolved under AAA rules.

Since 1996, AAA arbitrators have had the power to order discovery. Either employers or employees can be ordered to produce documents, answer written lists of questions, or appear and answer questions posed by an attorney. Under the 1996 rules, any party can be represented by an attorney. The arbitrator has a duty to make a decision and render a written award within 30 days of the end of the hearing. The arbitrator has the power to render whatever award he or she thinks is just, including ordering one side to pay the attorneys' fees and costs of the other side.

The arbitrator gets paid a fee for working on the case, and the AAA itself is entitled to an administration fee. The AAA fee depends on the size of the claim or counterclaim, determined at the time it is filed, not by any later amendments.

The AAA's general policy is that it will administer arbitration even if the employer unilaterally imposed the arbitration requirement as a condition of employment. However, the organization reserves the right to refuse to enforce unfair arbitration policies—policies that fail to provide basic due process protection to employees.

In a class action charging violations of the California Labor Code provisions about overtime, meal and rest breaks, payroll records, and itemized wage statements, the California Court of Appeal found in 2012 that an arbitration agreement was not unconscionable, even though the employer opposed class arbitration. Some factors supported procedural unconscionability: it was a preprinted form, required by the employer; the clause was on page 42 of a 43-page employment agreement; and the arbitration language was not highlighted. However, on balance the court found that the agreement was not substantively unconscionable. The plaintiff did not show that requiring individual arbitration violated any state or federal law or public policy. The California Court of Appeal held that the agreement was silent about class arbitration, so the employer could not be forced into class arbitration. The agreement referred to all claims "between myself and the employer," and the court of appeal said that class arbitration is not between the individual employee and the employer. [*Nelsen v. Legacy Partners Residential, Inc.*, 207 Cal. App. 4th 1115 (July 18, 2012)]

The Fourth Circuit refused to vacate an arbitration award that used the opt-out class certification rules under the AAA Supplementary Rules for Class Arbitration, and not the Fair Labor Standards Act opt-in class certification rules. (The case was brought by three former managers charging that the ex-employer violated the FLSA by failing to pay overtime.) The AAA Class Rules permit the arbitrator to decide if a case should proceed as a class. The Fourth Circuit ruled that the arbitrator rendered a reasoned award, and the arbitration agreement gave the arbitrator the power to render any relief that a court could provide. [*Long John Silver's Rests. v. Cole*, 514 F.3d 345 (4th Cir. 2008)]

## [C]  Securities Industry Arbitration

Workers in the securities industry have to sign a standard employment agreement called the U-4 as a condition of working in the industry. It was the only industry to have a uniform mandatory arbitration requirement, so it served as a kind of "test bed" for studying legal issues about arbitration.

As of August 7, 1997, the National Association of Securities Dealers (NASD) voted to eliminate mandatory arbitration of employment discrimination claims brought by registered brokers under federal and state antidiscrimination statutes.

The New York Court of Appeals ruled in early 2007 that a securities industry employer cannot be sued for defamation in connection with the contents of a NASD U-5 statement (reasons for termination of an employee). The forms are as absolutely privileged as ethics complaints against an attorney, because public policy calls for candor. [*Rosenberg v. MetLife*, 8 N.Y.3d 359 (2007); see Joel Stashenko, *N.Y. High Court Affirms Absolute Privilege for Securities Industry's Termination Notices*, N.Y.L.J. (Mar. 30, 2007)]

## [D] Getting Ready for Arbitration

To be prepared for arbitration, you should:

- Review how the dispute arose, and what has already been done to resolve it;

- Check all relevant work rules and policies and how they were applied, both to the grievant and the other employees;

- Makes copies of all relevant documents for your own file, for the employee, and for the arbitrator;

- Inform the employee of documents in the employee's possession that you want copies of, and that you want copies sent to the arbitrator;

- If necessary, ask the arbitrator to subpoena necessary documents that you have not been able to get by informal means;

- Make sure all the witnesses sound accurate and articulate, but not mechanical or coached;

- Anticipate questions that will be asked during cross-examination, and prepare the witnesses to answer them;

- Make a list of points that you want each witness's testimony to put into the record;

- Review collections of published arbitration decisions, because even though arbitrators don't absolutely have to follow past precedents, they will often be swayed by interpretations that other arbitrators have reached in similar cases.

The first stage in an arbitration hearing is the opening statement. Usually, in a case where the employer's termination or discipline is being challenged, the employer will present its case first, because the employer has to prove the justification for its actions. In other types of cases, the employee usually gives the first opening statement. Next comes the other opening statement, and then the side that goes first introduces the testimony of its witnesses; the other side has the right to cross-examine. Then, the parties sum up their cases, and it is up to the arbitrator to decide.

## [E] Appeals

In general, the court system tries to get involved with arbitration as little as possible, although arbitration awards can be enforced by the court system, and sometimes disputes about arbitrability or arbitration process are litigated. Especially because employees are often required to arbitrate claims that they would prefer to litigate, there are many instances in which the parties to an arbitration will want to appeal the decision. A 2003 California case is a good introduction to the problems of arbitration appeals. [*Little v. Auto Stiegler, Inc.*, 29 Cal. 4th 1064, 63 P.3d 979, 130 Cal. Rptr. 2d 892 (2003)] This case involves four interlocking questions:

- Is a provision in an arbitration agreement allowing either party to have any award over $50,000 reviewed by a second arbitrator unconscionable?

- If it is unconscionable, can it be severed from the agreement and the rest of the agreement enforced—or does it make the whole agreement invalid and unenforceable?

- Do the California rules for arbitration due process in statutory discrimination claims also apply to claims that an employee was wrongfully terminated contrary to public policy? (The plaintiff was a service manager of an automobile dealership, who claimed that he was demoted, and then fired, for discovering and reporting warranty fraud.)

- If these rules do apply, is the agreement's requirement that the employer pay all the costs of arbitration if it mandates arbitration still valid?

The California rules come from *Armendariz v. Found. Health Psychcare Servs., Inc.* [24 Cal. 4th 83 (2000)], which imposes minimum due process requirements that cannot be waived. The arbitration agreement must not limit damages that would normally be available under the relevant statute; the parties to arbitration must be allowed enough discovery to pursue their claims (although this will probably be far less than the often very intrusive discovery process allowed in litigation); the arbitrator must issue a written decision that is subject to enough judicial review to keep arbitrators in compliance with the relevant laws; and the employer must pay all the costs that are unique to arbitration.

Early in 2004, the Ninth Circuit tackled the question of whether the federal courts can hear appeals of arbitration awards in the employer's favor—in other words, whether an employee can challenge an award of $0. The Ninth Circuit said no: when it comes to deciding whether the amount in controversy is the $75,000 required for diversity jurisdiction (jurisdiction based on the parties being citizens of different states), the amount in controversy is the amount actually awarded in the arbitration proceeding, not the amount that the employee claimed he or she was entitled to. [*Luong v. Circuit City Stores Inc.*, 356 F.3d 1188 (9th Cir. 2004)] Later in the year, however, another panel of the Ninth Circuit allowed a $0 arbitration award to be judicially reviewed if the amount at stake in the underlying dispute satisfies the amount in controversy requirement. [*Theis Research Inc. v. Brown & Bain*, 386 F.3d 1180 (9th Cir. 2004, amended Feb. 18, 2005)]

## § 40.07  MANDATORY PREDISPUTE ARBITRATION CLAUSES

### [A]  "Predispute" vs. "Postdispute" Clauses

There are many ways to draft an arbitration provision. Predispute arbitration clauses specify in advance that future disputes, if they occur, will be arbitrable. Such a provision can be either voluntary or mandatory. If voluntary, arbitration is just one option available for resolving disputes. If mandatory, the employee is blocked from suing the employer. Postdispute arbitration clauses are an agreement between employer and employee after a claim has been raised, and the best way to handle it is via arbitration.

In 1998, the Supreme Court resolved some difficult issues in *Wright v. Universal Maritime Serv. Corp.* [525 U.S. 70 (1998)] In this case, an injured stevedore was denied employment because companies that might have employed him considered him permanently disabled. He sued under the ADA without filing a grievance or going through arbitration under the CBA. The district court dismissed his case because he did not exhaust his grievance remedies. The Fourth Circuit upheld the district court.

However, the Supreme Court reversed the Fourth Circuit. The *Gilmer* case permits compulsory arbitration of an ADA claim, but the Supreme Court ruled that a contract claim must be treated differently from a statutory claim. Contract claims are presumed arbitrable, but statutory claims are not. A CBA must be very explicit to prevent litigation of a claim under a civil rights statute. A general arbitration clause that does not list the civil rights statutes that are covered will not prevent litigation under those statutes.

Early in 2002, the Supreme Court returned to the subject of predispute arbitration mandates. The ruling in *EEOC v. Waffle House Inc.* [534 U.S. 279 (2002)] is that the EEOC can pursue employment discrimination litigation (in this case, involving the Americans with Disabilities Act) even if the employees themselves would be required to submit their disputes to arbitration. The decision is very important as an indicator of legal thinking about arbitration, but it will not have much practical effect, because the EEOC doesn't take on many cases a year, and not all of them involve companies with mandatory arbitration requirements.

On the grounds that not every employee who makes an EEOC charge proceeds with the case, the Eighth Circuit said that employers should be allowed to participate in the EEOC process without waiving the right to enforce arbitration clauses. Therefore, if an employee who is covered by an arbitration agreement brings a discrimination charge, the employer's participation in the EEOC investigation does not prevent the employer from enforcing the arbitration clause. [*McNamara v. Yellow Transp., Inc.*, 570 F.3d 950 (8th Cir. 2009)]

The two federal Courts of Appeals that have considered the question have both ruled that USERRA claims are subject to arbitration. *Garrett v. Circuit City Stores*, 449 F.3d 672 (5th Cir. 2006) holds that USERRA's preemption provision does not show that Congress intended to rule out arbitration, because arbitration does not waive any of the substantive rights protected by USERRA. *Landis v. Pinnacle Eye Care*, 537 F.3d 559 (6th Cir. 2008) uses a similar analysis; its concurring opinion says that Congress did not use the kind of unambiguous language that would be necessary to rule out arbitration. [Howard S. Suskin and Benjamin J. Wimmer, *Arbitrability of USERRA Claims: Battle on the Home Front*, special to law.com (Oct. 15, 2008)]

## [B]  Claims Other Than Discrimination

Mandatory predispute arbitration clauses are not limited to use in connection with discrimination claims. Five of the federal Circuit Courts have ruled that arbitration can be a proper way to handle ERISA claims. [*Bird v. Shearson Lehman/American Express*, 926 F.2d 116 (2d Cir. 1991); *Pritzer v. Merrill Lynch*, 7 F.3d 1110 (3d Cir. 1993); *Kramer v. Smith Barney*, 80 F.3d 1080 (5th Cir. 1996); *Amulfo P. Sulit, Inc. v. Dean Witter Reynolds, Inc.*, 847 F.2d 475 (8th Cir. 1988); *Williams v. Imhoff*, 203 F.3d 758 (10th Cir. 2000)]

The Second Circuit ruled in 2008 that Sarbanes-Oxley Act whistleblower claims are arbitrable, because the test is whether the parties agreed to arbitrate; the scope of the agreement; whether Congress meant that type of claim to be subject to arbitration; and, if only some claims in a complaint have to be arbitrated, whether the proceedings should be suspended until the arbitration has been held. [*Guyden v. Aetna*, 544 F.3d 376 (2d Cir. 2008); see Mark Hamblett, *Whistleblower Claims Arbitrable Under SOX, 2nd Circuit Determines*, N.Y.L.J. (Oct. 6, 2008) (law.com)]

The Tenth Circuit granted a motion to compel arbitration in a wrongful termination case. The plaintiff, who charged that firing him violated the Sarbanes-Oxley Act and Kansas common law, argued that his ex-employer, Ricoh, waived the right to demand arbitration by participating in the plaintiff's suit. The plaintiff, Hill, sued November 3, 2008; on April 3, 2009, after complying with discovery and serving its own discovery request, Ricoh moved to stay the case and compel arbitration. The Tenth Circuit said that the federal rule that describes "arbitration and award" as an affirmative defense that has to be pleaded by the defendant refers only to a case in which there has already been an arbitration award, not to one which a party wishes to arbitrate. The Tenth Circuit did not believe that Ricoh had waived the right to arbitrate: a four-month delay is not necessarily fatal, because the case had not progressed very far, and delaying the demand for arbitration did not prejudice the plaintiff. Although the plaintiff claimed that arbitrating the case would prevent him from exercising his rights under Sarbanes-Oxley as a whistleblower, the Tenth Circuit was not persuaded by his unsupported assumption that arbitrators are hostile to whistleblower claims. [*Hill v. Ricoh Americas Corp.*, 603 F.3d 766 (10th Cir. 2010)]

According to the California Court of Appeal, a job application clause that requires only the applicant, and not the employer, to agree to binding arbitration of all disputes that cannot be resolved informally is both procedurally and substantively unconscionable. The court found the clause procedurally unconscionable because the agreement lacked mutuality; job applicants are not in a position to negotiate, and the rules for arbitration were not disclosed. Applicants were not informed that they waived the right to a trial. In this case, plaintiffs were required to respond to off-hour calls within 20 minutes. They brought suit seeking overtime payment for the calls. Two of the plaintiffs did not sign an arbitration agreement; four of them signed one form, and another signed a second form. [*Wisdom v. Accentcare, Inc.*, 202 Cal. App. 4th 591(Cal. App. 2012)]

The usual way that questions of arbitrability arise is that an employee sues his or her employer or former employer and the employer then tries to terminate litigation and enforce an arbitration clause. A 2011 Third Circuit case took a more complex path. Former employer Gray Holdco Inc. demanded arbitration more than 10 months after suing ex-employee Randy Cassady and his new business for breach of Cassady's employment contract and interference with Gray Holdco's client relationships. Some ten months after this suit was filed, Gray Holdco filed a demand for arbitration under the arbitration clause included in Gray Holdco's stock option plan. Cassady argued that Gray Holdco had waived the right to arbitrate by active participation in litigation, including extensive discovery. The Third Circuit said that waiver of the right to arbitrate can be assumed only where the arbitration demand was made long after a suit was begun and both sides have participated in ongoing discovery. There are several factors in the determination, such as how timely the motion to arbitrate is, the extent to which the party now seeking arbitration participated in the litigation, and the extent of discovery. In this case, the Third Circuit concluded that Gray Holdco waived arbitration because there was no reason given for the 10-month delay in seeking arbitration and the drawn-out proceedings made it impossible to conserve resources or speed up the case by using arbitration instead of litigation. [*Gray Holdco Inc. v. Cassady*, 654 F.3d 444 (3d Cir. 2011)]

The Eighth Circuit held that ERISA does not apply to executive's employment contracts that are not part of an ERISA plan—even if the amount to be paid is determined by reference to terms of an ERISA plan. Therefore, a terminated CEO was allowed to arbitrate his claims that he was deprived of benefits to which he was entitled when he was terminated in anticipation of a merger. Although usually employers favor arbitration and employees favor litigation, in this case the employer argued that the dispute involved an ERISA plan and, therefore, had to be litigated in federal court. The Eighth Circuit's decision that it was a pure contract dispute over a free-standing agreement meant that the ex-CEO could arbitrate his claims, including state-law claims for double damages. Because his contract was not part of an ERISA plan, his state-law claims were not preempted. [*Dakota, Minn. & E. Railroad Corp. v. Schieffer*, 711 F. 3d 712 (8th Cir. 2013). See Jeffrey Russell, Jonathan Potts, and Carrie Byrnes,

*Eighth Circuit Clarifies the Scope of ERISA's Application to Severance Arrangements*, Bryan Cave ERISA & Benefits Litigation Blog (Apr. 11, 2013) (benefitslink.com)]

As a general rule, a biased arbitration panel is not a ground for refusing to arbitrate, because it is possible to use the bias to overturn the arbitrator's decision once it is rendered. However, the Sixth Circuit applied a different analysis to this situation in which the process of selecting the arbitrator was fundamentally unfair, because it prevented the arbitral forum from being an adequate substitute for the court system. In this instance, the fees paid by the defendant were a major source of revenue for the arbitration provider, causing an obvious conflict of interest. [*Walker v. Ryan's Family Steak Houses, Inc.*, 400 F.3d 370 (6th Cir. 2005)]

Accusations of bias were made against ex-judge Maureen Lally-Green, who now works as an arbitrator. She ruled against James Freeman in an ADEA case against Pittsburgh Glass Works. Freeman said that Lally-Green did not disclose that a company related to Pittsburgh Glass Works contributed $4,500 to her unsuccessful 2007 campaign for the Pennsylvania Supreme Court. The Third Circuit said that undisclosed campaign contributions do not prove bias: the campaign contributions are public records, and arbitrators have no duty to disclose readily available public information. Furthermore, the plaintiff's law firm also contributed to Lally-Green's campaign.

Freeman also said that Lally-Green failed to disclose that she taught a labor law class with the defendant's senior attorney. Pittsburgh Glass Works alleged that Lally-Green did disclose this fact; the court said that it was irrelevant because it was not strongly suggestive of bias. The Third Circuit used the same standard whether the challenger asserts actual bias or failure to disclose. According to the court, there is a high bar of proving actual bias that is evident to a reasonable person, not a mere appearance of partiality. This is not the same as the standard for recusal of a judge (any situation in which the judge's impartiality might reasonably be questioned). Arbitrators are often chosen because they are knowledgeable industry insiders, so it is common for arbitrators to already have dealt with some of the parties.[*Freeman v. Pittsburgh Glass Works*, 709 F.3d 240 (3d Cir. 2013); see Saranac Hale Spencer, *Contributions Not Enough to Show Ex-Judge and Arbitrator's Bias*, The Legal Intelligencer (Mar. 7, 2013) (law.com)]

The Third Circuit asserted an objective theory of contract formation to hold that a Spanish-speaking worker was bound by the arbitration clause in the English contract he signed—although the bilingual employee who translated the contract for him admitted that he did not translate the arbitration clause. The result was that, when the Spanish-speaking worker was fired and tried to sue for wrongful termination, the Third Circuit required the claim to be arbitrated instead. [*Morales v. Sun Constructors Inc.*, 541 F.3d 218 (3d Cir. 2008); No byline, *3rd Circuit: Agreement Can Be Enforced Despite Language Barrier*, The Legal Intelligencer (Sept. 9, 2008) (law.com)]

## [C]  Arbitration Costs

The court decided, in *Little v. Auto Stiegler, Inc.* [29 Cal. 4th 1064, 63 P.3d 979, 130 Cal. Rptr. 2d 892 (2003)], that an arbitration agreement's failure to specify an allocation for the costs of the process doesn't make the agreement void or unenforceable—it places the responsibility for paying all the arbitration costs on the employer. The court in the *Little* case ruled that this does not conflict with the Supreme Court's decision in a non-employment arbitration case [*Green Tree Fin. Corp. v. Randolph*, 531 U.S. 79 (2000)] holding that failure to allocate arbitration costs does not mean that an agreement is unenforceable on the grounds of failing to protect parties from excessively high arbitration costs. The *Little* court interpreted *Green Tree* to mean that someone who claims that the risk of excessively high costs prevents him or her from exercising the right to arbitration has the burden of proof as to the likelihood that such costs will be incurred.

According to the D.C. Circuit and the Tenth Circuit, a requirement that employees advance arbitration costs automatically denies them the right to arbitrate their grievances. In the Fourth Circuit, the test (under *Bradford v. Rockwell Semiconductor Systems Inc.* [238 F.3d 549 (4th Cir. 2001)]) is the effect on the individual claimant, but the Sixth Circuit looks at the effect not just on the individual but on other similarly situated employees. [*Morrison v. Circuit City Stores Inc.*, 317 F.3d 646 (6th Cir. 2003)] The Sixth Circuit said that when courts make this determination, they should also consider the possibility that the plaintiff will not have to pay the costs either because the arbitration agreement itself shifts the costs to the losing party, or because the arbitrator might impose the costs on the employer. In this case, the Sixth Circuit did find the fees excessive and possibly discouraging of the exercise of arbitration rights—the fees ranged from $1,125 to $3,000.

Late in 2003, the Ninth Circuit ruled that an employer who failed to pay for arbitration of an employee's claims of breach of the employment contract (the employee charged that payments, including stock options, were not made as promised) was in default under § 3 of the FAA. Therefore, the employer could not have the employee's suit stayed in order to get arbitration of the same claims, even though the employment contract that the employer allegedly violated contained an arbitration clause. [*Sink v. Aden Enterp. Inc.*, 352 F.3d 1197 (9th Cir. 2003)]

## [D]  Class Arbitration and Waivers

Throughout the legal system, there has been a trend for decades (encompassing both statutes and court decisions) to limit the availability of class actions. A number of compulsory arbitration agreements required by employers also require employees to waive the option of bringing employment-related claims as class arbitrations—so the court system has also had to determine the validity of such clauses.

California has ruled that, in at least some circumstances, waivers of class arbitration are invalid when employees charge violations of their statutory right to overtime pay under California Labor Code §§ 510 (time-and-a-half for overtime) and 1194 (forbidding contracts under which employees waive the right to overtime pay). Class waivers should not be enforced if the trial court determines that class arbitration would be significantly more efficient than individual arbitration. But the court also refused to set a general rule that it is always unlawful to waive class arbitration of overtime cases. The question is whether there is a community of interest: whether the common questions of law or fact are predominant, the class representatives' own claims or defenses are typical, and the class representatives adequately represent the class. [*Gentry v. Superior Ct. of L.A. County*, 42 Cal. 4th 443 (Cal. 2007)]

*Gentry* was an overtime case, and the California Supreme Court treated the right to overtime as a statutory right that cannot be waived. In 2012, the California Court of Appeal rejected the argument that *Stolt-Nielsen* and *Concepcion* had changed the law. In a class action about overtime and meal and rest breaks, the California Court of Appeal found that *Gentry* remains good law. Because it sets out the factors to be applied on a case-by-case basis to see if employees are barred from exercising statutory rights, it does not impose an invalid categorical rule against all class action waivers. [*Franco v. Arakelian Enters., Inc.*, 211 Cal. App. 4th 314, 149 Cal. Rptr. 3d 530 (2012) A case pending before the California Supreme Court, *Iskanian v. CLS Transp.*, No. S204032, involves the issue of whether *AT&T Mobility* preempts *Gentry*. [Cynthia Foster, *High Court Queues Up Number of Post-'Brinker' Cases*, The Recorder (Jan. 4, 2012) (law.com)]

## § 40.08  FACTORS THAT PROMOTE ADR SUCCESS

Most successful ADR systems embody several steps, including in-house procedures for resolving grievances before outside parties get involved. In-house resolutions can be quick and inexpensive. Using a mediator or arbitrator always involves some degree of delay and expense, even if it is far less than the ruinous effort of litigation.

Any ADR system should specify whether the matter will be heard by one mediator or arbitrator or by a panel. Panels usually have three members; it's definitely better to have an odd number to prevent 2–2 or 3–3 splits.

The ADR policy should specify not only the number but the qualifications of the decision makers. It should be clear which employees will be allowed to use ADR to settle disputes—and which ones will be compelled to use it. The policy should clarify which disputes are involved: All employment-related disputes? All federal statutory discrimination claims? Only certain federal claims? Only claims that would otherwise go to state court?

An appropriate policy is fair to employees, providing them with as much due process protection as litigation would offer. They should have an adequate opportunity to assert claims, get evidence about what the employer did, and receive adequate remedies if the mediator or arbitrator decides in their favor.

The American Bar Association's "Due Process Protocol" sets out these standards for fairness in mandatory arbitration matters:

- The employee is aware of the arbitration requirement and accepts it voluntarily;

- The employee can be represented at arbitration (e.g., by a lawyer or union representative);

- The employee has access to a full range of remedies;

The arbitrator has the power to make the employer pay the employee's arbitration-related costs. Some cases about arbitration take the position that, since the employer wanted arbitration in the first place, it should pay the full cost. The system could also be set up so that the employee never has to pay more than 50% of the cost of arbitration, or never has to pay more than one day's fee for the arbitrators.

CHAPTER **41**

# EEOC AND STATE ENFORCEMENT OF ANTIDISCRIMINATION LAWS

## § 41.01   INTRODUCTION

The Equal Employment Opportunity Commission (EEOC) is in charge of enforcing Title VII and the Americans with Disabilities Act (ADA). It also enforces the Equal Pay Act (EPA) and Age Discrimination in Employment Act (ADEA), although the enforcement provisions for these acts are slightly different because they reflect their derivation from the Fair Labor Standards Act. EPA complainants do not have to file an EEOC charge; the rules for ADEA charges are found in 29 C.F.R. § 1626.4.

The basic enforcement scheme is that people who believe they have been discriminated against file charges with the EEOC. The EEOC works with state antidiscrimination agencies, using methods ranging from informal persuasion to litigation to get employers to comply with the law and eliminate any discriminatory practices occurring in the workplace.

The EEOC can intervene in a suit brought by an employee or can bring its own lawsuits against employers. The EEOC has the power to collect data, investigate allegations of discrimination, view conditions in the workplace, and inspect records. It can also advise employers about how to comply with the law. The EEOC has the power to subpoena witnesses and documents, bring suits, and supervise the collection of damages that courts have ordered or that employers have agreed to pay under a settlement.

Therefore, the EEOC has a dual role. It investigates charges brought by employees, but it can also litigate as a plaintiff. The theory is that the EEOC acts as plaintiff to preserve the rights of all the employees within the workplace. The EEOC always has a right to investigate and, where it believes a cause of action exists, to litigate. So employees' waivers and releases, or their settlement of claims against the employer, can prevent those employees from suing their employers, but will not prevent a suit by the EEOC. Furthermore, waivers and releases are void as against public policy if they try to prevent employees from assisting in an EEOC investigation.

Similarly, the EEOC can pursue an ADA case (including seeking specific relief for an individual) even if the individual employee was covered by a mandatory predispute arbitration agreement (see § 40.07) and therefore could not sue the employer. [*EEOC v. Waffle House*, 534 U.S. 279 (2002)]

EEOC investigators assign cases to classifications of A (the most serious), B, and C. In an A-1 case, the EEOC itself may pursue the case as plaintiff. An A-2 case is likely to result in a finding of good cause, but no litigation by the EEOC itself. It's a bad sign if the EEOC sends out a questionnaire to potential plaintiffs; asks the defendant for a statement of its position; if the EEOC does not ask the employer to mediate; or if it's a deferral state (see below) but the first contact comes from the federal EEOC.

It is often helpful to demonstrate good faith by offering unconditional reinstatement to a charging party. There are many cases indicating that if the charging party rejects such an offer, he or she will not be eligible for various kinds of relief (back pay, front pay, possibly even court-ordered reinstatement).

The Department of Labor also has the right to sue federal contractors for remedies, including punitive damages, if the contractors are guilty of race, sex, or religious discrimination. Employees of federal contractors get a choice of filing their complaints with the EEOC or the DOL. The EEOC and DOL have a work-sharing plan.

It is often predicted that a poor economic climate will increase the number of discrimination charges filed because unemployed workers are willing to bring charges and risk getting reputations as troublemakers.

In FY 2012, there were a total of 99,412 EEOC charges filed: 33.7% (33,512 charges) of race discrimination, 30.5% sex discrimination (30,356 charges), 26,379 disability discrimination charges (26.5%), 22,857 age discrimination charges (23.0%), 10,883 charges of national origin discrimination (10.9%), 3,811 charges of religious discrimination (3.8%), 2,662 (2.7%) charges of discrimination on the basis of color, 1,082 (1.1%) Equal Pay Act charges and 280 charges (0.2%) under GINA. Retaliation charges were extremely common: there were 37,836 retaliation charges under all the statutes, and 31,208 Title VII retaliation charges. The percentages add up to far more than 100% because it is common for charging parties to allege more than one kind of discrimination. [EEOC, *Charge Statistics FY 1997 Through FY 2012*, <http://www1.eeoc.gov//eeoc/statistics/enforcement/charges.cfm?> (undated; last accessed Mar. 18, 2013)]

The EEOC won $365.4 million for discrimination victims in fiscal 2012. The EEOC's backlog increased every year from 2002 to 2011 but in both 2011 and 2012, the backlog was reduced. There were 78,136 pending charges at the end of FY 2011, 70,312 at the end of FY 2012. In its 2012 fiscal year, the EEOC filed 122 suits: 85 individual suits, 26 with multiple charging parties, and 10 alleging systemic discrimination. There were 254 resolutions of suits, involving more than 23,446 employees. Systemic discrimination is a focus for the EEOC, which completed 240 systemic investigations in FY 2012, leading to 46 settlements or conciliation agreements. [Andrew Ramonas, *EEOC Breaks Record for Amount Won for Workplace Discrimination Victims*, Nat'l LJ (Jan. 28, 2013) (law.com)]

In 2012, the EEOC announced a four-year strategic plan that focuses on systemic discrimination: pattern or practice cases with broad impact, but no specific percentage target was announced. The EEOC says that, with close to 100,000 individual private-sector charges a year and 14,000 requests from the federal sector for hearings and appeals, it is necessary to conserve resources—but individual discrimination charges will still be pursued. [Jenna Greene, *EEOC Releases New Strategic Plan, Vows to Fight Systemic Discrimination*, Blog of the Legal Times (Jan. 20, 2012) (law.com)]

Although in 2012, the EEOC reduced the number of suits filed (122 in fiscal 2012, 261 in FY 2011), it had four times as many systemic discrimination investigations under way as in the year before. Unless these cases settle, there will be many EEOC suits in 2013 and 2014. 2012 was the year in which the EEOC achieved record monetary recoveries: $365 million recovered in private sector administrative enforcement (including conciliation, mediation, settlement, and withdrawal with benefits). Approximately 10% was attributable to systemic discrimination cases, four times as high as the year before. The largest settlement of fiscal 2012 was $11 million, paid by YRC Inc. (formerly known as Yellow Transportation Inc.) for a racially hostile workplace where black employees were treated harshly and threatened. [Sue Reisinger, *EEOC 2012 Report Shows Fewer Discrimination Suits, More Investigations*, Corporate Counsel (Nov. 30, 2012) (law.com)]

In January 2013, the EEOC won two systemic discrimination cases. The Sixth Circuit finalized its decision to remand the EEOC's sex discrimination case about Cintas' hiring of sales representatives. The Sixth Circuit denied Cintas' motion for reconsideration and none of the judges voted in favor of rehearing en banc. Therefore, the EEOC did not have to pay the $2.6 million of the defendant's attorney's fees that the district court ordered, and the Sixth Circuit revived the EEOC's case. The Sixth Circuit held that the EEOC had acted in good faith and should not have to pay attorney's fees. The district court said that the EEOC erred by suing under § 706 of Title VII, not § 707 (which authorizes pattern-or-practice claims). The Sixth Circuit ruled that, even though there is no specific pattern-or-practice language in § 706, it can still be used in such cases. The EEOC applauded this decision, saying that it permitted a focus in the early stages of the case on whether the employer's ordinary practices were discriminatory rather than whether individual acts of discrimination were committed.

The EEOC sued UPS in 2009 for limiting leave of absence for disabled employees to 12 months and denying them reasonable accommodation. UPS protested that the EEOC named only two employees in its complaint and did not provide enough information about the unidentified workers on behalf the agency sought relief. The district court dismissed the first complaint and two amended complaints. However, when the EEOC moved to appeal the dismissal, the district court permitted the EEOC to file the second amended complaint, which includes detailed factual allegations about the effects of UPS' policy and charged that the policy was applied to all employees across the board. [Jenna Greene, *EEOC Scores Wins in Pair of Systemic Discrimination Cases*, The BLT (Jan. 18, 2013) (law.com)]

## [A]   Recent Settlements

Shortly before trial was scheduled to begin, Rite Aid agreed to pay $250,000 to settle EEOC charges of discrimination and retaliation against an epileptic employee. Rite Aid said that epilepsy is not an ADA disability; it did not regard the employee as disabled; and he posed a threat to himself and others during seizures. There were two instances when he was hospitalized after a seizure in the workplace. Three other EEOC settlements were announced on November 7, 2012.

Marriott settled sexual harassment charges for $155,000; a California hotel agreed to a $195,000 settlement of sexual harassment and retaliation charges; and a youth facility in Michigan entered into a 10-year consent decree to settle pregnancy discrimination charges. [Jenna Greene, *Rite Aid Settles EEOC Charges Regarding Employee With Epilepsy*, Nat'l L.J. (Nov. 8, 2012) (law.com)]

For recent examples of EEOC settlements, see, e.g., the following:

- Pepsi Beverages settled EEOC race discrimination charges, agreeing to pay $3.13 million and provide job offers and training. Most of the settlement goes to black job applicants, more than 300 of whom were denied access to permanent jobs. Pepsi also agreed to offer jobs to qualified applicants who still want to work there. The EEOC said that Pepsi's criminal background check procedure, which ruled out everyone who had ever been arrested even if no conviction resulted, discriminated against black applicants. Employment was also denied to people convicted of certain minor offenses. [Tara Cantore, *Pepsi to Pay $3.13M to Resolve Race Bias Charge*, plansponsor.com (Jan. 12, 2012)]

- Sparks Steak House agreed to pay $600,000 to settle EEOC charges of male/male harassment. The complaint accused some managers of regularly engaging in inappropriate touching and groping. The waiters complained but the harassment continued. The maitre d'hotel was the most serious harasser. Management imposed a last chance agreement on him but did not fire him. [Jenna Greene, *NYC Steakhouse Settles with EEOC over Male-on-Male Harassment Charges*, BLT (Nov. 16, 2012) (law-.com). Greene reports that the percentage of sexual harassment charges filed by men rose from 12% in 1997 to 16% in 2011.]

- Fishmonger M. Slavin and Sons settled an EEOC suit by paying $900,000 to 31 black workers who were routinely subjected to verbal and physical sexual harassment and sexual and racial slurs by supervisors. [Andy Newman, *Fish Seller Settles Harassment Suit Brought by Black Workers*, NYTimes.com (Dec. 20, 2011)]

- A federal magistrate judge in Chicago entered a $3 million consent decree to resolve EEOC's suit against Scrub, Inc., a janitorial service. The EEOC said that many black applicants were denied hiring for entry-level janitorial jobs, based on the company's subjective decision-making process that enabled discrimination. Approximately 550 job applicants will share the $3 million, and the decree also requires hiring of certain plaintiffs who still want to work for Scrub, Inc. [Rebecca Moore, *Janitorial Services Company to Pay $3M for Hiring Bias*, plansponsor.com (Dec. 2, 2010)]

- More than two dozen Somali Muslims working as Hertz drivers at Seattle-Tacoma International Airport were fired for refusing to clock out for their prayer breaks. Hertz said that the workers violated the CBA and a settlement reached two years earlier; the union said that the CBA did not require clocking out, The union filed a ULP complaint and EEOC charges. Eight of the 34 were re-hired after signing a clock-out agreement. [Rebecca Moore, *Union Suing Hertz After Firing of Two Dozen Muslims*, plansponsor.com (Oct. 21, 2011)]

- Las Vegas' The Sahara resort agreed to pay $100,000 to settle an EEOC national origin harassment/retaliation suit. Ezzat Elias, who worked for the hotel buffet, was harassed because he is Egyptian. Co-workers called him Bin Laden and made him the subject of graffiti. Managers did not stop the harassment and retaliated when he complained by increasing his workload, scrutinizing his work more intensively, disciplining him, and suspending him. Elias will receive $85,000 in monetary relief over a three-year period, and the hotel's owner will pay a further $15,000 to the Nevada Equal Rights Commission for education and outreach. [Plansponsor staff, *Sahara Hotel and Casino to Pay $85K to Egyptian Former Worker*, plansponsor.com (Dec. 7, 2010)]

- The Department of Labor's Office of Federal Contract Compliance Programs announced that Tyson Fresh Meats Inc. entered into two gender discrimination consent decrees, resulting in a total of $2.25 million in back wages, interest, and benefits to be paid to more than 1,650 qualified female job applicants who were denied hiring at four facilities. At least 220 plaintiffs will be offered jobs as openings arise at three of the plants (the fourth has already closed). The discrimination was discovered in the course of a compliance review assessing compliance with Executive Order 11246's ban on sex discrimination by federal contractors. [Tara Cantore, *Tyson to Pay $2.25M to Settle Discrimination Cases*, plansponsor.com (Sept. 20, 2011)]

- Advance Components (Texas) agreed to pay $201,000 to settle an EEOC suit. The company's executive vice president/general manager made biased comments to 64-year-old national sales manager, Dan Miller, and eventually fired him, saying he wanted to hire more "driven" young men who would earn less. The day after Miller was fired, he was replaced by a man in his 30s. The EEOC said that Miller was an effective salesman and popular with customers. [Rebecca Moore, *Company to Pay $201K for Firing Older Employee*, plansponsor.com (May 22, 2012)]

- Hawaii Healthcare Professionals, Inc. settled an EEOC ADEA suit by paying $193,000 to the 54-year-old office coordinator fired for "looking" and "sounding old." [Jay Polansky, *Hawaii Company Settles Age Discrimination Suit*, plansponsor.com (July 20, 2012)]

- Computer Systems LLC agreed to pay $32,500 to a 60-year-old billing specialist who was RIFed when a less qualified 34-year-old billing specialist was retained. [*EEOC v. Computer Systems LLC*, No. 2:11-cv-1178 (E.D. Wis. 2012); see *Rebecca Moore, Employer to Pay for Terminating 60-Year-Old*, plansponsor.com (Nov. 1, 2012)]

- Marymount Manhattan College settled an ADEA suit by paying $125,000 to Patricia Catterson. Catterson was already employed by Marymount. Because of her age, she was refused a job as a tenure-track assistant professor and passed over in favor of a less qualified, younger applicant. The school said that the younger candidate "was at the right moment of her life for commitment to a full-time position." [*Catterson v. Marymount*, No. 12-cv-2388 (JPO) (S.D.N.Y. settled 2013); see Jay Polansky, *Marymount Manhattan College Settles EEOC Suit*, plansponsor.com (Jan. 7, 2013); Rebecca Moore, *EEOC Sues College for Not Hiring 64-Year-Old*, plansponsor.com (Apr. 23, 2012)]

- The EEOC sued Wal-Mart for refusing let a long-term (22 year) employee with cerebral palsy return after medical leave for cerebral palsy-related surgery. Sales clerk Marcia Arney produced a doctor's note requiring periodic breaks. Her store manager would not permit her to come back to work without a full release with no restrictions. The EEOC sued for compensatory and punitive damages and injunctive relief, alleging that Wal-Mart could have accommodated her need for breaks. [Tara Cantore, *EEOC Sues Wal-Mart For Firing Disabled Employee*, plansponsor.com (Sept. 20, 2011)]

- Journal Disposition agreed to settle an EEOC suit for $55,000. The EEOC alleged that the company fired a long-term employee diagnosed with cancer when he used up his 26 weeks of short-term disability. Before the leave expired, he returned to work part-time while receiving chemotherapy and could perform the essential functions of the job. He was fired and made eligible for re-hire if he was once again able to work full-time. The EEOC said that he had sought accommodation: five months of part-time work while the chemotherapy proceeded. The company applied its policy restrictively without considering his ability to work, the reasonableness of his request, or whether it imposed undue hardship on the employer. [Tara Cantore, *Printing Company Accused of Firing Capable Worker with Cancer*, plansponsor.com (Nov. 21, 2011)]

- The Northern District of Illinois gave final approval in February 2010 to the largest ADA settlement in a single EEOC suit: Sears agreed to pay $6.2 million to settle a nationwide class action about firing of disabled workers. The suit began in 2004 with an employee's charge that he was fired for taking leave after being injured on the job, instead of being granted accommodations that would have permitted him to return to work. The EEOC's discovery revealed hundreds of other employees who were similarly treated. The named plaintiff received $122,500; 235 class members received amounts of $2,250 and up. [*EEOC v. Sears*, No. 04-C-7282 (N.D. Ill. Feb. 5, 2010); see Lynne Marek, *Sears Agrees to Multimillion-Dollar Settlement Over Firing of Disabled Workers*, Nat'l L.J. (Sept. 30, 2009) (la w.com); and *Judge Divides Up the Money in Sears' Record-Setting ADA Settlement*, Nat'l L.J. (Feb. 9, 2010) (law.com)]

- Comfort Suites agreed to pay $132,500 and change its policies to settle the EEOC's suit on behalf of hotel clerk with autism who was denied reasonable accommodation, disciplined, and eventually fired because of his disability; $125,000 went to the plaintiff, $7,500 as a donation to Partnerships with Industry, a local non-profit organization that supports employment of people with disabilities. Shortly after being hired at Comfort Suites, he applied for free job coaching from the state, which would have helped him with autism-specific training techniques. The hotel first denied him use of the job coach, then fired him. [*EEOC v. Tarsadia Hotels dba Comfort Suites*, No. 10-CV-1921-DMS-BGS (S.D. Cal. 2011); see Tara Cantore, *Comfort Suites to Pay For Discrimination Against Clerk with Autism*, plansponsor.com (Nov. 10, 2011)]

- United Insurance Co. of America agreed to pay $37,000 to resolve an EEOC disability discrimination lawsuit about Craig Burns, a recovering drug addict who had been in a methadone program since 2004. He was offered a job as an insurance agent in January 2010, contingent on passing a drug test. Of course the test showed methadone; he sent a letter from his treatment program saying that he was legally taking methadone as part of a program. The offer of employment was withdrawn. The EEOC brought suit in the Eastern District of North Carolina in August 2011. The settlement includes a two-year consent decree requiring training on need for individualized assessment of ADA disability and how to determine direct threat. [Tara Cantore, *United Insurance to Pay $37K for Failing to Hire Recovering Addict*, plansponsor.com (Jan. 25, 2012)]

- As part of the Obama administration's National HIV/AIDS Strategy, which includes removing barriers to employment of persons who are or who are perceived as being HIV-positive, the EEOC settled two suits on HIV status discrimination. Innershore Enterprises Inc. agreed to pay $20,000 to settle a suit over firing a female concession manager for being HIV-positive. Callaro's Prime Steak & Seafood, LLC agreed to pay $10,000 in an ADA suit for forcing an employee to resign because of her association with an HIV-positive family member. When the employee refused to get an HIV test at the employer's order, she was forced out by reducing her hours and impairing her working conditions. [Rebecca

Moore, *EEOC Announces Suits as Part of National HIV/AIDS Strategy*, plansponsor.com (Nov. 23, 2010)]

- Maverik Country Stores agreed to pay about $115,000 to settle the EEOC's suit charging Maverik with first refusing to accommodate then firing a bakery clerk whose HIV-positive status was disclosed in a Worker's Compensation proceeding. The EEOC's position is that the fact that a person is HIV-positive does not make it unsafe for him or her to work with food. [*EEOC v. Maverik, Inc. dba Maverik Country Stores* (D. Wyo. 2011); see Tara Cantore, *Maverik Ordered to Pay for Firing HIV-Positive Employee*, plansponsor.com (Nov. 7, 2011)]

- Imagine Schools, Inc., a nationwide charter school operator that has over 70 schools in 12 states, agreed to pay $570,000 to settle an EEOC suit in the Western District of Missouri. The EEOC alleged that Imagine Schools violated the PDA when it terminated two pregnant employees (an office manager and an administrative assistant) when it closed a charter school and re-opened a private school at the same location. [Rebecca Moore, *Charter School Operator Settles Pregnancy Discrimination Lawsuit*, plansponsor.com (Mar. 22, 2010)]

- Vanguard Group settled for $300,000 for refusing to hire an African-American woman as a financial planner because of her race. The applicant had an MBA in finance and 14 years of financial management experience; a less-qualified white man was hired instead. Vanguard did not admit fault, but agreed to give its managers and supervisors anti-discrimination training. [Fred Schneyer, *Vanguard Settles Racial Discrimination Case for 300K*, plansponsor.com (Jan. 6, 2010)]

- Lowe's Home Centers, Inc. agreed to settle a religious discrimination/retaliation lawsuit for $120,000; the EEOC said that Lowe's retaliated against a Christian who observed a Sunday Sabbath by assigning him to work 27 out of 28 Sundays. The settlement required giving the charging party a job without Sunday work. [Tara Cantore, *Lowes to Pay $120K to Settle Religious Bias and Retaliation Lawsuit*, plansponsor.com (Sept. 21, 2011)]

## [B]  Recent Litigation

The EEOC accused auto parts retailer AutoZone of harassment and failure to accommodate an employee's religion. Frank Mahoney-Burroughs converted to Sikhism. A manager asked him if he was a terrorist, belonged to al-Qaeda, or intended to blow up the store. Nor did AutoZone act when Mahoney-Burroughs was harassed by customers. Mahoney-Burroughs was not permitted to wear the turban and ritual bracelet required of male Sikhs, and eventually he was terminated because of his religion and in retaliation for his attempts to enforce his rights. [Rebecca Moore, *EEOC Case Shows Effects of 9/11 Still Creating Workplace Issues*, plansponsor.com (Sept. 29, 2010)]

The Third Circuit upheld summary judgment for the employer in an EEOC Title VII suit on behalf of female Muslim prison employees who wanted to wear khimars, a type of head covering, at work. The Third Circuit found that the khimars present at least a small danger because they could be used as a weapon against employees, or could be used by prisoners to impersonate guards, and it would be impractical to remove the khimars at each checkpoint. [*EEOC v. Geo Group Inc.*, 616 F.3d 265 (3d Cir. 2010); see *EEOC Wins Settlement of Suit on Behalf of Muslim,* plansponsor.com (Nov. 28, 2011) for Imperial Security's $50,000 settlement in favor of a security guard who was ordered to remove her khimar when she reported for work.]

The National Institute of Mental Health says that 5.7 million adults in the United States are affected by bipolar disorder each year, making it one of the top 10 causes of disability. In 2012, the EEOC won a case against Cottonwood Financial Ltd. in the Eastern District of Washington, one of the first cases involving bipolar disorder. Receptionist Kelly Ferris took medical leave to manage a flareup of her condition. She said that she was fired after five months, whereas company policy permits an 18-month leave. In September 2012, the EEOC sued the supermarket chain King Soopers for firing a bipolar worker. The year before, King Soopers settled another EEOC case for $80,000, for failing to stop the bullying of a mentally challenged worker. [Ashley Casas, *EEOC Sues Food Retailer for Firing Bipolar Worker*, plansponsor.com (Sept. 19, 2012)]

UPS Supply Chain Solutions agreed to pay $95,000 to settle a disability discrimination suit about denial of accommodation to Mauricio Centeno. Centeno was refused a sign language interpreter for training and staff meetings, although his employer knew that he had trouble reading written English. The case was settled after the Ninth Circuit held that employers must provide reasonable accommodations for employment conditions, such as staff meetings, even if they are not essential functions of the job. The settlement includes three years of non-monetary relief, including appointment of an ADA coordinator, prompt investigation of disability complaints, and ensuring that deaf and hearing-impaired employees receive effective accommodations. [*EEOC v. UPS Supply Chain Solutions*, No. CV 06-06210 ABC (Ex); see Tara Cantore, *UPS Unit to Pay $95K to Settle Disability Discrimination Lawsuit*, plansponsor.com (Dec. 15, 2011)]

The EEOC suffered defeat several times in its case against trucking company CRST Van Expedited Inc. The wider significance is that the EEOC may bring fewer cases on behalf of groups of plaintiffs.

The EEOC sued CRST, charging serious sexual harassment, including rape in some cases, of more than 200 female truck drivers by male drivers assigned to train them. The District Court for the Northern District of Iowa not only dismissed the EEOC's case, but also ordered the EEOC to pay more than $4.467 million in fees and expenses to CRST because the district court found that the defendant was the prevailing party in the suit. The district court found that the EEOC completely mishandled the preparation of the case. The EEOC was approached by a female driver who alleged severe harassment. The EEOC approached over 2,700 female former employees of CRST to get them to participate in the suit. The EEOC found over 200 potential class members. The district court gave the EEOC only three months for discovery, ruling that any woman for whom the EEOC did not get a deposition would be dismissed from the case. The EEOC took only 150 depositions, so 120 potential plaintiffs were excluded from the case. The district court also said that the EEOC improperly tried to pursue a case against CRST for maintaining a pattern or practice of sexual harassment—but had not provided evidence. The district court eliminated many other potential plaintiffs for various reasons (e.g., they did not allege severe and pervasive harassment; they did not list the potential recovery from the suit in their bankruptcy petitions; they did not complain to CRST and give the company a chance to eliminate the harassment).

After reducing the potential plaintiff class to 67, the district court dismissed all of those claims because the EEOC had failed to investigate or attempt conciliation of each individual claim. The district court treated this as a complete failure to satisfy Title VII's pre-suit procedural requirements. The district court also said that the trainers were not supervisors, so CRST was not vicariously liable for any harassment that occurred.

The EEOC appealed to the Eighth Circuit, which upheld most of the district court's findings. However, the Eighth Circuit ruled that claims of two of the plaintiffs—including the original complainant who went to the EEOC—should not have been dismissed. That meant that CRST was no longer a prevailing defendant—so the EEOC did not have to pay CRST's fees and costs immediately (although it might have to do so when the case is finally resolved). The EEOC asked the Eighth Circuit to re-hear the case. The Eighth Circuit agreed, but then, the next day, the Eighth Circuit re-issued its original opinion with only a minor change, and rejected the EEOC's request for another re-hearing by all of the judges of the Eighth Circuit. The Eighth Circuit agreed with the district court that the EEOC failed to meet its obligation to attempt conciliation of each claim. What the EEOC should have done was to investigate thoroughly before filing suit, and attempt conciliation of each claim uncovered during the investigation.

Then the Eighth Circuit remanded the case to the District Court for the Northern District of Iowa. History repeated itself as the district court reinstated the finding that CRST was a prevailing defendant, and once again ordered the EEOC to pay close to $5 million to CRST for attorneys' fees, court costs, and other expenses, reinstating the finding that CRST was a prevailing defendant because the EEOC brought 153 claims that were frivolous, unreasonable, or groundless. The district court excoriated the EEOC for the inadequacy of its investigation and failure to carry out the statutory duty of attempting conciliation. The district court treated the EEOC's pattern or practice claim as unreasonable because there was no foundation of statistics or legal citations to support the charges.

This decision opens up a defense argument for employers: that the EEOC denied the employer the chance to conciliate. The EEOC might respond by doing a better job of arguing pattern-or-practice allegations. [*EEOC v. CRST Van Expedited Inc.*, 679 F.3d 657 (8th Cir. 2012); *en banc rehearing denied*, June 8, 2012. The history of the case is discussed in, e.g., Jenna Greene, *Rocky Road for EEOC*, Nat'l L.J. (May 7, 2012) (law.com); and *Appeals Panel Rules Against EEOC in Trucker Harassment Case a Second Time*, The BLT (May 9, 2012) (la w.com); *EEOC v. CRST Van Expedited, Inc.*,No. 07-CV-95, 2013 U.S. Dist. LEXIS 107822 (N.D. Iowa Aug. 1, 2013); see Gerald L. Maatman, Jr. and Howard M. Wexler, *Time to Pay Up! EEOC Ordered to Pay $4.694 Million in Fees and Costs for Pursuing "Unreasonable" and "Groundless" Claims*,Lexology.com,   <http://www.lexology.com/library/detail.aspx?g=b02607dc-df4c-4db0-b6e8-d41731e59635> (Aug. 3, 2013)]

After this decision, the District Court for the Northern District of Illinois allowed an ADA case to proceed even though the EEOC attempted conciliation in two cases but not in the cases of 17 additional employees who were located during the investigation. The Northern District of Illinois focused on the validity of the claims rather than the correctness of the EEOC pre-trial procedure. In contrast, the District Court for the Eastern District of Washington cited the *CRST* case and ordered mediation because the court found that the EEOC's good-faith conciliation efforts were inadequate. [Compare *EEOC v. United Road Towing Inc.*, No. 10 C 6259 (N.D. Ill. May 11, 2012) with *EEOC v. Evans Fruit Co.*, No. CV-10-3033-LRS (E.D. Wash. May 24, 2012); see Jenna Greene, *Judge Allows EEOC Disability Discrimination Lawsuit to Move Forward*, The BLT (May 18, 2012) (law.com); Richard Tonowski, *Legal Update: EEOC Going Up and Down in Court Over Investigation Tactics,* <http://asr.ipma-hr.org/2012/07/legal-update-eeoc-going-up-and-down-in-court-over-investigation-tactics> (July 31, 2012)]

## § 41.02   EEOC ADR

At times, the EEOC itself will engage in ADR with employers and employees as an alternative to normal charge processing methods. The EEOC issued two policy statements on these subjects in 1997, although formal regulations were not issued at that time.

Under these policy statements, the EEOC said ADR was not appropriate in some cases. The agency did not treat ADR as fair or appropriate in important test cases where the EEOC wishes to establish policy or set a precedent; where the EEOC would have to maintain an ongoing presence to monitor compliance; or where the case has significant implications for people besides the parties to the individual charge—for instance, other employees and other companies in the same or different industries.

The EEOC took the position that ADR was fair and appropriate if:

- It is voluntarily elected, not compelled;
- The EEOC provides help to employees who are confused about the process;
- The decision maker (mediator or arbitrator) is truly neutral;
- The proceedings are confidential;
- The outcome of the process is an enforceable written agreement.

The EEOC's home page for mediation can be found at <http://www.eeoc.gov/eeoc/mediation/index.cfm>, containing a number of resources, including a video about the advantages of mediation.EEOC mediation was launched in 1991, with a pilot program in the Philadelphia, New Orleans, Houston, and Washington field offices; the pilot was later extended nationwide. An ADR program was in full operation by April 1999.

The agency says that between 1999 and 2010, close to 136,000 matters have been mediated. Close to 70% (more than 94,000 charges) were resolved. EEOC mediation involves not only EEOC personnel trained in-house and outside contract mediators, but volunteers as well. Mediation is offered as an option early in the process of handling a discrimination charge, but mediation is not provided after the EEOC determines that a charge is without merit, unless the parties request it. The EEOC has entered into 1,573 Universal Agreements to Mediate (UAM)s with local employers and 214 UAMs with regional or national employers. These agreements expedite the mediation process by setting up an ongoing relationship between the company and the EEOC. [EEOC, *History of the EEOC Mediation Program*, <http://www1.eeoc.gov//eeoc/mediation/history.cfm> (accessed Mar. 22, 2012)]

In fiscal 2012, the EEOC said that 11,376 mediations were conducted, leading to 8,714 resolutions, a resolution rate of over three-quarters (76.6%). Monetary benefits of $153.25 million were obtained for 7,488 persons (somewhat lower than the 2011 recovery of $170 million for 8,725 people) and 912 people received non-monetary benefits as a result of EEOC mediation. It took an average of 101 days to close a case in 2012. [EEOC, *EEOC Mediation Statistics FY 1999 Through FY 2012*, <http://www.eeoc.gov/eeoc/mediation/mediation_stats.cfm> (undated, accessed Mar. 22, 2013)]

## § 41.03   TITLE VII ENFORCEMENT

Both the EEOC and state antidiscrimination agencies have a role in investigating an employee's allegations of discrimination. Initial charges can be filed with either the EEOC or the state or local agency.

However, if the employee goes to the EEOC first, it generally "defers" to the state or local agency. That is, it sends the paperwork to the state or local agency, and gives it a 60-day deferral period to resolve the complaint. [See 29 C.F.R. § 1601.74 for a list of state and local agencies that are deemed to have enough enforcement power to handle a discrimination charge] Furthermore, some agencies (listed in 29 C.F.R. § 1601.80) are "certified" by the EEOC, based on a track record of at least four years as a deferral agency, during which time the EEOC found its work product to be acceptable.

Title VII and ADA charges must be filed within the EEOC within 180 days of the time of the alleged discrimination (if there is no deferral agency in the picture) or within 300 days of the alleged discrimination, or 30 days of the time the deferral agency terminates processing of the charge (if a deferral agency is involved).

However, these timing requirements are tricky and provide many opportunities for the employer to get cases dismissed. In a case involving a deferral agency, the filing period is really only 240 days, because of the 60-day period when the EEOC steps aside and lets the deferral agency handle the matter. However, most deferral agencies have what is called "work sharing" agreements with the EEOC. In the jurisdiction of those agencies, an employee's complaint is timely if it is made more than 240, but less than 300, days after the alleged discrimination occurred.

Many cases involve statute of limitations issues and call for determining timing issues of when a discriminatory act occurred. The Supreme Court ruled, in May 2007, that a Title VII pay discrimination charge must be filed within 180 days of the time the discriminatory employment decision was made and communicated to the employee. It is not acceptable to treat discriminatory pay as a continuing violation, for which a charge can be filed within 180 days of any paycheck. The Supreme Court said that if an employer engages in a series of intentionally discriminatory acts, each of which could support a separate charge, then each act counts as a new violation. But continuing to pay a female employee less than a comparable male reflects later effects of past discrimination—so the clock does not start again with each paycheck. [*Ledbetter v. Goodyear Tire & Rubber Co.* (550 U.S. 618 (2007)]

The first law signed by President Obama after his inauguration was the Lilly Ledbetter Fair Pay Act to reverse this ruling. The Ledbetter Act covers cases that had been filed or were pending on the day before the Supreme Court decision. As a result of the Ledbetter Act, a claim is timely if it is filed within 180 days (or 300 days, if applicable) of the adoption of a pay practice; when the worker becomes subject to the policy—or each time the policy is applied to an employee. Therefore, each new paycheck (or payment of benefits) can start the clock running.

The EEOC is also the agency responsible for enforcement of Title II of the Genetic Information Nondiscrimination Act of 2008 (GINA; Pub. L. No. 110-233, codified at 42 U.S.C. § 2000ff). Proposed Regulations were published at 74

Fed. Reg. 9056 (Mar. 2, 2009). However, OSHA is responsible for enforcing the laws protecting whistleblowers.

## § 41.04   EEOC INVESTIGATION

If the EEOC can't settle a charge informally, its next step is to investigate the facts and determine if there is reasonable cause to believe that the employee's complaint is well-founded. If it makes such a "reasonable cause" determination, it has an obligation to attempt to conciliate: to get the employer to improve its equal opportunity policies, sign a compliance agreement, and compensate the employee for past discrimination. The EEOC can't close its case file until it has evidence of the employer's actual compliance with the conciliation agreement.

The EEOC published a five-year plan for E-RACE for FY 2008–2013, with five main objectives:

1. Better collection and analysis of data, to identify and redress discrimination

2. Better charge processing by the EEOC itself

3. Training based on new strategies and legal theories to address new issues as they arise (e.g., conviction records, exclusion based on names or zip codes)

4. Improved visibility and a higher public profile for EEOC's efforts to combat race and color discrimination

5. Greater participation by members of the public in averting and eliminating discrimination. [EEOC, *E-RACE Goals and Objectives*, <http://www.eeoc.gov/eeoc/initiatives/e-race/> (Jan. 30, 2008) (accessed Mar. 22, 2013)]

As a general rule, an EEOC determination letter is admissible evidence in a suit later brought by the charging party. However, the determination letter is not automatically admissible: The court can keep it out, under Federal Rules of Evidence Rule 403, if the court determines that the probative value of the document is significantly outweighed by negative factors such as prejudice and risk of confusion. [*Coleman v. Home Depot Inc.*, 306 F.3d 1333 (3d Cir. 2002)]

If the EEOC believes that the employer is blocking the process, it sends a written notice demanding compliance. Title VII § 706(c) gives the EEOC discretion to sue the employer if an acceptable conciliation agreement cannot be reached within 30 days after the end of the period when the EEOC defers to state agency jurisdiction, or 30 days of the date a charge is filed with the EEOC. There is no statute of limitations for suits brought directly by the EEOC: They can sue even for events in the distant past.

If and when the EEOC concludes that there is no reasonable cause to believe that the facts are as charged by the employee, the EEOC will inform the charging party of this determination. In Title VII and ADA cases (but not Equal Pay Act or ADEA cases), the charging party can still sue the employer in federal court, but must get a "right to sue" letter from the EEOC indicating that the case has been closed. Usually, the EEOC gets 180 days to attempt conciliation, but the employee can ask for earlier termination of the EEOC's involvement, and earlier issuance of the right-to-sue letter. However, the employee can't bypass the conciliation process entirely.

Once the right-to-sue letter is issued, the employee has only 90 days to file the federal suit. If the 90 days pass without commencement of a suit, the EEOC can still bring suit, on the theory that the potential private plaintiff's inaction has reinstated the agency's own powers.

The EEOC's investigative powers generally end as soon as a right-to-sue letter has been issued. [*EEOC v. Federal Home Loan Mortgage Co.*, 37 F. Supp. 2d 769 (E.D. Va. 1999)] The exception is the case in which the EEOC thinks its investigation goes beyond the litigation, in which case it can intervene in the employee's private suit or file its own charges. However, the EEOC will not intervene in a suit, or bring a suit, if it makes a "no reasonable cause" determination.

Suits with the EEOC as plaintiff are limited to matters investigated as a result of a charge, not matters outside the scope of the matter for which the EEOC attempted to conciliate. In other words, the EEOC's efforts to conciliate one charge won't make the employer vulnerable to a host of other charges. Furthermore, because of the burden of its workload, the EEOC files only a few hundred suits a year.

## § 41.05  ADEA ENFORCEMENT

The rules for ADEA cases are similar, but not identical, to those for Title VII cases, so you should check to see if ADEA plaintiffs have violated any of the requirements for that type of suit. For example, in 2009, the Supreme Court ruled that the differences between the statutory language and case law of Title VII and the ADEA mean that ADEA plaintiffs who allege mixed motive discrimination (a combination of valid and illicit motivations for the adverse employment action) can win only if they prove, by a preponderance of the evidence, that the adverse action would never have been taken but for the plaintiff's age falling within the ADEA protected group. [*Gross v. FBL Fin. Servs., Inc.*, 557 U.S. 167 (2009)] The Ledbetter Act (see above) also applies to the ADEA.

In addition to suits brought by employees who charge that they have been subjected to age discrimination, the ADEA statute provides for enforcement by the Secretary of Labor; 29 U.S.C. § 26 gives the Secretary the power to investigate ADEA charges, including subpoenacing witnesses and inspecting employers' business records. (The DOL has delegated this power to the EEOC.)

Even criminal penalties can be imposed against anyone who "shall forcibly resist, oppose, impede, intimidate or interfere with" a DOL representative engaged in enforcing the ADEA. [See 29 U.S.C. § 629] The criminal penalty is a fine of up to $500 and/or up to one year's imprisonment, although imprisonment will be ordered only in the case of someone who has already been convicted of the same offense in the past.

Although the EEOC can become an ADEA plaintiff, it seldom does so. The cases it selects are usually large-scale, involving egregious practices, many employees, or a pattern or practice of discrimination. The EEOC can bring a suit even if no employee of the company has filed timely charges of age discrimination.

If the EEOC files suit after an employee has already sued based on the same conduct on the employer's part, the earlier individual suit can proceed. However, an individual who wants back pay or other monetary relief cannot file suit after the EEOC starts its own suit, because the EEOC litigates on behalf of all affected employees.

However, if the EEOC complaint covers a pattern or practice of discrimination lasting "up to the present time," this means the date when the EEOC filed its complaint, so an individual can file a private suit charging the employer with committing discrimination after the filing of the EEOC complaint.

The EEOC doesn't need written consent from employees to file a suit on their behalf. The EEOC can seek relief for all employees on the basis of a charge filed by one employee who only reported discrimination against him- or herself. The EEOC can also undertake a single conciliation effort for multiple charges, as long as the employer is notified that the charge involves more than one complainant.

No employee who has already sued the employer can get back pay or other individual relief as part of an EEOC suit involving the same facts. However, if an employee tried to sue, but the case was dismissed on the basis of untimely filing, then the EEOC can bring a suit to get an injunction against the employer, even if the EEOC's case is based on the same facts as the suit that was dismissed.

■ **TIP:**   The general rule is that a company that files for bankruptcy protection is entitled to an automatic stay—a period of time during which suits against the company cannot proceed. However, a suit by the EEOC is considered an exercise of the government's regulatory, policing function, and therefore can proceed even while the automatic stay is in place.

Certiorari was granted in 2007 in a case about the extent to which other employees will be permitted to "piggyback" their own charges in an ADEA case where another employee answered the EEOC questionnaire and made a statement (Form 283) but did not file a formal charge (Form 5). The Supreme Court held that employees should not be penalized for the EEOC's mistakes. The Court held that a valid ADEA charge requires only certain information (an allegation; the name of the charging party; and a request that the EEOC take remedial action or settle a dispute), and the intake questionnaire contained enough information to be adequate for this purpose. Although the informal dispute resolution procedure never occurred, the Supreme Court remanded the case to the district court to attempt to facilitate a settlement. [*Holowecki v. Federal Express*, 552 U.S. 389 (2008).]; see, e.g., Mark Sherman (AP), *Supreme Court Says FedEx Employees Can Sue Over Age Discrimination* (Feb. 28, 2008) (law.com); Fred Schneyer, *Supreme Court Clears FedEx Age Discrimination Case for More Hearings*, plansponsor.com (Feb. 28, 2008)]

## § 41.06   THE FEDERAL-STATE RELATIONSHIP

### [A]   ADEA Interaction

Unlike ERISA, which preempts whole classes of state laws dealing with certain retirement and employee benefit issues, the ADEA specifically provides for a joint working relationship between the federal government and state antidiscrimination agencies; 29 U.S.C. § 625(b) gives the Secretary of Labor the power to cooperate with state and local agencies to carry out the purposes of ADEA.

Section 633(a) provides that state agencies retain their jurisdiction over age-discrimination claims. However, federal ADEA suits supersede state age-discrimination enforcement efforts. A potential age-discrimination plaintiff has to go through enforcement procedures at both the state and the federal level. However, if the federal charge is filed on time, the complainant doesn't have to complete the state enforcement process—only to file a charge within the state system.

The federal ADEA provides that, if a state has a statute against age discrimination and has an enforcement agency, then potential plaintiffs have to file charges within both systems. The federal-state enforcement relationship revolves around the concepts of "referral" and "deferral."

Referral means that a state has a work-sharing arrangement with the EEOC, as provided by 29 C.F.R. § 1616.9. When an age-discrimination complaint is made to the state agency, the state agency refers it to the EEOC. If the state charge is dismissed, the EEOC has the power to conduct an independent investigation. Originally, the EEOC Regulations listed states that were identified as "referral" states because they had age discrimination laws. However, in August 2002, the EEOC proposed a set of regulations for ADEA litigation procedures: see 67 Fed. Reg. 52431 (Aug. 12, 2002), finalized at 68 Fed. Reg. 70150 (Dec. 17, 2003). The EEOC says that because most of the states now have laws to forbid age discrimination, it is no longer necessary to maintain these lists. The EEOC will simply make referrals to the state agencies as appropriate.

An additional group of states (Arizona, Colorado, Kansas, Maine, Ohio, Rhode Island, South Dakota, and Washington) are "conditional referral" states. They do have antidiscrimination statutes, but the terms of these state laws are quite different from the federal ADEA. This situation creates the possibility that employees will bring claims that are covered by the state law, but not by the federal law. In such instances, the state-only claims will not be referred to the EEOC. Claims that are covered only by federal law must be filed directly with the EEOC, within 180 days of the discriminatory act.

The deferral concept means that the EEOC defers to the state and does not process the charge for a period of 60 days after the referral, so that the state agency can take action.

Except in a deferral state, the charge must be filed no later than 180 days after the discriminatory act, or the latest act that forms part of a pattern. In a deferral state, the last permissible filing date is either 300 days after the discriminatory act (or last discriminatory act in a series) or 30 days after the state agency dismisses its charge and notifies the complainant of the dismissal—whichever comes earlier. Unlike Title VII plaintiffs, ADEA plaintiffs do not have to get a right-to-sue letter.

If a state has a law against age discrimination, 29 U.S.C. § 633(b) provides that employees may not bring ADEA suits in that state until they have waited 60 days for the state to resolve the charges. If state charges have been dismissed in less than 60 days, the employee doesn't have to wait for the full 60-day period to end. The 60-day period is imposed to allow for conciliation of the charge. [See 29 U.S.C. § 626(d)]

During this period, the EEOC's task is to decide if it has a "reasonable basis to conclude that a violation of the Act has occurred or will occur." If the answer is "yes," the EEOC makes a "good cause" or "reasonable cause" finding—i.e., that the employee had good cause to complain. Then the EEOC will probably issue a Letter of Violation. However, the mere fact that no letter is issued does not prove that the EEOC did not detect any violations.

Courts have reached different conclusions about what to do if the plaintiff does not wait 60 days as required. The Sixth Circuit says that the case should be dismissed (but without prejudice, so it can be refiled later). On the other hand, the Eighth Circuit says that the case should not be dismissed, only suspended pending the administrative disposition of the complaint. [Compare *Chapman v. City of Detroit*, 808 F.2d 459 (6th Cir. 1986), with *Wilson v. Westinghouse Elec. Co.*, 838 F.2d 286 (8th Cir. 1988)] The Final Rule calls for the EEOC to issue a Notice of Dismissal or Termination when the agency finishes processing a charge. A complainant can file suit in federal or state court at any time after 60 days have passed since the filing of the age discrimination charge—whether or not the EEOC has issued its Notice of Dismissal or Termination. But once the Notice is issued, the complainant has only 90 days from the date of the notice to bring suit; otherwise, the suit will be dismissed as untimely.

Next, the EEOC tries to get the company into compliance by informal persuasion. If the company and the EEOC reach an agreement that the agency believes will eliminate the discrimination, then the agreement will be written down and signed by the EEOC representative, a company representative, and the employee who charged the discrimination. If the charging party is not satisfied, he or she can withdraw the charge. The EEOC still has independent authority to settle on behalf of other employees affecting the discrimination.

On the other hand, if conciliation fails and no agreement is reached, possibly because there has been no discrimination, and therefore, the employer is unwilling to admit culpability and "admit" discrimination that never occurred in the first place, the EEOC and/or the charging party can sue. The charging party's suit must be brought no later than 90 days after receipt of notice from the EEOC that conciliation has failed, but it is not necessary to get a right-to-sue letter.

See 67 Fed. Reg. 52431 (Aug. 12, 2002) and 68 Fed. Reg. 70150 (Dec. 17, 2003). The notices inform the charging party that he or she has a right to sue the alleged perpetrator of age discrimination, but the right expires 90 days after the issue date of the NDT. Each aggrieved person will receive an individual NDT, but for multi-person charges, the NDT will not issue until proceedings end as to all of them.

Despite similarities, the NDT does not work in exactly the same way as a Title VII Right to Sue letter. A potential ADEA plaintiff can file suit at any time once 60 days have passed since the filing of the charge with the administrative agency, whether or not the NDT has issued. However, suit is untimely once 90 days have passed since the NDT date. To prevent confusion, the EEOC amended 29 C.F.R. § 1626.12 to clarify the difference between the notice that is issued when an EEOC conciliation attempt fails and this new type of notice.

The EEOC can terminate further processing of a charge if it discovers that a suit has been filed against the respondent of the charge, unless the agency determines that continued charge processing furthers the aims of the ADEA. However, the EEOC has the authority to investigate age discrimination cases and bring suit even if there is no individual charge filed. This is not true in Title VII or ADA Title I cases. When several people are involved in a charge, the EEOC will not issue an NDT until all the charges have been processed. The agency concluded that issuing a separate NDT to each charging party as his or her case was finished would lead to inefficient multiplication of court proceedings.

## [B]  State Laws Against Age Discrimination

Most of the states have some kind of law prohibiting age discrimination in employment. These laws may differ from the federal laws, in terms of coverage (e.g., they may cover employers too small to be subject to federal anti-discrimination laws).

Although the procedure varies from state to state, usually a person who claims to be a victim of age discrimination begins the state enforcement process by filing a charge with the state human rights/equal employment opportunity agency, within the time frame set out by the statute. Depending on the statute, this could be anywhere from 30 days after the alleged discriminatory practice to one year plus 90 days of the time the complainant discovered the employer acted illegally.

Most of the states, like the federal government, have a dual system of agency enforcement and private litigation. The agency investigates the charge and issues either a finding of good cause or a no-cause finding. If the agency deems that the charge is well-founded, then it tries to conciliate or sues the employer. On the other hand, if it makes a no-cause finding, or cannot resolve the matter promptly, the employee has the right to bring suit in state court, under the state antidiscrimination law. However, in some states, there is no agency enforcement, so employers are only at risk of private suit. Other states, however, give complainants a choice between going straight to state court without making an agency charge or filing an administrative complaint—but they must choose one or the other.

In 2010, the Tenth Circuit tackled timing issues when charges are filed with both the state agency and the EEOC. The district court dismissed a suit charging national origin, ancestry, and sex discrimination and retaliation because it was filed more than 90 days after the plaintiff, Rodriguez, received a right-to-sue notice from the Colorado Civil Rights Division. Three months after being fired, Rodriguez filed separate charges with the EEOC and the Colorado state agency. The Colorado agency decided that Rodriguez' sex discrimination charge was well-founded, but her other charges were unfounded. The sex discrimination charge was referred for mediation, which was unsuccessful. The Colorado agency issued a right to sue notice dated November 25, 2007.

The EEOC declined to pursue the case, but did not issue a right to sue notice until January 29, 2008. Rodriguez sued in district court, alleging only federal claims, on April 25, 2008—a date that was more than 90 days from the state right to sue notice, but within 90 days from the federal notice. The Tenth Circuit said that the Colorado right to sue notice did not start the filing period running within the federal system. Although Colorado has a work-sharing agreement with the EEOC, the agreement does not give the state agency the power to issue notices on the EEOC's behalf. The EEOC has a duty to give substantial weight to the Colorado agency's determinations, but is not bound by them. The Colorado notice did not inform Rodriguez of her rights under federal law; it included only the state charge number and explained Rodriguez' rights to sue in state court; and it did not mention the federal charge or state that the notice was binding on the EEOC. For all these reasons, the Colorado right to sue notice did not start the clock running for a federal suit. [*Rodriguez v. Wet Ink, LLC*, 603 F.3d 810 (10th Cir. 2010)]

# CHAPTER 42

# DISCRIMINATION SUITS BY EMPLOYEES: PROCEDURAL ISSUES

## § 42.01   INTRODUCTION

When it comes to litigating discrimination claims, it's understandable that both employers and employees feel vulnerable. Employers often feel that, no matter how little substance there is to a charge of discrimination, the employer will still have to fight the charge (which can be time-consuming and expensive) and might be ordered to pay immense damages. Employees feel that they are at the mercy of employers—that the only means of redress is complex and takes many years, by which time memories will have faded.

The Supreme Court held, in March 2011, that the "cat's paw" theory of liability, i.e., the allegation that an unbiased decision-maker acts on biased reports submitted by lower-level managers who are biased against the plaintiff, is viable. This decision reverses the Seventh Circuit, which had limited the employer's cat's paw liability to situations in which the biased supervisor exercised such singular influence over the decision-maker that the decision-maker engaged in blind reliance. This ruling was made in a USERRA case, but this interpretation of cat's paw liability is likely to apply to Title VII cases as well, because USERRA and Title VII use similar language about "motivating factors"for employment discrimination. However, the ADEA is drafted differently so this decision might not apply. [*Staub v. Proctor Hosp.*, 131 S. Ct. 1186 (2011); see Marcia Coyle, *Court Adds Claws to Cat's Paw Claims—But Hisses at Case Over Corporate Privacy*, Nat'l L.J. (Mar. 1, 2011) (law.com)]

Early in 2010, the Supreme Court ruled that a corporation's principal place of business is its executive office, and not where its products are sold. The case was brought in California state court by Hertz employees who said they were wrongfully denied overtime and vacation pay. Hertz, which is headquartered in New Jersey, wanted the suit tried in federal court as a diversity case. The Ninth Circuit rejected this argument, finding that Hertz does most of its business in California, so the case was not diverse. The Supreme Court reversed and remanded. The effect of this ruling is that more cases will go to federal court—which is more hostile to class actions than state courts. [*Hertz v. Friend*, 559 U.S. 77 (2010); see AP, *In Unanimous Ruling, Supreme Court Says Business HQ Is Where Executives Are* (Feb. 23, 2010) (law.com)]

The Ninth Circuit joined the Fourth, Fifth, and Tenth Circuits in holding that an FMLA front pay award is an equitable remedy. Therefore, it is set by the judge, not the jury. The Ninth Circuit held that liquidated damages do not have to be awarded in every case in which the plaintiff receives front pay: there could be cases where front pay is justified because there is too much hostility to reinstate the plaintiff, but the employer here acted in good faith so liquidated damages are inappropriate. [*Traxler v. Multnomah County*, 596 F.3d 1007 (9th Cir. 2010)]

## § 42.02  CAUSES OF ACTION

In legal parlance, a cause of action is something for which someone can be sued. Employees can charge employers with various kinds of wrongdoing, and the same suit can combine discrimination charges with other causes of action, such as:

- Violation of Title VII of the Civil Rights Act of 1964 (discrimination on the grounds of race, sex, nationality, or color—sexual harassment is considered a type of sex discrimination);

- Violation of the Pregnancy Discrimination Act (PDA), an addition to Title VII, which forbids treating a qualified pregnant employee on less favorable terms than a comparably situated, non-pregnant employee;

- Violation of the Age Discrimination Act (discriminating against an individual who is age 40 or over, in any term or condition of employment, including hiring, firing, promotion, and benefits);

- Violation of 42 U.S.C. § 1981, the Civil War-era statute that gives all citizens the same right to make contracts as "white citizens." Four Circuits allow § 1981 suits by at-will employees who claim they were discharged on the basis of racial prejudice—even though they had no written employment contracts. [*Lauture v. IBM,* 216 F.3d 238 (2d Cir. 2000); *Perry v. Woodward,* 199 F.3d 1126 (10th Cir. 1999); *Spriggs v. Diamond Auto Glass,* 165 F.3d 1015 (4th Cir. 1999); *Fadeyi v. Planned Parenthood,* 160 F.3d 1048 (5th Cir. 1998)] In 2009, the Third Circuit joined the First, Seventh, and Eleventh Circuits in applying 42 U.S.C. § 1981 to independent contractors, in a case involving alleged racist insults and cancellation of a black trainee's contract as a sales representative: *Brown v. J. Kaz Inc. d/b/a Craftmatic of Pittsburgh,* 581 F.3d 175 (3d Cir. 2009); see Zack Needles, *3rd Circuit Extends Civil Rights Protection to Independent Contractors,* The Legal Intelligencer (Sept. 17, 2009) (law. com)]

- Wrongful refusal to re-employ a military veteran, violating USERRA;

- Violation of the Equal Pay Act: paying women less than men for the same job. This law does not permit "comparable worth" claims that allege that a typically female job is more valuable than a different and higher-paid job that is typically performed by men;

- Retaliation against an employee who filed a discrimination claim (or exercised other legal rights, *e.g.,* in connection with unemployment benefits or Worker's Compensation) or cooperated in an investigation;

- Any act of wrongful termination for other reasons (e.g., discharging someone who "blew the whistle" on corporate wrongdoing);

- Violation of labor law (e.g., retaliating against someone for protected activity such as supporting the union or asserting a grievance against the employer). Nearly all labor law claims must be brought in federal, not state, court, because the federal statute the Labor Management Relations Act (LMRA) preempts state regulation—in other words, this is considered purely a federal matter;

- Breach of contract (either an explicit, written contract such as an employment contract or a collective bargaining agreement, or an implied contract);

- Defamation (in the context of an unfavorable reference or unfavorable statements in the press, and if the employer cannot assert a defense of truth);

- Interference with contractual relations, e.g., the employer prevents an ex-employee from getting a new job or establishing a business;

- Infliction of emotional distress (either negligent or intentional).

Frequently, employees will engage in several different proceedings, involving different statutes. Then, it becomes important to determine if the results of one proceeding will affect other proceedings (or prevent potential claims from being pursued). Denial of a person's FMLA claim for being fired while on maternity leave is *res judicata* to Title VII, ADEA, and the Florida Civil Rights Act claims. That is, the negative FMLA ruling is considered to have determined the other claims, because all the claims involve the same facts, which have already been litigated. [*O'Connor v. PCA Family Health Plan*, 200 F.3d 1349 (11th Cir. 2000)]

In mid-2013, the Supreme Court ruled on the important question of who is a "supervisor." The actual case involved a racially hostile workplace, although this concept is most often invoked in sexual harassment cases. The Supreme Court held that the employer is strictly liable if harassment is committed by a supervisor and involves a tangible employment action (e.g., hiring, firing, reassignment) against the victim. If the harasser is a supervisor, but there is no tangible employment action, then the employer can assert an affirmative defense under *Faragher/Ellerth*: that the employer took reasonable care to prevent and correct harassment, but the plaintiff unreasonably failed to take advantage of this procedure. The Supreme Court defined a supervisor as a person authorized to undertake tangible employment actions against the plaintiff. Therefore, the Supreme Court rejected the EEOC's broader definition of a supervisor as someone who either can undertake tangible employment actions, or exercises significant direction over the plaintiff's work. The narrower the definition of supervisor, the fewer cases in which the employer will be strictly liable or will be required to raise the *Faragher/Ellerth* affirmative defense. In this case, the alleged harasser was a co-worker of the plaintiff's, so the Supreme Court held that the employer would be liable only if it was negligent in controlling working conditions. [*Vance v. Ball State Univ.*, 133 S. Ct. 2434 (2013); see Marcia Coyle, *Supreme Court Makes It Harder to Prove Job Bias Claims*,Nat'l L.J. (June 24, 2013) (law .com)]

## § 42.03 STATISTICS ABOUT CHARGES AND RESULTS

In FY 2012, 99,412 EEOC charges of all kinds were filed: 33.7% (33,512 charges) of race discrimination, 30,356 charges sex discrimination (30.5%), 26,379 disability discrimination charges (26.5%), 22,857 age discrimination charges (23.0%), 10,883 charges of national origin discrimination (10.9%), 3,811 charges of religious discrimination (3.8%), 2,662 (2.7%) charges of discrimination on the basis of color, 1,082 (1.1%) Equal Pay Act charges, and 280 charges (0.2%) under GINA. Retaliation charges were extremely common: there were 37,836 retaliation charges under all the statutes, and 31,208 Title VII retaliation charges. The percentages add up to far more than 100% because it is common for charging parties to allege more than one kind of discrimination. [EEOC, *Charge Statistics FY 1997 Through FY 2012*, <http://www1.eeoc.gov//eeoc/statistics/ enforcement/charges.cfm?> (undated; last accessed Mar. 18, 2013)]

The EEOC won $365.4 million for discrimination victims in fiscal 2012. The EEOC's backlog increased every year from 2002 to 2011, but in both 2011 and 2012, the backlog was reduced. There were 78,136 pending charges at the end of FY 2011, 70,312 at the end of FY 2012. In its 2012 fiscal year, the EEOC filed 122 suits: 85 individual suits, 26 with multiple charging parties, and 10 alleging systemic discrimination. There were 254 resolutions of suits, involving more than 23,446 employees. Systemic discrimination is a focus for the EEOC, which completed 240 systemic investigations in FY 2012, leading to 46 settlements or conciliation agreements. [Andrew Ramonas, *EEOC Breaks Record for Amount Won for Workplace Discrimination Victims*, Nat'l L.J. (Jan. 28, 2013) (law.com)]

See Chapter 41 for more discussion of EEOC statistics on case filings and dispositions.

Recent studies show that the success rate for plaintiffs is lower in employment discrimination suits than in other civil cases, and judges tend to dismiss the cases faster. According to a study published in the Harvard Review of Law and Policy in February 2009, federal employment discrimination plaintiffs won only 15% of their suits—versus a 51% success rate for plaintiffs in other types of federal civil suits. A complicating factor is that the more meritorious a suit, the likelier it is that the defendant will settle rather than going to court. Many suits that are filed are terminated prematurely. In 2008, according to the Federal Judicial Center, 12% of employment discrimination cases ended in summary judgment (i.e., the court ended the case before there had been a full trial); in 90% of them, the employer moved for summary judgment, whereas only 3% of contract and 1.7% of personal injury cases ended in summary judgment. [Nathan Koppel, *Job-Discrimination Cases Tend to Fare Poorly in Federal Court*, <http://www.WSJ.

com> (Feb. 19, 2009). See *Bell Atlantic v. Twombly,* 550 U.S. 544 (2007), which increases plaintiffs' burden by allowing federal judges to dismiss a case unless the complaint includes enough facts to state a plausible claim; see Jess Bravin, *U.S. Courts Are Tough on Job-Bias Suits,* Wall St. J., July 16, 2001, at A2, concluding that, although there were regional differences, employers had a "huge advantage" over employee plaintiffs in all of the courts of appeals]

In contrast, in late 2009, Verdict Research reported more positive results for plaintiffs. Verdict Research said that the median award for all kinds of employment claims rose 60% between 2008 and 2009, from $204,000 to $326,640, whereas the median award for discrimination cases rose only 16% ($241,000 in 2009 versus $208,000 in 2008). The median settlement in 2009 was $90,000, the highest in a decade, and 20% more than in 2008. Employers won 39% of all employment cases—33% in age discrimination, 52% in disability discrimination. In federal court, employers won 43% of employment cases, more than the 37% win rate in state court. The median federal award to successful employee plaintiffs was 39% lower than the median state award: $165,000 and $270,000, respectively. The largest verdicts were in age cases, followed by disability, sex, and race cases. [LRP Publications, *Employment Practice Liability: Jury Award Trends and Statistics 2009 Edition* <http://www.shoplrp.com/product/p-2601.EPL09.html>; see *Employers More Often Losers in Discrimination Cases,* plansponsor.com (Nov. 16, 2009)]

## § 42.04    TITLE VII PROCEDURE

### [A]    Complaining Party

Federal antidiscrimination laws include extremely complicated procedures for bringing a complaint, and one of the employer's main lines of defense is that the potential plaintiff has failed to satisfy the procedural requirements.

42 U.S.C. § 2000e(l) defines "complaining party" in a Title VII case as either the private person who brings a case or the EEOC or the U.S. Attorney General.

### [B]    The Charging Process

Nearly every phrase or term in this section has already been extensively litigated. Individuals who think they have experienced an unlawful employment practice cannot simply go to the relevant federal court and file a complaint. Instead, they must file a written, sworn document called a "charge" with an administrative agency. Would-be plaintiffs cannot go to court until there has been an administrative investigation and attempts to settle the matter without getting the court system involved.

The EEOC notifies the employer of the charge within ten days, disclosing the date, place, and circumstances of the allegedly unlawful practices, and then starts an investigation to see if there is reasonable cause for the charge. The EEOC's duty is to complete the investigation as soon as possible—and within 120 days of the filing of the charge (or the referral date) "so far as practicable." (The EEOC has a big backlog and often misses the 120-day deadline.)

Grievance procedures under a CBA, or company-sponsored grievance procedures in a nonunion company, have no effect on Title VII suits. So the employee doesn't have to use those procedures before filing a charge with an antidiscrimination agency. On the other hand, ongoing grievances under the CBA won't prevent or delay a Title VII suit.

If the EEOC does not believe that the charge is supported by reasonable cause, it dismisses the charge, and the employee then has the right to sue. In fact, it is not even held against the employee that the EEOC made a "no-cause" finding. A no-cause determination does not prevent the employee from suing. It does not limit the suit, what the employee can try to prove, or even the remedies he or she can receive. The judge or jury makes its own independent inquiry into the facts and is not influenced by the EEOC investigation.

But if the EEOC does believe that the charge is supported, then the EEOC's job is to try to use "informal methods of conference, conciliation, and persuasion" to get the employer to change the employment practice. The conciliation process is confidential, and statements made during the process can only be publicized or used as evidence in litigation based on the written consent of the person making the statement. Violating this confidentiality can be punished by as much as $1,000 fine and/or a year in prison.

If the discrimination charges involve multiple employees, it may be necessary for the EEOC to attempt conciliation with respect to each employee. The agency lost a major case, *EEOC v. CRST Van Expedited Inc.*, 679 F.3d 657 (8th Cir. 2012), On remand, No. 07-CV-95, U.S. Dist. LEXIS 107822 (N.D. Iowa Aug. 1, 2013) for failure to attempt conciliation at the individual level. [See § 41.01[B]]

The EEOC's powers to investigate a charge include having access "at all reasonable times" to all evidence that is relevant to the charges, and the EEOC also is entitled to make copies. [42 U.S.C. § 2000e-8(a)]

Exhaustion of remedies is a requirement. The Tenth Circuit ruled that, in order to exhaust their administrative remedies, private sector employees have a duty to cooperate with the EEOC's investigation of their age bias charges before they file suit. (In this case, after filing a charge, the plaintiff and his attorney canceled three phone interviews scheduled with the EEOC investigator; wouldn't return the investigator's calls; and did not provide any information other than what was contained in the original charge.) Exhaustion of administrative remedies is a prerequisite to suing under the ADEA. Failure to exhaust administrative remedies does not justify summary judgment for the defendant but, according to the Tenth Circuit, will justify dismissal of the case for lack of jurisdiction.

[*Shikles v. Sprint/United Mgmt. Co.*, 426 F.3d 1304 (10th Cir. 2005); ADEA suits have also been dismissed for non-cooperation: e.g., *Rann v. Chao*, 346 F.3d 192 (D.C. Cir. 2003). It has been held, in the Title VII context, that failure to cooperate with the EEOC is failure to exhaust administrative remedies: *Brown v. Tomlinson*, 383 F. Supp. 2d 26, 29 (D.D.C. 2005); *Smith v. Koplan*, 362 F. Supp. 2d 266, 268 (D.D.C. 2005)]

A Title VII plaintiff has not exhausted administrative remedies if a suit refers to time frames, discriminatory conduct, or perpetrators different from the ones raised in the administrative charges. In this case, the Fourth Circuit held that evidence of derogatory racial epithets that was not raised until the summary judgment stage of trial was inadmissible; furthermore, the EEOC charges related to supervisors, whereas the epithets were allegedly used by co-workers. [*Chacko v. Patuxent Inst.*, 429 F.3d 505 (4th Cir. 2005)]

### [C]   State Agencies

In a Fifth Circuit case, procedural failures required dismissal of an age-discrimination judgment in favor of the plaintiff. He filed a complaint with the EEOC and did not check the box on the form indicating that he wanted the charge filed with both the EEOC and the Texas Commission on Human Rights. Therefore, he failed to go through the mandatory step of filing a state charge—and his federal lawsuit was invalid. [*Jones v. Grinnell Corp.*, 235 F.3d 972 (5th Cir. 2001)] Although Texas has a work-sharing agreement, this merely means that a single filing can cover both state and federal requirements—not that the state procedure can be ignored, even in a case where the charging party asserts only federal claims.

However, a 2010 case (where the plaintiff, Rodriguez, filed charges with both the state agency and the EEOC) held that a federal suit was timely when it was brought within 90 days of the date of the federal right to sue letter, even though it was filed more than 90 days after the state right to sue letter was issued. Colorado has a work-sharing agreement with the EEOC, but the agreement does not give the state agency the power to act on behalf of the EEOC. Furthermore, the state right to sue letter did not inform Rodriguez of her federal rights, and referred only to the state case. Therefore, Rodriguez' federal suit was timely because it was filed within 90 days of the date of the federal right to sue letter. [*Rodriguez v. Wet Ink, LLC,* 603 F.3d 810 (10th Cir. 2010)]

## § 42.05   TIMING REQUIREMENTS

### [A]   Generally

Section 2000e-5(c) says that if the state where the alleged unlawful employment practice occurred has a state antidiscrimination law, then EEOC charges may not be filed until 60 days have passed since commencement of state antidiscrimination charges. If the EEOC itself files a charge, it has an obligation to notify the appropriate state authority and give it sixty days to enforce the local law and eliminate the unlawful employment practice.

The basic rule is that, to avoid being dismissed as untimely, EEOC charges must be filed within 180 days of the date of the wrongful action. Then papers must be served on the employer within ten days. However, if the state has an anti-discrimination agency, the employee has 300 days from the date of the wrongful action to file with the EEOC. There is an additional requirement that the employee not wait more than 30 days after the state or local agency has dismissed a state charge to file with the EEOC. [42 U.S.C. § 2000e-5(e)(1)]

The charge has to be verified (the charging party has to state under penalty of perjury that the statements in the charge are true). [42 U.S.C. § 2000e5(b)] In March 2002, the U.S. Supreme Court upheld an EEOC regulation, 29 C.F.R. § 1601.12(b), that allows "relation back." That is, if a charge is made within the 300-day period but verified later, it will still be timely because the verification "relates back" to the timely charge. The Supreme Court ruled in *Edelman v. Lynchburg Coll.* [535 U.S. 106 (2002)] that Title VII requires both filing within 300 days and verification, but the two need not occur at the same time.

Although Title VII requires charging parties to verify their EEOC charges, the requirement is not jurisdictional, so a court can hear a case based on an unverified charge. Furthermore, if the employer responds to the charge without raising the fact that it is unverified, the employer will not be able to raise this issue later in the case. [*Buck v. Hampton Twp. Sch. Dist.*, 452 F.3d 256 (3d Cir. 2006)]

The Supreme Court resolved another timing issue. If the plaintiff's claim is for only one act of discrimination or retaliation, or for several separate acts, then the claim must meet the 180-day or 300-day requirement to be timely. However, if the plaintiff charges a number of acts that he or she claims made up part of the same practice creating a hostile work environment, then the claim is timely as long as there was at least one act in the series that occurred during the 180-day or 300-day period. [*National R.R. Passenger Corp. v. Morgan*, 536 U.S. 101 (2002)]

Five years later, the Supreme Court ruled that a Title VII pay discrimination charge must be filed within 180 days of the time the discriminatory employment decision was made and communicated to the employee. It is not acceptable to treat discriminatory pay as a continuing violation, for which a charge can be filed within 180 days of any paycheck. The Supreme Court said that if an employer engages in a series of intentionally discriminatory acts, each of which could support a separate charge, then each act counts as a new violation. But continuing to pay a female employee less than a comparable male reflects later effects of past discrimination—so the clock does not start again with each paycheck. [*Ledbetter v. Goodyear Tire & Rubber Co.*, 550 U.S. 618 (2007)]

Legislation was passed and signed in 2009 to reverse this result for Title VII, the ADA, the ADEA, and the Rehabilitation Act: The Lilly Ledbetter Fair Pay Act of 2009, Pub. L. No. 111-2. The Ledbetter Act provides that a charge is timely if filed within 180 days (or 300 days, in certain instances) of the adoption of a discriminatory practice; the employee's becoming subject to that practice; or the employee being affected by the application of the practice. Every paycheck that reflects discrimination can start the time running anew. A successful plaintiff can recover back pay for up to two years before the date of filing of the charge, for similar or related discriminatory acts during the filing period. The Ledbetter Act is retroactive for all cases that were pending on the day before the Supreme Court's decision, but not for cases that were already complete at that time. [Erin Kilgore, *Lilly Ledbetter Fair Pay Act Revives Pay Discrimination Claims,* Louisiana Law Blog (Feb. 13, 2009) (law.com); Sheryl Gay Stolberg, *Obama Signs Equal-Pay Legislation,* <http://www.nytimes.com> (Jan. 30, 2009); SCOTUS Blog, *Congress Overturns Court on Job Bias,* <http://www.scotusblog.com/wp/court-overturns-court-on-job-bias> (Jan. 28, 2009); Janell Grenier, Benefitsblog, *Lilly Ledbetter Fair Pay Act of 2009 Passes: Benefits Impacted,* <http://www.benefitscounsel.com/archives/002025.html> (Jan. 28, 2009)]

The Eastern District of Pennsylvania ruled that the Ledbetter Act applies only to charges of sex discrimination in compensation—it cannot be used to extend the time limit for a lawsuit alleging discriminatory denial of a promotion. The court said that each promotion that was denied constituted a separate discriminatory act, so the suit had to be filed within 300 days of the denial of promotion. The plaintiff was not allowed to allege that there was an ongoing pattern of discriminatory denials of promotions, so she could bring suit as long as she sued within 300 days of any act in the series. The court also rejected her argument that not being promoted reduced her compensation, so the Ledbetter Act should apply. [*Rowland v. CertainTeed Corp.,* No. 08-3671, 2009 WL 1444413 (E.D. Pa. May 19, 2009); see Shannon P. Duffy, *Judge: Ledbetter Act Doesn't Apply to Lost Promotion Suit,* the Legal Intelligencer (May 27, 2009) (law.com)]

Late in 2010, the EEOC ruled that the Ledbetter Act's expanded timetable for filing pay discrimination claims does not apply to pension payments. Therefore, a federal employee's claim of discrimination in pay and pension benefits, filed many years after retirement, was untimely because it would have had to have been filed within 45 days of retirement. The EEOC Compliance Manual allows courts to treat pension benefits as if they are paid at the time of retirement; each check is not considered a continuing violation that starts the clock anew. Section 2(4) of the Ledbetter Act says that the statute does not change the legal status of when pension distributions are considered paid. [*Brakeall v. EPA* (EEOC, Appeal No. 0120093805, Nov. 30, 2010); see Buck Consultants FYI, *EEOC Says Ledbetter Act Does Not Apply to Pension Payments* (Jan. 28, 2011) (benefitslink. com); Rebecca Moore, *Paycheck Rule of Fair Pay Act Doesn't Apply to Pension Payments,* plansponsor.com (Jan. 31, 2011) (benefitslink.com)]

In 2010, the Supreme Court ruled that discrimination charges brought by Chicago firefighters were not untimely. Although the promotion exam that allegedly had a disparate impact on black and Hispanic firefighters was given many years in the past, the Supreme Court ruled that the unlawful practice could be challenged every time it is used—i.e., every time a new promotion list is issued based on the allegedly biased examination. [*Lewis v. City of Chicago,* No. 08-974 (May 24, 2010)] In 2011, 19 white firefighters and one Hispanic firefighter began receiving payments under this decision; they will receive a total of $2 million in back pay, pension credits, and attorneys' fees. [Rebecca Moore, *Award Finally Decided in Connecticut Firefighters Suit,* plansponsor.com (Aug. 3, 2011)]

The City of Newark obtained summary judgment, affirmed by the Third Circuit, on § 1983 claims that a police officer suffered retaliation because of his assistance with a federal corruption probe. The courts found that there was insufficient proof of causal connection between participation in the investigation and the retaliatory acts alleged. The Third Circuit ruled that § 1983 actions are subject to the personal injury statute of limitations for the state in which the cause of action accrued; in New Jersey, that is two years. The Third Circuit said that after *Morgan,* there is a bright-line test for individually actionable discrete acts and acts that, linked together, form a pattern adding up to a hostile environment. Individually actionable claims can't be aggregated. In this case, nearly everything charged by the plaintiff was a discrete act (e.g., denial of promotion), so most of his allegations were untimely because they were made more than two years after the alleged retaliatory acts. [*O'Connor v. City of Newark,* 440 F.3d 125 (3d Cir. 2006). *Morgan* has also been applied to § 1983 by three circuits: *Sharpe v. Cureton,* 319 F.3d 259 (6th Cir. 2003); *Hildebrandt v. Ill. Dep't of Natural Res.,* 347 F.3d 1014, 1036 (7th Cir. 2003); *RK Ventures, Inc. v. City of Seattle,* 307 F.3d 1045, 1061 (9th Cir. 2002).]

In 2008, the Second Circuit said that, for statute of limitations purposes, a claim of discriminatory loss of seniority occurred on the date when an airline clerk learned he had lost seniority, not on the later date when he was fired: discharge was only the delayed, neutral effect of an alleged earlier act of discrimination. [*Alleyne v. American Airlines,* 548 F.3d 219 (2d Cir. 2008)]

The EEOC has 30 days after filing of a charge, or 30 days after the expiration of the period for referring charges from state agencies, to negotiate with the employer to produce a conciliation agreement that ends the unlawful employment practice. If the 30-day period expires without a conciliation agreement, the EEOC has the power to sue the employer in federal court.

On the other hand, if the EEOC makes a "no-cause" finding about the charge, or 180 days have passed since the charge was filed with the EEOC or referred from the state agency, and the EEOC has not filed suit and there has been no conciliation agreement, then the EEOC will notify the charging party. This is known as a "right-to-sue letter," because it enables the charging party to bring a federal suit.

Some employers draft their job applications to include a limitation on the time within which employees can bring employment-related claims (e.g., six months, rather than the state's statute of limitations, which is likely to be longer). Some courts have upheld these limitations, on the theory that signing the application and taking the job obligates the employee to abide by the limitation. [See, e.g., *Thurman v. DaimlerChrysler, Inc.*, 397 F.3d 352 (6th Cir. 2004)] However, the Eastern District of Michigan refused to apply contract limitations to an ADA or Title VII claim, when the employee's right to sue letter was issued after the limited time period expires; the employee was not allowed to sue before obtaining a right to sue letter. The court found that it would be unfair to apply the limitation—but the limitation would apply if the right to sue letter were issued during the limited period. [*Steward v. DaimlerChrysler Corp.*, 533 F. Supp. 2d 717 (E.D. Mich. 2008)]

In nearly all cases, the appropriate defendant is the employer company—there are virtually no situations in which Title VII suits can appropriately be brought against an individual person who is alleged to have performed discriminatory acts. For example, in 2007 the Eleventh Circuit held that individuals cannot be sued under either the ADA provision against retaliation in employment, or the Florida statute forbidding HIV/AIDS discrimination. The court held that the language of the employment provisions of the ADA is similar to that of Title VII and the ADEA, where individual suits have been ruled out; the Southern District of Florida has forbidden suits against individuals under the state HIV/AIDS statute. [*Albra v. Advan, Inc.*, 490 F.3d 826 (11th Cir. 2007)]

In rare cases, individual liability may exist under other federal statutes (e.g., the FLSA, EPA, or FMLA). In 2007, the First Circuit ruled that the president of a hotel was personally liable for wage and hour violations, because he had ultimate control over operations, and was instrumental in causing the corporation to violate the Fair Labor Standards Act. [*Chao v. Hotel Oasis Inc.*, 493 F.3d 26, 42 Cal. 4th (1st Cir. 2007)] The Fifth Circuit held that a supervisor can be personally liable for retaliation in an FMLA wrongful discharge case. [*Modica v. Taylor*, 465 F.3d 174 (5th Cir. 2006)] State courts may be more hospitable; even in a state that applies the concept of employment at will, it is possible that a supervisor would be held liable for discriminatory practices. [See, e.g., *Trau-Med of Am. Inc. v. All State Ins. Co.*, 71 S.W.3d 691, 703 (Tenn. 2002). These issues are discussed in Tresa Baldas, *Employment Litigation Gets Personal for Company Managers*, Nat'l L.J (Aug. 16, 2007) (law.com)] The Eastern District of Pennsylvania allowed an FMLA case to proceed naming three HR executives and a manager as defendants, based on evidence that the individuals tried to force the plaintiff out of the company, and they had the power to fire him. [*Narodetsky v. Cardone Indus.*, 2010 U.S. Dist. LEXIS 1613 (E.D. Pa. Feb. 4, 2010); see Shannon P. Duffy, *Federal Judge OKs FMLA Claims Against Individuals*, The Legal Intelligencer (Mar. 2, 2010) (law.com)]

Section 2000e-5(f)(3) provides that the suit can be filed in any federal District Court in the state where the alleged unlawful employment practice occurred. (The number of federal judicial districts in a state ranges from one to four.) The suit can also be brought in the judicial district where the relevant employment records are kept, or in the district where the plaintiff would have worked if there had been no unlawful employment practice. Finally, if the defendant company can't be found in any of those districts, the plaintiff can sue the defendant company in the judicial district where the company's principal office is located.

There is no explicit statute of limitations in 42 U.S.C. § 1981 (the federal law guaranteeing all persons within the jurisdiction of the United States the same rights to make and enforce contracts that "white citizens" have). Therefore, there was a circuit split on the proper statute of limitations to apply in § 1981 wrongful discharge cases. The split was resolved by the Supreme Court's May 2004 ruling: the statute of limitations is four years, because the current version of § 1981 was enacted by the Civil Rights Act of 1991 (CRA '91). Under federal law, the statute of limitations for all federal laws enacted after December 1, 1990, is four years, so that applies to CRA '91. [*Jones v. R.R. Donnelley & Sons Co.*, 541 U.S. 401 (2004)]

When there is no evidence of actual date on which a complainant received a right to sue letter, it will be presumed that delivery occurred three days after mailing—hence a suit, 98 days after issuance of the letter, was untimely, although the presumption can be rebutted by evidence of delayed receipt. Merely calling mail delivery unreliable is not enough. [*Payan v. Aramark Mgmt. Servs.*, 495 F.3d 1119 (9th Cir. 2007)]

## [B]  Tolling

In a limited group of circumstances, the statute of limitations can be tolled (suspended) when it would be unjust to insist on strict compliance. Tolling may be permitted if:

- The employer was guilty of deception or some other wrongdoing that prevented the employee from asserting Title VII rights;

- The employee tried to file a timely lawsuit, but the pleading was rejected as defective;

- The employee filed in time, but in the wrong court.

Tolling is usually considered a defense, which means that it is up to the plaintiff to prove that it was available, and not up to the defendant to prove that it was not.

The term "tolling" is sometimes used to cover two different but related concepts. "Equitable tolling" allows a delayed case to continue because, even though the plaintiff's excusable ignorance or oversight caused the delay, the defendant is not prejudiced (harmed) by the delay.

"Equitable estoppel" prevents the defendant from complaining about a delay that was caused in whole or part by the defendant's deceit or other conduct prejudicial to the plaintiff's interests, e.g., if the employee is afraid to approach the EEOC and endanger the internal investigation and grievance procedure that was being carried out. [*Currier v. Radio Free Europe*, 159 F.3d 1363 (D.C. Cir. 1998)]

## § 42.06  CLASS ACTIONS

Class actions are governed by Rule 23 of the Federal Rules of Civil Procedure, especially Rule 23(b). The various subsections of Rule 23 create several alternative methods of litigating a class action, but each method has its own procedural requirements that must be satisfied. The requirements relate to what the plaintiffs want (money damages, or just an injunction?) and how people become members of the class (are they automatically included unless they opt out, or do they have to opt in?). It can also be difficult and expensive for the potential plaintiffs to give the required notice to everyone who might want to join the class.

A case where restaurant waiters said they were forced to share their tips with ineligible employees and were also denied overtime pay raised federal claims via an FLSA collective action, which was combined with a putative class action under the New York labor law. The Second Circuit affirmed certification of the class action, even though the FLSA's collective actions are opt-in (i.e., an employee is involved only if he or she affirmatively agrees to be) and the New York class action was opt-out (all employees are involved unless they refuse to be). The restaurant said that Congress' intent in making FLSA collective actions opt-out would be hampered by combining the case with an opt-out class action, but the Second Circuit rejected this argument. Both suits involved the same fact situation—and the FLSA includes a provision that allows states to pass laws that are even more protective of employees' rights. The Seventh, Ninth, and D.C. Circuits have allowed FLSA collective actions to be combined with state-law class actions, but the Third Circuit has refused to do so. [*Shahriar v. Smith Wollensky Restaurant Group,* 659 F.3d 234 (2d Cir. 2011)]

Discrimination cases focusing on monetary damages can be hard to certify as class actions. Rule 23(b)(2) requires not only a common injury but uniform remedies for the whole class. Would-be plaintiffs who can't use Rule 23(b)(2) may have to fall back on Rule 23(b)(3), which requires them to prove that class-wide issues are more important in the case than individual issues. They must also prove that a class action is better than other methods of resolving the dispute. In some cases, a "hybrid" class action will be allowed. First a class is certified under Rule 23(b)(2) to decide if the employer is liable. If it is, damages are determined under Rule 23(b)(2). In recent years, many class actions have been denied certification, or have been certified and then de-certified, based on court findings that each claimant's assertions must be handled individually on a case-by-case basis.

### [A]  The Dukes Case and Its Implications

In mid-2011, the Supreme Court held that the massive sex discrimination class action against Wal-Mart was improperly certified. The plaintiffs alleged that Wal-Mart's broad corporate culture discriminated against women in pay and promotions, creating a company-wide discriminatory policy. In the view of the

Supreme Court majority, Wal-Mart gave store managers a significant amount of discretion, so the existence of sex discrimination would have to be assessed at the individual store level.

The Supreme Court majority opinion held that the plaintiffs failed to show a single policy rather than numerous acts of alleged discrimination against individuals, so there was no common employment decision that could be challenged under Rule 23(a)(2).

Nor could the plaintiffs use Rule 23(b)(2) to seek back pay, even if they called the back pay claims incidental to claims for injunctive relief. The Supreme Court held that Wal-Mart would be entitled to individual determinations of back pay eligibility—it would not be appropriate to determine a class-wide back pay award by extrapolating from a small sample.

Some commentators suggested that the lesson large companies can take from this is that if they establish an overall anti-discrimination policy but delegate significant power to regional managers, they will be able to use the *Wal-Mart* decision to defend themselves—possibly in contexts extending beyond discrimination cases. [*Wal-Mart v. Dukes*, 131 S. Ct. 2541 (2011); see, e.g., Tony Mauro, *Supreme Court Erects Major Barriers to Class Actions in Wal-Mart Ruling*, Nat'l L.J. (June 20, 2011) (law.com);]

The attorneys representing the *Dukes* plaintiffs announced a new strategy in late 2011: a series of regional suits, beginning with an amended complaint in the District Court for the Northern District of California, with the intention of certifying a class of approximately 95,000 California plaintiffs, with subclasses for injunctive relief and back pay. [Ginny LaRoe, *'Dukes' Back From the Dead* (law.com); (date unknown); Andrew Martin, *Women File New Class-Action Bias Case Against Wal-Mart*, NYTimes.com (Oct. 27, 2011)]

The reduced *Dukes* case survived a motion to dismiss. [Cynthia Foster, *Judge Certifies Class Suing Costco for Gender Bias*, The Recorder (Sept. 25, 2012) (law.com)]In September 2011, the Ninth Circuit ruled for Costco in a case that could have expanded a sex discrimination suit to hundreds of women. The Ninth Circuit reversed certification of a Title VII sex discrimination class. The case was remanded to apply the *Dukes* standard of commonality. The district court must consider whether the class members' claims for monetary relief require individual determinations. If so, a (b)(2) class action is inappropriate; if a class can be certified at all, it must fall under (b)(3). The Ninth Circuit said that a current employee was an adequate class representative because she is still employed and she has an incentive to pursue injunctive remedies. But ex-employees were not adequate class representatives because their sole interest was in monetary relief. The Northern District of California certified a class of approximately 700—the first post-*Dukes* sex discrimination class to be certified. Costco argued that the plaintiffs were denied promotion for personal reasons, but the district court held that concerns about family needs are universal, so defenses based on family or personal circumstances are appropriately resolved by class treatment. [*Ellis v. Costco Wholesale Corp.*, 657 F.3d 970 (9th Cir. 2011), *on remand*, No. 04-3341

(N.D. Cal. pending); see Karen Talley, *Costco Wins Appeal in Gender-Bias Suit*, WSJ.com (Sept. 16, 2011); Rebecca Moore, 9th *Circuit Uses WalMart Decision to Deny Class in Costco Case*, plansponsor.com (Sept. 26, 2011); Cynthia Foster, *Judge Certifies Class Suing Costco for Gender Bias*, The Recorder (Sept. 25, 2012) (law.com)]

After eight years and two Supreme Court appeals, a suit by a class of 700 black brokers against Merrill Lynch was settled in mid-2013. The class received $160 million, the largest race discrimination settlement to date. It was possible to certify a class in this case because Merrill Lynch imposed a system of uniform operations and strict centralized controls. [*McReynolds v. Merrill Lynch*, No. 11-01957 (7th Cir. settled 2013)/ *McReynolds v. Merrill Lynch*, No. 05-cv-06583 (N.D. Ill. settled 2013); see Patrick McGeehan, *Merrill Lynch in Big Payout for Bias Case*,NYTimes.com (Aug. 27, 2013)]

A late November 2011 article says, perhaps too optimistically, that after *Dukes* certification of a nationwide, multi-state, multi-business-location class action based on an employer's decentralized, subjective decision-making is "more challenging." The authors say that it is difficult to prove commonality across a wide geographic and operational scope. A multidistrict litigation (MDL) also has problems of coordinating discovery. To make the litigation more manageable, employers can seek a stay in one case until another one is resolved or use Federal Rules of Civil Procedure Rule 42 to consolidate discovery. Sometimes related cases can be brought together in one court as an MDL. The decision is made by the Judicial Panel on Multidistrict Litigation, which also decides which court will hear a consolidated case. First the cases are centralized in that court, then remanded for trial to the courts where they were originally filed. The Judicial Panel is a federal group; it does not have jurisdiction over state cases, although state cases can be removed to district court and then centralized. Cases are centralized if the cases have common questions of fact; centralization promotes the interests of justice and it is convenient for parties and witnesses. [Stephen P. Sonnenberg and Maria A. Audero, *Litigating Multidistrict Employment Actions After 'Dukes,'* N.Y.L.J. (Nov. 14, 2011) (law.com)]

## § 42.07  THE DISCRIMINATION COMPLAINT

Once the case is cleared for litigation in federal court, the plaintiff must draft a complaint to inform the defendant and the court system of the nature of the allegations against the defendant.

Late in 2001, the Eleventh Circuit adopted a position already held by the Third, Seventh, and Eighth Circuits: An EEOC intake questionnaire constitutes a "charge" if it is verified and has the information a charge would contain, and a reasonable person would consider the questionnaire to manifest an intent to seek Title VII remedies. [*Wilkerson v. Grinnell Corp.*, 270 F.3d 1314 (11th Cir. Oct. 22, 2001)]

A similar issue went to the Supreme Court in the ADEA context. The Court permitted an ADEA suit to proceed, after the complainant filed a Form 283 intake questionnaire with the EEOC, but did not file the official Form 5 (charge). The EEOC did not carry out informal dispute resolution with the employer. The Court held that a valid ADEA charge requires only a few items of information (the name of the charging party, the nature of the allegation, and a request that the EEOC settle a dispute or take remedial action). In this case, the employer was aware that the plaintiff and thirteen other employees had alleged age discrimination. The Court remanded the case to the district court, holding that the lower court can make up for the deficiency by attempting to reconcile the parties in a settlement. (The EEOC stated that it has improved its procedures to make sure the same problem will not recur.) [*Federal Express Corp v. Holowecki*, 552 U.S. 389 (2008); see Mark Sherman, AP, *Supreme Court Says FedEx Employees Can Sue Over Age Discrimination* (Feb. 28, 2008) (law.com); Fred Schneyer, *Supreme Court Clears FedEx Age Discrimination Case for More Hearings*, plansponsor.com (Feb. 28, 2008)]

A 2008 Third Circuit case finds that a two-page document, including EEOC Form 5, constituted a charge. The first page gave the plaintiff's date of birth and contact information for the charging party and his employer. The complainant checked the box alleging age discrimination and cross-referenced the second sheet. He signed it in two places, but did not check the box for dual filing with the state agency, and did not have the signatures notarized. The second page, described as an affidavit, described improper questions asked at the interview, leading the plaintiff to believe that he was not offered a job because of his age (59). The EEOC regulations provide that a charge should contain:

- The names, address, and phone numbers of the charging party;
- The name, address, and phone number of the defendant;
- A statement of the facts constituting the alleged discrimination;
- The number of employees the employer has (to establish that the employer is large enough to be subject to federal anti-discrimination statutes);
- Whether or not the charging party has already initiated state proceedings.

About two months later, the EEOC wrote to the plaintiff's attorney asking for more information, stating that the plaintiff would have to provide the information within 33 days. But, instead of submitting the information to the EEOC, the plaintiff brought suit 80 days after submitting the document to the EEOC. The defendant moved to dismiss the case for failure to exhaust administrative remedies; the Third Circuit accepted the two-page document as a charge because it gave notice of the nature of the plaintiff's allegations. [*Holender v. Mutual Indus. North Inc.*, 527 F.3d 352 (3d Cir. 2008)]

## § 42.08  MEETING BURDENS

In legal parlance, "the burden of production" means having to provide evidence to prove a particular point, and "the burden of proof" is the standard used to determine if adequate evidence has been supplied.

Section 2000e(m) says that "demonstrates" means "meets the burdens of production and persuasion." This covers the extremely important legal issue of who has to provide evidence of what. It is always easier to wait for the other party to produce evidence and then show that this evidence is incorrect, incomplete, not technically satisfactory, or inadequate to prove the case, than to have to submit independent evidence of one's own viewpoint.

Section 2000e-2(k) explains what the plaintiff has to prove in order to win a disparate-impact case. The complaining party must show that the employer's challenged employment practice has a disparate impact on a protected group. At this stage, the employer has a chance to prove that the employment practice is valid because it is job-related and consistent with the needs of the employer's business. However, if the employer demonstrates that the employment practice does not cause disparate impact, it is not necessary to prove business necessity for that practice. On the other hand, business necessity is only a defense against disparate impact claims, not against claims of intentional discrimination.

Another route for proving disparate impact is for the complaining party to demonstrate disparate impact and also show that the employer refused to adopt an alternative employment practice that would eliminate the disparate impact.

According to the Ninth Circuit, the 1991 amendments to Title VII, allowing proof of violation when discrimination was a motivating factor for the employer (rather than the sole motivating factor) does not require proof of the impermissible factor by direct evidence, because the statutory language does not include the phrase "direct evidence." A year later, the Supreme Court affirmed. [*Costa v. Desert Palace Inc.*, 299 F.3d 838 (9th Cir. 2002), *aff'd*, 539 U.S. 90 (2003)]

According to the Seventh Circuit, plaintiffs do not have to present evidence of better treatment of similarly situated employees. A law firm associate could present a "mosaic" of evidence to survive summary judgment in a case alleging religious and national origin discrimination. The rationale given for the associate's termination was that he was fired for "deficiencies in performance," but when he produced evidence that his work was fine—and that some partners were prejudiced against Muslims in the wake of the 9/11 attack—the firm changed its story and said he was fired for lack of work. The Seventh Circuit did not find this credible, because the firm continued to hire associates. The Seventh Circuit remanded the case for trial. [*Hasan v. Foley & Lardner*, 552 F.3d 520 (7th Cir. 2008); see Rebecca Moore, *No Need to Show Others Treated Better in Discrimination Suit*, plansponsor.com (Jan. 9, 2009)]

## § 42.09   RETALIATION CHARGES

A high percentage of discrimination cases also involve charges of retaliation. Indeed, in some cases, the judge or jury has ruled that the original charge of discrimination was not supported by adequate evidence—but there was enough evidence of retaliation for making the charge to subject the employer to retaliation liability.

Under a 2006 Supreme Court decision, liability for retaliation is broader than liability for underlying workplace discrimination, and a retaliation case can be sustained even if the employee is not demoted and his or her compensation remains the same—as long as the retaliation is severe enough that a reasonable employee would take it into consideration in deciding whether or not to pursue a discrimination complaint. [*Burlington Northern & Santa Fe Ry. Co. v. White*, 548 U.S. 53 (2006)]

However, in 2013, on another issue, the Supreme Court found that retaliation liability is narrower than Title VII liability in general. The 2013 case was brought by a Muslim professor, who alleged that his supervisor harassed him because of his religion and Middle Eastern national origin, and that his employer retaliated against him by interfering with a job opportunity to punish him for making discrimination charges. The Supreme Court required retaliation plaintiffs to prove that retaliation was the "but-for" cause of the adverse employment action taken against them: i.e., that they would not have been fired, demoted, etc. without a retaliatory motive. This is the same standard used in ADEA cases, but is more restrictive than non-retaliation Title VII cases, where the plaintiff can prevail by showing that discrimination was one of several motivations used by the employer. The Supreme Court held that mixed-motive cases are only proper in cases involving the five criteria based on personal characteristics specified in Title VII: race, color, religion, sex, and national origin. The Supreme Court noted that Title VII's retaliation provisions are in a separate section from the basic protection against discrimination, and considered the language of the retaliation section to be more like the ADEA, hence justifying applying the higher ADEA standard in retaliation cases. [*University of Tex. Sw. Med. Ctr. v. Nassar*, No. 12-484 (U.S. June 24, 2013); see Marcia Coyle, *Supreme Court Makes It Harder to Prove Job Bias Claims*, Nat'l L.J. (June 24, 2013) (law.com)]

The Supreme Court's 2009 *Crawford* decision holds that employees are protected against retaliation based on their answering questions during an internal investigation; it is not necessary for the employee to have volunteered the information or initiated the investigation, because participating in an investigation can constitute the type of active and consistent opposition to an unlawful practice that triggers entitlement to protection against retaliation. [*Crawford v. Metropolitan Gov't of Nashville & Davison County, TN*, 555 U.S. 271 (2009); see Rebecca Moore, *Employees Questioned in Workplace Sexual Harassment Investigations Are Protected*, plansponsor.com (Jan. 26, 2009)]

The Supreme Court ruled in early 2011 that Title VII forbids retaliation against someone who has filed a discrimination complaint if the retaliation takes the form of reprisals against a person who associates with the complainant. (In this case, it was the complainant's then-fiance who eventually became her husband.) The opinion says that Title VII's ban on retaliation extends to any action that would prevent a reasonable worker from making or pursuing a discrimination charge. Although it is difficult to draw firm lines, firing a close family member is very likely to be deemed retaliation; mild reprisal against an acquaintance is very unlikely to be; courts must find the balance in the intermediate areas. On the question of who is allowed to sue for retaliation, the Supreme Court said that as well as the person engaging in the protected activity, a suit can be brought by anyone within the zone of interests protected by Title VII. [*Thompson v. North Am. Stainless*, 131 S. Ct. 863 (Jan. 24, 2011)]

The Fourth Circuit held that the Fair Labor Standards Act (FLSA's) ban on retaliation applies only to employees, not to potential employees. Therefore, a job applicant cannot use this provision to sue a company that refused to hire her because of the FLSA suit she brought against a different employer. (The plaintiff got a job offer contingent on completing some forms; the offer was withdrawn after she disclosed the lawsuit on one of the forms.) [*Dellinger v. Science Applications Int'l Corp.* 649 F.3d 226 (4th Cir. 2011); see Sheri Qualters, *4th Circuit: Anti-Retaliation Provision of Wage Law Does Not Cover Job Applicants*, Nat'l L.J. (Aug. 15, 2011) (law.com)]

The Third Circuit ruled early in 2006 that retaliation claims can be premised on a hostile work environment. Most of the circuits allow retaliation claims premised on retaliation that takes the form of severe or pervasive harassment, but the Fifth and Eighth Circuits require an ultimate employment decision to sustain a retaliation claim. [*Jensen v. Potter*, 435 F.3d 444 (3d Cir. 2006)]

The anti-retaliation provisions of Title VII protect a person who is named as a voluntary witness in a Title VII case, even if he or she is not called to testify at the trial. [*Jute v. Hamilton Sundstrand Corp.*, 420 F.3d 166 (2d Cir. 2005)] In mid-2010, the Second Circuit rejected an original theory put forward by a plaintiff. The court ruled that declining to investigate an employee's complaint of workplace discrimination (in this case, race discrimination) does not constitute retaliation for making the charge. [*Fincher v. Depository Trust & Clearing Corp.*, No. 08-5013-cv (2d Cir. May 14, 2010)]

PPACA § 1558 amended the Fair Labor Standards Act to prevent employers from retaliating against employees who receive a subsidy or tax credit for purchasing health care coverage from an insurance Exchange. Employees are protected against retaliation if they provided or were about to provide information about PPACA Title I violations to the employer, the federal government, or a state attorney general. Retaliation is also forbidden for testifying or being about to testify in a proceeding about such a violation, assisting in or participating in a proceeding, or objecting to or refusing to participate in a proceeding. Title I is the portion of PPACA that forbids coverage limits, requires coverage of preventive services, the required summary of benefits and coverage, and mandatory inclusion of adult children in the plan to age 26. Retaliation is defined to include discipline, discrimination, threats, and the like with respect to compensation or terms and conditions of employment. Starting in 2014, employees are also protected against retaliation (such as termination of coverage) by EGHP insurers. However, retaliation complaints are processed by OSHA, not by the EEOC. [OSHA Fact Sheet, *Filing Whistleblower Complaints under the Affordable Care Act*, <http:// www.osha.gov/Publications/whistleblower/OSHAFS-3641.pdf > (Feb. 2013); see PLC Employee Benefits & Executive Compensation, *OSHA Rules Address Retaliation Complaint Procedures under Health Care Reform* (Feb. 25, 2013) (benefitslink.com)]

## § 42.10   TITLE VII LITIGATION

### [A]   Three-Step Process

A Title VII case is very different from other civil cases, because so much revolves around questions of intentions and statistics, not just the proof of simple facts.

The basic Title VII case is a three-step process. The plaintiff establishes a prima facie case: the basic facts that are suggestive of discrimination. This is sometimes referred to as "McDonnell-Douglas burden-shifting analysis" after the Supreme Court case that established this technique.

After the plaintiff submits a prima facie case, the defendant can ask the court to dismiss the case at that stage (summary judgment), if the prima facie case would not be good enough for the plaintiff to win if the defendant did not submit a case of its own.

On the other hand, if the prima facie case is strong enough to keep the case going, the defendant employer gets a chance to rebut the plaintiff's charge of discrimination. The employer can do this by proving a legitimate, nondiscriminatory reason for the job action against the plaintiff. The employer can also prevail by proving that its action was impelled by business necessity. If summary judgment is not granted, then there will have to be a full trial. The jury (or the judge, if there is no jury in the case) will have to decide the facts.

The third step is the plaintiff's again. At this stage, the plaintiff gets to show "pretextuality": that the employer's allegedly nondiscriminatory reasons are fabricated to hide its discriminatory motive.

Whether a company actually has 15 employees is a substantive element of the Title VII case, not a jurisdictional prerequisite. Therefore, if the issue is not raised in a timely fashion, it is waived. The Supreme Court held early in 2006 that the 15-employee requirement is not jurisdictional because it does not appear in the part of the Title VII statute that grants jurisdiction to the federal courts. The court's lack of subject matter jurisdiction can be raised at any point in the case.

[*Arbaugh v. Y&H Corp.*, 546 U.S. 500 (2006); similarly, *Minard v. ITC Deltacom Commc'ns Inc.*, 447 F.3d 352 (5th Cir. 2006) for the FMLA]

## [B]    Elements of the Prima Facie Case

The kind and amount of evidence that the plaintiff has to introduce to make a prima facie case depends on the kind of case (sex discrimination, sexual harassment, age discrimination, racial discrimination, etc.) and whether the plaintiff charges disparate treatment or disparate impact. Disparate treatment is a practice of intentional discrimination against an individual or group, whereas disparate impact is a practice that seems to be neutral and nondiscriminatory, but that has a heavier negative impact on some groups than others.

Furthermore, if the plaintiff charges that an employment practice has a disparate impact, and the employer responds by showing business necessity for that practice, the plaintiff can nevertheless win by proving that there was an alternative practice that would also have satisfied business necessity, but the employer refused to adopt that practice.

If a workplace decision involves many factors (for instance, promotion could be based on educational attainment, objective measures such as sales performance or departmental productivity, written tests, interviews, and assessments from supervisors), and the plaintiff challenges more than one of those criteria, the plaintiff has to be able to prove that each of those factors had harmful disparate impact on the plaintiff. If the various elements can't be separated and analyzed individually, then the whole decision-making practice can be treated as a single employment practice.

The "mixed motive" case works somewhat differently. It arises out of the situation in which several motivations influence the employer's decision. Some of them are lawful, others are discriminatory. The plaintiff can win a mixed motive case by showing that the discriminatory motive was influential. It is not necessary to prove that there were no legitimate motives involved. However, if the employer would have done the same thing even without a discriminatory motive being present, then the remedies available to the plaintiff will be reduced.

To establish the prima facie case, the plaintiff must show the following:

- That he or she belonged to a protected group;

- He or she had the necessary qualifications for the job (allegation of discriminatory failure to hire);

- He or she was doing an adequate job (if the allegation is improper discharge or failure to promote).

While disparate treatment cases usually depend on direct or indirect evidence of explicit discrimination, disparate impact cases usually turn on statistics about matters such as job applications and the composition of the workforce.

In mid-2003, the Supreme Court's *Desert Palace, Inc. v. Costa* decision [539 U.S. 90 (2003)] resolved a Circuit split. The First, Fourth, Eighth, and Eleventh Circuits had ruled that once the defendant meets its burden by articulating a legitimate non-discriminatory reason for the job action, the plaintiff can get a jury instruction on mixed motive only by showing direct evidence. But the Supreme Court sided with the Ninth Circuit and allowed the instruction to be given on the basis of circumstantial evidence. In this case, the plaintiff, a truck driver, said that the employer's stated reason for firing her (a fight with another employee) was another instance of being treated more harshly than male co-workers for the same conduct. She also alleged that she was discriminated against when overtime work was available, and that supervisors were aware of and tolerated sex-based slurs against her.

The Supreme Court agreed that a mixed-motive jury charge can be given whenever the amount of evidence (whether direct or circumstantial) is adequate. This ruling therefore means that more cases will be submitted to the jury, and more plaintiffs will have a chance of prevailing. [See Shannon P. Duffy, *High Court Paves Easier Road to Jury for Discrimination Plaintiffs,* The Legal Intelligencer (June 11, 2003) (law.com)]

A unanimous Supreme Court endorsed the "ministerial exception" in early 2012, holding that the First Amendment prevents courts from intervening when a minister is fired. All 12 of the circuits have recognized this exception, although this was the first time the Supreme Court dealt with the issue. The Court said that the ministerial exception is not a bar to a court's jurisdiction; it is an affirmative defense that has to be proved by the defendant raising it. The Supreme Court said that ministers can still sue for tortious conduct or breach of contract. The plaintiff, Cheryl Perich, alleged that she was fired in retaliation for threatening to file an ADA suit (she suffers from narcolepsy). The Sixth Circuit ruled for Perich, holding that she spent 45 minutes a day teaching religion and the rest of the time teaching secular subjects. The Supreme Court found this unpersuasive: all ministers have secular duties. [*Hosanna-Tabor Evangelical Lutheran Church v. EEOC* 132 S. Ct. 694 ( 2012); see Tony Mauro, *Unanimous High Court Finds for Church in EEOC Fight,* Nat'l L.J. (Jan. 11, 2012) (law.com)]

In a gender bias case, the District Court for the District of Massachusetts ruled in 2012 that a pattern-or-practice claim is a method of proving discrimination in a class action, not a free-standing cause of action. The plaintiff charged that CIGNA Healthcare's evaluation and promotion practices discriminated against women, violating Title VII and state law. CIGNA argued that the claims had to be arbitrated. The plaintiff said that the arbitration clause did not waive the right to litigate class-based or pattern-or-practice claims. The district court held that CIGNA's policies and procedures forbid class arbitration, so Karp had to pursue individual arbitration for her claim. [*Karp v. CIGNA Healthcare Inc.,* No. 11-10361-TSH, 2012 WL 1358652 (D. Mass. Sept. 14, 2012); see Sheri Qualters, *Judge Sends Gender Bias Case Against CIGNA To Arbitration,* Nat'l L.J. (Apr. 19, 2012) (law.com)]

## [C]  Evidence

Not only can each side introduce evidence about the course of the plaintiff's employment with the defendant company; in appropriate cases, the employer can introduce evidence about the plaintiff that the employer did not have at the time of the employment action.

The basic case on the use of after-acquired evidence is *McKennon v. Nashville Banner Pub. Co.* [513 U.S. 352 (1995)] In this case, the employer was allowed to introduce, at the trial, negative evidence about the plaintiff that the defendant learned after the employment action. Although the after-acquired evidence couldn't have motivated the employer, it was still relevant to the plaintiff's qualifications and credibility, so it can be introduced at trial.

In many cases, the plaintiff introduces statistics to show a pattern of discrimination by the employer. To prevail, a plaintiff must identify a specific employment practice that discriminates, not just rely on bottom-line numbers about the employer's work-force. The plaintiff must present statistical evidence of a kind and degree adequate to show that the practice has caused denial of promotion because of the applicants' membership in a protected group. When read in conjunction with the other evidence, adequate statistics must be of a kind and degree that reveals a causal relationship between the allegedly discriminatory practice and the disparity between actual promotions of group members, and the promotions that could be expected if there had been no discrimination.

In deciding whether to admit expert evidence at the class certification stage of an employment discrimination case, courts focus on whether the expert opinion meets the test of scientific validity. In employment discrimination cases, the plaintiffs usually want to introduce expert testimony consisting of statistics that show that there has been disparate impact or a pattern or practice of discrimination. [Elise M. Bloom and Amanda D. Haverstick, *Class Actions After 'Dukes,'* N.Y.L.J. (Oct. 24, 2011) (law.com)]

## [D]  Admissible and Inadmissible Evidence

The Second Circuit ruled that racist comments by a white employee can be used to show that the work environment was hostile to black people, even if the remarks were made after the black plaintiff resigned. [*Whidbee v. Garzarelli Food Specialties,* 223 F.3d 62 (2d Cir. 2000)] But testimony by four of the plaintiff's co-workers (that a supervisor's treatment of the demoted black employee was racially motivated) should not have been admitted. [*Hester v. BIC Corp.*, 225 F.3d 178 (2d Cir. 2000)] The witnesses could testify about their observations, but because they didn't know how good or bad the plaintiff's work performance actually was, they couldn't testify about the supervisor's motivation.

In mid-2011, the California Court of Appeal held that the trial court should have admitted "me too" evidence in a sexual harassment hostile work environment case. In other words, evidence that the defendant harassed other women should have been admitted because excluding it was prejudicial to the plaintiff's case. The Court of Appeal said that the evidence tended to show the defendant's bias against women and tended to disprove the legitimacy of his stated reason for firing the plaintiff. [*Pantoja v. Anton*, 198 Cal. App. 4th 87 (Cal. App. 2011); see Kate Moser, *Court OKs 'Me Too' Testimony in Sex Harass Suit Against Lawyer*, The Recorder (Aug. 9, 2011) (law.com)]

The New Jersey Appellate Division ruled in mid-2009 that defense lawyers cannot ask plaintiffs their immigration status during discovery in a wage and hour/overtime class action. (Several other courts have ruled the same way, on the grounds that it has a chilling effect on employees' attempts to enforce their rights.) Nor can they ask whether the plaintiffs made false statements or lied to the employer, unless the defense can show that the statements directly affect their credibility on the issue of their eligibility for back pay and overtime. [*Serrano v. Underground Utilities Corp.*, 407 N.J. Super. 253 (N.J. App. Div. 2009); see Michael Booth, *Court Sets "Don't Ask, Don't Tell" Rule for Illegal-Alien Class Action Plaintiffs*, N.J.L.J. (May 22, 2009) (law.com)]

In 2011, the District Court for the District of Massachusetts granted the plaintiffs' motion to make a restaurant owner answer written questions about possible members of the class—but denied the defendants' motion to require the plaintiffs to answer questions about their immigration status. Restaurant workers claimed that they were paid less than the Massachusetts minimum wage, because they routinely worked 60–80 hours per week but not only did not receive overtime but also were not paid for all the hours they worked. The district court concluded that the FLSA covers even illegal aliens; wages must be paid even if the worker is undocumented. [*Lin v. Chinatown Rest. Corp.*, Civil Action No. 09-11510-GAO, 2011 U.S. Dist. LEXIS 30626 (D. Mass. Mar. 23, 2011); see Sheri Qualters, *Plaintiffs' Immigration Status 'Irrelevant' to Their Wage Claims, Mass. Judge Rules*, Nat'l L.J. (Mar. 28, 2011) (law.com)]

Former contract attorney Kisshia Simmons-Grant sued Quinn Emanuel Urquhart & Sullivan in 2011, charging that, because she is black she was assigned less lucrative work than contract attorneys of other races, and that she was forced to quit when she complained. Simmons-Grant relied on statistical evidence that full-time black contract attorneys billed fewer hours than other full-time contract attorneys. The Southern District of New York granted summary judgment for the firm, holding that individual private plaintiffs must prove that they were individually subjected to intentional bias. The district court ruled that pattern or practice arguments are restricted to class actions; using them elsewhere would require employers to prove that they did not discriminate, whereas it is the plaintiff's burden to prove discrimination. [*Simmons-Grant v. Quinn Emanuel*, No. 1:11-cv-07706 (*dismissed*, S.D.N.Y.); see Christine Simmons, *Quinn Emanuel Wins Dismissal of Bias Suit*, N.Y.L.J. (Jan. 9, 2012) (law.com). See also *Chin v. Port*

*Auth.*, 685 F.3d 135 (2012) and *Parisi v. Goldman, Sachs & Co.*, 710 F.3d 483 (2d Cir. 2013): pattern or practice claims are limited to the class action context.]

## [E]  Other Litigation Issues

If the plaintiff files suit in state court, the employer often tries to get the case removed to federal court. State courts usually have less crowded calendars, so cases can be decided faster. Sometimes, state law permits the employee to assert additional causes of action, or to get remedies that would not be available in federal court. Sometimes, too, a particular action is subject to state but not federal law. For example, some states ban discrimination in workplaces that are too small to be covered by the federal law. Sexual-orientation discrimination is not covered by Title VII, but is covered by certain state or local laws.

In many cases, federal law preempts state law. In other words, certain matters, such as most of labor law and benefit law, are covered by federal law, and the states cannot interfere. Therefore, if a plaintiff's state-court claims operate in one of these preempted areas, the employer has a strong argument for getting the case removed to federal court, or even dismissed.

Norman Carpenter sued Mohawk Industries for wrongful termination. He alleged that, at a time when he was unaware that the company was the defendant in a pending class action charging the company with conspiring to use undocumented workers to drive down the wages of legal workers, he told Mohawk's HR department about undocumented aliens working at the company. Carpenter said that company lawyers pressured him to recant and he was fired when he would not. As part of his wrongful termination suit, Carpenter tried to get information from Mohawk about his meeting with the lawyer and the decision to fire him. Mohawk said that the information was protected by attorney-client privilege. The Supreme Court held in late 2009 that a court order requiring disclosure of allegedly privileged material is not a collateral order that is entitled to immediate appeal, because there are other measures, such as postjudgment review, that the party seeking to protect the information can use. [*Mohawk Indus., Inc. v. Carpenter*, 558 U.S. 100 (2009)]

As Chapter 40 shows, in many instances, a would-be plaintiff is subject to a mandatory arbitration clause that requires arbitration of all discrimination claims. The general principle is that pre-dispute arbitration requirements (i.e., an agreement to arbitrate disputes that arise in the future) will be enforceable even if the plaintiff charges a violation of rights under federal anti-discrimination laws.

## § 42.11  ADEA SUITS

### [A]  Generally

It is clear that the ADEA creates a private right of action—i.e., individuals can bring suit if they claim to have been subjected to age discrimination in employment. [See 29 U.S.C. § 626(c)] The statute is not very detailed. It says only that individuals can sue for "such legal or equitable relief as will effectuate the purposes" of the ADEA. However, a suit brought by the Secretary of Labor will terminate the rights of individuals to bring their own lawsuits involving their ADEA claims.

Under 29 U.S.C. § 626(d), would-be ADEA plaintiffs have to file their charges within 180 days of the alleged unlawful practice. In a "referral" state (a state whose antidiscrimination agency has a work-sharing agreement) the charge has to be filed within 300 days of the alleged unlawful practice. If the state-law proceedings are terminated, the potential plaintiff must file the charge within 30 days of the termination of the state proceeding.

When a charge is filed, all potential defendants are notified. In both the Title VII and ADEA contexts, the Secretary's duty is to "promptly seek to eliminate any alleged unlawful practice by informal methods of conciliation, conference, and persuasion."

In the federal system, whether a case can be heard by a jury (instead of just a judge) depends on several factors, including the preferences of the litigants and the nature of the suit itself. The basic rule is that juries are more appropriate for cases seeking money damages than those asking for purely equitable remedies such as injunctions or reinstatement. However, ADEA plaintiffs can demand a jury trial whenever they seek money damages, even if there are also equitable claims in the same suit.

When third parties, including independent contractors, are authorized to make hiring decisions on behalf of an employer, the Second Circuit held that the employer can be liable under the ADEA if the third party commits discrimination. General agency principles are used to assess the third party's authority. This is a fact inquiry, so summary judgment is not appropriate. [*Halpert v. Manhattan Apartments Inc.*, 580 F.3d 86 (2d Cir. 2009)]

### [B]  Timing Issues for ADEA Suits

The EEOC proposed regulations (67 Fed. Reg. 52431, Aug. 12, 2003) and finalized them at the end of 2003 (68 Fed. Reg. 70150, Dec. 17, 2003; effective January 16, 2004). Under the now-applicable regulations, the EEOC will dismiss (as untimely) charges filed more than 180 days after the discriminatory act—or more than 300 days in a referral jurisdiction. Extra time may be available if the charging party has a valid claim to waiver, estoppel, or equitable tolling.

The EEOC has a statutory obligation to try to eliminate alleged unlawful practices by means of informal conciliation. If the EEOC tries to conciliate but fails, it will give the charging party a notice—but the notice will be clearly labeled to distinguish it from the Notice of Dismissal or Termination, which is issued in ADEA cases as a rough parallel to the Right to Sue letter in other discrimination cases.

An age discrimination charging party does not have to wait until the NDT is issued to sue—as long as he or she waits at least 60 days after the charge was filed. But once the NDT is issued, the complainant has only 90 days to file suit (which can be filed in either federal or state court), or the case will be dismissed as untimely.

Federal employees are subject to some special rules. They can go straight to the District Court to assert ADEA claims without going through the normal administrative process. According to the First Circuit, when they do so, the appropriate statute of limitations is the one found in the Fair Labor Standards Act, not Title VII. [*Rossiter v. Potter,* 357 F.3d 26 (1st Cir. 2004)]

However, under 29 C.F.R. § 1614.407(a), suit must be brought within 90 days of the final agency action. A plaintiff's final agency action occurred on June 15, 2001, making the last day to file September 13, 2001. His attorney filed the complaint on the 12th, expecting it to be delivered the next day. However, it was not actually delivered until the 18th. The Eighth Circuit found the case untimely, and would not grant equitable tolling. The plaintiff was deemed to have had adequate notice of the filing requirements, he had a lawyer, and the delay was not the fault of the clerk's office; it was not reasonable to expect next-day delivery from 450 miles away. [*Hallgren v. U.S. Dep't of Energy,* 331 F.3d 588 (8th Cir. 2003)]

It is in the employer's best interest for the court to rule that the cause of action "accrued" earlier, i.e., that the clock started ticking when the employee had to file suit. The earlier the cause of action accrues, the more likely it is that a claim can be dismissed as untimely.

If the alleged discriminatory act is firing the employee, there is a single act of discrimination. Most cases hold that the discriminatory act occurs on the date the plaintiff is unambiguously informed that he or she will be fired. The important date is the date of this notice, and not the first warning the plaintiff receives of impending termination, and not the last day the employee works for the employer or the last date he or she is on the payroll. The notice does not have to be formal, or even written, but it must be a definite statement that a final decision has been made to terminate the employee.

It is harder to place other discriminatory acts on a time continuum. It has been held that a claim of failure to promote accrues when the employees know or should have known about the facts that support the claim—probably, that a younger individual received the promotion that the plaintiff wanted.

If there is only a single employment decision, there is only a single act that might be discriminatory. However, some courts allow a plaintiff to argue that there was a continuing violation lasting over a period of time—for example, that the plaintiff kept his or her job, but was denied promotions he or she deserved because of age discrimination. In a case where the court accepts the continuing violation theory, the cause of action accrues with the last discriminatory act in the series. A filing that is timely for one act of discrimination will be timely for all acts of discrimination in the same series.

A bad performance appraisal that makes an employee more vulnerable to being laid off or RIFed (but that is not an actual threat of dismissal unless performance improves) is generally not considered an employment action that could give rise to an ADEA claim.

For discriminatory layoff charges, courts reach different conclusions as to when the cause of action accrues. One theory is that accrual occurs on the actual date of layoff. The other is that the cause of action accrues later, when the possibility of reinstatement ends because the employer has filled the last job for which the plaintiff might have been recalled.

## [C]   Tolling the ADEA Statute of Limitations

The statute of limitations can be tolled (suspended), giving employees additional time to litigate, in various circumstances—usually as a result of deception or other misconduct on the part of the employer. However, certain circumstances have been held not to be wrongful conduct, and will not toll the statute of limitations:

- Putting an employee on "special assignment" until termination takes effect;

- Offering a severance benefits package. However, offering a lavish severance package, but preventing employees from discussing it, was held to discourage employees from vindicating their legal rights, and therefore to toll the statute of limitations.

■ **TIP:**  The statute of limitations is not tolled during the employer's in-house grievance procedure. However, a collective bargaining agreement provision is invalid if it terminates the employee's right to pursue a grievance once he or she files age discrimination charges with the EEOC or the local antidiscrimination agency. The clause is void because it punishes employees for exercising their legal rights.

Even if tolling occurs, it probably cannot last beyond the point at which an employee who took reasonable steps to investigate would have been aware of discrimination.

Do not forget that 29 U.S.C. § 627 requires the employer to post a notice of ADEA rights. The EEOC and Department of Labor distribute free copies of the mandatory notice; posters can also be purchased from many publishers. If the notice is duly posted, then the court will presume that the employee could have read the poster and become aware of at least basic ADEA rights.

However, if the information is not posted, the court may conclude that the employer deprived the employee of access to information about ADEA rights, thus tolling the statute of limitations. Yet some courts say that the real test is whether the employee actually was aware of what the ADEA says. Given actual knowledge, the court may decide that the absence of a poster in the workplace does not justify extending the time to bring suit.

## [D]  The ADEA Plaintiff's Burden of Proof

The *McDonnell-Douglas* pattern applies in ADEA cases. That is, first the plaintiff introduces evidence of a prima facie case of discrimination. If the evidence (taken at face value) is inadequate, the defendant employer can get summary judgment—that is, can have the case dismissed because of this inadequacy.

If, however, the case is good enough to survive a motion for summary judgment, it is the employer's turn at bat. By and large, proof is up to the plaintiff, but a BFOQ is an affirmative defense, which means that the employer has the burden of proving it. [*W. Air Lines Inc. v. Criswell,* 472 U.S. 400 (1985)] In non-BFOQ cases, the employer can rebut the prima facie case by showing a legitimate, non-discriminatory reason for the conduct challenged by the employee. Then the employee gets another chance, to demonstrate that the employer's justification is actually a pretext for discrimination. *Meacham v. Knolls Atomic Power Labs* [554 U.S. 84 (2008)], similarly holds that the reasonable factors other than age (RFOA) defense is also an affirmative defense.

It is not necessary in all cases for the plaintiff to prove that he or she was replaced by someone under 40 (i.e., outside the protected group). [*O'Connor v. Consol. Coin Caterers Corp.*, 517 U.S. 308 (1997)] It is possible, although difficult, for the plaintiff to win a case in which he or she was replaced by another person over 40, as long as improper age-related motives are shown.

In 1993, the Supreme Court set a new standard for proving ADEA cases based on age-related factors rather than on age itself. For instance, a 30-year-old cannot have 30 years' employment experience, but a 38-year-old employee might have worked for the company for 20 years, and therefore have more seniority than a 50-year-old hired only 10 years earlier. In that example, the allegedly age-related factors of higher salary and benefits would actually make the 38-year-old the more expensive employee.

The key case on this issue is *Hazen Paper Co. v. Biggins* [507 U.S. 604 (1993)] which requires the plaintiff to prove that the employer's decision was influenced by age, not merely by age-related factors.

In 2009, the Supreme Court agreed to hear a mixed motive age discrimination case, to determine the burden of proof. The Supreme Court ruled that, in order to win, a mixed-motive ADEA plaintiff must prove by a preponderance of the evidence that age was the "but-for" cause of the challenged employment action: that it would never have occurred but-for the plaintiff's age. The burden of persuasion is always on the plaintiff, and can be met by either direct or circumstantial evidence. The burden of persuasion never shifts to the defendant. This is not the same standard applied in Title VII, but the Supreme Court stressed the difference in wording and legislative history between the ADEA and Title VII [*Gross v. FBL Fin. Servs., Inc.*, 557 U.S. 167 (2009)]

Early in 2008, the Supreme Court did not fully resolve the question about whether ADEA plaintiffs can prove a corporate culture of discrimination by introducing testimony of employees who did not have the same supervisor as the plaintiff. The Court would not entirely rule out the use of such testimony, requiring instead that in each case, the facts should be examined to see if the probative value of the testimony outweighed the risk of possible prejudice. The Court ruled that, in general, the district court's determination is entitled to a high measure of deference, because the lower court hears testimony rather than merely relying on the record on appeal. The relevant provision of the ADEA is drafted similarly to Title VII, so the same principle should also apply in Title VII cases. [*Sprint/United Mgmt. Co. v. Mendelsohn*, 552 U.S. 379 (2008); see, e.g., Fred Schneyer, *Supreme Court Reverses Age Discrimination Ruling on Procedural Grounds*, plansponsor.com (Feb. 27, 2008)]

In mid-2010, the California Supreme Court permitted judges hearing discrimination cases to consider comments made by non-decision makers outside the personnel process. In other words, what might otherwise be excluded as "stray remarks" are admissible, because age-based remarks can provide relevant circumstantial evidence of discrimination. The plaintiff in the instant case was 52 when he was hired; he alleged that co-workers and managers called him obsolete, an old fuddy-duddy who lacked new ideas and did not fit into Google's corporate culture. [*Reid v. Google*, 50 Cal. 4th 512, 235 P.3d 988 (2010); see Fred Schneyer, *Court Rejects Stray Remarks Doctrine in Google Ageism Case*, plansponsor.com (Aug. 9, 2010)]

Direct evidence of age discrimination is hard to find—especially since even employers who do practice discrimination usually have enough sophistication to conceal it. As a practical matter, then, most ADEA cases will be based on statistical evidence in support of the allegation, with or without evidence about statements made by executives and supervisors. Statistics are especially prominent in disparate impact cases.

However, the legal trend has been to reduce the credence given to statistics. In *St. Mary's Honor Ctr. v. Hicks* [509 U.S. 502 (1993)], the court held that the plaintiff always has the "ultimate burden of persuasion." So if the fact-finder (which will be the jury or the judge in a nonjury case) doesn't believe the employer's explanation of why its conduct was legitimate, the plaintiff can still lose—if the plaintiff simply fails to offer enough evidence. The *Hicks* standard is sometimes called "pretext-plus": The plaintiff has to do more than just show that the defendant's excuses are a mere pretext for discrimination.

## [E]   The ADEA Prima Facie Case

The basic prima facie (initial) case for an ADEA lawsuit is:

- The plaintiff belongs to the protected group—that is, is over 40;

- The plaintiff was qualified for the position he or she held or applied for;

- The plaintiff was not hired, discharged, demoted, deprived of a raise, or otherwise disfavored because of age;

- (In appropriate cases) The plaintiff was replaced—especially by someone under 40, although it is not absolutely required that the replacement come from outside the protected age group. If the charge is a discriminatory RIF, plaintiffs must show that age was a factor (although not necessarily the only factor) in targeting them for termination, or at least that the employer was not age-neutral in implementing the RIF program. Employers can defend against an accusation of a discriminatory RIF by showing good economic reason for cutting back; it isn't necessary to show that the company would be at the brink of bankruptcy without the reductions.

Depending on the type of case, the court where it is heard and the individual facts, the plaintiff may have to prove that his or her own qualifications and/or job performance were satisfactory, or may have to prove that they were superior to those of the person who replaced him or her.

In 2012, the EEOC issued a Q&A explaining what employers must do to use a Reasonable Factors Other Than Age (RFOA) defense when practices that are neutral on their face but might have disparate impact on older workers are challenged. The employer is only required to prove an RFOA after an employee has identified a specific business practice with disparate impact on older workers. An RFOA is reasonably designed and administered to achieve a legitimate business purpose—for example, a physical test for police patrol officers.

Whether the factors are indeed reasonable depends on, e.g.:

- Their relation to the employer's stated business purpose;

- The extent to which the factor is accurately defined and fairly and accurately applied (application includes training managers and supervisors);

- Limits on supervisors' discretion, especially when the criteria are vulnerable to negative age-based stereotypes;

- The extent to which the employer assessed the adverse impact of the practice on older workers;

- The degree of harm to workers over 40—not just the number of people affected and the extent of the injury, but the employer's measures to reduce harm, balanced against the burden of the actual and potential measures.

- The EEOC stresses that these are not elements that all employers must prove in every case, merely characteristics of reasonable practices.

The EEOC said that, unlike an employment test that has been challenged under Title VII, it is not necessary for the employer to produce a validation study about the RFOA.

The EEOC says it is not unreasonble to use subjective decision-making (e.g., ranking an applicant or employee's qualities such as flexibility and willingness to learn new things) but it is useful to give supervisors evaluation criteria to help them avoid age-based stereotypes. The EEOC said that employers are not obligated to discover and use the least discriminatory method of achieving the purpose—but attempts to limit harm to older persons are not irrelevant. [EEOC, *Questions and Answers on EEOC Final Rule on Disparate Impact and "Reasonable Factors Other Than Age" Under the Age Discrimination in Employment Act of 1967*, <http://www.eeoc.gov/laws/regulations/adea_rfoa_qa_final_rule.cfm>; see Rebecca Moore, *EEOC Issues Final Rule Under ADEA*, plansponsor.com (Mar. 30, 2012)]

CBS ordered its affiliates to reduce budget by 10%. The plaintiffs, Schechner (age 66) and Lobertini (age 47) were laid off. They sued under California law for age and sex discrimination. The Ninth Circuit upheld the grant of summary judgment to the defendants, but ruled that a plaintiff can prove a prima facie case of disparate treatment age discrimination by statistical evidence, even if that fails to account for the defendant's legitimate non-discriminatory reason for discharge. Three other employees were laid off, all over 40 (at ages 51, 56, and 57). The plaintiffs submitted statistical reports showing disproportionate layoffs of older reporters. The station said that the news anchors could not be laid off because they didn't want the viewers to know about the station's financial problems. The plaintiffs offered statistical reports of on-air talent layoffs as compared to the entire on-air talent pool, showing disproportionate layoffs of older reporters. The Ninth Circuit ruled that to make a prima facie case entirely by statistics, the statistics must demonstrate a stark pattern of discrimination that cannot be explained any other way. In this case, the plaintiffs made a prima facie case, but the Ninth Circuit accepted the employer's reason (laying off general assignment reporters based on the dates their contracts expired) as legitimate and non-discriminatory. The defendant was also entitled to the same-actor inference (i.e., the decision-maker had hired the plaintiffs and must have been aware of their ages). [*Schechner v. KPIX TV CBS*, 686 F.3d 1018 (9th Cir. 2012)]

## [F]   ADEA Class Actions

Sometimes, an employee contends that he or she is the only person to suffer discrimination. Sometimes, however, it is alleged that the company engages in a pattern or practice of discrimination, affecting many people, and it becomes necessary to determine whether it is appropriate to certify a class action (i.e., to allow employees to combine their claims and present a single body of evidence).

The question of timing in class actions was addressed in *Armstrong v. Martin Marietta Corp.* [138 F.3d 1374 (11th Cir. 1998)] Certain employees were dismissed as plaintiffs from a pending ADEA class action. They brought their own suits. The Eleventh Circuit held that the statute of limitations is tolled (suspended) while a class action is pending, but starts all over again as soon as the District Court issues an order denying class certification.

Would-be plaintiffs who are thrown out of a class action because they are not similarly situated to the proper plaintiffs must file their own suits within 90 days of being removed from the class. Equitable tolling (i.e., permitting an action that would otherwise be too late to continue, on the grounds of fairness) can be granted only if the EEOC actually misinformed the plaintiffs about the statute of limitations, not if the plaintiffs simply failed to consider this issue or made an incorrect determination of how long they had to bring suit.

## § 42.12   TITLE VII REMEDIES

### [A]   Fundamental Remedies

Once the case gets to court and is tried to a conclusion (many cases are either settled along the way, or are dismissed before a full trial has occurred), and if the plaintiff wins (most employment discrimination cases are won by the employer), then the question becomes what remedies the court will order. Remedies are governed by 42 U.S.C. § 2000e-5(g).

The fundamental remedies under this section are equitable: hiring or reinstatement (plus up to two years' back pay for the time the plaintiff would have been working absent discrimination). Furthermore, the amount that the plaintiff earned in the meantime—or could have earned by making reasonable efforts—is offset against the back pay. In other words, plaintiffs have a duty to mitigate their damages. They have an obligation to use their best efforts to earn a living, instead of relying on the hope the defendant employer will eventually be ordered to pay up.

If the plaintiff further succeeds in proving disparate treatment (as distinct from facially neutral practices that have a disparate impact on the group the plaintiff belongs to), then compensatory damages can be awarded to the plaintiff as reimbursement for costs (such as job hunting or therapy) incurred directly as a result of the discrimination.

However, in cases of racial discrimination, the plaintiff must look to the Civil Rights Act of 1866 [42 U.S.C. § 1981], and not to Title VII, for compensatory and punitive damages. If the alleged discrimination consists of failing to accommodate a disability, the employer will not have to pay compensatory damages if it made a good-faith effort at reasonable accommodation, even if the offer of accommodation was later deemed inadequate.

If the court finds that the employer engaged in the unlawful employment practice that the plaintiff charged, it can enjoin the respondent from continuing that abusive practice. The court can order the defendant to take remedial steps, including but not limited to hiring an applicant or reinstating an ex-employee.

Employers cannot be ordered to hire, reinstate, or promote anyone, or pay back pay to him or her, if the employment action was taken "for any reason other than discrimination on account of race, color, religion, sex, or national origin" or unlawful retaliation. [42 U.S.C. § 2000e-5(g)(2)(A)]

In a mixed-motive case where the defendant demonstrates that, although a discriminatory motive was present, it would have taken the same action (e.g., fired or refused to promote the plaintiff) purely on the basis of the other motivations even if there had been no discrimination, then the court can grant a declaratory judgment (a declaration that the employment practice was unlawful), enjoin its continued use, or award attorneys' fees that can be traced directly to the mixed-motive claim. But, because the employer would have taken the same action even without discrimination, the court cannot award damages to the plaintiff or order the defendant to hire, rehire or promote the plaintiff. [42 U.S.C. § 2000e-5(g)(2)(B)]

The court has discretion, under 42 U.S.C. § 2000e-5(k), to order the loser—whether plaintiff or defendant—to pay the winner's attorneys' fees (including fees for expert witnesses, which can be very high) and court costs. However, losing defendants can't be ordered to pay fees to the EEOC. If the EEOC sues a company and loses, it can be ordered to reimburse the defendant for its fees and costs for the suit.

Also note that 42 U.S.C. § 2000e-2(n) provides that employees usually cannot challenge employment practices that were adopted based on a court order or to carry out a consent decree in an employment discrimination case, if the employees knew about the case and either had their interests represented or had a chance to voice their objections. However, employees who actually were parties in the case can enforce their rights under the order or settlement, and judgments and orders can be challenged on the grounds of fraud or the court's lack of jurisdiction over the case.

One important factor in analyzing employment cases is what claim(s) the employee raises. Some employment discrimination claims fit into the "breach of contract" category, but most of them are more like "tort" claims. The importance of the tort/contract distinction is that the remedies are different for the two categories. If a plaintiff proves breach of contract, the court's job is to put the plaintiff back in the position he, she, or it would have been in if the contract had been carried out. In the context of an employment contract, or implied employment contract, that probably means earnings and fringe benefits that were lost because of the breach, possibly plus out-of-pocket expenses for finding a new job. (The doctrine of mitigation of damages requires plaintiffs to do whatever they can to limit the amount of damages they suffer—which definitely includes finding a new job if at all possible, pending resolution of the claims against the former employer.)

Back pay is not limited to simple salary. It includes benefits, overtime, shift differentials, merit raises, and the like. However, if the employer can prove that the employee would have been laid off, or was unavailable for work, back pay will not be available for the time the employee would not have been working anyway.

Fringe benefits are valued at the cost the employee would have to pay to replace them, not the (probably lower) cost the employer incurred to offer them.

Amounts earned in the new job reduce what the ex-employer will have to pay in damages. On the other hand, to the extent that the plaintiff proves that the employer committed one or more torts, the successful plaintiff can be awarded back pay, front pay (moving from the end of the trial forward), lost earnings, medical expenses, and value of pain and anguish, and emotional distress. The plaintiff's spouse might be granted an award for loss of consortium (marital services that were not rendered because of the employer's wrongdoing). In most states, interest on the judgment, running from the time the case is decided, can also be ordered—which mounts up quickly if the award is in six or seven figures.

The Tenth Circuit ruled that to assure complete compensation in a Title VII case, prejudgment interest is an element of back pay awards. The calculation starts with the date of the adverse employment action, but does not accrue until actual monetary injury has been sustained (e.g., after severance pay runs out). The court ruled that the plaintiff (who alleged religious discrimination after being assigned to work on the Sabbath) was injured when he was terminated for failing to report to work as scheduled, but the injury did not occur all at once: It incurred as each pay period passed, so the interest should be calculated on each missed paycheck. [*Reed v. Mineta*, 438 F.3d 1063 (10th Cir. 2006)]

Sometimes, front pay and reinstatement can be combined, i.e., if the remedies don't overlap, chronologically or economically. Front pay can be awarded to get the plaintiff to the "point of employability," at which point he or she can be reinstated.

The equitable remedy of front pay can be denied to an employee whose conduct after termination renders her ineligible for reinstatement. This case involved a sexual harassment plaintiff who got another job at a bank, who was fired for attempting to process an unauthorized loan application. The case was remanded to determine if her misconduct in the second job would preclude reinstatement in the first job. [*Sellers v. Mineta*, 358 F.3d 1058 (8th Cir. 2004)]

Many discrimination cases can be brought by the plaintiff in federal court, because there is a federal question (alleged violation of a federal statute). If the plaintiff chooses to sue in state court instead, the issue arises of whether the defendant can get the case removed to federal court. Further issues arise when the reason for going to federal court is "diversity" (the plaintiff and defendant are citizens of different states). Federal courts have jurisdiction in diversity cases if, and only if, the amount in controversy is at least $75,000.

## [B]  CRA '91 Cap on Damages

The Civil Rights Act of 1991 (CRA '91) [Pub. L. No. 102-166] imposes a cap on total damages that can be awarded to a successful Title VII plaintiff: The amount depends on the size of the corporate defendant, not the number or seriousness of the charges. The cap applies to punitive damages and most compensatory damages (but not to medical bills or other monetary losses that the plaintiff incurred before the trial).

Companies with fewer than 15 employees are exempt from Title VII, so the cap calculation begins at the 15-employee level. The damage cap is $50,000 for a company with 15–100 employees. The cap is set at $100,000 for companies with 101–200 employees, $200,000 for 201–500 employees, and $300,000 for companies with over 500 workers.

The First Circuit ruled in mid-2011 that the number of employees for purposes of the CRA '91 damage cap is determined at the time of the discrimination, not at the time the court renders its decision. The District Court for the District of Puerto Rico awarded $300,000 in a sexual harassment case. The trial judge reduced this award to $50,000. On appeal, the First Circuit increased the compensatory damages to $200,000. The size of the employer's workforce had fallen dramatically between 2004 (when the alleged discrimination occurred) and the 2008 verdict. The First Circuit also held that the number of employees is an affirmative defense that has to be proved by the employer. [*Hernandez-Miranda v. Empresas Diaz Masso Inc.*, No. 10-1639 (1st Cir. June 29, 2011)]

In mid-2011, the Third Circuit reduced a $10 million jury award for racial discrimination received by three former police officers to $900,000. The officers brought only federal claims, so the $300,000 cap on damages applied. (If they had brought and prevailed on claims under Pennsylvania law, damages for those claims would not have been capped.) The plaintiffs, who are white, alleged that they suffered retaliation for protesting mistreatment of black co-workers. One of the plaintiffs was told that if he filed an EEOC charge, his supervisor would make his life "a living nightmare." In a separate opinion, $208,000 in back pay was awarded to one of the plaintiffs. [*McKenna v. Philadelphia*, 649 F.3d 171 (3d Cir. 2011); see Shannon P. Duffy, *3rd Circuit Upholds Slashing $10 Million Verdict to $900,000*, The Legal Intelligencer (Aug. 19, 2011) (law.com)]

## [C]  Punitive Damages

One of the most controversial questions is the matter of punitive damages. Theoretically, punitive damages are supposed to be quite rare, ordered only in those cases when the defendant's conduct has been worse than merely negligent or improper.

A defendant that has acted maliciously, or at least with reckless indifference to the plaintiff's rights, can be ordered to pay punitive damages. The employer's conduct need not be "egregious" for punitive damages to be available. [*Kolstad v. Am. Dental Ass'n*, 527 U.S. 526 (1999)]

The general rule in the federal system—not just in employment discrimination cases—is that "double digit" punitive damages (i.e., more than ten times the compensatory damages) are inappropriate, and that it is also inappropriate to impose punitive damages in a particular case because of the defendant's wrongful conduct in other cases or other states. According to the Fourth Circuit, it was permissible to award $100,000 to a wrongfully demoted employee who was not awarded any compensatory damages on her sex discrimination claim. The Fourth Circuit deemed the judge's award of $410,000 in back pay and interest to justify the punitive damage award, because the loss of income she suffered was actionable harm, the lost back pay was roughly equivalent to compensatory damages, and there is no explicit statutory condition under CRA '91 that punitive damages are dependent on compensatory damages. [*Corti v. Storage Tech. Corp.*, 304 F.3d 336 (4th Cir. 2002)]

There are not many instances in which very large punitive damages have actually been paid. Such awards are vulnerable to being reduced on appeal. Or the plaintiff may feel both emotionally vindicated and sick of litigating the case, and may settle the case post-trial for much less than the theoretical award. Nevertheless, even if the order is never carried out, it can be a real public relations disaster for a company to be ordered to pay millions of dollars as a punishment.

The EEOC's Compliance Manual lists appropriate factors for deciding whether the employer acted with malice or reckless indifference:

- Degree of unacceptability of the conduct;

- The nature, severity, and extent of the harm suffered by the complaining employee;

- The duration of the conduct: A practice that persists for years is more serious than one that is terminated after a short period of time;

- Whether there was an extensive pattern of past discrimination, or only a few isolated incidents;

- Whether the employer tried to remedy the situation, or exacerbated it by covering up or retaliating against complainants.

## [D]  Attorneys' Fees and Costs

Under appropriate circumstances, a court can award attorneys' fees and costs to the "prevailing party"—and there has been a good deal of litigation, inside and outside the employment discrimination context, on the issue of who has been successful enough to receive a fee award.

In 2010, the Supreme Court ruled that a specific section of ERISA (§ 502(g)(1)) gives the district court discretion to award attorneys' fees to either party, not necessarily to the "prevailing" party. (In contrast, ERISA § 502(g)(2), about delinquent contributions to a multi-employer plan, limits fee awards to the prevailing party.) Therefore, it was not an abuse of discretion to grant attorneys' fees to a claimant who went to court after being denied long-term disability benefits. The district court found that the insurer abused its discretion when it denied the benefits, and remanded for the insurer to reconsider; if it did not, the trial court said that it would enter judgment for the plaintiff. The benefits were granted, and the district court awarded attorneys' fees. The Fourth Circuit found that this was an abuse of discretion, because the plaintiff received only a remand, not substantive benefits. The Supreme Court reversed, citing the statutory language that does not require the party seeking fees to have prevailed. [*Hardt v. Reliance Ins. Co.,* 560 U.S. 242 (2010); see Workplace Prof Blog, *ERISA Supreme Court Attorney Fees Case Goes Way of Plaintiffs* (May 24, 2010) (benefitslink.com); Marcia Coyle, *Supreme Court Smooths Path to Plaintiff Fees in Disability Cases,* Nat'l L.J. (May 25, 2010) (law.com).

Shortly thereafter, the Fourth Circuit applied this case to award attorneys' fees to a claimant who was granted summary judgment when the district court found that she was entitled to long-term disability benefits for carpal tunnel syndrome. The Fourth Circuit found that there was no inherent bias in the termination of long-term disability benefits after two years—but the denial was not supported by substantial evidence, because the plaintiff's pain and loss of function continued: *Williams v. Metropolitan Life Ins. Co.,* 609 F.3d 622 (4th Cir. 2010); see Plansponsor Staff, *4th Circuit Upholds Award of Benefits and Attorneys' Fees in LTD Case,* plansponsor.com (July 2, 2010)]

Federal Rules of Civil Procedure Rule 68 provides that when the defendant makes a formal settlement offer before the trial; the plaintiff rejects the offer; and the plaintiff wins the case, but is awarded less than the offer, the defendant is entitled to reimbursement of litigation costs. However, the Third Circuit ruled that the defendant can never recover attorneys' fees under this provision, because the plaintiff's suit was not frivolous—the plaintiff merely made a bad strategic decision in a valid case. [*Tai Van Le v. Univ. of Pa.,* 321 F.3d 403 (3d Cir. 2003)]

## § 42.13   SETTLEMENT OF A DISCRIMINATION SUIT

### [A]   Generally

Suits can be settled at any time before a verdict or judicial decision is rendered. In fact, they can even be settled after the judge and jury have spoken. As long as there are appeal rights that could be exercised, the case is still open for negotiation. The objective of any settlement is to provide something for both parties: for the defendant employer, the chance to dispose of the case expeditiously and to eliminate the risk of a huge jury verdict; for the plaintiff, the chance to get at least some money quickly instead of many years later. At a very early stage, the matter might be resolved by an agreement to let the employee resign instead of being fired and receive severance pay, and perhaps some other benefits, in exchange for releasing the employer from all liability. Both sides must agree on how the matter will be treated for unemployment insurance purposes (based on counsel from a lawyer).

In a situation where the employer acknowledges that the plaintiff has a valid case, or at least that the claims have some validity, the employer may want to settle early to limit its possible liability exposure and bad publicity.

Even if the employer thinks the plaintiff's claims are fabricated, exaggerated, or legally invalid, it still might be prudent to settle the case because of the sheer cost and effort involved in litigating a major suit, even if the final result is victory for the employer.

Usually, cases are settled somewhere around halfway between the plaintiff's demand and the defendant's counter-offer. Of course, both sides know this, and it influences the amounts they suggest at the negotiating table. No one should ever engage in negotiations without authority actually to settle the case, and without a range of acceptable settlement figures.

Seyfarth Shaw's Annual Workplace Class Action Litigation Report published January 14, 2013 shows that *Dukes* immediately had a tremendous impact on private class action suits. Employers are taking a much harder line during settlement negotiations. The total involved in 2012's top 10 employment discrimination class settlements was approximately $46 million. This was the lowest figure since 2006, and much lower than the $346 million total from 2010. The EEOC has responded by increasing its systemic investigations, although it filed only half as many suits in 2012 as in 2011. The continuing problems of the economy will probably result in more class actions and collective actions alleging wage and hour violations. [Shannon Green, *Workplace Class Action Litigation Report Outlines a Post-Dukes World*, Corporate Counsel (Jan. 14, 2013) (law.com)]

On November 30, 2010, the Southern District of New York granted final approval to a major class-action settlement: a sex discrimination class action covering more than 6,000 women who are or were sales representatives for Novartis. The settlement consisted of $152.5 million in back pay and benefits, including incentive payments to the named plaintiffs. Attorneys' fees of $38.1 million, and costs of $2 million were awarded. Novartis also agreed to $22.5 million in non-monetary relief such as employing consultants to improve the company's culture and treatment of female representatives. Although this was the largest Title VII settlement of 2010, it was still far less costly for the employer than the $3.4 million in compensatory and $250 million in punitive damages awarded by the jury. [*Velez v. Novartis Pharm. Corp.*, No. 04-9194 (S.D.N.Y. settlement 2010); see Gerald L. Maatman, Jr. and Scott Velasquez, *Record Gender Discrimination Class Action Settlement and Fee Award Given Final Approval*, <http://www.workplaceclassaction.com/settlement-issues/record-gender-discrimination-class-action-settlement-and-fee-award-given-final-approval/> (Nov. 30, 2010); Chad Bray, *Approval Seen for Novartis Gender-Discrimination Pact*, WSJ.com (Nov. 19, 2010)]

> ■ **TIP:** Cases that are settled quickly are also often settled within the policy limits of the employer's liability insurance policy. Therefore, the insurer will assume the entire cost of settlement. Moreover, if the employer does a prompt investigation of the allegations, negotiates in good faith, and does not unduly delay the settlement, the employer has not acted outrageously and has not violated the norms of public policy. Therefore, there will probably be no grounds for assessing punitive damages against the employer.

When a settlement is reached, there are two major legal documents to be prepared. The first is a court order dismissing the case with prejudice (i.e., in a way that prevents it from being refiled later) and a release containing the terms of the settlement. It is usually prudent to try to provide the text of the release, in order to control the basic form of its terms. The 2009 Family and Medical Leave Act regulations (see Chapter 38) make it explicit that, while prospective waivers are forbidden (i.e., employees cannot give up the right to bring suit for violations that might occur in the future), employees can settle FMLA claims that have already accrued without court approval or the supervision of the Department of Labor.

Mid-2009 EEOC guidance includes a section on Older Workers Benefit Protection Act (OWBPA) waivers. A waiver covering a group or class of employees carries additional disclosure requirements. There are seven factors under the OWBPA for determining whether an ADEA waiver is knowing and voluntary. It must be written in a manner that can be clearly understood; must specifically mention ADEA rights or claims; must inform employees of the right to consult a lawyer; must give the employee at least 21 days to consider the offer and seven days to revoke acceptance; the waiver cannot cover claims to arise in the future; and the employee must receive some consideration for the waiver that would not otherwise be available. A waiver is invalid if obtained by fraud or undue influence, or if there has been a material mistake, omission, or misstatement.

[Rebecca Moore, *EEOC Issues Guidance on Waivers for Departing Employees*, plansponsor.com (Aug. 12, 2009)]

A settlement can be offered without admitting culpability. Also, under 29 C.F.R. § 1601.20(a), the EEOC has the power to dismiss an employee's discrimination charge if the employee rejects a written settlement offer from the employer that is a legitimate offer of "full relief" (i.e., adequate compensation for the discrimination suffered by the employee). The EEOC sends the employee a strongly worded form letter that gives him or her only two choices: to accept the settlement offer promptly, or have the EEOC charge dismissed. (This only means that the EEOC will not be involved in the case, not that the employee is prevented from suing.)

Full relief means that the employee gets full back pay, plus any out-of-pocket expenses related to discrimination (such as moving expenses after a wrongful termination, or psychological counseling for a stressed-out employee). Compensation must also be included for nonmonetary losses such as loss of sleep, anxiety, and indigestion.

However, the employer must be aware that settling with one employee is not necessarily the end of the problem. It is against public policy (and a court might issue an injunction forbidding this) to include a provision in a settlement agreement that forbids a current or former employee to cooperate with an EEOC investigation. A settlement can prevent a person from pursuing his or her own claims against the employer, but the EEOC's right to investigate workplace conditions, and pursue claims on its own behalf (and on behalf of other employees) continues.

## [B]    Tax Factors in Settling Discrimination Cases

The plaintiff's objective is to wind up with the best after-tax result from pursuing or settling a case. In some instances, appropriate structuring of the settlement can produce a better after-tax result for the plaintiff while reducing the cash-flow impact on the defendant.

Damages for breach of contract are taxable income for the plaintiff, because they are treated as delayed payment of compensation that the employee would have received earlier if there had been no breach of contract.

The treatment of tort damages is more complex. Damages are not taxable if they are payable because of the plaintiff's "personal injury." The Supreme Court has ruled that Title VII damages and ADEA damages are not received for personal injury, because they are not similar enough to the damages received in traditional tort cases (car crashes, for instance). [*United States v. Burke,* 504 U.S. 229 (1992); *Commissioner of Internal Revenue v. Schleier,* 515 U.S. 323 (1995)] Nevertheless, in 2006 the D.C. Circuit held that compensatory damages for emotional distress and loss of reputation are not taxable, and it was unconstitutional to apply section 104(a)(2) [the definition of "personal physical injury"] to the plaintiff, because compensation for non-physical personal injury should not have to be included in income if it is unrelated to lost earnings. [*Murphy v. IRS*, 460 F.3d 79 (D.C. Cir. 2006)]

Later, this anomalous result was reversed. The IRS asked for rehearing en banc (i.e., by all of the judges of the D.C. Circuit, not just a panel consisting of some of them). Instead of granting en banc rehearing, the original three-judge panel re-heard the case and reversed its earlier holding. This time around, the D.C. Circuit joined the other Circuits in treating the amount as taxable income. [*Murphy v. CIR*, 493 F.3d 170 (D.C. Cir. 2007); see, e.g. (AP) *D.C. Circuit: Damages for Emotional Distress Part of Gross Income* (July 5, 2007) (law.com). See also *Polone v. CIR*, 479 F.3d 1019 (9th Cir. 2007)]

The Small Business Job Protection Act of 1996 clarified the application of I.R.C. § 104(a)(2), the provision on taxation of damages. Starting August 21, 1996, damages received for "personal physical injuries" and physical illness are received free of tax—for instance, if the employer's wrongful conduct makes the employee physically ill. Damages for emotional distress are taxable except to the extent of medical expenses for their treatment.

Taxable damages that are wage replacements (under the FLSA, NLRA, Title VII, and ADEA, for example) may be FICA wages and may be subject to withholding. But see *Newhouse v. McCormack & Co.* [157 F.3d 582 (8th Cir. 1998)], where front and back pay awarded under the ADEA to a job applicant who was not hired was not considered "wages" subject to tax withholding.

A longstanding circuit split was resolved by the U.S. Supreme Court's January 2005 decision in *Comm'r v. Banks*, 543 U.S. 426 (2005). A judgment or settlement paid to a winning plaintiff's attorney under a contingent fee agreement must be included in the plaintiff's gross income, irrespective of whether state law gives the attorney special rights (over and above normal contract law rights) over amounts awarded to prevailing plaintiffs.

Section 703 of the American Jobs Creation Act (Pub. L. No. 108-357) makes attorneys' fees in employment discrimination cases an above-the-line deduction, although this is not true of attorneys' fees in other types of cases. *Banks* was decided after the enactment of this legislation, but the law is not retroactive.

In 2008, a Northern District of New York jury awarded back and front pay in a Title VII case. The plaintiff had been a New York State government employee, so the judgment was sent to the New York State Office of the Comptroller (OSC) for payment. The OSC considered the payment to constitute wages so it made deductions, including federal and state taxes, and sent Noel a check for the balance. He made a motion to require the state to pay the full, unreduced amount of the judgment. The district court granted the motion, holding that the state did not have the authority to make the deductions without prior court approval. The Second Circuit reversed, stating that the judgment replaced wages that the plaintiff lost due to discrimination and he would have had to pay taxes if there had been no discrimination and he had earned his ordinary salary. In this reading, both back pay and front pay are wages subject to income tax withholding and FICA tax. [*Noel v. New York State Office Of Mental Health Cent. New York Psychiatric Ctr.*, 697 F.3d 209 (2d Cir. 2012)]

The Third Circuit held that prevailing plaintiffs in employment discrimination cases (in this case, the winner of an ADA suit) can receive an additional award to make up for the negative tax consequences of receiving a back pay award in a lump sum. The Third Circuit's rationale was that anti-discrimination statutes seek to make the plaintiff whole for the losses suffered, and the tax problems are a result of the underlying discrimination. The Tenth Circuit has ruled similarly, but the D.C. Circuit has held that plaintiffs are never entitled to a supplemental award to improve their tax position. [*Eshelman v. Agere Systems Inc.*, 554 F.3d 426 (3d Cir. 2009); see Shannon P. Duffy, *Tax Needs May Require Additional Award in Employment Cases*, The Legal Intelligencer (Feb. 4, 2009) (law.com); the earlier cases are *Sears v. Atcheson, Topeka & Santa Fe R.R*, 749 F.3d 1451 (10th Cir. 1984) and *Dashnaw v. Pena*, 12 F.3d 1112 (D.C. Cir. 1994)]

CHAPTER 43

# INSURANCE COVERAGE FOR CLAIMS AGAINST THE EMPLOYER

## § 43.01    INTRODUCTION

It is only prudent for a company to maintain insurance against significant risks. However, although the potential risk exposure in a discrimination, harassment, or wrongful termination suit is quite large, it can be difficult to buy insurance that will fully cover these claims—or even cover them at all. In addition, the collapse of the financial markets beginning in 2008 has given rise to a wide variety of securities-related claims, including those brought by employees whose pensions were jeopardized.

A basic principle of insurance law is that you can't buy insurance to protect yourself against the consequences of your own intentional wrongdoing.

The current interpretation of this rule is that it does not violate public policy for companies to buy insurance covering employment-related liability, because this enhances the winning plaintiffs' chances to collect. This benefit is deemed to outweigh the risk that companies will be more willing to engage in improper employment practices if they know they are protected by insurance.

A related policy question is whether insurance can cover punitive damages. About two-thirds of the states that have decided cases about this say yes. However, punitive damages for intentional wrongdoing cannot be covered, and most punitive damages are imposed precisely because of the intentionality of the defendant's wrongful conduct.

One hundred twenty days before current coverage expires, insured companies should analyze their liability insurance portfolio, and confer with an insurance agent, the general counsel, and the risk manager to create a current risk profile for the company and determine what coverage is available at what cost to insure against this risk. Insurers issue Conditional Notice of Non-Renewal Letters about 90 days before a policy expires, indicating that they do not wish to renew a policy but that they might offer terms on receipt of additional information about the insured company. The outcome of the strategy meeting should assist the company in negotiating renewals where non-renewal has been threatened—or in seeking alternative coverage. [DeAndre Salter and Karen Kutger, *As Prices Rise on Executive Liability Coverage, Strategy and Negotiations Enter Tough Terrain*, N.Y.L.J. (Mar. 26, 2009) (law.com)]

## § 43.02    COMMERCIAL GENERAL LIABILITY

### [A]    Use of the CGL Policy

Most businesses get their basic liability coverage under the Commercial General Liability (CGL) policy. In fact, for most companies, this is the only liability insurance.

The CGL has two basic aims. The first is to provide a defense (i.e., supply a lawyer who will investigate, negotiate, and settle or try the case). The second is to pay whatever settlement or judgment the defendant company would otherwise have to pay to a successful plaintiff. The insurer's obligation is subject to the insured's obligation to pay a deductible. The insurer is not required to pay more than the limits of the policy. CGL policies are not really uniform. The Insurance Standards Organization (ISO) has published a very influential model policy, but insurers have the option of tailoring the model as they see fit.

Furthermore, the insurer must only pay for covered claims, not excluded ones. ISO has drafted an "employment-related practices exclusion," and the trend is for recent policies to follow this and simply exclude all claims related to a plaintiff's employment by a defendant. Even this is not as simple as it seems. For instance, a court might rule that the real injury to the plaintiff occurred after he or she was fired and therefore ceased to be an employee.

Even if the policy doesn't exclude all employment-related claims, there may be other factors that prevent the employer from collecting benefits under the policy.

The legal doctrine of "respondeat superior" makes employers liable for the negligence or misconduct of an employee committed in the scope of his or her employment—e.g., an automobile accident that occurs when the employee is driving on business. The "going and coming" rule says that the employer is generally not liable for conduct during the employee's regular commute because this is not within the scope of employment. However, California relaxes this rule when the employee's trip creates incidental benefits for the employer. The "special errand" rule makes the employer liable for the employee's actions while commuting if the employee is engaged on a special errand on the employer's behalf; for instance, returning from an out-of-town conference. The "required vehicle" exception is triggered when the employee expressly or impliedly makes his or her personal vehicle available as an accommodation to the employer, and the employer reasonably relies on the vehicle being used for business purposes. Companies for which this exception applies should be sure to amend their insurance coverage to cover employees' use of their own or company vehicles in the scope of employment, and ascertain that any employees for whom driving is part of their job duties have valid licenses and clean driving records. [Jennifer Brown Shaw and Alayna Schroeder, *Liability for the Regular Commute*, The Daily Recorder (Jan. 26, 2011) (benefitslink.com)]

## [B]  Bodily Injury and Personal Injury

Coverage A of the CGL provides liability insurance when the insured becomes liable to someone who has suffered "bodily injury." It's rare for employment plaintiffs to claim that they suffered physically. Usually, they assert that they lost economic benefits (such as salary and pension) because of the employer's wrongful conduct. CGL Coverage A will *not* apply to charges of breach of contract or other economic consequences.

For this and other reasons, plaintiffs often ask for damages based on their emotional suffering. Their complaints allege pain and suffering, intentional infliction of emotional distress, or negligent infliction of emotional distress. (The availability of these causes of action varies between the federal and state systems, and from state to state.)

Most courts that have dealt with this question say that there is no "bodily injury" in an emotional suffering case unless the plaintiff can prove that there was at least some physical consequence of the emotional injury: an ulcer or high blood pressure, for instance. Even if there are physical consequences, they could be considered basically economic and therefore outside the scope of Coverage A.

The CGL's Coverage B deals with liability that the insured encounters for "personal injury" (such as libel or slander) or advertising injury (such as defaming another company's products in your ads). Coverage B might get involved in an employment-related case if, for instance, the plaintiff claims that the employer not only fired him or her, but blacklisted him or her and used a campaign of lies to prevent the ex-employee from getting another job or establishing business relationships.

## [C]  CGL Case Law

Under liability insurance and Worker's Compensation insurance policies, asbestos-related disease is "bodily injury by disease" and not "bodily injury by accident." Asbestos exposure is not an accident because of its non-violent nature and because injuries develop over a latency period rather than manifesting immediately. [*Riverwood Int'l Corp. v. Employers Ins. of Wausau*, 420 F.3d 378 (5th Cir. 2005)]

A California court tackled some complex issues of successor liability and insurance in the early 2003 case of *Henkel Corp. v. Hartford Accident & Indem. Co.* [29 Cal. 4th 934, 62 P.3d 69, 129 Cal. Rptr. 2d 828 (2003)] The plaintiff, Henkel, bought Amchem's metallic products line and assumed all related liabilities. The question facing the court was whether Henkel also acquired the benefits of the insurance policies issued by Hartford to Amchem to cover lawsuits alleging injuries from exposure to chemicals during the policy period.

According to the superior court, there are three situations in which the buyer of corporate assets can become liable for the torts of the predecessor company (even without explicitly assuming the liabilities by contract). The buyer of assets can become liable if the transaction is a merger or consolidation, the purchasing corporation is a continuation of the selling corporation, or the transfer is fraudulent or undertaken to escape liability. The second possibility is that the acquirer of a product line can become liable for injuries caused by the predecessor's defective products if the acquisition extinguishes remedies against the predecessor business. There are also some statutes (such as the environmental statute CERCLA) that impose successor liability no matter what the contract says.

In mid-2007, the Indiana Court of Appeals reached a different result, holding that a company that becomes subject to liability as a result of a merger or acquisition can seek coverage under the acquired company's occurrence-based policy. The insurance company does not have to give prior approval to transfer of coverage to the acquirer. The Indiana Court of Appeals ruled that it would be a windfall for insurers if acquirers could not get coverage, and it would deter acquisitions if acquirers could not insure the liabilities incident to the new asset—clearly, insurers will not issue retroactive coverage for past losses. [*Travelers Cas. & Sur. Co. v. United States Filter Corp.*, 870 N.E.2d 529 (Ind. App. 2007); see Rebecca Moore, *Liabilities Acquired with New Firms Covered under Existing Policies*, plansponsor.com (July 27, 2007)] The victory was short-lived, however: In late 2008, the Indiana Supreme Court reversed (895 N.E.2d 1172 (Ind. 2008)), holding that the insurance policies all contained a ban on assignment of the policy without consent of the insurer. The Indiana Supreme Court found that policy rights can only be assigned if the insurer consents—or unless there has already been a loss that triggers the right to payment of a claim, in which case the right to payment can be transferred without the insurer's consent. But here, there was neither consent nor a post-loss assignment, so the Supreme Court ruled in the insurers' favor.

## § 43.03  OCCURRENCES AND THE PROBLEM OF INTENTION

Coverage under Coverage A depends on there being an "occurrence," which is defined as an accident that was neither intended nor expected by the insured. Coverage B does not have an occurrence requirement, but it does exclude coverage of personal injuries that stem from a willful violation of the law, committed by or with the consent of the insured company.

At first glance, it would seem that employment cases could never be covered under the CGL, because the plaintiff accuses someone of deliberately injuring him or her. The picture is far more complex. Some discrimination charges allege "disparate treatment" (roughly speaking, intentional discrimination), while others claim "disparate impact" (subtle negative effects on a protected group of employees). An employer's actions in adopting a policy or publishing an employee manual could have unintended consequences, which could possibly be treated as CGL "occurrences."

However, intentional discrimination would not be. Courts often treat some conduct (e.g., sexual harassment) as being so likely to have bad consequences for their victims that the consequences are presumed to have been intended, or at least expected, by the insured company.

Employment discrimination plaintiffs usually want the insurance company to be involved, because they know that liability insurance is another potential source of payment if they settle or win the case. In this instance, they are on the same side as the employer. They both want the CGL to cover the employee's claim. One simple strategy is for plaintiffs to add claims of negligent supervision by the employer, or negligent infliction of emotional distress, in the hope that these charges of negligence will be classified as covered "occurrences." The CGL exclusion of "intentional" conduct does not apply to conduct that is negligent, or even grossly negligent. However, this tactic usually fails because the negligence charges are treated as purely incidental to more important charges of intentional conduct.

In most instances, termination of an employee, even wrongful termination, does not involve the intention or expectation of harm, so the insurer will probably have a duty to defend. CGL personal injury coverage often excludes damage resulting from the willful violations of a penal statute or ordinance, committed by the insured or with the knowledge of the insured. Civil rights laws are not considered "penal statutes" for this purpose. Even if actions are "willful" for Title VII purposes, the criminal law exclusion will not be triggered.

Some CGL policies offer an endorsement or rider (at additional cost over the basic premium) that covers discrimination and harassment claims, often by broadening the underlying policy's definition of personal injury.

CGL policies typically exclude bodily injury to employees, arising out of and in the course of employment, whether the employer is liable as an employer or in other capacities. But that provision is probably included in the policy simply for coordination with Worker's Compensation. The employee could succeed in arguing that the tort claims they make do not arise out of or in the course of the employment relationship, because supervisors are not employed to commit discrimination or harassment. The insurer may have at least a duty to defend. Furthermore, occupational injuries could be treated as a known risk that employees are aware of, whereas discrimination and harassment are not risks of the same category.

## § 43.04  EMPLOYMENT PRACTICES LIABILITY INSURANCE

Because of the gaps in CGL coverage of employment matters, a separate form of policy, Employment Practices Liability Insurance (EPLI) evolved as of about 1990. The EPLI is designed to cover damages, judgments, settlements, defense costs, and attorneys' fee awards in the employment liability context (suits, proceedings, or written demands seeking to hold the employer civilly liable). Events included under the EPLI are discrimination, sexual harassment, and wrongful termination, but not "golden parachutes" (payments to top managers who lose their jobs because of corporate transitions) or contractual obligations to make payments to terminated employees. The EPLI policy generally excludes criminal charges, fines, punitive damages, retaliation, and any amounts that are uninsurable because of a relevant state law.

The usual coverage limit is $1 million–$5 million, but some insurers offer "jumbo" policies of up to $100 million in coverage.

EPLI owners can benefit even if they are never sued, because insurers require insured parties to audit their HR functions, improve their procedures, and add new procedures to minimize the risk of suit. The policy may offer access to valuable low-cost consulting services, and compliance advice that would otherwise carry a high price tag.

A claims-made policy is one that provides coverage when claims are made while the insured still has coverage, but not for claims made after coverage expires, even if the allegedly wrongful conduct occurred while the policy was still in force. The ISO EPLI form modifies this by covering claims made during the 30 days after policy expiration, unless another insurer is already in the picture. If the same employee makes multiple claims, they are all considered to have arisen on the date of the first claim, so coverage will be continuous, and it will not be necessary to figure out whether the initial or the later insurer is responsible. Sometimes, it is a false economy to replace a liability insurance policy if the new policy has a waiting period, creating a gap in coverage.

An HR blog looks at five main issues in researching and comparing EPLI policies:

**Coverage**—are only the standard issues (wrongful discharge, employment discrimination, harassment) covered, or are additional issues, such as negligent hiring, defamation, and infliction of emotional distress covered as well? Are claims covered only if asserted by full-time permanent employees, or are claims from independent contractors, part-time, temporary, seasonal, and temporary workers covered too?

**Exclusions**—all EPLI policies exclude punitive damages, and most of them list the statutes for which coverage will not be available, e.g., FLSA, WARN Act, NLRA, OSHA, or the ADA. The impact of an exclusion depends on the relevance of the topic to the company's business. Multi-state corporations may face a variety of risks under the different state laws, so it may be necessary to pay for coverage in multiple states to be protected against risks generated by individual state laws.

**Deductibles, policy limits**—these are usually applied on a per-claim as well as an aggregate basis, e.g., $250,000 per claim subject to a cap of $1 million on all claims. Accepting greater risk, by buying a policy with a higher deductible and/or lower cap, can be a cost-saving measure, but it leaves the insured vulnerable to more of the same risks that motivated buying the policy in the first place.

**Timing issues**—most EPLI policies are written on a "claims made" basis (i.e., to be covered, a claim must relate to conduct within the coverage period) and reported to the insurer during the prescribed reporting period. It is often necessary, even after discontinuing an EPLI policy, to purchase "long tail" coverage to account for claims that developed in earlier years but were not asserted until later. In some instances, long-simmering claims will be barred by statute of limitations and EEOC filing issues—but there are instances in which a claim covering many years of employment practices will be valid and will have to be defended. And, even if the claim itself is valid and requires a defense, if the insured fails to give timely notice to the insurer, the insurer may be relieved of responsibility.

**Defense counsel, defense costs, and settlement**—Generally, legal costs are included within the policy limit. If the claim is resolved in the employer's favor, this is not a problem, but if the employee prevails, amounts expended on defense are no longer available to pay the settlement or judgment awarded to the plaintiff or plaintiff class. Be aware that it is common for insurers to want to settle cases when the employer wants to fight to the last ditch, perhaps to clear its name and promote its good reputation. The policy might be drafted to give the insurer the right to settle even over the employer's objections. "Hammer clauses" are also common: i.e., the employer retains control over settlement—but if the employer rejects a settlement offer, insurance will not cover any discrepancy between the eventual settlement or judgment and the amount for which the employer could have settled the case. [Michael Moore, *Employment Practices Liability Insurance: Five Things Every HR Generalist Should Know*, <http://www.paemploymentlawblog.com/2008/02/articles/employer-liability/[ . . . ]> (Feb. 12, 2008)]

Two commentators suggest the following questions for evaluating an EPLI policy:

- Does it cover all employees? What about the liability consequences of actions of leased employees and independent contractors?

- Are former employees covered?

- Are claims for breach of explicit or implied employment contract covered by or excluded from the policy?

- Does the insurer have to provide you with a defense in administrative (e.g., EEOC and local antidiscrimination agencies) proceedings, or only at trial? (Only a small percentage of discrimination charges make it to the trial stage, but the investigative stage can be very unpleasant for the employer.)

- Are retaliation claims (including retaliation for filing Worker's Compensation claims) covered? (This is a large and growing part of the discrimination caseload.)

- Are injunctive and declaratory relief covered, or only money damages?

- Is the deductible imposed on a per-year or per-claimant basis? (If the latter is true, an insured employer might end up having to pay several deductibles a year.)

[Stephanie E. Trudeau and William Edwards, Employment Law Letter, archived at <http://www.ulmer.com>]

## § 43.05   OTHER INSURANCE

The business insurance portfolio could also include other types of insurance, such as excess liability (supplementing the CGL), umbrella coverage (with a broader definition of "personal injury"), Worker's Compensation insurance (see Chapter 33 for more detailed consideration of WC issues) and Directors' and Officers' (D&O) coverage.

### [A]   Excess Liability and Umbrella Coverage

Every CGL policy has limits: maximum amounts of coverage obtainable under particular circumstances. If your company already has maximum CGL coverage, but feels that more is necessary, there are two ways to supplement it.

The first is "follow-form" excess liability insurance, which increases the dollar amount of coverage available under your CGL, Worker's Compensation, and Business Automobile Liability coverage, but subject to the same terms and exclusions. For many companies, an "umbrella" policy is a better choice, because it is more broadly defined and may cover situations that were excluded by the underlying policy. This kind of "gap" coverage is generally subject to a "retained limit," another term for "deductible."

Umbrella policies offer coverage in more situations because their definition of "personal injury" is broader than Coverage A or Coverage B of the standard CGL. A typical provision includes both bodily injury and mental injury, mental anguish, shock, sickness, disease, discrimination, humiliation, libel, slander, defamation of character, and invasion of property. Therefore, many employment-related claims would be covered.

### [B]   Worker's Compensation

Specialized Worker's Compensation coverage is available to deal with the employer's obligation to pay benefits to employees who are injured in job-related situations. Of course, because of WC exclusivity, the employer does not have to worry about ordinary liability suits from injured workers, although there may be special situations in which suit can be brought (against the employer or another party, such as the manufacturer of unsafe factory machinery) even though Worker's Compensation is involved. In a WC employment liability policy, Worker's Compensation is Coverage A; the employment liability (e.g., bodily injury that is not subject to WC exclusivity) is Coverage B.

A company had two liability policies (covering bodily injury caused by accident) and a third, Worker's Compensation policy covering bodily injury caused by accident. The company and its president were sued by a former employee for wrongful termination, false imprisonment, interference with FMLA rights, and intentional infliction of emotional distress. The Seventh Circuit held that coverage was not triggered, because the employee alleged only intentional, not accidental, injuries. The plaintiff said that the company's president forced him to sit through a two-hour meeting after he fell at work and ruptured a muscle; the injury required an operation and five days of hospitalization. He claimed that the company president kept trying to get him to return to work before he was ready, and finally fired him. The company (Granite) tried to involve its CGL and WC insurers and its insurer under an Excess and Umbrella policy, characterizing the case as one about an accidental workplace fall. The Seventh Circuit, however, said that the case was about intentional acts (infliction of emotional distress, wrongful termination) so coverage was unavailable. [*Lucterhand v. Granite Microsystems*, 564 F.3d 809 (7th Cir. 2009)]

## [C]  Directors' and Officers' Liability (D&O)

D&O insurance covers the situation in which a corporation' directors and officers get not only themselves but the corporation into trouble. Frequently, executives will not agree to serve as directors or officers unless the corporation first promises them indemnification, i.e., that the corporation will pay the executive whatever amount he or she has to pay because of liability incurred while acting as a director or officer.

D&O insurance, in turn, reimburses the corporation for whatever it spends on indemnification, subject to a deductible and up to the limit of the policy.

According to Towers Watson's 2010 D&O Liability survey, businesses are increasing their liability limits. Multinational corporations are more likely than before to buy policies in non-U.S. jurisdictions. (One-quarter of respondents had a local D&O policy in another country, and the larger the company, the more likely it was to own a non-U.S. policy.) In 2008, 12% of respondents said that they increased their policy limits in the previous year—a percentage that rose to 21% in 2010. In 2008, 86% said they kept the same limits; 75% kept the same limits in 2010, and only 3% of respondents said they reduced their policy limits in 2010. [<http://www.towerswatson.com/united-states/press/3824>; see Rebecca Moore, *Survey Finds Companies Increasing D and O Liability Limits*, plansponsor.com (Feb. 22, 2011)]

In a case of first impression, the Second Circuit ruled in late 2010 that it is unlawful for a company to agree to indemnify its CEO or CFO for compensation or proceeds of stock sales that they are required to disgorge under Sarbanes-Oxley § 304 (the "clawback" provision that requires CEOs and CFOs to reimburse their employers for incentive compensation received or stock sale profits recognized in the 12 months after the filing of a financial statement that had to be restated due to misconduct). In this case, the indemnification clause was part of a settlement agreement, but the same argument could also be applied to forbid indemnification under the corporation's charter or through D&O insurance. The case arose when the stock price of a manufacturer of body armor dropped after the discovery that the company used inferior materials. In 2006, the CFO and Chief Operation Officer were charged with civil accounting fraud as well as criminal charges. In 2007, the company restated its financial statements for the years 2003–2005. A derivative and class action suit against the company was settled in 2008; the indemnification occurred at this time. After the federal prosecutor appealed, the Second Circuit overturned the settlement, agreeing that indemnification was inappropriate. Because there is no private right to sue under Sarbanes-Oxley § 304, all enforcement is done by the SEC, so indemnification was an attempt to relieve the CEO and CFO of their burdens under Sarbanes-Oxley. The SEC might make similar arguments against indemnification re Dodd-Frank Act clawbacks—although it is not clear if the Dodd-Frank clawback provision allows private suits. [*Cohen v. Viray*, 622 F.3d 188 (2d Cir. 2010); see McGuireWoods LLP, *2nd Circuit Rules That Companies May Not Indemnify Executives for SOX 304 "Clawback" Liability*, Legal Updates (Nov. 18, 2010) (benefitslink.com)]

### [D]   Errors & Omissions (E&O)

Errors and Omissions insurance pays, on behalf of the insured, all loss for which the insured person is not indemnified by the insured organization if the person is liable because of any wrongful act he or she committed or attempted. In general, committing disparate treatment discrimination will be considered a wrongful act that can be covered under the policy, unless the policy definition covers only negligent, and not intentional, acts and omissions.

In many companies, E&O insurance is complemented by D&O insurance that covers the company for losses it incurs when it indemnifies directors and officers acting in that capacity.

An important issue is whether or not administrative actions (such as state agency and EEOC proceedings, subpoenas, and federal grand jury target letters) are considered "claims or suits" for insurance purposes. Businesses also often encounter expenses for their own administrative or internal investigations. The insurer is likely to make the argument that back pay awarded to a prevailing plaintiff is equitable relief and not "damages" that could be covered under the policy.

However, many courts have rejected this argument and required liability insurers to handle back-pay awards against their policyholders. E&O insurers may also resist paying back pay if the policy excludes amounts owed under a "contractual obligation," but here again, the insured will probably prevail if a back pay award is made. D&O or E&O coverage for subpoena or investigation compliance must be negotiated before your company becomes a target. If the policy specifically refers to an indictment, a Grand Jury subpoena would probably not be treated as a "claim." Other decisions say that an investigation in and of itself is not a request for relief, but subpoenas and investigative demands have been found to be claims when the insured was required to produce testimony and documents as part of an ongoing investigation of the corporation. [Joseph D. Jean and Rachel M. Wrightson, *Ensuring Coverage for Actions in Response to Investigations*, N.Y.L.J. (July 10, 2009) (law.com)]

Another insurance form covers plans, administrators, and trustees against allegations of impropriety. Many employment-related claims involve ERISA allegations, so the employer should at least consider adding this coverage to its insurance portfolio.

## § 43.06   DUTY OF THE INSURANCE CONTRACT

### [A]   Duty to Defend

A lesser-known, but perhaps more important, part of the liability insurance policy is the insurer's duty to defend. That is, whenever a claim is made against the employer, the insurer has to provide a lawyer and take care of the case. However, usually the insurer is in control of the litigation, and decides how vigorously to defend the case and when to settle (although some policies return control of litigation to the insured). Most policies are drafted so that, if the insured company settles the case without consent and participation of the insurer, the insured company will not be able to recover any part of the settlement costs from the insurer.

The insurer's duty to indemnify is the duty to pay on the insured's behalf when the insured settles or loses a lawsuit. The duty to defend is much broader. If the allegations against an insured company are invalid, or can't be proved, then the liability insurer's role is to get the charge dismissed, even though there is no liability to indemnify. In general, if the charges combine claims that are covered by liability insurance with others that are not, the insurer has a duty to defend against all the charges, not just the covered ones.

Usually, the insurer's duty to defend is triggered by a "claim" made against the insured employer. This is usually interpreted as filing a complaint with a court. EEOC or local agency proceedings are not generally considered "claims," so an insured company is on its own for a significant part of the process before the duty to defend begins.

ERISA § 504 gives the DOL broad power to investigate ERISA violations, and responding to the investigation can be expensive in terms of legal fees and other expenses. A mid-2011 article points out that, if a notice of claim is filed relative to expenses of responding to a DOL investigation, the liability insurer can accept the notice as a claim; deny the notice of claim; or accept the notice as a circumstance that may give rise to a claim in the future. But there must be a claim to trigger defense coverage; a circumstance is not enough. Even if the claim is denied, having filed the notice helps the plan because it prevents the insurer from denying later claims on the grounds of late notice (i.e., that the plan did not give the insurer timely notice of a potential claim). The article says that the key is what the DOL tells the plan. If the DOL begins merely by requesting documents without identifying a possible violation that is under investigation, then the insurance carrier will probably state that there has been no claim because there is no allegation of a wrongful act. There might be a claim if the DOL identifies an official enforcement issue after investigation, and issues a Notice Letter, aka voluntary charging letter or 10-day letter, to the plan. However, by that time, the plan probably has incurred extensive legal fees in response to the investigation. The article suggests that plan fiduciaries can improve the odds of the situation being treated as a claim by contacting the insurer as soon as possible after the DOL begins to investigate. The situation is more likely to be treated as a claim if DOL has targeted a specific person of interest or target issue. If DOL issues any subpoenas, the insurer should be informed. [Segal, *Fiduciary Liability Policies May Not Cover Costs Associated with DOL Investigations,* The Fiduciary Shield (July 2011) (benefitslink.com)]

## [B]  Duties of the Insured

Insurance companies are relieved of their obligation to pay claims if the insured company fails to satisfy its obligations. The most obvious duty is paying premiums. Liability policies also require the insured to notify the insurer as soon as possible whenever a "claim" is made. Therefore, legal advice is necessary to determine which allegations have the legal status of a claim.

An Eighth Circuit case highlights these issues. The plaintiff, a cleaning service, was sued in 1997 in Hawaii state court for sexual harassment of a maintenance worker. The plaintiff (Interstate Cleaning Corporation—ICC) believed the case was just a nuisance suit, and didn't notify its insurer that it had been served with a complaint. The sexual harassment plaintiffs offered to settle the suit for $25,000, but ICC refused to settle. The jury ruled in favor of the sexual harassment plaintiffs. ICC was able to get the state court judgment amended to reduce the damages, and eventually the sexual harassment plaintiffs and ICC reached a settlement. In April 1999, ICC finally notified its insurer of the suit. The insurer refused to provide coverage on the grounds that the policy (a CGL policy with a self-insured endorsement, subject to a deductible of $50,000 per occurrence and $300,000 a year for multiple occurrences) did not cover the acts charged by the sexual harassment plaintiffs. ICC sued the insurer.

The Eighth Circuit found that, in general, insured parties have a duty to give immediate notice of claim to their insurers, although this requirement can be excused when it is not reasonably possible to provide notice. However, if an insurer is not prejudiced by the insured's failure to give notice, the insurer cannot use the notice failure as a reason not to defend or pay benefits. In this case, late notice did prejudice the insurer, because it was unable to investigate or participate in settlement negotiations. Therefore, it was not obligated to defend or indemnify the insureds. [*Interstate Cleaning Corp. v. Commercial Underwriters Ins. Co.*, 325 F.3d 1024 (8th Cir. 2003)]

## § 43.07   QUESTIONS OF TIMING

Liability policies are divided into "occurrence" and "claims-made" policies. If there is an "occurrence" covered by the policy (see above), all the occurrence policies in force at that time must make payments. But the insured doesn't get five times the amount of the liability. Coverage is coordinated (divided among them) to prevent windfalls.

A claims-made policy works differently. It covers only claims that are made during the policy term with respect to events that happened during the policy term. Because this can be a difficult standard to meet, claims-made policies are often extended to cover events after the policy's "retroactive date." There may also be an "extended reporting period" after the policy expires, where events are covered if they occurred while the policy was still in force, but were reported later.

Luciano Manganella, the former president of Jasmine Co., sought defense and indemnity on sexual harassment claims from Jasmine's liability insurer. Jasmine bought the policy in 1998, shortly after an employee charged Manganella with harassment. The policy excluded conduct that shows wanton, willful, reckless, or intentional disregard of law. Jasmine was sold to Lerner in mid-2005. Lerner gave Manganella an employment agreement, but $7 million of the purchase price was placed in escrow in case Manganella committed a major employment breach. The definition of major employment breach included refusal to comply with a significant policy of Lerner's. Shortly after the sale, Jasmine canceled the final installment of the policy but purchased coverage for an extended reporting period: claims made or reported during the 36 months after the effective date of the cancellation. Manganella was fired in mid-2006 after Jasmine investigated further sexual harassment charges against him. The dismissal letter said that the harassment constituted major employment breaches and that Lerner was entitled to the escrowed $7 million. The case went to arbitration. Although the arbitration panel held that Manganella was guilty of sexual harassment, the panel also held that he was entitled to the escrowed funds because Lerner did not give him notice or an opportunity to remedy his violations of company policy. The Southern District of New York confirmed the award. While the arbitration was pending, an employee filed Massachusetts sexual harassment charges against Manganella, Lerner, and Jasmine. The insurer denied Manganella's application for coverage on the grounds that the harassment was not limited to the period after the retroactive date. The district court ruled that the arbitration panel held that Manganella acted with wanton and willful disregard of Massachusetts law against sexual harassment, settling the issue so that it could not be relitigated. The First

Circuit agreed, holding that final arbitration awards are treated like court judgments to determine if an issue within a case has been finally determined. The insurer was justified in denying coverage. [*Manganella v. Evanston Ins. Co.*, 700 F.3d 585 (1st Cir. 2012)]

## § 43.08  FIDUCIARY LIABILITY INSURANCE

A fidelity bond makes a plan whole when it suffers losses from dishonest or fraudulent acts by employees who handle plan participants' money or securities. All qualified plans must maintain an ERISA fidelity bond in the amount of 10% of the amount handled. The typical duration of a fidelity bond is three years, and the amount must be adjusted each year to make sure the 10% requirement is satisfied. The PPA increases the maximum amount of the fidelity bond required for plans that hold employer stock, for plan years beginning after January 1, 2007, from $500,000 to $1 million. If the DOL discovers that the plan does not have the necessary bond, it can order the company to get a bond; permanently bar the fiduciary from ever serving as an ERISA plan fiduciary; remove the plan administrator and appoint an independent trustee; or impose penalties.

In contrast, fiduciary liability insurance protects the plan sponsor and its officers, directors, and employees from common-law, ERISA, and other statutory liability. [Janelle Sotelo, *Fidelity Bond v. Fiduciary Liability Insurance*, <http://www.preceptgroup.com/blog> (Feb. 19, 2009)] Where the policy covers the plan itself, the insurer can sue the fiduciary to recover the amount it had to pay out because of the fiduciary's conduct. Fiduciary liability insurance is usually available only in limited amounts, on a claims-made basis.

Other than banks, insurance companies, and broker-dealers, ERISA § 412 requires every fiduciary and every person who handles property of an employee benefit plan to be bonded. All plan trustees are fiduciaries; others can become fiduciaries through their relationship to a plan (discretionary authority or control over management of the plan—or any authority or control, discretionary or otherwise, over plan assets). Anyone who provides investment advice to the plan is also a fiduciary. DOL has required bonding of anyone whose duties involve receiving, keeping, or disbursing plan funds, having access to plan funds, or having the capacity to cause losses to the plan through fraud or dishonesty. Section 412 makes it illegal for any plan official to permit another plan official handle the plan's property without being bonded. In other words, anyone who has an obligation to be bonded must enforce this requirement on everyone else who has to be bonded. Several forms of fiduciary bond are available, so the plan must select the right form—and, if necessary, increase the bonding if the existing bond does not cover all the fiduciaries of the plan. [Joe Faucher, Reish & Reacher ERISA Controversy Report, *ERISA Fidelity Bonds—Who Needs Them, and Who is Responsible for Securing Them?* (February 2011) (law.com)]

Fiduciary liability insurance is an asset of the plan, but also protects trustees' personal assets. Furthermore, a fiduciary who breaches his or her duty may not be able to afford to reimburse the plan for its full losses.

For the policy to be truly useful, the definition of the "insured" should include the plan and/or trust, all past, present and future trustees and employees, and their successors. Coverage for the spouse of an insured if named as an additional defendant should also be included. The general rule is that most fiduciary liability policies don't cover third-party administrators or service providers who act as fiduciaries, although it may be possible to add them to the policy under an endorsement.

The definition of "loss" should include defense costs (including costs for investigators and expert witnesses) settlements, judgments, and pre- and post-judgment interest. Although liability insurance typically excludes coverage of fines and penalties, IRS Employee Plans Compliance Resolution System (EPCRS) penalties and amounts paid to the DOL when it wins or settles an ERISA § 502(l) case are usually either included in the basic coverage or added by endorsement.

> ■ **TIP:**  The entire policy has to be examined to see if there are additional limitations—for instance, the definition of "loss" may exclude fines and penalties.

Most fiduciary liability policies are claims-made policies. At each anniversary date, the insured can evaluate and adjust the policy limits and scope of coverage, bearing affordability in mind. Once a policy is purchased, it is hard to change carriers, because the application requires a warranty that there are no known claims or circumstances that would be excluded by the new insurer if they were fully disclosed—and it's very common for companies to face claims of this type!

Attorney Stephen Saxon published some suggestions about obtaining fiduciary liability insurance:

- Buy a "nonrecourse rider" if the plan pays for the insurance. ERISA prohibits fiduciaries from using plan assets to pay for fiduciary liability insurance, unless the plan has recourse against the fiduciary. The rider prevents the insurer from proceeding against the fiduciary in case there is a covered loss.

- Find out if the policy limits include defense costs, because if they do, an expensive defense can exhaust the policy.

- Check to see if the deductible applies to all the claims within a policy period or whether each allegation is subject to a separate deductible. Waiving the deductible for claims against individual fiduciaries is a common provision.

- The policy application will ask the trustees if they are aware of any potential claims (and there will be no coverage for claims that the trustees knew about but did not disclose), so obtain legal advice on how to answer the question completely and accurately.

- If the policy covers attorneys' fees on a "pay on behalf of" basis (i.e., the insured can select counsel rather than having to be represented by the insurer's attorneys) the policy will be much more useful if the fees are reimbursed as they are incurred, instead of only at the end of the case. [Stephen M. Saxon, *Insurance Policies: Tips on Securing Fiduciary Liability Insurance*, plansponsor.com, <http://www.plansponsor.com/magazine_type1_print.jsp?RECORD_ID=31594> (Apr. 2, 2006)]

A mid-2011 article points out some common misconceptions that fiduciaries often have about fiduciary liability insurance:

- That an ERISA fidelity bond protects their personal assets; the purpose of the fidelity bond is to protect the plan and its participants against misconduct by the fiduciary;

- That employee benefit liability policies cover fiduciaries fully; their errors and omissions in administration of the benefit plan itself are covered, but other aspects, such as investment of plan assets, are not necessarily covered;

- That D&O policies cover fiduciaries; this is true only with respect to activities in their capacity as directors and officers, not in their capacity as fiduciaries, and ERISA claims are usually excluded by D&O policies;

- Fiduciaries will be entitled to indemnification of all personal liabilities; this is not necessarily true, because ERISA prevents plans from indemnifying fiduciaries for breach of fiduciary duty. [Jerry Kalish, *Four Misconceptions About Fiduciary Liability Insurance*, Retirement Plan Blog (June 7, 2011) (benefitslink.com)

# INDEX

*References are to section number.*

## M

# U

USERRA (Uniformed Services Employment
and Reemployment Rights Act)
(*cont'd*)
failure to re-employ, 1.18[B]
FMLA leave and, 38.06[F]
pay planning, 1.18
recent cases, 1.18[B]
regulations, 1.18[A]
termination of protected employees, 1.18[A]
Uterus as preexisting condition, 18.02
Utilization review (UR), 18.13[E]
(UVBs) Unvested benefits, 10.05[A]


**V**

Vacations, 1.16, 2.02, 38.06[A]
Valuation and defined benefit plans, 5.05[H]
Variable pay, 1.05
Variable-rate premium (VRP), 5.08[B], 10.05
Variances, OSHA, 31.07
VEBAs (Voluntary Employee Benefit
Associations), 22.07
early retirement, 9.07, 9.09
Vertical partial termination of plan, 17.06[B]
Vesting
aggregate unvested benefits (UVBs),
10.05[A]
commissions, 1.05
defined contribution plans, 6.02[B]
layoffs, effect of, 14.01
pension plans, 4.01[A], 4.10, 4.14
graded vesting, 4.14[A]
service and, 4.14[C]
termination, vesting on, 4.14[B]
Veterans Benefits Improvement Act of 2004,
1.18[A]
Vicarious liability, sexual harassment,
35.03[B]
Video surveillance, 26.06[A]
Violence in the workplace, 31.05[D]
Visa holders, immigration status of
corporate transition, effect of, 16.01
Visa Reform Act of 2004, 23.11[E]
Voluntary Classification Settlement Program
(VCSP), 1.12[A], 2.05
Voluntary correction, 15.19[B]
expansion and updating of EPCRS,
15.19[B]
Voluntary Correction Program (VCP),
10.04[A]

Voluntary Employee Benefit Associations
(VEBAs), 22.07
early retirement, 9.07, 9.09
Voluntary exit programs, 1.04
Voluntary Protection Programs (VPP), 31.14
Voluntary termination of plan, 17.01
Voter eligibility, union, 30.04[E]
VPP (Voluntary Protection Programs), 31.14
(VRP) Variable-rate premium, 5.08[B], 10.05


**W**

Wage and hour issues, 1.06, 1.14
Wage bracket method of calculating income
tax withholding, 2.03[A]
Wage Theft Prevention Act, 1.06
Wagner Act, 30.02[B]
Walk-throughs, OSHA, 31.09[B]
WARN Act (Worker Adjustment and
Retraining Notification Act),
16.02[A], 30.10
faltering company exception, 30.10
guidance letter, 30.10
mass layoffs, 1.04
reduction in force, effect of, 30.10
severance pay, 3.03[C]
substantial cessation of operations, 30.10
unforeseen business circumstances
exception, 30.10
voluntary departure, 30.10
WC. *See* Workers' Compensation
Wearaway, 7.01, 7.06, 7.07, 7.07[A]
"Web 2.0," 27.05
Welfare benefit plans
administration, 22.09[A]
creation, 22.09[A]
EGHP as, 11.02[B]
ERISA, 22.09[A], 22.09[B]
SPDs, issuance to participants, 11.02[B]
taxation, 22.01
Wellness programs, 19.05[B], 36.10[D]
PPACA, 18.19[G]
WHCRA (Women's Health and Cancer Rights
Act), 18.03[C]
"Whipsaw," 7.07
Whistleblowers
discrimination actions by employees, 42.02
under Dodd-Frank Act, 15.11[B]
SEC's whistleblower rules 39.04[B]
jury trial right for, 39.04[B]